THE OXFORD
COMPANION
· TO THE ·

HIGH COURT
OF AUSTRALIA

The editors dedicate this book to
Emily Anne Coper-Jones and Edita Nova Dominello Grinbergs,
both born during the course of the project.

THE OXFORD COMPANION
· TO THE ·
HIGH COURT
OF AUSTRALIA

Edited by
TONY BLACKSHIELD
MICHAEL COPER
GEORGE WILLIAMS

Research Assistants
FRANCESCA DOMINELLO
SUSAN PRIEST
TROY SIMPSON

OXFORD
UNIVERSITY PRESS

OXFORD
UNIVERSITY PRESS

253 Normanby Road, South Melbourne, Australia

Oxford University Press is a department of the University
of Oxford. It furthers the University's objective of excellence
in research, scholarship, and education by publishing
worldwide in

Oxford New York

Athens Auckland Bangkok Bogotá Buenos Aires Cape Town Chennai
Dar es Salaam Delhi Florence Hong Kong Istanbul Karachi Kolkata
Kuala Lumpur Madrid Melbourne Mexico City Mumbai Nairobi Paris
Port Moresby São Paulo Shanghai Singapore Taipei Tokyo Toronto Warsaw

with associated companies in Berlin Ibadan

OXFORD is a trade mark of Oxford University Press
in the UK and in certain other countries

National Library of Australia
Cataloguing-in-Publication data:

The Oxford companion to the High Court of Australia.

Includes index.
ISBN 0 19 554022 0.

1. Australia. High Court—Dictionaries.
2. Courts of last resort—Australia—Dictionaries.
I. Blackshield, A. R. (Anthony Roland), 1937- .
II. Coper, Michael 1946- . III. Williams, George, 1969- .

347.94035

Edited by Trischa Baker
Cover designed by Patrick Cannon
Typeset by Desktop Concepts Pty Ltd, Melbourne
Printed by Kyodo Printing Company, Singapore

Contents

About the editors

Tony Blackshield is an Emeritus Professor at Macquarie University and an Adjunct Professor at the ANU and UNSW. He holds a masters degree in law from the University of Sydney and was a founding member of the Faculty of Law at UNSW. He has had a long interest in, and has written extensively about, the High Court as an institution and the nature of the judicial process. He is well known as a commentator on constitutional law, international law, and jurisprudence, among other areas. His works include, as coeditor, *The Judgments of Justice Lionel Murphy* (1986) and, as coauthor, *Australian Constitutional Law and Theory: Commentary and Materials* (2nd edn 1998).

Michael Coper is Dean of Law and Robert Garran Professor of Law at the ANU. A graduate in Arts and Law from the University of Sydney, he was a founding member of the Faculty of Law at UNSW. He was appointed to the Inter-State Commission in 1988, and, following the demise of the Commission, worked in private practice in Canberra from 1991 to 1995. His books include the prize-winning *Freedom of Interstate Trade Under the Australian Constitution* (1983) and *Encounters with the Australian Constitution* (1987, popular edn 1988). He has appeared as counsel in a number of High Court cases, including the landmark *Cole v Whitfield* (1988). In 1999, he was elected to membership of the American Law Institute.

George Williams is the Anthony Mason Professor and Director of the Gilbert & Tobin Centre of Public Law at UNSW. He was formerly based at the ANU. He has an economics degree and a law degree from Macquarie University, a masters degree in law from UNSW, and a PhD from the ANU. He has worked at the High Court as associate to Justice Michael McHugh and as a barrister has appeared in a number of High Court cases, including the *Hindmarsh Island Bridge Case* (1998). His books include *Human Rights Under the Australian Constitution* (1999) and *A Bill of Rights for Australia* (2000). He is a well-known media commentator on constitutional law issues and the High Court.

Preface

The High Court of Australia plays a fundamental role as an institution of Australian government. Yet, curiously, it has never been subjected to sustained scrutiny in that role. True, the law journals are replete with learned legal analyses, but these are addressed to a narrow audience, are mainly confined to particular areas of law, and, even within those boundaries, are largely doctrinal. This book examines the work of the Court as a whole: the way it operates, its historical development, the people who have contributed to that development, the leading cases, and, above all, the institutional role of the Court in Australian society. It will be of absorbing interest to lawyers, but it is not only for lawyers. It is for anyone whose life or work is touched by the Court, or who has a professional or intellectual interest in the way the Court shapes and develops Australian law, or who has even a modicum of curiosity about the role and record of the Court and its impact on Australian law, politics, and society.

The High Court's story, from A to Z, is told in 435 separate entries, by 225 authors, in about 650 000 words. Yet this is no mere compilation of known facts. The book is the product of a good deal of original research, and much of the information about the Court is published for the first time. Even more importantly, the book does more than merely present information, old or new; it provides fresh insights into the role and work of the Court through analysis, criticism, and reflection. It is not, after all, a dictionary, but a Companion; and like any good companion, it provides an honest appraisal, celebrating strengths and exposing weaknesses in equal measure.

In addition to the editors, who between them wrote about one-sixth of the book, the authors include current and former Justices of the Court, leading academics and practitioners, and others with special knowledge and expertise. Putting aside the shorter, factual entries, the wisdom of the authors is distilled into finely honed and literate mini-essays of up to 4000 words in length, which in some cases are gems of the genre. Like the Japanese *haiku* or the Shakespearean sonnet, these entries have a distinct form, their composition demanding a skill beyond expert knowledge of the subject matter. With some massaging from the editors, the entries taken as a whole display considerable virtuosity, and contain much to surprise and delight.

That is so partly because the editors, in addition to endeavouring to produce an original and authoritative work with a critical dimension, also encouraged diversity. The book does not 'run' any particular 'line'. The commentators come from all points on the socio-political spectrum, and the book is enriched by the resultant contrasts. That the entries are attributed to their particular writers signifies not merely authorship but also individual responsibility for a point of view. Many authors have not shrunk from expressing a point of view. The book is the better for it.

At one stage, the editors considered including entries directed specifically to evaluation of the Justices and evaluation of the Court's decisions. A well-known American commentator has, for example, identified what in his view are the ten 'best' and the ten 'worst' Justices, and the ten best and ten worst decisions, of the United States Supreme Court (Bernard Schwartz, *A Book of Legal Lists* (1997)). Although tempted to engage in this rather playful exercise, the editors ultimately resisted, for two reasons. First, the criteria by which this identification might be made are elusive and their application subjective. Is a decision good because, for example, its outcome is politically or socially desirable, or its reasoning elegant, or because it is faithful to precedent, or because it breaks new ground and departs from precedent? Secondly, there was in the end no need for discrete entries on these issues, as the whole book is an evaluation of the role and record of the Court in its first 100 years. We commend it to you on that basis.

The book was the brainchild of Michael Coper, who initiated the project when he first joined the Law Faculty of the Australian National University (ANU) on a part-time basis in 1994. The authors are multiple and diverse, but the project has significantly been an ANU project, with the editors all holding ANU positions, the project having been physically located in Canberra, and virtually all members of the ANU Law Faculty having made contributions as authors. Nevertheless, the book is the work of many hands, as is revealed emphatically by our acknowledgments below. The editors would, however, like to pay special tribute to their dedicated research assistants—first and foremost to Troy Simpson, who worked unstintingly on the book for almost three years, and secondly to Francesca Dominello and Susan Priest, who were each with the project for a little over a year. The book took its shape mainly from the collective effort of this team of six—the three editors and the three research assistants.

Of course, no single book on the High Court can be a comprehensive account of the Court's work over 100 years. Although there are entries on all of the Justices and most of the areas of substantive law to which the Court has contributed, the choice of particular cases to be accorded entries in their own right (many more are canvassed in other entries) was necessarily selective, and not a little subjective. The cases might have been selected because they were unarguably leading cases, or important milestones in the history of the Court or the nation, or because their facts or the identity of the litigants attracted some notoriety, or simply because the editors judged them to be interesting or instructive. If your favourite case is not there, you might write and let us know.

Indeed, we invite you, the reader, to write to us in relation to any aspect of this pioneering work. If you think we have fallen into any error, factual or legal, or have committed any serious sin of omission, and you can support your claim, we would be delighted to hear from you and to take account of your comments in the second edition.

The production of this book has been an extraordinary task. Liaising in a tight timeframe with more than 200 eminent (or in some cases soon-to-be-eminent) authors, who for the most part responded superbly to our rigorous editing process, was always going to be a challenge. In the context of this exquisite mix of pleasure and pain, every entry has its own story, though in the nature of things these stories are unlikely ever to be told. Instead, we offer to you in this book the end product of our labours: a companion to have by your side; to consult in times of need, or just for the pleasure of good company; to learn from and perhaps to be enriched by; to use as a point of reference or departure for further inquiry; or simply to enjoy. In any case, it is our hope that, in making the work of the Court better known and perhaps better understood, the book will truly be both *amicus curiae* and *amicus populi*.

TONY BLACKSHIELD
MICHAEL COPER
GEORGE WILLIAMS

JUNE 2001

Editors' acknowledgments

Many people have contributed in one way or another to the production of this book. The pivotal contribution came, of course, from our three full-time research assistants—Troy Simpson, Francesca Dominello, and Susan Priest—who worked creatively, tirelessly, and with good grace under constant fire. We also had the benefit of some excellent part-time research assistance, notably from Amelia Simpson and Rebecca Craske. We are grateful to all of these outstanding researchers for their commitment to, and enthusiasm for, the project.

Putting aside various sporadic, though recurrent, flickers of imagination, the first visible sign of the project was a meeting of a 'working group' in the staff library of the ANU Law School on 9 June 1994, convened by Michael Coper. In addition to the convenor, the group comprised Deborah Cass, Paul Finn, Nick Seddon, David Solomon, and Fiona Wheeler. Although the project was to develop in a different direction, we thank this group for its initial input. That direction crystallised when Michael Coper and George Williams met with Peter Rose of Oxford University Press in Melbourne on 16 February 1996. Tony Blackshield subsequently joined the team, and on Peter Rose's advice, a draft list of the headwords was sent to a select group of experts for comment and review. We are particularly grateful to the more than 60 people who assisted us in this task and helped us refine the headwords into a coherent, cohesive, integrated, and interesting list of key topics.

We then set about inviting the contributors, whose magnificent responses comprise the bulk of the book. We thank them for their scholarship and learning, in most cases for their punctuality, and for the good spirit with which they submitted themselves to the rigours of our editorial idiosyncrasies. We also thank those contributors, and others, who provided additional advice, read draft entries, answered queries, and made suggestions, especially JM Bennett, Lionel Bowen, Gerard Brennan, Clyde Cameron, Bruce Debelle, Peter Durack, Rae Else-Mitchell, RJ Ellicott, Gareth Evans, Malcolm Fraser, Harry Gibbs, John Gorton, Tom Hughes, Frank Jones, Michael Kirby, Laurence Maher, Anthony Mason, JD Merralls, John H Phillips, Gary Rumble, Michael Sexton, Simon Sheller, Ninian Stephen, Gough Whitlam, and the staff at the *Australian Dictionary of Biography*. We particularly thank Philip Ayres, who in addition to commenting upon various drafts, granted us access to the Dixon diaries.

The National Library of Australia provided magnificent support; we particularly thank Graeme Powell and Greg Wilson at the Manuscript Library and the staff at the Oral History Section. The staff of the National Archives of Australia were also unfailingly helpful, courteous, and professional. We are grateful as well to the state, overseas, and university libraries, the Australian War Memorial, and other archives, as well as the various media organisations and individuals, especially Hamish and Elizabeth Lindsay, who provided many of the *Companion*'s photographs.

Although this book is not in any sense authorised by the High Court, the Court itself provided invaluable assistance. We thank the Chief Justice and Justices and staff at the Court, particularly Chris Doogan, Carolyn Rogers, Lex Howard, Elisa Harris, Jacqueline Elliott, Rosemary Nicholson, and Janet Saleh for allowing our research assistants access to the Court's archives, for their comments on draft entries, and for their general support. Many of the Justices' associates, former associates, and other staff also provided assistance, particularly with the table of High Court associates. We also thank Kate Penhallurick for the work she did on the table of associates and Colin Fong for his advice and assistance with tables, citations, and proofreading.

Our publishers at Oxford University Press—Heather Fawcett, her predecessors Ray O'Farrell and Peter Rose, and our Managing Editor, Geraldine Corridon—were all sources of sound and helpful advice, and we thank them for their commitment, their goodwill, and their professionalism. Our OUP editor, Trischa Baker, worked closest to the coalface and consequently was in the greatest danger of editorial explosions, but she came through with great aplomb and rescued us from collapsing metaphors and other stylistic infelicities. We thank the entire team at Oxford, including the Delegates in the UK, who gave their consent to our joining the prestigious *Oxford Companion* series.

Individually, Michael Coper would like to thank Judy Jones for her personal sacrifice in supporting his work on this book, and George Williams would like to thank Emma Armson for her support and encouragement.

The Companion was made possible by generous grants from the Australian Research Council and the National Council for the Centenary of Federation, and by further financial and moral support from the Faculty of Law at ANU.

Contributors to the Companion

Margaret Allars
    Professor of Law, University of Sydney
        Entry: Writs

Nicholas Aroney
    Lecturer, School of Law, University of Queensland
        Entry: Implied constitutional rights: implications and inferences

Rosalind Atherton
    Professor and Head of the Division of Law, Macquarie University
        Entries: Deane, William Patrick; Succession law

Philip Ayres
    Associate Professor of English Literature, Monash University
        Entry: Dixon diaries

Peter Bailey
    Adjunct Professor of Law, ANU
        Entry: Civil liberties

Belinda Baker
    Legal Research Officer to the Solicitor-General for NSW
        Entries: Brennan, (Francis) Gerard; Strict liability

Peter Bayne
    Reader in Law, ANU
        Entries: Evatt, Herbert Vere; Northern Land Council Case; Uniform Tax Cases

Bryan Beaumont
    Judge, Federal Court of Australia
        Entries: Federal Court of Australia; Hierarchy of courts

Larissa Behrendt
    Professor of Law and Indigenous Studies and Director, Jumbunna Indigenous
    House of Learning, UTS
        Entries: Kruger v Commonwealth; Movement, freedom of

Juliet Behrens
    Senior Lecturer, Faculty of Law, ANU
        Entry: Family law

Andrew Bell

Barrister, NSW
Entries: Conflict of laws; Inter-State Commission

David Bennett

Solicitor-General for the Commonwealth
Entries: Argument before the Court; Orders; Overruling

JM Bennett

Historian and Barrister, NSW
Entries: Establishment of Court; Reporting of decisions

Tony Blackshield

Emeritus Professor of Law, Macquarie University; Adjunct Professor of Law, ANU
and UNSW

*Entries: Australia Acts; Authoritative legal materials; Bill of Rights; Caledonian
Collieries Cases; Constitutional basis of Court; Contract and tort; Cormack v
Cope; Corporations power; Counsel, notable; Deane, William Patrick; Dismissal of
1975; DOGS Case; Engineers Case; Federal Roads Case; Free Speech Cases;
Fullagar, Wilfred Kelsham; Inter se questions; Jacobs, Kenneth Sydney; Judicial
reasoning; Jurimetrics; Knox Court and arbitration; Litigants, notable, 1903–1945;
Litigants, notable, 1945–2001; Melbourne Corporation v Barry; 'Murphy affair';
Namatjira v Raabe; Obiter dicta; Papua and New Guinea; Parker v The Queen;
Precedent; Privy Council; Puisne Justices; Ratio decidendi; Realism; Removal of
Justices; Sankey v Whitlam; Seat of Court; Sovereignty; Tasmanian Dam Case;
Trident General Insurance v McNiece; Viro v The Queen*

Geoffrey Bolton

Emeritus Professor of History, Murdoch University and Edith Cowan University
Entry: Barton, Edmund

Keven Booker

Lecturer, Faculty of Law, UNSW
Entries: Reserved state powers; Trade and commerce power

Stephen Bottomley

Professor of Law and Director, Centre for Commercial Law, ANU
Entry: Corporations law

Frank Brennan

Director of Uniya (Jesuit Social Justice Centre); Adjunct Fellow, ANU; Visiting
Fellow, UNSW
Entry: Race

Gerard Brennan

Former Chief Justice of the High Court of Australia
*Entries: Bench, composition of; Common law; Decision-making process; Judicial
oath; Litigants in person; Values*

Simon Bronitt

Reader in Law, ANU
Entry: Sex

David Brown

Professor of Law, UNSW
Entry: Jury trial

Alex Bruce
Lecturer, Faculty of Law, ANU
Entry: Trade practices law

David Buchanan
Senior Counsel, NSW
Entry: X v Commonwealth

Henry Burmester
Chief General Counsel, Australian Government Solicitor
Entries: Interveners and amici curiae; Matters; Presumption of constitutionality; Standing

Fiona Burns
Senior Lecturer, Faculty of Law, University of Sydney
Entries: Muschinski v Dodds; Unconscionability; Undue influence

Christopher Caleo
Barrister, Victoria
Entry: David Securities v Commonwealth Bank

Ian Callinan
Justice, High Court of Australia
Entries: Ceremonial sittings; Webb, William Flood

Peter Cane
Professor of Law, Research School of Social Sciences, ANU
Entry: Proximity

Gerard Carney
Associate Professor of Law, Bond University
Entries: Attorney-General, role of; Parliamentary process, intervention in

John Carter
Professor of Commercial Law, University of Sydney
Entry: Restitution

Donald Chalmers
Professor and Dean of the Faculty of Law, University of Tasmania
Entry: Trusts

Hilary Charlesworth
Professor of Law and Director, Centre for International and Public Law, ANU
Entries: International law; Koowarta's Case; Stephen, Ninian Martin

Michael Chesterman
Emeritus Professor of Law, UNSW
Entry: Contempt

Michael Coper
Dean of Law and Robert Garran Professor of Law, ANU
Entries: Accountability; Amendment of Constitution; Cole v Whitfield; Concurring judgments; Constitutional law; Counsel, notable; Democracy, Court's role in; Dennis Hotels v Victoria; Excise duties; Intergovernmental immunities; Interstate trade and commerce, freedom of; Joint judgments and separate judgments; Marbury v Madison; National unity; Outcomes, effect of procedure on; Political institution, Court as; Privy Council; Territory Senators Cases; Tied vote

Zelman Cowen
Former Governor-General of Australia
Entries: Deakin, Alfred; Isaacs, Isaac Alfred; Latham, John Greig

Edward Cox
Barrister, NSW
Entry: Admiralty

Rebecca Craske
Associate, McKinsey & Company, NSW
Entries: Business of Court; Judgment production; Open court; Retirement of Justices; Tipstaves

Gregory Craven
Professor and Dean of Law, University of Notre Dame Australia, WA
Entry: Convention Debates

Robin Creyke
Reader in Law, ANU
Entries: Green v Daniels; Kioa v West; Legitimate expectation; Veterans' entitlements

Tina Crisafulli
Solicitor, Moray & Agnew, NSW
Entry: Conciliation and arbitration

Mary Crock
Senior Lecturer, Faculty of Law, University of Sydney
Entries: Immigration law; Immigration power

Gino Dal Pont
Senior Lecturer, Faculty of Law, University of Tasmania
Entry: Trusts

Erin Daly
Associate Professor of Law, Widener University
Entry: United States Supreme Court

Geoffrey Davies
Judge, Queensland Court of Appeal
Entry: Reasonableness

James Davis
Emeritus Professor of Law, ANU
Entries: Burnie Port Authority v General Jones; Donoghue v Stevenson; Occupiers' liability

Jessica Milner Davis
Visiting Fellow, Faculty of Arts and Social Sciences, UNSW
Entry: Humour

Bruce Debelle
Judge, Supreme Court of SA
Entry: Windeyer, (William John) Victor

Gim Del Villar
Associate to Justice Ian Callinan, High Court of Australia
Entries: Circuit system; Connotation and denotation; Originalism; 'Quick and Garran'

Katrine Del Villar
Research Specialist, Commonwealth Parliamentary Library
Entry: Court of Disputed Returns

Annemarie Devereux
Researcher, Centre for International and Public Law, Faculty of Law, ANU;
Human Rights Unit, UN Transitional Administration in East Timor
Entry: International Bill of Rights

John Devereux
Professor of Law, University of Queensland
Entry: Health law

Michelle Dillon
Solicitor, Baker & McKenzie, London
Entry: Mason Court

Francesca Dominello
Lionel Murphy Scholar, UNSW; Research Assistant, High Court Project, ANU
Entries: Background of Justices; Colonialism; Constitutional basis of Court; Contract and tort; Hannah v Dalgarno; Intergovernmental immunities and judicial reasoning; Papua and New Guinea; Popular culture; Popular images of Court; Race; Seat of Court; Sovereignty; Stereotypes

Christopher Doogan
Chief Executive and Principal Registrar, High Court of Australia
Entries: Administration of Court; Appeal book; Archives

Roger Douglas
Senior Lecturer, School of Law and Legal Studies, La Trobe University
Entry: Latham Court

John Doyle
Chief Justice, Supreme Court of SA
Entry: Mason Court

Peter Durack
Former Commonwealth Attorney-General
Entries: Administration of Court; Attorneys-General; Canberra, Court's move to; High Court of Australia Act; Wilson, Ronald Darling

John Eddy
Director, Australian Institute of Jesuit Studies, ACT
Entry: World War I

James Edelman
Lecturer in Law, St Edmund Hall, Oxford University
Entry: Toohey, John Leslie

Sandra Egger
Associate Professor of Law, UNSW
Entry: Criminal law defences

MP Ellinghaus
Associate Professor of Law, University of Melbourne
Entry: Contract law

Jacqueline Elliott
Librarian, High Court of Australia
Entry: Library

Simon Evans

Lecturer, Faculty of Law, University of Melbourne

Entries: Appointment of Justices; Inconsistency between Commonwealth and state laws

Mark Findlay

Professor of Criminal Justice, Faculty of Law, University of Sydney; Research Professor, Nottingham Law School

Entry: Criminology

Henry Finlay

Associate Professor of Law, University of Tasmania

Entry: Marriage and divorce powers

Simon Fisher

Associate Professor of Law, University of Queensland

Entry: Commercial law

Don Fleming

Professor of Law, University of Canberra

Entry: Social justice

Colin Fong

Associate Lecturer and Librarian, ATAX, UNSW; Research Librarian, University of Sydney Law Library

Entry: Citation of cases

Bill Ford

Dean of Law, University of WA

Entry: Labour relations law

Ian Freckelton

Barrister, Victoria; Adjunct Professor of Law, Monash University and La Trobe University

Entry: Expert evidence

Graham Fricke

Adjunct Professor of Law, Deakin University; Visting Professor of Law, University of Queensland

Entries: Counsel, notable; Gavan Duffy, Frank; Gavan Duffy Court; Isaacs Court; Knox, Adrian; Knox Court; Litigants, notable, 1903–1945; Litigants, notable, 1945–2001; Powers, Charles; Starke, Hayden Erskine; Williams, Dudley

Stephen Gageler

Senior Counsel, NSW

Entries: Brennan, (Francis) Gerard; Counsel, role of; Jurisdiction; Legalism

Brian Galligan

Professor and Head of Political Science, University of Melbourne

Entries: Political parties; Prime Ministers; World War II

Gertrude Gerard

Poet, NSW

Entry: AAP Case

Harry Gibbs

Former Chief Justice of the High Court of Australia

Entries: Business of Court; External affairs power: a critical analysis; Griffith, Samuel Walker; Law-making role: further reflections; Reform of Court: reflections

James Gillespie
Senior Lecturer, Department of Politics, Macquarie University
Entry: Federalism, Court's conception of

Murray Gleeson
Chief Justice of the High Court of Australia
Entry: Role of Court

Phillip Goad
Associate Professor and Reader in Architectural History and Theory, University of Melbourne
Entries: Architecture of Court building; Architecture of Court building: an analysis

John Goldring
Judge, District Court of NSW; Emeritus Professor of Law, University of Wollongong
Entry: Privy Council

Jeffrey Goldsworthy
Professor of Law, Monash University
Entry: Positivism

Morris Graham
Historian, NSW
Entry: Piddington, Albert Bathurst

Janice Gray
Lecturer, Faculty of Law, UTS
Entry: Men

Natalie Gray
Centre for Values, Ethics and Law in Medicine, University of Sydney
Entry: Toohey, John Leslie

Regina Graycar
Professor of Law, University of Sydney; Commissioner, NSW Law Reform Commission
Entries: Women; Women's work

Bhajan Grewal
Professor of Economics, Victoria University
Entry: Economy, impact of Court's decisions on

Gavan Griffith
Queen's Counsel, Victoria; former Commonwealth Solicitor-General
Entries: Cross-vesting; Solicitors-General

Katherine Guilfoyle
Barrister, NSW
Entry: McHugh, Michael Hudson

Richard Haigh
Senior Lecturer, School of Law, Deakin University
Entry: Judgment production

Elisa Harris
Deputy Registrar, High Court of Australia
Entries: Practice directions; Sittings of Court

Nicholas Hasluck
Judge, Supreme Court of WA; Novelist
Entries: Callinan, Ian David Francis; Kisch Case

Douglas Hassall
Senior Lecturer, Legal Workshop, ANU; Barrister, ACT
Entries: High Court Rules; Ziems v Prothonotary of the Supreme Court of NSW

Kenneth Hayne
Justice, High Court of Australia
Entries: Dixon, Owen; Menzies, Douglas Ian

Robert Heath
Barrister, Victoria
Entry: Buildings

Christine Henchman
Editor, CCH, NSW
Entry: Costs

Catherine Henry
Solicitor, Craddock Murray Neumann, NSW
Entry: Rogers v Whitaker

JD Heydon
Judge, NSW Court of Appeal
Entry: Evidence law

Graeme Hill
Counsel Assisting the Commonwealth Solicitor-General
Entry: Hayne, Kenneth Madison

Russell Hogg
Lecturer, School of Sociology and Justice Studies, University of Western Sydney
Entries: Chamberlain Case; Criminal procedure; Men

Ian Holloway
Professor and Dean of Law, University of Western Ontario
Entries: Aickin, Keith Arthur; Court attire; Higgins, Henry Bournes; House of Lords; Privative clauses

Christopher Horan
Barrister, Victoria
Entry: Territories

Bryan Horrigan
Professor of Law and Director, National Centre for Corporate Law and Policy Research, University of Canberra
Entries: Amadio's Case; Jurisprudence; Literalism; Natural law

Lex Howard
Marshal, High Court of Australia
Entries: Budget of Court; Courtrooms; Transcripts of argument

Helen Irving
Senior Lecturer, Faculty of Law, University of Sydney
Entries: Framers of the Constitution; Garran, Robert Randolph

David Jackson
Queen's Counsel, NSW
Entries: Brennan Court; Gibbs, Harry Talbot; Leave to appeal

Frank Jones
Magistrate, Victorian Magistrates' Court; former Registrar, High Court of Australia
Entries: Chief Executive and Principal Registrar; Court crier; Information technology; Marshal; Tipstaves; Unreported judgments; Vexatious litigants

Judith Jones
Lecturer, Faculty of Law, ANU
Entry: Environmental law

Henrik Kalowski
Solicitor, Mallesons Stephen Jaques, NSW
Entry: Gaudron, Mary Genevieve

Bryan Keon-Cohen
Queen's Counsel, Victoria
Entry: Mabo: counsel's perspective

Bruce Kercher
Professor of Law, Macquarie University
Entries: Deane, William Patrick; Reception of English law

Michael Kirby
Justice, High Court of Australia
Entries: Chambers; Etiquette; Ex tempore judgments; Kitto, Frank Walters; McTiernan, Edward Aloysius; Reserved judgments

Jeremy Kirk
Solicitor, Freehills, NSW
Entry: Proportionality

Linda Kirk
Lecturer, Law School, University of Adelaide
Entries: Boilermakers Case; Judicial power

Michael Kobetsky
Visiting Fellow, Faculty of Law, ANU
Entry: Taxation law

Rick Krever
Professor of Law, Deakin University
Entry: Taxation law

HP Lee
Professor of Law, Monash University
Entry: Cigamatic Case

Mark Leeming
Barrister, NSW
Entry: Fact finding

John Lehane
Judge, Federal Court of Australia
Entry: Gummow, William Montague Charles

Andrew Leigh
Frank Knox Scholar, John F Kennedy School of Government, Harvard University
Entries: Associates; Tenure

Geoffrey Lindell
Professor of Law, University of Melbourne
Entries: Justiciability; Nationhood, Court's role in building

Hamish Lindsay
Senior Technical Officer, High Court of Australia
Entries: Seal of Court; Symbolism of Court building

Katherine Lindsay
Lecturer, Faculty of Law, University of Newcastle
Entry: Discrimination

Stephen Lloyd
Barrister, NSW
Entry: Acquisition of property

Harold Luntz
Professor of Law, University of Melbourne
Entries: Damages; Tort law

Andrew Lynch
Lecturer, Faculty of Law, UTS
Entry: Dissenting judgments

Mark Mackrell
Solicitor, Norton White, NSW
Entry: Jacobs, Kenneth Sydney

Graham Maddox
Professor of Political Science, University of New England
Entry: Representative government

Laurence Maher
Barrister, Victoria
Entries: Cold War; Menzies, Robert Gordon

David Malcolm
Chief Justice, Supreme Court of WA
Entries: Legal profession, Court's relationship with; State Supreme Courts

Desmond Manderson
Associate Professor of Law and Director, Julius Stone Institute of Jurisprudence, University of Sydney
Entry: Theory and legitimacy

Henry Mares
Associate Lecturer, Faculty of Law, ANU
Entry: Sex

Anthony Mason
Former Chief Justice of the High Court of Australia
Entries: Barwick Court; Chief Justice, role of; Comparison with other courts; Form and substance; Griffith Court; Judiciary Act; Law-making role: reflections; Personal relations: a personal reflection; Policy considerations; Reform of Court: further reflections

Keith Mason
President, NSW Court of Appeal
Entries: Prospective overruling; Restitution

Penelope Mathew
Senior Lecturer, Faculty of Law, ANU
Entry: War Crimes Act Case

Russell Mathews (died 1 March 2000)
Former Director of the Centre for Research on Federal Financial Relations, ANU
Entry: Economy, impact of Court's decisions on

Robert McCorquodale
Professor of International Law and Human Rights, University of Nottingham
Entry: Teoh's Case

John McDonald
Former Head of Australian Art, National Gallery of Australia
Entry: Artworks of Court

Leighton McDonald
Senior Lecturer, Faculty of Law, ANU
Entry: Rule of law

Frank McGrath
Former Chief Judge of the Compensation Court of NSW
Entry: Workers' compensation

John Kennedy McLaughlin
Master, Supreme Court of NSW
Entry: Walsh, Cyril Ambrose

Stephen McLeish
Barrister, Victoria
Entry: Church and state

John McMillan
Alumni Professor of Administrative Law, ANU
Entries: Administrative law; Natural justice; Teoh's Case: some quandaries

Rob McQueen
Professor and Head of School of Law, Victoria University
Entries: History, Court's use of

Michael Meehan
Professor and Head of School of Literary and Communication Studies, Deakin University
Entries: Judicial style; Languages; Metaphor

Chris Merritt
Law Correspondent, *Australian Financial Review*
Entry: Public awareness

Andrew Mitchell
WM Tapp Scholar, Faculty of Law, University of Cambridge
Entry: Military justice

Jenny Morgan
Associate Professor of Law, University of Melbourne
Entries: Equality; Rights, critique of; Women

Marcia Neave
Professor of Law, Monash University
Entry: Land law

Garth Nettheim
Emeritus Professor of Law, UNSW
Entries: Mabo; Wik

Eddy Neumann
Solicitor, Craddock Murray Neumann, NSW
Entry: Background of Justices

David O'Brien
Solicitor, Minter Ellison, Queensland
Entry: Nauru

Graeme Orr
Lecturer, Law School, Griffith University
Entry: Electoral law

Rosemary Owens
Senior Lecturer, Law School, University of Adelaide
Entry: Characterisation

Andrew Palmer
Senior Lecturer, Law School, University of Melbourne; Barrister, Victoria
Entry: Causation

Archana Parashar
Associate Professor of Law, Macquarie University
Entry: Men

Christine Parker
Senior Lecturer, Faculty of Law, UNSW
Entry: Leeth v Commonwealth

Patrick Parkinson
Professor of Law, University of Sydney
Entry: Equity

Haig Patapan
Research Fellow, Key Centre for Ethics, Law, Justice, and Governance, Griffith University
Entries: Democracy, Court's conception of; Liberalism

Glenn Patmore
Lecturer, Faculty of Law, University of Melbourne
Entry: Disability discrimination

Dennis Pearce
Emeritus Professor of Law, ANU
Entry: Statutory interpretation

Rachel Pepper
Barrister, NSW
Entry: Judicial notice

Nye Perram
Barrister, NSW
Entries: Appearance, right of; Full Court; Superior court

Susan Phillips
Barrister, NSW
Entry: Native title

James Popple
Commonwealth Attorney-General's Department; Visiting Fellow, Faculty of Engineering and Information Technology, ANU
Entries: Information technology; Number of Justices; Seniority; Vexatious litigants

Graeme Powell
Manuscript Librarian, National Library of Australia
Entry: Private papers

Joan Priest
Biographer, Queensland
Entry: Gibbs, Harry Talbot

Susan Priest
Research Scholar, Macquarie University; Research Assistant, High Court Project, ANU
Entries: Bank Nationalisation Case; Irish Envoys Case; Jehovah's Witnesses Case; Strike of 1905

Richard Refshauge
Director of Public Prosecutions, ACT; Adjunct Professor of Law, ANU
Entry: Criminal law

Alexander Reilly
Senior Lecturer, Department of Law and Justice, Macquarie University
Entry: Cultural diversity

Henry Reynolds
Historian, Tasmania
Entry: Mabo: a historical perspective

Sam Ricketson
Professor of Law, University of Melbourne
Entries: Copyright; Patents and designs; Trade marks

Pauline Ridge
Lecturer, Faculty of Law, ANU
Entries: Garcia v National Australia Bank; Yerkey v Jones

Alan Robertson
Senior Counsel, NSW
Entries: Procedure; Remittal of cases from Court; Removal of cases into Court

Andrew Robertson
Senior Lecturer, Faculty of Law, University of Melbourne
Entries: Estoppel; Waltons Stores v Maher

Declan Roche
Lecturer in Law, London School of Economics
Entry: Dietrich v The Queen

Carolyn Rogers
Senior Registrar, High Court of Australia
Entries: Directions hearings; High Court Rules

Dennis Rose
Special Counsel, Blake Dawson Waldron, ACT
Entry: Leeth v Commonwealth: a critical analysis

Kim Rubenstein
Senior Lecturer, Faculty of Law, University of Melbourne
Entry: Citizenship

Peter H Russell
Emeritus Professor of Political Science, University of Toronto
Entry: Mabo: political consequences

Martha Rutledge
Research Editor, *Australian Dictionary of Biography*
Entries: Knox, Adrian; O'Connor, Richard Edward; Taylor, Alan Russell

Ronald Sackville
Judge, Federal Court of Australia
Entry: Activism

Cheryl Saunders
Professor of Law, University of Melbourne
Entries: Commonwealth–state relations; Dawson, Daryl Michael; Melbourne Corporation Case; Nationhood power

Hugh Selby
Senior Lecturer, Legal Workshop, ANU; Barrister, ACT
Entry: Expert evidence

Bradley Selway
Solicitor-General for SA
Entry: Responsible government

Michael Sexton
Solicitor-General for NSW
Entry: Defamation law

John Seymour
Adjunct Professor of Law, ANU
Entries: Children; Marion's Case

Robin Sharwood
Professorial Fellow, Faculty of Law, University of Melbourne
Entry: Fullagar, Wilfred Kelsham

Simon Sheller
Judge, NSW Court of Appeal
Entries: Kirby, Michael Donald; Rich, George Edward; Williams, Dudley

Amelia Simpson
Lecturer, Faculty of Law, ANU
Entries: Annual Reports; Attorneys-General; Litigants, notable, 1903–1945; Litigants, notable, 1945–2001; Personal relations; Reform of Court; Research assistance; World War I

Troy Simpson
Research Assistant, High Court Project, ANU
Entries: Appointments that might have been; Circuit system; Conferences; Counsel, notable; Humour; Irish Envoys Case; Personal relations; Tait's Case

Rob Sitch
Writer, Director, and Producer, Victoria
Entry: Castle, The

Russell Smyth
Senior Lecturer, Faculty of Business and Economics, Monash University
Entries: Citations by Court; Extrinsic materials

David Solomon
Contributing Editor, *Courier Mail*, Queensland
Entries: Federalism, impact of Court's decisions on; Political impact of Court's decisions; Public opinion

Peta Spender
Reader in Law, ANU
Entry: Civil procedure

Jim Staples
Former Deputy President of the Australian Conciliation and Arbitration Commission
Entry: Socialism

Ninian Stephen
Former Governor-General of Australia; former Justice, High Court of Australia
Entries: Independence, judicial; Televising of proceedings

Andrew Stewart
Professor of Law, Flinders University
Entry: Employment law

Cameron Stewart
Lecturer, Department of Law and Justice, Macquarie University
Entry: Deane, William Patrick

Daniel Stewart
Lecturer, Faculty of Law, ANU
Entries: Economics; Victoria Park Racing v Taylor

Adrienne Stone
Senior Lecturer, Faculty of Law, ANU
Entries: Constitutional interpretation; Implied constitutional rights; Political communication, freedom of

Margaret Stone
Judge, Federal Court of Australia
Entry: Property

Jennifer Taylor
Adjunct Professor, School of Design and Built Environment, Queensland University of Technology
Entry: Madigan, Colin Frederick

Anthony Thew
Adjunct Associate Professor of Law, University of Canberra
Entry: Judges' notebooks

James Thomson
Legal Officer, Attorney-General's Department, WA
Entries: Biographies and biographical writing; Commentators and commentary; Extra-judicial writings of the Justices

Margaret Thornton
Professor of Law and Legal Studies, La Trobe University
Entries: Feminism; Ideology; Women practitioners

Michael Tilbury
Professor of Law, University of Melbourne
Entry: Remedies

Sydney Tilmouth
Queen's Counsel, SA
Entry: Disqualification of Justices

John Toohey
Former Justice, High Court of Australia
Entries: Aboriginal peoples; Fiduciary obligations

Bruce Topperwien
Executive Officer, Veterans' Review Board
Entry: Foreign precedents

Anne Twomey
Lecturer, Faculty of Law, University of Sydney
Entry: Gibbs Court

Tania Voon
LLM Candidate, Harvard University
Entry: Military justice

Bret Walker
Senior Counsel, NSW
Entries: Cost of litigation; Gleeson, (Anthony) Murray

Kristen Walker
Senior Lecturer, Faculty of Law, University of Melbourne
Entries: Advisory opinions; Mason, Anthony Frank; Sexual preference

Jack Waterford
Editor, *Canberra Times*
Entries: Criticism of the Court; Media and the Court; Tuckiar v The King

Penelope Watson
Lecturer, Department of Law and Justice, Macquarie University
Entry: Strict liability

John Waugh
Senior Lecturer, Faculty of Law, University of Melbourne
Entry: State constitutions

Phillipa Weeks
Professor of Law, ANU
Entries: Owen, William Francis Langer; Patrick Stevedores Case

Fiona Wheeler
Senior Lecturer, Faculty of Law, ANU
Entries: Non-judicial functions; Separation of powers

Gough Whitlam
Former Prime Minister of Australia
Entry: Whitlam era

Graeme Wiffen
Senior Lecturer, Centre for Environmental Law, Macquarie University
Entry: Consumer law

Ernst Willheim
Visiting Scholar, Faculty of Law, ANU
Entry: Collective responsibility

George Williams
Anthony Mason Professor of Law and Director, Gilbert & Tobin Centre of Public
Law, UNSW; Barrister, NSW
*Entries: Bank Nationalisation Case; Communist Party Case; Defence power; Due
process; Express constitutional rights; Hindmarsh Island Bridge Case; Jehovah's
Witnesses Case; Judicial review; Langer v Commonwealth; Leeth v Commonwealth*

John Williams
Senior Lecturer, Law School, University of Adelaide
Entries: Barton, Edmund; Inglis Clark, Andrew; Murphy, Lionel Keith

George Winterton
Professor of Law, UNSW
Entries: Barwick, Garfield Edward John; Remuneration of Justices

Stanley Yeo
Professor of Law, Southern Cross University
Entry: Criminology

Leslie Zines
Emeritus Professor of Law, ANU; Visiting Fellow, Research School of Social
Sciences, ANU
*Entries: Commonwealth legislative powers; Depression of the 1930s; Dixon Court;
External affairs power; Gleeson Court*

How to Use the Companion

Entries in the Companion are arranged in alphabetical order according to their headword. This is self-explanatory for most entries. The headword for a case entry, however, may be the actual name of the case (for example, *Cole v Whitfield*) or the name by which it has become popularly known (for example, *Tasmanian Dam Case*). Case names are generally abbreviated. The year in brackets following the case name is the year in which the case was decided. Full citations appear in the table of cases, which includes all cases referred to in the book.

Words or phrases in **bold type** are cross-references to other entries, generally made on the first occurrence of the reference in a particular entry. The words in bold type might appear in a slightly different form in the course of the narrative of an entry, but the reference is always sufficiently similar to the headword to enable the entry to be located easily. The cross-referencing is also a guide to interesting groups of complementary entries.

Names of Acts are given in italics only on the first appearance in a particular entry. For subsequent references, italics are not used and the date and jurisdiction are omitted.

Most entries include a selection of suggested further reading. These are given in an abbreviated form sufficient for readers to locate the work.

The subject index helps the reader to find entries that might have appeared in other guises (for example, **Outcomes, effect of procedure on** might equally have been **Procedure, effect on outcomes**). It also gathers together all references to a particular topic. These topics—subject areas, issues, or themes—characteristically span a number of entries, even if they also have their own primary entry. As with the cross-referencing, the subject index, as well as the separate name index, enables readers to explore alternative patterns that differ from the book's organisation by topic, in alphabetical order.

Throughout the book, individuals are referred to without honorifics. A separate list of honours awarded to Justices appears on page 741 for ready reference. Justices of the Court and others with their own entries are referred to by surname alone, unless a given name is necessary to avoid confusion (as, for example, with Douglas and Robert Menzies).

The list of abbreviations on page xxix includes all abbreviations used in the text, apart from the most commonplace. A separate list of abbreviations of court reports appears immediately before the table of cases on page 745.

Abbreviations

ABC	Australian Broadcasting Corporation
AC	Companion of the Order of Australia
ACT	Australian Capital Territory
ADB	*Australian Dictionary of Biography*
Adel L Rev	*Adelaide Law Review*
AFL	Australian Football League
AFLG	*Australian Feminist Law Journal*
A-G	Attorney-General
AIF	Australian Imperial Force
AJFL	*Australian Journal of Family Law*
AJLL	*Australian Journal of Labour Law*
AK	Knight of the Order of Australia
ALB	*Aboriginal Law Bulletin*
ALJ	*Australian Law Journal*
ALP	Australian Labor Party
Alt LJ	*Alternative Law Journal*
ANU	Australian National University
ANZAC	Australian and New Zealand Army Corps
ANZSILP	*Australia and New Zealand Society of International Law Proceedings*
AO	Officer of the Order of Australia
APLJ	*Australian Property Law Journal*
AQ	*Australian Quarterly*
AT Rev	*Australian Tax Review*
ATAX	Australian Taxation Studies Program
Aust Bar Gaz	*Australian Bar Gazette*
Aust Bar Rev	*Australian Bar Review*
Aust J Leg Hist	*Australian Journal of Legal History*
Aust Jnl of Corp Law	*Australian Journal of Corporate Law*
Aust Lib J	*Australian Library Journal*
Australian J of Pol & Hist	*Australian Journal of Politics and History*
b	born
BA	Bachelor of Arts
BCL	Bachelor of Civil Law
BEc	Bachelor of Economics
BHP	The Broken Hill Proprietary Co Ltd
Bond LR	*Bond Law Review*
BSc	Bachelor of Science

C&SLJ	*Company and Securities Law Journal*
Canb LR	*Canberra Law Review*
CB	Companion of the Order of the Bath
CBE	Companion of the Order of the British Empire
ch/chs	chapter/chapters
CICJ	*Current Issues in Criminal Justice*
CJ	Chief Justice
CLQ	*Commercial Law Quarterly*
CMF	Citizen Military Forces
CMG	Companion of the Order of St Michael and St George
Commonwealth LR	*Commonwealth Law Review*
Comp Labor Law J	*Comparative Labor Law Journal*
CP	Country Party
Crim LJ	*Criminal Law Journal*
Crim LR	*Criminal Law Review*
CSIRO	Commonwealth Scientific and Industrial Research Organisation
Cth	Commonwealth
d	died
D Univ	Doctor of the University
DC	District of Columbia
DSO	Distinguished Service Order
ed/eds	editor/editors
edn	edition
et al.	and others
FL Rev	*Federal Law Review*
GCB	Knight Grand Cross of the Order of the Bath
GCMG	Knight Grand Cross of the Order of St Michael and St George
GCVO	Knight Grand Cross of the Royal Victorian Order
GLR	*Griffith Law Review*
HMAS	His/Her Majesty's Australian Ship
HMS	His/Her Majesty's Ship
ICLQ	*International and Comparative Law Quarterly*
Imp	Imperial
Int'l J Soc L	*International Journal of the Sociology of Law*
J	Justice
JBFLP	*Journal of Banking and Finance Law and Practice*
JCL	*Journal of Contract Law*
JCP	*Journal of Consumer Policy*
JCULR	*James Cook University Law Review*
JIR	*Journal of Industrial Relations*
JJA	*Journal of Judicial Administration*
JLIS	*Journal of Law and Information Science*
JSPTL	*Journal of the Society of Public Teachers of Law*
Jud Rev	Judicial Review
KBE	Knight Commander of the Order of the British Empire
KC	King's Counsel
KCMG	Knight Commander of the Order of St Michael and St George
Kt	Knight
LIC	*Law in Context*

LIJ	*Law Institute Journal*
LLB	Bachelor of Laws
LLD	Doctor of Laws
LLM	Master of Laws
LQR	*Law Quarterly Review*
LSB	*Legal Service Bulletin*
LSJ	*Law Society Journal*
MA	Master of Arts
MHR	Member of the House of Representatives
MLA	Member of the Legislative Assembly
MLC	Member of the Legislative Council
MLR	*Modern Law Review*
Mon LR	*Monash University Law Review*
MP	Member of Parliament
MULR	*Melbourne University Law Review*
NAA	National Archives of Australia
NCP	National Country Party
NLR	*National Law Review*
NPA	National Party of Australia
NSW	New South Wales
NT	Northern Territory
NYULR	*New York University Law Review*
NZ	New Zealand
OM	Order of Merit
Osgoode Hall LJ	*Osgoode Hall Law Journal*
PC	Privy Counsellor
PhD	Doctor of Philosophy
PLR	*Public Law Review*
PNG	Papua New Guinea
QC	Queen's Counsel
Qld	Queensland
QUTLR	*Queensland University of Technology Law Journal*
RAAF	Royal Australian Air Force
RAF	Royal Air Force
SA	South Australia/South Australian
SC	Senior Counsel
SS	Steamship
Syd LR	*Sydney Law Review*
TAB	Totalizator Agency Board
Tas	Tasmania
Texas LR	*Texas Law Review*
TLJ	*Torts Law Journal*
Tort L Rev	*Tort Law Review*
TPLJ	*Trade Practices Law Journal*
UAP	United Australia Party
UBCLR	*University of British Columbia Law Review*
UK	United Kingdom
UN	United Nations
UNESCO	United Nations Educational, Scientific and Cultural Organisation
UNRRA	United Nations Relief and Rehabilitation Administration
UNSW	University of New South Wales

UNSWLJ	*University of New South Wales Law Journal*
UQLJ	*University of Queensland Law Journal*
US	United States
USA	United States of America
USSR	Union of Soviet Socialist Republics
U Tas LR	*University of Tasmania Law Review*
UTS	University of Technology, Sydney
UWAL Rev	*University of Western Australia Law Review*
Vic	Victoria
Vic Bar News	*Victorian Bar News*
vol/vols	volume/volumes
WA	Western Australia/Western Australian
WIPO	World Intellectual Property Organisation
Yale LJ	*Yale Law Journal*

A

AAP Case (1975). The *Social Welfare Commission Act* 1973 (Cth) was an initiative of the **Whitlam era**. It established a Social Welfare Commission to investigate community social welfare needs, review the implementation and costs of social welfare programs, and formulate 'a nationally integrated social welfare plan' on 'a regional basis with localized administration'. Discussion papers prepared by the Commission developed a controversial 'Australian Assistance Plan': an experimental exploration of the ways in which social services might be channelled through regional councils, and what social services might be involved. The plan divided Australia into 17 regions, ignoring state boundaries. It included some forms of social welfare for which the Commonwealth had express power under section 51(xxiii) and (xxiiiA) of the Constitution, but others for which it had no such power. Apart from the discussion papers and a 1974 set of 'Guidelines for Pilot Programme', the plan had no formal charter and no statutory authority.

In 1974, the annual budget legislation (the *Appropriation Act (No 1)* 1974–75 (Cth)) authorised expenditures from Consolidated Revenue of $4 667 794 000, to be applied for the purposes set out in a schedule. The schedule allocated $141 637 000 to the Department of Social Security, including (in Division 530):

4. Australian Assistance Plan
01. Grants to Regional Councils
for Social Development — $5 620 000
02. Development and evaluation expenses — $350 000
Total — $5 970 000

The state of Victoria and its **Attorney-General** sued in the High Court for a declaration that this appropriation was beyond the powers of the Parliament, and for an injunction against expenditure of the money. In the absence of any other legislative provision, the attack was focused solely on the three-line item in the Appropriation Act.

The only **precedent** on the validity of an appropriation of money, the *First Pharmaceutical Benefits Case* (1945), had been inconclusive. It had seemed to establish that section 81 of the Constitution, requiring moneys in Consolidated Revenue 'to be appropriated for the purposes of the Commonwealth', was impliedly a *grant* of power to appropriate money, and also a *limitation* on the power (since any appro-

priation must be 'for the purposes of the Commonwealth'). But Chief Justice **Latham** and **McTiernan** had held that this was really no limitation (since any purpose to which Parliament appropriated money was thereby conclusively identified as a Commonwealth purpose); **Starke** and **Williams** had held that the specific grants of Commonwealth power in the Constitution must be treated as an exhaustive dictionary of permissible Commonwealth purposes; and **Dixon** and **Rich** had expressed no final view.

The *AAP Case* did nothing to resolve this issue. McTiernan (the only member of the 1945 Court still sitting) again affirmed that the Parliament itself had unlimited power to identify Commonwealth purposes, and hence that the appropriation was valid. **Murphy** now joined him in that view. Chief Justice **Barwick** and **Gibbs** took the opposite view: the permissible 'purposes' were limited by the Constitution, and did not include the Australian Assistance Plan. Hence, in their view, Victoria's challenge should succeed.

Mason agreed with McTiernan and Murphy that the meaning of 'purposes' was unrestricted, and hence that the appropriation was valid; yet he voted with Barwick and Gibbs in favour of an injunction, since he distinguished between the bare *appropriation and expenditure* of money, and 'the Commonwealth's engagement in the activities in connexion with which the moneys are to be spent'. The former were necessarily valid; the latter must be confined to activities within constitutional power. **Jacobs** seemed willing to assume that the meaning of 'purposes' in section 81 was constitutionally limited, but nonetheless voted with McTiernan and Murphy because, on his analysis of the powers assigned to the Commonwealth executive government (and the legislative powers incidental thereto), there was ample power to support the Australian Assistance Plan.

The deadlock was broken by **Stephen**, who (alone) held that neither Victoria nor its Attorney-General had **standing** to raise the issue, since 'the mode of expenditure of federal revenue' was merely a housekeeping matter between the Commonwealth Parliament and the Commonwealth executive, of no concern to the states. Thus, for the different reasons given by McTiernan, Stephen, Jacobs and Murphy, Victoria's action failed. Later, in *Davis v Commonwealth* (1988), Mason and others suggested that despite its divergent reasoning the *AAP Case* was 'authority for the proposition that the validity of an appropriation act is not ordinarily susceptible to effective legal challenge'.

Despite their inconclusiveness on the immediate issue, the judgments in the *AAP Case* (especially those of Mason and Jacobs) are a rich source of exploratory ideas concerning the scope of Commonwealth legislative and executive powers, especially the prerogative power and the **nationhood power**. Because of the diversity of opinion and the elusiveness of the issues, the case is one of the most complex in Australian **constitutional law**.

GERTRUDE GERARD

Further Reading
Gertrude Gerard, 'A Reply to the *AAP Case*' (1977) 2 *UNSWLJ* 105
Tom Roper, 'Social Welfare' in Hugh Emy, Owen Hughes, and Race Mathews (eds), *Whitlam Re-visited* (1993) 185

Aboriginal peoples. The first reported decision of the High Court in which an Aboriginal person was a party to the proceedings seems to have been *Tuckiar v The King* (1934). This was an appeal against conviction for murder by a 'completely uncivilised aboriginal native' whose lack of familiarity with the English language was a relevant consideration in allowing his appeal (compare *Ngatayi v The Queen* (1980)). Interestingly, *Tuckiar* does not appear under the heading 'Aboriginals' in the index to the *Commonwealth Law Reports*. The likely explanation is that the term does not appear in the headnote to the report.

It was not until the enactment of the *Aboriginal Land Rights (Northern Territory) Act* 1976 (Cth) that the attention of the Court was directed to aspects of Aboriginal life and culture. The Act gave rise to a number of proceedings in the Court, usually by way of prerogative **writ** challenging a decision of the Aboriginal Land Commissioner (see, for example, the *Northern Land Council Case* (1981)). The questions formulated for answer in these proceedings generally turned on **statutory interpretation**. Nevertheless, the Act contained definitions such as 'Aboriginal tradition', 'traditional Aboriginal owners' and 'sacred site', which led the Court to consider the content of these definitions even where that content was not critical to the outcome (see, for example, *R v Toohey; Ex parte Meneling Station* (1982)).

The coming into operation of the Land Rights Act coincided with a number of proceedings brought to the Court by indigenous peoples asserting their rights, while the enactment of the *Racial Discrimination Act* 1975 (Cth) led to claims against **discrimination**. A related issue in these proceedings was whether the respective plaintiffs had **standing** to bring the actions. In *Onus v Alcoa* (1981), an appeal on the question of whether the plaintiffs had standing under the *Archaeological and Aboriginal Relics Preservation Act* 1972 (Vic) to restrain the respondent from interfering with sacred relics, the Court moved beyond the standard common law requirement of a special or particular interest to include the spiritual significance of the relics to the plaintiffs. In *Wacando v Commonwealth* (1981), **Gibbs** (with **Murphy** and **Aickin** agreeing) found that 'having regard to the special connexion which exists between the plaintiff and Darnley Island ... the plaintiff has the necessary standing to raise the question relating to the constitutional position of

Darnley Island' (see also *Coe v Commonwealth (No 1)* (1979); *Koowarta's Case* (1982)).

The Land Rights Act was the Commonwealth's response to the judgment of Justice Blackburn in *Milirrpum v Nabalco* (1971), which rejected any doctrine of communal **native title** in Arnhem Land. Such a title was held to have no place in a settled colony like Australia, except under express statutory provisions. Blackburn held himself bound by the view of the **Privy Council** in *Cooper v Stuart* (1889) that Australia was 'a tract of territory practically unoccupied, without settled inhabitants or settled law'. He held that though the plaintiffs had established a recognisable system of law, it did not give rise to a relationship between the clans and the land that was acceptable as a proprietary right or interest.

There was no appeal from the judgment of Justice Blackburn, and the Land Rights Act applied only to the Northern Territory. But in *Coe (No 1)*, **Jacobs** and Murphy, in separate judgments, treated the relationship between Aboriginal people and the land as a live issue. Thereafter, it was only a matter of time before the Court would be called upon to determine its vitality. The occasion arose in an action brought by Eddie Mabo and others against Queensland and the Commonwealth claiming that the Crown's **sovereignty** over the Murray Islands in Torres Strait was subject to the land rights of the Mir people, based upon local custom and traditional native title. After the action was launched, the Queensland Parliament passed legislation that applied to the Murray Islands and had the effect of extinguishing any title to the land that the plaintiffs may have had. In *Mabo (No 1)* (1988), the Court held the legislation invalid on the ground of **inconsistency** with the Racial Discrimination Act.

After lengthy proceedings in which the taking of evidence was **remitted** to the Supreme Court of Queensland, the Court declared that, putting certain areas to one side, the Meriam people were entitled as against the whole world to possession, occupation, use and enjoyment of the lands of the Murray Islands. The Court rejected the long-standing view of the Privy Council that Australia was, at the time of white settlement, *terra nullius* (see **Mabo** (1992)).

Although the Court's formal declaration was necessarily limited to the Murray Islands, the judgments of the majority made it clear that the Court was enunciating principles applicable to the whole of Australia. The decision was significant primarily for its recognition of native title, but also for its place in the development of an Australian **common law**, freed from decisions of the English courts that were thought to be wrong or not acceptable, especially where a rule expressed in those decisions seriously offended contemporary **values** of justice and human rights, and where the rule itself was not an essential doctrine of the legal system in this country.

Mabo had two consequences for the work of the Court, one direct and the other indirect. The direct consequence was that, having given recognition to native title, the Court was called upon to consider the implications of that recognition. Inevitably the focus was on the status of native title in regard to other interests in the land in question—or, viewed another way, the circumstances in which native title might be extinguished. In *Wik* (1996), the Court held that the grant of certain pastoral leases under Queensland legislation did not necessarily extinguish all incidents of native title in respect of the areas covered by those leases; but that if there was an inconsistency between the rights and interests conferred by native title and those conferred under the statutory grants, the former must yield to the latter. Issues relating to 'extinguishment' will no doubt continue to arise, for example in relation to the consequences of the **acquisition** of land by the Crown subsequent to a grant of fee simple (see *Fejo v Northern Territory* (1998)).

The other consequence of *Mabo* for the Court arose from the legislative action taken by the Commonwealth following that decision. The *Native Title Act* 1993 (Cth) has initiated a complex scheme for the recognition of native title and has established a very considerable structure to give effect to that recognition. Questions have come before the Court concerning the validity of that legislation and the manner of its operation (see *Native Title Act Case* (1995); *Waanyi Case* (1996)).

The common law incidents of native title, in particular traditional hunting and fishing rights, have not been explored before the Court. The Native Title Act itself recognises those rights and the Court has upheld the efficacy of that provision (*Yanner v Eaton* (1999)). In *Walden v Hensler* (1987), an Aboriginal man who was convicted of an offence under the *Fauna Conservation Act* 1974 (Qld) relied upon section 22 of the *Criminal Code Act* 1899 (Qld) to assert an honest claim of right based upon Aboriginal custom. But the various answers turned very much on the language of the Code; the wider issues await determination.

The Court has rejected the argument that Aboriginal customary criminal law in some way survived British settlement. In *Walker v NSW* (1994), Chief Justice **Mason** upheld the power of the NSW legislature to enact criminal statutes of application to all persons, Aboriginal and non-Aboriginal. The criminal law of England, which this country inherited, said Mason, did not accommodate an alternative body of law operating alongside it; nor did the Australian **criminal law**. Thus, the recognition of traditional title to land stands in a special position and is not itself the springboard for a more general recognition of customary law.

Until 1967, section 51(xxvi) of the Constitution excluded 'the aboriginal **race** in any State' from the power of the Commonwealth to make laws with respect to 'the people of any race for whom it is deemed necessary to make special laws'. As a result of the referendum held that year, the reference to the Aboriginal race was deleted, with the result that it became competent for the Commonwealth Parliament to make special laws with respect to the people of that race (see *Koowarta's Case*). It has not been doubted that section 51(xxvi) authorises the making of laws for the benefit of the people of a particular race. What has not been clear is whether the provision will, at any rate in the case of the Aboriginal people, support legislation that is to their detriment.

The issue came before the Court in the **Hindmarsh Island Bridge Case** (1998), but no definitive answer emerged from the reasons of the Justices. It is for the Parliament to say whether a particular law is 'necessary', but that is not to say that no brake exists upon the exercise of the power. **Gaudron** held that the test of constitutional validity of a law enacted under the provision is not whether it is a beneficial law, but rather whether it is reasonably capable of being viewed as appropriate and adapted to a real and relevant difference that the Parliament might reasonably judge to exist. **Gummow** and **Hayne** contemplated the possibility that the character of a law purportedly based upon the provision will be denied to a law enacted in manifest abuse of the power of judgment. Only **Kirby** held that a law that was detrimental to and adversely discriminatory against people of the Aboriginal race by reference to their race fell outside the provision. The other members of the Court, Chief Justice **Brennan** and **McHugh**, found it unnecessary to determine that issue. The question remains a live one.

Thus the Court, which for most of its life has not been presented with issues relevant to Aborigines and Torres Strait Islanders, has been in the last decade greatly immersed in such issues, whether they have come before it as constitutional questions, as problems of statutory construction, or as part of the development of an Australian common law.

JOHN TOOHEY

Further Reading
John McCorquodale, 'Aborigines in the High Court' (1983) 55(1) *Australian Quarterly* 104

Accountability. The High Court is the end of the road for litigants; there is no further appeal to another court. Moreover, its Justices are appointed until **retirement** age, are not subject to recall by their appointers, and, not being elected, are not subject to recall by the people. Both the finality of its decisions and the **independence** of its Justices are deliberate and appropriate. The demise in 1986 of the last remaining **Privy Council** appeals appropriately placed the High Court at the apex of the Australian **hierarchy of courts**. And the **role** of the Court could not be properly discharged unless it was fearlessly independent: insulated from the threat of the executive and impervious to its favours; at arm's length from litigants; and, more subtly but just as importantly, possessed of a robustly independent mindset. How, then, is the Court accountable, to whom is it accountable, and for what?

These questions relate mainly to the Court's work: its decisions, its **decision-making process**, and the way in which it manages its **business**. But there are issues of accountability also in relation to individual Justices and their personal behaviour. In this context, and as a counterbalance to their security of **tenure**, the Constitution provides a procedure—only once invoked but never concluded—for the **removal of Justices** in extreme cases (section 72). Removal requires 'proved misbehaviour or incapacity' and an address by both Houses of Parliament. Every system needs an ultimate safeguard of this kind, but the one skirmish with it in Australia raised difficult and contested issues about the nature of the requisite behaviour and how, and to whose satisfaction, it had to be proved (see '**Murphy affair**').

In the context of the Court's work, there are three broad ways in which the Court is accountable. First, although it is the final court of appeal, the Court's decisions, at least so far as they lay down general principles of law, are capable of being overridden in other ways—though not commonly, and not without difficulty.

Decisions on the **common law** and **statutory interpretation**, if perceived to be wrong or inconvenient or otherwise inappropriate, may be overridden by Parliament (though not so as to affect the result as between the immediate parties, as that would be an unconstitutional interference with **judicial power**). A recent example is the amendment to the *Crimes Act* 1914 (Cth) to allow 'entrapment' by law enforcement officers in certain circumstances, responding to and overriding the decision of the High Court in *Ridgeway v The Queen* (1995) to exclude, or to uphold the trial judge's discretion to exclude, evidence obtained by unlawful conduct.

Interestingly, the prospect of legislative correction has had different effects on different Justices: some have been inhibited from exercising a broad law-making function by notions of deference to the democratic process, while others have been emboldened by the knowledge that their errors can be corrected. Both views assume that legislative correction is a practical proposition; in truth, legislative correction is sporadic, uncertain and relatively rare, and the theoretical prospect that it might occur does not relieve the Court of its responsibility to discharge its **law-making role**.

Decisions on the Constitution are in a somewhat different position, in degree if not in kind. They too can be overridden, not by the Parliament alone, but by the electorate voting at a referendum to amend the Constitution, following the passage of a Bill through the Parliament (Constitution, section 128). This has failed more often than not (as in the attempt in 1951 to overturn the Court's decision that the Commonwealth lacked power to ban the Communist Party (*Communist Party Case* (1951)). However, it happened, in a sense, in 1946, when the Commonwealth was given enhanced power over social services following the Court's finding of a lack of that power in the *First Pharmaceutical Benefits Case* (1945), and in 1977, when a retiring age for federal judges was introduced, overcoming the holding some sixty years earlier in *Alexander's Case* (1918) that the Constitution gave federal judges life tenure. However, correction or modification by the electorate is so rare, and is generally acknowledged to be so difficult, that the Court has, for all practical purposes, the final say on the interpretation of the Constitution, and thus a special responsibility in this area. One consequence of this is that the Court has been more open in constitutional cases to self-correction (see **Overruling**).

Apart from second-guessing decisions of the Court, parliament and the executive may seek to scrutinise and even regulate the Court's decision-making process and the way it manages its business (see **Annual reports**; *Judiciary Act*; **Tied vote**). Undue interference with the Court's independence in these matters may involve an unlawful intrusion into the province of judicial power and breach the Constitution's **separation of powers**, but some measure of accountability may be achieved as a result of the parliament and the executive acting within the limits of their lawful powers.

The second way in which the Court is accountable for its work resides in the simple but sometimes overlooked fact that, except in rare cases, it conducts its work in **open court** and it publishes its reasons for decision. Those reasons are then open to public scrutiny, appraisal and **criticism**. Despite a limited statutory duty on many administrators to provide a statement of reasons, this makes the Court significantly different from administrative decision makers, whose accountability rests primarily in correction on review or appeal. Moreover, the Court's reasons are generally elaborated at some length and in the context of sustained argumentation.

This is perhaps the key to the Court's accountability. The open court principle and the obligation to publish reasons are central elements in the idea of the **rule of law** that underpins our democratic system of government. The efficacy of published reasons as an accountability measure depends, however, on the existence of a community of vigorous, informed and attentive critics and **commentators**—in academia, the profession and the **media**—and a responsive Court. Informed and constructive criticism generally has an impact over time (see, for example, *Cole v Whitfield* (1988)), though in terms of legal method, the Court has gone, and is likely to continue to go, through cycles of **legalism** and pragmatism, with neither touchstone satisfying the proponents of the other.

It might be thought insufficient to meet the needs of accountability to lock up the criticism and debate about the Court and its work in a small, professional club (although the **legal profession** is today increasingly broad and diverse). However, the Court's decisions are now available almost instantaneously on the Internet, and more commentary is appearing in the media, although the interest of the media in the Court and the quality of the commentary have waxed and waned over the years. Public scrutiny is easier than ever, though it must be sustained and informed to have an impact.

Barriers nevertheless remain to informed scrutiny, notably the accessibility and intelligibility of the judgments, especially to the lay reader. The issues are often complex, but accountability demands that Justices write clearly and precisely and avoid impenetrable prose, long-winded repetition and loose organisation. Even then, it may be difficult to gauge the combined effect of multiple judgments, and there may be a case for a collective statement about the effect of a decision (see **Collective responsibility**; **Joint judgments and separate judgments**). Some Australian courts have taken the step of employing a public information or media liaison officer; the High Court (though evidently not for want of trying: see **Annual reports**) has not.

The third way in which the Court is accountable for its work comes from within itself and its own sense of responsibility. Accountability comes with the **appointment** of persons of integrity, whose professional ethos and sense of public service have been developed over many years of experience in an ethical profession. All the structural safeguards in the world cannot guarantee this. To some extent, we cross our fingers and rely on the appointers to be diligent and responsible, and on the appointees, in the relative loneliness of their large and demanding decision-making responsibility, to find their wellsprings of action as much in internal as in external constraints.

MICHAEL COPER

Further Reading
Frank Kitto, 'Why Write Judgments?' (1992) 66 *ALJ* 787
James Spigelman, 'Seen to be Done: The Principle of Open Justice' (2000) 74 *ALJ* 290, 378

Acquisition of property. One of the most fertile sources of constitutional litigation in the High Court has been section 51(xxxi) of the Constitution. This section, popularised in the movie *The Castle*, provides that the federal Parliament may make laws with respect to 'the acquisition of **property** on just terms from any State or person for any purpose in respect of which the Parliament has power to make laws'. In construing this provision, the Court has had to strike a balance between, on the one hand, the power of the federal legislature to provide for the acquisition of property to achieve its public purposes and, on the other hand, the protection of the property rights of private citizens (and of the states) by ensuring that any acquisition effected by the Commonwealth be on just terms.

Section 51(xxxi) was included in the Constitution to remove any doubt that might otherwise have existed about whether the Commonwealth did have power to acquire property for its purposes (**Dixon** in *Grace Bros v Commonwealth* (1946)). With the inclusion of the guarantee of just terms, however, the dual function of the provision as a **Commonwealth legislative power** and an **express constitutional right** has presented significant challenges.

The Court has had to develop a theoretical basis to explain the relationship between section 51(xxxi) and the other heads of power in section 51. On the one hand, if property could be acquired under other heads of power, the just terms guarantee in section 51(xxxi) could be rendered nugatory. On the other hand, if section 51(xxxi) were the only power to acquire property, and if all such acquisitions had to be on just terms, it would inhibit the capacity of the Commonwealth properly to pursue its public functions, such as the exercise of its power to tax—which necessarily cannot be 'on just terms' if that means that for any government taking there should be an equivalent government payment. Indeed, it may be this example that has led some Justices to suggest that money does not constitute 'property' for the purpose of this provision at all (see, for example, **Dawson** and **Toohey** in *Mutual Pools v Commonwealth* (1994)).

In *Burton v Honan* (1952), Dixon (for the Court) asserted flatly that a law that effects the forfeiture of illegally imported goods is not a law that comes within the ambit of section 51(xxxi). Forfeiture is not an acquisition of property so that it can be put to some 'purpose'; rather it is a means of enforcing a law that falls directly within the ambit of section 51(i) (the **trade and commerce power**). Nine years later, in *A-G (Cth) v Schmidt* (1961), Dixon (again for the Court) sought to explain that section 51(xxxi) did not apply to a range of laws that authorised the acquisition of property for reasons other than its intended application to a Commonwealth purpose, such as a law for the sequestration of the property of a bankrupt.

The Court's current 'explanation' of section 51(xxxi) is that it should be taken to extract from the other heads of power in section 51 all power to acquire property, whether or not that property be for the use of the Commonwealth itself. However, this approach is based upon a rule of construction—the conferral of an express specific power subject to limitations indicates that the same power is not also conferred as an incident of other general powers with no such limitations—and because this is only a rule of construction,

it does not apply where the language or incidents of some other power necessarily evince a contrary intention. Such an intention is likely to be found where the provision of just terms, as in the case of taxation, would defeat the very object of the acquisition (*Nintendo v Centronics Systems* (1994); *Mutual Pools* (1994)).

In *Teori Tau v Commonwealth* (1969), the Court held that the grant of power in section 122 of the Constitution to make laws with respect to the **territories** (in that case **Papua and New Guinea**) was not subject to the limitation contained in section 51(xxxi). Consequently, it was thought that in the territories, as in the states, it was constitutionally possible for a legislature to acquire property without just terms. This view was brought into doubt by *Newcrest Mining v Commonwealth* (1997). While only three of the four majority Justices were prepared to overturn *Teori Tau*, a significant blow was dealt to its authority.

Insofar as section 51(xxxi) provides a guarantee of just terms, the Court has insisted that it not be construed narrowly. It has repeatedly determined that the guarantee should not be defeated by 'indirect means' or 'circuitous devices' (see, for example, *Minister for Army v Dalziel* (1944) and the **Bank Nationalisation Case** (1948)). Because the guarantee is expressed as a qualification or limitation upon power, a failure to observe it will result in the challenged law being invalid, rather than confer a right of compensation.

The ambit of the guarantee depends upon three key elements: the breadth of 'property'; the breadth of 'acquisition'; and what is constituted by 'just terms'.

The Court has often approved the following statement by Dixon in the *Bank Nationalisation Case* about the breadth to be given to the notion of 'property':

> [Section] 51(xxxi) is not to be confined pedantically to the taking of title by the Commonwealth to some specific estate or interest in land recognized at law or in **equity** and to some specific form of property in a chattel or chose in action similarly recognized, but … extends to innominate and anomalous interests and includes the assumption and indefinite continuance of exclusive possession and control for the purposes of the Commonwealth of any subject of property.

The following have been held by the Court to be capable of falling within the ambit of 'property': 'any tangible or intangible thing' (*Dalziel*); 'land belonging to any State with all the minerals or metals that may be contained in such land' (*Commonwealth v NSW* (1923)); vested common law causes of action (*Georgiadis v Australian & Overseas Telecommunications Corporation* (1994)), even when they are time barred, if there is a mechanism for extending the limitation period or otherwise removing the bar (*Commonwealth v Mewett* (1997)); statutory debts and **copyright** (*Australian Tape Manufacturers Association v Commonwealth* (1993)); a broadcaster's licence (*Australian Capital Television v Commonwealth* (1992)); a mining lease (*Newcrest Mining*); and the assets of a business (*Bank Nationalisation Case*).

The list of matters claimed to be 'property' but which the Court has declined to protect is quite small: the liabilities of a company (*Bank Nationalisation Case*); an organisation's right to have members (*R v Ludeke; Ex parte Australian*

Building Construction Employees & BLF (1985)); and some statutory rights conferred when there was no similar right at common law (*Allpike v Commonwealth* (1948); *Health Commission v Peverill* (1994)).

An issue of some moment that the Court will be called upon to address in the near future is whether **native title** rights fall within the ambit of 'property'. In *Mabo* (1992), **Deane** and **Gaudron** indicated that native title rights would fall within the ambit of protection provided by section 51(xxxi). **McHugh**, in *Newcrest Mining*, appeared to have a similar view. However, also in *Newcrest Mining*, Toohey, **Gummow** and **Kirby** all appeared to be of the view that section 51(xxxi) would not offer protection to native title holders whose rights had been acquired, because native title rights are inherently susceptible to extinguishment.

The jurisprudence on what constitutes an 'acquisition' is still in a state of development. The classic formulation is that an acquisition of property occurs only when the acquirer receives a proprietary interest (*R v Taylor; Ex parte Federated Ironworkers Association* (1949)). The rights acquired need not be the same as the rights lost (*Georgiadis*). While the Court has not expressly deserted the classic formulation, it is now said that an acquisition occurs when a person receives 'a direct benefit or financial gain' (*Georgiadis*) or 'an identifiable benefit or advantage relating to the ownership or use of property' (*Newcrest Mining*). The Court appears to have relaxed the classic formulation in a way that provides broader protection to the property rights of states and individuals.

It has been said that a 'mere' extinguishment of rights is not an acquisition (see, for example, the *Tasmanian Dam Case* (1983)), although it is not clear when an extinguishment of rights will be said to be a 'mere' extinguishment. It is likely to be so characterised if there is no apparent beneficiary from the extinguishment of rights (*Commonwealth v WMC Resources* (1998)). Conversely, where there is a beneficiary from a law effecting the extinguishment of rights, it will not generally be characterised as 'mere' extinguishment (*Newcrest Mining*). However, where an extinguishment of rights does benefit a party from at least one perspective but is still not favoured by that party, it is not clear whether the extinguishment will be an acquisition or not (for example, in the *Tasmanian Dam Case*, Tasmania was 'freed' from the burden of having its parklands dammed, but as it did not see this as a benefit there was no suggestion that it had acquired anything; contrast *Newcrest Mining*, where the prohibition on mining was construed as conferring a benefit on the park owner).

The requirement that there be an *acquisition* of property distinguishes the Australian provision from that in the Fifth Amendment to the US Constitution, which provides that private property shall not 'be *taken* for public use, without just compensation'. That provision is satisfied simply by showing that the previous owner has been deprived of the property, whether or not some new owner has 'acquired' it.

The concept of 'just terms' has been said to involve 'full and adequate compensation for the compulsory taking' or 'a full measure of compensation' (*Johnston Fear & Kingham v Commonwealth* (1943)). But the Court has not insisted upon laws providing that every individual will in all respects be as well off as if the acquisition had not taken place. The measure of just terms has been said to involve a consideration of community interests as well as those of the individual (*Grace Bros*). Having said that, and in some respects in contradiction of it, the Court has indicated that terms will not be just if they do not provide for payment of the value of the property as at the date of expropriation (see, for example, *Commonwealth v Huon Transport* (1945)).

Finally, there is a body of judicial support for the view that just terms includes a notion of **natural justice** (*Australian Apple & Pear Marketing Board v Tonking* (1942); *Tasmanian Dam Case*), although this has not been authoritatively resolved.

Section 51(xxxi) has been one of the most litigated provisions in the Constitution. Yet many questions about its ambit and application remain unresolved, suggesting that no interpretation has gained sufficient judicial support to be regarded as settled doctrine.

STEPHEN LLOYD

Activism. Judicial activism is an expression coined in the US in the 1940s, which has since become a political slogan. Like many slogans, it bears different shades of meaning. In contemporary discourse in Australia, it is frequently used in a pejorative sense to describe judicial **law making**, especially of constitutional dimensions, that reflects the personal (usually liberal) **policy** preferences of unelected judges, rather than a neutral application by them of established principles (see **Liberalism**). In this sense, the expression implies that activist courts exceed the proper limits of the judicial function and, indeed, usurp the democratic authority of elected parliaments to make new laws. The pejorative effect of the term is made explicit in Ronald Dworkin's dictum: 'Activism is a virulent form of legal pragmatism'.

In a less pejorative sense, judicial activism describes a process of reasoning that openly takes account of contemporary but enduring community **values** when formulating legal rules or doctrines. Proponents of judicial activism accept that it is inevitable that courts, especially at appellate level, make new law, albeit in more limited circumstances and subject to greater institutional constraints than legislatures. It is better, they argue, to face the policy choices frankly and openly, rather than pretend that judicial decision making can be guided exclusively by neutral principles or by the often futile search for the original intention of the **framers of the Constitution** or of legislation (see **Originalism**).

The counterpoint to judicial activism is so-called judicial restraint. This expression, too, has different meanings. It is frequently used to describe **judicial reasoning** that follows established **precedent** (*stare decisis*) and endeavours faithfully to give effect to the text of the Constitution and of statutes. Judicial restraint emphasises the virtue of minimising, if not eliminating, the influence of the Justice's own policy preferences on the **decision-making process**. It implies that courts should defer to the expressed will of democratically elected parliaments. It also implies that, even where there is no settled rule that determines the outcome of a particular case, a judge will be able to resolve the question by the application of legal rules and principles, rather than policies. Thus used, the term 'judicial restraint' conveys a tacit approbation that tends to be played off against the pejorative effect of the term 'activism'. As Julius Stone has pointed out, the rhetorical effect of the terminology would quickly be reversed if, for example, what is called 'restraint' were described as 'abdication of judicial responsibility'. Stone argues that the virtue of 'judicial restraint' is primarily a function of deference between judicial and legislative institutions; and that what may be 'an impeccable principle of accommodation as between wielders of power may … leave the citizenry short-changed'.

Ironically, the expression 'judicial activism' was first used to describe decisions of the **United States Supreme Court** in the 1930s, when it struck down key elements of President Roosevelt's New Deal legislation. The Court adopted a process of **constitutional interpretation** that gave effect to a conservative philosophy of *laissez faire* capitalism. More recently, judicial activism has become associated with a quite different philosophy, one strongly protective of **civil liberties** and the rights of minorities.

In the US, the Warren Court of the 1950s and 1960s is usually seen as the clearest example of judicial activism, especially because of its decisions requiring the desegregation of schools, the reapportionment of gerrymandered electorates, and compliance with procedural safeguards in the course of criminal investigations. The Warren Court's reputation for judicial activism was enhanced by its expansive interpretation of the **Bill of Rights**, which forms part of the US Constitution.

The Australian Constitution contains few express protections of individual liberty. But the expression 'judicial activism' gained widespread currency in the early 1990s as a response to important decisions of the High Court during the period of the **Mason Court**. In particular, the recognition by the High Court of **native title** (*Mabo* (1992)) and of an implied constitutional freedom of **political communication** (*Nationwide News v Wills* (1992) and *Australian Capital Television v Commonwealth* (1992)—see *Free Speech Cases*) prompted critics to contend that the Court's judicial activism had exceeded permissible limits in its development of implied constitutional rights.

Despite the fierce and continuing debate about the limits of judicial creativity, the differences between judicial activism and judicial restraint may be less than the vehemence of the competing arguments might suggest. Under the common law doctrine of precedent, Justices always could make new law, and often did so. Their policy-making role was long obscured by the myth that Justices merely declared and applied the pre-existing law.

The doctrine of parliamentary **sovereignty** meant that in the UK judicial excesses, real or perceived, could be overturned by legislation. In countries with written constitutions, the scope for the 'counter-majoritarian' influence of the courts is considerably greater. The US Supreme Court asserted (in *Marbury v Madison* (1803)) its authority to declare invalid legislation transgressing the limits of the Constitution. In Australia, the principle of *Marbury v Madison* has been regarded from the beginning of federation as axiomatic (although as a matter of theory it is not).

In consequence, the High Court has been required to adjudicate on challenges to the constitutionality of federal and state legislation, and to do so by reference to language in the Constitution that is necessarily general and incomplete. After all, the framers of the Constitution could hardly have been expected to anticipate the great social, technological, geopolitical, and economic changes that have occurred in the century since federation. The task of constitutional adjudication sometimes must be undertaken with relatively little guidance from the text of the Constitution or the 'original intention' of the framers.

For many decades, the High Court functioned under the banner of a 'strict and complete **legalism**', the apparent antithesis of judicial activism. Yet that did not prevent it from declaring unconstitutional the Labor government's legislation nationalising the banks (*Bank Nationalisation Case* (1948)), or the Liberal–Country Party government's anti-Communist Party legislation (*Communist Party Case* (1951)) on the basis of reasoning not compelled by the constitutional text. More recently, the Court has invalidated the '**cross-vesting** scheme', endorsed by the democratically elected parliaments of the Commonwealth and every state, by reasoning suggesting (over a vigorous dissent) that a decision of such profound importance to the legal system could be made independently of policy considerations (*Re Wakim* (1999)).

Conversely, a frank recognition that courts can and do make law on the basis of policy considerations is by no means inconsistent with the qualities associated with judicial restraint: primacy accorded to the text of the instrument being interpreted; deference to the expressed will of parliament; and genuine adherence to precedent.

The fundamental question facing appellate courts is to determine the limits of the judicial law-making role and the criteria by which those limits are to be assessed. The label 'judicial activism' is not likely to assist in this task.

Ronald Sackville

Further Reading
Gregory Craven, 'The High Court of Australia: A Study in the Abuse of Power' (1999) 22 *UNSWLJ* 216
Brian Galligan, *Politics of the High Court* (1987)
Stephen Halpern and Charles Lamb (eds), *Supreme Court Activism and Restraint* (1982)
Kenneth Holland (ed), *Judicial Activism in Comparative Perspective* (1991)
Ronald Sackville, 'Continuity and Judicial Creativity' (1997) 20 *UNSWLJ* 145

Administration of Court. The administration of the Court underwent its most significant change in 1980. The reforms introduced by the *High Court of Australia Act* 1979 (Cth) replaced the long-standing arrangement under which the Attorney-General's Department provided for the Court's administration from funds under the Department's control, an arrangement that had led to dispute in the past (see, for example, **Strike of 1905**). The new system strengthened the administrative **independence** of the Court in return for greater **accountability** by way of **annual reports**.

The High Court of Australia Act gives the Court responsibility for its own administration, and, somewhat unusually, vests the power to administer the Court in 'the Justices or a majority of them'. Under **Barwick's** original proposal, power would have been vested in the **Chief Justice**. The power can be delegated by the Justices to any one or more of the Justices; no such formal delegation has ever occurred, although the Chief Justice has traditionally played a leading role, especially in relation to the listing of cases for hearing and the allocation of Justices to cases.

The day-to-day administration of the Court is performed by an official originally called the Clerk of the High Court but now called the **Chief Executive and Principal Registrar**. The Principal Registrar has a term of up to five years, which can be renewed. The Act makes it clear that the Principal Registrar carries out his or her duties 'on behalf of, and assisting, the Justices'. The Court can also appoint committees of Justices and other persons to advise the Court.

During the first week of each **sittings**, the Principal Registrar and all seven Justices meet formally to discuss important administrative and policy issues (see **Conferences**). Typically, such meetings include discussion of the Court's financial affairs, workload, and any legislative changes that will impact upon the administration of the Court. In between these formal meetings, the Principal Registrar meets informally with the Chief Justice as the need arises. The Senior Registrar also meets periodically with the Chief Justice to discuss the listing of cases for hearing. In recent times, the general practice has been for the Chief Justice to leave the administration of the Court to the Principal Registrar, though Barwick took a leading role in this area during his term as Chief Justice.

The Court's administration has three branches: the Registry Branch, the Library and Research Branch, and the Marshal's Branch. The Registry provides administrative services for the Court's judicial activities. Under the direction of the Principal Registrar, the Registry in **Canberra** coordinates the case-flow management of the Court's judicial workload. Apart from the Principal Registry in Canberra, offices of the Registry are located in Sydney, Melbourne, Brisbane, Adelaide, Perth, Hobart and Darwin. The Sydney, Melbourne and Canberra registries are staffed by officers of the Court. Registry functions in Adelaide, Hobart and Darwin are performed by officers of the Supreme Court of the respective state or territory under ministerial arrangements. Registry functions in Brisbane and Perth are performed by officers of the **Federal Court** by arrangement between the two Chief Justices.

The Library and Research Branch assembles and maintains **library** collections to assist the Court in its work. It also provides a reference and **research** service to the Justices, and library facilities for legal practitioners appearing before the Court.

The Marshal's Branch provides financial, personnel and corporate management services. It also provides Court **reporting** services and is responsible for the operation, security and maintenance of the High Court **building** and its precincts. The Marshal is also responsible for the service and execution of all **writs**, summonses, **orders**, warrants, precepts, process and commands of the Court that may be directed to him or her. This is provided for in section 27 of the Act, which also provides for taking, receiving and detaining all persons committed by the Court to the Marshal's cus-

tody, and for discharging all such persons when directed by the Court or otherwise required by law. In practice, it is rarely necessary for the Marshal to exercise these statutory powers.

Although revolutionary at the time, the system of independent administration established by the Court has been adopted over the past twenty years by other Australian **superior courts** (see also **Budget of Court**).

CHRIS DOOGAN
PETER DURACK

Administrative law is concerned with legal controls on government decision making. Those controls are mainly imposed by legislation, but the **common law** has always played an important role as well. Initially through prerogative **writs**, the courts developed a common law framework of principles—such as the duties to observe **natural justice** and to act in good faith—which government agencies were expected to observe in the absence of legislative provision to the contrary.

The **role** of the High Court in ensuring that government acts within the law is anchored in section 75(v) of the Constitution. This section confers original **jurisdiction** on the Court to grant three administrative law **remedies** against the Commonwealth. Despite the Court's concern that cases in its original jurisdiction lack the benefit of examination by a lower court or the filter of **leave to appeal**, it has nonetheless emphasised the importance of its original jurisdiction in administrative law. As **Dixon** observed in the *Bank Nationalisation Case* (1948), section 75(v) made it 'constitutionally certain that there would be a jurisdiction capable of restraining officers of the Commonwealth from exceeding Federal power'.

Nevertheless, most administrative law cases arise in the Court's appellate jurisdiction. They cover the full spectrum of Commonwealth, state, territory and local government activity. The legal obligations of government have been determined in areas ranging from **immigration** (*Kisch Case* (1934); *Kioa v West* (1985)), **Aboriginal** land rights (*Northern Land Council Case* (1981)) and freedom of assembly (*Melbourne Corporation v Barry* (1922)), to disclosure of government documents (*Sankey v Whitlam* (1978)) and recognition of international conventions (*Teoh's Case* (1995)).

Four themes established in the Court's early decisions have resonated throughout the Court's history. Some aspects of those themes emphasise judicial restraint in review of executive action; others point in an opposite direction.

The first theme is the Court's acceptance of the premise that legal authority is needed for all government action—a principle persuasively captured by **Latham's** observation that 'it is not the English view of law that whatever is officially done is law ... but, on the contrary, the principle of English law is that what is done officially must be done in accordance with law' (*Arthur Yates v Vegetable Seeds Committee* (1945)).

Government legal authority, the Court has accepted, can rest on the executive power—a non-statutory source of power that enables government to function in the world like other legal persons and entities. For example, the executive power has been considered as an adequate legal foundation for government to undertake inquiries (*Clough v Leahy*

(1904)), enter into contracts (*NSW v Bardolph* (1934)), appoint officers (*Marks v Commonwealth* (1964)), and form companies (*Davis v Commonwealth* (1988)).

Conversely, the Court has resolutely insisted that government action that is coercive, punitive or intrusive in nature must have an explicit statutory foundation. A government inquiry, for instance, cannot compel witnesses to give evidence unless authorised by statute (*Sorby v Commonwealth* (1983)). Moreover, all government officers must comply with the law, a point illustrated colourfully in *A v Hayden* (1984) (see **Humour**). There, the Court held that officers of the Australian Security Intelligence Service conducting a training exercise at the Sheraton Hotel in Melbourne had no inherent executive authority to ignore or break the law, and could be prosecuted accordingly. 'It is fundamental to our legal system', said **Gibbs**, 'that the executive has no power to authorise a breach of the law and that it is no excuse for an offender to say that he acted under the orders of a superior officer'. The requirement that government action be authorised by law is reflected in the Court's approach to **statutory interpretation**, notably in its reluctance to concede an expansive operation to legislative phrases of indeterminate scope. An early instance was the statement in *Potter v Minahan* (1908) that 'it is in the last degree improbable that the legislature would overthrow fundamental principles, infringe rights, or depart from the general system of law, without expressing its intention with irresistible clearness'. The principle was reaffirmed nearly ninety years later in *Coco v The Queen* (1994): 'An abrogation or curtailment of a fundamental right, freedom or immunity … must be clearly manifested by unmistakable and unambiguous language.'

That principle has always had a special significance in administrative law, as it allows a court considerable latitude in defining what constitutes a fundamental interest and what amounts to a legislative intention to override it. Instances abound in which Australian courts have declared government action invalid for interfering with common law freedoms in a manner not explicitly authorised by legislation. Law enforcement activity has been a regular casualty, with the Court holding that premises were searched, goods seized, offenders arrested or investigations undertaken in an unlawful manner (*George v Rockett* (1990); *Plenty v Dillon* (1991); *Coco*). Statutory authorisation for government **acquisition** of private **property** for a 'public purpose' has been narrowly construed (*Clunies-Ross v Commonwealth* (1984)). A person's common law right to expect that governments will observe the principles of natural justice can be extinguished only by a clear legislative statement to the contrary (*Commissioner of Police v Tanos* (1958); *Annetts v McCann* (1990)). Generally, the importance of this approach to statutory interpretation has grown with the developing recognition of human rights.

The second theme in the Court's administrative law jurisprudence is that interpretation of legislation is ultimately a judicial task. In one sense, there is nothing surprising about this: the judicial function of conclusively resolving the legal issues in any dispute to which the executive is a party is the central tenet of the **separation of powers**. The administrative law significance of this theme is to be found instead in its subsidiary implications.

One such implication has been the consistent judicial aversion to 'privative' or 'ouster' clauses. These clauses purport to confine **judicial review** by declaring that certain decisions cannot be reviewed by a court, or can be reviewed only on limited grounds or by a specified procedure. The enactment of **privative clauses** is prompted by a legislative concern that judicial review can have disruptive and counterproductive effects; for example, an unsuccessful party before an industrial tribunal may seek to use judicial review to prolong the matter and thus avoid the consequences of an adverse tribunal ruling. The Court, while acknowledging this concern, has been troubled by the potential of privative clauses to preclude courts from ensuring that the law is correctly administered by tribunals and executive bodies. Frequently, the Court has observed that it would be a contradiction if the limits imposed on such bodies by legislation could not be enforced by a court (*R v Murray; Ex parte Proctor* (1949); *R v Coldham; Ex parte Australian Workers Union* (1983); *Darling Casino v NSW Casino Control Authority* (1997)). The upshot has been a consistently narrow interpretation of privative clauses, as the Court wrestles to balance its respect for the **sovereignty** of the legislature against its desire to maintain the interpretive role of the judiciary (*R v Hickman; Ex parte Fox and Clinton* (1945); *Hockey v Yelland* (1984); *O'Toole v Charles David* (1991)).

The Court has also safeguarded its interpretive function by extending the boundaries of **justiciability** to include virtually all government administrative action. In *Church of Scientology v Woodward* (1982), the Court held that it had jurisdiction to examine whether the Australian Security Intelligence Organisation was acting beyond its statutory function of collecting and evaluating intelligence relevant to security. 'It would mock the will of Parliament', **Brennan** observed, if 'the functions which it has defined may be exceeded without restraint by the courts. Judicial review is neither more nor less than the enforcement of the **rule of law** over executive action'. The same view was adopted in the *Northern Land Council Case*, where the Court departed from its earlier view that administrative law writs were not available against a Governor-General or Governor (*Duncan v Theodore* (1917); **Communist Party Case** (1951)), and decided instead that statutory functions, by whomsoever exercised, are subject to judicial scrutiny. This outcome was significant in the Australian context, where routine statutory functions had commonly been exercised formally by state Governors.

Another offshoot of the Court's assumed responsibility for interpreting legislation is that, with occasional exceptions (*SA v Tanner* (1989)), it has declined to embrace the notion endorsed by North American courts that, in the construction of legislative phrases of uncertain meaning, courts should pay deference—or have special regard—to the interpretation adopted by the executive agency responsible for administering the legislation (*Enfield Corporation v Development Assessment Commission* (2000)).

The third theme in the Court's jurisprudence is its adherence to what is commonly referred to as the legality/merits distinction—that the role of a court is to define the boundaries of a statutory discretion, but not to examine whether a decision made within those boundaries was the preferable decision to make. This principle, as well as being enunciated explicitly in every era (*Randall v Northcote Corporation* (1910); *R v War Pensions Entitlement Appeal Tribunal; Ex parte Bott* (1933); **Green v Daniels** (1977); *A-G (NSW) v Quin* (1990)), has also been reflected more broadly. For example, in elaborating the common law criteria for evaluating whether an administrative decision was lawfully made, the Court shied away from indeterminate standards that would inevitably permit judicial intrusion into the merits of administrative judgment. Concepts such as 'uncertainty' and 'unreasonableness' were rejected by the Court as free-standing generic criteria, sanctioned only where they were an implicit requirement of the statutory power being exercised (*Williams v Melbourne Corporation* (1933); *King Gee Clothing v Commonwealth* (1945)). Latterly, despite legislative acceptance of those concepts as grounds for judicial review in the *Administrative Decisions (Judicial Review) Act* 1977 (Cth), the Court has remained reluctant to allow them to have any broader operation in its own original jurisdiction (*Minister for Immigration v Eshetu* (1999)).

The legality/merits distinction is at the root of judgments that define the approach to be adopted in construing the reasons for decision of an administrative tribunal or official. In *Minister for Immigration v Wu* (1996), the Court warned against 'over-zealous judicial review' in the close scrutiny of administrative reasons. A constrained philosophy of judicial review is similarly evident in other principles periodically affirmed by the Court. These include the principles that a court should generally defer to the decision of an inferior tribunal on an issue of jurisdictional fact (*R v Blakeley; Ex parte Association of Architects* (1950); *R v Ludeke; Ex parte Queensland Electricity Commission* (1985)); that errors occurring within jurisdiction are generally not subject to prerogative writ review (*Craig v SA* (1995)); that administrative fact finding is not ordinarily open to judicial review (*Australian Broadcasting Tribunal v Bond* (1990)); and that the executive is not restrained from the free exercise of a statutory discretion by a doctrine of administrative **estoppel** (*A-G (NSW) v Quin*).

A fourth and related theme has been the Court's approach to the construction of statutory discretions, particularly those cast in broad terms. It is in the nature of such a discretion, the Court has emphasised, that the decision maker 'has some latitude as to the decision to be made' (*Coal and Allied Operations v Australian Industrial Relations Commission* (2000)). An early exponent of this view was Dixon, whose statements of principle have repeatedly been affirmed (for example, *R v Australian Broadcasting Tribunal; Ex parte 2HD* (1979)). His approach emphasised the courts' obligation to work from the language of the statute: 'Courts of law have no source whence they may ascertain what is the purpose of the discretion except the terms and subject matter of the statutory instrument. They must, therefore, concede to the authority a discretion unlimited by anything but the scope and object of the instrument confirming it' (*Swan Hill Corporation v Bradbury* (1937)).

An illustration of that principle—controversial, perhaps, by modern standards—was the decision in *Water Conservation and Irrigation Commission v Browning* (1947), holding that there was no statutory inhibition against the Commission, in regulating the transfer of irrigation licences, applying a policy designed to prevent people of Italian birth from acquiring those licences. Another more recent illustration, attracting a different controversy, was the Court's decision in *Murphyores v Commonwealth* (1976), that a Commonwealth minister could refuse on environmental grounds to permit the exportation of mineral sands mined at Fraser Island under a licence granted by the Queensland government.

A non-interventionist view of statutory discretions and executive choice still resonates in the Court's jurisprudence, though in later years the Court has given equal emphasis to other countervailing principles. An example is the obligation of a decision maker to give consideration to relevant matters (*Minister for Aboriginal Affairs v Peko-Wallsend* (1986)). In applying that principle, Australian courts have readily inferred that administrators have an obligation of far-reaching potential to give close consideration to the aspects of a decision that will impact adversely on a member of the public. *Teoh* had a similar moderating effect on statutory discretions by requiring decision makers to consider the interaction between the legislative criteria and any relevant international conventions. Those techniques for moderating the exercise of statutory discretions, however broadly expressed, have added importance in the context of a growing judicial readiness to have explicit regard to human rights considerations in the review of executive decision making.

These four themes—the principle of legality, the judicial responsibility for legislative interpretation, the legality/merits distinction, and judicial appreciation of unconfined discretion—have guided the Court in delineating the legal powers and responsibilities of government. It is both a complex and a sensitive task, especially in a **democracy**. The themes and principles of administrative law provide only broad guidance on the way the balance between government power and the protection of community interests should be struck. Criticism and controversy can be expected from both sides—or, as commonly happens, from the disparate range of sectional interests, governmental and non-governmental, that impinge on policy formulation and administrative decision making.

It is perhaps not surprising, therefore, that the way the Court has fashioned the principles of administrative law in individual cases has never moved far from contemporary or prevailing trends in government and society. Government decisions have frequently been struck down, but the underlying rationale has rarely been antagonistic to governmental trends. The parallel movement of social, political and judicial attitudes is evident in many areas.

A noteworthy example is the judicial response to the efforts of unlawful immigrants to avoid deportation. For most of the twentieth century, the statutory powers of government to exclude, detain and deport aliens were construed broadly in favour of government, leaving little opportunity for those without Australian **citizenship** to contest an adverse decision (*Ah Yin v Christie* (1907); *Donohoe v Wong Sau* (1925); *Znaty v Minister for Immigration* (1972); *R v MacKellar; Ex parte Ratu* (1977)). By the mid-1980s, a time of growing acceptance in government practice and community expectations that procedural safeguards should apply in all areas of administrative decision making, the Court refashioned the established principles of administrative law to provide a far greater measure of protection to those facing expulsion (*Kioa*; *Haoucher v Minister for Immigration* (1990); *Teoh*).

The judicial response to national security claims evinces a similar trend. During **World War II**, the Court upheld the validity of subordinate legislation conferring extensive and intrusive powers on government (*Reid v Sinderberry* (1944); *Stenhouse v Coleman* (1944)). It also supported a limited view of the justiciability of executive action (*Communist Party Case*). Much later, in an era of heightened parliamentary and public appraisal of government defence and security intelligence operations, the Court had little difficulty in asserting its jurisdiction to enforce the rule of law throughout the full range of government activity (*Church of Scientology v Woodward*; *Alister v The Queen* (1984)).

The interaction of domestic and **international law** has been approached similarly. For decades, the Court unhesitatingly insisted that treaties, until adopted by Parliament, 'have no legal effect upon the rights and duties of subjects of the Crown' (*Chow Hung Ching v The King* (1948); *Simsek v Macphee* (1982)). By 1995, in *Teoh*, the Court was declaring that Australia's international commitments should not be disregarded by courts as merely 'platitudinous or ineffectual'. A short time later, amidst increased attempts by **commentators** and litigants to convert international standards into domestic legal criteria, the Court cautioned that 'many international conventions and agreements are expressed in indeterminate language ... Often their provisions are more aptly described as goals to be achieved rather than rules to be obeyed' (*Project Blue Sky v Australian Broadcasting Authority* (1998)).

The balance between government secrecy and public information rights has also shifted. Dixon, explaining in 1951 why the Governor-General was not subject to administrative law writs, observed that 'the counsels of the Crown are secret' (*Communist Party Case*). Thirty years later, **Mason**, rejecting the Commonwealth's attempt to restrain publication of leaked defence papers by invoking the protection given to confidential information in **equity**, remarked that 'it is unacceptable in our democratic society that there should be a restraint on the publication of information relating to government when the only vice of that information is that it enables the public to discuss, review and criticise government action' (*Commonwealth v John Fairfax & Sons* (1980)). In the same era, the Court held, in *Sankey v Whitlam*, that it is for the courts and not the executive to decide ultimately whether government documents should be produced for the purposes of judicial proceedings. Later still, the advent of freedom of information legislation was given by the Court as a reason for upholding the right of an upper house of the Parliament under a system of **responsible government** to suspend a minister who failed to comply with a resolution for the tabling of government documents (*Egan v Willis* (1998)).

The fabric of administrative law has also been repatterned to assimilate political trends towards public participation in government. Previously, **standing** to challenge the validity of government decision making had commonly been denied to individuals (*Anderson v Commonwealth* (1932)) and to public interest groups (*Australian Conservation Foundation v Commonwealth* (1980)). Before long, the added governmental recognition of accountability and public participation was reflected in a widening judicial recognition of the right of challenge (*Onus v Alcoa* (1981); *Bateman's Bay Local Aboriginal Land Council v Aboriginal Community Benefit Fund* (1998)).

The leeways of choice available to the Court, arising both from the plasticity of administrative law doctrine and from the variable weight to be attached to broader pressures impinging on government, are reflected not only in the shift of judicial attitudes over time, but also in split decisions within the Court. Thus, in *Salemi v MacKellar (No 2)* (1977), the Court split 3:3 in choosing whether to concede a broad operation to the Minister's power to deport a person unlawfully in Australia, or to require the Minister to observe natural justice in light of a government-declared amnesty for prohibited immigrants. Similarly, in *Foley v Padley* (1984), the Court split 3:2 in upholding the validity of a local council by-law that had the effect, if not the purpose, of preventing a fringe religious group from proselytising in a city plaza. A similar division of opinion was apparent in many earlier cases (*Melbourne Corporation v Barry*; *Clements v Bull* (1953)).

The significance of the Court's administrative law role is not simple to distil. Decisional trends and landmarks—and, for that matter, shortcomings—can be obscured by the predominance of technical questions of choice of remedy and statutory interpretation. In resolving disputes between government and the community, the Court is properly constrained by a need to respect legislative supremacy and executive discretion. And, however important, decisions of the Court are but a small element of a far larger mosaic of pressures, trends and objectives that impinge on and configure government.

Even so, it could be said that as a consequence of the Court's administrative law jurisprudence, government in Australia is better and fairer. It is more open. It is more responsive. It is more attuned to compliance with legal requirements. It is more considerate of the impact of its decisions on those whom it regulates. As a centennial landmark, that is a worthy achievement.

JOHN MCMILLAN

Further Reading

Mark Aronson and Bruce Dyer, *Judicial Review of Administrative Action* (2nd edn 2000)
Robin Creyke and John McMillan, *Control of Government Decision-Making* (forthcoming)
John McMillan, 'Parliament and Administrative Law' in Geoffrey Lindell (ed), *The Vision in Hindsight* (forthcoming)
Special Issue, 'Administrative Law in a Federal System' (2000) 28 *FL Rev* 169

Admiralty jurisdiction developed from the jurisdiction exercised by the Lord High Admiral in the fourteenth century, and later from the jurisdiction of the High Court of Admiralty in England. For matters arising on the high seas, the jurisdiction was exclusive; for matters arising between the ebb and flow of the tide, it was concurrent with the jurisdiction of the courts of **common law**.

Before federation, Admiralty jurisdiction was exercised in the Australian colonies by Vice Admiralty Courts pursuant to letters patent—from as early as 1787 in NSW, and later pursuant to the *Vice Admiralty Courts Act* 1863 (Imp). That jurisdiction included civil and criminal jurisdiction over 'all causes civil and maritime' in addition to 'offences … within our maritime jurisdiction', and some limited prize salvage jurisdiction at various times during wartime. In 1891, the Vice Admiralty jurisdiction was replaced with the commencement of the *Colonial Courts of Admiralty Act* 1890 (Imp) in all colonies except NSW and Victoria, where the Act was not brought into operation until 1911.

The scope and subject matter of this imperial jurisdiction in Admiralty had been restricted by legislation in the seventeenth and eighteenth centuries, and by **writs** of prohibition issued by the common law courts to restrict the Admiralty Courts' jurisdiction. However, notwithstanding these restrictions, the Admiralty Courts had developed distinctive procedures for the enforcement of claims against ships and other chattels, as actions *in rem* against the property itself. The nature and characteristics of jurisdiction *in rem* were examined by the High Court in *Aichhorn v The Ship MV 'Talabot'* (1974), where the Court rejected an application for service of a writ on a vessel outside the jurisdiction. But more interestingly, the Court approved the traditional conception of the action *in rem* adopted by the **House of Lords** in *The Henrich Björn* (1886), where Lord Watson said:

> The action is in rem, that being, as I understand the term, a proceeding directed against a ship or other chattel in which the plaintiff seeks either to have the res adjudged to him in property or possession, or to have it sold, under the authority of the Court … in satisfaction of his pecuniary claims.

This approach was followed in *Caltex Oil v The Dredge 'Willemstad'* (1976) where **Gibbs**, with whom the whole Court agreed on this point, further examined the nature of jurisdiction *in rem*, concluding that the action continues to be an action *in rem* even after the defendant has entered an appearance *in personam*. Further, he explained that where proceedings are *in rem*, the ship is the defendant, and as a consequence, a number of interested parties, such as the owner, charterer, mortgagee or master, may appear as defendants where they have an interest in the property arrested even though they would not be liable *in personam*. The Court thus maintained the separate existence of the action *in rem*, in contrast to the position in the UK (see *The Indian Grace* (1997)).

While the nature of the Admiralty action *in rem* has been consistently observed by the Court, the source of its jurisdiction has been more elusive. The High Court, as a court of unlimited civil **jurisdiction**, exercised original jurisdiction as a Colonial Court of Admiralty pursuant to section 2 of the Colonial Courts of Admiralty Act, but there was some confusion about the basis of that jurisdiction and its relationship with the *Judiciary Act* 1903 (Cth). Section 30A of that Act, inserted in 1914 after the outbreak of **World War I**, declared: 'The High Court is hereby declared to be a Colonial Court of Admiralty within the meaning of … the *Colonial Courts of Admiralty Act* 1890.' This declaration was unnecessary, since the Court already possessed jurisdiction under section 2 of the Imperial Act; but it did give rise to a number of issues regarding its validity and the consequences of that validity

for state jurisdiction. For one thing, the 1914 amendment was assented to by the Governor-General, and subsequently by King George V; and the proper formalities of reserving it for the King's pleasure may not have been observed. The High Court never decided the issue expressly, but in *John Sharp & Sons v The Katherine Mackall* (1924), **Isaacs** expressed doubt on the point. More interestingly, on a number of occasions the Court expressed concern about the consequences of the declaration: as **Dixon** put it in *Union Steamship Co of NZ v The 'Caradale'* (1937), 'a declaration specifying one court has the effect of confining the jurisdiction to that court', so that if section 30A was valid, the jurisdiction of the **state Supreme Courts** as Colonial Courts of Admiralty would be extinguished (see also *McArthur v Williams* (1936)).

The confusion over the source of Admiralty jurisdiction was further compounded by the independent conferral of federal jurisdiction on the High Court by section 30(b) of the Judiciary Act, also inserted in 1914. Section 30(b) purported to confer jurisdiction pursuant to section 76(iii) of the Constitution in relation to matters 'of Admiralty and maritime jurisdiction'. However, there was always some doubt as to whether the provision was constitutional because it was enacted prior to the *Statute of Westminster* 1931 (UK).

These dilemmas were ultimately resolved in 1939 when both section 30(b) and section 30A of the Judiciary Act were repealed. Thereafter, both the High Court and state courts continued to exercise jurisdiction as Colonial Courts of Admiralty under the Imperial Act (*McIlwraith McEacharn v Shell Co* (1945)). The only occasion when doubts were expressed as to whether the High Court was a Colonial Court of Admiralty was in *China Ocean Shipping v SA* (1979), where **Murphy** suggested that Australia was not a 'British possession' as required by the imperial legislation.

The High Court also exercised appellate jurisdiction pursuant to section 5 of the Colonial Courts of Admiralty Act as a local court of appeal, because the definition of 'British possession' included Australia and was not restricted to the relevant state (*McIlwraith McEacharn*). However, in reaching that conclusion the Court rejected the suggestion that federal jurisdiction in Admiralty had been conferred on state courts by section 39 of the Judiciary Act (which would have conferred an appeal under section 73 of the Constitution), because section 39 had been enacted prior to the Statute of Westminster.

By restricting itself to the Admiralty jurisdiction arising under the Imperial Act, the Court effectively restricted both its own jurisdiction, and that of the state Supreme Courts, to that which the High Court of Admiralty in England had exercised in 1890 (*Kanematsu v The Ship 'Shahzada'* (1956)). This in turn meant that the jurisdiction was restricted to that of the English High Court of Admiralty as it had been prior to the Judicature Acts of 1873 and 1875 (see the decision of the **Privy Council** in *The Camosun* (1909)). It followed that **remedies** dependent on **equity** (such as specific performance) were not available in the exercise of the imperial Admiralty jurisdiction, even though they had long been available in the UK. Similarly, the limits of the High Court's Admiralty jurisdiction were fixed as at 1890 notwithstanding legislation in the UK extending them.

The imperial Admiralty jurisdiction was also historically limited in respect of **criminal law**: it extended only to offences recognised by English law. Thus in *R v Bull* (1974), when a ship carrying cannabis was seized within three miles of the Northern Territory coastline and those aboard were charged with various statutory offences under the *Customs Act* 1901 (Cth), the question arose whether in trying those charges the Supreme Court of the Northern Territory was exercising 'ordinary' jurisdiction or Admiralty jurisdiction. In the latter event the prosecution must fail, since none of the statutory offences involved was known to English law. The High Court, after an extensive review of the historical scope and development of criminal jurisdiction in Admiralty, concluded that the charges were not within the scope of Admiralty jurisdiction, but that this was no barrier to the exercise of 'ordinary' jurisdiction.

Curiously, notwithstanding the imperial nature of the High Court's jurisdiction between 1903 and 1988, in *Huddart Parker v The Ship 'Mill Hill'* (1950), the Court held that section 79 of the Judiciary Act (requiring a court exercising federal jurisdiction in a state to apply the law of that state) was applicable to its Admiralty jurisdiction. This decision stands as a stark exception to the Court's adherence to the principle that this jurisdiction was conferred on it as a Colonial Court under the Imperial Act.

By 1988, it was clear that the Commonwealth Parliament had power to repeal the Imperial legislation, whether because of the High Court's decision in *Kirmani v Captain Cook Cruises (No 1)* (1985), or because of the *Australia Acts* 1986. Accordingly, after consideration by the Australian Law Reform Commission, the *Admiralty Act* 1988 (Cth) repealed the Colonial Courts of Admiralty Act in its application to Australia and introduced substantial reforms. Admiralty jurisdiction was expanded to include wider categories of subject matter jurisdiction, the enforcement of a claim against a ship by arrest of a sister ship, and other reforms following the 1952 International Convention for the Unification of Certain Rules Relating to the Arrest of Sea-Going Ships. The Act conferred jurisdiction concurrently on the **Federal Court** and the state Supreme Courts, but not on the High Court, which now retains only its appellate jurisdiction under section 73 of the Constitution.

In construing the Admiralty Act, the High Court has taken a wide view of the Commonwealth's legislative power and of the jurisdiction conferred by the Act. In *Owners of the Ship 'Shin Kobe Maru' v Empire Shipping* (1994), the Court rejected the suggestion that the power to confer federal 'Admiralty and maritime jurisdiction' under section 76(iii) of the Constitution should be limited to the scope that Australian Admiralty jurisdiction had in 1901 (see **Originalism**):

> Once it is accepted that 'maritime' in s 76(iii) serves to equate the jurisdiction there referred to with that of maritime nations generally, there is no basis for any qualification or limitation based on jurisdictional divisions peculiar to English law, which is the only basis on which it could be argued that there should be a limitation in the case of a claim for specific performance.

Most interestingly, in reaching this conclusion, the Court equated the scope of the power to confer Admiralty jurisdiction under section 76(iii) with that accorded by US courts to the similarly worded provision in Article III § 2 of the US Constitution (see *De Lovio v Boit* (1815)).

While the Court in *The Shin Kobe Maru* thus adopted a wide view of the legislative power in section 76(iii), in many of the earlier cases judicial comment had been less confident about the scope of that power or its independence from imperial restrictions. In *Nagrint v Regis* (1939), *McIlwraith McEacharn* and *China Ocean*, different Justices had expressed divergent views on the scope of section 76(iii) without deciding the issue. Similarly, Dixon commented in submissions to the Royal Commission to the Constitution in 1928 that 'Admiralty jurisdiction is a well known expression but no one seems to know what maritime jurisdiction is'.

This judicial reticence in moving beyond the colonial restrictions of Admiralty jurisdiction is most clear in the Court's first consideration of section 76(iii), in *Owners of the Ship 'Kalibia' v Wilson* (1910). In that case, the **Griffith Court** took an extremely narrow view of the scope and nature of section 76(iii), on the basis that when the Constitution was drafted it was understood that any legislation in relation to maritime regulation would be enacted by the Imperial Parliament. Accordingly, the Court at that stage rejected substantial **United States Supreme Court** authority in relation to the construction of section 76(iii). Notwithstanding the dubious imperial justification articulated in *The Kalibia*, the Court refrained from commenting in *The Shin Kobe Maru* on the correctness of the decision, even though it had been referred to in argument and by **Gummow** (in the Federal Court) at first instance.

EDWARD COX

Further Reading

Australian Law Reform Commission, *Civil Admiralty Jurisdiction*, Report No 33 (1986)

Zelman Cowen and Leslie Zines, *Federal Jurisdiction in Australia* (2nd edn 1978)

Frank Wiswall, *The Development of Admiralty Jurisdiction and Practice Since 1800* (1970)

Advisory opinions. An advisory opinion is, in its narrow sense, a judicial opinion on a point of law given at the request of the parliament or executive government. The opinion relates to a hypothetical situation, such as the validity of legislation enacted or to be enacted by the parliament, rather than to a concrete case or to litigation otherwise before the Court. In its broader sense, an advisory opinion is a judicial opinion in any case not involving the determination of the right, interest or duty of a person, regardless of whether the advisory opinion has been sought by the parliament or the executive or by an individual plaintiff.

Opinions differ as to whether an advisory opinion is an exercise of **judicial power**, but in any event the High Court, along with other federal courts, has no power to give advisory opinions. This lack of power is not stated expressly in the Constitution. Rather, it is the result of the Court itself holding that the giving of advisory opinions, although an exercise of judicial power, is not within the scope of the 'judicial power of the Commonwealth' conferred upon the Court by Chapter III of the Constitution.

The leading case on advisory opinions is *In re Judiciary and Navigation Acts* (1921). In that case, the Court considered the validity of the *Judiciary Act* 1903 (Cth), which purported to confer on the Court the power to decide questions referred to it by the Governor-General concerning the validity of any Commonwealth legislation. The Governor-General referred to the Court the question of the validity of certain sections of the *Navigation Act* 1912 (Cth). The Court refused to consider the question, however, holding that an advisory opinion did not involve a '**matter**' within sections 75 or 76 of the Constitution. The Court stated that: 'There can be no matter within the meaning of [section 76] unless there is some immediate right, duty or liability to be established by the determination of the Court.'

In the Court's view, it was beyond the power of the Commonwealth to confer jurisdiction on the Court 'to make a declaration of law divorced from any attempt to administer that law'. The Court went on: '[There is] nothing in Chapter III … to lend colour to the view that Parliament can confer power or jurisdiction upon the High Court to determine abstract questions of law without the right or duty of any person being involved.'

The Court has also refused to give advisory opinions in cases not involving a formal request from the parliament or the executive. For example, a majority of the Court refused to decide the effect of pastoral leases on **native title** in the *Waanyi Case* (1996), as there was no properly constituted proceeding in relation to which the Court could render a decision (see also *Wik* (1996)).

Because the question of whether a particular case involves a request for an advisory opinion turns on whether it affects a right, interest or duty of a person, it is closely related to the question of whether a plaintiff has **standing** to pursue his or her claim. If a plaintiff has standing then it is all but inevitable that the proceedings will involve the determination of some right, interest or duty of that plaintiff and that this determination will not constitute an advisory opinion. In *Croome v Tasmania* (1997), the plaintiffs challenged the validity of sections 122 and 123 of the *Criminal Code* 1924 (Tas), which criminalised sex between men (see **Sexual preference**). The plaintiffs had not been prosecuted under these laws and Tasmania argued that their challenge therefore involved no 'matter' and amounted to a request for an advisory opinion. Tasmania conceded, however, that the plaintiffs had standing to bring their action. In these circumstances the Court had no hesitation in holding that the case did not involve a request for an advisory opinion, noting the interdependence of the two issues.

The prohibition against advisory opinions has been moderated to some extent by the Court's practice. First, the Court may provide a declaratory judgment, which declares the rights and duties between parties, without providing further concrete relief. In some circumstances, a declaratory judgment resembles in substance an advisory opinion, although the Court has emphasised that there must be a real dispute between two parties and that it will not answer hypothetical questions by declaration (*Ainsworth v Criminal Justice Commission* (1992)).

Secondly, **Attorneys-General** at both state and Commonwealth level have considerable scope to seek a declaration that legislation is unconstitutional, even though there may be no controversy involving the application of legislation to particular individuals or to a concrete factual situation (*Marriage Act Case* (1962)). In the *First Pharmaceutical Benefits Case* (1945), for example, the Victorian Attorney-General was able to seek a declaration that the *Pharmaceutical Benefits Act* 1944 (Cth) was invalid before the Act had come into force, on the basis that it would operate within Victoria and affect the rights and obligations of Victorians. In addition, the Court held that a state itself has an ability to challenge the validity of Commonwealth legislation, without the participation of the Attorney-General as a party. In these circumstances, as **Jacobs** noted in the *Queen of Queensland Case* (1975), the Court's decision closely resembles an advisory opinion.

Thirdly, questions of **criminal law** referred to an appellate court after the acquittal of an accused can be validly decided by the Court, even though they do not affect the rights and duties of the accused. In *Mellifont v A-G (Qld)* (1991), the Court overruled earlier cases that suggested that such a question constituted an advisory opinion and could thus not be appealed to the High Court. Rather, a majority of the Court held that such a case was not 'divorced from the ordinary administration of the law' and did concern a matter within the meaning of Chapter III.

The High Court is not alone in rejecting the role of giving advisory opinions; courts in the US have taken a similar view. The reasons for refusing to render advisory opinions include the following. First, advisory opinions would lead to the politicisation of the courts and would undermine their **independence** and impartiality because they may appear to be giving assistance to the parliament or executive. Secondly, because an advisory opinion is not based on a concrete fact situation, the Court may render a judgment that is later seen to be defective or incomplete. Thirdly, an advisory opinion would not involve full argument from all interested parties and thus the Court may not be informed of all relevant issues and arguments. Fourthly, abstract questions may be framed in a misleading fashion or in such a way as to try to ensure a particular answer. Fifthly, an advisory opinion may result in a Justice taking a position on a particular legal issue in an abstract context and being unwilling to depart from that position if later confronted by a concrete fact situation.

The primary argument in favour of courts giving advisory opinions is that they provide an opportunity to invalidate unconstitutional legislation at an early stage, rather than at a later time when governments and individuals have acted in reliance on the legislation. In addition, those in favour of an advisory jurisdiction argue that the criticisms of such a jurisdiction are either incorrect or can be avoided by a careful structuring of the Court's power. In this respect, it should be noted that the Supreme Court of Canada has and regularly exercises an advisory jurisdiction, without any grave difficulties arising. In addition, the Judicial Committee of the **House of Lords** may provide advisory opinions, although it has rarely done so.

KRISTEN WALKER

Further Reading
Stephen Crawshaw, 'The High Court of Australia and Advisory Opinions' (1977) 51 *ALJ* 112

Patrick Gunning and Kristen Walker, 'The Judiciary', *The Laws of Australia*, subtitle 19.4

John Williams, 'Rethinking Advisory Opinions' (1996) 7 *PLR* 205

Aickin, Keith Arthur (*b* 1 February 1916; *d* 18 June 1982; Justice 1976–82) was a Justice cast in the Dixonian mould of precision in expression, dialectical method, and concern about faithfulness to principle in legal development. He was the last Justice of the Court to have been appointed with life **tenure**, prior to the **amendment** of section 72 of the Constitution in 1977.

Aickin was born in Melbourne at the height of **World War I**. His father was a teacher of mathematics and science at Melbourne Grammar School, which Aickin himself went on to attend. His contemporaries at Melbourne Grammar included the historian Manning Clark. From school, Aickin went to the University of Melbourne, from which he graduated in 1938 with the Supreme Court Prize in law and a first-class honours degree. He was admitted to practice in Victoria in 1939. That same year, he became **associate** to **Dixon**, in which position he served until 1941. From 1941–42, Aickin was, at the request of Dixon, who was their chairman, attached to the Central Wool Committee and the Commonwealth Shipping Control Board. In 1942, when Dixon was appointed Minister Plenipotentiary to the US, Aickin accompanied him as Third Secretary of the Australian legation. In 1944, on Dixon's return to Australia, Aickin went to London, where he served as legal adviser to the European Office of the United Nations Relief and Rehabilitation Administration (UNRAA). In 1948, he returned to the US where he was appointed to the newly formed legal department of the UN. During his time in London, Aickin had also read English law, and just prior to his return to America, he was called to the Middle Temple.

It was emblematic of the turbulent era in which he came of age that it was only in 1949, at the age of 33, that Aickin commenced his chosen profession as a barrister in the courts of Australia. Yet he was to rise quickly at the Victorian Bar. He was appointed QC in 1957, after just eight years practice as a junior. Typically for a capable young barrister of those days, Aickin's work was broadly cast, though he seldom appeared in criminal matters. His experience with the Central Wool Committee led to his being briefed to appear in many of the important wool realisation cases of the early 1950s. These include *Ritchie v Trustees Executors & Agency Co* (1951), in which he appeared alone, within two years of his call to the Victorian Bar; *Poulton v Commonwealth* (1953); *National Trustees Executors & Agency Co v FCT* (1954); and *FCT v Squatting Investment* (1954), in which he appeared in the **Privy Council** with Douglas **Menzies**. Aickin also enjoyed the rare experience for a member of the Australian Bar of having appeared before the **House of Lords** (in a **copyright** appeal for an Australian company). He acquired a substantial expertise in intellectual property, including **patent** law. Over time, Aickin also developed a significant reputation in **taxation** matters, and he appeared for the Commonwealth in the *Second **Uniform** Tax Case* (1957).

When Douglas Menzies was appointed to the Court in 1958, Aickin was widely acknowledged to be his successor as the leader of the Victorian Bar in constitutional and com-

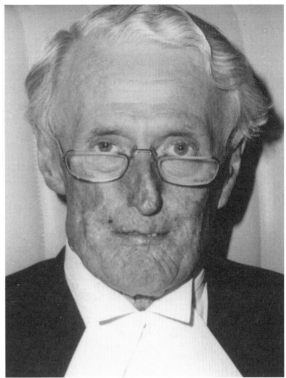

Keith Aickin, Justice 1976–82

mercial matters, and it has been said that by the time of his own appointment to the Court, Aickin was the undisputed leader of the tax Bar in Australia. He was consulted in commercial matters by arbitrators from across Australia and this was a step in the evolution of a nationally based **legal profession**. Dixon is said to have expressed disappointment that Aickin was not chosen to succeed him as **Chief Justice** when he retired in 1964 (the appointment going instead to **Barwick**; see **Appointments that might have been**). Aickin declined an invitation to succeed **Taylor** on his death in office in 1969, but accepted the offer to replace **McTiernan** on his **retirement** in 1976.

There can be no doubt that Aickin would have been considered a strong candidate for appointment when the opportunity arose in 1976, but a coincidence of timing led some to speculate on the motives of the newly elected Fraser government in making the appointment. In October 1975, shortly before the **dismissal** of the **Whitlam** government by Governor-General John Kerr, Aickin joined with **Gleeson** and Professor PH Lane to offer the opinion that the Governor-General might in appropriate circumstances be entitled to dissolve Parliament and call an election when a government which enjoyed the support of the House of Representatives was nonetheless unable to procure supply (*Ex parte JM Rothery* (1975); see Michael Sexton, *Illusions of Power* (1979) 218).

Despite his undisputed standing at the Bar, Aickin did not make a similar mark on the Bench. This certainly had something to do with the brevity of his tenure—he served as a Justice of the Court for less than six years. Yet it also was a function of his **judicial style**. He tended to write at considerable length (even for the High Court), employing the technique often found in the written opinions of **counsel**, of including extensive quotations from earlier authority. Moreover, the style which Dixon had embodied so well, and which contributed to his lionisation among the legal profession, was not so obviously suited for the temperament of the last quarter of the twentieth century, and had in any event a complex and enigmatic character in the hands of Dixon that was not easily replicated. As JD Merralls has put it, Aickin's judgments 'seldom cast the shaft of light for which one looks to the highest court'. One exception is provided by his judgments in patent matters, particularly in *Minnesota Mining & Manufacturing Co v Beiersdorf* (1980). Moreover, Aickin did not consciously court legal controversy, unlike some of his contemporaries on the Bench. An example can be seen in his analysis of the reviewability of Crown decisions in the *Northern Land Council Case* (1981). Aickin took greater pains than any of the other majority Justices to elucidate from the authorities the right to engage in **judicial review**. His approach stands in sharp contrast to that of **Mason**, in particular.

One of the more important cases in which Aickin participated was the second *Territory Senators Case* (1977). In the first *Territory Senators Case* (1975), a closely divided Court had upheld the validity of legislation providing for the ACT and the Northern Territory each to have two representatives in the Senate (McTiernan, Mason, **Jacobs** and **Murphy**; Barwick, **Gibbs** and **Stephen** dissenting). When Aickin replaced McTiernan in 1976, it was widely touted that had he been sitting on the 1975 case instead of McTiernan, the legislation would have most likely been invalidated. This may have been one of the factors that encouraged a second challenge to be mounted in 1977. In the event, the prediction about Aickin's likely stance was correct. He took what might be described as the more conservative view—the view that elevated **federalism** over populist **democracy**—and found the legislation to be invalid. But in one of those poignant moments in judicial decision making, Gibbs and Stephen—two of the three dissenters in the first case, with whose views Aickin was correctly predicted to agree—reacted against what they perceived to be an opportunistic exploitation by the litigants of the change in membership of the Bench and, although adhering to the views that had been earlier expressed, decided to follow the decision of the majority in the first case simply as a matter of **precedent**. Aickin's judgment contains a lengthy discussion of when it is appropriate for the High Court to **overrule** one of its earlier decisions; there is some irony in the fact that, in choosing to do so in this case, he was able to adopt the more conservative view of the Constitution only by taking the more radical path to that conclusion.

Aickin was conservative not only in his judicial views on the Constitution (see, for example, *Uebergang v Australian Wheat Board* (1980), where he foreshadowed his inclination to preserve the Dixonian view of section 92 (see **Interstate trade and commerce**) and *Koowarta's Case* (1982), where he joined the minority in a narrow view of the **external affairs power**), but also in his views on the dynamics of the curial process. He rarely intervened in the course of **argument** and he unfailingly treated counsel (especially younger members of the Bar) with courtesy and respect. Unlike some of his colleagues (most notably in this period Barwick and Murphy), Aickin did not consider it appropriate for Justices to engage with counsel in the thrust and parry of debate in the courtroom setting.

Yet Aickin's private views of the law should not be seen as antediluvian. One could not have achieved the level of professional respect that he did without forming critical views on the state of the law. His joint authorship of the controversial opinion on the political crisis of 1975 has already been noted. In 1967, Aickin spoke at length at the Australian Legal Convention as part of a panel discussing constitutional reform. Among other things, Aickin criticised fellow members of the panel for having been insufficiently ambitious in their terms of reference. He commented on the increasing inaccuracy of the theory of **responsible government** as a descriptor of the real working Constitution, and he mooted the desirability of Australia adopting an enshrined **Bill of Rights**. His strongest comments of all, however, were reserved for any move to increase the powers of the states within the Australian federation. He thought it essential that 'no constitutional change should be made which would tend to perpetuate [state rivalries] or to weaken federal control of the **economy** as a whole'.

Aickin died in June 1982 as a result of injuries sustained in a car accident. In 1952 he had married Elizabeth May Gullett, with whom he had two children: a son and daughter. Lady Aickin later achieved recognition in her own right in the High Court's story. It was she who designed the jabot the Justices wore until Mason introduced a change to the **Court's attire** in the 1980s.

IAN HOLLOWAY

Further Reading

Harry Gibbs, 'Tribute to the Late Sir Keith Aickin KBE' (1982) 56 *ALJ* 482

JD Merralls, 'Sir Keith Aickin' (1982) 12 *UQLJ* 3

'Proceedings of the Fourteenth Legal Convention of the Law Council of Australia' (1967) 41 *ALJ* 221

ICF Spry, 'Sir Keith Aickin' (1982) 11 *AT Rev* 133

Amadio's Case (1983) is a landmark in the protection of disadvantaged parties to commercial transactions. It establishes stringent expectations of what banks or other credit providers must disclose or explain to potential guarantors, especially if the guarantors are legally and financially vulnerable because of their personal relationship with the debtor. It reinforces the principle that those who give personal guarantees and mortgages to banks and credit providers to secure another person's debts have the legal right not to be taken advantage of by debtors or financiers, to know the true financial position, and to have adequate opportunity to receive independent advice. It stands with other examples of the High Court's use of the concepts and doctrines of **equity** (including **estoppel**, **undue influence**, constructive **trusts**, **restitution**, and relief against forfeiture of interests in land) to develop Australian **common law**, and establishes the notion of **unconscionability** as a unifying doctrinal rationale underlying much of that development.

In 1977, Giovanni and Cesira Amadio executed a mortgage and guarantee over their home in favour of a bank, as security for an overdraft for a company controlled by their son, Vincenzo. Both were aged in their seventies. Italian-born, they had lived in Australia for more than 40 years. Neither had received much formal education and both had some degree of difficulty in understanding written English. They had limited business experience and relied on Vincenzo to manage their financial affairs. He induced them to give the security.

Vincenzo traded as a land developer and builder through a number of companies he controlled. He had brought important business to the bank, and his company had a joint commercial building project with one of the bank's subsidiaries. Prior to the Amadios' mortgage, the bank had shown a degree of tolerance for the company's indebtedness and, anxious to keep Vincenzo's business, the bank agreed to give the company further assistance on conditions that included taking a mortgage over the parents' property.

Vincenzo wrongly told his parents that the mortgage would be limited to $50 000 and would only be for six months. Believing this, they signed the mortgage, at their home in the presence of a bank officer, without much opportunity to read it or to ask questions about it. The bank officer offered no explanation to them because he believed Vincenzo had done so, and nothing reasonably alerted him to their ignorance of its implications. However, Vincenzo and the bank knew that the transaction was financially unwise for the Amadios. They also knew that the mortgage was essential for the company to continue in business and knew that the Amadios had received no independent legal or financial advice. When the company went into liquidation, the bank served a demand on the Amadios and moved to exercise its power of sale.

The Amadios resisted the bank's action by proceedings in the Supreme Court of SA. Their **counsel** argued that the bank had acted unconscionably, that the mortgage was induced by undue influence, and that it was obtained by misrepresentation or concealment of information that the bank knew and should have disclosed. The trial judge decided in favour of the bank, but that decision was reversed on appeal. The bank's further appeal to the High Court was dismissed. The majority, with only **Dawson** dissenting, concluded that the personal circumstances of the Amadios and the circumstances surrounding execution of the mortgage were such that the Amadios were under a special **disability** or disadvantage; and that this was sufficiently evident to the bank to make it unconscionable for the bank to have obtained the mortgage without doing more to alleviate the injustice of the position. The Court ordered the transaction to be set aside.

The result is a striking development of the law of unconscionability as a ground for equitable intervention in contractual relations where a party in a superior bargaining position has unconscionably or unconscientiously taken advantage of another party's special disability or special disadvantage. As **Fullagar** had said in *Blomley v Ryan* (1956), cited by **Deane** in *Amadio*, the relevant special circumstances include but are not limited to 'poverty or need of any kind, sickness, age, sex, infirmity of body or mind, drunkenness, illiteracy or lack of education, and lack of assistance or explanation where assistance or explanation is necessary'.

More broadly, the case illustrates the High Court's use of equitable doctrines in contributing to Australia's development as a modern liberal **democracy** committed to fairness and justice, especially in the legal treatment of disadvantaged parties in commercial transactions. It represents a further significant step not only in the intermingling of common law and equity, but also in equity's displacement of the primacy of **contract** in response to contemporary developments in **consumer law**. The case might also be viewed as part of a wider anti-formalist trend in the High Court (see **Form and substance**).

BRYAN HORRIGAN

Further Reading
Anthony Mason, 'The Place of Equity and Equitable Remedies in the Contemporary Common Law World' (1994) 110 *LQR* 238

Amendment of Constitution. It is not the **role** of the Court to amend the Constitution. That role is given to the Australian people under section 128 of the Constitution. This section allows the Constitution to be amended if, and only if, a Bill for that purpose is passed by federal Parliament and approved at a referendum by a majority of the people and a majority in a majority of states. The role of the Court is to decide disputed questions of **constitutional interpretation**.

Yet the Court is sometimes accused of amending the Constitution. This happens when it adopts an interpretation that introduces, or appears to introduce, a significant change from the settled expectations of the accusers. The charge that the Court has effectively amended the Constitution is often merely a rhetorical way of characterising a decision with which the accusers happen to disagree, but it does give rise to the question of the extent to which the Court should be bold and progressive in adapting the Constitution to changing circumstances, or alternatively should be cautious and deferential to the historical intent of the written word, no matter how out of date and ill-adapted that might seem with the passage of time.

It is important first to understand the complex ways in which formal amendment through a referendum can interact with judicial decisions on the meaning of the Constitution. There are examples of referendums—some successful and some unsuccessful—designed specifically to overcome the effects of earlier decisions. Conversely, there are examples of judicial decisions that appear to be at odds with and may be seen to have undermined earlier referendum outcomes. And in addition to these practical though relatively few and often ambiguous examples, there remains the question—perhaps informed by such examples—of the ways in which the Court's approach to constitutional interpretation may be influenced by the ever-present hypothetical prospect of formal amendment.

The addition of section 51(xxiiiA) in 1946 expanded the power of the Commonwealth over social services after the Court had exposed limits to the power in the *First Pharmaceutical Benefits Case* (1945). The amendment of section 72 in 1977 to introduce a **retirement** age for federal judges overcame the decision in *Alexander's Case* (1918) that, on the proper interpretation of the original section, federal judges had life **tenure**. On the other hand, the **Menzies** government failed in 1951 to overcome by referendum the Court's decision in the *Communist Party Case* (1951) that its legislation banning the Communist Party was unconstitutional.

The converse cases of judicial decisions upholding the exercise of powers previously denied to the Commonwealth by the people are more intriguing. In 1937, a proposed amendment to extend Commonwealth power over aviation (itself a response to the Court's 1936 decision in *R v Burgess; Ex Parte Henry*) failed, yet some thirty years later, in *Airlines of NSW v NSW (No 2)* (1965), the Court found, in the light of the increased density and complexity of interstate air traffic, ample power for the Commonwealth in that area. More dramatically, the electorate rejected five referendum proposals between 1911 and 1944 to give the Commonwealth power to control monopolies (thus failing to overcome the decision in *Huddart Parker v Moorehead* (1909)), yet the power was effectively conferred in 1971 by the decision in *Strickland v Rocla Concrete Pipes*.

The conclusions that can be drawn from these examples are limited. The reasons why referendums fail are elusive, diverse, specific and time-bound. General explanations range from the cynical view that the electorate is typically ignorant and easily misled, to the more generous (but equally political) view that the electorate has typically had the innate good sense to know a bad proposal when it sees one. The Court interprets the Constitution according to a range of general principles, sometimes looking at the Constitution in a new light, sometimes even correcting past errors, but rarely speculating about the significance of past referendums. In the *Incorporation Case* (1990), counsel argued that the failure of the five referendum proposals from 1911 to 1944 supported a narrow interpretation of the **corporations power** that would preclude the Commonwealth from legislating in relation to the incorporation of companies. The Court adopted the narrow interpretation, but made no reference to the argument based on the failed referendum proposals.

Occasionally the Court has had to interpret a section of the Constitution amended as the result of a successful referendum. In the *Hindmarsh Island Bridge Case* (1998), for example, the issue was whether the 1967 amendment to section 51(xxvi) of the Constitution, to enable the Commonwealth to pass laws in relation to **Aboriginal peoples**, authorised only laws for their benefit or also laws to their detriment. The majority upheld a law facilitating the construction of a bridge from mainland SA to Hindmarsh Island that would allegedly violate a sacred site. **Kirby** dissented, placing particular emphasis on the intention of the 1967 amendment. The difference of opinion indicated that, whether it is the original Constitution or its amendments that fall to be interpreted, the same tensions will exist between textual and purposive considerations, and the same issue will arise of whether the living intentions of the drafters of and assenters to the text—old or new—have been sufficiently captured in their inert prose.

The more difficult question is whether, and how, the task of interpreting the Constitution is affected by the existence in the Constitution of a deliberate mechanism for formal amendment. Interestingly, the prospect of formal amendment has restrained some Justices and emboldened others, as

that prospect may be seen either as a legitimate brake on judicial creativity or as a safety valve for the correction of misplaced **activism**. Generally speaking, however, the historical difficulty of securing an amendment to the Constitution (in the 100 years from 1901 to 2001 only eight out of forty-four referendum proposals were approved) has meant that the fundamental task of judicial interpretation, with its inherent tensions and choices between progressivism and conservatism, between activism and restraint, between creativity and caution, has been little affected.

If anything, the difficulty in practice of formally amending the Constitution perhaps supports those Justices who would take more upon themselves in endeavouring to keep the Constitution up to date and in tune with modern and evolving needs, though that approach is often coupled with the more cynical view of why referendums fail. The practical difficulty of amendment does make the appeal of some Justices to the electorate to legitimise constitutional change seem overly theoretical. At least in relation to constitutional provisions and phrases of teasing generality rather than of limiting particularity, the Justices have a range of choices that are consistent with accepted principles and norms of constitutional interpretation. Even resort to **history** is not necessarily a straitjacket that binds the interpreter tightly to a particular perspective of the past, at least if it is acknowledged that progressive interpretation can itself be reasonably viewed as a part of what was historically intended. The truth is that individual approaches to constitutional interpretation, whether bold and imaginative or cautious and restrained, seem to owe little to the distant prospect of an amendment being submitted to—let alone approved by—the people.

MICHAEL COPER

Further Reading
Michael Coper, *Encounters with the Australian Constitution* (1987, popular edn 1988) Ch 9
Michael Coper, 'The People and the Judges: Constitutional Referendums and Judicial Interpretation' in Geoffrey Lindell (ed), *Future Directions in Australian Constitutional Law* (1994)

Annual Reports. The Court's obligation to furnish annual reports is designed to facilitate evaluation of its performance and to enhance its **accountability**. Annual reporting also ensures that a significant amount of information, otherwise unavailable, is placed on the public record. Nevertheless, the reporting obligation has generated disquiet from time to time, some seeing in it the potential to detract from judicial **independence**.

Before the commencement of the *High Court of Australia Act* 1979 (Cth), the **administration** of the Court was controlled by the Attorney-General's Department, with no requirement that the Court furnish annual reports. However, since 1979, section 47 of that Act has required the Court to present an annual report relating to the administration of the affairs of the Court. The Annual Report and accompanying financial statements are forwarded by the Court's **Chief Executive and Principal Registrar** to the **Attorney-General**, who then presents the Report to Parliament for consideration. Like all other public sector annual reports, the Court's reports are audited by the Commonwealth Auditor-General.

The Annual Reports from 1996 onwards are published on the Court's website.

As well as complying with the statutory requirements, the Annual Report provides general information about the Court, including a brief description of its operation, work and history; biographical details of the Justices and former Justices; an outline of its administration; financial statements for the financial year in question; and relevant statistical data. In addition, the Court has in recent years begun to use its Annual Reports as a vehicle for the expression of general concerns and more specific grievances. For example, the 1999–2000 Annual Report contains material under the headings 'Increased workload' and 'Unrepresented litigants'. It also expresses the Court's frustration at the government's denial of funding for a public information officer position, and funding for weekend openings of the Court building.

In practice, review of the Court's Annual Reports is undertaken by the Senate Standing Committee on Legal and Constitutional Affairs rather than directly by the Parliament. The Guidelines on reporting issued by that Committee are directed not only at the federal courts but also at a range of statutory authorities and other bodies such as the National Crime Authority, the Office of Parliamentary Counsel, the Human Rights and Equal Opportunity Commission, and the Administrative Appeals Tribunal. The High Court has, at various times, objected to being subject to the same reporting requirements as these other bodies, on the basis that the Court's status and **role** entitle it to a greater measure of independence.

In February 1986, the Committee wrote to the Court requesting the inclusion in Annual Reports of information about costs and delay, 'to dispel any misconceptions as to the efficient functioning of this distinguished Court'. For the Court, however, the Committee's request represented a threat to 'the independent position which the Constitution secures to the Court in its exercise of **judicial power**'. The Committee was unmoved, maintaining that 'there is a clear distinction to be drawn between judicial independence … and the accountability of institutions [funded by] public monies'. The Court ultimately acceded to the Committee's request and included in its 1985–86 Annual Report detailed information on costs and delay, including details of the expense incurred in maintaining **chambers** in various states, and in travelling to and hearing cases in the states (see **Circuit system**).

Since that episode, the Court has become more accepting of its reporting obligations—perhaps because it has recognised the potential of Annual Reports as a kind of lobbying and publicity tool, or perhaps because it has come to view them as part of the trade-off necessary to secure the advantages that have come with more direct control of its own administration under the High Court of Australia Act.

AMELIA SIMPSON

Appeal book. The documents that are to be considered in an appeal before the High Court are bound into a volume or volumes known as the appeal book. The documents include the pleadings, the evidence, and the judgments and reasons for judgment of the lower court or courts from which the appeal is brought. The formal and procedural requirements of the Court relating to appeal books are set out in the **High Court Rules** and in **practice directions** issued by the Court from time to time. One of those requirements is that ten copies must be filed: in addition to one for each of the seven Justices, the other three copies are used by staff in the Registry, the **Library** and the Court Reporting Service, which prepares the **transcript of argument**.

The Justices use the appeal book to prepare for oral **argument**. Then, during oral argument, frequent reference is made by the Justices and by **counsel** to the material contained in it. The Justices also draw upon the material in the appeal book in writing their judgments.

CHRIS DOOGAN

Appearance, right of. Section 55B of the *Judiciary Act* 1903 (Cth) confers a right of audience in all federal courts on practitioners who are entitled to practise in state or territory courts. This naturally includes a right of audience in the High Court. The right of practice conferred by section 55B is commensurate with the right of practice in the relevant state or territory. It cannot, however, be exercised until the practitioner's name has been entered in a register of practitioners maintained by the High Court. The High Court has a disciplinary jurisdiction over practitioners entered on the register under section 55C and can order that a practitioner's name be removed from the register. In practice, however, disciplinary matters are left to the state authorities and the High Court's jurisdiction is rarely invoked.

The right of audience conferred by section 55B also extends to cases before state courts exercising federal jurisdiction. A practitioner entitled to appear before federal courts is, therefore, also entitled to appear in any state or territory court exercising federal jurisdiction. Each **state Supreme Court** keeps a register of practitioners exercising that right of audience in which the practitioner's name must be entered.

The High Court Registry will enter a practitioner's name in the register of practitioners upon provision of copies of the practitioner's certificate of admission to a state or territory Supreme Court and, where applicable, the practitioner's practising certificate. The practitioner then receives a High Court practising certificate stamped with the **seal** of the Court.

NYE PERRAM

Appointment of Justices. The appointment of Justices to the High Court is frequently a matter of some speculation and, given the **role** of the Court, its nature as a **political institution**, and the impact of its decisions, has sometimes been controversial. Two enduring controversies concern the proper place of 'merit' in deciding on candidates for appointment, and the need for the appointment process to produce a more diverse Court that reflects or represents the society from which it is drawn.

Neither the Constitution nor the *High Court of Australia Act* 1979 (Cth) defines the process or the qualifications for the appointment of Justices to the High Court in any detail. Prior to **amendment** of the Constitution in 1977, Justices were appointed for life; since 1977, they are appointed until the age of 70 (Constitution, section 72; see **Tenure**).

Appointment of Justices

Justices of the High Court of Australia

Name	Born	Died	Period in office	Age on Court	Government at time of appointment	State of residence
Samuel Griffith	1845	1920	CJ 1903–19	58–74	Protectionist	Qld
Edmund Barton	1849	1920	1903–20	54–70	Protectionist	NSW
Richard O'Connor	1851	1912	1903–12	52–61	Protectionist	NSW
Isaac Isaacs	1855	1948	1906–30; CJ 1930–31	51–75	Protectionist	Vic
Henry Higgins	1851	1929	1906–29	55–77	Protectionist	Vic
Frank Gavan Duffy	1852	1936	1913–31; CJ 1931–35	60–83	ALP	Vic
Charles Powers	1853	1939	1913–29	60–76	ALP	Qld
Albert Piddington	1862	1945	1913	50	ALP	NSW
George Rich	1863	1956	1913–50	49–87	ALP	NSW
Adrian Knox	1863	1932	CJ 1919–30	55–66	Nationalist	NSW
Hayden Starke	1871	1958	1920–50	48–78	Nationalist	Vic
Owen Dixon	1886	1972	1929–52; CJ 1952–64	42–77	Nationalist–CP Coalition	Vic
Herbert Evatt	1894	1965	1930–40	36–46	ALP	NSW
Edward McTiernan	1892	1990	1930–76	38–84	ALP	NSW
John Latham	1877	1964	CJ 1935–52	58–74	UAP–CP Coalition	Vic
Dudley Williams	1889	1963	1940–58	50–68	UAP–CP Coalition	NSW
William Webb	1887	1972	1946–58	59–71	ALP	Qld
Wilfred Fullagar	1892	1961	1950–61	57–68	Liberal–CP Coalition	Vic
Frank Kitto	1903	1994	1950–70	46–67	Liberal–CP Coalition	NSW
Alan Taylor	1901	1969	1952–69	50–67	Liberal–CP Coalition	NSW
Douglas Menzies	1907	1974	1958–74	50–67	Liberal–CP Coalition	Vic
Victor Windeyer	1900	1987	1958–72	58–71	Liberal–CP Coalition	NSW
William Owen	1899	1972	1961–72	61–72	Liberal–CP Coalition	NSW
Garfield Barwick	1903	1997	CJ 1964–81	60–77	Liberal–CP Coalition	NSW
Cyril Walsh	1909	1973	1969–73	60–64	Liberal–CP Coalition	NSW
Harry Gibbs	1917		1970–81; CJ 1981–87	53–69	Liberal–CP Coalition	Qld
Ninian Stephen	1923		1972–82	48–58	Liberal–CP Coalition	Vic
Anthony Mason	1925		1972–87; CJ 1987–95	47–69	Liberal–CP Coalition	NSW
Kenneth Jacobs	1917		1974–79	56–61	ALP	NSW
Lionel Murphy	1922	1986	1975–86	52–64	ALP	NSW
Keith Aickin	1916	1982	1976–82	60–66	Liberal–NCP Coalition	Vic
Ronald Wilson	1922		1979–89	56–66	Liberal–NCP Coalition	WA
Gerard Brennan	1928		1981–95; CJ 1995–98	52–69	Liberal–NCP Coalition	Qld
William Deane	1931		1982–95	51–64	Liberal–NCP Coalition	NSW
Daryl Dawson	1933		1982–97	48–63	Liberal–NCP Coalition	Vic
John Toohey	1930		1987–98	56–67	ALP	WA
Mary Gaudron	1943		1987–	44–	ALP	NSW
Michael McHugh	1935		1989–	53–	ALP	NSW
William Gummow	1942		1995–	52–	ALP	NSW
Michael Kirby	1939		1996–	56–	ALP	NSW
Kenneth Hayne	1945		1997–	52–	Liberal–NPA Coalition	Vic
Ian Callinan	1937		1998–	60–	Liberal–NPA Coalition	Qld
Murray Gleeson	1938		CJ 1998–	59–	Liberal–NPA Coalition	NSW

Appointments are made by the Governor-General in Council (section 72), on the advice of the **Attorney-General** following a decision by Cabinet. Accordingly, appointment is in the gift of the executive government of the Commonwealth, though some consultation with the states has been required since the High Court of Australia Act was passed in 1979. The Constitution does not otherwise control the appointment process or specify the terms on which Justices are appointed, except to regulate **removal** and to prevent the Parliament from diminishing a Justice's **remuneration** during his or her term of office (section 72).

The High Court of Australia Act, and before it the *Judiciary Act* 1903 (Cth), regulates some aspects of the appointment process, though again these provisions are limited in scope and, moreover, are not constitutionally entrenched. First, as noted above, when there is a vacancy on the Court, the Commonwealth Attorney-General must consult the Attorneys-General of the states about the appointment to that vacancy. The manner and form of the consultation are not prescribed. (No consultation was required by law prior to the High Court of Australia Act, although some formal consultation had taken place since 1976 at least, and no doubt informal consultation before that.) Secondly, Justices are appointed by commission (in recent practice, at least, signed and sealed with the Great Seal of Australia). Thirdly, once appointed, Justices are not capable of accepting or holding any other office of profit within Australia. (The Judiciary Act had permitted a Justice to hold any other Commonwealth judicial office.)

The absence of detailed constitutional or statutory provisions for appointment means that the process rests mainly on convention and on practices adopted by individual governments. Currently, the Commonwealth Attorney-General writes to the state and territory Attorneys-General advising them of a vacancy or impending vacancy. They are invited to consult widely within their own jurisdictions and to identify and nominate candidates worthy of consideration. The Commonwealth Attorney-General then circulates to each state and territory Attorney-General a list of candidates under consideration. The list is based on the nominations received, together with any names the Commonwealth might wish to add to the list. In the ordinary course, the source of each nomination is not identified.

The Attorney-General also undertakes his or her own consultations within the states and territories, especially with members of the federal courts and others (including former judges, leaders of the legal profession and ministerial and other parliamentary colleagues). There is no formal consultation with the Opposition parties although the Attorney-General considers any submissions that they might make.

Following this process, the Attorney-General informs Cabinet of his or her recommendation. Cabinet considers the Attorney-General's recommendation and decides whom the Attorney-General should advise the Governor-General in Council to appoint. The Cabinet may decide on a person other than the person recommended by the Attorney-General (see, for example, **Appointments that might have been**). The Attorney-General, having obtained the agreement of the person chosen by Cabinet, advises the Governor-General in Council to issue a commission to that person. The High Court of Australia Act requires that the new Justice take a **judicial oath** or make an affirmation of allegiance and of office. The current practice is that the Justice does so at a **ceremonial sitting** of the Court at its **seat** in **Canberra**.

The Constitution is silent on the qualifications for appointment as a Justice, other than prohibiting the appointment of Justices who have reached the retiring age. The High Court of Australia Act provides that a person shall not be appointed unless he or she is or has been a judge of a federal, state or territory court, or has been enrolled for not less than five years as a legal practitioner of the High Court or of the Supreme Court of a state or territory. (The Judiciary Act restricted appointment to judges and *practising* barristers and solicitors of not less than five years standing.)

The lack of detailed criteria for appointment means that the executive government is subject to very few constraints on its choice. Despite this, the **background of Justices** has been remarkably homogeneous: almost all of those appointed have been middle-aged, male, Anglo-Saxon barristers or former barristers. However, the homogeneity has not been absolute—in particular, the first (though as yet the only) female Justice, **Gaudron**, was appointed in 1987—and there have been several contentious appointments.

The contentious appointments include **Piddington**, who, prior to his appointment in 1913, let it be known in response to a request from **Prime Minister** WM Hughes that he favoured Commonwealth over state power, and, following the controversy sparked in part by the revelation of that exchange, felt compelled to resign before taking his seat. The appointment of **Powers**, at the same time as Piddington, was also controversial, partly because he was not a practising barrister at the time (he was Commonwealth Crown Solicitor), and partly because he was trenchantly criticised in some sections of the press, as Piddington had been, for being mediocre in talent. The appointments of **Evatt** and **McTiernan** in 1930 resulted from a decision made by the Labor caucus, rather than by Cabinet, when Prime Minister James Scullin and Attorney-General Frank Brennan were overseas. Scullin and Brennan opposed the appointments as they feared that the appointees' Labor connections and the circumstances of the appointments would reduce the authority of the Court. The disagreement became known and was exploited by the Opposition. The appointment in 1975 of **Murphy**—a radical, reforming Labor Attorney-General—was heavily criticised by those who regarded a political background as unsuitable in general (notwithstanding that such a background had been a common feature of early appointments to the Court) and Murphy's politics—in substance and style—as undesirable in particular. Yet the politics of conservatism can also be controversial; **Callinan's** appointment occurred after National Party Leader and Deputy Prime Minister Tim Fischer had called publicly for the appointment of a 'capital-C conservative'.

In these cases, controversy arose, at least in part, because the appointments challenged the orthodox perception of the Court. That perception is that the Court is an independent, apolitical, and strictly legal institution, whose Justices are selected for their eminence as lawyers and not because of their social or political outlook (see **Accountability; Independence; Policy considerations; Political institution; Values**).

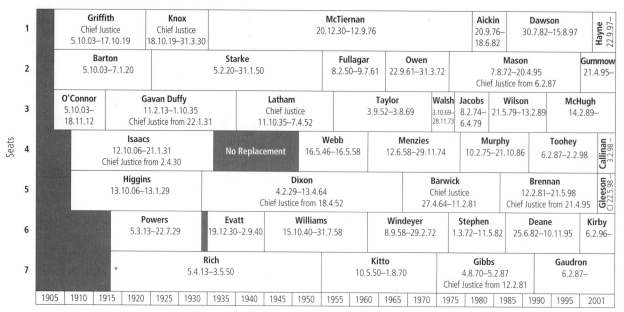

Seats / Period in office

Seat				
1	Griffith — Chief Justice 5.10.03–17.10.19	Knox — Chief Justice 18.10.19–31.3.30	McTiernan 20.12.30–12.9.76	Aickin 20.9.76–18.6.82 · Dawson 30.7.82–15.8.97 · Hayne 22.9.97–
2	Barton 5.10.03–7.1.20	Starke 5.2.20–31.1.50	Fullagar 8.2.50–9.7.61 · Owen 22.9.61–31.3.72	Mason 7.8.72–20.4.95 Chief Justice from 6.2.87 · Gummow 21.4.95–
3	O'Connor 5.10.03–18.11.12 · Gavan Duffy 11.2.13–1.10.35 Chief Justice from 22.1.31	Latham — Chief Justice 11.10.35–7.4.52	Taylor 3.9.52–3.8.69 · Walsh 3.10.69–28.11.73 · Jacobs 8.2.74–6.4.79	Wilson 21.5.79–13.2.89 · McHugh 14.2.89–
4	Isaacs 12.10.06–21.1.31 Chief Justice from 2.4.30 · No Replacement	Webb 16.5.46–16.5.58 · Menzies 12.6.58–29.11.74	Murphy 10.2.75–21.10.86 · Toohey 6.2.87–2.2.98 · Callinan 3.2.98	
5	Higgins 13.10.06–13.1.29 · Dixon 4.2.29–13.4.64 Chief Justice from 18.4.52	Barwick — Chief Justice 27.4.64–11.2.81	Brennan 12.2.81–21.5.98 Chief Justice from 21.4.95 · Gleeson CJ 22.5.98–	
6	Powers 5.3.13–22.7.29 · Evatt 19.12.30–2.9.40 · Williams 15.10.40–31.7.58	Windeyer 8.9.58–29.2.72 · Stephen 1.3.72–11.5.82	Deane 25.6.82–10.11.95 · Kirby 6.2.96–	
7	* · Rich 5.4.13–3.5.50	Kitto 10.5.50–1.8.70 · Gibbs 4.8.70–5.2.87 Chief Justice from 12.2.81	Gaudron 6.2.87–	

1905 1910 1915 1920 1925 1930 1935 1940 1945 1950 1955 1960 1965 1970 1975 1980 1985 1990 1995 2001

Period in office

* Piddington was a Justice from 6.3.13 to 5.4.13

Appointments made by Labor governments, particularly in earlier times, have regularly been criticised (often by a conservative **legal profession**) as 'political' and threatening the independence of the Court. But, as Geoffrey Sawer argued, such appointments are no less political than many appointments of eminent lawyers by non-Labor parties. 'The parties of the right habitually appoint social conservatives to such positions, but need to make no parade of it since most eminent lawyers are social conservatives.' Accordingly, in Sawer's view, 'Labor was entitled to seek to influence the general social outlook of the High Court by appointing men of a different background from those whom the non-Labor parties would normally choose for such positions'. In fact, however, Labor governments have tended to balance 'radical' appointments with appointments of eminent lawyers without party political affiliations or known 'radical' views. Even in 1945, when the Labor Cabinet decided initially to enlarge the Court to nine Justices (from the then six), with the evident purpose of appointing Justices sympathetic to Labor policies, Evatt—then Attorney-General and committed to the independence of the Court—persuaded Cabinet to reverse its decision and to enlarge the Court only to its former strength of seven Justices. Cabinet ultimately recommended the appointment of the generally conservative **Webb**.

In short, the executive's dominant practice of appointing skilled lawyers with high reputations for traditional legal expertise and the Court's dominant technique of **legalism** have supported each other throughout most of the Court's history. When legalism was challenged by **realism** as an account of the Court's **decision-making process** (as it was by Murphy and later by the **activism** of the **Mason Court** in decisions such as *Mabo* (1992) and the **implied constitutional rights** cases), it was inevitable that the appointment of

Justices would come under more critical scrutiny and that proposals for **reform** would be made.

There have in fact been proposals for change to the process of appointing Justices since the **establishment** of the Court and even before that time. The most radical was the proposal by SA delegates at the 1897 and 1898 meetings of the Constitutional Convention that the Court be composed of a **Chief Justice** and the Chief Justices of the states. That suggestion was renewed (and once again rejected) in the debate on the Judiciary Bill 1903.

In his 1977 'State of the Judicature' address, following the appointment of Murphy in 1975, **Barwick** argued that it was appropriate that the almost unlimited power of the federal government in relation to appointments be curtailed. He proposed that a body (composed of judges, practising lawyers, academic lawyers and lay people) advise the executive of the names of suitable candidates. In his view, such a body was more likely to have an adequate knowledge of the qualities of candidates than any minister. An appointment process involving such a body could take one of a number of forms; Barwick did not express any preference. The body could choose the person to be appointed; it could recommend candidates to the executive, which would retain an unlimited discretion as to the person it appointed; or it could recommend candidates to the executive, which would be obliged to provide reasons if it appointed a person other than one of the recommended candidates.

Appointments to the Court have so far been overwhelmingly from NSW and Victoria. It is not surprising, therefore, that some proposals have sought to add a substantive element to the consultation with the states. These proposals were aimed at increasing the number of Justices appointed from the less populous states, and, no doubt, at thereby increasing the number of Justices opposed to undue centralisation of power in the Commonwealth. For example, in 1973, the Victorian Delegation to the Australian Constitutional Convention proposed that the power to make appointments alternate between the Commonwealth and the states—and that the states' power rotate among the states—so that the Commonwealth would make every second appointment and each state every twelfth one. In the 1980s, the Queensland government proposed that three or more states together be able to veto an appointment.

Such proposals raise two issues: the appropriateness of appointing Justices with regard to their general social, political or legal outlook; and the appropriateness of seeking to have the Court (as the highest court in both the state and federal appellate **hierarchies** and the court that determines the boundaries between state and central power under the Constitution) represent or reflect the make-up of the federation. That issue is an example of a wider debate about whether the Court should represent or reflect the society from which its members are drawn.

In 1987, **Gibbs** argued that a judge should not be regarded as a *representative* of any section of society but should do—and be seen to do—justice to all. But he went on to acknowledge that a perception that any section of society was unfairly excluded from the Bench would be harmful to public confidence in the judiciary. In this sense, it was appropriate that the Court did *reflect* the make-up of the society from which it was drawn. Gibbs did not necessarily accept the realist account of the Court's decision-making process, but his proposal implicitly assumed that an observer might believe that the Justices' backgrounds could affect their decision making. Accordingly, he concluded that where a candidate, otherwise equally meritorious, belonged to a section of society that was not fairly reflected, the appointing government could take account of that fact.

Commentators tended to focus on Gibbs' criticism of a *representative* court and to ignore his argument that the Court could *reflect* the make-up of the society from which it is drawn. On the other hand, others challenged Gibbs' proviso that such a consideration could be taken into account only when candidates were otherwise 'equally meritorious', arguing that the concept of 'merit' was not a natural, apolitical concept but rather was constructed in a way that defined an unduly small cohort from which appointments could be made. In particular, the concept of merit underlying past appointment practices was said to reflect assumptions that practising barristers possessed *all* of the qualities required for judicial office and that *only* barristers possessed those qualities. Unpacking the concept of 'merit' demonstrates that others may possess the technical legal skills, independence and personal qualities required for appointment.

A further weakness in the Gibbs view is that it assumes that candidates who belong to under-represented sections of society will come to the attention of the executive and will be considered for appointment. In practice, such candidates are unlikely to belong to—or even be known to—the informal networks reached by the Attorney-General's consultations. Sean Cooney argues, therefore, that the Attorney-General should implement an affirmative action outreach program and a process of critical self-examination. Other commentators have preferred to combine Gibbs' proposal with Bar-

wick's and suggest that there be an appointment commission with an affirmative action mandate. Of course, this would not in itself solve the problems of accountability or necessarily result in a Court more reflective of the society from which it is drawn. Basic questions would remain: Who should appoint the appointments commission? Using what criteria? What criteria should the appointments commission use in making or recommending the appointment of Justices? Who should determine those criteria?

To answer these questions—and all questions regarding the appointment of Justices—requires a clear view of the role and decision-making processes of the Court. That remains elusive.

SIMON EVANS

Further Reading
Sean Cooney, 'Gender and Judicial Selection: Should There be More Women on the Courts?' (1993) 19 *MULR* 20
Harry Gibbs, 'The Appointment of Judges' (1987) 61 *ALJ* 7
Pip Nicholson, 'Appointing High Court Judges: Need for Reform?' (1996) 68(3) *Australian Quarterly* 69
Geoffrey Sawer, *Australian Federalism in the Courts* (1967)
Shimon Shetreet, 'Who Will Judge: Reflections on the Process and Standards of Judicial Selection' (1987) 61 *ALJ* 766
Daryl Williams, 'Judicial Independence and the High Court' (1998) 27 *UWAL Rev* 140

Appointments that might have been. Many have been considered for—even promised—**appointment** to the High Court, but not appointed. Who some of the candidates were, and why they were not appointed, reveals the influence on the selection process not only of 'merit', but also of politics, state of origin, friendships, and the views of sitting Justices, especially **Chief Justices**.

Given the paucity of records, the variable reliability of sources, and the inherent difficulty of researching events that did not happen, it is impossible to provide a comprehensive account; but the following canvasses instances of non-appointment for which reasonable evidence exists.

On 24 August 1903, **Attorney-General** Alfred **Deakin** wrote that he had always hoped to see five Justices on the inaugural Bench and had wanted Andrew **Inglis Clark** to be one of them. Josiah Symon was also on Deakin's list of appropriate appointees had five positions been available, but Parliament reduced the number of positions to three. Deakin was unsure whether **Barton** would relinquish the Prime Ministership to take the third position, so on 27 August Deakin wrote to Inglis Clark to determine whether Inglis Clark would accept a **puisne** Justiceship if offered it. Inglis Clark replied affirmatively, but Barton decided to take a seat on the High Court after all.

There had been pressure on Barton to appoint himself Chief Justice, but after consulting his friends, especially **O'Connor** (who also expected the Chief Justiceship, according to Chief Justice of SA, Samuel Way), Barton agreed that **Griffith** would be Chief Justice, with himself and O'Connor as puisne Justices. **Isaacs**, who was to join the Bench in 1906, wrote: 'I am sorry Barton took a puisne Justiceship. He should have been Chief or nothing and ought to have been Chief … I should have preferred O'Connor after Barton.'

Samuel Way, Chief Justice of SA 1876–1916, who was offered appointment to the High Court in 1906

According to Way, Symon and fellow South Australian John Downer were 'very angry' about not receiving a seat. Leader of the South Australian Bar and Chairman of the Judiciary Committee at the 1897–98 Federal **Convention**, Symon had probably hoped for the Chief Justiceship. South Australian politician and judge James Boucaut wrote to Griffith in 1901 about the position: 'I fancy Sir Josiah Symon is playing for it.' Symon was encouraged by his supporters who believed he would get the post, and he probably would have had a good chance, according to Sidney and Beatrice Webb in their *Australian Diary 1898*, 'were he not in one of the smaller Colonies'.

According to the *Argus*, when the Bench was increased to five in 1906, Ministers chose from 'Mr Isaacs, Mr **Higgins**, Sir Josiah Symon, Mr Justice Cussen, of Victoria, and Mr Justice Inglis Clark, of Tasmania, practically in that order'. According to South Australian lawyer and politician John Gordon, many in SA wanted Symon appointed so that, among other things, SA would be 'represented' on the Bench. On 29 August, SA barrister and later Commonwealth Attorney-General Patrick Glynn advised Deakin to appoint Symon. JA La Nauze has speculated that Deakin sought Glynn's advice as a 'gesture' to avoid 'the possible charge of having ignored Symon's claims'. Deakin admitted that Symon's qualifications were 'his difficulty' in making the appointment. He almost certainly did not want to foist Symon on the foundation Justices because of Symon's dispute with them as Attorney-General the previous year (see **Strike of 1905**).

On 10 September 1906, Deakin wrote to Way to determine whether Way would accept a formal offer of appointment to the High Court if it was made. According to Gordon, the invitation was 'obviously a ruse' and Way's rejection was 'a foregone conclusion'. Way, over 70 years old, replied on 13 September that when 'the formal offer is made I shall respectfully ask to be excused from accepting it'. The letter shows that before federation, Deakin had considered Way for the inaugural Bench. Deakin's diary suggests that he let Griffith know on 6 September that he would not appoint Symon. On 20 September, Barton wrote how glad he was not to have to suffer Symon as a colleague. Deakin made a formal offer of appointment to Way on 24 September. Deakin's invitation and Way's refusal were tabled in Parliament, allowing Deakin to use his offer—his 'gesture'—to deflect criticism that SA was not represented on the Bench.

On the day the Bill increasing the size of the Bench to five passed its third reading in the Senate, Deakin received a letter, signed by his entire Cabinet, expressing 'a hope that you will be willing to accept one of the positions' so that the Court would be 'exalted in the highest degree in public regard'. Deakin rejected the idea in Parliament on 4 July 1906 because such positions 'should be filled by better men'. In 1912, he wrote: 'I could not possibly have been CJ of the High Court or even a member of it. My professional life had not been nearly long enough to make that possible.' Isaacs and Higgins were appointed to the two vacancies.

O'Connor's death in 1912 and the increase of the Bench to seven created three High Court vacancies. In February 1913, Attorney-General WM Hughes stated publicly that he had first invited John Gordon to fill one of them. Gordon declined because of ill health, but wrote to Hughes about who might be appointed instead.

Gordon wrote that Glynn, whom Deakin tipped, was 'a good fellow', but his 'mental output always seems to … resemble scrambled eggs—wholesome enough, but messy'. Gordon, 'if I were A-G', would not hesitate to recommend a junior barrister like Thomas Bavin, later NSW Premier, 'rather than a doubtful KC'. Gordon also suggested NSW barrister Bernhard Wise and renowned scholar Jethro Brown, among others.

Journalist Hector Lamond recommended Robert **Garran**, Secretary of the Attorney-General's Department. It 'would leave the *SM Herald* without a word to say in protest'. In October 1920, Hughes said in Parliament that he would have appointed Garran to the judiciary at some stage, 'but for the fact that he is too valuable a man for us to lose. We cannot spare him'.

When the appointments were made in 1913, **Gavan Duffy** replaced O'Connor, and **Powers** and **Piddington** took the two other vacancies. When Piddington resigned, he suggested Hughes appoint Wilfred Blacket KC or **Knox**. In a letter to **Prime Minister** Andrew Fisher, Hughes considered **Starke** a good man, but someone 'quite opposed to our view'. In the end, **Rich** was appointed to replace Piddington.

According to **Dixon** in his **retirement** speech, when the government offered Starke a High Court seat in 1920, Starke immediately wrote to Leo Cussen about how it could be arranged to have Cussen appointed instead. 'Cussen found on the whole proposal that there were all sorts of difficulties in it—but most of all that they had asked Starke and had not asked Cussen.' Dixon said the failure to appoint Cussen to the High Court was one of 'two tragedies in the life of the High Court'. The other was the failure to appoint Chief Justice of NSW Frederick Jordan.

In April 1930, after Powers and Knox had resigned, and as expectation grew that Isaacs would be appointed Governor-General, Attorney-General Frank Brennan told the press that 'it seemed proper' to reduce the **number of Justices** to five. But when Brennan and Prime Minister James Scullin were overseas, Caucus demanded that the vacancies be filled by Justices politically acceptable to the Labor Party. Scullin was 'astounded'. He cabled the Acting Prime Minister from overseas:

It is a reversal of Cabinet decision, and means that Cabinet accepts political direction on appointments to the High Court judiciary. Political interference removing this matter from Cabinet responsibility strikes fatally at authority of Court. Attorney-General and I will be no party to that. Number of judges adequate … We ask party to reconsider appointments before it is too late.

Cabinet went ahead and appointed **Evatt** and **McTiernan** in Scullin's absence. Curiously, their appointments were pushed through during the Court's summer vacation (13 December 1930 to 9 February 1931). Evatt was appointed on 19 December 1930, McTiernan on 20 December. Newspapers such as the *Argus* explained why: 'As it is intended that Dr Evatt shall be the Chief Justice his commission will be issued one day before that of Mr McTiernan to ensure Dr Evatt's **seniority**.' The *Argus* believed that Scullin's return caused several Ministers to waver in their allegiance to Caucus, and Gavan Duffy was appointed Chief Justice instead. When Evatt and McTiernan were appointed, Dixon threatened to resign, but Starke talked him out of it.

In late April 1930, newspapers reported strong union pressure upon the federal Ministry to make the Commonwealth Court of **Conciliation and Arbitration** 'more democratic' by appointing the President of that Court, George Dethridge, to the High Court to make way for a more sympathetic judge in arbitration (possibly Piddington). On 1 May, Cabinet decided to hold over 'the question of altering the personnel of the [Arbitration] Court'. Isaacs' retirement in January 1931 created a third High Court vacancy. Cabinet minutes record that in early 1931, Scullin 'brought up matter of communications he received from ARU urging that the third vacancy on the High Court Bench be filled'. In the end, in a time of economic **depression** and controversy over the Evatt and McTiernan appointments, the Labor government left the vacancy unfilled.

Jordan was first offered the seat that went to **Williams** in 1940, but declined, citing age and difficulty of travel as the reasons. According to the **Dixon diaries**, Prime Minister Robert **Menzies** had commissioned the Commonwealth **Solicitor-General** to 'get the A-G [Hughes] to agree to appointing 1. Jordan, 2. W[illia]ms, 3. **Owen** to the Court'. Other names put forward to Hughes included 'Bonney, Nicholas, Maughan, Teece, Spender & Mitchell'. Dixon 'arranged to find out whether J[ordan] would consider it'. Dixon 'rang R[ich] who rang [Jordan]. Reply definitely no'. The diaries record Menzies saying later that 'he was in favour

of an immediate appointment to the HCA [of] Dudley Williams, WFL Owen & Napier (supposing Jordan against) favoured in that order. Weston, Mason & Mitchell discussed and excluded'.

On 2 October 1945, while Attorney-General Evatt was overseas, Cabinet decided to increase the number of Justices to nine. Arthur Calwell and Eddie Ward proposed the increase. At various times, Ward publicly advocated the appointment of people sympathetic to the Labor Party. After he returned, Evatt persuaded Cabinet, on 17 January 1946, to amend its decision. According to Calwell, Evatt feared the government would be accused of packing the Court if it increased the Bench to nine. Cabinet now decided to create one additional seat only. According to **Barwick**, Prime Minister Ben Chifley rejected Evatt's suggestions of Harry Alderman and Jack Barry, two senior **counsel** with Labor Party links:

Chifley wouldn't accept Evatt's nominations. He had Alderman and Jack Barry, but Chifley wouldn't have it. Chifley sent word to me, would I accept it, and I said no … Then the story came to me out of the Cabinet that Chifley said to Evatt, 'If you're not careful, I'll send for Barwick', and that was like a red flag to a bull to Bert. So he reached out and picked on Willy **Webb** … And he was a very nice chap, Willy Webb.

Former Labor Party MP Clyde Cameron has noted Alderman's proposed appointment in *The Cameron Diaries* (1990) and discussed it in an oral history recording with Mel Pratt in 1971. According to Cameron, the proposal to appoint Alderman was linked to his alleged engineering of the transfer of two radio broadcasting licences to the Labor Party. Menzies, who had already repeatedly pursued that allegation in Parliament, was likely to reopen the issue if Alderman was appointed. Others, such as former NSW Supreme Court judge Rae Else-Mitchell, who knew Alderman well, have shown less confidence about Alderman's candidature. Else-Mitchell has suggested that even if Alderman was considered for the appointment, it is unlikely that he would have accepted it.

Barry, a more serious contender, was an eminent Victorian barrister (later a Supreme Court judge), with a scholarly interest in **criminology**. For Geoffrey Sawer, the High Court would have gained from the presence of this 'gadfly … who would have set a brilliant nonconformist mind against the powerful but deeply conservative thought of Sir Owen Dixon'. But when rumours of Barry's appointment reached federal Parliament, his suitability was attacked by members of the Opposition, including Country Party Member for NSW HL Anthony (10 April 1946): 'I'm not challenging Mr Barry's probity, but does anyone suggest he would not be prejudiced if legislation by this Government came before him?'

The vacancy came up for Cabinet decision on 12 April 1946. Evatt now argued for Webb. According to Calwell, Evatt wanted Webb because his appointment would help attract the Catholic vote. Many in Cabinet, including John Dedman, Don Cameron, Jack Holloway, Calwell, and Ward, voted for Barry. The debate was fierce, but Evatt won.

In 1952, Dixon and Menzies discussed who might fill the vacancy caused by **Latham's** retirement. The Dixon diaries record that in early April, Dixon told Menzies that the Court 'had two passengers & we could not carry more'. Menzies said he would not agree to the appointment of Commonwealth Attorney-General John Spicer. Although Dixon thought Spicer a 'good fellow', 'high ability, law, and conduct were needed. I had no doubt of the third in his case but education and **background** counted so much'. After Dixon had discussed the matter with the other Justices, he suggested **Taylor**, Owen, Victorian Supreme Court judges Reginald Sholl and TW Smith, and Douglas **Menzies**. **Fullagar** added Alistair Adam, who had been Fullagar's pupil at the Bar; Latham added NSW Supreme Court Chief Judge in Equity, David Roper.

A month later, Menzies and Dixon reviewed the character of these men. 'Menzies asked me if I thought the idea of a balance between NSW & Vic mattered. I s[ai]d no.' Menzies thought Sholl 'overlaid a simple case with authorities'; his cousin, Douglas Menzies, 'c[oul]d wait'; and Smith was 'cold & unimaginative'. Dixon 'spoke of McT[iernan] and Webb & the possibility of their becoming diplomatists discussed'. In July 1952, Dixon wrote that 'we all thought Sholl less likely to be a success than when I last spoke. He seemed like a doctor so interested in the disease that he was indifferent to the fate of the patient'. Roper was ruled out because he was 'an **equity** man', and in that area, the Court already had Williams, Fullagar, and **Kitto**.

In August, Menzies told Fullagar that Spicer had wanted badly to be appointed but that Menzies had talked him out of it. Spicer and Solicitor-General Kenneth Bailey suggested Victorian QC PD Phillips as 'the only man to be appointed'. Fullagar viewed the appointment as 'entirely unsuitable', saying it 'w[oul]d wreck the Court'. Menzies insisted on Taylor, Owen, or Smith. Fullagar reported to Dixon that Douglas Menzies might have been appointed 'if his name had not been Menzies' and that Robert Menzies had in effect said this. The position was eventually filled by Taylor.

In April 1958, Dixon told Menzies that the Justices (Fullagar, Taylor, and Dixon) thought Douglas Menzies 'outstanding'. Robert Menzies said he had obtained favourable responses from some Cabinet members to Douglas Menzies' proposed appointment (as a replacement for Webb). Dixon told Menzies: 'We thought in NSW Owen J & [JK] Manning J the men. Smith J in Vic. Perhaps Burbury CJ in Tas. No one elsewhere ripe.' The position went to Douglas Menzies.

In May, Dixon and Robert Menzies discussed Williams' successor. Taylor recommended Manning but Dixon 'cast doubt on this' and suggested **Windeyer** or Owen. Menzies said his 'present view' was Owen but that he would enquire. In August, Menzies said that NSW Supreme Court judges Gordon Wallace, Bernard Sugerman, and **Walsh** had been proposed by various people. Dixon viewed Walsh's appointment as being 'without justification'. 'It would be a reflection on Owen, Windeyer, TW Smith in Victoria and so on. He might develop but there was no ground now. Owen and Windeyer were the men.' The appointment went to Windeyer.

In July 1961, Dixon proposed '**Aickin**, Smith, Adam & Owen' for the vacancy caused by Fullagar's death. Dixon and Menzies discussed these and referred to others—'Manning, Burbury CJ, **Jacobs**, Walsh (out) and **Gibbs**'. 'McT[iernan] was referred to as a difficulty.' Douglas Menzies canvassed his

cousin for Smith. Prime Minister Menzies apparently settled on Adam. By this time, Evatt was Chief Justice of NSW. In physical and mental decline, and embittered by Owen's role in the Petrov affair, Evatt had made Owen's life on the Supreme Court miserable. Before the matter went to Cabinet, the Prime Minister was apparently prevailed upon to appoint Owen.

According to Barwick's autobiography, Barwick told Menzies that while Aickin was the best candidate from the Victorian Bar to replace Dixon as Chief Justice in 1964, the Court needed a strong administrator. Barwick said he was willing to be appointed if Cabinet desired it. Dixon was devastated by Menzies' decision to appoint Barwick. His diaries contain several references to Dixon's suggesting to Menzies that he should consider taking the position himself. If Menzies refused, Dixon, wanting his successor to be from the Victorian Bar, had a clear preference for Aickin.

Cabinet papers confirm that in 1969, Aickin declined, for family reasons, the appointment that eventually went to Walsh. It is understood that Gibbs was also on the short list. When Gibbs was appointed in 1970, he was Attorney-General Tom Hughes' sole recommendation. Contrary to rumour, **Wilson's** name was not put forward.

There was speculation in 1972 about whether Nigel Bowen, the Minister for Foreign Affairs and former Attorney-General, would be appointed to fill the vacancy created by Owen's death. Prime Minister William McMahon had promised Bowen that he would be appointed. But the appointment would have necessitated a by-election for Bowen's marginal seat of Parramatta. A defeat there, in an election year, would have been a severe embarrassment to the government. According to the former Secretary of the Attorney-General's Department, Clarrie Harders, keeping Bowen in Parliament was also vital to McMahon because of Bowen's legal contribution to the government and the extent to which McMahon personally relied upon Bowen. The vacancy created by Owen's death was filled by **Mason**.

In the 1960s, Gough Whitlam evidently promised to appoint Else-Mitchell to the High Court if and when the opportunity arose. However, when the opportunity did arise (after Walsh's death in 1973), Else-Mitchell told Whitlam that he was no longer interested in a High Court seat, for a variety of personal and professional reasons. **Murphy** had at one stage proposed that Colin Howard be appointed, but Whitlam thought that Australians were not ready for an academic to be appointed to the Court. Whitlam and Murphy chose Jacobs instead.

In 1975, Murphy was appointed to fill the vacancy caused by Douglas Menzies' death. Solicitor-General Maurice Byers and NSW judge Robert Hope were the other major candidates for the post. It is widely believed that a promise of a seat was made to Byers, and that Byers was willing to accept it (but see **Whitlam era**).

Cameron has written in *The Cameron Diaries* about a Caucus meeting at which Whitlam discussed the government's proposal to introduce a compulsory retirement age for federal judges, Whitlam 'explaining that the proposed retiring age would not apply to existing judges, but that "when the Labor Government appoints Mr Justice Murphy as Chief Justice of the High Court, the new retiring age would apply to him"'. According to Cameron, 'it was generally accepted that when Murphy agreed to accept his appointment to the High Court there was a tacit understanding he would succeed Barwick'. Barwick gives an elaborate account in his autobiography, claiming that a meeting took place between Whitlam, Deputy Prime Minister Jim Cairns, and Murphy at which Murphy insisted that Whitlam give him a firm assurance that should the position of Chief Justice fall vacant Murphy would be appointed: 'Jim Cairns has assured Clyde Cameron that this took place.'

For Whitlam, 'it is unreal to suggest that Murphy would have sought or that Cairns or I could have given an assurance that Murphy would later be appointed Chief Justice … Cameron was not present when Cairns raised Murphy's appointment with me in December 1974 and when Murphy, Cairns and I discussed it on 9 February 1975. Cairns has assured me that he did not inform Cameron of our discussion.' Cairns has agreed: 'Whitlam never at any time gave Murphy an assurance that he would be appointed Chief Justice if the position became vacant. I never at any time assured Clyde Cameron that this took place.' Cameron, however, has reaffirmed what he wrote in *The Cameron Diaries*, asserting that his information came directly from Murphy as well as from Cairns.

When the vacancy caused by McTiernan's retirement arose in 1976, it was first offered to Wilson, from WA, because of a desire to encourage appointments from the less-populous states. Wilson declined for personal reasons. The position was then offered to Aickin, who accepted it.

There was much speculation about whether RJ Ellicott would be appointed to replace Barwick as Chief Justice in 1981. Ellicott had been offered, but had declined, the position that ultimately went to Wilson in 1979. Prime Minister Malcolm Fraser had asked Ellicott in 1979 whether he would accept the position of Chief Justice when Barwick retired. Ellicott said he would. When the position became vacant, Fraser and his senior Ministers canvassed widely the respective merits of Ellicott and Gibbs for the Chief Justiceship. The Labor Party attacked Ellicott's role in the **dismissal of 1975**; non-Labor states opposed Ellicott's appointment because of his 'centralist' stance; and newspapers attacked the appointment as an example of 'jobs for the boys'. In the end, Prime Minister Fraser offered Ellicott a puisne Justiceship, which Ellicott again declined.

In 1995, Foreign Minister and former Attorney-General Gareth Evans was seriously considered for a vacancy—evidently, the Chief Justiceship—created by the retirement of Mason. According to Keith Scott, Evans' biographer, at least one government Minister privy to discussions believed that Evans' appointment was a 'jobs-for-the-boys argument we could not afford to have'.

In 1997, the Commonwealth circulated to the states a short list of candidates to fill the vacancies created by the resignations of **Dawson** and **Toohey** and the imminent retirement of **Brennan**. This list was leaked to the *Sydney Morning Herald*. It included South Australian Chief Justice, John Doyle (the candidate who had been most favoured to replace **Deane** in 1995); Western Australian **state Supreme Court** judge Christine Wheeler (the sole woman on the list); the then President of the NSW Bar Association, David Bennett;

the President of the NSW Court of Appeal, Keith Mason; and the then Solicitor-General, Gavan Griffith. In the end, **Hayne** replaced Dawson. John von Doussa was evidently the Attorney-General's choice to replace Toohey, but Prime Minister John Howard preferred to appoint **Callinan**. Callinan's appointment occurred after Deputy Prime Minister and National Party leader Tim Fischer, responding to the *Wik* (1996) decision, publicly called for the appointment of 'capital-C conservatives'. Whether Callinan met that description (assuming such labels to be helpful) is another question.

TROY SIMPSON

Further Reading

J Myron Jacobstein and Roy Mersky, *The Rejected: Sketches of the 26 Men Nominated for the Supreme Court but not Confirmed by the Senate* (1993)

Architecture of Court building. The design of the High Court was developed on the basis of a grand and monumental urban design concept for a 400 metre square National Place within the Parliamentary Triangle in **Canberra**, Australia's national capital. That concept formed part of the design brief for the national architectural competition for the High Court building, held between 1972 and 1973 by the National Capital Development Commission on behalf of the Australian government. Six architectural firms proceeded into a second-stage development phase, and the competition was won by Edwards Madigan Torzillo & Briggs Pty Ltd, from a total submission of 158 designs.

A critical aspect of the design brief was the statement that 'the national functions of the High Court and the Parliament are strongly related. In simple terms, the former interprets Federal law established by the latter'. The brief went on to say that 'the locating of both the High Court and the Parliament in proximity to one another in the Federal Capital has strong symbolic significance. Together they represent the basis of government and justice at the national level'. Part of the design intention was that the High Court **building** be visually related to the Parliament in its setting but at the same time be seen as separate from, and independent of, the Parliament. As a reflection of the High Court's constitutional **independence**, its objectivity of deliberation and its freedom from political influence, the design of the High Court's first permanent home in Australia was intended to express directly through its architecture and **symbolism**, its unity of purpose and independent status.

When the competition was announced, Colin **Madigan** was senior director of Edwards Madigan Torzillo & Briggs, and responsible for the Australian National Gallery in Canberra (1968–82), which had just commenced construction. Madigan initiated the design work for the competition and an associate director of the firm, Chris Kringas, was appointed to head the design team. Tragically, Kringas died in March 1975 before construction work had commenced.

Madigan then resumed control of the design team, whose other main members included Feiko Bouman, Rod Lawrence, Michael Rolfe and Peter Simmonds. Design development work on the Australian National Gallery was already advanced and the firm's High Court team was drawn from the Gallery workforce, with direct access to all the design

Exterior view of the High Court, facing north, towards Lake Burley Griffin

evolution, engineering technology, and extensive design research knowledge that the Gallery project had developed for a building of similar scale and complexity. In many respects, therefore, the two buildings must be seen as in dialogue with each other, as well as being individual works of national architectural and cultural significance in themselves.

The High Court occupies a site near the south-east shore of Lake Burley Griffin in the Parliamentary Triangle, and is related in its landscape siting to the other major buildings of the precinct: Parliament House (1980–88); the Australian National Gallery (1968–82); and the National Library of Australia (1968). While earlier plans (1964) had intended that the High Court flank the nation's Parliament, such a direct relationship was severed with the adoption of the Court's new lakeside site and the move of the future Parliament House from Camp Hill to Capital Hill. Yet the eventual location of the large volumetric spaces of the **courtrooms** on the Parliament side of the building acknowledges that original symbolic relationship. There are two entry points to the High Court: one is for day-to-day business, the loop road off King Edward Terrace that also serves the National Gallery; the other is the forecourt at the level of the National Place. This latter approach is the High Court's ceremonial entrance, a long and gracious ramp with a rushing waterfall running the full length of its western side, with associated landscaping by Harry Howard & Associates. The paved forecourt, recessed in part, has car parking and archival storage beneath and is connected to the National Gallery by a pedestrian overpass bridge, which crosses the roads that give access to both buildings.

From the ceremonial forecourt, which has views back to Parliament House, one enters through a massive glazed wall into the Public Hall. This vast space, conceived as a semi-external space enclosed by enormous trussed glazed walls, is one of the most impressive post-war interiors in Australia. Punctuated only by two soaring concrete columns, which flare at their crowns to support a coffered concrete ceiling, the Public Hall is 24 metres high and forms the heart of the High Court building. Extending in height through eight levels, the Public Hall is the central gathering and circulation space for all the various activities in the building. Within this great volume, ramps that appear to continue the external landscape into the building give easy access to the central functions of the courts on the different levels: Courtroom No 1 on Level 2, Courtroom No 3 on Level 3, Courtroom No 2 on Level 4, and the Public Gallery to Courtroom No 1, also on Level 4. The public ramp system terminates at Level 4 (Courtroom No 2) and the visitor circuit returns to the Public Hall using a series of open stairs if desired.

This sequential route offers a multiplicity of varied perspectives for viewing the grand space of the hall and the various pieces of commissioned **artworks** by artist Jan Senbergs adorning the walls. This public route and progression through the building by ramps and stairs on the lower levels also provides a natural demarcation of the more private facilities at the higher levels, which are served by secure lifts and stairs. This demarcation reflects an expressive yet functional solution to the problems of security and the working processes of the courts. Hence the skylit **library** and the Justices' **chambers** and related spaces are on the uppermost level

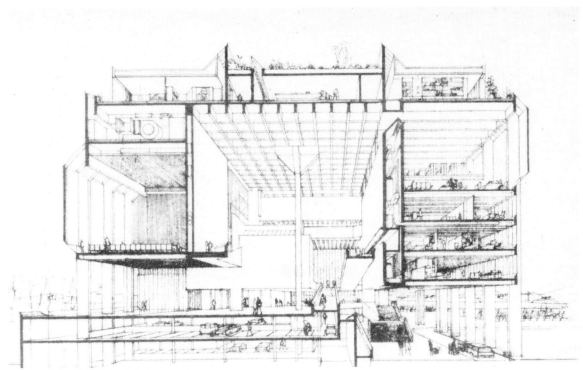

Sectional perspective of the High Court, facing south

(Level 9), and the Justices are able to descend to the **courtrooms** and enter and leave them in private.

The volumetric organisation of the building is expressed both internally and externally, with the three courtrooms, the Public Hall, and the administration wing stacked vertically and overlooking the lake, and the Justices' levels on the uppermost floors. A double-height public dining area is located on the northern side of the building and has views towards the lake. The vigorous functional expression is achieved by reinforced concrete, which is used extensively for the structural and architectural fabric of the building. Homogeneous, monolithic, off-white concrete, carefully designed and engineered, is the primary building element for floors, walls and ceilings. The engineers, Miller Milston and Ferris Pty Ltd, paid particular attention to the unusually extensive surfaces of unbroken panels of high-quality, off-form concrete. Externally and in various parts of the interior, the concrete surface was textured with a rough bush-hammered finish to highlight the warm off-white hue of the granite aggregate. Elsewhere the interiors are softened by the use of warm timbers for wall linings, court benches and associated furniture, as well as by the strategic placement of coats of arms and portraits of distinguished High Court figures of the past.

When the building was opened by Queen Elizabeth II on 26 May 1980, it was one of the most prominent buildings on the Canberra skyline when seen from the eastern side of Lake Burley Griffin. Its robust monumentality remains a tribute to the role of its initiator and major client, then Chief Justice of Australia, **Barwick**.

PHILLIP GOAD

Architecture of Court building: an analysis. In the Middle Ages and well after, the courts of justice were invariably located in the town hall. There was often no differentiation. Governance and justice were housed under the same roof. In London, the courts were in the Palace of Westminster and, more specifically, Westminster Hall. The architectural vocabulary chosen was Gothic—a very nationalistic choice even before the Houses of Parliament competition of 1835, when AWN Pugin and Charles Barry gave permanent Gothic form to the renewed visible evidence of British governance after the disastrous fire of 1834 had destroyed the Palace.

Separate monumental buildings for law courts had however existed in the English provinces since the early eighteenth century, and in France since the late eighteenth century. There, the favoured style for law courts was a grand form of Beaux Arts classicism. It was a style intended to evoke the appropriate sternness and even sacred quality of the law. Such courts were indeed palaces of justice, temples of severity intended to evoke both fear and respect. In Australia, many early courthouses such as those at Darlinghurst and Parramatta adopted the Greek Revival style, especially the Doric, for its austere sobriety. By contrast, George Edmund Street's 1866 design for the London Law Courts exemplified the climax of the Gothic Revival, a style of the utmost ethical and moral impunity. For these buildings and their subsequent heirs, the choice of style was paramount, evidence of the proper purpose and increasingly independent function of the law.

The High Court of Australia presents a not dissimilar image to its nineteenth-century counterparts, except that the image of the building is not one associated with historic styles but with the tenets of twentieth-century Modernism. More specifically, it was the functionalist ideals behind the emergence of a non-representational or non-symbolic architecture in the 1920s in Europe that, by the late 1960s, had been translated into an ethic of design that dictated truthfulness to material and structural expression, and clear and direct expression both internally and externally of the building's internal functions. Such an aesthetic of clarity and honesty seems eminently appropriate for a building devoted to justice. International critics were quick to label such architecture as Brutalism, especially when in the 1950s and early 1960s architects like Le Corbusier and Louis Kahn made bold sculptural uses of off-form concrete. However, the sources behind such architecture are infinitely more complex than a simple expression of function and use of off-form concrete.

In the design of the High Court, its dynamic asymmetry relates to its symbolic independence not just from the existing and dominant symmetry of John Smith Murdoch's Old Parliament House (1927) and Mitchell Giurgola Thorp's Parliament House (1980–88) at the very apex of Canberra's Parliamentary Triangle, but also from the insistent order of the plan and building forms proposed by the original designers of Canberra, expatriate American architects Walter Burley Griffin and Marion Mahony Griffin. The design of the High Court is an exercise in the sculptural deformation of a square. The Public Hall is a great hollowing out of a cubic solid. The law stands revealed and its workings open to scrutiny. The airy glazed volume is a gesture towards an open and accessible public reading of the legal system. The ramps and associated landscaping by Harry Howard (1931–2000), which cascade to the lakeside, are a reflection of the architects' understanding of the Griffins' concept of Canberra as a remediated landscape that was both urban and Arcadian. It is also a demonstration of the architects' desire to contribute to an urban landscape that eventually would have the persuasive monumentality of a place such as Teotihuacan, Mexico; Angkor Vat, Cambodia; or the Imperial Palace in Beijing.

At the same time, the choice of concrete for the material, and the emphasis in the composition of the forms both in plan and in three dimensions, recall the cosmic geometries and the interest in crystal structures that can be seen in the built work of the Griffins (see **Symbolism of building**). In this way, the design of the High Court building should not be seen as a reductive piece of Modernism but as an inclusive architecture that responds directly to its urban context and to the design methods of Canberra's initial planners. **Colin Madigan** himself describes the High Court and the National Gallery as having 'Promethean expression' and as holding 'a demanding asymmetrical balance, in some ways matching, in other ways threatening the illusionary safer symmetry' of the earlier buildings nearby. The grand scale of the ramp was conditioned to fit the scale of the National Place proposed in 1971 by Roger Johnson, then First Assistant Commissioner (Architecture) in the National Capital Development Commission from 1968–72.

That master plan did not eventuate and as a result some of the architectural gestures might, for some, today seem out of scale with the surrounding environment. Yet despite the complexity of the politics of the urban design of the surrounding precinct, the High Court remains one of the most robust and exhilarating pieces of 1970s architecture in Australia. For a court building, the High Court has become a benchmark in Australia for vital architectural expression that deliberately seeks to make the law visible, relevant, and accessible to the public. At the same time, it evokes an entirely fitting sense of monumentality, respectful of the image and also the scale of the law.

Phillip Goad

Further Reading
Edwards Madigan Torzillo & Briggs Pty Ltd and Harry Howard & Associates, 'The High Court of Australia: Architects' Statement' (July 1980) *Architecture Australia* 41
Roger Johnson, *Design in Balance* (1974)
Colin Madigan, 'Burley Griffin Lecture, 1983: The City's History, and the Canberra Triangle's Part in it' (January 1984) *Architecture Australia* 48
Jennifer Taylor, *Australian Architecture Since 1960* (1986)

Archives. The archives of the Court consist of its accumulated documents and records. The collection begins in 1903 and includes Registry files for every case that the Court has considered, files relating to the **administration** of the Court, and a variety of **judges' notebooks** left with the Court by some past Justices.

In early 1994, a Sydney consultancy firm, *Records Archives & Information Management Pty Ltd (RAIM)*, was engaged to conduct a survey of the records maintained by the Court and to provide a strategic plan for their management. The recommendations called for the Court to employ additional staff and incur additional expenditure. This did not occur.

With a large accumulation of paper dating back to 1903, the Court was running out of available space to maintain the records within the **building**. In late 1994, the **Chief Executive and Principal Registrar**, acting on behalf of the Court, entered into arrangements with the Director-General of Archives for Australian Archives to help the Court develop a long-term management program for its records. The work was undertaken by a Project Officer provided by Australian Archives, with the assistance of Registry staff within the Court.

Work proceeded throughout 1995, with the Court and Australian Archives agreeing on a records disposition program which prescribed arrangements for the retention or destruction of records. Experienced staff from Australian Archives worked during 1995 and 1996 to prepare the early records of the Court for transfer to the Australian Archives storage facilities located in Mitchell, an industrial suburb of **Canberra**. By the end of 1996, Court records covering the period 1903 to 1930 had been transferred to Australian Archives. All records after 1930 are currently retained by the Court, but it lacks the resources to comprehensively organise, index and manage them. A great challenge will confront future historians who wish to use the records in their research. Over time, records not immediately needed by the Court will be progressively transferred to Australian Archives.

Chris Doogan

Argument before the Court has been influenced both in style and substance by the Justices who have comprised the Bench during any given period of the Court's history. While **counsel** have rarely been able to present oral submissions without interruption from the Bench, the nature and degree of judicial involvement in argument has varied over time. Ideally, the object of oral argument is to enable the parties to present and refine their respective cases and, in conjunction with the Bench, to focus attention on the central and significant issues raised in the proceedings. As **Barwick** noted on his swearing-in as **Chief Justice** in 1964, 'the period of argument in court is an opportunity for the meeting of minds in the search for truth in relation to the matter at hand'.

Some periods during the Court's history have been characterised by a predilection for intense judicial interrogation of counsel—an approach favoured particularly by Justices such as **Isaacs**, **Gavan Duffy**, **Starke**, **Taylor**, and Barwick. Starke was even moved to observe rather dryly at the commencement of his judgment in *FCT v Hoffnung* (1928) that the appeal had been 'argued by this Court over nine days, with some occasional assistance from the learned and experienced counsel who appeared for the parties'.

Dixon recognised this practice and resolved to change it. On being sworn in as Chief Justice in 1952, he noted that the earlier methods of the Court 'were entirely dialectical, the minds of all the judges were actively expressed in support or in criticism of arguments', and that 'cross-examination of counsel was indulged in as part of the common course of argument'. Dixon came to regard this method as unsatisfactory:

> I felt that the process by which arguments were torn to shreds before they were fully admitted to the mind led to a lack of coherence in the presentation of a case and to a failure of the Bench to understand the complete and full cases of the parties, and I therefore resolved, so far as I was able to restrain my impetuosity, that I should not follow that method and I should dissuade others from it.

However successful Dixon may have been in curbing these judicial methods, there was a revival of the 'Socratic' approach to oral argument under the **Barwick Court**. This was no doubt largely due to the influence of Barwick himself, who on his **retirement** noted that 'no one has ever had to stretch himself much to make me talk, I'm afraid, and no one has had to work very hard to find out what the tendency of my mind may be'. Barwick regarded the time of hearing in court as 'work time', and stated:

> It is not a time for quiescence, it is a time for trying to move, first of all, to identify the problem, to isolate the irrelevant and to bend the mind to the centre and thereafter to begin to work towards a conclusion. You might not get there, but you would get on the way.

Although Barwick described this process as involving a 'dialogue between friends', his tendency to cross-examine counsel in the course of argument ensured that an appearance before the High Court during that period was not for the faint-hearted.

After Barwick's retirement, the Court retreated once again from this approach, as appears from the observation made by **Mason** in 1985 that 'the Court does not in general subject counsel to the gruelling interrogation, dignified by the description "Socratic dialogue", which was so fashionable in the 1960s and the first half of the 1970s'. Mason characterised the role of the Bench during oral argument as one of drawing attention to and seeking explanation of the critical aspects of counsel's case, and exploring the implications and consequences of the legal propositions advanced by the parties.

In more recent times, the Court appears to be returning to a more active and interventionist role during oral argument, and counsel are expected to deal with frequent questions and observations from the Bench.

The duration of oral argument for individual cases is generally shorter in modern times than it was at earlier periods in the Court's history. Although perhaps an extreme example, argument in the *Bank Nationalisation Case* (1948) occupied 39 hearing days before the High Court (and a further 36 hearing days on appeal to the **Privy Council**). Similarly, the *Communist Party Case* (1951) was argued over 24 hearing days. With its increased workload, the Court cannot afford to allow anything approaching this length of hearing in modern times. For example, significant cases such as *Wik* (1996), *Cole v Whitfield* (1988), or *Ha v NSW* (1997) (see **Excise duties**) were heard over three, four and five hearing days respectively. Most appeal hearings now occupy only one or two hearing days.

Unlike the **United States Supreme Court**, however, the High Court has never introduced formal time limits on oral argument in appeal hearings. In major cases involving numerous parties and **interveners**, the **Brennan Court** occasionally adopted a practice of giving directions that allocated time for oral submissions, dividing the available hearing days between the parties. However, this practice has not been continued under Chief Justice **Gleeson**. In contrast, time limits have been applicable since February 1994 to the hearing of applications for special **leave to appeal** to the Court. The **High Court Rules** currently provide that the applicant and the respondent each have a maximum of 20 minutes to present oral submissions, and the applicant has a maximum of five minutes in reply, although the Court has power to extend the time allocated to either party. Further, the Rules provide that a party may elect not to present any oral argument on a special leave application, instead relying exclusively on the written summary of argument prepared pursuant to the Rules.

The emphasis on brevity and efficiency in the presentation of oral submissions has been assisted by the discouragement of unnecessary repetition and of the practice of reading long passages from earlier judgments. The introduction of general requirements for written submissions has also enabled greater efficiency in the hearing of appeals. Judicial views on the utility of written submissions have differed over the years. Until recently, it was not the general practice for parties to prepare detailed written submissions, although a brief written outline of argument was usually handed to the Court by counsel at the beginning of his or her oral submissions.

As far back as the early 1950s, however, the High Court Rules provided a non-compulsory **procedure** by which a party to an appeal could prepare and file a 'written case' summarising the circumstances out of which the appeal arose, and setting out the contentions advanced by the party with supporting reasons. On his retirement in 1952, **Latham** drew attention to the new Rules and said that 'it is thought by the judges that if such a practice is established, and widely used, it will help towards clarity of argument and will save both Bench and bar a great deal of time'. Mason also supported the use of written submissions to complement oral argument, noting in 1985 that they would shorten the hearing without having to resort to fixed time limits, and 'would assist counsel in enabling the judge to appreciate more clearly the part which particular submissions play in the total context of the party's case'. **Gibbs**, on the other hand, observed in 1986 that 'written submissions are not as effective as oral argument in bringing the attention of the court quickly to the heart of the problem' and therefore 'can never … be a satisfactory substitute for oral argument'. Argument before the Court remains firmly in the oral tradition, in contrast with the practice of the US Supreme Court, which requires comprehensive written briefs and generally limits oral argument to half an hour per side.

Since February 1997, the Court has required the preparation of written submissions for appeal hearings, unless otherwise directed by the Court, a Justice or a Registrar. The stated objects of these requirements, set out in **practice directions** of the Court, are to enable the Justices to understand the contentions of the parties before the hearing of the appeal, to enhance the utility of oral argument (in particular by identifying and focusing attention upon the central issue or issues in the matter) and to avoid uncertainty about the documents relevant to the matter. To prevent the potential burdens involved in the receipt of unlimited written material, the practice direction limits both the length and the content of any written submissions.

Another innovation that has affected the conduct of oral argument before the Court is the introduction of hearings by video link, generally between the Bench sitting in **Canberra** and some or all counsel appearing in one of the state capital cities. The system of video link hearings has been designed, however, so as to minimise the impact on the style of oral argument, so that submissions generally proceed in much the same manner as in ordinary courtroom hearings.

Apart from the written submissions of the parties, the essential material relied on by the Court when hearing an appeal will be contained in an **appeal book**, which usually consists of the pleadings, the judgments of the court from which the appeal is brought, any relevant transcripts of the proceedings below, and other relevant primary documents. Each party must also file a list of the authorities it intends to cite during oral argument, to ensure that **associates** or **tipstaves** will have the relevant volumes or photocopies in court for reference by the Justices. These authorities will primarily consist of previous judicial decisions and relevant statutory provisions, but may also include (where appropriate) journal articles or historical material.

The conduct of proceedings in the original **jurisdiction** may raise different issues, not the least of which is the time involved in conducting trials at first instance (for example, the trial conducted by Isaacs in the *Coal Vend Case* (1911) lasted for 73 hearing days). It is now rare for the Court to con-

duct a trial, given that it has broad powers to **remit** matters commenced within its original jurisdiction to the **Federal Court** or to a state or territory court. Alternatively, particularly in constitutional cases, the Court may proceed by stating a case and reserving questions of law for consideration by a **Full Court**. The argument in relation to such questions is then conducted in a similar manner to an appeal proceeding.

DAVID BENNETT

Further Reading
Harry Gibbs, 'Appellate Advocacy' (1986) 60 *ALJ* 496
Anthony Mason, 'The Role of Counsel and Appellate Advocacy' (1984) 58 *ALJ* 537
Anthony Mason, 'Interveners and *Amici Curiae* in the High Court: A Comment' (1998) 20 *Adel L Rev* 173

Artworks of Court. From its opening in May 1980, the High Court **building** has been the home of a significant number of original artworks representing notable figures, and aspects of the Australian Commonwealth. Most of these works are owned by the Historic Memorials Collection of the federal Parliament. The collection, established in 1911, consists of commissioned 'portraits of the holders of certain parliamentary, judicial and vice-regal offices and certain commemorative paintings'.

The portraits of former **Chief Justices** and Justices of the Court that hang in the three **courtrooms** are on permanent loan to the High Court. In Courtroom No 1, the portrait of the first Chief Justice, **Griffith**, is a copy by William Dargie (*b* 1912) of an earlier work by Percy Spence (1868–1933), who was better known for his black-and-white illustrations in local publications such as the *Sydney Mail* and, later, *London Punch*. On the opposite wall hang a portrait of **Barton**, painted by John Longstaff (1861–1941), who enjoyed an outstanding reputation as a portraitist in Australia and England, and Spence's original portrait of **O'Connor**.

In Courtroom No 2 hang portraits of Chief Justices **Knox**, **Isaacs**, **Gavan Duffy**, **Latham** and **Dixon**, the most notable of the group being a likeness of Frank Gavan Duffy by WB McInnes (1889–1939), and a nicely understated portrayal of Dixon by Archibald Colquhoun (1862–1941). In Courtroom No 3 hang portraits of Chief Justices of more recent vintage: **Barwick** by Brian Dunlop (*b* 1938); **Gibbs** by Judy Cassab (*b* 1920); **Mason** by Brian Westwood (1930–2000), and **Brennan** by Robert Hannaford (*b* 1944). Hannaford has also completed a portrait of Chief Justice **Gleeson**, which hangs in the Justices' meeting room on Level 9. Upon Gleeson's **retirement**, the portrait will join those of his predecessors in Courtroom No 3. These artists, who are among the most experienced and distinguished portraitists in Australia, have approached their tasks in the conservative manner tacitly expected of such commissions. More avant-garde works of art may be found at the National Gallery of Australia, linked to the High Court by a concrete walkway.

Each courtroom also contains a coat of arms of Australia in a distinctive medium. Courtroom No 1 features a vibrant tapestry, from the Victorian Tapestry Workshop. The coat of arms in Courtroom No 2 was designed by Derek Wrigley (*b* 1924), and carved by Peter and Laurence Otto (*b* 1918 and 1946), while the version in Courtroom No 3, also designed

The Constitution Wall mural by Melbourne artist, Jan Senbergs

by Derek Wrigley, is made from hundreds of 3-millimetre copper rods.

Outside Courtroom No 1 hangs a wax mural by the Tasmanian artist Bea Maddock (*b* 1934), which uses text on a series of blackened tablets to describe the first **sitting** of the High Court in Melbourne on 6 October 1903. Nearby is a small, abstract metal sculpture by German émigré Erwin Fabian (*b* 1915), called *Curvilinear*. A gift from the Law Council of Australia in July 1981, the work's interlocking shards of metal may be taken as representing the hard and complex deliberations of the Court.

On the outside wall of Courtroom No 3 is a painting by the WA photorealist, Marcus Bielby (*b* 1951), depicting the *First Sitting of the High Court of Australia, Banco Court, Melbourne 6 October 1903*. The work shows the first three judges—Justices Griffith, Barton, and O'Connor—with an audience of other dignitaries including the Vice-Regal couple, Lord and Lady Tennyson, and the **Prime Minister** of the day, Alfred **Deakin**. Bielby's painting replaced Tom Roberts' massive *Opening of the First Parliament of the Commonwealth of Australia, May 9, 1901, by HRH The Duke of Cornwell and York, Exhibition Buildings* (1901–03), which hung in the High Court from 1981 to 1988, when it was moved to the new Parliament House.

By far the most important work of art in the High Court is the Constitution Wall mural by Melbourne artist Jan Senbergs (*b* 1939), which consists of six panels of diverse size, linked by a common theme. On an adjacent wall is Senbergs' States Wall mural, a group of twelve panels that contain references to mining, industry and agriculture, along with the emblems of the six states of Australia.

Senbergs won the commission in an open competition after conducting extensive preliminary research into the history and function of the High Court. He also consulted with the Chief Justice of the time, Barwick, and with historian Geoffrey Blainey. Having concluded that the two main activities of the Court were to deal with appeals from the states, and to decide weighty constitutional issues, he conceived the idea of the two related murals. While the States Wall aims to reflect the specific character of each region, the Constitution Wall is a mixture of historical documentation and lofty **symbolism**. Panel one, for instance, shows a lighthouse sending out light. In the words of the brochure handed to visitors to the Court, it 'represents the search for knowledge and justice', and is a symbol for the Constitution 'which sets out the framework for our Commonwealth'.

The second panel deals with the ongoing constitutional debate, as symbolised by the Australian flag and the banner of the Eureka stockade, with its familiar republican associations. Panel Three reproduces a photograph of the historical figures that helped shape the Constitution. Panel Four relates to the primeval forces that formed the continent, and to the nation's indigenous inhabitants. Panel Five depicts the old Parliament House as a symbol of **nationhood**, and draws attention to the relationship between government and the Court in the framing of legislation. The final panel shows the Murray River (which forms the border between Victoria and NSW); the rail link at Albury (the different rail gauges used by the colonies being one of the most tangible divisions that had to be overcome on the way to **national unity**); and the ship HMAS *Cerberus*, which arrived in Victoria in 1871, and became one of the principal vessels in the new Australian navy. The defence of Australia's shores was a crucial motivation behind federation.

It took two and a half years to fabricate the components of the two murals, which are contained within an aluminium armature of dynamic, interlocking forms. The images were screen-printed onto a resistant surface, etched onto large aluminium plates and anodised. The strong graphic nature of the work grew out of Senbergs' admiration for Japanese prints and old European engravings. In contrast to many of his peers, who became devotees of abstract art, Senbergs has remained attached to scenes of industry, urban sprawl and political allegory. He is, in many ways, a contemporary equivalent to the history painters of the eighteenth and nineteenth centuries. The High Court mural, which was unveiled to the public at the opening of the building in 1980, has been his major public commission.

JOHN McDONALD

Associates. When the High Court was **established**, each Justice was assigned both a **tipstaff** and an associate (also known as a law clerk). The first three associates were Percy Griffith (**Griffith's** son), Thomas Bavin (Secretary to the **Prime Minister** and later NSW Premier and Supreme Court judge) and George Flannery (Secretary to the Representative of the Government in the Senate and later QC).

Prior to 1972, when the Justices were allocated their own secretaries, associates were required to perform most of the administrative duties in the Justices' **chambers**. Until the 1930s, when a pool of typists was made available in each registry, this included typing and distributing the judgments. In the early stages, associates were permitted to keep the proceeds from selling the judgments—a perquisite that ceased in 1924.

Given the substantial administrative duties that the associate was required to perform, it is not surprising that many Justices chose to employ associates without legal qualifications, or with undistinguished academic records. Some associates were selected for their secretarial skills, others simply out of personal supportiveness for their careers. A few Justices chose associates because they were the children of friends. Several, like Griffith, employed close relatives as their associates. These included **Barton**, **O'Connor**, **Isaacs**, **Higgins**, **Gavan Duffy**, **Powers**, **Rich**, **Latham**, **Williams**, **Webb**, **Kitto** and **Jacobs**.

Yet from the beginning, some members of the Bench selected as their associates bright young lawyers who, they felt, might assist them in the process of preparing their judgments. Fresh from university, such associates also have the potential to act as conduits between academia and the Court. By the 1970s, it had become the norm for the judges to choose young lawyers as associates.

The duration of service for associates has varied substantially, with one associate, Edward Best, serving for over forty years (from 1906 to 1950). In general, those without legal training have been employed for an indefinite period, while young lawyers have generally been appointed for one or two years. Most associates today serve for a single year, although some chambers make different arrangements.

During the 1980s, most of the Justices came to question whether they needed a full-time tipstaff or whether they might be able to operate more efficiently with two associates. Since the early 1990s, nearly all Justices have employed two associates, who share the work of the tipstaff between them. The result has been more thoroughly footnoted judgments and more poorly maintained law reports.

Fewer associates are available to High Court Justices than to their colleagues on the **United States Supreme Court** (four clerks per judge) and the Canadian Supreme Court (three clerks per judge). However, the allocation is more generous than in the senior appellate courts in the UK, where several 'judicial assistants' are merely pooled between the judges.

High Court associates today perform a variety of duties. Before a case is heard, these may include preparing memoranda on the submissions by the parties and undertaking additional **research**. While a case is being heard, one of the Justice's two associates acts as tipstaff (attending to him or her in court). Once the court rises, the associate may act as a 'sounding board' for the Justice's views, carry out further research, and proofread the draft judgment. Proofreading requires the associate to check the draft for typographical and legal errors, and confirm that all **citations** are accurate. Occasionally, an associate may be asked by his or her judge to prepare a memorandum or draft judgment, but it is rare for this draft to be recognisable in the final judgment.

Since 1984, all appeals to the High Court have required the granting of special **leave**. This has meant that most associates now spend much of their time scrutinising applications for special leave, and preparing memoranda on these cases for their judges. Nonetheless, the volume of special leave applications is not so great that the Justices are unable to personally scrutinise the papers. This contrasts with the US Supreme Court, which receives around ten times as many applications for hearing as does the High Court. As a result, US Supreme Court clerks (the equivalent of High Court associates) perform a much more substantial role in vetting the incoming applications.

While each case is being heard, one of the associates who is not required to attend to his or her judge acts as clerk of the court. If a case is being handed down, this involves receiving copies of each of the judgments. During the hearing, the clerk sits at a table adjacent to the bench. He or she must record the names of the parties and **counsel**, and note the time at which each counsel commences and concludes speaking. The clerk is also responsible for handing up any material from the bar table to the Justices.

Although they are technically court officers, associates hold office at the discretion of their judge, and work entirely at the direction of that judge. Most Justices appoint their associates two or three years in advance. The positions are generally not advertised. Some Justices rely on particular academics to recommend talented students, while others simply select from among the applicants who have written to them over the course of the previous year. Unlike the US Supreme Court clerks, most High Court associates have not previously worked for a judge in a lower court.

In most years, there is a strong sense of collegiality among the associates, despite any differences that might exist between their judges. This is accentuated by **circuit** sittings,

which provide a further opportunity for the associates to socialise with one another.

While associates tend to be drawn from more diverse **backgrounds** than the Justices themselves, the pool is still relatively narrow. Only in the past few decades have a representative proportion of women been employed (on his **retirement** in 1981, **Barwick** thanked 'all those young men who were my associates over the past seventeen years'). Those from non-English speaking backgrounds and state schools continue to be under-represented. A substantial majority of associates are drawn from just five universities—the University of Sydney, the University of NSW, the Australian National University, the University of Melbourne and the University of Queensland.

In the US, there has been some discussion in the law journals of whether too much responsibility is delegated to Supreme Court clerks. The debate was fuelled by the publication in 1998 of *Closed Chambers: The First Eyewitness Account of the Epic Struggles Inside the Supreme Court*, written by Edward Lazarus, a former clerk to Justice Harry Blackmun. In Australia, the question of over-delegation to associates has seldom arisen. A number of systemic factors may help explain this. Compared with their US counterparts, High Court Justices have fewer associates to supervise and fewer appeal applications to sift through. They also have the benefit of longer oral **arguments**, in which associates do not play any role. There is also a different judicial culture in Australia, which is less favourable to the notion of delegating judicial work to associates than is the culture of the US Supreme Court.

If one compares the High Court to the legislative arm of government, it is perhaps surprising that a greater proportion of the work of the judiciary has not been delegated to associates. Australian parliamentarians today employ much larger staffs than they did at the time of federation—allowing modern politicians to delegate many of the tasks that their predecessors did themselves. Yet today's High Court Justices continue to operate with a similar number of assistants to their predecessors of 1903. No doubt the constitutional principle that **judicial power** can be exercised only by the Justices is a significant constraint on delegation, at least in relation to the Justices' ultimate responsibility for decision making.

Following their time at the High Court, many associates embark upon careers as barristers, solicitors or academics. They tend to remain in close contact with one another and with their judges. Many maintain an enduring interest in the institution itself. Two have even gone on to become Justices themselves. **McTiernan**, who served on the Bench from 1930–76, was **Rich**'s associate in 1916, and was with him on the Bench from 1930 until Rich's **retirement** in 1949. **Aickin**, who was a Justice from 1976–82, was **Dixon**'s associate from 1939–41.

ANDREW LEIGH

Further Reading
Philip Jamieson, 'Of Judges, Judgments and Judicial Assistants' (1998) 17 *Civil Justice Quarterly* 395
Andrew Leigh, 'Behind the Bench: Associates in the High Court of Australia' (2000) 25 *Alt LJ* 295

High Court Associates (1903–2001)*

Griffith (1903–19)	Barton (1903–20)	O'Connor (1903–12)
Percy Griffith	Thomas Bavin	George Flannery
George Wilson	Edmund Barton	Henry Manning
Norman McGhie	Norman Pilcher	Charles O'Connor Murray
Ralph Gore	Harold Jaques	Arthur O'Connor
John Rennick	Fenton Gibson	John Hughes
Wilfred Dovey	Edward Best	
	Neil McTague	
	Denis Kevans	

Isaacs (1906–31)	Higgins (1906–29)	Gavan Duffy (1913–35)
Edward Best	Brendan Gavan Duffy	(Desmond) Gavan Duffy
Nancy Isaacs	Mervyn Higgins	John Gavan Duffy
Roy Powers	Frank Officer	Mary Gavan Duffy
Frederick Salusbury	Franklin Petersen	Robert Cogswell
James Moloney	Egbert Reeves	Robert Curtain
John Keating	Allan McLennan	
	Edward Best	
	Graeme Castles	
	John Bourke	

Powers (1913–29)	Rich (1913–50)		Knox (1919–30)
Roy Powers	Arthur Campbell	George Rich	Richard Yates
Lionel Powers	Edward Best	Phillip Remington	Richard Dowse
	Edward McTiernan	T De Carteret Armstrong	

Starke (1920–50)		Dixon (1929–64)		Evatt (1930–40)
Wilfred Dovey	Peter Wickens	Alan Brooksbank	Howard Ednie	Jack Richards
Cedric Park	William Paul	Keith Aickin	Richard Searby	John Brennan
Percy Feltham	Eugene Healy	John McIntosh Young	Norman Coles	Geoffrey Davenport
Alistair Adam	John Doherty	Ivor Greenwood	JD Merralls	Keith Brennan
Ian Fitchett	Daryl Carty-Salmon	Philip Aitken	Paul Guest	
		John Reid	Sam Spry	

McTiernan (1930–76)		Latham (1935–52)	Williams (1940–58)
Francis Donovan	Graham Dethridge	John Paarman	Frank Treatt
George Tomlins	RD Lumb	Thomas Magney	Betty Kimpton
Gerald Donovan	Anthony Young	John Magney	Ross Williams
Raymond Triado	Denis Johnston	Basil Murphy	Charles Griffin
James Harney	Richard Horsfall	Charles Mason	Donald Morrison
Dermot Corson	Kevin Duggan	Louis Bickhart	David Lloyd
John Williams	Jeffrey Browne	Ivor Greenwood	Graham Crouch
John Kearney	Robert Wright	Winifred Latham	Peter Clay
Hugh Opello d'Apice	Michael Sexton		David Voss
David Cummings	Constantine Lucas		Simon Sheller
Wilfred Sheed	John Boultbee		
Timothy Cooper	Michael Cassin		
John Forbes	Eric Lucas		

Webb (1946–58)		Fullagar (1950–61)	Kitto (1950–70)
Richard Crane	John Ahern	Clarence Payne	Margaret Kitto
William Cuppaidge	Damian Lahz	Francis Curtain	Robyn Colquhoun-Thomson
John Webb	Michael O'Sullivan		Barbara Besley
Patrick Love	Jill Webb		

Taylor (1952–69)		Menzies (1958–74)		Windeyer (1958–72)	
Adrian Cook	Anthony Anderson	Simon Sheller	Richard Ladbury	Peter Henchman	Douglas Graham
Herbert Boardman	Rodney Craigie	John D Phillips	Chris Dane	Terence Hartman	David Tonge
Gordon Stewart	Denis Whiteman	Hugh Sutton	Paul Hobson	Bruce Debelle	Peter James
Brian Vaughan		Daryl Wraith	Mark Derham	David Hodgson	George Fryberg
		Jeffrey Fitzgerald		Michael Hodgman	Martin Cooper

Owen (1961–72)	Barwick (1964–81)		Walsh (1969–73)
HE Harrington	Vince Bruce	Bruce Collins	Bruce Donald
S Wheeler	Christopher Branson	Matthew Smith	Ian Cunliffe
Barbara Besley	Garry Downes	Peter McQueen	Peter Dwight
	Peter Rosier	Christopher Chapman	James Stevenson
	David Habersberger		

Gibbs (1970–87)		Stephen (1972–82)	Mason (1972–95)	
Alan Stewart	Nick Cowen	Ross Robson	Helen Casey	Brian Opeskin
William Heatley	Khory McCormick	Anthony North	John McMillan	Rod Hunter
John Morgan	Marian Gibney	Bill Wallace	Peter Lahy	Lynne Saunder
James Douglas	Douglas Campbell	Neil Young	Alan Sullivan	Stephen McLeish
Richard Vann	Timothy North	David McDonald	Sue Tongue	Michelle Healy
David Haigh	James McLachlan	John Middleton	Peter Comans	Andrew Bell
Peter Rowell	Elizabeth Stephen	John Connors	Kim Swan	Christopher Caleo
Donald Fraser		Susan Kenny	Jillian Segal	Simon Evans
		Hilary Charlesworth	Ian Davidson	Kristen Walker
			Alec Leopold	Mark Leeming
			Stephen Gageler	Jason Pizer

Jacobs (1974–79)

Rosemary Jacobs
Mark Mackrell
Gary Rumble
Richard Cogswell
Rebecca Davies

Murphy (1975–86)

Geraldine Kinnane
Angela Bowne
Elizabeth James
Gae Pincus

Jocelynne Scutt
Tom Faunce
Mark Cunliffe
Peter Renehan

Aickin (1976–82)

Robert Springall
Sally Walker
Peter Jopling
Garrie Moloney
Beverly Marshall

Wilson (1979–89)

Jeremy Allanson
Kenneth Martin
David Craig
Peter van Hattem
Melanie Sloss
Cameron Sweeney
Jennifer Wall
Richard Price

Brennan (1982–98)

Michael Fleming
Peter Power
Mary Molyneux
Gordon Brysland
John Bond
Roslyn Atkinson
Mark Snedden
Debbie Mortimer
James Elliott
Roger Derrington
Chris O'Grady
Catherine Lee
Vicki Mullen

Simonetta Astolfi
Sharon Erbacher
Christopher Horan
Katherine Merrifield
Kate Barrett
Della Stanley
Margaret Tregurtha
Kate Fitzgerald
Gerard Carney*
Richard Harris
Patrick Keyzer*
Daniel Clough
Michelle Rabsch

* = Executive Associate

Deane (1982–95)

Marcus Hutchinson
Michael Corrigan
Gregory Burton
Guy Reynolds
David Robertson
Rodney Brender
Robert Titterton
Peter Whitford
Michael Morehead
Bronwen Morgan
Anne-Marie Allgrove
Kathryn Graham
Jeremy Clarke

Dawson (1982–97)

Stephen O'Bryan
Trevor McLean
Joseph Tsalanidis
Mark Nicholls
Greg Lee
Pamela Tate
Grant Anderson
John Daley
Rachel Doyle
Robert Dann

Toohey (1987–98)

Clarke Hood
Anthony Darcy
Jeannine Purdy
Kathryn Rees
Stella Tarrant
Romanie Hollingsworth
Caroline Edwards
Jonathan Auburn

Catherine Paul
Georgina Adams
Su-Ann Teoh
Ingrid Cope
Lisa Wyman
James Edelman
Natalie Gray

Gaudron (from 1987)

Kevin Connor
Margot Stubbs
Peter Hamill
Kieran Smark
Fiona Wheeler
Frank Brennan
Kate Guilfoyle
Ronnit Lifschitz
Nicola Roxon
Philip Harrison
Richard McHugh
Fiona Phillips
Carmel Mulhern

James Popple
Vanessa Lesnie
Leighton McDonald
Eng-Lye Ong
Naomi Sharp
Susan Brown
Henrik Kalowski
Katrine Del Villar
Hung Ta
Haroon Hassan
Lucy Martinez
Janine Lapworth
Michael Wait

McHugh (from 1989)

Sarah Pritchard
Michelle Wright
Charlotte Steer
Joanna Bird
Laura Stephens
Lea Armstrong
David Fredericks
Simon Blewett
George Williams
Leanne Sharp
Adrienne Stone
Ian Cartmill
Kate Morgan
David Mossop

Elisabeth Peden
Rachel Pepper
Philip Breden
David Kell
Rowena Orr
Kirsti Samuels
Amelia Simpson
Patrick Flynn
Nick Kabilafkas
Lisa De Ferrari
Ross Foreman
Judith Levine
Anna Mitchelmore

Gummow (from 1995)

Paul Schoff
Justin Hewitt
Andrew Gotting
Joshua Thompson
Ben Kremer
Darrell Barnett

Kirby (from 1996)

Peggy Dwyer
Nicholas James
Bernard Quinn
Kirsten Edwards
Andrew Leigh
Jennifer Younan
Macgregor Duncan
Rebecca Craske
Joe Tan
Samantha Fradd
Jesse Clarke
Katie Young
Bruce Leishman

Hayne (from 1997)

Rowena Cantley-Smith
Graeme Hill
Kate Clark
Rachel Borny
David Bennett
Devika Hovell
Stephen Donaghue
Lisa Teasdale
Alistair Pound

Callinan (from 1998)

Robert Anderson
Jonathan Horton
Richard Scruby
Julian Leeser
Dominic Katter
Graham Connolly
Gim Del Villar

Gleeson (from 1998)

Helen Roberts
Daniel Gal
Nicholas Owens
Ben Olbourne
Simon Fitzpatrick
Helen Chisholm
Peter Kulevski
Anthea Roberts

*Note: This table has been compiled from interviews and a variety of documentary sources. The sources are incomplete and vary in reliability but every effort has been made to ensure that it is as accurate and complete as possible.

Attorney-General, role of. In Australia, the Commonwealth, all states, the Northern Territory and the ACT have Attorneys-General who are members of parliament and ministers of state, but who also exercise certain **common law** powers and functions as Chief Law Officers of the Crown. Although these powers and functions derive from the similar office in the UK, there is a significant difference between that office—which, despite being held by a member of parliament, is kept separate from the political arena—and the ministerial office in Australia, which is not similarly insulated. Consequently, certain tensions arise in Australia that are not found in the UK.

The Commonwealth Attorney-General, in particular, has ministerial responsibility for the High Court. This means that the executive's relationship with the Court is conducted through the Attorney-General, who must respect the constitutional importance of its **independence** from the other two branches of government. With one notable exception, Commonwealth **Attorneys-General** have generally understood this sensitive role. In 1905, the Court in effect threatened to **strike** over the failure of Josiah Symon as Commonwealth Attorney-General to provide adequate funds for the travel and administrative costs of the first three Justices of the Court. The relationship between the Court and the executive was severely fractured until a change of government later in 1905.

While the funding of the Court remains an issue today, the Court was accorded significant formal autonomy with the enactment of the *High Court of Australia Act* 1979 (Cth), which vests responsibility for the **administration** of the Court in the Justices (section 17). The Court provides the Commonwealth Attorney with an **annual report**, which relates only to the administrative affairs of the Court, together with financial statements; and these documents are tabled in Parliament (section 47). Administrative matters, including the Court's **budget**, are usually raised by the Court's **Chief Executive and Principal Registrar** with the Attorney-General and the Minister for Finance.

Apart from administrative concerns, there are few occasions where direct communications occur between the Commonwealth Attorney-General and the Court. When they occur, usually through the **chambers** of the **Chief Justice**, they are likely to relate to the **appointment** of new Justices or the enactment of legislation that pertains to the **jurisdiction** and powers of the Court, such as the *Judiciary Act* 1903 (Cth) and the High Court of Australia Act (but see **Canberra, Court's move to**).

Before the appointment of a new Justice is made by the Governor-General in Council pursuant to section 72 of the Constitution, the Commonwealth Attorney-General is required by section 6 of the High Court of Australia Act to consult with the Attorneys-General of the states. The level of consultation is left to the discretion of the Attorney-General. As this consultation is the only role accorded to the states in this process of appointment, it should be full and frank, with appropriate weight given to the views expressed by state Attorneys-General.

Traditionally, a further role of the Commonwealth Attorney-General has been to defend the Court from unjustified political attacks. This role, arising by virtue of the Attorney-General's ministerial responsibility for the Court, appears to have been abandoned after the refusal of Attorney-General Daryl Williams in 1997 to respond to **criticism** of the Court, particularly from state politicians in the aftermath of the *Wik* (1996) decision. Despite pleas from Chief Justice **Brennan** for the Attorney-General to assume this traditional role (see 'The State of the Judicature' (1998) 72 *ALJ* 33), Williams claimed that the political nature of his office denied him the capacity to respond objectively to political criticism of the Court, and argued that this role is more appropriately performed by the judiciary itself (see 'Who speaks for the Courts?' in *Courts in a Representative Democracy* (1994)). To some extent this has come about through the formation of the Australian Judicial Conference, which can respond to criticism of the judiciary, including the High Court.

Attorneys-General also play a significant role in relation to proceedings before the Court. Isaacs in *Kidman v Commonwealth* (1925) noted that 'this function of the Attorney-General is quite distinct from his political functions'. As Chief Law Officers of the Crown, the Attorneys-General of the Commonwealth and of each of the states and the two **territories** represent their respective governments in legal proceedings before the Court whether as plaintiffs or defendants or as **interveners**. Any Attorney-General may also be asked to grant a fiat by which parties who lack the necessary **standing** are enabled to institute proceedings in the Attorney-General's name. In such a case the action is formally brought by the Attorney-General 'on the relation of' ('*ex rel*') the real plaintiff; but the latter (the 'relator') has the control and conduct of the proceedings, and pays the **costs**. The Attorney-General's consent to such proceedings is usually given, though in the *DOGS Case* (1981), it is said that the plaintiff organisation ('Defence of Government Schools') had applied unsuccessfully to a number of Attorneys-General before the Victorian Attorney-General agreed to grant his fiat.

Pursuant to section 78A of the Judiciary Act, Commonwealth, state and territory Attorneys-General often intervene in High Court proceedings that involve a matter arising under the Constitution or involving its interpretation. This right is facilitated by the requirement under section 78B that they must be given notice whenever such a matter arises in any proceedings. Where those proceedings are other than in the High Court, an Attorney-General may require such a matter to be **removed** to the High Court under section 40(1). In non-constitutional matters, an Attorney-General may apply for removal to the Court under section 40(2).

Because they represent their respective governments and people, the Attorneys-General are accorded standing in all matters that involve an alleged breach of the law, even if the impugned law does not affect the interests of the relevant executive. In this respect, the Attorney-General is seen to represent the interests of all the people of his or her community. The Court looks beyond the private rights at issue (see *A-G (Cth) v T & G Mutual* (1978) where **Gibbs**, **Mason** and **Jacobs** said, in a joint judgment, 'such legislation is enacted in the interests of the community as a whole, and the Attorney-General has standing to take proceedings to protect those interests').

The Commonwealth Attorney-General can even challenge the validity of an exercise of power by a Commonwealth official or body. In *Commonwealth v Australian Commonwealth*

Shipping Board (1926), the Commonwealth and its Attorney-General (on the relation of an individual) sought a declaration that the Board had exceeded its powers in entering into an agreement to supply steam turbo-alternators to the Municipal Council of Sydney. The joint judgment of Chief Justice **Knox**, **Gavan Duffy**, **Rich** and **Starke** stated the principle: 'If a public body transgresses its statutory powers the Attorney-General on behalf of the public, whether private injury has been alleged or not, has the right to complain and to obtain a declaration to that effect.'

Whether the Commonwealth Attorney-General can seek a declaration as to the validity of Commonwealth legislation is doubtful. Although this was envisaged by Jacobs in the *Queen of Queensland Case* (1975), it may amount to the Commonwealth seeking an **advisory opinion**, which, according to *In re Judiciary and Navigation Acts* (1921), falls outside the Court's jurisdiction because of the absence of a '**matter**'. However, it is firmly established that the Commonwealth Attorney-General may grant a fiat for a challenge to Commonwealth legislation (*A-G (Cth); Ex rel McKinlay v Commonwealth* (1975)).

The Commonwealth Attorney-General also has standing to challenge the validity of a state statute under the Commonwealth Constitution (*Commonwealth v Queensland* (1920)). According to Isaacs and Rich, this arose by virtue of 'rights of a larger citizenship arising under and protected by the Australian Constitution'. In that case, a state attempt to tax the interest derived from Commonwealth stock was held invalid as contrary to a Commonwealth provision exempting such interest from both Commonwealth and state income tax.

Conversely, a state Attorney-General has standing to challenge the validity of a Commonwealth statute, at least when the statute operates within that state. Whether some link with the state is necessary remains unclear. In the *Union Label Case* (1908), Chief Justice **Griffith** acknowledged that an Attorney-General has standing to challenge an excess of power by any public official which is injurious to the public, and that a state Attorney-General has standing in the case of a Commonwealth official. The principle has been followed in several important decisions. In the *Clothing Factory Case* (1935), the Victorian Attorney-General granted a fiat to the Victorian Chamber of Manufactures to challenge the validity of the peacetime operations of a Commonwealth government clothing factory situated in Melbourne. Similarly, in the *First Pharmaceutical Benefits Case* (1945), Dixon held that a state Attorney-General has 'a *locus standi* to sue for a declaration wherever his public is or may be affected by what he says is an *ultra vires* act on the part of the Commonwealth or of another State' (see also the *Bank Nationalisation Case* (1948) and the *Marriage Act Case* (1962)).

More recently, the issue has arisen whether a state Attorney-General has standing to challenge Commonwealth legislative or executive action without necessarily establishing an effect on the people or interests of the state. No clear majority view has emerged. In the *AAP Case* (1975), Gibbs and Mason accepted that Victoria and its Attorney had standing to challenge a Commonwealth appropriation Act on the ground that a state has standing to challenge the validity of any exercise of Commonwealth power. Chief Justice **Barwick** regarded Victoria, rather than its Attorney-General, as the appropriate party. **Murphy** doubted the standing of the state to challenge an appropriation Act, while **Stephen** denied standing altogether because such an Act does not operate within a state or affect the rights of its public.

In the *DOGS Case*, Gibbs asserted the principle to be that

> even where no question arises as to the limits inter se of the powers of the Commonwealth and the State, the Attorney-General of a State may sue to compel the Commonwealth to observe the fundamental law of the Constitution, which the citizens of any State [have] an interest to maintain, although it may not be such a special interest as would enable them as individuals to bring the suit.

Although the majority in that case found it unnecessary to decide the issue of standing, it would be surprising and disappointing if the principle espoused by Gibbs were not accepted by the Court today.

It is evident that the wide scope given to the standing of the Attorneys-General in High Court proceedings has done much to alleviate the inconvenience arising from the High Court's refusal to give advisory opinions.

GERARD CARNEY

Further Reading
Gerard Carney, 'Comment: The Role of the Attorney-General' (1997) 9 *Bond LR* 1

Maxwell Foster, 'The Declaratory Judgment in Australia and the United States' (1958) 1 *MULR* 347

Queensland Electoral and Administrative Review Commission, *Report on Review of the Independence of the Attorney-General* (July 1993)

Attorneys-General. The first Commonwealth Attorney-General was Alfred **Deakin**, who held office from 1901 to 1903. Since then, the role of Attorney-General has greatly widened and has become more akin to that of a Minister of Justice. The Attorney-General has, however, always had the important responsibility of recommending the **appointment** of High Court Justices. Because of the demands of the Parliament, the Attorney-General's Department and the electorate, Attorneys-General have made few appearances in person before the Court (apart from **ceremonial** occasions), even where they have themselves previously been notable **counsel**. They have made an impact on the Court, however, not only through their role in appointments, but also as sponsors of legislation defining the Court's **jurisdiction** and as protagonists in disputes coming before or involving the Court. Of the 30 Attorneys-General since federation, a number have gained particular attention in their dealings with the Court.

Deakin was instrumental in the **establishment** of the Court. Among other things, he pioneered the *Judiciary Act* 1903 (Cth) and the *High Court Procedure Act* 1903 (Cth) required to establish the Court (but see **Constitutional basis of Court**); advocated relatively generous **remuneration** for the Justices; supported the **circuit system**; and secured the appointment of its foundation Justices, **Griffith**, **Barton** and **O'Connor**. Of all the Attorneys-General, Deakin's impact on the Court was probably the most enduring.

During James Drake's seven months as Attorney-General he represented the Commonwealth in *D'Emden v Pedder* (1904), where the Court upheld the Commonwealth's claim to immunity from a state law levying stamp duty. This outcome caused an uproar in the states, and was seized upon by federation sceptics as a vindication of their fears. Drake's win in that case was built upon soon after by his successor, **Higgins**, who convinced the Court in *Deakin v Webb* (1904) that Commonwealth officers could not be made liable to income tax under state law (see **Intergovernmental immunities**).

Not long after taking up their appointments, the foundation Justices became embroiled in a bitter dispute with Attorney-General Josiah Symon. Described as the **strike of 1905**, this feud over the Court's travelling expenses and other costs, accommodation, **library**, staff, the circuit system and the Court's 'true' **seat**, brought into focus the relationship between the Court and the executive and represented an early assertion of the Court's **independence**. Symon had been touted as early as 1898 for a seat on the Court—even as the Court's first Chief Justice—and was on Deakin's list of appropriate appointees had five positions been available. Symon was also a candidate for appointment in 1906, but his role in the dispute of 1905 made his appointment a practical impossibility (see **Appointments that might have been**).

A resolution to the 1905 dispute was brokered by Symon's successor, **Isaacs**. His term as Attorney-General lasted little over a year but was nonetheless characterised by vigour and enthusiasm. Isaacs made frequent appearances in the Court during his term as Attorney-General, though on none of these occasions did he represent the Commonwealth. Rather, his appearances were made on the behalf of private litigants or, more curiously still, the Crown in right of Victoria. Isaacs' term as Attorney-General ended when he accepted one of the two new seats on the Court—seats he had been instrumental in creating.

In his first term as Attorney-General (1906–08), Littleton Groom oversaw the enforcement of the minimum wage standard proclaimed by Higgins in his landmark 'Harvester judgment' (*Ex parte McKay* (1907)). He also represented the Commonwealth in *R v Barger* (1908), a formative case on the doctrine of **reserved state powers**. During his second term (1921–25), Groom's fear of subversive foreigners became evident in some of the deportation proceedings coming before the Court. He was personally involved in securing the deportation of the '**Irish envoys**' in 1923, and his poor handling of *Ex parte Walsh and Johnson; In re Yates* (1925) contributed to his forced resignation.

WM Hughes was perhaps the most colourful Attorney-General—and indeed one of the dominant politicians of the century. Between 1908 and 1941 he held the office of Attorney-General in different ministries over a total of 13 years, often simultaneously with the office of **Prime Minister**. Hughes gained the grudging respect of many of his detractors when, against his own clear self-interest, he departed from the tradition of appointing politicians to the High Court. Despite these honourable intentions, he was not very successful in his High Court appointments. As well as **Piddington**, who resigned in controversy, Hughes appointed (while Attorney-General) **Rich**, **Gavan Duffy**, **Powers**, **Knox**, **Starke** and **Williams**. Hughes aroused the Court's displeasure when, in

1910, he sponsored amendments to the Judiciary Act enabling the government to require **advisory opinions** from the Court concerning the validity of legislation. The Court ultimately declared this provision to be unconstitutional (*In re Judiciary and Navigation Acts* (1921)).

Latham's most notable achievement as Attorney-General was his success in persuading **Dixon** to take a seat on the Court. It appears that he may also have played a role in the **retirement** of Gavan Duffy from the Court in 1935 as part of a complicated deal between Latham, Gavan Duffy, Robert **Menzies**, and Joseph Lyons (see **Gavan Duffy**). Latham secured the passage of the *Judiciary Act* 1926 (Cth), which made two notable changes to the **administration** of the Court. The Act conferred upon the Justices pension entitlements that had originally been proposed in, but then deleted from, the Judiciary Bill 1903. It also postponed the commitment in section 10 of the Judiciary Act that the principal seat of the High Court 'shall be at the seat of government'. Addressing the Parliament on 21 May 1926, Latham explained that the amendment was 'necessitated by the impending removal of the seat of government to **Canberra**':

> At present the arrangements made for the transfer of the seat of government to Canberra do not include any provision for the High Court. It will be quite impossible for the High Court to function at Canberra until proper **buildings**, including a proper **library** and other accommodation are provided there, alike for the justices and the staff of the court.

As architect of the *Crimes Act* 1932 (Cth), Latham involved the Court in the government's efforts to stamp out communism. The Act empowered the Attorney-General to seek the Court's declaration that a particular association was seditious and hence unlawful. The first prosecution under the new provisions, which Latham had personally authorised, was overturned by the Court for lack of evidence (*R v Hush; Ex parte Devanny* (1932)).

As the Commonwealth's principal Law Officer, Latham played a key role in the dispute with the NSW Labor Premier Jack Lang over the latter's refusal to observe the 1928–29 Financial Agreement. The *Financial Agreement Enforcement Acts* (Nos 1, 2, 3 and 4) 1932 (Cth) enabled the Attorney-General to apply to the Court for judgment against a defaulting state. The High Court upheld the validity of this scheme in the *State Garnishee Case* (1932). As Attorney-General, Latham was also responsible for the *Conciliation and Arbitration Act* 1904 (Cth) amendments, which became the subject of the landmark *Boilermakers Case* (1956).

Apart from Robert Menzies' instrumental role in securing Latham's appointment as Chief Justice, as Attorney-General Menzies was notable for his continued appearances in the Court representing private litigants. For the Commonwealth, he presented argument in the **Privy Council** in *Payne v FCT* (1936) and *James v Commonwealth* (1936). In 1936, Menzies provided the driving force in the campaign for constitutional **amendment** to overcome the Court's decision in *R v Burgess; Ex parte Henry* (1936). Despite Menzies' efforts, that proposal failed at a referendum the following year.

Although Menzies rarely appeared before the Court when he was Attorney-General, he took a great interest in

Attorneys-General of Australia

Name	Period in office	Government in office
Alfred Deakin	1/01/01–24/9/03	Protectionist
James Drake	24/9/03–27/4/04	Protectionist
Henry Higgins	27/4/04–17/8/04	ALP
Josiah Symon	18/8/04–5/7/05	Free Trade–Protectionist Coalition
Isaac Isaacs	5/7/05–12/10/06	Protectionist
Littleton Groom	12/10/06–13/11/08	Protectionist
WM Hughes	13/11/08–2/6/09	ALP
Patrick Glynn	2/6/09–29/4/10	Protectionist–Free Trade–Tariff Reform Coalition
WM Hughes	29/4/10–24/6/13	ALP
William Irvine	24/6/13–17/9/14	Liberal
WM Hughes	17/9/14–21/12/21	ALP (17/9/14–14/11/16) National Labour/Nationalist (14/11/16–21/12/21)
Littleton Groom	21/12/21–18/12/25	Nationalist (21/12/21–9/2/23) Nationalist–CP Coalition (9/2/23–18/12/25)
John Latham	18/12/25–22/10/29	Nationalist–CP Coalition
Frank Brennan	22/10/29–6/1/32	ALP
John Latham	6/1/32–12/10/34	UAP
Robert Menzies	12/10/34–20/3/39	UAP/UAP–CP Coalition
WM Hughes	20/3/39–7/10/41	UAP–CP Coalition (20/3/39–7/4/39) CP–UAP Coalition (7/4/39–26/4/39) UAP (26/4/39–14/3/40) UAP–CP Coalition (14/3/40–7/10/41)
Herbert Evatt	7/10/41–19/12/49	ALP
John Spicer	19/12/49–14/8/56	Liberal–CP Coalition
Neil O'Sullivan	15/8/56–10/12/58	Liberal–CP Coalition
Garfield Barwick	10/12/58–4/3/64	Liberal–CP Coalition
Billy Snedden	4/3/64–14/12/66	Liberal–CP Coalition
Nigel Bowen	14/12/66–12/11/69	Liberal–CP Coalition
Tom Hughes	12/11/69–22/3/71	Liberal–CP Coalition
Nigel Bowen	22/3/71–2/8/71	Liberal–CP Coalition
Ivor Greenwood	2/8/71–5/12/72	Liberal–CP Coalition
Gough Whitlam	5/12/72–19/12/72	ALP
Lionel Murphy	19/12/72–10/2/75	ALP
Kep Enderby	10/2/75–11/11/75	ALP
Ivor Greenwood	11/11/75–22/12/75	Liberal–NCP Coalition
RJ Ellicott	22/12/75–6/9/77	Liberal–NCP Coalition
Peter Durack	6/9/77–11/3/83	Liberal–NCP/NPA Coalition
Gareth Evans	11/3/83–13/12/84	ALP
Lionel Bowen	13/12/84–4/4/90	ALP
Michael Duffy	4/4/90–24/3/93	ALP
Duncan Kerr	1/4/93–27/4/93	ALP
Michael Lavarch	27/4/93–11/3/96	ALP
Daryl Williams	11/3/96–	Liberal/NPA Coalition

appointments to the Court. As Attorney-General, his only appointment was that of Latham as Chief Justice. As Prime Minister, he was influential in the appointment of Williams, **Fullagar**, **Kitto**, **Taylor**, Douglas **Menzies**, **Windeyer**, **Owen** and **Barwick**.

Throughout his term as Attorney-General, **Evatt** also served as External Affairs Minister, with that role absorbing most of his energies during **World War II** and the immediate post-war years. His most notable achievement as Attorney-General was to secure a constitutional amendment in 1946 adding social security to the Commonwealth's powers. This amendment was pursued after the Court invalidated the Commonwealth's first attempt at a national pharmaceutical benefits scheme (*First Pharmaceutical Benefits Case* (1945)). In 1948, he appeared for the Commonwealth in the *Bank Nationalisation Case* (1948) before the High Court and then before the Privy Council in 1949, his extraordinarily lengthy argument proving unsuccessful in both instances. As Attorney-General, Evatt persuaded Cabinet against increasing the **number of Justices** to nine, advocating instead the appointment of one Justice only, to restore the number to seven. Evatt was instrumental in the selection of **Webb** in preference to the well qualified but politically affiliated John Barry (see **Appointments that might have been**).

Barwick's crowning achievement as Attorney-General was the passage of the *Matrimonial Causes Act* 1959 (Cth). In simplifying and standardising the grounds on which a divorce could be sought, the Act stemmed the flow of complex divorce suits coming before the Court in its appellate **jurisdiction**. Unfortunately for Barwick, that achievement was soon overshadowed by his sponsorship of controversial amendments to the Crimes Act, augmenting Commonwealth power to combat suspected traitors and subversives. Latham considered the proposals so draconian that he attacked the proposals in an open letter to Barwick.

It was Barwick who had, in 1963, secured the enactment of the legislation considered by the Court in *Re Bolton; Ex parte Beane* (1987). Section 19 of the *Defence (Visiting Forces) Act* 1963 (Cth) requires Australian police and armed forces to assist, in Australia, in locating and detaining any deserting members of another country's armed forces. In 1963, Barwick told Parliament that section 19 would apply to any deserter found in Australia, regardless of where the desertion had occurred. In *Ex parte Beane*, the Court disregarded Barwick's statement and found that the provision operated only where desertion had occurred in Australia.

Murphy was undoubtedly the most controversial Commonwealth Attorney-General. Prior to the Whitlam government's swearing-in, Labor had been out of office federally for 23 years. Even allowing for this, Murphy's reform agenda was vast and unrelenting. Murphy's hand-picked **Solicitor-General**, Maurice Byers, had unprecedented success in defending the government's legislative and other initiatives against the many challenges mounted in the Court (see **Whitlam era**). Two appointments to the Court were made during Murphy's term as Attorney-General. **Jacobs** was an appointment championed by Whitlam, though with Murphy's support. The second appointee, also at the urging of Whitlam, was Murphy himself. The announcement sparked outrage within influential sections of the **legal profession** and ensured that

Murphy's departure as Attorney-General was no less controversial than his incumbency.

The controversy was not abated when in several cases, including the *AAP Case* (1975), the *Seas and Submerged Lands Case* (1975) and the *First Territory Senators Case* (1975), he participated as a Justice in the hearing of challenges to legislation with which he himself had been associated as Attorney-General; his participation in the 4:3 decision in the *First Territory Senators Case* was particularly controversial. He took the view, however, that his previous participation in the legislative process merely to the extent of discharging his 'normal advisory functions … [as] the principal Law Officer of the Commonwealth' was not a reason for **disqualification**. On the other hand, in the *PMA Case* (1975), he did disqualify himself, with Barwick's approval (see (1975) 49 *ALJ* 110). Not only had he advised the Governor-General in April 1974 on the precise issue now to be determined by the Court, but he had himself appeared before the Court to argue the issue in **Cormack v Cope** (1974). He also did not sit in *Russell v Russell* (1976), because of his personal association as Attorney-General with the *Family Law Act* 1975 (Cth) there under challenge.

There have been two Commonwealth Attorneys-General named Bowen. Nigel Bowen held the office of Attorney-General between 1966 and 1969, during which time he appointed **Walsh** to the Court and argued the Commonwealth's position in relation to its territorial limits in *Bonser v La Macchia* (1969). In 1969, he became Foreign Minister. In 1972, Bowen was considered for appointment to the High Court, but he was probably too valuable for Prime Minister Billy McMahon to lose. Lionel Bowen was the longest-serving Attorney-General in the Hawke government and successfully negotiated the appointment of **Gaudron**, the first woman to sit on the Court, as well as that of **Toohey**.

Attorney-General Daryl Williams has held office since 1996 and has made three appointments to the Court. The vacancies were filled by **Hayne**, **Callinan** and **Gleeson**, though Callinan was not Williams' nominated candidate and represented instead the choice of Cabinet. Williams made a controversial speech at Gleeson's swearing in as **Chief Justice**, urging the Court to increase the frequency of **joint judgments**. By 2000, Williams had appeared twice before the High Court as Attorney-General, intervening in *Gould v Brown* (1998) to defend the national **cross-vesting** scheme and in *Re Patterson; Ex parte Taylor* (2000) to defend the delegation of ministerial decisions to parliamentary secretaries. He also intervened in the Family Court in *B and B: Family Reform Act 1995* (1997).

Since federation there have been six Commonwealth Attorneys-General who have also served on the Court—Higgins, Isaacs, Evatt, Latham, Barwick and Murphy. With the exception of Evatt, all have taken their places on the Court following their respective terms as Attorney-General. Evatt, by contrast, was appointed first to the Court and later resigned from his position to enter politics. However, the appointment of politicians to the Court may now be a thing of the past. There has not been such an appointment since that of Murphy in February 1975. Queensland Supreme Court Justice JB Thomas has suggested that the time has now come 'to recognise that a significant political career should be a barrier to judicial appointment, especially to a position as important and sensitive as that of High Court judge'. Many in the legal profession now share that view.

PETER DURACK
AMELIA SIMPSON

Australia Acts 1986 is the compendious name for twin statutes, each called the *Australia Act*, enacted respectively by the Australian and UK Parliaments in identical terms. Their primary effect was to sever the remaining links of law and government in the Australian states with the UK. Their particular effect on the High Court was to close the last avenues of appeal from state courts to the **Privy Council**, and to end a series of difficult cases concerning the continued operation of British law in Australia.

The Commonwealth of Australia, like other British Dominions, had been given independent Dominion status by the *Statute of Westminster* 1931 (Imp). This liberation did not, however, affect the position of the states, which thus retained some of the constitutional attributes of British colonies. The Australia Acts gave the states the same degree of independence from Britain as the Commonwealth had attained over 40 years earlier.

While making Australia's independence complete, the Acts also made it final. Section 4 of the Statute of Westminster had kept open the possibility that the UK might legislate for Australia at Australia's request and consent; section 9(2) had limited the Commonwealth's power to override British legislation; section 10(2) had permitted Australia to revoke its adoption of the Statute. The Australia Acts repealed these provisions.

The problem of ascertaining what English statutes were in force in Australia had been tackled after **World War I** by the Victorian judge Leo Cussen, whose 'years of patient and erudite labour' resulted in the *Imperial Acts Application Act* 1922 (Vic). A 1967 report by the NSW Law Reform Commission produced the *Imperial Acts Application Act* 1969 (NSW), and Victoria extended its 1922 legislation by passing the *Imperial Acts Application (Amendment) Act* 1971 (Vic). These initiatives were confined to the identification and rationalisation of English statutes 'received' in Australia through the **reception of English law**; they did not tackle the larger problem of Imperial statutes operating by 'paramount force' and beyond the power of the state parliaments to amend or repeal. But they drew attention to the problem, and from the early 1970s onwards, discussions among Commonwealth and state **Attorneys-General** and **Solicitors-General** were moving towards the eventual enactment of the Australia Acts. The final plan was settled by Premiers' Conferences in 1982 and 1984.

Three developments in the 1970s gave impetus to the discussions. The first was the 1973 Sydney session of the Australian Constitutional Convention. The second was a series of High Court cases drawing attention to the operation in the Australian states of long-outdated provisions in the *Merchant Shipping Act* 1894 (Imp) setting limits to the amount of compensation for injuries or damage sustained on or caused by a ship. The UK amendments increasing those limits to more realistic levels did not apply in Australia; and the states were effectively powerless to make any amendments themselves. The Court acknowledged the anachronism, but held that the slow evolution of Australian independence had not altered the legal situation (see **Stephen** in *China Ocean v SA* (1979)). **Murphy** (see *Bistricic v Rokov* (1976)) contended that the evolutionary process had merely worked out the implications of what happened conceptually when the Constitution came into force on 1 January 1901: from that moment on, Australia had been an independent nation, in which no remnant of 'imperial–colonial' relations could survive. But no other Justice accepted that view.

The third development was the Court's explication, in ***Viro v The Queen*** (1978), of the consequences of abolition of appeals from High Court to Privy Council. Since appeals to the Privy Council from the **state Supreme Courts** remained open, it might happen that, on the same legal issue, one litigant would appeal to the Privy Council and another to the High Court, with opposite results—by each of which the Supreme Courts would be bound. In *Southern Centre of Theosophy v SA* (1979), SA argued that the abolition of Privy Council appeals from the High Court had entailed, as a necessary logical consequence, the abolition of such appeals from state courts as well, since otherwise there would be what **Dixon** had called in *Ffrost v Stevenson* (1937) 'an antinomy inadmissible in any coherent system of law'. But only Murphy accepted the argument.

In 1979 the NSW Parliament passed a Privy Council Appeals Abolition Bill. NSW Governor Roden Cutler reserved it for the Queen's assent, which she refused on the advice of her British Ministers—specifically Lord Carrington as Secretary of State for Foreign and Commonwealth Affairs. It was said that at a subsequent cocktail party Murphy had raised the issue with Carrington, who explained that assent was withheld because the Bill might be unconstitutional: the NSW Parliament might have no power to abolish Privy Council appeals. Murphy agreed that this might be so, but observed that in such a case the proper course is for assent to be given so that the constitutional issue can be tested in the courts. Carrington replied: 'But the courts cannot pronounce on the validity of an Act of Parliament'—thus revealing that his advice to the Queen was based on a complete misapprehension of Australian constitutional practice.

On the issue of Privy Council appeals, as on all the issues covered by the Australia Acts, the locus of constitutional power to legislate was indeed uncertain. Perhaps it might be vested in the states, since their constitutional arrangements were affected; perhaps in the Commonwealth Parliament, since the matter affected the relationship between the UK and Australia and might therefore be an '**external affair**' under section 51(xxix) of the Constitution; perhaps in cooperative state and federal legislation under section 51(xxxviii) of the Constitution; or perhaps in the UK Parliament, since Imperial legislation operating by 'paramount force' was involved. But there were political and legal difficulties with all these suggestions.

In the end, the legislative strategy was comprehensive. The Commonwealth Parliament enacted its own version of the Australia Act, and also an *Australia (Request and Consent) Act* 1986 (Cth)—requesting the UK Parliament to enact its version, and consenting to that enactment, as section 4 of the Statute of Westminster envisaged. And both Commonwealth enactments had first been requested by legislation in every state (for example, the *Australia Acts Request Act* 1985 (NSW)).

In *Sue v Hill* (1999), the joint judgment of **Gleeson**, **Gummow** and **Hayne** reviewed the effect of the Australia Act by reference to the functions of government identified by the traditional **separation of powers**—legislative, executive and judicial. As to legislative power, the Australia Act made it clear that no future UK legislation could apply to any part of Australia (section 1), and vested in the Parliament of each state any legislative power which the UK Parliament might have retained in relation to that state (section 2(2)). Section 2(1) freed the state Parliaments from the dubious constraints of the doctrine of extraterritoriality, which denied or limited the operation of a state's legislation outside its own territory. (As the Court pointed out in *Union Steamship v King* (1988), judicial developments in cases such as *Pearce v Florenca* (1976) had rendered that supposed limit largely innocuous in any event.) More importantly, section 3 freed the state Parliaments from the limits on legislative power affirmed by the *Colonial Laws Validity Act* 1865 (Imp)—making that Act inapplicable to any state legislation, and specifically negating its concept that the states could not enact laws 'repugnant' to paramount British laws. Yet the foundation that the 1865 Act had provided for 'manner and form' provisions, by which **state constitutions** have been amended to impose effective limits on the power of future parliaments, was preserved and re-enacted: it now depends not on section 5 of the 1865 Act, but on section 6 of the Australia Act.

As to executive power, section 7 affirmed the position of state Governors as representing the Queen. The Queen (on the Premier's advice) appoints the Governor, and may exercise her powers and functions herself if 'personally present in a State'. Otherwise all her powers and functions are exercisable solely by the Governor, on advice tendered solely by the Premier. Sections 8 and 9 preclude any survival of the obsolete procedures by which legislation might be reserved for the Queen's assent or disallowed by her. By section 10, the UK government 'shall have no responsibility for the government of any State'. Finally, as to judicial power, section 11 abolished all remaining avenues of appeal to the Privy Council from any Australian court.

The joint judgment in *Sue v Hill* used these provisions to confirm that a British citizen is nowadays a citizen of a 'foreign power'. It conceded that Britain could not be regarded as a foreign power if its governing institutions retained any power in Australia, but used the Australia Act to demonstrate that this was no longer the case.

The Australia Act came into operation on 3 March 1986, after the Queen had travelled to Canberra in order to proclaim its commencement in her capacity as Queen of Australia. Yet much academic **commentary** has assumed that the effectiveness of the Act depended on its UK version. The implication is that the Australian version alone could not have achieved its objectives: that to sever the states' links with the UK, legislation by the UK was essential. The issue is symbolically important because, if the Australian version was sufficient, then even before 1986 Australia was arguably already independent: its **sovereignty** would not be negated by residual linkages with the UK, provided that the power to terminate them lay wholly within Australia. By contrast, if

Queen Elizabeth II gives royal assent to the Australia Acts on 2 March 1986 at Government House, Canberra, with Prime Minister Bob Hawke standing immediately behind

that objective could not be achieved without the assistance of UK legislation, then even in 1986 Australia was arguably not independent.

It is therefore significant that the joint judgment in *Sue v Hill* referred only to the Australian version—suggesting that the UK version was enacted 'out of a perceived need for abundant caution', and discounting any significance for Australia of the idea that, under the British conception of parliamentary sovereignty, the UK Parliament might retain the theoretical power to repeal its version of the Australia Act (and even the Statute of Westminster). If such a repeal were to happen, said the judgment, its effect in the UK would be a matter

for those adjudicating upon the constitutional law of that country. But whatever effect the courts of the United Kingdom may give to an amendment or repeal of the 1986 UK Act, Australian courts would be obliged to give their obedience to s 1 of the statute passed by the Parliament of the Commonwealth.

Moreover, the joint judgment (supported on this point by **Gaudron**) held specifically that the Australian version was valid under section 51(xxxviii) of the Constitution, which enables the Commonwealth Parliament to legislate with respect to 'the exercise within the Commonwealth, at the request or with the concurrence of the Parliaments of all the States directly concerned, of any power which can at the establishment of this Constitution be exercised only by the Parliament of the United Kingdom'. The decision accepted the broad view of section 51(xxxviii) unanimously taken in *Port MacDonnell Professional Fishermen's Association v SA* (1989) (see **Nationhood, Court's role in building**).

A year before the Australia Acts—after plans for the legislative package were far advanced—the decision in *Kirmani v Captain Cook Cruises (No 1)* (1985) pointed to other possible sources of power. One was section 2(2) of the Statute of Westminster, which enables a Dominion Parliament to repeal or amend any UK 'Act, order, rule or regulation in so far as the same is part of the law of the Dominion'. Another was the external affairs power, since it is commonly accepted that the expression 'external affairs' rather than 'foreign affairs' was chosen because the **framers of the Constitution** intended the power to extend to relations with the UK (see, for example, **Barwick** in the *Seas and Submerged Lands Case* (1975)). The four majority Justices in *Kirmani* agreed that, on one or both of these grounds, a Commonwealth enactment in 1979, amending the British Merchant Shipping Act in its application to the states, was valid. Yet with no clear majority for either ground and thus no clear *ratio decidendi*, the effect of the decision remains enigmatic.

If the Australian version of the Australia Act taken by itself was valid, it follows, as *Sue v Hill* implied, not only that the UK version was (from the viewpoint of Australian law) an unnecessary extra precaution, but that (for purposes of Australian law) any legal consequences must be derived solely from the Australian version. This is of practical importance in view of suggestions that the Australia Act, or the circumstances of its enactment, may have opened up an alternative method of amending the Constitution, bypassing the referendum process required by section 128.

The most frequent suggestion is as follows. Section 8 of the Statute of Westminster made it clear that the Commonwealth power to repeal or amend British legislation did not allow it to alter the Constitution or the *Commonwealth of Australia Constitution Act* 1900 (Imp); and section 5 of the Australia Act makes it clear that the power of the states to repeal or amend British legislation does not extend to either of those instruments, nor to the Statute of Westminster. But by section 15(1) of the Australia Act, the Commonwealth, 'at the request or with the concurrence of the Parliaments of all the States', can repeal or amend both the Statute of Westminster (in its Australian applications) and the Australia Act itself. The argument is that this procedure could be used to remove or modify the fetters imposed by section 8 of the Statute of Westminster and section 5 of the Australia Act, thus rendering the Constitution itself (or any specified part of it) open to legislative amendment. That amendment could then be achieved at a second stage—whether by further resort to cooperative legislation; or by Commonwealth legislation under section 2(2) of the Statute of Westminster; or by some wholly new procedure created by the initial amendment under section 15(1).

Clearly, no ordinary exercise of Commonwealth–state cooperation under section 51(xxxviii) of the Constitution could circumvent section 128, which emphatically declares: 'This Constitution shall not be altered except in the following manner.' To make sense of the argument about the Australia Act, we must assume that the formula used in section 15(1) (request or concurrence 'of all the States') is *different* from the formula in section 51(xxxviii) of the Constitution (request or concurrence 'of all the States directly concerned'). But this seems unduly strained. If, as seems likely, the Australia Act does not create a new independent alternative to section 51(xxxviii), but simply allows section 51(xxxviii) to be used for the specified purposes, any use of section 15(1) would still be 'subject to this Constitution'.

In any event, section 15(1) could create a new avenue for changing the Constitution only if the legislative powers used to enact it permitted such a result; and no possible basis for the Australian version could have that effect. The external affairs power, like section 51(xxxviii), is 'subject to this Constitution'. As for the power conferred by section 2(2) of the Statute of Westminster, no hypothetical future repeal of section 8 of that Statute could alter the fact that section 2(2) was effectively limited by section 8 when the Australia Act was passed. Accordingly, the supposed effect of section 15(1) must depend exclusively on its UK version. Moreover, the argument must assume that the UK version can have an effect which the Australian version cannot—that is, that the two identical texts of section 15(1) can be given different interpretations.

In any event, the power of the UK Parliament to legislate in the manner suggested would also be doubtful. Despite the theoretical possibility that the UK Parliament might assert a continuing Imperial power not limited by the Statute of Westminster, that is not what the UK version of the Australia Act purported to do. It purported to exercise the power retained by section 4 of the Statute of Westminster, to legislate for a Dominion provided that its request and consent is 'expressly declared'. That power, like the Commonwealth Parliament's power under section 2(2) of the Statute, would appear to be limited by the declaration in section 8 of the Statute that 'nothing in this Act shall be deemed to confer any power to repeal or alter' the Australian Constitution.

Of course, it might be said that section 2(2) of the Statute did not 'confer' a new power, but simply limited an existing power. And, in any event, the theory that the UK Parliament retains an inherent power to legislate inconsistently with the Statute of Westminster always lurks in the background. But the short answer to these conundrums is what *Sue v Hill* suggested: that these would be conundrums for British constitutional law, of no relevance in Australia.

In fact, the High Court's response suggests that far from undermining the democratic foundation of the Constitution, the Australia Act has reinforced it. Until 1986, the validity of the Australian Constitution was conventionally ascribed to its enactment by the UK Parliament at a time when that Parliament had Imperial authority over Australia. But a number of Justices—notably Mason in *Australian Capital Television v Commonwealth* (1992) and **McHugh** in *McGinty v WA* (1996)—have accepted that, since British legislation no longer has any relevance, the legitimacy of the Constitution must now depend on its foundation in popular sovereignty. As Mason put it, the Australia Act 'marked the end of the legal sovereignty of the Imperial Parliament and recognized that ultimate sovereignty resided in the Australian people'. Thus, although—as Gummow pointed out in *McGinty*—the Australia Acts were not themselves an exercise of popular sovereignty, they have led to an acceptance of that sovereignty as the foundation upon which Australia's constituent instruments must be construed. It is hardly likely that section 15(1), construed upon that foundation, would be found to have subverted that foundation.

Tony Blackshield

Further Reading

Michael Coper, *Encounters with the Australian Constitution* (1987, popular edn 1988) ch 1

Christopher Gilbert, 'Section 15 of the Australia Acts: Constitutional Change by the Back Door?' (1989) 5 *QUTLJ* 55

John Goldring, 'The Australia Act 1986 and the Formal Independence of Australia' [1986] *Public Law* 192

HP Lee, 'The Australia Act 1986—Some Legal Conundrums' (1988) 14 *Mon LR* 298

Bernard O'Brien, 'The Australia Acts' in MP Ellinghaus, AJ Bradbrook and AJ Duggan (eds), *The Emergence of Australian Law* (1989) 337

Authoritative legal materials may refer to the materials Justices *must* employ in **judicial reasoning**, or to those they *may legitimately* employ. The former sense refers primarily to legislation made by a parliament or under its authority, and to past judicial decisions rendered authoritative by the doctrine of **precedent**. Both kinds of material are 'authoritative' not only because they *must* be taken into account, but because there are precise legal criteria to determine what the authoritative material is.

In the **common law** tradition these authoritative sources were said to be accompanied by 'custom', particularly in the limited specialised contexts of a particular locality or trade. Here, too, precise legal criteria are used to determine whether a particular custom should be enforced. Resort to custom, however, now has limited significance in England, and would become significant in Australia only if the customary law of **Aboriginal peoples** were to be given recognition.

Whether textbooks or other academic or **extra-judicial writings** were 'authoritative', in the strong sense that their opinions would be accepted as decisive, was traditionally more doubtful. Perhaps a small number of classic texts from English legal history might make this claim, such as Thomas Littleton's *Treatise on Tenures* (*circa* 1480), or William Blackstone's *Commentaries on the Laws of England* (1765). In the High Court, almost from its earliest **sittings**, **Quick and Garran** achieved a similar status. For other less exalted scholarly writings, even the claim that they *may legitimately* be referred to has sometimes been controversial. At one stage the rule was that a book or article could be cited only if its author was dead—its 'authoritativeness' being established by the fact that it was still in use. Today, however, academic writers both living and dead are frequently cited by the Court (see **Citations by Court**; **Extrinsic materials**).

As a compendious summation from a more general jurisprudential viewpoint of the starting points that courts *may legitimately* employ for judicial reasoning, the phrase 'authoritative legal materials' was devised by the American jurist Roscoe Pound (1870–1964). He used it to demonstrate that, even within the confines of **legalism**, which insists that judges may refer *only* to legal materials such as cases and statutes, the range of ideas and intellectual strategies available is extremely diverse.

For example, Pound argued that what he called 'the precept element in law' embraces four different kinds of precept: rules, principles, precepts defining conceptions, and precepts defining standards. A rule is 'a definite detailed provision' prescribing 'a fixed and definite result for a fixed and definite

situation of fact'. 'Principles' have a higher level of generality, and a deeper level of analysis. They are

> premises for juristic deduction, to which we turn to supply new rules, to interpret old ones, to meet new situations, to measure the scope and application of rules and standards, and to reconcile them when they conflict. These principles are the living part of the legal system and are its most significant institution.

Dixon's fondness for resort to what he liked to call 'basal principle' pervaded most of his judgments. One striking example is his suggestion in *McDermott v The King* (1948) that 'the settled rule' excluding involuntary confessions had been applied too narrowly, through failure to give 'a sufficiently wide operation to the basal principle that to be admissible a confession must be voluntary, a principle the application of which is flexible and is not limited by any [particular] category' (see **Criminal procedure**). Another is his famous rebellion in *Commissioner for Railways (NSW) v Cardy* (1960) against the increasingly fictitious use of the rule-bound categories of **occupiers' liability** as a basis for duties of care: 'Why should we here continue to explain the liability … in terms which can no longer command an intellectual assent and refuse to refer it directly to basal principle?'

A 'conception', as Pound defined it, is a shorthand 'counter' lumping together all fact situations of a common type, along with the entire bundle of rules, principles and legal consequences pertaining to fact situations of that type. The result is 'an authoritative category into which cases may be fitted so that, when placed in the proper pigeonhole, a series of rules and principles and standards become applicable'. Examples range from overarching conceptions such as **contract and tort**, to more specific conceptions employed within those doctrinal frameworks, such as the notion of consideration in **contract law**. In **tort law**, the High Court's attempt (led by **Deane** from *Jaensch v Coffey* (1984) onwards) to encapsulate the principles and standards of negligence law within a unifying conception of **proximity** is a notable example. As a label for the kind of relationship which gives rise to an actionable 'duty of care', 'proximity' was a convenient shorthand expression: as a fascicle of criteria by which to identify the existence of such a relationship, it was unsuccessful. Finally, 'standards' in Pound's sense are 'measures of conduct' embedded in rules and principles and explicitly requiring an evaluative response, such as 'due care', **unconscionability**, **undue influence** and **reasonableness**.

In addition to this fourfold 'precept element', Pound insisted that the authoritative materials include 'the technique element in law': the practices and strategies that determine (for example) a court's approach to problems of **statutory interpretation**, **constitutional interpretation**, and the doctrine of precedent. These practices comprise:

> a body of traditional ideas as to how legal precepts should be interpreted and applied and causes decided, and a traditional technique of developing and applying legal precepts whereby these precepts are eked out, extended, restricted, and adapted to the exigencies of administration of justice … [These ideas] are not legal precepts; they are modes of looking at and hand-

ling and shaping legal precepts. They are mental habits governing judicial and juristic craftsmanship.

Finally, Pound spoke of 'the ideal element in law': 'a body of traditional or received ideals' embedded in the legal culture, which 'consciously or unconsciously … form the background of all judicial action'. By treating these ideals as themselves inherent in the body of legal materials, Pound gave weight to the role of **values** in **decision making**, while still insisting that the values by which 'legal precepts are continually moulded and reshaped' are inherited within the legal tradition, rather than extraneous to it. In the same way, **McHugh** has recognised that 'many of the values invoked to develop or modify the law derive from the legal system itself'; and that even when Justices invoke 'community values' this 'has usually been a reference to values such as freedom, equality before the law, good faith and reasonableness which already inhere in the legal system'.

TONY BLACKSHIELD

Further Reading

Michael McHugh, 'The Judicial Method' (1999) 73 *ALJ* 37

Roscoe Pound, 'The Theory of Judicial Decision' (1923) 36 *Harvard LR* 641

Roscoe Pound, 'The Ideal Element in American Judicial Decision' (1932) 45 *Harvard LR* 136

B

Background of Justices. There is a remarkable homogeneity in the 43 **appointments** that have been made to the High Court. Most Justices have come directly from the Bar or the judiciary. None has been a full-time academic, though many have taught in law schools part-time, and **Gummow's** long involvement with the University of Sydney Law School is a special case. **Gaudron** is the only woman to have become a Justice, while there has yet to be an appointment not of Anglo–Celtic background.

It is not surprising that leaders of the Bar often tend to be either apolitical or politically conservative. The predominance of this source of judicial appointments, compounded by the fact that appointments have mostly been made by the conservative side of politics, has yielded a Court with predominantly conservative Justices. That is not to assert any necessary connection between political conservatism and judicial decision-making, nor to characterise the Court as a whole, nor to deny the importance and fact of judicial **independence**. But it does challenge the view that only appointments by the radical side of politics are 'political'. As Geoffrey Sawer pointed out in 1958:

> The non-Labor parties do not have to make deliberately 'political' appointments to the Bench; they only have to choose from a small group of men whose professional eminence singles them out for judicial preferment, and those chosen will nearly all be as a matter of course supporters of non-Labor parties or apolitical men with middle-of-the-road or conservative temperaments.

Labor's position, as Sawer argued in 1967, is more difficult: 'The number of eminent lawyers favourable to the Labor outlook is small, and the deliberate choice of such a man by a Labor government at once produces howls of "packing the Bench".' Of the 35 appointments prior to 1987, only nine had been appointed by Labor governments: four (including **Piddington**) in 1913; **Evatt** and **McTiernan** in 1930; **Webb** in 1946; and **Jacobs** and **Murphy** in the **Whitlam era**. Of the total number of appointments, 14—about a third—have been appointed by Labor (see **Political parties; Prime Ministers**).

If, speaking generally, the Justices may fairly be described as conservative, that may, in part, be simply a product of their age. The youngest Justices at the time of appointment have been Evatt (36), McTiernan (38), and **Dixon** and Gaudron (43). The oldest has been **Owen** (almost 62); but **Gavan Duffy, Powers, Barwick, Walsh, Aickin**, and **Callinan** were all 60 or over. The average age at time of appointment has remained remarkably constant at 53 years.

The first five Justices had all been colonial politicians and **framers of the Constitution**, and all but **Griffith** (who in 1893 retired from state politics to become Queensland's Chief Justice) were members of the first federal Parliament. In Sawer's words they were 'eminent lawyers who had taken an active part in politics', like many members of the **United States Supreme Court**.

None of the Justices appointed since 1975 has had a background of direct political activity. By contrast, of the first 30 appointments (1903–75), 17—more than half—had some degree of party-political activity, including 13 who had served in state or federal legislatures. (Douglas **Menzies** had been a member of the Young Nationalists and Liberal Party, **Windeyer** a Liberal Senate pre-selection candidate, and Owen and Jacobs Liberal NSW parliamentary candidates; but they never held political office.) Of the 13 with parliamentary experience, only three had a background in Labor politics (Evatt, McTiernan, and Murphy). The others appointed by Labor governments (Piddington and Powers) were from the radical side of non-Labor.

Of those with parliamentary experience appointed by non-Labor governments, none displayed radical inclinations apart from the initial group of framers. **Isaacs** and **Higgins**, though radical in their politics, were appointed by **Deakin**, himself of the political centre. Isaacs, although 51 when appointed, seemed if anything to become more radical on the Bench. Griffith had radical sympathies earlier in his political career, but seems to have turned increasingly conservative with age. **Barton** and **O'Connor** were liberal conservatives from the Centre. **Knox** (who had sat in the NSW Parliament in the 1890s) was a liberal conservative, as were **Latham** and Barwick.

Until 1940, only two Justices out of 15 (Griffith and **Rich**) had been appointed directly from **state Supreme Courts**. Two others (O'Connor and Dixon) had prior experience as Acting Supreme Court Justices, but neither was serving judicially when appointed to the High Court. Of the five appointed between 1940 and 1952, only **Kitto** was *not* appointed from a state Supreme Court. Of the 23 appointments since 1958, nine came directly from state Supreme Courts or Courts of Appeal—seven from NSW (Owen, Walsh, **Mason**, Jacobs, **McHugh**, **Kirby** and **Gleeson**) and two (**Stephen** and **Hayne**) from Victoria. The first appointment from a federal court was **Gibbs**, from the Federal Court of Bankruptcy; prior to his appointment to that court he had been a judge of the Supreme Court of Queensland from 1961 to 1967. Since then, **Brennan**, **Deane**, **Toohey**, and Gummow have been appointed directly from the **Federal Court**. Thus, 14 of the 23 appointees since 1958 came directly from the judiciary. In addition, Gaudron, **Wilson** and **Dawson** were **Solicitors-General** of their respective states when appointed, while Mason had been Commonwealth Solicitor-General prior to his appointment to the NSW Court of Appeal. While only two of these 23 appointees (Barwick and Murphy) came directly from federal politics, it was equally true that only four (Menzies and Windeyer in 1958, Aickin in 1976, and Callinan in 1998) came directly from private practice at the Bar.

Of the 11 Chief Justices, two (Griffith and Gleeson) came directly from the position of Chief Justice in their respective state Supreme Courts. Six were appointed from within the High Court itself (Isaacs, Gavan Duffy, Dixon, Gibbs, Mason, and Brennan), and in each case the most senior **puisne Justice** was appointed (though whether there is any normative rule to that effect remains controversial). Only Knox, Latham, and Barwick were appointed from outside the judiciary, the latter two more or less directly from the position of Commonwealth **Attorney-General**.

With very few exceptions, those Justices appointed direct from a previous judicial position were appointed at both levels by governments of the same political colouring. That is not necessarily an indication of the appointee's political sympathies: Webb, for example, was appointed by Labor governments at both levels, and in 1942 (when appointed to chair the Federal Industrial Relations Council) had been accused of pro-Labor sympathies. But if that were the case, wrote Sawer in 1963, it 'never showed in his judgments'.

Isaacs, appointed as a Justice in 1906 by a Protectionist government and as Chief Justice in 1930 by a Labor government, is only an apparent exception to this pattern of same-party appointments, given the fluidity of party identification at the time of the earlier appointment. **Taylor** and Walsh are clearer exceptions—both appointed to the NSW Supreme Court by a Labor government, and subsequently (in Taylor's case almost immediately) to the Court by a non-Labor government. Toohey was appointed to the Federal Court by a Coalition government, but to the Court by the Hawke government. Mason and Brennan were appointed to the Court (and to their earlier judicial positions) by Coalition governments, but their promotions to Chief Justice were by the Hawke and Keating Labor governments respectively. Jacobs' appointments to the NSW Supreme Court and to the Court were by Labor governments, though his elevation in 1966 to the newly created NSW Court of Appeal was under a Coalition government.

For those appointed to the Court direct from an existing judicial position, the duration of their prior judicial experience varied considerably. Owen had been a Supreme Court judge for 24 years, and Webb for 21 years. The others can be rounded to the nearest whole year: Walsh (15 years); Jacobs

(14 years); Kirby (11 years); Griffith, Toohey and Gleeson (10 years); Gibbs (9 years); Gummow (8 years); **Fullagar**, Brennan, and Deane (5 years); McHugh and Hayne (4 years); Mason (3 years); Rich and Stephen (2 years). **Williams**, though appointed as an Acting Judge of the Supreme Court 11 months before his High Court appointment, had received his permanent tenured appointment only four months earlier; and similarly Taylor's High Court appointment came only four months after his Supreme Court appointment.

The cumulative total of prior judicial experience shared or pooled by the appointees of the last three decades is almost as great as that for those of the previous seven decades—and much greater if Webb and Owen are excluded. This reflects the growing tendency to look to the established judiciary as a source of High Court appointments. What is significant is that the kinds of judicial or quasi-judicial experience represented have become more diverse. Apart from their Federal Court positions, Brennan was the first President of the Administrative Appeals Tribunal (1976–79), Deane was President of the Australian Trade Practices Tribunal (1977–82), and Toohey was Aboriginal Land Commissioner for the Northern Territory (1977–82). Gaudron was a presidential member of the Conciliation and Arbitration Commission (1974–79). On resigning from that position she chaired the NSW Legal Services Commission (1979–80). Kirby was also a presidential member of the Conciliation and Arbitration Commission (1975–83), though his primary role throughout that time was as the founding Chairman of the Australian Law Reform Commission (1975–84). Brennan worked with him in the Commission (1975–77).

A number of Justices began their careers in government service. For example, O'Connor was a clerk of the NSW Legislative Council; Isaacs was in the Victorian Crown Law Department; Gavan Duffy was an officer in the Victorian State Treasury; McTiernan was a junior clerk in the Commonwealth Public Service and served as Rich's **Associate**; Fullagar was an interviewing officer in the Commonwealth Repatriation and Immigration Department; Kitto was in the NSW State Crown Solicitor's office; Powers was Queensland, then Commonwealth, Crown Solicitor; Webb held several legal offices under the Queensland government, including Public Defender and Solicitor-General; and Taylor began as a clerk in the Commonwealth Crown Solicitor's Office. Before going to the Bar, Aickin was Dixon's Associate (1939–41), then Third Secretary, Australian Legation Washington, DC (1942–44), Legal Adviser, European Regional Office UNRRA (1944–48), and worked for the UN Legal Department in 1948. Wilson began his working life as a messenger for the local courthouse, transferring in 1939 to the Crown Law Department in Perth, where he advanced through the positions of Assistant Crown Prosecutor (1954–59), Crown Prosecutor (1959–61), and Crown Counsel (1961–69) to appointment as Solicitor-General of WA in 1969. Callinan worked as a clerk in the Immigration Department before commencing his legal studies.

Ten Justices had prior military experience—Latham, Owen, Williams, Fullagar, Windeyer, Gibbs, Stephen, Mason, Jacobs, and Wilson. The only one who continued his military involvement after the World War in which he had served was Windeyer, who rose to the rank of Major-General in 1950 (retiring in 1957) and was CMF member on the Australian Military Board (1950–53). The only military involvement unconnected with wartime service was Dawson's position as Lieutenant-Commander in the Royal Australian Naval Volunteer Reserve.

Of the 43 appointments, six have been from Queensland, 23 from NSW, 12 from Victoria, and two from WA. The absence of appointments from SA and Tasmania and the disproportionate representation of NSW and Victoria have attracted recurrent political criticism. For example, in September 1961 George Munster's magazine *Nation* criticised Owen's appointment because it had failed to escape the tradition of appointing Sydney or Melbourne men only: in the absence of a 'Sydney–Melbourne man' of the calibre of Dixon, Latham or Fullagar, 'surely we could have got away from the dreadful preoccupation with the Sydney–Melbourne axis which has caused the High Court of Australia to be regarded as the High Court of NSW and Victoria'.

Since 1950, the Sydney side of the axis has been in the ascendant: of the 26 appointees during that time, 15 have been from Sydney as compared with six from Melbourne. The membership of the **Griffith Court** (1903–19), the **Gavan Duffy Court** (1931–35) and the **Latham Court** (1935–52) had been fairly evenly balanced between NSW and Victoria; the **Knox Court** (1919–30) had a composition ratio in favour of Victoria (2:1). Ironically, it was the **Dixon Court** (1952–64) that heralded the rise of the Sydney Bar. Since 1931, there have always been at least three Justices from NSW, except for a brief period in the **Gibbs Court** when (from 1981 to 1982) there were only two. By 1998, five of the seven Justices were from NSW and only one from Victoria.

These figures are calculated on the Justices' state of residence at the time of their appointments. It should not be assumed that they were born in that state—nor, for that matter, that they were all born in Australia. Griffith was born in South Wales, but left for Australia with his family at the age of eight. Higgins was born and raised in Ireland, arriving in Victoria at 18. Gavan Duffy was born in Dublin, arriving in Victoria with his father at three years old, and except for four years when he was sent back to England for his education, was raised in Melbourne. Stephen was born in England in 1923 and migrated to Australia in 1940.

Only one Justice, Isaacs, has been Jewish. Thirteen have been Roman Catholics or of Catholic background, though only four of these had been appointed in the Court's first 65 years. The rest have been at least nominally Protestant or from Protestant family backgrounds.

It is easy enough to say that there is no Jewish seat; but in earlier years the question was open as to whether there was a Catholic seat. There has always been at least one Catholic on the Bench: Gavan Duffy, the second Catholic appointed to the Court, succeeded to the seat of the first, O'Connor. However, McTiernan, the third Catholic, joined the Bench while Gavan Duffy remained; and both Webb (in 1946) and Walsh (in 1969) joined the Court while McTiernan was still sitting. Murphy came from an Irish Catholic background but was himself an agnostic—as was Mason, though with an Anglican father and a Catholic mother he was given a Catholic upbringing. By the time he became Chief Justice in 1987, five of the six puisne Justices also had a Catholic background:

Brennan, Deane, Toohey, Gaudron, and McHugh. Of these, Brennan, Deane, and Toohey remained devout practising Catholics. Gleeson, too, is a Catholic—as was his father; his mother was Presbyterian. On the whole, it does not seem that religion is, or has ever been, a factor in High Court appointments.

The ethnic origins of almost all Justices have been in the British Isles. Isaacs' father was a Polish Jew, but his mother was an English Jew. Knox's father was born in Denmark but of British parents. Williams' first forebear on his father's side in Australia was also the first American consul in Australia, his family having emigrated from England to the USA about 1637. His mother's grandfather was James Milson, the first settler in North Sydney. The Windeyer family, prominent in Australia since 1828, had been of Swiss origin, the first Windeyer migrating to England in about 1735. Brennan's grandfather had migrated from Ireland.

Most of the available information about the Justices' family backgrounds relates to their fathers or fathers-in-law rather than their mothers or mothers-in-law—a fact that reflects the position of women in society over most of the relevant period. In that context, a surprising number of Justices had ministers of religion as their fathers or fathers-in-law. Both Griffith and Higgins had fathers who had come to Australia to preach the gospel: Edward Griffith for the Congregational Church, John Higgins for the Methodist Church. Piddington's father, William Jones Piddington, had also begun his ministry as a Methodist, but ended it as Anglican Archdeacon of Tamworth. Powers was the son of a Methodist minister. Rich was the younger son of the Reverend Canon Charles Rich. Dixon married the daughter of an Anglican cleric, the Reverend H Brooksbank. Kitto, whose maternal grandfather was a Methodist minister, married the daughter of WH Howard, also a Methodist minister. Menzies was the son of a Presbyterian minister, Frank Menzies. His father-in-law William Borland was also a cleric (the Minister of Scots Church, Melbourne), as was his brother-in-law Francis Borland. Jacobs married a farmer's daughter, but both of her grandfathers were clergymen. Dawson's father had trained as a minister in the Church of Christ before taking up a career in journalism; he continued to preach at the Church of Christ in Swanston Street, Melbourne, until the family moved to Canberra in the late 1930s. Less surprisingly, several of the Justices had fathers or fathers-in-law in either the legal profession or politics, or both. Gavan Duffy came from a powerful Victorian family of politicians and lawyers. His father, Charles Gavan Duffy, had come to Australia from a celebrated background as an Irish rebel patriot and Irish member of the House of Commons. A Minister in Victoria's first **responsible government** in 1857, he became Premier in 1871, retiring to the Speakership in 1877.

Webb's father-in-law was George Agnew, a mechanical engineer who established his own carriage works. He entered the Queensland Parliament in 1888, and was twice re-elected. In 1895, he joined other members for country constituencies in forming a Farmers' Union to protect agricultural interests.

Dixon was the son of a Melbourne solicitor. Powers married the daughter of a Victorian solicitor. Williams was the son of a solicitor with a fairly large **admiralty** practice. Gibbs was the son of a prominent Ipswich solicitor. Wilson was the son of an English solicitor who migrated to WA about 1912 and set up a practice in Geraldton. Brennan's father was Frank Brennan—a sometimes controversial Justice of the Supreme Court of Queensland. Windeyer was the fifth generation of his family to practise law in Australia and the fourth to be active in Australian politics. His father, William Archibald Windeyer, was a prominent Sydney solicitor.

Owen also came from a prominent NSW legal family, following his grandfather (William Owen) and his father (Langer Meade Loftus Owen) to the NSW Supreme Court. Owen married the daughter of Thomas Rolin, thus becoming the only High Court Justice to have been the son of a judge and have married the daughter of a judge: Rolin was a judge of the first NSW Industrial Court and, after its abolition, an Acting Judge of the District Court. Through him, Owen also had a connection with Rich, since Rich and Rolin were close. Both born in 1863, in 1894 they had married sisters—the daughters of Richard Ryther Steer Bowker, an eminent surgeon and MLC. Thus Rich's sister-in-law Lydia was Owen's mother-in-law. Rich and Rolin had also edited a book together on company law.

In a better-known relationship between Justices' families, Gavan Duffy's niece (his brother John's daughter) married **Starke**. And, while many of the Justices had prominent relatives in law, politics, and business, the most notable was Douglas Menzies, who was a cousin of Prime Minister Robert **Menzies**.

Other Justices had fathers and fathers-in-law who held positions in the public service. Griffith's father-in-law was Commissioner of Crown Lands at East Maitland. O'Connor's father was Clerk to the first NSW Legislative Assembly and for many years 'Clerk of the Parliaments'. Kitto's father, James, began as a post office clerk but rose to become Deputy Director of the Postmaster General's Department in Sydney. Taylor's father was a customs officer. Dawson's father, after originally training for the ministry, became a journalist on the Melbourne *Argus* and moved to Canberra in the late 1930s as press secretary to Prime Minister Joseph Lyons and later to Robert Menzies. When **World War II** broke out, he became Editor of the Department of Information, and represented that department in New York and London in the latter years of the war. After the war, Dawson's mother worked in Canberra as a public servant.

Other Justices had fathers or fathers-in-law who were educated professionals. Higgins' father-in-law, George Morrison, was headmaster of Geelong Grammar School. Aickin's father had taught mathematics and science at Melbourne Grammar School. Mason's father was a surveyor; his father-in-law was a medical practitioner who had previously been headmaster of Presbyterian Ladies College, Croydon. Deane's father was an engineer in the Commonwealth **Patents** Office; his father-in-law was a medical practitioner. Dawson's father-in-law, too, was a medical practitioner, initially with a general practice in Victorian country towns but later as a specialist in industrial medicine in Melbourne.

Others had fathers or fathers-in-law who were leading businessmen. Barton's father, William, was Sydney's first stockbroker. Knox's father, Sir Edward Knox, was a wealthy businessman, the founder and chairman of directors of the Colonial Sugar Refining company, with other extensive business and pastoral interests. Williams married the daughter of Henry Webster, a company director who had come to Australia to set up Balm Paints. His mother-in-law was a daughter of Ross Fairfax, the youngest son of the founder of John Fairfax and Sons. Windeyer married a daughter of the wool manufacturer Robert Vicars. Jacobs' father was a managing director.

Other Justices came from more diverse and often humbler origins. Isaacs' father Alfred was a tailor who married the daughter of a wholesale tobacco and cigar merchant. McTiernan was the son of a sergeant of police who was active in Labor Party politics. Latham's father, Thomas, was the secretary of the Victorian Society for the Protection of Animals. Fullagar's father, Thomas, was a craftsman and partner in a firm of furniture makers. Barwick's father was a printer; his grandfather was a cobbler. Walsh was the son of a dairy farmer. Murphy's parents were publicans, initially at the Cricketers' Arms Hotel in Surry Hills and later in Paddington. Toohey's parents were also publicans, in rural WA; as a child he moved around with them from Meekatharra to Kojonup to Lake Grace. Gaudron's father was a railway worker in Moree. McHugh's father was a miner (in North Queensland) and a steelworker (with BHP in Newcastle). Kirby's father was a clerk, who had formerly had a small business manufacturing woodworking equipment. Hayne was born in Gympie, Queensland, where his father (Lancelot Eric Hayne) was a bank clerk. Callinan's father was an auctioneer and real estate agent. Gleeson's father was a garage proprietor; his father-in-law was a wool buyer.

Several Justices suffered childhood deprivation or family misfortune. Starke's father, Dr AG Starke, was a general practitioner who died when Starke was six. Webb's father was an accountant in a drapers' firm and later became a storekeeper, dying in 1898 when his son was eleven. When Stephen was only a few weeks old his father, who was a poultry farmer, died as a result of having been gassed during **World War I**; his widow obtained employment as a travelling companion to a wealthy woman from Queensland. Dawson's father, who was working for the Department of Information in London, died there in 1945 when Dawson was twelve. Gummow's father died before Gummow was born: a sailor on HMAS *Perth*, he was one of over 450 men who died when the *Perth* was torpedoed in the early hours of 1 March 1942 during the Japanese invasion of Java. Both Dixon's and Wilson's fathers were solicitors, but both of them grew up in virtual poverty. Dixon's father made poor investments and verged on alcoholism, while Wilson's father was disabled by a stroke when Wilson was seven, and died about five years later. Evatt's father, John Ashmore Hamilton Evatt, died when Evatt was seven; he had been the licensee of a small hotel in East Maitland. Evatt and his brothers (including Clive, a colourful jury advocate and a NSW government minister) were brought up, like Starke, in humble circumstances. Evatt, however, married Mary Alice Sheffer, the daughter of an American businessman who made his fortune in an agency for the supply of soap and toilet articles.

Most of the Justices' families were upper-middle class. Yet they did not, as a rule, come from the very top of the social hierarchy: they were the sons of solicitors rather than of barristers, or of ministers without university degrees rather than with university degrees. Nevertheless, most of them went to high-status schools and had a university education.

Of those who were educated at Sydney private schools, Barton, after two years at Fort Street, went to Sydney Grammar School, as did O'Connor, Piddington, Rich, Windeyer, Mason, and Gummow; Williams and Owen to Shore; and Jacobs to Knox Grammar. Of those who were educated at Melbourne private schools, Isaacs went to Beechworth Grammar School; Dixon went to Hawthorn College; Fullagar to Haileybury College; Starke, Latham and Hayne to Scotch College; and Aickin to Melbourne Grammar. Of those educated in Queensland, Powers and Callinan went to Brisbane Grammar School; and Gibbs to Ipswich Grammar.

Of those who were educated at Catholic schools, McTiernan went to a Sydney Marist Brothers School; Webb to Brisbane Catholic Schools; Brennan to Christian Brothers College (Rockhampton) and Downlands College (Toowoomba); Deane to St Christopher's College (Canberra) and St Joseph's College (Hunters Hill), which Gleeson later attended; Toohey went to St Louis School (Perth); Gaudron to St Ursula's (Armidale); and McHugh to Marist Brothers (Newcastle).

Of those who went to government schools, Griffith went to West Maitland High School; Menzies to Hobart and Devonport High Schools; Walsh to Parramatta High School; Barwick, Evatt, Taylor and Kirby to Fort Street Boys High School; Kitto to North Sydney High; Murphy to Sydney Boys High School; Wilson to Geraldton State School; and Dawson to Canberra High School.

Of those educated overseas, Knox went to Harrow; Gavan Duffy to the Lancashire Catholic school, Stonyhurst College; Higgins to a Dublin Wesleyan School; Stephen to a range of schools in Europe (George Watson's School (Edinburgh), Edinburgh Academy, St Paul's School (London), Chillon College (Switzerland)), and after migrating to Australia, Scotch College in Melbourne.

Thus, most of the Bench went to high-status schools. Indeed, only 11 of the 43 were educated at state schools, nine of these (Kitto, Taylor, Menzies, Barwick, Walsh, Murphy, Wilson, Dawson, and Kirby) being appointed since 1950.

All but four of the Justices (Powers, Starke, Owen, and McHugh) had university degrees. Knox was the only one to complete his undergraduate studies outside Australia, gaining his LLB at Cambridge. Of the Australian universities, the University of Sydney has produced 21 Justices, the University of Melbourne 11, the University of Queensland four and the University of WA two.

Many of those who graduated from Sydney or Melbourne universities prior to the 1950s had MA or LLM degrees. From Sydney, Griffith, Barton and O'Connor all had MA degrees, as did Rich, Evatt and Windeyer. From Melbourne, Higgins and Dixon had MAs, Isaacs and Fullagar had LLMs, and Latham had both. In the early years, however, such degrees often reflected little more than a BA or LLB with honours; Evatt's LLD—a research doctorate awarded for the thesis that later became his book *The King and His Dominion Governors* (1936)—was unique. Of the Justices appointed since 1970, Gibbs, Aickin, Gummow, and Kirby have had LLMs from their own Australian law schools, while four Justices have undertaken postgraduate studies overseas: Wilson

has an LLM from Pennsylvania, and Dawson from Yale; Deane studied at Trinity College, Dublin and then at the Hague Academy of International Law; and Hayne has a BCL from Oxford.

It would be simplistic to translate the Justices' social and political backgrounds into class sympathies. There are no unambiguous causal links between class background and judicial behaviour. Yet, undoubtedly, for the most part, appointments to the Court have been of conservative disposition. How one evaluates this fact is an issue in itself. Justice Robert Jackson of the US Supreme Court observed that: 'I, for one, do not complain that the contribution of the courts and of the legal profession to the balance of social forces should be on the conservative side'. In England, Lord Evershed defended conservatism as tending 'to promote a sense of stability in a rapidly changing world'. On the other hand, the merits of stability may depend on what is being stabilised.

FRANCESCA DOMINELLO
EDDY NEUMANN

Further Reading

Eddy Neumann, *The High Court of Australia: A Collective Portrait 1903–1972* (2nd edn 1973)

Bank Nationalisation Case (1948). Regarded as one of the most protracted legal battles in post-war Australia, this case opened to a crowded High Court in Melbourne on 9 February 1948. It was heard by the **Full Court** and concerned a legal challenge by 11 private trading banks and the governments of SA, Victoria and WA to the constitutional validity of the *Banking Act* 1947 (Cth).

The significance of the Banking Act was that it was designed to enable the Commonwealth to create a government monopoly over banking and to take over any private banks incorporated in Australia. The Act enabled the Commonwealth Bank to purchase shares in any private bank; provided for the management of the private banks to be placed in the hands of the Commonwealth; enabled the Commonwealth to acquire the assets and liabilities of private banks; and authorised the Commonwealth Treasurer to prohibit any private bank from carrying on business. The Banking Act was a central plank in the Labor government's agenda of **socialism** to nationalise sections of Australian industry.

In an effort to fend off this potentially lethal attack on their interests, the banks mobilised considerable resources and leading barristers of the day to block nationalisation and defeat the Labor government. **Counsel** acting on behalf of the private banks, led by **Barwick**, attacked the validity of the Act under the Constitution on five broad constitutional grounds. These grounds were that the Act was not authorised by any **Commonwealth legislative power** in section 51 of the Constitution; that the acquisition, management and prohibitory provisions of the Act were contrary to section 92 of the Constitution (see **Interstate trade and commerce**); that the Act breached an **express constitutional right** as it did not provide just terms for the **acquisition of property**; that the Act was an invasion of the constitutional integrity of the states; and that the Act was inconsistent with section 105A of the Constitution (which deals with agreements as to state debts).

The choice of **Evatt** to lead the case for the Commonwealth was not without controversy. As the current Attorney-General in the Chifley Labor government, he was responsible for drafting the Act, and from 1930 to 1940 had been a member of the High Court.

On the first day of proceedings, Evatt caused a stir in the courtroom when he sought the **disqualification** of **Starke** and **Williams**. Starke's wife and Williams were shareholders in private banks. Chief Justice **Latham** indicated that these circumstances would not affect a fair and impartial trial, declaring that 'the action will proceed'. After this opening, Evatt's relations with the Court did not improve. Evatt's behaviour became erratic. At one stage, he found himself in a dispute with Latham over whether, on a day of sweltering heat, the windows should be closed and a blanket provided to prevent Evatt from catching cold.

Sharp interchanges between Starke and Evatt were also reported in the newspapers in the early stages of Evatt's argument for the Commonwealth. On the seventeenth day of his address to the Court, Evatt was told by Starke that nothing he had said had added anything to what had been articulated the day before. Evatt replied that he had said more on a certain point 'if your Honour had been listening', to which Starke retorted 'I have been listening for two weeks'.

The case ran for 39 days. After 36 days in Melbourne, it was adjourned to Sydney for three days and ended on 15 April 1948. It was reported that this transfer meant 27 counsel travelled to Sydney along with eight volumes of official **transcript** typed on 2000 pages exceeding 1 000 000 words. The case captured headlines as the longest hearing in the High Court and as the biggest and easily the most expensive case in Australian constitutional history, at an estimated cost of £58 000. In a speech on 19 May 2000, **Gleeson** suggested it would be difficult to imagine that the High Court would ever again hear **argument** lasting as long as it did in the *Bank Nationalisation Case*.

The decision of the High Court was handed down in Sydney to a packed court on 11 August 1948. It made front-page headlines and was the cause for great celebration by the private banks and their supporters, both in Australia and overseas.

The key finding was by four members of the Court, with Latham and **McTiernan** dissenting, that the prohibition of business by private banks breached the freedom of interstate trade and commerce protected by section 92. Under the 'individual right' theory applied by the majority, each interstate trader was entitled to an immunity from legislative or governmental interference. Differently constituted majorities also held that sections of the Act were invalid on other grounds.

An appeal to the **Privy Council** was lodged by the Commonwealth on 13 August 1948. Although their Lordships held that they lacked the jurisdiction to determine the matter, since to do so might lead them into discussion of *inter se* questions, they thought 'it right to state their views' on section 92 since it had been so fully argued. Their Lordships then affirmed the 'individual right' theory adopted by the High Court. The argument in the Privy Council had indeed been long. It occupied 37 days, during which two of their Lordships, Lord Uthwatt and Lord du Parcq, died.

Many of the days were devoted to the arguments of Evatt, whose opening address alone lasted for 14 days.

The *Bank Nationalisation Case* has not stood the test of time, being effectively overruled some forty years later in *Cole v Whitfield* (1988). However, it was a major victory for Barwick. Sixteen years later, in 1964, he became the Chief Justice of the High Court. Other counsel for the private banks, Douglas **Menzies**, **Kitto** and **Taylor**, were also appointed. By contrast, the case was a severe blow to Evatt and the Labor government. It was a factor in the federal election a few months later, when Labor was voted out of office, not to return for another 23 years.

SUSAN PRIEST
GEORGE WILLIAMS

Further Reading
Brian Galligan, *Politics of the High Court* (1987) ch 4

Barton, Edmund (*b* 18 January 1849; *d* 7 January 1920; Justice, 1903–20). 'I shall never forget his kindness to me on many occasions during my career and most of all on my appointment as CJ. I doubt if any other man in his position would have gone out of his way as he did to convince me of his gracious feelings towards me.' So wrote **Knox**, the second **Chief Justice** of the High Court, to Lady Barton after the death of her husband in 1920. Barton, who had welcomed the newly appointed Chief Justice at Spencer Street railway station, was disappointed at having been passed over for the position after **Griffith's** retirement. Yet it is no small measure of the man that he displayed no rancour towards his new Chief Justice.

Edmund Barton was born in Glebe, Sydney. He was the youngest son of William and Mary Louisa (née Whydah). His father was an accountant, company secretary and stockbroker, though he suffered bankruptcy and the family fortunes were at times precarious. His mother was well educated and ran a girls' school in the 1860s. As a child, the young Barton was given the nickname 'Toby', a name that was to remain with him throughout his life. Barton was educated at Fort Street Model School for two years and then at Sydney Grammar School from 1857, where he struck up a lifetime friendship with **O'Connor**.

In 1865, he matriculated and entered the University of Sydney, enrolling in classics, mathematics and physics. He studied both law and French for only one term. In 1868, he graduated with a BA; in 1870, he was awarded his MA. Between 1868 and 1870, he studied law in the solicitor's office of Burton Bradley and in the chambers of GC Davis. He was admitted to the Bar in December 1871.

Among other pastimes, Barton loved fishing and playing cricket for the University. He was known as a handy batsman, but an atrocious fielder. He umpired a number of intercolonial cricket matches, and in 1879 he officiated at the Sydney Cricket Ground in a game between NSW and the visiting English cricket team captained by Lord Harris. The game ended in a riot and tension was further inflamed when Lord Harris attributed the Australians' behaviour to the 'convict stain'.

On a cricket tour to Newcastle, Barton was introduced to Jean Ross. He recorded in his diary: 'Jeanie Ross is beautiful and sings like a bird and is a dear.' He warned her of his prospects: 'You do not know the depths of my poverty or the slenderness of my chances.' They were engaged in 1872, but due to the slowness of his practice did not marry until 1877. With Jean, he was to have four sons and two daughters.

Barton gradually established himself at the Sydney Bar, appearing in a number of circuit courts. He was disappointed in 1875 in not being appointed parliamentary draftsman. The following year, he acted as the crown prosecutor for the Western Districts, a position that he was not able to make permanent. In 1876, Barton made his first attempt to enter politics for the seat of the University of Sydney. The electorate was composed exclusively of graduates of the University but he failed by six votes to unseat William Charles Windeyer, the Attorney-General. He was again unsuccessful in 1877, but in 1879 he won the seat. In Parliament he strongly supported Henry Parkes' *Education Act* 1880 (NSW)—an Act that would abolish his constituency. He was elected unopposed for Wellington and stood for the seat of East Sydney at the 1882 election. In 1883, he was elected the youngest ever Speaker in a turbulent Legislative Assembly.

In 1887, he resigned the speakership and took his place in the appointed Legislative Council. In 1889, he was briefly **Attorney-General** in George Dibbs' government and took silk. Although he and Dibbs agreed to differ over federation, he joined the government again as Attorney-General in October 1891, putting through 'one-man-one-vote' legislation in 1892–93 and drafting crucial banking legislation in the financial crisis of May 1893. As Acting Premier from April to September 1892, he incurred labour hostility because of the arrest and trial of Broken Hill strike leaders, but after some years he had largely lived it down. He resigned in December 1893.

With the coming of the federation movement, Barton's early promise was fulfilled. He endorsed Parkes' Tenterfield Oration, thus ensuring that the issue would have bipartisan support, and was chosen by the NSW Parliament as a delegate to the 1891 Australasian Federal Convention in Sydney. His contributions at the Convention were timely and informed. When **Inglis Clark** fell ill, he joined the Drafting Committee on the famous voyage of the *Lucinda* and won the admiration of Griffith.

With the retirement of Parkes as Premier in 1891, Barton was left to shoulder the burden of piloting the Constitutional Bill through the Legislative Assembly. His efforts were thwarted by a combination of local issues, and by the now obstructionist Parkes. Throughout the hiatus between 1891 and 1897, Barton was a tireless speaker and worker for federation. In December 1892, he toured the Riverina, stimulating the formation of the first Federation Leagues and helping to establish central organising committees. He attended the Bathurst People's Federal Convention, and was often supportive of the movement to the neglect of his legal practice.

At the March 1897 election for delegates to the Australasian Federal Convention in Adelaide, he topped the NSW poll and was elected as leader of the Convention and chair of the Drafting Committee. His capacity to mediate between the interests of the smaller and larger colonies, as well as his ability to work long hours, stamped his authority on proceedings. In the Referendum for the Bill in 1898, Barton

appealed for its adoption without change, in contrast to George Reid's famous 'yes–no' stance. At the same election, Barton unsuccessfully challenged Reid in his own seat. He was, however, returned at a by-election and became Leader of the Opposition.

In 1899, Barton resigned as party leader in favour of William Lyne, and in 1900 he left Parliament to join the delegation to London to monitor the passage of the Constitution through the Imperial Parliament. Despite the controversy relating to the compromise over appeals to the **Privy Council**, Barton emerged with an increased national profile and was appointed by the Governor-General, after the abortive approach to Lyne, as the first Commonwealth **Prime Minister**. Barton formed a strong ministry, and with the support of Labor was elected to form government in March 1901.

On 7 August 1903, the Senate had passed the Judiciary Bill and on that day Barton made a personal statement to the House quashing rumours that he would be appointing himself Chief Justice: 'It is not, and never has been my intention to do so.' By August 1903, it was clear that Griffith and O'Connor would be offered seats on the Court. The third remained open to speculation; Inglis Clark, Josiah Symon or even Samuel Way could harbour an expectation (see **Appointments that might have been**). Barton, by this stage, was in debt and unwell. The prospect of leaving the pressure of politics for a more measured lifestyle was encouraged by the Governor-General, Lord Tennyson, by Barton's friends, and by his doctor. Barton reluctantly left politics on 23 September 1903 and was sworn in as the senior **puisne Justice** of the High Court on 5 October 1903.

Barton's reputation for indolence has often been commented upon. **Deakin**, for instance, suggested that Barton's 'Apollo-like brow and brilliant capacities were to some extent chained to earth by his lazy love of good living'. These sentiments highlight Barton's fondness for his clubs and convivial nights. The theory of a lazy Barton is superficially supported by the regularity of his concurrences with Griffith. The *Commonwealth Law Reports* indicate that Barton shared Griffith's views in all 164 reported cases in the first three years of the Court.

Barton's **judge's notebooks** support the contrary view, argued by John Reynolds, that Barton was in fact a diligent worker. His notes on cases before him are copious and well informed. During oral **argument** he pressed **counsel** with apt and pertinent questions. His decision not to write separate judgments in cases where he agreed with Griffith could be seen as a mark of wisdom, in that subsequent interpretations could be confused by divergences even in the text of **concurring judgments** (see **Collective responsibility**).

The first Bench of the High Court set about laying down general principles and methods of **constitutional interpretation**. The Court enthusiastically applied American precedents in the area of intergovernmental relations, carefully attempting to give effect to the implied **intergovernmental immunities** that they saw as necessary to guide the coordinate federation (*D'Emden v Pedder* (1904); *Deakin v Webb* (1904); *Railway Servants Case* (1906)). This doctrine, coupled with the notion of 'reserved state powers' (*Peterswald v Bartley* (1904)), proved a restraint on the reach of the Commonwealth Parliament. In these seminal cases, Barton and

Edmund Barton, Justice 1903–20

O'Connor were enthusiastic supporters of the views usually expressed by Griffith.

All three judges were adamant that the **Convention debates** would have a restricted use in argument before the Court. As Barton cautioned: 'Individual opinions are not material except to show the reasoning upon which the Convention formed certain decisions' (*Municipal Council of Sydney v Commonwealth* (1904)).

The appointment in 1906 of the two Victorians, **Isaacs** and **Higgins**, dramatically changed the dynamics of the Court.

The role of the Privy Council in the judicial **hierarchy** was made newly contentious by the Privy Council's decision in *Webb v Outtrim* (1907). The High Court in *Baxter v Commissioners of Taxation (NSW)* (1907) refused to follow the Privy Council decision. In that case, Higgins rejected the implied immunities doctrine outright, with Isaacs limiting its application. Barton, who had first-hand experience of the Colonial Office's opinion of appeals to the Privy Council in 1900, was forthright in rejecting the ageing Lord Halsbury. He confided in a letter: 'Old man Halsbury's judgment deserves no better description than that it is fatuous and beneath consideration.' Barton continues, 'But the old pig wants to hurt the new federation and does not much care how he does it'.

From 1906 onwards, the High Court, usually with Isaacs and Higgins in the minority, picked its way through the Deakin and Labour 'New Protection' policy. There remained a solid constitutional position, which Barton supported, that the Commonwealth lacked the capacity to burden or interfere with the rights of the states. During this period, especially in the area of industrial relations, a schism developed between the original three members of the Court and the new appointees. In cases such as *Whybrow's Case (No 1)* (1910); *Allen Taylor's Case* (1912) and *JC Williamson v Musicians Union* (1912), Griffith and Barton maintained their view on the limits of the industrial power against the more expansive views of Isaacs.

Consistently with the judicial temperament of the times, Barton was willing to imply constitutional guarantees. In *R v Smithers; Ex parte Benson* (1912), he declared that 'the creation of a federal union with one government and one legislature in respect of national affairs assures to every free citizen the right of access to the institutions, and of due participation in the activities of the nation'.

In 1912, Barton's old friend O'Connor died. As his health declined, Barton had written to Deakin in insistent terms that the Commonwealth should make adequate provision for a pension in recognition of his years of service. O'Connor's replacement, **Piddington**, faced a storm of criticism over the undertakings he had given to WM Hughes prior to appointment. In his extremity, Piddington consulted Barton, who advised him to stand firm. The abortive appointment of Piddington and the expansion of the Court with the appointments of **Gavan Duffy**, **Rich** and **Powers** marked a break with the Court's members being exclusively founders of the Constitution.

Increasingly, Griffith and Barton found themselves in the minority. In 1913, Griffith went overseas for nine months, and Barton was Acting Chief Justice.

Ideological as well as personal differences were never too far below the surface. During Griffith's absence, Barton reported on his brethren, usually in less-than-glowing terms. In one of his notebooks, Barton reports: 'Mr Justice Barton concurred *silenter*. Mr Justice Isaacs concurred at great length.'

Griffith and Barton parted company on a number of critical issues. In the *Wheat Case* (1915), Barton, with Gavan Duffy, held that the Commonwealth Parliament could invest the **Inter-State Commission** with 'judicial functions' consistently with Chapter III of the Constitution. Barton, no doubt remembering the pre-federation border disputes, was dismayed by the majority decision. He argued that, once the Parliament had exercised its judgment in regard to the necessary adjudicative or administrative powers to be allocated to the Commission, it was not for the Court to prevent 'a body which was to perform the extremely important functions which the **framers of the Constitution** declared that this body was to exercise'.

In 1915, Barton visited England. He was sworn in as a Privy Counsellor by King George V, and sat on a number of cases. On his return, Barton again found himself in disagreement with Griffith. In *Foggitt Jones v NSW* (1916), Griffith, Barton, Isaacs and Rich held a NSW Act invalid on the grounds of section 92; but in the next case, *Duncan v Queensland* (1916), which dealt with substantially identical legislation, the majority overruled *Foggitt Jones*, leaving Barton and Isaacs in dissent. For Barton, the case marked a low point. He concluded that the majority view 'tends to keep up the separation of its people upon State lines by imputing to the Constitution a meaning which I venture to say was never dreamed of by the founders'. He ended by expressing his 'heavy sorrow' at dissenting from the majority.

He showed learning and common sense in the case of *Nelan v Downes* (1917). A Catholic widow bequeathed £50 to the parish priest of Colac, Victoria, for masses to be said for the souls of her deceased husband and herself. The Supreme Court of Victoria declared the bequest void on the grounds that the law of England (where Anglicanism was the established church) did not recognise such practices, so that the gift could not be described as charitable. Barton led Isaacs and Powers in overturning the Victorian decision, on the grounds that English law did not necessarily apply in the states of Australia, where all religious faiths stood on an equal footing. The verdict was received appreciatively by the Catholic community; it also showed Barton's unwillingness to be strictly bound by English practice.

In a case in which a Perth newspaper proprietor sought to appeal against an award to the Australian Journalists' Association, Barton delivered the Court's decision in what Clem Lloyd has described as a judgment of 'majestic simplicity': 'These **orders** *nisi* will be discharged. There will be no order as to **costs**. The Court does not think fit to make any further observations' (*R v Commonwealth Court of Conciliation and Arbitration; Ex parte Daily News* (1919)).

Griffith resigned in June 1919, six months after the Commonwealth Parliament finally legislated to award him a pension at half salary. Barton had not unrealistic expectations that he would be offered the vacant position. Higgins and Powers supported his claim; and Isaacs, Gavan Duffy and Rich agreed that it would be intolerable if an 'outsider' were appointed. Griffith, however, was active at this point in lobbying for Knox. Barton's poor health suggested the risk of an untimely death, which might allow Labor to replace him with a sympathetic Chief Justice such as Isaacs or Higgins. Griffith's thoughts were conveyed to the Governor-General, Munro Ferguson, who agreed to communicate them to Hughes. Ultimately, when Barton intimated his interest in the position to Hughes through Ferguson, it was too late. Cabinet had decided on Knox.

When Barton died in 1920 he was given a state funeral at St Andrew's Cathedral in Sydney. His immediate judicial legacy, like that of Griffith, was coming to an end. The Isaacs-inspired decision in the *Engineers Case* (1920) swept aside two of the doctrines that the members of the first Court had laboured so hard to defend. But the enduring legacy of Barton was as a nation builder, a task he performed in both Parliament and Court.

GEOFFREY BOLTON
JOHN WILLIAMS

Further Reading
Geoffrey Bolton, *Edmund Barton* (2000)
John Reynolds, *Edmund Barton* (1948)
Martha Rutledge, *Edmund Barton* (1974)

Barwick, Garfield Edward John (*b* 22 June 1903; *d* 13 July 1997; Chief Justice 1964–81), longest-serving **Chief Justice** of the High Court, achieved unrivalled pre-eminence as a barrister, but was less successful as a Commonwealth minister and as Chief Justice.

Born in Sydney, the son of Methodists Jabez Edward Barwick, a printer and former journalist, and Lily Grace Ellicott, Barwick attended St John's Parish School, Darlinghurst, and then state schools: Bourke Street Primary, Cleveland Street High and Fort Street High.

Barwick was not successful at sport, being slight in stature and considerably younger than his classmates. His Leaving Certificate results earned him a bursary to the University of Sydney, from which he graduated BA (1922) and LLB (1925) with honours and the University medal (shared). While studying law, Barwick served articles of clerkship with a Sydney solicitor, HW Waddell, but went to the Bar, being admitted in 1927. Legal practice had been an ambition from 'very early boyhood'.

Barwick married Norma Mountier Symons in 1929, a happy marriage that produced a son and a daughter. He first appeared in the High Court as early as 1929, but was initially reluctant to develop a practice in that court, apparently finding its Darlinghurst location inconvenient for a busy Supreme Court practice. Early High Court appearances included such non-constitutional cases as *Johnson v Buttress* (1936) and *Southwell v Roberts* (1940).

Taking silk in 1942, Barwick rapidly established an extensive High Court practice after the sudden death of Ernest Meyer Mitchell KC in April 1943. Mitchell had a large **constitutional law** practice, specialising in section 92 of the Constitution, and Barwick's practice developed similarly (see **Interstate trade and commerce**). Significant early High Court appearances include *R v Federal Court of Bankruptcy; Ex parte Lowenstein* (1938); *Colvin v Bradley Bros* (1943); *Reid v Sinderberry* (1944); *de Mestre v Chisholm* (1944); and *Gratwick v Johnson* (1945).

Barwick continued also to appear in the Supreme Court: a well-known case from this period was his (unsuccessful) challenge to the award of the 1943 Archibald Prize to William Dobell, in which he appeared against **Kitto** (*A-G (NSW) v Trustees of National Art Gallery of NSW* (1944)).

Barwick represented the plaintiffs in challenges to some of the Chifley Labor government's most important legislation: *Australian National Airways v Commonwealth* (1945), which invalidated essential aspects of airline nationalisation; the *Melbourne Corporation Case* (1947), which invalidated section 48 of the *Banking Act* 1945 (Cth), which effectively prohibited the states and their agencies from banking with private banks; and, most spectacularly, the *Bank Nationalisation Case* (1948), which struck down the nationalisation of private banks by the *Banking Act* 1947 (Cth). In that case, Barwick led the teams of leading **counsel** in both the High Court (1948) and the **Privy Council** (1949), while the Commonwealth was represented by Attorney-General **Evatt**. The tables were turned in their next encounter, when Evatt succeeded in having the *Communist Party Dissolution Act* 1950 (Cth) declared invalid (*Communist Party Case* (1951)).

Barwick's success in the *Bank Nationalisation Case* established his pre-eminence at the Australian Bar; for the next decade he appeared extensively, in both the High Court and the Privy Council, in virtually every significant constitutional case originating outside Victoria. High Court appearances include *Grace Bros v Commonwealth* (1946), *Nelungaloo v Common-*

wealth (1948), *Koon Wing Lau v Calwell* (1949), *Magennis v Commonwealth* (1949), *Wilcox Mofflin v NSW* (1952), *Wragg v NSW* (1953), *O'Sullivan v Noarlunga Meat* (1954), *Grannall v Kellaway* (1955), *Grannall v Marrickville Margarine* (1955), *Antill Ranger v Commissioner for Motor Transport* (1955), *Pioneer Express v SA* (1957), the *Second **Uniform Tax Case*** (1957) and *Browns Transport v Kropp* (1958). Privy Council appearances include *Nelungaloo* (1950), *Grace Bros v Commonwealth* (1950), *Hughes & Vale v NSW* (1954), *Antill Ranger* (1956) and *Noarlunga Meat* (1956).

In virtually all these cases, Barwick appeared for parties challenging the validity of state or Commonwealth legislation (the latter in cases before 1950, with the exception of the *Second Uniform Tax Case*). Frequently, the challenges relied on section 92. Attacking legislation was more congenial to Barwick than defence. His argument in the *Communist Party Case*, a rare example of the latter, was considered by Chief Justice **Latham** to be the worst he had heard from Barwick—a judgment with which Barwick concurred (see also **Dixon diaries**).

Barwick employed few notes in **argument** and sought dialogue between counsel and Bench, a practice he continued as a judge. He admitted to being a poor cross-examiner but was a superlative appellate advocate. Barwick conceded that over his career 'there would be many more losses than successes', but several of the latter were of great constitutional significance: *Australian National Airways*, *Melbourne Corporation*, *Bank Nationalisation* and *Hughes & Vale*. Barwick's final appearance as counsel was in 1961 as Commonwealth **Attorney-General** before the Privy Council in *Dennis Hotels v Victoria*.

Barwick was knighted (Knight Bachelor) in 1953, a signal honour for a barrister at a time when only three of the seven High Court Justices had knighthoods (though not unprecedented: Edward Mitchell KC of the Victorian Bar had been knighted (KCMG) in 1918). Barwick represented the Australian Security Intelligence Organisation before the Royal Commission on Espionage (1954–55).

With the encouragement of **Prime Minister** Robert **Menzies**, Barwick was elected to the House of Representatives in March 1958 as the Liberal Party member for Parramatta. He was appointed as Commonwealth Attorney-General that December, an office he held until December 1963. His most notable achievements in that office were the *Matrimonial Causes Act* 1959 (Cth), which allowed divorce on the ground of irretrievable breakdown of marriage with separation for five years, and preparation of anti-trust legislation based on the **corporations power**, ultimately enacted in amended form after he left the ministry. Indeed, Barwick believed that Menzies removed him from that portfolio under pressure from business interests opposed to strong **trade practices law**. From December 1961 to April 1964, when he became Chief Justice, Barwick was also Minister for External Affairs. Barwick claimed that Menzies pressed him to accept that ministry, but his successor, Paul Hasluck, reports Menzies' complaint that Barwick had strongly sought the office, for which he was unsuited. Hasluck remarked that Barwick 'knew law but not history' and 'had a poor understanding of international relations'. Barwick's most significant achievement in external affairs was to foster Australia's relationship with Indonesia, especially by pressing his colleagues to support

Garfield Barwick, Chief Justice 1964–81

Indonesia's claim to Irian Jaya, though President Sukarno disliked his adversarial style of diplomacy. The Australian Ambassador reported that Barwick had 'lectured, cross-examined and quoted documents to prove Sukarno wrong without giving Sukarno a chance to state his own case'.

It was widely assumed that Barwick had entered federal politics with a view to succeeding Menzies as Prime Minister; indeed, Barwick recorded that Menzies had alluded to that possibility when urging him to stand for Parliament. But, although one of the most competent ministers, Barwick was a poor politician, as he himself conceded. Hasluck noted that 'it soon became apparent' that Barwick was unsuited for parliamentary leadership. Barwick remarked that he 'had no burning ambition for the prime ministership … though I would have been more than pleased to have assumed it'. He stated that he would not have challenged Harold Holt for the leadership, though he doubted Holt's competence and may have entertained hope of succeeding Holt.

Barwick had secured Menzies' assurance that entering Parliament would not foreclose appointment to the judiciary, and he clearly hoped to succeed **Dixon** as Chief Justice, having declined to express interest in the **puisne Justiceship**, which went to **Windeyer** in September 1958. But Barwick's plans were disrupted by Dixon's decision to retire on grounds of failing health in April 1964, a decision from which Barwick (through Menzies) was unable to deflect him. Barwick was forced into a premature choice between gambling on the Prime Ministership (from which Menzies retired less than two years later) or the certainty of the Chief Justiceship. He chose the latter.

Barwick joined the High Court at the time of its transition to the apex of the Australian judicial system. Appeals to the Privy Council in federal matters were abolished in 1968 and appeals from the High Court in 1975, developments Barwick supported. He acknowledged the High Court's duty to 'declare the **common law** ... for Australia', noting that it 'will not necessarily be identical with [that] of England' (*MLC v Evatt* (1968)). As the 'final arbiter of ... the common law of Australia', the High Court bore a 'very heavy responsibility' to conduct 'its own close, critical and independent examination' to 'decide for itself upon principle what is the common law' (*R v O'Connor* (1980)). Regarding **precedent**, Barwick distinguished somewhat sophistically between correcting an earlier decision that was 'erroneous when made', which lay within the Court's power, and overturning accepted precedent, which must be left to parliament (*State Government Insurance Commission v Trigwell* (1979)).

Barwick contributed significantly to the development of Australian common law, especially in **criminal law**, in which his insistence that all elements of the offence be proved (influenced, possibly, by his general antipathy to the power of the state) led to surprising solicitude for defendants (*Croton v The Queen* (1967); *Ryan v The Queen* (1967); *R v Ireland* (1970); *Pemble v The Queen* (1971); *O'Connor*).

In constitutional matters, Barwick was moderately pro-Commonwealth. He construed the Commonwealth's **corporations power** liberally (*Strickland v Rocla Concrete Pipes* (1971); *Adamson's Case* (1979)), but would have invalidated the Whitlam government's more adventurous legislation (*PMA Case* (1975); *AAP Case* (1975); *Territory Senators Cases* (1975 and 1977); *Russell v Russell* (1976); *A-G (WA); Ex rel Ansett Transport Industries v Australian National Airlines* (1976); see **Whitlam era**). Barwick advocated an almost *laissez-faire* interpretation of section 92; his pressure for an extremely wide view of the 'freedom' of interstate trade and commerce eventually caused the Court to split (*Uebergang v Australian Wheat Board* (1980)), so that, ironically, Barwick's approach became the catalyst for *Cole v Whitfield* (1988), which he later condemned as 'terrible tosh'. He claimed to interpret the Constitution legalistically, but his approach was far more pragmatic and ideological than that of Dixon or Kitto.

Barwick, the archetypal self-made man, was a fervent believer in free enterprise, which required 'effective competition', and favoured small business. He rejected *laissez-faire*, believing in 'restraint of the exuberance of the marketplace'. He described himself as a modern liberal conservative. Barwick denied any moral duty to pay tax, the only obligation being legal. Tax *avoidance* was lawful, though *evasion* was not. A 1983 study concluded that Barwick demonstrated an 'exceptionally strong tendency ... to find for the taxpayer', deciding against the Commissioner to a greater degree than virtually any other Justice (see **Taxation law**).

Barwick held an exalted view of the High Court and of the position of Chief Justice, considering that Court 'the most important institution in the Australian federation'. He was instrumental in establishing a permanent **seat** for the Court with its own **building** in **Canberra**, serving on the panel judging architectural plans and supervising construction.

However, his endeavours to terminate **sittings** in the state capitals were overridden by his colleagues (see **Circuit system**), who also insisted that the Court's **administration** be vested in the Court as a whole, unlike the much larger **Federal Court** and the Family Court of Australia, which are administered by their Chief Justices. Barwick supported the establishment of the Federal Court to relieve the High Court from trial work, but opposed the abolition of appeals to the High Court as of right. He disapproved of the appointment of **Murphy** to the Court, and thereafter recommended **appointment** of judges by a commission chaired by the relevant Chief Justice.

Barwick twice tendered extra-judicial advice to the Governor-General. He advised Lord Casey on the appropriate course when Prime Minister Holt disappeared in December 1967 and, far more controversially, advised John Kerr on 10 November 1975 that Kerr had power to dismiss the Prime Minister on the ground that the Senate had denied Supply to his government (see **Dismissal of 1975**). Barwick defended both his advice and the propriety of giving it at the National Press Club the following year and in subsequent writings, maintaining that the issue could never have come before the Court. However, that is questionable; at the least, the question whether an issue is **justiciable** is itself justiciable.

Barwick served as judge *ad hoc* of the International Court of Justice in the *Nuclear Tests Cases* (1973–74), and occasionally sat on the Judicial Committee of the Privy Council (see, for example, *Frazer v Walker* (1966)). He persuaded the Privy Council to change its existing practice and to publish dissenting opinions.

Barwick retired in February 1981 aged 77, citing failing eyesight caused by diabetes, from which he had suffered since 1956, but had not previously publicly disclosed. He prided himself on being 'decisive' and possessed ferocious self-assurance. Hasluck, an astute observer, detected 'rapacity' and 'little generosity of mind'. He portrayed Barwick's intellectual sharpness memorably: 'He looks like a lawyer. This alertness, combined with his erect carriage and shortness of stature ... give an impression of an eager fox terrier who has come out to see what is going on.'

Barwick was a highly competent, though not great, judge. Ironically, the very qualities which contributed to his success at the Bar—self-assurance, combativeness and ability to identify the nub of an issue—detracted from his performance as a judge, making him appear insufficiently impartial and his judgments on occasion too simplistic or dogmatic. He had great technical mastery of the law and wrote clearly, though inelegantly. He was accurately described as 'very clever, but not deep'. Hasluck, again, expressed it well: 'He is far inferior to Owen Dixon in loftiness of intellect, depth of understanding and scope of humane studies ... He is inventive rather than creative.'

George Winterton

Further Reading
Garfield Barwick, *Sir John Did His Duty* (1983)
Garfield Barwick, *A Radical Tory* (1995)
Paul Hasluck, *The Chance of Politics* (1997), 93–99, 132–33
David Marr, *Barwick* (1980)
George Winterton, 'Barwick the Judge' (1998) 21 *UNSWLJ* 109

Barwick Court (27 April 1964-11 February 1981). The history of the Court during **Barwick's** term as **Chief Justice** may be divided into two periods. Initially, Barwick sat with Justices who were contemporaries and had sat on the **Dixon Court**. The character of the Court began to change with the **retirement** of those Justices. At first, the change was almost imperceptible. Later, it became more marked, as younger Justices were appointed.

There is reason to think that, in the earlier period, Barwick looked forward to sitting with younger Justices who would be less inclined to be 'slaves to **precedent**' and that, in the later period, his expectations were disappointed. In the earlier period, there were significant differences of judicial opinion between the Chief Justice and his colleagues, notably **Kitto**. Later, there were marked differences of opinion, not only about legal doctrine, but also about the move to **Canberra** and **administration** of the Court. One consequence of the marked differences of opinion about legal doctrine was that the Chief Justice was often in dissent. Barwick had a dominating intellect but his thinking was not always shared by other members of the Court.

Barwick's Chief Justiceship coincided with the Court's move to Canberra, which was Barwick's brainchild. The move provided the Court with a permanent base, and a courthouse with splendid facilities, including a comprehensive **library** and a recording system that produced complete **transcripts** of arguments promptly.

Contemporaneously with the move to Canberra, the High Court was given control of its own administration. The *High Court of Australia Act* 1979 (Cth) vested the administration of the Court in the Chief Justice and the Justices, despite Barwick's wish to have sole control. Giving the Court control of its own administration replaced the traditional system under which the Attorney-General's Department provided the Court's administration from funds under the control of the Department. The new system strengthened the **independence** of the Court.

The Chief Justice was a strong administrator, and believed that was what the Court needed. That belief carried through to the Court's judicial work. Barwick played an active part in the listing of cases, in determining the time allocated for oral **argument** and in ensuring, subject to some qualifications, that the time allocated was not exceeded. He controlled the oral argument, seeking to test the viability of propositions by reference to consequences, and discouraging the reading of long passages from decided cases. In this respect, he succeeded in changing the style of argument presented to the Court. There was, however, no disposition to move to written argument or to confine oral argument to rigid, invariant time limits (compare **United States Supreme Court**).

Barwick conducted a penetrating and, at times, destructive cross-examination of counsel's argument. In this, in the early period, he was sometimes abetted by other Justices. Presentation of argument to the High Court at that time was not an activity for the faint-hearted.

There was no disposition to move to a regular system of judicial **conferences**. The Chief Justice convened a judicial conference in a few cases, but this did not result in a bridging of differences. The outcome may have discouraged the Chief Justice from persisting with the initiative. Justices continued to work on their own, though there was a degree of cooperation between individual Justices. The lack of collegiality in the Court as a whole became more marked when **Murphy** joined the Court. His relationship with the Chief Justice was by no means an amicable one.

The Barwick period saw major jurisdictional changes that affected appeals to the **Privy Council** and both the original and appellate **jurisdiction** of the Court. The *Privy Council (Limitation of Appeals) Act* 1968 (Cth) confined the grant by the Privy Council of special **leave to appeal** to a decision of the High Court that was given on appeal from the Supreme Court of a state otherwise than in the exercise of federal jurisdiction, and did not involve the application or interpretation of a law, or an instrument made under a law, made by the Parliament.

Subsequently, the *Privy Council (Appeals from the High Court) Act* 1975 (Cth) abolished appeals from the High Court to the Privy Council altogether. The effect of the legislation was to place the High Court in a position in which it was able to declare finally what the law in Australia was, subject to the continuation of appeals from state **Supreme Courts** directly to the Privy Council. An unsatisfactory situation then obtained in which an unsuccessful litigant in a Supreme Court had an option of appealing to the High Court or the Privy Council. That situation was brought to an end by the *Australia Acts* 1986.

With the establishment of the **Federal Court** in 1976, the High Court was relieved of much of its original jurisdiction, notably in **taxation** and intellectual property. Section 35 of the *Judiciary Act* 1903 (Cth) was amended in 1976 to limit appeals as of right. The amendments, though at that stage preserving appeals as of right, reduced their number and better equipped the Court to focus on its constitutional and substantial appellate work.

The Barwick Court's contribution to **constitutional interpretation** centred on section 90 (which makes Commonwealth power over **excise duties** exclusive) and section 92 (which guarantees freedom of **interstate trade and commerce**). The contribution did not result in any greater clarity or certainty in the operation of these provisions. The **legalism** that characterised the approach of the Dixon Court to the interpretation of these sections was steadily eroded. The confusion created by *Dennis Hotels v Victoria* (1960) was reinforced by the decision in *Dickenson's Arcade v Tasmania* (1974), upholding by majority the possibility of a state tax on consumption of tobacco (though not the particular tax in question) and a state fee for a retail tobacconist's licence. The 'criterion of liability' test, which had been enunciated by Kitto in *Dennis Hotels* and unanimously adopted in *Bolton v Madsen* (1963), came under strong criticism from Barwick and later **Mason** on the ground that it was excessively formal, looking only to the legal operation of the legislation and not to its practical or substantial economic effects (see **Form and substance**).

The difference of opinion on excise was reflected in the Court's decisions on section 92. Barwick sought to enlarge the area of immunity conferred by section 92 by extending it to acts preparatory or antecedent to interstate trade and by holding that the first sale across the border formed part of interstate trade (*Damjanovic & Sons v Commonwealth*

(1968)). He also endeavoured to take account of the commercial, economic and practical consequences of a law in ascertaining whether it imposed a burden on interstate trade. In these endeavours, he was largely unsuccessful (see *Samuels v Readers Digest* (1969)), although he gained the support of Mason and **Jacobs** in expanding the narrow 'direct effect' test of the operation of a law (see *North Eastern Dairy Case* (1975)). However, his attempt to confine the concept of 'reasonable regulation' was strongly resisted by **Stephen**, Mason and Jacobs (see *Permewan Wright v Trewhitt* (1979); *Clark King & Co v Australian Wheat Board* (1978); *Uebergang v Australian Wheat Board* (1980)). The uncertainty surrounding section 92 was increased when Murphy sought to confine its operation.

The Court continued to adopt a legalistic approach to constitutional provisions that conferred rights on individuals, though Murphy took a different approach. *Henry v Boehm* (1973) on section 117 may be compared with the *DOGS Case* (1981) on section 116.

In other areas, the Court consistently upheld Commonwealth legislation, an exception being the *Petroleum and Minerals Authority Act* 1973 (Cth), which was passed at a joint sitting erroneously convened under section 57 (*PMA Case* (1975); compare *Cormack v Cope* (1974)). The *Seas and Submerged Lands Case* (1975) upheld the Commonwealth assertion of **sovereignty** over Australia's territorial sea and interpreted the **external affairs power** broadly. The *Family Law Act* 1975 (Cth) was upheld (*Russell v Russell* (1976)), as was Commonwealth legislation providing for territorial representation in the Parliament (see *Territory Senators Cases* (1975 and 1977)). The Court's decision in the *AAP Case* (1975) did not resolve the uncertainties surrounding the appropriation power in section 81.

In the area of non-constitutional law, the Court delivered important judgments, mainly relating to **criminal law**, elucidating substantive principles, providing guidance to trial judges and the profession and enhancing the fairness of the trial and trial procedures. *MLC v Evatt* (1968) was a notable decision on liability for negligent misstatement, though it was overruled by the Privy Council.

In a series of strongly expressed judgments, in which Barwick played the leading part, the Court upheld the right of the taxpayer to arrange affairs so as to minimise liability to tax, drawing a distinction between tax avoidance (legitimate) and tax evasion (illegitimate). The effect of these decisions was to deny to section 260 of the *Income Tax Assessment Act* 1936 (Cth), the general anti-tax avoidance provision, a wide-ranging operation. These decisions led to the commercial marketing of tax avoidance schemes and to very strong **criticism** of the Court—a criticism echoed by Murphy in his dissenting judgment in *FCT v Westraders* (1980).

The public image of the Court centred on Barwick and was associated with at times controversial aspects of his Chief Justiceship, notably the advice that he gave in 1975 to the Governor-General, John Kerr, that Kerr was entitled to dismiss the **Prime Minister** (see **Dismissal of 1975**).

ANTHONY MASON

Bench, composition of. The manner in which the High Court is constituted to exercise the **jurisdiction** vested in it by the Constitution or conferred upon it by the Parliament is governed by the *Judiciary Act* 1903 (Cth), supplemented by the **High Court Rules**. Appeals are heard and determined only by a **Full Court**. The minimum **number of Justices** required to constitute a Full Court is two, except in the case of an appeal from the Full Court or the Court of Appeal of a **state Supreme Court**, when the Act requires a minimum of three Justices to sit. Applications for special **leave to appeal** from a judgment of a Court other than the High Court may be determined by a single Justice or by a Full Court.

Subject to these and other provisions of the Act and the Rules, the jurisdiction of the Court may be exercised by any one or more Justices sitting in **open court**. In certain classes of case (chiefly cases dealing with practice and **procedure**), the jurisdiction may be exercised by a Justice sitting in **chambers**. A Justice sitting either in court or in chambers may state a case or reserve a question for the consideration of a Full Court or direct a case or question to be argued before a Full Court. When the Court sits as a **Court of Disputed Returns** under the *Commonwealth Electoral Act* 1918, the jurisdiction may be exercised by either the Full Court or a single Justice, but the Court may refer a question of fact to the **Federal Court** or to the Supreme Court of a state or territory. A single Justice may state a case for the consideration of the Full Court but no appeal lies from a decision of a Court of Disputed Returns constituted by a single Justice.

In practice, applications for special leave to appeal are determined by a Full Court. In applications for special leave in criminal cases prior to 1991, **counsel** for the applicant was permitted to argue as on an appeal in order that the Court could, if it saw fit, forthwith hear the respondent and determine an appeal in the matter. The treatment of criminal special leave applications as *de facto* appeals led to the Bench being constituted by five or more Justices. While the number of criminal special leave applications remained small, that procedure was satisfactory, but in the 1970s the number increased, and the volume of cases led to a change in procedure. As from 1 April 1991, no criminal appeals were heard unless the applicant had obtained a grant of special leave. Only three Justices determined applications for special leave.

Prior to 1984, many civil appeals were brought to the High Court as of right, but in that year the requirement of special leave to appeal in all civil cases was introduced. Civil special leave applications have generally been heard and determined by a Bench of three Justices. In 1994, the Court adopted a uniform procedure for applying for special leave in both civil and criminal cases, and the practice between that time and 1997 was for a Bench of three Justices to hear all applications for special leave.

In 1997, in an attempt to cope with the increasing number of special leave applications, the number of sitting Justices was reduced from three to two, unless it appeared desirable for a third Justice to sit to avoid the possibility of an even division. When the determination of a special leave application, whether civil or criminal, itself depends on an important point of law or practice, the Bench may be constituted by five or more Justices. If need be, the application will be adjourned by a smaller Bench until a larger Bench is constituted.

The number of Justices appointed to sit on an appeal has depended on a number of factors. When appeals were brought from a final judgment of a Supreme Court constituted by a single judge, the appeal was usually heard by a Court of three Justices. Since 1984, appeals from a single judge have been virtually unknown, and appeals from judgments of a Full Court or Court of Appeal are heard by Benches of five or more Justices. The ordinary 'working' Court of five Justices is constituted to determine appeals in which the only issue is the construction of a statute; a minor extension or modification of an existing principle; the correctness of the application of a principle by the court below; a question of procedural irregularity; or, rarely, the correctness of a finding of fact. But in general, all available Justices will sit if the issue in the appeal involves the construction of the Constitution; the correctness of an earlier decision of the High Court or a long-established **precedent**; a consideration of an important principle of law (not merely its application); a conflict between the decisions of two or more Australian **superior courts**; the decision of a Full Court or Court of Appeal consisting of five or more judges of an Australian superior court; or a question of exceptional public importance.

The Court tries to ensure that the opinions of all available Justices are secured to finally settle any questions of these kinds. It is unsatisfactory to have finely balanced questions resolved by fewer Justices than a majority of the whole Court. The factors that affect the number of Justices sitting in an appeal also affect the number of Justices sitting to determine issues arising in matters in the original jurisdiction—for example, issues of constitutional validity in a cause commenced in the High Court or **removed** into the High Court from another Court. On the return of an **order** *nisi* for **judicial review** of a non-judicial decision, three Justices are appointed to sit unless one or more of the factors earlier mentioned warrants a larger Bench.

On appeals from a judgment or order of a single Justice of the High Court, the practice has varied. On one view, an even number of Justices should sit so that, if there be an equal division in the opinion of the Justices sitting on appeal, the opinion of the Justice appealed from would prevail (see **Tied vote**). Another view is that the appellate Bench should be constituted by an uneven number of Justices so that the point is decided upon the opinion of the majority of the Justices who have heard the argument on appeal (see **Outcomes**). Generally, the former view has been followed. A single Justice presides at trials in the original jurisdiction.

The **Chief Justice** circulates a 'proposal' listing the cases to be heard at a **sittings** of the Full Court and nominating the Justices to sit on each case. Although a Justice who has not been listed to sit on a matter has a right to sit if he or she wishes to do so, an exercise of that right would be exceptional. If a Justice regarded a case as being of such significance as to warrant an exercise of the right, the proposal might be amended to include all available Justices. The proposal is designed to distribute the work of the Court evenly, taking into account judicial leave and other official judicial engagements. It is settled in consultation with the senior Deputy Registrar. Similarly, a roster of Justices to sit in chambers or in original jurisdiction matters is circulated by the Chief Justice. The roster ordinarily assigns matters pending in a District Registry other than Sydney to a Justice whose principal place of residence is in that district. Matters

not so assigned are heard by other Justices who are rostered by the week to determine applications listed for hearing during that week.

GERARD BRENNAN

Bill of Rights is an expression historically used for various solemn declarations of citizens' **rights** that governments are morally (and sometimes legally) bound to respect.

In English history, the reference is primarily to the *Bill of Rights* 1688, part of the political settlement defining the terms on which William and Mary of Orange agreed to accept the British Crown. This 1688 Bill of Rights remains in force in Australia through the **reception of English law**, and still resonates in contemporary case law—in particular for its historical importance as an affirmation of parliamentary privilege (see *Egan v Willis* (1998); *R v Murphy* (1986); **Gibbs** and **Stephen** in *Sankey v Whitlam* (1978)). In **taxation law**, its insistence on parliamentary consent to taxation has been invoked as excluding tax liabilities based on executive discretion rather than statutory criteria (*Commissioner of State Revenue (Vic) v Royal Insurance* (1994); *Commissioner of Stamps v Telegraph Investment* (1995)), while also underpinning the broader constitutional importance of parliamentary control of taxation (**Brennan** in *Northern Suburbs Cemetery v Commonwealth* (1993)). Its insistence on parliamentary consent to the maintenance of armed forces in peacetime was relied on by Brennan and **Toohey** in *Re Tracey; Ex parte Ryan* (1989) as supporting the view that military law could not oust 'the ordinary criminal law'. Its enjoinder against 'cruel and unusual punishments' was powerfully invoked by **Murphy** in *Sillery v The Queen* (1981), and its affirmation of the right to petition by **Kirby** in *Mann v O'Neill* (1997).

More vaguely, in *Williams v The Queen* (1986), **Wilson** and **Dawson** saw its affirmation of 'ancient and indubitable rights and liberties' as entrenching the right to the **writ** of habeas corpus, thus limiting police powers of detention. Generally, however, its affirmations of the rights of citizens (as distinct from the rights of parliaments) are no longer of practical significance (see Wilson in *Re Cusack* (1985) and **Hayne** in *Fyffe v Victoria* (2000)). Some of its affirmations now seem anachronistic, even offensive: its 'right to bear arms' is a right of Protestants to defend themselves against Catholics. Its enduring historical importance lies in its symbolism of, and absorption into, the evolutionary tradition of 'general constitutional principles' (**Dixon** in *Cam & Sons v Ramsay* (1960); compare **Isaacs** in the *Skin Wool Case* (1922) and Murphy in the *BLF Case* (1982)).

A more significant reference nowadays is to the US Bill of Rights, comprising the first ten amendments added to the US Constitution in 1791—originally intended only to limit the powers of the federal government, but in 1868 effectively extended by the Fourteenth Amendment to state powers as well. Far more pervasive in Australian law than the presence of the 1688 UK Bill of Rights is the absence of any equivalent to the 1791 US Bill of Rights. Though following much of the American model—and despite the powerful advocacy of **Inglis Clark**—the Australian drafters deliberately rejected any systematic Bill of Rights. **Commonwealth legislative powers** were to be limited by precise delineations of subject matter, but *not* by any systematic affirmation of rights and liberties by which Parliament would be legally constrained. As **Mason** said in *Australian Capital Television v Commonwealth* (1992), 'the **framers of the Constitution** accepted, in accordance with prevailing English thinking, that the citizen's rights were best left to the protection of the **common law** in association with the doctrine of parliamentary supremacy'. The only constraints on that doctrine were the conventions of **responsible government**.

Whether this was a mistake that should now be corrected—or whether, a century later, developments in legislative and executive powers and practices now require a different judgment—has been widely debated. Of ambiguous significance in that debate is the limited—sometimes nugatory—effect that High Court interpretation has given to the few sporadic examples of **express constitutional rights** the framers did accept. On the one hand, these examples are said to show that any more systematic attempt to rely on the Court for protection of 'rights' would simply be ineffectual. On the other hand, the Court's dispiriting record is explained as an understandable response to a random and anomalous scattering of isolated guarantees, lacking the supportive framework of any systematic commitment to rights. If the rarity of attempts to invoke or enforce these provisions has been a failure of the Bar as well as the Bench, a more systematic 'rights' jurisdiction might elicit more creative responses from both Bench and Bar.

The tentative experiments of the **Mason Court** with findings of **implied constitutional rights** were of equally ambiguous import. On the one hand, they were criticised as fundamentally incompatible with the deliberate choice of the framers. (Mason himself, in the passage already referred to, acknowledged that the framers' choice made it 'difficult, if not impossible, to establish a foundation for the implication of general guarantees of fundamental rights and freedoms'.) On the other hand, the Court's apparent willingness to make piecemeal findings of implied constitutional rights or freedoms was said to strengthen the case for a more explicit and more systematic statement of judicially enforceable rights.

This is not to say that a Bill of Rights must have constitutional force. The concept is broad enough to include any solemn written statement of fundamental rights, whether or not enshrined in the Constitution, and whether or not enforceable. Successive Labor **Attorneys-General** have tried to introduce a statutory Australian Bill of Rights: these proposals would not have had constitutional force, and how far they should be judicially enforceable was controversial. In the **Whitlam era**, Murphy introduced the Human Rights Bill 1973; in the first year of the Hawke government, Gareth Evans sought Cabinet approval for an Australian Bill of Rights Bill 1983; and eventually his successor, Lionel Bowen, introduced a modified version into Parliament as the Australian Bill of Rights Bill 1985. None of these measures succeeded.

Although these Australian proposals differed from the US model, two particular American provisions are often invoked in the Australian debate. One common argument against Bills of Rights is that—effectively in perpetuity—they may enshrine 'rights' that later generations come to perceive as anachronistic, or even socially harmful. The US Second Amendment ('the right ... to keep and bear Arms') is a telling example. Conversely, it is said that a Bill of Rights may be unduly restrictive, by failing to specify rights which future generations come to see as important. But the US Ninth Amendment ('The enumeration ... of certain rights, shall not be construed to deny or disparage others retained by the people') suggests that this problem can be foreseen and effectively countered. In *Griswold v Connecticut* (1965), for example, some Justices of the **United States Supreme Court** relied on this provision as the basis for a judicially enforceable 'right to privacy'. Beyond that, the US model suggests significant issues of policy and strategy that any Bill of Rights debate must resolve.

First, what the US model prevents is interference *by governments* with individual rights: it protects the community against the government. Legislation affecting human relationships within the community—reaching into the community to protect individuals against abuses by other individuals—is nowadays an important part of human rights regimes (see, for example, in Australia the *Racial Discrimination Act* 1975 (Cth), *Sex Discrimination Act* 1984 (Cth), and *Disability Discrimination Act* 1992 (Cth)); but the function of such legislation is generally understood as different from that of a Bill of Rights. Murphy's 1973 Bill sought to regulate private action as well as governmental action—but that was one of its more controversial features. On the other hand, some US decisions have extended the application of the Fourteenth Amendment to community practices, by finding that they were sanctioned or condoned by government in a way that involved 'state action'; and the High Court decision in *Street v Queensland Bar Association* (1989) may have opened the way for a similar extension in the operation of section 117 of the Australian Constitution.

Secondly, a Bill of Rights on the US model has constitutional force. Embedded in the Constitution itself, it imposes overriding constraints on the powers the Constitution confers on its legislative and executive organs. Thus the legislature is bound by judicial interpretations of those constraints. Short of judicial **overruling**, such interpretations can be overcome only by constitutional **amendment**.

By contrast, several countries have experimented (as the Murphy and Evans proposals did) with *statutory* Bills of Rights—enacted by the legislature itself, and thus open to legislative amendment. This may sometimes be the first step towards constitutional enshrinement: for example, while the *Canadian Bill of Rights* 1960 had only statutory force, the Canadian Charter of Rights and Freedoms in the *Constitution Act* 1982 has constitutional force. The Murphy and Evans proposals sought to initiate a similar development. In each case, the intention was that after the statutory regime had demonstrated its practical benefits (and any unexpected judicial interpretations had been overcome by amendment), a proposal for its constitutional enshrinement might be put to a referendum.

Thirdly, a Bill of Rights on the US model is judicially enforceable. It is not merely a high-sounding inspirational or exhortative statement of good intentions, or an education in civics. It is sometimes proposed that a 'Bill of Rights' confined to inspirational or educational functions would itself be of value. The 1983 Evans proposal was originally intended simply as a charter 'to hang on the schoolroom wall', though it also came to include limited provisions for judicial enforcement.

Assuming that judicial **remedies** are considered appropriate, they may still take different forms. The infringement of a constitutional Bill of Rights will normally result in a judicial declaration of invalidity; but under the *Human Rights Act 1998* (UK)—which gives effect within the UK to the European Convention on Human Rights—the only judicial remedy is a 'declaration of incompatibility', which may then prompt amendment of the legislation by executive order, if necessary without waiting for Parliament's approval.

The UK model does provide that persons who claim that a public authority 'has acted (or proposes to act)' incompatibly with their guaranteed rights may either rely on that claim as a defence in subsequent legal proceedings, or themselves initiate proceedings to test the issue. In common parlance, the Act may be used as a 'shield', but also as a 'sword'. But this, too, is a matter for strategic choice. The original conception of the 1983 Evans proposal was that it could only be used as a 'shield', though in the final draft, limited provision was made for affected individuals to take the initiative in seeking judicial relief. In the 1985 Bowen proposal, those provisions were watered down, but not wholly eliminated.

Finally, the US model is confined to a limited range of rights asserted by traditional **liberalism**. In the terminology of the **International Bill of Rights**, the focus is on 'civil and political rights' rather than 'social, economic and cultural rights'. Moreover, perhaps consequentially, the focus is on 'individual rights' rather than 'group rights'. Whether an Australian Bill of Rights should be similarly restricted is open to debate. On one view, that would prioritise a selective range of 'rights' derived from an outmoded **ideology**. Others would see the differentiation as a functional one—with 'civil and political rights' amenable to judicial enforcement through individual **matters** satisfying the requirements of **justiciability**, whereas 'social, economic and cultural rights' are less readily justiciable, and can effectively be realised only through 'progressive implementation' of legislative and executive policies.

Each of these aspects of the US model gives rise to strategic choices that advocates of an Australian Bill of Rights must resolve. The significant *content* of such a measure might well be of minimal scope: confined to protecting the 'civil and political rights' of individuals, and further confined to protecting them only against legislative and executive encroachments (leaving 'social, economic and cultural rights', and community respect for personal rights, to be dealt with by other legislative devices). The effective *implementation* of the protected rights might need to go further—with clear provision for enforceability through **judicial review**; with individuals having some degree of **standing** to initiate proceedings invoking the provisions as a 'sword' and not merely as a 'shield'; and with constitutional entrenchment at least as an eventual goal.

A constitutionally entrenched and judicially enforceable Bill of Rights would entail a significant power shift from the legislature to the judiciary, with implications for the **role** of the Court in a **democracy**. However, it might be argued that even a modest development along these lines would enhance the Court's capacity to effectively discharge its unavoidable role as a **political institution**. Judicial advertence to the **values** that underlie the **rule of law** would be more explicit, and judicial implementation of those values more sophisticated and confident. The increased sensitivity to human rights would benefit all the Court's work, not merely its Bill of Rights work. To the extent that such developments are already happening, those developments would be sanctioned and underpinned by a firm and legitimate foundation.

TONY BLACKSHIELD

Further Reading
Philip Alston (ed), *Towards an Australian Bill of Rights* (1994)
John Craig, 'The "Bill of Rights" Debates in Australia and New Zealand: A Comparative Analysis' (1994) 8(2) *Legislative Studies* 67
Catherine Henry and Francesca Dominello, 'The Case for an Australian Bill of Rights' (1998) 25 *Plaintiff* (Australian Plaintiff Lawyers' Association) 20
Murray Wilcox, *An Australian Charter of Rights?* (1993)
George Williams, *A Bill of Rights for Australia* (2000)

Biographies and biographical writing. Beyond a raconteur's delight in exposés, does the quest for and nurturing of first-rate biographies of Australia's judges matter? Yes—if beneath the rhetoric of judicial neutrality, autonomy, **independence**, and the concept of 'a government of laws and not of men' lurk personal **values**, preferences and choices.

In this context, perceptive judicial biographies can assist in understanding whether any and, if so, what correlation exists between a judge's personal commitments and **decision-making processes**, for example through the revelation, use and evaluation of previously undisclosed information (including draft judicial opinions; correspondence; memoranda; diaries and working files and **private papers**). They might also influence judicial **appointment** processes, whether by facilitating more confident prophesies about the likely post-appointment performance of potential judicial appointees, or by more clearly revealing the unreliability of those prophesies. Biographical ventures—book-length portraits, shorter monographs, theses, articles and reviews—can, therefore, add something more than a peripheral level of enjoyment and intellectual sustenance to most explorations of the law: they can make vividly clear that a difference, perhaps a good deal more than a significant difference, in the law may occur because one person, rather than another, was the judge.

Almost without exception, Australian judicial biographies make no overt attempt to confront such issues. Conventional, not interpretive, approaches are utilised. Chronological order predominates. Each stage of a judge's life, from birth to death, is reconstructed. Facts, public and private, are garnered. Evaluation—legal, psychological, political and ideological—is only infrequently included. Broader comparative perspectives are also often missing. How does the individual's contribution to legal doctrines, interpretive techniques and the more mundane work of courts relate to the efforts of their contemporaries and earlier or later judges? Such comparisons might extend beyond any one jurisdiction or country.

Any reasonably competent judicial biography exploring even some of these multi-dimensional facets would enhance the theoretical and pragmatic realms of legal literature.

Detailed analysis of an individual judge's opinions could contribute to **jurisprudence**, by applying, enriching, stimulating, changing or germinating theories of the judicial process. Insight into institutional working arrangements, revealed through exposition of a judge's daily routine, would add a touch of reality to studies of the history, practice, procedure and organisation of courts. Milieu does matter. Interaction of judges with their judicial brethren, **counsel**, **associates**, and litigants, and with less immediate influences emanating from the world outside the courtroom, requires comment and evaluation. A perceptive author might as a closing gesture endeavour to synthesise these fragments of a judge's life into an interpretive picture of larger themes and premises which may provide the unstated, but controlling and pervading, postulates behind judicial opinions.

What materials are needed to meet these diverse specifications? Obvious sources of information will not suffice. Opinions in law reports, scholarship in journals and books, parliamentary and other public addresses, and private papers, including personal letters and diaries, are among the usual litany of bibliographical material. However, more must be obtained. Unpublished and draft judicial opinions, court records, **transcripts of argument**, lawyer's briefs, the nature of the Justice's pre-appointment legal practice, law office opinions, files and cases, and a knowledge of the judge's personal library, must also be acquired and explored. Above all, the boundaries of research ought not to be set by law books and legal activities. Friendships and family relationships may be relevant to ascertaining what was influential in or shaped a Justice's decision-making processes. Social, economic, psychological and philosophical theories and practices must also be investigated. Biographers must embark upon an imaginative, patient and persistent quest to locate, synthesise and interpret.

Unfortunately, great biographies of Australian judges remain to be written. Compared to the US (and to a lesser extent Canada and England), biographies focusing on the lives, intellect and professional careers of Australian judges are rare. Excellent to routine biographies of **United States Supreme Court** Justices—not only the legendary but also the ordinary and even insignificant—have been and continue to be written. Of course, there are some Australian judicial biographies and biographical notes—including essays, reviews, anecdotes and obituaries—many of which are published in law journals; the *Commonwealth Law Reports*; the *ADB*; and *The Oxford Companion to the High Court of Australia*. Book length narratives are much rarer. The list, even in 2001, was short: **Griffith** (Roger Joyce), **Barton** (John Reynolds; Geoffrey Bolton), **Isaacs** (Zelman Cowen), **Higgins** (John Rickard), **Evatt** (Ken Buckley, Barbara Dale and Wayne Reynolds; Peter Crockett; Allan Dalziel; and Kylie Tennant), **Barwick** (David Marr), **Murphy** (Jenny Hocking) and **Gibbs** (Joan Priest). However, most of these focus primarily on the Justice's non-judicial life and work. Omissions from the list are obvious—particularly, **Dixon**, **Starke**, **McTiernan**, **Latham**, **Fullagar** and **Windeyer**. A dramatic increase in the quantity and quality of Australian High Court biographies is urgently required.

Movement from hagiographical narratives to comprehensive scholarly expositions, to increase quality, is, however, a more difficult task. Again, mere recitation of personal, 'warts and all' details will not suffice. Judicial biographies must provide explanations and analysis of, at least, the major cases; explore the judge's interpretive strategies and decision-making processes; expose intra-mural relationships—collegiality, collaboration and confrontation—with other Justices; trace the origins and development of the judge's character, beliefs, views and motivations; and delineate the influences—public and private—on the judge's opinions and decisions. Ultimately, the methodology and objectives of judicial biography should harmoniously support each other.

Major biographies of High Court Justices—Griffith, Barton, Isaacs, Higgins, Evatt, Barwick and Murphy—have a common characteristic: the intense involvement of those Justices in politics. For substantial periods of time, all were parliamentarians and Ministers of the Crown. Regrettably, especially from lawyers' perspectives, their biographies tend to be dominated by those 'political' aspects, with relatively little material, analysis or evaluation devoted to their judicial careers. Justices' papers, draft opinions, correspondence and diaries have not always been fully utilised. Many of their judicial decisions, arguments, basic premises and observations remain unnoticed. Consequently, connections, if any, between the diverse aspects of these Justices' multi-faceted lives are not discovered or discussed. Any illumination which biographies might offer of the interactions and operations of law, government and people, and what lessons or guidance this might convey to the present and future, remains to be realised. Given the influence exerted by the decisions and reasoning of most of these Justices, not only while on the High Court, but also, through the doctrine of **precedent**, on continuing legal development, the parlous condition of Australian judicial biography is disappointing.

Exacerbating this situation is the virtual absence of biographical scholarship devoted to other less 'political' Justices whose lives were perhaps more pedestrian, even more mundane. But did they or, at least, some of them live greatly in the law? Dixon is the pre-eminent example. His voluminous private papers, including diaries and letters to family members and colleagues, as well as his ongoing influence and 'brooding omnipresence' over vast tracts of Australian law, should entice a biography of comparable dimensions (quantitative and qualitative) to those of eminent American jurists such as Learned Hand (Gerald Gunther), Benjamin Cardozo (Andrew Kaufman), and Oliver Wendell Holmes Jr (Edward White). Hopefully that will be achieved by a Dixon biography being written by Phillip Ayres of Monash University (see **Dixon diaries**).

Extolling the 'greats', however, is not enough. The Court consists of more than one or even a few Justices. It is a collegial institution. Through comprehensive biographical studies intriguing questions might be answered. Does close association for many years, working together daily in a small group, lead to or necessitate compromises? Is there bargaining on decisions, opinions or doctrines? How does the Court operate? What are the **personal relations** among the Justices? Are less publicly notable Justices more dominant and influential within the privacy of judicial **chambers**? Particularly during the second half of Chief Justice Earl Warren's tenure, William Brennan epitomised this phenomenon through his influence in the nine Justices' chambers and the **conference** room of the US Supreme Court.

Cumulatively, judicial biographies of High Court Justices would add another important dimension to the apex of Australia's judiciary. As a contribution to Australian law and history, that would be a significant achievement. For those interested in the High Court as an institution of government in Australia, much work remains to be done.

JAMES THOMSON

Further Reading

JD Merralls, 'Biography of a Professional: Sir Owen Dixon' (Summer 1996) 99 *Vic Bar News* 26

Clifford Pannam, 'Judicial Biography: A Preliminary Obstacle' (1964) 4 *UQLJ* 57

Symposium: National Conference on Judicial Biography (1995) 70 *NYULR* 485

James Thomson, 'Judicial Biography: Some Tentative Observations on the Australian Enterprise' (1985) 8 *UNSWLJ* 380

James Thomson, 'Swimming in Air: Lionel Murphy and Continuing Observations on Australian Judicial Biography' (1998) 4 *Aust J of Leg Hist* 221

George Winterton et al., *Australian Federal Constitutional Law* (1999) 919–924 (bibliography of judicial biographies)

Boilermakers Case (1956) concerned a challenge by the Boilermakers' Society of Australia to sections 29 and 29A of the *Conciliation and Arbitration Act* 1904 (Cth), which empowered the Commonwealth Court of **Conciliation and Arbitration** ('the Arbitration Court') to issue orders of compliance with awards and to punish disobedience of such orders as **contempt** of court. The Society had been ordered by the Arbitration Court to comply with an award and, when it failed to do so, it was fined £500 for disobedience. It sought a **writ** of prohibition in the High Court directed at these orders. The Court, by a 4:3 majority (**Dixon**, **McTiernan**, **Fullagar** and **Kitto**; **Williams**, **Webb** and **Taylor** dissenting), held that the Arbitration Court, whose primary functions were arbitral (non-judicial), could not validly be invested with the **judicial power** of the Commonwealth because it was not permissible for Parliament to confer on a federal tribunal both judicial and non-judicial functions. The majority view was upheld on appeal to the **Privy Council** (1957).

The Court did not attempt to review the deeper justifications for the **separation of powers** in political theory, nor the long history of the doctrine in the US Constitution. The prohibition against an admixture of functions was said by the majority to be supported by the textual division of the legislative, executive and judicial powers in Chapters I, II and III of the Constitution. This textual arrangement was said to enshrine a legally enforceable distribution of powers. The reliance on textual divisions required the Court to address the established view that the Constitution permits the exercise of legislative and executive functions by the same persons, and that the legislature may validly delegate legislative powers to the executive. The majority explained this departure from the strict separation doctrine, as Dixon had earlier done in *Victorian Stevedoring & General Contracting Co v Meakes and Dignan* (1931), as a qualification based on British principle and practice.

The special role of the judicial branch in a federal system was seen by the majority as further supporting the strict separation of federal judicial power. This both justified and explained the existence of Chapter III, which was 'an exhaustive statement of the manner in which the judicial power of the Commonwealth is or may be vested'. It followed that the Commonwealth Parliament was denied the power to confer judicial functions upon a body that was not a Chapter III court, or to confer non-judicial functions on a Chapter III court, except insofar as those non-judicial functions were ancillary or incidental to the exercise of judicial power.

The dissenting judges were wary of the difficulties that a strict separation can create, as the American experience had shown. While conceding that only courts could exercise judicial power, they stressed that there was no express provision that they could not exercise other powers. Although there were some functions which could be exercised only by the appropriate branch of government, there were others, including the arbitral function, which could not be subject to exclusive delimitation. Its exercise was not incompatible with the exercise of judicial power, so long as that judicial power was vested in a body that was properly constituted as a Chapter III Court.

The majority judgments rested on a construction of the Constitution that marked a departure from previous development. Earlier cases had focused on the impermissibility of judicial power being exercised by bodies other than courts, and had thereby avoided a more general consideration of the admixture of judicial and non-judicial functions. It was clear from the earlier cases that judicial power could be exercised only by Chapter III courts, and, strictly speaking, the *Boilermakers Case*, by finding that the Arbitration Court was not a Chapter III court (in somewhat circular fashion, by emphasising its predominantly arbitral function) did not go beyond this established proposition. However, by couching its decision in terms of the impermissibility of combining judicial and non-judicial functions, the Court clearly established the converse proposition that Chapter III courts could exercise only judicial power.

The majority judgment bears the hallmarks of the constitutional vision of the **Chief Justice**, Dixon, who had long been convinced of the need for a strict separation of federal judicial power, but who had refrained from pursuing the issue while **Latham** (who had been responsible as **Attorney-General** for the 1926 amendments that reconstituted the Arbitration Court with arbitral and judicial functions) was a member of the Court. From his **extra-judicial** comments, it was clear that Dixon believed that public dissatisfaction with the Arbitration Court had the potential to affect the public perception of Chapter III courts generally. The prospect of wilful disobedience of Court orders and the further politicisation of the activities of the Arbitration Court, may have alerted the majority to the dangers of judicial involvement in industrial matters and persuaded them of the need for a strict separation doctrine.

The immediate consequence of the decision was the creation of two bodies: the Commonwealth Conciliation and Arbitration Commission and the Commonwealth Industrial Court, in which the arbitral and judicial functions of the old Arbitration Court were respectively vested. Although some members of the High Court have expressed dissatisfaction with the reasoning and result of the *Boilermakers Case*, the strict separation doctrine it established has endured.

LINDA KIRK

Further Reading

Deryck Thomson, 'The Separation of Powers Doctrine in the Commonwealth Constitution: The *Boilermakers' Case*' (1958) 2 *Syd LR* 480

Brennan, (Francis) Gerard (*b* 22 May 1928; Justice 1981–95; Chief Justice 1995–98). In many respects, Brennan embodied the tension that is at the heart of the **judicial oath**. He believed that it was a primary function of law to protect minorities and the disadvantaged, and his decisions struggled to achieve this result. Yet Brennan was also a strong adherent of the **rule of law**, believing that a Justice is limited in his or her ability to engage in judicial **law-making**. The tension between these imperatives characterised Brennan's judgments throughout his time as a Justice of the High Court.

Brennan was born in Queensland, the grandson of an Irish immigrant, and the son of Frank Brennan (a Justice of the Supreme Court of Queensland). He grew up in what he later described as a 'loving' Catholic household, attending the Range Convent School, the Christian Brothers College in Rockhampton, and Downlands College in Toowoomba. Brennan excelled at school, passing his exams so early that he was deemed too young to go to university (he was only 16 at the time). After waiting a year, Brennan enrolled in a combined BA/LLB degree at University of Queensland. While at university, Brennan was active in student affairs, and was elected President of the National Union of Students in 1949.

Brennan began work as an associate to his father at the Supreme Court of Queensland. On his own admission, Brennan's first day in this position was not a resounding success. Misreading an indictment, he mistakenly accused the prosecutor ('a most upright man') of sexual assault. Fortunately, counsel for the accused leapt to his feet, announcing 'Your Honour, I appear for My Learned Friend … We plead not guilty!'

After his father's death in 1949, he worked at the Australian National University and then as associate to Kenneth Townley, a newly appointed Justice of the Supreme Court of Queensland. Townley had recently been appointed to preside over the war crimes trials on Manus Island, New Guinea, and his work provided Brennan with an early insight into the complexities of **international law**.

Brennan was admitted to the Queensland Bar in 1951. His first reported case appears to have been a fairly humble matter involving letters of administration granted to a person outside the jurisdiction (*Re McKee* (1952)). Although modest, his early practice was diverse, consisting of matters ranging from committal proceedings to commercial disputes. In each of these matters, Brennan demonstrated his comprehensive knowledge of the law through his clear and lucid argument. His talent soon gained him respect, and he became one of the first Catholic barristers to cross the strong sectarian line that permeated the Brisbane Bar by receiving briefs from the Protestant end of town.

Brennan was appointed a QC in Queensland in 1965. He was later admitted in NSW, the Northern Territory, **Papua and New Guinea**, and Fiji. Notable cases in which he appeared included his 1969 representation of the Fijian Alliance Party in an arbitration matter before Lord Denning (concerning the Fijian sugar industry) and his 1972 prosecution in Rabaul of the murder of a District Commissioner. He was also one of the first advocates to argue a case for Aboriginal land rights, representing the Northern Land Council before the Woodward Royal Commission into Aboriginal Land Rights in the Northern Territory in 1974.

During his time at the Bar, Brennan played a leading role within the **legal profession**. He was elected President of the Bar Association of Queensland (1974–76), President of the Australian Bar Association (1975–76), and member of the Executive of the Law Council of Australia (1974–76). He also began to influence the development of Australian law through his position as a part-time member of the Australian Law Reform Commission (1975–77).

Despite these demanding positions, Brennan managed to be a dedicated father. In 1953, he married Dr Patricia O'Hara, with whom he had seven children (three sons and four daughters). His first child, Frank Brennan, born in 1954, would become a Jesuit Priest and achieve fame as an advocate for the rights of **Aboriginal peoples**.

One of Brennan's greatest achievements was the contribution he made to the development of Australian **administrative law**. In 1976, the Fraser government appointed him as the first President of the Administrative Appeals Tribunal. The Tribunal occupied a novel position at the time, straddling the divide between executive and **judicial power**. As the first President of the new institution, Brennan was in a unique position, able to develop the tribunal along lines consistent with either an administrative or judicial model. Brennan consciously adopted a judicial model, and, through his strong leadership, guided the tribunal through the difficult period of its establishment and early development. This, together with his work as the first President of the newly created Administrative Review Council (whose role was to advise the government on matters relating to administrative law), considerably strengthened the new administrative structures.

In 1979, Brennan retired from his position as President of the Tribunal to concentrate full-time on his duties as a judge of the **Federal Court**, to which he had been one of the original appointees in 1977. However, Brennan's service as a full-time member of the Federal Court was short-lived. In 1981, the Fraser government appointed him a Justice of the High Court (filling the vacancy created when **Barwick** retired and **Gibbs** became **Chief Justice**). Brennan had moved to **Canberra** shortly after his appointment as President of the Tribunal and remained there until his **retirement** from the High Court.

From his earliest days on the High Court, Brennan displayed characteristics that would stamp his **judicial style** for nearly two decades. Espousing a well-defined conception of a limited judicial **role**, Brennan strove for certainty in the exposition and application of legal principle. He was nevertheless willing to develop the law when he considered this to be necessary to achieve a just result consistent with the demands of modern society. As part of the majority in *Koowarta's Case* (1982) and the *Tasmanian Dam Case*

(1983), he gave wide scope to the **external affairs power**. In *Kioa v West* (1985), he expounded the importance of **natural justice** to the exercise of administrative power while emphasising its fundamental difference from judicial power. In *He Kaw Teh v The Queen* (1985), he carefully distilled a mass of conflicting case law into clearly expressed presumptions concerning the mental element of statutory offences.

Together with **Mason** and **Deane**, Brennan played a prominent role within the **Mason Court**. Yet his judicial method and his view of a limited role for the judiciary led him to frequent dissents. Unlike Mason and Deane, Brennan saw no place for social **policy** in the development of the law. He was prepared to embrace the notion of community **values** as a guide to judicial **decision making**, but only to a very limited extent. The fundamental difference between the role of the judiciary and the role of the parliament and the executive was to Brennan constantly to be borne in mind. Those values that could legitimately inform judicial decision making were confined to the 'relatively permanent values of the Australian community'. They were not the 'ephemeral opinions of the community' as they may exist from time to time.

Nowhere is the contrast in style better illustrated than in *Dietrich v The Queen* (1992), where Brennan in dissent argued against the power of a court to stay a criminal prosecution where an accused was indigent. While openly favouring the reform of **criminal procedure** to confer an entitlement to legal aid, Brennan vehemently rejected the ability of the Court to produce such a result through 'judicial legislation'. According to Brennan, the 'responsibility for keeping the **common law** consonant with contemporary values' did 'not mean that the courts have a general power to mould society and its institutions according to judicial perceptions of what is conducive to the attainment of those values'.

For Brennan, judicial method began with a thorough understanding of the existing case law. His judgments uniformly displayed great industry and attention to **history**. From the existing case law, Brennan sought to discern underlying values and principles. Those values and principles were weighed against the enduring values and principles of the Australian legal system as a whole. They were then applied to refine and where necessary reformulate the specific legal rules. Brennan saw that the courts could in this way legitimately develop the law to keep pace with contemporary social and **economic** conditions. However, for Brennan, the courts had no role in rejecting and replacing legal rules in the pursuit of social or economic ends. Nor could they bring about a change in the law simply to achieve tidiness or conceptual purity. **Overruling** was properly confined to those rare cases where specific legal rules had proved to be unworkable, or where to continue to apply them would perpetuate injustice.

In the formulation of the legal rules themselves, Brennan abhorred indeterminacy. He attempted wherever possible to pronounce the law in precise and even syllogistic terms. He drew upon and preferred to maintain traditional legal categorisations. These traits were evident in Brennan's sustained opposition to the doctrine of **proximity** as formulated by Deane. In place of proximity, Brennan favoured an 'incremental' development of the law of negligence by analogy

Gerard Brennan, Justice 1981–95; Chief Justice 1995–98

with existing categories of liability. Other striking examples of this approach were his insistence in dissent in *Australian Safeway Stores v Zaluzna* (1987) on preserving the separate categories of **occupiers' liability** for negligence, and in *Burnie Port Authority v General Jones* (1994) on preserving the rule in *Rylands v Fletcher* (1866 and 1868). In the same way, Brennan resisted the extension of discretionary judicial powers, believing that they 'tended to create a government of men rather than a government of laws'.

However, it was in **constitutional law** and administrative law that Brennan's considered and self-consciously restrained approach to the legitimate province of judicial decision making was most evident. In *A-G (NSW) v Quin* (1990), Brennan observed that the Court 'needs to remember that the judicature is but one of the three co-ordinate branches of government and that the authority of the judicature is not derived from a superior capacity to balance the interests of the community against the interests of an individual'. He declared that the 'duty and **jurisdiction** of the court to review administrative action do not go beyond the declaration and enforcing of the law which determines the limits and governs the exercise of the repository's power'. The 'merits' of an administrative decision were for the repository of power alone. In *McGinty v WA* (1996), Brennan led the Court in rejecting a constitutional implication of electoral **equality**.

'Implications', he said, 'are not devised by the judiciary; they exist in the text or structure of the Constitution and are revealed or uncovered by judicial exegesis'. The consequence was that no implication could be drawn from the Constitution that was not 'based on the actual terms of the Constitution or on its structure'.

To Brennan, the most important of the values and principles underlying the Australian legal system were the dignity of the individual and equality before the law. It was these that the institutional gulf separating the judiciary from the other branches of government was principally designed to protect. Indeed, Brennan saw the law as 'most needed when it stands against popular attitudes sometimes engendered by those with power and when it protects the unpopular against the clamour of the multitude'. In **Marion's Case** (1992), he stated that 'the law would fail in its function of protecting the weak' if it were to accept a policy of permitting sterilisation of the intellectually disabled simply to avoid the imposition of burdens on others.

This overarching concern for the dignity of the individual and for equality before the law lay at the heart of the most significant of Brennan's judgments and also the most controversial. In **Mabo** (1992), in a judgment that commanded the assent of a majority of the Court, Brennan rejected the common law doctrine of *terra nullius* as offensive to 'the values of justice and human rights (especially equality before the law) which are aspirations of the contemporary Australian legal system'. His careful formulation of a common law doctrine of **native title** involved tracing a path linking medieval **land law** with concepts of **sovereignty** that attended the age of European conquest. The resultant doctrine was deliberately and openly crafted to achieve a result that reversed a strongly perceived yet deep-rooted injustice within the Australian legal system without fracturing 'the skeleton of principle that gives the body of our law its shape and internal consistency'.

The measure of Brennan's restraint as a Justice can be seen by contrasting the result in *Mabo* with his judgment in *Wik* (1996), where he joined the minority in finding that pastoral leases extinguished native title. While acknowledging that the common law operated to produce a 'significant moral shortcoming', Brennan nonetheless considered that it was not open to him to alter the law. Rather, the shortcoming, he believed, should have been rectified by legislation.

Following the retirement of Mason in 1995, Brennan was appointed Chief Justice by the Keating government. The appointment was well received by the legal profession, and it was widely expected that under Brennan's leadership, the Court would consolidate rather than further develop the various directions that it had undertaken under the leadership of Mason. These predictions proved well-founded—as in *Lange v ABC* (1997), where the Court unanimously accepted Brennan's more limited formulation of the implied freedom of **political communication** (see *Free Speech Cases* (1992); **Implied constitutional rights**).

Consistently with his strong belief in a limited judicial role, as Chief Justice Brennan made few public statements other than on formal legal occasions. (Brennan's executive **associate** once joked that his standard reply to journalists was: 'No comment … and that's off the record'.) This was despite the sustained **criticism** from politicians and the **media** that attended the Court in the aftermath of *Mabo*. Brennan saw it as incumbent on the Commonwealth **Attorney-General** to defend the Court from this criticism—a view not shared by Daryl Williams, who became Attorney-General in the Howard government.

The criticism came to a head in early 1997, when Tim Fischer, then Deputy Prime Minister and leader of the National Party, publicly criticised the Court for delay in publishing its judgment in *Wik*. Brennan's response typified his quiet but forceful leadership of the Court. Shortly after the judgment was published, he wrote a private letter to Fischer (the letter was later published in a national daily newspaper) defending the Court. Brennan received an unreserved apology from Fischer shortly thereafter.

Brennan retired as Chief Justice in 1998. Although he took up a number of academic positions, he has generally refrained from public comment on contemporary legal issues.

BELINDA BAKER
STEPHEN GAGELER

Further Reading
Gerard Brennan, 'Limits on the Use of Judges' (1978) 9 *FL Rev* 1
Gerard Brennan, 'Judging the Judges' (1979) 53 *ALJ* 767
Gerard Brennan, 'The Christian Lawyer' (1992) 66 *ALJ* 259
Gerard Brennan, 'A Critique of Criticism' (1993) 19 *Mon LR* 213

Brennan Court (21 April 1995–21 May 1998). It was recognised that the Brennan Court would be short lived. What was not expected, however, was that in addition to the new Justice, **Gummow**, appointed in consequence of **Mason's** retirement, three further appointments would be made during the life of the Brennan Court. They were brought about by the early **retirement** of **Deane** (to become Governor-General), **Dawson** and **Toohey**. They were replaced by **Kirby** (appointed February 1996), **Hayne** (September 1997) and **Callinan** (February 1998). The continuity of membership implied in the term 'Brennan Court' was not present.

The changes caused administrative difficulties: **reserved judgments** in cases involving a departing Justice had to be delivered before the departure; scheduling of hearings had to take account of impending departures, including in the end that of **Brennan**; and six Justices (rather than seven) sat on some important constitutional cases. There was also no very long period where members of the Court became accustomed to sitting with each other, and thus used to each other's idiosyncrasies. Tensions among the members of the Brennan Court were sometimes unusually obvious.

Controversies arising outside the Court itself were also a distraction. A public difference of views emerged between Brennan and the Commonwealth **Attorney-General**, Daryl Williams, over the role of an Attorney-General in defending courts from attacks and ill-informed **criticism**. Williams' opinion was that the time had passed when such a defence could be expected; Brennan was an emphatic supporter of the traditional view. Deputy Prime Minister Tim Fischer also made a public attack—later withdrawn—on the Court for supposed delay in delivering judgment in *Wik* (1996). Remarks made in the **Federal Court** concerning evidence

The Brennan Court in 1996. Left to right: Toohey, Kirby, Dawson, Brennan, McHugh, Gummow and Gaudron

given by Callinan in litigation in that Court arising out of a matter in which he had been **counsel** also led to debate on whether steps should be taken against him in consequence. Nothing came of it.

Notwithstanding the difficulties and controversies, the volume of **business** dealt with by the Brennan Court was considerable, with many major cases being determined. They included *Grollo v Palmer* (1995), which confirmed the Parliament's power to confer *some* **non-judicial functions** on members of the federal judicature. This was further developed in *Wilson v Minister for Aboriginal and Torres Strait Islander Affairs* (1996), a case factually related to the **Hindmarsh Island Bridge Case** (1998). In *Kable v DPP* (1997), a case of the first importance, the states were held not to have unlimited legislative power in relation to their courts; they formed part of an integrated Australian judicial system and could not have conferred on them, even by the polities creating them, functions incompatible with the exercise of federal **judicial power**. *Commonwealth v Mewett* (1997) discussed the source of the Commonwealth's liability in **tort**, and the extent to which that could be diminished by providing for limitation periods.

Very important also were *Lange v ABC* (1997) and *Levy v Victoria* (1997), where the existence of a constitutionally protected freedom of **political communication** between the people concerning political or governmental matters was confirmed, its justification being to enable the people to exercise a free and informed choice as electors. *Lange* dealt with its application to **defamation** matters, *Levy* to forms of

non-verbal political protest. On the other hand, in *Kruger v Commonwealth* (1997), a majority prepared to endorse a separate implied constitutional freedom of **movement** and association was not achieved.

Henderson's Case (1997) dealt with the extent to which a Commonwealth authority might be subject to state laws in the absence of **inconsistent** Commonwealth legislation; it reduced the formerly perceived ambit of the *Cigamatic Case* (1962) doctrine of Commonwealth immunity (see **Intergovernmental immunities**). The states, however, suffered a severe financial blow in *Ha v NSW* (1997) when their tobacco taxes were held to be **excise duties**, and the adoption of a broad view of that term was confirmed. The effect of section 52(i) of the Constitution in invalidating state revenue laws operating in relation to Commonwealth places was confirmed in *Allders International v Commissioner of State Revenue* (1996). On the other hand, an instrument of one state was held to have no immunity from taxation by another (*State Authorities Superannuation v Commissioner of State Taxation (WA)* (1996)). *Gould v Brown* (1998), later not followed by the **Gleeson Court** in *Re Wakim* (1999), upheld the validity of **cross-vesting**, the Court of six Justices being equally divided (see **Tied vote**).

Newcrest Mining v Commonwealth (1997) held that the '**acquisition** on just terms' provisions of Constitution section 51(xxxi) could apply to the acquisition by the Commonwealth of **property** in a **territory** of the Commonwealth. In *Commonwealth v WMC Resources* (1998), however, the extinguishment of petroleum exploration permits issued by the

Commonwealth in the Timor Gap area was held not to attract section 51(xxxi).

The *Hindmarsh Island Bridge Case* in early 1998 attracted a great deal of publicity because of the long-running dispute concerning Aboriginal heritage claims in relation to the site of the proposed bridge, and because of the controversy surrounding the decision by the newly appointed Callinan to sit on the matter—a decision he later reversed. It also involved much discussion of the races power (see **Aboriginal peoples; Race**).

The *Industrial Relations Act Case* (1996) concerned the ambit of the **external affairs, conciliation and arbitration,** and **corporations powers** in the Constitution. The ability to make 'ambit claims' to create an industrial dispute in the federal sphere was again affirmed in *A-G (Qld) v Riordan* (1997). Other 'industrial' matters were *Byrne v Australian Airlines* (1995) (whether provisions of industrial awards became terms of contracts of employment) and *Re McJannet; Ex parte Minister for Employment* (1995) (the status of branches of a federal industrial organisation).

In relation to **constitutional interpretation,** in *Leask v Commonwealth* (1996) the Court reined in the operation of the doctrine of reasonable **proportionality** as a criterion of validity of Commonwealth laws made under a non-purposive power.

A number of issues arose in relation to elections. *Langer v Commonwealth* (1996) upheld the validity of the law prohibiting communications urging voters in elections for the House of Representatives to vote otherwise than in accordance with the preferential system prescribed by Parliament. A similar result was arrived at in relation to SA electoral laws in *Muldowney v SA* (1996). In *McGinty v WA* (1996), the WA Constitution was held not to require that there be equality of voting power. *Snowdon v Dondas* (1996) confirmed the Parliament's power to determine who could vote for the Northern Territory seats in the House of Representatives.

Breen v Williams (1996) held that the doctor–patient relationship conferred no entitlement on a patient to access to the doctor's records of treatment (see **Fiduciary obligations; Health law**). *Commissioner of Australian Federal Police v Propend Finance* (1997) held that legal professional privilege attached to copy documents in the possession of a solicitor if they were made for the purpose of obtaining or giving legal advice, or for use in legal proceedings, even where the original documents were not privileged.

In relation to **native title** claims, issues of procedure arose in the *Waanyi Case* (1996). Of great importance was *Wik,* which held that the grant of a pastoral lease (under the *Land Act 1962* (Qld)) did not of itself extinguish native title in the leased land; an examination of the terms and circumstances of each lease and of its authorising statute was necessary.

Hill v Van Erp (1997) held that a solicitor might be liable to a beneficiary disappointed by the solicitor's negligence in the manner of execution of the will. *Pyrenees Shire Council v Day* (1998) and *Romeo v Conservation Commission of the NT* (1998) explored the tests appropriate for determining the liability of public authorities for negligent inaction. *Northern Sandblasting v Harris* (1997) held that a landlord was obliged to make leased premises as safe for the intended purpose of entry as reasonable skill and care could make them.

The *Patrick Stevedores Case* (1998), one of the last cases of the Brennan Court, brought before it urgently a matter of great controversy in which the employer stevedoring group had sought to bring to an end the power of the maritime unions representing its employees.

Henry v Henry (1996) and *CSR v Cigna Insurance* (1997) laid down the Australian rules concerning stays of proceedings and anti-suit injunctions when there were parallel proceedings in a foreign court.

It is difficult to classify the Brennan Court. It was a time of transition for the Court, but one in which it handled a great deal of business, much of it of great significance.

DAVID F JACKSON

Budget of Court. The Court's funding and financial arrangements have in many ways been contentious. John Quick and others strongly opposed the **establishment** of the Court for reasons of cost. Financial arrangements, especially those concerned with travelling allowances, became an issue leading up to the **strike of 1905**. The reduction of Justices' allowances during the **Depression** also caused friction, at least among the judges. The funding of the Court again became an issue in the late 1970s and early 1980s. Many of these disputes reflect the tension between the government's concern about the Court's efficiency and **accountability** on the one hand, and the Court's concern about the erosion of its **independence** on the other.

The estimated cost of the Court for its first financial year of operation was £14 885. There were only three Justices (instead of the proposed five); the Court had no dedicated headquarters (see **Buildings**); and the Court was not even provided with a **library**. By contrast, the Court's current operating costs are around $10 million annually. About half of this amount is spent on salaries and related expenses for the seven Justices and Court staff. The other half is taken up mainly by the costs of operating and maintaining the High Court building in **Canberra** and the Court's offices in Sydney, Melbourne and Brisbane; maintaining the Court's extensive library collection; and travel expenses. Despite steadily increasing demands on the Court's services, its operating costs have remained relatively steady (in real terms) since 1980.

Until 1980, the Attorney-General's Department provided for the Court's **administration** from funds under the Department's sole control, and precise information about the allocation of funds for High Court purposes was hard to disentangle from the Department's overall budget for all federal courts and tribunals. **Barwick** saw the role of the Attorney-General's Department as posing a threat to the Court's independence: 'What if the High Court gave an unpopular decision against [the] government and it was dependent for its amenities on the government of the day? The government might hit back' (David Marr, *Barwick* (1980), quoting Kep Enderby). In 1978, Barwick proposed that the role of the Department in controlling the Court's budget be eliminated and that the **Chief Justice** be able to have direct access to Parliament to obtain the desired budget, as is the case with the **United States Supreme Court**.

At the same time, the increase in operating costs that the Court's move to Canberra entailed, and **criticism** from politicians and the public of the cost of the new Court building, made the Court's expenditure more vulnerable to public scrutiny than ever before. Barwick's proposal for direct access to Parliament to obtain his desired budget failed.

The system that succeeded was established by the *High Court of Australia Act* 1979 (Cth). Section 35 provides for moneys to be appropriated to the Court by the Commonwealth Parliament, and for the Minister for Finance to give directions on the amounts and timing of those appropriations. These moneys make up approximately 98 per cent of all funds available to the Court. Other sources of revenue include the interest received on deposits in bank accounts, rent from the Court's cafeteria, and income from the use of Court facilities by legal practitioners. Salaries and allowances for the Justices are paid out of Special Appropriations administered by the Attorney-General's Department.

Internally, general control of the Court's budget rests with the Justices. To assist in this task, a Finance Committee consisting of three Justices, together with the **Chief Executive and Principal Registrar**, considers significant new spending proposals and draft allocations of funds before they go to a meeting of all the Justices for approval. Day-to-day control of finances is centralised within the Marshal's Branch, with finance staff reporting regularly through the **Marshal** to the Chief Executive and Principal Registrar. The Chief Executive and Principal Registrar issues a monthly finance report to all Justices.

Section 47 of the Act requires the Court to prepare and submit to the **Attorney-General** an **annual report** on the administration of the Court, including audited financial statements. Since 1981–82, these statements have been prepared on a full accrual basis.

LEX HOWARD

Buildings. It is possible to trace the Court's development by reference to the buildings in which it has been housed. The Court's first **sitting** took place in the Banco Court of the Supreme Court of Victoria in 1903. It continued to occupy part of that building until a separate building in Melbourne was completed in 1928. In Sydney, it occupied part of the Darlinghurst Court House until a separate building was erected in 1923.

These arrangements created problems. By letter dated 28 February 1919, the Secretary of the Victorian Law Department informed **Gavan Duffy** that his **associate's** room had to be vacated in order to accommodate Judge Henry Winneke

Entrance to the old High Court building, 450 Little Bourke Street, Melbourne

Entrance to the old High Court building, Taylor Square, Darlinghurst, Sydney

of the County Court. After an exchange of correspondence, it was agreed that Gavan Duffy's associate would move to the newspaper room on the first floor of the Supreme Court library. The episode added weight to the concerns of those responsible for protecting and enhancing the standing of the young national Court. On the other hand, some critics continued to believe that the very existence of the Court was an extravagance, given the general satisfaction with existing state Benches and the preservation of a right to appeal to the **Privy Council**.

As the workload and the standing of the Court continued to rise, the Commonwealth government accepted the need to provide it with new buildings in Sydney and Melbourne. **Garran** played a considerable role in this development. The Melbourne building was erected in accordance with plans prepared by JS Murdoch, the Chief Commonwealth Architect from 1925 to 1929. The chief proponent of the 'Inter-War Stripped Classical Style', Murdoch also designed the old Parliament House, Gorman House and the Hotel Canberra. Like his other designs, this one is characterised by a symmetrical facade divided into bays; an entrance portal with vestigial columns and classical entablature; internal pavilions linked by corridors lit with natural light; and, generally, a strong emphasis on the horizontal line. It was opened on 20 February 1928 with scant ceremony.

The new building in Sydney—erected on a site adjacent to the Darlinghurst Court House—also helped to overcome the problems caused by the lack of space. Although extra space had been created, the design of the building conveyed an impression that the accommodation was temporary. The **circuit system** meant that, in other capital cities, the Court continued to rely on each **state Supreme Court** to provide **chambers** accommodation and **courtrooms**.

Barwick was sensitive to the problems relating to these arrangements. He proposed the abolition of circuits and the erection of a permanent building for the Court in **Canberra**. From the beginning, the *Judiciary Act* 1903 (Cth) had contemplated that the 'principal seat' of the Court should be at 'the seat of government' (see **Seat of Court**); and in 1926, when **Latham**, as **Attorney-General**, introduced amendments to the Judiciary Act to postpone that commitment, he envisaged that it would still be honoured as soon as 'the present pressure of building operations has been to some extent relaxed'. The matter was reopened by Gough **Whitlam** in 1957. Judges in the interim had held differing views about the desirability of accommodating the Court in Canberra. **Dixon**, with whom **Fullagar**, **Kitto**, and **Taylor** agreed, is known to have opposed the idea of the Court sitting permanently in Canberra; Douglas **Menzies** is known to have been in favour of the move.

Barwick's proposals were based on the belief that the Court's reputation hinged, in part, on the quality of the buildings in which it was housed. In generating support for his proposals, he often recounted the anecdote that, in order to gain access to the main courtroom, some of the Court's judges preferred to use the public entrance to Brisbane's Supreme Court building. This preference stemmed from the belief that the circular iron staircase connecting their chambers to the courtroom was unsafe.

The Commonwealth–State Law Courts Building in Sydney was opened in 1976, though until 1980 the Court continued to sit in the Darlinghurst building (now used by the District Court). The opening of the new building at the top of King Street marked a significant improvement in the Court's accommodation. Situated among some of Francis Greenway's famous buildings, it was designed to house both state and Commonwealth courts. The Supreme Court judges questioned the design, expressing the belief that their court should be housed in a separate and distinct building. The architects altered the design to ensure that the Supreme Court was separate from the Commonwealth courts. As part of this physical separation, the architects of this high-rise building located the various court registries on progressively higher floors, with the Federal Court higher than the state Supreme Court and the High Court highest of all. This change worked to reinforce the Court's position at the apex of the Australian judicial system. The location and design of the Court's building in Canberra conveys the same message (see **Architecture of Court building**).

The Court continues to schedule sittings of one week's duration in the state capitals other than Sydney and Melbourne. In almost all state capitals, the Commonwealth government has provided a separate building in which to house its courts. The Court uses these buildings on circuit visits. Like the older buildings in which the Court sits, these new buildings help to bolster its position as the federation's final court of appeal.

ROBERT HEATH

Further Reading
JM Bennett, *A History of the Supreme Court of New South Wales* (1974)
Robert Heath, '450 Little Bourke Street, Melbourne' (1999) 73 *ALJ* 124

Burnie Port Authority v General Jones (1994) is an example of the trend towards reforming **tort law** that was a feature of the Court's jurisprudence in the 1980s and early 1990s. Other examples of that trend include the rationalisation of **occupiers' liability**, the decision in *Rogers v Whitaker* (1992) concerning medical negligence, the protection of the privacy of a home-owner in *Plenty v Dillon* (1991), and the extension of a builder's duty of care to a subsequent purchaser of the dwelling in *Bryan v Maloney* (1995). In *Burnie Port*, the majority abolished a rule of **strict liability**, sought to reformulate aspects of vicarious liability, and declared inoperative an English statute that had been in force in Australia through the **reception of English law**.

The Port Authority had contracted out part of the renovation and expansion of its storage facilities. Through the negligence of one of the contractor's employees, frozen vegetables belonging to the respondent company were destroyed by fire. The respondent successfully sued both the Authority and the contractor in the courts in Tasmania. In the High Court, the respondent sought to retain its judgment against the Authority by the application of the rule in *Rylands v Fletcher* (1866 and 1868) and a special rule of liability relating to the spread of fire, as well as on the more general basis of the Authority's negligence. The majority (**Mason**, **Dawson**, **Toohey** and **Gaudron**; **Brennan** and **McHugh** dissenting), affirmed the Authority's liability in negligence, and in so doing concluded that both the rule in *Rylands v Fletcher* and the special rule relating to liability for fire had been subsumed within the general principles of negligence.

The rule in *Rylands v Fletcher*, developed from a decision of the Court of Exchequer Chamber in 1866 and the appeal

therefrom to the **House of Lords** in 1868, stated that an occupier of land, who brought onto the property some source of danger, was strictly liable for the damage that was the natural consequence of its escape, even if that damage had been caused by the negligence of an independent contractor. In *Burnie Port*, the majority of the Court considered that by 1994 the rule had become so qualified and limited that the time had come to do away with it as a separate head of liability.

But in so doing, the Court had necessarily to adjust other principles of liability for negligence. For one thing, the majority added to the categories of case in which a person will owe a personal and non-delegable duty to see that care is taken, even by an independent contractor. The central element that generated the non-delegable duty was seen to be control by one person and a special dependence and vulnerability by the other. That relationship could also be found between an occupier's introduction and collection of a source of danger, and the likelihood of harm to persons in the vicinity arising from the escape of whatever constituted that source of danger. For another thing, the majority treated the introduction and collection of a source of danger as a basis for imposing a higher standard of care on the occupier than would normally apply. But this feature of the decision invites the comment that, in jettisoning the rule in *Rylands v Fletcher*, the Court extended other aspects of the law of negligence to an unacceptable degree. Previously, some Justices had said, in both *Stoneman v Lyons* (1975) and *Stevens v Brodribb Sawmilling* (1986), that a personal and non-delegable duty will not be imposed on a person merely by reason of the fact that he or she is carrying on an ultra-hazardous activity. But in imposing a personal and non-delegable duty on an occupier who introduces and collects a source of special danger, the *Burnie Port* decision appears to come very close, at least in practical terms, to the notion thus earlier rejected.

It was also held in this case that any special rule relating to liability for fire had become obsolete, and that, as a consequence, an eighteenth-century English statutory provision (re-enacted in some jurisdictions in Australia) 'can be generally treated by the courts of this country as no longer applicable'. It may, however, be questioned whether the disapplication of statutes is a matter for the legislature rather than the High Court.

JAMES DAVIS

Further Reading
Kumaralingam Amirthalingam, 'Strict Liability Restricted' (1994) 13 *U Tas LR* 416
John Fleming, 'The Fall of a Crippled Giant' (1995) 3 *Tort L Rev* 56
Barbara McDonald and Jane Swanton, 'Non-delegable Duties in the Law of Negligence' (1995) 69 *ALJ* 323
Jeannie Marie Paterson, '*Rylands v Fletcher* into Negligence: *Burnie Port Authority v General Jones Pty Ltd*' (1994) 20 *Mon LR* 317
Jane Swanton, 'Another Conquest in the Imperial Expansion of the Law of Negligence: *Burnie Port Authority v General Jones Pty Ltd*' (1994) 2 *TLJ* 101

Business of Court. The business of the High Court has evolved significantly over time, reflecting Australia's development as a nation and its social, political and economic changes. The growth and change in the nature of the business has required the Court progressively to implement a number of jurisdictional reforms, with the result that the current business of the Court is significantly different from that of the early twentieth century.

The High Court was modelled in part on the **United States Supreme Court**. The jurisdiction of the Supreme Court, however, is far more limited as it does not act as a general appeal court from state courts except in federal matters. By section 73 of the Constitution, the High Court was made a general court of appeal from all federal courts, all **state Supreme Courts**, and all other state courts from which, in 1900, an appeal lay to the **Privy Council**. It was also given original **jurisdiction** (by section 75) in certain specified **matters** (including those between residents of different states) and by section 76 the Parliament was empowered to pass laws conferring original jurisdiction on the Court in certain other matters (including matters arising under any laws made by the Parliament).

The exercise of the Court's appellate jurisdiction is regulated by the *Judiciary Act* 1903 (Cth), which originally allowed an appeal as of right in matters involving £300 or more, and in matters affecting status under laws relating to aliens, marriage, divorce, bankruptcy or insolvency. In all other matters, special **leave to appeal** was required. Laws passed by the Parliament gave the Court original jurisdiction in matters relating to **patents** (1903), **trade marks** (1905) and **copyright** (1912), and provided for Justices to preside over the Court of **Conciliation and Arbitration** (1904) and to sit as the **Court of Disputed Returns** (1903). Later, original jurisdiction was conferred in other matters, including income tax (1915), and provision was made for Justices to sit as members of the ACT Supreme Court (1927).

It had been suggested in the parliamentary debates prior to the **establishment** of the Court that the Court would not have sufficient business. That did not prove to be the case. The Court's caseload has grown dramatically over the course of its history.

The early growth of business was reflected in the increase in the **number of Justices**. Attorney-General **Deakin** was forced to compromise in 1903, when the number of Justices was fixed at three rather than five. In 1906, however, the Judiciary Act was amended to increase the number of Justices to five, as the Court had been unable to cope with the increase in its business. In 1904, the Court heard 39 appeals, 40 motions and applications and 19 single Justice matters, and 37 original proceedings were instituted. In 1905, this had increased to 64 appeals, and 72 motions and applications, although the number of original proceedings instituted had fallen to 16. Early constitutional work largely concerned the ambit of Commonwealth and state legislative powers.

The growth continued and, at the end of 1912, the number of Justices was increased to seven. In that year, there were 89 appeals and 64 cases in the original jurisdiction, in addition to single Justice matters and the work O'Connor and **Higgins** had done in the Court of Conciliation and Arbitration. The **Depression** caused the Commonwealth Parliament in 1933 to reduce the number of Justices to six. It also affected the nature of matters before the Court, creating, for example, a sudden surge in bankruptcy appeals, and an increase in

industrial matters. At this time also, there was an increase in the number of cases raising issues of **interstate trade and commerce**, particularly in transport matters. The Court was not restored to seven Justices until 1946, when it became necessary to deal with the increased workload and to avert the likelihood of evenly divided decisions.

There have been occasional suggestions that the number of Justices should be increased to nine—including Labor's failed 'High Court Bench Reconstruction' plan of 1946—but this has not occurred despite a steady increase in the work of the Court, and in any event the Court has not favoured the notion of sitting in separate divisions (see **Bench, composition of**). To the end of 1965, about 3800 non-constitutional cases and 625 constitutional cases had been decided by the Court. Constitutional cases were still concerned primarily with Commonwealth and state powers. The Constitution contains no provisions corresponding to the first ten and the fourteenth amendments of the US Constitution (see **Bill of Rights**), although section 92, which protects freedom of interstate trade, commerce and intercourse, gave rise to many cases. However, it has been said that since the **Mason Court**, the Court is 'now recognised as playing a fundamental role in the protection of the rights and interests of the individual, in shaping and refining our constitutional arrangements and in maintaining integrity in government and public administration'.

In their 'State of the Australian Judicature' addresses, more recent Chief Justices have expressed concern at the heavy burden borne by the Court. To enable the Court to deal with its steadily increasing workload, it has, over time, been steadily divested of its less important jurisdiction. Although the Justices continue to sit occasionally as the Court of Disputed Returns (see **Electoral law**), they no longer sit as members of other tribunals such as the Court of Conciliation and Arbitration (since 1926), or the ACT Supreme Court (since 1933). Since the creation of the **Federal Court** in 1976, the Court has been divested of most of the original jurisdiction conferred on it by laws made by the Parliament, particularly in **taxation law** and matters involving patents, trade marks and copyright. By amendments to the Judiciary Act in 1976, appeals could no longer be brought from single judges of the Supreme Courts, or on a ground relating to the question of **damages** for death or personal injury, except by special leave. The amendments also made it no longer necessary to **remove** into the Court *inter se* **questions** pending in a Supreme Court; that requirement had originally been thought necessary to prevent appeals in such matters being taken direct from the Supreme Courts to the Privy Council, but it had proved inconvenient in practice.

There was one exception to the continuing reduction in the Court's jurisdiction. *The Nauru (High Court Appeals) Act* 1976 (Cth) provided for appeals to the Court from the Supreme Court of **Nauru**. Such appeals have been few in number.

Barwick wrote in 1979 that the 'workload of individual Justices [has] been considerably eased' by the amendments made in and after 1976. One hundred and forty-five matters, including special leave applications, were heard by the **Full Court** in 1977. By 1981, however, **Gibbs** was concerned that 'the volume of work [was] again increasing'. In 1982, the number of matters heard by the Full Court, including special leave applications, had jumped to 198. Gibbs wrote of a marked increase in the number of cases concerning **administrative law, constitutional law, criminal law, contract law** and **tort law**. Interstate commerce cases had declined considerably. The number of matters heard by single Justices had increased from 64 in 1980 to 151 in 1983.

In 1984, a further **reform** was made with a view to reducing the burden of the Court's appellate work. Amendments to the Judiciary Act in that year provided that no appeal could be brought from the Supreme Courts except by special leave, and the Court was given a wide power to remit matters to other courts. That power of **remittal** enabled the Court to remit to other courts matters arising in the jurisdiction given to the Court by section 75 of the Constitution—a jurisdiction that cannot be taken from the Court by legislation.

Since 1984, all appeals—civil and criminal—to the Court from the Federal Court and from the state and territory courts lie only by special leave of the High Court (different rules apply to appeals from the Full Court of the Family Court). Although some statutory criteria for the grant of special leave are set out in section 35A of the Judiciary Act, the grant or refusal of special leave is a matter of discretionary judgment and only brief reasons are provided by the Court when refusing leave.

The **legal profession** criticised the requirement of special leave, arguing that the **framers** would not have imagined that the Court, in its 'unfettered discretion', would ever be permitted to choose the cases that it puts aside or hears (see **Callinan**, 'An Over-Mighty Court?' (1994) 4 *Upholding the Australian Constitution* 81). Whatever may be the force of these criticisms, the special leave procedure has been found a valid exercise of Parliament's power in section 73 of the Constitution to make regulations (*Smith Kline & French Laboratories v Commonwealth* (1991)), and has helped to reduce the workload of the Court. In 1987, **Mason** wrote that special leave 'has placed a limit on our increasing burden of work by winnowing out those cases that have no general or public importance … The new system makes much better use of our time'.

The number of special leave applications rose from 88 in 1983, to 232 in 1988, to 237 in 1993, and to 251 in 1998–99. Many applications are heard using video conferencing techniques. The number of appeals heard by the Court grew from 39 in 1983, to 50 in 1998, to 38 in 1993 and to 61 in 1998.

The **annual reports** of the Court also illustrate the considerable increase in the non-appellate business of the Court. Constitutional matters heard rose from four in 1988 to 20 in 1993, but fell to 14 in 1998. Matters heard by single Justices rose from 87 in 1988 to 178 in 1993, falling to 120 in 1998–99. In the year ended 30 June 1999, in proceedings before single Justices, 28 per cent of litigants were unrepresented, appearing as **litigants in person**. The original requirement that an application for special leave should be made by **counsel** had been amended in 1993 to provide that such an application should, save with the leave of the Court, be presented by a barrister or solicitor. However, in 1996 this restriction was removed, and in the year ended 30 June 1999 the applicant was unrepresented in approximately 25 per cent of special leave applications. **Gleeson** said in 1999 that the appearance of litigants in person had caused 'delay, disruption and inefficiency' in the business of the Court and of its Registry, and was of concern to the Justices.

REBECCA CRASKE
HARRY GIBBS

Further Reading
Garfield Barwick, 'The State of the Australian Judicature' (1977) 51 *ALJ* 480
Harry Gibbs, 'The State of the Australian Judicature' (1985) 59 *ALJ* 522
Murray Gleeson, 'The State of the Judicature' (1999) 73(12) *LIJ* 67
Anthony Mason, 'The State of the Judicature' (1994) 68 *ALJ* 125

C

Caledonian Collieries Cases (1930). In the *Coal Vend Case* (1911), it was alleged that colliery owners in the NSW Hunter Valley were manipulating the interstate supply and price of coal. **Isaacs** made a finding to that effect; but the full High Court and the **Privy Council** reversed it (see *Adelaide Steamship Co v The King and A-G (Commonwealth)* (1912); *A-G (Commonwealth) v Adelaide Steamship Co* (1913)). During **World War I**, under the *War Precautions Act* 1914–16 (Cth), the Commonwealth government took over the output of mines in the Newcastle and Maitland area, and increased output, prices, and wages. The Act was repealed in 1920; but regulations relating to coal were extended to 1921.

From 1920 onward, the colliery owners insisted that under postwar conditions output, prices and wages must be reduced. Since 1912, industrial relations between owners and miners had depended on voluntary tribunals chaired by Charles Hibble. Under the *Industrial Peace Act* 1920 (Cth), the Commonwealth set up four tribunals (for miners; engine-drivers and firemen; engineers; and the coke industry), all chaired by Hibble. Despite applications for prohibition or injunctions against these tribunals (see, for example, *R v Hibble* (1920); *R v Hibble* (1921)), both owners and miners backed away from direct challenge to their validity.

In the miners' tribunal, a union log of claims in 1920 led to a further wage increase. In 1922 the owners filed a log of claims for wage reductions, which were refused. Strikes, lock-outs and temporary closures by the owners were common; the owners refused to ease the impact of sporadic unemployment by transferring men to another mine if their usual mine was closed. A major lockout in the Maitland area in 1923 left wages and conditions unchanged; but pit-top meetings without management consent were banned, and 'the legal right of the colliery manager to dismiss employees' was not to be questioned.

A further wage increase given by the Hibble tribunal in 1925 was largely negated by continued intermittent closures by the owners. In 1925 and 1926 the NSW Parliament (under Labor premier JT Lang) passed improved safety legislation; but after 1927, a new government (under conservative premier Thomas Bavin) took up the owners' demands. Conferences called by Bavin in August and October 1928 proposed a price reduction of 4/- per ton; NSW would forgo 2/- per ton in haulage and shipping charges, while owners' profits and miners' wages would be reduced by 1/- each. For export

coal, a further saving of 1/- a ton would be made by the Commonwealth government. In February 1929, the miners rejected the Bavin plan. Thereupon the owners gave the miners 14 days' notice: all the Hunter Valley mines would close down, to reopen only when the miners accepted a wage cut of 1/- per ton. The result was a stoppage that put ten thousand men out of work for 16 months.

Throughout 1929, efforts to get the mines reopened broke down. In the 1929 federal election, the Labor Party (led by JH Scullin and EG Theodore) promised that, if elected, their first action would be 'to secure a re-opening of the locked out collieries on the pre-lock-out basis'. Elected in October 1929, they called a conference chaired by Hibble. But against the miners' expectations Hibble failed to order resumption of work, and on 14 November he endorsed the Bavin plan. The NSW government gave the miners an ultimatum: if they did not now accept the plan, it would take over the mines at Cessnock, Pelton and Rothbury and reopen them on reduced wages.

On 16 December 1929, the NSW government reopened the Rothbury mine. A crowd of up to ten thousand miners assembled to try to prevent the reopening. Some had travelled all night. In the violence that followed, one miner was killed and others were wounded by police. Meanwhile, the threat of compulsory reopening had led to unrest in Victoria and Queensland, where the miners feared that reduction of wages in NSW would flow on to them. In Victoria, miners at Wonthaggi stopped work on 17 December; in Queensland there were stoppages on 17 and 19 December. On 17 and 18 December, in the Commonwealth Court of **Conciliation and Arbitration**, Judge George Beeby held a compulsory conference. When it failed, he found that 'an industrial dispute of which the Court can take cognizance exists or is threatened and impending'. By an interim award on 19 December, he set wages at pre-lockout rates.

On 22 January 1930, the High Court declared this award invalid (*Caledonian Collieries Case (No 1)* (1930)). In a joint judgment, **Gavan Duffy**, **Rich**, **Starke**, and **Dixon** held that there was no dispute 'extending beyond the limits of any one State'. The stoppages in Victoria and Queensland were only sympathy strikes; there was no actual dispute in those states, and none would be impending until the NSW dispute had been settled (since any 'flow on' of wage reductions would only then arise). Isaacs protested that the majority view was 'incomprehensible': it had been 'alarmingly evident that a great industrial conflagration was imminent', and in finding an industrial dispute of which he could take cognizance, Beeby was merely 'taking **judicial notice** of events that every rational adult in Australia was aware of':

> In my opinion, the circumstances not only justified, but loudly demanded, the intervention of the Arbitration Court. That intervention was the interposition of the national law to save the community from the loss and suffering of a national calamity, and it has been rightfully and properly exercised.

On 24 December 1929, as a 'second barrel' in case the attack on the award of 19 December succeeded, the miners' union served a log of claims on the mine owners. The matter was referred into court by Beeby on 20 January, two days before the High Court decision; his interim award, preserving wages at 1925 levels, was made on 23 January, one day after the High Court decision. The log of claims was largely based on one served in 1927 with a view to proceedings in the Hibble tribunal, but never pursued because Hibble was ill.

On 3 March 1930 the High Court held that this award, too, was invalid (*Caledonian Collieries Case (No 2)* (1930)). Again, Gavan Duffy, Rich, Starke and Dixon gave a joint judgment. They held that the log of claims of 24 December did not reflect a genuine dispute—it was simply a device to circumvent the problem in the previous case. Once again Isaacs was in sole dissent:

> This controversy has certainly reached an amazing position. For the second time … the coal-miners and the proprietors have been compulsorily brought into the Arbitration Court to compose by impartial methods a serious national industrial quarrel …; and for the second time … they are summarily ejected from that tribunal, with the conflict still active and its consequences unaverted … That a dispute must be 'real' or 'genuine' is in one sense undoubted. We know there are sham-fights, mere simulacra of battles, where everything is in show, and no one intends to strike a blow or fire a bullet … [But] when it is seen that the claims are in earnest and are persisted in to the fighting point, notwithstanding firm refusals, we are not to wait for casualties to convince us that the combat is real.

In *Munday v Gill* (1930), Isaacs—by then **Chief Justice**—found himself in dissent again. Nineteen of the miners who gathered at Rothbury to resist the reopening of the mine had been charged with having taken part in an unlawful assembly. Two of them, Timothy Patterson and Harold Mitchison, faced additional charges of carrying weapons 'likely to cause death or grievous bodily harm, to wit, a stick and a pit bottle'. When the defendants objected to being tried together, the magistrate heard one case, that of Edward Aubin, first; but then by consent heard the other 18 cases together. This meant that evidence given against Aubin was used against the other defendants. All the defendants were convicted, but all except Aubin, Patterson and Mitchison were granted a **writ** of prohibition by the NSW Supreme Court on the ground that the magistrate had had no jurisdiction to lump the cases together, even by consent.

The High Court reversed that decision. Gavan Duffy and Starke (in a joint judgment), and Dixon (in a separate judgment with which Rich agreed), held that the requirement of separate trials on indictment had no application to summary trials.

A separate issue arose from the statutory definition of an unlawful assembly as one seeking by intimidation or injury 'to compel any person … to abstain from doing what he is legally entitled to do'. It was said that the prosecution had failed to prove that the men employed to work at the reopened mine were 'legally entitled' to do so. But this argument, too, was rejected. 'Prima facie', said Gavan Duffy and Starke,

> a man is legally entitled to exercise his ordinary calling …, and the men employed at the Rothbury Colliery were simply attempting to exercise their right to work … The object of the assembly … was by means of intimidation and injury to prevent the men employed at Rothbury from working the colliery. And, but for the steady courage of the police officers there present, … that object would have been achieved.

Isaacs dissented on both grounds. He insisted that the need for separate trials applied to summary proceedings as well as to trials on indictment; any changes arising from the historical development of summary trials had been 'procedural only, and in no way destructive of the inherent principles of the **common law** safeguarding the liberty and the property of the individual'. The fact that the defendants had consented to the concurrent hearing of cases made no difference: 'A serious defect or error in criminal procedure is not one that can be waived or consented to.'

Moreover, the lumping-together of evidence assumed that the facts were 'the same in all cases'. Yet in fact they were 'very markedly different': for example, some of the evidence related to events after some of the accused had obeyed a police direction to leave the scene. 'No person can "continue" to be part of an assembly after he has severed himself from it', or be judged on the basis of what happened after he was gone.

Finally, as to whether the men attempting to work at the mine were 'legally entitled' to do so, Isaacs held that since this was an essential element of the offence, it should have been proved by the prosecution. Indeed, since some of the men had previously worked at the mine, they were probably union members, and hence *not* entitled to accept work on under-award conditions:

> It goes almost without saying that employees bound by an award cannot claim the legal right to aid and abet their employers to commit a breach of Commonwealth law … by infringing provisions of an award … We are not told what [the terms of employment] were, except that they were inconsistent with the award. How can such a contract be legal?

Five months after *Munday v Gill*, Isaacs resigned to take up his appointment as Governor-General. On the Hunter Valley coalfields, the events at Rothbury left a legacy of enduring bitterness: decades later, the abandoned mine was pointed out to children and visitors as a monument to injustice and oppression.

TONY BLACKSHIELD

Callinan, Ian David Francis (*b* 1 September 1937; Justice since 1998) was the sixth member of the High Court to be appointed from Queensland and the first direct **appointment** from private practice at the Bar for more than 22 years. His achievements as a writer add a further dimension to his legal career.

Callinan was born in Casino in northern NSW, the second of two sons. His parents moved to Queensland soon after his birth. His father enlisted in the RAAF, served in New Guinea, and in the post-war period went into business as an auctioneer and real estate agent, but ill-health arising from his war service forced him to retire in the 1950s.

Educated at Brisbane Grammar School, Callinan became a gifted cricketer, serving as captain of the school First XI and being selected as a member of the Queensland Colts. A large, burly man, his other sporting interests included rugby union and tennis.

In his first year after school, Callinan worked as a clerk in the Immigration Department. Guided by his mother, he obtained articles of clerkship with the city-based law firm of Feather, Walker & Delaney, and embarked upon five years of part-time study at the University of Queensland. He graduated in 1960. In the same year, he qualified as a solicitor and married Wendy Hamon, an unfailing source of encouragement in the years to come. He moved to Conwell & Co—a small firm active in the area of probate and inheritance law—and was soon admitted to the partnership. He has always maintained that service in a solicitor's office provided a valuable training for the Bar.

Callinan went to the Bar in 1965. His chambers in those days were in a three-level building—originally a boot factory dating back to 1919—on the present Inns of Court site. At that time, there were about ninety barristers in private practice in Brisbane, with a further five in Townsville and two in Rockhampton.

Increasing commercial activity in the region brought Callinan a retainer from the Queensland Cane Growers' Council, a link that was destined to last for 29 years. A fellow barrister on the 'sugar circuit' has said:

> Few tasks were more testing than the extraction of cohesive instructions, in the late hours of the night, from a mill suppliers' committee comprised of men with a strong sense of a dollar's worth and often with an idiosyncratic view of what the law was or ought to be. Ian Callinan always passed that test with admirable composure.

Callinan's practice, principally in civil litigation, expanded. He took silk in 1978. Actively involved in the affairs of the Queensland profession, he played a key role in organising the Australian Legal Convention held in Brisbane in 1983, served as a Director of Barristers Chambers Ltd for many years, and held various offices including Chairman of the Barristers Board and President of the Queensland Bar Association. He then became President of the Australian Bar Association.

Deregulation and the floating of the Australian dollar in the 1980s transformed the corporate landscape and set the scene for a wide variety of entrepreneurial activities, some of which fed into and prejudiced the ways of government.

These changes were inevitably reflected in the career of a leading advocate.

Briefed by the Commonwealth Director of Public Prosecutions (DPP), Callinan prosecuted businessman Brian Maher in the first of the 'bottom of the harbour' tax cases, and gained a conviction. When the DPP was looking for a senior barrister to prosecute High Court Justice and former Labor Attorney-General **Murphy** for allegedly attempting to pervert the course of justice, he turned to Callinan again as one who had the advantage of being from outside the Sydney Bar, where Murphy was well known.

Callinan cross-examined effectively and secured a conviction. In *R v Murphy* (1985), he fended off a challenge to the validity of the proceedings. When a new trial was ordered, he led for the prosecution again. On this occasion, however, Murphy was acquitted.

Callinan's involvement in the Murphy prosecution brought him to national prominence as an advocate. His association with a case that led to a parliamentary commission of inquiry into whether Murphy should be **removed** from the High Court under section 72 of the Constitution, on the ground of misbehaviour, was not forgotten by Callinan's critics when the Queenslander was appointed to the Court a decade later.

In court, Callinan spoke quietly, seldom raising his voice, and was not inclined to indulge in theatrical gestures. His technique in cross-examination has been described by those who have worked with him as 'death by a thousand whispers'. Nicholas Cowdery, a colleague in the Murphy trial, said: 'Callinan is remarkably quiet for such a big man. But the softness of his voice serves another purpose. It forces the witness to listen closely to what he is saying.'

In May 1986, an ABC *Four Corners* program made devastating claims about corruption in the Queensland Police Force. This led to the Fitzgerald inquiry and, later, to the resignation of Joh Bjelke-Petersen as Premier of the state. Callinan played an influential role in these events. As the government's principal legal adviser, he drafted terms of reference for a full and open inquiry. At a crucial stage, he was instrumental in arranging for the diaries of the Commissioner of Police—a man later found to be corrupt—to be made public. He also took steps to ensure that the interests of the government and the police were kept apart.

By now, Callinan was in constant demand. He was briefed to represent the high-flying Perth entrepreneur, Alan Bond, before the WA Inc Royal Commission. He defended Bond successfully against charges relating to secret commissions allegedly received during the government-backed rescue of Rothwells Ltd. He went to Majorca on behalf of the Australian government to seek an extradition order against Christopher Skase, head of the failed Qintex empire.

The list of reported cases in which Callinan appeared is long. It covers many jurisdictions—from the **Privy Council** to specialist bodies such as the Australian Broadcasting Tribunal—and embraces **constitutional law**, land acquisition claims, stamp duty issues, town planning, **trade practices** and insurance. The list includes various cases arising out of the notorious Mudginberri dispute of 1985, a pivotal moment in determining the boundaries of union power.

Callinan was also briefed in some widely reported **defamation** cases. These included claims brought by the

Ian Callinan, Justice since 1998

Duchess of York's sister, Jane Makim, and by leading rugby league player Andrew Ettingshausen. He held a retainer from Channel Nine, and successfully defended it in *Thiess v TCN Channel Nine* (1994), one of the longest defamation jury trials in Australian legal history.

Throughout his career at the Queensland Bar, Callinan affirmed the advocate's traditional role as an independent voice, available to either side. He was critical of the High Court's increasing **activism** in cases such as *Mabo* (1992), arguing that parliaments should do more to regain their authority over judicial law makers.

Callinan has a journalist son, and a daughter practising law. Since their marriage in 1960, he and his wife, Wendy, have been keen collectors of Australian art. This led to Callinan being appointed Chairman of the Queensland Art Gallery in 1996. He has also served as Chairman of the Queensland TAB.

Callinan's play *Brazilian Blue* was performed at the Twelfth Night Theatre in Brisbane in 1995 with leading actor Keith Michell in a key role. The play charts the demise of an entrepreneur embodying the greed and extravagance of the 1980s. *The Cellophane Ceiling* explores similar themes.

The first of Callinan's two novels, *The Lawyer and the Libertine* (1996), traces the fortunes of two boys brought up in Sydney during the Depression. Stephen Mentmore is eventually appointed Chief Justice of the High Court. His rival, George Dice, with some assistance from his Irish-Catholic friends, becomes Attorney-General in a Labor government. The plot centres upon recognisable political events such as the Petrov Commission and the Khemlani Affair in the **Whitlam era** (see **Popular images of Court**). The author's achievement is to give jurisprudence a human face and con-

nect **ideology** with the depths of the moral being. Dice regards bias as an inescapable fact of life and treats objectivity as an illusion to be ignored. Mentmore also acknowledges bias and prejudice as facts of life, but regards their existence as pressing reasons to insist on objectivity as the ideal. Ruminations about betrayal and loss also appear in *The Coroner's Conscience* (1999).

These plays and books were timely. In an era in which the Australian landscape was littered with reports by various royal commissions into governmental bungling, the arbiters of literary taste showed little interest in works illuminating the corridors of power. Callinan's fiction—annals of the prevailing disarray—brought extra colour to the literary scene. His characters are a reminder that Australian society is a vast, sprawling, unpredictable domain. His works affirm the wisdom of the **common law** in respecting individuality, and proceeding case by case.

Callinan was appointed to the High Court in December 1997. The *Hindmarsh Island Bridge Case* (1998) marked a contentious start to his judicial career, for shortly after being sworn in he was asked to **disqualify** himself on the ground that he had given advice about the statute in question. This brought into issue for the first time the question of whether a High Court judge could be disqualified by his colleagues. The issue fell away when Callinan, upon reflection, disqualified himself.

Other contentious moments followed, some of them resonating with issues Callinan had been associated with as an advocate. A ruling by a **Federal Court** judge from Melbourne expressed disquiet about the propriety of procedural advice Callinan was said to have given to solicitors representing a litigant involved in a dispute with a Queensland builder. **Commentators** were quick to draw attention to the Murphy precedent, and the President of the Law Council of Australia called for an inquiry. Did section 72 of the Constitution extend to conduct occurring prior to appointment? Was advice about procedural tactics to be judged by the standards of the Australian **legal profession**, by those of the wider community, or, more specifically, by the standards of the Queensland Bar in the 1980s when the advice was given?

Again, the issue fell away. The Commonwealth **Attorney-General** declared emphatically that there were no grounds for an inquiry. When the original decision was taken further, the appeal court was not required to explore the implications of the ruling in the court below.

In the controversial *Patrick Stevedores Case* (1998), Callinan concluded—unlike the majority of the High Court—that orders reinstating sacked waterside workers should be set aside. Courts should not make de facto business decisions under the guise of supervisory orders. In *Yanner v Eaton* (1999), his dissenting judgment, which countenances the reduction of **native title** rights by statute, reflects his earlier views about the respective roles of parliament and the High Court. His judgments generally display the wide range of experience he brought to the Bench, especially in the area of **commercial law**.

Before his appointment, Callinan was one of a small group of advocates who built up a truly national reputation. He was well qualified to assume the burdens of high judicial office. His plays and novels link him to some equally notable lawyers with literary skills who came to prominence while the Commonwealth of Australia was taking shape: Alfred **Deakin**, Robert **Garran**, **Griffith**, **Piddington**, and later, **Evatt**.

NICHOLAS HASLUCK

Further Reading
Nicholas Hasluck, 'Deconstructing the High Court' (1998) 42
    Quadrant 12

Canberra, Court's move to. It was always intended that the **seat** of the Court should be at the national capital. In fact, the effect of section 10 of the *Judiciary Act* 1903 (Cth) was that when the seat of government was moved to Canberra in 1927, the principal seat of the Court would follow as a matter of course. A government amendment in 1926 that prevented the automatic removal of the Court to 'the airy and healthy, but somewhat bleak, plains of … Canberra' was treated by Frank Brennan MP as 'an act of mercy'. The government would reconsider providing the Court with a headquarters in Canberra, said Attorney-General **Latham**, 'when the present pressure of building operations has been to some extent relaxed'.

Forty-two years later, **Barwick** persuaded the government of the day that the Court should have a home of its own in Canberra alongside the other arms of government, the Parliament and the executive. It would have a dedicated **building** of its own for the first time in its already long life. The move would also involve the transfer of the principal registry of the Court from Sydney to Canberra, and the closure of the state registries, which had a major role in the **administration** of the Court and supported the **circuit system**.

The next ten years were spent in planning the building, finding a suitable site, organising a design competition, inviting tenders, letting the contract, and finally, in 1975, beginning construction. The building was completed in 1980, and opened by the Queen on 26 May of that year. The Governor-General, Zelman Cowen, did not look favourably upon the government's decision that he should not attend (the Governor-General was the Queen's representative and, with the Queen in attendance, she did not need a representative).

The opening occasioned much criticism. Politicians argued about the building's cost (the budget blew out from $10.9 million in 1974 to $50 million upon completion); architects and others questioned the building's style; and many lawyers held grave doubts about the move. This controversy was nothing, however, compared to the reaction of the **puisne Justices** in 1979 and early 1980 to Barwick's plans for the Court.

The full detail of Barwick's plans became apparent towards the end of 1978. Over the previous 75 years, the practice had developed of allowing Justices to decide where they would live and could most conveniently work on their judgments. From the beginning, the Court adopted the practice of visiting all the capital cities at least once a year, but the vast majority of their work was in Sydney or Melbourne.

Conveniently, most Justices had lived in Sydney or Melbourne before their **appointment** to the Court, and remained in the same city thereafter. There were few appointments outside that magic circle, and there was no pressure on those appointed to move to Sydney or Melbourne, although some did so.

Under Barwick's plan, however, not only was there going to be a very expensive building and the provision of only one central registry in Canberra, but all the Justices would move to Canberra. Only one of them (**Murphy**) lived there. Furthermore, a suitable 'homestead' style residence outside the city would be acquired by the government for the use of the Chief Justice (but see **Humour**). The other Justices would have to find homes of their own. To round off this plan, Barwick also proposed that the Court should have access to Parliament via the treasury to obtain its desired **budget**. The role of the Attorney-General's Department in determining the

The Queen at the opening of the High Court, 26 May 1980 with, from left to right, Wilson, Murphy, Gibbs, Barwick, Stephen, Mason and Aickin

The Queen declares the High Court open, 26 May 1980

Court's budget was to be eliminated. This proposal was soon abandoned.

Justices of the Court, traditionally and properly, keep at arm's length from both the executive and the Parliament and deal as little as possible with the **Attorney-General** or the Department. Dealings were almost always conducted by the **Chief Justice**. Barwick established a right to deal directly with **Prime Minister**, Malcolm Fraser. Naturally, he had to deal with departmental officers as well, but he rarely dealt with the Attorney-General. It must have been some surprise for Barwick when the six puisne Justices sought a meeting with the Attorney-General about his proposal that they should all live in Canberra when the new Court was set up there. The approach came through the Secretary of the Department, Clarence Harders.

The meeting took place in March 1979, and was held in the very limited accommodation afforded the High Court at the Darlinghurst Court building in Sydney. Barwick was told of the meeting, and raised no objection. It was held in the common room, which only just accommodated the eight people present. There was a long agenda, and the meeting lasted for some time. There was no transcript of the discussion but Harders kept notes.

The discussion focused on the requirements of five of the Justices following the Court's move to Canberra. Two Justices were uncertain about whether they would at some stage move to Canberra, but the other three were firm about retaining their present homes and travelling to Canberra for **sittings**. This, of course, required a travelling allowance to be paid and there was also some discussion about compensa-

tion for living both in Canberra and their home cities. One of their main concerns was retaining **chambers** and **library** facilities in their home bases. A good part of their judgments would be written where they lived. Various views were expressed about staff, but it appeared that at least some staff would travel with their judge, as he decided, and the rest would be based in Canberra.

There was a second meeting with the Justices, apart from **Gibbs**, who was overseas, in October 1979. By that time Harders and **Jacobs** had retired. The new Secretary of the Department, Alan Neaves, and the newly appointed **Wilson** (who lived in Perth), were in attendance. It was just a follow-up of the earlier meeting and was required to finalise the Justices' submissions to Cabinet. Barwick also submitted his case for the Justices' move to Canberra. No member of the Court appeared before Cabinet.

Cabinet considered the submission early in December 1979. Its result was a bombshell for the Justices. Cabinet did agree that the current Justices would not be required to move their homes to Canberra, but ruled that they would not be allowed travel expenses to and from Canberra after June 1981. Furthermore, no Justice would be provided with chambers and library facilities in their home cities, and all staff would be based in Canberra.

Wilson was placed in a particularly difficult situation. He decided to live in Perth and commute to Canberra for sittings. The WA government provided him with chambers in Perth, but the cost of travel to Canberra would be prohibitive. Furthermore, he would have no staff in Perth. Clearly he would be forced to move to Canberra or resign.

Was it in the nation's interest for all the High Court Justices to be forced to live in Canberra? This question went beyond the problems of the present Justices and involved the future quality of the Court. Protests came strong and swift from four states—Queensland, WA, SA and Tasmania. It was bad enough for the executive to be based in Canberra, but the High Court should keep in touch with the Australian community, particularly as it decides cases on state laws as well as federal. The Attorney-General of WA commented: 'The fact that judges have lived in their home states and have kept in touch with the shades of thought and attitude around the nation has helped keep the Court in tune with the federal nature of Australia.'

There were other major issues as well. Would potential candidates for the Court—who are rarely appointed before the age of 50, and by then have strong roots in their own cities—be prepared to move to such a different environment? It would be hard to persuade top lawyers to join the Court in Canberra as well as give up their much higher incomes.

Clearly, something had to be done about this decision. Another submission was considered by Cabinet within a fortnight, and it resulted in one significant change. Existing Justices of the High Court who did not move to Canberra would be entitled to travel allowance between their home and Canberra for both themselves and their spouses. Further, the Attorney-General was requested to examine the question of payment of a Canberra allowance for such Justices. This was also agreed.

Although a major concession had been made to the Justices, and Barwick's plan greatly changed, the problem was not resolved. The denial of chambers, library, and staff assistance in their home states was dealt with by the newly independent administration of the Court. However, concerns about the quality of future appointments to the Court remained. Finally, in April 1982, the government conceded that future appointees to the Court would retain the option of residing in their home state, with the further provision of a hearing room for urgent applications.

PETER DURACK

Castle, The. The Working Dog film *The Castle* was released in 1997, and has been one of Australia's most successful films. It is a sweeping saga that takes the harsh Australian outback, the rugged characters of the ANZAC legend, the spirit of Banjo Patterson—and ignores them in favour of a greyhound-racing tow-truck driver who never meant to be a hero. *The Castle*'s connection to the High Court came through what we at Working Dog thought at the time was a relatively benign piece of individual insurrection: what if someone challenged a compulsory **acquisition**?

These acquisitions seemed relatively normal if you grew up in Australia during the 1960s and 1970s. The country was growing fast and the infrastructure needed was barely catching up. Whole properties were compulsorily acquired—for new dams for example—and this was deemed by most to be unfortunate but necessary. In the case of the Kerrigan family portrayed in the film, the acquisition was to expand an airport.

The idea of a challenge to the acquisition led us to the Constitution. This document has been ridiculed over the years for its dry nature. Whereas you would imagine such a grand and important document might start with 'We the people...' it actually starts with 'Whereas...'. Santo Cilauro (one of the co-creators of *The Castle*) remarked that its dry nature was its great strength. He did not like flowery preambles (advocating instead the simple statement, 'Here it is...') and felt that its straightforward style made clear its intentions: to be fair. He then said the now infamous words 'fairness is the "vibe" of the document'. The idea that a lawyer would argue his or her case on the basis of the 'vibe' of the Constitution made everyone laugh out loud. When we stopped laughing, the notion still seemed to resonate.

The next step was to decide which section of the Constitution could be the basis for a challenge. A friend of Santo's—a QC specialising in **land law** (quite handy)—suggested section 51(xxxi). The producers' reactions to each of these stages provided new ideas for the script. Rob Sitch remarked that persisting with Roman numerals was irrelevant, awkward and pompous. Santo wondered what it would be like to be in a higher court as a lawyer struggling with Roman numerals. That ended up in the film too.

Section 51(xxxi) states that the Parliament has power to make laws with respect to 'the acquisition of **property** on just terms from any state or person for any purpose in respect of which the Parliament has the power to make laws'. One phrase immediately sticks out: 'on just terms'. What does that mean? We assumed a monetary focus, but since the film's theme was non-monetary values, that was just the opening needed. Lawyers advised that this point had not been seriously tested, but that it would probably fail if it did go all the way.

The notion of testing the interpretation of the Constitution touches on powerful stuff in this country. High profile cases in the High Court have entered the popular consciousness. The impression is that the decisions are made in a rather faceless, slow, deliberate fashion, after a process devoid of the usual political and social manipulations that pervade almost every other part of our lives. A challenge in the High Court quickly became the film's end point.

From there, we looked at where cracks could be opened up a little. So much of the law seems definite and clear—but, of course, it has been drafted by human beings. Words do not necessarily nail down the intentions of the legal drafter. Time tests the grey areas. It occurred to us that the High Court Justices would have to consider, privately at least, the intention of the writers as much as the literal meaning.

We had no idea how a challenge based on this section would proceed in the High Court, but liked to think that one of the less legal arguments would hold some weight. This is summed up in the statement made by Bud Tingwell's character: 'I can't speak for those who wrote this document but I'll bet when they put in the phrase "on just terms" they hoped it would stop anyone short-changing someone like Darryl Kerrigan'.

That struck us as being about right. If you sat down to write a constitution today, you would like to think that it protects decent people in the future from being out-manoeuvred or unfairly dealt with by the laws of the country.

The film records that the High Court found in favour of the Kerrigans. It will be interesting to see if the application of section 51(xxxi) to the kind of situation depicted in the film is put under the microscope in the future. We would all find it interesting to have the finest legal minds in the country wrestle with what values underpin the notion of being 'just'. It would be nice to think that in the end, the Justices of the High Court had to base their decision on the 'vibe' of the document. Then Dennis Denuto, the small-time suburban lawyer who initially represented the Kerrigans, would be proved as smart as the best of them.

The internal scenes of *The Castle* were filmed in the Court of Appeal in Melbourne, and the exteriors at the High Court itself. If there was one sour note, it was that the powers that be at the High Court refused to let filming take place inside the building. Some reasons were given, but we found them unconvincing. The fact is that filming in public locations and in publicly owned buildings is now considered to be part of the public amenity. It is done all over the world.

ROB SITCH

Causation. In many branches of the law, a litigant must prove that a particular result has been caused by an act or omission of the opposing party. This is because, in general, the law holds people responsible only for the harm that their acts or omissions have caused. Proof of murder, for example, requires that the prosecution prove that an act of the accused caused the death of the deceased; similarly, to succeed in a negligence action, the plaintiff must prove that the defendant's breach of duty caused the plaintiff to suffer loss or damage. The causation inquiry in law is not, therefore, an open-ended inquiry into the reasons why an event occurred, but a method of deciding where to attribute legal responsibility for harm. Unfortunately, as **McHugh** observed in *Royall v The Queen* (1991), 'judicial and academic efforts to achieve a coherent theory of **common law** causation have not met with significant success'.

As the Court has frequently pointed out, the approaches taken by science and philosophy to questions of causation produce unsatisfactory and unacceptable results in the context of apportioning legal responsibility. In explaining the occurrence of a given phenomenon, for example, a scientist might argue that the cause of the phenomenon is the sum of all of the conditions necessary to produce it. Adapted for the purposes of the law, this would lead to the 'but for' test, under which a wrongful act would be regarded as a cause of an event if, but for the wrongful act, the event would not have occurred, so that it was a *causa sine qua non*.

Used as an exclusive criterion for attributing legal responsibility for an event, however, the 'but for' test is both over- and under-inclusive. It is over-inclusive in that it would, for example, suggest that a wrongful act that merely brings a person to a place where some harm then befalls them is a cause of that harm, even if the harm was no more likely to happen there than anywhere else. Its under-inclusiveness can be seen in cases where two or more independent events occur, each of which would be sufficient on its own to cause the harm (often referred to as 'multiple sufficient causes'). The 'but for' test suggests that neither event can be regarded as a cause of the harm.

The Court's main method for avoiding results such as these has been to declare that causation is essentially a matter of 'common sense': see, for example, *Fitzgerald v Penn* (1954); *Timbu Kolian v The Queen* (1968); *March v Stramare*

(1991); *Royall v The Queen*; *Bennett v Minister of Community Welfare* (1992); *Chappel v Hart* (1998). In doing so, it has frequently cited the influential textbook by HLA Hart and Tony Honoré, *Causation in the Law* (1959; 2nd edn 1985). Like Hart and Honoré, the Court has premised its 'common sense' approach to causation on the idea that a wrongful act should not be regarded as a cause of harm unless an ordinary person, applying their common sense, would so regard it. The objection that there is no such thing as a consistent 'common sense' notion of what constitutes a cause was raised by McHugh in *March v Stramare*, where he argued for the adoption of the 'but for' test as the exclusive test of causation (except in cases of multiple sufficient causes), and for all other limitations on liability to be recognised as policy-based rules relieving persons of responsibility for harm regarded by the law as too remote. The 'common sense' approach to causation, argued McHugh, was arbitrary in its operation, since it effectively gives courts an 'unfettered discretion' to 'use subjective, unexpressed, and undefined extra-legal **values** to determine legal liability'.

McHugh's objections had no influence on the majority in *March*, who were happy to acknowledge that causation in law was based not only on 'common sense', but also on 'value judgments and **policy considerations**'. The 'common sense' approach to causation endorsed by all members of the Court, including McHugh, in *Bennett v Minister of Community Welfare*, can now be seen as operating in two distinct ways. Occasionally, 'common sense' has been cited as the actual justification for a decision: see, for example, the judgment of **Kirby** in *Chappel v Hart*. Both Kirby and **Hayne** claimed in that case that decisions on causation will often be made fairly intuitively, and may not therefore be susceptible to detailed analytical justification. On this approach, the 'ordinary person's common sense' seems almost to be a *test* of causation—a development that would fully justify McHugh's warnings in *March*.

The more usual way in which 'common sense' operates is as an umbrella justification for a number of far more concrete and specific principles used to determine whether a wrongful act will be regarded as a cause of harm. The first of these is to sanction the 'but for' test as a negative test of causation, in all cases except for those where there are multiple sufficient causes; that is, if a wrongful act fails to satisfy the 'but for' test, it will be eliminated as a cause (*March*). The Court has been adamant, however, that satisfaction of the 'but for' test is not in itself an adequate basis for a positive finding of causation in law. For example, the Court has held that a wrongful act that merely serves to bring a person to a time and place where an otherwise unrelated injury occurs is not to be regarded as a cause of that injury (see *Lindeman v Colvin* (1946)).

It has been far more difficult for the Court to develop a satisfactory doctrine of *novus actus interveniens*. Under this doctrine, a person may be relieved of responsibility for harm that would not have occurred but for their wrongful act, when there has been a subsequent 'intervening act' which is also a necessary condition of the harm, and 'breaks the chain of causation' between the earlier wrongful act and the harm. The Court has struggled, however, to identify the features distinguishing those subsequent acts or events that 'break the chain of causation' from those that do not. In *Mahony v Kruschich* (1985), *March*, and *Bennett*, the judgments suggested that the question turns on matters such as the voluntariness and foreseeability of the subsequent act or event. In *Chapman v Hearse* (1961), in a passage approvingly quoted by **Mason** in *March*, the Court had declared that reasonable foreseeability was not a test of causation, although it did mark the limits beyond which a person would be relieved, on grounds of remoteness, of responsibility for damage resulting from their wrongful act. Despite Mason's approval of this *obiter dictum*, however, *Mahony*, *March* and *Bennett* suggest that reasonable foreseeability is now part of the test of causation.

In *Royall*, the criminal counterpart to *March*, a similar confusion of concepts appears. **Brennan** reiterated the orthodox position that 'causation of death is concerned solely with the external elements of homicide: it is not a mental element of any crime of culpable homicide'. The judgments, however, suggest that the boundary this implied between *actus reus* and *mens rea* of a criminal offence is a little more blurred than the orthodox position would have it. Mason claimed that the test was whether the subsequent event—in this case, the deceased jumping out of a window to her death to escape a violent attack by the accused—was the 'natural' consequence of the accused's acts; and he acknowledged that this test was linked both to the foreseeability of the subsequent event and to the accused's state of mind, namely whether the accused intended the consequences that resulted from the subsequent event. Yet he argued that it would generally be better to avoid directing a jury in such terms. A similar ambivalence can be seen in the judgments of Brennan, **Deane**, **Dawson**, **Toohey** and **Gaudron**. Only McHugh argued that reasonable foreseeability and intention should be explicitly recognised as the tests for whether a subsequent act constituted a *novus actus interveniens*. There can be no doubt that the **criminal law**, like the civil law, needs some mechanism for limiting liability for harm that is too 'remote'. The question posed by *Royall*, however, is whether the causation inquiry, in its present form, provides a conceptually coherent vehicle for achieving this.

Another situation in which the Court has indicated a possible willingness to depart from the results of the 'but for' test arises in cases where causation is inherently difficult to prove. Several members of the Court have stated that in such situations, proof of a wrongful act, coupled with proof of the kind of damage likely to be caused by such an act, will lead to an inference that there was a causal connection between the two. The result will be the shifting of the evidentiary onus to the party denying the connection (see *Betts v Whittingslowe* (1945); Mason, **Wilson**, Brennan and Dawson in *McLean v Tedman* (1984); Gaudron in *Bennett*; and McHugh, **Gummow** and Kirby in *Chappel v Hart*).

Even more difficult are cases where the wrongful act has merely increased an existing risk—for example, an increased risk of developing cancer through exposure to a carcinogen; or where the wrongful act, typically a negligent medical procedure, has deprived the plaintiff of what would otherwise have been a chance of survival or cure. In the first category of case, it may be impossible to prove that the plaintiff would not have developed the condition or disease if not exposed to the risk; in the second category, it may be impossible to prove

that the plaintiff would have been cured. Indeed, if the chance of a cure is less than 50 per cent, the ordinary application of the standard of proof to the question of causation suggests that the plaintiff has suffered no harm. Although similar cases have arisen in **contract** (see *Commonwealth v Amann Aviation* (1991)) and under the *Trade Practices Act 1974* (Cth) (see *Sellars v Adelaide Petroleum* (1994)), personal injury litigation is likely to present far greater difficulties for the Court. So far, tentative views have been expressed by Gummow in *Chappel v Hart*, and by **Callinan** in *Naxakis v Western General Hospital* (1999), but it is still too early to discern how the Court is likely to deal with these challenges to conventional notions of causation.

ANDREW PALMER

Further Reading
David Hamer, '"Chance Would be a Fine Thing": Proof of Causation and Quantum in an Unpredictable World' (1999) 23 *MULR* 557
Nick Mullaney, 'Common Sense Causation: An Australian View' (1992) 12 *Oxford Journal of Legal Studies* 431
Andrew Palmer, 'Causation in the High Court' (1993) 1 *TLJ* 9
Jane Stapleton, 'Legal Cause: Cause-in-Fact and the Scope of Liability for Consequences of Tortious Conduct' (2001) 54 *Vanderbilt Law Review* 941

Ceremonial sittings occur to mark occasions of importance to the High Court and its members, past and present. Ceremonial sittings are also held at the beginning of each year for new silks to inform the Court of their appointments and commissions; on the **appointment** of a new Justice of the Court; to welcome new Justices to a state capital in which they have not yet sat; on the **retirement** of the **Chief Justice** and **puisne Justices**; on the death of a Justice; and to mark other special occurrences. Instances of the last are the opening of the High Court building by Her Majesty the Queen, and the cessation of hostilities in **World War I** in 1918 (see 25 *CLR* v).

The *Commonwealth Law Reports* record the proceedings of most of these **sittings**. However, there are some regrettable omissions. The record of ceremonial sittings noting the death of all Justices has been reported except for **Griffith**, **Powers** and **Evatt**. Justices who have died in office seem to have been accorded somewhat longer obituary speeches than deceased retired Justices. The speech to mark **McTiernan's** death occupies only one page of the Reports (168 *CLR* v).

A ceremonial sitting is recorded for the retirement of the ailing Chief Justice Griffith in 1919 (26 *CLR* v), but nothing appears in the Reports on the appointment or retirement of Justices until 1952, when **Latham** retired as Chief Justice and **Dixon** succeeded him (85 *CLR* vii and xi). Thereafter, the appointment or retirement of a Chief Justice has always been recorded in the Reports.

The format of ceremonial sittings for the appointment or retirement of a Justice is well settled. Counsel wear wigs, unless they come from states and territories that have abandoned them; and until 1988, Justices wore full-bottomed wigs. Speeches or brief comments are customarily made by the Chief Justice or presiding Justice, the Commonwealth **Attorney-General**, the President of the Law Council of

Opening of the first High Court, Melbourne, 6 October 1903. Left to right: Barton, Griffith (Chief Justice), and O'Connor

Australia, the President of the Australian Bar Association, and the President of the Bar Association and Law Society of the Justice's state of residence. These are followed by a speech from the Justice, customarily acknowledging former Justices of the Court and members of other jurisdictions present, frequently expressing gratitude to family, friends and colleagues for their support and assistance, and also perhaps making some general observations about the **role** of the Court or the **rule of law**. A similar but abbreviated procedure occurs in each of the states where a welcome is held for a Justice who has not previously sat there. Only one **Prime Minister** has spoken at a ceremonial sitting: Robert **Menzies**, who came to speak at the retirement of Dixon in 1964 (110 *CLR* v). Menzies sought and obtained the permission of his former pupil-master to appear without wig or gown. In his speech, he said: 'it must be of all things most embarrassing to have good things said about you to your face.'

Ceremonial sittings serve the useful and valuable purpose of manifesting the role of the Court at the pinnacle of the whole of the judicial **hierarchy** of the Commonwealth and the states, and as the judicial arm of the polity.

IAN CALLINAN

Chamberlain Case (1984). On 29 October 1982, in the Northern Territory Supreme Court, Lindy Chamberlain was convicted of murdering her nine-week-old daughter, Azaria, by cutting her throat in the front seat of the family car at a camping area beside Uluru (Ayers Rock) in central Australia.

Her husband, Michael, was convicted as an accessory. Appeals to the **Federal Court** and the High Court were unsuccessful. The convictions were quashed in 1988 after a judicial inquiry.

Few cases have generated as much public controversy. The **role** of the High Court in this drama was, however, a minor one. Controversy did not stem from the novelty and significance of the doctrinal issues raised by the case but from the 'facts': the question of what had happened to Azaria on the night of her disappearance. Attempts to answer that question were to see law and science become embroiled in an intense polarisation of opinion that permeated Australian society. Unlike the names **Mabo** and **Wik** for example, which were not widely known until the High Court decisions were handed down, the name Chamberlain had assumed legendary significance by the time of the High Court appeal in November 1983.

This process began a short time after Azaria Chamberlain disappeared from the family tent at Uluru on the evening of 17 August 1980. Her body was never found, although her heavily blood-stained singlet, jumpsuit and nappy were discovered a week later. Lindy Chamberlain alleged that a dingo had taken the baby. This allegation aroused public disbelief as widespread as it was ill-informed; but this was only the first sign that ignorance and prejudice would run ahead of the **evidence** and ultimately dictate its direction in critical ways. Out of bigotry concerning the Chamberlains' adherence to the Seventh Day Adventist faith and a seemingly

Michael and Lindy Chamberlain holding photograph of baby Azaria

endless stream of bizarre rumours—such as the claims that the name Azaria meant 'sacrifice in the wilderness' and that the Chamberlains had expressed no grief at the loss of their daughter—was forged the urban myth that Azaria's death was a sacrificial rite carried out by religious fanatics. In vital respects this formed the unstated subtext of the police investigation and prosecution case.

The rumour mill left the vital evidence that would have supported Lindy Chamberlain's claims adrift in its wake. This consisted of the observations of a large number of manifestly honest and disinterested witnesses who were present in the camping area at the time the baby disappeared or who joined the search soon after. It appears that none of these witnesses—campers, rangers, trackers, searchers or local police who initially attended the scene— doubted that the baby had been taken by a dingo. Reports of dingo attacks on children had led to officially notified concerns about the problem only weeks before. On the night Azaria disappeared, dingoes were seen close to the camping area, and witnesses in a tent next to that of the Chamberlains heard a growl just before Lindy raised the alarm. Dingo tracks were observed leading away from the tent. There was blood on the interior of the tent. And none of these witnesses, some of whom were with the Chamberlains immediately before or after Azaria's disappearance, detected anything suspicious in their conduct. They observed Lindy to be a devoted and affectionate mother to the baby and to her two young sons—a conclusion backed by a wealth of evidence from other witnesses, and contradicted by none.

The Crown faced yet more acute obstacles. One witness, a stranger to the Chamberlains until a short time before Azaria's disappearance, gave clear and unwavering evidence that she heard the baby cry at a time when, according to the Crown case, the baby must already have been dead. It is also remarkable that if the baby's throat was cut in the front seat of the car, no eyewitness saw any blood on Lindy's clothing or in the car. These witnesses included a district nurse who, later that night, helped the Chamberlains pack and unpack the car and at their invitation occupied the front seat during a trip from the camping area to a motel.

With no body, no evidence of motive and no eyewitness evidence that even vaguely incriminated the Chamberlains, the Crown case was wholly circumstantial, and supported in the main by the claims of expert witnesses to the effect that the state of Azaria's clothing was inconsistent with a dingo attack, that there was a bloody handprint on the jumpsuit; and that substantial quantities of blood, including the blood of an infant, had been found throughout the Chamberlain car.

There were many problems with the methods and findings of these witnesses, only some of which, however, could be effectively communicated to a jury in a criminal trial. The Crown invited the jury to infer that in a space of five to ten minutes, during which Lindy returned to the tent with the baby and six-year-old Aidan, she had cut Azaria's throat and stuffed the body into Michael's camera case while her son apparently stood by. She had then raced Aidan back to the barbecue area, where normal life was resumed, and displayed no signs of unease or distress until the opportunity presented itself of blaming a dingo for the baby's disappearance. The Chamberlains were said to have later buried the body, then exhumed it so that the clothing could be placed in a strategic location to lend further credibility to the dingo tale.

In February 1984, the High Court refused Lindy Chamberlain's appeal by majority (**Murphy** and **Deane** dissenting). Earlier, **Brennan** (sitting alone) had refused her application for bail while the appeal was pending (*Chamberlain v The Queen (No 1)* (1983)).

The Court was asked to quash the convictions on the ground that the verdicts were unsafe and unsatisfactory. The majority were in substantial agreement on the principle to be applied. The Court had to decide whether, on the evidence before it, the jury, acting reasonably, could have been satisfied of the guilt of the accused beyond a reasonable doubt. If so, the appeal must fail. Deane took the view that if the appellate court itself was persuaded that a reasonable doubt remained as to the guilt of the accused, it must find that the verdict was unsafe, even though the jury had been persuaded otherwise. Murphy did not explicitly address this issue, although his reasoning and conclusions suggest that he was more inclined to the position adopted by Deane. In most cases, not much will turn on the differences between the two approaches; they both leave the Court with substantial discretion to review the evidence.

The judgments in *Chamberlain* are largely consumed with this task. For the most part, this involved weighing the scientific evidence suggesting guilt against the conflicting scientific evidence offered by the defence, the latter including substantial eyewitness evidence that a dingo had taken

Azaria, evidence of the Chamberlains' good character, and lack of evidence of any motive for the crime.

As to the Crown allegation that foetal blood was found in the car, three Justices (**Gibbs, Mason** and Murphy) agreed that the evidence did not justify the jury in safely finding that there was in fact foetal blood in the car. However, Gibbs and Mason concluded that the jury was nevertheless entitled to convict on the whole of the evidence, even if they could not safely have accepted this fact as proven. This was the key point upon which Murphy dissented. He argued that there was no way of disentangling the general assessment of the safety of the verdict based on the totality of the evidence from a consideration of the role this one vital piece of evidence may have played in the jury's deliberations. If the jury accepted this evidence as reliable (which it was not) this may have coloured its consideration of all the exculpatory evidence and resolved any doubts about the other incriminating evidence. For Murphy, this was the fatal flaw in the Crown case that justified overturning the convictions.

Deane also dissented. In weighing all the evidence and concluding that it did not in his mind establish guilt beyond reasonable doubt, he seemed particularly struck by the force of the eyewitness evidence that the baby was heard to cry by three separate witnesses (one of them completely independent of the Chamberlains) at a time when, according to the Crown, she had already been murdered by her mother.

With Lindy Chamberlain's supporters disappointed by the outcome but buoyed by the **dissenting judgments** in the High Court, their campaign for her release continued to grow. After the discovery of Azaria's matinee jacket at Uluru in early 1986, the Northern Territory government released Lindy and established an inquiry into the convictions chaired by Federal Court Justice Trevor Morling. In finding that the convictions were unsafe, the inquiry relied on new evidence, but it also substantially discredited the evidence relied upon by the Crown at the trial.

The relatively minor points of law and nuances in their application aside, the enduring significance of this remarkable case in the annals of High Court jurisprudence lies in the sobering example it provides of the limited capacity of the appellate process to remedy injustice where it stems from a source other than manifest legal error—in this case from prejudice, incompetence, misplaced zeal and excessive confidence in the certitudes of science.

RUSSELL HOGG

Further Reading
John Bryson, *Evil Angels* (1985)
Ken Crispin, *The Crown Versus Chamberlain 1980–1987* (1987)

Chambers. The rooms in which Justices of the High Court and their staff conduct their work are called chambers. Before the Court's move to **Canberra** in 1980, the Justices had permanent chambers in Little Bourke Street, Melbourne, and subsequently in a wing of the law courts complex in Darlinghurst, Sydney. The Melbourne and Sydney chambers were large but somewhat gloomy. Because of inadequate **library** facilities, the chambers were surrounded, floor to ceiling, by bookshelves, and there were few facilities for staff or for interaction among the Justices.

The Chief Justice's chambers at the High Court building in Canberra

When the Court went on **circuit** to state capitals, it usually sat in the Banco Court of the Supreme Court of each state. Supreme Court judges ordinarily vacated their chambers, as required, during the week of the High Court circuit. This arrangement is still followed in SA and Tasmania. In Queensland and WA, the Justices have chambers in the Federal Courts building. In Melbourne and Sydney, where special **leave** hearings are regularly held, the High Court itself provides chambers for visiting Justices and their staff without the need to impose upon, or disrupt, other courts.

At the more recently constructed Court **building** in Canberra, the chambers of the **Chief Justice** and the six **puisne Justices** are found on level 9. Chambers are provided on other levels for visiting retired Justices of the Court, as well as offices for the **Chief Executive and Principal Registrar**, the federal **Attorney-General** and **Solicitor-General**, other law officers, and lawyers with cases before the Court.

Each Justice not permanently resident in Canberra is also provided with chambers in the city where he or she lives. The personal assistants to the Justices do most of their work in the Canberra chambers, although a few Justices prefer to have their personal assistants in the chambers of their city of residence. Most of the **associates** to the Justices work permanently in the Canberra chambers. All the associates are present in Canberra when the Court sits in that city.

Typically, a Justice's chambers comprise four rooms—one each for the Justice, the personal assistant and two associates. The chambers in Canberra are panelled in different types of Australian timber, and each has a balcony overlooking either Lake Burley Griffin or Parliament House (see **Architecture of Court building**). The decoration of individual chambers, however, is largely a matter for each Justice. The largest chambers in the Court building in Canberra are those of the Chief Justice, with facilities for a staff of four officers and an adjoining room for a **research** officer or additional associate.

The chambers in Canberra open to a central area housing part of the High Court library. This area contains basic law reports, journals, texts and reference works in regular use. With the elimination of spaces presently devoted to library and **conference** facilities on level 9, it would be physically possible to expand the number of judicial chambers to accommodate nine Justices. The possibility of increasing the **number of Justices** to nine is also reflected in the provision for expansion of the benches in **Courtrooms** No 1 and No 2.

The operation of chambers varies with the methods of work of the Justice concerned. However, the principal functions in all chambers include the writing, checking and finalisation of draft reasons for publication when a **reserved judgment** is delivered. Under the **High Court Rules**, certain applications to a single Justice may be heard and determined in chambers. In particular, applicants for **writs** of prohibition or other constitutional writs and like relief will normally proceed by way of application in chambers for an **order** *nisi* returnable before the **Full Court**. In practice, even these 'chamber applications' are now usually heard in Courtroom No 3 (sometimes by video link to another city), or, between **sittings** of the Court in Canberra, in a courtroom in Sydney, Melbourne or Brisbane.

The chambers tend to reflect the personality of their occupants. A good working relationship usually exists between staff in the different chambers. They enjoy social, sporting and other contacts out of court hours. However, all are places of intensive work, and this is particularly true of the chambers in Canberra during sittings of the Court.

MICHAEL KIRBY

Characterisation is a term described by **Windeyer** in *Worthing v Rowell & Muston* (1970) as 'uncouth for grammarians and those who care for English undefiled, [but] accepted and useful in the jargon of Australian **constitutional law**'. It refers to the process of determining whether a Commonwealth statute is 'with respect to' one of the subject matters of **Commonwealth legislative power** enumerated in section 51 or 52 of the Constitution. The nature of the required connection between the statute and the Constitution has been variously described as 'not insubstantial, tenuous or distant' (*Bank Nationalisation Case* (1948)), 'reasonable' (*Burton v Honan* (1952)) or 'sufficient' (*Leask v Commonwealth* (1996)).

An emphasis in other jurisdictions on the 'true nature and character' of the law (see, for example, the **Privy Council** decision in *Russell v The Queen* (1882)) might have suggested that it was necessary to give the law a single character. This approach would restrict the range of laws the Commonwealth Parliament could enact. Indeed, concern for the so-called 'federal balance' (see **Federalism**) has influenced some Justices to consider characterisation as involving the identification of the predominant character of the statute (see **Higgins** in *Huddart Parker v Moorehead* (1909); **Latham** in *West v Commissioner of Taxation (NSW)* (1937) and the *Melbourne Corporation Case* (1947); **Barwick** in the *Payroll Tax Case* (1971)).

However, the High Court has rejected this and generally engaged in a process of 'dual' characterisation (see the authorities cited by **Mason** in the *Tasmanian Dam Case* (1983)). Dual characterisation acknowledges that, as long as a Commonwealth law can fairly be described as 'with respect to' one of the subject matters enumerated in sections 51 and 52 of the Constitution, it is of no consequence either that it can also be described as a law with respect to a subject matter not so included or that there is no independent connection between the subject matters of the law, provided always that the other subject matter is not expressly or impliedly prohibited by the Constitution (see Mason and **Deane** in *Re F; Ex parte F* (1986)).

In characterising a statute, the Court often focuses on its direct legal effect, identifying whether the rights, duties, powers or privileges it changes or creates come within one of the constitutional subject matters (see the *First Uniform Tax Case* (1942); *Airlines of NSW v NSW (No 2)* (1965); *Fairfax v FCT* (1965); *Actors Equity v Fontana Films* (1982)). In this process, the fact that Parliament may have been motivated by a desire to control other matters lying beyond its power is not relevant, even where the law might be characterised as also concerning them (see *Fairfax*; *Herald & Weekly Times v Commonwealth* (1966); *Murphyores v Commonwealth* (1976)). Thus, in *Fairfax* the Commonwealth was able to use its tax power to influence investment decisions, and in *Murphyores* the Commonwealth was able to use its export power to prevent sandmining on Fraser Island.

The practical effect of a statute is, however, significant in characterisation. This is especially so when the issue is one of the validity of a law enacted under the implied incidental power (see the US decision in *McCulloch v Maryland* (1819); and see *Grannall v Marrickville Margarine* (1955)), or under a purposive power such as the **defence power**. These cases often require recourse to the purpose of the statute, and to an assessment of it as a means to that end (see the *Second Uniform Tax Case* (1957); *Bank Nationalisation Case*). On other occasions—for instance, in characterising the legislative implementation of international treaties under the **external affairs power**—the Court has looked to whether the law is 'appropriate and adapted' to achieve the ends that are in power (see the *Tasmanian Dam Case*; *Richardson v Forestry Commission* (1988)). Here, too, it is the purpose of giving effect to the treaty that brings the law within power.

Given the purposive aspect of characterisation in these instances, it is not surprising that some Justices have also resorted to the idea of reasonable **proportionality** (see especially Mason in *Nationwide News v Wills* (1992)). However, a majority of Justices have drawn back from this approach, preferring to emphasise sufficiency of connection to the Constitution (*Leask*).

A recurring concern of the Court has been to maintain the distinction between legislative and judicial functions (see **Separation of powers**), emphasising that it is not the **role of the Court** to determine the validity of a law by reference to the desirability of the policy choices made by the legislature. For some Justices, this is the very danger inherent using a criterion of reasonable proportionality: as **Toohey** observed in *Leask*, 'the Court would be drawn inexorably into areas of **policy** and of **value** judgments'. The Court insists that the judicial role should involve an objective determination of whether the statute conforms to constitutional requirements.

So far as characterisation is based on a formal examination of the constitutional and statutory texts, this elevation of **form** over substance has been considered to be one of the hallmarks of **legalism**. The modern approach to characterisation certainly owes much to the influence of **Dixon** (see especially the *Bank Nationalisation Case*), who reiterated the *Engineers* (1920) principle that Commonwealth legislative powers should be interpreted broadly and without regard to the notion of **reserved state powers**. This, coupled with the recognition of dual characterisation, has produced an expansive approach to Commonwealth power. However, a significant number of Justices have consistently recoiled from the logical consequences of broad **constitutional interpretation** coupled with dual characterisation. In their judgments, what would once have been an inquiry into 'the true nature and character' of the legislation is refigured as a narrower interpretation of the power.

Although the process of determining the validity of a Commonwealth Act has traditionally been separated into two distinct issues (first, the meaning of the head of power, and secondly, the process of characterising the statute), in reality, as Mason noted in the *Tasmanian Dam Case*, it is difficult to separate them. The prior question of interpretation is always examined through the example of the particular law, the validity of which is at issue. Thus even determining 'sufficiency of connection' involves matters of judgment on which there will inevitably be disagreement.

ROSEMARY OWENS

Further Reading
Jeremy Kirk, 'Constitutional Guarantees, Characterisation and the Concept of Proportionality' (1997) 21 *MULR* 1
Leslie Zines, *The High Court and the Constitution* (4th edn 1997) chs 2 and 3

Chief Executive and Principal Registrar. The *Judiciary Act 1903* (Cth) provided for the appointment of a Principal Registrar to be located at the Principal Registry of the High Court, with a District Registrar at every District Registry and such other officers as were necessary. The Judiciary Act also provided for the appointment of a **Marshal**, a position that the Principal Registrar occupied from 1950 to the period of the **Barwick Court**.

The Judiciary Bill had attracted parliamentary opposition and press **criticism** in 1902, the proposal to create the High Court being referred to as 'a splendid luxury'. While vigorously defending the Bill, **Attorney-General** Alfred **Deakin** agreed with members of the House of Representatives that 'the question of expense must be taken into account'. He indicated to members that, on the estimates, an amount of £6000 had been provided for the Registrars, Marshals, and other court officers and for other contingencies. 'I believe that for the first few years we should be able to get State officers to perform the duties of registrars and marshals. Consequently, the outlay should be very small.'

The first appointment made was that of Principal Registrar. Gordon Castle, formerly Chief Clerk of the Commonwealth Attorney-General's Department, was appointed on 2 October 1903. Castle held the position in Melbourne until 7 May 1913. He was paid an allowance of £40 per annum in addition to his salary. On 5 October 1903, William O'Halloran, the Prothonotary of the Supreme Court of Victoria, was appointed to be Deputy Registrar in the Principal Registry without salary. Other state officers were subsequently appointed to the positions of District Registrar and Deputy District Registrars in each of the District Registries in the other states.

Shortly after 11.30 am on Wednesday, 6 October 1903, Castle carried out his first official function in the Banco Court in the Supreme Court Building in Melbourne. **Griffith**, **Barton**, and **O'Connor** entered the packed courtroom and handed Castle their commissions of appointment as **Chief Justice** and Justices of the High Court. After reading aloud each commission, Castle administered the Oath of Office to their Honours in turn. The completion of that ceremony marked the formal constitution of the Court. The Justices had taken the Oath of Allegiance to the King before Governor-General Lord Tennyson at a meeting of the Executive Council held in Melbourne on 5 October 1903. The oaths were handwritten on pieces of foolscap.

The reading of the commission of each newly appointed Justice remains the ceremonial function of the Principal Registrar, although after the initial swearing in, the oaths of allegiance and of office are administered by the Chief Justice, or when a new Chief Justice is sworn in, by the senior **puisne Justice**.

There was little change in the functions of the Principal Registrar until the **seat** of the Court moved to **Canberra** in 1980. The Principal Registrar was responsible both to the

Secretary of the Commonwealth Attorney-General's Department and to the Chief Justice. The Attorney-General's Department had administrative and financial responsibility for the Court until the proclamation of the *High Court of Australia Act* 1979 (Cth) in early 1980.

The Principal Registrar arranged and attended all **sittings** of the Court outside Melbourne. It was the practice that when on **circuit**, and on occasions in Melbourne and Sydney, the Principal Registrar would sit in court as clerk to the **Full Court** to note up the Court minute book. **Barwick** thought this wasteful of resources, and directed that the Justices' **associates** carry out this function on a roster prepared by the associate to the Chief Justice.

The Registrars and registry staff of the Court provide advice to the **legal profession**, federal, state, and territory law offices, **litigants in person**, and members of the public on the practice and **procedure** of the Court. The Registrars supervise the preparation of the material to be put before the Court in the application books and **appeal books**. The Principal Registrar, in consultation with the Chief Justice, arranges the sittings of the Court in Canberra, on circuit, and where necessary, by video link from capital cities other than Sydney and Melbourne.

Under the Judiciary Act, there were nine Principal Registrars: Gordon Castle (1903–13); John O'Halloran (1915–22); Seaforth Mackenzie (1922–36); John Gardner (1937–40); James Hardman (1943–57); Michael Doherty (1957–62); Neil Gamble (1962–73); Leslie Foley (1973–79); and Frank Jones, who served (1979–80) as Acting Principal Registrar pending the proclamation of the High Court of Australia Act, then as Registrar under that Act from 1980–94. Christopher Doogan has served as Chief Executive and Principal Registrar (as the title became) under the High Court of Australia Act since April 1994. The title 'Chief Executive and Principal Registrar' was introduced in part to combine the functions of the Clerk of the Court (who was effectively the executive officer of the Court) with those of the Registrar.

FRANK JONES

Chief Justice, role of. The commission held by the Chief Justice appoints him or her to the office of Chief Justice of the High Court of Australia. It follows that, subject to some qualifications, the legal powers and responsibilities of the Chief Justice are confined to the Court and its activities. Despite the precise terms of the commission, the Chief Justice is seen today as 'Chief Justice of Australia'—the term by which William Cullen addressed **Knox** when Knox was appointed Chief Justice in 1919. Cullen probably had in mind the Chief Justice's *Pension Act* 1918 (Cth), which provided for the grant of a pension to 'the First Chief Justice of Australia'. The chairmanship of the Council of Chief Justices of Australia and NZ is another recognition of this wider role. The Council is a non-statutory body, comprising the Chief Justices of federal and state **superior courts** and the Supreme Court of NZ. It deals with a range of matters of interest to the **superior courts** and the judiciary.

The Chief Justice administers the oath when a new Governor-General takes office, and acts as delegate of the Governor-General in opening a new Parliament and administering the oath to members of the House of Representatives. The Chief Justice is also generally a member and Chairman of the Australian National Group in the Permanent Court of Arbitration, whose function is to make nominations to the International Court of Justice under its statute. The Chief Justice was, but no longer is, a member of the National Debt Commission and Chairman of the Council of the Order of Australia.

The Chief Justice is *primus inter pares* (first among equals)—and thus in a position that differs very little from that of any other Justice. One difference arises from section 23(2) of the *Judiciary Act* 1903 (Cth), which establishes a general rule that, if the Court is equally divided, the opinion of the Chief Justice or, if the Chief Justice is absent, the opinion of the senior Justice present, prevails (see **Tied vote**). However, the rule does not apply in cases where an earlier decision by a Justice of the High Court, a state or territory Supreme Court, the **Federal Court** or the Family Court, 'is called in question by appeal or otherwise': in those cases, if the High Court is evenly divided, the judgment below stands. The *High Court of Australia Act* 1979 (Cth) vests the **administration** of the Court in the Chief Justice and the Justices. The person responsible for the day-to-day administration of the Court is the **Chief Executive and Principal Registrar**, who consults closely with the Chief Justice. Important administrative issues are dealt with at regular meetings of the Justices at which the Chief Justice presides.

The Chief Justice represents the Court in discussions with government and is consulted by the **Attorney-General** or the **Prime Minister** in relation to **appointments** to the Court and, on occasions, to other courts or tribunals. The Chief Justice may discuss **budget** difficulties with the Attorney-General, the Minister of Finance or the Prime Minister. Although the Chief Executive meets with officers of the Department, there was one occasion when **Mason** met the Departmental officers. Early in 1997 **Brennan** had occasion to write to Deputy Prime Minister Tim Fischer taking exception to **criticism** that Fischer had made of the Court in connection with the delivery of judgment in *Wik* (1996).

The annual **sittings** are proposed by the Chief Executive and Principal Registrar in consultation with the Chief Justice and approved by the Justices. The listing of cases before the **Full Court** and the composition of the Benches is prepared by the Chief Justice and circulated to the Justices in the form of a 'proposal'. The estimated duration of a case is determined by the Chief Justice on advice from the senior Deputy Registrar, who consults with the parties. In constitutional cases—which often take the form of a stated case or reservation of questions settled at a **directions hearing**, generally before the Chief Justice—counsel will provide an estimate of hearing time.

The Chief Justice also circulates a roster of Justices to sit in **chambers** or original **jurisdiction**. Matters pending in a District Registry are assigned to a Justice whose principal place of residence is in that district.

The role of the Chief Justice varies with time, circumstance and personality. At one end of the spectrum stands the legendary image of **Gavan Duffy** at the Weld Club, Perth, waving his colleagues off to work at the Supreme Court on the other side of the street. This image is not inconsistent with the comments about Gavan Duffy made by **Dixon** on the occasion of Dixon's **retirement** from the High Court (see 110 *CLR* v). At the other end is the image of Dixon himself. He provided leadership by writing judgments of such quality that they commanded the concurrence of his colleagues or emerged as **joint judgments**. Dixon was the outstanding exemplar of a Chief Justice who dominated the Court of his era by virtue of outstanding judicial ability and reputation (see also **Dixon Court**).

The Court's character as a collective or cooperative institution has consequences for the relationship between the Chief Justice and the Justices. The Chief Justice has a responsibility to maintain effective working relationships within the Court. Frank and open discussion of all matters relevant to the Court is essential to that end.

Although it is for the Court itself to determine its mode of work, it is for the Chief Justice to take the initiative in ensuring that an appropriate system and methodology is in place. Today, after discussion in **conference** about the issues in the case following the oral **argument**, the Chief Justice will usually seek to secure agreement that the writing of a judgment should be allocated to a particular Justice or Justices, and will also be responsible for monitoring progress in the preparation of the judgment and its ultimate and timely acceptance. The Chief Justice may be able to speed the process and encourage consensus through discussion with other Justices. But time constraints and, to a lesser extent, geographical separation, limit opportunities for discussion. Extended oral **argument** at the hearing, in which the Justices participate, may reveal their tentative thinking.

It is for the Chief Justice to control oral argument, to ensure that it is directed to the points at issue and that time is not wasted. Otherwise, the Chief Justice's role depends upon the Court's mode of work and its approach to the writing of judgments. The English tradition of individual judgments was followed for a long time. The main exceptions were in the first High Court, which delivered a number of joint, unanimous judgments, and the Dixon Court, which saw an increase in the number of joint judgments. The tradition of individual judgments was associated with the conviction that each Justice had an obligation to work out the answer for himself or herself—an obligation which would not be fully discharged if the Justice sacrificed any part of the personal responsibility for evolving the answer. The tradition may have gathered strength from the Court's conception of a Justice's obligation as transcending the limitations inherent in counsel's arguments and the materials by which they are supported.

In recent times, the tradition of delivering individual judgments has attracted adverse criticism. The Court is a collective institution; it is the Court, rather than the individual Justices, that decides the case and declares the law. There is now an expectation that the Court will declare the law in clear terms in order to provide guidance for trial judges, the **legal profession** and the community. So the Court, and especially the Chief Justice, has a strong responsibility to explore the possibility of delivering a 'judgment of the Court' or, at least, a joint majority judgment, and in a timely fashion (see also **Collective responsibility**).

But the obligation cannot be stated higher than that. In the modern world, there is basic disagreement about the

limits of the judicial role and the **role** of the Court. Such disagreements were strongly expressed in some individual judgments of the **Mason Court**. Not all Justices believe in the virtues of 'strict and complete **legalism**' or agree upon what it entails. Granted this basic disagreement, it is idle to speak of an obligation to deliver judgments of the Court. Quite apart from this problem, no judge can be expected to compromise his or her intellectual integrity. The notion that Court judgments are a matter of bargaining is beset with difficulties. And the great pressure of work imposes time constraints on the capacity of Justices to resolve all the tangential points of difference that may arise between the authors of judgments which **concur** in the result.

The account just given discloses greater interaction between the Chief Justice and the Justices than prevailed in the **Barwick Court**, where the tradition of working on one's own was still very strong and Barwick was anxious not to attempt to influence the views of other Justices otherwise than by the circulation of his own reasons for judgment.

In some cases, the Chief Justice may convene a conference before the hearing in order to canvass questions that may require determination during the hearing. Here the delivery of written argument in advance of the hearing is an advantage.

As the leader of the Australian judiciary, the Chief Justice speaks and writes in that capacity as well as in the official capacity as Chief Justice of the High Court. Communication with the **legal profession** and the community has become an important part of the role of the Chief Justice—the more so since federal Attorney-General Daryl Williams made it clear in 1997 that he did not regard it as part of the role of the Attorney-General to speak for or defend the judiciary. It therefore falls to the Chief Justice to explain the function of the courts and express views on matters of interest to the judiciary, the legal profession and the public. This may be done by means of speeches, papers delivered at conferences and seminars, and even by interviews. The Chief Justice also represents the Court by making official visits to foreign courts and jurisdictions.

The Chief Justice has from time to time advised the Governor-General on constitutional matters, most controversially in 1975 when Barwick advised John Kerr. Opinion is divided on whether the giving of such advice is appropriate (see **Dismissal of 1975**; **Dixon diaries**).

ANTHONY MASON

Children. The questions that courts are required to answer regarding persons under the age of 18 arise in many contexts. Much litigation occurs following the breakup of a family: frequently the proceedings involve disputes about parental rights and obligations, and thus require courts to do their best to safeguard the welfare of the children. Less commonly, courts are asked to protect a child in an intact family—for example, by determining whether medical treatment should be undertaken. Apart from domestic litigation, actions in **contract** or **tort law** sometimes raise problems relating to children's legal powers and responsibilities.

In many proceedings involving children, two contrasting perceptions of childhood are open to the courts. One takes as its starting point the assumption that the essential feature of childhood is incapacity, and that before the age of majority is attained, a child should be regarded as vulnerable and in need of protection. The other makes no such assumption; instead it rests on the view that in many circumstances a child possesses the capacity to make decisions and accept responsibility. Whether this is so will be determined case by case. In the past, judicial decisions tended to reflect the former perception, and accordingly to emphasise the protective role of the law. Recently, however, the adoption of the language of children's rights has led courts to be more willing to consider the desirability of promoting children's autonomy.

If a court is to recognise a child's autonomy it must address the question of parental rights. In England, this task was undertaken in *Gillick v West Norfolk Area Health Authority* (1985), where the **House of Lords** accepted that a parent's power over a child is not absolute. It diminishes as a child matures, with the result that the law will now acknowledge that in some circumstances a child with sufficient intelligence and understanding may make his or her own decisions, such as whether to consent to medical treatment. This conclusion reflected recognition not only of the gradual development of a child's capacities, but also of the social fact of the increasing independence of the young.

The High Court has indicated that the *Gillick* analysis should be adopted in Australia. In *J v Lieschke* (1987), **Wilson** suggested that it might be followed to allow a child with sufficient intelligence and understanding to instruct a solicitor in court proceedings. He added that no right which a parent may have to arrange legal representation for a child can override the right of a child to make his or her own decision on the matter. *Marion's Case* (1992) offered a fuller discussion of the law's willingness to acknowledge children's autonomy. The majority (Chief Justice **Mason**, **Dawson**, **Toohey**, and **Gaudron**) described *Gillick* as 'of persuasive authority' and accepted that it should be followed in Australia as part of the **common law**. As **Deane** put it, the authority of parents with respect to a young person is 'limited, controlled and varying'. Similarly, **McHugh** observed: 'Modern case law makes it impossible … to assert that parents have a natural right of almost absolute control over the person, education, conduct and property of their children.'

These comments, however, should be read in the light of other views expressed in *Marion's Case* and *Lieschke*. These suggest that, in spite of its changing perceptions of childhood, the law will continue to accept that normally the natural right of parents to exercise authority over their children should be recognised. *Lieschke* endorsed this view by ruling that, where practicable, a parent is entitled to be heard in court proceedings in which his or her rights as a custodial parent and guardian are challenged. The principal judgment (by **Brennan**) saw the parent's right to be heard as flowing from 'the natural parental right to discharge parental duties and to exercise parental authority'. This judgment—in which all members of the Court concurred—suggested that it is usually in a child's interests to accept the authority of a parent: 'There is a natural reciprocity between the duty and authority of parents with respect to the nurturing, control and protection of their child and the child's rights and its interests in being nurtured, controlled and protected.' This is to assert that the maintenance of parental rights can further children's rights. Perhaps it was this consideration that prompted Brennan in his **dissenting judgment** in *Marion* to express reservations about the decision in *Gillick*, commenting that he doubted if it sufficiently recognised 'the primacy of parental responsibility'. Similarly, McHugh underlined the need for recognition of parental authority, noting that the common law gives parents control over their children because 'it perceives them to be the most appropriate repository of such a power'.

Thus, in *Lieschke* and *Marion's Case*, the High Court acknowledged both the need (in appropriate circumstances) to recognise children's autonomy, and the law's long-established support of parental authority. Other decisions articulate principles designed to take account of children's diminished capacity. *McHale v Watson* (1966) involved a **damages** claim against a boy of 12. While playing, he had negligently injured a girl aged nine. The Court was required to rule on the standard of care that could reasonably be expected of him. This required a decision as to whether his age should be taken into account in determining his liability. While it is clear that a very young child who is incapable of appreciating the existence of a risk could not be liable in tort, all the Justices accepted that there could not be a general immunity for twelve-year-old boys. The majority (**McTiernan**, **Kitto**, and **Owen**) also decided that the boy's liability could not be determined by reference to the standard of care reasonably expected of an adult. After noting that in the case of an adult, liability for negligence arises from a failure to show a 'proper' standard of care, Kitto explained:

> It does not follow that [a child] cannot rely in his defence upon a limitation upon the capacity for foresight or prudence, not as being personal to himself, but as being characteristic of humanity at his stage of development and in that sense normal … In regard to the things which pertain to foresight and prudence—experience, understanding of causes and effects, balance of judgment, thoughtfulness—it is absurd, indeed it is a misuse of language, to speak of normality in relation to persons of all ages taken together. In those things normality is, for children, something different from what normality is for adults; the very concept of normality is a concept of rising levels until 'years of discretion' are attained.

On this basis, Kitto held that the standard of care set by the law was the standard expected of an ordinary child of comparable age. This, he said, allows for the 'deficiencies of foresight and prudence that are normal during childhood'. To resolve the problem in this manner is to make concessions to youth—to see immaturity as a mitigating factor—but to do so in a way that avoids reliance on rigid age-based rules. In this respect, the decision anticipated *Gillick* in its willingness to adopt a flexible approach to the question of whether children should be regarded as legally responsible. Similar flexibility was seen in *Hamilton v Lethbridge* (1912), where **Isaacs** accepted that, although minors may bind themselves by contract, their ability to do so is not unlimited. In Isaacs' words, a minor 'can no more dissolve a contract which the Court sees is beneficial to him than he can make one which the Courts sees is to his prejudice'. This is a further example of the law acknowledging that children have certain legal capacities, but that the courts will endeavour to protect them by taking account of their immaturity.

In contrast with the small number of cases dealing with children's rights and responsibilities is the larger number of matters in which the High Court has focused on the use of the law for purely benevolent and protective purposes. In these cases, children are viewed as vulnerable beings and the issue is whether—and, if so, when—legal intervention should be employed to safeguard them from harm. One of the recurring questions relates to the appropriateness of intervention in the private world of the family. This in turn raises a further question as to the power of the state to supplant parents. The fundamental problem is the identification of the nature and limits of the state's power to intervene in order to promote children's welfare.

It is well established that the state has broad powers of intervention exercisable by way of the *parens patriae* jurisdiction. This jurisdiction was originally exercised by the English Court of Chancery, and was inherited by the **state Supreme Courts**. A more recent development was the acquisition by the Family Court of the power to make orders with regard to the welfare of the child of a marriage. *Marion's Case* accepted that the effect of this had been to confer on the Family Court a jurisdiction similar to the *parens patriae* jurisdiction. This view was reaffirmed in *P v P* (1994) and *ZP v PS* (1994). The exercise of the ancient jurisdiction and of its newer counterpart must be guided by the principle that the welfare of the child is the paramount consideration.

Courts and **commentators** regularly stress the breadth of the *parens patriae* jurisdiction. The analysis offered by the High Court identifies some of the problems arising from the assumption that a court exercising the *parens patriae* jurisdiction has virtually limitless powers to do what is best for a child. The view that the jurisdiction is purely derivative and therefore allows a court to do no more than exercise the powers possessed by a natural parent was rejected by the majority in *Marion's Case*. It was held that a court exercising the jurisdiction may make decisions on matters beyond parental power as well as on matters within parental power. Brennan dissented on this point and rejected the conclusion that—at least on matters affecting a child's bodily integrity— a court possessing the *parens patriae* jurisdiction could lay claim to powers greater than those of a parent. He also challenged the view that the Family Court's welfare jurisdiction corresponds with the *parens patriae* jurisdiction. In his opinion, 'the jurisdiction with respect to welfare can hardly be construed as authorising the Family Court to make whatever order a judge may deem to be for the welfare of a child'.

In *P v P* (like *Marion*, a sterilisation case), Brennan reconsidered the limits of the Family Court's welfare jurisdiction. He repeated his opinion that it was unacceptable for a judge to authorise such an invasion of a person's physical integrity on the basis of no more than a personal view that the operation was in the girl's best interests. 'It is erroneous to assume that a power is reposed in a court merely because it is thought desirable or convenient that the power be available.' He thus challenged the notion that a benevolent court, intent on promoting a child's welfare, has virtually limitless powers. Similarly, in *AMS v AIF* (1999), Gaudron, speaking of the welfare jurisdiction of the Family Court of WA, remarked

that it would be 'reading too much' into the statute conferring this jurisdiction to interpret it 'as authorising any **order** that would promote the child's welfare'.

Comments like these identify a number of competing considerations. In the future, there is likely to be increasing recognition of children's autonomy. Yet regard must be had to the vulnerability and dependence of the young and to the fact that their capacities vary. When children are incapable of making their own decisions, the issue is where authority in respect of their welfare should properly reside. The High Court has confirmed that the state has the power both to exercise a supervisory jurisdiction over parents and to exercise powers over children greater than those possessed by a natural parent. Yet some members of the Court have expressed reservations about a law permitting a court to intervene in a child's life whenever a judge decides that this course is in a child's best interests.

JOHN SEYMOUR

Church and state. The Court has generally kept a discreet distance from matters religious. While it has emphasised the importance of religious **equality** and tolerance, it has at the same time given a restrictive operation to section 116 of the Constitution—the only constitutional provision about religion. Although it embodies an express constitutional recognition that the Commonwealth has limited powers concerning religion, section 116 has rarely been invoked in the Court in support of religious rights or even as a restriction on Commonwealth power. It provides:

> The Commonwealth shall not make any law for establishing any religion, or for imposing any religious observance, or for prohibiting the free exercise of any religion, and no religious test shall be required as a qualification for any office or public trust under the Commonwealth.

As the Court deals increasingly with other questions of individual rights, it may come to address issues regarding religion more frequently.

The 'establishing' clause and the 'free exercise' clause in section 116 have close similarities to those in the First Amendment to the US Constitution, but have never received the generous interpretation that provision has enjoyed. The High Court has noted textual differences rather than similarities, and the different constitutional **history** in the two countries. For example, the 'establishing' clause of section 116 has never been held to require any general separation between church and state beyond prohibiting the Commonwealth from legislating for the purpose of establishing a state religion. In the *DOGS Case* (1981), a majority upheld the Commonwealth's power to direct federal funding to religious-denomination schools. **Murphy**, in dissent, would have followed the American authorities and required a clear line between church and state, forbidding such funding. The majority judgments closely examined the constitutional text rather than searching for any underlying policy in interpreting the section. They relied especially on the word 'for'— absent from the First Amendment—so that even if a law had the tendency or effect of establishing a religion it would not offend section 116 unless that was what it was 'for' (that is, unless that was its purpose). The language was construed as a restriction on legislative power first and a guarantee of individual freedom second.

Likewise, the 'free exercise' clause of section 116 has never been used to strike down a Commonwealth law. In *Krygger v Williams* (1912), it was relied on in an attempt to justify conscientious objection to **military** service. Both **Griffith** and **Barton** described the claim as 'absurd'; Barton thought it 'as thin as anything of the kind that has come before us'. The Court looked only at whether military service prevented the appellant from doing acts required in the practice of his religion. In *Judd v McKeon* (1926), an elector claimed a conscientious objection to compulsory voting on political grounds. The majority of the Court held that the voter's objection was not a 'valid and sufficient reason' for failing to vote. Only **Higgins**, in dissent, explored the analogy with section 116. He thought the earlier decision in *Krygger* had taken too narrow a view of religious freedom, and said that 'if abstention from voting were part of an elector's religious duty, as it appeared to the mind of the elector, this would be a valid and sufficient reason for his failure to vote'.

A more extensive analysis was undertaken in the *Jehovah's Witnesses Case* (1943). The sect was declared by Order in Council in 1941 to be prejudicial to the defence of the Commonwealth and the efficient prosecution of **World War II**. Their premises were seized and occupied pursuant to regulations. The Jehovah's Witnesses proclaimed and taught that the British Empire and other organised political bodies were organs of Satan, although they took no part in world politics and their religion required them not to interfere in war between nations. The Court found against them on the section 116 issue, but in their favour on other grounds. **Latham** stated that section 116 proclaimed 'the principle of toleration of all religions, but also the principle of toleration of the absence of religion'. Further, it was intended especially to 'protect the religion (or absence of religion) of minorities, and, in particular, of unpopular minorities'.

Latham saw the purpose of the free exercise clause as one of keeping the historical recurrence of conflict between religious and political duty to a minimum, seeing it as being 'based upon the principle that religion should, for political purposes, be regarded as irrelevant'. However, the Court found that free exercise of religion must yield to interests of public safety and defence—matters in which the Court deferred to the opinion of the executive government (at least in time of war). Foreshadowing the approach of the *DOGS Case*, the Court did not look at the effect of the laws in question on any person's religious freedom, but only at the laws themselves, to see whether they were laws 'for' prohibiting the free exercise of religion. The same emphasis on the purpose of a challenged law appears in *Kruger v Commonwealth* (1997), where the Court held that a law enabling **Aboriginal** children to be placed in the care and custody of a government authority had not had the purpose of prohibiting the free exercise of any religion. **Toohey** noted the existence of material tending to show that it had exactly that purpose, insofar as it sought to remove children from the influence of tribal 'superstitions', but he held that any reference to those materials was excluded by the way the proceedings had been structured.

The 'religious test' clause of section 116 has only once been considered by the Court: when the election of a Roman Catholic member of the federal Parliament was challenged on the ground that he was under acknowledgment of allegiance, obedience or adherence to a foreign power (the Vatican) and therefore ineligible for election under section 44(i) of the Constitution. **Fullagar** held that to accept this argument would amount to the adoption of a religious test for public office contrary to section 116 (see *Crittenden v Anderson* (1950)).

The Court has sometimes needed to consider how far it should look into questions of religious belief and practice (see, for example, the *Chamberlain Case* (1984)). Some members discussed the nature of religion in the course of deciding that the Church of Scientology was a religious institution for pay-roll tax purposes in *Church of the New Faith v Commissioner of Pay-roll Tax (Vic)* (1983). **Mason** and **Brennan** attempted to define the essential features of a 'religion'. Murphy was prepared to accept that any body 'which claims to be religious, and offers a way to find meaning and purpose in life, is religious'. He was reluctant to become involved in deciding what was a religion, but paused to nominate tax exemption for religious bodies as a cause of 'severe social problems'. **Wilson** and **Deane** also declined to nominate any essential features of a religion, and held that what mattered was the sincerity of a religion's adherents rather than the internal consistency of their beliefs. It is worth noting that in passing, Mason and Brennan described section 116's function as being to 'preserve the dignity and freedom of each man so that he may adhere to any religion of his choosing or to none'—perhaps suggesting a focus on individual rights absent from earlier decisions. They described freedom of religion as 'the paradigm freedom of conscience', and 'of the essence of a free society'.

In the *Red Book Case* (1948), the Court was asked to decide whether certain liturgical practices endorsed by the Bishop of Bathurst were in breach of **trusts** on which Church of England property was held. The Court divided equally (see **Tied vote**). Latham accepted jurisdiction since, there being no ecclesiastical courts in Australia, there would otherwise be no **remedy** for breach of trust. Although it was not for the Court 'to determine the soundness of any particular doctrine or the wisdom of a particular ritual', he held after a detailed discussion of Church doctrine that the practices in question were deviations from the Book of Common Prayer and hence unlawful. The injunctions that had been granted in the Supreme Court of NSW should be formulated more narrowly in order to confine them to the proven deviations, but with that variation the Supreme Court's decree should be affirmed. **Williams** agreed, but described the adjudication as 'distasteful'. In contrast, **Dixon** would have held that courts of **equity** lacked jurisdiction to deal with matters of liturgy. **Rich** saw the controversy as unfit for a civil court and would have declined on discretionary grounds to deal with 'abstract questions involving religious dogma'.

The Court ruled on the legality of a union of churches enabled by statute in *A-G (NSW) v Grant* (1976), noting that its concern was 'with matters of law, and not with matters of individual faith and conscience'. However, Murphy warned that 'courts should not decide questions of doctrine, practice or procedure in ecclesiastical government'; to do so would 'exceed the judicial sphere and interfere with religious freedom'. He would have deferred to the governing body of the church on such issues. The Court has not been called upon again to decide whether it should examine the legality of particular religious doctrines or practices.

The Court's focus on legislative purpose under section 116 rather than the effect of a law upon religious freedom or upon the relationship between church and state is best understood by recalling that the Court is more familiar with questions of legislative power in a federation than with issues of individual rights. Perhaps, as the Court deals with more cases of the latter kind (see **Implied constitutional rights**; **Political communication**), the law will evolve to clarify the operation of section 116 and articulate an understanding of its underlying function in the Australian constitutional structure. This evolution may be accompanied by a reassessment of the criteria by which the Court should become involved, if at all, in questions of religious doctrine or practice.

STEPHEN MCLEISH

Further Reading
FD Cumbrae-Stewart, 'Section 116 of the Constitution' (1946) 20 *ALJ* 207
Stephen McLeish, 'Making Sense of Religion and the Constitution: A Fresh Start for Section 116' (1992) 18 *Mon LR* 207
Clifford Pannam, 'Travelling Section 116 with a US Road Map' (1963) 4 *MULR* 41
Joshua Puls, 'The Wall of Separation: Section 116, The First Amendment and Constitutional Religious Guarantees' (1998) 26 *FL Rev* 139

Cigamatic Case (1962). In this case, the High Court held that the Commonwealth enjoyed a wide immunity from state law; this spawned an intense and continuing controversy about the precise extent, and the appropriateness, of such an immunity (see **Intergovernmental immunities**). The *Engineers Case* (1920), which jettisoned the immunity of the states from the operation of Commonwealth laws, had suggested that the rule that Commonwealth law was generally binding on the states was reciprocal, so that state law would generally be binding on the Commonwealth (except when Commonwealth legislation prevailed over **inconsistent** state law by virtue of section 109 of the Constitution). *Cigamatic* suggested otherwise.

Cigamatic represented the culmination of **Dixon's** efforts to provide a notion of **federalism** in which the position of the Commonwealth would necessarily be stronger than that of the states. The Commonwealth had claimed that certain taxes and charges owed to it by a company in liquidation must be paid in priority to debts owing to ordinary unsecured creditors, notwithstanding NSW companies legislation prescribing an order of priority incompatible with the claim of the Commonwealth. On the strength of the then prevailing authority of *Uther's Case* (1947), which had raised a similar issue, and in the absence of any relevant Commonwealth legislation overriding the state law, the Commonwealth's claim would have been defeated. However, in *Cigamatic*, Dixon, in his penultimate year as **Chief Justice** and perhaps at the height of his powers, forged a

majority view that adopted his dissenting judgment in *Uther*.

In *Uther*, Dixon had doubted the capacity of the states to legislate so as to affect the rights of the Commonwealth in relation to its own subjects. He added that the fact that the priority claimed by the Commonwealth sprang from one of the prerogatives of the Crown was 'an added reason, a reason perhaps conclusive in itself' for saying that it was a matter lying completely outside state power. He also said: 'But there is the antecedent consideration that to define or regulate the rights or privileges, duties or disabilities, of the Commonwealth in relation to the subjects of the Crown is not a matter for the States.'

In *Cigamatic*, Dixon preferred to describe the prerogative right to priority of payment as 'one of the fiscal rights of government' and therefore to say that 'to treat those rights as subject to destruction or modification or qualification by the legislature of a State must mean that under the Constitution there resides in a State or States a legislative power to control legal rights and duties between the Commonwealth and its people'. Such a power, he said, was not available to the states.

The enigma of *Cigamatic* lies in the width of the principle that it purported to establish. Should it be confined only to immunising a Commonwealth Crown prerogative? Or should it provide immunity to the Commonwealth only when it is exercising its 'fiscal' or other 'governmental' rights in relation to its subjects? Or should it be viewed as enunciating the broadest proposition that the states simply lack the power to make laws binding on the Commonwealth?

Cigamatic adds to the perplexities by providing an exception to the rule. Reflective of the exception also mentioned by him in *Uther*, Dixon said:

> It is not a question of the authority of the power of a State to make some general law governing the rights and duties of those who enter into some description of transaction, such as the sale of goods, and of the Commonwealth in its executive arm choosing to enter into a transaction of that description.

A similar exception was proffered in *Commonwealth v Bogle* (1953) by **Fullagar**, who also asserted that a state parliament had 'no power over the Commonwealth', a view endorsed by Dixon and three other Justices in *Bogle*.

The 'entering into a transaction' exception or the 'affected by' doctrine reiterated in *Cigamatic* was problematic, for a distinction had to be drawn between those state laws that 'affect' and those that 'bind' the Commonwealth. This distinction was refashioned by a majority of the High Court in *Henderson's Case* (1997), in which the Commonwealth had invoked the principle articulated in *Cigamatic*.

Dawson, **Toohey**, and **Gaudron**, in a joint judgment, interpreted *Cigamatic* as involving a distinction to be drawn between 'the capacities of the Crown on the one hand, by which we mean its rights, powers, privileges and immunities, and the exercise of those capacities on the other'. **Brennan** adopted a similar distinction. The Commonwealth would thus be immune from state legislation relating to its capacities, but not from state legislation 'which assumes those capacities and merely seeks to regulate activities in which the Crown may choose to engage in the exercise of those capacities'.

Two of the Justices in *Henderson*, **McHugh** and **Gummow**, did not find this new distinction helpful. The distinction, as Leslie Zines has suggested, 'does nothing to remove uncertainty' and 'seems to raise difficulties at least as great as the binding/affecting dichotomy'. Despite the dissenting view of **Kirby** in *Henderson* that *Cigamatic* should be 'reverently laid to rest', the principle in *Cigamatic* continues to play an enigmatic role in determining the nature of the Australian federal system.

HP LEE

Further Reading

John Doyle, '1947 Revisited: The Immunity of the Commonwealth from State Law' in Geoffrey Lindell (ed), *Future Directions in Australian Constitutional Law* (1994)

RP Meagher and WMC Gummow, 'Sir Owen Dixon's Heresy' (1980) 54 *ALJ* 25

Igor Mescher, 'Wither Commonwealth Immunity?' (1998) 17 *Aust Bar Rev* 23 (commentary by Bradley Selway, 42, and Alan Robertson, 45)

George Winterton, HP Lee, Arthur Glass and James Thomson, *Australian Federal Constitutional Law: Commentary and Materials* (1999) ch 9

Leslie Zines, *The High Court and the Constitution* (4th edn 1997) ch 14

Circuit system. 'The circuit system' refers to the Court's practice of undertaking regular **sittings** in the various states. Since 1903, High Court Justices have travelled not only as single Justices, but also as a **Full Court**. Over the years, supporters of this system have drawn attention to the public's enhanced perception of the Court, and the benefits for litigants and the **legal profession**. Opponents have also focused on public perceptions, and on the inconvenience and expense of the practice. Examining the history of the circuit system clarifies these arguments and highlights the conflicting, sometimes passionate, views of former Justices and **Attorneys-General** on how the Court should operate.

The circuit system was strongly supported by Commonwealth Attorney-General Alfred **Deakin**, and was facilitated by legislation in 1903. The *Judiciary Act* 1903 (Cth) provided that the Court should sit not only at the principal **seat** of the Court, but wherever there was a District Registry. The Act enabled the Court to hear a case at one place, and pronounce judgment at another. On the introduction of the Judiciary Bill 1902, Deakin eloquently described his vision for the Court, including his desire that the Court be 'a reality to every State … and not merely a name'. While the idea of an itinerant Court attracted strong **criticism** from other members of Parliament, mainly on the grounds of inconvenience and alleged inefficiency, the Judiciary Act was eventually passed, helping give effect to Deakin's vision. Together with the **High Court Rules**, the Act enabled the Court to begin its practice of sitting regularly in each of the state capitals.

In 1905, the circuit system was one of the major issues in a bitter and personal dispute between Commonwealth Attorney-General Josiah Symon and the foundation Justices. Symon argued that circuits were unnecessary, too expensive, and never envisaged by Parliament or the Constitution. Symon also questioned the extent of public support for circuits. The Justices, in response, strongly defended circuits on a variety of grounds. They argued that while circuits were inconvenient and costly, they gave the Justices knowledge of local conditions, enhanced **national unity**, and enabled litigants to employ their own state's **counsel** without the expense of sending them to the principal seat of the Court. These arguments proved unacceptable to Symon, who threatened severe curtailment of the Justices' travelling allowances. As a result, the Court, for the only time in its history, went on 'strike'.

The view of the Justices prevailed with the end of Symon's term as Attorney-General. The attitude of the Justices was supported by new Attorney-General **Isaacs**, who maintained that the intention of Parliament was to enable the Court to undertake circuits to the states 'as may be required'. In a series of published opinions (see 'The Home of the High Court and a High Court Bar' (1905) 3 *Commonwealth LR* 49), leading lawyers representing all the states supported circuits, for similar reasons to those of the foundation Justices. In November 1905, Symon introduced from Opposition the Judiciary Act Amendment Bill 1905 to phase out circuits, but the Bill was never passed. Early attempts to give the Court a permanent, fixed location thus failed. Except for a period during the **Depression of the 1930s** and **World War II**, when circuits were restricted as an austerity measure, circuits were not reviewed again until the establishment of the Court's **seat** in Canberra.

Not all Justices in the interim supported circuits. **Starke** was notorious for his opposition. At various times, he argued that circuits did not affect the public's perception of the Court, that they caused too much personal inconvenience to the Justices, that there was often insufficient **business** in the smaller state capitals to warrant circuits, and that the accommodation provided—in Queensland, Tasmania, and WA, **state Supreme Court** judges offered their chambers; but in SA, the Justices had to squat in the associates' rooms—detracted from the Court's prestige. On one occasion, Starke described the Court's sitting schedule as 'preposterous' and stated that the Justices 'are like and are treated like Carpet Baggers roaming the country'. As a result, Starke often refused to sit beyond Sydney or Melbourne, offering a variety of excuses for his unwillingness to travel. In 1936, for example, Starke offered the following justifications to Chief Justice **Latham** for why the Court, and Starke in particular, should not travel to Perth: the small amount of business in Perth; the possibility that travel might affect Latham's health; Starke's need to attend to other Court business in Melbourne; and because, in Starke's words, 'my boy would be alone in the house and I am not prepared … to leave him for so long a time'. Starke's 'boy', who was almost 23 years of age, once sold the family wood-heap while Starke was on circuit, to obtain extra pocket money.

Even those Justices who generally favoured the practice were sometimes reluctant to go on circuit. Travel to Sydney or Melbourne was arduous enough; and travel to the outlying capitals was worse. The Justices did not have to ride on horseback as their US counterparts had done or cope with a murder attempt by an angry litigant while on circuit (as **US Supreme Court** Justice Stephen Field had), but the Justices did have to endure long voyages to Perth (by train as far as Adelaide and from Adelaide to Perth and back by boat), rough trips on small steamers across Bass Strait to Hobart, and uncomfortable train trips to other states, often late at night. Arriving in Melbourne at 2.00 am, having been delayed because of floods, **Rich** noted sourly to Latham: 'Water everywhere, but no drinks on train.' **Dixon**, who clearly possessed a strong sense of duty, on one occasion considered it as a 'piece of luck' if sitting in WA proved unnecessary. Even **McTiernan**, who was normally extremely cooperative with circuit scheduling, on one occasion raised an objection to sitting in WA. McTiernan stated that he 'would not be sorry' if he was not required to travel to WA, and described the Court's sitting schedule as 'too revolutionary'. Despite these occasional misgivings, the general view was that the circuit system was valuable and should not be replaced despite the personal inconvenience caused.

Barwick, however, took a very different view. In 1968, he had emphasised to the government that establishing a permanent location for the Court at the seat of government in Canberra would advance public awareness of the Court as one of Australia's most important institutions. In accordance with this belief, in 1979 Barwick proposed that all state registries be closed, that Justices be obliged to live in Canberra, and that circuits be abolished altogether.

The mooted abolition of circuits provoked strong resistance. Various members of Parliament expressed the desire that the circuit system be maintained, primarily for the sake of saving litigants expense. Newspapers pressed for the maintenance of circuits on a variety of grounds. They claimed that the Court would take an increasingly centralist position; that it would be perceived as more remote; and that a specialised Bar would emerge. The legal profession was similarly concerned. Members raised the prospect of a specialist Bar, increased litigation costs, and inconvenience to counsel. Perhaps most importantly, the Commonwealth Attorney-General and some of his state colleagues were strongly opposed to abolishing circuits. In deference to such views, in late 1979 the government announced that the Court would be able to continue sitting in the states as the Court saw fit (see section 15 of the *High Court of Australia Act 1979* (Cth)).

The Court no longer hears appeals and other cases before the Full Court in Sydney and Melbourne, though it conducts sittings for special **leave** applications there. It has full sittings in Hobart, Brisbane, Adelaide, and Perth, if business warrants it.

The long-term future of the circuit system is unclear. Although members of the legal profession and the Bench value circuits as a way of maintaining the Court's links with the outlying states, many of the arguments for circuits have less cogency today. Travel from the state capitals is quicker and cheaper than in previous years; the amount of business done in the outlying states is small; and cases from all around Australia are commonly heard in Canberra, which suggests that litigants find it inconvenient to wait for the annual sittings. The potential for greater use of video links may further reduce demand. The concern that having a Court based permanently in Canberra could 'centralise' its decisions appears overstated: a century of circuits has not prevented the federal

balance from shifting steadily in favour of the Commonwealth. This suggests that there are more important factors affecting the Court's propensity to take a centralist stance than where it sits.

If the future of the circuit system is unclear, its historical impact is otherwise. Circuits reduced the **cost of litigation**, contributed to professional acceptance of the Court, and probably advanced national unity. Whether or not the circuit system, or some modified version of it, is out of place in the twenty-first century, for many years it served its function well.

Gɪᴍ Dᴇʟ Vɪʟʟᴀʀ
Tʀᴏʏ Sɪᴍᴘsᴏɴ

Further Reading
JM Bennett, *Keystone of the Federal Arch* (1980) 99–105
Commonwealth, *Correspondence Between the Attorneys-General and the Justices of the High Court Re Sittings Places and Expenses of the Court*, Parliamentary Paper No 26 (1905) 1119
Commonwealth, *Parliamentary Debates*, House of Representatives, 18 March 1902, 10962 (Alfred Deakin)
Commonwealth, *Parliamentary Debates*, Senate, 2 November 1905, 4471 (Josiah Symon)
WG McMinn, 'The High Court Imbroglio and the Fall of the Reid–McLean Government' (1978) 64 *Journal of the Royal Australian Historical Society* 14

Citation of cases. The citation of cases may differ slightly according to whether the cases are cited by academics in books or articles, by practitioners providing legal advice, or by the courts in their judgments.

Traditionally, High Court decisions were cited by referring to a particular publisher's series of law reports. The authorised reports of the Court (those checked and approved by the Justices) are the *Commonwealth Law Reports* (CLR). The unauthorised reports include the *Argus Law Reports*, *Australian Argus Law Reports*, *Australian Law Journal Reports* and *Australian Law Reports*. Numerous subject-specific law reports also regularly report High Court cases.

An example of a High Court decision cited in full is *The Commonwealth of Australia v WMC Resources Limited* (1998) 194 CLR 1. Cases like this may sometimes appear in an abbreviated form (for example, as *Commonwealth v WMC Resources Ltd*). The full citation shows that the judgment was handed down in 1998, that it can be found in volume 194 of the CLRs and that the judgment commences on page one. A 'pinpoint' reference (a reference to a particular page) would usually be cited as (1998) 194 CLR 1 at 32. If a CLR reference is unavailable, the unauthorised reports may be cited. The citation would include the year the case was handed down, the volume number of the report (if there is one), the abbreviation for the law reports series and a page reference number.

The High Court adopted a medium-neutral and vendor-neutral citation for its judgments in 1998, beginning with the first judgment delivered in that year. 'Medium-neutral' means that the citation is not tied down to a particular publisher's series of law reports—nor, indeed, to a printed 'hard copy' at all. This followed the trend in Canada and many US states, which encouraged the use of medium-neutral citations for their judgments. Paragraph numbers were incorporated into the body of the Court's judgments for pinpoint citation. This is because electronic page references often differ, and may be lost altogether in a different electronic medium.

The above case, when first handed down in pamphlet form or electronically, was therefore cited as *Commonwealth v WMC Resources Ltd* [1998] HCA 8. This citation shows that the judgment was handed down in 1998, the designated court is the High Court of Australia, and that this was the eighth judgment for that year. Medium-neutral citations now appear on the first page of each case reported in the published law reports. To give a pinpoint reference, the citation would be [1998] HCA 8 at [69], which corresponds with the CLR pinpoint reference provided above. The correct citation for multiple-paragraph references is: 'at [19]–[21]'.

Traditionally, if a High Court judgment was cited from a series of law reports, a researcher would look on the library shelves to find it. With the introduction of medium-neutral citations, judgments may now be found on numerous Internet sites such as the Australasian Legal Information Institute (AustLII), SCALEplus, and LawNet; by subscription to Butterworths Online or LBC Online; or through various CD ROM products such as *Federal Cases on CD-ROM*. Many Australian courts and tribunals have followed the High Court's lead and have introduced their own designated medium-neutral modes of citation for their judgments and rulings.

A second way a lawyer 'cites' a case is by referring to a case during **argument**. When **counsel** refers to the cited case, the **tipstaff** or **associate** hands the report to the Justice open at the relevant page. When appearing before the High Court, practitioners are expected to cite High Court judgments in the CLRs when available. If the case is not yet published in the CLRs, practitioners may cite a judgment using the medium-neutral mode of citation or one of the various unauthorised law reports.

COLIN FONG

Further Reading
Colin Fong, *Australian Legal Citation* (1998)
Pearl Rozenberg, *Australian Guide to Uniform Legal Citation* (1998)
Anita Stuhmcke, *Legal Referencing* (2nd edn 2001)

Citations by Court. Judges, especially appellate judges, are expected to give reasons for their decisions. In the course of giving these reasons, the judges generally cite authorities in support of their conclusions. So far as these authorities are earlier judicial decisions (see **Authoritative legal materials**), the rationale for citing them lies in the rules of **precedent**. Some previous decisions are cited because they are binding, others are cited because they are persuasive, and others are cited only to be distinguished or rejected.

The table that follows presents statistics on the citation practice of the High Court in five sample years—1920, 1940, 1960, 1980 and 1996. There is nothing special about these years, except that they denote different stages in the history of the Court. In the absence of a comprehensive survey covering several decades, it is impossible to know whether these particular years are representative of successive High Courts. But there is no reason to believe that the sample years are not

Citations by the High Court (based on Commonwealth Law Reports)

Cited Court	1920		1940		1960		1980		1996	
	Number	%	Number	%	Number	%	Number	%	Number	%
High Court	452	24	192	13.4	841	33	1227	44.6	4095	47.4
Federal/Family Court	NA	NA	NA	NA	NA	NA	16	0.6	612	7.1
State/territory Supreme Court	72	3.8	93	6.6	341	13.4	269	9.8	1038	12
Total Australian courts	**524**	**27.8**	**285**	**20**	**1182**	**46.4**	**1512**	**54.9**	**5745**	**66.5**
House of Lords	324	17.2	135	9.5	225	8.8	330	12	422	4.9
Privy Council	254	13.5	81	5.7	157	6.2	98	3.6	194	2.2
English Court of Appeal	187	9.9	349	24.4	197	7.7	232	8.4	504	5.8
Lower English courts	436	23.1	377	26.4	462	18.1	228	8.3	402	4.7
Total English courts	**1201**	**63.7**	**942**	**66**	**1041**	**40.8**	**888**	**32.3**	**1522**	**17.6**
Courts in other countries	89	4.7	66	4.6	69	2.7	159	5.8	470	5.4
Secondary authorities	72	3.8	129	9	255	10.1	193	7	904	10.5
Other	NA	NA	6	.4	NA	NA	NA	NA	NA	NA
Grand Total	**1886**	**100**	**1428**	**100**	**2547**	**100**	**2752**	**100**	**8641**	**100**
Citations per case	22.7		32.4		29.6		55		240	
Citations per page	3.1		2		2.3		2.6		6.4	
Citations per judgment	6		8.4		7.1		10.6		43.9	

representative. With the exception of 1940, both the absolute number of citations, and the citation rate on a per case, per judgment and per page basis, increased over the sample period.

The table shows which authorities have been cited most over time, in absolute terms and as a percentage of total citations. (For a measure of the proportion of *cases* in which foreign precedents have been cited, see **Foreign precedents**.) Some general trends are observable. First, with the exception of 1940, the High Court has cited its own previous decisions more than those of any other single court. This is consistent with several studies of other courts. Secondly, in 1920 and 1940 the High Court cited English decisions more than decisions of Australian courts, but in 1960, 1980 and 1996, there were increases both in the number of Australian cases cited by the Court and in the proportion of Australian cases relative to the proportion of English cases. Thirdly, citations of foreign precedents other than those of English courts have been fairly constant at around 5 per cent, but there were slight increases in 1980 and 1996. Fourthly, case law, as opposed to secondary authorities, has accounted for most of the citations, although the proportion of secondary authorities cited increased after 1920.

What factors explain these observed trends—if they are trends—and what do they tell us about the High Court as an institution? The increasing proportion of citations of Australian cases and, at the same time, the declining proportion of citations of English cases, including **Privy Council** cases, reflect the changing precedent value of English decisions. In 1920, the Privy Council received 13.5 per cent of total citations, but in 1996 the comparable figure was just 2.2 per cent. In contrast, citations to previous decisions of the High Court increased from 24 per cent in 1920 to 47.4 per cent in 1996 (by which time there were of course many more High Court decisions to cite). This is evidence to support the view that since the abolition of appeals from the High Court to the Privy Council, a new Australian jurisprudence is emerging, in which the Court's **role** as a final court of appeal has been enhanced.

Turning to the relative citations of each of the English courts, lower English courts have generally been cited the most, followed by the Court of Appeal, **House of Lords** and Privy Council. This may seem surprising, because their importance in terms of persuasive value is the reverse. But one reason is that there are many more lower-court decisions to draw on than there are decisions of the higher courts. A further factor is that, in some subject areas such as probate and **trusts**, there are numerous old lower-court English decisions on which the law has built, and these are often cited when discussing the way the law has developed. Nevertheless, the percentage of decisions of lower English courts that the High Court cites dropped in 1980 and 1996; this reflects the fact that several of the old doctrines have been incorporated into Australian cases, which are now cited instead.

Studies of the citation practice of the **United States Supreme Court** suggest that it cites few foreign precedents, even from Canada. When English cases are taken into account, the High Court is nowhere near as isolated from legal opinion outside Australia, although it is still true that for most of its history, citations by the High Court to courts

in countries other than England have been relatively insignificant. One explanation, at least in the past, has been that cases from other **common law** jurisdictions are considered to have little persuasive value, or perhaps were difficult to locate. It also seems fair to suggest that in most instances, **counsel** appearing before the Court would cite decisions from jurisdictions other than Australia or England only if there were no relevant local or English authorities. The citation rate to foreign courts other than England increased slightly in 1980 and 1996. In part this reflects the fact that the Internet and other electronic search tools have made it easier to access foreign cases. However, a more important explanation is that in recent times several High Court Justices have expressed the view that cases decided in countries such as NZ and the US have the same persuasive value as prior decisions of English courts. This is consistent with the view put forward by **Mason** that it is appropriate for the High Court to draw on foreign case law in order to 'fashion a common law for Australia that is best suited to our conditions and circumstances'.

Various explanations could be offered for the higher number of secondary authorities cited by the Court in recent years. One of the main factors is organisational change in the court system. The number and breadth of secondary authorities available to Justices in the High Court's own **library** has increased over time, particularly during the period of the **Mason Court**. The creation of the **Federal Court** has also freed the High Court to concentrate on cases raising issues of general importance, especially, though by no means exclusively, in the constitutional area. These are the kinds of cases where the opinions of **commentators** and textbook authors are most valuable.

In general, the changing citation pattern of the Court is suggestive of a newly emerging Australian jurisprudence, in which the High Court will cite its own decisions or decisions of other Australian courts before looking to guidance from English cases. At the same time, recent willingness to cite foreign decisions other than those of English courts, and secondary authorities, signifies a readiness to be open to foreign legal opinion and academic writing in developing a common law suited to Australia's needs.

RUSSELL SMYTH

Further Reading
Anthony Mason, 'Future Directions in Australian Law' (1987) 13 *Mon LR* 149
Russell Smyth, 'Other than "Accepted Sources of Law"? A Quantitative Study of Secondary Source Citations in the High Court' (1999) 22 *UNSWLJ* 19
Paul von Nessen, 'The Use of American Precedents by the High Court of Australia, 1901–1987' (1992) 14 *Adel L Rev* 181

Citizenship, as **Gaudron** reminded us in *Chu Kheng Lim v Minister for Immigration* (1992), is not a constitutional term at all. The use of the concept in Australian law 'is entirely statutory, originating as recently as 1948'. Although the concept 'can be pressed into service for a number of constitutional purposes', it is not 'constitutionally necessary', and has no 'immutable core element' that might ensure its constitutional relevance. Indeed, the term was deliberately omitted from the Australian Constitution. While John Quick was keen to include a reference to national citizenship, **Isaacs** successfully pressed for its omission (see **Framers of the Constitution**).

The absence of any explicit use of the term has been a constraining factor in the High Court's approach to Australian citizenship. The Court has had no constitutional foundation for securing the concept of citizenship held out by **liberalism**, which treats political membership as the source of protection for human rights. Similarly, the plaintiffs in *Kruger v Commonwealth* (1997) were unable to rely on any constitutional foundation in a concept of citizenship. Bereft of any aspirational statement about citizenship, and without a **Bill of Rights**, our Constitution does not guide us in understanding which notions of citizenship apply, and when. Thus, the Court's views on citizenship have mainly been expressed in legislative and **common law** contexts.

Ironically, the Constitution's sole use of the word 'citizen' is in section 44, which disqualifies any 'citizen of a foreign power' from eligibility for Parliament. In *Sue v Hill* (1999), by tracing the gradual transformation of Australia's relationship with the UK, the Court reached the conclusion that for this purpose, Britain is now a 'foreign power' (see **Nationhood**). Gaudron emphasised the change in the meaning and attribution of the status of 'British subject' as the British Empire was transformed into independent nation states with the former British subjects as their citizens. She referred in particular to the effect of the *Nationality and Citizenship Act* 1948 (Cth), now the *Australian Citizenship Act* 1948, and to the statutory removal of the status of 'British subject' in 1987. From that time on, Australians were solely Australian citizens. The decision bestows upon citizenship an important republican dimension, in that the concept of Australian citizenship contributed to the Court's recognition of Australia's independence from Britain.

The Constitution does include terms casting shadowed light on the meaning and shape of Australian citizenship, including 'people of the Commonwealth' (section 24), 'subjects of the Queen' (sections 34 and 117) and 'aliens' (section 51(xix)). The Court's strongest attempt to deal with citizenship has been through section 117, which protects 'a subject of the Queen' resident in any state from **discrimination** in another state on the basis of that out-of-state residence. In *Street v Queensland Bar Association* (1989), **Mason**, though he did not directly address the meaning of citizenship, saw section 117 as designed to enhance 'national unity and a real sense of national identity'. **Brennan** and **Toohey** deemed it unnecessary to determine whether the term 'subject of the Queen' was synonymous with 'Australian citizen', and referred to the **Convention Debates**, where the former expression was consciously chosen in preference to the latter because, as Toohey put it, 'the term "citizen" carried a distinctly republican flavour'. The question both left open was whether there might be 'subjects of the Queen' to whom the protection of section 117 would extend even though they were not Australian 'citizens'. By contrast, **Deane** explicitly employed the word 'citizen', asserting that the purpose of section 117 was to 'protect the citizen resident in one State from being subjected in another State to "disability or discrimination"'. More fundamentally, he saw the section as directed to

the 'promotion of national economic and social cohesion and the establishment of a national citizenship'. Clearly, Deane was implying a concept of Australian citizenship from the Constitution. The equation of citizenship and **equality** was also a theme for **Dawson**, who saw section 117 as intended to ensure that persons from one state were treated in another as citizens of the one nation, not as foreigners.

Among the questions left unresolved by *Street* was that raised by Toohey: 'Whether a person living in Australia, but not a natural born or naturalised Australian citizen, is entitled to the protection accorded by s117 is a matter to be considered when the occasion arises.' When that occasion does arise, the Court will have to determine the difference between the legal status of 'citizen' and the broader notion of 'member of the Australian community'.

Since the legal notion of 'citizenship' in Australia has developed mainly through legislation, the High Court's role has been limited to responses to the legislative schema, themselves largely directed by the Parliament. Most obviously, this issue arises in the context of **immigration law**, and particularly in deportation and detention cases, because of the centrality of 'citizenship' in the *Migration Act* 1958 (Cth). The Court has affirmed the sovereign right of the executive government to determine who is allowed to become a member of the Australian community, and has been reluctant to find constitutional limits on the power to control immigration. This was highlighted particularly in *Chu Kheng Lim*, where the Court affirmed the executive's power to detain non-citizens in contexts where it would have been unconstitutional to detain citizens.

A similar distinction was drawn in *Cunliffe v Commonwealth* (1994), another migration law case, involving a challenge to amendments to the Migration Act, which restricted migration lawyers in providing advice to clients. The challenge rested on **implied constitutional rights**, and in particular on the freedom of **political communication**. Some Justices addressed the question of whether such an implied freedom could be claimed by non-citizens. Only Mason embraced the idea that non-citizens in Australia were entitled to the protection afforded by the Constitution and by the laws of Australia. Relying on *Re Bolton; Ex parte Beane* (1987), he said that non-citizens within Australia were entitled to invoke the implied freedom of communication, 'particularly when they are exercising that freedom for the purpose, or in the course, of establishing their status as entrants and refugees or asserting a claim against government or seeking the protection of the government'. Brennan and Deane, on the other hand, while affirming the right of non-citizens to the protection of the law, distinguished this from the right to invoke the implied constitutional freedom of communication, since the latter was grounded in their view in a concept of **representative government** or representative **democracy**. The limits of that concept meant, for Brennan, that aliens 'have no constitutional right to participate or be consulted on matters of government in the country' and 'the Constitution contains no implications that the freedom is available to aliens who are applying for or who have applied for visas … Nor is there any basis for implying that aliens have a constitutional right'. While Deane accepted part of Mason's argument, and included aliens in the scope of some constitutional protections—such as section 80 (**jury trial**), section 92 (freedom of **interstate trade and commerce**), and section 116 (freedom of religion)—he distinguished rights implied from the concept of representative democracy, concluding that 'any benefit to an alien must be indirect in the sense that it flows from the freedom or immunity of those who are citizens'. The distinction is crucial in highlighting the extent to which the rights of citizenship are viewed as flowing from political membership.

It was for this reason that **McHugh** argued in *Kruger* that residents of the Northern Territory had no constitutional claim to freedoms of association and **movement**, although he was prepared to recognise those freedoms as entailed in political membership. Conversely, Gaudron argued that precisely because the residents of the Territory had a limited political membership they were in need of greater constitutional protection than other Australians.

In *Air Caledonie International v Commonwealth* (1988), the Court affirmed that citizenship provides a person with a right of entry to Australia, stating that 'the right of an Australian citizen to enter the country is not qualified by any law imposing a need to obtain a licence or "clearance" from the Executive'. This is not an **express constitutional right**, and the Court does not indicate from where it believes such a right might be derived. Along with the common law cases mentioned below, such a decision shows the Court developing some 'rights of citizens', though in this instance the right is reserved to legal citizens only. In *Teoh's Case* (1995), in determining the rights of the individual whom the government sought to deport, Gaudron focused on the citizenship status of the deportee's **children**. In her view, 'citizenship carries with it a common law right on the part of the children and their parents to have a child's best interests taken into account, at least as a primary consideration, in all discretionary decisions by governments … directly affecting the child's individual welfare'.

In these migration cases, the distinction between citizens and non-citizens is essential. But in common law cases, the Court has often spoken of 'citizens' rights' in contexts where the person referred to may not be a citizen, but simply an Australian resident.

In **tort law**, the Court has often invoked the concept of citizenship when talking about a person's rights in negligence and trespass cases. In **criminal law**, the terminology of citizenship is often used when common law principles are discussed. This 'citizenship' is invoked in *Mortimer v Brown* (1970) (discussing a person's right to refuse to answer incriminating questions); in *Bunning v Cross* (1978) (where the 'right to immunity from arbitrary and unlawful intrusion into … daily affairs' arose in the context of illegally obtained evidence); and in *Ousley v The Queen* (1997) (discussing the intrusion of listening devices on individual liberty and privacy). In *Clough v Leahy* (1904), **Griffith** asserted that officials asking questions were not exercising a prerogative power, but simply 'a power which every individual citizen possesses'. In *Victoria v Australian Building Construction Employees and BLF* (1982) (on the right of a state to establish a Royal Commission), Griffith's concept was more critically examined, with **Stephen** suggesting rather that often 'the only available safeguard of the citizen' is 'the fair and proper

administration of justice'; but in the *Waanyi Case* (1996), McHugh returned to Griffith's original conception, asserting that the President and Registrar of the **Native Title** Tribunal 'had the common law right of every citizen to ask questions'.

Reference to persons as 'citizens' has also been made in *R v Marks; Ex parte Australian Building Construction Employees* (1981) (on an individual's right to a hearing); and in *Carter v Managing Partner Northmore Hale Davy & Leake* (1995) (where the common law protection of legal professional privilege was also referred to as a 'fundamental right of the citizen'). In all these cases, the reference might more accurately have been to 'persons': the reference is not to any specific legal status, but simply to a rights-bearing person.

The word 'citizenship' is used in popular discourse in vastly different ways. The above examples show that the High Court has also used the term variously. In the constitutional and legislative context, it mainly denotes a strict legal status (contrasted with that of visitors or permanent residents). This is because citizenship has primarily been a statutory concept. In common law cases, however, where the Court is less constrained by legislative parameters, 'citizenship' is used in a broader sense. This may lead one to speculate on what the Court might do if citizenship were recognised in the Constitution. A constitutional concept of citizenship might give the Court more flexibility in using the term in the broader sense of rights-bearing persons, endowed with rights that might extend well beyond the common law.

KIM RUBENSTEIN

Further Reading
John Chesterman and Brian Galligan (eds), *Defining Australian Citizenship: Selected Documents* (1999)
Kim Rubenstein, 'Citizenship in Australia: Unscrambling its Meaning' (1995) 20 *MULR* 503
Kim Rubenstein, 'Citizenship and the Constitutional Convention Debates: A Mere Legal Inference?' (1997) 25 *FL Rev* 295
Kim Rubenstein (ed), *Individual, Community, Nation: 50 Years of Australian Citizenship* (2000)
Kim Rubenstein, *Australian Citizenship Law in Context* (2001)

Civil liberties. In the British **common law** tradition, an emphasis on the legal **sovereignty** of Parliament was combined with a conception of 'civil liberties' as distinct from 'civil rights'. The major task of the High Court, as inheritor of the British tradition, has been to adapt these conceptions to a very different Australian legal system. Essentially, the Court has had to adapt the traditions of the common law to a written and rigid Constitution that establishes a federal system and incorporates a limited number of **express constitutional rights**. More recently, the Court has had to respond to a growing expectation of positive rather than negative rights.

The Court's response to these challenges has been uneven: at times maddeningly conservative, and at times surprisingly innovative. It cannot be described by superficial labels such as 'conservative' or 'liberal'; broadly speaking, it has operated within the grand but cautious tradition of the common law, Australian style. To those concerned with promotion of human rights in the Australian legal system, it has probably been a disappointment. Yet to others it has been a body that has seriously undermined the doctrine of parliamentary supremacy and the traditional protection of **property** rights.

The term 'civil liberties' is not much used nowadays, but it refers essentially to civil and political rights. The word 'liberties', however, denotes rights often described as 'negative'. They provide a 'shield' to protect a person against deprivation of rights, but not a 'sword' by which offending legislation or administrative action may be struck down. The word 'rights', on the other hand, connotes legal enforceability, and usually also a means for claiming compensation for breach.

The common law approach is based on the view that each individual has freedom to do what he or she likes, unless there is a law that prevents the action. 'Common law rights' are therefore, in a sense, residual, and the terminology of rights is a somewhat rhetorical device that judges (or academic writers of textbooks) have invented to make sense of recognised common law **remedies**. For reasons that lie deep in British history, the focus is on what the state, rather than individuals, has done to curtail freedom. If, for example, the claim is of breach of privacy by the government, it is the common law cause of action for trespass or false imprisonment, not the 'right', that gives the remedy. The government and its agents may be restrained from further breaches, but there will be no positive remedy.

How far then has the Court, steeped in the common law tradition, been willing to carry forward the development of common law liberties? The answer is, not very far. The reason lies partly in deference to the legislatures. Thus in *State Government Insurance Commission v Trigwell* (1979), the protection of the freedom of persons to travel on the highway was not extended to cover liability, in Australian conditions, of adjoining owners for damage caused by their straying animals. The majority of the Court considered that changing the inherited common law rule was an action that only the legislatures should take, even though the rule had been developed in very different conditions from those of Australia in the late twentieth century. Though the common law had traditionally protected liberty of the person, the majority of the Court decided as recently as *Halliday v Nevill* (1984) that a person backing a car out of a neighbour's driveway, who chanced to be recognised by the driver of a passing police car as a disqualified driver, could be pursued into the private driveway and arrested there without a warrant, since the police have an implied licence to enter private property for such a purpose. The decision effectively diminished the belief that a citizen's 'home is his castle' (*Entick v Carrington* (1765)). Only **Brennan** dissented, on the grounds that the case was about 'privacy in the home, the garden and the yard', and that no person may trespass on the land of another without clear legal warrant. Again, the Court has not, in the sensitive matter of interrogating and apprehending suspects, been willing to follow the lead of the British Courts (and now Parliament) in adopting the so-called Judges' Rules (*Van der Meer v The Queen* (1988)).

On the other hand, the Court has been adventurous in developing the common law relating to criminal trials. In *Dietrich v The Queen* (1992), it held that a person has a right to a fair trial, and that this entails in serious cases a right to **counsel**, or the trial will not proceed. Although **Mason** and **McHugh** observed that the right is 'more accurately expressed in negative terms as a right not to be tried unfairly or as an immunity against conviction otherwise than after a fair trial', the 'negative' nature of the common law right has to some degree been superseded, since the practical effects of the decision have been that a trial can be avoided rather than simply being declared later to have been ineffective, and that governments have felt obliged to provide substantial additional legal aid funding in cases involving serious criminal charges.

On the whole, the Court has been conservative in developing the common law for the better protection of civil liberties. In any event, much of the common law has today been superseded by legislation. But it still falls to the Court to interpret that legislation, and the rule of **statutory interpretation** that a very clear indication must be given before traditional civil and political rights will be taken to be diminished indicates a certain sensitivity to civil liberties. Sometimes this sensitivity has manifested itself also in **constitutional interpretation**, spectacularly so in the *Communist Party Case* (1951)—certainly in the result (the Court struck down legislation banning the Communist Party), and possibly in the motivation, if not overtly in the reasoning.

In interpreting the few rights expressly included in the Constitution, including section 80 (**jury trial**); section 92 (freedom of **interstate trade and commerce** and intercourse); section 116 (freedom of religion); section 117 (**discrimination** against residents of another state); and section 51(xxxi) (right to just compensation for government **acquisition of property**), the Court might have felt itself free to make generous (rights-extending) interpretations. However, influenced by the negative concept of rights and the doctrine of the supremacy of Parliament, from the beginning the Court gave most of these rights a narrow interpretation.

The early aversion to robust positive rights is partly illustrated by *R v Smithers; Ex parte Benson* (1912), where **Griffith** and **Barton**, although creative in their use of an implied freedom of **movement**, found it appropriate to determine the issue by reference to the common law doctrine of necessity. The question was whether Benson, a resident of Victoria who had served a prison term there and then left for NSW to find work, could be prosecuted under the *Influx of Criminals Prevention Act* 1903 (NSW). Griffith and Barton saw the NSW Act as an exercise of the common law 'police power', though in the end not justified by the doctrine of necessity. The less senior and more liberal-minded Justices, **Isaacs** and **Higgins**, went straight to the Constitution (section 92) and declared the NSW provision inoperative. Isaacs noted that the section 92 freedom is 'absolute'. One can see here the capacity of the Court to begin to use the new Constitution to achieve rights, and the arguably less tendentious basis on which they were able to proceed. On the other hand, this overtly rights-based start was not followed through. Despite the outcome of the *Communist Party Case*, only four Justices (**Latham, Dixon, Fullagar** and **McTiernan**) even mentioned 'civil rights', and all decided the case on abstract constitutional grounds. Only McTiernan made more than a perfunctory reference to rights. (He actually used the term 'civil liberties'.)

In *Krygger v Williams* (1912), the constitutional guarantee of freedom of religion (section 116) was in effect ignored in deference to the *Defence Act* 1903 (Cth). In *Davies and Jones v WA* (1904), the protection against discrimination given by section 117 to out-of-state residents was read down to mean virtually nothing. In *Muramats v Commonwealth Electoral Officer (WA)* (1923), the potential right to vote (section 41) was made simply a historical blip (see also *R v Pearson; Ex parte Sipka* (1983)). In *R v Archdall and Roskruge* (1928), the apparent guarantee of trial by jury in section 80 was in effect rendered extinguishable by Parliament.

The Court has more recently begun to shift, both in the language of rights and in the substance of rights protection. The later section 80 cases have shown a strengthening minority view in favour of higher protection, and in *Cheatle v The Queen* (1993), a requirement of unanimity among jurors was constitutionally enshrined against state legislative provisions permitting majority verdicts. The Court gave a broad interpretation to the meaning of religion in the *Jehovah's Witnesses Case* (1943) and later in *Church of the New Faith v Commissioner of Pay-roll Tax (Vic)* (1983), though the ambit of the right was restricted by a narrow interpretation of the permissible extent of its 'free exercise'. The most rights-recognising decision was in *Street v Queensland Bar Association* (1989), where the Court gave life to section 117, interpreting it as an effective guarantee of substantive **equality**, and thereby introducing to its repertoire a new approach grounded in equality and linked to discrimination law. The Court has sometimes been commended for its recognition of the 'right' to just compensation where the Commonwealth acquires property (section 51(xxxi) of the Constitution). However, the protection given has been limited in various ways. Imbued with the common law regard for the sacred right to property, the Court has interpreted section 51(xxxi) expansively by exposition of the twin concepts of 'acquisition' and 'property'. But it has refrained from extending the guarantee to cover acquisitions by the states with Commonwealth funds (*Pye v Renshaw* (1951)), the exercise of legislative powers other than section 51(xxxi) (*Nintendo v Centronics Systems* (1994)), and the adjustment of competing rights (*Mutual Pools v Commonwealth* (1994)). It has also, by the decision in *Cole v Whitfield* (1988), reversed the earlier rights-based interpretation of section 92 that gave individuals freedom of interstate trade and commerce, although it left open the possibility of more comprehensive protection for the purely personal freedoms of movement and communication that might be covered by the word 'intercourse' in section 92.

The Court's narrow reading of the express constitutional provisions relating to rights has probably stemmed from a variety of causes: the cautious instincts and practices of common law courts; the negative rather than positive conception of rights; the inclusion of only a relatively few, and in some senses random, selection of express rights in the Constitution; and in some cases (such as section 92), the counterbalancing effect of persuasive constitutional arguments against an individual rights focus.

However, the Court has been innovative in reconciling the supremacy of Parliament with the operation of the fundamental provisions of the Constitution. It has developed, by implication from sections 7 and 24, a doctrine of **responsible government** or **representative government** that prevents the executive and legislature from restricting freedom of **political communication**. It has perceived, beyond the formulas used in the late 1890s to embody in the Constitution the

British common law structures, the values lying behind those structures. In interpreting the meaning of the written Constitution, it has converted the common law freedoms to act politically by way of speech, and possibly demonstration, association and assembly, and freedom of movement, into a set of underlying constitutional freedoms. The common law negative freedoms have in effect been transformed into a common law of the Constitution. This new mode of the common law (the implied constitutional freedom) has protected **political parties** from being excluded by legislation from free electoral television (*Australian Capital Television v Commonwealth* (1992): see **Free Speech Cases**) and in principle may protect persons demonstrating on political matters by action rather than words (*Levy v Victoria* (1997)). In *Lange v ABC* (1997), the Court unanimously confirmed this **implied constitutional right** to freedom of political communication, though retreating somewhat from its earlier decision in *Theophanous v Herald & Weekly Times* (1994) to transform aspects of the common law of **defamation** into part of the constitutionalised freedom. These cases show that the Court is capable of applying the written Constitution in a way that, while true to the common law tradition, gives new force to old common law rights.

The legal concept of 'human rights' has, as is appropriate for universal fundamental rights, been developed primarily through **international law** (see **International Bill of Rights**). Three relatively recent cases are of particular significance in the incorporation of international human rights principles into Australian common law. One, ***Mabo*** (1992), can be seen as relating to economic, social and cultural rights; another, *Dietrich*, to civil and political rights. In *Mabo*, the Court established that the common law of Australia recognises the existence of **native title** for indigenous inhabitants. In what has been accepted as the leading judgment in *Mabo*, Brennan noted the importance of the views of the international community, and carefully stated the relevant parameters. On the one hand, 'the common law does not necessarily conform with international law, but international law is a legitimate and important influence on the development of the common law, especially when international law declares the existence of universal human rights'. On the other hand, 'recognition by our common law of the rights and interests in land of the indigenous inhabitants of a settled colony would be precluded if the recognition were to fracture a skeletal principle of our legal system'.

In *Dietrich*, references were made in all the judgments to the right to a fair trial contained in the International Covenant on Civil and Political Rights. However, the Covenant goes further in that it envisages an enforceable right to assistance where a person's means do not otherwise enable representation. Accordingly, the Covenant was not cited as the basis for settling the principle. Here, the Court has struck a compromise between what is in effect an enforceable right and the altogether ineffective decision in the earlier case of *McInnis v The Queen* (1979). But it left unused the key international right, arguably showing greater respect for common law tradition than for the rights of those without means.

In *Teoh's Case* (1995), the respondent claimed protection from deportation by referring to the Convention on the

Rights of the Child, to which Australia is a party. The Convention provides that it is in the child's best interests not to be separated from his or her parents. The Court held if an official decision maker does not intend to observe the Convention, the affected parties should be notified so that they have an opportunity to object. The Court was prepared to mandate only that the matter be reconsidered, not what the outcome should be (except that it be according to law). The negativity of common law remedies, while potentially effective (at least where there is good faith all round), can too easily be found deficient or incomplete.

To establish a wider range of enforceable rights, a first step would be to follow up the developing thinking revealed in *Newcrest Mining v Commonwealth* (1997). In that case, **Kirby** built on earlier pronouncements about the use of international law in cases of ambiguity by Brennan, **Deane** and **Dawson** in *Chu Kheng Lim v Minister for Immigration* (1992); Mason and Deane in *Teoh*; and **Gummow** and **Hayne** in the *Hindmarsh Island Bridge Case* (1998). Kirby suggested that in such cases there be an interpretive principle that would recognise the importance of international law, and particularly human rights law, where constitutional provisions are involved and 'fall short of giving effect to fundamental rights'. He noted that 'the Constitution not only speaks to the people of Australia who made it and accept it for their governance. It also speaks to the international community as the basic law of the Australian nation which is a member of that community'.

A second step would be to introduce a legislative **Bill of Rights**. Although common law doctrines about the supremacy of parliament may prevent the full effectiveness of such a Bill, since the orthodox view is that mere legislation cannot limit the power of a future parliament to legislate inconsistently, the Canadian experience suggests that the orthodox view is not necessarily conclusive. Long before 1982, when the Canadian Charter of Rights and Freedoms was given constitutional force, the purely statutory provisions of the Canadian Bill of Rights 1960 were considered by the Supreme Court of Canada in *R v Drybones* (1969). In a daring decision, the Court allowed the equality provisions of the Bill of Rights to prevail over a later (federal) law discriminating against indigenous Canadians.

Ironically, the majority of the High Court, in *University of Wollongong v Metwally* (1984), took the view that the Parliament could prospectively, but not retrospectively, enact provisions to remove prior section 109 **inconsistency** between its *Racial Discrimination Act* 1975 (Cth) and the *Anti-Discrimination Act* 1977 (NSW). Metwally was accordingly deprived of a Tribunal finding and award in his favour under NSW law. In denying the Commonwealth the capacity to reverse a prior finding of inconsistency between Commonwealth and state law, Deane, for the majority, saw section 109 as in part a guarantee for the citizen against the double application of laws.

A third step would be to recognise that, in the longer term, great issues are at stake. The lessons of the past, the scrutiny of the outside world, the inexorable pressures of globalisation, and the broad sentiment of the Australian people seem likely to combine to encourage the Court to continue on the path of building human rights principles into Australian law.

There is a long way to go, and the fact that international human rights law is itself gender-biased, and in part tilted towards the values and modes of expression of Western democracies, suggests that the way is not necessarily clear. However, the Court may be able to incorporate further human rights standards into the Constitution through a more sympathetic and 'rights-aware' interpretation of the provisions explicit and implicit in the Constitution and in the common law, and through greater use of the rich seams available in international human rights law.

PETER BAILEY

Further Reading
Peter Bailey, *Human Rights: Australia in an International Context* (1990)
Peter Bailey, 'Civil and Political Rights', *Halsbury's Laws of Australia* (1998) title 80
Nick O'Neill and Robin Handley, *Retreat from Injustice: Human Rights in Australian Law* (1994)
George Williams, *Human Rights under the Australian Constitution* (1999)

Civil procedure. The High Court deals with matters of civil procedure both at first instance and on appeal. Section 38 of the *Judiciary Act* 1903 (Cth) imposes an exclusive original **jurisdiction** on the High Court, and it has its own Rules of Court covering these matters. The **High Court Rules** are remarkably antiquated, perhaps because the High Court is not ordinarily a trial court, and proceedings involving contentious issues of fact are nowadays invariably **remitted** to a trial court (*Robinson v Shirley* (1982)).

As an appellate court, the High Court has been relatively less influential in developing policy about civil procedure than it has in other areas of law. The **role** of the appellate court in procedural matters is more restricted than it is in substantive law. Although there is a large volume of civil disputes that could be described as 'procedural', such issues are usually dealt with at the interlocutory stage and judges are generally granted wide discretionary powers. The role of an appellate court in this context is limited to reviewing the exercise of discretion to determine whether it has miscarried (*Adam Brown Male Fashions v Philip Morris* (1981); *House v The King* (1936)). Interestingly, the intermediate appellate courts have decided many of the influential precedents in Australian procedural law. The special **leave** requirements of the High Court may now create a particular incentive for parties to focus on substantive issues.

However, as the final appellate court, the High Court has played an important role in the development of principles for the evolution of procedural law, and has had an opportunity to reflect on the wider issues that arise in this context. This role is accompanied by responsibilities to mediate the relationship between the courts and the parties, to balance the rights and interests of parties to litigation, and to show leadership in effecting change in procedural law.

As far as mediating the relationship between the courts and the parties is concerned, until the 1980s the High Court, and Australian courts generally, favoured an adversarial model of civil litigation in which control of the process rested with the parties, particularly the plaintiff. This approach is demonstrated by decisions of the Court dealing with discovery (*Mulley v Manifold* (1959)) and with summary judgment (*General Steel Industries v Commissioner for Railways (NSW)* (1964)).

However, by the mid-1980s, the failure of trial courts to curtail the adversarial behaviour of litigants had led to chronic delays and calls for strict caseflow management. Although caseflow management confronts the traditional adversarial model by requiring courts to control the progress of litigation, judges adapted quickly and favourably to the new regime. However, ardent implementation of caseflow management challenges notions of individual justice. The Court in two decisions has acknowledged that both of these demands are legitimate. In *Sali v SPC* (1993), it was recognised that a court is entitled to consider the effect of a request for adjournment on court resources and on other litigants waiting in the court lists as well as the interests of the parties. However, in *Queensland v JL Holdings* (1997), the Court held that justice is the paramount consideration. While case management is a relevant consideration, it should not prevail over proper adjudication of issues between the parties.

Zealous reformers such as Justice David Ipp of the Supreme Court of WA condemned *JL Holdings* as a 'major limitation to reform' and considered that it would be 'hailed by some with the enthusiasm akin to that displayed by the supporters of Louis XVIII when the Bourbon king re-entered Paris'. Although some practitioners may truly 'yearn for a less demanding time when efficiency and professionalism were not at an optimum', the High Court's assertion of the pivotal role of individual justice was critical to the reform process.

As is inherent in civil procedural law, the High Court has also had to balance the interests of the plaintiff and defendant. The Court has at times striven to maintain this fine balance against the upheaval in procedural law caused by short-term legislative change.

This difficulty is clearly demonstrated by the law of limitations—statutes that set down strict time frames within which cases must be commenced. Limitation law is highly susceptible to legislative tinkering. Traditionally the Court interpreted the limitation legislation formally and strictly. However, the strict interpretation caused grave injustice in cases where a plaintiff suffered from latent disease, as the plaintiff's right to commence proceedings might be barred before the plaintiff was aware of the disease. The statutes contained clumsy provisions that allowed an extension in limited circumstances. The Court wrestled with these statutes to attempt to provide justice to plaintiffs (*Do Carmo v Ford Excavations* (1984)).

A rise in the number of cases involving dust disease such as asbestosis caused state legislatures to amend the statutes to provide more flexibility and judicial discretion. But after the passage of the new provisions, the balance swung to the plaintiff, and the lower courts became increasingly permissive in allowing plaintiffs to extend the limitation periods. The High Court arrested this trend in *Brisbane South Regional Health Authority v Taylor* (1996), thereby reinstating the integrity of the legislative decree. But opportunistic applications for special leave on limitation matters continued, especially from NSW. This led **Gummow** to comment that the Court 'has set its face somewhat against … dealing

with issues arising out of the New South Wales limitation legislation' (*Nominal Defendant v Warren* (1998)).

During the same period, the Court attempted to preserve the conceptual integrity of limitation law against short-term legislative measures designed to discourage forum shopping (for example, sections 55–57 of the Limitation Act (ACT)) (see *McKain v Miller* (1991), *Gardner v Wallace* (1995), and *Commonwealth v Mewett* (1997)), although it ultimately retreated from the challenge in *John Pfeiffer v Rogerson* (2000).

On the demerit side, the expedient operation of the statutory rules on service of process was delayed for many years by an indeterminate decision in *Laurie v Carroll* (1958), and an effective system to conduct litigation in a federal system was struck down in *Re Wakim* (1999) (see **Cross-vesting**). Further, despite several attempts (*Grant v Downs* (1976) and *Esso v Commissioner of Taxation* (1999)), the Court has failed to develop an effective conceptual framework to analyse legal professional privilege. Finally, in *John Pfeiffer v Rogerson*, the Court potentially unhinged the entire operation of procedural law by declaring, in a statement that was wider than was necessary for the immediate context of choice of law in **conflict of laws**, that all 'laws that bear upon the existence, extent or enforceability of remedies, rights and obligations should be characterised as substantive and not as procedural laws'. A general conversion of procedural law into substantive law would disrupt the fundamental underpinning of civil procedure, challenging procedural concepts such as caseflow management, the power to punish for **contempt**, and the inherent jurisdiction of **superior courts**. From a practical perspective, the plaintiff bears the burden of proof of matters of substantive law. So, for example, the plaintiff would need to affirmatively prove compliance with limitation statutes rather than relying on the defendant to raise the issue, and must do so without recourse to **estoppel** or waiver (*Commonwealth v Verwayen* (1990)). Placing this obligation upon the plaintiff will invite confusion about the nature of the 'substantive right' held by the plaintiff where the limitation statute has expired, even if the statute grants the discretionary power to the court to extend the limitation period.

The High Court has played a role in encouraging innovation in procedural law, encouraging, in particular, judges in lower courts to embrace change. The most striking example is *Carnie v Esanda Finance* (1995), where a group of farmers sought to bring a class action in the Supreme Court of NSW. The NSW Court of Appeal held that such a claim was impermissible in the absence of detailed legislative prescription. By contrast, the High Court held that the existing Supreme Court Rules could sustain the action, and that it was important to do so in order to facilitate the administration of justice. The *Carnie* decision was instrumental in developing both the doctrine and the jurisprudence of class actions in Australia.

However, no such leadership was demonstrated when the High Court refused to grant special leave in *Qantas Airways v Cameron* (1996), another group proceeding. In that case the Full **Federal Court** had held that the applicants could not rely on their public interest purpose as a reason to avoid liability for **costs**, since **damages** were being sought in the private interests of the group members. Arguably, the damages sought were minimal, and conducive to the principal aim of establishing a duty to the public based in negligence. In a subsequent decision (*Oshlack v Richmond River Council* (1998)), the High Court upheld an exercise of discretion by which the NSW Land and Environment Court had relieved a plaintiff who was pursuing public interest litigation of liability for costs. The issue of costs in class actions is important from both practical and public interest viewpoints.

In *Levy v Victoria* (1997), **Brennan** and **Kirby** took the opportunity to encourage participation by third parties in litigation as **interveners and *amici curiae***. In carefully considered judgments, they encouraged intervention by third parties where their rights were directly affected. Kirby went further and recognised that perceptions of the judicial role have evolved to a point where the declaratory theory of judgment is no longer unquestioningly accepted (see **Law-making role**). He stated that courts have unavoidable choices in determining the law, and that the assistance of *amici* and interveners should therefore be encouraged. Whether the **Gleeson Court** will adhere to that attitude seems less clear.

PETA SPENDER

Further Reading

Mark Aronson and Jill Hunter, *Litigation: Evidence and Procedure* (6th edn 1998)

Australian Law Reform Commission, *Managing Justice: A Review of the Federal Civil Justice System*, Report No 89 (1999)

Bernard Cairns, *Australian Civil Procedure* (5th edn 2001)

Stephen Colbran et al., *Civil Procedure* (1998)

Cold War is the term commonly used to describe the dominant geopolitical condition in the second half of the twentieth century. Originating in the Bolshevik Revolution of 1917, it flared up after the allied victory in 1945 and, through a series of irreconcilable conflicts, escalated to global proportions, thus fundamentally reordering international power relationships. Its causes, still hotly debated, included the inability of the Soviet Union and the Western powers led by the USA to effect the cooperative reconstruction of devastated Europe, the West's fear of global communist expansionism, and traditional Russian insecurity about vulnerability to attack from the east. It divided Germany, and produced instability in western Europe and the Mediterranean, the extension of Soviet hegemony in eastern Europe, an arms race, and fluctuating fears of a world war involving atomic weapons. Tensions abated with *détente* in the 1970s, but increased in the 'Star Wars' anti-missile weapons phase in the 1980s. Ending with the Soviet bloc's collapse in 1989, the Cold War influenced the development of Australian law and the work of the High Court.

Australia's Cold War involvement underwent a change with the Chifley Labor government's defeat in 1949. This reflected the rivalry between, and the contrasting temperaments and ideas of, two highly gifted and ambitious lawyer-politicians, **Evatt** and Robert **Menzies**, each intimately connected with the High Court.

Evatt's commitment to the UN, his singular determination to play a decisive international role as External Affairs Minister, and his undulating attitudes to communism, foreign and domestic, provoked a rupture in Australia–US relations cul-

minating, in 1948, in an embargo on supplying Australia with classified military information. Washington's perception that the Australian government was 'soft on communism' and a security risk persisted—notwithstanding Chifley's establishment in 1949, at Westminster's behest, of the Australian Security Intelligence Organisation (ASIO). Evatt's participation in controversies about Australian communism reached back to his days as **counsel** in *Ex parte Walsh and Johnson; In re Yates* (1925), and as a member of the Court in *R v Hush; Ex parte Devanny* (1932) and the *Kisch Case* (1934).

For Menzies, Australia's survival in a deteriorating world situation demanded unequivocal resistance to Soviet aggression and subversion, loyal support for the UK, and a defence treaty with the USA (1951). Menzies participated in the *Kisch* episode, which originated in his attempt as **Attorney-General** to prevent the entry of left-wing speakers into Australia for a peace conference. In 1940, he went on to ban the Communist Party of Australia (CPA)—a ban lifted by Evatt in 1942. His anti-communism, driven, as it typically is, by a loathing of socialist regimentation, of the **ideology** of class struggle, and of atheism, along with a fear of Russian world conquest, led him to denounce the CPA as a treacherous integer of the Moscow-controlled worldwide communist apparatus. By 1948, Menzies was part of a mounting chorus of demands for the outlawing of the CPA.

Unlike the **United States Supreme Court**, which became enmeshed in controversies about the constitutional rights of communists and suspected communists arising out of the hysteria fanned by the eponymous Senator Joseph McCarthy, the High Court was only occasionally drawn into the Australian anti-communist crusade. It was, however, no less an arbiter of the political freedom of Australians.

Chief Justice **Latham**, long a political scourge of the CPA, remained a committed anti-communist. **McTiernan**, a former state and federal parliamentarian for the Australian Labor Party (ALP), was supportive of Chifley's interventionist post-war reconstruction reforms, but like **Rich**, **Starke**, **Williams** and **Webb**, had no sympathy for communism. Similarly unsympathetic, **Dixon** was, like Latham, no stranger to behind-the-scenes politicking. Exposed to international power politics as Australian Minister in Washington (1942–44) and UN mediator in the Kashmir dispute (1950), Dixon maintained close contacts with Menzies, influential world figures including US Secretary of State Dean Acheson, and local diplomatic and military circles. Dixon acted as a sounding board for, and provided inside information to, Frederick Shedden, the Defence Department Secretary, on the eve of Shedden's departure for Washington in 1949 on what proved to be an unsuccessful mission to lift the US embargo.

The Cold War atmosphere encouraged constitutional litigation and the Court thwarted Chifley's legislative controls on transportation, pharmaceutical services, and banking (*Australian National Airways v Commonwealth* (1945); the *Pharmaceutical Benefits Cases* (1945 and 1949); the *Melbourne Corporation Case* (1947)). Chifley's announcement in 1947 of nationalisation of the private banks, branded by conservatives as a step along the path to communism, produced the first of two major Cold War constitutional contests. With **Barwick** leading the banks' attack, Attorney-General Evatt defending, and McTiernan and Latham dissenting, the Court (whose decision the **Privy Council** affirmed (1949)) invalidated the legislation (*Bank Nationalisation Case* (1948)). Henceforth, section 92 of the Constitution would stand as a bulwark against Labor's socialisation objective (see **Interstate trade and commerce**).

International tensions worsened throughout 1947. In 1948, a Soviet-backed coup succeeded in Czechoslovakia, a communist insurgency commenced in Malaya, and, in a ruthless show of strength, the Soviet Union instituted a land blockade of Berlin that lasted until mid-1949. By that year's end, the Soviets had detonated their first atomic device and the communist People's Republic of China (PRC) was proclaimed. In June 1950, communist North Korea invaded South Korea and PRC forces followed in December. Australia swiftly committed forces to the UN response.

Amid intensifying controversy about the political legitimacy of Australian communism, the Court upheld the imprisonment for sedition of senior CPA officials who had been induced to state, hypothetically, that Australian workers would welcome 'liberating' Soviet forces entering Australia. The appeal in *Burns v Ransley* (1949) was dismissed by a **tied vote** with Dixon and McTiernan dissenting; in *R v Sharkey* (1949) only Dixon dissented. In *R v Taylor; Ex parte Federated Ironworkers Association* (1949), the Court sustained the validity of the *National Emergency (Coal Strike) Act* 1949 (Cth), which Evatt had swiftly secured to crush the long and debilitating CPA-inspired coal miners' strike.

In 1950, **Fullagar** and **Kitto** replaced Starke and Rich. In the other great Cold War constitutional case—with Evatt again pitted against Barwick—the Court (Latham dissenting) invalidated the *Communist Party Dissolution Act* 1950 (Cth). Evatt was at the forefront of the narrow defeat of the subsequent referendum intended by Menzies to reverse the Court's decision (1951). Latham, on the other hand, advised Menzies on the conduct of the government's referendum campaign. The majority decision in the High Court depended primarily on a restricted **positivist** conception of the **defence power**; but it also involved a rejection of Menzies' claim that, by the device of deeming the country to be at war, Parliament could outlaw persons allegedly pledged to destroy **democracy** (*Communist Party Case* (1951)).

Yet, in *Marcus Clark v Commonwealth* (1952)—ironically a case about economic controls—the Court by a majority (Williams and Kitto dissenting) deferred to Menzies' claim of an unmistakable danger of world war by the end of 1953 in upholding the validity of a central provision of the *Defence Preparations Act* 1951 (Cth) which, like the 1950 Act, contained a chilling preamble reciting Australia's determination to resist international (that is, communist) aggression.

By the end of 1953, when the 1951 Act ceased to operate, there was an uneasy Korean War armistice, and the threat of world war was receding, as was the Court's immediate impact on the domestic Cold War. Although enjoying minuscule electoral success, the CPA exerted considerable influence over the union movement. The Court effectively monitored this influence through its regular supervision of the Commonwealth Court of **Conciliation and Arbitration**, notably curbing the CPA in cases concerning court-supervised union elections (*R v Commonwealth Court of Conciliation and Arbitration; Ex parte Federated Clerks Union* (1950);

Federated Ironworkers Association v Commonwealth (1951)), and in confining union attempts to restrict management decision making (*Melbourne Tramways Cases* (1965–67)). It sustained a leading communist union official's imprisonment for **contempt** of the lower court (*R v Taylor; Ex parte Roach* (1951)), and decided two minor cases involving CPA-related protest activities (*Waters v Commonwealth* (1951); *Clements v Bull* (1953)).

Fear of Soviet espionage—an abiding Cold War preoccupation—was most dramatically manifested when Vladimir Petrov, a Soviet spy operating under diplomat cover, defected in Canberra in 1954. The ensuing bitter clash between Menzies and the increasingly erratic Evatt hastened the latter's unravelling. Dixon declined Menzies' invitation to conduct the ensuing Royal Commission into Espionage, but in letters to Viscount Simonds he revealed his continuing close political proximity to Menzies and fierce partisan opposition to Evatt, some of whose staff were implicated in Petrov's espionage revelations. The Court became involved when a prominent communist unsuccessfully sought to prevent enforcement of a Commission subpoena issued to him (*Lockwood v Commonwealth* (1954)).

The presiding Commissioner, **Owen**, was appointed to the Court in 1961, as was senior counsel assisting the Commission, **Windeyer**, in 1958. **Barwick**, who had represented ASIO in the Commission, succeeded Dixon as **Chief Justice** in 1964. In 1960, as Commonwealth Attorney-General, he had introduced controversial amendments to the *Crimes Act* 1914 (Cth)—amendments designed primarily to combat the CPA.

The Petrov affair precipitated a disastrous split in the ALP (1954–55) and its affiliated trade union movement. This led to an appeal in a *cause célèbre*, *Williams v Hursey* (1959), involving two union supporters of the breakaway movement known initially as the ALP (Anti-communist) and later as the Democratic Labor Party. In its latter guise, it was long to vex the ALP by capturing Senate seats, thus provoking several **electoral law** cases (*Kane v McClelland* (1962); *Re Lack; Ex parte McManus* (1965); *Cole v Lacey* (1965)). Accusations of communist perfidy or affiliations prompted several **defamation** appeals (*Uren v John Fairfax & Sons* (1966); *Australian Consolidated Press v Uren* (1966); *Turner v Bulletin Newspaper* (1974)).

The construction of the Berlin Wall in 1961 gave the East-West divide menacingly concrete form, and in 1962 the Cuban missile crisis heightened anxiety about nuclear war. Despite the CPA's fragmentation in the wake of the Sino-Soviet split in 1961, communism was still portrayed as imperilling Australian democracy. Much later, the registration of a militant union with a pro-Peking leadership was cancelled (*R v Winneke; Ex parte Gallagher* (1982); *R v Ludeke; Ex parte Australian Building Construction Employees and BLF* (1985)). Three decades after *Roach*, a majority of the Court, **Murphy** dissenting vigorously, rejected an appeal against the union leader's conviction for contempt of court stemming from his rhetorical assertion that the **Federal Court** had succumbed to union pressure in deciding a case (*Gallagher v Durack* (1983)).

The reintroduction of conscription and opposition to Australian participation in the Vietnam War generated a series of unsuccessful challenges to decisions under the

National Service Act 1951–64 (Cth) (*R v District Court; Ex parte White* (1966); *R v District Court; Ex parte Thompson* (1968); *Collett v Loane* (1966); *Zarb v Kennedy* (1968); *Giltinan v Lynch* (1971)), and, perhaps surprisingly, only one case on the right to demonstrate, *Samuels v Stokes* (1973).

Placed under the command of a military officer in 1950, ASIO was dedicated to systematic covert anti-communism. The Court deferred to the Commonwealth's absolute determination to shield the national security apparatus from public gaze and **judicial review** (*Commonwealth v John Fairfax & Sons and Walsh* (1980); *Church of Scientology v Woodward* (1982); *Alister v The Queen* (1984)). In the last two cases, Murphy—who, as Attorney-General in the **Whitlam** government, had controversially exerted his authority over ASIO—again dissented vigorously. However, deference was limited, and when the foreign espionage agency, the Australian Secret Intelligence Service (ASIS), spectacularly bungled a training exercise, the Court declined to prevent disclosure of the ASIS participants' identities to the Victoria Police, whose concern was that criminal offences had been committed (*A v Hayden* (1984)).

At the Cold War's end, the Court rejected the UK government's attempt to suppress ex-MI5 agent Peter Wright's book, *Spycatcher* (1987) (*Spycatcher Case* (1988)), and began reviewing refugee status cases involving PRC citizens complaining about the communist regime's human rights record (*Chan v Minister for Immigration* (1989); *Applicant A v Minister for Immigration* (1997)). Well after the domestic Cold War had passed, there was a faint echo of earlier controversies about toleration of radical political dissent in the Court's disposition of a free speech claim by a notable Marxist agitator of the 1960s (*Langer v Commonwealth* (1996)).

Laurence W Maher

Further Reading

Michael Kirby, 'HV Evatt, The Anti-Communist Referendum and Liberty in Australia' (1991) 7 *Aust Bar Rev* 93

Clem Lloyd, 'Not Peace but a Sword! The High Court under JG Latham' (1987) 11 *Adel L Rev* 175

Laurence W Maher, 'Tales of the Overt and the Covert: Judges and Politics in Early Cold War Australia' (1993) 21 *FL Rev* 151

George Williams, 'Reading the Judicial Mind: Appellate Argument in the *Communist Party Case*' (1993) 15 *Syd LR* 3

George Winterton, 'The Significance of the *Communist Party* Case' (1992) 18 *MULR* 630

Cole v Whitfield (1988). When David Wayne Whitfield, operations manager of the Boomer Park Crayfish Farm in southern Tasmania, was charged under Tasmanian law in January 1983 with being in possession of 60 male and 37 female undersized crayfish, he probably had no idea that his litigation would lead to one of the greatest upheavals of **constitutional law** in the history of the High Court.

The so-called 'Everett defence' was no longer open to him—that loophole had been closed by legislation. (Former Tasmanian **Attorney-General** and **Federal Court** Justice Mervyn Everett had once, as a young barrister, argued successfully for a defendant in a similar position that, if the crayfish were measured from end to end, not in a straight line but along the humps and ridges, they were not actually undersized.) Instead, Whitfield pulled out a constitutional thunderbolt: since the crayfish had been brought in from SA (where, with faster growth to maturity in warmer waters, the required minimum size was smaller, so possession of the same crayfish in that state was lawful), he argued before an unsuspecting magistrate that he was protected by section 92 of the Constitution. Section 92 provides that 'trade commerce and intercourse among the States … shall be absolutely free'.

The magistrate, doing the best he could with an impossibly confused area of the law (see **Interstate trade and commerce**), acquitted Whitfield. That would normally have been the end of the matter. Somewhat unusually, however, the Crown appealed against the acquittal. The case was subsequently **removed** from the Supreme Court of Tasmania into the High Court.

Then followed the usual **procedure** by which the Attorneys-General of all Australian jurisdictions consider, as is their right under the *Judiciary Act* 1903 (Cth), whether or not to **intervene**. Sensing that the case might be a suitable vehicle to ask the High Court for a major review of the law relating to section 92, the Attorneys-General of all of the states and of the Commonwealth decided to intervene.

The sensing mechanisms of the Attorneys-General, or rather of their advisers and advocates, primarily the **Solicitors-General**, were right. The stars were in the right constellation. The diversity of opinion on the Court had become extreme. Academic commentary had developed into a crescendo of **criticism**. There were two new Justices (**Toohey** and **Gaudron**). **Mason**, latterly himself a critic of the state of the law, had become **Chief Justice** and might be expected to exert some intellectual leadership. Most importantly, the nub of the criticism was not merely that the law was confused; it was that the Court had, for most of the century, gone down a fundamentally wrong track by detaching the interpretation of section 92 from its intended purpose of preventing state protectionism.

The case was vulnerable to disposal on narrow grounds. There were technicalities surrounding the capacity of the Crown to appeal against an acquittal. There was an issue as to the existence and sufficiency of transactions constituting interstate trade. But, after some initial wavering from Victoria, which was attracted to the second of the narrow grounds, and Tasmania, which was inclined to want to keep alive some of the old law on section 92, the Solicitors-General grasped the nettle and decided to present a united front in asking the Court to abandon the old law and to substitute a test of validity that turned on the presence or absence of protectionism.

With all the planning and precision of a military campaign, the states and the Commonwealth (usually on opposite ends of the Bar table) divided up the tasks for the major assault. SA would focus on the drafting history of section 92. NSW would elaborate on the comparative position in the USA. The Commonwealth, for its part, would prepare a comprehensive list of every decided case on section 92 and indicate how each would or might have been decided on the new approach. Amidst all this firepower, and overshadowed by the importance of the case, Whitfield cut a lonely figure. He could, however, take comfort from the fact that, as his case had metamorphosed into a test case with much wider significance, the Crown had agreed not to persist with the prosecution should its appeal be successful.

The appeal was successful. Ironically, so too was Whitfield. Excused from the prosecution that should in theory have followed the reversal of the magistrate's decision, he soon afterwards expanded his thriving business to supply gourmet seafoods up and down the east coast of Australia. More importantly, in a unanimous decision handed down on 3 May 1988, the Court overturned nearly a hundred years of case law and made a fresh start to the interpretation of section 92 along the lines submitted by the Solicitors-General.

The Court held that, henceforth, only discriminatory laws of a protectionist kind would infringe section 92. The constitutional history, presented so ably by SA Solicitor-General John Doyle, was compelling. The earlier cases had proceeded on incorrect principles (though whether some or all of them were wrongly decided—an issue the Court did not engage—depended on how the new law would have applied to their particular facts: an imponderable that would in many cases require an investigation that had never been undertaken). The old 'individual right' theory, and necessarily with it such landmark decisions as the *Bank Nationalisation Case* (1948), was swept away.

Only two brief paragraphs at the end of a long judgment were devoted to actually applying the new test of validity to the crayfish law—almost as if the Court had run out of energy after its groundbreaking elaboration of the reasons for a fresh start. The law was upheld, though on the basis of a brief agreed statement of facts rather than a comprehensive factual inquiry. The law did not give local crayfish a competitive or market edge. Even if it had, the hint was (anticipating a line of reasoning explained more fully, though not applied successfully, in *Castlemaine Tooheys v SA* (1990)) that the law was appropriate and adapted to the pursuit of a non-protectionist object—in this case, the need for effective law enforcement—and was not disproportionate to the achievement of that object. In order to conserve local stocks, the law needed, strictly, to apply only to the possession of Tasmanian crayfish; but as fisheries inspectors would find it impossible to distinguish crayfish according to their state of origin, the law was appropriately applied to the possession in Tasmania of any undersized crayfish.

The decision in *Cole v Whitfield* does not represent the end of difficulty in the interpretation of section 92, but rather a new, and sensible, beginning. It was a significant achievement by the Court to jettison the baggage of the past and to make a new start with a single voice. It is probably no coincidence that, since *Cole v Whitfield*, there has been a dramatic drop in the volume of section 92 litigation.

Cole v Whitfield also marked the beginning of a new willingness on the part of the Court to allow reference in argument to a broader range of historical materials (see **Convention debates**; **History**). This has had an impact on **constitutional interpretation** well beyond the result of the case itself.

MICHAEL COPER

Further Reading
Michael Coper, *The Curious Case of the Callow Crayfish: The New Law Relating to Section 92 of the Australian Constitution*

(1989–90), Discussion Paper No 1, Legislative Research Service, Department of the Parliamentary Library
Michael Coper, 'Section 92 of the Australian Constitution Since *Cole v Whitfield*' in HP Lee and George Winterton (eds), *Australian Constitutional Perspectives* (1992) 129

Collective responsibility. The strong tradition of judicial **independence** is the source both of the High Court's strength and arguably of its greatest weakness. Although its decisions often give rise to public controversy and sometimes attract strong **criticism**, the independence of the Court from other arms of government is not seriously questioned. Less attention has, however, been focused on the independence of the Justices from each other. Misplaced emphasis on independence in this sense may detract from the Court's **role** as a **law-making** institution.

The Court's role extends beyond settling particular disputes. Its reasons establish legal principles that bind other courts. It declares the law for Australia. When the Court issues a single judgment, or even a single majority judgment, the outcome of a case, and the law emerging from it, will generally be clear. Frequently, however, the Court's view is expressed in a multiplicity of judgments (see **Joint judgments and separate judgments**). Yet apart from the Court's formal **orders**, it is only rarely that the Court itself or the members of the Court will indicate or explain the combined effect of multiple judgments. In this respect, the Court has failed to recognise its role as a law-making institution and thus its responsibility to make a clear and intelligible statement of the law.

The potential problems with multiple judgments are many. Separate judgments may reach similar conclusions for different reasons. Individual Justices may not address arguments on which other Justices rely. Personal writing styles vary. Judgments may use different language, different expressions, and different emphases, without reference to the other judgments and without explanation of whether differences of substance are intended. The difficulty of extracting a clear *ratio decidendi* is compounded. And separate statements of the facts may give rise to uncertainty about whether different conclusions turn on different views of the facts. In cases where multiple judgments create acute and avoidable uncertainty, the administration of the law is brought into disrepute.

There is a strong case for saying that the members of the Court should see themselves as having a collective **accountability**, as an institution, for the Court's law-making function, and thus as being accountable not only for their individual judgments but also for the combined effect of their judgments. It is in the public interest that lower courts, legal advisers and the community be able readily to ascertain the legal principles established by the Court's decisions. Arguably, this requires appropriate identification and explanation of differences between the members of the Court. The Justices may have given too much weight to their independence from each other. It is one thing to reach independent conclusions; it is another thing to write judgments in isolation.

It does not follow that members of the Court should not write individual judgments. At the highest appellate level there is value to the community in the identification of different lines of thought. Differences in judicial thinking at the highest level should not be subsumed in the compromises that are sometimes necessary to secure agreement to joint judgments. Justices who **concur** in a judgment written by another may not subject the reasoning to the same careful scrutiny as they would their own. Significant differences in judicial philosophy and **judicial reasoning** should not be hidden. Indeed, the High Court owes much of its undoubted status to the richness of the independent thought of its Justices. These are not, however, arguments against coordination. Genuine differences between judgments can and should be identified and explained.

Two particular situations warrant special mention. First, in the area of **criminal law**, there is special need for certainty. Trial judges need clarity in the legal principles from which they draw their directions to juries. Secondly, at the highest appellate level there should rarely be occasion for multiple statements of the facts.

The frequency of multiple judgments in the High Court may be contrasted with the pattern in the intermediate courts of appeal—the **Federal Court**, the Family Court, and the **state Supreme Courts**. In many of these, a strong culture of joint judgments has developed. Often, arrangements are made for the preparation of a first or leading judgment. Other judges who agree will generally avoid writing separate judgments. Where they are in substantial but not complete agreement, they will often supplement the first judgment with a separate judgment dealing only with areas of difference. Articulation of difference in this way may achieve greater clarity than an entirely separate judgment.

Implementation of the principle of collective responsibility of the Court as an institution would require a higher level of communication between Justices than has often appeared to be the case (see **Conferences; Personal relations**). There may be advantage in consultation to identify issues and areas of agreement and disagreement prior to writing judgments. Whether or not such a practice is adopted, individual reasons for judgments would need to be circulated in draft form. Justices who have prepared individual judgments would need to consider whether differences in expression reflect substantive differences. Individual judgments might need revision—for example, to align terminology, to clarify the significance of different terminology, or to identify and explain substantive differences. An agreed 'addendum' by the Court, explaining the combined effect of the judgments, might be appropriate. In some cases, albeit rare, it might be appropriate for such an addendum to state explicitly that no single view of the applicable legal principle commands a majority. Coordination of this kind is consistent with judicial independence and very much in the public interest. Reduction of uncertainty would enhance the standing of the Court.

All this would have resource implications. Workload pressures would be increased. At times when the Justices are widely scattered, travel costs might be increased. (Those increases might be avoided, however, if the 'Canberra allowance' were paid only to Justices who established permanent homes in Canberra, rather than to those who live elsewhere, as is now the case.)

Greater recognition of the principle of collective responsibility would not require deference of any one member of the Court to any other member or members. It would, however, require recognition, by all of the Justices, of the Court's law-making function, and of the need to clarify the precise effect of the Court's decision—whether in a separate statement on behalf of the Court (as in the *Tasmanian Dam Case* (1983)), or by the inclusion of a summary in the judgment of the **Chief Justice** (as in *Mabo* (1992) and *Dietrich v The Queen* (1992)) or of the senior majority Justice (as in *Wik* (1996)). These examples represent a welcome initiative.

Development of collegiate or institutional responsibility might not come easily to individual Justices. Prior professional practice as **counsel** is likely to have inculcated an individualistic approach. Perceptions of judicial independence may enhance an already entrenched individualistic culture. But that culture fails to give adequate recognition to the institutional role and law-making function of the Court. The notion of collective responsibility would not override or displace the duty of each Justice to bring his or her own mind to bear on each case and to reach his or her own decision. It would merely require that the final expression of opinion of each Justice should acknowledge and respond to the opinions of each of the others and be presented on a coordinated basis. The public interest in the administration of justice would be enhanced without any diminution of judicial independence.

ERNST WILLHEIM

Colonialism, a term initially used by the citizens of an imperial power to disparage settler populations, acquired widespread currency after **World War II** as a label for the tendency of the settler populations themselves to disparage and exploit indigenous peoples. In the postwar decolonisation movements, particularly in the former French colonies, 'colonialism' was a powerful conceptual tool for analysing the relationship between colonisers and colonised—perhaps most vividly in Aimé Césaire's version of *The Tempest*, which interpreted the relationship between Prospero and Caliban in these terms (*Une Tempête* (1969)). In this modern usage, 'colonialism' has 'the derogatory sense of an alleged policy of exploitation of backward or weak peoples by a large power' (*Oxford English Dictionary*). In Australia, this 'policy' was implemented by European settlers, and had a legal impact on indigenous peoples on the mainland of Australia, in the Torres Strait and in the Territories of **Papua and New Guinea** (while under Australian control).

Closely linked with the White Australia Policy for most of the twentieth century, colonialism both emphasised and sought to eliminate the cultural differences of the indigenous populations from the European (usually Anglo-Celtic) population. Administered by the use of force and combined with the writing of history from the perspective of the 'white man', it operated to silence and make invisible the experiences of the indigenous populations in Australia. The law was pervasively complicit in the process—denying Aboriginal **sovereignty**, supporting dispossession through the doctrine of *terra nullius*, and maintaining a protectionist regime of subordination and dependency for indigenous peoples.

Ironically, the most eloquent expression of colonialist attitudes in the High Court came from **Dixon** in the *Kisch Case* (1934). Although he reached a liberal outcome as far as Egon Kisch was concerned, he did so by holding that Scottish Gaelic is not a European language, noting that:

the remnant of people who speak this language is fast diminishing … In a modern community it has not been found a practicable medium for carrying on the affairs of daily life … It is a speech which probably contains a vocabulary ill-fitted to deal with modern conditions. It is spoken by a people who appear to lead somewhat special lives, and do not move about and mix in the general life of the whole community of Great Britain.

That English colonial attitudes towards the Scots had survived the Act of Union in 1701 is notorious; and if Dixon, always an Anglophile, shared such attitudes, that may merely reflect his cultural heritage.

Implicit in **Isaacs'** judgment in *R v Bernasconi* (1915), that the constitutional guarantee of **jury trial** (section 80 of the Constitution; see **Express constitutional rights**) did not extend to the territory of Papua, was the attitude that 'the population, … whether German or Polynesian', was too inferior to warrant protection by the superior British system. Cruder perceptions of indigenes in New Guinea were apparent in **Starke's** judgment in *Cranssen v The King* (1936), where Cranssen, a Roman Catholic priest, appealed against the severity of a sentence of five years imprisonment with hard labour for burning three native dwellings. The alleged arson arose from a history of rivalry between Roman Catholic and Lutheran missionaries. In a joint judgment, Dixon, **Evatt** and **McTiernan** found the sentence manifestly excessive, and reduced it to six months imprisonment. Starke agreed that it should be reduced, but only from five years to two. His central concern appeared to be for consistency in sentencing—especially, it seems, when sectarian implications were involved. A few days earlier, in *Foege v The King* (1936), where a Lutheran missionary had been sentenced to two years imprisonment for 'unlawfully depriving an uncivilised native of his personal liberty by holding him in custody against his will', the High Court had declined to interfere.

Starke appeared also to be concerned with deterrence. On the one hand, he was conscious that Cranssen

> has devoted his life to civilising and educating the savages of the territory, and, so far as I can judge, at great sacrifice and with some success. He is not a wicked man, but a good man who has blundered, seriously and dangerously, but who is never likely … to repeat his mistake.

On the other hand, Starke saw the sentence as 'a warning to persons in the uncivilized parts of New Guinea against taking the law into their own hands and doing acts which might excite dangerous savages and arouse them into action'. His appraisal of Cranssen suggests an inherent acknowledgment of Cranssen's capacity for reason—a capacity Starke apparently found inherently lacking in the 'uncivilised natives'.

The treatment of colonised peoples by their colonisers is driven, as these examples suggest, by a sense of their inferiority, symbiotically linked with a heightened sense of the colonisers' superiority. The ways in which the inferiority of the colonised manifests itself may begin in the colonisers' own imaginations; but imagination alone would be impotent were it not for the crucial difference in power between the two. The colonisers' uses of power to make real their perceptions of the inferiority of the colonised have differed

around the world. Invariably, however, constructing the inferiority of colonised peoples has served important ideological purposes, and also an immediate practical purpose—the accumulation of wealth.

In Australia, the promise of land and wealth necessitated that the original inhabitants be treated as inferior to facilitate their dispossession. The legal doctrine of *terra nullius*—the understanding that the territory belonged to no one—enabled the settler population to expand as if there had never been any dispossession in the first place. The dispossession experienced by indigenous peoples has had such a far-reaching, negative impact on indigenous culture and familial ties that many people of Aboriginal descent now claim to have been victims of genocide. Such claims are yet to be accepted by the Court (see *Kruger v Commonwealth* (1997)). The extreme example of the colonialist attitudes underlying the *terra nullius* thesis was in *In re Southern Rhodesia* (1918), where the **Privy Council** said: 'Some tribes are so low in the scale of social organization that their usages … are not to be reconciled with the institutions or the legal ideas of civilized society. Such a gulf cannot be bridged.'

The doctrine of *terra nullius* did not apply in Papua, but when the Court heard an appeal involving the recognition of **'native title'**, a perception of the 'savage' and 'barbarous' nature of the indigenous Papuans was used to defeat a claim that the town of Port Moresby had been acquired from the wrong traditional owners. If there had been any truth to that claim, said **Barwick**, the true owners would not have stood idly by—since they were self-evidently 'belligerent people given to quite savage, at times quite inhuman, acts of revenge or reprisal'. Besides, the missionaries, who were 'highly solicitous for the land interests of the Papuans', would have intervened (*Administration of Papua and New Guinea v Daera Guba* (1973)). Previously, in *Custodian of Expropriated Property v Tedep* (1964), the Court had interpreted a provision of the Lands Registration Ordinance 1924 (PNG) to mean that the absence of any explicit reference to native title on the Register of Titles had the effect of excluding any possibility of a native title claim, though the provision was clearly intended to have precisely the opposite effect.

It is sometimes said that in these two cases the **Barwick Court** had recognised native title for Papua and New Guinea a generation before the **Mason Court** did so for Australia in *Mabo* (1992). It might be more accurate to say that both cases reflect the judicial attitudes inherent in Australian colonialism. In each case, the Court dealt with difficult questions arising from the recognition in the relevant Territory of traditional entitlements to land. But in each case, while the indigenous claim was recognised by the Supreme Court of Papua and New Guinea, it was then rejected by the High Court.

Within Australia, the first challenge to the doctrine of *terra nullius* was in *Coe v Commonwealth (No 1)* (1979), although in that case only a minority (**Murphy** and **Jacobs**) would have allowed the issue to be argued. The challenge finally received majority support in *Mabo*. Yet, as **Mason** was to emphasise in *Walker v NSW* (1994), *Mabo* did nothing to undermine a conception of British sovereignty that excludes any possibility of coexistence with Aboriginal sovereignty. Moreover, claims for native title must still be determined according to Australian law, and this law still operates to favour non-indigenous interests over those of indigenous peoples. Only time will tell if the elaborate legislative regime now in place will simply be another vehicle for further dispossession.

The legal hypothesis of *terra nullius* survived for so long in Australia because the image of **Aboriginal peoples** as primitive and without social organisation was so strong in the Australian consciousness. This image was perpetuated in a multitude of ways, not least by the protectionist or welfare legislation of the various states and territories. An explicit sense of their inferiority pervaded the legislation; their depiction as an inferior race of people was chillingly reflected in the legislative use of blood lines to categorise them into groups. While the legislation reinforced the image of Aboriginal peoples as 'other'—that is, as the absolute binary opposite of the European population—the legislative categorisation on blood lines sowed division and disunion among them. One effect of these statutes was the removal of entire families from their traditional lands, disingenuously facilitating dispossession and making the land more easily available for settlement by new British migrants—a central objective of the **immigration** policy of the time (see the *Federal Roads Case* (1926), and Barwick's review in the *Seas and Submerged Lands Case* (1975) of the pre-federation use of colonial legislation to facilitate British settlement).

The racial categories incorporated in the welfare legislation were uncritically accepted by the Court (see **Race**), nor were there any direct attempts to challenge their protectionist purposes until *Kruger*. The challenge in that case failed in part because the Court held that on its face the Aboriginals Ordinance 1918 (NT) was paternalistic in intent, not genocidal as the plaintiffs claimed. Paternalism was perceived as a legitimate purpose, genocide was not. Yet paternalism (if that is what it was) still denied Aboriginal peoples equal status as human beings, and depended on a construction of their collective identity as a child race in need of benevolent protection. By treating paternalism as a legitimate purpose, the Court failed to identify all of the forms that colonialism (and genocide for that matter) may take. Nor does the *Kruger* decision give any hint of recognition that paternalism towards these peoples was simply another mechanism to compound their inferior status.

Given the high representation of indigenous peoples in Australia in the criminal justice system, it is no coincidence that the first reported High Court judgment involving an indigenous person, *Tuckiar v The King* (1934), was a criminal appeal. The case is a striking illustration of how the protectionist policy in the Northern Territory, supposedly administered for the benefit of Aboriginal peoples, operated in fact to their detriment. The unremitting racism pervading the jury trial, as reported in the joint judgment of **Gavan Duffy**, Dixon, Evatt and McTiernan, was displayed most overtly by the trial judge and by counsel for the accused (instructed by the Protector of Aborigines, Dr Cecil Cook). Effectively in collusion with the prosecution, they were able to manipulate the jury to convict Tuckiar of murder. The cumulative flouting by Tuckiar's counsel of his professional duty to his client, combined with the trial judge's misdirections, led the High Court to quash the conviction. Moreover,

since counsel's public statements had made a fair trial impossible, no order for a new trial was made.

The decision was important for all accused persons because of its emphatic restatement of counsel's duties to a client. It was particularly important, however, in showing how the protection regime had subjected indigenous peoples to discriminatory treatment fundamentally inconsistent with the **rule of law**. Starke appeared quite sympathetic to the difficulties that Tuckiar faced at trial: 'He lived under the protection of the law in force in Australia, but had no conception of its standards. Yet by that law he had to be tried. He understood little or nothing of the proceedings or of their consequences to him.' But the judgments made no attempt to explore the systemic **discrimination** involved, relying simply on a colour-blind application of established **common law** principles. In this respect Tuckiar was fortunate. By faithfully applying common law standards of fairness the Court (unlike the trial judge) declined to treat Tuckiar's Aboriginality as a basis for departure from those standards.

Similarly, in wrestling with the sentencing difficulties in *Veen v The Queen* (1979) and *Veen v The Queen (No 2)* (1988), the Court's racially neutral approach to the fair administration of criminal justice enabled it to be sensitive to the tragic circumstances of Robert Veen's personal history, though not to the systemic deracination of Aboriginal peoples that lay behind that history—although the trial judge at Veen's first trial had noted 'that the prisoner had at one time a strong personality that gradually deteriorated as the impact of the problems of a black person in a white society was felt by him'. But such cases were exceptional. The **equality** of treatment that was possible in the common law context of *Tuckiar* was less helpful in statutory contexts. **Fullagar**, who had been Tuckiar's **counsel** in his appeal to the High Court, subsequently sat alone to determine *Waters v Commonwealth* (1951). The plaintiff, 'an aboriginal', was seeking an injunction restraining the Director of Native Affairs for the Northern Territory from continuing to restrain him against his will at an Aboriginal reserve about one hundred miles from Alice Springs. Fullagar noted that in the absence of statutory authority, the Director's order to restrain the plaintiff would have been ineffective. He found, however, that the Director's power to restrain the plaintiff was amply provided for in the Aboriginals Ordinance. Furthermore, in response to the plaintiff's claim that the Director had abused his powers, Fullagar found that in exercising his discretion under the Ordinance, the Director 'may legitimately take into consideration a number of other factors in addition to the welfare of the particular aboriginal concerned … these include the welfare of other aboriginals and the general interests of the community in which the particular aboriginal dwells'. In concluding that the power had not been abused, Fullagar attached significant weight to the plaintiff's leading role in causing 'disturbances among the natives at and about Darwin, in the course of which they had been incited not to work and subjected to threats if they continued to work'.

By the time of *Namatjira v Raabe* (1959), the 1918 Ordinance had been replaced by the Welfare Ordinance 1953 (NT); but the continuity of the earlier protectionist purpose was positively confirmed by the Court, and persuaded the Court to acquiesce in administrative procedures that allowed an Aboriginal person no say in being declared a ward of the state. The Court was content to subordinate the will of the individual Aboriginal person to that of his or her protectors.

Even where legislative intent could be interpreted favourably to Aboriginal persons, the Court has had difficulty in accepting that interpretation. In *Ngatayi v The Queen* (1980), it was open to the Court under section 631 of the *Criminal Code* (WA) to find that the appellant, 'a full blood aboriginal' with no comprehension of the defences available under Australian **criminal law** to a charge of murder, was wrongfully tried and should have been discharged. In interpreting the requirement that an accused be 'capable of understanding the proceedings', the joint judgment of **Gibbs**, Mason and **Wilson** reduced his inability to comprehend the possibility of **criminal law defences** to a mere incapacity to understand legal doctrine, and in doing so elided the real problem. They recognised the problem of applying Australian law to Aboriginal peoples brought up and living under tribal law, but dismissed the problem as one of 'high legislative policy'.

Murphy's dissent acknowledged more fully the 'serious problems' arising from 'the existence of two systems of law side by side, the prevailing one and Aboriginal customary law, with their very different attitudes to guilt and responsibility'. Mason stated the law most intractably in *Walker*, when he found that Aboriginal customary law cannot coexist with Australian criminal law at all. Applying *Mabo*, he declared that even if Aboriginal customary criminal law had survived British settlement, its operation had been extinguished 'by the passage of criminal statutes of general application'. Although he did not suggest that the whole of Aboriginal customary law had thus been extinguished, the postulated extinguishment of customary criminal law would represent another significant erosion of Aboriginal culture (see **Cultural diversity**).

Throughout Australia's colonial history indigenous peoples have reacted against the colonisation process. As part of the movement towards self-determination, indigenous peoples have increasingly looked to the High Court to assert their rights (see **Litigants, notable, 1945–2001**). Although the Court's reactions have been mixed, indigenous Australians have experienced significant breakthroughs in the areas of land rights (*Northern Land Council Case* (1981); *Mabo (No 2)*; *Wik* (1996)), cultural heritage (*Onus v Alcoa* (1981); the *Tasmanian Dam Case* (1983)) and discrimination (*Koowarta's Case* (1982); *Gerhardy v Brown* (1985); *Mabo (No 1)* (1988)). Many of these breakthroughs have flowed from legislative initiatives such as the *Aboriginal Land Rights (Northern Territory) Act* 1976 (Cth) and the *Racial Discrimination Act* 1975 (Cth).

Moreover, **Brennan**'s judgment in *Davis v Commonwealth* (1988) is a powerful affirmation of the right of indigenous peoples to peaceful expression of their political views. In that case, the Court unanimously decided that the celebratory expenditures authorised by the *Australian Bicentennial Authority Act* 1980 (Cth) were valid under the **nationhood power**; but that this validity did not extend to provisions that effectively prevented Lou Davis, an Aboriginal activist, from marketing T-shirts he had designed in protest against the 1988 bicentennial celebrations. According to Brennan:

The form of national commemoration of historical events usually reflects the significance which the majority of people place upon the event. But there may well be minority views which place a different significance on the same event … It is of the essence of a free and mature nation that minorities are entitled to equality in the enjoyment of human rights. Minorities are thus entitled to freedom in the peaceful expression of dissident views.

This was a significant victory for indigenous peoples. In 1938, at the sesquicentennial celebrations, officials had shepherded a group of Aboriginal men into demeaning supportive roles as servile accessories to triumphal re-enactments of British 'settlement'. Brennan's sympathetic insight in *Davis* officially sanctions the right of indigenous peoples to articulate *their* experiences of colonialism. Unfortunately, Davis himself was unable to take full advantage of the decision because it came only in December 1988.

The movement for self-determination and reconciliation has contributed to decolonisation in more recent times. Yet colonialism has not ended in Australia. Indigenous peoples still face many challenges. For many of them the outcomes will depend upon the High Court. The result of the *Hindmarsh Island Bridge Case* (1998) was equivocal as to whether the races power enables Parliament to make laws that discriminate against indigenous people. The Court's answer to this question will be vital to the future working out of colonial relations in Australia.

Francesca Dominello

Further Reading
Commonwealth of Australia, *Aboriginal Welfare: Initial Conference of Commonwealth and State Aboriginal Authorities* (1937)
Greta Bird, Gary Martin, and Jennifer Nielsen (eds), *Majah: Indigenous Peoples and the Law* (1996)

Commentators and commentary. Two major themes—explorations of past performances and guidance towards or prophecies of future endeavours—flow from analyses and evaluations of the High Court, its Justices and judicial opinions. Quantitatively and qualitatively, the result is an exponentially expanding edifice of private and public law commentary. Contributions come from a wide and diverse range of commentators: legal scholars, historians, journalists, lawyers and judges (including High Court Justices). Initially, English legal treatises and textbooks, especially on **common law** and **statutory interpretation** issues, provided the framework within which the High Court's decisions and reasons were measured, explained and, to some extent, criticised. Gradually, with the cessation of appeals from Australia to the Judicial Committee of the **Privy Council** and the proliferation of Australian law schools, together with the High Court's increasing (though not exclusive) focus on Australian law and precedents, a more authentic antipodean legal scholarship has emerged. Publication of more and better Australian textbooks and casebooks has been the inevitable result. Of course, as might be expected, in the realm of Australia's **constitutional law**—colonial, state and Commonwealth—this pre-eminence of Australian commentators and commentary occurred earlier and with fewer traces of hesitation or deference to England.

Even before the Australian Constitution came into force, commentators were investigating, probing and dissecting its text, structure and omissions. **Constitutional interpretation** and publications about the Constitution, its origins, status and significance, began with a roar, not with muted murmurs. **Framers** and opponents of the Constitution produced a significant (though subsequently under-utilised) corpus of writings about most of its aspects. Writings by **Griffith**, **Inglis Clark**, **Garran** and **Higgins** are prominent examples, as well as articles and letters published by the radical journal *Tocsin*. Joining this initial pre-1901 foray were also scholars. William Harrison Moore's four lectures on the 1897 Constitution Bill are, perhaps, the most notable in this category.

Almost immediately after its inception on 1 January 1901, the Constitution was the subject of three classic expositions: **Quick and Garran's** *The Annotated Constitution of the Australian Commonwealth* (1901); Inglis Clark's *Studies in Australian Constitutional Law* (1901, 2nd edn 1905) and Harrison Moore's *The Commonwealth of Australia* (1902, 2nd edn 1910). All pre-date the High Court's first **sitting** on 6 October 1903, and all have been utilised—Quick and Garran leading by an impressive margin—in High Court Justices' opinions.

Indeed, Quick and Garran continues to dominate the judicial, though not the academic, terrain of constitutional law. Written from the perspective of proponents of the Constitution, and participants in its making, *The Annotated Constitution* is not only a historical survey and comparative exegesis (principally with the US Constitution) but also a section-by-section analysis of the Constitution in its pristine unamended form. Quietly, a sense of celebration is advanced: under a federal Constitution Australia would prosper. One mystery remains: what was the fate (and why) of the book by **Isaacs** and JE Mackey, *The Constitution of Australia*, advertised in 1899 by Charles F Maxwell, Law Publishers, as being 'in the press'?

Subsequent pre-1939 commentators (for example, Donald Kerr, HS Nicholas, Thomas Brennan, Edward Mitchell and Kenneth Bailey) were able to focus on, explain and criticise a growing array of judicial decisions interpreting the Constitution. A leading publication of this era was W Anstey Wynes, *Legislative and Executive Powers in Australia* (1936, 5th edn 1976). 'Judicial Powers' was added to the title from the second edition (1956) onwards. Eschewing an emphasis on the Constitution's political and financial dimensions, this treatise was case-oriented and legalistic. Reference to comparative Canadian and American judicial decisions added to, rather than detracted from, its **legalism**. A perhaps unintentional impetus, sustaining and inculcating this case-oriented approach and its legalistic consequences, was subsequently provided by Australia's first constitutional law casebook: Geoffrey Sawer, *Cases on the Constitution of the Commonwealth of Australia* (1948, 4th edn 1982).

Some movement towards other than legal perspectives—for example, those of political scientists and economists—gained momentum through Sawer's other writings and publication of conference and seminar papers in *Federalism in Australia* (1949) and *Federalism: An Australian Jubilee Study* (1952). In turn, that assisted the development of a more nuanced approach to High Court opinions and decisions. If constitutional law was not, as American legal **realism** might advocate, purely politics or judges' personal preferences, neither was it exclusively tethered to the constitutional text. Some room (and the question always is: how much?) remains for other factors, including doctrine, **precedent**, interpretive methodologies, historical and current contexts, **policy considerations** and **values**, to be influential. Clearly within this category is Sawer's later scholarship, exemplified by *Australian Federalism in the Courts* (1967) and *Federation Under Strain: Australia 1972–1975* (1977).

Indeed, the constitutional crisis surrounding the **dismissal of 1975** liberated constitutional scholarship from a High Court fetish to a more panoramic vision of the whole Constitution, encompassing all of its institutions, their structures and, importantly, their relationships. Consequently, a plethora of publications—books, essays and articles—plunged into constitutional politics, the existence and exercise of the 'reserve' powers, and basic themes such as parliamentary majoritarian **representative government** and **responsible government** and the source of the Constitution's authority. The judiciary was not banished, but merely given a less pivotal role. This commentary included Gareth Evans (ed), *Labor and the Constitution 1972–1975* (1977) and George Winterton, *Parliament, the Executive and the Governor-General: A Constitutional Analysis* (1983).

Other scholars have maintained a steadfast gaze on the law reports. Consequently, the creation, development and disintegration of judicial doctrine dominates their explication of the Constitution. PH Lane's doctrinal publications, for example, *Lane's Commentary on the Australian Constitution* (2nd edn 1997), and Michael Coper's *Freedom of Interstate Trade Under the Australian Constitution* (1983), analysing the historical development of doctrine and recommending its future direction, symbolise this vigilance. Similarly, student texts have generally emphasised case analysis and close examination of the Justices' reasons, principles and premises. Such expositions include Colin Howard, *Australian Federal Constitutional Law* (1968, 3rd edn 1985); Peter Hanks, *Constitutional Law in Australia* (1991, 2nd edn 1996); and the more sophisticated doctrinal approach in Leslie Zines, *The High Court and the Constitution* (1981, 4th edn 1997). What the Justices have said about the Constitution, its operation and other Justices' opinions is, from this perspective, the most important, perhaps the only, substantive component of constitutional law. Therefore, these commentaries tend to create the impression that exclusive and ultimate power to interpret and apply the Constitution resides with the High Court, or at least a majority of Justices (currently four out of seven) and that the views and opinions of other institutions or officials, including the Commonwealth Parliament and Governor-General, are (despite non-**justiciable** areas of the Constitution) irrelevant.

Refusal to cabin commentary (and, thus, the Constitution) merely within the law's domain has been a slow, but developing, movement. Although focused primarily on the Constitution and the High Court, publications by Brian Galligan—*Politics of the High Court* (1987) and *A Federal Republic* (1995), David Solomon—*The Political Impact of the High Court* (1992) and *The Political High Court* (1999)—and

Michael Coper—*Encounters with the Australian Constitution* (1987, popular edn 1988)—encompass a wider panorama of the multi-dimensional relationship between politics, the people, finance, culture, the Court and the Constitution.

Some commentaries (including Justices' **extra-judicial writings**) cover institutional and biographical aspects of the Court: the history, procedures, **decision-making processes**, and judicial **appointment** and **tenure** arrangements. JM Bennett, *Keystone of the Federal Arch* (1980) narrates the Court's institutional history. More technical aspects are considered in other books, including Harold Renfree, *The Federal Judicial System of Australia* (1984), David O'Brien, *Special Leave to Appeal* (1996), Brian Opeskin and Fiona Wheeler (eds), *The Australian Federal Judicial System* (2000) and practical looseleaf services: *Australian High Court and Federal Court Practice* (1978) and *Practice and Procedure: High Court and Federal Court of Australia* (1991).

Of course, the High Court's jurisdictional parameters extend well beyond constitutional issues into litigation involving a vast array of public and private law. Not unexpectedly, an abundance of commentary covers these domains. Again, however, much of this scholarship is doctrinal and legalistic, concentrating on specific decisions or synthesising larger segments or topics where the High Court has exerted its authority over the law, such as in **contracts**, **torts**, **criminal law**, **equity** and **trusts**. Unlike much of the commentary on constitutional law, this commentary has focused more on the law than on the High Court's **role**, especially where the law's development has mainly occurred in other courts and parliaments (see, for example, **Environmental law**; **Trade practices law**).

Books and treatises are not the only sources of commentary. Speeches, essays, reviews and articles published in journals, including non-legal periodicals; unpublished theses and dissertations; and parliamentary papers and committee reports must also be taken into account. Even newspaper bricolage, at its best exemplified by Sawer's regular and pithy 'Between the Lines' compositions in the *Canberra Times* (from 1967 to 1992) and (in the US) Anthony Lewis's columns in *The New York Times*, should not be forgotten.

Of course, commentary is essential in any quest to understand not only the High Court's functions and powers but also its effect, beneficial and detrimental, on Australian law and society. It is also essential in keeping the Court **accountable** in a constitutional **democracy**. Unfortunately, especially when compared to the US and Canada, much—particularly the continuous production of more and better commentary—remains to be done.

JAMES THOMSON

Further Reading

Andrew Inglis Clark, *Studies in Australian Constitutional Law* (1901, reprint 1997) i–xxxix
William Harrison Moore, *The Constitution of the Commonwealth of Australia* (2nd edn 1910, reprint 1997) i–ixix (includes bibliography)
Geoffrey Lindell, 'Introduction' in *Future Directions in Australian Constitutional Law* (1994) vii, viii–x
A Schick, 'Bibliography of Works by Geoffrey Sawer' (1980) 11 *FL Rev* 271
James Thomson, 'Quick and Garran's Australian Constitution in Retrospect' (1998) 1 *The New Federalist* 74
George Winterton et al., *Australian Federal Constitutional Law* (1999) 905 (select bibliography)

Commercial law governs transactions relating to the supply of goods and services. It includes the law of agency, bailment, banking and finance, consumer protection, insolvency, insurance, intellectual property, negotiable instruments, personal **property**, sales, securities and supply of services. Commercial law is a branch of private law, even if some commercial legal actors are governmental business enterprises. The Court's **role** in commercial law is to order and rationalise legal doctrines and resolve collisions between legislation and the **common law**.

The Court's impact on the large body of commercial law has been and is likely to continue to be modest compared with its **role** and impact in the field of **constitutional law** and **constitutional interpretation**. One of the Court's tasks is to ensure uniformity in the content of commercial legislation. In areas governed by national or uniform legislative schemes (see **Corporations law**), the Court has assumed responsibility for directing the way lower courts are to interpret and apply those schemes (see, for example, *Australian Securities Commission v Marlborough Gold Mines* (1993)). The same reasoning should apply to national legislative schemes not yet considered by the Court, such as the *Consumer Credit Code* regime (see **Consumer law**).

The *Australia Acts* cemented the Court's role at the apex of the Australian **hierarchy of courts**, and ended the possibility of Australian commercial disputes going before the **Privy Council** (see *Maynegrain v Compafina Bank* (1984) as an example of a case that bypassed the Court, going before the Privy Council on appeal from the NSW Court of Appeal). Australian commercial law is now self-sustaining and self-generating, and the High Court is free to select or discard **foreign precedents** on commercial law (*Kenny & Good Co v MGICA (1992)* (1999)). Moreover, the requirement, since 1984, that appellants must obtain special **leave to appeal** enables the Court to confine its appellate **jurisdiction** to matters of public importance. Commercial law matters enjoy no special pre-eminence in the granting of special leave.

In addition to resolving particular disputes, the Court's role in this area is to order and reorder commercial law. This has taken place by incremental and measured steps rather than by paradigm shifts. The Court's judgments do not collectively display any particular philosophy or distinctive overarching conception. In commercial law, the Court adheres to the same conventions of **judicial reasoning** as in other fields. Indeed, its activity has centred on the process of judicial reasoning as much as on substantive commercial legal doctrines themselves.

Some Justices have developed overarching themes that have figured prominently in some branches of commercial law. For example, in *David Securities v Commonwealth Bank* (1992), the organising principle of unjust enrichment (see **Restitution**) was employed to do away with the dichotomy between 'mistake of fact' and 'mistake of law' that had fissured the law governing recovery of mistaken payments of money. Other judgments have focused on consumer welfare as an element of adjudication, and that concept has proved to have a normative influence in the judicial elaboration of section 52 of the *Trade Practices Act* 1974 (Cth) (see *Concrete Constructions v Nelson* (1990); *Qantas Airways v Aravco* (1996); **Trade practices law**).

Pitted against consumer welfare is the **ideology** of individual freedom. In *Darlington Futures v Delco* (1986), for example, the Court upheld the efficacy of an exemption clause in a **contract** between a futures trader and a commercial customer. The ideologies of consumerism and contractual freedom clash, and where there is an applicable statutory regime the Court is guided by its philosophy. The result is a fragmentation of ideologies, rather than any systematic ranking of ideologies. The explanation lies in the sheer diversity of commercial law and the need for the Court to make measured, if sometimes cautious, pronouncements on particular issues. These tend to concern the systematic ordering of commercial law.

Hewett v Court (1983) is an example. The Court there considered the interplay between the law of equitable liens and bankruptcy law. The parties were a trustee in bankruptcy (representing the bankrupt estate of a builder) and the owners of a partly constructed, prepaid, prefabricated building. The Court held that the property owners held an equitable lien that survived the bankruptcy of the builder to secure the prepaid purchase price, and the equitable lien was not struck down as a voidable preference. In the same case, the Court also had occasion to consider and settle tests for the characterisation of some common commercial transactions—which, as **Gibbs** and **Murphy** acknowledged, is important so that lawyers and commercial actors know which part of the body of commercial law applies to their transactions. In *Pitt Son & Badgery v Proulefco SA* (1984), the Court calibrated the standard of care of commercial bailees of goods consistently with the standard of care under negligence law. In *Parsons v The Queen* (1999), the Court considered differences between Australian and English banking practice concerning the retention of paid cheques, preferring the former to the latter. The Court was attuned to modern Australian commercial practice in reaching its decision. While such rulings do not have a broad or deep social impact, they rationalise and order commercial law doctrines and regimes, and resolve the collision of different commercial and regulatory regimes that serve distinct and sometimes opposing social purposes. They tend to promote consistency and predictability in the adjudication of legal disputes. They can also be seen as favouring coherency in commercial law.

The quest for overarching philosophical themes or ideologies of the Court only ever yields simple platitudes, such as noting the commitment of Justices to the free enterprise system (see **McHugh** in *Hill v Van Erp* (1997)). **Dixon's** dissenting judgment in *O Gilpin v Commissioner for Road Transport (NSW)* (1935) (on section 92 of the Constitution) evinced his support for freedom of commerce (see **Interstate trade and commerce**). While this idea is important to a liberal democratic society like Australia, it is not a licence for libertine commercial behaviour. To illustrate, in *Perre v Apand* (1999) (see **Tort law**), McHugh posited that 'the common law has generally sought to interfere with the autonomy of individuals only to the extent necessary for the maintenance of society'.

In the adjudication of commercial disputes, members of the Court have displayed a sound knowledge of the business environment and the operation of commercial techniques and practices. Good examples are the judgments of **Stephen** and **Wilson** in *Morris & Sons v Bank of Queensland* (1980) and McHugh in *Coles Myer Finance v FCT* (1993). This reinforces the confidence of commercial litigants that the Justices have the necessary commercial acumen to understand the implications of their decisions for business people and commercial transactions.

That confidence is not always reciprocated. In *Hewett*, Murphy lamented the narrow approach to the resolution of commercial disputes taken by commercial litigants: 'As so often happens in commercial and conveyancing cases, the Court was not assisted by any "commercial impact statement", that is, of what would be the effect in commerce generally, of charges [equitable liens] arising in such circumstances.' It is doubtful that this remark could be marshalled as compelling evidence of legal **realism**; it reflects no more than a general concern with the consequences of judicial decision. And the conduct of commercial litigation before the Court has shown little sign of response to Murphy's challenge, though the **transcripts** of hearings of appeals and special leave applications reveal other occasions when Justices have inquired about the broader impact of the dispute on the workings of commerce and on society generally. These isolated instances apart, there is no discernible adherence to legal realism as a distinct legal philosophy informing the Court's outlook on commercial law—by contrast with the **United States Supreme Court**, where for many Justices a commitment to legal realism has been part of their judicial philosophy. The most that can be said is that the High Court is mindful of the consequences of its decisions beyond the immediate confines of the case. The Court is cautiously consequentialist.

Where commercial disputes are governed by international commercial treaties that have been incorporated into domestic Australian law, the Court's response is guided by international judicial commercial comity. The Court has regard to authoritative foreign decisions on international treaties in areas such as the original Hague Rules under the *Sea-Carriage of Goods Act* 1924 (Cth) and the amended Hague Rules under the *Carriage of Goods by Sea Act* 1991 (Cth)—see *Shipping Corporation of India v Gamlen Chemical (A/Asia)* (1980) and *Great China Metal Industries v Malaysian International Shipping Corporation* (1998). In these cases, the Court emphasised the need for uniformity with leading foreign courts of final jurisdiction in the interpretation of international commercial treaties, and for lower Australian courts to follow the lead set by the Court. In *Great China Metal Industries*, **Gaudron**, **Gummow** and **Hayne** expressly adverted to the positive commercial implications of this quest for uniformity, saying 'insurance markets set premiums efficiently and the cost of double insurance [is] avoided'.

The Court has not had a strong role in promoting business ethics in the field of commercial law, particularly in the 1970s and 1980s. For example, in *Crabtree-Vickers v Australian Direct Mail* (1975), the Court lamented the lack of 'business ethics' displayed by some officers of a company in resiling from a purchase of equipment, yet adhered to the positive tenets of agency law requiring company officers to have actual or implied authority to bind the company to a transaction. This was a lost opportunity for the Court to elevate morality (or at least commercial morality) above positive, decisional law. In *Keith Henry & Co v Stuart Walker & Co* (1958), the Court rejected a company's claim for equitable relief against another company which had obtained governmental approval to import goods, contrary to an inter-company agreement not to do so. The appeal to 'commercial ethics' by the unsuccessful applicant failed to generate a sufficient cause of action. The nadir of the role of ethics and its relationship with positive law is perhaps the **Barwick Court's** response to tax evasion in the form of the 'bottom of the harbour' tax schemes, which had an influence on commercial law and corporate law (see **Corporations law; Taxation law**).

Two distinctive features characterise the institutional role of the Court in the field of commercial law. First, the Court has attuned commercial law to modern conditions and striven to promote certainty, predictability, consistency and stability in legal doctrine. Secondly, the Court has demonstrated an awareness of the impact of commercial law on the broader social, political and economic goals of individuals, corporations and polities in Australia, and on the cross-pollination of these goals. Commercial law has not been a vehicle for judicial **activism**, nor has any distinctive ethical conception marked its commercial law jurisprudence. Nevertheless, on the whole, the Court's role in commercial law has been positive and beneficial.

SIMON FISHER

Further Reading

Gerard Brennan, 'Commercial Law and Morality' (1989) 17 *MULR* 100

JW Carter and Andrew Stewart, 'Commerce and Conscience: The High Court's Developing View of Contract' (1993) 23 *UWAL Rev* 49

Roger Giles, 'Commercial Law: What is it?' (1997) 11 *CLQ* 16

Brenda Marshall, 'Liability for Unconscionable and Misleading Conduct in Commercial Dealings: Balancing Commercial Morality and Individual Responsibility' (1995) 7 *Bond LR* 42

Anthony Mason, 'Law and Morality' (1995) 4 *GLR* 147

Anthony Mason, 'An Australian Common Law?' (1996) 14 *LIC* 81

Common law is the law developed by judges through the cumulative effect of judicial decisions, as distinct from the law contained in statutes or in statutory instruments. In this sense, the term includes the law developed in courts of **equity**, though in a narrower sense 'common law' and 'equity' are contrasted.

The common law is the basis of the Australian legal system. It developed from the common law of England which, so far as it was locally applicable, was brought to each of the Australian colonies by English settlers and became the law of the territory for want of any other system of settled law (see **Reception of English law;** *Cooper v Stuart* (1889); *State Government Insurance Commission v Trigwell* (1979); *Mabo* (1992)). The English judges of the twelfth and thirteenth centuries laid the foundations of the common law by drawing on English custom, but it is characteristic of the common law that it develops to meet changing circumstances.

When the High Court was constituted in 1903, appeals lay from each of the **state Supreme Courts** to the Judicial Committee of the **Privy Council**, which could hear appeals from the High Court as well (subject to section 74 of the Constitution: see *Inter se* questions). Thus the Judicial Committee possessed the ultimate authority to declare the common law for Australia. Through it, the common law of Australia and other parts of the British Empire was kept in substantial harmony with the common law of England. But, as the authority of the decisions of the High Court grew, the Privy Council accepted that the common law of Australia might diverge from the common law of England, at least where the divergence was occasioned by Australian judicial opinion on the policy of the law (*Australian Consolidated Press v Uren* (1967); *Geelong Harbor Trust Commissioners v Gibbs Bright & Co* (1974); see now *Invercargill City Council v Hamlin* (1996)). For its part, the High Court ceased to regard itself as bound by decisions of the **House of Lords** (see *Parker v The Queen* (1963)) and, once appeals from the decisions of the High Court were terminated, the Court no longer regarded itself as bound by the decisions of the Privy Council (see *Viro v The Queen* (1978)). The Court had assumed the responsibility for declaring authoritatively the common law of Australia. But until appeals from state courts to the Privy Council were abolished by the *Australia Act* 1986, it was possible that the High Court and the Privy Council would address the same issue in proceedings arising from the same judgment, and reach different conclusions.

Once the High Court assumed the ultimate responsibility of declaring the common law of Australia, it sought local wellsprings from which to refresh the common law and to maintain its serviceability. The contemporary but enduring **values** of the Australian people were invoked, together with the principles of **international law** (see **Murphy** in *Dugan v Mirror Newspapers* (1978); **Brennan** in *Mabo*), thus reflecting both Australian custom and Australian membership of the family of nations (see *Teoh's Case* (1995) for the influence of international treaties on the exercise of statutory powers). English decisions and the decisions of courts in other common law countries are now accorded only persuasive authority.

Although the several states and **territories** of the Commonwealth are distinct law areas, the common law is uniform throughout Australia. The uniformity of the common law of Australia, like the common law of England, depends on the doctrine of **precedent** and the authority of a centralised, final court of appeal. As the High Court declares the law to be observed by all Australian courts, the principles of the common law are uniform throughout the territory in and over which Australian courts exercise their jurisdiction, albeit subject to local statutory variations in the several law areas. Local statutes may modify the common law in differing ways but the uniformity of the underlying common law is not shaken by statutory differences. In this way, the Australian conception of a uniform common law in all Australian jurisdictions differs from the conception adopted by the **United States Supreme Court** in *Erie Railroad v Tompkins* (1938), according to which each state has its own common law. The Australian conception was spelled out by **Griffith** in *R v Kidman* (1915); and although it has sometimes been challenged (see, for example, LJ Priestley, 'A Federal Common Law in Australia?' (1995) 6 *PLR* 221), it has now been strongly reaffirmed by the High Court (see *Lipohar v The Queen* (1999); *John Pfeiffer v Rogerson* (2000)).

The common law of Australia must conform with the Constitution, but is itself the legal matrix of the Constitution and informs its construction (see *Lange v ABC* (1997)). Thus the common law freedom of expression on matters of government and politics (see **Political communication**) is shielded by the constitutions of both the Commonwealth and the states. The Constitution from which the Commonwealth and the states derive their existence and functions was enacted by the Imperial Parliament, which the English common law invested with 'supreme and unlimited legislative power' (see **Dixon**, 'The Common Law as an Ultimate Constitutional Foundation' (1957) and 'The Law and the Constitution' (1935), both reprinted in *Jesting Pilate* (1965)).

From its earliest days, the High Court's judgments have contained scholarly expositions of the common law (see, for example, *Clissold v Perry* (1904) (real **property**); *Anning v Anning* (1907) (gifts); *Niesmann v Collingridge* (1921) (contract)). In *McDonald v Dennys Lascelles* (1933), the **Depression of the 1930s** led to a notable re-examination of the consequences of the failure of a contract for sale of land. In *Telegraph Newspaper v Bedford* (1934), **Evatt** illuminated the effect of the Queensland Criminal Code upon civil actions for **defamation** by historical analysis of the English case law on the defence of qualified privilege. In *Willey v Synan* (1937), the finding of a concealed bag of coins by the boatswain of a ship in mid-ocean led to a significant reappraisal of the English and American 'finders' cases', while in the same year the dispute over gold-mining rights in *Grundt v Great Boulder Gold Mines* (1937) led Dixon to an important restatement of 'the basal purpose' of the doctrine of **estoppel**. In the decades after **World War II**, the Court established new precedents of enduring significance in many areas: *Penfolds Wines v Elliott* (1946) (trover); *Peters American Delicacy v Patricia's Chocolates* (1947) (restraint of trade); *McRae v Commonwealth Disposals Commission* (1951) (mistake in contract); *Commissioner for Railways (NSW) v Cardy* (1960) (negligence); *Latec Investments v Hotel Terrigal* (1965) (mortgages). In 1975, Lord Denning opined that, during what he described as the 'Golden Age' of the Court when Dixon was Chief Justice, its reputation 'overtopped even that of the House of Lords'.

In the years following the abolition of appeals from the High Court to the Privy Council, the Court revisited many fields of the common law, introducing changes of a distinctly Australian character. In *Mabo*, the Court rejected the conventional view that **native title** did not survive English settlement of the Australian colonies. The **tort** of negligence has been redefined and expanded through a series of landmark cases including *Caltex Oil v The Dredge 'Willemstad'* (1976); *Hackshaw v Shaw* (1984); *Jaensch v Coffey* (1984); *Sutherland Shire Council v Heyman* (1985); *San Sebastian v Minister* (1986); *Australian Safeway Stores v Zaluzna* (1987); *Nagle v Rottnest Island Authority* (1993); *Bryan v Maloney* (1995); *Hill v Van Erp* (1997); and *Perre v Apand* (1999). Other significant changes in the common law have included the enlarging of the **remedies** in judicial review (*Northern Land*

Council Case (1981)); the acknowledgment of a third party's right under an insurance contract (*Trident General Insurance v McNiece* (1988)); the relaxing of the common law presumption that the Crown is not bound by the general words of a statute (*Bropho v WA* (1990)); the denial of the notion that marriage created an irrevocable consent to sexual intercourse by a spouse (*R v L* (1991)); and the abolition of the rule in *Rylands v Fletcher* (1866 and 1868) (*Burnie Port Authority v General Jones* (1994); see **Strict liability**).

Equitable relief has been expanded in several cases. These include the extension of relief against forfeiture in contracts for the sale of land (*Legione v Hateley* (1983) and *Stern v McArthur* (1988)); the widening of the relief available to guarantors under a **disability** (*Amadio's Case* (1983) and *Garcia v National Australia Bank* (1998)); and the defining of the remedy of a constructive **trust** (*Muschinski v Dodds* (1985)). The Court developed doctrines of estoppel and waiver (*Waltons Stores v Maher* (1988) and *Commonwealth v Verwayen* (1990)), of **restitution** (*Pavey & Matthews v Paul* (1987)), and of recovery of money paid under a mistake of law (*David Securities v Commonwealth Bank* (1992)).

In the absence of a **Bill of Rights**, the Court has found in the common law a measure of protection of human rights (see **Civil liberties**). The starting point is the common law's assumption of a general freedom to do anything, subject only to the provisions of the law. Statutes are not construed as diminishing rights or freedoms unless the language is unmistakable and unambiguous (see, for example, *Sargood Bros v Commonwealth* (1910); **Melbourne Corporation v Barry** (1922); *Coco v The Queen* (1993); **Statutory interpretation**). Accordingly, the Court has confined the power of public officials to enter premises (*Plenty v Dillon* (1991)), to carry out searches (*George v Rockett* (1990)), to demand information (*Sorby v Commonwealth* (1983)) and to prevent publication of information on the workings of government (*Commonwealth v John Fairfax & Sons* (1980)). The Court has asserted the common law right of an accused person to a fair trial within a reasonable time (*Dietrich v The Queen* (1992); *Jago v District Court (NSW)* (1989)). The right to a fair trial may require the provision of legal representation for an indigent accused in a serious case, or the warning of a jury against conviction on uncorroborated police evidence of a confession (*McKinney v The Queen* (1991)).

The making of changes in the common law has challenged the theory that judicial decisions merely declare the common law as it is and has been, but the High Court has never applied that theory so absolutely as to prevent a new departure when new circumstances or more accurate perceptions so require (see **Law-making role**). The law may be declared to be different from what it had been understood to be, but the Court does not admit an authority to overrule an earlier case prospectively, for that would alter existing rights and obligations and thereby go beyond **judicial power** (see **Prospective overruling**).

The Court develops the common law by stating a new principle or restating an existing principle to govern the case in hand and future cases. **Policy considerations** play a part, taking account of a variety of factors: precedent, the justice and efficiency of existing rules, their conformity with underlying principle, the implications of change and the capacity of society to absorb change. In considering a change in the common law, the Court is conscious, as it stated in *Trigwell*, that it is 'neither a legislature nor a law reform agency'. Changes are not made in the common law if they would fracture the skeleton of principle that gives the body of the common law its shape and internal consistency (see *Mabo*).

GERARD BRENNAN

Further Reading
Leslie Zines, *The Common Law in Australia: Its Nature and Constitutional Significance* (1999), Law and Policy Paper No 13, Centre for International and Public Law, ANU

Commonwealth legislative powers. The Constitutions of the USA and Canada provided, for the **framers** of the Australian Constitution, two different models of **federalism**. The effect of the Canadian scheme, in the *British North America Act* (1867) (Imp), was to confer two separate lists of exclusive legislative powers, one on the Canadian Parliament and one on the provincial legislatures. Any residuary power was given to the former. The US Constitution conferred express and specific powers on the federal Congress only, leaving all the residue of legislative power with the states. This model was preferred by the Australians, and was embodied in the first of four resolutions moved by Henry Parkes at the first Constitutional **Convention** in 1891:

> That the powers, privileges and territorial rights of the several existing colonies shall remain intact, except in respect of such surrenders as may be agreed upon as necessary and incidental to the power and authority of the National Federal Government.

Most of the Commonwealth Parliament's legislative powers are contained in the 40 paragraphs in section 51 of the Constitution. Included are those usually regarded as necessary for a central government: **trade and commerce** with other countries and among the states, **defence**, **immigration**, naturalisation and aliens, **external affairs**, and currency, coinage, and legal tender. Also granted are powers relating to a variety of commercial and financial subjects such as banking, insurance, bills of exchange, bankruptcy, forms of intellectual property, and foreign, trading, and financial corporations. Two powers outside the areas of public or commercial matters are those with respect to **marriage and divorce**. The exercise of all these powers is subject to express and implied limitations in the Constitution (see **Constitutional law**).

Only two **amendments** have been made to the list of Commonwealth legislative powers. The first, in 1946, conferred power with respect to a variety of social benefits and services relating to health, family, students, and unemployment. Power with respect to invalid and old-age pensions was already included. In 1967, the Commonwealth gained power with respect to **Aboriginal people** by the deletion of words excepting them from a power to make laws with respect to 'the people of any **race** for whom it is deemed necessary to make special laws'.

Most subjects that Australians in 1900 associated with government regulation were not included in section 51. These included Crown lands, education, public health,

roads, railways (except with state cooperation), police, mining, local government, factory laws, and licensing of occupations. That was also the case with the general **criminal law** and civil law, including **tort**, **contract** and **property**. As for economic matters, the Commonwealth appeared to lack direct power in relation to manufacture, agriculture, **labour relations** (apart from **conciliation and arbitration** of interstate industrial disputes) and intrastate trade and commerce.

In the first decade, the Commonwealth attempted to use several of its powers to regulate matters regarded as primarily within state control. The **taxation** power was used to force manufacturers to provide specified conditions of employment (*R v Barger* (1908)). The **corporations power** was relied on to control restrictive practices in, and monopolisation of, trade (*Huddart Parker v Moorehead* (1909)). The **trade marks** power was the vehicle for a law to strengthen trade unionism by providing for a union mark to be placed on goods produced by union members (*Union Label Case* (1908)). In all these cases, the laws were held invalid because they were purporting to regulate matters deemed to be within the implied **reserved state powers**.

In 1920, the doctrine of reserved state powers was overruled by the ***Engineers Case*** (1920), which laid down the principle that federal powers were to be given their 'ordinary and natural meaning'. That principle, together with recognition that the Constitution was to endure for a long time, led to a broad construction of federal powers without regard to what would remain within the exclusive power of the states. As a result, the power with respect to 'postal, telegraphic, telephonic and other like services' was held to include radio and television services, and no doubt it covers all modern forms of electronic communication (*R v Brislan; Ex parte Williams* (1935); *Jones v Commonwealth* (1965)). The corporations power was held to provide authority for the regulation of all the trading activities of trading corporations (*Strickland v Rocla Concrete Pipes* (1971)). It also extends to acts such as manufacture if they are done for the purposes of trade (*Tasmanian Dam Case* (1983)). By virtue of the external affairs power, Parliament can pass laws to give effect to an international convention to which Australia is a party, whatever its subject matter. Laws upheld in this way include the prohibition of development of the national parks of southwest Tasmania (*Tasmanian Dam Case*), the control of virtually all aspects of air navigation (*Airlines of NSW v NSW (No 2)* (1965)) and of labour relations (*Industrial Relations Act Case* (1996)), and the prohibition of racial **discrimination** (*Koowarta's Case* (1982)).

It is clear from the above cases that the fact that a law can reasonably be described as one with respect to a subject not within federal power, such as the **environment**, restrictive **trade practices**, racial discrimination, or labour relations, is irrelevant if it can also be characterised as falling within the scope of a federal power (see **Characterisation**).

The Commonwealth's powers may also be used to achieve indirectly objects that seem to be outside the areas it can regulate directly. By means of the imposition of taxation, the Commonwealth can ensure that persons act or refrain from acting as it wishes, even though it cannot directly prohibit the action or inaction and subject it to a penalty (*Fairfax v FCT* (1965); *Northern Suburbs Cemetery v Commonwealth* (1993)).

Any attempt, however, to limit the taxation power to laws that have no other principal purpose than the collection of revenue would cause great difficulty and complexity and invalidate many provisions on which the community has relied. A glance at the exemptions, rebates, deductions and other provisions of the income tax legislation makes that clear.

The use of federal powers to further ulterior objects is not confined to taxation. Throughout its history the Commonwealth has used the trade and commerce power to prohibit imports in the interest of health or morality. Similar policies are pursued in postal and broadcasting legislation. In the face of the Queensland government's encouragement of the mining of Fraser Island, the Commonwealth prohibited the export of minerals obtained from there. That made the mining not viable commercially. The object was to preserve the island's environment. The High Court held that any law prohibiting exports was a law with respect to overseas commerce, and that the policy giving rise to the prohibition was a political rather than a constitutional question (*Murphyores v Commonwealth* (1976)).

This approach is sometimes criticised on the ground that it ignores social consequences and enables the Commonwealth to do indirectly what it cannot do directly. However, if one assumes the validity of laws prohibiting the importation of specified drugs, or the sending through the mail of undesirable literature or goods, or the regulation of broadcasting of advertisements for medicines, and so on, it is impossible in principle to distinguish other policies, such as environmental protection or labour relations, for purposes of constitutional validity. Any distinction could be based only on social or ideological predilection.

In most circumstances, the Court has refused to give a restricted meaning to a particular power by reference to the existence of another power. The corporations power was held in *Strickland v Rocla Concrete Pipes* to authorise laws controlling the intrastate trade of corporations, even though the commerce power is confined to interstate and overseas trade. Conversely, the commerce power supports the creation of a corporation for the purpose of engaging in interstate trade (*Australian National Airways v Commonwealth* (1945)) even though it does not specifically refer to incorporation, while the banking power does expressly include the incorporation of banks.

A different approach, however, is adopted where the description of a power includes an express exception or restriction and another power would, on an ordinary construction, enable the Commonwealth to avoid the restriction or to legislate in the excepted area. The most important example is the power in section 51(xxxi) with respect to 'the **acquisition of property** on just terms from any State or person for any purpose in respect of which the Commonwealth has power to make laws'. On their ordinary constructions, the other powers (combined with the incidental power) would authorise laws to acquire property for their purposes. To so construe them, however, would avoid the requirement of 'just terms' in the acquisition power and so defeat what is clearly intended to be a constitutional guarantee. It has been held, therefore, that the acquisition power fetters all the legislative powers of the Commonwealth by forbidding acquisitions on terms that are not just (*Bank*

Nationalisation Case (1948); *A-G (Cth) v Schmidt* (1961)), unless there is a clear indication to the contrary in respect of any particular power (*Nintendo v Centronics Systems* (1994)).

LESLIE ZINES

Commonwealth–state relations. The Australian federal model involves two spheres of government: the Commonwealth and the states. Each sphere has a complete set of governing institutions: legislative, executive and, with some necessary qualifications, judicial. The qualifications are that section 77(iii) of the Constitution authorises the Commonwealth to use state courts for the exercise of federal jurisdiction and that under section 73 the High Court performs the final appellate function for both Commonwealth and states.

In practice, Australian **federalism** is characterised by a complex and sophisticated network of intergovernmental arrangements. These arrangements involve interaction between the spheres of government in a manner that departs from a strictly coordinate federal model. Some are specifically authorised by the Constitution. These may be categorised as executive (for example, the use of state prisons for federal prisoners under section 120); legislative (primarily through state legislation for referral of powers to the Commonwealth Parliament under section 51(xxxvii) and through Commonwealth legislation with 'the concurrence of the Parliaments of all the states directly concerned' under section 51(xxxviii)); judicial (through the vesting of federal jurisdiction in state courts); and financial (sections 94, 96, 105 and 105A). Most intergovernmental arrangements are not specifically contemplated by the Constitution; they must, however, be legally compatible with it.

In Australia, as in other federations, intergovernmental arrangements have implications for the rest of the structure of government. The democratic processes of both Commonwealth and states rely principally on parliamentary **responsible government**. A parliamentary system in which the executive generally controls the Parliament assists in the implementation of intergovernmental arrangements, in the sense that agreements between governments can readily be implemented if legislative action is required. At the same time, however, such arrangements often detract from the accountability of government to Parliament and to voters. Generally, the arrangements are complex. Important detail is not always public. The arrangements tend to present parliaments with a *fait accompli*. In this sense they reinforce the potential for conflict between federalism and responsible government, foreshadowed by some of the **framers of the Constitution** during the original Conventions and by **Quick and Garran** shortly thereafter, with particular reference to the powers of the Senate.

Many Commonwealth–state arrangements by their nature are non-**justiciable**, embodying agreements that are political and inappropriate for enforcement through courts. Even where the arrangement itself is non-justiciable, however, questions of constitutionality may arise (see, for example, *Railway Standardisation Case* (1962)). Over the past hundred years, the High Court has frequently been required to determine constitutional questions affecting Commonwealth–state arrangements in some way. Some of these cases demonstrate the difficulty of striking an appropriate balance between the demands of federalism and other constitutional principles, particularly where intergovernmental cooperation is involved.

Most of the arrangements that have a base in the Constitution have been the subject of judicial interpretation. In a series of cases on the reference power (section 51(xxxvii)), the Court confirmed that states retain concurrent power to legislate on a referred matter, subject to the possibility of **inconsistency** under section 109 of the Constitution (*Graham v Paterson* (1950)); and that a matter may be referred in terms that enable the reference to be revoked (*R v Public Vehicles Licensing Appeal Tribunal; Ex parte Australian National Airways* (1964); *Airlines of NSW v NSW (No 1)* (1964)). The continuing uncertainty in those cases about whether an apparently unlimited reference can be revoked may have contributed to state hesitation about referring power to the Commonwealth. The key provision for revenue sharing in section 94 of the Constitution, which might have provided a basis for a more principled financial relationship between the Commonwealth and the states, was interpreted out of existence in the first decade of federation (*Surplus Revenue Case* (1908)). Shortly thereafter, a course of decisions began which made the power of the Commonwealth to attach conditions to state grants under section 96 of the Constitution almost unlimited in scope (*Federal Roads Case* (1926); *Moran's Case* (1939), affirmed by the **Privy Council** in 1940; *Uniform Tax Cases* (1942 and 1957)). The decision in *Sankey v Whitlam* (1978) that the Financial Agreement was a contract without constitutional force undermined the capacity of states to enforce it against the Commonwealth.

By contrast, in determining that the Commonwealth must generally take state courts as it finds them for the purposes of investing them with federal jurisdiction under section 77(iii) (see, for example, **Griffith** in the *Woodworkers Case* (1912); **Knox**, **Rich** and **Dixon** in *Le Mesurier v Connor* (1929)), the Court has attempted to strike an effective balance between the interests of the Commonwealth and the states (see, for example, *Russell v Russell* (1976)).

The balance between federalism and other constitutional principles has arisen in different ways in relation to extra-constitutional Commonwealth–state arrangements. In the middle decades of the twentieth century, the Court heard a series of cases concerning the validity of legislative schemes with intergovernmental implications. The Court's approach to these was characterised by **literalism** and an inclination to examine component parts of such schemes in isolation from each other when determining constitutional validity. This technique was influential, although ultimately not determinative, in dismissing the challenge to the uniform tax scheme in the *First Uniform Tax Case*. A similar approach in *Moran* showed how other constitutional provisions might be evaded through complementary statutes of the Commonwealth and the states, unless the Court were prepared to read them as an integrated whole. Despite warnings in *Moran* itself that the limits might be exceeded, there has been only one case (*Magennis v Commonwealth* (1949)) in which legislation has been invalidated on these grounds, and in that instance the problem was readily cured (see *Pye v Renshaw* (1951)).

More recently, a different set of issues has emerged in relation to the constitutionality of intergovernmental schemes. A common theme of these cases has been the relevance of cooperative action to the constitutionality of Commonwealth or state laws. This issue was explored most extensively in a series of cases dealing with the legal effects of the operation of the Coal Industry Tribunal, established jointly by the Commonwealth and NSW to provide a comprehensive **conciliation and arbitration** regime for all disputes in the coal mining industry (see, for example, *Aberdare Collieries v Commonwealth* (1952); *Australian Iron & Steel v Dobb* (1958); *R v Lydon; Ex parte Cessnock Collieries* (1960); *Re Cram; Ex parte NSW Colliery Proprietors Association* (1987)). The principal constitutional challenge to the arrangement was in *R v Duncan; Ex parte Australian Iron & Steel* (1983). The challenge failed. In the course of their judgments, various Justices referred to the cooperative nature of the arrangements in positive terms, suggesting, in the words of **Deane**, that cooperation was a 'positive objective of the Constitution'.

The constitutional validity of cooperative commodity marketing schemes was upheld in *Wilcox Mofflin v NSW* (1952) (hides and leather) and in *Clark King & Co v Australian Wheat Board* (1978) (wheat). Reference to the relevance of cooperation has also been made in other contexts. In particular, in *Port MacDonnell Professional Fishermen's Association v SA* (1989), in upholding the validity of the Commonwealth–state arrangements for the areas offshore, entered into pursuant to section 51(xxxviii), the Court referred to the cooperative nature of the exercise. Similar references have been made in relation to other constitutional provisions; for example the observation in *Cole v Whitfield* (1988) that legislation enacted pursuant to an intergovernmental scheme is unlikely to transgress section 92.

By the 1990s, the joint arrangement that had survived challenge in relation to the coal-mining industry was adapted and extended to a range of other schemes. Most significantly, after the Commonwealth's loss in the *Incorporation Case* (1990), this became a key component of the new cooperative Corporations Scheme. A central agency, which eventually became the Australian Securities and Investment Commission, was created by the Commonwealth Parliament and invested with power by all participating jurisdictions. To deepen the practical uniformity of the scheme, other Commonwealth agencies, including the Director of Public Prosecutions, were invested with comprehensive power as well, under both Commonwealth and state law.

In a parallel development, relying on the principle of cooperation, the Commonwealth Parliament authorised the conferral of state jurisdiction on federal courts, both generally, in the context of a comprehensive scheme of **cross-vesting** arrangements, and for the purposes of the Corporations Law. After one challenge in which a Court of six was evenly divided (*Gould v Brown* (1998)), the conferral of state jurisdiction on federal courts was held invalid by a 6:1 majority in *Re Wakim* (1999). According to the majority, Chapter III of the Constitution is an exhaustive statement of the jurisdiction that can be conferred on federal courts. In any event, they concluded that the Commonwealth Parliament lacked the necessary power to authorise the states to confer jurisdiction, or to consent to its conferral, so as to counter the effects of section 109.

This decision made it clear that the principle of cooperation is essentially passive. There is no constitutional impediment to cooperation; but the principle will not supply power that otherwise does not exist, even in small doses.

This decision had further repercussions. The most significant was a challenge to the validity of the conferral of a duty on the Commonwealth Director of Public Prosecutions to prosecute offences under state Corporations legislation. In *R v Hughes* (2000), the challenge was dismissed, but on grounds specific to the circumstances of the case, raising an apprehension that intergovernmental schemes of this kind were more generally at risk. It is not yet clear whether there is a more general basis on which such schemes might be upheld by reference to, for example, the executive power in section 61 of the Constitution, underpinned by legislation based on the incidental power (section 51(xxxix)).

The outcome in *Hughes* raises the question whether the Constitution should more explicitly provide a framework for Commonwealth–state arrangements. A properly drafted provision would have the advantage of meeting some of the accountability problems associated with such arrangements while providing a more secure constitutional foundation for them.

CHERYL SAUNDERS

Communist Party Case (1951). In the years after **World War II**, communism was viewed by many as a dire threat to Australian **democracy**. Community apprehension swelled as the union movement became subject to communist infiltration. Events such as the seven-week coal strike of 1949 demonstrated the effectiveness of the industrial power of the Australian Communist Party. The strike saw heavy industry come to a standstill and led to rationing of electricity and domestic gas in some states.

Robert **Menzies** capitalised on community fear of the 'red menace' by campaigning strongly for the suppression of communism. In the election held on 10 December 1949, Menzies led the Liberal and Country Party coalition to a convincing win. As **Prime Minister**, Menzies' first significant piece of legislation was the *Communist Party Dissolution Act* 1950 (Cth).

The Dissolution Act was prefaced by nine recitals in which the federal Parliament set out its view of communism and sought to expose the Australian Communist Party as a peril to the Australian nation. The recitals were followed by the operative provisions of the Act. Section 4 declared the Australian Communist Party to be an unlawful association, provided for its dissolution, and enabled the appointment of a receiver to manage its property. Section 5 provided the machinery for declarations by the Governor-General that organisations other than the Party were also unlawful. This provision targeted bodies that supported or advocated communism, were affiliated with the Party, or whose policies were substantially shaped by members of the Party or by 'Communists'. 'Communist' was defined by the Act to mean 'a person who supports or advocates the objectives, policies, teachings, principles or practices of communism, as expounded by Marx and Lenin'. Once declared to be unlawful, an association would be dissolved under section 6 and a receiver appointed under section 8.

An organisation could be declared unlawful under section 5(2) where:

> the Governor-General is satisfied that a body of persons is a body of persons to which this section applies and that the continued existence of that body of persons would be prejudicial to the security and defence of the Commonwealth or to the execution or maintenance of the Constitution or of the laws of the Commonwealth.

Under section 9(2), the Governor-General could declare any person to be a 'communist' or member of the Australian Communist Party by applying a similar discretion to that laid out in section 5(2). Once such a declaration was made, section 10 meant a person could not hold office in the Commonwealth public service or in industries declared by the Governor-General to be vital to the security and defence of Australia. Should a person wish to contest a declaration by the Governor-General, he or she could do so under section 9(4), although section 9(5) reversed the onus of proof by providing that 'the burden shall be on him to prove that he is not a person to whom this section applies'.

The Australian Communist Party, ten unions and several communist union officials took little time to challenge the validity of the Dissolution Act. On the day the Act came into force, eight actions were commenced in the High Court seeking a declaration that the Act was unconstitutional.

Evatt, a former Justice of the High Court and then the Deputy Leader of the Opposition and an avowed anti-communist, astonished all concerned by announcing that he would represent the communist-led Waterside Workers' Federation and its communist official, James Healy, in the High Court. This action exposed deep divisions in the Australian Labor Party, the Victorian branch passing a motion condemning Evatt. However, in Parliament, the Leader of the Opposition, Ben Chifley, vigorously supported Evatt's actions as being consistent with Evatt's long championship of **civil liberties**. Nevertheless, Harold Holt, for the government, summed up what could be the only political result of Evatt's decision: 'rightly or wrongly the people of Australia will read into the appearance of the right honourable gentleman a sympathy and support for the cause which he seeks to defend.' JA Ferguson, the NSW President of the Labor Party, said that Evatt's acceptance of the brief was 'ethically correct, professionally sound, and politically very, very foolish'.

The High Court began hearing the *Communist Party Case* on 14 November 1950. **Argument** continued over 24 days with Evatt opposed by **Barwick**, who argued on behalf of the Commonwealth that the law was validly passed under the **defence** and **nationhood** powers. In response, Evatt and others forcefully submitted that the Act was invalid due to its derogation of civil liberties and the democratic process. **Dixon** went so far as to note in his diary of Evatt: 'I had never heard him to more advantage & he made a considerable impression.' Five days later, however, Dixon wrote: 'Evatt continued. A dreary repetitious argument.'

On 9 March 1951, the High Court, with Chief Justice **Latham** in sole dissent, declared the Dissolution Act invalid. The decision was a great victory for Evatt and the most significant defeat of Barwick's distinguished career as a barrister.

The majority did not find the Act invalid because it breached constitutionally entrenched civil liberties, but because it could not be **characterised** as law falling within Commonwealth power. This conclusion rested on two findings. First, the Court refused to accept the Parliament's view of the legislation and the Australian Communist Party as expressed in the recitals. The recitals could play no role in determining whether the Act fell within power. That was a decision for the High Court as part of its function of **judicial review**.

Secondly, the Court found that the Act lacked a sufficient connection with a **Commonwealth legislative power**. The Governor-General's power to make declarations under sections 5(2) and 9(2) was found by the Court to be unreviewable; effectively the power amounted to an unfettered discretion to determine the scope of Commonwealth power by declaring certain persons or organisations to be 'prejudicial to the security and defence of the Commonwealth'. According to **Fullagar**, these sections were invalid because they imposed 'legal consequences on a legislative or executive opinion which itself supplies the only link between the power and the legal consequences of the opinion'.

Underpinning both findings was the view that responsibility for determining the scope of Commonwealth power lay with the High Court alone. The attempt by the Parliament to determine the ambit of its own power breached the cryptic maxim that 'a stream cannot rise higher than its source'.

In what Zelman Cowen described as a 'lone, vehement and incredulous dissent', Latham took a very different view of the **role** of the Court. He held that the defence and nationhood powers were entrusted to the federal Parliament for the purpose of ensuring the continued existence of the Commonwealth. Paraphrasing Oliver Cromwell, Latham asserted that 'being comes before well-being' and that in times of crisis the Court must not prevent parliamentary action. For Latham, the real issue of the *Communist Party Case* was, in times of crisis: 'By what authority—by Parliament or by a court?'. For him, the answer was that the Parliament should have a free hand to deal with the communist threat as it saw fit. Dixon reacted strongly to this line of reasoning, noting in his diary: 'After Court Latham read to me the beginning of a judgment which he had prepared. It sickened me with its abnegation of the function of the Court & I said so.'

George Winterton has described the decision in the *Communist Party Case* as 'probably the most important ever rendered by the Court'. In the result, the decision held invalid legislation that would have significantly impeded the political liberties of Australians. Moreover, the arguments of **counsel** on issues of civil liberties did find some voice in the Court's decision. In a departure from the **legalism** pervading the judgments, Dixon stated:

History and not only ancient history, shows that in countries where democratic institutions have been unconstitutionally superseded, it has been done not seldom by those holding the executive power. Forms of government may need protection from dangers likely to arise from within the institutions to be protected. In point of constitutional theory the power to legislate for the protection of an existing form of government ought not to be based on a conception, if otherwise adequate,

adequate only to assist those holding power to resist or suppress obstruction or opposition or attempts to displace them or the form of government they defend.

Despite such rhetoric, however, the *Communist Party Case* cannot be cast as a great civil libertarian decision. The Court did strike down a law that infringed basic freedoms; but in spite of the majority's clear dislike of the Act, the finding of invalidity did not depend on the Act having breached any express or implied constitutional guarantee of human rights. The real significance of the *Communist Party Case* lies in the fact that the Court, in striking down the Dissolution Act, entrenched its own position as an independent check on the power of the legislature and the executive. In particular, the mantra 'a stream cannot rise higher than its source' can be seen as a bulwark against the exercise of arbitrary governmental power.

A week after the Court's decision, Menzies called an early election. Communism remained the issue of the day and the Liberal Party's campaign slogan in Tasmania was 'Menzies or Moscow'. Menzies won the poll held on 28 April 1951. Evatt was opposed in his seat by World War II hero Nancy Wake, who campaigned on the slogan 'I am the defender of freedom; Dr Evatt is the defender of communism'. Evatt retained his seat by 243 votes.

After the election, Menzies set out to gain the constitutional power to ban the Australian Communist Party by way of a referendum under section 128 of the Constitution that would overcome the decision in the *Communist Party Case*. There is evidence to suggest that Menzies received support in drafting the proposed amendments from an unlikely (and arguably inappropriate) source: Latham. Journalist and historian Clem Lloyd has uncovered correspondence in which Latham remarks that he has had 'an informal talk with the Prime Minister' regarding constitutional **amendments** and that he had 'made some suggestions to him'.

The referendum put to the people on 22 September 1951 sought to add a new section to the Constitution. Section 51A would have allowed the Commonwealth to legislate with respect to communists and communism, to enact the Dissolution Act and to amend that Act within certain limits. Menzies argued for a 'Yes' vote on the ground that communism was a threat that had to be countered and that, as the High Court had set the limits of Commonwealth power, the Constitution was inadequate and had to be altered. Initially, the referendum proposal attracted massive electoral support.

In Parliament, Evatt, now Leader of the Opposition after the death of Chifley, described the proposal as 'one of the most dangerous measures that has ever been submitted to the legislature of an English-speaking people'. In four weeks of campaigning, he turned the tide of support for a 'Yes' vote towards a 'No' vote. The referendum failed to gain the support of a majority of electors by a narrow margin, 2 317 927 'Yes' votes to 2 370 009 'No' votes. Menzies was bitter about the loss, accusing the proponents of a 'No' vote of misleading the public with a 'wicked and unscrupulous' campaign.

Despite his loss in the High Court and at the referendum, Menzies' anti-communist measures led to a decline in membership of the Australian Communist Party. Moreover, while Menzies' crusade to suppress the Party failed, it did contribute to the breaking of its industrial power and the Party never again played a major role in Australian politics. The Party survived until December 1989, when it was voluntarily disbanded.

GEORGE WILLIAMS

Further Reading

Michael Kirby, 'HV Evatt, The Anti-Communist Referendum and Liberty in Australia' (1991) 7 *Aust Bar Rev* 93

Clem Lloyd, 'Not Peace But a Sword!—The High Court under JG Latham' (1987) 11 *Adel L Rev* 175

George Williams, 'Reading the Judicial Mind: Appellate Argument in the *Communist Party Case*' (1993) 15 *Syd LR* 3

George Williams, 'The Suppression of Communism by Force of Law: Australia in the Early 1950s' (1996) 42 *Australian J of Pol & Hist* 220

George Winterton, 'The Significance of the *Communist Party Case*' (1992) 18 *MULR* 630

Comparison with other courts. The courts with which the High Court is most often compared are the Judicial Committee of the **Privy Council**, the **House of Lords**, the Supreme Court of Canada and the **United States Supreme Court**. The High Court makes more use of the decisions of these courts than of the decisions of other courts (see **Citations by Court**; **Foreign precedents**).

The comparison between the High Court and the Judicial Committee is of jurisdictional and historical interest. The Judicial Committee is strictly a committee of judges (including senior judges of the UK), not a court. It advises rather than decides, though its advice is treated as binding. It had a wide-ranging appellate jurisdiction. Like the High Court, it decided constitutional questions as well as general appeals. Most appeals are heard by a committee of five Law Lords. Justices of the High Court were appointed as Privy Counsellors and sat from time to time on Privy Council appeals until the last remaining appeals from Australian courts were abolished in 1986. The Privy Council was, as the High Court is today, the final court of appeal from Australia. An appeal lay, as of right or by special leave, from the Supreme Courts of the Australian colonies to the Privy Council. The continuation of that appeal was not affected by the Australian Constitution except in so far as the Privy Council ordinarily declined to grant special leave otherwise than from a decision of the highest court in the dominion or colony. In the case of Australia, that was the High Court.

The High Court was normally bound to follow Privy Council decisions because of the possibility of appeal to the Privy Council from the High Court. But for *inter se* questions there was no such appeal in the absence of a certificate given by the High Court. This exception gave rise to an early conflict when the High Court in *Baxter v Commissioners of Taxation (NSW)* (1907) refused to follow the Privy Council's decision in *Webb v Outtrim* (1906) because that decision rejected the doctrine of implied prohibitions on which *Baxter* was based (see **Intergovernmental immunities**). Ultimately, the Privy Council's rejection of that doctrine was vindicated by the *Engineers Case* (1920), even if the rejection had come about because the Privy Council trespassed into the forbidden field of *inter se* questions.

The difference of opinion over implied prohibitions reflected a deeper difference about resort to American authority. The Australian Constitution was partly modelled on the US Constitution, and the early Justices of the High Court, who had participated in the federal Conventions, were well acquainted with the US Constitution and its interpretation. They cited decisions of the US Supreme Court, which held little attraction for their Lordships in the Privy Council either at that time or for many years to come. With the **retirement** of the early members of the Court, the High Court did not make as much use of American authority and began to interpret the Australian Constitution, as the Privy Council did, as a statute of the Imperial Parliament.

Following the appointment of **Dixon** and **Evatt** to the High Court in 1929 and 1930, and later **Latham**, the High Court began to deliver judgments of very high quality. Privy Council judgments then compared unfavourably with those of the High Court and the House of Lords. No doubt the Privy Council practice of delivering a collective advice, as opposed to individual opinions, was a contributing factor to this unfavourable comparison (see **Joint judgments and separate judgments**). In 1966, largely on the initiative of **Barwick**, the Privy Council adopted the practice of allowing its dissentient members to publish a **dissenting** opinion. Dissenting opinions, however, have been infrequently delivered.

Privy Council decisions on Australian constitutional questions encountered criticism. One such was Lord Normand's judgment in *Nelungaloo v Commonwealth* (1950), where he spoke of the states before federation exercising sovereign powers of legislation. Another was the judgment of Lord Diplock in *Oteri v The Queen* (1976) where, in the context of an offence committed outside territorial waters, he boldly and incorrectly stated: 'The legislative power of the Commonwealth … does not extend to **criminal law**.' Geoffrey Sawer once observed that, in relation to constitutional cases, the Privy Council never had a sufficient flow to enable it to really understand the Australian Constitution, but had enough to do significant damage.

The judgments of Dixon were particularly influential in the Privy Council and never more so than when Viscount Simonds was sitting. In his Lordship's eyes, the attribution to Dixon of error appeared to verge on sacrilege. Dixon's influence extended beyond constitutional to other legal questions.

With the limitation and subsequent abolition of appeals from the High Court to the Privy Council, the High Court began to develop an Australian **common law**. In doing so, the High Court has regarded itself as no longer bound to follow Privy Council decisions (see *Viro v The Queen* (1978)). In *Mabo* (1992), the High Court refused to follow the Privy Council view, in *Cooper v Stuart* (1889), that NSW was 'practically unoccupied, without settled inhabitants or settled law'.

Membership of the House of Lords is not based on geographical representation, though by convention there is at least one Scottish judge. There is usually also at least one Chancery judge. From time to time there is a judge from Northern Ireland. Most appeals are heard by a Bench of five Law Lords. The number varies and it includes peers who are not Lords of Appeal in Ordinary.

Although the High Court was not bound by decisions of the House of Lords, the Court did invariably follow these decisions until the 1960s. The Law Lords sat on the Privy Council. So there was good reason to think that the view of the House of Lords on a question would be adopted by the Privy Council. In *Parker v The Queen* (1963), Dixon acknowledged that the Court had followed decisions of the House of Lords at the expense of the Justices' own opinions and previous High Court decisions. Nonetheless, in *Parker*, Dixon, with the concurrence of all other members of the Court, refused to follow *DPP v Smith* (1960) on intention in criminal law because he considered the propositions on which it rested to be fundamentally wrong. This was an exceptional step. Until the final abolition of Australian appeals to the Privy Council, the High Court formulated the Australian common law in line with the English common law. *R v Hickman; Ex parte Fox and Clinton* (1945), relating to **privative clauses** and the powers of administrative tribunals, was an exception to this general approach. Today, House of Lords decisions are not binding and are useful only so far as their reasoning is persuasive: *Cook v Cook* (1986).

The House of Lords has adhered to the tradition of delivering individual judgments. In recent decades, it has made more use of comparative law and of academic writings. The law of the European Union is having an increasing impact upon the work of the House of Lords, which will now include the application of the *Human Rights Act* 1998 (UK). That Act will bridge the gulf between English law and the European Convention on Human Rights.

The Supreme Court of Canada resembles the High Court more than any other court. The Supreme Court is both a constitutional court and a general court of appeal. As in the High Court, an appeal lies by special **leave**, though in certain criminal cases an appeal lies as of right. Unlike the High Court, the Court does not assign a ground for the refusal of special leave. The High Court's use of a video link for special leave hearings was based on a Supreme Court model. These applications are now presented to the Supreme Court in writing, not orally. The number of applications substantially exceeds the number in the High Court, which totalled 407 in the year ended 30 June 1999 and increased significantly in 2000. The High Court also deals with a large number of prerogative **writ** applications.

Unlike the High Court and other courts, the Supreme Court is vested with statutory jurisdiction to give an **advisory opinion** at the request of the Governor-General in Council. In 1912, the Privy Council refused to read into the Canadian Constitution a limitation precluding the conferring of such a jurisdiction, there being no express constitutional **separation of powers** (*A-G (Ontario) v A-G (Canada)* (1911)).

Decisions of the Supreme Court were subject to appeal to the Privy Council, without any limitation corresponding to section 74 of the Australian Constitution. The appeal was abolished in 1949. Since that time, the membership of the Court has been nine Justices. The membership has reflected a pattern of regional representation (three from French-speaking Quebec, three from Ontario, two from the Western provinces, and one from the Atlantic provinces). Before the adoption of the *Constitution Act* 1982 (Can) incorporating the Canadian Charter of Rights and Freedoms, the pattern of the Supreme Court's work was not unlike that of the High

Court. Since then the Supreme Court has dealt with many fundamental rights issues.

Like the High Court, the Supreme Court makes considerable use of comparative law, particularly in relation to **constitutional law**, common law and fundamental rights. In the last two decades, judgments of the Supreme Court have been influential in many jurisdictions outside Canada, notably in relation to issues concerning fundamental rights, common law and **equity**.

To some of the prominent **framers** of the Australian Constitution and to **Attorney-General** Alfred **Deakin**, the US Supreme Court was a vision of what the High Court might become. That vision has not been realised, largely because the Supreme Court today, heavily engaged as it is with fundamental rights issues, is very different from what it was at the end of the nineteenth century.

There is and always has been a fundamental difference between the two courts in that the Supreme Court never has been a general court of appeal. It is essentially a constitutional court, though it has a jurisdiction to deal with federal matters. One outcome of this difference is that there is no uniform American common law, while there is a uniform Australian common law (see, for example, *Lipohar v The Queen* (1999)).

In modern times, the US Supreme Court has been the preeminent court, at least in the common law world. It has done more than any other court to shape the jurisprudence of fundamental rights and **due process**. Its judgments on federal constitutional issues have contributed significantly to the development of Australian constitutional law. Whether we should regard ourselves as indebted to the Supreme Court for all these developments—notably, the Byzantine complexities of federal jurisdiction—is a matter of debate. More recently, the High Court's development of the Australian common law (including equity) has drawn upon American learning, though that learning is not substantially expressed in Supreme Court decisions.

The Supreme Court's jurisprudence, unlike that of the other courts discussed, has been relatively insular. Little account was taken of decisions in other jurisdictions, though this attitude may be changing. On the other hand, the Supreme Court has led the way in taking account of academic writings.

Regional representation plays no part in the appointment of the nine Justices of the Court. They run the gauntlet of a confirmation hearing before the Senate Judiciary Committee before the Senate consents to the Presidential nomination.

Unlike the High Court, the Supreme Court relies extensively on written **argument**, with very limited time for oral argument. The Justices also make extensive use of their clerks (or, in Australia, 'associates'). Each Justice has four clerks, who prepare drafts of opinions. The clerks are responsible for filtering the certiorari petitions, amounting to over 6000 per annum (of which approximately 100 are granted).

In the early 1800s, the Supreme Court adopted the convention of delivering a single majority opinion and minority opinion, thereby avoiding the spread of views sometimes exhibited in High Court judgments. In recent times, however, the Supreme Court has departed from this convention.

Anthony Mason

Further Reading

John Goldring, *The Privy Council and the Australian Constitution* (1996)

Louis Blom-Cooper and Gavin Drewry, *Final Appeal: A Study of the House of Lords in its Judicial Capacity* (1972)

Kermit Hall (ed), *The Oxford Companion to the Supreme Court of the United States* (1992)

Robert Stevens, *Law and Politics: The House of Lords as a Judicial Body, 1800–1976* (1979)

Paul Weiler, *In the Last Resort: A Critical Study of the Supreme Court of Canada* (1974)

Conciliation and arbitration. As the consequence of an awkward compromise between those who desired full Commonwealth power over industrial relations and those who desired none, section 51(xxxv) of the Constitution enables the Commonwealth to make laws with respect to 'conciliation and arbitration' for the prevention and settlement of 'industrial disputes' extending 'beyond the limits of any one state'. Each element in this circumscription of power has been interpreted by the High Court. Many cases have been politically contentious, with the Court becoming the forum where unions, employers, and state and federal governments have argued their divergent interpretations of the power as a means of implementing their own industrial and economic agendas.

Initially, section 51(xxxv) was seen as empowering the Commonwealth to establish a specialist industrial tribunal to conciliate and arbitrate industrial disputes. The traditional role of the tribunal was to establish industry-based awards covering the terms and conditions of employment for Australian workers. Since the 1980s, with the shift towards enterprise bargaining, workers are also covered by Enterprise Agreements, certified by the tribunal.

Originally known as the Court of Conciliation and Arbitration (which also acted judicially), the tribunal was reconstituted after the *Boilermakers Case* (1956) as the Conciliation and Arbitration Commission, with its former judicial functions exercised by a separate court. In 1993, it was renamed the Australian Industrial Relations Commission. Unions have traditionally favoured the role of the tribunal, whereas some employers have resisted it, arguing that there should be little or no intervention by a third party—let alone an organ of government—in the bargaining processes between employers and employees. Thus, most of the cases before the High Court have involved attempts either to extend or to limit the powers of the tribunal.

The inclusion of section 51(xxxv) by the **framers of the Constitution** was part of an experiment unique to Australasia. (NZ had led the way with the *Industrial Conciliation and Arbitration Act* 1894 (NZ), creating regional Boards of Conciliation and a Court of Arbitration presided over by a Supreme Court judge.) The bitter industrial disputes throughout the Australian colonies in the 1890s (such as the maritime and shearers strikes of 1890–94) led the framers to explore ways of using the new Constitution and the new Commonwealth to help prevent industrial unrest. While this industrial unrest was not unique to Australasia—indeed, the late nineteenth century had seen moves towards compulsory arbitration in North America—one important factor in the

Australian response was the influence of the Labor Party, with its links to the trade union movement.

This is not to say that the arbitration system was designed to benefit the trade union movement in the interests of workers. Unions were (and still are) required to register as organisations in order to appear in the tribunal; and since registration could be revoked, both registration and deregistration became a means of monitoring the trade union movement. Indeed, in 1986, the Australian Building Construction Employees and Builders Labourers Federation (BLF) was deregistered by legislation held valid under section 51(xxxv) in *Australian Building Construction Employees and BLF v Commonwealth* (1986).

In the early years of federation, both liberals and conservatives were primarily concerned with preserving industrial peace, and supported the novel approach to arbitration for that reason. Liberals were also willing to give limited support to unionism because of their concern with **social justice**. Yet that concern was primarily expressed through other legislation—such as the provision in the *Excise Tariff Act* 1906 (Cth) for certification of 'fair and reasonable' wages, struck down by the High Court in *R v Barger* (1908). **Higgins**, as President of the Arbitration Court, had used that provision in his 'Harvester judgment' (*Ex parte HV McKay* (1907)) to formulate the 'minimum wage'—an enduring Australian icon of social justice, but not dependent on conciliation or arbitration. As **Deakin** said as **Prime Minister** in his second reading speech (22 March 1904), the object of the *Conciliation and Arbitration Act* 1904 (Cth) was industrial peace; it was aimed just as much at 'the tyranny of trade unions' as 'the tyranny of employers'.

Thus, while the factors leading to the acceptance and implementation of the conciliation and arbitration power were complex, they involved a degree of consensus among divergent political groups. The trade union movement saw arbitration as an adjunct to other methods of collective bargaining; liberals and conservatives were willing to support the experiment in the hope of industrial harmony.

Whether that experiment worked, and how far the High Court's judicial supervision has helped or hindered its working, have always been controversial. Pursuant to the constitutional purpose—'the prevention and settlement of industrial disputes'—the original Arbitration Act listed first among its 'chief objects' the prevention of lock-outs and strikes. But another 'chief object' was 'to facilitate and encourage' the submission of industrial disputes to the Arbitration Court by organisations: any registered organisation could 'submit to the Court any industrial dispute in which it is interested'. The practice soon developed that a union would serve on employers and their organisations a 'log of claims' enumerating demands for wages and working conditions; the employers would reject those demands; and the disagreement thus crystallised would be submitted to the Arbitration Court as a 'dispute'. This procedure also circumvented the constitutional restriction of Commonwealth power to disputes 'extending beyond the limits of any one state'—since a log of claims served in different states, and rejected by employers in different states, became 'an interstate dispute'.

Griffith and **Barton**, anxious to protect what they saw as **reserved state powers**, resisted these developments; but theirs was a rearguard action. In the *Woodworkers Case* (1909), a union log of claims was rejected independently by 13 employers in different states. Their failure to act in concert did not prevent the recognition of a single dispute; but Griffith warned that 'in the case of a mere paper demand … some combination or preconcert in resisting it may be necessary'. He insisted on 'real community of action' on both sides. If that element was present, it 'need not be formulated in any written document'; if not, 'mere mischief-makers' could not create it 'by the expenditure of a few shillings in paper, ink, and postage stamps'. In the *Felt Hatters Case* (1914), he again insisted that the constitutional purpose was to minimise 'real' disputes, not 'to facilitate the creation of fictitious disputes'. Barton agreed: 'It could not be intended that the tribunal should be paltered with by means of merely fabricated or paper disputes.' Again, however, the majority held that employer rejection of union demands gave rise to a genuine dispute. Higgins protested that the whole anxiety about 'paper disputes' had been whipped up by 'partisan journals'.

The recognition of paper disputes was further validated in the *Burwood Cinema Case* (1925). **Overruling** the contrary decision in *Holyman's Case* (1914), the Court held that employers whose employees were satisfied with their working conditions could nevertheless be joined as respondents, and bound by the ensuing award. Importantly, employers using only non-union workers, whose interests the union did not represent, were similarly held to be bound. Initially, Griffith had insisted that the joinder of employers must depend on their actual involvement, either in united resistance to union demands or in direct dispute with their workers. Now both **Isaacs** and **Starke** insisted that the only 'nexus' was participation in 'the industry itself'.

Although all *employers* in an industry could now be made parties to arbitration and bound by the resulting award, it did not follow that an award could regulate the working conditions of all *employees* in an industry, whether union members or not. A union was a representative party only on behalf of its members; and the nature of 'arbitration' was such that the rights and obligations it settled must be those of the parties only. The divergent judgments in *Alderdice's Case* (1928) had held, by a bare and unstable majority, that as a matter of **statutory interpretation** the Act had not in fact authorised an award extending to non-union members; but in the *Metal Trades Case* (1935), *Alderdice* was overruled. The Court held that although non-unionists were not themselves parties to a dispute, a demand in respect of 'all persons employed' gave rise to an arbitrable dispute between union and employers; and in settlement of that dispute, an award could bind the respondent employers in respect of all employees, including non-unionists.

The familiar notion of an 'ambit claim' is also a product of 'paper disputes'. Particularly in disputes about wages, the identification by demand and response of the minimum that a union will accept, and the maximum that employers will offer, sets precise limits to the area of dispute; and conciliation or arbitration must proceed within those limits. In *Ex parte Whybrow* (1910), Higgins had awarded certain apprentices higher wages than the union had claimed. Since this was not within the 'ambit' of the dispute, it was held invalid.

The effect of *Burwood Cinema* and the *Metal Trades Case* was reaffirmed in the *Aberdeen Beef Case* (1993). The employers in that case had questioned the *Burwood Cinema* emphasis on 'the industry itself' as the 'nexus' drawing employers and employees in different states and with differing circumstances into a single 'dispute'—not only because diversification and specialisation had made the concept of a single 'industry' less relevant, but because in the *CYSS Case* (1983) the Court itself had moved away from the concept of 'industry' as a touchstone of 'industrial disputes'. The majority conceded that the underlying requirement is that of 'community of interest'—but continued to assert that it would most commonly be satisfied by participation in a single industry, especially where (as here) there was a history of collective demands affecting the disparate work categories involved. Only **McHugh** would have shifted the focus more directly to 'community of interest'; but he too saw participation in 'a common industry or calling' as a significant factor.

Ironically, while service of a log across state boundaries was usually sufficient to establish an interstate 'paper dispute', direct industrial confrontation still posed jurisdictional problems. Strikes, lock-outs, or stoppages at particular worksites were often perceived as confined to a particular location, and hence to a particular state (see, for example, the first **Caledonian Collieries Case** (1930) and the *Pinkenba Case* (1957)). Occasionally, however, the Court acknowledged a pattern linking individual confrontations in a wider campaign transcending state boundaries (see, for example, *R v Turbet; Ex parte Australian Building Construction Employees and BLF* (1980)).

Even in relation to 'paper disputes', there remained a tendency to insist that disputes must be 'genuine'. In the second *Caledonian Collieries Case*, a log of claims was rejected because it was perceived as a mere device to circumvent the absence of arbitral power. In *Re State Public Services Federation* (1993), a claim to flat minimum remuneration of $7500 per week was dismissed by **Toohey** as 'lacking all industrial reality', and therefore not 'genuine'. The rest of the Court interpreted the claim as inviting the Commission to fix whatever rates it thought appropriate; but this interpretation led to no arbitrable dispute, either, since it lacked any definite 'ambit'. However, *A-G (Qld) v Riordan* (1997) made it clear that the Court was not abandoning the conception of 'paper disputes'—which **Kirby**, in particular, strongly defended—nor its tolerance of 'ambit claims'. **Brennan** and McHugh stressed that the 'apparent extravagance' of demands is not inconsistent with 'reality or genuineness', though a 'legitimate ambit claim' could not exceed 'what might reasonably be thought to be attainable by negotiation, conciliation and arbitration in the immediate future'.

The Court has repeatedly insisted that section 51(xxxv) does not extend to industrial relations as such, but only to the specified methods of 'conciliation' and 'arbitration'. As Higgins pointed out in *Australian Boot Trade Employés' Federation v Whybrow & Co (No 2)* (1910), these are 'means to an end':

> But they are the only means to that end provided by the Constitution … It is not enough for [laws] to be directed to the prevention and settlement of industrial disputes; they must be

directed to the particular method of prevention and settlement mentioned.

In that case, the Court unanimously struck down as invalid a provision empowering the Arbitration Court to make its award 'a common rule' of industry-wide application. To do so would effectively be to legislate; and 'arbitration' was not legislation. The practical effect of that decision was largely negated or circumvented by the *Metal Trades Case*; but the conceptual exclusion of a 'common rule' has steadfastly been maintained (see *R v Kelly; Ex parte Victoria* (1950)).

With the shift in the 1980s and 1990s towards enterprise bargaining, the traditional reliance on arbitration has been scaled down. Though many provisions of the old Conciliation and Arbitration Act remain, its name was changed to the *Industrial Relations Act* in 1988 and to the *Workplace Relations Act* in 1996, thus eliminating the very language of section 51(xxxv). The 1996 amendments directed the Commission to rely 'so far as possible' on conciliation, with arbitration 'as a last resort'. Furthermore, the issues that may now be submitted to arbitration are restricted to a specified list of 'allowable award matters' (job classification, working hours, wages, leave entitlements and so on).

Similar restrictions were imposed on existing awards. The 1996 amendments declared that, after an 'interim period' of 18 months, any existing award provision not dealing with 'allowable award matters' would cease to have effect. During the interim period, the Commission was empowered to vary awards so as to deal only with 'allowable award matters'; and 'as soon as practicable after the end of the interim period', the Commission was required to review all existing awards, and to vary them by removing any provisions no longer allowable.

In the *CFMEU Case* (2000), the Court assumed that the restrictions on future awards were valid. As **Gleeson** explained, section 51(xxxv) allows Parliament to 'establish and maintain' a system of conciliation and arbitration; but also to 'vary, modify, or abrogate' that system. On that basis, Parliament could simply have cancelled all existing awards. But as to the compulsory variation of existing awards—deleting some provisions while maintaining others—the Court divided 4:3.

Although the issue was perceived as 'transitional', its effect was far-reaching because of the large number of existing awards of long standing. Ironically, they had been maintained in force by the direct operation of a legislative provision—currently section 148, which provides that, after an initial term fixed by the arbitral tribunal and until it orders otherwise, 'an award dealing with particular matters continues in force until a new award is made dealing with the same matters'. When the predecessor of this provision, section 28(2) of the 1904 Act, was held to be valid in *Waterside Workers' Federation v Commonwealth Steamship Owners' Association* (1920), Isaacs and **Rich** dissented—protesting that the constitutional power was limited to 'arbitration', and that by extending the operation of awards by legislation the Parliament was 'departing from arbitration', effectively enacting 'new and independent obligations outside the arbitrator's award'. Now, in the *CFMEU Case*, essentially the same com-

peting arguments that had been deployed in 1920 for and against a legislative provision for the extension of awards, were deployed in 2000 for and against a legislative provision for their dismemberment.

The dissenting judges (**Gaudron**, McHugh and Kirby) maintained that in each case, the settlement resulting from 'arbitration' was the balance struck by the entire package of provisions in the existing award; and that, by mandatory deletion of some parts of that package, the legislature was in effect substituting its own package for that arrived at through arbitration. As Gaudron put it, the Parliament was no longer

> legislating with respect to the outcome of the processes of conciliation and arbitration. It is creating a new outcome from the combined process of legislation and arbitration … A law which substitutes an outcome that is different from the outcome of the processes of conciliation and arbitration is not a law with respect to conciliation and arbitration.

The majority were unmoved by this argument. The **joint judgment** of **Gummow** and **Hayne** emphasised the contemporary policy of shifting the emphasis of **labour relations law** away from awards. In that context, they said, the legislative command that certain award provisions should cease to have effect should be understood merely as withdrawing the legislative effect conferred by the Act (leaving untouched any effect arising, for example, from specific incorporation in employment contracts). Thus understood, it fell comfortably within the principle that what Parliament giveth, Parliament can take away. Arguments that the deletion of provisions might 'upset the balance' of the original award were simply irrelevant. **Callinan** had no sympathy with such arguments either, pointing out that the original award may well have contained 'elements repugnant to parties bound by it' and may even have been 'anathematical in whole to some parties'. In any event, the remaining award provisions on 'allowable award matters' could be adjusted by further variations.

Also controversial throughout much of the century was the meaning of 'industrial disputes'. Initially, the *Jumbunna Coal Case* (1908) had endorsed a broad 'common sense' meaning: notably, **O'Connor** held that the constitutional power was 'not confined to industries connected directly or indirectly with manufacture or production'. Yet, over the next decade, as the struggle over the supposed immunity from Commonwealth law of state governments as employers continued, the question whether particular state employees could be said to work in an 'industry' led repeatedly to limiting arguments: for example, that 'industry' entailed manual labour, or profit-making in the private sector. In response to such arguments Isaacs and Rich, in the *Municipalities Case* (1919), defined 'industrial disputes' as relating to the terms and conditions of 'co-operation' between capital and labour 'for the satisfaction of human wants or desires'.

Though this definition was intended to enlarge the scope of the arbitral power, it proved to have a restrictive effect. In the *Insurance Staffs Case* (1923), the majority (with **Knox** and **Gavan Duffy** dissenting) held that employees of banks and insurance companies could have 'industrial disputes' because banking and insurance, as sources of capital, were 'indispensable portions of the general industrial mechanism', even if they were not themselves 'industries'. But in the *School Teachers Case* (1929), it was held (over Isaacs' passionate dissent) that teachers in state government schools were not engaged in an 'industry' and therefore could not initiate an 'industrial dispute'. Thereafter, workers in various occupations, including fire fighters (*Pitfield v Franki* (1970)), were excluded from arbitration because they did not work in an 'industry'.

In the 1970s, this artificial restriction on the scope of section 51(xxxv) was increasingly questioned (initially by **Mason** in the *Federated Clerks Case* (1975)). Finally, in the *CYSS Case* (1983), a unanimous judgment returned to the original broad definition of 'industrial disputes' in *Jumbunna Coal*.

In recent years, the Court has acknowledged that the Commonwealth may also use other powers to regulate industrial relations. For example, in the *Industrial Relations Act Case* (1996), the Court upheld aspects of the *Industrial Relations Reform Act 1993* (Cth), which relied upon the **external affairs power** by giving effect to international instruments (particularly to Conventions of the International Labour Office). Likewise, the *Workplace Relations and Other Legislation Amendment Act 1996* (Cth) relies upon the external affairs power to validate its provisions relating to freedom of association, but also utilises the **trade and commerce power** and the **corporations power**—the latter in providing the Commission with additional jurisdiction to certify non-union enterprise agreements, and establishing a new form of agreement (the 'Australian Workforce Agreement') between an employer corporation and individual employee.

The Court, in interpreting the meaning of 'conciliation and arbitration', augmented the evolution of industrial relations throughout the twentieth century. While the chief objective of the power was to prevent industrial unrest, ironically the Court was infrequently called upon to interpret the parameters of the legislature's power with respect to cases involving strikes and lock-outs. For example, in a recent bitter dispute, the *Patrick Stevedores Case* (1998), the validity of legislation for freedom of association was seen as turning on the external affairs power rather than on section 51(xxxv). Instead, through a focus on 'paper disputes' and increasingly broad interpretations of the meaning of 'genuineness', 'interstateness' and 'industry', section 51(xxxv) was used to develop a system of bargaining based on industry-wide awards and a strong, centralised tribunal. While there has been significant pressure to move towards a decentralised system, awards and the tribunal still underpin Australian industrial relations. By supporting that system, the Court has endorsed an industrial process that is uniquely Australian.

TINA CRISAFULLI

Further Reading
HB Higgins, *A New Province for Law and Order* (1922)
Martin Vranken, 'Demise of the Australasian Model of Labour Law in the 1990s' (1994) 16 *Comp Labor Law J* 1
Ronald McCallum, 'The New Millennium and the Higgins Heritage: Australian Industrial Relations in the Twenty-First Century' (1996) 38 *J Industrial Relations* 294
WJ Ford, 'Reconstructing Labour Law: A Constitutional Perspective' (1997) 10 *Aust J Labour Law* 1
Laura Bennett, *Making Labour Law in Australia: Industrial Relations, Politics and Law* (1994)

Concurring judgments. A Justice who agrees in the result of a particular case may either join in the judgment of the Court, or of the majority, or may write a separate judgment expressing his or her concurrence. A separate judgment expressing agreement in the result is called a concurring judgment. If the concurring Justice's reasoning differs from that of the other Justices who agree in the result, that does not make his or her judgment a **dissenting judgment**; that term is reserved for a judgment in which disagreement is expressed with the result (as encapsulated, generally speaking, in the **order** of the Court). Yet a Justice may, in a concurring judgment, disagree strongly with the reasoning of other Justices notwithstanding their common conclusion. Indeed, that is often precisely why a Justice chooses to write a separate concurrence.

Whether a Justice should or should not write a separate concurring judgment is part of a wider debate about the relative merits of **joint judgments and separate judgments**. On one hand, joint judgments—especially those of the Court as a whole or of a majority—are said to serve the interests of clarity and certainty, and thus to provide better guidance to lower court judges, legal advisers, and others who have to apply the law. On the other hand, separate judgments are said to have the advantage of revealing latent differences of opinion, the temporary suppression of which may make the certainty claimed for the joint judgment somewhat illusory; they are said also to offer the best assurance that each Justice is discharging his or her individual responsibility for judging; and they are said, finally, to reflect realistically the complexity of the law and the diversity of perspectives open to a final appellate court, as well as the diversity of the **values** and **policy considerations** underlying those perspectives.

While the dissenting judgment has a respectable place in the law (bolstered by celebrated examples of dissenting judgments later vindicated by a change in the law), the concurring judgment is often criticised as an unnecessary gloss, and inconsistent with the Court's **collective responsibility**. That is certainly so if the concurring judgment merely engages in a further recitation of uncontroversial facts or the statutory framework, or even of the legal principles, if they are relatively straightforward. Yet disagreement in a concurring judgment on matters of principle may be just as important to the development of the law as if it were contained in a dissenting judgment—and to that extent, agreement on the **outcome** of the particular case may be incidental.

The subtleties of concurrence and dissent often complicate the search for the elusive *ratio decidendi* of a case and pose questions about the value of a decision as a **precedent**. Where there is no clear majority reason for a particular result, the decision might not be easily generalisable beyond its particular facts (but see *Dennis Hotels v Victoria* (1960)). Sensitive to that concern, Justices sometimes express their views in the alternative. Conscious of the extreme diversity of opinion that had emerged within the Court in the late 1970s in relation to the interpretation of section 92 of the Constitution (see **Interstate trade and commerce**), both **Barwick** and **Murphy** did so in *Uebergang v Australian Wheat Board*

(1980). With unusually explicit pragmatism, Murphy said: 'While adhering to my own view of s92, I would, as an alternative, support that which seems to be the nearest to mine in order to obtain or increase the vote for that view and to reject a more extreme alternative.'

The effectiveness of this strategy was never really tested, as eight years later the Court found unanimity in *Cole v Whitfield* (1988). A similar strategy employed by **Deane** in *Theophanous v Herald & Weekly Times* (1994), however, was singularly unsuccessful. Deane agreed with **Mason**, **Toohey**, and **Gaudron** that the implied constitutional freedom of **political communication** precluded liability for **defamation** in the instant case, but went much further in expounding the impact of the constitutional guarantee. Nevertheless, he declared that he would 'lend his support for the answers which their Honours give to the question reserved by the stated case' (although those answers set out propositions of law with which Deane disagreed). In *Lange v ABC* (1997), the Court found this to be insufficient to create a majority of the kind that established a precedent that, if it were to be departed from, would need to be **overruled**.

At some point, a Justice may move from adhering to his or her own view and expressing agreement with others in the alternative, to capitulating to the majority view. The occasion for separate concurrence will then generally have passed. Yet in *Hughes & Vale v NSW (No 2)* (1955), **McTiernan** could not quite let go. Though a party to the joint judgment of **Dixon**, himself and **Webb** in that case, he noted in a separate 'addendum' that he desired to make 'some brief observations for myself':

> In the joint judgment to which I am a party there is stated, as I believe adequately, with respect to the particular problem these cases raise, what appears to be the true operation of the views which in the past I had found myself unable to share. But perhaps I may be permitted to say that I remain personally far from convinced that the result is one which the framers of s92 either intended or foresaw.

(If this conjunction of agreement and disagreement were not odd enough in itself, in a bizarre twist it appears from the **Dixon diaries** that this expression of lingering discontent with the Dixon view of section 92 was actually written for McTiernan, at McTiernan's request, by Dixon himself.)

Sometimes (and particularly in *ex tempore* **judgments**) a concurring judgment is as brief as 'I agree'. This kind of concurring judgment is no different in substance from being a party to a joint judgment, although care must be taken to leave no doubt about what it is with which the Justice agrees. If that brief expression of agreement is immediately preceded by the concurring judgment of another Justice who has said something like 'I have read the opinion of the learned Chief Justice and there is nothing I can usefully add', the simple 'I agree' (whether innocent or mischievous) may easily be misunderstood.

The concurring judgment does open up the potential for confusion, though usually as a result of what is said beyond 'I agree'. An extreme example occurred in *R v Murray and Cormie; Ex parte Commonwealth* (1916). The **Full Court** of seven Justices heard an application for **leave to appeal** from the District Court of NSW outside the time permitted for such appeals. Chief Justice **Griffith**, with whom **Barton** and **Powers** agreed, held that the Court had no jurisdiction to grant leave, and that, in any event, it ought not to exercise its discretion to do so. **Isaacs** said that 'as to the question of discretion, personally I do not take the same view as that expounded by the learned Chief Justice'. Notwithstanding this disagreement, **Higgins** stated somewhat unhelpfully: 'I agree with what has been said by the Chief Justice and my brother Isaacs.' **Rich** did perceive that there was a disagreement, but said with an air of resignation: 'As at present advised, I do not feel the same certainty about the matter as the majority of the Court do, but the expression of the reason for my doubts will be of no avail.' But **Gavan Duffy's** three-word judgment was even more unhelpful. In a faintly oxymoronic statement that would be difficult to classify as either concurring or dissenting, Gavan Duffy said: 'I say nothing.'

The separate concurring judgment is born of the desire to say something, whether in elaboration, supplementation, qualification, or negation of the pronouncements of those who happen, in the circumstances, to reach the same conclusion. In many cases, this will be a helpful gloss that provides an alternative viewpoint, underlines the dynamic nature of the development of the law, and gives a possible indication of what the law might become. In some cases, it will be an unhelpful repetition or a source of unnecessary ambiguity (particularly if it fails to deal at all with some of the issues). In discharging their individual and personal responsibility to make their own independent decisions on the cases that come before them, the Justices must weigh up the relative merits of speaking with one voice or many.

MICHAEL COPER

Conferences. After a hearing has ended and judgment has been **reserved**, the practices of collegiate courts vary widely. The High Court, unlike the **United States Supreme Court**, has had no regular system of conferences. The extent to which on a formal or informal collegiate basis Justices have conferred, circulated their reasons, become partners to **joint judgments**, or written **concurring judgments**, has depended on the Justices' personalities and **personal relations**, their **sitting** arrangements and places of residence, and the role and influence of the **Chief Justice**.

Consultation in the **Griffith Court** from 1903 to 1906 was probably informal, consisting of discussion among friends. After February 1905, **Griffith**, **Barton**, and **O'Connor** all lived in Sydney, allowing a certain degree of face-to-face discussion. They lunched together on working days and resided together on **circuit**. From 1903 to 1906, there were only four formal **dissenting judgments**, all of them by O'Connor.

The atmosphere and approach changed in 1906 when **Isaacs** and **Higgins**, who both lived in Melbourne, were appointed. Thereafter, such consultation as did occur was impeded by ideological differences and by the mix of the Justices' temperaments—for example, by Griffith's dominant personality and disapproval of Isaacs' and Higgins' views on **constitutional law** and **constitutional interpretation**; by Barton's antipathy to Isaacs and Higgins; by Isaacs' intransigence and incredulity that there could be another view; and by Higgins' pride. Acting Chief Justice Barton wrote to Griffith about the *Engine-Drivers Case* in 1913: 'I think the end of it will be that four will agree upon one view, and that the most mischievous one. We have not consulted together since the **argument** closed so that I am not quite sure how they stand' (Isaacs, Higgins, **Gavan Duffy**, and **Rich** adopted 'the mischievous' view; Barton and **Powers** dissented). Barton wrote about a time when the Justices did meet to discuss a case: 'We consulted as to the judgement last Saturday'; but because of the diversity of opinion among the Justices on different aspects of the case, 'the whole affair collapsed'. Despite the differences of opinion, the exchange of reasons after 1906 was not confined to Griffith, Barton, and O'Connor. Griffith sent a copy of his draft judgment in *Barnes v Sharpe* (1910) to Higgins, for example.

In 1924, Gavan Duffy described to Higgins the procedure in the **Knox Court**: 'Isaacs & Rich retire to their tents (or perhaps I should say to Isaacs's tent) and excogitate judgments which I never see till they are delivered.' **Knox**, **Starke**, and Gavan Duffy himself

> exchange views as we go to or leave Court and on the strength of this interchange of ideas produce something which does not exactly express the opinion of any one of us, but endeavours to say nothing to which any one of us objects. I am beginning to think that I could render most service by limiting my observations to a statement that I think the appeal should, or should not, be allowed.

In *Commonwealth and Commonwealth Oil Refineries v SA* (1926), Higgins confirmed the lack of consultation between the Justices: 'I had no idea that any of my colleagues [Knox, Isaacs, and Starke] wished to **overrule** *Duncan's Case* until their judgments were published' (see also *Roughley v NSW; Ex Parte Beavis* (1928)).

When **Latham** became Chief Justice in 1935, he 'at once endeavoured to make a change by introducing a sensible system of consultation'; but by 1939, 'the position … remained unchanged … in spite of my endeavours to improve it'. The lack of consultation prompted **Evatt** to ask Latham to amend the **High Court Rules**, so as to require the Justices to exchange their reasons:

> The present position as to consultation and inter-change of opinions has become very unsatisfactory. While **Dixon** is away, you, and you alone, receive all the opinions. You communicate to the other judges as much or as little as you choose of any opinion of which you become possessed … But all judges should have the judgments of all others made available … I am not content with your oral interpretations to me of the judgments of others, or of mine to others.

Latham agreed that there was a lack of proper consultation, but reminded Evatt:

> You would not attend conferences with a certain justice [Starke] … Other justices hold similar views and they similarly decline to confer … Each justice makes his own distribution [of their reasons]. You do not send your reasons to one justice and he does not send his to you. If you agree to send yours to

him I will do my best to get him to receive them and to reciprocate, as he ought to do.

According to Evatt, the situation was a good deal worse than when Gavan Duffy was Chief Justice. Evatt asserted that in the **Gavan Duffy Court**, it was 'practically understood' that the Justices would not be 'deprived of the light and learning' of those who held differing opinions 'except on grounds of overwhelming urgency'. Starke gave a different, probably more accurate, description of Gavan Duffy's practice as Chief Justice—'He had none'.

Although Latham was not immediately successful in introducing a system of formal conferences, the **Dixon diaries** show that in the 1930s informal meetings were common. These included discussions between Rich, Dixon, Evatt, and **McTiernan** for the *Metal Trades Case* (1935) and the *Tramways Case* (1935); a meeting about *Riverina Transport v Victoria* (1937) and *Hartley v Walsh* (1937); and a meeting between Latham, Rich, Dixon, and Evatt over *Evans v Evans* (1939), 'an application for special **leave** in a custody case where the fight is over religion'. By the end of the period of the **Latham Court**, the Justices had developed a practice of regularly circulating their judgments to others who had sat on the case, a practice that, in the absence of conferences, Justices appreciated. Writing from Tokyo in 1948, **Webb** told Latham that it was 'such a handicap to write judgments without having conferences with the other judges', but 'it is something to get copies of the reasons of the other judges'.

Formal conferences were held in the late 1940s and early 1950s. A conference—'the first for many years', as Dixon noted—was held in June 1948 for the **Bank Nationalisation Case**. The Justices met in the High Court **library** to discuss a long memorandum Latham had circulated in which he had outlined the questions requiring decision, his own answers, and counter arguments. Despite the conference, Latham failed to persuade a majority of Justices to support his views on the case. There was a more successful conference for *R v Foster* (1949), in which the Court delivered a unanimous judgment. **Williams** thanked Latham and Dixon for 'moulding the result of the conference into such excellent shape. It is a great thing that the Court is able to speak with one voice on these important cases'. Similar techniques used for the *Bank Nationalisation Case* were applied to the *Communist Party Case* (1951). Dixon made a note about the conference in his diary: 'At 3.30 we had a judges' conference. The CJ began by wasting time over a request for a cooler uniform made by the tipstaffs, about which he was very strange: hostile to the tipstaffs and extreme in his expression. We then got to the case, but got nowhere.' After **Fullagar** and **Kitto** were appointed, Latham found ways to save time by 'consultation and by assigning one judge to write a judgment'. It was now possible to 'adopt this method more frequently', but 'it has to be watched in order to prevent a tendency which … has at times been most odious in the **Privy Council**, to leave it to one judge to do all the work and really make up the mind of the Court'.

In the **Dixon Court**, informal meetings were held regularly during sittings. The conversation—often over cups of tea in Dixon's **chambers**—ranged over current cases and judgments in the course of preparation. Dixon, Fullagar, and

Douglas **Menzies** were among the first to circulate their judgments; **Windeyer** often circulated his judgment later, not for want of diligence, but because of his keen interest in the **history** of issues. Arrangements for joint judgments were ad hoc, but in some cases, especially criminal appeals, there was a general preference for unanimity.

NSW **Solicitor-General** and former High Court **associate**, Michael Sexton, described in *Uncertain Justice* (2000) the procedure in the early 1970s:

> After tolerating the greatest possible degree of inefficiency in the presentation of a case, the court then seemed to compound this by its method of producing a decision. At no time did all the judges of the court ever sit collectively except to actually hear a case in the **courtroom**. After the hearing each judge retreated to his own rooms to prepare an individual judgment in each case. This way of operating no doubt resulted from a life at the bar where there is a lot of solitary work.

Each Justice arranged for the circulation of his own judgment to the other Justices who sat in the case. **Mason** was often the first to circulate his draft; **Jacobs** completed his judgments early as well. Sexton continued:

> There were some joint judgments but the overall duplication of effort raised a real question about the efficiency of the court's operations. It was certainly a source of concern to Sir Garfield **Barwick** … He was interested in the US Supreme Court's system of conferences—attended by all judges—to discuss cases and allocate the writing of majority decisions to one member of the court. But Barwick found no real support for this idea among most of his colleagues.

Barwick did later convene a few conferences, but they did not work well, and were abandoned. Because of the complexity of the issues and because he thought some degree of consensus was desirable, Barwick convened a lengthy conference for *R v Bull* (1974). According to Mason, the conference consisted of lengthy and unsuccessful attempts by Barwick and Douglas Menzies to change the views of the other. The other Justices contributed little to what seemed to be, in Mason's words:

> a ritual joust between two old gladiators. The array of disparate and conflicting views in the judgments was the outcome of that conference. I think it highly unlikely that Barwick thought that a system of regular discussion failed because he sought to impose his views on others. His efforts to influence the thinking of other Justices were confined largely to his interventionist conduct of oral argument in the hearing of a case. Otherwise I did not feel that he was attempting to impose his views on me. Sometimes in discussion with me he would express his view strongly, if my view did not coincide with his, but that was all. It is more likely that he thought the conference discussion failed because others did not share his views—his judgments were never influential like Dixon's—and because *he felt* that others thought he was trying to impose his views on them. In his early days, **McTiernan**, Kitto, **Taylor**, Menzies, and Windeyer may well have thought that. In any event, at the end of the day, why persevere when the discussions generate dis-

agreement rather than consensus? That was my reaction years later after *Bull*.

There was no conference system in the **Gibbs Court**. Often, at the end of a case, Justices discussed the outcome. Meetings were convened rarely, when unanimity was thought especially desirable. Usually, a Justice worked alone to prepare his judgment; but once it had been circulated, others sometimes discussed it to indicate agreement or to suggest amendments.

Meetings were held each month in the **Mason Court** to monitor progress in judgment writing and to exchange views about particular judgments, especially to ascertain whether a joint judgment was possible. Sometimes, a special meeting was convened to discuss important or complex cases or if unanimity was perceived as particularly desirable. In such cases, Mason, or the presiding Justice, with the concurrence of the Justices sitting in the case, would invite a particular Justice or Justices to write the first judgment, the designated author or authors sometimes discussing the draft in progress with other Justices.

Collegiate decisions during the Mason Court such as *Cole v Whitfield* (1988) and *Voth v Manildra Flour Mills* (1990) were presumably the result of these meetings. In *Voth*, Mason, **Deane**, **Dawson**, and **Gaudron** said that in light of the diversity of opinion expressed in *Oceanic Sun Line v Fay* (1988), they had 'put aside individual differences of emphasis in order to participate in this majority judgment', in order to 'enunciate authoritatively the principles and criteria to be applied by Australian courts in future cases' (see **Collective reponsibility**). The procedures adopted by the Mason Court continued through to the **Brennan Court**.

In the **Gleeson Court**, informal meetings commonly follow the hearing of argument and, when there is extended argument, continue during adjournments. With five of the seven Justices based in Sydney, informal discussions sometimes take place in Sydney chambers and with other Justices by telephone or facsimile. For special leave applications, meetings are convened by the presiding Justice and take place shortly before the hearing. These involve discussion, necessarily tentative, of the responses to each application, based on the written arguments filed by the parties in accordance with the High Court Rules. The procedure of analysis of the application and of the arguments of the parties is quite formal, and responsibility for each case is, by convention, assigned among the participating Justices by the presiding Justice. It not infrequently happens that a tentative view expressed at the special leave meeting is changed following oral argument. Formal conferences are now held, with all Justices participating, in the week following each sitting of the Court, to discuss reserved judgments. Commonly held in Sydney or Melbourne, these conferences are often combined with a short special leave hearing in the city of the meeting. The Court commented on the conferences in its 1998–99 **Annual Report**:

> The discussion has contributed in some cases to agreement upon single opinions for the Court, following the concurrence of opinion amongst the Justices both as to the result and as to the reasons for the result. It has also facilitated arrangements

for the acceptance of obligations, on the part of particular Justices, to prepare a first draft for the Court's consideration. Such a division of labour promotes efficiency. It can also assist in the early delivery of decisions … The discussions will not always secure agreement between the Justices and this is not their purpose. Even where important differences exist, discussion can help clarify and refine opinions and reasoning. Such meetings also contribute to the collegiality of the Court and to relationships between the Justices and their understanding of their respective opinions.

Given the availability of modern **information technology**, it is possible that in the future these meetings will be conducted by video link.

TROY SIMPSON

Further Reading
High Court of Australia, *Annual Report 1998–99*, 5–6
Robert J Janosik, 'Conference, The' in Kermit Hall (ed), *The Oxford Companion to the Supreme Court of the United States* (1992) 174
Clem Lloyd, 'Not Peace but a Sword! The High Court under JG Latham' (1987) 11 *Adel L Rev* 175
GPJ McGinley, 'The Search for Unity: The Impact of Consensus Seeking Procedures in Appellate Courts' (1987) 11 *Adel L Rev* 203
Senate Standing Committee on Legal and Constitutional Affairs, *Examination of Annual Reports: High Court of Australia* (Official Hansard Report) (1986)

Conflict of laws. Sometimes known as 'private international law', the doctrines developed under the rubric 'conflict of laws' are designed to resolve the complex practical issues that arise when the laws of more than one jurisdiction impact upon a given factual situation. Few of these issues have remained untouched by the High Court.

One issue is whether the matter in question is sufficiently connected with a particular jurisdiction to allow the courts of that jurisdiction to hear the matter. Cases of this kind have come before the High Court in both transnational and federal contexts. Thus, *Parker v Parker* (1908) involved the question whether the NSW Supreme Court had jurisdiction in divorce proceedings over a husband alleged to have deserted his wife in circumstances where it was held that, although the wife and child of the marriage had acquired a domicile in NSW, the husband had never lost his Victorian domicile of origin. By contrast, *Gillett v National Benefit Life & Property Assurance Co* (1918) involved the question whether an English company registered as a foreign company in NSW was amenable to the jurisdiction of the NSW Supreme Court after it had ceased to carry on business in that state.

Another issue is what law should apply when a matter has elements involving more than one jurisdiction (the 'choice of law' issue). As with questions of jurisdiction, the choice of law problem in **contract** has been considered by the Court both in transnational contexts and in federal or interstate contexts. The transnational examples include *Barcelo v Electrolytic Zinc* (1932), *Wanganui-Rangitikei Electric Power v AMP* (1934), *Bonython v Commonwealth* (1948, affirmed by the **Privy Council** in 1950) and *Akai v People's Insurance Co* (1996). In *Akai*, an insurance policy issued in Singapore, but

insuring a NSW company in respect of its NSW business, was held to be governed by NSW law. The earlier cases involved debentures, and, in each of them, the applicable law was held to be that of the jurisdiction where the debentures were issued.

Examples in a federal context include *Merwin Pastoral Co v Moolpa Pastoral Co* (1933) and *Wragge v Sims Cooper* (1933). Both cases involved the sale of land in NSW. In *Merwin Pastoral* the contract of sale was held to be governed by NSW law; in *Wragge* the purchase price had been secured by a promissory note issued and payable in Victoria, which was held to be governed by the law of Victoria.

In the area of **tort**, *Voth v Manildra Flour Mills* (1990) is an important decision in the transnational context on the manner in which the *locus* (place) of a tort for conflict of laws purposes is identified—an exercise of especial complexity when the tortious conduct alleged involves an omission or failure in one jurisdiction to perform or carry out a particular act or duty with consequences in another jurisdiction. In *Voth*, two NSW companies had employed an American accountant, resident and practising in Missouri, as their taxation adviser. They sought to sue him for negligent advice. The majority (with **Brennan** in sole dissent) held that, even if the matter were to be litigated in NSW, the relevant law would be that of Missouri, since it was in Missouri that the negligence, if any, had occurred.

The vexed question of the choice of law rule for tort—which depends, at least in part, on identifying the *locus* of the tort—has been considered by the Court, directly or in passing, on no fewer than nine occasions, from *Musgrave v Commonwealth* (1937) to *John Pfeiffer v Rogerson* (2000). Significantly, all of these cases have arisen in the Australian federal context.

Until *Pfeiffer*, there was little difference in the Court's approaches to conflict of laws problems in the transnational and the federal contexts. In *Potter v BHP* (1906), the preoccupation of the **Griffith Court** with the **sovereignty** of the states had led it to repudiate any distinction between 'Sovereign States' and 'foreign Powers'. The result, for most purposes in the conflict of laws, was that each Australian state was treated as a distinct and separate country or 'law area': see, for example, **Williams** in *Chaff and Hay Acquisition Committee v Hemphill* (1947) and **Windeyer** in *Pedersen v Young* (1964).

On the other hand, **Rich**, **Dixon** and **Evatt** had suggested in the *Merwin Pastoral* case in 1933 that an alternative basis for the decision might be found in section 118 of the Constitution, which requires that 'Full faith and credit shall be given, throughout the Commonwealth to the laws, the public Acts and records, and the judicial proceedings of every State'. Section 118 was not, but conceivably could have been, relied upon by the Court in *Chaff and Hay Acquisition Committee v Hemphill*; instead, the Court relied upon the notion of comity of nations, imported into the context of federal interstate relations, in allowing the Chaff and Hay Acquisition Committee, an unincorporated body created by SA legislation, to be sued in the NSW Supreme Court.

In *Laurie v Carroll* (1958), the Court noted parenthetically that the fiction of separate Australian 'law areas' must be 'subject to the Commonwealth Constitution and legislation under it such as the *Service and Execution of Process Act*'. But it was not until *Breavington v Godleman* (1988) that the relevance of the constitutional provisions was explored in any detail. In that case, a clear and profound division emerged between those Justices who regarded the fiction of separate 'law areas' as inconsistent with the text and structure of the Constitution, and those who saw the Constitution as having no role to play in the resolution of such questions. This fundamental difference of approach was reiterated in *McKain v Miller* (1991) and in *Stevens v Head* (1993), with the fiction of separate countries commanding majority support. That fiction was at last exploded, however, in *Pfeiffer*, a decision that greatly curtails the scope for 'forum shopping' within Australia.

The appellant company in *Pfeiffer* carried on business in the ACT, where it employed Rogerson as a carpenter. He was injured, however, while working on a project at Queanbeyan, in NSW. Under ACT law he was entitled to common law **damages**; under NSW law, his damages would be limited by the *Workers Compensation Act* 1987 (NSW). On the basis of *Stevens v Head*, the applicable law was the law of the forum (that is, of the ACT); but the Court (with **Callinan** dissenting) departed from *Stevens v Head* to hold that, in all such cases in Australia, the applicable law should be determined by the *locus* of the tort. In a powerful joint judgment, Chief Justice **Gleeson**, **Gaudron**, **McHugh**, **Gummow** and **Hayne** rejected the older **common law** decisions as decided 'in a context far removed from that of the Australian federal compact'. Applying *Lange v ABC* (1997), they held that 'the common law of Australia must adapt to the Constitution'. Whatever else section 118 of the Constitution might mean, it meant 'that, as between themselves, the States are not foreign powers as are nation states for the purposes of **international law**'. They concluded that 'within the federal system, it is appropriate that each State and Territory recognise the interest of the other States and Territories in the application of their laws to events occurring in their jurisdiction'.

Oceanic Sun Line Special Shipping v Fay (1988), decided in the same year as *Breavington v Godleman*, also produced strong differences of opinion within the Court as to the proper role and scope of the Scottish doctrine of *forum non conveniens*, adopted by the **House of Lords** two years earlier in *Spiliada Maritime Corporation v Cansulex* (1986) and subsequently adopted in a number of other common law jurisdictions. *Oceanic Sun Line* was the first case since *Maritime Insurance v Geelong Harbor Trust* (1908) in which a question of the discretion to exercise jurisdiction had arisen in a transnational case for the Court's consideration. The issue was whether the NSW Supreme Court should stay proceedings commenced in that Court by an Australian plaintiff injured on a cruise in the Greek Islands, to allow the issue to be determined by litigation in Greece. A stay was refused by a majority of 3:2. Subsequently, in *Voth*, the differences of opinion in *Oceanic* were put aside in favour of a single formulation of the test for the discretionary exercise of jurisdiction. It was held that an Australian court should decline to exercise jurisdiction only if that court was clearly inappropriate as a forum for the resolution of the particular case. In that case, given the majority view that the accountant could be liable only if he were liable under the law of Missouri, it

was held that NSW was clearly an inappropriate forum, and the proceedings were stayed.

The 1990s saw four further cases concerned with the exercise of jurisdiction in a transnational context: two in the area of **family law** (*ZP v PS* (1994) and *Henry v Henry* (1996)) and two in the area of commercial insurance (*Akai* and *CSR v Cigna Insurance* (1997)). These cases—involving respectively an international child custody dispute, nullity proceedings with litigation and assets in multiple jurisdictions, anti-suit injunctions restraining foreign proceedings and exclusive jurisdiction agreements, and their interaction with beneficial municipal legislation—were in part products of technological developments in the second half of the twentieth century facilitating the international movement of goods, services and persons and the globalisation of the world economy. Like *Oceanic* and *Voth*, these cases considered the role of international comity, and developed a sophisticated body of principles designed to identify a suitable forum for the resolution of transnational disputes in any given case, while minimising the possibility of a multiplicity of suits.

In the *Spycatcher Case* (1988), which attracted general public attention because of its subject matter, the doctrines of public and private international law overlapped and interacted, and the question of jurisdiction merged into that of **justiciability**. The Court refused to entertain an application by the UK **Attorney-General** for an injunction to restrain the publication of a book by a former member of the British intelligence services. The publication was said to be in breach of a contractual and equitable obligation of confidence owed by the author to the British government. The injunction was refused by reference to the doctrine that a domestic court should not entertain a suit to enforce the public laws of a foreign state. A similar theme, though not directly referred to in *Spycatcher*, had underpinned the Court's earlier decisions in **patents** cases—that the validity of a patent can only be challenged (*Potter v BHP*) and the monopoly it confers can only be enforced (**Fullagar** in *Norbert Steinhardt v Meth* (1961)) in the courts of the sovereign state responsible for granting the patent.

In considering the various issues raised by the conflict of laws, members of the Court have consistently drawn upon academic writings. For example, in one of its earliest decisions in the field, *AMP v Gregory* (1908)—where a Tasmanian assignor, the beneficiary of a **trust** established by his father's will in respect of land in Tasmania, had assigned his interest to a Tasmanian assignee who was unaware that the assignor had been declared bankrupt in South Africa—the Justices, in deciding that the assignee was entitled to priority over the South African trustee in bankruptcy, drew variously upon the writings of AV Dicey, Joseph Story, John Westlake, JA Foote, Henry Wheaton and John Erskine of Carnock. The detailed consideration in *McKain v Miller* of the dichotomy between substance and procedure in the conflict of laws is a later illustration of the influence of scholarship on the Court in this field. The decisions of the **United States Supreme Court** in the area of conflict of laws have also been an important source of authority and ideas for the Court (see **Citations by Court; Extrinsic materials**).

ANDREW BELL

Connotation and denotation. The distinction between connotation and denotation is a tool used by the High Court in **constitutional interpretation**. The technical distinction adopted by modern logicians comes from the second edition of John Stuart Mill's *A System of Logic* (1846). In that usage, as adopted by the High Court, the 'connotation' of a word used in the Constitution is the set of attributes to which the word referred in 1900, when the Constitution was enacted. Its 'denotation' refers to things in the world which may now be seen to possess those attributes, so as to justify applying the word to them. In the *Tasmanian Dam Case* (1983), **Dawson** used the terms in the opposite sense found in literary and popular usage; however, in *Street v Queensland Bar Association* (1989), he repented of having done so, since Mill's usage was 'more or less consistently' entrenched in High Court judgments, and seemed 'to offer a precision which the popular usage [did] not'.

Accordingly, in the entrenched constitutional usage, the connotation of a word is constant, whereas its denotation changes over time. Thus, to take an uncontroversial example, the word 'vehicle' connoted 'a means of transport' in 1900 and at that time it included trains and carriages. That connotation has not changed, but the denotation of the word now includes jet aircraft, although they were unknown at the turn of the century.

Commentators have both attacked and defended the Court's reliance on this distinction in constitutional interpretation. On one view, the distinction itself, and the concept of 'attributes' on which Mill's stipulative definitions depend, are philosophically outdated, and the Court has engaged in a fruitless task by attempting to define the essential attributes of constitutional terms. Leslie Zines, for instance, contends that there is no logical way of determining what the essential attributes of a term are when borderline cases are involved. He argues that, in relation to the extent of Commonwealth power, the advantage or otherwise of a matter being under federal control should be the deciding factor, and that this should be articulated. On another view, represented by Jeff Goldsworthy, the Court's usage of 'connotation' and 'denotation' reflects similar distinctions that continue to be drawn in the philosophy of language, such as intension and extension, and sense and reference.

It is hard to accept that the distinction between connotation and denotation is untenable simply because its application fails to solve borderline cases. Even the clearest of terms, such as 'man' and 'woman', can have doubtful applications, as the existence of hermaphrodites demonstrates. But that does not make the distinction between these terms any less real. Nor does the existence of difficult cases necessarily obviate the distinction between connotation and denotation. It does, however, mean that when the Court is called upon to decide whether borderline cases fall within the ambit of a constitutional description, language will not be decisive, and it will be legitimate to have regard to **policy** factors.

Perhaps a more telling argument against the distinction is that the Court has misapplied it. In several judgments, the Court seems to have relied on something akin to Ronald Dworkin's distinction between concepts and conceptions while using the language of connotation and denotation.

According to Dworkin, the US Constitution embodies abstract and contested moral concepts such as '**equality**', the meaning of which depends on the political theory that is used to explain it. Judges must give effect to their conceptions of what these abstract concepts require, even if this results in the invalidation of practices that were accepted as valid by the founders.

In *McGinty v WA* (1996), **Toohey** and **Gaudron** (dissenting) decided that a constitutional requirement of 'representative **democracy**' invalidated a WA law that created inequality of voting power. Each stated that the essence or connotation of representative democracy remained unchanged from 1900, but the content varied according to the changes in society. On that basis, they concluded that inequality of voting power was now forbidden, even though it was not forbidden at the turn of the century. Their reasoning here overlooks the fact that 'representative democracy', unlike 'vehicle', is a contested concept; its essence depends on the political theory that one uses to explain it. This makes it difficult to say that the connotation of representative democracy has remained the same throughout the twentieth century, and only its denotation has altered.

Even more problematic is *Cheatle v The Queen* (1993). In that case, the Court unanimously held that a Commonwealth law could not provide for majority verdicts in criminal cases, because section 80 of the Constitution imposed a requirement of 'trial by jury'. The Court noted that majority verdicts were unknown to the **common law** in 1900, and said that there were sound policy reasons for ensuring that verdicts were unanimous. This reasoning ignores the distinction between connotation and denotation. By claiming that unanimity was an essential feature of 'trial by jury', the Court in effect found that the connotation *and* denotation of that term required unanimous verdicts. This was puzzling, to say the least. Majority verdicts had been used in cases across Australia and around the world for years, and it could not plausibly be said that, as a matter of language, trials decided by majority verdict were not 'trials by jury'. *Cheatle* thus reveals a Court that has been unable, or unwilling, to apply the distinction between connotation and denotation in a coherent manner.

The distinction between connotation and denotation helps to explain how constitutional language applies to events and circumstances that were not foreseen at the time of federation. The distinction itself seems sound. However, the Court's use of the distinction has been questionable. Members of the Court have occasionally confused the distinction with that between concepts and conceptions. At other times, they seem to have ignored the distinction altogether, perhaps because it would lead to uncongenial outcomes. If the distinction cannot be coherently applied, one is driven to ask what purpose it serves. There seems little point in having a distinction that conceals the Court's policy preferences under the guise of linguistic analysis.

GIM DEL VILLAR

Further Reading
Michael Devitt and Kim Sterelny, *Language and Reality* (1987)
Ronald Dworkin, *A Matter of Principle* (1985)

Jeffrey Goldsworthy, 'Originalism in Constitutional Interpretation' (1997) 25 *FL Rev* 1

David Tucker, 'Textualism: An Australian Evaluation of the Debate between Professor Ronald Dworkin and Justice Antonin Scalia' (1999) 21 *Syd LR* 567

Leslie Zines, *The High Court and the Constitution* (4th edn 1997)

Constitutional basis of Court. Section 71 of the Constitution provides that the **judicial power** of the Commonwealth 'shall be vested in a Federal Supreme Court, to be called the High Court of Australia, and in such other federal courts as the Parliament creates'. Clearly these last words did not themselves do anything to establish federal courts, but merely empowered the Parliament to do so. By contrast, the provision that judicial power 'shall be' vested in a High Court seems capable of having some operation independently of legislative implementation. Yet section 71 stops short of saying that there 'shall be' a High Court (unlike, for example, section 101, which declares categorically that there 'shall be' an **Inter-State Commission**). Did section 71 create a High Court, or did it not?

Article III of the US Constitution was expressed in similar terms. But in the USA, it was always assumed that the constitutional provision 'was, of course, not self-executing. Before the federal courts, including the Supreme Court, could come into existence, they had to be provided for by statute' (Bernard Schwartz, *A History of the Supreme Court* (1993)). Yet the use of the word 'existence' raises a metaphysical question, as to which the position in Australia was less clear.

Section 4 of the *Judiciary Act* 1903 (Cth) declared that the High Court 'shall be a **superior court** of record' consisting of the **Chief Justice** and two other Justices. (The Constitution had specified this as a minimum, but had otherwise left the **number of Justices** to be 'as the Parliament prescribes'.) But section 4 did not purport to say that there 'shall be' a High Court, any more than section 71 of the Constitution had done. The legislative provision was expressed as if it was to operate upon a High Court already in existence. Similarly, while section 30 exercised the Parliament's power to give the High Court original **jurisdiction** under section 76(i) of the Constitution, it noted that the jurisdiction thereby conferred was 'in addition to' that 'conferred on the High Court by the Constitution'. The language clearly imports an implication that whatever the Constitution has done has already been done; but that implication does not answer the question of what exactly it is that the Constitution has done. For example, section 75 of the Constitution (like section 71) does not say that there 'shall be' a High Court, but only that 'the High Court shall have original jurisdiction' in certain specified classes of **matters**.

During the **Convention Debates** in 1897, Bernhard Wise had insisted that the High Court would be 'independent of Parliament; that is to say, it comes into existence by the Constitution and not by Act of Parliament'; and it was Wise who, as **counsel** in *Hannah v Dalgarno* (1903), invited the Court to adopt that view by holding that his client's right of appeal had arisen from the direct operation of the Constitution itself, even before the Judiciary Act had formally structured the Court. The respondent's counsel, Richard Sly, replied that there was no right of appeal (and in effect no High Court) until the Judiciary Act came into force. There could be no appeal to a High Court that did not yet 'exist'. By posing the question of when, and why, the High Court could be said to 'exist', these arguments opened up a yawning gap in the Court's authority at the very moment when it began to manifest its judicial presence.

At that moment the Court could hardly be expected to question its own existence: like the basic norm in Hans Kelsen's pure theory of law, the Court's authority had simply to be assumed. That **Griffith** took the question seriously is remarkable; that he declined to answer it is unsurprising. The gap between ontology and law was unbridgeable; and if Griffith finally evaded the metaphysical question, it might simply have been because judges must give pragmatic answers to practical problems. Yet something more was involved. Once the issue was posed as requiring a choice between alternative sources for the Court's authority, to choose either of the proffered sources would seem to discount the other. Thus, whether Griffith was conscious of it or not, either answer would have undermined part of the authority from which the Court derived its existence.

Section 10 of the Judiciary Act purported to establish the **seat** of the Court—though only in an ambulatory way, since initially it was to be 'at such place as the Governor-General from time to time appoints'. On one view of ontology, until the Court had a geographical 'home' or 'place'—even a variable and moveable 'place'—it could not be said to exist. For Martin Heidegger, human existence is defined ontologically by its having 'place', historically and sociologically determined. As William Kluback and Jean Wilde put it in 1959 in their translation of Heidegger's *Über 'die Linie'*, 'To have "place" ontologically and empirically is to have a house in which being can unfold itself and manifest its Being'.

If the High Court could not exist without Justices or without a 'home', it might follow that all the Constitution did was to create the mechanism by which the Court could be brought into being. The Constitution establishes Parliament's procreative capacity but it is Parliament that procreates, and exercises the parental right to determine where the High Court will live.

On either view, by the time *Hannah v Dalgarno* was argued, it might have seemed unnecessary to answer the metaphysical question, since the Court was itself a fully fledged legal and institutional being. Yet perhaps even this was uncertain. The Court had been given the capacity to exercise judicial power, but arguably that power was not perfected until the capacity was actually exercised—just as, despite the rule that 'there is no **equity** … to complete an imperfect gift', such a gift may sometimes be perfected where the donee, without further external intervention, is able to act in a way that manifests full 'control and possession' (**Dixon** in *Brunker v Perpetual Trustee Co* (1937)), or perhaps where the subject matter of the gift is 'a mere expectancy or possibility', perfected when the objects of the expectancy 'come into existence' (**Windeyer** in *Norman v FCT* (1963)). Since *Hannah v Dalgarno* was the Court's first judgment, one might argue that it was by the process of delivering that judgment that the Court perfected its inchoate power and constituted itself as judicial. The institutional equivalent of Descartes' *cogito ergo sum* might be *judico ergo sum*.

Yet behind that first judgment lay a chain of events, any one of which might be said in a sense to have given the High Court 'existence'. From the moment it was first suggested that the federal arrangements might include a High Court, the idea of such a court was present in the federal discourse. The Court was talked about and thought about; its coming, and the desirability of its coming, pervaded constitutional discourse. There followed a series of landmarks: the agreement of the **framers** in 1897 that there was to be a High Court; the agreement of the people of the colonies, when they voted to approve the draft Constitution, that Commonwealth judicial power 'shall be' vested in a High Court; the enactment of the *Commonwealth of Australia Constitution Act* 1900 (UK); the commencement of the Judiciary Act on 25 August 1903; the appointment of the first three judges and their swearing into office on 5 October 1903; the Court's inaugural ceremony on 6 October 1903 (when the judges took the **judicial oath**); and the first working **sittings** for argument and judgment in *Hannah v Dalgarno* itself. Any one of these might be singled out as the point at which the Court assumed a definite form and existence; or, better, the Court's emergence as an existing authoritative institution might be seen as the cumulative result of all these steps. From the viewpoint of legal **positivism**, however, the Court's foundational origin could only lie in one of two steps, one English and one Australian: the enactment (or perhaps the proclamation) of the Constitution Act, and the enactment of the Judiciary Act.

The dichotomous choice between these alternatives presented in *Hannah v Dalgarno* no doubt reflects the adversarial arguments from which the issue arose. Yet it also reflects the conceptual paradigm of divided sovereignties which was to permeate the **Griffith Court's** judgments. That paradigm meant not only that, within the new Australian Commonwealth, **sovereignty** was seen to be vested in separate states, armed with **intergovernmental immunities** and **reserved state powers**; it also meant that the sovereignty from which the Constitution, and hence the institutions of Commonwealth government, had derived their authority must necessarily be seen as external to that of the Commonwealth itself. After the *Engineers Case* (1920), with its emphasis on the one and indivisible Crown, such notions of divided authority could no longer be sustained in either context. Neither could the authority behind the Constitution be seen as separate or divided from the authority behind the Judiciary Act.

Wise's argument in *Hannah v Dalgarno* ascribes to the authority behind the Constitution an omnipotent being, like God: the pronouncement that there 'shall be' a High Court is like God's commands in the first chapter of *Genesis*. Of course, those commands were self-executing: as soon as God said 'Let there be light', there was light. But that theological concept supposes an omnipotent sovereignty, whereas the Australian Constitution both creates and was created by divided and multiple sovereignties. What is intriguing about Griffith's dilemma in *Hannah v Dalgarno* is that he makes no attempt to analyse the problem as one of the cumulative exercise of several sovereignties: whether the High Court was brought into being by the Constitution or the Judiciary Act, the assumption is that it must owe its being to one sovereign act of genesis.

A decade later, in *Delph Singh v Karbowsky* (1914), **Isaacs** and **Higgins** had no such problem. They took it for granted that the appellant had a 'statutory right of appeal under the Constitution as modified by … the Judiciary Act'. On that basis, where the appellant had failed to give security for costs within the time prescribed by the **High Court Rules**, they felt able to grant an extension of time, on the basis that by the cumulative operation of the Constitution and the Judiciary Act the Court was seised of a 'matter'. Ironically, Griffith, **Barton** and **Gavan Duffy** insisted that there was no such 'matter': only when the Rules had been fully complied with could the appeal be said to exist. On the other hand, they cheerfully granted special **leave to appeal**, though for this Isaacs and Higgins could see no statutory basis. On both sides of the argument, ontology had given way to law.

TONY BLACKSHIELD
FRANCESCA DOMINELLO

Constitutional interpretation, the process of giving meaning to the Constitution, is one of the most important tasks of the High Court. In Australia, it seems always to have been assumed that the Constitution was enforceable by judges by the means of **judicial review** (compare the US position stated in *Marbury v Madison* (1803)). It was inevitable, therefore, that it would be judges (and principally the judges of the highest court) who would be charged with the task of applying the general terms of the Constitution to specific circumstances. Indeed, this is a role that the High Court has jealously guarded. Its decision in the *Communist Party Case* (1951) is a strong statement of the Court's determination that the judiciary, not the Parliament or the executive, is to be the final arbiter of constitutional meaning.

The task of constitutional interpretation is, however, dogged by the question of the democratic legitimacy of judicial review (see **Democracy, Court's role in**). Put simply, the question is why unelected and unaccountable judges should have the power to set aside laws made by the elected arms of government. The 'counter-majoritarian difficulty', as American constitutional theorists have described this conundrum, remains at the heart of much constitutional debate.

As a result, many judges and constitutional theorists have been attracted to methods of constitutional interpretation that seem to give the task some legitimacy. Principal among these are textualism (or **literalism** as it is often described in Australia) and originalism. Textualism gives the Constitution the plain meaning conveyed by its text; originalism gives it the meaning the **framers** intended it to have (or perhaps the meaning that others would have understood it to have at the time it was drafted). One of the principal attractions of these methods of constitutional interpretation is that they appear to exclude the subjective preferences of judges and appeal to the 'true' meaning of the Constitution—a meaning that gains its democratic legitimacy from adoption of the Constitution by referendum of citizens and from the democratic **amendment** process provided for in section 128.

It is not surprising, then, that Australian constitutional interpretation has long been dominated by a strong commitment to text-based interpretation. This commitment received its most influential expression in the famous *Engineers Case* (1920), in which the Court rejected the doctrine of implied immunity of instrumentalities (and by implication the related doctrine of **reserved state powers**) by asserting the primacy of constitutional text. Nor is it surprising that textualism has always been supplemented with originalist analysis. Indeed, on some analyses, literalism and originalism go hand in hand. One rationale for literalism is that giving the text its plain or literal meaning will ensure adherence to the original meaning of the Constitution. The importance of the originalist method was confirmed by the High Court's decision in *Cole v Whitfield* (1988) to allow reference to the **Convention Debates** at which the Constitution was drafted.

The legacy of the *Engineers Case* has, however, proved to be more complex. On one view, *Engineers* was itself informed by the kinds of considerations it purported to exclude: that is, by a judicial conception of 'the spirit of the compact', the nature of the society established by the Constitution. **Windeyer** argued that the real explanation for the decision was the need to allow for the growth of Commonwealth power by abolishing doctrines that had previously confined it: see, for example, Windeyer in the *Payroll Tax Case* (1971). The centralisation of power to the Commonwealth has certainly been one of the most marked consequences of constitutional interpretation ever since, perhaps reaching its climax in the expansive interpretation of the **external affairs power** in the *Tasmanian Dam Case* (1983). Whether this has been an accidental or intended consequence of literalism, the outcome is not in doubt (see **Commonwealth legislative powers**).

Further, other interpretive methods have challenged the primacy of textualism and originalism. Although textualism and originalism do contemplate that the meaning of the Constitution might change over time (see the general principles of interpretation expounded by **O'Connor** in *Jumbunna Coal Case* (1908) and the concept of **connotation and denotation**), they also assume a core of meaning that is fixed. Contrary to this assumption, some Justices have been prepared to 'update' the Constitution in a more overt manner.

The pressure to update the Constitution has been felt most acutely in relation to the protection of individual rights, a matter on which the text of the Australian Constitution is noticeably restrained and an idea to which the framers were rather hostile. The bold rights-oriented approach of **Murphy**, seen in decisions such as *R v Director-General of Social Welfare (Vic); Ex parte Henry* (1975) and *Miller v TCN Channel Nine* (1986) is perhaps the clearest example. Declaring that 'it is a Constitution for a free society', Murphy appeared willing to 'read in' a wide range of protections for the individual.

Few judges have found this level of boldness attractive; but in the late 1980s and early 1990s there was a clear shift in the High Court's interpretive approach. First, the Court was more concerned with substance and less with form (see **Form and substance**). That is, when assessing the constitutional validity of an impugned law, the Court began to focus on what a law actually *did* rather than the form in which it was expressed. The preference for substance over form is seen clearly in *Street v Queensland Bar Association* (1989). In that case, the Court replaced the established interpretation of section 117 (prohibiting **discrimination** on the basis of state residency) with a doctrine that focused on the position of the

person claiming discrimination rather than on the form of the impugned law.

The focus on substance was accompanied by an invigorated sense of the importance of individual rights. In *Street*, section 117 was described as 'a constitutional *right* not to be subject to a certain disability or discrimination', and a provision 'directed towards *individuals* and their protection' (emphasis added). This new approach stands in marked contrast to the Court's traditionally narrow interpretation of the few constitutional provisions that might protect the individual (in relation to section 117, see *Henry v Boehm* (1973); in relation to the guarantee in section 80 of a **jury trial**, see *R v Bernasconi* (1915) and *R v Archdall and Roskruge* (1928); see also **Express constitutional rights** and **National unity**).

That *Street* heralded a new era in constitutional interpretation seemed to have been confirmed in *Australian Capital Television v Commonwealth* (1992) and *Nationwide News v Wills* (1992) (see *Free Speech Cases*). These decisions combined the established interpretive method of constitutional implication—that is, the recognition of doctrines unexpressed in the Constitution but implied by its text and structure, as explained in the *Melbourne Corporation Case* (1947) and the *Boilermakers Case* (1956)—with the new emphasis on individual rights. The result was a doctrine known as the freedom of **political communication**. The essence of the Court's reasoning in these cases was: the Constitution establishes a system of **representative government** and **responsible government**; it therefore impliedly prohibits legislative and executive action that interferes with the political expression necessary for the proper operation of such a system of government.

These cases gave rise to the hope in some (and fear in others) that the High Court would move from recognising a limited right of freedom of expression to developing an extensive rights jurisprudence. The expectations were ultimately not realised. In reality, these decisions were relatively moderate. Most members of the Court stressed the relationship between the implied freedom and the text of the Constitution, and voiced scepticism about the possibility of comprehensive rights protection. Only a minority of judges mounted a full-scale challenge to traditional modes of constitutional interpretation. **Deane** and **Toohey** in particular began to make adventurous arguments for the recognition of individual rights, even where this appeared to contradict historically accepted and originally intended meaning. As Deane put it in *Theophanous v Herald & Weekly Times* (1994), 'the Constitution must be construed as "a living force" representing the will and intentions of all contemporary Australians, both **women** and **men**, and not as a lifeless declaration of the will and intentions of men long since dead'. The boldness of the approach of Deane and Toohey can be seen in their recognition in *Leeth v Commonwealth* (1992) of an implied right to legal **equality**.

Even though this kind of progressive constitutional interpretation was first advocated at the time of the drafting of the Constitution (for example by **Inglis Clark** in his *Studies in Australian Constitutional Law* (1901)), it remains an unorthodox approach to constitutional interpretation. Indeed, there has been a retreat from the adventurousness of some decisions of the late 1980s and 1990s. In *Lange v ABC*

(1997) much of the controversy over the freedom of political communication was brought to a close by a unanimous decision of the Court which, though it affirmed the freedom of political communication, reiterated a strong commitment to traditional methods of interpretation. The process of drawing implications was, the Court stressed, to be tightly confined by the 'text and structure' of the Constitution. That is, implications could be drawn only where logically or practically necessary to give effect to the structure of the Constitution as revealed in its text. They should not be drawn simply from the vague notions of representative and responsible government that permeate and inform the text.

It may seem that Australian constitutional interpretation has come full circle, from conservative orthodoxy to progressive **activism** and back again; but although there certainly has been a return to restraint, it would be unwise to dismiss progressive methods of interpretation entirely.

First, it is important not to overstate the effect of the conservative reiteration of textualism in *Lange*. If *Lange* was meant to suggest that constitutional interpretation is to be entirely governed by text, it is clearly wrong. It is doubtful that constitutional text alone could ever provide a sufficient basis for constitutional interpretation, and recent cases in the High Court confirm this. The judges continue to read the Constitution in light of its **history**, traditional concepts of the **common law**—including, it seems, the **rule of law**, as in the *Hindmarsh Island Bridge Case* (1998)—with regard to changing circumstances (see, for example, the finding in *Sue v Hill* (1999) that in the light of developments in Australia's status as a nation and in the constitutional arrangements of the UK, the expression 'foreign power' in section 44 now includes the UK) and, in some cases at least, with an eye to the practical consequences of its decisions: see *Abebe v Commonwealth* (1999).

Moreover, despite a moment of unanimity in *Lange*, the Court remains divided on matters of constitutional interpretation. Striking in this context is the approach of **Kirby** (who was not a member of the *Lange* Court). Generally more progressive than other members of the Court, his most distinctive position is his argument that, where it is ambiguous, the Constitution should be interpreted consistently with **international law**, specifically international human rights norms: see, for example, *Newcrest Mining v Commonwealth* (1997).

Whether it likes it or not, the Court seems set for a continuing struggle between the competing claims of certainty and democratic legitimacy on the one hand, and flexibility and adjustment to changing circumstances on the other.

ADRIENNE STONE

Constitutional law is the law that 'constitutes' the nation, and therefore occupies a primary place in any national legal system. This is especially so in a federal system, where the law defines the nation's 'constituent' parts, their respective powers and the restrictions on those powers, and their legal relationships. Those powers and those relationships are generally set out—inevitably in a federal system—in a written document called a Constitution. Again inevitably (though not necessarily explicitly—see *Marbury v Madison*), it falls to the courts to interpret and apply that Constitution, and the High Court has played a major **role** in the interpretation and application of the Australian Constitution.

Constitutional law in Australia is not, however, merely about the judicial interpretation of the Australian (or 'Commonwealth' or 'federal') Constitution. For one thing, the states also have their own **state constitutions**, which have generated a body of state constitutional law; so, in a sense, do the **territories** of the ACT and the Northern Territory, in the form of their self-government Acts, which, although merely legislation of the Commonwealth (made pursuant to the Commonwealth's territories power in section 122 of the Constitution), are the constituent documents for those territories. For another thing, not all constitutional law is made by judges. Some parts of constitutional law are not **justiciable** (the Court has taken this view, for example, of most aspects of section 53 of the Constitution, which governs the powers of the two Houses of the Commonwealth Parliament in relation to money Bills), and the arms of government to which those parts relate form their own view of the law and act upon it. Moreover, academics opine, writers expound and advisers advise. In the absence of **authoritative** pronouncements, these opinions, expositions and advices may, in appropriate cases (see **Commentators**), be taken as a good guide to what the law is or is likely to become.

The Constitution must also be understood against a background of practices, customs, traditions and conventions, especially those of **responsible government**. Many of its provisions, particularly those conferring power upon the Governor-General, are otherwise unintelligible. Again, the courts have generally not intruded into this area of political activity, although since the rediscovery by the High Court in the 1990s of **implied constitutional rights**, some writers have suggested that responsible government might be treated not merely as an assumption but as an implication of the Constitution. In the great political upheaval of 1975, the convention that the Governor-General should act only on the advice of the Prime Minister was not followed (see **Dismissal of 1975**), but the High Court was not called upon to adjudicate. Controversially, however, and precisely because he perceived the issue to be non-justiciable, the **Chief Justice** had earlier advised, in some kind of quasi-personal capacity, that the Governor-General's proposed course of action would be appropriate (see **Barwick**; **Whitlam era**).

The major part of constitutional law is, however, the body of doctrine that emerges from the accumulation of High Court decisions on the meaning of the Constitution, in addition to its role as the final appellate court in the Australian legal system (at least since the abolition by the *Australia Acts* 1986 of the last of the remaining **Privy Council** appeals), is that of **constitutional interpretation**. The Court's approach to constitutional interpretation, and the resulting doctrine, has gone through several distinct phases.

The early High Court, despite a generous view of the Commonwealth's **defence power** during **World War I**, took a generally narrow view of the scope of **Commonwealth legislative powers**, largely because of the adoption by **Griffith**, **Barton** and **O'Connor** of the doctrine of **reserved state powers**. Thus, for example, the **corporations power** could not extend to the regulation of corporate activity in intrastate trade (*Huddart Parker v Moorehead* (1909)), and the **taxation** power could not be used indirectly to influence labour conditions in the states (*R v Barger* (1908)). Drawing on nineteenth-century American precedents, Griffith, Barton and O'Connor also invented a doctrine, which they said was implicit in the nature of **federalism** as a system of government, of reciprocal **intergovernmental immunities**. Thus, for example, the states could not tax the Commonwealth (*D'Emden v Pedder* (1904)), and the Commonwealth could not apply its industrial law to the states (*Railway Servants Case* (1906)). These two doctrines were the hallmarks of the early **Griffith Court**, although O'Connor opined famously in the *Jumbunna Coal Case* (1908) that the Court should 'always lean to the broader interpretation' of an expression in the Constitution 'unless there is something in the context or in the rest of the Constitution' that favours the narrower interpretation.

The easy harmony of the early Court dissipated with the addition in 1906 of the discordant voices of **Isaacs** and **Higgins**. Neither accepted the idea of reserved state powers or of implied immunities, and in due course Isaacs was able to marshal a majority in the landmark *Engineers Case* (1920)—by which time Griffith, Barton and O'Connor had all gone—to overturn both doctrines. Commonwealth industrial law was now applied to the states; and the words of the Constitution were to be given their ordinary and natural meaning, without restrictions implied from vague assumptions of continuing state power or vague theories of political necessity. Retrospective views of the *Engineers Case* have generally seen its outcome and its philosophy as appropriate and timely in the context of the growth of **nationhood** following World War I; yet Isaacs, despite the irony of his reliance on the unwritten doctrine of responsible government, got there with a unique brand of **literalism** that reverberated down the years and has had a lasting, though not always coherent, influence upon many areas of constitutional interpretation.

That influence can be seen in the wide view subsequently taken in the **characterisation** of Commonwealth legislation for the purpose of determining whether it falls within Commonwealth power, as in the case of the **trade and commerce power** (*Murphyores v Commonwealth* (1976)), the taxation power (*Fairfax v FCT* (1965)), the corporations power (*Strickland v Rocla Concrete Pipes* (1971)), and, most controversially, the **external affairs power** (*Tasmanian Dam Case* (1983)); in the contortions later judges had to go through in order to reintroduce a more limited doctrine of implied intergovernmental immunities (*Melbourne Corporation Case* (1947)); and in the silencing for some seventy years of any attempt to imply personal rights or freedoms of the kind with which Griffith and Barton had been comfortable in *R v Smithers; Ex parte Benson* (1912) (see freedom of **movement**).

Yet although the literalism of *Engineers* tended to magnify Commonwealth power and inhibit the making of restrictive implications, the elevation of text over context, of **form** over substance, and of plain meaning over purpose, policy or pragmatism, was equally capable of narrowing power or, where the restrictions on power were express, enlarging those restrictions. Thus, for example, the interstate element of the trade and commerce power has constricted the operation of the power far more than that of its US counterpart (*A-G (WA); Ex rel Ansett Transport Industries v Australian National Airlines* (1976)); emphasis on the word 'formed' as

used in relation to the corporations the Commonwealth can regulate under the corporations power has prevented the Commonwealth from dealing with company incorporation (the *Incorporation Case* (1990)); and the words 'absolutely free' in section 92's guarantee of freedom of **interstate trade and commerce** were allowed to catapult that section out of its proper context and so to remain until sanity prevailed in *Cole v Whitfield* (1988).

The early Court's generally narrow view of Commonwealth power was not manifest only in relation to the scope or reach of the powers granted in section 51. The supremacy of Commonwealth law under section 109 in cases of **inconsistency** with state law did not disable Commonwealth and state laws from operating side by side unless simultaneous obedience to both was impossible (*R v Brisbane Licensing Court; Ex parte Daniell* (1920)). But again under the influence of Isaacs, and later of **Dixon**, the Court excluded state law, with wide effect, where the Commonwealth had 'covered the field' (*Clyde Engineering v Cowburn* (1926); *Ex parte McLean* (1930))—provoking the Commonwealth Parliament, in recent times, typically to spell out in its legislation an intention that state law is not to be excluded where it is 'capable of operating concurrently' with Commonwealth law. The range of taxes excluded from the states because of their categorisation as **excise duties** under section 90 of the Constitution was also initially conceived narrowly (*Peterswald v Bartley* (1904)), but once more the hands of Isaacs (*Commonwealth and Commonwealth Oil Refineries v SA* (1926)) and Dixon (*Matthews v Chicory Marketing Board* (1938); *Parton v Milk Board* (1949)) can be seen in the steady broadening of the definition, which has thus far prevailed against vigorous and persistent dissent (*Ha v NSW* (1997)).

Engineers and other contemporaneous cases (notably *McArthur v Queensland* (1920), which confined the operation of section 92 to the states until it was overruled by the Privy Council in *James v Commonwealth* (1936)), presented the Commonwealth with significant opportunities to capitalise on the Court's more favourable approach to Commonwealth power following World War I, but the federal conservative governments of the 1920s failed to take advantage of those opportunities. When the more activist federal Labor governments of the 1940s pushed closer to the limits of constitutional power, the Court was no longer in such an expansive mood. Although in a wartime context the Commonwealth's takeover of income tax from the states survived challenge (*First Uniform Tax Case* (1942), building on the **Federal Roads Case** (1926)), the Commonwealth's pharmaceutical benefits scheme was struck down (*First Pharmaceutical Benefits Case* (1945)), as were the Commonwealth's attempts to nationalise the airlines (*Australian National Airways v Commonwealth* (1945)), to centralise the banking system (*Melbourne Corporation Case*), and, subsequently, to nationalise the banks (*Bank Nationalisation Case* (1948, affirmed by the Privy Council in 1949)). Section 92 was here the main destroyer of the nationalisation schemes, the section having been held at bay in the 1930s largely by **Evatt** and **McTiernan**, and to an extent **Gavan Duffy** and later **Latham**, thus allowing, during the **Depression** and beyond, the survival of severe restrictions on the emerging road transport industry, designed to protect the railways (*R v Vizzard; Ex parte Hill* (1933)), and the survival also of at least some of the multitude of organised marketing schemes (*Milk Board (NSW) v Metropolitan Cream* (1939)).

In 1951, in one of its most significant and celebrated constitutional decisions, the Court challenged the perception that it was driven by hostility to Labor by invalidating the **Menzies** conservative government's attempt to outlaw the Communist Party (*Communist Party Case* (1951)). Paradoxically, at the same time the **United States Supreme Court** upheld a similar ban (*Dennis v US* (1951)), notwithstanding the presence in the US Constitution of explicit guarantees of freedom of speech and association and their corresponding absence in Australia. The High Court's decision (Latham angrily dissenting) was not overtly based on the protection of these freedoms, but rather on the Court's insistence on its right and duty to judge the sufficiency of the connection between a Commonwealth law and the alleged source of constitutional power (in this case, defence), rather than allow that judgment to be pre-empted by the Parliament and the Court's function of **judicial review** to be usurped.

Dixon's accession to the Chief Justiceship shortly afterwards ushered in a period of overt **legalism** yet subtle incorporation of **policy considerations**, with the emphasis of the *Communist Party Case* on judicial **independence** accentuated by the seminal decision in the *Boilermakers Case* (1956) requiring a strict **separation of powers**, at least in relation to federal **judicial power**. Earlier cases had identified that federal judicial power could not be exercised except by courts established or invested with **jurisdiction** under Chapter III of the Constitution (the *Wheat Case* (1915); *Alexander's Case* (1918)), but *Boilermakers* reformulated the principle more broadly by precluding the combination of judicial and non-judicial power in the same body, thus bringing into sharper focus the corollary or obverse of the original proposition: not only could federal judicial power be exercised only by Chapter III courts, but those courts and those judges could not exercise any other kind of power, and in particular could not undertake **non-judicial functions** (see *Hilton v Wells* (1985); *Grollo v Palmer* (1995)).

The insulation of judicial power was derived from the textual separation of the respective chapters of the Constitution dealing with legislative, executive and judicial power, but was also bolstered by a concern to protect the integrity of the judicial function. Lamented in some quarters as arid, technical and inconvenient, especially in the context of *Boilermakers* itself and its forced separation of the functions of **conciliation and arbitration** from supervision and enforcement, the doctrine has flowered in recent times as a source of individual rights of **due process** (*Dietrich v The Queen* (1992); *Chu Kheng Lim v Minister for Immigration* (1992)). Yet criticism of the unrelieved purity of the doctrine has re-emerged, now in the context of its role in preventing the federal judiciary from exercising state judicial power and thus inhibiting practical Commonwealth–state cooperative schemes for the **cross-vesting** of jurisdiction (*Re Wakim* (1999); *R v Hughes* (2000)).

The 1950s saw a continuation of the wide effect produced by a contextually anchorless interpretation of section 92, with the ultimate victory of road transport companies against discretionary state licensing (*Hughes & Vale Cases* (1953 and 1955)). These cases confirmed the 'individual right' interpretation of section 92 established in the *Bank Nationalisation Case*, and the **Dixon Court** and its successors struggled to find intelligible and doctrinally coherent limits. The *Second Uniform Tax Case* (1957), however, confirmed the hands-off approach of the first case, even in the absence of the **World War II** context, and pretty much conceded the absence of legal limits on the ability of the Commonwealth to use its financial powers—particularly its power to make conditional grants to the states under section 96—as a medium through which to browbeat the states and, as **Deakin** had foreseen, to make or influence policy in areas beyond its direct legislative control. This development was reinforced by the *AAP Case* (1975), where a narrow majority declined to put limits on the range of objects of direct expenditure open to the Commonwealth under its appropriations power in section 81. The financial dimension of **Commonwealth–state relations** is now played out primarily in the political arena, though the legal boundaries of the notion of excise duties continue to affect the states' independent revenue raising capacity (see *Dennis Hotels v Victoria* (1960)).

The Dixon period drew to a close with Dixon's success, in the *Cigamatic Case* (1962), in establishing the dissenting view he had expressed in *Uther's Case* (1947)—namely that, notwithstanding *Engineers*, the states lacked the capacity to bind the Commonwealth, at least in matters 'directly affecting the Commonwealth's relationship with its subjects'. Dixon had also been instrumental in the revival of implied limits on the power of the Commonwealth to bind the states (*Melbourne Corporation Case*). The latter crystallised into two propositions—that the Commonwealth must not **discriminate** against the states, nor threaten their capacity to function (*Payroll Tax Case* (1971); *Queensland Electricity Commission v Commonwealth* (1985); *Re Australian Education Union; Ex parte Victoria* (1995))—and both appear to have become doctrinally well-entrenched, despite their air of unreality in the broader context in which the Court abandoned any attempt to put legal limits on the Commonwealth's ability to flex its financial muscle. The existence and scope of the Commonwealth's *Cigamatic* immunity remain controversial, especially since it seems unnecessary in the light of the Commonwealth's ability to protect itself through legislation that will prevail over inconsistent state law under section 109; yet it withstood challenge in *Henderson's Case* (1997), and continues to create uncertainty, as the Court and advisers alike struggle to pin down its limits.

The revival of both of these modified versions of intergovernmental immunities seemed largely to depend on abstract reasoning and the pull of **precedent**, in contrast with the broad fashioning by the early Court of principles seen to be implicit in the concept of pre-existing polities coming together, for limited purposes, to form a federal system. With the growth in **national unity**, these principles became less compelling and were superseded; yet their metamorphosis is a testament to their resilience and to the ongoing debate about the true nature of a federal system.

Barwick succeeded Dixon as Chief Justice in 1964, and immediately made his presence felt by insisting that the proper identification of excise duties under section 90 and of infringements of the freedom of interstate trade under section 92 required the Court to take greater account of 'practical considerations' (see, respectively, *Anderson's v Victoria* (1964) and *Samuels v Readers Digest* (1969)). Despite this, Barwick remained a legalist—or at least an avowed legalist—and seemed all the more so when set against the even more robust approach and iconoclastic conclusions of **Murphy** from 1975 on; but his approach in these areas gave both sections a wider impact and unsettled existing doctrine. Neither Barwick's nor Murphy's view of section 92 prevailed but both were catalysts for change.

Barwick also found himself in frequent dissent on key issues, if not always in the result, in the flurry of cases about the composition and operation of the federal Parliament and the **parliamentary process** that characterised the 1970s, most arising out of the activities and initiatives of the Whitlam government (see, for example, *Cormack v Cope* (1974); the *PMA Case* (1975); the *Territory Senators Cases* (1975 and 1977); *A-G (Cth); Ex rel McKinlay v Commonwealth* (1975); *A-G (NSW); Ex rel McKellar v Commonwealth* (1977)). In the eyes of many, this perceived tendency of Barwick to hold idiosyncratic views (in this respect having much in common with Murphy) only underscored the questioning of the wisdom of his actions in advising the Governor-General in relation to the **dismissal** of the Prime Minister in 1975.

The appointment of Murphy to the Court in 1975 opened up new vistas for the protection of **civil liberties.** He approached the reinterpretation of the Constitution's handful of **express constitutional rights** and the rediscovery of implied constitutional rights with a vigour not previously seen—as if to compensate for the Constitution's absence of a **Bill of Rights.** Murphy was in dissent even more than Barwick, but he showed what was possible, and helped to create a climate for change. The express guarantee in section 80 of **jury trial** remains an unfulfilled promise (*Kingswell v The Queen* (1985); *Cheng v The Queen* (2000)); the right to vote that might have been extracted from section 41 has been consigned to the dustbin of transitional provisions (*R v Pearson; Ex parte Sipka* (1983); see **Electoral law**); and the guarantee of religious freedom in section 116 has not been much litigated (see **Church and state**), perhaps reflecting a lack of need as much as a judicial dampening (but see *Kruger v Commonwealth* (1997)). On the other hand, the **Mason Court** breathed new life into section 117's prohibition of **discrimination** based on state residence (*Street v Queensland Bar Association* (1989)), and continued the Court's traditional sympathy for **economic** rights with a robust view of section 51(xxxi)'s guarantee of just compensation for the compulsory **acquisition of property** (*Georgiadis v Australian & Overseas Telecommunications Corporation* (1994); see also *Newcrest Mining v Commonwealth* (1997)). The Mason Court did, however, correct the earlier Court's misinterpretation of section 92 as a guarantee of an individual economic right and thus of free enterprise as such, narrowing it to a prohibition of laws that discriminate against interstate trade in a protectionist sense—overturning (if not **overruling**) nearly a century of case law in the process (*Cole v Whitfield*).

In overturning **precedent** to this degree in *Cole v Whitfield*, the Mason Court entered a period of judicial **activism**, nowhere better exemplified than in *Australian Capital Television*

sion v Commonwealth (1992) and *Nationwide News v Wills* (1992), where the Court implied a freedom of **political communication** from the Constitution's establishment of a system of **representative government** (see *Free Speech Cases*). Yet the contrast between these two areas of judicial law-making revealed a degree of ambivalence about the role of **history** and the place of **originalism** in constitutional interpretation. While the Court laboured to justify the discovery of implied rights in the face of the deliberate omission by the **framers of the Constitution** of a comprehensive list of express rights, in *Cole v Whitfield* the major justification given was reversion to the historical intention, and, indeed, that reversion was facilitated by a lifting of the long-standing taboo on reference to the **Convention Debates**. The decisions in each area could be justified on other grounds: the implied rights cases turned on the evolving nature of the concept of representative government anchored in section 24 of the Constitution, particularly in the phrase 'chosen by the people', and in any event the cases on intergovernmental immunities had entrenched the legitimacy of implications; and *Cole v Whitfield*, for its part, made good institutional as well as historical sense. But the resurgence of history was potentially constraining rather than liberating, and played a significant role in the narrow view of the corporations power taken in the *Incorporation Case.*

The insistence on fidelity to the framers' intentions seems unlikely to trump the techniques of progressive interpretation such as the distinction between **connotation and denotation**, or the resort to plain meaning, supplemented by policy and institutional considerations, that proved decisive in, for example, the *Tasmanian Dam Case.* In any event, the framers may be taken in at least some instances to have intended that phrases of appropriate generality be interpreted broadly enough to embrace changing circumstances. But the renewed emphasis on history was a reminder of the range of weapons in the armoury of constitutional interpretation, including not only historical or purposive intention, textual exegesis, contextual epexegesis, structural analysis, institutional considerations and precedent, but also, in more recent times, guidance from the norms of **international law** (see **Kirby** in *Newcrest Mining v Commonwealth* (1997); *Hindmarsh Island Bridge Case* (1998)).

The High Court's interpretation of the Constitution has passed through many phases, from the political theory of the early Court, to the textual focus of the post-*Engineers* period, to the revival of implications, to renewed dependence on the safe harbour of the text (*Lange v ABC* (1997); *Re Wakim*)—though always with cross-currents, diversity of opinion, accidental or fortuitous majorities that take the pomp out of general theory, and differing developments in different areas, all of which challenge generalisation. Precedent has played a smaller role in constitutional law than in the **common law** and **statutory interpretation**, because of the perception (and reality) that the Constitution is harder to amend—although, even so, the advocates of judicial restraint often point to the mechanism in section 128 for constitutional **amendment** as the more legitimate avenue for constitutional change (while the advocates of judicial activism point to it as a safety valve should the activism not be acceptable). In any event, the Court's constitutional responsibility has kept it in touch with social issues and social change, which it has sometimes retarded and sometimes advanced. In recent times, the Court's involvement with issues of **race** and with **Aboriginal peoples** as litigants has made it a significant player in indigenous politics (see **Litigants, notable, 1945–2001**) and its decisions in *Mabo* (1992) and *Wik* (1996), while not involving 'constitutional law' in the narrow doctrinal sense, have had a profound impact on our constitutional arrangements in the broadest sense (see **Political institution**).

Moreover, the volume of constitutional litigation has steadily increased, particularly since the introduction in 1984 of the requirement of special **leave** for all appeals; the climate thus created for accentuating the Court's role generally as law maker in difficult cases that raise important issues of principle appears to have made both the Court and **counsel** more creative in raising constitutional issues. It seems likely that the Court's ongoing role in constitutional law and its place in Australian **democracy** will continue to confound Geoffrey Sawer's 1967 observation—perhaps true enough at the time—that, constitutionally speaking, Australia was the 'frozen continent'.

Michael Coper

Further Reading
Michael Coper, *Encounters with the Australian Constitution* (1987, popular edn 1988)
Geoffrey Sawer, *Australian Federalism in the Courts* (1967)

Consumer law gives effect to policies of consumer protection. However, while consumer protection is a useful concept for organisations in the consumer movement, and for consumer affairs agencies in the federal, state and territory bureaucracies which have an advocacy role, it is more difficult for courts. Those who set out to review the work of the High Court by reference to its advancement of consumer protection will be disappointed. Consumer protection has not been adopted as an organising principle by courts and other arbitral bodies—not even, it might be said, by tribunals that are identified as consumers' arenas. This is because such an organising principle may be seen as at odds with the law's ideal of evenhandedness.

Consumer law strives to achieve a beneficial outcome for a particular group, however vaguely defined. Yet the idea of consumer protection is eclectic. It is pluralistic in that it can be used to aid decision making in many areas of law; it is autonomous in being directed at a particular desired outcome. From a partisan view, the role of the judge is to be engaged in the project. As Thierry Bourgoignie puts it: 'Judges are henceforth expected to participate in the development of specific policies, to perform "political work" in the broad sense of the term. They are no longer merely the custodians of the law; but they become co-agents of legal change.'

The High Court most obviously considers law and the consumer in its interpretation of the *Trade Practices Act* 1974 (Cth). To treat this as the extent of the High Court's contribution would, however, do the Court a disservice.

In the Trade Practices Act, the Commonwealth Parliament for the first time enacted a comprehensive national consumer protection law. The Court's interpretation of the Act—and particularly of section 52, the most frequently litigated section—fills consumer advocates with dismay and lawyers and business with bemusement. The disappointment of the consumer advocate is that the Court has not approached the interpretation of the Act with a view to furthering consumer protection as a co-agent of political change.

On one view, the intention of Parliament was clear. **Murphy**, in his speech as **Attorney-General** when he introduced the Bill in the Senate, located the legislative purpose firmly within a perhaps romantic view of the development of **contract**. There may have been a time, in medieval markets, when consumers and traders could contract with confidence and in something like **equality**. Goods were simple, quantities small and skill levels approached equality. The industrial revolution of the nineteenth century and the rise of mass consumption in the twentieth changed this, with relative equality changing to relative inequality.

Consumer protection and the Trade Practices Act were to alleviate these effects. Sadly, perhaps, the **Federal Court** was nominated as the consumers' forum. It is now apparent that for many reasons consumers do not take their problems to the courts. Thus, the High Court was faced with interpreting a consumer protection statute when the parties in the few cases before it, and in the many cases before the Federal Court, rarely included consumers.

The words of section 52 are disarmingly direct:

> (1) A corporation shall not in trade or commerce engage in conduct that is misleading or deceptive or likely to mislead or deceive.

The initial cases before the High Court considered the threshold question of who could seek a remedy under the Act—in particular, who could seek an injunction against the behaviour prohibited by the section. 'Any … person' may be granted an injunction under the Act (section 80). Did this apply in respect of section 52? In *Hornsby Building Information Centre v Sydney Building Information Centre* (1978), the Court decided that since the words of section 52 were not ambiguous there was no need for recourse to the heading of Part V of the Act, 'Consumer Protection'. Thus there was no scope for restricting section 52 to operation as a consumer remedy. Murphy, who as Attorney-General had introduced the legislation, agreed with this interpretation in his role as a Justice of the Court.

Thus the pattern of section 52 cases was set: a business attempts to enjoin the commercial operations of a competitor on the basis that the conduct was misleading or deceptive.

Consumer advocates mourned the loss of a consumer remedy. However, in this context the words of Chief Justice **Gibbs**, much criticised in the consumer movement, may not be unreasonable. In *Parkdale Custom Built Furniture v Puxu* (1982) he said:

> The section may have been designed to protect the weak from the powerful, but it may be used by a large and powerful corporation to restrain the activities of a smaller competitor. I am, with all respect, unable to see any reason why a section so broadly expressed and so drastic in its possible consequences should be beneficially construed.

There have been important gains for consumers in the interpretation of the Act, but perhaps more in the Federal Court than the High Court. The Australian Competition and Consumer Commission (formerly the Trade Practices Commission), is, when its budget permits, a vigorous litigant, and pursues a sophisticated pro-consumer policy. Others who might use the Act in 'political work' have not been significant players. Consumer groups cannot afford to risk an adverse order for costs, and we still await the evolution of an effective model of class and representative actions that would allow entrepreneurial lawyers to organise consumers into litigants.

The main effect of the consumer protection provisions of the Trade Practices Act has been the creation of a new stream in **commercial law**, which provides alternatives to other forms of action in commercial litigation.

Justices had foreseen this development as far back as *Hornsby*, and the High Court grappled with it most clearly in *Concrete Constructions (NSW) v Nelson* (1990), when asked whether incorrect instructions from a foreman to a worker on a building site that led to the worker being injured gave the worker an action under section 52. The Court said not, but only the minority gave as its reason the fact that the worker was not a consumer. The majority considered that to use consumer protection as a rationale would be discriminatory. An advocate might say that consumer law should be discriminatory, but the majority, in an echo of Gibbs' words, refused to impose any artificial limitation on the possible users of the Act. Their joint judgment rejected the idea of confining the general words of the section

> to cases involving the protection of consumers alone. So to constrict the provisions of s52 would be to convert a general prohibition of misleading or deceptive conduct by a corporation, be it consumer or supplier, in trade or commerce, into a discriminatory requirement that a corporate supplier of goods or services should observe standards in its dealings with a corporate consumer which the consumer itself was left free to disregard.

This is not, however, the full extent of the High Court's influence on consumer law. Ultimately, any formulation of consumer protection is designed to combat inequality of bargaining power between parties in contractual situations who may not be negotiating in an area of their professional competence.

Milestones in consumer law include the imposition of new obligations to inform the consumer in pre-contractual negotiations; the extension of liability to consumers on the part of retailers, manufacturers or providers of services; and the establishment of abstract controls of fairness in contractual relations. Much has been achieved by statute, but much also by the courts—and the High Court's interpretation of the Trade Practices Act may not be the place to look.

Consumer law challenges the **common law** ideal of the objectified legal subject (often referred to as 'the reasonable man'), whose hypothetical conduct and attitudes are used to set a standard of behaviour that parties are expected to meet. Consumer law substitutes the subjective conduct and attitudes of the actual party involved. It is here that the High Court has been so important.

The Court's contribution to consumer law is not found in the section 52 cases, nor in the small number of cases under other parts of the Trade Practices Act. It is found in other areas where the Court has responded to the subjective needs of the party it perceives to be in an unequal position—Mrs Amadio in *Amadio's Case* (1983), Mr Maher in *Waltons Stores v Maher* (1988), and others in a line of cases invoking the principles of **equity** in areas previously the preserve of the common law (see also **Unconscionability**; **Undue influence**). These cases have rewritten consumer protection law in the Australian jurisdictions and have brought the gains into the mainstream (see also **Trade practices law**).

GRAEME WIFFEN

Further Reading
Thierry Bourgoignie, 'Characteristics of Consumer Law' (1992) 14 *JCP* 293

Anne Hurley and Graeme Wiffen, *Outline of Trade Practices and Consumer Protection Law* (2nd edn 1999)

Bruce Kercher and Richard Thomas, 'The Reform of Insurance Law: Caveat Emptor Survives' (1987) 10 *UNSWLJ* 173

Contempt. In several of the thirty-odd cases in which the High Court has dealt at any length with issues related to contempt of court, it has sought to preserve judicial control over both the development of the principles involved and their application in specific cases.

This desire for control is apparent in several rulings linking **common law** contempt with the Australian constitutional version of the doctrine of **separation of powers**. The argument stems from two long-standing principles of English contempt law: first, that only 'courts'—meaning bodies that exercise **judicial power**—have the power to punish for contempt; and secondly, that in the case of **superior courts** of record, these powers form part of the court's 'inherent jurisdiction'. In *Re Colina; Ex parte Torney* (1999), **Gleeson** and **Gummow** stated that the contempt powers of any federal court that is a superior court of record should be viewed as 'an attribute of the judicial power of the Commonwealth which is vested in those Courts by section 71 of the Constitution'. Earlier, in *R v Federal Court of Bankruptcy; Ex parte Lowenstein* (1938), Chief Justice **Latham** had even suggested that a presiding judge's decision to initiate proceedings for contempt in the face of his or her court was an exercise of judicial power, notwithstanding that, seen in isolation, an act of this nature seems anything but judicial.

Some individual Justices—for example, **Deane** in *Hammond v Commonwealth* (1982)—have also suggested that, since the judicial power of the Commonwealth is vested only in 'courts' falling within Chapter III of the Constitution, the Commonwealth Parliament might not be competent to abolish or reduce the contempt powers of these courts. This proposition appears to be at odds with the Court's decision in *R v Metal Trades Employers Association; Ex parte Amalgamated Engineering Union* (1951). Yet the mere fact that the idea has been proposed within the Court illustrates the importance that it attaches to contempt powers as being integral to the concept of a 'court'.

In similar vein, the Court has preserved the rule that contempt cases should be tried summarily—that is, by one or more judicial officers sitting without a jury. In *Porter v The King; Ex parte Chin Man Yee* (1926), **Isaacs** described the power of superior courts to try contempts in this way as 'a power of self-protection or a power incidental to the function of superintending the administration of justice'. In *John Fairfax & Sons v McRae* (1955) and *James v Robinson* (1963), the Court rejected the argument that charges of contempt arising from the publication of prejudicial matter relating to a pending criminal trial (*sub judice* contempt) should themselves be tried by a jury. Similarly, a majority of the Court in *Colina* held that because statutory provisions conferring contempt powers on the High Court and the Family Court of Australia were merely declaratory of the common law, contempts of these courts were not offences against a 'law of the Commonwealth'. They therefore could not be subject to the requirement of **jury trial** contained in section 80 of the Constitution.

In general, the Court has also maintained, if not enhanced, the deterrent role of contempt law in relation to conduct posing a threat to judicial authority. In *Gallagher v Durack* (1983), a majority of the Court reaffirmed the traditional formulation for the form of contempt known as 'scandalising the court': namely, that it covers 'baseless attacks on the integrity or impartiality of courts or judges', which might undermine 'public confidence' in 'the authority of the law'. **Murphy** was alone in maintaining that the applicable test should be the much narrower one, developed under the First Amendment to the US Constitution, of 'clear and present danger' to the administration of justice. In *Australasian Meat Industry Employees Union v Mudginberri Station* (1986), the Court held that past disobedience to an order could attract sanctions imposed solely by way of punishment. This, it said, might be necessary 'to protect the effective administration of justice by demonstrating that the court's orders will be enforced'. By contrast, in the earlier case of *Australian Consolidated Press v Morgan* (1965), **Windeyer** had described the purpose of sanctions for civil contempt as 'primarily coercive or remedial'.

On two occasions, publications allegedly scandalising the High Court itself have been the subject of contempt proceedings in the Court. In *R v Nicholls* (1911), a newspaper article stated that **Higgins** had been appointed to judicial office on account of having 'well served a political party' and that he was not prepared to permit any criticism of those who appointed him. Dismissing the motion for contempt on behalf of the Court, **Griffith** characterised this allegation as a fair comment on remarks Higgins had made while presiding in the Commonwealth Court of Conciliation and Arbitration. Griffith implied that these remarks might themselves have been such as to impair public confidence in judicial impartiality. On the other hand, the Court seemed distinctly more sensitive to **criticism** in *R v Dunbabin; Ex parte Williams* (1935). It imposed a fine for contempt on the publisher of an editorial that ridiculed the Court in a sarcastic tone, saying it was unduly keen to invalidate legislation through ingenious hair splitting and that its decision in the *Kisch Case* (1934) would please only 'the Little Brothers of the Soviet and kindred intelligentsia'. Only **Starke** considered it wrong to impose a penalty, though he agreed that contempt had been committed. He said that the Court should 'leave to public opinion the reprobation of attacks or comments derogatory to or scandalising it'. The editorial had asked whether, if the Act were amended, 'the ingenuity of five bewigged heads' might 'discover another flaw'. Starke, who had dissented in the *Kisch Case* and who never wore a wig, told his son that if it had referred to 'four bewigged heads' it would not have been contempt at all.

Not all the Court's contempt decisions have been overtly protective of judicial authority. In *Nationwide News v Wills* (1992), one of the first of the **Free Speech Cases**, the Court emphasised that the idea of contempt by scandalising the court is limited by the defences of truth and fair comment. In *Lewis v Ogden* (1984), it overturned the conviction of a barrister for a statutory offence broadly equivalent to contempt in the face of the court. It held that even 'discourteous' and 'offensive' remarks to a judge might not constitute contempt because 'the freedom and responsibility which counsel has to present his client's case are so important to the administration of justice'.

In *McRae* and again in *Hinch v A-G (Vic)* (1987), the Court narrowed the scope of liability for *sub judice* contempt in order to provide greater leeway for freedom of speech. These are, however, decisions dealing with threats to the impartiality of juries rather than to judicial authority.

Finally, while the Court has retained summary trial procedures for contempt, it has insisted that, since penal sanctions may be imposed, the safeguards associated with **criminal procedure** must be observed. Its decisions in *Coward v Stapleton* (1953), *Keeley v Brooking* (1979), and *Macgroarty v Clauson* (1989) superimposed basic principles of **natural justice**—the right to proper notice of charges laid and the opportunity to prepare and present a case in reply—on the summary procedure for contempt in the face of the court. In *Doyle v Commonwealth* (1985), the Court held that a notice of motion to commit for civil contempt must name the alleged contemners individually and must normally be served personally. In *Witham v Holloway* (1995), it held that in proceedings for civil as well as for criminal contempt, the case must be proved by the instigating party beyond reasonable doubt.

To sum up, the High Court has adhered to traditional perceptions of contempt as an array of special rules and procedures controlled and deployed by judges in order to punish affronts to judicial authority, along with other forms of interference with the administration of justice. But it has been careful to ensure that basic standards of procedural fairness apply when these powers are actually put into operation.

MICHAEL CHESTERMAN

Further Reading
Australian Law Reform Commission, *Contempt*, Report No 35 (1987)
Michael Chesterman, 'Contempt: In the Common Law but not the Civil Law' (1997) 46 *ICLQ* 521
Brendan Edgeworth, 'Beneath Contempt' (1983) 8 *LSB* 171
Sally Walker, 'Freedom of Speech and Contempt of Court: The English and Australian Approaches Compared' (1991) 40 *ICLQ* 583

Contract and tort are the two main foundations recognised by the **common law** for awards of monetary **damages** for breaches of legal duty, though their clear doctrinal differentiation came only in the nineteenth century. Much of the modern law of contract developed at around the same time, partly under French influence and partly through the prevalent *laissez faire* free market **ideology**. According to that ideology, duties in **tort law** were imposed upon defendants by the law of the land, whereas those in **contract law** were voluntarily assumed by contractual parties as free-willing individuals.

In cases where plaintiffs have a choice between suing in tort and in contract, one cause of action may sometimes be more favourable than the other. But in *Winterbottom v Wright* (1842), the possibility of using tort law to overcome the limits of contract law was specifically excluded: it was held that where a defendant's activity was regulated by contract, the contractual duties must exhaustively determine the defendant's potential liabilities, to avoid the 'injustice' of allowing the contractual relationship to be 'ripped open' by an action in tort.

The celebrated *Balmain Ferry Case* (1905–09) reflected a similar ideological preference. There the contractual element arose from a notice: persons who had entered the ferry wharf by putting a penny in the turnstile, but who then wished to leave the wharf, were required to insert another penny. The plaintiff maintained that this restriction on his freedom to leave the wharf constituted the tort of false imprisonment. On that basis, a NSW jury awarded him £100 damages; but as the case moved up the appellate ladder, the tort analysis was progressively displaced by a contract analysis. In the High Court, all three Justices (**Griffith**, **Barton**, and **O'Connor**) used a contract analysis to defeat the plaintiff's claim. The **Privy Council** was even more emphatic, condemning his behaviour as 'thoroughly unreasonable throughout'.

In *Donoghue v Stevenson* (1932), the **House of Lords** adopted an expanded conception of tort liability in negligence and overruled *Winterbottom*. In *Grant v Australian Knitting Mills* (1932–35), the SA Supreme Court was quick to recognise the significance of *Donoghue v Stevenson*; but in the High Court only **Evatt** did so. It was left to the Privy Council to extend the *Donoghue* analysis, holding that a plaintiff who suffered dermatitis after purchasing underpants with insufficient washing instructions, was entitled to sue both the manufacturer (in the tort of negligence) and the retailer (in contract, on an implied warranty of reasonable fitness for wear).

In that case, the claims in tort and contract were against different defendants. But increasingly, as negligence liability expanded, the same claim against the same defendant could be formulated either way, resulting in 'concurrent liability'. For example, most workplace accidents entitled the worker to sue the employer both in negligence (for lack of reasonable care) and in contract (on an implied promise of a reasonably safe system of work). And as cases such as *Hedley Byrne v Heller* (1963) (in England) and *MLC v Evatt* (1968) (in Australia) expanded the law of negligence to cover mere economic loss (with no physical injury), and mere negligent professional advice (with no physical action), the scope of tort liability moved even further into professional and commercial relationships in which liability had previously been regulated solely by contract, or even excluded by contract. By

the 1970s, some academic writers were predicting that contract and tort liability might merge in a hybrid 'contort'. Others even predicted 'the death of contract', as traditional contract doctrines came under other pressures as well (see *Trident General Insurance v McNiece* (1988)).

It was just at this very point in history, however, that increasing uncertainties at the outer limits of the concept of negligence seemed likely to halt or even reverse the process of its expansion. At the same time, the resurgence of free market ideologies in **economics** evoked countervailing tendencies: an increasing resort to negligence claims as a corporate strategy for minimising economic loss to risk capital in development and investment programs (as in *San Sebastian v Minister* (1986)); but also a tendency for the contract model to assume the same kind of privileged status as it had done a century earlier. Predictions of 'the death of contract' seemed increasingly premature.

The tension remains unresolved. In *Hawkins v Clayton* (1988), **Deane** asserted that in areas of 'concurrent liability', where the contractual solution would merely duplicate that of tort law, the latter should 'cover the field' to the *exclusion* of the contract analysis. In *Astley v Austrust* (1999), **Gleeson, McHugh, Gummow,** and **Hayne** argued precisely the reverse: 'Why should the law of negligence have any say at all in regulating the relationship of the parties to the contract? … There is no reason why the contract should not declare completely and exclusively … the legal rights and obligations of the parties.'

It may not be strictly accurate to say that the expression of these attitudes in *Astley v Austrust* involved an **overruling** of *Hawkins v Clayton*. The actual decision in *Hawkins v Clayton* was simply that a solicitor who prepared and held a client's will had no contractual duty to inform the executor about the will when the client died, but did have such a duty under tort law. The whole Court agreed that there was no relevant contractual term.

In *Astley v Austrust*, the respondent trustee company (the former Elders Trustees), attempting to diversify into new entrepreneurial roles, had undertaken the management of a piggery. The scheme was improvident, and neither the company nor its advising solicitors had adequately assessed the risks involved. The actual decision was that the solicitors had 'concurrent liabilities' in both tort and contract, and that the company's own contributory negligence would reduce the damages recoverable in tort, but *not* those available in contract.

Astley does, however, signify a clear move away from any tendency towards merger of tort and contract—both by its affirmation of a clear distinction between the two, and by its continued tolerance of concurrent liabilities arising under both heads. On the latter point, *Astley* follows the House of Lords in *Henderson v Merrett Syndicates* (1994), where Deane's argument against the need for an implied contractual term was rejected. Moreover, both *Henderson* and *Astley* reaffirm that where concurrent liabilities exist, plaintiffs may choose the cause of action most advantageous to them.

To some extent, these issues have been overtaken by statute. For example, on a complaint of misleading or deceptive conduct under section 52 of the *Trade Practices Act* 1974 (Cth), it is immaterial whether the context is one of tort or of contract. Whatever the future relationship between the two, it may be that further statutory developments will render both common law foundations of liability, and the precise distinctions between them, increasingly irrelevant.

TONY BLACKSHIELD
FRANCESCA DOMINELLO

Contract law comprises the rules formulated by judges to prescribe what a contract is and how it is made, what obligations it imposes, who can enforce it, what constitutes a breach of it, when its performance is excused, how it is terminated, and the **remedies** for breach.

The High Court heard several contract cases in its first full year of operation (1904), and has decided about 770 since. Probably no court at the apex of any other **common law** jurisdiction has so intensively engaged with contract doctrine. The Court has carved out a strong identity for contract as an independent category of private law, with empirical and legal foundations distinct from those of **tort**, **restitution** and **equity**. It has insisted on the unique nature of **damages** for breach of contract as seeking to place the injured party in the same situation as if the contract had been performed. In cases such as *Gates v City Mutual* (1986), *Commonwealth v Amann Aviation* (1991), *Marks v GIO* (1998) and *Astley v Austrust* (1999), the Court has emphasised the greater ambit of contract-based 'expectation' damages when compared with 'reliance' damages in tort and under **trade practices law** (see **Contract and tort**).

A notable aspect of High Court case law has been the predominance—now diminishing—of contracts of sale of land. Because such contracts create an equitable title and are enforced by an equitable decree of specific performance, their ubiquity may explain the Court's willingness to apply equitable principles, culminating in landmark decisions of the **Mason Court** on estoppel and **unconscionability**. Paradoxically, as such contracts are usually in a formal signed document, this may also have contributed to the Court's rather rigid approach to issues of formation and construction.

Although the High Court has from its inception relied heavily on English contract law, this dependency has gradually lessened. References to other common law jurisdictions (notably the USA, Canada, and NZ) and to European and **international law** have increased, with open divergences from English law on several points. Nevertheless, English precedents are still routinely cited and analysed. As a result, Australian contract law often has a second-hand quality. Even its elite practitioners still keep an ear permanently cocked towards London.

The mass of cases on contract defies brief exposition. In a series of early decisions, *Mooney v Williams* (1905), *Barrier Wharfs v Scott Fell & Co* (1908), *Heppingstone v Stewart* (1910), *McBride v Sandland* (1918) and *Farmer v Honan* (1919), the Court entrenched the conception of a contract as a bargain or exchange, consisting of a promise given in consideration of a counter-promise or in consideration of an act. Its key elements are the concepts 'offer', 'acceptance' and 'consideration'. In *Australian Woollen Mills v Commonwealth* (1954), the Commonwealth had announced to woollen manufacturers a subsidy on purchases of wool from growers. A manufacturer bought quantities of wool in reliance on the

announcement, but the Commonwealth refused to pay the subsidy. The Court held that no contract had been made. The government had not intended any promise, nor proposed an exchange; it merely wished to keep down the price of woollen goods. As a result there was no offer, no acceptance, and no consideration.

Implicit in this conception is the idea that a contract springs forth fully articulated at the precise moment of acceptance. This is often difficult to apply in practice, as shown by such cases as *Lang v James Morrison* (1911), *Robertson v Martin* (1956), *MacRobertson Miller Airline Services v Commissioner of State Taxation (WA)* (1975) and *Sindel v Georgiou* (1984). The demand for precision sometimes has ludicrous results. In *R v Clarke* (1927), Clarke claimed a reward offered by the police for information about a murder. Clarke knew of the reward, but admitted that when he gave the information he was thinking only of clearing his own name. The Court held there was no contract. The offer had not been accepted because Clarke was not thinking of it at the relevant time.

By adopting a conception of contract based on promise and exchange, the High Court excluded conduct falling short of promise, even if justifiably relied on. However, in **Waltons Stores v Maher** (1988), the Court held that a party who has reasonably relied on an assumption induced by another party may be able to enforce the assumption on the ground of estoppel. In *Giumelli v Giumelli* (1999), the Court insisted that the liability so imposed is not contractual, but equitable and discretionary, arising only if no contractual promise has been made. Thus the formal conception of contract was kept intact, though liability was expanded.

The emphasis on promise has also left its mark on the rules determining content, leading to a fine distinction between 'warranty' (promise) and 'representation' (not a promise). In *Ross v Allis-Chalmers* (1980), the seller of a harvesting machine told the buyer that he 'should budget on 90 acres per day'. The Court held this was a representation, not a warranty. **Aickin** acknowledged that the distinction 'depends in many cases on niceties of language in conversations recounted, often years afterwards, by persons who would not have been conscious of the significance of the particular words used'. Nevertheless, that was the law.

If a contract is fully formed at a precise moment, its content must be determined as at that moment. Hence statements made in negotiations are often excluded, and if a document was signed, such statements may not even be admissible in **evidence**. The 'parol evidence rule' excludes evidence given 'to subtract from, add to, vary or contradict the language of a written instrument'. It was first applied in *Rankin v Scott Fell* (1904) and has often been invoked since, notably in *Life Insurance v Phillips* (1925), *Hope v RCA Photophone* (1937), and *Codelfa Construction v State Rail Authority of NSW* (1982).

The Court has accepted that a pre-contractual promise may be enforceable as a 'collateral' contract. However, since *Hoyt's v Spencer* (1919), this approach has been severely hampered by the rule that a collateral contract cannot be inconsistent with the 'main' contract. In *Hoyt's*, a lease provided that the lessor could terminate it at any time. Before it was signed, the lessor promised not to do so except in defined circumstances. The Court held that the promise was not enforceable as a collateral contract because the consideration for it was the lessee's entry into the lease as it stood, and the promise therefore negated the consideration. Despite the arid circularity of this argument and its unfair effect, *Hoyt's* was affirmed in *Gates v City Mutual* (1986).

The Court has similarly restricted the scope of rectification, an equitable remedy for the correction of documents. It has refused rectification even where the parties' expectations are demonstrably at odds with their written contract. In *Pukallus v Cameron* (1982), both parties believed that the land described in a contract of sale included a bore pointed out to the buyer during an inspection of the property. The Court nevertheless declined to rectify the contractual boundaries, which excluded the bore.

In contrast with this strict approach to the express terms of a contract, the Court has constructed a powerful framework for implying terms. It has made clear that contractual obligations are not limited to what was expressly agreed. Implied terms operate at three levels: universal terms implied in all contracts, generic terms implied in classes of contract, and specific terms implied in individual contracts. All three kinds of implication are well established in the Court.

Pre-eminent among universal terms endorsed by the Court is the duty of the parties to cooperate. Initially, this was defined as requiring whatever was necessary 'to give efficacy to the agreement' (*O'Keefe v Williams* (1910)). In *Secured Income Real Estate v St Martins Investments* (1979), the Court adopted a more precise formula: 'each party agrees to do all such things as are necessary to enable the other party to have the benefit of the contract', taken from a judgment by **Griffith** in the Supreme Court of Queensland (*Butt v M'Donald* (1896)). In *Secured Income*, an amount under a contract of sale of a commercial building was payable only if the income from the building reached a nominated level. To achieve this, the seller offered himself as a tenant. The buyer refused. The Court held that this would have breached the implied duty to cooperate, but for the existence of reasonable doubts about the seller's financial position. The *Butt* formula has since become entrenched.

Other universal duties have also been proposed, including a duty to act reasonably (*Electronic Industries v David Jones* (1954)) and a duty not to impair the basis of the contract (*Ansett Transport Industries v Commonwealth* (1977)). Since *Canning v Temby* (1905), the Court has held that if no time is fixed for performance a reasonable time is implied. The Court has not yet had an opportunity to consider whether a duty to act in good faith is implied in all contracts, as other Australian courts have suggested.

Many decisions illustrate the implication of generic terms. In *Cavallari v Premier Refrigeration Co* (1952), the Court spelt out the implied content of contracts of sale of land. Doctors owe an implied obligation to their patients to exercise reasonable care and skill in giving advice and treatment (*Breen v Williams* (1996)). A carpark owes its customers such a duty in parking their cars (*Sydney City Council v West* (1965)). The organisers of a sporting event owe a duty to spectators to make the premises safe (*Australian Racing Drivers Club v Metcalf* (1961)). The duty is distinct from and concurrent with that imposed by the law of negligence.

Since *Bowden Bros v Little* (1907), the Court has repeatedly recognised that specific terms may be implied in contracts if required by 'business efficacy'. In *Secured Income*, the Court adopted a five-point test laid down by the **Privy Council** in *BP Refinery v Shire of Hastings* (1977): a term is implied if it is necessary, reasonable, obvious, clear, and consistent with the express terms of the contract. The Court has shown some inclination to retreat from over-rigorous application of this test, especially where there is no formal document. While it has often said that courts are slow to imply terms, it has done so as often as not.

The Court recognises the right of parties to exclude obligations otherwise implied in their contract, and to limit liability for breach. It has refused to place substantive limits on the limitation of liability, leaving it to the legislature to do so (see **Consumer law**). In *Bergl v Moxon Lighterage* (1920) the defendant's vessel sank while carrying the plaintiff's goods. The Court held that a clause denying liability for loss or damage protected the defendant even against breach of the fundamental obligation to provide a seaworthy vessel. Since then the efficacy of such clauses has frequently been affirmed. However, reasonable notice of such clauses is required when making the contract. In *Oceanic Sun Line Co v Fay* (1988), the Court held that clauses on a ticket could not be relied on because the contract with the passenger had been made before the ticket was issued. In *Sydney City Council*, the Court said that handing a ticket to a driver in a stream of traffic entering a parking station was not reasonable notice. Moreover, a party relying on such a clause must show that its words cover the situation (*Tozer Kemsley v Collier's Interstate* (1956)); ambiguities will be resolved against that party ('*contra proferentem*'). So in *Sydney City Council* a generalised denial of liability did not cover an act not authorised by the contract (delivering a car to a person who had no ticket). In *TNT v May & Baker* (1966), the Court denied protection to a carrier of goods whose driver, instead of taking them to the depot, took them home, where they were lost in a fire. But it has declined to interpret a clause *contra proferentem* (against the interests of the party who drafted it) as between commercial parties aware of the risks of a transaction (*Van der Sterren v Cibernetics* (1970)); *Darlington Futures v Delco* (1986); *Nissho Iwai v Malaysian International* (1989)).

An important question is whether a clause limiting liability protects not only the parties to a contract but others involved in its performance, for example subcontractors or employees. In *Wilson v Darling Island Stevedoring* (1956) and *Port Jackson Stevedoring v Salmond & Spraggon* (1978), the Court rejected this notion; but, on appeal in the latter case, the Privy Council (1980) held that by appropriate drafting a carrier of goods can circumvent the doctrine of privity of contract and protect its employees, agents and subcontractors. The Court has since reaffirmed the doctrine of privity—though only by majority, and with willingness to accept a range of devices by which to circumvent its operation in insurance cases—in **Trident General Insurance v McNiece** (1988). In *Nissho Iwai*, the Court granted **leave to appeal** because it thought that policy arguments relied on in *Port Jackson Stevedoring* would arise for examination (in the event they did not). These developments suggest that the point remains unresolved.

The duty to perform a contract is not absolute. The parties may be excused from performance on various grounds including lack of mental capacity, mistake, **undue influence**, duress, misrepresentation, unconscionability, and public policy. In *Gibbons v Wright* (1954), the Court laid down comprehensive rules on mental incapacity. In *Johnson v Buttress* (1936), it likewise settled the law of undue influence, holding that it was presumed in contracts between unequal parties such as solicitor and client, doctor and patient, guardian and ward. However, the doctrine of duress (coercion) has received little attention. In particular, 'economic duress' (illegitimate commercial pressure) has not been considered since *Smith v William Charlick* (1924), where it was held that a seller's threat to stop supplies unless more money was paid was not illegitimate pressure. The decision conflicts with developments in other Australian courts, and awaits re-evaluation.

The right to avoid a contract induced by misrepresentation has been considered in many decisions, including *Holmes v Jones* (1907), *Ritter v North Side Enterprises* (1975), *Alati v Kruger* (1955), *John McGrath Motors v Applebee* (1964), *Sargent v Campbell* (1972), *Gould v Vaggelas* (1985), *Vadasz v Pioneer Concrete* (1995) and *Krakowski v Eurolynx* (1995). Despite or perhaps because of the number of cases, an important issue remains unresolved: is subjective inducement enough, or must a misrepresentation be objectively 'material'?

In dealing with the excuses so far described, the Court has not ventured beyond the limits of orthodoxy established in other common law jurisdictions. However, this is not true of its treatment of unconscionability. This equitable doctrine allows the rescission of a contract made by a party at a 'serious disadvantage *vis-à-vis* the other'. In several powerful cases, the Court has endowed unconscionability with a unique status in Australian contract law. *Amadio's Case* (1983) is regarded as the leading case, but its precursor *Blomley v Ryan* (1956) should not be forgotten. There the Court annulled a contract by which Ryan sold his farm to Blomley in the course of a drinking bout. **Fullagar**, in a much-quoted passage, stated that a 'great variety' of disadvantages may justify rescission of a contract, including 'poverty or need of any kind, sickness, age, sex, infirmity of body or mind, drunkenness, illiteracy or lack of education, and lack of assistance or explanation'.

Since *Amadio*, the Court has applied the doctrine of unconscionability on three occasions. In *Louth v Diprose* (1992), it annulled the gift of a house obtained by taking advantage of the donor's infatuation with the donee. In **Garcia v National Australia Bank** (1998), it set aside a mortgage of a matrimonial home securing business loans to the husband, because the wife did not understand the transaction and the bank made no effort to explain it to her or to find out whether she had independent advice. The Court endorsed an earlier decision, **Yerkey v Jones** (1939), in which **Dixon** invoked an equitable principle specifically protecting married women, as a particular application of unconscionability. Finally, in *Bridgewater v Leahy* (1998) the Court annulled transfers of land by a farmer to his nephew because the nephew had taken advantage of his uncle's 'strong emotional dependence and attachment'.

More than any other factor, the High Court's commitment to the doctrine of unconscionability (despite **criticism** from **commentators** who believe that it undermines the security of contracts) distinguishes Australian contract law from that of other common law jurisdictions. The Court has warned against reading the doctrine as legitimising idiosyncratic notions of conscience. But it has also stressed that unconscionability cannot be defined exhaustively. As **Mason** pointed out in *Amadio*, and the whole Court acknowledged in *Vadasz*, unconscionability is the integrative rationale of other invalidating factors such as duress, undue influence and misrepresentation—'they all constitute species of unconscionable conduct'. It may also be a means for rationalising the law of mistake. The Court has long struggled to develop coherent rules to regulate contracts made under a mistaken belief not induced by misrepresentation. In *Goldsbrough Mort v Quinn* (1910), it accepted that a mistake about the meaning of words resulting in an absence of consent could be a reason for not enforcing a contract. However, in *Cameron v Slutzkin* (1923) and *Life Insurance v Phillips*, it held that the parties to a contract were bound by its objective meaning as determined by the Court. In *McRae v Commonwealth Disposals Commission* (1951) and in *Svanosio v McNamara* (1956), mistakes about the subject matter of a sale were disregarded, in one case because the mistake was self-induced, in the other because it did not result in a 'total failure of consideration'. But in *Petelin v Cullen* (1975), the Court held invalid an option signed in the belief that it was a receipt for money, saying that the defence '*non est factum*' is available to persons unable to understand what they have signed. And in *Taylor v Johnson* (1983), it held that a contract made by a party seriously mistaken about its content (in that case the price) is voidable if the other party has acted unconscionably, for example by deliberately failing to correct the mistake. *Taylor* points the way to the adoption of unconscionability as a general criterion of operative mistake.

A contract may also be invalid because it is against public policy. Despite recurrent attacks on this doctrine, a long line of decisions from *Kerridge v Simmonds* (1906) to *Fitzgerald v FJ Leonhardt* (1997) has unequivocally affirmed it. In *Wilkinson v Osborne* (1915), the Court declined on this basis to enforce a contract by two members of Parliament to lobby the government to buy their client's property. **Isaacs** said that reliance on public policy must identify 'some definite or governing principle which the community as a whole has already adopted'. Here that principle was that legislators must act independently and for the public welfare. In *A v Hayden* (1984), the Court held that a promise by the government not to disclose the identity of its employees was against public policy because it prevented the investigation of a crime. A contract involving unlawful conduct is normally against public policy (*Hutchinson v Scott* (1905)). A contract involving conduct prohibited by statute may be against public policy even if the statute itself does not prohibit contracts (*North v Marra Developments* (1981)), but this is unlikely if the statute imposes specific penalties, such as fines (*Yango Pastoral v First Chicago* (1978); *Fitzgerald*).

While the Court has thus endorsed a range of invalidating factors, it has shown a strong inclination to uphold contracts validly made. So breach does not justify termination of a contract unless it relates to an essential term or deprives the other party substantially of the benefit of the contract

(*Associated Newspapers v Bancks* (1951); *Carr v JA Berriman* (1953); *Progressive Mailing v Tabali* (1985); *Ankar v National Westminster Finance* (1987)). In particular, failure to perform on time does not justify termination unless otherwise agreed (*Laurinda v Capalaba Park Shopping Centre* (1989)). The Court has similarly restricted termination for failure of a specified contingency (such as obtaining a loan or a permit). In a long line of decisions, including *Maynard v Goode* (1926), *Suttor v Gundowda* (1950), *Gange v Sullivan* (1966), *Perri v Coolangatta Investments* (1982), and *Meehan v Jones* (1982), it has held that termination in such cases is generally not automatic, and that failure of a contingency does not avail a party who made insufficient efforts to bring it about. Moreover, a right to terminate, whether for breach or failure of contingency, is lost by conduct affirming the contract, waiving the right or giving rise to an estoppel. In *Sargent v ASL Developments* (1974), the Court held that a party can lose a right to terminate even if unaware of its existence, although *Immer v Uniting Church* (1993) suggests some retreat from this position.

While the Court has accepted that a contract may confer a right to terminate where the law would not, it has subjected such rights to strong control. In *Shevill v Builders Licensing Board* (1982), it held that a party exercising such a right can only claim limited damages. Moreover, in cases such as *Godfrey Constructions v Kanangra Park* (1972), *Pierce Bell Sales v Frazer* (1973), *Stern v McArthur* (1988) and *Foran v Wight* (1989), the Court has invoked an equitable discretion to prevent the unconscionable exercise of such rights. Other cases, including *Commonwealth v Amann Aviation*, suggest that such rights are limited by an implied obligation to act reasonably.

A touchstone of any contract law is the extent to which it excuses performance of a contract because subsequent events have impeded it or made it more costly. The Court has acknowledged what is now called the doctrine of 'frustration' since *Hart v MacDonald* (1910), but has rarely applied it. In such cases as *Ockerby v Watson* (1918), *Firth v Halloran* (1926), *Scanlan's v Tooheys* (1943) and *Meriton Apartments v McLaurin & Tait* (1976), the Court held that an event could frustrate a contract only if there was an implied term to that effect. However, in *Brisbane City Council v Group Projects* (1979), following English authority, the Court adopted a test of frustration based on an objective comparison between circumstances then and now. This new approach was affirmed in *Codelfa Construction v State Rail Authority*. In both cases, it was held that a contract had been frustrated, in the one by compulsory acquisition of land by the government, in the other by court orders severely restricting hours of work. These decisions may signal an expansion of the doctrine of frustration.

Although the Court has adhered to many features of classical contract doctrine, the Mason Court altered its shape in two vital respects. On the one hand, it invoked estoppel to impose obligation where none existed under classical rules. On the other hand, it increased reliance on unconscionable conduct as a reason for not enforcing a contract. As these developments counteract one another it is likely, notwithstanding some contemporary apprehensions, that there has been no fundamental shift in the tilt of Australian contract law.

It is superficially tempting to discern a transition from the formulary of the early Court to the more fully wrought **legal**-ism of the **Dixon Court**, and thence to the equity-based jurisprudence of the Mason Court, with a return to modified legalism perhaps in prospect under the **Gleeson Court**. But on closer inspection, such transitions are merely changes in the choice of doctrinal means. The enduring substance of High Court contract law was expressed by **Windeyer** in *Placer Development v Commonwealth* (1969): 'A basic assumption of our law is that bargains are to be kept.' The Court's commitment to this principle spans its history. In *Balmain New Ferry Co v Robertson* (1906), a ferry company stipulated that passengers must pay a penny on entering or leaving the wharf, whether they travelled on the ferry or not. Robertson paid a penny to enter the wharf but decided not to travel. He was kept from leaving unless he paid a further penny. The Court held that the company could detain him to enforce the contract. The principle that bargains must be kept still animates the Court. In *Pan Foods v ANZ Banking Group* (2000), **Kirby** said: 'Business is entitled to look to the law to keep people to their commercial promises. In a world of global finances and transborder capital markets, those jurisdictions flourish which do so.'

MP ELLINGHAUS

Further Reading
MP Ellinghaus, 'Towards an Australian Contract Law' in MP Ellinghaus, AJ Bradbrook, and AJ Duggan (eds), *The Emergence of Australian Law* (1989)
MP Ellinghaus, *The High Court of Australia on Contract* (1999)

Convention Debates. The expression 'Convention Debates' is used to refer to the printed Hansard debates of the two great Conventions that met to frame the Australian Constitution between the years 1891 and 1898. The first of these was the National Australasian Convention that met in Sydney in 1891, while the Australasian Federal Convention assembled in Adelaide and Sydney in 1897 and, finally, in Melbourne in 1898.

The Debates comprise five large volumes, amounting in total to some 7000 pages and roughly 3.5 million words of debate. In the standard manner of Hansard of the time, they were published with a sessional index to the speeches of the individual members of the Convention, together with an index to debate on particular clauses of the draft Constitution Bill. As clause numbers changed between and within sessions, the latter can be extremely hard to follow. No general index accompanied any of the original volumes, nor was there any overall index spanning the different sessions. All of these factors combined to render the Debates, in the past, a relatively cumbersome interpretive tool.

This has been unfortunate, as the Debates are in fact a remarkable resource. As a verbatim Hansard record of a public assembly, they are vastly more informative and reliable than any of the highly partial and incomplete sources relating to the drafting of the US Constitution. Moreover, the fact that the Australian **framers** were, with the exception of those from WA, directly elected to the Convention of 1897–98, gives to their formal utterances a degree of democratic authority denied to the parents of the American document.

In 1985, the chronically scarce Debates were made vastly more accessible through their republication in a modern

The Federal Convention that drafted the Australian Constitution, sitting in Sydney 1897–98

edition by Sydney publisher Legal Books. This edition was accompanied by a sixth volume, which contained—in addition to commentaries, a consolidated index of speeches and a selective general index—a comprehensive guide to the evolution of each of the Constitution's provisions throughout the different sessions of the Conventions (Gregory Craven, *The Convention Debates 1891–1898: Commentaries, Indices and Guide* (1985)). In 1999, the Debates reached a new level of public accessibility through their publication in searchable form at the web site of the Commonwealth Government (www.aph.gov.au/senate/pubs/records.htm).

Naturally, the extent of use and influence of the Debates will depend upon the methodology of **constitutional interpretation** adopted by the High Court and its individual Justices. Thus, for example, a strictly literalist judge will have little occasion to turn to the Debates. A progressivist judge, committed to interpreting the Constitution according to the contemporary needs of the Australian people, should prove similarly immune to the Debates' blandishments. However, any judge who sees his or her duty as being to interpret the Constitution according to the intentions of its authors is likely to find delving into the Debates an irresistible pathway to enlightenment.

Despite some flirtation with the idea (not revisited until *Cole v Whitfield* in 1988) that the Debates might be referred to, not as direct evidence of intention but as an indication of the 'mischief' that was being addressed (*Municipal Rates Case* (1904)), the Court's original attitude to the use of the Debates was one of frosty disapproval, expressed early and sternly by the High Court in *Tasmania v Commonwealth*

(1904). Although their strictures were expressed in terms of literalist norms of **statutory interpretation**, there can be little doubt that at the heart of the disinclination of such figures as **Griffith** and **Barton** to allow resort to the Debates was the understandable conviction that they knew their own minds as framers without any need for recourse to a written record.

In any event, the first High Court's interpretive method, highly intentionalist in basis and federalist in effect, did not produce results markedly different from those that would have ensued from a heavy reliance upon the Debates. Consequently, the Court's early denial of the Debates was of limited importance. However, this altered after the *Engineers Case* (1920), when the Court, dominated by **Isaacs**, embarked upon an ultra-literalistic, centralising interpretation of the Constitution. The Debates, with their constant reiterations of the federal principle and states' rights would have been an obvious counter-balance to Isaacs' constitutional nationalism. Ironically, however, Isaacs' judicial opponents on the first High Court had firmly removed them from the equation.

Throughout the years of unchallenged **literalism** between *Engineers* and *Cole v Whitfield*, the Convention Debates remained an unploughed field, though reference was allowed by the Court to the successive drafts of the Constitution Bill and—bizarrely—to **Quick and Garran's** own secondary account of the development of provisions through the Convention. It was not until the Court was impelled to untangle the impossibly twisted skein of section 92 (see **Interstate trade and commerce**) that the ban on the Debates themselves was lifted.

In *Cole v Whitfield*, the Debates were used decisively and enthusiastically to restore a historically derived, anti-protectionist reading to section 92. At the same time, the Court was concerned not to subject the words of the Constitution themselves to a general overlordship of the framers' utterances. The Court opined that the history of constitutional provisions might be resorted to, not with a view to substituting for the meaning of the words actually used the scope and effect subjectively intended by the framers, but rather for the purpose of establishing the contemporary meaning of those words, the subject matter of the provision and the general objectives of the federation movement. In reality, the Court comprehensively ignored this nostrum in *Cole v Whitfield*, and used the Debates precisely for the purpose of extracting out of the vague words of section 92 the anti-protectionist operation envisaged by the founders. Nevertheless, the false dichotomy between forbidden 'subjective meaning' and permissible establishment of 'purpose' continues to bedevil the use of the Convention Debates (see, for example, *Re Wakim* (1999)).

The Court's subsequent use of the Debates has been equivocal. Arguably, their first use to reconstruct the jurisprudence of section 92 in *Cole v Whitfield* was their high-water mark. Nevertheless, the Debates (or curial reflections of them in *Huddart Parker v Moorehead* (1909)) were also critical to the outcome of the *Incorporation Case* (1990), where the majority denied to the Commonwealth power to legislate with respect to the incorporation of constitutional corporations. The Debates are now routinely referred to, with whatever effect, in the major constitutional decisions of the Court.

Use of the Debates has most recently been compromised by the Court's pursuit of **implied constitutional rights**. Given that the Debates are quite clearly hostile to the existence of judicially enforceable rights, it is not surprising that their use does not feature prominently in the majority judgments in such cases as *Australian Capital Television v Commonwealth* (1992) and *Theophanous v Herald & Weekly Times* (1994), although they have been used by some judges in an attempt to moderate the claims of their more adventurous brethren (for example **Brennan** in *Nationwide News v Wills* (1992); see **Free Speech Cases**). At the same time, judges more supportive of the development of constitutional rights were impelled to devise an alternative constitutional **history** in an effort to fend off obvious ripostes based on the Debates. The most obvious example here was **Deane's** elevation of the sympathetic **Inglis Clark** to the status of a constitutional Moses (see, for example, *Theophanous*).

One obvious question concerning the Debates is how illuminating they are likely to prove on any given issue. Generally speaking, the Debates are far more comprehensive than has often been recognised; they frequently provide an excellent insight into the scope and purpose of the provision concerned. So much is abundantly illustrated in relation to section 92 in *Cole v Whitfield*; but the Debates on, for example, section 51(xx) (the **corporations power**), section 51(xxvi) (the **races power**) and section 41 (qualification of electors) are similarly illuminating. Less transparent are the Debates concerning section 90 (**excise**), where the framers seem to have used that term to cover a number of different imposts; but even here the central meaning of a tax on the

local production or manufacture of goods does emerge reasonably clearly (see *Capital Duplicators v ACT (No 2)* (1993)). Sometimes, however, the Debates are opaque—a good example being those portions relating to section 109, where little assistance may be derived concerning the nature of constitutional **inconsistency**.

As to future use, the judicial deployment of the Debates will depend, realistically, upon the extent to which individual Justices believe their contents to be congenial. For example, were the Court to resume its pursuit of implied rights, the place of the profoundly embarrassing Debates presumably will be downplayed. Similarly, in crucial areas of Commonwealth power—such as corporations, **external affairs** and excise—the Debates are either unhelpful or downright hostile to an expansionist reading, and so are unlikely to recommend themselves to the Court. Nevertheless, the Debates will certainly be resorted to by constitutionally conservative judges eager to find material with which to combat unhistorical interpretations (see, for example, the minority judgment in *Capital Duplicators (No 2)*). Moreover, given the conceptual and political difficulties of overt progressivism on the High Court, the Debates will doubtless be resorted to by more adventuresome judges for the purpose of providing a respectable historical strand to what is essentially an argument of constitutional policy.

GREGORY CRAVEN

Further Reading
Gregory Craven, *The Convention Debates 1891–1898: Commentaries, Indices and Guide* (1985)

Copyright. Since 1912, when the *Copyright Act* 1911 (UK) was declared to be in force in Australia by the *Copyright Act* 1912 (Cth), the High Court has dealt with most aspects of copyright law. For most of this time, it has been concerned with questions of fundamental principle. More recently, it has had to come to grips with the application of these principles to new information technology.

The 1911 legislation, for the first time, included the requirement of 'originality' as a precondition for the copyright protection of literary and artistic works, and it was unclear whether this embodied a standard similar to that of inventiveness or novelty in **patent** law. In two important early judgments, by the **Full Court** in *Sands & McDougall v Robinson* (1917) (involving maps) and by **Starke** in *Blackie & Sons v Lothian Book Publishing* (1921) (involving compilations), it was confirmed that a relatively low level of originality was required for protection. Later decisions, both before and after the *Copyright Act 1968* (Cth), have continued to display a similar generous approach and have extended protection to a broad range of subject matter, particularly of a factual and informational kind. Instances include *Australian Consolidated Press v Morgan* (1965) (public opinion polls), *O'Brien v Komesaroff* (1982) (unit trust deeds) and *SW Hart v Edwards Hot Water Systems* (1985) (drawings for solar heating panels).

Cases where the level of originality has been insufficient to qualify for protection have been rare (the racing information in *Victoria Park Racing v Taylor* (1937) provides one example), and the influence of the High Court's approach to this question on lower courts (**state Supreme Courts** and, more recently, the **Federal Court**) has been profound.

In several instances, issues of copyright law have become enmeshed with wider questions of **constitutional law.** As noted above, the Copyright Act 1911 (UK) was a piece of imperial legislation that was declared to be in force in its own right by the Copyright Act 1912 (Cth) (*Gramophone Co v Leo Feist* (1928)). This led to the unusual situation where the High Court held that the Copyright Act 1911 continued in force in Australia after its repeal by the UK Parliament: see *Copyright Owners Reproduction Society v EMI* (1958). This continued to be the case until the Commonwealth Parliament finally adopted its own legislation (the Copyright Act 1968) in the exercise of its plenary power under section 51(xviii) of the Constitution. On a later occasion, copyright reform ran foul of the Constitution when the Court struck down the legislature's attempt to compensate copyright owners for losses from private and domestic copying of sound recordings through the imposition of a blank tape levy. This was on the basis that the levy was a taxation measure that did not comply with section 55 of the Constitution (see *Australian Tape Manufacturers Association v Commonwealth* (1993)), which requires a law imposing taxation to be in a separate Act from a law dealing with any other matter.

In other decisions, the Court has highlighted difficulties that have required subsequent legislative amendment. In *Interstate Parcel Express v Time-Life International* (1977), the Court contrasted the rights of patentees with those of copyright owners (and exclusive licensees) in relation to the parallel importation of copies of works made lawfully abroad. Although the decision was doctrinally sound, its possible anti-competitive and anti-consumer effects were abundantly clear, as **Murphy** outlined in his judgment. Subsequent amendments have significantly reduced the rights of copyright owners to control the parallel importation of books, sound recordings and accompanying labels and packaging, and the government has announced that it intends to remove these controls almost completely.

In the same way, the Court's decision on the scope of authorisation of infringement in *University of NSW v Moorhouse* (1975) led ultimately to the introduction of statutory licensing schemes directed at compensating copyright owners for the reproduction of their works within educational and similar institutions. More recently, the decision in *Telstra v Australasian Performing Right Association* (1997) highlighted the complexity of the provisions of the Copyright Act dealing with broadcasting and diffusion rights, and these matters have now been resolved by the introduction of a right of communication to the public in the *Copyright Amendment (Digital Agenda) Act* 2000 (Cth).

The Court has also considered the copyright status of computer programs on a number of occasions. *Computer Edge v Apple Computer* (1986) was one of the earliest instances where this was done by a national court anywhere in the world. A majority held that programs in object code were incapable of protection as original literary works, because of their failure to convey anything meaningful to a human reader or user of the program. In terms of copyright principle, this was undoubtedly correct, although a strong minority view to the contrary was expressed by **Mason** and **Wilson**. Even though, by the time of the Court's decision, Parliament had already legislated specifically to protect computer programs (in both source and object code) as literary works, the majority decision remains of great significance and underlines the fact that this is a specific extension of protection that would not have been justified under normal principles. Many difficulties that have subsequently arisen in the application of copyright protection to computer programs might possibly have been avoided had the Australian government opted for a non-copyright *sui generis* solution at this early stage, when the appropriate form of protection had not yet been resolved at the international level (see now article 10(1) of the Trade-Related Intellectual Property Rights Agreement 1994 and article 4 of the WIPO Copyright Treaty 1996, not yet in force). It is worth noting that, in the late 1970s, the World Intellectual Property Organisation had produced an alternative model for protection, in the form of a Model Law on Computer Software that sought to provide a more custom-made and limited form of protection that would have sat outside both the copyright and patent systems. This initiative was subsequently swamped in the headlong national rush into copyright, with all the attendant problems that have now become apparent, particularly with respect to such matters as the scope and duration of protection, and the limitations and exceptions to its operation.

The Court's subsequent decisions on computer programs have been more mixed in character. In *Autodesk v Dyason (No 2)* (1993), after hearing an application to review its decision in *Autodesk v Dyason (No 1)* (1992), the Court held that there had been a reproduction of a substantial part of the plaintiff's Widget C program where a 127-bit look-up table had been taken by the defendant. Although this was a minute part of the program, the majority held that it was still substantial because it was 'essential' to the running of the plaintiff's program. Such an approach can be extremely limiting in the case of computer programs, as they will generally not operate if even one digit has been altered. In *Data Access v Powerflex* (1999), a somewhat differently constituted Court therefore took pains to repudiate the 'but for' essentiality test which had been 'effectively invoked' by the *Autodesk v Dyason (No 2)* majority, saying this was not practicable for computer programs. It held that, in determining whether something is a reproduction of a substantial part of a program, its 'essential or material features' should be ascertained by 'considering the originality of the part allegedly taken'. Where this was only data or related information, it would be unlikely that these would form a substantial part since they would ordinarily be irrelevant to the program's structure, choice of commands and combination and sequencing of commands (these being the crucial parts of a program). This holding brings computer programs back into line with the approach taken by courts in other areas of copyright infringement.

In other ways, too, the High Court has developed or confirmed the application of basic copyright principles. In *Avel v Multicoin Amusements* (1990), it held that the exclusive publication right was confined to 'first publication' and was not to be viewed as a *de facto* distribution right. In *SW Hart*, the Court made it clear that substantive objective similarity was required for the purposes of an infringing reproduction, in this case a reproduction of a two-dimensional artistic work in three dimensions. Again, in *Telstra v APRA*, the Court endorsed prior judicial decisions on the meaning of the term 'public' in the context of both performing and broadcasting rights.

Copyright is one of the great balancing acts of the law. Many balls are in play and many interests are in conflict. On one side, there stand the creators, each with strong claims to protection for their endeavours. Alongside the creators, and often at odds with them, are the investors and entrepreneurs, who take these creative products into the marketplace. On yet another side, there are trade competitors who would like to do the same things and who assert their right to do so as competitors in a free market. And then there is the general public, which wants ready access to all this material. Overriding all these competing interests is the relentless pressure of technological change, which constantly challenges the present framework of protection. The conflicts are often intense, and frequently require legislative and judicial intervention to resolve. In all of this, the High Court's contribution to the development of Australian copyright jurisprudence has been constructive, though inevitably restricted. If, at times, the Court has faltered (as in *Autodesk*), it has soon repaired the damage (as in *Data Access*). On other occasions (as in *Computer Edge*), it has been prescient in foreshadowing the difficulties that may arise in seeking to apply the copyright template to subject matter for which it is not wholly appropriate. The dance proceeds, and there can be little doubt that, as the twenty-first century unfolds, the Court will be called upon to adjudicate some of the complex struggles that are occurring as authors, investors and users come to grips with the implications of the online environment.

SAM RICKETSON

Cormack v Cope (1974) was a last-minute attempt to prevent the joint sitting of both Houses of the Commonwealth Parliament which followed the double-dissolution election of 1974. Double dissolutions and joint sittings are both departures from the normal parliamentary process; they form part of the special procedure laid down in section 57 of the Constitution for the resolution of disagreements between the two Houses. The **Whitlam era** saw two double dissolutions (the third and fourth in Australian history), the second imposed by Governor-General John Kerr as a condition of his **dismissal** of the **Prime Minister** on 11 November 1975. The first, granted to Prime Minister Gough Whitlam on 11 April 1974, resulted in the federal election of 18 May 1974 and thereafter in the joint sitting of Tuesday 6 August 1974—still unique in Australian history.

The plaintiffs in *Cormack v Cope* were two Coalition senators from Victoria: Magnus Cormack, formerly President of the Senate, and James Webster (see *In re Webster* (1975)). Their writ was issued on Thursday 1 August, five days before the scheduled sitting. On Friday 2 August, Chief Justice **Barwick** immediately referred the matter to the **Full Court**, which heard argument throughout that day and much of the following Monday, with **Murphy** as **Attorney-General** arguing the case for the defence. For an hour and a half on Monday afternoon the six Justices gave *ex tempore* **judgments**. The Court's order dismissing the motions for injunctions was pronounced at 5.15 pm.

The whole Court agreed that no injunctions should issue, but for different reasons. **McTiernan** flatly denied the **justiciability** of the issues, which he saw as 'intrinsically of concern' to the Houses of Parliament only. By contrast, though Barwick conceded that the Court would not interfere in the Parliament's 'intra-mural deliberative activities', he insisted that where the Constitution prescribes a special law-making process, 'the courts have a right and duty to ensure that that law-making process is observed'. He indicated that, given a fuller hearing, he might well have been disposed to grant an injunction. But he held that as a matter of discretion, no interlocutory injunction should issue. He was influenced by the pressure of time, by the difficulty of framing an appropriate injunction, and by the knowledge that if section 57 had not been fully complied with, any resulting legislation could later be declared void 'at the instance of a proper plaintiff'.

The views of the other four judges were subtly shaded between these extremes. **Gibbs** agreed with Barwick that the Court had **jurisdiction** 'to interfere at any stage', but ought not to do so in this case. He framed the result expressly as an exercise of the Court's 'discretion', though speaking also of its 'settled practice'. **Mason** did not 'find it necessary to decide' whether the Court had jurisdiction or not. Assuming that there was such a jurisdiction, he thought there was no case for its exercise.

Douglas **Menzies** stated categorically that the High Court 'does not' intervene in the **parliamentary process**. Though speaking in terms of High Court practice, he appeared to regard it as an invariant practice from which the Court could not depart, since it has no 'authority' to prevent the passage of unconstitutional laws. Referring to **Dixon's** expressions of doubt in *Hughes & Vale v Gair* (1954) and in *Clayton v Heffron* (1960) as to the use of injunctions in such cases, he stressed that Dixon had spoken not of judicial discretion but of 'the relationship between the courts and Parliament in Australia'. He left open what might happen if the law-making process were being used to exclude the Court's later scrutiny, saying only that such a situation 'is unlikely to arise'.

Stephen (with a similar reservation about the possible exclusion of **judicial review**) also stated that the Court 'does not' intervene in the law-making process, but stressed that in his view this 'depends not upon discretionary but on jurisdictional grounds'. Like Menzies, he did not think the earlier statements in *Hughes & Vale v Gair* and *Clayton v Heffron* could be explained away as mere statements of discretion.

All six Justices emphasised that if the joint sitting went ahead, the validity of any resulting legislation could subsequently be challenged, without the extraordinary pressures of time involved in this last-minute hearing. The joint sitting passed six enactments, four of which the Court later scrutinised. One, the *Petroleum and Minerals Authority Act*, was held to be invalid, since the Senate's adjournment of debate on 13 December 1973 had not constituted a 'failure to pass' within the meaning of section 57 (the *PMA Case* (1975)). Three pieces of electoral legislation (notably the *Senate (Representation of Territories) Act*) were held to be valid primarily because there was no constitutional objection, at the time of the double dissolution in April 1974, to reliance on Bills which had been deadlocked up to seven months earlier (*First Territory Senators Case* (1975)). Even Barwick, who in *Cor-*

mack v Cope had raised serious doubts about the 'stockpiling' or 'staleness' of triggers for double dissolution, was not prepared to say that such a lapse of time was unreasonable.

Though **Murphy** in the *PMA Case*, and **Jacobs** in *Territory Senators*, agreed with McTiernan's original denial that issues arising under section 57 are justiciable at all, the results in these cases clearly confirm their justiciability.

TONY BLACKSHIELD

Corporations law. It would not be accurate to say that the High Court has led the development of corporations law in Australia. The bulk of corporate law cases have been handled by the **state Supreme Courts** and, over the last quarter-century—though since *Re Wakim* (1999) to a declining extent—by the **Federal Court**. Nevertheless, the High Court has made significant contributions to the fabric of corporations law both in the interpretation and application of relevant statutes and in the development of **common law** principles.

In the second half of the twentieth century the focal point of corporate law development in Australia shifted gradually from the courts to the legislature. As the High Court has recognised, this statutory development entailed a series of oscillations between the recognition of commercial concerns and the imposition of regulatory requirements. In *Australian Consolidated Press v Australian Newsprint Mills* (1960), for example, **Fullagar** and **Menzies** observed in a joint judgment that the drafter of a particular section of the *Companies Act 1920–57* (Tas) had been 'content to use the imprecise, but no doubt generally understood, language of business rather than to express himself in words which refer accurately to clearly recognised legal conceptions'. Thirty years later, **Mason** commented on the reverse problem: the proliferation of overly complex legislative provisions that 'can obscure the identification of policy goals and guidelines, reducing the role of the courts to an application of the statutory language which, on its own, does not always make much economic, social or practical sense'.

Only a few High Court decisions have led directly to reform of corporate law statutes. For example, in *Corporate Affairs Commission v Drysdale* (1978), the Court held that the statutory definition of 'director' included a de facto director, a ruling later recognised expressly in the new definition in the *Companies Act* 1981 (Cth). More often, however, the Court's impact on legislative reform has been less direct; its decisions have provided law reformers with authoritative demonstrations of the need for statutory reform. A good example of this is the law concerning liability for pre-incorporation contracts (contracts created by a company's promoter prior to incorporation). The common law required a court to determine the validity of a pre-incorporation contract by examining the intention of all parties. Frequently, as in the High Court decision in *Black v Smallwood* (1966), judges concluded that no contract had been created, thereby causing problems of commercial uncertainty. This problem was eventually remedied in 1981 by provisions in the new Companies Act.

The High Court's contribution to the common law of corporations has largely been to confirm or clarify existing principles. Few decisions have suggested or established new principles or directions for legal development. This can be seen by examining the High Court's contribution to three

fundamental issues for corporate law: directors' powers and responsibilities, majority rule and minority protection, and the concept of corporate status.

The High Court has been a notable advocate of judicial non-intervention in directors' decision making. This principle—sometimes referred to as the business judgment rule—surfaced early in the Court's corporate law jurisprudence. In *Australian Metropolitan Life Assurance v Ure* (1923), **Isaacs** referred to the uncontrolled discretion of the directors: 'Acting entirely within the scope of their power, honestly basing their action on their own business opinion, they were exercising a function with which no court can interfere, and over which no court has any jurisdiction of review or appeal.' During the period of the **Latham Court**, the non-intervention principle became mixed with what might be called a theme of commercial realism. In *Mills v Mills* (1938), for example, the Court examined the potential for conflicts of interest when a director holds shares in his or her own company. **Latham** stressed that 'it would be ignoring realities and creating impossibilities in the administration of companies to require that directors should not advert to or consider in any way the effect of a particular decision upon their own interests as shareholders'. He went on to make the often-cited reminder that a director is not 'required by the law to live in an unreal region of detached altruism and to act in a vague mood of ideal abstraction'.

The non-intervention principle is used to mark out the boundaries between judicial expertise and corporate expertise, but it certainly has not meant that the Court has adopted a *laissez faire* approach to directors' conduct. In *Furs v Tomkies* (1936), for example, the High Court heard an argument that a director should not be liable to account for a personal profit because, in that case, the company had not suffered any unfairness. In reply, the Court upheld the strict rule that requires a director to account for personal profits. The Court took the view that it was not in a position to determine what was fair for the company: 'no court is equal to the examination and ascertainment of the truth' in such a case.

The application of the non-intervention principle continued in the **Barwick Court**. In *Harlowe's Nominees v Woodside Oil* (1968), the Court expounded a clear version of the business judgment rule. In a passage that was subsequently approved by the **Privy Council** in *Howard Smith Ltd v Ampol Petroleum* (1974), the Court said:

> Directors in whom are vested the right and the duty of deciding where the company's interests lie and how they are to be served may be concerned with a wide range of practical considerations, and their judgment, if exercised in good faith and not for irrelevant purposes, is not open to review in the courts.

A reminder that this principle is not to be equated with a *laissez-faire* approach can be found in *Whitehouse v Carlton Hotel* (1987), a decision of the **Mason Court**, where a majority stressed that it is the courts—not company directors—who are the arbiters of what constitutes a proper or relevant purpose.

Turning to the exercise of majority voting power by shareholders, we can see the slow emergence of a distinct contribution to corporate legal doctrine by the High Court. In *Peters*

American Delicacy v Heath (1939), the Court considered the power of majority shareholders to amend the corporate constitution against the wishes of minority shareholders. Ever since the English Court of Appeal decision in *Allen v Gold Reefs of West Africa* (1900), it had been accepted in Australia that the exercise of that power would be valid only if it was exercised 'bona fide for the benefit of the company as a whole'. In *Peters American Delicacy*, Latham and **Dixon** each questioned the utility of this test, although without rejecting it. Latham, consistently with his non-interventionist approach, stressed that 'it is not for the court to impose upon a company the ideas of the court as to what is for the benefit of the company'. However, he then noted that:

> the benefit of the company as a corporation cannot be adopted as a criterion which is capable of solving all the problems in this branch of the law … In cases where the question which arises is simply a question as to the relative rights of different classes of shareholders the problem cannot be solved by regarding merely the benefit of the corporation.

Dixon's judgment carefully analysed the policy issues raised when one group of shareholders seeks to alter the terms that affect all shareholders in a company. As he put it:

> To say that the shareholders forming the majority must consider the advantage of the company as a whole in relation to such a question seems inappropriate, if not meaningless, and at all events starts an impossible inquiry. The 'company as whole' is a corporate entity consisting of all the shareholders.

The doubts expressed in *Peters American Delicacy* were a key factor in the decision in *Gambotto v WCP* (1995), a case that completely—and controversially—reformulated the law governing amendments to corporate constitutions, at least where this involves the expropriation of minority shares. In *Gambotto*, the High Court rejected the *Allen* test and substituted a test that imposes on majority shareholders requirements of both proper purpose and procedural and substantive fairness. In a joint judgment, Mason, **Brennan**, **Deane** and **Dawson** expressed their concern that the law should not be tilted 'too far in favour of commercial expediency', adding that the law as it stood had failed 'to attach sufficient weight to the proprietary nature of a share'.

The decision in *Gambotto* generated widespread critical debate. Concerns were expressed that the Court had tilted the balance too much in favour of minority shareholders. Another concern was that *Gambotto* relied on the concept of fairness, which might lead to the erosion of the idea of judicial non-intervention in corporate affairs. This argument was prompted by the existence of a 'fairness' criterion in the statutory remedy for oppressive or unfair conduct, which was considered in *Wayde v NSW Rugby League* (1985). There, the Court suggested that the reference to fairness might permit a court to intervene in a decision made by directors even where that decision had been made in good faith and for a proper purpose.

To a much lesser extent, the debate about *Gambotto* also took up the challenge implicit in the High Court's decision: to examine the values and ideas that underlie the modern concept of the corporation. This raises philosophical, political and economic questions which have, for the most part, remained buried in Australian corporate law jurisprudence. The very few express references to this issue in the High Court have tended towards a theory that regards corporations as individual entities created by the state and possessing powers that are limited by law. In *Northside Developments v Registrar General* (1990), for example, Brennan stated that: 'a company, being a corporation, is a legal fiction. Its existence, capacities and activities are only such as the law attributes to it.' In *Environment Protection Authority v Caltex Refining* (1993), Mason and **Toohey** approved the view that 'the corporation is a creature of the State. It is presumed to be incorporated for the benefit of the public'. In the same case, **McHugh** categorised the corporation as 'an artificial entity' and 'the creature of the law'.

The Court has also used the entity approach to emphasise that each corporation must be regarded as an isolated entity. Even though the phenomenon of the corporate group—a number of companies linked by shareholdings or common directorships so that one company effectively controls the remainder—is commonplace, the Court has consistently declined to give legal recognition to the concept. In a much-cited judgment in *Walker v Wimborne* (1976), Mason stated that 'to speak of the companies as being members of a group is something of a misnomer'. One year later, a similar argument decided the case of *Industrial Equity v Blackburn* (1977). The persistence of this approach has prompted proposals to reform the corporation law statute to recognise corporate groups.

The High Court's role in the development of corporations law has been a combination of consolidation, clarification and, occasionally, establishing new directions. Perhaps the biggest impact that the Court has had on corporations law has resulted from its **constitutional law** decisions on the scope of the **corporations power** (*Incorporation Case* (1990); *R v Hughes* (2000)) and the invalidity of the **cross-vesting** scheme (*Re Wakim*).

STEPHEN BOTTOMLEY

Further Reading

Anthony Mason, 'Corporate Law: The Challenge of Complexity' (1992) 2 *Aust Jnl of Corp Law* 1

Ian Ramsay (ed), *Gambotto v WCP Ltd: Its Implications for Corporate Regulation* (1996)

Peta Spender, 'Guns and Greenmail: Fear and Loathing after *Gambotto*' (1998) 22 *MULR* 96

Corporations power. Section 51(xx) of the Constitution grants power to the Commonwealth to make laws with respect to 'Foreign corporations, and trading or financial corporations formed within the limits of the Commonwealth'. This collocation of words has always been difficult to interpret. In 1906, the **Deakin** government relied on the power to support sections 5 and 8 of the *Australian Industries Preservation Act* 1906 (Cth), an early Australian equivalent of American antitrust law or contemporary **trade practices law**; but in *Huddart Parker v Moorehead* (1909) those sections were held to be invalid. The majority judgments were heavily influenced by the doctrine of **reserved state powers**; but

Higgins agreed on the basis that a broad reading of the power would be 'extraordinary, big with confusion'. All the judgments struggled to find some intelligible meaning of the power.

The Australian Industries Preservation Act had an unexpected revival in *Redfern v Dunlop Rubber* (1964), when three small private tyre-retailing firms used it to complain of price fixing by major tyre manufacturers. The **Dixon Court** held that those sections of the Act based on the **trade and commerce power** in section 51(i) of the Constitution were valid. The decision added impetus to the campaign **Barwick**, as **Attorney-General**, had been waging for new trade practices legislation; and in 1965 (after Barwick's departure) the *Trade Practices Act 1965* (Cth) was passed. In *Strickland v Rocla Concrete Pipes* (1971), a majority of the **Barwick Court** held, for technical drafting reasons, that the 1965 Act was invalid; but, more importantly, the whole Court held that the corporations power could be used to support such legislation. The immediate result was the *Trade Practices Act* 1972 (Cth), replaced and extended in 1974.

Although the *Concrete Pipes Case* overruled *Huddart Parker*, it made no attempt to explore the full scope of the corporations power; Barwick explained that a fuller exploration must await the case-by-case development 'familiar in the **common law**'. At the very least, however, the power could be used for 'regulating and controlling the trading activities of trading corporations'.

Much of the ensuing litigation arose under the Trade Practices Act. An initial focus was on the criteria that determine whether a particular corporation is a 'trading corporation' so as to fall within Commonwealth power. In *R v Trade Practices Tribunal; Ex parte St George County Council* (1974), a 3:2 majority held that the St George County Council was *not* a trading corporation; despite its extensive trading activities, it had been formed as a 'municipal corporation'. In *Adamson's Case* (1979), a 5:2 majority went the other way: although the clubs and leagues administering Australian Rules football had been formed essentially for sporting purposes, their extensive commercialisation meant that they were now 'trading corporations'. Generally, in these cases, those Justices seeking to limit Commonwealth power (and thus to exclude particular corporations) favoured the 'original purposes' test; those Justices taking a broader view of the power (and thus tending to include particular corporations) favoured the 'current activities' test. But this dichotomy is too simplistic. In *Fencott v Muller* (1983), the corporation in question was a pure 'shelf company', formed to facilitate the sale of a wine bar. It was therefore impossible to characterise it by its 'current activities', since it had none. In that situation **Mason**, **Murphy**, **Brennan** and **Deane** fell back on the 'original purposes' test to classify it as a 'trading or financial corporation'; **Gibbs**, **Wilson** and **Dawson** held that it failed to satisfy either test, since it had never engaged nor 'been intended to engage' in trading or financial activities.

In *State Superannuation Board v Trade Practices Commission* (1982), similar principles were applied to the identification of 'financial corporations'. The judgments made it clear that, to satisfy the activities test, the 'trading' or 'financial' activity of a corporation need not be its 'predominant' activity; it is sufficient if it is 'substantial' and 'forms a significant part' of the overall activities. *How* substantial or significant it must be remains a question of degree.

The more fundamental question is what kind of laws the Commonwealth can enact under this power (see **Characterisation**). Attention has been largely focused on 'trading corporations', and initially two main views emerged. One is that the corporations power is a 'person' power, sufficiently attracted by the fact that the law is to operate upon the specified type of legal person: on this view any law imposing entitlements or duties of any kind upon trading corporations (or foreign or financial corporations) will be valid. This is precisely the far-reaching view that caused Higgins such concern in *Huddart Parker*. On the other view, what the Commonwealth can enact in relation to a corporation must have something to do with the characteristics that bring it within Commonwealth power: if it is a trading corporation, the law must in some significant way relate to its trading activities. On this view, the *Concrete Pipes* formula ('regulating and controlling the trading activities of trading corporations') is the core or typical case.

That formula was extended in *Actors Equity v Fontana Films* (1982) when the whole Court held that the 'secondary boycott' provisions in section 45D of the Trade Practices Act were valid. Those provisions sought to prevent industrial action by trade unions aimed not at the employer with whom an industrial dispute had arisen, but at other corporations dealing with the employer if they thereby suffered 'substantial loss or damage' in their business, or 'substantial lessening of competition'. On the narrow view, these provisions were valid as *protecting* the trading activities of trading corporations. The requisite nexus with 'trading activities' was thus still present.

Again, in the *Tasmanian Dam Case* (1983), the Tasmanian Hydro-Electric Commission was characterised by the majority as a 'trading corporation' because of its extensive commercial supply of electricity, and its reason for wishing to dam the Gordon River was to generate electricity for the purpose of commercial supply. Thus, although the building of the dam was not a trading activity, it was an activity that the Commission was undertaking 'for the purposes of its trading activities'. The legislation had prohibited foreign or trading corporations from undertaking (except with ministerial approval) a wide range of acts such as excavation works, building works, cutting down trees, and using explosives. On the broad 'person' view of the power, each of these prohibitions would be valid, simply because it was directed to a foreign or trading corporation. Mason, Murphy and Deane so held. But the legislation also made it unlawful ('without prejudice' to those prohibitions) for a foreign or trading corporation to undertake any such action 'for the purposes of its trading activities'. Brennan, the crucial fourth member of the majority, held that since this provision was valid, it was unnecessary to decide the validity of the other provisions; and Gibbs, though dissenting because in his view the Commission was not a 'trading corporation', agreed that if it had been, this provision would have been valid.

One difficulty with the narrower view was that although it postulated that the 'trading activities' of a trading corporation are what bring it within Commonwealth power, it tended to be adopted by those who, in identifying the nature of the relevant corporations, preferred to rely on the 'purposes' test rather than the 'activities' test. Another difficulty, emphasised by Mason in the *Tasmanian Dam Case*, is that although section 51(xx) identifies three distinct classes of 'constitutional corporations', it is framed as a single grant of power, so that the principles to be applied in construing it should operate consistently for corporations of all three kinds. However plausible it may be to focus on 'the trading activities of trading corporations', a focus on 'the financial activities of financial corporations' is less plausible, and a focus on the foreignness of foreign corporations less plausible still.

In fact, however, the Court has moved beyond that entire debate. In *Re Dingjan; Ex parte Wagner* (1995), all the judgments seemed to agree that the critical question is not one of charting the outer limits of legislative power, but of what degree of relevance or connection to 'constitutional corporations' will justify characterisation as a law 'with respect to' those corporations. The semantic differences between the judgments turned on whether this connection must be with the corporate characteristics of the corporation, or with its 'business', and on whether the connection must be 'significant', or 'substantial', or merely 'sufficient'. (Mason, in his dissenting judgment, managed to use all three of these epithets.) If 'substantial' seems too strong a criterion, 'significant' too ambiguous, and 'sufficient' too question-begging, the inquiry on which these epithets appear to converge is one in which abstract questions about the outer limits of the power need no longer be resolved.

A different issue arose in the *Incorporation Case* (1990), where the Court held that the power did *not* extend to the incorporation of corporations, so that the Commonwealth could not by its own legislative power enact a uniform national Corporations Law. The result is that the operation of a uniform Corporations Law has depended on a complex package of enactments adopted cooperatively (pursuant to the Alice Springs Agreement of 29 June 1990) by all state and federal governments. More recently, the difficulties and gaps in that package have been highlighted in *Re Wakim* (1999), *Byrnes v The Queen* (1999), *Bond v The Queen* (2000), and *R v Hughes* (2000). In these cases, the Court expressed its distaste for the complexity of the legislation—and even the *Incorporation Case* may have had similar undertones. When **Solicitor-General** Gavan Griffith exhorted the Court in the *Incorporation Case* to adopt a broad approach to constitutional grants of power, McHugh responded: 'But why should you, when it leads to an Act like this?'

The result in that case can perhaps be justified: if section 51(xx) is a 'person' power, so that any law directed to or operating upon a corporation is valid, and if by regulating and defining the process of incorporation the Commonwealth also has power to determine what is a corporation, then the Commonwealth would in effect be able to determine the limits of its own power—a prospect the Court has consistently refused to entertain, most dramatically in the *Communist Party Case* (1951). This, however, was not the reason the majority judgment gave. It depended in part on the use of the word 'formed': if 'formed' is a past participle, then the power applies only to corporations already formed, and hence cannot extend to their formation. Beyond that, the

Court relied primarily on **obiter dicta** in *Huddart Parker*—as Deane put it in a scathing dissent, 'disinterred and selectively dissected for the occasion'.

Recent attempts by successive Commonwealth governments to move industrial relations away from **conciliation and arbitration** to contract-based mechanisms of 'workplace relations'—notably in Laurie Brereton's *Industrial Relations Reform Act* 1993 (Cth) and in Peter Reith's *Workplace Relations and Other Legislation Amendment Act* 1996 (Cth)—have relied heavily on the corporations power (as well as the **external affairs power**). That the limits of the conciliation and arbitration power (section 51(xxxv) of the Constitution) can be bypassed by relying on other heads of power was established in *Pidoto v Victoria* (1943) (in relation to the **defence power**). On the current approach to characterisation, it seems clear that any attempt to regulate the internal workplace relations of a corporate enterprise has sufficient connection with its corporate identity or with its 'business' to be valid under the corporations power. Accordingly, both the existing legislation and projected future extensions of it are generally assumed to be valid. However, the Court's decision in the *Industrial Relations Act Case* (1996), while consonant with this prevailing assumption, in fact did little to confirm it. Although in that case three states had combined to challenge the validity of the 1993 legislation, only WA had challenged those provisions based primarily on the corporations power; and that challenge was abandoned at the hearing.

TONY BLACKSHIELD

Cost of litigation. Although the High Court appears remote from the mass of litigation, it knows that the cost of litigation presents a constant policy dilemma. Before a High Court appeal, a trial and one appeal have already incurred significant **costs**. Other cases originating in the Court are constitutional conflicts involving government or large disputes where the costs are relatively unimportant. The issue nonetheless affects, and is affected by, the jurisprudence of the Court.

The 1990s saw a crescendo of governmental, professional and public attention to the prohibitive cost of litigation, often seen as an obstacle to justice, especially for individuals. The Senate's *Cost of Justice* reports of 1993 and the 1994 *Access to Justice Action Plan* commissioned by the Commonwealth **Attorney-General** identified elaborate curial procedures as one of the causes of expense in litigation, and assumed that cheaper justice would be better justice because more people could litigate if the cost were reduced.

In its earliest days, the Court supervised the enforcement of the loser-pays rule, including its limit of reasonableness. Thus, in *Donohoe v Britz* (1904), **Barton** stated the 'general rule that, as between party and party, the luxuries of litigation must be paid for by those who indulge in them, [while] the necessaries only are to be paid for by the losing side'. But the Court also recognised the financial burden of being sued, and reaffirmed the 'general rule that a wholly successful defendant should receive his costs unless good reason is shown to the contrary': *Milne v A-G (Tas)* (1956).

Expenses peculiar to litigation in a Court hearing cases from anywhere in the Commonwealth were early appreciated. In *Western Australian Bank v Royal Insurance* (1908),

Griffith commended the Court's sitting in 'the several States endeavouring to give suitors in all the States, however distant from the seat of Government, equal facilities for obtaining its judgment' (see **Circuit system**), and allowing the costs of interstate practitioners so as to put 'suitors in all parts of the Commonwealth on an equal footing as far as practicable'. But the federal judicature represented an additional level of appeal, and so in *King v Commercial Bank of Australia* (1920), **Rich** ruled against an impecunious applicant, on security for costs, who was 'indulging in the luxury of an appeal to this Court and is dragging the respondent from one Court to another'.

Inflation obscures any comparison of the cost of litigating in the High Court at different periods. In 1931, in *Huddart Parker v Commonwealth* (1909), with Robert **Menzies** as leading **counsel**, the costs of proceedings heard for two days in the original **jurisdiction** were taxed at £217 4s 9d. In Menzies' heyday as **Prime Minister**, 1957, the costs of a typical appeal were taxed at £110 12s 11d. Roughly equivalent work in the appellate jurisdiction was assessed as costing $1130 in 1975, $8009.46 in 1989, and $37 771.83 in 1997 in typical cases.

The Court has recently ventured towards a more substantive role in relation to the cost of litigation. In joining the majority decision in *Dart Industries v Decor Corporation* (1993), **McHugh** sought to reduce 'the prospect of contested litigation … and the cost and length of the hearing while the parties and their witnesses investigated and debated the hypothetical' in relation to an account of profits for infringement of a **patent**. In *Carnie v Esanda Finance* (1995), McHugh regarded increased liberalism in allowing representative proceedings as proper in 'the Age of Consumerism', where otherwise the 'cost of litigation often makes it economically irrational for an individual to attempt to enforce legal rights arising out of a consumer contract'.

Realistically, the Court noted in *Cachia v Hanes* (1994) that the award of costs was 'never intended to be comprehensive compensation for any loss suffered by a litigant', describing the era as 'these days of burgeoning costs', when the risk of costs was 'a real disincentive to litigation'. The Court has thus ensured that the salutary power to award costs extends to orders against non-parties where it is in the interests of justice (*Knight v FP Special Assets* (1992)). The perennial tension between justice and cost emerged in *Queensland v JL Holdings* (1997), where the majority affirmed 'that the ultimate aim of a court is the attainment of justice and no principle of case management can be allowed to supplant that aim', although **Kirby**, agreeing in the result for different reasons, noted the now-accepted view that 'costs orders are not necessarily an adequate balm to the other party'.

As to crime, in *Latoudis v Casey* (1990), the majority permitted a departure from the former practice of no costs orders, in light of the possibly 'substantial, perhaps crippling' financial burden of defending 'a criminal charge which, in the event, should not have been brought'.

In these ways, the High Court has contributed to the broader debate on the political problems raised by the cost of litigation. Its firm refusal to countenance the direct judicial distribution of legal aid in *Dietrich v The Queen* (1992) illustrates the limitations on its capacity to solve those problems.

BRET WALKER

Costs. The primary source of the High Court's power to order one party to pay the costs of another lies in the *Judiciary Act* 1903 (Cth) and also in the **High Court Rules** made pursuant to that Act. It is a very broad power, in the discretion of the Court, although subject to other Commonwealth legislation. The Court also has power under the Rules to order security for costs in an appeal. In the Court's original **jurisdiction**, there is no provision in the Rules for the ordering of security for costs, but the Court enjoys a broad inherent or implied power to make such an order (*Merribee Pastoral Industries v ANZ Banking Group* (1998)).

Under the **common law** rule, costs generally follow the event: the loser pays the costs of both sides. The ordinary qualification to that rule is that where a party has succeeded only upon a portion of its claims, the circumstances may make it reasonable for that party to bear its own costs, and sometimes those of the other party, in respect of the unsuccessful claims. In any event, a party awarded 'party and party costs' receives far less than full compensation for the costs actually incurred. Even where indemnity costs are ordered, the usual court order will restrict the allowable amounts to those reasonably, as opposed to actually, incurred.

Particularly in the last decade, the overuse of the Court's resources and the ever-increasing costs to litigants have become issues of major concern. There are several ways in which the Court can use its costs powers, and has done so, to deter unmeritorious litigation and prolonged trials, and to ensure a measure of justice on costs issues. These ways include:

• Ordering security for costs against the party initiating the proceedings. Earlier English case law developed the general rule that poverty was to be no bar to a litigant—though an exception was made in the case of appeals (which comprise most of the High Court's caseload) since an insolvent applicant, having had his or her day in court and lost, should not be permitted to drag the opponent from one court to another. In *Lucas v Yorke* (1983), **Brennan** said that the discretion in the High Court Rules was not to be fettered by a rule that security for costs would ordinarily be required from an insubstantial appellant, but acknowledged that poverty and earlier failures continue to be relevant factors. The grant of special **leave to appeal** will generally introduce another relevant factor: namely, that the case is one of public importance, as evidenced by the grant of leave (**Mason** in *Devenish v Jewel Food Stores* (1991)). Indeed, an appellant who has persuaded the Court to grant special leave to appeal is not lightly to be shut out because of his or her financial position: *Webster v Lampard* (1993); *Perre v Apand* (1999). However, it may well be that in a case where costs follow the event, the need to bring action in a foreign court to enforce an order for costs will weigh very heavily in favour of an order for security (*Singer v Berghouse* (1994)).

• Ordering costs, even indemnity costs, against a non-party. The power to order costs against a non-party in certain categories of cases was recognised in *Knight v FP Special Assets* (1992). The particular category there relied on arises where the party 'is an insolvent person or man of straw', while the non-party 'has played an active part in the conduct of the litigation and … has an interest in the subject matter of the litigation'. In such a case, the costs order will be made if the interests of justice require it. In *Helljay Investments v Deputy Commissioner of Taxation* (1999), not only were costs awarded against a director of the applicant company, but they were awarded on an indemnity basis. **Hayne** found that the applicant's claims were 'untenable and obviously so', and that the director had persisted with the application despite the express opposition of the company's liquidator.

- Declining to give public interest groups an automatic immunity from costs. In *Oshlack v Richmond River Council* (1998), a costs power was contained in environment protection legislation. The state court held that as the proceedings were brought in the public interest, the challenge was an arguable one, and the case had resolved significant issues of **statutory interpretation**, the applicant, though unsuccessful, should not be ordered to pay the costs of the respondent local council. The High Court saw no error in that decision, holding that the true question was not whether the proceeding was 'public interest litigation' but whether the trial judge had erred by taking into account objects extraneous to the legislation. The Court emphasised that the costs provision in question related to a new species of litigation, and that the exercise of the discretion it conferred should allow for the varied interests at stake in such litigation. This the trial judge had done, and his decision on costs should stand. In *South-West Forest Defence Foundation v Department of Conservation* (1998), **Kirby** confirmed that nothing in *Oshlack* required that every time an individual or body brought proceedings asserting a defence of the public interest and protection of the environment there should be a new costs regime exempting that individual or body from the conventional rule.

- Ordering costs against solicitors in certain circumstances— a power to be exercised 'sparingly' (**Gummow** in *McKewins Hairdressing v FCT* (2000)). In *McKewins*, not only were the grounds for the application for **removal** into the High Court untenable, but the application had been made by a solicitor who was not the person named as applicant and who was instructed only by a stranger to the litigation. In that respect, the solicitor was in breach of a basic professional requirement. The proceedings were dismissed and costs ordered against the solicitor on an indemnity basis.

- Refusing to be drawn beyond the basic purpose for which costs are ordinarily awarded—namely, to provide some compensation for legal costs actually incurred. Thus, even a wide statutory provision permitting an order 'as to' costs, as opposed to one permitting an order 'for' costs, is not so wide as to permit the making of an order that a legal aid body provide costs for legal representation, since in reality that would be an order for legal aid (**Gaudron** in *Re JJT; Ex parte Victoria Legal Aid* (1998)). The confining of costs orders to costs actually incurred also means that a litigant who acts for himself or herself, although successful, cannot be recompensed for the work done in the preparation and conduct of the case; nor could the loss of earnings resulting from preparation time be treated as a disbursement (*Cachia v Hanes* (1994)). The Court even doubted the English cases allowing an exception in the case of a solicitor acting for himself.

- Avoiding penalising parties by costs orders in certain cases where the moving party no longer proceeds with the litigation. Thus, in *Re Minister for Immigration; Ex parte Lai Qin* (1997), **McHugh** declined to make costs orders in favour of a would-be appellant in a migration case where the Minister had granted the desired visa during the appeal. He explained that proceedings that do not go to trial present the Court with a difficulty: the general rule is that a successful party is entitled to its costs, yet in such a case, with no hearing on the merits, 'the court is deprived of the determining factor'. He said that if it appears that both parties have acted reasonably in commencing and defending the proceedings, and their conduct continues to be reasonable until the litigation is settled or its further prosecution becomes futile, the proper order will generally be no order as to costs.

The Court has not yet dealt with the issue of security for costs in 'class actions' where a representative party applies on behalf of members of the group. The courts are reluctant to use an order requiring security for costs to prevent an insubstantial applicant from getting to trial; but if others, with means, stand behind the applicant, the situation may be different. The **Federal Court** has held that, particularly in the light of statutory restrictions on its powers to award costs against group members, this factor is not so significant in representative proceedings: *Woodhouse v McPhee* (1997); *Tobacco Control Coalition v Philip Morris* (2000). In *Tobacco Control*, the representative party was a company with no assets, incorporated only a few days before the commencement of the proceeding, and the proceedings had allegedly been structured to immunise certain organisations of substance from liability to costs. It was held that although the contrived immunity should be given weight, security for costs ought not to be ordered if the proceedings were in the public interest and had a high prospect of success. However, since the prospects of success were far from evident, security for costs was ordered.

Given the growing number of class actions in Australian litigation, and the likely financial impact on class action applicants of orders requiring security for costs, the High Court's approach to these issues will be of considerable importance. Its liberal approach to the scope of 'class actions', evident in *Carnie v Esanda Finance* (1995), would suggest that its response may be at least as fair and non-restrictive as that of the Federal Court.

CHRISTINE HENCHMAN

Counsel, notable. Although the High Court is sometimes confronted with **litigants in person**, most cases are argued by **counsel**, whose advocacy of their clients' cases contributes, to some extent, to the formulation and shaping of the legal doctrines ultimately adopted by the Court. Over the years, in Arthur Dean's phrase, 'a multitude of counsellors' have come and gone, with varying degrees of success. These have included most Justices of the Court at earlier stages of their careers (see table), though **Evatt** also appeared in some celebrated cases after leaving the Court (in particular, the *Bank Nationalisation Case* (1948 and 1949) and the *Communist Party Case* (1951)). As the Justices have been drawn mainly from the ranks of barristers (see **Appointment of Justices**), and then from among the most prominent or successful, it is not surprising that most—and not only those with the prodigious reputations of **Dixon**, **Barwick**, and **Aickin**—would take their place in any account of the notable counsel who have appeared before the Court. Their stories are told in their respective biographical entries.

Even among the counsel who have not been appointed to the Court, it would be invidious to attempt to identify, by some objective criterion or criteria, those who might be described as notable. Opinions vary widely among the peer group of Justices, former Justices, counsel, and former counsel, as to both the criteria and their application. What follows is a selective survey, with a particular emphasis on the Court's early years, of some of the many counsel—other than those who later themselves became Justices—who, for diverse reasons, may be considered worthy of notice.

The first reported case in the High Court—*Hannah v Dalgarno* (1903)—pitted Wise against Sly. Bernhard Ringrose Wise (1858–1916) had returned to Sydney in 1883 after a brilliant academic career in England. Associated in NSW politics with Henry Parkes and the free trade movement, he was also a strong supporter of the emerging Labor movement. A powerful campaigner for federation and a **framer of the Constitution**—he was one of the celebrated *Lucinda* party in 1891—he failed to win election to the first federal Parliament, but remained active in NSW politics. His strong support for the High Court in its first year of sittings helped to **establish** its reputation. Although unsuccessful in *Hannah v Dalgarno*, he persuaded the Court to adopt a narrow definition of **excise duties** in *Peterswald v Bartley* (1904), and to uphold the powers of a Royal Commission in *Clough v Leahy* (1904). After an extended absence in England (1904–08), he resumed his High Court practice in 1909—representing the Commonwealth in the *Coal Vend Case* (1911), and the Speaker of the NSW Legislative Assembly in *Willis and Christie v Perry* (1912). He died in London in 1916.

Richard Sly (1849–1929) was one of three lawyer brothers—including George, a founder of the firm of Sly and Russell—who, unusually for the time, all had LLD degrees. As a barrister, Sly was notoriously nervous, constantly fiddling with a piece of pink tape while addressing the Court. After *Hannah v Dalgarno*, he made relatively few High Court appearances, and became a judge of the Supreme Court of NSW in 1908. In *Boxall v Sly* (1911), his award in a land compensation case was unsuccessfully challenged by Wise.

Wilfred Blacket (1859–1937), a celebrated barrister and law reformer, was equally known for his literary talents—as a frequent contributor to the *Bulletin* and its first subeditor—and for his zest as a legal raconteur, preserved in his book *May It Please Your Honour* (1927). His early High Court appearances were mainly in customs and **immigration** matters and in minor **criminal** cases, but with briefs in **constitutional** cases such as *R v Sutton* (1908) and *Osborne v Commonwealth* (1911), his reputation grew. He took silk in 1912, and continued to appear in the High Court until 1924. His greatest triumph was his victory in the *Wheat Case* (1915).

Walter Coldham (1860–1908), a champion tennis player and all-round athlete, had been admitted to the Melbourne Bar in 1884. With expertise in mathematics, engineering, and science, he had a flourishing **patents** practice (see, for example, *Potter v BHP* (1906); *Cullen v Welsbach Light Co* (1907)), and frequently indulged the Court with lengthy scientific dissertations in other cases—for example, in a detailed explanation of the chemical and geological properties of guano in *Cuming Smith v Melbourne Harbour Trust* (1905). On one such occasion, **Griffith** remarked that, having heard Coldham at great length, he was 'none the wiser'—to which Coldham replied: 'Not wiser, your Honour, but perhaps better informed.'

Initially, not all leading counsel thought it particularly important or prestigious to appear before the nascent High Court. Julian Salomons (1935–1909), for example, the acknowledged leader of the Sydney Bar at the time, had opposed the Court's creation; and after five appearances in the Court's first few months of sittings, including *Clissold v Perry* (1904) and *McLaughlin v Fosbery* (1904), returned only in 1907—to argue (successfully) in *R v Governor of SA* (1907) that the Court had no power to issue a **writ** of mandamus to a state Governor, and (singularly unsuccessfully) in *Baxter v Commissioners of Taxation* (1907) that the High Court as 'an inferior Court' was bound by the **Privy Council** decision in *Webb v Outtrim* (1906), and that in any event Griffith, **Barton**, and **O'Connor** should **disqualify** themselves because, as residents of NSW, they were potentially liable to pay the tax whose validity was under challenge. His early appearance in *Saunders v Borthistle* (1904) did, however, launch a remarkable High Court career for his junior, Richard Windeyer (1868–1959), uncle of the future High Court Justice Victor **Windeyer**.

Among the most successful counsel of the early years were two who became Chief Justices of their **state Supreme Courts**: William Cullen (1855–1935), later Chief Justice of NSW (1910–25), and William 'Iceberg' Irvine (1858–1943), later Chief Justice of Victoria (1918–35). Like many barristers of his generation, Cullen—another LLD—was active in the federal movement, in state politics, and in university life: he was Chancellor of the University of Sydney from 1914 to 1934. An early proponent of the abolition of Privy Council appeals, he supported the Court strongly from the time of his early appearances in the *Municipal Rates Case* (1904) and *Clissold v Perry*. Often appearing for the Commonwealth—for instance, in *Commonwealth v NSW* (1906) and *Baxter v Commissioners of Taxation (NSW)*—he also appeared for NSW, notably (though unsuccessfully) in the *Surplus Revenue Case* (1908). But his practice was diverse: he appeared for the Sydney solicitor John McLaughlin (see **Litigants, notable, 1903–1945**) in *McLaughlin v Daily Telegraph* (1906) and *McLaughlin v Freehill* (1908), and for Lever Bros in a successful defence of their **trade mark** 'Sunlight soap' (*Lever Bros v Abrams* (1909)). According to John Peden, Griffith regarded him 'as being in the first rank' of the barristers then practising before the Court.

Irvine, who in 1886 had written a book with **Gavan Duffy** on *Law Relating to the Property of Women*, had been active in Victorian politics since 1894—as Attorney-General (1899–1900), Leader of the Opposition (1901–02), and Premier (1902–04). It was during his two years as Premier that he acquired the soubriquet 'Iceberg', attributed to his appearance of prim austerity and his 'monosyllabic, incisive method of speech'. On losing office in February 1904, he

William Cullen, regarded by Griffith as one of the best barristers to appear before the High Court

resumed his practice at the Bar, and had a flourishing High Court practice from that time on—often as a leader to **Starke** (whose own High Court practice was extremely large). He was active in the Victorian resistance to the **Griffith Court's** doctrine of **intergovernmental immunities**, urging the Court in *Flint v Webb* (1907) to settle the matter by granting a certificate for appeal to the Privy Council.

In 1906, he began a controversial career in federal politics. Alfred **Deakin**, forming a ministry in 1909, was advised: 'This man must be excluded at all costs.' In **World War I**, he was a strong supporter of conscription. Throughout this time, he maintained an active practice in the High Court. As Commonwealth **Attorney-General** in 1913–14, he narrowly survived a censure motion because, while Attorney-General, he had represented the Italian Marconi company in litigation against the Commonwealth (see *Marconi's Wireless Telegraph Co v Commonwealth (No 2)* (1913)). In the same period, he also appeared for the Colonial Sugar Refining company in *Merchant Service Guild v Commonwealth Steamship Owners Association* (1913), and for Schweppes in *Schweppes v Rowlands* (1913), successfully opposing the grant of a trade mark for 'Sarilla' ginger beer. In the major case of the period on the **defence power**, *Farey v Burvett* (1916), he led Starke in an unsuccessful challenge to government regulations fixing the price of bread. His involvement in wartime controversies ended only when he became Chief Justice of Victoria in March 1918.

No such judicial advancement awaited Arthur Feez (1860–1935), who in 1901, after 20 years at the Bar, was firmly established as Queensland's leading barrister. In 1882, he had been the best man at Nellie Melba's wedding. His appeals to the High Court often had a distinctive Queensland flavour or background: among his more important cases, he appeared on behalf of the Brisbane Tramways Company in the *Union Badge Case* (1913) and the *Tramways Cases* (1914); on behalf of Laura Duncan in *Duncan v Queensland* (1916) and *Duncan v Theodore* (1917); on behalf of members of the Queensland Legislative Council, seeking unsuccessfully to block constitutional moves for its abolition, in *Taylor v A-G (Qld)* (1917); and on behalf of Queensland pastoral employers in *Waddell v Australian Workers Union* (1922). In many of these cases, he appeared to be swimming against a socialist tide. Indeed, his determined resistance to **socialism** found him frequently at odds with the Labor-dominated political establishment in Queensland—most notably when he spearheaded the opposition to the appointment of Thomas McCawley to the Supreme Court of Queensland (see *McCawley v The King* (1918))—and led ultimately to his being passed over for appointment to the Supreme Court himself. When Frank Brennan—the father of the future High Court Chief Justice—was appointed to the Supreme Court in 1925, Feez moved in protest to Sydney, where he had some late High Court successes—persuading the Court in *Mathews v Foggitt Jones* (1926) that a sausage was not a 'carcase' or 'portion of a carcase', and in *Roman Catholic Archbishop of Sydney v Metropolitan Water, Sewerage & Drainage Board* (1928) that St Patrick's College at Manly was entitled to an exemption from water rates.

No less vehement in their opposition to socialism were EF Mitchell (Edward) (1855–1941), from Melbourne, and EM Mitchell (Ernest) (1875–1943), from Sydney. Both were among the leaders of their respective state Bars, and made regular appearances in the High Court during its first four decades: sometimes, as in *McArthur v Queensland* (1920), the two Mitchells appeared together.

Edward Mitchell, admitted to the Bar in 1881 and appointed KC in 1904, dominated the Court's constitutional work in its early years, and was also a notable **equity** lawyer. As Chancellor of the Anglican diocese of Melbourne, he encouraged Archbishop Henry Clarke to sue successfully for **defamation** in *Norton v Clarke* (1911). In the High Court, especially in constitutional cases, he and 'Iceberg' Irvine frequently appeared together—for example, in *Huddart Parker v Moorehead* (1909), *SA v Victoria* (1911), and *A-G (Qld) v A-G (Cth)* (1915)—or for different parties in the same interest, as in *R v Barger* (1908) and in the *Woodworkers Case* (1909). On other occasions, they were on opposite sides: for example, in *Webb v Syme* (1910)—as to income tax on the trust estate of the late David Syme—and in *Packer v Peacock* (1912), an early case on **contempt** of court.

Ernest Mitchell was admitted to the NSW Bar in 1906 and became a KC in 1925. As counsel, he played a leading role in the great cases of the 1930s on section 92 of the Constitution (see **Interstate trade and commerce**), and also appeared on behalf of the aviator Henry Goya Henry in both of his High Court appeals.

Despite their 20-year age difference and their different state backgrounds, the two Mitchells were united in their opposition to NSW Premier Jack Lang. Edward Mitchell led the public campaign against Lang, both through articles in the Melbourne *Argus* and through his book *What Every Australian Ought to Know* (1931). Ernest Mitchell appeared (free of charge) for the plaintiffs in *A-G (NSW) v Trethowan* (1931), successfully blocking attempts to abolish the NSW Legislative Council. He also appeared on behalf of the Commonwealth in the *State Garnishee Cases* (1932). From 1933 to 1943, he was himself a NSW Legislative Councillor.

During the Court's earliest years, Leo Cussen (1859–1933) was another leading barrister with a wide-ranging practice, although, like Starke, he never took silk. His appearances in the High Court were mostly as a junior, for example to **Isaacs** in *Bond v Commonwealth* (1903) and *Deakin v Webb* (1904). Appointed to the Supreme Court of Victoria in 1906, he sat as a judge of that Court until his death in 1933. A second Leo Cussen, admitted to the Bar in 1908, was also a notable advocate, though his health failed early. Initially he, too, appeared mostly as a junior—to Gavan Duffy in *Peacock v The King* (1911), to Irvine in *R v Bernasconi* (1915), and frequently to Starke. But by 1917, he was appearing on his own. In *Lennon v Scarlett & Co* (1921), he appeared as leading counsel opposed to **Latham** and Robert **Menzies**; and in *Horne v Barber* (1920), he led Dixon—though in later cases, after Dixon became a KC, those roles were reversed.

Menzies described the elder Cussen as 'one of the great judges of the English-speaking world'; and Dixon expressed regret that, like Frederick Jordan, Cussen was never appointed to the High Court (see **Appointments that might have been**). A similar regret was expressed by the **legal profession** in SA over the non-appointment of Francis Villeneuve Smith (1883–1956), whose West Indian grandmother was descended from Nelson's great adversary at the battle of Trafalgar, the French admiral Pierre-Charles Villeneuve. Admitted to the SA Bar in 1906, and appointed KC in 1919, Villeneuve Smith was one of the leading advocates of the next generation of High Court counsel. That generation also included Wilbur Ham (1883–1948) and Robert Menzies (1894–1978).

Ham, related on his mother's side to the Latham family, appeared frequently in the 1930s and 1940s, particularly in cases involving **taxation law** and constitutional law (see, for example, the *First Uniform Tax Case* (1942)), but also in other landmark cases such as *Clements v Ellis* (1934) and *Australian Knitting Mills v Grant* (1933). His children bore the surname 'Wilbur-Ham'. Menzies—who remembered Ham fondly as 'a master of polished profanity'—secured his own place in Australian legal folklore with his appearance at the young age of 25 in the landmark *Engineers Case* (1920)—alone against a range of opposing counsel including Ham, Edward Mitchell, Latham, and Evatt—and perhaps even more with his colourful recounting, if not embellishment, of that appearance in his University of Virginia lectures, published in 1967 as *Central Power in the Australian Commonwealth*. Menzies opened by relying upon a distinction that had emerged from earlier decisions. On being told by Starke that his **argument** was 'nonsense', he responded somewhat brashly that it was a nonsense forced upon him by the decisions of the Court, and that he would be happy to advance a more sensible argument if the Court were prepared to question any of those earlier decisions. The Court retired briefly and then announced that

it would hear argument on the reopening of the earlier cases. It was therefore little surprise when those cases were **overruled**—with the changes in the composition of the Bench, it was a case that was waiting to be won (see **Intergovernmental immunities**)—but it cemented Menzies' place in Australian legal history.

Menzies was not the only young political aspirant in the early twentieth century who decided that the way to political success lay through practice at the Bar. The young activists in Sydney at the turn of the century who honed their political skills at the Bar included another future **Prime Minister**, WM Hughes (1862–1952), and two future Premiers of NSW, William Holman (1871–1934) and Thomas Bavin (1874–1941). Hughes appeared as a barrister before the High Court only rarely, and only in industrial cases (see, for example, *Trolly, Draymen and Carters Union v Master Carriers Association* (1905)). Holman was NSW Attorney-General from 1910 to 1913, and Premier from 1913 to 1920. A brilliant orator, he was also among the leading theoreticians of the Labor movement in Australia, which he had joined in 1890 along with Hughes and George Beeby (1869–1942), later Chief Judge of the Commonwealth Court of **Conciliation and Arbitration**. In later years, Holman fell out with Hughes, primarily because of his commitment to state politics rather than federal politics. Admitted to the Bar in 1903, he soon developed a general practice that included some of the most important industrial cases of the time: *Clancy v Butchers' Shop Employés* (1904); the *Railway Servants Case* (1906), as junior to **Higgins**; the *Union Label Case* (1908); and *Ex parte Whybrow* (1910). After his defeat as Premier in 1920, he became a KC and again appeared in the High Court from 1922 onwards, notably in the *Limerick Steamship Case* (1924).

Bavin's political allegiances, like those of Hughes, were less enduring. Admitted to the Bar in 1897, he shared chambers with Wise and was befriended by Barton. After a brief career as a law academic (at the universities of Sydney and Tasmania), he joined Barton in Melbourne in 1901 as Barton's private secretary, and in 1903 moved with Barton to the High Court as his **associate**, while simultaneously continuing as a private secretary to the new Prime Minister, Deakin. Returning to the Sydney Bar in 1906, he quickly developed a flourishing practice. In *Smith v Watson* (1906), he and Holman appeared together; six years later, in *R v Smithers; Ex parte Benson* (1912), they were on opposite sides. By that time, Bavin had appeared—often as a junior to Cullen and often on behalf of the Commonwealth—in important cases including *Baxter v Commissioners of Taxation (NSW)*, the *Steel Rails Case* (1908), and the *Union Label Case*. In *Baxter v Ah Way* (1909), he was junior to Wise and Blacket; in 1911 in the *Coal Vend Case*, he was junior to Wise.

After entering NSW politics in 1917 as a member of Holman's Nationalist Party (then still aligned with Hughes), he increasingly quarrelled with Holman. In 1920, after unsuccessfully moving a motion of no confidence in Holman's leadership, he resigned from the party and joined the Progressive Party (which Beeby had founded in 1915). From 1922 to 1925, he was Attorney-General in the Nationalist government of Premier George Fuller. Even after entering politics, Bavin had maintained his private practice at the Bar, and had appeared in *R v Brisbane Licensing Court; Ex*

Table of Reported High Court Appearances by Counsel Later Appointed as Justices

(**bold** = CLR volume; followed by page number)

Starke (211)

1 460, 632, 693 **2** 684 **3** 117, 132, 460, 467, 516, 557, 799, 1028 **4** 835, 864, 913, 941, 990, 1453, 1489, 1569, 1668, 1719 **5** 188, 480, 647, 856 **6** 41, 194, 647 **7** 34, 76, 133, 146, 179, 752 **8** 33, 54, 146, 170, 187, 225, 262, 330, 419, 779 **9** 247, 301, 773 **10** 1, 176, 207, 266, 482, 607, 742 **11** 1, 100, 258, 311, 462 **12** 13, 165, 398, 667 **13** 32, 35, 129, 302, 577, 676 **14** 141, 183, 387 **15** 32, 65, 235, 333, 389, 407, 426, 685, 721, 731 **16** 27, 92, 178, 245, 344, 384, 591, 715 **17** 1, 55, 60, 90, 261, 499, 514, 524, 601, 615, 680 **18** 17, 54, 88, 152, 209, 493, 540, 553, 560, 578, 646 **19** 43, 288, 349, 356, 457, 521, 544, 562, 620, 629, 681 **20** 21, 54, 118, 148, 201, 261, 277, 282, 490, 526, 552, 573 **21** 124, 142, 157, 172, 205, 225, 268, 376, 379, 407, 422, 433, 503, 509 **22** 40, 103, 142, 187, 203, 206, 261, 268, 288, 367, 402, 437, 545, 556 **23** 5, 9, 78, 220, 226, 358, 422, 438, 504, 576, 589 **24** 34, 303, 318, 324, 331, 334, 339, 360, 369, 462 **25** 234, 381, 394, 434, 506 **26** 5, 9, 87, 110, 175, 231, 336, 348, 404, 410, 508 **27** 72, 105, 119, 194, 207, 231, 236, 245, 289, 294

Dixon (175)

13 461 **15** 373 **17** 55, 60, 549 **18** 540, 560 **19** 237, 562 **20** 15, 201, 277, 418, 490, 570 **21** 149, 268, 469 **22** 103, 268 **23** 185, 226, 589 **24** 303, 309 **25** 9, 144, 434 **26** 180, 302, 404, 410, 460, 508 **27** 31, 60, 119, 231, 286, 289, 331, 400, 436, 445, 494, 532, 560 **28** 1, 51, 209, 278, 305, 419, 456, 508, 530, 588, 602 **29** 1, 39, 55, 98, 106, 134, 154, 186, 243, 257, 305, 321, 325, 329, 347, 396, 406, 527, 537, 579 **30** 16, 34, 132, 144, 198, 353, 362, 450 **31** 1, 76, 290, 394, 421 **32** 95, 509, 596, 602, 606 **33** 267, 369, 426, 491, 517 **34** 38, 198, 234, 283, 420, 482 **35** 143, 186, 275, 355, 422, 449, 462 **36** 31, 41, 60, 88, 119, 230, 322, 378, 410, 442, 464, 526, 585 **37** 1, 305, 351, 363, 393, 432, 466, 569 **38** 48, 63, 153, 325, 586 **39** 139, 158, 190, 363, 411, 455, 533, 570, 595 **40** 1, 98, 135, 142, 148, 156, 217, 246, 481, 510, 566 **41** 1, 75, 83, 99, 102, 107, 167, 254, 282, 331, 402 **42** 1, 39, 66 46 413

Barwick (173)

51 300 **55** 253 **56** 113 **57** 765 **59** 556 **63** 581 **64** 461, 588 **66** 161, 603 **67** 266, 461, 488, 496, 567, 599, 619 **68** 151, 428, 504 **69** 18, 51 **70** 1, 100, 405, 459, 561, 598, 635 **71** 29, 161, 545 **72** 1, 37, 141, 269, 409, 435, 575 **73** 19, 39, 157, 213, 459, 549 **74** 31, 204, 375 **75** 1, 203, 218, 293, 409, 430, 436, 480, 495 **76** 1, 414, 431, 453, 463, 501, 584 **77** 123, 574, 601 **78** 336 **79** 428, 442, 477 **80** 11, 382, 533 **81** 64, 161, 263, 537, 585 **82** 208, 267, 423, 645 **83** 1, 314, 402, 413, 539, 617 **84** 13, 58, 140, 177, 328, 442, 460 **85** 20, 55, 336, 386, 423, 467, 488, 545 **86** 46, 183, 540 **87** 353, 501 **88** 67, 177, 353, 450, 476, 509, 523, 529 **89** 138, 327, 540, 608, 636 **90** 295, 583 **91** 1, 193, 288, 628 **92** 17, 200, 317, 424, 467, 483, 565, 605 **93** 36, 55, 83, 351 **96** 35, 154, 261, 397, 429 **97** 23, 36, 89, 202, 633, 667 **98** 93, 151, 345, 398, 460, 495 **99** 155, 227, 521, 575 **100** 66, 95, 117, 170, 352, 478, 537, 597 **101** 119 **102** 147 **103** 256 **106** 186

Knox (138)

1 158, 243, 283 **2** 387 **3** 27, 344, 393, 912 **4** 97, 324, 944, 1364, 1395 **5** 33, 56, 68, 737, 789, 818, 879 **6** 214, 243 **7** 51, 100, 179, 629 **10** 180, 341, 365, 391, 417, 434, 539, 722 **11** 148, 347, 432, 492, 550, 601, 620, 667, 723, 738 **12** 1, 39, 321, 579, 653 **13** 152, 197, 326, 438, 490, 592, 704 **14** 1, 54, 114, 387 **15** 65, 576, 586, 636, 661 **16** 50, 285, 404, 705, 715 **17** 720 **18** 142, 224, 331, 360, 381, 433, 640 **19** 19, 33, 180, 197, 267, 298, 381, 499, 510, 515, 641, 698, 714 **20** 49, 54, 114, 242, 258, 580, 615 **21** 317, 336, 357, 559, 582, 636 **22** 84, 352, 381, 420, 490 **23** 1, 22, 58, 102, 292, 322, 337, 351, 426, 443 **24** 21, 120, 166, 189, 197, 209, 399, 409, 413 **25** 172, 183, 241, 325, 416, 552 **26** 135, 205, 316 **27** 294

Fullagar (132)

31 148 **33** 174 **34** 225, 420 **35** 69 **36** 41, 165, 230 **38** 308, 399, 477 **40** 510 **41** 484, 569 **42** 145, 384, 481, 582 **43** 77, 105, 185 **44** 254, 297 **45** 282, 406, 573 **46** 1, 470 **47** 274 **48** 266, 316, 391, 565 **49** 37, 84, 171, 220, 349, 382, 480 **50** 30, 131, 568 **51** 217, 387, 619 **52** 157, 335, 383, 533, 701 **53** 206, 322, 409, 463 **54** 361, 445, 463, 614 **55** 110, 144, 276, 367, 459, 483 **56** 20 57 147, 233, 327, 448, 461, 666 **58** 1, 146, 618 **59** 230, 709, 729 **60** 263, 633, 741 **61** 584 **62** 687 **63** 503, 619 **64** 65, 421 **65** 118, 134, 320, 373 **66** 43, 432, 488, 557 **67** 1, 116, 314, 335, 347, 413, 434 **68** 29, 51, 67, 87, 199, 261, 344, 354, 391, 436, 455, 485, 504, 525, 613, 628 **69** 185, 476, 501, 539, 613 **70** 23, 141, 293, 362, 441 **71** 388, 596 **72** 189, 480

Aickin (131)

82 408 **84** 532, 553 **86** 536, 570 **87** 335 **88** 23, 141, 285, 413 **89** 177, 196, 540 **91** 42, 209, 540 **92** 529 **93** 127, 247, 264 **94** 1, 182, 367, 419, 470, 614 **95** 300, 353 **96** 35, 177, 294, 390, 577 **98** 187, 424, 444, 637 **99** 28, 132, 185, 212, 431, 575 **100** 5 **102** 29, 147, 252, 561, 661 **103** 650 **104** 508 **105** 126, 473 **106** 318 **107** 208 **108** 130 **109** 243, 276, 407, 475, 501, 649 **110** 9, 194, 264, 387, 419, 592, 644 **111** 41, 86, 353 **112** 1, 206 **113** 54, 207, 475, 520 **114** 185, 283, 537 **115** 177, 353, 418 **116** 124, 613, 628 **117** 253, 613, 631 **118** 219, 325, 331, 504, 618, 644 **119** 16, 318, 564 **120** 42, 74, 92, 240, 285, 437, 603 **121** 1, 483 **122** 13, 152, 353 **123** 361, 418, 648 **127** 529 **128** 171, 199 **129** 521, 650 **130** 177, 276, 461 **131** 1 **132** 463 **133** 191, 483 **135** 337 **137** 86 **138** 492 **140** 92, 247

Latham (90)

14 220, 341 **15** 355, 389, 625, 725 **16** 591, 664 **17** 8 **18** 440, 553 **19** 681 **20** 137, 490 **21** 205, 433 **22** 136, 206, 556 **24** 348 **27** 286, 327, 334, 350, 436, 526, 560 **28** 1, 129, 209, 278, 294, 395, 436, 508, 530, 588, 595 **29** 1, 55, 106, 347, 396, 491, 499, 515 **30** 34, 132, 353, 362, 450, 498, 585 **31** 1, 46, 122, 136, 148, 174, 490, 503, 511 **32** 81, 159, 252, 362, 596, 606 **33** 1, 229, 297, 329, 452, 517 **34** 225, 234, 294, 404, 420, 558 **35** 132, 143, 186, 275, 449 **36** 31, 60, 230, 442, 464

Deane (73)

98 383 **101** 11, 184, 568 **104** 394 **106** 186 **110** 9 **111** 599 **112** 113, 125, 483 **113** 177, 265 **114** 194 **115** 389 **117** 52, 390 **118** 271 **120** 191, 400, 664 **121** 177, 353, 432, 483 **122** 69, 139, 237 **123** 71, 361, 476 **124** 220, 317, 367, 468, 605 **125** 52, 84, 353 **126** 177, 449, 471 **127** 62, 106, 174 **128** 1, 28, 63, 645 **129** 177, 446, 477 **130** 177, 245, 533 **131** 409, 432 **132** 270 **134** 81, 201, 338, 559 **135** 337, 507 **136** 475, 529 **137** 545 **138** 106, 283, 346, 492 **139** 117, 527

Taylor (73)

39 22 **52** 1, 221, 234, 260 **54** 97, 262 **55** 499, 608 **56** 381 **59** 254 **60** 97 **61** 534, 557, 735 **63** 489 **65** 373 **66** 1, 77, 198, 344, 624 **67** 116 **68** 165, 428, 553 **69** 227, 509 **70** 175, 598 **71** 184, 531 **72** 269, 435, 634 **73** 39, 237 **74** 375 **75** 59, 140, 218, 320, 436, 480, 495, 628 **76** 1, 431, 463, 584 **77** 78, 363, 387, 432 **78** 410, 464 **79** 43, 201 **83** 1, 322, 344, 402 **84** 126, 285, 328, 421 **85** 110, 189, 336, 488, 545 **86** 46 **87** 375

Gleeson (70)

110 177 **113** 177 **115** 10, 570 **116** 81, 233 **117** 288 **121** 1 **122** 353 **123** 71, 327, 361 **124** 27, 220, 468 **125** 52 **129** 151, 617 **130** 245, 533 **131** 378, 409, 432, 477 **132** 535 **133** 459 **134** 81 **135** 337, 632 **136** 214 **137** 567 **138** 467 **140** 120 **142** 375 **143** 440 **147** 169 **148** 42 **150** 258 **151** 599 **152** 281, 460 **153** 491, 644 **154** 1 **156** 296, 522 **158** 1, 447, 622 **159** 1 **160** 55, 226, 330 **161** 1, 98, 543 **163** 140, 303, 421, 656 **164** 261, 513 **165** 55, 71, 197, 346 **166** 417 **167** 177 **168** 147 **180** 459

Menzies (68)

49 25 **55** 459 **57** 372 **60** 263 **61** 665 **70** 587 **71** 623 **73** 66, 119, 435, 583 **74** 31 **76** 1 **77** 299 **79** 201 **80** 1, 229, 269, 432 **81** 64 **82** 349, 372, 463 **84** 177, 460 **86** 463, 570 **87** 501 **88** 1, 23, 285, 353 **89** 66 **90** 348, 552 **91** 209, 540 **92** 17, 245, 529 **93** 127, 247, 472, 528, 645 **94** 182, 193, 254, 353, 367 **95** 344 **96** 390, 529, 577 **98** 35, 367, 424, 637 **99** 28, 132, 185, 212, 227, 575 **100** 155, 277, 312, 324

Kitto (65)

40 394 **43** 247 **44** 211, 394 **47** 369, 402 **49** 160 **52** 110 **53** 235, 571, 587 **54** 23, 657 **55** 127 **56** 774 **57** 89 **58** 316, 341 **61** 337, 534 **63** 52, 232, 382 **64** 15, 241, 361, 492 **65** 29, 338, 351, 572 **66** 198 **67** 455, 529 **69** 1, 121, 257, 389, 407 **71** 125, 283, 309, 407 **72** 37, 134, 262, 269, 608 **73** 19, 187, 490, 549 **74** 204, 508 **75** 361 **76** 1 **77** 143, 184, 574 **78** 224 **80** 177, 304, 382 **81** 263, 396

Dawson (60)

107 381 **111** 353 **113** 54 **118** 562 **119** 564 **120** 353 **122** 353 **123** 547 **131** 50, 432 **132** 258 **133** 390 **134** 81, 201, 338, 495 **135** 1, 92, 337, 507 **136** 62, 475 **137** 20, 40, 545, 633 **138** 194, 346, 492 **139** 338 **140** 364, 615 **142** 237, 308 **143** 162, 376 **144** 120, 633 **145** 1, 107, 172, 246, 266, 330, 438 **146** 64, 447, 559 **148** 337, 383, 457, 668 **149** 227 **150** 49, 615 **151** 342 **152** 25, 211 **153** 168, 650

Mason (53)

83 424 **87** 375 **88** 523, 529 **90** 353 **92** 157 **94** 489 **95** 132 **98** 93 **99** 155, 177 **100** 342, 566 **101** 11 **102** 629, 650 **104** 164, 381 **105** 303, 361 **106** 186, 623 **108** 651 **109** 59, 163, 169, 434 **110** 177, 194 **111** 169, 344, 529 **112** 152, 177, 564 **113** 54, 177, 475 **114** 1, 537 **115** 166, 342, 418 **117** 383, 390, 539 **118** 90, 305, 488 **119** 584 **120** 240 **122** 177 **123** 28

Gavan Duffy (53)

2 684, 735, 768 **3** 196, 516, 529 **4** 895, 946, 990, 1195, 1338, 1569, 1572, 1668 **5** 174, 188 **6** 41, 202, 309, 382, 469 **7** 34, 277 **8** 146, 170, 178, 262, 330, 465 **9** 231, 301, 347, 474, 510, 773 **10** 43, 266, 607 **11** 1, 63, 311 **12** 256, 321, 549 **13** 577, 619 **14** 17, 180, 675 **15** 182, 355, 685 **16** 245

McHugh (52)

108 372 **114** 153 **115** 413 **116** 397, 453 **117** 665 **118** 171 **122** 25, 237, 493 **123** 89 **124** 303 **126** 212 **130** 1 **133** 37, 507 **134** 81, 201 **135** 569 **136** 619 **137** 388 **138** 164, 194 **139** 499, 585 **140** 63, 470, 487 **141** 257, 296, 632, 648, 672 **142** 1, 509, 583 **143** 242, 549 **144** 633 **145** 78 **146** 40 **148** 72 **149** 293 **150** 169 **151** 57 **152** 632 **153** 514, 521 **154** 531, 632 **156** 364 **180** 404

Wilson (49)

105 172, 630 **107** 142, 208, 494 **108** 433 **109** 225, 593 **111** 327, 353 **112** 30 **113** 54, 365 **115** 575 **116** 273, 506 **120** 42, 74, 92 **121** 1 **123** 89 **125** 93, 138 **126** 576 **130** 177, 245 **132** 611 **133** 125 **134** 81, 201, 338, 495 **135** 1, 337, 507 **136** 406, 475 **137** 545 **138** 182, 194, 283, 346, 492 **139** 527, 585 **140** 120 **142** 211 **144** 633 **145** 107

Piddington (47)

1 181 **2** 214, 744 **3** 50, 150 **4** 694, 716 **5** 217, 263, 405, 445, 737 **6** 406 **7** 213 **9** 496, 534 **10** 391, 655 **11** 1, 123, 171 **12** 321, 653 **13** 114, 152, 438 **32** 138 **33** 538, 555 **35** 1, 260, 528 **37** 451, 466 **38** 74 **50** 258 **52** 221, 234, 248, 739 **53** 434 **54** 262, 626 **56** 580 **58** 146 **59** 140, 150

Windeyer (46)

37 375 **43** 208 **45** 359 **46** 284, 494 **48** 128 **53** 1 **55** 523 **56** 390 **58** 670 **60** 111 **61** 596, 735 **73** 549 **74** 31, 375 **75** 487 **79** 477 **81** 27, 199 **82** 1 **83** 1 **84** 58, 249 **85** 138, 423 **86** 402 **87** 375, 524 **88** 54, 322, 529, 646 **89** 152, 286, 353, 540 **91** 112, 368 **92** 424 **96** 35 **97** 379 **98** 625 **99** 521 **100** 246 **101** 56

Gummow (43)

138 1 **143** 410 **144** 45 **145** 438 **147** 39, 61 **148** 1, **150**, 262, 457 **151** 101, 491, 575, 599 **152** 254 **154** 1, 261, 311 **155** 186, 474 **156** 41, 170, 228, 249, 337, 414 **157** 1, 57, 351 **158** 622, 678 **159** 351, 461, 636 **160** 171, 371, 475 **161** 47, 217, 376, 556 **162** 74 **180** 322

Gaudron (37)

125 166, 332, 529 **127** 11 **149** 107 **150** 49, 169, 282 **151** 302, 491, 599 **152** 632 **153** 280 **154** 1, 261, 311, 404, 579 **155** 72, 368 **157** 57 **158** 1, 447, 535, 596 **159** 22, 351 **160** 315, 330, 430, 548 **161** 60, 217, 556, 639 **162** 447, 574

Evatt (37)

27 100 **28** 129, 330, 386, 436 **29** 219 **30** 1 **31** 286, 552, 583 **32** 518 34 141 35 69 37 36 **39** 139, 381 **40** 209 **41** 385, 519, 540 **42** 162, 209, 258, 527, 558 **43** 53, 440, 472 **44** 1, 29, 38, 166, 319 **76** 1 **79** 201 **81** 537 **83** 1

Williams (36)

34 174 **36** 310 **37** 161 **39** 16, 139 **40** 169, 467 **41** 316 **42** 277 **45** 68, 82 **49** 293 **50** 317 **51** 422, 653 **52** 609 **54** 97, 583 **56** 177, 605 **57** 186 **58** 155, 316, 689, 773 **59** 30 **60** 111, 396, 468, 583, 798 **61** 149, 337, 457, 534 **64** 312

Stephen (32)

92 157 **97** 599 **98** 187 **100** 273, 664 **103** 177 **104** 508 **105** 126, 537 **106** 318, 448, 472 **107** 46, 529 **109** 243 **110** 275, 419 **111** 303, 353 **113** 54, 475 **114** 283 **117** 111, 631 **118** 177, 529 **119** 72, 365 **120** 396 **121** 283, 483 **122** 546

Gibbs (28)

83 453 **86** 1 **88** 54 **90** 140, 598 **91** 642 **94** 531 **95** 11 **96** 131 **98** 228 **99** 94 **100** 117, 146, 422, 582 **101** 56 **102** 177, 340, 574 **103** 194 **104** 456, 609 **105** 164, 379 **106** 48, 377, 395 **107** 521

Isaacs (27)

1 13, 406, 460, 585, 668, 693 **2** 277, 315, 684, 716, 768, 787 **3** 196, 467, 479, 516, 608, 632, 846, 1018, 1028, 1099, 1170 **4** 1, 71, 78, 488

Murphy (26)

89 653 **96** 317 **97** 71 **99** 177, 285, 505 **100** 163, 277, 312 **102** 363 **103** 341, 368 **105** 42 **106** 23, 95 **111** 518 **114** 20 **115** 443 **117** 78 **118** 600 **121** 406 **122** 237 **125** 502 **127** 374 **128** 221 **131** 432

Callinan (25)

121 149 **144** 413, 596 **145** 266, 485 **146** 165 **147** 677 **151** 117 **154** 106 **155** 107, 288, 306 **156** 605 **157** 124, 215 **158** 596 **160** 156 **161** 98, 254 **163** 164, 221, 545, 611 **165** 306, 642

Brennan (22)

103 452 **106** 377 **108** 106 **111** 177 **113** 170 **116** 518 **117** 1, 173 **118** 144, 540 **123** 295 **124** 60 **125** 383 **129** 252 **131** 338, 592, 623 **132** 473 **133** 209, 260, 641 **134** 298

Hayne (16)

133 483 **134** 338 **136** 475 **137** 153 **138** 492 **140** 236 **142** 113 **145** 68 **146** 559 **151** 302 **153** 650 **157** 277 **160** 492, 540 **169** 41 **172** 167

Toohey (15)

106 60 **108** 230 **114** 98 **118** 292 **119** 118, 612 **121** 137 **125** 494 **128** 158, 595 **129** 332, 629 **130** 276 **134** 640 **139** 28

Rich (15)

1 283 **2** 74, 190, 387 **4** 57, 548 **5** 349 **6** 243 **7** 100, 232, 710 **8** 241 **9** 547 **11** 492 **12** 579

Jacobs (13)

85 467 **87** 177 **88** 177, 476 **89** 507 **92** 565 **95** 190, 420 **96** 429 **97** 310 **100** 392 **101** 119, 265

Owen (11)

39 46, 330 **47** 471, 497, 520, 618 **48** 649 **50** 520 **51** 351 **54** 134, 657

Walsh (10)

64 382 **66** 624 **67** 529, 567 **73** 404 **85** 20, 386 **88** 67, 168, 215

McTiernan (8)

23 49 **27** 133, 355 **33** 386 **37** 252 **39** 139, 411 **43** 70

Higgins (8)

1 585 **2** 252, 315, 565 **3** 316, 479 **4** 1, 488

Kirby (5)

121 375 **127** 1, 374, 617 **131** 432

Webb (3)

31 66, 382 **33** 76

Griffith, Barton, O'Connor, Powers (0)

parte Daniell (1920); but as Attorney-General, his choice of briefs appeared to reflect his changing politics. In earlier industrial cases, he had often appeared for trade unions—particularly for the Merchant Service Guild in a series of cases in 1913, in *Holyman's Case* (1914), and (with Menzies) in *Merchant Service Guild v Commonwealth Steamship Owners Association* (1920), a sequel to the *Engineers Case*. But as Attorney-General, he represented employers in some of the most important cases of the 1920s (see **Knox Court and arbitration**): *George Hudson v Australian Timber Workers Union* (1923); *Waterside Workers Federation v Gilchrist, Watt & Sanderson* (1924); *Hillman v Commonwealth* (1924); and the *Burwood Cinema Case* (1925).

When Labor took office in 1925 under Lang, Bavin became Leader of the Opposition. Himself becoming Premier in 1927, he committed NSW to that year's Financial Agreement, which was ultimately to be Lang's downfall. He also introduced the amendments to the *Constitution Act 1902* (NSW), which in *Trethowan's Case* were held to have effectively blocked Lang's attempt to abolish the Legislative Council. After losing the 1930 election, he returned to his High Court practice (see, for example, *Telegraph Newspapers v Bedford* (1934)); but by the time he was appointed to the Supreme Court of NSW in 1935, he was ailing, and confined himself mainly to hearing chamber applications.

The politician–barristers are notable mainly for their contributions to Australian politics, and in later careers of this kind the political element quickly overshadowed the nascent legal career. Gough Whitlam, for example, had five reported appearances as a barrister in the High Court. In *Brady v Thornton* (1947), he appeared as a junior to **Taylor**. In *Saffron v The Queen* (1953), Whitlam and **Mason** appeared together as juniors, opposing Barwick; in *Grannall v Marrickville Margarine* (1955) and in *Owen v Woolworths Properties* (1956), Whitlam was Barwick's junior. In *Thompson v Easterbrook* (1951), he appeared on his own. Peter Costello had two High Court appearances, in the *Ranger Uranium Case* (1987) and the *Wooldumpers Case* (1989), before his election to Parliament in 1990. On the other hand, a distinguished career at the Bar has sometimes been interrupted by a relatively brief interlude in politics. Tom Hughes, who first took silk in 1962, returned to a position of leadership at the Sydney Bar after serving as Attorney-General in the Gorton government (1969–71); while RJ Ellicott, after regular appearances in the High Court as Commonwealth **Solicitor-General** (1969–73), went on to become Attorney-General in the Fraser government (1975–77), and—after a brief period as a judge of the Federal Court (1981–83)—has continued to play a prominent role among senior High Court counsel.

Other eminent counsel over the years have been notable for their contributions to the formation of legal doctrine. The extent to which the ideas and doctrines adopted by the Court may be sheeted home to the argument of particular counsel is always difficult to judge; few Australian counsel can claim to have had an influence on the development of the law comparable to that of Daniel Webster on the doctrines espoused by the **United States Supreme Court** in the nineteenth century. But in the generation that included JD

Holmes (1907–73), Rae Else-Mitchell (1914–), Bruce Macfarlan (1910–78), and Nigel Bowen (1911–94) from Sydney and PD Phillips (1897–1970) from Melbourne, the standard of argument before the High Court was consistently high; and in any generation, Maurice Byers (1917–99) must be regarded as outstanding. As Commonwealth Solicitor-General from 1973 to 1983, and later in major cases such as *Australian Capital Television v Commonwealth* (1992) (see *Free Speech Cases*; **Implied constitutional rights**), *Kable v DPP* (1996), and *Wik* (1996), he had an extraordinary success rate. Like those of Robert Menzies, his arguments may have fallen on the ears of a receptive Court; but in his genial avuncular style, he projected his inner character and made the Court comfortable with what still appears to some as a radical proposition that the Constitution contains an implicit guarantee of the freedom of **political communication**. Melbourne barrister Ron Castan (1939–99) also had to win the confidence of the Court in the landmark **native title** case of *Mabo* (1992) in order to persuade it to depart from long settled expectations about **land law** in Australia, and this he did with the *sine qua non* of all successful counsel: thorough preparation and careful scholarship.

Apart from the Solicitors-General of the Commonwealth and the states—who, in the latter part of the twentieth century, came virtually to monopolise argument in constitutional cases—two counsel with significant, if not dominating, High Court practices in recent times have been David F Jackson (originally from Brisbane) and David Bennett (from Sydney), the latter taking up appointment as Commonwealth Solicitor-General in 1998. Jackson, who began his career as **Gibbs'** associate in the Supreme Court of Queensland, and represented the Queensland government in most of the great constitutional cases of the 1970s, returned to the Bar in 1987 after a brief period as a judge of the **Federal Court**, and since 1996 has practised mainly from Sydney.

Although the ranks of prominent High Court counsel have been dominated by those who were later elevated to the Bench—including not only Dixon, Barwick, and Aickin but also, for example, Isaacs, Gavan Duffy, **Knox**, Starke, Evatt, Latham, **Kitto**, Taylor, Douglas **Menzies**, Mason, **Deane**, **McHugh**, and **Gleeson**—not all those who have appeared before the Court have fitted the mould of being white, Anglo-Celtic males. The first woman to appear before the Court was Roma Mitchell (1913–2000), who was only 25 when she argued *Maeder v Busch* (1938), a patents case. Mitchell went on to be Australia's first woman QC, first woman judge (of the Supreme Court of SA), and first woman state governor (SA). Joan Rosanove (1896–1974), of the Melbourne Bar and a specialist in **family law**, appeared before the Court shortly after Mitchell, in *Briginshaw v Briginshaw* (1938). **Gaudron** made regular appearances as NSW Solicitor-General in the 1980s, but **women** entered this field late and remain underrepresented (see **Women practitioners**). Chinese Australians, however, were represented from the very beginning. William Ah Ket (1876–1936) joined the Melbourne Bar in 1903 and often appeared in the High Court for Chinese Australian litigants in cases involving **discrimination** of one kind or another: see, for example, *Ah Yick v Lehmert* (1905), *Potter v Minahan* (1908), and *Ingham v Hie Lee* (1912).

As far as can be ascertained, and despite the Court's increasing contact with issues involving **race** and **Aboriginal peoples,** no indigenous Australian, from among the still very small number of the legally qualified, has yet appeared as counsel before the High Court.

TONY BLACKSHIELD
MICHAEL COPER
GRAHAM FRICKE
TROY SIMPSON

Further Reading

JM Bennett (ed), *A History of the New South Wales Bar* (1969)

Arthur Dean, *A Multitude of Counsellors: A History of the Bar of Victoria* (1968)

HV Evatt, *Australian Labour Leader: The Story of WA Holman and the Labour Movement* (1940)

Graham Fricke, *Judges of the High Court* (1986)

Counsel, role of. The presentation of **argument** before the Court has traditionally been the role of counsel representing the parties or appearing as **interveners** or *amici curiae.*

In recognition of their role, the names of counsel and summaries of their arguments before the Court are shown at the beginning of the official report of each decision of the Court reported in the *Commonwealth Law Reports.*

The role of counsel is formally facilitated by provisions of the *Judiciary Act* 1903 (Cth), which allow parties to appear personally or by barristers or solicitors, and give persons entitled to practise as barristers or solicitors in any state the right to practise in the Court, subject only to their names first being entered on a register of practitioners maintained by the Court (see **Appearance, right of**).

Appearance before the Court has been confined in practice almost exclusively to barristers, who by training and experience are specialist advocates. With the notable exceptions of **Attorneys-General** and **Solicitors-General** and counsel appearing for the prosecution in criminal cases, those barristers have been predominantly from the independent Bars. Independent Bars existed in NSW, Victoria and Queensland before the **establishment** of the Court and developed in other states and **territories** during the second half of the twentieth century. In important cases, counsel have usually appeared in teams of two or more barristers led by a senior counsel. Senior counsel, colloquially referred to as 'silk' by reference to their silk gowns, historically held commissions granted by the Governor of a state—or, more rarely, by the Governor-General—designating them as King's Counsel or Queen's Counsel. However, since the mid-1990s new silk in most states and territories have simply been designated as 'senior counsel' under the rules of their respective professional associations.

The adversary system of justice inherited by the Court places a heavy emphasis on the role of counsel. The system, in its idealised form, relies on all available arguments being put to the Court on behalf of the parties or by *amici curiae* so that the task of the Court is simply to evaluate the competing arguments and choose between them. The role of counsel appearing for each party is to marshal the arguments available and present them in a form most likely to persuade the

Court to a result favouring the client. The proper performance of that role involves winnowing out arguments that have little prospect of acceptance as much as honing those that seem more promising. The system in reality has always seen the Court take a significant part in shaping the form of the arguments presented to it. The Court has also been inclined—to different degrees at different times—to formulate its own solutions to problems independently of the arguments presented.

Dixon recounted that when he first began to practise as counsel before the **Griffith Court** its methods were 'entirely dialectic', 'the minds of all judges were actively expressed in support or in criticism of arguments' and 'cross-examination of counsel was indulged in as part of the common course of argument'. The same was true of the **Knox Court.** The lengths to which this was taken were sometimes extreme. **Starke** commenced his reasons for judgment in *FCT v Hoffnung* (1928) by observing that the appeal in that case had been 'argued by this Court over nine days, with some occasional assistance from the learned and experienced counsel who appeared for the parties'. Dixon in particular felt that 'the process by which arguments were torn to shreds before they were fully admitted to the mind led to a lack of coherence in the presentation of a case and to a failure of the Bench to understand the complete and full cases of the parties'. He resolved when appointed to the Court not to follow the practice and to 'dissuade others from it'.

By the time of the **Latham Court** there was less judicial intervention in the argument of counsel. But this had only led to those arguments getting longer. **Latham** reminisced on the occasion of his **retirement** that he 'always sought to secure that every argument had a fair hearing' but that it had 'sometimes been hard to hear repetition of argument when the same proposition ha[d] been advanced six times'. Less judicial intervention had also led to what Dixon acknowledged at his swearing in as **Chief Justice** to be a tendency on the part of the Court 'to work out new and possibly unexplored solutions of cases after the argument [had] finished'.

The **Barwick Court** saw a reversion to the robust practices of the past. **Mason** described its methods as subjecting counsel to 'gruelling interrogation, dignified by the description "Socratic dialogue"'. This reversion was thankfully relatively short-lived. Argument by the time of the **Mason Court** had again come generally to be presented and received with equanimity. However, the pressure of **business** led inevitably to the curtailment of lengthy oral argument. At the same time, the tendency of the Court to work out its own solutions to cases independently of the arguments of counsel became accentuated. The availability to the Court of improved **research** facilities following the establishment of the Court's **library** in **Canberra** contributed to this tendency. So too did the increasing desire of members of the Court to have the benefit of foreign legal materials then neither generally familiar to, nor readily accessible by, counsel.

Although mooted much earlier, written argument was introduced only during the Mason Court. Comprehensive written argument became a standard requirement for all cases argued before the Court only during the **Brennan**

Court. Written argument prepared by counsel for a party is normally required to be provided to the Court and to other parties at a specified time in advance of a hearing, and is normally restricted in its length. Corresponding with the introduction of written argument, a strict time limit of 20 minutes on the presentation of oral argument in special **leave** applications was also introduced towards the end of the Mason Court. That time limit continues to be applied and is normally policed by the prominent display of a red light when the limit is reached. An attempt by **Brennan** in a number of cases to introduce strict time limits more generally on the presentation of oral argument before the Court proved unpopular with counsel and other members of the Court and was ultimately abandoned.

STEPHEN GAGELER

Further Reading
David Jackson, 'Practice in the High Court of Australia' (1997) 15 *Aust Bar Rev* 187
Anthony Mason, 'The Role of Counsel and Appellate Advocacy' (1984) 58 *ALJ* 537
Geoffrey Sawer, 'Division of a Fused Legal Profession' (1966) *University of Toronto Law Journal* 245

Court attire. The dress worn by members of the **legal profession**—especially the wig—is something about which most people associated with the law hold definite views. One school of thought sees legal dress as a harmful anachronism—and as something that serves to set the law apart from the people. Another school sees legal dress as a kind of uniform that helps to depersonalise the **rule of law**, so that it seems less like the rule of an unelected despot. A third school acknowledges the lawyer's costume to be anachronistic, but charmingly and harmlessly so.

The rules governing judicial dress were set out in the Judges Dress Rules of 1653, which, with some modification, govern the attire worn by English judges even today. According to the accepted understanding of the **reception of English law**, these Rules would have been received as part of NSW law, subject to their suitability 'to the needs of the infant colony'. It is for that reason that when the first Chief Justice of NSW, Francis Forbes, decided not to wear a wig, he stated his reasons in Blackstonian terms: that the wig was 'unsuited to the conditions of a young community'.

When the High Court was created, the decision was made to emulate the working costume of the English Court of Appeal, which was also the costume customarily worn at *nisi prius* in England: the black silken gown of the King's Counsel. JM Bennett attributes this to the fact that the Court was a creature of statute with a defined **jurisdiction**, in contrast to the inherent jurisdiction of the **state Supreme Courts** (see **Establishment of Court**). A similar explanation was also offered by **Barwick** in his autobiography. This explanation does not sit easily, however, with the fact that judges of the Supreme Court of Canada, which is also a creature of statute, wear scarlet robes lined with ermine for ceremonial occasions.

Whatever the case, the Court's dress has had several fine changes in detail over the years. In photographs of the first **sittings** of the Court, the Justices can clearly be seen wearing the bands of the barrister at the neck. In other contemporary photos, they can sometimes be seen wearing a white bow tie as well. But formal portraits of both **Isaacs** and **Gavan Duffy** show each wearing lace *jabots* in lieu of bands. Gavan Duffy is also seen wearing lace cuffs. Nonetheless, bands seem to have been the ordinary dress for the Justices up to 1980, when a *jabot* (designed by Lady Aickin) was adopted as formal dress at the formal opening of the Court's **building** in **Canberra**. It is thought that **Gibbs** brought the idea of the *jabot* back from a visit to South Africa. Up to the 1970s, Justices wore 'Windsor court dress', that is, breeches, silk stockings and buckled shoes, as part of their ceremonial costume, but during Barwick's Chief Justiceship, striped morning trousers came to be the norm.

As for wigs, it was the custom for Justices to wear the full-bottomed wig for ceremonial occasions, and the 'bench wig'—similar to the short barrister's wig—for daily work. Much has been made, especially by those who oppose judicial costume as a matter of principle, of the decision by **Murphy** to cease wearing a wig in the late 1970s, but in fact the first Justice of the Court not to wear the wig was **Starke**, who ceased to wear one in his later years. And Forbes had chosen not to wear a wig as early as 1824. Intriguingly, given that much of the colour associated with English legal dress has been eschewed by the Court, Justices formerly used to carry the tricorne hat carried (though seldom worn) by English judges on state occasions. The view has been expressed that the tricorne was adopted as a mark of status as a member of the **Privy Council**, and that when Justices of the Court stopped being appointed to the Privy Council, the right to wear the tricorne was lost. One wonders about this, though, for a photograph exists of a young **Dixon** carrying the tricorne, at a time before he had been appointed PC. Moreover, Justices of the Supreme Court of Canada continue to carry the tricorne even though they are not members of the Privy Council.

Barristers appearing before the Court wear the robes they would wear in the Supreme Courts of their states or territories. Similarly, solicitors who are addressing the Court robe if they would do so to appear in the Supreme Courts of their states or territories. Court officials, **associates** and **tipstaves** wear simple black robes and morning dress.

For the Justices, the greatest change in court dress came during the Chief Justiceship of **Mason**, when wigs were abandoned, and the QC's gown was discarded in favour of a shapeless style of gown similar to that worn by the Justices of the **United States Supreme Court**. With the new gown, neither bands nor *jabot* are worn. The reason for the change was to modernise the Court's costume, though one wonders whether the change could have pleased anyone. For the first school of thought referred to earlier, the new dress may still cause offence in principle (though undoubtedly less so than an overtly English costume). For the second, the new dress has little of the dignity associated with inherited tradition. For the third, the dress must seem neither charming nor anachronistic.

IAN HOLLOWAY

Further Reading
J Derriman, *Pageantry of the Law* (1955)
WN Hargreaves-Mawdsley, *A History of Legal Dress in Europe Until the End of the Eighteenth Century* (1963)

Victor Windeyer, 'Of Robes and Gowns and Other Things' (1974) 48 *ALJ* 394

Court Crier is the title given to an officer who makes public announcements in a court of justice. The public announcements made are the opening and closing of each session of the Court. **Dixon** approved various forms of proclamation when he became Chief Justice in 1952, and redefined the position of Court Crier. The proclamation to be used at an opening of the Full Court was 'All persons having business before the High Court of Australia are now commanded to draw nigh, give their attendance, and they shall be heard. God Save the Queen!'

Prior to 1952, the duties of Court Crier were limited to the opening and closing of the Court, and were performed by officers of the Supreme Courts in those states where the Court had occasion to sit. Dixon thought that the duties were not being performed to a standard that was acceptable to the Court. For establishment purposes, the newly created position was designated 'Court Attendant'. In addition to the duties of Court Crier, the person occupying the position carried out other duties such as setting up the **courtroom**, exhibiting daily court lists on notice boards and delivering copies to the Justices' **chambers**. The duties later expanded to encompass the photocopying of judgments.

The first full-time Court Crier was V Webb, who started in 1952 and retired in early 1965. William (Bill) Coles began as Court Crier on 3 May 1965 and held the position until after the first sitting of the Court in the new **building** in **Canberra** in June 1980, when he retired at the age of 77. When Bill Coles was appointed he was 62, the recommendation for his appointment noting that he would have to retire in August 1968. The Public Service Board was no match for Barwick, who managed to keep Coles past normal retirement age by various ploys.

Many barristers who went on to be judges, including High Court Justices, will remember Coles fondly for his words of encouragement after their first appearance in the High Court: 'That was well done sir!' **Barwick** referred to the silver-haired Coles as 'the old fellow', although he was older than Coles. He also tolerated Coles' habit of nodding off towards the end of the day. On one occasion, Barwick tapped at the top of the bench above Coles' head to wake him, and asked him to adjourn the Court. Coles sprang up and mistakenly gave the proclamation to open the court. He was mortified to see everyone in the court grinning—including the Justices.

In 1964, Barwick personally designed a distinctive form of attire for the Court Crier. The uniform consisted of a long black frock coat with accompanying Windsor striped trousers, a black tie, and a white shirt. The uniform changed with the appointment of Sheila Mumberson as the first female Court Crier in 1986. She designed a uniform that retained the frock coat, with a skirt of Windsor material, and a white blouse with an Elizabethan-style frilly collar. The current uniform is that worn by attendants at the Court, namely short black jacket and grey flannel trousers. Mumberson retired in 1994 and was replaced by Antoinette Breddels (1994–97), who in turn was replaced by Rex Avis (1997–98) and Alfred Slater (from 1998).

FRANK JONES

Court of Disputed Returns. Under the *Commonwealth Electoral Act* 1918 (Cth), and formerly under the *Commonwealth Electoral Act* 1902 (Cth), the High Court is designated as the Court of Disputed Returns. It is invested with the **jurisdiction** initially granted to the Houses of the federal Parliament under section 47 of the Constitution in relation to the qualifications of candidates, vacancies in parliamentary seats, and disputed electoral matters. The jurisdiction derives from that conferred on the Court of Queen's Bench in England and Ireland by the *Parliamentary Elections Act* 1868 (UK), and is similar to jurisdiction exercised by courts in Canada, NZ and in the Australian states.

Although on occasion the Court of Disputed Returns has been constituted by several High Court Justices sitting together (*Mulcahy v Payne* (1920); *In re Porter* (1923)), it is generally constituted by a single Justice. Matters are frequently referred from that Justice, sitting as the Court of Disputed Returns, to the **Full Court** of the High Court (for example, *Chanter v Blackwood (No 1)* (1904); *Evans v Crichton-Browne* (1981); *Snowdon v Dondas* (1996)). The Court also has power to refer a petition to the **Federal Court** or to a state or territory Supreme Court for trial, particularly if the case involves disputed matters of fact.

Petitions to the Court of Disputed Returns may be brought by electors or unsuccessful candidates challenging the validity of an election or return. The Electoral Commission is also entitled to file a petition disputing an election, although this has never occurred. Grounds for bringing an election petition include allegations that candidates were not constitutionally qualified, allegations of bribery, corruption or undue influence, and allegations of errors made by electoral officials. The Court will declare an election void only for those errors that would affect its result, not for mere technicalities. The Court of Disputed Returns is statutorily prohibited from inquiring into the correctness of the electoral roll. Thus it may not entertain allegations that persons entitled to vote were wrongly removed from the roll (*In re Berrill's Petition* (1976)), or allegations that persons enrolled to vote were not living in the electorate (*Perkins v Cusack* (1930)).

Petitions, often brought by unsuccessful candidates, frequently raise intensely political questions, including matters that specifically impugn the character of the elected candidate. For example, in *Crouch v Ozanne* (1910), a defeated candidate made numerous allegations of bribery and illegal canvassing, including the claim that Ozanne had offered a female voter a silk dress if she voted for him. Recurring unsuccessful complaints to the Court of Disputed Returns include allegations that political advertising makes false or misleading statements about a rival party's policies (*Evans v Crichton-Browne*; *Webster v Deahm* (1993)) and that sitting members or Senators are using parliamentary entitlements to conduct election campaigns (*Robertson v Australian Electoral Commission* (1993); *Pavlekovich-Smith v Australian Electoral Commission* (1993)).

Especially in the early years of the Court, the jurisdiction has sometimes involved the Justices in the painstaking task of personally examining ballot papers to determine whether irregularly marked papers were valid or were informal. A recount of disputed ballot papers has led in some close elections to the successful candidate's election being declared void (*Chanter v Blackwood (No 2)* (1904); *Kennedy v Palmer* (1907)). However, in *Cameron v Fysh* (1904), the election of Phillip Fysh by the narrow margin of 32 votes survived a recount of all 255 ballot papers initially rejected as informal.

In several early cases, errors by electoral officials led to some narrow electoral victories being invalidated, including the 1920 election of Edwin Kerby to the House of Representatives seat of Ballarat by a majority of just one vote (*Kean v Kerby* (1920); see also *Blundell v Vardon* (1907)).

The Court of Disputed Returns has also declared the election of other candidates void for non-compliance with constitutional requirements. Section 44 of the Constitution contains a number of grounds on which candidates for election may be disqualified. It has been successfully invoked to invalidate the election of candidates with dual **citizenship** (*Sykes v Cleary (No 2)* (1992); *Sue v Hill* (1999)) and candidates employed by the Crown, whether as a teacher in a state public school (*Sykes v Cleary (No 2)*) or as an officer in the defence force (*Free v Kelly* (1996)). Section 163 of the Electoral Act prescribes that a candidate must be at least 18 years old, and must have Australian citizenship—a requirement that was used to invalidate the election of a candidate with American citizenship in *In re Wood* (1988).

Since 1907, the High Court sitting as the Court of Disputed Returns has also had jurisdiction to hear, on a reference by one of the Houses of Parliament, matters respecting the qualifications of any Senator or Member of the House of Representatives. The Houses of Parliament retain a concurrent jurisdiction to determine disputes relating to the election, return and qualifications of their members (*In re Wood*). In contrast to the frequency with which electoral petitions are brought, the reference jurisdiction of the Court has only been exercised twice: in *In re Webster* (1975) and *In re Wood*. The Opposition called for a third reference in June 1999, when it was revealed that the parliamentary secretary to the Minister for Industry, Warren Entsch, had an interest in a company that had won a lucrative contract to supply concrete for a RAAF base in far north Queensland. The reference was not forthcoming, because the House of Representatives passed a resolution declaring that Entsch's interest did not amount to a pecuniary interest in an agreement with the Commonwealth Public Service, and therefore did not violate section 44(v) of the Constitution. This highlights the dependence of the Court's reference jurisdiction on the existence of political will to refer such questions to the Court.

The decision of Chief Justice **Barwick** in *In re Webster* has been the subject of some **criticism**. The case involved a reference from the Senate as to whether Senator James Webster should be disqualified under section 44(v) of the Constitution for having a pecuniary interest in an agreement with the Commonwealth Public Service. Senator Webster was managing director and a shareholder of a family company that operated a timber business. The company contracted to supply timber to the Commonwealth Department of Housing and Construction. Barwick, a former member of Parliament who had belonged to the same party as Senator Webster, heard the case alone, and declined to refer it to the Full Court. In what has been described as a narrow and strained interpretation of section 44(v), Barwick held that section 44(v) applied only to executory contracts and to con-

tracts of a permanent and continuing character, not to contracts of limited purpose and duration. He thus concluded that there was no reason to disqualify Webster. The criticism of Barwick for sitting alone was difficult to answer.

The validity of the High Court's jurisdiction to sit as the Court of Disputed Returns has been challenged in recent years. It was first contended that the Court's jurisdiction over disputed elections and its jurisdiction over qualifications and vacancies were mutually exclusive. Thus, it was said, petitions could only be brought challenging the machinery of elections, including illegal practices in relation to elections, whereas the qualifications of candidates could be determined only by Parliament itself or the Court of Disputed Returns on a reference from either House. This argument was rejected by a single Justice, **Dawson**, in *Sykes v Cleary (No 1)* (1992). In *Sue v Hill*, a bare majority of the Court upheld his decision, although three Justices would have invalidated the Court's long-standing practice of hearing and determining petitions disputing an election based on the qualifications of candidates. **McHugh**, **Kirby** and **Callinan** held that the qualifications of candidates could be raised in the Court only on a reference from the relevant House—although McHugh, with whom Callinan agreed on this point, accepted that the issue could also arise incidentally in the determination of an election petition alleging that a candidate had committed an illegal practice by falsely declaring he or she was qualified to be elected. All three of these judges held (in dissent) that the Court's jurisdiction over election petitions related only to 'the validity of any election or return'. They based this conclusion on the history of parliamentary law and practice, and the textual consideration that election petitions and references were contained in separate Divisions of the Commonwealth Electoral Act. However, despite this structural division, **Gaudron**, with whom **Gleeson**, **Gummow** and **Hayne** agreed on this point, saw nothing to suggest that the separate jurisdictions thus conferred were mutually exclusive.

A more fundamental objection to the High Court's electoral jurisdiction is that it involves the exercise of non-**judicial power** contrary to the doctrine of the **separation of powers** between the legislature, executive and judiciary. This objection was first raised before (but not determined by) **Mason** in *Re Brennan; Ex parte Muldowney* (1993). In *Sue v Hill*, the majority convincingly upheld the validity of the Court's electoral jurisdiction. The Court examined historical and textual considerations and concluded that the power to determine disputed returns was neither essentially legislative nor essentially judicial in nature, but could be exercised by either the Parliament or the judiciary.

The High Court's jurisdiction over electoral matters, sitting as the Court of Disputed Returns, has been described as 'peculiar': *Webb v Hanlon* (1939). Certainly it is an unusual jurisdiction to be exercised by a court, as it inevitably involves the Court in overtly political decisions, including frequent invalidation of election results. However, the jurisdiction has withstood recent constitutional challenges. While some would consider it inappropriate for the Court to exercise such a political function, it could equally be said that the Court's role as overseer of the election process is integral to its role as upholder and defender of the Constitution.

Arguably, judges' integrity and **independence** from party politics make them more suited to exercise such powers than what **Barton** in 1897 termed 'a fallacious tribunal, a Committee of the Houses of Parliament'.

KATRINE DEL VILLAR

Further Reading
Gareth Evans, 'Pecuniary Interests of Members of Parliament under the Australian Constitution' (1975) 49 *ALJ* 464
Peter Hanks, 'Parliamentarians and the Electorate' in Gareth Evans (ed), *Labor and the Constitution 1972–1975* (1977) 178
Paul Schoff, 'The Electoral Jurisdiction of the High Court as the Court of Disputed Returns: Non-Judicial Power and Incompatible Function?' (1997) 25 *FL Rev* 317
Kristen Walker, 'Disputed Returns and Parliamentary Qualifications: Is the High Court's Jurisdiction Constitutional?' (1997) 20 *UNSWLJ* 257

Courtrooms are used for the presentation of oral **argument** before the Court, and for the announcement of the Court's decisions. The High Court building in **Canberra** has three courtrooms of varying sizes (see **Architecture of Court building**), and the Commonwealth Law Courts buildings in both Sydney and Melbourne each contain one dedicated High Court courtroom. In the other Australian states, by a longstanding arrangement, the **Federal Court** or **state Supreme Courts** provide the High Court with courtrooms and **chambers** when the Court is on **circuit**. Prior to the opening of the building in Canberra, this was the arrangement in all states (see **Buildings**).

In Canberra, Courtroom No 1 is the High Court building's focal point. A huge, wood-panelled room with public seating, on two levels, for almost 200 people and a 17-metre-high ceiling, it is used for all **ceremonial sittings** and for all cases where a Full Bench of seven Justices sit. The long, curved bench and bar table are both made from marble and WA jarrah timber. The bar table will comfortably accommodate up to twenty **counsel**. A large representation of the Australian Coat of Arms in tapestry, 11 m^2 in area, hangs on the western wall of the courtroom. Large paintings of the first three Justices of the Court also hang on the walls (see **Artworks of Court**).

Courtroom No 2 is the venue for the majority of hearings—generally appeals from lower courts involving a Bench of five Justices. It is similar in design and accoutrements to Courtroom No 1, but on a smaller scale. This is the venue for the majority of hearings by video link, and special equipment has been installed to allow these hearings to take place. Paintings of former Chief Justices of the Court hang on the eastern wall.

Courtroom No 1

Courtroom No 2

Courtroom No 3 is the smallest of the three courtrooms in the building. It is used for hearings involving a single Justice (for example, **directions hearings** and chamber applications) and, like Courtroom No 2, is equipped for hearings by video link. Interestingly, this courtroom has also been built with a jury box and witness stand for the rare occasion when a **jury trial** may need to be conducted before the High Court (the last such occasion was evidently *R v Brewer* (1942)). Again, paintings of former Chief Justices of the Court hang on the walls.

The doors to each of the three courtrooms feature silvered bronze shields partly recessed into laminated glass panels. The shields represent the Court's function as protector of the Australian Constitution and the liberties of the Australian citizen.

All courtrooms have sophisticated sound reinforcement equipment. Audio and video signals from the courtroom are reticulated to a remote monitoring room, from where the audio is fed to the court reporting area for production of the daily **transcript** of proceedings.

The layout of the two major courtrooms is identical. The bench area is wide enough for the Justices to be seated with their respective **associates** or **tipstaves** behind them. Each associate or tipstaff has a trolley containing the authorities to be referred to in the case being heard. The Justices sit at the bench in a set order: the Chief Justice, or presiding Justice, in the middle and the other Justices alternating in order of **seniority** from the right of the **Chief Justice** to the left of the Chief Justice. Thus, in a **Full Court** of seven, the most junior Justice is always seated on the far right (as one faces the bench).

To the side of the bench are seated the Court Clerk and the **Court Crier**. In front of the bench is the bar table, with a lectern in the middle. Counsel for the applicant or appellant sit to the left of the lectern, and counsel for the respondent to the right. Behind the bar table are tables for instructing solicitors.

Courtroom No 3 is designed slightly differently, due to the different nature of proceedings in that room. It is customary for a Court Registrar to attend all hearings in this courtroom (in case there is a need to provide advice to the presiding Justice on registry procedure) and this officer sits directly in front of the bench, alongside the Justice's associate or tipstaff. This courtroom, unlike the other two, has the court reporting monitoring facilities located in the courtroom itself, alongside the jury box. This is in case of a trial, where taped evidence may need to be played back in open court. Another peculiarity of Courtroom No 3 is that there is no central lectern. Instead, counsel stand to address the Bench without leaving their places at the bar table.

Courtroom No 3

All courtrooms contain a public gallery, of varying size, at the back of the room, and all hearings are open to the public (see **Open court**).

LEX HOWARD

Criminal law. At the time of the High Court's **establishment**, the conditions for it to make a significant impact on the infant federation's criminal law were promising. The new Chief Justice, **Griffith**, had completed a Criminal Code for Queensland only six years earlier. The Court was also a court of general appeal from the **state Supreme Courts**, unlike its model, the **United States Supreme Court**, which hears criminal appeals only when they involve a federal or constitutional issue.

Despite this, the Court's criminal casework started very slowly. The first reported decision in a criminal case was on 4 April 1905, when special leave was refused to appeal from the NSW Supreme Court's decision not to issue prohibition to a magistrate who had convicted the applicants for gaming offences (*Ex parte Spencer* (1905)).

The first reported hearing in a criminal case—on 21–23 March 1905, though judgment was not delivered until 10 April 1905—was in *Quan Yick v Hinds* (1905), which also related to gambling. This, too, was an appeal from the NSW Supreme Court, which had heard a challenge to a magis-

trate's decision, this time on a case stated. As would continue to be the case, the Court's decision was more significant to **constitutional law** than to criminal law. It became the leading case on the **reception of English law**.

That these early appeals came before the High Court from decisions of magistrates was not surprising. The notion of appeals from **jury trials** had not yet been developed. Various devices, such as the writ of error and the reservation of questions of law, had been used to review the legal issues arising from jury trials, and had sometimes reached the High Court on appeal. But it was not until 1912 that NSW, and later other states, followed the UK in introducing appeals from convictions and sentences following jury trials.

The other limiting factor was that, from the beginning, an appellant in a criminal case had to seek special **leave to appeal**. Initially, the Court adopted the restrictive criteria for leave to appeal established by the **Privy Council** in *In re Dillet* (1887). Thus, in *Millard v The King* (1906), the Court pronounced itself 'very reluctant to grant special leave to appeal in criminal cases', adding that it would do so only on 'some point of great general importance ... which, if wrongly decided, might seriously interfere with the administration of justice'.

In *Eather v The King* (1914), **Isaacs** protested that the Court had no authority to limit its role in this way, and that Privy Council analogies were irrelevant under the Australian

Constitution. The difference of opinion was ultimately resolved by a ruling that, on the one hand, 'the Court has an unfettered discretion to grant or refuse leave in every case', but that, on the other hand, in criminal as in civil cases, 'the term "special leave" connotes the necessity for making a *prima facie* case showing special circumstances' (*In re Eather v The King* (1915); see also *R v Snow* (1915)).

This negative stipulation was later doubted by **Evatt** and **McTiernan** (in dissent) in *Craig v The King* (1933). To say that the Court 'is not a court of criminal appeal', they argued, is true 'only … in the sense that there is no appeal as of right to this Court in criminal matters. If special leave is granted, the functions of the High Court are assimilated precisely to those of … [a] Court of Criminal Appeal'. In *Cornelius v The King* (1936), however, **Starke** reaffirmed that the Court should be 'slow to interfere' in criminal proceedings except in cases of 'substantial and grave injustice', adding that the Court 'is no more a court of criminal appeal' than the Privy Council.

Since then, this restrictive approach has been followed, using the negative stipulation to refuse special leave (see, for example, *Liberato v The Queen* (1985)). Accordingly, the Court has consistently refused to consider fresh evidence on appeals (*Mickelberg v The Queen* (1989); *Eastman v The Queen* (2000)).

It is not surprising, therefore, that the criminal appeals that were heard often had a significance far beyond their importance to the criminal law. *R v Kidman* (1915) stands for the general proposition that statute law prevails over the **common law**, and includes an important discussion of the relationship of the common law to the Commonwealth. *Viro v The Queen* (1978) represented a significant statement of Australian **nationhood**, the Court no longer being bound by Privy Council decisions. The nature of courts under the Constitution has recently been elucidated in criminal cases (*Kable v DPP (NSW)* (1996) and *Re Governor, Goulburn Correctional Centre; Ex parte Eastman* (1999)). Criminal cases have also featured prominently in the social history of the Court. A criminal case, *Peacock v The King* (1911), was the first in which **Barton** disagreed with Griffith.

The Court initially used criminal decisions to assert the independence of Australian jurisprudence from its British origins. Although the Court had never quite seen itself as bound by the English Court of Criminal Appeal, it had, as late as *Piro v Foster* (1943), expressed its allegiance to decisions of the **House of Lords**. It was in criminal cases that this bond was first breached. In *Parker v The Queen* (1963), the Court expressly disapproved the House of Lords view in *DPP v Smith* (1960) that a defendant is regarded as intending the natural or probable consequence of his or her acts, and ruled that the case 'should not be used as authority in Australia at all'. Later, in *R v O'Connor* (1980), the Court expressly departed from the House's view in *DPP v Majewski* (1976) of self-induced intoxication as a limited defence.

Through its criminal jurisdiction, the Court also gradually introduced a body of principles applicable throughout Australia. As a general appellate court from all jurisdictions, it could achieve this—despite the existence of the criminal Codes alongside the common law, and despite the Commonwealth's own limited criminal power—and it did so particu-

larly in the 1980s and 1990s. In *He Kaw Teh v The Queen* (1985), for example, the Court examined the nature of possession and offences of strict responsibility, formulating 'general principles' to apply comprehensively to Code, Commonwealth and common law offences.

It is not easy to discern general trends. Before the 1970s, the annual number of applications for special leave to appeal in criminal matters was usually in single figures. In 1972, there were three applications; two were granted. Since then, the number has increased very substantially, particularly in the late 1980s and the 1990s. In a conference address in 1990, **Dawson** attributed the increase to the decision to grant special leave and allow the appeal in *Morris v The Queen* (1987). That decision (from which he and **Mason** had dissented) had, he said, been 'viewed by the profession as an encouragement to make application for special leave in criminal cases involving only matters of fact and to dispute the rejection by the court [below] … of any submission that the verdict of the jury was unsafe or unsatisfactory'.

This state of affairs led the Court in 1996 to change the way it dealt with such applications. Previously, a **Full Court** would consider the application for leave and the substantive appeal in one sitting, after which it would either refuse special leave, or grant the leave and allow the appeal. In 1996, however, criminal cases were brought into line with civil cases: the application for leave is a separate hearing, now usually before two Justices. If leave is granted, the appeal is later heard by a Full Court.

Criminal appeals had increased substantially by the mid-1980s and remain a significant part of the Court's **business**. Between 1980 and 2000 the Court delivered more than a hundred criminal judgments, on procedure, **evidence** and jurisdiction, as well as on substantive law. Many of these decisions are applied on a daily basis in the criminal courts of all Australian jurisdictions, at all levels. Many are relied upon as persuasive authority throughout the common law world.

Until about 1980, the Court, although not bound by English decisions, remained strongly influenced by them. Its decisions were, by and large, legally conservative, and somewhat less influential than those of state Courts of Criminal Appeal, which often sought rather impudently to distinguish High Court decisions into irrelevance.

This did not mean that the Court forged no criminal jurisprudence before the 1980s. Since *Hardgrave v The King* (1906), it had grappled with the notion of strict responsibility and the **criminal law defence** of reasonable mistake of fact. Generally, offences of **strict liability** were limited to those whose purpose is to 'protect a civil right by a drastic means of enforcement' (*Brown v Green* (1951)). A 'civil right' meant one giving rise only to action in a civil court—'social and industrial regulation' or 'economic and social regulation'. This approach led to the *locus classicus*, namely *Proudman v Dayman* (1941), of the defence of an honest and reasonable belief in facts which, if they existed, would make an accused's act innocent. This decision, formulating a tripartite division of *mens rea*, strict liability and absolute liability, has had a wide influence internationally in British Commonwealth jurisdictions, particularly Canada.

Other decisions in this period have also had a significant and ongoing influence. *House v The King* (1936) is still the leading Australian case on appellate review of a discretionary judgment. 'Griffiths bonds'—named after *Griffiths v The Queen* (1977)—are still regularly granted to offenders deemed worthy of an opportunity for rehabilitation. Discussion of the discretion to exclude illegally obtained evidence would be incomplete without reference to *R v Ireland* (1970) and *Driscoll v The Queen* (1977) (see now *Ridgeway v The Queen* (1995)).

Despite the general influence of English decisions up to the 1980s, it was in criminal cases that the Court came most effectively to express its independence from the British courts, well before legislation severing the formal bond by abolishing appeals to the Privy Council. In particular, the judgments of **Dixon** and Evatt in *Sodeman v The King* (1936) evinced a clear determination to extend the defence of insanity beyond the limits maintained by the English Court of Criminal Appeal in cases such as *R v Flavell* (1926); and although on appeal the Privy Council in *Sodeman* refused to entertain the prospect of 'different standards of law prevailing in England and the Dominions', it was clear that in cases involving 'uncontrollable' or 'irresistible' impulse, different standards did in fact prevail. Thus, the High Court effectively adhered to its view in *Brown v The Queen* (1959), though again admonished by the Privy Council (*A-G (SA) v Brown* (1960)). Throughout this period, the Court continued to follow House of Lords decisions until it decisively abandoned that practice in *Parker*. This set a trend that effectively created an Australian common law.

That trend was motivated more by the Court's fidelity to legal principle than by patriotic independence. *Parker* simply reinforced earlier decisions of the Court such as *Stapleton v The Queen* (1952) and *Smyth v The Queen* (1957), which developed general principles of fault that the later English authorities were regarded as violating. The Court has often delved into **history** to discern the principles underpinning the law in order to develop it in a coherent way, for example in *Saraswati v The Queen* (1991), *Wilson v The Queen* (1992) and *R v L* (1991).

Nevertheless, the Court was at first reluctant to recognise a common law of Australia as distinct from that of the individual jurisdictions. This was particularly evident in criminal matters: the Court would initially not bridge the gulf between the Code states and the common law, and was not committed to providing unifying principles that could be termed an Australian common law of crime. From time to time, there were isolated statements about 'a common law of Australia', building on Griffith's identification in *Kidman* of a 'common law of the Commonwealth' (see, for example, **Webb** in *R v Sharkey* (1949)). But the Court took no steps to give reality to such a concept until much later, at a time of mounting dissatisfaction with the incoherence of separate state systems of criminal law and the movement in the 1980s and 1990s towards a unified Model Criminal Code.

In short, until the mid-1980s, the Court remained relatively conservative and, despite its independence, deferential to English authority. There were, however, strong dissents, especially from **Murphy**, which were often later adopted by the **Mason Court**. For example, Murphy's dissent in *McInnis v The Queen* (1982) became, substantially, though with little acknowledgment, the decision in *Dietrich v The Queen* (1992).

Sentencing does not often reach the Court, but was considered in *Veen v The Queen* (1979) and *Veen v The Queen (No 2)* (1988), which emphatically asserted a principle of **proportionality** in sentencing (that is, 'that a sentence should not be increased beyond what is proportionate to the crime in order merely to extend the period of protection of society from the risk of recidivism on the part of the offender')—while balancing this with recognition that 'the protection of society' may be a material factor in the exercise of a sentencing discretion.

In the 1980s, the Court became generally more active in criminal law, grappling with difficult issues considered as technical 'lawyers' law' but heavily influenced by **policy considerations**. Two main themes were evident: the subjective fault principle and the fair trial principle.

The subjective fault principle first received express recognition in the seminal decision on complicity, *McAuliffe v The Queen* (1995), where three youths acting in concert had assaulted two men, one of whom died as a result. The Court noted that 'the test of what fell within the scope of the common purpose' had formerly been determined objectively, so that the participants would in fact be liable for the consequences of the common action whether or not they had those consequences in contemplation. However, in deference to 'the emphasis which the law now places on the actual state of mind of an accused person', the Court held that the test of what came within the common purpose must now be subjective. At the same time, this subjective understanding extended to a merely possible consequence of the joint enterprise: a participant who foresaw it as a possible consequence but continued to participate would share the responsibility for that consequence if it ensued.

In a series of cases including *Giorgianni v The Queen* (1985), *Bahri Kural v The Queen* (1987) and *Pereira v DPP* (1988), the Court hammered out a jurisprudence of the knowledge necessary to found criminal liability, with particular reference to how 'wilful blindness' by deliberate abstention from inquiry fitted into the traditional requirement of a 'guilty mind' for all but strict-liability offences. The Court enunciated a clear view that while knowledge may be inferred from a defendant's wilful blindness to facts, it was still necessary to infer that there was actual, rather than imputed, knowledge.

In developing the principle of subjective fault, murder received not unexpected attention; but the development was neither uniform nor particularly radical. A line of cases leading to *Stingel v The Queen* (1990) confirmed the test for provocation as objective: the provoking conduct must be capable of causing the ordinary person to lose self-control. The offender must actually have lost self-control and acted before regaining control. *Stingel* involved the Tasmanian Code, but the Court repeated this test in the common law decision of *Masciantonio v The Queen* (1995)—thus developing a convergence between Code and common law, a trend continued in the Court's criminal jurisprudence to the end of the century. The Court further refined these principles in *Green v The Queen* (1997), treating the accused's subjective circumstances as relevant to the **reasonableness** of the gravity of provocation.

In *Meyers v The Queen* (1997), the Court reaffirmed that intent must accompany any fatal acts. In *Osland v The Queen* (1998), the Court first considered the 'battered woman syndrome', though with little enthusiasm.

Consideration of the accused's fault was not, of course, confined to murder. In *Jiminez v The Queen* (1992), the Court held that a sleeping driver could be excused from culpability for a car accident; in *Meissner v The Queen* (1995), the Court required the accused to have intended to pervert the course of justice when engaging in the relevant conduct.

The concept of a fair trial initially referred largely to permissible modes of proof. The Court considered the evidentiary hearsay rule on numerous occasions, balancing the need to exclude contestable evidence of debatable provenance against the desirability of including evidence of probative value. In the 1990s, the Court also grappled in at least seven cases with the admissibility of 'similar fact' evidence, taking the view that such evidence is admissible, not because of any probative value, but as evidence of propensity.

Late in this period, the Court established a broad pattern of strengthening traditional liberties and broadening the right to a 'fair trial'. It paid increasing attention to international and comparative jurisprudence and steadily absorbed norms from sources such as the **International Bill of Rights**.

In reaffirming the impermissibility of inferring guilt from silence or denying credibility to a late explanation (in *Petty v The Queen* (1991)), the Court strengthened the accused's right to silence. In *McKinney v The Queen* (1991), the Court required that juries be instructed of the danger of convicting an accused solely on the evidence of a confession made in police custody. In this, the Court intervened to meet community expectations ignored by legislatures. In *Dietrich*, the Court held that a trial would be unfair if an indigent, who without fault had exhausted all access to legal assistance, had to face a serious charge without representation. Again, the Court, revolutionising legal aid, met community demands unmet by government (but see **Women**). In *Pollitt v The Queen* (1992) and later in *R v Swaffield* (1997), the Court recognised the dangerousness of the evidence of police informers, and limited the use of such evidence to circumvent the right to silence.

This period also saw the rise of the appeal ground that a jury verdict was 'unsafe and unsatisfactory', perhaps as an aspect of the concern for a fair trial. In *M v The Queen* (1994), the Court concluded that an appeal court must consider the whole of the trial evidence to determine whether it experienced a doubt that a reasonable jury ought to have entertained, allowing for the advantages of a jury in actually seeing and hearing the evidence.

In the late 1990s, the **activism** seems to have moderated. The Court turned back from a policy-influenced to a technical approach. This is seen in such cases as *Byrnes v The Queen* (1999), *Bond v The Queen* (2000) and *R v Hughes* (2000), where a restrictive construction of legislation meant that otherwise fair trials were set aside. However, the Court did not retreat far from the concern for fairness and the interests of the accused; in *RPS v The Queen* (2000), the accused's right to silence was jealously guarded. The Court has also shown signs of consolidating the move for an independent, unified Australian jurisprudence, and in *Lipohar v The Queen* (1999) clearly articulated a view of the common law as uniform throughout Australia.

The Court has not been immune from **criticism**. Many of its members have had little, sometimes no, criminal trial experience, occasionally leading to decisions that are impossible to apply in practice. For example, the result of the elucidation of self-defence in *Viro* was a complicated, difficult process for the jury. Nine years later, the Court recognised the difficulties and substituted a single question, 'whether the accused believed upon reasonable grounds that it was necessary in self-defence to do what he did': *Zecevic v DPP* (1987).

Nevertheless, the Court's increased output has led some to complain that the quite specific directions now required add significantly not only to the task of a trial judge in directing a jury, but also to the number and detail of the directions with which the jury must comply. With more fertile ground for appeals and more frequent retrials, the result may be an increase in the cost of trials and the cost to the system as a whole.

The Court has become an important part of the criminal justice system. The importance the Justices attach to criminal justice and to fair results for the community is evidenced by the number and nature of their **extra-judicial** comments in papers and speeches. There is no doubt that the Court will continue to have a significant influence upon criminal justice, upholding fairness and increasing public confidence in the criminal law.

RICHARD REFSHAUGE

Further Reading
Daryl Dawson, 'Recent Common Law Developments in Criminal Law' (1991) 15 *Crim LJ* 5
Anthony Mason, 'Fair Trial' (1993) 19 *Crim LJ* 7
Anthony Mason, 'Opening Remarks, Fourth International Criminal Law Congress' (1993) 17 *Crim LJ* 5

Criminal law defences. Notwithstanding the differences in the laws that create the criminal defences in each state and territory, the High Court has frequently attempted to state rules and principles of general application. An example of this approach is *Stingel v The Queen* (1990), an appeal raising the defence of provocation under section 160(2) of the *Criminal Code* (Tas). The Court noted 'a perception that, in this particular field of the **criminal law**, the common law, the Codes and other statutory provisions, and judicial decisions about them, have tended to interact and to reflect a degree of unity of underlying notions'. The Court added that it shared that perception. The ambit of the decision was extended to the **common law** and to the statutory provisions in NSW.

A similar approach was adopted for the defences of automatism and insanity in *R v Falconer* (1990) and for self-defence in *Zecevic v DPP (Vic)* (1987). The judgments in both cases contained references throughout to the similarity of principle in the code provisions and in the common law. In keeping a watchful eye on the 'unity of underlying notions', the Court has developed a greater **national unity** of criminal defences than would otherwise have occurred in Australia with its nine discrete jurisdictions, each with its own set of criminal laws. The 1991 decision of the Standing Committee of **Attorneys-General** to draft and adopt a Model

Criminal Code reflects a wider political concern with the fragmentation of criminal law in a relatively small nation.

The Court's consideration of criminal defences has been disproportionately skewed towards the defence of provocation, and to a lesser extent, self-defence. Over the last forty years the Court has examined the defence of provocation on at least twelve separate occasions. The defence exists in all Australian jurisdictions, although the precise rules differ according to whether it is governed by the common law or by statutory provisions. It originated in the common law in the seventeenth century and has been described over the centuries as a concession to human frailty. The modern defence was recently stated in *Masciantonio v The Queen* (1995) by **Brennan, Deane, Dawson**, and **Gaudron**:

> Homicide, which would otherwise be murder, is reduced to manslaughter if the accused causes death whilst acting under provocation. The provocation must be such that it is capable of causing an ordinary person to lose self-control … The provocation must actually cause the accused to lose self-control and the accused must act whilst deprived of self-control.

The Court has examined the defining elements on a number of occasions. The time interval between the provocative conduct and the killing (suddenly, in the heat of passion) was examined in *Parker v The Queen* (1963). **Dixon** (in dissent) held that the twenty or so minutes intervening between the adulterous deceased's insults and the fatal stabbing did not constitute a 'delay in which the blood might cool'. He concluded that 'the jury might find all of the elements of suddenness in the unalleviated pressure and the breaking down of control as the prisoner came to the end of his pursuit of the man taking away his wife'. His compassionate approach was subsequently approved by the **Privy Council**.

The element in provocation that has received most attention both judicially and in academic, legal and community debate is the 'ordinary person' test. The issue is the extent to which the 'ordinary person' may incorporate the personal attributes of the accused. Prior to *Stingel* the Court allowed the ethnic origin of the accused to be considered (see *Moffa v The Queen* (1977)). In various decisions, the **state Supreme Courts** had also allowed the conception of the ordinary person to develop in a manner consistent with a pluralist society. He or she was endowed with the age, sex, race, culture and religion of the accused. This trend came to an end with the reformulation of the test in *Stingel*. The Court held that 'the personal characteristics or attributes of the particular accused may be taken into account for the purpose of … assessing the gravity of the wrongful act or insult' for the ordinary person, but that personal characteristics (with the exception of age) are not relevant in assessing the power of self-control of the ordinary person.

The decision in *Stingel* generated widespread debate, much of it critical of the Court's failure to respect the ethnic and **cultural diversity** of Australian society. These criticisms were accepted by **McHugh**, who subsequently stated in a compelling **dissenting judgment** in *Masciantonio*: 'Real **equality** before the law cannot exist when ethnic or cultural minorities are convicted or acquitted of murder according to

a standard that reflects the **values** of the dominant class but does not reflect the values of those minorities'.

Further controversy was generated by the decision of the Court in *Green v The Queen* (1997). The provocative conduct was a sexual advance, the gravity of which was aggravated by the defendant's special sensitivity arising from a history of violence and sexual assault within his family. The majority of the Court applied *Stingel* and held that the special sensitivity to sexual assault was relevant to the assessment of the gravity of provocation but not to the power of control of the ordinary person. In a scholarly dissenting judgment, **Kirby** examined the 'textual, historical and policy reasons' for declining to disturb the jury verdict, noting that the 'ordinary person in Australian society is not so homophobic as to respond to a non-violent sexual advance by a homosexual person as to form an intent to kill' (see **Sexual preference**).

In *Osland v The Queen* (1998), the Court dealt with another issue of wider public concern: the admission of evidence pertaining to the battered woman syndrome (see **Feminism**). While rejecting the defence in this case, the majority approved the trial judge's direction and held that the battered woman syndrome is a proper matter for **expert evidence**, and is relevant to the assessment of the gravity of provocation in the ordinary person test.

The defence of self-defence has been reformulated and refined twice by the Court in the second half of the century. The central concern is whether the force used was a reasonably necessary reaction to the threat faced. The Court in *R v Howe* (1958) and later in *Viro v The Queen* (1978) formulated the test for self-defence and developed the doctrine of excessive self-defence as a basis for reducing criminal liability from murder to manslaughter. **Mason's** judgment in *Viro* is famous for its complexity, although many regarded it as 'fair and just'. The majority in *Zecevic*, although not asked to by either party, abolished the doctrine of excessive self-defence and laid down a deceptively simple test: 'whether the accused believed upon reasonable grounds that it was necessary in self-defence to do what he did'.

The test has been widely discussed and its simplicity both praised and criticised. The difficulties in raising self-defence faced by **women** who kill in the context of long-term domestic violence have been a particular focus of the wider legal and social debate.

The mental or psychiatric defences have not received the same degree of attention from the Court. The defence of insanity is still largely governed by the common law rules articulated in *M'Naghten's Case* (1843) and has been infrequently examined by the Court. Of interest is the fact that *R v Porter* (1933) is still regarded as a significant statement of the law of insanity although Dixon's 'judgment' was only a direction to the jury in a trial in the original **jurisdiction** of the Court. In recent times the Court has examined the defence of insanity in *Falconer*, a case more concerned with the distinction between insanity, insane automatism and non-insane automatism. In *Falconer*, the Court confirmed that where the cause of the defendant's involuntary act was a mental disease, the defence of insane automatism applied and that insanity and insane automatism were governed by the same rules. The majority also held that a dissociative state brought on by a psychological blow (such as severe stress) could constitute non-insane automatism, but that the presumption of capacity could be displaced only by medical evidence as to the cause of the involuntary acts. The effect of the majority decision is to broaden the ambit of non-insane automatism in a cautious but compassionate way. The defence of diminished responsibility is still awaiting a comprehensive examination by the Court, notwithstanding the controversy associated with the defence in some states and territories.

The principles underlying the common law defence of intoxication were laid down in *R v O'Connor* (1980). In endorsing principle rather than policy, the Court rejected the **precedent** set by the **House of Lords** in *DPP v Majewski* (1976) and held that evidence of self-induced intoxication may be admitted to negate the element of voluntariness and intent in crimes of specific intent. Although the decision has been criticised as a 'drunk's charter', its continuing operation is narrow because of extensive statutory reformulation in most jurisdictions.

The old common law defences of necessity and duress are yet to be considered by the Court and there is considerable uncertainty as to their ambit. But for statutory offences apparently imposing **strict liability**, state Supreme Courts (especially in SA) have developed an intricate range of defences stemming ultimately from *Maher v Musson* (1934) (honest and reasonable ignorance) and from Dixon's reworking of it in *Proudman v Dayman* (1941) (honest and reasonable mistake of fact).

SANDRA EGGER

Criminal procedure. In *Hussien v Chong Fook Kam* (1969), Lord Devlin suggested that the investigation of crime begins with the awakening of suspicion and ends when the investigators have obtained prima facie proof. That process may include such familiar steps as entry, search and seizure, arrest, bail, pre-trial detention, identification of suspects and interrogation in custody. Frequently, these pre-trial procedures give rise to procedural issues at trial, though the focus is then on the laws of **evidence** and the inherent power of most courts to control their own process.

The **common law** accusatorial framework for investigation and prosecution of crime differs fundamentally from that of the civil law systems of continental Europe, where investigation is directly supervised by a judicial officer. The common law process is often described as a contest between the parties, conducted (with limited exceptions) in **open court** before an impartial tribunal of fact and law.

The High Court has affirmed the essential foundations of this accusatorial model. These include 'the elementary right of every accused person to a fair and impartial trial' (**Isaacs** in the *Irish Envoys Case* (1923); see also *Dietrich v The Queen* (1992)); the presumption of innocence and the requirement of proof beyond reasonable doubt (*Environment Protection Authority v Caltex Refining* (1993)); the privilege against self-incrimination (*Sorby v Commonwealth* (1983)); the right of an accused to know the particulars of the charge he or she must face (*John L v A-G (NSW)* (1987)); and the safeguard of **jury trial** for serious offences (*Brown v The Queen* (1986); *Cheatle v The Queen* (1993)). The Court has held that the right to a fair trial extends to the 'whole

course of the criminal process' (**Mason** in *Jago v District Court (NSW)* (1989)), and that its practical content must adapt flexibly to changing conditions such as the availability of appropriate recording technologies when police interrogate suspects in custody (*McKinney v The Queen* (1991)). In *Dietrich*, the Court held that the right to a fair trial required that an accused facing a serious criminal charge be represented in all but exceptional circumstances.

It is intrinsic to the accusatory structure of criminal procedure that the material placed before the court—the selection of charges, the choice of evidence and witnesses—is up to the parties (see *R v Apostilides* (1984); *Maxwell v The Queen* (1996)). Party control and the trial-centredness of common law procedure has meant that such control as judges exercise over pre-trial procedures tends to be limited, indirect and negative in effect. It is exercised through exclusionary rules of evidence and powers to control the conduct of the trial, including powers to warn a jury in respect of certain categories of evidence, to grant an adjournment, and to stay proceedings temporarily or (in exceptional circumstances) permanently (*R v Glennon* (1992); *Barton v The Queen* (1980); *Dietrich*). These powers are designed to guard against the admission of irrelevant or unreliable material and to ensure the fair treatment of accused persons. They are mostly powers to *exclude* evidence, to *temporarily suspend* or ultimately to *stop* the proceedings, rather than positively directing the process in the interests of fairness and justice.

Challenges to the exercise of such powers commonly provide the basis for appeals to the High Court. Appeal is by special **leave**, granted only where a question of law of general importance is involved. For this and other reasons (including **cost** and delay), appeals to the High Court do not afford a satisfactory remedy for miscarriages of justice in individual cases. This remains the primary responsibility of state **Supreme Courts**.

This distinctive system of criminal procedure, with its enduring tensions and controversies, has its roots in English constitutional arrangements, which historically vested civil authority in lay and decentralised institutions such as the jury, local justices of the peace and private prosecutors. Difficulties arise in modern societies where these institutions have been largely supplanted by bureaucratic state law enforcement agencies. For all the talk of the enhanced rights of criminal suspects in the modern criminal justice system, the most striking feature is perhaps the growing tension between the egalitarian premises of the common law and the reality of the substantial advantage in resources, power and authority enjoyed by modern law-enforcement agencies over the typically poor and ill-educated objects of their attention. Recent attempts by the High Court to redress this inequality—by using the limited means at the Court's disposal to extend judicial scrutiny to procedures controlled by the executive government, such as the provision of legal aid to accused persons and arrangements for recording the interrogation of suspects in custody—have in the eyes of some sorely tested these constitutional boundaries. **Brennan's** careful dissents in *McKinney* and *Dietrich* are instructive in highlighting the constitutional and practical constraints on the Court's capacity to achieve legal and policy objectives with which he was fully in sympathy.

The police forces established in the common law world during the nineteenth century, primarily to prevent crime and keep the peace by a visible uniformed street presence, came to occupy centre stage in the investigation and prosecution of crime not by constitutional design but by piecemeal evolution. According to Laurence Lustgarten, they came to exercise quite 'awesome' power, including the power 'alone to decide whether to investigate, how to conduct the investigation, whether to charge a suspect and what charges to lay'—all this within a common law framework which, consistently with the constitutional vision of AV Dicey, continued to treat them as simply 'citizens in uniform'. This has served to obscure the fact that modern methods of policing—with their near monopoly over access to criminal sanctions, their paramilitary organisational structures, the resources and technology they command and the authority and special legal powers they exercise—raise questions of regulation and accountability entirely different from those of the old local constabulary system.

These points are as relevant in the Australian as in the English context. The advent of independent prosecution agencies in both countries in the last fifteen years has made little difference: unlike the US District Attorney system, these new agencies lack any independent investigative arm of their own, and exercise no effective supervision over police investigations.

The resultant legal controversies have engaged the High Court's attention throughout its history, and are something of a litmus test of its impact in the field of criminal procedure. Judicial disquiet in the late nineteenth and early twentieth centuries about the new roles, powers and methods of police investigators gave way to acceptance and accommodation in the formative years of the Court. Initially, in both Australia and England, judges had expressed concern at the recourse to increasingly inquisitorial methods such as custodial investigation and interrogation. That a police officer might cross-examine a suspect in a police station and record the fruits of the investigation for use as evidence against the person—a power denied to judges and magistrates in open court—was seen by some as profoundly un-English (*R v Rogerson* (1870); *Ah Hoy v Hough* (1912)). Some judges expressed particular scepticism when the evidence thus obtained was later repudiated by the suspects at trial (*R v Thompson* (1893)).

However, in *Hough v Ah Sam* (1912), the High Court confirmed the legality of such practices. In reality, their developing systematisation, in the hands of increasingly bureaucratically organised police investigators, was something that the common law had simply not contemplated. The common law regulation of such practices was limited to the requirement that any statement adduced in evidence against its maker be shown to have been made voluntarily, in the sense that it was not induced by threat or promise by a person in authority. This was the position affirmed in *Hough v Ah Sam*, and also in the English courts (*Ibrahim v The King* (1914); *R v Voisin* (1918)).

This principle of voluntariness became the touchstone for testing the legal admissibility of confessional evidence throughout the twentieth century, until the introduction of uniform *Evidence Acts* in the 1990s. In his influential formulation of the principle in *McDermott v The King* (1948),

Dixon doubted whether Australian courts had given it 'a sufficiently wide operation'—perhaps highlighting the gap separating the Court's occasional affirmations of high legal principle from routine police practices, as well as from the more accommodating attitudes of many lower courts.

As a judicial means of regulating police conduct, the voluntariness rule was a blunt, reactive, and vague instrument, remote from its target and capable only of intermittent deployment. Given the complexities of modern police work, it was clearly inadequate. Where police had available to them myriad tactics for sanctioning the non-cooperation of suspects and ordinary citizens, how could it confidently be said that cooperation was voluntary in any meaningful sense?

This regulatory deficit with respect to emerging police methods and powers was made apparent when in 1912—just as the High Court affirmed the legitimacy of police questioning in *Hough v Ah Sam*—the judges of the King's Bench Division in Britain, in response to a request from the Home Secretary, produced a set of rules intended to give guidance to police in the exercise of their powers and duties. The 'Judges' Rules', as they came to be known, were adopted as the basis for administrative standing orders in Australian police forces as well (sometimes under other names, such as Commissioner's Instructions). Revised and expanded over the century, they were superseded by legislation in England in 1986. They never carried the force of law in Britain or Australia, though frequently adverted to in Australian courts. Their status and purpose was made clear in the English case of *R v Voisin*: 'they are administrative directions the observance of which the police authorities should enforce upon their subordinates as tending to the fair administration of justice.' The clear implication was that the task of regulating police powers was first and foremost the responsibility of police forces themselves, and that the courts could and would assume only a secondary role.

These administrative instruments were closely linked to the High Court's steady development of discretionary rules for the exclusion of evidence (especially evidence of admissions) obtained by what were seen as improper means, or which it would otherwise be unfair to admit against an accused (see *Cornelius v The King* (1936); *McDermott*; *R v Lee* (1950); *R v Ireland* (1970); *Bunning v Cross* (1978); *Cleland v The Queen* (1982)). These discretionary rules served to supplement the traditional requirement of voluntariness. Their hallmark, however, was their complete lack of specificity as to which norms and standards of police conduct would be treated by the courts as imperative, so as to render inadmissible evidence obtained in their breach. It was the trial judge's responsibility to decide admissibility, if necessary by conducting a *voir dire* (a preliminary investigation of admissibility) in the absence of the jury (see *Cornelius*; *Basto v The Queen* (1954); *MacPherson v The Queen* (1981)). Enormous discretion was thus entrusted to trial judges to admit evidence, however obtained, and whether in contravention of police standing orders or even of the common law itself.

The consequence was that general judicial affirmations of abstract principle—of the importance of fairness and warnings against the dangers of unchecked police power—were repeatedly accompanied by reasons why, in the instant case, it would not be unfair to admit the illegally or improperly obtained evidence. In practice, the exceptions might seem to have swallowed the rule, except that they could always be cast in terms of the peculiar circumstances of the individual case. The high-sounding principles were allowed to stand, attracting ritual judicial obeisance, while frequently rendered nugatory in their application to specific instances of police misconduct.

The High Court was not free from this tendency. In the case of Jean Lee, the last woman to be hanged in Australia (see *R v Lee*), the Court spelled out the principle that thereafter governed the application of the discretionary exclusion rules: judgments of impropriety or unfairness 'must depend upon the circumstances of each particular case, and no attempt should be made to define and thereby to limit the extent or the application of these conceptions.' Although repeating time-honoured sentiments as to the 'vital importance that detectives should be scrupulously careful and fair', the Court restored the murder conviction and death sentence of Lee and her accomplices, concluding that there was no 'serious breach' of the Commissioner's Standing Orders. The Court reasoned that although the accused had not been cautioned in the police station and certain other rules had not been complied with, these were not material infringements, since at the material time the suspects were probably not 'regarded by the detectives as being in custody: they had not been arrested or charged: the matter was still in the stage of police inquiry and investigation'. It was strange as well as erroneous for the Court to base its view of the suspects' legal status at the relevant time on speculations about the thought processes of the detectives accused of impropriety, rather than on the available evidence of the objective legal position—especially given the Court's earlier description of how the accused 'were *taken* to Police Headquarters ... and separately questioned' for about three hours in the middle of the night (emphasis added).

The gulf opened up between the common law and routine police practice has no clearer illustration than in this question of the police detention of suspects for purposes of interrogation and other investigative procedures. The common law position was straightforward. Police officers were not permitted to detain a suspect solely for the purposes of questioning or the conduct of other inquiries (*Clarke v Bailey* (1933); *Bales v Parmeter* (1935)). The requirement for an arrested person to be taken before a justice without unreasonable delay reflected the common law solicitude for the liberty of the subject, 'the most elementary and important of all common law rights' (**Fullagar** in *Trobridge v Hardy* (1955)), as well as the related conception of the constable as an adjunct to the judicial process, and especially to the role of justices in the initiation of criminal proceedings. As Mason and Brennan later observed, affirming the common law rule in *Williams v The Queen* (1986), 'the jealousy with which the common law protects the liberty of the subject does nothing to assist the police in the investigation of criminal offences.' In other words, the formal position was that the common law made no concession to the entrenched routines of police investigation.

Yet, despite occasional expressions of appellate judicial concern (see, for example, *Bales v Parmeter*), illegal and improper police practice appeared to be indulged by the courts, as in *Lee*,

for reasons of expedience. The tension between the common law and police practice was reconciled by effectively neutralising the law rather than outlawing the practice.

As time went on, this tension became more obvious. In *Williams* and in *Foster v The Queen* (1993), for example, the police conduct, although in blatant defiance of the law of arrest, had apparently been regarded by the police themselves as routine and acceptable practice. The Court in *Foster* condemned the police conduct and overturned the conviction. Perhaps more surprising was that it had attracted no adverse comment at the trial, nor in the NSW Court of Criminal Appeal. The price of judicial indulgence and political expedience was substantially to leave to police themselves the task of regulating those of their powers that touched the most cherished of common law rights—the individual right to freedom from arbitrary detention.

By the 1980s, some Justices (for example, **Murphy** and **Deane** in *Cleland*) were manifesting increasing frustration at the unchecked abuse of police powers, and a corresponding willingness to strengthen the exclusionary rules. When the *Williams* case was appealed in 1986, some expected that the Court would follow English decisions such as *Dallison v Caffery* (1964) by seeking to adjust the common law to conform to police practice, rather than *vice versa*. However, the Court affirmed the old common law position—though significantly without clarifying the law governing the discretionary exclusion of evidence obtained by illegal detention and questioning.

Williams was an important moment in the Court's recent more activist phase in relation to criminal procedure, during which it entertained an increasing number of such appeals—no doubt fuelled by government inquiries and public debates concerning police misconduct and the reform of pre-trial investigative procedures. In a series of cases, including *Carr v The Queen* (1988), *Duke v The Queen* (1989), *McKinney* and *Foster*, Justices began to grapple seriously with issues of the detention and questioning of suspects in police custody, and allegations of police fabrication of confessional evidence. They demonstrated a keen understanding of the realities of police work and their implications for the rights of suspects, and a determination to utilise the limited means at their disposal to uphold those rights against the claims of executive expedience. In *McKinney*, the Court drew attention to how the power imbalance between police and suspect in the closed world of the police station militated against a fair trial in cases where the evidence against the accused comprised only the uncorroborated fruits of police questioning.

The Court's decisions during this period added to the pressure on Australian governments to regulate police custodial procedures, to give statutory expression to various rights of suspects, and to require the electronic recording of police interrogations—a pressure that in the 1990s led to reforms in a number of Australian jurisdictions.

Yet, just at the time when Australian governments and courts appear belatedly to be coming to grips with the common law's inadequate ability to regulate the institutions of modern criminal justice, developments in law enforcement herald an era of fresh challenges for the Court. We are witnessing a growing reliance on technology (particularly computers, electronic surveillance and new forensic technologies such as DNA testing) and more proactive law enforcement in areas such as drug trafficking and white-collar and organised crime. New law enforcement agencies have been established: the National Crime Authority, the Criminal Justice Commission in Queensland and the Independent Commission Against Corruption in NSW, for example. There has been a proliferation of special legislative regimes covering technologies such as listening devices and the interception of communications. We are seeing the spread of novel techniques of investigation and evidence-gathering such as integrity testing, undercover policing, and controlled 'sting' operations.

Many of these developments await consideration by the High Court, though some have already been addressed. *Ridgeway v The Queen* (1995) involved a 'controlled importation' of drugs illegally conducted by authorities in order to apprehend the recipient of the drugs in Australia. The two cases heard and decided together in *R v Swaffield* (1998) involved covertly recorded confessional evidence obtained, it was argued, in contravention of the suspects' right to silence: in one case by a police officer working undercover and in the other by a civilian recruited as an agent of the police.

The approach in these cases suggests the Court will continue its more robust attitude to the scrutiny of executive power in law enforcement and the defence of traditional rights and liberties, although the responsibility for effective accountability in the administration of criminal justice will rest primarily on the governments and parliaments of Australia.

RUSSELL HOGG

Further Reading

David Dixon, *Law in Policing: Legal Regulation and Police Practices* (1997), ch 5

Laurence Lustgarten, *The Governance of Police* (1986)

Criminology. Classical notions of criminal responsibility require courts to regard all accused persons as rational and reasonable individuals who have acted voluntarily. In this context, the accused is viewed as an autonomous and free-willing individual, responsible for his or her actions and therefore liable to just punishment. Conventional theorising about the causes of crime is compatible with this model of **judicial reasoning** to the extent that it focuses on the behaviour and characteristics of the individual offender. Each accused is assumed to act in a self-determined rather than a socially constructed environment, and prevailing judicial notions of criminal justice are conceptually committed to confronting and resolving individual criminal responsibility. Therefore, judicial interpretations of crime and its causes are inextricably centred on 'model' individuals and their behaviour—failing to recognise, or recognising only peripherally, the explanations that emphasise social determinism and the consequences of legal intervention.

The High Court has reaffirmed this view of crime and the individual by its insistence on an inquiry into the mental state of the accused (see *Parker v The Queen* (1963)) and on voluntary conduct being an essential requirement of criminal responsibility (see *R v Falconer* (1990); **Criminal law**). It is rare, however, to see the Court expressly endorse any theory about crime and its causes. Rather, its judgments are more likely to contain statements in favour of a particular rationale for punishment or a principle of sentencing. These, in turn, are likely to be based on assumptions about crime and responsibility, including the significance of social determinism on the accused's conduct and mental state.

The High Court has been resolute in maintaining its **common law** approach to problem solving. This approach, involving a heavy reliance on judicial **precedent** coupled with deductive and inductive reasoning, creates a major obstacle to the Court's adoption of criminological theory and research. This seems strange, given that criminology as a discipline seeks to inform the courts, among others, about criminal behaviour and community attitudes to such behaviour, and attempts to provide constructive ways of dealing with the behaviour. Very occasionally, individual Justices may espouse a criminological finding, but this is far from saying that the Court as a whole is open to these 'non-legal' sources of ideas and information.

A good starting point is the Court's treatment of the contention by **Aboriginal peoples** that their customary criminal laws operate alongside the common law. **Mason** emphatically rejected this contention in *Walker v NSW* (1994) with the comment that 'English criminal law did not, and Australian criminal law does not, accommodate an alternative body of law operating alongside it'. Mason would certainly have known of criminological studies showing that some indigenous Australian communities continue to maintain their customary criminal laws to this day. However, adherence to the Court's common law approach made him deliver the *coup de grâce* by saying that 'even if it be assumed that the customary law of Aboriginal people survived British settlement, it was extinguished by the passage of criminal statutes of general application'.

The Court has carried this negative stance towards indigenous Australian customary law into its rulings on substantive criminal law. For instance, in *Walden v Hensler* (1987), the Court rejected the defendant's argument that he believed, in accordance with Aboriginal custom, that he was entitled to take bush turkeys and that he was committing no offence in doing so. The Court affirmed that there is a defence of an honest claim of right under the law governing **property** offences; however, the 'right' had to be a right which was recognised by Australian law and not one which owes its existence to some non-legal regimen such as the defendant's customary law. This reveals not only the limitations imposed by common law principles on the Court's frame of reference, but also suggests that distortions may accompany a consideration of individualised responsibility divorced from notions of collective responsibility.

The strongest inroad made by criminology into the Court's deliberations has been in the realm of **criminal law defences**. Yet a survey of the Court's decisions reveals that it has been slow to embrace criminological theories and research into its deliberations. Thus far, the Court's recognition of the 'battered woman syndrome' is arguably the high point. For many years, the legal approach to abused partners was that they should rely on the police and legal injunctions ordering the battering partner to stay away; that they could walk out of the relationship, and so on. Criminological research has shown these expectations to be unrealistic, and that many **women** who have experienced long-term physical and emotional abuse from their domestic partners suffer from battered woman syndrome. The relationship between the accused person and the victim is evidence of a conflict-theory explanation of crime, in which power, dominance and submission are socially constructed within a private environment where criminal justice has traditionally been reluctant to intervene and provide protection (see also **Rights, critique of**). The social determinants of conflict within these relationships need to be recognised if defences such as provocation and self-defence are to have reality for the victim. Appreciation of the unique dangers inherent in domestic relationships and settings is consistent with the trend of opportunity theory within criminology. Interestingly, it was the **state Supreme Courts**, not the High Court, which first recognised the syndrome as having a significant role in jury deliberations on the defences of provocation and self-defence. While the High Court had several opportunities to embrace criminological research on the syndrome, it was not until *Osland v The Queen* (1998) that it finally, if somewhat ambiguously, did so.

A recognition of battered woman syndrome by the whole Court is highly unusual. Rather, the trend is for only one or two individual judges, if any, to go out of their way to invoke criminological research in their judgments. For instance, in *Masciantonio v The Queen* (1995), the Court was asked to reconsider the distinction in the law of provocation between those personal characteristics of the accused that were relevant to determining the gravity of the provocation and those that were relevant to determining the issue of self-control. Only **McHugh** was prepared to acknowledge that the distinction is inconsistent with criminological studies showing that the defendant's personality must be taken as a whole, and cannot be dissected into the way a person perceives some provocative conduct on the one hand, and the way that person would respond emotionally to such a perception on the other. Consequently, McHugh delivered a dissenting judgment in which he held that the law should take into account a defendant's ethnic or cultural characteristics in both respects—in determining not only the gravity of the provocation, but also the issue of lost self-control (see **Stereotypes**).

Another example of a degree of influence exerted by criminological research is *Green v The Queen* (1997). The main issue before the Court was the significance to be given to the 'homosexual advance' defence claimed by the defendant (see **Sexual preference**). Only **Kirby** reviewed the criminological writings on the subject in great detail. That perspective contributed materially to his decision that the ordinary Australian male was not so homophobic as to form a murderous intent in response to a non-violent sexual advance by a homosexual person. This led him to reaffirm the defendant's conviction for murder. In contrast, in attaching little or no significance to the criminological writings on the homosexual advance defence, the majority judges quashed the conviction.

In some respects, it is not the outcome of the case but rather the contested consideration of social determinants on the mind and conduct of the accused that engages criminological theory. The High Court's recognition that determinism is a factor in assessing criminal responsibility shows the Court moving away from a purely individualist or behaviourist position in explaining and founding criminal responsibility. Furthermore, placing the formulation of criminal intent (or its explanation) in the context of community sentiment has resonance beyond the conflict between subjective and objective determinants of criminal responsibility. In *Green*, the Court expressed concern over both the behavioural *and* the social influences that contribute to such responsibility.

A final example is the High Court's recent rulings on the criminal law doctrine of complicity—particularly, the extent to which common purpose or joint enterprise might rest on the implicit agreements between participants in a crime. Although in an unarticulated way, the Court in *McAuliffe v The Queen* (1995) was evidently influenced by the criminological theory of differential association, which stipulates that a person's criminality can only be contextualised through the manner in which he or she chooses to relate to the other deviants.

The same reticence in the Court's approach to criminological theory and research is to be found in its sentencing decisions. To be fair, there have been few occasions when the Court has been asked to alter a sentence on account of some criminological research having a bearing on the sentencing decision. However, this may be explained by the Court's practice of rarely granting special leave applications in relation to sentencing appeals, preferring instead to leave the field to the Courts of Criminal Appeal of the states and territories. This practice is questionable, especially in cases where the lower appellate courts have failed to consider relevant criminological research affecting the sentencing decision. **Murphy** made the same point in *Veen v The Queen* (1979) when he urged his fellow judges 'to break [with] the "hands-off" sentencing tradition which has so far been followed' and argued that the Court should 'develop principles and give guidance to other courts in the same way as it does in other branches of the law'.

In the few cases where the Court has granted **leave to appeal** against a sentence, reliance on such research is sparse. Murphy's judgment in *Neal v The Queen* (1982) is a notable and rare exception, and accords with his view that the Court should be more actively involved in sentencing matters. The applicant was an indigenous Australian who was convicted by a magistrate of assaulting the complainant, the Caucasian manager of the local store. In allowing the applicant's appeal, Murphy referred in detail to criminological studies on the appalling social conditions in Aboriginal reserves such as the one in which the applicant lived, and the strained **race** relations between Aborigines and white people. Murphy regarded these as significant mitigating factors and held that the magistrate and the Queensland Court of Criminal Appeal had failed to take them into account when sentencing the applicant.

The Court has also resisted ranking the aims of sentencing in some order of priority, contrary to criminological theory and research. A comment in *Veen v The Queen (No 2)* (1988) illustrates this judicial eclecticism:

The purposes of criminal punishment are various: protection of society, deterrence of the offender and of others who might be tempted to offend, retribution and reform. The purposes overlap and none of them can be considered in isolation from the others when determining what is an appropriate sentence in a particular case.

Numerous criminological studies have shown that this lack of a coherent structure of sentencing aims produces disparate and consequently unjust sentences.

The Court's position on the connection between theories of sentencing, and penalty and punishment, has been simplistic and often dichotomous. For instance, the limited mention in the joint judgment in *Veen (No 2)* of the prevailing debate between just deserts and protective (reform) motivations for sentence tended to suggest that punishments that have a preventive dimension might not be permissible. No doubt the ultimate justification for capital punishment (when it existed in Australian jurisdictions) was preventive as far as the individual offender was concerned. The court may not have supported such forms of punishment if community protection inherent in the penalty (or prevention) were to challenge proportionality.

Overall, the record of the High Court has been poor in embracing criminological research or permitting criminological theory to influence its reasoning process. While it is understandable that the Court would feel constrained by the common law tradition (including the contradictions inherent in classical notions of criminal responsibility), greater openness to the ideas and findings of social research would do much to improve the quality of Australian criminal justice. Such research would challenge judges to re-evaluate their preconceived notions about criminal behaviour, criminal responsibility and the sentencing of offenders. It would also educate them about the factual dimensions of the issues at stake, and the different views held by others in relation to those issues, and would expand the range of possible solutions. It is hoped that the few instances where the High Court has been prepared to be influenced by the discipline of criminology will multiply and become, not just the interest of a few individual judges, but of the entire Court. This is particularly relevant in Australia, where a distinctive criminology, with its feet firmly grounded in applied critical social policy, flourishes.

MARK FINDLAY
STANLEY YEO

Further Reading
John Braithwaite, *Crime, Shame and Reintegration* (1990)
Russell Hogg and David Brown, *Rethinking Law and Order* (1998)
Rob White and Fiona Haines, *Crime and Criminology: An Introduction* (1999)

Criticism of the Court. Any institution called upon to decide major issues of **Commonwealth–state relations**, questions of the extent of governmental power, disputes between government and the citizen, and even disputes between citizens, is bound to attract criticism from those who disagree with its decisions, not least frustrated politicians—particularly when the answers must often depend on **value** judgments, and are effectively beyond appeal. Adherence to strict **legalism** may disguise the fact that judges are making choices; it can never entirely conceal it (see **Law-making role**).

The High Court, at the apex of Australia's judicial **hierarchy**, has always been subject to critical scrutiny. Indeed, this is an important element in its **accountability**. But in recent times, as other public institutions have also come under increasing attack, the tenor of criticism has been far more frank, and often much less respectful—to an extent, some think, that poses a threat to the authority and the standing of the Court. In controversial cases such as *Mabo* (1992) or *Wik* (1996), attacks have come from both disappointed politicians and interested parties. Moreover, the Court can no longer rely on traditional defenders such as the **Attorney-General** to answer such criticisms. The Court has, to a degree, responded to this change by a greater willingness to discuss its work publicly, and even to address some of the criticisms; but there are obvious limits to what it can do or say.

Particular Justices who have come under strong criticism over the years include **Piddington**, **Evatt** and **McTiernan** (over their **appointments**), **Barwick** (over interventions characterised as political), **Murphy** (over his appointment and style), **Brennan, Deane** and **Gaudron** (over their judgments and writing styles in *Mabo*) and **Callinan** (over his appointment and career at the Bar). The Court's judgments in the *Engineers Case* (1920), the *Bank Nationalisation Case* (1948), the *Communist Party Case* (1951), cases in the 1970s on **taxation law**, cases in the 1980s on the **external affairs** power (such as *Koowarta's Case* (1982) and the *Tasmanian Dam Case* (1983)), and, generally, cases that pit assertions of Commonwealth power against claims to states' rights, have excited criticism of the Court or of particular Justices.

Past criticism was probably more muted because the Court itself, in actions for **contempt** of court, placed clear limits on the tenor of criticism allowed. In *R v Dunbabin; Ex parte Williams* (1935), for example, **Rich** categorised as contempt not only 'any matter … which has a tendency to deflect the Court from a strict and unhesitating application of the letter of the law, or, in questions of fact, from determining them exclusively by reference to the evidence'. Contempt could also arise, he said, from publications which tended

> to detract from the authority and influence of judicial determinations, publications calculated to impair the confidence of the people in the Court's judgments because the matter published aims at lowering the authority of the Court as a whole or that of its Judges and excites misgivings as to the integrity, propriety and impartiality brought to the exercise of the judicial office.

The jurisdiction to punish for contempt, he added, was not given to protect the judges personally 'from imputations to which they might be exposed as individuals', but 'in order that the authority of the law as administered in the Courts may be established and maintained'.

In fact, the Court has generally had a more robust attitude to reasoned criticism than this case would suggest—at least so long as the criticism was expressed in reasonably rational terms and not accompanied by abuse, or generalised accusations of partiality or bias, or suggestions that the courts had bowed to external threats (compare *A-G (NSW) v Mundey* (1972) and *Gallagher v Durack* (1983)). In more recent times, the Court's acceptance of a constitutional commitment to freedom of **political communication** (see *Free*

Speech Cases (1992)) has led to a clear extension of the ambit of criticism it will allow.

Some would trace the modern increase in criticism to a generally declining respect for public institutions, and to public disapproval of a supposed trend towards judicial **activism**. It is, however, more complicated than that. The **Federal Court**, which now hears most first instance Commonwealth cases, was established only in 1976. Until then, the High Court did an enormous amount of first-instance work and appellate work in which appeals lay as of right. Although it had achieved some independence from the **Privy Council**, the continued existence of Privy Council appeals put considerable pressure on the Court for uniformity of approach with settled British law, even when it was not necessarily well adapted to Australian conditions.

Now the Court does very little first-instance work, except in constitutional cases, and all appeals are by special **leave**. Generally, the Court will not grant leave unless the issue involves a question of law of public importance, and even then only if the factual situation is suitable for the resolution of conflicting points of principle, interpretation or approach. The fence is high, and many fail to clear it. Yet the volume of the Court's **business** has not dropped off. The special leave system means that the Court is now called upon to resolve an important issue of principle in almost every case it determines.

This does not necessarily mean that the Court is always called upon to be 'adventurous', to perform acts of judicial legislation, to reverse centuries of **precedent** or to forge a new path in the law—generally the sort of thing most likely to attract criticism (even if inaction will often do the same, though from different quarters). But it does mean that the need and the opportunity for creativity are now far greater.

Moreover, there is now statutory encouragement for judges to take a purposive approach to **statutory interpretation**, rather than interpreting a law simply by consulting a dictionary. Many Acts also require the Court to determine disputes in accordance with vague and undefined phrases such as 'the best interests of the **child**' or 'the public interest', or use key words such as '**unconscionable**', or 'misleading or deceptive'. Similarly, in many areas of **administrative law**, wide discretions are given to decision-makers, often with little legislative guidance on how such discretions are to be exercised. In all of these cases, Parliament has invited the judiciary to flesh out the law but has given little guidance. If this produces results with which politicians disagree, it is not always the judges' fault.

In these and other cases, the Justices have increasingly acknowledged that they must make conscious policy choices. They have to take into account matters such as the nature of the **economy**, general commercial expectations, ideas about the status of families, the balance of rights, notions of **equity** and **fiduciary obligation** and community expectations. Many of them have observed that such considerations are difficult to receive as evidence (see **Fact finding**; **Judicial notice**), but nevertheless insist that the need to deal with them is endemic.

The past thirty years, moreover, have seen a marked development of Australia into a single economy, increasingly affected by the global economy. Some centrist decisions by the High Court may themselves have spurred this process along; but the shifts were inevitable and affect the way judges must approach cases, whether in **contract** or **tort law**, in equity or administrative law. There is more pressure now to adapt the law to the needs of modern commerce, and to recognise new types of relationships between citizens, and new forms of transactions between people who communicate with each other in ways the old law could never have contemplated, or have understandings or expectations of each other which previously did not exist.

There have also been fundamental changes in the legal relationship between the citizen and the state. Much of this relationship is not intrinsically political. It involves tax, or social security, or employment, or industrial or other obligations; and, typically, it involves legislation that entrusts high discretions to non-elected decision-makers and results in some structural imbalance of rights between decision-makers and citizens. It is noteworthy that some of the most significant judicial initiatives in this field have been taken by judges often accused of being conservative (for example, **Aickin** and **Dawson**).

Moreover, there have been marked developments in notions of human rights and community expectations of fairness. A number of international treaties are explicitly recognised in legislation. There is a host of rights-conferring statutes, not only in the field of **discrimination**, but also in **labour relations law**, health and safety law, privacy, and **corporations law**. The legislation is buttressed by executive action in fields such as legal aid, social security legislation and much welfare legislation. Judges often look to such developments in attempting to articulate community expectations. Moreover, the decisions of courts in other countries, while admittedly only persuasive, are now far more accessible by way of the Internet. And there is a greater general pressure for conformity, because the world is, in fact, a much closer place.

Some of the criticism of the High Court—particularly for its supposed undermining of parliamentary **sovereignty**—fails to recognise that Australia is a hybrid of different models of government. The **framers** of the Australian Constitution consciously decided to follow the Westminster model of **responsible government**, with an executive formed from within the legislature, and rejected more republican models. But they also consciously borrowed from republican models too. Unlike Britain, Australia has a written constitution. The Constitution establishes a mechanism of **separation of powers** that owes much to the US model, though necessarily adapted to our executive system. Parliamentary sovereignty cannot exist in Australia as it does in Britain. Parliament is constrained by the Constitution, which consciously (though not explicitly) gave powers of **judicial review** to the judiciary. Australia was able to develop a system of administrative and **constitutional law** much more quickly than Britain, and went further than the British courts have been prepared to go. The framers consciously decided not to have a **Bill of Rights**, confident to leave the protection of rights to a parliament which, if it usurped them, could be thrown out by the people; but another reason for that confidence was that there was a check and balance in an **independent** judiciary. Yet one might think, from some of the criticisms of the Court—drawn misleadingly from British textbooks—that it was never contemplated that judges would have any constitutional **role** beyond the mechanical application of statutes and precedents to instant sets of facts.

Of course, notions of checks and balances, and of separation of powers, do involve issues of the right combinations of adventurism and restraint, and of mutual respect among different arms of government, and a need for each arm of government to appreciate the limits of its role. A parliament acting within its areas of constitutional power is entitled to respond to circumstances as it sees fit, and it should not be for the courts to substitute their own view of correct policy or practice. Courts need to exercise particular care if the effect of a decision is to appropriate public resources but parliament has made no provision for it (see *Dietrich v The Queen* (1992)). Moreover, if the executive is given a discretion, and it is exercised within its proper jurisdiction, that discretion includes the right to make the wrong decision.

Nevertheless, there are gaps. If parliament is inactive in adapting the law to changing circumstances, the courts are likely to shift—often not boldly, but incrementally. Sometimes parliament acquiesces, whether passively by failing to override the change, or actively, by adopting legislation that embraces change already introduced by the judiciary. On other occasions, parliament may override particular judgments, as in **family law** and **immigration law.**

In short, the resort by judges to **policy considerations**, and sometimes to their own views of what seems right and just, is not merely a matter of personal impulse. It is part of a system and process that is necessary in the modern state if there are to be sound, just and reasonably certain relationships among individuals, or between individuals and the state.

Over the years, the Justices have responded to such demands in different ways. They now acknowledge, to a greater extent, that policy does matter, and that questions of general attitude, approach and temperament—sometimes even broad political views—can be significant. Understandably, in the light of this, there are criticisms that the pool from which judges are selected is too narrow, so that, even if politicians were not consciously choosing judges for their imagined support of the government's own predilections, they are not sufficiently representative and sometimes not sufficiently diverse (see **Appointment of Justices; Cultural diversity**).

By and large, however, the style of writing judgments—even those laden with value and policy choices—still tends to operate by a form of legal syllogism that often disguises the choices. High in the list of criticisms of *Mabo*, for example, was the claim that some Justices (notably Deane and Gaudron) had used emotive language. Indeed they had; yet their process of formal reasoning was as replete with conventional syllogism as any other. There is, in fact, equally a problem of judges tending to seem too detached. The strict legalism preached by **Dixon** as the appropriate style of Australian judgment is well designed to give an impression of inevitability and infallibility about the result; and in an environment of deep respect for (and little understanding of) the law, this may be effective. But more people now see through the veils. While most judges would appreciate a better-informed or more respectful debate, most recognise that they cannot expect to be immune from strong criticism, particularly when it comes to their policy choices. Those policy choices have to operate and be justifiable in a free market of ideas, and acquire no particular cachet simply because they have been adopted on the Bench.

JACK WATERFORD

Further Reading
Michael Coper, 'The High Court and Its Critics' (1998) 20 *Adel L Rev* 11

Cross-vesting. The Australian cross-vesting scheme had its genesis in an initiative of the Commonwealth and state **Attorneys-General** to address the need for jurisdictional reforms of the courts of Australia, identified at the 1985 Constitutional Convention in Brisbane. The Attorneys-General mandated the Special Committee of **Solicitors-General** to devise means to eliminate the 'arid jurisdictional disputes' that had become apparent with the establishment of the Family Court and the Federal Court. Unsatisfactory High Court decisions had highlighted the incapacity of the Family Court to resolve all issues in family court disputes involving ex-nuptial **children** and **property** matters, and the *Trade Practices Act* 1974 (Cth) was often found to require separate proceedings in related matters in both state and federal courts.

The Solicitors-General recommended and drafted a cooperative solution, enacted by each of the parliaments of the Commonwealth and states and the **territories**, in the scheme constituted by the *Jurisdiction of Courts (Cross-Vesting) Acts* 1987.

The scheme was directed to achieve two aims. The first was to ensure that jurisdictional disputes would be eliminated from all Australian courts and that entire disputes could be resolved in one court, to avoid a multiplicity of proceedings in matters over which more than one court had jurisdiction. This was achieved by each state and territory vesting the entire jurisdiction of its own Supreme Court in the Supreme Court in each of the other states and territories, and in the Federal Court and the Family Court. A complementary Commonwealth law vested most of the federal jurisdiction of one federal court in the other federal court, and the jurisdiction of both of them in each of the Supreme Courts of the states and territories.

The second aim was to ensure that matters would be heard and entirely disposed of in the most appropriate court. This was achieved by enabling any court, upon the application of a party or on its own motion, to transfer a matter commenced in it to a more appropriate court for hearing and determination. Procedural delays were prevented by eliminating appeals from orders of transfer, and by providing for any steps taken in the transferor court to remain effective on the continuance of the hearing in the transferee court. Appropriate provision was made on choice of law issues (see **Conflict of laws**).

The scheme came to be accepted as a striking example of the effective workings of cooperative **federalism**, whereby each part of the federation had joined to eliminate the unsatisfactory consequences of the establishment of the federal courts.

The judges of Australia gradually overcame their initial anxieties and cooperatively supervised the effective operation of the scheme. For 12 years, jurisdictional disputes were eliminated from litigation throughout the ten **superior courts** in nine legal jurisdictions (the two federal courts and the Supreme Courts of each state and territory).

When they created the scheme, the Solicitors-General appreciated that there was a residual constitutional risk that, even with the specific statutory consent and authority of the Commonwealth law, the High Court might not recognise the constitutional capacity of state courts to vest state jurisdictional power directly in federal courts. However, given that the Constitution already provided for the complete admixture of state and federal jurisdictions in state courts, and that issues of jurisdictional competence had emerged as a practical difficulty only on the creation of the federal courts, it might fairly have been suggested that authority for a similar joinder of state and federal jurisdiction in the federal courts might be implied in the Constitution. In *Gould v Brown* (1998), the High Court held the scheme valid by a statutory majority of 3:3 (see **Tied vote**). But in 1999, a confident 6:1 majority held that Chapter III of the Constitution implicitly prohibited the vesting of state **judicial power** in federal courts, in a way that could not be overcome by consent in a Commonwealth Act (*Re Wakim* (1999)).

The vesting of the entire jurisdiction of the courts of the states and territories in each of the other state and territory courts remains effective, as does the complete vesting of federal jurisdiction in the state and territory courts. It is the jurisdiction of the federal courts that is affected, to the extent that the non-federal jurisdiction may be exercised only within the more limited doctrines of 'accrued' and 'associated' jurisdiction, as determined controversy by controversy (see **Federal Court of Australia**). The integrity of the entire scheme was fractured.

As the High Court has confirmed that state judicial power may constitutionally be invoked on a case-by-case basis by federal courts without any statutory conferral of jurisdiction by the states, it is surprising that it found it constitutionally impermissible for that same state judicial power to be entirely vested in the federal courts by cooperative Commonwealth and state laws. Also, given that the rejected effect of the scheme was limited to the exercise of the judicial power of the states, the Court could usefully have found that there was sufficient constitutional underpinning in the consent by the Commonwealth Parliament to the vesting of such power in federal courts. The dissenting opinion of **Kirby** contains a persuasive argument that it was unnecessary for the majority to derive from Chapter III an implied requirement that created, rather than remedied, a constitutional mischief. The decision also marks a departure from the Court's earlier more robust view of the permissibility of cooperate efforts to avoid constitutional gaps (*R v Duncan; Ex parte Australian Iron & Steel* (1983)).

Cross-vesting was also adapted to underpin the Corporations Law, as part of the cooperative scheme for the regulation of corporations enacted to overcome the adverse effects of the High Court's 6:1 decision in the *Incorporation Case* (1990). *Re Wakim* also attacked the constitutional underpinnings of the Corporations Law and the related capacity for the Federal Court to exercise national jurisdiction in matters pertaining to corporations. Although the *Incorporation Case* may possibly be reversed upon reconsideration by the Court, for some time it is likely that the integrity of the cross-vesting scheme will be restored, if at all, only by constitutional **amendment**.

GAVAN GRIFFITH

Further Reading

Garrie Moloney, 'Cross-vesting of Jurisdiction: Nationalism Versus Robust Individualism' (1994) 3 *Journal of Judicial Administration* 229

Dennis Rose, 'The Bizarre Destruction of Cross-Vesting' in Adrienne Stone and George Williams (eds), *The High Court at the Crossroads* (2000) 186

Cultural diversity. Decisions of the High Court have had a considerable impact on cultural diversity in Australia, particularly in the areas of **race**, ethnic origin and religion. The extent of cultural diversity reflected in the membership of the Court itself is also an issue.

In *Mabo* (1992), the Court made one of the most radical pronouncements of cultural diversity in Australian law, holding that Australia's **Aboriginal peoples** possess a right to land called **native title**. Native title has its origin in the traditional laws and customs observed by the indigenous inhabitants, and can coexist with statutory land grants under the Crown. The decision has provided new ways for indigenous Australians to protect their traditional connections to the land. Parliament responded to *Mabo* by enacting the *Native Title Act* 1993 (Cth), which established a scheme for claiming native title to land, but leaves most of the details of the nature, proof and extinguishment of native title to the **common law**, and thus ultimately to the High Court. Since *Mabo*, there have been a number of significant decisions in relation to the nature of native title and its relationship with other land grants. In particular, *Wik* (1996) articulated the important principle of coexistence of native title with non-exclusive statutory grants to land such as pastoral leases. This decision has ensured that a diversity of land rights will continue to exist over vast areas of Australia into the future.

Under the races power, the Commonwealth Parliament can pass laws with respect to 'the people of any race for whom it is deemed necessary to make special laws'. This is an unusual power in a modern Constitution that potentially has great implications for cultural diversity. Though its original purpose was to allow **discrimination** against people from the South Pacific, Asia and Africa, it was never used for this purpose. After its amendment by referendum in 1967 to bring Aborigines and Torres Strait Islanders within its ambit, the Commonwealth Parliament has invoked the power on a number of occasions. In the *Hindmarsh Island Bridge Case* (1998), the Court was divided on the proper interpretation of the power, with two Justices prepared to read it narrowly so that effectively it could be used only to *benefit* people identified on the basis of race, and two Justices reading it more broadly. It remains for a future High Court to determine the ambit of the power.

The Court has had an influence on the way governments have managed migration to Australia, especially from poor, undeveloped and non-English speaking countries. It has done so through determining the constitutionality of legislation embodying restrictive immigration policies and the legality of administrative practices under that legislation. Decisions on who is an immigrant and whether tests of eligibility for entry into Australia have been fairly administered have brought the Court into direct conflict with government policies on occasions, and have led to outspoken public **criticism** of the Court's **role**. More recently, the High Court has upheld several controversial laws under the **immigration power**—including, in *Cunliffe v Commonwealth* (1994), a law restricting access to the advice or assistance that can be given to people entering Australia without a visa, and in *Abebe v Commonwealth* (1999), a law restricting **judicial review** of the decisions of the Refugee Review Tribunal by the **Federal Court**. The ominous implications of the *Abebe* decision for the workload of the High Court, whose own jurisdiction is guaranteed by section 75(v) of the Constitution, are still being worked out (see *Re Minister for Immigration; Ex parte Durairajasingham* (2000); *Herijanto v Refugee Review Tribunal* (2000); *Re Refugee Review Tribunal; Ex parte Aala* (2000)).

An important form of cultural expression is the practice of religion (see **Church and state**). In *Church of the New Faith v Commissioner of Pay-roll Tax (Vic)* (1983), the Court defined religion broadly, emphasising a universal spirituality over particular religious doctrine. **Murphy** went so far as to say that the very attempt to define religion posed a threat to religious freedom. However, in the *DOGS Case* (1981), the Court dismissed an argument that government funding of private religiously based schools amounted to the 'establishment' of religion in contravention of section 116 of the Constitution. Six Justices (with Murphy dissenting) defined establishment narrowly. The Court thus endorsed a role for the state in the promotion of religious education.

In several decisions in the area of **criminal law**, the Court has pronounced on the relevance of an accused person's cultural background to the objective 'ordinary person' test in the **criminal law defence** of provocation. A majority held in *Stingel v The Queen* (1990) that the only characteristic of an accused person relevant to the objective test is their age. Other characteristics such as ethnicity and gender are relevant only to determining the gravity of a particular provocative act to the accused person.

There have been some strong dissents from this position. In *Masciantonio v The Queen* (1995), **McHugh** asserted that construing the objective test so narrowly imposes a 'standard of control of a middle class Australian of Anglo-Saxon-Celtic heritage' on accused persons. Earlier, in *Moffa v The Queen* (1977), Murphy had held:

> the objective test is not suitable even for a superficially homogenous society, and the more heterogeneous our society becomes, the more inappropriate the test is. Behaviour is influenced by age, sex, ethnic origin, climatic and other living conditions, biorhythms, education, occupation, and above all, individual differences … The objective test has no place in a rational criminal jurisprudence.

Overall, the Court has been sensitive to the issue of cultural diversity in a number of areas, but has failed to give a clear pronouncement on the position of race in the Constitution, and its explanation of the role of culture in the defence of provocation is not completely convincing. The Court's decisions determine the attitude of the law to important issues of cultural diversity and affect the rights and freedoms of every Australian citizen. They therefore deserve close attention and constructive commentary and criticism.

The membership of the Court itself also deserves comment in this context. Of the 43 Justices appointed to the Court since 1903, all but one have been male, and all have had British or Irish origins (see **Background of Justices**). Most went to private schools, and were raised and practised law in NSW or Victoria. Nearly all were practising barristers. The membership of the Court has been remarkably homogeneous, and clearly not representative of the Australian community in terms of gender, religious tradition, socioeconomic background or ethnic identity (see also **National unity**).

Two proposals in particular have been mooted periodically as ways of diversifying the membership of the Court. The first is to replace the secretive executive **appointment** process with appointment by a judicial commission representative of the community. The second is to make appointments from a broader pool of lawyers that includes solicitors and academics as well as barristers. But whether there needs to be a greater cultural diversity (among other types of diversity) on the Bench is controversial, and depends on one's understanding of the process of **constitutional interpretation** and **decision-making**. Is legal interpretation immune from cultural considerations? Is a judgment simply the correct application of a consistent and logical method of interpretation to a set of facts? Or does a judgment necessarily reflect the cultural affiliations and personal prejudices of its author?

In 1987, Chief Justice **Gibbs** argued that 'There are some who assert that it is right to endeavour to ensure all sections of society … are fairly represented on the bench. However, judges should not seen to be representatives of particular groups; they are there to do justice to all manner of people'. In the same year, an Advisory Committee to the Constitutional Commission considered that there was no need to change the current system of appointment (*Report on the Australian Judicial System* (1987)). It is beyond doubt that Justices of the High Court do not 'represent' any sectional interests. That, however, is not necessarily inconsistent with an argument for greater cultural diversity on the Court, as that diversity could inform and enhance both the Court's understanding of cultural issues and their impact on legal issues, and the sense of ownership and participation by the Australian community in the nation's highest court.

ALEXANDER REILLY

D

Damages. Section 6 of the *Judiciary Amendment Act* 1976 (Cth) introduced a requirement that special **leave to appeal** be obtained from the High Court before an appeal might be brought from a judgment of a state court on a ground that related to the quantum of any damages in respect of death or personal injury. Before the amendment, an appeal had lain as of right once a monetary threshold, which had become very low with the passage of time, was passed. The Court had thus been dealing with many cases where the only issue was the adequacy or excessiveness of damages.

Barwick regarded such appeals, at least in personal injury cases, as a waste of the Court's valuable time (see **Tort law**), and before the amendment came into effect, he did what he could to discourage them. In several cases, of which *Planet Fisheries v La Rosa* (1968) is the most notorious, he, along with several of his colleagues, 'emphatically' rejected submissions that the Court should seek out in its decisions a norm or standard for the assessment of general damages and make comparisons between the award in the case before it and such standard. The refusal to articulate such a standard, together with his urging of 'judicial restraint' by appellate courts in dealing with findings of negligence or no-negligence by trial judges, was strongly castigated at the time by a judge of an intermediate appellate court, Frank Hutley. **Kirby**, when a member of the NSW Court of Appeal, lost few opportunities to criticise the doctrine (see, for example, *Moran v McMahon* (1985)). Many judges have called for a reconsideration of the issue by the High Court. **Mason** appeared to be sympathetic to the **criticism**, and was able to obtain a narrow majority in a case that opened the way for a comparison of **defamation** damages with the scale of values in personal injury cases (*Carson v John Fairfax & Sons* (1993)).

Carson contains a valuable discussion of the purposes of damages awards in defamation, not least in a **dissenting judgment** by **McHugh**, who generally seems to display a strong predilection towards accepting awards made by juries. Defamation law provided the battleground for the High Court in *Uren v John Fairfax & Sons* (1966) and *Australian Consolidated Press v Uren* (1966) to assert its independence of the **House of Lords** by refusing to follow *Rookes v Barnard* (1964) in restricting the type of case in which exemplary (or punitive) damages might be awarded. This challenge to the authority of English law in Australia was given the imprimatur of the **Privy Council**, which, on appeal from the latter

decision, held that where the law in Australia had been regarded as settled, it was open to the High Court to decide not to change it (*Australian Consolidated Press v Uren* (1967)).

The issue of whether exemplary damages could be awarded in a case where the defendant was compulsorily insured came before the High Court in *Lamb v Cotogno* (1987), where it held unanimously that the deterrent object of such an award is not confined to the defendant alone, but extends to like-minded people, and would not be defeated by the fact that the defendant would not pay the damages personally. Many legislatures have disagreed, denying courts the power to award exemplary damages in such cases (for example, *Motor Accidents Compensation Act* 1999 (NSW), section 144). In *Gray v Motor Accident Commission* (1998), Kirby and **Callinan** indicated that they would not be averse to a reconsideration of this issue, but the majority were of the opinion that any challenge would have to call in question the whole notion of awarding, in a civil action, damages that are designed in part to punish. A clear majority held that exemplary damages may not be awarded where the defendant has already suffered substantial punishment at the hands of the **criminal law** for substantially the same conduct. The Court refused to stray beyond the facts of the case before it and speculate on whether exemplary damages may be awarded where the criminal punishment is less than 'substantial'—or, indeed, where the defendant has been acquitted. Such restraint is to be contrasted with a wide-ranging judgment of the NZ Court of Appeal given shortly beforehand and subsequently upheld by the Privy Council (*Daniels v Thompson* (1998); affirmed *sub nom W v W* (1999)) .

Exemplary damages are an exception to the general rule that damages are compensatory. The High Court has on many occasions reiterated the fundamental principle that damages should as nearly as possible put the party who is injured in the position he or she would have been in if no wrong had been suffered. In **contract law**, this requires that damages be awarded to put the plaintiff in the position he or she would have been in if the contract had been performed. Consequently, the loss is different in **contracts and torts**. Contract law allows recovery of the expectation interest, whereas in tort, the diminution in value is usually the appropriate measure of damages.

Very early in its history, the Court recognised this distinction in *Holmes v Jones* (1907), which held that in the tort of deceit a plaintiff could recover damages only for actual loss (for example, if he was induced to buy property for more than it was worth), whereas even if there was no actual loss he might have received some damages for breach of warranty if suing in contract. In contract, the Court allowed the owner of a house not built in accordance with the specifications to recover the cost of putting the house right, even though the plaintiff would have suffered little loss if the house had been sold (*Bellgrove v Eldridge* (1954)). Similarly, under an exception to the general rule that damages for breach of contract do not ordinarily allow recovery of non-pecuniary loss, it allowed a plaintiff whose holiday cruise ended when the ship sank to recover damages for distress and disappointment (*Baltic Shipping v Dillon* (1993)). The Court also held that a plaintiff suing in contract who cannot prove that the contract would have been profitable is not confined to recovery of the uncertain expectation interest, but may recover damages for expenditure incurred in performance of the contract—that is, for the reliance interest (*McRae v Commonwealth Disposals Commission* (1951); *Commonwealth v Amann Aviation* (1991)). Earlier, the Court had stressed that mere difficulty in estimating the damages is not to stand in the way of an award: *Fink v Fink* (1946). It had also applied the fundamental compensatory principle in preference to rules of thumb in the tort of conversion in *Butler v Egg and Egg Pulp Marketing Board* (1966). In many of these judgments, the Court was ahead of developments elsewhere. However, its decision in *Astley v Austrust* (1999)—that contractual damages may not be reduced for contributory negligence—has provoked universal condemnation and speedy legislative reversal in one state.

In *Skelton v Collins* (1966), the High Court actually departed for the first time from a decision of the House of Lords. This was a personal injury action in which the plaintiff had been made permanently unconscious. Declining to follow *H West & Son v Shephard* (1963), the Court held that damages for non-pecuniary loss were to be moderate. At the same time, it refused to follow a decision of the English Court of Appeal, *Oliver v Ashman* (1961), which had held that damages for loss of earnings could be awarded only for the period that the plaintiff was now expected to live. The House of Lords subsequently agreed with the High Court on that issue in *Pickett v British Rail Engineering* (1978).

On some other personal injury damages issues, the High Court and the House of Lords continue to disagree. Where the defendant to the action has voluntarily provided nursing care and domestic assistance to the plaintiff, the High Court allows the plaintiff to recover the value of the services by way of damages, whereas the House of Lords refuses to do so (compare *Kars v Kars* (1996) with *Hunt v Severs* (1994)). The decision of the High Court flows from the principle it established in *Griffiths v Kerkemeyer* (1977), and reaffirmed in *Van Gervan v Fenton* (1992), that a plaintiff may recover the value of such care and assistance even though there is no cost to the plaintiff. It has refused to adopt the English law that a plaintiff who recovers such damages holds them on trust for the provider of the services. Unlike the English courts, it insists that the measure of the value will ordinarily be found in the commercial cost of supplying them. Once again, legislatures have not been happy with these decisions and have

often sought to reduce the damages payable in such circumstances (for example, Motor Accidents Compensation Act, section 128).

Another difference between the High Court and English courts is the local insistence on the concept of 'loss of earning capacity', as opposed to 'loss of earnings' (see, for example, *Medlin v State Government Insurance Commission* (1995); *Husher v Husher* (1999)). The emphasis on this concept by Barwick, in particular, led to the Court temporarily departing, in a wrongful dismissal case, *Atlas Tiles v Briers* (1978), from the English rule of deducting income tax on wages that would have been earned. The division of opinion in this case led to chaos in the lower courts on what had to be done in personal injury cases. Once again, some legislatures intervened. Sanity was soon restored in *Cullen v Trappell* (1980).

Perhaps the leading case on damages for personal injuries, *Sharman v Evans* (1977), manifests a number of curiosities. First, its importance was initially not recognised by the official reporters, who would have relegated it to the status of an **unreported judgment** (see (1977) 51 ALJR 376). Secondly, the formal **order** of the Court, upholding the appeal and reducing the damages by a specified amount, was agreed to by only two members of the five-judge Bench. No explanation was offered as to how this came about—nor as to how the Court came to make the order as to **costs**, which was contrary to the view of Barwick, the only Justice to discuss the matter.

At a time when inflation was sweeping the world, the High Court gave two notable judgments: *Pennant Hills Restaurants v Barrell Insurances* (1981) and *Todorovic v Waller* (1981). Although the differences of opinion among the Justices could not be resolved, the Court took the unusual course in *Todorovic* of issuing a short statement on the effect of the decision (see also **Public opinion**), which settled the discount rate to be used in the calculation of future loss. At an earlier stage, the Court had taken the view that it was not appropriate for an appellate court to lay down a discount rate for lower courts (*Hawkins v Lindsley* (1974)), a view shared by the Supreme Courts of the USA and Canada. In the decision of the **United States Supreme Court** to this effect (*Jones & Laughlin Steel Corporation v Pfeifer* (1983)), the judgments in the *Pennant Hills* case were cited—a rare if not unique occurrence. When the House of Lords in *Wells v Wells* (1998) decided to lay down a similar guideline to that adopted in *Todorovic*, **Stephen's** dissenting judgment drew the following accolade from Lord Lloyd of Berwick: 'The approach to the basic calculation of the lump sum has been explained in many cases, but never better than by Stephen.'

The *Trade Practices Act* 1974 (Cth) has given the Court the opportunity to make contributions to the law of damages on matters such as loss of a commercial opportunity (*Sellars v Adelaide Petroleum* (1994)) and the nature of the loss sustained by someone who enters into a contract on the basis of a misrepresentation (*Marks v GIO* (1998)).

HAROLD LUNTZ

Further Reading
FC Hutley, 'Appeals within the Judicial Hierarchy and the Effect of Judicial Doctrine on Such Appeals in Australia and England' (1976) 7 *Syd LR* 317

David Securities v Commonwealth Bank (1992). In this seminal decision for the development of the law of **restitution** in Australia, all seven Justices of the High Court concluded that the traditional rule precluding the recovery of money paid under a mistake of law should be held not to form part of Australian law. The Court decided that payments made under a mistake of law should be *prima facie* recoverable in the same way as payments made under a mistake of fact. In so deciding, the Court adopted an analytical structure for approaching cases of unjust enrichment that provided significant guidance for all subsequent restitutionary claims, whether based on mistake or not. The decision was characteristic of a general thrust of the **Mason Court** to rationalise and simplify legal doctrine by abandoning inherited distinctions seen as artificial and difficult to justify.

The plaintiffs sued the Commonwealth Bank, among others, in the **Federal Court**, alleging that they had suffered significant losses by entering into foreign currency borrowing arrangements at the inducement of the bank. The bank cross-claimed for recovery of money due under the borrowing arrangements. The plaintiffs argued that they were entitled to set off against the amount claimed by the bank the money they had paid to the bank pursuant to clause 8(b) of the relevant loan agreements, on the ground that the clause was void by virtue of section 261 of the *Income Tax Assessment Act* 1936 (Cth).

The plaintiffs were unsuccessful at trial. On appeal, the Full Court of the Federal Court found that clause 8(b) was indeed rendered void by section 261 and that consequently, in paying moneys pursuant to clause 8(b), the plaintiffs had made a mistake of law or of mixed law and fact. However, by applying earlier authorities according to their traditional interpretation, the Full Court concluded that the plaintiffs were not entitled to a set-off for the reason that an action for money 'had and received' did not lie in cases of payment made under a mistake of law.

The plaintiffs appealed to the High Court. On appeal, the bank challenged the Full Court's findings both as to the applicability of section 261 and as to the existence of a relevant mistake. The Court unanimously rejected the bank's argument in relation to section 261, and, subject to the determination of the plaintiffs' appeal, unanimously ordered the **remittal** of the proceedings to the trial judge for further consideration of the issue of mistake. For the purpose of determining the principal issue raised by the plaintiffs' appeal, however, the Court proceeded on the basis that the alleged mistake was as to the existence of section 261 and its legal operation to render void the purported contractual obligation in clause 8(b).

The principal judgment of the Court was delivered by Chief Justice **Mason**, joined by **Deane**, **Toohey**, **Gaudron** and **McHugh**, with **Dawson** delivering a short, **concurring judgment** and **Brennan** dissenting in part. All Justices rejected the traditional rule precluding the recovery of money paid under a mistake of law. They did so for three main reasons. First, the Court showed that, notwithstanding its eventual acceptance as an immutable rule, the principle precluding recovery had sprung from clearly erroneous origins. Secondly, the Court concluded that three previous decisions of the Court (*York Air Conditioning v Commonwealth* (1949), *Werrin v* *Commonwealth* (1938) and *South Australian Cold Stores v Electricity Trust* (1957)), on which the bank relied as demonstrating acceptance of the traditional rule, could be reconciled with the narrower principle that payment made voluntarily in settlement of an honest claim is irrecoverable. Thirdly, the Court was influenced by the numerous calls from both judges and **commentators** for abolition of a rule that enshrined artificial distinctions and gave rise to numerous exceptions. In rejecting the traditional rule, the Court nevertheless emphasised that the burden lies on a plaintiff to identify and prove a mistake which is causative of the payment. The Court was not unanimous on the precise nature of the causative mistake that must be established.

Further, all members of the Court accepted, in principle, that the law should recognise a defence of 'change of position', to ensure that enrichment of the recipient of a payment is prevented only in circumstances where it would be unjust. The central element of this defence is that the recipient of the money has acted to his or her detriment on the faith of having received it. The existence of the defence had not previously been supported by any appellate court in Australia. The bank sought to rely on the defence. Determination of that question was included in the remitter to the trial judge.

CHRISTOPHER CALEO

Further Reading
Peter Birks, 'Modernising the Law of Restitution' (1993) 109 *LQR* 164
Keith Mason and JW Carter, *Restitution Law in Australia* (1995) 117–125

Dawson, Daryl Michael (*b* 12 December 1933; Justice, 1982–97) was born in Melbourne and educated at Canberra High School. He graduated with a first class honours degree in law from the University of Melbourne, then attended Yale University with a Fulbright Scholarship and graduated LLM. He signed the Roll of Counsel of the Victorian Bar in 1957 and was appointed as a QC in 1971. He served as **Solicitor-General** for Victoria from 1974 to 1982 and was an active member of the Council for Legal Education during this time. In 1982, he was **appointed** as a Justice of the High Court. After **retirement** from the High Court, he was appointed as a Non-Permanent Judge of the Hong Kong Court of Final Appeal in 1998.

As both Solicitor-General and Justice of the High Court, Dawson was involved in some of the most critical formative events in the development of Australian law. His period as Solicitor-General for Victoria began during the **Whitlam era**. This was a time of change in Australian law and constitutional practice. Federal legislation and administration challenged the boundaries of **Commonwealth legislative powers**. Divisions between the government and the opposition in the Parliament produced a spate of litigation. As Solicitor-General, Dawson argued some of the central constitutional cases of the time. These included challenges to the validity of the Australian Assistance Plan in the *AAP Case* (1975), the validity of Commonwealth claims over offshore areas in the *Seas and Submerged Lands Case* (1975), and defence of the constitutionality of Commonwealth electoral boundaries in *A-G (Cth); Ex rel McKinlay v Commonwealth* (1975). The issues

Daryl Dawson, Justice 1982–97

highly regarded for their breadth of legal understanding, technical legal analytical skill and clarity of expression. He was a masterful exponent of the **common law** method in the sense that he sought resolution of each case before the Court through rigorous application of existing rules involving, at most, incremental judicial development of the law. He was a strong defender of judicial **independence**, but believed that this required courts to confine their own **role**, leaving both law reform and public **policy** to the legislature.

On the Bench, Dawson had a reputation as a conservative, though he might not have been perceived that way in earlier times. In a Court that typically reflected a diversity of views, he was generally to be found at the end of a spectrum that was less **activist** and more supportive of what previously had been assumed to be the status quo. Thus, in *Mabo* (1992) he was the sole dissentient from the view that the common law now recognised the **native title** of Australia's indigenous inhabitants, despite the long-held Australian assumption of *terra nullius*. Similarly, in the *Free Speech Cases*, beginning with *Australian Capital Television v Commonwealth* (1992), in which a majority of the Court accepted that the Constitution placed limits on power to restrict freedom of **political communication**, Dawson took the more narrow ground. He agreed that some limitation on power might be drawn from the requirement in sections 7 and 24 of the Constitution that the Parliament be directly 'chosen' by the people. At the same time, however, he rejected any suggestion that the Constitution provided more generally for representative democracy or **representative government**, from which constitutional implications might be derived. Ironically, he applied the narrower limitation more rigorously than the majority: see his dissent in *Langer v Commonwealth* (1996). To a degree, his view of the narrower basis of the principle ultimately prevailed, in the unanimous decision of the Court in *Lange v ABC* (1997), which drew this line of authority to a close, at least for the time.

Dawson took a similar approach to the related development of a concept of **proportionality** as an analytical tool for determination of the scope of legislative power by reference to unexpressed rights. With characteristic thoroughness, he undertook a study of the doctrine in European law as a basis for repudiating its broad application in Australia, other than in relation to powers that clearly were purposive or to give effect to express constitutional limits on power (*Cunliffe v Commonwealth* (1994); see also *Nationwide News v Wills* (1992)). His views were influential in the decisions of the Court in *Cunliffe* and *Leask v Commonwealth* (1996), which substantially restricted the use of the doctrine in circumstances that might encourage further implied limits on power.

Dawson sometimes was typecast also by the trend of his decisions on issues affecting the constitutional power of the states. Soon after his appointment, he joined a minority who would have invalidated the World Heritage Conservation legislation of the Commonwealth in the *Tasmanian Dam Case* (1983). In taking that position, he refused to accept that the power with respect to 'external affairs' authorised the implementation by the Commonwealth of all international treaties that imposed obligations on Australia. He also would have required a more substantial connection between a law and the

raised in these and other cases foreshadowed themes that were to be significant for the High Court over the next two decades: the scope of the **nationhood power** of the Commonwealth, the meaning and operation of the Commonwealth power with respect to **external affairs**, and the extent to which principles of representative **democracy** are embodied in the Constitution.

Changes in Australian law and the context in which it operates were no less dramatic during Dawson's 15 years on the Bench. The passage of the *Australia Acts* 1986, by both Australia and the UK, to sever the final, formal colonial links between the two, precluded any practical possibility of further Australian appeals to the **Privy Council**. The High Court thus became the ultimate court of appeal in Australian law. With hindsight, this also was the period during which the forces of globalisation and internationalisation began to have a major impact on Australia. A new range of issues, including the **environment**, human rights and national treatment of **Aboriginal peoples** became subjects of international debate. Australia ratified the International Covenant on Civil and Political Rights and, subsequently, the First Optional Protocol. During this period, also, the forces of international economic competition placed particular pressure on federations, such as Australia, where power is divided between different spheres of government and responses inevitably are slower and more complex. Inevitably, these developments were reflected in issues raised before the Court and in the Court's responses to them.

Dawson's approach to judicial **decision making** was in the best classical tradition of the Court. His judgments were

corporations power, in which the fact that a constitutional corporation was subject to the law was significant in the way the law related to it. He was a consistent critic of the more expansive definition of 'external affairs' thereafter, even where, in form, he followed what had become established precedent (*Richardson v Forestry Commission* (1988)). And in *Re Dingjan; Ex parte Wagner* (1995), his views on the corporations power prevailed to the extent that he was a member of a majority which invalidated a law for insufficient connection with the power. Famously, Dawson also was a consistent member of a minority of Justices who espoused a narrower view of the Commonwealth's exclusive power to impose excise duties, until the battle was lost in *Ha v NSW* (1997); atypically, in this area he was prepared to depart from precedent and to give effect to his view of basic principle.

The High Court is not a specialist constitutional court and deals with appeals in a wide variety of other matters, in both federal and state jurisdiction. Dawson's legal skills and broad professional experience served him well across all fields. In particular, his deep understanding of criminal law and practice, derived from his period as a state Solicitor-General, made him a valuable member of a Court in which not all Justices have acquired experience of this kind. Decisions of note include *Zecevic v DPP* (1987), in which he delivered a joint judgment with Wilson and Toohey, *Wilson v The Queen* (1992), in which with Brennan and Deane he was in dissent, and his individual dissent in *Dietrich v The Queen* (1992). Service as Solicitor-General also provided Dawson with an understanding of the workings of executive government, evidenced in some of his decisions in administrative law, including *Haoucher v Minister for Immigration* (1990) and *A-G (NSW) v Quin* (1990).

It would be a mistake to exaggerate Dawson's position as a dissentient in the courts of which he was a member. The point can be demonstrated by reference to constitutional decisions, typically most likely to give rise to differences of view and to attract public interest and attention. At a rough estimate, approximately a hundred such cases were decided by the High Court during 1982 and 1997. In half of these, the Court was in broad agreement. These included landmark cases on the meaning of the freedom of interstate trade for which the Constitution provides (*Cole v Whitfield* (1988)); on discrimination on the grounds of state residence (*Street v Queensland Bar Association* (1989)); on the position of government under statute (*Bropho v WA* (1990); *Jacobsen v Rogers* (1995)); and on the need for a unanimous verdict to satisfy the jury trial requirement of section 80 of the Constitution (*Cheatle v The Queen* (1993)). In another thirty cases or so, Dawson was with the majority, in outcome if not in reasoning. He was in clear dissent in only about twenty constitutional cases over a period of 15 years. His dissents were often a salutary reminder of alternative viewpoints, and his position in some of these cases, at least, appears to have influenced other Justices in subsequent cases.

Dawson was on the Bench at a time of vigorous intellectual debate about future directions for Australian law, particularly constitutional law, and the role of the High Court in relation to it. Dawson espoused a traditional approach, at a time when some other Justices were attracted by new ideas and new approaches, sometimes drawn from international

experience, in response to new challenges. The rigour of his analysis earned respect for his judgments, irrespective of outcome. They contributed to the intellectual calibre of the distinguished courts of which he was a distinguished member.

CHERYL SAUNDERS

Further Reading
Daryl Dawson, 'The Constitution: Major Overhaul or Simple Tune-up?' (1984) 14 *MULR* 353
Daryl Dawson, 'Judges and the Media' (1987) 10 *UNSWLJ* 17
Daryl Dawson, 'Intention and the Constitution: Whose Intent?' (1990) 6 *Aust Bar Rev* 93
Daryl Dawson, 'Recent Common Law Developments in Criminal Law' (1991) 15 *Crim LJ* 5
Daryl Dawson, 'Do Judges Make Law? Too much?' (1996) 3 *Jud Rev* 1

Deakin, Alfred (*b* 3 August 1856; *d* 7 October 1919). As first Attorney-General and second Prime Minister of the new Commonwealth, Deakin's influence on the early High Court was profound, particularly in relation to the first five appointments and, above all, the successful enactment of the *Judiciary Act* 1903 (Cth) (see Constitutional basis of Court).

Born in Melbourne, Deakin was the son of English immigrants of modest means. He was educated at Melbourne Grammar School and the University of Melbourne, from which he graduated with an LLB. He commenced practice as a barrister, but preferred journalism, and established a relationship with David Syme, publisher of the *Age*. (Later, from 1900 to 1910, he was to write an anonymous column for the London *Morning Post*, often commenting upon events in which he played a leading role.) Entering the Victorian Legislative Assembly in 1879, Deakin held office from 1883 to 1890. He took up the cause of federation, becoming a member of the federal Conventions of 1891 and 1897–98 and a member of the Australian delegation which went to the UK to promote the passage of the Constitution Bill. Deakin was elected to the first federal Parliament in 1901 as member for Ballarat. As deputy to Barton and as Attorney-General in that Parliament, on 18 March 1902 Deakin introduced the second reading of the Judiciary Bill. The Bill, which sought to fulfil the establishment of the High Court as laid down by the Constitution, was Deakin's most 'cherished measure'.

O'Connor described Deakin's three and a half hour speech as: 'Magnificent. The finest speech I have *ever heard*.' The acting Leader of the Opposition, William McMillan, in immediate response, said a 'more comprehensive speech … both in regard to the principles and details of a great Bill, has not been heard in the House'. Deakin's address was not only a superb piece of oratory and advocacy; it was also a masterly analysis of the principles of federalism.

He began by describing the Bill as 'a fundamental proposition for a structural creation which is the necessary and essential complement of a federal Constitution'. He then went on to outline, with great subtlety and prescience, the reasons why the Court would be 'necessary and essential'. He pointed out that the Constitution had deliberately been drawn on 'large and simple lines … because it was felt to be an instrument not to be lightly altered, and … to apply under circumstances probably differing most widely from the expectations now cherished by any of us'. Consequently, 'it opens an immense field for exact definition and interpretation'.

Further, the Constitution 'involves a series of compacts' between the states and the Commonwealth relating to the finances of the states, and to the boundaries of **Commonwealth legislative power**. These compacts, 'dealing with all classes and interests, are to be interpreted and safeguarded by this court'. He asked: 'How many of us yet realise … the complex character of every federal system, and the specially complex character of that created by our Federal Act.' The use of general language meant that the division of powers between the Commonwealth and Imperial Parliaments were 'vaguely defined'. There was 'a large area of disputable territory, which has yet to be marked, either to our relative gain or relative loss of power and authority'.

The High Court 'exists to protect the Constitution against assaults'. It was also necessary if the Constitution was to remain a living document. 'I would say that our written Constitution, large and elastic as it is, is necessarily limited by the ideas and circumstances which obtained in the year 1900. It was necessarily precise in parts, as well as vague in other parts.' That Constitution could be altered only by the 'difficult' process of **amendment**:

> But the nation lives, grows, and expands. Its circumstances change, its needs alter, and its problems present themselves with new faces. The organ of the national life which preserving the union is yet able from time to time to transfuse into it the fresh blood of the living present, is the Judiciary … It is as one of the organs of Government which enables the Constitution to grow and to be adapted to the changeful necessities and circumstances of generation after generation that the High Court operates.

Deakin was well aware that in many quarters the Court was seen as a 'splendid luxury'. It had been argued that in the interests of economy the work should continue to be done by the state courts, with appeals going to the **Privy Council**. He described this as an attempt 'to conduct a federal system upon purely provincial lines, which must inevitably fail'. As to suggestions (made even by **Griffith**) that a 'scratch court' of state Chief Justices would serve as an alternative, it seemed to him 'wholly unsatisfactory' to commit the national Parliament and national interests 'to courts constituted at the convenience and pleasure of the states out of a shifting body of judges'. It was at the 'absolute behest' of the Constitution that a High Court be established, 'not in State Courts, not in a combination of State Judges, not in the Privy Council'. Writing for the *Morning Post* the following year, Deakin expressed the imperative need for a federal court in succinct terms— the Court was essential for the interpretation and enforcement of the many constitutional compacts. 'Without this third co-ordinate power the State Courts would be left to settle some of them and the Privy Council the rest, no thorough investigation being given to the merits of the compacts from the Australian as distinguished from the provincial points of view.'

In his second reading speech, Deakin made what has been described as 'his most celebrated pronouncement' about the new Court:

Alfred Deakin, who as Australia's first Attorney-General introduced the Judiciary Bill in 1902

> The Constitution is to be the supreme law, but it is the High Court which is to determine how far and between what boundaries it is supreme. The federation is constituted by distribution of powers, and it is this court which decides the orbit and boundary of every power. Consequently, when we say that there are three fundamental conditions involved in federation [a Constitution; distribution of powers under it; and a judicial authority to interpret it], we really mean that there is one which is more essential than the others—the competent body which is able to protect the Constitution, and to oversee its agencies. That body is the High Court. It is properly termed the 'keystone of the federal arch'.

Despite the praise given to his exposition, Deakin had no illusions as to the future of the Bill. The conclusion of his *Morning Post* article on the subject was: 'In the circumstances, whilst warmly applauding the Minister's speech, the majority appear to have tacitly decided not to pass his measure until it has been closely examined, and probably curtailed to more modest dimensions.' His forecast was precisely correct. The Bill was not reintroduced until June 1903, and then it had to be fought for every inch of the way in a climate of opinion that had grown steadily more unfavourable towards it. State resentment of Commonwealth powers was increasing; and severe nationwide drought brought new demands for retrenchment and fresh antagonism towards any federal 'luxuries'.

The Bill was attacked strenuously by three eminent lawyers: Patrick Glynn, **Higgins**, and John Quick. Each complained that the High Court could not truly be the 'keystone of the federal arch' while the right to appeal to the Privy Council remained. Higgins believed that the Court would be docked of power and shorn of dignity. The time, therefore, was not yet ripe for its creation. State courts could carry out its functions. In any case they rejected the argument that the Constitution *required* the creation of a High Court. Glynn also put forward a popular argument—which turned out to be utterly wrong—that the Court would have very little **business** to conduct.

The Bill reached the committee stage with a majority of only nine—several Opposition members had supported the measure, but a greater number of government members had deserted it. Deakin privately threatened to resign if the measure was not passed. In committee, the Bill was treated severely, despite constant and vigorous attempts to defend it by Deakin and **Isaacs**. The principal loss was the extended original **jurisdiction** of the Court. This was struck out, and the Court was made a court of appeal only, except in five expressly defined areas. Parliament also retained the right to confer original jurisdiction on the Court. Notwithstanding the reduction in its original powers, the Court still retained an original jurisdiction far more extensive than that of the **United States Supreme Court.**

Other amendments saw the **number of Justices** reduced from five to three; and, in a blow of peculiar pettiness, the provision for their pensions was abandoned (see **Remuneration of Justices**). As Deakin later wrote, the Bill was 'fiercely assailed to the last by economists, the States' right militants, and the Opposition guerrillas. Twice its fate in the House depended in critical divisions on a single vote, while defeat was evaded again and again by postponements or recommittals'. Even the third reading was pressed to a division, much to Deakin's disappointment. Given gentler treatment in the Senate, the Bill received assent on 27 August 1903. In Deakin's words: 'No measure yet launched in the Federal Parliament was so often imperilled, skirted so many quicksands, or scraped so many rocks on its very uncertain passage.'

The passing of the Judiciary Act—and of its companion machinery measure, the *High Court Procedure Act* 1903 (Cth)—was by no means the end of Deakin's troubles. The appointment of Justices to the new Court would prove vexing, and was an issue of some delicacy for Deakin's own career. The choice of O'Connor, at least, was widely expected and did not arouse controversy. Deakin had wished to offer a place to Andrew **Inglis Clark**, but the reduction in the number of Justices from five to three had diminished Inglis Clark's chances. Deakin was definite in his preference for Griffith as **Chief Justice**, despite strong opposition from those in Cabinet who believed that no state judge should be appointed.

Deakin was apparently prepared to consider resignation over the issue. The most likely candidate for the final seat was generally agreed to be the Prime Minister, Barton. However, he was hurt by public criticism that he was merely seeking 'a fat billet' for his old age. Also, the retirement of Barton from politics would leave Deakin as the logical choice to succeed to the Prime Ministership. In late August 1903, with Barton still wavering, Deakin wrote to Inglis Clark about the last seat

on the Court. Inglis Clark said he would accept if offered a position. Finally, on 24 September Deakin, now Prime Minister, was able to announce the appointment of Griffith as Chief Justice with Barton and O'Connor as his colleagues.

The Court lost no time in establishing itself as a formidable constitutional instrument. It immediately began hearing constitutional cases; asserted its power over the state courts, reversing them on occasion, and showed no disposition to accept challenges to its constitutional authority from the Privy Council. All this was as Deakin had intended by the appointment of men eminent in the cause of federation as well as in the law.

The success of the Court was reflected in the rapid increase in the volume of its workload. In 1906, an amending Judiciary Bill, introduced by Attorney-General Isaacs, provided for the appointment of two more Justices, thus meeting Deakin's original intention that the Court should have five members. As it was well known that Isaacs was a leading contender for one of the vacancies, he could not be closely involved with the selection. There were rumours that Prime Minister Deakin might be appointed. They were given substance by a letter addressed to him from all his Cabinet colleagues, including Isaacs. The letter expressed the hope that Deakin might accept one of the positions. The request was based 'on public grounds'—that the High Court ought to be 'exalted in the highest degree in public regard, and that those who occupy seats upon it shall be (as in your case) not only learned in the law but also distinguished and held in public esteem, both as public men and private citizens'. This startling gesture towards investing a criterion of being 'distinguished in public life' with equivalent value to strictly legal eminence, was stillborn. In later years, Deakin was most emphatic that his relative lack of professional experience entirely ruled him out of consideration for any place on the Court. His 'jealous regard' for the standing of the High Court could lead him to no other conclusion.

As a matter of courtesy, the first offer was made to Samuel Way, the aged Chief Justice of SA—and also one of the firmest opponents of the Court's creation. Deakin also consulted Glynn about the claims of another South Australian, Josiah Symon. This inquiry must have been a matter of form. Despite Symon's undoubted professional and public standing, his case for appointment had been tarnished irretrievably by his acrimonious disputation with the High Court Bench over questions of cost and location during his term as Attorney-General in the Reid Government (see **Strike of 1905**). When Way declined, as expected, the positions were offered to Isaacs and Higgins, and were warmly accepted.

Deakin was Prime Minister until 1908 and then again in 1909–10. He retired from Parliament in 1913. His last years were clouded with illness, and after 1916 he lived as a recluse. Deakin died in October 1919, but his legacy endured, for his 'cherished measure' concerned an institution that would last as long as the federation Deakin helped to create.

ZELMAN COWEN

Further Reading
JA La Nauze, *Alfred Deakin* (1965)

William Deane, Justice 1982–95

Deane, William Patrick (*b* 4 January 1931; Justice 1982–95) was a leading member of the **Mason Court** and staunch defender of human rights. His career has been an unpredictable mix of conservative and radical elements. While many described him as intensely private and reserved during his time on the Bench, his judgments blazed trails in the areas of human rights, **tort law**, and **equity**. They reflect a desire to reform archaic and unjust law, while using methods that remain consistent with past judicial approaches. This desire often led him to take bold new approaches—not always with the support of his colleagues.

Deane was born in Melbourne to a strictly Catholic family in 1931; the family moved to Canberra soon after. He attended St Christopher's Convent School before boarding with the Marist brothers at St Joseph's College in Sydney, and went to the University of Sydney where he obtained a BA and LLB. He then studied at Trinity College, Dublin and later at the Hague Academy of International Law, from which he graduated *summa cum laude*.

During the 1950s, Deane's anti-communism led him to join the Democratic Labour Party for a brief dalliance with party politics. However, the infighting he experienced during this period 'cured him of politics'.

Deane was admitted to the Bar in 1957 and practised mainly in equity, **taxation**, **trade practices**, and **commercial law**. He married Helen Russell in 1965 and they have one daughter (Mary) and one son (Patrick). He took silk in 1966.

In February 1977, he was appointed to the Equity Division of the Supreme Court of NSW. After less than two months in that position, he accepted an appointment to the **Federal Court** to sit as President of the Australian Trade Practices Tribunal. He was appointed to the High Court by the Fraser government in 1982.

Soon after joining the Court, Deane almost single-handedly transformed the law of negligence by introducing the concept of **proximity**. At that time, the question of when to impose a duty of care in negligence had become a vexed and difficult issue, particularly in relation to claims for pure economic loss and psychiatric injury. Dissatisfaction with the concept of reasonable foreseeability in cases of pure economic loss led **Stephen** in *Caltex Oil v The Dredge 'Willemstad'* (1976) to call for 'some control mechanism based upon notions of proximity between tortious act and resultant detriment'. Deane, who had appeared as **counsel** in the *Caltex* case, attempted to develop this idea in *Jaensch v Coffey* (1984) through a new duty concept based on closeness of time, space, or relationship. According to Deane, a duty of care could be established in cases of physical proximity (closeness of space and time), circumstantial proximity (close or overriding relationships), or causal proximity (close or direct causal links between acts and injuries or losses).

In *Jaensch*, Deane stood alone in his formulation of proximity; but subsequent decisions saw growing acceptance of the concept (see *Sutherland Shire Council v Heyman* (1985); *San Sebastian v Minister* (1986); **Burnie Port Authority v General Jones** (1994); *Bryan v Maloney* (1995)). The concept was not without criticism from other Justices, especially **Brennan**, who favoured the incrementalist approach of finding a duty of care by reference to established categories.

As in other areas, the Court has since turned away from the trails that Deane blazed. 'Proximity' as the touchstone of a duty of care has now been discarded (see *Hill v Van Erp* (1997); *Pyrenees Shire Council v Day* (1998); *Perre v Apand* (1999)).

In *Hawkins v Clayton* (1988), Deane showed once again that he was willing to take a creative line of his own. The question concerned the concurrent liability in **contract and tort** of professional people such as solicitors. Traditionally, solicitors had been liable only in contract (*Groom v Crocker* (1938)), but the development of recovery of pure economic loss arising from negligent misstatement gave rise to the possibility of their being concurrently liable in contract and tort. This led to conflicting decisions. Would the principles of assessment of **damages** in contract and tort merge, so that the cause of action chosen did not dictate the result? Or would contract and tort principles remain separate, allowing the plaintiff to take the benefit of whichever remedy he or she found most advantageous?

In *Hawkins v Clayton*, Deane took a third path. He held that if a person was liable in tort for negligent misstatement, there was no need to imply a term into the contract requiring that reasonable care be taken. He thought that concurrent liability was better described as conflicting liability, and ought to be avoided where possible. In doing so, he would have preferred to remove professional liability from the individualist **values** of **contract law** into community values as expressed in tort law. This was a radical step because it ignored the long line of cases holding solicitors negligent in contract.

Deane's initiative in *Hawkins v Clayton* suffered the same fate as his proximity principle. The **House of Lords** rejected it in *Henderson v Merrett Syndicates* (1994), and then the Full High Court did the same. In *Astley v Austrust* (1999), the Court decided by a 4:1 majority that Deane was wrong to deny liability in contract, both in legal principle and as a matter of **history**. In the past, said the majority, professional people had been liable in contract, and the addition of tort liability should not affect that. Plaintiffs should be able to recover under whichever remedy was the more advantageous.

Particularly in his judgments in equity, Deane sought to forge new synergies and blaze new trails. Though not entirely alone in this, he was firm in his own path. In *Waltons Stores v Maher* (1988), he was an advocate of **estoppel** as an active doctrine in the absence of pre-existing legal relationships. With **Mason**, he sought to harmonise existing categories of estoppel through the merging of promissory and proprietary estoppel. More radically, he proposed a merger of **common law** and equitable estoppel—a development that orthodox legal scholars might consider heretical. These ideas are evident in *Foran v Wight* (1989) and *Commonwealth v Verwayen* (1990), in both of which the Court charted new territory in articulating a broader notion of estoppel.

Deane also broke new ground in the field of constructive **trusts**. In *Muschinski v Dodds* (1985), his judgment laid the foundation for a constructive trust, which could be imposed quite apart from the parties' intention, that was based upon the need for a remedy where one party's attempted retention of the other's contribution to a joint relationship was unconscionable. In *Baumgartner v Baumgartner* (1987), the Court (including Deane) took this approach further. The key element in the new constructive trust was **unconscionability**. The issue for the future is how far this idea can go: in particular, whether it can be used as a remedy, in the absence of statute, taking into account the whole range of contributions, financial and domestic, in relationships.

In **constitutional law**, Deane's arrival quickly established a new majority (Mason, **Murphy**, Brennan, and Deane, with **Gibbs**, Wilson, and Dawson dissenting), usually in favour of the Commonwealth—as in *Hematite Petroleum v Victoria* (1983) and *Gosford Meats v NSW* (1985) (**excise duties**); *Fencott v Muller* (1983) (trading corporations); and above all, the *Tasmanian Dam Case* (1983), where Deane's contribution was distinctive. On the one hand, his concurrence in the principal majority holding—that the legislative implementation of treaties under the **external affairs power** can extend to any treaty whatsoever, regardless of subject matter—was based on the doubtful contention that *R v Burgess; Ex parte Henry* (1936) had already established that proposition (see *Ratio decidendi*). On the other hand, he joined Gibbs, Wilson, and Dawson in finding that the Commonwealth's initial attempt to prevent construction of the dam by regulations was invalid—for Deane, because (as he alone held) the assertion of Commonwealth power over Tasmanian bushlands entailed an **acquisition of property** with no adequate compensation scheme. Moreover, he joined Brennan in holding that most of the relevant statutory provisions were also invalid, as insufficiently tailored to the purpose of protecting this particular river. The idea that legislation implementing a treaty must be suitably tailored to its purpose had

been present in all the earlier cases; but Deane gave it a novel formulation and focus, absorbing it into a conception of **proportionality** that was to reverberate with growing significance through the Court's constitutional work.

Deane's analysis of the *Tasmanian Dam* regulations as an acquisition of property was an early indication of his concern for constitutional rights. Thereafter, this took many forms. In *Evda Nominees v Victoria* (1984), he dissented from the Court's new rule that any argument for the **overruling** of an earlier High Court decision required the prior leave of the Court, protesting that counsel should be free to advance any argument at any time. In *University of Wollongong v Metwally* (1984), he joined Gibbs, Brennan, and Murphy in holding that amendments to the *Racial Discrimination Act* 1975 (Cth), designed to rescue state anti-discrimination legislation from **inconsistency** with Commonwealth law, could not apply retrospectively. That the state Act had been rendered inoperative by inconsistency (see *Viskauskas v Niland* (1983)) was for Deane a 'fact of history' that no legislative power could undo. The decision did little to advance Mohamed Metwally's right to freedom from **discrimination**; but Deane saw it as protecting a more basic constitutional right of every Australian. The inconsistency provision in section 109 of the Constitution is not, he wrote, a mere device for adjusting competitive assertions of power by state and federal parliaments, but protects the individual from 'the injustice' of being expected to obey contradictory Commonwealth and state legislation simultaneously. For Deane, this was a right of **citizenship**, linked with ideas of **nationhood** and popular **sovereignty**. The Australian federation 'was and is a union of people'; and all constitutional provisions should be understood 'as ultimately concerned with the governance and protection of the people from whom the artificial entities called Commonwealth and States derive their authority'.

In *Kirmani v Captain Cook Cruises* (1985), Deane analysed the Commonwealth's ability to repeal British legislation still in force in the states by relying, like Mason and Brennan, on what he called the 'traditional legal theory' that Australia's constituent instruments derive their authority from enactment by the Imperial Parliament. Deane added, however, that if ever that theory needed to be examined more closely, the true underlying basis of Australia's independent sovereignty might be found in the external affairs power (enabling the Commonwealth to exclude legal interference by any other country, including the UK), and in the power of the Australian people to amend their own Constitution—so that 'ultimate authority in this country lies with the Australian people'.

In *Breavington v Godleman* (1988), Deane (supported by Wilson and **Gaudron**) reinterpreted section 118 of the Constitution (requiring recognition of state laws 'throughout the Commonwealth') as a substantive assurance of **national unity** and 'a unitary national system of law'. Though Deane's approach was rejected in *McKain v Miller* (1991) and *Stevens v Head* (1993), his continued dissents (and Gaudron's) were ultimately vindicated in *John Pfeiffer v Rogerson* (2000).

Especially where separate state regimes might fragment legal uniformity, Deane read **Commonwealth legislative powers** expansively—for example (in **joint judgments** with Mason) the **marriage** power in *Re F; Ex parte F* (1986) and *Fisher v Fisher* (1986), and (in sole dissent) the **corporations** power in the *Incorporation Case* (1990). But when the Court upheld a Commonwealth–state cooperative scheme in *R v Duncan; Ex parte Australian Iron & Steel* (1983), Deane stressed that this was, in part, an affirmation of the continuing legislative power of the states, freed from 'outmoded doctrines appropriate to times that are gone'. When *Street v Queensland Bar Association* (1989) breathed new life into section 117 of the Constitution, which prohibits state discrimination against residents of other states, Deane emphasised that this fostered both national unity and individual rights. Yet his was the broadest concession that sometimes, consistently with section 117, a state might validly confine the provision of benefits to its own residents.

In *Kingswell v The Queen* (1985), Deane's powerful **dissenting judgment** was alone in calling for reinterpretation of the guarantee of **jury trial** in section 80 of the Constitution. Brennan dissented on more technical grounds; but Deane endorsed the dissenting view of **Dixon** and **Evatt** in *R v Federal Court of Bankruptcy; Ex parte Lowenstein* (1938), interpreting section 80 as an effective guarantee of trial by jury for serious offences. Unlike Dixon and Evatt, he declined to adopt a mechanical definition of 'serious offences', holding rather that whether an offence is serious 'in the sense that it is not capable of appropriately being dealt with summarily by justices or magistrates is, ultimately, a question of law to be determined by the courts'. While later cases such as *Cheng v The Queen* (2000) have anxiously re-examined Brennan's dissent in *Kingswell*, Deane's more radical challenge remains unanswered.

The conception of **judicial power** in Chapter III of the Constitution was, for Deane, a further protection of liberty. In the *War Crimes Act Case* (1991), he held that a retrospective **criminal law** would be unconstitutional, since 'it is basic to our penal jurisprudence' that conviction depends on a judicial finding of failure to obey a law applicable 'at the time the act was done'. In *Re Tracey; Ex parte Ryan* (1989), *Re Nolan; Ex parte Young* (1991), and *Re Tyler; Ex parte Foley* (1994), he insisted that the system of **military justice** must deal only with 'exclusively disciplinary offences' and must not 'supplant the jurisdiction or function of the ordinary courts'. In *Re Bolton; Ex parte Beane* (1987), he proclaimed that judicial safeguards such as habeas corpus are 'the very fabric of the freedom under the law which is the prima facie right of every citizen and alien in this land'.

His willingness to find **implied constitutional rights** was not limited to rights of **due process**. In *Leeth v Commonwealth* (1992), he and **Toohey** proposed that **constitutional interpretation** should assume that the **framers of the Constitution** chose systematically 'to incorporate underlying doctrines or principles by implication'—including a 'general doctrine of legal **equality**' importing not merely the formal idea of 'equality before the law', but substantive protection against any legislative infringement of the inherent equality of all 'people of the Commonwealth'. In *Kruger v Commonwealth* (1997), most Justices rejected that notion; but in *Nationwide News v Wills* (1992) and *Australian Capital Television v Commonwealth* (1992), a majority of the Court discerned an implied constitutional freedom of **political communication** (see *Free Speech Cases*). Deane and Toohey grounded this freedom in a 'doctrine of representative gov-

ernment', which they saw (along with **federalism** and **separation of powers**) as one of 'three main general doctrines of government' pervading the Constitution. They interpreted this doctrine as a powerful version of popular sovereignty, in which all the powers of government—'legislative, executive or judicial'—are 'ultimately derived from the people themselves', to be exercised in a representative capacity on the people's behalf.

Deane was appointed Governor-General in 1995; his initial five-year term was extended until mid-2001. Despite the quality and impact of his work on the Bench, he is arguably better known and more popular for his role as Governor-General, in which he proved to be an uncharacteristically outspoken commentator on social issues.

Deane's role as Governor-General has not been without controversy. His advocacy of the rights of indigenous peoples is consistent with his judgment with Gaudron in *Mabo* (1992), where the dispossession of **Aboriginal peoples** was identified as 'the darkest aspect of the history of this nation'. His defences of multiculturalism, the reconciliation process, **native title**, and **social justice** have attracted criticism. However, in the main, his social commentary has served only to increase his popularity. During the period of republican speculation, he was touted by many as a suitable candidate for appointment as Australia's first president.

Deane has a love of horse racing and has bred racehorses, including the relatively successful Man about Town, for more than three decades—not without the criticism of Lady Deane, who calls his horses 'slow'. He is also known to love tennis, and to follow Essendon in the AFL and Parramatta in the Rugby League. However, his greatest love may be Rugby Union—a game that led to the loss of the sight of his right eye in a match in Canberra after he had graduated from Sydney University.

Deane will be remembered by those who know him personally, and by Australians generally, with great affection. There is a reason for his popularity. He is an enormously talented, yet humble, man of great convictions and integrity. His career serves to remind us that, in the words of Donald McNicol, 'idealism is not the prerogative of the young or of the recently learned'.

ROSALIND ATHERTON
TONY BLACKSHIELD
BRUCE KERCHER
CAMERON STEWART

Decision-making process. The making of a judicial decision cannot be delegated or transferred. Each Justice must make a decision in his or her own way. A tentative view can be, and often is, formed on reading the court papers. The reasons for a judgment that is under appeal, or the reasons for a decision that is under review, will usually identify and discuss the issue to be decided by the Court. A Justice's tentative view can be, and often is, modified when written submissions are furnished by the parties, by **interveners** or by *amici curiae*, but no final view is formed until after the oral **argument** is concluded.

The practice of the Court has been to rely heavily on oral argument. The dialectic of advocacy and exchanges between Bench and Bar illuminate the issues for decision and usually identify the material on which the decision is based. But the written and oral submissions do not necessarily limit the material considered by the Court. As the final court of appeal responsible for declaring the law of Australia, the Justices conduct their own research and may, in particular cases, follow their own line of reasoning. However, if a majority of the Court come to consider a question which it would be unfair to decide against a party without hearing the party on that question, the matter is relisted for further argument.

Until 1982, the Court was constrained to rely solely on oral argument and the research carried out by the individual Justices or their **associates**. The oral argument in difficult or important cases often extended over lengthy periods. From February 1982, the Court required **counsel** at the beginning of their oral submissions to hand to the Bench written summaries of argument succinctly stating the contentions to be made. In 1984, the Court permitted the summaries to contain a list of the principal authorities to be cited and a chronology. In time, the summaries became more extensive and many were replete with argument and the citation of authority. In 1997, the Court called for detailed written submissions for appeals in order to allow the Justices better to understand the parties' contentions before oral argument commenced. The time for oral argument could thus be shortened. In complex or important cases, **directions hearings** are held and **orders** are made for the delivery of full outlines of argument at specified times before the date of hearing.

In the course of oral argument, the current—albeit still tentative—views of Justices are likely to become manifest to their colleagues, if not to counsel. During adjournments and after most hearings, there are brief discussions among the Justices in which their current opinions are exchanged. Those of similar opinion may agree that one of their number should either write the first judgment or prepare a draft for their joint consideration. In many cases, however, a Justice is unable to express an opinion until he or she has worked through the propositions in writing.

In the years prior to 1998, a formal post-hearing discussion was scheduled only for particular cases. Brief discussions by all Justices who sat on a case took place at the Court meetings held during the monthly **sittings** to review the list of **reserved judgments**, but Justices did not meet formally between sittings unless resident in the same city. Since 1998, more formal discussions of judgments are scheduled between the sittings, to permit a fuller exchange of views and to identify more closely opportunities for the writing of **joint judgments** (see **Conferences**).

To reach a decision, each Justice endeavours to apply not a personal but an external standard derived chiefly, but not always exhaustively, from the existing body of law. Where statutory language is uncertain or ambiguous or where the application of some other legal norm would be either of doubtful validity or unjust, decision making may require a Justice to determine the better interpretation or application. **Precedent**, analogical reasoning, legal **policy** and the enduring **values** of society may legitimately influence the decision in such cases. It is not possible to attribute a priority among these factors in every case, nor to define the weight that individual Justices accord to these factors. Decision making may allow a Justice a certain leeway of choice in particular cases,

but the process is not idiosyncratic; it is constrained by the judicial method, which demands both a reasoned and a public exposition of the steps leading to judgment (see also **Law-making role**).

The preparation of a judgment in a Justice's **chambers** depends entirely upon the practice in those chambers. A Justice may dictate, write or type a judgment drawing solely on the contents of the **appeal book** or application book, the written summary of argument, the **transcript** of oral argument and the authorities cited by counsel. Or a Justice might first ask an associate to prepare a paper on a particular aspect of the case, to find a line of authority or to conduct a search of the relevant literature. **Research assistance** by associates was supplemented and enhanced when the Court **library** appointed a research officer in 1983 to provide references to relevant legal sources and to prepare papers on areas of the law arising in litigation.

It has been the general practice of the Justices to draft their own judgments. The associate may be invited to discuss the draft before it is circulated. When a Justice has completed a draft, it is proofread by an associate, who checks all references. When a judgment is drafted as a joint judgment, the draft may first be circulated to the participating Justices for comment and possible amendment.

When a judgment is fully prepared, it is circulated to the other Justices who sat on the case. Those Justices who **concur** with the judgment circulate their concurrences or are invited by the author of the judgment to join in it as co-authors. If a Justice is in general agreement but has a reservation upon or qualification of the circulated judgment, the author of the judgment may incorporate the reservation or qualification with the approval of all participants in the judgment, or the reservation or qualification will be expressed in a separate judgment. In the former case, it is usual for the Justice proposing the amendment to join in the judgment.

When the judgments of all the Justices who sat in the case have been circulated, they are sent to the **judgment production** section. The proofreader discusses any suggested changes to a judgment with the associate of the relevant Justice. The Justice may make the suggested changes and, if material, circulate the changes to other Justices. The case is listed for delivery of judgment when all proofreading changes are complete.

GERARD BRENNAN

Defamation law. Cases of libel and slander have come on appeal to the High Court from its earliest days. In the first volume of the *Commonwealth Law Reports*, for example, the Court heard an appeal from the Supreme Court of NSW on the ground that excessive **damages** had been awarded to a country storekeeper for a publication by his bank to the effect that he had been bankrupted (*Miles v Commercial Banking Co* (1904)).

Until 1984, when a general requirement of special **leave to appeal** was imposed, appeals in civil actions, including libel and slander, could be brought to the Court as of right if a relatively modest financial threshold was met. If, in the course of hearing those appeals, the Court ruled on a particular aspect of defamation law, that decision was, of course, binding on all other Australian courts. There are, however, numerous points of law in this area that have not been considered by the Court and are still governed by English or other Australian authorities.

The starting point of a plaintiff's case in a libel action is the existence of a defamatory imputation or meaning. For example, in *Readers Digest v Lamb* (1982), the plaintiff was a journalist who had reported a sensational crime. He complained that an account of his actions had reflected on his journalistic ethics. Specifically, the jury found an imputation that he had exploited his personal friendship with the victim's family to secure a sensational newspaper story. The defendant's appeal was dismissed. **Brennan** explained the process by which it is decided whether an imputation is defamatory as follows:

> The issue of libel or no libel can be determined by asking whether hypothetical referees—Lord Selborne's reasonable men or Lord Atkin's right-thinking members of society generally or Lord Reid's ordinary men not avid for scandal—would understand the published words in a defamatory sense. That simple question embraces two elements of the cause of action: the meaning of the words used (the imputation) and the defamatory character of the imputation.

The associated process of determining meaning was referred to by **Mason** in *Mirror Newspapers v Harrison* (1982), where the Court found that a story conveying the meaning that the plaintiff had been arrested and charged with a criminal offence did not carry with it an imputation that the plaintiff was guilty of that offence:

> A distinction needs to be drawn between the reader's understanding of what the newspaper is saying and judgments or conclusions which he may reach as a result of his own beliefs and prejudices. It is one thing to say that a statement is capable of bearing an imputation defamatory of the plaintiff because the ordinary reasonable reader would understand it in that sense, drawing on his own knowledge and experience of human affairs in order to reach that result. It is quite another thing to say that a statement is capable of bearing such an imputation merely because it excites in some readers a belief or prejudice from which they proceed to arrive at a conclusion unfavourable to the plaintiff. The defamatory quality of the published material is to be determined by the first, not by the second, proposition.

The other major elements in the plaintiff's case are publication and identification. Liability for publication was analysed by the Court in *Webb v Bloch* (1928). In that case, it was found that a circular distributed on behalf of the organising committee for a political campaign by wheat growers in Victoria, commenting on the failure of a similar campaign in SA, was defamatory. Three of the four committee members had not seen the circular, but all had authorised its circulation and all were held to be responsible. The issue of identification—that is, whether the defamatory statement can be understood as referring to the plaintiff—was dealt with in *David Syme v Canavan* (1918), where **Isaacs** noted: 'The test of whether words that do not specifically name the plaintiff refer to him or not is this: Are they such as reasonably in the circumstances would lead persons acquainted with the plaintiff to believe that he was the person referred to?'

In *Lee v Wilson* (1934), it was held that two police officers, Arthur and Clifford Lee, had been defamed in a newspaper article reporting the payment of a bribe to 'Detective Lee'. There was evidence that in fact the original allegation referred to a different police officer, also named Lee; but the Court held that the intention of the publisher was not relevant to this inquiry.

As to the major defences available to a libel action, the most potent of these, if available, is that of justification: the defendant admits that a publication is defamatory but contends that it is true in substance and in fact. The Court as a whole has not yet considered the variant of this defence established by the series of English decisions beginning with *Polly Peck (Holdings) v Trelford* (1985).

The defence of fair comment has been modified by statute in a number of Australian jurisdictions but still retains the basic **common law** elements. The crucial distinction between statements of fact and expressions of opinion was examined by the Court in *O'Shaughnessy v Mirror Newspapers* (1970). The plaintiff, the actor Peter O'Shaughnessy, had starred in the title role of his own production of *Othello*, which was the subject of a scathing review including the sentence: 'But the waste and dishonesty of this production, or rather recitation, make me very angry indeed.' The trial judge ruled that the whole article was 'comment' but left to the jury the question of whether it was fair comment. On appeal, however, **Gaudron** (as counsel for O'Shaughnessy) persuaded the Court that the word 'dishonesty' was capable of imputing a 'dishonourable motive' as a statement of fact, so that the issue of fact or comment should have been left to the jury.

So far as the defence of common law qualified privilege is concerned, the Court confirmed in one of its early decisions, *Howe & McColough v Lees* (1910), that this category of 'privilege' to speak freely arises when the speaker has a 'social or moral duty' to make the statement to the person to whom it is made, and both speaker and hearer have a legitimate interest (**Griffith** called it a 'community of interest') in conveying and receiving the information. This test of 'reciprocity of interest' has since been applied in a number of cases (see *Mowlds v Fergusson* (1940) and *Guise v Kouvelis* (1947)); but it was in *Lang v Willis* (1934), involving a by-election feud between former NSW Premier Jack Lang and his former supporter AC Willis, that the issue received most public notoriety (see **Litigants, notable**). Lang had attacked Willis as 'a concealed enemy sailing under the flag of a Labor independent candidate', 'a subtle and insincere politician' who 'when the ship was sinking … rushed for the shore without warning his mates'. Willis sued Lang for defamation. The jury supported Lang on all counts, and although the Full Court of the Supreme Court of NSW ordered a new trial, **Rich** joined **Evatt** and **McTiernan** in allowing Lang's appeal. **Dixon** and **Starke** (both from Melbourne) dissented; but Dixon agreed with Evatt's statement that 'the theory that privilege attaches to *every* occasion upon which speakers at election meetings choose to broadcast before large gatherings opinions or information about one or other of the candidates cannot be supported'.

The Court has also considered on occasions the protection accorded to publications by the defence of qualified protection in the Code jurisdictions of Queensland and Tasmania (*Telegraph Newspaper v Bedford* (1934)). In *Calwell v Ipec Australia* (1975), similar provisions in the *Defamation Act* 1958 (NSW) were regarded as applicable to a newspaper article, published in 1971, which alleged that Gough Whitlam's leadership of the Labor Party was being undermined by 'a narrow and embittered gerontocracy' including the former leader Arthur Calwell. Years earlier, in *Loveday v Sun Newspapers* (1938), the Court had noted that the defence might extend to defamatory statements made by the defendant in response to an original attack made by the plaintiff (see also *Penton v Calwell* (1945)).

In the absence of economic loss, damages in libel actions fall under two headings, injury to reputation and hurt to feelings. The nature of an award for damage to reputation was described by **Windeyer** in *Uren v John Fairfax & Sons* (1966):

> When it is said that in an action for defamation damages are given for an injury to the plaintiff's reputation, what is meant? … It seems to me that, properly speaking, a man defamed does not get compensation for his damaged reputation. He gets damages because he was injured in his reputation, that is simply because he was publicly defamed. For this reason, compensation by damages operates in two ways—as a vindication of the plaintiff to the public and as consolation to him for a wrong done. Compensation is here a solatium rather than a monetary recompense for harm measurable in money.

This was one of two cases in which Labor Party shadow minister Tom Uren had sued over a defamatory report that he had allowed himself to be manipulated by 'the Rusian spy, Ivan Skripov'. In the parallel case, *Australian Consolidated Press v Uren* (1966), Uren had based his claim not only on the Skripov allegation, but on a series of earlier defamatory statements, including an editorial assertion that he and other named members of the Labor Party 'would have difficulty running a raffle for a duck in a hotel on Saturday afternoon'. These cases represented one of the first occasions when the Court declined to follow a decision of the **House of Lords**—in this instance, by refusing to limit the award of exemplary damages to the categories to which they had been confined in *Rookes v Barnard* (1964). In the *Fairfax* case, the Court held that, in Australia, exemplary damages could be awarded for what all the Justices referred to as 'conscious wrongdoing in contumelious disregard of another's rights', though they added that this was not such a case. Windeyer stressed that, in any event, a 'firm distinction between aggravated compensatory damages and exemplary or punitive damages' was impossible. In the *Consolidated Press* case, the Court held that the earlier publications did not warrant exemplary damages, but ordered a new trial. Since this left open the possibility that exemplary damages might be awarded, the defendants appealed to the **Privy Council**—which held that, the law on exemplary damages having been settled in Australia long before *Rookes v Barnard*, there was no reason why Australian courts should follow the latter case (*Australian Consolidated Press v Uren* (1967)).

On the question of directions a jury might be given in arriving at an award of compensatory damages, the majority stated in *Carson v John Fairfax & Sons* (1993) that there was 'no significant danger in permitting trial judges to provide to the jury an indication of the ordinary level of the general damages component of personal injury awards for comparative purposes, nor in counsel being permitted to make a similar reference'. The same issue had been considered in *Coyne v Citizen Finance* (1991), where it was said by the majority that the trial judge might invite the jury to consider the investment or buying power of any sum that it was minded to award.

The requirement for an award of aggravated compensatory damages was set out in *Triggell v Pheeney* (1951). Such an award might be made 'if there is a lack of bona fides in the defendant's conduct or it is improper or unjustifiable'.

A major development in the Court's treatment of the law of defamation occurred in the 1990s, when the defence of common law qualified privilege became enmeshed with the freedom of **political communication** held to be implied in the Constitution by the decisions in the *Free Speech Cases* (1992). In *Theophanous v Herald & Weekly Times* (1994), a majority, albeit not for the same reasons, considered that the Constitution protected political discussion if the publisher met certain requirements. This decision was, however, effectively overruled in *Lange v ABC* (1997), when the Court ruled that the common law defence of qualified privilege existed in relation to publications concerning government and political matters subject to a requirement of **reasonableness** in relation to the conduct of the publisher (and, of course, to an absence of malice). This approach was rejected by the NZ Court of Appeal in *Lange v Atkinson* (1998), where it was held that such a publication was only defeated by a demonstration of malice, but essentially accepted by the House of Lords in *Reynolds v Times Newspapers* (1999).

The **role** of the Court in this area of the law has, therefore, largely been as a final appellate tribunal engaged in the ratification and development of common law principles. These have traditionally embodied a balance between freedom of speech and protection of individual reputation. The Court's attempt to strike a new balance in the context of the Constitution for one category of publications, political discussion, has again illustrated the difficulty in reconciling these two conflicting values.

Michael Sexton

Defence power. In times of war, particularly during **World War I** and **World War II**, the Commonwealth's power over defence under section 51(vi) of the Constitution has assumed prime importance. It has enabled the Commonwealth to meet the exigencies of war and to assume powers otherwise only within the competence of the states.

The central High Court doctrine concerning the defence power is that the power waxes and wanes. It is a fixed concept with a changing content because its scope depends on Australia's defence needs at any given time, and as these needs fluctuate, so does the scope of the power. Hence, at the height of a global war the measures which the Commonwealth Parliament can enact in the exercise of this power may extend into virtually every aspect of Australian life, and may involve far greater control and coordination of the national **economy** than is normally possible. According to **Isaacs** in *Farey v*

Burvett (1916), the scope of the power during a war in which the existence of Australia is threatened is virtually unlimited. It becomes a 'paramount' source of power, the scope of which is 'bounded only by the requirements of self-preservation'.

In times of what might be called 'profound peace', the scope of the defence power is far more limited. It enables the Commonwealth to maintain 'defence preparedness', and therefore to deal with 'such matters as the enlistment (compulsory or voluntary) and training and equipment of men and women in navy, army and air force, the provision of ships and munitions, the manufacture of weapons and the erection of fortifications' (**Communist Party Case** (1951)).

Although the power is 'elastic', it does not immediately snap back at the end of a period of international conflict to its limited peacetime scope. The transition back into peacetime conditions may justify a continuation of some wartime measures and new measures may be needed to cope with the process of transition (*R v Foster* (1949)).

The defence power is a 'purpose' power. It authorises the Commonwealth to legislate not on a specified subject matter, but for a specified purpose. A law can be **characterised** as a law under the power not because it is a law on the topic of defence, but because it is, or reasonably may be, conducive to the purpose or object of defence. Although this analysis is widely accepted, it has not been unanimous. Throughout World War II, **Starke** insisted that 'defence' is a subject matter for legislation, to be approached much like other heads of **Commonwealth legislative power**. Thus, throughout that period, High Court majorities commonly upheld regulations because they were for the *purpose* of defence, while Starke dissented because they were not on the *topic* of defence (see, for example, *Australian Woollen Mills v Commonwealth* (1944)).

The conditions that determine the scope of the power as it 'waxes and wanes' are factual conditions, such as, for example, whether Australia is currently at war or facing a real or perceived threat of invasion, and the immediate military and economic needs of Australia at such a time. The most obvious facts are external to Australia, but internal conditions are also important. Most of these circumstances are political, international, economic and social in nature and are likely to be notorious as matters of common knowledge. They are thus the kind of facts of which courts take 'judicial notice'—that is, facts that judges can draw from their personal knowledge without requiring evidentiary proof.

Where judicial notice is insufficient to show that a measure is for the purpose of defence, there are obvious difficulties of inference and proof. The success of military and other policies is rarely certain, and a demonstration that a particular measure will contribute to victory, or will enhance defence preparedness, cannot reasonably be expected. Such 'facts' are likely to be matters of opinion or judgment; and their nature is such that the **separation of powers** requires that the judgment be made by the executive and not by the courts. Hence, the Court has accorded substantial deference to legislative and executive judgment, thereby giving very wide latitude to government policies that might be conducive to defence (see also **Fact finding**).

In times of total war, the Court has deferred almost completely to the needs of the country as perceived by the government, rather than take too pedantic a line on the constitutional limits of power. During World War II, **Latham** and **Dixon** experienced the problems faced by the executive first hand as Ministers respectively to Japan (1940–41) and the USA (1942–44). It is not surprising that they took a liberal approach to the power to be afforded to the government.

Despite such deference, the question of whether a particular law is authorised by section 51(vi) is ultimately one to be decided by the Court in its function of **judicial review**. The separation of powers means that neither the legislature nor the executive can pre-empt the judicial function by purporting itself to determine the constitutional question. Evidence of the beliefs and intentions of the legislature or executive may assist the Court, but the Court itself remains the only authoritative interpreter of the Constitution. The Parliament cannot be the judge of its own constitutional power (*Communist Party Case*).

GEORGE WILLIAMS

Further Reading
Geoffrey Sawer, 'The Defence Power of the Commonwealth in Time of War' (1946) 20 *ALJ* 295

Democracy, Court's conception of. The High Court's conception of democracy was fundamentally shaped by the English political and legal traditions that informed and continue to influence Australian constitutionalism. Far from representing a radical break from Imperial authority, the claims for independence and self-determination advanced by the Australian colonies were articulated in terms of securing and adopting local versions of English institutions. The pivotal institutions in this context were Parliament and the **rule of law**. It is not surprising, therefore, that the **framers of the Constitution** retained the parliamentary institutions already established in the colonies, and adopted a system of representative parliamentarianism for the Commonwealth. Importantly, they secured and entrenched judicial **independence** as an essential aspect of democracy in Australia. Nevertheless, the Court's conception of Australian democracy has as its centre and core the parliamentary conception of **representative government**.

It is easy to overlook the conventional dimension of parliamentary democracy in Australia. An essential feature of Australian democracy, based on Westminster traditions, was its implicit adoption and recognition of **responsible government**. That the cabinet and executive were responsible to parliament, which in turn was subject to the people, was seen to be one of the most important means for securing individual liberty. Combined with the inheritance of the **common law** and the rule of law, a system of representative and **responsible government** was regarded as a complete answer to the encroachments and threat of an overreaching executive.

Not only was representative parliamentary government a means for securing liberty, it also had the considerable advantage of providing a place for public deliberation and debate, a forum for proposing innovations and evaluating outcomes. Parliament, in other words, was the principal means for advancing the frontiers of thought and therefore assuring progress.

To the extent that this understanding of Australian parliamentary democracy was informed by John Stuart Mill, who greatly influenced the founders, the Court's conception of democracy can be said to be Millian, though mediated by the **jurisprudence** of Albert Dicey and James Bryce. Ironically, this is a conception of democracy that silences its own judicial articulation, since it holds that the appropriate place for the explication and evolution of political ideas is the Parliament. As **Stephen** noted in *A-G (Cth); Ex rel McKinlay v Commonwealth* (1975), 'the particular quality and character of the ... ingredients of representative democracy ... is not fixed and precise':

> Representative democracy is descriptive of a whole spectrum of political institutions, each differing in countless respects yet answering to that generic description. The spectrum has finite limits and in a particular instance there may be absent some quality which is regarded as so essential to representative democracy as to place that instance outside those limits altogether; but at no one point within the range of the spectrum does there exist any single requirement so essential as to be determinative of the existence of representative democracy.

Accordingly, it was not the Court's **role** to determine precisely what form the franchise or the electoral system might take: 'The Constitution leaves this to legislatures to determine', and 'so long as what is enacted is consistent with the existence of representative democracy', it is 'not for this Court to interfere'. In the result, the majority (**Murphy** dissenting) declined to find that the Constitution embodied the principle 'one vote, one value'—that is, there was no strict requirement that the single-member electorates in the House of Representatives had to be equal in size.

The Court in *McGinty v WA* (1996) also emphasised the Millian nature of democracy in Australia, again leaving to the discretion of the Parliament the determination of such core concepts as voting rights and **citizenship**. In particular, **McHugh** insisted that the Court has no jurisdiction 'to determine what representative democracy requires. That is a political question and, unless the Constitution turns it into a constitutional question for the judiciary, it should be left to be answered by the people and their elected representatives acting within the limits of their powers as prescribed by the Constitution' (see also the *Engineers Case* (1920), the *Boilermakers Case* (1956) and *Levy v Victoria* (1997)). The strict demarcation of politics from law has been considered essential for preserving both the authority of parliament and the independence of the judiciary.

It is true that this view of parliamentary democracy, with its inherent basis of parliamentary **sovereignty**, did not sit easily with the theory and practice of **federalism**—an innovation the founders appropriated from the USA. That Australia was a constitutional democracy meant that sovereign parliaments were now subject to the Constitution. Significantly, the boundaries of their sovereignty—and particularly the boundaries defining the relationship between state and Commonwealth parliaments—were now subject to the determination of the Court. To a large extent, however, the Court continued to adapt, accommodate and absorb aspects of **federalism** into the prevailing parliamentary traditions. As far as possible, the Court interpreted parliamentary authority broadly and extensively, construing narrowly specific limitations on parliamentary power. When exercising federal **judicial review**, the Court consistently denied that any 'political' decision was involved in declaring parliamentary enactments unconstitutional; it was no different from any other legal exercise of interpreting an enactment, in this case the Constitution as an Imperial Act. Yet, as **Dixon's** enigmatic affirmation and denial of the 'political' arguments in the *Melbourne Corporation Case* (1947) acknowledged, the judicial view both of legislative authority and of the limitations upon it inevitably reflected political conceptions.

The result is that, despite the Court's insistence on **legalism**, federal judicial review has had a major bearing on the nature of Australian democracy, especially in determining the relative authority of state and Commonwealth parliaments, the development and standing of Australia as a sovereign nation, and the character of liberal democracy in Australia (see also **Liberalism**).

The Court's decisions on **implied constitutional rights** have confirmed the importance of representative and responsible parliamentary democracy in Australia. In *Australian Capital Television v Commonwealth* (1992) and later in *Theophanous v Herald & Weekly Times* (1994), the Court held that the representative democracy secured in the Constitution implied a freedom of **political communication** (see *Free Speech Cases*). In *Stephens v WA Newspapers* (1994), the Court accepted that such a freedom could also be discerned in the **state Constitutions**. By declaring representative democracy a constitutional principle, these decisions appeared to allow the judiciary greater scope to derive a range of further limits on parliamentary democracy. But subsequent decisions have confirmed that the implied right of political communication is derived from the terms of the Constitution, not from the concept of representative democracy as a free-standing principle (*Lange v ABC* (1997)). In *Levy*, the Court acknowledged the need for a reasonable accommodation between the implied freedom and Parliament's other legitimate concerns.

The Court's implied rights decisions have clearly sought to confirm the liberal democratic nature of Australian parliamentary democracy. Importantly, they have emphasised the deliberative character of Australian parliamentary democracy. In this light, the Court's 'rights' decisions may perhaps be understood as a form of 'representation-reinforcing' judicial review, where the judiciary ensures the integrity of the processes, if not the substance, of parliamentary democracy (John Hart Ely, *Democracy and Distrust* (1980)).

Although this conception of Australian democracy has dominated the Court's jurisprudence, there are competing views that challenge or are in tension with it. Perhaps the most notable of these is the recent rejection by some Justices of the declaratory theory of adjudication as a 'fairy tale' (Mason, 'The Judge as Law-Maker' (1996) 3 *James Cook ULR* 1; Brennan, 'A Critique of Criticism' (1993) 19 *Monash ULR* 1). The acknowledgment that the Court does not simply declare the law, but also makes the law, has necessitated a theoretical accommodation with the notion of a representative and responsible democracy. The response, which appears to be based on a form of sociological **jurisprudence**, has sought to justify judicial **law-making** as a way of keeping laws up-to-date with changing community **values**.

The Court's recent interpretation of the **separation of powers** secured in the Constitution has also challenged the dominant notion of responsible government. Its decisions on the rights to **natural justice**, a fair trial, and counsel in serious cases, and its rejection of bills of attainder, emphasise the liberal democratic dimension of separation of powers—designed to provide checks and balances and to disperse power, and thereby to protect individual liberty. By augmenting Blackstone's notion of judicial separation of powers with the American conception of institutional checks and balances—most clearly outlined by Alexander Hamilton, John Jay and James Madison in *The Federalist Papers* (1788)—the Court implicitly elevates the role of the judiciary as an institution that will supervise and, if necessary, check parliament. The very requirement for dispersal of powers, which is inherent in this notion of separation of powers, suggests a redefinition of parliament's traditional role as the principal institution for shaping politics in Australia.

Finally, the Court's increasing reliance, in developing the common law and interpreting the Constitution, on certain enduring 'values' such as those of the common law (*Mabo* (1992)), on the norms of **international law** and the **International Bill of Rights** (*Mabo*; *Dietrich v The Queen* (1992); *Teoh's Case* (1995); *Newcrest Mining v Commonwealth* (1997)), and even on popular sovereignty (*Australian Capital Television*), points to a theoretical limitation of the principle of parliamentary democracy. Arguably, it represents the tentative first steps in a fundamental redefinition of the character of representative and responsible government. It certainly reinterprets the role of the judiciary within Australian constitutionalism. By locating sources of authority outside parliament and making the judiciary their interpreters and guardians, the Court moves beyond representation-reinforcing judicial review—which is intended to secure the efficiency of parliamentary government—to a more substantive judicial review in which it exercises greater moral, political and legal authority.

The range and scope of these competing views illustrates the extent to which democracy in Australia has become a contested and contestable notion. It is also an important reminder of the continually changing and evolving nature of Australian constitutionalism. In this light, the increasingly important role of the Court in engaging and mediating these differing notions of democracy suggests that the Court's conception and articulation of democracy will have profound consequences for the place of the Court within the polity, and more generally for the character of Australian constitutionalism.

HAIG PATAPAN

Further Reading
Haig Patapan, *Judging Democracy: The New Politics of the High Court of Australia* (2000)
John Uhr, *Deliberative Democracy in Australia* (1998)
George Williams, *Human Rights Under the Australian Constitution* (1999)

Democracy, Court's role in. Our constitutional origins are an uneasy mix of British and American influences. From the British, we inherited the notions of **responsible government** and parliamentary **sovereignty**—the latter, in particular, relegating the courts to a subordinate role of declaring the **common law** and of merely interpreting, yet always remaining subject to, the will of parliament. From the Americans, we inherited the notions of a written Constitution and the institution of **judicial review**, the latter empowering the courts, particularly the High Court, to override the will of parliament and to declare invalid legislation made, or other acts done, without proper constitutional authority. Though obscured for many years by the simultaneous presence of the more familiar British strand of the inheritance, and compounded by the Court's own natural reticence about its **law-making role** and its function as a coordinate institution of government, the American inheritance posed a fundamental question for Australian democracy that had been hotly debated in the USA since *Marbury v Madison* in 1803: how could it be consistent with democratic government for an unelected court to have, and to exercise, the power to invalidate the acts of democratically elected parliaments?

The early answers were not unlike those given in *Marbury v Madison* itself, emphasising **form** over substance. The written Constitution was a higher law. The Court's mechanical role was simply to compare an Act of parliament with the dictates of the higher law, and to declare it invalid if it was inconsistent with, or unauthorised by, that higher law. As **Higgins** self-effacingly observed in *R v Smithers; Ex parte Benson* (1912):

> It is our duty meekly to ascertain the meaning and application of the words used in our own Constitution, as they stand, as the words of an instrument which is complete in itself, and which has to be construed, as a will is construed, by an examination of its own language within its own four corners.

Griffith, **Barton**, and **O'Connor** were more comfortable about using broad implications from the notion of federal government to restrain what the elected governments and parliaments could do, and accordingly more ready to draw upon American precedents of the nineteenth century; but the triumph of the **legalism** of **Isaacs** and **Higgins** in the *Engineers Case* (1920) set the tone for the next 70 years. As Albert Dicey had said, **federalism** is legalism; and it seemed only natural that, if the federal Constitution limited the lawful powers of the parties to the Constitution, those limits should be enforceable by the courts. Indeed, according to **Dixon**, strict and complete legalism was the key to the Court's legitimacy and the only way of maintaining the confidence of the parties in the great conflicts over their constitutional powers.

If the mechanical model were correct, it would provide a complete answer to the question of how, consistently with democracy, an unelected court can second-guess the will of an elected parliament. For one thing, there is more than one parliament. There are Commonwealth, state and territory parliaments, and the Court is the neutral umpire of their conflicting demands, resolving them according to the law that it authoritatively pronounces. For another, the law provides the framework within which all of these parliaments operate. The law precedes democracy and makes it possible, and the courts are merely the voice of the law.

The truth is a good deal more complicated. The courts have difficult choices to make in **constitutional interpretation**, often involving **values** and **policy considerations**. Respectable and legitimate arguments may be marshalled on both sides of a question—for example, for a broad or narrow view of **Commonwealth legislative power**—and a court's decision creates constitutional policy. The legalism of Isaacs was not policy-neutral; probably intentionally—but whether intentionally or not—it facilitated the growth of national power and the development of **national unity** (see also **Political institution**). From this perspective, the courts, although still confined to determining the parameters of legality, share power with the democratically elected policy makers. Moreover, they do so not merely by virtue of the accidental consequences of strict and complete legalism; they exercise choices, upon which values and policy considerations insistently impinge.

This gives a clue to how courts exercising judicial review can be a component of a more sophisticated concept of democracy than simple majority rule. Democracy is partly about the sharing and diffusion of power—in Australia, between levels of government (Commonwealth and states); between different institutions (legislature, executive and judiciary); and within institutions (legislative power in most instances being distributed between two Houses, executive power generally being wielded collectively by Cabinet, and **judicial power** generally suppressing idiosyncrasy through majority opinion and moderating error through appeal). This sharing of power gives us the familiar idea of checks and balances in the **separation of powers**. The judiciary may keep the government and the parliament within the law, but the government appoints the judges; the parliament can, to an extent, affect the courts' **jurisdiction** and modus operandi; and, in extreme cases, the parliament may effect the **removal** of a recalcitrant judge.

But the diffusion of power is by no means the complete answer to the question of how judicial review is consistent with democratic government. It is not a naked power struggle between the respective institutions. Each institution exercises power according to the principles and mores that inform our understanding of democracy. For the judiciary, this particularly means elaborating the reasons for decision, which are then open for scrutiny, **criticism** and debate (see **Accountability**). In a substantive rather than a procedural sense, it may also mean using objective principles of interpretation; these principles may not control outcomes, given the choices open to the judges, but they should provide guidance to the judges and points of reference for that critical debate.

Interestingly, the dominant principles have been textual (for example, 'give the words their ordinary and natural meaning') rather than overtly policy-oriented; only **Murphy** favoured a strong **presumption of constitutionality**, at least for Commonwealth legislation, although deference to legislative judgment has emerged from time to time in different contexts. Close textual analysis has been the traditional way for the Court to distance itself from the perception that it is subjectively making policy. Thus, it is not surprising that the **implied constitutional rights** decisions of the **Mason Court** were so controversial. How could the Court justify striking down legislation of a democratically elected parliament if it

could not point to any of the traditional touchstones—explicit language and relatively clear **history**—that identified objective constraints?

The Court's answer—that to invalidate legislation on the ground of freedom of **political communication** was to enhance rather than to diminish **representative government**—was not sophistry. The same reasoning has been applied in identifying minimum standards for the democratic integrity of the electoral system and the very composition of the Parliament itself. Although the Court has not gone so far as to interpret 'chosen by the people' in section 24 of the Constitution so as to mandate the idea of 'one vote, one value' for the single-member electorates of the House of Representatives (*A-G (Cth); Ex rel McKinlay v Commonwealth* (1975)), there is a certain appeal in the principle that deference to parliament is somewhat hollow in a situation in which its current members have a direct vested interest in the outcome. Yet in each case, an unelected court must be sensitive to developing notions of representative democracy, and must not arrogantly pre-empt the solutions that may be evolving in a political context. **Brennan's** deference to political judgment in his dissent in *Australian Capital Television v Commonwealth* (1992) (see *Free Speech Cases*) indicated that a range of approaches is possible in this area, as in others.

In brief, the Court's **role** in our democracy reveals the tensions inherent in our dual British and American origins. The former helped to give a particularly legalistic flavour to the justification of the key idea derived from the latter, the notion of judicial review. The dominant tradition of legalism has inhibited the growth of perceptions of the High Court as a coordinate institution of government, which the **activism** of the Mason Court first made manifest in any sustained way. But the Court is a coordinate institution of government, and its reasoned decisions are an important part of the public dialogue about how we best structure our system of government. That dialogue is itself one of the key ingredients of Australian democracy.

MICHAEL COPER

Further Reading
Tony Blackshield, 'Judicial Innovation as a Democratic Process' in *Future Questions in Australian Politics* (Meredith Memorial Lectures, La Trobe University, 1979)

Michael Coper, 'The High Court and Free Speech: Visions of Democracy or Delusions of Grandeur?' (1994) 16 *Syd LR* 185

John Hart Ely, *Democracy and Distrust* (1980)

John Toohey, 'A Government of Laws, and Not of Men?' (1993) 4 *PLR* 158

Dennis Hotels v Victoria (1960). Anyone who has served on a committee will understand that, when the different components of a motion receive varying support, the result may be an uneasy compromise that does not coincide exactly with the view of any individual. Judicial **decision making** in multi-member courts is no different. The more the Justices write individual rather than **joint judgments**, the more likely it is that different propositions will receive different degrees of support. For some decisions, there may be no single reason that commands majority support; indeed, for any single reason, taken separately, there may be a majority against. In

Dennis Hotels, a decision later described by **Murphy**, although for different reasons, as a 'blot on our constitutional jurisprudence', the extraordinary outcome was reached that the proposition for which the case appeared to be authority was in fact rejected by six of the seven Justices.

The case concerned the constitutional validity of two distinct liquor licence fees in Victoria. Licensees who sold liquor from permanent premises (such as hotels) had to pay an annual licence fee based essentially on the value of the liquor purchased for the premises in the preceding licence period. Licensees who sold liquor from temporary premises (such as sporting grounds) had to pay a licence fee based on the value of the liquor sold under the licence.

Dixon, **McTiernan** and **Windeyer** held that both fees were duties of **excise** and thus invalid under section 90 of the Constitution, which makes the power to levy taxes in the nature of customs or excise duties exclusive to the Commonwealth. **Fullagar**, **Kitto** and **Taylor** held that neither fee was a duty of excise and thus that both were valid. **Menzies** held that the fee for permanent premises was valid, but that the fee for temporary premises was invalid, thus generating a differently constituted majority of four to three on each issue. His judgment therefore determined the result of the case, even though six of the seven Justices had rejected the materiality of any distinction between the two fees.

One distinction was that the fee for permanent premises was levied by reference to the preceding licence period, whereas the fee for temporary premises was levied by reference to the current licence period. There was nothing surprising about this. The former fee, and the more significant of the two, had been in place for many years and was a convenient method of collecting revenue from ongoing businesses at fixed premises. The latter reflected the exigencies of collecting revenue from sporadic activities. But for six Justices, nothing turned on the distinction. Three thought that both fees were duties of excise because they effectively taxed the sale of goods in Victoria. Three thought that neither was a duty of excise, although for more diverse reasons: for Fullagar, only taxes on production were duties of excise; Kitto thought that the fees were the price of engaging in the business at all rather than taxes on the actual sales of the goods themselves; and Taylor was influenced in part by the overall regulatory context of which the fees were a part. Only Menzies drew the distinction between fees based on past transactions and fees based on current transactions.

It was the validity of the fee based on prior dealings that assumed significance. Although not originally conceived as such, it was now perceived by the states as a way of circumventing section 90 and as opening up real revenue-raising possibilities in other areas. But how generalisable was the decision? For what proposition was it authority?

Given the absence of a reason common to the majority, one might have thought that the authority of the case was confined to its immediate facts: the validity of prior period licence fees for selling liquor from permanent premises in Victoria. However, Justices in subsequent cases—some attracted to the legalistic elements of the reasoning of Kitto and Menzies, some anxious to keep faith with the Menzies distinction notwithstanding its idiosyncrasy, and some possibly sympathetic to state revenue needs—purported to

extract a more general proposition about prior period licence fees. The more general proposition was based on the reasoning that the 'criterion of liability' for the imposition of the tax was not any particular dealing with goods but rather the renewal of the licence, so that individual transactions were not directly taxed as such, but were used merely to determine the quantum of a tax that was really on the permission to carry on the business.

Dennis Hotels never acquired, however, the status of an authority for a general proposition about the validity of prior period licence fees. Yet neither has it been **overruled** or even confined strictly to its own facts. Fortified by the decision, a number of states imposed tobacco taxes and petrol taxes based on the prior period licence fee, but those taxes were not challenged until 1974 (*Dickenson's Arcade v Tasmania*) and 1977 (*HC Sleigh v SA*). By this time, the prior-period licence fees had become an important source of state revenue (and, significantly, a source independent of Commonwealth largesse), and even those Justices uncomfortable with the decision or reasoning in *Dennis Hotels* were clearly reluctant to invalidate taxes on which the states had come to rely. But their determination to uphold the tobacco and petrol taxes without conceding that *Dennis Hotels* stood for any readily discernable general proposition about prior period licence fees led them to make tenuous and shifting distinctions. Fees for processing fish (*Kailis v WA* (1974)) and slaughtering meat (*Gosford Meats v NSW* (1985)) were struck down, suggesting a distinction (otherwise intelligible but not if confined to licence fees) between sale and production, as was a fee for selling X-rated videos (*Capital Duplicators v ACT (No 2)* (1993)), suggesting a distinction based on the nature of the product. And when tobacco fees were again upheld in 1989 (in *Philip Morris v Commissioner of Business Franchises (Vic)*) but ultimately struck down in 1997 (in *Ha v NSW*), *Dennis Hotels* was narrowed even further, with emphasis this time on the traditional regulatory context for alcohol and tobacco, leaving uncertain whether the petrol tax upheld in *HC Sleigh v SA* in 1977—clearly an unabashed revenue-raiser—would survive a new challenge. *Dennis Hotels* remained intact, but despite their initial protectiveness towards the states, the Justices were not prepared, ultimately, to turn a blind eye to what was increasingly revealed as (and was in truth) a mere device for raising revenue.

Murphy regarded *Dennis Hotels* as a blot on the constitutional landscape because of the artificial reasoning it contained, the fine distinctions it spawned, and the convoluted legislative schemes it encouraged. To have accepted it as authority for a general proposition about prior licence fees would have allowed widespread evasion of section 90. To have accepted it as authority for anything less was logically flawed. Yet no judge except McTiernan was prepared to overrule the decision or to confine it strictly to its own facts. In trying to steer a middle course between fidelity to **precedent** and sensitivity to outcomes, the Court succeeded only in tying itself in knots.

But for Murphy, all this was irrelevant. For him, the holding in *Dennis Hotels* that the prior period licence fee was valid was correct, for reasons that had nothing to do with the method of calculation. In his view, and as Fullagar had thought in *Dennis Hotels*, excise duties were confined to taxes on production and did not extend to taxes on sale, whether the tax on sale was in the form of a licence fee or any other impost. That view narrowly failed to become established in *Ha*. If it ever does, *Dennis Hotels* will be able to be consigned to the dustbin of constitutional history.

MICHAEL COPER

Depression of the 1930s. The collapse of the New York stock market in October 1929 led to what became known as the Great Depression. The economic recovery began in about 1934, but was not fully achieved by the time of **World War II**. The start of the Depression roughly coincided with the election in Australia of a Labor government under **Prime Minister** James Scullin in 1929. **Powers** had resigned from the High Court in July of that year and **Knox** resigned in April 1930. **Isaacs** succeeded Knox as **Chief Justice**. As a result of the economic downturn, the **business** of the Court in 1930 was considerably reduced, so the government decided, as an austerity measure, to keep the Bench at five Justices for the time being.

While the Prime Minister and the **Attorney-General**, Frank Brennan, were abroad, however, caucus resolved that **Evatt** and **McTiernan** should be appointed to the two vacant positions. Cabinet went ahead with the appointments, despite the protests of the Prime Minister cabled from London (see **Appointments that might have been**). There was an outcry in conservative political and legal circles at these appointments on the ground that there were many distinguished and experienced barristers who were senior to them. The Bar of Victoria condemned the appointments as 'political rewards'. In the case of Evatt, however, there was no doubt that he was a leading silk with a high professional standing, even though he was, at 36, the youngest person ever to be appointed to the Court. In January 1931, Isaacs resigned to become Governor-General. The vacancy was not filled, and the Court continued with six Justices until 1947. **Gavan Duffy** was appointed Chief Justice.

In 1931, when Parliament enacted legislation to reduce the salaries of public servants and federal office-holders, the Act could not apply to the Justices because section 72 of the Constitution prevented their **remuneration** from being 'diminished during their continuance in office'. The Justices were therefore asked to accept a reduction in salary. They formally refused, on the ground that there should be no encroachment on their **independence** by means of executive pressure. Nevertheless, some agreed to forgo travelling allowances, and others said they would make cash payments into the treasury. The Justices pointed out that their position differed from that of public servants in another respect: their salaries had not changed since 1903.

During the Depression years, the Court produced a number of constitutional judgments that had long-term significance. In 1928, the Bruce government had enacted the *Transport Workers Act* for the purpose of breaking a strike of stevedores. The Act authorised the making of regulations in respect of the employment of transport workers in relation to interstate and overseas trade. The power extended to the overriding of other Acts of Parliament. Regulations were made requiring the licensing of waterside workers at proclaimed ports. Many non-unionists were licensed, while members of the striking union were not. The strike col-

lapsed. When the Scullin government came to power, regulations were made for the opposite purpose of giving preference to members of the union. They were challenged as being beyond the **trade and commerce power** because membership of a trade union had no relevance to trade and commerce. A majority of the Court upheld the regulations on the ground that any law that prescribed who could engage in an activity essential to interstate or overseas trade was within the power. The clear industrial policy of the legislation was constitutionally irrelevant (*Huddart Parker v Commonwealth* (1931)). This case was followed four decades later to uphold the use of the commerce power to protect the **environment** (*Murphyores v Commonwealth* (1976)).

A further challenge was made to the Transport Workers Act on the ground that the broad delegation of legislative power breached the **separation of powers**. The argument was rejected. **Dixon**, in particular, perceived a tension between the separation of powers discerned in the text of the Constitution and the practical need to have delegated legislation. British constitutional concepts and practices prevailed (*Victorian Stevedoring & General Contracting Co v Meakes and Dignan* (1931)). It is difficult to see how these considerations justify a provision that enables different governments to pursue opposing policies by delegated legislation without reference to Parliament. Nevertheless, the case remains a leading authority.

The Labor government fell at the end of 1931 and was followed by the Lyons government, which was concerned about what were perceived to be threats to society from communists at home and abroad who might take advantage of the misery caused by the depression. The *Crimes Act* 1914 (Cth) made illegal those associations with subversive or seditious objects. An amendment in 1932 gave power to the Attorney-General to obtain a declaration that an association was unlawful. He was also authorised to compel persons to answer questions and disclose documents to assist him in preparing the case. The editor of a communist newspaper was charged under the Act in respect of soliciting money for a demonstration against 'war and fascism'. The information alleged that the Communist Party was an unlawful association. Allegations by the prosecution contained in the information ('averments') were prima facie evidence. The editor was convicted but on appeal the conviction was quashed by the High Court. Despite an information of 68 pages containing 61 averments, the Court held that all that was shown was that the contributions were for a 'United Front' demonstration which could not be assumed to be the Communist Party or to have its alleged treasonable objects. Gavan Duffy and **Starke** called the information 'an amazing document well calculated to embarrass the proper trial of the accused'. Evatt said it was 'one of the most amazing documents in the whole history of the law' (*R v Hush; Ex parte Devanny* (1932)). The government later found itself similarly thwarted by the High Court in its attempt to prevent a left-wing Czech writer, Egon Kisch, from entering Australia and later in attempting to deport him (see *Kisch Case* (1934)).

In 1930, an attempt was made to reduce the significance of the *Engineers Case* (1920) by arguing that an industrial award could not bind state railway authorities because any expenditure by them depended, in accordance with basic constitutional principle, on Parliament appropriating the funds. The Court accepted that principle, but held that the award itself was binding on the state, although its enforcement was conditional on parliamentary appropriation (*ARU Case* (1930)).

That case was the prelude to the *State Garnishee Case* (1932). The Premier of NSW, Jack Lang, opposed payment of interest to British bondholders for the duration of the Depression. He refused to satisfy the state's obligation in that regard—an obligation arising from the Financial Agreement between the Commonwealth and the states. The Commonwealth paid the interest owing and enacted legislation to create an involuntary assignment of prescribed revenues of the state to the Commonwealth in execution of a judgment of the Court regarding its debt under the Agreement. The validity of most of the legislation was upheld by a majority as incidental to federal **judicial power** and the power in section 105A(3) of the Constitution to make laws 'for the carrying out by the parties thereto' of the Agreement (Gavan Duffy and Evatt dissenting). In reply to the argument that execution of a judgment could not issue against a state without appropriation of money, the majority relied in part on section 105A(5), which made obligations under the Agreement binding 'notwithstanding anything contained in … the Constitutions of the several States'. That included the requirement of appropriation by parliament. Lang's attempts to avoid the application of this Act led to his dismissal by the Governor.

Because of the crisis, some states enacted moratorium legislation enabling a person who had personal liability in respect of a mortgage or hire purchase agreement to postpone payment. The *Moratorium Act 1930* (NSW) required leave of the court before making a demand for such payment. The High Court held that the Act applied to action on a promissory note given as collateral security. It was argued that the state legislation was to that extent invalid under section 109 of the Constitution, because of **inconsistency** with the *Bills of Exchange Act* 1909 (Cth). The latter Act provided that the holder 'may sue on the bill in his own name' and recover the amount thereof with interest. The success of this argument would have destroyed the moratorium legislation, as all lenders would demand promissory notes. Yet only the state could enact general moratorium legislation. The Court held (Dixon dissenting) that there was no inconsistency (*Stock Motor Ploughs v Forsyth* (1932)), as the legislation was not intended to be a complete code; it left many matters to be determined under the general law.

Leslie Zines

Further Reading

Geoffrey Sawer, *Australian Federal Politics and Law 1929–1949* (1963)

Leslie Zines, 'Social Conflict and Constitutional Interpretation' (1996) 22 *Mon LR* 195

Dietrich v The Queen (1992). In *Dietrich*, a majority of the High Court (**Mason, McHugh, Deane, Toohey** and **Gaudron; Brennan** and **Dawson** dissenting) held that the lack of legal representation for an accused charged with a serious crime may result in an unfair trial.

Olaf Dietrich had been convicted in the Melbourne County Court of offences relating to the importation of a trafficable quantity of heroin in contravention of the *Customs Act* 1901 (Cth). Throughout the 40-day trial the defendant was unrepresented, unable to afford private representation and unsuccessful in attempts prior to trial to obtain representation at public expense. The High Court unanimously granted the applicant **leave to appeal** against his conviction, the application being made solely on the basis that the applicant's trial miscarried by virtue of the fact that he was not provided with legal representation.

The High Court dismissed the argument that there was a right to **counsel** at public expense. The majority, however, held that the right of an accused to receive a fair trial according to law (more accurately stated as a right not to be tried unfairly) is a fundamental element of Australian **criminal law**. Moreover, as Mason and McHugh held in a joint judgment, the 'courts possess undoubted power to stay criminal proceedings which will result in an unfair trial'. They continued: 'The power to grant a stay necessarily extends to a case in which representation of the accused by counsel is essential to a fair trial, as it is in most cases in which an accused is charged with a serious offence.' Thus a trial judge faced with an indigent unable to obtain legal representation should adjourn, or stay the proceedings until legal representation is available. Where an application to do so is refused, and the defendant's lack of representation makes the defendant's resulting trial unfair, an appellate court must quash any conviction that results. It was on this basis that that the applicant's conviction was quashed.

By way of *obiter dicta*, Deane and Gaudron held that the right to a fair trial was entrenched in Chapter III of the Constitution, which requires **judicial power** to be exercised in accordance with judicial process. Consequently, as Fiona Wheeler has noted, they 'would regard the inherent power of a court exercising federal jurisdiction to stay or adjourn proceedings to prevent what would otherwise be an abuse of its process—an unfair trial of a criminal offence—as immune from legislative abrogation'.

A significant aspect of *Dietrich* was the Court's preparedness to look to **international law** in the development of **common law**, the Court accepting that the International Covenant on Civil and Political Rights, albeit an unincorporated treaty, could, as Mason later said, 'influence the development of the common law, though in the end result it did not do so'. Perhaps more significant, however, was the controversial budgetary impact of the Court's decision, which indirectly exerted significant influence on political decisions about the level and allocation of funding for legal aid.

Dietrich is one of a series of important decisions of the **Mason Court**; it builds on Brennan's conception of a fair trial in *Jago v District Court (NSW)* (1989) as 'the onward march to the unattainable end of perfect justice'. The concept of a fair trial is crucial to the prevention of wrongful convictions, and the maintenance of public confidence in the judicial system. *Dietrich*, however, leaves many questions unanswered. The nature of judicial **law-making** is such that there has been 'no judicial attempt to list exhaustively the attributes of a fair trial' (Mason in *Dietrich*). The decision raises immediate questions about what is a serious offence and when is a person indigent. As Justice Jeremy Badgery-Parker points out, 'competent legal representation in criminal proceedings is so expensive as to be beyond the reasonable means of most people'. More broadly, it raises the question whether the concept of a fair trial applies not just to legal proceedings, but throughout the criminal process, including the way evidence is collected. Subsequent international human rights decisions suggest that the concept may have a more extensive application. In *Teixeira de Castro v Portugal* (1998), for example, the European Court of Human Rights held that evidence obtained by police entrapment violated the defendant's right to a fair trial.

DECLAN ROCHE

Further Reading

KP Duggan, 'Reform of the Criminal Law with Fair Trial as the Guiding Star' (1995) 19 *Crim LJ* 258

George Zdenkowski, 'Defending the Indigent Accused in Serious Cases: A Legal Right to Counsel?' (1994) 18 *Crim LJ* 135

Directions hearings. Traditionally, the procedure of making an application or issuing a summons for directions was designed to overcome unusual or difficult procedural problems, and was usually set in motion by a party. There is a tendency now for directions procedures to be used more broadly to assist the prompt, complete, and effective determination of court proceedings.

Order 31 of the **High Court Rules** provides that a party may take out a summons for directions at any time before judgment. Affidavits are not to be used on the hearing of a summons for directions except by the leave of the Court or a Justice. Upon the hearing, the Court or a Justice may give such directions with respect to the proceedings as the Court or Justice thinks fit. Although Order 31 contemplates a summons for directions being heard by the Court or a Justice, it is usually brought on for hearing before a single Justice.

In actions to be tried in the High Court, a party might take out a summons for directions relating to the interlocutory features of the action including discovery and inspection of documents; delivery of interrogatories; inspection of real or personal **property**; admissions of fact or of documents; and the place, time and mode of trial. The Court or a Justice might also pronounce **orders** as to the mode of evidence to be given at the hearing or trial; the number of expert witnesses each party may call; the appointment of a Court expert; the setting down of the action for trial; the pleadings and particulars; or an order that a written offer of contribution by one party be treated as a notice of payment into court.

Actions involving the trial of issues of fact are, however, generally **remitted** to another Court for trial pursuant to section 44 of the *Judiciary Act* 1903 (Cth). Directions hearings are now more likely to be held in matters involving discrete questions of law to be determined by the **Full Court** of the High Court. In these circumstances, the directions hearing involves judicial management of the action to ensure that the hearing before the Full Court is conducted effectively and efficiently.

Once the pleadings have closed in matters to be referred to the Full Court, the parties apply to a single Justice for orders stating a case or reserving a question for the consideration of a Full Court pursuant to section 18 of the Judiciary Act or for orders stating a special case pursuant to Order 35 of the High Court Rules. The parties frequently apply at the same time for directions as to the conduct and hearing of the matter before the Full Court.

In other instances, matters referred to the Full Court for determination are listed for directions at the instigation of the Court itself. This type of directions hearing is often required in matters involving a large number of parties or raising issues attracting the intervention of the Commonwealth, state or territory **Attorneys-General** pursuant to section 78A of the Judiciary Act. If it is considered appropriate, the matter is listed before a single Justice so that a timetable can be fixed for the filing and exchange of comprehensive written submissions in advance of the Full Court hearing. Directions might also be made as to the allocation of hearing time between all participants (including any applicants for leave to be heard as **interveners** or *amici curiae*) for the presentation of oral **argument** before the Full Court.

CAROLYN ROGERS

Disability discrimination is controversial. Is a visually impaired person entitled to the services of a tram conductor to advise him or her of a stop? Should a person be dismissed from employment because he or she suffers from a particular disease? Under the regime of anti-discrimination legislation, the High Court has been asked to provide answers to these questions. In such legislation, certain forms of less favourable treatment based on personal characteristics such as **race**, sex, **sexual preference** and disability, are declared to be unlawful.

Discrimination in these contexts may be defined as direct or indirect. Direct discrimination occurs when a person is treated less favourably on the basis of an irrelevant or impermissible reason. Indirect discrimination occurs when a requirement or condition is imposed which does not overtly differentiate on the basis of an irrelevant or impermissible reason, but has substantially the same or similar effect. Such an imposition, however, may be made if it is reasonable.

In *Waters v Public Transport Corporation* (1991) the critical issue was whether the decision of the Public Transport Corporation of Victoria (PTC) to remove conductors from most of its trams and to introduce a 'scratch ticket' system amounted to indirect discrimination. People with disabilities found it exceedingly difficult, if not impossible, to use the new system; and the absence of conductors meant that no one had been provided to help them. A challenge to the PTC's action was heard before the Equal Opportunity Board and then on appeal by the High Court.

The case turned on a number of issues of **statutory interpretation** arising from the definition of 'discrimination' in section 17(5) of the *Equal Opportunity Act* 1984 (Vic), and particularly on the meaning of the word '**reasonableness**'.

Mason and **Gaudron** (dissenting) interpreted the test of reasonableness as requiring the Court to identify a limited range of cases in which an imposed requirement or condition would not be rendered impermissible by the Equal Opportunity Act. For this purpose, it would be inappropriate to take into account the financial or economic considerations that may have motivated the PTC's decision, since considerations of that kind might permit the very kind of differential treatment that the Act was intended to prohibit.

For example, if it were more expensive to operate trams with conductors, it might be considered reasonable to remove conductors, despite the disproportionate impact on people with disabilities.

By contrast, **Dawson**, **Toohey**, **Deane**, and **McHugh** held that the term 'reasonableness' in this context involved a weighing of all relevant factors, including the financial or economic considerations of the defendant. This 'balancing of interests' is the familiar approach of contemporary **liberalism** to the problem of ascertaining the meaning of 'reasonableness'—especially when, as here, a general rule is made subject to reasonable exceptions. However, as Mason and Gaudron point out, the effect of such an approach in this statutory context is open-ended. On their approach, the precise statutory wording—'[if] the requirement or condition is not reasonable'—was to be understood as part of the definition of discrimination: its function was only to exclude 'those cases in which a requirement or condition serves to effect a genuine distinction'. If that approach were rejected, they argued, the legislative purpose might be defeated: 'If "reasonable" is not limited by the concept of "discrimination", there is nothing else in the Act to limit the considerations to be taken into account in reaching a decision on that issue.'

The Court returned the issue of reasonableness to the Board for its reconsideration. By the time the Board heard the matter, however, the Victorian government had changed its policy, making further consideration unnecessary. Following *Waters*, the Victorian parliament enacted the *Equal Opportunity Act* 1995 (Vic), replacing the 1984 Act. The majority's view of reasonableness in *Waters* is reflected in section 9(2) of the 1995 Act, and in other state Acts.

In *X v Commonwealth* (1999) the issue was one of direct discrimination. The appellant had been discharged from the Australian Defence Force (ADF) because he was HIV-positive. The discharge was made pursuant to the ADF's 'Policy for the Detection, Prevention and Administrative Management of HIV Infection' (1989). X (whose actual name was suppressed: see **Open court**) challenged the ADF policy on the basis that it amounted to discrimination on the basis of disease, contrary to the *Disability Discrimination Act* 1992 (Cth).

The Commonwealth conceded that the dismissal fell within the Disability Discrimination Act's definition of discrimination, but sought to justify its action by reference to an exemption in section 15, which provided that discrimination is justified if the employee 'would be unable to carry out the inherent requirements of the particular employment'. For example, in *Qantas Airways v Christie* (1998), a similar statutory reference to 'inherent requirements' was held to be satisfied (for the purposes of discrimination on the basis of age) by the fact that many countries would not allow aircraft operated by pilots over sixty years of age to enter their airspace.

Similarly, the Court held (**Kirby** dissenting) that X's disability did not relate merely to the 'incidents' of army service, but to its 'inherent requirements'. His appeal was dismissed. The majority (**Gleeson**, McHugh, **Gummow**, **Hayne** and **Callinan**) adopted a broad interpretation of 'inherent requirements', as including operational and practical considerations, thereby giving wide scope to an employer's argument that the disabled employee could not perform the inherent requirements of the position.

Kirby adopted a narrow interpretation of 'inherent requirements'. He included only those duties that are permanent and essential to the employment. The employer, therefore, must demonstrate that because of the disability, the employee is unable to perform these requirements, not merely that the employee may have difficulties in doing so. This narrow definition would mean that employers could dismiss employees only on the basis of permanent and essential duties ascertained in accordance with the objects of the Disability Discrimination Act, rather than by reference to the employer's criteria or interests.

In *X* and *Waters*, the majority defined the parties' rights according to broader economic and social considerations. If liberal notions of 'reasonableness' are allowed to dictate the definition of indirect discrimination, and if operational considerations are allowed to dictate the inherent requirements of a job, the protection offered by the legislation is significantly limited. Operational considerations and reasonableness may, as Anna Chapman has commented, simply affirm dominant standards and practices. The experiences of people with disabilities are thereby excluded or marginalised.

In yet another recent case, the High Court failed to accommodate the experience of people with disabilities. Unlike the decisions in *X* and *Waters*, the majority decision depended on technical legal argument. It was claimed in *IW v City of Perth* (1997) that the refusal of planning approval for a support centre for people with HIV attracted the statutory prohibition of discrimination on the ground of impairment under the *Equal Opportunity Act* 1984 (WA). A majority of the High Court quite beneficently held that a local government council, when dealing with a planning approval, is providing a 'service' for the purpose of that Act. Nonetheless, the claim was dismissed. The judges expressed divergent views regarding the meaning and application of key terms in the WA legislation. These included whether the council had 'refused' that service or provided it in a discriminatory 'manner'. Another issue was whether IW, the plaintiff, was 'the aggrieved person' or the person entitled to bring the claim.

These differing opinions are an indication of conflicting views over the scope of anti-discrimination laws in Australia, which in part stem from the unclear wording of such legislation. A further difficulty is posed by the Australian federal framework. For instance, in *AMP v Goulden* (1986), the Court had little choice but to hold that the Commonwealth's comprehensive regulation of life insurance, including provision for actuarial assessment of risk, was **inconsistent** with, and therefore prevailed over, state law prohibiting discrimination on the basis of physical disability (see section 109 of the Commonwealth Constitution).

Apart from questions involving the federal framework, the **role of the Court** in these cases is to give effect to the purpose of anti-discrimination legislation—to remedy or prevent disability discrimination. However, in neither *Waters*, nor *X*, nor *IW*, when it had the opportunity to do so, did the majority give the legislation its full effect. As Justice WR McIntyre pointed out in the Supreme Court of Canada in *Andrews v Law Society of British Columbia* (1989), true equality requires the accommodation of difference, not its marginalisation. Furthermore, the fact that the majority interpretation of 'reasonableness' in *Waters* was later enshrined in Victorian legislation is a matter for regret, and underscores the important relationship between the High Court and the Australian parliaments on matters of discrimination.

There is a pressing need for progressive reform of current anti-discrimination legislation. Fortunately, some guidance is offered by the **dissenting judgments** in *Waters* and *X*.

GLENN PATMORE

Further Reading

Anna Chapman, 'The Impact of the Equal Opportunity Act 1995 (Vic) on Paid Work Relationships' (1996) 9 *Aust J Labour Law* 1

Glenn Patmore, 'Moving towards a substantive conception of the anti-discrimination principle: *Waters v Public Transport Corporation of Victoria* reconsidered' (1999) 23 *MULR* 121

Discrimination. The notion of discrimination has at its heart the drawing of distinctions and the recognition of differences. The dominant contemporary use of the notion is in its pejorative guise: our concern to avoid 'adverse discrimination' is highlighted in the legislative framework of equal opportunity or anti-discrimination statutes.

The High Court has considered the meaning of 'discrimination' in a variety of contexts, ranging from the constitutional prohibition on discrimination against out-of-state residents in section 117 of the Constitution to the interpretation of various provisions of federal and state anti-discrimination and equal opportunity statutes. Other constitutional prohibitions of discrimination are present in sections 51(ii) and 99 of the Constitution, while the *Engineers Case* (1920) suggested that the general principle subjecting state and federal governments to each other's laws might be confined to laws 'which apply generally to the whole community without discrimination'. That reservation was developed in the *Melbourne Corporation Case* (1947), where **Dixon** held that **Commonwealth legislative powers** could not be exercised in a way 'which discriminates against States, or … which places a particular disability or burden upon an operation or activity of a State'.

The diverse manifestations of the notion of discrimination do have a core of common content. However, the interpretations by the High Court may be distinguished according to whether the context is that of a constitutional constraint upon the exercise of legislative power or that of some statutory measure of protection for an individual against defined classes of discriminatory behaviour.

The limited provisions in the Constitution which expressly prohibit the discriminatory exercise of Commonwealth legislative powers are confined to the powers to legislate with respect to **taxation**, bounties, and **trade and commerce**. In *Moran's Case* (1939), **Latham** sought to limit the constitutional relevance of 'discrimination' to those specific contexts. He said:

> There is no general prohibition in the Constitution of some vague thing called 'discrimination'. There are the specific prohibitions or restrictions to which I have referred. The word 'discrimination' is sometimes so used as to imply an element of injustice. But discrimination may be just or unjust. A wise differentiation based upon relevant circumstances is a necessary element in a national policy.

Section 51(ii) prohibits discrimination between states or parts of states in taxation, while section 99 prohibits the giving of a 'preference' to a state or part of a state in 'trade, commerce, or revenue'. Leslie Zines has noted that sections 51(ii) and 99 were inserted 'because of the fears of the smaller States that New South Wales and Victoria would use their numbers to gain benefits for themselves at the expense of others'. The desire at federation to remove discriminatory burdens upon trade and commerce, particularly when imposed by the states, is also reflected in section 92, which has been characterised as a 'rallying call for federationists'. The High Court held in *Cole v Whitfield* (1988) that although section 92 proclaims that **interstate trade** shall be 'absolutely free', what it actually prohibits is 'discrimination of a protectionist character'.

The object of sections 51(ii) and 99 was to promote uniformity throughout the nation in respect of revenue, trade and commerce. However, in interpreting these sections the Court has placed emphasis upon form without considering the differing effects throughout the nation that a uniform rule may have (see **Form and substance**). Thus, **Higgins** stated in *James v Commonwealth* (1928) that in order to satisfy the requirements of sections 51(ii) or 99 a 'rule' should simply be 'general, applicable to all States alike'. He specifically rejected the idea that the unequal operation of a law in different states might offend the prohibitions against discrimination and preference. In *Elliott v Commonwealth* (1936), the concept of 'preference' to one state over others was given a similar restricted meaning.

This legalistic interpretation has had implications for the interpretation of other provisions, such as section 96 (the grants power). Latham in *Moran's Case* endorsed the use of section 96 as a mechanism for 'adjusting inequalities' which might arise out of the operation of a 'non-discriminatory' uniform provision. And, as Australia has grown to maturity, the legalistic interpretation of sections 51(ii) and 99 and consequent narrowing of those sections has been seen by some to be justified in policy terms (see Advisory Committee on Trade and National Economic Management, *Report to the Constitutional Commission* (1987) 200–04). On the other hand, given that the threat of fragmentation is more likely to come from the states than from the Commonwealth, the substantive notion of discrimination adopted for section 92 in *Cole v Whitfield* has generally been applauded.

The 'discrimination' which Dixon identified in the *Melbourne Corporation Case* as calling for an exception to the principles of the *Engineers Case* has been considered in many subsequent cases. In *Queensland Electricity Commission v Commonwealth* (1985), an attempt by the Commonwealth government to subject a Queensland government authority to specialised procedures for the resolution of industrial disputes was held to offend the prohibition. The Court confirmed that the Commonwealth is prohibited from enacting laws that either discriminate against the states (or a particular state) by imposing special burdens or disabilities, or, although of general application, operate, when applied to the states, to destroy or curtail their continued existence or their capacity to function as governments (see **Intergovernmental immunities**).

Section 117 is found in Chapter V of the Constitution, which is headed 'the States'. However, unlike the other sections in that chapter, it is not addressed to the Commonwealth or states as a direct limitation upon the exercise of power. In contrast, it provides a guarantee for the individual ('a subject of the Queen') of protection against discrimination on the ground of out-of-state residence. The focus on the individual has been described by **Gaudron** as 'a particular subtlety in the language of s 117'. Until 1989, the section had been given a narrow interpretation by the Court (*Davies and Jones v WA* (1904); *Henry v Boehm* (1973)). These authorities were described by **Deane** in *Street v Queensland Bar Association* (1989) as 'a triumph of form over substance'. Street's challenge to the Supreme Court of Queensland Rules, which precluded a barrister from obtaining admission in Queensland unless he or she practised principally in that state, was the vehicle by which the Court gave substance to the section 117 guarantee.

The seven lengthy judgments in *Street* provide detailed and diverse analyses of the section's federal purpose and its objective of equal treatment. In some of the judgments, notably those of **Mason** and Gaudron, assistance in interpreting section 117 was found in anti-discrimination jurisprudence drawn from a number of jurisdictions including the UK, Canada and the USA. However, **McHugh** sounded a note of caution with his view that section 117 'was not intended as a human rights charter for interstate residents'. The Court accepted, however, that section 117 requires an assessment of the practical effect of a law upon an out-of-state resident. As with section 92, this approach is in contrast to that taken in respect of sections 51(ii) and 99, and reflects the different positions in the federation of the Commonwealth and the states, as well as a range of influences upon **constitutional interpretation** during the 1980s.

In a small number of significant cases, the Court has considered both the constitutional validity and the interpretation of federal and state anti-discrimination statutes. In *Koowarta's Case* (1982), a narrow majority of the Court upheld the validity of the *Racial Discrimination Act* 1975 (Cth) as a law with respect to **external affairs**. This decision was followed by *Viskauskas v Niland* (1983) and *University of Wollongong v Metwally* (1984), which explored the constitutional relationship between federal and state statutes that sought to provide redress for unlawful discrimination on the ground of **race**. The result in those cases, however, depended on the **inconsistency** provision in section 109 of the Constitution rather than on the anti-discrimination objectives of the state and federal legislature. Indeed, the end result in both cases was that these objectives were defeated: the existence of the Commonwealth Act was seen as excluding the operation of state legislation with the same objectives. In order to avoid that operation of section 109, the Commonwealth amended its race, sex and **disability discrimination** legislation to permit the concurrent operation of state and territory anti-discrimination laws.

A further constitutional issue concerning the practical operation of anti-discrimination law arose in *Brandy v Human Rights and Equal Opportunity Commission* (1995), where the mechanisms for enforcement of determinations by the Commission were held to be invalid because they had the effect of ascribing to Commission determinations the essential attributes of **judicial power**. That decision, too, has

required the government to re-examine the Commonwealth statutory framework.

Jurisprudence in the area of anti-discrimination law has developed slowly, with most decisions confined to tribunals or the lower courts. Some Justices have expressly counselled caution in the development of legal principle in this area. For example, **Brennan** in *Qantas Airways v Christie* (1998) said: 'The experience of the courts in this country in applying anti-discrimination legislation must be built case by case. A firm jurisprudence will be developed over time; its development should not be confined by too early a definition of its principles.' However, some **commentators** (for instance, Wojciech Sadurski) have urged the need for a more robust and principled, and less mechanical, approach to the interpretation of anti-discrimination statutes.

Brennan and McHugh in *IW v City of Perth* (1997) recognised explicitly that the task of interpreting anti-discrimination statutes is far from easy, in part because in many such statutes both 'discrimination and the activities which cannot be the subject of discrimination' are defined 'in a rigid and often highly complex and artificial manner'—a point made earlier in *Waters v Public Transport Corporation* (1991). In such circumstances, some Justices feel that even if they try to give a purposive and beneficial construction to an anti-discrimination statute, it 'will not always be capable of applying to acts that most people would regard as discriminatory'. The Court has sought assistance in the interpretation of anti-discrimination statutes from analogous provisions elsewhere, especially in the UK and North America.

The Court has decided a modest number of cases in the areas of race, sex and disability discrimination. Most of the cases since *Ansett Transport Industries v Wardley* (1980) have been appeals from **state Supreme Courts**. Perhaps the most significant of these has been *Australian Iron & Steel v Banovic* (1989), in which the High Court considered the requirements for proof of indirect sex discrimination in employment: that is, proof that an apparently neutral criterion may nevertheless have 'a disparate impact'. In that case, the retrenchment of workers on a 'last on, first off' basis, though not in itself inappropriate, was held to be discriminatory because of its 'exacerbation of the adverse effects of past discriminatory practices'. **Dawson** agreed with the **joint judgment** of Deane and Gaudron; Brennan and McHugh dissented. The joint judgment insisted that, in determining whether the policy had a disproportionate impact on **women**, 'a calculation made by reference to the aggregate workforce' was insufficient. Instead, the number of **men** affected and the number of women affected must each be ascertained as a proportion of a relevant base group, selected in such a way that the base groups 'do not themselves incorporate the effect of allegedly discriminatory practices'. This method of determining whether an apparently neutral requirement will have a discriminatory impact has attracted numerous commentaries. The *Banovic* **precedent** was applied by the Court in *Waters*, where a group of disabled persons complained that the use of 'scratch tickets' on Melbourne trams, combined on most trams with the removal of conductors who might have been able to offer assistance, had made it impossible or extremely difficult for them to travel. Remitting the complaint to the Victorian Equal Opportunity

Board for further consideration, the Court held that 'conduct which is "facially neutral" may nevertheless amount to, or result in, "less favourable" treatment'; and that 'material difference in treatment' may constitute discrimination notwithstanding the absence of any discriminatory 'intention or motive'.

As the overlap between anti-discrimination and industrial relations jurisdictions has become more apparent, the courts have also had to interpret anti-discrimination provisions in industrial laws. For example, in *Qantas Airways v Christie*, the Court had to determine whether an industrial agreement requiring Qantas pilots to retire at 60 was overridden by a provision in the *Industrial Relations Act* 1988 (Cth) prohibiting termination of employment on the ground of age, except where the use of an age criterion was 'based on the inherent requirements of the particular position'. The fact that Qantas flies to many countries which exclude pilots over 60 from their airspace was a material factor in the decision that the provision had not been infringed. In many other instances, workplace relations statutes now explicitly include issues of discrimination in employment within the definition of 'industrial matters'. The relationship between discriminatory practices and industrial matters is thus a dynamic one, of a kind not previously envisaged—indeed, it had been explicitly rejected by **Stephen** in 1980 in his judgment in *Wardley*.

In this malleable environment, the need for High Court guidance in matters of legal principle and **statutory interpretation** becomes ever more pressing.

KATHERINE LINDSAY

Further Reading
Rosemary Hunter, *Indirect Discrimination in the Workplace* (1992)
Wojciech Sadurski, '*Gerhardy v Brown* v The Concept of Discrimination: Reflections on the Landmark Case that Wasn't' (1986) 11 *Syd LR* 5
Leslie Zines and Geoffrey Lindell, 'Form and Substance: "Discrimination" in Modern Constitutional Law' (1992) 21 *FL Rev* 136

Dismissal of 1975. The events of 11 November 1975, when Governor-General John Kerr brought the **Whitlam era** to an end by dismissing **Prime Minister** Gough Whitlam, left many unresolved questions. Two of them affected the High Court. *Could* the Court have intervened in the events leading up to the dismissal? And *should* Chief Justice **Barwick** have intervened by advising the Governor-General that he had the power and duty to act? The questions are related, since Barwick in part defended his extra-judicial role by insisting that there was no way the Court could have become involved judicially.

Dismissed Prime Minister Gough Whitlam listening as the Governor-General's secretary, David Smith, reads the proclamation dissolving Parliament in 1975

Throughout the Whitlam government's term of office it faced a hostile Senate. The possibility that the Senate might fail to pass annual Appropriation Bills, in an endeavour to force the government to an election, was repeatedly raised. On 10 April 1974, when the government moved to debate an Appropriation Bill in the Senate, Opposition Senator Reg Withers moved an amendment that the debate be deferred until 'the Government agrees to submit itself to the judgment of the people at the same time as the forthcoming Senate election'. His motion adduced various justifications, primarily that 'because of its maladministration, the Government should not be granted funds until it agrees to submit itself to the people'. **Murphy**, as government leader in the Senate, moved that the question be put. He announced that if that motion failed, or if Withers' amendment were carried, 'the Government will treat that as a denial of Supply'. Murphy's motion was lost. Whitlam immediately advised the Governor-General to dissolve both Houses of Parliament (see *Cormack v Cope* (1974)) and the Labor government was returned at the ensuing election.

On 16 October 1975, when the government moved to debate an Appropriation Bill in the Senate, Opposition Senator Robert Cotton moved an amendment that the debate be deferred 'until the Government agrees to submit itself to the judgment of the people, the Senate being of the opinion that the Prime Minister and his Government no longer have the trust and confidence of the Australian people'. Again his motion adduced justifications, primarily 'the continuing incompetence, evasion, deceit and duplicity of the Prime Minister and his Ministers as exemplified in the overseas loan scandal'.

While the turbulence of the so-called 'loans affair' provided the immediate impetus for the opposition (see *Sankey v Whitlam* (1978)), another factor was the High Court's decision in the *Territory Senators Case* (1975). That decision was announced on 10 October 1975, on the eve of a Liberal Party Federal Council meeting. It meant that, at the next half-Senate election, the Northern Territory and the ACT would elect two senators each. Three of these four new seats were likely to be won by Labor. Moreover, the elected senators would take their seats immediately, not waiting until the next July as new senators normally do. The Whitlam government would thus obtain a majority in the Senate.

Presumably, this calculation was present to Whitlam's mind also, for throughout the ensuing confrontation he maintained that the appropriate solution was a half-Senate election at a time of his choosing. But he also took high constitutional ground, maintaining that the Senate's strategy was unconstitutional, and that his duty to the Constitution and to future governments was to defy it. That view also had some support in Liberal Party ranks, and as the confrontation dragged on there were rumours that Liberal senators might cross the floor and allow the budget to pass.

On 11 November 1975, Whitlam went to advise the Governor-General that the time had come for a half-Senate election. Before he could do so, Kerr informed him that he had been dismissed. Kerr's rationale was essentially that Whitlam was unable to secure Supply; that a Prime Minister who cannot obtain Supply must resign; and that if in such circumstances he fails to resign, the Governor-General has the

constitutional power and duty to remove him. Yet in terms of the conventions of **responsible government**, each of these propositions was debatable; and if the Senate strategy was unconstitutional, it could hardly be unconstitutional for a Prime Minister to resist it.

On the morning of 10 November, Barwick had called on the Governor-General in response to a telephone invitation the previous evening. Kerr outlined his proposed plan of action and asked whether Barwick was prepared to advise upon its propriety. After a further lunchtime consultation, Barwick delivered his written advice to Kerr that afternoon. It asserted all the crucial propositions on which Kerr's action depended: that 'the Senate has the constitutional power to refuse to pass a money bill'; that 'a Prime Minister who cannot ensure Supply … must either advise a general election … or resign'; that if the Prime Minister 'refuses to take either course, Your Excellency has constitutional authority to withdraw his Commission'; and that in that event 'Your Excellency's constitutional authority and duty would be to invite the Leader of the Opposition to form a caretaker government'.

The Senate's powers relating to money Bills, particularly those 'appropriating revenue … for the ordinary annual services of the Government', are set out in the first four paragraphs of section 53 of the Constitution. The Senate cannot originate or amend such a Bill, though it may return it to the lower house with a request for amendments. The fifth paragraph reads:

> Except as provided in this section, the Senate shall have equal power with the House of Representatives in respect of all proposed laws.

On an orthodox reading, this paragraph means that the Senate does have the legal power to defer or reject Supply. But on another reading, advanced in particular by FW Eggleston, though with few supporters, the first four paragraphs are an exhaustive code of the Senate's powers with respect to money bills. On that view, the fifth paragraph should be read as if it begins: 'Except as to money bills …'.

More commonly, critics of the Senate strategy conceded the Senate's *legal* power to defer or reject Supply, but asserted a *convention* that the power should never be exercised, or only under special conditions. The argument rested in part on unbroken Senate practice from 1901 to 1974, and in part on analogies with the **House of Lords** in the UK Parliament. Section 53 was broadly understood as intended to reproduce the British conventions of responsible government, and in 1901 these included a convention that the House of Lords should not reject Supply. When the House of Lords broke that convention in 1908, the *Parliament Act* 1911 (UK) took away its *legal* power to reject Supply.

The analogy between House of Lords and Senate was imperfect. Barwick's letter to Kerr denied it altogether. The Senate is—as the Lords were not—democratically elected. Yet the basis for Senate elections is not (as it is in the House of Representatives or the UK House of Commons) direct proportional representation of the population.

On the morning of 11 November 1975, I participated in a conference with **counsel** in which we began to draft a statement of claim asking the High Court to declare that the

Senate strategy was unconstitutional. To say that it was in breach of convention would not in itself have provided a basis for the Court to act, since conventions are not directly enforceable by the courts—though some **commentators** have argued, at least since the *Free Speech Cases* (1992), that the conventions of responsible government may now be thought to be constitutional implications. But if Eggleston's argument was sufficiently tenable to show that section 53 was ambiguous, the Court could be asked to resolve the ambiguity; and in such a case the courts can take notice of the conventions of responsible government, preferring a reading that accords with convention to one that does not (see, for example, *Copyright Owners Reproduction Society v EMI* (1958)).

There were, however, other practical problems. One was to find a plaintiff with appropriate **standing**. Another was the strong judicial tradition of non-intervention in the **parliamentary process**, as specifically developed by the High Court in relation to the **justiciability** of provisions in Chapter I, Part V of the Constitution. In *obiter dicta* in *Osborne v Commonwealth* (1911), the Court had contrasted section 55 with sections 53 and 54, suggesting that section 55 is justiciable, but that sections 53 and 54 are not.

One reason for this suggestion is that, if it is infringed, section 55 prescribes a specific legal consequence. Another is that section 55 refers to 'laws' (measures that have completed their passage through Parliament), while sections 53 and 54 refer to 'proposed laws' or 'the proposed law' (measures whose parliamentary passage is not yet complete). But in 1975, that distinction was weakened: the High Court decided that section 57 is justiciable, though it refers to a 'proposed law' throughout (see *Cormack v Cope*; *Territory Senators*; *PMA Case* (1975)).

Thus, Barwick's belief that the Court could never have become judicially involved was unfounded. The view of section 53 taken in *Osborne* may well have been reaffirmed, as it subsequently has been (see *Northern Suburbs Cemetery v Commonwealth* (1993); *Native Title Act Case* (1995)). But at least the Court would have had to rule on the threshold question of whether it could intervene.

The idea that judges should not espouse a position extrajudicially on issues they might have to determine judicially was only one consideration affecting the propriety of Barwick's advice. For one thing, it was hardly conducive to **personal relations** within the Court. On 12 November, before his letter to Kerr was released to the public, he circulated it to the other Justices for their 'confidential information'. Murphy responded in a memorandum protesting both against Barwick's advice and against his decision to give it, concluding: 'I dissociate myself completely from your action in advising the Governor-General and from the advice you gave.' Barwick replied:

> I note your remarks. I fundamentally disagree with them, both as to any legal opinion they involve and as to any matter of the propriety of my conduct. I see no need to discuss with you either question.

The views of the other Justices then became a matter for conjecture. Barwick asserted in his memo to Murphy: 'I do not regard any Justice as having confirmed or approved my action.' But in January 1994, he told a television interviewer that he had discussed his letter with **Mason**. Newspaper columnist Gerard Henderson then wrote that both Kerr and Barwick had previously told him of Mason's involvement (*Sunday Age*, 9 January 1994).

Some critics of Barwick's role at the time invoked the Court's decision in *In re Judiciary and Navigation Acts* (1921) that it cannot give **advisory opinions**. In fact that case is irrelevant to what judges as individuals might do extra-judicially. But in *Grollo v Palmer* (1995), the Court echoed the concern of the **United States Supreme Court** in *Mistretta v US* (1989) that judges as individuals should not 'assume extrajudicial duties' not 'compatible with, or appropriate to, continuing service on the bench', but should rather avoid any 'entanglement' which 'undermines public confidence' in their 'disinterestedness'. In *Wilson v Minister for Aboriginal and Torres Strait Islander Affairs* (1996), the joint majority judgment used these criteria to hold that a judge could not directly advise a minister where 'the function is an integral part of, or is closely connected with, the functions of the Legislature or the Executive Government'. In that context, the Court did think it relevant to recall that 'the giving to the executive of advisory opinions on questions of law is quite alien to the exercise of the **judicial power** of the Commonwealth'.

Barwick's involvement had ample precedents. Chief Justices **Griffith**, **Latham** and **Dixon** had all given sensitive political advice to Prime Ministers or vice-regal officers (see **Non-judicial functions**). As the majority in *Wilson* recognised, its 'criteria of incompatibility … have not always been observed in practice'. As Queensland Justice JB Thomas has said of other historical examples (*Judicial Ethics in Australia* (2nd edn 1997), Barwick may have been 'caught on the ebbtide of a previously acceptable practice'. But as Thomas adds, quoting US debates on past instances of judicial involvement with executive government, 'it is now asserted that "the practice of judicial advisement on matters of state is not tolerable", although it formerly had been'.

TONY BLACKSHIELD

Further Reading

Jeffrey Archer and Graham Maddox, 'The 1975 Constitutional Crisis in Australia', in D Woodward, A Parkin and J Summers (eds), *Government, Politics and Power in Australia* (3rd edn 1985) 50–67

Garfield Barwick, *Sir John Did His Duty* (1983)

Michael Coper, *Encounters with the Australian Constitution* (1987, popular edn 1988) ch 7

Paul Kelly, *November 1975* (1995)

John Kerr, *Matters for Judgment* (1978)

Gough Whitlam, *The Truth of the Matter* (1979)

Disqualification of Justices. Since the earliest days of the High Court, it has been thought desirable that, so far as possible, all Justices should sit on important cases, and particularly desirable that they should do so in major constitutional cases (see **Bench, composition of**). Thus, it is the frequent, though not invariable, practice for all seven to sit on important cases involving the interpretation of the Constitution (*Commonwealth v Colonial Combing, Spinning & Weaving* (1922)).

However, it is a fundamental principle of the **common law** that **natural justice** requires that judges not sit on matters in which they might have an interest in the outcome and that they should be free of bias in favour of or prejudice against any party to the proceedings. This means in essence that judges must be impartial and be seen to be impartial. These requirements, which are designed to maintain respect for the dignity and integrity of the judicial process, are regarded as essential aspects of **due process** and the structure of the Australian judicature erected by Chapter III of the Constitution.

Accordingly, it is open to a party to litigation to challenge a decision of a judge on the ground of partiality if in all the circumstances the parties, or a member of the public, might entertain a reasonable apprehension that the judge might not or did not bring an impartial and unprejudiced mind to the resolution of the matter (*Livesey v NSW Bar Association* (1983); *Grassby v The Queen* (1989); *Webb v The Queen* (1994)).

These fundamental principles apply to any court or judge sitting at any level in the **hierarchy** of Australian Courts. In the case of the High Court, they flow directly from the federal **jurisdiction** vested by Chapter III of the Constitution, which imports traditional judicial procedures, **remedies** and methodology: *War Crimes Act Case* (1991). Accordingly, it has been held by the High Court itself that Chapter III of the Constitution preserves the integrity, **independence** and impartiality of the federal courts in which Parliament invests federal jurisdiction: *Kable v DPP* (1996). Indeed, the concepts of independence and impartiality of the judiciary are considered integral to the doctrine of **separation of powers** in Australia: *Grollo v Palmer* (1995). Similar concepts inhere in Article 3 of the US Constitution, which has also been interpreted as containing a guarantee of judicial impartiality: *Northern Pipeline v Marathon Pipe Line* (1982); *Harris v Caladine* (1991).

There is no clear role or established practice of the High Court to govern the process by which a Justice might be disqualified from hearing a case. Commonly, a Justice might indicate a potential conflict and offer to withdraw if objection is taken by any of the parties; or **counsel** for one of the parties might indicate in a letter to the Registrar that they will seek to have a Justice disqualified, giving the Justice a chance to withdraw before the case is heard. On other occasions, such as the *Bank Nationalisation Case* (1948) and *Langer v Commonwealth* (1996), objections to a Justice hearing a matter have been raised in **open court**.

It is not unusual for a Justice to disqualify himself or herself because of a conflict of interest or the possibility that he or she might not be viewed as impartial in deciding the matter. The Justice might, for example, have acted previously as counsel for one of the parties to the proceedings, or may be a close personal friend of one of the parties, or may have a financial interest in the outcome of the case. **Dawson** did not sit in *Hematite Petroleum v Victoria* (1983) because as **Solicitor-General** he had advised the Victorian government on the likely result in the matter.

Ordinarily, the appropriate remedy when a judge otherwise disqualified by the principles of natural justice continues to sit in a case lies either in an appeal to the court next in the hierarchy, or in proceedings in the nature of prerogative writs or **judicial review** seeking **orders** disqualifying the judge concerned or quashing the judgment.

However, because the High Court is the ultimate court of appeal for Australia, such conventional remedies are unavailable. There is no tribunal to whom a disaffected litigant can further appeal, and the High Court does not have the power to make an order in the nature of judicial review against itself: *Federated Engine-Drivers and Firemen's Association v Colonial Sugar Refining Co* (1916). Further, a determination of a single judge refusing to stand down from a case is not a judgment within the meaning of section 73(i) of the Constitution from which an appeal lies to the **Full Court** of the High Court (*R v Watson; Ex parte Armstrong* (1976)).

Although the question of the Court's power to disqualify one of its own number from sitting in a particular case has not yet been authoritatively determined, it might be open to the party aggrieved to apply to the remaining Justices of the Court for an order effectively preventing that Justice from sitting. That avenue of redress might arise either as an exercise of the inherent jurisdiction of the Court or as an integral component of original jurisdiction empowering the Court to enforce and uphold the essential requirements of the **judicial power** devolved by Chapter III of the Constitution, including that of impartiality.

This very situation arose in the *Hindmarsh Island Bridge Case* (1998). In that case, **Callinan**, sitting alone, after a short hearing declined to disqualify himself from sitting to hear the full arguments. After the hearing before the full complement of seven Justices was completed, but before judgment had been delivered, an application was made to the Full Court—to be constituted by the other six Justices—for an order forcing Callinan to retire from further deliberating on the matter and from participating in the ultimate judgment of the Court. As it happened, Callinan disqualified himself from any further participation in the deliberations before the application to have him removed could be heard.

A similar situation coincidentally arose in the *Pinochet Case* (1998) before the **House of Lords**, itself the ultimate court of appeal for England. The Lords as originally constituted ruled by a 3:2 majority that it was competent for a British court to extradite former Chilean head of state Augusto Pinochet for trial on human rights offences. It later came to light that one of the Law Lords participating in this decision had links with an intervening party, who advocated a position adverse to that of Pinochet. An application was then made before an entirely differently constituted panel of Law Lords to set aside the first order on the basis of partiality of the member concerned. In due course, it was held that the first decision could not stand. The House had no difficulty in determining that it had the jurisdiction to rescind or vary an order previously made by it as the ultimate court of appeal or that it retained the power necessary to correct an injustice caused by an earlier order as an exercise of its unfettered inherent jurisdiction (*R v Bow Street Magistrate; Ex parte Pinochet (No 2)* (1999)). The result is a clear illustration of the principle that disqualification must follow in cases where a judge has an interest in the subject matter of the litigation, and is ultimately an application of the more fundamental principle of natural justice, which should be equally applicable in Australia, because 'justice should not only be done, but manifestly and undoubtedly be seen to be done' (*R v Sussex Justices; Ex parte McCarthy* (1923)).

These principles, however, are yet to be tested in Australia. In *Superclinics v CES* (1996), **Brennan** refused to disqualify himself from hearing an application by members of the Catholic Church to intervene in the proceedings, despite his admission that he was personally acquainted with members of the Catholic Bishops Conference, one of the organisations seeking to intervene. The proceedings, which centred on the legality of abortion, were settled shortly after the hearing began. The Catholic Church groups, however, had been successful in their application to intervene. The Court had divided 3:3 on that question, but Brennan's vote as Chief Justice, in favour of the application, determined the end result (see **Tied vote**).

SYDNEY TILMOUTH

Further Reading

Gerard Brennan, 'Why be a Judge?' (1996) 14 *Aust Bar Rev* 89

John Frank, 'Disqualification of Judges' (1947) 56 *Yale LJ* 605

Gregory Henry, 'Pinochet: In Search of the Perfect Judge' (1999) 21 *Syd LR* 667

'High Court Practice as to Eligibility of Judges to Sit in a Case' (1975) 49 *ALJ* 110

Sydney Tilmouth and George Williams, 'The High Court and the Disqualification of One of its Own' (1999) 73 *ALJ* 72

Dissenting judgments. A dissenting judgment is one delivered by a Justice who disagrees with the majority as to the final **order** resolving the litigants' dispute. There is a tendency, however, to describe parts of judgments that differ from the majority view as 'dissenting' on particular issues, even when there is no disagreement as to the outcome of the case. Such a judgment is more accurately classified as **concurring**. A truly dissenting judgment is opposed to the result reached by the majority of the Court.

A Justice who disagrees with his or her colleagues generally writes a separate judgment to justify the contrary conclusion. In doing so, the Justice may helpfully refer to the reasoning of the majority and explain why that view is not shared. The primary function of a dissenting judgment is for a member of the Court to make it clear why he or she disagrees with the outcome reached by the majority and to put forward a contrary solution. Unfortunately, however, dissenting Justices often prefer to explain simply why they think the conclusion they have reached is correct rather than why that of their colleagues is wrong. **Commentators** despair when the Justices fail to engage in this way and question whether the Court's **conferencing** practice over the years has been adequate (see **Collective responsibility**).

From the viewpoint of the immediate parties to the action, especially since the abolition of appeals to the **Privy Council**, dissenting judgments of the High Court are valueless—cold comfort for the vanquished at best. However, to those outside the immediate dispute the dissent may hold more interest. Critics may champion the dissent as the view that should have prevailed in a controversial case. Whether the dissent is simply used as part of a broader attack upon the Court through the **media** or is used more specifically and

constructively as a basis for a legislative response to the majority's decision depends upon a number of factors, not least of which are the nature of the issue and the source of the **criticism**.

In the longer term, dissent provides rich material for academic analysis of the Court's decisions. Debate about the correctness of the various stances adopted may ensure that the issues remain alive well after the decision is handed down. The Court may have cause to return to these issues in a later case, and the commentary made on earlier decisions may help its members to a consensus. Two significant constitutional cases of recent years illustrating the combined effect of dissenting opinions and academic criticism are *Cole v Whitfield* (1988), which finally resolved the Court's meaning of section 92 of the Constitution after decades of uncertainty (see **Interstate trade and commerce**) and *Lange v ABC* (1997), which confirmed the existence of an implied freedom of **political communication** after a much briefer, yet perhaps even more controversial, period of debate. The process can occasionally work in reverse, with commentary causing dissension where there was none before, as is demonstrated by **McHugh's** dissent in *Masciantonio v The Queen* (1995) from the reasoning of a unanimous judgment in which he had participated in *Stingel v The Queen* (1990). In the subsequent case, he attributes his defection substantially to his reading academic criticism of the *Stingel* judgment.

Justices who dissent often write with a view to convincing their colleagues to abandon their own opinions and adopt those of the dissenter. The stronger the conviction of the Justice that he or she is right, the more likely it is that the Justice will persist in dissent over a series of cases rather than defer to the majority as a matter of **precedent**. Perhaps the most significant function of dissent is that it may be persuasive in the formulation of future judgments of the Court. As Chief Justice Charles Evans Hughes of the **United States Supreme Court** once observed:

> A dissent … is an appeal to the brooding spirit of the law, to the intelligence of a future day, when a later decision may possibly correct the error into which the dissenting judge believes the court to have been betrayed.

This sentiment was echoed by **Mason, Wilson, Dawson** and **Toohey** in *Federation Insurance v Wasson* (1987).

The close participation of **Griffith, Barton,** and **O'Connor** as **framers of the Constitution** resulted in a relatively harmonious beginning to the Court's proceedings when they formed its original Bench. From 1903 to 1906, there were only four dissents (all by O'Connor, and none in a constitutional case). However, the addition of **Isaacs** and **Higgins** in 1906 resulted in dissenting judgments becoming a regular occurrence—especially in matters of **constitutional interpretation**. Although both newcomers had also been prominent in the **Convention Debates**, neither had been on the Drafting Committee. That they were less enamoured of the final form of the Constitution than their colleagues (indeed, Higgins had advocated a 'No' vote on the finished Bill) was to prove a significant factor in establishing a tradition of dissent. Their repeated dissents from decisions applying the doctrines of intergovernmental immunities and reserved state powers were eventually vindicated in the *Engineers Case* (1920).

Isaacs was the Court's first great dissenter, but there has been no shortage of dissenters on the Court since then. The rate of dissent in the **Knox Court** was high. Of the 561 collegiate decisions reported during the period, divisions of opinion occurred in 209 cases, or 37 per cent of the total. In 1926 and 1927, the proportion was 50 per cent, and the following year it rose to 57 per cent. In the 1930s, **Starke's** hostile attitude towards some of his colleagues may well have contributed to a particularly high rate of dissent. But there was competition—the **Latham Court** was notable for acrimonious **personal relations**, with **Evatt**, **McTiernan** and Latham himself all being frequent dissenters as well. Of the 789 collegiate decisions reported, divisions of opinion occurred in 42 per cent of these, reaching 72 per cent in 1944, dropping back to 39 per cent in 1945, but rising again to 65 per cent in 1946.

The only member of this Court still sitting when his colleague **Dixon** assumed the office of **Chief Justice** in 1952 was McTiernan, who was to be a continual dissenter throughout his 46 years on the Court. But with that exception, the **Dixon Court** was probably the most harmonious the Court has known, with disagreements in only 27 per cent of the collegiate decisions reported. With some notable exceptions, particularly in relation to early cases concerning freedom of interstate trade, Dixon himself was seldom in dissent and the Justices who served on his Court and into the early **Barwick Court** all had low incidences of dissent.

The tide turned in the 1970s, and McTiernan ended his **tenure** in a Court just as fractured as that in which he first sat. **Murphy's** propensity to dissent is legendary, although, even so, his rate of dissent was only about one case in six—a reminder that dissent must be seen in context and that, despite the impression given by spectacular examples to the contrary, any particular Justice is much more often in agreement with his or her colleagues than in disagreement. Of course, the proportion of dissents for any individual Justice will be much lower than the overall proportion of non-unanimous decisions to unanimous ones.

Murphy was not the only notable dissenter. Although **Barwick** had dominated the Court in the latter half of the 1960s, he dissented with increasing frequency throughout the 1970s as he rapidly lost influence over the newer Justices. Murphy's reputation as a dissenter is well deserved, but Barwick, **Aickin** and **Jacobs** were all high dissenters in their own right. Generally, quieter times seemed to prevail in the **Gibbs Court**, despite the number of high-profile constitutional cases that split the Court during these years.

At first glance, the **Mason Court** seemed to mark a return to the levels of consensus achieved under Dixon's leadership in the 1950s, but the true picture was slightly more complex. **Mason** himself was a rare dissenter—almost from his arrival in 1972 he was regularly the voice of the majority. Unlike Barwick, this was something he was able to sustain throughout his time on the Bench and until his **retirement** in 1995. The number of unanimous judgments led by Mason as Chief Justice is striking when compared with the extent of unanimity under his two predecessors, yet there was still room for individual voices during these years. **Deane** and McHugh

were notable dissenters in this period, but the other Justices also had healthy rates of dissent. The present Court has Justices at each end of the spectrum. **Gummow** has dissented only a handful of times since his appointment in 1995, while **Kirby** is a much more frequent dissenter.

The fluctuation in dissenting judgments across the Court's history is due to a myriad of factors, including the role played by the Chief Justice. What is clear is that dissent is a relational concept. The propensity to dissent is not (or is probably not) an inherent characteristic of a Justice—he or she finds that role by virtue of the characteristics of the other Justices and the dynamics of the Court as a whole, in addition to his or her individual qualities.

It is not surprising that most dissenting judgments do not have long-term impact. While the Court is not strictly bound by precedent, adherence to past decisions, even if only majority decisions, promotes certainty and stability; thus majority opinions inescapably command more respect. Nevertheless, some dissenting judgments have later assumed a much greater importance. The rejection by Isaacs and Higgins of the Court's early constitutional implications and the eventual acceptance of that view in the *Engineers Case* is a striking example. The subsequent vindication of many of Murphy's dissents may be another, although whether there is a causal connection between those dissents and the subsequent shifts in the law is hotly debated.

Conversely, it is not uncommon for Justices to defuse any potential impact of their minority view by concurring in the final result nonetheless. Such a judgment is deprived of its status as a dissent. The justification given for this approach is to avoid divisive uncertainty over an important issue. The deference by Dawson to the majority view after his own view of the **external affairs power** was defeated in the *Tasmanian Dam Case* (1983) is instructive and is to be contrasted with the continuing dissent of other Justices on comparable issues. One of the most poignant examples of abandonment of dissent is Dixon's judgment in *Hughes & Vale v NSW (No 1)* (1953). With the Court poised 3:3, he cast his lot, on the basis of precedent, for the view with which he personally disagreed—only to be overturned by the Privy Council, which preferred his reasoning and restored his original view.

The likelihood of persistence or capitulation depends upon various factors, including the size of the majority, the passion with which the dissenting view is held, and the perceived importance of the issue and likelihood of its recurrence. In *Peters v The Queen* (1998), Kirby put aside his own opinions on conspiracy to defraud so that a majority view could be reached, yet it is clear that in regard to other matters he would maintain a stoic dissent at all costs. Conversely, a Justice may persist in his or her view, but agree with another view in the alternative so as to form a majority (see, for example, Murphy in *Uebergang v Australian Wheat Board* (1980)).

Finally, what of the impact of dissent upon the dissenters themselves? Many of the judgments betray no hint of their author's reaction to the rejection of his or her views beyond bland acknowledgment of the fact. As **Stephen** said upon retirement, 'it's not a matter of great zeal and enthusiasm that my view should prevail … If it doesn't happen to be the majority view, so be it'. However, there are some memorable judgments whose status as dissenting must have been deeply disappointing to their author. Evatt's moving quotation of poetry and fiction to convey the anguish of a parent whose child is lost indicates a depth of feeling absent from the majority in *Chester v Waverley Corporation* (1939), which dismissed a claim for nervous shock from a mother who witnessed the recovery of her drowned son from a drain. A more direct, yet no less poignant, sentiment of regret is found at the end of Barton's dissenting judgment in *Duncan v Queensland* (1916): 'To say that one regrets to differ from one's learned brethren is a formula that often begins a judgment. I end mine by expressing heavy sorrow that their decision is as it is.' In *Re Wakim* (1999) (see **Cross-vesting**), Kirby cited Barton and concluded his opinion with the statement, 'So, in this case, do I'.

ANDREW LYNCH

Further Reading
John Alder, 'Dissents in Courts of Last Resort: Tragic Choices?' (2000) 20 *Oxford Journal of Legal Studies* 221
Michael Coper, *Encounters with the Australian Constitution* (1987, popular edn 1988) ch 3
Michael Coper and George Williams (eds), *Justice Lionel Murphy: Influential or Merely Prescient?* (1997)
GPJ McGinley, 'The Search for Unity: The Impact of Consensus Seeking Procedures in Appellate Courts' (1987) 11 *Adel L Rev* 203
Cheryl Saunders (ed), *Courts of Final Jurisdiction: The Mason Court in Australia* (1996)

Dixon, Owen (*b* 28 April 1886; *d* 7 July 1972; Justice 1929–52; Chief Justice 1952–64) was the only son of Joseph William Dixon, a barrister who, becoming deaf, left the Bar to practise as a solicitor. Dixon received his secondary education at Hawthorn College. Academically bright, he did well in his matriculation examinations.

At the University of Melbourne, his examination results were not outstanding, but his studies were profoundly influential on the development of the man. Two scholars were of particular importance: Thomas George Tucker, under whom he studied classical **language** and literature for his arts degree, and William Harrison Moore, who held the chair of law. From Tucker, he acquired a love of classical literature and a sympathy with classical thought that affected the cast of his mind. It instilled in him an appreciation of 'strict logic and high technique' that came to characterise his work as a Justice. On his death, it was said that 'all his work as a judge was marked by habits of scholarship in no small part derived from these early studies, though undoubtedly the natural bent of his mind was scholarly. He habitually exhibited what he called "the scholar's instinct to verify"'. Dixon took his BA in 1906 and his MA in 1909.

From Harrison Moore, a scholar whose chief interests were English and US constitutional law, Dixon obtained a complete grasp of legal principle and a lively interest in constitutional and legal development.

Having graduated LLB in 1908, and having served articles of clerkship with Crisp & Cameron in the following year, he signed the roll of **counsel** of the Victorian Bar on 1 March

Owen Dixon, Justice 1929–52; Chief Justice 1952–64

1910. Pupillage was not then compulsory and, because of the poor financial circumstances of his family, Dixon did not read with anyone. Even so, he soon made his name at the Bar. In his early years, he was one of three juniors commissioned by Leo Cussen to work on the 1915 consolidation of Victorian statutes. As a junior, he took three pupils—Robert **Menzies** (later **Prime Minister**), Henry Baker (later a Tasmanian politician) and James Tait.

In 1922, after 12 years at the Bar, he was appointed a KC. While he remained at the Bar, he was its acknowledged leader, exercising 'absolute dominance' as its outstanding lawyer and greatest advocate. His style was distinctive:

His wide smile, happy in its unconcern, lights up his face when he is listening to his learned brother put the case he is soon to reduce to powder. When His Honour calls upon him to reply to a proposition, Dixon hitches his gown over his right shoulder, coughs nervously, gives a short, staccato laugh, of which he appears entirely unconscious, and then, however unawares he seems to have been taken, delivers a reply which is complete to six decimal places.

Both as junior and as silk, Dixon appeared often in the High Court and in all jurisdictions in Victoria; as silk, he appeared before the **Privy Council**. The High Court of the day was said to be 'a Court of judges contentiously holding individual convictions which were pungently expressed'. It was said of Dixon that 'he would with diabolical skill set one judge against another in dialectical combat in the course of persuading the majority to decide in his favour'.

He enjoyed his work at the Bar. He was to say, when acknowledging the Victorian Bar's welcome on his **appointment** as **Chief Justice**: 'For my part, I have never wavered in the view that the honourable practice of the profession of advocacy affords the greatest opportunity of contributing to the administering of justice according to law.' His skills as a barrister were recognised wherever he appeared. When he went to the Privy Council, John Simon KC (later Viscount Simon) suggested that he take chambers in London and practise there, but he did not, presumably for a mixture of personal and professional reasons.

In July 1926, Dixon was appointed an acting judge of the Supreme Court of Victoria. Although pressed to take a permanent seat, he did not, as he did not enjoy judicial work. In that same year, he was offered the position of Chief Judge of the Commonwealth Court of **Conciliation and Arbitration**, but again he declined.

In 1928, Dixon and two other members of the Victorian Bar were appointed by the Bar to give evidence to the Royal Commission on the Constitution. The evidence he gave revealed a deep and clearly formed understanding of the Constitution.

In 1929, at the age of 42, he was appointed a Justice of the High Court. More than once, Dixon was to express the view that judicial work 'is the most difficult, most exacting and least satisfying of any work which I have had to attempt' and that it was 'hard and unrewarding work'. The Court of the 1930s was not happy (see **Personal relations**). No doubt this did not ease any difficulty Dixon felt about the work, but it certainly did not diminish the amount of work he did. Many of the **joint judgments** to which Dixon was party during the 1930s bear the mark of his authorship.

In the early years of **World War II**, Dixon continued to perform his duties as a Justice, but he accepted appointment as chairman of several war-related committees: the Central Wool Committee (1940–42); the Australian Shipping Control Board (1941–42); the Marine War Risks Insurance Board (1941–42); the Salvage Board (1942); and the Allied Consultative Shipping Council of Australia (1942). His work on these bodies was seen as that of 'a very practical administrator'.

In April 1942, he was appointed Australian Minister to Washington, and took leave of absence from his judicial duties. As Australian Minister, he had the usual duties of the head of a diplomatic mission, but his chief task was to ensure that the war in the Pacific, and Australian interests, were not neglected in Washington. **Aickin** served as Third Secretary. Dixon was an Anglophile and did not regard the USA with great affection. Nevertheless, he formed very good relationships with a number of holders of high office in the USA including Justice Felix Frankfurter of the **United States Supreme Court**, with whom he was to establish a long correspondence.

Evatt, who had sat with Dixon on the Court, was Minister for External Affairs in the Australian government during Dixon's time in Washington. Evatt had not supported Dixon's appointment. Dixon, in turn, had required that he be responsible to the Prime Minister, not Evatt. Dixon eventually became frustrated with Evatt's conduct and in 1944

sought to be, and was, relieved of his post. On Dixon's departure from Washington, Dean Acheson, then Assistant Secretary of State, said that Dixon would be greatly missed. Acheson also said of Dixon that he would be an adornment to the Bench of the Supreme Court if it were possible to appoint him to it.

Washington was not the only diplomatic mission Dixon undertook. In 1950, he was nominated as UN representative to mediate in the dispute between India and Pakistan about Kashmir. He spent some months seeking to resolve the conflict but was unable to do so, despite the fact that he was highly regarded by both sides.

In 1952, Dixon was appointed the sixth Chief Justice. He served in that office for 12 years (see **Dixon Court**). In the 35 years he spent on the Court, interrupted by the diplomatic service just mentioned, he produced a body of work that was widely admired. For many, he was the greatest judicial lawyer in the English-speaking world and the most distinguished exponent of the **common law**—a fact reflected in the many honours given to him. He was awarded honorary doctorates by the universities of Oxford, Harvard, Melbourne and the ANU. In 1955, Yale University awarded him the Harry E Howland memorial prize 'for services to mankind'. He was appointed to the Privy Council in 1951 and appointed GCMG in 1954. In 1963, he was appointed to the Order of Merit. In 1970, he became a corresponding Fellow of the British Academy.

That he was the pre-eminent common lawyer of his time is commonly accepted. The reasons for that pre-eminence, and the effect his work continues to have, repay close consideration. At the end of the twentieth century, Dixon's name was often associated with a reference to 'strict and complete **legalism**' and a suggestion that his approach to the law, and his decisions, are therefore out of date, if not irrelevant. The reference derives from his statement, upon being sworn as Chief Justice, that

close adherence to legal reasoning is the only way to maintain the confidence of all parties in Federal conflicts. It may be that the court is thought to be excessively legalistic. I should be sorry to think that it is anything else. There is no other safe guide to judicial decisions in great conflicts than a strict and complete legalism.

In its own terms, the statement now so often associated with his name was directed to the resolution of federal conflicts and the avoidance of any suggestion of political influence on that task. Moreover, to understand it as advocating a mechanistic approach to the law would be simplistic and wrong.

Central to his view of the common law and its methods was his understanding of the **rule of law**. That had several consequences. First, the rule of law implied an external standard of legal correctness by which a decision could be adjudged to be right or wrong. Secondly, it led Dixon to condemn the judicial innovator as 'bound under the doctrine of **precedents** by no authority except the error he committed yesterday'. Thirdly, and most importantly, it found its reflection in the course of events in *Tait's Case* (1962). Tait was a convicted murderer who had been condemned to death. The time of Tait's execution was fixed, and announced, despite an application to the High Court challenging the legality of his execution being pending. The **Full Court**, presided over by Dixon, enjoined the executive government of Victoria, under whose laws the execution was to be carried out, from doing so before the hearing and determination of the application pending in the Court. On behalf of the Court, Dixon said that this was done 'without giving any consideration to or expressing any opinion on the grounds upon which [the applications] are to be based but entirely so that the authority of the Court may be maintained and we may have another opportunity of considering it'.

The doctrine of precedent did not, in Dixon's eye, or under his hand, lead to the stultification of development of the law. In Dixon's view, adherence to precedent was desirable as promoting the development of a body of common law uniform within the British Commonwealth, but the processes of deduction and induction central to the techniques of the common law would allow for adaptation of that law.

Adherence to precedent was not, however, an end in itself, sufficient to withstand all contrary argument. Dixon was to lead the High Court's break, in *Parker v The Queen* (1963), from its previous practice of unfailingly following the **House of Lords**, and on occasion he joined in refusing to follow the Court's own previous decisions—for example, in the *Second Uniform Tax Case* (1957) and in the *Cigamatic Case* (1962). But, as the section 92 cases which culminated in *Hughes & Vale v NSW (No 2)* (1955) show, precedent was central to his judicial technique.

Many of the constitutional issues that occupied the Court in Dixon's day are now settled. Most if not all of the section 92 learning that owed so much to Dixon was made obsolete by *Cole v Whitfield* (1988). The learning on **excise duties**, so much of which was built up through the decades in and after the 1930s, was largely settled by the Court's decisions in Dixon's day. (Some, at least, of the problems associated with licence fees remaining after *Dennis Hotels v Victoria* (1960) were considered in *Ha v NSW* (1997)). The reduction in, if not elimination of, constitutional litigation on these subjects in more recent years should not, however, be taken as suggesting that Dixon's legacy in constitutional cases is now reduced in value.

His legacy in relation to Chapter III of the Constitution can be traced from his argument (as a junior) for the Attorney-General for Victoria in *In re Judiciary and Navigation Acts* (1921) about the meaning of **matters**, through his discussion of the nature of the appellate **jurisdiction** of the Court in *Victorian Stevedoring & General Contracting Co v Meakes and Dignan* (1931) (soon after his appointment as a Justice), to the discussion of **separation of powers** and of the **judicial power** of the Commonwealth in the *Boilermakers Case* (1956). His conception of federation and the consequences of the adoption of a federal system, as reflected in the *Melbourne Corporation Case* (1947) and the *Cigamatic Case*, remains of continuing importance.

Just as important, however, as his legacy in the field of **constitutional law** is his enduring influence in many other areas of the law, including subjects as diverse as the law of **evidence** about hearsay and expert witnesses in *Ramsay v Watson* (1961), the duties of counsel for an accused in *Tuckiar v The King* (1934), the equitable principles applicable to voluntary transactions and **undue influence** in *Yerkey v Jones* (1939), the common law doctrine of **estoppel** in *Grundt v Great Boulder Gold Mines* (1937), and the law relating to nuisance expounded in *Victoria Park Racing v Taylor* (1937). That so many of these cases warrant separate treatment in this work reveals something of the nature and continuing extent of the influence of Dixon's work.

Dixon resigned his commission in 1964 because, as he said, 'I believe I ought'. For much of the time after his **retirement**, he was in poor health and he took no part in public life. In 1920, he married Alice Crossland Brooksbank, who died in 1971. They had four children.

KENNETH HAYNE

Further Reading
'Articles in Honour of Sir Owen Dixon' (1985–86) 15 *MULR* 543
Douglas Menzies, 'The Right Honourable Sir Owen Dixon, OM, GCMG' (1973) 9 *MULR* 1
JD Merralls, 'The Rt Hon Sir Owen Dixon, OM, GCMG, 1886–1972' (1972) 47 *ALJ* 429
Alan Watt, *Australian Diplomat* (1972)
'Retirement of the Chief Justice' (1964) 110 *CLR* v
'The Chief Justice of the High Court' (1952) 26 *ALJ* 2
'The Late Sir Owen Dixon' (1972) 126 *CLR* v
SHZ Woinarski (ed), *Jesting Pilate* (1965)

Dixon Court (18 April 1952–13 April 1964). During this period, the Court's prestige was very high, not only in Australia, but in other **common law** countries. Lord Denning described it as the Court's 'Golden Age' and declared it had established a reputation that 'overtopped even that of the **House of Lords'**. It was referred to by the Victorian Bar Association as 'the finest court in the English-speaking world'. The authority of **Dixon** over the Court was immense, made even more significant by the presence of other Justices, particularly **Fullagar** and **Kitto**, who were respected and admired. In contrast with the **Latham Court**, **personal relations** between the Justices were harmonious, and there were many more **joint judgments**. In contrast with earlier courts and with the later **Barwick Court**, the **Chief Justice** ensured that **counsel** were given an opportunity to present a coherent **argument**, rather than be subject to frequent judicial cross-examination.

In the last years of the Latham Court, major policies of federal governments under **Prime Ministers** Ben Chifley and Robert Menzies had been aborted as a result of the Court's constitutional decisions. By comparison, the period of the Dixon Court was fairly tranquil in that regard, partly because the government was generally content to live within the core of the Commonwealth's expressly granted powers, and did not generally attempt to test the limits of those powers. Cases that involved the interpretation of **Commonwealth legislative powers** were usually decided in the Commonwealth's favour. Direct regulation of the slaughtering of meat intended for export was upheld under the **trade and com-**

The Dixon Court on Dixon's retirement. Left to right: Windeyer, Taylor, McTiernan, Dixon, Kitto, Menzies and Owen

merce power (*O'Sullivan v Noarlunga Meat* (1954)). That power was also held to authorise the exemption of a Commonwealth statutory shipping corporation from state taxation (*Australian Coastal Shipping Commission v O'Reilly* (1962)). The **territories** power was held to provide authority to control activities in a state as long as there was a sufficient nexus with a territory (*Lamshed v Lake* (1958)). A state law impairing the freedom of trade between the state and a territory was, therefore, held invalid under section 109 of the Constitution because it was **inconsistent** with a federal law, made under the territories power, providing for such freedom of trade.

A second challenge was made to the uniform income tax scheme, first upheld in 1942. The Court reaffirmed the power of the Commonwealth under section 96 of the Constitution to make financial grants to the states on condition they did not levy income tax, but held invalid a provision making it unlawful to pay state income tax before paying federal tax. On the main point, Dixon expressed a personal view in favour of a more limited interpretation of the grants power, but followed past cases. In invalidating the other provision, the Court made it clear that any legislative reliance on incidental powers required the Court to consider the purpose of the legislation and its connection with the subject of the power (*Second Uniform Tax Case* (1957)).

While this case preserved a scheme that had operated for 15 years, the *Boilermakers Case* (1956) put an end to a system that had existed for 30 years. The admixture of arbitral and **judicial power** exercised by the Court of **Concilia-**tion and **Arbitration** was held to be inconsistent with the separation of the judicial power of the Commonwealth implied from Chapter III. The Court expounded a theory of **separation of powers** that was stricter than had hitherto been applied. After *Boilermakers*, many challenges were brought to the Court testing whether particular powers of federal courts were in breach of Chapter III. While *Boilermakers* was deplored by many as making more difficult the development of a sound system of **administrative law**, the Court, both under Dixon and later, allowed a large overlap of power that could validly be exercised by either courts or administrative tribunals. Ten years after Dixon retired, **Barwick** and **Mason** cast doubts on *Boilermakers* (*R v Joske; Ex parte BLF* (1974)), but it remains a leading authority.

The most striking constitutional development of the Dixon Court was in relation to section 92, which provides that trade, commerce and intercourse among the states shall be absolutely free. The Court followed an earlier minority interpretation by Dixon to the effect that section 92 guarantees to each individual a constitutional right to engage in **interstate trade**, subject to reasonable regulation. The **Privy Council** upheld that view in a judgment that consisted almost entirely of long quotations from the judgments of Dixon and Fullagar (*Hughes & Vale v NSW* (1954)). In the aftermath of that decision, state laws regulating transport and rationalising road and rail transport were invalidated (*Hughes & Vale v NSW (No 2)* (1955)), though limited taxes designed to compensate for wear and tear on the roads were upheld in *Armstrong v Victoria (No 2)* (1957). A state marketing scheme for fish was held inapplicable to fish from another state in *Fish Board v Paradiso* (1956).

Technical distinctions were common. A law limiting the production of margarine was held applicable to margarine intended to be sent interstate, on the ground that production preceded trade and therefore was not protected by section 92: *Grannall v Marrickville Margarine* (1955). Similarly, a state law prescribing the price of goods was held applicable to the first sale within the state of imported potatoes because the sale occurred after the interstate trade had ended: *Wragg v NSW* (1953). The **economic** effect on the trade was referred to as irrelevant. As time went on, this interpretation collapsed because of varying applications by the Justices, and was eventually overthrown in *Cole v Whitfield* (1988).

The Dixon Court was divided on the meaning of duties of 'excise', the imposition of which is made exclusive to the Commonwealth by section 90 of the Constitution. Most of the Court accepted an earlier view of Dixon in *Parton v Milk Board* (1949) that the concept of 'excise' extended to taxes not only on the production of goods but on all later transactions down to the point of receipt by the consumer. However, the Justices differed over whether the incidence of a tax was to be determined in accordance with the formal criterion of liability laid down in the Act, or by examination of the commercial and economic effects of the tax. A decision by a narrowly divided Court allowing a state to impose a licence fee on sellers of liquor provided it was quantified by reference to the value of past business purchases (**Dennis Hotels v Victoria** (1960)) led in later years to the Court holding valid many state licence fees on sellers of liquor, tobacco and petrol, using a similar technique, even though the fees had the same practical effect as (invalid) sales taxes. Most of these cases were effectively discredited in *Ha v NSW* (1997), though technically even then the Court stopped short of **overruling** them.

Implications from the federal nature of the Constitution resulted in the Court declaring that the Commonwealth had greater immunity from state law than was earlier thought to be the case. In the *Cigamatic Case* (1962), it was held that a state companies law could not affect the Commonwealth's priority over other creditors in the liquidation of an insolvent company. The decision vindicated the view that Dixon had earlier expressed in dissent in *Uther's Case* (1947) (see also **Intergovernmental immunities**).

The Dixon Court was in later years seen as characterised by **legalism**, and Dixon spoke in favour of that concept when he was sworn in as Chief Justice. Nevertheless, the Court was not hidebound or rigid when basic principles were at stake; instead it called for a creative approach. For many years, the Court had followed decisions of the House of Lords and, usually, the English Court of Appeal, in preference to its own decisions. Other Australian courts were instructed to do the same, even in the face of an earlier inconsistent High Court decision (*Piro v Foster* (1943); *Waghorn v Waghorn* (1942)). The purpose was to achieve a uniform interpretation of the common law throughout the British Commonwealth. In 1963, however, the Court for the first time refused to follow a decision of the House of Lords for the reason that it was fundamentally wrong (**Parker v The Queen** (1963)). This led

increasingly to the development of a common law of Australia distinct from that of England.

In **Tait's Case** (1962), the Court stayed the execution of a convicted man pending the hearing of an appeal, in the face of a refusal by the Crown to give an undertaking that the execution would be postponed. Dixon declared that the Court had power to 'preserve any subject matter, human or not, pending a decision'. An adjournment was ordered 'entirely so that the authority of this Court may be maintained'.

The Court attempted a more rational and principled approach to the issue of **children** harmed while on property without permission. Although strictly trespassers, these children had often been deemed 'licensees' in order to obtain the benefit of a higher duty of care by the occupier. The Dixon Court saw this as the use of a fiction, which created confusion and lacked intellectual conviction. Building on earlier initiatives by Dixon (*Thompson v Bankstown Corporation* (1953)) and Fullagar (*Rich v Commissioner for Railways* (1959)), the Court held that there should be applied a duty of care based on the general law of negligence (*Commissioner for Railways (NSW) v Cardy* (1960)). In the 1980s, the Court was to take this approach further, abolishing the special categories of **occupiers' liability** and analysing all such cases in terms of a general duty of care under the ordinary law of negligence (*Australian Safeway Stores v Zaluzna* (1987)).

LESLIE ZINES

Further Reading
SHZ Woinarski (ed), *Jesting Pilate* (1965)

Dixon diaries. During 1911, during the first two months of 1929, and in each of the years from 1935 to 1965, **Dixon** kept a diary. He may have kept other diaries that were lost or later destroyed, though there are no cross-references to non-surviving diaries. The 1935 diary, one should note, does not begin as though it were a new venture. In addition, he kept travel journals, written up daily like diaries: from 27 November 1923 to 22 March 1924 during his second trip to London to appear before the **Privy Council**, and again from 20 May to 5 September 1939 during his trip to Britain and the USA with his two sons, Franklin and Ted.

His chief purpose in compiling the diaries seems to have been to make a daily record that could be checked later if necessary, and there are examples of retrospective cross-referencing. However, they are more than *aides-mémoires*—if he is depressed, or has sinus pain, or if one of the children is ill or being troublesome, he notes it. Many of the pages are written in minute handwriting and great detail. They record most of the books he read for the periods they cover, most of the cases that came before him, and many significant discussions with colleagues and friends. Those for 1942–44, covering his years as Minister to Washington, provide pocket summaries of all his important discussions with President Roosevelt, Harry Hopkins, Assistant Secretary of State Dean Acheson, members of the Joint Chiefs of Staff, heads of legations, Felix Frankfurter, and others. The 1950 diary provides the same detail of record for his period as UN mediator between India and Pakistan over Kashmir. The diaries give Dixon's view of, and contributions to, a large part of twentieth-century

The Dixon diaries, kept meticulously for more than 30 years

Australian history and those who made it, his circles of acquaintance being wide and powerful. They offer a unique interior perspective for a biographical study, being frequently personal, even deeply private, in content.

The Dixon they reveal is largely consistent with the public persona—intensely hard-working (regularly to 1.00 am, frequently to 3.00 am or later), civic-spirited, sceptical, ironical, dry in wit, classical in sensibility (a reader of Greek and Latin literature in the original **languages**), devoted to a wife and children from whom his work separated him more than he would have liked, an Anglophile through and through, a leading light in the English Speaking Union and the Australian Institute for International Affairs, supportive of a White Australia like almost everyone else. The diaries also reveal a Dixon easily depressed, even over little matters. For instance, after a day on the Bench putting up with **Starke's** rudeness and **Latham's** depressing 'political' statements, he was looking forward to seeing his barrister friend TS Clyne, whom he had invited to tea through his **associate**, but there was no answer—'another example of the hopeless condition I have attained' (4 November 1937).

In the diaries, he writes about his colleagues with critical frankness. In the 1930s, they were the chief reason he hated his life on the Court, and by 1935 he was looking for a way out. On 8 February of that year, an opportunity of returning to the Bar presented itself when his former pupil, **Attorney-General** Robert **Menzies**, asked him to chair a Royal Commission on Banking and Finance, decided on at the previous day's Cabinet meeting. Dixon told him it was contrary to

proper judicial conduct but agreed to consider it, noting in his diary that 'it seems to present an opportunity of resigning in order to do this work and then of returning to the bar'—then turned it down. He dissuaded **Fullagar** and Wilbur Ham (see **Counsel, notable**) from accepting positions on the Supreme Court of Victoria, telling the latter that 'no one could get any pleasure out of judicial work' and that he hated it (1 October 1935; he said the same to Norman O'Bryan). He knew that **Gavan Duffy** would have to go if the High Court were to be improved, taking it on himself to urge him to resign (15 February 1935). To judge from Gavan Duffy's 'amazed' reaction, no one, not even his son, had previously broached the matter. Dixon was aware of the rumours that the Chief Justiceship had been promised to Latham and he resented his friend Robert Menzies' continued silence on the matter, and his ultimate **appointment** of Latham (17 and 19 October 1935).

The earlier diaries reveal a Court hopelessly compromised by divided personalities (see **Personal relations**). For instance, Starke's antipathy towards **Rich** and **McTiernan** meant that he could never be left in Sydney to form a Court of three with them, and for that reason Dixon cancelled a trip to Melbourne for the first convention of the Law Council of Australia at the end of October 1935, his two papers having to be read for him (see also **Circuit system**). Numerous entries show him regularly helping Rich with his judgments (even when Dixon had not sat on the case), and occasionally he helped McTiernan with his. Later entries state that he wrote some of Rich's judgments for him, though it is possible that Dixon meant he was writing *sections* of Rich's judgments. He was no admirer of Latham, though he thought the Court happier for his presence. He considered him coarse in sensibility, with a cynical, condoning view of political immorality (14 September 1937), a low sense of **humour** (30 April 1938), and unbearable egotism (26 November 1938). He was at first prepared to give **Evatt** the trust and confidence appropriate to a fellow Justice, but over the decade he lost faith in his probity. Later, as a diplomat, he found it almost impossible to deal with the political Evatt. He respected the quality of some of his judgments (for instance, his dismissal of the application to commit *The Sydney Morning Herald* for **contempt** over **criticism** of the Court's role in the *Kisch* saga), but was frequently critical of him, seeing his and McTiernan's appointments as blatantly political. He believed that former politicians were bad choices for the High Court. That went for Latham, too, a man Dixon thought sometimes hasty in reaching conclusions, as during the hearing of *Sodeman v The King* (1936)—'It seemed apparent that Latham had made up his mind on grounds of public **policy** to dismiss the appeal' (30 March 1936)—and frequently political in his conduct of cases, exemplified early on in what Dixon saw as his pro-Commonwealth statements during the hearing of *Radio Corporation v Commonwealth* (1938) (4 November 1937). In the *Bank Nationalisation Case* (1948), Dixon noted that Latham 'seemed openly to espouse the government and met every contention of the Bank with initial disfavour', the product of his 'habitual bias for the government' (23 February 1948). He was even harsher on Latham's conduct and judgment in the hearing of the *Communist Party Case* (1951).

Of his later colleagues he was less critical, though the diaries indicate that he thought **Webb** incompetent and **Williams** lazy. In April 1958, as **Owen** told Dixon, Williams 'seemed very neurotic and psychologically disturbed. Quite incapable of decision about his resignation'. Dixon replied that 'the Court could not go on any longer without a judge in his place. It was unfair to the other judges. I had gone to the utmost lengths with him over the last four years. Said that he had written only 12 judgments in the last 12 months' (23 April 1958). There are few criticisms of Owen in the diaries, and Dixon was reasonably close to him. **Taylor** emerges as less than diligent. In 1957, he was 'reported to have returned the Privy Council judgments in the *Boilermakers Case* and the long service leave case without reading them. No mention by him to me of the cases' (26 March 1957). Some of Taylor's judgments were 'superficial and obviously dictated' (2 April 1959). It surprised Dixon a little that Douglas **Menzies**, who had been a dazzling advocate, did not make the grade as a High Court Justice and found the work 'unexpectedly defeating' (24 December 1962). On the other hand, he regarded **Kitto** and **Windeyer** as of real High Court mettle and Fullagar as nonpareil.

While acknowledging the general quality of **Barwick's** advocacy, Dixon was not always impressed. During the *Communist Party Case*, Barwick 'did his case a great deal of harm by his approach, based on impossible constructions to save the Act' (11 December 1950). Dixon felt obliged to outline to Barwick the case he could have made to support the validity of the legislation, but Barwick 'made no fist of it' (14 December 1950). When Evatt's reply 'made hay' of Barwick's arguments, Dixon 'felt it necessary to say that there was another case' than the one that Barwick had argued, and that Barwick's 'unexpected course' had placed the Court 'in a position of peculiar responsibility' (15 December 1950). Nor did Dixon like him: 'Barwick proposed the toast of Bar and Bench in terms which threw me off balance. I tried to deal with the offensive undertones or implications of his speech but did it all badly … I said [to Kitto] I thought [Barwick] was a declared enemy of the Court and of me particularly and said how I hated being a judge for such reasons' (19–20 September 1952). Needless to say, he deplored Barwick's appointment as his successor.

Many entries reveal his high standards of judicial propriety. Three examples must suffice. He thought no High Court Justice should sit on a Royal Commission, believing that they should avoid involvement in controversial matters other than those that could not be avoided in the performance of judicial duty. The Petrov Commission is a case in point. **Prime Minister** Menzies asked him to chair it, saying 'that it was of the greatest international and domestic consequence. I was known in Washington and in London and would carry weight'. Dixon refused, the majority of his colleagues endorsing his decision (21–22 April 1954). He believed that, ideally, every Justice on the Court should write a judgment for each case on which he sat (10 October 1937), though in certain areas of the law he considered that, if possible, the Court should speak with a single voice, for instance in some **crimi-**

nal law cases to avoid confusion at the trial level. However, he did not believe a judge should compromise his views to facilitate **joint judgments**. And, as a third example, he refused to discuss with counsel matters that might conceivably come before the Court (7 June 1962). On the other hand, he felt free to advise the Governors of Victoria and WA, and the Governor-General (in each case, very significantly, a non-lawyer), how they might resolve both real and putative constitutional crises (30 October 1952, 2 April 1955, 6 January 1956, 6 March 1960, 3 March 1961), discussed the Petrov Royal Commission with its chairman, Owen (several entries in the second half of 1954), and discussed it too with Colonel Charles Spry, head of the Australian Security Service (17, 25 August 1954). Some, certainly not all, would consider these as breaches of propriety, but to Dixon, a commanding judicial figure with an undeniable sense of propriety, the circumstances outweighed any niceties.

These diaries were never intended for the eyes of all and sundry. Shortly before Dixon died, the National Librarian wrote to say that the Library had received Latham's **private papers**—might it one day have Sir Owen's? Dixon refused the request, expressing concern that his private letters to Latham were available to any prying stranger who might ask to see them. He would almost certainly have destroyed the diaries had he believed they would ever end up there, for they contain intimate details of family life, not all of them happy. Nevertheless, he preserved them.

Philip Ayres

DOGS Case (1981). Seeking to challenge the constitutional validity of state aid for church schools, but concerned about their own **standing** to do so, members of the DOGS organisation ('Defence Of Government Schools') approached a number of **Attorneys-General** asking them to institute a relator action on the organisation's behalf. Although the Attorneys-General in every other state refused to grant a fiat for such an action, the Victorian Attorney-General agreed. Other plaintiffs included members of the organisation suing in their own right, claiming standing as parents or teachers of children in government schools, as residents of Victoria, or simply as taxpayers.

The package of legislation under challenge included the annual *Appropriation Acts* (insofar as they appropriated money for non-government schools), and also, in particular, the *States Grants (Schools Assistance) Acts* 1976–79 (Cth). The Acts provided for ministerial approval of a list of non-government school systems and a list of individual schools; and for each of them the Minister for Education was authorised to fix an appropriate level of financial assistance (based on numbers of students enrolled, and on six different levels of 'need'). Pursuant to the 'grants power' in section 96 of the Constitution (as interpreted in the *Uniform Tax Cases* (1942 and 1957)), this amount was then granted to the state as 'financial assistance'—on condition, first, that it be paid to the school authority 'without undue delay' and identified as Commonwealth funding; and, secondly, that the state should first procure an agreement from the school authority to apply the money solely to recurrent expenditure, and to furnish to the Commonwealth Minister an accountant's certificate to that effect, along with 'such other financial and statistical information' as the Minister might require.

In March, April and June 1979, **Murphy** sat in Melbourne to take detailed evidence from witnesses for the plaintiffs and for the non-government schools. In January 1980, he ordered that the case be argued before the **Full Court**.

The plaintiffs' main argument was that direct state aid to church schools violated section 116 of the Constitution ('The Commonwealth shall not make any law for establishing any religion'). The argument relied on decisions of the **United States Supreme Court** interpreting the First Amendment to the US Constitution ('Congress shall make no law respecting an establishment of religion …') as prohibiting any direct governmental support for religious institutions.

Only Murphy accepted that argument, interpreting the Australian section 116, like the US First Amendment, as importing Thomas Jefferson's conception of 'a wall of separation' between **church and state**. The majority Justices emphasised the verbal differences between the two clauses—arguing, for instance, that the Australian phrase '*for* establishing any religion' was confined to laws enacted for the *purpose* of establishing a religion. Against that background, the Australian provision was read as confined to prohibiting the official identification of government with any one religion (as the monarchy in the UK is identified with the Church of England and the Church of Scotland). Only **Stephen** took a more flexible view, extending section 116 not only to the establishment of a national church but to 'the favouring of one church over another'. In argument, the hypothetical case was put of a Commonwealth grant to a particular church to enable it to build a cathedral in Canberra: the majority reasoning suggests that such a grant would not infringe section 116.

The plaintiffs also argued that the Grants Acts were not a legitimate use of the 'grants power'; but the Court unanimously rejected this argument. **Wilson** expressed 'great sympathy' with the argument as a matter of principle: he pointed out that the device of granting the allocated moneys to the states was a matter of **form**, not substance, since in reality the grants 'give no assistance to a State as a body politic but use it merely as a conduit or an agency by which moneys are distributed to schools and school systems upon conditions fixed by the Commonwealth'. He emphasised, however, that the plaintiffs had not sought an **overruling** of the Court's earlier decisions on the grants power (the *Uniform Tax Cases* and particularly *Moran's Case* (1939)); and that as long as those cases stood unchallenged the argument could not be pursued.

Since the plaintiffs' claim failed on both main grounds, most Justices did not discuss the issue of standing. Stephen and Wilson expressly refused to do so. **Gibbs** held that the Victorian Attorney-General had standing, but that individual plaintiffs (even parents) probably did not. For Murphy, given the traditional duty of an Attorney-General to defend the validity of legislation, it was 'incongruous and unrealistic' to say that he alone could challenge validity. 'A citizen's right to invoke the **judicial power** to vindicate constitutional guarantees should not … depend upon obtaining an Attorney-General's consent. Any one of the people of the Com-

monwealth has the standing to proceed in the courts to secure the observance of constitutional guarantees.'

On the main issue concerning the effect of the 'establishment' clause in section 116, Murphy's dissent is a striking example of his **activism** in giving effect to **express constitutional rights**. Conversely, the majority view reflects the Court's consistent tendency to interpret such provisions narrowly. Indeed, both **Mason** and Wilson argued that on principle, *grants* of legislative power should be broadly construed, while *limitations* on legislative power should be strictly construed. **Barwick**, however, explicitly denied this distinction; and any such distinction may nowadays be difficult to maintain, especially if limitations on power are alternatively characterised as 'rights'. Some Justices have treated the terminology of 'rights' and 'limitations' as giving rise to a further distinction, so that 'a constitutional guarantee of the rights of individuals' should be construed more broadly than a 'restriction on power'. But this distinction, too, may be difficult to maintain. Stephen relied on it in the *DOGS Case*, as he had done earlier in *King v Jones* (1972); yet he also noted that section 116 is 'a constitutional provision of high importance', providing 'important safeguards for religious freedom for Australians'.

TONY BLACKSHIELD

Further Reading

Australian Council for the Defence of Government Schools, *DOGS and the High Court Case*, http://www.ozemail.com.au/~adogs/dogs_high_court_case1.htm

Michael Coper, *Encounters with the Australian Constitution* (1987, popular edn 1988) 317–21, 406–08

Donoghue v Stevenson (1932), a decision of the **House of Lords** concerning an alleged snail in a bottle of ginger beer, is probably the best-known judgment in the **common law** world. Although formally the decision resolved no more than an issue of the Scots law of delict, its influence has been such that it is still regarded as the foundation of the law of negligence throughout the British Commonwealth.

The issue was whether David Stevenson, a manufacturer of ginger beer, owed a duty of care to May Donoghue, who had consumed some of Stevenson's ginger beer. Mrs Donoghue alleged that the ginger beer was contaminated by the decomposing remains of a snail, the presence of which she had discovered only after she had drunk some of the ginger beer. When she commenced proceedings against Stevenson in Edinburgh, Stevenson raised as a preliminary point the argument that, even if Donoghue's allegations were proved correct, he would not be liable, as his duty of care did not extend to each and every consumer of the products he manufactured. Stevenson's argument was rejected at first instance, but upheld on appeal to the Inner House of the Court of Session. On further appeal to the House of Lords, a bare majority held that, on the alleged facts, Stevenson did owe a duty of care to the consumer of his products.

The immediate principles to be derived from the majority judgments were, first, that a manufacturer owes a duty of care to consumers of the products of that manufacture, and, secondly, that the fact that a manufacturer may have a contractual obligation to some people does not preclude the imposition of a duty in **tort**, to exercise reasonable care, to others with whom the manufacturer has no contractual relationship. As a case about manufacturers' liability, *Donoghue v Stevenson* was raised in argument before the High Court a little over a year later in *Australian Knitting Mills v Grant* (1933), where the respondent argued that he had suffered considerable physical injury from sulphides contained in long woollen underpants manufactured by the appellant. A majority of the Court held that *Donoghue v Stevenson* was not applicable, as the respondent had not sufficiently proved that the appellant had failed to exercise reasonable care in the process of manufacture. However, Dr Grant's further appeal to the **Privy Council** was successful (see **Litigants, notable, 1905–1945**).

But *Donoghue v Stevenson* was also recognised as having relevance far beyond the area of manufacturers' liability. The landmark judgment of Australian-born Lord Atkin was seen in particular as furthering the development of negligence as a separate tort. Liability for harm caused through another's lack of care had previously depended on the plaintiff establishing the existence of some relationship, falling into a well-recognised category, between the defendant and the plaintiff. *Donoghue v Stevenson* dispensed with the need to establish such a relationship. Lord Atkin, at least, asserted that a duty to exercise reasonable care was owed to all persons who 'are so closely and directly affected by my act that I ought reasonably to have them in contemplation as being so affected when I am directing my mind to the acts or omissions which are called in question'. Such persons were to be regarded as the 'neighbours' of the defendant by reason of their **proximity** to the effects of the latter's acts or omissions.

Evatt wrote to Atkin in 1933:

> The Snail Case has been the subject of the keenest interest and debate at the Bar and in the Sydney and Melbourne Law Schools: on all sides there is profound satisfaction that, in substance, your judgment and the opinion of Justice Cardozo in the USA (in *MacPherson v Buick Motor Co*) coincide, and that the common law is again shown to be capable of meeting modern conditions of industrialisation, and of striking through forms of legal separateness to reality.

As a statement of a general principle of liability, *Donoghue v Stevenson* was first relied on by the High Court in its attempt, in the 1950s and early 1960s, to free the law relating to **occupiers' liability** from its historical shackles so as to ameliorate the lot of trespassers who were injured while on another's land. The decision was also the basis of the Court's subsequent successful move to rationalise and simplify the principles relating generally to occupiers' liability. It was the foundation of the Court's development of liability for nervous shock brought about by the sudden perception of physical injury to another (*Jaensch v Coffey* (1984)), and the Court's determination of the circumstances in which a person might owe a duty of care to guard against another's purely financial harm, whether that harm was caused by the defendant's negligence in word or deed (*MLC v Evatt* (1968)). The case provides the ultimate authority for determining the

circumstances in which one may be liable for having failed to act to avert harm to another, and for setting the boundaries of one's liability for injuries caused by the acts of a third party.

An example of the way in which *Donoghue v Stevenson* has affected all aspects of liability for injury caused through another's lack of care may be found in the development of the law relating to a landlord's liability (or lack thereof) towards persons other than the tenant who are injured by some defect in the premises. In *Cavalier v Pope* (1906), the House of Lords held that a landlord was immune from such liability, and the judgments in *Donoghue v Stevenson* did not seek to change that position. *Cavalier v Pope* was assumed by the High Court, in *Voli v Inglewood Shire Council* (1963), to be part of the law of Australia. But when the issue of a landlord's liability next came before the High Court, in *Northern Sandblasting v Harris* (1997), **counsel** for the landlord conceded that any principle to be derived from *Cavalier v Pope* had been overtaken by the broad statement, based on *Donoghue v Stevenson*, of a duty being owed to all those who are reasonably foreseeable as likely to be affected by one's acts or omissions.

Whenever the issue arises of whether a person should be regarded as owing a duty to take reasonable care for the protection of another, it is the judgments of the majority of the House of Lords in *Donoghue v Stevenson* that form the basis of the answer, whether reference is made to the case itself or to the many subsequent cases that have applied it. And yet, curiously, it never was established whether there was a snail in the bottle of ginger beer.

JAMES DAVIS

Further Reading

Peter Burns (ed), *Donoghue v Stevenson and the Modern Law of Negligence: The Paisley Papers* (1991)

RFV Heuston, '*Donoghue v Stevenson* in Retrospect' (1957) 20 *MLR* 1

Geoffrey Lewis, *Lord Atkin* (1983)

Alan Rodger, 'Mrs Donoghue and Alfenus Varus' (1988) 41 *Current Legal Problems* 1

Due process. The contemporary notion of 'due process' is derived from US **constitutional law**, where it is seen as having two distinct aspects. Procedural due process refers to the way a judicial or administrative function is undertaken, and suggests that a court may ensure that such tasks are carried out by following the appropriate procedures. Substantive due process refers to the content of a law and suggests that laws on certain subjects—such as, in the USA, abortion—may be reviewed by a court to ensure that the legislature has observed 'due process' by giving sufficient consideration to fundamental **values** and liberties. This latter aspect is the more controversial, because it gives a court the power not only to ensure that the correct procedures are followed, but to scrutinise the acceptability of legislative **policy** judgments.

The idea that the Australian Constitution should contain a guarantee of due process has a long history. At the 1891 **Convention**, Andrew **Inglis** Clark, the Tasmanian **Attorney-General**, argued that the Constitution should protect fundamental rights, and proposed a clause that would require 'the equal protection of the laws'. This was incorporated as part of the draft Constitution adopted by the 1891 Convention. It remained unamended until the 1898 Convention in Melbourne. By 1898, Inglis Clark had become convinced that the provision needed to be bolstered. He proposed, through the Tasmanian Parliament, that the Convention insert a new clause that would in addition provide 'nor shall a state deprive any person of life, liberty, or **property** without due process of law'.

Inglis Clark's proposal was based on the Fourteenth Amendment to the US Constitution, which had been inserted after the Civil War to prevent racial **discrimination** and to entrench a measure of **equality** for the newly freed slaves (see **Bill of Rights**). The clause did not survive in the Australian Constitution in the form Inglis Clark had proposed. The Convention instead inserted a new provision: it became section 117 of the Constitution, which prevents discrimination on the basis of state residence—a mere shadow of Inglis Clark's original vision.

It is ironic that Inglis Clark's battle to insert an **express constitutional right** of due process was lost, yet the High Court has since discovered that some rights of this kind might in any event be implied from the **separation of powers**, and in particular from the separation of **judicial power**, brought about by the Constitution. In *Re Tracey; Ex parte Ryan* (1989), **Deane** suggested that the separation of judicial power effected by the Constitution is 'the Constitution's only general guarantee of due process'.

In the *War Crimes Act Case* (1991), Deane summarised the requirements of Chapter III of the Constitution, which achieves the separation of judicial power:

> The Parliament cannot, consistently with Ch III of the Constitution, usurp the judicial power of the Commonwealth by itself purporting to exercise judicial power in the form of legislation. Nor can it infringe the vesting of that judicial power in the judicature by requiring that it be exercised in a manner which is inconsistent with the essential requirements of a court or with the nature of judicial power.

The final sentence amounted to a guarantee of procedural due process that has since been accepted by other Justices (see, for example, **Brennan**, Deane and **Dawson** in *Chu Kheng Lim v Minister for Immigration* (1992)). For Deane, Chapter III implied not only that judicial power could be vested only in Chapter III courts, but also that any power thus vested must be exercised in accordance 'with the essential requirements of a court'. By this means, for example, Chapter III might give constitutional entrenchment to the fundamental **common law** elements or postulates of **criminal procedure**, such as the presumption of innocence.

In short, the Court has recognised that the Constitution contains an implied guarantee of procedural due process, although exactly which rules and procedures are guaranteed remain unclear. In *Leeth v Commonwealth* (1992), Deane and **Toohey**, with possible support from Brennan, suggested that a guarantee of substantive due process might also be implied. They held that the Constitution, as informed by the common law, entrenches a right to 'legal equality', which would override inconsistent laws. In the *War Crimes Act Case*, Deane had argued that Chapter III prevents the federal Parliament from requiring a court to act otherwise than in accordance with the essential attributes of a court. In *Leeth*, these attributes were taken to include 'the duty of a court to extend to the parties before it equal justice, that is to say, to treat them fairly and impartially as equals before the law and to refrain from discrimination on irrelevant or irrational grounds'. This limitation was said to be only one aspect of a broader requirement that the Commonwealth observe the principle of equality under the law.

In the same case, **Gaudron** also recognised a guarantee of due process, but limited it to its procedural aspects. She found that 'it is an essential feature of judicial power that it should be exercised in accordance with the judicial process' and that 'the concept of equal justice' is basic to that process. Any concept of equality under the law was, for Gaudron, rooted in the concept of judicial process. Thus it only applied where a federal court was being asked to exercise a power granted by the federal Parliament.

Deane and Toohey did not seek to limit their implication in this way. For them, equality under the law was not restricted to the judicial process but operated as a standard for review of any Commonwealth law. Its source was not merely in Chapter III, but in a 'general doctrine of legal equality' derived not only from Chapter III, but from 'the inherent equality of the people' as parties to the federal compact. What was entrenched was a standard of equality to be determined by judicial perception. There is nothing in the text of the Constitution to give guidance on the content of such a standard. It might ultimately mean that judges would be faced with difficult social and political questions similar to those before the **United States Supreme Court**, such as whether affirmative action programs on the basis of race or gender meet the standard of equality required by the Constitution.

In their **joint judgment** in *Leeth*, **Mason**, Dawson and **McHugh** agreed that there might be some limitations on the way in which a court might be required to exercise its powers. For example, an attempt 'to cause a court to act in a manner contrary to **natural justice** would impose a non-judicial requirement inconsistent with the exercise of judicial power'. Hence, they accepted that the Constitution does support some form of due process guarantee. However, while they were prepared to support some limits on Commonwealth power in 'essentially functional or procedural' respects, they rejected the substantive limitation asserted by Deane and Toohey. This left the Court split on whether a substantive guarantee of equality can be discerned in the Constitution.

The question was raised again in *Kruger v Commonwealth* (1997), where the Court was asked to determine whether the Aboriginals Ordinance 1918 (NT) had validly authorised the forced removal of **Aboriginal** children from their families and communities. One argument was that the treatment of Aboriginal children authorised by the Ordinance was discriminatory and unequal, and therefore breached the concept of legal equality developed in *Leeth*. That argument failed.

Only Toohey adhered to the approach which he and Deane had taken in *Leeth* (Deane by this time having left the Court to become Governor-General). By contrast, a majority composed of Dawson, Gaudron, McHugh and **Gummow** clearly rejected that approach. They held that a general guarantee of equality under the law could not be derived from the Constitution, nor from the common law. However, they did recognise that some form of procedural due process is guaranteed by Chapter III in relation to the exercise of judicial power by federal courts. Moreover, while the direct effect of this guarantee would be limited to the functions that Commonwealth legislation can impose upon federal courts, the decision in *Kable v DPP* (1996) suggests that there might effectively be similar limitations on the functions which state legislation can impose on state courts, since what *Kable* decides is that state courts cannot be required to act in any way that is 'incompatible' with the fact that those courts sometimes exercise the judicial power of the Commonwealth.

This means that safeguards of procedural fairness will continue to be explored in the context of determining specific issues as to the form of judicial process required by Chapter III of the Constitution. The most obvious focus for this exploration will be the criminal trial process for federal offences. The concept of due process might, for example, be a means of implying a right to a **jury trial**, even in the absence of an effective express right, or of holding that a person charged with a serious criminal offence has a constitutionally protected right to be represented by **counsel**.

GEORGE WILLIAMS

Further Reading
Christine Parker, 'Protection of Judicial Process as an Implied Constitutional Principle' (1994) 16 *Adel L Rev* 341
Fiona Wheeler, 'The Doctrine of Separation of Powers and Constitutionally Entrenched Due Process in Australia' (1997) 23 *Mon LR* 248
George Winterton, 'The Separation of Judicial Power as an Implied Bill of Rights' in Geoffrey Lindell (ed), *Future Directions in Australian Constitutional Law* (1994)

E

Economics is essentially concerned with the production, distribution and consumption of scarce resources. It has often been applied as a basis both for a descriptive or predictive examination of the behavioural incentives created by legal rules, and for prescriptive or normative judgment of those rules. However, the High Court's explicit use of economic analysis has been largely restricted to those areas of law defined in terms of economic concepts. In other areas, the Court has found itself restricted both analytically and procedurally from incorporating the economics of its decisions.

Much of economic analysis derives from assumptions about individual, institutional or social behaviour. For example, individuals are commonly assumed to be rational and self-interested. On that basis, deductions from their expected behaviour in the context of the legal constraints they face can provide both a positive framework for examining the operation of legal principle, and a normative conception of efficiency against which to evaluate it. That framework provides one common form of analysis of the way the legal system acts to modify and ultimately to define the markets in which individuals act, and hence of the way the legal system may regulate the decisions made by those individuals.

The impact and outcomes suggested by such a framework have had considerable influence on the formation and structure of legislative and regulatory policy. However, such an analysis is only one of the many competing and often controversial methodologies adopted in pursuing the varied goals and ideological values inherent in different economic theories. Economic theories extend from the libertarian individualism of the Austrian school to the empirical political economics of John Maynard Keynes through to the dialectical materialism of Marxism. Thus the questions raised by the contemporary 'law and economics' movement—how distinctions or developments in legal principles might introduce transaction costs, distort incentives or reduce the efficiency of existing resource allocations—are only specific examples of the use of economic theory from a particular economics perspective.

In any event, the Court has generally been reluctant to ask any such questions, even in areas where an economic framework forms the basis of the statutory provisions being interpreted. In many fundamental **taxation** cases decided in the **Barwick Court**, the Court adopted what has been termed a strictly literal interpretation of the tax legislation, which systematically resolved uncertainties in favour of taxpayers. Graeme Cooper is one of the writers who have suggested that 'while the High Court may have a very developed sense of the private claims of individuals to immunity from tax, it has never displayed a similar appreciation of the economic foundations of the income tax'. This is further illustrated in subsequent cases such as *FCT v Myer Emporium* (1987) and *Hepples v FCT* (1991), where the Court continued to draw distinctions between the terms under consideration without economic justification.

Perhaps the clearest use of economic theory has come in the interpretation of the *Trade Practices Act* (1974) (Cth) (see **Trade practices law**). In *Queensland Wire Industries v BHP* (1989), the Court considered the question of 'market definition' at length, for the purpose of assessing whether there had been substantial use of market power. Although the various Justices made reference to economic literature on the question of market definition, there was little consideration of how such a definition might affect broader considerations of consumer welfare or market efficiency. Economic analysis was adopted on the basis that the explicit objective of the legislation was to put into effect a particular economic principle. Even then, some elements of economic analysis, such as the use of empirical evidence or the institutional relationship between a company and its wholly owned subsidiary, were not adopted by the Court.

The Court has also explicitly utilised what may be termed economic concepts in determining questions such as profit (see, for example, *Colbeam Palmer v Stock Affiliates* (1968)) or in the assessment of compensatory **damages** (see, for example, *Pennant Hills Restaurants v Barrell Insurance* (1981)). These, along with terms such as fair value or costs, are interpreted as explicitly involving particular economic conceptions. However, even in these cases there is little analysis or acknowledgment of the differing economic rationales for any particular definition.

The use of economics in **constitutional interpretation** has been similarly constrained. The early Court engaged in the debate of protectionism or free trade without reference to the then-developing economic consensus of the losses associated with an isolationist view. Section 92 of the Constitution seemed to embody this sentiment at least as between the states (see **Interstate trade and commerce**). Yet it took until

Cole v Whitfield (1988) for the Court to reach a settled view—and then it was with regard to **precedent** and the **history** of the **Convention Debates** rather than economic analysis. Justices in subsequent cases such as *Bath v Alston Holdings* (1988) have continued to disagree over distinctions between economically equivalent fees based on what they considered to be the required interpretation of section 92.

In defining the meaning of 'excise' in section 90, the Court has similarly found itself concerned with interpreting an essentially economic concept. Early considerations of section 90, leading up to cases such as *Matthews v Chicory Marketing Board* (1938), incorporated the discussion of the meaning of 'indirect taxes' as that conception had been used in several Canadian cases. However, these attempts at definition avoided reliance on the ultimate economic impact of the excises under consideration. This may have prevented the Justices from recognising the inconsistencies in the distinctions they were drawing. More recent expansions of the meaning of excise in cases such as *Ha v NSW* (1997) have referred to economic debates at the time the Constitution was drafted in preference to any current analysis.

Similar confines of constitutional interpretation may be seen in the interpretation of the word 'industrial' in section 51(xxxv). In not acknowledging the place of education in industrial organisation, the majority in the *School Teachers Case* (1929) explicitly rejected any 'thesis upon economics', as did **Isaacs** in dissent. Even the expansion of 'industrial' to cover all employment situations in the *CYSS Case* (1983) was due to an application of its ordinary meaning rather than to an assessment of the economic effects of any distinction.

Terms such as 'free trade', 'excise' and 'industrial' all suggest economic implications, yet as **Mason** has suggested, they are not explicitly premised on any particular economic rationale. Even more recent cases such as *Airservices Australia v Canadian Airlines International* (1999) illustrate how economic analysis may be referred to when inherent in a previously determined interpretation, without any real economic analysis of the wider implications of such an interpretation or its appropriateness for meeting the objectives of the statutory provision in question.

Beyond the sphere of constitutional or **statutory interpretation**, economics has had even less explicit impact. Development of the principles relating to, for example, **land law** and other **property** law, **contract**, **estoppel** and **tort law** has been premised on fixing responsibility or liability, with only limited explicit reference to economic analysis of inalienability, risk, loss spreading or efficiency. For example, the various justifications for not expanding liability for negligence to purely economic loss included elementary economic arguments suggesting the potential indeterminacy of the affected class. However, such arguments played little part in *Perre v Apand* (1999), when the Court attempted to formulate principles by which that class could be determined.

The use of economics by the Court may therefore have been mainly at a less explicit, primarily ideological level. For example, it may be possible to trace the influence of JS Mill's *Principles of Political Economy* (1848) in early 'excise' decisions, or the *laissez-faire*, survival-of-the-fittest teachings of Herbert Spencer in the views of **Dixon** and **Barwick**. In some decisions, clashes of economic **ideologies** may be clearly

apparent, as in the judgments of Barwick and **Murphy** in *FCT v Westraders* (1980). In other cases, such as *Johns v Australian Securities Commission* (1993), *Gambotto v WCP* (1995) or the taxation cases mentioned above, economic analysis is subject to the other individual interests being considered by the Court. Any influence that may have been exerted by the work on transaction costs by Ronald Coase, the work on incentive structures by Guido Calabresi, or the more recent work of Richard Posner, Frank Easterbrook and Richard Epstein on contract, property and other areas of the law, remains largely unexpressed by the Court.

Even if it were accepted that various forms of economic analysis could contribute to an effective resolution of cases before the Court, there would remain difficulties with the Court's capacity to apply them, and the appropriateness of doing so. The Court has not adopted what in the **United States Supreme Court** are referred to as 'Brandeis Briefs', designed to place before the judges information about the social and economic consequences of a decision. The ability of **interveners** to present such information before the Court has been considered (see, for example, *Levy v Victoria* (1997)), but the position generally remains unfavourable. Nor has the Court generally been receptive to the submission of *amicus curiae* briefs to assist it in considering implications of its decisions going beyond the immediate fate of the parties. And there has been little consideration of the use of the **Inter-State Commission** to engage in economic **fact finding** to assist the Court, despite the evident intention of the **framers of the Constitution**.

Therefore, while there has been acceptance of the Court's **role** in developing rather than merely declaring applicable legal principles, the Court has yet to embrace alternative economic methodologies to construct or assess those principles. The Court has limited its use of economic analysis, perhaps to avoid reaching instrumental or normative conclusions, and in so doing has distinguished itself from the other arms of government for which economics has become an increasingly influential tool. However, precisely because economics presents the Court with methodologies so far largely foreign to the judicial method, it provides another potentially effective way to analyse the legal environment. The challenge for the Court remains how best to utilise the benefits of the different types of economic analysis without undermining its judicial role.

Daniel Stewart

Further Reading
HW Arndt, 'Judicial Review under Section 90 of the Constitution: An Economist's View' (1952) 25 *ALJ* 667 and 706
Anthony Mason, 'Law and Economics' (1991) 17 *Mon LR* 167
Note, 'The Inter-State Commission and Section 92 of the Constitution' (1988) 62 *ALJ* 586
Megan Richardson and Gillian Hadfield (eds), *The Second Wave of Law and Economics* (1999)

Economy, impact of Court's decisions on. The decisions of the High Court on the constitutional validity of Commonwealth and state laws have had a significant impact on the Australian economy. The operation of the federal system and the development of Australian **federalism** have been shaped by the Court's judgments on the power of the Commonwealth to make grants to other governments, and on the **taxation** powers of the Commonwealth and the states. Some of its judgments have permanently changed the course of economic activity in particular regions. Other judgments have had a significant impact on the quality of the **environment**. All of its judgments have an economic effect of one kind or another.

Australia's centralised taxation system is a direct consequence of the Court's decisions on uniform income tax and on section 90 of the Constitution, which prohibits the states from imposing duties of **excise**. As there is no clear definition of such duties in the Constitution, the task of determining what constitutes an excise duty rests with the Court. The Court has been inclined to interpret section 90 so as to exclude the states from the broad field of commodity taxation. Thus, from *Parton v Milk Board* (1949) onwards, the view that increasingly tended to prevail was that any state tax on goods, imposed at any stage from manufacture to consumption, was an excise duty. As a result, the Court has invalidated many state taxes falling on the sale or, in effect, the consumption of goods. Consequently, Commonwealth–state financial arrangements have often been adjusted in response to the Court's judgments.

The outcome of the June 1970 Premiers' Conference and the transfer of payroll tax to the states in 1971 were determined, for example, in the shadow of three decisions by the Court between 1969 and 1971. In *WA v Hamersley Iron* (1969), the Court held that certain state receipt duties were unconstitutional. A year later, in *WA v Chamberlain Industries* (1970), the Court extended that principle to a tax imposed by reference not to receipts but to periodic returns of trade. In the *Payroll Tax Case* (1971), the Court established that state government departments and their instrumentalities were not exempt from liability for Commonwealth payroll tax.

In recognition of their loss of revenue due to these judgments, the states won major concessions at the 1970 Premiers' Conference, including additional financial assistance grants, a higher betterment factor for determining the growth in real terms of these grants, the transfer of $1000 million of state debt to the Commonwealth over five years, and an interest-free capital grant of $200 million in 1970–71. The Commonwealth also agreed to transfer the payroll tax to the states from September 1971.

The states had also developed in the 1970s new taxes, which came to be known as 'business franchise fees', on petroleum products, tobacco and alcohol. The legislation was carefully structured so as not to offend the Court's previous interpretations of section 90, particularly in *Dennis Hotels v Victoria* (1960). In due course, these fees grew into a significant source of revenue for the states. Although levied at increasingly high rates, the fees were considered to have satisfied the criteria expounded by the Court in previous cases until they were struck down as unconstitutional in *Ha v NSW* (1997).

The immediate effect of *Ha* on the state budgets was an annual loss of nearly five billion dollars. The Commonwealth introduced a rescue package to protect the state budgets from the shock: it imposed additional excise duties on the three commodities, and used these as the basis for compensatory revenue payments to the states. These revenue-sharing arrangements in turn contributed to the states' support for the Liberal Party's proposal, during the 1998 general election, to introduce a goods and services tax from 1 July 2000.

Although there is no constitutional prohibition on the states' authority to impose income tax (indeed, they levied income taxes simultaneously with the Commonwealth until 1942), the Commonwealth forced the states out of this field, initially as a wartime measure in **World War II** and eventually permanently. This fundamental change in Australia's public finances and fiscal federalism could not have occurred without High Court authority, which was given in the *Uniform Tax Cases* (1942 and 1957).

The Court's judgments have thus helped to create a severe vertical fiscal imbalance (between the tax powers and spending responsibilities of the two levels of government) in Australia. This imbalance has in turn resulted not only in excessive reliance by the states on Commonwealth grants, but also in the development by states of a plethora of small, inefficient and mostly regressive taxes in their search for independent sources of revenue.

In recent years, the states have exploited gambling taxes aggressively. This has attracted widespread criticism on account of community concerns about the social impact of gambling. **Gibbs**, speaking from **retirement** in 1997, observed that gambling taxes have 'the unfortunate consequence that the States, in the hope of deriving the greatest possible revenue from this source, have encouraged the establishment of large casinos, to the detriment of society generally'.

Naturally, the vertical fiscal imbalance has been a welcome source of power over the states for the Commonwealth government. As former federal Treasurer and **Prime Minister** Paul Keating stressed in an address to the National Press Club in October 1991, the national perspective dominates Australian political life largely because the national government dominates revenue raising.

Others have criticised the vertical fiscal imbalance as responsible for loss of efficiency and accountability in public sector decision making. The point is that excessive reliance of the states on Commonwealth funding is undesirable for both levels of government because neither is fully accountable for its fiscal decisions.

Some of the Court's judgments in the 1970s were exploited for income tax avoidance and evasion in Australia on a large scale. The Court's judgments in *Curran v FCT* (1974), *Slutzkin v FCT* (1977) and *FCT v Westraders* (1979) had validated a series of artificial and contrived schemes, including the so-called 'bottom of the harbour' scheme. The issue was brought to a climax in 1982 in separate reports of the McCabe–Lafranchi Inquiry and the Costigan Royal Commission. Legislation was passed in 1982, with the support of the Labor Opposition, to recover retrospectively the unpaid company tax from those found guilty of evasion.

The **Knox Court's** judgment in the *Federal Roads Case* (1926) laid the foundation for the tremendous growth of Commonwealth specific purpose grants to the states in subsequent years, and helped in expanding the Commonwealth's spending power into state activities. In that case, the Court rejected Victoria's challenge to the constitutional validity of the *Federal Aid Roads Act* 1926 (Cth), under which the Commonwealth proposed to provide grants to assist the states in building roads. Victoria had submitted that the intention and effect of the Act was to enable the Commonwealth to engage in road construction, which was not an activity included in the list of **Commonwealth legislative powers** under section 51. The High Court rejected the state's objection, stating simply that the Act was warranted by section 96 of the Constitution, and did not contravene any other provision. This broad approach to the power to make financial grants to the states was affirmed—and indeed was the foundation of the decisions—in the *Uniform Tax Cases*. The Commonwealth has also been able to influence policy in areas otherwise within state power through use of its power under section 81 of the Constitution to appropriate funds directly to recipients, bypassing the states (see *AAP Case* (1975)).

The decision in *Murphyores v Commonwealth* (1976) put an end to sand mining on Fraser Island and was a major victory for environmental protection in Australia. The Court upheld the Commonwealth's refusal to grant a licence for the export of zircon and rutile concentrates recovered from the mining of mineral sands on Fraser Island on the ground that, although the purpose of the refusal was to protect the environment (over which the Commonwealth has no express power), the focus on export meant that the law fell squarely within the Commonwealth's overseas **trade and commerce power.**

For much of the twentieth century, Commonwealth regulation of the corporate sector was inhibited by the narrow meaning given to the **corporations power** in *Huddart Parker v Moorehead* (1909); but when *Huddart Parker* was **overruled** in *Strickland v Rocla Concrete Pipes* (1971), a new regulatory era began, particularly through the *Trade Practices Act* 1974 (Cth). Thereafter, the range of corporate activities coming within reach of the power seemed steadily to expand. The use of the corporations power in the *Tasmanian Dam Case* (1983), along with the **external affairs power**, enabled the Commonwealth to stop the construction of a dam proposed by the Tasmanian Hydro-Electric Commission to flood the Gordon–Franklin river system for the purpose of generating electricity. This had a direct and immediate impact on the Tasmanian economy.

The Court's judgment in the *Incorporation Case* (1990), that the Commonwealth could not use the corporations power for the incorporation of companies, made necessary and resulted in the National Corporate Regulation Scheme for the administration of company law and the regulation of the securities and futures industries. The scheme, which came into force on 1 January 1991, depended on complementary legislation passed by the Commonwealth and all the states. Recent decisions have cast doubts on the validity of the scheme (see *R v Hughes* (2000)). Whatever arrangements are devised to overcome these doubts, they are driven in large part by decisions of the High Court.

All decisions of the Court—in private law as well as public law—have an economic impact. Its decisions on the law of **contract**, for example, and on the law of **tort**, determine where economic loss falls and the nature and incidence of insurance arrangements. Its decisions on restrictive **trade practices** go to defining markets and affect levels of competition. Its decisions on intellectual property law affect the degree to which inventions and innovations can be commercially exploited (see **Copyright; Trade marks; Patents and design**). Its decisions on **constitutional law** affect the framework for the federal balance in Australia. Whether this means that the Court should have expertise in **economics**, or be better equipped to receive **expert evidence** from economists, is another question.

BHAJAN GREWAL
RUSSELL MATHEWS

Further Reading
Russell Mathews and Bhajan Grewal, *The Public Sector in Jeopardy* (1997)

Electoral law encompasses various regulatory and constitutional issues concerning voting at elections and referendums. These include: the franchise; boundaries and redistributions; the voting system; the campaign, polling and scrutiny; party registration, funding and disclosure; and challenges to returns, members' qualifications and, through **judicial review**, the validity of legislation.

The referendum jurisdiction has generated little work for the High Court, although the *Referendum (Machinery Provisions) Act* 1984 (Cth) vests it with jurisdiction in relation to disputed returns. The paucity of this work is attributable to the infrequency of referendums, their generally clear outcomes, and the fact that voters (as opposed to governments) are not empowered to petition referendum results.

Federal Parliament's power to enact laws relating to its own elections was read expansively, beyond the mere official conduct of polls, in *Smith v Oldham* (1912). This power is augmented, through, for example, the Commonwealth's broadcasting power, and can extend to aspects of state and local elections. It extends to the representation of **territories** through the territories power (see *Territory Senators Cases* (1975 and 1977)). The introduction of territory representation in the Commonwealth Parliament, however, does not affect state representation or the numerical nexus between the House of Representatives and the Senate (*A-G (NSW); Ex rel McKellar v Commonwealth* (1977)).

The jurisdiction over disputed elections and qualifications had formerly been exercised by parliamentary committees in both colonial and Westminster parliaments—a tradition reflected in section 47 of the Constitution. But mirroring the late Victorian belief that the policing of free and fair elections and unlawful and corrupt electoral practices was best left to independent judges, federal Parliament has largely ceded its power in this respect to the Court.

Thus, from its foundation, the Court was vested with federal power to try electoral petitions (*Commonwealth Electoral Act* 1902 (Cth), Part XVI). It does so as the **Court of Disputed Returns**, generally constituted by a single Justice, but with occasional questions referred to the **Full Court** and with issues of fact potentially referable to lower courts. While the disputed returns jurisdiction is naturally sporadic, it featured significantly in the earliest reports. The 1903 federal election (Australia's first under uniform laws) gave rise to four challenges. The most significant was resolved in *Chanter v Blackwood (Nos 1 and 2)* (1904), where the Court adopted liberal readings of formality provisions, reasoning that the importance of the franchise should not be defeated by technical interpretations.

More controversial has been the power to disqualify a member of federal Parliament. A bare majority in *Sue v Hill* (1999) held that the Court could determine a petition challenging a successful candidate's qualifications, without a reference from the relevant House. The decision in *Sue* also confirmed the validity of the vesting of electoral jurisdiction in the face of claims that it did not involve **judicial power**.

In general, electoral law in Australia, as in other **common law** countries with political institutions influenced by the UK model, has given priority to stability of governance over more fluid practices. This is primarily born of statutory choices, many of which reinforce a two-party system. Examples include the predominance of the constituency system over proportional representation for lower Houses; compulsory enrolment and preferential voting; Senate group-ticket voting; and short time limitations for petitions.

The Court's decisions in this area have largely served to reinforce these priorities. This reflects a *laissez-faire* attitude which, aside from the enforcement and interpretation role of the disputed returns **jurisdiction**, leaves electoral law largely to the political and parliamentary realm. Even when the Court has decided that statutory provisions fall short of constitutional requirements, it has tended to assume that in a **democracy**, the holding of an election is sufficient to cure any irregularities (see *A-G (Cth); Ex rel McKinlay v Commonwealth* (1975)).

The compulsory voting system, pioneered in Australia, has consistently been upheld, even against those with no preference between the candidates on offer (see *Judd v McKeon* (1926) and *Faderson v Bridger* (1971)). Compulsory expression of full preferences was also upheld in **Langer v Commonwealth** (1996), although it was noted that in the secrecy of the ballot box, a voter is effectively able to vote informally. Compulsory voting helps the established parties by minimising their need to encourage voters to the polls, and compulsory preferences require voters ultimately to make a choice between the dominant parties.

Senate group-ticket voting has been upheld in a string of single-Justice decisions, starting with *McKenzie v Commonwealth* (1984), despite repeated complaints that the system discriminates against independents.

In a line of cases starting with *Cameron v Fysh* (1904), the Court held that time limitations for filing petitions are strict, and allow no subsequent substantive amendment. Keeping these periods short allows little time for the gathering of facts to draft a petition, but reinforces stability by requiring finality of challenges. Further, a petition cannot impugn a whole election. If irregularities are widespread, the result must be challenged seat by seat (or, in the Senate, state by state: *Muldowney v Australian Electoral Commission* (1993)). Aside from minimising eccentric ambit claims, this also reinforces post-election parliamentary stability. Further, since *Bridge v Bowen* (1916), the Court has evinced a robust attitude to petitions and the purity of elections, requiring more than a mere numerical possibility of the result being affected by irregularities before a member will be unseated.

One area where the Court has adopted a strict interpretation *despite* its potential to disrupt stable representation concerns the disqualification provisions in section 44 of the Constitution—in particular, those dealing with offices of profit under the Crown and relationships with foreign powers. Thus, in *Sykes v Cleary* (1992), the Full Court unseated a member despite his having taken leave without pay from the state teaching service to nominate and campaign. *Sykes* also held that candidates are ineligible to nominate unless they have taken all reasonable steps to renounce any foreign **citizenship**. These constitutional impediments mean that several million Australian electors with dual citizenship or public service positions cannot nominate for election. Conversely, in the matter of the disqualification of members with pecuniary interests in agreements with the Commonwealth, **Barwick** in *In re Webster* (1975) took a narrow view that effectively avoids disbarring candidates with diverse or significant business interests.

The formal recognition of political parties is a recent phenomenon in electoral law. The *Commonwealth Electoral Act* 1918 (Cth) now contains detailed provisions governing party registration, disclosure and public funding. Questions arising from these provisions are chiefly based in **administrative law**, and hence within the province of the Administrative Appeals Tribunal and **Federal Court**. However, the emergence of party registration and public funding threatens the status of the famous associations case, *Cameron v Hogan* (1934), in which the Court took a non-interventionist approach to the political realm by denying the **standing** of party members seeking judicial enforcement of party rules.

The leeway the High Court has left to parliaments to shape the law governing their members' election is, in part, a consequence of the absence of a **Bill of Rights**, and contrasts with the pivotal role played by US courts (in particular the **United States Supreme Court**) in shaping and administering electoral law. In part, it also reflects inherited Westminster ideas of non-interference with parliamentary **sovereignty**, especially in matters closely touching democratic structures. This approach may be criticised on two grounds.

The first is methodological consistency. In *Australian Capital Television v Commonwealth* (1992), the Court boldly invalidated federal laws prohibiting paid electoral broadcasting during campaigns. The provisions were intended to reduce the cost of electioneering and minimise the danger of corruption, and they mirrored long-established UK practice. The Court found them unduly restrictive of a freedom of **political communication** implied from the Constitution to support **representative government**. While this implication was extended to reshape **defamation law**, it proved a false dawn for the reshaping of electoral law. Later Courts were reluctant to apply it, upholding in *Langer* a prohibition on advocating optional preferential voting, and declining in *McGinty v WA* (1996) to generate further implications enshrining any particular democratic theory or electoral system. In *McGinty*, a state redistribution system, which permitted a disparity of up to 291 per cent in the number of voters in Lower House electorates, was upheld, mirroring the rejection of any constitutional principle of 'one-vote, one-value' at the federal level in *McKinlay*.

The second criticism concerns democratic theory. Reluctance to interfere with matters close to parliament's internal affairs, and a faith in parliament's reasonableness and sensitivity to the democratic instincts of voters, are laudable sentiments. However, it is arguable that, since electoral law is so fundamental to democratic process and of such personal interest to parliamentarians and parties, it requires heightened judicial scrutiny. Of course, electoral law has far-reaching political ramifications, and the Court must be wary of allegations of partisanship. Nevertheless, its record in applying judicial method to the resolution of often intensely disputed petitions has insulated it from perceptions of partiality. Judicial review also involves abstract and general questions that frequently transcend the particular issues in individual petitions.

Nor has the Court embraced creativity in the fundamental question of defining the franchise. While recent jurisprudence on sections 7 and 24 of the Constitution (the Houses of Parliament to be 'directly chosen by the people') may suggest otherwise, the traditional approach has been to see voting as a privilege (or even duty) delimited by legislation, rather than a positive or constitutionally protected civil right. This explains the formalistic decisions in *Muramats v Commonwealth Electoral Officer (WA)* (1923)—a case that failed to question racially discriminatory exclusions—and in two cases where the Court's historical reading of section 41 of the Constitution denied the section any role as a contemporary guarantee of voting rights (*King v Jones* (1972) and *R v Pearson; Ex parte Sipka* (1983); see **Express constitutional rights**).

The 1980s and 1990s have seen an increase in the volume of the Court's electoral work, led in part by an increase in matters brought by candidates as **litigants in person**. Although litigants in person present challenges to the Court's processes, in the field of democratic rights their appearance may be a healthy sign.

GRAEME ORR

Further Reading

Adrian Brooks, 'A Paragon of Democratic Virtues? The Development of the Commonwealth Franchise' (1993) 12 *U Tas LR* 208

Graeme Orr, 'Electoral Regulation and Representation' (1998) 7 *GLR* 166

Graeme Orr, 'The Conduct of Referenda and Plebiscites in Australia: A Legal Perspective' (2000) 11 *PLR* 117

Michael Sexton, 'The Role of Judicial Review in Federal Electoral Law' (1978) 52 *ALJ* 28

George Williams, 'Sounding the Core of Representative Democracy: Implied Freedoms and Electoral Reform' (1996) 20 *MULR* 848

Employment law. The High Court has exerted a profound influence on the regulation of the employment relationship (and hence of the labour market) in Australia. Yet that influence has for the most part been indirect because of the unusual nature of Australian employment law, and because the Court's major **role** has been to define the constitutional limits that determine the scope and shape of employment legislation (see **Conciliation and arbitration; Labour relations law**).

Arrangements for paid work in Australia are governed by a complex mix of rules and processes stemming from a number of different sources. A majority of the employed workforce is covered by a mixture of awards and registered collective agreements—instruments with statutory force that typically regulate matters such as wages and working hours. There is also a growing body of federal and state legislation that directly regulates working conditions and practices. Aside from statutes dealing with employment in the public sector, such legislation covers matters such as **workers' compensation**, workplace safety, various forms of leave, **discrimination**, and unfair dismissal.

Then there is the agreement of the parties themselves. The extent to which the parties to an individual **contract** are free to determine wages and conditions of employment by negotiation has fluctuated over time, as **Dixon** noted in *A-G (NSW) v Perpetual Trustee* (1952). But, particularly in relationships not covered by awards or registered agreements, the parties generally have a fair degree of autonomy.

It is in this respect that the courts have most direct control over the employment relationship. They determine the basic rules of contracting that establish how agreements can be made, varied and terminated, and indeed what sort of agreements are to be regarded as legally binding. And perhaps most importantly in the employment context, they may formulate default rules that are implied into contracts to deal with matters that the parties have not explicitly addressed. This is especially significant in practice in relation to employee obligations.

Yet despite the potential for employment law to be shaped through the High Court's authority over these **common law** rules, its contribution to their development has been limited. Although the Court has put its stamp on many aspects of **contract law** in the past two decades, it has had relatively few opportunities over that period to apply those principles in the specific context of employment. Of the many contract cases that came before the Court in 1982 and 1983, for example, none involved an employment relationship. And in the few employment cases that have reached it since that time, the Court has not had the occasion to apply any of the doctrines of **equity**—particularly those relating to **unconscionability**—that have become so central to its modern contract jurisprudence.

Moreover, even where the Court has been called upon to consider the common law of employment, it has generally been content to apply established principles of English law. This is despite the fact that, as **McHugh** and **Gummow** observed in *Byrne v Australian Airlines* (1995), 'social conditions, the **history** of **labour relations**, and the relative legislative schemes differ significantly' between the two countries—and have done since the beginning of the twentieth century. Even on issues that have regularly been before the Court—such as the scope of the employer's duty to provide a safe workplace, or the validity of restrictions on freedom of employment—it is hard to find a decision that does not have its antecedents in English authority, or would have been decided any differently by an English court.

One possible exception, and indeed a case that remains perhaps the Court's most distinctive contribution to the common law of employment, is *Automatic Fire Sprinklers v Watson* (1946). The decision is significant in analysing both the nature of the wage–work bargain that lies at the heart of any employment relationship, and the effect of a wrongful termination of the employment contract. The plaintiff, who had been dismissed without proper notice, continued to turn up for work for some months. His action for wages in respect of this period succeeded, because of the effect of certain regulations in force during **World War II**. However, a majority of the Court indicated that he would not have succeeded at common law. As **Dixon** put it: 'The common understanding of a contract of employment at wages or salary periodically payable is that it is the service that earns the remuneration and even a wrongful discharge from the service means that wages or salary cannot be earned however ready and willing the employee may be to serve.'

In effect therefore, at least at common law, the plaintiff could only claim **damages** for loss of wages, rather than claiming wages as such—the distinction being that a claim for damages is affected by the principle that the plaintiff should mitigate the loss by seeking alternative employment. On the other hand, the Court also made it clear that even if the wrongful dismissal had effectively brought the employment *relationship* to an end, it had not automatically terminated the employment *contract*. The employee still had the option of electing to keep the contract alive—even if he could not earn wages and the making of any **order** requiring the parties to re-establish the relationship was extremely unlikely. The decision settled Australian law on this point, though years later the English courts were still debating the merits of 'elective' and 'automatic' theories of termination of employment.

A further area in which Australian law has diverged from its English antecedents is in the definition of what constitutes a 'contract of service', as opposed to a 'contract for services' or any other kind of relationship that cannot properly be characterised as one of employment.

The High Court was originally content to apply what for many years was the established test of an employment relationship under English law: whether the 'employer' had sufficient power of control over the worker in question. It did, however, endeavour to refine that test by emphasising that what mattered was the *right* to exercise control, even in incidental matters, not the actual exercise of detailed control over task performance. This enabled the Court to find that skilled workers such as actors and circus trapeze artists could be employees, despite their employer's inability to tell them exactly how to do their job (*FCT v J Walter Thompson* (1944); *Zuijs v Wirth Bros* (1955)). By contrast, in cases such as *Humberstone v Northern Timber Mills* (1949), the Court emphasised that control of itself could never be sufficient: there must be a commitment on the part of the worker to perform the promised services personally. A worker who was permitted by the contract to delegate the relevant tasks must be a contractor rather than an employee.

With the decision in *Stevens v Brodribb* (1986), the Court formally abandoned the control test and embraced a 'multi-factor' approach. This requires the presence or absence of an employment relationship to be determined by reference to a range of factors, of which the extent of any right of control is merely one. Again, the decision settled Australian law at a time when English law was unclear—as indeed it remains unclear today—on the appropriate test to apply.

Notwithstanding *Watson* and *Stevens v Brodribb*, many of the leading authorities on the common law of employment are still English, or are decisions of the lower courts in Australia. Some key issues have never been before the High Court for decision. These include the enforceability of unregistered collective agreements; the extent to which obligations of confidentiality can be invoked to restrain former employees from using information they acquired on the job; and the emerging principle that the employer is under an implied obligation not to damage the 'trust and confidence' between the parties.

Moreover, in stark contrast to its willingness over the past few decades to refashion the general principles of contract law—and indeed many other aspects of the common law—the Court has been distinctly conservative in its approach to the employment contract. This is particularly evident in *Byrne v Australian Airlines* (1995). The plaintiffs claimed damages for breach of an award term that prohibited their employer from dismissing them unfairly, even though the governing legislation made no provision for such a remedy. Their principal argument was that the award term had become incorporated into their employment contracts, so that they could sue for damages for breach of contract.

During the first part of the twentieth century, the Court had established in cases such as *Mallinson v Scottish Australian Investment* (1920) that the existence of a contract of employment was a prerequisite to the operation of an award as between employer and employee, and that, at least in some cases, an amount owed under an award could be recovered as a civil debt. The Court had also ruled that a contract may validly impose an obligation on an employer that exceeds the minimum required by an applicable award (*Kilminster v Sun Newspapers* (1931)). However, the precise relationship between an award and an employment contract had never been fully addressed.

In *Byrne*, the Court settled the issue by holding that award terms do not automatically become imported into employment contracts, either by force of statute or by reason of an implied term. It held that such incorporation was not strictly 'necessary' either to the functioning of the award system or to the operation of the contracts in question. This was doubtless correct, but it is notable that the Court made little or no reference to broader **policy considerations**. Strangely too, it ignored a substantial body of Australian scholarly literature on the subject, at a time when reference to such literature in High Court decisions had become the norm rather than the exception (see **Extrinsic materials**).

The Court's lack of enthusiasm for breaking new ground in the common law of employment is also apparent in more recent cases. In *FAI v AR Griffiths & Sons* (1997), the Court refused even to hear an argument that a term should be implied requiring employers who are adequately insured against the consequences of negligent work performance to rely on that insurance rather than bring proceedings against their employees. The **House of Lords** had rejected such a term 40 years earlier, but some Australian judges had cast doubt on the decision and the matter had never been before the High Court. Nonetheless, the Court stated that 'it is desirable that a legislative rather than a judicial solution be found' to any problems caused by the House of Lords decision.

Similarly, in *Concut v Worrell* (2000) the Court failed to resolve the most important issue of principle raised by the case—and presumably the reason for **leave to appeal** being granted in the first place—namely, whether an employee is under an implied duty to disclose previous misconduct.

The judgments in *Concut* are also notable for their repetition of the mantra that the employment relationship is inherently fiduciary in nature: that is, that *employees* owe **fiduciary obligations** to their employer. While this seems appropriate in the case of workers holding very senior positions of trust and responsibility (as was the case in *Concut*), it does not appear to have occurred to the Court that it might not (or should not) always be true of lower level workers, especially those employed by large organisations.

The Court's essentially static view of the nature of employment obligations can partly be attributed to its view of the relationship as a social and economic construct. Although it has been prepared to accept the legitimacy of trade union activities, as is apparent from decisions as diverse as the *Jumbunna Coal Case* (1908) and *McKernan v Fraser* (1931), it is rare to find the relation of employer and employee discussed in anything other than strictly hierarchical terms. Employers are entitled to expect 'obedience' to their 'orders' (*Adami v Maison de Luxe* (1924)), while an employee must avoid any conduct which 'involves an opposition, or conflict between his interest and his duty to his employer, or impedes the faithful performance of his obligations, or is destructive of the necessary confidence between employer and employee' (*Blyth Chemicals v Bushnell* (1933)).

There have occasionally been exceptions to this strictly 'unitary' view of employment relations. In *Federated Clerks Union v Victorian Employers Federation* (1984), a case concerning the validity of an award provision dealing with the introduction of new technology, **Wilson** noted that consultation between management and labour 'is not only sensible but essential if commerce and industry are to meet the challenge of progress in a spirit of harmony and with some regard for human dignity'. **Murphy** in the same case spoke of a demand by workers 'to be emancipated from the industrial serfdom which will otherwise be produced by the domination of the corporations; a demand to be treated with respect and dignity'. Yet just two years later, a majority of the Court in *Stevens v Brodribb* were still describing the relationship as one of 'master and servant' without any hint that these terms might be outmoded.

If the High Court's impact on the common law of employment has been rather limited, it has had more to say about some of the statutes that directly regulate working conditions. Cases arising out of the workers' compensation systems have frequently been before the Court, and it has regularly been called upon to settle issues arising out of the legislative framework governing public sector employment—especially the relationship between that framework and the concept of Crown prerogative, which, as cases such as *Commonwealth v Quince* (1944) and *Coutts v Commonwealth* (1985) reveal, still constitutes the basis for 'employment' in the armed forces and perhaps even the police.

Outside these categories, however, it is relatively rare to find the Court ruling on the interpretation (as opposed to the constitutional validity) of statutory employment conditions. It is remarkable, for instance, that despite the vast growth in unfair dismissal claims over the past 20 years, *Byrne v Australian Airlines* remains the only case in which the Court has had occasion to consider directly the principles relating to what constitutes a 'harsh, unjust or unreasonable' dismissal. The Court held that a dismissal for misconduct should not be found to be unfair merely because of a lack of procedural fairness on the part of the employer, without at least considering whether the worker's conduct nonetheless warranted dismissal.

Similarly, there are many aspects of the burgeoning law of employment discrimination that have not been before the Court. However, it did make an important ruling on the concept of 'indirect' discrimination in *Australian Iron & Steel v Banovic* (1989), and more recently has had two opportunities to consider the circumstances in which an employer may defend what would otherwise be unlawful discrimination by asserting that a particular characteristic is an 'inherent requirement' of the job in question. In both cases, the Court took a broad view of the defence: in *Qantas v Christie* (1998), the requirement was an age limit for pilots; while in *X v Commonwealth* (1999), it was the capacity of members of the armed forces to 'bleed safely' in combat—something they could not do if HIV-infected.

In the **Patrick Stevedores Case** (1998), the Court had its first opportunity to consider the 'freedom of association' provisions in Part XA of the *Workplace Relations Act* 1996 (Cth)—provisions which are surely destined to come before the Court again. However, the case is perhaps more notable for the nature of the interlocutory order that the Court (largely) upheld, and for its impact on the underlying dispute between Patrick Stevedores (and its supporters in business and government) and the Maritime Union.

In many ways, the High Court's most significant contribution in relation to the statutory regulation of employment conditions has been to determine whether that regulation applies at all. The application of many of these statutes is triggered by the presence of an employment contract or 'contract of service'. In the absence of a detailed statutory definition, the common law principles will be decisive. Awards and enterprise agreements in particular tend to be applicable only to employees, rather than independent contractors—as determined according to the principles adopted in *Stevens v Brodribb*.

This is just one example of the High Court influencing the scope and development of the most distinctive feature of Australian employment law: the federal and state systems for the conciliation and arbitration of industrial disputes. That influence has been felt not just at the level of **statutory interpretation**, but also through the Court's constitutional rulings.

It was, after all, the Court that, by taking a broad view of the concept of 'dispute' from 1914 onwards, facilitated the transformation of the federal industrial system. What was originally intended to be a system of last resort for large-scale disputes rapidly became an administrative regime for the regulation of minimum wages and conditions across whole industries and occupations. And the Court has influenced the demarcation between federal and state industrial systems through important decisions over the years on **inconsistency** under section 109 of the Constitution, such as *Clyde Engineering v Cowburn* (1926) (see **Knox Court and arbitration**). More recently, the Court's generally liberal approach to **Commonwealth legislative powers**, notably in the *Industrial*

Relations Act Case (1996), has encouraged successive federal governments to base the federal industrial system primarily on the **corporations power** and the **external affairs power** rather than on the more constricted 'conciliation and arbitration' power.

ANDREW STEWART

Engineers Case (1920) has been regarded as the foundation of Australian **constitutional law** ever since it was decided. As he retired in 1981, Chief Justice **Barwick** dwelt on the 'need to be very wary that the triumph of the *Engineers' Case* is never tarnished'. The **Griffith Court's** approach to **constitutional interpretation** had been based on a doctrine of implied **intergovernmental immunities**, and a doctrine of **reserved state powers**. The *Engineers Case* swept both doctrines aside, at least in their early rigorous form.

The doctrine of intergovernmental immunities had asserted that, in order to preserve the **sovereignty** both of the Commonwealth and of its component states, neither level of government could ever be subject to laws made by the other. Initially, in *D'Emden v Pedder* (1904), that doctrine was applied to protect Commonwealth agencies against state interference. But from the beginning, the Court foreshadowed that it should equally protect the states against Commonwealth interference, and in the *Railway Servants Case* (1906) it was used to hold that state railways authorities, in their capacity as employers, were not subject to the system of federal industrial awards established by the Commonwealth under its **conciliation and arbitration** power. The original Court—comprising **Griffith**, **Barton**, and **O'Connor**—was speaking for the last time; **Isaacs** and **Higgins** had both been appointed to the Court by the time the case was decided. Both of them, as **counsel** in the case, had argued *against* the application of the immunities doctrine: Isaacs as Commonwealth **Attorney-General**, and Higgins on behalf of the union. Thenceforth, under Isaacs' influence, the application of the doctrine to industrial arbitration cases was gradually eroded, particularly by the *Engine-Drivers Case* (1913) and the *Municipalities Case* (1919), which held that the immunity of state instrumentalities extended only to their exercise of governmental functions, and not to trading or commercial functions.

That might have been enough to dispose of the *Engineers Case*. A union of employed engineers was seeking an award against 843 employers throughout Australia. In WA, the respondent employers included the State Sawmills; the State Implement and Engineering Works; and the Minister for Trading Concerns. Higgins, sitting in **chambers** as a High Court Justice, found that an 'industrial dispute' existed in relation to most of the 843 employers; but he stated a case for the **Full Court's** opinion on whether there could be an 'industrial dispute' with the three 'governmental' employers. Victoria, NSW, Tasmania and SA obtained leave to intervene.

The union's argument that the three employers *could* be subject to an award was presented by Robert **Menzies**, who recalled in his 1967 lectures on *Central Power in the Australian Commonwealth* that he had initially argued simply that the three employers' functions were not 'governmental'. According to Menzies' recollection, **Starke** (himself newly appointed to the Bench) interjected: 'This argument is a lot of nonsense!'

Menzies replied: 'Sir, I quite agree.' But he added that the argument was 'compelled by the earlier decisions of this Court. If your Honours will permit me to question … these earlier decisions, I will undertake to advance a sensible argument'. Thereupon, after a short adjournment, Chief Justice **Knox** announced that when the case was relisted in Sydney, 'counsel will be at liberty to challenge any earlier decision of this Court'. The **judges' notebooks** suggest that Menzies may have embroidered his anecdote, since in fact a challenge to the earlier decisions had been clearly raised at the outset.

In the result, the 'implied immunities' doctrine was rejected—primarily in a judgment written by Isaacs, which Geoffrey Sawer has described as 'one of the worst written and organised in Australian judicial history'. Isaacs was given to rhetoric and repetition, and here he gave those habits full rein.

Knox, **Rich** and Starke joined in Isaacs' judgment. Higgins gave a separate **concurring judgment**, focusing more closely on the immediate issue concerning the scope of the conciliation and arbitration power. **Gavan Duffy** dissented. The **joint judgment** dismissed the 'implied immunities' doctrine as

an interpretation of the Constitution depending on an implication which is formed on a vague, individual conception of the spirit of the compact, which is not the result of interpreting any specific language to be quoted, nor referable to any recognized principle of the **common law** of the Constitution, and which, when started, is rebuttable by an intention of exclusion equally not referable to any language of the instrument or acknowledged common law constitutional principle, but arrived at by the Court on the opinions of Judges as to hopes and expectations respecting vague external conditions.

The actual result in *D'Emden v Pedder* (that a Commonwealth salary receipt was exempt from state stamp duty) was explained as depending on **inconsistency** under section 109 of the Constitution. The other 'implied immunities' cases, including *Railway Servants*, were **overruled**.

Both 'implied immunities' and 'reserved state powers' had been fashioned by the Griffith Court by analogy from American sources including the Tenth Amendment to the US Constitution, which declares that: 'The powers not delegated to the United States … are reserved to the States.' The Griffith Court had purported to find a similar reservation in section 107 of the Australian Constitution, which provided that when the colonies became states, their existing legislative powers 'shall … continue'. It had argued that **Commonwealth legislative powers** under section 51 of the Constitution must be read narrowly to avoid encroachment on the legislative powers of the states. Isaacs and Higgins had consistently resisted that doctrine, and in the *Engineers Case* Isaacs' judgment disposed of it also: 'It is a fundamental and fatal error to read sec 107 as reserving any power from the Commonwealth that falls fairly within the explicit terms of an express grant in s 51, as that grant is reasonably construed, unless that reservation is as explicitly stated.'

The overruling of these particular doctrines represented a Cartesian turn in the Court's approach to the federal distribution of powers. The doctrine of implied immunities was later to return in a modified form (see *Melbourne Corporation Case* (1947)). The idea that reserved state powers should restrict the interpretation of Commonwealth powers continues to influence cases on section 51(i) of the Constitution (the **trade and commerce power**), and traces of it have sometimes been detected in other contexts as well. **Windeyer** in the later *Professional Engineers Case* (1959) heard 'muffled echoes of old arguments'; **Murphy** in *A-G (WA); Ex rel Ansett Transport Industries v Australian National Airlines* (1976) complained that the majority approach in that case 'keeps the pre-Engineers ghosts walking' (see also *Gazzo v Comptroller of Stamps* (1981)). But the reaction to such echoes only confirms that the principles of *Engineers* are accepted as axiomatic.

Even more far-reaching in its effects has been the insistence of *Engineers* on **literalism** in construing the constitutional text. According to *Engineers*:

> The one clear line of judicial inquiry as to the meaning of the Constitution must be to read it naturally in the light of the circumstances in which it was made, with knowledge of the combined fabric of the common law, and the statute law which preceded it, and then *lucet ipsa per se.*

In short, the approach of the **Privy Council** in *A-G (Ontario) v A-G (Canada)* (1911) should apply: 'If the text is explicit the text is conclusive, alike in what it directs and what it forbids.'

Tony Blackshield

Further Reading

Michael Coper and George Williams (eds), *How Many Cheers for Engineers?* (1997)

Stephen Gageler, 'Foundations of Australian Federalism and the Role of Judicial Review' (1987) 17 *FL Rev* 162

George Williams, '*Engineers* is Dead, Long Live the Engineers!' (1995) 17 *Syd LR* 62

Environmental law. The High Court's **role** in developing the principles of environmental law in Australia has been relatively limited. This is largely because, with the exception of some **common law** actions in **tort**, 'environmental protection' laws are almost exclusively embodied in federal, state, and territory legislation, most of which has been enacted since the early 1970s.

The common law, in many cases, proved to be an unsuitable source of environmental **remedies**. In general, the anticipatory ('*ex ante*') planning, preventive, and regulatory tools in legislation are preferable to *ex post* remedies as a means of environmental protection. The only common law remedy that persisted to any real degree was 'the rule in *Rylands v Fletcher*' (1866 and 1868); but in **Burnie Port Authority v General Jones** (1994), this specialised rule about **strict liability** for the escape of dangerous things from land was effectively ended and subsumed into the general law of negligence.

Although the common law was the original source of **property** and resource rights, such as riparian rights, today these rights are largely embodied in—and sometimes eroded by—statutes. Similarly, rights to maintain existing uses of property arise from statute. Thus, the primary role of the Court today is to determine the extent of these rights through **statutory interpretation**. This is well illustrated by *Woollahra Municipal Council v Banool Developments* (1973), where the Court con-

sidered the extent to which, in relation to the use of a building, the expression 'continuance of the use' in the *Local Government Act* 1919 (NSW) could accommodate breaks or interruptions in that use. Similarly, in *Dorrestjin v SA Planning Commission* (1984), the Court considered whether SA planning legislation permitted the clearing of large trees remaining after a fire without obtaining development consent. The majority (**Mason, Deane,** and **Dawson; Brennan** and **Murphy** dissenting) held that, although the clearance was not a clearance of regrowth and was therefore a 'development' within the meaning of the legislation, the clearance fell within the concept of 'continued use'.

Among the most vexed issues in environmental law has been the definition of the relevant environment. Mostly, in Australia, reliance is placed on statutory definitions, so the task is again one of statutory interpretation. The Court has held that, even when aided by expansive legislative definitions, the word 'environment' must find its meaning through its application in specific contexts. In 1990, for example, the Court had to interpret the *Local Government Act* 1936 (Qld) to determine what was the relevant environment for the purposes of considering whether a subdivision would have a deleterious impact upon it, and more particularly, upon a coastal turtle rookery (*Queensland v Murphy* (1990)). The Court (Mason, Brennan, Deane, **Gaudron,** and **McHugh**) gave a unanimous judgment. After noting the ordinary meaning of 'environment' as 'that which surrounds', and acknowledging the broader meaning as 'the conditions under which a person or thing lives', they traced the broader meaning back to Thomas Carlyle's 1827 usage as 'the aggregate of external circumstances, conditions and things that affect the existence and development of an individual, organism or group'. They then held that, in the context of the particular statute, what constitutes the relevant environment 'must be ascertained by reference to the person, object or group surrounded or affected'. In this case, the relevant environment, or object, included the land adjacent to the proposed subdivision, and thus the turtle rookery; consequently, the more restrictive interpretation adopted by the **state Supreme Court** was overturned.

One consequence of the legislative dominance of this area is that the Court has not developed a body of doctrine that might be characterised purely as 'environmental law'. Rather, the so-called environmental law cases can be so described only because of the facts from which the legal issues emerge. While the facts have concerned environmental protection, the legal issues have been those of other, familiar areas of substantive law. Thus, the leading cases that typically appear in environmental law textbooks will invariably be equally at home in texts on **constitutional law** (*Murphyores v Commonwealth* (1976) and the *Tasmanian Dam Case* (1983)); **administrative law** (*Sinclair v Maryborough Mining Warden* (1975) and *Australian Conservation Foundation v Commonwealth* (1980)); and **land law** (*Newcrest Mining v Commonwealth* (1997)). However, environmental lawyers inevitably view those cases from a different perspective, particularly that of their outcomes.

The most significant High Court cases relating to environmental legislation are the constitutional cases considering the extent of **Commonwealth legislative power**. Despite the absence of a specific head of power relating to environmental matters, the Court, through expansive interpretation of the **trade and commerce power**, the **taxation** power, the **corporations power** and the **external affairs power**, has made it clear that the Commonwealth has broad powers to enact legislation dealing with the environment. In *Murphyores*, the Court held that the Commonwealth could make an export licence conditional upon environmental considerations and thus effectively stop sand mining on Fraser Island. In the *Tasmanian Dam Case*, a narrow majority upheld the Commonwealth's attempt to stop the construction by Tasmania of a dam that would have flooded the Gordon River below the Franklin. The decision demonstrated the potential of the external affairs power, given the broad range of treaties and international agreements on environmental matters to which Australia is a signatory.

The Court made it clear in *Koowarta's Case* (1982) and in the *Tasmanian Dam Case* that there are restrictions: the Commonwealth must enter into any treaty *bona fide* and, more significantly, any legislation must be consistent with the provisions of the treaty. But given the Court's confirmation of wide Commonwealth powers to legislate on environmental matters, what impact has this had on the extent to which successive Commonwealth Parliaments since the 1970s and 1980s have actually enacted legislation to secure positive environmental outcomes?

In short, environmental outcomes, whether conservationist or development-oriented, are determined largely by politics. Despite the opportunities created by the Court, the Commonwealth has not taken advantage of its broad powers so as to increase centralised environmental management. Although progressive for its time, the Commonwealth's environmental legislation passed in the **Whitlam era**—covering an impressive-sounding list of subjects such as environmental impact assessment, world heritage, flora and fauna and the Great Barrier Reef Marine Park—has on the whole proved relatively limited when measured against the wide range of environmental matters that subsequent experience has shown could and should be addressed. Four of the five major pieces of legislation enacted in the 1970s have since been repealed and replaced by the *Environment Protection and Biodiversity Conservation Act* 1999 (Cth), the application of which, in general terms, is limited to 'matters of national environmental significance'—a phrase that the Court may be called upon to interpret in due course. The notable exception to Commonwealth reluctance to intervene in environmental matters was of course the Hawke government's role in securing the passage of the *World Heritage Properties Conservation Act* 1983 (Cth), which brought the Tasmanian dam dispute before the High Court. Otherwise, the environmental legislation of the last 25 years has been generated largely by state and territory governments, which are generally considered to be more pro-development in orientation, and to have more pro-development policies, than the federal government.

Other constitutional cases have been significant for environmental law. First, section 90 of the Constitution makes Commonwealth power exclusive in relation to customs, **excise** and bounties. Two noteworthy cases dealing with state laws affecting natural resources are *Hematite Petroleum v Victoria* (1983) and *Harper v Minister for Sea Fisheries*

(1989), respectively involving a licence fee to operate Bass Strait pipelines for the transmission of hydrocarbons, and a royalty for the exploitation of abalone. The former fee was held to be an excise and therefore invalid; the latter was upheld. The distinction appears to lie in the finite nature of the abalone resource, the relationship between the royalty imposed and the benefit granted through access to the resource, and thus the relevance of the royalty to protecting the resource. The Court has thus opened the way for state charges on the exploitation of finite natural resources. While the imposition of a charge may sometimes result in the rationing of a scarce resource, it is not clear whether this would always have an environmentally protective consequence. In the absence of that protective consequence, *Harper* may have been differently decided.

Secondly, section 92 of the Constitution provides that **interstate trade and commerce** shall be 'absolutely free'. Although the focus in *Cole v Whitfield* (1988) was on the law rather than the facts, in the result the Court upheld Tasmania's right to conserve its crayfish stocks by prohibiting the possession of undersized crayfish, even when the prohibition extended to crayfish brought in from interstate. Even if this gave some incidental protection to the local industry—and in the absence of evidence, the Court thought it did not—the law was justified because local and interstate crayfish were indistinguishable, and to have confined the law to possession of the former would have made the law practically unenforceable.

In *Castlemaine Tooheys v SA* (1990), the Court decided that SA legislation imposing a 4¢ deposit on refillable bottles (generally produced, used and recycled locally), and a 15¢ deposit for non-refillable bottles (generally produced and sourced from interstate), was discriminatory and protectionist, and thus infringed section 92. SA argued that the object of the legislation was to encourage the use of refillable bottles in order to reduce litter and conserve energy. The Court was not satisfied that there was sufficient evidence to demonstrate that the legislation genuinely achieved these goals rather than simply protecting local industry. Importantly, however, the Court added that the legislation would not have infringed section 92 if it had been 'appropriate and adapted to the protection of the environment in South Australia from the litter problem and to the conservation of the State's finite energy resources', provided that the impact on interstate trade was 'incidental and not disproportionate to the achievement of those objectives'. Although the particular measure in question did not pass scrutiny, the Court thus left the door open for states to adopt economic incentives for positive environmental outcomes.

As environmental legislation is predominantly state-based, it is no surprise that a pervasive issue has been the extent to which the Commonwealth is bound by state environmental regulation. In *Botany Municipal Council v Federal Airports Corporation* (1992), the Court held, by a relatively straightforward application of section 109 of the Constitution, that the purported state regulation was **inconsistent** with Commonwealth legislation, and that the environmental consequences of building the third runway at Sydney airport must therefore be assessed according to federal law. Where there is no applicable Commonwealth legislation and the issue is one of Crown immunity, the issue is more difficult (see **Intergovernmental immunities**). In *Henderson's Case* (1997), the Court, following the *Cigamatic Case* (1962), acknowledged the existence of the immunity but left its limits unclear, thus making it incumbent upon the Commonwealth to legislate explicitly if it wants to put beyond doubt whether its agencies are or are not to be bound by state law. Whether state or Commonwealth law is binding on the Crown in any capacity, state or Commonwealth, can also involve threshold issues of statutory interpretation, and in *Bropho v WA* (1990) the Court moved away from an inflexible presumption that if legislation is silent there is no intention to bind the Crown, concluding in the circumstances of that case that **Aboriginal** heritage legislation of WA did apply to WA government activities.

If one tries to discern a general trend in relation to outcomes, it would be that the results of the Court's constitutional decisions have frequently been sympathetic to, or facilitative of, environmental protection. This is so, whether in relation to the reach of Commonwealth power; the extent of restrictions on state power (where resource protection has been accommodated within section 90 and appropriate environmental measures within section 92); the application of Commonwealth and state laws to their own and each other's agencies; or the ability of Commonwealth and state laws, where appropriate, to operate side by side. On the last point, and despite *Botany Municipal Council* where the Commonwealth appears to have sought deliberately to oust state law to facilitate construction of the third runway, an instructive case is *Commercial Radio Coffs Harbour v Fuller* (1986), where the Court held that the possession of a Commonwealth broadcasting licence did not preclude state environmental controls on the construction of broadcasting facilities.

The accumulation of these results is not necessarily coherent in terms of constitutional law doctrine. Yet the outcomes, whether deliberate or accidental, do cast the Court in a positive light from an environmentalist's outcome-oriented perspective. But the Court can achieve only so much—it is up to the legislators to make the laws for which the Court has created the opportunity (see also **Commonwealth–state relations**).

In the area of administrative law, one of the values cherished by most, perhaps all, environmentalists is public participation in decision making. Here the Court has played a significant role. First, it has enforced the values implicit in the giving of proper public notice where required by statute (*Scurr v Brisbane City Council* (1973)). Secondly, environmental litigants in the early 1980s brought important cases that led the Court to define the boundaries of the law of **standing** for mainstream administrative law—particularly the 'special interest' requirement for members of the public to challenge the actions of regulatory agencies. In *Australian Conservation Foundation*, the ACF sought to complain that the Commonwealth had not complied with environmental impact statement and foreign exchange control requirements in approving plans for the development of a tourist resort by a Japanese company. The Court held (Murphy dissenting) that the ACF, in seeking to enforce a public right rather than a private right, could not show more than a 'mere intellectual or emotional' interest, which was insufficient to distinguish it from the position of any other concerned member of the public. However, in *Onus v Alcoa* (1981), the Court did recognise the special interest of a local indigenous group in enforcing Aboriginal heritage legislation in relation to a proposal to construct an aluminium smelter. The Court declined, in *Australian Conservation Foundation*, to liberalise the rules of standing by according a sufficient 'special interest' to ACF, but *Onus v Alcoa* very soon afterwards offered environmental litigants more encouragement.

Access to the courts for environmental litigants has been confirmed by two recent decisions. In *Oshlack v Richmond River Council* (1998), in a remarkable 3:2 decision (Gaudron, **Gummow**, and **Kirby**; Brennan and McHugh dissenting), the Court upheld a disputed order as to **costs** which favoured the unsuccessful public interest litigant—initially made by Justice Paul Stein, then of the NSW Land and Environment Court, but reversed by the NSW Court of Appeal. In the High Court, Kirby relied on the expanded or 'open standing' provisions in the *Environmental Planning and Assessment Act* 1979 (NSW) and on discretionary costs provisions in the *Land and Environment Court Act* 1979 (NSW), both designed to facilitate public interest environmental litigation. In the *Truth About Motorways Case* (2000), the Court upheld the ability of the legislature to expand the common law requirements in relation to standing.

However, while the Court has increased the ease with which public interest litigants can get into court, the remedies available to them are often limited by the courts' inability to intervene on the merits. Whether at common law or under the Commonwealth's *Administrative Decisions (Judicial Review) Act* 1977, litigants can seek only judicial review on grounds of legality rather than full review of the merits.

The grounds of review commonly relied upon in environmental matters in inferior courts and in the **Federal Court** frequently raise difficult questions of both fact and law. This raises the issue of the proper scope of **judicial review** of factual determinations made not only by administrators in general, but also in particular by specialist environmental decision-making bodies. In the USA, the courts have developed a doctrine of deference to the views of specialised agencies on the interpretation of the legislation they administer (the so-called 'Chevron doctrine', after the decision of the **United States Supreme Court** in *Chevron USA v Natural Resources Defense Council* (1984)). The High Court has preferred to approach the issue on the basis of whether the **fact finding** by the lower court or tribunal is jurisdictional (reviewable) or non-jurisdictional (not reviewable). In *Australian Heritage Commission v Mt Isa Mines* (1997), the Court held that the Australian Heritage Commission was the final arbiter of whether a place was properly considered to be part of the 'national estate', and thus properly registered under the *Australian Heritage Commission Act* 1975 (Cth). In *Enfield Corporation v Development Assessment Commission* (2000), the Court confirmed that jurisdictional facts must be for the courts to determine, but left the door open—at least where the evidence before the court was the same as that before primary decision maker—to the possibility of the court giving weight to the findings of a body equipped with specialist expertise.

These issues are pervasive in environmental regulation, and raise the critical institutional question of who is best equipped to make the relevant decisions. Given the flexibility with which issues can be characterised as issues of fact or issues of law, and the elusiveness of the distinction between jurisdictional and non-jurisdictional error, the courts have a wide discretion in choosing whether or not to intervene. Again, the ardent environmentalist will be tempted to assess the record of the courts on the extent to which the outcomes are favourable to environmental protection.

As to property rights in natural resources, several High Court cases have the potential to impact upon environmental regulation. The decision in *Newcrest Mining* held a prohibition on mining to be an **acquisition of property** within section 51(xxxi) of the Constitution, and thus subject to the constitutional requirement of just compensation (see also *Commonwealth v WMC Resources* (1998)). Although the Australian requirement that there be an 'acquisition' of property does not go as far as the US doctrine of 'regulatory takings' (see the *Tasmanian Dam Case*), one consequence of an expansive interpretation of section 51(xxxi) is that governments may become more reluctant to protect the environment where the direct cost of doing so is prohibitive or at least significant.

The ownership and conservation of natural resources is an important part of environmental law, and since *Mabo* (1992), **native title** has become an important part of any consideration of property in natural resources. As the conservation of threatened flora and fauna is regulated by environmental statutes in all jurisdictions, the question arises from a conservation perspective of whether a holder of a native title can exercise hunting and fishing rights over protected flora and fauna. In *Yanner v Eaton* (1999), the Court held (**Gleeson**, Gaudron, Gummow, Kirby, and **Hayne**; McHugh and **Callinan** dissenting) that Murrandoo Yanner could lawfully hunt and take protected juvenile crocodiles without first obtaining a licence under the *Fauna Conservation Act* 1974 (Qld). The case turned primarily on whether, as a matter of interpretation, fauna had become 'property of the Crown' within the meaning of the Queensland Act, but so far as the outcome of the case reflected a balancing of conflicting interests in native title and conservation, it was the former that prevailed.

In a wide range of areas of law, the High Court has made significant decisions affecting the environment. As the Court is concerned primarily with doctrine rather than outcomes (see **Rule of law**), it is not surprising that some decisions have favoured environmental protection and some have not. Yet—given that the outcomes have been predominantly benign—is it not possible that, as the environmental movement has swept the world, a new awareness of the imperatives of environmental protection has reached even into the consciousness of the High Court?

JUDITH JONES

Equality. The Constitution contains no explicit guarantee of equality, or exclusion of differential treatment based on criteria such as gender, **race**, or sexuality, of the type that is commonly found in countries with a **Bill of Rights**. However, notions of equality have clearly been part of the High Court's jurisprudence. The Court's understanding of the concept of equality is evident from its flirtation with, and subsequent rejection of, a doctrine of equality as an **implied constitutional right**. That episode invites us to reflect on the Court's attitude to gender equality and, to a lesser extent, racial equality.

In *Leeth v Commonwealth* (1992), **Deane** and **Toohey**, relying on the **common law** doctrines and political principles underlying the Constitution, implied into it a constitutional principle of substantive equality. However, their approach was roundly rejected in *Kruger v Commonwealth* (1997). All the Justices who rejected Deane's and Toohey's approach (**Brennan**, **Dawson**, **Gaudron**, **McHugh** and **Gummow**) relied on the fact that the Constitution clearly contemplated inequalities of treatment—through express constitutional provisions such as section 51(xxvi), which authorised the enactment of special (and discriminatory) laws against the people of 'any race'; section 51(xix), similarly authorising discriminatory laws against aliens; and section 127, which until its removal in the 1967 referendum directed the exclusion of **Aboriginal people** from the census. Historically, it is difficult to argue that the **framers of the Constitution** had any interest in protecting individuals against discriminatory treatment by a broad-based right to equality. Indeed, the very opposite is the case (see **Race**).

Regardless of the acceptance or rejection of an implied general equality right, it is still important to consider how the Court understands 'equality'. If the Court has only a limited understanding of equality, agitation for constitutional entrenchment of a broad equality right may be somewhat misguided. In other words, the more important question is what such a right to equality might mean. Deane and Toohey had argued in *Leeth* that the formal notion of 'equality before the law' may not be enough: that 'in some circumstances, theoretical equality under the law sustains rather than alleviates the practical reality of social and economic inequality'. Yet the pull of a merely formal conception of equality is very strong.

The Supreme Court of Canada has developed a sophisticated understanding of both equality and **discrimination** in the course of interpreting section 15 of the Canadian Charter of Rights and Freedoms. That section provides, in part, that 'every individual is equal before the law and has the right to equal protection and equal benefit of the law without discrimination'. The Supreme Court has consistently affirmed that the question whether an individual's equality rights have been denied requires a contextual and purposive analysis. The current state of equality jurisprudence is summarised in *Law v Canada* (1999), which involved a pension plan for surviving spouses, graduated so that able-bodied surviving spouses without dependent children were not eligible for a pension until age 35, and could not receive full benefits until age 45. The Supreme Court held that this was not an impermissible discrimination on the basis of age. The Court explained that mere differential treatment is not a breach of section 15, unless it

reflects the stereotypical application of presumed group or personal characteristics, or otherwise has the effect of perpetuating or promoting the view that the individual is less capable, or less worthy of recognition or value as a human being … Differential treatment will not likely constitute discrimination within … s 15(1) where it does not violate the human dignity or freedom of a person or group in this way, and in particular where the differential treatment also assists in ameliorating the position of the disadvantaged within Canadian society.

In assessing whether a law or practice disadvantages a group or individual, the Court suggested that regard may be had to the history of disadvantage experienced by the group, together with its current situation and the purpose and effect of the challenged law or practice. In this way, the Canadian Court has avoided the pull of mere formal equality—the notion that identity of treatment regardless of context ensures equality.

Avoiding the simplicities of formal equality requires a recognition of substantive inequality. Interestingly, in developing their analysis of an implied equality right, in particular its common law origins, Deane and Toohey found it necessary to gloss over 'the past anomaly' of discrimination against **women**. This dismissal of the continuing effects of entrenched inequality between women and **men** does not augur well for the Court's capacity to recognise and respond to that inequality.

In the **Gleeson Court**, **Kirby** is perhaps the Justice who has most strongly engaged with the meaning of (gender) equality. In *Osland v The Queen* (1998), he said: 'As evidence of the neutrality of the law it should avoid, as far as possible, categories expressed in sex specific or otherwise discriminatory terms.' At first glance, this appears to be a failure to recognise that if context and purpose are taken into account, sex-specificity may well be appropriate as a response to a sex-specific problem. However, Kirby went on to say: 'Such categories tend to reinforce **stereotypes**. They divert [attention] from the fundamental problem which evokes a legal response to what is assumed to be the typical case.' Here, he may well be recognising the increasing awareness of **feminism** that claims on behalf of 'women' can sometimes ignore differences among women, and may set up a new stereotype or merely reinforce traditional ones.

In both *Osland* and *Garcia v National Australia Bank* (1998), Kirby criticised arguments made from 'gender loyalty or sympathy', contrasting such arguments (in *Osland*) with those based on 'ethical and legal principle'. Kirby was not suggesting that ethical principles do not require equality between genders. The real question is how this can best be achieved. There is a danger, however, that Kirby's preoccupation with principle will simply reinforce the 'pull' towards formal equality, clearly present in the Court's decisions more generally.

In Australia, one of the few provisions in the Constitution which protects individuals is section 117. It provides:

A subject of the Queen, resident in any State, shall not be subject in any other State to any disability or discrimination which would not be equally applicable to him if he were a subject of the Queen resident in such other State.

This section had effectively been rendered nugatory in *Henry v Boehm* (1973), when the Court, faced with a challenge to a requirement of residence in SA before a lawyer from interstate was allowed to practise there, decided that since both residents and non-residents of SA had to comply with the residence requirement, there was no discrimination for the purposes of section 117. In other words, the Court (with a strong dissent from **Stephen**) applied a 'strict equal treatment approach': equality or non-discrimination is achieved if everyone is treated in precisely the same way.

However, in *Street v Queensland Bar Association* (1989), the Court overruled this approach and indicated a willingness to recognise a contextualised approach to equality for the purposes of section 117. Once again faced with a challenge by an out-of-state lawyer to restrictive residence rules for admission to practice in a state, **Mason**, for example, recognised that while a provision as to residence 'applies equally to all', its disadvantages could 'apply unequally'. He concluded that if a provision's *effect* was to discriminate, this was enough to breach section 117. For Gaudron, discrimination for the purposes of section 117 meant 'discrimination against', rather than a mere difference in treatment. McHugh recognised that 'discrimination can arise just as readily from a law which treats as equals those who are different as it can from a law which treats differently those whose circumstances are not materially different', while Brennan recognised that what matters is not whether

the character of the law is discriminatory … but the impact which the law has … A law which does not have a discriminatory character may produce an impermissible discrimination in a particular case, and a law which does have that character may not do so in a particular case … The absence of discrimination consists as much in the unequal treatment of unequals as in the equal treatment of equals.

All of the Justices recognised that, in some circumstances, it might be necessary for a state to discriminate against non-state residents—for example, when enshrining the franchise for electing state legislatures and state members of the Senate, the 'states' House'. This explicit recognition that explicit discrimination or preference may sometimes be justified indicates a willingness, once again, to take account of context in assessing discrimination or inequality.

Street is not isolated in its move away from a merely formalised understanding of equality. The focus on substance rather than **form** has also occurred, for example, in recent decisions on section 92 of the Constitution (see **Interstate trade and commerce**). In *Cole v Whitfield* (1988), the Court found that 'it does not follow that every departure from equality of treatment imposes a burden or would infringe a constitutional guarantee of the freedom of interstate trade and commerce from discriminatory burdens'. The Court looked to the 'practical operation of the law in order to determine its validity'. With the more recent changes in the Court's membership, however, there has been a move back to formalism (see, for example, *Re Wakim* (1999); **Cross-vesting**).

In any event, understanding equality in a contextualised sense and applying that understanding are two different matters: the pull of formal equality is extremely strong. It is worth emphasising, as the Court has recognised, that although section 117 is on its face directed to individuals, it in fact has much more in common with provisions such as section 92. In both contexts, equality between states and 'national unity' are pre-eminent values. Where the Court has to deal squarely with equality between groups of Australians whose group identification is not state-based, its understanding may well be more inhibited.

For example, in *Gerhardy v Brown* (1985), the Court found that the *Pitjantjatjara Land Rights Act* 1981 (SA), which excluded non-Pitjantjatjara from an area of land amounting to about one-tenth of SA, did discriminate against non-Pitjantjatjara under the Commonwealth *Racial Discrimination Act* 1975. The Court held the legislation valid, but only because it amounted to a 'special measure' designed for the benefit of the Pitjantjatjara. Although the Court recognised the benefits of the Land Rights Act, it is of concern that the Court could see the Act as discriminatory in the first place. Mere difference of treatment does not amount to discrimination, a point recognised by the Court in *Gerhardy*, but not fully applied. As Wojciech Sadurski put it: 'By suggesting that racially protective measures and invidious racial classifications are discriminatory alike and therefore must either stand or fall together, the Court refuses to include the analysis of purposes into the discussion of discrimination.' The effect of such an approach was starkly illustrated by **Wilson's** dissent in *Mabo (No 1)* (1988), where the Queensland Parliament had passed legislation for the retrospective extinguishment of traditional rights of **native title**. Wilson thought that this did not 'create an inequality' on racial grounds, but operated 'to remove a source of inequality formerly existing', since only the peoples of indigenous races had enjoyed traditional rights in the first place. On his view, by ensuring that the peoples of indigenous races 'will enjoy the same rights with respect to the ownership of **property** and rights of inheritance as every other person in Queensland', the legislation would achieve 'equality before the law'.

Private law litigation has also provided opportunities for the Court to explore the meaning of 'equality', and we can see some similarities in the understanding of equality in 'public' and 'private' law. For example, in *Garcia*, the Court recognised structural inequality between women and men, but refused to base its decision on this recognised inequality.

In that case, the Court reconsidered the rule in *Yerkey v Jones* (1939), which had established a 'special rule' for married women who signed guarantees to support their husbands' businesses. Such guarantees would not be enforced against the wife if her signature had been obtained by the husband's **undue influence** on her, nor equally if she did not understand the nature of the guarantee, unless the lender had itself explained the effect of the guarantee (rather than relying on the husband). The Court's reaffirmation of this 'special rule' in *Garcia* failed to evince a complex understanding of equality. Gaudron, McHugh, Gummow, and **Hayne** acknowledged that, despite changes in the position of women over the last 60 years, 'there are still a significant number of women in relationships which are, for many and varied reasons, marked by disparities of economic and other power between the parties'. However, the rule was not upheld on this basis, but on the basis of the 'trust and confidence … between marriage partners', and there were indications that the rule should apply in a gender-neutral way, to husbands and to same-sex couples. Thus the Court offers, in a manner reminiscent of the approach in *Gerhardy*, a recognition (albeit undeveloped), of inequality between husbands and wives, but a disavowal of such inequality as justifying or, indeed, being relevant to the decision.

To recognise this inequality fully would not necessarily dictate any particular outcome; but, as Kristie Dunn has pointed out, if the decision is to contribute to an understanding of equality in a substantive sense, a fuller exploration is required. For the Court to contribute to an understanding of equality in a substantive sense, as applied to groups rather than 'states', the Court must demonstrate that it can apply its understanding of substance rather than form outside the conventional contexts. Such an analysis will not dictate a foregone conclusion in a particular case, but it could lead to an informed debate on equality when it really matters.

JENNY MORGAN

Further Reading
Kristie Dunn, '"Yakking Giants": Equality Discourse in the High Court' (2000) 24 *MULR* 427
Gareth Evans, 'Benign Discrimination and the Right to Equality' (1974) 6 *FL Rev* 26
Wojciech Sadurski, '*Gerhardy v Brown* v The Concept of Discrimination: Reflections on the Landmark Case that Wasn't' (1986) 11 *Syd LR* 5
Cheryl Saunders, 'Concepts of Equality in the Australian Constitution' in Geoffrey Lindell (ed), *Future Directions in Australian Constitutional Law* (1994)

Equity. There is perhaps no area of law in which the High Court has made as great a contribution to the jurisprudence of the **common law** world as in its judgments on equity. 'Equity' is not a discrete area of law in the same way as might be said of **contract law**, **corporations law**, **tort law**, or **land law**. Rather, this branch of the law includes a variety of doctrines and **remedies**, all of which originated in the jurisdiction of the Court of Chancery, and many of which have wide-ranging applications. Equitable principles may be involved in decisions to set aside transactions or gifts procured in an unfair manner, to hold people to their word when the general rules of the law would allow them to avoid it, to moderate the consequences of applying certain rules where those consequences would be **unconscionable**, and to ensure that the competing claims of justice are properly weighed in the granting of certain remedies. Equitable doctrines also affect the law of **property** in various ways, notably through the operation of express, resulting, and constructive **trusts**.

The High Court's contribution to equity jurisprudence has been particularly marked since the early 1980s, and this period coincides with the growing recognition that Australian law might need to diverge from the law as laid down by the **House of Lords** and the **Privy Council**. Mason, Deane, and **Gummow** have been particularly influential in this renaissance of equity jurisprudence in recent years.

The High Court's equity jurisprudence provides a window on the **values** that underpin its perception of justice. Equity cases often require the application of principles rather than rules, and they demand that courts choose between competing values. For example, equity cases concerned with setting aside transactions often raise the question of the balance to be found between personal responsibility and the protection of the vulnerable. To what extent should people be relieved from the consequences of disadvantageous transactions which they entered into without duress or improper pressure? What is the right balance to be found between the law's legitimate requirement that all land transactions should be in writing (for the sake of certainty) and the need to protect people who trusted too much in the spoken assurances of another? Courts in different jurisdictions have offered different answers to these questions at different times.

In dealing with such questions, the High Court's jurisprudence in equity is dominated by a concern with the conscience of the defendant as the principal justification for equitable relief. The term 'unconscionability', which is the *leitmotif* of Australian equity jurisprudence, is not given the same emphasis in any other country of the common law world. In contrast to jurisdictions which are strongly influenced by **restitution** theory, the emphasis in the High Court's decisions on equity is not upon whether the defendant has acquired an enrichment without juristic reason, but whether his or her conduct has violated the dictates of conscience as the law interprets them. In such cases, there may or may not have been an enrichment. It follows that in the High Court's judgments on **undue influence**, there is no requirement of manifest disadvantage to the plaintiff from the transaction such as exists in Britain (*National Westminster Bank v Morgan* (1985)). It is enough that the transaction was procured through what is presumed to have been an improper exercise of influence by a person who was in a position of trust and confidence (*Johnson v Buttress* (1936)). In some situations, it is a claim to the retention of benefits in circumstances which would make this unconscionable that justifies equitable relief. That is, the dictates of conscience determine whether an enrichment is unjustified (see, for example, *Muschinski v Dodds* (1985)).

This line of reasoning explains the Court's approach on a number of issues: for example, the question whether a contract should be set aside for unilateral mistake. In *Taylor v Johnson* (1983), the Court set aside an option contract where the vendor was mistaken as to the agreed price, not merely because the vendor's misfortune would have led to a windfall gain for the purchaser, but because the purchaser knew of this mistaken apprehension and made efforts to conceal it from the vendor.

As the conscience of the defendant is usually the key issue in determining whether the plaintiff is entitled to equitable relief, so it may also be a ground for excusing the defendant from liability in equity. The Court has indicated, through *obiter dicta* in *Warman International v Dwyer* (1995), that it is not inclined to follow English **precedent** on the strict application of **fiduciary obligations** where the fiduciary has acted honestly and has not sought to harm the interests of those to whom the obligations are owed. On this basis, the High Court would not have decided the landmark case of *Phipps v Boardman* (1966) in the same way as did the House of Lords. Deane marked out the basis of disagreement with a number of English decisions on the law of fiduciary obliga-

tions when he wrote in *Chan v Zacharia* (1984) that the 'over-enthusiastic and unnecessary statement of broad general principles of equity in terms of inflexibility may destroy the vigour which it is intended to promote … and convert equity into an instrument of hardship and injustice in individual cases'.

Just as the High Court has been concerned with the conscience of the defendant, so has it been concerned that equitable doctrines not be invoked in a way that results in the unmeritorious enrichment of plaintiffs. This concern led the Court to reconsider the conventional rules on illegality in the law of trusts in *Nelson v Nelson* (1995). In that case, a plaintiff, who was complicit in her mother's plan to obtain an illegal benefit from the government, would have obtained a windfall gain if those rules had prevented her mother from relying on the presumption of a resulting trust. In reformulating these rules, the Court clearly rejected both the majority and minority approaches of the House of Lords in *Tinsley v Milligan* (1993). In regard to the law of fiduciary obligations, the Court, in *Warman International v Dwyer* (1995), quoted Deane's statement in *Chan v Zacharia* that the 'liability to account for a personal benefit or gain obtained or received by use or by reason of fiduciary position, opportunity or knowledge will not arise in circumstances where it would be unconscientious to assert it'. In saying this, the Court distanced itself from English authority on the subject (*Regal (Hastings) v Gulliver* (1942)). A similar concern to avoid the unmeritorious enrichment of plaintiffs has influenced the Court in fashioning equitable relief. In *Maguire v Makaronis* (1997), the Court granted the rescission of a mortgage procured in breach of fiduciary duty, but only on condition that the plaintiffs repaid the principal and interest.

When is behaviour unconscionable, in the view of the High Court? A major theme in the Court's equity jurisprudence is to treat the exploitation of another person's vulnerability or weakness as grounds for equitable intervention. In *Stern v McArthur* (1988), Deane and **Dawson** summarised this theme in the Court's interpretation of unconscionable conduct when they wrote that 'a person should not be permitted to use or insist upon his legal rights to take advantage of another's special vulnerability or misadventure for the unjust enrichment of himself'. This principle underlies not only the expansive view of special **disability** or disadvantage in the doctrine of unconscionable dealing (*Blomley v Ryan* (1956); *Louth v Diprose* (1992)) but also a number of other important decisions of the Court.

Nowhere is this concern for the protection of the vulnerable more evident than in relation to third party guarantees. The Court has shown itself willing to set aside guarantees on a range of grounds, and this jurisdiction long predates the modern legislation providing for guarantees to be set aside in certain circumstances. The Court has adopted a test of constructive notice in determining whether banks have sufficient notice of the possibility of undue influence to invalidate a guarantee where there was no independent advice (*Bank of NSW v Rogers* (1941)); it has treated old age and a limited capacity in written English as a sufficient disadvantage even where the parents who guaranteed their son's debts had extensive business experience (*Amadio's Case* (1983)); it has also reaffirmed the doctrine of *Yerkey v Jones*

(1939) that the relationship between husbands and wives is such that banks or other lenders need to ensure that the wife understands the nature and effect of a guarantee of her husband's debts (*Garcia v National Australia Bank* (1998)). These decisions reflect a view that the onus is on financial institutions which receive the benefit of guarantees to ensure that those who sign such guarantees do so without pressure, improper influence, or misunderstanding, and that they have received independent advice.

This concern to protect the vulnerable from exploitation and to ensure that risky financial transactions are entered into with full information, reflects Australian values, which may be seen also in unique Australian legislation on consumer protection and fair dealing in commerce. Statutes such as the *Contracts Review Act* 1980 (NSW) and the *Trade Practices Act* 1974 (Cth) give courts considerable scope to set aside contracts that have been unfairly procured, or to award a range of other remedies. Australian courts also have a broad jurisdiction to relieve against misleading or deceptive conduct in commerce. As the case law on guarantees demonstrates, the notion that in the law of contract each party is responsible to look after its own interests, and that the court's role is only to ensure that there has been a valid contract freely entered into, has never taken root in Australia. This contrasts with the view taken in nineteenth century England, and with the underlying rationale of much contemporary law-and-**economics** theory. The High Court has been assiduous in protecting the vulnerable from the full discipline of the market. Consequently, the doctrines of unconscionable dealing and relief against forfeiture have retained their vigour in Australia when at times they have largely disappeared from view in other common law countries.

While the Court is mainly concerned with the conscience of the defendant, there is in certain of its decisions a discernible tendency to exercise a jurisdiction of mercy in order to relieve parties from obligations that have become unduly burdensome in light of changed circumstances. **Brennan** protested in *Stern v McArthur* (1988) that the concept of unconscionability is not a charter for judicial reformation of contracts, but his was a dissenting voice.

Indeed, respect for the sanctity of contract as a governing principle for private law is much less entrenched in the jurisprudence of the Court than it is in other parts of the world. As a consequence, contracts are more likely to be set aside in Australian courts on the grounds of unfairness than in many other jurisdictions, and there is an increasing tendency for Australian courts to recognise rights arising from express or implied assurances which do not depend for their validity on the existence of a contract.

This may be seen in a number of famous High Court decisions. In *United Dominions Corporation v Brian* (1985), the Court held that fiduciary obligations may arise even prior to the signing of a joint venture or partnership agreement where a relationship of trust and confidence can be shown to exist in which one party is in a position of vulnerability. In *Waltons Stores v Maher* (1988), the Court held that legal obligations could arise from assumptions induced as a consequence of pre-contractual negotiations, and *Commonwealth v Verwayen* (1990) held that rights could arise from assurances made by the other side in the early stages of litigation.

The Court has also invoked equitable doctrine to challenge a fundamental tenet of the classical law of contract: the doctrine of privity. Early indications of a willingness to rethink traditional notions of privity were seen in **Windeyer's** judgment in *Coulls v Bagot's Executor & Trustee* (1967). A major qualification on the doctrine of privity emerged in *Trident General Insurance v McNiece* (1988). The Court indicated that in principle, a trust could be inferred in favour of a third party who was identified as a possible beneficiary of an insurance contract but who had not given consideration for the insurance.

These challenges to orthodox contract theory do not represent a repudiation of the need for commercial certainty, nor a rejection of traditional concepts concerning the enforcement of promises. Rather, the Court has indicated that traditional understandings of contract law do not provide a sufficient basis for doing justice concerning interpersonal or commercial arrangements in modern society. The Court has also indicated, through the development of equitable principles, that moral obligations, and therefore legal obligations, may arise in dealings between persons or corporations from circumstances other than the conclusion of a contractual arrangement. Equity, in this view, plays its traditional view of supplementing, not displacing, common law rules.

An unresolved issue in the Court's equity jurisprudence is how to deal with equitable claims which, if recognised, would require the Court to ignore the clear terms of a statute. This issue typically emerges in the law of equitable assignments where the court is asked to recognise a purported transfer as valid despite the fact that the statutory formalities have not been complied with. Surprisingly, the Court's justification for departing from the terms of a statute is not predicated only on the need to prevent fraud. In *Corin v Patton* (1990), the Court confirmed by a majority (albeit in *obiter dicta*), that a court may give effect to a gift despite the absence of the requisite formalities if the donor has done everything that he or she needed to do to effectuate the gift. In such cases, it is apparent that equity is departing from the maxim that 'equity does not assist a volunteer' (the 'volunteer' being the beneficiary), or is at least not allowing the statute to be invoked to hinder volunteers from asserting their title. The justification for ignoring the clear terms of the statute—which aims to ensure that all valid property interests appear on the land titles register—was not explained in terms of equitable principle.

A similar willingness to allow a person to evade the terms of the statute may be seen in the early High Court decision in *Anning v Anning* (1907). The Court held, by a 2:1 majority, that a dying man's wishes to transfer property to his family, expressed in the form of a deed, could be given effect even though in many cases the formalities for that form of property had not been fulfilled, either because in some instances he had taken sufficient steps of his own to complete the transactions, or because he could be held liable in **damages**. **Griffith** and **Isaacs** reasoned that the estate could be held liable for damages in seeking to 'derogate from the grant' (that is, to prejudice or destroy it) since the estate, in seeking clarification of the legal position from the court, had taken a position in the litigation in opposition to the claims of the

children. It had thereby violated an 'implied covenant' in the deed. Such a recourse to legal fictions to achieve a result demonstrates again the jurisdiction of mercy evident in certain decisions of the Court. There is a tendency in the High Court for such decisions to favour individuals over the collective entitlements of taxpayers where these are the competing interests (see for example, *Commissioner of Stamp Duties (Qld) v Jolliffe* (1920)). There is room for more than one opinion about what is a just result in such cases.

These cases are unusual examples of the abdication of principle. In general, the Court's judgments in equity over the last century have been characterised by a concern to search for principle and to articulate the law's underlying values. Deane reflected the mood of the Court for generations in criticising the invocation of equitable doctrines as a means of indulging in 'idiosyncratic notions of fairness and justice' (*Muschinski v Dodds*). The Court has been assiduous in maintaining the clarity of equitable principle and not allowing it to be confused by mistaken notions about the effects of fusion of the administration of law and equity (*Chan v Cresdon* (1989)). It has asserted orthodox propositions concerning the nature and purpose of fiduciary obligations (*Breen v Williams* (1996)) in the wake of departures from that orthodoxy in other jurisdictions.

Adherence to precedent has, however, always been less important to the Court than articulating the principles of equity that lie behind that precedent. In articulating those principles, the High Court has ensured that equitable doctrine will retain both its vigour and its compelling moral power as a major influence on Australian law in the twenty-first century.

PATRICK PARKINSON

Further Reading

Malcolm Cope (ed), *Equity: Issues and Trends* (1995)

Gino Dal Pont and Don Chalmers, *Equity and Trusts in Australia and New Zealand* (1996)

Paul Finn (ed), *Essays in Equity* (1985)

RP Meagher, WMC Gummow, and JRF Lehane, *Equity: Doctrines and Remedies* (3rd edn 1992)

Patrick Parkinson (ed), *The Principles of Equity* (1996)

Establishment of Court. The primitive court arrangements brought to Australia on British settlement included avenues of appeals, in the modern sense, from early quasi-judicial officers to the colonial Governor and thence to the **Privy Council.** Those appeals were permitted partly by statute and partly by the royal prerogative. With the creation, from the 1820s, of colonial Supreme Courts having jurisdictions akin to those of the Superior Courts at Westminster, supervisory and corrective powers over lower courts were exercised by prerogative **writs** and other non-statutory procedures. The concept of 'appealing' from one court to another developed in nineteenth-century Australia due largely to the creation of such intermediate tribunals as District and County Courts.

Appeals to the Privy Council, which had been possible since the first settlement, fell into disuse for a time after statutory changes made at Westminster from 1828. Orders in Council to grant, or confirm the continuance of, such

appeals were overlooked and not implemented for most Australian colonies until the 1850s or 1860s. Francis Forbes, first Chief Justice of NSW, never had to consider the question of a common Australasian court of appeal; but he disapproved of a similar proposal, then contemplated for the West Indies, on grounds of expense and difficulty of access.

In 1849, at the instigation of Earl Grey, the Privy Council constituted a Committee on Trade and Plantations, the report of which was drafted by, and reflected the powerful influence of, James Stephen (Jr), latterly Under Secretary of State for the Colonies. The committee virtually recommended Australian federation and proposed that one of the Australian Governors be designated 'Governor-General of Australia' with authority to convene 'the General Assembly of Australia', which was to have ten specified powers, including:

6. The establishment of a General Supreme Court, to be a Court of Original Jurisdiction, or a Court of Appeal for any of the inferior Courts of the separate provinces.

The determining of the extent of the jurisdiction and the forms and manner of proceeding of such Supreme Court.

The proposal, although embodied in a parliamentary Bill, was criticised on the same grounds Forbes had applied to the West Indies concept. It was abandoned.

Nevertheless, the broad notion of pursuing federal arrangements was carried over into proceedings of various Australian colonial committees, and advocated by influential individuals, during the 1850s and 1860s. A South Australian proposal, made in 1856, for a 'General Court of Appeal' that would visit the Australian capital cities in rotation, won little support, especially because it aimed to 'diminish, if not entirely put an end to, appeals to the Privy Council'.

Despite overwhelming parochialism that disposed the Australian colonies to issue their own postage stamps, impose customs barriers at frontiers, and adopt incompatible railway gauges, Inter-Colonial Conferences were regularly convened from the 1880s. They provided a forum for canvassing federal possibilities, but were concerned increasingly with matters of high constitutional principle and feasibility rather than with creating courts in a federation.

In 1870, a Victorian Royal Commission examining opportunities for greater cooperation between the Australian colonies reported that a common regional court of appeal had become 'almost a matter of necessity'. With its creation, it was thought, colonial laws would inevitably become more uniform. Draft legislation accompanying the report postulated a 'High Court of Appeal for Australia' having final **jurisdiction** on all **matters** referred to it by the participating colonies. The Privy Council Office thought the proposal insulting, and caused it to be stifled for a decade.

In 1880, a draft Bill for 'An Act to provide for the establishment of an Australasian Court of Appeal' was adopted; the Imperial Parliament was invited to enact it, but declined. The Bill contemplated a court exercising 'appellate civil jurisdiction within and throughout' all the Australian Colonies and NZ. Further appeal to the Privy Council was expressly retained. Just as that Bill failed to command support, so too did the suggestion, aired at ensuing Federation Conferences, that there should be an 'Australian Privy Council'.

At the 1890 Inter-Colonial Conference, attention moved away from a regional court of appeal to creating, within the proposed federation, a 'Supreme Court' with original jurisdiction like that of the **United States Supreme Court**. Andrew **Inglis Clark**, of Tasmania, stimulated the change of emphasis. He advanced his own draft of a possible Australian Constitution, based on his study of the Constitutions of the USA and Canada. Thus began a flirtation in Australia with the US federal system that, particularly at the court level, has continued since in greater or lesser degree. The constitutional chapter on the courts, as drafted by Inglis Clark, referred to 'the Federal Judicatory' consisting of a federal Supreme Court with a defined original jurisdiction and a final appellate jurisdiction—that finality creating a distraction threatening the success of the whole.

Inglis Clark may be likened to a surveyor, or draftsman of building plans. He prepared the way: but what was built followed instead the 'architectural' skills of **Griffith**, incumbent Premier and future **Chief Justice** of Queensland, who—by force of his intellect, persuasive powers and political understanding—largely shaped the High Court. He became chairman of a Constitutional Committee, and personally assumed carriage of the drafting of a constitutional instrument developed from refinements of Inglis Clark's original text. Under Griffith's superintendence, Chapter III of the Constitution was similarly settled. Its title was changed to 'The Judicature'. It was generally understood as not calling into being any immediate court or judge, but rather as enabling the prospective Commonwealth Parliament to create 'a Federal Supreme Court, to be called the High Court of Australia' in which 'the **judicial power** of the Commonwealth shall be vested' (an understanding the correctness of which was left open in *Hannah v Dalgarno* (1903); see **Constitutional basis of Court**). The 1849 preference for a 'Supreme Court', coupled with deference to the American usage, was thus retained, but only nominally—thereby placating the Australian colonies, most of which feared that the authority of their established Supreme Courts might be diminished.

One American precedent did prevail. The Court was to be constituted by judges described as 'the Justices of the High Court' (section 72), the expression 'Justice', in that sense, being then anomalous in Australia, as it ordinarily designated magistrates and others in the commission of the peace. The Constitution itself (section 71) prescribed that there would be a Chief Justice 'and so many other Justices, not less than two, as the Parliament prescribes'.

The question of appeals to the Privy Council became more vexed when the Imperial Parliament declined to accept a draft clause regulating them. Eventually, at a conference with Australian delegates in London, a compromise was settled (Constitution, section 74). Its effect was to preserve Privy Council appeals subject to the power of the High Court to control, by issuing or withholding a certificate, such appeals on *inter se* questions.

After much controversy, debate, and political excitement, Australian federation was agreed to by referendum, and the provisions of a new Constitution received legal force through section 9 of the *Commonwealth of Australia Constitution Act* 1900 (Imp), to which royal assent was given on 9 July 1900.

However, bringing the High Court into being had to await the passage of the *Judiciary Act* 1903 (Cth)—achieved only after much energetic parliamentary debate from those still opposed to the very idea of the Court. Many politicians remained convinced that it would be a tribunal of mere ceremony, having scant **business** to transact. Many lawyers were affronted that the majesty of the **state Supreme Courts** would be impaired. As late as June 1900, Frederick Darley, Chief Justice of NSW, remained satisfied that High Court appeals 'will be few and far between'. Samuel Way, Chief Justice of SA, declared privately that the High Court was no more wanted than a fifth wheel to a coach. It fell principally to Alfred **Deakin** and **Barton** to press the Bill for the Judiciary Act upon an uncommitted legislature. From its introduction until its assent, the Bill was before the Parliament for more than a year.

The Judiciary Act declared the High Court to be a **superior court** of record. It left the **number of Justices** (after an earlier draft had provided for five) at the bare minimum permitted by the Constitution of three, and provided for their **remuneration** without pensions. Among other provisions, it specified the nature and manner of exercise of the Court's original and appellate jurisdictions. An extraneous jurisdiction as the **Court of Disputed Returns** was added by the *Commonwealth Electoral Act* 1902. In pursuance of the Judiciary Act, Griffith was appointed as the first Chief Justice, Barton and **O'Connor** as the **puisne Justices**. The Court sat for the first time in Melbourne on 6 October 1903 (see **Sittings of Court**).

Institutionally, the High Court has changed little since its foundation. Doctrine and symbols have altered, but the body itself has stood fast. The most significant change was the opening, in 1980, of a national courthouse in **Canberra**. Vast and pretentious in scale (but see **Architecture of Court building**), it anchored the Court to the Commonwealth's capital. Previously, the Court had its own **buildings** in Melbourne and Sydney, and used state accommodation on **circuit**. The introduction, in the 1980s, of hearings by video link throughout the continent, particularly for interlocutory and **chamber** matters, added to the sense of centrality afforded by the Canberra location.

Four statutory changes materially augmented the Court's supremacy. First, the *Privy Council (Limitation of Appeals) Act* 1968 (Cth) and the *Privy Council (Appeals from the High Court) Act* 1975 (Cth) had the practical effect (when supplemented by the *Australia Acts* 1986) of abolishing Australian appeals to the Privy Council—a matter that had been in contention since the earliest contemplation of federation. Secondly, the *Federal Court of Australia Act* 1976 (Cth) was passed after much parliamentary diffidence and the airing of 'states' rights' concerns very similar to those of the colonies about federation itself (see **Federal Court of Australia**). The 1976 Act divested the High Court of much jurisdiction that was handicapping the due discharge of its major functions. The Court was thus left free to concentrate on its primary **role** as interpreter of the Constitution, expositor of the **common** law of Australia, and final arbiter of nationally important questions of legal principle. Thirdly, an amendment to the Judiciary Act in 1984 required special **leave to appeal** to be sought in most cases. With this added shield, the numerical strength of the Bench—increased to five in 1906 and to seven in 1913, with a temporary reduction in the **Depression of the 1930s**—was able to sustain the Court's vast amount of judicial business for the remainder of the twentieth century. Fourthly, the *High Court of Australia Act 1979* (Cth) gave the Court considerable administrative independence from the executive government. In return, more public disclosure was sought from the Court, by way of **annual reports**, as to its **administration**: a course resisted for a time as being a possible threat to judicial **independence**.

Although the Justices were left for many years without pension entitlements, their salaries, along with most state superior judicial salaries in the early twentieth century, were relatively generous (see **Remuneration**). In 1926, Attorney-General **Latham** sponsored amendment of the Judiciary Act to provide for pensions in limited circumstances. Latham's amendment was embellished from time to time, and, in due course, carried across into the *Judges' Pensions Act* 1948 (Cth) and later amendments, and then to the *Judges' Pensions Act* 1968 (Cth).

In response to perceived community discontent at life **tenure** of public offices, and after a referendum as to federal judicial offices, section 72 of the Constitution—which had been assumed to guarantee **appointment** for life—was amended in 1977 so as to impose a judicial retiring age of 70 years.

At its inception, the Court, in keeping with the times, was an all-male preserve. By the end of the twentieth century, there was one female Justice, **Gaudron**, while at hearings, **women practitioners** regularly attended as **counsel** or instructing solicitors. A more symbolic change occurred in **court attire**. When founded, the Court, as a creature of statute, adopted not the colourful robes of the superior Common Law Courts, but the black gown, with wig, customarily worn at *nisi prius* in England. In the period of the **Mason Court**, that attire was discarded in favour of gowns, without wig, after the American pattern: another instance, perhaps, of the seductive American influences evident since the days of Inglis Clark.

The achievements of the Court over a short span of time have been remarkable. From a body that was, at the outset, thought by credible critics to have neither a place nor a future in the Commonwealth, the High Court has become recognised as a greatly respected source of judicial authority throughout the common law world and beyond. Of the many factors contributing to that result, not the least, but one frequently overlooked, was the genius of Griffith as first Chief Justice. However prickly his temperament or vain his character, he was not merely the architect of the Court in prospect, but the grand conductor of the Court in being. He silenced the critics; he prevailed over inward-looking states; he compelled a reluctant profession to look to legal substance rather than to procedural technicality; and by force of his own example, he ensured the Court's stature as Australia's 'Federal Supreme Court'. When, at the very outset, the Supreme Court of Victoria challenged the juridical pre-eminence of the High Court by distinguishing one of its pronouncements and purporting to prefer Privy Council advice on the Constitution of Canada, Griffith remarked in *Deakin v Webb* (1904):

If the reasons [of the High Court] may be disregarded and treated as mere *obiter dicta*, because, in the opinion of the [state] court, the same conclusion might have been reached by another road, the value of judgments as expositions of the law would be sensibly diminished.

So might the Court itself have been diminished had not Griffith stood in the path of its detractors. To no other individual does the Court as an institution owe so much.

JM BENNETT

Further Reading
JM Bennett, *Keystone of the Federal Arch* (1980)
Roger Joyce, *Samuel Walker Griffith* (1984)
JA La Nauze, *The Making of the Australian Constitution* (1972)
John Quick and Robert Garran, *The Annotated Constitution of the Australian Commonwealth* (1901)

Estoppel. The High Court has developed a uniquely Australian approach to estoppel by conduct, based on preventing **unconscionable** conduct and protecting against the detrimental consequences of reliance on the conduct of others. The Court's development of the principles of estoppel during the 1980s and 1990s exemplifies its willingness to expand equitable doctrines in the interests of creating a fairer system of private law obligations.

Estoppels by conduct create rights where one person (the representee) relies on an assumption induced by the conduct of a second person (the representor) in such a way that the representee will suffer harm if the representor turns out to act inconsistently with the assumption. The two broad categories of estoppel by conduct are those arising from assumptions of fact (often called **common law** estoppel) and those arising from assumptions as to the way in which the representor will behave in the future (equitable estoppel). The distinction between the two is illustrated by *Waltons Stores v Maher* (1988), where the Mahers carried out building work on their land on the faith of an assumption either that Waltons had signed a lease (an assumption of fact) or would sign a lease (an assumption as to future conduct). That action proved detrimental when Waltons indicated that it had not, and would not, sign the lease.

In his judgments in *Thompson v Palmer* (1933) and *Grundt v Great Boulder Gold Mines* (1937), **Dixon** identified the 'basal purpose' or foundation of what would now be called common law estoppel. He said the foundation of the estoppel is the representee's change of position on the faith of the assumption induced by the representor. The 'basal purpose' of the doctrine is to prevent the detriment to the representee that would flow from that change of position if the representor were allowed to desert the assumption. The focus on the representee's detrimental reliance is evident in numerous other High Court decisions of the period, including *Craine v Colonial Mutual* (1920), *Donaldson v Freeson* (1934), and *Newbon v City Mutual* (1935). In more recent years, those early judgments have greatly influenced the Court as it has attempted to rationalise the principles of estoppel by conduct and to unify different types of estoppel.

In accordance with English orthodoxy, the Court assumed in early cases such as *Ferrier v Stewart* (1912) and *Craine v*

Colonial Mutual that an estoppel could arise only from reliance on an assumption of fact. Two exceptions to that rule were recognised in **equity**. First, a 'proprietary estoppel' could arise from reliance on an assumption that an interest in land would be granted to the representee. Secondly, a 'promissory estoppel' could arise from an assumption that contractual rights would not be enforced. Promissory estoppel was first recognised by the Court in *Legione v Hateley* (1983).

In *Waltons Stores*, the High Court recognised the unity of principle between proprietary and promissory estoppel. In each case, equity grants relief on the basis that it is unconscionable to depart from an assumption which one has induced another to adopt and rely upon to their detriment. On one view, the unified equitable estoppel recognised by the Court is a new substantive doctrine which can create independently enforceable rights in a wide range of situations not previously covered by promissory or proprietary estoppel (see, for example, *W v G* (1996)).

The expansion of equitable estoppel in *Waltons Stores* has been seen as a very positive development. The Court has not adequately explained the nature of the new doctrine, however, despite considering its effect in six decisions during the 1980s and 1990s (*Legione v Hateley*; *Waltons Stores*; *Foran v Wight* (1989); *Commonwealth v Verwayen* (1990); *Australian Securities Commission v Marlborough Gold Mines* (1993); and *Giumelli v Giumelli* (1999)). In *Verwayen*, the Court exacerbated the confusion by handing down seven separate judgments expressing widely diverging views on the nature and effect of estoppel by conduct and its relationship with the doctrine of waiver. The Court has left several fundamental questions unresolved. First, is equitable estoppel capable of operating in relation to any promise, or just a promise relating to an existing or proposed legal relationship? Secondly, does equitable estoppel operate as an independently enforceable source of rights—that is, does it provide a cause of action? Thirdly, how should a court exercise its discretion in giving effect to the estoppel? Should it generally fulfil the representee's expectations, or go no further than is necessary to prevent detriment being suffered as a result of the representee's reliance? Fourthly, how many different doctrines of estoppel by conduct now operate in Australia? The Court's failure to resolve these issues has resulted in confusion and inconsistency in the state **Supreme Courts** and in the **Federal Court**.

Although the Court has left important practical questions unresolved, the development of the principles of estoppel has been informed by detailed consideration of the purpose of the doctrine and its relationship with the law of **contract**. The Court developed the principles of estoppel on the basis of concerns with preventing unconscionable conduct and protecting against the harmful consequences of reliance on the conduct of another person. The focus on detrimental reliance (harm resulting from reliance on a given state of affairs or on another person's conduct), which has underpinned developments in estoppel, has also shaped the 'change of position' defence to restitutionary claims, which was recognised by the Court in *David Securities v Commonwealth Bank* (1992).

The recognition of a broad doctrine of equitable estoppel such as that developed by the High Court can be seen as an intrusion into the territory of contract. Both contract and estoppel are concerned with the enforcement of promises: promises that form part of a mutual exchange are enforced through contract, while unilateral promises that have simply been relied upon are enforced through equitable estoppel. The Court has been careful to ensure that the recognition of a substantive doctrine of estoppel does not upset the balance and structure of the law of obligations by undermining the law of contract. In *Giumelli*, for example, the Court accepted that no estoppel could arise from reliance on a contractual promise, and adopted suggestions that the focus on reliance, rather than promise, together with the discretionary nature of the remedy, is sufficient to maintain an adequate distinction between equitable estoppel and contract.

ANDREW ROBERTSON

Further Reading

Patrick Parkinson, 'Estoppel' in Patrick Parkinson (ed), *The Principles of Equity* (1996)

Andrew Robertson, 'Satisfying the Minimum Equity: Equitable Estoppel Remedies after *Verwayen*' (1996) 20 *MULR* 805

Andrew Robertson, 'Situating Equitable Estoppel Within the Law of Obligations' (1997) 19 *Syd LR* 32

Andrew Robertson, 'Estoppel by Conduct: Unresolved Issues at Common Law and in Equity' (1999) *NLR* 7, www.nlr.com.au

Etiquette. In keeping with Australia's generally egalitarian society, the rules of etiquette for dealings with the Justices of the High Court are relatively relaxed. But there are rules.

It is normal in referring collectively or individually to judges of the High Court, past and present, to describe them as 'Justices', that being the word appearing in section 71 of the Constitution. A Justice met on a social occasion, however, will ordinarily be addressed as 'Judge' (or 'Chief Justice', as the case may be). Only if the Justice is known personally, or has invited this degree of informality, will he or she normally be addressed by a given name. Even then, members of the **legal profession** meeting the Justice will evaluate whether such familiarity is appropriate to the occasion. Particularly in circumstances in which non-lawyers are present, it may be prudent to use the more formal salutation. In Court, and in public **chambers**, all Justices are addressed as 'Your Honour'. Australian judges, like those of NZ or **Papua and New Guinea** (and unlike those of most parts of the Commonwealth of Nations) have never been addressed in Court as 'Your Lordship', 'Your Ladyship', 'My Lord', or 'My Lady'. Thus the High Court has not had to face, as the Supreme Court of Canada has, the abolition of lordly titles. The only place where a Justice would be described in that way was, in the past, if he sat on the **Privy Council** or, today, if he or she were, after office, to accept appointment in Commonwealth countries where those titles are used.

While holding office, all the Justices are entitled, in accordance with convention and their commissions, to the designation 'The Honourable'. Upon a Justice's **retirement**, the Queen may (and invariably does) agree to the retention of that title. The retired Justice is then known as 'The Honourable John Toohey AC', for example. In ordinary speech, he reverts to 'Mr Toohey'. The abolition of knighthoods, once customary for Justices of the High Court, has ordinarily left retired Justices without title after retirement. Sometimes, however, the retired

Justice may hold office as a judge in the courts of other countries. **Mason**, **Brennan**, and **Dawson**, for example, are judges of the Hong Kong Final Court of Appeal. In such a case, it would not be incorrect to continue to describe them as 'Justice' and in polite social conversation as 'Judge'.

A presently serving Justice should be referred to in oral **argument** as 'Justice **Gaudron**' and in written submissions as 'Gaudron J'. This is also the correct mode of reference to past Justices and should normally be followed. While it is strictly incorrect to describe them as, for example, 'Sir Isaac **Isaacs**' or 'Sir Owen **Dixon**', even experienced **counsel** occasionally refer to them in that way. However, where the judgments or other writings of past Justices are referred to in argument, the Justices should be described by their judicial and not by their civil title.

Although the **Chief Justice's** commission formally appoints him or her as 'the Chief Justice of the High Court of Australia', since 1918 the Chief Justice of the Court has commonly been described as 'the Chief Justice of Australia'. This is a courtesy normally attributed to the Chief Justice of a nation's apex court. In the increasing contacts between judges of different nations, any other title might be confusing, especially where the 'High Court', in the English tradition, is a first-instance **superior court**, not an appellate court. In India, NZ and elsewhere, the 'High Court' is an intermediate court. Chief Justice **Barwick** preferred the title 'Chief Justice of Australia'. On the other hand, Chief Justice **Gibbs** ordinarily described himself as 'Chief Justice of the High Court of Australia'. His successors have reverted to Barwick's style, which appears in permanent form on the brass plate attached to the doors of the Chief Justice's chambers in **Canberra**. Constitutional support for the shorter title may be found in the provision for the appellate **jurisdiction** of the High Court—which supervises all other Australian courts (section 73 of the Constitution)—and in the fact that the Court is now the court of last resort in all Australian matters. On the other hand, some purists regard 'Chief Justice of Australia' as a misnomer, in that the Chief Justice of the High Court possesses no powers with respect to the **administration** of lower courts and no say in the **appointment**, **removal**, or regulation of judges of those courts.

High Court **puisne Justices** observe each other's **seniority** in accordance with the dates of their commissions. The separate constitutional office of Chief Justice takes primacy over puisne Justices. In some final courts (for example, the Supreme Court of India), a firm convention has been established that when the Chief Justice dies or retires, the office automatically devolves upon the most senior puisne Justice. When Indira Gandhi breached this rule in 1973 and 1977, major controversies ensued, and the rule has since been strictly adhered to. No similar rule or convention has been established in Australia, although on those occasions when a sitting Justice has been appointed Chief Justice, the appointment has in fact invariably gone to the senior Justice of the Court.

Seniority governs the seating arrangements of the Justices. When the Chief Justice is present, the holder of that office presides. Otherwise, the most senior of the participating Justices presides. The other Justices are seated in accordance with seniority alternately to the right and left of the presiding Justice, the most senior being seated on the immediate right.

Before the Court moved to its permanent **seat** in Canberra, the Justices followed the conventional rule of entering and retiring from the **courtroom** in order of seniority. In Canberra, for convenience, they enter the courtroom behind the Chief Justice or presiding Justice and then in order of their seats on the Bench. However, on retirement from a hearing, they fall out to follow the Chief Justice or senior Justice, in accordance with their seniority.

In **conference** and in other formal meetings within the Court, no rule of seniority is observed in the Justices' seating arrangements. Nor, in discussing **reserved judgments**, do they follow the convention—observed by the Privy Council, the International Court of Justice, and the **United States Supreme Court**—by which the most junior Justice in order of commission speaks first as to his or her opinion about a case. Discussion in conference in the High Court is entirely informal; this accords with the Court's general approach, which is less formalised than those adopted in other final courts.

The **judicial oath**, which is provided for by section 11 of the *High Court of Australia Act* 1976 (Cth), follows the form in the schedule to that Act. Alternatively, an affirmation in that form is taken. It requires a public declaration of allegiance to the Queen and a promise to serve her in office doing 'right to all manner of people according to law without fear or favour, affection or ill-will'. The same form is observed by judicial officers throughout Australia and it has an ancient lineage. In the High Court, the oath or affirmation is taken in a public ceremony, normally in Canberra. The last Justice to be sworn into office outside Canberra was Dawson, who took his oaths in Adelaide during the Court's **circuit** there. Other **ceremonial sittings** of the Court include the annual ceremony to welcome new QCs and Senior Counsel (held in February each year), and ceremonies for the retirement of Justices or to mark the death of a Justice. On the last-mentioned occasion, by convention, the Chief Justice or presiding Justice makes a formal speech in the nature of an obituary, and this is published in the *Commonwealth Law Reports*.

Dress before the High Court is formal. Legal practitioners are expected to robe in accordance with the rules governing their appearance before the Court of Appeal or Full Court of the state in which they primarily practise. If in that state it is normal for the legal practitioner to wear a wig when addressing the Court of Appeal or Full Court, that is how counsel should be attired when addressing the High Court. In consequence of this rule, it is not unusual for some counsel at the Bar table to be wigged and robed and others to be wigless. In some states and territories, different rules govern the wearing of wigs in civil and criminal appeals. The High Court Justices have not worn wigs since 1986 (see **Court attire**). Legal practitioners appearing before the Court in public chambers may appear unrobed. Nevertheless, the mode of dress is usually sober.

Before and after the hearing of a matter before the Court, communications to the Justices are strictly limited. Any legal practitioner wishing to place additional matter before the Court in relation to a proceeding should secure leave to do so during the hearing, or should seek to do so through the **Chief Executive and Principal Registrar**. Upon signification that all parties or their representatives consent to the communication, it may, if uncontroversial, be passed on to the Justices' **associates**. It is a serious breach of professional ethics to speak to a Justice about a pending or reserved decision out of Court. Rules of this kind are strictly observed by legal practitioners, who should not presume upon past professional friendships with a Justice to break them. The need for careful adherence to the rules about communication of materials to the Court after a hearing is illustrated by what happened in *Stuart v The Queen* (1959). There the Court rebuked the prosecution for attempting to forward material to the Principal Registrar after the matter stood for judgment.

Communications with Justices about other matters will depend upon past acquaintance and the nature of the matter in question. Normally, communications should be addressed to the Justice's associate, although some of the current Justices correspond regularly with other judges, professional colleagues, and academics by email and other informal means.

In correspondence with a Justice, it is usual to include any applicable post-nominals after the Justice's name. Thus, Justices who have been appointed Companions of the Order of Australia will have the letters 'AC' after their names. During office as a Justice, the post-nominals 'QC' are not included if the Justice held that commission, being taken to merge in the judicial commission. The salutation in a letter (depending on the degree of personal acquaintance) will be 'Dear Chief Justice' or 'Dear Judge' or 'Dear Justice Gaudron', as the case may be.

Orders of precedence are established for both federal and state official occasions. They regulate the detail of the precedence to be accorded to Justices in relation to other public holders at such events. Under the Commonwealth order of precedence, the Governor-General, state Governors, **Prime Minister**, Premier or Chief Minister within his or her own state or territory, and the President of the Senate and Speaker of the House of Representatives according to the date of appointment, take precedence over the Chief Justice. Further down the list, puisne Justices take precedence over the Chief Justices of the **Federal Court** and state **Supreme Courts**. The leader of the Opposition, former Governors-General, and former Chief Justices of the High Court, are among those who take precedence over currently serving puisne Justices.

The Justices of the High Court, depending on temperament, are unlikely to be unduly concerned about the foregoing rules of etiquette, except in relation to irregular communication about cases before them. But if such rules are observed, as they easily can be, they help to avoid embarrassments. Lawyers soon learn that there have to be rules, and that most of them have a rational foundation.

MICHAEL KIRBY

Evatt, Herbert Vere (*b* 30 April 1894; *d* 2 November 1965; Justice 1930–40). Evatt was born at Maitland, NSW. His father died when Evatt was seven. Evatt's mother moved the family to Sydney, where Evatt attended Fort Street Model (Boys High) School and the University of Sydney. He graduated BA (1915), MA (1917), and LLB (1918), all with the highest honours. In 1924, he was awarded an LLD on the basis of work that became the book *The King and His Dominion Governors* (1936).

Herbert Vere Evatt, Justice 1930–40 (circa 1928)

Evatt volunteered for service in **World War I**, but was rejected because of his astigmatism. In 1916, he became associate to NSW Supreme Court Chief Justice William Cullen. In the 1920s, Evatt developed a very successful career as a barrister, including a High Court practice. While his politics generated much work from unions, he sometimes appeared for employer interests in industrial matters, most famously in the *Engineers Case* (1920). Evatt was elected to the NSW Legislative Assembly in 1925 as the Member for Balmain, and re-elected as an independent in 1927. He was appointed a KC in 1929.

Evatt's greatest contribution as **counsel** was his successful advocacy of propositions fundamental to the High Court's **role** of **judicial review**. In *Ex parte Walsh and Johnson; In re Yates* (1925), Evatt argued, as **Isaacs** paraphrased it, that 'an act founded on the belief of a Minister as to the extent of a power was not an act in respect of the subject of the power'. Thus, Evatt said, 'the **judicial power** of the Commonwealth is protected from complete subversion by the legislative power, because the shutting off of access to the Courts may be strong or conclusive evidence that Parliament has gone outside the field indicated in secs 51 and 52 of the Constitution'. He saw this as a corollary of *Engineers*, for 'while admitting the full scope of **Commonwealth legislative power** within the enumerated fields, it is impossible for Parliament to trespass outside those fields directly by itself or indirectly through the executive organs of the Government'. A majority accepted Evatt's argument.

Evatt's **appointment** to the High Court was criticised as politically motivated. At 36, he was the youngest person ever appointed to the Court. But there is little question that his stature in the profession warranted the appointment.

As a Justice, Evatt used sociological **jurisprudence** and conceptions of legal and moral **rights** to achieve what he thought were socially desirable results. Dissenting in *Victoria Park Racing v Taylor* (1937), he and **Rich** found against the defendants, who had erected a tower to overlook the plaintiff's racecourse for the purpose of broadcasting their races. While accepting that there was no general 'right to privacy', Evatt was prepared to extend the law of nuisance to cover the plaintiff's complaint. His reasons largely eschewed the majority's analytical approach. He displayed moral indignation at the defendants' behaviour, and noted that it facilitated illegal off-course betting. Insisting that the principles he formulated were 'embodied in the **common law**', he agreed with Lord Macmillan in *Donoghue v Stevenson* (1932) that conceptions of legal liability must adapt to 'altering social conditions and standards', and with Lord Esher in *Emmens v Pottle* (1885) that 'the common law of England' could not be 'wholly unreasonable and unjust'.

Evatt was particularly concerned with workers' rights. Workers and employers were entitled to exercise their common law liberty of contract (*Huddart Parker v Commonwealth* (1931)), but, for both, this right was qualified by statutory schemes that regulated employment. Evatt approved such schemes, but mitigated the effects of laws that treated workers more harshly than employers. His long judgment in *McKernan v Fraser* (1931) contains many references to academic and US judicial **criticism** of the benevolent application by English courts of the **tort** of conspiracy to combined action by employers, in contrast to their more restrictive attitude towards trade union activity. Evatt insisted that the same principles 'should apply uniformly' to employers and unions alike. In other contexts, he was solicitous to protect social rights, such as a person's right to livelihood or vocation (*Kahn v Board of Examiners (Vic)* (1939); *R v Mahony; Ex parte Johnson* (1931)).

Evatt was concerned about defendants' rights in the criminal process. He stated the notion that an accused has a right to a fair trial most clearly in *Johnson v Miller* (1937). In contrast to the minority, he took a rights approach, raising a wide range of issues. He was more inclined than his contemporaries to criticise the conduct of a criminal trial (see *Craig v The King* (1933)). Yet he recognised that rights analysis had its limits. Dissenting in *Thomas v The King* (1937), for example, Evatt did not adopt the presumption that *mens rea* is an essential element in bigamy. He was concerned to protect the interests of persons other than the defendant, and of the public.

Evatt was a common law reformer. On his **retirement** from the Court, he said that 'very important branches of jurisprudence' are 'capable of further … development or of adjustment to the changing needs of modern society', adding: 'I have always searched for the right with a lamp that was lit by the flame of humanity.' In 1932, he wrote to Lord Atkin that in *Donoghue v Stevenson*, 'the common law is again shown to be capable of meeting modern conditions of industrialisation, and striking through forms of legal separateness to reality'. In *Australian Knitting Mills v Grant* (1933), Evatt embraced *Donoghue*, taking the widest view of its *ratio*. The majority avoided discussing the case. In *Cowell*

v Rosehill Racecourse (1937), he agreed that a licence to enter **property**, given for value, did not create a proprietary interest in land, but a contractual duty only. But he maintained in sole dissent that **equity** could preclude the land owner from revoking the licence or relying on its revocation. He followed the English decision in *Hurst v Picture Theatres* (1915), noting the *Law Quarterly Review's* praise of that decision for remedying an injustice in trespass law. In *Bunyan v Jordan* (1937), Evatt alone applied *Wilkinson v Downton* (1897) to permit recovery by a plaintiff whose terror at her employer's drunken threats had induced a neurasthenic illness, even though she did not apprehend physical injury to herself.

Evatt's dissent in *Chester v Waverley Corporation* (1939) was prescient. He held that a local council was liable in negligence for nervous shock suffered by a mother who saw her son's body being recovered from a water-filled trench that council workmen had left uncovered. Evatt rejected the view that the mother's reaction was not reasonably foreseeable. Later English and Australian decisions have endorsed Evatt's view and praised his judgment. Evatt acknowledged 'the risk of too wide an extension of liability in cases where proof is beset with special difficulties', and sought to meet it by a **proximity** test, which has since had its own rise and fall.

The judgment typifies Evatt's **judicial style** in common law areas. It is written in essay form, with many references to North American authority. There is literary allusion—he quotes William Blake to capture the mother's mental state, and Tom Collins (Joseph Furphy) to describe the 'agony of fearfulness caused by the search for the lost child'. There is reference to political outcome, in the sense of who would benefit—he referred to 'the unfortunate but notorious fact that **children** of workpeople are frequently compelled to play in the streets'. His observation that common law principles 'are not to be rejected or evaded merely because they have introduced … an element of humanity and common sense', is both a statement of what he thought he was doing, and a criticism of the majority Justices.

As politician and Justice, Evatt promoted a view of **administrative law** that was premised on limited government. His very acceptance of an expanded role for state power led him to be concerned both with the proper limits of such power and with the role that judicially fashioned administrative law might play in setting those limits. He generally accepted the deferential attitude of the time towards ministerial responsibility. But he was prescient of the modern approach, which rejects the efficacy of ministerial responsibility as a means for control and subjects even ministerial discretion to judicial review. In *R v Carter; Ex parte Kisch* (1934) (see *Kisch Case*), he showed how the law can check the substantial outcome of an exercise of power. Elsewhere, he stressed the practical utility of according **natural justice** to those affected by the exercise of administrative power.

Evatt's pro-union and pro-worker stance no doubt influenced his approach to the Commonwealth's **conciliation and arbitration** power. His decisions bear out the observation of C Hartley Grattan, who knew Evatt well from 1937 to 1960, that 'Evatt's questions from the Bench proceeded from the assumption that the management was always wrong and the workman right'. It was partly a desire to bypass the limits of Commonwealth power in this area that underlay Evatt's **joint** judgment with **McTiernan** in *R v Burgess; Ex Parte Henry* (1936), holding that the **external affairs power** authorised Commonwealth legislation giving effect to international treaties or Conventions. This proposition, with which **Latham**, who had also been a practising politician, agreed, was not settled until 1983 (see the *Tasmanian Dam Case* (1983)). Evatt's and McTiernan's view that section 51(xxix) can be used to give effect to a mere recommendation by an international body (citing in particular the International Labour Organisation) has not yet been applied.

Evatt's contribution to **constitutional law** was wide-ranging and is far from played out. Evatt and **Dixon** in *West v Commissioner of Taxation (NSW)* (1937) arguably presaged the **implied constitutional rights** theories of the late twentieth century when they held, in Evatt's words, that 'principles of the Constitution which are not immediately discoverable in its words' limit the exercise of both Commonwealth and state power. Their acceptance that this had consequences for people's rights may be indicated by aspects of Evatt's advocacy in the *Communist Party Case* (1951), and by Dixon's comment in that case (perhaps inspired by Evatt) that the '**rule of law**' is assumed by the Constitution.

In *R v Federal Court of Bankruptcy; Ex parte Lowenstein* (1938), in a rare joint judgment, Evatt and Dixon recognised that protecting personal liberty by constitutional restrictions on government power had not been 'a guiding purpose' of the Constitution's **framers**. However, Evatt and Dixon read expansively the explicit guarantee of **jury trial** in section 80 of the Constitution. They also derived from the **separation of powers** a limitation on legislative and executive power that indirectly protected individual rights, by holding that a statute could not authorise or require a federal court to assume the double role of prosecutor and judge, since this was 'outside the conception of judicial power'. Their judgment was arguably a precursor to the modern '**due process**' jurisprudence. When Evatt returned to the Court in a different capacity—as counsel in the *Communist Party Case*—he argued that 'under the Constitution, Acts of Attainder and Bills of Pains and Penalties are impliedly prohibited … because they would represent an exercise of judicial power by the Parliament'. Three Justices rejected the argument, but in the light of the *War Crimes Act Case* (1991), it might now be accepted.

In *Victorian Stevedoring & General Contracting Co v Meakes and Dignan* (1931), Evatt disagreed that the Constitution implied a strict separation of mutually exclusive Commonwealth powers. He accepted that non-judicial power might be assigned to a federal court. He was less clear on the extent to which judicial power might be assigned to administrative tribunals, saying that functions 'resembling those of a strictly judicial character' might lawfully be vested in them, but that 'strictly judicial power' must be vested in a court. As between the legislature and the executive, he held that the legislature could vest in the executive 'some power to pass regulations' (since otherwise 'effective government would be impossible'), but added that 'the extent of the power granted will often be a very material circumstance' in determining the validity of the legislation granting the power. While agreeing with Dixon that a grant of legislative power in relation to a head of power might be so wide that the law was not one 'with respect to' that head of power, he went further than Dixon in delineating the factors relevant to that judgment. His conception is often dismissed as a theoretical limit having no practical utility, but has not been tested.

Generally, Evatt was concerned with balancing the interests involved in Commonwealth and state legislative action. He accepted the discarding of **reserved state powers**, and sometimes read Commonwealth powers expansively (*Ex parte Henry*). But he also gave effect to constitutional guarantees of individual rights and sought to protect the role of the federal courts. He also sought to protect the states (see especially the *State Garnishee Case* (1932); *Elliott v Commonwealth* (1936); *Moran's Case* (1939)). He was critical of the Court's approach to section 109 **inconsistency** (*Stock Motor Ploughs v Forsyth* (1932)).

In *West's Case*, Evatt insisted that the 'existence and independence of the States … could not be ignored in deciding on the validity of Commonwealth legislation', and that 'the Constitution left room for implications arising from the co-existence side by side of seven legislatures', each sovereign within its limits. He held that a law with respect to state powers could not be a law with respect to some subject matter that was within power. In less abstract terms, he said that

> it must be implied in the Constitution, as an instrument of Federal Government, that neither the Commonwealth nor a State legislature is at liberty to direct its legislation toward the destruction of the normal activities of the Commonwealth or States.

Dixon broadly agreed; but Evatt went further, saying that even a non-discriminatory law might so burden another government as to be invalid as a 'serious impediment' to its governmental activities. Their views were precursors to the 'two limbs' of the 'revived' **intergovernmental immunities** doctrine in the *Melbourne Corporation Case* (1947).

Evatt was a nationalist and an internationalist. Uniquely for the time, he thought about Australia's place in the world and, in contrast to non-Labor politicians, saw Australia's role as not simply determined by the UK government after consultation with the Dominions. The influence of these views was evident most clearly in *Jolley v Mainka* (1933) (see **Papua and New Guinea**).

While on the Court, Evatt took a scholarly interest in legal questions, and in legal **history**. His works include *Injustice Within the Law* (1937), *Rum Rebellion* (1938), and *William Holman: Australian Labour Leader* (1940).

In 1940, Evatt resigned from the Court to re-enter politics. After 1940, he became the federal member for Barton, serving both as **Attorney-General** and Minister for External Affairs in three ALP governments (1941–49). He became Deputy Prime Minister in 1946. His role in creating the UN was conspicuous. He participated actively in its affairs, and became the President of the General Assembly for its third session (1948–49). After the ALP lost office in December 1949, Evatt became Leader of the Opposition (1951–60). In 1960, he became Chief Justice of NSW, but soon became ill and resigned in 1962.

In politics, Evatt still had an influence on the Court. He successfully resisted the 'court-packing plan' of 1945 (see **Appointments that might have been**). As Attorney-General, he unsuccessfully led the government's defence of the *Bank Nationalisation Case* (1948). In this and other cases, Evatt saw Dixon's theory of section 92 prevail over his own (see **Interstate trade and commerce**). Over strong opposition within the ALP, Evatt took a brief in the *Communist Party Case* from a Communist-led union to seek, successfully, the invalidation of the law proscribing the party and those thought sympathetic to its aims. He then took the leading role in the successful campaign against the attempted **amendment** of the Constitution to give validity to that Act. Those efforts may well be Evatt's most significant contribution to Australian public life. They did, however, undermine his position in the ALP, and created the conditions for his becoming embroiled, at great personal cost, in the Petrov Royal Commission, which investigated the activities of agents of the USSR in Australia.

In the *Communist Party Case*—Evatt's last appearance before the Court—he placed *Ex parte Walsh and Johnson* at the forefront of his argument and returned to it repeatedly. **Fullagar's** statements that 'the legislative power of the Commonwealth Parliament is limited by an instrument emanating from a superior authority', so that 'in our system the principle of **Marbury v Madison** is accepted as axiomatic', built directly on Evatt's argument. Twenty-five years after Evatt had first expressed that idea in *Walsh and Johnson*, the majority decision in the *Communist Party Case* made it effective.

PETER BAYNE

Further Reading

Peter Bayne, 'Mr Justice Evatt's Theory of Administrative Law: Adjusting State Regulation to the Liberal Theory of the Individual and the State' (1991) 9 *LIC* 1

Zelman Cowen, 'Mr Justice HV Evatt and the High Court' (1966) 2(1) *Aust Bar Gaz* 3

Peter Crockett, *Evatt: A Life* (1993)

Michael Kirby, 'HV Evatt, The Anti-Communist Referendum and Liberty in Australia' (1991) 7 *Aust Bar Rev* 93

Kylie Tennant, *Evatt: Politics and Justice* (1970 revised edn 1972)

Leslie Zines, 'Mr Justice Evatt and the Constitution' (1969) 3 *FL Rev* 153

Evidence law. When the High Court was created, the **common law** of evidence applied in Australia was indistinguishable from the English common law, was not characterised by the use of explicit judicial discretion, and was little affected by statute. In the succeeding century, in certain respects the common law has diverged from English law, many explicit discretions have been introduced, and statute has had a significant impact in every jurisdiction—to the point that there is a partly successful but also partly stalled movement towards a kind of codification. The first two of these developments have been actively fostered by the High Court. The third has not prevented its **role** in the law of evidence from having continuing vitality, and in significant respects it has refused to modify the common law by analogy to statute (*Esso Australia v FCT* (1999)).

Australia has produced three judges whose names are distinctively associated with mastery of the law of evidence—three judges to whose opinions on that subject any informed inquirer, in Australia or elsewhere, would pay immediate regard and respect. Of these three—**Gibbs**, Harold Glass in NSW, and Andrew Wells in SA—only the first sat on the

High Court, and some of his most penetrating expositions of the law were not delivered there. Yet certainly, many of those who have sat on the High Court have offered classical expositions of the law of evidence.

Some cases are of outstanding importance because they give lapidary expression to the results of a long line of settled authority: they state what oft was thought but ne'er so well expressed. An example is *Briginshaw v Briginshaw* (1938) (standard of proof of serious allegations in civil proceedings). Some authorities are important because they analyse conflicting authority from all over the common law world and arrive at a synthesis suitable for Australian conditions. Examples are *Domican v The Queen* (1992) (jury directions on identification evidence) and *Alexander v The Queen* (1981) (photographic identification and hearsay aspects of out of court identification). Some authorities are important because of their originality—their fashioning of legal principle and application of it to a novel problem, such as *Butera v DPP* (1987) (admissibility of tape recordings). And some authorities are important because though the problem considered has been analysed elsewhere, the Court's resolution of it has led to the creation of a 'doctrine' or 'rule' repeatedly thereafter applied in Australian courts to facts which, when they arise abroad, evoke a less conscious and articulate response. An illustration is the exposition in *Jones v Dunkel* (1959) of the inferences to be drawn where one party fails to testify or to call available evidence. There are English cases, for example, that apply similar principles to those stated in *Jones v Dunkel*, but those principles have been subjected in Australia to a degree of refined analysis in later authorities that has resulted in a distinctive and rich local body of doctrine. The same is true in relation to the freedom of appellate courts to reverse a trial judge's inferences from admitted or undisputed facts (*Warren v Coombes* (1979)) and their reluctance to reverse factual findings based on an assessment of credibility (*Abalos v Australian Postal Commission* (1990); *Devries v Australian National Railways Commission* (1993); *State Rail Authority of NSW v Earthline Constructions* (1999)). Authorities of each of these kinds can be found at all periods of the history of the Court, and apart from those just mentioned, there are many fields in which the decisions of the Court are outstanding.

One is **estoppel** by record (*Blair v Curran* (1939) (issue estoppel); *Jackson v Goldsmith* (1950) (res judicata); *Administration of Papua and New Guinea v Daera Guba* (1973) (estoppel arising from decisions of tribunals which are not courts); *Port of Melbourne Authority v Anshun* (1981) (estoppel arising from abuse of process); and *Rogers v The Queen* (1994) (no issue estoppel in criminal cases)).

In relation to the burden and standard of proof, important authorities are *Purkess v Crittenden* (1965) (distribution of legal and evidential burden); *Robinson v The Queen* (1991) (error in directing jury about accused's interest in the outcome); *Palmer v The Queen* (1998) (permissibility of inquiries about the motive of a complainant for lying); *Dowling v Bowie* (1952) and *Vines v Djordjevitch* (1955) (impact on burden of proof of distinction between provisos and exceptions); *Thomas v The Queen* (1960) (jury direction on standard of proof); and *Plomp v The Queen* (1963) (significance of motive, and jury directions on circumstantial evidence).

The problems that arise during the course of the trial have been illuminated by *R v Apostilides* (1984) (power of judge at criminal trial to call witness); *Richardson v The Queen* (1974) (role of Crown prosecutor in calling witnesses); *Dairy Farmers Co-Operative Milk v Acquilina* (1963) (tender by cross-examiner of documents used to refresh memory); *Kilby v The Queen* (1973) (evidentiary significance of failure to complain); *Nominal Defendant v Clements* (1960) (recent invention); *McLellan v Bowyer* (1961) (hostile witnesses); *Wakeley v The Queen* (1990) (power of court to control cross-examination); *Shaw v The Queen* (1952) and *R v Chin* (1985) (the rule against case-splitting); and *Doney v The Queen* (1990) (illegality of direction to acquit where there is some, albeit weak, evidence capable of supporting guilty verdict).

In cases where the admission of evidence is resisted on grounds of privilege, there has been a distinctive contribution on the possibility of waiver of privilege (*A-G (NT) v Maurice* (1986)). There are significant authorities on the application of the privilege against self-incrimination in non-judicial proceedings and the construction of statutes that apparently collide with it (*Pyneboard v Trade Practices Commission* (1983); *Sorby v Commonwealth* (1983)). The Court has cast light on some difficult areas of legal professional privilege, such as the application of the privilege to copies of documents (*Commissioner of Australian Federal Police v Propend Finance* (1997)), its role in preventing access by an accused person to documents that might raise a reasonable doubt about guilt (*Carter v Managing Partner Northmore Hale Davy & Leake* (1995)), and its defeat if used in furtherance of a deliberate abuse of statutory power (*A-G (NT) v Kearney* (1985)). On public interest immunity, there are several leading authorities, such as **Sankey v Whitlam** (1978); *Alister v The Queen* (1984); and *Commonwealth v Northern Land Council* (1993).

In relation to confessions, there are many leading cases, exemplified by *MacPherson v The Queen* (1981) (procedure in relation to determining voluntariness and burden of establishing grounds for discretionary exclusion); *Wendo v The Queen* (1963) (standard of proof of facts justifying finding of voluntariness); *McKinney v The Queen* (1991) (rule of practice that warning be given of the dangers of convicting on the uncorroborated evidence of police officers that a confession was made where the confession is the only basis for inferring guilt); *R v Lee* (1950) (discretion to exclude a voluntary confession where in all the circumstances it would be unfair to use it against the accused); and *Cleland v The Queen* (1982) (discretion to exclude a voluntary confession that was unlawfully obtained, even where its use might not be unfair). Related to the latter discretion is the discretion to exclude non-confessional evidence that was unlawfully obtained (*Bunning v Cross* (1978)), the discretion to exclude evidence of an offence the commission of which was brought about by unlawful conduct on the part of law enforcement officers (*Ridgeway v The Queen* (1995)), and the discretion to exclude evidence the prejudicial effect of which exceeds its probative value (*R v Swaffield* (1998)).

In the field of opinion evidence, there have been important statements about the distinction between fact and opinion (*Clark v Ryan* (1960)) and the capacity of a witness's theory to be admissible as **expert** opinion even though it is unproven and not accepted by others (*Commissioner for Government Transport v Adamcik* (1961)).

The Court has made many contributions to the exposition of the rule against hearsay. These include *Hughes v National Trustees Executors & Agency Co* (1979) (classification of testator's reasons for disinheritance of applicant for testator's family maintenance as original evidence; otherwise inadmissible evidence admitted without objection); *Ahern v The Queen* (1988) (statements by co-conspirators); *Lustre Hosiery v York* (1936) (admissions by conduct and by agents); *Fraser Henleins v Cody* (1944) (implied authority to make admissions); *R v Grills* (1910) (admissions by silence in criminal cases); *Thatcher v Charles* (1961) (admissions by silence in civil cases); and *Laws v Australian Broadcasting Tribunal* (1990) (non-reception of admissions in pleadings).

The Court has authoritatively pronounced on the meaning of 'character' evidence both in general (see, for example, *Melbourne v The Queen* (1999)) and in statutes controlling the cross-examination of accused persons on their convictions (*Attwood v The Queen* (1960)). It has rigorously analysed the construction of those statutes in relation to the accused's good character (*Donnini v The Queen* (1972)), in relation to the making of imputations on the prosecution (*Curwood v The King* (1944); *Dawson v The Queen* (1961); *Phillips v The Queen* (1985)), and in relation to the giving of evidence against a co-accused (*Matusevich v The Queen* (1977)).

In the field of documentary evidence, the Court has delineated the limits of the secondary evidence rule (*Commissioner for Railways (NSW) v Young* (1962)), prevented proof of inconsistent collateral agreements (*Hoyt's v Spencer* (1919)), prevented proof of collateral agreements and implied terms in the face of 'entirety of the contract' clauses (*Hart v MacDonald* (1910)), expounded the principles affecting the admissibility of extrinsic materials (*Codelfa Construction v State Rail Authority of NSW* (1982)) and subsequent conduct (*Daera Guba*) in construing contracts and in establishing their existence (*Howard Smith & Co v Varawa* (1907); *Barrier Wharfs v Scott Fell & Co* (1908)).

There are also topics on which, though the Court cannot be said to have decided leading cases, the scantiness of authorities throughout the common law world means that corresponding importance attaches to what individual Justices have said. Examples include **Dixon's** opinions on the permissible types of cross-examination on credit in relation to convictions (*Bugg v Day* (1949)), **judicial notice** (***Communist Party Case*** (1951)), and business records (*Potts v Miller* (1940)).

However, there are some fields in which judging by the number of appeals within quite short periods, the Court has not succeeded in stating the law authoritatively in a manner permitting easy application by lower courts. One of these, where the Court has encountered problems akin to those experienced by the English courts for the last century, is the difficult field of similar fact evidence: despite numerous earlier cases in the High Court, **House of Lords**, and **Privy Council** over the past century and copious juristic analysis, there were at least 11 appeals between 1982 and 1999, with considerable diversity of opinion not only overall, but in each case (see, for example, *Perry v The Queen* (1982) and *De Jesus v The Queen* (1986)).

There has not been universal applause for the Court's efforts, particularly its recent efforts, in relation to the definition of hearsay (*Walton v The Queen* (1989) and *R v Benz* (1989)); the application of the rule to interpreters (*Gaio v The Queen* (1960)); and the creation of new exceptions based on reliability, for example the reception of A's evidence of what B said about a telephone conversation between B and C before, during or after it (*Pollitt v The Queen* (1992)). There are also instances of extensive though pointless quasi-academic debate about such controversies as the reception of admissions against interest by deceased persons—pointless because no decisive conclusion was arrived at (*Bannon v The Queen* (1995)).

Edwards v The Queen (1993), a case on the use of lies as corroboration, has spawned an extraordinarily large amount of intermediate appellate controversy. There is here a resemblance with the impact of the **Chamberlain Case** (1984) upon jury directions about circumstantial evidence prior to the Court's restatement in *Shepherd v The Queen* (1990).

The Court's handling of claims to legal professional privilege, as a result of which such claims have increased substantially in the last generation, has produced instability. In *O'Reilly v Commissioners of the State Bank of Victoria* (1983), the Court held 3:1 that the privilege did not apply outside litigation. In *Baker v Campbell* (1983), barely six months later, by a 4:3 majority, the Court held that it did. In *Grant v Downs* (1976), the Court held that the privilege applied only to documents brought into existence for the sole purpose of obtaining legal advice or use in legal proceedings. In *Esso Australia v FCT*, the Court abandoned the sole purpose test for a dominant purpose test.

Some of the Court's innovations have experienced legislative reversal in a number of jurisdictions, sometimes speedily, as in the response to the Court's assertion of a discretion to exclude evidence of an offence the commission of which has been brought about by unlawful police conduct (*Ridgeway*). Another example is the 'rule' in *Walker v Walker* (1937). Conversely, some legislative innovations have been received unenthusiastically by the Court (see *Longman v The Queen* (1989); *Bull v The Queen* (2000); **Feminism**).

Particularly since the mid-1970s, and perhaps as a consequence of the termination of appeals as of right, the Court has increasingly appeared to entertain criminal appeals as a significant proportion of its work, and among them many appeals on evidentiary issues. The Court has thus come to have a more dominant influence on the law of evidence than in former times, and has exercised this influence during a period when its members have necessarily had less trial experience than their predecessors, and particularly less jury experience. The increased influence of the Court has not increased the certainty of the law in its day-to-day application, because the Court has been instrumental in creating, recognising, approving, or widening discretions of all kinds to exclude otherwise admissible evidence and to give various warnings. This has reduced predictability for trial counsel and greatly increased the length and complexity of jury directions. To some extent, these trends were stimulated by, and to some extent they triggered, statutory changes which have reinforced their unsettling effect. Nor has the increased dominance of the High Court always increased the certainty

of the law as a matter of doctrinal statement, because there are fields in which some Justices have contradicted not only each other, but also themselves.

Not even the increased role of statute law is likely to weaken the significant role of the Court. The language of the Commonwealth and NSW *Evidence Acts* of 1995 is of a generality that calls for decisive and rigorous construction, and this it has tended to receive from the Court in the early cases on the legislation.

There have been changes in the definition and application of Australian evidence law in the twentieth century. It has moved away from the English common law. It has increasingly tended to incorporate a wide range of discretions. It has revealed its propensity to generate or continue difficulties in some areas. Despite all this, the record of the Court in the first century of its existence has been an enviable one in the field of evidence. No final appellate court in the common law world in that period has surpassed it.

JD Heydon

Excise duties. The Court's attempt to define 'duties of excise'—a kind of tax which, along with duties of customs, section 90 of the Constitution forbids to the states—has not been one of its spectacular successes. This is the fault neither of any individual Justice, nor of the Court at any particular time. It is rather the cumulative consequence, over time, of interaction among three distinct layers of complexity: diverse perceptions of constitutional purposes and policies (and of their relevance at all); contrasting approaches to legal method; and differing attitudes to **precedent**, the tangled web of which has been neither wholly decisive nor wholly escapable.

Unlike that of section 92 (see **Interstate trade and commerce**), the constitutional purpose of section 90 is not altogether clear, at least as to excise. As to customs, it is clear enough that any external tariff had to be a uniform national tariff. Section 92 secured an internal common market by eliminating tariffs on goods passing between the states; section 90, by prohibiting state customs duties, prevented the states from distorting the flow of goods into Australia and from undermining national policy on the appropriate level of protection for Australian industry from overseas competition. In this context, a ban on state excise—that is, on taxation of goods produced within rather than imported into the state—might be seen as a corollary of the ban on customs: if state customs duties could disrupt national policies of free trade, state excise duties could disrupt national policies of protection.

Had this plausible hypothetical history been the guiding light, excise might have been confined to taxes on goods of a kind subject to customs duties; or, less narrowly but judicially more manageably, to taxes only on local manufacture. Moreover, the idea of customs as taxes on imports and excise as taxes on local production reflected the symmetry of their constitutional collocation. On this view, a state tax on goods—irrespective of their origin—would be neither customs nor excise: since it would not affect the cost differential between imports and local manufacture, it would not disrupt Commonwealth tariff policy, whether that policy be free trade or protection (though it might interfere with some wider national economic policy).

The **Griffith Court** defined excise, consistently with this view, as 'a duty analogous to a customs duty imposed on goods either in relation to quantity or value when produced or manufactured and not in the sense of a direct tax or personal tax' (*Peterswald v Bartley* (1904)). But **Dixon** had a different view. Echoing his submission 20 years earlier to the 1929 Royal Commission on the Constitution, he led a narrow majority in *Parton v Milk Board* (1949) to hold that the purpose of section 90 was to give the Commonwealth 'a real control of the taxation of commodities'. Since 'a tax upon a commodity at any point in the course of distribution before it reaches the consumer produces the same effect as a tax upon its manufacture or production', *Parton* established a significant extension of excise from production taxes to sales taxes, thus abandoning any attempt to confine section 90 to the protection of Commonwealth tariff policy.

Dixon's theory that a tax on goods at any point in their distribution has the same effect as a tax on manufacture was not tested by either theoretical analysis or empirical evidence; the proposition that all of these taxes would be passed on and add to the cost of the goods in the hands of the consumer was a hypothetical generalisation based on common experience. Neither was there any historical evidence supporting his view of the purpose of section 90. Yet the Dixon view has persisted, despite recurrent dissents that have narrowly failed, at critical times, to muster enough support to metamorphose into orthodoxy. It was affirmed most recently, and received its most vigorous and sustained defence, by a 4:3 majority in *Ha v NSW* (1997).

One consequence of the Dixon view was to exacerbate the problem of 'vertical fiscal imbalance' in the Australian federation; that is, the imbalance between Commonwealth and states in terms of governmental responsibility and independent revenue-raising capacity. The general effect has been to increase the financial dependence of the states on the Commonwealth and to drive them, in their search for independent revenue sources, to impose cumbersome taxes such as business franchise licence fees, or economically undesirable taxes such as payroll tax.

Perhaps partly through sensitivity to the financial impact on the states of an overly wide view, but also because of the perceived demands of legal formalism in defining a term left undefined by the Constitution, the Court insisted that an excise was not a tax merely 'related to' goods but must be a tax 'on' goods. Thus, although Dixon had established in *Matthews v Chicory Marketing Board* (1938), again by a narrow majority, that no precise mathematical relationship between the tax and the quantity or value of the goods was required, an excise had to be 'directly related' to the goods, and to take some dealing with the goods as its 'criterion of liability' (*Bolton v Madsen* (1963)). A relatively uncontroversial example of an insufficiently direct relationship was *Anderson's v Victoria* (1964): Victorian stamp duty on hire-purchase agreements was held not to be an excise on the goods subject to those agreements but rather a tax on the agreements by which they were sold (since the quantum of the tax depended on the amount of credit extended rather than the value of the goods, and the same goods could be purchased in other ways without attracting tax).

Yet in that case, **Barwick** warned against undue **legalism** and insisted that whether a tax was an excise was essentially a practical question. Mirroring a similar tension at the time in section 92 cases, this dichotomy between **form and substance** was a major source of divided opinion. A striking example was the fate of the so-called 'consumption' tax in *Dickenson's Arcade v Tasmania* (1974). A majority having agreed on the principle that a tax on consumption was not a duty of excise, three Justices held that the tax in question—a $7^1/2$ per cent tax on the consumption of tobacco—was indeed a tax on consumption, because that was its criterion of liability; yet Barwick and **Mason** (who, with **McTiernan**, formed a statutory majority (see **Tied vote**)) held that, since for all practical purposes the tax would be paid only at the point of purchase, it was in reality a tax on that purchase and not on the act of consumption (that is, on the smoking or chewing of the tobacco).

Of course, the idea of a tax on smoking, payable by the smoker and calculated on the amount of tobacco smoked, was slightly absurd, and Barwick had a field day in ridiculing the suggestion that this could have been intended. Exploiting the absurdity, he was able to conclude that the tax was not really what it seemed. In truth, Tasmania was using the tax as a bargaining chip in a wider battle with the Commonwealth over financial support for the state. But the Court's decision did reveal that, despite the exclusion of consumption taxes from the definition of excise, the practical problem of enforcement made the possibility of the states actually levying such taxes more theoretical than real.

Non-lawyers are frequently puzzled by the lawyers' distinction between sales tax and consumption tax, the two taxes being synonymous in common parlance, sharing in particular the feature of being borne ultimately by the consumer. Given that shared feature, it is difficult to comprehend why the wide Dixonian view of excise should have stopped short of the point of consumption. The Court seems to have allowed itself to be hypnotised by an abstract distinction (derived from a very different Canadian context) between 'indirect' and 'direct' taxes—another victory here for form over substance.

However, the major battle between form and substance was fought out in the area of business franchise licence fees. In *Dennis Hotels v Victoria* (1960), a narrow majority (Dixon dissenting on this point) held that a fee for a licence to sell liquor, calculated on the value of liquor purchased for the premises in the previous licence period, was not an excise. The decision encouraged the states to resort to similar fees as a major new source of revenue, and before long state licence fees calculated by a '*Dennis Hotels* formula' were widely adopted, particularly for the sale of tobacco and petrol. The first challenge to these taxes (*Dickenson's Arcade*, involving a different part of the legislation from that imposing the consumption tax) came only in 1974, and the intervening 14 years of reliance on *Dennis Hotels* inhibited those Justices who doubted its correctness from being prepared to depart from it. A majority upheld the licence fee in *Dickenson's Arcade*, and thus began a long and tortuous line of cases involving grudging adherence to precedent and finer and finer distinctions, as the Justices struggled to keep faith with *Dennis Hotels* and yet to prevent it from totally subverting the post-*Parton* approach to section 90.

The difficulty was apparent immediately. In *Kailis v WA* (1974), decided on the same day as *Dickenson's Arcade*, a narrow majority, although for no common reason, declined to follow *Dennis Hotels* in relation to a fee for a licence to process fish, and held it to be a duty of excise. Three years later, however, in *HC Sleigh v SA* (1977), a majority (**Jacobs** dissenting) could not distinguish a fee for a licence to sell petrol from the fees in *Dennis Hotels* and *Dickenson's Arcade*. For a time, it seemed that *Kailis* was an aberration and that the states could get away with their taxes on alcohol, tobacco, and petrol. This was so despite a significant loosening in other cases of the requisite connection between the amount of the tax and the quantity or value of the goods: in *Logan Downs v Queensland* (1977), a statutory majority struck down a Queensland stock tax that had stood for 60 years, despite what **Stephen** described in dissent as its 'eccentricity of incidence' in relation to the diversity of products of the stock; and in *Hematite Petroleum v Victoria* (1983), a majority struck down a flat fee for operating pipelines that appeared to have no quantitative relationship at all with the volume or value of the gas passing through those pipelines.

Buoyed by the Court's approach in *Hematite*, a second challenge was brought to the tobacco tax the following year, but was thrown out peremptorily, the Court refusing to allow the question to be reopened (*Evda Nominees v Victoria* (1984)). Yet the issue would not go away: a year later, a narrow majority held in *Gosford Meats v NSW* (1985) that *Dennis Hotels* was inapplicable to a fee for a licence to slaughter meat, which was therefore invalid as an excise. This provoked a third challenge to the tobacco tax (*Philip Morris v Commissioner of Business Franchises* (1989)), which, although again unsuccessful, revealed sufficient diversity of opinion to leave the issue more unsettled than settled. In *Capital Duplicators v ACT (No 2)* (1993), a 4:3 majority confined *Dennis Hotels* to licence fees imposed in traditional areas of social regulation. An ACT fee for a licence to sell X-rated videos was struck down as a mere revenue raiser, though one might have thought that, like alcohol, the sale of X-rated material was also a traditional area of social regulation. (A differently constituted majority had held in *Capital Duplicators v ACT (No 1)* (1992) that section 90 applied to the **territories**: see **Outcomes**.) In *Ha*, the fourth tobacco tax challenge, the plaintiffs finally succeeded: NSW had so increased the fee that it was now manifestly a mere revenue raiser. Yet even then, though *HC Sleigh* (the petrol case) was doubted, *Dennis Hotels* and *Dickenson's Arcade* were affirmed 'as authorities for the validity of the imposts therein considered'.

In both *Capital Duplicators (No 2)* and *Ha*, a strong minority failed by just one vote to re-establish the narrower, pre-*Parton* view of excise as a tax on production or manufacture. On that view, *Dennis Hotels* and all the subsequent cases upholding fees for retail licences were correctly decided, although for the wrong reasons. Interestingly, so too were *Kailis* and *Gosford Meats*, as the fees there struck down were for licences to produce or manufacture rather than to sell—a distinction that made no sense in the context of the focus of *Dennis Hotels* on the calculation of fees by reference to transactions in an earlier period, but does make sense when dis-

joined from that context. The trouble, on this view, lay in the *Parton* extension from taxes on production to taxes on subsequent transactions. The line of dissent from that extension had been strong and persistent—from **Fullagar** in *Dennis Hotels*, to **Murphy** in *HC Sleigh* and *Logan Downs*, to **Dawson**, **Toohey**, and **Gaudron** in *Capital Duplicators (No 2)* and *Ha*. The issue cannot be regarded as settled, though the new dispensation linking state revenues to the Commonwealth goods and services tax may reduce state reliance on franchise fees and thus make future litigation in this area less likely.

In summary, the Court has been unable to agree on the meaning of 'duties of excise'. In the absence of significant textual guidance, the narrow view that the purpose of section 90 was to protect Commonwealth tariff policy has competed not only with the Dixon view that its purpose was to maximise Commonwealth economic control, but also, more recently, with the view that 'free trade' somehow requires equality of taxation of goods throughout the country. Cutting across these divergent views has been the battle between form and substance, with the formalists sometimes denying the relevance of the debate about constitutional purpose, but sometimes using form as a pragmatic constraint on an overbroad view of excise, which would otherwise impact unduly harshly on state revenues. Compounding these divergences of purpose and method has been the pull of precedent. Making sense of the accumulation of cases, themselves reflecting the jumble of diverse and shifting views, has been a major challenge for any Justice striving to be faithful to the incremental methods of the **common law**.

After intense examination of the subject, the Constitutional Commission concluded in 1988 that the federation would survive perfectly well with no ban on state excise duties. Local sales tax was commonplace in other federations. Vertical fiscal imbalance would be reduced. The ban was a narrow and incomplete way of protecting Commonwealth policy, and the Commonwealth could in any event legislate to protect itself from state interference by relying on section 109 of the Constitution (see **Inconsistency**). The Commission's discussion disclosed considerations relevant not only to constitutional reform but also to the choices that the Court has to make between competing interpretations of the existing section (most of those **policy considerations** supporting the narrower view). Yet, given the nation's poor record of constitutional **amendment** and the Court's inability to reach consensus, it is a toss-up where salvation lies.

MICHAEL COPER

Further Reading

Michael Coper, 'The High Court and Section 90 of the Constitution' (1976) 7 *FL Rev* 1

Michael Coper, *Encounters with the Australian Constitution* (1987, popular edn 1988) 208–25

Michael Coper, 'The Economic Framework of the Australian Federation: A Question of Balance' in Gregory Craven (ed), *Australian Federation—Towards the Second Century* (1992) 144–47

Final Report of the Constitutional Commission (1988) vol 2, 820–29

Rowan McMonnies, '*Ngo Ngo Ha* and the High Court v New South Wales: Historical Purpose in History and Law' (1999) 27 *FL Rev* 471

Expert evidence. Addressing a medico-legal gathering in 1933 on 'Science and Judicial Proceedings', **Dixon** observed: 'Questions of fact, raised by the standards of legal liability, which formerly might have appeared simple, are now shown to contain ingredients calling for close and complicated examination. Where the rough and ready answers of the practical man might once have sufficed, an exact and reasoned solution is now called for.'

Speaking the next year on 'The Law and the Scientific Expert', he added: 'The courts are there to administer the law … They are not tribunals fitted for the determination of disputed questions of science. They are not skilled in science. They must depend upon those who are skilled in such matters.'

In *Adhesives Pty Ltd v Aktieselskabet Dansk Gaerings-Industri* (1935), where **Evatt**, in a judgment affirmed by the **Full Court** on appeal, had laboured mightily (with the assistance of two Court-appointed assessors) to understand the chemical processes involved in the fermentation of yeast, **Rich** made the same point.

Granted that the courts need experts for many aspects of their **fact-finding** tasks, the problem is to reconcile the primary authority of the scientifically inexpert decision makers with their dependence for the required scientific knowledge upon the quality of the expert and of his or her opinion. Defining and refining the elements of this tension is an undercurrent in every decision of the Court about expert **evidence**.

Judges and jurors cannot delegate decision-making to experts. They must form their own opinions. In *Adelaide Stevedoring Co v Forst* (1940), Rich was emphatic: 'I do not see why a court should not begin its investigation, ie, before hearing any medical testimony, from the standpoint of the presumptive inference which this sequence of events would naturally inspire in the mind of any commonsense person uninstructed in pathology.' After describing a fatal heart attack during strenuous activity at work, he asked: 'Why should not a court say that here is strong ground for a preliminary presumption of fact … that the work materially contributed to the cause of death?'

After hearing the experts, judges or juries must form their own opinions on the issues they alone must resolve. This is so, even though the witness is regarded as being of the highest authority and of unimpeachable credit, and can cite authoritative textbook support for interpretations of facts. In the medical negligence case of *Hocking v Bell* (1945), a jury verdict in favour of the plaintiff had been set aside by the Supreme Court of NSW, and the High Court dismissed her appeal. **Latham** and Dixon, dissenting, stressed that the questions of fact involved must be resolved by the jury—as the **Privy Council** also emphasised when it ultimately allowed the plaintiff's appeal (*Hocking v Bell* (1947); see also *Ramsay v Watson* (1961)).

In the *Chamberlain Case* (1984), in the context of a not uncommon conflict between experts, **Brennan** reaffirmed the same principle:

> There were opposed scientific opinions … The jury, having the duty to decide whether the tests were sufficient and having credible evidence either way from acknowledged experts, were

not precluded from acting upon the opinion of the prosecution witnesses because the defence witnesses gave credible evidence to contradict it … Conflicts of evidence are to be resolved by the jury.

Judges must be vigilant to ensure that a purported expert has sufficient expertise and stays within it. Evaluating the appropriateness of qualifications or experience, or both, involves an exercise of personal judgment on the part of the judge, for which the authorities provide little help. Some typical cases demonstrate how the High Court has moved from examining *how* the expert's knowledge was acquired, to a concentration upon what is known, and whether it might help the trier of fact. The Court is receptive to soundly based evidence from experts, whether of fact or opinion, but is affronted by speculation that is passed off as the product of expert knowledge.

In *Bugg v Day* (1949), an experienced motor vehicle repairer was permitted at trial to give expert evidence about the condition of a motorcycle that had been damaged in a collision. However, he went on to assert that his examination of the motorcycle enabled him to deduce that the car that struck it had been travelling at 40 miles per hour. On appeal, this was held to be inadmissible. As Dixon explained: 'His conclusion would involve a problem far beyond his capacity and qualifications and one to which he did not purport to address himself. It was not evidence based upon a branch of knowledge or an art in which the witness was skilled but a wild and unsophisticated conjecture.'

In *Clark v Ryan* (1960), a witness for the plaintiff, testifying as an expert, gave evidence that a vehicle such as the defendant's had a characteristic of jackknifing. This witness had no formal engineering qualifications but had some 50 years of engineering experience, and for many years had been engaged in investigating road accidents. Dixon held that 'if technical evidence of the physics involved in such collisions were called … it might have been given by someone more highly academically qualified than this expert'. He found that the witness's evidence was partly opinion evidence, which lay outside any qualifications that he could be said to possess. He declared it inadmissible. **McTiernan** would have allowed the evidence, emphasising that the question of its value or weight was entirely a question for the jury.

However, in *Weal v Bottom* (1966), a case that turned on the possibility that the rear end of a trailer had been over the midline of the road at the critical time, **Barwick** endorsed the taking of evidence from those with practical experience, saying:

> It would be very surprising if a course of study by reading and instruction warranted the admission of a statement as to the behaviour of a vehicle derived from its nature whereas a long course of actual experience in the use of the vehicle or of observation of its actual behaviour in relevant circumstances did not qualify a person to speak of such behaviour.

The evidence of psychologists has been particularly problematical. In *Murphy v The Queen* (1989), Brennan and **Dawson** affirmed a trial judge's rejection of a psychologist's evidence for the defence. If accepted, it threw doubt upon the accused's confession. Brennan held that neither the psychologist's report nor his statement of qualifications revealed any expertise that would have permitted him to form a view about the accused's understanding of particular questions or his use of particular words or phrases. Dawson thought that the psychologist's qualifications, as presented in evidence, would equip him only to express the view that the accused was poorly educated and of limited intellectual capacity.

More recently, in *Osland v The Queen* (1998), **Kirby**, in discussing the utility of expert evidence of 'battered woman syndrome', made the point that while diagnosis in terms of that syndrome does not enjoy universal support (see **Feminism**), there is considerable agreement that expert evidence about the general dynamics of abusive relationships is admissible if relevant to the issues in the trial.

In *HG v The Queen* (1999), **Gleeson** rejected a psychologist's evidence as failing to satisfy the Commonwealth and NSW statutory requirement that opinion evidence be wholly or substantially based on specialised knowledge. He found the evidence to be 'based on a combination of speculation, inference, personal and second-hand views as to the credibility of the complainant, and a process of reasoning which went well beyond the field of expertise of a psychologist'.

At **common law**, experts cannot expound to the finders of fact on matters regarded as common knowledge. On the other hand, Australian courts have conceded that advancing knowledge has displaced some notions of what 'everyone knows'. As Dixon remarked in 1933, 'an exact and reasoned solution is now called for'. This is especially the case when notions of 'normal' and 'abnormal' mental states are involved.

In *Jackson v The Queen* (1962), the Court pointed out that where the mental condition of a person who makes a confession is relevant in assessing the weight to be given to the confession, 'all the circumstances surrounding the making of it which tend to show either that it can safely be relied upon or that it would be unwise to do so are admissible'. In *Murphy v The Queen* (1989), the trial judge had rejected the proposed expert evidence on the basis that, once the psychologist's report had excluded brain damage and mental retardation, what remained related to matters of human nature and behaviour within the limits of 'normality'—about which the jurors were competent to form their own views, it being common knowledge. Departing from that traditional approach, the High Court, by a bare majority, held that the evidence should have been admitted. **Mason** and **Toohey** held: 'It does not follow that, because a lay witness can describe events and behaviour, expert evidence is unavailable to explain those events and behaviour. Expert evidence will often build upon lay observations.'

When rival experts are pitted against each other in support of opposing sides in an adversary trial process, judges are sometimes sceptical of the objectivity of their claims. In *Vakauta v Kelly* (1989), the trial judge had referred to three medical witnesses as 'doctors who think you can do a full week's work without any arms or legs'. Brennan, Deane, and **Gaudron** noted that trial judges inevitably form views about frequently seen witnesses. But when listening to and assessing the evidence of such witnesses, a judge is expected to

maintain the 'professional detachment of an experienced judge' in order to preserve the 'impartial administration of justice'.

The Court has always been ambivalent about the capacity of jurors to be impartial and competent assessors of the material before them. As Dixon observed in 1933:

> When a judge is confronted with some question which depends upon a scientific inquiry however ill equipped he may be for the task, he is expected to acquire from the evidence of experts a sufficient knowledge of the subject to enable him to appreciate and even form a critical judgment upon the scientific facts, inferences and deductions which contribute to a correct solution of the question. No one expects a jury to do this … For the most part, it is useless to expect a jury to form any reasoned judgment on scientific or technical questions.

Compare, however, his view in *Hocking v Bell*.

At the other extreme, more than half a century later, Mason and Toohey observed, in *R v Glennon* (1992): 'In the past too little weight may have been given to the capacity of jurors to assess critically what they see and hear and their ability to reach their decisions by reference to the evidence before them.'

Traditionally, expert evidence upon a witness's credibility was not allowed unless the witness suffered a mental illness or an intellectual disability. In all other cases, credibility was regarded as the exclusive province of the triers of fact. In *Farrell v The Queen* (1998), this restriction was relaxed. The psychiatrist called on behalf of the accused expressed the opinion that persons such as the complainant, suffering from an antisocial personality disorder, 'are inherently less truthful than the average person'. The trial judge directed the jury to scrutinise the complainant's evidence with particular care, but commented that the psychiatrist's opinion 'really does not count for anything because he did not get to the stage of diagnosing an actual medical condition which would be [beyond] your experience and mine'.

The Court held, by a majority, that the accused had been wrongly deprived of the chance of an acquittal that was fairly open to him because the case against him depended on the jury's acceptance of the complainant's evidence. The ground-breaking aspect of the decision was that it opened up the potential for expert evidence to be led about matters that might affect evaluation of credibility. Kirby, for instance, held that, while expert evidence on the ultimate credibility of a witness is not admissible, expert evidence on psychological or physical conditions that may induce behaviour relevant to credibility is admissible. This is subject to the jury being given a firm warning that the expert cannot determine matters of credibility, which it remains the ultimate obligation of the jury to determine. The extent to which expert evidence will now be admissible to assist jurors to appreciate how a range of personality characteristics may affect credibility remains to be seen.

Notwithstanding the range of judicial opinions, there is a clear trend by which the Court has reduced the scope of some longstanding exclusionary rules. There is a preparedness to allow experts to tread where once they would have been excluded, subject to the exercise by trial judges of strict control to avoid the jury being overborne or misled by purported 'expertise'. As Dixon said: 'True science has nothing to fear from law. But *nemo nascitur artifex* [no one is born a skilled workman]'.

IAN FRECKELTON
HUGH SELBY

Further Reading
Owen Dixon, 'Science and Judicial Proceedings' (1933) and 'The Law and the Scientific Expert' (1934), in SHZ Woinarski (ed), *Jesting Pilate* (1965) 11, 24

Express constitutional rights. The Australian Constitution does not contain a **Bill of Rights**. The **framers of the Constitution** were largely unconcerned with the protection of **civil liberties**. They were more interested in rights of a different kind: namely, states' rights.

Nevertheless, the Constitution does contain a few, scattered rights. This is mainly due to the efforts of one drafter, Andrew **Inglis Clark**, the Tasmanian **Attorney-General**, who argued that the Constitution should protect fundamental freedoms. Even Inglis Clark did not argue for a Bill of Rights, but merely for an idiosyncratic list of individual rights. For example, he argued for guarantees of freedom of religion and trial by jury, but nothing that would protect freedom of speech or association.

The list of rights expressed in the Constitution is short. It includes the following civil and political rights: a right to vote in federal elections for persons entitled to vote in state elections (section 41); a right to **jury trial** for the 'trial on indictment of any offence against any law of the Commonwealth' (section 80); four guarantees relating to freedom of and from religion (section 116); and a freedom from any 'disability or **discrimination**' imposed on the basis of state residence (section 117). The Constitution also contains two important economic freedoms: the Commonwealth cannot acquire **property** except on just terms (section 51(xxxi), as popularised in *The Castle*—see **Acquisition of property**); and 'trade, commerce, and intercourse among the States … shall be absolutely free' (section 92; see **Interstate trade and commerce**).

The fact that the Constitution contains so few rights has led to the idea that it, and the High Court as its interpreter, can have little or no role to play in the protection of fundamental freedoms in Australia. However, the absence of a Bill of Rights in the Constitution can be misleading. As **Deane** stated in *Street v Queensland Bar Association* (1989):

> It is often said that the Australian Constitution contains no bill of rights. Statements to that effect, while literally true, are superficial and potentially misleading. The Constitution contains a significant number of express or implied guarantees of rights and immunities … All of those guarantees of rights or immunities are of fundamental importance in that they serve the function of advancing or protecting the liberty, the dignity or the **equality** of the citizen under the Constitution.

Although the list of express rights is short, it does concern some very significant topics. Robustly interpreted, such rights could provide significant protection in important areas.

While the Court has recently been willing to recognise **implied constitutional rights** relating to topics such as freedom of **political communication** and **due process**, it has, with one exception, not interpreted the express civil and political rights in the Constitution to provide any meaningful protection for civil liberties. Thus, in *R v Pearson; Ex parte Sipka* (1983), the Court held that section 41 was merely a transitional provision that preserved a person's right to vote where it had been acquired before the passing of the *Commonwealth Franchise Act* 1902 (Cth). It therefore operated only at the first federal election; and even if the persons then affected acquired a permanent constitutional right, they must by 1983 have been at least 103 years old! (See Michael Coper, *Encounters with the Australian Constitution* (1988) at 335: 'The Right to Vote: Centenarians Rejoice'.) That year, the Constitutional Commission described the section as a 'dead letter' and recommended that it be removed from the Constitution.

Similarly, the guarantee of a right to a jury trial in section 80 has been transformed into a provision that provides no meaningful guarantee or restriction on Commonwealth power. The Court has interpreted the provision to allow the Commonwealth Parliament itself to determine whether a trial is to be on indictment, and thus whether there need be a jury trial. According to **Barwick** in *Spratt v Hermes* (1965), 'what might have been thought to be a great constitutional guarantee has been discovered to be a mere procedural provision'. The guarantees of religious freedom in section 116 have also been ineffective, the Court never having upheld a claim based upon that provision (see **Church and state**).

It was only in 1989 that one of the express guarantees was successfully invoked in the High Court. That was in *Street v Queensland Bar Association*, where the Court **overruled** its earlier restrictive approach to section 117 in *Henry v Boehm* (1973). The earlier approach had given the provision almost no work to do at all; the new approach gave substantive and meaningful protection to Australians against discrimination on account of the state in which they live. The Court found that section 117 was not necessarily satisfied by the finding that 'a law, administrative policy or judicial practice' was 'of general application'; it was necessary to consider 'the actual impact which a law, policy or practice produces on the persons to whom it is directed'.

The judgments in *Street* provided a powerful contrast to the reasoning in earlier decisions on section 117, and indeed to the course of decisions on sections 41, 80, and 116. No longer was section 117 characterised as a narrow provision seemingly incapable of substantive operation. Instead, it was conceived by **Mason** as 'one of the comparatively few provisions in the Constitution which was designed to enhance **national unity** and a real sense of national identity by eliminating disability or discrimination on account of residence in another State'. The provision was seen as integral to the federal purpose of creating 'one nation and one people'.

The decision in *Street* marked a profound break with the earlier approach of the Court to express civil and political rights. It appeared to herald a new approach in which the Court might re-evaluate its interpretation of the other rights. This has not proved to be the case. For example, in *Kruger v Commonwealth* (1997), the Court showed few signs of willingness to develop the protection of religious freedom in section 116 as a meaningful guarantee.

Until the Court reinterpreted section 117 in the *Street* case, none of the express civil and political rights in the Constitution protective of personal liberty had been successfully invoked by a plaintiff to strike down a state or federal law. On the few occasions that the Court had interpreted these provisions, it had chosen an approach that rendered the relevant provision largely meaningless. On the other hand, when similar opportunities arose to interpret the express economic rights in the Constitution (the guarantee of freedom of interstate trade and commerce and the protection of property rights), they were construed as substantial and effective limitations on governmental power.

A clear difference in approach can be identified between the case law on civil and political rights, and the case law on economic rights. The different interpretive approaches to these different classes of rights reveal a 'double standard' that has spanned the decision making of generations of High Court Justices. At least until the late 1980s, the Court preferred to implement economic over civil and political rights. This double standard was never articulated by any member of the Court, but is clearly implicit in the pattern of decisions.

In the 1970s, **Murphy** sought to reverse this preference. While advocating a creative and progressive approach to the protection of rights such as trial by jury in section 80, he repudiated the same approach in the interpretation of section 92. In a series of decisions culminating in *Uebergang v Australian Wheat Board* (1980), he construed section 92 narrowly to avoid the assumption by the Court of 'a super-legislative role' in the area of economic regulation. Yet in the same case, he emphasised that 'in human rights and other non-economic areas, courts have applied tests of **due process, natural justice, reasonableness** and fairness': that is, courts could appropriately have recourse to 'public **policy** tests'.

GEORGE WILLIAMS

Further Reading

George Williams, *Human Rights under the Australian Constitution* (1999)

***Ex tempore* judgments** (from Latin, meaning 'on the spur of the moment, without premeditation') are those given without preparation (contrast **reserved judgments**). *Ex tempore* judgments are comparatively rare in the High Court, but can occur in particular circumstances: first, to dispose of an appeal or application considered to be urgent or straightforward and upon which each participating Justice is prepared to have the reasons stated immediately, orally, and in **open court**; and, secondly, to dispose of applications for special **leave to appeal**. Where such an application is dismissed, the presiding Justice invariably states the **order** of the Court and the reasons for it briefly, usually immediately after the conclusion of **argument**. Since the earliest days, short reasons at least have been given in such cases (see, for example, *Newcastle Coal v Firemen's Union* (1908)). Occasionally, other participating Justices add short oral reasons of their own. Thirdly, to dispose of matters including directions or applications made pursuant to the **High Court Rules**. Such applications are usually heard by a single Justice, who normally gives an immediate oral statement of the orders made and the reasons for them. Those reasons are recorded in the **transcript** of the proceedings. Because they may settle disputed questions concerning the practice of the Court, or indicate probable approaches to that practice, they may later be published in the law reports. They are in that event taken directly from the transcript, and are not usually issued by the Court in pamphlet form.

Occasionally, important points of constitutional principle are established by *ex tempore* judgments. An example is *Teori Tau v Commonwealth* (1969). The report of that decision reveals that the judgment of the Court was delivered by **Barwick** after 'the judges left the Bench for a short time to consult'. The correctness of the decision was questioned by later authority (see *Newcrest Mining v Commonwealth* (1997), where **Gummow** referred to the fact that the reasons in *Teori Tau* were given *ex tempore* and that they contained 'neither discussion nor analysis nor, indeed, citation, of previous authority').

In *Hughes & Vale v Gair* (1954), for reasons given *ex tempore* principally by **Dixon**, the Court refused to grant an injunction to restrain the presentation to the Governor of Queensland for the royal assent of a Bill that had been passed by the state Parliament. In *R v Richards; Ex parte Fitzpatrick and Browne* (1955), involving applicants who had been imprisoned for breach of the privileges of a House of Parliament, the judgment of a unanimous Court was delivered *ex tempore* by Dixon. In *Tait's Case* (1962), for reasons shortly stated by Dixon, the Court adjourned an application for special leave to appeal and ordered that the execution of the prisoner convicted of a capital offence, fixed for the following day, should not be carried out but be stayed pending disposal of the application by the High Court. In rare cases, where the application of a recently decided constitutional point is involved in an appeal, the Court, for brief reasons given *ex tempore*, may grant special leave and allow the appeal immediately without requiring **remedies** to be pursued in an intermediate appellate court (see *Aston v The Queen* (1995)). The same procedure is adopted where an obvious injustice has occurred requiring immediate intervention in the case of a prisoner in custody (see, for example, *Thornberry v The Queen* (1995)).

On rare occasions, when it appears on the papers that an appeal may raise a short point involving the application of settled law, one of the Justices may prepare draft notes which, subject to discussion, elaboration, and amendment, can be agreed to by all of the Justices participating and read as the reasons of the Court. Occasionally, a concession made during argument may leave only one possible outcome. In such a case, short reasons will be agreed and pronounced by the presiding Justice (see, for example, *Markovina v The Queen* (1999)). Special leave previously granted may sometimes be revoked, the Justices proceeding to give immediate *ex tempore* reasons for favouring, or opposing, that course (see *South-West Forest Defence Foundation v Department of Conservation* (1998)). Very occasionally, it may be considered that some point referred to in disposing *ex tempore* of a special leave application with more extended reasons than usual is worthy of report in the authorised reports of the Court (see, for example, *R v Elliott* (1996)). Nowadays, however, it is rare for matters concluded by *ex tempore* reasons to be included in the *Commonwealth Law Reports*.

Ex tempore disposal of appeals and substantive applications is now comparatively rare in the High Court. The requirement of special leave means that cases generally raise issues of complexity or importance. Proceedings in the original **jurisdiction** of the Court may involve a constitutional question or some other matter of complexity or importance. Because such questions are not normally suitable for instantaneous disposal, *ex tempore* judgments in such cases are infrequent. If any member of the Court asks that a matter be reserved for the later publication of reasons, by convention that must be done.

Sometimes, particularly in criminal appeals where the appellant is in custody, orders disposing of an appeal will be pronounced with reasons reserved for later publication. The inclusion of High Court judgments in many published series, and the attention paid to them by courts throughout Australia and beyond, impose inhibitions upon the disposal of matters by *ex tempore* reasons.

MICHAEL KIRBY

Further Reading
Michael Kirby, '*Ex tempore* Reasons' (1992) 9 *Aust Bar Rev* 93

External affairs power. Section 51(xxix) of the Constitution confers power on the Commonwealth Parliament to make laws with respect to 'external affairs'. The scope of the power was regarded as uncertain for many decades, since the Commonwealth was at its inception a colony with no independent power of entering into treaties or sending or receiving diplomatic representatives. Matters of foreign affairs and declarations of war and peace were within the exclusive province of the Imperial government. As a result of the evolution of Australia to **nationhood**, the Crown prerogatives relating to foreign affairs and defence came to be exercised by the Governor-General on the advice of Commonwealth ministers. They are now regarded as conferred by section 61 of the Constitution as part of the executive power of the Commonwealth. As the states did not develop international personality and as other countries recognise the Commonwealth as representing Australia, those prerogatives never passed to the state Governors (*Seas and Submerged Lands Case* (1975); *Bonser v La Macchia* (1969)). The result is that the Commonwealth's treaty-making power is unlimited in subject matter. However, a treaty, though binding at **international law**, does not change domestic law. If the treaty requires such a change it must be done by legislation (but see *Teoh's Case* (1995)).

If the subject matter of the treaty comes within a federal power other than external affairs, such as **taxation** or overseas **trade and commerce**, that power authorises a law to implement the treaty. If it is not within such a power, the issue—which was uncertain for decades—was whether the external affairs power authorised legislation giving effect to the treaty. It was not until 33 years after the High Court began its work that it made an extensive examination of the power. The only clear result that emerged was that some treaties not otherwise within federal power (including the Convention on Air Navigation) could be implemented under

section 51(xxix) (*R v Burgess; Ex parte Henry* (1936)). Some Justices (**Latham, Evatt,** and **McTiernan**) thought that the power extended to all treaties. **Dixon** suggested it was confined to treaty subjects that were 'international in character', while **Starke** suggested that it might be confined to treaty subjects 'of sufficient international significance' to warrant international cooperation and agreement. The issue was not resolved for another 50 years because Commonwealth governments adopted a policy of not ratifying a treaty outside the normal subjects of power unless all state laws were in conformity with it.

The matter next came to a head, but was not fully resolved, in 1982 when the Court by a narrow majority upheld under section 51(xxix) some provisions of the *Racial Discrimination Act* 1975 (Cth), which gave effect to a Convention prohibiting **discrimination** on the basis of **race** (*Koowarta's Case* (1982)). The majority Justices, however, differed in their reasoning. **Mason, Murphy,** and **Brennan** held that, whatever the subject matter of the Convention, the existence of the Convention gave rise to an external affair. **Stephen** did not go so far; he thought that the Convention had to be on a topic of 'sufficient international concern' (which, in his view, this Convention was). **Gibbs, Aickin,** and **Wilson** dissented, disagreeing with both lines of reasoning.

The issue was settled in the *Tasmanian Dam Case* (1983), where the Court upheld the validity of federal legislation giving effect to the World Heritage Convention. The legislation was used to prevent Tasmania building a dam in a national park that was part of the 'natural and cultural heritage' within the meaning of the Convention and the Act. This time a clear majority (Mason, Murphy, Brennan, and **Deane**) held that the Commonwealth could give effect to any international obligation imposed by a bona fide treaty or by customary international law. They all indicated that the power was not limited to the fulfilment of obligations. The dissenting Justices (Gibbs, Wilson, and **Dawson**) preferred the view that the subject must be seen as 'external affairs' apart from any international obligation or concern; but, in the light of *Koowarta*, they applied the test whether the subject was of sufficient international concern. They held it was not.

All of the Justices had resort to—but drew different conclusions from—textual considerations, historical perspectives, and **policy** factors. In relation to the text, the majority relied on the plain meaning of the words, while the minority insisted that the power had to be read in context (see **External affairs power: a critical analysis**). In relation to **history**, the majority indicated that it had always been envisaged that the power would be used for treaty implementation and that what had changed was simply the range of matters now the subject of international agreement (see **Connotation and denotation**); the minority could not accept, however, that the consequential imbalance of power in Australian **federalism** could have been intended. And in addition to the traditional criteria of **constitutional interpretation**, all the Justices relied on policy grounds. The majority were concerned with the position of Australia in relation to the world. National need and interests in matters of international affairs were emphasised, and the need to prevent a 'crippling' of Australia in its dealings with other nations and its participation, generally, in world affairs. The major concern of the dissenters was the need to preserve the federal system. For them the broad view threatened the complete destruction of any exclusive state legislative power.

The *Tasmanian Dam Case* has since been followed. It was applied, for example, to uphold a federal Act imposing industrial relations obligations that had been prescribed by an International Labour Convention (*Industrial Relations Act Case* (1996)). One important limitation on federal power, despite its unlimited subject matter, is that the Act must be seen as an appropriate means to give effect to the treaty. In the *Tasmanian Dam Case*, for example, the majority Justices were divided on that issue in respect of some of the legislative provisions.

The cases concerning treaties all make it clear that one of the major purposes of section 51(xxix) is to give power to the Commonwealth to legislate in respect of international relations. Some matters are of this nature, although no treaty or rule of international law is involved. A definition of sedition that included exciting disaffection against the government of any of the King's dominions was upheld on that ground (*R v Sharkey* (1949)). A law that dealt exclusively with the rights and duties of foreign nations, enterprises, or governments would clearly come within the power. Indeed, the dissenters in *Koowarta* would have confined the power to such matters. It has also been held that if a law is confined to actions or things geographically external to Australia it is within the external affairs power, without the necessity of showing that it has any effect on international relations, or arises under a treaty (*Horta v Commonwealth* (1994); see also the **War Crimes Act Case** (1991)). Like all the powers in section 51, the external affairs power is subject to express and implied limitations such as section 92 (freedom of **interstate trade**), section 116 (freedom of religion), and principles that prevent the Commonwealth discriminating against states or attempting to impair their independent existence and governmental organisation (*Koowarta*; see **Intergovernmental immunities**).

Leslie Zines

Further Reading
Michael Coper, 'The Role of the Courts in the Preservation of Federalism' (1989) 63 *ALJ* 463

External affairs power: a critical analysis. By majority decisions, the Court has given a dual operation to the power conferred by section 51(xxix) of the Constitution. First, the power extends to persons, matters, things, and conduct outside the boundaries of Australia (**War Crimes Act Case** (1991)). Secondly, the power has been held to support a law whose purpose is to implement an international treaty entered into by Australia in good faith, even though the law has an entirely domestic operation and the subject matter of the treaty is not of international character or concern (*Tasmanian Dam Case* (1983)). The power extends to the carrying out of recommendations of international bodies, draft international conventions, and international recommendations and requests (*Industrial Relations Act Case* (1996)).

The opinion of the majority in the *War Crimes Act Case* accords with the natural meaning of the words of section 51(xxix), but the opinion of the majority in the *Tasmanian Dam Case* is arguably wrong. The majority, in construing paragraph (xxix), gave no regard to the context in which the paragraph appears. The **Engineers Case** (1920) decided that the Constitution did not reserve to the states any particular heads of power, but is no authority for disregarding the rule of **statutory interpretation** that a statute should be considered as a whole and that the words of one section should be construed in the light of their context and so as to avoid inconsistency or repugnancy with other parts of the statute. The executive government has power to enter into international agreements on any subject, whether or not that subject lies within the legislative powers granted to the Commonwealth by provisions other than section 51(xxix). If the majority view is correct, the executive can, by making treaties, determine the scope of **Commonwealth legislative power** and can enlarge that power so that it embraces all forms of domestic activity. Such a construction gives no weight to the fact that the other paragraphs of section 51 specifically define the heads of Commonwealth power. It renders meaningless the division of powers between the Commonwealth and the states effected by the Constitution. It ignores the federal nature of the Constitution; in a federation, the states must have at least some powers that are exclusive—but on this view, the states have none.

The context in which paragraph (xxix) appears, and the words of the paragraph themselves, support the conclusion that to fall within the power the law itself must relate to an external affair. It does not follow that because a treaty is a matter of external affairs, legislation which gives effect to a treaty must therefore be a law with respect to external affairs. A law which gives effect to a treaty, but which operates entirely within Australia, will be a law with respect to 'external affairs' only if the subject of the law has itself the character of an external affair. A law which forbids the building of a dam (*Tasmanian Dam Case*) or the cutting down of trees (*Richardson v Forestry Commission* (1988)) within a state, or that regulates industrial relations within Australia (*Industrial Relations Act Case*), cannot properly be characterised as a law with respect to an external affair, even though the law may have been enacted to give effect to an international obligation. On the other hand, a law dealing with fugitive offenders or aerial navigation, although domestic in its operation, might involve international relations, and, if so, would fall within the power.

The qualification suggested by the majority, that the power will not be available if the treaty was not entered into in good faith is, for practical purposes, meaningless.

An alternative suggestion, that it is enough if the law deals with a matter of international concern, should also be rejected. The fact that a domestic issue gives rise to international concern does not convert a law with respect to a domestic issue into a law with respect to external affairs.

The better view is that a law which gives effect within Australia to an international agreement or recommendation will be a law with respect to 'external affairs' only if the law itself has the character of an external affair; that is, if it involves in some way a relationship with other countries or with persons or things outside Australia. The argument that if the power were limited in this way Australia could not fulfil its international obligations is unsustainable, as the experience of other federal nations has shown.

HARRY GIBBS

Extra-judicial writings of the Justices. Reclusiveness has not characterised High Court Justices' willingness to publish articles and papers. Even so, several questions remain largely unexplored. For example, from the perspective of constitutional propriety and, perhaps, law, should Justices be confined to the litigation process, including publication of judicial opinions?

At least as a matter of tradition and practice, an unambiguous answer has evolved. Apparently without reticence or hesitation, Justices publish articles and chapters in books. Some—especially **Mason** and **Kirby**—have done so with regularity. Indeed, **Dixon**, as demonstrated in Severin Woinarski's compilation *Jesting Pilate* (1965), is an exemplary model. In quantity, and sometimes in quality, the corpus of Justices' extra-judicial writings is significant.

Predominantly, such writing deals with issues of law, the legal system and courts, and especially the High Court. A recurring example is the Chief Justice's annual 'State of the Judicature' address. Within the confines of **constitutional law**, famous examples include Dixon, 'The Law and the Constitution' (1935) 51 *LQR* 590 and 'The Common Law as an Ultimate Constitutional Foundation' (1957) 31 *ALJ* 240 (both reprinted in *Jesting Pilate*); **Latham**, 'Interpretation of the Constitution' in Rae Else-Mitchell (ed), *Essays on the Australian Constitution* (2 ed 1961); and Mason, 'The Role of a Constitutional Court in a Federation: A Comparison of the Australian and United States Experience' (1986) 16 *Fed LR* 1. A recent example that ranges over a number of areas is **Gummow**'s *Change and Continuity: Statute, Equity and Federalism* (1999).

Of course, on some issues Justices are uniquely qualified to write, and can do so effectively only in an extra-judicial capacity. How judgments are written, and what it is like to be a High Court Justice, are obvious examples. The opposite extreme is even clearer. Justices must not write extra-judicially about specific cases which are or may be litigated. Apart from the judges' sense of propriety, **disqualification** or recusal (though not, except in extreme cases, **removal** from office) are strong deterrents and sanctions. In other areas, to assess whether extra-judicial writing is appropriate may require a balance between preserving the judiciary's impartial, non-political and independent stature and upholding judges' freedom, as citizens and community members, openly to express their views on all matters of public interest. Also, care must be taken to ensure that extra-judicial expressions of opinion do not raise apprehensions of bias (actual or perceived) and, as a result, contribute to the politicisation of judicial office.

Clearly, like other citizens, Justices should have outlets for creative activity. However, time devoted to extra-judicial writings (whether on legal or non-legal topics) should not impinge upon or detract from judicial functions and duties. Famous examples of non-legal writings include **Griffith's** Latin and Italian translations including Dante, **Evatt's** historical and biographical scholarship, and **Callinan's** novels and plays (see **Popular images of Court**).

What, if any, significance should be attributed to extra-judicial writings? Strictly, as a matter of law, they have no precedential value or force. Even so, extra-judicial writing may be persuasive and influential, especially if it clarifies, extends or exposes the underlying premises of a judge's views or the reasoning previously enunciated in a case or series of cases. Relatively, at least in Australia, a comparative evaluative survey of the use in judicial opinions of judges' extra-judicial writings and the scholarship of others may well reveal the former to have been, even if less frequently cited, the more influential.

If greater refinement is required, a tripartite division might be drawn between writings published before, during and after a judge's **tenure**. The first category might reveal the extent, if any, to which a Justice's views have developed or changed (and why that has occurred) after joining the Court. **McHugh's** writings on **proximity** and his apparent change of approach once appointed to the High Court may be an illustration. Measured by frequency of publication, Kirby commands the middle category and Mason leads in post-**retirement** writings.

In contrast with the attention given to **United States Supreme Court** Justices, no extensive bibliographic compilation of High Court Justices' extra-judicial writings has been published. Their existence and location must be ascertained predominantly from two sources: bibliographies in **biographies** of individual Justices and indexes to legal and non-legal periodicals. Essays and chapters in books, together with unpublished lectures or papers, may be more difficult to locate.

A comprehensive compilation of the Justices' extra-judicial writings should be undertaken with all deliberate speed. Perhaps, beyond providing intellectual pleasure, the resulting list might have other utilitarian benefits, such as assisting in the assessment of judicial performance. Given the American experience, one prediction can be safely ventured: this will not dampen the Justices' penchant for extra-judicial writing.

JAMES THOMSON

Further reading
Tony Blackshield, 'Judicial Essays by Sir Owen Dixon', *Sydney Morning Herald*, 5 March 1966, 16

Nicholas Hasluck, 'Deconstructing the High Court' (1998) 42 *Quadrant* 12 (reviewing Ian Callinan, *The Lawyer and the Libertine* (1997))

High Court of Australia: Speeches, http://www.hcourt.gov.au/speeches.htm

Michael Kirby, *Through the World's Eye* (2000)

Clifford L Pannam, 'Dante and the Chief Justice' (1959) 33 *ALJ* 290

Kylie Tennant, *Evatt: Politics and Justice* (1970, revised edn 1972) 397–9 (bibliography of Evatt's books and articles published while a Justice)

Extrinsic materials. All courts, when deciding questions of **common law**, **statutory interpretation**, and **constitutional interpretation** draw upon a range of sources and materials. Primary sources are the relevant statutory and constitutional texts, as well as earlier cases (see **Precedent**). Yet courts also draw upon secondary sources and materials to elucidate the meanings of those texts, and to develop the common law; sometimes they go even further and cite secondary material in order to support observations or conclusions about relevant **policy considerations** and **values** that underpin their decisions or impinge upon the **decision-making process**. The question of which materials are **authoritative legal materials** is not uncontroversial, particularly in relation to the exegesis of texts, which many have argued should stand by themselves and reveal their meaning only through their chosen words (see **Legalism**; **Literalism**). More recently, however, it has become accepted that a range of extrinsic materials—that is, materials extrinsic to the texts themselves—is relevant and helpful in coming to conclusions about intended meanings.

In relation to statutes, the question of what extrinsic materials could or should be resorted to became more pressing with the shift towards a purposive approach to meaning, as now embodied in section 15AA of the *Acts Interpretation Act* 1901 (Cth), added in 1981. It was one thing to require courts to have regard to the overall purpose of statutes rather than to adopt their literal meaning; it was another thing to explicate the materials on which a search for the statutory purpose could be based. Thus, section 15AB of the Acts Interpretation Act, inserted in 1984, provides, in relation to Commonwealth statutes, for resort to a range of extrinsic material, including Australian Law Reform Commission (ALRC) discussion papers, ALRC reports, ministerial second reading speeches, parliamentary committee reports, parliamentary debates, and Royal Commission reports. This list is not exhaustive; however, reference under section 15AB in practice is normally limited to ministerial second reading speeches.

A parallel development, generated by the High Court itself rather than by the Parliament, occurred in relation to constitutional interpretation. In *Cole v Whitfield* (1988), the Court legitimised greater use of the **Convention Debates** as an aid to interpretation. Those debates are to be used not as a direct guide to intended meaning itself, but rather as an indication of the nature of the problem the **framers** sought to address and of the solutions they had in mind; the line between permissible and impermissible use is, however, not easy to draw.

The circumstances in which the Court can refer to extrinsic materials in the interpretation of statutes are not unfettered. Recourse to extrinsic material under section 15AB is legitimate only if the relevant statutory provision is 'ambiguous or obscure' or the ordinary meaning conveyed by the text 'is manifestly absurd or is unreasonable'. The Court has tended to adopt a restrictive view of section 15AB, allowing only limited recourse to extrinsic materials under this provision. The leading judgment in *Re Bolton; Ex Parte Beane* (1987) states the limits on the use to which a Minister's second reading speech can be put:

> The words of a Minister must not be substituted for the text of the law... It is always possible that through oversight or inadvertence the clear intention of the Parliament fails to be translated into the text of the law. However unfortunate it may be when that happens, the task of the Court remains clear. The function of the Court is to give effect to the will of Parliament as expressed in the law.

If extrinsic material is not admissible under section 15AB, it might still be admissible at common law—as, for example, in *Newcastle City Council v GIO* (1997). The basis for admitting extrinsic materials at common law was explained in *CIC Insurance v Bankstown Football Club* (1997), where the Court observed that 'it is well settled that at common law, apart from any reliance on s 15AB of the *Acts Interpretation Act* 1901 (Cth), the court may have regard to reports of law reform bodies to ascertain the mischief which a statute is intended to cure'.

The main argument advanced in favour of using Hansard and committee reports is that when the text is ambiguous, use of such materials is likely to produce interpretations that are closer to the true intention of the legislature. However, at the same time, several criticisms have been made of the use of extrinsic materials. One argument is that reference to Hansard, committee reports, and the like can prolong a hearing; but on the restrictive view of section 15AB adopted in the High Court, this argument seems exaggerated. Because the Court has placed limitations on the use that can be made of Ministers' second reading speeches, **counsel** appearing in the High Court now refer to them much less frequently than in the first year of the Act. A second argument is that Hansard and other extrinsic materials such as committee reports are not as readily available as the statutes themselves; but again this seems overstated, and, in any event, may have more force in relation to lower courts than in relation to the High Court.

A third and more significant argument, as it goes to the heart of the concept of the meaning of a statute, is that speeches in parliament merely express the personal views of individual members and do not necessarily represent the collective view. **Mason** has expressed a similar concern about the Convention Debates: 'They rarely reveal the extent to which the expressed views of a speaker are shared by the other delegates.' While this argument has more force than the first two, it has to be seen in the context of the cautious view the High Court has adopted on the use of Hansard and similar materials.

There are no formal restrictions on the use of journal articles and textbooks in the High Court. In the past, there was a rule in England that a living author could not be cited, but this no longer applies and even casual inspection of the law reports suggests that the views of academic **commentators**, living and dead, are often cited. Indeed, the use of this material has increased over time (see **Citations by Court**), partly as a result of the increase in the number of **associates** and the degree of **research assistance**, enhancement of the Court's **library**, and the Court's relatively recent shift in **judicial style** to the use of footnotes.

Judicial views on the extent to which it is appropriate to use and cite academic authorities as an aid to interpretation in the High Court have been mixed. Several Justices have supported the use of academic authorities. For example, **Dixon** observed in an address he gave at Yale University in 1955 that 'textbooks and other works of authority' are important components 'of a definite system of accepted knowledge or thought' ('Concerning Judicial Method' (1956) 29 *ALJ* 468). **Barwick**, on the other hand, thought that 'to bolster the judge's conclusions by citation of the views of others, however eminent and authoritative, may reduce the authority of the judge and present him as a research student recording by citation his researched material' (*A Radical Tory* (1995)).

Academic views have also been mixed. Most academic comment critical of the use of journal articles and textbooks points to their indiscriminate use. In his tome on **evidence**, John Wigmore stated with irony: 'Almost any printed pages, bound in law-buckram and well advertised or gratuitously presented constitutes authority fit to guide the courts' (*Evidence* (3rd edn 1940)). No doubt the best view is that the weight given to journal articles and textbooks should depend on the reputation of the author and the standard of the scholarship in each case.

Generally, the focus is on material drawn directly from a context in legislative processes or legal discourse, and thus bearing in some direct way on the interpretation of the primary legal materials. Occasionally, however, Justices wishing to locate their analysis of a legal problem in its sociological or cultural context have drawn on a wider literature. For example, **Isaacs** in the *School Teachers Case* (1929) drew extensively on contemporary writings in **economics** for his understanding of the organisational structure of an industrial economy; **Jacobs** in *Russell v Russell* (1976) relied on Edward Westermarck's *History of Human Marriage* (3rd edn 1903) for a sociological approach to the **marriage** power; and **Murphy** on two occasions supplemented his judgments with a wide-ranging bibliography: in *Koowarta's Case* (1982), a list of 31 items on **discrimination** against **Aboriginal peoples**, and in *Church of the New Faith v Commissioner of Pay-roll Tax (Vic)* (1983), a list of 133 items on social, psychological, and other aspects of religion.

Russell Smyth

Further Reading

Attorney-General's Department, *Symposium on Statutory Interpretation* (1983)

Patrick Brazil, 'Legislative History and the Sure and True Interpretation of Statutes in General and Constitution in Particular' (1961) 4 *UQLJ* 1

Patrick Brazil, 'Reform of Statutory Interpretation: The Australian Experience of Use of Extrinsic Materials: With a Postscript on Simpler Drafting' (1988) 62 *ALJ* 503

Anthony Mason, 'Trends in Constitutional Interpretation' (1995) 18 *UNSWLJ* 237

Russell Smyth, 'Other than "Accepted Sources of Law"? A Quantitative Study of Secondary Source Citations in the High Court' (1999) 22 *UNSWLJ* 19

F

Fact finding is the principal occupation of most trial courts. In its appellate **jurisdiction**, with the rare exception of cases where fresh **evidence** is adduced, the High Court, like intermediate courts of appeal, does not itself find facts but rather tests whether the process of fact finding and legal reasoning in the reasons for judgment of the court below was affected by appealable error.

The concept of appellate review of facts was unknown at **common law**, where the resolution of disputed facts was, in virtually every case, the province of the jury. However, by a doctrine whose origins lie in the nineteenth-century Courts of Chancery (see **Equity**) and **Admiralty**, appellate courts considered themselves able to review findings of fact (see *State Rail Authority of NSW v Earthline Constructions* (1999)). Nevertheless, conscious of the advantages enjoyed at trial, especially when assessing the credibility of witnesses, appeal courts show great deference to the findings of fact at first instance (see *Abalos v Australian Postal Commission* (1990); *Devries v Australian National Railways Commission* (1993)). If a finding depends to any substantial degree on the credibility of a witness, the finding must stand on the appeal unless it can be shown that the advantages enjoyed by the judge at first instance have been 'palpably misused', or that the judge acted on evidence inconsistent with facts incontrovertibly established, or made findings that were 'glaringly improbable'. The High Court has criticised intermediate appellate courts that have not applied those principles (see, for example, *Boland v Yates Property Corporation* (1999)).

The Court is more directly confronted with the problem of fact finding in its original jurisdiction. The Court has an extensive original jurisdiction directly conferred upon it by section 75 of the Constitution—extending far beyond constitutional cases—and by Parliament pursuant to section 76 of the Constitution. For example, any suit between residents of different states, or between a citizen and the Commonwealth, may be commenced and heard in the High Court. In former days, the trial might be heard by a single Justice of the High Court, and many important decisions arose in that manner (see, for example, *Little v Commonwealth* (1947); *Suehle v Commonwealth* (1967)). *Little* remains a leading case on the liability of the Commonwealth for actions of its agents beyond authority. *Suehle*, although on the facts a simple case on whether an employer had breached its obligation to take reasonable care for the safety of its employee,

contained **Windeyer's** valuable contribution to the source of liability of the Commonwealth in **tort**—a matter not resolved until *Commonwealth v Mewett* (1997).

Mewett, too, was commenced in the High Court but was remitted to the **Federal Court**, thus illustrating what is nowadays the almost invariable fate of proceedings involving contested questions of fact that are commenced in the High Court's original jurisdiction (see **Remittal**). Now that the Federal Court has a very large federal jurisdiction (following the amendments to section 39B of the *Judiciary Act* 1903 (Cth) in 1983 and 1997), in almost every High Court case there will be another court having jurisdiction to determine the case, to which the matter will be remitted. Indeed, this was one of the reasons for creating the Federal Court. **Barwick**, as **Attorney-General** in 1964 and one of the proponents of a federal **superior court**, perceptively foresaw the need to free the High Court 'for the discharge of its fundamental duties as interpreter of the Constitution and as the national court of appeal untrammelled by some appellate and much original jurisdiction with which it need not be concerned'.

Formerly, the High Court also had original jurisdiction, pursuant to section 76 of the Constitution, to hear certain matters arising under Commonwealth laws; the two most important categories were intellectual property cases and certain **taxation** appeals. *Colbeam Palmer v Stock Affiliates* (1968), a **trade mark** action tried by Windeyer over five days, is a leading decision on the remedy of an account of profits that deals with several complex questions of accounting evidence. There are some hundreds of such cases reported in the *Commonwealth Law Reports*.

There remain two significant areas where the High Court constituted by a single Justice makes findings of fact. The first is its jurisdiction as the **Court of Disputed Returns** for Commonwealth elections under the *Commonwealth Electoral Act* 1918. The second arose by reason of amendments to the *Migration Act* 1958 (Cth) in 1995: the High Court now has sole jurisdiction to review **immigration** and refugee decisions for want of **natural justice**, ostensible bias, *Wednesbury* unreasonableness, and taking into account irrelevant considerations, or failing to take into account relevant considerations. In a majority judgment in *Abebe v Commonwealth* (1999), the Court upheld the legislation, which significantly restricted the scope of review of such decisions by the Federal Court. The entirely unsurprising consequence, predicted in *Abebe*, has been a very significant number of proceedings commenced in the High Court. As **Gleeson** and **McHugh** observed in *Abebe*: 'The effect on the **business** of this Court is certain to be serious.' In *Re Minister for Immigration; Ex parte Durairajasingham* (2000), McHugh again questioned the rationale for legislation that effectively requires the High Court—unlike any 'other constitutional or ultimate appellate court of any nation of which I am aware'—to perform of such trial work. Further interpretation in *Minister for Immigration v Yusuf* (2001) may afford some relief.

In other cases where facts need to be found, the High Court will remit all or part of the proceeding to an appropriate court to make findings of fact. Those findings bind the Court. For example, in *Mabo v Queensland* (1986), **Gibbs** remitted all issues of fact to the Supreme Court of Queensland. One reason Eddie Mabo was represented separately from the other plaintiffs when the legal issues were finally argued before the High Court in *Mabo* (1992) was that the Queensland Supreme Court judge to whom factual issues had been remitted had found that Mabo himself, contrary to his claims, was not a descendant of the traditional leaders of the Meriam people, was not adopted as heir by his (landowning) aunt and uncle, and generally was not a credible witness (see also *Mabo*: **counsel's perspective**).

In constitutional litigation, questions of constitutional fact arise—for example, whether a law is discriminatory against **interstate trade and commerce** in a protectionist sense, as forbidden by section 92 of the Constitution as construed in *Cole v Whitfield* (1988), or whether a law regulating **political communication** is reasonably appropriate and adapted to achieve an object compatible with the system of government prescribed by the Constitution (see *Lange v ABC* (1997)). The phrase 'constitutional facts' was defined by **Mason** and **Brennan** in *Richardson v Forestry Commission* (1988) to mean facts 'the existence of which is necessary in law to provide a constitutional basis for legislation'. Neither the Parliament nor the executive can deprive the High Court of its function of determining constitutional facts (**Communist Party Case** (1951); and compare the US notion of 'independent inquiry' in *Norris v Alabama* (1935)). Sometimes those facts can be agreed and presented to the Court by way of a stated case (see, for example, the economic facts in *Cole v Whitfield* and *Ha v NSW* (1997)). In other cases, and notwithstanding, as **Dixon** said in *Commonwealth Freighters v Sneddon* (1959), that it was 'highly inconvenient' for the Court to be engaged in making factual inquiries, there is no alternative when a criterion of validity is a particular fact. There remains considerable controversy as to how constitutional facts are to be proved in constitutional litigation, and it is generally agreed that the High Court has not clearly enunciated what is required (see also **Inter-State Commission**).

The phrase 'constitutional fact' was borrowed from the USA, where it appears first to have been used by the **United States Supreme Court** in *Jacobellis v Ohio* (1964), a case on the outer limits of the protection to free speech afforded by the First Amendment. Coincidentally, that decision is most commonly known for Justice Potter Stewart's frank confession of inability to elucidate the finding of fact relevant to the case. A criminal law can validly prohibit the publication of material that can be described as 'hardcore pornography'. But as to what was involved in making that finding of fact, Stewart could say only 'I know it when I see it'.

MARK LEEMING

Further Reading
Andrew Bell, 'Section 92, Factual Discrimination and the High Court' (1991) 20 *PLR* 240
Susan Kenny, 'Constitutional Fact Ascertainment' (1990) 1 *PLR* 134
Leslie Zines, *The High Court and the Constitution* (4th edn 1997) 471–82

Family law decisions in the High Court may reveal the Justices' attitudes to gender, marriage, and family. They have also provided a context for the development of principles relating to discretionary decision making. However, the Court's decisions reflect a certain remoteness from the everyday work of the Family Court.

The Commonwealth first exercised its **marriage and divorce powers** in 1959, though **Isaacs** had urged that legislation was needed as early as 1913 (*Fremlin v Fremlin*). Before 1959, the Court heard appeals on family law (particularly on the dissolution of marriage) from state and territory courts. Even before then, many cases related to the scope of the trial judge's discretion. In *Pearlow v Pearlow* (1953), a husband successfully appealed against a discretionary refusal to grant a dissolution under the *Matrimonial Causes and Personal Status Code 1948* (WA)—which, uniquely for Australia at the time, incorporated five years separation as a ground for divorce. The Court held that the trial judge had based his decision on irrelevant factors. While acknowledging that the Code conferred an 'absolute discretion', **Dixon** stressed that it was 'a judicial discretion' that depended 'upon considerations affecting the justice or injustice, the desirability or undesirability, the expediency or inexpediency, of maintaining the marriage union between the parties or in some other way relevant to the propriety of granting or withholding … the relief sought'.

In other states, divorce could be granted only on proof of fault, which was often narrowly defined. For example, in *Gough v Gough* (1956), the Court had to determine whether the ground that 'during one year' the husband had 'repeatedly assaulted and cruelly beaten' the wife had been established. The wife brought **evidence** of four assaults but, largely because only one involved substantial physical injury, the Court agreed with the trial judge that the grounds had not been established. There is evidence in this decision of a tendency to perceive the violence as a mode of conflict resolution, rather than as a common pattern of abuse involving the escalation of violence and the use of both physical and emotional violence to dominate and control. There is also evidence of a tendency to discount the significance of the violence. In one incident, the husband, while driving a car, had hit the wife 'three or four times across the face with the back of his left hand, telling her that he should drive her to the Gap but she was not worth hanging for'. Both the trial judge and **Webb** concluded that this did not constitute cruelty. None of the Justices recognised the intimidation involved in the words. At least the Court did not require evidence of recurrent violence throughout the whole year, although on the basis of different statutory wording a later Court did (*Tilney v Tilney* (1968)).

The standard of proof required for a finding of adultery was a troublesome issue. In *Briginshaw v Briginshaw* (1938), the Court required 'reasonable satisfaction' rather than 'satisfaction beyond reasonable doubt'. Dixon's insistence that 'reasonable satisfaction' must vary with 'the nature and consequence of the fact or facts to be proved'—with 'the seriousness of an allegation made, the inherent unlikelihood of an occurrence of a given description, or the gravity of the consequences flowing from a particular finding'—has often been quoted.

Briginshaw was affirmed in *Watts v Watts* (1953). The Court held that despite a 12-day trial, the wife's alleged adultery had not been proved on either standard, but that the trial judge had misdirected himself by requiring satisfaction 'beyond reasonable doubt'. The judge had applied a **House of Lords** decision (*Preston-Jones v Preston-Jones* (1950)) in preference to *Briginshaw*. **Kitto** and **Taylor** explained that in *Preston-Jones* a finding of adultery would have operated 'to bastardize the respondent's child', and that such a serious consequence demanded a very high standard of proof.

After 1959, the Matrimonial Causes Act was considered in a handful of appeals from state **Supreme Courts**. In *Cominos v Cominos* (1972), the respondent husband argued that the discretions conferred by the Act relating to maintenance, **property**, and **costs** were too widely expressed to fall within the concept of **judicial power**—the court could 'make such order as it thinks proper', having regard to 'all other relevant circumstances'. The argument was dismissed, but it resonates intriguingly in current debates about the desirability of discretion in contemporary Australian family law.

Repeatedly, since the Family Court was established, the High Court has demonstrated a willingness to overturn its decisions. Nevertheless, the appellate success rate should be kept in perspective. Appeals have been relatively few, and cases that pass through the net—including the restrictions imposed by the special **leave** procedure—tend to be exceptional. The litigation must usually be funded from the parties' own resources, and there are inherent difficulties in appealing discretionary decisions. Many controversial issues—including the relevance of the parties' conduct to property disputes, and the relevance of sexuality, violence, **race**, and culture to decisions concerning **children**—have never reached the High Court. Whole areas such as dissolution of marriage, nullity, and child and spousal support, have remained untouched by the Court since the enactment of the *Family Law Act* 1975 (Cth).

An early decision under the Family Law Act demonstrated the Court's willingness to overturn a Family Court attempt to make family law more workable. The extent to which Family Court decisions can bind parties outside the marriage is partly a constitutional question, but it also depends on the powers conferred by the Act. In *Ascot Investments v Harper* (1981), the majority (**Murphy** dissenting) reversed the Family Court's decision that in property proceedings between spouses it had power to bind a company that was not a party to the proceedings. Specifically, a family company could not be required to register a transfer of shares to secure a maintenance order in favour of the wife and children. (The husband had persistently failed to comply with the order and had been imprisoned for doing so.) The majority did, however, leave open the possibility that a third party could be bound if it were a 'mere puppet' or a 'sham' created by one of the spouses, and the Family Court has often used this to overcome the difficulties that *Harper* would otherwise pose. Reaffirmed in *R v Ross-Jones; Ex parte Green* (1984), *Harper* continues to limit the Family Court's power over third parties—adversely affecting **women** in particular, since they are more likely to be affected by denial of access to third-party resources.

Mallet v Mallet (1984) and *Norbis v Norbis* (1986) explored the roles of appellate courts and trial judges in discretionary decision making. The legislation gives the Family Court a very wide discretion to do what is 'just and equitable' in the division of matrimonial property having regard to the parties' contributions and other factors, including needs. The Full Court had developed a rule of thumb, widely used in practice, that, in a long marriage, equality was a useful starting point for determining the spouses' respective contributions. In *Mallet*, this approach was rejected.

Gibbs demonstrated some appreciation of the difficulties of working in a discretionary system. He found it understandable that practitioners advising clients might 'treat the remarks of the court in such cases as expressing binding principles', and even that judges 'seeking certainty, or consistency, should sometimes do so'. He insisted, however, that individual decisions can 'do no more than provide a guide; they cannot put fetters on the discretionary power which the Parliament has left largely unfettered'. He emphasised that the respective values of the parties' contributions must depend entirely on the facts of the case.

Mason, **Wilson**, and **Dawson** also condemned the idea of a 'starting point'. Because they did so in different language, the combined effect of their judgments had a certain lack of clarity about the differences between 'guidelines', 'rules', 'principles', 'starting points', and 'presumptions', and which of these (if any) could legitimately assist the exercise of judicial discretion. Only **Deane** was willing to accept the Family Court's conception of a starting point as being different from 'the enunciation … of a legal principle or presumption'. He found it permissible and desirable for Family Court judges to look to prior cases 'for assistance and guidance in determining what is just and appropriate in the differing circumstances of subsequent cases'; and that 'shared experience and accumulated expertise' should lead to 'generally accepted concepts of what is prima facie just and appropriate'.

The language used in *Mallet* has been criticised from the viewpoint of **feminism** as embodying assumptions that women and **men** do work, and should work, in separate spheres. (For Wilson, equality was an appropriate starting point only if 'the respective contributions of husband and wife, each judged by reference to their own sphere, are equal'.) The judgments have also been criticised as devaluing **women's work**. (Mason and Dawson suggested that equality of contribution might not be appropriate if the husband has conducted a business while the wife has assumed responsibilities in the home.) Yet the judgments did note that homemaking and parenting contributions must be recognised in a substantial, not a token way, and acknowledged the role of domestic labour in freeing the other party to earn income and acquire assets.

In *Norbis*, Mason and Deane acknowledged the difficulties of a discretionary system, and conceded that the **Full Court** could give guidance to avoid inconsistency and arbitrariness, though still allowing 'little or no scope' for binding rules. They added that though failure to apply a guideline would not of itself be an error, it might 'throw a question mark over the trial judge's decision and ease the appellant's burden of showing that it is wrong'. If this was a minor retreat from *Mallet*, Wilson and Dawson made no such retreat, continuing to emphasise the case-by-case approach.

The practical effect of these decisions is debatable. Practitioners still work with rules of thumb, which may differ between registries. Clearly, however, the decisions make it harder to challenge trial judges' decisions.

The appellate response to discretionary decisions has also been a principal focus in cases relating to children. In *Gronow v Gronow* (1979), the Court (Murphy dissenting on this point) reaffirmed the view that a trial judge's discretion should be overturned only if the discretion had been improperly exercised. That principle was referred to in *Mallet* and *Norbis*, and has since been reiterated (*CDJ v VAJ* (1998); *AMS v AIF* (1999)).

Under the Family Law Act, the paramount consideration in any decision affecting a child is the welfare (or, more recently, the best interests) of the child. Again, the Court has rejected rules of thumb in applying this test, although again not in very clear language. In *Gronow*, the Court rejected the 'mother principle' as a presumption in custody disputes. In Mason's and Wilson's words:

> The principle invoked by the respondent—that a young female child is best left in the custody of the mother—is not, and never has been, a rule of law. It is, or was, a canon of common sense founded on human experience. The weight … to be given to it has varied with the times and from case to case.

Where the language in *Mallet* embodies a 'story' that men and women work in separate spheres, *Gronow* can be criticised for presenting a different picture: one of shared parenting and housework that is not supported by empirical evidence.

In **Marion's Case** (1992), **Brennan** said the focus on the child's best interests does 'no more than identify the person whose interests are in question: it does not assist in identifying the factors which are relevant to the best interests of the child'. More recently, in *AMS v AIF*, **Kirby** and **Hayne** pointed out that the paramount consideration need not be the 'sole' consideration. Kirby observed that 'a statutory instruction to treat the welfare or best interests of the child as the paramount consideration does not oblige a court … to ignore the legitimate interests and desires of the parents'. Before this decision, Family Court judges had considered such factors only to the extent that they might affect the children's best interests (see, for example, *B and B* (1997)). In *A v A* (2000), however, the Full Court accepted *AMS v AIF* as authority for the proposition that, in relocation cases, the child's best interests are the paramount but not the sole consideration.

Most High Court appeals do not involve the actual application of the 'best interests' test or discussion of its detailed content. *Marion* is an exception. The Court held that the sterilisation of an intellectually handicapped girl could not be authorised by parental consent, but only by a court. Mason, Dawson, **Toohey**, and **Gaudron** stated that such a decision should be 'confined by the notion of "step of last resort"'. The decision is consistent with the feminist argument that the interests of individuals within a family may not necessarily best be determined within that family, while the careful limitations placed upon the sterilisation of girls show some movement towards a position consistent with women's rights to control their own fertility.

Both in *Marion's Case* and in *AMS v AIF*, the Court gave greater emphasis to human rights arguments than the Family Court had done. In *Marion*, Mason, Dawson, Toohey, and Gaudron asserted a 'fundamental right to personal inviolability existing in the **common law**'. They stressed, however, that the decision did not rest upon a right to reproduce, which they saw as problematic if it extended beyond a right to bodily integrity. These comments demonstrate some sensitivity to gender issues. In *AMS v AIF*, the Court upheld a mother's appeal against a restriction on her taking the child outside WA; the trial judge had erroneously required her to show 'compelling reasons' why continued residence in the Perth area would not better promote the child's welfare. **Gleeson**, **McHugh**, and **Gummow** stated that, when the matter was reheard, care should be taken to avoid any greater impediment on **freedom of movement** 'than that reasonably required to achieve the objects of the … legislation'. The decision may offer some gains for women, though rejecting a minority approach in the Supreme Court of Canada in *Gordon v Goertz* (1996), which would have created a presumption in favour of the residence parent in the absence of good reason to the contrary relevant to the best interests of the child.

Again, the judgments show some gender sensitivity. Kirby rejected an argument that the mother's movement had not been restricted by the order: 'As a matter of practicality, the only way the mother's freedom of movement could be fully restored would be by her surrendering the custody of the child … She had made it perfectly plain that she regarded this as an intolerable price.' However, none of the judgments conveys much appreciation of the contexts within which women may make relocation decisions, or of the effects that restrictions on relocation may have upon women.

Allegations of sexual abuse were considered in *M v M* (1988) and *B v B* (1988). In each case, the Court rejected an argument by the appellant father that a court must only consider the risk of possible future abuse if it has first made an affirmative finding that sexual abuse has occurred. The Court stated that custody or access should not be granted if it would pose an 'unacceptable risk of abuse' to the child. This is not a particularly helpful test, and the Family Court has continued to struggle with its application.

The relationship between the Family Law Act and state legislation has caused some problems. In *P v P* (1994), the Court found that provisions of the *Disability and Guardianship Act* 1987 (NSW) making sterilisation unlawful unless approved under that Act were **inconsistent** with the Family Law Act. More recent decisions, however, have tended to limit the powers of the Family Court. In *Northern Territory v GPAO* (1999), the Court held that the Family Court's powers of subpoena did not extend to relevant records of the territory's

Child and Protective Services unit, but were limited by provisions of the *Community Welfare Act* 1975 (NT) requiring persons acting under that legislation to preserve strict confidentiality 'except for the purposes of this Act'. The decision turned partly on the relationship between the 'best interests' principle, and procedural limitations under state or territory legislation. For the majority, the 'best interests' principle does not apply to preliminary evidentiary matters.

In *Re JJT; Ex parte Victoria Legal Aid* (1998), Family Court Justice John Faulks had ordered that Victoria Legal Aid provide the future costs of a child's separate representation, or provide such representation. The High Court majority held that he had no power to make such an order, although section 117(2) of the Family Law Act confers power to 'make such order as to costs … as the court considers just'.

In *CDJ v VAJ* (1999), the issue was whether common law restrictions on the admission of fresh evidence on appeal applied to the Full Family Court. In view of the discretionary appellate powers conferred on that Court by section 93A(2) of the Family Law Act, the High Court held that the common law restrictions do not apply. However, the power to admit further evidence on appeal was not unfettered: it should be exercised only if it was found that the additional evidence, if tendered at trial, would have been likely to produce a different result, and that the best interests of the children required a rehearing notwithstanding the stress, inconvenience, and uncertainty that it would cause. The Court recognised that the first of these requirements might be waived in exceptional cases (for example, cases involving allegations of abuse), where there is a real risk to the child's welfare if the trial judge's orders are allowed to stand. Because the Full Court had not followed this approach, the appeal was successful.

JULIET BEHRENS

Further Reading
John Dewar, 'Reducing Discretion in Family Law' (1997) 11 *AJFL* 309

Federal Court of Australia, created by the *Federal Court of Australia Act* 1976 (Cth), began to exercise its jurisdiction on 1 February 1977. It assumed a miscellany of statutory jurisdictions formerly exercised by the High Court, and the whole of the jurisdiction formerly exercised by the Australian Industrial Court and the Court of Bankruptcy. One of the principal reasons for setting up the Federal Court was the recognition that, with more and more matters arising under federal laws, the High Court could not act as a federal trial court and still have adequate time for **research** and reflection in important areas of its constitutional and appellate **jurisdiction** (*Re Minister for Immigration; Ex parte Durairajasingham* (2000); and see Commonwealth, *Parliamentary Debates*, House of Representatives, 21 October 1976, 2110–13). **Barwick**, who as **Attorney-General** had advocated the creation of a Federal Court, said in 1964 that his objective was to free the High Court for the discharge of its fundamental duties as interpreter of the Constitution and as the national court of appeal, untrammelled by some appellate and much original jurisdiction with which it need not be concerned (see also **Whitlam era**). This view prevailed against the fears of some that the creation of a federal court might introduce costly and unnecessary jurisdictional disputes of the kind that have marked the division between federal and state courts in the USA.

In addition to the other jurisdictions vested in the Federal Court by the Commonwealth legislature, the High Court has power under section 44 of the *Judiciary Act* 1903 (Cth) to **remit** certain matters commenced in its original jurisdiction to both state and federal courts (*State Bank of NSW v Commonwealth Savings Bank* (1984)). In 1983, the High Court was further empowered to remit to the Federal Court most claims for prerogative relief by way of prohibition or mandamus.

The Federal Court is a **superior court** of record and a court of law and **equity**. It sits in all capital cities and elsewhere in Australia from time to time. Its original jurisdiction is conferred by more than 120 statutes (see the Court's Annual Report 1998–99, Appendix 5). Its jurisdiction is broad and unlimited in amount. It covers almost all civil matters arising under Australian federal legislation and some summary criminal matters. Its jurisdiction, which is often exclusive (except for the High Court), embraces **Admiralty**; bankruptcy; **judicial review** of federal administrative action, including appeals from federal tribunals (see **Administrative law**); **copyright**, **patents and designs**, and **trade marks**; federal **labour relations**; **consumer law**; anti-competitive **trade practices**; human rights; **native title**; federal **taxation** appeals; and misleading or deceptive conduct in corporate trade or commerce.

The Federal Court also has jurisdiction with respect to associated matters (section 32 of the Federal Court of Australia Act) and an accrued jurisdiction in respect of an attached non-severable claim (*Stack v Coast Securities* (1983)). The former provision allows the Federal Court to decide federal matters related to a claim within its jurisdiction even though no express jurisdiction over those matters is conferred by the relevant statutes. The latter relates to matters arising under state jurisdiction or the **common law** that are not of themselves matters of federal jurisdiction, but are related to a Federal Court claim. As a result of the High Court's decision in *Re Wakim* (1999) on the **cross-vesting** scheme, the Federal Court lost a substantial part of its jurisdiction over **corporations law**, and must again deal with difficult issues of associated and accrued jurisdiction.

The Federal Court has a substantial and diverse appellate jurisdiction. It hears appeals from decisions of single judges of the Court and also exercises general appellate jurisdiction in **criminal law** and civil matters on appeal from the Supreme Court of the ACT and the Supreme Court of Norfolk Island.

Under section 33(2) of the Federal Court of Australia Act, no appeal lies to the High Court from a judgment of a single judge of the Court. But section 33(3) of the Act permits an appeal to the High Court from a judgment of the Full Court if the High Court grants special **leave to appeal**. The High Court has jurisdiction to grant the **writ** of prohibition against the Federal Court, whether or not there is a right to appeal to the High Court (*Adamson's Case* (1979)). The High Court has jurisdiction to grant certiorari (calling up the records of a lower court) directed to a judge of the Federal Court (*R v Gray; Ex parte Marsh* (1985); *Durairajasingham*).

In managing its litigation, the Federal Court has developed some innovative techniques, especially in the area of **expert evidence**. The Court is self-administered and autonomous. Part IIA of the Federal Court of Australia Act now makes provision for its management along lines similar to the *High Court of Australia Act* 1979 (Cth), with one exception: powers of **administration** are conferred upon the **Chief Justice** of the Federal Court, not the Justices as a whole. But in practice, there is little difference in the ways the two courts are administered: both have embraced the spirit of collegial governance.

The establishment of the Federal Court was not without controversy. As well as the fear, in some quarters, that there would be jurisdictional disputes, there was fear in some states about the Federal Court's impact on **state Supreme Courts**. However, as the first Chief Justice of the Federal Court, Nigel Bowen, said in 1985:

> The fact is that the Federal Court has slotted into the Australian legal system very smoothly. It has dealt with specialized federal areas of jurisdiction not previously dealt with by State courts. It has not to any appreciable extent taken work away from State courts. It has prevented them from being invested with a substantial body of new federal jurisdiction which would overload their already strained resources.

The Court's place in the Australian legal system has been reinforced by the appointment of a number of judges of the Federal Court to the High Court, namely **Brennan**, **Deane**, **Toohey**, and **Gummow**.

BRYAN BEAUMONT

Further Reading

Garfield Barwick, 'The Australian Judicial System: The Proposed New Federal Superior Court' (1964) 1 *FL Rev* 1
Bryan Beaumont, 'The Self-Administering Court: From Principles to Pragmatism' (1999) 9 *JJA* 61
Bryan Beaumont, 'Managing Litigation in the Federal Court' in Fiona Wheeler and Brian Opeskin (eds), *The Australian Federal Judicial System* (2000)

Federal Roads Case (1926). By the *Federal Aid Roads Act* 1926 (Cth), the Commonwealth government was authorised to make agreements with the states for the making and remaking of roads with Commonwealth financial support. A draft agreement annexed to the Act defined Federal Aid Roads as main roads which open up and develop new country; trunk roads between important towns; and arterial roads to carry traffic away from main or trunk roads. It envisaged an allocation to NSW of £5 520 000; to WA £3 840 000; Queensland £3 760 000; Victoria £3 600 000; SA £2 280 000; and Tasmania £1 000 000—a total of £20 million over ten years. Three-fifths of the allocation was by population, and two-fifths by area. The Act created a Federal Aid Roads Trust Account to which the allocated funds would be transferred from Consolidated Revenue.

Victoria and SA sued for declarations that the Act was invalid and an injunction to prevent any payments. In its written defence, the Commonwealth tried to bring the scheme within both the **defence power** and the **immigration power** by adducing facts 'arising out of and/or connected with the Great War and/or the defence and/or the need for the immigration into and settlement of the people of Great Britain [*sic*] in Australia'. But the Court held that no such argument was needed: the scheme had a sufficient foundation in section 96 of the Constitution ('the grants power'), which authorises financial assistance to the States 'on such terms and conditions as the Parliament thinks fit'.

The Court's judgment—perhaps its shortest ever, certainly in a significant constitutional case—read in its entirety as follows:

> PER CURIAM. The Court is of opinion that the *Federal Aid Roads Act* No 46 of 1926 is a valid enactment.
>
> It is plainly warranted by the provisions of sec 96 of the Constitution, and not affected by those of sec 99 or any other provisions of the Constitution, so that exposition is unnecessary.
>
> The action is dismissed.

Despite its brevity, this judgment was to be the foundation for a virtually unchallengeable series of **precedents**, notably the *Uniform Tax Cases* (1942 and 1957), establishing that the grants power has no effective constitutional limits, even when it allows the Commonwealth to assume effective policy control of matters such as roads, education, or hospitals for which it otherwise lacks constitutional power. In the *Federal Roads Case*, Robert **Menzies** (as **counsel** appearing for Victoria) tried to avoid that outcome by the technique of **characterisation** used in *R v Barger* (1908): since this was *really* a law about roads, it was not *really* a law about financial aid to the states. More convincingly, NSW (as **intervener**) argued that the grants power was limited to 'loans for temporary purposes'—relying on **Quick and Garran**, who noted that the 1899 Premiers' Conference had added section 96 to the Constitution to deal with 'exceptional circumstances … from time to time'. It was 'not intended to be used, and ought not to be used, except in cases of emergency'. But such arguments were simply brushed aside.

TONY BLACKSHIELD

Federalism, Court's conception of. Federalism as a system of government is generally thought to require a constitutional guarantee of the integrity and viability of each level of government. Cases concerning **Commonwealth–state relations** have been one of the High Court's most political areas of judgment, and its decisions have played a major part in shaping the institutions of national governance.

From the beginning, there has been a tension between attempts to use the law to establish clear boundaries between the powers of the Commonwealth and those of the states, and acceptance of the messier realities imposed by the Australian model of concurrent powers. How far should judicial decisions be shaped by an *a priori* model of federalism? And can governmental powers be defined without excessive judicial intrusion into the prerogatives of parliaments and executives, state and Commonwealth? The problem was posed bluntly by **Starke** in 1937 in *R v Poole; Ex parte Henry (No 2)* (1939). Insisting that Commonwealth power to regulate aviation 'must be construed liberally' rather than by 'inflexible and rigid adherence' to the exact wording of the relevant international Convention, he warned: 'No more impracticable tribunal can be imagined than a court of law for determining what regulations are desirable or necessary for carrying out an international air convention.'

The two decades after federation were dominated by doctrines of dual federalism. Drawing on American constitutional theory of the late nineteenth century, federalism was seen as a contract between equal, coordinate partners. The Constitution, in this view, had assigned to the Commonwealth and the states distinct powers and **intergovernmental immunities**. The duty of the High Court was to police the boundaries of their coordinate authority. Neither could tax or regulate the other, nor its employees, unless assigned an explicit power in the Constitution. Much of the intellectual energy of the **Griffith Court** was expended on locating, and defending, residual **reserved state powers**. This procedure was attacked acidly by **Isaacs** and **Higgins** as akin to identifying the residue of a deceased estate before assigning legatees their portions. The majority's reasoning set limits on Commonwealth powers, blocking attempts by the **Deakin** (Liberal) and Fisher (Labor) governments to extend federal industrial relations and economic regulation.

This first phase was not a simple defence of 'states' rights'—although that was one effect. Several of the key judgments restrained the states as well. The rule of *D'Emden v Pedder* (1904) held that 'when a State attempts to give its legislative or executive authority an operation which would fetter, control, or interfere with the free exercise of the legislative or executive power of the Commonwealth, the attempt, unless expressly authorised by the Constitution, is to that extent invalid and inoperative'. Nor was the Court's defence of federalism welcomed by its supposed beneficiaries. Several key judgments—including *D'Emden v Pedder*—were so administratively impracticable that the states and Commonwealth cooperated to avoid implementing them. The design of Australian federalism made the dualist model unworkable. Section 109 of the Constitution, which resolves **inconsistency** between Commonwealth and state laws, and the vagueness of **Commonwealth legislative powers** in section 51, made the task of defining the separate spheres of state and federal governments impossible.

Dual federalism began unravelling from the start. If the Court's majority remained unsympathetic to wider interpretations of the enumerated Commonwealth powers, it was more susceptible to indirect means of expanding central power. The *Surplus Revenue Case* (1908)—the key to establishing a national state—enabled Deakin to push ahead with his naval and pension plans. Similarly, during **World War I**, the Court adopted a very generous construction of the **defence power**. In *Farey v Burvett* (1916), the Court decided that the defence power gave the Commonwealth Parliament sweeping powers of economic regulation in wartime. When the Commonwealth curtailed the civil rights of enemy aliens, the Court gave it more power than had been sought. These defence power cases were more significant than their limited impact as legal precedents might indicate. It was far from inevitable, in the very limited mobilisation of World War I, that the Commonwealth would require a defence power beyond the ability to raise troops and conduct military operations.

The *Engineers Case* (1920) marked the end of dual federal doctrines. The Court overturned implied immunities and—more significantly, if only implicitly—abandoned the doctrine of reserved state powers. Decisions on the distribution of power between rival levels of government were to be decided by narrow principles of **statutory interpretation**, not by reference to *a priori* models of federalism. In practice, the Court accepted a more extensive use of concurrent powers, a cooperative federalism that cemented the role of the states as junior partners. In the *Federal Roads Case* (1926), the Commonwealth's use of section 96 to intrude into formerly exclusive state areas was accepted without argument. The **Latham Court** took this further, widening the regulatory powers of the national government over radio broadcasting (*R v Brislan; Ex parte Williams* (1935)).

The second great turning point in federal–state relations came with the first *Uniform Tax Case* (1942), which overshadowed *Engineers* in its practical consequences. Deciding the case in the darkest days of **World War II**, when the prospect of invasion by Japan still seemed possible, the Court allowed the Commonwealth's monopoly over the field of income **taxation**. In a narrow reading, the Court refused to look behind each of the four Acts establishing the new tax system to the clearly stated intentions of the legislation—blocking the states from access to a revenue source they had previously shared with the Commonwealth.

Uniform Tax had massive effects on the practice of Commonwealth–state relations, but it was not an opening to a wider revaluation of federalism. As though shocked by its implications, the Court spent the next decade cavilling at attempts to broaden Commonwealth powers. From the *First Pharmaceutical Benefits Case* (1945) to the *Bank Nationalisation Case* (1948), Commonwealth appropriation, spending, and regulatory powers were interpreted narrowly, constraining the Chifley Labor government's reconstruction program. Leslie Zines suggested in 1965 that **Dixon** had revived a federal theory based on implied immunities—the return of an implicit *a priori* theory of federalism. State and Commonwealth legislation could be upheld only after looking at its implications for federalism. Actions of the Commonwealth that substantially undermined the effective functioning of the states could violate this principle. The central government was also protected: indeed, in the *Cigamatic Case* (1962), the Court held that in some areas (obscurely defined in the judgments) the Commonwealth was altogether immune from state legislation. Dixon's judgment in the second *Uniform Tax Case* (1957) gave support to the view that had he been sitting on the Court in 1942, the first case would have gone differently. He accepted that the lapse of time and the manner in which uniform taxation had become 'a recognised part of the Australian fiscal system' obliged the Court to uphold a generous definition of section 96 that departed from what had evidently been envisaged by the **framers of the Constitution**.

From the late 1960s and into the 1980s, the Court's approach to federalism became more sympathetic to expanding national powers. In the *Payroll Tax Case* (1971), **Windeyer** waxed lyrical on the significance of the *Engineers Case* as reflecting 'a growing realisation that Australians were now one people and Australia one country and that national laws might meet national needs'. While the implications of the *AAP Case* (1975) were rather cloudy, it strengthened the view that additional powers derived simply from the 'character of the Commonwealth as a national government' (see **Nationhood power**). This national reading of federalism was clearer in the *Seas and Submerged Lands Case* (1975), upholding Commonwealth legislation to control offshore mineral resources. In a second line of cases from *Koowarta's Case* (1982) to the *Tasmanian Dam Case* (1983), national powers were enhanced through the use of the **external affairs power** to intervene in matters otherwise within state jurisdiction.

The 1990s marked a new approach to intergovernmental relations. Starting with the Hawke government's New Federalism, governments moved towards bargained consensus rather than litigation to demarcate their powers. Initial attempts to use administrative—rather than constitutional—criteria failed to achieve a tidy-minded elimination of overlapping powers. However, with the formation of the Council of Australian Governments (1992), conflicts were increasingly sorted out on an administrative level, or by joint legislation, in a new spirit of cooperation.

Ironically, after several 'black-letter' **appointments**, the Court was becoming more narrowly legalistic in its judgments. The result was open tension between the **legalism** of the Court and the new cooperative federalism. The Court now favoured a cleaner legal theory, leaning towards a clear demarcation of powers, drawing a firm line between the spheres of each level—just as public policy was heading in the opposite direction. If the rigidity of a narrow reading of the Constitution frustrated government, so be it.

By this time, the parlous position of state government finances was again at issue. The states and Commonwealth had long been unhappy with the broad definition the Court had given to **excise duties**, which, under section 90 of the Constitution, only the Commonwealth can impose. Consistently with the doctrine of reserved powers, the early High Court had taken a very narrow reading of 'excise'; but in a line of cases from *Parton v Milk Board* (1949) to *WA v Chamberlain Industries* (1970), the Court widened the meaning of the term. Denied access to the most lucrative growth taxes, the states used complicated and inefficient licensing schemes to get around the prohibition in section 90 (see also *Dennis Hotels v Victoria* (1960)). From the mid-1970s, the Court accepted this rather unsatisfactory compromise. But in *Ha v NSW* (1997), the Court extended its already wide reading of excise to prohibit state fees that it perceived as effectively imposing sales taxes.

In *Re Wakim* (1999), **Kirby** echoed the worries of Starke and Dixon over excessively detailed judicial intervention in the work of government—in this case, the **cross-vesting** scheme—suggesting that the Court hesitate in the face of the 'rare (if not unique) governmental and legislative unity' of the New Federalism. He was rebuffed by the majority. **McHugh** argued 'the judiciary has no power to amend or modernise the Constitution … That necessarily means that decisions, taken almost a century ago by people long dead, bind the people of Australia even in cases where most people agree that those decisions are out of touch with the present needs of Australian society'.

JAMES GILLESPIE

Further Reading
Gregory Craven, *Australian Federation: Towards the Second Century* (1992)
Brian Galligan, *A Federal Republic* (1995)
Geoffrey Sawer, *Australian Federalism in the Courts* (1967)

Federalism, impact of Court's decisions on. The federal balance in Australia bears little relationship to that which existed at the beginning of the twentieth century or which seemed to be envisaged by the **framers of the Constitution**. It was inevitable that the centralising ambitions of national politicians would test the extent of **Commonwealth legislative powers**. However, the initial High Court resisted most of their efforts. It was not until the *Engineers Case* (1920) that the Commonwealth's political and constitutional supremacy was made possible. That decision was later reinforced by others allowing the national government to determine, either directly or indirectly, the policies that states should adopt, even in fields clearly within the states' constitutional responsibility. Ultimately, the Commonwealth's dominance was established by a series of decisions that enhanced the **taxation** power of the Commonwealth at the expense of the states, and ensured that the states became largely dependent financially on the Commonwealth.

The Court has not given its approval to every attempt by the Commonwealth to increase its powers at the expense of the states. But to a large degree, the history of federalism in Australia is a record of the history of High Court decisions, either approving or disapproving particular legislative attempts by the Commonwealth to increase its powers. Most of those decisions have favoured the Commonwealth.

After the Court's **establishment** in 1903, it quickly developed two principles that it applied in determining the constitutional validity of Commonwealth and state laws. The first, the doctrine of implied immunity of instrumentalities, held that where two governments, federal and state, were operating in the same territory, each would normally be immune from the laws of the other (see **Intergovernmental immunities**). The doctrine first emerged in *D'Emden v Pedder* (1904), when the Court held that Tasmania could not levy a stamp duty on a Commonwealth official resident in Tasmania. The second was the doctrine of **reserved state powers**, which required the courts to give a narrow construction to any Commonwealth powers where to do otherwise would reduce the traditional governmental powers of the states. That reasoning was stated explicitly in *R v Barger* (1908). The majority (**Griffith**, **Barton**, and **O'Connor**—the first three Justices) said: 'The scheme of the Australian Constitution, like that of the United States of America, is to confer certain definite powers upon the Commonwealth, and to reserve to the states … all powers not expressly conferred upon the Commonwealth.' They added that in interpreting the Commonwealth's taxation power, 'it must be considered not only with reference to other separate and independent powers, such as the power to regulate external and **interstate trade and commerce**, but also with reference to the powers reserved to the States'. They said that the regulation of labour conditions was reserved to the states, and that therefore the taxation power could not be used to regulate domestic concerns of the states, which had been denied to the Commonwealth Parliament.

The doctrine of implied immunities involved a vision of federalism under which the Commonwealth and the states were separate and independent of each other; the doctrine of reserved state powers went further in protecting the states against the exercise of federal powers in relation to their domestic affairs.

Both doctrines were abandoned in the *Engineers Case*. In essence, the Court decided that the legislative powers of both the Commonwealth and the states should be interpreted to give them full effect. When they were in conflict, the issue would be settled by applying section 109 of the Constitution, which provides for the supremacy of Commonwealth law (see **Inconsistency**). The result was that the Commonwealth Parliament could pass laws without regard to whether its laws interfered with the powers of the states. The courts would give—and subsequently mostly have given—full effect to the list of Commonwealth powers stated in the Constitution. How those powers would be used was a political question, for determination by the Parliament, not a legal one for the courts. It was not the business of the High Court to try to balance the respective powers of the Commonwealth and the states—to impose its own vision of federalism and the federal balance. The Court has, however, subsequently added qualifications, including the important one that the Commonwealth's powers could not be used to destroy the basic governmental structures of the states (see *Melbourne Corporation Case* (1947)).

One consequence of the *Engineers Case* was that in the field of **conciliation and arbitration**, with which *Engineers* was directly concerned, there was at first a certain contraction and later a wholesale expansion of the Commonwealth's powers. Now the power extends to awards covering state public servants, school teachers, and even firemen, though each of these categories of workers was at one stage held to be outside the reach of the conciliation and arbitration power.

According to **Windeyer**, in his judgment in the *Payroll Tax Case* (1971), where the Court allowed the Commonwealth to impose payroll taxes on all employers including state governments, the effect of *Engineers* was to divert 'the flow of **constitutional law** into new channels … In 1920 the Constitution was read in a new light, a light reflected from events that had, over 20 years, led to a growing realisation that Australians were now one people and Australia one country and that national laws might meet national needs' (see also **Nationhood**).

The result of *Engineers* was felt particularly in the last quarter of the twentieth century, when the Parliament used the **corporations power** to control aspects of the national **economy**, although in 1990, in the *Incorporation Case*, the Court rejected Parliament's attempt to enact a single national **corporations law**, on the ground that it did not have the power to control the incorporation of companies. That decision provoked a complex Commonwealth–state cooperative scheme that has been replicated in many other areas where the Commonwealth has been held to lack the power to act unilaterally—indicating that even the Court's negative decisions have also had an impact on the practical operation of the federation, and on the shape and structure of the political arrangements devised to make it work (see also **Commonwealth–state relations**).

The effect of *Engineers* was also felt in relation to the Court's decisions on the **external affairs power** that allowed the Commonwealth Parliament to make laws about any matters covered by international treaties. Perhaps the most significant expansion of power was attributable to the Court's decisions (initially by a 4:3 majority) to allow the Commonwealth to use the external affairs power to override state laws in the field of human rights and **property** rights and then of the **environment** (*Koowarta's Case* (1982) and the *Tasmanian Dam Case* (1983)).

In 1902, **Attorney-General** Alfred **Deakin** wrote in a remarkably prescient, anonymous piece of journalism for the London *Morning Post* that the 'independence of our States is doomed' and that the Constitution had left the states 'legally free, but financially bound to the chariot wheels of the central government'. The first indication of the Commonwealth's financial strength came in 1908, when the government, of which Deakin was by then **Prime Minister**, found a way around a constitutional provision requiring the Commonwealth to pay at least three-quarters of its net revenue from customs and **excise duties** to the states, until the Parliament determined otherwise. Deakin's government—mindful of the future costs of a new pension scheme and a new Australian navy—appropriated surplus revenue into trust funds. The Court held that this siphoning off of surplus revenue was valid. Griffith said 'if a sum of money is lawfully appropriated out of the Consolidated Revenue for a specific purpose, that sum cannot be regarded as forming part of a surplus until the expenditure of it is no longer lawful or no longer thought necessary by the Government' (*NSW v Commonwealth* (1908)).

The next step in binding the states to the purposes of the Commonwealth came in 1926. In a judgment only three sentences long, the Court rejected a challenge to Commonwealth legislation making grants to the states for road construction purposes. The law was held to be valid as an exercise of the Commonwealth's power under section 96 of the Constitution to 'grant financial assistance to any state on such terms and conditions as the Parliament thinks fit'. The Court rejected an argument that the law was a law relating to road making in the states, and hence outside Commonwealth power (see *Federal Roads Case* (1926); **Menzies, Robert Gordon**).

The next crucial step came in 1942, at the height of **World War II**, when the Commonwealth decided to increase its own income taxes and force the states out of that field of taxation. It passed four laws, together constituting what was acknowledged to be a scheme to eliminate state income taxes. One law provided for grants to the states each financial year under section 96, approximately equal to the taxes they were then collecting, but subject to their not collecting their own taxes on income. The second provided for a complete takeover of all the state tax-collecting offices. The third gave the Commonwealth priority in the collection of tax. The fourth imposed very high rates of taxation. By a majority, the Court held that all four Acts were valid. Only one Justice did so by relying on the **defence power** (see *Uniform Tax Cases* (1942 and 1957)).

Despite a significant political campaign by the Opposition and by the states, the uniform tax system remained in place after the war. Eventually, NSW and Victoria challenged the scheme, but the Court decided that the scheme had achieved its permanent character in 1946, and that the Court should not reconsider its approval.

The states sought in vain to find other growth taxes that would allow them to fund their ordinary budget programs without reliance on special grants made by the Commonwealth to the states for specific purposes in fields such as education, health, and infrastructure development. Not even the so-called tax reimbursement grants (grants made in lieu of the income taxes the states had forfeited) were sufficient to fund normal state expenditures. Gradually, the Commonwealth came to dictate the way the state universities would be run and the policies that the states had to adopt in return for Commonwealth grants in a host of other areas where the Commonwealth did not have any direct constitutional responsibility.

The states experimented with the introduction of other taxes, but most were invalidated by the Court on the ground that they were excise duties. Section 90 gives the Commonwealth the 'exclusive' power to impose customs and excise duties. In 1960, the Court approved a device to allow the states to collect taxes on alcohol by means of licensing fees based on past sales (see *Dennis Hotels v Victoria* (1960)). But the licensing fees, later extended by analogy to tobacco and petrol, grew to such a point that the Court finally determined that they should be characterised as taxes rather than licence fees, and in *Ha v NSW* (1997) the Court, by a 4:3 majority, ruled that they were excises and therefore could not be imposed by the states. The 1990s marked an important philosophical change in the Court, culminating with the *Ha* decision—though that result had been foreshadowed in *Capital Duplicators v ACT (No 2)* when **Mason, Brennan, Deane**, and **McHugh** said that sections 90 and 92 of the Constitution 'taken together with the safeguards against Commonwealth **discrimination** in section 51(ii) and (iii) and section 88, created a Commonwealth economic union, not an association of states, each with its own separate economy'. The minority in *Ha* denied this proposition, saying that the union that was meant to be achieved was a customs union— 'not an economic union if what is meant by that term is a single economy'.

While state revenues may become healthier following the introduction of the goods and services tax, that tax is a federal tax, and its reach and extent is determined by the Commonwealth. The states remain more firmly tied than ever before to Deakin's chariot wheel.

DAVID SOLOMON

Further Reading
Michael Coper, 'The Role of the Courts in the Preservation of Federalism' (1989) 63 *ALJ* 463
David Solomon, *The Political High Court* (1999)

Feminism incorporates a range of positions that evince a concern with the omission of the perspectives and experiences of **women** from the construction of knowledge. Inspired by an inclusive social vision, legal feminism has been critical of the way assumptions about law from a masculinist perspective, presented as universal truths, have sys-

tematically impeded equal representation of women in legal and political processes; appreciation of women's differences from **men** and from each other; and full recognition of those differences in law. Feminist critiques have been directed to the sex of the agents of legality, the underlying philosophy of adjudication, and the nature of law itself, as well as to the injustices arising within substantive areas of law.

For most of its history, the High Court has been an unrelievedly masculinist institution in which all the *dramatis personae* have been male. Women rarely appeared as **counsel** (see **Women practitioners**), they were unwelcome as **associates**, and, until the **appointment** of Gaudron in 1987, no woman had ever been appointed as a Justice. In view of their domination of the public sphere generally, it is perhaps unsurprising that most **litigants** have been men, or male-dominated corporations. Even when women have been parties to proceedings, the Court has found it difficult to modify legal principles to account for the distinctive experiences of women, or has simply confirmed sexist **stereotypes**. The conjunction of numbers and social power has enabled masculine interests to shape the jurisprudence of the Court. Mainstream scholarship has also remained resistant to feminist critiques of this tilted world, presumably because most constitutional and legal theorists have also been men, or adherents of a masculinist world view.

A persistent factor identified by some feminists as contributing to the suppression or elision of the specificity of women's experiences has been the dichotomy between the public and the private spheres associated with **liberalism**. One of the tenets of liberalism is the notion of **equality** for all in the public sphere. Yet the very emphasis on the public sphere has meant that the notion of equality has systematically been distorted, since that emphasis has consistently ignored the significant responsibilities in the private sphere undertaken by many women. Indeed, the freedom of men to participate in public life, civil society, and the workplace has been predicated on women taking primary responsibility for households, **children**, the elderly, and the infirm. When women themselves have sought to enter the public sphere, they have rarely been supported in the performance of these tasks. For example, in *Lodge v FCT* (1972), the Court disallowed the cost of childcare as a legitimate work-related expense for taxation purposes. Even though the expenditure was necessary for the purpose of gaining assessable income, **Mason** deemed it to be of a 'private or domestic' nature. This ruling has continued to be upheld (see, for example, the **Federal Court** decision in *Jayatilake v FCT* (1991)).

Property rights grounded in non-monetary contributions by women represent a provocative example of different treatment under both legal and equitable principles. **Murphy** led the way in acknowledging the economic value of **women's work** in the home in *Sharman v Evans* (1977). This principle had been built into the *Family Law Act* 1975 (Cth) as a basis for effecting an equitable property settlement on dissolution of **marriage**, but the Justices have generally been hesitant about accepting its full implications (*Mallet v Mallet* (1984)). Murphy, however, was prepared to extend the principle to women living in de facto relationships (*Calverley v Green* (1984)). In other contexts, the Court has been more willing to give a monetary value to what has traditionally been women's work, and unpaid (see *Griffiths v Kerkemeyer* (1977)).

Concerned primarily with the allocation of public powers within a federation, the Constitution appears to be a gender-neutral document, but this appearance obscures the masculinist partiality that subtly informs the adjudication of constitutional cases. The very preoccupation with government power rather than citizens' rights is an example. The absence of a **Bill of Rights** has inhibited the legal scrutiny of gender issues. Guarantees of individual rights of the kind found in the US Constitution—such as those relating to equality—have provided scope for the **United States Supreme Court** to address contemporary issues that impact more directly on the lives of women. The erasure of difference is less easily effected if it represents the precise focus of a constitutional issue.

The conventional approach to constitutional cases in Australia has involved a narrow and technical focus on precise issues of constitutional doctrine regardless of their wider social context. For example, in *Ansett Transport Industries v Wardley* (1980), only **Stephen** acknowledged sex **discrimination** as a 'social evil'; the rest of the Bench focused solely on whether there was a formal **inconsistency** between Commonwealth and state laws. The pros and cons of whether women should become airline pilots, and the social significance of the exclusion of all women of child-bearing age from a specific sector of the workforce, were not perceived as relevant issues. The vital issue of the intersection between ethnicity and gender in discrimination cases was similarly ignored in *Dao v Australian Postal Commission* (1987); that case was also disposed of simply on the basis of inconsistency of laws.

The **implied constitutional rights** approach has sought to overcome perceived limitations of the Constitution arising from the absence of express guarantees. In *Leeth v Commonwealth* (1992), **Deane** and **Toohey** were prepared to read an (inchoate) equality guarantee into the Constitution, but the approach has not won favour with the Court as a whole (see *Kruger v Commonwealth* (1997)).

Given the vagaries of judicial interpretation, it does not follow that substantive equality for women would flow from the inclusion of an equality guarantee, either express or implied. Some Justices might opt for a narrow procedural interpretation in accordance with the universal prescript of equality before the law, as **Wilson** did in *Mabo (No 1)* (1988), when he argued that the extinguishment of **native title** rights would remedy an inequality between indigenous and non-indigenous peoples. As Deane and Toohey recognised in *Leeth*: 'In some circumstances theoretical equality under the law sustains rather than alleviates the practical reality of social and economic inequality.'

The High Court's general appellate **jurisdiction** has afforded it some opportunity for responding to feminist criticisms of exclusion. However, the mode of adjudication favouring **form** over substance has meant that substantive factors tend to be sloughed off, as in constitutional cases. In *Australian Iron & Steel v Banovic* (1989), the Court had to confront the meaning of indirect discrimination on the ground of sex, which involved an intricate test of sex-based proportionality under the *Sex Discrimination Act* 1984 (Cth). As with *Wardley*, the problem of systemic discrimination against women in non-traditional areas of employment was given little consideration.

The dominant discourse of the Anglo–Australian legal tradition has fostered the belief that disputes between individuals should be resolved objectively and at a high level of abstraction, transcending or suppressing the specificity of the individual case and the particular and subjective interests of the individuals involved. The result is that the identifying characteristics of the individual, including sex, **race**, sexuality, able-bodiedness, class, and so on, are relegated to the background or disappear altogether. The suppression of these characteristics, and the drive to make legal propositions universal and objective, produces the construct of a supposedly neutral legal subject. Yet a feminist critique of that construct reveals that *he* is likely to be modelled on an Anglo-Celtic, heterosexual, able-bodied, middle-class man—what Ngaire Naffine refers to as 'the man of law'. While the erasure of difference appears to be fair on its face because it suggests that everyone is treated the same, equal treatment ignores the disproportionate impact of treating the same those who are in fact differently situated from the normative legal subject.

Judicial responses to legislative expressions of a feminist consciousness have been reluctant. The amendments in 1976 and 1985 to the *Evidence Act* 1906 (WA) were typical of the 'rape shield' laws of the 1970s and 1980s. But in *Longman v The Queen* (1989), the new section 36BE (excluding the need for trial judges to warn juries against reliance on uncorroborated accusations of sexual assault) was unanimously read down because it could not have been intended to 'sterilise the trial judge's ability to secure a fair trial'; and in *Bull v The Queen* (2000), by two entirely different processes of reasoning, the new section 36BA (excluding '**evidence** relating to the disposition of the complainant in sexual matters') was read down to permit such evidence if it would have been admissible at **common law**.

Glimpses of a feminist consciousness in the work of the Court itself have been few and far between. Apart from Isaacs' dissent in *Wright v Cedzich* (1930), where the majority reaffirmed that **tort** actions for loss of consortium of a spouse can be brought by husbands but not by wives, they became significant only in the late 1970s—particularly in Murphy's judgments. Even then, the influence of feminist critiques of law has not been deployed solely to acknowledge the experiences and entitlements of women, and at times has even operated adversely to such an acknowledgment. Feminist advocacy of less-abstract principles and greater recognition of specificity in the law was to some extent accepted by the majority in *Moffa v The Queen* (1977). Yet the result in that case—and in subsequent cases regarding provocation as a **criminal defence**—may have been unsettling for feminists. Michele Moffa, an Italian immigrant, had killed his Australian wife, and was convicted of murder. On appeal, a majority of the Court substituted a verdict of manslaughter for the verdict of murder, accepting the accused's claim that he had been provoked by his wife's admissions of adultery. The case is significant for two reasons: it extended the defence of provocation to the utterance of words; and Murphy (and to a lesser extent **Barwick**) sought to modify the objective test of what would provoke a 'reasonable man' by allowing for the subjective reactions and cultural background of the accused. Murphy's view was that the 'reasonable man' had 'no place in a rational jurisprudence'. Thus the case paved the way for an appreciation of the subjectivity of the accused, and signalled a move to a more inclusive use of language. Yet later references to the 'reasonable person' or 'ordinary person' have still turned out too often to be a proxy for the reasonable or ordinary *man*.

In any event, whether subtly gendered or not, the model referred to by gender-neutral expressions such as 'reasonable person' cannot escape the tendency to rely on abstract legal constructs. Indeed, later cases such as *Stingel v The Queen* (1990) and *Masciantonio v The Queen* (1995) have shown that the attempt to incorporate subjective elements into an objective model leads to irresolvable contradictions. Other contradictions abound. The claims to provocation by men in cases such as *Moffa* or the Victorian case of *R v Dincer* (1982) are more readily accepted by judges than the analogous claims by abused women who kill their violent partners, despite the fact that the former claims are uncorroborated and the latter are corroborated by medical evidence concerning the 'battered woman syndrome'. Yet that concept remains contentious among feminist scholars themselves, since it suggests that women's reactions have been pathologised, while those of men have not. Women's experience is still perceived as deviant from the norm. The contradictions remain unresolved. Although in the particular circumstances of *Osland v The Queen* (1998) the Court rejected a defence of provocation based on the battered woman syndrome, Gaudron, **Gummow**, and **Kirby** at least signified a willingness to address some of the feminist literature.

The meaning of autonomous subjecthood for women living in intimate heterosexual relations remains contradictory. On one hand, the free will of a wife to consent to marital **sex** has been finally recognised in the abolition of the immunity for husbands accused of rape (*R v L* (1991)). On the other hand, a married woman may be deemed to be in need of special protection in financial dealings—which suggests that her autonomy remains less than that of her husband. 'Sexually transmitted debt', in which a guarantee may be repudiated if a woman had been pressured by her partner to sign, is illustrative (*Garcia v National Australia Bank* (1998), following the pre-war decision of *Yerkey v Jones* (1939)). While ostensibly well-intentioned, the residual paternalism of this manifestation of **equity** is anachronistic, and significantly detracts from the Court's prevailing rhetoric of equality between the sexes.

The High Court's tentative acknowledgment of feminist critiques of law is a *fin de siècle* phenomenon in which the views of the Justices tend either to ignore gender issues or, in a somewhat reductive and over-inclusive way, to treat women as a homogeneous and slightly inferior class. Addressing the differences *between* women is a more challenging project on which the Court has not yet ventured. The concern is that the swing back to conservatism in the **ideology** of the Court may result in a resiling from the modest gains made to date.

Margaret Thornton

Further Reading
Ngaire Naffine, *Law and the Sexes* (1990)

Margaret Thornton (ed), *Public and Private* (1995)
Margaret Thornton, 'The Development of Feminist Jurisprudence' (1998) 9 *Legal Education Review* 171

Fiduciary obligations. The decisions of the High Court where issues of fiduciary duty have arisen—including the scope of **remedies** available where such a duty has been breached—reveal an insistence upon precision in this area of the law.

In large part, these decisions emphasise the distinction between fiduciary obligations and other relationships that may give rise to actions in **contract** or in **tort**. A person in a fiduciary relationship may well be liable in such an action—but for the reason that there has been a breach of a contractual obligation or a duty of care, not because the parties stand in that relationship.

In these respects, the Court aligns itself more closely with the English courts than with the courts of Canada and of the USA. Indeed, in *Breen v Williams* (1996), **Gaudron** and **McHugh** said the Canadian cases reveal 'a tendency to view fiduciary obligations as both proscriptive and prescriptive', while 'Australian courts only recognise proscriptive fiduciary duties'. The distinction is between a positive obligation to act in the best interests of another and an obligation to avoid a conflict between one's duty and personal interest. The distinction is perhaps most apparent in *Breen v Williams*, where the Court rejected a claim that the relationship of doctor and patient gave rise to a fiduciary obligation on the part of the doctor to make available to the patient a copy of all medical records (see also *Birtchnell v Equity Trustees, Executors & Agency Co* (1929); *Consul Development v DPC Estates* (1975); *Chan v Zacharia* (1984)).

The Court has been at pains to keep open the categories from which a fiduciary relationship may be inferred, but at the same time to emphasise the factual inquiry needed in order to draw that inference (see *Birtchnell*; *Jenyns v Public Curator* (1953)). This is well illustrated by two decisions delivered within 12 months of each other. In *Hospital Products v US Surgical Corporation* (1984), the Court held, by majority, that there was no fiduciary relationship between the parties to an exclusive distribution agreement for the sale of surgical stapling products. In *United Dominions Corporation v Brian* (1985), the Court held unanimously that such a relationship existed between joint venturers in land development.

In both cases, the Court was careful to leave the category of fiduciary relationships open. Differences in the characterisation of the relationships between the parties in the two cases led to different results. In *Hospital Products*, a majority found that the arrangement between the parties was purely commercial: they had dealt with each other at arm's length and on an equal footing, and were each directed at making their own profit. The Court has consistently held that no fiduciary duty arises in these circumstances: see *Jones v Bouffier* (1911); *Dowsett v Reid* (1912); *Para Wirra Gold & Bismuth Mining Syndicate No Liability v Mather* (1934); *Keith Henry & Co v Stuart Walker & Co* (1958). By contrast, the Court in *United Dominions*, in discussing the factual circumstances in that case, found that the parties were negotiating partners in a joint venture—a characterisation it held to be conducive to a finding of a fiduciary relationship between them. **Mason**, **Brennan**, and **Deane**, in a **joint judgment**, applied **Dixon's** judgment in *Birtchnell*, where he had found the participants in each of the then-proposed joint ventures were 'associated for … a common end', and the relationship between them was 'based … upon a mutual confidence' that they would 'engage in the particular … activity or transaction for the joint advantage only'.

In those cases where the plaintiff has sought to establish a breach of fiduciary obligation, the intention has usually been to obtain some form of **restitution**, whether by way of a declaration of constructive **trust** or otherwise, and thus to secure an advantage over unsecured creditors. The current limits on obtaining that kind of advantage in other causes of action inevitably increase the likelihood of plaintiffs arguing that a fiduciary relationship exists. A narrowing of those limits might well shift the focus to some extent; but as things stand, the Court has drawn a discernible line between breach of fiduciary obligation and other causes of action.

Any emphasis on restitution as the relief available for a breach of such an obligation must recognise the conditions the Court may attach to granting relief of that kind. This is shown by the decision in *Maguire v Makaronis* (1997). The plaintiffs were husband and wife; the defendants were their solicitors in the execution of a mortgage to secure bridging finance. The mortgage was in favour of the defendants, who did not draw their clients' attention to that fact or tell them that they should obtain independent legal advice. On default, the defendants claimed possession of the mortgaged property and the plaintiffs sought by counterclaim a declaration that the mortgage was void. The Court held that the mortgage was liable to be set aside as a result of the defendants' breach of fiduciary duty in entering into the mortgage in the absence of the informed consent of their clients, but that the mortgage could only be set aside if relief were conditional upon repayment by the plaintiffs of principal and interest. The basis of the decision was that the equity of the plaintiffs to have the whole transaction rescinded and the parties remitted to their original position could not be achieved without conditioning relief; otherwise, the plaintiffs would be left with the fruits of the transaction of which they complained.

This approach echoed what the Court had said earlier in *Warman International v Dwyer* (1995), when it observed that the stringent rule requiring a fiduciary to account for profits could be carried to extremes, and that, in cases outside the realm of specific assets, liability of the fiduciary should not be transformed into a vehicle for the unjust enrichment of the plaintiff.

The full scope of fiduciary relationships and obligations remains to be further explored. In particular, the Court has not been required to consider, to any extent, the position of the Crown as a fiduciary.

The Court's recognition of **native title** in *Mabo* (1992) carried with it acceptance of the power of the Crown to extinguish that title, whether by alienation of the land or otherwise. The plaintiffs in that case had argued that if they failed to establish native title, Queensland was 'under a fiduciary duty' to protect their rights and interests in the Murray Islands. Because the plaintiffs succeeded in establishing title, the Court did not have to rule on that claim. However, **Brennan**—with whom **Mason** and McHugh agreed—suggested that if native

title were surrendered to the Crown in expectation of a grant of a tenure to the indigenous title holders, there may be a fiduciary duty on the Crown to grant a tenure to meet that expectation. **Toohey** held that the vulnerability of native title gave rise to a fiduciary obligation on the part of the Crown.

The plaintiffs in *Wik* (1996) had also made a claim of breach of fiduciary duty owed to them by Queensland, but on this occasion it was unanimously rejected by the Court. The breach, it was argued, was authorised by statutory enactments by Queensland that had caused the plaintiffs to lose rights they might otherwise still enjoy. As **Kirby** reasoned, however, 'the fact that other persons (such as the Wik) may thereby have lost rights previously belonging to them is simply the result of the operation of legislation, the constitutional validity of which is not impugned'. Thus, although the assertion of a fiduciary duty was defeated by the statutes, the question of whether such a duty might exist in the absence of statute was left unresolved.

The question whether the Crown owed a fiduciary duty to **Aboriginal** children in the Northern Territory who had been placed in institutions did not arise directly in *Kruger v Commonwealth* (1997) because it was the validity of an Ordinance that was at issue. However, proceedings have been taken against the Crown in other courts by those who were removed from their homes as children: see *Cubillo v Commonwealth* (2000); *Williams v The Minister* (2000). Clearly, the role of the Crown as a fiduciary will require the attention of the Court at some time.

JOHN TOOHEY

Further Reading
Paul Finn, *Fiduciary Obligations* (1977)
Patrick Parkinson, 'Fiduciary Law and Access to Medical Records' (1995) 17 *Syd LR* 433
David Tan, 'The Fiduciary as an Accordion Term: Can the Crown Play a Different Tune?' (1995) 69 *ALJ* 440

Foreign precedents. The High Court regularly cites cases from England, the USA, Canada and NZ, and occasionally from other **common law** countries. The Court rarely cites cases from non-common law countries. It is not bound to follow foreign cases as **precedent**, but uses them as aids to formulating questions and legal issues, proposing solutions to those issues, and testing and justifying or rejecting the proposed solutions.

Until the last remaining appeals to the Judicial Committee of the **Privy Council** were abolished in 1986, that body was at the pinnacle of the Australian court **hierarchy** and, as such, could not properly be regarded as a foreign court. It was also at the pinnacle of the judicial system of most other dominions and colonies within the British Commonwealth of Nations, and in relation to cases from these other dominions and colonies, it could have been seen, in Australia, as a foreign court. However, until *Viro v The Queen* (1978), the High Court regarded Privy Council decisions relating to other dominions and colonies as binding on it to the extent that they were applicable. Reflecting notions of a unified common law and the indivisibility of the Crown, the Privy Council was regarded as the ultimate arbiter for the common law of the Commonwealth of Nations.

Notwithstanding that there was no appeal from English courts to the Privy Council, in *Brown v Holloway* (1909), **O'Connor** noted that judgments of the **House of Lords** were regarded 'in judicial courtesy' as binding on the High Court, as it was 'the tribunal of highest authority in the British Empire'. Decisions of the English Court of Appeal were also highly regarded, and would usually be followed.

In *Davison v Vickery's Motors* (1925), **Isaacs** considered courts within the British Empire as sister courts, within a single common law system, whose judgments were to be highly regarded and usually followed. Decisions of Canadian and NZ **superior courts** were, for the High Court, of similar status to decisions of the Australian **state Supreme Courts**, from which appeals could be taken directly to the Privy Council. In this sense, they were not regarded as 'foreign'— but neither were they binding.

As the British Empire developed into the Commonwealth of Nations and various colonies gained their independence, the doctrines of a unified common law and the indivisibility of the Crown became less important and began to disappear. There was no longer any need to promote consistency between the common law of the various dominions, and the High Court felt freer to develop a common law more appropriate for Australia.

Until 1920, the High Court cited American cases extensively in **constitutional law** matters. The Australian Constitution was modelled to a greater extent on the US Constitution than on the *British North America Act* 1867 (UK), which federated the Canadian Provinces, so it was natural to look to US precedents to assist the Court in interpreting the Australian Constitution. American cases frequently cited with approval included *Marbury v Madison* (1803), concerning **judicial review** of legislation; *McCulloch v Maryland* (1819), concerning **intergovernmental immunities**; and *Gibbons v Ogden* (1824), concerning **interstate trade and commerce**.

In the *Engineers Case* (1920), the Court overturned the doctrine of **intergovernmental immunities**, which it had borrowed from US cases such as *McCulloch v Maryland*, and adopted **literalism** as the proper approach to **constitutional interpretation**. The majority said, 'American authorities … are not a secure basis on which to build fundamentally with respect to our own Constitution [but] on secondary matters they may … afford considerable light and assistance'. By adopting literalism (an approach developed later by **Dixon** as 'strict **legalism**'), the Court limited the extent to which implications could be drawn from the Constitution. These factors significantly limited the extent to which US cases were cited to and by the Court for the next 60 years; they were occasionally used for comparative purposes in **tort law** and **immigration law** matters, and sometimes in constitutional law matters, but they were not often followed. Of the total number of citations of US cases by the Court before 1980, about 35 per cent occurred before 1920. While the table that follows indicates that the number of cases in which the High Court cited US precedents did not significantly reduce after 1920, there was, however, a significant reduction in the extent of the reliance on and citation of US cases by the Court in those cases.

In the 1980s and 1990s, the High Court moved away from literalism and changed the focus of its use of foreign precedent, reflecting its new-found independence and the maturing of Australian **nationhood**. The abolition of appeals to the Privy Council encouraged the Court to look for fresh approaches in other countries. It also meant that previous Privy Council cases could be regarded as though they were foreign cases, having persuasive effect, but no longer binding. The table indicates that during this time, the proportion of cases in which the Court cited US, Canadian, and NZ precedents greatly increased.

The *Free Speech Cases* (1992) saw the emergence of a new paradigm to displace some of the influence of the *Engineers Case*. They emphasised notions of popular **sovereignty** and **representative government** rather than parliamentary sovereignty and **responsible government**, and recognised certain **implied constitutional rights**. The result was to bring the Australian Constitution a little closer to the American, promoting greater use of US case law.

Canadian cases relating to the Canadian Charter of Rights are often cited in relation to human rights matters—for example, in relation to the right to a fair trial considered in *Dietrich v The Queen* (1992). Canadian and NZ cases are most often cited in relation to cases concerning **native title**, tort law, and **evidence law**.

The table below measures the percentage of High Court cases in which various foreign precedents have been cited

Percentages of High Court Cases in which Foreign Precedents have been Cited
(based on Commonwealth Law Reports (1903–99); Australian Law Reports (1972–99))

Cases from	1903–10 (%)	1911–20 (%)	1921–30 (%)	1931–40 (%)	1941–50 (%)	1951–60 (%)	1961–70 (%)	1971–80 (%)	1981–90 (%)	1991–99 (%)
England	83	70	82	88	78	81	86	89	85	88
USA	14	10	11	12	10	9	8	13	25	41
Canada*	4	4	7	7	5	6	6	10	21	37
NZ*	5	4	7	13	10	8	13	15	20	33
Any foreign†	88	75	87	89	91	84	92	91	88	92

* including Privy Council appeals from those countries
† any non-Australian cases, including Privy Council appeals from Australia

(that is, the proportion of cases with citations of foreign precedents to the total number of cases). For the relative percentages of citations of Australian and foreign precedents (that is, the proportion of different categories of citations to the total number of citations), see **citations by Court**.

BRUCE TOPPERWIEN

Further Reading

T Allen and B Anderson, 'The Use of Comparative Law by Common Law Judges' (1994) 23 *Anglo-American Law Review* 435

GL Davies and MP Cowen, 'The persuasive force of decisions of United States Courts in Australia' (1996–97) 15 *Aust Bar Rev* 51

Paul von Nessen, 'The Use of American Precedents by the High Court of Australia, 1901–1987' (1992) 14 *Adel L Rev* 181

Form and substance. The word 'substance' is a philosophical term with a long history, generally used to denote the basic feature or features of reality. Aristotle defined substance as that which possesses attributes but is itself the attribute of nothing. In philosophical terminology, it also means the 'substrate', the 'essence', the 'thing in itself' (see Chief Justice of NZ Robert Stout in *Hills v Stanford* (1904)).

The **common law**, like other legal systems, has drawn a fundamental distinction between substance and form. The distinction is so well entrenched that, in deciding whether, for the purposes of section 49(1) of the *Acts Interpretation Act* 1901 (Cth), a new regulation was 'the same in substance' as a disallowed regulation, **Rich** considered that the words 'in substance' were sufficient to indicate 'that in making the necessary comparison form should be disregarded' (*Women's Employment Case* (1943)).

The distinction between substance and form has been applied not only in the interpretation of the Australian Constitution and statutes, but also in the characterisation of private transactions. In **constitutional law**, it is now accepted that guarantees of rights and prohibitions are generally concerned with substance not form: *Georgiadis v Australian & Overseas Telecommunications Corporation* (1994). So, in the judgments on sections 51(xxxi), 80, 90, 92, and 117 of the Australian Constitution, there have been repeated references to substance and form, chiefly by Justices who considered that the relevant provision should be given a substantive operation rather than an operation that is merely procedural or formal.

In the first case on section 90 relating to **excise duties**, *Peterswald v Bartley* (1904), **Griffith** said: 'In considering the validity of laws of this kind we must look at the substance and not the form. If the Statute is good in substance, the Court will regard the substance, and hold the law to be valid, whatever the form may be.'

In the context of excise duties, however, the distinction between substance and form is of little assistance. This is because, according to one school of thought, duties of excise are a narrow form of tax on goods with particular characteristics, whereas, according to the opposing school of thought that presently prevails, duties of excise form a broader category of taxes, the purpose of section 90 being to give the Commonwealth a substantial measure of control of the taxation of commodities to ensure that whatever policy it adopted would not be hampered or defeated by state action: *Parton v Milk Board* (1949); *Ha v NSW* (1997).

A variant of the narrow view was the attempt to determine whether or not a tax was an excise by reference to the 'criterion of liability' specified in the taxing statute. This approach, as advocated by **Kitto** in *Dennis Hotels v Victoria* (1960), and briefly adopted by a unanimous Court in *Bolton v Madsen* (1963), gave exclusive emphasis to the terms of the statute as the determinant of an excise duty. Another variant was the distinction drawn by **Menzies** in *Dennis Hotels* between a licence fee calculated by reference to the value of sales made under a licence (an excise) and a licence fee calculated by reference to the value of sales made in a period antecedent to the grant of the licence (not an excise). Both these approaches were criticised by adherents of the broad view on the ground that they relied on form not substance, and were artificial (*HC Sleigh v SA* (1977); *Philip Morris v Commissioner of Business Franchises* (1989)). Justices who give emphasis to substance also insist that the validity of the tax in question depends upon the practical operation of the statute (*Ha*), whereas those who emphasise form look to the terms of the statute (*Bolton v Madsen*).

In the context of section 92, the 'criterion of operation' served a similar purpose to that served by the 'criterion of liability' in relation to section 90 (*Hospital Provident Fund v Victoria* (1953)). The criterion of operation also gave emphasis to the legal operation of the terms of the statute, as distinct from its practical operation, as the determinant of validity. The criterion of operation was not as susceptible to **criticism** on substance and form grounds because it was accompanied by the qualification that legislation might impair freedom of **interstate trade**, commerce, and intercourse 'by circuitous means or concealed design': *Grannall v Marrickville Margarine* (1955).

However, in its unanimous judgment in *Cole v Whitfield* (1988), the Court criticised the criterion of operation on the grounds that it was highly artificial, that it depended upon the formal and obscure distinction between the essential attributes of trade and commerce and those facts, events, or things that are inessential, incidental, or preparatory to that trade and commerce, and that it looked to the legal operation rather than the practical operation of a law. After noting that **Dixon** drew support for his judgment in the *Bank Nationalisation Case* (1948) from the opinion of Justice Felix Frankfurter of the **United States Supreme Court** in *Freeman v Hewit* (1946), the Court pointed out that in *Complete Auto Transit v Brady* (1977), the Supreme Court, in overruling *Freeman v Hewit*, had described that decision as 'a triumph of formalism over substance'.

Echoing this comment, **Deane** characterised the earlier decisions of the High Court on section 117 of the Constitution (protecting against **discrimination** on the ground of out-of-state residence) as representing 'a triumph of form over substance' (*Street v Queensland Bar Association* (1989)). In *Street*, the Court **overruled** its previous decision in *Henry v Boehm* (1973), which, in accordance with earlier decisions, had held that a law would infringe section 117 only if its criterion of operation was permanent residence in the state. So, in *Henry v Boehm*, admission rules for legal practitioners in SA were held to apply validly to a Victorian practitioner seeking admission, although they required an applicant to have 'continuously resided' in SA for a period before admission.

The rules were upheld because the criterion in the rules was temporary residence. The Court in *Street* regarded this formalistic approach as emasculating an important constitutional guarantee, the purpose of which was to enhance **national unity**. Again, the Court refused to confine its attention to the legal operation of the law, and looked to its practical effect.

Similar trends have been apparent in the Court's approach to the prescription in section 80 that the trial on indictment of an offence against a Commonwealth law 'shall be by jury' (see **Jury trial**). The Court has clung to the early interpretation given to section 80, namely that it is a procedural provision whose only effect is to regulate the mode of criminal trial when it has been initiated by indictment (*R v Archdall and Roskruge* (1928); *R v Federal Court of Bankruptcy; Ex parte Lowenstein* (1938); *Kingswell v The Queen* (1985)). This interpretation has encountered strong criticism from dissenting Justices on substance and form grounds: 'The Constitution is not to be mocked' (Dixon and **Evatt** in *Lowenstein*); 'the words "trial on indictment" … should be construed by reference to substance rather than mere procedure or form' (Deane in *Kingswell*).

Justices who favour a broad rather than a narrow construction sometimes resort to stating that the narrow construction amounts to a mockery of the Constitution. An instance is the *War Crimes Act Case* (1991), where Deane said of a narrow construction of Chapter III of the Constitution that it would 'convert [Chapter III] into a mockery, rather than a reflection, of the doctrine of **separation of powers**'.

The Court's approach to section 51(xxxi) of the Constitution—the acquisition power—is a striking illustration of the principle that an interpretation favouring substance over form will be preferred, at least when individual rights are at stake. The provision, which is in form the grant of a power subject to a condition, has been construed as a guarantee of just terms in cases of **acquisition of property** by the Commonwealth (*Georgiadis*).

The maxim 'you cannot do indirectly what you are forbidden to do directly', often invoked in a constitutional context (see, for example, *Wragg v NSW* (1953)), is in essence a guide to the interpretation of guarantees and prohibitions, indicating that they are concerned generally with substance rather than form (*Georgiadis*).

The tension between form and substance has also been evident in the **characterisation** of Commonwealth legislation in order to determine whether it falls within the scope of **Commonwealth legislative power**. Early suggestions that this should turn on the legislation's 'pith and substance' have not been favoured (see especially **Latham** in the *Bank Nationalisation Case*), and ulterior motives and indirect effects have been disregarded in favour of whether the law simply answers the relevant description (*Murphyores v Commonwealth* (1976)); but the *Communist Party Case* (1951) inhibited one kind of formalism by preventing the Parliament from 'reciting itself' into power and pre-empting the right of the Court to make the necessary connection. Nevertheless, that connection continues to be made under the heavy influence of the course set by the literal approach to interpretation adopted in the *Engineers Case* (1920).

In a constitutional context, the distinction between substance and form often reflects a conflict between purposive interpretation and literal or formalistic interpretation (see **Legalism**; **Literalism**). But it should not be assumed that literal or formalistic interpretation never serves purposive and **policy** goals. Dixon's interpretation of section 92, involving the criterion of operation and the distinction between essential and incidental attributes, served to reduce the detrimental expansive operation of the section, while the criterion of liability narrowed the concept of 'excise duties' and potentially preserved a larger taxing power for the states. Conversely, the literal approach to interpretation, applied in *Engineers* and *Murphyores*, served to expand the reach of Commonwealth legislative power.

The distinction between form and substance is also related to another fundamental distinction made by the common law between substance and procedure. The latter distinction constitutes a broad, dichotomous classification with many legal consequences, depending upon which classification is chosen for a particular provision (for an illustration in the area of **conflict of laws** see *John Pfeiffer v Rogerson* (2000)). The conjunction of the two distinctions is clearly seen in the controversy over the interpretation of section 80.

The distinction between substance and form is also of vital importance in the characterisation of private transactions. Courts are concerned to ascertain and identify what is the real transaction intended by the parties. To that end, they will disregard the form of a transaction if its form was intended to be a cloak for another and different transaction (*Boydell v James* (1936); *Vicars v Commissioner of Stamp Duties* (1945)). So the **House of Lords** has held that an ostensible sale may serve as a cloak for a loan (*Maas v Pepper* (1905)) and the **Privy Council** has held that a purported conveyance on sale may serve as a cloak for a mortgage (*Barton v Bank of NSW* (1890)). The device of sale and purchase is sometimes employed as a means of making money available to a person who needs it. In one form of this device, the person who wants the money buys a chattel from a complaisant vendor for a price payable in the future and immediately resells it to the vendor for a much lower price, paid in cash. In the Supreme Court of NSW, Chief Justice Frederick Jordan once described this as '*le truc du crocodile empaillé*' (*Boydell v James*). Another illustration is the hire-purchase agreement that serves as a cloak for an unregistered bill of sale (*Price v Parsons* (1936)).

To be distinguished from this category of transactions are cases in which the parties seek by an express provision in their **contract** to create or negate a particular relationship, whether it be a lease, a licence, or a partnership. In these cases, regard for substance in preference to form means characterising the legal effect of the contract according to its operative provisions and disregarding the express provision dealing with the relationship if it is inconsistent with the operative provisions.

A transaction intended not to operate according to its terms, but to serve as a cloak for the underlying real transaction, is often described as a sham or colourable transaction. Although it is of no legal effect, the underlying real transaction will have legal effect unless it is rendered void by statute or the general law.

Taxation law has a particular concern with sham transactions—that is, transactions intended by the parties to give to third parties and the court the appearance of creating legal rights and obligations that are different from the actual legal rights and obligations the parties intended to create. The fact that an arrangement is artificial or contrived is not enough to make it a sham; it may nevertheless be intended to operate according to its terms.

Whether an arrangement is a sham depends upon the **evidence** as to the parties' intention. Because that evidence may be unclear, the question may be difficult to determine. *Jaques v FCT* (1924) is an example (**Knox** considered that the scheme was a sham but the majority held otherwise). Sham transactions are to be distinguished from transactions that are avoided by statutory provisions directed at tax avoidance schemes, such as section 260 of the *Income Tax Assessment Act* 1936 (Cth).

ANTHONY MASON

Further Reading

Owen Dixon, 'The Law and the Constitution' (1935) 51 *LQR* 590

Nabil Orow, *General Anti-Avoidance Rules: A Comparative International Analysis* (2000) 53–55, 329–34

Leslie Zines and Geoffrey Lindell, 'Form and Substance: "Discrimination" in Modern Constitutional Law' (1992) 21 *FL Rev* 136

Leslie Zines, *The High Court and the Constitution* (4th edn 1997) ch 17

Framers of the Constitution. The processes by which the Australian Constitution came into being were protracted and complex. The Constitution was framed, in the form of a Bill, over a nine-year period. Its first full draft was completed at the Australasian Federal Convention, which met in Sydney from 2 March 1891 to 9 April 1891. A second Bill was drawn up at the second Federal Convention, which opened in Adelaide on 22 March 1897, met for a second session in Sydney in September 1897, and concluded in Melbourne on 17 March 1898. Certain provisions in that Bill were amended by the colonial parliaments following an agreement reached at a Premiers' Conference in January 1899, and several further amendments were made to the Covering Clauses and to section 74, immediately prior to the Constitution's passage as an Act of the Imperial Parliament in July 1900.

Who then were the Constitution's framers? There are several alternative responses. That title might be applied to all the members of the Federal Conventions, irrespective of their level of contribution to debate or committee work. Forty-six attended the 1891 Convention (seven from each Australian colony, three from NZ, plus one Victorian replacement). Fifty-four attended the second (ten delegates from each Australian colony except Queensland, plus four replacements from WA). Allowing for the 17 who attended both, this is a total of 83 men.

Members of the first Convention were elected from and by the colonial parliaments. The second Convention was chosen

Delegates to the Federation Conference, Melbourne, 1890. Left to right (standing): Andrew Inglis Clark; William Russell; Samuel Griffith; Henry Parkes; Thomas Playford; Alfred Deakin; Stafford Bird; GH Jenkins (Secretary). Left to right (sitting): William McMillan, John Hall, John Macrossan; Duncan Gillies; John Cockburn; James Lee-Steere

by direct, popular election in Victoria, NSW, SA, and Tasmania, and by parliamentary election (from an open field of candidates) in WA. All of the successful candidates, with one exception (James Walker (1841–1922) from NSW), were sitting or former politicians. One alone (William Trenwith (1846–1925) from Victoria) represented the labour movement. The majority were Australian-born. With two exceptions (George Grey (1812–98), born in Portugal, and Simon Fraser (1832–1919), born in Nova Scotia), the remainder were all born in Britain. By birth, there were five Catholics and two Jews, with the others spread across the Protestant denominations. The majority were in their forties; the youngest at the time of becoming a member (Andrew Henning (1865–1947)) was 32, and the oldest (Adye Douglas (1815–1906)) 82. Almost one third of them were lawyers.

This response to the question 'who were the framers?' tells us something of their general characteristics but it is too broad to be useful, since many of these 83 men left no impression upon the Constitution and some were virtually invisible even in the Conventions. At the other extreme, the narrowest response would be to confine 'framers' to those who served on the Conventions' Drafting Committees. This list is small but mighty. The 1891 Drafting Committee was chaired by Queensland Premier (and future Queensland Chief Justice, subsequently first High Court **Chief Justice**) **Griffith**. Other members included the Tasmanian Attorney-General (and later Tasmanian Supreme Court judge) Andrew **Inglis Clark**, and the Leader of the SA Opposition (and soon-to-be Premier) Charles Cameron Kingston (1850–1908), both of whom had prepared draft Constitution Bills prior to the Convention. During the Easter break, while drafting continued on board the Queensland government ship, the *Lucinda*, the Committee was joined by former Queensland Justice Minister, Andrew Thynne (1847–1927), Henry Wrixon QC (1839–1913) from Victoria, and (during Inglis Clark's temporary absence) **Barton**. Bernhard Wise (1858–1916), a former NSW Attorney-General (later an elected member of the second Convention but not a member in 1891), was an unofficial guest and may well have taken part in discussions (see **Counsel, notable**). At the 1897–98 Convention, the Drafting Committee consisted of the Chair, John Downer (1844–1915), Barton, and his future fellow Justice of the first High Court, **O'Connor**. Secretary to this Committee was the young Robert **Garran**, already emerging as one of Australia's leading constitutional authorities.

Of all of these men, it is Griffith who left his mark most clearly upon the 1891 draft and, indirectly, upon the final Constitution. Griffith was not a member of the second Convention (his colony was unrepresented and, in any case, he was probably ineligible, being Chief Justice of Queensland). While his 'terse, clear style' (in Alfred **Deakin**'s words) did not altogether survive the Constitution Bill's redrafting between 1897 and 1900, the arrangement of the provisions, the major themes, and the relations between the parts, retain much of his imprint. It is sometimes claimed that Inglis Clark's own draft was the foundation of the Constitution and that he, rather than Griffith, deserves the attribution of authorship. There are certainly many similarities between the Constitution of today and Inglis Clark's version, although these should not be exaggerated. They can partly,

perhaps largely, be explained by reference to the US Constitution, the *British North America Act* 1867 and the *Federal Council of Australasia Act* 1885, which not only Inglis Clark but also other members of the Convention had studied and drawn upon.

This narrower approach to identifying the framers has the appeal of precision, but it would rule out many active members. More meaningfully, framers may be defined as those who directly or indirectly made successful suggestions for provisions in the Constitution or for amendments to the Constitution in its final stages. While the majority of provisions emerged from the Conventions' select Committees (Constitutional, Finance, and Judiciary) and were given form by the Drafting Committee, certain significant sections can be attributed to the initiative or advocacy of individuals. Among others, James Howe (1839–1920) proposed the old-age and invalid pensions power (section 51(xxiii)) in 1897–98. Kingston proposed the **conciliation and arbitration** power (section 51(xxxv)) in 1891, and this was successfully promoted at the second Convention by Victorian delegate **Higgins**. Richard Chaffey Baker (1841–1911) from SA (who also prepared a useful 'Manual' on federal systems for the 1891 Convention) proposed the 'nexus' requirement between the two Commonwealth Houses of Parliament (section 24). John Gordon (1850–1923) proposed the **Inter-State Commission** (section 101) in 1891. Higgins proposed section 116 in 1898, prohibiting the Commonwealth from establishing a religion or imposing a religious test for public office. John Quick (1852–1932) was unsuccessful in 1898 in having 'citizenship' defined, or alternatively a Commonwealth head of power over 'citizenship' inserted in the Constitution, but his attempt led to the inclusion of section 117, prohibiting **discrimination** on the ground of out-of-state residence. Quick also proposed what became known as the Corowa Plan, leading to the Convention of 1897–98 and the eventual adoption of the Constitution. Edward Braddon (1829–1904) proposed in 1898 what was to be known by opponents of federation as the 'Braddon Blot': section 87, which provided that three-quarters of all Commonwealth customs and excise revenue should be returned to the states for a ten-year period after federation. Joseph Abbott (1842–1901) proposed a Commonwealth head of power over astronomical and meteorological observations (section 51(viii)) in 1891. Henry Wrixon (1839–1913) in 1891 was first to propose that the Senate should not be allowed to amend money Bills (section 53) and that there should be no tacking-on of taxation laws to other Bills (section 55).

The sections of the Constitution that describe the High Court went through various stages of drafting, with a range of authors. Prior to the Convention's opening, Henry Parkes (1815–96) suggested that there should be 'a Judiciary, consisting of a Federal Supreme Court of not fewer than ten Judges' but, following consultation with other Premiers, his resolution was changed to omit any reference to numbers. In the event, the 1891 draft referred to a Chief Justice and no less than four others, while ultimately section 71, as it emerged in 1898, provided for a Chief Justice and no less than two others (see **Number of Justices**).

Inglis Clark's draft for the relevant section began in words almost identical to the US Constitution: 'The **Judicial power** of the federal Dominion of Australia shall be vested in one Supreme Court.' To Inglis Clark's dismay, this mandatory formula was not adopted in the 1891 draft, which provided instead that 'The parliament of the commonwealth shall have power to establish a court, which shall be called the Supreme Court of Australia'. His construction was, however, reinserted in 1897, with the name of the Commonwealth and the High Court added. The name 'High Court' emerged from the Convention's Judiciary Committee. It is not known which member first proposed it. Inglis Clark provided for the establishment of other federal courts, but the original idea of investing state courts with federal jurisdiction, found in section 77(iii)—what the High Court was later to call the 'autochthonous expedient'—was provided at the second Convention by a young WA lawyer, Walter James (1863–1943).

Significantly for the Constitution's later development, Inglis Clark's draft included a provision ruling out appeals from the High Court to the **Privy Council** altogether. This was effectively followed in 1891 and largely retained, although modified, in 1897–98. In 1900, the provision emerged as a point of serious disagreement between the Australians and Britain's Colonial Secretary, Joseph Chamberlain (1836–1914), who wanted to preserve appeals to the Privy Council from all Australian courts and in all classes of matter. Ultimately, a compromise formula was suggested (both Griffith and Chamberlain are credited with this) and is now found in section 74. The majority of other Chapter III provisions were the work of the Judiciary Committee at the second Convention, its members consisting of Josiah Symon (1846–1934) (Chair, SA); Wise and Walker (NSW); Alexander Peacock (1861–1933) and Higgins (Victoria); Patrick Glynn (1855–1931) (SA); Matthew Clarke (1863–1923) and Henry Dobson (1841–1918) (Tasmania); and Walter James (1863–1943) and George Leake (1856–1902) (WA). All but Walker, Clarke, and Peacock were lawyers, but the level of individual contribution is likely to have been very uneven.

Some of the leading federalists were notable both for particular contributions and for their broader involvement in the process. Parkes was the instigator of the 1891 Convention and the Convention's President. There he moved the series of resolutions that served as general principles to guide the Constitution's design. He proposed the name 'Commonwealth' and his use of the expression 'absolutely free' found its way into section 92 of the Constitution (see **Interstate trade and commerce**). Deakin—perhaps the most insightful of the framers—spoke frequently and eloquently in **Convention debate**, and was very active in suggesting and supporting amendments. He proposed section 113, allowing the states to regulate the alcohol trade, notwithstanding the guarantee of 'absolutely free' trade among the states in section 92. Temperance was a powerful political force in the 1890s, but this can now scarcely be considered a key section. But Deakin's later role as a member of the Australian delegation in London in 1900 was crucial in assisting the vigorous defence of the Constitution Bill and the negotiations over its amendment. John Forrest (1847–1918), Premier of WA, brought his colony into the Commonwealth. Several of the other delegates, such as Thomas Playford (1837–1915), **Isaacs**, William Trenwith (1846–1925), and James Munro (1832–1908), made major contributions to debate that appear to have had a significant impact upon the outcome of divisions.

All of these men may be considered 'Founding Fathers' or even 'fathers of the Constitution' (as the historian, JA La Nauze, called them). But some have a greater claim to the title of 'framer' than others. If, in the words of Griffith, the Constitution was 'the work of many men in consultation with each other' rather than 'any one man', we can be confident that some of these men, including Griffith himself, stand out as framers because, in consultation, they had most to say.

The impact of the framers upon the High Court was not of course confined to their contributions to the drafting of the Constitution in the 1890s. Some of them were subsequently appointed as Justices of the Court (Griffith, Barton, O'Connor, Isaacs, and Higgins, the first five Justices), some were **appointments that might have been** (notably Inglis Clark, Symon, and Gordon), and some attained positions such as **Prime Minister** or **Attorney-General**, from which they continued to influence or attempt to influence the Court (notably Deakin and Symon). The intimate personal knowledge they possessed of the drafting process might have been thought to give the first Justices unique insights into the intended meaning of the Constitution. Yet the disagreements on the Court, at least after 1906 when Isaacs and Higgins were appointed, were immediately to demonstrate the diversity of views amongst the framers themselves and the complexity of **constitutional interpretation**.

HELEN IRVING

Further Reading
Helen Irving (ed), *A Woman's Constitution? Gender and History in the Australian Commonwealth* (1996)
Helen Irving (ed), *The Centenary Companion to Australian Federation* (1999)
JA La Nauze, *The Making of the Australian Constitution* (1972)

Free Speech Cases (1992). Despite much controversy over the possibility of the High Court giving effect to **implied constitutional rights**, one example now clearly accepted is the Court's recognition of an implied constitutional freedom of **political communication**. This freedom of *political* communication stops short of 'free speech' in general, and is not strictly a 'right', since its only legal operation is to limit legislative and executive power (and presumably **judicial power**). That such a freedom exists, and avails against Commonwealth legislation, was first clearly articulated in two cases decided on 30 September 1992: *Nationwide News v Wills* and *Australian Capital Television v Commonwealth* (*'ACTV'*).

Nationwide News concerned the *Industrial Relations Act* 1988 (Cth), which replaced the *Conciliation and Arbitration Act* 1904 (Cth), reconstituting the Conciliation and Arbitration Commission as an Industrial Relations Commission. The new section 299 shielded the Commission against contempt by creating offences roughly similar to **contempt** of court. Most of section 299 could be read as limited to actual disruption of Commission hearings; but by subsection (1)(d)(ii) it was an offence to speak or write anything that might bring the Commission or its members into disrepute.

On 14 November 1989, the *Australian* published an article by Maxwell Newton headed 'Advance Australia Fascist', depicting Australian **labour relations** as stifled by a bureaucratic regime 'enforced by a corrupt and compliant "judiciary" in the official Soviet-style Arbitration Commission'.

Other paragraphs spoke of 'pliant "judges"' and 'corrupt labour "judges"'. The publishers were prosecuted under section 299(1)(d)(ii).

The whole Court held that section 299(1)(d)(ii) was invalid, but only four Justices (**Brennan, Deane, Toohey,** and **Gaudron**) based this result directly on the implied freedom. By contrast, **Mason, Dawson,** and **McHugh** declared that, while some reasonable protection for the Commission could validly be enacted as incidental to the exercise of legislative power with respect to **conciliation and arbitration**, what was reasonably incidental could not extend to such a wholesale restriction on freedom of speech. Mason gave even this approach an innovative twist, arguing that where the validity of a law depends upon incidental power, it is always the *purpose* of the law that supplies the necessary connection with the primary subject matter—and that, in every case where the validity of a law depends on its *purpose*, the Court can apply a test of **proportionality** to that purpose. Dawson emphatically rejected this argument, though he agreed with Mason and McHugh that the law was not 'within power'.

Gaudron also agreed with much of what Mason and McHugh had said. Although she based her decision on the implied freedom, she agreed that the question whether a law is incidental to a legislative power will 'very often' depend on its purpose, and that it was so in this case. She also agreed that the law was not 'appropriate and adapted' to its purpose. But she saw this as bearing on compatibility with the implied freedom, not on **characterisation**.

Brennan agreed with Gaudron that the law *was* 'within power'. For both of them, therefore, it was necessary to rely on the more fundamental ground that the Commonwealth cannot use its legislative powers incompatibly with the implied freedom. For Deane and Toohey, the incompatibility with the implied freedom was so obvious that there was no need to consider whether the law was 'within power' or not.

ACTV concerned the *Political Broadcasts and Political Disclosures Act* 1991 (Cth), which amended the *Broadcasting Act* 1942 (Cth) by inserting a new Part IIID, headed 'Political Broadcasts'. By section 95B, the broadcasting of political advertisements on radio or television during a federal election was prohibited. Section 95C extended the ban to territory elections; section 95D to state or local government elections. Section 95A made exceptions for news and current affairs items, talkback radio programs, and advertisements for charities that did not 'explicitly advocate' a vote for any one candidate or party. Section 95S added an exception for policy launches.

Division 3 of Part IIID established a scheme for 'free time' to be allocated to **political parties** by the Australian Broadcasting Tribunal. Of the total time available, 90 per cent was reserved for parties contesting the election with 'at least the prescribed number of candidates', after having been 'represented by one or more members' in the previous Parliament (section 95H(1)). Units of 'free time' could be used for a two-minute telecast or one-minute radio broadcast 'that consists of words spoken by a single speaker (without dramatic enactment or impersonation)', accompanied (in a telecast) 'by a transmitted image … of the head and shoulders of the speaker' (who must be a candidate or sitting member). There must be 'no other vocal sounds' and no other image (or 'a single … static background image only') (section 95G). By

section 95H, the computation of 'free time' was dependent on regulations; by section 95J, the whole of Part IIID 'does not apply in relation to an election … until [such] regulations are made … that relate to that election'. By section 95Q, once free time was allotted, the broadcaster was required to make it available, and had to do so free of charge.

Mason, Deane, Toohey, Gaudron, and McHugh all held this scheme invalid as an unacceptable restriction of the freedom of political communication. Brennan agreed that such a freedom existed, but thought this particular scheme was not incompatible with it, since he was prepared to give the Parliament a 'margin of appreciation'. Only Dawson dissented outright, protesting that any talk of 'implied freedoms' was incompatible with the Court's consistent approach to **constitutional interpretation** ever since the *Engineers Case* (1920).

Deane and Toohey saw the freedom of political communication as arising from a broad constitutional doctrine of **representative government**. Mason also invoked this conception, impliedly contrasting it with a narrower doctrine of **responsible government**. (The latter might imply that the fundamental liberties and values of the people are implemented through electoral and legislative processes, the former that they are safeguarded by the courts, acting on the people's behalf.) Brennan spoke of 'representative **democracy**', though like Gaudron, he also invoked the **common law** as a source of constitutional freedoms—and of their limitations. McHugh found a narrower textual basis in sections 7 and 24 of the Constitution, which require that the Houses of Parliament be 'chosen by the people', and hence require a meaningful choice, based on full information and discussion.

The lasting effect of these cases is unclear. In *Theophanous v Herald & Weekly Times* (1994) and *Stephens v WA Newspapers* (1994), the Court was deeply divided over whether the constitutional protection of freedom of political communication meant that the Court should now constitutionalise the law of **defamation** by devising a constitutional defence for published statements on political matters (as the **United States Supreme Court** had done in *New York Times v Sullivan* (1964)), or whether a similar result should be reached by development of the **common law** defence of qualified privilege (an option that had not been available to the American Court). The sharp divisions of opinion surrounding this and related issues were resolved by a unanimous Court in *Lange v ABC* (1997) in favour of the common law solution. But the constitutional freedom of political communication was reaffirmed as a limitation on state and federal legislative power: legislation may now afford greater protection to freedom of speech than the Constitution requires, but it cannot give less. The essential underlying concepts of representative and responsible government were also reaffirmed. But the practical significance of these reaffirmations remains to be seen.

TONY BLACKSHIELD

Full Court is defined by section 19 of the *Judiciary Act* 1903 (Cth) to mean a **sitting** of the Court consisting of at least two Justices. A number of areas of the High Court's **jurisdiction** are required to be exercised by a Full Court, and in some cases by a Full Court with a particular prescribed composition. The jurisdiction not required by the Judiciary Act to be exercised by a Full Court can be exercised by a single Justice.

Applications for special **leave to appeal** are generally heard by a Full Court consisting of two or three Justices. Although there is a residual possibility of special leave being granted by a single Justice, this does not occur in practice. Appeals from state or federal courts (including single Justices of the High Court) must be heard by a Full Court by force of sections 20 and 21 of the Judiciary Act. In practice, the Court nowadays sits as a Bench of five Justices on such appeals, though in the past Benches of three were common. If the appeal involves one party asking the Court to **overrule** one of its prior decisions, the Court will generally sit as a Bench consisting of all available Justices (seven, unless one or more is unavailable). Likewise, if the case involves a particularly important issue, all available Justices will sit. In constitutional cases, all available Justices invariably sit.

While applications for **removal** into the High Court from another Court under section 40 of the Judiciary Act can, as a matter of **procedure**, be made to a single Justice, in practice the Court always makes such applications returnable before a Full Court. (See also **Bench, composition of; Number of Justices.**)

NYE PERRAM

Fullagar, Wilfred Kelsham (*b* 16 November 1892; *d* 9 July 1961; Justice 1950–61) was born in Malvern, Victoria, the first child and only son (there were two younger daughters) of Thomas Kelsham Fullagar, merchant, and his wife Sarah Elizabeth, née Law, both born in Australia. Sons of the Fullagar family had been given the middle name 'Kelsham' since William Fullagard (*sic*) married Agnes Kelsham, the daughter of the Lord of the Manor of Headcorn, Kent, in 1565.

After schooling at Haileybury College, Brighton, under the gifted classics teacher and headmaster Charles Henry Rendall, who regarded him as the most brilliant boy to have gone through the College, Fullagar studied arts and law at Ormond College, the University of Melbourne, 1910–16. His achievements in classics gained him the Wyselaskie Scholarship in Classical and Comparative Philology and Logic. In law, he graduated with first-class honours and the Supreme Court Prize.

Fullagar's love of the classics was lifelong. He continued to read Greek and Latin literature (see also **Languages**), and to compose Latin poetry. **Dixon**—who, like Fullagar, had studied classics at Melbourne under the illustrious Professor TG Tucker—considered that Fullagar's classical training gave 'an added distinction to his writings'.

Following graduation, Fullagar became an articled clerk to Melbourne solicitor JW McComas, but did not complete his term of articles. Instead, in October 1916, he enlisted in the Australian Imperial Forces. In November 1917, he sailed for France, where he served with the 27th Battery, Australian Field Artillery, obtaining the rank of sergeant. For six months in 1919, while still in England, he was granted 'non-military employment leave to study law', during which he met and married his first wife. He returned to Australia in January 1920, and was discharged on 8 February.

For two years, Fullagar held positions in the Repatriation Department and the Commonwealth Immigration Office, feeling that, as a young married man, he could not afford to go to the Bar. In April 1922, however, with financial assistance pressed on him by **Latham** and Dixon, he took that step, read-ing with Charles Lowe. He was rapidly successful and repaid his advances from Latham and Dixon within the year. He was at his best in **equity**, and also developed a formidable reputation in **constitutional law**. As his Victorian judicial colleague Arthur Dean later wrote, he 'was not an advocate in the accepted sense, and no one would think of briefing him in the Criminal Court or before juries', but 'as a sound and learned lawyer, as a brilliant expositor of the law, he was unrivalled'. He was appointed a KC in September 1933, after a mere 11 years at the Bar. In 1945, he accepted appointment to the Supreme Court of Victoria, reportedly after having declined previous offers of appointment on financial grounds.

His five years in the **state Supreme Court** produced several notable judgments. His decision in *Harris v Harris* (1946) was for many years the leading authority on the 'full faith and credit' provision in section 118 of the Constitution. His analysis in *In re Panter* (1947) of the rule in *Lassence v Tierney* (1849), as to the consequences of an invalid exercise of a power of appointment, became the basis of the High Court judgments (including his own) in *Russell v Perpetual Trustee Co* (1956), *Duncan v Cathels* (1956), and *Duncan v Equity Trustees Executors & Agency Co* (1958). Two cases in which he sat in the Full Supreme Court attracted public notoriety. In *R v Close* (1948), where the Court upheld a jury verdict that Robert Close's novel *Love Me Sailor* (1945) was 'obscene', Fullagar observed that 'everything in human life is the object of legitimate human interest' (adding, in his beloved Latin, '*Nihil humanum a me alienum puto*'), and left open 'the debateable question whether anything is gained in the long run by the prosecution and punishment of such things as "Love Me Sailor"'. But he also thought the book contained passages which no amount of literary merit 'could transmute from filthiness to cleanness or from beastliness to humanity'. The other case, the *Whose Baby Case* (1949), involved a claim that newborn babies were inadvertently exchanged at the hospital. Fullagar gave the principal judgment, carefully reviewing what should happen when **expert evidence** shades into opinion **evidence**, and concluding (contrary to the view of the trial judge, John Barry) 'that the *only direct* scientific evidence ... suggests that Nola is the child of Mr and Mrs Jenkins' (see also **Webb**).

Appointed to the High Court in the last months of the **Latham Court**, Fullagar remained on the Bench through most of Dixon's term as **Chief Justice**. Their relationship was unusually close, both philosophically and personally. The period was one of transformation in the Court's approach to freedom of **interstate trade** under section 92 of the Constitution; the 'transport cases' of the 1930s—beginning with what Fullagar called the *fons et origo malorum* of *R v Vizzard; Ex parte Hill* (1933)—were finally **overruled** in favour of Dixon's dissenting view in those cases. Within a month of joining the Court, Fullagar had sat in *McCarter v Brodie* (1950), where he and Dixon maintained (in dissent) that the transport cases were incompatible with the **Privy Council** decision in the *Bank Nationalisation Case* (1949). When the Privy Council finally endorsed that view, in *Hughes & Vale v NSW* (1954), the judgment consisted largely of extensive quotations from *Bank Nationalisation* and from Dixon and Fullagar, including a five-page quotation from Fullagar's judgment in *McCarter v Brodie*. In the series of High Court decisions that followed, beginning with *Hughes & Vale v NSW (No 2)* (1955), he usually wrote separate judgments—**concurring** with the **joint**

Wilfred Fullagar, Justice 1950–61

(1955) condemned the 'interference with the plaintiff's person and liberty' as 'a grave infringement of the most elementary and important of all **common law** rights'.

His **liberalism** extended to the rights of trade unions, though not necessarily to militant or disruptive industrial action. In the Supreme Court of Victoria, when the Melbourne Harbour Trust Commissioners had made it an offence to 'hold any meeting or address any assemblage' in the port area without their consent, Fullagar had held this regulation invalid (*Kenneally v Berman* (1949)). In the High Court, presented with a substantially similar regulation, Fullagar (joined by Webb and **Taylor**; **Williams** and **Kitto** dissenting) again held it invalid (*Clements v Bull* (1953)). At the same time, he was anxious not to seem 'lacking in appreciation' of the Commissioners' problems: he found it 'not difficult to understand that gatherings may and do take place which … are a real source of disturbance and annoyance in the port'.

This aversion to 'disturbance and annoyance' perhaps explains why in *Waters v Commonwealth* (1951), in upholding the power of the Northern Territory's Director of Native Affairs to confine the **Aboriginal** plaintiff to a remote reserve, he appeared to attach particular weight to 'disturbances among the natives' in which the plaintiff had not only 'taken a leading part', but had been 'incited thereto by officers of the union, into whose motives I see no need to inquire' (see **Colonialism**). Perhaps, too, it explained his eagerness (along with Dixon) in *Australian Boot Trade Employees v Commonwealth* (1954) to uphold the validity of Commonwealth legislation making it an offence for trade union officials to 'advise, encourage, or incite' their members on a wide range of industrial matters—an issue the rest of the Court dismissed as hypothetical and premature.

The real test of these attitudes came in *Williams v Hursey* (1959). When Frank Hursey and his son decided to join the Democratic Labor Party (DLP), the Hobart branch of the Waterside Workers Federation had been plunged into months of turmoil. Initially, the Hurseys refused to pay a union levy supporting the Australian Labor Party; later, they refused to pay any political levy at all, even when told that they could pay it to the DLP. In a powerful judgment (with which Dixon and Kitto agreed), Fullagar held that the political levy, and the deeper connection between unionism and political action, were valid, and that the Hurseys' union membership had validly been terminated. He also held that the **damages** awarded to the Hurseys in an action in **tort** for their exposure to constant picketing should be reduced from £2500 to £1000, in part because their 'provocative' conduct and 'unjustified' refusal to pay the political levy had been 'the ultimate source of all the trouble'.

Dennis Hotels v Victoria (1960) found Dixon and Fullagar on opposite sides. Dixon adhered to the broad view he had taken in *Parton v Milk Board* (1949) of the Commonwealth's exclusive power to levy duties of **excise**; Fullagar argued powerfully for a return to the original, narrow conception in *Peterswald v Bartley* (1904) that an excise duty is a 'tax upon goods' and 'the necessary relation is to be found in the manufacture or production of goods'. While never attracting majority support, his argument has been kept alive by repeated strong dissents.

In other contexts, Fullagar took a strong view of the Commonwealth's powers and supremacy. In *O'Sullivan v*

judgments delivered by Dixon, but emphasising his own conception (first expounded in *McCarter v Brodie*) of the regulatory charges that might be imposed on interstate road transport consistently with section 92. He also insisted—as he himself had argued unsuccessfully as **counsel** in *Riverina Transport v Victoria* (1937)—that section 92 was infringed by discriminatory administrative action as well as by legislative action.

Another landmark soon after Fullagar's appointment was the *Communist Party Case* (1951). His judgment was notable for its pithy explanation of the inutility of legislative recitals: 'Parliament cannot recite itself into a field the gates of which are locked against it by superior law'; his innovative exploration of the 'secondary aspect' of the **defence power**; his equally innovative exploration (along with Dixon) of what is now called the **nationhood power** (referred to by Fullagar as 'the constitution-preservation power', or simply as 'the other power'); his explanation of the Delphic **metaphor** 'that a stream cannot rise higher than its source'; his analysis of what is required to support the validity of a law singling out specific or named individuals (what Fullagar called a *privilegium*); and his proclamation that 'in our system the principle of *Marbury v Madison* is accepted as axiomatic'.

Fullagar was generally protective of **civil liberties**. His dissent with Dixon in *Hall v Braybrook* (1956) protested against the disclosure of prior convictions to a magistrate in committal proceedings because it was 'fundamental in the administration of criminal justice' that a tribunal concerned with guilt or innocence be not informed of the prior convictions or bad character of the accused. His vehement disapproval of the abusive police conduct in *Trobridge v Hardy*

Noarlunga Meat (1954), his explanation of why the Commonwealth could control the quality of meat for export was a classic statement of the reach of the 'incidental power'. In a famous passage in *Commonwealth v Bogle* (1953), he insisted that it was 'a fundamental misconception' to think that state laws could ever bind the Commonwealth (though the Commonwealth might, he conceded, be 'affected by' state laws). Though eventually disapproved in *Henderson's Case* (1997), this passage was treated for many years as amplifying and explaining the view of Commonwealth immunity developed by Dixon in *Uther's Case* (1947) and the **Cigamatic Case** (1962) (see also **Intergovernmental immunities**). Fullagar's view, like Dixon's, depended on a distinctive view of the relationship between the Crown and its subjects as fundamentally different from the ordinary litigious relations between individual subjects (see, for example, his judgments in *Rural Bank v Hayes* (1951) and in *George v FCT* (1952)).

In many other areas, Fullagar's judgments were influential in the development of distinctive Australian doctrines, including the gradual subsumption of the special categories of **occupiers' liability** within the general conception of negligence flowing from *Donoghue v Stevenson* (1932) (see *Watson v George* (1953); *Rich v Commissioner for Railways* (1959); *Commissioner for Railways (NSW) v Cardy* (1960); and Fullagar's last reported judgment, *Commissioner for Railways (NSW) v Anderson* (1961)). In *Blomley v Ryan* (1956), he gave what is still the classic formulation of the kinds of impairment or disadvantage that might lead to a contract being set aside for **unconscionability**. His analysis, in *Wilson v Darling Island Stevedoring* (1956), of apparent exceptions to the doctrine that a **contract** cannot legally benefit those who are not parties to it, has been deeply influential. His judgment in *Gorringe v Transport Commission* (1950), exploring both the historical origins and the 'very curious' anomalies of the rule that a highway authority cannot be sued for nonfeasance, remained the leading authority on the subject for half a century, until the nonfeasance rule was finally overruled in *Brodie v Singleton Shire Council* (2001). His dissenting judgment in *Jackson v Goldsmith* (1950) developed a distinctive Australian concept of issue **estoppel**, which he traced back to **Higgins** in *Hoysted v FCT* (1920) and Dixon in *Blair v Curran* (1939). As further developed by Fullagar in *Brewer v Brewer* (1953), the doctrine reached its fullest development (in Fullagar's absence) in *Mraz v The Queen (No 2)* (1956).

Fullagar's judicial work was of the highest quality. He has always been regarded as one of the most brilliant judges to have sat on any Australian Bench. At his death, **Prime Minister** Robert **Menzies** acknowledged 'his mastery of the law', while Dixon said: 'He combined with a remarkable erudition great resources of scholarship. His judgments commanded the admiration of lawyers not only for their penetration, their soundness and their correctness, but for the exposition of legal principles in an almost unequalled English style.'

His stature was recognised internationally. Justice Felix Frankfurter, of the **United States Supreme Court**, who had not actually met him, nevertheless told Dixon that he felt Fullagar's death 'as a personal loss', so close had been his sense of 'professional communion'. In *Midland Silicones v Scruttons* (1961), Viscount Simonds told the **House of Lords**, five months after Fullagar's death and in reference to his judgment in *Wilson v Darling Island Stevedoring*, that he 'entirely agreed ... with every line and every word of it, and, having read and reread it with growing admiration, I cannot forbear from expressing my sense of the loss which not only his colleagues in the High Court of Australia but all who anywhere are concerned with the administration of the common law have suffered by his premature death'. Such tributes are rare.

Fullagar was of medium height, thick-set, with a full face, blue eyes, and dark hair touched with ginger. A quiet, modest, gentle, friendly man, with a delicious sense of **humour** and (as Dixon put it) 'a most lovable nature', he commanded the respect and warm affection of all who knew him. Arthur Dean recalled him as 'a most genial and friendly man with whom it was impossible to fall out', and added:

> His sense of humour and fondness for a good story saved him from becoming a dry lawyer and he had the true humourist's ready response to a good story or a witty remark in or out of Court, employing as the occasion appeared to demand, a hoot of delight or a soft chuckle.

The chuckle was infectious: Menzies recalled him as 'a remarkably learned lawyer, who had been a notable classical scholar, and a lovely chuckling humourist'.

His principal recreations in later life were reading, gardening, bowls, walking, and trout fishing, with a fondness for the writing of light verse, the bagpipes, and Gilbert and Sullivan. In the High Court, he appeared to find tax avoidance cases especially Gilbertian. Of the scheme in *War Assets v FCT* (1954), he wrote: 'The dramatist who conceived Utopia Ltd and the Duke of Plaza-Toro Ltd might have found material for satire in the highly artificial structure which was erected. But I have to treat it as presenting a serious legal problem.' And in *FCT v Newton* (1957): 'I would not suggest that the great complexity of what was done ... was designed with no other object than to give artistic verisimilitude to what otherwise might have seemed bald and unconvincing.' As for the **evidence** in *Paff v Speed* (1961) of an injured policeman's lost career prospects, Fullagar could not refrain from commenting that the jury had been asked to assume 'that a policeman's lot is a very happy one indeed'.

On 11 October 1919, Fullagar married Marion Lovejoy at the Fulham Registry Office, London. She died in 1941, and on 4 July 1942, at South Yarra Presbyterian Church, he married Mary Taylor, who survived him. He had five sons, all from his first marriage, of whom four survived him. One son, Richard Kelsham Fullagar (1926–), followed his father to the Bench of the Supreme Court of Victoria in 1975.

Fullagar died suddenly of a cerebral thrombosis on 9 July 1961. A lecture series to honour his memory was established by Monash University in 1968.

TONY BLACKSHIELD
ROBIN SHARWOOD

G

Garcia v National Australia Bank (1998). In this case, the High Court was confronted with an anachronistic rule based upon controversial assumptions about the vulnerability of married **women**.

Garcia concerned the circumstances in which **equity** would allow a lender to take security for a loan from someone related to the borrower. The particular issue was whether a guarantee given by the appellant wife in relation to her husband's business debts, from which she derived no financial gain, could be enforced by the respondent bank when it had not explained to her the effect of the guarantee. In *Yerkey v Jones* (1939), **Dixon** had held that equity would prevent a creditor enforcing a security given by a wife in several situations. The outcome of *Garcia* depended upon whether Dixon's judgment in *Yerkey v Jones* should be followed.

Critics said *Yerkey v Jones* was paternalistic, demeaning of women, discriminatory, and anachronistic, given changes to the status of women since the 1930s. Conversely, empirical research pointed to the continued vulnerability of many women to make ill-advised financial decisions on inadequate information for the financial benefit of a partner or spouse.

In *Garcia*, the Court decided unanimously for the appellant wife. **Gaudron**, **McHugh**, **Gummow**, and **Hayne**, in a **joint judgment**, affirmed *Yerkey v Jones*, located it within equity's jurisdiction to prevent unconscionable insistence on legal rights, and specified the requirements for **unconscionability** in this context. The **criticisms** of *Yerkey v Jones* were addressed by restating the rationale for equitable intervention as the protection of sureties in relationships of trust and confidence, though its application to relationships other than marriage was left open. The majority favoured sureties over lenders by making securities unenforceable wherever the lender had not taken the necessary precautions, regardless of the particular surety's need for protection.

Callinan applied *Yerkey v Jones* without elaboration. Although agreeing in the result, **Kirby's** judgment stands alone. He rejected Dixon's statement of the law as 'a discriminatory rule expressed in terms which are unduly narrow, historically and socially out of date and unfairly discriminatory'. Instead, he proposed non-discriminatory protection of all vulnerable sureties.

The case sheds light on the Court's **law-making role**. As well as considering academic commentaries and law reform findings concerning *Yerkey v Jones*, the Court heard submissions on behalf of a consumer credit organisation (see **Interveners and** *amici curiae*). At the hearing, McHugh had been resistant to that course:

> People may not like to hear it but our essential function is to decide cases between parties. We are not here to reform the law generally … As an incident in deciding cases we may have to develop the law, but our primary function is to decide cases between parties.

Nevertheless, within those constraints, McHugh's judgment avoided the discriminatory and demeaning overtones of *Yerkey v Jones* without lessening the protection given to vulnerable sureties. But the joint judgment left the scope of equity's protection unresolved, and offered no guidance as to the requisite advice to be given potential sureties. Those questions were left for future courts before whom full submissions could be made.

A division of opinion was apparent as to the doctrine of **precedent**. The joint judgment disagreed with the NSW Court of Appeal's findings that Dixon's judgment in *Yerkey v Jones* was not the *ratio decidendi* of the case, or had somehow impliedly been overruled or subsumed by *Amadio's Case* (1983), and emphasised that the **overruling** of a High Court decision was a matter for the High Court alone. But as Kirby pointed out, this was inconsistent with the 'recent encouragement given by this Court to the appellate courts of Australia to play their part in the refinement, development and re-expression of legal principle which cannot, in the nature of things, be wholly left to this Court'.

Garcia is a landmark case in the thriving equitable jurisdiction to prevent unconscionable insistence on legal rights. It demonstrates the Court's ability to mould equitable doctrine creatively to accord with contemporary **values**, even within the self-imposed restrictions on the Court's law-making function.

PAULINE RIDGE

Further Reading

Australian Law Reform Commission, *Equality Before the Law: Women's Equality*, Report No 69 Part II (1994)

Belinda Fehlberg and Richard Ingleby, 'Surety Wives and Australian Law' (1998) 4 *Current Family Law* 207

GFK Santow, 'Sex, Lies and Sureties: Touching the Conscience of the Creditor' (1999) 10 *JBFLP* 7

Garran, Robert Randolph (*b* 10 February 1867; *d* 11 January 1957) was one of Australia's leading constitutional authorities and longest-serving Crown officers. He is remembered for several distinct and remarkable contributions to the Australian Commonwealth: as one of the most active and influential of the NSW federationists in the 1890s; as Secretary to the Drafting Committee of the 1897 Federal **Convention**; as co-author, with John Quick, of *The Annotated Constitution of the Australian Commonwealth* (1901) (see **Quick and Garran**); and as first Secretary of the Attorney-General's Department and later as Commonwealth **Solicitor-General** from 1916 to 1932. In addition, he served on or advised a number of commissions and committees of inquiry, represented Australia on international bodies, was active in musical, literary, and educational circles in Canberra, and was a founder of the ANU. His autobiography, *Prosper the Commonwealth* (1958), completed only days before his death, records his long and distinguished life with much warmth and humility.

Born in Sydney, Garran was the sixth child and only son of Andrew Garran and Mary Isham, née Sabine. He was educated at Sydney Grammar School and the University of Sydney, and was admitted to the NSW Bar in 1891. In 1902, he married Hilda Robson; their long and happy marriage produced four sons. From 1873 to 1885, Garran's father served as editor of the *Sydney Morning Herald*, taking a strong pro-federation line, as well as covering the many social and political reform movements of the day. Mary Garran was an energetic promoter of **social justice** and women's education. Their son grew up in a comfortable, educated household, committed to social and political improvement. In 1887, Henry Parkes appointed Andrew Garran to the NSW Legislative Council. There he actively supported industrial and social reforms, serving as Chair of the 1890 Royal Commission on strikes and Chairman of the NSW Council of Arbitration.

During the 1890s, Robert Garran followed his father's interests, becoming increasingly active in the federal movement as it shifted from an exclusively parliamentary process to a popular movement. He observed the 1891 Federal Convention in Sydney, and thereafter (possibly uniquely) attended every other key federal conference. He joined the Australasian Federal League at its formation in 1893 and became a League Council member. As League representative, he attended the Conference organised by the Riverina Federation Leagues and Australian Natives' Association branches, in Corowa, in mid-1893, which was to prove critical in the federation story. There, for the first time, he met his future collaborator, Quick, and served as a member of the small *ad hoc* committee that formulated Quick's celebrated resolution (thereafter known as the Corowa Plan). When the resolution was put, he acted as Quick's seconder. The resolution called for a new, directly elected Convention, which would be charged with writing a Constitution Bill, to be followed by a referendum on the Bill. The Corowa Plan was adopted at a Premiers' Conference in 1895, and was followed to its conclusion over the next six years. Again as representative of the Australasian Federation League, Garran attended the Bathurst People's Federal Convention in November 1896 and, ten days after his thirtieth birthday, chaired the Young Men's Federal Convention in Sydney in February 1897.

Garran's influential book, *The Coming Commonwealth* (written from his notes for a University of Sydney extension course on federal systems that had failed to attract any enrolments) appeared in the same month and found him instantly in demand as, in his own words, 'a junior authority on the subject'. NSW Premier George Reid, who had just been elected a delegate to the 1897 Convention, invited the younger man to accompany him to the Convention as his Private Secretary. Once there, Garran was seconded by the Convention Leader, **Barton**, to serve as Secretary to the Convention's Drafting Committee, and he worked strenuously and effectively, advising and assisting. Over the years, Garran also composed and published poems and doggerel (in the *Bulletin* and elsewhere), much of it commenting on the federation movement and its leading personalities.

In mid-1898, the completed Constitution Bill was sent for the voters' approval at referendums in four colonies. Garran was an energetic participant in the campaign, speaking, writing, and circulating pro-Bill literature for the Federation League. Following the referendum's failure in NSW, a Premiers' Conference took place in Melbourne in early 1899, and amendments to the Bill were agreed. Garran was again invited by Reid to provide assistance, but at that time he had begun working with Quick on the *Annotated Constitution* and found himself too busy to accept. (Alfred **Deakin's** memoir, *The Federal Story*, inaccurately records Garran as having attended the Conference.)

'Quick and Garran', dedicated to 'the people of Australia', appeared in 1901. More than 1000 pages in length, it contains a long historical introduction setting out the complex progress of the federation movement. This is followed by a detailed analysis of each section of the Constitution, including its historical background and relevant international comparisons, provenance, and evolution at the various Convention sessions. This work, as its authors intended, has continued to serve as an undisputed authority for students of **constitutional law**, historians, lawyers, and judges, and has been more influential in shaping Australians' understanding of the origins and working of the Commonwealth than probably any other single work.

Following a successful round of referendums in 1899, the Constitution Bill was enacted and the Commonwealth inaugurated. On 1 January 1901, Garran received the award of CMG for services to the federation movement. At the same time, he was appointed Secretary to the Attorney-General's Department, thereby becoming the first, and for a short time the only, Commonwealth public servant. His immediate task was to write the first *Commonwealth of Australia Gazette*, which he did by hand, delivering it in person to the printers. Next, he set in train the machinery for the first federal elections in late March 1901. He also supervised the transfer of the departments of defence, customs, and posts and telegraphs, among others, from the colonies to the new Commonwealth. He acted, in his own words, as 'both head and tail' of his department. Garran became the Department's permanent Head, eventually serving 16 governments, under ten **Prime Ministers** and 11 **Attorneys-General**. In 1916, Prime Minister WM Hughes appointed him first Solicitor-General for the Commonwealth, an office he retained for 16 years. In 1917, Garran was made a knight, and in 1937 awarded the GCMG.

process. Premiers' Conferences, he stated, 'might almost be said by this time to form an unwritten part' of the Constitution. The most serious difficulty with Australia's federal Constitution, Garran argued, lay in attempting to ascertain with precision the boundaries of the spheres of the state and the central governments.

These views were reiterated in his later writings; among other things, he called for urgent amendment to unify Australia's transport system under the Commonwealth. He also urged amendment to the **conciliation and arbitration** power on the grounds that it entrenched a particular method for resolving industrial disputes, and had contributed to a tendency for employers and employees to be organised into hostile groups.

Garran retired on 9 February 1932, but continued to work, taking up legal practice once more and occasionally appearing at the Bar, serving public authorities, promoting the establishment of the ANU, writing, singing, and playing music. In 1934, he assisted in preparing *The Case for Union*: the Commonwealth's reply to WA's secessionist movement. It argued that, contrary to the secessionists' claims, the High Court had rarely invalidated state laws and that it had been far from a one-sided arbiter of the Constitution. *The Case for Union* bears Garran's style, characterised by a lightness of touch, economy of expression, and, even in such a context, wit. In 1946, at the age of nearly 80, he won a national ABC song competition.

Garran's death in 1957 broke the last direct link with the making of Australia's Constitution. But, more than this, it marked the end of a generation of public men for whom the cultural and the political were natural extensions of each other and who had the skills and talents to make such connections effortlessly.

HELEN IRVING

Further Reading
Robert Garran, *Prosper the Commonwealth* (1958)

Gaudron, Mary Genevieve (*b* 5 January 1943; Justice since 1987) has, since February 1998, been the Court's senior **puisne Justice**. She was the first—and remains the only—female Justice of the High Court. In that sense, her appointment is remarkable. Yet Gaudron's career is a classic example of talent and industry triumphant over limited opportunity.

Gaudron was born in the NSW country town of Moree, daughter of Edward, a train driver, and Grace ('Bonnie'), née Mawkes. In 1951, a watershed experience occurred in her life. **Evatt** visited Moree, campaigning from the back of a truck for the 'No' case in the referendum that, if passed, would have permitted the banning of the Australian Communist Party (see *Communist Party Case* (1951)). Eight-year-old Gaudron inquired what was this 'Constitution' the 'Doc' kept on about? Evatt sent her a copy.

Gaudron had her secondary education at St Ursula's, Armidale, a Catholic school run by nuns. One recalled her as a 'quick-witted girl … determined to make the best of her abilities'. Those abilities secured Gaudron a scholarship to the University of Sydney. She arrived in 1960 with 'high hopes and a shiny new briefcase', graduating BA in 1962. At university, Gaudron married. In 1965, mother to a baby

Robert Garran, first Commonwealth Solicitor-General

Over the years, in addition to drafting Bills (noted for their spare, economical style) and giving legal advice to governments and Commonwealth departments, Garran appeared for the Commonwealth in some constitutional cases, including an appearance before the **Privy Council** for the Commonwealth as **intervener** in *Webb v Outtrim* (1906). He held strong views about the meaning of certain constitutional provisions—later writing, for example, that 'the violence of the oscillations in the interpretation' of section 92 was unnecessary, since the section appeared clearly to intend 'an absolute prohibition directed to the Commonwealth and to States against the re-erection of any form of barrier to interstate trade' (see **Interstate trade and commerce**). In December 1912, an adviser to Attorney-General Hughes recommended that Garran be appointed to the High Court to fill the first of three vacancies created by the death of **O'Connor** in 1912 and by the increase of the **number of Justices** to seven in 1913. In 1920, Hughes said in Parliament that Garran would have been appointed to judicial office 'but for the fact that he is too valuable a man for us to lose. We cannot spare him' (see **Appointments that might have been**).

In 1927, Garran was invited to give evidence to the Royal Commission on the Constitution, established that year by the Nationalist government under Prime Minister Stanley Bruce. There, he took pains to trace the historical evolution of the Commonwealth, including the establishment of Commonwealth departments and a Commonwealth judiciary. This 'quarter of a century', he told the Commission, 'has been very largely a period of beginnings and getting things in order' and federal cooperation had been crucial to this

Mary Gaudron, Justice since 1987

daughter, she graduated LLB with first-class honours and the University medal in law. She was the first female part-time student to receive the medal, and only the second woman (the first being Elizabeth Evatt) to do so. Later, Gaudron would receive Honorary Doctorates in Law from Macquarie University (1988) and the University of Sydney (1999).

Law students' publication *Blackacre* thought Gaudron displayed 'all the attributes of the thoroughly disconcerting ... a keen analytical mind, a magnificent command of the language and sheer audacity'. University friends remembered her as 'brilliant', 'good fun' or both. Gaudron's law lecturers included **Mason** and, for **succession law**, Frank Hutley, later a renowned judge of the NSW Court of Appeal. Hutley remembered Gaudron's near-perfect succession exam paper as the finest he ever marked. He became an important early mentor at the Bar.

Gaudron lectured in succession at her *alma mater*, completed her articles, and was admitted to the Bar in October 1968. Stellar results should have facilitated early admission to membership of a floor. Instead, she experienced hostility. Initially, she shared a room with Janet Coombs, to whom Gaudron has paid tribute as a pioneer among **women practitioners**.

Despite those early difficulties, Gaudron's talent quickly began to shine. By the mid-1970s, she enjoyed a busy practice in all jurisdictions of the NSW Supreme Court, with a focus on industrial and **defamation law**. Appearances in the High Court during that time included her successful argument of *O'Shaughnessy v Mirror Newspapers* (1970). She was led by Hutley in *R v Flight Crew Officers' Industrial Tribunal; Ex parte Australian Federation of Air Pilots* (1971), and in *Leslie v Mirror Newspapers* (1971) by Harold Glass, also to become a distinguished judge of the NSW Court of Appeal.

In 1972, Gaudron became the first woman appointed to the NSW Bar Council. In 1973, she successfully appeared for the Commonwealth before the Arbitration Commission in the *Equal Pay Case*. That led in April 1974 to appointment as a Deputy President of the Commission. She was just 31.

Commission decisions she participated in included the *Maternity Leave Case*, which she has remembered as a highlight of her career to that point. From 1979 to 80, Gaudron also served as foundation Chair of the NSW Legal Services Commission. In May 1980, she resigned from the Arbitration Commission. Newspaper reports suggested it was a protest over the attempted demotion of Commission colleague Justice Jim Staples, with whom Gaudron had worked at the Bar.

Following her resignation, Gaudron took up a visiting lectureship at the University of NSW Law School. But not for long. In February 1981, she was appointed NSW **Solicitor-General**. She was the first woman to occupy that office in any Australian state. Shortly afterwards, she was appointed NSW's first female QC. As Solicitor-General, Gaudron appeared frequently before the High Court in some of its most significant constitutional cases, including *Actors Equity v Fontana Films* (1982), the ***Tasmanian Dam Case*** (1983), *Hematite Petroleum v Victoria* (1983), *Stack v Coast Securities (No 9)* (1983) and *Miller v TCN Channel Nine* (1986). She developed a wide reputation for what the *Australian Law Journal* described as 'outstanding and ingenious' advocacy.

Murphy died in late 1986. Gaudron spoke powerfully at his memorial service at the Sydney Town Hall, to a packed audience. His death created a vacancy on the Court and, following the retirement of **Gibbs**, **Toohey** and Gaudron were appointed in 1987. She was just 43, among the youngest Justices ever (see **Background of Justices**). Gaudron's appointment was widely welcomed by the profession. Only the NSW legal gossip sheet *Justinian* dissented, charging her, in what today seems undisguised sexism, with 'an emotional disposition inappropriate in a holder of judicial office'. By contrast, the speeches made at a NSW Bar Association Dinner held in Gaudron's honour show the depth of enthusiasm for her appointment, and the affection for her personally, felt among her colleagues.

Since her appointment, Gaudron has contributed to the development of every important area of Australian law, from a workable theory of section 92 (*Cole v Whitfield* (1988)) to recognition of **native title** (*Mabo* (1992); *Wik* (1996)), as well as greater resolution of the implications of Chapter III for the federal system (*Re Wakim* (1999)—see **Cross-vesting**); identification of an implied freedom of **political communication** (*Australian Capital Television v Commonwealth; Nationwide News v Wills* (1992)—see *Free Speech Cases*); progression of **administrative law** in areas including **standing** (*Bateman's Bay Local Aboriginal Land Council v Aboriginal Community Benefit Fund* (1998)) and **natural justice** (*Ainsworth v Criminal Justice Commission* (1992)); and reform of both **criminal procedure** (*Dietrich v The Queen* (1992)) and **conflict of laws** (*John Pfeiffer v Rogerson* (2000)).

Gaudron's judgments have been particularly influential in developing the **criminal law**. They combine technical mastery with a general tendency to insist on strict compliance by trial judges with their obligations in directing juries—a tendency that seems motivated by an interest in ensuring both procedural fairness for the accused and due respect for the function of the jury in the administration of criminal justice (see, for example, *Zecevic v DPP* (1987); the joint judgments in *Doney v The Queen* (1990) and *Edwards v The Queen* (1993); *Farrell v The Queen* (1998); *HG v The Queen* (1999)). Perhaps Gaudron's most significant contribution, however, is her theory of **discrimination**, applied to section 117 of the Constitution in *Street v Queensland Bar Association* (1989) (see **Express constitutional rights**) and to section 92 in her joint judgment with McHugh in *Castlemaine Tooheys v SA* (1990) (see **Interstate trade and commerce**) and encapsulated in the statement in that case that 'discrimination lies in the unequal treatment of equals, and … the equal treatment of unequals'. Non-discrimination emerges in her judgments as an organising principle of the federal compact (see, for example, *Ha v NSW* (1997); **Excise duties**).

Gaudron's formulation of the principle of non-discrimination—'equal treatment under the law that allows for relevant difference'—has proved a key theme of her Chapter III jurisprudence. There, Gaudron has identified equal treatment as a fundamental characteristic of the judicial process required for the proper exercise of **judicial power**. In *Leeth v Commonwealth* (1992), she would have invalidated a law having the effect of requiring that courts designated to exercise the judicial power of the Commonwealth were to sentence certain Commonwealth offenders differently according to the state or territory they were tried in. In Gaudron's view, by failing to treat like offences against Commonwealth laws in a like way, the power created by the law exhibited an impermissibly discriminatory character repugnant to the judicial process, and therefore precluding its conferral on section 71 courts (see also **Equality**).

Gaudron's Chapter III judgments have also emphasised how effective resolution of controversies involving exercise of the judicial power of the Commonwealth depends on public confidence that courts and judges will act, and be seen to act, independently according to a judicial process: in short, that ordinary people will receive equal treatment under the law with government and other institutions of power. In *Wilson v Minister for Aboriginal and Torres Strait Islander Affairs* (1996), Gaudron therefore joined the majority in holding a law invalid to the extent it directed the performance by judges exercising the judicial power of the Commonwealth of functions threatening to compromise that public confidence.

The principle of equal treatment similarly underscores Gaudron's view of independent **judicial review** of the exercise of administrative and executive powers as a fundamental feature of the **rule of law** (*Enfield Corporation v Development Assessment Corporation* (2000)).

Gaudron's judgment in *Re Tracey; Ex parte Ryan* (1989) suggests a broader principle of independent judicial power, describing as part of the 'general pattern of constitutional and legal arrangements obtaining in Australia' that ordinarily it is for the properly constituted civil courts alone to determine whether conduct offends against the general law and what if any penalty should be imposed for such conduct (see **Military justice**).

That the law under challenge in the *War Crimes Act Case* (1991) departed from that principle explains why Gaudron would have invalidated it as a usurpation of judicial power. By leaving it to the courts to determine only whether a person answered the description of someone already declared guilty by parliamentary enactment, Gaudron considered that the law foreclosed the exercise of the fundamental feature of judicial power in criminal proceedings: determination of guilt or innocence by application of the law to facts as found.

Gaudron's method of **constitutional interpretation** typically involves a search for the meaning required by text or necessarily comprehended by context. Accordingly, because the Constitution 'mandates whatever is necessary for the maintenance of the democratic processes for which it provides', Gaudron has held that, to that extent, there exist limited freedoms of association and of **movement** (*Kruger v The Commonwealth* (1997)).

From the principle that judicial power must be exercised according to a judicial process, Gaudron has also held that there arises from Chapter III a limited guarantee of fair trial of those Commonwealth offences that must be tried in the courts named or indicated in section 71 (*Re Nolan; Ex parte Young* (1991)).

In her judicial method generally, Gaudron is a rigid logician, as her persuasive dissenting joint judgment with **Gummow** in *Osland v The Queen* (1998) demonstrates. Gaudron's judgments also reflect a respect for *stare decisis* (adherence to precedent), revealed as a reluctance to depart from authority without careful reconsideration of its correctness (see, for example, her reappraisal of *McInnis v The Queen* (1979) in *Dietrich*). That respect for *stare decisis* explains Gaudron's ungrudging adoption of views that have prevailed over hers (see, for example, her acceptance in *Nicholas v The Queen* (1998) of the 'minimum' position decided in *Ridgeway v The Queen* (1995)). Gaudron's preference for correctness over dogmatism also accounts for occasional revision of her own earlier opinions in later cases (compare her view of section 51(xxvi) in the *Hindmarsh Island Bridge Case* (1998) with that in *Chu Kheng Lim v Minister for Immigration* (1992)).

Gaudron has, however, also applied the principles that the Constitution prevails over inconsistent judicial pronouncements, and that existing decisions on questions of **constitutional law** are of limited authority if not based on a principle or reasoning that has commanded majority support (see, for example, *Re Tyler; Ex parte Foley* (1994)).

Gaudron's writing style is emphatic but not emotive—a rare exception being the passage in her joint judgment with **Deane** in *Mabo* (1992) identifying dispossession of **Aboriginal peoples** of their traditional lands as 'the darkest aspect of the history of this nation'. Increasingly, her judgments strive to build consensus of opinion in the interest of clarity and certainty (for example, the summation in her own judgment of the others in *Marks v GIO Australia Holdings* (1998)).

Gaudron lives in Sydney. She has a son with her husband, and two daughters from her previous marriage. She also has a superb sense of **humour**, which is often evident in her speeches, her dealings with her judicial colleagues, her **associates** and other staff.

In her speeches, and not inconsistently with her duties as a Justice, Gaudron has sought to draw attention to the status of **women**, particularly women in the legal profession (see, for example, (1998) 72 *ALJ* 119). Her speeches have also paid tribute to pioneering women lawyers including the late Dame Roma Mitchell. Where appropriate, Gaudron has also drawn attention in her judgments to the need in various areas of the law for greater recognition of women's paid and unpaid work (for example, *Baumgartner v Baumgartner* (1987) and *Singer v Berghouse* (1994)).

Gaudron has, in speeches, sometimes expressed impatience with suggestions that the discriminatory attitudes of some male lawyers will improve over time and with greater experience of their female colleagues. Ironically, many male lawyers have felt their own such attitudes transformed by exposure to Gaudron's enormous intelligence, efficiency, kindness, infectious good humour, and the respect and admiration for her that that combination produces.

HENRIK KALOWSKI

Gavan Duffy, Frank (*b* 29 February 1852; *d* 29 July 1936; Justice 1913–31; Chief Justice 1931–35) was the first son of the second marriage of Charles Gavan Duffy (to Charles' first cousin, Susan Hughes). When Charles became tired of facing treason trials in Ireland, he left with his family, including the three-year-old Frank, for the recently established colony of Victoria. They arrived at Port Phillip on the *Ocean Chief* in early 1856.

A decade later, Frank sailed back to Great Britain for his secondary education at Stoneyhurst College, Lancashire. He returned to the colony in 1869 to study law and arts at the University of Melbourne. By the time he was called to the Melbourne Bar in 1874, his father had served in three governments as a minister, including one term as Premier, and had been knighted. In 1880, he married Ellen Torr. They were to have three sons—including one they named Charles, who was later to achieve judicial office as well as a knighthood.

At the Bar, Frank soon emerged as a distinguished advocate and dialectician; in 1901, he was appointed a KC. We have the authority of **Dixon** for the view that Gavan Duffy was a man who 'could make bricks without straw in open court'. He was better regarded as a jury advocate than as a man of deep legal learning, but he developed a reasonable proficiency in legal analysis by lecturing at his old law school, writing texts, and editing law reports.

Although his practice thrived in the first decade of federation, Gavan Duffy was not generally perceived as High Court material. But in 1913, WM Hughes, as **Attorney-General** in a Fisher Labor government, needed to replace one of the original members, **O'Connor**, who had died in 1912. He appointed Gavan Duffy, who at the age of almost 61, was the oldest person then to have been appointed to the Court.

According to **Higgins'** biographer, John Rickard, there was some suggestion that the Court's token Catholic was being replaced by another. The fact that Gavan Duffy was perceived by his contemporaries at the Bar to be a radical may have improved his prospects of **appointment** by a Labor government. If Hughes had looked behind Gavan Duffy's radical rhetoric and appreciated his innate conservatism, he might have thought twice about the appointment.

Griffith and **Barton** immediately found their new sexagenarian colleague congenial, for he supported their position on **reserved state powers** and **intergovernmental immunities** (he was to be the lone dissenter in 1920 when the doctrines were abolished in the *Engineers Case*). In 1913, Barton wrote to Griffith, who was overseas, that he, Gavan Duffy, and **Rich** were going to Perth, and that when the trio sat together 'business gets along fairly well'. Barton wrote critically about **Isaacs** and Higgins, but described Gavan Duffy as 'honest'. Hughes, who had been so keen to discover whether

Frank Gavan Duffy, Justice 1913–31; Chief Justice 1931–35

Piddington looked 'favourably on the national side of things', must have been chagrined to observe that Gavan Duffy not only supported the doctrines that had been swept aside by *Engineers*, but consistently dissented from Isaacs' sweeping interpretations of federal power.

Gavan Duffy could be proud and imperious. At a Victorian Bar dinner to celebrate his appointment to the High Court, the Bar's most junior member impudently asked in his speech whether the new appointee would be 'Frank the fair, Gavan the garrulous, or Duffy the diabolical?' Gavan Duffy was not amused. 'I am not acquainted with Mr Junior', he snorted, 'but I sincerely hope that he will never appear in my court'. Soon after that, Gavan Duffy reacted so strongly to perceived slights by staff at Government House that Griffith, who himself often displayed similar sensitivity, was constrained to write to the Governor-General seeking some sort of social amends.

But although he was sensitive, Gavan Duffy was renowned for his sense of **humour**. And Mr Junior may have got close to the bone in one aspect of his rhetorical question, for Gavan Duffy could be garrulous. On one occasion, Rich—who was notorious for adopting the easy course of **concurring** in judgments written by his colleagues—took Gavan Duffy to task for his loquacity in court. 'Small wonder', replied Gavan Duffy, 'since I have to talk for two'.

Despite his demonstrated conservatism and lacklustre performance on the Court, Gavan Duffy was, in his late seventies, promoted to the Chief Justiceship by another Labor government in 1931. The circumstances were somewhat unusual. The Scullin government had endured a good deal of criticism over the appointment of **Evatt** and **McTiernan** in 1930 and the appointment of Isaacs as the first Australian-born Governor-General. It was also reeling from attacks based on its handling of the economic effects of the **Depression**. Perhaps the safest course was to promote the ageing senior **puisne Justice**.

Gavan Duffy remained **Chief Justice** into his early eighties (although he was fond of saying that he had not yet turned 21, as he had been born on 29 February). He then demonstrated his pride and wiliness as a negotiator. According to a story with wide anecdotal support, Gavan Duffy was pressured into resigning in order to make way for the ambitious **Latham**, who had had enough of politics. Gavan Duffy extracted a number of conditions. One was that his son Charles should be appointed a Justice of the Supreme Court of Victoria. Robert **Menzies**, who was the Victorian Attorney-General, and had an interest in this game of musical chairs, since he wanted to succeed Latham as the federal member for Kooyong (and as federal Attorney-General), was able to oblige. Charles Gavan Duffy was appointed to the Supreme Court of Victoria in 1933. But the Chief Justice had not exhausted his bargaining chips. He had merely said that he was 'prepared to consider' retiring if his son was appointed to the Bench. Gavan Duffy spread the word that if he were to retire, he thought it would be fitting that a portrait of him should be commissioned.

Robert Menzies, who had carried out the first part of the deal, but who still had not achieved his own goals, fell in with the need to satisfy the vanity of the elderly jurist. He solicited donations from the Victorian Bar, of which he was a member, towards the commissioning of a portrait of Gavan Duffy.

Satisfied that the cost of the portrait would be met, and that Latham was about to retire from federal politics, Menzies resigned from the Victorian Legislative Assembly in July 1934. Two days later, when the House of Representatives rose for the elections, Latham announced that he would not be contesting the seat of Kooyong at the next elections. He gave as his reasons that he 'had had enough of politics', and that he wanted to return to his practice as a barrister in order to 'attend to his material fortunes which had been so long neglected in politics'.

Menzies was elected to the federal Parliament in September 1934, and succeeded Latham as federal Attorney-General in the following month. Latham obviously expected that Gavan Duffy would then announce his **retirement**. But he had to endure further delay. According to Gough Whitlam, Gavan Duffy refused to stand down, in the hope that **Prime Minister** Joseph Lyons and Attorney-General Menzies, on their visit to England in August 1935, would arrange for him to make his debut on the **Privy Council** (Gavan Duffy had been appointed Privy Counsellor three years earlier). Lyons and Menzies failed to meet Gavan Duffy's wish. Gavan Duffy did not resign until October 1935. A relieved Latham was appointed Chief Justice by the Lyons government, courtesy of its Attorney-General, Robert Menzies.

Gavan Duffy was not a great lawyer in the technical sense, although he showed remarkable prescience and a good instinct for a sound result in his dissent in *McArthur v Queensland* (1920) concerning section 92 of the Constitu-

tion (see **Interstate trade and commerce**). He had been an effective **counsel**, and his major skill in his early years on the Bench involved debating the issues. He also penned a delightful poem entitled 'A Dream of Fair Judges', written in 1892 but published years later in the *Australian Law Journal*, in which he spoke memorably of the 'full immunity from doubt/Of the judicial mind', and of 'laboured judgments lucidly obscure,/Perspicuously wrong'. It was perhaps unfair to expect that he would exercise great authority or administrative abilities when he was appointed Chief Justice well beyond the age at which he would now be compelled to retire. The challenges were enormous. He spent the first part of his new office enjoying the prestige and the second part manoeuvring for personal and family advantage. Having achieved the appointment of his son to the Bench and the commissioning of his own portrait, he left the management and intellectual challenges to the younger Latham.

GRAHAM FRICKE

Further Reading
Frank Gavan Duffy, 'A Dream of Fair Judges' (1945) 19 *ALJ* 43

Gavan Duffy Court (22 January 1931 to 1 October 1935). Amid the economic and political turbulence generated by the **Depression**, the Court was wracked by deteriorating **personal relations** and manoeuvres over **appointments**, from both within and outside the Court. There were also generational factors: by 1931 **Rich** had been on the Court for almost 18 years and **Starke** for over a decade, but **Dixon** had been there only two years and **Evatt** and **McTiernan** barely a month. **Gavan Duffy's** elevation as **Chief Justice** rebuffed those in the Labor Caucus who had hoped to see Evatt in that role. Yet Starke was openly hostile to Evatt's presence even as a **puisne Justice**, and Dixon, while outwardly civil, had been equally distressed. Within the new conservative government elected in January 1932 under **Prime Minister** Joseph Lyons, with **Latham** again as **Attorney-General**, there were rumours of plots and sub-plots aimed at achieving Latham's appointment as Chief Justice.

In 1931, the controversy over the appointments of Evatt and McTiernan, the decline in the Court's **business**, and the need to economise, led the Labor government of JH Scullin to leave the seventh place on the Court unfilled; and in 1933, the Lyons government formally amended the *Judiciary Act* 1903 (Cth) to reduce the **number of Justices** to six. To economise further, the **circuit system** was suspended, and the government asked the Justices to accept reduced **remuneration**. (They refused, but made voluntary payments to the Treasury or forwent their travelling allowances).

With the Court reduced to six Justices (an even number), there were frequent applications of the Judiciary Act provisions determining the result of **tied votes**—most graphically in the case of Harold Williams, originally sentenced to 18 months' imprisonment for counterfeiting (a federal offence). The Supreme Court of NSW had increased Williams' sentence to five years (on appeal by NSW prosecution authorities), then to four years (on appeal by the Commonwealth). The High Court set the first increase aside because the NSW procedure for prosecution appeals against sentence could not be used by state authorities in relation to federal offences

(*Williams v The King (No 1)* (1933)). As to whether the Commonwealth could use the procedure, the Court was evenly divided. Under section 23(2)(a) of the Judiciary Act, the four-year sentence was affirmed, although Gavan Duffy, Evatt and McTiernan would have allowed Williams' appeal (*Williams v The King (No 2)* (1934)).

As soon as the original sentence of 18 months was completed, Williams applied for a **writ** of habeas corpus (*Ex parte Williams* (1934)). He argued that since this involved the Court's original rather than appellate **jurisdiction**, section 23(2)(b) of the Judiciary Act would apply, and Gavan Duffy's view would prevail (as the view of the Chief Justice). But the whole Court held that, since a Supreme Court decision was still in question, section 23(2)(a) would still apply. The order nisi for habeas corpus was refused.

Gavan Duffy was 78 when he became Chief Justice. His capacity for effective input was minimal. Weak and ineffectual in **administration**, he did nothing to facilitate **conferences** or exchange of draft judgments, let alone to assist or influence the Court by circulating his own draft judgments. His judicial contribution was scanty in the extreme. Leaving aside cases finally disposed of by a single Justice—usually by Starke or Dixon, and including Dixon's influential judgment on **occupiers' liability** in *Lipman v Clendinnen* (1932)—the Court sat in collegiate benches in 294 reported cases. The *Commonwealth Law Reports* record 118 unreported collegiate cases. Of these 412 cases, Gavan Duffy sat in 168—just over 40 per cent. The burden thus imposed on the puisne Justices was especially onerous in 1933 (when Gavan Duffy sat in 8 out of 55 reported cases and 10 out of 30 unreported cases) and in the first nine months of 1935 (when he sat in 8 of the 57 reported cases and in none of the 23 unreported). In his last four months as Chief Justice, he did not sit at all. When his son Charles Gavan Duffy was appointed to the Supreme Court of Victoria in 1933, the father could not sit to hear appeals from the son; but this explained very few of his abstentions.

The 124 reported cases where he did sit included 16 in which he delivered the Court's unanimous judgment. In six of them he did so in four sentences or less—including *McNamara v Langford* (1931), a bankruptcy case, where after announcing the result he added characteristically 'that, although I do not dissent from that view, I do not wish to state my formal adherence to it'. In 14 cases, he delivered a joint majority judgment with only one other Justice (usually Starke) separately concurring or dissenting; and in four, he spoke for himself and three other Justices, with the other two writing separately. These unanimous or near-unanimous judgments accounted for 34 of the cases in which Gavan Duffy sat.

In another 52 cases, he gave a joint judgment with one or more other Justices—including eight with Dixon, three with both Dixon and Rich, and 23 with Starke. In eight of those cases Gavan Duffy and Starke were the only dissenters, and in *Metropolitan Gas Co v FCT* (1932) their judgment prevailed in a 2:2 tied vote. Even when in the majority, their judgments were often distinctive: in *Transport Commissioners v Barton* (1933), which generally affirmed the restrictive **common law** categories of occupiers' liability, it was Gavan Duffy and Starke who most clearly left open an alternative approach through 'the more general principle of the duty of care'. But after May 1934, there were no more joint judgments with Starke; their personal estrangement had become too bitter.

Previously, Gavan Duffy had given three joint judgments with Evatt and McTiernan. Now, from May 1934 to May 1935, there were another seven such judgments. There was also a joint judgment with Evatt in *Roman Catholic Archbishop of Melbourne v Lawlor* (1934)—which, with McTiernan's separate concurrence, prevailed in another tied vote. On the same day, in *Donaldson v Freeson* (1934), Gavan Duffy gave his last joint judgment with Starke. Earlier, there were three other joint judgments with Evatt, including the dissents in *Smith v FCT* (1932) and *Commissioner of Stamp Duties v Millar* (1932). In April and May of 1932, a brief rapprochement had produced four joint judgments by Gavan Duffy, Starke, and Evatt, including the tied vote in *Deputy FCT v Wheat Pool of WA* (1932).

In seven cases, Gavan Duffy delivered no judgment at all—delegating to another Justice (as he had often done in the **Knox Court**) the task of announcing his concurrence. Initially courteous, these announcements grew noticeably more terse. In the end, Dixon was saying simply: 'The Chief Justice agrees in this judgment.'

In only 31 reported cases did Gavan Duffy, as Chief Justice, actually express his own view. In 21 of them, his judgment was only one or two sentences; in another five, it was less than a page. Only in the five remaining cases—an average of one a year—did Gavan Duffy give a full judgment; and in three of those (*R v Vizzard; Ex parte Hill* (1933), *Public Trustee v FCT* (1934) and *Williams (No 2)*), it was less than three pages. His longest judgments—each in dissent, and each about three pages—were in *A-G (NSW) v Trethowan* (1931) and the *State Garnishee Case* (1932).

Both cases reflected the turbulence of NSW Labor politics under premier Jack Lang. *Trethowan* concerned Lang's attempt to abolish the NSW Legislative Council. A previous attempt in 1926, when McTiernan was Lang's Attorney-General, had failed; and in 1929 the conservative government of premier Thomas Bavin had introduced amendments to the *Constitution Act* 1902 (NSW) to prevent abolition of the Legislative Council without a referendum. The question in *Trethowan* was whether the NSW Parliament could effectively limit its own future legislative powers in this way; the majority, with Gavan Duffy and McTiernan dissenting, held that it could. The decision (affirmed by the **Privy Council** in *A-G (NSW) v Trethowan* (1932)) depended on section 5 of the *Colonial Laws Validity Act* 1865 (Imp), which recognised the power of colonial parliaments to alter their own constitutions, provided it was done in the 'manner and form' required by any 'law in force'. The majority treated the referendum provision as a 'manner and form' requirement—not excluding the possibility of abolishing the Legislative Council, but merely prescribing the procedure by which that objective must be pursued. In a haunting passage, Dixon hinted at a deeper constitutional principle: even in the UK Parliament, with its undoubted assumption of illimitable parliamentary **sovereignty**, a question might arise whether legislative power 'had in truth been exercised in the manner required for its authentic expression and by the elements in which it had come to reside'.

The *State Garnishee Case* (*NSW v Commonwealth (No 1)*) arose from the Lyons federal government's action against NSW under the *Financial Agreements Enforcement Act* 1932 (Cth), which created a drastic summary procedure for High Court 'declarations' of state indebtedness to the Commonwealth, to be enforced (without further judicial proceedings) by seizure of the revenues (including unpaid taxes) of the defaulting state. McTiernan joined Rich, Starke, and Dixon in holding the legislation valid; Gavan Duffy and Evatt dissented. Attacking the decision in the NSW Parliament, Lang reserved his most potent venom for Dixon (who, he said, had helped to draft the legislation and had then upheld its validity), and for McTiernan (whose judgment, said Lang, had been written by a well-known Sydney QC). In *NSW v Commonwealth (No 2)* (1932), the Court refused a certificate for appeal to the Privy Council (see *Inter se* **questions**). Only Evatt dissented. In *NSW v Commonwealth (No 3)* (1932), the Court dismissed a separate challenge to section 15 of the Act, involving a compulsory takeover of all bank accounts 'standing to the credit of the State'; Gavan Duffy and Evatt again dissented. Later, when the amount of NSW debt was declared (*In re NSW; Ex parte A-G (Cth)* (1932)), the Court rejected the state's claims to a set-off (for example, of Commonwealth grants withheld from it under the Loan Council and **Federal Roads** schemes).

Three weeks after the *State Garnishee Case*, Lang was dismissed from office by Governor Phillip Game. But before leaving office he had personally authorised a series of advertisements for the NSW Government Tourist Bureau in the *Labor Weekly*. The new government of premier Bertram Stevens refused to pay for the remaining advertisements; but the paper's owner, Kenneth Bardolph, continued to insert them. Once the contract period was over, he sued for the full amount of the agreed advertising rates (*NSW v Bardolph* (1934)). Evatt found an enforceable contract. On appeal the other five judges agreed: the contract was binding, though a parliamentary appropriation of money (in this case already made) would be necessary before the judgment in such a case could be enforced.

The political and financial turmoil engulfing Labor administrations was not confined to Scullin and Lang. Edmund Hogan was Labor premier of Victoria from 1929 to 1932. Because he had supported the 1931 'Premiers' Plan' to deal with the Depression, the Labor Party's central executive withdrew his endorsement as a parliamentary candidate and expelled him from the party. Re-elected to the Victorian Parliament as an independent, he sued for a declaration that his expulsion and disendorsement were wrongful, and for **remedies** by way of injunctions and **damages**. In the Supreme Court of Victoria, Charles Gavan Duffy awarded him one shilling in damages. The High Court took even that away (*Cameron v Hogan* (1934)): the Labor Party was a voluntary association whose rules created no enforceable rights, and membership conferred no 'tangible or practical' basis for an injunction.

The Depression produced numerous appeals involving bankruptcy, **taxation law**, **corporations law**, **property**, tenancy, and agricultural liens. All governments had enacted provisions for emergency financial relief, and in cases such as *Barcelo v Electrolytic Zinc* (1932), *Merwin Pastoral Co v Moolpa*

Pastoral Co (1933), *Wragge v Sims Cooper* (1933), and *Wanganui-Rangitikei Electric Power Board v AMP* (1934), attempts to evade or attract those provisions raised issues in the **conflict of laws** as to the law governing particular contracts or debentures. The *Moratorium Act* 1930 (NSW) made hire purchase agreements (apparently including promissory notes) unenforceable except by leave, while the *Bills of Exchange Act* 1909 (Cth) gave a specific statutory right to sue on a promissory note. But in *Stock Motor Ploughs v Forsyth* (1932), the Court upheld the state legislation. Only Dixon found an **inconsistency** under section 109 of the Constitution.

The depreciation of the Australian pound—hitherto treated as equivalent to the English pound—led to unfamiliar problems. In *Payne v FCT* (1934), the joint judgment of Gavan Duffy, Evatt, and McTiernan held that a payment in England of £5671 sterling must be taxed on the basis of its Australian yield (at the new exchange rate) of £6768: in a tied vote, Rich, Starke, and Dixon were left in Anglophile dissent. The new exchange rate also led to an increase (in Australian currency) in earnings from sales of gold in London; and in 1931, when Britain went off the gold standard, the price of gold went up. In *Cominelli & Bonazzi v Lake View & Star* (1934), the Court held that the tributers who worked the WA gold mines and supplied ore to the owners were entitled to the whole of the unexpected additional earnings: their rights were protected by the *Mining Act* 1904 (WA), and their compromise agreement to accept a lesser amount was invalid, since their statutory protection was a matter of public policy that could not be varied by agreement.

The general pressure for reductions in wages dominated **labour relations**. In *Australian Insurance Staffs Federation v Atlas Assurance* (1931), the majority (with Gavan Duffy and Starke dissenting) held that award wages could not be reduced below the parameters set by the 'ambit' of the original dispute (see also *Australian Tramway Employees v Commissioner for Road Transport* (1935)). But in *Australian Workers Union v Graziers Association* (1932), it was held (with Evatt and McTiernan dissenting) that a reduction in shearers' pay *was* within the original 'ambit', since the employers' log of claims had envisaged 'such lower rates as may from time to time the Court seem just' (see also *Federated Millers v Butcher* (1932)).

The *Transport Workers Act* 1928 (Cth) was litigated three times. Initially devised by the conservative Bruce–Page government to break the power of the Waterside Workers Federation (WWF) on the Melbourne waterfront, the Act had set up a licensing scheme for waterside workers that was used to promote a rival union, the Permanent and Casual Wharf Labourers' Union (PCWLU). In December 1930, while Labor Prime Minister Scullin was overseas, his Cabinet decided to use the Act in reverse: under new regulations, licences were given to the WWF and not to the PCWLU. In *Huddart Parker v Commonwealth* (1931), Rich, Dixon and Evatt held the Act and regulations valid under the **trade and commerce power**. Starke dissented; Gavan Duffy avoided the constitutional issue by holding that the new regulations did not conform to the Act. A protracted parliamentary struggle ensued: as often as the Senate disallowed the regulations, the government reintroduced them. In *Dignan v Australian Steamships* (1931), a Senate opposition manoeuvre to disallow the latest regulations was upheld by Rich, Starke and Dixon, with Gavan Duffy and Evatt dissenting. In *Victorian Stevedoring and Meakes v Dignan* (1931), the Court affirmed again that the legislation was valid: the very broad power given by the Act to make regulations overriding 'any other Act', though delegating substantial legislative power to the executive government, did not infringe the **separation of powers**.

The case arose from a prosecution for giving preference to a member of the PCWLU. By the time the case reached the High Court, the relevant regulation had been disallowed by the Senate. Nevertheless, the Court upheld the conviction, since the magistrate had correctly applied the law in force at the time. On the other hand, when a PCWLU member complained that he was denied a licence because of his union membership (*R v Mahony; Ex parte Johnson* (1931)), the whole Court held that this was not a legitimate reason, and that a **writ** of mandamus should issue. Indeed, the majority moulded the writ to *compel* the issue of a licence—though Starke, dissenting on that point, would have used the usual formula requiring only that the matter be reconsidered according to law.

The tensions within the Court produced a series of shifting alliances, most enduringly between Rich and Dixon. Despite his relatively recent appointment, Dixon's influence was already apparent; but Evatt was a formidable rival. Evatt's erudition was evident, for example, in his learned dissertations on the **history** of 'conspiracy', both in **criminal law** in *R v Weaver* (1931), and in **tort law** (as applied to trade unions) in *McKernan v Fraser* (1931). In *R v Hush; Ex parte Devanny* (1932) it was Rich's turn to use history: in a prosecution of the *Workers Weekly* for soliciting funds for an unlawful association (the Australian Communist Party), the information set out massive 'averments' of the Party's organisational links and 'unlawful' proclivities. The prosecution proposed to use these averments to discharge its onus of proof. Rich found historical precedents for this in trials for treason and sedition; but Evatt castigated the strategy as scandalous, while Gavan Duffy and Starke found the information an 'amazing document, well calculated to embarrass the proper trial of the accused'. Dixon and McTiernan held that, even at face value, the averments disclosed no offence. Rich was left in sole dissent.

Evatt's influence was manifest elsewhere. His joint judgment with McTiernan in *Maher v Musson* (1934)—holding that a chemist should not be convicted of selling illicit spirits if he neither believed nor had reason to believe that they were illicit—contributed to the Court's growing reluctance to treat statutory offences as imposing **strict liability** (see also Rich in *Bond v Foran* (1934)). In **immigration law**, the Court cut back on the operation of the deeming provisions in the *Immigration Act* 1901 (Cth), by which elements in immigration offences were established simply by averments (see *Ali Abdul v Maher* (1931); *Griffin v Wilson* (1935)). The Court's most spectacular encounter with Commonwealth immigration policy was the *Kisch Case* (1934), where Evatt's role was pivotal, both at first instance and in the Full Court.

The struggle for intellectual leadership between Dixon and Evatt was particularly evident in cases under section 92 of the Constitution (see **Interstate trade and commerce**).

Evatt maintained that what was protected was the total volume of trade: so long as the interstate movement of persons and goods as a whole was unimpaired, individual participation in the process was not guaranteed. Dixon maintained that the protection extended to any individual 'act or transaction' forming part of interstate trade. Sometimes section 92 was infringed on either test, especially where state legislation or executive action appeared to protect a local interest—as in *Vacuum Oil v Queensland (No 1)* (1934), where vendors of motor spirit were required to purchase power alcohol from Queensland manufacturers who extracted it from molasses, or *Tasmania v Victoria* (1935), where Tasmanian potatoes were barred from Victoria because of an alleged risk of disease. In both cases, Starke dissented (joined in *Vacuum Oil*, in a separate judgment, by Gavan Duffy). In *Crothers v Sheil* (1933), the whole Court agreed that statutory control of supplies of milk for the Sydney metropolitan area, including compulsory vesting in the Milk Board, did not infringe section 92. But in *Peanut Board v Rockhampton Harbour Board* (1933), a majority sided with Dixon, holding a compulsory marketing scheme unconstitutional (over Evatt's dissent) because 'the provisions operate directly upon the individual grower's liberty of disposing of the peanuts he produces for sale'.

By contrast, in the series of 'transport cases' beginning with *Willard v Rawson* (1933), state legislation protecting state railways against competition by interstate road transport was held valid over Dixon's dissent. The battle lines were drawn most clearly in *R v Vizzard; Ex parte Hill; Gilpin v Commissioner for Road Transport* (1935); and *Bessell v Dayman* (1935). In all three cases, Starke and Dixon dissented. In *Duncan v Vizzard* (1935), Starke again dissented, but Dixon accepted the earlier cases as binding. His previous dissents, especially in *Gilpin*, would be vindicated—at least until *Cole v Whitfield* (1988)—when the Privy Council **overruled** the 'transport cases' two decades later. For the time being, however, Evatt's view had prevailed—though ironically, when the same legislation was used in Victoria to protect the railways by discriminating against road carriage of goods on wholly Victorian journeys, the Court held that this was an improper exercise of the licensing discretions involved (*Victorian Railways Commissioners v McCartney* (1935)).

Clearly, the collapse in the Knox Court of the near consensus in *McArthur v Queensland* (1920) had left the newer Justices divided and the older ones disoriented. In *James v Commonwealth* (1935), *McArthur* was reaffirmed. Gavan Duffy, who had dissented in *McArthur*, did not sit. The scene was set for a challenge to *McArthur* in the Privy Council. Meanwhile, on section 92 as elsewhere, the Court was in disarray.

GRAHAM FRICKE

Gibbs, Harry Talbot (*b* 7 February 1917; Justice 1970–81; Chief Justice 1981–87) brought to the High Court great strength of intellect, wide knowledge and experience, a swift grasp of complex issues, a strong underlying sense of fairness and justice, and outstanding clarity of expression.

Elder son of Harry Victor and Flora Macdonald Talbot Gibbs, Gibbs was born in Sydney, but grew up in Ipswich, Queensland, where his father was a prominent solicitor.

Harry Gibbs, Justice 1970–81; Chief Justice 1981–87

Gibbs attended Ipswich Grammar School, excelling in English and History and then attended the University of Queensland where, despite presenting as an unassuming, almost shy, man he became inaugural president of the Law Students' Society, vice-president of Emmanuel College, and president of the Students' Union, as well as being the editor of the literary magazine *Galmahra*. An early interest in constitutional matters was shown when he secured the presidency of the university's Women's Club, having discovered that there was no requirement that its members, or its president, be a woman. Chivalrously, he and the supporters who had procured his election resigned shortly afterwards.

In 1937, he graduated BA with first-class honours in English literature, and in 1939 was one of the university's first two graduates in law to be awarded first-class honours. That achievement allowed them—but only after a contested hearing in the state's Full Supreme Court (*In re Mathews; In re Gibbs* (1939))—remission of the fees payable on their admission to the Queensland Bar.

Gibbs had barely begun legal practice when **World War II** intervened. He enlisted immediately, serving from 1939–45, and was discharged with the rank of major. He saw active service in New Guinea, where he was mentioned in despatches. In 1944, he assisted in planning unified post-war government for **Papua and New Guinea**; the knowledge he acquired was reflected in his thesis on the subject resulting in his LLM (and perhaps also in his judgment in *Administration of Papua and New Guinea v Daera Guba* (1973)).

In 1946, Gibbs resumed practice at the Queensland Bar. He rapidly developed a formidable reputation, extending beyond Queensland, particularly in appellate, constitutional, and opinion work. He also lectured at the University of Queensland in **commercial law**, **evidence**, and legal interpretation. He was personally very popular and was highly regarded by his peers—to whom he was known as 'Bill'—for his companionship, erudition, and good **humour**. He took silk in 1957.

In his last case as **counsel**, he appeared in the High Court (*Whitehouse v Queensland* (1960)) and the **Privy Council** (1961) for the Queensland government in proceedings brought by licensed victuallers challenging the validity of the Queensland liquor licensing fees, as being duties of **excise** (see also *Dennis Hotels v Victoria* (1960)). In both courts, Gibbs' argument prevailed, extracting a compliment from **Dixon** (in the minority in the High Court) in his reasons. Gibbs enjoyed appearing in the Privy Council; later he was to be a member. On his return, Gibbs was appointed to the Queensland Supreme Court. He was 44. He was welcomed enthusiastically for his legal and scholarly attributes and his 'characteristic modesty'.

The work of the **state Supreme Court** was varied. Gibbs presided with facility and distinction in all areas, criminal or civil, appellate or at first instance, of the Court's jurisdiction. He was highly regarded for his conduct of criminal trials—an area where his experience had earlier been limited.

During his period as a judge of the Supreme Court, he served on two inquiries, one as Royal Commissioner into the conduct of police in connection with the enforcement of laws in relation to Brisbane's National Hotel, the other as Chairman of the Committee of Inquiry into Expansion of the Australian Sugar Industry. In later years, the conduct of the National Hotel Inquiry was criticised as too legalistic, and not sufficiently investigative. It was, however, a reflection of the times, and perhaps of the formidable legal representation ranged against those making the accusations. The Sugar Industry Inquiry recommended expansion, which proved advantageous to that industry.

In early 1966, the Chief Justiceship of Queensland became vacant when Alan Mansfield retired to become Governor of that state. Many thought that Gibbs was the obvious replacement, but that was not to be.

Shortly afterwards, a different career path emerged. In 1967, he was appointed judge of the Federal Court of Bankruptcy and a judge of the Supreme Court of the ACT. He was based in Sydney, and the Gibbs family moved there. The appointments were made and taken in the expectation that he would thereafter become the first Chief Justice of a new superior court of the Commonwealth—a court that was to have a much wider jurisdiction than the then existing federal courts.

The proposal, however, did not go ahead. Indeed, such a court did not come into being until the establishment of the **Federal Court** by the *Federal Court of Australia Act* 1976 (Cth). For the next three years, Gibbs—as his friends thought—languished in the bankruptcy jurisdiction, with occasional forays into the ACT Supreme Court. His talents were noted, however, and the pause in his career was short-lived. In August 1970, he was appointed to succeed **Kitto** on the High Court. Sadly, his father died shortly before the appointment, something which caused him great regret.

Gibbs' period on the Court saw great change in its membership and in its **role** and the nature of its **business**. In just over six years, Gibbs became its most senior member other than **Barwick** (**Windeyer** retired in 1972, **Owen**, **Walsh**, and Douglas **Menzies** died in 1972, 1973, and 1974 respectively, and **McTiernan** retired in 1976). Four of the Justices appointed subsequently to Gibbs also ceased to hold office before he left the Court (**Jacobs** resigned in 1979, **Aickin** died in 1982, **Stephen** resigned in 1982 to become Governor-General, and **Murphy** died in 1986).

Public appreciation that the Court was Australia's ultimate constitutional court had been reawakened with the conflicts arising from the 1974 double dissolution of the federal Parliament and from the legislative activism of the **Whitlam era**. Notable examples were the double dissolution cases (*Cormack v Cope* (1974); the *PMA Case* (1975); the *First Territory Senators Case* (1975)); the attack by Victoria on the appropriation of Commonwealth funds for the Australian Assistance Plan (*AAP Case* (1975)); the challenges to the ambit of the *Family Law Act* 1975 (Cth) (*Russell v Russell* (1976); *R v Demack; Ex parte Plummer* (1977); *R v Lambert; Ex parte Plummer* (1980)); and the challenge by all the states to the Commonwealth's claims to rights in relation to offshore areas (the *Seas and Submerged Lands Case* (1975)). The *First Territory Senators Case* involved a challenge by WA to the legislative power to enact the *Senate (Representation of Territories) Act* 1973 (Cth), a challenge renewed (again unsuccessfully) in the *Second Territory Senators Case* (1977). There were also the **electoral law** cases (*A-G (Cth); Ex rel McKinlay v Commonwealth* (1975) and *A-G (NSW); Ex rel McKellar v Commonwealth* (1977)). A curiosity was Queensland's unsuccessful attempt to entrench the Privy Council as part of the Australian legal system by the enactment of the *Appeals and Special References Act* 1973 (Qld) (*Queen of Queensland Case* (1975)).

In addition to the cases deriving from the Whitlam era, the Court heard many other constitutional cases during Gibbs' membership of the **Barwick Court**. They included *Strickland v Rocla Concrete Pipes* (1971) concerning the Commonwealth's **corporations power**, in which Gibbs' dissent was an early indication of his independence of thought; section 92 cases (such as the *North Eastern Dairy Case* (1975); *Buck v Bavone* (1976); and *Perre v Pollitt* (1976)) and excise challenges (for example, *Logan Downs v Queensland* (1977)).

In relation to non-constitutional matters, at the time of Gibbs' **appointment**, most civil appeals were as of right, and were sometimes from a single judge of a Supreme Court. These were usually heard by a Court of three Justices. Justices sitting alone heard a number of matters, principally revenue appeals. The range of appeals to the Court that could be instituted as of right was reduced in stages, until in 1984 the requirement of special **leave** became general. The transfer of **jurisdiction** to the Federal Court on its establishment effectively removed the single-Justice cases. The restriction and ultimate abolition of appeals to the Privy Council, and the extension of the requirement of special leave to appeal, changed the role of the Court significantly. It had become the final court for Australia and it could select the appeals that it heard. It became very rare for an appeal to be from other than an intermediate appellate court.

The impending move of the High Court to its new **building** in **Canberra** gave rise to differences of view within the Court. Gibbs and some other Justices were opposed to Barwick's decision that in consequence of the move the Court should cease its annual **sittings** in the state capitals (see **Circuit system**). In the event, those sittings continued, but they are much shorter; video link hearings were also introduced.

When Barwick retired in 1981, the Fraser government appointed Gibbs as the new **Chief Justice**. He had been Acting Chief Justice on many occasions. The appointment was well received by the **legal profession** and by the press, which described him as 'Sir Harry the Healer'.

Gibbs presided over the Court with dignity, fairness, and efficiency. A particular problem he encountered was the strain imposed on the Court by the '**Murphy affair**', particularly when Murphy insisted on returning to the Bench while inquiries into the allegations against him were still pending.

Gibbs believed in development of the law—and change, when necessary, by judicial decision—but he did not regard the Court as a vehicle for major social change (see **Lawmaking role**). It is unlikely that he would have decided the *Mabo* cases in the same way as their majorities; he would have regarded so significant an alteration as a matter for the legislature. From his early days as a judge (see, for example, *R v Industrial Court of Queensland; Ex parte Federated Miscellaneous Workers Union of Employees* (1967)), he favoured following previous decisions unless very clearly persuaded that they were wrong. Not long after appointment to the High Court, he dissented in *Kotsis v Kotsis* (1970). Shortly afterwards, in *Knight v Knight* (1971), he observed in relation to *Kotsis*: 'I could not agree with this conclusion but I am bound by the decision.' The same respect for **precedent** can be seen in the *Second Territory Senators Case*, when, on a very politically charged issue, he held he should follow the earlier decision 'notwithstanding that I believe it to be wrong', and, while recognising that the Court had power to **overrule** its previous decisions, added the memorable observation: 'No Justice is entitled to ignore the decisions and reasoning of his predecessors, and to arrive at his own decision as though the pages of the law reports were blank, or as though the authority of a decision did not survive beyond the rising of the Court.'

The 1980s saw a number of major constitutional cases involving the reach of Commonwealth power, notably the ***Tasmanian Dam Case*** (1983) (see also **Gibbs Court**). Gibbs, generally in dissent in these cases, took a relatively narrow view of the scope of Commonwealth power, endeavouring to maintain what he described—in a way that attempted to distance his view from the long-rejected doctrine of **reserved state powers**—as 'the federal balance' (see **External affairs power: a critical analysis**). As ever, he expressed his views with great clarity. Ironically, this exposed him to **criticism** from those who disagreed—criticism that Justices who wrote with more obscurity were often able to avoid.

By accepting office as Chief Justice, Gibbs became subject to the retiring age—introduced by constitutional **amendment**—of 70. In **retirement**, he remained active. In 1987–91, he was Chairman of a committee reviewing the Commonwealth's **criminal laws**; he served from 1988 to 1999 as President of the Kiribati Court of Appeal; in 1989, he was Chairman of an inquiry established by the Queensland Parliament in relation to the conduct of two judges (Supreme Court judge Angelo Vasta and District Court judge ECE Pratt); and in 1990 and 1991, he conducted for NSW an Inquiry into Community Needs and High Voltage Transmission Line Development. He was also the Menzies Lecturer at the University of Virginia in 1987 and in the same year Chief Adjudicator in the BHP Pursuit of Excellence awards. Since 1990, he has been Chairman of the Australian Tax Research Foundation. After retirement, perhaps partly as a response to the **activism** of the **Mason Court**, he also became active in public discussion of **constitutional law** and related issues. A particular interest has been the presidency, since 1992, of the Samuel Griffith Society, a conservative body formed to promote the discussion of such matters. He also took an active part against the proposal for an Australian republic in the campaigns leading to the 1999 referendum.

He has been the recipient of many honours: he was created KBE in 1970, GCMG in 1981, and AC in 1987. He was appointed a Privy Counsellor in 1972 and on three occasions went to London to sit on the Privy Council. He is also an Honorary Bencher of Lincoln's Inn. He holds honorary doctorates from the University of Queensland and Griffith University.

In 1944, Gibbs married Muriel Dunn, whom he had met at the Queensland University Law School. They have been very much partners in a happy marriage of more than half a century's duration, taking great pride in their three daughters and son.

DAVID JACKSON
JOAN PRIEST

Further Reading
Joan Priest, *Sir Harry Gibbs: Without Fear or Favour* (1995)

Gibbs Court (12 February 1981 to 5 February 1987). The Gibbs Court bridged the transition from the more conservative **Barwick Court** to the more liberal **Mason Court**. When **Gibbs** was appointed **Chief Justice** in 1981, the Court comprised Gibbs, **Stephen**, **Mason**, **Murphy**, **Aickin**, **Wilson**, and **Brennan**. During the term of the Gibbs Court, Stephen resigned in 1982 to take up the position of Governor-General, Aickin died in 1982, and Murphy died in 1986. The new Justices who joined the Court were **Deane** and **Dawson**. Murphy was not replaced until after the **retirement** of Gibbs.

The High Court became the subject of political controversy during this period. In part, this was due to the allegations against Murphy, which resulted in two trials, appeals and parliamentary inquiries into his fitness for office (see 'Murphy affair'). This led to strained **personal relations** between the Justices, particularly in regard to Murphy's return to the Court.

However, the Court was also required to play a **role** in the major political and social controversies of the day, such as the proposal to dam the Franklin River (the *Tasmanian Dam Case* (1983)), the Australian Security Intelligence Service exercise at the Sheraton Hotel (*A v Hayden* (1984)), the Mudginberri industrial dispute (*Australasian Meat Industry Employees Union v Mudginberri Station* (1986)), and the *Chamberlain Case* (1984). The involvement of the Court in these controversies raised its public profile significantly.

The most significant procedural change was the abolition of a right of appeal to the Court for cases involving a prescribed amount of money, and its replacement with a system requiring special **leave to appeal**. This amendment to the *Judiciary Act* 1903 (Cth) took effect from 1 June 1984. In deciding whether to grant special leave to appeal, the Court now considers whether: the question in issue is a matter of public importance; there are differences of opinion between courts that must be resolved by the final appellate court; or the interests of the administration of justice require consideration of the matter by the High Court. To limit the expense of adding an additional layer of proceedings, the Court agreed to sit in Sydney and Melbourne to hear special leave applications. This development gave the Court far greater control of its workload—especially of the types of cases it heard—thus allowing it to focus on the development of the law.

There were a number of significant constitutional cases during the period, with Gibbs himself frequently in a minority. For the most part, the decisions further supported the ascendancy of the Commonwealth over the states, and were often characterised by a 4:3 split, with Mason, Murphy, Brennan, and Deane in the majority, and Gibbs, Wilson, and Dawson in dissent.

The most crucial development was the interpretation of the extent of the **external affairs power** (section 51(xxix) of the Constitution). In *Koowarta's Case* (1982), the Court was divided on the extent to which the power to implement treaties could be used to legislate with respect to matters internal to Australia over which the Commonwealth Parliament would not otherwise have power. Gibbs, Aickin, and Wilson took a narrow view of section 51(xxix), while Mason, Murphy, and Brennan took a broader view. Stephen took the intermediate position that the subject matter of the legislation must be of 'international concern'. The *Tasmanian Dam Case* finally settled the matter. Stephen had been replaced by Deane, who joined the majority to adopt the broad view of section 51(xxix). Given the large range of treaties in the world today, the consequence is that **Commonwealth legislative power** has significantly expanded, allowing it to override the states on most subjects.

Another area of expansion was the **corporations power**. Section 51(xx) of the Constitution had previously been little used, because its scope had been narrowly interpreted. In *Actors Equity v Fontana Films* (1982), the Court held that the power extended to the regulation and protection of the trading activities of trading corporations. *Fencott v Muller* (1983) and the *Tasmanian Dam Case* reinforced and further extended the scope of section 51(xx) to cover other activities of trading corporations undertaken for the purposes of their trading activities. This expansion of the interpretation of section 51(xx) led to its far more extensive use by the Commonwealth Parliament.

The **conciliation and arbitration** power in section 51(xxxv) was also expanded in scope by the Gibbs Court. Previously, the Court had taken a narrow view of the meaning of an 'industrial' dispute, requiring such a dispute to be 'in an industry'. In the *CYSS Case* (1983), a unanimous **joint judgment** took a broader view of 'industrial', giving it its popular meaning of any dispute between employer and employee, thus extending it to white-collar workers generally. In *Re Lee;*

Ex parte Harper (1986), the Court further extended this Commonwealth power to cover state employees such as school teachers, thereby substantially diminishing state industrial powers.

Another series of judgments that fundamentally affected the relationship between the states and the Commonwealth concerned the application of section 109 of the Constitution. In *Viskauskas v Niland* (1983), the Court held that the Commonwealth *Racial Discrimination Act* 1975 covered the field, leaving no application for state anti-**discrimination** laws. The Commonwealth then legislated to make it clear that state and Commonwealth anti-discrimination laws were to operate concurrently where there was no **inconsistency**. In *University of Wollongong v Metwally* (1984), the Court held that such legislation could not retrospectively change the effect of the Constitution. The issue arose again in *Gerhardy v Brown* (1985), where it was argued that SA laws giving **Aboriginal people** exclusive access to land were in breach of the Racial Discrimination Act. This time, however, the Court was more flexible, finding that the laws amounted to 'special measures' permitted by the Commonwealth Act.

The Court also expanded the meaning of **excise** in *Hematite Petroleum v Victoria* (1983). Section 90 of the Constitution prohibits the states from imposing an excise, so any expansion in the meaning of excise reduces the power of the states to raise revenue. However, the Court had some sympathy for the financial position of the states in *Evda Nominees v Victoria* (1984). It continued to uphold an artificial device to avoid the section 90 prohibition—a device involving 'licence fees' based on past sales (see *Dennis Hotels v Victoria* (1960)). It did so in recognition of the fact that the states had organised their financial affairs in reliance on the earlier cases. However, the Court has now severely restricted this approach (see *Ha v NSW* (1997)).

During the time of the Gibbs Court, the *Australia Acts* 1986 were negotiated and enacted. Their progress influenced not only the Court's approach to matters concerning constitutional relations with Britain, but also the hierarchy of **precedent** in the Australian legal system. In *Caltex Oil v XL Petroleum (NSW)* (1984), the High Court held that a contemporaneous order of the **Privy Council** would not prevail over an order of the High Court with respect to the same subject matter. In *Kirmani v Captain Cook Cruises (No 2)* (1985), the Court held that although appeal to the Privy Council from the High Court in *inter se* questions was still 'theoretically possible' under the Constitution, this jurisdiction was now spent and the High Court would not abdicate its responsibility for the final decision of questions affecting the boundary between Commonwealth and state powers. Appeals from **state Supreme Courts** to the Privy Council were abolished by the Australia Acts. The High Court was now the highest source of authority on Australian law.

Other relations with Britain became more distant. British subjects could be characterised as 'aliens' under the naturalisation and aliens power (section 51(xix) of the Constitution; see *Pochi v MacPhee* (1982)) and British laws that applied by paramount force in the states could be repealed by the Commonwealth Parliament (*Kirmani v Captain Cook Cruises (No 1)* (1985)). The Australia Acts later allowed the states to repeal these laws.

On the **separation of powers** and the scope of **judicial power**, the Gibbs Court showed itself to be more flexible than its successors. It held, in *Pioneer Concrete v Trade Practices Commission* (1982), that an administrative body can exercise powers to compel the production of evidence without breaching the separation of powers. In *Hilton v Wells* (1985), it permitted judges to exercise non-judicial powers as *personae designatae* (that is, in their personal capacity), and in *Australian Building Construction Employees and BLF v Commonwealth* (1986) it held that Parliament may alter rights at issue in pending litigation without breaching the separation of powers.

The Gibbs Court also handed down a number of landmark judgments in other areas of law. In **administrative law**, the most significant judgment was *Kioa v West* (1985). Here the Court expanded on the notion of **natural justice** and the applicability and extent of the necessity for procedural fairness in decision making. *FAI Insurances v Winneke* (1982) was a forerunner to *Kioa* in establishing that natural justice must be applied even to decisions made by the Governor-in-Council.

Developments in **evidence law** included *Baker v Campbell* (1983) on the nature of legal professional privilege, *Chamberlain* on circumstantial evidence and inferences of guilt, and *Perry v The Queen* (1982) on similar-fact evidence. A new test for **standing** to bring civil proceedings was outlined by the Court in *Onus v Alcoa* (1981).

Two important decisions based in **equity** were *Amadio's Case* (1983), which expanded the equitable principles relating to relief against **unconscionable** dealing, and *Muschinski v Dodds* (1985), which applied equitable principles to non-fiduciary domestic relationships. In **tort law**, *Jaensch v Coffey* (1984) extended the duty of care to those not at the scene of an accident who may later be affected by it. While this limited the role of physical **proximity** in establishing liability for nervous shock, Deane's judgment introduced a wider theory of 'proximity' that was to be accepted as the touchstone of liability for negligence generally for the next decade. *Commonwealth v Introvigne* (1982) expanded upon contributory negligence and the duty of care of the Commonwealth in relation to schools operated by the state. In *Hackshaw v Shaw* (1984), Deane picked up the threads of the line of cases in which the **Dixon Court** had been moving towards the subsumption of the separate restricted categories of **occupiers' liability** into the broad general principles of negligence. The Privy Council had cut that development short in *Commissioner for Railways v Quinlan* (1964). Deane's judgment revived it.

Cases that developed **contract law** included *Codelfa Construction v State Rail Authority of NSW* (1982) on implied terms and frustration of contract, *Hospital Products v US Surgical Corporation* (1984) on implied terms and **fiduciary obligations** in commercial transactions, and *Meehan v Jones* (1982) on implied terms and certainty of contracts. Important cases on **land law** included *Legione v Hateley* (1983) on promissory **estoppel** and *Heid v Reliance Finance Corporation* (1983) on the priority of interests.

One marked difference of the Gibbs Court from the previous Barwick Court was the way it treated the subject of **taxation**. The Barwick Court had become controversial for its decisions favourable to taxpayers, which almost completely negated the effect of anti-avoidance provisions such as section 260 of the *Income Tax Assessment Act* 1936 (Cth). The Gibbs Court began to alter this approach. It no longer took a literal approach, and sought the intention of the provisions (*Cooper Brookes v FCT* (1981)). It revived the effectiveness of section 260 as an anti-avoidance provision in *Commissioner of Taxation v Gulland* (1985), and upheld the penalties for 'bottom of the harbour' schemes in *MacCormick v FCT* (1984).

In summary, the Gibbs Court moved away from 'strict legalism', took a more expansive view of Commonwealth legislative power, and asserted its own role as the pre-eminent judicial authority for Australia.

ANNE TWOMEY

Gleeson, (Anthony) Murray (*b* 30 August 1938; Chief Justice since 1998) was the first Chief Justice of a **state Supreme Court** to be appointed as **Chief Justice** of the High Court since **Griffith**, whose Queensland Chief Justiceship predated the High Court.

Gleeson was born at Wingham on the north coast of NSW, the son of a local garage proprietor. From the age of 11, he was educated at St Joseph's College, Hunters Hill in Sydney, where he excelled at cricket (as a spin bowler) and at the more vocational debating and oratory. After gaining a first-class honours degree at the University of Sydney and spending a year as a solicitor with Messrs Murphy & Moloney, he was called to the Bar in 1963, reading with Laurence Street, on the same floor as another leading **equity** and commercial junior, **Mason**. Gleeson thus started his career in chambers with his future predecessor as Chief Justice of NSW and in company with one of his future predecessors as Chief Justice of Australia.

The demand for Gleeson as a junior **counsel** was high—as was the quality of his practice. He appeared in the High Court frequently, from his first year, mainly in **taxation** and commercial cases, along with important constitutional arguments. His leaders included Maurice Byers, **Dawson**, and, more often, **Deane**. Opponents included **Aickin** and **Wilson**.

Murray Gleeson, Chief Justice since 1998

His public law briefs included *R v Anderson; Ex parte Ipec-Air* (1965) concerning government contracts, the *Payroll Tax Case* (1971) concerning the Commonwealth taxing the states, the *Tasmanian Breweries Case* (1970) concerning **judicial power**, *Strickland v Rocla Concrete Pipes* (1971) and *R v Trade Practices Tribunal; Ex parte St George County Council* (1974) concerning the **corporations power**, *Kailis v WA* (1974) on state licence fees as **excise duties**, and *Barton v Commonwealth* (1974) confirming the prerogative right to extradition. These were a tiny fraction of his industry as a junior, largely in the robust world of Sydney commercial litigation.

Ironically, in the days before section 78A of the *Judiciary Act* 1903 (Cth) (added in 1976) entitled the Commonwealth, states, and eventually the **territories** to **intervene** as of right in constitutional litigation in the High Court, Gleeson's early briefs for the Commonwealth and for NSW seeking to intervene in constitutional cases both resulted in the High Court refusing to hear him.

Gleeson took silk early, in 1974. His career as senior counsel remains second to none. He dominated wherever his varied practice took him. The emphasis remained heavily commercial and constitutional, but his success before a jury in defending Ian Sinclair, Federal Leader of the National Party, against criminal charges, showed that his skills were versatile. The law reports record his dominance of appellate and other High Court cases, but his standing was based equally on his impact at trial. His trademark analytical skills reduced legal propositions to aphoristic principle, and citation of authority to the truly essential. As a cross-examiner, his precision was displayed to a high degree—not always appreciated by the witnesses, but leaving an economical **transcript** full of facts. In appellate **argument**, the transcripts of Gleeson's addresses have a coherence that many other lawyers could hope to attain only in their written submissions.

Constitutional arguments in which Gleeson appeared as silk include the *PMA Case* (1975) concerning the double-dissolution trigger under section 57 for the 1974 re-election of the **Whitlam** government; the *Seas and Submerged Lands Case* (1975) concerning the territorial limits of states; *Hematite Petroleum v Victoria* (1983) concerning pipeline fees as an excise; *Pioneer Concrete v Trade Practices Commission* (1982) and *Re Cram; Ex parte Newcastle Wallsend Coal* (1987) concerning judicial power; *MacCormick v FCT* (1984) concerning the taxation power and 'bottom-of-the-harbour' companies; *University of Wollongong v Metwally* (1984) and *AMP v Goulden* (1986) concerning section 109 **inconsistency** and anti-**discrimination** law; *Northern Land Council v Commonwealth* (1986) concerning the territories power and the Ranger uranium project; and the *Tasmanian Dam Case* (1983) and *Richardson v Forestry Commission* (1988) concerning natural heritage legislation and the **external affairs power**, among other important issues.

Gleeson appeared for William McMahon, former **Prime Minister**, in *Evans v Crichton-Browne* (1981), successfully preventing the rhetoric of political debate from being subjected to judicial scrutiny under the Commonwealth *Electoral Act* 1918. He argued the application of the privilege against self-incrimination in *Sorby v Commonwealth* (1983), the requirements of **natural justice** in *National Companies* and Securities Commission v News Corporation (1984), the availability of **contempt** powers in *Australasian Meat Industry Employees Union v Mudginberri Station* (1986), and fundamental matters of market power in *Queensland Wire Industries v BHP* (1989). Commercial briefs included *Carlton & United Breweries v Castlemaine Tooheys* (1986) concerning defences arising from the *Trade Practices Act 1974* (Cth) in Supreme Court proceedings, and *Oceanic Sun Line Co v Fay* (1988) concerning the stay of proceedings because another jurisdiction is more suitable. The commercial field of football litigation saw Gleeson against the Western Suburbs Rugby League Club in *Wayde v NSW Rugby League* (1985).

Meantime, Gleeson continued to appear in the High Court regularly in taxation and other commercial cases, his practice being truly national. His opponents in the High Court included future members of and colleagues on the High Court, namely Aickin, Deane, Dawson, Wilson, **McHugh**, **Gaudron**, and **Gummow**. Gleeson's practice was not confined to Australia, and he won the last appeal by leave to the **Privy Council** from the High Court, being *Port Jackson Stevedoring v Salmond & Spraggon* (1980). (Appeals by leave to the Privy Council were abolished in 1975, apart from cases already commenced.)

Gleeson became President of the NSW Bar Association in 1984. The next year, he received the AO for service to the law. His direct approach proved effective. Answering a criticism that abolition of the two-counsel rule (which made a junior compulsory whenever a silk appeared) threatened the established social order, Gleeson stated the case for modernised professional regulation—'That rule was necessary only for cases where it should not exist'.

Allied with Gleeson's crisp vigour professionally was, and is, a sense of **humour** shared mostly in private with friends, family, and colleagues. However, as a leading barrister—and frequently during his judicial life—his characteristic dry wit and mordant understatement have been displayed in nearly all his public speeches.

Gleeson's appointment as Chief Justice of NSW—the first barrister to be thus elevated directly since Frederick Jordan in 1934—was popular, although the prospect of the continuation of his cross-examination skills was daunting for advocates. The next decade saw considerable change as the Supreme Court grappled with the spiral of growing demand, cost stringencies, and delay, all in a climate of heightened consumer scrutiny. On many occasions, Gleeson set out to mark, in public utterances, appropriate boundaries for the political debate concerning litigation: he insisted that the administration of justice was no mere consumer service, but rather an integral part of civilised government, and decried suggestions that supposed the invisible hand of the market, or productivity measures, to have any legitimate claim to dictate the way improvement of the legal system should proceed. In an era where mercantile functionalism sometimes appeared to dominate thinking about the profession, Gleeson continued and deepened the tradition of the Supreme Court Chief Justice declaring and explaining the elementary idealism and duties that should characterise the profession.

Gleeson also continued the tradition of the Chief Justice presiding frequently in the Court of Criminal Appeal—an area of work in which he was much more heavily involved on

the Bench than he had been at the Bar. A notable decision was *R v Birks* (1990), where the availability of trial counsel's incompetence as a ground of appeal was explained. Another was *A-G (NSW) v Milat* (1995), where the Court refused to allow the issue of representation, as a basic requirement of fairness in a serious criminal trial, to be determined by current rates of professional remuneration. Strong statements of principle concerning criminal contempt by media publication came from Gleeson in *A-G (NSW) v TCN Channel Nine* (1990), and in *A-G (NSW) v Dean* (1990), concerning a confessed murderer.

Despite the extent of his commitments to **criminal law** and to administration, Gleeson also presided relatively frequently in the Court of Appeal, where his strength of analysis and enunciation of doctrine, coupled with logical presentation of argument (often exceeding the logic shown by counsel), are displayed in areas including **constitutional law**, **administrative law**, **commercial law**, and equity. He presided in *Greiner v Independent Commission Against Corruption* (1992), which exculpated (too late) a Premier of statutory corruption. His concern for the necessary tensions and balance in a system of **responsible government** is shown in *Egan v Willis* (1996)—upheld by a Bench of six in the High Court, after his own **appointment** to the High Court—concerning the power of a house of parliament to compel the executive to produce documents. In *Ballina Shire Council v Ringland* (1994), Gleeson noted the High Court's implied freedom of **political communication** as reinforcing the conclusion that local councillors could not sue for **defamation** on statements about their performance.

Systemic issues concerning the overlapping or fragmentation of jurisdictions received attention from Gleeson in the Court of Appeal in *National Parks and Wildlife Service v Stables Perisher* (1990), concerning the limited powers of the Land and Environment Court and the important doctrine of accrued or pendent jurisdiction, *Goliath Portland v Bengtell* (1994), concerning so-called forum shopping and extra-territorial jurisdiction, and *Falls Creek Ski Lifts v Yee* (1995), concerning the territorial restrictions on the District Court.

In the area of **civil liberties**, he addressed the limits of arrest without warrant in *Lippl v Haines* (1989), the balance between public hearings and damage to reputation in *Independent Commission Against Corruption v Chaffey* (1993), and the publication of telephone taps in *John Fairfax Publications v Doe* (1995), where he called in aid European human rights jurisprudence. Concerning the **legal profession**, he addressed immunity of advocates in *Keefe v Marks* (1989)—in a way side-stepped a decade later in the High Court in *Boland v Yates Property Corporation* (1999)—and the inappropriateness of charging solicitors' costs on a 'simple flat, hourly rate' in *NSW Crime Commission v Fleming and Heal* (1991).

Unsurprisingly, Gleeson's Court of Appeal jurisprudence includes notable commercial and **property** cases. Significantly, he used the ambit of **law-making** permitted to an intermediate appellate court to update case law in light of changed social circumstances. Thus, in *Green v Green* (1989), he declined to count the lack of formal marriage against an equity arising in circumstances of cohabitation, and in *Brown v Brown* (1993), he refused to distinguish between fathers and mothers concerning presumptions arising from the advancement of money. As to the burgeoning use of mediation, he emphasised the limits imposed by its consensual nature in *Gain v Commonwealth Bank* (1997).

Too short a time has passed since Gleeson's translation to Chief Justice of the High Court on 22 May 1998 to generalise about his individual jurisprudence in that Court. One striking feature of his first two years has been the very large majority of **joint judgments**. Nearly all of Gleeson's judgments so far have been together with other Justices—and no pattern has emerged of repeated alliance with one or other of his colleagues. Relatively frequently, he is party to a majority judgment that plainly provides the High Court's *ratio decidendi*. A good example is *John Pfeiffer v Rogerson* (2000), where Gleeson joined with Gaudron, McHugh, Gummow, and **Hayne** in a joint judgment changing the **common law** governing choice of law in intranational **torts**. A number of his judgments efficiently summarise and argue for the majority conclusion. Gleeson's judgment in *Re Wakim* (1999), where he joined with other Justices in rejecting the **cross-vesting** scheme, is an ideal explanatory exposition of the problems with this solution to the politically difficult issue of separate jurisdictions in a federation. His judgment in *Katsuno v The Queen* (1999) about the fundamental requirements for **jury trial** is in the same mould.

So far, Gleeson has very rarely dissented. The dangerous task of attributing judicial prose in a joint judgment to one of its declared authors should not be attempted; nevertheless, the pellucid exposition of issues and statement of determinative principles at the commencement of judgments to which Gleeson has been party is unlikely to be free of his influence. Nor is the stern limitation of the role of a Chief Justice, in relation to judicial **independence**, in *Re Colina; Ex parte Torney* (1999).

It is nonetheless possible to discern a continued attention by Gleeson to bright lines between legislative, executive, and judicial power, particularly where merit review is sought (for example, *Bachrach v Queensland* (1998); *Re East; Ex parte Nguyen* (1998); *Northern Territory v GPAO* (1999); *A-G (Cth) v Breckler* (1999); *Abebe v Commonwealth* (1999); and *Minister for Immigration v Eshetu* (1999)).

In 2000, the Australian Law Reform Commission suggested the establishment of an Australian Judicial College. As head of the Australian judicature, Gleeson's approach to that suggestion is likely to be important, and his energetic role as President of the NSW Judicial Commission would give him unparalleled insights into such an innovation. His Chief Justiceship may, therefore, be marked by a contribution off the Bench as enduring as service on the Bench.

BRET WALKER

Gleeson Court (22 May 1998–). At the end of 2000, **Gleeson** remained the most recently appointed Justice. A few months before his appointment, **Dawson** and **Toohey** retired and were replaced by **Hayne** and **Callinan**. Four members of the Gleeson Court were, therefore, also members of the **Brennan Court** throughout all or most of its duration (**Gaudron, McHugh, Gummow,** and **Kirby**).

It is too early to discern any pronounced characteristics or trends in the judgments of the Court, although there has been some tendency to place more emphasis on 'the text and structure' of the Constitution or a statute as a basis for interpretation. In an address to the Australian Bar Association in New York in 2000, the **Chief Justice** extolled the virtues of '**legalism**' and '**legal reasoning**' in a manner reminiscent of **Dixon** and **Barwick**. He did not explain how it differed from other forms of reasoning or examine the problem of choice of interpretation where more than one result is possible. This address contrasted with those given by **Mason** as Chief Justice (see also **Law-making role: reflections**). Similarly, Gummow and Hayne distinguished arguments based on

The Gleeson Court in 2000. Left to right: Hayne, Gummow, Gaudron, Gleeson, McHugh, Kirby and Callinan

social 'convenience' and 'efficiency' from 'legal analysis and the application of accepted constitutional doctrine' (*Re Wakim* (1999)). At a press conference on his appointment, Callinan said his aim would be to decide cases in an 'orthodox' manner. The impression was gained that many members of the Court were endeavouring to distinguish themselves from the more **policy**-oriented and **value**-based judgments of the **Mason Court**.

Much of the change, however, seems to be more a matter of tone and style than of substance. In *Egan v Willis* (1998), the Court upheld the power of the NSW Legislative Council to suspend the Treasurer for refusing to produce non-privileged documents. The Court relied on the function of each House of Parliament in making the executive government accountable. Reference was made to political, historical and constitutional works relating to **responsible government** in Australia and Britain. Similarly, in *Sue v Hill* (1999) it was held that Heather Hill, being a British citizen at the time of her nomination for election to the Senate, was a citizen of a 'foreign power' within section 44(i) of the Constitution, and therefore not eligible for election. There was much in the text of the Constitution that could be regarded as justifying the opposite result; but the Court looked to the evolution of Australia's status as a **sovereign** state, and interpreted the Constitution in accordance with modern political perceptions (see also **Nationhood**).

With respect to the **characterisation** of Commonwealth laws, the Court has generally followed the long-standing principle that the Constitution should be interpreted in a manner that would enable it to embrace new situations and developments that the **framers** could not have envisaged. Applying that principle, the *Plant Varieties Act* 1987 (Cth) was upheld under the power relating to 'patents of invention' (*Grain Pool of WA v Commonwealth*) (2000)).

The Court has, however, avoided the issue of whether the power with respect to 'the people of any **race** for whom it is deemed necessary to make special laws' (section 51(xxvi)) was confined to laws benefiting the people of any race, or of the **Aboriginal** race in particular (see *Hindmarsh Island Bridge Case* (1998)). The Court held valid the *Hindmarsh Island Bridge Act* 1997 (Cth), which removed the area of the bridge from the scope of an Act providing a scheme of protection for places of particular significance to Aborigines. It did not have to decide the issue of whether the race power was limited to beneficial laws because the Act simply reduced the scope of operation of a law that conferred benefits. Having enacted a benefit, the Parliament was not disabled for all time from repealing the legislation, wholly or partly. Gummow and Hayne, however, expressed a view rejecting a restrictive interpretation of the power, while Kirby (who dissented) held to the contrary.

Chapter III of the Constitution, relating to the judicature, continued to be the subject of litigation (see **Separation of powers**). In *Abebe v Commonwealth* (1999), a majority upheld the power of the Commonwealth Parliament to limit the grounds on which an administrative decision could be reviewed by the **Federal Court**, even though full review by the High Court was available under section 75(v) of the Constitution. The majority were influenced by practical considerations such as permitting the Commonwealth, if it

wished, to establish specialist courts. The result has been a significant increase in the Court's workload (see also **Fact finding**; **Immigration law**).

In *Re Wakim*, on the other hand, six members of the Court (Kirby dissenting) overruled an earlier decision (*Gould v Brown* (1998)) and proceeded to hold invalid a large part of a scheme that had operated successfully for 12 years—a scheme under which there had been a **cross-vesting** of jurisdiction among the federal, state, and territory courts. The majority held that the provisions of Chapter III prohibited the states from vesting state jurisdiction in federal courts, even with the statutory approval of the Commonwealth, and that the Commonwealth Parliament had no power to consent to those courts exercising the jurisdiction. The reasoning contrasted with *R v Duncan* (1983), where it was said that cooperative arrangements between the Commonwealth and the states were 'a positive object of the Constitution'. By contrast, in *Re Wakim*, cooperative **federalism** was reduced by some Justices to a 'slogan' having no legal significance. In *R v Hughes* (2000), where Chapter III was not involved, the Court held that the Commonwealth could use its incidental power to permit officers to perform state functions. If, however, the question was the performance of a duty under state law, it was necessary for the Commonwealth to have a substantive power. The Court expressly left open whether such arrangements were within the scope of the executive power and the express incidental power in section 51(xxxix).

The Court has upheld, as consistent with Chapter III, a broad view of **standing**. In *Truth about Motorways* (2000), it held that provisions of the *Trade Practices Act* 1974 (Cth) giving standing to any person to institute proceedings under specific provisions of the Act proscribing unlawful conduct were valid. On the other hand, the Court has taken a much stricter stance in refusing to determine issues that are not based on facts that are established by evidence or agreed by the parties (*Bass v Permanent Trustee* (1999)). The determination of such issues was regarded as an **advisory opinion** even though it was part of very complex litigation involving numerous parties.

The Gleeson Court has developed an earlier trend of characterising the **common law** as a single Australian system of law rather than as separate state systems (*Lipohar v The Queen* (1999). The Court also held that the common law of Australia should be developed so that the law of the place where a **tort** has occurred should be the governing law in respect of torts committed in Australia (*John Pfeiffer v Rogerson* (2000)). The Court relied on the nature of a federal system and the policy reflected in section 118 of the Constitution that each state recognise the interest of other states in the application of their laws to events occurring within their jurisdiction.

LESLIE ZINES

Further Reading
Adrienne Stone and George Williams (eds), *The High Court at the Crossroads* (2000)

Green v Daniels (1977). The significance of *Green v Daniels* as a foundation case in Australian public law was only belatedly recognised. The case totally failed to capture legal interest when it first appeared—perhaps because it appeared to raise only matters of **statutory interpretation**—and as a consequence it is not reported in the *Commonwealth Law Reports*.

That its significance was appreciated—albeit belatedly—is fitting, given that it was the first case on social security law to reach the High Court; it was responsible for a finding that income support payments are not gratuities that can be made or withdrawn at will by the government; it established that the executive can breach the law as much by inflexible application of departmental policies as by failing to follow the letter of the law; it demonstrated that a court, even with a limited law-declaring **role**, can lay down rules about how the executive should approach its task; and it was a foretaste of the burst of litigation on social security matters, which continues unabated.

Karen Green was a 16-year-old who applied for unemployment benefit in December 1976, soon after she left school. She was told that, despite being unemployed, she could not qualify for payment until February the following year because of a departmental policy that prevented teenagers of school-leaving age from receiving the benefit until after the long vacation. She challenged the refusal in the original **jurisdiction** of the High Court, as a test case instituted by the Fitzroy Legal Centre. Sitting as a single Justice, **Stephen** found that despite the policy's being prefaced with the words 'as a general rule', in practice it was administered inflexibly, and was an unlawful gloss on the Act. The policy had become in effect another hurdle to be met by unemployed school leavers—but one not sanctioned by the Parliament.

The finding did not enable Green to receive backpayments of unemployment benefit. As Stephen noted, the role of the Court was limited to finding whether the Director-General had made the decision according to legal principle; it did not extend to deciding the factual question of whether Green had taken reasonable steps to obtain work and hence could qualify for unemployment benefit. The answer to that question—or the merits of the decision—was a matter for the Director-General, not for the Court.

For these reasons, Stephen had no option but to return the case to the Director-General with a direction to reconsider the claim according to law, though he did specify with precision which matters the Director-General should consider. In response to his criticism of the Director-General's undue reliance on policy, the *Social Security Act* 1947 (Cth) was amended in 1977 to add to the formal statutory tests that no school leaver could receive unemployment benefit in the six weeks following the end of the school year.

When Green's claim was reconsidered, it was refused a second time on the basis that she had not taken reasonable steps to obtain work. So she was again denied payment. At the same time, the issue of the treatment of school-leavers during the long vacation was taken to the Commonwealth Ombudsman and led to a lengthy investigation. During this phase, the Ombudsman formally requested the Director-General to seek an **advisory opinion** on a legal issue that arose during the inquiry from the Commonwealth's pre-eminent tribunal, the Administrative Appeals Tribunal. The advice—provided by the Tribunal's then President, **Brennan**, later to become **Chief Justice** of Australia—was the first, and by 2000, the only occasion the advice-giving procedure had been activated. The result was a leading ruling

on the difference between decision by a delegate and decision by an agent in **administrative law** (see *In Re Reference under Section 11 of Ombudsman Act 1976 for an Advisory Opinion; Ex parte Director-General of Social Services* (1979)).

When the Director-General failed to act on the Ombudsman's recommendations relating to the denial of unemployment benefits for school leavers, the Ombudsman, in March 1980, made the first formal report to the **Prime Minister** on the issue—a step reserved for recalcitrant agencies. Ultimately, the Prime Minister, Malcolm Fraser, recommended a gratuitous payment of arrears of unemployment benefit to certain of the school leavers denied payment over the 1976–77 summer vacation. Thus, in the end, the combination of remedies produced a positive outcome, but by a complex route that would never have been foreseen.

ROBIN CREYKE

Griffith, Samuel Walker (*b* 21 June 1845; *d* 9 August 1920; Chief Justice 1903–19) had a political and legal career of great distinction. He was twice Premier of Queensland, and then Chief Justice, before becoming the first **Chief Justice** of the High Court.

The son of the Reverend Edward Griffith, a Congregational minister, and Mary Griffith, he was born in Wales and in 1853 accompanied his parents to Australia. After attending schools in Ipswich, Sydney, and Maitland, he was admitted to the University of Sydney, from which he graduated in 1863 as BA with first-class honours in classics, mathematics and natural science and as MA in 1870. Subsequently, he was awarded honorary degrees of LLD from the University of Queensland (1912) and the University of Wales (1913). After serving articles with an Ipswich solicitor—interrupted when in 1865 he visited Europe on a travelling scholarship—he passed the Bar examination, and was admitted to the Queensland Bar on 14 October 1867.

In 1870, Griffith married Julia Janet Thomson. They had two sons and four daughters, all of whom, except one son, survived him. Although generally regarded as cold and austere, Griffith was devoted to his family.

Griffith soon had a busy practice, which he maintained during his parliamentary career. He took silk in 1876. He was elected to the Queensland Parliament in 1872 and before long dominated its proceedings. He was Attorney-General from 1874 to 1879, but even before his appointment to the ministry he introduced legislation effecting significant reforms to legal **procedure**. As Attorney-General, he was responsible for the passage of the *Judicature Act* 1876 (Qld). As Secretary for Public Instruction (an office he held together with that of Attorney-General from 1876), he was responsible for introducing a system of scholarships. He lost office in 1879 and became Leader of the Opposition. From 1883 to 1888, he was Premier of Queensland. He was liberal and humanitarian and was regarded as a radical. He secured the passage of the *Crown Lands Act* 1884 (Qld), under which large pastoral holdings were resumed for closer settlement; the *Pacific Islanders Labourers Act of 1880 Amendment Act* 1885 (Qld), which prohibited the recruitment of Pacific Islanders after 1890; and statutes to recognise trade unions and to provide for **workers' compensation**.

Samuel Griffith, Chief Justice 1903–19

In 1888, he was again Leader of the Opposition. He then introduced a Bill, The Elementary Property Law of Queensland, which, under the influence of Karl Marx, would have given workers a share of the net value of their produce in addition to a fair wage. He did not proceed with the Bill when he again became Premier, although the fact that after his retirement he wrote a pamphlet repeating similar views shows that he was sincere, although naive, in introducing the Bill. During his second term as Premier (from 1890 to 1893), he lost some of the widespread support he had previously enjoyed and was branded by critics as insincere and untrustworthy. He procured the repeal of the Pacific Islanders Labourers Act, possibly because of the financial difficulties of the sugar industry and the state generally. He used an armed force to restore order during the shearers' strike of 1891.

As a minister, Griffith showed considerable political skills as well as remarkable energy. He closely supervised the work of his officers, perhaps because he found it difficult to delegate his authority.

In the 1880s, Griffith became one of the leaders in the movement towards federation. At a conference held in Sydney in 1883 to discuss European expansion in the Pacific, Griffith persuaded the delegates to agree to form a Federal Council. He drafted a Bill that, in substance, became the *Federal Council of Australasia Act* 1885 (UK); its provisions describing the legislative powers of the Federal Council later appeared (with some changes) in section 51 of the Constitution.

A Colonial Conference held in London in 1887, which Griffith attended, commissioned a report that emphasised the danger of divided colonial control of the armed forces. As a consequence, a conference was held in Sydney in 1891 to draft a Constitution to federate the colonies. Griffith was vice-president of the conference and Chairman of the Constitu-

tion Committee, and he exercised a commanding influence over the whole proceedings. He produced a draft Bill for a Constitution. Although Griffith was helped by others, the Bill, as Alfred **Deakin** wrote, 'as a whole and in every clause bore the stamp of Sir Samuel Griffith's patient and untiring handiwork, his terse, clear style and force of expression'. The colonial parliaments took no action on the Bill at that time.

In 1893, Griffith became Chief Justice of Queensland, having first negotiated, with the government of which he was Premier, an increase in salary. From 1899 to 1903, he was also Lieutenant-Governor of Queensland. As Chief Justice, he revealed the mastery of legal principle and soundness and promptness of decision that later marked his career on the High Court. During his Chief Justiceship of Queensland, Griffith produced a codification of the **criminal law**—a considerable undertaking of lasting value—and drafted new Rules for the Supreme Court, on which the **High Court Rules** were largely modelled.

Griffith maintained his interest in federation, and although he could not attend a further Constitutional Convention held in 1897–98, he was consulted by some delegates and produced 'Notes on the Draft Federal Constitution', in which he criticised the new draft Bill and suggested amendments, some of which were adopted. The final form of the Constitution contains much of his original draft and of his later corrections to the draft of 1897–98. The Constitution Bill was approved in Australia, but the Imperial government objected to the restrictions on appeals to the **Privy Council** it contained, and suggested a compromise that was acceptable to the Australian delegates to London, but was strongly opposed in Australia—by Griffith among others. Griffith's objections to the compromise were inconsistent with the views he had expressed in 1891. The controversy that resulted threatened to delay or even prevent federation, but it was resolved when Griffith made a suggestion for a form of words for what is now section 74 of the Constitution, which (as Deakin said), 'provided the golden bridge over which the delegates passed to union'. Subsequently, Griffith drafted the *Judiciary Act* 1903 (Cth).

Griffith's **appointment** in 1903 as the first Chief Justice of the High Court was applauded generally by the press, but was strongly criticised by a minority of politicians on the grounds, among others, that he was unreliable and self-seeking. The **establishment** of the Court itself met with opposition, and with resentment from some judges of the state **Supreme Courts**. Griffith soon demonstrated that his critics were wrong, and ensured that the Court became recognised as the pre-eminent legal authority in Australia. When presiding in Court, Griffith was dignified, but firm and decisive. He was quick to grasp the point, intolerant of ill-prepared arguments, and impatient of mere technicalities. He commenced the practice, followed ever since, of intervening in **argument** by questioning **counsel**. He raised the standard of legal argument in Australia. He was prompt in giving judgment.

The Court, accepting the correctness of American doctrine, asserted its right to determine the validity of an attempted exercise of legislative power by a state (*D'Emden v Pedder* (1904)) or by the Commonwealth (*Railway Servants Case* (1906)). It freely overruled judgments of the state courts. It refused to give a certificate to allow an appeal to the

Privy Council although five states supported the application for it *(Deakin v Webb; Lyne v Webb* (1904)). It refused to follow a decision of the Privy Council on an *inter se* question where no certificate had been given by the Court *(Baxter v Commissioners of Taxation (NSW)* (1907)). It held that an order of the High Court could not be stayed by a Supreme Court pending an appeal to the Privy Council and rebuked the Chief Justice of Victoria for asserting that the Court could not direct an officer of the Supreme Court to conduct an inquiry *(Bayne v Blake* (1908)). The respect the Court acquired was due not only to decisions such as these, which reflected Griffith's strength of character, but also to the cogency of the reasons for judgment and to the fact that Griffith was recognised (as **Barton** said) as 'the greatest lawyer in the Commonwealth'.

From 1903 until 1906, most of the judgments of the Court were written by Griffith with the concurrence of his colleagues Barton and **O'Connor**. This unanimity of judgment ceased when **Isaacs** and **Higgins** were appointed in 1906 and the dominance of Griffith's influence came to an end when further Justices were appointed in 1913. But he had secured the reputation of the Court in the early years of its operation.

When the Court first sat, in 1903, Griffith declared that the Court would hold **sittings** in all states. However, in 1905, the **Attorney-General**, Josiah Symon, tried to ensure that the Court would sit only in Melbourne, and for this purpose proposed—among other things—to limit the Court's travelling expenses. Griffith refused to hold sittings of the Court until proper expenses were paid (see **Strike of 1905**). Later that year, when Isaacs replaced Symon as Attorney-General, the dispute was resolved and the **circuit system** affirmed.

Griffith's approach to **constitutional interpretation** has not stood the test of time. In endeavouring to balance the respective powers of the Commonwealth and the states, Griffith, with the support of Barton and O'Connor, held that there was to be implied in the Constitution a doctrine of immunity of instrumentalities, which prevented a state from interfering with the exercise of the legislative or executive power of the Commonwealth, and vice versa (see, for example, *D'Emden v Pedder; Railway Servants Case*; see also **Intergovernmental immunities**). More generally, the Constitution was to be understood as impliedly prohibiting the Commonwealth from interfering with **reserved state powers** *(R v Barger* (1908); *Union Label Case* (1908)). When Isaacs and Higgins joined the Court in 1906, they dissented from these views, and in the *Engineers Case* (1920) the doctrines Griffith had enunciated, and the method of interpretation that supported them, were finally rejected. Griffith's views were extreme, but the *Engineers Case*, which greatly increased **Commonwealth legislative power**, itself may be criticised for giving too much weight to the literal meaning of individual provisions, and too little to the context in which those provisions appear.

Griffith's approach to the interpretation of the Constitution led him to give a restrictive effect to some of the paragraphs of section 51, and influenced his construction of section 90 of the Constitution. However, his definition of 'duties of **excise**' in *Peterswald v Bartley* (1904) was clear and practical, and the departure from that definition has caused uncertainty and inconvenience.

Nevertheless, Griffith's judgments provide the basis for the understanding of many sections of the Constitution. Some examples are *Farey v Burvett* (1916), which gave a wide effect to the **defence power**; *Osborne v Commonwealth* (1911) (the **taxation** power); *Potter v Minahan* (1908) (**immigration**); and *Huddart Parker v Moorehead* (1909) which, although disapproved on one aspect of the effect of the **corporations power**, has proved influential on another aspect of that power, and in any case has been followed in relation to the **judicial power**.

In cases not concerning the Constitution, Griffith stated the principles clearly and authoritatively (see, for example, *Spencer v Commonwealth* (1907); *Holmes v Jones* (1907); *R v Snow* (1915)).

As Chief Justice, on a number of occasions Griffith gave advice to Governors-General as to the exercise of their powers (see also **Non-judicial functions**). Griffith was created KCMG in 1886 and GCMG in 1895. He was made a Privy Counsellor in 1901 and was sworn in and sat on the Board in 1913.

In 1917, Griffith had a stroke; he did not sit again that year and sat on only a few cases thereafter. By that time, the original harmony of the Court had been lost (see **Personal relations**). Griffith had found recreation in continuing his translation of Dante, which he had commenced while Chief Justice of Queensland. Critics said that he had 'succeeded in rendering the poetry of Dante into the language of a Parliamentary enactment'. When finally a pension was provided, Griffith retired in 1919. He had lived in Sydney during the sittings of the High Court but returned to Brisbane on his **retirement**. He died within a year, after a life of notable achievement, in the course of which he had played an important part in the federation of the Australian colonies, the framing of the Constitution, and the attainment by the Court of its high standards of integrity, learning, ability, and industry.

HARRY GIBBS

Further Reading
Alfred Deakin, *The Federal Story* (1944)
Austin Douglas Graham, *The Life of the Right Honourable Sir Samuel Walker Griffith GCMG PC* (1939)
Roger Joyce, *Samuel Walker Griffith* (1984)

Griffith Court (5 October 1903 to 17 October 1919). The challenges that faced the High Court upon its **establishment** in 1903 were many and varied and, in all probability, more troublesome than anyone then appreciated. Yet expectations for the Court's success were very high. And, as we look back over the gulf of more than 80 years at the Court's achievements, we can say without any question that those high expectations were not disappointed. The Griffith Court laid firm foundations on which the Court was able to build in later years—most notably in interpreting the legislative powers of the Commonwealth.

Deakin's grand vision of the Court saw it enjoying a status and reputation equal to that of the great **common law** courts in other jurisdictions, the **United States Supreme Court**, the **House of Lords**, and the **Privy Council**. The personalities of **Griffith**, **Barton**, and **O'Connor** might have caused some to

The first three Justices of the High Court in 1903. Left to right: Barton, Griffith, and O'Connor

doubt whether they would work together effectively. Not without ambition, each of them had contemplated the possibility of becoming the first **Chief Justice** of Australia. Griffith was an uncompromising and enigmatic personality, and was regarded by his critics as a self-seeker. Moreover, he had been strongly critical of Barton's role in the London negotiations that led to agreement on the form the Constitution was to take.

They succeeded, however, in putting the past and disappointed ambitions behind them and working as a team. They lunched together daily until **Isaacs** and **Higgins** joined the Court, when the practice was discontinued. The credit for their success must be shared between them. Griffith possessed, in **Dixon's** words, 'a dominant and decisive legal mind', a 'mind of the Austinian age, representing the thoughts and learning of a period which had gone'. Barton, though generally considered a lesser lawyer than Griffith, with a less extensive reservoir of legal knowledge, was highly regarded by no less a judge than Leo Cussen for his sagacious and well-written constitutional judgments. Dixon's judgment was that O'Connor's 'work has lived better than that of anybody else of the earlier times'. The writer agrees with that judgment, so long as it is confined to the foundation Justices. Despite the felicity of O'Connor's thought and style, his influence and output do not match that of Isaacs. The judgments of the foundation Justices exhibit a perceptive appre-

ciation of the relationship between the various branches and institutions of government and of the workings of government and administration. They brought to their work their experience in the Constitutional Conventions that preceded federation.

Griffith was the dominant Justice on the early Court. It was his leadership and wide-ranging knowledge of the law, exhibited in well-reasoned judgments, particularly in private law, that won for the Court its reputation as an appellate court, as well as its acceptance by the **legal profession** and the state judges who had been opposed to the creation of the Court. To give three examples: Griffith's definition of **judicial power** in *Huddart Parker v Moorehead* (1909) has frequently been cited as the classic statement upon that topic; his judgment on assignments of choses in action in *Anning v Anning* (1907) has likewise been regarded as a classic statement and has been preferred to the judgment of Isaacs; and his judgments on **defamation** have also been influential.

Until the appointment of Isaacs and Higgins in 1906, Griffith wrote most of the judgments of the Court with the concurrence of his colleagues, though they not infrequently elaborated additional reasons. Very infrequently, O'Connor dissented. The unanimity of the Court's decisions contributed to the acceptance of its decisions and the establishment of its authority. The practice of sitting in the state capitals (see **Circuit system**)—strongly supported by Deakin but opposed by the **Attorney-General** Josiah Symon in 1905—was probably influential in gaining professional acceptance for the Court and in promoting **national unity**. The Court's threat to 'go on **strike**' on that occasion demonstrated its willingness to stand up to the executive.

The Court was quickly confronted with attempts by the Commonwealth Parliament to exercise legislative power over matters that the Australian colonies had considered to be their own preserve, and with countervailing claims by the states to regulate those matters to the exclusion of the Commonwealth. The tension became manifest in two areas, those of taxation and industrial relations. Indeed, much of the Court's constitutional **jurisprudence** in the time of Griffith was concerned with the preservation of the powers and status of the states.

In the first important constitutional case, *D'Emden v Pedder* (1904), the Court embraced the doctrine of **intergovernmental immunities** enunciated by US Supreme Court Chief Justice John Marshall in *McCulloch v Maryland* (1819). According to this doctrine, state laws could not 'fetter, control or interfere with the free exercise of the legislative or executive power of the Commonwealth', and vice versa. So Tasmanian stamp duty could not be imposed upon a receipt given by a Commonwealth official for his Commonwealth salary. In argument, Griffith suggested that if the doctrine applied, section 109 of the Constitution (see **Inconsistency**) 'would appear to be unnecessary'. In fact, that was the central thrust of the opposing argument, which led to the later demise of the immunities doctrine in the *Engineers Case* (1920). The Griffith Court reaffirmed the doctrine in *Deakin v Webb* (1904) and *Baxter v Commissioners of Taxation (NSW)* (1907), notwithstanding that the **Privy Council** in *Webb v Outtrim* (1906) had purported to overrule *Deakin v Webb*. But with the dissents of Isaacs and particularly Higgins in *Baxter*, the storm signals had been hoisted for the doctrine of intergovernmental immunities.

Linked to the immunities doctrine was the doctrine of **reserved state powers**, according to which the legislative powers conferred upon the Commonwealth Parliament were to be construed by reference to the powers of the states reserved by the Constitution—for example, sections 106 and 107 (the *Union Label Case* (1908)). This doctrine played a part in restrictive interpretations of the **corporations power** (*Huddart Parker*), the **trade and commerce power**, and the taxation power (*R v Barger* (1908)). The doctrine also contributed to a narrow conception of 'excise' in section 90 of the Constitution (*Peterswald v Bartley* (1904)). Though supported by the foundation Justices, the doctrine of reserve powers was also swept away by the *Engineers Case*. That decision ushered in what was described as interpretation according to the natural and ordinary meaning of the words of the Constitution (**literalism**) and the paramountcy of Commonwealth law as provided for in section 109 of the Constitution.

The two doctrines, by preserving a balance between the constituent elements of the Australian federation, probably conformed to community sentiment, which at that stage was by no means adjusted to the exercise of central power. It was only after **World War I** had created a strong sense of national unity that the Court rejected those doctrines in the *Engineers Case*.

The decision in *Baxter's Case* marked a definitive stage in the Court's relationship with the Privy Council. In the judgments in that case, the Court was able to point to errors in the Privy Council's approach, in *Webb v Outtrim*, to section 39(2) of the *Judiciary Act* 1903 (Cth), and to the relevance of US **constitutional interpretation** to a proper understanding of the Australian Constitution. Earlier, the Court in *Deakin v Webb* had sternly rebuked the Supreme Court of Victoria for following its own decision in *Wollaston's Case* (1902) in preference to the Court's decision in *D'Emden v Pedder*. By refusing, in *Deakin v Webb*, to issue a certificate under section 74 authorising an appeal to the Privy Council, the Court asserted its exclusive authority to determine *inter se* questions. *Baxter's Case* established that exclusive authority for the future and cemented the Court's position at the apex of the Australian judicial **hierarchy**, subject only to the appeal to the Privy Council.

Industrial relations became the main constitutional battleground at a very early stage. It was to remain so for most of the century. Early on, the Court adopted a very constructive approach to the **conciliation and arbitration** power (section 51(xxxv)) when it held in the *Jumbunna Coal Case* (1908) that the power extended to the incorporation and registration of associations of employers and employees, and implicitly recognised that associations formed in different states might make common cause to formulate a demand across state boundaries. In the *Felt Hatters Case* (1914) and the *Builders Labourers Case* (1914), Griffith and Barton protested that this did not mean that associations of employees cooperating across state boundaries could create an arbitrable dispute merely through the service of a log of claims to which employers did not agree; but by this time, Isaacs was in the ascendancy and Griffith and Barton were alone in dissent. By decisively recognising in *Builders Labourers* that the non-acceptance by employers of a demand for terms and conditions of employment by an association of employees could give rise to an interstate industrial dispute, the Court effectively endorsed the creation of paper disputes, thus ensuring that the arbitration power would have very considerable regulatory scope. In this way, the constructive interpretation of the power in *Jumbunna* became the foundation of the federal system of industrial conciliation and arbitration. The interpretation has stood the test of time.

Jumbunna, however, was an exception. Generally the foundation Justices took a far more restrictive view of the arbitration power. For example, in the *Woodworkers Case* (1909), Griffith and O'Connor insisted that the arbitration process must operate within the limits set by state legislation and statutory authorities, including State Wages Boards. In *Whybrow's Case (No 1)* (1910), Barton joined them in reaffirming that view, with Isaacs and Higgins dissenting, while in *Whybrow's Case (No 2)* (1910), the whole Court struck down a provision enabling an award to be declared as a 'common rule' applicable throughout a whole industry.

Indeed, the Court's approach to most issues of constitutional interpretation was orthodox and conservative. The Court refused to have recourse to the **Convention Debates** in interpreting the Constitution (*Municipal Council of Sydney v Commonwealth* (1904))—a view overturned in *Cole v Whitfield* (1988). The Court rejected a broad interpretation of section 116 in *Krygger v Williams* (1912) and of section 117 in *Davies and Jones v WA* (1904) and *Lee Fay v Vincent* (1908): two provisions that guarantee individual rights. Section 117 was reinterpreted more broadly in *Street v Queensland Bar Association* (1989). The Court, like its successors, had difficulty in enunciating a consistent and coherent view of section 92 (*Fox v Robbins* (1909), *Duncan v Queensland* (1916); see **Interstate trade and commerce**).

With the advent of Isaacs and Higgins, Griffith's dominating influence began its steady decline. The decline gathered pace with the death of O'Connor in 1912, his replacement by **Gavan Duffy**, and the appointment of **Powers** and **Rich** as additional Justices in 1913—although Griffith did not dissent in a constitutional case until the *Felt Hatters Case*. Isaacs' knowledge of the law was just as comprehensive as Griffith's. Isaacs was an outstanding constitutional and **equity** lawyer whose influence has continued to the present day. He was just as determined and as energetic as Griffith had been. He was a prolific judgment writer; his judgments were encyclopaedic but prolix. The days of friendly concurrences were a thing of the past. The tensions within the Court culminated in Griffith's success in having **Knox** appointed as his successor, thereby frustrating Isaacs' hopes, for the time being at any rate.

Anthony Mason

Further Reading

Austin Douglas Graham, *The Life of the Right Honourable Sir Samuel Walker Griffith GCMG PC* (1939)

Roger Joyce, *Samuel Walker Griffith* (1984)

Anthony Mason, 'The High Court in Sir Samuel Griffith's Time: Contemporary Parallels and Contrasts' (1994) 3 *GLR* 179

John Williams, 'Samuel Griffith and the Australian Constitution: Shaking Hands with the New Chief Justice' (1999) 4 *The New Federalist* 37

Gummow, William Montague Charles (*b* 9 October 1942; Justice since 1995) was born and educated in Sydney. He had what he described, at his swearing in as a Justice, as the benefit of 'a vigorous education' at the Sydney Grammar School. He proceeded to the University of Sydney, where he graduated in arts and, with first-class honours, in law. Later, he graduated LLM, also with first-class honours.

From the year of his graduation until his **appointment** as a Justice, Gummow taught in the Faculty of Law of the University of Sydney. From 1966 until his appointment, in 1986, as a judge of the **Federal Court**, he taught the intellectual property course. From 1970 until 1995, he lectured also in **equity**. He has written extensively. He is joint author, with RP Meagher and JRF Lehane, of *Equity: Doctrines and Remedies* (3rd edn 1992); wrote, with JD Heydon and RP Austin, several editions of *Cases and Materials on Equity and Trusts* (4th edn 1993); and is joint editor, with RP Meagher, of *Jacobs on Trusts* (6th edn 1997). He has written numerous essays and articles, several of which appear in published collections of essays or in learned journals. In 1992, the University of Sydney marked Gummow's contributions to the University and to legal scholarship by conferring on him an LLD, *honoris causa*. He became a member of the American Law Institute in 1997.

William Gummow, Justice since 1995

His essay 'Legal Education' (1988) presented a number of themes evident elsewhere in his approach to the law: notably, an emphasis on the importance of statutes and a high regard for legal **history**, both of which were and are insufficiently taught in Australian law schools. He also advocated teaching by practitioners exposed to 'the law in action', and noted in his swearing-in speech that **Mason** (who had retired the previous day) had taught both himself and **Gaudron**.

Gummow began his professional career as an articled law clerk with the Sydney firm of solicitors, Allen Allen & Hemsley. He was admitted as a solicitor in 1966 and in 1969 became a partner of the firm. In those days, specialisation, among partners of large firms, was by no means as much the norm, or as strict, as it has become; thus the diversity of the practice which Gummow developed, though striking, was not unique. It included banking law, **trusts** and revenue law, intellectual property litigation, commercial documents and transactions (many of considerable size and complexity), and some **constitutional law**.

In 1976, Gummow was admitted to the Bar. He developed a diverse and heavy practice. It included equity, **commercial**, **tax** and intellectual property litigation. Notably, it extended also to cases involving large constitutional issues, in many of which Gummow appeared as junior to the then Commonwealth **Solicitor-General**, Maurice Byers. Gummow took silk in 1986. Shortly thereafter, he was appointed a judge of the Federal Court, an office he held until his appointment as a Justice of the High Court in 1995. In 1997, he was appointed AO.

Gummow has delivered—and participated in—a number of leading judgments on aspects of intellectual property law and related subjects, both as a judge of the Federal Court and since his appointment to the High Court. They are marked both by a close attention to statutory language and context and by a careful examination of the evolution of principle and doctrine. So, the **joint judgment** in *CCOM v Jiejing*

(1994) contains a close analysis of the historical background from which the statutory concept of 'fair basing' emerged in **patent** law and of what the concept involves in the various contexts in which it operates. Gummow's judgment in *Werner & Co v Bailey Aluminium Products* (1989) includes a detailed exposition of the emergence, development and origin, again in patent law, of the separate concepts of lack of novelty and obviousness (as to which, and the extent of any 'threshold' requirement of inventiveness, see the joint majority judgment, in which Gummow participated, in *Advanced Building Systems v Ramset Fasteners* (1998)). In *Prestige Group v Dart Industries* (1990), Gummow discussed, with detailed reference to history and authority (including US authority both ancient and modern), the meaning and effect of 'false suggestion or misrepresentation' in patent law.

Likewise, in *ConAgra v McCain Foods* (1992), Gummow examined the elements of the passing-off action—offering, particularly, a precise analysis of the relevance of fraud, of the nature of the relevant fraud, and of the character of the reputation (or 'goodwill') that the passing-off action protects. Previously, in *NSW Dairy Corporation v Murray-Goulburn Cooperative* (1989), Gummow had analysed the distinction between the reputation or distinctiveness necessary to maintain passing-off and the distinctiveness, or lack of it, that is relevant for various purposes under the **trade marks** legislation (some controversies surrounding that topic were laid to rest by the joint judgment of all members of the High Court in *Campomar Sociedad v Nike International* (2000)).

The approach evident in those intellectual property cases (and numerous others) is evident equally in Gummow's judgments in other areas of the law. Four equity cases may be mentioned. In *Re Australian Elizabethan Theatre Trust; Lord v Commonwealth Bank* (1991), there is an analysis of the basis, in the established principles of the law of trusts, of the so-called Quistclose trust. Gummow's judgment in *Breen v Williams* (1996) includes a consideration of the nature and limits of the **fiduciary** duties owed by medical practitioners to patients and of aspects of the duties of express trustees which of their nature ought not to apply—and do not apply—to fiduciaries generally (a subject on which there was little prior learning). The joint judgment of **Deane** and Gummow in *Nelson v Nelson* (1995) contains an important exposition of the effect of 'illegal purpose' on trusts, particularly implied or resulting trusts, and an insistence on the flexibility of equitable doctrine and on the importance, where the asserted illegality is based on a statutory provision, of a search for the underlying policy or purpose of the statute in question. The fourth equity case is *Garcia v National Australia Bank* (1998). The majority judgment, in which Gummow participated, considered some of the principles underlying the law of **undue influence** and unconscientious conduct and the place of *Yerkey v Jones* (1939) within each.

Finally, Gummow has contributed considerably to the development of public and constitutional law. His constitutional judgments display the same approach: a careful textual analysis, highly sensitive to historical context and the evolution of principle. His judgments have been highly influential, particularly in the areas at the core of the Australian federation: the interplay of different polities within the federation and, especially, the elaboration of the consequences of the

separation of powers and insulation of federal **judicial power** in Chapter III (see, for example, the reformulation of choice of law rules in *John Pfeiffer v Rogerson* (2000), the striking down of the **cross-vesting** scheme in *Re Wakim* (1999), the restrictions on the legislative capacity of the states in *Kable v DPP* (1996), and the holding in *Commonwealth v Mewett* (1997) that the Commonwealth's liability to suit arises from the Constitution). In the area of public law, mention may be made of his treatment of **standing** in *Alphapharm v SmithKline Beecham* (1994), *Bateman's Bay Local Aboriginal Land Council v Aboriginal Community Benefit Fund* (1998) and the *Truth About Motorways Case* (2000); his discussion, in *Minister for Immigration v Eshetu* (1999) of *Wednesbury* unreasonableness and 'jurisdictional fact'; and his analysis of the **writs** of mandamus and prohibition in the joint judgment with Gaudron in *Re Refugee Review Tribunal; Ex parte Aala* (2000). But it would not do him justice to single out examples; Gummow's contribution has been sustained and comprehensive.

Gummow was invited, in 1999, to deliver the Clarendon Law Lectures at Oxford University. The series of three lectures has been published under the title *Change and Continuity: Statute, Equity and Federalism* (1999). The lectures draw together a number of important themes: among them, in the first lecture, 'The Common Law and Statute', the interplay between statute, the **common law**, and equity (seen, for example, in the 'long administration of the patent law and of charitable trusts [which have] provided a source of vitality of old law'); and the processes of reasoning by which courts have construed statutes imposing norms of conduct as conferring also private rights of action. The second lecture, 'Equity Follows the Law', contrasts with the antiquity of pervasive equitable principle the relatively recent conceptual development of **contract and tort**; draws attention to the evolutionary development of equitable principle, so that 'the lineage of an idea may be quite clear and its persistence through changing circumstances all the more readily applicable'; and emphasises the importance of 'clarity of thought and an understanding of the conceptual roots of living equitable doctrine'.

The third lecture, '**Federalism**', discusses what the **legalism** implicit in a federal system actually involves and the perspective it offers in 'the comprehension of the legal system as a complex whole'; the part played by 'constitutional historicism' in **constitutional interpretation** and the relationship—and distinction—between the judicial process and the methods of historical scholarship; and the accommodation of 'basic common law concepts and techniques' (including the doctrine of parliamentary supremacy) to a federal system—as to which see the joint judgments in *Lange v ABC* (1997) and in *John Pfeiffer v Rogerson*.

It is not difficult to see in the lectures an elaboration—and a further and perhaps more speculative consideration—of a number of themes evident in judgments and earlier writings.

JOHN LEHANE

Further Reading
WMC Gummow, 'Legal Education' (1988) 11 *Syd LR* 439
WMC Gummow, *Change and Continuity: Statute, Equity and Federalism* (1999)

H

Hannah v Dalgarno (1903). The first case to be decided by the High Court had started off quite simply. On 9 August 1901, while Commonwealth telephone wires were being repaired in Elizabeth Street, Sydney, a wire fell across an electric tramline, electrocuting the horse that drew Robert Hannah's hansom cab. The cab was damaged, and Hannah was injured. In an action in the Supreme Court of NSW (exercising federal jurisdiction under the *Claims against the Commonwealth Act* 1902 (Cth)), Hannah sued the Deputy Postmaster-General for NSW, James Dalgarno, as a nominal defendant representing the Commonwealth. The main issue was whether the plaintiff could recover **damages** despite the absence of any real **evidence** of negligence. The trial judge ruled that according to *Scott v London and St Katherine Docks* (1865), the jury might infer negligence from the nature of the accident itself. The plaintiff was awarded £200 in damages. The defendant applied to the Full Court of the Supreme Court of NSW for the verdict to be set aside on the ground that there had been no evidence of negligence. The application was rejected in a 2:1 decision dated 20 August 1903.

On 25 August, the *Judiciary Act* 1903 (Cth) received the royal assent. On 15 October, the High Court granted the defendant special **leave to appeal**. The plaintiff then brought a motion to rescind the grant of leave. His **counsel**, Richard Sly, supported the motion on the grounds, first, that 'the Court has no **jurisdiction** to grant leave ... because the judgment appealed from was pronounced before the passing of the *Judiciary Act*', and secondly, that 'the judgment did not decide a matter or question of great public importance'.

On the first ground, Sly argued that the source of the Court's jurisdiction was the Judiciary Act. The grants of appellate jurisdiction in section 35 of that Act were expressed to operate retrospectively in certain circumstances—but not, as here, where appeal to the **Privy Council** would have required a grant of special leave and no such leave had been sought. Subject to the possibility of such leave being granted, the plaintiff had a vested right to his judgment, which the Judiciary Act could not take away retrospectively except by unambiguous words.

On the other hand, NSW **Attorney-General** Bernhard Wise, appearing for the defendant, argued that the Judiciary Act 'does not constitute the Court ... The Court existed potentially from the date of the establishment of the Constitution'. Moreover, its appellate jurisdiction was created by

section 73 of the Constitution; thus it was the defendant who had a vested right (to seek leave) unless the plaintiff could show that the Judiciary Act was intended to take that right away. Sly responded that notwithstanding section 73 of the Constitution, 'there was no right of appeal to the High Court, because there was no Court in existence' at the time of the Supreme Court decision. In his view of section 73, no right could exist until Parliament created the Court.

Griffith, for the Court, acknowledged the 'difficulty and importance' of the question but left it undecided (see **Constitutional basis of Court**). On the one hand, he noted that in this case the Supreme Court of NSW was invested with federal jurisdiction. He saw 'much force' in the contention that when a state court exercised federal jurisdiction (as distinct from state jurisdiction), it was intended to be subject to the right of appeal to the High Court—a right that could not be lost or taken away by mere parliamentary inaction or delay. The source for this right was to be found in the Constitution itself. He noted also that section 7 of the Claims against the Commonwealth Act had empowered the Attorney-General in certain circumstances to postpone an appeal from a **state Supreme Court** until the end of 1903—that is, said Griffith, to 'a time when ... the High Court would probably have been established'.

On the other hand, Griffith noted the difficulties posed by initiating an appeal to a Court that does not yet exist. He cited *Ex parte Walker* (1903), where the Privy Council had stressed that 'a successful litigant is entitled to know when he can regard the litigation as at an end'. He conceded that the words 'shall be' and 'shall have' in sections 71 and 73 of the Constitution might merely be 'words of futurity'. As for section 35 of the Judiciary Act, if its wording reflected an opinion in Parliament that appellate jurisdiction could sometimes be retrospective and sometimes not, he thought that such an opinion might or might not be correct.

Exercising his discretion, Griffith disposed of the matter in the plaintiff's favour by rescinding the grant of special leave to appeal on the basis of the plaintiff's second argument: that such leave should be granted only in cases of public importance (*Prince v Gagnon* (1882)).

Francesca Dominello

Hayne, Kenneth Madison (*b* 5 June 1945; Justice since 1997) was appointed to the High Court in September 1997 from

Kenneth Hayne, Justice since 1997

method' (if you don't like the question, challenge the question), a useful technique for advocates in dealing with questions from the Bench. Other memorable aspects of Oxford included Dworkin's lectures on the legitimacy of civil dissent and the Clarendon Building being occupied by students. Even English beer became tolerable with practice. Hayne graduated in 1971 with a BCL with first-class honours.

On his return, Hayne went to the Victorian Bar. He read with John D Phillips who, years later, was his colleague on the Victorian Supreme Court and Court of Appeal. Hayne's practice was mainly in **commercial law**, although he also appeared as junior **counsel** in several important constitutional cases. These included the *AAP Case* (1975) and *HC Sleigh v SA* (1977), both with Dawson, the then **Solicitor-General** of Victoria, *A-G (WA); Ex rel Ansett Transport Industries v Australian National Airlines* (1976), with **Deane**, and the *DOGS Case* (1981).

Hayne took silk in 1984 and his practice came to be dominated by large commercial disputes. Largest of all was a dispute over Bass Strait oil royalties, which led to two cases in the Victorian Supreme Court as well as arbitration, and also brought Hayne into contact with **Gleeson**. Hayne also represented BHP during an inquiry by the National Companies and Securities Commission into cross-investments between BHP and Elders, which resulted in a High Court challenge (*BHP v National Companies and Securities Commission* (1986)). In addition to this commercial work, Hayne represented the plaintiff in the conflict of laws case *Breavington v Godleman* (1988). He returned to these issues as a High Court Justice in *John Pfeiffer v Rogerson* (2000). The difference between the views he expressed as counsel and those he expressed as a Justice reflects the difference between these roles.

After 21 years at the Bar, Hayne was appointed to the Supreme Court of Victoria in 1992. He began with trial work, including murder trials, which provided something of a contrast to his practice as a barrister. More familiar subject-matter was found in the Supreme Court's commercial list, which Hayne managed from 1993 to 1995. Notwithstanding his prodigious output and what some have termed 'disconcerting promptness', his judgments have stood the test of time and continue to influence the development of company law today.

Hayne was appointed as a foundation member of the Victorian Court of Appeal in 1995. In addition to his busy court schedule, Hayne was also heavily involved in the Supreme Court's reform of **civil procedure**. His workload did not, however, prevent him from developing legal principle, particularly in the area of **criminal law**. His discussion of indefinite sentencing provisions in *R v Moffatt* (1997) was recently referred to with approval by the High Court in *Lowndes v The Queen* (1999). Indeed, the only times when judgments of his on the Victorian Supreme Court (either at first instance or in the Court of Appeal) have been overturned by the High Court have occurred *after* his **appointment** to the High Court (*Palmer v The Queen* (1998); *Naxakis v Western General Hospital* (1999)).

In hindsight, the path from the University of Melbourne to the High Court might seem to have been a natural progression. The pace of Hayne's ascent through the judicial **hierarchy** is demonstrated by the fact that he was precluded

the Victorian Court of Appeal to replace **Dawson**. Although born in Gympie (the Queensland newspaper the *Courier Mail* proclaimed 'Queenslander rises to High Court'), Hayne, like his predecessor, is proudly a product of the Victorian **legal profession**.

Hayne's connection with the High Court began in 1911 when his grandfather provided **O'Connor** with use of the public library on Thursday Island, for which he received a letter of thanks and a donation of '*Prescott's Mexico* and *Prescott's Peru*, four volumes in all'. Then, as a first-year law student at Melbourne University, Hayne attended a packed Court in Melbourne for the farewell of **Dixon** as **Chief Justice** of the High Court. His lecturers at the University of Melbourne included Harold Ford in company law—which may explain Hayne's continuing interest in the subject, although he regrets that he studied **constitutional law** one year too late to be taught by Zelman Cowen. In 1968, Hayne graduated with first-class honours in law and was awarded the Supreme Court Prize and the EJB Nunn Scholarship. For this reason, perhaps, many of his contemporaries thought he was destined for a career in academia. He did not share these expectations and was admitted to practice in 1969.

Hayne was awarded a Rhodes Scholarship in 1969, and was accepted into Exeter College at Oxford, whose alumni include legal theorist Julius Stone. This period was tremendously influential in Hayne's legal development. He was taught by some of the great minds of the **common law** world, including JHC Morris in **conflict of laws**, Ronald Dworkin and Anthony Honoré in **jurisprudence**, Rupert Cross in **evidence**, and Otto Kahn Freund in **labour relations law**. He learnt the 'Oxford

from sitting on the first constitutional case to be determined by the High Court after his appointment (*Commonwealth v WMC Resources* (1998)) because, as counsel, he had signed the statement of claim. At his swearing in, however, Hayne professed with characteristic modesty that he had found each successive step in his legal career more daunting than the last. As he observed in his keynote address at the Judicial Conference of Australia in November 1999, all judges are 'compelled to reduce a complex slice of human experience with all its subtlety, to what is, in essence, a one line answer: "A wins, B loses"'. The difficulty of this task is magnified on the High Court, where each judgment is, in effect, a statement of a broader principle that people in the position of A win, and people in the position of B lose.

It is of course premature to speculate on what Hayne's contribution to the High Court's jurisprudence will be. Perhaps the judgment that has had the greatest impact so far is his **joint judgment** with **Gummow** (effectively the judgment of the Court) in *Re Wakim* (1999), which held that key provisions of the **cross-vesting** scheme were invalid. Nonetheless, even at this early stage, two themes emerge strongly.

The first is a strong preference for cautious incremental development of the law (what **McHugh** in *McGinty v WA* (1996) termed 'bottom up' reasoning). Like McHugh, Hayne has a particular interest in the common law. Judgments to which Hayne is party rarely develop the law beyond the extent necessary to decide the case (see, for example, the joint judgments in *Garcia v National Australia Bank* (1998) and *Fejo v Northern Territory* (1998)). This caution does not prevent Hayne from having regard to **policy considerations** or academic writings—but, as he reiterated at the Judicial Conference in 1999, 'our search must always be for principles that guide the making of decisions'. For this reason—as exemplified in his **dissenting judgment** in *Perre v Apand* (1999)—he dislikes tests dependent upon criteria such as 'fair, just and reasonable' that do not provide any guidance as to how they should be applied.

The second is a concern that High Court judgments promote the effective working of the Australian legal system—although Gummow and he stated in *Re Wakim* that convenience does not supply absent constitutional power. This concern exhibits itself in a variety of ways. First, Hayne has a preference for joint judgments where possible; this enables the *ratio decidendi* of a case to be more readily identified. In his first two years on the Court, he was party to joint majority judgments in more than half of the cases he decided. Secondly, Hayne is acutely aware that the rules formulated by the High Court must be capable of being understood and applied by judges below, often in the stress of a trial. This is reflected in the statement of McHugh, Hayne, and **Callinan** in *Pearce v The Queen* (1998) that the criminal law must avoid 'excessive subtleties and refinements'. Finally, Hayne has explicit regard to the demands that the Court's judgments will place on the resources of the courts below (see in particular Gummow and Hayne (dissenting) in *Jackamarra v Krakouer* (1998) and McHugh and Hayne (dissenting) in *Gipp v The Queen* (1998)).

In a speech delivered in May 1999, Hayne noted that 'those who win or lose will see the legal process through the prism of that result'. For this reason, he agrees with Dixon that the most important person in a court is the unsuccessful party, in the sense that the judge must ensure that that party comes away feeling that his or her arguments were given a fair hearing. The careful and patient manner in which he dealt with legally untenable arguments in *Joosse v Australian Securities and Investment Commission* (1998) pays tribute to this philosophy. Unfortunately perhaps, the need to preserve the dignity of the Court means that parties are deprived of his whimsical sense of **humour** and gift for mimicry. Hayne is married to Michelle Gordon, a barrister, and they have a son. He has a daughter and three sons from a previous marriage.

GRAEME HILL

Health law. The High Court's contribution to health law has been relatively recent but by no means modest: significant not only for the outcomes of particular cases, but also for the underlying rationale of the decisions. In three important areas, the Court has made a distinctively Australian contribution: capacity to consent to medical treatment, medical negligence, and a patient's right of access to medical records.

Until 1992, there was uncertainty about whether a child under the age of 16 could consent to his or her own treatment, or whether the consent of a parent was always needed. In *Marion's Case* (1992), the Court held that a child of sufficient maturity to understand fully what was proposed could herself give consent to most treatments. At first blush, the decision was no more than an adoption of the earlier English case of *Gillick v West Norfolk Area Health Authority* (1985). The significance of *Marion* was that, although the Court came to the same conclusion as the **House of Lords**, it did so on a different basis. The Court relied on psychological studies of the way in which **children** develop, as well as on academic writing suggesting that the law should apply this developmental approach. These underpinnings from another discipline seem not to have been relevant to the House of Lords finding in *Gillick*.

Secondly, unlike *Gillick*, *Marion* acknowledges that some decisions on medical treatment involve such far-reaching consequences that neither a competent child nor a parent should ever be able to consent, such matters requiring the prior approval of a court. There is some uncertainty, following *Marion*, about what decisions would require such approval. **McHugh** suggested that abortion and sterilisation would fit into this category. A later case in the Family Court, *GWW and CMW* (1997), suggested that bone marrow harvests would be included. The Queensland Law Reform Commission's Report *Consent to Health Care of Young People* (1996) suggests that the removal of life support or gender reassignment would also qualify. An additional uncertainty following *Marion* is exactly what 'understanding fully' involves.

In determining the standard of negligence by which a medical practitioner should be assessed, Australian courts had long adopted the English 'profession-centred' standard: provided the practice adopted by a medical practitioner was consistent with that of a reasonably competent band of medical practitioners, then the practice was not negligent. Though some disquiet with this approach can been seen in the earlier SA decision of *F v R* (1983), the break from the profession-centred approach was made in *Rogers v Whitaker*

(1992). In that case, the Court noted that a doctor owed one comprehensive duty to a patient, encompassing diagnosis, advice, and treatment. The Court suggested that while it might be guided by the profession's practice in assessing whether a doctor had been negligent in diagnosis or treatment, the correct approach was to ask the objective question: did the doctor advise of material risks?

The Court held that a risk was material if a reasonable person, warned of the risk, would attach significance to it, or if the medical practitioner was or should reasonably have been aware that the particular patient, if warned of the risk, would be likely to attach significance to it.

A less frequently noted though equally important aspect of *Rogers v Whitaker* is that the Court suggested for the first time that the level of specialisation of medical practitioners is critical when assessing whether a particular practitioner is negligent. The Court reiterated that the standard of care expected of a medical practitioner is that of the ordinary skilled person exercising and professing to have that skill. Ian Freckelton pointed out in 1999 that, in *Rogers v Whitaker*, the High Court determined the skill base not according to the level of care to be expected of a medical practitioner, nor by a surgeon, nor even by an opthalmic surgeon—but according to the level of skill expected of a surgeon specialising in corneal and anterior segment surgery. The Court, Freckelton noted, arguably acknowledged the increasing specialisation of the profession and required higher standards of those who profess greater skill.

Following *Rogers v Whitaker*, there were conflicting NSW Court of Appeal decisions as to whether *Rogers v Whitaker* applied also to cases involving negligent treatment and diagnosis (*Lowns v Woods* (1996)), or whether the principle was limited to negligent advice (*Howarth v Adey* (1996)).

In *Naxakis v Western General Hospital* (1999), the High Court appeared to abandon the profession-centred approach to negligence even in respect of diagnosis and treatment. It held that the standard of negligence is not determined solely or even primarily by reference to the practice followed or supported by a responsible body of opinion in the relevant profession or trade; rather, the standard is that of the ordinary skilled person exercising and professing to have that special skill. This is a question to be determined not by the profession, but by the court.

The vexed issue of access to medical records was determined by the Court in *Breen v Williams* (1996). That case, too, was important not only for deciding that patients had, at law, no right of unfettered access to their records, but for the basis on which the decision was reached. The appellant submitted that there were a number of possible grounds on which a right of access could be based. The first, a proprietary right, was rejected by the Court as it was clear that the doctor owned his or her own medical records. The second—that right of access was part of an implied contractual term—raised squarely, for the first time in Australian case law, the question of what terms would be implied in the doctor–patient relationship. The Court adopted the approach favoured by English courts that a term would be implied only where a reasonable bystander would have assumed that such a term was implied, and that it was necessary to give the contract business efficacy. This test was derived from *The Moorcock* (1889), and its application led the Court to find that there was no implied term granting a patient access to records. The Court also rejected the argument that there was an innominate **common law** right that accorded a right of access, or that 'the general trend' of decisions such as *Rogers v Whitaker* implied that patients had a growing right to know.

The most interesting part of the Court's judgments in *Breen v Williams* was the question of whether the doctor–patient relationship was fiduciary in nature, and, if so, whether on that ground a patient had a right of access to medical records. The fiduciary argument was a strong one: Canadian cases such as *Norberg v Wynrib* (1992) and *McInerney v MacDonald* (1992) had held that the doctor–patient relationship is fiduciary in nature—a stance that has been used as the basis of the patient-centred test of negligence adopted by some North American jurisdictions. It is clear that patients have a special kind of trust in their doctors, and that this is sufficient to give rise to a presumption of conflict of interest in respect of gifts between doctor and patient. The High Court declined, however, to find that a doctor owed broad-based **fiduciary obligations** to a patient.

A number of health law issues await the High Court's consideration. Chief among them is the vexed area of abortion law. An appeal from the NSW Court of Appeal's judgment in *CES v Superclinics* (1995) was settled by the parties, denying the High Court the chance to determine authoritatively when a woman may lawfully seek an abortion. Another is the question of whether a doctor owes a duty to attend and treat a person with whom he has no prior doctor–patient relationship. Though the NSW Supreme Court has twice stated that a doctor may owe a duty in such circumstances (*Lowns v Woods* (1996); *BT v Oei* (1999)), it is not clear that the High Court would take the same approach.

John Devereux

Further Reading
John Devereux, *Medical Law* (1997)
Ian Freckelton and Kerry Petersen, *Controversies in Health Law* (1999)

Hierarchy of courts. The structure of Australia's court system has changed significantly over the past century. At the time when the Commonwealth was established in 1901, each of the self-governing colonies had its own court structures, modelled on the English system. Each had a Supreme Court, some had intermediate District or County Courts, and all had courts of summary jurisdiction, constituted by police or stipendiary magistrates or justices of the peace.

In civil cases, the **state Supreme Courts** had a general, unlimited civil jurisdiction. District or County Court jurisdiction was limited by amount and, to some extent, by the type of action. The jurisdiction of courts of summary jurisdiction was further limited in these respects. An appeal could ordinarily be brought from a judgment of a Supreme Court judge, sitting alone or with a jury, to a Full Supreme Court, or to the **Privy Council** if a sufficient amount was in issue or the Privy Council granted special leave. Appeals from intermediate courts (District or County Courts) lay to the Supreme Court of that state. Appeals from courts of summary jurisdiction lay to the District or County Court in that state, if there was one, or to the Supreme Court.

Indictable offences were tried by a Supreme Court (or a District or County Court) judge sitting with a jury. Less serious offences were dealt with by courts of summary jurisdiction without a jury; those courts also determined whether a person should be committed for trial on indictment. An appeal upon conviction by a jury lay to a Full Supreme Court. The Privy Council could grant special leave to appeal in criminal cases. Appeals from summary convictions lay to the District or County Courts or, sometimes, to a single judge of the Supreme Court.

The establishment of the Commonwealth did not itself have a major impact on the basic structures of the courts of the colonies—which became the states of the federation—but it did have significant effects upon their place in the Australian legal system and upon the laws they were to apply. At the level of the Supreme Courts, except for the creation of permanent Courts of Appeal in NSW, Victoria, and Queensland, the structures remain basically the same. (Tasmania has never had an intermediate court.) Since federation, the states have set up many specialist courts and tribunals, over which the Supreme Courts exercise appellate or supervisory jurisdiction. One significant innovation after federation was the Commonwealth's adoption of the 'autochthonous expedient' of conferring federal jurisdiction upon state courts pursuant to the provisions of section 77(iii) of the Constitution (*Boilermakers Case* (1956)).

Federation brought about many other fundamental changes to the landscape of the court system. Most importantly, by section 71 of the Constitution, the Commonwealth's **judicial power** was vested 'in a Federal Supreme Court, to be called the High Court of Australia, and in such other federal courts as the Parliament creates, and in such other courts as it invests with federal jurisdiction'.

Sections 73, 75, and 76 of the Constitution invested the High Court with a special original **jurisdiction** and a comprehensive appellate jurisdiction. Writing in 1900, **Quick and Garran** observed:

> The High Court is the crown and apex, not only of the judicial system of the Commonwealth, but of the judicial systems of the States as well … It is a court of appeal from federal courts and courts exercising federal jurisdiction … But … the High Court is [also] a court of appeal from all decisions of the Supreme Courts of the States, utterly irrespective of the subject-matter of the suit or the character of the parties. In this respect it resembles the Supreme Court of Canada, and differs from the Supreme Court of the United States.

They went on to say that the High Court, like the **United States Supreme Court**, is the 'guardian of the Federal Constitution'; but that unlike the Supreme Court it is also 'the guardian of the Constitutions of the several States'.

The status of the appeal to the Privy Council was a contentious issue during the **Convention Debates**, and the main subject of dispute between the Australian delegates and the Colonial Secretary, Joseph Chamberlain. Under a compromise, the prerogative appeal by special leave was preserved by section 74 of the Constitution, with two exceptions: first,

unless the High Court certified (a rare event), there was no appeal on *inter se* questions; and secondly, the Commonwealth Parliament was granted power to enact legislation that would 'at once curtail the royal prerogative to grant special leave to appeal and render [the High] Court—"the highest judicial organ created by the Australian people"—a court of final resort': *A-G (Cth) v T & G Mutual* (1978). The exercise of this prerogative had been much regulated by statutes and by Orders in Council, but the *Commonwealth of Australia Constitution Act* 1900 (UK) marked the first occasion upon which, in the case of any court in the Empire overseas, there was a statutory denial of all access to the Queen in Council from certain of its judgments, effected by Imperial Act (*T & G Mutual*). By this method, appeals from the High Court were eventually 'limited' to the point of abolition. The effect of the *Australia Acts* 1986 was to abolish all remaining appeals to the Privy Council from Australian courts.

The High Court's appellate jurisdiction is as follows. An appeal lies from a judgment of a Justice exercising original jurisdiction (Constitution, section 73(i); *Judiciary Act* 1903 (Cth), section 34). An appeal may be brought from a Supreme Court but only with the special **leave** of the High Court (Judiciary Act, section 35(2)). In the case of a decision by a single judge, leave will be granted only in exceptional circumstances. An appeal to the Full Supreme Court from a single judge may be removed to the High Court. **Removal** may be ordered at the request of a party or an **Attorney-General**. Removal is discretionary, save that any Attorney-General (Commonwealth or state) has a right to have a constitutional matter removed (Judiciary Act, section 40).

With the special leave of the High Court, an appeal lies from any decision of a Court exercising federal jurisdiction (Judiciary Act, section 39(2)(c)), or from a decision of the Full **Federal Court** (*Federal Court of Australia Act* 1976 (Cth), section 33(2)). An appeal lies from a decree of the Family Court by special leave of the High Court, or if the Full Court of the Family Court certifies that an important question of law or of public interest is involved (*Family Law Act* 1975 (Cth), section 95; see *DJL v Central Authority* (2000)).

The Full Federal Court has appellate jurisdiction in relation to the decisions of single judges of that Court, decisions of the **territory** Supreme Courts (except the Northern Territory), decisions of the federal magistracy, and certain decisions of state courts exercising federal jurisdiction (Federal Court of Australia Act, section 24). An appeal to the Full Family Court lies from decrees of a single judge of that Court, from a state Family Court exercising federal jurisdiction, and from decisions of the federal magistracy (Family Law Act, section 94).

Several eminent jurists have argued that a dual system of courts, federal and state, is not an essential ingredient of **federalism**, and that the constitutional provisions in Chapter III providing for that division were misconceived; that is, there is a single Australian legal system even though the rules and principles of law may vary in different states. In his evidence before a Royal Commission on the Constitution in 1927, **Dixon** mentioned the possibility of a national judicial system, saying 'it would appear natural to endeavour to establish the Courts of justice as independent organs which were neither Commonwealth nor State'.

The possibility of a national judicial system was considered, but rejected, by the Constitutional Commission in 1988, notwithstanding the difficulties that arise from jurisdictional conflicts. At that time, legislation for the **cross-vesting** of jurisdiction had only recently been introduced. The Commission said:

> It is clear to us, as it was to all members of the Advisory Committee, that ... the conflict of jurisdiction difficulties that can still arise do not in themselves warrant such a great change to our system that would result from the establishment of an integrated national court structure. Certainly one should first wait to examine the effectiveness of the legislation relating to the cross-vesting of jurisdiction.

That legislation did, in fact, operate effectively for 12 years, but was held to be beyond power in June 1999 (*Re Wakim* (1999)). The temptation to take a jurisdictional point for its own sake, in order to avoid an adjudication on the merits, will undermine a legal system if it becomes common practice. There are disturbing indications that this is happening. Yet the idea of a single system of law is central to this nation's sense of itself. It is time to revisit Dixon's proposal.

BRYAN BEAUMONT

Further Reading
James Crawford, *Australian Courts of Law* (3rd edn 1993)

Higgins, Henry Bournes (*b* 30 June 1851; *d* 13 January 1929; Justice 1906–1929) was one of two Justices of the Court born in Ireland (the other being his close friend, **Gavan Duffy**). He was one of those Justices whose greatest mark on Australian life was made not through their work on the High Court Bench, but through ancillary work—in Higgins' case, through his presidency of the Commonwealth Court of Conciliation and Arbitration.

Higgins was born in midsummer 1851, in Newtownards, County Down. He was educated at a boarding school in Dublin, but as a consequence of a serious chest infection, he left school at the age of 14. Following a lengthy convalescence, Higgins was sent to work in a draper's warehouse—an experience he did not enjoy. In 1869, the Higgins family migrated from Ireland to Australia, arriving in Melbourne in early 1870. Higgins' illness led him to develop a life-long love of strenuous exercise.

Higgins enrolled in the University of Melbourne, where he was a student of the extraordinary polymath Professor WE Hearn, to whom AV Dicey was to offer credit for the original encapsulation of the essence of English constitutionalism as the **rule of law**. Higgins' time at university was one of great personal growth for him, but he was plagued throughout by self-doubt, associated in part with a rejection of some of his inherited religious beliefs, engendered by Hearn's lectures on comparative religion. Higgins' contemporaries at university included Alfred **Deakin**.

In 1875, Higgins unsuccessfully applied for a Chair in **history** at the university. He was called to the Victorian Bar in 1876, and began to develop a practice in **equity**. Initially, Higgins' fortunes did not seem any greater at the Bar than in the academy. In his first year of practice, he earned only 24

Henry Higgins, Justice 1906–29

guineas; in his second year, his income dropped to just 13 guineas. It was not until the 1880s, when a number of the leading equity **counsel** were appointed to the Bench, that Higgins' practice began to flourish. With the upturn in his professional fortunes came a return of sorts to the university, for in 1887, Higgins was elected to the Council—a position he was to occupy for 36 years. Higgins took silk in 1903, after an earlier refusal in protest against the appointment as QC of Crown Law officers who had not practised at the Bar.

Possibly because of the rigorous self-examination to which his views had been subjected at university, Higgins was a man of independent spirit and intellectual courage. As **Isaacs** was to say of him after his death, his 'was a thoroughly independent mind. He sought his own solution of every problem that was brought before him and, having reached his conclusion and considered it right, it mattered not to him whether it found favour or failed to find favour in the eyes of others'. Like most of his generation, Higgins was a supporter of White Australia, but he also urged legal protection for **Aboriginal** interests. Controversially for a Protestant, Higgins was a firm supporter of Home Rule for Ireland (see *Irish Envoys Case* (1923)). He also opposed the Boer War—a stance that was largely responsible for his defeat in the election for the Victorian Parliament in 1900. On the question of Empire relations generally, Higgins was an early advocate of the sort of informal partnership that eventually came to be enshrined in the Balfour Declaration of 1926. It was in recognition of this freedom of spirit that Higgins' biographer, John Rickard, subtitled his book *The Rebel as Judge*.

Most interestingly of all, perhaps, Higgins opposed the form of the Constitution that came to be adopted by the

Australian federation. He was a keen proponent of the union of the Australian colonies, and served as one of the Victorian delegates to the 1897–98 Federal Convention, but he disagreed both with the principle of equal representation in the Senate and with the notion of constitutional entrenchment. Constitutional entrenchment, he thought, would lead to an ossified constitutional system. In this regard, Higgins viewed the US Constitution in a negative light, unlike many others. And he considered equal representation in the Senate to be a sop to colonial parochialism that would effectively preclude any move towards a unitary form of government. In Higgins' view, the constitutional structure of the new entity should have been, in his words, 'susceptible to growth'. On the question of the division of legislative power in the proposed Constitution, Higgins' contributions to the **Convention Debates** generally leaned towards the federal government. One particular legacy of his, which emerged from the Melbourne session of the Convention, and would later provide a basis for his own career in arbitration, was the inclusion of the **conciliation and arbitration** power, which came to be enshrined in section 51(xxxv) of the Constitution.

Despite his position on the Constitution, Higgins was elected to represent the seat of North Melbourne in the new Commonwealth Parliament. Though he was not a member of the Labor Party, he served as **Attorney-General** in the first, short-lived Labor administration of John Watson. Higgins' sympathies with labour were deep, and in the Victorian Parliament and elsewhere, he had argued for improved wages and conditions of employment for the working classes. When he was a member of parliament, Higgins had introduced a private member's Bill to call upon the states to hand over industrial relations jurisdiction to the Commonwealth.

In 1906, at the time of its expansion from three Justices to five, Higgins was offered a seat on the High Court by his old university contemporary, Deakin. Higgins and Isaacs took their seats on the Bench at the same time—hence their occasional description as 'the judicial twins' (though Isaacs' **appointment** was dated a day before Higgins', giving Isaacs **seniority**). Higgins was asked by Deakin to take over the presidency of the Court of Conciliation and Arbitration from **O'Connor**, but because of his political links to labour, Higgins asked if his appointment could be delayed for a year. Higgins served as President of the Arbitration Court for 14 years, from 1907 to 1921. He remained a champion of the system of industrial arbitration at a very turbulent time, and in the face of hostility from various **Prime Ministers**, especially WM Hughes. In the post-war period, Hughes increasingly sought means of bypassing the Arbitration Court through the use of special tribunals, and in protest against the government's policy, Higgins resigned.

Quite apart from anything else, Higgins' lasting impact on Australian law was confirmed in his judgment in the famous *Harvester* case of 1907, where he defined the expression 'fair and reasonable wage' appearing in the *Excise Tariff Act* 1906 (Cth). Higgins formally protested against what he described as Parliament's 'shunting of responsibility' in leaving the question of definition to the Arbitration Court. In his view, this placed the Court 'within the range of political fire'. Yet it is clear from reading his judgment that Higgins took to the task with relish.

Higgins engaged in what today would seem like a crude method of calculation, but he attempted to define a fair and reasonable wage by reference to the actual cost of living, 'in frugal comfort', of a working-class family of five. This required, in Higgins' judgment, 7s per day or £2.2s per week. The idea underlying this calculation—the sense that in a civilised society wages ought to be related to need rather than simply to relative bargaining power—served as the principle that guided the fixing of wages in Australia for most of the twentieth century. Higgins' judgment represented a genuine defining moment in Australian **social justice**, and his approach was for a long time thought by Australians to render their system of wage settlements superior to others.

As a High Court Justice, Higgins was something of a loner in methodological terms. He consistently wrote his own judgments, even when he concurred with his brethren in the result. It is partly as a consequence of his insistent individualism that his impact as an appellate judge is not as frequently remarked upon as that of some of his contemporaries. Yet it should not be thought that he was isolated or removed in an intellectual sense from the judicial temperament of his times. Probably most significantly of all, he was consistently allied with Isaacs in the fundamental shift in approach to **constitutional interpretation** finally consummated by the *Engineers Case* (1920)—which, as President of the Arbitration Court, he had referred to the High Court. His willingness to embrace progressivism in interpretation (which, notwithstanding the disclaimers in Isaacs' judgment, lay at the heart of the *Engineers Case*) was also made plain by his approach in *Gillen v Laffer* (1925), an early post-**World War I** case on the doctrine of **natural justice**. Applying nineteenth-century case law, the majority of the Court (**Knox** and **Rich**) held that natural justice should apply as a matter of course to any statute that purported to divest someone of an interest in **property**. In contrast, Higgins—with whom the **Privy Council** ultimately agreed (*Laffer v Gillen* (1927))—held that with modern legislation, one had to engage in a more textured approach to interpretation in order to ascertain the real intention of the legislature. His judgment in this case is sadly not well known today, but it presaged the drift of **administrative law** in Australia and the Empire for the next 40 years.

Despite his progressive values, Higgins' **judicial style** was often surprisingly legalistic and technical, although he did have a flair for curious **metaphors**. In *Clyde Engineering v Cowburn* (1926), for example, he offered the following approach to the test for **inconsistency** under section 109 of the Constitution, in opposition to Isaacs' more enduring 'covering the field' metaphor: 'The State law is like the Nile river, which covers the whole area with its flood, except that part of the area which is appropriated to the villages. The State law fills, as it were, all the sponge except the fibre.'

Higgins died at his home, Heronswood, which had formerly been the home of his revered teacher, Hearn, in the evening of Sunday 10 January 1929. Fittingly, he had spent his last day with his two passions: a walk, followed by an afternoon spent reading.

IAN HOLLOWAY

Further Reading
John Rickard, *HB Higgins: The Rebel as Judge* (1984)

High Court of Australia Act 1979 (Cth). The High Court of Australia Act—enacted contemporaneously with the Court's move to **Canberra**—had been drafted in the Attorney-General's Department in preparation for the move. To cooperate with the plans of the Court and the government, Parliament gave the legislation a bipartisan and timely passage.

Although the Court had been established by the Constitution (see **Constitutional basis of Court**), it required the *Judiciary Act* 1903 (Cth) and the *High Court Procedure Act* 1903 (Cth) to enable it to operate. Alfred **Deakin** was the driving force behind this legislation, and he ensured that the Court would have an appropriate federal structure: it would have both a Principal Registry and District Registries, and would sit at all of these. This created the highly successful **circuit system** which, in a modified form, is still a feature of the Court: although section 15 of the High Court of Australia Act provides that the **seat** of the Court is to be in the ACT, it allows the Court to sit at other places within Australia. The Court determines these matters itself, although both the government and the Parliament, which determine the Court's **budget,** can and do express their views from time to time.

The centrepiece of the Act was a new form of **administration** of the Court. Section 17 gives the Court responsibility for its own administration and provides it with associated powers. It reads like the creation of a statutory authority except that any property held by the Court is deemed to belong to the Commonwealth. Section 46 makes it clear that it is 'the Justices or a majority of them' that exercise these powers. The new system strengthened the administrative **independence** of the Court and was the most cherished reform in **Barwick's** long list of proposals (see **Whitlam era**), although he was thwarted in his desire to have the power of administration vested in the **Chief Justice.**

Section 47 provides, among other things, that the Court must present an **Annual Report** relating to 'the administration of the affairs of the Court'. This provision was the subject of contention in the mid-1980s, when the Clerk of the Court refused to deal in its Annual Report with questions of cost and delay, arguing that such matters were outside the ambit of administration. More fundamentally, the Court saw the requirement of reporting on such matters as posing a threat to its independence.

There is one other major **reform** in the Act. Section 6 states: 'Where there is a vacancy in an office of Justice, the **Attorney-General** shall, before an **appointment** is made to the vacant office, consult with the Attorneys-General of the States in relation to the appointment'. This requirement arose from a commitment to follow such a procedure made by the Attorney-General at the Constitutional Convention in 1978.

There had been long-standing complaints by the states about High Court appointments, which the Constitution assigns to the federal government. The state governments pointed out that they, too, had a major interest in the Court's decisions. There had similarly been complaints from many quarters about political appointments. These were greatly activated by the appointment of **Murphy** in 1975. The long tradition of appointing politicians or former politicians had by then become unfashionable, despite the quality of many such appointments.

Wilson's appointment in May 1979 provided the first opportunity to test how such consultation might work on an informal basis. It proved to be a success and it was decided to give it statutory effect. By and large, it has worked well although there have been some criticisms from the states about the extent of the federal Attorney-General's cooperation, and, more fundamentally, about the inherent weakness of the right to be consulted as compared with a more determinative role.

Peter Durack

High Court Rules. In the High Court's embryonic period from 1901 to 1903, the effect of state rivalries extended, perhaps inevitably, even to opinions about what form the new national Court's practice and **procedure** should take. **Griffith's** powerful and dominant personality ensured that the Court's first Rules of 1903 were modelled largely on those of the Supreme Court of Queensland, revised in light of English experience. It was said of Griffith that as a young barrister starting a practice in Brisbane, he had learned the Rules of the Queensland Supreme Court by heart.

Adoption of the Queensland model in 1903 led to initial outbursts of protest by lawyers in the other states, particularly those of the oldest and most populous colony, NSW. However, there was a certain federal balance in the joint authorship of the first textbook dealing with the High Court Rules, *The Judicial Power of the Commonwealth* (1903) by John Quick, a Victorian barrister, and Littleton Groom (later Commonwealth **Attorney-General**) of the Queensland Bar.

Despite the state rivalries, as JM Bennett has noted, when the High Court Rules were laid before the federal Parliament in Melbourne, they attracted little interest—at least once it became clear that the Justices would have the power to alter or make such new Rules for the conduct of the Court's functions as they might from time to time see fit (always subject, of course, to due parliamentary scrutiny).

One remnant of the original Rules is the demurrer procedure. The High Court, even today, retains this procedure, traditionally used in England for the taking of objections in point of law—though the state and territory jurisdictions have modified forms of procedure for that purpose. Demurrers have been found useful for taking constitutional points (see **Kirby** in *Levy v Victoria* (1997)).

The current law and practice relating to the making and alteration of the Court's Rules are governed by the *Judiciary Act* 1903 (Cth). The Act provides that the Justices, or a majority of them, 'may make Rules of Court necessary or convenient to be made for carrying into effect' the provisions of the Judiciary Act *and* of any other Act conferring **jurisdiction** on the High Court or relating to its practice or procedure.

Proposed Rules of Court are drafted and reviewed by a Rules Committee of three Justices, after which they are presented to the entire Court for consideration. Proposed amendments to the Rules are distributed for comment to members of the **legal profession** through the Australian Bar Association and the Law Council of Australia.

Once approved by the Justices, Rules of Court are forwarded to the Office of Legislative Drafting in the Attorney-General's Department for printing. After printing, the signatures of the Justices are endorsed, along with that of the

Chief Executive and Principal Registrar, and the signed Rule of Court is impressed with the **seal** of the Court. A copy of the Rule of Court is then returned to the Office of Legislative Drafting for notification and tabling in accordance with the provisions of Part XII of the *Acts Interpretation Act* 1901 (Cth). Rules of Court made by the Justices are subject to all the requirements of Part XII, including the requirement that they be laid before each House of the Parliament within 15 sitting days of that House after the making of the Rule of Court, and be subject to resolutions by either House of the Parliament disallowing the Rule.

Section 86 of the Judiciary Act identifies a number of matters that may be the subject of Rules of Court. These include appointing and regulating the **sittings** of the Court. The sittings of the Court, including **Full Court** sittings in **Canberra** and on **circuit,** and motion days to hear applications for **leave** or special leave, are prescribed by a Rule of Court issued by the Justices for each calendar year.

The High Court Rules in force in 2000 were introduced in 1952 as a result of a project initiated by **Latham.** The 1952 Rules were largely due to the work of **Dixon** and RL Gilbert of the Victorian Bar. They superseded the older Rules, which had relied heavily on English precedents, and sought to adapt them to the typical arrangement and presentation of Rules of **state Supreme Courts,** then universally familiar throughout Australia, while replacing antiquated drafting expressions with a style considered to be more modern. As to appeals, the object of the 1952 **reform** was to establish a uniform procedure regardless of the source from which an appeal originated. As the High Court Rules now stand, Orders 1 to 73 regulate practice and procedure in civil and criminal matters coming before the High Court in its original and appellate jurisdiction.

The next detailed review of the Rules was initiated by **Barwick** in 1978. Barwick seconded District Registrar Frank Jones to prepare a draft of new trial and appellate Rules that would be in place by the time the Court moved to Canberra. Jones worked closely with Barwick over 15 months to prepare a draft of the proposed Rules. The draft was formally settled by Parliamentary Counsel Bronte Quayle. During the period, Barwick engaged in discussions with Nigel Bowen, Chief Justice of the **Federal Court,** with a view to the Federal Court adopting the proposed High Court Rules in order to have a unified set of federal Rules. Nothing came of this proposal, as Bowen favoured Rules based on the Rules of the Supreme Court of NSW. Barwick then attempted to have the Justices adopt the proposed new Rules, but they opposed the adoption because the Rules were based on the Court sitting only in Canberra. Jones subsequently prepared a set of appellate Rules at the direction of **Gibbs.** These Rules were considered and reviewed by a Rules Committee comprising **Wilson** and **Dawson,** and were ultimately adopted by the Court. Notable changes to the Rules in the latter decades of the Court's first century included limitations upon time for oral **argument** and Rules relating to applications for special leave to appeal. In 1999–2000, the Rules were rewritten by **Toohey,** in consultation with the Chief Executive and Principal Registrar and the Senior Registrar, for adoption after comment by the legal profession.

Although the making of the Rules by the Court is a quasi-legislative function, this has never been seen as an issue for the constitutional **separation of powers** between the legislature, the executive, and the judiciary.

DOUGLAS HASSALL
CAROLYN ROGERS

Further Reading
FJ Bethune and SA Thompson, 'High Court Rules' (1903) 1 *Commonwealth LR* 208

Hindmarsh Island Bridge Case (1998). Hindmarsh Island (Kumarangk) is in the Murray River delta in SA. During the 1980s, there was commercial development on the island, and in 1989, construction of a bridge from the island to the mainland was proposed as a condition of planning approval for a marina.

This proposal met strong opposition on Aboriginal heritage grounds, since the island and the Goolwa Channel area in which it was located were part of the traditional home of the Ngarrindjeri people. The Minister for Aboriginal and Torres Strait Islander Affairs was urged to exercise his powers under the *Aboriginal and Torres Strait Islander Heritage Protection Act* 1984 (Cth) for the protection and preservation of the area. Ngarrindjeri women claimed to be the custodians of secret women's business for which the island had traditionally been used, and which could not be disclosed to Ngarrindjeri men, nor to other men.

In 1994 and 1996, the claim was the subject of two reports to the Minister, one by Professor Cheryl Saunders and one by Justice Jane Mathews. Each report ended in a controversy that failed to resolve the underlying issue—the latter because of the High Court decision in *Wilson v Minister for Aboriginal and Torres Strait Islander Affairs* (1996) that, for reasons of **separation of powers,** the statute did not permit the report to be obtained from a judge. The *Hindmarsh Island Bridge Act* 1997 (Cth) was then enacted by the newly elected Howard government to preclude any further possibility of a protection order under the 1984 Act. The Hindmarsh Island Bridge Act amended the 1984 Act so that it no longer applied to 'the Hindmarsh Island bridge area' and thus prevented any further possible claim that the area had secret or sacred significance for Ngarrindjeri women.

The Ngarrindjeri women responded by bringing an action in the High Court challenging the validity of the Hindmarsh Island Bridge Act. They argued that the Act could not be passed under the races power (section 51(xxvi) of the Constitution) because that power extended only to laws for the benefit of a particular **race,** and could not be used to impose a detriment on the people of a race. That argument was of momentous political significance because, if accepted, it might have provided a legal platform from which to challenge the Howard government's 'ten point plan' for **native title** (as enacted in the *Native Title Amendment Act* 1998 (Cth) in response to the High Court decision in *Wik* (1996)).

In the High Court, the Commonwealth argued that there were no limits to the races power: so long as the law affixed a consequence based upon race, it was not for the High Court to examine the positive or negative impact of the law. On the afternoon of the first day of the hearing, the Commonwealth **Solicitor-General,** Gavan Griffith, suggested that the races power was 'infused with a power of adverse operation'. He acknowledged 'the direct racist content of this provision' in the sense of 'a capacity for adverse operation'. The following exchange then occurred:

Kirby J: Can I just get clear in my mind, is the Commonwealth's submission that it is entirely and exclusively for the Parliament to determine the matter upon which special laws are deemed necessary ... or is there a point at which there is a **justiciable** question for the Court? I mean, it seems unthinkable that a law such as the Nazi race laws could be enacted under the race power and that this Court could do nothing about it.

Griffith QC: Your Honour, if there was a reason why the Court could do something about it, a Nazi law, it would, in our submission, be for a reason external to the races power. It would be for some wider over-arching reason.

The case was decided by only six Justices because **Callinan**, after some initial reluctance, had **disqualified** himself from deciding the matter, since he had previously advised the Commonwealth that the Act was constitutionally valid. The challenge failed by 5:1, with **Kirby** dissenting, because, in the words of **Brennan** and **McHugh**: 'Once the true scope of the legislative powers conferred by s51 [is] perceived, it is clear that the power which supports a valid Act supports an Act repealing it.' It was common ground that the 1984 Act was valid. Hence, it necessarily followed that a later modification of its operation must also be valid. This conclusion meant that Brennan and McHugh did not need to address the scope of the races power.

The other four Justices did address that issue. **Gummow** and **Hayne** held that the power could be used, as in this case, to withdraw a benefit previously granted to **Aboriginal people** (and thus to impose a disadvantage). More generally, they pointed out that the use of 'race' as a criterion—which section 51(xxvi) not only permits but requires—is inherently discriminatory, and that any discriminatory measure that benefits some may disadvantage others. They did, however, leave open the suggestion, made earlier in the *Native Title Act Case* (1995), that the Court might retain 'some supervisory jurisdiction to examine ... the possibility of a manifest abuse of the races power'. Moreover, they hinted at the possible relevance in such a case of the ultimate power of **judicial review** under *Marbury v Madison* (1803), and of Dixon's suggestion in the *Communist Party Case* (1951) that in the Australian Constitution 'the **rule of law** forms an assumption'.

Kirby's **dissenting judgment** held flatly that the power 'does not extend to the enactment of laws detrimental to, or discriminatory against, the people of any race (including the Aboriginal race)'. He argued that the 1967 constitutional **amendment** 'did not simply lump the Aboriginal people of Australia in with other races as potential targets for detrimental or adversely discriminatory laws', but reflected the Parliament's 'clear and unanimous object', with 'unprecedented support' from the people, that the operation of section 51(xxvi) 'should be significantly altered' so as to permit only positive or benign **discrimination**.

Gaudron, who had previously suggested that a limitation of the power to beneficial purposes might have 'much to commend it' (*Chu Kheng Lim v Minister for Immigration* (1992)), concluded that on closer examination such a limita-

tion could not be sustained—in part because the suggestion that the original effect of the power had been changed by the 1967 amendment was too weighty a consequence to ascribe to a 'minimalist amendment'. (The deletion of eight words could not change the meaning of the words that remained.) She went on, however, to examine more closely the requirement in section 51(xxvi) that the Parliament must deem it 'necessary' to make special laws for the people of a race. Applying the analysis of discrimination that she had developed in other contexts, she argued that any such judgment of the 'necessity' for a law must be based on some 'relevant difference between the people of the race to whom the law is directed and the people of other races'; and hence that the resulting legislation 'must be reasonably capable of being viewed as appropriate and adapted to the difference asserted'. These tests, she suggested, might give operable meaning to the concept of 'manifest abuse'. Further, she found it 'difficult to conceive' that any adverse discrimination by reference to racial criteria might nowadays satisfy these tests—and 'even more difficult' in the case of a law relating to Aboriginal Australians, since any obvious 'relevant difference' in their situation is one of 'serious disadvantage', including 'their material circumstances and the vulnerability of their culture'. On the face of it, therefore, 'only laws directed to remedying their disadvantage could reasonably be viewed as appropriate and adapted to their different circumstances'.

Although this analysis differed from an assertion that section 51(xxvi) is confined to beneficial uses, in any practical context it might well yield the same result. The overall effect of the judgments was therefore inconclusive. Gaudron's approach specifically excluded Kirby's approach; but that of Gummow and Hayne does not necessarily exclude Gaudron's approach. Brennan and McHugh were silent on the issue.

This left open the question of whether the Commonwealth has power under the Constitution to enact racially discriminatory laws. The possibility has reinforced calls for an Australian **Bill of Rights**.

GEORGE WILLIAMS

History, Court's use of. The use of history as an aid to interpretation has, until recently, been largely eschewed by the High Court. The reluctance of the Justices to draw upon historical documentation has its origins in the prevailing belief that, as judges, they were not well placed to make judgments on the veracity or otherwise of historical evidence brought before them. The predominant view, at least until the 1980s, was that **extrinsic material** had little or no role to play in the determination of questions brought before the Court. Such questions were to be resolved by **precedent** and by a general policy of **literalism** in **statutory interpretation**. In the words of **Dixon's** famous pronouncement in 1952, 'there is no other safe guide to judicial decisions in great conflicts than a strict and complete **legalism**'.

Despite repeated statements by members of the Court, during the long period from its **establishment** to the **appointment** of Murphy in 1975, that extrinsic material had no role to play in **decision making**, historical material was in fact, on occasion, relied upon by individual Justices. This was particularly so in **constitutional law**. However, because such reliance upon historical materials was unsystematic, it did not lead to the establishment of a historiographical tradition.

Also, those Justices who chose to use historical materials generally did so within a narrow historiographical framework. In Bain Attwood's words in 1996, Justices assumed 'that the past belongs to another realm of time which is separate from the present, and that consequently … it is possible for the historian … to show the past as it really was and to understand it on its own terms'. 'History' was considered by those Justices who relied upon it to support their judgments as a tool by which 'truth' could be better ascertained. Most Justices who used historical evidence did so both selectively and uncritically. History itself was not generally conceived of as a discipline that creates its own ambiguities.

The Justices, when they have chosen to rely upon historical evidence, have generally demonstrated their limited appreciation of historical method. For instance, in **constitutional interpretation** Justices have often been prepared to rely solely upon a limited array of historical evidence such as the annotations to the Constitution by **Quick and Garran**. However, such a selective reliance upon a solitary account of historical events defies all historiographical logic. Historians tend to piece together accounts of historical events from a diverse range of sources. Also, historians generally qualify their accounts, considering them subject to revision in the light of further evidence. But the courts have revealed a particular attitude to the use of history: they have tended to take notice of historical events as if they were incontestable truths.

For example, in the *Communist Party Case* (1951), Dixon said that courts may, in certain circumstances, 'use the general facts of history as ascertained … from the accepted writings of serious historians' to inform themselves of certain matters, such as the specific beliefs and general doctrines of communism. However, there is an assumption in Dixon's statement that a historical study can be sufficiently 'serious' and 'accepted' to avoid polemics—and therefore to offer 'objective' information, in contrast to other accounts that are simply 'ideological' in nature. He also assumes that a judge is in a good position to distinguish the 'serious' from the fanciful.

Courts are ill-prepared to make judgments on the 'seriousness' or otherwise of particular historical accounts. Any choice between particular historical accounts is ideological in nature, and should be identified as such. Murphy's contribution to the use of history by the Court was not so much in his technical adroitness in handling historical evidence, but rather in his identification of history as **ideology**. This is particularly apparent in cases such as *Bistricic v Rokov* (1976) and *China Ocean Shipping v SA* (1979). In the latter case, Murphy's insistence that Imperial laws ceased to apply in Australia at the very moment of federation is a very different version of history from that advanced by **Stephen** in the same case, which considers the *Statute of Westminster* 1931 (Imp) and the *Statute of Westminster Adoption Act* 1942 (Cth) as the defining events in Australia's **nationhood**. Which version is correct is beside the point. The difference between them illustrates that the choice between historical narratives is inevitably ideological in nature.

A number of legislative developments and the changing climate of constitutional jurisprudence have made reference to history more compelling for the Justices in recent years.

The enactment in 1984 of section 15AB of the *Acts Interpretation Act* 1901 (Cth), which authorised reference to extrinsic materials, such as historical documentation, in interpreting statutory provisions, was one important turning point. Another was the decision in *Cole v Whitfield* (1988), which legitimised the use of historical documents and other extrinsic materials in constitutional jurisprudence. This case also sparked a continuing debate about the respective merits of **originalism** and progressivism as interpretive approaches in ascertaining the intention and meaning of particular constitutional provisions. Recent cases in which these issues are discussed are *Grain Pool of WA v Commonwealth* (2000) and *Eastman v The Queen* (2000). **Kirby** provides a particularly eloquent exposition of the progressivist approach in his judgment in the *Grain Pool* case.

The originalist approach was the subject of scrutiny by **Gummow** in his 1999 Clarendon lectures. Gummow drew upon a number of recent critiques of originalism in the USA to suggest that in such accounts, past reality is frequently rendered in a form in which it becomes nothing more than a rhetorical device to support the resolution of a present dispute. He suggests that the use of history in judicial proceedings should be seen for what it is—a pragmatic device used to support a particular line of argument before the court. However, he also notes that when a court employs history in its reasoning, it attaches the force of legal precedent to that particular version of history, which is then transmitted throughout the body politic as constitutional doctrine. Such historical renderings are fraught with danger: they may bring both history and law into contention, and possible disrepute. But they may also contribute to a more adventurous jurisprudence.

Perhaps the single greatest challenge to the Court in relation to its use of historical documentation as evidence has been presented by the burgeoning litigation of issues concerning **Aboriginal peoples**, such as the claims for compensation by the 'stolen generation' in *Kruger v Commonwealth* (1997) and **native title** claims (as in *Mabo* (1992) and *Wik* (1996)). These cases have demanded that serious attention be paid to the ways in which historical narratives might be used as evidence. They have also highlighted dangers associated with a court engaging in 'history' and then reaching a 'legal' conclusion on the basis of their 'historical' understanding of the particular issue in question.

The pressure on the High Court to make more and more use of historical material is occurring against a backdrop in which historians themselves are less prepared to consider the product of their researches as leading to some version of the 'truth'. Historians are less prepared than ever to present the fruits of their labour as the unqualified 'truth'. Historical accounts are increasingly seen as provisional and, at least to some degree, fictitious. Nevertheless, while there is a growing realisation, among both historians and lawyers, that historical truth is hardly ever more than a descriptive hypothesis, it is also recognised that once a particular version of history is given the imprimatur of 'authenticity' by a **superior court** it becomes *the* definitive account of the particular event. Once a particular version of history is enshrined in precedent it becomes legal truth, which has a performative nature.

The Justices continue to be divided about the Court's use of history. However, as pressure continues to grow for the

Court to accept historical material in a wide variety of areas—ranging from 'ownership' issues in native title to the determination of what division of responsibilities the **framers of the Constitution** intended in relation to **corporations law,** as evidenced in the *Incorporation Case* (1990) and the scrutiny of the **cross-vesting** scheme in *Re Wakim* (1999)—pressure also grows for the Court to develop a coherent approach to the use of history in court proceedings. There is a certain urgency to this need for coherence: the litigation of matters relating to reconciliation continues apace, and important issues of constitutional identity and nationhood continue to be raised by cases brought before the Court.

ROB McQUEEN

Further Reading

Enid Campbell, 'Lawyers' Uses of History' (1968) 6 *UQLJ* 1

Michael Coper, 'The Place of History in Constitutional Interpretation' in Gregory Craven (ed), *The Convention Debates 1891–1898: Commentaries, Indices and Guide* (1986) 5

Jonathan Fulcher, 'Sui Generis History? The Use of History in *Wik*' in Graham Hiley (ed), *The Wik Case: Issues and Implications* (1997) 51

WMC Gummow, *Change and Continuity: Statute, Equity and Federalism* (1999)

Rowan McMonnies, '*Ngo Ngo Ha* and the High Court v New South Wales: Historical Purpose in History and Law' (1999) 27 *FL Rev* 471

Rob McQueen, 'Why High Court Judges Make Poor Historians' (1990) 19 *FL Rev* 245

Alexander Reilly, 'The Ghost of Truganini: Use of Historical Evidence as Proof of Native Title' (2000) 28 *FL Rev* 453

House of Lords. The House of Lords is both the upper house of the British Parliament and the highest court of appeal in the UK. Further putting the lie to Montesquieu's description of the **separation of powers** in the British Constitution, the presiding officer in the House of Lords is the Lord Chancellor, who is not only also the senior judge in the kingdom, but a member of Cabinet as well.

While the judicial practice of the Lords is of recent development, the judicial authority of the House is shrouded in the mists of history. There are records of Parliament exercising an original civil jurisdiction in the thirteenth century, and as early as the mid-fourteenth century, there are references to the jurisdiction of the Lords to amend errors by the **common law** courts. The present-day judicial authority of the Lords, however, is based in the alliance between Parliament and the common law against the rival jurisdiction of the specialised courts created by the Tudor and Stuart monarchs. For reasons not altogether certain, the adjudicative power of Parliament came to be seen as exercisable by the Lords. By the seventeenth century, the Lords' jurisdiction came to be accepted as a feature of the Constitution—though in fact jurisdiction remains vested formally in the Crown in Parliament. It is for that reason that an appeal to the Lords is formally styled as being to 'Her Majesty the Queen in her High Court of Parliament'.

The current appellate jurisdiction of the Lords is founded in the *Appellate Jurisdiction Act* 1876 (UK). The intention of the original *Judicature Act* of 1873 (UK) was to vest exclusive jurisdiction to hear appeals in the new Court of Appeal (section 20). This had the support of both Liberals and Conservatives, but entrenched interests forced both parties to abandon the attempt to wrest judicial authority from the Lords. Interestingly from an Australian perspective, section 21 of the 1873 Act provided for the jurisdiction of the Judicial Committee of the **Privy Council** to be transferred to the Court of Appeal as well.

Formerly, the judicial business of the Lords was conducted in the main by those hereditary peers who had held high judicial office. In 1856, to assist with the burdens of judicial work, an attempt was made to create the first life peer—Baron Parke—but in the *Wensleydale Peerage Case* (1856), life peerages were held to be unconstitutional. Parke was accordingly given a regular peerage, but life peers were provided for in the Appellate Jurisdiction Act. These judicial life peers are known colloquially as 'Law Lords'.

Under the 1876 arrangements, the House of Lords has jurisdiction to hear both civil and criminal appeals. By custom, membership of the Lords includes two Law Lords from Scotland, and appointments have occasionally been made from Ireland. A quorum of the House for judicial business is three. Counsel are wigged and robed (see **Court attire**), but the Lords hear appeals in mufti. Likewise, since **World War II**, appeals have no longer been heard in the Lords' chamber, but in a committee room upstairs. Judgments are delivered in the chamber, however—for which reason they are properly known as 'speeches'. Following delivery of the speeches (often in an abridged form), a vote is taken on the motion that the appeal be allowed. It was only in 1844, in *O'Connell v The Queen*, that it was held inappropriate for lay Lords to vote in judicial matters—though it is thought that a lay peer may have made up the quorum with Lords Cairns and Cranworth in *Rylands v Fletcher* (1868). A lay peer attempted to vote in *Bradlaugh v Clarke* (1883), but he was ignored by the Lord Chancellor.

Custom allows the Lords to summon judges of the (English) High Court to provide them with advice, but this has not happened since *Allen v Flood* (1897).

The Lords' attitude towards the doctrine of *stare decisis* has altered over the years. Up to the latter part of the nineteenth century, **precedent** was conceived of as a guide rather than a source of binding authority. But in *London Tramways v London County Council* (1898), the House held that it was absolutely bound by its own decisions—although the only authority for this was *London Tramways* itself. That was the rule until 1966, when the House issued a Practice Statement in which it asserted the authority to 'depart from' its own previous decisions in exceptional circumstances.

The relationship between the House of Lords and Australian law has been curious, given that the House of Lords has never formed part of the Australian judicial **hierarchy**. It was not until *Parker v The Queen* (1963) that the High Court held that it would follow one of its own decisions in preference to a conflicting decision of the Lords (see also *Skelton v Collins* (1966)). The earlier view, stated by **Latham** in *Piro v Foster* (1943), was that in cases of conflict between the High Court and the Lords on questions of legal principle, the High Court should defer to the Lords. One reason sometimes given for this was that, because of the overlap in membership between the House of Lords and the Privy Council, the views expressed by the Lords were likely to be echoed in the Privy Council, by whose decisions the High Court was, at that time, bound. Some Australian state courts continued as recently as the 1980s to consider themselves bound to follow judgments of the House of Lords in cases where there were no conflicting decisions of the High Court or Privy Council (see, for example, *R v Darrington and McGauley* (1979); *Life Savers (Australasia) v Frigmobile* (1983); *Horne v Chester and Fein Property Developments* (1986)—though compare the comments of **Kirby** to the contrary in *X v Amalgamated Television Services (No 2)* (1987)).

On the other hand, there have been a number of instances where the High Court did not consider recent decisions of the House of Lords, even in important cases. One of the most notable is the Court's judgment in *Testro Bros v Tait* (1963), in which it failed to refer, except in passing, to *Ridge v Baldwin* (1963).

Australia had a significant connection with the House of Lords through Lord Atkin, who was born in Brisbane, and who was the Australian nominee to the War Crimes Commission until his death in 1944.

IAN HOLLOWAY

Further Reading

Louis Blom-Cooper and Gavin Drewry, *Final Appeal: A Study of the House of Lords in its Judicial Capacity* (1972)
Alan Paterson, *The Law Lords* (1982)
Robert Stevens, *Law and Politics: The House of Lords as a Judicial Body, 1800–1976* (1979)

Humour can manifest itself in a variety of ways. It may be oral, written, or visual. It may be cerebral or visceral; subtle or heavy-handed; gentle or harsh; ironic, sardonic, whimsical, or satirical. It may be based on puns or word play, or on incongruous juxtaposition, or on the shock of the unexpected. Or it may be black—as in the case of **Starke's** legendary remark to **Rich** at Isaacs' funeral in 1948: as they passed by the open grave, Starke leant over to Rich, who was 85 years old, and asked him: 'George, are you sure it's worth your while to go home?'

Humour in the High Court may arise in the written judgments of the Justices or in the cut and thrust of **argument**. Deliberate attempts to be humorous in written form, embedded as they are in the detached permanence of inert prose, often die a quick death; by contrast, the spontaneous wit of the quick riposte in oral argument thrives on the immediacy and transience of the moment. Thus, one finds humour, or at least wit, more often in oral exchanges between Bench and Bar than in written judgments, and especially in applications for special **leave to appeal**, where argument is restricted to 20 minutes.

Mason has recalled that a **Solicitor-General** once concluded his argument with the words: 'That concludes the first branch of my argument', when Douglas **Menzies**—the 'laughing cavalier' of the Court—responded: 'Mr Solicitor, would not "twig" be a more appropriate word?' Mason, known for his acerbic wit, himself showed no mercy in one case when **counsel** conceded: 'Your Honour has me on the ropes', to

which Mason responded: 'On the canvas would be a more accurate expression.' When in *Livingstone v Willox* (1997) the applicant asked: 'May I just point very briefly, your Honour, to the problem of voodoo?', **Brennan** responded that, as if by magic, her time had unfortunately expired. And in *Shields v ANZ* (1998), the applicant asked a startled **McHugh**: 'You are not Justice **Toohey** by any chance?', to which McHugh replied: 'He has retired. When I sit on special leave days I think sometimes I should be retired.'

Dixon possessed an acid wit. He is credited with the quip: 'It was not until I heard **Powers** deliver a judgment that I fully understood the meaning of the phrase *ultra vires*' (beyond powers). In a case in the 1960s, Dixon had little patience with the advocacy of Dr FC Louat QC. When counsel addressed a particular point, Louat got to his feet and said: 'I can throw some light on that.' Dixon remarked to the other counsel: 'Dr Louat believes he has a lantern.' Louat proceeded to quote the detailed facts of a quite irrelevant case, pausing as he realised his mistake. Dixon remarked, alluding to Gilbert and Sullivan's *The Mikado*: 'Detail adds verisimilitude to an otherwise bald and unconvincing narrative.'

Sometimes a humorous remark may be misunderstood or taken too seriously. In the course of hearing *Lanyon Pty Ltd v Commonwealth* (1974), Douglas Menzies visited the historic homestead Lanyon, near Canberra. Menzies joked to counsel: 'This would be a great place for Gar' (a reference to **Barwick**). Some say that this is the source of the widespread belief that Barwick wanted the homestead as the official residence of the **Chief Justice** when the Court moved to **Canberra**.

The humour in the High Court's permanent legacy of written judgments is frequently unconscious, arising simply from the oddity or comical nature of the issues. This is particularly so in **statutory interpretation**, as in *Deputy FCT v Zest Manufacturing* (1949), where the issue was whether goldfish were livestock; *Herbert Adams Pty Ltd v FCT* (1932), where the issue was whether a sponge was a pastry or a cake; and *Mathews v Foggitt Jones* (1926), where the issue was whether a sausage could be a portion of a carcass.

These kinds of oddities can of course be exploited for comic effect, as in *Slattery v Bishop* (1919), where **Gavan Duffy** made fun of the lower court's difficulty in distinguishing between a grocery shop and a butcher's shop that sold tea and pickles; *Dickenson's Arcade v Tasmania* (1974), where Barwick played up the absurdities of a 'plain meaning' approach to state legislation that, on its face, purported to tax each consumer for every individual instance of the actual consumption of tobacco (see **Excise duties**); and *A v Hayden* (1984), where Mason likened a security exercise at the Sheraton Hotel that went wrong to 'a Law School moot based on an episode taken from the adventures of Maxwell Smart'.

Patent, **copyright**, and **trade mark** cases also sometimes provide the opportunity for Justices to create humorous effect by giving minute and abstract descriptions of ordinary and everyday objects, such as Dixon's elaborate account of a ball-point pen in *Martin v Scribal* (1954) (see **Popular culture**) and **Windeyer's** descriptions of the 'Shell Oil-drop man' in *Shell v Esso Standard Oil* (1963).

In recent times, **Kirby** is probably the most noted humorist. In *Phonographic Performance Co v Federation of Commercial*

Television Stations (1998), he drew attention to the limits of judicial responses to new technologies by adding in a footnote: 'Courts cannot always, in the manner of *Star Trek's* Captain Jean-Luc Picard, say "Make it so!"' His judgment in *Johnson v American Home Assurance Co* (1998) begins:

The ninety-first Psalm reflects the common human fear of injury to the foot. The Psalmist promises rescue from various misfortunes. The angels, we are assured, will take charge over the righteous:

'They shall bear thee up in their hands, lest thou dash thy foot against a stone.'

Unfortunately, angels did not intervene to protect the appellant's foot. But he had an insurance policy. This case concerns his attempt to obtain earthly rescue from the insurer.

Humour in the High Court can occasionally be visual, even bordering on the practical joke. Barwick once wound the Court's clock forward by one hour so that he could leave early. In the 1960s, it was common knowledge among **associates** that although **Fullagar** fell asleep within minutes of the Court resuming at 2.15 pm, he was usually awake about half an hour later. The associate who was sitting as clerk of the Court could always tell when Fullagar awoke because the judge would move his feet. But Fullagar—a 'lovely chuckling humorist', as Robert **Menzies** described him—would appear to remain asleep for another five or ten minutes and then, still not lifting his head, would ask some incisive question in an attempt to demonstrate that he had never been to sleep at all. On one occasion, Dixon proposed placing a hotel 'Do Not Disturb' sign in front of the sleeping judge during his nap on the Bench. According to **Evatt's** biographer Peter Crockett, Evatt once told his associate, John Brennan, to sprinkle breadcrumbs between Starke's bed sheets when Evatt and Starke were travelling on **circuit**. Brennan declined.

Starke was himself the victim of the subversive and levelling effect of visual humour. Starke was renowned for giving counsel a hard time. In *FCT v Hoffnung* (1928), for example, he observed drily that the appeal had 'been argued by the Court over nine days with some occasional assistance from the learned and experienced counsel who appeared for the parties'. But on one occasion, counsel had the last laugh. One cold May, with the Court sitting in the old **building** at Little Bourke Street in Melbourne, Starke kept a rug over his knees to keep himself warm. Appearing before him was Eric Miller QC, and Starke was giving him a very hard time. When Miller protested: 'Your Honour is very rude to counsel', Starke retorted: 'With justification.' Miller demanded to know: 'Is Your Honour suggesting some constitutional justification?', at which point Chief Justice **Latham** intervened: 'The Court will adjourn for a few minutes.' As they got up to leave, Starke tripped over his rug and fell flat on his face.

Gleeson has cautioned against the temptation for judges to indulge in humour. In 1998, he said: 'Some judges, out of personal good nature, or out of a desire to break the tension that can develop in a courtroom, occasionally feel it appropriate to treat a captive audience to a display of wit'. When it is not appreciated, 'the consequences can be very unfortunate. Judges and legal practitioners may underestimate the seriousness which litigants attach to legal proceedings, and they can become insensitive to the misunderstandings which might arise if the judge appears to be taking the occasion lightly'.

On the other hand, as Kirby has noted: 'Judges are supremely individuals. Their expression is, in part, a reflection of their personalities and individual **values**.' Just as humour can be effective in the ordinary communications of life, so it has a place in judicial communication. For the judge, a moment of humour can break the tension of a case or relieve the tedium of writing a judgment. For the barrister, it can help relieve monotony, stress, and frustration. The issues in litigation are serious. Too serious, perhaps, not to be occasionally taken light-heartedly.

JESSICA MILNER DAVIS
TROY SIMPSON

Further Reading

Murray Gleeson, 'The Role of the Judge and Becoming a Judge', National Judicial Orientation Programme, Sydney, 16 August 1998 (www.hcourt.gov.au)

Michael Kirby, 'On the Writing of Judgments' (1990) 64 *ALJ* 691

I

Ideology refers to any systematic set of beliefs, usually political, through which attitudes to particular issues are predetermined by their consistency with a perceptual framework, and which the closure of the belief system shields from critical scrutiny. Without even being aware of it, the proponents of an ideology may accept their ideological perspective as the only legitimate point of view from which to judge an issue. A range of ideologies has flourished in Australia since the High Court was **established**, although not all ideologies have had equal influence on the **decision-making process**.

Very early in Australian history, a crucial clash of ideologies concerning material wealth divided politics between the left and the right. The left, or working-class wing, is supported primarily by the Labor Party, while the right, or free-market wing, is now supported primarily by the Liberal Party, although positioning on the continuum is fluid, and at times it has been difficult to distinguish the politics of one party from those of the other. The difficulty may reflect the fact that the dominant political philosophy of both major parties is **liberalism**, though the Labor Party has emphasised its egalitarian strand and the Liberal Party its free-market strand. The similarities and differences between the parties may also depend on their respective responses to other ideological pressures: the racism of the White Australia Policy, which was discarded by mainstream politics only in the 1960s; welfare state ideology in response to the **Depression of the 1930s**; anti-communism, especially throughout the **Cold War**; and the range of ideologising movements generated by the alternative politics of the Vietnam era, including **Aboriginal** rights campaigns, the second wave of **feminism**, environmentalism, multiculturalism, consumerism, and more recently, postmodernism.

Because of the property interests involved in most legal disputes and because of the **cost of litigation**, the Court plays a central **role** in preserving existing social relations, not only in their economic and class dimensions but in attitudes to sex, **race**, sexuality, and able-bodiedness, which may intersect with class in particular ways. The Court also facilitates free-market activities, which is apparent from the extensive litigation involving sections 90 and 92 of the Constitution (see **Excise duties** and **Interstate trade and commerce**). Law nevertheless holds itself out to be an impartial guardian of the interests of citizens.

Legal **positivism** has enabled law to present a value-free and apolitical mien to the world. For much of its history, the High Court has consciously favoured a positivistic approach, dubbed 'strict and complete **legalism**' by **Dixon**, so that in the struggle of **form** versus substance the focus has been on form. Strict legalism has operated to disguise the play of power beneath the neutral veneer of technocratic rules. Hence, ideology tends to be covert, so that the homologous relationship between the Court and powerful interests appears to be normal, neutral, and even natural.

The Justices themselves have been inclined to espouse ideological positions that favour the status quo. With one exception, they have all been white **men**, and have generally been the middle-class products of private boys' schools (see **Background of Justices**). Even for those from a less privileged background, like **Barwick**, a preference for practice in **commercial law** and **equity** at the senior Bar, together with a professional milieu populated by politically conservative men of wealth and influence, has conduced to the generation of a somewhat skewed world view. While this world view is perceived as apolitical, Justices who have been advocates of reform, such as **Evatt**, **Murphy**, **Gaudron**, and **Kirby**, have been characterised as 'radical', even though they have not necessarily been equally progressive on all issues.

Generally speaking, there has not been a vast ideological gulf between Liberal and Labor appointees to the Court. In fact, Labor governments have been somewhat reticent about making left-wing appointments, although Liberal governments do not appear to have felt similarly constrained about making right-wing appointments. Both Barwick and **Latham**, for example, were appointed as **Chief Justices** directly from political positions by Liberal governments, but their support for an untrammelled free market, together with their social conservatism, rendered their **appointments** less controversial than the Labor appointments of Evatt and **McTiernan** in 1930 or Murphy in 1975.

The fact that Barwick was appointed by a Liberal government did not prevent his persistent subversion, in cases such as *FCT v Westraders* (1980), of attempts by a later Liberal government to reform **taxation law**. His overt clash with Murphy in that case is a rare example in which starkly opposing ideologies were made explicit, while still perhaps sharing a deeper ideological base. Both sought to promote the liberal ideal of a free society—though Barwick equated this with freedom to maximise wealth, Murphy with freedom from government oppression and rejection of a taxation regime that was 'optional for the rich'. The conflict was thus rooted in a shared tradition of underlying liberalism, and was thinly veiled as a conflict about the virtues of strict **literalism** in **statutory interpretation.**

As in Western liberal democratic states generally, a significant political development in Australia after the Depression of the 1930s was the emergence of an inchoate welfare state, the legislative implementation of which was sought primarily through Labor legislation. Challenges to the constitutional validity of the legislation provoked a clash between the legislature and the Court. Far from being neutral and autonomous, the Court's efforts to thwart such reforms reveal it to have been imbricated in contemporary politics and to have evinced a conservative bias (see **Socialism**). The most notable examples occurred during the period of reconstruction following **World War II**, when the Chifley Labor government sought to enact a raft of regulatory legislation with a socialist flavour. The preference of the **Latham Court** for *laissez-faire* individualism resulted in its consistently striking down this legislation in cases such as the *First Pharmaceutical Benefits Case* (1945); *Australian National Airways v Commonwealth* (1945); the *Melbourne Corporation Case* (1947); and the *Bank Nationalisation Case* (1948).

Nevertheless, neither the ideological positions of the Justices nor the outcomes of disputes are always clear-cut or predictable. A notable example is the *Communist Party Case* (1951), which invalidated the *Communist Party Dissolution Act* 1950 (Cth), designed specifically to outlaw communism. The decision represented a challenge both to the Liberal government of Robert **Menzies** and to prevailing orthodoxy at the height of the Cold War. Furthermore, the *Communist Party Case* enhanced the status of the Court as a champion of **civil liberties**. Yet the decision is explicable in terms of strict legalism, since the constitutional basis for the legislation was slight; it by no means represents an ideological *volte face* on the part of the majority.

Generally speaking, comparatively few civil liberties cases stand out. Although in part this reflects the personal conservatism of the Bench and the absence of a **Bill of Rights**, it may also reflect a more basic divergence between an American political tradition founded on distrust of government and a British tradition of deference to government authority. The exceptions include the early case of *Melbourne Corporation v Barry* (1922) and the later case of *Davis v Commonwealth* (1988) (see **Colonialism**). One notable exception is *Neal v The Queen* (1982), a case involving a gaol sentence of six months with hard labour imposed by an appellate court on an Aboriginal man for spitting at a white man. The Court unanimously upheld the application for **leave to appeal**, and Murphy's eloquent judgment linked the right to political dissent with human progress.

Like the Chifley government, the Labor government of the **Whitlam era** also sought to effect a significant reform agenda, but it was not thwarted by the Court in the same way. Times had changed with the demise of the **Dixon Court**: adherence to strict legalism no longer commanded the same respect; the Labor appointments of **Jacobs** and Murphy had changed the Court's composition; and the Whitlam legislation, while socially progressive, did not directly threaten the free market to the same extent.

Over the Court's first three decades, **Isaacs** had advanced a version of Australian nationalism consonant with the cultural traditions of the UK, and resonant with the xenophobia of the White Australia Policy. The Court did very little to advance an alternative version of nationalist sentiment, and the internationalism of Evatt in the 1930s received little support. But the Court did slowly begin to develop an innominate **nationhood power**, and gradually gave the country a sense of identity separating it from the mother country (see **Nationhood**). It was not until the 1970s that there was a radical shift in social and foreign policy—away from the racist White Australia Policy to multiculturalism and **cultural diversity**—and an extension of the **external affairs power** to accommodate legislation bringing Australian policies on race and ethnicity into line with international concerns. A majority of the Court responded positively to these developments in *Koowarta's Case* (1982) and the *Tasmanian Dam Case* (1983). Both have been hailed as victories for anti-racism, and the latter—along with *Murphyores v Commonwealth* (1976), which unanimously upheld legislation pertaining to centralised environmental controls—as a victory for environmentalism as well.

The change in the Court's approach to race perhaps best exemplifies the new ideology that emerged in the 1980s, as well as the subsequent resiling from it. In the late 1970s, **Gibbs** described an Aboriginal claim that challenged proclamations of **sovereignty** made on behalf of the British Crown as 'absurd and vexatious' (*Coe v Commonwealth (No 1)* (1979)). Soon afterwards, *Koowarta* confirmed the validity of the *Racial Discrimination Act* 1975 (Cth). On a different issue, in 1983, **Brennan** was able to say in the *Tasmanian Dam Case* that the 'odious practices of oppression and neglect of Aboriginal people were at an end'. In *Mabo* (1992), the majority recognised **native title** for the first time, and categorically rejected the long-standing fiction that Australia was *terra nullius*. Of particular interest is the Court's passionate denunciation of racism—a **judicial style** that contrasts sharply with the dry legalism of most constitutional adjudication.

Mabo, together with *Wik* (1996), elicited trenchant attacks on the Court by free marketeers, politicians, landholders, and conservative **commentators** for allegedly usurping the role of the legislature. The outcry demonstrated that the ideology of the Court becomes an issue only when it deviates from the conservative position. *Mabo* and *Wik* led to the appointment of several conservative Justices by the Howard government, including **Hayne** and **Callinan** and Chief Justice **Gleeson**, with a correlative movement away from a strong anti-racist stance. Narrow readings relating to race are apparent in *Kruger v Commonwealth* (1997) and the *Hindmarsh Island Bridge Case* (1998), in which legislation excluding the plaintiffs' community from the benefit of the *Aboriginal and Torres Strait Islander Heritage Protection Act* 1984 (Cth) was challenged. The plaintiffs argued that the races power (section 51(xxvi) of the Constitution) can be used only for the benefit of Aborigines, not for their detriment. The legislation was upheld, but on another ground. As to the scope of the races power, the case was inconclusive; only Kirby (dissenting) could unreservedly commit himself to the plaintiffs' argument. Contemporaneous decisions evince a tightening-up in respect of other vulnerable groups, namely refugees (*Minister for Immigration v Eshetu* (1999)), people with disabilities (including people with HIV; see *X v Commonwealth* (1999)), and homosexuals (*Green v The Queen* (1997); see **Sexual preference**).

Kirby has been a notable dissenter in such cases. Generally, when a Justice is moved by an ideology that conflicts with the prevailing ideology of the Court, he or she is forced to give a **dissenting judgment** (see, for example, Isaacs' feminist-inspired protest in *Wright v Cedzich* (1930) or **McHugh's** defence of multiculturalism in *Masciantonio v The Queen* (1995)). The dissenting judgment stands as evidence that the majority could have decided differently. As a dissent, it remains on the margins of the law: even so, it remains articulated in the law reports as a challenge to the status quo. For the future, it is open to the Court to choose from a range of ideological positions.

Although the ideology of the High Court is never entirely static, conservatising influences have always exercised a powerful centripetal pull, even when progressivism has been in the ascendancy. The favoured adjudicative style of strict legalism has itself also played an ideological role in seeking to disguise the fact that the Court has generally been associated with dominant interests and a desire to maintain the status quo.

MARGARET THORNTON

Further Reading
Jean and Richard Ely (eds), *Lionel Murphy: The Rule of Law* (1986)
Brian Galligan, *Politics of the High Court* (1987)
Valerie Kerruish, *Jurisprudence as Ideology* (1991)
Laurence W Maher, 'Tales of the Overt and the Covert: Judges and Politics in Early Cold War Australia' (1993) 21 *FL Rev* 151

Immigration law. The **role** played by the High Court in the evolution of Australian immigration law evinces a complex relationship between the Court and the legislative and executive branches of government in Australia. There has been a continuing pattern of deference in cases involving constitutional challenges to migration legislation. At the level of **statutory interpretation** and administration of the law, however, the Court's approach has shown greater variation. It has responded to changing community **values** and developments in **international law**—on occasion, placing itself at loggerheads with both the administration and the legislature. The Court's recent rulings have placed immigration law at the cutting edge of both **administrative law** and **constitutional law** in Australia.

There are a number of reasons why the Court has been deferential in its approach to immigration matters. Despite the contrary view of some academics such as WF Craies, the **Griffith Court** accepted that the power to admit, exclude, or expel aliens was a prerogative of government, and inherent in the Austinian concept of **sovereignty** (*Robtelmes v Brenan* (1906); see also the *Kisch Case* (1934)). Moreover, until relatively recently, the Court regarded any decisions made by a minister of the Crown in the exercise of a statutory discretion as an inappropriate subject for **judicial review**. For example, in *Lloyd v Wallach* (1915), the Court held it contrary to public policy to inquire into the **reasonableness** of the minister's belief that the applicant alien represented a threat to Australia's national security (see **World War I**).

From the outset, the Court gave wide scope to Parliament's power to legislate pursuant to the **immigration power** in section 51(xxvii) of the Constitution. It extended the meaning of the term 'immigration' to include both the process of permanent settlement and the regulation of movement into and out of Australia. While views differed on whether the power justified enactments affecting immigrants absorbed into the Australian community, the Court accepted laws imposing conditions on the grant of residence or preventing 'absorption' altogether.

The Court has consistently upheld provisions relating to the exclusion, deportation, or removal of illegal immigrants and (after 1949) non-citizens. It supported the validity of the dictation test that was the primary vehicle for the racially selective White Australia Policy (see *Chia Gee v Martin* (1905); *Potter v Minahan* (1908)). It upheld other racially protectionist legislation such as the *Pacific Island Labourers Act* 1901 (Cth), which facilitated the removal of imported Kanak labourers (see *Robtelmes*) and the controversial *Wartime Refugees Removal Act* 1949 (Cth) (see *Koon Wing Lau v Calwell* (1949)). Indeed, it appears that the Court has never declared unconstitutional a deportation or removal provision.

The Court's early immigration rulings played a significant role in determining the nature and composition of the emergent Australian community. The omission of any constitutional reference to Australian **citizenship** meant that membership of the Australian polity turned on whom the High Court characterised as an 'immigrant' for the purposes of the *Immigration Act* 1901 (Cth). While there were some vigorous dissents—see, for example, the comments of **Knox** and **Gavan Duffy** in *Williamson v Ah On* (1926)—the language used by some of the Justices suggests a ready acceptance of the government's White Australia Policy. **Isaacs** provides some choice examples of judicial scaremongering, referring to illegal migrants in *Williamson's* case as 'loathsome hotbeds of disease' who conspire to 'defy and injure the entire people of a continent'. In *Potter*, the same Justice made it clear that a person's characterisation as an immigrant had everything to do with his or her conformity to Anglo-Saxon norms of culture and appearance—legal concepts such as nationality and domicile being mere evidentiary facts. After **World War II**, as Immigration Minister, Arthur Calwell launched his drive to populate Australia with the right sorts, the Court upheld legislation passed simultaneously to rid the country of Asian refugees who had sought refuge here. In *Koon Wing Lau*, **Webb** likened the refugees to 'unrepaired damage done by enemy bombing to an Australian city [that] may be as validly dealt with under the **defence power**'.

On the other hand, there are some notable examples of judicial intervention to correct misuse or abuse of the powers conferred on immigration officials. For example, in the early 1930s, the dictation test was applied in an attempt to exclude an activist travelling the world to warn against the dangers of fascism. Egon Kisch was fluent in so many European languages that the immigration officer resorted to dictating a passage in Scottish Gaelic. The High Court issued a **writ** of prohibition on the ground that Scottish Gaelic was not a European language for the purposes of the immigration legislation.

As the era of the new administrative law dawned in the 1960s and 1970s, immigration remained one of the last bastions of closed government. The *Migration Act* 1958 (Cth) had replaced the dictation test by investing the Minister for Immigration (in his various appellations) with sweeping discretionary powers both to admit and to expel non-citizens. The amplitude of the minister's powers operated as a barrier to judicial review so long as the Court maintained traditional views about the non-**justiciability** of prerogative powers and the non-applicability of the rules of **natural justice** to administrative decision making. The Court did not acknowledge the hearing rights of migrants until the landmark decision in **Kioa v West** (1985), 19 years after the English Court of Appeal had done so: compare the English development in *Re HK (An Infant)* (1966) with the narrow approach of the High Court in *Salemi v MacKellar (No 2)* (1977) and *Simsek v Macphee* (1982).

The breakthrough came in the mid-1980s with a series of cases that reached the Court from the newly created **Federal Court**. In 1984, the High Court greatly expanded the range of justiciable migration decisions when it held, in *Minister for Immigration v Mayer* (1985), that certain ancillary rulings made by the Minister were 'decisions made under an enactment' for the purposes of the *Administrative Decisions (Judicial Review) Act* 1977 (Cth). In the following year, the decision in *Kioa* cut through much of the older case law and recognised that an illegal migrant had a right to be heard before being deported. Jason Kioa was an individual who could point to no right or expectation to remain in Australia; indeed, it is difficult to identify in the case any basis for a legal entitlement to procedural fairness other than a rather inchoate notion of 'good administration' or fairness writ large.

Kioa proved something of a revolution for administrative lawyers. Once the Court had recognised the illegal migrant's right to a hearing, it became much easier to mount legal arguments on matters of relevancy and reasonableness in administrative decision making. The case was not just a boon for persons wishing to challenge a migration decision. It benefited anyone aggrieved by an administrative decision made in the exercise of the most apparently unfettered of powers. The government responded to the litigation explosion by amending the Migration Act so as to replace the broad discretions with closely codified or regulation-based decision making. In 1994, more radical changes were made. A new Part 8 of the Migration Act set drastic limits to the grounds on which the Federal Court can judicially review migration decisions. In *Abebe v Commonwealth* (1999) and *Minister for Immigration v Eshetu* (1999), the High Court upheld this legislation; but in practice, these decisions have merely resulted in an enormous increase in the number of migration cases coming before the High Court for review (see *Re Minister for Immigration; Ex Parte Durairajasingham* (2000)).

After *Kioa*, the most significant contribution of the Court to the development of Australian immigration law came in *Chan v Minister for Immigration* (1989). That was the first case in which the Court considered in any detail the provisions of the international instruments governing the recognition and protection of refugees in Australia: the 1951 UN Convention relating to the Status of Refugees and its subsequent 1967 Protocol. The Court's willingness to grant refugee status if there was a 'real chance' of persecution made that criterion the touchstone for the development of a uniquely Australian refugee jurisprudence. This has grown exponentially with the creation of a specialist refugee tribunal.

The new sensitivity of the Court to international law and comparative immigration jurisprudence became apparent in two subsequent cases that met with a strong response from the government of the day. In *Chu Kheng Lim v Minister for Immigration* (1992), a successful challenge was mounted against legislation that affected the powers of the Court and the interpretation of the **judicial power** in Chapter III of the Constitution. The case arose out of a constitutional challenge to legislation passed initially to mandate the detention of asylum-seekers and illegal migrants who came to Australia by boat in and after 1989. While the Court upheld the constitutionality of the new detention regime as a whole, it struck down a provision prohibiting *any court* from ordering the release of certain non-citizens in immigration detention. Moreover, it held that up to the time of the 1992 amendments, the plaintiffs' detention had been unlawful. Parliament responded by passing legislation declaring that immigration detainees held without legal warrant would be entitled to no more than one dollar per day as compensation.

The second case, **Teoh's Case** (1995), involved a Thai national who sought residence in Australia on grounds of marriage but was rejected after being convicted of serious drug offences. In the High Court, he argued that the decision to deport him was unlawful because the minister had failed to consider the interests of his seven Australian children as required by Article 3 of the 1989 UN Convention on the Rights of the Child. The Court confirmed the basic principle that Australia's obligations at international law do not bind decision makers until translated into domestic law by statute. However, while accepting that this Convention had *not* been so incorporated, the majority found that it gave rise to a **'legitimate expectation'** that the decision would be made in accordance with the Convention, with the further consequence that if the decision was not to be made in that way, Teoh should have been given an opportunity to argue that it should be. The government responded with a policy statement negating any such expectation, and successive governments introduced Bills to the same effect.

Most recently, the Court has returned to a more constrained and deferential approach to the review of migration cases—a trend that may reflect an upsurge in the community's concern about illegal immigration and the perceived impropriety of the actions of proactive refugees in disregarding immigration laws. But the Court has divided sharply on a number of the more contentious cases. In *Applicant A v Minister for Immigration* (1997), a narrow majority rejected the contention that fugitives of China's One Child Policy could meet the definition of refugee. However, the effect of that decision has been modified by the further holding, in *Chen Shi Hai v Minister for Immigration* (2000), that although Chinese parents who disobey the One Child Policy do not qualify as refugees on the basis of their exposure to potential persecution as a 'social group', their children may do so. On the other hand, the Court has refused to entertain arguments about fine matters of interpretation of the Refugee Convention and has sent a strong message to the Federal Court that it has been too ready to intervene and question the legality of migration decisions (see *Minister for Immigration v Wu* (1996) and *Eshetu*). These cases sit uneasily with statements made in other contexts (for example in *Craig v SA* (1995)) about the distinction that should be drawn between decisions of inferior courts and those made by tribunals or administrative review bodies.

MARY CROCK

Further Reading
WF Craies, 'The Right of Aliens to Enter British Territory' (1890) 6 *LQR* 27
Mary Crock, 'Judicial Review and Part 8 of the *Migration Act*: Necessary Reform or Overkill?' (1996) 18 *Syd LR* 267
Mary Crock, *Immigration and Refugee Law in Australia* (1998)
Freda Hawkins, *Critical Years in Immigration: Australia and Canada Compared* (1988)
Myra Willard, *History of the White Australia Policy* (1923)

Immigration power. Section 51(xxvii) of the Constitution empowers Parliament to legislate with respect to '**immigration** and emigration'. After federation, the High Court's interpretation of this provision played a vital role in shaping Australia's social and cultural identity.

The early significance of the provision was that the powers in section 51 of the Constitution made no mention of Australian **citizenship**. At the time of federation, there was no concept of Australian citizenship even for British settlers (who still regarded themselves as British subjects). Moreover, the text of the Constitution displays a general reluctance to embrace as Australian the **Aboriginal peoples** and others of non-European background. Rather than conferring power to make laws with respect to citizenship, section 51(xxvii) was used as a substitute to enable the federal legislature to control admission to and membership of the Australian community.

A continuing **role** for the High Court was ensured by the absence in the early statutes of any explicit criteria defining those who could enter or remain in the country. The *Immigration Restriction Act* 1901 (Cth) provided simply for the exclusion or removal of six classes of 'prohibited immigrants', among them those who failed to pass a dictation test administered at any time within three years of entry (see *Kisch Case* (1934)). It fell ultimately to the High Court to pronounce on which people were, and which were not, 'immigrants' for the purposes of this test. The Court's determination of this issue in many cases suggests a strong awareness of, if not deference to, the commitment of Australian governments to a White Australia policy. **Isaacs** described the 'ultimate fact to be reached' as whether an individual was 'a constituent part of the community known as the Australian people' (*Potter v Minahan* (1908)). He added: 'Nationality and domicil are not the tests; they are evidentiary facts of more or less weight in the circumstances.' In a number of cases, it is difficult to see that some Justices used anything other than the applicant's skin colour and ethnic heritage as the critical determinant of community membership (see **Race**). Little else can explain the different rulings in the otherwise parallel cases of *Potter v Minahan*, involving a man of Anglo–Chinese heritage, and *Ah Yin v Christie* (1907), where the young woman's parents were both ethnic Chinese.

Generally, the Court has treated immigration legislation with deference, accepting that the power to admit, exclude, or expel aliens is a prerogative of government and an inherent part of state **sovereignty** (see *Robtelmes v Brenan* (1906)).

It expanded the common meaning of immigration—leaving an old home in one country to make a new home elsewhere—to cover all acts of permanent or temporary entry into Australia by non-citizens (see *Chia Gee v Martin* (1905)), whether they be controversial visitors charged with sedition (*Irish Envoys Case* (1923)) or wartime refugees (*Koon Wing Lau v Calwell* (1949)).

The Court also upheld Parliament's power to impose conditions on the admission of persons on a temporary or permanent basis (see *Robtelmes*; *O'Keefe v Calwell* (1949)). It endorsed legislative use of the power to revoke permission to remain in Australia even when such permission had formerly been granted (see *R v Kidman* (1915)). The Court held that the power authorises the regulation and prohibition of an immigrant's absorption into the community, but split on the question of whether an 'absorbed' immigrant could pass beyond the reach of the power. Isaacs and **Rich** favoured an expansive interpretation of the power, postulating that an immigrant could never lose his or her immigrant status, and accordingly remains susceptible to government control: see Isaacs' notorious epigram: 'Once an immigrant, always an immigrant' in *Irish Envoys* and *Ex parte Walsh and Johnson; In re Yates* (1925). The opposing, narrow view is that the power cannot be used to justify laws affecting persons absorbed into the community. However, the Court agreed that retrospective legislation could not be used to remove dissenters such as the trade unionist Walsh in *Ex parte Walsh and Johnson*, who had been part of the community since before federation.

The Court has always accepted the validity of statutes empowering the Minister to exclude or deport aliens (see *Chia Gee*; *R v Green*; *Ex parte Cheung Cheuk To* (1965); *R v Forbes; Ex parte Kwok Kwan Lee* (1971)).

By the mid-1970s, most issues relating to the extent of the immigration power were well settled. Although some debate remained as to whether the power remained available as a means of continuing legislative control of immigrants who had been 'absorbed' into the Australian community, the prevailing wisdom favoured the narrow view of the power. In *R v Director-General of Social Welfare (Vic); Ex parte Henry* (1975)), a case involving an immigrant child, **Jacobs** alone suggested that the power could be used to benign effect where Parliament intended to protect or confer a benefit on an 'absorbed' person who was once an immigrant.

Since *Ex parte Henry*, the constitutional discourse has shifted steadily. The *Nationality and Citizenship Act* 1948 (Cth) (now the *Australian Citizenship Act* 1948 (Cth)) established for the first time a separate Australian citizenship, while at the same time the *British Nationality Act* 1948 (UK) reduced the significance of the old Imperial notion of 'British subjects'. Against that background, the judgments in *Nolan v Minister for Immigration* (1988) again endorsed the narrow view of the immigration power, implying that 'absorbed' non-citizens *can* pass beyond the reach of the immigration power. However, in the same breath, the Court reduced the significance of section 51(xxvii) by invoking other heads of power to justify legislation affecting 'absorbed' immigrants. The most important are the aliens power (section 51(xix)) and the **external affairs power** (section 51(xxix)). As a result, notions of absorption have become irrelevant in determining the constitutionality of immigration laws—even in cases involving British nationals, who once enjoyed quasi-citizen status in Australia (see *Nolan*; *Wiggan v Minister for Immigration* (1988); and *Kenny v Minister for Immigration* (1993)).

MARY CROCK

Further Reading

Michael Coper, 'The Reach of the Commonwealth's Immigration Power: Judicial Exegesis Unbridled' (1976) 50 *ALJ* 351

PH Lane, 'The Immigration Power' (1966) 39 *ALJ* 302

Jean Malor, 'Deportation Under the Immigration Power' (1950) 24 *ALJ* 302

Implied constitutional rights. The Australian Constitution contains comparatively few provisions that expressly limit government power in a manner that could be described as conferring a right on an individual. However, during the late 1980s and early 1990s, the High Court seemed to respond to the dearth of such provisions with a reading of the Constitution that was notably more protective of rights. In the earliest cases of this type, such as *Street v Queensland Bar Association* (1989), the Court gave provisions that conferred **express constitutional rights** a more robust reading. The more innovative feature of the Court's reasoning during this time was, however, the use of the concept of implied rights—that is, rights not expressed in the Constitution's text, but implied therefrom. This method of **constitutional interpretation** was also more controversial, raising accusations that the Court had departed impermissibly from the meaning of the constitutional text and the original intention of the **framers** of the document (see also **Originalism**).

The implied rights recognised during this period can be roughly divided into three kinds. First, there are rights that arise from the interpretation of specific provisions. The best-established of the implied rights—the freedom of **political communication** arising from provisions of the Constitution implementing aspects of **representative government** and **responsible government**—is of this type. Since *Lange v ABC* (1997) in particular, the Court has been careful to tie the freedom to the constitutional text and necessary implications from the text.

This interpretive technique may also give rise to other implied rights. Although it has yet to attract a clear majority of the Court, there has been some judicial recognition that the existence in the Constitution of the institutions of representative and responsible government might also imply a certain level of freedom of **movement** and freedom of association (see *Kruger v Commonwealth* (1997); *Levy v Victoria* (1997)). The former 'right' (perhaps in an even broader form) could also be grounded in the requirement of section 92 that 'intercourse' among the states be 'absolutely free'.

Perhaps the acceptance of the freedom of political communication and its related freedoms is not surprising when it is recalled that argument for these kinds of rights is an old phenomenon. Indeed, an argument of this kind can be found as early as *R v Smithers; Ex parte Benson* (1912). In that case, two Justices, **Griffith** and **Barton**, found that an implied freedom of movement between states arose out of the creation of a federation, and that this protected a right to come to the seat of government.

However, other kinds of implied rights are so far less well-developed. Another type of implied right can be seen as emerging, in several ways, from the establishment of federal courts under Chapter III of the Constitution and the separation of **judicial power**. Most fundamentally, it might be said that individual rights are served by the Court's firm reassertion of its **role** as the arbiter of the constitutionality of laws in the *Communist Party Case* (1951), especially the invocation in that case of the **rule of law** as an assumption on which the Constitution is founded.

Secondly, it has been argued that the judicial power conferred on federal courts can be exercised only in a manner that observes some essential requirements, some of which protect individuals. Most prominently, **Deane** and **Gaudron** have held that certain features of a criminal trial are constitutionally entrenched because they are inherent in the notion of judicial power (see *War Crimes Act Case* (1991); *Dietrich v The Queen* (1992)). Finally, there are arguments that the **separation of powers**, by requiring that certain functions (classified as inherently judicial) can be performed only by courts and not by the Parliament or executive, can protect individuals. The Court accepted this kind of argument (subject to some exceptions) with respect to the 'adjudgment and punishment' of criminal guilt under a Commonwealth law in *Chu Kheng Lim v Minister for Immigration* (1992), although it conferred the protection only upon Australian citizens.

For the most part, these kinds of rights have so far attracted only minority support on the Court (as in the case of the constitutionalisation of aspects of the trial process) or have been stated at a high level of generality that makes the scope of any right difficult to predict (as in the case of implications from the rule of law). However, even less well developed are arguments in favour of a third type of implied right. These arguments rely on the nature of the Constitution as a whole or on the **common law**, and the rights they support are rights such as those found in the judgment of Deane and **Toohey** in *Leeth v Commonwealth* (1992). In *Leeth*, Deane and Toohey implied a right of **equality** between citizens from the agreement of the people to unite into a federation, evidenced in the preamble. This argument was further supported by reference to fundamental conceptions of equality in the common law, thus picking up on suggestions that some common law doctrines are too deeply embedded in the law to be abridged by Parliament. A similar form of argument, perhaps even more broadly stated, can be found in the early judgments of **Murphy**, who asserted, for example, that the Constitution was 'a Constitution for a free society' (*R v Director-General of Social Welfare (Vic); Ex parte Henry* (1975)).

For the moment, arguments for this third type of implied right are very unlikely to garner majority support. Apart from judicial and academic **criticism** of this kind of reasoning (see, for example, **Dawson's** judgment in *Kable v DPP* (1996)), the Court has since adopted a more cautious approach to rights generally—an approach that has constrained even the use of representative and responsible government as a source of rights. Indeed, since the decision in *Lange*, there has been little discussion of the freedom of political communication in the High Court, and lower courts have overwhelmingly dismissed challenges based on that doctrine.

Thus the judicial development of implied rights has slowed down, if not stalled. However, the debate over the place of implied rights in Australian **constitutional law** is likely to continue, and the lessons of our constitutional **history** so far should caution us against assuming that the issue is dead. It is entirely possible that a differently minded Court may resurrect these doctrines, heralding a period of further development of implied constitutional rights.

ADRIENNE STONE

Further Reading

Stephen Donaghue, 'The Clamour of Silent Constitutional Principles' (1996) 24 *FL Rev* 133

Jeffrey Goldsworthy, 'Implications in Law, Language and the Constitution' in Geoffrey Lindell (ed), *Future Directions in Australian Constitutional Law* (1994) 150

Symposium: Constitutional Rights for Australia? (1994) 16 *Syd LR* 145

George Winterton, 'The Separation of Judicial Power as an Implied Bill of Rights' in Geoffrey Lindell (ed), *Future Directions in Australian Constitutional Law* (1994) 185

George Winterton, 'Constitutionally Entrenched Common Law Rights' in Charles Sampford and Kim Preston (eds), *Interpreting Constitutions* (1996) 121

Implied constitutional rights: implications and inferences. Implications are an unavoidable aspect of **constitutional interpretation**. The implication of constitutional rights is objectionable, however, when the supposed implication is not warranted by the relevant source of **constitutional law**— be that the text of a written Constitution or statute, or the 'unwritten' **common law** relating to the Constitution.

Constitutional implications can be distinguished by reference to the degree to which their existence and substantive content is demonstrably derived from the relevant constitutional text. A first degree or order of implication occurs where the inference arises as a matter of *syllogistic logic*. A second degree of implication occurs where the inference is considered 'necessary' in order to give *practical effect* to a provision or set of provisions of the Constitution. A third degree of implication occurs where the inference is considered necessary in order to give a provision or provisions a *normatively desirable* operation. A fourth category of *purported* implication may arise in two different kinds of ways. The first is that a right based on a normative theory external to the Constitution might simply be applied by the judiciary without showing how that freedom or normative theory arises as a matter of interpretation of the Constitution. The second is that the normative elements in a series of third-order inferences are relied on to construct a particular implied right.

Putting aside a discussion of the legitimacy of third-order implications, the fourth category of purported implication is not warranted by the Constitution because such implications rely on normative propositions wholly extraneous to the Constitution. For example, in a line of cases starting with *Australian Capital Television v Commonwealth* (1992) (see *Free Speech Cases*), the High Court held that a guarantee of freedom of **political communication** implied by the Commonwealth Constitution limited the legislative powers of the federal Parliament. In coming to this conclusion, the Court made use of the normative elements in a succession of third-

order inferences to construct a particular implied freedom, amounting to this fourth category of purported implication. The reasoning began with the provision in sections 7 and 24 that the Parliament should consist of members 'chosen by the people'; the provision in section 128 for the **amendment** of the Constitution by popular referendum; and the Constitution's facilitation of a system of **responsible government**. These sections were said to require, by implication, the existence of a system of '**representative government**' or 'representative **democracy**'. It was then argued that such a system necessarily required the existence of freedom of communication in respect of political matters. Next, it was reasoned that it was necessary that such freedom be protected by a judicially enforced limitation on the powers of the Commonwealth. Finally, the premise that no freedom can be absolute was introduced to reduce the scope of the implied freedom so as not to invalidate exercises of Commonwealth power using 'reasonably appropriate and adapted' or '**proportionate**' means to the achievement of a 'legitimate objective'.

Each of these steps in reasoning involved the incorporation of normative elements. Each successive inference drew on the normative elements of the inference that preceded it. Thus, the inference of a system of representative and responsible government, as expressed in the judgments, incorporated a range of normative propositions concerning, for example, the ideas of 'effective' representation, 'accountability' and 'government by the people'. In turn, the inference of the necessity of freedom of communication about political matters rested on these normative propositions, and involved an additional inference regarding the normative desirability of free communication between the people and their representatives. Next, the inference concerning the judicial enforcement of a limit on the legislative power built on these propositions a further assertion regarding the normative desirability of judicial control. Finally, the proposition that no freedom can be absolute, but must be limited by reference to other legitimate factors, involved a further normative claim. The entire chain of reasoning was thus a series of successive, compounding third-order inferences, amounting to a result far removed from its supposed constitutional foundations.

In addition to these objections, Tom Campbell, Andrew Fraser, Gerald Rosenberg, and John Williams have demonstrated the problems involved in the Court's selective adoption of a particular normative interpretation of representative democracy when other interpretations were available. Jeffrey Goldsworthy has demonstrated the difficulty in purporting to rely on the **framers**' general intention to establish a representative democracy, but not on their intimately linked intention to do so only by particular means. Those means included the common law, constitutional conventions, parliaments, and the electoral process; they did not include a judicially enforced guarantee of freedom of political communication. In this context, Leslie Zines has expressed concern that the related 'extraordinary upsurge in judicial boldness in challenging legislatures', when not based on any specific provisions, 'provide[s] no guidance or check to judicial aggrandisement or personal predilections'.

In *Lange v ABC* (1997), the Court restated the basis for the implied freedom as being limited to what the text and structure of the Constitution requires. This insistence on 'text and structure' was apparently intended to eliminate or reduce the degree of reliance on normative propositions external to the text of the Constitution. This, in turn, would restrict the content of the ideas of representative and responsible government and of free political communication to that which may be gathered from specific provisions of the Constitution, read in light of the **Convention Debates** and contemporary understandings. Adopting a dictum of **Dawson**, a dissenting Justice in *Australian Capital Television*, the Court appeared in *Lange* to draw back from the notion of a free-standing conception of representative democracy, limiting the freedom to that involved in the constitutional imperative that members of Parliament be chosen by the people.

Michael Chesterman has argued that in *Lange* the Court successfully avoided the problem of cumulative third-order inference. However, in two further cases, *Levy v Victoria* (1997) and ***Kruger v Commonwealth*** (1997), the unanimity of *Lange* was fractured: some Justices adopted a narrower view of the freedom, others reverted to the 'wider' conception apparently based on a series of successive, compounding third-order inferences, again amounting to a result far removed from its basis in the text of the Constitution.

NICHOLAS ARONEY

Further Reading

Nicholas Aroney, *Freedom of Speech in the Constitution* (1998)

Tom Campbell, 'Democracy, Human Rights, and Positive Law' (1994) 16 *Syd LR* 195

Andrew Fraser, 'False Hopes: Implied Rights and Popular Sovereignty in the Australian Constitution' (1994) 16 *Syd LR* 213

Jeffrey Goldsworthy, 'Constitutional Implications and Freedom of Political Speech: A Reply to Stephen Donaghue' (1997) 23 *Mon LR* 362

Gerald Rosenberg and John Williams, 'Do not Go Gently into that Good Right: The First Amendment in the High Court of Australia' [1997] *Supreme Court Review* 439

Leslie Zines, 'A Judicially Created Bill of Rights?' (1994) 16 *Syd LR* 166

Inconsistency between Commonwealth and state laws. Every federation in which the central and constituent polities have concurrent law-making powers over some subject matters—and are therefore able to make inconsistent laws in relation to the same topic—requires a rule to identify which of the inconsistent laws prevails and which its citizens must obey. Almost inevitably, the rule is that the laws of the central polity prevail over the inconsistent laws of the constituent polities. The way the federation's courts, particularly its apex constitutional court, interpret the rule will play an important part in shaping the federal balance.

So it is in Australia. The Commonwealth and the states have concurrent law-making power in relation to most of the subjects on which the Commonwealth can make laws. Where those powers are exercised concurrently and produce inconsistent laws, section 109 of the Constitution operates to resolve the conflict in favour of the Commonwealth law:

> 109. When a law of a State is inconsistent with a law of the Commonwealth, the latter shall prevail, and the former shall, to the extent of the inconsistency, be invalid.

The High Court's wide interpretation and application of section 109 has played an important role—alongside the Court's wide interpretation of the **Commonwealth's legislative powers** in section 51—in shifting the federal balance in favour of the Commonwealth.

Section 109 has been relied on, sometimes successfully, in attempts to oust the operation of state laws regulating subjects as diverse as **discrimination** on grounds of sex and **race**, the working conditions of shearers and **women** in factories, the removal of shipwrecks, and the licensing requirements for airlines and the slaughter of meat for export. Three major questions arise when it is argued that section 109 applies to invalidate such state laws: what are 'laws' for the purpose of section 109; when are state laws and Commonwealth laws 'inconsistent'; and what is the effect of inconsistency when it is found to exist?

Section 109 addresses inconsistencies between state and Commonwealth *laws*. But many of the inconsistencies that arise in practice are inconsistencies between state and Commonwealth industrial awards, judicial orders, and statutory rules. Characteristically, in *Ex parte McLean* (1930), **Dixon** devised an explanation that reconciled the narrow language of section 109 with the practical necessity that it apply to such inconsistencies, and owed much to the Court's dominant **legalism** and **literalism**. Notwithstanding recent support for other explanations from some members of the Court, Dixon's explanation—that the inconsistency lies strictly in the laws that authorise the various instruments made under them—remains preferable.

By 1930, the Court had also identified three approaches to determining whether Commonwealth and state laws were inconsistent.

Under the first approach, a Commonwealth law and a state law were inconsistent only if it was not possible to obey both laws. Consistently with the approach of a majority of the Court in the period before the ***Engineers Case*** (1920), this narrow test of inconsistency—which caught only conflicting positive commands and not prohibitions or authorisations—increased the instances of concurrent regulation, favoured the continued operation of state legislation, and limited the power of the Commonwealth to oust state legislation.

Under the second approach, a Commonwealth law and a state law were inconsistent if the Commonwealth law conferred a right, power or privilege, and the state law took away that right (or vice versa), even though it was possible to obey both laws.

These types of inconsistency are generally referred to as instances of direct inconsistency. The third approach to inconsistency—metaphorically defined in terms of a Commonwealth law 'covering the field'—is referred to as indirect inconsistency. In *Clyde Engineering v Cowburn* (1926), **Isaacs** said: 'If … a competent legislature expressly or impliedly evinces its intention to cover the whole field, that is a conclusive test of inconsistency where another legislature assumes to enter to any extent upon the same field.'

This type of inconsistency 'does not lie in the mere coexistence of two laws which are susceptible of simultaneous obedience'; rather it 'depends upon the intention of the [Commonwealth] Legislature to express by its enactment, completely, exhaustively, or exclusively, what shall be the law governing the particular conduct or matter to which its attention is directed': *Ex parte McLean*. A state law that purports to regulate that conduct or matter is regarded as inconsistent with the Commonwealth law and as attracting the operation of section 109. Laws may not be inconsistent on this basis if they relate to different subject matters. Moreover, there is no inconsistency if it appears that the Commonwealth law was intended to be 'supplementary to or cumulative upon' the state law.

The 'covering the field' approach to inconsistency can invalidate state legislation in a broad-brush fashion, even when the Commonwealth legislation is silent on the particular matters regulated by the state law, and can prevent the states from exercising significant parts of their law-making function. It fits well with the centralising tendency of High Court jurisprudence since the *Engineers Case*.

Nonetheless, the Court's adoption of that approach is not the naked embodiment of an institutional preference for central power. All the approaches to inconsistency can be applied in a way that favours either validity or invalidity of state legislation. Like the other approaches, the test of covering the field depends on the Court's identifying the intention of the Commonwealth Parliament: did the Parliament intend to cover the field that the state law is said to have invaded? Similarly, the second approach can be cast in the form: did the Parliament intend to create a right or privilege that the state law is said to alter, impair, or detract from?

Although the Court will give effect to explicit legislative statements that a Commonwealth law is not intended to cover a particular field, more commonly the Parliament's intention is unstated and elusive. The jurisprudence of section 109 therefore leaves ample scope for Justices to project their own centralist or federalist preferences into the reconstruction of the Parliament's intention. Nonetheless, in practice, some **commentators** have argued that the Court has tended to find a parliamentary intention to exclude the operation of state law rather more readily than is necessary. There is more widespread agreement that the Court has failed adequately to descend from lofty **metaphor** to concrete particularity and spell out the way the field of Commonwealth legislation is determined, when an intention to cover that field will be found to exist, and when the state legislation can be said to invade that field.

When section 109 operates, the state law is invalid 'to the extent of the inconsistency'. When the inconsistency ceases to exist—for example, if the inconsistent Commonwealth law is repealed or is amended prospectively to provide that the law is not intended to cover the relevant field—the state law once again operates according to its terms. To this extent, the Court has minimised the invalidating effect of section 109.

However, the Court has held that the Commonwealth cannot remove an inconsistency that has already arisen by *retrospectively* legislating to provide that its laws were not intended to cover the relevant field (or presumably to remove any direct inconsistency). The state law remains invalid unless and until new consistent and retrospective legislation is enacted by the state (and perhaps also by the Commonwealth): *University of Wollongong v Metwally* (1984). *Metwally* provides rare recognition from the Court that section 109 has a role other than 'adjusting the relations between the legislatures of the Commonwealth and the

States'. A bare majority approached section 109 on the footing that it has a role in 'providing a degree of real protection to the citizen faced with the otherwise impossible predicament of contemporaneous and conflicting demands of Commonwealth and State laws'. How sound that is as a general proposition may be doubted when in practice most inconsistency is characterised as being of the 'covering the field' type, which does not depend on establishing that the citizen is faced with such an impossible predicament. Nonetheless, the case shows that occasionally, the High Court is capable of regarding the Constitution as an instrument concerned with individual rights rather than simply as an instrument allocating power between levels of government (see also **Commonwealth–state relations; Federalism**).

SIMON EVANS

Further Reading

Michael Coper, *Encounters with the Australian Constitution* (1987, popular edn 1988) chs 1 and 4

Gregory Craven, 'The Operation of Section 109 of the Commonwealth Constitution', Appendix F to Australian Constitutional Convention, *Fiscal Powers Sub-Committee Report to Standing Committee* (July 1984)

Allan Murray-Jones, 'The Tests for Inconsistency Under Section 109 of the Constitution' (1979) 10 *FL Rev* 25

Gary Rumble, 'The Nature of Inconsistency Under Section 109 of the Constitution' (1980) 11 *FL Rev* 40

Independence, judicial. Judicial independence is an essential attribute of any worthwhile judicial system. More than that, it is also critical to the existence of modern democratic government. Without the guarantee of such independence, the very essence of any justice system—that it be just and fairly administered—cannot be ensured. Moreover, without an independent judiciary, a democratic government, however otherwise guaranteed, is unlikely to long remain democratic.

In Australia, judicial independence owes its origin to the development in England, over the centuries, of the independence of judges as the keepers of the **rule of law**. In the late twelfth century, the royal courts were largely staffed by royal clerks, drawn from the ranks of clerics of the minor religious orders. By the end of the thirteenth century, however, there had come into existence a thriving **legal profession** of barristers. It was from that profession that in the early fourteenth century judges of the royal courts came to be appointed, displacing the royal clerks. The mere fact that English judges were recruited from the profession, and had thus begun their careers not as servants of the Crown but as self-employed members of an independent profession, was evidence of a move towards independence.

Until Queen Mary's reign, the judiciary kept relatively clear of politics and possessed a real measure of independence. All judges—except the barons of the Exchequer, who alone had **tenure** during good behaviour—held office only during royal pleasure; they could be, and were on occasion, dismissed from office if they incurred royal displeasure. In 1640, as a result of parliamentary pressure, all judges began to hold office not during pleasure but during good behaviour, and so it remained throughout the Commonwealth.

However, the restoration of the Stuart monarchy brought with it a return to appointment during pleasure, and both Charles II and James II removed from office numerous judges who displeased them.

On the abdication of James II and the accession of William and Mary, judicial tenure reverted in practice to the holding of office during good behaviour. By the *Act of Settlement 1701*, their commissions were formally expressed to be during good behaviour, their salaries ascertained and established, and their removal being lawful only upon address of both Houses of Parliament. Judicial tenure has remained thus for now almost 300 years. The existence of an independent judiciary has been regarded as a basic principle of England's unwritten Constitution and as a cornerstone of freedom ever since the Act of Settlement. It was from these English origins that section 72 of the Australian Constitution took its inspiration, although it goes further, with its requirement of proven misbehaviour or incapacity as the only ground for **removal** (see also **Murphy affair**).

Judicial independence in the **superior courts** of Australia is primarily ensured by legislation conferring upon judges security of tenure and **remuneration**. Once appointed, judges hold office until reaching the age of **retirement** and may only be removed for misbehaviour or, in the case of the Commonwealth and some states, also for incapacity. The tenure of the Justices of the High Court and of federal superior courts is, if anything, more amply safeguarded. The terms of tenure entrenched in section 72 of the Constitution can be altered only by referendum. Section 72 provides only one means for the removal from office of such a Justice: on an address of both Houses of Parliament on the ground of proven misbehaviour or incapacity. They hold office until retirement, now fixed, in the case of the High Court, at age 70, and their remuneration may not be diminished during their continuance in office.

The ensuring of judicial independence depends, however, on more than security of tenure and of salary. While that security removes obvious sources of influence which might otherwise be brought to bear, much still depends upon the individual Justice and his or her determination to maintain independence and repel all efforts to affect the exercise of impartial **judicial power**.

The essence of judicial independence is that the holders of judicial office be free to render impartial justice in their communities, protected from the power and influence of the state and made as immune as humanly possible from other influences that might affect their impartiality in the **decision-making process**.

The doctrine of the **separation of powers**—a doctrine entrenched in the Constitution in the case of federal courts—powerfully supports judicial independence by operating to strictly separate the federal judiciary from the other two arms of government: the legislature and the executive, the two political arms of government. An important function of the courts of law, including the High Court, is to protect the citizen from unlawful acts of government agencies and public officials. The doctrine of the separation of powers and consequent removal of the judiciary from any association with the other two arms of government leaves the judiciary free to exercise their protective function.

In a federation such as Australia, with a written Constitution, and with the High Court as its interpreter and reviewer of the constitutionality of legislation, the independence of the Justices of that Court is of quite special significance. In *Kable v DPP* (1995), **McHugh** described it as a basic principle of the Australian Constitution 'that the judges of the federal courts must be, and must be perceived to be, independent of the legislative and the executive governments'; and, as **Gaudron** observed in her judgment in *Wilson v Minister for Aboriginal and Torres Strait Islander Affairs* (1996), the judicial power of the Commonwealth must be exercised with an impartiality that is and is seen to be 'completely independent of the legislatures and executive governments of those polities' that make up the federation. In that case, the majority judgment cited Viscount Simonds' statement in the *Boilermakers Case* (1956) that 'in a federal system the absolute independence of the judiciary is the bulwark of the Constitution against encroachment whether by the legislature or by the executive'. The majority judgment in *Wilson* went on to cite the judgment of McHugh in *Harris v Caladine* (1991), emphasising the need for litigants to have their cases decided by judges 'free from potential domination by the legislative and executive branches of government'.

Judicial independence is further supported by the immunity of the judiciary from civil liability for any act done by them in the exercise of the Court's **jurisdiction**, even if it involves gross error. The remedy of someone injured by such an act lies not against the individual judge, but rather through appeal; of course, this immunity does not extend to criminal acts, such as, for example, corruption. This immunity of the judiciary has been explained as ensuring that judges may do their duty with complete independence and free from fear of adverse consequences.

Again, protection of individual Justices from exposure to **criticism** in Parliament supports judicial independence. Standing orders require that no offensive words be used against any member of the judiciary, and the practice has long been that, unless based upon a substantive motion, aspersions should not be cast in debate upon the conduct of a Justice. This has been described as one side of the coin, Justices being required at the same time not to become involved in matters of political controversy. Parliament's regard for this particular immunity from criticism was justified more than 150 years ago by Lord John Russell in the Commons, when he said that the independence of judges was so sacred that nothing but the most imperious necessity should induce the House to adopt a course that might weaken their standing or endanger their authority.

In Australia, both federally and in the states, the **appointment of Justices** has always been a matter for the government of the day. In the case of appointments to the High Court, the **Attorney-General** is required by the *High Court of Australia Act* 1979 (Cth) to consult with state Attorneys-General about any proposed appointment. There has been much recent debate about alternative methods of appointment designed to remove from the act of appointment what some regard as a taint of political influence—and with it, a threat to subsequent judicial independence.

Other **common law** countries have a variety of other systems of appointment of Justices: for instance, by popular election, by the use of advisory judicial appointment commissions, by a requirement for senate approval of appointments, or by a process of independent assessment of proposed appointees. Whether any of these systems would be an improvement on the present system in Australia remains open to debate.

Ninian Stephen

Information technology. The Court has come a long way in its use of information technology, or in the old terminology, 'equipment', since 1903. A perusal of correspondence between the District Registrar in NSW and the Principal Registrar in Melbourne reveals that office requisites then included such items as ink wells, steel nibs for wooden pens, chalk (presumably for the drying of ink), and typewriter ribbon.

Court proceedings and the Register of Practitioners were recorded in traditional leather-bound registers. The entries were made in ink, using steel-ribbed pens, until about 1973, when entries by fountain pen or ball point pen were permitted. The Court's registers were retained until the installation of computer systems in the Registry and in the Justices' **chambers** in the early 1980s.

Judgments were typewritten by secretaries, with carbon copies being taken at the same time. The carbon copies gave way to stencils that could be printed on a hand-operated machine that produced any number of printed ink copies. This form of reproduction of judgments continued into the early 1970s, when it was replaced by the photocopy process.

The photocopier was perhaps the first major technology introduced to the Court. It enabled the more efficient distribution of draft judgments between chambers, and a more rapid dissemination of the Court's judgments to the **legal profession**, the press, and the general public. The photocopier also relieved the pressure on the **library** resources of the Court. Copies could be made of authorities, which enabled Justices to work at home without needing to transport bound law reports to their homes or, even more inconveniently, when they went on **circuit**. As copiers have become more sophisticated, reliance on printed law reports has declined.

The production of judgments was changed from automated typewriters to IBM Magcard machines in the late 1970s. **Barwick** had seen the machines in England during a visit, and had asked IBM to demonstrate them. The Magcard machine used special cards that were sent from the Justices' various chambers. The machine collated the cards, enabling the judgment to be produced as a single continuous judgment, rather than as separate judgments stapled together. The Court introduced computerised word processing in the early 1980s, later moving to stand-alone personal computers. The Justices initially resisted the introduction of a linked network because of what they perceived to be a lack of security in respect of their individual judgments while in draft form.

The Court now uses information technology not only to facilitate its internal operations, but as an important part of its interaction with the public. It has a local area network that connects personal computers in its premises in **Canberra**, Sydney, and Melbourne. The network makes use of 'thin-client' technology to provide remote access to networked applications over standard telephone lines. Word processing applications are used for **research** and in the preparation of judgments. Database applications and web browsers are used to assist in research by Justices' staff and by the library. Other applications (for example, accounting packages) are used by staff in the management of the Court.

The Court's Registry uses a purpose-built case management system that tracks matters from the time the first documents are filed until a decision is handed down and (if necessary) **costs** are taxed. The system also generates standard correspondence from Registry staff to parties, as well as providing statistical data for the Court's **annual reports**. The case management system also holds contact information for the firms that represent parties in cases and for **litigants in person**, and a database of legal practitioners (barristers and solicitors).

Video links, introduced in March 1988, enable **counsel** to appear in a state capital and have their argument **televised** live to the Bench **sitting** in Canberra. After some initial reluctance by counsel, who feared that video links would impact adversely on the style of their oral **argument**, the video link system has been accepted by both the Justices and counsel, and is used regularly throughout the year for applications for special **leave to appeal**, chamber matters, and some administrative matters.

In January 1997, the Court launched an Internet home page <www.highcourt.gov.au>. The site has information about the Court and the Justices, including its annual reports and its business lists. There are also links to judgments and **transcripts** of hearings. These are hosted by the Australasian Legal Information Institute at <www.austlii.edu.au>; the Institute receives e-mailed copies of judgments from the Court minutes after they are handed down, and transcripts soon after they are prepared; it automatically adds hypertext links to legislation and cases referred to in those decisions and transcripts before making them available on the web.

As a consequence of the increased availability of electronic copies of its judgments, the Court adopted paragraph numbering in its judgments from the beginning of 1998 to facilitate 'medium neutral' **citation** of the Court's decisions: that is, citation that does not rely on the pagination of a document by a particular word processing or page layout application.

The Court's case management system has been designed to facilitate future enhancements. If the Court approved it, much of the data held in the system could be regularly published on the Internet. This would allow parties, practitioners, and interested members of the public to follow the progress of cases using a web browser. The system has also been designed with the possibility of the electronic filing of documents in mind. At present, the **High Court Rules** require that parties file documents in paper form at an office of the Registry. If the Court were to approve a change to those Rules, documents could be submitted electronically (by e-mail or using a web browser), stored in the case management system and, once accepted for filing, made publicly available on the Internet with other information about cases. This would make widely and readily available information that is currently publicly available, but only through examination of the Registry's paper files.

The principal area of the Court's activities in which there is still scope for further use of information technology is in the **courtrooms** themselves. Material that is now handed up to the Court in paper form could be electronically made available to the Court during the hearing. The bench and the bar table could also have access to databases of legislation, cases, and articles referred to during the hearing—for individual perusal, or to bring to the attention of all present. The **appeal book** (selected material from the courts below, currently put before the Court in paper form) could also be provided electronically. This would require some standardisation of the electronic document formats used by lower courts, and by the practitioners who appear in them. It would also require a significant change in practice by the Court, whose members have, of course, been used to receiving this material on paper.

FRANK JONES
JAMES POPPLE

Further Reading

Tony de la Fosse, 'The Application of Remote Control Software in a Judicial Environment' (1997) 8 *JLIS* 320

James Popple and Tony de la Fosse, 'Escaping the Relational Database Paradigm: Case Management in the High Court of Australia' (1998) *Proceedings of the Australian Institute of Judicial Administration 'Technology for Justice' Conference*

Inglis Clark, Andrew (*b* 24 February 1848; *d* 14 November 1907). 'So you are not to be one of the High Court Judges', wrote William Harrison Moore to Inglis Clark on 12 October 1906. Harrison Moore continued: 'For many reasons I am sorry. But I fear that you could have taken it too hard, and that the want of any permanent settlement, and the break up of your family life would have left you little of joy in the office. Both **Isaacs** and **Higgins** will I am sure feel this very much'.

Inglis Clark was born in Hobart, the youngest son of Alexander Russell Clark and Ann, née Inglis. His family were of Scottish stock, emigrating to Australia in 1832. Inglis Clark was a frail child who acquired much of his early education at home from his formidable mother. He completed his secondary education at Hobart High School. Initially, he qualified as an engineer and joined the family business; but at 24, he decided that his interests lay in the law, and was articled to the **Solicitor-General**, Robert Adams. In 1877, he was called to the Bar.

The 1870s marked an important period in the young lawyer's life. He converted from the family's Baptist heritage to Unitarianism and began to promote his progressive ideas through the pages of his short-lived journal, *Quadrilateral*. He was prominent in a number of clubs and societies and championed progressive ideas on moral and social issues.

In 1878, he decided to enter politics, and stood for the electorate of Norfolk Plains. His nomination was heralded by the Hobart *Mercury* in less than effusive terms: 'Mr AI Clark will be a candidate as a rising young lawyer—very young, some 17 months standing, and is credited with holding such very ultra-republican, if not revolutionary, ideas that we should hardly think he will prove acceptable to the electors of Norfolk Plains.'

Inglis Clark was elected unopposed. He rejected the *Mercury's* claim that he was 'one who finds his proper place in a band of Communists', replying that he 'believed in the theory of Government which was propounded by the late A Lin-coln—"Government of the people, for the people, and by the people"'.

As a backbencher, in 1880 Inglis Clark introduced a number of private member's Bills in an attempt to reform the *Master and Servant Act* 1856 (Tas) and Tasmanian criminal law. He lost his seat in Parliament at the 1882 election and was unsuccessful in East Hobart in 1884 and 1886.

Out of Parliament, Inglis Clark established himself at the Bar in a number of criminal and civil matters. His reputation as a reformer continued to expand as he founded the Southern Tasmanian Political Reform Association.

In 1887, he was elected in a by-election to the seat of South Hobart and became **Attorney-General** in the Phillip Fysh government—a position he held until 1892. He was again Attorney-General to the Braddon government from 1894 to 1897. Consistent with his activities outside the Assembly, he set about implementing a law reform agenda that included amendment of the Master and Servant Act, legalisation of trade unions, and reform of the electoral system (the introduction of the 'Hare–Clark' system). In all, Inglis Clark initiated over 150 ministerial Bills in his short parliamentary career, 'one less than Sir Henry Parkes during his whole career'.

Inglis Clark's interest in federation was theoretical as well as practical. The customs walls that impeded interstate trade would have been evident from the activities of the family business. As a lawyer, he was keenly aware of the limitations associated with a colonial Australia. Writing to **Barton** in 1889, he noted the obstacles that Parkes had placed in the way of federation. However, he noted, 'his day of authority and obstruction will come to an end like that of other Ministers, and … I have no doubt that you will then be in a position to effectually assist the cause of Australasian federation'. In the same letter, Inglis Clark raised the failures of colonial administrations to deal with joint stock companies, executor and trustee companies, and deceased estates with property in several colonies, as well as the need for mutual recognition of the orders of other colonial jurisdictions.

Federation was in the air in 1890. Inglis Clark joined the delegates from the other colonies assembled in Melbourne for the Federation Conference. He made a bold push for the American constitutional model, rather than the Canadian model (the *British North America Act* 1867 (Imp)). In doing so, he was at odds with **Griffith**, one of two delegates from Queensland.

In 1891, Inglis Clark represented Tasmania in the **Privy Council** appeal from *Main Line Railway v The Queen* (1889). The appeal was settled, but gave him an opportunity to observe at first hand the 'grand and august tribunal' where 'only one of the judges was awake and the other three were all dozing'.

Inglis Clark's preference for the USA as a federal template is not surprising. As Alfred **Deakin** noted, it was 'a country to which in spirit he belonged'. He was consumed by all things American and studied its history, law, and politics. His three visits to the USA established friendship with leading public figures including Oliver Wendell Holmes Jr, with whom he corresponded. It is said that his adulation of Holmes extended to the installation of a window from Holmes' house into the study of Inglis Clark's Battery Point house in Hobart.

Andrew Inglis Clark, who was considered for appointment to the first High Court

The decision to proceed to a larger **Convention** in Sydney in 1891 provided his finest hour. Prior to the Convention, Inglis Clark had prepared a complete draft Constitution for consideration by the delegates. It became a critical foundation upon which the drafting process was built. At the Convention, he chaired the Judiciary Committee, where he oversaw the design of his precious High Court. He was adamant that the Court should be the final arbiter of Australian law and condemned attempts to retain appeals to the Privy Council. With Griffith and Charles Kingston, Inglis Clark made up the Drafting Committee that laboured over the Constitution. The Committee's work included revising the draft Constitution on the famous voyage of the *Lucinda*, but ill health prevented Inglis Clark's attendance for most of it. In later years, Inglis Clark lamented the way that the 'picnic on the pleasure yacht' had 'messed' with his clauses relating to the judicature.

After 1891, federation was put by until 1897. Inglis Clark returned to Tasmanian politics and continued his reforming efforts. He was not a candidate for election to the second Federal Convention at Adelaide in 1897. Why he declined what would have been certain election remains something of a mystery.

His failure to attend in Adelaide did not prevent him from taking a close interest in the events. He corresponded with delegates, and through the Tasmanian Parliament offered numerous amendments, including the proposal of a protection for the citizens of Australia modelled on the US Fourteenth Amendment (see **Bill of Rights**).

Disillusionment with the financial clauses of the draft Constitution, coupled with his appointment to the Supreme

Court of Tasmania in 1898, meant that Inglis Clark remained silent during the referendum campaigns. It was this partial withdrawal from the cause that allowed writers such as Deakin and Bernhard Wise to underplay Inglis Clark's role in the federation process.

Outside the law, Inglis Clark developed a close following among Tasmania's liberal thinkers. His home in Battery Point, with its well-stocked library, was a meeting place where vibrant intellectual exchanges took place. Inglis Clark's sympathies were republican; according to his son, they were 'early formed [and] strengthened with the years'.

Inglis Clark's interest in the development of the Constitution included his decisions as a Supreme Court judge in a number of constitutional matters before the **establishment** of the High Court. In *Pedder v D'Emden* (1903), he held in dissent that Tasmania could not require Commonwealth public servants to pay stamp duty on their salaries. He supported the **Griffith Court's** developments of the doctrines of **intergovernmental immunities** and **reserved state powers**, writing to Griffith to congratulate him on the Court's early decisions. His *Studies in Australian Constitutional Law*, first published in 1901, linked the development of Australian **constitutional law** to its American precedents, and has often been cited by the High Court (see, for example, **Dixon**, **McTiernan**, **Fullagar**, and **Kitto** in the *Boilermakers Case* (1956), **Stephen** in the *BLF Case* (1982), **McHugh** in the *War Crimes Act Case* (1991), and **Gleeson**, **Gummow**, and **Hayne** in *Sue v Hill* (1999)). In particular, Inglis Clark promulgated a 'living force' approach to **constitutional interpretation**. This approach has been influential among a number of High Court Justices, and remains a dynamic source of constitutional method (see **Deane** in *Theophanous v Herald & Weekly Times* (1994), **Toohey** in *McGinty v WA* (1996), and **Kirby** in *Eastman v The Queen* (2000)).

In 1903, Inglis Clark was tentatively offered a position on the High Court. However, the decision to reduce the **number of Justices** from five to three meant that he was unsuccessful (see **Appointments that might have been**). He was considered again in 1906.

Patrick Glynn wrote of Inglis Clark's sense of occasion at the inauguration of the Commonwealth in 1901. For Inglis Clark, 'his nationality had been created or won, not acquired'. It is fitting that Deane in *Theophanous* described Inglis Clark as the 'primary architect of our Constitution'.

JOHN WILLIAMS

Further Reading

Marcus Haward and James Warden (eds), *An Australian Democrat: The Life, Work, and Consequence of Andrew Inglis Clark* (1996)

Andrew Inglis Clark, *Studies in Australian Constitutional Law* (1901, reprinted 1997)

FM Neasey, 'Andrew Inglis Clark Senior and Australian Federation' (1969) 15 *Australian J of Pol and Hist* 1

John Reynolds, 'AI Clark's American Sympathies and his Influences on Australian Federation' (1958) 32 *ALJ* 62

John Williams, '"With Eyes Open": Andrew Inglis Clark and Our Republican Tradition' (1995) 23 *FL Rev* 149

Intergovernmental immunities. All federal systems give rise to complex and subtle issues concerning the legal relationships between their component parts. One of the most vexed of those issues in Australia and elsewhere has been the extent to which the parties to the federation can make laws binding on each other: can the nation pass laws binding on the states, and can the states pass laws binding on the nation?

Although the text of the US Constitution was silent on the matter, the answer given in nineteenth-century America was clear: using the model of **sovereign** states at **international law**, Chief Justice John Marshall held in *McCulloch v Maryland* (1819) that a state had no power to tax the operations of the national bank in the state. The controversy generated by this invented limitation on the power of the states abated somewhat when Marshall's reasoning was later extended for the benefit of the states and converted into a reciprocal immunity from national law (*Collector v Day* (1870)).

The text of the Australian Constitution was not silent on the matter—in section 114, the Commonwealth and the states were forbidden to tax each other's **property**—and this specific restriction could easily have been seen as an exception to an otherwise general rule against immunity. But the early High Court picked up Marshall's idea as well as his reasoning, and in the first constitutional case of *D'Emden v Pedder* (1904), **Griffith**, **Barton**, and **O'Connor** held unanimously—reversing the Supreme Court of Tasmania (**Inglis Clark** dissenting)—that Tasmania could not lawfully impose stamp duty on forms signed by Commonwealth public servants in acknowledgement of receipt of their salary. Section 114 would have to be regarded not as an exception to, but as an example of, the general rule.

Shortly afterwards, the **Griffith Court** held further—this time reversing the Supreme Court of Victoria and overruling a previous decision of that court (*Wollaston's Case* (1902))—that the states could not impose income tax upon the income of Commonwealth public servants (*Deakin v Webb* (1904)). Then followed one of the most celebrated clashes in Australian judicial history. In 1906, an appeal was taken from the Supreme Court of Victoria direct to the **Privy Council**, which held that Commonwealth public servants *were* liable to state income tax (*Webb v Outtrim* (1906)). In a decision handed down 11 days later, the High Court ignored *Webb v Outtrim* altogether, affirmed the immunities doctrine, and indeed extended it by making it reciprocal, holding Commonwealth industrial law to be inapplicable to state railway employees (*Railway Servants Case* (1906)). Then, in mid-1907, the High Court again held—though now with the dissenting voices of **Isaacs** and **Higgins**—that the states could not tax Commonwealth public servants: *Baxter v Commissioners of Taxation (NSW)* (1907). Despite the fundamental doctrinal difference between them, the High Court Justices were united in their view that the issue was no business of the Privy Council (see *Inter se* questions). Amendments were made to the *Judiciary Act* 1903 (Cth) in an endeavour to cut off appeals direct from **state Supreme Courts**, and *Webb v Outtrim* continued to be either ignored or distinguished. Ironically, the Privy Council decision anticipated the rejection of the immunity doctrine in the watershed *Engineers Case* in 1920, but it proceeded largely on the basis that the King could disallow inappropriate statutes—a ground that even then was both theoretical and repugnant.

The early Griffith Court was comfortable, as the Marshall Court had been in the USA, in going beyond the language of the Constitution to draw broad implications from the nature and structure of federal government. Griffith and Barton did so outside the context of intergovernmental immunities in *R v Smithers; Ex parte Benson* (1912), where they implied a citizen's right of access, involving freedom of **movement**, to the institutions of the national government. But it suited Isaacs' curious combination of **literalism** as an interpretive methodology and nationalism as a political **ideology** to disavow the doctrine of implied immunities, and in the *Engineers Case*—by which time Griffith, Barton, and O'Connor had all gone—he led the majority (**Gavan Duffy** dissenting) in holding that Commonwealth industrial law did apply to the employees of WA state sawmills and engineering works.

The Court also took the opportunity to overturn the Griffith Court's doctrine of **reserved state powers**. This, in combination with the Court's liberation of the Commonwealth from the implied restriction on its ability to apply its laws to the states (and also, in *McArthur's Case* (1920), from the guarantee in section 92 of the freedom of **interstate trade**), left the Commonwealth poised, in the period of growth in Australian national identity following **World War I**, to exploit its legislative powers to the full. Yet a period of conservative government followed, and when **Commonwealth legislative powers** were next seriously tested by the Labor governments of the 1940s, a differently composed Court in 1947 breathed life back into the doctrine of implied immunity—and a year later reapplied section 92—so as to thwart completely the Commonwealth's post-**World War II** plans for restructuring the banking system through centralisation (*Melbourne Corporation Case* (1947)) and then nationalisation (*Bank Nationalisation Case* (1948)).

In *Engineers*, Isaacs had stressed the importance of giving effect to the express words of the Constitution, superimposing no qualifications based on vague implications derived from extraneous political theory, either as to the explicit powers of the Commonwealth (the reach of which should not be restricted by vague assumptions about the intended scope of state power) or as to the explicit restrictions on those powers (the exercise of which should not be further restricted by vague notions of political necessity). Despite his strong association with the more subtle tenets of **legalism**, **Dixon** was never a proponent of Isaacs' brand of literalism; indeed, according to Geoffrey Sawer, he 'disliked *Engineers*; its literary style set his teeth on edge, and he never mentioned it without a touch of asperity'. In *Melbourne Corporation*, Dixon led the Court in reinventing a modified form of the implied immunity of the states from Commonwealth law. The Commonwealth, in the exercise of its express powers, could neither single out the states (or a state) for special treatment (the 'non-**discrimination**' rule), nor, according to some Justices—even in a law of general application—threaten the existence of the states (or a state) or impair their capacity to function. Accordingly, a majority held, applying the non-discrimination rule, that the Commonwealth, by a law otherwise within its power in section 51(xiii) of the Constitution to legislate with respect to banking, could not compel the states to bank with the Commonwealth Bank.

The non-discrimination rule has since had further authoritative explication and application in *Queensland Electricity Commission v Commonwealth* (1985)—different procedures could not be applied by the Commonwealth to expedite the resolution of industrial disputes involving state instrumentalities—and the more controversial general limb of the post-*Engineers* immunity was first applied unambiguously in *Re Australian Education Union; Ex parte Victoria* (1995): the Commonwealth could not, in the course of resolving an industrial dispute, control hiring and firing in the state public service or regulate the terms and conditions of senior state public servants.

The Griffith Court saw the immunity as reciprocal, and the Court in *Engineers* appeared to see its abolition in the same terms. But if Dixon was uncomfortable with the unqualified literalism of *Engineers* in relation to the ability of the Commonwealth to bind the states, he was even more uncomfortable with the idea that the states could bind the Commonwealth. Dissenting in *Uther's Case* (1947), he observed that:

> The Colony of New South Wales could not be said at the establishment of the Commonwealth to have any power at all with reference to the Commonwealth. Like the goddess of wisdom the Commonwealth *uno ictu* sprang from the brain of its begetters armed and of full stature. At the same instant the Colonies became States; but whence did the States obtain the power to regulate the legal relations of this new polity with its subjects? It formed no part of the old colonial power. The Federal constitution does not give it.

Significantly, Dixon avoided the language of immunity and approached the issue squarely in terms of a lack of state power. One may doubt whether, as a matter of logic, his argument from historical impossibility is compelling; but his view was vindicated, and *Uther* overruled, when the Court held in the *Cigamatic Case* (1962) that the states could not alter the priority of the Commonwealth in the order of payment of debts in a company winding up. Despite **criticism**, the decision withstood a full-frontal challenge in *Henderson's Case* (1997), a majority (**Kirby** dissenting) seeking to make palatable its anarchic mandate for the exemption of the Commonwealth from state legal systems with an elusive, if not incomprehensible, distinction between state law affecting the capacities of the Commonwealth (invalid) and state law affecting the exercise of those capacities (valid).

The original doctrine of reciprocal immunity, based as it was upon a doubtful analogy with sovereign states at **international law**, was rather unsophisticated and, although arguably appropriate in the political climate of the nascent Commonwealth, also—if applied in its full rigour—somewhat impractical. Thus, it was not surprising that even the Griffith Court had carved out exceptions: Commonwealth customs duty applied to goods imported by a state (*A-G (NSW) v Collector of Customs (NSW)* (1908)); the Commonwealth could waive its immunity from state law (*Chaplin v Commissioner of Taxes (SA)* (1911)); and a state could be bound by Commonwealth law if it was acting in a 'trading' capacity rather than a 'governmental' capacity (*Engine-Drivers Case* (1913)). These exceptions perhaps prepared the ground for the overthrow of the doctrine in *Engineers*, which replaced it with the opposite assumption of the absence of immunity. The *Engineers* thesis was as singular and uncom-

plicated as its antithesis had been in *D'Emden v Pedder*, but its threefold justification for the absence of an implied restriction on the Commonwealth was powerful: give the text its natural meaning; let the nation prosper; and let not the Justices lightly interfere with the wishes of the democratically elected legislatures and the operation of the political process.

Nevertheless, each justification adduced a persuasive response, as Dixon and others engaged in their more sophisticated overlay of exceptions, qualifications, and modified assumptions. Words must take their meaning from their context, and *Engineers* had itself relied freely on the Constitution's implicit assumption of **responsible government**; the argument for integration of the nation, however desirable, could not ignore the federal nature of the Constitution; and, taken too far, judicial self-restraint would amount to an abdication of the Court's duty to uphold the Constitution.

Ultimately, an assessment of the record of the Court in relation to intergovernmental immunities turns on the legitimacy of constitutional implications and the **role** of the Justices. It is probably common ground that implications are unavoidable in **constitutional interpretation**; the real question is whether, in each case, they are persuasive. In relation to recent developments in **implied constitutional rights**, reasonable minds may differ. So, too, with implications from **federalism**—although the case for judicial protection of the states from a predatory Commonwealth is probably stronger than the case for judicial immunisation of the Commonwealth government and its agencies from state law, given that the Commonwealth can always protect itself by legislation that will prevail over **inconsistent** state law under section 109 of the Constitution. Even in its modern guise, the doctrine of implied intergovernmental immunities is a controversial judicial invention, which, at least in its more extreme forms, arguably pays insufficient attention to two principles: first, that all governments should be subject generally to the law (see **Rule of law**) and, secondly, that not every political problem must have a judicial solution.

MICHAEL COPER

Further Reading

Lawrence Claus, 'Federalism and the Judges: How the Americans Made Us What We Are' (2000) 74 *ALJ* 107

Michael Coper and George Williams (eds), *How Many Cheers for Engineers?* (1997)

Henry Higgins, '*McCulloch v Maryland* in Australia' (1905) 18 *Harvard Law Review* 550

RP Meagher and WMC Gummow, 'Sir Owen Dixon's Heresy' (1980) 54 *ALJ* 25

Ronald Sackville, 'The Doctrine of Immunity of Instrumentalities in the United States and Australia: A Comparative Analysis' (1969) 7 *MULR* 15

Intergovernmental immunities and judicial reasoning. In the *Engineers Case* (1920), the Court **overruled** the doctrines of implied immunity of instrumentalities and **reserved state powers**. Both doctrines were created by the **Griffith Court**— the former having its origins in *D'Emden v Pedder* (1904) and the latter in *Peterswald v Bartley* (1904), as more fully elaborated by **Griffith** in the *Union Label Case* (1908).

The 'implied immunity' doctrine reflected John Austin's understanding of **sovereignty** in *The Province of Jurisprudence Determined* (1832) as requiring a determinate superior which does not itself owe obedience to any other superior. Translated literally into the Australian context, this would have meant that neither level of government could be subject to any interference whatsoever by the other, and that each was absolutely immune from the other's laws. Although the Griffith Court was soon forced to acknowledge exceptions to these immunities, the Austinian conception remained at their base.

Significantly, this conception was treated as *implied* in the Constitution, and for this very reason the Court in the *Engineers Case* felt able to overrule the earlier cases as depending on 'a vague, individual conception' of the 'spirit' of the Constitution. Yet, simultaneously, the Court insisted that the Constitution be interpreted by reference not only to its actual language but to 'acknowledged **common law** constitutional principle[s]', thus substituting one vague method of interpretation for another. Moreover, the new reasoning relied in part on the principle of '**responsible government**'—an implication in its own right.

Dixon obviously did not regard *Engineers* as prohibiting him from making implications in the Constitution. Building on exceptions and qualifications in the very text of the *Engineers Case* itself, he reaffirmed intergovernmental immunities in cases involving the royal prerogative; or the impact on state legislative and executive powers of particular Commonwealth powers such as **taxation**; or **discrimination** by one level of government against another (which the relevant passage in *Engineers* had contrasted with laws 'which apply to the whole community, without discrimination'). In the *ARU Case* (1930), he restated *Engineers* in these terms, and in *West v Commissioner of Taxation* (1937) he used language from **Isaacs'** dissent in *Pirrie v McFarlane* (1925) to support his restatement.

In this, as in his repeated insistence on limiting *Engineers* to what it actually decided, he demonstrated the classic common law technique by which Justices are able to follow **precedent** and yet to change the law. In context, the passage from *Pirrie v McFarlane* had been used by Isaacs to reaffirm a rigorous literal interpretation of the Constitution, whereas Dixon used it to support the making of implications. Yet each of their approaches claimed a source in *Engineers*.

The key unlocking Dixon's understanding of intergovernmental immunities was his command of language—his ability to drive and direct it. Yet it took him years of patient reworking to refine his version of intergovernmental immunities: only with the *Cigamatic Case* (1962) was his work complete.

In the wartime context of the first *Uniform Tax Case* (1942)—and in Dixon's absence—only **Starke** was prepared to make an implication denying the Commonwealth's power effectively to deprive the states of their ability to levy income tax. But in the post-war context of the *Melbourne Corporation Case* (1947), **Rich**, Starke, and Dixon each formulated separate tests to limit Commonwealth power over the states. Dixon elaborated on the discrimination element of his trilogy of exceptions to *Engineers*, finding that a Commonwealth law, even if validly made under an express power in the Constitution, will be invalid if it 'discriminates against States, or ... place[s] a particular disability or burden upon

an operation or activity of a State, and more especially upon the execution of its constitutional powers'. Starke rejected a test based on the concept of discrimination, finding that legislative or executive action by either level of government would be invalid if it 'curtails or interferes in a substantial manner with the exercise of constitutional power by the other'. Rich saw the implied immunity as arising in 'two classes of case': a Commonwealth law will be invalid if it 'singles out the States or [their] agencies' and imposes on them restrictions that prevent or impede them from performing 'the normal and essential functions of government'; or alternatively, if its general application would have that effect when applied to the states or their agencies.

In a Court of six, these three Justices decided that the challenged law was invalid on the basis that it infringed their respective versions of the states' implied immunity. **Latham** and **Williams** agreed in the result, but on different grounds.

The individual approaches in *Melbourne Corporation* differed markedly from that of the Griffith Court. For that Court, the implied immunities doctrine was a two-way doctrine, immunising each level of government to the same extent against interference by the other. For Rich, Starke, and Dixon, it is *constitutional power* that is being protected—as distinct from any activity that is governmental or happens to be conducted by a government officer. Starke's test is still a two-way test; yet it differs from the Griffith Court's approach by stressing that only 'substantial' interference with one level of government by the other will be invalid. Dixon tailors his test to apply to specific laws 'singling out governments and placing special burdens upon the exercise' of their constitutional functions, while Rich's test applies to both specific and general Commonwealth laws (the former 'singling out governments', the latter if they impose 'special burdens').

Yet Rich's test did not resolve a problem that had plagued the Griffith Court: that of identifying a distinction between essential and non-essential functions of government. And the tests devised by Dixon and Starke introduced new problems—in Starke's case, the formula to be used in deciding how much interference was 'substantial', and in Dixon's case, the meaning to be ascribed to the concept of 'discrimination' when applied to laws dealing only with one class of persons without reference to the treatment of any comparable person or class. None of these problems was made any easier when in the *Payroll Tax Case* (1971) **Gibbs** acknowledged the difficulty of the tests proposed by Rich and Starke, and found that while Dixon's test should be accepted, its focus on the effect of specific laws on the states was too narrow, since this was not the only way discrimination against the states could manifest itself. He found that 'a general law of the Commonwealth which would prevent a State from continuing to exist and function' would also be invalid. Implicit in his test of invalidity relating to general laws was an insight into the way their application may give rise to issues of formal and substantive inequality. Less satisfactory was his conclusion that the test of invalidity was 'to some extent' a matter of degree—so that, in the context of the legislation in its entirety, even specific provisions that formally discriminated between state and non-state employers did not impose such a 'special burden' as to be unacceptable.

In the *Tasmanian Dam Case* (1983) and *Queensland Electricity Commission v Commonwealth* (1985), **Mason** reduced the different approaches in *Melbourne Corporation* to an explicitly two-tiered test that has since been accepted as authoritative. The first tier is a translation of Dixon's 'discrimination' test; the second, prohibiting legislation that 'inhibits or impairs the continued existence of a state or its capacity to function', is a translation of Starke's approach; and the bifurcation into 'two classes of case' is drawn from Rich. In *Tasmanian Dam*, the state's claim to immunity was rejected on the basis of the second tier, while in *Queensland Electricity*, Queensland's claim to immunity succeeded on the basis of the first. In *Re Australian Education Union; Ex parte Victoria* (1995), issues arose under both tiers; and while the state had some success on the second tier, it failed on the first.

In focusing the second tier on a state's 'capacity to function', Mason in *Tasmanian Dam* distinguished between this 'capacity' and the mere 'functions' through which it is exercised, permitting the Commonwealth to interfere with the latter but not with the former. The language of 'capacity' and 'functions' can be traced back to Isaacs' dissent in *Pirrie v McFarlane*, as reinterpreted by Dixon in *West's Case*—though, interestingly enough, neither Isaacs nor Dixon had thought to contrast the two terms in this way. **Dawson** in *Australian Education Union* rejected such a distinction for its artificiality, while the majority went one step further, translating the state's 'capacity to function' as preserving its 'integrity' or 'autonomy'. For Dixon in *Melbourne Corporation*, what was protected was simply 'the State's exercise of its executive power'.

More broadly, the protection of the states from discrimination and from interference with their capacity to function derives from a judicial concern to preserve their existence as constitutional polities. In 1901, section 107 of the Constitution had declared that state legislative powers 'shall … continue'; and the Griffith Court had treated that as if it were an express grant of power. After the *Engineers Case*, that interpretation of section 107 was no longer tenable—as Dixon repeatedly insisted. He rested the implied protection of the states not on their powers, but on 'their position as separate governments in the system exercising independent functions'.

The Griffith Court had postulated a balanced relationship between Commonwealth and states, with equal and reciprocal immunities. Dixon recognised that such a relationship of **equality** was impossible (although a somewhat confused passage in *West's Case* suggests that at that time, he assumed the reciprocal operation of a single undifferentiated principle). The express grants of **Commonwealth legislative power** in section 51 of the Constitution, the grants of *exclusive* Commonwealth power in section 52, the merely residual nature of state powers under sections 107 and 108, and above all, the capacity of Commonwealth laws to override **inconsistent** state laws under section 109, all pointed, in his view, to an inherently unequal relationship in which the Commonwealth has supremacy.

For Dixon, therefore, the impact of Commonwealth laws on the states and vice versa 'are two quite different questions … affected by considerations that are not the same'. In *Melbourne Corporation*, his position was that the states' implied immunity was relevant only when the law in question was

properly characterised as falling within Commonwealth legislative power. In *Uther's Case* (1947), he insisted in dissent that in areas of Commonwealth immunity, the states simply lacked legislative power.

These areas of Commonwealth immunity were defined in Dixon's *Uther* judgment partly by reference to the royal prerogative, but primarily by reference to the states' inability to affect 'the rights or privileges … of the Commonwealth in relation to [its] subjects'. In *Cigamatic*, when Dixon's advocacy of Commonwealth immunity was accepted as the majority view, his reference to prerogative rights was translated (in language he thought more suited to 'modern times') into a reference to 'the fiscal rights of government'; but his fundamental argument remained that the states could not 'directly derogate from the rights of the Commonwealth with respect to its people'. Apart from these clues, Dixon did little to describe the area of Commonwealth immunity from state legislative power, instead reiterating a series of instances of what it is not.

Since 1962 the *Cigamatic* doctrine has never been applied by the Court, and there has been no unanimity in identifying the area of Commonwealth immunity. Dixon—with notable support from **Fullagar** in *Commonwealth v Bogle* (1953)—had been concerned to ensure that the states did not interfere with the Commonwealth's 'legal relations … with its subjects'; but this did not give the Commonwealth total immunity from state laws, since both Dixon and Fullagar conceded that the Commonwealth could be 'affected by' state laws. Again, however, this was a distinction wracked by difficulties.

In *Henderson's Case* (1997), Dawson, **Toohey**, and **Gaudron**, in a **joint judgment**, performed consecutive linguistic somersaults in order to bring *Cigamatic* into line with *Melbourne Corporation*. First, they introduced a distinction between 'the capacities of the Crown … and the exercise of those capacities'—equating this with Dixon's use in *West's Case* of Isaacs' phrase 'capacity or functions', and extending it to his *Cigamatic* conception of the 'legal rights of the Commonwealth in relation to its subjects'. The distinction between the Commonwealth's 'capacities' (which the states cannot regulate) and their exercise (which they may) appears to mirror Mason's distinction in *Tasmanian Dam* and *Queensland Electricity* between states' 'capacity to function' and their functions, and thus to suggest that what is protected is the same in each case.

Secondly, they insisted that the 'fundamental principle' was the same in *Cigamatic* as in *Melbourne Corporation*, though conceding that 'the application of the principle' was necessarily different. Yet although their explanation of different 'applications' closely followed Dixon's judgment in *Uther*, his purpose was to show that the starting points for limits on state and Commonwealth power are inherently unequal.

Lastly, they recast Dixon's conception of 'the legal rights of the Commonwealth in relation to its subjects' in the language of equality and discrimination. They argued that the *relationship* between the Commonwealth and its subjects was sometimes one of equality and sometimes not. Where the relationship is one of equality the states may regulate the Commonwealth along with its subjects, but may not 'discriminate' against it. Where the relationship is rendered unequal by Commonwealth power or privilege, any state law must accept and accommodate that unequal situation.

Other members of the Court found it difficult to accept this reduction of the differences between *Cigamatic* and *Melbourne Corporation* to a unified whole. Even **Brennan**, who accepted a distinction between 'capacities and functions' and their exercise, protested that, in a case where the Commonwealth claimed immunity from state legislation, the *Melbourne Corporation* principle could have no application, since that principle 'is irrelevant to the scope of any State legislative power'. **Kirby**, in dissent, called for *Cigamatic* to be overruled so that *Melbourne Corporation* could have a two-way operation. It would seem to be only in that way that the two immunities—Commonwealth against state and state against Commonwealth—could be convincingly unified.

FRANCESCA DOMINELLO

International Bill of Rights. This expression is used to describe not one document but a collection of UN instruments dealing with human rights. It comprises the Universal Declaration of Human Rights (UDHR), the International Covenant on Civil and Political Rights (ICCPR), and the International Covenant on Economic, Social, and Cultural Rights (ICESCR). Particular rights within these instruments and their application to particular groups have been made the subject of further human rights instruments including the Convention on the Elimination of all Forms of Discrimination Against Women (CEDAW), the Convention on the Elimination of all Forms of Racial Discrimination (CERD), the Convention on the Rights of the Child (CROC), and the Convention Against Torture (CAT).

The earliest connection between the High Court and the International Bill of Rights was indirect. One of its former members, **Evatt**, was President of the General Assembly at the time of the UDHR's adoption in December 1948. At that time, Evatt declared, in welcoming the UDHR, that it would become an inspirational touchstone for millions of **men**, **women**, and **children**. Yet despite this connection and Australia's close involvement with the drafting of the international instruments, High Court members have shown little enthusiasm for extensively quoting from or using the international guarantees. Preferring to rely on articulations of traditional freedoms recognised in the **common law**, the Court's use of the International Bill of Rights has remained isolated and sporadic.

In the period from **World War II** until the 1970s, only one Justice cited the UDHR in a judgment. In *R v Wallis* (1949), as early as six months after the adoption of the UDHR, **Latham** referred in passing to its protection of the right to belong to an association and the right not to be compelled to do so. The issue in *Wallis* was whether the Commonwealth *Conciliation and Arbitration Act* 1904 authorised an award that gave a monopoly of employment in an industry to the members of a union. The Court concluded that it did not, the power under section 56 of the Act being limited to the granting of preference in employment. Latham referred to the UDHR to support his contention that closed-shop policies involved complex issues extending beyond industrial relations, while emphasising that the declaration was not part of the law of Australia.

It was not until the late 1970s that another Justice, **Murphy**, made frequent reference to international standards of human rights in his judgments. In dissent in *Dugan v Mirror Newspapers* (1978)—a case dealing with whether the English doctrine of civil death formed part of the common law—Murphy drew upon the ICCPR's articulation of **equality** before the law and right of access to tribunals. Similarly, in *Dowal v Murray* (1978), Murphy quoted from the UDHR and ICCPR provisions concerning the welfare of children to support his interpretation of the **Commonwealth legislative powers** over **marriage** and **external affairs**, while in *R v Director-General of Social Welfare (Vic); Ex parte Henry* (1975), he cited provisions of the Declaration on the Rights of the Child as part of the background against which to read provisions dealing with the guardianship of children.

With Australia's ratification of the ICCPR and ICESCR in 1980 and 1975 respectively, and the ensuing legislative program embarked upon by Commonwealth and state parliaments to implement these obligations, the Court's consideration of the domestic implications of the International Bill of Rights has increased. This trend has been pronounced in relation to **race** and **immigration** issues. In *Koowarta's Case* (1982), for instance, the Court upheld the validity of the *Racial Discrimination Act* 1975 (Cth) as an exercise of the 'external affairs' power of the Commonwealth, given that it implemented the obligations within CERD. In so doing, the Court, particularly **Stephen**, recognised the global concern with human rights matters and displayed a receptiveness to considering non-treaty international human rights obligations (those within customary **international law** such as the prohibitions of genocide and slavery). Obligations within CERD were also the subject of examination in the case of *Gerhardy v Brown* (1985)—in particular, the concepts of equality and special measures as adopted in the Racial Discrimination Act.

In developing the concepts of 'relevant considerations' and **natural justice** in **administrative law**, the Court has also displayed an increasing openness to human rights obligations under international instruments. In *Kioa v West* (1985), for instance, the Court held that decision makers were entitled to have regard to international obligations as relevant considerations, but were not bound to do so. In *Teoh's Case* (1995), the Court went further, and stated that Australia's ratification of various international instruments (in that case, CROC) and the undertaking of international obligations therein gave rise to a **legitimate expectation** that administrative decision makers would make decisions that accorded with those international obligations. Where decision makers intended to make a decision contrary to those obligations, the applicant was entitled to a hearing on the matter of that intention. Although stopping short of mandating that decisions be in accordance with international obligations (including human rights), *Teoh* demonstrated the indirect impact of international human rights standards on the administration of government.

The most innovative use of the International Bill of Rights in recent years similarly involved the issue of racial **discrimination** and displayed the potentially transformative effect of international human rights norms on the common law. In *Mabo* (1992), as part of his explanation for the rejection of *terra nullius* and recognition of **native title, Brennan** approved recourse to international standards of human rights in developing the common law:

> The opening up of the International Covenant on Civil and Political Rights brings to bear on the common law the powerful influence of the Covenant and the international standards it imports. The common law does not necessarily conform with international law, but international law is a legitimate and important influence on the development of the common law, especially when international law declares the existence of universal human rights.

The ICCPR has also been quoted in cases such as *Dietrich v The Queen* (1992) to support particular interpretations of the right to a fair trial.

Perhaps more than any other Justice, **Kirby** has carried on from Murphy in using the International Bill of Human Rights in a creative fashion, asserting in particular its relevance to **constitutional interpretation**. While the majority of the Court have resisted using this source for functions other than the interpretation of legislation or the development of the common law, Kirby has concluded that where a question of constitutional interpretation is fairly evenly divided, international norms are a legitimate source of help in resolving the interpretive question (see *Newcrest Mining v Commonwealth* (1997); *Hindmarsh Island Bridge Case* (1998)). Given Kirby's frequent commendation of the Bangalore Principles, which advocate the integration of international human rights norms into domestic legal systems, it is likely that his use of such standards will continue to develop.

Equally revealing are the situations in which the Court has not referred to international standards of human rights. Particularly neglected have been economic, social, and cultural rights under the ICESCR. No reference, for instance, has been made to the right to social security in interpreting social security legislation in such landmark cases as *Green v Daniels* (1977). Given that in *Mabo*, Brennan justified recourse to international human rights standards in part by noting that Australia, in ratifying the Optional Protocol to the ICCPR, had accepted the jurisdiction of the UN Human Rights Committee to consider individual complaints of breaches of civil and political rights, the absence of an individual complaints mechanism for the ICESCR might have been thought to provide a possible explanation for the distinct treatment of ICESCR rights. However, this distinction is not persuasive in light of the Court's use of other international human rights obligations for which no complaints mechanism exists—for example, those within CROC. Similarly, the Court has made little reference to international standards when considering the extent to which human rights guarantees apply to non-citizens (*Chu Kheng Lim v Minister for Immigration* (1992)).

Even in the **implied constitutional rights** cases involving **political communication**, the Court has tended to rely on historic articulations of traditional common law rights rather than using contemporary human rights standards to inform the nature of implications to be drawn. In so doing, the Court has displayed an enduring commitment to dualist notions of the separation of international and domestic law. Thus, in the majority of cases, the International Bill of Rights remains little more than a rhetorical tool in the hands of the Court. The system of law and jurisprudence that has developed in the international arena, and regionally, has as yet made little impact on the thinking or methodology of the High Court.

ANNEMARIE DEVEREUX

International law. Over the past century, the High Court has shown ambivalence towards international law. At times it has embraced, at other times spurned, the 'law of nations'. The variable often appears to be the personal experience and familiarity of individual Justices with the international legal system. The Court is yet to establish a clear framework for the use and interpretation of international legal principles.

International law, traditionally understood, is the body of rules and principles that regulates relationships between countries. Increasingly, international law has come to have an impact upon areas of activity that occur primarily within countries. The international law of human rights and of the **environment** are examples of this development. The great advances in communications and trade have also given international law considerable significance in all national legal systems. The two major sources of international law are international agreements (such as treaties and conventions) and customary law (practices of states that are regarded as binding). Australia has generally been an enthusiastic supporter of international regulation and is a party to a great range of treaties. This enthusiasm has caused some tension in the Australian legal system.

At federation, international law did not appear to be an important source of domestic law. Moreover, it was accepted that Australia did not have the power to enter into treaties itself; Great Britain would act on its behalf. The Constitution contains only indirect references to international law such as the **external affairs power** in section 51(xxix) and the ineffective grant of **jurisdiction** to the High Court by section 75(i) in matters 'arising under any treaty'. The 1891 draft of the Constitution, however, included a startlingly broad provision (adapted from the US Constitution) that would have made all treaties entered into by the Commonwealth 'binding on the courts, judges and people of every state, and of every part of the Commonwealth' and capable of overriding **inconsistent** state law. That provision did not survive into the final version of the Constitution because of its implication that Australia had the power to enter into international agreements independently of Great Britain.

Australia's acquisition of full international status occurred gradually over the first part of the century, culminating in the *Statute of Westminster* (UK) in 1931 and legitimating Australia's capacity to enter into treaties. Although the Constitution does not provide explicit authority for the Commonwealth to be the only Australian entity to enter into treaties, the general executive power in section 61 has been accepted as including this function. As **Dawson** observed in the *Tasmanian Dam Case* (1983), the Commonwealth executive is assumed to have unlimited treaty-making power. As a corollary of Australia's development of full international status, the constituent states are assumed to lack international personality, and thus to lack any independent treaty-making capacity. Putting aside trade agreements, this effectively gives the Commonwealth exclusive power to represent the nation in international affairs.

What is the relationship between the Australian legal system and international law? The High Court has given a series of rather confused answers. With respect to international agreements to which Australia is a party, it has generally insisted that for a treaty or convention to have any domestic effect, the agreement must have been adopted into Australian law through legislation (the 'transformation' approach). *Teoh's Case* (1995), however, goes beyond such strictures. In the case of customary international legal principles, the Court has wavered on whether there needs to be specific domestic legislative implementation or whether Australian law already incorporates such principles. In *Chow Hung Ching v The King* (1948), **Dixon** spoke of customary international law as a source rather than a part of Australian law, but **Starke** implied a closer relationship by suggesting that a universally recognised rule of international custom should be applied by Australian courts, unless it was in conflict with statute or the **common law** (the 'incorporation' approach). The Court wrestled with the problems of determining the status of an asserted norm of customary international law in both *Chow Hung Ching* and the *War Crimes Act Case* (1991), indicating that an uncontroversial, widely accepted norm of custom will be more readily regarded as part of Australian law by the Court.

In general, the Court has adopted a 'dualist' approach that regards national and international legal systems as quite separate. An example is the case of *Horta v Commonwealth* (1994). East Timorese resistance leader Jose Ramos Horta challenged Commonwealth legislation implementing a bilateral maritime boundary treaty with Indonesia on the ground that the treaty was invalid at international law and thus not properly a matter under the external affairs power. He argued that the treaty, which created a regime for exploitation of the sea bed between Australia and East Timor, contravened the basic principle of international law that territory could not be acquired through the use of force. Indonesia's 1975 invasion of East Timor thus could not give it valid title over the East Timorese sea bed. The High Court unanimously and briefly dismissed the challenge. It held that the external affairs power did not require that the treaty being implemented be consistent with international law.

The Court has encountered international law in an increasing range of contexts. Much of this has been in its jurisprudence on the external affairs power. But international law has also been more recently invoked in the contexts of the common law and of techniques of **statutory interpretation** and **constitutional interpretation**.

Mabo (1992) emphasised the significance of international law in the development of the common law. **Brennan** described the relationship in this way, drawing on both the transformation and incorporation approaches: 'The common law does not necessarily conform with international law, but international law is a legitimate and important influence on the development of the common law, especially when international law declares the existence of universal human rights.' He argued that if a common law doctrine was based on an outdated notion of international law (such as *terra nullius*), the common law could lose its legitimacy.

The influence of international human rights law on the common law is also evident in *Dietrich v The Queen* (1992), in which the Court discussed the possibility of a common law right to a fair trial based on international standards. **Mason** and **McHugh**, who identified such a common law right, rejected the idea that international guarantees of legal representation were part of the Australian common law in the absence of specific legislation. Brennan, by contrast, presented international law as a 'legitimate influence' on the common law as a method of tapping into the contemporary **values** of the community, although in the end he found that there was no common law right to a fair trial.

In *Teoh*, the **Mason Court** identified a significant role for treaties in the context of **administrative law**. At issue was the status of the Convention on the Rights of the Child, a treaty ratified by Australia but not specifically incorporated into Australian law. A majority (**McHugh** dissenting) held that there was a '**legitimate expectation**'—departure from which without advance warning would violate **natural justice**—that administrative decision makers would consider the treaty in reaching their decisions. Mason and **Deane** said that the influence of international legal principles on the common law would depend on factors such as the nature and purpose of the international legal norm, its degree of international acceptance, and its relationship with existing principles of domestic law. Although the Court emphasised the need for a cautious approach to the use of international treaties in developing the common law, the decision caused an uproar. It was condemned by politicians as an inappropriate excursion into the political realm. The Minister for Foreign Affairs, Gareth Evans, and the **Attorney-General**, Michael Lavarch, sought to override the impact of the decision in an unprecedented formal statement—a move repeated in 1997 by their Liberal Party successors, Alexander Downer and Daryl Williams. Both the Keating and Howard governments unsuccessfully attempted to legislate to overcome the effect of the decision. This reaction was parodied by **Mason** after his **retirement**: 'So when an Australian convention ratification is announced, they may dance for joy in the Halmaheras, while here in Australia we, the citizens of Australia, must meekly await a signal from the legislature, a signal which may never come. Of course, this concept of ratification involving a statement to the international community but no statement to the national community is quite unsupportable.'

Various members of the Court have articulated a role for international law both in statutory interpretation and in interpreting the Constitution. In *Polites v Commonwealth* (1945), a majority of the Court accepted that statutes should be interpreted in accordance with international law, unless Parliament clearly indicates a contrary intention. This principle of construction has a long history in British courts and is based on the presumption that Parliament will legislate consistently with international law. A somewhat weaker version of this principle was endorsed in *Chu Kheng Lim v Minister for Immigration* (1992), where Brennan, Deane, and Dawson referred to the use of treaty provisions accepted by Australia in the case of statutory ambiguity. In *Teoh*, Mason and Deane reiterated the principle and gave it greater impact by arguing that the notion of ambiguity should be broadly understood. They stated that 'if the language of the legislation is susceptible of a construction which is consistent with [international law], then that construction should prevail'.

At the beginning of the twenty-first century, by far the keenest exponent of the value of international legal principles in High Court jurisprudence is **Kirby**. Influenced by his extensive experience working with the UN and other international organisations, Kirby has argued for recourse to international law, particularly in cases involving gaps in the common law or textual ambiguity in statutes or the Constitution. Kirby was a key participant at the Bangalore Colloquium of Commonwealth judges (1988), where the Bangalore Principles on the relationship between international and domestic law were developed. His approach as President of the NSW Court of Appeal was evident in a series of decisions. Kirby's **appointment** to the High Court has given his views a broader stage and allowed him to apply them in constitutional interpretation. His extensive **extra-judicial writings** have often been devoted to the theme of harmonising international and domestic law, and a similar theme is evident also in many of his decisions.

Kirby's interest in international law is particularly strong in the area of international human rights law. For example, his dissent in the ***Hindmarsh Island Bridge Case*** (1998) accepted the plaintiff's argument that the races power should be read in the light of international standards of non-discrimination. He spoke of an interpretive principle that, where the Constitution is ambiguous, the High Court 'should adopt the meaning which conforms to the principle of universal and fundamental rights rather than an interpretation which would involve a departure from such rights'. The Kirby approach goes further than the accepted principle of construction in the case of ambiguity. In *Newcrest Mining v Commonwealth* (1997), Kirby said: 'To the full extent that its text permits, Australia's Constitution, as the fundamental law of government in this country, accommodates itself to international law, including insofar as that law expresses basic rights.' He also introduced the idea, repeated in *Hindmarsh*, that the Constitution spoke not just to the people of Australia but also to the international community, and in *Hindmarsh*, he referred to a 'strong presumption' that the Constitution is not intended to violate fundamental human rights and human dignity—implying that the Constitution should be interpreted in light of international law whether or not an ambiguity could be identified. The radical nature of this approach emerges in contrast with that of members of the majority. Although **Gaudron** was prepared to acknowledge the inherent claim to human rights of all people and the fundamental nature of the international law prohibition on racial **discrimination**, she argued that the norm could not restrain **Commonwealth legislative power**. For their part, **Gummow** and **Hayne** accepted that Australian laws should be interpreted as far as possible in conformity with international law, but held that 'unmistakable and unambiguous' language will override international law.

While **Murphy** (in external affairs power cases) and Kirby have been the most enthusiastic members of the High Court in their recourse to international law, other members of the Court have sometimes portrayed international law as dangerous and uncertain. The indeterminacy of the language of international agreements is a regular theme in High Court encounters with treaties (see, for example, *Project Blue Sky v Australian Broadcasting Authority* (1998)). Even Mason, who demonstrated a willingness to use international legal principles in his judgments, has recommended a conservative approach to the engagement with international law. Since leaving the Bench, he has written that international law should be used not to impose new or imported values on Australian law, but as an expression of existing common law principles or community values. Brennan's use of international law in *Mabo* was similarly tempered by his statement that international law could not be used to interfere with the 'skeleton of principle which gives the body of our law its shape and internal consistency'.

The Court has certainly displayed more interest in international law than has been evident in the isolationist tradition of the **United States Supreme Court**. By **comparison with other courts**, such as the Indian and Canadian Supreme Courts and the NZ Court of Appeal, however, the High Court has been wary of the international legal system.

International law is likely to have a growing, if subtle, effect on the Court's jurisprudence. With the expansion of international law, few areas of social and commercial life will be untouched by international standards and norms. It is increasingly important that the High Court develop more creative and consistent approaches to the significance of the international legal system for Australian law.

HILARY CHARLESWORTH

Further Reading

Sam Blay, Ryszard Piotrowicz, and Martin Tsamenyi (eds), *Public International Law: An Australian Perspective* (1997)

Brian Opeskin and Don Rothwell (eds), *International Law and Australian Federalism* (1997)

KW Ryan (ed), *International Law in Australia* (2nd edn 1984)

Cheryl Saunders, 'Articles of Faith or Lucky Breaks?: The Constitutional Law of International Agreements in Australia' (1995) 17 *Syd LR* 150

Amelia Simpson and George Williams, 'International Law and Constitutional Interpretation' (2000) 11 *PLR* 205

***Inter se* questions** are those involving potential competition or conflict between the constitutional powers (particularly the legislative powers) of the Commonwealth and the states—or alternatively, between two or more states, though this proved of little importance. The concept identifies the exceptional class of constitutional cases reserved by section 74 of the Constitution for the High Court, with appeals to the **Privy Council** excluded 'unless the High Court shall certify' that such an appeal is appropriate. Only one certificate was ever granted, in *Colonial Sugar Refining Co v A-G (Cth)* (1912). The Privy Council's erratic response (*A-G (Cth) v Colonial Sugar Refining Co* (1913)) made any repetition unlikely.

The extent to which the High Court should displace the Privy Council as an arbiter of Australian law was controversial throughout the Federal Conventions of the 1890s; but by 1897, most delegates agreed that certain disputes arising from **federalism** should be reserved for decision in Australia. As

Dixon observed in *Whitehouse v Queensland* (1960), the delegates had anticipated what experience confirmed: that 'only those who dwell under a Federal Constitution … can become adequately qualified to interpret and apply its provisions'.

Even then, the identification of such cases remained controversial. The compromise formula finally adopted was imposed by the British government, with connivance behind the scenes by influential Australians such as **Griffith**. It refers to 'any question, howsoever arising, as to the limits inter se of the Constitutional powers of the Commonwealth and those of any State or States'. The Latin phrase '*inter se*' was not used in the Australian draft, but had previously been used in Colonial Office correspondence.

The compromise draft had a loophole. It did not exclude the possibility that a **state Supreme Court** might grant leave to appeal to the Privy Council in an *inter se* matter. The original section 40 of the *Judiciary Act* 1903 (Cth), providing for **removal** of constitutional issues into the High Court, sought to block that loophole. It was reinforced by section 39, which deprived state courts of any *state* jurisdiction in such matters, and invested them with equivalent *federal* jurisdiction on the basis that—by section 39(2)(a)—their decisions would be 'final and conclusive' apart from appeal to the High Court.

The early conflict over **intergovernmental immunities** tested these provisions. In *Deakin v Webb* (1904), where **Isaacs** appeared on behalf of the Victorian government, his application for a section 74 certificate was emphatically rejected; but he then obtained leave to appeal to the Privy Council on the issue from Justice Henry Hodges of the Supreme Court of Victoria, who ruled that section 39 of the Judiciary Act was itself invalid (*In re the Income Tax Acts* (1905)). The Privy Council agreed, and allowed the appeal (*Webb v Outtrim* (1906)).

In *Baxter v Commissioners of Taxation (NSW)* (1907), the High Court simply refused to acknowledge the Privy Council's decision, protesting that it had usurped the Court's own exclusive domain. In *Flint v Webb* (1907), the Court refused a certificate on the issue. The legislative response (suggested by Griffith) was to strengthen the Judiciary Act by a new section 40A, providing that upon an *inter se* question arising 'in any cause pending in the Supreme Court of a State … it shall be the duty of the Court to proceed no further in the cause'. Instead, the cause was automatically removed into the High Court. Moreover, a new section 38A made High Court **jurisdiction** exclusive in all matters involving *inter se* questions (apart from certain criminal cases).

In *Lorenzo v Carey* (1921) and the *Limerick Steamship Case* (1924), the Court upheld the overall structure of section 39 as valid, but skirted over the validity of section 39(2)(a). The issue came to a head in the *Skin Wool Case* (1926), when the plaintiffs in an action against the Commonwealth appealed to the Full Court of the Supreme Court of Victoria from a single judge of that Court. When the Commonwealth objected that under section 39(2)(a) the appeal lay only to the High Court, the Full Court held that section invalid, and proceeded to hear the appeal. The High Court responded by holding not only that section 39(2)(a) was valid, but that the moment it was invoked in the Full Court an *inter se* question had arisen, and the entire cause had been removed into the High Court. Isaacs' impassioned judgment linked the neces-

sity for Australian control of federal *inter se* questions with the theory of **responsible government**.

In *Pirrie v McFarlane* (1925), the Victorian government (advised by FW Eggleston, Robert **Menzies**, and Dixon) mounted an audacious challenge. The state Supreme Court, obediently to section 40A, had transmitted the papers to the High Court; but from that decision the Victorian government went direct to the Privy Council, which informed the High Court by cable that it had granted special leave to appeal. Eggleston explained to an angry High Court that the object was to secure a ruling that section 40A was invalid— in which event the cause had *not* been removed into the High Court. Asserting 'the manifest duty of this Court to proceed on the assumption that the section is valid', Chief Justice **Knox** directed that the matter be heard.

In due course, the Court ruled that sections 38A and 40A were valid. It identified an *inter se* question not only in the substantive issue (whether Victorian traffic laws bound a Commonwealth defence officer), but also in the antecedent question of whether section 40A was valid. The Privy Council, having waited until the High Court had spoken, thereupon announced that the Court's decision had rendered the issue moot.

The operation of section 40A was initially unclear. When the Supreme Court of Queensland transmitted the papers in *R v Maryborough Licensing Court* (1919), the High Court held the transmission premature. The matter could have been determined independently of the constitutional issue; and, even if section 40A applied, the High Court would be seised of the specific *inter se* question only. Though both these limiting propositions were ultimately discarded, they generated uncertainty for many years, particularly for state Supreme Courts.

Ironically, the Privy Council itself took the lead in defining and enforcing the limits of its own jurisdiction. In *Jones v Commonwealth Court of Conciliation and Arbitration* (1917), their Lordships refused to entertain an appeal in the *Builders Labourers Case* (1914). Since the **Commonwealth legislative power** with respect to industrial disputes 'extending beyond the limits of any one State' (section 51(xxxv) of the Constitution) did not correspond to any equivalent state extraterritorial power, it was argued that decisions on the Commonwealth power had no *inter se* implications. Their Lordships rejected that argument. Even though no direct conflict arose, it was sufficient that the High Court had 'decided that the frontier of the Commonwealth power reaches … into the State'.

The *Bank Nationalisation Case* (1948 and 1949) went further. The High Court had decided the case on multiple grounds; but the Commonwealth's appeal to the Privy Council was confined to the effect of section 92 of the Constitution, which according to *James v Cowan* (1932) had no *inter se* implications. Yet their Lordships held that, since no order could be made concerning the validity of the legislation without considering the *inter se* questions, they simply had no jurisdiction. Ironically, they then reviewed the section 92 issue at length.

By this time, **Barwick** was representing the Nelungaloo wheat growers in their campaign for compensation for wheat compulsorily acquired under the National Security (Wheat

Acquisition) Regulations 1945. The initial claim, concerning the harvest of 1945–46 (*Nelungaloo v Commonwealth* (1948)), involved two possible bases for compensation: regulation 14, which converted the growers' rights into 'claims for compensation', presumably as causes of action; and regulation 19, which set out an elaborate formula for compensation to growers who submitted their claims to the Australian Wheat Board in the prescribed form. **Williams** awarded compensation under regulation 19, holding that the plaintiffs' conduct excluded any claim under regulation 14. An evenly divided **Full Court** dismissed an appeal.

In *Nelungaloo v Commonwealth* (1950), the Privy Council also dismissed an appeal, since an *inter se* question was involved. One way for the plaintiffs to bring the case within regulation 14 was to argue that regulation 19 was invalid; and that would involve a determination of the Commonwealth's power of **acquisition of property** under section 51(xxxi) of the Constitution. The plaintiffs had not pressed that issue in the High Court, but now proposed to do so. Their Lordships ruled that they had no jurisdiction. Building on the 1917 *Jones* case, they affirmed that *any* question as to the scope of Commonwealth powers under section 51 of the Constitution is an *inter se* question. Building on *Bank Nationalisation*, they affirmed that where an *inter se* question was only one among several issues decided by the High Court, they could entertain the other issues if the *inter se* question were excluded. Even then, if such a question later emerged they would have to abandon the case. In this case, where the *inter se* question appeared at the outset, no appeal could be entertained. In *Grace Bros v Commonwealth* (1950), their Lordships took a similar view.

Barwick then took the *Nelungaloo* case back to the High Court for an *inter se* certificate (*Nelungaloo v Commonwealth* (1952)), arguing that the Privy Council decisions had radically altered the basis on which previous applications had failed. But the whole Court agreed with Dixon 'that the obligation of the Court to accept the responsibility for the final interpretation of the Constitution in its distribution of powers should be treated as paramount'. The certificate was refused.

The *Nelungaloo* plaintiffs sued again in the Supreme Court of NSW over the harvests of 1946–48. They relied on regulation 14, thus avoiding any *inter se* question. However, the Commonwealth based its defence on regulation 19, and moved for removal into the High Court—arguing that although section 40A could not operate until an *inter se* question emerged, removal under section 40 was possible at any time (*Nelungaloo v Commonwealth* (No 4) (1953)). The Court held that section 40A was already applicable: an *inter se* question already arose, essentially for the same reasons as before.

The most obvious *inter se* questions, as *Jones* and *Nelungaloo* made clear, are those affecting the validity of Commonwealth legislation. On issues solely of Commonwealth concern (like the Commonwealth **separation of powers**) no *inter se* question arises. (Hence the Privy Council appeal in the *Boilermakers Case* (1956).) Whether freedom of **interstate trade** under section 92 of the Constitution gave rise to *inter se* questions was initially unclear. In *Ex parte Nelson (No 2)* (1929), Isaacs and **Starke** thought so; Dixon and **Rich** disagreed. Knox and **Gavan Duffy** expressed no opinion. At that time, section 92 was not regarded as binding the Common-

wealth, so that the Commonwealth **trade and commerce power** (section 51(i) of the Constitution) was perceived as effectively exclusive. Dixon's reasoning implied that an *inter se* question could never arise for Commonwealth exclusive powers, but only for areas of concurrent power where Commonwealth and state powers meet. But in *James v Cowan*, the Privy Council held that no *inter se* question arose whether the Commonwealth was bound or not, since on either basis 'there are no boundaries' between Commonwealth and states that come into question.

The status of **inconsistency** issues under section 109 of the Constitution was more problematic. In *Ex parte McLean* (1930), Dixon asserted flatly that such an issue is not an *inter se* question; but the issue was settled only in the aftermath of the High Court decision in *O'Sullivan v Noarlunga Meat* (1954). The challenge in that case to the validity of the Commonwealth's Commerce (Meat Export) Regulations was clearly an *inter se* question; but what of their inconsistency with SA legislation?

When the Privy Council granted leave to appeal excluding any *inter se* question, the appellant sought a section 74 certificate (*O'Sullivan v Noarlunga Meat (No 2)* (1956)). Dixon repeated his earlier view that the question was 'not between powers, but between laws made under powers'. **Kitto** suggested that, although no *inter se* question could arise while the underlying interpretation of section 109 was clear, any challenge to that interpretation would be an *inter se* question, since 'when a court is called upon to decide what is the correct test of inconsistency, the answer given must have a direct bearing upon … the location of the boundary' between state and Commonwealth power.

The appellant thereupon amended his pleadings in the Privy Council to exclude any challenge to the High Court's view of 'the meaning of section 109'. On that basis, their Lordships finally ruled that the application of section 109 did not involve an *inter se* question, for the reason given by Dixon: namely, that the conflict was between *laws*, not between legislative *powers* (*O'Sullivan v Noarlunga Meat* (1956)).

Questions involving *exclusive* Commonwealth powers were also problematic. For many years, it was thought that no *inter se* question arose in such cases: there could be no question of a 'boundary' between powers where the state has no power at all. That view, based on **obiter dicta** by Dixon in *Ex parte Nelson*, was endorsed by the Privy Council in *Nelungaloo*, and again in *Boilermakers*. But in 1952, Dixon's own *Nelungaloo* judgment began to question the settled understanding; and finally, in **Dennis Hotels v Victoria** (1961), the Privy Council ruled that a question concerning section 90 was an *inter se* question, since it 'bears at one and the same time upon the limits of the Commonwealth's powers in this field and upon the limits of the State's powers in everything that is not within this field'.

Over the years, the High Court's approach to section 40A grew more rigorous. In response to the divorced wife's **property** claim in *Lansell v Lansell* (1962) in the Supreme Court of Victoria, the husband contended that section 86(1) of the *Matrimonial Causes Act* 1959 (Cth) was invalid. When Justice Reginald Sholl pointed out that this raised an *inter se* question, the husband conceded that the provision was valid, but attempted to read it down. Sholl ruled that this still involved an *inter se* question, and the case was removed into the High Court (*Lansell v Lansell* (1964)). Kitto took the opportunity to suggest that the Supreme Courts should emulate the Privy Council: as soon as an *inter se* question emerged, section 40A should operate. It was 'immaterial' that there might be ways to decide the case without considering the *inter se* question. In *WB Hunter v Forshaw* (1971), Barwick agreed, removing a lingering ambiguity in Kitto's fomulation by stressing that 'if the matter *may* be decided wholly or partly by a decision of [the *inter se* question]', that question 'will have arisen and the jurisdiction of the State Court lost'.

Clearly, the original cautious approach of *Maryborough Licensing* had gone. In *R v Green; Ex parte Cheung Cheuk To* (1965), Justice Oliver Gillard of the Supreme Court of Victoria revived that approach. He held that, although the validity of provisions in the *Migration Act* 1958 (Cth) had been questioned, he still had jurisdiction so long as it seemed possible to reach a decision without addressing that issue. Once he concluded that that was impossible, he announced that the cause was removed. The High Court held that section 40A had operated the moment validity was mentioned: 'So soon as the *inter se* question arises, whether by pleading, by submission, or by the Court's own perception of it, the Supreme Court loses jurisdiction to hear the matter any further or to decide any point involved in it.'

The *Australia Acts* 1986 abolished Privy Council appeals from state courts. The identification of *inter se* questions no longer matters. Yet until section 74 of the Constitution is amended, the theoretical possibility remains that the High Court might certify that an *inter se* question 'is one which ought to be determined' by the Privy Council. Clearly it will never happen. Yet the final irony remains that *only* for *inter se* questions does Australian law still allow for the possibility of a Privy Council appeal.

TONY BLACKSHIELD

Inter-State Commission. According to the conception of the **framers of the Constitution**, the Inter-State Commission was to have played an institutional role in the development of the new federation second only in importance to that of the High Court itself. The mandatory language of section 101 of the Constitution, providing that 'there shall be an Inter-State Commission, with such powers of adjudication and administration as the Parliament deems necessary for the execution and maintenance, within the Commonwealth, of the provisions of this Constitution relating to trade and commerce, and all laws made thereunder', makes its absence for the greater part of the twentieth century—and its continuing absence—one of the great constitutional curiosities.

Section 101 of the Constitution is at the heart of Chapter IV entitled 'Finance and Trade'. That chapter contains section 92, which is concerned with freedom of **interstate trade and commerce**, and was designed to eliminate protectionist colonial border tariffs that had their physical manifestation in the much-loathed Customs Houses. Chapter IV also contains section 102, which was specifically directed to the subject of differential and preferential railway rates, which had been a particular source of tension between NSW and Victoria. So politically controversial were questions relating to freedom of interstate trade and commerce that it was thought unde-

sirable to reserve them to the High Court. Thus, during the course of the 1898 Melbourne **Convention Debates**, Josiah Symon, referring to the clause that would become section 92 of the Constitution, stated that 'it would introduce political questions and matters of **policy** that would tend to derogate from the position which the High Court should occupy under this Constitution'. The anticipated difficulty of the issues likely to arise under section 92 had led **O'Connor** to advise delegates at the Adelaide Convention during the previous year that 'the practical working of this principle of freedom of trade throughout the Commonwealth would be a very difficult thing indeed, unless it is in the hands of some skilled body of persons'. The Commission was to be that body. Section 73(iii) of the Constitution conferred **jurisdiction** on the High Court to hear and determine appeals from its judgments, decrees, orders, and sentences, 'but as to questions of law only'.

In a policy speech delivered on 17 January 1901, **Prime Minister**-designate **Barton** described the Commission as a body 'next in importance to the High Court' and observed that these 'two tribunals will give confidence everywhere to the people of the Commonwealth that justice will be done for them'. Notwithstanding this sentiment and John Quick's similar observation that the Commission was 'the necessary adjunct to the Constitution', the Commission was not established until 1913. Bills introduced in 1901 and 1909 for its establishment lapsed in the face of competing priorities, some opposition from the states, and active lobbying by vested interests such as shipowners and agents opposed to regulation.

Notwithstanding strong rumours that **Attorney-General** (later Prime Minister) WM Hughes would be appointed its first head, **Piddington** was appointed Chairman of the Commission, only months after resigning his **appointment** to the High Court without ever taking up his commission. The other Commissioners were George Swinburne, formerly a minister in the Victorian government, and Nicholas Lockyer, former head of Customs for NSW and the Commonwealth. Under Piddington's leadership, the Commission embarked upon a major inquiry into the tariff, receiving 666 submissions and taking evidence from more than 1200 witnesses. Another inquiry led directly to the creation of the Advisory Council for Scientific Research, the precursor to the Commonwealth Scientific and Industrial Research Organisation. The Commission also produced reports on 'British and Australian Trade in the South Pacific' and an 'Investigation into the Causes of Increased Prices'.

In 1915, there came before the Commission a challenge to the *Wheat Acquisition Act* 1915 (NSW), which permitted the compulsory acquisition of wheat in NSW in return for prescribed compensation. The soon to become familiar question was whether such legislation violated section 92 of the Constitution. A majority of the Commission (Piddington dissenting) answered this question in the affirmative. The Commonwealth, acting on behalf of several Riverina wheat growers, appealed against this decision to the High Court by way of a case stated by the Commission (the *Wheat Case* (1915)). Of several questions that came before the Court, the first was whether the Commission could validly exercise **judicial power** under the Constitution to hear and determine the wheat growers' petition and grant the injunction and **order** for **costs** made in their favour. In answering this question in the negative, a majority of the Court effectively stultified the Commission and its potentially central role in the working of Chapter IV of the Constitution and section 92 in particular, reducing it, in essence, to a permanent commission of inquiry.

The *Wheat Case*, which subsequently assumed central importance in the *Boilermakers Case* (1956), has been analysed in terms of institutional competition, Colin Howard observing that 'the High Court disposed of the invasion of its own area of interest by deciding that section 101 did not mean what it said'. Certainly the result of the *Wheat Case* coincided with **Isaacs**' desire expressed some 17 years earlier at the Melbourne Federal Convention to 'eliminate the constitutional creation of the Interstate Commission', describing it as a 'great mistake that we should erect this body, a fourth branch of government'. No further Commissioners were appointed following the completion of Piddington's seven-year term in 1920.

One consequence of the Court's decision in the *Wheat Case* was to ensure that what was conceived to be an essential component of the constitutional machinery designed to ensure freedom of interstate trade, commerce, and intercourse was henceforth unavailable. Geoffrey Sawer described the decision as not only 'effectively killing the Commission' but also 'with it, the possibility of the sensible administrative policing of section 92'. The vexed history of section 92 throughout the first century of federation at the very least founds an inference that the Court might not have struggled so desperately with this section had the Commission been permitted to play the constitutional role described by Barton in his powerful dissent in the *Wheat Case*. This point was expressly acknowledged by **Latham** in *Riverina Transport v Victoria* (1937) and repeated by Gough Whitlam in his 1957 Chifley lecture 'The Constitution versus Labor'. The Court's belated recognition in *Cole v Whitfield* (1988) that section 92 essentially raises factual questions of **discrimination** and protectionism only strengthens this supposition.

Pursuant to legislation introduced during the **Whitlam era** and passed by the Parliament in 1975 but never proclaimed to come into force, the Hawke government re-established the Commission in 1984. Over the next five years, it produced a series of reports, principally in relation to interstate transportation and waterfront reform. Despite its continuing constitutional resonances (its members included economist Keith Reid, grandson of founding father George Reid, and constitutional lawyer Michael Coper), this incarnation of the Commission was also short-lived, its functions being subsumed in late 1989 into those of the non-constitutional Industries Assistance Commission.

ANDREW BELL

Further Reading
Michael Coper, 'The Second Coming of the Fourth Arm: The Role and Functions of the Inter-State Commission' (1989) 63 *ALJ* 731
Note, 'The Inter-State Commission and Section 92 of the Constitution' (1988) 62 *ALJ* 586

Interstate trade and commerce, freedom of. No area seems to have bedevilled the work of the High Court like the inter-

pretation of section 92 of the Constitution, which insists that 'trade, commerce, and intercourse among the States … shall be absolutely free'. It took around 140 cases, some extraordinary twists and turns of legal doctrine, and over three million words of commentary and **criticism** before the High Court, in the landmark case of *Cole v Whitfield* (1988), returned the interpretation of section 92 to its evident origins and ushered in a period of stability that seems likely to endure.

The interpretive problem is obvious. The section cannot be taken absolutely literally—no one could seriously contend that the resultant chaos from liberating interstate trade from all legal restrictions could possibly have been intended—yet, somewhat unhelpfully, the section stops virtually in midsentence. It fails to spell out the kinds of restrictions from which interstate trade was to be absolutely free.

The **framers of the Constitution** were well aware of their ellipsis. But the idea that interstate trade should be 'absolutely free' was a popular political slogan, and its lure was too strong. The framers knew what they meant. They wanted no customs taxes or other tariff or like barriers between the states. The creation of an internal 'common market' through the eradication of these generally protectionist barriers (sometimes overtly intended as such, sometimes disguised (as 'inspection' fees and the like) and sometimes the incidental consequence of revenue raising—but in any case generally protectionist in effect) was the *sine qua non* of federation. As George Reid put it, the section was 'a little bit of laymen's language which comes in here very well'.

The very early cases were consistent with the idea that a state should not erect protectionist barriers—whether in the form of monetary imposts or broader measures—against the trade of another state. But a series of cases during **World War I** proved more difficult. NSW and Queensland commandeered certain food supplies, ostensibly to assist the war effort but with an unmistakable whiff of looking after their own citizens first in a time of scarcity. **Isaacs**, who had protested unsuccessfully during the drafting of the Constitution that the bare words of section 92 were prone to be given a far wider effect than was really intended, proceeded on the Bench, in a remarkable example of self-fulfilling prophecy, to give those words precisely that effect. The states could make no law on the subject of interstate trade. They could compulsorily acquire a product, as that involved a law on the subject of 'ownership' and left the product free to be traded by its new owner, the state (the *Wheat Case* (1915)); but they could not legislate at all for the control of the interstate trade of others (*Duncan v Queensland* (1916)).

Isaacs' reasoning was artificial, literal, and potentially devastating for sensible, non-discriminatory regulation by the states of trade within their borders, including interstate trade. His salvation for the regulation of interstate trade lay with the Commonwealth. In *McArthur v Queensland* (1920), he led the Court in holding that section 92 applied only to the states, and not at all to the Commonwealth. Coming only three months after the decision in the *Engineers Case* (1920), this left the Commonwealth poised for a significant expansion of its powers.

The Commonwealth's exemption from section 92 lasted, however, only until 1936, when that aspect of Isaacs' theory was overruled by the **Privy Council** in *James v Commonwealth*, one of a series of cases brought by intrepid SA fruit grower Frederick Alexander James against the orderly marketing of his 'Trevarno' brand of dried fruits (see **Litigants, notable, 1903–1945**). Once section 92 applied both to the Commonwealth and the states, the destructive **literalism** of Isaacs' 'subject matter' approach was clearly unsustainable; yet, although detached from their original context, elements of the Isaacs theory lingered—most significantly, the alleged irrelevance of the absence of **discrimination** against interstate trade. The idea of section 92 as directed only to the prevention of discriminatory or protectionist barriers to interstate trade—embraced, interestingly, by **Gavan Duffy** in his long-forgotten dissent in *McArthur*—was not to be seriously revisited for another 50 years.

From the standpoint of knowing how the story was to unfold in *Cole v Whitfield*, it must seem odd that it took so long to restore what appears to have been originally intended, and even odder that the original intent was not unambiguously embraced by the early High Court, which was entirely composed of former framers of the Constitution. One reason has already been suggested: whether or not as a payback for his rebuff at the Conventions, and whether or not as a smokescreen for his ardent nationalism, Isaacs' literalism had a significant impact on the Court's jurisprudence, in this area as elsewhere. And literal or not, the Court had cut itself off from the **Convention Debates** and had striven for methods of interpretation that were largely textual, as if the Constitution were an ordinary Act of Parliament. This, together with the then-undeveloped state of **administrative law**, made it almost impossible for the Court to deal with the hints of state protectionism in the wartime cases, because such protectionism as there was appeared to infect not the legislation itself, but the way it was being applied.

Cut off from being understood in the context of its origins, the interpretation of section 92 in the 1930s spawned many and diverse theories, from **Evatt's** unworkable proposition that what was protected was the overall flow or volume of trade (*R v Vizzard; Ex parte Hill* (1933)) to **Dixon's** emerging view that what was important was the trade of individuals (*O Gilpin v Commissioner for Road Transport (NSW)* (1935)). Evatt had the greater success in the 1930s, staving off in particular the challenges to road transport licensing and, for 20 years at least, pragmatically saving the state railways from ruinous competition; but it was Dixon's view that was vindicated by the Privy Council at the end of the 1940s. In the celebrated *Bank Nationalisation Case* (1949), the Privy Council invalidated Commonwealth legislation prohibiting the operation of private banks and conferring a monopoly on the Commonwealth Bank. Following the High Court's invalidation of the Chifley government's attempt to nationalise the airlines (*Australian National Airways v Commonwealth* (1945)), this detached section 92 so far from its origins that it had become (notwithstanding the *Wheat Case*) a guarantee not of free trade but of free enterprise, and a major inhibitor of the platform of one side of federal politics.

This result may have been congenial to the more politically conservative Justices, but the Court still had to confront the task of distinguishing permissible from impermissible restrictions on interstate trade. The **Dixon Court** attempted

to elaborate the two criteria adopted by the Privy Council in the *Bank Nationalisation Case*: that only 'direct' interferences were impermissible, and that, in any event, laws that were merely 'regulatory' would not infringe. Neither criterion was successful in stemming the flow of seemingly irreconcilable decisions. The more the **legalism** of the test of directness limited the destructive impact of section 92, the more it raised questions about whether the Court was, in truth, achieving its stated object of guaranteeing the freedom of individual traders; and the more the Court asked whether a law was merely 'regulatory', the more it seemed to be merely second-guessing the political judgment of the elected legislatures. Regulation did not, however, permit prohibition, and first the Privy Council and then the Dixon Court struck down on this basis (as individuals without licences were prohibited from operating) the discretionary state road transport licensing schemes that had been upheld over the previous 20 years (*Hughes & Vale v NSW* (1954), *Hughes & Vale v NSW (No 2)* (1955)).

The succession to the Chief Justiceship of **Barwick**, who had made his name particularly as an advocate in section 92 cases, only made matters worse. Barwick would have alleviated the artificial legalism of the Dixon Court with greater recognition of practical considerations, so that, for example, a law operating on an intrastate sale of goods might nevertheless directly affect interstate trade because of its practical impact on prior importation (and indeed, the sale itself might, for the same practical reasons, be regarded as part of interstate rather than intrastate trade). He would also have given a narrower scope to the concept of regulation, allowing only what was necessary for the mutual accommodation of interstate traders rather than for the vindication of some overriding public interest. But he could not carry with him a majority of his colleagues (clashing particularly with **Kitto** in *Samuels v Readers Digest* (1969)), and when challenges were brought in the late 1970s to long-standing national wheat marketing arrangements (*Clark King & Co v Australian Wheat Board* (1978); *Uebergang v Australian Wheat Board* (1980)), the judge-made law of section 92 began to collapse under the weight of its own internal contradictions and endemic diversity of opinion. This state of near-collapse underscored the lack of a credible anchoring point in terms of the constitutional purpose the section was intended to serve.

With faint echoes of the similar result in the *Wheat Case* in 1915, the wheat marketing scheme survived challenge—this time partly because, on one view, it fell within an exception foreshadowed in the *Bank Nationalisation Case* to the otherwise inevitable unconstitutionality of government monopoly: although the scheme was a prohibition of individual trade, it was, in the circumstances, 'the only reasonable and practical' method of regulation. This, more than anything else, underlined the political nature of the task the Court had set for itself under current doctrine. But change was in the air: the unsatisfactory state of the current doctrine had not escaped the attention of either the **commentators** or the more introspective of the Justices (**Deane** observing in *Miller v TCN Channel Nine* (1986) that 'many voices of authority have been speaking differently at the same time'); **Murphy** had confined section 92 to fiscal burdens in the nature of customs duties, which, although idiosyncratic and unacceptably narrow, served to refocus attention on the historical core purpose of the framers of the Constitution; and the mid-1980s saw important changes in the composition of the Bench, particularly the elevation to **Chief Justice** of **Mason**, who, with Deane, had in the preceding cases expressed extreme discomfort with the existing state of the law.

The opportunity came in *Cole v Whitfield*, and a unanimous Court threw out the old 'individual right' theory of section 92 and replaced it with the principle that the section is infringed only by the imposition of discriminatory burdens of a protectionist kind. A Tasmanian law prohibiting the possession of undersized crayfish was upheld. The question of whether the freedom of intercourse in section 92 might still connote some kind of individual right of movement or communication was left to another day. Shortly afterwards, in *Bath v Alston Holdings* (1988), the Court divided on whether a Victorian tobacco tax was discriminatory in a protectionist sense; but the difference of opinion, although a salutary reminder that the new law would not be free from difficulty, did not call into question the basic principle. In *Castlemaine Tooheys v SA* (1990), the Court unanimously struck down a SA law that set different mandatory deposits for refillable and non-refillable bottles; although on its face it was non-discriminatory against interstate trade, it was discriminatory in its impact (as the locals mainly used refillable bottles and the outsiders non-refillable), and that impact was disproportionate to any non-protectionist object (such as litter prevention or energy conservation) that the law might have been thought to serve. In *Barley Marketing Board (NSW) v Norman* (1990), limited aspects of the NSW barley marketing scheme were upheld as non-discriminatory.

Otherwise, the flow of section 92 cases seems to have slowed to a trickle, perhaps suggesting that a greater degree of certainty has at last been achieved. Certainly, it is now much harder for a challenge to succeed, partly because the area of operation of section 92 has been narrowed, and partly because future litigation is likely to involve difficult problems of proof in relation to the factual impact of a law. The Court has not fully addressed the **fact finding** processes by which factual discrimination or protectionism must be proved, at least where the issues are contested. In *Cole v Whitfield* and *Castlemaine Tooheys*, the Court was fortunate to have agreed statement of facts between the parties.

Although the concept of discrimination in a protectionist sense—especially when not evident from the face of legislation—is likely to be somewhat elusive and problematic (perhaps disclosing a further explanation for its failure to emerge initially as the guiding principle for the interpretation of section 92), it makes sense of section 92 historically and institutionally. The historical justification is given in *Cole v Whitfield*; institutionally, the Court assumes a narrower and more workable role as the enforcer of one aspect of the achievement of economic unity in a federal system, the prevention of state protectionism resulting from the imposition of discriminatory burdens on interstate trade. If this be thought to be too narrow, it should be remembered that other kinds of laws or practices that detract from the achievement of an internal common market or otherwise threaten national economic unity (usually state laws or actions, though not inevitably) may require different reme-

dies, such as overriding national legislation or uniform agreement among the states (as in the case of the former protectionist rules for tendering for state contracts). *Cole v Whitfield* also avoids the political interventionism of the *Bank Nationalisation Case* and leaves the large battle between **socialism** and capitalism to be fought out in the political arena.

It took many years for the High Court to make sense of section 92. As early as *James v Cowan* (1930), **Rich** cried out with eloquent despair that 'some hint at least might have been dropped, some distant allusion made, from which the nature of the immunity intended could afterwards have been deduced by those whose lot it is to explain the elliptical and expound the unexpressed'. **Latham**, in his **retirement** address in 1952, observed that 'when I die, section 92 will be found written on my heart'. Yet the hints and allusions were always there, had not the Court—fuelled by Isaacs' natural inclinations and ulterior motives—embarked on an abstract exercise of giving an almost context-free meaning to the words of the section. Despite a number of unproductive fresh starts, the continuing accumulation of **precedent** ultimately became oppressive and unsustainable, and in *Cole v Whitfield* the Court took section 92 back to its roots. The earlier law had become detached from those roots and had not only wrongly elevated private enterprise into a constitutionally protected value, but more generally had placed interstate trade in a privileged position as compared with intrastate trade (rather than merely in a position of **equality**), producing an array of distortions, including, for example, the 'border-hopping' cases of the 1950s and 1960s, which saw truck operators unnecessarily diverting across state borders simply to attract the protection of section 92.

In **constitutional interpretation**, **history** is often an unwelcome constraint that demands an interpretation perceived to be out of touch with modern needs. In *Cole v Whitfield*, the High Court discovered history as a tool of liberation and brought forth an interpretation which, judged in a broader institutional context, struck a sensible balance in resolving the inherent tension between the Constitution's twin goals of achieving national economic unity and preserving state autonomy and diversity.

MICHAEL COPER

Further Reading
Michael Coper, *Freedom of Interstate Trade Under the Australian Constitution* (1983)
Michael Coper, *Encounters with the Australian Constitution* (1987, popular edn 1988)
Michael Coper, 'The Economic Framework of the Australian Federation: A Question of Balance' in Gregory Craven (ed), *Australian Federation: Towards the Second Century* (1992) 144–47
Michael Coper, 'Section 92 of the Australian Constitution Since *Cole v Whitfield*' in HP Lee and George Winterton (eds), *Australian Constitutional Perspectives* (1992)

Interveners and *amici curiae*. The High Court has taken a restrictive approach to the role of interveners and *amici curiae* (friends of the Court) in matters before it. This approach is in contrast to that of certain other final appellate courts, such as the Canadian Supreme Court and **United States Supreme Court**, where participation by such persons is a regular practice.

In the absence of statutory provision, intervention occurs by leave as a discretionary matter pursuant to the inherent power of the Court. As an intervener becomes a party to the proceedings, intervention is normally only permitted where a special interest in the subject matter of the proceedings can be shown by the person seeking to intervene. A desire to have the law declared in particular terms is not a sufficient interest. However, if a substantial effect on a person's interest is demonstrable (as it is for a party to pending litigation) this will suffice to support a grant of leave to intervene. The practice of the Court in this regard is supported by the historical practice of other courts, particularly courts of **equity**, and derives from the Court's responsibility for the administration of justice and its inherent power to control its own proceedings. **Brennan** conveniently states the position in *Levy v Victoria* (1997).

Attorneys-General of the Commonwealth, the states, or internal **territories** are the main interveners in constitutional cases. This now occurs pursuant to statutory entitlement. Prior to 1976, it occurred in the discretion of the Court. As **Dixon** indicated in the *ARU Case* (1930), intervention was permitted in cases where some right, power, or immunity of the body politic of the Attorney-General seeking intervention was involved, especially in matters related to the diminution or enlargement of powers the states or Commonwealth may exercise. Intervention was not, however, automatic in all constitutional cases, and was sometimes refused. Since 1976, Attorneys-General of the Commonwealth and states (and more recently those of the internal territories) have been provided by section 78A of the *Judiciary Act* 1903 (Cth) with an express right of intervention in proceedings in the High Court or any other court 'that relate to a matter arising under the Constitution or involving its interpretation'. In most constitutional cases before the High Court (other than some **inconsistency** cases), one or more Attorneys-General will intervene. The Commonwealth Attorney-General intervenes more often than state or territory counterparts. To allow Attorneys-General to consider possible exercise of their statutory right of intervention, notices specifying the nature of the constitutional matter are required to be given a reasonable time before the hearing, and a court is not to proceed in the cause until satisfied that notice has been given and a reasonable time has elapsed for consideration of the notice (section 78B of the Judiciary Act). In non-constitutional cases, Attorneys-General are generally treated the same as any other applicant to intervene.

Intervention by private parties has been allowed in relatively few cases. Examples include *Gerhardy v Brown* (1985), where an **Aboriginal** association intervened in a case involving racial **discrimination** issues; and *Lange v ABC* (1997) and *Levy*, where a number of media proprietors were granted leave to intervene to put arguments about the implied constitutional freedom of **political communication**. This was on the basis that their interests were likely to be substantially affected by any decision to reopen the earlier *Free Speech Cases* (1992). **Native title** cases have also seen a relaxed approach to the granting of leave to intervene to governments, whose **property** interests are significantly affected, as well as to native title claimants in other litigation where similar issues arise.

The discretion to allow intervention by an *amicus curiae* is exercised on a different basis. It is designed to allow a person to be heard where that person is able to assist the Court, because the parties are either unwilling or unable adequately to do so. The time and cost of intervention should not be disproportionate to the assistance to be derived. *Amici* are often limited to making written submissions. The High Court has been reluctant to allow intervention of this type, although its approach remains largely ad hoc and pragmatic, giving rise to considerable uncertainty about what has to be shown to attract a grant of leave to appear as *amicus*. For instance, in *Kruger v Commonwealth* (1997), the Court refused to allow the International Commission of Jurists to intervene because the Court already had before it persons able and willing to provide adequate assistance. By contrast, leave was granted to the Tasmanian Wilderness Society in the *Tasmanian Dam Case* (1983) and to eleven film or television bodies or persons related to the industry in *Project Blue Sky v Australian Broadcasting Authority* (1998). In *A-G (Cth) v Breckler* (1999), the Court, by majority, refused to allow the Association of Superannuation Funds of Australia to intervene as *amicus*, despite the interest of the members of the Association in the validity of the complaints regime governing them. In his judgment in that case, **Kirby** criticised what he said may seem to an outsider to be the unpredictable and inconsistent approach to allowing intervention adopted in recent cases. He has argued that the Court must adapt its procedures, particularly 'in constitutional cases and those where large issues of legal principle and legal policy are at stake'.

The High Court has no special procedures governing applications to intervene or appear as an *amicus*. The result has been that parties seeking to intervene usually file detailed written submissions in support of their application, and also on the substantive issues. Decisions on applications to intervene are not usually made until the time of the actual hearing. Where intervention results in the hearing of a matter being significantly extended, the Court has in some cases ordered interveners to pay the additional **costs** incurred by the parties. This has occurred in some constitutional cases, and it is reflected in the discretionary power conferred on the Court to order costs against the Commonwealth or a state whose Attorney-General intervenes under section 78A of the Judiciary Act. It is, however, as stated in *O'Toole v Charles David* (1991), 'only in special circumstances' that it is appropriate to make an order for costs against an intervener.

HENRY BURMESTER

Further Reading

Enid Campbell, 'Intervention in Constitutional Cases' (1998) 9 *PLR* 255

Susan Kenny, 'Interveners and Amici Curiae in the High Court' (1998) 20 *Adel L Rev* 159

Christopher Staker, 'Application to Intervene as *Amicus Curiae* in the High Court' (1996) 70 *ALJ* 387

George Williams, 'The *Amicus Curiae* and Intervener in the High Court of Australia: A Comparative Analysis' (2000) 28 *FL Rev* 365

Irish Envoys Case (1923) immersed the Court in a major political, religious, and public controversy. It is notable for the impassioned judgment of **Isaacs**, the manifest anxiety of **Higgins**, and the advocacy of **Evatt**.

Sinn Fein representatives Father Michael O'Flanagan and Joseph O'Kelly came to Australia in March 1923 seeking support for the Irish Republican cause—a cause that had just been defeated in the Irish Civil War (1921–23). The Civil War followed the Anglo–Irish Treaty of 1921 and the establishment of a moderate government in the Irish Free State. That government remained within the Commonwealth, whereas Sinn Fein demanded complete Irish independence.

One of Australia's most controversial churchmen, Archbishop Daniel Mannix, welcomed the envoys at Melbourne's annual St Patrick's Day celebrations. The St Patrick's Day procession had been the subject of controversy the previous year (see *Melbourne Corporation v Barry* (1922)). At first, the envoys met with mild criticism, but as they circulated about the archdiocese promoting their cause, feeling against them grew.

Mannix was the only Catholic bishop to have supported the envoys. The rest of the Catholic hierarchy made them unwelcome, supporting the Irish Free State and viewing the delegates' visit as divisive. Father William Mangan, editor of one of Melbourne's two Catholic papers, the *Tribune*, led the attack: 'The good people in their Catholic halls are being asked to contribute to propagating the work of extremists. The burnings and shootings, the stab in the back, the looting of homes and sacking of defenceless villages … These are the gentle aims and objects of Fr O'Flanagan.'

Irish Envoys' arrival in Sydney from Melbourne, Central Railway Station, 20 April 1923

Melbourne's other Catholic paper, the *Advocate*, controlled by Mannix, retaliated. It labelled Mangan a 'cawstle Cawtholic' and his views 'a whining and slavish doctrine'. Mangan responded sarcastically, suggesting sacrificing the envoys at the zoo 'or in the stadium'.

At a 'monster' Irish Republican demonstration, O'Kelly attacked 'the Papish little mosquito editor' of 'that so-called Catholic paper', the *Tribune*. Even Mannix thought O'Kelly's personal abuse of Mangan was going too far. Religious and political groups, members of the public, and Commonwealth **Attorney-General** Littleton Groom called for the envoys' deportation.

The envoys were arrested in April and charged with sedition under the *Crimes Act* 1914 (Cth). While criminal charges were still pending, O'Flanagan and O'Kelly were summonsed to appear before the Immigration Board to show cause why they should not be deported for advocating 'the overthrow by force or violence of the established Government of a civilised country other than the Commonwealth, to wit, the Irish Free State'. Mannix opened a fund for the envoys' defence.

O'Flanagan and O'Kelly commenced proceedings in the High Court. Evatt, led by Andrew Watt KC, acted for the envoys. Evatt and Watt argued that the use of section 8A of the *Immigration Act* 1901–1920 (Cth), under which the Immigration Board was appointed, was invalid and sought a declaration to that effect. They also sought a **writ** of prohibition, certiorari, or quo warranto, or an injunction to restrain the Board from proceeding. Evatt's biographer Kylie Tennant has described the hearing: 'The argument was tortuous and interminable and cases came hurtling across the court from the bench to the Bar and back above the bewildered heads of the two Irish gentlemen.'

Since the conduct of the Board's hearing might prejudice the envoys in their choice of tactics in the criminal proceedings against them, Isaacs held (**Knox** and **Rich** agreeing) that, if the hearing had been unlawful, an injunction would have been appropriate. After a passionate speech about the High Court's **role** in protecting individual liberty, Isaacs concluded: 'I consider that the clear assertion of the power of the Court to protect individual rights of liberty from unauthorised violation, particularly when asserted in the name of the law, is, even among the many important features of this case, by far the most important.'

The Court in any event held unanimously that intervention by prerogative writ was not appropriate, since the Board was not exercising **judicial power**. Higgins—who was Irish-born, Protestant, and a firm supporter of Home Rule—expressed anxiety:

> I have … anxiously sought to find in these provisions … something which would justify me in holding that this Board of inquiry has the essential qualities of a judicial tribunal, and that these men cannot be ejected from Australia without a trial of some sort … [But by weight of **precedent**] I am compelled to say that this Board is not a judicial tribunal to try these men in any sense for the offence; and in my opinion, therefore, the rules nisi for prohibition must be discharged.

On the constitutional issues, Evatt and Watt argued that section 8A exceeded the **immigration power** in section

51(xxvii) of the Constitution. They argued that the immigration power did not extend to British subjects, or that it was limited to migrants intending permanent settlement, or that it could apply only at the point of entry in Australia. Four Justices rejected these arguments. They took a wide view of the immigration power, spelled out most emphatically by Isaacs.

Isaacs held that the concept of immigration is not limited to permanent settlers but extends to the entry into Australia of any person who in so entering is not 'coming home'. Any concept of 'visitors' who were outside the immigration power would leave the Commonwealth unable to control the entry of crime, prostitution, and infectious disease, and would undermine a sentiment 'of paramount significance, a determination to preserve a White Australia'. In another flight of rhetoric, Isaacs said:

> Unless the recited power is sufficiently broad to meet, not only possible, but very probable, movements of population from other parts of the world towards Australia, we have but a crippled Constitution wherewith to meet the necessities of the future. That it is ample, in relation to this power, to protect people of Australia physically, racially, industrially and socially, is, to my mind, perfectly clear … Who could imagine that, when 'immigration' was entrusted to the Commonwealth Parliament, Chinese visitors were to be henceforth free from interference? Such a contention puts back the clock of Australian history a quarter of a century.

Isaacs also held that the power is not limited to the 'act' of immigrating. If entry into Australia can be prohibited, it can be allowed on conditions: deportation for reasons arising *after* entry is valid. In a phrase that in later cases became inseparably linked with Isaacs' name, he said, of anyone whose first home was elsewhere, 'the rule holds "Once an immigrant always an immigrant"'.

Even Higgins, in *obiter dicta*, somewhat ambiguously held that the Immigration Act could apply to British subjects, though in *Potter v Minahan* (1908) he had spoken of all British subjects throughout the Empire as belonging to 'one great society' with 'one tie of allegiance to the one Sovereign'.

It may be that some lingering wish on Higgins' part to maintain the freedom of all British subjects 'to move at will throughout the Empire' contributed to his dissent on the other two constitutional issues involved. Higgins held that the immigration power did *not* extend to a person entering Australia merely as a temporary visitor with no intention of permanent settlement; and also that the power was applicable *only* to 'the act of immigrating'—that is, that it could only be exercised at the point of entry into Australia, so that once having been allowed to enter the country, the Irish envoys had passed beyond the reach of the 'immigration' power. On these points, Higgins was in sole dissent.

Having failed in the High Court, the envoys were deported in June 1923. Their deportation was delayed after Evatt arranged for their temporary release when the government found there was no ship available to deport them. Mannix later paid tribute to Evatt's defence of the envoys.

In *Ex parte Walsh and Johnson; In re Yates* (1925), Evatt (opposing Robert **Garran**) attempted to impose some limits on the immigration power. In a strenuous challenge to Isaacs' contrary view, Evatt argued that a person who was once an immigrant might pass beyond the reach of the power by being absorbed into the Australian community. Although Evatt managed to persuade Knox and **Starke**, Isaacs' uncompromising view remained to haunt the Court for decades (see **Immigration law**).

SUSAN PRIEST
TROY SIMPSON

Isaacs, Isaac Alfred (*b* 6 August 1855; *d* 11 February 1948; Justice 1906–30; Chief Justice 1930–31) was a lawyer and judge of great ability who was born in humble circumstances. He was the first child of poor migrants, Alfred and Rebecca Isaacs, who arrived in Melbourne in 1854, the year before his birth. Alfred, the father, was a tailor who was born

Isaac Isaacs, Justice 1906–30; Chief Justice 1930–31

in Russian Poland, and made his way to London, where he met and married Rebecca in 1849. Little is directly known about her, though it is clear from correspondence with her son that she was an extraordinary person; she exercised a powerful influence on him until her death in 1912. Letters from her to him, and his letters to her, provide a glimpse of the extraordinary mind and character of this woman whose opportunity for formal education must have been extremely limited. The story is told that when Isaacs went with his mother to choose a barrister's wig, she told the wig-seller that she would be back in due course for a judge's wig—and made good the undertaking.

In 1859, the family moved from Melbourne to Yackandandah in north-east Victoria. Isaacs went to school there, and later to the common and then the grammar school in the larger town of Beechworth. After a short period as a teacher, he secured an appointment in 1874 as a clerk in the Crown Law Department in Melbourne. He left the family in Beechworth until 1886 when, having acquired a house, he brought them to Melbourne. In 1876, he had entered the University of Melbourne, where he began his law studies as a part-time student. He was a very good student, and graduated LLB with first-class honours. Having received his degree, he began his practice at the Victorian Bar in 1882.

Isaacs continued to practise until his **appointment** to the High Court in 1906. His work steadily built up, and he established a reputation for thorough and detailed preparation. He was a very well-furnished lawyer, with a remarkable range of learning and an intellectual capacity that brought him to the very top of the profession. He was appointed QC in 1899.

Isaacs was a Jew, and in his early adult years played some part in the affairs of the organised Jewish community. It is judged by those well qualified to know that he was not religious—as evidenced by synagogue attendance and observances. He did, however, see Jewishness as a matter of religion, and he sternly and emphatically repudiated notions of distinct Jewish ethnicity. As his correspondence and personal associations reveal, he had a strong and continuing interest in Jewish and other religious and historical cultures.

He married Daisy Jacobs in July 1888. She was the daughter of a well-known Melbourne merchant. The marriage was long-lasting; Lady Isaacs survived her husband and died in 1960. There were two daughters of the marriage, Nancy and Marjorie. Marjorie, who married David Cohen, had one son, Tim.

In 1892, Isaacs entered colonial politics and was elected for the seat of Bogong. In 1893, he accepted office as **Solicitor-General**, only to resign it after differing with the Attorney-General, Bryan O'Loghlen, over the issue of prosecution of well-known figures involved in the failure of the Mercantile Bank. The best that can be said of this unseemly affair is that both Isaacs and the government with which he quarrelled were, for different reasons, wrong. Isaacs stood again and was re-elected. In 1894, he became Attorney-General in the Turner Ministry, and held office, with only a short interruption, until he resigned to enter federal politics as member for Indi in the first federal Parliament. He had been elected to the Constitutional Convention of 1897–98, and played a prominent part in its proceedings, as Alfred **Deakin** recounts in some detail in his account of the Convention's work. After

a period of hesitation, the Victorians resolved to support the vote for federation; Isaacs exhorted his fellow citizens to do so, and it carried.

Isaacs actively participated in the work of the early federal Parliaments. In 1905 he was appointed **Attorney-General** in the second Deakin administration; Robert **Garran** testifies to the enormous energy he devoted to the discharge of the functions of the office (*Prosper the Commonwealth* (1958)). He also maintained a private practice which, despite criticism, he declined to give up. A month before his appointment to the High Court he appeared for the Commonwealth as Attorney-General in the *Railway Servants Case* (1906); he then appeared as a member of the private Bar in three more cases, including the prosecution of an unregistered dentist on behalf of the Dental Board of Victoria (*Joske v Lubrano* (1906)).

Although his judgment in the *Engineers Case* (1920) was to be associated with an emphasis on **legalism** and **literalism**, Isaacs was one of the earliest of Australian federal judges to give explicit recognition to the social implications of decision making; in his judgments he spelled out social policies—and, where appropriate, economic policies—often in detail. There are many examples of this; those in **family law** and divorce law (*Fremlin v Fremlin* (1913)), or in the field of factory legislation and legislation designed to protect employees (*Cofield v Waterloo Case Co* (1924); *Bourke v Butterfield & Lewis* (1926)), are typical. He spoke of the need for the courts to be 'living organs of a progressive community' (*Wright v Cedzich* (1930)). In relevant areas, as a judge, he showed an awareness of social issues. He read widely in social and economic literature; he supported his judgments with references to such writings as well as with copious legal authority, which he mustered as a formidable artillery in support of his position.

His technique and his **judicial style** were not so appealing. His speaking style was often rhetorical and verbose, like his judgments; worse was his unshakeable conviction of the rightness of his opinion, and the utter and complete inability to see merit in any other view. It comes out strongly in his judgments, and it came out in the course of his speeches and his polemical and controversial writings in later years. There was also an unwillingness to confess error in cases where he simply had to reverse course and withdraw from a position that had been dogmatically stated and was wrong. His technique was not simply to confess error, but to sweep it aside as if it had never been firmly asserted by him. He was a very learned and widely read lawyer and judge, but he never ceased to be a committed advocate, and the achievement of the desired result justified too much.

As a member of the Court, in deciding great constitutional issues, he said it was the duty of the Court interpreting the Australian Constitution to declare, regardless of consequences, 'the preeminence of the Constitution over any attempted legislation unauthorized' (*R v Hibble; Ex parte BHP* (1920)), and he moved steadily to a position of strong, almost undeviating support for the exercise of national—that is to say, central—power. In 1952, Ross Anderson spoke of 'an aggressive nationalism' burning through his judgments. In one of the cases touching the federal **conciliation and arbitration** power, he put it that the issue was 'whether the Commonwealth as a whole is empowered to deal with its most momentous social problem on its own broad scale unimpeded by the sectional policies of particular States' (*Clyde Engineering v Cowburn* (1926); see also **Knox Court and Arbitration**).

For almost a decade and a half from 1906, he was a dissenter in important constitutional cases; but with the passing from the scene of **Griffith**, the first **Chief Justice**, the balance shifted. The *Engineers Case* was a great monument to Isaacs' achievement. The precise issue in that case—whether a dispute between unions and WA state authorities was subject to the federal arbitration power—could have been decided on quite narrow ground; the majority, in a judgment that indisputably reveals Isaacs' hand, took much higher ground, and sought to minimise the role of vague implications from the federal nature of the Constitution in favour of the plain meaning of the text. That decision, in turn, attracted some strong opposition. Over a range of issues, he asserted a wide reach for national power. During **World War I**, he claimed a greater reach for such power than did his brethren (see especially *Farey v Burvett* (1916)); in cases involving the arbitration power, he claimed, both in a majority position and in dissent, a very wide scope for Commonwealth authority (see especially the *Burwood Cinema Case* (1925))—with a mixture of nationalism and literalism, the latter often serving the ends of the former. So it was also in relation to the **immigration power** and other powers (see also **Knox Court**).

In the Constitutional Convention of 1897–98, he had warned against the loose wording of section 92, which affirms that **interstate trade and commerce** shall be absolutely free; at that stage, he had some concern about the impact of such a clause on Victorian interests. In early cases calling for interpretation of the section, he construed its restraints as applicable both to Commonwealth and to states, but by 1920 he had taken the position that it had a broad scope, but that it bound only the states, leaving the Commonwealth free from its far-reaching constraints (*McArthur v Queensland* (1920)). Once he reached that position, he asserted that no other conclusion was credible. After his **retirement** from the High Court, the **Privy Council** held in *James v Commonwealth* (1936) that section 92 bound both Commonwealth and states; as soon as Isaacs' retirement from the office of Governor-General left him free to speak, he denounced the Privy Council decision as palpable error.

Knox, who had succeeded Griffith as Chief Justice, resigned at the end of March 1930, and Isaacs was appointed Chief Justice in his place. His tenure as Chief Justice was very short, and overshadowed by the issue of the Governor-Generalship. Isaacs resigned as Chief Justice on 21 January 1931, and the next day assumed the office of Governor-General. In such a short period, it was not possible for him to place a distinctive mark on the Chief Justiceship.

The Australian Commonwealth government, under **Prime Minister** James Scullin, had resolved to recommend the appointment of Isaacs as Governor-General in succession to Lord Stonehaven. The King, George V, declared himself to be firmly opposed to this appointment—a principal reason being the undesirability of appointing a 'local' man, as Isaacs was. Scullin remained firm in his recommendation of Isaacs. It was agreed to refer the matter to the Imperial Conference, which was in session in London; the Conference resolved that the Governor-General should be appointed on the advice of the Dominion government concerned, after informal consultation with the King. The King then appointed Isaacs. The central point established in this case is that the source of appointment is the Commonwealth government concerned and not the UK government. It has also been clear since the appointment of Lord Casey in 1965 that *only* an Australian will be appointed.

Isaacs turned 80 during his term of vice-regal office, but he undertook the heavy demands of travel and speech-making with relish, and earned general respect for his dignified conduct of the office. In retirement, over a long period, he continued to work almost to the end of his life. He made many speeches, and wrote articles and papers. He was active in his advocacy of constitutional reform, remaining always a strong supporter of central power. His writings on 'political Zionism', as he described it, were, however, intemperate, dogmatic, and insensitive, and they put him at odds with the Australian Jewish community.

The great period of Isaacs' career was as a Justice of the High Court over a quarter of a century. **Dixon**, writing in 1963 on the basis of his own impressions as **counsel** and judge over a long period, acknowledged the diversity of Isaacs' contributions to Australian public life, but concluded that Isaacs should be remembered primarily as a 'greatly talented … judge of the High Court of Australia, an office to which he … devoted himself with an energy, a learning, a concentration of mind and an intellectual resourcefulness which can seldom have been equalled'.

ZELMAN COWEN

Further Reading
Zelman Cowen, *Isaac Isaacs* (2nd edn 1993)
LF Crisp, *The Unrelenting Penance of Federalist Isaac Isaacs, 1897–1947* (1981)
Max Gordon, *Sir Isaac Isaacs: A Life of Service* (with an introduction by Owen Dixon) (1963)

Isaacs Court (2 April 1930–21 January 1931). **Isaacs** was a **puisne Justice** for more than 23 years and **Chief Justice** for 42 weeks. **Gavan Duffy**, **Rich**, and **Starke** were still members of the Court, and **Dixon** had replaced **Higgins** 14 months before Isaacs became Chief Justice; but the vacancies created by **Powers**' resignation and Isaacs' elevation to the Chief Justiceship were filled only by the **appointments** in December 1930 of **Evatt** and **McTiernan**, who did not sit until Gavan Duffy became Chief Justice (see **Gavan Duffy Court**). Effectively, therefore, this was a Court of five (see **Number of Justices**).

Initially there was an interregnum. Knox's resignation was accepted on 31 March 1930, while Isaacs' appointment was not announced until 2 April. The explanation has been provided by Dixon, who suggested to Isaacs that 1 April might not be an auspicious day on which to commence his new role.

The issue of Isaacs' Governor-Generalship dominated the period, as did changes, proposed and actual, in the Court's membership (see **Appointments that might have been**). **Personal relations** may have been strained, but worse was to follow when Evatt and McTiernan were appointed (see **Latham Court**). Relations with the **Privy Council** also remained prickly: in *Hobart Savings Bank v FCT* (1930)—where the Court concluded, after an elaborate review of the **history** of the savings bank movement, that savings banks were not 'charitable' institutions for purposes of taxation exemptions—it emerged that when *Adamson's Case* (1928) was argued before the Privy Council, Lord Dunedin had noted an apparent divergence between English and Australian courts on the meaning of 'charitable' and added condescendingly: 'But, of course, this is Australia.' Both Rich and Dixon bridled at this, and Rich was moved to quote 1 *Corinthians* 14.11:

> There are, it may be, so many kinds of voices in the world, and none of them is without signification. Therefore if I know not the meaning of the voice, I shall be unto him that speaketh a barbarian, and he that speaketh shall be a barbarian unto me.

Although Isaacs had another 17 years of vigorous public life ahead of him, for much of his time as Chief Justice he was uncharacteristically ill. After the Brisbane sittings in June, he did not sit again to hear argument until the end of September. At the Perth and Adelaide sittings, Gavan Duffy presided as Acting Chief Justice. There are only 20 reported cases in which Isaacs gave judgment as Chief Justice (including the belatedly reported *Fieman v Balas* (1930)), and five of them had been argued before he assumed the Chief Justiceship. In 13 of the 20 cases, the result was reached unanimously (including five where the Court gave a single joint judgment, one where Starke concurred separately with what was otherwise a joint judgment, and two where Rich did so). Isaacs dissented in four cases and Rich in one, while in two cases—*McArthur v FCT* (1930) and *Stephen v Federal Commissioner of Land Tax* (1930)—Isaacs' view prevailed in a **tied vote**. In both cases, it was Starke who voted with Isaacs; in *McArthur v FCT* Rich and Gavan Duffy dissented, while in *Stephen* Rich concurred with Dixon (as he now increasingly did).

As a result of the **Depression**, the **business** of the Court was considerably reduced. In addition to the 20 cases in which Isaacs sat, there were 22 other reported cases (including two single-judge matters); and the *Commonwealth Law Reports* record an additional 28 unreported cases, in 12 of which Isaacs sat (see 45 CLR 600). The Court's traditional diet of **taxation law** was beginning to be varied by bankruptcies, failed hire purchase transactions, mortgagees exercising powers of sale, and purchasers of land who were now unable to pay and sought unsuccessfully to set aside the contract on technical grounds (as in *Leske v SA Real Estate Investment Co* (1930)). A more ingenious argument of that kind was in *Land Development Co v Provan* (1930), where the contract had been signed on a Sunday: the purchaser claimed that the contract was illegal since by working on Sunday the estate agent had infringed the *Sunday Observance Act* 1677, in force in NSW through the **reception of English law**. The Court held that the statutory language of 1677—'noe tradesman, artificer workeman labourer or other person'—did not include a real estate agent.

Dixon's influence was already dominant. It was Isaacs who, in *Clyde Engineering v Cowburn* (1926), had first clearly proclaimed the 'cover the field' test of **inconsistency** under section 109 of the Constitution; but it was Dixon whose explanation and analysis in *Ex parte McLean* (1930) gave the test its authoritative form. (Isaacs and Starke concurred in a separate judgment.) In the *ARU Case* (1930), the immediate issue concerned a legislative attempt to displace the powers of the Court of **Conciliation and Arbitration** by 'conciliation committees'; but it was Dixon who, from the beginning, took charge of the proceedings and converted them into a re-examination of the *Engineers Case* (1920).

The case was a virtuoso display of Dixon's capacity to direct and control the course of litigation. The new committees (with power to vary existing awards) had been established by a new section 34 of the *Conciliation and Arbitration Act* 1904 (Cth), and a new section 33 provided that once such a committee had been appointed, the Arbitration Court would have no power to vary the relevant award. The Australian Railways Union had obtained awards in March, but in August invoked the new provisions to seek a variation of those awards by conciliation committees. The committees were appointed on 11 September; but later that day the state Railways Commissioners began proceedings in the Arbitration Court in which parts of the awards were subsequently set aside. By summons under section 21AA of the Arbitration Act, the union challenged that decision, arguing that, once the committees were appointed, the Arbitration Court could no longer interfere.

The case was argued initially (by **Evatt** for the Commonwealth and Robert **Menzies** for the employers) as one of **statutory interpretation**; but Dixon intervened from the bench to suggest that section 34 might be invalid as purporting to authorise settlement of a dispute without arbitration—and that if it was invalid, section 33 might fall as well. Menzies willingly adopted this argument, submitting that parts of section 34 were invalid and that since they were not 'severable', sections 33 and 34 must wholly fail. But Dixon intervened again. The *Acts Interpretation Act* 1901 (Cth) had recently been amended by adding section 15A (which directs judicial 'severance' to ensure that as much as possible of an enactment survives); but Dixon observed that this amendment 'does not appear to have been proclaimed', and was therefore not in force. The amendment was hastily proclaimed later that day, and came into force three days later. Finally, Dixon intervened again to ask: 'Is it intended to raise the question of the power of the Arbitration Court to bind State Railways Commissioners?' Menzies replied that this had 'not been considered'.

On 31 October the Justices announced their tentative views. Rich, Starke, and Dixon agreed that sections 33 and 34 were invalid. Gavan Duffy was 'disposed to adopt the same view'; Isaacs strongly opposed it. It would follow that the Arbitration Court's variations to the awards were valid, but that the original awards would otherwise remain on foot. But the Court desired further argument on whether the awards were initially valid: that is, whether Commonwealth legislative power under section 51(xxxv) of the Constitution extended to the making of awards binding on state Railways Commissioners. It was this issue that directly reopened the *Engineers Case*, since the one decision clearly overruled by *Engineers* was the *Railway Servants Case* (1906), where the **Griffith Court** had held that Commonwealth arbitration could not extend to state railways (see **Intergovernmental immunities**).

The issue was reargued on 19–21 November. Menzies argued that the *Railway Servants Case* had depended in part on a point not affected by *Engineers*: namely, that the specific powers relating to state railways in section 51(xxxii), (xxxiii) and (xxxiv) of the Constitution 'excluded [their] implied inclusion … in the other powers'.

In the event, Rich, Starke, and Dixon held in a joint judgment that section 33 was invalid. Isaacs and Gavan Duffy dissented, the latter treating section 33 as saved by the new 'severance' provision. The whole Court also held that the original awards had been valid. On this issue, Starke and Dixon delivered separate judgments—in which Dixon, by an elaborate dissection and reinterpretation of *Engineers*, laid the foundation for the later return in the **Melbourne Corporation Case** (1947) to a modified version of intergovernmental immunities.

Isaacs protested that 'speaking personally, after the searching examination given to the whole subject [in the *Engineers' Case*] …, I should have thought the question had been defi-

nitely settled'. Yet perhaps the dissent he would have found most galling was in the very first reported case in which he sat as Chief Justice. In January and March, while Knox was still Chief Justice, Isaacs had dissented in the **Caledonian Collieries Cases** (1930), where the rest of the Court had refused to allow the Arbitration Court to intervene in the NSW government's compulsory opening of the Rothbury coal mine. Now, in *Munday v Gill* (1930), 19 of the miners who gathered at Rothbury to resist the reopening of the mine had been charged with having taken part in an unlawful assembly. One case had been tried separately; the others had been tried together. The majority held that this was acceptable: the requirement of separate trials had no application to summary proceedings. Again Isaacs was in sole dissent.

McArthur v FCT was Isaacs' last reported judgment. At the age of 75, he left the Court to take up his new role as the first Australian-born Governor-General. Dixon, at the age of 44, was preparing for another 34 years on the Court.

GRAHAM FRICKE

J

Jacobs, Kenneth Sydney (*b* 5 October 1917; Justice 1974–79), the elder son of Albert Sydney Jacobs and Sarah Grace Aggs, was born on Sydney's north shore at Gordon, then rural bushland. His childhood centred on his local preparatory school, St John's Anglican church and the cub and scout troops, meeting at the church hall. He was educated at Knox Grammar School and from 1935 at the University of Sydney, residing at St Andrew's College. In 1938, after graduating BA with honours in Latin and Greek, he commenced his LLB and was articled to Duncan Barron.

World War II interrupted his studies. Enlisting in the Australian Imperial Forces in May 1940, he served with the 9th Division in Egypt at the battle of El Alamein in 1942 and in New Guinea in 1943; he was at the landings at Lae and Fin-

Kenneth Jacobs, Justice 1974–79

schhafen. He was then appointed as an intelligence officer. He later said that, after a rather sheltered early life, his army years had enabled him to learn much more about human behaviour, and that this, and the added years, had aided his success at the Bar.

Resuming his law studies in 1945, Jacobs graduated LLB in 1947, with first-class honours and the University Medal. In his last year at law school, he was associate to Justice Leslie Herron, later Chief Justice of NSW. Admitted to the Bar in February 1947 as a pupil of Kenneth Asprey, he quickly developed a general practice, particularly in **commercial law**, **taxation law**, and **equity**, and later in **constitutional law**. He was junior **counsel** in the High Court in *Marcus Clark v Commonwealth* (1952), and junior to **Barwick** before the **Privy Council** in *Johnson v Commissioner of Stamp Duties* (1956). Thereafter, he appeared increasingly in constitutional cases, mostly as junior to Barwick.

In 1952, he married Eleanor Mary Stewart, née Neal. They had one daughter, Rosemary. Peter Stewart, Jacobs' stepson, was aged six at the time of the marriage.

From 1953 to 1961, Jacobs lectured in equity at the University of Sydney Law School. Even after judicial duties compelled him to relinquish that role, he retained his association with the Law School as patron of the student law society. In 1958, he published his influential work, *The Law of Trusts in NSW* (sixth edition by Roderick Meagher and **Gummow**, 1997).

As a former student of the Professor of **Jurisprudence**, Julius Stone, Jacobs had been greatly impressed by Stone's analysis of the doctrine of **precedent**, which was to influence him throughout his judicial career. In a tribute to Stone's influence, written in 1967, he argued that legal certainty could best be achieved if 'the actual elements which go into the creative choice' were explicitly stated, so that 'the true scope of the decision may be … directly observed'. His steadfast adherence to this conception, and the tension between the subtlety of his legal reasoning and his unpretentious insistence on 'common sense', were the keys to his judicial method.

In November 1958, Jacobs was appointed a QC and in early 1959 appeared before the Privy Council on briefs returned by Barwick on his appointment as a federal minister. Soon after Jacobs returned from England, the Liberal Party leader in the NSW Parliament asked him to stand for a vacancy in the Legislative Council. The Liberal Party was divided at the time, and Jacobs failed by one vote to be elected. This was his only foray into politics.

The state Labor government appointed Jacobs as an acting judge of the Supreme Court of NSW in July 1959. In March 1960, he became a judge of that Court, sitting at **common law** and as an additional Judge in Equity. In 1966, the state Liberal government appointed him to the newly created NSW Court of Appeal, where his colleagues included **Walsh** and later **Mason**. Jacobs became its President in 1972.

In 1963, Barwick, as Australia's Minister for External Affairs, had asked Jacobs to accept a three-year appointment as President of the Constitutional Court of Cyprus. The appointment was announced in London, Canberra, and Nicosia—but before it could be implemented, fighting broke out between the Greek and Turkish Cypriots. The constitutional settlement collapsed, and the Constitutional Court never sat again.

Addressing the Australian National University Law Society in May 1968, Jacobs referred ironically to the 'great leap forward' NSW was to make in 1970 by adopting the judicature system of 1875. Questioning the adequacy of that system for 1970, he suggested that this should be the opportunity for 'novel' reforms to aid the pursuit of truth—including the use of expert assessors, procedures compelling parties to provide **evidence** on oath at an early stage, prior submission of evidence in writing, and limits on cross-examination. He deplored the Australian tendency to treat judges as immune from **criticism**, suggesting that it reflected 'the "touchiness" of a colonial judiciary rather than the sophistication of a nation grown to **nationhood**'. The Courts, he said, 'need the full glare of the public spotlight upon them just as parliament and the executive need it, and in a vigorous country one should expect vigorous language.' He also questioned the conventional division of the **legal profession**, asking why solicitors involved in vast and complex financial transactions and increasing specialisation should still regard the Bar as the 'senior branch' of the profession.

As a Supreme Court judge, Jacobs was best known for his judgments in equity. Among those attracting public attention were his judgment at first instance on the bequest to St Vincent's Hospital from the Resch brewing fortune (*Perpetual Trustee Co v Sisters of Charity* (1966)), and his dissenting judgment in *Barton v Armstrong* (1971), both upheld by the Privy Council (*In re Resch's Will Trusts* (1967); *Barton v Armstrong* (1973)). There were other cases in which his rational and objective approach reflected the more advanced thinking of the day. In *Ex parte McKay; Re Crowe* (1967), his joint judgment with Justice JD Holmes struck down convictions for indecent publications that the High Court later reinstated (*Crowe v Graham* (1968)). In *R v Portolesi* (1973) and *R v Sloane* (1973), Jacobs joined the Chief Justice, John Kerr, in holding that sentencing judges should fix a comparatively short non-parole period, giving the Parole Board the earliest opportunity to consider each case—not so that the period fixed would be automatically accepted, but to permit the body with the best expertise and resources to determine as early as possible whether a prisoner should remain incarcerated, or serve the balance of sentence under supervision outside the prison.

In January 1974, the Whitlam Labor government appointed Jacobs to the High Court. Richard Ackland's article in the *Australian Financial Review* of 24 January 1974 was perceptively headed: 'A liberal Liberal fills High Court Bench.'

Upon **appointment**, Jacobs quickly became involved in the turmoil of litigation surrounding the end of the **Whitlam era**, including the aftermath of the joint sitting of August 1974 (see *Cormack v Cope* (1974)). In the *PMA Case* (1975), he alone accepted an interpretation of section 57 of the Constitution that would enable the Court to avoid the invidious task of deciding whether the Senate had 'failed to pass a Bill'; in the *Territory Senators Case* (1975), he accepted **McTiernan's** earlier view that the section 57 procedures were simply not **justiciable**. Those procedures include an 'expression by the people of their preference in the choice of their elected representatives'; and 'no court in the absence of a clearly conferred power has the right to thwart or interfere with the people's expression of their choice'. His principled yet pragmatic approach to **democracy** was also evident in his **joint judgment** with McTiernan in *A-G (Cth); Ex rel McKinlay v Commonwealth* (1975)—agreeing that the words 'chosen by the people' did not require **equality** in electoral distributions, but insisting that the franchise must be 'wide enough to satisfy the description "popular"'.

In *Viro v The Queen* (1978), he agreed, for his own distinctive reasons, that Privy Council decisions no longer bound the High Court. Where other Justices sought an orderly approach to precedent, Jacobs perceived an anarchic breakdown: 'The law of precedent depends upon … a **hierarchy of courts** and now there is no longer a hierarchy.' Similarly, his conclusion that **state Supreme Courts** should now invariably follow the High Court rested on a subtle conceptual argument about the belated fulfilment of section 73 of the Constitution, proclaiming that 'the High Court is the court of appeal' from those courts.

Though Mason and Jacobs often delivered joint judgments, the *AAP Case* (1975) found them on opposite sides. Jacobs found the impugned appropriation of money valid; Mason did not. Yet their judgments explored the same uncharted areas in an eerily parallel way. Both distinguished a bare appropriation from the actual 'threatened expenditure', the validity of which might be impugned. Both explored a novel range of **Commonwealth legislative powers**, including the prerogatives encompassed in Commonwealth executive power and the so-called **nationhood power**. Jacobs added an ingenious but abstruse distinction between the 'incidental power' implied in every grant of legislative power in section 51 of the Constitution (limited to 'incidents of' the primary subject of power), and the 'incidental power' expressly granted by section 51(xxxix) (extending to what might be done 'incidentally' when legislating on that subject).

In general, his approach to Commonwealth powers reflected a conception of legislative power as 'sovereign' and 'plenary' within its specified areas (see *Berwick v Gray* (1976)). In *Russell v Russell* (1976), he alone would have upheld the challenged provisions of the *Family Law Act 1975* (Cth) in their entirety. While acknowledging the deep involvement of **family law** with 'personal and private rights' traditionally left to state law, he countered this with a broad conception of the **marriage** power in relation to **children**, bolstered by a sociological understanding of marriage as primarily concerned with the procreation, nurture, and protection of offspring.

The 1970s witnessed stirrings towards future High Court developments, not only through **Murphy's** radical challenges to settled understandings, but through the increasing questioning of those understandings by Justices such as Mason, Jacobs, and **Stephen**. Their gradual, cautious repudiation of Barwick's view of section 92 of the Constitution (see **Interstate trade and commerce**) was both a symptom and a catalyst of change. In the *North Eastern Dairy Case* (1975), Jacobs emphasised that decisions in this area must vary with the 'economic, social and other circumstances' of the community; yet also that such decisions must 'result in a pattern emerging'. He accepted as a unifying thread the distinction between direct and indirect impediments to interstate trade; but argued that a direct impediment would typically involve **discrimination** against interstate trade— sometimes 'gleaned from its express terms', but 'more commonly' from 'its actual operation'. In *Bartter's Farms v Todd* (1978), he identified two factors as crucial: 'the element of discrimination', and the role of section 92 in preventing 'attempts by one unit of a federation … to give itself and its residents economic advantages over other units of a federation'. The themes of discrimination and protectionism, ultimately to prevail in *Cole v Whitfield* (1988), had clearly been sounded.

Similarly, in *HC Sleigh v SA* (1977), Jacobs sought a coherent pattern in the precedents defining **excise duties** under section 90 of the Constitution. The majority held that a licence fee for retail sales of petrol, calculated by reference to prior sales, was not an 'excise duty', thereby following *Dennis Hotels v Victoria* (1960) and *Dickenson's Arcade v Tasmania* (1974). Jacobs, in a dissenting judgment many found disconcerting at the time but which proved to be prescient, saw those cases as a 'bulge' in the otherwise 'coherent pattern of decision', sending 'a danger signal' of 'strain and distortion'. Unless this tendency was 'curbed', he warned, the Court must face 'the virtual supersession of s90 or a need at some later time to cry halt'.

While stressing that the Court should depart from its own decisions only in response to 'social, economic or political consequences which cannot be tolerated by the nation', he stressed also that 'any case is only authority for what it actually decides'. Later cases may always be decided by *distinguishing* the earlier precedent. He emphasised, in an echo of his tribute to Stone, that the making of such distinctions is a matter of judicial choice, the reasons for which must be explored to clarify the emerging principle. He protested (in language echoed by **Deane** in *Jaensch v Coffey* (1984) and *SA v O'Shea* (1987)) that his emphasis on judicial choice was not a charter for 'individual predilections ungoverned by authority', since such choices must be guided and limited by 'training, tradition, respect for the opinions of other members of the Court, past and present, and the ordinary intellectual processes of argument'.

Ultimately, Jacobs distinguished *Dennis Hotels* and *Dickenson's Arcade* on the basis later adopted in *Capital Duplicators v ACT (No 2)* (1993) and *Ha v NSW* (1997): namely, that in the original cases 'a concatenation of factors' had allowed the calculation of the licence fee to be treated as 'no more than a

method of quantification of that licence fee and not a tax upon the product dealt with'. That could not be said where the licence was merely 'a mechanism for collection of a tax'.

There was prescience, too, in Jacobs' sensitivity to issues of human rights. His judgment in *R v Quinn; Ex parte Consolidated Foods Corporation* (1977), linking the historical conception of **judicial power** with the basic rights traditionally defended 'by that independent judiciary which is the bulwark of freedom', was a harbinger of the resort to Chapter III of the Constitution for guarantees of **due process** of law. In *Coe v Commonwealth (No 1)* (1979), he foreshadowed the common law argument that ultimately succeeded in *Mabo* (1992); and his exposition of the statutory defence of 'public good' in *Calwell v Ipec Australia* (1975) (see **Defamation law**) foreshadowed the language in which the Court would ultimately discern an implied constitutional freedom of **political communication** (see *Free Speech Cases* (1992)).

Particularly in cases involving **trusts** (for example, *ANZ Banking Group v National Mutual* (1977); *A-G (Qld); Ex rel Nye v Cathedral Church of Brisbane* (1977)) or land law (see *Commonwealth v Oldfield* (1976); *Housing Commission v San Sebastian* (1978)), Jacobs often gave the leading judgment. In other cases such as *Pigram v A-G (NSW)* (1975), *Equity Trustees Executors & Agency Co v Commissioner of Probate Duties (Vic)* (1976) or *Quadramain v Sevastapol Investments* (1976), his view of equitable principles or commercial realities led him into dissent, and sometimes into sole dissent. Repeatedly in such cases, he appealed to 'a fair and reasonable interpretation' of community experience and business expectations by judges 'representing the community of which they are part' (*Helicopter Sales v Rotor-Work* (1974)), or to 'business sense' and 'substance, not legal **form**' (*LJ Hooker v WJ Adams Estates* (1977)); or argued that the majority approach was 'unfair and unsatisfactory', whereas his would 'operate more fairly and more in accordance with the business expectations of ordinary men and women' (*Brien v Dwyer* (1978)).

These criteria led him to consistent support for workers' **compensation** claims (see *Dowell Australia v Archdeacon* (1975); *Higgins v Jackson* (1976); *Commonwealth v Muratore* (1978); *Public Trustee v State Energy Commission* (1979))— but also, in taxation cases, to frequent agreement with Barwick in upholding taxpayers' claims (see, for example, *Gauci v FCT* (1975); *FCT v Bidencope* (1978)). Sometimes it was Barwick who agreed with Jacobs (see *Lister Blackstone v FCT* (1976); *Brambles Holdings v FCT* (1977)). Often these results reflected a distinctive approach to **statutory interpretation** and construction of documents, combining scrupulous sensitivity to the nuances of words with insistence on 'rational' or 'common sense' meanings. In *Public Transport Commission v J Murray-More* (1975), where the Court held that an employer liable for workers' compensation could not claim indemnity from another defendant, Jacobs agreed because of 'the impossibility of applying the section coherently' on one construction, and the 'irrationality' of another. In *R v Halton; Ex parte AUS Student Travel* (1978), he rejected a suggested construction because 'it just would not make sense'.

In **tort law**, Jacobs' approach to precedent, and his own long experience in a state jurisdiction, led him to focus scrupulously on the facts of particular cases. In *Caltex Oil v The Dredge 'Willemstad'* (1976), the Court held Caltex entitled to **damages** when dredging operations in Botany Bay severed the underwater pipeline from the Caltex refinery to its terminal. Jacobs based the liability on the precise physical circumstances: the severing of the pipeline was a direct physical effect on the plaintiff's **property**, and all of the consequences arose from the 'physical propinquity' of the terminal and the refinery.

In 1979, it seemed that Jacobs' health would not permit him to sit regularly on the Court for some months. Although he was urged to take leave, his experience as President of the Court of Appeal had made him deeply conscious of the burden placed on other judges when a member of a court is unable to bear his share of the work. Rather than continue as a less than fully effective member of the Court, he retired on 6 April 1979.

Tony Blackshield
Mark Mackrell

Further Reading
KS Jacobs, 'Lawyers' Reasonings: Some Extra-Judicial Reflections' (1967) 5 *Syd LR* 425

Jehovah's Witnesses Case (1943). On 17 January 1941, as **Word War II** was being fought overseas, the Governor-General declared the Jehovah's Witnesses, who claimed that 'all organised political bodies were agents of Satan' and who opposed involvement in world political affairs or 'wars between nations', to be 'prejudicial to the defence of the Commonwealth' and to the 'efficient prosecution of the war' under the National Security (Subversive Associations) Regulations 1940. On the same day, police officers moved across Australia to occupy premises belonging to the group.

Within hours, these dramatic events captured newspaper headlines. Reports were filed of bungled raids that had resulted in injury to officers and led to charges of assault and grievous bodily harm. The Jehovah's Witnesses responded by stating that accusations of hampering the war effort were 'malicious and entirely unfounded'.

On 4 September 1941, the Adelaide Company of Jehovah's Witnesses sought an injunction in the High Court to restrain the Commonwealth from continuing or repeating the trespass; they also sought **damages**. In 1943, before five members of the High Court, with **Fullagar** as their leading **counsel**, they contended that the regulations contravened section 116 of the Constitution. This section, an **express constitutional right**, excludes religious **discrimination** at Commonwealth level in four distinct ways, including a denial of Commonwealth power to enact legislation for prohibiting 'the free exercise of any religion'.

The High Court had examined section 116 on only one prior occasion. In *Krygger v Williams* (1912), it had defined the provision narrowly, holding that compulsory **military** training did not intrude upon 'the free exercise of any religion'. Krygger had stated: 'I decline to render military service because it is opposed to the word of God … Attendance at drill is against my conscience and the will of God.' **Griffith** responded: 'It may be that a law requiring a man to do an act which his religion forbids would be objectionable on moral grounds, but it does not come within the prohibition of sec 116.' **Barton** reached the same conclusion, stating that

'this objection is as thin as anything of the kind that has come before us'.

In the *Jehovah's Witnesses Case*, the Court unanimously held that the regulations did not infringe section 116. While the concept of 'religion' for the purposes of the guarantee was construed very widely, the protection actually afforded was minimal. Indeed, the latter conclusion flowed naturally from the former. In the leading judgment of the Court, **Latham** set out some of the practices that during periods of human **history** have been regarded as religious, including the 'essentially evil and wicked', such as 'human sacrifice or animal sacrifice'. By including these within the scope of section 116, he was able to reason that the protection offered by the section could not be absolute, or even very broad. This reasoning had particular force where the free exercise of religious belief would threaten ordered government under the Constitution.

Latham found that the regulations could be characterised as 'a law to protect the existence of the community' rather than 'a law "for prohibiting the free exercise of any religion"'. The other Justices also held that section 116 was not infringed by a law that enabled the Commonwealth to suppress persons and bodies prejudicial to the defence of the Commonwealth. As **Rich** put it: 'Freedom of religion may not be invoked to cloak and dissemble subversive opinions or practices and operations dangerous to the common weal.'

Despite these findings on section 116, the Adelaide Company of Jehovah's Witnesses succeeded in arguing that the regulations were invalid on the ground that they exceeded the scope of the Commonwealth's **defence power** in section 51(vi) of the Constitution. Describing the regulations as 'arbitrary, capricious and oppressive', the Court found they exceeded 'what was reasonably necessary for the protection of the community and … the interests of social order'.

The High Court has had few opportunities since the *Jehovah's Witnesses Case* to interpret section 116 (see **Church and state**; *DOGS Case* (1981); *Kruger v Commonwealth* (1997)). This may be due in part to the fact that attempts at reliance upon the provision have invariably failed. The *Jehovah's Witnesses Case* thus stands as central to a line of authorities in which the religious freedom proclaimed by the Constitution has been judicially narrowed.

Importantly, other recent decisions of the Court concerning minority faiths now exist outside the realm of section 116: see for example, *Church of the New Faith v Commissioner of Pay-roll Tax (Vic)* (1983). While the Court has adopted a more protective and sensitive approach to religious freedom in such cases, this has not led the Court to re-examine its decision in the *Jehovah's Witnesses Case*.

Susan Priest
George Williams

Further Reading
Stephen McLeish, 'Making Sense of Religion and the Constitution: A Fresh Start for Section 116' (1992) 18 *Mon LR* 207
James Richardson, 'Minority Religions, Cults and the Law' (1995) 18 *UQLJ* 183

Joint judgments and separate judgments. Courts decide legal disputes between parties. In so doing, they must frame

orders that dispose of the disputes. But courts also frame rules of more general application in the course of publicly discharging their function of deciding those disputes 'according to law'. They therefore issue not only particular orders but also more discursive 'judgments' (referred to also as 'opinions'), designed to encapsulate the reasons behind their decisions.

Practices in relation to the delivery of reasons for judgment vary widely. In multi-member courts, the court may publish a single opinion of the whole court, or of a majority of the court; groups of judges may join together to write joint opinions; or individual judges may issue their own individual opinions, whether in concurrence or dissent. The **United States Supreme Court** has favoured a consolidated opinion of the Court or of the majority; the High Court has been marked by rugged individualism, though with bursts of collective effort from time to time. In both countries, the relative merits of joint and separate judgments are hotly contested.

The perceived advantage of a joint judgment—particularly of the whole court—is that clarity is enhanced by the absence of diverse views or diverse ways of saying the same thing. As the final appellate court in Australia, the High Court has a responsibility to declare the law; this is obviously assisted if the Court can speak with one voice. Yet the High Court has generally spoken with many voices, and at considerable length, much to the chagrin of the law students, **commentators**, practitioners, and judges who have to spend many hours sifting the sediment to find the gold. At the very least, the Court could avoid tedious repetitions of the facts and unnecessary differences of opinion on minor points of **statutory interpretation**, reserving its differences for important points of legal principle. And whereas **dissenting judgments** have an honourable place in the law—the reputation of many a great judge having been built upon the eventual vindication of a point of view that once seemed idiosyncratic—separate **concurring judgments** often seem merely self-indulgent (see **Collective responsibility**).

On the other hand, there are very good reasons for separate opinions. First, the clarity and certainty allegedly achieved by joint opinions may be illusory. A joint opinion can sometimes be a rather bland compromise that tends to paper over and disguise rather than resolve real differences of opinion—differences that can leap up and bite the unwary when the joint opinion is put to the test in a later case. The aggregation of separate opinions, their nuances more patent than latent, may in fact, although initially more demanding for the reader, be a surer guide to future development. The *realpolitik* of prediction is, here, a counterbalance to naive faith in the productiveness of an abstract search for the elusive *ratio decidendi*.

Secondly, and more importantly, each judge has, as part of the **judicial oath,** a separate and individual responsibility for decision, and that responsibility is most obviously discharged by the writing of a separate opinion. Joint opinions may encourage laziness or undue influence of some judges over others. In 1950, **Latham** observed:

A great deal of time can be saved by consultation and by assigning one judge to write a judgment. I am now finding it possible to adopt this method more frequently, but it has to be watched in order to prevent a tendency which, I suggest, has at times been most odious in the **Privy Council**, to leave it to one judge to do all the work and really make up the mind of the Court.

The practice of the Judicial Committee of the Privy Council was, of course, an extreme example of the use of joint opinions. Until 1966, when, in his capacity as a sitting member to hear appeals from countries other than Australia, **Barwick** instigated a change, it refused to countenance the publication even of a dissenting opinion on the historical but now quaint basis that, as opinions of the Judicial Committee were formally tendered as 'advice' to the monarch, he or she would be confused or embarrassed if the advisers did not speak with one voice.

In similar vein to Latham, in 1820, when John Marshall was Chief Justice of the US Supreme Court, Thomas Jefferson had written in disapproval of the idea of an opinion reached by Justices

huddled up in a conclave, perhaps by a majority of one, delivered as if unanimous, and with the silent acquiescence of lazy or timid associates, by a crafty Chief Justice, who sophisticates the law to his own mind by the turn of his own reasoning.

Whatever the potential dangers of joint opinions, separate opinions may well enhance the integrity of the **decision-making process**, in fact and in appearance.

Thirdly, it should not be forgotten that diversity of opinion in the Court is a reflection of the complexity and openness of most of the issues that come before it; of the wide range of **values** that underlie those issues; and, to an extent, of analogous diversity in the wider community. As Oliver Wendell Holmes of the US Supreme Court observed, 'certainty generally is illusion, and repose is not the destiny of man'. Once it is accepted that the law develops with a balance of certainty and flexibility, and that the achievement of certainty is one but not the only object of the law, then endemic diversity of opinion, as manifested in the tendency to separate opinions, becomes more understandable, and consequently more palatable.

Tendencies of judges to be parties to joint opinions or to write separate opinions, and the style of those opinions, vary between different legal cultures and over time. In the High Court, these tendencies have varied over the years with variations in individual temperament, the Justices' **personal relations**, the interest and persuasiveness of different **Chief Justices** in seeking consensus, and the pressure of **business**. The caseload of the US Supreme Court probably necessitated the system of a single opinion of the Court, though that had been the inclination of Chief Justice Marshall in any event. On the other hand, time pressures can inhibit rather than encourage a corporate approach: the seven individual (and long) judgments in the *Tasmanian Dam Case* (1983) appear to have been the product of shortage of time to explore the potential for agreement. By contrast, in *Cole v Whitfield* (1988), the 11 months between **argument** and decision no doubt facilitated the production of a single, unanimous, joint judgment, in a case in which, after 80 years of cacophony, speaking with one voice was seen to be particularly important.

Separate opinions indulge idiosyncrasy and allow scope for individual difference, whereas joint opinions, like reports of committees, tend to be more bland and less interesting. Functionally, joint opinions are associated with consensus, clarity, certainty, and stability, whereas separate opinions are associated with individual responsibility, fluidity, difference, and diversity, and more openly presage change. The reality is that appellate courts worth their salt must achieve a balance between attaining certainty and maintaining flexibility, between ensuring continuity and permitting change, between seeking consensus and tolerating difference, between making corporate decisions and preserving individual **independence**, between achieving efficiency and allowing due deliberation. No single model for arriving at and pronouncing judgment—whether it be that of one voice or many—can be right for all times and for all occasions and for all judges.

Michael Coper

Judges' notebooks. High Court Justices, like other holders of judicial office, receive notebooks in which to record their notes of **argument** and (rarely) of evidence taken in the original **jurisdiction** of the Court. The preparation of a daily **transcript** of extremely high quality has overtaken the need for the detailed judges' notes which, in earlier times, performed a more valuable role.

Judges' notebooks are maintained by the Justices as an *aide-mémoire* in the matters coming before them for determination. Prior to the introduction of shorthand **reporting** in about 1920, judges' notebooks represented (in some matters at least) the authentic record of judicial proceedings. They usually consisted of short statements of what transpired in the course of the trial or proceedings. This included statements of the testimony of witnesses, lists of documents admitted into evidence, notes as to argument before the Court, and useful **citations**. The notebooks of some Justices, such as **Isaacs**, contain notes made in shorthand, sketches of **counsel**, and abstract doodles.

The use made of the notebooks currently depends on the practice of each individual Justice. Some Justices record appearances and **orders** and take detailed notes. Most record important points—especially matters of impression they wish to use later to supplement the transcript and stimulate recall of ideas developed during argument. Still others take few notes at all. Some Justices keep rudimentary notes in their notebook but supplement these with a record on plain paper of a first draft of the outline of their reasons for judgment, as it develops in their mind in the course of the hearing. Some Justices take the view that the hearing should be used efficiently to plan the structure of their subsequent reasons or at least to identify the issues that will have to be addressed in the judgment when it is later prepared.

As with Justices' **private papers**, there has not been a uniform practice as to the preservation of notebooks. To the extent that they have been maintained, judges' notebooks have been retained by each Justice during their period of office, and handed to the Registrar of the Court on their **retirement**. Many notebooks of retired Justices were kept in the Court's **archives** in the basement of the Court's Canberra **building** until the late 1990s, but most of these are now kept at the National Archives of Australia. Some early notebooks, such as **Barton's** notebook of 1903, are held at the National Library of Australia. Barton's notebook records, in point

form, the events that transpired at the Court's first **sitting** on 6 October 1903, and includes details of other early cases such as *Hannah v Dalgarno* (1903). Some Justices reportedly had their notebooks destroyed on retiring from office. Notebooks of current Justices are kept in **chambers**.

The notebooks of early High Court Justices may have been under-utilised by legal historians. As part of an address to mark the seventy-fifth anniversary of the *Engineers Case* (1920), **Brennan** referred to entries made by Knox and Isaacs in their notebooks for that case. So far the only major use of High Court notebooks, Brennan's findings cast a new light on the legal history of *Engineers*. Containing unedited—though usually brief and sometimes sparse—references to the issues and argument before the Court, early High Court notebooks are a potentially useful and largely untapped resource.

Tony Thew

Further Reading

Gerard Brennan, 'Three Cheers for *Engineers*' in Michael Coper and George Williams (eds), *How Many Cheers for Engineers?* (1997) 145

Judgment production. Where decisions have been **reserved**, judgment production is the process beginning with the research and writing of reasons for judgment and concluding with their publication. Written reasons have always been highly valued. As **Kitto** has said, 'the very exercise of writing ensures more careful thinking and rethinking, gives greater opportunity for detecting hidden fallacies, and reduces the chance that some relevant point has been missed or glossed over in the argument'. Written reasons also explain to parties not only whether they have won or lost, but how the Justices reached that conclusion. Moreover, written reasons are considered integral to the open administration of justice (see **Open court**).

Most Justices follow a similar procedure during the early stages of judgment production, although there is significant variation later on. All Justices start the preparation of reasons for judgment after the oral hearing, with the assistance of **appeal books** prepared by the parties (including the judgments in the lower courts); written submissions; **transcripts** of proceedings; and case, legislative and **extrinsic materials**.

Justices rarely act alone in developing their reasons for judgment. A Justice may be assisted by the opinion of colleagues who have already circulated their proposed reasons, or by discussions or **conferences** with other Justices. A Justice may also be assisted by an **associate**, or by the Court's **research** staff, who provide research and memoranda. But unlike the **United States Supreme Court**, for example, the High Court has developed no practice whereby the first draft of a Justice's reasons is written by the Justice's associate.

After the initial draft is prepared, the next stage is its circulation and proofing. Each Justice circulates his or her proposed reasons to colleagues who participated in the hearing of the matter. When all changes to the initial draft have been marked, it is recirculated. Reasons may be withdrawn and recast, or even entirely discarded. Agreements and joinders may be tendered. At the end of this process, an associate proofs the draft produced by his or her judge, using the Style Manual of the Court. The associate offers comments to the

Justice on the reasoning, structure and syntax of the opinion, as well as reviewing the accuracy and relevance of quotations and citations. During this period, both minor and substantive changes may be made as the Justices reflect on their own and each other's reasons.

When all the members of the Court who have participated in the hearing of the matter have circulated their proposed reasons, and these have been proofed within **chambers**, the **Chief Justice** circulates a proposal for delivery of the case on a certain date. The Court's publishing officers then begin their own proofing process, which involves a secondary review of syntax and citations. At the end of this process, the publishing officer may liaise with each Justice's associate and propose final amendments. These proposals are reviewed by the associate, and then sent to the Justice for approval or rejection.

Draft **orders** and catchwords are then produced within the chambers of the presiding Justice (should there be an opinion of the Court) or, otherwise, within the chambers of the most senior majority Justice. Once drafted, orders and catchwords are then circulated for amendment and approval by each Justice who participated in the matter. The proposed orders and catchwords are also reviewed by the Court's publishing officers, who review all amendments made after the completion of the proofing process. These procedures are relatively recent. Until the Court appointed a publication officer, proofing was done only within chambers, and only recently have catchwords been prepared within the Court. Moreover, before a Court research officer was appointed in 1976, associates and Justices did all the research.

All that then remains is for the final form of the manuscript of each Justice's reasons to be signed by the Justice, handed down in open court, and deposited in the Court Registry. Under the supervision of the publishing officer, the finished reasons are also published in pamphlet form, to be provided to the interested parties and the public. These judgment pamphlets have been generally available only since July 1977, though ever since the Court's **establishment** most of its judgments have subsequently been published by various legal reporting services (see **Reporting of decisions**). Nowadays, judgments are quickly uploaded to the Court's website (see **Information technology**).

In complex or controversial cases, the judgment production process may take months—sometimes more than a year—although, as **Gleeson** has noted, the present Court has been able to maintain a relatively quick turnover of most of its workload. The Court does not usually append any statement explaining its decision in addition to the catchwords and judgments, though a number of people, including **Stephen**, have suggested the systematic release of press statements summarising the effect of decisions (see **Media and the Court**).

In earlier times, the technical aspects of the process were vastly different. Written submissions from the parties were not expected, and rarely offered, so that Justices relied more heavily on their own notes of oral **argument**; but with the changes in court procedures and increased levels of complexity in most modern litigation, extensive written materials are now commonplace. There were also fewer rules of practice governing the need for appeal books and written submissions. The typing of draft and final judgments—done

manually, with carbon copies—was an arduous task. The difficulty of correcting typed copies meant that Justices would often make final edits and changes by hand on the copies to be read out in open court. (In the early years of the Court, judgments were read from the Bench in their entirety.) This practice made the actual manuscript of the judgment look quite different from today's word-processed documents. Justices' idiosyncrasies were much more apparent; and the judgment manuscripts much less homogeneous. Some Justices, including **Latham**, **Dixon**, and **Rich**, preferred to have their judgments typed on short sheets (approximately equivalent to A5 size today) so that they could maintain eye contact with people in the courtroom while reading a judgment aloud. Other Justices—**McTiernan**, **Evatt** and **Starke**, for example—used foolscap-size paper. Some preferred triple-spacing, others double-spacing. And some used high-quality, watermarked vellum, while others preferred onion skin.

But these past differences have more to do with technological changes than with differences in the nature of the task. Many aspects of the process have remained relatively constant. There have almost always been informal discussions between the Justices—by oral communication or letter, privately or in conference—which have been conducive to **joint judgments** and **concurring judgments**. Judgments have always been delivered in open court, as the delivery of reasons is an integral aspect of the open administration of justice.

REBECCA CRASKE
RICHARD HAIGH

Judicial notice. When a court takes judicial notice of a particular fact (during the course of either a criminal or a civil matter) it declares that the fact exists notwithstanding that specific evidence of it has not been tendered. In *Holland v Jones* (1917), **Isaacs** identified two main instances where a court has recourse to the doctrine:

> wherever a fact is so generally known that every ordinary person may be reasonably presumed to be aware of it, the Court 'notices' it, either simpliciter if it is at once satisfied of the fact without more, or after such information or investigation as it considers reliable and necessary in order to eliminate any reasonable doubt.

The doctrine is a product of the adversarial system in which a court, unlike the courts in an inquisitorial system, generally adjudicates only on the evidence before it, and does not embark on its own factual inquiry into the completeness of such material. The rationale for the doctrine is essentially the efficient administration of justice: it is designed to expedite the hearing of a matter by eliminating the need for evidence to be adduced, especially where it would be disproportionately costly and difficult to obtain.

In the High Court, the doctrine has been much less frequently employed in its appellate **jurisdiction** than in its original jurisdiction, since appeals are normally conducted on the basis that all the material facts have been fully established at trial level. Even in its appellate jurisdiction, however, the Court has taken judicial notice of the fact that the fingers of the human hand have unique and individual fingerprints (*Parker v The King* (1912)), that a particular individual is a minister (*Holland*), and that a consequence of acute alcoholism is paranoia (*Timbury v Coffee* (1941)).

In the Court's original jurisdiction, the doctrine is often employed (although not always with clarity) where the constitutional validity of legislation depends on the establishment of certain facts ('constitutional facts'). This exercise can often be difficult, because such issues typically arise in the absence of any preliminary factual contest between the parties, and also because of the very general nature of the facts in question. In such cases, the Court is not concerned with facts peculiar to the parties before it, but rather with the factual background that may bear on the process of **judicial reasoning** required to determine the constitutional validity of a given law. Once the law is declared valid, the decision is binding with respect to that law, and the Court will rarely revisit its underlying factual basis (*Commonwealth Freighters v Sneddon* (1959); *Breen v Sneddon* (1961)).

Examples include the ***Communist Party Case*** (1951) where, in the course of determining the constitutional validity of legislation seeking to ban the Australian Communist Party, the Court took judicial notice of what were commonly accepted to be the principal tenets of communism—but not of the content of the Constitution of the former USSR: the former being a matter of general public knowledge, the latter not. In *Stenhouse v Coleman* (1944), the issue was whether or not certain regulations imposed on bakers were a necessary wartime measure. In that case, the Court took notice of the fact that the minister regarded bread as an essential article, and upheld the validity of the regulations pursuant to the **defence power**.

In earlier cases, the Court—no doubt conscious of the tension between the concept of judicial notice and the other rules of evidence—expressed a more cautious view of the ambit of the doctrine (see, for example, *Stenhouse*). In more recent times, however, the Court has resiled from this conservative sentiment and adopted a more flexible and pragmatic approach to **fact finding** in the interests of expediency (see, for example, *Todorovic v Waller* (1981); *Gerhardy v Brown* (1985); and even *Lange v ABC* (1997)).

But the broader the scope of the doctrine, the more problematic its application becomes. Greater judicial initiative may result in greater uncertainty for litigants as to the facts of which a court will take notice. Likewise, where judicial notice goes beyond facts that are incontrovertible, parties may be denied **natural justice** by not being permitted the opportunity to challenge the view of the court as to the facts found.

The **United States Supreme Court** has partly resolved these problems by accepting what is commonly referred to as a 'Brandeis brief'. A Brandeis brief is essentially a dossier—including such material as reports of committees, research materials, papers by academics, and laws of other jurisdictions—submitted to the Supreme Court by one of the parties to give the Court access to social and **economic** facts and other information deemed relevant to the matter before it.

While an advantage of the Brandeis brief is that it affords an opposing party the opportunity to reply to the material contained within it, it is clear that evidence presented in this way is subjected to little, if any, testing or scrutiny, and may be incorrect or misleading. In any event, the type and breadth of the facts presented to the Supreme Court in a Brandeis brief go much further than the doctrine of judicial notice currently espoused by the High Court. Consequently, this device has not been formally adopted in Australia. Rather, the Court may allow itself to be informed of certain matters, or to have relevant material put before it, by granting leave to interested persons or organisations to appear as **interveners** or *amici curiae*.

As debate continues over the extent to which it is appropriate for the High Court to construct the factual matrix upon which the constitutional validity of laws may depend, some **commentators** have suggested that the Court should establish formal procedures for the ascertainment of facts. Irrespective of the merits of such an approach, the **role** of the Court as the ultimate arbiter of constitutional matters will ensure that the task of fact finding in such contexts will remain an inescapable and unenviable burden.

RACHEL PEPPER

Further Reading
Patrick Brazil, 'The Ascertainment of Facts in Australian Constitutional Cases' (1970) 4 *FL Rev* 65
Sanford Kadish, 'Judicial Review in the High Court and the United States Supreme Court' (1959) 2 *MULR* 127
Susan Kenny, 'Constitutional Fact Ascertainment' (1990) 1 *PLR* 134
PH Lane, 'Facts in Constitutional Law' (1963) 37 *ALJ* 108

Judicial oath. The *High Court of Australia Act* 1979 (Cth) requires a person appointed as a Justice, before proceeding to discharge the duties of the office, to take an oath or make an affirmation that he or she will 'bear true allegiance to Her Majesty Queen Elizabeth the Second, Her Heirs and Successors according to law' and will 'well and truly serve Her in the Office of Chief Justice [or Justice] of the High Court of Australia and … will do right to all manner of people according to law without fear or favour, affection or ill-will'. The prescribed form combines an oath of allegiance with an oath of office. Both oaths have a long history.

The oath of allegiance has its origin in the feudal duty of fidelity owed to the liege lord, though the tie between subject and King was personal rather than tenurial. Allegiance is the duty owed by a subject to the King, the binding tie between the subject and the Sovereign. Under early English law, natural-born subjects over the age of 12 were required to swear allegiance, but the *Promissory Oaths Act* 1868 (UK) permitted only judges and certain other officers of government to take the oath. In the present day, the Oath of Allegiance to the Queen as the Head of State of the Commonwealth has been seen as a promise of fidelity and service to the Australian people in whom the constitutional **sovereignty** of the Commonwealth is vested.

The oath of office derives from a statute of Edward III in 1346. That statute fixed the form of the oaths of allegiance and of judicial office that were used until more modern forms were prescribed by the Promissory Oaths Act. The oath or affirmation of office imposes a solemn obligation on the Justice to exercise the **jurisdiction** of the Court or Justice ('will do right'), to be impartial and not to be a partisan for a cause or section of society ('to all manner of people'), to apply the law ('according to law'), to be independent ('without fear or favour'), and not to be influenced by emotion or by improper considerations ('without … affection or ill-will'). Thus the oath reflects the qualities expected to be exhibited by a Justice in the performance of his or her judicial duties.

The practice of the Court is for an incoming **Chief Justice** or a newly appointed Justice to present his or her Commission of Appointment and to take the oath or make the affirmation in **open court**. A printed form of the oath or affirmation is tendered by the Chief Justice to a newly appointed Justice—or by the senior Justice to an incoming Chief Justice—and the appointee is invited to swear the oath or make the affirmation and to subscribe the printed form. When the form is subscribed, it is filed in the Court records.

GERARD BRENNAN

Judicial power. From an early date, the High Court made clear that the judicial power of the Commonwealth—vested by section 71 of Chapter III of the Constitution in the High Court, the federal courts, and state courts invested with federal jurisdiction—is of a special nature. However, despite the Court's attempts to identify the characteristics of judicial power, it remains an elusive concept.

Through its interpretation of the jurisdictional limits of federal judicial power and its conception of the distinction between judicial and **non-judicial functions**, the Court has limited both the subject matter and the content of the jurisdictions which can be invested by the Commonwealth and state parliaments in Chapter III courts—including the High Court itself—and which cannot validly be invested in bodies other than these courts. The Court's conception of judicial power has enabled it to determine the jurisdictional demarcation between Chapter III courts and other non-judicial bodies.

The outer limits of federal judicial power are determined by the terms in which the appellate and original **jurisdiction** of the High Court is defined in Chapter III. In *In re Judiciary and Navigation Acts* (1921), the High Court declared invalid Part XII of the *Judiciary Act* 1903 (Cth), which purported to empower the Governor-General to refer to the High Court for determination any question of law as to the validity of any Act. The Court held that the giving of an **advisory opinion** was a judicial function, but that it was not part of the judicial power of the Commonwealth as it was not a 'matter' within section 75 or section 76 of the Constitution.

In *Re Wakim* (1999), *In re Judiciary and Navigation Acts* was relied upon by the High Court to find that the federal courts are insulated against the possibility of being invested by state parliaments with state jurisdiction. The Court held unconstitutional section 9 of the *Jurisdiction of Courts (Cross-vesting) Act* 1987 (Cth), by which the Commonwealth purported to consent to the vesting of state jurisdiction in federal and territory courts. The majority found that the provisions of Chapter III were 'intended as a delimitation of the whole of the original jurisdiction' that could be invested by the Commonwealth Parliament, and gave rise to the negative implication that no other jurisdiction could be invested in these courts. The decision had the effect of invalidating a critical feature of the **cross-vesting** scheme, which had operated to avoid the inconvenience and expense occasioned by jurisdictional conflict.

In *Huddart Parker v Moorehead* (1909), the Court asserted that section 71 of the Constitution does not give Parliament power to entrust the exercise of judicial power to any body other than a Chapter III court. In the *Wheat Case* (1915), this principle was invoked by the majority to invalidate Part V of the *Inter-State Commission Act* 1912 (Cth), which conferred adjudicatory powers on the **Inter-State Commission** established by section 101 of the Constitution. The majority found that, despite the terms of section 101, the adjudicatory functions conferred on the Commission by the Act went beyond what were incidental to its executive and administrative functions, and amounted to an invalid conferral of the judicial power of the Commonwealth inconsistent with the requirements of Chapter III. The effect of this decision was to preclude the Commonwealth from establishing a 'third class' of courts, and saw the demise of the Inter-State Commission. In *Alexander's Case* (1918), the High Court declared that a central characteristic of a federal court is the **tenure** provided for its members, and that a body constituted otherwise than in accordance with section 72 (in that case by appointment for a limited seven-year term of office) cannot validly be invested with federal judicial power.

The lines of reasoning developed in the *Wheat Case* and *Alexander's Case* were extended in the ***Boilermakers Case*** (1956) to preclude the vesting of non-judicial functions in Chapter III courts. The High Court held that the Commonwealth Court of **Conciliation and Arbitration** could not validly exercise the judicial power of the Commonwealth on the ground that it was not permissible for Parliament to confer on one body both judicial and arbitral (non-judicial) functions. The case established the requirement for a strict separation of federal judicial power and the prohibition against an admixture of judicial and non-judicial functions in Chapter III courts.

An important consequence of these cases has been the need to draw a sharp distinction between judicial and non-judicial functions so as to distinguish between judicial and non-judicial power. The High Court has acknowledged the 'difficulty, if not impossibility, of framing a definition of judicial power that is at once exclusive and exhaustive'. This arises from the fact that many of the typical attributes of judicial power are not conclusive of the characterisation of a power as judicial. The High Court's approach has been to have regard to a number of indicators of judicial power which, in combination, provide guidance on whether a particular power is judicial. These focus on the process by which the power is exercised, the product of that process, historical considerations, and the status and trappings of the body exercising the power.

In *Huddart Parker*, **Griffith** described judicial power as the power to make binding and authoritative determinations that settle controversies about rights. In *Alexander's Case*, the Court suggested that what distinguishes judicial from non-judicial power is the adjudication of existing rights and obligations, as distinct from the *creation* of rights and obligations. However, several functions involving the creation of new rights—for example, the power to create new **property** rights for the benefit of a party to a marriage or dissolved marriage (*Cominos v Cominos* (1972))—have been held to be part of the judicial power of the Commonwealth.

The High Court has insisted that judicial power involves the application of established legal standards. A decision-making power that requires the application of **policy considerations** or involves a substantial degree of discretion is less likely to be characterised as judicial. This was seen as a critical factor in *R v Spicer; Ex parte Australian BLF* (1957), where the High Court found that section 140 of the *Conciliation and Arbitration Act* 1904 (Cth), which authorised a federal court to disallow an 'unreasonable' rule of an industrial organisation, was an invalid conferral of non-judicial power on the court.

In difficult cases, the High Court has considered the historical treatment of functions in order to characterise a particular power as judicial or non-judicial. The functions traditionally given to courts of law under English law, even when there is no dispute between parties, have been classified as judicial where they were treated as such by the legislation conferring the function—for example, the power to make a voluntary sequestration order (*R v Davison* (1954)). The historical practice of committing the trial of **military** offences to courts martial has been recognised as placing this function outside the constitutional concept of judicial power (*R v Bevan; Ex parte Elias and Gordon* (1942)). The Court has recognised that some functions are of an innominate nature, in the sense that their characterisation as judicial or non-judicial may depend on the character of the repository of the grant of the power. In determining how such a function is to be classified, the Court has considered whether Parliament intended to confer judicial or non-judicial power on the body.

In *R v Quinn; Ex parte Consolidated Foods Corporation* (1977), **Jacobs** noted that this historical approach to the characterisation of functions reflects the traditional, protective concern that 'basic' rights be determined by an independent judiciary. This concern for the protection of individual rights has caused the Court in more recent times to identify 'exclusively judicial functions' that can only be exercised by Chapter III courts and cannot be the subject of interference by the legislature. In the *War Crimes Act Case* (1991), a majority of the Court held that a law that declares a named person to be guilty of a crime and imposes a penalty on that person (a Bill of Attainder) would be an invalid usurpation of judicial power.

The Court has recognised that the nature of the product of the decision-making process is a key factor in determining whether the power exercised by a body is judicial. A judicial decision conclusively settles the rights and liabilities of the parties to the decision and is not open to collateral challenge in, for example, proceedings for its enforcement. The characteristic of conclusiveness has been used by the Court to determine the jurisdictional demarcation between Chapter III courts and administrative tribunals. In *Brandy v Human Rights and Equal Opportunity Commission* (1995), the binding and conclusive nature of the determinations resulting from amendments to the *Racial Discrimination Act* 1975 (Cth) was a significant factor in the conclusion that the amended provisions had invalidly conferred judicial power on the Commission, a non–Chapter III body. However, *Rola Co v Commonwealth* (1944) demonstrates that this characteristic is not decisive of the question whether the decision-making function is an exercise of judicial power, particularly where the conclusive determination is as to matters of fact.

Linda Kirk

Further Reading
Leslie Zines, *The High Court and the Constitution* (4th edn 1997) ch 10

Judicial reasoning refers both to the process of thought by which a judge reaches a conclusion as to the appropriate result in a case, and to the written explanation of that process in a published judgment. The latter is the principal mechanism of judicial **accountability**: an explanation of the reasons for decision is owed not only to the unsuccessful litigant, but to everyone with an interest in the judicial process, including other institutions of government and ultimately the public. No other public decision makers are under such a heavy obligation to explain the reasons for their decisions. Yet the specialised nature of legal discourse means that the function of public justification is often imperfectly realised: the explanations are designed to be understood primarily by other judges and by the **legal profession** in general.

While the published reasons for decision lend themselves to objective analysis, the underlying processes of thought involved in exploring and resolving a legal problem are so complex and variable that neither judges nor writers on **jurisprudence** have been able to reduce them to an adequate explanatory or prescriptive model. Ideally, the written reasons for judgment not only provide an accurate mirror of the underlying reasoning process, but may actually help to shape it: the task of reducing one's thinking to writing is itself an aid to thinking, and sometimes a decisive aid. The **Dixon diaries** record several instances in which **Dixon**, on completing his written judgment, found that he had reached the opposite conclusion to that which he expected to reach when he began to write.

A typical written judgment begins by outlining the facts of the case, and then proceeds to a discursive exploration of the relevant legal doctrines and principles. Implicit in this structure, though rarely spelled out explicitly, is the idea that the final stage in the process of judicial reasoning can be reduced to a syllogism: the relevant propositions of law provide the major premise, the facts of the case are the minor premise, and the conclusion follows simply from the application of the law to the facts. The difficulty is that neither premise is given: both premises need to be established, and tailored to each other in such a way that the explicit or implicit construction of the final syllogism is possible. Moreover, while the syllogistic model might imply that the legal and factual premises can be formulated independently, this is rarely the case. The mental processes of apprehending the facts and formulating the relevant propositions of law unavoidably shape each other.

In trial courts, the **fact finding** process is onerous and uncertain, involving the sifting and interpretation of complex and often contradictory **evidence**. In the High Court that burden is far less demanding. In the Court's appellate **jurisdiction**, the facts on which the Court must base its conclusions have already been established at the trial level; only rarely does the Court go behind the established findings to reappraise the facts for itself (see *Edwards v Noble* (1971);

Warren v Coombes (1979)). Even then, the reappraisal goes not to the raw or 'primary' facts established by the evidence, but to the inferences to be drawn from those facts, or their evaluative interpretation. In cases where the facts have been found by a **jury**—especially in **criminal law**—appellate reluctance to interfere with the findings is even stronger, since the jury represents community perceptions more directly than appellate judges can do. The appellate concern with 'facts' is then at a further remove: the **role of the Court** is not to determine whether the jury's findings are 'true', but to satisfy itself whether a properly instructed jury could reasonably or 'safely' have arrived at such findings (see, for example, the *Chamberlain Case* (1984)).

Yet the rarity of explicit reappraisal of 'the facts as found' is misleading. In every case, the apprehension of the primary facts involves processes of inference, evaluation and selection. Even when the Court is presented with a frozen record of findings, the mental process of absorbing it is neither mechanical nor instantaneous. The first rough apprehension of the fact situation will already trigger tentative intuitions of the area of law that might be relevant—prompting scrupulous attention to some aspects of the facts, and dismissal of others as irrelevant. But as a fuller picture unfolds, those initial impressions may change. Different configurations of the facts may suggest different legal issues, in turn suggesting different perceptions of what are the relevant facts. Moreover, the legally relevant 'facts' may themselves be value-laden. A finding of 'fact' that the defendant was fraudulent, or negligent, or **unconscionable** in the exercise of **undue influence**, involves complex judgments of fact and value, guided partly by propositions of law and partly by the Justices' own understandings of human experience. The divergent perceptions of the 'facts' in *Louth v Diprose* (1992) (see **Men**; **Stereotypes**) are an extreme example.

For all this, the main concern of appellate courts is not with the difficulties of finding the facts, but with formulating the principles that determine their legal consequences. In the High Court's original jurisdiction, the need to establish the relevant 'facts' is even less important—at least now that single Justices are no longer routinely required to sit as trial judges or make findings of fact for the Court. In cases involving **constitutional law**, the relevant framework is often supplied simply by the text of the statute whose validity is challenged; the Court has no effective machinery for establishing other 'facts' that might be relevant, for example as to the social or economic effects of legislation (see **Judicial notice**). Yet even when the provisions of a statute are themselves the primary 'facts', judicial perceptions of which provisions are relevant will interact selectively with perceptions of the constitutional issues. In the *Communist Party Case* (1951), for example, the crucial issues turned not on the primary legislative goal of suppressing communism, but on the absence of judicial safeguards for executive judgments under sections 5 and 9 of the Act, and on the effect of the statutory recitals in the preamble (see **Judicial review**).

Despite these pervasive interactions with 'the facts', the primary role of the Court, in appellate and original jurisdiction alike, is the formulation of legal principles—not only because the **authoritative legal materials** must be interpreted and manipulated to yield a major premise suitably tailored to the immediate problem, but because, through the system of **precedent**, the propositions thus formulated will themselves be added to the authoritative materials for future cases in the High Court itself and in all Australian courts. For this reason, each Justice is conscious of the need to formulate the relevant law in a way that will be an acceptable basis for decision not only in the immediate dispute, but in similar cases thereafter.

Although this may sometimes involve the **overruling** of an unsatisfactory precedent, that is a last resort. The more usual objective is to formulate the law for disposal of the instant case by arriving at a fair interpretation of the existing legal materials. Accordingly, the process of judicial reasoning depends almost entirely on an exhaustive review and reinterpretation of earlier judicial decisions and judgments, including *obiter dicta*.

In **popular images** of the Court, this distinctive mode of reasoning is often not understood—and when it is understood, it may often provoke negative reactions. As **Mason** observed extra-judicially in 1988:

> Precedent brings in its train corresponding detriments—a mode of argumentation which appears to be excessively formal because it is preoccupied with past decisions and dicta, and an inability to respond to the need for change. The examination of past authorities dominates the process of legal reasoning ... The attention lavished on the discussion of decided cases is often disproportionate to discussion of the inherent considerations which might influence an outcome one way rather than another. This characteristic of legal reasoning, for it is as evident in academic writings as it is in judgments, conveys the impression that the law superimposes its own standards on the processes of reason. And it conveys the impression that law is a remote discipline, a realm for specialists, removed from decision-making processes as they are understood by non-lawyers.

Yet while the analysis of previous judgments may appear to be narrowly focused, the analytical methods are extremely diverse—ranging from mere cut-and-paste collage of quotations from earlier judgments, to wide-ranging reflective essays on the problems of legal ordering in the spheres of human action involved. Even if the end result is the explicit or implicit formulation of a legal proposition that can be applied syllogistically, the interpretive process cannot itself proceed along linear or logical lines. Indeed, philosophers who have tried to analyse legal reasoning have been struck by its lack of linearity. John Wisdom, in 1944, found 'not a *chain of demonstrative reasoning*', but 'a presenting and representing of those features of the case which *severally co-operate* in favour of the conclusion ... The reasons are like the legs of a chair, not the links of a chain.' Chaim Perelman, in 1958, compared a persuasive argument to 'a piece of cloth', with a total strength 'vastly superior to that of any single thread which enters into its warp and woof'.

If the process cannot be reduced to simple deductive logic, it cannot be reduced, either, to less formal methods of reasoning such as induction or analogy. While each of these plays a significant part, their functions are very different. Judges wanting to extend an earlier approach are likely to reason by induction; those who want to avoid or confine it are likely to reason by analogy. Inductive reasoning extrapolates the implications of a precedent beyond its particular facts; analogical reasoning can be and often is used to confine it to its particular facts.

It is sometimes said that inductive reasoning tends to produce legal 'principles', while analogical reasoning produces more narrowly defined legal 'rules'. Yet the very same intuitive idea may sometimes provide the broad inspirational guidance of a 'principle' and sometimes the more specific constraint of a 'rule'. As Martin Golding observed in 1963, what matters is not whether the Court is applying a 'rule' or a 'principle', but whether it is engaged in a process of 'principled decision-making'—in which choices between wider or narrower views of the precedents are guided by an explicit or intuitive sense of **policy considerations** and **values**, and concern for the good order of the body of legal doctrine as a whole. This concern for 'good order'—sometimes explained in terms of the 'coherence' or 'consistency' of the legal system, sometimes more pretentiously in terms of its 'integrity' or 'pattern maintenance'—is part of the Court's role in every case, since each new litigious problem requires the Court to revisit a particular area of legal doctrine, and to reappraise or restate it to ensure that it remains in good working order.

In inductive reasoning, one particular decision—or more frequently, as George Paton suggested in 1946, a series of decisions 'plotting the points on a graph'—will be used to extrapolate a broad hypothesis that can also be tailored in such a way as to bear on the instant case. The facts of the previous cases become less important, except to the extent that a series of cases can now be seen to involve a set of common fact-elements (not always apparent at the time). In analogical reasoning, the facts of the previous case assume greater importance. In the narrowest instances where only an 'actual decision' is treated as binding, it will not be followed unless its factual analogy with the instant case is exact. More commonly, what is important is not the presence but the absence of analogy. A precedent case will be distinguished because, although its facts partly correspond to those now presented, the analogy is incomplete: the previous situation involved a fact-element now perceived as 'material'—whether or not it was so perceived by the precedent judge—which is absent from the present case. If the earlier decision depended on that fact-element being present, it should be followed only in a case where that fact-element is reproduced.

This process of 'distinguishing' a case on its facts may sometimes be an artificial or spurious way of avoiding a result that no longer fits the judge's perception of 'good order'. More often, such 'distinctions' are a legitimate way of clarifying the presuppositions of the earlier approach, and thus clarifying the scope or rationale of an emergent rule or principle. As **Jacobs** insisted in *HC Sleigh v SA* (1977), 'the point or points of distinction must be relevant to the subject matter upon which the Court has given its decision', and the reasons for the distinction 'must be explored so that the course which is emerging … can be the better predicted'.

In all this, the Court has a double purpose: to formulate a clear and persuasive basis for decision in the instant case, and to shape and restate the developing body of relevant legal doctrine in a way that is both just and 'coherent'. All judges in a common law system are conscious that what they do in any one case is one step in a continuing process of legal evolution and revision. They are conscious, too, that it is only one step: as **Barwick** said in *Strickland v Rocla Concrete Pipes* (1971), 'the law develops case by case, the Court in each case deciding so much as is necessary to dispose of the case before it'.

Yet how broad or narrow a proposition should be to supply the foundation that is 'necessary' for a particular decision is a question on which judicial perceptions may differ (see *Ratio decidendi*); and in any event, the reluctance to pronounce upon matters not immediately 'necessary' is no more than a canon of judicial restraint, with varying weight for different judges or in different cases. If judges have to guard against unduly wide propositions, it may also be necessary to guard against unduly narrow ones. In *Actors Equity v Fontana Films* (1982), Mason, having decided that the challenged legislation was valid on a relatively narrow understanding of the **corporations power**, added that he would not 'wish it to be thought' that the power was confined to that narrow scope, and proceeded to outline a broader conception of what he understood to be the power's essential content. **Brennan**, on the other hand, expressly refrained from committing himself to any view of the broader question either way:

> Hewing close to the issues raised by each case, the Court avoids the possibility of having its judgment applied to issues which were not envisaged in the arguments before it and which may have implications emerging only in the future. The development of principle from the concrete issues of particular cases may be slow, but it gives assurance that the principle will not be unsuited to the solution of practical problems. It follows that it is undesirable to answer a question left open in an earlier case unless an answer is evoked by the issues in the case in hand.

In 1986, Justice Shirley Abrahamson of the Supreme Court of Wisconsin told Australian interviewer Garry Sturgess:

> I like to compare writing an opinion with writing the next chapter of a book that has already been written … We do not write the final chapter, we just write the next scene, and then the next opinion writes another scene, and so it goes. And forever in the law there is this movement … the law is stable and yet law changes to meet societal needs.

The same idea has been developed more fully by Ronald Dworkin (*Law's Empire* (1986)). Lawrence Lessig ('Fidelity in Translation' (1993) 71 *Texas LR* 1165) offers a different metaphor: the judge's reformulation of the existing legal materials is like translation from a foreign language. Just as the translator has to adapt the original text to the needs of a different language, so the judge in interpreting an authoritative text must adapt it to a new context—either because of new factual circumstances, or because the underlying presuppositions and values have changed. At the same time, in adapting the original text to its altered setting, the translator-judge must still observe the requirements of fidelity to the original.

Yet these analogies understate the complexity of the interpretive processes involved. The legal materials are intensely intertextual: each judgment to be interpreted itself contains interpretations of many other judgments or statutory provisions, which may or may not be directly relevant to the case at hand. Lessig's translator-judge must interpret not just one existing text but a multitude of texts, whose meanings must be adjusted to each other as well as to the needs of the instant case. Dworkin's chain novelist is not simply writing the next chapter in a single unfolding story, but is drawing together and seeking to harmonise a multitude of plot lines tied together only by the legal conception that the judge is trying to discern.

The legal issues to be determined, along with the relevant precedents and their relevant interpretations, are usually identified for the Court by the **arguments** of **counsel**—though occasionally an issue may be raised from the Bench, like the **inconsistency** issue in *Hume v Palmer* (1926) (see **Knox Court and arbitration**) or the retrospectivity issue in the *War Crimes Act Case* (1991). Occasionally, too, a Justice will simply adopt counsel's argument, restated in the Justice's own words. But, almost always in the High Court, the opposing arguments will present alternative lines of reasoning, drawing on different precedents or different interpretations of the same set of precedents, with opposite results. When the arguments are equally persuasive, the Court must choose between them; and even if a Justice finds one view clearly more persuasive, the explanation of reasons for the decision should include an explanation of why the alternative argument fails.

Because judicial reasoning must always be grounded in the existing legal materials, it lends itself to analysis in terms of **legalism**. Because the existing materials must always be reinterpreted in a way that entails choices between alternatives, guided by different perceptions of how best to serve the functional needs of society or ensure just outcomes, the process lends itself to analysis in terms of **realism**. The precise balance that would give the most coherent account of judicial reasoning has yet to be found. One reason it is elusive is that no two judges strike quite the same balance.

Tony Blackshield

Further Reading
Tony Blackshield, 'Five Types of Judicial Decision' (1974) 12 *Osgoode Hall LJ* 539
Karl Llewellyn, *The Common Law Tradition: Deciding Appeals* (1961)
Neil MacCormick, *Legal Reasoning and Legal Theory* (1978)
Julius Stone, *Legal System and Lawyers' Reasonings* (1964)
Julius Stone, *Precedent and Law* (1985)

Judicial review involves the High Court assessing governmental action for consistency with the Constitution. Where, for example, the federal Parliament or a state parliament has passed a law that is contrary to the Constitution, the High Court will exercise its power of judicial review to hold the law invalid. The law will then be of no effect. This amounts to a check by the Court on the exercise of arbitrary power and thus implements the **rule of law**, as well as providing fundamental protection against the infringement of human rights.

This form of judicial review may be contrasted with that exercised by courts as part of **administrative law**, whereby judges assess the lawfulness of administrative decision making against statutes and the **common law**. The underlying conception is the same: a specific governmental power is conferred by a superior instrument, and the Court scrutinises the exercise of the power to ensure its conformity to the superior instrument. But judicial review on constitutional grounds of powers conferred on a democratically elected law-making body has more profound implications for constitutional and democratic theory.

It is widely accepted by **commentators** that the Court may exercise the power of judicial review to strike down legislation for non-compliance with the Constitution. Far more controversial is the question whether certain common law rights are so fundamental or 'deeply rooted' as to be beyond interference by the exercise of legislative power. In *Dr Bonham's Case* (1610), Chief Justice Coke famously wrote:

It appears in our books that in many cases the common law will control acts of Parliament and sometimes adjudge them to be utterly void; for when an Act of Parliament is against common right and reason, or repugnant, or impossible to be performed, the common law will control it and adjudge such Act to be void.

The power asserted here to hold legislation void because it is inconsistent with the common law has not been exercised by an English, let alone an Australian, court. In 1885, AV Dicey in his book *Introduction to the Study of the Law of the Constitution* declared the alleged power to be 'obsolete'.

Although a common law power of judicial review has not been applied by the High Court, it has nevertheless been suggested from time to time that the common law might afford a basis for judicial review in extreme cases where fundamental rights are breached—such as Dicey's example of a law that provided 'all blue-eyed babies should be murdered'. This suggestion is sometimes reinforced by resort to the opening words of section 51 of the Constitution, which provide that the Commonwealth Parliament has power to make laws for the 'peace, order, and good government of the Commonwealth' with respect to the 40 topics enumerated in that section. In *Building Construction Employees & BLF v Minister for Industrial Relations* (1986), Chief Justice Laurence Street of the Supreme Court of NSW held that similar words in the *Constitution Act* 1902 (NSW) did not confer 'unlimited legislative power' and that the 'ringing words of Lord Coke … may even yet provide encouragement for courts in putting down tyrannous legislation'. **Kirby**, then President of the NSW Court of Appeal, rejected this as inconsistent with accepted notions of parliamentary **sovereignty**. He found that the words did not afford a power of review, and that 'unbroken law and tradition has repeatedly reinforced and ultimately respected the democratic will of the people as expressed in Parliament'.

The High Court has not finally resolved the different approaches of Street and Kirby and has left open the faint possibility of a common law power of judicial review. In *Union Steamship v The Queen* (1988), the Court said: 'Whether the exercise of … legislative power is subject to some restraints by reference to rights deeply rooted in our democratic system of government and the common law … is another question which we need not explore.' In subsequent decisions, such as *Durham Holdings v NSW* (2001), it has yet to close off this possibility. The idea that the common law might be applied to strike down legislation played a role in the much criticised and now disfavoured judgment of **Deane** and **Toohey** in *Leeth v Commonwealth* (1992), in which they held that a right to **equality** could be discerned in the Constitution; and Toohey has given support to a similar idea in his **extra-judicial writings**.

Even where the common law does not afford a power of judicial review, it has been applied by the Court to protect **civil liberties**. The Court has developed common law rules of **statutory interpretation** that reflect a presumption against the invasion of fundamental rights by the legislature. According to **Mason**, **Brennan**, **Gaudron**, and **McHugh** in *Coco v The Queen* (1994): 'The courts should not impute to the legislature an intention to interfere with fundamental rights. Such an intention must be clearly manifested by unmistakable and unambiguous language.' When in the late 1970s **Murphy** revived interest in discovering **implied constitutional rights**, he frequently used them to read legislation down as an alternative to (and to some extent a precursor of) the more drastic step of invalidating the legislation.

The Court's power to exercise judicial review to uphold the Constitution is nowhere expressed in the Constitution. It can, however, be implied from Chapter III, which achieves a **separation** of **judicial power** from that of legislative and executive power. Section 75 establishes certain '**matters**' as being within the **jurisdiction** of the Court—matters such as those 'in which a **writ** of Mandamus or prohibition or an injunction is sought against an officer of the Commonwealth'. Section 76 states that 'the Parliament may make laws conferring original jurisdiction on the High Court' in any of the matters then listed. Strangely, matters 'arising under this Constitution, or involving its interpretation' are listed under section 76(i) as among those in which the Parliament may confer jurisdiction upon the Court, rather than being listed in section 75 among the matters in which the Court 'shall have' jurisdiction. Despite this, it is clear that the Constitution vests power in the High Court to review legislative and executive action for consistency with its requirements. In 1955, **Dixon** argued extra-judicially that the words of section 76(i) 'impliedly acknowledge the function of the courts' to engage in judicial review.

The **Convention Debates** of the 1890s indicate that the **framers** of the Constitution intended, or perhaps simply assumed, that the High Court would be the ultimate arbiter of the Constitution. In the main, this has been uncritically accepted ever since. Unlike the situation in the USA, where both the historical basis and the contemporary exercise of the Supreme Court's function of judicial review have been hotly contested and debated (see, for example, Charles Black, *The People and the Court* (1960) and John Hart Ely, *Democracy and Distrust: A Theory of Judicial Review* (1980)), there has been comparatively little written in Australia on the justification—historical, philosophical, or instrumental—of judicial review. The question of whether it might infringe basic principles of **democracy** for the Court to strike down laws enacted by a duly elected legislature has been touched upon rhetorically, but the conflicting arguments have rarely been explored in depth.

On the one hand, it can be argued that it is inappropriate for an unelected, unrepresentative and largely unaccountable institution to declare legislation that represents the considered will of a majority of the representatives of a duly elected parliament to be unlawful. On the other hand, it can be argued that democracy does not mean majoritarianism, and that the Court has an important role to play in ensuring that parliaments comply with the basic law-making rules set out in the Constitution, and perhaps in protecting the rights of minorities vulnerable to populist action by parliaments. Acceptance of such arguments has varied according to the different areas in which judicial review has been applied. While it is generally accepted that the Court may appropriately strike down legislation because it breaches the division of powers between the Commonwealth and the states, the legitimacy of the Court's actions has been strongly contested when it has struck down legislation by relying upon its own derivation of **implied constitutional rights**. In purporting to keep the other arms of government within lawful boundaries, the Court may itself overstep the mark and be vulnerable to the accusation of exercising arbitrary power if it lacks an objective basis for its holdings.

In *Marbury v Madison* (1803), the **United States Supreme Court** held that it possesses the power to declare legislation to be inconsistent with the US Constitution and therefore invalid. There is no equivalent single decision in Australia that establishes the authority of the High Court to review legislation for unconstitutionality.

The closest that the High Court has come to positively declaring its role is the *Communist Party Case* (1951), where the Court upheld a challenge to legislation introduced by the newly elected **Menzies** coalition government in an attempt to suppress the Australian Communist Party. The legislation amounted to an attack on fundamental liberties including freedom of association and expression. More subtly, it also undermined the position of the High Court, since the federal Parliament had sought to 'recite itself' into power—that is, to pre-empt the question of validity by purporting to declare in preliminary recitals that there was a necessary connection between the legislation and the **defence power**. For example, the ninth recital stated Parliament's belief that 'it is necessary, for the security and defence of Australia and for the execution and maintenance of the Constitution and of the laws of the Commonwealth, that the Australian Communist Party … should be dissolved'.

These recitals implicitly asserted a claim that the Court should take **judicial notice** of the Parliament's belief that its legislation was constitutionally valid, whether under its implied power to legislate about Australian **nationhood** or under its defence power in section 51(vi) of the Constitution. The recitals were thus a challenge to the High Court's power of judicial review, and the Court's position as the final arbiter of the scope of Commonwealth power under the Constitution.

The Court responded with a strong affirmation of its function of judicial review. With only **Latham** dissenting, the Court held the legislation to be invalid. It refused to accept the conclusiveness of Parliament's view of the Australian Communist Party as expressed in the recitals. The recitals might be of some use in ascertaining the intention of the Parliament in passing the Act, but could not determine whether the Act actually fell within power. That was a decision for the High Court.

The enduring significance of the case lay in the fact that the Court, in striking down the legislation, reinforced its own position as the ultimate arbiter of the Constitution, and thus as an independent check on the power of the legislature and the executive. The doctrine of judicial review was emphatically affirmed. As stated by **Fullagar**, 'in our system the principle of *Marbury v Madison* is accepted as axiomatic'.

GEORGE WILLIAMS

Further Reading

Tony Blackshield, 'The Courts and Judicial Review' in Sol Encel, Donald Horne, and Elaine Thompson (eds), *Change the Rules! Towards a Democratic Constitution* (1977) 119

Brian Galligan, 'Judicial Review in the Australian Federal System: Its Origin and Function' (1979) 10 *FL Rev* 367

James Thomson, 'Constitutional Authority for Judicial Review: A Contribution from the Framers of the Australian Constitution' in Gregory Craven (ed), *The Convention Debates 1891–1898: Commentaries, Indices and Guide* (1986) 173

John Toohey, 'A Government of Laws, and Not of Men?' (1993) 4 *PLR* 158

George Winterton, 'Constitutionally Entrenched Common Law Rights: Sacrificing Means to Ends?' in Charles Sampford and Kim Preston (eds), *Interpreting Constitutions* (1996) 121

Judicial style. George Orwell once wrote that professional English style should be as transparent as a window pane; that it should give such quick and untrammelled access to ideas and information as to be invisible to the reader. It is not easy to describe the literary devices that promote invisibility; it is far easier to identify those who are in breach of Orwell's principle than it is to honour those who are observant. Those High Court Justices whose linguistic devices and strategies are often highly conspicuous, such as **Rich, Isaacs**, and **Windeyer**, will attract attention as having a distinct 'style', to be traced in their flights of **metaphor**, their analogies, rhetorical questionings, extended narratives, appeals to emotion, personifications, literary and historical allusions, literary quotations (whether in Greek, Latin or English), grandiloquence, and circumlocution. Those whose stylistic devices represent the art that disguises art—who aim to reduce, as far as possible, the intrusion of style upon content and who try to approach Orwell's ideal of transparency, invisibility and impersonality—are less likely to figure in an account of judicial style, and must generally be content with the quiet gratitude of thousands of legal readers rather than the acclamations of literary critics.

In the Australian context, the interpretive bias of the High Court towards 'strict and complete **legalism**' and 'the literal sense of the words' in the constitutional arena has imposed constraints upon stylistic excess. The relatively plain language of the Australian Constitution—the spare style, rather in the nature of an instruction manual—imposes a dour model that in itself may have discouraged stylistic flights. Moreover, the antipathy expressed in the *Engineers Case* (1920) to the proliferation of 'principles', 'spirits', and 'alien' and 'exotic' doctrines from elsewhere may have fostered caution about extravagant speculations or vague but evocative incantations of abstract principle of the kind that have elsewhere enriched judicial style.

There was wisdom in this. In those one or two awkward moments where the Constitution does achieve 'lift-off', as in the use of the word 'absolutely' in section 92, it has been an incitement not only to some of the High Court's most contorted and elusive reasoning, but also to some of its most heavily worked judicial prose—the most notorious being Rich's extended passage, in *James v Cowan* (1930), responding in kind to the perceived 'obmutescence' of the section:

The rhetorical affirmation of sec 92 that trade, commerce and intercourse between the States shall be absolutely free has a terseness and elevation of style which doubtless befits the expression of a sentiment so inspiring. But inspiring sentiments are often vague and grandiloquence is sometimes obscure. If this declaration of liberty had not stopped short at the high-sounding words 'absolutely free', the pith and force of its diction might have been sadly diminished. But even if it was impossible to define precisely what it was from which inter-State trade was to be free, either because a commonplace definition forms such a pedestrian conclusion or because it needs an exactness of conception seldom achieved where constitutions are projected, yet obmutescence was both unnecessary and unsafe. Some hint at least might have been dropped, some distant allusion made, from which the nature of the immunity intended could afterwards have been deduced by those whose lot it is to explain the elliptical and expound the unexpressed. As soon as the section was brought down from the lofty clouds whence constitutional precepts are fulminated and came to be applied to the everyday practice of trade and commerce and the sordid intercourse of human affairs, the necessity of knowing and so determining precisely what impediments and hindrances were no longer to obstruct inter-State trade obliged this Court to attempt the impossible task of supplying an exclusive and inclusive definition of a conception to be discovered only in the silences of the Constitution … After many years of exploration into the dark recesses of this subject I am content to take the decided cases as sailing directions upon which I may set some course, however unexpected may be the destination to which it brings me, and await with a patience not entirely hopeless the powerful beacon light of complete authoritative exposition from those who can speak with finality.

'High-sounding words' have appeared in other areas. Early members of the High Court had strong literary credentials. **Griffith** was a translator of Dante (we may overlook the judgment of one early critic that he made Dante read like a statute) and Isaacs is notorious still for his extravagant analogies and his flamboyant use (and sometimes insistent accumulation) of rhetorical questions in his judgments. In the first *Caledonian Collieries Case* (1930), for example, he renewed his sustained attack on what he saw as the misuse of section 21AA of the *Conciliation and Arbitration Act* 1904 (Cth) (see **Knox Court and arbitration**) by writing:

In the present intricate state of legislation, awards brought into this Court and under cover of that section subjected to the attacks of destructive criticism of all kinds, and sometimes meticulous technicalities suggested by ingenious legal minds, who as the law stands are only doing their duty to those they represent, have very much the same chance of escape as had the victims in the arena of the ancient Roman Colosseum. How is a statute of this nature, so uncertain, contradictory and deceptive, to achieve its declared object?

Later in the same paragraph, we find the same characteristic probing combination of disorienting analogy and insistent question: 'Can such a system, giving with one hand and taking back with the other, conserve or promote peace? It invites thousands to a peaceful journey on a *Lusitania*, and then provides the torpedo that destroys the vessel.'

Narratives of various kinds occur frequently in legal judgments, whether they be narratives of 'the facts', narratives offering historical evidence and explanation—as in **Deane's** extensive account, in *Kingswell v The Queen* (1985), of the origins and history of **jury trial**—or even 'narratives of law', tracing various 'streams of authority' to and from their legal source. The narrative of facts, in the High Court, has generally been stylistically restrained, though there have been some distinguished exceptions, as in the judgment of Windeyer in *FCT v Casuarina* (1971), where a particularly complex set of facts is recounted through an extended theatrical metaphor. References to 'scenarios' and 'actors' occur frequently in legal judgments, but in *Casuarina*, the metaphor is developed in intricate (and finally cumbersome) detail, with producer, scenes, scenarios, entries, exits, parts to play, and *dramatis personae* to play them. The Court has not adopted the ostensibly simple and folksy but in fact calculatedly emotive and highly manipulative narrative style of a Lord Denning—'It was bluebell time in Kent'—but there are certainly memorable instances of strong and emotive narratives, such as Isaacs' account of the 'months of struggle and endurance', of 'severe privations', that preceded the reopening of the Rothbury coal mine—'Disorder arose, and life was lost'—in the *Caledonian Collieries Case*, or in **Evatt's** extended evocation, with literary support, of a mother's feelings on the loss of her child in *Chester v Waverley Corporation* (1939)—'During this crucial period the plaintiff's condition of mind and nerve can be completely understood only by parents who have been placed in a similar agony of hope and fear with hope gradually decreasing'.

 Appealing vignettes abound, as in the homely social realism of Isaacs' discourse on the quintessential nature of the sausage, in *Mathews v Foggitt Jones* (1926)—'If the internal portion of the sausage is itself before envelopment portion of a carcase, I utterly fail to see how the mere fact that it is covered with an intestine makes it cease to be what it was immediately before it was covered. Its identity remains, just as much as the identity of a man remains whether he is a soldier in uniform, a barrister in robes or a cricketer in flannels'—and in Chief Justice **Barwick's** long disquisition on a pipeful of tobacco, in *Dickenson's Arcade v Tasmania* (1974). These narratives and parables are all stylistically intrusive in a sense, but they represent far more than mere linguistic play or idle storytelling: their vividness is integral to a more widely significant style of judgment in which a firmer and more tactile grasp of the 'facts'—which may, as in *Chester v Waverley Corporation*, include the emotions attached to those facts—is presented as a powerful prelude (in *Chester*, in a forward-looking **dissenting judgment**) to the subversion of the majority's facile imposition of inherited legal categories (see **Popular culture**).

The High Court's use of metaphor is rich and extensive. While much of the stock of metaphor is traditional and inherited, the resource that vivid metaphor provides—for adding emphasis to **argument** and for reframing legal thinking—has always been richly developed in the Court's judgments, with resounding instances such as **Brennan's** description of inherited English law as merely the 'skeleton of principle', or Deane's apocalyptic vision of the Commonwealth collapsing into 'a bedlam of a Babel' in *Breavington v Godleman* (1989), tapping deeply into national legal and social sensitivities, and representing far more than mere linguistic garniture. The highly inventive use of spatial metaphor, too—the exploring of Rich's 'lofty clouds', and the probing of those 'silences of the Constitution'—has been a significant and enduring element in Australian approaches to **constitutional interpretation**.

There has, however, been a gravitational pull, in more recent years, towards a plainer professional style, away from the Edwardian cadences of early High Court prose—perhaps as a result of new levels of linguistic self-consciousness in the profession generally, as evidenced in the extent of discussion of linguistic issues in legal professional journals and the appearance of articles, such as that of **Kirby**, on the business of judgment writing. **Gaudron** uses a plain, highly technical and contracted style in her judgments—for example, in *Leeth v Commonwealth* (1992)—to the point where sentences are almost artificially shortened, resulting in the repeated use as sentence-openers of conjunctions and demonstrative pronouns, more characteristically found mid-sentence—'that', 'thus', 'but' and 'and'; 'That is so because …', 'But a law making that the dominant consideration …', 'And other differences are only to be expected …'. Precedents for a truncated syntax of this kind (though in the context of the traditional extended legal paragraph) are to be found in the more concise judgments of **Dixon**, as in *A-G (NSW) v Trethowan* (1931). What is lost in stylistic euphony is no doubt gained in precision and comprehensibility, though it can be argued that a plain style, pushed to these lengths, begins to build, in Orwellian terms, towards a new kind of visibility and even opacity of its own.

 Still, an increased legal professional attention to clear and effective communication—one that looks to its reader as well as to its legal subject—has led the Court towards a simpler style and an increased attention to the effective conceptual organisation of judgments and sentences within judgments alike. No doubt we will see, in the future, the persistence in the Court of the broad characteristics of legal writing in English—the long sentences, the latinate phrasing, the laboured stylistic objectivity, forged through the use of passive and impersonal constructions—'It is convenient to consider …', and 'The questions are to be answered as follows …', and the wholesale refuge in 'one': 'That is not, of course, to *close one's eye to reality* and assert that the traditional criminal trial by jury is without any identifiable weaknesses.' No doubt, too, if there are to be further instances of 'unrestrained language' of a more personal and emotional hue, as in the joint judgment of Deane and Gaudron in *Mabo* (1992), they will still be accompanied by the same kind of apology we find in the conclusion to that judgment—and apology for the use of language that 'some may think to be unusually emotive for a judgment of this court'. Flamboyant moments may recur, but, as has always been the case in the High Court, they will tend to appear as tiny, exotic islands in a sea of restrained, relatively invisible, carefully crafted English prose.

MICHAEL MEEHAN

Further Reading
Michael Kirby, 'On the Writing of Judgments' (1990) 64 *ALJ* 691

Judiciary Act 1903 (Cth). The Judiciary Act, enacted in August 1903 after vigorous and prolonged debate (see **Deakin**), makes comprehensive provision for the exercise of federal **judicial power** under Chapter III of the Constitution. It also provides for the rights of barristers and solicitors to practise (Part VIIIA), suits by and against the Commonwealth and the states (Part IX), suits relating to the Northern Territory (Part IXA), the exercise of criminal jurisdiction, including the jurisdiction of state and territory courts in criminal cases, and appeals in such cases (Part X), and the **procedure** of the High Court (Part 10A).

The Act declares the High Court to be a **superior court** of record with power to punish for **contempt** (section 4). It provides that the Court's process is to run, and its judgments and **orders** are to have effect and may be executed, throughout the Commonwealth (section 25).

The Act regulates the exercise of the original and appellate **jurisdiction** of the High Court. It provides that, in addition to the original jurisdiction given to the Court by the Constitution, the Court shall have original jurisdiction in all matters arising under the Constitution or involving its interpretation and in trials of indictable offences against Commonwealth laws (section 30). The Act enumerates five classes of case in which the Court's original jurisdiction is to be exclusive: (a) matters arising directly under any treaty; (b) suits between states, or between persons suing or being sued on behalf of different states, or between a state and a person suing or being sued on behalf of another state; (c) suits by the Commonwealth, or any person suing on its behalf, against a state, or any person being sued on its behalf; (d) suits by a state, or any person suing on its behalf, against the Commonwealth, or any person being sued on its behalf; and (e) matters in which a **writ** of mandamus or prohibition is sought against an officer of the Commonwealth or a federal court (section 38).

The Act provides for the exercise of original jurisdiction by one or more Justices (section 16) and enables a Justice to state any case or reserve any question for consideration of a **Full Court** or direct any case or question to be argued before a Full Court (section 18). Much of the Full Court's constitutional work has come to it by this route.

The Act did not create any federal court, though the Court of **Conciliation and Arbitration** was constituted by the *Conciliation and Arbitration Act* 1904 (Cth). Section 39 of the Act did, however, invest comprehensive federal jurisdiction in state courts. That section was the central element in limiting appeals to the **Privy Council**. The section deprived state courts of non-federal jurisdiction in the matters in which federal jurisdiction was invested. The section then made the exercise of that federal jurisdiction by a **state Supreme Court** final and conclusive, except for an appeal to the High Court.

The operation of the section became a source of conflict. In *Webb v Outtrim* (1906), the Privy Council held that the section was ineffective to block an appeal from a state court to the Privy Council in the exercise of invested federal jurisdiction. Because *Webb v Outtrim* involved an ***inter se* question**—a factor the Privy Council failed to consider in its ruling on section 39—the High Court refused to follow it, holding that, in matters of federal jurisdiction, the section had validly eliminated appeals from state courts to the Privy Council (*Baxter v Commissioners of Taxation (NSW)* (1907)). The impediments to an appeal from state courts were strengthened by the introduction of section 40A of the Act, which provided for automatic **removal** to the High Court of a cause pending in a state Supreme Court involving an *inter se* question. Section 40A played an important part in removing cases to the High Court in the decades in which it was in operation. The section was replaced in 1976 by section 40, which enables constitutional and other important questions to be removed into the High Court by order.

The residual doubts as to the validity of section 39(2)(a) were finally dispelled by the Court's later decisions in appeals against orders made by state Supreme Courts purporting to grant leave to appeal to the Privy Council under the Imperial Orders in Council regulating such appeals (*Skin Wool Case* (1926)). By these means, and by the refusal of certificates under section 74 of the Constitution, the determination of *inter se* questions was restricted to the High Court. In 1968, appeals to the Privy Council in matters of federal jurisdiction were excluded, and in 1975, the appeal from the High Court was abolished.

Once the **Federal Court** was established, a large part of the High Court's statutory original jurisdiction was vested in the Federal Court by other statutes. The original jurisdiction of the Federal Court includes, subject to exceptions, jurisdiction with respect to any matter in which a writ of mandamus or prohibition or injunction is sought against a Commonwealth officer (section 39B).

The Act confers upon the High Court an extensive power of **remitter** to any federal court, court of a state, or court of a territory (section 44). Where the High Court remits a matter falling within certain categories of federal jurisdiction, the remitter operates to confer jurisdiction on the court to which the matter is remitted (section 44(3)).

The Act initially provided for appeals as of right and appeals by leave and special leave to the High Court (section 35). Appeals as of right were subject to a pecuniary qualification that was increased from time to time. In 1984, amendments to the Act abolished appeals as of right and prescribed the grant of special **leave to appeal** as a condition of an appeal to the High Court. The validity of the 1984 amendments was unanimously upheld by the High Court (*Smith Kline & French Laboratories v Commonwealth* (1991)). In considering applications for special leave, the Court is required to consider whether there is a question of law of public importance, whether a High Court decision is necessary to resolve differences of opinion in courts below, and whether the interests of the administration of justice, either generally or in the particular case, require reconsideration of the judgment (section 35A).

The Act contains important provisions dealing with the substantive liability of the Commonwealth, the courts in which it can be sued (section 56), the rights of parties in a suit to which the Commonwealth or a state is a party (section 64), the application of state laws to courts exercising federal jurisdiction (section 79) and, in the last resort, the application of the **common law** of England as modified by the Constitution and by the statute law of the state in which the jurisdiction is exercised (section 80).

Mention should be made of section 64, if only because there has been continuous controversy about its interpretation, particularly in relation to its effect on **intergovernmental immunities**. It provides: 'In any suit to which the Commonwealth or a State is a party, the rights of parties shall as nearly as possible be the same, and judgments may be given and costs awarded on either side, as in a suit between subject and subject.' The section applies to substantive as well as procedural rights (*Maguire v Simpson* (1997); *Commonwealth v Evans Deakin Industries* (1986)).

The Act also confers rights of **intervention** on the **Attorney-General** of the Commonwealth and of a state in constitutional matters (section 78A) and requires a court not to proceed to deal with such a matter unless and until such a notice is given (section 78B).

Anthony Mason

Further Reading

Commonwealth, *Parliamentary Debates*, House of Representatives, 18 March 1902, 10962; 9 June 1903, 587 (Alfred Deakin, Attorney-General)

Zelman Cowen and Leslie Zines, *Federal Jurisdiction in Australia* (2nd edn 1978)

Leslie Zines, *The High Court and the Constitution* (4th edn 1997) 366–72

Jurimetrics is a term coined by Lee Loevinger in the late 1940s and popularised in the early 1960s. The term refers to any law-related use of statistical analysis or symbolic logic; and since most of those techniques are nowadays computer assisted, its connotation has expanded to include any interaction between law and computer technology.

Within that broad genre, two lines of inquiry bore particularly upon the judicial process. The first, more practical in orientation, sought to arrive at a mathematical prediction of future results in cases of a particular type by giving numerical weights to the recurrent material facts in such cases and using these as a basis for formulaic prediction. Notable among the American pioneers of this approach was Fred Kort; in Australia, Alan Tyree has done related work.

A second approach, more theoretical in orientation (though it, too, sometimes aspired to predictive capacity) involved the analysis of judicial voting patterns in non-unanimous cases—partly to identify the attitudinal factors predisposing the judges to vote as they did, and partly to represent their collegiate relationships in terms of their psychological distance from one another within a shared psychological space. Among the various methodologies deployed to this end, the most influential were those of Glendon Schubert in his seminal study of the **United States Supreme Court**, *The Judicial Mind* (1965).

In order to verify his findings and methods, Schubert then undertook a comparative study of the High Court of Australia, chosen for both its similarities and its dissimilarities to the US Supreme Court. His study of the **Dixon Court** for 1952–61 was reported most comprehensively in an unpublished paper ('The High Court and the Supreme Court: Two Styles of Judicial Hierocracy'), presented to the American Political Science Association on 10 September 1966. Particular aspects of the study were later published separately. For his attitudinal analysis, Schubert used the scalogram technique devised by Louis Guttman (sometimes called 'Guttman scales'); for his spatial modelling of the judges' relationships he initially used factor analysis, and later more sophisticated methods of 'smallest space analysis'. Schubert continued to develop these methods in his later two-volume comparative study of Swiss and South African judges, *Political Culture and Judicial Behavior* (1985).

In 1969, Roger Douglas applied Schubert's scalogram technique to the **Latham Court** for 1935–49. My own work, much of it unpublished, explored both scalogram and factor analysis, and included two published studies of the **Barwick Court**: in 1972, for the period 1964–69; and in 1978, for the period 1972–76.

The simple example of a scalogram below displays the voting patterns in non-unanimous cases concerning freedom of **interstate trade** in 1964–69. Each column represents a Justice (**Barwick, Windeyer, Owen, Kitto, Taylor, Menzies, McTiernan**) and each row represents a case. The 'item' numbers are abbreviated **citations** to the *Commonwealth Law Reports*: thus 120001 is *Samuels v Readers Digest* (1969) 120 CLR 1. Votes for and against the application of section 92 are scored as '+' and '-' respectively.

Initially, the cases are arranged according to the type of voting division (1:4, 2:4 and so on), and within each such group in chronological order. Both rows and columns may then be reshuffled to minimise the number of inconsistent votes. In this instance, the only inconsistent votes are Owen's in 120092 (*Associated Steamships v WA* (1969)) and Windeyer's in 115177 (*O'Sullivan v Miracle Foods* (1966)). A

Scalogram of voting patterns

Item	Bw	Wn	Ow	Ki	Ta	Me	Mc	Scale Type
114361	+		-		-	-	-	1-4
117353	+		-	-	-	-		1-4
120001	+			-	-	-	-	1-4
120092	+	-	(+)	-		-	-	2-4
112353	+	+		-		-		2-3
112374	+	+	-		-	-		2-3
115177	+	(-)	+		+	-		3-2
114341		+	+	+		+	-	4-1
118581	+	+	+			+	-	4-1
118644	+		+	+		+	-	4-1
Pro	09	04	05	02	01	03	00	
Con	00	02	04	03	05	07	06	
NP	01	04	01	05	04	00	04	

stepped diagonal line (the 'breakline') separates consistent positive from consistent negative votes, and indicates for each Justice the point at which his support for the postulated value ceases. (The implicit postulate is that the cases at the bottom of the scale are those where the claims of interstate traders are strongest.)

This example strikingly demonstrates the strength of Barwick's support for such claims, and the depth of McTiernan's lack of support. It also suggests that Windeyer tended to support Barwick's position, and Menzies to support McTiernan's. However, the scalogram does not allow us to distinguish among Owen, Kitto, and Taylor. A stronger scalogram would differentiate clearly among all seven Justices, ranking them in a definite order.

In general, High Court scalograms tend to be weak because of the high rate of absences ('non-participation' or 'NP'). In this example, only one case was decided by a Court of six, and none by a **Full Court** of seven. Any equivalent scalogram for the US Supreme Court would normally contain no blank spaces, since usually all nine judges sit in every case.

To overcome this and other statistical problems in the scaling of High Court data, particular attention focused on the accumulative compilation of much larger scalograms, bringing together cases involving many different issues from diverse doctrinal areas, simply by reference to their common voting patterns. The aim was to generate the largest possible consistent scale from all non-unanimous decisions in a given period; then the largest possible scale from the cases that remain; and so on. *After* these cumulative scales were assembled, the cases thus collated were examined inductively in search of an interpretive explanation for the similarity of voting patterns. Repeatedly, over different periods of High Court history, this procedure has appeared to generate one large scale broadly corresponding to the conventional left–right political spectrum, and another reflecting judicial attitudes to the legal ordering and legal control of hierarchies of power ('the X and Y Scales'). My 1978 paper identified four scales (X, Y, Z, and N), and analysed their content in detail.

Objective verification of these results was sought through the psychological modelling techniques (in my own work, through factor analysis). The starting point is a table of correlation coefficients, measuring the strength or weakness of correlation in voting behaviour for every possible pair of Justices. The correlations are analysed mathematically as the product of a series of 'factors', which are then used to generate a spatial representation, showing the location of each Justice within the psychological space they all inhabit.

Each factor is represented as an axis in a two-dimensional graph or a spherical or hyperspherical space of three or more dimensions. The Justices' positions along each axis are represented by 'loadings' between +1.0 and -1.0; their spatial positions are determined by plotting these loadings against each other as in a Cartesian graph. Plotting two such axes together defines a circular plane; plotting three of them together defines a spherical three-dimensional space, which represents the outer limit of our capacity for visualisation. But mathematical analysis knows no such limit: the same technique can be extended to any number of dimensions.

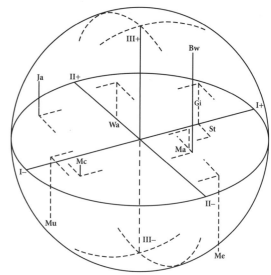

Three-dimensional view

In the result, some Justices will appear to be clustered closely together, while others will appear spatially (and hence psychologically) more remote from each other. The example displays, in a three-dimensional space, the relationships among all nine Justices in 1972–76 (including both **Walsh** and Menzies, who died in office respectively in 1973 and 1974, and **Jacobs** and **Murphy**, who replaced them). The two-dimensional plane lying flat in the centre of the sphere is determined by Axes I and II. In that plane, **Mason**, Barwick, **Stephen**, and Menzies lie in the same quadrant (I+, II-); Walsh and Gibbs in the same quadrant (I+, II+); Jacobs and Murphy in the same quadrant (I-, II+); and McTiernan in a quadrant by himself (I-, II-). The addition of the third vertical axis changes these relationships: in particular, it sharply differentiates Barwick from Menzies and Murphy from Jacobs.

The assumption is that the varying relationships thus represented are determined by the Justices' attitudes to the 'factors' affecting judicial **decision making** in a non-mathematical sense: for example, by their varying degrees of commitment to a distinctive legal conception of individual rights. These varying attitudes might themselves be represented by 'loadings' along a spectrum ranging from extreme commitment to extreme indifference. That series of loadings might itself be represented by an axis passing through the centre of the factorial space. To identify such axes would allow us to *explain* the Justices' voting behaviour in a way that the purely mathematical plotting of the space does not.

Assuming that the cumulative scalograms (for example, the X and Y Scales) have identified significant attitudinal patterns, it should be possible to represent them in the factorial space by axes of the kind just described. From the scalogram one can compute for each Justice a 'score' between +1.0 and -1.0; and if, within the factorial space, it is possible to locate an axis on which the Justices' loadings approximately correspond to these scores, then the factor analysis and the scalogram analysis will tend to confirm each other. Replication within the factorial space will supply the cumulative scales with the scientific rigour they lack. Conversely, the cumulative scales will provide the factor analytic space with the explanatory and interpretive content it lacks.

My own further work at the University of Melbourne in 1984 resulted in the following findings. First, the appropriate space for an exhaustive representation of *all* the information in a correlation table for a group of seven Justices is a six-dimensional space. Secondly, within such a space it is possible to locate an *exact* replication of each of the X, Y, Z, and N Scales, marking out the Justices' relationships at precisely the intervals postulated by the scales.

Thirdly, however, the first proposition is a mere mathematical triviality. The relations among any set of points, no matter how complex and unwieldy, can always be exhaustively represented in a number of dimensions one fewer than the number of points. The relationship between any two points can be represented in one dimension: that is, by a single straight line. The relationship between any three points can be represented in two dimensions: that is, it is always possible to devise a plane that passes through all three points. The relationship between any four points can be encompassed within a three-dimensional space, and so on. Fourthly, the possibility of exact replication within a six-dimensional space of the rankings from a set of cumulative scales is also mathematically trivial, since through any space with a number of dimensions one fewer than the number of significant points, it is always possible to project an axis upon which the significant points are projected in *any* postulated ranking, and at any precisely postulated set of mathematical intervals. A scale derived from scalogram rankings can be precisely identified; but so can a scale derived from the Justices' shoe sizes or telephone numbers. Fifthly, if any set of rankings and intervals derived from a cumulative scale can be *precisely* located in a six-dimensional space, it is also unsurprising and insignificant that a reasonably good approximation of the same set of rankings and intervals can be located in a space of lesser dimensionality, such as a two- or three-dimensional space. In short, the mathematical modelling of the Justices' psychological space (at least by the factor analytic methods employed in the work described above) adds nothing of significance to the scalograms.

The scalograms themselves remain of some interpretive value. The simpler Guttman scales can be used to verify or falsify hypotheses about judicial voting behaviour, and the larger cumulative scales offer fruitful possibilities for interpretation of groupings of cases which might never be thought of under more conventional methods. Nevertheless, the potential of such modes of analysis has largely remained unexplored—partly because of the need for mastery of sophisticated mathematical techniques, partly because of scepticism about whether any mathematical technique is capable of capturing the ultimate subjectivity of the judicial process, and partly because of scepticism about whether quantitative analysis can, in any event, add anything to informed qualitative observation and intuition. Indeed, the scaling techniques are of greatest value only when it is recog-

nised that they are merely a stimulus and aid to subjective interpretation of the cases themselves.

TONY BLACKSHIELD

Further Reading

Tony Blackshield, 'Quantitative Analysis: The High Court of Australia, 1964–1969' (1972) 3 *Lawasia* 1

Tony Blackshield, 'X/Y/Z/N Scales: The High Court of Australia, 1972–1976' in Roman Tomasic (ed), *Understanding Lawyers* (1978) 133

Roger Douglas, 'Judges and Policy on the Latham Court' (1969) 4 *Politics* 20

Fred Kort, 'Predicting Supreme Court Decisions Mathematically' (1957) 51 *American Political Science Review* 1

Fred Kort, 'Simultaneous Equations and Boolean Algebra in the Analysis of Judicial Decisions' (1963) 28 *Law and Contemporary Problems* 143

Glendon Schubert, 'Political Ideology on the High Court' (1968) 3 *Politics* 21 (Australasian Political Studies Association)

Glendon Schubert, 'Judicial Attitudes and Policy-Making in the Dixon Court' (1969) 7 *Osgoode Hall Law Journal* 1

Alan Tyree, 'The Geometry of Case Law' (1977) 4 *Victoria University of Wellington Law Review* 403

Alan Tyree, 'Fact Content Analysis of Case Law: Methods and Limitations' (1981) 22 *Jurimetrics Journal* 1

Jurisdiction is the power and authority of a court to hear and determine a **justiciable** controversy. The jurisdiction of the High Court derives from Chapter III of the Constitution and comprises both original and appellate jurisdiction.

A defining characteristic of the Court's jurisdiction is that it exists only in respect of **matters**. That ordinary word of common usage has become in the Court a term of art. There can be no matter 'unless there is some immediate right, duty or liability to be established by the determination of the Court' (*In re Judiciary and Navigation Acts* (1921)). On this basis, the Court has repeatedly held that it has no original or appellate jurisdiction to give **advisory opinions** or to entertain proceedings in which the issues are moot or hypothetical.

The Court's original jurisdiction is conferred in part directly by section 75 of the Constitution and in part by laws made by the Commonwealth Parliament under section 76 of the Constitution. The original jurisdiction conferred directly by section 75 is in respect of five categories of matter. The most significant are matters 'in which the Commonwealth, or a person suing or being sued on behalf of the Commonwealth, is a party' (section 75(iii)) and matters 'in which a **writ** of Mandamus or prohibition or an injunction is sought against an officer of the Commonwealth' (section 75(v)). They also include matters between states, between residents of different states, or between a state and a resident of another state (section 75(iv)). More obscure in conception and irrelevant in practice is the inclusion within the Court's constitutionally entrenched original jurisdiction of matters arising under a treaty (section 75(i); see *Re East; Ex parte Nguyen* (1998)) and matters affecting consuls or representatives of other countries (section 75(ii)).

While the Court has taken a very broad view of who may be identified as representing the Commonwealth or a state for jurisdictional purposes, it has taken a narrow view of who may be a resident. The Commonwealth and the states are treated as organisations or institutions of government in accordance with 'the conceptions of ordinary life' so as to include corporations that are agencies or instrumentalities of government (*Bank Nationalisation Case* (1948)). A corporation, however, cannot be a resident of a state (*Australasian Temperance & General Mutual v Howe* (1922)). The result is that what is sometimes called the 'diversity jurisdiction' of the Court in matters between residents of different states is limited to suits between natural persons (see, for example, *McDermott v Collien* (1953)).

The constitutional entrenchment of jurisdiction over applications for a writ of mandamus or prohibition or an injunction against an officer of the Commonwealth gives the Court a pivotal **role** in ensuring the compliance of officers of the Commonwealth executive government with the **rule of law**. The Court has held that officers of the Commonwealth also include Commonwealth judicial officers (*Adamson's Case* (1979)), but not state judicial officers exercising federal jurisdiction (*R v Murray and Cormie; Ex parte Commonwealth* (1916)). The consequence is that writs of mandamus and prohibition may be sought to correct jurisdictional error on the part of federal courts in the original jurisdiction of the High Court. This is in addition to the Court's ability to correct such errors in the exercise of its appellate jurisdiction.

The matters in respect of which original jurisdiction was left to be conferred on the Court by the Commonwealth Parliament include, most significantly, matters arising under the Constitution or involving its interpretation (section 76(i)) and matters arising under laws made by the Parliament (section 76(ii)). They also include matters of **admiralty** and maritime jurisdiction (section 76(iii)), and matters relating to the same subject matter claimed under laws of different states (section 76(iv)).

A matter arises under a law made by the Parliament only where a right or duty in question in the matter owes its existence to Commonwealth law or depends on Commonwealth law for its enforcement (*LNC Industries v BMW (Australia)* (1983)). The notion of a matter arising under the Constitution or involving its interpretation is broader. It encompasses not only matters in which constitutional validity is in issue but also matters in which the interpretation of the Constitution is relevant to an issue of **statutory interpretation** (*A-G (NSW) v Commonwealth Savings Bank* (1986)).

Although the Court's original jurisdiction in constitutional matters was not constitutionally entrenched but was left to be conferred by the Parliament (making an odd contrast with the relatively less important diversity jurisdiction, which was constitutionally entrenched), it was given to the Court from its inception by section 30(a) of the *Judiciary Act* 1903 (Cth) and has always been retained. The Court also had, for many years, original jurisdiction in respect of matters arising under a plethora of Commonwealth laws including the *Income Tax Assessment Act* 1936 (Cth), the *Patents Act* 1952 (Cth), and the *Trade Marks Act* 1955 (Cth). The Court was largely relieved of this workload when the **Federal Court** was established. The only significant original jurisdiction conferred by Commonwealth legislation now retained by the Court is that which it exercises in its capacity as the **Court of Disputed Returns** under the *Commonwealth Electoral Act* 1918 (Cth).

The Court for some years had original jurisdiction in matters of **admiralty** and maritime jurisdiction conferred by the Commonwealth Parliament under section 30(b) of the Judiciary Act. This jurisdiction existed concurrently with the additional—and constitutionally anomalous—jurisdiction of the Court as a Colonial Court of Admiralty under the *Colonial Courts of Admiralty Act* 1890 (Imp). The former was repealed in 1939 and the latter was terminated by the *Admiralty Act* 1988 (Cth). The Court has never been given jurisdiction in matters relating to the same subject matter claimed under laws of different states (section 76(iv)) and, given that the meaning and application of this potential source of jurisdiction has never been elucidated, it is never likely to be.

In all matters in which it has original jurisdiction, the Court has full power under the Judiciary Act to pronounce such judgments and to grant such legal or equitable **remedies** as may be necessary to do complete justice. This includes the making of binding declarations of right and the granting of habeas corpus. The exception is that in matters arising under the Commonwealth Electoral Act, the powers of the Court are governed by that Act.

Subject to a power of **remittal**, the Judiciary Act makes the original jurisdiction of the Court exclusive of that of state courts in two classes of matters. The first class involves suits between states or between the Commonwealth and a state. The second class involves matters in which a writ of mandamus or prohibition is sought against an officer of the Commonwealth. The Federal Court now has concurrent jurisdiction in relation to some matters in the second class but not in the first. The jurisdiction of the High Court in matters arising under the Constitution or involving its interpretation is not exclusive of the jurisdiction of other courts, but the Court has power upon application to order the **removal** from other courts of proceedings or parts of proceedings pending in those courts that raise constitutional issues.

The Court's appellate jurisdiction is conferred by section 73 of the Constitution. That section provides that the Court has jurisdiction 'to hear and determine appeals from all judgments, decrees, **orders** and sentences' of five specified categories of tribunal. The three main categories of tribunal are any Justice or Justices exercising the original jurisdiction of the High Court, any other federal court or court exercising federal jurisdiction, and **state Supreme Courts**. Categories now of only historical interest are any other state court from which an appeal lay to the **Privy Council** at the establishment of the Commonwealth and the **Inter-State Commission**.

The reference to 'all judgments, decrees, orders and sentences' includes any formal order of a court, irrespective of its form and irrespective of its subject matter. Unlike its original jurisdiction, the appellate jurisdiction of the Court is therefore unlimited as to subject matter. With the abolition of appeals to the Privy Council, this means that the Court is constituted as the ultimate court of appeal of general jurisdiction for Australia. Despite earlier holdings to the contrary, the Court has now accepted that it is not necessary that a judgment or order from which an appeal is brought be one that finally determines the rights of the parties. An appeal may be brought from the preliminary determination of separate questions (*O'Toole v Charles David* (1991)) or from the answer of a court of criminal appeal to a question referred by the prosecution following the acquittal of an accused (*Mellifont v A-G (Qld)* (1991)).

To hear and determine an 'appeal' under section 73 of the Constitution is 'to consider and determine whether the judgment of the court appealed from was right on the materials before that Court': *Davies and Cody v The King* (1937). The Court has for this purpose full power to redetermine the facts and the law. However, the Court has no power to receive fresh evidence on an appeal (*Mickelberg v The Queen* (1989); *Eastman v The Queen* (2000)) and must apply the law that existed at the time of the judgment from which the appeal is brought (*Victorian Stevedoring & General Contracting Co v Meakes and Dignan* (1931)).

The appellate jurisdiction conferred by section 73 of the Constitution is expressed to be subject to such exceptions and regulations as the Commonwealth Parliament prescribes. The Parliament has imposed a requirement for the grant of **leave to appeal** from an interlocutory judgment of a Justice or Justices exercising the original jurisdiction of the High Court and, since 1984, for the grant of special leave to appeal from judgments of all other courts.

The jurisdiction of the Court to hear and determine appeals from the Supreme Courts of the **territories** is conceptually problematic (see also **Nauru; Papua and New Guinea**). The jurisdiction has traditionally been treated as lying outside section 73 of the Constitution and as depending on the exercise of **Commonwealth legislative power** under section 122 of the Constitution (*Capital TV & Appliances v Falconer* (1971)). Consistently with this perception, provision for appeals to the High Court from judgments of the Supreme Court of the Northern Territory is now made in section 35AA of the Judiciary Act and is subject to the requirement for special leave. There is currently no similar provision for appeals from the Supreme Court of the ACT. Legislative provision now exists for appeals from that Court only to the Full Court of the Federal Court with a further appeal, by special leave, then lying to the High Court under section 73 of the Constitution.

STEPHEN GAGELER

Further Reading
Zelman Cowen and Leslie Zines, *Federal Jurisdiction in Australia* (2nd edn 1978)
RJ Ellicott, 'The Exercise of Federal Jurisdiction: A Revision of the Federal Structure' (1977) 1 *Crim LJ* 1
Final Report of the Constitutional Commission (1988), vol 1, 373–391

Jurisprudence. The term 'jurisprudence' most commonly means legal philosophy and legal theory or, more particularly, theories about law, legal reasoning, and justice. It informs understanding and **criticism** of the High Court as an organ of government, including the Court's institutional **role** and impact as well as the reasoning of its Justices and critics alike.

For Julius Stone in *The Province and Function of Law* (1946), 'jurisprudence' embraced the whole range of perspectives and insights that might be brought to bear on the theory and content of law from disciplines other than law, including **history**, philosophy, political science, sociology, and **economics**. Jurisprudence was 'the lawyer's extraver-sion', 'the examination of law in the light of other disciplines than the law'. Other conceptions postulate almost the converse of this: 'jurisprudence' refers to the theoretical component within the discipline of law, parallel to but distinct from the theoretical component of other disciplines. On either view, the range of jurisprudential theories includes **natural law** and 'fundamental rights' jurisprudence; **positivism**; American legal **realism**, **jurimetrics**, sociological jurisprudence, and socio-legal studies; **liberalism**, utilitarianism, relativism, Marxism, and other politico-justice theories; law and economics; and critical legal studies, **feminism**, critical race theory, post-modernism, post-structuralism, deconstruction, neo-pragmatism, and other critique-based theories.

Jurisprudential theories explain decision-making as well as other aspects of legal systems. According to some theories of natural law: law's ultimate justification lies outside law and the legal system in the form of objective **values** or human goods; law both shapes and is shaped by those values; some of those values (such as legal fairness) can only be pursued through law; and judges must inescapably use both law and some forms of 'non-law' (policies, principles, and community values) to justify their decisions.

According to some theories of positivism: law's ultimate justification lies outside law and the legal system in the form of popular acceptance of the legitimacy of the system for making legal rules; rules of law are separate from political and moral standards; rules of law are identified primarily by reference to their source or pedigree; and judges can occasionally use both law and some forms of 'non-law' (policies, principles, and community values) to justify their decisions.

According to the contemporary liberalism of Ronald Dworkin: law's justification is internal rather than external; law consists of 'rules' and 'principles' but not 'policy'; whatever forms part of an interpretation or account of the law that best 'fits' and morally 'justifies' the community's legal record as a matter of political morality counts as 'law' and is consistent with the judicial obligation to decide according to law; in that sense, judges are confined to 'law' in their **decision making** and never justifiably use 'non-law'; and there is always 'one right answer' in adjudication according to the 'rules' and 'principles' of the settled law. In *Re Wakim* (1999) (see **Cross-vesting**), **McHugh** endorsed Dworkin's theory of 'constructive interpretation' of constitutions.

According to some economic theories of law: the best legal systems and laws maximise economically effective behaviour and overall well-being as the sum total of the rational exercise of individual preferences; this is facilitated by creating appropriate conditions (including laws) that encourage people to pursue their individual preferences in reasoned ways; transaction costs and other economic consequences resulting from unrestricted rational choices by individuals must be factored into decision making; and these economic considerations inform legal, social, and political reasoning. In a conference paper published in 1999, McHugh candidly admits the influence of economic and other values:

Extrinsic values and practical experience derived from democracy, economics, science, social and political forces, public morality and contemporary conceptions of justice are often relevant factors in shaping the development of the law.

Such theories do not necessarily meet the challenges of contemporary theories which explore issues of authority and legitimacy, and the construction of hierarchies of power and normative legal subjects. These contemporary theories treat legal interpretation as involving the construction of meaning from texts, thus seeking to demonstrate that complex value judgments of various kinds are involved. On this view, even claims about the Court's progression in its own jurisprudence from literalistic and legalistic reasoning to purposive and policy-oriented reasoning do not go far enough, as a reinterpretation of legal reasoning itself is needed.

Thus, according to some critique-based theories building on legal realism: law's doctrines and rules are often irretrievably in conflict; the legal system and its laws reflect the values and interests of dominant power groups in society; and under the impartial shield of **legalism**, judges as well as legislators wield significant power, which needs to be analysed not only in strictly 'legal' terms, but in terms of social categories such as class, **race**, and gender (see **Men**; **Women**).

According to some post-structural theories: law's ultimate justification is grounded in the use of official force or violence (see Michel Foucault, *Discipline and Punish* (1977)); the limits of law and legal argument are contingent, arbitrary, and artificial boundaries or constructs, which impose an illusory distinction between 'legal' and 'non-legal' discourse; every legal decision or act is a creation, re-creation, and justification of law and its authority and power afresh in each new legal situation; and the legal system's participants (including judges) should acknowledge and confront these features of their institutional role in their decision making.

The term 'jurisprudence' may be used in various other ways. It may refer simply to the body of case law developed by a particular court ('the jurisprudence of the High Court') or in a particular country. Thus, in *Mabo* (1992), reference is made to 'English jurisprudence' and 'the various systems of native jurisprudence throughout the Empire'. Cases such as *Levy v Victoria* (1997), *Kruger v Commonwealth* (1997), and *Re Colina; Ex parte Torney* (1999) use 'jurisprudence' in a similar way, referring (for example) to English law, American law, or colonial law. In *Lange v ABC* (1997), the term 'jurisprudence' is used to signify one integrated body of Australian law: 'The Constitution, the federal, State and territorial laws, and the **common law** in Australia together constitute the law of this country and form "one system of jurisprudence".'

The Court's 'jurisprudence' may also refer simply to its approach to **judicial reasoning**. In this sense, the Court's jurisprudence has evolved from literal and legalistic approaches to interpretation—based on strictly defined categories and forms of legal analysis and argument—to include purposive and policy-oriented interpretation. In the last few decades of the twentieth century, the Justices started acknowledging **policy considerations** more openly in their decisions—especially in landmark cases such as *Bryan v Maloney* (1995) (liability in negligence of a builder of a home to its subsequent purchasers), *Pyrenees Shire Council v Day* (1998) (liability in negligence of public authorities such as local councils), and *Garcia v National Australia Bank* (1998) (status of married women under the law of guarantees). Indeed, in *Wik* (1996), **Kirby** illustrated the desirable judicial methodology (in his view) by canvassing considerations of 'legal principle' and 'legal policy' as well as considerations of 'legal authority' and **precedent**.

This reflects a more general trend away from complete reliance upon first-order reasoning about precise rules, towards second-order reasoning about underlying principles, policies, and values. At the same time, both the Court and the Australian community are yet to confront fully the value-laden elements inherent within legal interpretation and the contingent assumptions surrounding the framework within which legal arguments and actions proceed.

For much of the twentieth century, legal analysis in Australia and High Court decision making were dominated by an orthodox liberal-democratic framework often associated with what is called 'strict legalism'. The historical dominance of narrow forms of legal positivism produced narrow forms of the declaratory theory of law that determined legal and community views about the role of judges, thus establishing a self-reinforcing pattern that has proved resistant to change. In this model, judges were thought simply to declare pre-existing law rather than engage in **law-making**; law was regarded as being objectively embodied solely in the text of legislation and precedent; its interpretation was a technical process often guided by **literalism**, without much regard to context, consequences, and non-legal influences; legal reasoning consisted largely of strict induction, deduction, and analogy from existing rules of law; and the law was regarded as containing an answer for every problem without regard to 'non-legal' factors such as economic, social, and political conditions and other 'policy' considerations.

Related to the prevalence of these forms of positivism in Anglo–Australian jurisprudence was an emphasis on formalism (see **Form and substance**). Its most obvious manifestation in the High Court was the doctrine of 'strict legalism', often attributed to **Dixon**. In his landmark address in 1952 upon first sitting as **Chief Justice** in Sydney, Dixon strongly endorsed the idea that 'there is no other safe guide to judicial decisions in great conflicts than a strict and complete legalism'; elsewhere he defended legal reasoning as a 'system of fixed concepts, logical categories and prescribed principles of reasoning'. Yet, as **commentators** and Justices such as **Mason** have indicated, 'strict legalism' does not necessarily prevent judges from having regard to 'deeper, more ordered, more philosophical and perhaps more enduring conceptions of justice'—to use Dixon's own descriptions (see **Realism**)—which they say derive from the law.

The Court's adherence to strict legalism diminished with Dixon's departure. The tensions among competing conceptions of the judicial process between **Kitto** and **Barwick**, and later between Barwick and **Murphy**, which emerged in the **Barwick Court** had begun by 1987 to generate a new consensus, with commentators having mixed reactions to the judicial **activism** of the **Mason Court**. In that year, Mason defended the Court's approach, saying:

We are developing an Australian common law. In the pursuit of this goal we must necessarily depart, in some respects at least, from the philosophy of legalism or legal formalism which, so it is said, the High Court followed in past years.

Although 'strict legalism' strives for the application of objective rules and principles of interpretation, grounded in the law rather than idiosyncratic judicial views or values (see **Deane** in *Muschinski v Dodds* (1985)), Mason noted in 1986 that this ignores the reality that no act of interpreting law can ever be completely value-free, and that 'the ever present danger is that "strict and complete legalism" will be a cloak for undisclosed and unidentified policy values'. Similarly, in a conference paper published in 1988, McHugh commented that 'if, as I believe is the case, policy factors are decisive in hard cases, then the judiciary should not be composed exclusively of those who are masters only of a strict and complete legalism'.

Charges against the Court for being 'activist' or 'conservative' are something it now shares with other courts such as the **House of Lords** and the **United States Supreme Court**, both of which have been described in different eras as activist or conservative to varying degrees. While this dichotomy between 'activism' and 'conservatism' refers to the Court's institutional capacity for law-making, and is itself an aspect of the Court's jurisprudence, the notion that a court has its own 'jurisprudence' may also refer to other theoretical issues, which are equally controversial. These include debates about **constitutional interpretation**—where implications are made or resort is had to the **Convention Debates** for clarifying constitutional provisions (see **Originalism**), or arguments are advanced based on the 'text' and 'structure' of the Constitution. They may also include debates about **characterisation**, particularly where a head of power is read to expand **Commonwealth legislative power** at the expense of state power; the battle between literal and purposive constitutional and **statutory interpretation**; the changing judicial meanings given to the concept of **sovereignty**; the scope for constitutional and non-constitutional limits on legislative capacity and parliamentary supremacy; and the capacity for interpreting ambiguous constitutional provisions according to the norms of the **International Bill of Rights**.

Yet another conception of 'jurisprudence' refers to the higher order principles and conceptions that serve to order and unify the body of legal doctrine. Thus, in some judgments, jurisprudence and legal theory are linked to conceptual thinking in law, as correctives to the occasional infelicity of fit between conceptual soundness and the law's incremental development.

In other judgments, as in the *War Crimes Act Case* (1991), the term is used to describe the principles of a particular body of law—in that instance, the principles of 'criminal jurisprudence' requiring that criminal liability should not attach to something that was not a crime at the time of its commission. In *Trident General Insurance v McNiece* (1988), 'jurisprudence' is referred to in the context of precedent and overturning settled doctrines.

In his 1988 paper, McHugh speaks of 'general legal principles and jurisprudential concepts' as guiding the process of adjudication. In *Wik*, Kirby refers to the 'unifying simplicity' from the perspective of 'legal theory' of the body of Australian **property** law prior to *Mabo*. In *Hill v Van Erp* (1997), McHugh uses the term 'doctrinal integrity' in refusing to 'quarantine' the professional liability of lawyers from the general law of negligence. In *Trident*, **Dawson** refers to **Windeyer's** comment in *Olsson v Dyson* (1969) about perceptions of 'the rigidity of conceptual thinking', from the perspective of 'jurisprudence and legal theory'.

While some Justices have been willing to admit, in their judgments or **extra-judicial writings**, that law is neither completely objective nor completely value-free, most of those acknowledgments have still occurred within the framework of a liberal **ideology** that assigns particular limited roles in adjudication to values, policies, and principles. On one view (that of Dworkin), judges may draw upon those values, policies, or principles they perceive as being embedded in society's legal framework and its laws, or alternatively supported by a majority of the community as 'consensus values' or 'community values', as part of a justification for adjudication in those so-called 'hard cases' where the effect of legal text and precedent is unclear. There are two important problems with this approach. It asserts the possibility of gauging a consensus on the meaning of law or of community values, and its focus on 'hard cases' simultaneously affirms and marginalises the acknowledgment of evaluative judgment—the response of legal realism being that every case is a 'hard case'.

A deconstruction of the High Court's decision-making processes would reject the idea of a linear progression from the ontology of 'legalism' to the teleology of 'policy', revealing instead a perennial oscillation from the **Griffith Court** onwards between the poles of 'legalism' and 'policy'—even though explicit support for the latter may appear to have gained majority acceptance only in the Mason Court. For example, despite Dixon's proclamation in his 1952 speech of the importance of 'strict and complete legalism', his judgment in the *Melbourne Corporation Case* (1947) reveals that he himself found it difficult to disentangle politics from law: 'the Constitution is a political instrument [and] deals with government and governmental powers', so that 'nearly every consideration arising from the Constitution' can be described as political, the real question being whether it is 'compelling'.

However, what neither the language of 'legalism' nor that of 'policy' is able to achieve (and indeed what they may serve to exclude) is a critical questioning of the source of judicial and legislative power, and the consequences of its exercise. Both seek legitimation either from within (judicial impartiality) or from without (social norms or presumed consensus). Neither fully confronts the challenges and insights of contemporary theories of jurisprudence and their exploration of authority, legitimacy, and interpretation (see **Theory and legitimacy**).

The Court continues to locate responsibility for its wielding of legal and institutional power impersonally in the law and the Constitution, with the more controversial outcomes eliciting the more insistent disclaimers. Thus in the *Tasmanian Dam Case* (1983), the Justices accompanied their reasons for judgment with a public statement emphasising that the Court was concerned with 'strictly legal questions' and 'in no way concerned with the question whether it is desirable or undesirable … that the construction of the dam should proceed'. Nor is this an unusual disclaimer. Dixon sought to emphasise in his 1952 speech that the Court's 'sole function is to interpret a constitutional description of power or restraint upon power and say whether a given measure falls on one side of a line consequently drawn or the other, and that it has nothing whatever to do with the merits or demerits of the measure'. **Latham** similarly denied that any choice was involved in his dissent in the *Bank Nationalisation Case* (1948). In *Mabo*, Deane and **Gaudron** seemed to go beyond mere clinical legal analysis of the issues towards articulating the historical operation of the legal system 'to dispossess, degrade and devastate the **Aboriginal peoples**', leaving 'a national legacy of unutterable shame'. Yet their explanation for having adopted such an emotive tone was grounded in legalism: they explained that they had done so only because 'the full facts of that dispossession are of critical importance to the assessment' of the Queensland government's arguments. The judgment of Kirby in *Green v The Queen* (1997) (see **Sexual preference**) is an example of challenging the legitimating process underlying the policy-oriented approach by challenging notions of community consensus.

Finally, the Court's jurisprudence in the various areas of law has been shaped by influential legal philosophers throughout its history. The Griffith Court based its analysis of **intergovernmental immunities** on a theory of sovereignty derived from the positivism of John Austin. Sometimes, the Court has referred expressly to leading jurisprudential works and thinkers of the twentieth century, including theorists such as Stone, Dworkin, HLA Hart, Hans Kelsen, John Finnis, and Richard Posner, as well as the jurisprudential influence of Justices such as Dixon. In *Kable v DPP* (1996), there are references to John Salmond on *Jurisprudence* (2nd edn 1907), to Hart's *The Concept of Law* (1961), and to Kelsen's concept of a *grundnorm*; and again in the *War Crimes Act Case* to Kelsen's *General Theory of Law and State* (1949). In *Trident* and in *Gala v Preston* (1991), there are references to Stone's *Precedent and Law* (1985); and in *Trident* also to Dixon's 1955 speech 'Concerning Judicial Method' (see **Realism**). Finnis's *Natural Law and Natural Rights* (1990) is cited in *Marks v GIO Australia Holdings* (1998); Posner's *The Problems of Jurisprudence* (1990) is cited in *Wik*; and Dworkin's books *Taking Rights Seriously* (1977) and *Law's Empire* (1986) are cited in *Re Wakim*. In particular, Stone's notion of the 'leeways for choice' available to appellate court judges has been an important influence on the Court: for example, see Kirby's judicial use of 'leeways for choice' in *Northern Sandblasting v Harris* (1997), and his extra-judicial homage to Stone's influence upon the High Court in 'Julius Stone and the High Court of Australia' (1997) 20 *UNSWLJ* 239.

In summary, 'jurisprudence' has a number of contextual meanings in Australian law and High Court adjudication.

BRYAN HORRIGAN

Further Reading

Owen Dixon, 'Concerning Judicial Method' (1956) 29 *ALJ* 468, reprinted in SHZ Woinarski (ed), *Jesting Pilate* (1965) 152

Anthony Mason, 'The Role of a Constitutional Court in a Federation: A Comparison of the Australian and the United States Experience' (1986) 16 *FL Rev* 1

Anthony Mason, 'Future Directions in Australian Law' (1987) 13 *Mon LR* 149

Anthony Mason, 'The Interpretation of a Constitution in a Modern Liberal Democracy', in Charles Sampford and Kim Preston (eds), *Interpreting Constitutions: Theories, Principles and Institutions* (1996) 13

Michael McHugh, 'The Law-Making Function of the Judicial Process: Part II' (1988) 62 *ALJ* 116

Michael McHugh, 'The Judicial Method' (1999) 73 *ALJ* 37

Jury trial as a **common law** institution has been variously 'traced to Roman, Saxon, Frankish or Norman origins' (**Deane** in *Kingswell v The Queen* (1985)) and is often sourced—erroneously, according to Deane—to the Magna Carta provision that: 'No free man shall be taken and imprisoned or disseised of any free tenement or of his liberties or free customs or outlawed or exiled, or in any other way destroyed … except by the lawful judgment of his peers or by the law of the land.'

Currently, jury trial involves a panel of 12 citizens, randomly selected from the electoral roll. The qualifications, eligibility, summonsing, empanelling, swearing, and general regulation of juries are spelt out in individual state and territory legislation. The High Court itself can hold jury trials under section 77B of the **Judiciary Act** 1903 (Cth), although this has rarely been done; for examples see *R v Porter* (1933) and *R v Brewer* (1942). When it does occur, the law governing juries in the state or territory in which the case originates is applicable (section 77D).

Whatever its exact origins, jury trial was being proclaimed as an ancient right in England by the fourteenth century. The notion of jury trial as a central element of political **citizenship** and a check against monarchical, executive, or judicial dictate was further entrenched in the eighteenth-century trials of dissenters such as John Wilkes. In a number of celebrated treason and sedition trials, individual juries refused to follow judicial directions to convict despite threats to lock them up without food and water until they did.

In the early Australian penal colonies, juries were composed of military officers, and some of the first political petitions in the fledgling colonies put the right to 'trial by a jury of peers' at the top of the list. In the political struggles between emancipists and exclusivists that followed, the right to jury trial was seen as central to demands for full citizenship on the part of emancipated convicts. By the time of federation, jury trial was established in all states and **territories** and section 80 of the Australian Constitution provided: 'The trial on indictment of any offence against any law of the Commonwealth shall be by jury'—one of the few provisions in the Australian Constitution creating **express constitutional rights** in the manner of a **Bill of Rights**.

Deane captured the impetus for jury trial well in *Kingswell*:

> The guarantee of section 80 of the Constitution was not the mere expression of some casual preference for one form of criminal trial. It reflected a deep-seated conviction of free men and women about the way in which justice should be administered in criminal cases. That conviction finds a solid basis in an understanding of the history and functioning of the common law as a bulwark against the tyranny of arbitrary punishment. In the history of this country, the transition from military panel to civilian jury for the determination of criminal guilt represented the most important step in the progress from military control to civilian self-government.

Nevertheless, section 80 has traditionally been given an exceedingly narrow and literal interpretation by the High Court. Such an interpretation—described as 'mocking' by **Dixon** and **Evatt** in their joint minority judgment in *R v Fed-*

eral Court of Bankruptcy; Ex parte Lowenstein (1938)—would leave it in the hands of the legislature to bypass jury trial simply by providing in legislation that particular offences be triable summarily. As Evatt had told the Australian Legal Convention in 1936, section 80

has certainly been given a very narrow interpretation, so narrow that the safeguard may be rendered illusory at the will of the very Parliament whose action it was intended to restrict by safeguarding the rights of the citizen. If anyone is possessed of an ambition to fill up 'gaps' in the Constitution by restoring safeguards to the people, he may start by endeavouring to secure that the right of trial by jury in serious cases should be made effective.

No such ambitions were demonstrated by **Barwick** in *Spratt v Hermes* (1965) when he declared that 'whereas s 80 might have been thought to be a great constitutional guarantee, it has been discovered to be a mere procedural provision'; nor by **Menzies** in *Zarb v Kennedy* (1968) when he stated that

it is well established that s 80 does not mean that trial for any offence, or what may be called a serious offence, against any law of the Commonwealth shall be by jury: this section means no more than it says, i.e. that every trial on indictment shall be by jury.

The challenge to 'restore safeguards to the people' mounted by Dixon and Evatt in *Lowenstein* was taken up by **Murphy** (a great defender of and believer in the jury even, and especially, throughout his own travails) in the 1970s (see *Beckwith v The Queen* (1976); *Jackson v The Queen* (1976); *Yager v The Queen* (1977); *Li Chia Hsing v Rankin* (1978)) and further developed in a powerful and passionate dissent by Deane in *Kingswell*. Deane viewed the 'narrow' procedural interpretation as concealing 'circuity or obvious error or leading to tautology'. In his opinion, section 80 should apply to all 'serious' Commonwealth offences, which Dixon and Evatt had tentatively defined as those offences carrying a maximum penalty of more than one year's imprisonment.

In the same year, in *Brown v The Queen* (1986), a 3:2 majority held that in any case where section 80 does apply, it guarantees jury trial irrespective of the defendant's wishes, so that a right to waive jury trial on indictment provided by the law of a state (in that case, SA) is inapplicable to Commonwealth offences tried on indictment in that state. Even the minority view accorded section 80 the status of a fundamental individual right under the Constitution which, because it was vested in an individual, could be waived by that individual. The majority argued that it was not merely an individual right, but a fundamental part of the constitutional structure. On either view, it seemed that some life was being breathed back into section 80—a diagnosis confirmed by a unanimous High Court seven years later in *Cheatle v The Queen* (1993).

That case involved a challenge to a SA provision that allowed a trial judge to accept a majority jury verdict. It was held that the provision could not apply in a trial of a Commonwealth offence. The Court unanimously declared that '**history**, principle and authority combine to compel the conclusion' that in Commonwealth cases tried on indict-

ment, section 80 requires a unanimous verdict. In addition to reliance on the historical understanding of the phrase 'trial by jury' in 1900 (see **Connotation and denotation**), central to the decision was the view that a unanimous verdict 'ensures that the representative character and the collective nature of the jury are carried forward into any ultimate verdict'. Unlike an electoral process in which voters express their own individual views, the jury 'only exists as a collectivity, and not as a group of individuals'. The requirement of unanimity 'promotes deliberation and provides some insurance that the opinions of each of the jurors will be heard and discussed', thereby reducing the prospect of 'hasty and unjust verdicts' and reflecting the 'fundamental thesis … that a person accused of a crime should be given the benefit of any reasonable doubt'.

The cumulative effect of *Brown* and *Cheatle* was further reinforced by *Katsuno v The Queen* (1999) and *Re Colina; Ex parte Torney* (1999); and in *Cheng v The Queen* (2000), it was argued that the time had come to **overrule** the majority decision in *Kingswell*. The argument was rejected. **Gleeson**, **Gummow**, and **Hayne** held that since the defendants had pleaded guilty, there was no legislative denial of trial by jury in relation to any element of the charge, and therefore it was not an appropriate occasion to reopen *Kingswell*. **Gaudron** held that section 80 ought to be read as a constitutional guarantee, or 'more precisely a constitutional command' but that on the facts no question arose as to the infringement of that command. **Callinan** expressed 'disquiet' that under the narrow interpretation of section 80 Parliament was left to decide 'what is, and what is not to be an offence charged on indictment and its elements' but went on to hold that as there had not been any 'oppressive misuse of the statutory power to define offences' *Kingswell* should not be overturned.

It is in the opposed judgments of **McHugh** and **Kirby** that we find the substantive issue most fully argued. McHugh engaged in a detailed analysis of the origins of section 80 in the 1898 **Convention Debates**, coming to the conclusion that section 80 'was enacted in the form in which it was for the purpose of enabling the Parliament to have the right to say whether an offence was to be indictable or punishable summarily and for ensuring that the right to trial by jury would depend on Parliament's classification of the offence'. It followed that the construction of section 80 accepted by the majority in *Kingswell* was correct, and section 80 'is not a great guarantee of trial by jury for serious matters'. Kirby, in dissent, held that the decision in *Kingswell* should be reopened, noting that 'the disadvantages and inconvenience of correcting earlier errors of constitutional doctrine are usually exaggerated so that they appear as "apocalyptic scenarios" designed to frighten judges "into submission"'. He adopted **Brennan's** definition of 'offence' in *Kingswell* and drew support from the decision of the **United States Supreme Court** in *Apprendi v New Jersey* (2000), quoting Justice John Paul Stevens' conclusion that 'any fact that increases the penalty for a crime beyond the prescribed statutory maximum must be submitted to a jury, and proved beyond reasonable doubt'. Kirby concluded:

The constitutional guarantee of trial by jury … would be a puny thing indeed if the Parliament could so easily circumvent jury determination of matters in contest by classifying some facts as 'sentencing enhancement' factors when in truth they constitute the ingredients of a much more serious variety of 'offence'.

Section 80 appears in the Constitution. It has been mocked and evaded in Australia for too long. It is time for this Court to give the section a constitutional construction.

Some of the Court's strongest expressions of the importance attached to jury trial tend to emerge in the course of majority opinions refusing **leave to appeal** or dismissing an appeal on the ground that to allow the appeal would 'usurp the functions of the jury': Brennan in the *Chamberlain Case* (1984); see also *Doney v The Queen* (1990); *Chidiac v The Queen* (1991). Such comments are problematic in two respects. First, they can result in a downplaying of the appellate function and a tendency to collapse the various grounds of appeal into one 'unsafe and unsatisfactory' ground that is not even in the terms of the 'common form' statutory formula specifying grounds for appeal—see Kirby in *Gipp v The Queen* (1998). The focus on this single, compendious ground elides the existence of the separate 'miscarriage of justice' ground, and hinders the development of a sceptical judicial sensibility attuned—as Murphy's, Deane's, and Kirby's have been—to possible miscarriages. The tendency is well illustrated in the majority judgments denying the *Chamberlain* appeal.

Secondly, the expressed reluctance to 'usurp' the role of the jury tends to portray the overturning of a jury verdict as an attack on the jury system itself. But the answer to this argument is provided by Deane in *Chamberlain*:

> The principle that no person should be convicted of a serious crime except by a jury on the evidence has no corollary requiring that every person who is found guilty by a jury's verdict should remain so convicted. The safeguard provided by trial by jury is not dependent on any assumption of infallibility of the verdict of the jury. It would be foolish to deny that a jury may be prejudiced, perverse or wrong. Any notion that a jury's verdict of guilty should be given the degree of finality which the principle of double jeopardy requires to be accorded to a verdict of acquittal has long been rejected: it is, for example, quite inconsistent with the existence of the 'common form' ground of appeal that the verdict of the jury 'is unreasonable or cannot be supported having regard to the evidence'. Nor is the cause of the continued acceptance of jury trial likely to be served by treating a jury's verdict of guilty as unchallengeable or unexaminable. To the contrary, so to treat a jury's verdict of guilty could sap and undermine the institution of trial by jury in that it would, in the context of modern views of what is desirable in the administration of criminal justice, be liable to be seen as a potential instrument of entrenched injustice.

The right of jury trial has been undermined in various ways. First, section 80 has been given a narrow interpretation. Secondly, a number of jurisdictions (Victoria, WA, SA, Tasmania, and the Northern Territory) have legislated to permit majority verdicts, despite the reasoning in *Cheatle* that unanimity is an essential feature of jury trial. Thirdly, some jurisdictions (NSW, SA, WA, and the ACT) have provided for judge-only trials at the election of the accused and with the prosecutor's consent, despite the importance given to jury trial in *Brown*. Moreover, judges generally do not wel-

come judge-only trials, as they require the judges to be finders of fact, require a full written judgment, and remove the element of popular participation in the process, thereby weakening community confidence in the verdicts that the popular participation generates.

Fourthly, some jurisdictions have allowed versions of the pernicious practice of jury-vetting to disfigure the random basis of jury selection. Whereas jurors were formerly drawn from lists of ratepayers and therefore had a predominantly male and middle-class character, most jurisdictions now draw juries from electoral rolls, and **women** now make up approximately 50 per cent of jurors. Certain categories of citizen are disqualified from jury service (for example, by a prior prison sentence), are ineligible (for example, if their occupations are connected with the criminal justice system), or are exempt as of right (a disparate category including those aged over 65, pregnant women, and those living at a distance from the court). Prospective jurors are summonsed to attend and are empanelled in a process that allows both prosecution and defence to challenge individual jurors 'for cause' (infrequent) or by way of a specified number of 'peremptory' challenges—the number varies across the jurisdictions—that are usually exercised on the basis of **stereotypes** based on class, gender, dress, demeanour, and other such signifiers.

It emerged in the UK in the 1980s that the practice of vetting jurors—the standing aside of potential jurors on the basis of advice given to the prosecution by police or security services that particular citizens were undesirable or untrustworthy because of non-disqualifying convictions or suspicions that they might be ill-disposed to authority—had been widespread for decades (see *R v Sheffield Crown Court; Ex parte Brownlow* (1980); compare *R v Mason* (1980); Practice Note (1988) 3 All ER 1086).

The level of jury vetting in Australia is unclear but the practice is possible in jurisdictions that permit prosecution access to jury panel lists (Victoria, Tasmania, Queensland, WA, and the ACT). It has been held in Victoria that jury vetting on the basis of information of non-disqualifying convictions supplied to the Department of Public Prosecutions by police is not unlawful (*R v Robinson* (1988); *R v Su* (1995); compare *In the Trial of D* (1988)). The High Court in *Katsuno v The Queen* (1999) unanimously held that the practice was unlawful, but a majority went on to find that such unlawfulness did not involve a defect in the criminal process, and did not deny the accused his constitutional right to trial by jury. In strong dissent, McHugh found that 'a breach of the requirements of the criminal process in a fundamental respect occurred once the prosecution was able to obtain an unfair advantage by using information received in breach of the Act to select the jury panel', and Kirby held that 'the trial was flawed because the constitutional tribunal which conducted it was shown not to have been lawfully chosen'. The reasoning of the majority resonates with a contemporary version of 'convict taint', illustrating the continued pertinence of colonial agitation by emancipist convicts for full citizenship.

Finally, not only has summary jurisdiction been massively expanded, but formerly indictable offences triable by judge and jury have been legislatively classified downwards so that they, too, are triable summarily by magistrates. Such reclassification is usually justified in technocratic terms as faster, more efficient, and less costly.

Inasmuch as summary trial diminishes access to trial by jury, such claims are true. Whether such developments are desirable is another matter. Doreen McBarnet argued in 1981 that 'legal policy has established two tiers of justice', the exceptional higher court form where the 'ideology of justice is put on display' and the lower courts where the bulk of criminal law is acted out without due process.

Whatever weight we give to the argument from efficiency, jury trial is in relative decline as a mode of trial: in NSW, for example, jury trials comprise less than 1 per cent (it is 0.65 per cent) of all criminal cases in all criminal courts and 5 per cent of all hearings where the defendant has pleaded 'Not guilty'. But the institution of jury trial cannot be evaluated solely in instrumental and technocratic terms: it is vital to understand jury trial in terms of politics, citizenship, and the organisation and distribution of power rather than simply by reference to its practicality, expertise, economy, or efficiency as a legal institution. As Lord Devlin put it in 1991: 'The jury is invested with a dispensing power to be used when their respect for the law is overridden by the conviction that to punish would be unjust.' While tending at a general level to assert the historical importance of the jury as a social and political institution, the High Court has failed to follow through on the implications of this in practical contexts and has so far declined (over vigorous dissents) to read section 80 of the Constitution as a broad guarantee of jury trial.

DAVID BROWN

Further Reading
JM Bennett, 'The Establishment of Jury Trial in New South Wales' (1959–60) 3 *Syd LR* 463
Michael Chesterman, 'Criminal Trial Juries in Australia: From Penal Colonies to a Federal Democracy' (1999) 62 *Law and Contemporary Problems* 69
Lord Devlin, 'The Conscience of the Jury' (1991) 107 *LQR* 402
HV Evatt, 'The Jury System in Australia' (1936) 10 *ALJ* Supplement 49
Mark Findlay and Peter Duff (eds), *The Jury Under Attack* (1988)
David Neal, 'Law and Authority: The Campaign for Jury Trial in NSW' (1987) 8 *Journal of Legal History* 107

Justiciability, and its opposite, 'non-justiciability', can mean different things in different contexts. It may refer to whether, as a matter of strict law, a court has **jurisdiction** to determine an issue, or it may refer to whether the issue is a suitable one for judicial resolution. These different meanings are not unrelated, for whether a court *ought* to deal with an issue may well have an important bearing on the way in which a court will (and should) expound the relevant principles of law to avoid the determination of issues considered unfit for judicial determination.

In the first sense, an issue may be non-justiciable for one of three analytical reasons. First, a court may simply lack jurisdiction to deal with the issue—because of the subject matter of the dispute or the nature of the parties involved, or because of the court's inability to grant appropriate judicial relief. Secondly, it may be that a court has jurisdiction but is not obliged to exercise that jurisdiction—although the soundness of this argument is open to serious question if it is meant to suggest anything more than the exercise of the traditional discretions attached to the grant of prerogative **writs**

and the forms of judicial relief grounded in **equity**. Thirdly, it may be unnecessary for a court to determine the issue because the application of the relevant principles of law does not depend on that determination—for instance, because the parliament or government has acted within the scope of its legal powers and there is no relevant legal limitation on the exercise of those powers.

In the second sense of justiciability—whether an issue is considered to be appropriate and fit for judicial determination—the issue may be non-justiciable because it is thought to be peculiarly political and better fitted for determination by the non-judicial agencies of government. Alternatively, it might be thought that the consequences of legal invalidity would produce an unacceptable degree of uncertainty about the existence of constitutional authority in a community. Whatever the precise reason, the issues posed by the notion of justiciability highlight the need to identify the limits of the institutional competence of the judicial process. They require courts to strike an appropriate balance between the potentially conflicting demands of the **rule of law** and the **separation of powers**.

There has been little judicial discussion of justiciability in Australia, although some members of the High Court have recently shown an awareness of its importance. A learned and helpful analysis of the subject appears in **Gummow's** judgment in the **Federal Court** in *Re Ditfort* (1988), where he noted the potential importance of justiciability in determining the scope for **judicial review** of the Australian government's conduct of foreign affairs under section 61 of the Constitution. He warned, however, that the limits on justiciability accepted by courts in the UK might not necessarily apply in Australian courts, given their obligation to uphold a written Constitution. **Kirby** has indicated that the subject raises large and controversial questions, and that the relevant law is in a state of development (*Lindon v Commonwealth* (1996); *Thorpe v Commonwealth (No 3)* (1997)).

The mere fact that a matter is political does not place it beyond the scope of judicial review. This is not surprising, since 'the Constitution is a political instrument': **Dixon** in the *Melbourne Corporation Case* (1947). Unlike the **United States Supreme Court**, the High Court has yet to evolve an articulate doctrine for isolating the kind of political issues that are not justiciable. This is not to deny, however, the use that can be made—and has been made—of the factors that inform the 'political questions doctrine' in the USA, as expounded, for example, in the famous case of *Baker v Carr* (1962). The same underlying factors may be replicated in Australia in different forms—for instance, in the reluctance of Australian courts to deal with various aspects of the conduct of foreign affairs and the internal proceedings of parliament. It is, however, the American doctrine that provides perhaps the most comprehensive analysis of the political issues that would universally be regarded as unfit for judicial determination because of their peculiarly political nature.

The High Court's willingness to pronounce upon issues in **constitutional law** that, because of their highly political nature, might once have been classified as lying beyond the scope of judicial review, is illustrated by the Court's decisions as to the requirements for a joint sitting of both Houses of Parliament under section 57 of the Constitution (*Cormack v Cope* (1974); *PMA Case* (1975)); and as to the composition of the House of Representatives under section 24 (*A-G (Cth); Ex rel McKinlay v Commonwealth* (1975); *A-G (NSW); Ex rel McKellar v Commonwealth* (1977)). In both contexts, the Court has been careful to stipulate that its decisions would not invalidate previous elections or deny that past and current parliaments were validly constituted.

Nevertheless, there is an ample range of analytical techniques by which the High Court can abstain from deciding certain political issues. The concept of '**matters**' in Chapter III of the Constitution prevents federal courts from dealing with disputes that do not involve 'principles of law' (*Truth About Motorways* (2000)) and, more controversially, with disputes not comparable to those that 'could arise between individual persons' in 1900 (*Boundary Dispute Case* (1911)). The provisions of sections 47 and 49 operate to commit a range of issues to determination by the Australian Parliament, at least until Parliament itself provides otherwise. These include questions concerning the qualifications of members of Parliament, filling of vacancies, disputed elections, and parliamentary privilege (see **Electoral law**). Some of the constitutional provisions concerning the respective powers of the two Houses of Parliament and the relationship between them with respect to money Bills (but not those in section 57 relating to deadlocks between the two Houses) have been treated as non-justiciable because they are expressed as relating only to 'proposed laws': *Osborne v Commonwealth* (1911), reaffirmed in *Northern Suburbs Cemetery v Commonwealth* (1993) and the *Native Title Act Case* (1995). The *Railway Standardisation Case* (1962) suggests that some agreements between federal and state governments are political, and are not intended to give rise to enforceable legal obligations—though it is unclear whether this is genuinely a matter of justiciability or is rather the result of the application of the ordinary principles of **contract law**. Indeed, a similar result has often been reached in relation to governmental dealings with private individuals by denying any enforceable government contract (see, for example, *Australian Woollen Mills v Commonwealth* (1954); *Administration of Papua and New Guinea v Leahy* (1961); *Placer Development v Commonwealth* (1969)). In any event, section 64 of the *Judiciary Act* 1903 (Cth) may limit the enforceability of governmental agreements to those that would have been capable of enforcement between private individuals.

Perhaps the area most affected by the need to limit judicial review concerns the conduct of foreign affairs, reflecting limitations on the institutional competence of the courts in this area. That is reflected in the courts' reliance on executive certificates (normally conclusive) for determining such matters as the extent of acquisition of foreign territory; the existence of war, belligerency, and neutrality; and the recognition of foreign governments. It is also reflected in the unreviewable status of matters arising from the width of the prerogative powers entrusted to the executive. This is illustrated by the 'act of state' doctrine; by the general inability of domestic courts to give effect to treaties and other international agreements that have not been incorporated into domestic law; and by the inability of domestic courts to deal with disputes involving foreign governments, even if those disputes arise in the course of

resolving disputes between private persons: *Spycatcher Case* (1988), approving the principle established by the **House of Lords** in *Buttes Gas v Hammer* (1981). However, the mere fact that a matter involves foreign affairs is not sufficient by itself to place the matter beyond the scope of judicial review.

Although the High Court has considerably widened the scope of **administrative law** powers of review, in part reflecting statutory developments, some doubt remains as to the extent to which some **common law** prerogative powers may still be treated as falling beyond the scope of judicial review. It is now accepted that the principles of such review govern the exercise of statutory powers vested in the Queen's representatives in Australia (**Northern Land Council Case** (1981)). While this suggests that prerogative powers will not automatically be regarded as immune from judicial review, the High Court may, and possibly should, continue to take that view in relation to some prerogative powers by reason of their subject matter—for example, those relating to the making of treaties, the defence of the realm, the grant of honours, the dissolution of parliament, and the appointment and dismissal of ministers. Review of Cabinet decisions has been seen as giving rise to peculiarly sensitive issues because they are 'primarily concerned with the "political, economic and social concerns of the moment"': *SA v O'Shea* (1987).

Mason has suggested that the concept of justiciability may provide the limits on the scope of judicial review in such areas. This requires attention to whether an issue lends itself to judicial rather than political decision. That, in turn, will depend on a number of factors such as the nature and importance of the **policy considerations** and the degree to which the decision is determinative of the rights or interests of an individual.

Much remains to be done in identifying the proper use of justiciability in limiting judicial review and the precise factors that help to explain why some issues do not lend themselves to judicial adjudication. The criteria suggested by Mason will not be sufficient by themselves if the concept of justiciability is to be much more than a discretionary and subjective tool by which a court may abstain from deciding difficult issues in cases where it is otherwise properly seised of jurisdiction at the instance of a competent litigant.

GEOFFREY LINDELL

Further Reading

Alex Castles, 'Justiciability: Political Questions' in Leslie Stein (ed), *Locus Standi* (1979) ch 8

House of Representatives Legal and Constitutional Affairs Committee, *The Third Paragraph of Section 53 of the Constitution* (1995)

Geoffrey Lindell, 'The Justiciability of Political Questions: Recent Developments' in HP Lee and George Winterton (eds), *Australian Constitutional Perspectives* (1992) ch 7

Geoffrey Lindell, 'Judicial review of International Affairs' in Brian Opeskin and Donald Rothwell (eds), *International Law and Australian Federalism* (1997)

Cheryl Saunders, 'The Concept of Non-justiciability in Australian Constitutional Law' in DJ Galligan (ed), *Essays in Legal Theory* (1984)

K

Kioa v West (1985) is a landmark decision that extended the application of the doctrine of **natural justice** in administrative decision making. It revitalised the rules of natural justice and heralded a period of **activism** of the Court in relation to this ground of review. Prior to *Kioa*, natural justice applied to a narrow band of decisions, mostly those made by tribunals or involving the deprivation of an existing right or interest such as a licence. Although there were signs that the Court was disposed towards applying natural justice more broadly—notably in *Banks v Transport Regulation Board (Vic)* (1968), *Twist v Randwick Municipal Council* (1976), *Heatley v Tasmanian Racing and Gaming Commission* (1977), *Bread Manufacturers of NSW v Evans* (1981), and *FAI Insurances v Winneke* (1982)—it was *Kioa* that firmly set the new direction.

Kioa concerned a decision to deport a Tongan family who had unlawfully overstayed their short-term resident visas. Although the personal impact of deportation would be significant, in other respects their claim proceeded from a weak foundation, namely, unlawful residence, and was measured against the right of Australia to admit or exclude those whom it chose. The force of these countervailing factors had been recognised by the Court in two earlier cases, *Salemi v MacKellar (No 2)* (1977) and *R v MacKellar; Ex parte Ratu* (1977), in which the High Court had ruled (though in *Salemi* by a **tied vote**) that the obligation to observe natural justice did not apply to a decision to deport a person. In those cases, the Court had stressed the discretionary nature of the decision, and the absence of any recognised legal interest on the part of the deportee. In *Kioa*, the High Court reversed that position and found that the rules of natural justice did apply; moreover, they had been breached in that case by reason of a failure to disclose a particular allegation against the Kioas that was in one of the departmental briefing papers.

In explaining why the majority (**Mason, Wilson, Brennan**, and **Deane**; Chief Justice **Gibbs** dissenting) had changed its mind, two points were common to many of the judgments. The first was the emphasis that had come to be placed on whether a decision related to, and had an impact on, a particular individual—in this case, deportation from the country. The second was the introduction into Australian **administrative law** of the obligation on the government to provide, on request, reasons for its decisions. The change of mind was the more striking since, arguably, the Kioas had had an opportunity (see **Federal Court** Justices RM

Northrop and Murray Wilcox in *Kioa v Minister for Immigration* (1984)) to address the adverse information in the briefing paper recommending deportation—Jason Kioa's alleged involvement with other 'illegals'—which was said to be unfair.

The result of this change has been that, since *Kioa*, it has been much easier to establish that natural justice applies. Subsequent developments have borne this out, since natural justice now commonly applies to most decisions by government, including visa decisions. This was foreshadowed in *Kioa* in the universalist approach to the application of natural justice that Mason developed in that case. Although his view did not command majority support in *Kioa* itself, subsequently other Justices came to accept the Mason view (**Dawson** in *A-G (NSW) v Quin* (1990); Deane in *Haoucher v Minister for Immigration* (1990); Deane and **McHugh** in *Annetts v McCann* (1990)). It is now accepted as the broad principle for applying natural justice.

The development of this principle had apparently led the Justices to assume that post-*Kioa*, the focus would switch to the form of natural justice to which citizens are entitled. In practice, as the judgments in cases such as *SA v O'Shea* (1987), *Quin, Haoucher, Annetts, Johns v Australian Securities Commission* (1993), and *Teoh's Case* (1995) have shown, that shift in focus has not occurred.

Kioa did, however, herald another change. Mason and Wilson abandoned the expression 'natural justice' in favour of 'procedural fairness'—a move that has subsequently been widely adopted. The change distinguishes the less-demanding fair process obligations on the executive from the more extensive natural justice required of the courts.

Though the decision of the High Court in *Kioa* was of benefit to the family (they were ultimately given permanent residence in Australia), the main thrust of the argument they took to the High Court was not accepted. The arguments in *Kioa* were premised on the right of the Kioas' Australian-born daughter, Elvina, as a citizen of Australia, to remain in the country: a right said to be grounded in an international convention, the 1989 UN Convention on the Rights of the Child. The majority (Brennan dissenting) held it had no obligation to consider such a claim. It was ten years before the Court showed greater willingness to take account of interests grounded in **international law**. In *Teoh*, the Court held that the impact of deportation on a child of a person unlawfully in the country attracted a right to a hearing before deportation, at least in relation to whether a minister should have regard to a relevant international treaty (a treaty to which Australia was a party, but which it had not implemented in domestic legislation) before making a decision.

ROBIN CREYKE

Kirby, Michael Donald (*b* 18 March 1939; Justice since 1996). When appointed to the High Court, Kirby had already held judicial office for more than 20 years: from 1975, as Deputy President of the Australian **Conciliation and Arbitration** Commission; from 1983 to 1984, as a judge of the **Federal Court**; and from 1984, for 11 years as President of the NSW Court of Appeal. On several occasions, he had acted as Chief Justice of NSW. Between 1995 and 1996, he was President of the Court of Appeal of the Solomon Islands.

In March 1939, Australia was emerging from the **Depression**. In September 1939, **World War II** was declared. Religious and racial intolerance flourished, often unrecognised, not merely in the attitudes of many Australians but also in the nation's policies. Parenting was difficult. Kirby's mother, Jean Langmore Knowles, was an Australian of Anglican Ulster stock. Kirby's father, Donald Kirby, also Australian-born, was an Anglican from a mostly Catholic Irish family, hard-working and devoted to his young family. Typically of the time, both parents venerated the monarchy and its place at the heart of the British Empire. The family, though never in want, was not well off. Their sympathies were generally with the Australian Labor Party. Jean Kirby was ambitious

for her children, and lived long enough to see those ambitions for Kirby and his surviving brothers and sister fulfilled.

From childhood, Kirby was exceptional. An iron discipline and relentless application drove him towards set goals. One brother has described his routine of daily study as intellectual weightlifting. Kirby has said of himself: 'I don't think I was ever young.' The slightest failure at school fuelled only greater determination. His interests extended to the theatre, debating, and refereeing rugby union—the last a gesture towards being the rounded person. Kirby's school was Fort Street Boys High, one of Australia's oldest, and renowned for its teaching; its former students included **Barton**, **Evatt**, and **Barwick**. Kirby achieved the highest grades and carried into the University of Sydney intellectual muscle built on discipline and concentration. He graduated BA in 1959, LLB in 1962, BEc in 1965, and LLM in 1967.

In June 1961, Kirby's classmate **Gleeson** nominated him as the law representative on the Students' Representative Council. In 1962, he became President. The many issues he spoke about included the 'essential barbarity of capital punishment' and the mistreatment of **Aboriginal peoples**. He became President of the University Union and a Fellow of the University Senate. His success in student politics was founded on his mastery of any subject of debate. Politics was the obvious career choice for him.

The future that called was one of austere self-sufficiency, in part the price of his homosexuality. The law at the time forbade him open love and companionship. But the experience of forced isolation taught him the pain and distress that **discrimination** causes. That experience combined with his Labor Party links and stringent upbringing to fire a champion of anti-discrimination and human rights. Kirby became a radical. And he chose to be a lawyer.

Both in and away from the Court, Kirby has protested against the injustice that discrimination breeds. He has said that to discriminate against people because of their **sexual preference** is like discriminating against people because they are left-handed. In 1991, he was the winner of the Australian Human Rights Medal. In 1998, he was named Laureate of the UNESCO Prize for Human Rights Education.

Such enlightenment seemingly sits uncomfortably with a monarchist. Kirby has remained unmoved by proposals that Australia become a republic. No doubt part of his attachment to constitutional monarchy derives from his upbringing. But he has explained his support for the present constitutional arrangements as being based on the success of constitutional monarchy as the least dangerous form of government, and on his distaste for nationalism. He has portrayed adherence to a constitutional system with an absentee international monarch as the radical option. But in fundamentals (Crown, **religion**, and the **rule of law**), Kirby's attitudes reveal a conservative element in his **values**.

Kirby was admitted to practice as a solicitor in NSW in 1962 and as a member of the Bar in 1967. However, he saw himself as a mediator rather than gladiator, and after only eight years at the Bar accepted judicial office. His role in education continued. Between 1965 and 1993, he was a member of the governing bodies of Sydney, Newcastle, and Macquarie Universities, and from 1984 to 1993 Chancellor of Macquarie University. The honorary degrees of LLD (Macquarie,

Michael Kirby, Justice since 1996

Sydney, National Law School of India and Buckingham), D Litt (Newcastle and Ulster), D Univ (SA), and Honorary Fellowship of the Academy of Social Sciences in Australia recognised his services to education both in Australia and beyond.

Kirby pursued reform as the foundation Chairman of the Australian Law Reform Commission for nine years, until 1984. He worked to take law reform proposals beyond lawyers and experts to the community at large, using surveys, laymen's discussion papers, public hearings, interdisciplinary consultations, consultation with special groups, and—something of a novelty for a judge—the **media**.

Law reform brought Kirby to the interface between scientific developments and the law. The Human Genome Project, the largest cooperative scientific activity in history, established in 1990, was an international effort over 13 years to find and determine the biochemical nature of all genes on every chromosome in the human body. One unique goal of the project was to address its ethical, legal, and social consequences. Kirby became a member of the Ethics Committee of the Human Genome Organisation—work he regarded as among his most important.

For two and a half years until 1 May 1996, he was the special representative of the Secretary-General of the UN for Human Rights in Cambodia. Kirby measured the laws and practices of Cambodia against the UN's principles of human rights and reported departures to the Secretary-General and the government of Cambodia. That country's protection of cultural rights, and the rights of its people to health, education, a healthy environment, and sustainable development came under his scrutiny. The work was dangerous. In his last mission, he concentrated upon the human rights of **women**, and made recommendations about providing school education for women, teaching judicial officers about the particular vulnerability of women, and establishing shelters for victims of sexual, physical, or mental violence.

Kirby has written books, articles, and papers and spoken about a huge range of topics. Library catalogues list hundreds. In 1983, he gave the six Boyer Lectures about the judiciary. In July 1987, the *Australian Law Journal* noted that Kirby had completed a ten-day visit to NZ, during which he took a seat on the Court of Appeal, delivered lectures at Victoria University (Wellington) and Canterbury University (Christchurch), and addressed the annual dinners of the NZ Law Society in Wellington and the Southlands Law Society in Invercargill. His themes included the future of the judiciary, the impact of science and technology upon the law, and the possible entry of NZ into an Australian federation. For Kirby, this was a common pattern. Between 1984 and 2000, he was a member (and in 1992–95, President) of the International Commission of Jurists.

A feature of Kirby's written judgments is the attention they give to the **argument**. When presiding in the Court of Appeal, he helped to develop counsel's argument, particularly if it was not well put or seemed the weaker argument. This characteristic is carried into his reasons, where arguments are presented in all their force. Kirby's mastery as an advocate puts each argument at its highest. Detailed analysis follows. To the reader, the solution often seems inevitable.

Kirby is a judicial innovator, and his perceived judicial **activism** has brought its critics. In *Osmond v Public Service Board* (1984), he was part of a majority in the Court of Appeal that extended the **common law** to impose upon a statutory tribunal an obligation to give reasons despite the absence of any statutory requirement to do so. To many **commentators**, this was desirable in the interests of fairness and good administration. Kirby did not see this development as constrained by any binding **precedent**. But, allowing the appeal, the **Gibbs Court** unanimously held that Kirby's conclusion was contrary to overwhelming authority. Any such change, even if beneficial, involved a departure from settled rules on grounds of **policy**, and was for the legislature to make.

Kirby is an admirer of Evatt and **Murphy**, whom he sees as examples of Australia's general rejection of its prophets. Australia 'reserves its special humiliations for intellectuals and men and women of learning and idealism'. Though a flawed human being, Evatt was a libertarian warrior, a man of gigantic intellect, courageous and tenacious, an architect of the Charter of the UN and the Universal Declaration of Human Rights, and, in Australia, a defender, at great personal and political cost, of the fundamental freedom threatened by the attempt to amend the Constitution to dissolve the Communist Party of Australia and to 'declare' its adherents (see *Communist Party Case* (1951)). Kirby's admiration of Evatt typifies his inclination to stress the goodness and downplay the frailty of his fellow beings.

Kirby gave character evidence at Murphy's first trial during the '**Murphy affair**'. He knew Murphy well, and much admired him. To him, Kirby attributes the new impetus in the High Court to learn from and use the decisions of courts in other jurisdictions, not merely those of England, and, when interpreting legislation, to pay greater regard to human rights and explanatory materials (see **Foreign precedents**; **Extrinsic materials**). Murphy 'was an early herald of an important creative period in the work of the High Court'. He broke the spell of unquestioning acceptance of old rules where changes in social circumstances and community attitudes had made those rules inappropriate and inapplicable.

The affinity between Murphy and Kirby was not born of like interests but from Kirby's admiration of a man of ideas, often heterodox at the time, often expressed in **dissenting judgments** that have subsequently become accepted doctrine in Australia. 'Powerful ideas, simply expressed can work within our legal system to plant their seeds of doubt until, in due time, the once dissenting view becomes accepted. This is the beauty of our common law system with its judicial right to dissent.' Dissent in the final appellate court is neither a badge of honour nor a mark of dishonour but an appeal to the future.

Kirby dissents from his colleagues more often than any other current or past Justice of the High Court. That was also the case in the Court of Appeal. To Kirby, the nature and dimensions of a problem are often different from those perceived by others. He has been more inclined than some of his colleagues to pay regard to international views about human rights and the need to fashion the common law in Australia to attend not only to Anglo–American traditions, but to those of other common law countries—particularly Australia's neighbours in the Pacific, Indian Ocean, and near-Asia. The breadth of experience and research revealed in his judgments and other writings is awesome.

Inevitably, Kirby's difference in approach has led him to dissent and often to be in sole dissent. Dissent against powerful counter-arguments brings out the polemicist in Kirby. In *Commissioner of Taxation v Ryan* (2000), he saw the majority reasoning as a return to 'the dark days of **literalism**' in **statutory interpretation**. Kirby added: 'It is hubris on the part of specialised lawyers to consider that "their Act" is special and distinct from general movements in statutory construction … The Act in question here is not different in this respect. It should be construed, like any other federal statute, to give effect to the ascertained purpose of the Parliament.'

Four cases in particular reveal Kirby's underlying judicial philosophies. In the High Court, Kirby has reiterated that it is permissible, indeed requisite, to resolve ambiguities in Australia's Constitution, its statutes, and common law in ways consistent with the norms of international rights law. The first case, *Newcrest Mining v Commonwealth* (1997), concerned the **acquisition of property** in the Northern Territory. Section 51(xxxi) of the Constitution requires that any such acquisition must be 'on just terms'; but *Teori Tau v Commonwealth* (1969) had held that this requirement did not apply in the **territories**. Kirby was one of a strong minority arguing that *Teori Tau* should be **overruled**. Noting the international recognition of rights to **property**, he held that where there is an ambiguity in the meaning of the Constitution, it should be resolved in favour of upholding such fundamental and universal rights. There can be no estoppel against the Constitution: its true meaning prevails, no matter how long, and at what level in the **hierarchy**, error in the decided cases has persisted.

Section 51 (xxvi) of the Constitution, 'the **race** power', was considered in the second case, the *Hindmarsh Island Bridge Case* (1998). The High Court upheld the validity of legislation that removed the Hindmarsh Island Bridge area from the scope of the *Aboriginal and Torres Strait Islander Heritage Protection Act* 1994 (Cth). Kirby alone dissented. In his view, the race power permitted special laws for people on the grounds of their race, but not so as to discriminate adversely against such people on that ground. In part, his reasons proceeded on common assumptions against the background of which he thought the Constitution should be read. Those assumptions were reinforced in his view by the resolute stand of **international law** against discrimination. The Constitution should not be interpreted so as to condone an unnecessary withdrawal of the protection of such rights.

In the third case, *Re Wakim* (1999), the second and successful challenge to the **cross-vesting** legislation, Kirby, in dissent, lamented the revisiting of constitutional issues addressed but a few months previously in *Gould v Brown* (1998). He disagreed with the view that the Court's function in **constitutional interpretation** was to give effect to the intention of the **framers** as evinced by the terms in which they expressed their intention. Kirby was rather of the opinion that once the framers' draft was settled and approved by the Australian people and enacted by the Imperial Parliament, it took upon itself its own existence and character as a constitutional charter. The framers did not intend—nor did they have the power to require—that their wishes and expectations should control those who now live under its protection. The Constitution is read by today's Australians to meet, so far as its text allows, their contemporary governmental needs.

The fourth case was *Green v The Queen* (1997). The appellant had been convicted of murder. At his trial, he relied on a defence of provocation claiming that the victim, a person he looked up to and trusted, had made a homosexual advance towards him. There was evidence that the accused was especially sensitive to matters of sexual abuse because of childhood memories of his father's assaults on his sisters and mother. The trial judge had directed the jury that this evidence was not relevant to the issue of provocation. **Gummow** and Kirby, in dissent, held that the trial judge's view was correct. They said that the gravity of the affront may help to explain whether the accused was *in fact* provoked. But provocation in law conventionally required a second element that is measured against the objective standard of the ordinary person's self-control. However unwarranted the provocation, the common law has always set its face against extending mercy to extreme loss of self-control.

In 1983, Kirby was made a CMG for service to the law and in 1991 an AC for service to the law and law reform. Since 1969, Kirby's partner and companion has been Johan van Vloten, who was born in The Netherlands and migrated to Australia in 1963. Although *Who's Who* describes Kirby's recreation as work, he has developed a keen interest in photography. Typically, when he meets people he produces a camera and arranges for photographs to be taken of everyone present—a habit that will no doubt one day enrich the High Court's **archives**.

SIMON SHELLER

Further Reading
Michael Kirby, 'Lessons for Life as a Solicitor' (1999) 37(11) *LSJ* (NSW) 62
Michael Kirby, 'Seven Ages of a Lawyer' (2000) 26 *Mon LR* 1
Michael Kirby, *Through the World's Eye* (2000)

Kisch Case (1934). Egon Kisch, a left-wing journalist, was refused entry to Australia in November 1934. Various rulings by the High Court contributed to the ensuing controversy but did not determine why the ban was imposed. Kisch remains an enigmatic figure in Australian history, viewed as a martyr by those on the left of politics and as an *agent provocateur* by those on the right.

Born and educated in Prague, Kisch worked as reporter for the German-language newspaper *Bohemia*. His early writings portray the underworld in his native city and are still regarded as pioneering works in the genre known as reportage. He added to his reputation as an investigative journalist on the eve of **World War I** by revealing that a high-ranking officer in the Habsburg empire, Chief of Staff General Alfred Redl, had been caught spying for the Russians.

Kisch served on the Serbian front as a corporal. A trenchant critic of imperial wars, he commanded a group of Red Guards in Vienna when the Habsburg empire was overthrown. Throughout the 1920s, in Berlin, Moscow, Shanghai and New York, the widely travelled reporter, who was fluent in many languages, moved with artists and intellectuals of

Egon Kisch, a celebrated litigant, circa 1935

the left, including Stalin's principal agent and propagandist in middle Europe, Willi Münzenberg.

Kisch's credentials as an opponent of Fascism were established in early 1933 when he and other writers were imprisoned by the Nazis after the Reichstag fire in Berlin. Kisch later fled to Paris, where the ingenious Münzenberg was busy publishing *The Brown Book of the Hitler Terror* (1933) and organising the Reichstag Fire Counter Trial to be held in London—a forum set up to show that the Nazis started the fire as a ploy to seize power. When Kisch tried to attend this forum, he was stopped at Dover and had his name placed on a British blacklist.

In 1934, the Australian branch of the Congress Against War and Fascism applied to its head office in Paris for a speaker to address an anti-war rally being organised in Melbourne on Armistice Day. Delegated to attend the rally, Kisch arrived at Fremantle on the P&O liner *Strathaird* shortly before the appointed date. He was prevented from landing by a ministerial declaration made under the *Immigration Act 1901 (Cth)* concerning undesirable persons. When the ship reached Port Melbourne, Kisch jumped ashore: a dramatic leap to the quay below that earned the ebullient journalist some additional notoriety (and a broken leg) but did not overcome the ban. He was seized, hustled back on board, and forced to travel on.

The ship's arrival in Sydney marked the beginning of an extraordinary series of court cases. **Piddington** KC, instructed

by the Anti-War Congress, managed to persuade **Evatt** of the High Court to issue a **writ** of habeas corpus on the grounds that the sources of information underlying the ministerial declaration had not been properly specified.

In the meantime, the Kisch case was being debated in the federal Parliament. Speakers for the conservative Lyons government, such as the **Attorney-General**, Robert **Menzies**, pointed to the events preceding the earlier ban in Great Britain, and the possibility that left-wing agitation could lead to an overthrow of democratic government. Supporters of the Anti-War Congress contended that Menzies and his colleagues, like their Tory counterparts in England, found Hitler and Mussolini more acceptable than defenders of freedom such as Kisch. That view was an article of faith on the left for decades after the controversy.

The respite afforded by Evatt's ruling proved illusory. Bundled off the ship, by then on crutches, Kisch was arrested for failing to pass a dictation test of the kind used to underpin the White Australia policy—in this case a test in Scottish Gaelic—as a way round the unwanted visitor's formidable skills as a linguist. Out on bail, Kisch addressed various rallies on the east coast; he was present on one memorable occasion in the Domain, in Sydney, when a veteran of pacifist protests going back to the Boer War, the white-headed Reverend Albert Rivett, fell dead at the end of a feverish speech condemning the government's actions.

Soon afterwards, in *R v Wilson* (1934), the High Court ruled that the dictation test given to Kisch was invalid. The NSW Attorney-General, HE Manning KC, appearing for the Commonwealth Crown Solicitor, claimed that Scottish Gaelic was a European language within the meaning of the Immigration Act. **Dixon** disagreed, holding that the test had to be given in a language recognised as the ordinary means of communication among the inhabitants of a European community for all purposes of the social body. The Gaelic language was simply 'an ancient form of speech spoken by a remnant of people inhabiting the remote portion of the British Isles' (see **Colonialism**). This view was supported by **Rich**, **Evatt**, and **McTiernan**. **Starke** dissented.

Menzies then made a further declaration of undesirability, relying on updated information that Kisch was banned from entering England 'on account of his known subversive activities'. When the new charge was brought before the Court of Petty Sessions, the tenacious Piddington insisted that Manning should relinquish his brief from the Commonwealth, arguing that as the Attorney-General of NSW Manning was the employer of the magistrate hearing the matter. During the course of these angry exchanges, Piddington, exhausted by the struggle, collapsed in court.

Kisch was convicted, although the exact nature of the 'subversive activities' the subject of the charge remains unclear to this day. Undaunted, Piddington promptly lodged a fresh notice of appeal; Kisch remained out on bail.

The controversy brought with it various collateral rulings. Indignant Scottish patriots wrote letters to the press protesting the High Court's supposed denigration of Scottish culture. A letter written by Mungo McCallum, Chancellor of the University of Sydney, under the pseudonym *Columbinus* was particularly vitriolic, contending that members of the High

Court had made themselves 'dictators of all language and above linguistic facts'. In *R v Fletcher* (1935), Evatt dismissed an application to have the editor of the *Sydney Morning Herald* punished for **contempt** of court.

R v Dunbabin (1935) shows that the editor of the *Sun* was not as fortunate. He was fined for asserting that the law that was intended to keep Australia white was in a state of suspended animation owing to the ingenuity of 'five bewigged heads' who had managed to discover a flaw in the Immigration Act. 'To the horror of everybody except the Little Brothers of the Soviet and kindred intelligentsia, the High Court declared that Mr Kisch must be given his freedom.'

In *Griffin v Wilson* (1935), the High Court quashed the conviction of another delegate to the Anti-War Congress for lack of evidence.

After four months of controversy and constant litigation, the government compromised. Kisch left Australia voluntarily in March 1935, legal costs paid, his passport returned to him. He wrote a book about his misadventures down under, fought in the Spanish Civil War, emigrated to Mexico, and eventually went back to Prague, where he died of a stroke in 1948. Two years later, a Royal Commission into the 'Aims and Activities of the Communist Party in Victoria' found that Kisch had come to Australia as an agent of Stalin's Comintern.

NICHOLAS HASLUCK

Further Reading

Manning Clark, *A History of Australia* vol 6 (1987) at 459–82

Nicholas Hasluck, *Our Man K* (1999)

Nicholas Hasluck, 'Waiting for Ulrich: The Kisch and Clinton Cases' (1999) 43(4) *Quadrant* 28

Egon Kisch, in AR Yarwood (ed), *Australian Landfall* (1969)

Stephen Koch, *Double Lives* (1994)

Kitto, Frank Walters (*b* 30 July 1903; *d* 15 February 1994; Justice 1950–70) was a Justice with a powerful analytical mind and a reputation for **legalism** and conservatism. Eldest son of James Kitto and Adi Lilian Kitto (née Carey), Kitto was born in Melbourne and moved to Sydney at about ten years of age. He grew up in a strict Methodist household. Kitto attended Mosman Primary School and later North Sydney Boys High School. He did not excel in sport, and reportedly found mathematics and science difficult. He must have performed well in his matriculation exams, however, since he won a scholarship to the University of Sydney that exempted him from fees.

Kitto graduated with a BA in 1924, majoring in Greek and Latin, his mastery of which often exhibited itself in his fine prose style. He graduated with an LLB with first-class honours in 1927. He completed his studies while working part-time at the NSW Crown Solicitor's Office (1921–27). He was admitted to the NSW Bar in 1927 and embarked upon a legal practice that took him mainly into **equity** with, in due course, a large number of tax cases and some constitutional work.

In 1929, Kitto collaborated with JH Hammond KC on the third edition of *Law of Landlord and Tenant in New South Wales*. His *Summary Digest of Statute Law Cases (New South Wales) 1825–1931* was published in 1932. These undertakings demonstrated his capacity for painstaking

Frank Kitto, Justice 1950–70

and technical work, his insistence on accuracy and his love of clear prose.

Outside the law, Kitto's major commitment was to his wife, born Eleanor Howard. She, like Kitto's mother, was the child of a Methodist Minister. Engaged in 1925 and married in 1928, the couple enjoyed, in Kitto's words, 'almost fifty-four years of the happiest marriage that one could imagine on this earth'.

Kitto had a strong sense of duty to the legal profession, his family, his church, and his community. When his mother died in 1927, Kitto took over responsibility for his four younger brothers and sister. Kitto was not, however, a gregarious man. According to his daughter, he shunned publicity and 'barriers of reticence affected even his closest relationships. His emotions were deeply felt and deeply buried'. The sudden death in 1969 of Kitto's eldest child created for Kitto 'pain [that] persisted for the rest of his life'.

Kitto's legal career continued to flourish. He became Challis Lecturer in bankruptcy and probate law at the University of Sydney (1930–33). While still at the junior Bar, in 1930–31 he appeared as counsel for the NSW Attorney-General in *Trethowan's Case*, a leading constitutional case that went to the **Privy Council** in 1932.

Soon after appointment as KC in 1942, Kitto was briefed by the trustees of the Art Gallery of NSW to defend the award of the 1943 Archibald Prize to William Dobell. Kitto's performance in this case was described by Dobell as brilliant. During the period that followed, Kitto became involved in some of the most important litigation of the time. In many of the cases, as with the Dobell case, he appeared against **Barwick**. In some, he was led by Barwick.

In the *Bank Nationalisation Case* in 1948–49, Kitto went to the Privy Council as leading counsel and in the same cause as Barwick. Commentaries suggest that the success of the banks' position before the Privy Council resulted, in no small way, from Kitto's 'masterminding of content and strategy'. Barwick and Kitto worked together in a constructive way. Barwick, rarely generous in his praise of others, later paid tribute to Kitto's contributions to the respondent banks' arguments. While their relationship remained always amicable, significant differences in judicial viewpoints later developed between Kitto and Barwick, especially on federal and state constitutional powers and section 92 of the Constitution (see **Interstate trade and commerce, freedom of**).

Their success in the *Bank Nationalisation Case* in defeating the prized legislative scheme of the Chifley Labor government was well timed for Kitto. The return of the **Menzies** government in 1949 produced the retirements of **Rich** and **Starke**. Starke's seat was filled by **Fullagar**, who, along with **Dixon**, was to be among Kitto's most admired colleagues. Kitto was appointed a week after the resignation of Rich. According to contemporary notes in the *ALJ*, Kitto's **appointment** was 'received with pleasure and satisfaction by the profession'. Commentators observed that 'no two judges could have been temperamentally more dissimilar' than Kitto and Rich. Less than six months after his **appointment**, Kitto contributed his opinion to the *Communist Party Case* (1951).

Kitto's judgment in the *Communist Party Case* is written in his characteristic way. The logic of the structure and reasoning is compelling; the text is dense; no help whatever is provided by way of headings or layout. Kitto's long and complex sentences conformed with his view of the law as constituting a technical enterprise, and illustrate the complexity of Kitto's mind itself. Statements in Kitto's opinion indicated his dedication to upholding the **rule of law**. The solution to the problem, however, was found in a strict analysis of past decisions, rather than any reliance on bold general conceptions or implications derived from the structure of the Constitution.

Kitto's decision against the Menzies government's legislation, so soon after his arrival at the Court, also demonstrated his allegiance to no political side and no social philosophy—only to his view of the Constitution and the law. The standards of independence and neutrality Kitto displayed during his judicial service represent one of the major and enduring contributions he made to the law, and to Australia, while on the Bench and subsequently.

Kitto's opinions—the writing of which he later described as 'sheer toil' and a 'soul-searing tedium'—also demonstrate legal excellence. Examining his judicial opinions in virtually any legal field always brings enlightenment. He shared with **Griffith** a confident command of nineteenth-century English jurisprudence. He shared with **Isaacs** the deployment of powerful language in the cause of persuasion. He shared with Dixon the philosophy of judicial restraint. While he did not have **Windeyer's** inquisitive fascination for the policies that lay behind the common law principles, or for legal **history**, he wrote in every area of the law he touched with accuracy and precision.

Kitto possessed particular expertise in the field of equity. The assurance with which he wrote in this area may be illustrated by many cases (see, for example, *Latec Investments v Hotel Terrigal* (1965); *Blomley v Ryan* (1956); *Shepherd v FCT* (1965); *Olsson v Dyson* (1969)). He was also a major figure in the Australian case law on intellectual property. His style and substance in this area can be seen in such cases as *Wolanski's Registered Design* (1953); *Southern Cross Refrigerating v Toowoomba Foundry* (1954); *Tub Happy Case* (1956); *Shell Co v Esso* (1963); *Bayer Pharma v FBA* (1965); *Carl Zeiss* (1969). He was also a notable contributor to the law of **taxation** in Australia (see, for example, *Clowes v FCT* (1954); *NSW Associated Blue-Metal Quarries v FCT* (1956); and *FCT v Western Suburbs Cinemas* (1952)). Kitto's judgments in these and other areas are still often cited. His explanation of the nature of **judicial power** in *R v Trade Practices Tribunal; ex parte Tasmanian Breweries* (1970) is perhaps the most often cited. It represents a clear exposition of his syllogistic view of law. He generally preferred writing individual judgments rather than **joint judgments**, believing that the individual judgment 'tends to produce the better work'.

Kitto expounded and practised his conception of the judicial role. Denunciation of malleability in the law and of the suggested influence of social forces was a recurring theme of Kitto's opinions. For Kitto, the only legitimate judicial **lawmaking** function was one strictly limited to developments formed 'by applied logic from within principles already established'. Dixon's dictum about complete legalism was one that Kitto wholeheartedly endorsed. In *Rootes v Shelton* (1967) he said:

> If I may be pardoned for saying so, to discuss [a] case in terms of 'judicial policy' and 'social expediency' is to introduce deleterious foreign matter into the waters of the common law—in which, after all, we have no more than riparian rights.

While quiet and understated in personal dealings, in court Kitto could often be extremely direct. According to former SA Supreme Court judge Andrew Wells:

> He had a way of bringing out the best and worst of an argument, when counsel was in full flight, by interposing the one word 'Why'? If counsel answered well, he was allowed to continue; if not, Kitto continued his interrogation until counsel was brought face to face with a proposition which counsel's argument could accommodate. If it could not, the argument, at that stage was destroyed. He very rarely allowed exchanges with the Bar to become heated—once only I remember such an occasion, when he systematically took submissions by Barwick QC (on interstate trade) apart … If he judged that an argument was soundly based he took up his pen and began to take notes. [This] was the highest compliment he could give counsel.

Kitto was not devoid of **humour**; he often displayed an acid but subdued wit.

Kitto made a special contribution to tertiary education and public affairs. During his service on the Court, Kitto began his long association with the University of New

England—first as Deputy Chancellor (1968–70) and later as Chancellor (1970–81). After his **retirement**, Kitto served as first Chairman of the Australian Press Council (1976–82). In that capacity, he vigorously defended the role and privileges of the media.

After the conclusion of his service on the Court, Kitto settled in the Armidale district of NSW. After the death of his wife in 1982, he devoted his time 'to a mass of reading that … had to be put aside through the years of [his] professional life'. This reading ranged over subjects 'from history and biography … and philosophy to fiction, both light and classical'. He even spoke of the enjoyment of selected programs on television. It was only towards the end of his life that he severed his links with the Methodist Church to explore the beliefs of the Quakers. He was reportedly impressed by the absence of dogmatic insistence on doctrinal imperatives, and greatly taken by the atmosphere of silent reverence in the presence of God. There are ironies in these reports, for in court Kitto could be sharp and cutting, and his career in the law was marked by the search for imperatives.

MICHAEL KIRBY

Further Reading

Michael Kirby, 'Kitto and the High Court of Australia' (1999) 27 *FL Rev* 131

Frank Kitto, 'Why Write Judgments?' (1992) 66 *ALJ* 787

Knox, Adrian (*b* 29 November 1863; *d* 27 April 1932; Chief Justice 1919–30) was born in Sydney, the fourth son and youngest of eight surviving children of Edward Knox, Danish-born founder and managing director of the Colonial Sugar Refining company (CSR), and his wife Martha, née Rutledge, from Ireland. Apart from his commitment to CSR, Knox's father, Sir Edward, had pastoral interests in Queensland and was chairman of the Commercial Banking Company of Sydney, a director of the Royal Exchange, and a foundation member of the Sydney Chamber of Commerce. He was chairman of the board of Royal Prince Alfred Hospital, and a member of the Legislative Council from 1881 to 1894.

Adrian Knox attended Waverley House, Sydney, and HE Southey's school at Mittagong. In 1878, he went to England to continue his education at Harrow and Trinity College, Cambridge, graduating with an LLB in 1885. He was called to the Bar in England at the Inner Temple on 19 May 1886. Two months later, on his return to Australia, he was admitted to the Sydney Bar. He read with his eldest brother, George, a successful barrister, who had established a flourishing practice at Lyndon Chambers.

On George's death in 1888, Knox, a barrister for only two years, inherited much of his practice and was briefed by leading solicitors. In 1888–90, he reported **equity** cases for the NSW Law Reports. From the early 1890s, he had rooms in Northfield Chambers. Standing on a platform of free trade and non-payment of members, Knox was elected to the Legislative Assembly for Woollahra in 1894 and held his seat the following year. The *Daily Telegraph* reported that he was 'an excellent speaker, of a style none too common, being precise, easy, deliberate, and possessing the constitutional gift of engaging rather than irritating his auditors'. Soon becoming disillusioned with politics, he did not seek re-election in 1898. By this time, he was also a director of the Australian Mutual Provident Society and an original member of the Walter and Eliza Hall Trust. At Christ Church, Bong Bong, near Moss Vale, on 5 February 1897, he had married Florence Lawson.

'No mean cricketer' when young, Knox played for I Zingari cricket team in Australia, and later enjoyed golf, sailing, and fishing on the south coast. He handled an automobile 'in expert fashion'. His great interest, however, was the turf. From 1896, he served on the committee of the Australian Jockey Club (AJC) and owned some good horses—Crown Grant, Popinjoy, and Vavasor (winner of the 1910 Sydney Cup)—but gave up racing his own horses during **World War I**. His iron discipline as chairman of the AJC in 1906–15 and 1916–19 raised the tone of racing in NSW to a high level. While he was in office, Randwick racecourse was 'practically rebuilt' and prize money increased from just over £23 000 to more than £80 000. He revised the rules of racing and encouraged country racing associations.

By the 1900s, Knox was recognised as a leader at the Bar and took silk in February 1906. He served on the NSW Bar Council from its foundation in 1902 until 1919 (except in 1910 and 1916). His 'capacity for work was enormous' and from 1903, as he steadily enhanced his reputation before the High Court, his practice became largely appellate. His first flurry of briefs in **constitutional law** came in 1908, when he appeared in the High Court for the NSW government in *R v Sutton*, the *Steel Rails Case*, the *Public Service Case* and the *Surplus Revenue Case*. His next constitutional case did not come until *Osborne v Commonwealth* (1911), but he continued to appear before the Court regularly in other cases.

In the *Coal Vend Case* (1911), he appeared for the Associated Northern Collieries. In the trial before **Isaacs**, which occupied 73 sitting days spread over four months, two other colliery companies, J & A Brown and John Brown, were separately represented by JL Campbell KC and Wilfred Blacket.

Adrian Knox, Chief Justice 1919–1930

But Knox had established a friendship with John Brown through their common horse racing interests; and at the appeal before the **Full Court**, Campbell and Blacket withdrew, leaving Knox to represent all the coal owners. In a brief judgment, the Full Court rejected Isaacs' reasoning and allowed the owners' appeal (*Adelaide Steamship Co v The King and A-G (Cth)* (1912)).

According to the newspaper tributes published at the time of Knox's death, Knox was 'a consummate advocate', 'suave, persuasive, clear and short' in **argument**. 'Before Courts of Appeal, he had no equal in his generation.' Although his all-round knowledge of the law was unusually deep and wide, he found it 'more congenial to argue abstruse issues in the placid atmosphere of Equity' than to browbeat an untruthful witness.

A foundation member (1914) of the executive of the British (Australian from 1916) Red Cross Society, Knox abandoned his lucrative practice to go to Egypt with Norman Brookes as Australian Red Cross commissioners in August 1915. They 'flung themselves with the greatest zeal into the work', opened an office at Shepherd's Hotel, Cairo, established depots, and reached an agreement with the British Red Cross to solve the problem of getting stores to the forward bases at Lemnos and Gallipoli. Knox showed great organising ability and worked 'amid many difficulties and not a few risks'. Returning to Sydney early in 1916, he was an official visitor to internment camps and served on a Commonwealth advisory committee on legal questions arising out of war problems. He was appointed CMG in June 1918 and an officer of the Ordre du Mérite Agricole by the French government in 1924. In December 1918, he made a celebrated appearance at the Bar of the Legislative Assembly to defend the members of the Public Service Board against charges arising from a Royal Commission report.

With his antecedents and associations, Knox must have been seen as an inappropriate person for WM Hughes as **Attorney-General** in a Labor government to appoint to the Court in 1913, though **Piddington** had suggested Knox when he tendered his own resignation. But by 1919, Hughes had come to lead a conservative government, to which Knox was plainly acceptable. **Griffith** helped to secure Knox's **appointment** as the Court's second **Chief Justice**, by preferring him to Isaacs and **Barton**. Sworn in as Chief Justice on 21 October 1919, Knox was appointed to the **Privy Council** in 1920 and KCMG in 1921.

Upon becoming Chief Justice, he immediately resigned from the committee of the AJC and sold all his shares (including his CSR inheritance) to avoid any conflict of interest. Nevertheless, in *Automatic Totalisators v FCT* (1920), when the Federal Commissioner of Taxation gave notice of intention to seek details from the AJC of all winners on the totalisators at Randwick, Canterbury, and other racecourses, with a view to taxing the winnings as 'prize[s] in a lottery', Knox did not hesitate to lead **Gavan Duffy** and **Starke** in holding that a totalisator is not a lottery, since 'a person investing on the totalisator' makes a personal selection of a horse after forming 'a judgment to the best of his ability, having regard to his knowledge and experience, and to such information as he may acquire, as to the probability of that horse winning the race'.

Despite his brilliant gifts, Knox made little individual mark on Australian law. **Dixon** later recalled him as 'a conspicuous advocate' but 'a type that you do not often meet: a highly intellectual man without any intellectual interests'. He was 'capable of almost anything … yet he was not capable of taking a really serious intellectual interest'. Within months of his becoming Chief Justice, the Court was to hand down its historic decisions in the *Engineers Case* (1920) and *McArthur v Queensland* (1920)—the latter (for a time) freeing the Commonwealth's **trade and commerce power** from any limitations imposed by section 92 of the Constitution (guaranteeing freedom of **interstate trade**), and the former freeing all **Commonwealth legislative powers** (but especially the **conciliation and arbitration** power) from the **Griffith Court's** doctrines of **intergovernmental immunities** and **reserved state powers**. Yet on both occasions, and in many cases thereafter, Knox simply participated in a **joint judgment**—initially (as in *Engineers* and *McArthur*) with Isaacs and Starke, but increasingly as the decade went on with Gavan Duffy, who had dissented in both *Engineers* and *McArthur*.

The great landmarks of the 1920s were not Knox's successes or failures, but those of the senior **puisne Justice**, Isaacs. Occasionally, especially in cases involving equity or **taxation law**, Knox delivered his own full judgments; yet even then, he tended to confine himself to bland elaborations of general principle, avoiding detailed analysis of **precedent**. Partly under the influence of *Engineers*, and partly through the Justices' own predilections, argument and decision in the High Court increasingly became 'a matter of syllogistic or casuistical reasoning from dogmatic jural postulates'. Knox's own judgments, said a judiciously worded obituary in the London *Times*, were 'almost without exception short and to the point. Neither at the Bar nor on the Bench was he discursive'. Instead, 'he reduced a problem to its simplest terms with a marked facility'.

His reluctance to engage in lengthy discussions of constitutional questions was attributable partly to his strong belief that the Court should decide such questions only if was absolutely necessary to do so. Increasingly, under his leadership, cases involving potential disagreements on constitutional issues were decided on other grounds such as those of **statutory interpretation**, leaving the constitutional questions unanswered (see, for example, *Alderdice's Case* (1928)). Even when answers were given, they were not always explained. In the *Federal Roads Case* (1926)—the first major case concerning Commonwealth grants of assistance to the states under section 96 of the Constitution—the Court delivered a six-line judgment describing its conclusions as so self-evident 'that exposition is unnecessary', thereby laying the foundation for the first *Uniform Tax Case* (1942). In *R v Archdall and Roskruge; Ex parte Carrigan* (1928), a joint judgment delivered by Knox rejected an argument that the category of indictable offences must be frozen as the **framers of the Constitution** had understood it in 1901 (see **Originalism**); but the argument was rejected in such broad and vague terms—again with the pronouncement that 'its rejection needs no exposition'—as to lead to the future emasculation of the guarantee of **jury trial** in section 80 of the Constitution. If Knox's intention was to leave constitutional questions open, such simplistic and dismissive *ex cathedra* pronouncements had the opposite effect.

Yet Knox was an astute and conscientious administrator of the Court's **business**, and on the whole managed to steer the Court through Isaacs' domineering flights of rhetoric, **Higgins'** prickly independence, and Starke's pragmatic impatience, to a remarkable degree of consensus. In this, the less forceful personalities of the other members of the Court were both a help and a hindrance. **Rich** was a weathervane, joining or concurring with the judgments of others according to the prevailing wind; when he did deliver a separate judgment, it was frequently indecisive. **Powers** was largely absent from the Court from 1921 to 1926; he had replaced Higgins as President of the Court of Conciliation and Arbitration when Higgins resigned from that position in June 1921, and himself resigned in June 1926 on the day that **Latham's** legislation reconstituting the Arbitration Court received the royal assent. On returning to full-time sittings in the High Court, he sometimes gave long judgments, but they were stronger on recitals of fact than on expositions of law. As for Gavan Duffy, he had never wholly abandoned his dissenting views in *Engineers* and *McArthur*; and increasingly towards the end of the decade he and Knox found themselves in the majority, leaving Isaacs in dissent and sometimes even in sole dissent. Yet, even more than Rich, Gavan Duffy was increasingly indecisive and unable or unwilling to commit himself, often delegating to another Justice the task of reporting Gavan Duffy's concurrence, and sometimes giving no judgment at all (see, for example, *FCT v S Hoffnung & Co* (1928)).

In this atmosphere of conflict and uncertainty, Knox's predilection for joint judgments was an effective management strategy. **Conferences** involved no more than a quick exchange of views among the Justices: the result did not exactly express the opinion of any of them, but said nothing to which anyone objected. Of approximately 500 reported cases in which Knox participated in judgment, he was in the majority in almost 94 per cent. Furthermore, he participated in an astonishing 260 joint judgments in which he was a member of the majority—more than half of the total number of cases heard by the Full Court during the period.

Moreover, Knox was vigilant in guarding the Court from encroachments on its **independence** or embroilment in political controversy. On the very day after his appointment, he refused a request from **Prime Minister** Hughes to nominate or permit a Justice of the Court to conduct a Royal Commission. Thereafter, he consistently refused all such requests—notably in a letter to Hughes' successor Stanley Bruce in August 1923 echoing that year's 'Irvine Memorandum', in which Victorian Chief Justice William Irvine had enunciated a similar policy for the Supreme Court of Victoria. Knox reiterated his own position in 1928.

He did, however, visit England in 1924 at the request of the Commonwealth government to sit in the Privy Council at a hearing relating to the constitutional powers of the Irish Boundaries Commission to settle the disputed boundary between the Irish Free State and Northern Ireland. In 1927, he advised Latham, the Attorney-General in the Bruce government, on proposed amendments to the *Judiciary Act* 1903 (Cth). He questioned the wisdom of a single Justice hearing constitutional cases, as this would reduce the Full Court to six, with the possibility of a **tied vote**. He firmly resisted repeated demands that other Commonwealth tribunals should use the High Court's **buildings** in Sydney and Melbourne, telling the **Solicitor-General** in 1928 that he found it 'quite difficult enough to manage the work of this court so as to avoid delays and other unpleasantness without the additional complications now thrust upon me' (see also **Circuit system**).

In impaired health and ineligible for a pension, Knox resigned as Chief Justice on 30 March 1930 on learning that he was a residuary legatee under the will of his 'old and intimate friend' John Brown. He explained to Isaacs that acceptance of the legacy 'involved a direct, if not an active participation by me in a business carried on in Australia … [that] was incompatible with the retention by me of any judicial office' not only on ethical grounds but because 'the duty of a Judge is to devote the whole of his time and energy, and to confine his attention, to his judicial duties'. Brown's estate (sworn for probate at £640 380) left Knox an immediate legacy of £10 000, the Darbalara estate with all fittings and bloodstock, and (after minor bequests) an equal half share in the residuary estate. The bequest included a large stable of valuable racehorses; Balloon King won the Victoria Derby in 1931. He became a director of the Bank of NSW and the Commercial Union Assurance Company, rejoined the board of the AMP Society and in 1931 was chairman of the Primary Producers' Advisory Council.

Clean-shaven, with neatly parted, almost smooth hair, Knox had a long, straight nose, brown eyes, bespectacled, and a firm mouth and chin. Unlike his brothers, he never built a large house, living after his marriage at eight different addresses at Woollahra and Potts Point; but he gave his wife beautiful jewellery. He liked entertaining, and frequenting the Union Club, which he had joined in 1886, and was an excellent bridge player. From 1915, he also belonged to the Melbourne Club. He was held in affection by his family.

Governor-General Munro Ferguson recorded in 1917 that Knox was an 'ill-tempered person … a worthy man, but sees the disagreeable side of things first'. But although to some Knox appeared 'brusque in manner', others, especially juniors at the Bar, found him kind, patient, and helpful. According to Gavan Duffy's eulogy in 1932, the more the Justices had seen of Knox 'in intimate companionship', the more 'we liked and esteemed him'. Bred 'in a society which does not encourage the display of exuberant emotion', Knox did not 'wear his heart upon his sleeve', but he had 'a kind and generous heart, and his friendships once formed were warm and lasting'. the *Sydney Morning Herald* recorded that Knox, as Chief Justice at a time of consolidation, had conducted his Court with great dignity and brought to it 'a wide knowledge of the world'.

Knox died of hypertensive arteriosclerosis on 27 April 1932 at his home at Woollahra. His wife, son and two daughters survived him; his younger daughter Elizabeth married Lewis Joseph Hugh, 12th Baron Clifford of Chudleigh. Rarely at home when Chief Justice, in his later years he spent much time in his garden (and would not permit anyone else to prune his roses).

GRAHAM FRICKE
MARTHA RUTLEDGE

Knox Court (18 October 1919 to 31 March 1930). **Griffith's** retirement as **Chief Justice** marked the end of an era; and when **Barton** died in January 1920, within three months of **Knox's** arrival, the last link with the original Court of 1903 was gone. **Isaacs** was now the senior **puisne Justice**; and for much of the next decade his forceful personality dominated the Court. **Rich** had already fallen into a pattern of frequent **joint judgments** with Isaacs; and when **Starke** was appointed to replace Barton, both he and Knox initially followed suit. But as different majorities formed and divided, Isaacs was increasingly left in dissent.

In the *Engineers Case* (1920), Knox and Starke joined Isaacs and Rich in a judgment that radically altered the direction of Australian **federalism**—disavowing the earlier Justices' conception of **intergovernmental immunities**, and focusing **constitutional interpretation** on the text of the document to the apparent exclusion of political or other considerations. Three months later, Isaacs had another victory in *McArthur v Queensland* (1920). Again, Knox, Isaacs, and Starke gave the leading judgment; Rich added a brief separate concurrence. *McArthur* gave sweeping effect to the guarantee in section 92 of the Constitution of freedom for **interstate trade and commerce**, but declared that section 92 did not bind the Commonwealth—so that any legitimate need for regulation of interstate commerce could be met by Commonwealth legislation under section 51(i) of the Constitution (the **trade and commerce power**). In thus enhancing the Commonwealth's power and seeking to release it altogether from the trammels of section 92, *McArthur* reinforced the centralism of *Engineers*.

Yet neither *Engineers* nor *McArthur* could settle these issues. **Gavan Duffy** dissented in both cases, and followed them only with reluctance. At times he seemed increasingly disinclined to deliver any judgment at all. Often he aligned himself with Knox in joint judgments—particularly as to the powers of the Commonwealth Court of **Conciliation and Arbitration**, or of the High Court itself (see, for example, their joint dissents in the *Limerick Steamship Case* (1924) and *Porter v The King* (1926)). The *Engineers Case* had ended one chapter in the struggle surrounding federal arbitration, but on other fronts of that struggle, Isaacs was increasingly isolated as the decade went on (see **Knox Court and arbitration**). His apparent victory in *McArthur* was even more unstable: when it came to section 92, neither Commonwealth omnipotence nor state impotence could be a basis for lasting consensus.

When Queensland's fruit marketing scheme was challenged in *Committee of Direction of Fruit Marketing v Collins* (1925), the Court avoided the constitutional issue, confining itself to questions of **statutory interpretation** and an injunction narrowly tailored to the individual case. In *Commonwealth and COR v SA* (1926), the section 92 issue was overshadowed by the finding of **excise duties** under section 90 of the Constitution: significantly, Knox declined to deal with the section 92 issue at all. In *James v SA* (1927), only **Powers** supported Isaacs' view that executive as well as legislative action might infringe section 92; and in *James v Commonwealth* (1928), an attempt to reopen *McArthur* was rejected because only four judges were sitting. In *Roughley v NSW* (1928), only Starke was prepared to hold that a licensing scheme for farm produce agents infringed section 92—and even his judgment suggested a shift in his understanding of *McArthur*, prompting Isaacs to comment that Starke had understood it perfectly well in *Commonwealth and COR*. When the issue finally came to a head in *Ex parte Nelson (No 1)* (1928), the result was a **tied vote**. Knox, Gavan Duffy and Starke supported the legitimacy of state regulation consistently with section 92 (characterising restrictions on the importation of diseased cattle as a regulation of health); Isaacs, Higgins, and Powers denied it (characterising those restrictions as a regulation of trade).

By 1929, with Higgins' death and Powers' resignation, Isaacs' isolation seemed complete. At first instance in *James v Cowan* (1930), Starke went back to the *Wheat Case* (1915) to hold that compulsory acquisition of dried fruits did not infringe section 92. On appeal, Knox and Gavan Duffy agreed in a joint judgment of only three sentences; Rich eloquently lamented the 'obmutescence' of section 92, and spoke wistfully of clarification by the **Privy Council** (see **Judicial style**); and Isaacs was left alone in dissent. Ten days later, Knox resigned as Chief Justice.

The Court had some difficult encounters with **immigration law**. Both the *Irish Envoys Case* (1923) and *Ex parte Walsh and Johnson* (1925) arose from specific amendments to the *Immigration Act* 1901 (Cth) designed to achieve the expulsion from Australia of perceived troublemakers. For judges committed to maintaining the width of the **immigration power**, but committed also to traditions of **civil liberties** and **natural justice**, such cases presented a dilemma.

In *Irish Envoys*, where a special board to recommend deportation was convened while criminal charges of sedition were pending, only Higgins maintained that such a procedure was unconstitutional. In *Walsh and Johnson* the Court held—unanimously as to Tom Walsh, who had come to Australia before federation, and (with Isaacs and Rich dissenting) as to Jacob Johnson also, in effect because he had been absorbed into the Australian community—that neither man was within the reach of the immigration power. Isaacs, as he had done in *Irish Envoys*, insisted on the maxim 'once an immigrant, always an immigrant'; but the judgments of Knox and Starke as to Johnson clearly rejected that view. The actual result was unanimous, since Isaacs and Rich found a valid exercise of constitutional power, but held that the summonses to Walsh and Johnson were an insufficient exercise of the ministerial powers that the legislation conferred.

Although these cases did not involve the White Australia Policy, Isaacs' fulminations about the 'power of a great people to control its own destiny' reflected his conviction of the 'paramount' need 'to preserve a White Australia'. He protested in *Irish Envoys* that the Constitution would be 'crippled' and 'grotesque' if it failed to ensure 'sufficiently broad' control of 'movements of population from other parts of the world … to protect the people of Australia physically, racially, industrially and socially'. In *Williamson v Ah On* (1926), the White Australia Policy was directly involved, and Isaacs' insistence on giving it 'effective force' was even more strident. The case involved the 'deeming' provisions by which the essential elements of immigration offences could be proved by prosecution averments unless the defendant disproved them. First introduced in 1910, those provisions had been extended and strengthened in 1924; applied uncritically by the Court in *Gabriel v Ah Mook* (1924); and strengthened again in 1925. In *Williamson*, only Knox and Gavan Duffy (dissenting) considered them unconstitutional.

Even in *Potter v Minahan* (1908), Isaacs and Higgins had dissented from the view that the Victorian-born Chinese James Minahan, returning after years in China, was not a prohibited immigrant because he was 'coming home' (though, characteristically, they had found procedural reasons to join in allowing Minahan's appeal). In *Donohoe v Wong Sau* (1925), the Victorian-born Chinese Lucy Wong Sau, also returning after years in China, had no such luck: the whole Court held that she was *not* 'coming home'. (Higgins snorted: 'She could not even speak a word of English.') In *Wall v The King: Ex parte King Won and Wah On (Nos 1 and 2)* (1927), Justice Donald Roberts of the Northern Territory Supreme Court held that the applicants *were* 'coming home'. Charged with being prohibited immigrants, they had been committed to gaol while awaiting a hearing; but Roberts issued **writs** of habeas corpus (to secure their release from gaol), and followed them with writs of prohibition (to prevent any further hearing of the charge). The High Court held that it had no power to interfere with habeas corpus, since its own appellate jurisdiction could not 'deprive the subject of an ancient and universally recognized constitutional right'; but in separate proceedings allowed the prosecution's appeal against prohibition, ruling (in a collateral attack on the writs of habeas corpus) that Roberts 'was undoubtedly in error throughout'. This time, Isaacs' sense of British justice prevailed: he declined to be associated with 'the first occasion on record, at least for 300 years', where 'a British Court' had allowed a person to be prosecuted with a view to imprisonment after an 'unimpeachable' declaration of innocence and release on habeas corpus.

Knox had become Chief Justice less than a year after the Armistice. In *Roche v Kronheimer* (1921), the *Treaty of Peace Act* 1919 (Cth) and regulations were held valid under the **defence power** (section 51(vi) of the Constitution)—with immense unperceived implications. Higgins based his concurrence primarily on the **external affairs power** (section 51(xxix)), thus proclaiming for the first time the principle—whose limits were debated six decades later in the *Tasmanian Dam Case* (1983)—that the power extended to legislation giving effect within Australia to an international treaty. The decision that the Governor-General was validly authorised to make regulations rested only on uncritical acceptance of cases decided during **World War I**—such as *Farey v Burvett* (1916) and *Sickerdick v Ashton* (1918)—but was later treated as conclusive authority that Australian adherence to the British practice of delegating legislative power to the executive government did not infringe the **separation of powers** (or, rather, that in this respect a strict separation of powers would not be insisted upon: see *Victorian Stevedoring and Meakes v Dignan* (1931)).

Roche v Kronheimer was by no means the end of the Court's postwar hangover. A steady stream of questions under the *War-time Profits Tax Assessment Act* 1918 (Cth) engaged the Justices' attention throughout the decade. There was also a protracted sequel to *Lloyd v Wallach* (1915), where the **Griffith Court** had endorsed the internment, on suspi-cion of disaffection or disloyalty, of the German-born (but naturalised British subject) Franz Wallach, the manager of a British company trading in Australia. Following his internment the **Attorney-General** had declared the company to be 'managed or controlled' by 'persons of enemy nationality' within the meaning of the *Trading with the Enemy Act* 1915 (Cth). When the company was wound up, the claims of its creditors moved repeatedly back and forth between single Justices and the Full Court (see *In re Australian Metal Co* (1921), *Broken Hill Pty Co v Warnock* (1922), *In re Australian Metal Co* (1923) and *Sydney Municipal Council v Australian Metal Co* (1926)). Another notable series of cases involved the wartime arrangement between the British and Australian governments for marketing Australian wool. In *John Cooke & Co v Commonwealth and Central Wool Committee* (1922), the Court accepted **Dixon's** argument that this was a purely political arrangement, 'not cognizable by Courts of law, creating no legal rights and duties and depending entirely for its performance upon the constitutional relationship between those Governments and their good faith towards one another'. But that did not prevent a series of later cases raising major issues both of **constitutional law** (for example, the *Wooltops Case* (1922)) and of liability for estate duty (*Watt's Case* (1926)).

There was other unfinished business from the past. As the generation of public servants transferred from the states to the Commonwealth in 1901 reached retirement age, questions about their entitlements reached the Court in *Le Leu v Commonwealth* (1921), *Lucy v Commonwealth* (1923), *Bradshaw v Commonwealth* (1925), and *Schedlich v Commonwealth* (1926). Yet, in other ways, the Court was groping towards the future. In **tort law**, it was slowly acknowledging the need to modernise the **common law** of negligence—and particularly the effect of the rule that any degree of contributory negligence would wholly defeat a plaintiff's claim. In *Bond v SA Railways Commissioner* (1923), a plaintiff who fell off a railway platform was held to be protected by **occupiers' liability** to invitees, as defined in *Indermaur v Dames* (1866); but Isaacs took care to leave open the possibility of a 'higher duty'. In *Cofield v Waterloo Case Co* (1924), the plaintiff was the widow of a factory worker killed by a dangerous machine. Isaacs, quoting Roscoe Pound's critique of contributory negligence (*The Spirit of the Common Law* (1921)), suggested that in factory accidents involving an employer's breach of statutory duty, the defence of contributory negligence might not be available at all. In *Bourke v Butterfield & Lewis* (1926), the whole Court accepted that view—though the joint judgment of Knox, Gavan Duffy and Starke studiously avoided any reference to Isaacs' earlier suggestion in *Cofield*, and in *Piro v Foster* (1943), the **Latham Court** was to **overrule** *Butterfield & Lewis* in deference to the more conservative view of the **House of Lords**.

In *Healing & Co v Harris* (1927), a three-judge Court (Isaacs, Higgins, and Starke) accepted a finding that the defendant's negligence was 'the cause' of the motor car collision, as conclusively excluding any question of the plaintiff's contributory negligence. In *SA Railways Commissioner v Barnes* (1927), the Commissioner had inherited responsibility for what was formerly a private railway line, in the middle of a street in Port Adelaide. The woodblocks surrounding the rails were worn and the wheels of the plaintiff's horse-drawn trolley were caught in the resulting grooves. Higgins and Starke found a statutory duty to keep the line in good repair; Isaacs found a common law duty. While acknowledging that a road authority is not ordinarily liable for 'mere non-feasance', he held that 'non-repair of an artificial work' resulting in danger 'is not *mere* non-feasance, and is actionable where damage ensues'. In *Victorian Railways Commissioners v Speed* (1928), a widow had sued, under statutory compensation provisions, after her husband was killed in a fire caused by sparks from a railway engine. The *Railways Act* 1915 (Vic) required that 'all actions for losses caused by sparks from railway engines' be referred to arbitration; but the Court held this provision inapplicable. Knox made the point most succinctly: this was 'not an action for losses caused by sparks from railway engines', but 'an action for losses caused to the family of the deceased by his death', with different issues and a different measure of damages.

Finally, in *Hoyt's v O'Connor* (1928), James O'Connor, a pedestrian, had been injured when a five-ton corrugated-iron verandah, suspended over the footpath in Bourke Street, Melbourne, collapsed under the weight of some forty people who had clambered onto it to watch a procession. The verandah, supposedly capable of holding up to 170 people, had often been used for such purposes, with the owners' tacit permission. O'Connor sued the owners for negligence both in the construction of the verandah and in allowing spectators to use it, and obtained a jury verdict of £1500. In a tied vote, the High Court held that the verdict should stand. Isaacs and Powers invoked the support of Bracton's *De Legibus et Consuetudinibus Angliae* (*circa* 1259) for the incremental extension of the common law to 'new and unaccustomed cases', in response to 'the multiform and changing aspects of life in a progressive society'.

In cases such as *Bain v Bain* (1923) and *Cook v Cook* (1923), the Court displayed some sensitivity to the rights of **women**. *Watkins v Combes* (1921) was an important case on **undue influence**: a 69-year-old woman was so much under the influence of the couple who took her into their home that her transfer of property to them was set aside. Her mind 'was entirely under the dominion of the defendants'; she was 'incapable of dealing with them on a footing of equality'.

A surprising number of women came before the Court as property owners—including the lessors in *Mulcahy v Hoyne* (1925) and *National Trustees, Executors & Agency Co v Boyd* (1926); the original subdivider and the present owner in *Dabbs v Seaman* (1925); the complainants in *Webster v Mosman Municipal Council* (1926) and *Werribee Shire Council v Kerr* (1928); the transferors and the intermediate or ultimate transferees in *Royal Insurance v Mylius* (1926) and *Currey v Federal Building Society* (1929); the lessee in *Major v Bretherton* (1928); the hotelier in *Daniell v FCT* (1928); and the testator in *FCT v Taylor* (1929). Yet in two cases involving a court-ordered sale of property to satisfy a judgment debt, the Court struggled mightily with the fact that the defendant whose property was thus sold was a *feme covert* (married woman), and thus incapable of giving a good title to land. The sale in *McCormick v Allen* (1926) had taken place before the *Married Women's Property Act* 1893 (NSW), the sale in *Registrar-General v Wood* (1926) after it; yet even in the latter

case Knox and Higgins (dissenting) held that the sale was ineffective, because 'the wife has no separate interest that can be taken in execution'. In *Symons v Stacey* (1922), a wife was injured when her husband's horse-drawn cart collided with a car. The Court ordered a new trial on whether her husband's contributory negligence should defeat her claim, but shied away from confronting the assumption that her separate identity was so merged in that of her husband as to make such an outcome possible. And in *Wright v Cedzich* (1930), at the very end of Knox's term as Chief Justice, the Court refused to hold that the ancient action by which a husband could sue for the loss of his wife's consortium could also be invoked by a wife seeking damages for the loss of her husband's. Only Isaacs dissented. Quoting *The Taming of the Shrew* ('I will be master of what is mine own: She is my goods, my chattels'), and eloquently reviewing the advancement of women in most areas of public and professional life, he concluded that it was time 'to abandon the assertion that in the eye of the law they are merely the adjuncts or property or the servants of their husbands'.

Knox's own disinclination to engage in lengthy analysis, especially in constitutional cases, was reflected in the Court's sometimes perfunctory approach to its business, and in judgments of surprising brevity: *Roche v Kronheimer* was an early example. In *Muramats v Commonwealth Electoral Officer (WA)* (1923), where a naturalised Japanese in WA was refused admission to the Commonwealth electoral roll (see **Race**), only Higgins gave a full judgment: Knox, Gavan Duffy and Starke were 'clearly of opinion that the order of the magistrate was right'. In *Mainka v Custodian of Expropriated Property* (1924), Knox and Gavan Duffy had sat but delivered no judgments at all, leaving Isaacs (with one-sentence concurrences from Rich and Starke) to explain the Court's appellate jurisdiction for **Papua and New Guinea**. On the vexed topic of the provisions in the *Judiciary Act* 1903 (Cth) designed to prevent appeals on *inter se* questions from state courts to the Privy Council, Knox spoke fiercely on behalf of his Court at the hearings in *Pirrie v McFarlane* (1925); but on the crucial issue of whether section 39(2)(a) of the Judiciary Act was valid, he and Gavan Duffy expressed no opinion. In the *Limerick Steamship Case* they would have left that question to the Privy Council; in the *Skin Wool Case* (1926), where the Supreme Court of Victoria had held that section 39(2)(a) was invalid, the joint judgment of Knox, Gavan, Duffy and Powers ignored the substance of that proposition, holding simply that, since the case had been removed into the High Court automatically before the Supreme Court spoke, the latter had no jurisdiction. The extreme example was the six-line judgment in the *Federal Roads Case* (1926), asserting that since the impugned legislation was 'plainly warranted', 'exposition is unnecessary'; but *R v Archdall and Roskruge* (1928) used the same approach, and almost identical language.

Despite occasional pointed or disdainful comments, the tensions between Justices rarely boiled over into public displays of animosity. The frequency of joint majority judgments, while sometimes resulting in simplistic reasoning, enhanced the clarity and digestibility of the results. Among the Court's procedural changes was an amendment to the **High Court Rules** permitting Justices to announce their judgments simply by stating their opinion, without reading their reasons aloud. Handing the written opinion to the Registrar or to an **associate** in **open court** was henceforth to be deemed 'publication', avoiding the perceived tedium of long judgment-readings.

The Court managed to avoid any direct involvement with the 1928–29 Royal Commission on the Constitution (see **Reform of Court**): Knox made it clear to the federal government that he would not supply a Justice to preside over the Commission. To the Court's undoubted relief, most of the recommendations concerning its operation and jurisdiction were supportive. In particular, the Commission resisted considerable pressure from the **legal profession** to lift restrictions on appeals to the Privy Council—recommending instead that the High Court remain the ultimate arbiter of *inter se* questions.

Yet, having successfully evaded controversy in connection with the Royal Commission, the Court was soon plunged into greater controversy when Knox announced his resignation to take control of the horse breeding and racing empire bequeathed to him by the NSW coal baron John Brown. For a Court still struggling to achieve real credibility and respect, it was an inglorious end to an era.

GRAHAM FRICKE

Further Reading
Graham Fricke, 'The Knox Court: Exposition Unnecessary' (1999)
  21 *FL Rev* 121

Knox Court and arbitration. The immediate effect of the *Engineers Case* (1920), in **Knox's** first year as **Chief Justice**, was to bring state government agencies, as employers, within the system of **conciliation and arbitration** established by the *Conciliation and Arbitration Act* 1904 (Cth). On the same day, in *Merchant Service Guild v Commonwealth Steamship Owners (No 2)* (1920), the decision was applied to the Sydney and Melbourne Harbour Trusts and various NSW government shipping enterprises. **Gavan Duffy**—seeing no point in repeating his *Engineers* dissent, and not having 'had an opportunity' to consider how the majority decision applied—announced: 'Accordingly I do not propose to deliver any judgment.'

The case exposed continuing tensions over how far the concept of 'industrial disputes' in section 51(xxxv) of the Constitution could be limited by a restrictive definition of 'industry'. The *Municipalities Case* (1919) had taken a relatively broad view of 'industry'; but Gavan Duffy had dissented there, too. In *Merchant Service Guild*, the *Municipalities Case* was followed, as 'a standing decision not overruled', but with emphasis that it was not to be 'taken as the opinion' either of Gavan Duffy (given his earlier dissent) or of Knox and **Starke** (as new members of the Court).

The same three Justices had already avoided the issue in *Daily News v Australian Journalists Association* (1920), where Isaacs treated the matter as one of **connotation and denotation**. (The 'basic meaning' must remain the same, but 'the progress of industry itself, its advancing reliance on science and art, must bring more and more instances within the ambit of the clause'.) In that case, Isaacs, **Higgins**, and **Rich** held that journalism was an 'industry'. Knox, Gavan Duffy, and Starke, allowing the employer's appeal on other grounds, expressed no opinion.

The looming possibility of a narrower view of arbitral power was averted in the *Insurance Staffs Case* (1923), where Starke, Higgins, and **Powers** joined Isaacs and Rich in holding that banking and insurance employees could initiate 'industrial disputes'; Knox and Gavan Duffy dissented. Starke explained (perhaps tautologically) that 'the Constitution must receive an interpretation which will enable Parliament to exercise that power effectively over the whole area of industrial service within the ambit of the power'. But the reasoning was at best equivocal as to whether banking and insurance were 'industries'; and in the *School Teachers Case* (1929) Starke (joining with Knox and Gavan Duffy) and Rich (concurring separately) swung back to a restrictive conception of 'industry', leaving Isaacs in sole dissent.

As to governmental employers, whether state or Commonwealth, the Court insisted that any award that was to bind them must identify them with precision. In *Railway Commissioners v Orton* (1922), the Court held that the NSW Railway Commissioners were not bound by an award that did not name them as parties, even though the state of NSW and His Majesty the King in right of NSW had been so named. In *Hillman v Commonwealth* (1924), an award for naval dockyard workers was made binding on the Naval Board, the Minister for Navy and the Minister for Defence (the Ministers responsible for the dockyards at the time). But two days later, the administration of the dockyards was transferred to the Prime Minister's Department—ostensibly to enable them to expand their commercial operations. Starke held at first instance that the award could no longer be enforced. On appeal, in a brief joint judgment, Knox and Gavan Duffy agreed. Isaacs concurred, but found it 'difficult to believe that the Commonwealth is taking shelter behind such a technicality'.

The range of employers who could be bound by awards was contested throughout the decade. Isaacs had another notable victory in the *Burwood Cinema Case* (1925), where Powers, Rich, and Starke joined him in **overruling** *Holyman's Case* (1914) to hold that an award could bind all employers in a particular industry, even those who employed no union members or whose employees were content with their existing terms of employment. Ironically, given the tendency to use the concept of 'industry' to restrict the range of 'industrial disputes', both Isaacs and Starke, building on their judgments in *George Hudson v Australian Timber Workers Union* (1923), used the concept of 'industry' as the 'nexus' drawing all employers in the same industry into a common dispute. But again, in *Burwood Cinema*, Knox and Gavan Duffy dissented. Participation in an 'industry' remained an uncertain nexus.

The range of employers who could be bound had also been extended by statute. Since 1914, section 29(ba) of the Arbitration Act had provided that where an employer's business changed hands, 'any successor … assignee or transmittee' of the original employer would be bound by the relevant award. That provision did not apply in *Hillman v Commonwealth* (the dockyard case) because there had been no relevant change. The employer was still the King; only his agents (his Ministers) had changed. But in the *Daily News* case, the effect of section 29(ba) had produced a **tied vote**; and in cases such as *Shaw v United Felt Hats* (1927), its operation was bitterly contested. In *Carter v Roach & Milton* (1921), the majority

(Knox, Gavan Duffy, Powers, and Rich) refused to regard the 'successor' provision as caught by section 24 of the Act, which gave registered agreements the same effect as awards. Thereupon, Parliament inserted a new 'successor' provision directly into section 24 itself. The 1923 *George Hudson* case held that to be valid; but Knox and Gavan Duffy dissented.

In the *North Melbourne Tramways Case* (1920), the effect of section 24 was acknowledged less grudgingly; and in *Monard v HM Leggo & Co* (1923), the Court accepted that it brought conciliation agreements within section 28(2) of the Act—which provided that, after an initial period fixed by the arbitrator, 'the award shall, unless the Court otherwise orders, continue in force until a new award has been made'. But in *Waterside Workers Federation v Commonwealth Steamship Owners* (1920), section 28(2) was itself held valid only by a 4:3 majority. Isaacs and Rich, supported by Powers, dissented—maintaining that, since the award thus extended depended on a legislative pronouncement, rather than that of the arbitrator, it was not an outcome of 'arbitration' and thus not within constitutional power. The inclusion in section 28(2) of the words 'unless the Court otherwise orders' was probably essential to its validity; but in *Alderdice's Case* (1928), those words proved controversial.

In response to a claim by the Amalgamated Engineering Union, Judge George Beeby in the Arbitration Court had awarded a 44-hour week for 'all employees'. Later, he clarified his award by saying that it extended to fitters and turners 'covered by the Gas Employees' award'. In effect, he had varied the Gas Employees Award at the instance of a different union. The High Court unanimously held that this variation was not binding, but for diverse reasons. (For Isaacs, it was only because a later full bench decision in the Arbitration Court had superseded the Beeby award.) Higgins and Powers found an implication in the words of section 28(2) ('unless the Court otherwise orders') that any variation of an award must be in the same proceeding, and between the same parties: Powers found it unthinkable that 'an outside union could *in another dispute in another industry*, without any notice to the union or its members to be affected, obtain awards binding on the other union … conflicting with existing awards'. Gavan Duffy and Starke (supported by Knox) rejected that argument, but held that the Arbitration Act did not authorise an award that would bind employers in respect of any employees other than members of the claimant union.

This opened up a potential challenge to the *Burwood Cinema Case*. Robert **Menzies** (for the union) had argued that it followed from *Burwood Cinema* that an award could impose obligations for the benefit of all employees in an industry, whether union members or not. **Dixon** (for the employers) argued the contrary, leading Isaacs to interject: 'Is this a denial of the *Burwood Cinema Case*?' Dixon answered that the case could be distinguished. Given the tangle of other issues in *Alderdice*, the result was inconclusive. In denying that Beeby could make an award in respect of non-union members, Knox, Gavan Duffy, and Starke held only that as a matter of **statutory interpretation** the Arbitration Court had not been given such a power; they did not decide whether such a power was constitutionally possible. But *Amalgamated Clothing and Allied Trades Union v Arnall & Sons* (1929) appeared to reaffirm *Alderdice*; and this time, with

Higgins dead and Powers resigned, Isaacs was in sole dissent. Only when the **Latham Court** overruled *Alderdice* in the *Metal Trades Case* (1935) was the full effect of *Burwood Cinema* realised.

Another controversy that resurfaced in *Alderdice* related to section 21AA of the Arbitration Act, which provided that 'when an alleged industrial dispute is submitted to the Court', the High Court could be asked to answer questions of law, in particular as to whether an arbitrable dispute existed. Originally inserted in response to a suggestion by Isaacs in the *Tramways Case (No 1)* (1914)—after that case and the *Builders Labourers Case* (1914) had confirmed that the Arbitration Court was amenable to **writs** of prohibition—the provision was meant as a simple and expeditious procedure for obtaining preliminary legal rulings at an early stage. But in *Ince Bros v Federated Clothing and Allied Trades Union* (1924), the Court held in a tied vote (Knox, Gavan Duffy, and Starke, with Isaacs, Powers, and Rich dissenting) that the procedure could be used at any time, even after an award had been made. In effect, section 21AA had become an additional means of attacking an award.

In *R v Hibble; Ex parte BHP Co* (1920), the Court had held that, under the *Industrial Peace Act* 1920 (Cth), prohibition could issue to a tribunal even after it had discharged its duty and was *functus officio*; but in *Ince Bros*, the new extended use of section 21AA led Isaacs and Rich (supported by Higgins) to embark on a fresh campaign to establish that, once the Arbitration Court had given its award, it was *functus officio* and hence no longer amenable to prohibition. They explained the grant of prohibition in cases such as *Builders Labourers* by saying that those cases had assumed that the Arbitration Court had continuing functions after an award was made: that assumption, they said, had been exploded when *Alexander's Case* (1918) denied the Arbitration Court's power to enforce its own awards. They renewed the argument in *Waterside Workers Federation v Gilchrist, Watt & Sanderson* (1924), maintaining that the *Hibble* case had been overtaken by a **House of Lords** decision (*In re Clifford and O'Sullivan* (1921)) that prohibition should not issue when 'nothing remains to be done'.

In making this argument in the *Gilchrist, Watt* case, Isaacs and Rich maintained that Higgins and Powers would support them; but Higgins was overseas and Powers, as President of the Arbitration Court, had, by convention, not sat. This attempt to include the absent Justices in a headcount was unavailing: Starke supported Knox and Gavan Duffy in holding that prohibition could issue at any time. But when Knox and Gavan Duffy further held that prohibition should issue, on the basis that an award provision was not within the 'ambit' of the dispute, Starke joined Isaacs and Rich in rejecting that argument and affirming that the award was valid.

In *Alderdice*, Isaacs returned to the issue of section 21AA, complaining that what was 'designed as a prophylactic' was 'being used as an irritant', and urging that the section be amended: if awards could be 'summarily' nullified

at any distance of time … no proper reliance can be placed upon them. Private or public confidence must be wanting respecting awards that constantly have hanging over them a sword of Damocles that is suspended, it may be, by the frailest hair of legal technicality.

Many of these cases arose from the enforcement of awards. For example, the award in the *Gilchrist, Watt* case was challenged by an employer against whom the union had sought an injunction to restrain alleged breaches of the award. In the end, the injunction was granted; Knox and Gavan Duffy dissented. In *Mallinson v Scottish Australian Investment Co* (1920), the Court recognised the individual right of a union member to sue for full award wages: although the scheme of the Act was 'collective bargaining', unions represented their members 'for the purpose of obtaining benefits for them as individuals'. But in *Bishop v Ford & Petrie* (1925) and *Australian Timber Workers Union v George Hudson* (1925), individual claims to award entitlements failed on technical grounds. In both cases, Knox and Starke were in the majority—supported in one case by Higgins (with Isaacs and Rich dissenting), in the other by Isaacs (with Higgins dissenting). In *Fletcher v AH McDonald & Co* (1927), Rich joined Knox and Starke in holding (with Isaacs and Higgins dissenting) that an award for apprentices' wages could not apply to apprenticeships that had already begun.

In *Waddell v Australian Workers Union* (1922) an injunction was granted—with a poignant expression of reluctance and disappointment by Higgins—to prevent the union from encouraging or inciting a strike. But in *Metropolitan Gas Co v Federated Gas Employees* (1925), Isaacs, Higgins, and Rich held that a statutory ban on strikes by unionists bound by an award did not prevent a strike against an employer not so bound. In *Commonwealth Steamship Owners v Federated Seamen's Union* (1923), the Court held that a prosecution of the Seamen's Union for breach of an award was rightly dismissed, since actions by the union's officers—including its president, Tom Walsh (see **Litigants, notable 1903–1945**)—could not be imputed to the union; but in *Australian Commonwealth Shipping Board v Federated Seamen's Union (No 1)* (1925), Isaacs and Starke did not hesitate to grant an injunction against Walsh and the Sydney branch secretary Jacob Johnson to prevent them from engaging in or advocating a strike. Even then Higgins dissented, finding no evidence that the union or its officers had incited the refusal to work.

Two months later, the registration of the Seamen's Union was cancelled. In the Arbitration Court Dixon, **Latham**, and Robert Menzies put the case for deregistration, while Tom Walsh represented the union. The High Court held unanimously that the deregistration was valid. It was not beyond the powers of the Arbitration Court, since it did not involve **judicial power**; and since the *Jumbunna Coal Case* (1908) had treated registration as incidental to conciliation and arbitration, the same must follow for deregistration (*Australian Commonwealth Shipping Board v Federated Seamen's Union (No 2)* (1925)). Four days later, on Walsh's appeal against convictions arising from his attempt to involve the Waterside Workers Federation in industrial action by the Seamen's Union, the joint judgment of Knox and Starke (supported by Rich) held that evidence of Walsh's intervention through a branch secretary was so 'loose and unsatisfactory' that the conviction should be set aside—but that as to his own direct intervention, the conviction should stand (*Walsh v Sainsbury* (1925)). Isaacs and Higgins, dissenting, would have set aside both convictions.

An essential element in the package that Isaacs had put together in *Engineers* was the idea that the Commonwealth could always prevail over state legislation—not through any implied immunity, but through the express constitutional override of state laws by Commonwealth laws in cases of **inconsistency** (section 109 of the Constitution). But there was as yet no coherent analysis of how section 109 was to operate. *R v Brisbane Licensing Court; Ex parte Daniell* (1920) was a simple example of directly contradictory laws—though it did enable Higgins to explain that a state law overridden by section 109 is not nullified, but merely dormant. As he put it, indulging his penchant for simile and **metaphor**, the state law 'still lives, subject to the pressure of the Federal Act—like Jack-in-the-box under his lid'.

The finding of an inconsistency in *Commonwealth v Queensland* (1920)—between state and federal provisions for the tax implications of interest on Commonwealth bonds—still elicited no real analysis. Only Dixon's argument on behalf of the Commonwealth foreshadowed the 'cover the field' test: since the Commonwealth had 'shown an intention to cover all the rights and obligations' involved, any state legislation imposing obligations must be inconsistent. 'The Federal Parliament has appropriated the particular field of legislation.' In *Pirrie v McFarlane* (1925), the majority denied any Commonwealth defence exemption from state road licensing laws: even Isaacs and Rich, who in separate judgments did assert inconsistency, significantly relied not only on section 109 but also on an implied immunity—attaching, said Isaacs, to the 'actual performance of Commonwealth official duty'. (For example, he suggested, a state law could not validly prescribe that federal **judges' notebooks** should have red covers.) Like Dixon in *Commonwealth v Queensland*, he foreshadowed the 'cover the field' test: the Commonwealth might

> legislate on its own field in such a way that, whether from its express terms or [by] the legitimate implication of the language and scheme adopted, its enactment so occupies that field that the operation of the state law in question would be incompatible.

The breakthrough came in *Clyde Engineering v Cowburn* (1926). A federal award (made by Powers) prescribed a working week of 48 hours; NSW legislation prescribed a 44-hour week. According to *Ex parte Daniell* there was no inconsistency, since it was possible to obey both laws: an employer who observed a 44-hour week would obey the state law without disobeying the federal award. Higgins and Powers, adhering to that simple test, held in dissent that the state law was enforceable; but the majority found an inconsistency. To Rich the two laws seemed inconsistent simply because they were 'different'. But Knox and Gavan Duffy accepted that statutes are inconsistent when one 'takes away a right' conferred by the other, while Starke agreed that the state law 'alters the rights and obligations of the parties', and undoes 'what the Commonwealth tribunal considered a right and just settlement'. Isaacs seized the opportunity to proclaim the 'cover the field' test: if a Commonwealth law evinces an intention exhaustively to regulate a topic, what is inconsistent with that intention is the presence of any state law at all on that topic.

The full significance of these judgments was not immediately apparent. In *Cowburn*, a federal award had prevailed over more generous state provision for working hours; *HV McKay v Hunt* (1926) applied *Cowburn* to hold that a federal award prevailed over more generous state minimum wages. But the brief judgments added nothing to the principles involved. In *Hume v Palmer* (1926), argued almost four months after *Cowburn*, **counsel** seemed unaware that a section 109 issue was involved: it was raised only from the Bench. The SS *Wear*, on her way to Darling Harbour, had collided with the ferry *Kalibia* while the ferry was crossing between Milsons Point and Circular Quay. Both Commonwealth and state regulations made it clear (in identical terms) that the *Wear* should have given way. Her captain, William Hume, was prosecuted under the state regulations—but the Court held them inoperable. The regulatory duplication gave rise to an inconsistency, not merely because offences were triable by different procedures and with different penalties, but because (as Isaacs put it) 'the Commonwealth's general supersession of the regulations of conduct' should be seen as 'displacing the State regulations, whatever those may be'. Only Higgins, still clinging to *Ex parte Daniell*, thought that since ships' officers were not 'perplexed by conflicting directions', there was no inconsistency.

The immediate point of *Clyde Engineering v Cowburn* was to establish that federal awards prevailed over inconsistent state laws—overruling the converse rule (from which Isaacs and Higgins had dissented) in the *Woodworkers Case* (1909) and *Whybrow's Case (No 1)* (1910). In *Whybrow*, the **Griffith Court** had softened its insistence on the supremacy of state law by holding that there was no inconsistency between different minimum wages, since payment of the higher minimum satisfies both requirements. (Hence Higgins' determination in the 1920s to cling to a narrower test of inconsistency.) Even before *Engineers*, a joint judgment by Knox, Gavan Duffy, and Starke in *Federated Engine-Drivers v Adelaide Chemical and Fertilizer Co* (1920) had cast doubt on both aspects of *Whybrow*—applying both its priority rule and its saving for different minimum wages, but emphasising that in the absence of a direct challenge, 'it must not be said hereafter' that *Whybrow* had been reconsidered or affirmed. Confronted with different minimum wages in *John Heine & Son v Pickard* (1921), Knox, Rich and Starke had given effect to the higher federal minimum, but still with no real analysis. In the *Gilchrist, Watt* case, Starke alone had considered whether an award provision for preferential employment of ex-service personnel was inconsistent with NSW legislation on that subject. He thought at that stage that, if *Woodworkers* and *Whybrow* were still good law, this would be a problem: but that it was 'impossible' to reconcile those decisions with *Engineers*. Foreshadowing an analysis later made clear in *Ex parte McLean* (1930), he explained: 'An award made under the authority of the Commonwealth legislation takes its sanction and its force from that legislation, and has, therefore, supremacy over the State law.'

The overruling of *Woodworkers* and *Whybrow* in *Clyde Engineering v Cowburn* had firmly established the supremacy of federal awards; and *Burwood Cinema* had entrenched the use of 'paper disputes' to transcend 'the limits of any one state'. Yet in cases of direct industrial confrontation, occurring at a particular location (and thus within a particular

state), federal encroachment was still vigilantly resisted. When the Arbitration Court's power to intervene in such conflicts was tested in the ***Caledonian Collieries Cases*** (1930), Gavan Duffy, Rich, and Starke (joined by the newly appointed Dixon) denied that there was any such power. Isaacs' sole dissents blazed with genuine anger and distress.

TONY BLACKSHIELD

Koowarta's Case (1982) illustrates a recurring tension in the High Court's jurisprudence between a desire to preserve broad state legislative powers and a yearning to respond to palpable injustice. *Koowarta* is a landmark in the interpretation of the Commonwealth's **external affairs power**. It is significant also as the first invocation by the High Court of international human rights principles in response to human rights abuses.

John Koowarta was a member of the Winychanam group of **Aboriginal people** who lived near Aurukun in Northern Queensland. The Aboriginal Land Fund Commission contracted to purchase a pastoral lease for use by the Winychanam people, but the Queensland government refused to approve transfer of the lease because of a 1972 Cabinet policy that viewed unfavourably 'proposals to acquire large areas of additional freehold or leasehold land for development by Aborigines or Aboriginal groups in isolation'. Koowarta then brought a claim for **damages** under the *Racial Discrimination Act* 1975 (Cth) against Queensland Premier Joh Bjelke-Petersen and other government members. In response, Queensland sought a declaration in the High Court that the Act was invalid as outside the Commonwealth's legislative power. Queensland's action was supported by Victoria and WA.

The case provoked intense speculation in the **media** and in legal and political circles. It was a challenge by a powerful, conservative state government—a government that had unabashedly entrenched racially discriminatory policies in a range of areas—to the single successful legislative legacy of the **Whitlam** government in the area of human rights. It was seen from one perspective as a battle for states' rights over the forces of meddling do-gooders, and from another as a duel between the fundamental norm of non-discrimination and systemic violations of that principle.

The outcome of the case was hard to predict, as the scope of the major head of legislative power relied on by the Commonwealth, the external affairs power, was uncertain. (The Commonwealth also invoked the power to make laws 'with respect to the people of any **race**' (section 51 (xxvi)), but this argument failed because the Act was about racial **discrimination** generally rather than being directed to a particular race). The Racial Discrimination Act was a domestic implementation of the 1965 United Nations Convention on the Elimination of All Forms of Racial Discrimination. Did the external affairs power extend to legislation, implementing an international treaty, whose primary operation was within Australia and was not otherwise within Commonwealth power?

The High Court was crowded for the oral arguments, remarkable particularly for the passionate advocacy of Ron Castan QC as counsel for John Koowarta. In the end, the Court decided that the Racial Discrimination Act was valid as a law 'with respect to ... external affairs' by a 4:3 majority. **Stephen**, **Mason**, **Murphy**, and **Brennan** (each writing separate judgments) held that that the notion of 'external affairs' had expanded beyond matters physically external to Australia. For Mason, Murphy, and Brennan, the mere presence of an international treaty to which Australia was a bona fide party was enough to generate an external affair. Stephen suggested that the subject matter of the treaty must also be a matter of 'international concern', although he stated that it would be 'very exceptional' for a treaty not to fulfil this requirement. On either view, the founding of the UN in 1945 and the development of an **international law** of human rights were regarded as critical in the transformation of the power. The majority acknowledged that this interpretation would encroach to some extent on state legislative powers, but it was concerned that to hold otherwise would unduly fetter Australia's actions internationally. Murphy expressed this fear most vividly when he commented that a more limited view of the power in the manner urged by the states would make Australia 'an international cripple unable to participate fully in the emerging world order'.

The minority Justices (**Gibbs**, **Aickin**, and **Wilson**) rejected the contention that race discrimination could be more than a purely domestic matter. Their chief concern was the maintenance of the Australian federal system. This anxiety is captured in Gibbs' statement that 'the distribution of powers made by the Constitution could in time be completely obliterated; there would be no field of power which the Commonwealth could not invade, and the federal balance achieved by the Constitution could be entirely destroyed'. Wilson's concern for the preservation of states' powers over international human rights principles in *Koowarta* is a considerable contrast to his later ardent advocacy of Aboriginal rights as President of the Human Rights and Equal Opportunity Commission.

The decision was controversial. Critics regarded it as a serious threat to the federal system, while its supporters celebrated it as providing a firm constitutional basis for Commonwealth human rights legislation in an era when few states had enacted such laws. Shortly after the decision, Stephen left the Court to become Governor-General, and Aickin died. The narrowness of the *Koowarta* majority, the apparent diversity of the reasoning within the majority, and the change in the High Court's membership prompted another state, Tasmania, to test the limits of the decision within a year in the *Tasmanian Dam Case* (1983). That case cemented the broad view of Mason, Murphy, and Brennan.

Apart from its political and doctrinal significance, *Koowarta* also illustrates the pyrrhic nature of many legal victories for the human beings involved in litigation. John Koowarta died destitute in 1991. He never gained possession of the Archer River lease, which was converted into a National Park by the Queensland government in pique at the High Court decision, nor received compensation under the Racial Discrimination Act—an outcome deplored by Ninian Stephen in a speech in 1991.

HILARY CHARLESWORTH

Kruger v Commonwealth (1997). The 'Stolen Generations Case' was the first opportunity for the High Court to consider the legal infringements and **remedies** resulting from the policy of the forcible removal of indigenous children. The

Court was asked to consider questions relating to the validity of the Aboriginals Ordinance 1918 (NT) and its subsequent amendments in 1939 and 1953. The plaintiffs—five people who had been taken from their families under the Ordinance, and one parent whose child had been taken from her under the same provision—sought a declaration that the Ordinance was invalid. Section 6 of the Ordinance allowed the Chief Protector of Aborigines to take into 'care, custody, or control … any Aboriginal or half-caste, if, in his opinion it is necessary or desirable in the interest of the Aboriginal or half-caste for him to do so'. Under section 7, the Chief Protector of Aborigines was made legal guardian of indigenous children until the age of eighteen, regardless of the existence of parents or other living relatives. He was empowered to keep **Aboriginal people** on reserves under section 16. Regulations were made under section 67.

The plaintiffs attacked the validity of the Ordinance on many grounds. For instance, they argued that it contravened the protection of the freedom of religion in section 116 of the Constitution; infringed an implied **freedom of movement**; authorised involuntary detention of a 'penal' or 'punitive' character that was a decision of a judicial nature (and could therefore only be made by a court); and contravened the International Convention on the Prevention and Punishment of the Crime of Genocide. The claims based on freedom of religion met with a mixed response from the Court. **Dawson** and **McHugh** held simply that section 116 did not apply to the **territories**. The majority of the Court found that to breach section 116, the law must, on its face, show that its object or purpose is to prohibit the exercise of religion and that the Ordinance did not have that express purpose. **Toohey**, **Gaudron**, and **Gummow** (and Chief Justice **Brennan** by implication) held that section 116 did apply to the territories. **Gaudron**, accepting the plaintiffs' argument in principle, considered that, since there was no constitutional provision for self-government in the territory, this provided an exceptionally strong reason for saying that legislation for the territories (under section 122 of the Constitution) should be subject to express constitutional guarantees and freedoms unless their terms clearly indicate otherwise. She avoided answering the question of whether Aboriginal cultural beliefs constituted a religion for the purposes of section 116, holding that this was a question of fact and could not be decided at the stage of the proceedings then before the Court.

The majority of the Court declined to invalidate the Ordinance on the basis of an implied freedom of movement. However, Gaudron, Toohey, and McHugh reaffirmed their recognition of an implied freedom of movement as incidental to the implied freedom of **political communication** derived from the constitutional requirement of a **representative government**. McHugh found that, since at the time the Ordinance was passed the residents of the Northern Territory had no part to play in the constitutionally prescribed system of government or the amendment procedure, there was no implied freedom of movement.

In dissent, Gaudron and Toohey found that the implied freedom of movement applied to the territories. Gaudron held that sections of the Ordinance infringed the freedom of movement and could be valid only if they were 'necessary for the attainment of some overriding public purpose or for the satisfaction of some pressing social need'.

The Court also considered whether the Ordinance interfered with an implied right of **due process** in the exercise of the **judicial power** of the Commonwealth under Chapter III of the Constitution. One aspect of this argument was that the Ordinance purported to confer judicial power on persons other than Chapter III courts. A majority decided that the Ordinance was non-punitive in nature, and therefore was not an exercise of judicial power—and that, even if it was, the requirements of Chapter III did not extend to the territories. Dawson and McHugh held that courts created under section 122 of the Constitution (the territories power) are not federal courts and accordingly that the **separation of powers** doctrine has no applicability in a territory. Gaudron found that there was 'no convincing reason' for not applying Chapter III to the territories, but concluded that the power to deprive people of their liberty was not necessarily a judicial power and was therefore not offensive to Chapter III. An argument based on an implied right of legal **equality** was also rejected with a majority finding that there was no such guarantee within the Constitution.

Arguments that the Ordinance breached the International Convention on the Prevention and Punishment of the Crime of Genocide were rejected, on the grounds, among others, that the Convention came into force in 1951 and the Ordinance was in place in 1918, thirty years before, rejecting the plaintiffs' argument that the Convention merely gave expression to an existing international norm. According to the Convention, a necessary element in genocide is an 'intent to destroy' an ethnic, racial or religious group. The paternalistic wording of the Ordinance defeated the argument of genocide, since it did not show any such intent.

The Court held that even if the Ordinance had been unconstitutional, entitlement to **damages** would be reliant on **tort law**: that is, there is no cause of action against the Commonwealth or its officers for a breach of constitutional rights. Even Gaudron, in relation to her finding of a breach of freedom of movement and section 116, referred to common law remedies.

The plaintiffs failed to show that, on the face of it, the Ordinance was in breach of any express or implied limitation on the power of the legislature. The plaintiffs' arguments were often defeated by the benevolent nature of the statute. As Brennan noted, power under the Ordinance was 'conferred to serve the interests' of those to whom the Ordinance applied. While review of a decision made under the Ordinance could be made on administrative grounds, it could not be done on constitutional grounds, even if the effects have 'profoundly distressed the nation' and now breach 'contemporary community standards'. Because the plaintiffs' claims had been limited to a challenge to what was evident from the face of the Ordinance, the High Court considered the legislation as a matter of fact, devoid of its ideological, social and historical context. This was a sad irony, since the beneficial language of the legislation was used in a way that furthered the **ideologies** of assimilàtion, racial inferiority, and 'breeding out'; but this remained outside the sphere of judicial consideration. This detachment from social context occurred despite the findings of the Human Rights and Equal Opportunity Commission's *Bringing them Home* report on the strength and depth of the emotions aroused, and the physical and psychological harm caused by the removal policy contained in the Aboriginals Ordinance.

The *Stolen Generations Case* drew attention to the undecided nature of the races power. Gaudron gave weight to the argument that the races power only authorises laws for the benefit of the people of a **race** for whom it was necessary to make special laws. On the other hand, Gummow observed that the races power had permitted detrimental as well as beneficial legislation.

The case also emphasised the fact that rights protection is primarily the responsibility of the legislature and highlighted the inability of the present Constitution to provide adequate protection for indigenous rights—and rights generally. The limitations in the Constitution in relation to rights in turn restricted the ability of the High Court to protect indigenous Australians. The case thus revealed the limits of the judicial process, particularly when the Court is called upon to deal with issues arising out of events long past and, moreover, confined to abstract issues arising from the face of the legislation. Indigenous people seeking redress in the High Court for rights violations have had disappointing results, and understandably have gravitated instead towards negotiation with the legislature.

LARISSA BEHRENDT

L

Labour relations law. The distinctive, even defining, feature of Australian federal labour law has been its institutionalised focus on compulsorily conciliated or arbitrated industrial awards as instruments for regulating relations between employers and employees. The scope and content of these awards has been the responsibility of the Australian Industrial Relations Commission and its predecessors, exercising powers under legislation made almost exclusively pursuant to section 51(xxxv) of the Constitution. The High Court's principal involvement in this complex regulatory scheme has been in supervising the limits—constitutional and statutory—of the specialist tribunal's jurisdiction. In this role, the Court had a fundamental influence on Australian labour relations.

The first comprehensive statute establishing the federal system of labour regulation was the *Commonwealth Conciliation and Arbitration Act* 1904 (Cth). Its key provisions almost immediately became the subject of repeated constitutional challenges, requiring the Court to consider and expound the meaning of the grant authorising the federal Parliament to make laws 'with respect to **conciliation and arbitration** for the prevention and settlement of industrial disputes extending beyond the limits of any one State'. The nature and frequency of those challenges prompted **Higgins**, the second President of the Commonwealth Court of Conciliation and Arbitration, to comment somewhat pointedly, in the *Felt Hatters Case* (1914), on the degree of ingenuity which, even by then, had been applied 'in considering the meaning of the plain, ordinary English words' of the power, particularly the phrase 'industrial disputes'.

From one point of view, the primary jurisdictional fact specified in section 51(xxxv) is that of industrial dispute. As **Barton** pointed out in *Allen Taylor's Case* (1912), in the absence of that condition being satisfied, 'to consider the question of extension beyond the limits of one State' would simply be 'a waste of time'. What constituted a dispute for these purposes, however, was a question that seriously divided the Court for some years. That division of opinion was precipitated by the union practice of serving written logs of claims on employers in different states in order to secure arbitrated federal awards, a practice described, somewhat disapprovingly, as the creation of paper disputes.

Some Justices—until 1914 the majority—adopted the position that, as **Griffith** continued to insist in *Felt Hatters*, a dispute within the meaning of section 51(xxxv) had to be 'something more than a claim to have the conduct of an industry regulated'. They regarded as necessary the existence of a state of affairs 'of such a nature as to indicate a real danger of dislocation of industry if it is not settled'. Although resort to actual strike or lock-out was not essential, mere discontent or dissatisfaction did not suffice unless it threatened the industrial peace of the community, the intention of the Constitution (as Griffith understood it in *Allen Taylor*) being in this respect not 'to foment industrial war, or to interfere with the domestic affairs of the States, but to prevent or compose disturbances of industrial peace likely to affect the whole Commonwealth'.

For those Justices who subscribed to this meaning of dispute, setting up 'some tribunal to regulate the conditions of industry … with a jurisdiction co-extensive with any series of claims that can be made by employees on employers, may or may not be an entirely desirable thing', but it was not what the Constitution authorised (Barton in *Felt Hatters*). To seek to invoke federal arbitration 'not for the real purpose of preserving industrial peace but for the purpose of taking the control of industry out of the hands of employers' amounted, in Griffith's words, to 'a fraud upon the Constitution'.

The opposing view, which finally commanded clear majority support in the *Builders Labourers Case* (1914), interpreted section 51(xxxv) as referring not to industrial dislocation or disruption but rather to disagreement or difference between parties in an industrial relationship. That the disagreement did not raise the immediate prospect of actual industrial conflict or warfare was not to the point, so long as the differences were seriously held and persisted in by the parties. Formal demands for altered conditions not acceded to by those on whom they were served, although not actually constituting an industrial dispute, were nonetheless prima facie evidence that one existed. On this argument such demands were simply a convenient means of proving a necessary jurisdictional fact, and therefore constitutionally unexceptionable.

As Barton foresaw in *Allen Taylor*, the almost inevitable consequence of this 'broad' construction of dispute was that the further and associated jurisdictional condition, that such a dispute extended beyond the limits of any one state, became for most practical purposes a requirement 'merely of nominal effect'. The requirement of interstateness in section 51(xxxv) was designed to confine the federal jurisdiction to those industrial disputes that could not effectively be dealt with by any one state. The proposition that this might limit the Commonwealth to a few industries that crossed state boundaries, or involved individual employers who operated in two or more states, was never seriously entertained by the Court. As Higgins pointed out in the *Jumbunna Coal Case* (1908), the constitutional condition applied not to the employment but to the dispute, 'the only difficulty' being that 'a "dispute" is something intangible and abstract' whereas the tribunal and the Court had 'to measure it by things concrete and tangible—by States, areas of territory'. The stipulation was satisfied if disputants in different states combined to make common cause. But the result had to be a single interstate dispute, not a series of separate intrastate disputes whose only true connection was temporal. Formal organisation or combination was not essential; nor was trade competition between the employers, so long as the relevant parties shared a community of interest. A nexus of sympathy, however, was not enough.

Opponents of the 'paper disputes' doctrine objected to the jurisdictional sufficiency for this purpose of claimants merely serving identical demands on various parties in two or more states. Thus, Griffith protested in *Builders Labourers*, were this to be approved, 'it is plain that the whole subject matter of the regulation of any and every branch of industry can be taken out of the hands of the State and transferred to the Commonwealth Arbitration Court' by the simple expedient of disputants consolidating their separate disagreements into a single document and then making a joint demand.

In the event, this issue, like the definition of 'dispute', was also authoritatively resolved in the *Builders Labourers Case*, the majority holding (as **Gavan Duffy** and **Rich** put it in their **joint judgment**) that 'a dispute extends beyond the limits of any one State when it exists in more than one State, that is to say, extends over an area which embraces territory of more than one State'. To this end, the existence of demands in the form of a common log of claims served upon, and definitely and finally refused by, employers in different states, was evidence of the existence of an interstate dispute. Whether in any particular case that sufficed to establish that 'a given industrial dispute answers the requisite geographical character'—covered Australian territory transcending the limits of any one state—was, said **Isaacs** in *Builders Labourers*, 'a pure question of fact', to be determined in the first instance by the tribunal and ultimately, if necessary, by the High Court. In the decades since *Builders Labourers*, however, even this comparatively undemanding interpretation of the requirement has been progressively relaxed by the Court to the point where it now rarely presents an impediment to the exercise of federal jurisdiction.

Acceptance of the 'paper disputes' principle greatly facilitated proof of the existence of an interstate dispute and, as **Barwick** observed in *R v Heagney; Ex parte ACT Employers Federation* (1976), thereby 'added significance to the constitutional power'. Later decisions recognising that trade unions acted as parties' principals, rather than as mere agents of their members, were a further turning point in federal labour law: *Burwood Cinema Case* (1925) and *Metal Trades Case* (1935). As **Windeyer** said in the *Professional Engineers Case* (1959), together these cases had brought 'a great part of the Aus-

tralian economy directly or indirectly within the reach of Commonwealth industrial law and … of the Commonwealth Industrial Tribunal'. They certainly ensured, as **Kirby** observed in *A-G (Qld) v Riordan* (1997), that the procedure of creating interstate paper disputes rapidly became the standard method of invoking federal power. But although the industrial disputes referred to in section 51(xxxv) do not have to be of a kind that threatens breaches of the industrial peace of the community, they must be 'real and genuine' in the sense that the claims being advanced and resisted have genuinely to reflect what the claimants really want. Reality and genuineness in this sense, while perhaps more appropriately descriptive of the particular claims than of the dispute, are not negatived by proof that those advancing the claims also want to attract the exercise of federal jurisdiction and have therefore assiduously sought to meet and satisfy all the formal conditions precedent to any such exercise (*Builders Labourers Case*).

The Court's continued insistence on this particular requirement, however, has had to be sufficiently flexible to accommodate the competing requirements of the doctrine of ambit, a notion long regarded as inherent in the constitutional conception of arbitration. And since the requirements of the ambit doctrine 'not only promote, but necessitate, the making of inflated demands' (as the Court observed in *R v Ludeke; Ex parte Queensland Electricity Commission* (1985)), the practical effect of its application has been largely to emasculate reality and genuineness of all serious content. As it has long been held 'unnecessary for an organization to insist that its demands be implemented immediately in order that they be bona fide', extravagantly optimistic claims, intended to establish the widest possible margins to a dispute not inconsistent with highly attenuated notions of industrial fancifulness, quickly became an established feature of the award process.

The Court's acquiescence in this practice of serving ambit claims, combined with its endorsement of the proposition that formal written demands should normally be viewed, prima facie at least, as real and genuine, has meant that parties seeking to oppose the exercise of jurisdiction are faced with an almost Herculean task. Seldom have prosecutors succeeded in disproving reality and genuineness, although very occasionally formal demands have been shown to be so inflated and extravagant as to amount to no more than bare claims for regulation by the specialist tribunal, a matter incapable of giving rise to an interstate industrial dispute under section 51(xxxv) (*Re State Public Services Federation* (1993)).

According to the Court, the requirement that the interstate dispute be 'industrial' has two separate aspects, the first going to the nature or identity of the parties and the second to the subject matter of the issue between them. From the beginning, there was a question of whether the constitutional power covered independent contractors as well as employees—a long-established, if curiously artificial and anachronistic, **common law** distinction that nevertheless remains of central importance in Australian **employment law**. Classifying contemporary work relationships on this basis has proved to be increasingly difficult and unsatisfactory, from both a doctrinal and a policy perspective. The Court has now acknowledged as much in its rejection of the so-called 'control' test, in favour of a more flexible multi-factorial approach to the identification of employees engaged under contracts of service (see *Stevens v Brodribb Sawmilling* (1986)). This development has been paralleled by a relaxation of the formal requirements for implying terms into contracts of service. It is, however, debatable whether that change will have any significant practical impact in the case of parties covered by awards and statutorily sanctioned agreements, collective or individual—since although the terms of an award or collective agreement may expressly incorporate award conditions, the Court has rejected any suggestion that such conditions are incorporated by implication in individual contracts (*Byrne v Australian Airlines* (1995)).

Even more contentious than this issue of employment categorisation and coverage, however, was whether the tribunal could validly be authorised to deal with disputes between state government agencies or instrumentalities and their employees. In the *Engineers Case* (1920), in the context of section 51(xxxv), the Court appeared emphatically to reject its earlier implication of **intergovernmental immunities**. Paradoxically, however, the **overruling** of that doctrine led not to an expansion but a contraction of the power, and after the decision in the *School Teachers Case* (1929), saw the issue of the federal regulation of state government employment again become confused and unclear. That situation continued until, in the *CYSS Case* (1983), the Court signalled a return to the broad approach to the interpretation of section 51(xxxv) evident in many of the earlier cases, particularly *Jumbunna Coal*. The expression 'industrial dispute' was to be given its popular meaning—which extended beyond, but certainly included, 'disputes between employees and employers about the terms of employment and the conditions of work'. The unanimous judgment completely rejected 'any notion that the adjective "industrial" imports some restriction which confines the constitutional conception to disputes in productive industry and organised businesses carried on for the purpose of making profits'. Even so, some important difficulties were left unresolved, including the position of employees engaged in the so-called administrative services of the states. This has since begun to be addressed by the Court as an issue involving the application of implied limitations deriving from the federal structure of the Constitution, as spelled out in the *Melbourne Corporation Case* (1947) (see *Re Australian Education Union; Ex parte Victoria* (1995)).

Disputes between employers and employees, however, are only within federal power if the subject matter of the dispute is also industrial in character. So, for example, some matters were thought for a time not to be capable of being the subject of an industrial dispute because they concerned managerial prerogatives. Although this particular criterion no longer has any constitutional currency, and notwithstanding the insistence of Isaacs and Rich in the *Union Badge Case* (1913) that the words of section 51(xxxv) 'stand unabridged by any specified subject matter of dispute', the Court has continued to insist that some issues may be too indirect or remote in their connection with the industrial relationship of the parties to be within power (*Re Manufacturing Grocers' Employees Federation* (1986)). In this regard, however, the influence of the terms of the legislation has been especially important and cannot be ignored.

The predominance of paper disputes as a means of invoking federal jurisdiction led almost inevitably to an overwhelming preoccupation by the Court with the scope of the 'settlement' limb of section 51(xxxv), to the relative neglect of the power to conciliate and arbitrate for the 'prevention' of interstate industrial disputes. Until recently, the decisions holding invalid legislative attempts to authorise any arbitration imposing a common rule (*Whybrow's Case (No 2)* (1910)) were taken as suggesting a very limited scope for the preventive aspect of the power. Lately, however, there have been strong judicial indications to the contrary, albeit by way of *obiter dicta*—with several Justices appearing to attribute the difficulties thus far encountered in this regard to the structure of the legislation, rather than to the language of the constitutional grant. It is now clear that section 51(xxxv) authorises laws conferring powers of conciliation and arbitration exercisable if the tribunal considers that an interstate industrial dispute is otherwise likely to occur. According to some Justices, it might even permit legislation conferring a jurisdiction 'merely conditioned upon the opinion of the tribunal that circumstances exist in which [its] conciliation and arbitration procedures may be conducive to the prevention and settlement of interstate industrial disputes' in the abstract (**Gaudron** and **Gummow** in *A-G (Qld) v Riordan*, quoting Deane in the *Wooldumpers Case* (1989)).

It is somewhat ironic that the apparent return in the *CYSS Case* to the more expansive and less technical reading of section 51(xxxv) adopted in the very early years of federation should occur at about the same time as the system of industrial conciliation and arbitration has fallen, politically, into such evident disfavour and decline. And while some aspects of the scope of the federal power remain unsettled (see, for example, *Re Australian Education Union*), it is now beyond question that the grant is broad enough to support even a regime of collective agreements having the force of awards and negotiated by parties using protected industrial action (the *Industrial Relations Act Case* (1996)), although the continued significance of the industrial **torts** should not be underestimated (see *Williams v Hursey* (1959); *Patrick Stevedores Case* (1998)).

The focus of attention has very noticeably begun to shift in the last two decades, however, to various other constitutional powers as potential sources of legislative authority for regulating industrial relations. For a brief period during the 1990s, the **external affairs power** occupied centre stage for this purpose; but political considerations have since seen it supplanted by an almost total preoccupation with section 51(xx), the **corporations power**. Since 1996, the reach of the corporations power as now interpreted by the Court has been relied upon by the federal coalition government to enact legislation facilitating the making of individual and (non-union) collective agreements between employees and those employers falling within the presently accepted conception of constitutional corporations. All the indications are that future industrial relations regulation may rest as much or more on the Court's construction of these other heads of constitutional power, including and in particular section 51(xx), as on section 51(xxxv). Be that as it may, for good or ill the High Court has played, and will continue to play, a major role in shaping the institutional foundations, and even the course, of Australian labour relations.

BILL FORD

Land law. It is generally accepted that land law requires a high degree of certainty and stability. With the notable exception of *Mabo* (1992) and *Wik* (1996), the High Court's land law decisions have attracted little controversy, and have rarely resulted in significant legal change.

There are still substantial similarities between Australian and English land law. Heavy reliance on English authorities, combined with the Court's emphasis on 'a strict and complete **legalism**', particularly during the period of the **Dixon Court**, has helped to maintain this continuity. In decisions in the first half of the century, some Justices displayed greater familiarity with arcane aspects of English land law than with Australian conveyancing practice. For example, in *Wright v Gibbons* (1949), a case concerning whether two sisters who were joint tenants had defeated a third sister's right of survivorship by transferring their interests to each other, **Dixon** cited Bracton, Coke, and several nineteenth-century English conveyancers before examining the relevant provisions of the NSW *Real Property Act* 1900.

This deference to English authority, which appears to be stronger in Australia than in other **common law** countries such as Canada, may in part reflect the technical nature of the questions that the Court has had to decide. Cases involving recovery of compensation for improvements by co-owners (*Brickwood v Young* (1905)), the creation of easements (*Commonwealth v Registrar of Titles* (1918)), and the rights conferred by possession of land (*Allen v Roughley* (1955)) provide little scope for judicial innovation. In migrant groups, it has often been observed that language in the settler community does not evolve in the same way as the language in the home country. A parallel exists in Australian land law, where courts have continued to apply principles that have been abandoned or substantially modified by English courts. For example, the requirements of the doctrine of part performance became less rigorous in England after the **House of Lords** decision in *Steadman v Steadman* (1974); but in *Regent v Millett* (1976), the High Court abstained from any conclusion as to how far that decision might affect its own established view in *McBride v Sandland* (1918) and *Cooney v Burns* (1922): see the **Federal Court** discussion in *ANZ Banking Group v Widin* (1990). Again, a licence to enter or remain on land has been held to be enforceable by injunction against the licensor in England (see *Winter Garden Theatre (London) v Millennium Productions* (1947) and *Hounslow London Borough Council v Twickenham Garden Developments* (1970)). By comparison, the High Court's approach to licence disputes not involving use of Crown land remains under the shadow of *Cowell v Rosehill Racecourse* (1937) (see *Forbes v NSW Trotting Club* (1979))—although, where the government terminates a licence, resort to **administrative law** may produce a different outcome.

When the High Court has had the opportunity to reshape the law to make it more appropriate to Australia it has sometimes declined to do so. An early example is *Moore v Dimond* (1929), where the Court applied the ancient presumption

that a tenant under an informal fixed-term lease who paid rent on a weekly basis was a yearly tenant. A more recent example is *Corin v Patton* (1990), where the Court applied the traditional rule prohibiting unilateral severance of a joint tenancy instead of following more recent English authority (*Burgess v Rawnsley* (1975)).

Although the advent of the Torrens system gave the Court an opportunity to develop distinctively Australian land law principles, this did not always occur. Some Justices read down the Torrens legislation in the light of common law principles it was intended to replace. It was the **Privy Council** (in *Frazer v Walker* (1966)) rather than the High Court that decided that a person who became registered under a void instrument gained indefeasible title (compare the judgments of Dixon and **McTiernan** in *Clements v Ellis* (1934)), though once this principle was established, the High Court faithfully applied it (see, for example, *Breskvar v Wall* (1971)). In *Dabbs v Seaman* (1925), a majority of the Justices applied the general law conveyancing principle according to which the purchaser of land described in the conveyance as 'abutting' a lane acquires an easement over that lane, even though the purchaser had not intended to purchase the easement and the easement was not registered on the title. (**Higgins** delivered a strong **dissenting judgment**.)

In deciding priority disputes between holders of unregistered interests in Torrens system land, the Court has usually preferred to reason by analogy from pre-existing equitable principles, rather than develop principles to take account of statutory mechanisms such as caveats by which holders of unregistered interests can protect themselves. An exception is the judgment of Chief Justice **Griffith** in *Butler v Fairclough* (1917), which held that the holder of an unregistered interest who failed to caveat should lose priority over the holder of a later unregistered interest. Although Griffith compared possession of title deeds under the general law system with 'a clear title on the register' under the Torrens system, he relied on this analogy to set a new standard for Torrens system conveyancers. Later cases undermined this approach by placing greater emphasis on protecting the holder of the first equitable interest than on safeguarding holders of later interests who deal on the faith of the register (see, for example, Chief Justice **Barwick's** judgment in *J & H Just (Holdings) v Bank of NSW* (1971)). The inclusion of an expert conveyancer on the Bench might have led to a different emphasis. Unfortunately, this approach has tended to encourage the creation of equitable interests outside the register.

In recent years, the Court has been more inventive. Reliance on equitable principles during the period of the **Mason Court** assisted claimants who could not satisfy the formal requirements for the transfer of a legal or equitable interest in land, with positive effects for those (often **women**) who made substantial contributions of money or labour to land in which another person holds legal title. In *Baumgartner v Baumgartner* (1987), for example, the Court imposed a constructive **trust** to prevent the owner of a house from unconscionably retaining the benefit of contributions of money and domestic labour made by his former de facto wife on the assumption that their relationship would continue. Although the *Baumgartner* principle gives the contributor an *in personam* entitlement against the legal title holder—an entitlement that is not necessarily enforceable against third parties—in practical terms, it allows the contributor to gain a share of the value of land held during the relationship. Similarly, in *Legione v Hateley* (1983) and *Stern v McArthur* (1988), it was held that **equity** would provide relief against forfeiture to a purchaser of land in breach of the **contract**, in circumstances where it was **unconscionable** for the vendors to rely on their strict legal rights.

The tension between the Torrens goal of simplifying conveyancing, and the High Court's increased reliance on equitable principles in response to individual claims for justice, is illustrated by *Bahr v Nicolay (No 2)* (1988), where the Court held that a registered proprietor who had bought the **property** on the basis of an undertaking to the vendor that a third party would be able to purchase it, could not rely on his registration to defeat the third party's interest. At a formal level, this does not conflict with the indefeasibility principle, which permits enforcement of *in personam* claims against registered proprietors. However, a generous application of this principle could undermine indefeasibility and seriously affect the security of titles. In the future, the Court's enthusiasm for equity should be tempered by realisation of the potential for such principles to undermine the title registration system. Otherwise, the infusion of equity could bring Australian land law closer to the general law system that Robert Torrens sought to overturn.

In contrast to the incremental effects of this equitable infusion, the Court's 1992 decision in *Mabo* overturned principles that had been regarded as central to land law from the time of English colonisation. Prior to *Mabo*, the 'subtle and elaborate system highly adapted to the country in which the people led their lives' that regulated the relationship between Aboriginal groups and their land was ignored in Australian law. It was assumed—though it had never been decided, at least by the High Court—that the feudal doctrine of tenure, under which proprietary interests in land are normally derived from a Crown grant, precluded recognition of **native title**. It followed that when Australia was settled, the Crown not only acquired **sovereignty** over, but beneficial title to, all land in Australia.

In *Mabo*, all members of the Court except **Dawson** followed earlier US and Canadian authorities that recognised native title. In his influential judgment, **Brennan** reasoned that the notion that the Crown acquired beneficial title as well as sovereignty over land was based on the factually false and discriminatory legal fiction that indigenous people 'were so low in the scale of social organisation' that they had no system of law or recognisable interests in land. The doctrine of tenure did not preclude recognition of native title, which continued in existence unless it was extinguished by loss of connection between **Aboriginal people** and their land, by legislation or an executive act expressing a clear intention to extinguish, or by an inconsistent Crown grant to a third party.

In *obiter dicta*, Brennan suggested that grant of a fee simple or a leasehold estate to a third party would extinguish native title. Although other members of the Court expressed themselves more cautiously, the *Native Title Act 1993* (Cth) reflected the assumption that leases, including various statutory leases, extinguished native title. This assumption was rejected by the High Court in *Wik*, which held that Queensland pastoral leases did not extinguish native title, because they did not confer exclusive possession on lessees and their legal incidents were not otherwise inconsistent with native title rights.

Mabo and *Wik* reflect both continuity and change. Despite the fundamental break with the past made in *Mabo*, the majority in both *Mabo* and *Wik* draw heavily on traditional land law doctrines, including the doctrine of tenure, the property rights conferred by possession, and the nature of leasehold interests. Reflecting the theme of change, **Gummow** warns in *Wik* against giving 'traditional concepts of English law … a fascination beyond their utility in instruction for the case at hand'. Both cases are characterised by their close attention to 'the unique developments not only in common law, but also in statute which mark the law of real property in Australia'.

MARCIA NEAVE

Further Reading

Brendan Edgeworth, 'Tenure, Allodialism and Indigenous Rights at Common Law: English, United States and Australian Land Law Compared After *Mabo v Queensland*' (1994) 23 *Anglo-American Law Review* 397

Mary-Anne Hughson, Marcia Neave, and Pamela O'Connor, 'Reflections on the Mirror of Title: Resolving the Conflict Between Purchasers and Prior Interest Holders' (1997) 21 *MULR* 460, 479

Andrew Lokan, 'From Recognition to Reconciliation: The Functions of Aboriginal Rights Law' (1999) 23 *MULR* 65

JG Tooher, 'Muddying the Torrens Waters With the Chancellor's Foot?' (1993) 1 *APLJ* 1

Langer v Commonwealth (1996). In 1996, Albert Langer was imprisoned for ten weeks for distributing leaflets encouraging voters in a federal election to put the candidates of the Australian Labor Party and the Liberal–National Party Coalition equal last. Amnesty International described him as 'the first prisoner of conscience in the country for over 20 years'.

Sections 7 and 24 of the Constitution provide that the members of the Senate and the House of Representatives shall be 'directly chosen by the people'. The system of **representative government** recognised by these provisions is implemented by the detailed provisions of the *Commonwealth Electoral Act* 1918 (Cth). That Act provides for a system of compulsory voting at federal elections. By section 240, 'In a House of Representatives election a person shall mark his or her vote' by numbering every square '1, 2, 3, 4 …'. Under section 329A, it was an offence attracting up to six months jail to encourage voters to fill in a ballot paper in any other way. Despite this, section 270 provided that a ballot paper 'shall not be informal' if it includes a sequence of consecutive numbers beginning with '1', even if numbers are duplicated and even if one square is blank. Thus a paper numbered '1, 2, 3, 3 …' would be counted as indicating a preference for candidates '1' and '2'.

Langer had been a well-known political activist since the 1970s. In *R v Langer* (1971), the Supreme Court of Victoria quashed a conviction arising from a speech at a May Day march for which he had been sentenced to 18 months imprisonment. At the 1990 federal election, he sought to make voters aware of the option of voting '1, 2, 3, 3 …', and encouraged them to exploit it by placing the major parties equal last on their ballot papers, thereby ensuring that preferences would not be distributed to those candidates. In 1992, section 329A was added to the Electoral Act in response to Langer's campaign; but at the 1993 election, he renewed his campaign. The Electoral Commission's counter-publicity emphasised that a formal vote must number every square. Langer sued in the High Court for an injunction to stop the Commission's advertisements, arguing that they were 'misleading and intimidating', and would 'have an effect … on the Election such that it will no longer be free or fair'. His application for urgent relief was refused, but the question whether section 329A was valid was reserved for the **Full Court's** opinion. It came on for hearing in October 1995.

Langer directed his main attack to the validity of section 240, arguing that its stipulations as to voting method were inconsistent with the constitutional requirement that representatives be 'freely chosen by the people'. He argued that the people, if voting freely, must be free not to choose—that is, not to number every square. It followed, he said, that section 329A was also invalid, since it 'cannot validly prohibit the encouragement of voters to exercise that right of choice which the Constitution allows'. He argued that as a result of those sections, there had not been a 'free election', and hence that the Parliament elected at the 1993 election was invalid. This led him on the day of the **argument** in the High Court, where he was a **litigant in person**, to assert (unsuccessfully) that **Gummow** should be **disqualified** from hearing the matter. Gummow had been appointed in 1995 by the government formed from the Parliament elected in 1993. Langer argued that if that Parliament had not been validly elected, Gummow's commission as a High Court Justice could not be valid either. The same argument applied to **Brennan's** appointment as **Chief Justice**; Langer conceded, however, that Brennan's **appointment** as a **puisne Justice** in 1981 had been valid, and accordingly that Brennan could continue to hear the case, although not as Chief Justice.

To focus the argument on section 240 proved to be a tactical error. The Court unanimously held that section 240 was valid, since the Constitution leaves to the Parliament a broad discretion in selecting the means by which its members are chosen. As Brennan put it, section 240 was valid because it could 'reasonably be regarded as prescribing a method of freely choosing members of the House of Representatives'. It followed that section 329A was also valid, as 'a law which is appropriate and adapted to prevent the subversion of that method'.

Ironically, the only dissenter from this latter conclusion was **Dawson**, who held that section 329A infringed the implied freedom of **political communication**. When the Court had first declared the existence of that freedom in the *Free Speech Cases* (1992), Dawson had dissented; and he still maintained that any such freedom must be limited to 'what is necessary for the conduct of elections by direct popular vote', as section 24 of the Constitution envisaged. But he held that, even on that basis, the people's choice 'must obviously be a genuine, or informed, choice', which 'requires access on the part of the voter to the available alternatives in the

making of the choice'. It followed that section 329A was invalid as 'a law which is designed to keep from voters information which is required by them to enable them to exercise an informed choice'.

The issue no longer arises. After the 1996 election, the federal Parliament repealed section 329A and amended section 240 to include the words 'consecutive numbers, without the repetition of any number'. This latter change made it clear that '1, 2, 3, 3 …' no longer counts as a formal vote. Langer, however, has continued to insist through a website campaign (www.neither.org) that the new section 240 is both unconstitutional and ineffective, since section 268 of the Act requires merely that a formal vote should indicate 'an' order of preference.

GEORGE WILLIAMS

Further Reading

Chris Field, '"Tweedledum and Tweedledee 1, 2, 3, 3": The Albert Langer Story', Parliamentary Research Service, Commonwealth Parliament, *Current Issues Brief*, No 14, 1995

Anne Twomey, 'Free to Choose or Compelled to Lie? The Rights of Voters After *Langer v The Commonwealth*' (1996) 24 *FL Rev* 201

Languages. The reasons of the High Court are given solely in the English language—the language of the majority of Australian citizens and of the **legal profession**. In this respect, the problems of translation that arise in other final appellate courts of the Commonwealth (for example, Canada and South Africa) do not arise in Australia. However, from time to time the reasons of the Justices have included use of foreign languages. In one recent decision, Chinese characters appeared (see **Kirby** on 黑孩子 or 'black children' in *Chen Shi Hai v Minister for Immigration and Multicultural Affairs* (2000)). Although they were used in the pamphlet version of the Court's reasons, they proved too difficult for the publishers of non-authorised reports; in the *Australian Law Reports* and the *Australian Law Journal Reports*, the characters were deleted by the editors.

The most frequent judicial resort to foreign languages is to the 'dead' languages, Latin and classical Greek. **Dixon** often demonstrated his command of classical Greek. In *Commissioner for Railways (NSW) v Scott* (1959), for example, and without the benefit to his readers of translation, he wrote that 'there is no reason for distinguishing between the case of the οἰκέτης and that of the περίοικος even if the latter were a εἱλώτης'; there are anecdotal reports, too, of Dixonian dinner-table story-tellings spiced with classical Greek, and of judicial irritation when the punch-line went unappreciated. Dixon's mastery of Greek and classical learning was shared by **Fullagar**: sometimes they exchanged notes in Greek in court, often asking **Williams**, who sat between them, to pass them. Williams was not amused. In *FCT v Newton* (1957), a group of motor car companies had sought to minimise tax liability by channelling shareholding and dividend transactions through a holding company called Pactolus Pty Ltd. 'Pactolus' was a Phrygian river, supposedly in the time of the mythological King Midas, which brought down golden sands. Fullagar's judgment showed his appreciation of the classical allusion involved. 'The sands of the Lydian river', he wrote, 'were indeed golden, but there was no gold which did not come from the profits of the motor companies'. Fullagar also prided himself on his knowledge of French: when documents translated from the French were produced to the Court in evidence, Fullagar often checked the translation against his own understanding of the original (see, for example, *In re Usines de Melle's Patent* (1954); *Compagnie des Messageries Maritimes v Wilson* (1954)).

The use of Latin has been far more pervasive, going beyond mere literary allusion or analogy to the heart of legal **argument**. Until the 1950s, most Australian law schools included Roman Law among their compulsory subjects, and matriculation in Latin was required as a precondition of entry into Australian law schools. Virtually every Justice during the twentieth century would have studied Latin at school, and some at university. An ability to produce a Latin quotation was one way of showing membership of an educated elite, of investing one's writing with a character that seemed to elevate it beyond the vagaries of place and time. The use of Latin in the reasons of the early High Court was thus not uncommon, and quotations from Latin writings, from literature, philosophy, and from a wide range of legal sources and traditions, were frequently incorporated, untranslated, into the structure of legal argument.

It is possible to delineate a range of uses of Latin from this era, some of which have persisted to our own time, when Latin no longer serves as a *lingua franca* even among the educated elite. In some instances, the invocation of a principle, maxim or aphorism is closely integrated into legal argument. On other occasions, it provides the basis for some kind of illustrative analogy (often rather strained) between the facts of the case and some mythical or legendary event. Sometimes it offers wisdom or insight from an ancient and purportedly authoritative source, and sometimes it seems to offer little more than gentlemanly coloration or garniture, establishing the cultural credentials of the legal writer but throwing little light on the legal issues at hand.

There are many examples of the early High Court's use of Latin. In *Union Steamship of New Zealand v Commonwealth* (1925), **Higgins** quoted Cicero's *Topica*, section 53, in untranslated Latin, to convey the sense in which a Commonwealth law would be 'repugnant' to a British Act by virtue of the *Colonial Laws Validity Act* 1865 (Imp). As with the Court's early conception of **inconsistency** under section 109, the word 'repugnant' covered a narrow ground, requiring direct hostility between two laws to support its application so that simultaneous obedience was impossible, 'as in Cicero Top XII, fin—*quicquid repugnat, id ejusmodi est, ut cohoerere nunquam possit*' ('whatever is repugnant is of such a kind as to be always incapable of being consistent'). If Higgins quoted from his own reading of Cicero's *Topica*—a little-read reworking of Aristotle's treatise of the same name—he was a scholarly man indeed, though the passage can be found, it is true, in what was for a long time the standard Latin dictionary: CT Lewis and C Short, *A Latin Dictionary* (1879).

In the *Jehovah's Witnesses Case* (1943), **Latham**, including 'evil' or 'wicked' practices within the scope of 'religion' for the purposes of section 116 of the Constitution and therefore giving that section's protection of 'religion' a narrow operation, quoted Lucretius's *De Rerum Natura* (*On the Nature of the Universe*) book one, line 101, in untranslated

Latin—*Tantum religio potuit suadere malorum*: 'Such enormity of evil only religion could prompt'. **Windeyer** often also displayed his skills in Latin (see, for example, *Commissioner For Railways (NSW) v Scott*; *National Insurance of New Zealand v Espagne* (1961); *Da Costa v Cockburn Salvage & Trading* (1970); and, especially, *Smith v Jenkins* (1970)).

The use of Latin was sometimes confined to well-known legal phrases (for example, *inter alia* (among other things)). Sometimes particular categories have become commonly used in Australian legal writing, such as *forum non conveniens* (an inappropriate venue for the proceedings), *lex loci delicti* (the law of the place where the wrong occurred), or *lex fori* (the law of the jurisdiction in which the proceedings are brought). Sometimes it extended to legal aphorisms such as *expressio unius est exclusio alterius* (express reference to one is the exclusion of the other (*Ainsworth v Criminal Justice Commission* (1992)) or *audi alteram partem* (hear the other side; see, for example, *Kioa v West* (1985)). Sometimes the Latin tag is traced to its source: in *Commissioner of Police v Tanos* (1958), **Dixon** traced *audi alteram partem* to Seneca's play *Medea*, apparently first cited in *Boswel's Case* (1583)—*Quicunque aliquid statuerit, parte inaudita altera, Aequum licet statuerit, haud aequus fuerit* ('Whoever passes sentence with the other party unheard has not acted justly, even if the sentence is just'). At other times, the familiarity of the Latin maxim within an educated community is comfortably assumed. In *D'Emden v Pedder* (1904) Griffith observes: 'It is only necessary to mention the maxim, *quando lex aluquid concedit, concedere videtur et illud sine quo res ipsa valere non potest*'—though he goes on to paraphrase its meaning ('In other words, where any power or control is expressly granted, there is included in the grant, to the full extent of the capacity of the grantor, and without special mention, every power and every control the denial of which would render the grant itself ineffective'). In *Pioneer Express v Hotchkiss* (1958), Dixon is content to leave the same maxim untranslated; and in *Arnold v Mann* (1957), Fullagar thinks it sufficient to say: '*quod semel in electionibus*, etc' (referring to the maxim that an election once made cannot be repudiated).

Increasingly, response to the use of Latin in legal argument has been one of scepticism and caution. Ironically, the gravest warnings about undiscriminating submission to the power of the Latin phrase have come from those most adept in the area, and most given to Latin quotation, such as Dixon and Windeyer. Here, it is true, objections to Latin are mixed in with wider cautions and reservations about so-called 'principles' of interpretation that happen to be phrased in Latin, and most references to Latin in the High Court, in more recent decades, have been in judicial attempts to limit their application. Reference has often been made to the fact that, because they are expressed in Latin, they may seem to carry more authority than is their due. In *Anchor Products v Hedges* (1966), Windeyer warned against attributing special status to the *res ipsa loquitur* doctrine because it was expressed in the Latin phrase, and in *Crowe v Graham* (1968), he made scathing reference to 'those who like Latin tags or rules of construction'. In his longest discussion on the issue, in *Smith v Jenkins*, those 'who like to interlard English law with Latin' come under similar criticism. In *Franklin v Victorian Railways Commissioners* (1959) **Dixon**, too, cautioned that 'the day for canonising Latin phrases has gone past', and quoted with approval Lord Shaw of Dunfermline's comment on the phrase *res ipsa loquitur*, that 'if it had not been in Latin, nobody would have called it a principle' (*Ballard v North British Railway* (1923)). This mood of scepticism has been picked up extensively in subsequent judgments. **Barwick**, in *Nominal Defendant v Haslbauer* (1967), blames the 'resort to Latin' for 'elevating a reason for logical inference, grounded on the common experience of mankind, into a principle or doctrine'. **Taylor** wrote, in *Iannella v French* (1968), that the 'epigrammatic formulation of a doctrine does not suffice to determine its application in particular cases. And it gets no more precision by being put in Latin'. And **Deane** has referred to ways in which the 'disarming mystique' of Latin offers a 'warrant for essential misdescription', in *Kern Corporation v Walter Reid Trading* (1987).

Despite these criticisms, the legacy of the long tradition of education in Latin is still felt in the Court. Close syntactical parsing remains a significant element in Australian legal argument, and for this, it is likely that traditional grammar—the kind most thoroughly acquired in school Latin classes—will long remain the basis, with the Justices still probing English sentences for pluperfects, gerunds and even gerundives. Quotation from classical texts, and even from classical literary sources of no particular legal relevance, still carries with it an authority and cultural resonance to which modern and local literary allusion will never accede. The strong scepticism expressed in the High Court about 'Latin tags' and the importation of 'exotic Latin maxims' (Windeyer in *Smith v Jenkins*) has perhaps moderated the use of the apt Latin phrase, but has not proscribed it. We must now generally be content with English language translations, but the classics still provide an evocative source of quotation and, sometimes, illustrative analogy, as in the strong overture to Kirby's judgment in *Grincelis v House* (2000), which offers Virgil's *Georgics* not just as illustration but as authority:

> We have it on the authority of Virgil [*Georgics*, book I, line 281] that when an endeavour was made in ancient times to pile Ossa on Pelion and then 'to roll leafy Olympus on top of Ossa', the Gods scattered the heaped-up mountains with a thunderbolt. Their divine anger may have been occasioned by irritation with the logic of height being pressed too far. This appeal explores the limits of logical deduction in the legal context of compensation for the unpaid care provided by a family member to a person injured as a result of a legal wrong.

MICHAEL MEEHAN

Latham, John Greig (*b* 26 August 1877; *d* 25 July 1964; Chief Justice 1935–52) brought to the office of **Chief Justice** highly developed powers of logical analysis, a clear grasp of legal principles, and a generally conservative cast of mind.

He was the first of five children of Thomas and Jean Latham. The economic circumstances of the family were austere and Thomas was a strict Methodist. John Latham, however, was throughout his adult life an unswerving rationalist, and was for some years President of the Rationalist Society of Victoria.

John Latham, Chief Justice 1935–52

He went to Scotch College with scholarships, and then entered the University of Melbourne, where he graduated in arts in 1897 with particular distinction in Philosophy and Logic. He then taught for a short period, but returned to study law, and graduated in 1902, when he shared the Supreme Court Prize. He supported himself with teaching in philosophy and logic, and in law. He went to the Victorian Bar in 1905, and made a slow start, but by the outbreak of war in 1914, he was established. His work was distinguished by a rigorously logical style of **argument**.

In 1907, John Latham married Eileen Mary Tobin, who was also a graduate of the University of Melbourne. She was a vigorous woman who enjoyed public life with her husband, and she was herself active in hospital work, for which she was awarded the CBE. The marriage was long-lasting and successful; their tragedy was to suffer the loss of two of their three children. Richard, who was establishing a high reputation in the law in Oxford, was killed in service with the RAF in 1943, and their daughter, Freda, died in 1953.

Latham volunteered for service in **World War I** and was appointed Lieutenant Commander in the Naval Reserve. He went to England as a member of the Australian Prime Minister's party in 1918, and was designated as adviser to Joseph Cook, Minister for the Navy. He attended the Imperial Conference in London in 1918, and was a member of the Australian delegation to the Peace Conference in Paris in 1919. For his work, he was appointed CMG.

On his return to Australia, Latham set about restoring his legal practice, which developed well and was wide-ranging. He was appointed KC in 1922. In that year, he stood for and was elected to the federal House of Representatives for Kooyong. He stood as an independent liberal union candidate, in vehement opposition to the Hughes government. Having won Kooyong, he worked very closely with Earle Page, leader of the Country Party, in planning the steps by which Hughes was forced from office in 1923. This achieved, Latham joined the Nationalist Party, and in December 1925 was appointed **Attorney-General** in the Bruce–Page coalition, with Stanley Melbourne Bruce as **Prime Minister**.

In a continuing struggle with militant unions, earlier attempts to deport the leaders of the seamen's strike had been struck down by the High Court in *Ex parte Walsh and Johnson; In re Yates* (1925). Latham acted to amend the *Crimes Act* 1914 (Cth) to provide for the deportation of offenders not born in Australia. His amendments also struck at various associations seen as revolutionary and subversive. In the event, the most contentious clauses of the Act were not invoked.

The complexities and constraints of the **conciliation and arbitration** system also contributed to the turbulent years when Latham was Attorney-General. His amendments to the *Conciliation and Arbitration Act* 1926 (Cth) reconstituted the Arbitration Court in a way which was intended to overcome the constitutional problem exposed by *Alexander's Case* (1918), but which in fact perpetuated the problem finally dealt with in the *Boilermakers Case* (1956). A 1926 referendum seeking to delineate federal and state arbitration powers more clearly was defeated. In 1928, he produced an amended Arbitration Act. In 1929—by which time he was also Minister of Industry—he helped bring forward a proposal that the federal government abandon the regulation of industrial relations. That proposal was the key issue in the 1929 general election, in which the government was decisively defeated and Prime Minister Bruce lost his seat.

With the departure of Bruce from political life, Latham became Leader of the Opposition. When Joseph Lyons quit the Labor Party and joined the Nationalists, Latham, well aware of Lyons' greater popular appeal, ceded the leadership of the newly formed United Australia Party to him. Labor was defeated at the general election of December 1931, and Latham again assumed office as Attorney-General and Minister for External Affairs and for Industry.

Latham had a keen interest in international affairs. With Bruce, he attended the important Imperial Conference in London in 1926, and then joined the Australian delegation to the League of Nations Assembly in Geneva. He was a warm supporter of Imperial links, but was wary of attempts to give them precise legal definition. He attacked the appointment of **Isaacs** as Governor-General in 1930, complaining that appointment of an Australian would weaken the ties of Empire. He also opposed the procedures adopted by Prime Minister James Scullin in securing the King's appointment of Isaacs.

Latham's interest in Asia was ahead of its time. In 1934, he led a goodwill mission through East Asia, including China and Japan. On returning, he asserted that Australia 'should speak and think of the Near North instead of the Far East'. This was the first expression of an independent Australian diplomacy in Asia. In 1940, when Chief Justice, he accepted an appointment as Minister to Japan, seeking leave from the High Court to do so, but his mission came too late for his embassy to be effective.

In appearance, tall and austere, with rimless pince-nez; in manner, grave, precise, and unemotional, Latham's public face was that of a 'coldly logical personality'. His activities multiplied. He was Chancellor of the University of Melbourne in 1939–41. His unrelenting work ethic and sense of duty found him an active member of the committees of many public bodies and societies. When nearly 86, he said that he gave up six presidencies to allow himself more time for reading and letter-writing. He could sometimes unbend, displaying an unexpected taste for social evenings—most notably, perhaps, in the company of fellow-members of the 'Boobooks' dining club.

Latham retired from politics at the end of 1934, and on 11 October 1935 he was appointed Chief Justice of the High Court in succession to the aged **Gavan Duffy**. Latham said that he had returned to the Bar in order to restore his neglected finances, but it is likely that he also had the impending vacancy in his sights.

At that time, the High Court had been without an effective Chief Justice for almost 20 years since **Griffith's** departure in 1919, and it was not a harmonious Bench (see **Personal relations**). Its members were not given to cooperation in the preparation of their judgments. Latham was at times sorely tried by the difficulties on the Bench, but he managed the **business** of the Court efficiently, and displayed 'unfailing courtesy, dignity and a firm control'. He was, however, given 'to interrupting the argument of counsel too often and at too great length'.

In constitutional issues, Latham consistently emphasised the purely legal function of the Court. In the first *Uniform Tax Case* (1942), he was aware of the threat which the scheme posed to the financial independence of the states, but ultimately affirmed the superiority of the Commonwealth. Like the majority of Justices, he insisted 'that the problems before the court should be approached as strictly legal questions'. Latham expressed this principle with great simplicity in the *Bank Nationalisation Case* (1948), saying that it was not for the Court to have 'any opinion with respect to the merits and demerits' of bank nationalisation. The Court, he declared, was concerned exclusively with the 'legal question', which was whether bank nationalisation was within the powers of the Commonwealth Parliament.

Latham's logical and literal mind caused him to react against the formulation of broad principles not explicitly stated in the constitutional text. He did so in criticising Isaacs' judgment in the *Engineers Case* (1920). In an extra-judicial comment on Isaacs' proposition that the two pervasive features of the Australian Constitution were the common **sovereignty** of all parts of the British Empire and the principle of **responsible government**, Latham wrote, 'it is difficult to see precisely what effect these cardinal principles had upon the decision in the *Engineers Case* or in any other case'. As to the former principle, of indivisible sovereignty, he observed in *Minister for Works v Gulson* (1944) that 'when stated as a legal principle, it tends to dissolve into impressive verbal mysticism'. In the *Melbourne Corporation Case* (1947), he agreed that Commonwealth legislation that sought to regulate the use of private banking by state instrumentalities was invalid. But unlike other majority Justices, he did not rely on notions of implied **intergovernmental immunities**:

instead, he based his decision on his **characterisation** of the provision as a law with respect to state rather than Commonwealth functions.

In his interpretation in the *Jehovah's Witnesses Case* (1943) of section 116 of the Constitution, which protects 'the free exercise of any religion', Latham joined the rest of the Court in according to the section a very narrow degree of protection. However, while denying constitutional protection to the sect under section 116, he joined other Justices in holding the relevant regulations invalid under the **defence power** (section 51 (vi)).

In general, Latham was sympathetic to an expansive view of **Commonwealth legislative power**, especially in the defence context. Between 1945 and 1950, the **Cold War** escalated dramatically, and Australian troops fought in the Korean War. The scope and boundaries of the Commonwealth defence power became an increasingly important constitutional question. This was the background to Latham's last great case, the *Communist Party Case* (1951), where he alone in the Court strenuously maintained the right of the Parliament to ban the Communist Party under the defence power. He failed to carry with him any of his six colleagues on the Bench.

At his **retirement**, Latham declared that 'when I die, Section 92 will be found written on my heart'. That vexed section (see **Interstate trade and commerce**) occupied his attention on many occasions, and in the *Bank Nationalisation Case*, he dissented, maintaining that section 92 was no barrier to the *Banking Act* 1947 (Cth).

His judgment in *R v Burgess; Ex parte Henry* (1936) ranged widely over the power to legislate with respect to **external affairs**, spelling out in very broad terms the domestic implications of the right of the Commonwealth to make law in implementation of treaties to which the Commonwealth was a party. After leaving the Bench, he maintained his speculative interest in this, and in other constitutional questions. He argued for substantial constitutional **amendment** and clarification in areas such as section 92, the **corporations power**, and the taxing powers of the states.

Much the greater part of Latham's work on the Court was taken up in deciding a wide variety of non-constitutional matters. It has been aptly said that his contributions in these fields were often felicitous; he strove to provide lucid expression of general legal principles. Latham was a very capable judge and judicial administrator, and his stewardship of the High Court left it in better condition than he found it.

In old age, Latham liked to reminisce at length about events and activities in his remarkable career. He seemed forever surprised, but very pleased, that it was all really happening to him. He often spoke of his time in politics, rather more often indeed than of his time as Chief Justice. In the decade and more before his death, when I was Dean of the University of Melbourne Law School and he was visiting, as he did quite often, I taxed him with questions. 'Why do you so often say … "When I was a Minister" rather than "When I was Chief Justice of the High Court"? Did you enjoy politics more than your judicial activity?' He would answer that it was not proper to do, in respect of his work as a judge, what he might very properly do and discuss in his life in politics. I think the truth was that he enjoyed his politics.

ZELMAN COWEN

Further Reading
Zelman Cowen, *Sir John Latham, and Other Papers* (1965)

Latham Court (11 October 1935 to 7 April 1952). Latham's term as **Chief Justice** was punctuated by a brief interregnum in 1940–41. He was given leave of absence from his judicial duties and served as Minister to Japan, **Rich** serving as Acting Chief Justice. In addition, for a year prior to the official end of his term, he heard almost no cases. The Court was, in effect, the **Dixon Court**, Part I. It was the last Australian High Court to include three former politicians among its members, and it is the only High Court to have had two of its members engaged in mid-term stints as diplomats.

In one sense, the Latham Court was remarkably stable. It included all four of Australia's longest-serving High Court Justices, and while Latham's term on the Bench was brief compared with those of his brothers **McTiernan**, Rich, **Dixon**, and **Starke**, his term as Chief Justice is exceeded only by that of **Barwick**, and then only narrowly. Between 1935 and 1949, there was only one resignation (**Evatt** in 1940), and only two new **appointments**—**Williams** in 1940 and **Webb** in 1946. Webb, however, did not become an active member of the Court until 1948.

It was also a fragmented court, especially prior to 1940. The most bitter conflicts were those between Starke on one hand and the two former Labor politicians, Evatt and McTiernan on the other—but Starke was also resentful towards Dixon, somewhat contemptuous of Rich, and cool towards Latham. Evatt reciprocated Starke's hostility, and his relations with Latham could sometimes be prickly (see **Personal relations**). With Evatt's resignation, relations seem to have improved, but even in the years that followed, the Court did not become an effective social unit until after Starke and Rich had been replaced by **Fullagar** and **Kitto**.

The fragmented nature of the Court is reflected in the rarity of **joint judgments**. Joint judgments were delivered in only a fifth of **Full Court** decisions, with Dixon and Evatt being the only Justices of the early Latham Court to give joint judgments with any degree of frequency, usually joining with each other. Starke virtually never delivered joint judgments. Only during Dixon's acting Chief Justiceship did joint judgments become more common. Indeed, for the first time since 1906, single judgments by the whole Court (or all members of the majority) became common.

A strong sense of judicial individualism minimised Latham's capacity to provide leadership to the Court. Even in relation to basic administrative matters, **puisne Justices** could prove recalcitrant (see **Conferences**). Starke simply refused to go on **circuit** to WA, and responded vituperatively to reprimands from Latham. Rich, having been given leave for six months, managed to stretch it to nine, albeit at minimal intellectual cost to the Court. Evatt periodically complained at being slighted. Latham did, however, provide a degree of intellectual leadership. He took judgment writing seriously, and his judgments are generally detailed and comprehensive. Only Dixon wrote longer judgments (and more of them). While Latham's judgments did not usually attract concurrence, only Dixon's attracted a higher rate of concurrence.

Despite personality clashes, and the Justices' different political and social **backgrounds**, the Court managed to achieve unanimity in almost two-thirds of reported Full Court decisions. In fewer than a sixth was there more than one **dissenting judgment**. Dissent rates do not seem to mirror the level of personal tensions on the Court: there was somewhat more unanimity in the years 1935–39 (prior to Evatt's resignation) than during the period 1941–49.

Voting patterns in split decisions reflect the well-documented hostility between Starke and Evatt and McTiernan, Starke being less likely than any other Justice to agree with Evatt and McTiernan in split decisions. However, voting patterns varied according to the type of issue before the Court, and the outwardly cordial relationship between Dixon and Latham coexisted with a relatively high level of disagreement between them in the cases.

The Latham Court made only a limited contribution to the development of private and **criminal law**. Generous provisions for appeals as of right meant that many cases which reached the Court were of little doctrinal importance. The Court's capacity for creativity was further constrained by its continued acceptance of the overriding authority of decisions of the **House of Lords**, by its subordination in the judicial **hierarchy** to the **Privy Council**, and by its commitment to a relatively strict doctrine of **precedent**. Nonetheless, within these constraints, the Court clarified, developed—and occasionally complicated—the law in a number of areas. When faced with apparently conflicting authorities, the Court was free to choose the direction in which the law was to develop, and in situations where the problem involved applying rules rather than interpreting them, it also enjoyed the luxury and burdens of choice.

The Court tended to be wary of extending the degree to which **equity** could be employed to alleviate the rigours of the **common law**. Thus in *Cowell v Rosehill Racecourse* (1937), only Evatt was prepared to draw upon equitable principles to mould adequate relief for a ticket holder wrongly ejected from a racecourse. The Court was, however, willing to allow scope for equity to operate in more traditional contexts. It upheld the setting aside of transactions flawed by the beneficiary having exercised **undue influence**, as against both the influential beneficiary and third parties who ought to have realised that a beneficiary was exercising undue influence (*Johnson v Buttress* (1936); *Yerkey v Jones* (1939); *Bank of NSW v Rogers* (1941); *Wilton v Farnworth* (1948)). In *Slee v Warke* (1949), it held that so long as a common intention existed, a written **contract** to the contrary could be rectified, notwithstanding the absence of an antecedent contract. In *Turner v Bladin* (1951) it was prepared to order specific performance in an action founded on *indebitatus assumpsit* (the old form of action for debt).

The Court was also prepared to apply and develop the common law so as to avoid clearly unjust results, as in *McRae v Commonwealth Disposals Commission* (1951), where the plaintiff was allowed to recover the expenses of a salvage expedition on which he had embarked in reliance on a contract for the sale of a non-existent tanker. In criminal cases, it extended the range of situations in which honest and reasonable mistake of fact could constitute a defence (*Thomas v The King* (1937); *Proudman v Dayman* (1941)). However, it was not willing to preserve or create artificial distinctions as a basis for achieving what might have been the just result in

particular cases (see, for instance, *Cowell*). And in accordance with English authority, the emerging **tort** of negligence was given only a narrow operation by the majority (over a notable dissent by Evatt) in *Chester v Waverley Corporation* (1939). The Court also (with Evatt again dissenting, joined in this instance by Rich) refused to recognise a tort of invasion of privacy (*Victoria Park Racing v Taylor* (1937)).

In **administrative law**, the Court's greatest contribution was Dixon's development of a coherent approach to **privative clauses** in *R v Hickman; Ex parte Fox and Clinton* (1945). In **constitutional law**, the Court struggled to develop a coherent interpretation of section 92 without ever achieving a consensus (see **Interstate trade and commerce**). In relation to **Commonwealth legislative powers**, its most important decision was the *Uniform Tax Case* (1942) which, by effectively allowing the Commonwealth to deprive the states of their capacity to levy income taxes, left the states critically weakened. Less dramatic in its immediate implications was *R v Burgess; Ex parte Henry* (1936), in which the Court began the process by which the **external affairs power** has come to be such a fruitful basis for the expansion of Commonwealth powers.

Historically, the significance of the Latham Court lies in its role in dealing with the legal dimensions of the great political and social issues generated by the period of war and post-war reconstruction (see **Defence power**; *Jehovah's Witnesses Case* (1943); **World War II**). Its most dramatic decisions were those which undermined the post-war plans of the Labor government. The *First Pharmaceutical Benefits Case* (1945) and the *Second Pharmaceutical Benefits Case* (1949) complicated Labor's attempt to establish a comprehensive health insurance scheme. *Australian National Airways v Commonwealth* (1945) and the *Bank Nationalisation Case* (1948) effectively precluded the nationalisation of entire industries. In 1945, the Court's perceived anti-Labor bias provoked a move to pack the Court by adding three more Justices, but nothing came of this, and Labor's sole appointee, Webb, was not—and was not perceived as—particularly sympathetic to Labor (see **Appointments that might have been**). In the *Communist Party Case* (1951), the Court struck down legislation that gave effect to a major plank in the Liberal–Country coalition's 1949 electoral platform. Latham was the sole dissenter. This was his last hurrah.

ROGER DOUGLAS

Further Reading

Roger Douglas, 'Judges and Policy on the Latham Court' (1969) 4 *Politics* 20

Clem Lloyd, 'Not Peace but a Sword! The High Court under JG Latham' (1987) 11 *Adel L Rev* 175

Laurence W Maher, 'Tales of the Overt and the Covert: Judges and Politics in Early Cold War Australia' (1993) 21 *FL Rev* 151

Law-making role: reflections. The central function of the courts is the adjudication of disputes. However, in the **common law** system, the adjudication of disputes necessarily involves the creation of rules and standards by reference to which disputes are to be resolved. The creation of such rules and standards may be seen as legislative in character, as indeed it is when undertaken by the legislature. When undertaken by the courts, it is seen as an exercise of the courts' law-making **role**.

Courts—more particularly appellate courts and even more so the High Court—make law in many situations: when they interpret a constitution or a statute; when they enunciate, extend, or qualify a common law rule or principle; even when they apply a rule to a new fact situation. The extent of the courts' law-making activities may be gauged from the vast corpus of law contained within the ever-expanding volumes of *Halsbury's Laws*. Virtually every judgment of the High Court makes law.

Judicial law-making is strongly constrained by judicial respect for **precedent** and by other factors, including the **separation of powers**, the need for certainty or predicability in the law, and the fact that courts are ill-equipped to engage in major law reform activity (*State Government Insurance Commission v Trigwell* (1979)). When an appeal lay from the High Court to the **Privy Council**, the High Court was bound by decisions of the Privy Council. Since the appeal was abolished in 1975, the High Court has no longer been so bound. As the High Court has never considered itself to be bound by its prior decisions, it is not as constrained by precedent as other courts that are bound by the decisions of higher courts or by their own prior decisions.

Although the Court has power to review and depart from its previous decisions, such a course is not lightly undertaken (*Second* **Territory Senators Case** (1977); *John v FCT* (1989)). Four matters have been identified as justifying the **overruling** of earlier High Court decisions. The first is that the earlier decisions do not rest upon a principle carefully worked out in a significant succession of cases. The second is a difference between the reasons of the Justices constituting the majority in an earlier decision. The third is that earlier decisions have achieved no useful result, but on the contrary have led to considerable inconvenience. The fourth is that earlier decisions have not been independently acted on in a manner that militates against reconsideration (*Commonwealth v Hospital Contribution Fund* (1982); *John v FCT*).

In **constitutional law**, the policy of *stare decisis* (adherence to decided precedents) has less force than elsewhere because Parliament cannot rectify the consequences of a decision on the Constitution (*Perpetual Executors and Trustees Association of Australia v FCT* (1949); *Second Territory Senators Case*; see **Amendment of Constitution**). There is a tension between the paramount judicial responsibility to give effect to the text of the Constitution, not the **judicial reasoning**, and the principle of *stare decisis*—a tension brought out by **Windeyer** in *Damjanovic & Sons v Commonwealth* (1968). That tension is heightened by a concern that the authority of the Court will be weakened if it departs too readily from its earlier decisions.

In the context of judicial law-making, **constitutional interpretation** and **statutory interpretation** differ from decisions on the common law. In matters of interpretation, the function of the Justice is restricted; it is essentially to decide what the words of the Constitution or the statute mean. In discharging this function, although the Justices are not at liberty to depart from the policy of the Constitution or the statute, they may apply a purposive rather than a literal interpretation and have regard to **extrinsic** evidence (see, as to statutes, *Acts Interpretation Act* 1901 (Cth) sections 15AA

and 15AB). They may also apply presumptions, one of which is that a statute will not be read as abrogating or curtailing a right or value protected by the common law, such as liberty of the individual or freedom of expression, unless there is an unambiguous indication of intention to do so (*Coco v The Queen* (1994)).

On occasions, the Court has engaged in major shifts in constitutional interpretation. An early example was the famous rejection of the doctrine of implied **intergovernmental immunities** and the adoption of a more literal approach to constitutional interpretation (the *Engineers Case* (1920)). More recent examples were the rejection of earlier interpretations of section 92 in favour of the view that the section prohibits discriminatory burdens of a protectionist kind (*Cole v Whitfield* (1988)) and the implication of a freedom of communication as to government and political matters that enables the people to exercise a free and informed choice as electors (*Australian Capital Television v Commonwealth* (1992); *Lange v ABC* (1997); see *Free Speech Cases*; **Political communication**). *Street v Queensland Bar Association* (1989) and *Ha v NSW* (1997) are other cases that departed from earlier decisions (see respectively **Discrimination** and **Excise duties**).

Major shifts in statutory interpretation rarely occur, perhaps because an unacceptable judicial interpretation can be reversed by the legislature. But if an appellate court is convinced that a previous interpretation is plainly erroneous, it cannot allow previous error to stand in the way of declaring the true intent of the legislature (*John v FCT*).

Criticism on the ground that High Court decisions amount to judicial legislation has mainly been directed to decisions on the common law. In declaring and formulating common law rules, the judicial function is less restricted than it is in matters of interpretation. The function will extend, where appropriate, to an evaluation of relevant **policy considerations** and to taking account of the enduring **values** of the community (*Mabo* (1992); *Dietrich v The Queen* (1992)). But it has been said that policy considerations cannot justify abrupt or arbitrary change involving the abandonment of settled principle in favour of a result perceived as desirable (*Breen v Williams* (1996)). In other words, the courts should not fracture 'the skeleton of principle' (*Mabo*). It is because the Justice's function in articulating common law rules is less restricted that the judicial function in this area more closely resembles the legislative function, thereby generating controversy.

Various models of judicial law-making have been advanced without attracting general acceptance. One model is that judicial law-making can be undertaken only when it proceeds upon the basis of a community consensus as to the values to be applied. So judges do not engage in major reforms; the changes they make are generally incremental, involve 'lawyer's law', and relate to matters where legislatures rarely intervene.

Another model, favoured by Ronald Dworkin, is that judges make decisions according to the rights that persons have, not on the basis of what is best for the collective welfare (*Taking Rights Seriously* (1978)). A third model recognises that there is no essential difference between judicial and legislative law-making except that judicial law-making is confined to gaps or interstices in the law, and that the rule enunciated must fit within the existing rules of law (John Bell, *Policy Arguments in Judicial Decisions* (1983)).

Attempts have been made to distinguish the judicial function from the legislative function by suggesting that judicial reasoning proceeds by way of analogy and induction rather than deduction. But this is too narrow a view. In *R v L* (1991), the Court held, contrary to what had long been thought, that a husband could be guilty of the rape of his wife. The old view was unsuited to today's circumstances, conditions, and values—a point strongly made by the **House of Lords** in its decision on the same question (*R v R* (1991)).

In *Environment Protection Authority v Caltex Refining* (1993), **Deane**, **Dawson**, and **Gaudron** suggested that if the desire to deny the privilege against self-incrimination to natural persons or corporations tends to be 'dictated by pragmatism rather than principle, then it is more appropriately a matter for the legislature than the courts'. This statement appears to recognise that there is no essential distinction between judicial and legislative law-making, but that some aspects are better left to the legislature than the courts. In similar vein, in *Breen v Williams* (1996), Dawson and **Toohey** said: 'There is more than one view upon the matter and the choice between those views, if a choice is to be made, is appropriately for the legislature rather than the court.'

Lord Goff of Chieveley acknowledged, as this writer would, that he never quite knew where to locate the boundary between legitimate judicial development of the law and legislation (*Woolwich Equitable Building Society v IRC* (1992)). His Lordship pointed out that if the boundary were to be too tightly drawn, *Donoghue v Stevenson* (1932), modern **judicial review**, and *Mareva* injunctions would not have taken place. Location of the boundary in a given case appears to be a matter of discretion or value judgment rather than principle. And leaving the matter to the legislature may, in some cases, create an impression of wishing to avoid controversy.

There have been conspicuous instances of judicial law-making in recent times. *Mabo* recognised for the first time **native title** in certain unalienated Crown lands. As the Court had not previously decided the question, it was at liberty, if not bound, to decide the question for itself. By doing so, the Court brought the Australian common law more in line with the common law as it had developed in relation to indigenous land rights in Canada, NZ, and the USA. Another decision was *Dietrich v The Queen*, where the Court held that an indigent accused person charged with a serious offence could apply for a stay of proceedings to enable legal representation to be provided by the state. This entitlement was held to be an element in the accused's right to a fair trial.

Other decisions have developed the principles of **equity** and **contract**: *Taylor v Johnson* (1983) on mistake; *Amadio's Case* (1983) on **unconscionable** conduct; *Waltons Stores v Maher* (1988) on **estoppel**; *Legione v Hateley* (1983) on rescission of contract and relief against forfeiture; and *Trident General Insurance v McNiece* (1988) on privity of contract. There has also been an array of decisions on **administrative law** and the general duty of care in negligence, one effect of which has been to subsume the particular duties owned to specific categories of entrants upon premises into the general duty of care (*Australian Safeway Stores v Zaluzna* (1987); see **Occupiers' liability**). A number

of these decisions have endeavoured to achieve greater symmetry in the law.

ANTHONY MASON

Further Reading

John Doyle, 'Implications of Judicial Law-Making' in Cheryl Saunders (ed), *Courts of Final Jurisdiction* (1996) 84

Anthony Lester, 'English Judges as Law Makers' [1993] *Public Law* 269

Michael McHugh, 'The Law-making Function of the Judicial Process' (1988) 62 *ALJ* 15 (Part 1), 116 (Part 2)

Lord Reid, 'The Judge as Lawmaker' (1972) 12 *Journal of Public Teachers of Law* 22

Law-making role: further reflections. From one point of view, the Court engages in a law-making **role** in almost every case. It is now generally accepted that a court makes law when it applies an existing rule to a new set of circumstances, or develops a settled principle, or gives a definitive meaning to an ambiguous statute. The claim that in such a case a court is merely finding and declaring the law is now regarded as a fairy tale. In that sense, a court makes law where it does anything more than apply an established principle to facts of a kind to which it had already been held to be applicable. It follows that the High Court makes law by most of its decisions, since the nature of its **jurisdiction** is such that a case rarely calls for the routine application of a settled principle to a familiar class of facts.

More obviously, a court engages in law-making when by its decision it abandons established principle or refuses to follow clear **precedents** of its own. The law-making role of the Court, in this latter sense, has been freely exercised in the course of **constitutional interpretation**. In many cases, the Court has **overruled** earlier authority and given a new meaning to provisions of the Constitution (see, for example, the *Engineers Case* (1920); *Strickland v Rocla Concrete Pipes* (1971); *Cole v Whitfield* (1988); *Street v Queensland Bar Association* (1989); *Ha v NSW* (1997)). Although there is no doubt that the individual opinions of the Justices have influenced these decisions, they may be justified on the view that the first loyalty of the Court is to the Constitution and that the Court's conclusion as to the correct interpretation of the Constitution must prevail over earlier, erroneous decisions. On the other hand, some Justices have felt bound to follow decisions they believed to be erroneous. Thus in the *Second Territory Senators Case* (1977), two Justices followed the *First Territory Senators Case* (1975) although they disagreed with that decision, whereas two other Justices refused to follow it. There is no fixed rule that governs the question whether an earlier constitutional decision should be reconsidered.

In some cases, the Court makes law by enunciating a new constitutional principle in a case not governed by previous authority—for example, by finding in the words of the Constitution an implication whose existence was not previously suspected, as the Court did in *Australian Capital Television v Commonwealth* (1992) and other cases considered in *Lange v ABC* (1997) (see *Free Speech Cases*; **Political communication**).

Although some of these decisions have given rise to controversy, the question of the limits that should be observed by the Court in exercising a law-making role arises more frequently in relation to the rules of **common law** and **equity** than in cases of constitutional interpretation. Development of principle must necessarily occur, but the traditional doctrine is that it should be predictable and consistent; the Court's conclusion should not be subjective or personal to the Justices. The Court may, as Chief Justice **Dixon** suggested, 'extend the application of accepted principles to new cases or … reason from the more fundamental of settled legal principles to new conclusions or … decide that a category is not closed against unforeseen instances which in reason might be subsumed thereunder', but should not 'deliberately … abandon [long accepted legal] principle in the name of justice, or of social necessity or of social convenience'. In other words, the law may be developed by logic and analogy, but should not be changed simply because altered social conditions or community **values** seem to require a change.

This view has more recently been rejected by some Justices in favour of the theory that the Court may differ from a settled principle if it regards it as operating unsatisfactorily or unjustly, particularly if it is thought to be outmoded and unsuited to modern conditions or inconsistent with contemporary values. Clearly, when the law allows a discretionary judgment to be made, a court must exercise its judgment in the light of contemporary values and beliefs. Thus the question whether a publication is defamatory, a performance is obscene, or an action is negligent, must be decided according to the values of the day. There are, however, a number of objections to the assertion that a new principle of law may be created or an old one rejected to give effect to the Court's subjective notions of justice or to what the Court believes to be the values of the time. To decide in that way introduces an element of uncertainty into the law, whereas certainty—or at least a reasonable predictability—is an essential feature of any sound legal system. To frame a rule that will do justice, it is often necessary to weigh conflicting considerations, and in many cases this can be done most efficiently by the legislature, since a court is ill-equipped to inform itself of all the matters that should be taken into account in determining **policy** or to predict the social and **economic** consequences of its judgments. It is not always clear what are the contemporary values of Australian society, and there is a temptation for Justices to think that their own values are generally accepted.

Two cases in particular illustrate the difficulties of making the law on the basis of a subjective judgment. In *Dietrich v The Queen* (1992), the Court held that a person accused of a serious offence would not generally have a fair trial unless he or she had legal representation. Here, the Court had to balance the desirability of legal representation against the expense to the community of providing it and the consequences of adjourning or of aborting trials where representation is not provided. It may be thought that the government concerned—with its knowledge of the resources of and demands on the Treasury and on the judicial system—is better able to make such a judgment.

In *Mabo* (1992), the Court held that the common law recognised **native title**. In doing so, it departed from principles that had been settled for over a century, but which the Justices regarded as unjust and discriminatory, and at variance with contemporary values. It may be argued that the community was deeply divided on the question, and that the Court was not well placed to weigh the claims to native title against other conflicting interests, particularly since the legal and social consequences of the decision were unpredictable.

Other cases in which the Court has made a pronounced departure from settled principle because the authorities on which it was based were regarded as unsatisfactory include *Trident General Insurance v McNiece* (1988), *David Securities v Commonwealth Bank* (1992), *Bryan v Maloney* (1995), and *Northern Sandblasting v Harris* (1997). In a rather different category is *R v L* (1991), because the earlier authorities there considered were not so compelling.

In some other cases, the law-making activity of the Court, although exercised courageously, may be regarded as complying with the traditional theory of legal development. In *Waltons Stores v Maher* (1988), the Court extended the doctrine of promissory **estoppel** to allow the enforcement of voluntary promises, but did so by relying on the equitable rules regarding **unconscionable** conduct. The Court has subsumed special rules under the general principles of negligence (*Australian Safeway Stores v Zaluzna* (1987); *Burnie Port Authority v General Jones* (1994); see **Occupiers' liability**). Also, where no precedent covers the situation before the Court, the Court must of necessity make law. *Marion's Case* (1992) was one of this kind.

There is no doubt that the Court will continue to exercise its law-making role, and in doing so will develop the fundamental principles of the common law; but as **Mason** said in *State Government Insurance Commission v Trigwell* (1979), there are powerful reasons why the Court should be reluctant to depart from a settled rule and replace it with a new rule. The suggestion has been made that there are procedural limitations which are sufficient to confine judicial law-making within proper grounds; limitations of that kind are only as effectual as the Justices wish them to be, as *Mabo* illustrated. The limits to the law-making power of the Justices are to be found in the Constitution, existing statutes, and the fundamental principles of the common law. It is not their role to reshape those laws to make them consistent with their own ideas of justice or with what they think are contemporary values.

Harry Gibbs

Further Reading

Daryl Dawson, 'Do Judges Make Law? Too Much?' (1996) 3 *Jud Rev* 1

Owen Dixon, 'Concerning Judicial Method' (1956) 29 *ALJ* 468, reprinted in SHZ Woinarski (ed), *Jesting Pilate* (1965) 152

Michael Kirby, 'Judicial Activism' (1998) 16 *Aust Bar Rev* 10

Michael McHugh, 'The Judicial Method' (1999) 73 *ALJ* 37

Leave to appeal. By section 73 of the Constitution, the High Court's **jurisdiction** to hear and determine appeals from all judgments, decrees, **orders**, and sentences of Justices exercising its original jurisdiction, of federal courts and courts exercising federal jurisdiction, and of the Supreme Courts of the states, is conferred 'with such exceptions and subject to such regulations as the Parliament prescribes'. No such exception or regulation, however, was to prevent the Court from hearing and determining an appeal from a **state Supreme Court**

if, at federation, an appeal lay from that Court to the Judicial Committee of the **Privy Council**.

Appeals from state Supreme Courts were at first the major part of the Court's appellate jurisdiction, and the *Judiciary Act* 1903 (Cth) initially provided for appeals as of right from final judgments of Supreme Courts in civil matters where the monetary sum involved or the value of the matter at issue was £300 or more; where any **property** or civil right of that value was directly or indirectly involved; or where the outcome might affect a person's status under laws relating to aliens, marriage, divorce, bankruptcy, or insolvency. Leave to appeal was required in cases where the judgment appealed from was interlocutory, even if it otherwise satisfied those criteria. Special leave was required in all other civil cases; it has always been required in criminal cases. Apart from some increases in the monetary amounts involved, these requirements were unchanged for 70 years.

With the movement towards abolition of appeals to the Privy Council—the High Court becoming in consequence the final appellate court for Australia—and with the establishment of the large federal courts (the **Federal Court** and the Family Court), legislative changes culminating in the *Judiciary Amendment Act (No 2)* 1984 (Cth) brought about a radically different situation. No appeal now lies to the High Court as of right from a decision of the Supreme Court of a state; special leave to appeal must be obtained from the High Court (Judiciary Act, section 35(2)). A similar situation obtains in relation to the Federal Court (*Federal Court of Australia Act* 1976 (Cth), section 33(3)) and the Family Court (*Family Law Act* 1975 (Cth), section 95(a)). There is an exception in the case of the Family Court, since section 95(b) of the Family Law Act allows the Full Court of the Family Court to grant a certificate that an important question of law or public interest is involved (see *DJL v Central Authority* (2000)). No appeal lies to the High Court from a judgment of a federal Magistrates Court (*Federal Magistrates Act* 1999 (Cth), section 20(1)). Appeals from the Supreme Courts of the **territories** also require special leave (Judiciary Act, section 35AA; Federal Court of Australia Act, section 24(2)). Leave, as distinct from special leave, remains as a requirement for appeal from an interlocutory judgment of a Justice or Justices exercising the Court's original jurisdiction (Judiciary Act, section 34(2)). Such appeals are now rare. The High Court may also grant special leave to appeal from *any* court of a state exercising invested federal jurisdiction, notwithstanding that the law of the state may prohibit any appeal from that court (Judiciary Act, section 39(2)(c)).

The constitutional validity of the requirement for special leave to appeal was upheld in *Smith Kline & French Laboratories v Commonwealth* (1991) in relation to the Federal Court, and in *Carson v John Fairfax & Sons* (1991) in relation to the Supreme Courts of the states.

The requirement for special leave means that the High Court has a discretion to choose the appeals it will hear. The selection of the cases in which special leave is granted identifies the areas in which the law may be changed or confirmed, and also the possible extent and pace of any change. For example, one result of the expanded requirement for special leave is that criminal appeals have become a significantly larger part of the Court's work (see **Business of Court**). The mix of cases plays a part in determining the extent to which the Court attracts a description such as **activist** or conservative.

Cases where special leave to appeal is granted fall into two broad categories—those in which a sufficiently important legal issue is involved, and those where there has been a significant irregularity in the way in which the matter was dealt with in the courts below (*Morris v The Queen* (1987); *Smith Kline & French*; *Carson*). The second category has been of particular importance in criminal cases, but is also important in ensuring that civil cases at all levels are conducted according to law (see, for example, *State Rail Authority of NSW v Earthline Constructions* (1999)). The Judiciary Act, by section 35A, requires that the Court, in determining whether to grant special leave, shall have regard to whether the proceedings involve a question of law of public importance, or one on which a High Court decision is needed to resolve differences of judicial opinion; and to whether a judgment already given requires consideration by the High Court in 'the interests of the administration of justice, either generally or in the particular case'. In most cases, special leave is granted only where a point of law of importance is involved.

Applicants for special leave ordinarily need to demonstrate that the issue they seek to agitate is of sufficient importance to merit the grant of special leave; that the case is a suitable vehicle for the resolution of that issue; and that their contentions on that issue are sufficiently arguable.

A case may not give rise to an issue of sufficient importance if it involves only a question of construction of a particular contract, or of a statute of limited application, or a question that is otherwise unlikely to arise again, or if the decision sought to be appealed from is interlocutory, or if in reality only a question of fact is involved. A case may not be a 'suitable vehicle' if the resolution of the issue is not essential to the ultimate determination of the litigation, or is premature, or if the necessary findings of fact have not been made, or have been made against the applicant (so that an appeal would also be necessary on the factual issue). Special leave will not be granted if the decision appealed from is not sufficiently attended by doubt. Even if the reasoning of the court below may be dubious, special leave will not be granted if the *result* arrived at by that court is not sufficiently in doubt.

An application for special leave may be dealt with by the Court on the papers if no party seeks to be heard by oral **argument**. Oral argument is limited to 20 minutes for each party, with five minutes for an applicant's reply. The Court can, but rarely does, extend the time. At the oral hearing, the Court endeavours to get to the heart of the case as quickly as possible. The two (occasionally three) Justices hearing the application have read the written arguments before the hearing. Sometimes the respondent will be called on first. Sometimes the respondent is not called on at all.

The Court does not usually give reasons for granting special leave, although the reasons should be obvious enough from the dialogue that has taken place. Instead, the presiding Justice will say: 'There will be a grant of special leave in this matter', or something along the lines: 'There will be a grant of special leave limited to Grounds 1 and 2 in the draft notice of appeal filed in support of the application.' When refusing special leave, the Court gives short reasons such as: 'The decision in the Court below is not attended by sufficient doubt to merit the grant of special leave', or: 'The case is no more than an attempt to reagitate an issue of fact, and involves no question of law meriting the attention of this Court'. The decision is normally given immediately following the conclusion of oral argument.

Special leave may be granted on terms. It may be a condition of special leave that the applicant pay the respondent's **costs** of the appeal in any event, or that the costs orders below not be disturbed if the appeal succeeds. Again, a course sometimes adopted by the Court, particularly if the applicant seeks to **overrule** one of the Court's earlier decisions, is to refer the application for special leave to a Bench of seven Justices. On the hearing of that application before the larger Bench, the parties have to be prepared to argue the matter as if on appeal.

A grant of special leave may be rescinded at, or before, the hearing of an appeal. Its importance may have disappeared—as where the statute giving rise to the issue has been repealed or amended. Closer examination of the case by the Court may also make it apparent that only a question of fact is involved.

The view adopted by the Court is that until the grant of special leave, 'there are no proceedings *inter partes* before the Court' (*A-G (Cth) v Finch (No 2)* (1984)). This means that refusal of an application for special leave does not produce a final judgment, and does not preclude the reopening of the application (*DJL v Central Authority*). Although attempts to reopen applications for special leave to appeal are very unusual, they are sometimes successful. Exceptional circumstances must be shown (*Aston v The Queen* (1995); *Burnell v The Queen* (1995); *Cachia v St George Bank* (1993)).

The number of special leave applications heard each year has been increasing; in the 1999–2000 financial year, 275 civil and 112 criminal applications were decided. Of these, 52 civil and 14 criminal applications succeeded. Many applications are now heard by video link with the Court **sitting** in **Canberra**, one or more of the parties being in another capital city. While cases may sometimes be won by oral argument 'on the day', in general the importance of the written argument has increased.

Respondents, as well as appellants, may require special leave to appeal. When a respondent desires to appeal from part of the judgment below or to vary part of that judgment, special leave to proceed with a cross-appeal is necessary. The leave may be sought at the hearing of the appeal, but it is not granted as a matter of course (*DPP v United Telecasters Sydney* (1990)).

DAVID JACKSON

Further Reading

David Jackson, 'Appellate Advocacy' (1991) 8 *Aust Bar Rev* 245

David Jackson, 'Practice in the High Court of Australia' (1997) 15 *Aust Bar Rev* 187

Anthony Mason, 'The Regulation of Appeals to the High Court of Australia: The Jurisdiction to Grant Special Leave to Appeal' (1996) 15 *U Tas LR* 1

David O'Brien, *Special Leave to Appeal* (1996)

David Solomon, 'Controlling the High Court's Agenda' (1993) 23 *UWAL Rev* 33

Leeth v Commonwealth (1992). People jailed for offences against Commonwealth law are generally housed in state jails, as envisaged by section 120 of the Constitution. Although later amended, section 4 of the *Commonwealth Prisoners Act 1967* (Cth) provided that, on sentencing federal offenders, judges should fix a minimum non-parole period by applying the practices of the relevant state. The rationale was that a single parole regime applied to all inmates in the state would minimise conflict in prisons. However, a further consequence was that federal prisoners' parole expectations would vary—often greatly—depending on the state in which they were convicted.

Richard Leeth was convicted under the *Customs Act* 1901 (Cth) for importing cannabis in commercial quantities; he was sentenced to 25 years imprisonment. Applying section 4 and the law of Queensland, a minimum non-parole period of 14 years was set. Leeth challenged the validity of section 4 in the High Court, claiming that it violated a constitutional requirement of equal treatment under the law.

Arguably, a majority in the case—**Brennan**, **Deane**, **Toohey**, and **Gaudron**—supported an approach which drew from the Constitution an implication of a doctrine of legal **equality**. There were three bases for the implication.

The first argument asserted a right to procedural equality in proceedings before courts exercising jurisdiction under Chapter III of the Constitution. This was said to flow from a requirement implicit in the **separation of powers** not only that all Commonwealth power of a judicial nature must be vested in 'courts', but that the power so vested must be exercised in a judicial manner, which obliges 'a court to extend to the parties before it equal justice … and to refrain from **discrimination** on irrelevant or irrational grounds'. This was most fully expounded by Gaudron, who found section 4 unconstitutional on this ground. **Mason**, **Dawson**, and **McHugh** also indicated a willingness to see processes that respect **natural justice** as 'fundamental' to the exercise of **judicial power**.

The second argument asserted a right of all citizens to equal treatment by Commonwealth laws implied from the free agreement of the people to unite in one Commonwealth under the Constitution. **Isaacs** had stated in the *Skin Wool Case* (1926) that 'it is the duty of this Court, as the chief judicial organ of the Commonwealth, to take **judicial notice**, in interpreting the Australian Constitution, of every fundamental constitutional doctrine existing and fully recognized at the time the Constitution was passed'. In *Leeth*, Deane and Toohey quoted this passage, and continued: 'The doctrine of legal equality is in the forefront of those doctrines.' They then sought to tie this principle into a foundation constructed from the **common law**, saying:

> Putting to one side the position of the Crown and some past anomalies, notably, discriminatory treatment of **women**, the essential or underlying theoretical equality of all persons under the law and before the courts is and has been a fundamental and generally beneficial doctrine of the common law and a basic prescript of the administration of justice under our system of government.

Deane and Toohey then held that this common law principle of 'equality of all persons under the law' could be derived by necessary implication from the Constitution, and therefore that it acted as a limitation on legislative power. They held that this limitation invalidates Commonwealth laws that fail to recognise equality by discriminating against a class of persons on irrelevant or unreasonable grounds, except where the express words of the Constitution authorise or contemplate such discrimination. According to Deane and Toohey, this principle is implicit in the free agreement of the people to the Constitution, as recited in the preamble and in section 3 of the *Commonwealth of Australia Constitution Act* 1900 (Imp). They struck down section 4 of the Commonwealth Prisoners Act because there was no 'rational and relevant basis for the discriminatory treatment' that it brought about.

Similarly, Brennan saw equality under law as implicit in 'the constitutional unity of the Australian people "in one indissoluble Federal Commonwealth"'. However, he declined to find section 4 unconstitutional. He suggested that the plaintiff might have succeeded if section 4 had prescribed different maximum penalties for the same offence.

The third argument relied on the existence of a number of specific provisions that were said to reflect a general doctrine of legal equality. Deane and Toohey cited sections of the Constitution that attempt to facilitate equality in the operation of Commonwealth laws, including provisions prohibiting discrimination between people of different states (sections 51(ii) and (iii), 86, 88, 90, and 99), the guarantee of direct suffrage and equality of voting rights for all those already recognised as qualified to vote (sections 24 and 25), and the guarantee that no religious test be required as a qualification for public office (section 116). To these could be added the constitutional dynamic towards greater equality expressed in constitutional **amendments**, which have removed provisions authorising discrimination against **Aboriginal peoples**. Deane and Toohey argued that 'once it is appreciated that it is the ordinary approach of the Constitution not to spell out the fundamental common law principles upon which it is structured', the absence or presence of specific provisions bearing on the issue will merely provide examples of, or limits to, the doctrine of legal equality. Such provisions cannot affect the fundamental implication of the principle itself.

While Mason, Dawson, and McHugh found that there might be some limitations on the way a court might be required to exercise its powers, they strongly rejected any constitutionally implied guarantee of equality. They held that there is nothing in the Constitution that requires Commonwealth laws to have a uniform operation throughout Australia.

Brennan joined Mason, Dawson, and McHugh in holding section 4 valid. Therefore, the section was upheld by a majority of 4:3.

Leeth proved intensely controversial in its suggestion that the Constitution might, by implication, incorporate some form of equality. In *Kruger v Commonwealth* (1997), the approach of Deane and Toohey in *Leeth* was rejected by a majority of the High Court. The Court did, however, leave open the correctness of the more limited approaches of Brennan and Gaudron.

CHRISTINE PARKER
GEORGE WILLIAMS

Further Reading
Michael Detmold, 'The New Constitutional Law' (1994) 16 *Syd LR* 228
Christine Parker, 'Protection of Judicial Process as an Implied Constitutional Principle' (1994) 16 *Adel L Rev* 341
Fiona Wheeler, 'The Doctrine of Separation of Powers and Constitutionally Entrenched Due Process in Australia' (1997) 23 *Mon LR* 248

Leeth v Commonwealth: a critical analysis. In *Leeth*, **Deane** and **Toohey** (jointly), and **Gaudron**, supported an approach which drew an implication of 'substantive **equality**' from the Constitution. With the greatest of respect, the reasons given in their judgments lacked substance. They failed to deal adequately or at all with arguments against the implication. Their judgments contained illogical inferences and referred to materials that, when examined in their full contexts, give no support to the uses made of them.

This is particularly disturbing given the enormous consequences that such an implication would have. In the version proposed by Deane and Toohey, the implication would give the High Court a veto on any Commonwealth legislation—and also (given the reliance on Chapter III) on any state legislation—which distinguishes between persons on grounds not considered by the Court to be 'rational and relevant' having regard to the nature of the powers being exercised. (They seem to have meant 'relevant and sufficient' rather than 'rational and relevant'.) The implication would be serious enough even if limited (as Gaudron held) to legislation conferring discretionary powers on courts, or if limited (as **Brennan** suggested) to legislation discriminating on geographical grounds.

Whether it would be desirable for the High Court to have such powers (as the **United States Supreme Court** has, though with an explicit textual basis), is questionable (see, for example, Frank Brennan, *Legislating Liberty—A Bill of Rights for Australia* (1998)). However, that issue is irrelevant to an evaluation of the *Leeth* judgments unless there is sufficient uncertainty to justify resort to such considerations as a 'tie breaker'. No such uncertainty was demonstrated in any of the *Leeth* judgments (and none exists). For instance, Deane and Toohey said that **judicial power** under Chapter III is a power to do 'justice' and that Chapter III therefore does not permit the courts to apply laws that 'discriminate' between persons. Gaudron similarly saw Chapter III as precluding substantive laws under which exercises of judicial discretion would have discriminatory results. This argument ignores the fact that a judge's duty is to do justice 'according to law'—that is, *valid* law—and cannot yield any criteria for the validity of a substantive law. The vesting of federal judicial power in courts does not justify the conclusion that legislative powers to make laws for the 'peace, order, and good government' of the Commonwealth or a state are subject to an implied requirement of substantive equality in any of its claimed versions.

Deane and Toohey asserted that a 'general doctrine of legal equality' not limited to procedural matters was implied since it is a 'fundamental and generally beneficial doctrine of the **common law**' and the **framers** envisaged the Constitution as embodying such doctrines. This proposition is belied by the materials cited. One example is the incorrect assertion that AV Dicey's **rule of law** included a concept of substantive equality. There is also the remarkable proposition that **discrimination** against **women** should be 'put to one side' as an 'anomalous' exception. It defies belief that the Constitution was intended to imply a requirement of substantive equality on the basis of a common law that denied such equality between half the population and the other half, and made unjust distinctions between many other categories of people.

Equally unconvincing is the proposition by Deane and Toohey that no impediment to the implication was created by the express provisions of the Constitution that prohibit various kinds of discrimination (sections 51(ii) and (iii), 92, 99, and 117). They brushed these aside with the remark that the maxim *expressio unius est exclusio alterius* (the express mention of one thing is the exclusion of the other) can be a 'dangerous master'. What was needed was a balanced examination of the contexts relevant to the application of that maxim. It is wholly unpersuasive to see the express provisions as merely manifestations of a general underlying requirement of substantive equality. As Leslie Zines has pointed out, this is like arguing that the express powers of the federal Parliament are manifestations of a general legislative power.

If the Court had endorsed the implication it would have been a most serious usurpation of the powers of the elected parliaments and of the people (in referendums). However, at least in the broad form stated by Deane and Toohey, it was clearly rejected in *Kruger v Commonwealth* (1997) by a majority, including **Dawson** and **Gummow**, whose judgments include trenchant criticisms of the claimed implication.

DENNIS ROSE

Further Reading
Dennis Rose, 'Judicial Reasonings and Responsibilities in Constitutional Cases' (1994) 20 *Mon LR* 195

Legalism. The dominant theme of the **judicial style** of the Court for much of the twentieth century and the antithesis of **realism**, legalism was openly embraced as a judicial virtue by **Dixon** on the occasion of his swearing-in as **Chief Justice** in 1952. 'There is no other guide to judicial decisions in matters of great conflict', he said, 'than strict and complete legalism'.

The meaning of these often-quoted words can be fully appreciated only by considering the historical context in which they were uttered. The Court had the previous year decided the *Communist Party Case* (1951), in which legislation banning the Communist Party was invalidated. Dixon had been in the majority. A constitutional alteration to reverse the effect of that decision proposed by the government of Robert **Menzies** had just been defeated in a referendum. Yet the same government had chosen to appoint Dixon as Chief Justice. The 'matters of great conflict' to which Dixon referred would have been immediately apparent to those attending his swearing-in. So too would have been the poignancy of Dixon's prefatory remark that 'close adherence to legal reasoning is the only way to maintain the confidence of all parties in Federal conflicts'.

Legalism was never a denial of the practical impact of the Court's decisions, nor of the political character of the consid-erations informing those decisions. It was rather an approach to judicial **decision making** that relied on the strict analytical and conceptual techniques of formal legal argument to form an interpretive judgment as to the meaning of a constitutional or statutory text or the scope of a judicial **precedent**. The **role** of the Court was to ascertain that meaning and then simply to apply it to the circumstances of the case at hand. Dixon explained that 'the Court's sole function' in constitutional adjudication was 'to interpret a constitutional description of power or restraint upon power and say whether a given measure falls on one side of a line constitutionally so drawn or the other'. The question was not whether the considerations bearing on the formation of such a judgment were political, for as Dixon also explained in the *Melbourne Corporation Case* (1947), 'nearly every consideration arising from the Constitution can be so described'. The question was whether they were 'compelling'.

The function of the Court was to declare, not to make, the law. However, legalism was not confined to **literalism**. The Court was not limited in the process of interpretation to a consideration of the letter of the text. Implications were to be drawn where (but only where) they were perceived to be inherent in its language or structure. Nor did legalism involve a slavish adherence to precedent. Earlier decisions were to be **overruled** when considered to be in error. The search was in all cases for legal truth. That legal truth was to be found within the body of the **authoritative legal materials** as correctly understood. It was not to be found in social or **economic** policy. The role of the Court was essentially one of revelation: to discern and expound the law. The law existed independently of its exposition. There was perceived to be a 'definite system of accepted knowledge or thought': 'judgments and other legal writings' were merely 'evidence of its contents'. Within that system of knowledge or thought, there was no room for **policy considerations** and no scope for choice in judicial decision making. Divergences in judicial opinion were attributed to differences in perception and not to differences in **values**. To the extent that the law might have appeared to develop over time, this was properly explained as nothing more than the result of its interstitial and incremental revelation.

Legalism reached its apogee in the period of the **Dixon Court** and continued to be influential for some time afterwards. It was repeatedly espoused (though not always implemented) by Chief Justice **Barwick**; Chief Justice **Gibbs**, however, was prepared to acknowledge a limited role for judicial creativity. The influence of legalism waned markedly in the period of the **Mason Court**. Chief Justice **Mason** in particular came to be a strong advocate of the recognition of the inevitability of policy choices in judicial decision making. The death knell for legalism was sounded (at least in its traditional form) in a series of decisions notably including *Cole v Whitfield* (1988), *Mabo* (1992), and *Dietrich v The Queen* (1992) in which the High Court, while continuing to apply analytical and conceptual techniques, more openly acknowledged the policy choices being made.

As subsequently explained by Chief Justice **Brennan** on the occasion of his **retirement**, the central flaw in legalism lay in its presupposition of the existence of law as a system of knowledge or thought independent of its exposition. The reality is that law 'is not an ever-expanding cosmos containing rules for the solution of the problems of every generation and awaiting only a judicial telescope to capture their text. As each generation faces new problems, the rules must be crafted by the judges of the time'. Contrary to the central premise of legalism, the evaluation and development of legal principle in the light of contemporary needs and values is now almost universally recognised and accepted as the legitimate and pre-eminent role of the Court.

STEPHEN GAGELER

Further Reading
Stephen Gageler, 'Foundations of Australian Federalism and the Role of Judicial Review' (1987) 17 *FL Rev* 162
Jeremy Kirk, 'Constitutional Interpretation and a Theory of Evolutionary Originalism' (1999) 27 *FL Rev* 323

Legal profession, Court's relationship with. Since the first **sitting** of the High Court in Melbourne on 6 October 1903, the Court has had a strong commitment to establishing and maintaining a social as well as a legal relationship with the legal profession, from which **appointments** to the Court are drawn (see **Background of Justices**). Section 10 of the *Judiciary Act* 1903 (Cth) contemplated that the principal **seat** of the Court be at the seat of government or at such place as the Governor-General appointed. Melbourne was appointed. It followed that from the beginning, the Court established close links with the profession in Melbourne. The Court also frequently sat in Sydney, and likewise developed close links with the profession in that city.

The **Full Court** heard the first reported case, *Hannah v Dalgarno* (1903), in Sydney during the first week of November 1903. The Court first heard a case in WA on 8 December 1903: *D & W Murray & Co v Collector of Customs* (1903). The Court sat in Hobart on 24 February 1904 to hear *D'Emden v Pedder* and in Brisbane on 16 May 1904 to hear *Dixon v Todd*. The Court soon established a pattern of annual visits to each state capital (see **Circuit system**).

The Court's annual visits to the state capitals have been seen as very special occasions by the local judiciary and the profession. The Court continues to sit in the capital cities of each state once every year, provided there is sufficient business. The Justices consider this an invaluable experience both for the Court, in that a Commonwealth 'presence' is maintained, and, as **Dixon** said in 1952 on first sitting in Perth as **Chief Justice**, so that litigants may 'have the advantage of the services of their own **counsel**, and the advantage of seeing for themselves how their cases fare'. Although the introduction of the video link means that there is no longer a physical necessity for the Court to travel to the states, the annual visits remain important events on the legal calendar. They create an opportunity for the members of the Court to meet lawyers in the various jurisdictions, keeping open the lines of communication, and maintaining and developing personal relationships with the profession and the local judiciary. In 1972, **Windeyer** said that the visits were invaluable as a means of meeting the legal profession, judges, and members of the community and promoting 'a sense of unity of the nation through the basic unity of its laws'.

In WA, for example, each High Court visit is marked with a dinner organised by the Law Society. The WA Bar Association organises a cocktail party prior to the dinner. In the early years, it was customary for the President of the Law Society to call upon the Chief Justice of the High Court to report in an informal way on relevant developments. In the last 25 years, a toast to the High Court has been proposed by the most junior QC. More recently, this has become a toast to the judiciary, with a response from a member of the High Court. In addition, an annual High Court Dinner is hosted alternatively by the Supreme Court and the High Court. Similar functions take place in other jurisdictions.

The Court also has an impact on the profession through its decisions, and has been called upon to decide such matters as professional standards of conduct and immunity from suit. For example, in *Ziems v Prothonotary of the Supreme Court of NSW* (1957), the appellant was a barrister who had been convicted of manslaughter and imprisoned for two years. At first instance, the Supreme Court of NSW had struck the barrister from the roll of counsel upon conviction. The Full Court of the Supreme Court had upheld this decision on the sole ground of his conviction and imprisonment, with no consideration of the circumstances of the case. In a 3:2 decision (Dixon and **McTiernan** dissenting), the Court upheld the appeal. The appellant was suspended from practising for the duration of his imprisonment only. The decision acknowledges the possibility that a convicted person may reform and once again become a fit and proper person.

The Court discussed the virtues of a fit and proper person that are necessary to maintain the honour and high standards required of a barrister. Dixon said: 'If counsel is adequately to perform his functions and serve the interests of his clients, he should be able to command the confidence and respect of the court, of his fellow counsel and of his professional and lay clients.' Great emphasis is placed on the barrister's responsibilities not only to clients, but also to the Court and to colleagues.

In *Giannarelli v Wraith* (1988), a majority of the Court (with **Deane** dissenting) reaffirmed the traditional rule that a barrister (or a solicitor when acting as an advocate) cannot be sued for negligence in respect of his or her courtroom performance, nor in respect of preliminary work directly related to the court hearing. The scope of that rule has since been questioned (see *Boland v Yates Property Corporation* (1999)), but the rule remains in force.

Justices of the High Court are periodically subject to **criticism** by various sections of the community. This criticism was traditionally responded to by the **Attorney-General**, whose ministerial responsibility it was to defend the Court. This role has recently been abandoned. It is recognised that the Chief Justice of a court may speak on behalf of the judges of that court in court-related matters, but it is rare that a Chief Justice will do so. The role of responding to criticism of the judiciary has been taken up, in part, by the Australian Judicial Conference, limited to comments on matters of 'general principle affecting the judiciary', the 'administration of justice', and statements made upon request by the Chief Justice or a judge of the Court.

The relationship between the High Court and the Law Council of Australia is an important one. The Law Council is the national organisation of the legal profession; it consists of representatives from the various Bar Associations and Law Societies from each state and territory. Since the first State of the Judicature address was given by **Barwick** at the Australian Legal Convention in 1977, it has been customary for the Chief Justice of the High Court to give a similar address. In particular, since the 1950s, representatives of the profession, including the Presidents of Bar Associations and Law Societies—and, more recently, of the Law Council and the Australian Bar Association—have been invited to speak at welcome and farewell ceremonies at the High Court.

The annual ceremony at which newly appointed QCs announce their appointments was first held in 1986 at the High Court in **Canberra**. It lapsed for a few years but was resurrected in 1996. This ceremony followed a suggestion made by the Australian Bar Association, and it has become an important tradition. This ceremony is followed by an Annual Dinner of the Association held at the High Court. In earlier years, counsel would announce their appointment at the first sitting of the Court in the state after receiving their commission—a procedure determined by the Justices in 1941.

The importance of the relationship between the High Court and the legal profession has not diminished since 1903. It provides a vital link between the states, **territories**, and the Commonwealth, the maintenance of which is a necessary and desirable feature of the administration of justice and the work of the legal profession.

DAVID MALCOLM

Legitimate expectation is a concept applied in **administrative law** to determine whether a person has a right to a hearing under the doctrine of **natural justice**—or, as it is now known, procedural fairness. A common assertion is that government should provide a hearing before it resiles from a promise or a regular course of action on which someone has, or could have, relied. Any change of position by government can give rise to complaints that the new rule is operating retrospectively, which is regarded as unfair. At the same time, to impose a hearing obligation on government can complicate, if not encumber, its freedom to develop and adapt policy. Hence, there are conflicting interests at stake—interests which have led the High Court to take a cautious approach to the recognition of the doctrine.

From the time of its acceptance by the Court in *Heatley v Tasmanian Racing and Gaming Commission* (1977) to *Teoh's Case* (1995), the doctrine of 'legitimate expectation' has been controversial. The Court has been divided about its suitability as a factor conditioning government procedural practice, the division of opinion stemming principally from the lack of precision of the doctrine and from the fact that, at its most controversial, it has tended to obscure the division of the judicial **role** from that of the executive, and even perhaps from that of the legislature.

Lord Denning fashioned the doctrine of legitimate expectation in an English case, *Schmidt v Secretary of State for Home Affairs* (1968). He did so in response to the significant expansion in the twentieth century of government involvement in citizens' lives. Denning held that decision-making which involved the discretionary denial of government benefits and privileges warranted a degree of protection parallel to that accorded to rights in the strict sense. The result marked a significant rebalancing of interests in the citizen's favour.

The first High Court case on legitimate expectation was *Salemi v MacKellar (No 2)* (1977). Significantly, the Court split evenly on whether the doctrine applied. Ignazio Salemi had claimed that he met the criteria for an amnesty offered to prohibited immigrants, and accordingly that he had a legitimate expectation that he would not be deported without a hearing. While the Court was divided on whether the Minister was obliged to provide procedural fairness to Salemi, only **Barwick** expressed opposition to legitimate expectation as the foundation for the action. Two months later, the opportunity to accept the doctrine arose in *Heatley*. On that occasion, the Court (Barwick again dissenting) found that a legitimate expectation existed. The majority held that a person could not be 'warned off' a racecourse without a hearing. The national pastime—betting—was sufficiently important for any member of the public who paid the entrance fee to have a legitimate expectation of not being excluded from a racecourse by a government agency without fair process.

The doctrine was cemented in Australian law five years later in *FAI Insurances v Winneke* (1982), the Court holding that an application to renew a **workers' compensation** insurance licence gave rise to a legitimate expectation that the licence would not be refused without an opportunity for comment. Subsequently, in *Haoucher v Minister for Immigration* (1990), the Court, by majority, held that the Minister could not reject a recommendation by the Administrative Appeals Tribunal against deportation without first providing a hearing. Finally, in *Teoh*, the most controversial of all of the legitimate expectation cases, ratification by the executive of an international convention—even though the convention had not been incorporated by statute into Australian domestic law—was held to create a legitimate expectation that, in the absence of a legislative or executive indication to the contrary, the requirements of the convention would be observed by the executive, or at least that they would not be departed from without giving affected persons the right to be heard.

This chronology indicates, as **Brennan** pointed out in *Kioa v West* (1985), that the legitimate expectation seed 'has grown luxuriantly' in Australia. It has been held to apply to government decisions that are inconsistent with a government representation or promise; that depart from a regular practice; that decline renewal of a benefit or privilege; or that reject an application because it does not satisfy statutory criteria. The growth has, however, not been without detractors. Barwick recognised in *Heatley* that a person might have an expectation that was 'justifiable in human terms' but would not necessarily be 'lawful'. He appreciated the 'literary quality' of legitimate expectation 'better than I perceive its precise meaning and the perimeter of its application'. Brennan, too, has argued that the notion 'is of uncertain **connotation**' and 'may be misleading' as a touchstone for procedural fairness: it is not a person's subjective expectation but objectively determined interest that should determine whether fair process is required (for example, *Kioa*; *SA v O'Shea* (1987); *A-G (NSW) v Quin* (1990); *Annetts v McCann* (1990)). **Dawson** and **Deane** in *Haoucher* expressed concern about the lack of clarity of the notion, and Dawson noted in *Quin* that legitimate expectation could be a circular concept, if the subject of the expectation was claimed to be a government practice of offering a hearing. Further, **Mason** and Dawson in *Quin* affirmed that legitimate expectation is only a procedural right: in other words, satisfying the expectation does not mean that there is a right to the privilege or benefit the subject of the expectation.

McHugh joined the critics when, in a strong minority judgment in *Teoh*, he argued that a relevant provision of an international instrument, signed but not incorporated into domestic law, should not give rise to a legitimate expectation. In his view, to impose the obligation of a hearing in these circumstances would unduly tax officials, would usurp the role of the executive and of Parliament, could intrude upon the **sovereignty** of state governments, and might undermine the role of the body implementing the convention (in *Teoh's Case*, the Human Rights and Equal Opportunity Commission).

Despite these criticisms, legitimate expectation continues to be accepted by Australian courts. Though the concept remains unclear, legitimate expectation is likely to cause less difficulty as a filter for procedural fairness because there is now a tendency to oblige officials to accord procedural fairness in all administrative decisions. Accordingly, the need to establish a legitimate expectation has become correspondingly less important. At the same time, development of the concept is likely to continue. In particular, aligning legitimate expectation with comparable doctrines in **equity** and under the *Trade Practices Act* 1974 (Cth) may lead to the broader protection of expectation interests in Australian law.

ROBIN CREYKE

Further Reading

PP Craig, 'Legitimate Expectations: A Conceptual Analysis' (1992) 108 *LQR* 79

Paul Finn and Kathryn Smith, 'The Citizen, the Government and "Reasonable Expectation"' (1992) 66 *ALJ* 139

Graeme Johnson, 'Natural Justice and Legitimate Expectations in Australia' (1984) 15 *FL Rev* 39

Pamela Tate, 'The Coherence of "Legitimate Expectations" and the Foundation of Natural Justice' (1988) 14 *Mon LR* 15

Liberalism. The Court's understanding of Australian liberalism has been significantly influenced by the evolutionary changes in Australian constitutionalism. Instead of a radical break from British rule, independence for the Australian colonies generally meant the local adoption of English institutions. Along with the traditions of the **common law** and judicial **independence**, the emerging doctrines of **representative government** and later of **responsible government** were seen as hallmarks of local self-reliance and maturity, though still within an overall framework of **colonialism**.

The British tradition transplanted within this framework had been nourished by several theoretical streams of thought. They ranged from the common law of Hale, Coke, and Blackstone, to Lockean constitutionalism, Burkean prescriptive rights, and the utilitarianism of Jeremy Bentham. In particular, at the founding and later, Australian constitutionalism was significantly shaped by the liberal utilitarianism of John Stuart Mill.

The liberal character of this constitutionalism, with its emphasis on **civil liberties** and individual freedom, seemed inconsistent with the apparently unconstrained and unlimited power of parliament, recognised in the notion of parliamentary **sovereignty**. Yet the emphasis on conventional or unwritten limits on parliament, evident in commitment to the principle of responsible government, confirmed the underlying belief in the liberal democratic and progressive nature of parliamentarianism. Parliament was thought to secure liberty by enabling individuals, through their representatives, to debate and enact legislation. Significantly, parliament was thought to provide an additional protection for liberty by supervising the executive—traditionally the greatest threat to individual freedom. In this way, responsible parliamentary government, combined with the **rule of law**, secured the liberal nature of the political settlement.

The Court's view of this liberal democratic constitutionalism was decisively shaped by AV Dicey's influential *Introduction to the Study of the Law of the Constitution* (1885). Importantly, Dicey's interpretation of parliamentary sovereignty, the rule of law, and constitutional conventions influenced the Court's understanding of its own **role** within the regime. This role was potentially problematic because of the introduction of **federalism** into Australian constitutionalism. Derived from an American constitutionalism based on inalienable rights, institutional checks and balances, and limited government, federalism presented a subtle challenge to the liberal constitutional orthodoxy. In particular, it directly challenged the concept of parliamentary sovereignty, especially by allowing **judicial review**, the power of the courts to strike down parliamentary enactments as unconstitutional. Federalism also introduced the notion of a written—or, in James Bryce's terms, 'rigid'—constitution, to be contrasted with the 'elastic' English constitution. The Australian Constitution provided express limitations on parliaments, not only through a federal division of powers but also (albeit to a limited extent) through **express constitutional rights**: see, for example, sections 51(xxxi), 80, 116, and 117. Thus, from the beginning, the Court had to negotiate and mediate differing liberal traditions in interpreting the Australian Constitution (see also **Democracy, Court's role in**).

The Court's response was to favour and uphold the prevailing view that liberty was effectively secured by representative government (through the people's control of the parliament), responsible government (through the parliament's control of the government), and the rule of law (as an exclusion of arbitrary power). In the context of federal judicial review, this meant a strict demarcation between the 'political' role of parliament and the 'legal' role of the Court, and an insistence on **legalism** as the appropriate hermeneutic principle for the judiciary. Thus the Court gave limited scope to the few express rights provided in the Constitution. Such provisions were seen as unnecessarily restrictive and an inappropriate reflection on the motives of parliament; the Court considered responsible government and the common law as sufficient to protect individual rights and freedoms. The two major exceptions were the Court's interpretation of section 92 of the Constitution as a guarantee of *laissez-faire* liberalism (see **Interstate trade and commerce**) and its reading of the section 51(xxxi) requirement that the Commonwealth can only acquire **property** on 'just terms' (see **Acquisition of property**). Arguably, these exceptions reflected the strand in traditional liberalism that placed particular emphasis on the economic freedoms and property rights of individuals, both as the ultimate underpinnings of a system of law and government, and as the objects of its special solicitude.

The Court's recent jurisprudence suggests that it is reappraising the theoretical and institutional foundations of Australian liberalism. There are a number of reasons for this shift in perspective. The Australian community is now different, better educated, more diverse, and pluralistic. A parliament dominated by **political parties** and by the executive, and hence by an expanding and unelected bureaucracy, raises profound questions concerning the efficacy of responsible government. At the same time, the increasing importance of **international law**, and in particular the **International Bill of Rights**, has contributed to a greater awareness of natural rights or human rights. These changes have coincided with the growing independence of Australia from Britain—acknowledged and formalised in the enactment of the *Australia Acts* 1986—and with the High Court's increasing authority as effectively a final court of appeal (see **Nationhood, Court's role in building**).

Consequently, emphasis has shifted from parliament as the sole source and guardian of rights and freedoms to a more significant role for the judiciary. This is not unique to Australia: similar changes can be discerned in many other Western liberal democracies. What is unusual in the Australian case is the absence of an entrenched **Bill of Rights** and the relatively few human rights treaties and conventions that have been implemented in the domestic regime. These factors have significantly influenced the way in which the Court has augmented its federal judicial review with a jurisprudence that engages such fundamental liberal democratic issues as **citizenship**, civil liberties, and **separation of powers**.

The Court's delineation of Australian liberalism has a number of aspects. Its new assessment of parliament's role has meant that it is now prepared to give greater force to the express rights specified in the Constitution (see, for example, *Street v Queensland Bar Association* (1989)). In addition, starting with the *Free Speech Cases* (1992), it has determined that the institutions of representative and responsible government established by the Constitution implicitly guarantee a freedom of **political communication** (see also *Theophanous v Herald & Weekly Times* (1994); *Levy v Victoria* (1997); and *Lange v ABC* (1997)). It has construed the Judicature provisions (Part III) of the Constitution as a constitutional guarantee of separation of powers and **due process** of law, and therefore as an essential means for protecting liberty by checking and balancing power (*Kable v DPP* (1996); *Wilson v Minister for Aboriginal and Torres Strait Islander Affairs* (1996)). In its interpretation of **judicial power**, the Court has elaborated a number of rights and freedoms including the right to counsel in serious criminal cases (*Dietrich v The Queen* (1992)) and the freedom from Bills of Attainder (*War Crimes Act Case* (1991)). Perhaps the most politically contentious aspect of the Court's rights jurisprudence has been its recognition of **native title** in Australia (see *Mabo* (1992); *Wik* (1996)). These decisions have been made in the context of the willingness of several Justices to dismiss as a fiction or a fairy tale the old idea that the Court

simply declares a pre-existing law. By acknowledging that in one sense it 'makes' law, these Justices have justified the role of the Court as one way of helping to keep the laws up to date with community **values**.

In addition, the Court has stated that the **implied constitutional rights** it has discerned in the 'text or structure' of the Constitution are not individual or personal rights but rather freedoms necessary and incidental to the institutions on which the operation of the Constitution depends. To that extent, it would appear that the Court has, after all, not moved far from its initial Millian liberalism, and is in effect seeking to support it. Nevertheless, the Court's increasing reliance on international human rights law may point to a future jurisprudence of natural and human rights, which will entail a progressive re-evaluation not only of the Court's place within the regime, but of the notions of citizenship, sovereignty, and liberal democracy generally (see *Mabo*; *Teoh's Case* (1995); and *Newcrest Mining v Commonwealth* (1997)).

In assuming a more prominent role in defining Australian liberalism, the Court has confronted a number of theoretical and practical difficulties. The principal theoretical tension concerns the need to reconcile a judicial **law-making role** with the principles of rule of law, separation of powers, and democratic governance. Related to this difficulty is whether the Court, as an institution with changing membership and constrained by the demands of litigation, can entertain and implement any overarching liberal vision for Australia. These tensions inevitably articulate themselves in specific practical concerns. Which cases should the Court hear? Which rights and freedoms deserve recognition? What is the best way the Court can inform itself in its deliberation—that is, who should appear before the Court, who should make submissions to it, and importantly, given the wider political implications of its judgments, how should the Court deliver its opinions to encourage thoughtful reflection, deliberation, and debate?

These difficulties, which are not unique to Australia, raise a more subtle and profound question. At a time of increasing dissatisfaction with other institutions of governance, the judiciary is exerting greater influence and asserting greater authority. Significantly, it is doing so by appropriating, developing, and relying on decisions from other jurisdictions (see **Citations by Court**; **Foreign precedents**). This ongoing conversation in ideas and decisions across jurisdictions by the judiciary points to an evolving international liberal democratic constitutionalism transcending the specific boundaries of any one regime. The participation of the High Court in this evolution highlights the subtle yet powerful role of the judiciary everywhere in confronting, mediating, and shaping international challenges to liberalism.

Haig Patapan

Further Reading

Haig Patapan, *Judging Democracy: The New Politics of the High Court of Australia* (2000)
George Williams, *Human Rights under the Australian Constitution* (1999)

Library. When the High Court began its **sittings** in October 1903 there was no provision for a library. In the early years, the Justices relied on their own books and a handful of law reports. The earliest records show that on 24 June 1904, three copies of **Quick and Garran's** *Annotated Constitution of the Commonwealth of Australia* were purchased for the Justices. On 17 October of the same year, CR Walsh, NSW District Registrar, requested authority from the Principal Registrar 'to subscribe to the *Commonwealth Law Reports* and *The Commonwealth Law Review*'. At the same time, correspondence passed between **Griffith** and Josiah Symon, **Attorney-General** from August 1904, concerning the lack of library facilities and the failure of the Commonwealth to provide shelving in Sydney **chambers** (see **Strike of 1905**).

On 12 March 1906, the District Registrar in Sydney sent the Principal Registrar in Melbourne 'a list showing the books (other than record books), in this Registry, and a list of the books in Mr Griffith's Chambers at Darlinghurst which are the property of the Commonwealth'. The holdings then comprised 35 texts, one set of *Commonwealth Law Reports*, *United States Reports*, *Commonwealth Law Review*, several statutes, *Encyclopaedia of the Laws of England*, and 37 volumes of Commonwealth *Parliamentary Debates*: a total of 306 volumes. The District Registrar added that there may be 'some books belonging to the Commonwealth in the Chambers of the **Chief Justice** and Judges' but this was not certain because the Justices and their staff were away at the time.

Up to the time of **Barwick**, the library was largely built up by purchasing Justices' libraries as they retired. The Law Book Company would give a valuation of the books and the Court would buy them. No librarian was assigned to look after the Court's collection of books. Instead, an allowance called 'the Custodian of the Library Allowance' was paid to one of the **tipstaves** to maintain the library. This situation continued until well after **World War II**. The Senate Hansard of 21 October 1965 records that Senator John Gorton, in reply to a question on the High Court Library from Senator **Murphy**, answered that 'up to the present time, the personal staffs of the High Court Justices have provided the library services for the High Court'.

In Sydney, the Court was not prepared to make library facilities available to barristers. With no particular part of the **building** set aside for the purpose, the Court library was housed in its entirety in secure areas of the Court, such as the anterooms to Justices' chambers, which were not areas that could be open to **counsel**. In Melbourne, the barristers had access to a set of CLRs and the *Authorised Reports (UK)* in the robing room.

Early in 1965, at the instigation of Barwick, Athol Johnson, Assistant National Librarian, inspected the collections in Sydney and Melbourne. On 10 March 1965, he submitted a report recommending the secondment of a librarian for three or four months to establish a framework for an efficient library service for the Justices. Johnson found that the collections in Melbourne and Sydney were respectively 10 000 and 15 000 volumes, inadequately organised, and that library services were at a minimum or unavailable. Subsequently, Barbara McDonough did a thorough report on both libraries, which resulted in a recommendation for the appointment of a permanent librarian.

Sixty-four years after the High Court's **establishment**, on 20 March 1967, Rob Brian was seconded from the National Library to fill the new position of High Court Librarian, located in the old buildings at Taylor Square, Darlinghurst, Sydney. The Court at this time had a disparate and inadequate collection of material of about 45 000 volumes, including 20 sets of CLRs and many other duplicates. The books were not only divided between Sydney and Melbourne, but within the Sydney quarters, they were dispersed among chambers and various rooms—wherever accommodation was available.

One of the new librarian's main duties was to plan for the integration of the collection and its move to the **Canberra** headquarters where the **seat** of the Court was eventually to be located. In 1970, there were no specific plans for a new building, but ten years later, the then librarian, Mark Powell, was able to accomplish the move.

The two collections from Melbourne and Sydney were brought together to establish the new library. High up in the new building on the shores of Lake Burley Griffin, the library was at last able to display all its holdings in one location, where the beautifully designed furniture and fittings are still much admired. The High Court building in Canberra was opened on 26 May 1980; it included provision for the Judges' Library (on two floors) and a Bar Library for visiting counsel.

The Library now has 14 staff, including three engaged in **judgment production**, and occupies three floors of the High Court building, with the main collection located on Level 9 outside the Justices' chambers. The rest of the Judges' Library is on Level 8, with the Bar Library and library workroom on Level 7. The Bar Library contains a duplicate collection of basic primary and secondary materials, which counsel use for Court. The Library includes a rare book collection, and a special High Court Collection containing books and articles by and about the High Court Justices. The Sydney and Melbourne Registries and interstate chambers also have working collections of law reports.

The Library currently consists of approximately 150 000 volumes, many of which are duplicates, and has access to a wide range of electronic resources through CD-ROMs and the Internet (see **Information technology**). The library has one of the most extensive collections of US law reports in Australia and a comprehensive collection of UK material, as well as extensive holdings of Canadian, Indian, NZ, and general Commonwealth material. The library has very little foreign **language** material.

JACQUELINE ELLIOTT

Further Reading
JM Bennett, *Keystone of the Federal Arch* (1980) 105–07
Rob Brian, 'The High Court Library' (1970) 19 *Aust Lib J* 222

Literalism is an approach to legal interpretation. It applies to legal instruments with a 'public' authorship, such as constitutions and other legislation, but also to instruments with a 'private' authorship, such as wills or contracts (see **Succession law; Contract law**). Broadly, it assumes that the meaning of any legal instrument can be found in its language and framework, understood in its historical context—but otherwise unaffected by anything beyond the instrument itself. In its most basic form, literalism emphasises the literal and plain meaning of words according to their natural sense—to be understood within the text, structure, and context of the legal instrument in which they appear, but without regard to external factors such as political or social **values** and needs. Throughout the High Court's history, the Justices themselves, and politicians and **commentators** responding to their decisions, have frequently relied on literalism.

The opinions of judges in previous cases, given legal effect by the doctrine of **precedent**, are usually not construed in this way. There is far less attention to particular words, and far more attention to factual context and underlying principles and purposes. When **counsel** in *Caltex Oil v Feenan* (1981) spoke of 'construing' the High Court judgments in *Stevenson v Barham* (1977), they were reprimanded by the **Privy Council**:

> To speak of 'construing' the words in which judges have chosen to express the reasons for their judgment involves … a misuse of language that is all too common and reflects a mistaken approach to the use of judicial precedent. The only words that require to be 'construed' are those of the statute itself.

Particularly in relation to legal instruments such as constitutions and statutes, the judicial predilection for literalism provokes many critical questions. Do such instruments have meanings limited to the literal sense of their words? Can that meaning be established wholly in terms of what is in the instrument itself, without regard to anything external to the document such as **policy considerations**, values, and consequences? Should the Australian Constitution be understood as 'a monolithic block of determinate meanings', in Greg Craven's colourful 1992 phrase? There is much contemporary debate about the extent to which legal instruments *can* have self-contained meanings that are literal and value-free; and about whether the inherent ambiguities of language *can* be resolved by reference to the language, terms, and structure of legal instruments in a wholly self-contained way. There is also endless debate about precisely what it means to construe a legal instrument according to its 'text and structure', whether literalistically or otherwise.

These questions have important political as well as legal implications. As commentators such as Craven and **Mason** have noted, the increasing **criticism** of the Court since the time of the **Mason Court**, and the more overt exposure of policy choices in many of the Court's judgments, may suggest that in previous decades, the presence of policy choices had been cloaked by the rhetoric and methodology of literalism—or at least of the broader notion of **legalism**, of which literalism is sometimes viewed as a component part.

While literalism is not confined to **constitutional interpretation**, its most important influence on the Court has been in **constitutional law**. Many legal theorists assume that the meaning of a constitution or statute is the meaning intended by its **framers**, and that this intended meaning is to be found in the literal meaning of the language they used. Some commentators point to strong connections between literalism, legalism, and **originalism**, as well as between literalism and the recently discredited declaratory theory of law.

A resort to literalism may be motivated, however, by two very different assumptions. One is that the task of the Justice in interpreting any legal instrument is to give effect to its makers' intentions, and that the best guide to their intentions is found in the words they actually used. The other is that the task of the Justice is to ascertain the legal effect of the instrument that its framers actually produced, regardless of whether this corresponds to their original intentions—those intentions being neither readily discoverable nor legally relevant. On either basis, a literalist approach to constitutional and **statutory interpretation** requires close attention to the legal effect of the language that was actually used, rather than to its authors' subjective intentions and expectations—and still less to anything external to the actual text, such as contemporary social needs and values. Of course, some contemporary theories grounded in postmodernism challenge that orthodox approaches such as literalism assume to be 'internal' and 'external' to the text of law (see **Jurisprudence**).

In political terms, the adequacy and effectiveness of literalism as a strategy of constitutional interpretation raise fundamental questions about political and legal authority and legitimacy. In part, these questions depend on the precise extent to which literalism allows the Court to look beyond the constitutional text. Does it prohibit or permit reference to **extrinsic material** such as the pre-federation **Convention Debates** to interpret the Constitution? Does it preclude or allow reference to the historical context in which the Constitution was framed, and the political and legal problems to which it was directed? Does it enable High Court Justices, while focusing on the words of the Constitution, to construe those words in the light of contemporary problems, values, and contexts, as an organic document that is capable of adapting to evolutionary changes in Australia's development on a range of political, economic, social, and legal levels? Should the words of the Constitution be read and applied according to their literal meaning as understood in 1901, or alternatively, can the meaning of the words change over time? (see **Connotation and denotation**). For example, is the meaning of constitutional terms such as 'marriage', 'foreign power', 'trade and commerce', and 'copyrights, patents … and trade marks' confined literally to what those terms meant in 1901, long before anyone imagined a world of married and unmarried partners, Australian independence from Great Britain, computerised information, e-commerce, and the Internet? (compare, for example, the *Union Label Case* (1908) with *Grain Pool of WA v Commonwealth* (2000)).

Different Justices from different eras have strongly disagreed on these questions, alternating between literalist and non-literalist approaches at different times. Among the interpretive approaches that contrast most strongly with literalism is what **Deane** and **Kirby**, following Andrew **Inglis Clark**, have called the 'living force' doctrine of constitutional interpretation (see Deane in *Theophanous v Herald & Weekly Times* (1994); Kirby in *Eastman v The Queen* (2000)). That doctrine views the Constitution as an organic and evolving document whose text remains constant but whose operation changes with time and circumstance to meet the contemporary governmental and social needs of the Australian people. The doctrine has emerged against the background of a wider shift in the Court's institutional **ideology**, away from formalism or legalism—reflected, for example, in the contrast between literalist and purposive approaches to statutory and constitutional interpretation (see **Form and substance**).

The *Engineers Case* (1920) is commonly regarded as a landmark in the Court's commitment to literalism because of its emphasis on 'the natural meaning of the text of the Constitution' and its legalistic and literalistic rejection of vague constitutional implications that might limit **Commonwealth legislative power** in favour of the states. Yet the *Engineers Case* does not necessarily preclude reference to external sources such as the Convention Debates. The majority judgment written by **Isaacs** expressly permitted reference to the background and **history** of the Constitution, and argued that because the Constitution is permeated by fundamental doctrines such as the principle of **responsible government**, and the common and indivisible **sovereignty** of the British Empire, they 'must be taken into account in determining the meaning of its language'. These qualifications make the *Engineers* judgment more complex than a simple charter for rigid literalism, and increase the complexity of interpretation, even on a literalist view. It must also be remembered that the literalism of *Engineers* served the policy end of expanding the power of the Commonwealth.

In any event, the interpretation of the *Engineers Case* solely in terms of literalism is undergoing review. In the *Payroll Tax Case* (1971), **Windeyer** wrote that the *Engineers Case*, 'looked at as an event in legal and constitutional history, was a consequence of developments that had occurred outside the law courts': what happened was that 'the Constitution was read in a new light, a light reflected from events that had, over twenty years, led to a growing realisation that Australians were now one people and Australia one country and that national laws might meet national needs'. In *Eastman*, three decades later, **McHugh** suggested:

> The traditional approach to constitutional interpretation in Australia is probably better described as textualism or semantic intentionalism. It is not literalism, if by literalism is meant no more than [that] a statute is to be interpreted by reference to its words according to their natural sense and in the context of the document … Although the majority justices in the *Engineers' Case* emphasised the necessity to construe the words of the Constitution, their approach is probably better regarded as one of legalism with textualism the instrument of that legalism.

However great its past impact may have been on the Court's decision making, the ideology and methodology of literalism are difficult to reconcile with recent landmark decisions such as *Cole v Whitfield* (1988) on section 92 of the Constitution; *Street v Queensland Bar Association* (1989) on section 117 of the Constitution; *Bropho v WA* (1990) on executive government immunity from legislation; *Wik* (1996) and *Yanner v Eaton* (1999) on statutory regimes and **native title** rights; or *Sue v Hill* (1999) and *Re Refugee Review Tribunal; Ex parte Aala* (2000) on interpretation of constitutional terms according to their contemporary meaning. As **Gaudron** and **Gummow** remarked in *Aala*—in language that rejected literalism in its narrowest form—to examine the understanding of a constitutional term 'at the time of the commencement of the Constitution and thereafter … is not to adopt the proposition that the Constitution should be interpreted merely with the text in one hand and a dictionary in the other'. Yet, in spite of such observations, vestiges of the literalist approach still remain in some contemporary advocacy and judgments; and it may be unrealistic to expect that they will ever be wholly eradicated.

BRYAN HORRIGAN

Further Reading
Gregory Craven, 'The Crisis of Constitutional Literalism in Australia' in HP Lee and George Winterton (eds), *Australian Constitutional Perspectives* (1992) 1
Michael Kirby, 'Constitutional Interpretation and Original Intent: A Form of Ancestor Worship?' (2000) 24 *MULR* 1
Anthony Mason, 'The Interpretation of a Constitution in a Modern Liberal Democracy' in Charles Sampford and Kim Preston (eds), *Interpreting Constitutions* (1996) 13

Litigants, notable, 1903–1945. Litigants might be described as 'notable' for any number of reasons. Noteworthy litigants during the first decades of the Court's life included many well-known public figures, and many others who became notable precisely because of their involvement in litigation that attracted public notoriety. Other litigants have been notable for the persistence of their approaches to the Court, or for having some personal connection with the Justices.

While governments, corporations, and organisations are sometimes unavoidably 'repeat players' in High Court litigation, individual 'repeat players' have been rare. The first of them was John McLaughlin, whose resentment at his confinement to a lunatic asylum fuelled four separate appeals to the Court. McLaughlin, a respected and influential Sydney solicitor who had acted for Henry Parkes, was committed to an asylum by his wife, who then set about dealing with his assets during the months of his committal. On being certified sane and released, McLaughlin pursued a series of legal battles against several of the protagonists in his drama: the police officers who transported him to the asylum (*McLaughlin v Fosbery* (1904)), a solicitor who had unsuccessfully sought his release (*McLaughlin v Freehill* (1908)), a bank from which his wife had borrowed (*McLaughlin v City Bank of Sydney* (1912)), and a company in which he had held shares (*McLaughlin v Daily Telegraph* (1904)). In the *Daily Telegraph* case, the **Privy Council** refused special leave to appeal; in two other cases, it dismissed McLaughlin's appeals (*McLaughlin v Westgarth* (1906, on appeal from the Supreme Court of NSW) and *McLaughlin v City Bank of Sydney* (1914)).

Other Sydney identities of the time, many of them immortalised in Cyril Pearl's book *Wild Men of Sydney* (1958), were more reluctant to embrace the new Court. Richard Denis Meagher, the Sydney solicitor struck off the rolls in 1896 for his vigorous defence in *R v Dean* (1895) of a client whom he knew to be guilty, came before the Court only once, when the NSW Law Institute successfully appealed against the NSW Supreme Court's decision to readmit him to practice (*Incorporated Law Institute v Meagher* (1909)). In holding that Meagher was unfit to be readmitted, **Higgins** dwelt on his role in the *Dean* case; **Griffith** and **Isaacs** dwelt rather on Meagher's apparent involvement with William Nicholas Willis MLA in a series of corrupt land deals investigated by Royal Commission in 1906. Both of them took **judicial notice** of the notorious facts found by the Royal Commission. Isaacs found it difficult to believe that Meagher had been 'a mere dupe of Willis', and added that if that were the case, it would demonstrate that Meagher was 'much too simple and confiding to bear the heavy strain of responsibility required of … a solicitor'.

The evidence related particularly to what Griffith called 'Rea's leases': Crown leases procured by Willis ostensibly in the name of Patrick Rea, a jockey, with mortgages to Willis's wife Mary. Litigation involving Rea's leases, with Mary Willis as a party, came before the Court twice, in *Willis v Trequair* (1906) and *Wingadee Shire Council v Willis* (1910)—though Willis himself did not, having fled to South Africa at the time of *Willis v Trequair*. Mrs Willis's involvement was itself regarded as a ground for suspicion: as Chief Justice Frederick Darley put it in the Supreme Court of NSW, Rea 'was merely a dummy', and 'long experience has shown that where large sums of money or large properties have been placed by a man in the possession of his wife … the object is to carry out a fraud' (*Trequair v Willis* (1906); see **Women**).

Despite his High Court rebuff, Meagher went on to become president of the Australian Labor Party (1914) and Lord Mayor of Sydney (1916–17). He was finally readmitted to practice by Act of Parliament, the *Legal Practitioners Amendment Act 1920* (NSW).

Thomas Ernest Rofe was struck off the roll of solicitors in 1895 after a jury convicted him of conspiracy with a client in a divorce case. Through a long and prosperous life as entrepreneur and philanthropist, he maintained that he had had the misfortune to be caught up in the aftermath of the *Dean* case, when juries were disposed to believe the worst of any legal practitioner accused of unethical conduct. He was ultimately readmitted to practice in 1933, having been largely vindicated in an appeal to the Privy Council (*Rofe v Smiths Newspapers* (1926)). His appearances in the High Court were less dramatic: in *Rofe v Deputy Federal Commissioner of Land Tax* (1920) in relation to his father's will, and in *Rofe v Campbell* (1931) in relation to his liability as a preference shareholder in the liquidation of a theatre company. In the High Court, he successfully denied liability; but that decision was reversed by the Privy Council on appeal (*Campbell v Rofe* (1932)).

Even the pugnacious John Norton, the editor of *Truth*, appeared in the High Court only infrequently. When the information which he laid against the Lord Mayor of Sydney for corruption was dismissed by a magistrate, Norton unsuccessfully applied to the High Court for special **leave to appeal** (*Norton v Taylor* (1905)), and then appealed to the Privy Council (*Norton v Taylor* (1906)) with no greater success. His only other High Court appearances were interlocutory appeals arising from **defamation** proceedings in the Supreme Court of Victoria. In *Norton v Clarke* (1911), he was sued for defamation by the Anglican Archbishop of Melbourne (whom Norton had pilloried in *Truth* as 'the Anglican Archnightman of Smellbourne'); in *Norton v Herald* (1913), he was sued for professional costs by the Melbourne solicitor who had acted for him in *Norton v Clarke*. In 1913, Norton (writing in *Truth*) and a Melbourne journalist, Benjamin Hoare (writing in *The Tribune*), attacked each other in print and then sued each other for defamation. Two interlocutory appeals to the High Court (*Norton v Hoare (Nos 1 and 2)* (1913)) produced only one point of general interest: that Norton, in his defence against

Hoare's suit for defamation, was entitled to plead the *Tribune's* attack on him by way of justification.

The most tenacious and successful of the Court's repeat players was Frederick Alexander James. His dried fruit business at Berri, SA, had been established in 1914: but after **World War I**, he faced competition from a growing number of ex-soldiers in the Riverina and elsewhere whom the Commonwealth and the states had sought to establish in the dried fruit industry in a cooperative postwar resettlement scheme. In the 1920s, when the resulting oversupply of dried fruit resulted in a glut on the world market, both Commonwealth and states sought to protect the ex-soldiers by quotas and marketing schemes: the Commonwealth for overseas markets and the states for domestic markets. For more than a decade James contested these schemes, primarily as an interference with his freedom of **interstate trade**.

In *James v SA* (1927), he failed in a challenge to SA's compulsory acquisition of all dried fruit produced in the state, but successfully challenged the imposition of marketing quotas on growers. When the Commonwealth tried to fill the gap, James' challenge under section 92 failed (since *McArthur v Queensland* (1920) had held that section 92 imposed no limit on Commonwealth power), but his challenge based on unequal treatment of the states (see **Discrimination**) succeeded: the failure to provide an administrative licensing apparatus in Queensland and Tasmania was held to give a 'preference' to the other four states, even though Queensland and Tasmania produced no dried fruits (*James v Commonwealth* (1928)). A further challenge to the compulsory seizures of James' fruit under the SA scheme failed in the High Court (*James v Cowan* (1930)), but succeeded in the Privy Council (*James v Cowan* (1932)).

Thus encouraged, James embarked on a further challenge to the Commonwealth's seizures, this time tackling directly the authority of *McArthur v Queensland* on which he had foundered in 1928. Again, he failed in the High Court (which did, however, reject the Commonwealth's claim that his suit was **vexatious**: *James v Commonwealth* (1935)), but succeeded in the Privy Council (*James v Commonwealth* (1936)). By this time, his Victorian suppliers had been drawn into the fray: the appellants in *Hartley v Walsh* (1937) had been prosecuted for supplying Victorian fruit to James' packing sheds in SA. James himself returned to the High Court in *James v Commonwealth* (1939) to claim **damages** under **tort law** for the various seizures of his dried fruits. **Dixon**, sitting alone, allowed the claim, though rejecting a separate claim to damages for breach of constitutional rights.

A less successful attempt to rely on section 92 had been made by Laura Duncan, the surviving owner of the Mooraberrie cattle station in Queensland. Her attempt to drove 600 fat cattle to SA (where they would fetch a better price than in Queensland) was initially blocked when the Queensland government acquired the cattle under the *Meat Supply for Imperial Uses Act 1914* (Qld). Encouraged by the High Court's decision in *Foggitt Jones v NSW* (1916) that equivalent NSW legislation infringed section 92, she and the other executor of her husband's estate sued in the High Court for damages; but in *Duncan v Queensland* (1916), the Court changed its mind, **overruling** *Foggitt Jones* and declaring that the Queensland legislation was valid. In any event, the Queensland government had pre-empted the High Court decision: while *Duncan v Queensland* was pending, the government again acquired the cattle—this time under the *Sugar Acquisition Act* 1915 (Qld), after two proclamations extending the operation of the Sugar Act to cattle. Mrs Duncan and her co-plaintiff sued again. This time, the principal defendant was himself a notable litigant: the acquisition under the Sugar Act had been ordered by the Queensland Treasurer, 'Red Ted' Theodore, later to be Premier of Queensland and a controversial federal Treasurer. Challenging the validity of the proclamations, and the alleged ulterior motive for the seizure, Mrs Duncan claimed that the seizure was wrongful, and that liability in damages should attach to the Queensland government, to the policeman who had taken possession of the cattle, and to Theodore personally. She succeeded at trial and was awarded £2900 in damages. Thereafter, in a seesaw series of appeals, the defendants succeeded in the Full Supreme Court of Queensland; the plaintiffs in the High Court (*Duncan v Theodore* (1917)); and the defendants in the Privy Council (*Theodore v Duncan* (1919)). In the High Court, Isaacs and **Powers**, in dissent, protested that the defendants had merely attempted 'to carry out, for the benefit of the whole community, what they believed to be the law'.

Dulcie Williams, the wife of the NSW trade unionist Frank Graham, was another woman who came before the Court twice—most notably in *R v Brislan; Ex parte Williams* (1935), when she was prosecuted for listening to the Labor Party station 2KY without a wireless listener's licence. The prosecution was seized upon as a test case to challenge **Commonwealth legislative power** relating to radio broadcasts, and **Piddington** was briefed on her behalf. He persuaded Dixon (but not the rest of the Court) that the Commonwealth power in respect of 'posts and telegraphs and other like services' did not extend to broadcast technology, but was limited to the transmission and reception of messages between individuals under conditions of 'mutuality of exchange' and non-disclosure to other persons. It was while that case was pending that the Sydney *Sun* launched a scathing attack on the High Court's decision in the **Kisch Case** (1934). (Egon Kisch was himself, of course, a notable litigant.) Piddington, who had been Kisch's **counsel**, persuaded the Court that the *Sun* and its editor should be punished for **contempt** of court; again, Dulcie Williams agreed to put her name to the application (*R v Dunbabin; Ex parte Williams* (1935)).

Another husband and wife prominent in left-wing circles, until in the 1930s they turned to fascism, were Tom Walsh and his wife Adela Pankhurst. Walsh, as President of the Federated Seamen's Union, and his union ally Jacob Johnson, had repeated confrontations with shipowners on the waterfront and in the Commonwealth Court of **Conciliation and Arbitration**, several of which reached the High Court. In *Australian Commonwealth Shipping Board v Federated Seamen's Union (Nos 1 and 2)* (1925), the Court first granted injunctions against both Walsh and Johnson to prohibit them from inciting strike action, and then upheld the Arbitration Court's power to deregister the union. In *Walsh v Sainsbury* (1925), Walsh appealed to the Court against two convictions arising from a dispute at Fremantle: his union had declared a ship 'black' and had tried to persuade Joseph

Morris, the secretary of the Waterside Workers' Federation, to have that union do likewise despite a 'no strike' clause in its award. Walsh had put his case to Morris directly and (by telegram) had asked his own branch secretary John O'Neill to do so as well. He was convicted of one charge of urging Morris to commit an offence against a law of the Commonwealth, and another of unlawfully inciting O'Neill to counsel such an offence. On appeal, **Latham** appeared for Walsh, and Dixon for the informant. The majority, with Isaacs and Higgins dissenting, upheld the first conviction despite the 'very meagre' evidence, but found the evidence concerning O'Neill so 'loose and unsatisfactory' that the conviction should be set aside.

By this time, the militancy of Walsh and Johnson had so angered the government that new provisions, aimed at 'any person not born in Australia', were added to the *Immigration Act* 1901 (Cth) to procure their deportation. The whole Court held that the provision could not apply to Walsh, who was born in Ireland in 1871 but had migrated to NSW in 1893, well before federation. Johnson, born in Holland, had not arrived in NSW until 1910; but the majority held that the provision could not apply to him either. Isaacs and **Rich**, who dissented on that point, held the deportation proceedings invalid on other grounds (*Ex parte Walsh and Johnson; In re Yates* (1925); see **Immigration power**).

Adela Pankhurst, the daughter of Emmeline Pankhurst and the sister of Christabel and Sylvia Pankhurst, appealed to the Court twice against convictions arising out of her protest activities during World War I. In *Pankhurst v Porter* (1917), heard by the High Court two days after her marriage to Walsh, her appeal was successful: charged with taking part in a meeting of persons assembled 'on a pretext of making known their grievances', she persuaded the Court that because her protest was genuine, it was not a 'pretext'. She was less successful a few weeks later in *Pankhurst v Kiernan* (1917): only Higgins accepted her argument that the *Unlawful Associations Act* 1916 (Cth), which made it an offence to advocate or incite 'the destruction or injury of property', was unconstitutional because it lacked a sufficient connection with the **defence power**. Ironically, after a series of ideological transitions that led her from the Communist Party to her own right-wing 'Australian Women's Guild of Empire' and ultimately to the Australia First movement, she finished up being interned for a seven-month period during **World War II** at the instance of **Evatt** as **Attorney-General**.

For some litigants, notoriety is tinged with bemusement, and even perhaps with ridicule. Archibald Nugent Robertson may be remembered forever as the barrister who went to the Privy Council for a penny—and lost. Robertson had missed a ferry and was refused egress from the wharf unless he paid a penny to exit through a turnstile. He refused to pay, and the resulting altercation prompted him to sue the ferry company for false imprisonment. He initially obtained £100 damages, but saw that result overturned in the High Court (*Balmain New Ferry Co v Robertson* (1906)). The Privy Council dismissed his appeal, declaring that his behaviour had been 'thoroughly unreasonable' throughout; and the English law reports got his name wrong, reporting the case as *Robinson v Balmain New Ferry Co* (1910). Robertson was no stranger to setbacks: at the 1897 NSW election for delegates to that year's

Henry Goya Henry, notable litigant, in his famous Australian-made plane, *Genairco*, circa 1935

Federal Convention, he had come forty-ninth out of 49 candidates. After his defeat in the Privy Council, he remained at the Bar, eking out his income with assignments as Crown Prosecutor on country circuits, and with 31 years of service as Visitor to the NSW system of hospitals for the insane. He wrote bad Kiplingesque verse and a Mills and Boon novel, *Her Last Appearance* (1914).

Dr Richard Thorald Grant, a young Adelaide general practitioner, became notable for his long woollen underwear. Grant, who had suffered acute dermatitis after wearing the underwear, sued the manufacturer and retailer of the garments. His success in the Supreme Court of SA, where Chief Justice George Murray upheld his claim and awarded him £2450, was due partly to Murray's appreciation of the relevance of *Donoghue v Stevenson* (1932), decided a bare six months earlier. In the High Court, only Evatt was similarly perceptive: Dixon, in the leading judgment allowing the defendants' appeal, was preoccupied with exhaustive critical scrutiny of the **expert evidence** on the medical and scientific aspects of Dr Grant's itches (*Australian Knitting Mills v Grant* (1933)). The subsequent decision of the Privy Council allowing Grant's appeal (*Grant v Australian Knitting Mills* (1935)) was a major landmark in the recognition (and expansion) of the new approach to negligence which *Donoghue v Stevenson* had pioneered. May Willis, whose heel came off her new shoes the third time she wore them, had an easier time in establishing an implied contractual warranty that the shoes were reasonably fit for their purpose (*David Jones v Willis* (1934)). She had somewhat more difficulty, however, in establishing that the relevant purpose was 'walking': she had told the shop assistant that she only wanted 'a shoe which would come up over her bunion'.

One particularly colourful litigant in the 1930s was the aviator Henry Goya Henry—the first person with a wooden leg to be granted a flying licence—who delighted in stunt-flying under Sydney Harbour Bridge. Even more provocative was his habit of taking members of the public for short joyrides in a light plane along the perimeter of Mascot airport. For this, his licence was suspended for 14 days from 28 September 1934, but two days later he offended again and was charged with unlicensed flying. The offence was so minor that it was heard in a Court of Petty Sessions; but Goya Henry's response had far-reaching consequences that were still being felt decades later when the *Tasmanian Dam Case* (1983) was fought.

Upon conviction, Goya Henry sought a **writ** of prohibition to restrain any further proceedings. His counsel argued that the regulation under which he was charged was invalid. The Air Navigation Regulations had been passed purportedly under the *Air Navigation Act* 1920 (Cth), which in turn derived its support from the Aerial Navigation Convention entered into in Paris in 1919 (see **International law**). After a five-day hearing, the High Court upheld the argument that the regulations did not carry out and give effect to the Convention; but in the course of their reasons, Latham, Evatt, and **McTiernan** formulated a wide view of the ambit of the **external affairs power**.

Not one to count his blessings, Goya Henry resumed his joyrides. But in 1937, the regulations were amended to prohibit low flying anywhere in the airport (including the perimeter area), and in 1938 Goya Henry was charged again under the new regulations. This time, although the regulations went further than the Convention (which prohibited low flying only in the actual landing area), the High Court accepted them as a reasonable means of giving effect to the Convention (*R v Poole; Ex parte Henry (No 2)* (1939)). Henry later quit Sydney and became captain of a trawler in New Guinea.

The Pope was an appellant before the Court in a 1934 **succession** dispute (*His Holiness the Pope v National Trustees, Executors & Agency Co* (1934)). A wealthy Victorian, Patrick Lawlor, had made generous bequests to the Catholic Church for various purposes, some of which were of doubtful validity under the law of **trusts**. The executors of Lawlor's will commenced a Supreme Court action seeking to clarify the will. The Pope was one of the defendants, and he appealed against part of the decision. The Court found in the Pope's favour, significantly boosting the share of Lawlor's estate destined for the Church.

Walt Disney (referred to in the *Commonwealth Law Reports* as 'Walter E Disney') became a respondent in *Radio Corporation v Disney* (1937) when the appellants attempted to register the names 'Mickey Mouse' and 'Minnie Mouse' as **trade marks** for radio sets. Arguably, the true protagonists in the High Court's deliberations were Mickey and Minnie Mouse (see **Popular culture**).

A defamation case in 1934 involved former NSW Labor Premier Jack Lang as the defendant (*Lang v Willis* (1934)). Willis, an estranged former supporter of Lang's, sued Lang for comments made in the course of a by-election campaign. Willis contested the seat of Bulli as an independent, prompting Lang to attack him as 'a concealed enemy sailing under the flag of a Labor independent candidate', 'a subtle and insincere politician' who 'when the ship was sinking … rushed for the shore without warning his mates'. A Sydney jury found for Lang at trial, but on appeal a new trial was ordered. The High Court majority overturned that order, finding that the jury had been entitled to accept Lang's defence of 'no likely injury'.

Occasionally, the Court was required to adjudicate in disputes involving litigants with whom the Justices had some personal acquaintance. The first Justices, Griffith, **Barton**, and **O'Connor**, had taken leading roles in the federal Conventions at which the Constitution was framed. Alfred **Deakin** had been a fellow-traveller in that endeavour and later, as the first Commonwealth Attorney-General, had fought a long parliamentary battle for the **establishment** of the Court. He came before the Court in a different capacity in 1904, arguing that as a Commonwealth officer he enjoyed immunity from state income tax laws (*Deakin v Webb* (1904)). In accepting Deakin's argument, the Court put further flesh on its fledgling doctrine of **intergovernmental immunities**.

In 1939, the Court had to determine the appeal of a man who could easily have become a colleague—Piddington—who had been appointed to the Court in 1913 but resigned without sitting. At the age of 76, he had been struck by a motorcycle in Sydney and had sued the cyclist's employer. At the trial, a witness who claimed to have seen the accident was asked how he came to be at the scene. He replied that he had attended a nearby bank to do business for a Major Jarvie. The trial judge permitted the manager of the bank to testify that

Major Jarvie's account had not been operated on during that day. The jury returned a verdict for the defendant.

Piddington appealed ultimately to the court to which he had been appointed 26 years earlier, but on which he had never sat. The Court considered the argument based on the finality of answers to collateral questions and allowed Piddington's appeal, with Latham and **Starke** dissenting (*Piddington v Bennett and Wood* (1940)). Starke observed sternly that friendship and sympathy for 'an old and distinguished member of the legal profession' should not sway the judgment of the Court.

Tony Blackshield
Graham Fricke
Amelia Simpson

Litigants, notable, 1945–2001. In Australia's sombre postwar years, the colourful individualism sometimes displayed by litigants of the inter-war period came to be less apparent. Some categories of notable litigant remained constant: there were, as before, those litigants having pre-existing celebrity status and those whose notoriety instead grew from their encounters with the law. For many in the latter category, though, the **Cold War** generated notoriety of a deeply serious nature. New varieties of notoriety also emerged. Increasingly, litigants became notable because their case gave rise to an important legal principle, thereafter bearing that litigant's name. The profile of indigenous litigants, too, has been rising steadily, with some of the Court's most notable litigants in recent years being of Aboriginal or Torres Strait Islander descent.

The first of the identifiable Cold War cases to come before the Court involved the unfortunate fate of one Gilbert Burns. Burns was charged with sedition after statements he made, at a public debate on communism in Brisbane, in response to a hypothetical question about the allegiance of the Australian Communist Party should the Soviet Union go to war with the West. He appealed his conviction to the High Court, arguing that an answer to a hypothetical question could not establish the seditious intention required by the *Crimes Act* 1914 (Cth). **Dixon** (supported by **McTiernan**) accepted that argument; **Latham** (supported by **Rich**) rejected it. Latham's view prevailed—not on the ground that an appeal must fail unless it gains a majority, but because, since the appeal came only from a magistrate, the Chief Justice's view was decisive (*Burns v Ransley* (1949)) (see **Tied vote**). On the same day, with only Dixon dissenting, the Court confirmed the conviction of Laurence Louis Sharkey, general secretary of the Australian Communist Party, who had expressed similar sentiments in a statement prepared for a journalist—again in response to a hypothetical question (*R v Sharkey* (1949)). The divisive effect of these prosecutions was an important precursor to the **Menzies** government's failed attempt to ban the Communist Party altogether (see *Communist Party Case* (1951)).

The Cold War produced other notable litigants. When Rupert Lockwood, the author of the infamous 'Document J', received a subpoena requiring him to appear before the Petrov Commission, his application for an injunction to prevent the Commission from proceeding was dismissed by **Fullagar**, sitting alone (*Lockwood v Commonwealth* (1954). Fullagar agreed that the appointment of the three Commissioners was

Deborah Wardley, Australia's first female commercial pilot

focused particularly on the scientific dispute about a spray pattern on the dashboard of the Chamberlains' car, which the prosecution witnesses had identified as baby's blood. It turned out to be not even human blood, but sound-deadening material sprayed on the dashboard during manufacture. Chamberlain was released from prison and eventually compensated.

Other High Court litigants who have attained notoriety in recent years include Deborah Wardley, whose application for employment as a pilot was rejected by Ansett on the basis of her gender (*Ansett Transport Industries v Wardley* (1980); see **Discrimination**); Ivan Polyukhovich, the defendant in Australia's first, and perhaps last, war crimes prosecution (see **Due process**; *War Crimes Act Case* (1991)); and Bernard Verwayen, whose **damages** claim for injuries sustained in the HMAS *Voyager* collision hinged on whether the Commonwealth could renege on its promise not to rely on the statute of limitations (see *Commonwealth v Verwayen* (1990); **Estoppel**).

An entirely different class of notable litigant comprises public figures and celebrities—people well known to the public independently of their encounters with the law. **Taxation law** has been a fertile source of such cases. After Jon Cleary's novel *The Sundowners* was filmed in 1960 starring Robert Mitchum, Mitchum's resulting liability for income tax in Australia reached the High Court in *FCT v Mitchum* (1965). The Court acknowledged him as 'an actor who … had acquired a considerable reputation in the motion picture industry and with motion picture audiences'. Again, after the death of the novelist Nevil Shute, the continuing international income from his novels gave rise to the taxation appeal in *Union-Fidelity Trustee Co v FCT* (1969).

The University of Sydney physics professor Harry Messel was well known to the public, but was also regarded by Murphy as an intimate personal friend. When Messel was convicted of offences relating to the taking of protected fauna in the Northern Territory, Murphy raised an issue of his **disqualification** to hear the case because of his 'close association with [Messel] for many years'. He agreed to sit only because 'issues of great public importance' were involved, and because 'the members of this Court who initially considered the application directed that it should be heard by all seven members' (*Davern v Messel* (1984)). Messel had argued that a complicated series of appeals and rehearings in the courts below had attracted the rule against double jeopardy: in a Court of seven, only Murphy and Deane accepted that argument.

Some of the most widely known individual litigants have been politicians. The case of *Sankey v Whitlam* (1978) concerned a private prosecution, launched by Sydney solicitor Danny Sankey, in which the defendants were former **Prime Minister** Gough **Whitlam** and three of his Cabinet ministers, including Murphy. There was speculation that the real target was Murphy, since a conviction might have provided grounds for his **removal** from the High Court Bench. Murphy was later to be a notable litigant in his own right (see '**Murphy Affair**'), but in *Sankey v Whitlam* his name was tactfully removed from the record for purposes of the High Court proceedings. Sankey had charged the defendants with conspiring to effect an illegal purpose, in part involving an alleged contravention of the 1927 Financial Agreement. The Court held that on two of the four charges the prosecution must fail, as

not authorised by the *Royal Commission Act* 1954 (Cth), which clearly envisaged the appointment of only one Commissioner; but he held that the appointments were valid under the *Royal Commissions Act* 1902 (Cth). Lockwood's separate action against **Windeyer** for **defamation**, based on allegations made by Windeyer as counsel assisting the Commission, never went to trial. When Frank Hursey and his son Denis joined the Democratic Labor Party and refused to pay a union levy to support the Australian Labor Party, the ensuing turmoil on the Hobart waterfront occupied the headlines for months, and gave rise to litigation in three separate cases, which the Court eventually disposed of together in *Williams v Hursey* (1959). Again, it was Fullagar who gave the leading judgment, substantially vindicating the position of the union officials against the Hurseys, since their own provocative action was 'the ultimate source of all the trouble'.

Few court cases outside this ideological context have caused bitter divisions of opinion within Australian society. However, one case that did produce considerable division was that of Lindy Chamberlain. Chamberlain had been convicted of the murder of her baby Azaria at Ayers Rock (Uluru) in August 1980. She insisted that the baby had been taken from a tent by a dingo. No body was ever found, nor did the Crown produce a weapon or suggest a motive. Nevertheless, the High Court dismissed her appeal, with **Murphy** and **Deane** dissenting (*Chamberlain Case* (1984); see **Popular culture**; **Popular images of Court**). Lindy began her prison sentence, but public disquiet continued, and eventually Justice Trevor Morling of the **Federal Court** was appointed to conduct a wide-ranging inquiry. Morling

the information laid did not disclose any offence known to the law. The remaining charges were later dismissed.

On several occasions, defamation cases brought by politicians have found their way to the Court. In 1963, federal Labor MP Tom Uren was drawn into a scandal involving allegations of Soviet spying in Australia. It was alleged that Uren and another Labor MP had been befriended by Ivan Skripov, a Soviet spy, and at his instigation had asked probing questions in Parliament concerning the location and function of Australian defence bases. The allegations were devoured by the press and an incensed Uren brought libel proceedings against two publishers. On appeal before the High Court, both cases turned on whether, in the circumstances, exemplary damages were warranted. The Court in each case found that they were not (*Uren v John Fairfax & Sons* (1966); *Australian Consolidated Press v Uren* (1966)). Uren himself, as Minister for Territories in the Hawke Labor government, returned to the Court as one of the defendants in *Clunies-Ross v Commonwealth* (1984).

Apart from the notoriety gained from his vigorous implementation of the 'White Australia Policy' as Minister for Immigration in the Chifley government after **World War II** (see *O'Keefe v Calwell* (1949); *Koon Wing Lau v Calwell* (1949)), Arthur Calwell also came before the Court in two defamation cases. *Penton v Calwell* (1945) was the climax to a long-running public dispute between Calwell and Frank Packer's *Daily Telegraph* over wartime censorship. After the 'Cowra breakout' of Japanese prisoners of war in 1944 was reported by the *Daily Telegraph*, Calwell publicly suggested that the report had defied a censorship order. The paper replied with an editorial headed 'Calwell Can Sue on This', denying the imputation and calling Calwell 'maliciously and corruptly untruthful' and 'a dishonest, calculating liar'. Thereupon, in the High Court's diversity **jurisdiction**, Calwell (in Melbourne) sued the editor (in Sydney).

The editor pleaded in justification a long history of prior exchanges in which Calwell had attacked the press in general and the Packer press in particular. At first instance, Dixon ordered that a number of the pleas be struck out; an appeal from that **order** was allowed in part. The whole Court agreed with Dixon that, while specific attacks made by Calwell on the Packer press might result in a qualified privilege for statements made by way of reply or defence, his criticisms of newspapers generally could not be used for that purpose. Only McTiernan accepted Dixon's suggestion that the publication of accusations by way of a challenge or invitation to sue 'is inconsistent with the very basis and rationale of the protection which the privilege gives'.

Thirty years later, Calwell's reputation was again at issue in *Calwell v Ipec Australia* (1975), this time in response to an article in the *Sunday Review* in April 1971. At that stage, Whitlam had succeeded Calwell as Leader of the Opposition, and the article alleged that Calwell and others had 'deteriorated into a narrow and embittered gerontocracy', undermining Whitlam's leadership. A jury found that the article was defamatory and awarded damages of $18 000, but the NSW Court of Appeal set that verdict aside and ordered judgment for the defendant (*Calwell v Ipec Australia* (1973)). Calwell had died while the defendant's appeal was pending in the Court of Appeal; the appeal to the High Court was brought by

his widow, as executrix of his estate. The whole Court agreed that the statutory defences of qualified privilege under section 17 of the *Defamation Act* 1958 (NSW) were applicable, while **Jacobs** and **Stephen** added that, regardless of their truth or falsity, the dissemination of such views was for the 'public good'. This view of politicians' defamation actions has since found expression through the implied freedom of **political communication**, which has influenced defamation law in a way unfavourable to plaintiff politicians.

The publisher of *Sunday Review* was the Sydney businessman Gordon Barton, whose challenges to the establishment reached the High Court on several occasions. Although many of these high-profile cases were prosecuted through his corporate interests, rather than in his personal capacity, they remained synonymous with Barton in the public mind. Barton's interstate transport business, Ipec Australia Ltd, had begun in October 1951 when Barton, then a recent law graduate, established the business with a second-hand truck in anticipation of the **Privy Council** decision in *Hughes & Vale v NSW* (1954), and adopted a policy of paying under protest the fees which the NSW government still imposed upon interstate transport. Following the *Hughes & Vale* decision, in which the Privy Council held the NSW law to infringe the freedom of **interstate trade and commerce** guaranteed by section 92 of the Constitution, he sued to recover the fees (*Barton v Commissioner for Motor Transport* (1957)). The Court held that an attempt to defeat the claim by a retrospective statute of limitations was itself invalid. In 1965, Barton's attempt to challenge the 'two airlines policy' by establishing his own interstate air freight service was defeated in *R v Anderson; Ex parte Ipec-Air* (1965). The Court held that the Director-General of Civil Aviation had exceeded his powers when he refused a charter licence for Ipec to fly interstate, but had acted within his powers in refusing a licence to import the necessary aircraft; and, since there could be no flights without aircraft, the Court declined to issue a **writ** of mandamus in respect of the charter licence either. Again, in *Interstate Parcel Express v Time-Life International* (1977), after Barton's corporate holdings had expanded to include Angus & Robertson, he challenged the use of **copyright** restrictions to maintain monopolistic practices in the importation of books; but again, his attempt was unsuccessful.

Fresher in the public mind are the entrepreneurial activities of Alan Bond. Bond was unsuccessful in his challenge to a decision by the Australian Broadcasting Tribunal that he was unfit to hold a broadcasting licence (*Australian Broadcasting Tribunal v Bond* (1990)); but in the same year, his brewing companies achieved two notable victories. An attempt by several banks to put the companies into receivership was rejected by the Supreme Court of Victoria, and the High Court dismissed the banks' appeal (*National Australia Bank v Bond Brewing Holdings* (1990)). An attempt by SA legislation to discourage the use of non-refillable beer bottles was held to be invalid because, in practice, the only non-refillable beer bottles sold in the state were those supplied from interstate by the Bond companies: in effect, the Court held that discrimination against non-refillable bottles was discrimination against Bond's business (*Castlemaine Tooheys v SA* (1990)). More recently, Bond himself succeeded in his constitutional challenge to part of a sentence imposed for corporate fraud offences (*Bond v The Queen* (2000)).

A businessman of a different kind was the Sydney identity Abe Saffron, who first appeared as a litigant in the Court in 1953, when he was represented by **Barwick** in an unsuccessful application for special **leave to appeal** against a legal ruling that might assist the Crown in future prosecutions against him. The Court found that Saffron could not appeal the ruling, as he had been acquitted of the relevant charges (*Saffron v The Queen* (1953)). Saffron failed again when he appealed a finding that he had not paid for goods supplied to him (*Saffron v Société Minière Cafrika* (1958)).

Two of Australia's best-known talkback radio hosts have brought appeals to the High Court. Derryn Hinch appealed following his conviction for **contempt** of court in Victoria: *Hinch v A-G (Vic)* (1987). Hinch was found to have prejudiced the fair trial of a former Catholic priest accused of child molestation. He had made a series of statements on air about the man's previous conviction for sex offences, in the course of questioning the man's suitability to remain director of an organisation running camps for children. On appeal, he argued that the trial judge, in finding contempt, had failed to take proper account of the public interest in this disclosure. The High Court not only dismissed Hinch's appeal unanimously, but also ordered that he bear substantial accumulated **costs**.

In 1990, John Laws appealed to the Court in the course of his protracted feud with the Australian Broadcasting Tribunal: *Laws v Australian Broadcasting Tribunal* (1990). Three members of the Tribunal had made a determination that Laws was in breach of the Tribunal's programming standards. Laws responded with a defamation suit, and then sought to use the Tribunal's vigorous defence of that suit as proof of the Tribunal's likely bias in its ongoing inquiry into Laws' conduct. The High Court found that, while it might be reasonable to fear bias on the part of the three members issuing the original determination, the remainder of the Tribunal's members could not reasonably generate any such fear. Laws thus failed in his challenge to the validity of the inquiry.

Some litigants' names are known through their association with a landmark case. A recent example is Olaf Dietrich, whose case established an effective right to counsel in serious criminal cases (***Dietrich v The Queen*** (1992)). Ironically, having established that right, Dietrich some years later dismissed his counsel at the start of an armed robbery trial, and proceeded to conduct his own defence. He behaved so abusively towards the Bench and prosecutor (during a segment recorded on videotape) that he was subsequently sentenced to 18 months imprisonment for contempt of court, in addition to his sentence for the armed robbery. Other litigants lending their names to landmark cases include Giovanni and Cesira Amadio, who succeeded against a bank that had acted unconscionably in relation to a loan guarantee (***Amadio's Case*** (1983)); Mohamed Naguib Fawzi Ahmed Metwally, the Egyptian postgraduate student whose complaint against the University of Wollongong under the *Anti-Discrimination Act 1977* (NSW) was defeated by the Court's insistence that the **inconsistency** of that Act with Commonwealth law could not be cured retrospectively (*University of Wollongong v Metwally* (1984)); Shawar Kirmani, who was knocked unconscious on a Sydney harbour cruise when another passenger fell on her from the upper deck, and who thereby triggered a reassessment of the Commonwealth's power to liberate itself from Imperial law (*Kirmani v Captain Cook Cruises* (1985); see ***Australia Acts***); Ah Hin Teoh, whose case established that a failure to consider the relevance of **international law** to administrative decisions may give rise to issues of procedural fairness (***Teoh's Case*** (1995)); and Giancarlo Gambotto, a self-represented small shareholder, who successfully argued that a forced buyout of his shares had been conducted oppressively and so was invalid (*Gambotto v WCP* (1995)). Encouraged by his success, and still self-represented, Gambotto then sought to challenge other takeovers on constitutional grounds, including arguments relating to freedom of interstate trade and **acquisition of property**, to which **Gummow** (sitting alone) gave short shrift (*Gambotto v Resolute Samantha* (1995)).

The Court has seen only a handful of Aboriginal and Torres Strait Islander litigants, distressingly often in criminal cases. Only one such case appears to have reached the High Court prior to World War II (***Tuckiar v The King*** (1934)); but as the consequences of Aboriginal degradation and exclusion from mainstream society have become more apparent, there have been a number of such cases (see, for example, *Ngatayi v The Queen* (1980); *Veen v The Queen (Nos 1 and 2)* (1979 and 1988); and see **Colonialism**). The case that attracted most public disquiet was *Stuart v The Queen* (1959), where the **Dixon Court** simply refused special leave to appeal, though noting that 'certain features of this case have caused us some anxiety'. In that case, Rupert Max Stuart, described in the High Court judgment as 'an aboriginal of the Arunta tribe, not quite of the full blood', had been convicted of the shocking rape and murder of a nine-year-old girl. The conviction depended largely upon a written confession supposedly dictated by Stuart; the evidence before the High Court included an affidavit from the respected anthropologist TGH Strehlow, who testified on the basis of his knowledge of the Arunta language and his own lengthy interview with Stuart that the supposed confession could not in fact have been dictated by him.

Prompted by the High Court's expression of 'anxiety', **Evatt**, in his capacity as Leader of the Opposition in the federal Parliament, then intervened on Stuart's behalf. An appeal to the Privy Council was rejected, and a subsequent SA Royal Commission affirmed that Stuart was guilty. But the controversy over his guilt or innocence was never resolved. John Starke, who represented Stuart before the Royal Commission, told the radio broadcaster Jon Faine in 1991 that he still believed Stuart was 'probably innocent', and had no doubt that the confession was 'bashed ... out of [him]'.

Three months before its refusal of special leave in the *Stuart* case, the Court had also dismissed an appeal from the distinguished watercolourist Albert Namatjira (see *Namatjira v Raabe* (1959)). Namatjira's ensuing prison sentence was thought to have hastened his death later that year. The celebrity that Namatjira enjoyed at the time may now be eclipsed by that of Eddie Koiki Mabo who, along with other Murray Islanders, challenged the *terra nullius* principle and posthumously gave his name to the Court's recognition of **native title** (*Mabo* (1992)). However, attempts to persuade the Court to recognise the rights of **Aboriginal peoples** have had a long history. The oppressive powers conferred by the Northern Territory's Aboriginals Ordinance 1918, now well-known through *Kruger v Commonwealth* (1997), had already been unsuccessfully challenged in *Waters v Commonwealth* (1951). Fred Waters, a union activist also known as Fred Nadpur, was detained involuntarily on an Aboriginal reserve. An injunction application seeking his release came before Fullagar, the claim being that the detention proceeded from the improper motive of stifling trade union action on behalf of Aboriginal peoples. Fullagar refused the application on jurisdictional grounds. Nevertheless, he declined to make an order for costs, since he did not wish 'to discourage any person, who thinks that a real injustice has been done to an aboriginal, from invoking the assistance of the courts even against the Director'.

Greater success was enjoyed by a later activist, Percy Neal (*Neal v The Queen* (1982)). A stipendiary magistrate had convicted Neal, a community leader on the Yarrabah Aboriginal Reserve in North Queensland, of assaulting an officer of the Queensland Department of Aboriginal and Islanders Advancement (Mr Collins) who managed the community store. Neal had allegedly spat on Collins, whom he accused of exploiting the dependency of the community. Neal appealed his two-month prison sentence to the Queensland Court of Criminal Appeal, but that Court considered the sentence 'manifestly inadequate' and increased it to six months. The increased sentence was quashed by a unanimous High Court, with all Justices expressing concern, in varying degrees, at the factors motivating the exercise of sentencing discretion in the courts below. Murphy's judgment showed particular empathy with Neal's objectives, declaring famously that 'Mr Neal is entitled to be an agitator'.

Other notable indigenous litigants include John Koowarta, who took on the Queensland government and established the validity of the *Racial Discrimination Act* 1975 (Cth) (*Koowarta's Case* (1982)); Paul Coe and his sister Isobel Coe, who sought, unsuccessfully, to establish that white settlement in Australia was unlawful (respectively in *Coe v Commonwealth (No 1)* (1979) and *Coe v Commonwealth (No 2)* (1993)); Lorraine Onus, who established that Aboriginal people have a 'cultural' or 'spiritual' interest in protecting Aboriginal relics, giving them the necessary **standing** to take legal action (*Onus v Alcoa* (1981)); Lou Davis, whose right to market Bicentennial T-shirts denouncing '200 years of suppression and oppression' was upheld in *Davis v Commonwealth* (1988); Denis Walker, the son of the poet Oodgeroo Noonuccal, who suggested that Aboriginal criminal law had remained in force in the same way as Aboriginal native title (*Walker v NSW* (1994)); Doreen Kartinyeri, the Ngarrindjeri woman who challenged the constitutionality of the *Hindmarsh Island Bridge Act* 1997 (Cth) (*Hindmarsh Island Bridge Case* (1998)); Alec Kruger, who along with other members of the 'Stolen Generation' of indigenous Australians failed to establish any grounds for redress in *Kruger v Commonwealth*; and the Wik People, whose successful native title claim confirmed that such title is not necessarily extinguished by the grant of a pastoral lease (*Wik* (1996)). While the climate of **public opinion** at the beginning of a new century may in some respects have become less conducive to the vindication of Aboriginal rights, the Court will still have a **role** as final arbiter in native title claims.

In cases like these, the Court's response to the claims of notable litigants may help to focus public attention on significant social issues, though the consequent shifts in public opinion may be both positive and negative. In other cases, aside from adding an element of human interest, the presence of notable litigants ensures that the High Court itself is at least periodically a focus of public attention. Without them, the average person might have little occasion to reflect on the existence and role of the Court.

TONY BLACKSHIELD
GRAHAM FRICKE
AMELIA SIMPSON

Litigants in person. The right of audience before the High Court has usually been exercised by members of the **legal profession**—more frequently by those practising as barristers than by those practising as solicitors. On numerous occasions, the Court has noted the assistance given to it by the legal profession. That assistance has enabled the Court to dispose efficiently of its caseload. Usually, but not universally, litigants in person are disadvantaged by an absence of familiarity with the Court's **procedure** and with legal principles. That absence of familiarity imposes significant burdens on both the Court and its Registry when litigants conduct their matters in person.

Litigants in person have always had a right of audience in all matters save in applications for leave and special **leave to appeal**. Under the early Rules of Court, when leave or special leave could be given on applications by motion *ex parte*, the Court heard litigants in person. They would be called on after the motions by **counsel**. The procedure was not always efficient. Thus Ebenezer Cox, a litigant in person, moved *ex parte* on 2 June 1932 for special leave to appeal in a matter in which he had applied once before. **Starke** refused the application and told him that he must not come before the Court in the same matter again, lest his action be treated as **contempt**. Then, in *Collins v The Queen* (1975), the Court held that the provisions of order 70 as it then stood validly required applications for special leave to appeal to be made by **counsel**, though written applications from persons in custody had been received. When the procedure was reformed in 1986, the requirement for such applications to be made by counsel was retained. When the procedure was reformed again in 1993, litigants in person were allowed to make such applications to the **Full Court** orally only 'in exceptional circumstances'. But provision was made for litigants in person to file a written case and for a Court or Justice to decide whether the case should be served on the opposing party and whether an oral hearing should follow.

This procedure proved to be extremely oppressive. The examination of written cases consumed much judicial time. In 1996, the Rules were amended once more. The distinction between applications by counsel and applications by litigants in person was eliminated, but summaries of **argument** were required to be filed; a party was entitled to elect not to present oral argument and the time for oral argument was limited. Applications by litigants in person for special leave to appeal are quite numerous and it is estimated that 25 per cent of Registry time is occupied in dealing with such applications. Examination of the application books and the consideration of the issues that might arise are more anxious duties for the Justices than they would be if they had the assistance that is expected from counsel.

The proportion of applications made by litigants in person in matters coming before a single Justice has increased in recent years—it is now of the order of between one-quarter and one-third. In appeals or in original **jurisdiction** matters heard before the Full Court the proportion is lower and, if the case is one that raises a difficult question of law, the Court might invite the Registrar to enquire about the availability of legal aid or other professional assistance to conduct the proceeding. If legal aid is not available, Bar Associations, or their members, have often assisted both the Court and the litigant in person by preparing and delivering full argument.

Some litigants in person have been declared **vexatious litigants**. On the other hand, some litigants in person have had success in the conduct of their proceedings (see, for example, *Gambotto v WCP* (1995)).

The public right of access to the Court has to be balanced against the preservation of the Court's ability to dispose effectively of its case load without being occupied by cases brought without an appreciation of their lack of legal merit. With the increase in the Court's workload, that balance has proved to be difficult to strike.

GERARD BRENNAN

M

Mabo (1992). In 1982, Eddie Koiki Mabo, James Rice, and David Passi (together with Celuia Salee and Sam Passi, who later withdrew) commenced proceedings in the High Court against Queensland and the Commonwealth, seeking declarations that in respect of lands and waters in the Murray Island group in the Torres Strait, they held a traditional **native title** which had not been extinguished by Queensland's annexation of the islands in 1879, nor by subsequent actions of government. A preliminary hearing before **Deane** on 28 October 1982 decided that the parties should try to agree on a statement of facts; but that attempt failed. In February 1986, **Gibbs** directed that the issues of fact be remitted to the Supreme Court of Queensland (*Mabo v Queensland*) (1986)). The proceedings in the Supreme Court were allocated to Justice Martin Moynihan, who began taking evidence on 13 October 1986.

Meanwhile, the Queensland Parliament had enacted the *Queensland Coast Islands Declaratory Act* 1985 (Qld). This Act declared retroactively that the legislature's intention in 1879—when, with Imperial authority, it annexed the islands—was that any pre-existing land rights were extinguished, without compensation. When Queensland pleaded this Act as a defence to the *Mabo* litigation, the plaintiffs demurred; and after a further **directions hearing** before Deane on 13 February 1987, the hearings before Moynihan were adjourned until the issues arising on the demurrer were determined. In *Mabo (No 1)* (1988), the High Court held by a 4:3 majority that the 1985 Act was invalid for **inconsistency** with section 10 of the *Racial Discrimination Act* 1975 (Cth). **Wilson** and **Dawson** dissented, while **Mason** thought the issue could not be resolved on demurrer—that is, in the absence of any findings as to the plaintiffs' rights.

Moynihan then resumed his hearings. On 5 June 1989, he found that the plaintiffs' claims could not be sustained in relation to offshore areas and accordingly made an order dismissing the Commonwealth from the action. However, in three volumes handed down on 16 November 1990, he found that there was a continuing system of customary rights in respect of land and also made findings about the particular lands claimed by the plaintiffs. The High Court heard argument on 28–31 May 1991 and gave judgment on 3 June 1992. Six Justices (Dawson dissenting) declared that (except for two small areas as to which further evidence was needed) the Meriam people were entitled against the whole world to the possession, occupation, use and enjoyment of the Murray Islands.

The majority held that Australian **common law**, in common with the law in other lands colonised by the British, recognises the pre-existing land rights of indigenous peoples. Statements to the contrary in earlier cases relating to Australia had not involved indigenous parties, with the sole exception of the decision of Justice Richard Blackburn of the Supreme Court of the Northern Territory in *Milirrpum v Nabalco* (1971), which the High Court effectively overruled.

Brennan (with whom Mason and **McHugh** concurred) emphasised the limits on the Court's power to overturn long-held assumptions. 'Rules that accord with contemporary notions of justice and human rights' could not be adopted if to do so 'would fracture the skeleton of principle which gives the body of our law its shape and internal consistency'. Nevertheless, he held that within these limits the Court faced a choice. 'The proposition that, when the Crown assumed **sovereignty** over an Australian colony, it became the universal and absolute beneficial owner of all the land therein, invites critical examination.'

As Brennan understood it, the manner in which a sovereign state might acquire new territory primarily depends on **international law**, with which the common law had marched in step. For the acquisition of sovereignty over uninhabited lands, international law had adopted the Roman law notion of *terra nullius*. Thereafter, the European colonial nations had justified their acquisition of sovereignty over territories inhabited by 'backward' peoples—especially if the land was uncultivated—by 'enlarging' this concept. But this 'enlarged concept of *terra nullius*', by which 'the settlement of an inhabited territory is equated with settlement of an uninhabited territory', had 'depended on a discriminatory denigration of indigenous inhabitants', treating them as 'barbarous or unsettled and without a settled law' (see **Colonialism**). Since that perception was both 'false in fact' and 'unacceptable in our society', its supposed legal consequences needed to be re-examined.

In the International Court of Justice, that re-examination had already occurred (*Advisory Opinion on Western Sahara* (1975)). That Court had held that the classification of territory as *terra nullius* 'would be possible only if it were established that … the territory belonged to no-one'. Brennan noted that 'international law is a legitimate and important influence on the development of the common law', especially in the area of universal human rights.

to prescribe what parcels of land and what interests in those parcels should be enjoyed by others and what parcels of land should be kept as the sovereign's beneficial demesne … But if the land were occupied by the indigenous inhabitants and their rights and interests in the land are recognized by the common law, the radical title … cannot itself be taken to confer an absolute beneficial title to the occupied land.

He explained that 'the radical title, without more, is merely a logical postulate': it supports the grant of tenures derived from the Crown, and supports the Crown's beneficial ownership of those lands that it chooses to acquire. But where the Crown has not exercised its sovereign power in either of these ways, 'there is no reason why land … should not continue to be subject to native title. It is only the fallacy of equating sovereignty and beneficial ownership of land that gives rise to the notion that native title is extinguished by the acquisition of sovereignty'.

Nevertheless, native title is a more limited and vulnerable form of title than titles granted by government. The holders of native title cannot transfer or otherwise dispose of their title, except by surrender to the Crown: it is 'inalienable'. More importantly, a sovereign government has the power effectively to 'extinguish' native title, as decisions of the **United States Supreme Court** had recognised since the early nineteenth century. A government may exercise this power either by making grants of interests in land, or by allocating land to public purposes (see *Wik* (1996)). To the extent that such acts are inconsistent with the continued exercise and enjoyment of native title rights and interests, those rights and interests are extinguished. It was on this basis that the Court was able to recognise native title without disturbing two centuries of land grants. However, as Brennan said, 'the exercise of a power to extinguish native title must reveal a clear and plain intention to do so'.

In several ways, the equally elaborate judgment of **Toohey** went further. For example, he emphasised that, once the common law was received into a new colony, the common law itself insisted that any compulsory **acquisition of property** by the Crown required legislative authority. Again, while courts in other countries had found that the native titles in those countries were inalienable, Toohey questioned how far (or in what precise sense) that had been the case in Australia. He noted that in one case he had heard as Aboriginal Land Commissioner, there was evidence of land being 'given' by one group to another.

More importantly, he held that precisely because a state government has the power to extinguish native title,

> this power and corresponding vulnerability give rise to a **fiduciary obligation** on the part of the Crown. The power to destroy a people's interests in this way is extraordinary and is sufficient to attract regulation by **Equity** to ensure that the position is not abused. The fiduciary relationship arises, therefore, out of the *power* of the Crown to extinguish traditional title.

Whether such a fiduciary obligation—which Toohey equated with a constructive **trust**—can be said to exist remains unresolved. **Deane** and **Gaudron** envisaged that 'actual or threatened interference' with native title might

Torres Strait Islander and litigant Eddie Mabo

It was 'only by fastening on the notion that a settled colony was terra nullius', said Brennan, that it was possible to assume that the acquisition of sovereignty over the Australian colonies had carried with it the 'universal and absolute' beneficial ownership 'of all the land therein'. It was 'only on the hypothesis that there was nobody in occupation' that it could be said—as NSW Chief Justice Alfred Stephen had said in *A-G (NSW) v Brown* (1847)—that the Crown became the absolute owner of 'all the waste and unoccupied lands of the colony; for … there is no *other* proprietor'. 'If that hypothesis be rejected', said Brennan, 'the notion that sovereignty carried ownership in its wake must be rejected too'.

He conceded that any distinction between 'sovereignty' and 'ownership' must be reconciled with the feudal doctrine of tenures, since this was a fundamental principle of English **land law** which was received on the settlement of the Australian colonies (see **Reception of English law**), and 'could not be overturned without fracturing the skeleton which gives our land law its shape and consistency'. According to this doctrine, all land tenures derive ultimately from a grant from the Crown; and the Court agreed that this had been the essential basis for the **property** rights acquired by the settler population. But the necessary underpinning for these derivative tenures was only that, along with its sovereignty, the Crown had acquired the 'radical title', which was not necessarily to be equated with the beneficial ownership of land.

The radical title is a postulate of the doctrine of tenure and a concomitant of sovereignty. As a sovereign enjoys supreme legal authority in and over a territory, the sovereign has power

attract equitable **remedies**, in particular 'the imposition of a remedial constructive trust'; and that where native title was extinguished 'wrongfully', that might also give rise (subject to limitations provisions) to a claim for compensatory **damages**. The force of the moral assessment underlying these suggestions was indicated earlier in their judgment, when they wrote of 'the conflagration of oppression and conflict which … spread across the continent to dispossess, degrade and devastate the **Aboriginal peoples** and leave a national legacy of unutterable shame'. At the end of their judgment, they defended this use of 'language … which some may think to be unusually emotive for a judgment in this Court' by disclaiming any intention 'to trespass into the area of assessment or attribution of moral guilt', explaining that an appreciation of the 'full facts' of the dispossession of Australian Aborigines was 'of critical importance to the assessment' of the fiction of *terra nullius*. Despite this disclaimer, their 'unrestrained language' was seized upon by critics of the decision as evidence of a departure from the usual judicial standards of objectivity and impartiality.

Brennan conceded that there might be a fiduciary duty in the special case where native title was 'surrendered to the Crown in expectation of a grant of a tenure to the indigenous title holders'; but beyond that, while the legal validity of any particular act of extinguishment might be open to review under 'the general law', he emphasised that the courts 'cannot review the merits, as distinct from the legality', of an exercise of sovereign power—whether or not it displayed 'solicitude for the welfare of indigenous inhabitants'. Mason and McHugh also rejected any suggestion that an extinguishment of native title could be 'wrongful', suggesting that this rejection was a majority view since it was also supported by Dawson's dissent.

Further, while Toohey agreed with the analysis by which prior 'traditional native title' survives the acquisition of sovereignty and is recognised by (though its incidents are not defined by) the common law, he also considered an alternative argument that in any event, *after* the acquisition of sovereignty, the continued occupation by indigenous peoples might give rise to a 'possessory' title ('common law aboriginal title'), arising from (and defined by) the operation of the common law itself. Without reaching a firm conclusion, he held that this, too, was a tenable argument.

Finally, Toohey drew particular attention to the Racial Discrimination Act—which, as *Mabo (No 1)* had shown, gives native title the same level of protection as other forms of title. The point was also made, though less elaborately, in other judgments: Deane and Gaudron invoked *Mabo (No 1)* as showing that the Racial Discrimination Act imposes 'an important restraint upon State or Territory legislative power to extinguish or diminish common law native title', while Brennan noted that this power is 'subject to the valid laws of the Commonwealth, including the *Racial Discrimination Act*'.

Indeed, it was concern about the combined effect of the *Mabo* decision with the Racial Discrimination Act on post-1975 acts of governments, and the perceived need to validate such acts, that was the major motivation for the enactment of the *Native Title Act* 1993 (Cth). That legislation was enacted after a year of intense public debate about the issues, including the **role** of the Court itself, and whether the *Mabo* deci-

sion represented a 'judicial revolution', or merely a 'cautious correction' of the common law (see also **Law-making role**).

GARTH NETTHEIM

Further Reading
Richard Bartlett, *The Mabo Decision* (1993)
Essays on the Mabo Decision (1993), substantially reprinted from 15 *Syd LR* 119
Nonie Sharp, *No Ordinary Judgment* (1996)
Special Issue, 'Indigenous Peoples: Issues for the Nineties' (1993) 16 *UNSWLJ* 1
Margaret Stephenson and Suri Ratnapala (eds), *Mabo: A Judicial Revolution* (1993)

***Mabo*: a historical perspective.** When Governor Arthur Phillip arrived in Australia in 1788 with the First Fleet, he had no instructions relating to the status of Aboriginal **property** rights. No reason was given for this omission. Historians have attempted to account for it, but the lack of contemporary documentation precludes any definitive answer. Two interpretations have been adduced. One suggests that the British believed Australia to be practically uninhabited—literally, a *terra nullius*. The other proposes that the Imperial government took the view that the **Aboriginal peoples** were too primitive to negotiate with, and that their nomadism did not give them a legitimate claim to the land.

Later evidence supports the first interpretation. In 1822, James Stephen, the legal adviser to the Colonial Office, declared that Australia had been acquired 'neither by conquest nor cession, but by the mere occupation of a desert or uninhabited land'.

But experience in the Australian colonies led to a reassessment of early assumptions. The indigenous population proved to be greater than expected. Aborigines provided abundant evidence that they lived in clearly defined territories and regarded the land as theirs. The impact of increased knowledge was apparent in the case of Stephen, who in 1840, as Under Secretary of the Colonial Office, noted on a despatch from SA: 'It is an important and unsuspected fact that these Tribes had Propriety in the Soil—that is, in particular sections of it which were clearly defined and well understood before the occupation of their country.'

Opinion in Britain about the rights of indigenous people changed rapidly in the wake of the successful crusade against slavery. In 1837, the *Report of the House of Commons Select Committee on Aborigines (British Settlements)* declared: 'It might be presumed that the native inhabitants of any land have an incontrovertible right to their own soil: a plain and sacred right, however, which seems not to have been understood'.

Colonial Office policy incorporated this recognition of **native title** during the 1830s and 1840s. Its most important manifestation was the creation, between 1848 and 1850, of pastoral leases providing for the preservation of Aboriginal rights to remain on the subject land.

With the achievement of **responsible government** in eastern Australia between 1856 and 1859, control of Aboriginal affairs passed to the new legislatures. On several occasions, Aboriginal groups petitioned the colonial parliaments seeking to have their rights to traditional lands respected—or, more commonly, they fiercely resisted the incursion and settlement of European pioneers. But land rights did not become a central issue again until the 1960s. The impetus for the modern movement came from several different sources.

In 1959, the Federal Council for Aboriginal Affairs, at its second annual conference, adopted as policy the 1957 International Labour Organisation Convention 107, article 11 of which read: 'The right of ownership, collective or individual, of the members of the populations concerned over the lands which these populations traditionally occupy shall be recognized.'

In 1963, the Yolngu people of north-eastern Arnhem Land sent a bark petition to the federal Parliament expressing their concern about the excision of land from their reserve for a mining venture. Failing to receive the response they sought, they took action in the Supreme Court of the Northern Territory in the case of *Milirrpum v Nabalco* (1971). Justice Richard Blackburn found that there had never been any recognition of customary title in Australia, and that the Yolngu relationship with the land could not be construed as ownership. But land rights emerged as a major political issue with the erection of the Tent Embassy on the lawns in front of Parliament House in Canberra in 1972, and their recognition was adopted as government policy in the **Whitlam era** of 1972–75.

Eddie Koiki Mabo took an interest in indigenous politics from the time of the Inter-Racial Seminar in Townsville in 1967. But his focus on land rights only became pronounced and personal when he learnt that in the eyes of the law Murray Island was Crown land. This was for him an extraordinary situation. He had grown up in a community where few Europeans lived and where families were sharply aware of their property rights over their gardens and residential land.

His disquiet found an outlet during a conference on land rights at James Cook University in 1981, where he met visiting speakers who had the expertise to advise him and his associated plaintiffs how to advance a case through the courts. The litigation in *Mabo* began in May 1982.

HENRY REYNOLDS

Further Reading
Alan Frost, 'New South Wales as *Terra Nullius*: The British Denial of Aboriginal Land Rights' (1981) 19 *Historical Studies* 513
Henry Reynolds, *The Law of the Land* (2nd edn 1992)

Mabo: counsel's perspective. Forty thousand years inhabiting this continent is a long time: so is ten years of litigation for all those involved, whether litigants, lawyers, or the Court. The *Mabo* litigation, resulting in two separate **Full Court** decisions, was commenced in the original **jurisdiction** of the High Court in May 1982: the final decision was handed down on 3 June 1992. The plaintiffs' legal team over that period comprised Ron Castan, Greg McIntyre, Barbara Hocking, and myself. This period saw an unusually high level of development in the Court's attitudes and change in its membership, leading, on one view, to *Mabo* as the high point of the **Mason Court's** 'activist' period.

From my own perspective as one of the **counsel** in the case, this lengthy, hard-fought, and fragile 'test case' litigation was founded on, and strategically guided by, three principles in particular.

Ron Castan, counsel in *Mabo*

The first arose from our instructions, which led us to the belief that a compelling injustice—recorded ultimately in the Court's judgment in clear and unequivocal terms—should be confronted and, if possible, corrected.

Secondly, the plaintiffs and their lawyers were convinced that Australia's highest court should, for the first time since 1901, be squarely presented with the critical legal issues. These were, in essence, whether Australian **common law** at the end of the twentieth century should recognise the social and cultural realities of the Meriam people (that is, whether the existence of customs and traditions incorporating traditional rights and interests to the lands and surrounding seas of the Murray Islands delivered enforceable **property** rights known to the common law); and in particular whether, upon colonisation of Australia, the common law of England extinguished, arbitrarily and without compensation, the prior traditional property rights of the indigenous inhabitants, or recognised and accommodated those rights in the new legal regime. For 200 years, colonial, state and federal politicians had failed to resolve these issues; the High Court (now free from **Privy Council** supervision) was the plaintiffs' only hope of redress.

Thirdly, numerous precedents and good arguments were available in 1982 from Australian colonial courts, from the High Court itself, and from equivalent common law jurisdictions—especially the Privy Council on appeal from Africa, NZ, and Canada—to support the plaintiffs' central claim.

In *Mabo*, counsel's dictum—'know thy court'—became significant for two reasons. First, it was decided, so far as possible, to ensure that the case was heard in the High Court, or otherwise in federal jurisdiction. This would conserve limited resources and maximise the impact of any success as a **precedent**; moreover, rightly or wrongly, it was thought that the case would receive a more favourable reception from federal judges, who might arguably have wider jurisprudential and constitutional horizons and be more sensitive to national consequences.

Accordingly, the claim was issued in the Court's original jurisdiction; included a claim not only against Queensland but also against the Commonwealth as a second defendant; and pleaded an international treaty—the Torres Straits

Treaty, entered into with Papua New Guinea. All this attracted jurisdiction under section 75 of the Constitution.

After argument, on 27 February 1986, Chief Justice **Gibbs** remitted the trial of the factual issues raised by the pleadings (though not the legal issues) not to a **Federal Court** judge, as the plaintiffs had sought, but to the Supreme Court of Queensland (*Mabo v Queensland* (1986)). It was important, however, that in this **remittal** the state court was exercising federal jurisdiction. Among other things, this enabled the High Court to supervise the trial judge's decisions made along the way—some of which arguably exceeded the limited terms of the remitter. It ensured that the High Court retained its place as sole determiner of the legal issues, and enabled Victorian counsel to appear in the Queensland Supreme Court. In hindsight, that 'federal' strategy, which also avoided costly intermediate appeals, worked to the plaintiffs' advantage. But it meant that the trial judge, Justice Martin Moynihan, was denied the opportunity to determine the legal issues, and found the limited remitter experience 'enriching and rewarding … [but] essentially both unsatisfactory and unsatisfying'.

Moynihan conducted the trial in two stages between October 1986 and September 1989, and delivered his determination of facts on 16 November 1990. Those findings, and all the evidence, were returned to the High Court for ultimate **argument** on the legal issues, which occurred in Canberra during 28–31 May 1991.

Secondly, 'know thy court' had a further significance: over the period 1982–92, the changes in the Court's membership and the developments in its jurisprudence were both considerable—as they have been again in the decade since. One wonders how the *Mabo* case might be received today. In May 1982, the Court comprised Gibbs, **Stephen**, **Mason**, **Murphy**, **Aickin**, **Wilson**, and **Brennan**. Over the ensuing decade, two Justices died (Aickin and Murphy), two resigned (Stephen and Wilson) and one retired (Gibbs). A new **Chief Justice**—Mason—was appointed, along with a total of five new **puisne Justices** (**Deane**, **Dawson**, **Toohey**, **Gaudron**, and **McHugh**). Thus a differently constituted Full Court heard argument, in March 1988, in *Mabo (No 1)*, from the Bench that heard argument, in April 1991, in *Mabo (No 2)*. And of course, Eddie Mabo himself died from cancer on 21 January 1992, while awaiting judgment. Such are the fortunes of history for courts, and litigants. There were many delays—early procrastination and denial by Queensland; two years spent arguing the demurrer leading to *Mabo (No 1)*; a lengthy trial; and a further wait of one year for the trial judge to deliver his determination of facts. However, given the development, through the 1980s, of the 'activist' character of the Mason Court, the delay worked, arguably, to the plaintiffs' advantage.

From counsel's perspective, although our instructions, our central objectives, and the test case implications were all blindingly clear, and although the legal difficulties and practical logistics were somewhat burdensome, the burdens were always leavened by the knowledge that the plaintiffs' cause was unquestionably just. From the earliest **directions hearings**, the path was strewn with obstacles—jurisdictional, evidential, logistical, doctrinal—not to mention the difficulties of resources. No such claim had previously been litigated in the High Court—and very rarely in lower courts.

Over the decade, several forensic crises came and went, any one of which could have defeated the case. Human and financial resources were a constant problem: so much so that counsel's families were called upon to assist at various points, especially during the trial. At times, the battle between the plaintiffs and Queensland erupted, in court and elsewhere, into serious trench warfare. After years of delay, demands for yet further particulars, and general denial, the Bjelke-Petersen Queensland government decided enough was enough, and hurriedly passed an Act that purported—retrospectively, and without compensation—to abolish any traditional rights to land that may have survived British annexation of the Torres Straits in 1879, and thereby kill the case. The plaintiffs thereupon filed a demurrer bringing on the central question of whether the state law was valid. This was argued in March 1988. By the narrowest of majorities (4:3), and on only one of several arguments presented, the Court, in December 1988, declared the Queensland law to be **inconsistent** with section 10(1) of the *Racial Discrimination Act* 1975 (Cth) and thus inoperative because of section 109 of the Constitution. Thus the *Mabo* litigation survived.

After this play within the play, the trial resumed in Brisbane in May 1989, with Eddie Mabo continuing the evidence in chief he had begun two and a half years earlier, in October 1986. As history now shows, the heavy-handed legislative intervention by the Queensland government backfired in another significant way: the importance of the Racial Discrimination Act as a legislative protection to the otherwise fragile nature of **native title** became clear to all governments after *Mabo (No 2)*.

Another point of crisis arose in May 1989, at the resumed trial in Brisbane. Two key plaintiffs, without any forewarning, sent a message advising that they had withdrawn from the proceedings. After new instructions had been obtained—and after considerable argument before Moynihan—one of these two plaintiffs, Father Dave Passi, was readmitted. This was a fortuitous ruling. Without the findings in relation to Passi's claims—and given that Eddie Mabo failed at the trial to prove his interests, which meant that he had to be represented separately before the High Court—the findings of fact presented to the High Court as the foundation for final legal argument would have been much weaker. As it was, Queensland argued on the first day of the final hearing in the High Court that the Court should not further entertain the matter, since insufficient findings of traditional rights and interests in the claimed land had been recorded by the trial judge. The Court considered this argument seriously. I well recall that at the end of this first day of argument, the plaintiffs' legal team was seriously depressed—and not for the first time.

Some say that *Mabo* was a 'strong' case—a relatively easy native title claim. That had not been counsel's view from the trenches over the decade.

BRYAN KEON-COHEN

Further Reading
Bryan Keon-Cohen, 'The Mabo Litigation: A Personal and Procedural Account' (2000) 24 *MULR* 893

Mabo: political consequences. The High Court's decision in *Mabo* (1992), which incorporated the **common law** doctrine of **native title** into Australian law, was undoubtedly a landmark case in law. But it was much more than that. The Court's recognition of the legitimacy of an indigenous legal order predating the arrival of Europeans challenged the prevailing understanding of Australian **history** and **nationhood**. In rejecting the idea that before European settlement Australia was *terra nullius*, the Court was overturning much more than a legal doctrine. In settler Australia, *terra nullius* had become a state of mind. Overcoming that state of mind—not just ideologically but also in practical legal and constitutional arrangements that give due recognition to Aborigines and Torres Strait Islanders as Australia's first peoples and original proprietors—was bound to be a wrenching experience for the country.

The first step in coming to terms with *Mabo* was enactment of the *Native Title Act* 1993 (Cth) by the federal Parliament. Pressure to enact legislation came primarily from the mining and pastoralist industries, which wanted the removal of any threat that native title might pose to their interests. Miners and pastoralists were particularly concerned about the validity of titles or leases issued to them after the coming into effect of the *Racial Discrimination Act* 1975 (Cth). While not indifferent to these concerns, **Prime Minister** Paul Keating made it clear in a speech at Redfern Oval on 12 December 1992, inaugurating Australia's participation in the International Year of the World's Indigenous Peoples, that his government would only support legislation that respected *Mabo* as 'an historic turning point … for a new relationship between indigenous and non-Aboriginal Australians'.

The legislative process did not get under way until after the federal election of March 1993, when the Keating Labor government was returned to office. From early April until final passage of the Native Title Act three days before Christmas, the issue dominated Australian politics. On one side of this struggle were the state and territory governments—particularly those of WA, Queensland, and the Northern Territory—which had the largest exposure to native title claims and the strongest connections with the mining and pastoralist industries. On the other side, a remarkable coalition of indigenous leaders emerged to press the case against massive and unilateral extinguishment of native title and the case for a process that would facilitate the processing of native title claims.

The Keating government was caught in the middle, and the legislative product of this intense and protracted political struggle was very much a compromise. In the final stages, the government abandoned any effort to accommodate the Liberal–National Opposition, which had lined up with the states and the mining industry. To achieve passage of the legislation in the Senate, it accepted amendments supported by Green senators in close touch with Aboriginal leaders.

Nonetheless, the Native Title Act was a bitter disappointment to much of the indigenous community. It read more like an Act legitimating indigenous dispossession than an instrument for recognising native title. Not only did it remove any doubts about acts of dispossession without compensation before 1975, which had generally been expected, but it also provided for the validation of grants made since 1975. On the other hand, the Act established a National Native Title Tribunal and a nationwide process for establishing and asserting native title in those large areas of the country where it still had not been extinguished. However, faced with future acts encroaching on their lands, including grants to the mining industry, native title holders would not have a power of veto but only a 'right to negotiate'.

The complex land tenure provisions of the Native Title Act were not the whole of the initial legislative response to *Mabo*. The initial package of reforms contained some other, less controversial, measures to promote justice for Australia's **Aboriginal peoples.** An Indigenous Land Corporation was set up to purchase land for descendants of indigenous people who had long been dispossessed and would not be able to meet the criteria for native title claims. Over the next decade, $1.5 billion would be allocated to the fund. Also, in 1993 the position of Aboriginal and Torres Strait Islander Social Justice Commissioner was established within the Human Rights and Equal Opportunity Commission. The Social Justice Commissioner would promote public awareness of the human rights of indigenous Australians, including their entitlements under the Native Title Act. The first Commissioner, Mick Dodson, played a leading role in representing indigenous interests in negotiations leading up to the Native Title Act.

The emergence of a highly visible and articulate group of indigenous leaders onto the Australian political stage was one of the major consequences of the intense and protracted political storm that raged around the legislative response to *Mabo*. This group included persons such as Lowitja O'Donoghue, Chair of the Aboriginal and Torres Strait Islander Commission; Patrick Dodson, Chair of the Council for Aboriginal Reconciliation; Noel Pearson of the Cape York Land Council; and leaders of various other Land Councils who, like Mick Dodson, held leading positions in statutory bodies established to promote justice for indigenous Australians. It also included leaders such as Michael Mansell and Geoff Clark from organisations such as the Aboriginal Provisional Government with independent roots in the indigenous community. In August 1993, 400 Aboriginal and Torres Strait Islander representatives met at the Eva Valley Station in the Northern Territory to formulate a united position on the proposed native title legislation. This was the largest country-wide assembly of indigenous leaders in Australian history. Although, in the end, the Native Title Act fell far short of the position set out by Aboriginal and Torres Strait Islander leaders at Eva Valley, the strength of their intervention in the debate over the legislation ensured them a permanent and prominent place in Australian political life.

The intensity of the political struggle over the Native Title Act demonstrated how difficult it would be to translate the Court victory of *Mabo* into tangible gains for indigenous Australians. The Act itself—a dense, 127-page statute of 253 sections—not only validated indigenous dispossession up to 1994, but also imposed a much more complex and limiting set of tests and procedures on any future native title claims than exists in other English-settler countries. Even this legislation was too much for the Opposition, for the Northern Territory, and for some state governments. In marked contrast to the unity that marked the 1967 referendum campaign removing discriminatory provisions from the Constitution, the Native Title Act debate left non-indigenous Australia deeply divided along both partisan and federal lines on the recognition of native title. Clearly, it was easier for a consensus to form around a general commitment to equal justice for indigenous Australians than to recognise their special rights as the country's original proprietors.

The Native Title Act, despite all its details and complexity, left at least one major issue unresolved—did the mere granting of a pastoral lease automatically extinguish native title? In December 1996, in the *Wik* case, the High Court, by a majority of four to three, answered this question in the negative: where native title holders and graziers could coexist, the native title was not extinguished by the mere grant of the pastoral lease. Given that 42 per cent of continental Australia was leased for sheep and cattle grazing, in many instances on lands still used by Aboriginal people, much was at stake in this dramatic sequel to *Mabo*.

The political reaction to *Wik* was as intense and vitriolic as the response to *Mabo*. A Liberal–National government led by Prime Minister John Howard was now in power in Canberra; it promised to amend the Native Title Act in ways that would remove uncertainty for the holders of pastoral leases, and for other industrial interests potentially affected by native title claims. Again, a prolonged legislative debate over this effort to circumscribe native title rights was the central issue in Australian politics for many months. In order to obtain passage of its legislation in the Senate in July 1998, the Howard government had to back down a little from the full force of its 'ten-point plan' to reduce native title rights. One critical issue was the right of native title holders to negotiate with miners; that right was retained, but could become subject to state-based tribunals and regulatory systems.

Mabo and *Wik* did much to heighten political interest in the High Court. The decisions demonstrated, perhaps more clearly than ever before, that although court decisions are rarely self-executing, the outlook of judges on fundamental issues of principle could make a great difference in the development of the country's public law. After *Wik*, members of the Howard government attacked the Court and vowed to appoint more conservative Justices. There were also renewed calls to give the states a major role in making High Court **appointments**.

The Court's decision in *Mabo* was a major turning point in Australian history. Its challenge to prevailing assumptions at the core of Australian identity as well as to major economic and political interests meant that it would not be an untroubled turning point. The journey towards reconciliation between indigenous and non-indigenous Australians would continue, but *Mabo* ensured that reconciliation would have to recognise the unique status and rights of Aborigines and Torres Strait Islanders. The political struggle following *Mabo* and *Wik* demonstrated that there was still a long way to go in building a consensus on the terms of that recognition.

PETER H RUSSELL

Further Reading
Bain Attwood (ed), *In the Age of Mabo: History, Aborigines and Australia* (1996)
Frank Brennan, *One Land, One Nation: Mabo—Towards 2001* (1995)
Murray Goot and Tim Rowse, *Make a Better Offer: The Politics of Mabo* (1994)

Madigan, Colin Frederick (*b* 22 July 1921). The High Court **building** in **Canberra** is among the major works of **architecture** of the twentieth century in Australia. It was completed in 1980 to the design by architects Edwards Madigan Torzillo and Briggs, Sydney, winners of the competition of 1972. The competition design team was led by Christopher Kringas, who died in 1975; design responsibility was then assumed by Colin Madigan, and held by him until the completion of the building.

Born in Glen Innes on the New England Tableland in 1921, Madigan grew up in Inverell, where his father was an architect. As his father's assistant, he was introduced to architecture at the age of 14, and in 1937 he began his studies at the Sydney Technical College, gaining practical experience in the office of David King. After two years training, he joined the Navy as an anti-submarine rating, and served in the Pacific arena for five years. Madigan was one of the survivors of ten days in the water after the sinking of HMAS *Armidale* in the Timor Sea. He says that it was as a result of his reflective thinking and questioning during that ordeal that he first began to develop the philosophical stance that deeply conditions his architecture—a stance he explored initially through the writings of George Bernard Shaw. After the war, he returned to his studies and graduated in 1950. The firm of Edwards Madigan and Torzillo was founded in 1954, and was joined by Briggs in 1966.

Since the 1960s, Madigan has been acknowledged as one of Australia's leading designers. The firm was awarded the Sulman Medal twice—for the Warringah Library at Dee Why (1967) and the Mitchell College, Bathurst (1970)—and the Blackett Award for a library for Warren Shire (1969). It won the competition for the National Art Gallery in 1968 (completed in 1982) and the competition for the High Court in 1972; the firm was also included as a finalist for the 1980 Parliament House Competition. Madigan was awarded the Gold Medal of the Royal Australian Institute of Architects in 1981.

Madigan is a concerned and creative architect, committed to ideals of the human condition and to the ability of architecture to express and enhance that condition. On the one hand, he is a pragmatist dedicated to the integrity and direct expression of the work; on the other, he is a social philosopher, seeking meaningful architecture that moves beyond **symbolism** to capture the essence of the institutions it houses and represents. His work is conditioned by deep convictions, and while his buildings are sometimes controversial, Madigan's sincerity is never in doubt.

Madigan is a highly literate man, widely read in philosophy, Fabian political theory, astronomy, and physics. In his early career, he was influenced by the modern architecture of Mies van der Rohe and the Bauhaus School, and, after a visit to North America and Europe in 1963, by the work of Louis Kahn.

A fundamental principle of Madigan's work is to provide for clear communication between the building and those who use it. The architecture is strong and confident, with a complexity that arises from an uncompromising functional expressionism. Structure is exploited for effect, and materials and services are commonly left exposed. Through the expression of its parts and its purpose, Madigan seeks to impart to the building an integrity that can be read, and to which people will relate. He believes that architecture must act as a mode of cultural communication, must challenge old ideas and preconceptions, and must 'portray new forms to the public for their understanding and acceptance'.

Architect of the High Court Colin Madigan, pictured in front of the National Gallery of Australia, which he also designed

The High Court and the National Art Gallery stand as focal buildings on adjacent sites on the edge of Lake Burley Griffin. They make major statements about the role of public architecture in a way that defies the conventions of symmetry and rationalist simplicity. The High Court is especially expressive, and its articulated exteriors, enlivened with the complex profiles of the building's parts, are matched in the interior by the vast spaces of the Public Hall and **Courtroom** No 1. The Court building is intended to embody a spirit of nationalism and pride, through a heroic architecture of wilful individuality. To Madigan, architecture's most important role is to encapsulate and extend the experiences of humanity.

JENNIFER TAYLOR

Further Reading

Colin Madigan, 'AS Hook 1982: The AS Hook Memorial Address' (1982) 71 *Architecture Australia* 70

Jennifer Taylor, 'Madigan and Architecture' (1982) 71 *Architecture Australia* 32

Marbury v Madison (1803). In a private dining room in the **United States Supreme Court** in Washington, DC, two portraits hang side by side. One is of William Marbury, one of a number of last-minute appointments to the federal judiciary made by the outgoing Federalist administration of President John Adams in March 1801. The other is of James Madison, framer of the US Constitution, Secretary of State under the incoming Republican administration of President Thomas Jefferson, and later himself President of the USA (1809–17). This whimsical juxtaposition and visual presentation of 'Marbury and Madison' commemorates the landmark case that established **judicial review** in the USA and exerted considerable influence, directly and indirectly, on the **framers** of the Australian Constitution.

In the last two weeks of his term, President Adams created 16 new circuit court judgeships and appointed 16 Federalists to fill them—these were the so-called 'midnight judges'. Then, less than a week before the end of his term, Adams secured the passage of a further Act, under which Marbury, among others, was appointed as a Justice of the Peace for the District of Columbia. Marbury was named as a Justice on 2 March 1801 and confirmed by the Senate on 3 March 1801, Adams' last day in office. His commission was signed and sealed but had not been delivered to him by the end of the day. The incoming Jeffersonian Republicans were hostile to what was perceived as entrenchment of partisan Federalists in the judiciary, and the new Secretary of State Madison refused to deliver Marbury's commission, treating it as a nullity. With three others in a like position, Marbury sought a **writ** of mandamus from the Supreme Court to compel Madison to deliver the commission.

Ironically, Chief Justice John Marshall, who had been appointed Chief Justice only in February 1801 and was therefore akin to a 'midnight judge' himself, had, as Adams' Secretary of State, been the person who signed and sealed Marbury's commission; but, because of the pressure of time, he had failed to arrange its delivery. He did not, however, **disqualify** himself from participating in the decision (though he did so later in a different context in *Martin v Hunters Lessee* (1816)). The case was not heard until February 1803, as the Republican Congress repealed the Federalist legislation under which the 'midnight judges' had been appointed and also abolished the remaining Supreme Court terms in 1802, evidently to delay a constitutional challenge to the repeal legislation. (The repeal legislation was held to be valid shortly after the decision in *Marbury v Madison*: see *Stuart v Laird* (1803)).

The Supreme Court held that Marbury had a right to his commission, and that, since the government of the USA was a 'government of laws and not of men' (see **Rule of Law**), he was entitled to a remedy for the violation of that right. But the remedy that he sought—the writ of mandamus—was one the Court pronounced itself unable to give. Its power to do so was purportedly given by section 13 of the *Judiciary Act* of 1789; but that Act, said Marshall, was inconsistent with the Constitution, as it sought to expand the Court's original jurisdiction, the limits of which were stated exhaustively in the Constitution and did not include the issuing of mandamus against public officers. Section 13 of the Judiciary Act was to that extent unconstitutional, and Marbury's petition failed.

The Supreme Court had faced a difficult decision. Had it found for Marbury and ordered the delivery of the commission, its order would almost certainly have been ignored. If it did not find for Marbury, it risked being seen to be complicit in Jefferson's pursuit and denunciation of the 'midnight judges'. Thus, the Court's combination of, on the one hand, declaring unlawful the executive act of refusal to deliver the commission, and, on the other, declining to remedy that refusal, was seen by Robert McCloskey in 1960 as a 'masterwork of indirection, a brilliant example of Marshall's capacity to sidestep danger while seeming to court it, to advance in one direction while his opponents are looking in another'—though Gerald Gunther noted in 1997 that this observation 'needs to be taken with a grain of salt'.

The Republicans were focused on the immediate question of Marbury's commission, and took issue with the Court's assertion that the executive action was illegal; but the larger question was the Court's assertion of its authority to declare Acts of Congress unconstitutional. The larger question did not go unnoticed—indeed, there was trenchant criticism from Judge Spencer Roane of Virginia (in the newspapers) and Judge John Gibson of Pennsylvania (see his dissent in *Eakin v Raub* (1825))—but the Court's avoidance of confrontation by failing to find a remedy to vindicate Marbury took the sting out of both assertions. As Tony Blackshield has observed, Marshall's judgment was 'a Solomonic blend of diplomacy and defiance'. Moreover, the Court, by basing its finding *against* Marbury and *for* Madison on the unconstitutionality of section 13 of the Judiciary Act, had, in McCloskey's words, 'rejected and assumed power in a single breath'.

It is Marshall's eloquent statement that laws repugnant to the Constitution must be void, and that the duty of the Court must be to declare such laws unconstitutional, for which *Marbury v Madison* is remembered and for which it remains significant. Its logic was not inevitable, and the Jeffersonian view of the **separation of powers** in which each branch would authoritatively interpret the Constitution in its own sphere was widely supported. Moreover, it was not the first assertion of the power of judicial review—*Dr Bonham's Case* (1610) had been drawn upon by American colonial lawyers, and Alexander Hamilton's writing on limited government in *The Federalist (No 78)* in 1788 was clearly influential—and it was not picked up and applied again, at least in relation to federal law, for another 50 years (see *Dred Scott v Sandford* (1857); as to state law, see *Fletcher v Peck* (1810) and *Martin v Hunters Lessee*). But it was the first such assertion by the US Supreme Court, and its message has resonated through the ages—as a direct consequence, no doubt, of the assertion's success.

It is some measure of its success that the power of judicial review has prevailed, notwithstanding its lack of any explicit basis in either the US Constitution or the Australian Constitution. There is not a little irony in this, given that the reason for the holding in *Marbury v Madison* that section 13 of the Judiciary Act was unconstitutional was that there was no explicit basis in the Constitution for the Court to be given original jurisdiction in addition to that conferred directly by the Constitution. But by the time the Australian Constitution came to be drafted, the principle of the 'great case' of *Marbury v Madison* was, according to **Fullagar** in the *Communist Party Case* (1951), 'accepted as axiomatic'. In an address at Harvard in 1955 on the occasion of the bicentenary of Marshall's birth, **Dixon** made the same point:

> To the framers of the Commonwealth Constitution the thesis of *Marbury v Madison* was obvious. It did not need the reasoned eloquence of Marshall's utterance to convince them that simply because there were to be legislatures of limited powers, there must be a question of ultra vires for the courts.

Dixon drew, persuasively, upon the experience of Australian courts in the nineteenth century with the limited powers of colonial legislatures, notwithstanding (or perhaps in contrast with) the doctrine of parliamentary supremacy in the UK. Yet there were few express references to *Marbury v Madison* in the course of the **Convention Debates** surrounding the drafting of the Australian Constitution. Only **Griffith** and **Inglis Clark** had intimate knowledge of the US Constitution, and even Inglis Clark argued for the power of judicial review more as a necessary implication from the notion of the supremacy of law than as a product of particular historical precedents. However, Inglis Clark had clearly read *Marbury v Madison*, and he included in his own draft Bill a clause designed specifically to overcome the result of the case by ensuring that the High Court would have the power to issue mandamus against a minister of the Crown. Such a clause was included in the Convention's draft Bills of 1891 and

1897, but omitted from the 1898 draft. On hearing of this, Inglis Clark protested to **Barton**, who replied:

> I have to thank you further for your telegram … None of us here had read the case mentioned by you of *Marbury v Madison* or if seen it had been forgotten—It seems however to be a leading case. I have given notice to restore the words on the reconsideration of the clause.

The words were indeed restored, and became part of section 75(v) of the Constitution, which expressly provides that the High Court shall have original **jurisdiction** in matters in which a writ of mandamus is sought against an officer of the Commonwealth.

Nevertheless, on the broader point, there is no express provision conferring or authorising the exercise of the power of the Court to invalidate Commonwealth or state legislation. There seems little doubt that the power was intended, but **commentators** have been troubled by the absence of explicit authorisation. James Thomson concluded, after a comprehensive study in 1986, that attempts to imply the power from the text were 'endeavours to rest a prodigious power on a slender reed', though Geoffrey Sawer had observed some 20 years earlier that the Constitution 'has many provisions which are unintelligible unless such a power was intended'.

To criticise or attempt to restrain the High Court on the basis that its power of judicial review lacks express constitutional justification is an exercise in futility. Nevertheless, the charge that judicial review is a usurpation of power has coloured the debate about the legitimacy of unelected Justices striking down the Acts of elected legislatures and the actions of elected governments (see **Democracy**), and may also have had a formative influence upon those Justices who lean towards judicial self-restraint (see **Activism**). Acknowledgment of the written Constitution as higher and binding law is not inconsistent with respect for, and a degree of deference to, the interpretation of that higher law by the other branches of government.

Marbury v Madison has been cited many times by the High Court. Barton acknowledged in *Ah Yick v Lehmert* (1905) that the insertion in the Australian Constitution of section 75(v) was attributable to the decision. It has also been relied upon to support similar conclusions about the exhaustiveness of the High Court's original jurisdiction under sections 75 and 76 (*Ex parte Whybrow* (1910); *Tramways Case (No 1)* (1914)), and seems to have been found useful in the **cross-vesting** cases to support the view that an affirmative statement can have negative implications (*Gould v Brown* (1998); *Re Wakim* (1999)).

More broadly, **Gibbs** relied on *Marbury v Madison* in the *AAP Case* (1975) to conclude that the constitutionality of an Appropriation Act was **justiciable**, citing Marshall's statement that 'In some cases, then, the constitution must be looked into by the judges. And if they can open it at all, what part of it are they forbidden to read or to obey?' And in *A-G (NSW) v Quin* (1990), **Brennan** recalled Marshall's 'memorable words': 'It is, emphatically, the province and duty of the judicial department to say what the law is.'

So it is. But that simple statement unleashed two centuries of controversy and debate about the legitimacy of judicial review, the politics of judicial **decision making**, the plausibility of **legalism**, the degree of room for judicial choice, the place of **values** and **policy considerations**, and the role of the Justices in a democracy. In a vibrant democracy with a written Constitution and a separation of powers, that controversy is unlikely to abate.

MICHAEL COPER

Further Reading

Tony Blackshield, 'The Courts and Judicial Review' in Sol Encel, Donald Horne, and Elaine Thompson (eds), *Change the Rules! Towards a Democratic Constitution* (1977) 119

Robert Clinton, *Marbury v Madison and Judicial Review* (1989)

Owen Dixon, 'Marshall and the Australian Constitution' (1955), reprinted in SHZ Woinarski (ed), *Jesting Pilate* (1965) 166

Geoffrey Sawer, *Australian Federalism in the Courts* (1967) 76

James Thomson, 'Constitutional Authority for Judicial Review: A Contribution from the Framers of the Australian Constitution' in Gregory Craven (ed), *The Convention Debates 1891–1898: Commentaries, Indices and Guide* (1986) 173

John Williams, '"With Eyes Open": Andrew Inglis Clark and Our Republican Tradition' (1995) 23 *FL Rev* 149

Marion's Case (1992) considered whether the parents of a 14-year-old intellectually disabled girl had the power to authorise the performance of a hysterectomy and ovariectomy and, if not, whether the Family Court could do so. To answer these questions, the Court had to confront ethical issues of a kind not normally brought before it. The problem posed by the proceedings was whether it was appropriate for the law to determine what was best for a person who lacked the capacity to manage her own life. In dealing with this problem, the Court had to confront the central dilemma of child welfare law: how to decide when the law should be invoked to protect vulnerable **children** and when legal intervention should be rejected as insensitive interference in a matter better left to the family.

For all the Justices, the crucial feature of the proposed operation was that it would result in the sterilisation of the girl. Though the surgery involved much more than this, they therefore characterised the operation as a sterilisation. In their majority judgment, **Mason**, **Dawson**, **Toohey**, and **Gaudron**, after accepting that a parent has the power to give valid consent to medical treatment that is in a child's best interests, asked whether special considerations applied to sterilisation. They concluded that the factors involved in a decision to authorise the sterilisation of another person were such that the decision 'should not come within the ordinary scope of parental power to consent to medical treatment'. Family Court authorisation was necessary to ensure that the interests of the child would be protected.

The other Justices offered different answers. **Deane** distinguished between a parent's power to authorise surgery on a child for conventional medical purposes and the power to authorise surgery for other purposes. Because surgery for conventional medical purposes would always be in the child's best interests, he accepted that a parent could authorise it. Surgery for other purposes, however, might not be in the child's best interests, and this raised the question of how, and by whom, the decision should be made. In Deane's view, there were some situations in which the sterilisation of a severely disabled child would, according to general community standards, obviously be necessary for the welfare of the child. In these situations, he held, the parents should be able to give the necessary authorisation. In others, when there is doubt about what is in the child's best interests, scrutiny by the Family Court was required. **McHugh** took a similar approach, ruling that if the circumstances were sufficiently compelling, the parents could give lawful consent to a sterilisation procedure. The criterion to be applied was whether the performance of the procedure would advance or protect the welfare of the child. In doubtful cases, he accepted that the Family Court had the power to give the necessary consent.

Brennan's dissenting judgment adopted a distinctive starting-point. While the analysis offered by the other Justices reflected the assumption that the task was to decide who could give a valid consent to the sterilisation procedure, Brennan saw the problem as being to decide whether *anyone* had the power to give consent. 'Neither parents nor other guardians nor courts have power to authorise sterilization simply because a child is intellectually disabled.' He stressed the law's role in upholding a person's right to physical integrity, a right that is not diminished by intellectual **disability**. In his view, there was a need for 'some compelling justification' to be offered before a major violation of this integrity could be authorised. He accepted that such a justification would exist if a proposed procedure was therapeutic. In the absence of a therapeutic justification, however, he ruled that neither a parent nor a court had the power to authorise sterilisation.

Brennan did not agree that the law could fulfil its protective function by applying the 'best interests' criterion when surgery on a child was being contemplated. He regarded this criterion as providing no guiding principle and allowing an outcome determined by the **value** system of the decision maker. He was therefore unwilling to accept that a court should make decisions on the basis of what it considered to be the child's best interests. To permit this would allow the exercise of a virtually unfettered discretion; he expressed concern about the danger of creating an 'imperial judiciary'. These doubts were to be reiterated in *P v P* (1994).

The significance of *Marion's Case* lies primarily in the questions that it raises regarding the appropriateness of legal intervention in the normally private world of the family. Mason, Dawson, Toohey, and Gaudron accepted that legal procedures and concepts could be employed to resolve the problem. Underlying this view were a number of assumptions: that in some circumstances authorisation could be given for a non-therapeutic sterilisation; that parents lacked the power to give that authorisation; and that the law could effectively protect people like Marion by identifying the course that was in her best interests. Deane and McHugh saw less need for legal intervention. In their view—in the absence of exceptional circumstances—parents should be recognised as the ones best suited to make decisions of the kind required in this case. Like the members of the majority, they regarded the 'best interests' criterion as a valid basis for such decisions (whether by parents or a court). Brennan rejected the use of this criterion by a court. He saw it as opening the way for orders based on the personal views of the judiciary. This fear was part of a more fundamen-

tal concern. He challenged the arguments in favour of non-therapeutic sterilisation and placed the primary emphasis on Marion's right to physical integrity. Brennan regarded it as the law's task to protect this right.

The case reveals two very different approaches to the use of state power to protect people who are incapable of protecting themselves. On the one hand, there are the judgments reflecting the view that a court such as the Family Court can be relied on to make wise decisions about the necessity for all forms of medical treatment of such persons. On the other hand, there is Brennan's fear of the recognition of a jurisdiction under which the Family Court can exercise powers not possessed by a parent whenever a judge concludes that this would be in a child's best interests. 'Courts, for all their independence and wisdom, are not appropriate repositories of so awesome a power.'

JOHN SEYMOUR

Further Reading
Patrick Parkinson, 'Children's Rights and Doctors' Immunities: The Implications of the High Court's Decision in *Re Marion*' (1992) 6 *AJFL* 101

Marriage and divorce powers. The list of **Commonwealth legislative powers** in section 51 of the Constitution includes powers to legislate with respect to 'Marriage' (section 51(xxi)) and 'Divorce and matrimonial causes; and in relation thereto, parental rights, and the custody and guardianship of infants' (section 51(xxii)). That wording reflects a nineteenth-century view of legal relationships that failed to anticipate the important role family relationships were to assume in the twentieth century. The interpretation of both powers has since been the subject of conceptual change, and of growth in judicial recognition of social and community **values** relating to the family within the constraints of traditional **legalism**. It also illustrates an orthodoxy in **constitutional interpretation**: that the **connotation** of a given term remains fixed as in 1901, while its denotation changes with circumstances (*Union Label Case* (1908)).

The result is a much greater complexity in meaning than originally appeared possible. Moreover, while the terms of the divorce power expressly include certain ancillary matters, the very fact of their inclusion was to create lasting problems of interpretation because of the implied exclusion of other matters not expressly referred to.

'Marriage' in section 51(xxi), on the other hand, has raised questions because of its very simplicity. The early commentary in **Quick and Garran** (1901)—suggesting that the minimum content of the marriage power would embrace both the establishment of the relationship, and its proximate consequences, such as the mutual rights and obligations of the parties—reflected a traditional view of marriage grounded in **property** and personal status. Discussion thus centred on issues of inheritance, legitimacy, and inter-jurisdictional recognition of marital status.

Upon federation, the Commonwealth did not initially exercise these powers. It was not until the *Matrimonial Causes Act* 1959 (Cth) and the *Marriage Act* 1961 (Cth), introduced by **Barwick** as **Attorney-General**, that a federal law of marriage and divorce emerged. Even then, its administration remained in the **state Supreme Courts** under section 77(iii) of the Constitution. When the High Court came to consider the new law, discussion went well beyond the views of the early **commentators** (*Marriage Act Case* (1962)). The majority upheld the Commonwealth's power to provide for the legitimation of **children** by the subsequent marriage of their parents (section 89 of the Marriage Act), and for the validity of an otherwise invalid marriage which at least one party believed to be valid (section 91, the 'putative marriage'). **Dixon's** dissent as to both provisions saw them as standing outside the legislative topic of 'marriage', and therefore as unconstitutional intrusions into exclusive state powers. The majority view was reflected in **Kitto's** statement that the provisions merely regulated the legal consequences of marriage, or limited the legal consequences of invalidity.

One important principle emerged. Legitimation of children had been a matter for state legislation, but it now resulted from the operation of a federal law. This brought into play the operation of section 109 of the Constitution, which provides that, in cases of **inconsistency** between state and federal laws, the latter prevail over the former. The statement by Douglas **Menzies** that 'the marriage power must extend to the regulation of the mutual rights and obligations of spouses' foreshadowed later cases on the nature and quality of the mutual obligations of the parties to a marriage.

The Court also took a wide view of the divorce power in its application to matrimonial property settlements and their relationship with maintenance (*Sanders v Sanders* (1967)). In *Lansell v Lansell* (1964), the provision of ancillary relief as to property was upheld as incidental to or consequential upon dissolution of marriage, and hence authorised by the matrimonial causes power.

Following these changing perceptions, Attorney-General **Murphy** grasped the nettle in introducing the *Family Law Act 1975* (Cth), based on no-fault divorce and administered by a federal Family Court. Internationally the time was ripe, coming within a decade of the UK Law Commission Report *The Field of Choice* (1966), which recommended irretrievable breakdown as the sole ground for divorce, and of the Californian no-fault *Family Law Act* 1969. The Australian Family Law Act was promptly challenged in *Russell v Russell* (1976), putting in issue the extent to which either the matrimonial causes power or the marriage power had enabled the Parliament to legislate for proceedings relating to children or property—including, in relation to children, claims to custody, guardianship, maintenance or access—in cases where the proceedings were not merely ancillary to proceedings for 'principal relief' such as divorce. **Jacobs** took the broadest view of the scope of Commonwealth power, holding that, in relation to the children of a marriage, it was not confined to authorising only proceedings between the parties to a marriage.

Against the dissent of Barwick and **Gibbs**, **Mason** (with whom **Stephen** agreed) took an intermediate position and upheld the Act under the marriage power by reading down its provisions (which were unlimited as to parties) so as to apply only to proceedings between the parties to a marriage and in relation to the natural or adopted children of the marriage. That view may have been unduly narrow, but at least the Act, as read down, survived. But in *Gazzo v Comptroller of Stamps* (1981), the **Gibbs Court** (Gibbs, Stephen, and

Aickin) fell into downright error, invalidating a provision exempting property transfers between spouses or former spouses pursuant to a Family Court order from payment of state stamp duty; Mason and Murphy dissented. Gibbs held that the requisite connection with marriage—and whether the law was 'in truth' one as to that relationship—was a matter of degree and closeness of connection, which were lacking here.

The reasoning in *Gazzo* was disapproved in *Fisher v Fisher* (1986) as 'fundamentally unsound'. That decision upheld a provision in the Family Law Act for property proceedings to be continued after one of the parties to the marriage had died. Gibbs still sought the constitutional nexus in closeness or strength of connection between the law and the marriage relationship. Mason and **Deane**, on the other hand, focused on the primary scope of the legislative power to create and continue to enforce rights arising out of the marital relationship, even after it has been terminated by divorce or death. A number of other decisions (*Dowal v Murray* (1978); *R v Lambert; Ex parte Plummer* (1980); *Vitzdamm-Jones v Vitzdamm-Jones* (1981); *Fountain v Alexander* (1982); *V v V* (1985)) have also affirmed the reach of the power in its effect on third parties.

In *Re F; Ex parte F* (1986), Mason and Deane, in dissent, took a much wider view of the marriage power than did the remainder of the Court. The case concerned the status of a child who was 'deemed' to be a child of the marriage on the basis of acceptance as 'ordinarily a member of the household of husband and wife', though born to the wife ex-nuptially. The provision reflected similar legislation in some of the states and in England, recognising the reality of modern family relationships. Gibbs, **Wilson**, **Brennan**, and **Dawson** held that such a child could have no connection with the marriage power.

In a joint dissent, Mason and Deane viewed such a child, when born during the period of the wife's marriage, as being within the marriage power. They concluded that the earlier cases had paid 'insufficient attention' to the distinction between the direct operation of a given law and its operation within the 'penumbra of things that are incidental, consequential and ancillary' to the power in question (borrowing a phrase used by Dixon in the *Marriage Act Case*). In their focus on 'incidental' or 'ancillary' connections, Mason and Deane now argued, the earlier majorities had failed to give 'any real consideration' to the possibility that the challenged provisions might fall within 'the primary or central area of the marriage power'.

In reaching this conclusion, Mason effectively accepted the argument Deane had advanced (in dissent) in *R v Cook; Ex parte C* (1985)—that, by being accepted as an ordinary member of the household, an ex-nuptial child of one spouse 'acquires a special familial relationship' with the other spouse 'by reason of the marriage itself'. The recognition of such a relationship as that of step-parent and stepchild conformed to 'well-established social custom'.

Deane's view was couched in more conventional terms than Murphy's dissent on the same subject in an earlier case, *In the Marriage of Cormick* (1984). It points the way towards a possible future extension of the concept of marriage through the social acceptance of de facto and in vitro parent–child relationships.

After *Fisher*, the **Mason Court** came to treat the marriage and divorce powers as part of an integral system as far as the Constitution allows. So in *P v P* (1994), dealing with the sterilisation of an intellectually incompetent minor, and following *Marion's Case* (1992), the majority held that the Act had in fact, if not in so many words, conferred a *parens patriae* or wardship jurisdiction on the Court. As a Commonwealth law entrusting the Family Court with a welfare jurisdiction over an incapable child of a marriage, this was held to prevail over a state Guardianship Act.

Despite the increasingly liberal attitude of the Court towards family relationships in its interpretation of the marriage and divorce powers, Australian **family law** must remain fragmented while significant areas such as adoption and ex-nuptial relations remain outside federal power. The referral in 1987 of state powers with respect to children (except in WA, which has its own Family Court), although revocable, has made the jurisdiction more complete for the time being. The invalidation by the High Court in *Re Wakim* (1999) of the 1988 **cross-vesting** scheme between state and federal jurisdictions, however, has underlined the absence of a firm constitutional basis for the reciprocity on which such ventures in cooperative **federalism** depend. This reminder of the incomplete nature of federal jurisdiction in family law sounds a warning that a more comprehensive statutory scheme is likely to be achieved only by constitutional **amendment**.

HENRY FINLAY

Further Reading

Zelman Cowen and Mendes Da Costa, *Matrimonial Causes Jurisdiction* (1961)

Henry Finlay, 'A Commonwealth "Family Law"?' (1982) 56 *ALJ* 119

Ronald Sackville and Colin Howard, 'The Constitutional Power of the Commonwealth to regulate Family Relationships' (1970) 4 *FL Rev* 30

Marshal. The original role of the Marshal was the service and execution of process, including warrants for the arrest of ships under the Court's **Admiralty** jurisdiction. It was also his responsibility to receive and detain any person who might be committed to his custody by the Court.

Walter Bingle was appointed the first Marshal of the Court on 2 October 1903. Bingle held the position until 1926, when Colonel Richard Dowse, **associate** to Chief Justice **Knox**, was appointed to the position. Thereafter, associates held the position, until 1950 when the person appointed as Principal Registrar also held the position of Marshal. This was changed by Chief Justice **Barwick**, and the position was then held by a succession of Superintendents of the Commonwealth Police, who delegated their powers to the persons performing the function of Sheriff in the Supreme Courts of the various states and territories.

The office now has a dual role under the *High Court of Australia Act* 1979 (Cth). The Marshal has retained the statutory responsibilities for service and execution of

High Court staff picnic, with Chief Justice Griffith (centre), and Justices Barton and O'Connor, date unknown

process, but also assumes a role in the **administration** of the Court.

FRANK JONES

Mason, Anthony Frank (*b* 21 April 1925; Justice 1972–87; Chief Justice 1987–95) was a member of the High Court for 23 years and is regarded by many as one of Australia's greatest judges, as important and influential as **Dixon**. The ninth **Chief Justice**, he presided over a period of significant change in the Australian legal system, his eight years as Chief Justice having been described as among the most exciting and important in the Court's history.

Mason grew up in Sydney, where he attended Sydney Grammar School. His father was a surveyor who urged him to follow in his footsteps; however, Mason preferred to follow in the footsteps of his uncle, a prominent Sydney KC. After serving with the RAAF as a flying officer from 1944 to 1945, he enrolled at the University of Sydney, graduating with first-class honours in both law and arts. Mason was then articled with Clayton Utz & Co in Sydney, where he met his wife Patricia, with whom he has two sons. He also served as an associate to Justice David Roper of the Supreme Court of NSW. He moved to the Sydney Bar in 1951, where he was an unqualified success, becoming one of **Barwick's** favourite junior **counsel**.

Mason's practice was primarily in **equity** and **commercial law**, but he also took on a number of constitutional and appellate cases. After only three years at the Bar, he appeared before the High Court in *R v Davison* (1954), in which he successfully persuaded the Bench that certain sections of the *Bankruptcy Act* 1924 (Cth) invalidly purported to confer **judicial power** upon a registrar of the Bankruptcy Court. Although such appearances involved much hard work, there were occasional moments of levity. In one case, Mason erroneously referred to the English case *Ogdens v Nelson* as *Ogden v Nash*. **Dixon** pointed out the mistake, implying that Mason had (mis)spent his youth reading Ogden Nash.

Perhaps more influential on Mason's development as a lawyer, however, was his unsuccessful attempt to appear in the House of Representatives to defend newspaper owner Raymond Fitzpatrick against charges of **contempt**. The House ordered Fitzpatrick and journalist Frank Browne jailed for three months without allowing their counsel to make submissions on their behalf. The case went to the High Court (*R v Richards; Ex parte Fitzpatrick and Browne* (1955)), with Mason appearing as junior to PD Phillips QC, but the Court declined to interfere with the warrant issued by the House. These events left an indelible impression on Mason's mind: that the protection of individual rights is better left in the hands of judges than it is in the hands of politicians. This view, however, is more evident in his later judgments than in his earlier ones.

During his time at the Bar, Mason also lectured in equity at the University of Sydney Law School from 1959 to 1964; he taught both **Gaudron** and **Gummow**. Mason was appointed **Solicitor-General** for the Commonwealth in 1964, two days after he took silk. In that capacity, he appeared regularly for the Commonwealth in constitutional cases. He was also heavily involved in the development of federal **administrative law**, in particular as a member of the Administrative

Anthony Mason, Justice 1972–87, Chief Justice 1987–95 in academic dress

Review Committee (ARC). The work of the ARC led to the creation of the 'new administrative law': the *Administrative Appeals Tribunal Act* 1975 (Cth); the *Ombudsman Act* 1976 (Cth); the *Administrative Decisions (Judicial Review) Act* 1977 (Cth) (ADJR Act); and the *Freedom of Information Act* 1982 (Cth). In addition, Mason was the leader of the Australian delegation to the UN Commission on International Trade Law from 1966 to 1969; he was its Vice-Chairman in 1968. In 1969, he was appointed to the NSW Court of Appeal—though his tenure in that Court was short-lived because of his elevation to the High Court in 1972.

During Mason's early years on the Court, he and Barwick issued quite a number of **joint judgments**. During this period, Mason was not a particularly adventurous judge. His approach to judicial decision making was relatively conservative, as is evidenced by his judgments in areas such as development of the **common law** and **constitutional interpretation**. An example is *State Government Insurance Commission v Trigwell* (1979), which concerned the development of the law of negligence. While acknowledging a **law-making role** for the courts, Mason said:

> But there are very powerful reasons why the court should be reluctant to engage in such an exercise. The court is neither a legislature nor a law reform agency. Its responsibility is to decide cases by applying the law to the facts as found. The court's facilities, techniques and procedures are adapted to that

responsibility; they are not adapted to legislative functions or to law reform activities.

This may be contrasted with later cases such as *Trident General Insurance v McNiece* (1988), *Burnie Port Authority v General Jones* (1994), and *Bryan v Maloney* (1995), where Mason adopted a more active judicial **role**.

Mason's earlier, restrictive approach to constitutional interpretation can be seen most clearly in *Miller v TCN Channel Nine* (1986), where he said:

> There was an alternative argument put by the defendant, based on the judgment of **Murphy** J in *Buck v Bavone*, that there is to be implied in the Constitution a new set of freedoms which include a guarantee of freedom of communication. It is sufficient to say that I cannot find any basis for implying a new s 92A into the Constitution.

Some six years later, however, Mason joined a majority of the Court in the *Free Speech Cases* (1992) to find an implied freedom of **political communication** in the Constitution. His views on the value of a **Bill of Rights** have also changed over time; although initially opposed to a Bill of Rights, he has more recently acknowledged that there could be some benefits in such a development.

The development in Mason's judicial approach over the years has been noted by various **commentators**. In an interview on Radio National in 1994, Mason responded to those observations:

> I think that the extent of the change on my part has been somewhat exaggerated … It is inevitable, with the passage of time, that the views of an individual are likely to change. In my case, I have been a judge for 25 years. It would be strange indeed, if all my views remained static over that period of time. If they did, I would regard that as a worthy subject of criticism.

In 1987, Mason was appointed Chief Justice. Shortly afterwards, the Court decided two of the most important cases of Mason's career: *Cole v Whitfield* (1988) and *Mabo* (1992). In *Cole v Whitfield*, the Court, after 80 years of uncertainty, resolved in a unanimous judgment the problem of the meaning of section 92 of the Constitution (see **Interstate trade and commerce**). This illustrates well one of Mason's key roles on the Court, both as a Justice and as Chief Justice: to provide a central point around which a majority of the Justices could coalesce. Unfortunately, this success was not matched in the area of section 90, where the Court was to remain divided on the limits placed on the states' ability to levy various fees (see **Excise duties**). In *Mabo*, the Court (by a 6:1 majority) overturned nearly 200 years of apparently settled law to recognise that the prior occupation of Australia by its **Aboriginal peoples** could be a source of title to land. *Mabo* and the *Free Speech Cases* were probably the most controversial of the Court's decisions during Mason's time, attracting significant **criticism** as well as considerable praise.

As Chief Justice, Mason became associated with a move away from the strict **legalism** of Dixon's day. Rather than seeing legal reasoning as the simple application of precise rules or formulae, Mason saw **precedent** as 'an exercise in

judicial **policy** which calls for an assessment of a variety of factors in which judges balance the need for continuity, consistency and predictability against the competing need for justice, flexibility and rationality'. He took a similar attitude towards constitutional interpretation, again emphasising the importance of policy. Mason was also known for the use of **foreign precedents** in his judgments.

Other notable public law cases on which Mason sat include the *Tasmanian Dam Case* (1983), where a majority of the Court adopted a wide approach to the **external affairs power**; *Dietrich v The Queen* (1992), concerning the right of an indigent accused to counsel in a criminal trial; and *Teoh's Case* (1995), where a majority gave an expanded role to **international law** in domestic law. In addition, in cases such as *Kioa v West* (1985), *Australian Broadcasting Tribunal v Bond* (1990), and *A-G (NSW) v Quin* (1990), Mason continued his role in the development of administrative law. In private law, Mason was also influential, as is evidenced by the subsequent adoption by a majority of the Court of his **dissenting judgment** in *Hospital Products v US Surgical Corporation* (1984), concerning **fiduciary obligations**, and by other equity cases such as *Waltons Stores v Maher* (1988) and *Baumgartner v Baumgartner* (1987).

Significant procedural changes to the Court's operations also occurred during Mason's tenure as Chief Justice (see **Procedure**). These include the abandonment of wigs and the adoption of a less formal robe (see **Court attire**); an increase in the use of written submissions (see **Argument before the Court**); and the introduction of time limits for special leave arguments (see **Leave to appeal**). Another noteworthy development was Mason's increased engagement with the **media** during his time as Chief Justice. He spoke in public quite often about the role of judges and about some of the more controversial decisions of the Court, taking the view that, if the Court was to be properly understood by the public, it was necessary for judges to play a role in cultivating **public awareness**.

Since leaving the Court, Mason has remained active both judicially and academically. He sat as a Judge of the Supreme Court of Fiji, as President of the Solomon Islands Court of Appeal, and as a long-serving member of the Permanent Court of Arbitration. He currently sits as a Non-Permanent Judge of the Hong Kong Court of Final Appeal, where he sat on the controversial right of abode cases.

In the academic arena, Mason was Chancellor of the University of NSW, a National Fellow at the ANU Research School of Social Sciences, and Chairman of the Advisory Board of the National Institute for Law, Ethics and Public Affairs at Griffith University. He is currently a member of the Advisory Board of the Centre for Comparative Constitutional Studies at the University of Melbourne. Mason's reputation and activities also extend internationally. In 1996–97, he was Arthur Goodhart Professor in Legal Science at Cambridge University, and in 1989 he was the Leon Ladner Lecturer at the Universities of British Columbia and Victoria in Canada. During his career, he has written and published an extraordinary number of **extra-judicial** articles and papers.

Mason has received several honours: a CBE in 1969, a KBE in 1972, and an AC in 1988. He received honorary degrees in law from the Australian National University and University of NSW, and from Sydney, Melbourne, Oxford, Monash,

Griffith, and Deakin Universities. He was made an Honorary Bencher of Lincoln's Inn in England and a Fellow of the Academy of Social Sciences in Australia. Outside the law, Mason's interests are in tennis and gardening, and he maintains close relationships with his children and grandchildren.

Praise for Mason has been frequent since his **retirement**. He is known for his keen intellect and acerbic wit. David Jackson QC, who made frequent appearances before the Court, described Mason's court persona as follows:

> He said relatively little, but was very good at progressing the business of argument. The combination of a commanding intelligence, vast experience, and an ability to convey by facial expression the fact that the shelf-life of an argument had expired made him very effective in that regard. At the same time he was good-humoured and encouraged even the most junior practitioners who had done their work.

KRISTEN WALKER

Further Reading
David Jackson, 'Personalia: Sir Anthony Mason AC, KBE' (1995) 69 *ALJ* 610

Anthony Mason, 'Reflections on the High Court of Australia' (1995) 20 *MULR* 273

Mason Court (6 February 1987 to 20 April 1995). The Mason Court was described by Maurice Byers in 1996 as one of 'the most gifted and courageous High Courts in our history'. Certainly, much was achieved during **Mason's** eight years as **Chief Justice**—a period characterised by a series of landmark decisions evincing not only significant doctrinal development but also broad changes in the approach taken by the Court.

The membership of the Court during Mason's time as Chief Justice was remarkably stable, the only change being the **retirement** of **Wilson** in February 1989 and the **appointment** of **McHugh**. The other members of the Mason Court were **Brennan, Deane, Dawson, Toohey,** and **Gaudron**. The use of the expression 'Mason Court' should not disguise the important contributions of all members of the Bench during this period.

That the Mason Court would be both productive and adventurous was evident almost immediately. Shortly after Mason's appointment as Chief Justice, the Court delivered the unanimous decision in **Cole v Whitfield** (1988), bringing to

The Mason Court in 1987. Left to right: Mason, Wilson, Brennan, Dawson, Gaudron, Toohey, and Deane

an end the confusion that had long surrounded the interpretation of section 92 of the Constitution (see **Interstate trade and commerce**). It was a decision that saw the Court abandon the legalistic tests previously applied to section 92 in favour of a test that looked to the historical purpose of the section—namely, to provide a free trade area throughout Australia.

Cole v Whitfield set the pattern for the following years, although not all of the Court's landmark decisions would be unanimous. A number of elements in *Cole v Whitfield* were repeated in later judgments: the examination of the **history** of provisions of the Constitution; the use of the **Convention Debates**; the adoption of an approach (in this case, protectionism) that used open-ended and qualitative concepts; and a willingness to overturn established doctrines and **precedents** perceived to be no longer working, rather than relying on Parliament or constitutional **amendment** to make the necessary changes. The decision appeared to mark the end of the Court's preoccupation with **legalism** and the beginning of an approach that looked to the purpose and intent of constitutional provisions. This approach had consequences beyond **constitutional law**. It was indicative of a trend towards greater judicial creativity and increased willingness to acknowledge the Court's **law-making role** and the influence of **policy considerations** (see also **Activism**).

The Mason Court's more policy-oriented and purposive approach to **constitutional interpretation** was also used to discover freedoms and rights implied from the text of the Constitution. The discovery of **implied constitutional rights** is seen most clearly in the *Free Speech Cases*. In *Australian Capital Television v Commonwealth* (1992) and *Nationwide News v Wills* (1992), a majority of the Court held that elements of the principle of **representative government** are recognised in certain provisions of the Constitution, and that these provisions necessarily presuppose a freedom of **political communication**. This theory was extended in *Theophanous v Herald & Weekly Times* (1994) and *Stephens v WA Newspapers* (1994). Not all members of the Mason Court were comfortable with this development; Dawson in particular adopted a more legalistic view and declined to imply constitutional freedoms in the absence of an explicit **Bill of Rights**. Dawson's more traditional approach was to be repeated in several **dissenting judgments** over the following years.

The last formal legal ties between Australia and the UK were severed in 1986, the passage of the *Australia Acts* removing the last avenues of appeal to the **Privy Council**. The influence of the British courts had by then waned significantly. Nevertheless, the formal confirmation of the High Court as Australia's ultimate appellate court saw the Court become more independent of English legal authority and refer more frequently to decisions of other **common law** systems, gradually developing a uniquely Australian body of law (see also **Citations by Court; Foreign precedents**). The Court also began to pay increasing attention to developments and trends in **international law**—in particular, to the content of international treaties and to decisions of the International Court of Justice and the European Court of Human Rights. The decisions in *Mabo* (1992), *Teoh's Case* (1995), and *Dietrich v The Queen* (1992) are illustrations of the Mason Court's development of the law by reference to principles expressed in international conventions.

A number of the Mason Court's judgments were controversial, receiving high praise and stringent **criticism** in equal measure. Perhaps the most controversial of the Mason Court's landmark decisions was *Mabo*. The Court there held that, under certain conditions, the common law of Australia recognised the **native title** interest in land of **Aboriginal peoples**. *Mabo* was applauded by many for its rejection of false and discriminatory legal doctrine; but it also unleashed a torrent of protest, revealing deep divisions within the Australian community on the issue of the recognition of indigenous land rights and the **role** of the Court in that process. The legislative response to *Mabo* brought with it significant political, social, and **economic** consequences for many Australians.

Teoh was similarly controversial, although it did not inspire nearly as much public—as opposed to political—controversy. The Court there held that an international treaty could create a **legitimate expectation** that a decision maker would exercise a statutory discretion in conformity with the terms of that treaty. That was despite the fact that the treaty had not been implemented by Parliament and could thus have no direct legal effect on domestic Australian law. The government of the day vehemently disagreed with the Court's decision and moved quickly to introduce legislation to ameliorate the aspects of the judgment relating to legitimate expectation. The legislation was not at that stage passed by Parliament. This tension between the various arms of government was to be a recurring theme during the Mason Court years.

Dietrich received less attention at the time it was delivered. Nevertheless, the practical impact of the decision and its far-reaching implications for the criminal justice system have since made this judgment similarly controversial. In *Dietrich*, a majority of the Court found that the power of a court to order a stay to avoid an unfair trial may be exercised where an accused is charged with a serious offence and, through no fault of his or her own, is unable to obtain legal representation.

The Mason Court was responsible for important doctrinal developments in other less contentious, but no less important, areas of the law. The period of the Mason Court saw, for example, the continued development of the concept of **natural justice** or procedural fairness (*Haoucher v Minister for Immigration* (1990); *Annetts v McCann* (1990)), the expansion of equitable doctrines in **commercial law** (*Waltons Stores v Maher* (1988); *Trident General Insurance v McNiece* (1988); *David Securities v Commonwealth Bank* (1992)), and significant rationalisation and expansion of the law of **torts** (*Burnie Port Authority v General Jones* (1994); *Rogers v Whitaker* (1992); *March v Stramare* (1991)). A unifying theme of the Mason Court's decisions in these areas was a preference for solutions involving discretionary elements rather than the application of apparently absolute general rules—a movement **Gleeson** described in 1995 as the 'individualisation of justice'.

A wider issue raised by the more adventurous decisions of the Mason Court was the legitimacy of the Court's law-making role. Although it was by that stage widely acknowledged and understood by informed observers that judges make law, the question raised by the policy-oriented approach of the Mason Court was how far the Court should go in reformulating legal principle and the method by which it should do so. The open acknowledgment by the Court of its law-making role also caused considerable discomfort among those who were not so well informed. A number of the cases that came before the Mason Court invited consideration of what was best for the welfare of society, and thus a consideration of the **values** of society. The more explicit recognition of policy considerations meant, however, that the Court was more frequently and more openly criticised both in respect of the outcome in particular decisions (for example, *Mabo*) and for general doctrinal change (for example, *Teoh*). **Commentators** questioned the Court's ability to understand or identify the 'relatively permanent values of the Australian community', by reference to which the Court was increasingly justifying its law-making role, and whether the different roles of the Court, the Parliament, and the **executive** were being respected. Concern was also expressed that the Court had not stated clearly how it drew the line between the role of the Court and the role of Parliament, nor clearly articulated when it was appropriate for it to change the law and on what materials the Court could or should draw in reaching such a decision.

There were other significant changes during this period, unrelated to doctrinal developments but important in modernising the manner in which the Court undertook its work. The video link system was introduced (see **Information technology**), allowing applications for special **leave** to be heard with one or both parties in Brisbane, Perth, or Adelaide before a Court **sitting** in Canberra. The traditional wigs and robes were discarded in favour of simpler **court attire**, and greater use was made of written **argument** provided to the Court prior to oral submissions. The Mason Court also engaged in dialogue with the **media** to a greater extent than had previously been the case. Late in his time as Chief Justice, Mason showed a willingness to talk about the work of the Court and its role in Australian society, appearing several times on television and radio. In so doing, he gave a public face to the Court and made its work both more relevant and more understandable to the public.

MICHELLE DILLON
JOHN DOYLE

Further Reading

Michael Kirby, 'AF Mason: from Trigwell to Teoh' (1997) 20 *MULR* 1087

Cheryl Saunders (ed), *Courts of Final Jurisdiction—The Mason Court in Australia* (1996)

Matters. The word 'matter' is used in Chapter III of the Constitution in the provisions defining the **jurisdiction** of the High Court. It was chosen by the **framers of the Constitution** in preference to the words 'cases and controversies' used in the US Constitution. The word was accepted by the first High Court as denoting the widest range of controversies that might arise for judicial adjudication. However, the Court has subsequently given the word a significance that is belied by its apparent simplicity and everyday meaning. In the constitutional context, the meaning of the word remains to some extent elusive. The Court uses the requirement that there be a 'matter' to define the limits on the judicial **role** that it sees as appropriate in particular circumstances, having

regard to its conception from time to time of what the **separation of powers** requires. It provides the peg on which judicially created barriers or limitations on the exercise of federal **judicial power** can be hung.

In *In re Judiciary and Navigation Acts* (1921), the Court used the requirement that there be a 'matter' to reject the idea that the federal courts might be asked to give **advisory opinions**. It concluded, in what has become the accepted meaning of the word, that 'matter' does not denote a legal proceeding, but rather the subject matter for determination in a legal proceeding involving some immediate right, duty, or liability to be established by the determination of the Court. Abstract questions of law divorced from any attempt to administer the law do not give rise to a matter. The word 'matter' therefore has two elements: the subject matter itself, and the concrete adversarial nature of the dispute sufficient to give rise to a justiciable controversy. The rejection of advisory opinions was on the basis that they did not involve a matter—not that the giving of such opinions was not a judicial function.

The requirement that there be a matter is also relevant to the consideration of issues of **standing**, as well as to mootness and **justiciability**. The word has also assumed a major role in defining the accrued jurisdiction of federal courts. In this latter role, the word 'matter' has been interpreted expansively. By focusing on the scope of the controversy (the matter) that gives rise to the federal claim, the Court has allowed non-federal claims to be heard by the federal courts as part of the resolution of a single controversy. This aspect has gained new importance with the demise of key parts of the **cross-vesting** scheme.

In *Fencott v Muller* (1983), the Court acknowledged that it is a question of impression and of practical judgment whether a non-federal claim and a federal claim joined in one proceeding are within the scope of one controversy, and thus within the ambit of a matter. A single matter can embrace different claims arising out of a common substratum of facts, or can be discerned if the determination of one claim is essential to the determination of the other. Completely distinct and unrelated claims are not part of the same matter.

The definition of a 'matter' also assumed significance in *Abebe v Commonwealth* (1999), in relation to attempts to limit the jurisdiction of federal courts to review **immigration** decisions by restricting the grounds on which such review can be sought. The majority considered it was possible to limit the grounds available for **judicial review** in a federal court (other than the High Court) without infringing the requirement that there be a matter. It was relevant for the purpose of identifying the matter to have regard to the **remedies** available in the court where it is litigated. The minority, however, considered that by limiting the grounds of review available in a particular court, the law in question had failed to confer jurisdiction in relation to a matter. In their view, the concept of 'matter' refers to the whole justiciable controversy, which encompasses all claims made within the scope of the controversy independently of the proceedings brought. To disaggregate such a compendious matter by permitting judicial scrutiny of only some aspects of it did not identify a 'matter' at all.

The concept of 'matter' has also served as a reason not to answer questions of general legal or constitutional interest when the Court's decision on other issues has rendered the question hypothetical or moot. Thus, in the *Waanyi Case* (1996), the Court declined to deal with the effect upon **native title** of pastoral leases, considering that to do so would be to deliver an advisory opinion, given that the Court had already decided for other reasons to set aside the order of the **Federal Court**. A similar restrictive approach to answering questions with no agreed facts was taken in *Bass v Permanent Trustee Co* (1999). This approach has not always been unanimous. **Kirby** in particular has expressed the view that the judicial function is not frozen in time, and provision of assistance to parties by answering questions that arise incidentally to the determination of an appeal ought not to be viewed as going beyond the appropriate judicial role.

The requirement that there be a 'matter' has also led to disagreement as to what cases can be brought on appeal to the High Court from state courts, which are not constrained in the same way as federal courts in relation to the cases they can hear. This has been particularly an issue when a case is stated for a Court of Criminal Appeal in order to clarify the law after a trial and acquittal. A willingness to hear an appeal in such a case was shown in *Mellifont v A-G (Qld)* (1991), which overturned more restrictive earlier decisions. In *DPP v B* (1998), the relationship between the question reserved and the factual issues at the trial was regarded as critical to establishing jurisdiction. Where questions are reserved in general terms unrelated to facts, there is unlikely to be a 'matter'.

In relation to standing, the Court has acknowledged the link between the interest relied on by the plaintiff and the existence of a matter. This is reflected in cases such as *Croome v Tasmania* (1997), where a generous approach to standing was taken but in the context that there was a concrete dispute capable of judicial resolution concerning the validity of state laws. Where issues concerning compliance with international obligations or the legality of particular foreign policy decisions are raised, the Court will often use the absence of a 'matter' as the basis for rejecting the claim without needing to rely directly on grounds such as standing or justiciability.

HENRY BURMESTER

Further Reading

Henry Burmester, 'Limitations on Federal Adjudication' in Brian Opeskin and Fiona Wheeler (eds), *The Australian Federal Judicial System* (2000) 227

McHugh, Michael Hudson (*b* 1 November 1935; Justice since 1989) was the product of a strong working-class tradition. His father had felt the bite of the **Depression** and valued loyalty to his friends, family, and fellow workers. The son of Jim and Moira McHugh, McHugh was born in Cooks Hill, a suburb of Newcastle. In 1942, his family moved to Collinsville, in North Queensland, where his father was employed as a miner. When McHugh was 13 years old, his family returned to Newcastle, where his father worked as a steelworker with BHP. Jim McHugh was a physically strong and confident man and an avid reader. He had the legacy of an Irish Catholic upbringing, which resulted in a firm adherence to his principles. In his son, Jim McHugh's sometimes rigid adherence to rules was balanced by a respect for **civil**

Michael McHugh, Justice since 1989

liberties. This balance permeates McHugh's view of the law and his application of legal principle.

McHugh went to school at Marist Brothers in Newcastle, where he played rugby league for the Marist Brothers premiership teams. Although he excelled academically, the young McHugh profoundly disappointed his father by leaving school at the age of 15 without attaining his Leaving Certificate. He worked in a variety of jobs, including labourer, telegram boy, crane chaser, sawmill worker, and clerk. In 1957, at the age of 22, he enrolled in evening classes for the Leaving Certificate at Hamilton Public School, and in 1958 he began the study of law through the Barristers' Admission Board. In July 1960, he married Jeanette Goffet, who later became the Labor Party member for Phillip in the House of Representatives and Minister for Consumer Affairs. For the duration of his studies with the Barristers' Admission Board, McHugh was in full-time employment as a clerk with BHP. Nevertheless, he completed the course in three years, and was called to the Bar on 28 July 1961.

After McHugh's admission to the Bar, he and Jeanette moved to Sydney, where McHugh read with JM Williams and John Kearney. Although he appeared as junior **counsel** in the High Court before the year was over, as a newcomer to Sydney he took time to establish a successful practice.

In 1962, with a young family to support, McHugh decided to return to Newcastle. There, he caught the eye of Jack Smyth, who was renowned for his formidable cross-examination and tactical skills. Thereafter, McHugh was regularly retained as a junior to that legendary advocate, from whom he learnt through observation. In the same year, he appeared before the **Dixon Court** as a junior to JM Williams and FJ Gormly for the defendants in the *Cigamatic Case* (1962), a leading authority on **intergovernmental immunities** and the Crown's right to priority in payment of debts. In 1965, with the encouragement of Smyth, McHugh returned to Sydney and took a room in University Chambers, which he shared with John Nader. Initially, McHugh commuted weekly between Newcastle and Sydney. Eventually, however, the family decided to move permanently to Sydney.

In 1966, with Harold Glass, McHugh co-wrote the standard work *The Liability of Employers in Damages for Personal Injury*. In undertaking this enterprise, and through an enduring professional relationship with Glass, McHugh was a beneficiary of Glass's profound understanding of legal principle and argument, which was always given clear and cogent expression in his written texts. When Glass wrote as a novelist (under the pen name 'Benjamin Sidney'), his fictional protagonist, Paul Sherman, was based in part on McHugh.

As a junior, McHugh's practice was extremely broad, encompassing **tort law**, intellectual property law, **criminal law**, **labour relations law**, and the law of landlord and tenant, and eventually including a formidable **defamation** practice. As an advocate in defamation proceedings, McHugh was influenced by Clive Evatt, with whom he frequently appeared as a junior on behalf of plaintiffs. At his peak, Evatt's superb oratorical skills and tactical ability gave him a commanding presence over a jury.

In 1973, McHugh was appointed QC. From 1977 to 1984 he served on the NSW Bar Council, becoming President of the NSW Bar Association (1982–83) and President of the Australian Bar Association (1983–84). He was one of the recognised leaders of the NSW Bar, and his appearances during this period attest to his versatility and skill. In 1983, he appeared as counsel for the Commonwealth government in the Hope Royal Commission on the Australian Security Intelligence Organisation. He also acted for Lindy and Michael Chamberlain in their appeals to the **Federal Court** and the High Court against their respective convictions as principal and accessory in the murder of their daughter Azaria (see *Chamberlain Case* (1983)). In the same year, he appeared in *Hospital Products v US Surgical Corporation* (1983), which became a leading authority on **fiduciary obligations**.

On 30 October 1984, McHugh was appointed a Judge of Appeal of the NSW Court of Appeal, where he quickly established a reputation for soundly reasoned judgments and a readiness to challenge established doctrine. His influence on the development of the **common law** has been exhibited in a number of cases. For instance, in *Trident General Insurance v McNiece* (1987), McHugh (with whom Justices Robert Hope and LJ Priestley agreed), in a judgment affirmed by the High Court in 1988, expressly recognised the injustice of a rigid application of the doctrine of privity of **contract**, and held that a third party was entitled to enforce a contract with no need to establish the existence of a **trust**. In *Bus v Sydney County Council* (1988)—in a **dissenting judgment** which the High Court upheld on appeal (*Bus v Sydney County Council* (1989))—McHugh held that the defendant had a duty to protect an experienced tradesman against risks that were part of his daily work, even where the tradesman had the skills to identify those risks. In *Bropho v WA* (1990), the High Court approved McHugh's reasoning in *Kingston v Keprose* (1987), where McHugh, again in dissent, expounded what has become the contemporary approach to **statutory interpretation**, with its emphasis on legislative purpose.

On 14 February 1989, McHugh was sworn in as a Justice of the High Court upon the **retirement** of **Wilson**. As a Justice of the High Court, he has shown a willingness to address issues where change is seen by him to be required, tempered by a conservative or cautious approach in application. His judgments characteristically reveal clarity of expression, together with a clear exposition of principle. Throughout his judgments there is a dichotomy between two clearly discernible strands: a recognition of the rights of the individual, but also a consciousness of the need for certainty and predictability in the law, and hence for adherence to, and application of, binding rules.

In *Mabo* (1992), the High Court, by majority, recognised the existence of **native title**. McHugh was among this majority, and agreed with the leading judgment of **Brennan**. In a speech delivered in London in 1998, he said that the recognition of native title in *Mabo* was 'merely a belated recognition in this country of an interest long recognised by the common law of England and other countries'. However, in *Wik* (1996), he again agreed with the reasoning of Brennan, this time in dissent—holding that the common law recognition of native title did not extend to the grant of pastoral leases, and that such leases conferred grants of exclusive possession on the grantees.

In the *Free Speech Cases* (1992), a majority of the High Court held that the system of **representative government** established by the Constitution implied constitutional protection for freedom of **political communication**. McHugh's view—narrower than that of the other majority Justices—was that such implications must be closely tied to specific constitutional provisions. Accordingly, in *Theophanous v Herald & Weekly Times* (1994) and *Stephens v WA Newspapers* (1994), McHugh, together with Brennan and **Dawson**, dissented from the majority view that the constitutional protection of freedom of political discourse extended to actions for defamation. In McHugh's view, the implied freedom of political discourse existed only to protect a narrow concept of representative government—namely, the direct election of the federal Parliament by the people. He insisted that the Constitution 'does not adopt or guarantee the maintenance of the institution of representative government or representative **democracy**' as such: those ideas were not available as independent starting-points for **judicial reasoning**, but only as tools for explicating the electoral processes directly required by the constitutional text. There could therefore be no foundation for a constitutional defence to actions for defamation.

In *Stephens*, the majority based its conclusion not on a constitutional defence but on the common law defence of qualified privilege, which arises where a potentially defamatory communication is both made and received in pursuit of a legitimate interest or duty. While denying that this common law defence was available at all on the particular facts in *Stephens*, McHugh emphasised that, under modern conditions, 'the general public has a legitimate interest in receiving information concerning … the exercise of public functions and powers vested in public representatives and officials'; and that this legitimate interest should, in principle, be regarded as sufficient to found a defence of qualified privilege. Thus, his refusal to adopt a constitutional defence in *Theophanous* and *Stephens* was combined, in *Stephens*, with an apparent willingness to extend the common law protection to political communication in the media—utilising the capacity of the common law to implement change by an incremental approach, and acknowledging the importance of the open discussion of public affairs. In a powerful passage adopted by the whole Court in *Lange v ABC* (1997), he emphasised that the concern of the common law is for the 'quality of life and freedom of the ordinary individual', which he identified as 'highly dependent on the exercise of functions and powers vested in public representatives and officials by a vast legal and bureaucratic apparatus funded by public moneys'.

The protection of civil liberties at many levels and in the legal process itself is an enduring theme of McHugh's judgments. In *Kable v DPP* (1996), McHugh recognised the need to protect the judicial system created by Chapter III of the Constitution from legislative or executive interference. In *Dietrich v The Queen* (1992), the High Court declared that a trial court has power to stay criminal proceedings where a lack of legal representation would jeopardise a fair trial—the right to which was stated by Mason and McHugh to be a 'central pillar of our legal system'. In *Brisbane South Regional Health Authority v Taylor* (1996), McHugh addressed with compelling clarity the dangers of prejudice to the right to a fair trial arising from the effluxion of time, a danger that may be avoided by the strict application of limitation provisions. In such circumstances, the strict application of the rules may protect the rights of the individual.

McHugh's desire to protect civil liberties has, however, been accompanied by a clear acknowledgment of the necessity of judicial adherence to decided principle. For example, in his judgment in *Burnie Port Authority v General Jones* (1994), in which he defended the *Rylands v Fletcher* rule of prima facie **strict liability**, McHugh distinguished the **law-making** function of the Court from that of the legislature, and cautioned against a too-ready willingness to depart from settled rules of common law.

This insistence on adherence to legal principle and caution against change can be seen as a conservative approach to judicial law-making, yet many of the cases in which this approach has been applied reveal a liberal concern with the welfare of the individual. McHugh's decision in *Burnie Port Authority* reflected a recognition of the vulnerability of the average person to exposure to toxic substances in modern times; his reluctance in *Hill v Van Erp* (1997) to broaden the law of torts in the area of economic loss reflected a concern to avoid increasing costs to the legal profession that would be passed on to the ordinary consumer; and he warned in *Perre v Apand* (1999) that the increased cost of litigation would be a bar to the average person's access to justice. The duality of McHugh's conservative approach to legal method and his liberal recognition of the rights of the individual is one of the most interesting facets of his judicial decision-making, and, when properly understood, challenges the observation sometimes made that McHugh, as a Justice of the High Court, has adopted a more circumspect view of the judicial role than he has expressed in his extra-judicial writings.

KATE GUILFOYLE

Further Reading

Michael McHugh, 'The Law-Making Function of the Judicial Process.' (1988) 62 *ALJ* 15 (Part 1), 116 (Part 2)

Michael McHugh, 'The Law-Making Function of the Judicial Process. Part 2' (1988) 62 *ALJ* 116

Michael McHugh, 'The Judicial Method' (1999) 73 *ALJ* 37

McTiernan, Edward Aloysius (*b* 16 February 1892; *d* 9 January 1990; Justice 1930–76), the longest serving Justice (46 years), was the second of three children of Irish immigrants Patrick McTiernan and Isabella Diamond. Born in Glen Innes, NSW, in humble circumstances, he grew up in a strict Catholic household. He spent his early childhood in Metz, a small NSW goldmining town, and attended the local public school at Glen Innes.

At age seven, McTiernan fell off the verandah of his family's home and suffered a severe injury to his left arm. The injury may have saved his life, since it later exempted him from service in **World War I**, for which he had volunteered. It also made possible his appointment as **associate** to **Rich**, who had insisted on employing only someone who had volunteered for military service and been rejected. At the time, the fall was also one of the reasons why the family moved from the goldmining town to Leichhardt, an inner suburb of Sydney.

Settled in Leichhardt, McTiernan attended the Christian Brothers School at Lewisham and Marist Brothers School, Darlinghurst. He matriculated in 1908. With no financial support for attending university, and with sectarian prejudice pervading employment in the commercial houses of Sydney, McTiernan decided to follow his father's advice and work in the new federal public service. His father had predicted that the federal service would grow in size and importance. McTiernan would later help to realise his father's forecasts through his judgments in such cases as the *Uniform Tax Cases* (1942 and 1957) and the *AAP Case* (1975).

Employed as a clerk, McTiernan used his small wages to study Arts part time at the University of Sydney. He achieved excellent results. He was also selected to be a member of the University debating team that was sent to England. After completing his BA, he resigned from the public service in order to enter the legal profession. He worked part time as a junior clerk at a firm of solicitors—a position he discovered quite by chance—and studied law after office hours. He applied himself diligently, and graduated in 1915 from the University of Sydney with first-class honours.

In 1916, during his service as associate to Rich, McTiernan was admitted to the NSW Bar. Having joined the political Labor League in 1911, he stood for parliament at the 1920 NSW state election. Aged 28, he became a member of the NSW Legislative Assembly and retained his seat until 1927, holding the posts of Attorney-General and Minister of Justice under Premiers James Dooley (1920–22) and Jack Lang (1925–27). Lang's biographer Bede Nairn records that McTiernan was 'the most effective reformer in an active cabinet', one 'whose social conscience and great knowledge of the law were indispensable to all ministers'. In 1926, he played a leading role in Lang's attempt to abolish the NSW Legislative Council—to the extent of travelling to London to persuade the Secretary of State for the Colonies, LS Amery, that Governor Dudley de Chair must accept his ministers' advice on the matter.

Edward McTiernan, Justice 1930–76

In the 1927 crisis over the adoption by the Labor Party Conference of the so-called 'Red Rules', McTiernan and his fellow-Catholic, Carlo Lazzarini, previously among Lang's strongest supporters, parted company with him. In the Cabinet reshuffle that followed in May, McTiernan was replaced as Attorney-General by Andrew Lysaght. At the state election in October, McTiernan did not renominate, but returned to full-time practice as a barrister and to lecturing in Roman law at the University of Sydney.

McTiernan resumed his political career in 1929, when he stood for election for the seat of Parkes in the federal House of Representatives. He won the seat handsomely for the Labor Party, and held it until his **appointment** to the High Court in 1930 at the age of 38.

McTiernan was appointed a day after **Evatt**. Some members of caucus would not agree to Evatt's appointment unless it was balanced by the more temperate McTiernan. The appointments were controversial, and made against the wishes of the **Prime Minister** and the **Attorney-General**, who were out of the country at the time. Much of the criticism was directed at McTiernan, who had never taken silk, though the option had been available to him when he was NSW Attorney-General. The thrust of the criticism was that he lacked the distinction to deserve the office and that his only apparent claim to it was his faithful service to the Labor Party. Bar associations and law societies around the country shunned him. **Starke**, also believing that McTiernan's appointment was purely political, was often offensive towards him (see **Personal relations**). Yet throughout the difficult period of the **Latham Court**, McTiernan absorbed the hurts

heaped upon him and rarely complained. He was ever a gentleman, in and out of court.

McTiernan restricted his circle of friends to a small number of people of similar **background**, political views, and religion. He was shy and stubborn by nature. He filled his private life with his associations in the Catholic Church. In 1928, before his appointment to the High Court, he had taken an active part in the Eucharistic Congress held in Sydney in that year. He was one of the founders of the Red Mass, which annually opens the Law Term in Sydney. He was also one of the founders of the St Thomas More Society. For his loyalty and devotion to the Church, he was awarded a high papal honour. In the largely Protestant environment of the Court and the legal profession, his visible allegiance to the Catholic Church added to the isolation caused by the circumstances of his appointment and the subsequent severance of his former political friendships.

The early cases in which McTiernan sat saw him quite frequently in concurrence with **Gavan Duffy** and Evatt. The three provided a core of opinion in the Court that promised to advance federal power and respond sympathetically to the concerns of Australian working men and women. Issues of NSW state politics were more divisive, however. In 1929, a conservative state government led by Premier Thomas Bavin had attempted to forestall any future attempt to abolish the Legislative Council by inserting a new section 7A in the *Constitution Act* 1902 (NSW). In *A-G (NSW) v Trethowan* (1931), with Lang again in power and challenging the effectiveness of this new constitutional barrier, Rich, Starke, and **Dixon** held that it was effective. The normal rule that a parliament cannot 'bind its successors' by limiting their future options was satisfied, they held, because section 7A did not exclude the possibility of Legislative Council abolition, but merely prescribed the 'manner and form' by which it must be achieved.

Gavan Duffy and McTiernan dissented. While McTiernan's position recalled his own role in the 1926 attempt to abolish the Legislative Council, his argument that 'manner and form' requirements could not be imposed without a reduction in substantive legislative powers has continued to reverberate in later cases exploring the capacity of a parliament to fetter its subsequent legislative freedom (see, for example, the Supreme Court of SA in *West Lakes v SA* (1980)).

A year later, however, in the *State Garnishee Case* (1932), the High Court held that Part 2 (Enforcement against State Revenue) of the *Financial Agreement Enforcement Act* 1932 (Cth) was valid. The decision had vital financial, constitutional, and political implications for Lang's tenure of office, leading inexorably to his dismissal three weeks later. Evatt joined Gavan Duffy in dissent, but McTiernan decided with the majority. The Commonwealth, he wrote, 'is a Government, not a mere confederation of States, and no State within the Commonwealth is entitled to decline to fulfil … any obligation imposed upon it by the Constitution'. From that day on, Lang, regarding McTiernan's decision as a betrayal, refused to speak to him.

During the 1930s, McTiernan joined in many **joint judgments** with Dixon, whom he greatly admired, although often finding his prose obscure. He also participated, but to a lesser extent, in joint judgments with Evatt. McTiernan and Evatt most commonly agreed in cases concerning **workers'**

compensation and trade unions. McTiernan also adopted a similar approach to that of Evatt in the cases of the 1930s on freedom of **interstate trade**. As Ken Buckley has noted, McTiernan seems to have been sensitive to claims that he was too strongly influenced by Dixon, and maintained that he always thought for himself. Occasionally, the leadership role between Dixon and McTiernan was reversed (see, for example, *Dickson v FCT* (1940)).

Following the outbreak of **World War II**, the Court generally supported the extension of **Commonwealth legislative powers**, a tendency that comfortably accorded with McTiernan's own views. However, when the threat to Australia declined in the mid-1940s, the Court reverted to a narrower interpretation of the federal legislative powers. By now often in dissent, McTiernan was the only Justice to uphold the validity of the *Pharmaceutical Benefits Act* 1944 (Cth) (see the *First Pharmaceutical Benefits Case* (1945)), while he and **Latham** alone supported the validity of the nationalisation measure in the *Bank Nationalisation Case* (1948).

McTiernan's support for federal power and his tendency to be in favour of the underdog in litigation were consistent throughout his career. His decisions were the least 'pro-employer' in industrial accident compensation cases. They were the most 'pro-accused' in criminal appeals. They were the least 'pro-*laissez faire*' in cases under section 92 of the Constitution. Next to **Windeyer**, his decisions were the least 'pro-defendant' in road accident cases. Yet in applications to review government decisions by constitutional **writs**, his judgments were the most sympathetic to government and least supportive of the applicant challenging the benevolent state. His judgments were generally shorter than those of his brethren, as he clearly placed more importance on outcomes than on the development of doctrine; yet the results he arrived at were often sound and sometimes prophetic—as in *FCT v Casuarina* (1971), where McTiernan held in sole dissent that the respondent company was engaging in tax evasion and should be assessed to tax. From this perspective, his judicial contribution may have been underrated.

In 1948, McTiernan, aged 56, married Kathleen Lloyd. The marriage took place three years after the death of McTiernan's father, with whom McTiernan maintained almost daily contact. There were no children of the marriage. Instead, McTiernan tended to treat his associates as part of his family. The associate would eat with him in his **chambers**; usually dine at the McTiernan home at least once a week; and discuss politics with him.

McTiernan was not devoid of **humour**. His associates have told of how McTiernan could become animated and have bursts of energy and enthusiasm. But it was generally over history or politics, not the law. He also had a legendary reputation for frugality.

Although McTiernan's strong opposition to communism went back to the days of the 'Red Rules', in 1951 he aligned himself with the majority in striking down the *Communist Party Dissolution Act 1950* (Cth) in the **Communist Party Case** (1951). As he told Frank Brennan, he was 'most relieved' when he realised that he would not be alone in declaring the Act invalid. He played an active role in the case to help ensure its result. In the same year, he was appointed a KBE.

While Dixon dominated the Court during the relatively uneventful period of the 1950s and later, there were significant differences in judicial viewpoints between McTiernan and Dixon during this period. Often McTiernan was more concerned with the practical and social effects of the Court's decisions than were other members of the Bench (see, for example, *Mason v NSW* (1959), one of many cases where McTiernan was the sole dissentient). Although he remained personally opposed to Dixon's approach to section 92 of the Constitution, the **Privy Council** decision in *Hughes & Vale v NSW* (1954) constrained him to accept that approach. In the subsequent cases beginning with *Hughes & Vale v NSW (No 2)* (1955), he (like **Webb**) joined in the judgments in which Dixon expounded the effect of the Privy Council decision on the 'transport cases' of the 1930s; but McTiernan attached to the joint *Hughes & Vale* judgment a poignant 'Addendum'— citing his own judgments in the earlier cases as showing that his contrary view had been held 'for many years', but accepting that the Privy Council had found that view 'not to be acceptable … and it is incumbent upon me to work out as best I may the results and implications of the contrary views which commended themselves to their Lordships'. He went on:

> In the joint judgments to which I am a party there is stated, as I believe adequately … what appears to be the true operation of the views which in the past I had found myself unable to share. But perhaps I may be permitted to say that I remain personally far from convinced that the result is one which the **framers** of s 92 either intended or foresaw.

The 'Addendum' becomes even more poignant when the **Dixon diaries** reveal that, in a telephone conversation a week earlier, McTiernan had asked Dixon 'to write a supplementary explanation or apologia for him to deliver, which I did'.

Similarly, when Dixon's broadening view of duties of **excise** had prevailed in *Matthews v Chicory Marketing Board* (1938) and in *Parton v Milk Board* (1949), Latham and McTiernan had dissented. But in *Dennis Hotels v Victoria* (1960), McTiernan agreed with Dixon's view that both of the liquor licensing fees involved were excise duties. The only **precedent** he cited was *Parton v Milk Board*, and once again he explained: 'I feel that it would be contrary to the decision of the majority in that case for me to adhere to the opinion which I expressed in that case.'

In *Hughes & Vale (No 2)* and *Dennis Hotels*, McTiernan's personal statements were characterised by gentle understatement. Those close to him detected a similar understatement in *Giltinan v Lynch* (1971), a challenge to the balloting system by which young men were conscripted for service in the Vietnam War. The case was heard on **circuit** in Brisbane. On the second day of the hearing, **Barwick** announced that the Justices had considered the matter overnight and were ready to deliver judgment. In a series of short *ex tempore* judgments, the challenge was unanimously dismissed. McTiernan agreed that the ballot was 'an appropriate means' of exercising the Commonwealth's executive power, but added meaningfully: 'The question whether it is a moral or ethical means does not arise in these proceedings. I do not pass any opinion on that aspect.'

In 1972, McTiernan took a long journey around the world, which his wife had organised. He insisted on being accompanied by his associate on the journey. While in England, he sat in the Privy Council, of which he had been made a member in 1963 (see *Edwards v The Queen* (1972)).

In the 1960s and 1970s, there were times when McTiernan's enthusiasm and energy seemed to be waning and the number of his **dissenting judgments** fell. But from time to time, his vigour reasserted itself: when **Taylor** died in 1969 and **Kitto** resigned in 1970, McTiernan responded to rumours that he, too, was about to retire by buying a new judicial robe. In some of the cases of the **Whitlam era**, he played an important role—particularly in the first *Territory Senators Case* (1975). In the *AAP Case*, the Court revisited the 1945 *Pharmaceutical Benefits Case*: McTiernan was the only member of the Bench to have sat in both cases, and in both of them he held that the Commonwealth scheme under challenge was valid. In *Cormack v Cope* (1974) and the *PMA Case* (1975), he maintained that the special legislative procedures prescribed by section 57 of the Constitution were not **justiciable**.

At times during these years, his interventions in oral **argument** were as sharp as ever, though his fine, quavering voice was often difficult for counsel to understand. At other times, especially during a long hearing, he appeared distracted. On one occasion, as Acting **Chief Justice**—an office McTiernan had held on many occasions, having been the senior **puisne Justice** since 1952—he swore in new members of the Senate. The members of Parliament were uniformly shocked at McTiernan's age and apparent feebleness. Bipartisan support for the 1977 amendment of the Constitution imposing a compulsory retirement age for federal judges followed shortly thereafter.

McTiernan would probably have remained on the Bench until his death and served for over 50 years, but for another accident. In 1976, in his room at the Windsor Hotel in Melbourne, he overbalanced while trying to kill a cricket with a rolled-up newspaper, and broke his hip. Chief Justice Barwick, sensing an opportunity to fill McTiernan's post with someone younger and closer to his own world view, is said to have declined to alter the accommodation of the Court to provide for a judge in a wheelchair. He persuaded McTiernan to retire.

In 1990, McTiernan died in Sydney, just short of his ninety-eighth birthday. Legal commentators paid handsome tributes to him. Despite initial adversity, he attained high legal and political office through diligence, luck, and ability.

MICHAEL KIRBY

Further Reading
Michael Kirby, 'Sir Edward McTiernan: A Centenary Reflection'
  (1991) 20 *FL Rev* 165

Media and the Court. In its first two decades, the High Court, as an element in the new institutional structure of the new federation, was the subject of intensive and detailed newspaper reportage, especially in the Melbourne *Argus*. But as the nation matured, media attention to the Court declined. By mid-century, media scrutiny of the Court was fitful and unsophisticated.

It was only when the Court moved to **Canberra** in the early 1980s that any major media organisation regularly reported it, and, even now, although major decisions are reported by senior and qualified journalists, the volume of material coming from the Court has not been thought to justify the assignment of full-time journalists to that beat. During much the same period, with a declining focus on law reform, and with the 1970s activism of the Attorney-General's Department subsiding in the 1980s and 1990s, the idea of combining such a round with Canberra legal commentary has also foundered.

The Court is now reported by journalists who are essentially specialists, but for whom coverage of the Court is only a part of their duties. That their other duties generally include political coverage gives a flavour to their reporting that may tend to accentuate the Court's **role** as the third arm of government: there is a far stronger focus on constitutional than on **common law** matters, and considerable attention is given to the politics, or supposed politics, of the Court, the **appointment** process, and the impact of decisions on government. The disadvantage is that the more routine work of the Court, particularly its common law and general appellate work, gets little attention, unless, as in cases such as *Mabo* (1992), there are obvious political consequences. The Court's work in high-profile **criminal law** matters has, of course, always been covered, but more in the tradition of general court reporting, and with much less focus on the Court's reasoning than on results.

That the first three-quarters of a century of the Court saw little specialist coverage was not merely a matter of its want of a base. Cases with a significant **political impact**, such as the *Bank Nationalisation Case* (1948) and the *Communist Party Case* (1951), were reported—though again with more focus on outcomes than on the Court's reasoning—sometimes directly by journalists, and sometimes by legal academics as direct or quoted **commentators**. Newspapers have been generally conscious of the significance of the Court in the constitutional framework and its role as a referee in disputes between the Commonwealth and the states, or between the state and its citizens in framing rights, and far from unsophisticated in recognising the importance of the Justices' predispositions and **values**. But a number of factors inhibited the development of sustained reporting or deeper analysis.

The peripatetic nature of the Court did not help (see **Circuit system**). Neither did the fact that the Court dealt with a considerable volume of trial work, much of little general interest, nor that, even in relation to the appellate work, there was often little in the way of new law, as much of it came to the Court as of right. The denseness of judgments, the self-conscious **legalism** and legalistic writing style of many of the Justices, and the fact that it was often difficult to discern a governing principle from different judgments in the majority did not assist confident reporting. The Justices made few concessions to reporters, and did not appreciate even respectful **criticism**, which in any event tended to come only from editorials. Deference was, generally, the order of the day. When commentary came, it tended to take decisions, even unexpected ones, as read, or at least as infallible, and was largely the domain of reporters covering that particular field of activity. The essence of good general court reporting was in skilfully summarising the facts—something relatively unimportant in the work of the Court; and even skilful reporters were not well trained in the law. Just as significantly, there was comparatively little legal activism on the part of either executive or legislative government, and it was only rarely that a matter came before the Court in a way that put the Court itself at centre stage.

That began to change in the mid-1960s as the Commonwealth became more active in seeking for itself a role in national **economic** regulation and in **trade practices**, which cast a renewed spotlight on the character of Justices as either centrists or states'-righters. It developed further with the advent of the **Whitlam era** in 1972. Whitlam's government had an agenda of law reform, human rights reform, **administrative law** reform, a more activist role for the Commonwealth in economic and social affairs, and a bigger role for government generally. There were constitutional as well as political obstacles, and the importance of the Court as arbiter of the limits of Commonwealth power was frankly recognised. There was also considerable political commentary on the role of Chief Justice **Barwick** in inviting a rehearing of the issue in the *Territory Senators Cases* (1975 and 1977) and, later, on his decision to offer formal advice to the Governor-General, John Kerr, over the **dismissal** of the Whitlam government in 1975. At the same time, the Whitlam government's appointment of its **Attorney-General, Murphy**, to the Court in 1975, caused a storm of controversy, particularly in conservative political circles, and the politics of filling the Senate vacancy arising from his appointment were themselves among the precipitating factors of the dismissal. The Murphy appointment was not, of course, the first controversial appointment to the Court, but the journalistic coverage and commentary were of a frankness not previously seen.

Murphy himself quickly developed a **judicial style** that was warmly welcomed by reporters; it tended to give his judgments, even in minority, a coverage that other, more densely reasoned, judgments did not get. The increased open discussion of the constitutional basis of government programs, the focus that this put on the predilections of Justices, the increased willingness of political players to discuss judicial personalities, and the Barwick and Murphy controversies, set the stage for more active reporting. So did the fact that the same period was witnessing a revolution in journalism. Radio and television were changing the roles of newspapers and putting more focus on analysis and commentary, and journalists were becoming better educated and more professional. Three of the journalists assigned to the High Court **building** when it opened in Canberra in 1980 were qualified as lawyers, and as confident in their capacity to comment on the political, social, and economic impact of the Court's decisions as on the strict legal points resolved. The Justices remained aloof from the press, but had to become used to being treated as players.

There were other changes. Both Barwick and Murphy spoke at the National Press Club and answered questions. For Barwick, this almost invariably involved heated discussions about his role in 1975—debates he would enter with zest; Murphy, while careful to avoid making comments about current controversies before the Court or direct party-polit-

ical matters, freely canvassed human rights and other live political issues. Over the same period, Barwick found himself under direct attack in the Senate over his personal share dealings, and the press was highly critical of the Court's majority decisions on **taxation** evasion and avoidance. Later, the various controversies arising out the '**Murphy affair**', including one initiated by Chief Justice **Gibbs** about whether Murphy should sit, led to an increased focus on personalities—a focus echoed years later in controversies about **Callinan**. The aloof and dignified Court of, say, 50 years before, was now far closer to centre stage in politics and government. If it was still generally treated respectfully, there was little pretence, even by the Justices themselves, that decisions emerged by formula or did not involve value choices.

The Court's arrival in Canberra coincided with changes in the nature of its **business**. Progressively, appeals to the **Privy Council** were being abolished, as were appeals as of right to the Court. Apart from constitutional and section 75 matters, most cases were coming to the court by **leave**. Old first-instance work was being handled by the **Federal Court**, or, in some cases, by administrative tribunals. Judicial and administrative review work was becoming more significant, as were cases involving human rights issues, particularly as a result of Commonwealth **discrimination** legislation. Many old staples of the High Court diet—bankruptcy and **succession**, and the mere passing of the ruler over the quantum of common law **damages**—virtually disappeared. The material before the Court was now intrinsically more political and newsworthy, and, often, already in the centre of major controversy. A number of cases which might have come before the Court at any time—the *Chamberlain Case* (1984), for example— probably received additional coverage from the attention now being given the Court. Commentary, whether from reporters, academics, or senior lawyers, was becoming more robust and less respectful. The *Mabo* decision—and later *Wik* (1996)—brought an avalanche of criticism upon the Court, particularly from conservative elements of the legal profession, but also from politicians. Increasingly, there was a personal, even a bitter aspect to this, which would have astonished observers only a few decades before. It was all eagerly reported by the press.

The Court was at centre stage in the *Tasmanian Dam Case* (1983) and in *Koowarta's Case* (1982), as well as a range of other constitutional matters, including those arising from the *Family Law Act* 1975 (Cth). At the same time, less noticed and commented upon by journalists, the Court was streamlining the law of **torts**, becoming more purposive in disputes about **contract** and **equity**, and more concerned about procedural fairness in criminal law matters. The comparative lack of attention to such developments, as well as to the significance of decisions such as *Shaddock v Parramatta City Council* (1981) and the *Northern Land Council Case* (1981), in part reflected the difficulties that journalists had in summarising the Court's reasoning in ways to which ordinary readers (and news editors) could relate: the outcomes, and their significance, were clear enough. One result of this is that the role of the Court as an appellate court is generally less well understood than its role as a constitutional court. It is not widely appreciated, for example, that *Mabo* was a common law, rather than a constitutional, case.

The Court has very good facilities for journalists, even if no journalists now base themselves there. From the opening of the Canberra building, the Court has had state-of-the-art video **transcription** facilities—allowing reporting to occur from outside the Court—and an excellent registry system, permitting access to documents and **appeal books**. Some of the Court's requirements, particularly in relation to summaries of the parties' arguments, are helpful to journalists seeking to comprehend the issues. In recent years, the Court's decisions have been quickly available on the Internet, giving even journalists physically remote from the Court (and academics and others who may wish to comment) ready access to judgments and to research on older cases. Although the Court has not been able to obtain funding for the employment of a public information officer, major cases now sometimes involve joint statements by the Court in which an effort is made to summarise the issues and the Court's decision in simple terms (see **Collective responsibility**). Although most Justices are extremely cautious about contacts with the media, recent Chief Justices—and not a few Justices—have addressed and answered questions at the National Press Club and have taken opportunities in public speaking to discuss the work of the Court and some of the criticisms of its workings.

One criticism by journalists, in part being addressed by summaries of decisions, involves the way the Court communicates its decisions. There are often seven judgments, many simply repeating the facts: some extend to many pages, often with very tight legal reasoning. Although the proportion of **joint judgments** is increasing, cases involving separate judgments make it difficult even for experts to ascertain the principles upon which a majority is agreed. The pressures upon journalists—including broadcast journalists—to produce quick summaries of decisions are increasing. Judges such as former Chief Justice **Brennan** have pointed to the risk of plain English summaries becoming the decision itself, and of the danger of different processes of reasoning being submerged by pressure to produce an outcome upon which a majority can agree, but there can be little doubt of the media appetite for clear expression, and for Justices whose judgments are easy to understand.

JACK WATERFORD

Further Reading
Jack Waterford, 'The Role of the Chief Justice: A Media View' in Cheryl Saunders (ed), *Courts of Final Jurisdiction* (1996)
George Williams, 'The High Court and the Media' (1999) 1 *UTS Law Review* 136

Melbourne Corporation Case (1947) is one of the principal blocks on which the legal nature of the Australian federation is constructed. To *Melbourne Corporation* can be traced the doctrine—often invoked, if rarely applied—that there are limits drawn from the fact of **federalism** on the scope of express **Commonwealth legislative powers**. As an implied limit on Commonwealth power, the *Melbourne Corporation* principle also represents a **precedent** on which reliance may be placed in implying limits on Commonwealth power in other parts of the Constitution.

The case arose from an attempt on the part of the Chifley Labor government to nationalise the Australian banking

system. One measure that it adopted to this end was to prohibit banks other than the Commonwealth bank (or, necessarily, state banks) to conduct banking business on behalf of the states or their authorities. The Corporation of the City of Melbourne, as a local governing authority of the state of Victoria, challenged the validity of the legislation on a series of grounds. The challenge was successful (**Latham**, **Rich**, **Starke**, **Dixon**, and **Williams**; **McTiernan** dissenting).

The *Melbourne Corporation Case* is now taken to stand for the proposition that limits on the scope of express Commonwealth legislative powers can be implied from the federal character of the Constitution. Two limits now are accepted to exist, separately or, sometimes, in combination. These are that the Commonwealth may not discriminate against the states (or particular states) and that it may not exercise its powers so as to threaten the continued existence of the states or their capacity to function. *Melbourne Corporation* itself represents an application of the first of these in the sense that, on its face, section 48 of the *Banking Act* 1945 (Cth) discriminated against the states. These two limbs of the **intergovernmental immunities** doctrine became accepted as a qualification of the hard-line doctrine in the *Engineers Case* (1920) that Commonwealth powers should be read literally and given full effect.

The proposition for which *Melbourne Corporation* is generally now accepted to stand is less obvious from the judgments themselves. Part of the explanation may lie in the composite form in which the argument that Commonwealth power was limited was put to the Court by **Barwick** as **counsel** for the Melbourne Corporation. In the final outcome, some Justices placed emphasis on the discriminatory character of the legislation, and others on its impact on essential government activities and thus on the capacity of governments to function. While most identified **discrimination** against the states as the fatal flaw in the legislation, Justices differed among themselves over why the flaw was fatal. Latham, for example, avoided endorsing the development of a new stream of federal immunity by **characterising** the legislation as 'really … with respect to a State or State functions as such'. Williams, in more heretical mode, argued that 'if the law is in pith and substance a law which seeks to give directions to the States … it is not a law for the peace, order and good government of the Commonwealth'.

It is Dixon's formulation of principle and analysis of the reasons why legislation which discriminates against the states is likely to offend the Constitution that has endured and been attributed to the Court as a whole. Even this judgment has difficulties in its reasoning, however. One is the suggestion (which Dixon had developed in a series of earlier cases beginning with the *ARU Case* (1930)) that legislation which discriminates against the states is a 'reservation' to the doctrine laid down in *Engineers*. On closer inspection, the reservation lies in no more than Dixon's own logic and his negative proposition that *Engineers* has 'nothing to say … in *support*' of such a use of the power'.

Following the decision in *Melbourne Corporation*, the government pursued its policy in less discriminatory form (*Banking Act* 1947 (Cth))—in the belief, following a hint in the decision itself, that a law of general application that prohibited banks other than the Commonwealth bank from conducting any banking business would not infringe the implied limitation. The hint was right—but this time the legislation foundered on the obstacle of section 92, amongst others, in the *Bank Nationalisation Case* (1948). The immunities doctrine endured, however. That part of the doctrine that prohibits discrimination has been relied on by the Court on several occasions, most notably in *Queensland Electricity Commission v Commonwealth* (1985). Even the prohibition against impairing the capacity of the states to function has been given effect, albeit in limited form, in decisions about the scope of Commonwealth power to prescribe industrial relations arrangements for states and their employees (*Re Australian Education Union; Ex parte Victoria* (1995); *Industrial Relations Act Case* (1996)).

CHERYL SAUNDERS

Melbourne Corporation v Barry (1922). In Melbourne in the 1880s, city and suburban council bylaws prohibited street processions except with prior written consent from the mayor or town clerk, and with 24 hours advance notice to police. In *Rider v Phillips* (1884) and *Bannon v Barker* (1884), both involving marches by the Salvation Army, the Supreme Court of Victoria accepted these bylaws as a valid exercise of statutory powers 'for regulating traffic and processions'.

The provision for consent by the mayor or town clerk was justified as enabling march organisers to obtain permission promptly at any time. But in 1920, the Melbourne City Council resolved that the Council itself should make such decisions. In November 1921, its by-laws (now made under the *Local Government Act* 1915 (Vic)) were amended accordingly.

On 6 February 1922, the Council used the new bylaw to *refuse* permission for the annual St Patrick's Day procession. The 17:11 vote was celebrated by Protestants and execrated by Catholics. The Council refused to budge, and invoked the *Unlawful Assemblies and Processions Act* 1915 (Vic), which prohibited processions reflecting 'religious or political differences between any classes of His Majesty's subjects'.

On Saturday 18 March, a large and peaceful procession was held. Archbishop Daniel Mannix rode in the leading car, accompanied by Father John Barry, the Administrator of St Patrick's Cathedral and Chancellor of the Melbourne archdiocese. Police took their names but made no arrests. Instead, Father Barry instituted proceedings to have the by-law quashed as invalid.

The significant issue was whether power to *regulate* processions included power to *prohibit* them. For the Council, **Latham** and **Dixon** argued that it did; and that in any event the 1884 cases were conclusive. The original power of 'regulating traffic and processions' had been re-enacted in the *Local Government Act* 1903 (Vic), and consolidated in 1915; and these repetitions of the earlier language must be meant to have the effect judicially stated in 1884.

The Victorian Supreme Court rejected these arguments by a 2:1 majority (*Barry v City of Melbourne* (1922)). The 1884 cases had not *directly* held that 'regulation' includes 'prohibition'. Insofar as they did, they were overridden by later contrary decisions of the **Privy Council** and the High Court.

The appeal to the High Court was heard by a three-judge Bench. Chief Justice **Knox** accepted the 1884 decisions as binding, but **Isaacs** and **Higgins** rejected them. Each of them seized the occasion for a strong defence of **civil liberties**.

Isaacs stressed that any legitimate regulation of marches must be carefully circumscribed, since 'citizens are entitled to know to what extent their **common law** rights are restricted' and to be protected against 'total surrender of their right innocently and unaggressively to use the King's highway in company' for 'great and important national, political, social, religious or industrial movements or opinions'. Higgins insisted that, wherever possible, statutes should be interpreted to avoid 'any interference with a common law right'; that 'the liberty of procession is … a safety valve'; and that nothing would produce more bitterness or divisiveness than 'to allow a mere majority of the councillors to forbid processions of bodies whose nature or purposes are not acceptable to the majority'.

Although Latham had argued *against* the idea that 'regulation is not prohibition', he was later to use that idea effectively in cases on freedom of **interstate trade**, for example *Milk Board (NSW) v Metropolitan Cream* (1939).

TONY BLACKSHIELD

Men. The preponderance of men in all aspects of High Court life—as Justices, **counsel**, **litigants**, and the (usually unstated) subjects of legal reasoning—is partly a historical legacy of the **common law** culture, in which only men were thought competent to participate in the exercise of public authority, whether as voters, political candidates, jurors, or legal practitioners. Although the formal exclusion of **women** from most of these roles ended many years ago, some Australian jurisdictions did not, for example, admit women to jury service until the 1970s.

The masculine orientation of the law and legal institutions is perhaps so obvious that it has largely passed unnoticed, except during the two great waves of **feminism**. Even then, the central concern has been with the exclusion of women rather than with the related yet distinct fact of the masculinist nature of law. To focus solely on the former issue may obscure the full implications of the latter by continuing to assume the presence of men in familiar and unquestioned roles, arguing only that these roles should now be open to women.

While the masculinity of law might be said to privilege men as a group overwhelmingly, this is an incomplete view. Men, like women, come in many kinds. Yet the culture and conventions of the law have tended to project a very uniform image of the male subject of law: one which by definition has excluded women, but also within which only certain limited forms of masculinity are recognisable. The constructions of men in High Court jurisprudence can be detected in areas as diverse as **equity**, **common law**, **family law**, and **criminal law**.

The 'Reasonable Man'. The 'reasonable man' test, as a referential standard both at common law and in equity, has frequently been criticised for its non-incorporative nature—parading as an objective test in a way that thinly veils the use of a male perspective as the benchmark for everyone's conduct. The image of man underpinning the test usually displays the stereotypical characteristics associated with white, middle-class men: autonomous and engaging with the world objectively and without emotion. Behaviour falling short of the **stereotype** ordinarily fails the test.

In *Legione v Hateley* (1983), the Court used the 'reasonable man' test to determine whether a particular representation was 'clear'. A purchaser of land had sought to extend the date for payment of the purchase price. His solicitor had contacted the vendors' solicitor to seek an extension, but had spoken to his secretary, who said: 'I think that'll be all right, but I'll have to get instructions.' Hearing nothing further, the purchaser assumed that an extension of time had been granted. If the question is whether a reasonable man would have thought the words unambiguous, the answer will depend in part on the template of men that is used. A template that values objectivity, crisp definition, and autonomy might well produce a different result from a template acknowledging reticence, diffidence, and deference.

The question in *Consul Development v DPC Estates* (1975) was whether a constructive **trust** arose when an employee's disclosure of confidential information enabled that employee to share with an entrepreneurial acquaintance the profits of a real estate venture resulting from the disclosure. Again, the 'reasonable man' test was used: the acquaintance would be a constructive trustee only if he had 'knowledge of circumstances which would indicate to an honest and reasonable man' that the scheme was dishonest, or would put him on inquiry whether that were the case.

The Court has invoked the 'reasonable man' to help it calibrate facts and judge conduct in many other cases (see, for example, *Laurinda v Capalaba Park Shopping Centre* (1989)). Although the word 'man' is supposed to act as a substitute for 'all people', it conceals the systemic and substantive **discrimination** that such a usage implies. If the experiences of reasonable men are equated with those of women and of non-stereotypical men, experiences are homogenised so that all people are treated the same. While **equality** before the law is a cornerstone of our legal system, treating all experiences as the same is not necessarily treating them equally. The 'reasonable man' test can result in unfairness because different experiences are not taken into account: **Latham's** Spartan acceptance of the death of a child in *Chester v Waverley Corporation* (1939) as 'not an unusual event' may perhaps have reflected a masculine model of stoical fortitude under adversity, but did less than justice to the anguish of the bereaved and traumatised mother. Furthermore, the use of such a benchmark tends to ignore social context, preferring to view events as disaggregated and leading to individualised harm. This is particularly ironic where equitable principles are being applied, since equity historically operated to individualise justice through contextualisation.

With the influence of feminist theories, the rise of cultural studies, and the passing of legislation to outlaw discrimination on the basis of sex and **race**, many courts, including the High Court, have consciously tried to remove the 'reasonable man' test from their lexicon, rewriting it instead as the 'reasonable person' test. **Mason's** test of **unconscionability** in *Amadio's Case* (1983) is an example. By asking whether the known facts would raise doubt 'in the mind of any reasonable person', Mason appeared to neutralise the test of a 'reasonable man', substituting a gender-inclusive test. Yet in going on to explain his test he relied on Lord Cranworth's words in *Owen and Gutch v Homan* (1853), which hark back to the experiences of men by asking whether 'the dealings are such as fairly to lead a reasonable man to believe that fraud must have been used'. The 'reasonable person' becomes the 'reasonable man' in disguise, and men's experiences are still the benchmark.

Mercatorial man. A more specific type of 'man' is frequently the benchmark in cases with a commercial context. 'Mercatorial man', as he might usefully be called, is one whose business transactions should not be meddled with by the Court. He is competent, astute, and demonstrates commercial acumen in his transactions. He is responsible for his own bargains: if he chooses to enter into a bargain that seems unfairly weighted against the other party, that is his business. Only if there is unconscionability amounting to some recognised ground for relief—through fraud, mistake, misrepresentation, or taking advantage of another's weakness—will the Court intervene (see *Commonwealth Bank v Quade* (1991); *ANZ Banking Group v Westpac* (1988); **David Securities v Commonwealth Bank** (1992)).

Even where 'man' is not specifically mentioned, in cases concerning commercial transactions the experience of mercatorial man pervades the legal discourse. In *Hospital Products v US Surgical Corporation* (1984), **Gibbs** stated: 'The fact that the arrangement between the parties was of a purely commercial kind and that they had dealt at arm's length and on an equal footing has consistently been regarded by this Court as important, if not decisive, in indicating that no **fiduciary** duty arose.' Business practices reflecting male paradigms can be seen to underpin the reasoning: the US company was 'under no pressure' since it was free 'to include in its contract whatever terms it thought necessary to protect its position'. The Court upheld a *laissez faire*, free-market approach to business transactions, focusing on freedom of contract and autonomous, dispassionate decision-making practices associated with male standards.

In *Taylor v Johnson* (1983) and *Harrington v Lowe* (1996), the High Court applied the English Court of Appeal decision in *Riverlate Properties v Paul* (1974). In that case, the Court of Appeal explained equity's reluctance to intervene in commercial cases by asking: 'If conscience is clear at the time of the transaction, why should equity disrupt the transaction?' It went on:

> If a man may be said to have been fortunate in obtaining a property at a bargain price … because the other party unknown to him has made a miscalculation or other mistake, some high minded men might consider it appropriate that he should agree to a fresh bargain to cure the miscalculation or mistake, abandoning his good fortune. But if equity were to enforce the views of those high minded men, we have no doubt that it would run counter to the attitudes of much the greater part of ordinary mankind (not least the world of commerce), and would be venturing on the field of moral philosophy in which it would soon be in difficulties.

Although neither of the two High Court decisions expressly endorsed this view, the willingness to apply *Riverlate* suggests indirect acceptance of mercatorial man as a dominant figure whose values correspond with those of the wider community.

Men in relationships. The use of male standards is not unrelated to the way men are constructed in their relationships with others, notably women and **children**. In the context of family business affairs, the man is typically portrayed as a powerful paterfamilias. The image of the husband in *Yerkey v Jones* (1939) as a dominant influence, overbearing his wife's 'apparent or real comprehension', was only slightly softened in *Garcia v National Australia Bank* (1998). In *Amadio's Case*, the husband and wife were Italian immigrants, with little formal education. He had some limited business experience; she had none. In the Supreme Court of SA, Justice Andrew Wells had summarised the relationship in language that effectively incorporated the wife's identity into that of the husband: 'Mr Amadio senior was, in effect, spokesman for himself and his wife, who nevertheless … comprehended, in a general way, what was happening.' This allowed **Deane** to conclude that 'Mr and Mrs Amadio, viewed together, were the weaker party'. Instead of their having independent voices, hers was subsumed in his.

Louth v Diprose (1992) presents a contrasting image of the besotted and lovesick man, whose attentions to the appellant extended to buying a house in her name, but who then wanted it back. The man, Louis Diprose, is seen to be under a special disability arising from his infatuation with Mary Louth, exacerbated by a 'false atmosphere of crisis' when she said she was facing eviction and was suicidal. As Lisa Sarmas's analysis has shown, Louis is depicted as powerless in the face of love—so beguiled by Mary that he cannot restrain his generosity, even though he receives few or no sexual favours in return.

Inevitably, this construct relies on the interpretation of facts by the courts below. That interpretation required that Louis be seen as the weaker party, with his education and financial strength de-emphasised in order to portray him more easily as a duped and defenceless male, making Mary's manipulation more plausible. Hence, although he was a solicitor, with extensive assets including a plane, his financial position and education were downplayed. The disparity with Mary's dependence on a supporting mother's pension was not emphasised. Further, his written outpourings to her were characterised as the 'Mary Poems', connoting romance and love, rather than invasive conduct amounting to sexual harassment. All this assisted in his construction as a pathetic, lovesick victim.

As husbands and fathers, men are perceived as responding to changing times and expectations. But the idea that men are the real owners of **property** because they are the owners of real property remains entrenched. The couple in *Martin v Martin* (1959) had lived and worked on their land together. The husband had paid for the land but had bought it in the name of his wife. The Court upheld the trial judge's decision to give one-third of the land to the husband—not because any equitable trust had been established, or because the judge in his discretion considered it just and equitable, but because that had been the husband's intention. The husband was given only one-third of the land because that was all he had asked for.

In *Mallet v Mallet* (1984), the Court restored the trial judge's order—that the husband and wife have 50 per cent each of the jointly held assets and the wife receive 20 per cent of the assets in the sole name of the husband—partly because equality of contribution could more readily be inferred for a matrimonial home, superannuation benefits, or pension entitlements than for assets acquired by the husband: his ability and energy had enabled him to conduct an extensive business, while his wife had made no financial contribution but was merely a homemaker and parent. The Court held that the business was built by the husband, who put in long hours of work, seized opportunities as they arose, and made careful investments. The wife had played no direct part and could not claim equality of contribution.

The changing role of men as fathers is presented as one of increasing involvement in housework and child-rearing, though they seem to be depicted as being less reliable as single parents (see *M v M* (1988)). In *Gronow v Gronow* (1979), **Stephen** observed that 'the increase in the proportion of working mothers in the community has no doubt led to significant changes in the respective roles of husband and wife', though he cited no empirical support for this view. In any event, his point was to insist on the need for parenting orders to be based on 'a full investigation of the relevant circumstances in the individual case', rather than on 'any arbitrary presumption or rule' in favour of either parent.

In *AMS v AIF* (1999), **Kirby** (citing sociological literature) acknowledged that in separated families most non-resident parents are men, and that any undue restrictions on the mobility of the resident parent would unfairly favour these men. In this case, if the mother was not allowed to move with the child, the father would suffer no such constraint: he could live where he chose, and effectively require his former partner to remain nearby to maximise his contact with their child. The Court held that such a restriction on the mother's freedom of movement was unjustified.

The Violence of 'Ordinary Men'. In some other domains, images of masculinity remain far less open to change. In *Green v The Queen* (1997), a 3:2 majority (**Gummow** and Kirby dissenting) decided that the extremely violent killing of a homosexual man, prompted by his non-violent sexual advances to the killer—who was his friend—might be regarded as falling within the law of provocation, thus entitling the jury to convict the accused of manslaughter rather than murder. The majority decided that unwelcome homosexual advances might cause an *ordinary* man to lose self-control and form an intention to kill or cause serious bodily injury. This affords a quite striking example of how the objective benchmark or standard of the ordinary man may endorse a very particular model of masculinity, while symbolically and practically disqualifying others. As Kirby argued in dissent: 'The "'ordinary person" is a fiction. However, that person represents someone exhibiting a measure of self-control in unwanted situations equal to that which society expects of those living within it and to which its system of criminal justice lends it[s] aid.'

In treating a murderous retaliation to a non-violent sexual advance as consistent with the reactions of an ordinary man, the majority set certain boundaries both to permissible masculine violence and to permissible masculine sexual identity. The ordinary man, it appears, is not only assuredly heterosexual, but possesses a limited capacity to peaceably withstand unwanted sexual advances by others of a different sexual disposition. His capacity for forbearance is far short of that legally expected of women confronted with unwanted sexual conduct by heterosexual men. The asymmetry in

Green's legal treatment of homosexual and heterosexual men is mirrored elsewhere in the Court's approach to the sexual conduct of women and men. It was, for example, the long-accepted common law view that a wife gave irrevocable consent to sexual intercourse with her husband, who could therefore never be guilty of raping her. This principle was overturned by statute in many jurisdictions only in recent times, and by the High Court in *R v L* (1991) (see **Sex**).

In *Bull v The Queen* (2000), the Court quashed the convictions of three men accused of handcuffing a young woman (a friend of one of the men) and, over a three-hour period, inflicting multiple acts of sexual violence and humiliation upon her. The jury had acquitted the men in relation to the handcuffing and several of the alleged acts, but found each of them guilty on four charges, including one in which the woman was subjected to aggravated sexual penetration involving the use of a frozen tube of toothpaste. The men claimed that all the acts were performed with the woman's consent. The convictions were quashed on the ground that **evidence** tendered by one of the accused, relating to the woman's alleged sexual fantasies and sexual frustration, was relevant to the question of consent and had wrongly been excluded. The Court faced a formidable task of circumventing the apparently clear and absolute statutory exclusion of evidence of sexual disposition on which the trial judge had relied.

Of interest here is the way in which this issue served to focus attention on the sexualised conduct (and alleged fantasies) of the young woman as the possible driving force behind these events, to the total exclusion of any consideration of the conduct and sexual intent of the men. This is even more obvious from the **transcripts** of the **argument** in the case. The condemnatory language used by the majority Justices to describe the sexual conduct of the deceased in *Green* makes an interesting contrast with the silence surrounding the admitted conduct of the three young men in this case. Heterosexual male sexual desire of itself attracts no legal interest, even when manifested in the form evidenced by the acts of the accused here. Particular forms of male desire and agency are so normalised—so taken for granted—as to require no comment. Instead, the focus is shifted to the issue of the woman's consent, to be resolved by drawing inferences from her alleged expression of sexual fantasies and sexual frustration. The clues to events are sought in the conduct of others: the female complainant in *Bull*, the homosexual male victim in *Green*. These others are suddenly overburdened with agency, but only for the negative purpose of wholly or partly effacing the violence of ordinary men.

It might be said that the Court in *Bull* was confronted only with narrow legal issues of **statutory interpretation** and admissibility of evidence, the weighing and interpreting of such evidence being matters for the jury. But the judgments ultimately turned on the Justices' unquestioning acceptance of the *relevance* of this evidence—which is both a legal and a factual question, and one that serves to reveal just how fossilised within legal discourse are the asymmetrical assumptions about male and female sexuality.

There is nothing natural or immutable about these legal constructions. The boundaries of permissible and impermissible subjectivity (male, female, and transgender) are drawn and redrawn in the interplay between the life of the Court and the life of society. Yet, as these recent cases attest, the movement in some areas can at best be glacial.

Janice Gray
Russell Hogg
Archana Parashar

Further Reading

Jacques Derrida, 'Women in the Beehive: A Seminar with Jacques Derrida' in Alice Jardine and Paul Smith (eds), *Men in Feminism* (1998)

Ngaire Naffine, *Law and the Sexes* (1990)

Ngaire Naffine and Rosemary Owens (eds), *Sexing the Subject of Law* (1997)

Wendy Parker, 'The Reasonable Person: A Gendered Concept?' (1993) 23 *Victoria University of Wellington Law Review* 105

Lisa Sarmas, 'Storytelling and the Law: A Case Study of *Louth v Diprose*' (1994) 19 *MULR* 701

Carol Smart, 'Rape: Law and the Disqualification of Women's Sexuality' in Carol Smart, *Feminism and the Power of Law* (1989)

Alison Young, 'The Wasteland of the Law, the Wordless Song of the Rape Victim' (1998) 22 *MULR* 442

Menzies, Douglas Ian (*b* 7 September 1907; *d* 29 November 1974; Justice 1958–74) was born in Ballarat, Victoria, the eldest son of a Congregational Minister (the Reverend Frank Menzies). Educated at the Clemes School in Hobart (later known as The Friends' School), Hobart High School, and Devonport High School, he moved to Melbourne in 1925 to study law at the University of Melbourne. At first, he boarded with his uncle, James Menzies, but later became a resident of Queen's College. An outstanding student, he won the Jessie Leggatt Scholarship in 1927 and, in 1928, the EJB Nunn Scholarship and the Supreme Court Prize for the candidate placed first in the final honours examinations in law. He graduated LLB in 1928 and LLM in 1929.

Admitted to practice in May 1930, he signed the Roll of Counsel of the Victorian Bar in February 1932, reading in the Chambers of EH Hudson, later a judge of the Supreme Court of Victoria. It was an unwelcoming decade in which to start a career at the Bar, but a little over five years after he had signed the roll, Menzies first appeared in a constitutional matter in the High Court as junior **counsel** in *Hartley v Walsh* (1937). There then followed appearances in *Matthews v Chicory Marketing Board* (1938) and in *Hopper v Egg and Egg Pulp Marketing Board* (1939). In all three cases, Menzies appeared for the party seeking to defend a compulsory marketing scheme for agricultural products against attacks based on sections 90 and 92 of the Constitution (see **Excise duties; Interstate trade and commerce**). In the *Chicory* case, **Dixon's** contrary view prevailed; in the other two cases, Menzies' client succeeded.

In 1939, Bernard O'Dowd and Menzies wrote *Victorian Company Law and Practice*. It took the form of annotations to the provisions of the *Companies Act* 1938 (Vic) but soon became a standard work on company law and practice.

During **World War II**, Menzies acted from 1941 to 1945 as Secretary to the Australian Defence Committee and the Chiefs of Staff Committee.

On his return to practice, Menzies was soon very busy, practising principally in **commercial law** and **constitutional law**.

Douglas Menzies, Justice 1958–74

Volumes 70 to 76 of the *Commonwealth Law Reports* record several matters in which he appeared as junior counsel, most notably the *Melbourne Corporation Case* (1947) and the *Bank Nationalisation Case* (1948). In *Parton v Milk Board* (1949), where Dixon expanded the broad view of duties of excise which he had taken in *Matthews v Chicory Marketing Board*, Menzies again appeared as junior counsel for the unsuccessful defendants, as he had done in the *Chicory* case.

In 1949, he took silk, and thereafter appeared in many important commercial and constitutional cases in the High Court and in the **Privy Council**, including the *Boilermakers Case* (1956), where he appeared for the Commonwealth. He, **Barwick**, and a few others, dominated the Australian work done in the Privy Council.

He did not confine his energies to the Bar. From 1948, he was a director of the Australasian Temperance and General Mutual Life Assurance Society, and between 1954 and 1957, he was an honorary area commissioner of Toc H Victoria. In his last years at the Bar, he held office in key professional associations: President of the Law Council of Australia from 1956 to 1958; Chairman of the Victorian Bar Council in 1958; and President of the Medico-Legal Society of Victoria from 1957 to 1958.

By 1958, he was an acknowledged leader of the Bar. So eminently qualified was he to fill the vacancy on the Court caused by the resignation of **Webb** that his relationship as first cousin to the **Prime Minister** of the day, Robert **Menzies**, though noted at the time of his **appointment** in June 1958, caused no controversy whatever. Ironically, it was only because of apprehension that the relationship might cause

controversy that he had not been appointed six years earlier, after Dixon became **Chief Justice** (see **Appointments that might have been**).

The Court Menzies joined was dominated by Dixon, but its members also included **Fullagar** and **Kitto**, men of powerful intellect and great scholarship. It is therefore not surprising that in the six remaining years of Dixon's Chief Justiceship, Menzies' work on the Court was less prominent than that of some other members of the Court. Perhaps this was aggravated by his suffering a severe cardiac illness within one year of his appointment. One case from this period with which Menzies is often associated is *Dennis Hotels v Victoria* (1960). He alone held in that case that a distinction could be drawn between the licence fees imposed by a Victorian statute for two different forms of liquor retailing licence, and decided that the statute contravened section 90 of the Constitution (which gives the Commonwealth exclusive power to impose duties of excise) in the case of one form of licence but not the other. The distinction that Menzies drew was less arbitrary than is sometimes supposed. Unhappy with the approach adopted by Dixon in *Parton v Milk Board*, he felt bound to follow it in the case of the so-called 'temporary licence fee', but seized on the opportunity to distinguish it in the case of the 'victualler's licence fee'.

Menzies was later to say that he differed from Dixon only with hesitation and foreboding. It was, nevertheless, a period that Menzies found 'stimulating and enlarging in his understanding of the work of the court'.

It was inevitable that the **personal relations** within the Court would change when Dixon retired and **Barwick** was appointed Chief Justice. Barwick and Menzies had often been opposed in the High Court and the Privy Council. Over the years, they had formed a close friendship. Menzies brought features of collegiate life to the Court which had not previously obtained. No longer was the work of the Court the only thing that brought its members together. Menzies organised dinners and other social events at which members of the Court and their wives met and exchanged views on more than the cases of the time.

Frequent reference is to be found to Menzies' good **humour** and gaiety relieving the otherwise austere life of the Court. Expressions such as 'clubbable', 'witty', 'raconteur', and the 'laughing cavalier' of the Court, were used about him, just as often as expressions applauding his diligence and determination.

The judgments he wrote between the time of Barwick's appointment and his own death in 1974 reflect the issues of the day. Some, notably those in *Spratt v Hermes* (1965) and (to a lesser extent) *Anderson v Eric Anderson Radio & TV* (1965), have been influential in the development of constitutional law about federal jurisdiction and the **territories**. In *Strickland v Rocla Concrete Pipes* (1971), the Court held that the **corporations power** enabled the Commonwealth to enact a **trade practices law**, but nevertheless that the *Trade Practices Act* 1965 (Cth) was invalid. It was Menzies who explained most incisively why the complex legislative drafting had been unacceptable: 'Parliament cannot direct courts to reconstruct out of the ruins of one invalid law of general application a number of valid laws of particular application.' His other work of that time is referred to less often, but that is largely because the issues the Court must now resolve are different from those that were agitated in the 1970s.

In cases where taxes imposed by the states were challenged as duties of excise, the surgical precision of Menzies' approach continued to be distinctive, as it had been in *Dennis Hotels*. In *WA v Hamersley Iron* (1969) and *WA v Chamberlain Industries* (1970), he drew a distinction between a tax imposed upon the issuing of a document called a receipt and a tax imposed upon the actual receipt of money, in relation to which the issuing of a receipt was but the machinery for collecting the tax. In *Dickenson's Arcade v Tasmania* (1974), though four other Justices reluctantly joined him in following *Dennis Hotels*, only Menzies did so on the ground that he thought that the decision was right. And yet, in a vivid example of the complexity of the excise cases, on the same day he joined **Mason** and **McTiernan** in *Kailis v WA* (1974) in declining to apply *Dennis Hotels*, evidently because of the particular form in which the statute in question had been drafted.

An *obiter dictum* by Menzies in *Fairfax v FCT* (1965)—a landmark decision on the **characterisation** of Commonwealth laws—attracted some attention over the years, especially from law students endeavouring to understand the true limits of the Commonwealth's **taxation** power. The Court held that a Commonwealth law which, through tax incentives, encouraged (but did not compel) certain kinds of investment, was, because the only obligations it imposed were to pay tax, truly a law with respect to taxation. Menzies suggested that, by contrast, a tax upon income 'derived from the sale of heroin or from the growing or treatment of poppies for the production of heroin' might not be 'a law with respect to taxation', but rather 'a law made for the suppression of the trade in that drug … It would simply be that its true character is not a law with respect to taxation'. The suggestion was difficult to reconcile with the actual decision in the case and the reasoning given for that decision, and in the *Second Fringe Benefits Tax Case* (1987) Menzies' dictum was disapproved by a majority of the Court.

Menzies was sworn as a Privy Counsellor in 1964, and in that year sat as a member of the body before whom he had so often appeared as counsel.

In 1969, he became Chancellor of Monash University. These were times of student unrest and rebellion against authority, but Menzies was later to be described as 'an ideal Chancellor—wise, urbane, dignified, and influential; detached from day-to-day affairs but deeply concerned with the long-term development of the university'.

Menzies died in November 1974, shortly after collapsing as he was about to go in to the annual dinner of the NSW Bar Association. His wife, Helen Borland, whom he had married in 1936, had died in 1966. They had four children.

Kenneth Hayne

Menzies, Robert Gordon (*b* 20 December 1894; *d* 15 May 1978). In its breadth and duration, Menzies' individual influence on the High Court—as **counsel**, state and Commonwealth **Attorney-General**, and **Prime Minister**—is unrivalled. It extended from his first appearances as counsel aged 24, in *Troy v Wrigglesworth* (1919) (without a leader) and *Moors v Burke* (1919), to the **retirement** in 1981 of Chief Justice **Barwick**, whom he had appointed in 1964.

Robert Menzies as a young barrister, in chambers

The son of a rural shopkeeper turned state parliamentarian, Menzies graduated from the University of Melbourne (LLB and Supreme Court Prize in 1916; LLM in 1918). Commencing practice in 1918 at the Victorian Bar as **Dixon's** pupil, Menzies swiftly demonstrated his intellectual calibre and forensic talents. He rose to immediate national professional prominence when, again without a leader, he successfully pressed the applicant's case for full interpretation of **Commonwealth legislative powers** in the *Engineers Case* (1920), in which **Evatt**, soon to be a regular opponent as counsel and later an implacable political adversary, also appeared. Menzies' advocacy in that case alone assures him of an enduring place in the annals of Australian **federalism**.

Appearing frequently in the Court over three decades, Menzies was, by all accounts, an outstanding advocate; he was, in every sense, an all-rounder, equally as effective when appearing before juries as he was in complex appeals. Apart from his decisive role as a constitutional lawyer, his clients had him plead their causes in the Court in appeals about local government, **employment**, **commercial law**, insurance, shipping, intellectual property, wills, **taxation**, bankruptcy, **defamation**, and **contempt** of court.

In the evolving and turbulent area of industrial **conciliation and arbitration**, he frequently appeared for employers, but, as in the *Engineers Case*, solicitors were quick to recognise and employ his talents on behalf of their union clients as well (*Insurance Staffs Case* (1923); *Federated Engine-Drivers and Firemen's Association v A1 Amalgamated* (1924)). Menzies was a favourite with state and Commonwealth Crown Solicitors (his brother FG Menzies was Victorian Crown Solicitor from 1926) (see, for example, *John Fairfax & Sons v NSW* (1927)), and with larger capital city law firms outside Melbourne (*Cuthbertson v Hobart Corporation* (1921); *Adelaide Corporation v Australasian Performing Right Association* (1928)). As a junior, he was as often led by Dixon (who took silk in 1922) as he was opposed to him without a leader. He was also a close professional (and later political) colleague of **Latham**, and they frequently appeared together or opposed to each other in the Court.

When appointed a KC in 1929, Menzies had long been a leader of the High Court Bar and had recently embarked on his remarkable career as a conservative politician. His forensic career continued along its stellar path (*School Teachers Case* (1929); *Huddart Parker v Commonwealth* (1931); *Victorian Stevedoring & General Contracting Co v Meakes and Dignan* (1931)).

Elected as a Nationalist candidate to the Victorian Legislative Council in 1928 and the Legislative Assembly in 1929, Menzies became state Attorney-General in 1932. Interestingly, amid political controversy, he retained a right of private practice, which he freely exercised, appearing in the Court for various clients including the Federal Commissioner of Taxation (*Metropolitan Gas Co v FCT* (1932); *Blyth Chemicals v Bushnell* (1933); *Williams v Melbourne Corporation* (1933); *Roman Catholic Archbishop of Melbourne v Lawlor* (1934)).

Elected in 1934 to the House of Representatives seat which Latham had vacated to resume practice at the Victorian Bar, Menzies also immediately succeeded Latham as **Attorney-General** in the new United Australia Party government and was thus instrumental in Latham's **appointment** as **Chief Justice** in 1935 (see also **Gavan Duffy**). As Commonwealth Attorney-General, he went to London to plead the Commonwealth's cause in the **Privy Council** in *James v Commonwealth* (1936) and *Payne v FCT* (1936). Again, as Commonwealth Attorney-General, he retained and exercised a right of private practice (*Palmer v Dunlop Perriau Rubber Co* (1937)).

Menzies' political accomplishments, fuelled by ambition, outstanding oratory, and mastery of detail, led to his becoming Prime Minister in succession to Earle Page who served in the interim following the death of Joseph Lyons in 1939. However, amid gruelling wartime pressures and party in-fighting, Menzies was forced to resign in 1941 and went into Opposition. He resumed appearing regularly in the Court (*Carter v Egg and Egg Pulp Marketing Board* (1942); *Footscray Corporation v Maize Products* (1943); *Rola Co v Commonwealth* (1944)), but his political aspirations regained dominance with the United Australia Party's rebirth as the Liberal Party in 1944. His last appearance as counsel was in *Essendon Corporation v Criterion Theatres* (1947), by which time he had appeared before all the Justices except **Griffith** and **O'Connor**.

By 1948, as the **Cold War** worsened, Menzies was devoting himself fully to rallying conservatives in the mounting struggles for free enterprise and against the democratic **socialism** espoused by the Australian Labor Party—which had provoked the *Bank Nationalisation Case* (1948)—and the interrelated threats of domestic and international communism. Menzies led the Liberal–Country Party coalition to a resounding electoral victory in 1949. The Court's decision in the *Communist Party Case* (1951) was a rebuff to Menzies; ultimately, however, it was his masterly political exploitation of anti-communism that contributed so much to his record term of office.

As Prime Minister (1939–41; 1949–66), Menzies was responsible for the appointment of Chief Justices **Dixon** (1952) and **Barwick** (1964), and Justices **Williams** (1940), **Fullagar** (1950), **Kitto** (1950), **Taylor** (1952), his cousin Douglas **Menzies** (1958), **Windeyer** (1958), and **Owen** (1961). He was also instrumental in the appointment of six Commonwealth Attorneys-General, including Barwick (1958).

Through the combined effect of his vigorous commitment to the full development of the national capital and the appointment of Barwick as Chief Justice, Menzies deserves more credit than is customarily given to him for the Court's move to a permanent location in **Canberra** in 1980.

Menzies was always particularly close to Latham and Dixon. He had Latham take leave to serve as Australian Minister in Tokyo (1940–41) and persuaded Dixon to act as the UN mediator in the Kashmir dispute (1950); he failed, however, to convince Dixon to chair the fateful Royal Commission into Espionage (1954–55) which precipitated Evatt's tragic decline.

It was Menzies' remorseless determination to have the House of Representatives imprison a journalist and newspaper proprietor for breach of parliamentary privilege—unmoved by Evatt's plea that the imposition of a fine would suffice—that prompted the historic case of *R v Richards; Ex parte Fitzpatrick and Browne* (1955).

In the *Federal Roads Case* (1926), in a failed attempt on behalf of Victoria to restrict the grants power in section 96 of the Constitution, Menzies unsuccessfully relied on a **characterisation** of Commonwealth legislation authorising the execution of agreements granting financial assistance to the states for road construction as 'a law relating to road-making' and therefore 'not a law for granting financial aid to the states'.

Rejection of the fallacy of state **sovereignty** and a pragmatic commitment to the establishment of what he called 'a priority for national consciousness' were the hallmarks of Menzies' treatment of the federal compact as an organic political instrument. It necessarily followed, in his view, that the centralising impact of section 96 grants and the *Uniform Tax Cases* (1942 and 1957) had helped and not hindered the states. This also reflected his realistic appreciation of the formidable obstacles to formal constitutional **amendment**, stretching from the 1926 referendum and the stormy Evatt-led opposition to the referendum on communism (1951) to his creation of the parliamentary Joint Committee on Constitutional Review (1956–59), and beyond.

Menzies' attitude to Australian federalism as *realpolitik* probably accounts for his determined preference for reserving seats on the Court exclusively for members of the NSW and Victorian Bars; it was scarcely calculated to inspire confidence in the four less-populous states. Menzies was no stranger to the talent displayed by the conservative leaders of the Bar in those other states, but with a few exceptions, he generally preferred to entrust important public offices to those from the two most populous states whom he knew well, and to trusted confidants—especially those from his Young Nationalists days such as **Solicitor-General** Kenneth Bailey, Attorney-General John Spicer, and PD Phillips of the Victorian Bar, who served as Chairman of the Commonwealth Grants Commission (1960–66). Bailey and Phillips had appeared for the Commonwealth in the *Second Uniform Tax Case*.

The pro-Commonwealth dimension of Menzies' attitude to federalism was best exemplified, first, in the creation of the Australian Universities Commission (1959) and the use of section 96 grants to give the Commonwealth the leading role in tertiary education, and, secondly, in the passage of the *Matrimonial Causes Act* 1959 (Cth) and the *Marriage Act* 1961 (Cth) (*Marriage Act Case* (1962)). His most politically opportunistic use of section 96 was the implementation of his astute electoral promise of government aid to private religious schools (1963), which eventually survived a challenge under section 116 of the Constitution (see *DOGS Case* (1981)).

Renowned as a proud 'Britisher' and passionate supporter of the British Empire (and Commonwealth), he was a strong supporter of retention of Privy Council appeals in non-constitutional cases.

His last appearance before the Court—unrobed ('locusts or something have dealt with my robe')—was when he delivered an encomium to Dixon on his retirement in 1964.

LAURENCE W MAHER

Further Reading

Arthur Dean, *A Multitude of Counsellors: A History of the Bar of Victoria* (1968)

Allan Martin, *Robert Menzies: A Life*, vol 1 1894–1943 (1993), vol 2 1944–1978 (1999)

Robert Menzies, 'The Challenge to Federalism' (1961) 3 *MULR* 1

Robert Menzies, *Central Power in the Australian Commonwealth* (1967)

Robert Menzies, *Measure of the Years* (1970)

Metaphor. Many years ago, the High Court nailed its colours to the mast, instituting, through the *Engineers Case* (1920), an emphasis on the language of the Constitution itself that would determine the course of adjudication for generations to follow. The 'language itself', however, has proved to offer either an oversupply of meanings—in the ambiguities that have emerged even from the spare provisions of the Constitution—or an undersupply—in areas of legal conflict unforeseen by the **framers** in their 'gaslight era' and their 'horse and buggy' document. In this context, the 'strict', 'legal', and 'literal' approach—appealing to the 'ordinary meaning of the words'—has not always provided the materials necessary for interpretation and adjudication, and the Court has been richly inventive in providing a supplement, in metaphor, which has effectively extended the meanings of the original document; made its 'silences' speak (**Isaacs** in the *Skin Wool Case* (1926), evoking Lord Watson's 'silent operation of constitutional principles' in *Cooper v Stuart* (1889)); brought up 'dormant' and 'buried' meanings from the 'recesses' of the text (**Rich** in *James v Cowan* (1930)); and facilitated access to richer and more durable constitutional 'fabrics' below the flawed and ephemeral writing that makes up the existing document (Isaacs in *Pirrie v McFarlane* (1925); see also **Murphy** in *Sillery v The Queen* (1981)).

Almost every area of human learning is, in the ancient **common law** phrase, 'raked up in the ashes of the law', and a vast range of human activity is incorporated, perhaps colonised, through the metaphorical reaches of Australian legal writing. Despite all High Court appeals to **legalism** and **literalism**, its rhetoric in all areas of the law has always been richly enhanced by metaphors, with many of these—and perhaps the most subliminally potent—so entrenched as to be invisible, even to the 'eye of the Law' itself.

The language inherited by the Court was already deeply metaphorical—a rich domain of 'fields of operation' watered by pure and 'unpoisoned' streams of power, justice, and authority; flowing from a higher imperial source (**Brennan** in *Kirmani v Captain Cook Cruises (No 1)* (1985)); haunted

by a ghostly clutch of 'spirits', 'spectres', and 'silences'; and presided over by the ruling personification, the Law itself, richly personified in countless judicial allusions, the Law invested with 'skeleton', 'hand', 'arm', 'limbs', 'organs', 'face', 'heart', 'soul', 'spirit', and, most evocatively, most authoritatively, with an 'eye', and with a 'voice'. Much of this may be mere garniture, mere incantatory repetition of phrases and tropes long hallowed in the common law. Some of it acts as strong rhetorical emphasis; a 'spirit' is more elusive, less assailable than a black-letter provision, and a 'stream of authority' less resistible than a mere set of legal cases.

Many areas of the common law, and indeed the idea of the common law itself, have been illuminated and even developed by the richness of metaphor. **Windeyer**, perhaps the Court's leading exponent of metaphor, drew on his military background in *Benning v Wong* (1969) to articulate his conception of the common law's reconciliation of constancy and change:

> Those who insist that the common law is still on the move should remember that it must always march in step. Decisions in cases passing at the moment must be in step with those which have just gone past, although not necessarily with those at the head of the column. Moving the metaphor from the parade ground to the field, it is as sound a maxim for law as for war that operations should be from a firm base, that an advance must be from a position which has been securely established.

In *Rootes v Shelton* (1967), **Kitto** used metaphor to convey his view of the role of **policy considerations** in developing the common law: 'If I may be pardoned for saying so, to discuss [a] case in terms of "judicial policy" and "social expediency" is to introduce deleterious foreign matter into the waters of the common law—in which, after all, we have no more than riparian rights.'

Brennan in *Mabo* (1992) resorted to the idea of the common law's 'skeletal principle', which should not be 'fractured'. **Kirby**, however, has favoured a more robust view, preferring to 'avoid that metaphor, which suggests both a morbidity and fragility in the foundational principles of the Australian legal system which I do not detect' (*Fejo v Northern Territory* (1998); see also **Activism**).

In *Uther's Case* (1947), **Latham** and **Dixon** used metaphor to convey their opposing conceptions of **intergovernmental immunities**. For Latham, the Commonwealth was subject to the *Companies Act* 1936 (NSW) because 'Australia was not born into a vacuum. It came into existence within a system of law already established', to much of which the Commonwealth became subject like any other newborn legal person. Dixon, on the other hand, argued that the Commonwealth was immune from the NSW law: 'Like the goddess of wisdom the Commonwealth *uno ictu* sprang from the brain of its begetters armed and of full stature.' NSW, as a colony, had no power over this new polity once the Commonwealth was established; nor did NSW, when it became a state, ever acquire such power.

Higgins frequently resorted to metaphor, often of the utmost obscurity. Not content with Isaacs' elaboration of **inconsistency** under section 109 of the Constitution with the metaphor that Commonwealth law would prevail over state law if it 'covered the field' (*Clyde Engineering v Cowburn*

(1926)), Higgins opined that 'The State law is like the Nile River, which covers the whole area with its flood, except that part of the area which is appropriated to the villages. The State law fills, as it were, all the sponge except the fibre.'

Six years earlier, in *Federated Engine-Drivers and Firemen's Association v Adelaide Chemical & Fertilizer Co* (1920), he had likened an industrial dispute to a 'cheese which has to be disposed of ... by the silver knife of conciliation and ... the steel knife of arbitration; by cutting vertically as between respondents, or horizontally as between subjects.'

Moreover, action by the Court did not change the character of the dispute: 'As well might it be contended that if a domestic be authorised to cut up any cheese with a red rind round it, the cutting authority ceases as soon as the first cut has been made, and the red rind has been broken.'

While much of this may be mere garniture and rhetorical emphasis, the Court has often taken the process of metaphoric elaboration a stage further. Its richest metaphoric inventiveness has been more integral to the process of interpretation and adjudication, and the century since the Court was established has seen the evolution of an ingenious interpretive language, which has populated the 'bleak and barren prosescape' of the Constitution with supporting, enlivening metaphors that have played a central role in extending the life of the Constitution.

Commentators, academic and judicial, have long recognised the important role of metaphor in legal argument, and warnings have been sounded—most authoritatively by Benjamin Cardozo, in his comment, sometimes cited in the High Court, that 'Metaphors in law are to be narrowly watched, for starting as devices to liberate thought, they end often by enslaving it' (*Berkey v Third Avenue Railway Co* (1926)).

In the Australian context, the drama of liberation and enslavement has been extensively rehearsed within the realm of metaphor. The inherited language of the law was rich in reference to 'bonds', 'fetters', and 'shackles', inevitable products of a legal culture eager to set the 'living body of the law' in motion, and yet to direct it to the interests of restriction, order, and control. Our judicial literature is so dense in reference to statutory 'limbs' that have been 'fettered', to 'bonds' and to 'shackles', that the metaphoric foundation of such terms has largely been lost. Where this train of 'dead metaphor' has taken on a more striking and more indigenously Australian hue is where the imperial legacy has been addressed, and the references to fettering, bonding, and shackling become comments upon the powers of the High Court and the legislature itself.

In the writings of Murphy, who always used his metaphors for more than their legal content, the metaphor of the 'straitjacket' informed this wider saga of legal liberation. In *China Ocean Shipping v SA* (1979), as in *State Government Insurance Commission v Trigwell* (1979) and *Dugan v Mirror Newspapers* (1978), it seemed that the living body of Australian law was shackled to a legal corpse, in this instance, to nineteenth-century English laws for the regulation of colonies. To affirm the validity of such laws, Murphy suggested, was to bring down the threat of an Australia 'doomed indefinitely to live in a constitutional straitjacket'. Such 'liberationist' inventiveness in High Court metaphor, sifting through the complex strands of residual imperial authority, has achieved a cultural currency beyond the usual readership

for legal professional literature, and this movement of High Court metaphor out into the general culture was enhanced in *Mabo*. Brennan's description in *Mabo* of Australia as a 'prisoner of its **history**', and his reduction of the imperial legal tradition to a 'skeleton of principle' was a neat way, in effect, of maintaining a tradition, an authority, while consigning it to the legal knacker's yard.

Throughout the history of the Court, there have also been many metaphors which have been more dynamic and more essentially legal in their function, providing interpretive tools and intellectual perspectives that have facilitated analysis and judgment. How can so spare a text as the Constitution, cobbled together so long ago, contain within itself all meanings necessary to regulate a society, a century later? 'Metaphor and analogy', Jeremy Webber wrote in 1999, 'are basic building blocks of our political or legal arguments. When we define our concepts, we often do so by refining our metaphorical arsenal'.

One such refinement in the Court has been in this domain of 'containment'. One of the devices used to extend the meanings of the original document, while paying due respect to the perimeters established by the original text, has been to explore the secret and hidden spaces of the Constitution, and through a considerable metaphorical ingenuity, to capture those meanings that exist within, above, below, and between the Constitution's provisions. The language of the Court has thus been rich in 'probings' and 'soundings' and ingenious exhumations, resuscitating the legal wisdom that lies 'beneath' the text (**Deane** in *Thompson v The Queen* (1989)), or 'buried' within the text, or sleeping 'behind' the text (Windeyer in the *Payroll Tax Case* (1971)), or hiding within the 'interstices' of the text (Murphy in *Groves v Commonwealth* (1982)), with the richest excursions of all being those that burrow 'below' the text, to explore the various 'fabrics' on which the constitutional text is written (Isaacs in *Pirrie v Macfarlane*), or to commune, in this legally enriched subterranean territory, with the spirits and indeed, the 'silences' of the Constitution (Isaacs in the *Skin Wool Case*).

Legal metaphor in its more conventional and incantatory forms can indeed reinforce postures of submission and obedience. Into this category fits the whole tradition of legal personification: a branch of metaphor and an ancient trope in legal writing that has been passed on in an undistilled form to the Court, so common still in its invocation as to be largely invisible even to those who employ it, but potent still in its quasi-religious implications, implying wisdom, omniscience, a clear and unified 'voice', and a patriarchal authority.

Legal metaphors used in this way may be incarcerative in ways that Justice Cardozo scarcely thought of. But in the history of the High Court, it has more often been against various forms of 'enslavement'—the 'skeletons' of the legal past, the 'shackles' and 'straitjackets' of the legal tradition, and the confines and limitations of the constitutional text itself—that its 'metaphorical arsenal' has been most inventive, and most strongly 'refined', as a liberating device working towards transition in thinking, creating, in a visually enriched and rhetorically persuasive fashion, the 'spaces' necessary, 'above', 'within', 'between', 'below', for adaptive legal thinking.

Metaphor is, finally, inescapable. The *Engineers Case*, to do with the power of the Commonwealth to make laws binding on the states with respect to **conciliation and arbitration**, has been described by Leslie Zines as the 'keystone of the arch of Australian **constitutional interpretation**' and as our principal defence of the constitutional text against the assaults of a whole panoply of spirits, principles, implications, interpolations, and 'exotic' and alien doctrines from without. And against, one might think, the vagaries and distracting flights of legal metaphor.

The *Engineers Case*, however, is actually one of the most richly articulated and most deeply figurative in our judicial history, with its 'spirits' and 'fabrics', its 'bindings' and its 'fetterings', its 'lights' and its 'labyrinths'. It indicates, perhaps more clearly than any other case, and with all the emphasis that paradox imports, the potency of metaphoric elaboration. 'We have endeavoured' wrote **Knox, Isaacs**, Rich, and **Starke**, 'to remove the inconsistencies fast accumulating and obscuring the comparatively clear terms of the national compact of the Australian people; we have striven to fulfil the duty the Constitution places upon this court *of loyally permitting that great instrument of government to speak with its own voice*'.

The whole tradition of Australian High Court literalism thus has its roots in an inventive, and almost ecstatic, metaphor. The central case for a literal and 'legal' approach—for an abandonment of exotic legal fantasy and for a return to the 'language of the Constitution'—is founded squarely on one of the richest and most evocative personifications in our legal culture. A critical history of the High Court must also be, and centrally, a history of its metaphors.

MICHAEL MEEHAN

Further Reading
Milner Ball, *Lying Down Together: Law, Metaphor, and Theology* (1985)
Michael Meehan, 'The Poetics of Literalism: Mythology, Metaphor and Australian Constitutional Interpretation' in John Barnes (ed), *Border Crossing: Studies in English and Other Disciplines* (1991) (special issue of *Meridian*, vol 10(2))
Jeremy Webber, 'Constitutional Poetry: The Tension between Symbolic and Functional Aims in Constitutional Reform' (1999) 21 *Syd LR* 260

Military justice refers chiefly to the trial and punishment of members of the defence forces for disciplinary offences. The Commonwealth Parliament's power to legislate in respect of military justice derives from section 51(vi) of the Constitution: the **defence power**. Despite the difficulties involved in determining the scope of this head of power in the abstract, it seems clear that the establishment of military service tribunals to maintain discipline in the defence forces falls within it, in both peace and war. So much is generally accepted by the High Court. The greater difficulty lies in determining the powers that such tribunals may exercise. The main source of contention, and the primary basis for the High Court's **role**, has been in defining the boundaries of the jurisdiction of service tribunals where conduct of a defence force member constitutes both a disciplinary offence and an offence against ordinary civilian laws.

The Australian system of military justice is drawn from the *Defence Force Discipline Act* 1982 (Cth), which creates service offences and service tribunals to hear and punish Australian Defence Force personnel who commit service offences. The Act creates three kinds of offences: offences peculiar to the defence forces (for example, endangering morale, absence without leave, and disobedience of command); offences that are analogous to ordinary civil offences (for example, destruction, damage to or unlawful possession of service property, and dealing in narcotic goods); and offences imported directly from the general law. Punishments under the Act extend, at the extreme, to life imprisonment. There is no provision for review of service tribunal decisions by the Commonwealth Administrative Appeals Tribunal or under the *Administrative Decisions (Judicial Review) Act* 1977 (Cth), although appeals to the Defence Force Discipline Appeals Tribunal and the **Federal Court** are available in some circumstances.

One difficulty with these service tribunals is that, on their face, they appear to be exercising **judicial power** in breach of the constitutional doctrine of the **separation of powers**. No matter how fair they are in practice, they have not been created in accordance with Chapter III of the Constitution and therefore lack the constitutional protections imposed on federal Chapter III courts.

The overlap between offences under the Defence Force Discipline Act and those under the general law also creates some difficulty. The Act initially included provisions intended to avoid double jeopardy, by prohibiting a civil court from trying an offence that a service tribunal had already tried. However, in *Re Tracey; Ex parte Ryan* (1989), the High Court held these provisions invalid as falling outside the defence power, and severed them from the rest of the Act. Section 109 of the Constitution could potentially be used to allow service tribunals to prevail over civil courts, but the High Court has held that there is no **inconsistency** between the Defence Force Discipline Act and a state law that purports to govern conduct of a defence member that also amounts to an offence under the Act, even if the penalties applicable under the two laws are different (*McWaters v Day* (1989)).

These decisions of the High Court have profound implications for defence force members alleged to have engaged in conduct that constitutes both a civil and a disciplinary offence. Australian Defence Force policy aims to resolve jurisdictional issues in a practical manner and requires consultation with civilian prosecution authorities in cases of doubt. However, except in cases of serious offences such as murder and manslaughter (in relation to which section 63 of the Act precludes service tribunal jurisdiction except with the consent of the Commonwealth Director of Public Prosecutions), a defence member could conceivably be tried twice for the same offence—once by a service tribunal and once by a civil court. This fact underscores the importance of ensuring that the jurisdiction of service tribunals is properly defined in accordance with the Constitution.

In the past 50 years, the High Court has scrutinised the constitutional validity of military service tribunals on several occasions. The issue arose in *R v Bevan; Ex parte Elias and Gordon* (1942) and *R v Cox; Ex parte Smith* (1945) (in relation to courts martial established under previous defence legislation), and more recently in *Ex parte Ryan; Re Nolan; Ex parte Young* (1991); and *Re Tyler; Ex parte Foley* (1994). On each occasion, the authority of service tribunals to conduct trials and impose punishment in relation to the particular offence has been upheld on the basis that it derives from a proper exercise by the legislature of its defence power. On no occasion has this been considered by the Court as a whole to involve a breach of the separation of powers doctrine.

Yet most Justices have agreed that service tribunals exercise what would ordinarily be seen as falling within the definition of 'judicial power', and there has been no unifying and satisfactory explanation of why this does not breach the separation of powers doctrine. In addition, no clear majority position has emerged regarding the limits of the functions of service tribunals or the criteria for determining which offences can be properly dealt with by service tribunals without usurping the role of the courts. In particular, there is no consensus on whether it is acceptable for defence legislation to provide simply (as in section 61 of the Act) that all civil offences in a particular jurisdiction automatically constitute disciplinary offences for defence purposes and therefore fall within the jurisdiction of service tribunals.

Many nations have grappled with the conflict between notions of separation of powers and individual rights, and the practical need for a flexible and effective defence force. Several European countries have abolished their separate military justice systems, typically as a result of criticism of their operation during **World War II**. For two decades, the USA restricted military jurisdiction to 'service-connected' crimes. However, the doctrine of service connection was overruled in *Solorio v USA* (1987) when the **United States Supreme Court** upheld the legislative expansion of the jurisdiction of military service tribunals to virtually all crimes, based solely on the military status of the accused.

The US system of military justice derives from Article I, Section 8 of the US Constitution, which specifically grants Congress power to make rules and regulations for the governance of the armed forces. This power has long been regarded as extending to provision for trial and punishment of defence force members, independently of the judicial power conferred by Article III (*Dynes v Hoover* (1858)). Most Justices of the High Court have drawn a similar distinction between judicial power *per se* (which is exercised by service tribunals) and 'the judicial power of the Commonwealth' under Chapter III of the Constitution (which is not). However, this is a difficult distinction to draw, and the High Court has not yet agreed on an appropriate rationale for drawing it.

The US doctrine of service connection can also be compared to various tests used in the High Court cases to determine the scope of a service tribunal's powers: whether there is a 'sufficient connection' between the exercise of the power and the good order and discipline of defence members (**Mason**, **Wilson**, and **Dawson**); whether particular service tribunal proceedings 'substantially serve the purpose' of maintaining or enforcing service discipline (**Brennan** and **Toohey**); whether the exercise of the power is 'appropriate and adapted' to the object of controlling the defence forces (**Gaudron**); and whether persons subject to military law are deprived of the benefits and safeguards of administration of justice by independent courts only 'to the extent necessary' to enforce military discipline (**Deane**).

Since the latest relevant High Court case in 1994, the composition of the High Court has changed dramatically. Only two of the present Justices, Gaudron and **McHugh**, have delivered judgments on this issue in that Court, and on those occasions both Justices indicated that they disagreed with the reasoning of the majority in the prevailing authorities. In addition, the separation of powers doctrine has acquired a sharper bite in recent years, exemplified by cases such as *Brandy v Human Rights and Equal Opportunity Commission* (1995). Finally, the Commonwealth Parliament Joint Standing Committee on Foreign Affairs, Defence, and Trade recently completed its inquiry into military justice in Australia. These factors present an appropriate opportunity for the High Court to reassess its position on military justice and provide a clear framework for the operations of service tribunals in the near future.

ANDREW D MITCHELL
TANIA VOON

Further Reading

RA Brown, 'The Constitutionality of Service Tribunals under the *Defence Force Discipline Act* 1982' (1985) 59 *ALJ* 319

Commonwealth Parliament Joint Standing Committee on Foreign Affairs, Defence, and Trade, *Military Justice Procedures in the Australian Defence Force* (1999)

Andrew Mitchell and Tania Voon, 'Defence of the Indefensible? Reassessing the Constitutional Validity of Military Service Tribunals in Australia' (1999) 27 *FL Rev* 499

D Schlueter, 'The Court-Martial: An Historical Survey' (1980) 87 *Military Law Review* 129

Edward Sherman, 'Military Justice Without Military Control' (1973) 82 *Yale LJ* 1398

Movement, freedom of. Freedom of movement within Australia—at least freedom of movement interstate—is to some extent an integral aspect of the freedom of **interstate trade**, commerce, and intercourse guaranteed by section 92 of the Constitution. In *R v Vizzard; Ex parte Hill* (1933), the High Court held that 'movement of persons and things is the very thing to which absolute freedom is given'. That principle was applied in *Gratwick v Johnson* (1945), where the Court held that a young woman who had travelled by train across the Nullarbor Plain, to visit her sailor boyfriend who was on shore leave in Perth, was protected by section 92. National security regulations during **World War II** had required a permit for such a journey; but the Court held that requirement invalid. As the *Sydney Morning Herald* summed up in a headline: 'Love Triumphs over National Security Regulations.'

In *Cole v Whitfield* (1988), the Court developed a more stringent conception of the freedom of interstate 'trade' and 'commerce', but recognised (citing *Gratwick v Johnson*) that the freedom of interstate 'intercourse' might be more nearly absolute, extending to a personal freedom 'so immune from legislative and executive interference' that a similar immunity for commercial freedom would result in 'anarchy'. That suggestion has not yet been taken up. Indeed, individual Justices have tended to limit this conception of personal freedom precisely by insisting that it must involve 'movement' (see **Brennan** in *Nationwide News v Wills* (1992) and **Dawson** in *Australian Capital Television v Commonwealth* (1992); see *Free Speech Cases*).

In a series of cases from 1976 onwards, **Murphy** had taken a limited view of the freedom of trade and commerce, but had sought to balance this by asserting a broad implied right of personal freedom of movement and communication. In *Buck v Bavone* (1976), he argued that this was 'a fundamental right arising from the union of the people in an indissoluble Commonwealth'—'so fundamental that it is not likely it would be hidden away in section 92'. In *Ansett Transport Industries v Commonwealth* (1977), he argued that the electoral provisions in the Constitution 'require freedom of movement, speech and other communication, not only between the States, but in and between every part of the Commonwealth'. Moreover, these requirements did not operate only at election times: 'The proper operation of the system of **representative government** requires the same freedoms between elections.' He added that the same freedoms were 'also necessary for the proper operation of the Constitutions of the States', and argued once again that these freedoms are 'so elementary that it was not necessary to mention them in the Constitution'.

In *McGraw-Hinds v Smith* (1979), Murphy bolstered his argument by an extensive review of the willingness of past Justices to find constitutional 'implications'. Although the past emphasis had been particularly on implications from **federalism** and **responsible government**, he argued that the scope for constitutional implications was much wider: 'From the nature of our society, reinforced by parts of the written text, an implication arises that there is to be freedom of movement and freedom of communication. Freedom of movement and freedom of communication are indispensable to any free society.'

Finally, in *Miller v TCN Channel Nine* (1986), he again asserted that 'implied guarantees of freedom of speech and other communications and freedom of movement not only between the States and the States and the **Territories** but in and between every part of the Commonwealth' were 'fundamental to a democratic society', and 'a necessary corollary' of **national unity**.

In one respect, Murphy's argument had a respectable pedigree going back to the **Griffith Court**. In *R v Smithers; Ex parte Benson* (1912), **Griffith** and **Barton** had recognised an implied right of access to government, and hence to the seat of government. As Barton put it, 'the creation of a federal union with one government and one legislature in respect of national affairs assures to every free citizen the right of access to the institutions, and of due participation in the activities of the nation'. Similarly, in *Pioneer Express v Hotchkiss* (1958), where the Court held that section 92 did not protect the carriage of passengers from Sydney to Canberra, **Dixon** suggested 'a much more solid foundation' in 'a constitutional implication protecting the citizens of Australia … from attempts on the part of State legislatures to prevent or control access to the Capital Territory and communications and intercourse with it on the part of persons within the States'.

In *Miller v TCN Channel Nine*, the rest of the Court rejected Murphy's argument, though only on the basis that as section 92 included an express guarantee of interstate freedom of communication and movement, there was no room

for an implied guarantee to the same effect. As **Mason** put it, 'it is sufficient to say that I cannot find any basis for implying a new s 92A into the Constitution'. At the same time, **Deane** emphasised that this rejection depended on 'the wide operation which current authority gives to s 92'. With the reinterpretation of section 92 in *Cole v Whitfield*, that objection lost its force; and in the *Free Speech Cases*, a majority of the Court accepted that the Constitution implied a freedom of **political communication**. As a necessary corollary of that conception, some members of the Court envisaged the possibility of an **implied constitutional right** to freedom of movement. In *Australian Capital Television*, for example, **Gaudron** drew upon Murphy's earlier arguments to suggest that the 'notion of a free society governed in accordance with the principles of representative parliamentary **democracy** may entail freedom of movement'.

In *Kruger v Commonwealth* (1997), the plaintiffs sought a declaration that the Aboriginals Ordinance 1918 (NT), and the powers it conferred for the removal and institutional confinement of Aboriginal children, were invalid because they infringed an implied freedom of movement and association. Although the majority of the Court declined to invalidate the Ordinance on this basis, members of the Court had the opportunity to consider the extent to which such a right may exist.

Gaudron, **Toohey**, and **McHugh** expressly reaffirmed their recognition of an implied freedom of movement based upon the implied freedom of political communication: thus, for McHugh, the reasons that had led to the implication of a freedom of political communication 'lead me to the conclusion that the Constitution also necessarily implies that "the people" must be free from laws that prevent them from associating with other persons, and from travelling, inside and outside Australia for the purposes of the constitutionally prescribed system of government'. However, since these implications depended on the 'constitutionally prescribed system of government', and since until 1977 the Constitution had made no provision for the people of the territories to participate in that system, he, along with Dawson, held that the implications did not operate in the territories.

By contrast, Gaudron and Toohey held that the implied freedom of movement did apply to the territories. For Toohey, to the extent that the Ordinance authorised restrictions on freedom of movement, its validity depended on the **proportionality** of those restrictions to the purpose of 'protection and preservation of the **Aboriginal people** of the Northern Territory', in the light of 'the standards and perceptions prevailing at the time of the Ordinance'. He did not suggest that the standards and perceptions of the time would be decisive; 'the infringement of a relevant freedom may be so fundamental that justification cannot be found in the views of the time'. But the issue could be resolved only by a further inquiry, which was not possible on the basis of the questions and materials before the Court.

In Gaudron's view, the plaintiffs were entitled to succeed on this ground. She, too, recognised that the freedoms of movement and association were 'subsidiary to' the freedom of political communication, but stressed that this was so 'only in the sense that they support and supplement that latter freedom and not in the sense that they are inferior to or less robust than it'. In her view, if the purpose of a law 'is to restrict those freedoms', the law is invalid; and questions of 'compelling justification, necessity and proportionality' are merely instruments for ascertaining its purpose. If a law directly interferes with those freedoms, that will be taken to be its purpose, unless the interference is 'necessary for the attainment of some overriding public purpose' or to satisfy what Deane had referred to in *Cunliffe v Commonwealth* (1994) as some 'pressing social need'. On that basis, the relevant provisions were invalid.

Brennan and **Gummow** held that even if there were such an implication, the ostensible purposes of the Aboriginals Ordinance were not incompatible with it. Accordingly, the question whether such an implication existed was one they did not need to decide. However, both of them made it clear that they would be cautious about such an implication.

In *Levy v Victoria* (1997), Gaudron reaffirmed her view that the Constitution implies freedom of movement as an 'aspect of freedom to engage in political communication or as a subsidiary to that freedom'. In that case, again relying on her notions of 'overriding public purpose' or 'pressing social need', she found that regulations which prevented a person approaching within five metres of a duck hunter had not infringed freedom of movement because they were reasonable restrictions in the interests of public safety.

More recently, in *AMS v AIF* (1999), the High Court cautioned the Family Court to take into account, in framing any custody orders it might make, the need not to impose upon the freedom of interstate movement of either parent 'an impediment greater than that reasonably required to achieve the objects of the applicable legislation' (see **Family law**). The Court based this enjoinder primarily on the freedom of movement envisaged by section 92, noting that this is 'an aspect of s 92 doctrine which is being developed from case to case'.

Though on uncertain ground, members of the High Court, particularly Gaudron, have sown the seeds for an implied freedom of movement. However, the uncertainty points to the vulnerability of any rights dependent on implication, and to the need for more formal structures, such as a **Bill of Rights**, to provide a better framework of protection.

LARISSA BEHRENDT

Murphy, Lionel Keith (*b* 30 August 1922; *d* 21 October 1986; Justice 1975–86), as a lawyer, politician, Commonwealth **Attorney-General**, and High Court Justice, was an advocate of reform for Australia's legal and political institutions. His career was studded with achievement and dogged with controversy. No other member of the Australian judiciary has provoked such divided opinions. Whether this was a product of the message, or of the colourful nature of the messenger, remains an open question. Whatever the case, as Ross McMullin has observed, 'Murphy polarised people'.

Murphy was the youngest son of Lily and William Murphy, and grew up in Sydney. Through the 1910s, his parents entered a period of gradual estrangement from the Catholic Church. Murphy's primary education was at Kensington Public School, of which he was dux in 1935. From there, he went to Sydney Boys High, where he demonstrated some athletic aptitude. In 1941, he arrived at the University

Lionel Murphy, Justice 1975–86

of Sydney, where he studied organic chemistry, graduating with honours in 1945. The next year, he commenced his study of law, ultimately graduating with honours in 1949. Two years into his degree, Murphy took the unusual decision to sit the NSW Bar exam before he had taken out his degree. He passed, and was admitted on 2 May 1947, establishing himself initially at University Chambers and then at Wentworth Chambers.

The fourth floor of Wentworth Chambers had among its ranks a number of rising labour lawyers including Neville Wran, Bill Fisher, Jack Sweeney, and Tony Bellanto. Murphy, however, with his command of the law and his industriousness, was its leader. His extensive personal library, and devotion to books, made his chambers a meeting place for the floor.

While not exclusively in an industrial practice, Murphy became involved in some of the critical trade union struggles of the **Cold War** period. His professional association with left-wing members of the Federated Miscellaneous Workers Union of Australia in their battles against the incumbent industrial group helped to establish not only his legal reputation but also his political base. In a series of cases representing Jack Dwyer and Ray Gietzelt, Murphy tested his legal capacities against advocates such as John Kerr and Hal Wootten.

Murphy's first High Court appearance was in 1953, as a junior in a **taxation** case before **Kitto** in *Berry v FCT* (1953). He was unsuccessful. In July 1954, Murphy married Nina Morrow at St John's Church in Darlinghurst. Their daughter, Lorel Katherine, was born in 1955 at a time when Murphy's career was burgeoning.

In 1959, Murphy made his first attempt to enter federal politics, but was unsuccessful in gaining preselection for the Australian Labor Party (ALP) in the seat of Phillip. A year later, he succeeded in securing the second position on the NSW ALP Senate ticket behind Joe Fitzgerald. In the same year, he was appointed as a QC after 13 years at the Bar.

Murphy was elected at the 1961 federal election, taking up his Senate seat in 1962. His time in Parliament can be divided into three periods. From 1962 to 1967, he was a backbencher. From 1967 onwards, he was elected Leader of the Opposition in the Senate. In the same year, his marriage to Nina ended in divorce. In 1969, Murphy married Ingrid Gee (Grzonkowski) with whom he had two sons, Cameron and Blake. With the election of the **Whitlam** government in 1972, he became Leader of the Government in the Senate, Attorney-General, and Minister for Customs and Excise. He held these ministries until his resignation from the Commonwealth Parliament on 10 February 1975.

As a backbencher, he interested himself in issues of censorship, the role of the UN, human rights, **Aboriginal** health, and **discrimination**. As Leader of the Opposition in the Senate, he was influential in changing the Labor Party's traditional hostility to the role of the Senate. Murphy realised that the Senate could be used as a key institution of change in Australian governance. To this end, he obtained caucus approval for a full system of Senate Standing Committees. Senator Reg Withers, a critical figure in the events of 1975 in which the Senate played a key role (see **Dismissal of 1975**), no doubt appreciated the irony that (as Withers had acknowledged in 1973) it was Murphy who administered the 'kiss of life' to the 'sleeping beauty' that was the Australian Senate before 1970.

As Attorney-General, Murphy was, as his Senate colleague Jim McClelland recalled, a 'passionate and indefatigable promoter of his reforms'. Reflecting on Murphy's contribution, Whitlam—who was not always an enthusiastic supporter—told the Parliament in 1975 that Murphy 'has been unquestionably the most creative and effective legislator that we have ever had as an Australian Attorney-General'. During his time as Attorney-General, he secured the passage through Parliament of 20 Acts, including the *Death Penalty Abolition Act* 1973 (Cth), the *Law Reform Commission Act* 1973 (Cth), and the *Trade Practices Act* 1974 (Cth). Other legislation that he introduced included the Corporation and Securities Industry Bill, the Family Law Bill, the Racial Discrimination Bill, the Human Rights Bill, the Superior Court of Australia Bill, and the legislation establishing the Australian Legal Aid Office.

His time as Attorney-General involved his politically damaging 'ministerial visit' in March 1973 to the Melbourne offices of the Australian Security and Intelligence Organisation (ASIO). He also argued, with Maurice Byers and Elly Lauterpacht, the legality of French nuclear testing in the Pacific before the International Court of Justice in July 1974.

Murphy's **appointment** to the High Court was far from extraordinary. He was not the first Commonwealth parliamentarian to be appointed to the High Court; **Barton, O'Connor, Isaacs, Higgins, McTiernan, Latham,** and **Barwick** had all crossed the constitutional divide. Yet the event, as with so many things related to Murphy, was controversial. His elevation to the Bench after the death of Douglas **Menzies** was greeted with predictable disquiet. **Chief Justice** Barwick declared privately to Whitlam that Murphy was 'neither competent nor suitable for the position'. Whatever the facts and speculation of the appointment, it was obvious to all that the Senate and the High Court would not be the same again.

Murphy joined a Bench that included Barwick, McTiernan, **Gibbs, Stephen, Mason,** and **Jacobs**. It was a High Court that was entering a period of transition. By the time of his death in 1986, the High Court would be freed of oversight by the **Privy Council**, and be confirmed as the ultimate court of appeal for Australia.

At first glance, Murphy's methodological approach would appear to be contradictory. He was a staunch nationalist, yet consistently acknowledged the importance of international trends in the law. He argued for the rights of the individual, yet had an expansive approach to the power of the Commonwealth Parliament and a more deferential attitude to the executive government than his fellow Justices.

His judgments, especially his constitutional ones, usually involved discussion of, or reference to, fundamental principles of governance. Within a republican tradition, Murphy conceived of the Constitution in Jeffersonian terms. He frequently quoted Thomas Jefferson's enjoinder: 'Our peculiar security is the possession of a written Constitution. Let us not make it a blank paper by construction' (see, for example, *Li Chia Hsing v Rankin* (1978)).

In terms of judicial method, Murphy was scornful of the doctrine of *stare decisis* when rigid adherence to it would result in what he considered to be an unfair, irrational, inhumane, or unjust decision. Slavish adherence to **precedent**, he suggested, was 'a doctrine eminently suitable for a nation overwhelmingly populated by sheep'. He argued with great passion against the binding nature of precedent when it compelled conclusions that were irrational or unjust (*Dugan v Mirror Newspapers* (1978)) or simply outmoded (*State Government Insurance Commission v Trigwell* (1979)).

Murphy conceived of the Constitution as a document 'designed for a democratic society' (*First* **Territory Senators** *Case* (1975)). Within the fabric of the Constitution, he argued, there were 'silent constitutional principles' that informed its operation (*Sillery v The Queen* (1981)). His focus on rights and their protection was one of the hallmarks of his time on the Court. In terms of the few express guarantees in the Constitution, he took a robust interpretation. He alone held that section 41 of the Constitution provided a right to vote, a right that was 'so precious that it should not be read out of the Constitution by implication' (*R v Pearson; Ex parte Sipka* (1983)). He agreed with the view expressed by **Dixon** and **Evatt** in *R v Federal Court of Bankruptcy; Ex parte Lowenstein* (1938) that section 80 was more than just a 'mere procedural provision' (*Beckwith v The Queen* (1976)). On the basis of the freedom of and from religion protected by section 116, Murphy would have constructed an impressive wall between **church and state** following the First Amendment jurisprudence of the **United States Supreme Court** (*DOGS Case* (1981)).

It was in the area of **implied constitutional rights** that Murphy was at his most adventurous. He argued that some 'implications arise from consideration of the text; others arise from the nature of the society which operates the constitution' (*McGraw-Hinds v Smith* (1979)). The nature of Australian society was such that guarantees could be found against 'slavery or serfdom' (*R v Director-General of Social Welfare (Vic); Ex parte Henry* (1975), against 'cruel and unusual punishment' (*Sillery*), and in favour of a right to 'freedom of **movement**, speech and other communications' (*Ansett Transport Industries v Commonwealth* (1977)). No Justice, before or since, has been so expansive in the articulation of an implied **Bill of Rights**.

Murphy was a judicial nationalist. He argued that Australia had been an independent sovereign state from 1 January 1901 (*Bistricic v Rokov* (1976)). This view has scant historical or judicial support and is generally regarded as untenable. However, consistent with such a view of judicial and national independence was his forthright opinion of the paramount authority of the High Court. State courts, according to Murphy, should in all cases follow the authority of the High Court rather than the Privy Council, which he described as 'an eminent relic of **colonialism**' (*Viro v The Queen* (1978)).

While Murphy asserted Australia's **sovereignty**, he remained committed to an internationalisation of Australian law. He drew heavily on other jurisdictions and renewed interest in US precedents.

Murphy supported the constitutional capacity of the Commonwealth Parliament, subject to restrictions protecting individual and democratic rights. He often noted that as an 'authentic expression of the will of the people' there was 'a strong **presumption of constitutionality** or validity of every Act' (*Tasmanian Dam Case* (1983)).

Within the tradition of the *Engineers Case* (1920), he was ever vigilant against any perceived backsliding that would keep 'the pre-Engineers ghosts walking' (*A-G (WA); Ex rel Ansett Transport Industries v Australian National Airlines* (1976)). Thus, he expressed broad interpretations of the **trade and commerce power**, the **corporations power**, and the **external affairs power**. The last was essential to Australia's ability to fulfil its international obligations. A narrow reading of the section, he cautioned, would leave Australia 'an international cripple unable to participate fully in the emerging world order' (*Seas and Submerged Lands Case* (1975)).

While sceptical about arguments predicated upon the notion of a federal balance, Murphy remained a democrat. The state parliaments, like the Commonwealth, had electoral commitments and required the ability to implement them. His view of section 90 (see **Excise duties**), which would have increased the ability of the states to raise revenue, would have strengthened the federalist principle in the Constitution (*HC Sleigh v SA* (1977); *Logan Downs v Queensland* (1977)).

As with so many things about Murphy, his legacy is hotly debated. Many of the constitutional notes struck by Murphy, from the freedom of **political communication** to the rights of the accused, have resonated through contemporary jurisprudence (*Australian Capital Television v Commonwealth* (1992); *Dietrich v The Queen* (1992)). Yet subsequent High Court Justices who have moved in similar directions rarely start with Murphy, and often fail even to acknowledge his precur-

sory views. It may be that Murphy's greatest legacy was his ability to increase the category of the possible.

His legacy has, to a greater or lesser degree, been affected by the events relating to the so-called '**Murphy affair**'. The publicity surrounding his trial, conviction, and ultimate acquittal further stamped his career as being extraordinary. His decision to return to the Court after stepping aside for the period of his trial brought him into conflict with Chief Justice Gibbs. Murphy, who was terminally ill, maintained that it was his constitutional right to sit; he did so for one week in August 1986. The two cases argued during that week were *King v The Queen* (1986) and *Miller v TCN Channel Nine* (1986). In order that Murphy's judgments could be delivered (the convention is that when a Justice dies any undelivered judgment dies with him), the other Justices expedited the preparation of their judgments, and both cases were listed for judgment on Wednesday 22 October. At lunchtime on the Tuesday, Ingrid Murphy telephoned the Court to say that Murphy would not live until then. At 3.00 pm, Gibbs and **Brennan** constituted a special **Full Court** to hand down the judgments in both cases. At 4.00 pm, Murphy died.

Murphy came to the High Court with a comprehensive outlook on the law and its operation. He laid down, rather than developed, his view of the law while on the Court. In grappling with fundamental concepts, he eschewed many of the traditional strictures of judicial methods. His judgments were usually short, with sparse reasoning. This, combined with reactions of discomfort if not outright disapproval to his **judicial style**, would make it difficult to replicate the 'Murphy view'. He remains inimitable.

JOHN WILLIAMS

Further Reading
Tony Blackshield et al. (eds), *The Judgments of Justice Lionel Murphy* (1986)
Michael Coper and George Williams (eds), *Justice Lionel Murphy: Influential or Merely Prescient?* (1997)
Jenny Hocking, *Lionel Murphy: A Political Biography* (1997)
Jocelynne Scutt (ed), *Lionel Murphy: A Radical Judge* (1987)
John Williams, 'Revitalising the Republic: Lionel Murphy and the Protection of Rights' (1997) 8 *PLR* 27

'**Murphy affair**' refers to the series of investigations and criminal trials, relating to alleged improprieties by **Murphy**, that began with the publication of the '*Age* tapes' on 2 February 1984, and ended with Murphy's death on 21 October 1986.

'*Age* tapes' was itself a misnomer. The reference was to a large body of material, allegedly transcribed from tapes of telephone conversations illegally recorded by the NSW police, and allegedly containing evidence of widespread corruption in NSW. Tangentially, the material included excerpts from Murphy's telephone conversations with Sydney solicitor Morgan Ryan, obtained through a tap on Ryan's telephone.

Murphy had been briefed by Ryan during the 1950s and 1960s. In 1979, their acquaintance was renewed when Ryan acted as solicitor for Murphy's co-defendant Dr Jim Cairns in the *Sankey v Whitlam* prosecution. The tap on Ryan's phone was placed a month after that prosecution failed, and the transcripts included alleged conversations between Ryan

Lionel and Ingrid Murphy outside the Supreme Court of NSW after Murphy's acquittal of controversial criminal charges

and Murphy commenting adversely on participants in that prosecution. These comments, taken out of context, were the basis of the Melbourne *Age*'s front page story 'Secret Tapes of Judge'.

After Murphy was identified as the judge in question (in the NSW Parliament, on 21 February 1984; in the Queensland Parliament, on 6 March 1984), a Senate Committee to investigate the allegations against him was established on 28 March 1984.

The Committee cleared Murphy of any allegations arising from the '*Age* tapes', but heard evidence from Clarrie Briese (Chief Stipendiary Magistrate for NSW) which included a new allegation on which the Committee could not agree. That became the focus for a second Senate Committee, appointed on 6 September 1984 and comprising four Senators assisted by two retired judges, John Wickham and Xavier Connor. This time, it was Judge Paul Flannery (of the NSW District Court) whose evidence yielded a new allegation, lending possible corroborative support to 'the Briese allegation', and leaving the second Committee again unable to agree.

The Briese and Flannery allegations related to the prosecution of Morgan Ryan for alleged conspiracy in immigration matters. Briese's story was that on 6 January 1982, while Ryan's committal for trial was pending before magistrate Kevin Jones, Murphy and his wife dined at Briese's home. The Ryan matter was mentioned over dinner. Briese offered (on his version) to 'make some inquiries', or (on Murphy's version) to 'have a look to see how it's going'. Although this offer was volunteered without direct prompting from

Murphy, the '*Age* tapes' had led Briese to believe in retrospect that Murphy had been inviting him to put pressure on Jones to decide against committing Ryan for trial.

On Saturday 9 July 1983, Flannery in turn had attended a dinner at Murphy's Darling Point home. Ryan's trial (with Flannery presiding) was due to commence the following Monday. The dinner conversation made no direct reference to Ryan, but during a general discussion of the dangers of conspiracy charges, Murphy referred to his judgment in *R v Hoar* (1981). Two days later, Ryan's counsel cited that case in his opening argument.

Conceivably, the Senate committees might have disposed of the affair more effectively with fuller cooperation from Murphy. For the three Labor members of the first Committee, 'the Briese allegation' did *not* establish a *prima facie* case of misbehaviour; and its two Liberal members found a *prima facie* case only on the basis that Murphy's *written* denials should carry less weight than Briese's evidence, which was 'tested' by questioning. The remaining member, Senator Chipp, felt unable, without evidence from Murphy, to make any finding at all.

Chipp saw the issue as Senate power; Murphy saw it as judicial **independence**. He had given the Committee one written statement responding to the '*Age* tapes' materials, and another after Briese's evidence. He refused to submit to questioning for three distinct reasons.

First, he maintained that any such hearing would violate the rules of **natural justice** unless his counsel were permitted to cross-examine Briese. Under Senate Standing Order 304, this was not permissible. (Only Chipp was willing to resolve this impasse by suspending the Standing Order.)

Secondly, Murphy maintained that the questioning of a High Court Justice by a Senate Committee would infringe the **separation of powers**. Thirdly, he maintained that the Committee's 'investigative' function was being taken too far. In his view, any decision on **removal of Justices** is entrusted by section 72 of the Constitution exclusively to the Parliament. For the Senate Committee to contemplate summoning or interrogating a High Court Justice was not only an attempt by the legislative branch to assert coercive power against the judicial branch, but a misconception of any role that could be delegated to a Committee consistently with section 72.

The second Senate Committee's procedures sought to meet these objections. Elaborate evidentiary rules were devised to ensure fairness to Murphy if he chose to appear. The new procedures specifically authorised cross-examination of witnesses, and stipulated that 'Justice Murphy shall not be summoned to give evidence', though after all other evidence had been heard he could be invited to do so.

Again, however, when that invitation was given, Murphy declined it; and this time, a strict interpretation of the new evidentiary rules meant that not even his *written* denials could be considered. The Committee was left to assess the allegations as if they stood uncontested.

The political context was unfortunate. By the time of the Committee's invitation to Murphy, the Hawke government had called an early election. On 26 October 1984, the Parliament was to be dissolved. In that situation, Murphy's counsel (Tom Hughes) informed the Committee on 12 October that the Justice would refuse to appear, for two principal reasons. First, in the time frame now remaining, there was no possibility that any proceedings under section 72 could be completed before the Parliament rose. Any further inquiry could therefore 'be seen as a futile step taken solely for political reasons', and as 'an unjustifiable attempt … to pre-empt the proper role of the new Parliament'. Secondly, the Committee proceedings were now being conducted 'in a highly politicised environment … as a factor in the opening stages of an election campaign. If the judge gives evidence, it is virtually inevitable that he may become a political football in the election. This would be intolerable.'

It was after the failure of the second Senate Committee that Ian Temby, as Commonwealth Director of Public Prosecutions, recommended on 21 November 1984 that Murphy be prosecuted on charges (the Briese and Flannery allegations) of attempting to pervert the course of justice. Two weeks earlier, Temby had argued in a seminar paper that in such a case criminal prosecution would help to 'clear the air'; and when his opinion in the Murphy matter was later released to the press, it confirmed that that had been his intention. Murphy, for his part, 'welcome[d] the fact that the allegations will be tried by judge and jury and not by the **media**'. Hitherto, he had continued to sit in the High Court as usual; now he announced that he would not take part in any new cases until the criminal proceedings were over, though he emphasised that he was 'not standing down or aside'. In cases already argued, he continued to deliver judgments (see, for example, *Kirmani v Captain Cook Cruises* (1985)).

On 5 July 1985, the jury at Murphy's first trial (presided over by Justice Henry Cantor and prosecuted by **Callinan**) acquitted him of 'the Flannery allegation' but convicted him of 'the Briese allegation'. There followed an extraordinary sequence of events in which members of the jury came forward to protest that Cantor's directions had led them to understand that they must convict, despite their belief that Murphy had done nothing wrong. Murphy contested the conviction in three ways: a conventional appeal; a challenge to jurisdiction (ultimately heard by the High Court after **removal** from the Supreme Court of NSW); and a referral to the High Court of 21 questions of law. The High Court refused to answer the 21 questions, remitting them to the NSW Court of Criminal Appeal to be dealt with along with the appeal. The Court did, however, dismiss the jurisdictional challenge (*R v Murphy* (1985)). Murphy had argued that the Briese allegation, even if proven, would not entail an attempt to pervert the course of justice 'in relation to the **judicial power** of the Commonwealth'; and that the relevant provisions investing state courts with federal jurisdiction were unconstitutional. Even if these arguments had succeeded, the substantive issues would have remained unresolved.

Finally, on 28 November 1985, a specially constituted five-judge Bench of the NSW Court of Criminal Appeal quashed the conviction on the Briese allegation and ordered a new trial: *R v Murphy* (1985).

On Monday 28 April 1986, the jury at the second trial (presided over by Justice David Hunt) acquitted on 'the Briese allegation' as well. The acquittal did not necessarily exclude the possibility of sufficient impropriety to warrant parliamentary proceedings for Murphy's removal from the Bench; but over the next few days, politicians of all parties issued statements that the matter was over.

On Friday 2 May, however, a discussion between Chief Justice **Gibbs** and **Attorney-General** Lionel Bowen led Bowen to believe that the High Court Justices were themselves proposing to deliberate on whether Murphy's return to the Bench was acceptable to them. Convinced that the Justices themselves had no constitutional authority to make a pronouncement on such an issue (since only the Parliament has power to seek a Justice's removal from office), Bowen resolved to reassert the Parliament's exclusive authority by appointing a Parliamentary Commission of Inquiry to review the entire affair. In a press release the following Monday, Gibbs protested that the Court had had no such intention. But whatever processes may have been unfolding within the Court had been overtaken by events. On Wednesday 7 May, Bowen announced that the new Parliamentary Commission would be constituted by three retired judges (George Lush, Richard Blackburn, and Andrew Wells). They were not to reconsider the Briese and Flannery allegations (except where that might be 'necessary for the proper examination of other issues'), and their charter was limited to 'specific allegations made in precise terms'. But within those limits, the Commission was to consider 'any conduct' by Murphy that might amount in its opinion to 'proved misbehaviour'.

By 31 July 1986, the Commission had assembled 42 allegations; had determined that 28 of them were wholly lacking in substance; and was poised to consider the remaining 14. But on that day, Murphy announced that he was dying of incurable cancer, and intended to return to the Court for as long as he could. The work of the Commission was immediately halted, and its constituent statute was repealed. Murphy returned to the Court for one week of sittings. He died on 21 October 1986. How the Commission would have dealt with the remaining 14 allegations will never be known.

Although the Briese and Flannery allegations were the focus of the criminal trials, other allegations had continued to circulate throughout. Some of the original imputations arising from the *Age* tapes, though already investigated and rejected by the first Senate Committee, repeatedly resurfaced as fresh allegations—for example, that Murphy and Ryan had discussed the possibility of reprisals against David Rofe, the prosecuting counsel in *Sankey v Whitlam*; that Murphy had suggested that Ryan should seek to avert his own impending prosecution by asking a member of the NSW Parliament to announce that investigation had left Ryan 'smelling like a rose'; that Murphy had offered to help Ryan put improper pressure on Milton Morris, a member of the NSW Parliament; that Murphy had answered a question from Ryan by asserting that two federal police officers, David Lewington and Robert Jones, were not open to improper influence because 'they were both very straight'; and that Murphy had approached NSW Premier Neville Wran seeking (unsuccessfully) to procure the reappointment of Wadim Jegorow in the NSW Ethnic Affairs Commission. A new allegation in the *National Times*, after Murphy's second trial, was that in December 1979, prior to the formation of the Australian Federal Police, Murphy had spoken to a Commonwealth police officer, Donald Thomas, and offered to procure his promotion in the new force in exchange for inside information. Though this allegation recurred in numerous versions, all of them entailed irreconcilable contradictions in chronology. Other repeated rumours linked Murphy's name with the Sydney identity Abe Saffron—for example, that Murphy had sought Saffron's intervention to procure the withdrawal of the prosecutions in *Sankey v Whitlam*; or that Murphy had made 'representations' in support of tenders by Saffron for the remodelling of Sydney Central Railway Station and for a lease of Luna Park.

Criticisms of Murphy's conduct during his criminal trials gave rise to further allegations. In particular, his exercise at the second trial of his right to make a statement from the dock (rather than going into evidence) was said to be inappropriate. (Moreover, it was said that when Murphy recounted in his statement a remark that Briese's allegation had come 'out of the blue', that was an imputation against Briese infringing the rule in *Browne v Dunn* (1893), which requires that allegations against a witness should be raised during cross-examination so that the witness has a chance to respond.) Others insisted that at the first trial Murphy had given false evidence—for example, by understating the extent of his association with Ryan, or by misrepresenting the chronological sequence of his contacts with NSW District Court Chief Judge JH Staunton and with Justice (formerly Senator) Jim McClelland. The admitted purpose of these contacts was to procure an expedited trial for Ryan; and this in itself was said to be an exercise of improper influence. Again, since the evidence of the dinner conversation with Briese on 6 January 1982 had

disclosed that Murphy and Briese had discussed the so-called 'Greek conspiracy case', then pending in Briese's court, it was said that this in itself, apart from any reference to the Ryan case, was an attempt to pervert the course of justice.

For some, even if all of these allegations had been disproved, their cumulative effect would have generated such an aura of impropriety that for that reason alone Murphy should have been removed from the Bench. For others, the frenzied piling of allegation upon allegation and rumour upon rumour was a frightening echo of the communal hysteria of the *Chamberlain Case* (1984).

TONY BLACKSHIELD

Further Reading
Tony Blackshield, 'After the Trial: The Free Speech Verdict' (1985) 59 *LIJ* 1187
Tony Blackshield, 'Murphy: Return to the Court' (1986) 76 *Arena* 28
Jenny Hocking, *Lionel Murphy: A Political Biography* (1997)
Garry Sturgess, 'Murphy and the Media', and Tony Blackshield, 'The "Murphy Affair"' in Jocelynne Scutt (ed), *Lionel Murphy: A Radical Judge* (1987) chs 11 and 12
JB Thomas, *Judicial Ethics in Australia* (2nd edn 1997)

Muschinski v Dodds (1985) was one of a series of important decisions in the 1980s, including **Waltons Stores v Maher** (1988) and **Amadio's Case** (1983), where the High Court addressed and refashioned principles of **equity** in the light of new social relationships and conditions.

In *Muschinski*, a de facto wife had provided almost the whole of the purchase price for a block of land. She and her de facto husband were registered as tenants in common. They were unable to develop the land commercially as originally planned, and ultimately the relationship ended. The woman sought a declaration that she was the sole beneficial owner of the land. In order to sustain her claim, she had to prove that she had a proprietary interest in her partner's share. However, she could not rely on a 'common intention constructive **trust**' or 'a resulting trust' because there was clear evidence that she had intended that he should have his share. It appeared that she had no legal basis for her claim.

However, **Deane** (with whom **Mason** agreed) identified a new kind of constructive trust that would arise over **property** where a joint endeavour has come to an end without attributable blame, and where it had not been intended that the recipient would benefit in such circumstances. Deane ascertained and legitimised this constructive trust by reference to analogous situations where the law provided relief to recover contributions, and to the equitable principle of **unconscionability**. He showed that a constructive trust could arise in cases where the unconscionable conduct took place after the receipt of the disputed property and where there were no pre-existing **fiduciary obligations**. He held that the dichotomy between 'institutional' and 'remedial' constructive trusts was a superficial one, particularly as both arise without the need for a court order and in the absence of the intention of the parties to create a trust.

Although the relationship in question was both a commercial and personal one, Deane recognised that de facto relationships were becoming more commonplace and that it was necessary, in the absence of statutory schemes, for courts to adjudicate a fair distribution of assets, taking into account both direct financial contributions and indirect contributions such as homemaking and family care. In *Baumgartner v Baumgartner* (1987), the Court endorsed Deane's judgment, applied this constructive trust in a domestic relationship, and grappled with the practical evaluation of contribution.

However, Deane clearly indicated that the development of modern equity jurisprudence demanded a principled basis for judicial intervention. In order to sustain and nurture a coherent and rational legal system, it was inappropriate for judges to adopt idiosyncratic or vague notions of justice and fairness. Therefore, he expressly rejected the 'new model' of a constructive trust that had been devised by Lord Denning in the English Court of Appeal. Moreover, he emphasised the need, when fashioning the remedy, to take into account the competing claims of third parties.

In *Muschinski* and *Baumgartner*, the Court boldly charted a new direction for the constructive trust. It balanced the urgent need to redress new forms of unconscionable conduct with an emphasis on the importance of legal reasoning and **precedent**.

Fiona Burns

Further Reading

Barbara McDonald, 'Constructive Trusts' in Patrick Parkinson (ed), *The Principles of Equity* (1996) 209

Marcia Neave, 'The New Unconscionability Principle: Property Disputes Between De Facto Partners' (1991) 5 *AJFL* 185

Pamela O'Connor, 'Happy Partners or Strange Bedfellows: The Blending of Remedial and Institutional Features in the Evolving Constructive Trust' (1996) 20 *MULR* 735

Patrick Parkinson, 'Doing Equity Between De Facto Spouses: From *Calverley v Green* to *Baumgartner*' (1988) 11 *Adel L Rev* 370

N

Namatjira v Raabe (1959). Albert Namatjira (1902–59) was the first Aboriginal artist to attract widespread popularity. In the 1950s, his watercolours of Central Australian landscapes hung in thousands of Australian homes.

In the 1950s, the treatment of **Aboriginal people** in the Northern Territory changed. Under the Aborigines Ordinance 1918, they were all effectively wards of the government. Under the Welfare Ordinance 1953, the Administrator could *declare* them to be wards. In 1957, no fewer than 15 711 Aboriginal people were 'declared' to be wards—most of them in a single declaration on 30 May 1957. Namatjira and his wife were not included.

Their exclusion was widely, but misleadingly, reported as meaning that they had been granted 'Australian **citizenship**'. It did mean that they were free to vote, to purchase alcohol, and to live where they chose. But their children were still wards, and the family remained at the tribal camp.

In 1958, there were frequent reports of drunkenness at the camp. In August, a young woman was killed there, and at the inquest the coroner, magistrate JE Lemaire, publicly warned Namatjira that if caught supplying liquor he would be gaoled. Three weeks later, Namatjira was arrested on such charges. Lemaire recused himself, and magistrate Stuart Dodds dismissed all charges but one: that on 26 August, while sharing a taxi to Hermannsburg, Namatjira had shared a bottle of rum with a fellow Aranta tribesman and artist, Henoch Raberaba.

Under the Licensing Ordinance 1939–57, the supply of liquor to 'a person who is a ward within the meaning of the Welfare Ordinance' was an offence. Dodds found that the offence was proved: at the least, Namatjira had deliberately left an open bottle of rum on the seat of the taxi. In deference to Namatjira's position, Dodds imposed the minimum sentence open to him: a mandatory six months imprisonment with hard labour. On appeal, the Supreme Court of the Northern Territory exercised its appellate discretion and reduced the sentence to three months.

In 1959, a further appeal to the High Court was dismissed. By then, the case had attracted a public outcry, led by most state Premiers; and the Minister for Territories, Paul Hasluck, had promised that if Namatjira did have to serve his sentence, it would be in open country under supportive conditions. But the only issue engaging the High Court's attention was a technical one.

The offence under the Licensing Ordinance depended on Raberaba's being subject to a declaration of wardship under section 14 of the Welfare Ordinance. That section empowered the Administrator to make such declarations in respect of persons needing special care or assistance by reason of (*a*) manner of living; (*b*) inability to manage their own affairs; (*c*) social habits and behaviour; and (*d*) personal associations. In Raberaba's case, there was no evidence of any individualised assessment of these factors; his name had simply been included in a job lot of 15 200 persons on 30 May 1957.

Did the careful specification of criteria mean that individualised assessment was required? Speaking *ex tempore* for a unanimous Court, Chief Justice **Dixon** thought that this

Albert Namatjira, who was gaoled for supplying liquor to a ward of the state

491

might normally follow, but that here there were countervailing factors.

First, the Welfare Ordinance did allow a right of appeal, as 'an immediate remedy [if] a person declared to be a ward ... objects to his status'. Dixon spoke of this as a right of appeal against 'an adverse conclusion'. He acknowledged that declarations of wardship were intended as 'beneficial and not adverse', but found it 'easy ... to understand' that a ward 'might not so view the matter'.

Secondly, though the wardship system was not limited to Aboriginal people, extensive exclusions in section 14(2) left it applicable only to them. The regime of the Welfare Ordinance was 'analogous to' and continuous with that of the Aboriginals Ordinance, and reflected an approach to Aboriginal people 'as a class'. If Aboriginals were a collective problem, a collective solution was appropriate.

The Court heard the appeal on 12 March and gave judgment on 13 March. Namatjira was taken into custody on 18 March. He served most of his sentence at Papunya Native Reserve, received one month's remission for good behaviour, and was released on 19 May. On 8 August, less than three months later, he died.

TONY BLACKSHIELD

Further Reading
Nadine Amadio, *Albert Namatjira: The Life and Work of an Australian Painter* (1986)
Joyce Batty, *Namatjira: Wanderer Between Two Worlds* (1963)

National unity. The High Court has played a significant **role** in the achievement of national unity, particularly through its **common law** and **constitutional law** functions (even though the actual membership of the Court has been dominated by **appointments** from NSW and Victoria and thus might be said not to have had a genuinely national base).

Most obviously, the Court has played a unifying role in the Australian legal system, simply by virtue of its general **jurisdiction** to hear appeals from the states and **territories** (unlike the **United States Supreme Court**, which has only federal jurisdiction). Through its function of finally declaring the law for Australia—at least once it was freed from the shackles of **Privy Council** appeals, and had freed itself from the self-imposed shackles of British **precedent**—the Court has played a pivotal role in fashioning the unity of Australian law, and indeed a uniquely Australian common law.

Initially, the **establishment** of the Court was met with doubt, criticism, and even outright hostility—fanned by the suspicion of lawyers, predictions of a lack of **business**, concern about states' rights, and in some instances satisfaction with the Privy Council (see also **Deakin**; *Judiciary Act*). The doubts were overcome by the quality of the original Bench, led by **Griffith**; by insistence on high standards at the Bar and in lower courts (whose decisions the **Griffith Court** was more than ready to overturn); and by the Court's insistence on its constitutional right to have the final say on matters of peculiarly Australian concern (see *Inter se* questions). Once established, the Court quickly settled into place at the apex of the Australian judicial **hierarchy**. Even the symbolism reflected this; as early as 1919, the **Chief Justice** was sometimes referred to as the 'Chief Justice of Australia'.

In its common law work, it took some time, because of deference to British precedents, for the Court to focus on national unity rather than the unity of the common law as a whole; and although from the beginning the Court was prepared to revisit its own precedents, the idea of actively remoulding the common law to meet modern needs was less readily accepted. Even when it was accepted, in dramatic examples such as *Mabo* (1992), the promotion of national unity was not necessarily the same as the achievement of a national consensus; it was rather a display of national leadership, which a majority of the Court judged essential to the future of the nation. But, over time, the Court has made a major contribution to national unity through development of the general law.

The Court's other major role is to interpret the Constitution. That Constitution is a federal Constitution. The Constitution itself thus seeks to balance national unity and local diversity, and the Court's interpretation of the Constitution is therefore critical in determining where the balance lies.

The constitutional scheme for balancing national unity and local diversity works partly by directly depriving the states of power to do parochial things to the detriment of the nation, and partly by identifying particular areas of national legislative competence, leaving it to the Commonwealth Parliament to exercise its power in those areas according to the politics of the day. Examples of the former approach include section 92, which prevents the states from engaging in economic protectionism (see **Interstate trade and commerce**), and section 117, which prevents them from discriminating against residents of other states.

It was only in the late 1980s that the Court came to see these provisions in terms of the balance between national unity and local diversity. Initially, **Isaacs** had pushed a strongly nationalist approach to section 92; between 1920 and 1936, this resulted in the complete liberation of the Commonwealth from its constraints. But a literal approach to the words of the section—perhaps reinforced by subtle ideological preferences or predispositions—had resulted in an interpretation that protected free enterprise rather than free trade. In *Cole v Whitfield* (1988), the Court returned section 92 to its core constitutional purpose, and set about the conscious task of balancing local autonomy against the demands of nation.

The Court had always endeavoured to be alert to recognise and prevent state protectionism (see, for example, *Fox v Robbins* (1909); *Tasmania v Victoria* (1935); *North Eastern Dairy Case* (1975)); but its predominantly literal approach not only went further than necessary but may at the same time have fallen short of what was necessary, so that state protectionism could pass unchecked even when it was present. In *Cole v Whitfield*, the Court refocused on state protectionism and developed a two-pronged test: first, is the impugned law discriminatory in a protectionist sense, and secondly (as elaborated in *Castlemaine Tooheys v SA* (1990)), if so, is it nonetheless valid as a reasonable and **proportionate** pursuit of a non-protectionist purpose? The new test recognised, on the one hand, that the very point of state governments is to promote the welfare of their people—and yet, on the other, that some measures the states might adopt are simply inconsistent with the higher demand of national unity. Although it has never found a satisfactory way of undertaking the **fact finding** relevant to competing claims in this area, the Court has come to terms with the unavoidable need to balance these principles. It is not necessarily a task for which a court is best equipped (see **Inter-State Commission**), but it is fundamental to the concept of federation.

Just as section 92 has been recognised as a pillar of national economic unity, so in 1989 the Court belatedly recognised section 117 as a pillar of national social unity. In *Street v Queensland Bar Association* (1989), a unanimous Court breathed new life into section 117 by holding that Queensland's Bar admission rules infringed the section's prohibition of **discrimination** based on state residence. The early cases on section 117 had been quite restrictive (*Davies and Jones v WA* (1904); *Lee Fay v Vincent* (1908)), but none more so than *Henry v Boehm* (1973), where the Court, with **Stephen** in sole dissent, upheld the SA Bar's admission rules on the highly artificial basis that it was equally open to residents and non-residents to satisfy the requirement of continuous residence in SA for a certain period prior to admission. Clearly the requirement had a greater impact on non-residents (who had to move to SA to comply with it), and in *Street* the Court swept away this formalism, holding that the appropriate comparison was not between the hypothetical situation of the plaintiff as a resident and the situation of other residents, but between the hypothetical situation of the plaintiff as a resident and his or her situation as it was in fact.

Yet, as with section 92, section 117 requires a balance to be struck. In instances such as voting rights and welfare entitlements, state residential criteria are generally accepted as appropriate. The Court was ambivalent about whether these instances were 'exceptions' based on necessity, or on the integrity of the states as autonomous units, or whether they were simply entailed in a proper understanding of the words 'disability or discrimination' in section 117. On either view, the same tension was manifest as in the case of section 92 between the countervailing demands of national unity and state autonomy. That tension will always be present, but it took the Court until 1989 to find the right starting point.

An important factor in the achievement of national unity has been the Court's willingness to allow the Commonwealth an expansive interpretation of its legislative powers. Until 1920, under the influence of Griffith, **Barton**, and O'Connor, the Court had limited the reach of Commonwealth power by starting with the assumption that certain powers were 'reserved' to the states; thus, for example, the **corporations power** was limited so as not to intrude into purely intrastate trade, and national anti-monopoly legislation was thereby made impossible (*Huddart Parker v Moorehead* (1909)). But in 1920, with persistent dissenters Isaacs and **Higgins** now in the ascendancy, the Court held in the landmark *Engineers Case* that the several categories of **Commonwealth legislative power** should be given their ordinary and natural meaning, without any limiting assumptions about the intended ambit of state power. Although it took another 50 years to confirm that the Commonwealth could now regulate corporate anti-competitive behaviour (*Strickland v Rocla Concrete Pipes* (1971)), this was a major step in facilitating national economic and other legislation.

Despite occasional pleas that Commonwealth powers must be read in the context of a federal Constitution, the *Engineers Case* has ensured a broad reading of those powers.

Interestingly, the Court's expansive view in 1920 ran ahead of the Commonwealth's willingness at that time to exploit its powers; and by the time a more adventurous government sought to do so in the 1940s, a changed Court found other ways of cutting it back—notably, by using section 92. But with broad readings of the corporations power and the **external affairs power** in the *Tasmanian Dam Case* (1983), coupled with a broad reading of the Commonwealth's financial powers (*Fairfax v FCT* (1965); *Uniform Tax Cases* (1942 and 1957); *AAP Case* (1975)), the Court has, since 1920, consistently tilted the federal balance towards the nation and away from its component parts.

That is not to say there are no limits and gaps. And the Court has in recent times taken a miserly view of the capacity of Commonwealth–state cooperative schemes to overcome those limits and gaps (*Re Wakim* (1999); *R v Hughes* (2000)). But even this miserly view has scarcely made a dent in the national unity established over the course of the twentieth century; indeed, it has tended rather to provoke creative thinking about alternative solutions, including references of power by the states to the Commonwealth, and constitutional **amendment**. Sometimes even adverse judicial decisions can be a catalyst for national unity.

The *Engineers Case* did not inhibit the **Mason Court** from reinvigorating some of the **express constitutional rights**, including section 117, nor from discovering a range of **implied constitutional rights**, notably the freedom of **political communication**. In a sense, these rights decisions are also a contribution to national unity; individual rights, despite their relative paucity under the Constitution, transcend state boundaries and attach to **citizenship** on a national basis. Section 117, too, is a reflection of the idea of national citizenship.

Many things contribute to a country's sense of national unity: shared **values**, common heritage, growth in communications, the pressure of external events, the trauma of war, the celebration of national icons, success on the world stage, and a myriad of other factors—social, political, cultural, and psychological. The part played by the legal system, and by the role of the highest court in the structure of that legal system, is perhaps relatively small. Nevertheless, it is not insignificant, particularly in a federal system, which, almost by definition, has an inbuilt capacity for fragmentation. In Australia, the High Court has played a significant role in the achievement of national unity, partly through its general appellate jurisdiction and partly through its general tendency to accentuate the national and downplay the local when interpreting the Constitution.

That tendency is evident in a wide range of areas, including, in addition to those discussed, the scope of **intergovernmental immunities**, the ambit of **inconsistency** under section 109 of the Constitution, and the implication of a general (though limited) **nationhood** power in addition to the express powers of the Commonwealth. Moreover, the Court's position at the apex of the Australian judicial hierarchy, as well as ensuring the unity of the common law, has itself had constitutional implications: in *Kable v DPP* (1996), a majority relied on the integrated national court system to conclude that a state court could not be invested with functions incompatible with its federal judicial functions (see **Separation of powers**).

The idea of national unity has also prevailed, finally, in the long-standing controversy over whether, in the context of federal **conflict of laws**, the relevant law should be the law of the state or territory where the legal proceedings were commenced or that of the state or territory where the event giving rise to the proceedings occurred. In *Breavington v Godleman* (1988), **Deane** relied on Australia's 'unitary national system of law' to adopt the latter; it was inconsistent with national unity to resort to the traditional 'choice of law' rules of private international law as if the states were separate countries. This was accepted (and 'forum shopping' significantly inhibited) in *John Pfeiffer v Rogerson* (2000).

The Court's doctrinal contribution to national unity has been strengthened by aspects of its modus operandi. For example, the Court was prepared from the beginning to be peripatetic, and still shows the flag around the country despite having had a permanent home in **Canberra** since 1980 (see **Circuit system**). Moreover, the Court has generally consisted of Justices of high calibre, and sometimes of Justices, like **Dixon**, with significant international reputations. The respect it has earned has made the impact of its work all the more effective.

The respect the Court has generated and maintained as an institution seems to have been sufficient to overcome both the fierce **criticism** provoked by its **activism** in the early 1990s, and the less strident but more persistent criticism of the predominance of appointments from NSW and Victoria. The idea that a state or territory should be 'represented' on the Court has rightly been resisted; yet a wider geographical spread of appointments would arguably increase the sense of national participation in the nation's highest court. Despite the Court's contribution to national unity through its common law and constitutional roles, national unity could be further enhanced if, without any compromise of excellence, the diversity of the nation were better reflected in the composition of the Court itself.

Michael Coper

Further Reading

Michael Coper, 'The Role of the Courts in the Preservation of Federalism' (1989) 63 *ALJ* 463

Nationhood, Court's role in building. The High Court has played an important role in recognising the attainment and effect of Australia's independence as a nation, especially given the absence, for the most part, of any formal declaration of that status. That role was highlighted in *Sue v Hill* (1999), when the Court decided that whatever the position may have been at federation, a UK subject was now to be treated as a citizen of a 'foreign power' within the meaning of section 44(i) of the Constitution, and thus as incapable of being chosen as a member of the Commonwealth Parliament.

By applying progressive principles of **constitutional interpretation**, the Court has recognised the evolutionary and somewhat fragmented way independence was acquired, as well as the corresponding evolutionary change in the position of the Queen as the constitutional Head of State of Australia and other British Commonwealth countries. The nature of the process has made it difficult for the Court to state the precise moment at or by which the status of independence was obtained—especially because, though it may seem paradoxical, Australia obtained international recognition as a separate nation before it achieved full legal and constitutional autonomy over its internal affairs. Independence was also achieved at different times for the federal and state levels of government.

The process has not necessitated **amendment** of the Australian or **state Constitutions**. Nor has it resulted in a break in **sovereignty** or a disruption of the continued existence of the institutions that were previously in place, despite the location of their origin and source in legislation enacted by the British Parliament at a time when Australia formed part of the British Empire (*Joosse v Australian Securities and Investment Commission* (1998)).

The use of progressive principles of interpretation, combined with the operation of constitutional conventions and practices, also accounts for the Court's acceptance that the 'executive power of the Commonwealth' in section 61 of the Constitution contained from its inception a latent power to encompass the **common law** prerogative powers of the Crown to conduct Australia's foreign relations—for example, entry into treaties, declarations of war and peace, and the sending and receipt of ambassadors. That latent power grew as Australia attained its independence, though it could not be fully expressed while Australia remained part of the British Empire (*Industrial Relations Act Case* (1996)). This illustrates the observation made by **Isaacs** that 'it is the duty of the Judiciary to recognise the development of the Nation and to apply established principles to the new positions which the Nation in its progress from time to time assumes' (*Wooltops Case* (1922)), as well as his belief in 'the silent operation of constitutional principles' (*Skin Wool Case* (1926)).

The Court has also played an important part in the abolition of appeals to the **Privy Council**, and thereby in its own emergence as Australia's final court of appeal. It upheld the power of the Australian Parliament to enact valid legislation for the prevention of appeals to the Privy Council from its own decisions in all matters (*A-G (Cth) v T & G Mutual* (1978)). Earlier, it had upheld the validity of legislation enacted by the Australian Parliament for the prevention of appeals from other Australian courts in matters involving the exercise of federal jurisdiction; and also for the ouster of state jurisdiction in respect of such matters—the state courts being invested instead with federal jurisdiction in respect of those matters so as to prevent appeals lying direct to the Privy Council on the same matters (*Limerick Steamship Case* (1924); *Pirrie v McFarlane* (1925); *Skin Wool Case*). The Court has granted only one certificate under section 74 of the Constitution to allow a question of the limits *inter se* of the powers of the Commonwealth and the states to be determined by the Privy Council. It has since made clear its determination never to grant any such certificate in the future, thereby rendering section 74 obsolete in that regard (*Kirmani v Captain Cook Cruises (No 2)* (1985)). Chapter III of the Constitution has also been interpreted as preventing **advisory opinions** being obtained from the Privy Council in relation to matters of federal jurisdiction (*Queen of Queensland Case* (1975)).

Before the adoption of the *Statute of Westminster* 1931 (Imp), the Court took the view that even the Commonwealth was unable to pass laws inconsistent with British legislation, which operated by paramount force—for example, legislation designed to protect the interests of the British Empire on such matters as merchant shipping (*Union Steamship Co of NZ v Commonwealth* (1925))—though apparently the disability did not extend to legislation affecting Privy Council appeals in matters that involved the exercise of federal jurisdiction (*Limerick Steamship*; *Skin Wool*). By section 2 of the Statute of Westminster, the **Commonwealth's legislative powers** were freed from any such restriction. But a series of cases in the 1970s made it clear, despite suggestions to the contrary by **Murphy**, that British legislation having 'paramount force' still operated to limit the legislative powers of the states (see *Bistricic v Rokov* (1976); *China Ocean Shipping v SA* (1979); *Southern Centre of Theosophy v SA* (1979)).

Subsequently, in *Kirmani v Captain Cook Cruises (No 1)* (1985), some members of the Court suggested that the Australian Parliament had power to abolish these and other restrictions on the autonomy of the Australian states. The suggestions may have hastened the enactment of the ***Australia Acts*** 1986 by the Australian and British parliaments, acting with approval of the states. These Acts terminated all such limitations, including any residual right of appeal to the Privy Council in relation to state matters. The Australian version of the Act relied in part on the power of the Australian Parliament under section 51(xxxviii) of the Constitution to exercise powers that in 1901 could be exercised only by the UK Parliament, provided this is done 'at the request or with the concurrence' of the parliaments of the states. Subsequently, in *Port MacDonnell Professional Fishermen's Association v SA* (1989), the Court confirmed that the mechanism in section 51(xxxviii) should be given 'the broad interpretation which befits it as a constitutional provision with a national purpose of a fundamental kind'. Again, the rationale was an evolutionary one:

> In the early days of the Constitution, there may well have been some inhibition against giving that grant of legislative power its full scope and effect in that it could have been seen as controlled by the then status of the Commonwealth itself within the British Empire. Today, any room for such inhibition has long been denied by 'the silent operation of constitutional principles' in the context of complete independence and international sovereignty.

The Court has also recognised that the Commonwealth has an implied power to engage in enterprises and activities that can only be undertaken by the Commonwealth as the Australian national government. **Brennan** has suggested that the power enables the Commonwealth to deal with 'many of the symbols of nationhood—a flag or anthem, for example—or the benefits of many national initiatives in science, literature and the arts' (*Davis v Commonwealth* (1988); see **Nationhood power**).

Dawson has emphasised that in the light of the attainment of Australia's independence, 'an interpretation of the Constitution which denies the completeness of Australian legislative power is unacceptable in terms of constitutional theory and practice' (*War Crimes Act Case* (1991)). It remains for the Court to apply that view regarding the ability of the Australian parliaments (possibly with the approval of the elec-

tors at a referendum) to deal with the remaining matters that reflect Australia's former colonial status—namely, the rules of succession to the British Crown and the 'covering clauses' of the Australian Constitution—matters that affect Australia's ability to become a republic.

GEOFFREY LINDELL

Further Reading
Final Report of the Constitutional Commission (1988) vol 1, 2.112–2.174
Leslie Zines, 'The Growth of Australian Nationhood and its Effect on the Powers of the Commonwealth' in Leslie Zines (ed), *Commentaries on the Australian Constitution* (1977) ch 1

Nationhood power. The concept of an implied federal 'nationhood' power draws on two distinct lines of authority. The first, older, line comprises decisions in which the High Court has confirmed that the Commonwealth has power to protect the country against internal insurrection in addition to its express power for **defence** of the country against external threats (section 51(vi) of the Constitution). Thus in *R v Sharkey* (1949), it was accepted that Commonwealth power to create an offence of inciting insurrection arose 'out of the very nature and existence of the Commonwealth as a political institution' (see also *Burns v Ransley* (1949); ***Communist Party Case*** (1951)).

A second, more recent and more pervasive line of authority, stems from the *AAP Case* (1975). In that case, the question for the Court was whether the Commonwealth could unilaterally give effect to a policy to promote social development throughout Australia on a regional basis. The Plan was not supported by legislation, although funds for the purpose had been appropriated in the *Appropriation Act (No 1)* 1974–75 (Cth).

The Australian Assistance Plan was challenged by the state of Victoria. In the event, the challenge was dismissed—without, however, endorsing the validity of the Plan or identifying a clear proposition for which the decision stood. As to the substantive validity of the scheme, the Court divided 3:3, while the seventh Justice, **Stephen**, held that the state lacked **standing** to bring the action, and did not deal with the substance.

One approach to the resolution of the issue, which involved recourse to an implied 'nationhood' power, proved persuasive in subsequent cases. This approach was articulated most clearly in **Mason's** judgment. In his view, the central question was whether the executive power of the Commonwealth (section 61 of the Constitution) supported implementation of a program of this kind. He accepted that although, for the most part, federal executive power was coextensive with the heads of **Commonwealth legislative power**, it also included responsibilities that could be ascertained from the 'character and status of the Commonwealth as a national government'. Matters that he identified as potentially falling within the nationhood power thus understood included scientific research and inquiries in relation to public health. In his view, however, the Australian Assistance Plan did not fall within the power. The nationhood power did not support action by the Commonwealth merely because it was more convenient for the Commonwealth, rather than the states, to act.

The nationhood power has some potential to undermine the division of power between the Commonwealth and the states. That potential in turn depends on the extent to which the executive power to act for implied national purposes can be translated into legislative power as well. At the very least, this is possible through reliance on the express incidental power in section 51(xxxix) of the Constitution, to legislate with respect to matters incidental to the execution of power vested by the Constitution in the government of the Commonwealth. In *Davis v Commonwealth* (1988), three Justices—Mason, **Deane**, and **Gaudron**—were prepared to accept that, in appropriate circumstances, the Parliament might directly exercise an implied nationhood legislative power. In doing so, they invoked the earlier line of authority dealing with protection against insurrection. **Wilson** and **Dawson** expressly disagreed with this view, however. As matters stand at the beginning of the twenty-first century, there is no acknowledged authority of the Parliament to legislate by reference to nationhood, other than as an incident to the executive power or for limited security purposes. The issue was avoided in the *Tasmanian Dam Case* (1983), where the Court upheld the validity of the challenged legislation by reference to other, express, legislative powers.

Even the combination of the nationhood power with the express incidental power has some capacity to undermine the federal division of power. Possibly for this reason, the Court has limited its scope in various ways. Most notably, it has been said (by Mason, Deane, and Gaudron in *Davis*) that Commonwealth action is more likely to be supported by reference to nationhood where there is no likely competition with state power. This was the case in relation to the establishment of an Authority to commemorate the bicentennial of European settlement, which was in issue in *Davis*.

The incidental power may also have other limitations that affect the nationhood power in practice. *Davis* itself showed that the incidental power may be vulnerable where it is used in a way that affects **common law** rights, indicating that the limits of the power have been exceeded—a conception that was extended in *Nationwide News v Wills* (1992) (see *Free Speech Cases*). In *Davis*, **Brennan** also suggested that the power could not be used to create offences, save where this was necessary to protect the effective execution of executive power. Similarly, in the *Tasmanian Dam Case*, Wilson had suggested that any resort to a 'nationhood' power could not be 'coercive', while Deane had implied that the power was limited to 'the protection, preservation or promotion' of 'particular physical **property** or artistic, intellectual, scientific or sporting achievement'—in short, to what Brennan in *Davis* called 'an essentially facultative function'.

At the beginning of the twenty-first century, at least one important question about the use that may be made of the nationhood power remained unanswered. It is the extent to which the power authorises the Commonwealth to enter into agreements with the states on subjects not otherwise within Commonwealth power. Assuming that such agreements fall within the power, there is a connected question whether the Commonwealth Parliament may rely on the express incidental power to authorise or require Commonwealth agencies to exercise state power for the purposes of the agreement. These questions were left unanswered in *R v Hughes* (2000), where the challenge to the authority of the Commonwealth Director of Public Prosecutions was able to be resolved by reference to a substantive head of power. If and when an answer is given, it will be significant for the operation of intergovernmental cooperative schemes that rely on shared administration.

CHERYL SAUNDERS

Native title. In *Mabo* (1992), the High Court recognised that some of the plaintiffs held native title over land on the Murray Islands in the Torres Strait. The decision was both radical and conservative. It was radical in the sense that, in order to recognise the title held by the plaintiffs, the Court abandoned the legal fiction, which had gradually come to be relied upon in the colony, that when the British monarch acquired **sovereignty** over Australia the land was *terra nullius* (land empty of law—not necessarily of people). It was conservative in that it essentially preserved the status quo: native title survived only over those lands where it had not been extinguished by the grant of inconsistent interests. The Court also held (by a 4:3 majority) that there was no basis for compensation where native title had been extinguished before the passage of the *Racial Discrimination Act* 1975 (Cth). The Court found that, consistently with basic **common law** rules—the 'skeleton of principle'—native title could be defined as the interest in land held by people who had descended from the original inhabitants, and who, 'so far as practicable', had maintained the laws and customs which connected them to that land. Even where these two conditions were satisfied, it could only exist where no other interest adverse to its survival had been created.

Since the acquisition of sovereignty over Australia by the British Crown and the **reception of English law** in the colony, colonial judges had wrestled from time to time with the basis upon which the law empowered them to deal with **Aboriginal people** brought before them, almost always as defendants (see, for example, *R v Ballard* (1829); *R v Bonjon* (1841)). The *Mabo* decision resolved this dilemma by finding within the common law an ancient mechanism of general application where sovereignty was acquired by the British Crown (or indeed by other European colonial powers): that local law survived except where it was inconsistent with the law of the new sovereign, in which case the incoming law prevailed over the local law to the extent of the inconsistency. The decision clarified the distinction between sovereignty and interests in land; it involved a significant statement about how tenures are created and how they can coexist with interests that do not derive from the devolution of power from the Crown.

After *Mabo*, it was possible for the courts to recognise that indigenous law may survive, continuing to bind the people who maintain it according to its own attributes, although subject, where there is any inconsistency, to the laws made by the Australian sovereign. The Court made it clear that the *content* of the indigenous law is outside the cognisance of the common law. What the Court described in *Mabo* was the common law mechanism that allowed for the recognition of indigenous laws. It said nothing about the nature or incidents of native title, which lie only within the knowledge of the people observing and keeping the local law and custom.

In *Mabo*, the Court departed from its earlier, tacit confirmation of *terra nullius* as the basis for the acquisition of sovereignty in *Coe v Commonwealth (No 1)* (1979)—although the powerful **dissenting judgments** of **Jacobs** and **Murphy** in that case had foreshadowed the resolution found in *Mabo*. Other indications of the path the Court would take had emerged in *Mabo (No 1)* (1988), where Queensland legislation purporting to extinguish any traditional rights that might have survived annexation of the islands was held to be invalid because of the protection afforded by section 10 of the Racial Discrimination Act. The plaintiffs in *Mabo* avoided the sovereignty issue, although the Court felt it necessary to reiterate that the acquisition of sovereignty by the British Crown was not municipally **justiciable**. It has consistently done so since *Mabo* when Aboriginal applicants, relying on the recognition of native title, have sought to reintroduce arguments that challenge the acquisition of sovereignty (see *Coe v Commonwealth (No 2)* (1993); *Walker v NSW* (1994); *Thorpe v Commonwealth (No 3)* (1997)).

Since the *Mabo* decision, the Court has had a limited number of opportunities to further develop the jurisprudence of native title in Australia. Like *Mabo* itself, several of the later decisions have also required examination of the fundamental principles on which the common law and the Constitution are founded.

In the *Native Title Act Case* (1995), the Court held not only that the *Native Title Act* 1993 (Cth) was valid, but that the rival state legislation, the *Land (Titles and Traditional Usage) Act* 1993 (WA), was invalid or ineffectual. The state Act had purported to work initially by extinguishing all native title in WA—thus wholly negating the common law as declared in *Mabo*—and by then replacing each title thus extinguished with statutory 'rights of traditional usage', equivalent in principle to those recognised by *Mabo*, but subject to specific statutory modifications. The High Court rejected this solution because, when the modified statutory rights thus conceded to indigenous peoples were compared with the equivalent rights of non-indigenous **property** holders, the indigenous rights were consistently more limited. Thus, the WA Act was **inconsistent** with the Racial Discrimination Act.

In this context, the Court further explored the principles underpinning the vesting of title to land in the Crown, and the circumstances in which extinguishment will occur. The Court held that where legislation had been passed creating interests in land, it must express a clear and plain intention to extinguish native title before such an effect would be presumed. The Court also held that the Commonwealth's Native Title Act could not, as it had purported to do, declare the common law to have 'the force of a law of the Commonwealth'. By this declaration, the Parliament had attempted to elevate the *Mabo* decision to the status of 'a law of the Commonwealth', so that any inconsistency with *Mabo* in subsequent state legislation would render that legislation inoperative under section 109 of the Constitution. The High Court held that this was not possible, primarily because the provision 'attempts to confer legislative power upon the judicial branch of government. That attempt must fail either because the Parliament cannot exercise the powers of the Courts or because the Courts cannot exercise the powers of the Parliament'.

The development of Australia's native title jurisprudence is taking a distinctive line, which, although referable to North American (both Canadian and US) and NZ jurisprudence, is developing its own characteristics. The Court has found that interests in land that are less than exclusive possession may coexist with native title (*Wik* (1996)). However, it has also found that native title is extinguished for all time by the grant of an interest that confers exclusive possession (*Fejo v Northern Territory* (1998)). This differs from the approach of the Canadian Supreme Court, which assumes that although native title will be burdened to the extent of the inconsistency, it may revive once the burdening interest ceases (*Delgamuukw v British Columbia* (1997)). The Canadian courts have developed a three-stage test for extinguishment requiring, first, a clear and plain expression of parliamentary intention to bring about extinguishment; secondly, a legislatively authorised act which demonstrates the exercise of permanent adverse possession; and thirdly, the actual use of the land by the holder of the tenure in a way that is permanently inconsistent with the continued existence of aboriginal title rather than its mere suspension. This approach has been distinguished by the High Court (for example, by **Gummow** in *Wik* and by **Kirby** in *Fejo*), in part because of constitutional differences between the jurisdictions.

There are many unresolved questions about the relationship of native title to the legal system within which it is now recognised. One analytical perspective asks whether native title is a relationship, of the fullest kind capable of recognition by the non-indigenous legal system, between indigenous peoples and the land. Seen from this perspective, native title will be diminished only to the extent of the creation of adverse interests. The other perspective regards native title as akin to a bundle of rights, each of which must be demonstrated to have survived. The High Court has thus far avoided being drawn into choosing between these perspectives; instead, it has returned to the issue of consistency of interests as its criterion of whether native title survives, but without commenting on its attributes.

The difference between these approaches may be decisive when different stakeholders seek clarification of whether and to what extent interests coexist with native title. Knowing the attributes of the native title held in a particular area will be important where future acts in that area are proposed. The attributes of the title will be significant, for example, in determining who can be a party to an agreement that a future act may be done, or to proceedings to determine whether native title exists. The problem may also arise when compensation for extinguishment is sought. Cases currently on appeal to the High Court—*Commonwealth v Yarmirr* (1999) and *WA v Ward* (2000)—may provide guidance in this area.

Yanner v Eaton (1999) provided the Court with an opportunity to distinguish between regulation and extinguishment of native title by reference to the test to be applied to executive and parliamentary acts, requiring a clear and plain intention to burden native title. The appellant, a Gangadilla tribesman in far-north Queensland, was prosecuted under the *Fauna Conservation Act* 1974 (Qld) for killing two juvenile crocodiles. He pleaded that he had been exercising traditional hunting and fishing rights under tribal law, and that the taking of juvenile rather than adult crocodiles had tribal totemic significance. The High Court held that the traditional rights thus asserted were protected as 'native title rights and interests' under the Native Title Act, and that the prosecution had been rightly dismissed. In *Yanner*, as in *Mabo*, the Court set out its understanding of a fundamental concept underpinning the common law. In this case, the concept of property as a legal relationship to an object, rather than an attribute of the object, appears to have influenced the Court.

Another question still not conclusively determined is whether the Crown has a **fiduciary obligation** towards Aboriginal people. This question was the subject of consideration by **Toohey** in *Mabo (No 2)* and *Wik*, and by Kirby in *Thorpe*. The lack of resolution of this question is a further point of departure between the High Court and the North American jurisdictions. In both the USA and Canada, the courts have held that governments owed fiduciary duties to indigenous peoples with respect to the creation of interests in their lands. In the **United States Supreme Court**, the existence of such a duty had been powerfully asserted by Chief Justice John Marshall in the 1830s; it has since been reaffirmed in *US v Mitchell* (1983). In Canada, the decisions in *Guerin v The Queen* (1984) and *R v Sparrow* (1990) have established that a fiduciary duty existed with respect to the lands of the aboriginal peoples.

Since *Mabo*, the High Court has focused very precisely on the facts of each case before it. It has reviewed fundamental common law principles on several occasions, guided always by whether or not the interests held under the two systems can coexist. The variety of contexts in which native title now arises for consideration will gradually provide opportunities for the Court to elaborate the distinctive nature of native title in Australia.

SUSAN PHILLIPS

Further Reading

Australian Institute of Aboriginal and Torres Strait Islander Studies, Native Title Research Unit, Native Title Issues Papers, and *Native Title Newsletter* (www.aiatsis.gov.au/)

Australian Research Council Collaborative Research Project on Governance Structures for Indigenous Australians on and off Native Title Lands, *Discussion Papers* (www.austlii.edu.au/au/special/rsjproject/rsjlibrary/arccrp/index.html)

Richard Bartlett, *Native Title in Australia* (2000)

State Library of NSW, Legal Information Access Centre, *Native Title* (Hot Topic 27, June 2000 or later update) (www.slnsw.gov.au/liac/hothead.htm)

Natural justice is among the oldest and most renowned phrases in English public law. At base, it is a doctrine of the **common law** stipulating two procedures to be observed in administrative decision making in the absence of explicit legislative displacement. One is the hearing rule—*audi alteram partem* (hear the other side)—which requires that a person be told the case to be met, and be heard in reply, before a decision is made depriving that person of an existing legal right, interest, or expectation. The other is the bias rule—*nemo debet esse judex in propria sua causa* (no one can be judge in his own cause)—which **disqualifies** a decision maker as to whom there is a reasonable apprehension of bias

arising from a conflict of interest, partiality, prejudgment, or something similar. A breach of either rule causes the affected decision or proceeding to be invalid.

Natural justice is a doctrine of 'procedural fairness'—an alternative phrase more commonly used nowadays, principally at the suggestion of **Mason** in *Kioa v West* (1985). However, to relegate the doctrine to the realm of procedural law is to understate its importance to **administrative law** and government. It is, in essence, a code of justice for tempering and civilising the administrative process, formulated by the judiciary and read into the powers that are conferred on government officials to impinge on the lives and fortunes of others. The legislative intention to exclude natural justice 'is not to be assumed nor is it to be spelled out from indirect references, uncertain inferences or equivocal considerations … [but] must satisfactorily appear from express words of plain intendment' (*Commissioner of Police v Tanos* (1958)).

The basic features of the doctrine—its common law origin, adaptability, and undefined boundaries—make it a legal chameleon. It straddles the divide between legislative and **judicial power**, between executive discretion and judicial **values**. To what government decisions should natural justice apply? What kind of hearing should be given? Has it been displaced by contrary legislative intent? What constitutes apprehended bias? The judicial answers to those questions define the meaning of natural justice and, in the process, delineate the boundary between judicial, executive, and legislative power. Unsurprisingly, many High Court decisions on natural justice have broader appeal as seminal pronouncements on administrative law and the scope of **judicial review** of executive action.

The early natural justice decisions of the Court, though heavy with the language of fundamental justice, dealt mostly with the protection of business and **property** interests. A government agency could not, it was held, exercise power to demolish a building, restrict building rights, or close a restaurant without giving prior notice to the proprietor and affording an opportunity to be heard in reply (*Municipal Council of Sydney v Harris* (1912); *Delta Properties v Brisbane City Council* (1955); *Tanos*). It was similarly accepted that an administrative tribunal adjudicating pension rights or taxation claims must observe natural justice—though not, it was emphasised, in the formal manner of a court (*R v War Pensions Entitlement Appeal Tribunal; Ex parte Bott* (1933); *Mobil Oil v FCT* (1963)).

The constrained influence or operation of natural justice during this period is illustrated by decisions that denied its operation. Thus, an obligation to provide a hearing did not apply to a government decision to terminate a contract to provide shipping services to the Commonwealth (*Boucaut Bay v Commonwealth* (1927)), to a declaration of wardship against **Aboriginal people** (*Namatjira v Raabe* (1959)), to the preparation of an adverse investigation report on a company's affairs (*Testro Bros v Tait* (1963)), or to a decision to deport an unlawful immigrant (*R v MacKellar; Ex parte Ratu* (1977)).

The platform for extending natural justice rights was initially laid by a **House of Lords** decision, *Ridge v Baldwin* (1963), declaring invalid a decision to dismiss a police constable for suspected corruption without first affording him a hearing. The significance of the decision lay in its insistence that natural justice applies generally to administrative decisions that affect individual rights, and not only where a procedure of a judicial nature had already been created by legislation. The importance of the decision was quickly acknowledged in Australia, **Barwick** expressing 'entire agreement' in *Banks v Transport Regulation Board (Vic)* (1968) (see also *Heatley v Tasmanian Racing and Gaming Commission* (1977)).

Judicial moves to extend rights of natural justice in Australia coincided with a growing parliamentary interest in administrative law reform. A pivotal event was the report in 1971 of the Commonwealth Administrative Review Committee (of which Mason was a member, while Commonwealth **Solicitor-General**). The report's implementation gave rise to the Administrative Appeals Tribunal (1975), the Commonwealth Ombudsman (1976), the *Administrative Decisions (Judicial Review) Act* 1977 (Cth), and a general statutory right to written reasons for administrative decisions.

The tide of judicial innovation in this era included some seminal natural justice cases. *FAI Insurances v Winneke* (1982) was significant on two counts: the Court held that an obligation to observe natural justice applied to a decision of the Governor-in-Council; and it did so because the decision—to refuse annual renewal of a **workers' compensation** insurance licence—impinged on the licensee's **legitimate expectation** of renewal. *Kioa v West*, another significant decision, reversed an established line of authority in holding that a hearing should ordinarily be given before deportation is ordered. The protection against deportation was taken a step further in *Haoucher v Minister for Immigration* (1990), the Court holding that the Minister, before rejecting a recommendation of the Administrative Appeals Tribunal against deportation, must first give a further hearing to the person in addition to that already given by the Tribunal.

The interests thought worthy of natural justice protection were now conceived broadly. In *Annetts v McCann* (1990), the parents of two boys who had perished in the desert in WA were granted a right to full participation in the coronial inquest, in line with a principle that natural justice should apply to any power conferred 'upon a public official to destroy, defeat or prejudice a person's rights, interests or legitimate expectations'. Business reputation was protected in *Ainsworth v Criminal Justice Commission* (1992) and *Johns v Australian Securities Commission* (1993), both cases requiring that a hearing be given to a company officer before information damaging to his business affairs was passed from one agency of government to another. A less tangible interest—the expectation held by all Australians that government decision makers should decide consistently with Australia's international obligations—was recognised in **Teoh's Case** (1995).

It was acknowledged that there were special situations in which natural justice would not apply. The principle that natural justice could be excluded by the legislature was applied in *Twist v Randwick Municipal Council* (1976) to a housing demolition decision that was subject to a full right of appeal to a court. In *Bread Manufacturers of NSW v Evans* (1981), the Court held that a decision by a State Prices Commission to set the maximum selling price of bread affected the whole community—consumers, sellers, and manufac-

turers—and accordingly, there was no obligation to give special hearing rights to manufacturers above and beyond those stipulated by statute. In *Coutts v Commonwealth* (1985), the dismissal of an officer of the armed forces was held to be a dismissal from an appointment enjoyed 'at the pleasure of the Crown, an appointment which was liable to be terminated at any time for good or bad reason or for none'. Finally, in *SA v O'Shea* (1987) the Court held that the Governor-in-Council did not have to provide a hearing before making an indefinite detention order against a person convicted of repeated paedophile offences. The factors emphasised by the Court (though without unanimity on any point) were the hearing earlier given to O'Shea by the parole board, the public interest orientation of the Governor's decision to protect the community welfare, and the involvement of the Cabinet in preparing a recommendation to the Governor.

Despite those restrictions, the current position is that an obligation to observe natural justice presumptively applies to most executive decision making. Often the more important question is what is required to satisfy the obligation—a point emphasised in *Kioa*. The guiding principle, articulated plainly by **Kitto** in *Mobil Oil v FCT*, is that decision making must be procedurally fair, the detailed content of the obligation depending upon the circumstances of the individual case and the statutory framework being administered (see also *National Companies and Securities Commission v News Corporation* (1984)). Usually an exchange of letters or submissions is adequate, without the need for oral hearings, legal representation or cross-examination. If any standard is paramount it is the need for full and prior disclosure of 'the critical issue or factor on which the administrative decision is likely to turn', and especially for disclosure of 'adverse information that is credible, relevant and significant to the decision to be made' (respectively, Mason and **Brennan** in *Kioa*). By contrast, natural justice does not impose an obligation to provide reasons *after* a decision has been made (*Public Service Board (NSW) v Osmond* (1986)).

The rule against bias has not engaged the Court's attention as often as the hearing rule, nor have there been the same shifts in its meaning and operation. The most frequent issue is whether the comments or demeanour of a court or tribunal indicated prejudgment of the issue to be decided. In that as in other areas, the test applied is whether the circumstances would excite a 'reasonable apprehension or suspicion' of bias or prejudice in 'the ordinary reasonable member of the public' (*Webb v The Queen* (1994)). The test has a flexible content, adjusting to the circumstances of each case and the nature of the decision maker.

The Court, though continually stressing the importance of maintaining public confidence in the integrity and impartiality of judicial and administrative processes (*Webb*; *Ebner v Official Trustee* (2000)), has been robust in applying the bias rule. Adjudicators are encouraged to make known their preliminary thoughts or views (*Vakauta v Kelly* (1989)). Prior engagement with an issue or the parties to a dispute will not of itself disqualify a person (*R v Commonwealth Conciliation and Arbitration Commission; Ex parte Angliss Group* (1969); *Re Polites; Ex parte Hoyts Corporation* (1991)). A judge can own shares in a public company that is a party to litigation before the judge, provided the value of the shares will not be affected by the decision (*Ebner*). There is also guarded support for a principle of necessity where there is no alternative decision maker practically available (*Laws v Australian Broadcasting Tribunal* (1990); *Ebner*).

What of the future of natural justice? Will it retain its provisional status, always subject to legislative displacement, albeit only by words of unambiguous meaning? There are *obiter dicta* suggesting that it would be inconsistent with the separation of judicial power in Chapter III of the Constitution for Parliament to require a federal court to proceed in breach of natural justice (**Leeth v Commonwealth** (1992); *Ebner*). As to executive power, it has been suggested that the original **jurisdiction** of the Court to grant a remedy under section 75(v) of the Constitution to restrain unlawful Commonwealth action embodies some substantive meaning as to what is unlawful (*Abebe v Commonwealth* (1999); *Re Refugee Review Tribunal; Ex parte Aala* (2000)). Perhaps the bias rule could be anchored in section 75(v), on the premise that it would be inconsistent with the spirit of that section for Parliament to authorise a decision maker to proceed in bad faith, with a closed mind, or in a spirit of prejudice. Could it also be said that the hearing rule, hallowed and shaped by the Court for a century as a principle of fundamental justice, is a minimum condition for the lawful exercise of Commonwealth executive power?

JOHN MCMILLAN

Further Reading
Mark Aronson and Bruce Dyer, *Judicial Review of Administrative Action* (2nd edn 2000)

Natural law has been a recurrent idea in **jurisprudence** throughout the history of Western thought. Assertion and denial of its presence as an immanent foundation for human law, and competing views of its content and of its relationship to human law, have been the subject of endless debate. For its adherents, natural law is the ultimate source of the validity and content not only of a legal system as a whole, but also of its particular laws and judicial decisions. It therefore provides a moral standpoint from which judicial **decision making** may be evaluated.

The basic premise underlying all natural law theories is that there exists a necessary relationship between law and morality. In this relationship, moral **values** provide the criteria for evaluating whether a particular law is a 'good' law. This evaluation determines whether a law is worthy of obedience by the community at large. In this way, law's validity is made to depend on conformity to minimum moral requirements, and not just on factors internal to the legal system itself, as postulated by **positivism**.

Accordingly, while some positivists limit their analysis of law and legal reasoning to what the law *is* as determined by **authoritative** sources, natural lawyers broaden the scope of the analysis: in their view, questions about what the law *ought to be* are not merely of moral or political interest, but provide an essential basis for judgments about the identification and validity of 'law'. They argue that objective human values should be reflected in institutional and personal decision making, which are shaped by and (in some natural law theories) may also help to shape those values. These values include ultimate or absolute values such as respect for life,

treating people with fairness and justice, doing good rather than evil, and so on. For natural lawyers, these values should underlie the legal system and its institutions as a whole and should also be reflected in the detailed content of its rules, particularly its **common law** rules. Indeed, some values, such as fairness and justice, may include both procedural and substantive components that the legal system is uniquely capable of respecting and delivering (see **Form and substance**).

There are times when the High Court makes value judgments with both legal and moral dimensions because of the facts of a particular case. This occured, for example, in *Marion's Case* (1992) (dealing with issues of human dignity, bodily integrity, and personal inviolability in relation to the legally sanctioned sterilisation of an intellectually disabled young woman); *R v L* (1991) (the landmark 'rape in marriage' case, where the Court rejected the idea that marriage means that a woman automatically gives irrevocable consent to **sex** with her husband); *A-G (Qld); Ex rel Kerr v T* (1983) (on whether a biological father has a legal right to an injunction to prevent abortion of an unborn child); *Mabo* (1992) (rejecting the *terra nullius* doctrine, which denied legal recognition of the **native title** rights of **Aboriginal peoples** in Australia, as inconsistent with the contemporary values of the Australian people); and even *Green v The Queen* (1997) (on whether a homosexual advance is an understandable basis for an ordinary person losing self-control to the point of killing someone; see **Sexual preference**). Regardless of their particular outcomes, all of these examples involve consideration of fundamental human values such as respect for life and for human dignity. Similarly, legislation promoting human rights and prohibiting **discrimination** may be viewed from a natural law perspective as recognising the existence and importance of fundamental human values underlying Australia's legal system and laws—though, in contrast to the examples given above, the Court has been less inclined to confront the underlying moral issues directly when addressing the legal issues arising from such legislation (see **Feminism; Inconsistency between Commonwealth and state laws**).

John Finnis, in his landmark work *Natural Law and Natural Rights* (1980), has summarised the fundamental nature and operation of natural law principles in the following way:

> What are *principles of natural law*? ... There is: (i) a set of basic practical principles which indicate the basic forms of human flourishing as goods to be pursued and realised, and which are in one way or another used by everyone who considers what to do, however unsound his conclusions; and (ii) a set of basic methodological requirements of practical **reasonableness** (itself one of the basic forms of human flourishing) which distinguish sound from unsound practical thinking and which, when all brought to bear, provide the criteria for distinguishing between acts that (always or in particular circumstances) are reasonable-all-things-considered (and not merely relative-to-a-particular-purpose) and acts that are unreasonable-all-things-considered, ie between ways of acting that are morally right or morally wrong—thus enabling one to formulate (iii) a set of general moral standards ...The principles of natural law, thus understood, are traced out not only in moral philosophy or ethics and 'individual' conduct, but also in political philosophy and jurisprudence, in political action, adjudication, and

the life of the citizen. For those principles justify the exercise of authority in community.

On this view, principles of natural law may be apprehended by our recognition of basic human goods, which we value as desirable for their own sake and not because of any instrumental use or value. Among these basic goods, Finnis identifies 'life', 'knowledge', 'play', 'aesthetic experience', 'sociability' or 'friendship', 'religion' (in the sense of the relationship between the human and the divine), and 'practical reasonableness' (as a way of thinking about these basic human goods). Practical reason about what fulfils or enhances these basic human goods, and thereby maximises the conditions for human flourishing, then dictates the extent to which judicial decisions and legislative outcomes deserve moral criticism as 'good' or 'bad' results.

In judgments to which **Gummow** was a party in the **Federal Court**, Finnis's book has been cited in *Secretary, Department of Foreign Affairs v Styles* (1989) (for its understanding of reasonableness), and in *Tobacco Institute v Australian Federation of Consumer Organisations* (1988) (curiously, for its summation of WN Hohfeld's 'fundamental legal conceptions'). A repetition of the latter passage led to a derivative **citation** in the High Court in *Marks v GIO* (1998). In other High Court judgments, notably during the time of the **Mason Court**, there have sometimes been more direct allusions to natural law ideas. In *Kable v DPP* (1996), **Dawson** referred (though he stressed that he did so as a matter 'of academic or historical interest only') to the seventeenth-century suggestions 'that courts might invalidate Acts of Parliament which conflict with natural law or natural equity'. In *Australian Broadcasting Tribunal v Bond* (1990), **Deane** emphasised the need to avoid confusion of the technical requirements of '**natural justice**', embodying the 'common law requirements of fairness and detachment', with 'the jurisprudence of wider theological and civilian perceptions of natural law'. In both these instances, the point of the allusion to 'natural law' was to differentiate the Court's immediate task from anything that a natural law approach might have seemed to require. Yet in *Marion's Case*, natural law ideas inform much of the discussion about the 'rights' of parents, the 'natural human attribute' destroyed by irreversible sterilisation, and the responsibility of parents to care for **children** as a fundamental principle of natural law. In *Mabo*, there is much discussion of the extent to which common law doctrines and assumptions concerning land tenure should give way if they are repugnant to fundamental principles of justice concerning recognition of the unextinguished land rights of indigenous people, with particular emphasis on the recognition of the land rights of native inhabitants in the natural law tradition of English and European jurisprudence.

In other cases, the influence of natural law has been even more indirect. For example, in *Baker v Campbell* (1983), Deane referred to legal professional privilege as a fundamental principle of justice that 'represents some protection for a citizen—particularly the weak, the unintelligent and the ill-informed citizen—against the leviathan of the modern state'. A similar concern with what **Dixon** called 'deeper and more enduring conceptions of justice' can be seen in the shift away from formalism in the form and substance debate, and in the intermingling of principles of common law and **equity**. In 1994, **Mason** summarised these developments in a way that crystallised the influence of underlying natural law ideas in the Court's decisions:

> The ecclesiastical natural law foundations of equity, its concern with standards of conscience, fairness, **equality** and its protection of relationships of trust and confidence, as well as its discretionary approach to the grant of relief, stand in marked contrast to the more rigid formulae applied by the common law and equip it better to meet the needs of the type of liberal democratic society which has evolved in the twentieth century.

Overtones of the perennial battle between natural law jurisprudence and other schools of jurisprudential thought continue to echo both within the Court and in wider public debate in relation to judicial **activism** and the role of fundamental values in the law; in divergent interpretations of **express constitutional rights** and the possible enunciation of **implied constitutional rights**; and, more generally, in differences over how far **constitutional interpretation** should be guided by international human rights principles (or by what legal philosophers such as Ronald Dworkin call the 'moral' reading of constitutions). In a conference paper delivered in Darwin a few days after the handing down of the *Free Speech Cases* (1992), **Toohey** spoke explicitly of 'a revival of natural law jurisprudence'. Although he recognised the constraints Justices might feel about appealing directly to such a concept, he argued that 'a court which is established as guardian of a written constitution', and adjudicating upon 'an entrenched federal structure … conducive to the maintenance of the **rule of law**', might well adopt 'an approach to constitutional adjudication … [that] would over time articulate the content of the limits on power arising from fundamental common law liberties'.

Traditionally, in common law history, appeals to the underlying values and principles of the common law tradition have often been a surrogate for natural law ideas, particularly through the assumptions that the common law was the embodiment of reason, and that just solutions are often inherent in the facts of particular cases. Today, the surrogate for natural law ideas is more likely to be an appeal to **international law**, not only in the constitutional context but also in the continuing debates about whether the principles of international law should be incorporated in judge-made rules of **statutory interpretation** to preserve fundamental human rights from erosion by ambiguous legislation, and whether the Court in its **law-making role** should make normative use of fundamental values derived from international human rights law to develop Australian common law at the expense of settled **precedent**. In such contexts, some Justices—for example, **Gaudron** in *Teoh's Case* (1995)—have preferred to limit the influence of international human rights instruments to cases where they are 'in harmony with community values and expectations' in Australia: in that case, what was significant for her about the 1989 Convention on the Rights of the Child was that it 'gives expression to an important right valued by the Australian community', 'to a fundamental human right which is taken for granted by Australian society, in the sense that it is valued and respected here as in other civilised countries'. But that, too, is a conception that could readily be accommodated and appropriated by some theories of natural law.

BRYAN HORRIGAN

Further Reading
John Finnis, *Natural Law and Natural Rights* (1980)
Anthony Mason, 'The Place of Equity and Equitable Remedies in the Contemporary Common Law World' (1994) 110 *LQR* 238
John Toohey, 'A Government of Laws, and Not of Men?' (1993) 4 *PLR* 158

Nauru. The only country other than Australia from whose courts an appeal lies to the High Court is the Republic of Nauru.

Nauru was proclaimed a territory of Germany on 2 October 1888. By Article 119 of the Treaty of Versailles, Germany renounced all rights and titles in respect of 'her overseas possessions', including Nauru, in favour of the allied powers. On 2 July 1919, the governments of Great Britain, Australia, and NZ concluded an Agreement that provided for their joint administration of Nauru. Pursuant to various Instruments, these countries effectively administered Nauru until the Republic of Nauru was formed on 30 January 1968.

From 1967 to 1968, Commonwealth legislation regulating Nauruan affairs conferred **jurisdiction** upon the High Court of Australia to determine appeals from Nauruan courts (*Nauru Act* 1965 (Cth), section 54). This purported jurisdiction was, however, never exercised. Eight years after independence, on 6 September 1976, the governments of Nauru and Australia entered into an Agreement stating that certain appeals would lie from the Supreme Court of Nauru to the High Court of Australia.

Nauru's Constitution provides that the Nauruan Legislative Assembly may legislate for an appeal avenue from decisions of the Nauruan Supreme Court to 'a court of another country'. Pursuant to this Article and anticipating the 1976 Agreement, the Legislative Assembly in 1974 amended the *Appeals Act* 1972 (Nauru), to provide that appeals may lie to the High Court of Australia. However, as **Gummow** and **Hayne** pointed out in *Re Wakim* (1999), 'Nauruan law may provide for appeals to [the High Court] but if jurisdiction is validly conferred on the Court it is conferred by legislation of the Commonwealth Parliament, not by any Act of the Nauruan legislature'.

Although the Australian Constitution does not expressly confer jurisdiction upon the High Court to hear appeals from other nations, nor expressly empower the Australian Parliament to confer such jurisdiction, Parliament has purported to do so by the *Nauru (High Court Appeals) Act* 1976 (Cth). According to that Act, the High Court has since 21 March 1977 had jurisdiction to hear and determine appeals from the exercise by the Supreme Court of Nauru of its appellate and original jurisdiction in both criminal and civil cases. The Act provides that some appeals require the leave of the High Court, or in some instances the trial judge, before they may proceed. Others may proceed as of right. Order 70A of the **High Court Rules** governs procedural aspects of these appeals.

The source of the Commonwealth's power to confer this jurisdiction is unclear. If the jurisdiction conferred is original, Parliament may derive suitable power from section 51(xxix) or (xxx), and section 76(ii) of the Constitution, or perhaps from section 75(i). If, as seems more likely, the jurisdiction was intended to be appellate, it must fall within the description of the High Court's appellate jurisdiction in Chapter III of the Constitution (particularly section 73), in order to be a valid conferral. This appears doubtful. The theory—evident for example in the **Federal Court** decision of *WA Psychiatric Nurses Association v Australian Nursing Federation* (1991)—that the legislative power to confer jurisdiction might sometimes lie wholly outside Chapter III appears to have been discredited by the majority reasoning in *Re Wakim*.

Even if Commonwealth legislation does validly confer jurisdiction, there are provisions in the Nauruan legislation that purport to regulate the High Court's exercise of that jurisdiction, and which find no reflection in Commonwealth legislation. For example, section 42(1) provides that a party sentenced to imprisonment is not entitled to be present at the hearing (contrast *Ex parte Eastman* (1994)); and section 49(2) allows for the admission of evidence by the High Court in a criminal appeal (contrast *Mickelberg v The Queen* (1989)).

Since 1977, the High Court has twice heard and determined appeals from the Supreme Court of Nauru (*DPP (Nauru) v Fowler* (1984), which was brought pursuant to the leave of the High Court; and *Amoe v DPP (Nauru)* (1991), which was an appeal as of right). In neither case was the High Court's jurisdiction questioned.

DAVID O'BRIEN

Non-judicial functions. Section 71 of the Constitution states that the **judicial power** of the Commonwealth is vested in the High Court, federal courts created by the Commonwealth Parliament, and courts invested with federal jurisdiction. In this setting, the capacity of the High Court and its Justices to exercise non-judicial functions is limited by a constitutionally binding doctrine of **separation of powers** and by certain conventions or ethical practices traditionally associated with judicial office. The constraints imposed by these considerations have evolved over the life of the Court. However, the touchstone for the application of each has remained constant—the need to preserve judicial **independence** and impartiality—values that in turn underpin the **rule of law**.

In the early years of the High Court, a broad view of the non-judicial functions that could legitimately be discharged by members of the Court prevailed. Between 1905 and 1926, **O'Connor**, **Higgins**, and **Powers** each served as President of the Commonwealth Court of **Conciliation and Arbitration**. This was in accordance with section 12(1) of the *Commonwealth Conciliation and Arbitration Act* 1904 (Cth), which until 1926 required the President of the Arbitration Court to be chosen 'from among the Justices of the High Court'. Other members of the High Court, including **Isaacs** and **Starke**, served as Deputy Presidents. Despite its name and judicial trappings, the Court of Conciliation and Arbitration's functions were predominantly non-judicial, and included the quasi-legislative power of making industrial awards. Thus Higgins—President of the Arbitration Court from 1907 to 1921—played a significant and often controversial role in

Dixon, as Australian Minister to Washington 1942–44, presents US President Franklin D Roosevelt and his wife Eleanor with a copy of Captain Cook's journal

shaping Australian wages policy. Nonetheless, he continued to sit on High Court cases.

The involvement of early members of the High Court in non-judicial functions was not confined to the industrial domain. During **World War I**, both **Griffith** and **Rich** conducted Commonwealth Royal Commissions: in 1915, Rich examined allegations of maladministration at the Liverpool Military Camp, and in early 1918 Griffith reported upon the size of the Australian Imperial Force. Shortly after the war, Rich served as a delegate to the League of Nations. In addition, Griffith and **Barton**, while members of the High Court, provided advice to successive Governors-General on a range of constitutional issues. The frequency of these consultations between the Crown's representative and the nation's two most senior Justices suggests there was little doubt about the propriety of the practice at the time (see Don Markwell, 'Griffith, Barton and the Early Governor-Generals' (1999) 10 *PLR* 280). However, as Markwell points out, the practice appears not to have continued beyond the first few decades of federation—at least to any significant extent. The notable exception is **Barwick's** advice to John Kerr during the **dismissal of 1975**. But **Latham's** informal advisory activities were extensive (see Clem Lloyd, 'Not Peace But a Sword! The High Court Under JG Latham' (1987) 11 *Adel L Rev* 175), while **Dixon** on several occasions advised the Governors of Victoria and WA on constitutional matters, and discussed the Petrov Royal Commission with **Owen** during the latter's chairmanship of that Commission (see **Dixon diaries**).

In the early 1920s, the Commonwealth established the National Debt Commission. Under section 6 of the *National Debt Sinking Fund Act* 1923 (Cth), the members of the Commission included the **Chief Justice** of the High Court—a situation that remained unchanged until 1989. In other respects, however, the 1920s signalled a shift in approach. JM Bennett records that as Chief Justice, **Knox** declined at least four federal government requests to supply a Justice to conduct a

Royal Commission. Later requests were also turned down, leading Dixon to comment in 1955 that the Court 'has always, with only one very trifling exception during the war of 1914–1918, maintained the position that its judges ought not to be Royal Commissioners'. There is no evidence that the High Court has departed from this view. Thus, although members of other federal courts have conducted Royal Commissions, notably in the 1970s and 1980s, Griffith is the last High Court Justice to have assisted the government in this way.

Perhaps surprisingly, the Court's approach to Royal Commissions in the 1920s and 1930s did not prevent individual members of the High Court undertaking a range of executive functions during **World War II**. In an extraordinary example of the deployment of Justices outside the courtroom, Latham served in 1940–41 as Australian Minister in Japan, and Dixon between 1942–44 as Australian Minister in the USA. During the war, Dixon also served on a number of non-judicial bodies such as the Central Wool Committee and the Allied Consultative Shipping Council. **McTiernan** was appointed by the federal government to inquire into a controversy over aircraft production.

The participation of Latham, Dixon, and McTiernan in these activities must be understood in the context of the crisis of 1939–45. A decade on, in less turbulent times, Dixon offered a surprisingly personal account of his involvement in 'other work'. He confessed that initially he had felt 'very depressed' about the outcome of the war:

> In those conditions, feeling very restless indeed and finding it difficult to accommodate myself to sitting on the Bench throughout the war, I agreed to do other work. Looking back from this point of view, I am not sure that it was right. I do not wish it to be thought that, looking in retrospect, I altogether approve of what I myself did.

Nonetheless, in 1950 Dixon travelled to South Asia to mediate, on behalf of the UN, between India and Pakistan in relation to Kashmir. He met with the Prime Ministers of both countries and produced a report on the issue.

In more recent decades (and putting aside the statutory anomaly of the Chief Justice's membership of the National Debt Commission), members of the High Court have abstained from involvement in legislative and executive functions, suggesting the consolidation of a convention that High Court Justices no longer engage in these types of activities (see Murray McInerney and Garrie Moloney, 'The Case Against' in Glenys Fraser (ed), *Judges as Royal Commissioners and Chairmen of Non-Judicial Tribunals* (1986) 32–33). This is in contrast to members of other federal courts, many of whom serve on federal administrative tribunals, including the Administrative Appeals Tribunal, the Australian Competition Tribunal, and the Copyright Tribunal (see, for example, **Federal Court of Australia**, *Annual Report 1999–2000* ch 1). The High Court's status, coupled with the special nature of its constitutional and appellate work, presumably accounts for this difference. Nonetheless, there are those who argue that it is today undesirable for any Australian **superior court** judge to engage in non-judicial work, and that in the interests of judicial independence and impartiality all judges should decline to participate in such activities.

In tandem with gradually tightening ethical restraints, the High Court, in an interesting reflection on its own recent practice, has now stated that the Constitution sets strict limits on the non-judicial functions that may validly be exercised by federal judges even in their personal capacity (see *Wilson v Minister for Aboriginal and Torres Strait Islander Affairs* (1996)). In particular, such functions must not be incompatible with judicial office. Although the leading judgment in *Wilson* did not comment directly on past use of federal judges in non-judicial roles, it recognised there had not always been strict compliance with the separation of powers. Thus, the historical examples of High Court Justices serving in non-judicial roles may today be regarded not only as contrary to convention, but, at least in some cases, as contrary to the positive commands of the Constitution.

An issue that has not been widely addressed is the extent to which High Court Justices can legitimately engage in extra-judicial activities that are not strictly legislative or executive in nature. Based on the recent practice of members of the Court, there seems to be more leeway here. For example, Barwick was successively President and Vice-President of the Australian Conservation Foundation (1965–70 and 1970–73 respectively). He was also Chancellor of Macquarie University (1967–78). **Wilson** served as Chancellor of Murdoch University and towards the end of his period on the Court became President of the Uniting Church of Australia. While on the Bench, **Dawson** was a member of the Council of the University of Melbourne (1976–86). He also served on the Australian Motor Sport Appeal Court (1974–87). **Kirby**, who joined the Court in 1996, was President of the International Commission of Jurists (1995–98).

Fiona Wheeler

Further Reading

JM Bennett, *Keystone of the Federal Arch* (1980)

AJ Brown, 'The Wig or the Sword? Separation of Powers and the Plight of the Australian Judge' (1992) 21 *FL Rev* 48

Fiona Wheeler, 'Federal Judges as Holders of Non-judicial Office' in Brian Opeskin and Fiona Wheeler (eds), *The Australian Federal Judicial System* (2000) 442

George Winterton, 'Judges as Royal Commissioners' (1987) 10 *UNSWLJ* 108

Northern Land Council Case (1981) is the foundation of the modern approach to **judicial review** of administrative action. Contrary to the theory in earlier case law, the Court held that a regulation made by a representative of the Crown was amenable to challenge on the ground that the representative had pursued a purpose not authorised by the empowering statute.

Some High Court decisions had already undermined the earlier law. In *Television Corporation v Commonwealth* (1963) and *Murphyores v Commonwealth* (1976), the Court had held that a ministerial discretion was reviewable—in *Murphyores* on the ground that the act was done for an improper purpose. In *Northern Land Council*, some judges reasoned that it made no sense to distinguish the position of a minister from that of a Crown representative, since when exercising statutory powers the latter acts upon the advice of the former. **Stephen** quoted **Latham** in the *Communist Party Case* (1951); he had

said that the opinion of the Queen's representative 'is really the opinion of the Government of the day'.

The *Northern Land Council Case* involved an unusual regulation made by the Administrator of the Northern Territory. The *Aboriginal Land Rights (Northern Territory) Act* 1976 (Cth) does not apply to 'land in a town', as defined in Northern Territory town planning laws. **Toohey**, as Land Rights Commissioner, had held that he could not hear a claim, because a regulation made by the Administrator had expanded the 'town' of Darwin from 142 km^2 to 4350 km^2. The High Court held that this was not decisive: even if the Administrator represented the Crown, the regulation could be challenged for ulterior motive or want of good faith. The matter was remitted to the Commissioner.

At this stage, the Northern Territory resisted the discovery of documents relating to the making of the regulations, on the ground that the documents were subject to legal professional privilege. However, Toohey's successor as Land Rights Commissioner, Justice William Kearney, ordered that the documents be produced, and the High Court upheld that order (see *A-G (NT) v Kearney* (1985)). The next Commissioner to hear the application—Justice Michael Maurice—was held by the **Federal Court** to be disqualified on the ground of apprehended bias (*R v Maurice; Ex parte A-G (NT)* (1987)). The fourth Commissioner, Justice Howard Olney, held that the regulations were invalid on the ground of improper purpose, a decision sustained by the Federal Court (*A-G (NT) v Olney* (1989)). The High Court refused **leave to appeal**.

After a lengthy inquiry in 1989 and 1990, Olney found that there were no traditional owners of the land, but in 1992 the Federal Court found that that this decision was vitiated by legal error (*Northern Land Council v Aboriginal Land Commissioner* (1992)) and remitted the matter to the Commissioner. The hearing was conducted by the new Commissioner, Justice Peter Gray, who in December 2000 recommended to the Minister that with some excision, the land claimed be granted to a land trust for the benefit of all **Aboriginal people** entitled by Aboriginal custom to the use or occupation of the land. Early in 2001, this decision was under appeal to the Federal Court. In the event that the decision stands, it will remain for the Minister to determine whether the land should be granted to a land trust. The Minister must take into account the detriment that a grant may occasion to others, including the government of the Northern Territory. At this stage, further consideration is likely to be given to the need to expand the boundaries of Darwin.

However, the original 1981 decision that the regulation redefining the 'town' of Darwin could be challenged for bad faith or ulterior motive had implications far beyond its significance for the particular claimants. Broadly, the decision rests on the principle stated by Stephen that, unless the Parliament has, acting constitutionally, excluded judicial review, the courts may review an exercise of a statutory power on all the grounds of review, whether the power be vested in a representative of the Crown, a minister, or some other person or body. But some Justices went further.

Wilson said that the matter raised 'a question of great importance to the relationship of the courts to the executive government'. The earlier case law needed review because:

the steadily expanding role of the State in recent decades provides increasing occasion for the individual citizen to feel aggrieved as the result of administrative action with a consequent need to ensure that the principles of **administrative law** relating to judicial review of such action remain sufficiently flexible to meet the requirements of justice without imposing unreasonable restraints on the freedom of government action.

Apart from the general principle stated by Stephen, the significance of the decision lies in the manner in which the Justices disposed of the justifications for judicial deference stated in the older case law.

A major influence had been the view that the scope for judicial review of decisions by ministers or by the Crown was qualified. **Isaacs** had declared in *Williamson v Ah On* (1926) that '**responsible Government** is the constitutional check on arbitrary administration'. In the *Communist Party Case*, **Williams** had said that, generally speaking, an unfettered discretion vested in a minister was 'a matter with which the courts are not concerned at all'. The Court rejected this premise of the older cases. **Mason** declared:

> the doctrine of ministerial responsibility is not in itself an adequate safeguard for the citizen whose rights are affected. This is now generally accepted and its acceptance underlies the comprehensive system of judicial review of administrative action which now prevails in Australia.

This reasoning may illustrate the occasionally symbiotic relationship between legislative and judicial reform of the **common law**. Mason's comment alludes to the reforms to Commonwealth **administrative law** made by the legislation creating the Ombudsman, the Administrative Appeals Tribunal, and the jurisdiction of the Federal Court under the *Administrative Decisions (Judicial Review) Act* 1977 (Cth). Mason had, prior to judicial **appointment**, played a role in such developments, and may well have been aware of the substantial progress made, by 1981, towards the enactment of a freedom of information law. One may speculate that some of the Justices were, without saying so, employing reasoning often summed up by the notion of the 'equity of a statute' to reform the common law. On the other hand, the reform of the case law achieved in *Sankey v Whitlam* (1978) had been a fillip to Parliament's progress on the freedom of information law.

Sankey v Whitlam was taken by the Court as reason to reject another premise of the case law overruled in *Northern Land Council*. **Dixon** had justified Crown immunity by saying (in the *Communist Party Case*) that 'the counsels of the Crown are secret'. Rejecting this, Mason said that 'the old rule does not conform to the modern notions of freedom of information and secrecy'. This reference to freedom of information was a signal, at least from Mason, that this notion, so opposed to the long tradition of government secrecy, was henceforth to be taken more seriously.

A third ground of justification for the older case law was that 'the courts should not substitute their views for those of the executive on matters of policy'. **Gibbs** said that while this was true, it did 'not mean that the courts cannot ensure that a statutory power is exercised only for the purpose for which

it is granted'. Wilson accepted that 'it is not for the courts to assume any responsibility for oversight of the policy expressed through the decisions of the executive government'. The Justices did not indicate, however, how a court was to draw the relevant line. Mason said that the question was whether 'the particular exercise of power is not susceptible of the review sought'. This restates the question, although it does suggest a factor to address in answering it. After the reform of the common law built on *Northern Land Council*, the question of the limits of judicial review remains to be adequately addressed by the High Court.

Murphy emphatically disagreed with the majority approach. He affirmed the older cases to the extent that 'inquiry by the judicial branch into the misuse of legislative powers (at least except where authorised by Parliament) is inconsistent with the **separation** of legislative and **judicial powers**'. He foresaw challenge to 'a multitude of laws so as to extend greatly the possibilities of conflict between the judicial and legislative branches'. It was preferable that 'misuse of legislative power may be dealt with by Parliament or by the electorate'. He did agree with the majority result, but on narrower statutory grounds. In *FAI Insurances v Winneke* (1982) and *Bread Manufacturers v Evans* (1981), he spelt out more clearly the difficulty with judicial review of decisions made collectively by politicians, and sought to have the Court take more seriously the role of ministers in administrative decision making. There is no doubt a reflection here of Murphy's experience as a minister and parliamentarian.

His general approach has not, however, been a significant influence on the Court. On the basis of the *Northern Land Council Case*, and the two companion cases just mentioned, the scope for judicial review of administrative action was transformed over the last decades of the twentieth century.

PETER BAYNE

Number of Justices. Section 71 of the Constitution provides that the High Court 'shall consist of a **Chief Justice**, and so many other Justices, not less than two, as the Parliament prescribes'. When the *Judiciary Act* (Cth) came into force in 1903, it made provision for the smallest Bench possible: three Justices. The government had originally intended that the Court comprise five Justices, but it yielded to opponents in Parliament who voiced concerns about the Court's cost and, indeed, whether there was yet a need for the Court at all (see **Establishment of Court**). The first **appointments** were made in October 1903: **Griffith** as Chief Justice, **Barton** and **O'Connor** as **puisne Justices**.

In 1906, the Justices made representations to Parliament to increase their number. The increase was said to be necessary because of the Court's heavy workload and its extensive itinerary. The number was increased to five in response to these concerns, but, as **Prime Minister** Alfred **Deakin** wrote anonymously in an English newspaper, 'above all things to add to [the Court's] dominance in constitutional questions and all interpretations of the Constitution'. Two additional appointments, **Isaacs** and **Higgins**, were made in October that year.

When O'Connor died in November 1912, **Attorney-General** WM Hughes rushed amending legislation through the Parliament to increase the number of Justices to seven,

505

allowing the government to make three appointments to the Court in its last few months of office. As had been done six years earlier, Hughes pointed to the Court's workload and its itinerary—which had taken it to 'every part of the continent' in that year—as reasons for appointing more Justices. He also argued that the Court 'should not be less numerous than the Courts appealed from' and the Supreme Court of NSW, he said, had six Justices (in fact, it had eight —and if this argument were applied today, the High Court would need more than 40 Justices). Further, Hughes pointed out, 'with seven Justices, it will be practicable for **business** of minor importance to hold two **Full Court** sittings at the same time in the different capitals'. The legislation was passed in 1912, and the three vacant positions were filled early the following year: **Gavan Duffy**, **Powers**, **Piddington** (briefly), and then **Rich**.

Powers retired from the Bench in July 1929; **Knox** retired in March 1930, and was replaced as Chief Justice by the senior puisne Justice (Isaacs). For reasons of economy, and because the Court's workload had decreased with the start of the **Depression**, these two positions were not immediately filled. They were filled only in December 1930, when **Evatt** and **McTiernan** were appointed at the instigation of the Labor caucus, despite the opposition of Prime Minister James Scullin and Attorney-General Frank Brennan, who were overseas at the time (see **Appointments that might have been**). When Isaacs retired one month later and the senior puisne Justice (Gavan Duffy) was made Chief Justice, the resulting vacancy was not filled. It remained unfilled and the Judiciary Act was amended in 1933, formally reducing the number of Justices to six.

The Court comprised six Justices until 1946, when the number provided in the Judiciary Act was changed back to seven and an additional appointment, **Webb**, was made. Cabinet had wanted to increase the size of the Court to nine, but Evatt, then Attorney-General, persuaded Cabinet to make it seven—an increase that was said to be justified by an increased workload and problems caused by decisions in which the Court was equally divided (see **Tied vote**). In 1980, provision for the number of Justices was removed from the Judiciary Act and made, instead, in the *High Court of Australia Act* 1979 (Cth).

The Court has comprised seven Justices since 1946. There have, however, been several gaps between appointments during that period—gaps of more than four months on two occasions: between **Dixon's** elevation to Chief Justice (upon the **retirement** of Latham) and **Taylor's** appointment in 1952, and between **Owen's** death and **Mason's** appointment in 1972.

The Advisory Committee on the Australian Judicial System, in its 1987 report to the Constitutional Commission, noted that the desirable number of Justices had been variously put at seven, eight, nine, and eleven. The Committee took the view that seven was satisfactory because 'the greater the number of Justices the greater would be the scope for divergence of views and the greater the difficulty in reaching a consensus'. This assumes the continuation of the practice of all available Justices sitting on important cases, particularly constitutional cases—a practice that is not strictly required. All that is required is that a sufficient number sit to comply with existing legislative requirements (assuming those requirements to be constitutionally valid: see **Separation of powers**). These requirements include section 23 of the Judiciary Act, which provides that at least three Justices must concur in a decision on a question affecting the constitutional powers of the Commonwealth, and section 21, which provides that appeals from Full Courts of **state Supreme Courts** must be heard by no fewer than three Justices (though in practice, that **jurisdiction** is usually exercised by five or more Justices). Section 21 also provides that applications for special **leave to appeal** may be heard by a single Justice or a Full Court; in practice, these are generally heard by either two or three Justices (see **Bench, composition of**).

The possibility of nine Justices (as in the **United States Supreme Court**) was allowed for in the design of the Court's **building** in **Canberra**. Increasing the total number of Justices to nine would increase the scope for several Benches to sit simultaneously so as to deal with an increased workload. However, the Court has defended its practice of assigning all available Justices to important cases on the ground that unsuccessful litigants should not be able to speculate that they might have fared better had the Bench been differently constituted.

JAMES POPPLE

Obiter dicta—*obiter* meaning 'by the way', and a *dictum* being something that is said—are observations made by judges, in the course of their judgments, which are not essential to the immediate decision but may nevertheless be influential as expressions of judicial opinion. The contrast is with the *ratio decidendi* of a case (the 'reason for deciding'), which refers to the proposition or propositions of law explicitly or implicitly relied upon as the basis for decision. Under the doctrine of **precedent**, a court *must* follow the *ratio decidendi* of an earlier decision by which it is bound, but is free to reject its *obiter dicta* or to treat them as merely persuasive.

Whether a statement is ratio or obiter is often itself debatable. The basic principle, as expressed by **Stephen** and **Jacobs** in *Li Chia Hsing v Rankin* (1978), is that 'anything which is said … beyond what is strictly necessary for a decision on the particular facts is necessarily *obiter dicta*'. By contrast, in *R v Cook; Ex parte C* (1985), **Gibbs** insisted that comments in *In the Marriage of Cormick* (1984) were 'a necessary part of the reasoning leading to the conclusion', and were therefore not merely obiter.

Even if it is clearly obiter, any explicit expression of judicial opinion should be considered once the issue arises for decision. In *Johnson v The Queen* (1976), when the Court decided that the onus of proof of provocation as a **criminal defence** rested wholly on the accused, contrary dicta in *Parker v The Queen*, in both the High Court (1963) and the **Privy Council** (1964), were rejected. Gibbs rejected them only 'after the most anxious consideration', observing: 'We are not bound by an expression of opinion in the Judicial Committee which is merely *obiter*, although we should of course give the greatest weight to any considered dictum of the Board.' In *De Jesus v The Queen* (1986), the failure of the trial judge and the WA Court of Appeal to consider some obiter observations in *Sutton v The Queen* (1984) was for **Dawson** a sufficient reason to grant special **leave to appeal**.

A court may sometimes think it appropriate to expatiate on questions that strictly do not arise for decision. The result may be an *obiter dictum* of a peculiarly authoritative kind. For example, the appeal to the Privy Council in the **Bank Nationalisation Case** (1949) was confined to the High Court's holding on section 92 of the Constitution (see **Interstate trade and commerce**); and the Privy Council declined jurisdiction lest it be drawn into other issues debarred to it as *inter se* questions. Yet their Lordships thought it 'right to

state their views' on the section 92 question, and did so in a massive and profoundly influential *obiter dictum*. Five years later, when their Lordships determined in *Hughes & Vale v NSW* (1954) that section 92 protected interstate road transport, the states were in turmoil. In *Hughes & Vale v NSW (No 2)* (1955), an initial attempt by NSW to devise a licensing and taxing system compatible with section 92 was held to be invalid. But five judges then offered elaborate suggestions for a taxing strategy that might be permissible; and in *Armstrong v Victoria (No 2)* (1957), those suggestions were applied. **Williams** conceded that they were only *obiter dicta*, but thought that since 'they were only expressed after careful consideration' and because the states 'were urgently in need of such guidance', they should be accepted 'as a correct statement of the law'. Even **Kitto**, who had disagreed with the earlier dicta, conceded that they were 'considered pronouncements', and obediently 'studied them with a desire to accept and apply any principle which I could see commanded the approval of a majority of the Court'.

Again, in *Strickland v Rocla Concrete Pipes* (1971), the High Court held that the intricate drafting of the *Trade Practices Act 1965* (Cth) was unconstitutional. Yet the judgments were mainly devoted to showing that a differently drafted enactment would be valid under the **corporations power** (section 51(xx) of the Constitution). In a paradoxical example of **overruling** by *obiter dictum*, the contrary decision in *Huddart Parker v Moorehead* (1909) was rejected as no longer correct. More recently, in *Sykes v Cleary* (1992), the Court held that the successful candidate in a by-election had been disqualified by section 44(iv) of the Constitution. That meant that a fresh election would be needed, in which the candidates who had not been elected were likely to stand again. Accordingly, the Court expressed its opinion that they, too, would be disqualified by a different provision in section 44.

In such cases, the obiter pronouncements are almost **advisory opinions**. At the least, the Court regards itself as having a kind of incidental power once it is seised of a **matter**.

By contrast, in the *Waanyi Case* (1996), where the Court had been expected to settle the controversial issue of whether the mere grant of a pastoral lease extinguished **native title**, the majority declined to do so. The ruling that the Native Title Tribunal had exceeded its powers by addressing that question was not only sufficient to dispose of the case, but had left the High Court with no jurisdictional footing from which to speak. Only **Kirby**, in dissent, thought an obiter answer to the question appropriate.

Some Justices are especially wary of obiter pronouncements on constitutional issues, maintaining that constitutional issues should not be reached at all if a non-constitutional ground is available, and even when reached, should be explored no further than the case requires. **Brennan** was a strong and consistent exponent of this approach. In *Actors and Announcers Equity v Fontana Films* (1982), he extolled

> the practice of this Court in interpreting the Constitution case by case, deciding only so much as is necessary to decide the case in hand … Hewing close to the issues raised by each case, the Court avoids the possibility of having its judgment applied to issues which were not envisaged in the arguments before it.

Such an approach reflects an awareness that the influence of *obiter dicta* may sometimes be profound. The obiter remarks of **Fullagar** in *Commonwealth v Bogle* (1953) were frequently relied on as helping to explain the *Cigamatic Case* (1962), until *Henderson's Case* (1997) took a different view of *Cigamatic*, and dismissed them as merely obiter. The inference drawn from *Cooper v Stuart* (1889) that the laws and entitlements of **Aboriginal peoples** had not survived European settlement was never more than obiter; yet, as **Deane** and **Gaudron** conceded in *Mabo* (1992), the accumulation of *obiter dicta* in that and other cases had acquired 'formidable' authority. When **Isaacs** excluded any effective guarantee of **jury trial** from section 80 of the Constitution (by saying in *R v Bernasconi* (1915) that 'if a given offence is not made triable on indictment at all, then sec 80 does not apply'), and when **Higgins** said in *R v Archdall and Roskruge* (1928) that although section 80 requires a jury 'if there be an indictment', there is 'nothing to compel procedure by indictment', they were speaking obiter. Yet, despite the formidable challenges by **Dixon** and **Evatt** in *R v Federal Court of Bankruptcy; Ex parte Lowenstein* (1938), and by Deane in *Kingswell v The Queen* (1985), the effect of their passing comments has been treated as settled law.

Thus, the Court has been ambivalent in its attitude to *obiter dicta*, sometimes treating them as authoritative and sometimes dismissing them as superfluous. The ambivalence is likely to continue, and underscores the breadth of the choices open to an appellate court in developing the law of the land.

TONY BLACKSHIELD

Occupiers' liability refers to the duty lying upon an occupier of land to take reasonable care for the safety of an entrant to the land from harm arising from the state of the land or structures on it. It is an aspect of **tort law** that the Court rationalised and simplified in a series of decisions in the 1980s. Prior to that simplification, the extent of the duty owed by the occupier generally depended on the characterisation of the injured party as falling into one or other of the recognised categories of entrant. In *Lipman v Clendinnen* (1932), **Dixon** identified five such categories—one who enters 'in the execution of an independent authority given by law'; one who enters in pursuance of a contract with the occupier; one who enters for purposes connected with the occupier's business (known as an invitee); one who enters

merely with the permission of the occupier or for a social purpose (described as a licensee); and a person who enters without the occupier's consent—a trespasser. In *Aiken v Kingborough Corporation* (1939), Dixon identified a sixth category: one who uses premises under the control of a public authority and enters those premises as of common right. At one end of the scale of liability to a trespasser, the occupier was originally liable only for injuries wilfully inflicted. At the other end of the scale, an occupier owed to a contractual entrant a duty described by **Windeyer** in *Voli v Inglewood Shire Council* (1963) as a duty to ensure that the premises were as safe as reasonable care and skill could make them.

The liability (or lack thereof) of an occupier vis-à-vis a trespasser underwent considerable development in the middle years of the twentieth century. In some English cases, the lot of a child trespasser had been ameliorated by classifying him or her as a licensee, especially if the occupier had placed on the land something that might be an allurement to a person of tender years. But in a trilogy of cases, *Thompson v Bankstown Corporation* (1953), *Rich v Commissioner for Railways (NSW)* (1959), and *Commissioner for Railways (NSW) v Cardy* (1960), the Court rationalised these earlier decisions by concluding that, as well as the special duty described above, the occupier might also owe to an entrant the general duty of care based on *Donoghue v Stevenson* (1932). Any development along these lines was, however, delayed by the decision in *Commissioner for Railways v Quinlan* (1964)—an appeal taken directly from the Full Supreme Court of NSW to the **Privy Council**. Their Lordships' opinion restored the earlier, draconian, rule that an occupier was liable to a trespasser only for injuries wilfully inflicted. This approach did not last for long. In *Cooper v Southern Portland Cement* (1972), the High Court, by an imaginative interpretation of *Quinlan*, went a long way towards restoring the principles enunciated in its earlier trilogy, and, on appeal, the Privy Council required of an occupier a duty, if not of reasonable care, then at least of 'common humanity' (*Southern Portland Cement v Cooper* (1973)). But a wholesale reformation of the law had to wait until the 1980s.

The first attempt at this reformation was made by some members of the Court in *Hackshaw v Shaw* (1984) and *Papatonakis v Australian Telecommunications Commission* (1985). That move culminated in the decision of the majority in *Australian Safeway Stores v Zaluzna* (1987) that any distinction between the so-called special duty resting on an occupier and the general duty imposed by *Donoghue v Stevenson* should be abandoned, and that the liability of an occupier of land or structures to any person entering thereon should be determined solely by the application of general principles of negligence. The new synthesis was urged primarily by **Deane** and resisted primarily by **Brennan**. The majority of the Court thus achieved a result that had been arrived at only by legislation in England, NZ, and four of the nine **common law** Provinces of Canada. Prior to the *Zaluzna* decision, legislation based on the English model had been passed in SA, Victoria, and WA. While the courts of those states still rely on that legislation, such reliance now seems unnecessary. The Australian Law Reform Commission, asked whether the law in the ACT relating to occupiers' liability was adequate and appropriate, concluded in 1988 that no legislative reform was necessary in the light of the *Zaluzna* decision.

The *Zaluzna* case has considerably simplified the law. Thus, in *Nagle v Rottnest Island Authority* (1993), it was accepted that the respondent's liability should be based on the application of ordinary principles of negligence, and not on the fact that the appellant was an entrant as of right onto land under the control of the Authority. But *Zaluzna* left some matters outstanding, and they have not always been clarified in later decisions. Pre-*Zaluzna*, an occupier might, in some ill-defined circumstances, have been liable to an invitee even though the danger had been created by an independent contractor employed by the occupier. The Court has not yet had the opportunity to decide whether an occupier now owes such a personal and non-delegable duty to invitees in all circumstances, or even to licensees or trespassers. One who, under the old law, was classified as a contractual entrant, was in all circumstances owed a personal and non-delegable duty. It may be that this rule has survived *Zaluzna*. In *Calin v Greater Union Organisation* (1991), although the question was not directly in issue, a majority of the Court said that 'it would not be right' to treat *Zaluzna* and its predecessors as **overruling** the cases establishing that non-delegable duty. And, if a person has entered premises in pursuance of a contract to which he or she is a party, the decision of the majority in *Astley v Austrust* (1999) now establishes that the occupier cannot seek to have the **damages** reduced on account of the entrant's contributory negligence.

JAMES DAVIS

Further Reading

Australian Law Reform Commission, *Occupiers' Liability*, Report No 42 (1988)

O'Connor, Richard Edward (*b* 4 August 1851; *d* 18 November 1912; Justice 1903–12) was born in Glebe, Sydney, the third son of Irish-born Richard O'Connor and Mary Ann, née Harnett. His father became a librarian of the NSW Legislative Council in 1843, clerk of the Legislative Assembly in 1856, Clerk of the Legislative Council in 1860, and in 1864 was designated as 'clerk of the parliaments'. Brought up to be a devout Roman Catholic, the young O'Connor was educated by the Benedictines at St Mary's College, Lyndhurst, the non-denominational Sydney Grammar School, and the University of Sydney, graduating BA in 1871 and MA in 1873. From boyhood, his closest friend was **Barton**.

While working as a copying clerk in the Legislative Council from 1871 to 1874, O'Connor frequented the Sydney School of Arts Debating Club. In 1874, he began to study law, and the following year read with Frederick Darley, later Chief Justice of NSW. O'Connor was admitted to the Bar on 15 June 1876. He 'devilled' for Darley for two years and eked out his income by law **reporting** and by contributing to various newspapers. From 1878 to 1883, he was Crown prosecutor for the Northern District and built up a successful practice, mainly in **common law** and in appellate matters, from his chambers in Wentworth Court, Sydney. On 30 October 1879, he married Sara Jane Hensleigh (*d* 1925) at St Joseph's Church, Delegate.

O'Connor was nominated to the Legislative Council on 30 December 1887. From 23 October 1891, he served as Minis-

Richard O'Connor, Justice 1903–12

ter for Justice, with the right of private practice, in George Dibbs's Protectionist Cabinet; he was also **Solicitor-General** (July to September 1893). Before taking office, O'Connor and Barton, the Attorney-General, had accepted briefs to act for George Proudfoot in litigation against the Railway Commissioners (who retained their own solicitor). The case dragged on, and in November 1893 the propriety of ministers of the Crown acting against a government agency (albeit a statutory authority) was questioned in Parliament. They immediately relinquished their briefs and, after a motion for adjournment was carried against them in the Legislative Assembly on 7 December, resigned their portfolios. The case was eventually settled. O'Connor travelled overseas in 1894, visiting Egypt, Italy, England, and Ireland. Returning invigorated and freed from the constraints of office, he took silk in 1896. From November 1898 to March 1899, he was an acting Supreme Court judge.

O'Connor had been a founder of the Australasian Federation League of NSW in 1893 and a delegate to the People's Federal Convention at Bathurst in 1896. The next year, he was elected to the Australasian Federal **Convention**. Like Barton, he had studied **constitutional law** and was familiar with the American, Canadian, and Swiss Constitutions. When the Convention met in Adelaide, O'Connor was elected to the constitutional and drafting committees. Anxious to preserve the checks and balances carefully embodied in the Constitution, he was the author of section 24, which by providing that the members of the House of Representatives would be 'as nearly as practicable, twice the number of senators' sought to preserve the 'strength and power of the Senate'.

The first draft Constitution Bill failed to achieve the necessary majority in NSW. After fruitlessly campaigning throughout the colony for its acceptance, O'Connor resigned from the Legislative Council on 22 July 1898 to contest (unsuccessfully) the Legislative Assembly seat of Young. In 1899, he campaigned less widely for the second referendum on the Constitution Bill, as he found that he 'had to stick to my business as it began to come back or I would have been in a disastrous plight', but he still managed to speak 'four or five nights a week' in Sydney. On Christmas Day 1900, Barton announced his Cabinet: O'Connor was vice-president of the Executive Council (an honorary portfolio). In March 1901, he was elected to the Senate at the top of the poll—the only Protectionist senator returned for NSW.

The first Barton ministry faced a hostile Senate and as government leader, O'Connor displayed hitherto unsuspected dexterity in managing three very stormy sessions without any major defeats. From the opening of Parliament, he discouraged the Senate from voting as the states' house and convinced the majority of members that it was their duty to bow to the wishes of the House of Representatives. His greatest achievement was steering the *Customs Tariff Act 1902* (Cth) through the Senate virtually unaltered. O'Connor's control was the more remarkable as he struggled to maintain his practice in Sydney between parliamentary sessions in Melbourne, but found there was no longer 'the same continuous stream that used to make my business so good'. The *Catholic Press* believed he had sacrificed an income of £4000 a year to accept office, and in June 1901 he reluctantly told Alfred **Deakin** that he could not continue without some remuneration. As the number of salaried ministers was limited by the Constitution, each agreed to contribute £200 a year to a fund for honorary ministers.

O'Connor's last major task in the Senate was the carriage of the *Judiciary Act* (1903), which **established** the High Court. In the House of Representatives, the Bill had been bitterly attacked as an unnecessary extravagance, and had been amended so as to reduce the **number of Justices** and remove **retirement** pensions (see **Remuneration of Justices**). O'Connor resigned his portfolio on 24 September and resigned from the Senate on 27 September. On 5 October, he and Barton were appointed to the High Court with **Griffith** as **Chief Justice**. The liberal-minded O'Connor brought to the Bench 'sound common sense'.

For three years, the Justices worked harmoniously. Griffith later claimed that his and O'Connor's 'minds ran … in similar grooves' perhaps due to 'our early training at our common University of Sydney'. The foundation Justices shared a balancing view of the Constitution, defending the states' legislative powers but at the same time devising the doctrine of 'implied immunity of instrumentalities' to prevent the states taxing Commonwealth officials (see **Intergovernmental immunities**). They jealously guarded the High Court's supremacy over the **Privy Council** on constitutional matters. In *Deakin v Webb* (1904), O'Connor forthrightly stated that it was the duty of the High Court to defend the 'Constitution from the risk of what we consider a misrepresentation of its fundamental principles'. He was outraged when the Privy Council rejected the doctrine of implied immunities in *Webb v Outtrim* (1906); he wrote to Deakin that Deakin could 'take

it for certain that the High Court will not allow itself to be overruled by the Privy Council in any matter involving the interpretation of the Constitution'. In the *Jumbunna Coal Case* (1908), he argued that 'it must always be remembered that we are interpreting a Constitution broad and general in its terms'. Aware that the Court's decisions would be 'a guide throughout the Commonwealth', he took 'almost too anxious care' in preparing his judgments, which were always written. On the rare occasions that the three foundation Justices disagreed—four times in all—it was O'Connor who dissented.

The Court sat in all the state capitals to deal with more appellate work than expected, and caused passing resentment by applying scholarly standards to their judgments and demanding a high level of advocacy and proficiency from the Bar. Frequently, decisions of the **state Supreme Courts** were overturned. Josiah Symon, on becoming **Attorney-General** in December 1904, tried to move the High Court's principal **seat** from Sydney to Melbourne, and humiliated the Justices by cutting travelling and other expenses. O'Connor believed that abolishing **tipstaves** and messengers would 'materially affect the efficiency of the Court'. Angry and voluminous correspondence was exchanged, and in May 1905 he cancelled a sitting of the Court in Melbourne without due notice (see **Strike of 1905**). A compromise was not reached until **Isaacs** took office as Attorney-General in July 1905.

In February 1905, O'Connor had reluctantly accepted the additional office of President of the Commonwealth Court of **Conciliation and Arbitration**, 'so long as the work of the High Court was not seriously hampered or delayed'. He had to devise the procedure of the Arbitration Court, and he took a 'good deal of trouble with the decisions', since he was conscious that they covered 'the beginnings of things in the working of the court'. He soon found that the High Court's appellate and **circuit** work left little time for arbitration matters, and in April 1906 complained to Isaacs that 'I find myself obliged to take a course which would suspend all the appeal business of the High Court for a month, or postpone hearing of this most important dispute indefinitely'.

After O'Connor had resigned from the Arbitration Court late in 1907, he sometimes agreed on industrial matters with Isaacs and **Higgins**, whose appointments to the High Court in December 1906 destroyed its initial unanimity. **Dixon** later remarked that O'Connor's work on the Bench 'lived better than that of anybody else of the earlier times'. O'Connor twice declined a knighthood; he was, however, disappointed that he was not appointed to the Privy Council.

From childhood, O'Connor had been fascinated by the romantic story of his grandfather Arthur O'Connor's involvement in the 1798 Irish rebellion, and had ardently supported the Home Rule movement. He stood above sectarianism and was respected by Protestants as well as by Catholics. Well-read and a lover of Shakespeare, he belonged to the Athenaeum and Australian clubs in Sydney. He was a fellow (1890–91 and 1893–1912) of the Senate of the University of Sydney. Tall, with dark hair and eyes, a trim beard, and a luxuriant moustache, O'Connor was 'somewhat grim-visaged, but possessing a ready smile that illumined his countenance with irresistible good humour'. His 'conversational voice was rich and musical'. Moderate and careful in his mode of living, he walked long distances every day and was never happier than when gardening at his country home at Moss Vale. He loved trout-fishing in the Snowy Mountains and regarded Dalgety as 'an ideal site for a Federal capital'.

Troubled by chronic nephritis and unable to retire because he was pensionless, O'Connor went overseas in 1907–08 and in 1912. He died of pernicious anaemia on 18 November 1912 in St Vincent's Hospital, Sydney, and was buried with Catholic rites in the Anglican section of Rookwood cemetery. His wife, four sons, and two daughters survived him; two of his sons were killed in action on the Western Front in **World War I** and a third fought with the Light Horse, Australian Imperial Force, at Gallipoli and in the Middle East.

O'Connor's premature death was widely lamented. Barton, grief-stricken, firmly believed 'that assiduous toil did much to shorten a life that was most precious'. Griffith spoke of O'Connor as 'absolutely fearless in the performance of his judicial duties ... in the rarer sense of not shrinking from the enunciation of first principles which are sometimes rather obscured than elucidated by judicial decisions'. A portrait of O'Connor, by famous Australian artist Percy Spence, is held by the High Court in Canberra.

MARTHA RUTLEDGE

Open court, a principle entrenched in the law and practice of the High Court, guarantees the access of the public to proceedings. Section 15 of the *Judiciary Act* 1903 (Cth) provides that the 'jurisdiction of the High Court may ... be exercised by any one or more Justices sitting in open Court'. Section 16 of the Judiciary Act sets out the circumstances in which jurisdiction may be exercised by a Justice sitting in **chambers**.

The inauguration of the High Court was witnessed on 6 October 1903 by a capacity crowd in the Supreme Court of Victoria. Since then, the Court has made several pronouncements emphasising the fundamental importance of open court. First, in *Dickason v Dickason* (1913), the Court rejected an application for an appeal to be held in camera. **Barton**, with the concurrence of the other members of the Court, relied upon the decision of the **House of Lords** in *Scott v Scott* (1913), 'the effect of which is that there is no inherent power in a Court of justice to exclude the public, inasmuch as one of the normal attributes of a Court is ... the admission of the public to attend the proceedings'. He stated further that the Judiciary Act clearly evidenced 'an intention on the part of the legislature that the jurisdiction of this Court should be publicly exercised'.

In *Russell v Russell* (1976), the original *Family Law Act* 1975 (Cth) had provided that 'all proceedings in the Family Court ... shall be heard in closed court'. Chief Justice **Barwick** and Justices **Gibbs** and **Stephen** held that in its application to state courts, the essential nature of which the Commonwealth must take as it finds, this provision went beyond mere procedure and was invalid; **Mason** and **Jacobs** dissented. Gibbs observed that it was 'the ordinary rule of the ... courts of the nation, that their proceedings shall be conducted "publicly and in open view". This rule has the virtue that the proceedings of every court are fully exposed to public and professional scrutiny and **criticism**, without which abuses may flourish undetected'.

He did not deny that a **matter**, or part thereof, might occasionally need to be heard in closed court. He concluded,

however, that 'the public administration of justice tends to maintain confidence in the integrity and **independence** of the courts. The fact that courts of law are held openly and not in secret is an essential aspect of their character'.

On the night of 8 November 1988, **Deane** was hearing an urgent application by the Commonwealth government for an injunction to restrain the publication of allegedly sensitive material. Counsel for the Commonwealth stated that the Court might need to be closed during parts of the hearing, given the sensitivity of the material. Deane did not grant the application and no further request was made.

The application was made at about 8.00 pm and the High Court **building** would normally have been closed at about 5.00 pm. But Deane had instructed the Court staff to keep the building open and publicly display a notice that the matter was being heard. The Commonwealth officers involved in the application were unaware that those directions had been given.

Some days later, Deane was informed that before the hearing of the application, a Commonwealth officer had spoken to members of Court staff in the public gallery and had made a list of their names. Deane convened another hearing at which he required an explanation (*Commonwealth v Toohey* (1988)). The explanation given was that, prior to the application for the Court to be closed, a Commonwealth officer had attempted to compile a list of persons who would be permitted to remain if the application was granted. The names of the Commonwealth officers directly involved were listed, and Court staff in the public gallery were asked if they intended to remain. If so, they were asked to give their names so that they could be added to the list.

Upon receiving this explanation, together with appropriate undertakings and apologies, Deane took no further action. He emphasised, however,

> that the open and public administration of justice by the country's final Court is a safeguard of judicial independence and conducive to public trust. To subject members of the public exercising the right to be present at a public sitting of the Court to questioning about their identity or the reasons for their presence would represent a qualification of that right and could be seen as a discouragement of its exercise.

He went on to stress that 'as a general rule no government officer is entitled, without the authority of the Court, to subject persons in the public gallery of the Court ... to [such] questioning'. If a case involves a government agency, that

> can only serve to underline the importance of ensuring that the right of members of the public to attend the public sittings of the Court be not compromised and that the independence of the Court from the control of the Executive Government ... be vigilantly safeguarded and publicly proclaimed.

The principle that the public have access to all aspects of the judicial process apart from its deliberative phase is manifested in various ways. All **sittings** are open to the public, including those held on **circuit**, and since the Court's move to **Canberra**, the building itself has been a significant tourist attraction. As JM Bennett wrote in 1980, the 'High Court of

Australia, in its functional and symbolic home in Canberra, [has become] a more visible institution than it has been in the past to average men and women who have no occasion to enter its doors as litigants'. Due to funding cuts, and only with great reluctance, the building was closed to the public on weekends and public holidays from 1 July 1997, although the Justices have continued to encourage public access, including visits by schoolchildren and use of the Court's public areas for concerts and exhibitions.

Judgments and **transcripts** of hearings are made available to the public (see **Accountability**). Initially distributed only through the registries of the Court, they are now available on the High Court web page, established in January 1997. Given the publicity inherent in open court and in the availability of transcripts and judgments, the Court is willing to suppress the names of certain parties in sensitive proceedings by the use of initials or a pseudonym.

Although hearings are not presently transmitted outside the building, the Court is considering broadcasting its Canberra sittings (either live or edited versions of significant cases) on its web site. Initially, this would be only an audio transmission, but plans to broadcast videos of proceedings over the Internet are also being evaluated. The cameras are already installed in the **courtrooms** as they are used in producing the transcript, although video records of proceedings have thus far been confined to **ceremonial sittings** such as the swearing in of newly appointed Justices (commencing in 1982 with Deane). **Television** crews were first permitted to enter Courtroom No 1 in February 1987 to produce footage of the **retirement** of Gibbs and the swearing in of Chief Justice Mason and Justices **Toohey** and **Gaudron**. They are sometimes allowed to film general news items (see **Media and the Court**). The Court is yet to appoint a public information officer, although this idea has been discussed for several years, and was promoted by the Justices in the Court's 1998–99 **Annual Report**.

Rebecca Craske

Further Reading
Frank Kitto, 'Why Write Judgments?' (1992) 66 *ALJ* 787
James Spigelman, 'Seen to be Done: The Principle of Open Justice' (2000) 74 *ALJ* 290, 378

Orders. The decision of the Court on the issues between the parties to a proceeding is expressed in the judgment or order of the Court. The judgment or order is given or pronounced by the Court either at the end of the hearing, or, when the decision is **reserved**, at a subsequent date. Occasionally, the Court may hear further **argument**, either when judgment is handed down or on a later date, as to the form of the orders to be made.

In matters heard by a **Full Court**, the orders will reflect the reasons for judgment of a majority of Justices, and are generally formulated by the senior Justice in the majority in consultation with the other majority Justices. Where there is a **tied vote**, either the decision appealed from is affirmed or, in cases within the Court's original **jurisdiction**, the opinion of the **Chief Justice** (or the most senior Justice) prevails.

In its original jurisdiction, the Court may make and pronounce all judgments necessary for doing complete justice, and has power to grant all **remedies** to which the parties are entitled so that as far as possible all **matters** in controversy between the parties may be completely and finally determined. In addition to declarations and injunctions, the Court has power in matters falling within its original jurisdiction to grant **writs**, including mandamus, prohibition, certiorari, quo warranto, and habeas corpus. An application for these writs is generally made by way of application to the Court or (more usually) to a Justice in **chambers** for an order *nisi* (that is, an order calling on the respondent to show cause why the writ should not be issued). If granted, an order *nisi* is ordinarily returnable before a Full Court, which may either discharge the order or make the order absolute (that is, complete and unconditional). When an order is made absolute, the applicant or prosecutor becomes entitled to the grant of the writ or other relief sought.

In its appellate jurisdiction, the Court may affirm, reverse, or modify the judgment appealed from; may give such judgment as ought to have been given in the first instance; and may **remit** the cause to the court from which the appeal was brought.

The Court also has power to make interlocutory orders, both in its original and appellate jurisdiction—for example, where necessary to preserve the subject matter of the proceedings or to prevent the proceedings from being rendered futile.

The drawing up and entry of judgments and orders is dealt with in orders 43 and 44 of the **High Court Rules**. This is sometimes referred to as 'taking out' or 'perfecting' the orders of the Court. The party having carriage of the matter must generally take out formal orders within seven days after the judgment is finally made or pronounced. The orders are then drawn up by (or under the direction of) a Registrar, if necessary after consideration of draft orders and submissions by the parties.

In exceptional cases, the Court (as a final court of appeal) has power to vary or reopen its orders after they have been made or pronounced. At least before an order has been entered, an application may be made to vary or reopen the order in order to avoid injustice—for example, where the Court has proceeded on a misapprehension as to the facts or the law, or a party has been denied a proper opportunity to be heard (see *Autodesk v Dyason (No 2)* (1993)). The Court is much less willing to vary or reopen an order after it has been entered, but there are cases where it has done so. In particular, order 29 rule 11 of the High Court Rules permits the correction of a clerical mistake or an accidental slip or omission in any judgment or order (the 'slip rule'). Further examples may be cases where the order fails to reflect the Court's true intention as revealed in the reasons for judgment, or where there has been misdescription of a party. In *De L v Director-General of NSW Department of Community Services (No 2)* (1997), the Court permitted the reopening of a **costs** order before it had been entered, but ultimately declined to alter its initial order. In *Re Brown; Ex parte Amann* (1999), a Justice allowed an application to amend a writ of prohibition after it had been entered so as to reflect more accurately the reasons for judgment given by the Court.

Where the parties to a proceeding file a consent order, the Registrar may bring the matter before a Justice, who may direct the Registrar to draw up, sign, and seal an order in accordance with the terms of the consent. A consent order can be set aside (in a fresh proceeding) on any ground on which the underlying agreement between the parties can be set aside, such as fraud, mistake, or duress (*Harris v Caladine* (1991)).

DAVID BENNETT

Originalism is a theory of **constitutional interpretation** that requires judges to discern and give effect to the evident intentions of those who framed and enacted the Constitution. A corollary is that judges are not to give the Constitution a current, as opposed to a historical, meaning except in quite limited circumstances. This theory has been perhaps the most debated theory of constitutional interpretation in the USA over the last 30 years. In Australia, it has become a focus of recent debate among judges and academics about the role of **history** in interpreting the Constitution.

The catalyst for this debate was the Court's abandonment of what had been perceived to be a long-standing prohibition on the use of the **Convention Debates**. The question arose in argument in the early constitutional cases, and following some adverse though inconclusive observations by the Court, it was clear that reference to the Debates would not be favoured (*Municipal Council of Sydney v Commonwealth* (1904); *Tasmania v Commonwealth* (1904)). Although it appears to have remained possible to cite the Debates as evidence of the 'mischief' that was being addressed rather than as direct evidence of intention, the received wisdom became that the Debates were inadmissible. While the Court occasionally cited the Debates in its judgments (see, for example, *In re Webster* (1975); *Brown v The Queen* (1986)), this remained the perception—and the practice—until 1988. During this time, the Court effectively denied access to the Debates, but allowed reference to draft Bills of the Constitution, historical episodes, and early commentaries such as **Quick and Garran**. In *Cole v Whitfield* (1988), however, the Court announced a new attitude to the use of history. Sweeping aside the perceived prohibition on referring to the Debates, the Court declared:

> Reference to the history … may be made, not for the purpose of substituting for the meaning of the words used the scope and effect—if such could be established—which the founding fathers subjectively intended the section to have, but for the purpose of identifying the contemporary meaning of the language used, the subject to which that language was directed and the nature and objectives of the movement towards federation from which the compact of the Constitution finally emerged.

Ironically, the lifting of the ban on use of the Debates, and the difficulty of applying a distinction between impermissible 'subjective' intentions and 'objective' historical meaning, has only kindled deep disagreements about the use of history. Justices had traditionally regarded history as vital to constitutional interpretation; in cases such as the *DOGS Case* (1981), the Court justified the ban on the Debates on the pragmatic ground that these materials (unlike the words of the Constitution) were poor guides to the intention of the **framers**. Yet the availability of the Debates has prompted some Justices to question the importance of the founders' intentions. In the *Incorporation Case* (1990), the majority's reliance on the Debates to support a narrow reading of the

corporations power caused **Deane** to retort: 'It is not permissible to constrict the effect of words which were adopted by the people as the compact of a nation by reference to the intentions or understanding of those who participated in or observed the Convention Debates.'

In *Theophanous v Herald & Weekly Times* (1994), Deane went further, rejecting reliance on the Debates as a basis for denying the existence of an implied right of freedom of **political communication**, and stating that the Constitution should be construed as a 'living force' and not as 'a lifeless declaration of the will and intentions of men long since dead'. On the other hand, **Dawson** relied on the well-known antipathy of the founding fathers towards judicial enforcement of rights to conclude that the implied freedom was not part of the Constitution.

These disagreements have multiplied. In cases such as *Grain Pool of WA v Commonwealth* (2000) and *Eastman v The Queen* (2000), **Kirby** has argued that history, while occasionally helpful, cannot impose 'unchangeable meanings' upon the words of the Constitution. For him, the Constitution 'is to be read according to [today's] contemporary understandings of its meaning, to meet, so far as the text allows, the governmental needs of the Australian people'. In many of the same cases, **McHugh** has taken a different view. He has indicated that he would look to history and the intentions of the founding fathers to determine the 'concepts' that the Constitution embodies, although the particular application of those concepts may generate results not envisaged at the turn of the last century. **Callinan**, likewise, appears to place a great deal of weight on the intentions of the founders as evidenced in the Debates. As a result, it appears that the Court's attitude to history is now more divided than ever.

Both sides of the debate agree that the Constitution is not frozen in time; both treat the Constitution as applying to new circumstances that were unforeseen at federation. Originalists claim, however, that the meaning of the Constitution is largely fixed in the past, that it evolves only through the operation of existing concepts and traditional interpretive tools such as **connotation and denotation** and the distinguishing or extension of **precedents**. On the other hand, advocates of a 'living' Constitution (progressivists) regard the Constitution as a more fluid entity. In their view, the words and concepts of the Constitution may change meaning to suit the temper of the times.

The arguments arrayed in support of the 'living force' approach are several. Deane and Kirby argue that history is not decisive, because the founding fathers did not intend future generations to be bound by the meaning they attributed to the Constitution, but rather to leave future generations free to interpret the Constitution in light of changed **values** and needs. This argument makes an empirical claim. To date, however, the historical support for it has been based largely on ambiguous comments by Andrew **Inglis Clark**, cited by Deane in *Theophanous* and Kirby in *Eastman*. This hardly seems sufficient.

Advocates of the 'living force' view also maintain that the notion of a collective intention attributable to the founding fathers, as the product of a collective mind, makes no sense. To this, originalists answer that people can share intentions, and commonly do. Statements such as 'the Australian nation wants X' or 'the founding fathers intended X' mean only that the relevant intention is shared by all or most members of the group. Thus, where there is good evidence that a particular intention was held by most of the founders, it is appropriate to speak of the founders' intentions.

Still other progressivists have contended that Justices (perhaps because they are not subject to the same constraints as professional historians) are apt to conceal their **policy** preferences under the guise of objective historical analysis. In other words, they contend that the use of history is suspect because it often serves as little more than window dressing for decisions reached on other grounds.

Originalists note that this argument fails to explain what distinguishes the use of history from other, well-accepted aspects of **judicial reasoning**. The **citation** of authority is an example. Justices sometimes cite misleading or inaccurate authorities to support their claims; but this is hardly a basis on which to ban the practice. For instance, both **Mason** and **Brennan** decided in *Australian Capital Television v Commonwealth* (1992) that the Constitution contained an implied freedom of political discussion that restricted Commonwealth power. They each reached this conclusion after referring to Canadian cases which, they said, had recognised that an implied freedom of speech was indispensable to the efficacious working of Canadian representative parliamentary **democracy**. However, those cases were decided in the context of the division of powers between the Provinces and the central government. They had simply held that the Provinces had no power to affect political speech, which was a matter left exclusively to the federal legislature. Seen in this way, the cases offered scant support for the conclusions that were drawn from them. Yet this does not establish that Justices should have no recourse to authority. The question is why history should stand in a different position.

Proponents of the 'living Constitution' approach argue against the dead hand of the past. They claim that a historically fixed view of the Constitution must regard the Constitution's legitimacy as depending on a social contract that binds today's Australians and commits them to accepting the intentions of the founders. They then observe that this notion has severe flaws: the moral force of the original compact is undermined by the fact that **women** and minorities had no say in the framing or ratification of the Constitution; the parties that ratified any contract in 1900 are long since dead; and the notion denies the fact that the Constitution depends for its legitimacy on the consent of present-day Australians.

Unfortunately, this argument suffers from flaws as great as those it purports to uncover. At least if it is understood as an empirical proposition, the premise that the legitimacy of the Constitution depends on the consent of present day Australians is unsustainable given the well-documented and widespread ignorance about the Constitution and the way it operates. But more importantly, the social contract argument overlooks other justifications for treating the Constitution as having a fixed, historical meaning. A focus on the historical meaning of the Constitution may be justified by reference to the certainty and stability that historical rules offer—not only to government, but to individuals. It may also be justified by noting that a small group of eminent lawyers, who are neither **accountable** to an electorate nor experts in **economics** or moral philosophy, are not well placed to undertake the task of bringing the Constitution up to date. All things considered, it may be better to have a Constitution containing rules that are not optimally desirable rather than giving a coterie of lawyers the power to remould our basic law whenever they divine that the *Zeitgeist* requires it.

For much of the twentieth century, the Court took a selective and in some ways incoherent approach to the use of history in interpreting the Constitution. It banned access to the Debates, but permitted resort to other **extrinsic materials** such as Quick and Garran and the draft Bills of the Constitution. Despite these anomalies, the Court never regarded history as anything other than a vital element of constitutional interpretation. The lifting of the prohibition on the use of the Debates has, however, seen a shift from hypothetical history to actual history, although this in itself does not make the notion of collective intention any the less elusive. The Court is engaged in a struggle, echoing that in the USA, over the respective merits of originalism and progressivism. Which side in the debate ultimately prevails, and the use to which the Court will put history in the future, depends ultimately on (and itself will influence) the Court's conception of its own **role**.

GIM DEL VILLAR

Further Reading

Henry Burmester, 'The Convention Debates and Interpretation of the Constitution' in Gregory Craven (ed), *The Convention Debates 1891–1898: Commentaries, Indices and Guide* (1986) 25

Michael Coper, 'The Place of History in Constitutional Interpretation' in Gregory Craven (ed), *The Convention Debates 1891–1898: Commentaries, Indices and Guide* (1986) 5

Jeffrey Goldsworthy, 'Originalism in Constitutional Interpretation' (1997) 25 *FL Rev* 1

Jeremy Kirk, 'Constitutional Interpretation and a Theory of Evolutionary Originalism' (1999) 27 *FL Rev* 323

Carl McCamish, 'The Use of Historical Materials in Interpreting the Commonwealth Constitution' (1996) 70 *ALJ* 638

Outcomes, effect of procedure on. To give effective legal advice, lawyers need to know more than simply what the law is. They also need to know what the law is likely to become, and thus to engage in the subtle art of prediction, drawing upon or being guided by perceived trends, judicial hints of preferred outcomes, the weight of accumulated **criticism**, changes in the composition of the Bench, and even the personal characteristics and **background** of the Justices. But they also need to give serious consideration to issues of **procedure**, as litigation frequently throws up procedural choices that can have a dramatic effect on substantive outcomes (see also *Mabo*: **counsel's perspective**).

For example, in the days when appeals from a single Justice of the High Court to a **Full Court** of the High Court were common, a choice could arise between taking that course or, alternatively, asking the single Justice to state a case for the full Bench, of which he or she could then be a member. If only six Justices were available in total, an appeal from a single Justice would be determined by the majority view of three of the five Justices constituting the appellate Bench.

Thus, if three of the five disagreed with the Justice at first instance, the appeal would succeed and the view of the Justice at first instance would be overturned. Yet if the single Justice were to state a case for and be a member of the full Bench of six, and the two otherwise minority Justices who agreed with the single Justice's view were to include the **Chief Justice**, that view would now prevail because of the effect of the *Judiciary Act* 1903 (Cth) in giving a casting vote to the Chief Justice in the case of an equal division of opinion in the Court's original **jurisdiction** (see **Tied vote**).

The quirky impact of procedural choices is not merely hypothetical. Litigation frequently involves multiple issues. Strikingly different outcomes can occur according to whether the issues are consolidated or separated. Two constitutional cases provide spectacular examples.

In *Miller v TCN Channel Nine* (1986), television station Channel Nine had erected and maintained a microwave transmitter at Somersby in NSW in order to improve the quality and reliability of its transmission to Queensland, and was prosecuted under the *Wireless Telegraphy Act* 1905 (Cth) for doing so without having obtained the necessary licences. In its defence, Channel Nine made two arguments: first, that the Act was invalid because it infringed the freedom of **interstate trade**, commerce, and intercourse guaranteed by section 92 of the Constitution ('argument A'), and, secondly, that the Act was invalid because it infringed an implied constitutional freedom of communication ('argument B').

In relation to the charge of maintaining the transmitter without a licence, a majority of four (**Mason, Murphy, Brennan,** and **Deane**) to three (**Gibbs, Wilson,** and **Dawson**) held that argument A failed. On the same charge, a majority of six to one (Murphy dissenting) held that argument B failed. On the basis, therefore, of separate consideration of the two arguments, Channel Nine failed in its defence. Yet (as the percipient Murphy pointed out) had the issue been framed in terms of a single question—'does Channel Nine have a good defence to the charge?'—there would have been a majority of four to three for yes: Gibbs, Wilson, and Dawson on the basis of section 92 (the dissenters on argument A) and Murphy on the basis of the implied freedom (the dissenter on argument B). In other words, a majority of four (Gibbs, Wilson, Dawson, and Murphy) can be constructed in favour of the proposition that Channel Nine was protected by *either* section 92 *or* by the implied freedom. On this basis, Channel Nine had a good defence, although for no common reason.

Channel Nine could count itself unlucky, therefore, not to have been acquitted (although it was unambiguously convicted on the different charge of erecting the transmitter without a licence). After all, the practice in appeals (which *Miller v TCN Channel Nine* was not) is to decide whether the appeal succeeds or fails, not whether it succeeds on any particular ground. The consequence, however, is that an appeal may succeed even though there is a majority of Justices against any particular reason that supports that outcome. But this is an endemic hazard of diversity of individual opinion within group decision making on multiple issues (see especially *Dennis Hotels v Victoria* (1960)).

In similar vein, the division of one question into two enabled the plaintiffs in the notorious pornography litigation in the ACT in the early 1990s to succeed where they would otherwise have failed. The plaintiffs asserted that the prohibitive fees charged by the ACT for their licences to sell X-rated videos were invalid by reason of section 90 of the Constitution, which gives the Commonwealth exclusive power to levy duties of **excise**. In *Capital Duplicators v ACT (No 1)* (1992), a majority of four (Brennan, Deane, **Toohey,** and **Gaudron**) to three (Mason, Dawson, and **McHugh**) held (overruling the defendant's demurrer) that section 90 applied to prohibit not only the states but also the **territories** from levying duties of excise. In *Capital Duplicators v ACT (No 2)* (1993), a majority of four (Mason, Brennan, Deane, and McHugh) to three (Dawson, Toohey, and Gaudron) held (again on demurrer) that the particular licence fees in question were indeed duties of excise. Thus, the plaintiffs succeeded consecutively on each issue and consequently in the result (that the licence fees were invalid).

Had the case been heard at a single hearing, however, the plaintiffs' claim would have been dismissed by a majority of five to two: Mason and McHugh on the ground that section 90 did not apply to the territories; Toohey and Gaudron on the ground that the licence fees were not duties of excise; and Dawson on both grounds. Splitting the case into two issues was understandable from the perspective of saving hearing time and **costs**; the second issue might not arise at all, and, even if it did, the states could confine their intervention to that issue, in which they had a more direct interest. But splitting it into two also changed the outcome.

It is interesting that the puzzle of how a question is framed, and whether it is consolidated or broken down, reflects the tension between the dual functions of the highest court in any judicial **hierarchy**. On the one hand, the **role** of the Court is to settle disputes between parties. From this perspective, the question must be whether the plaintiff or appellant wins or loses. On the other hand, it is also the function of the Court to state authoritatively the law for Australia. From this perspective, it is understandable that the Court is asked to pronounce upon abstract questions of law. But particularly when procedures are used such as demurrer, case stated, or questions reserved, the way in which those abstract questions are constructed (or deconstructed) can have a profound effect on how the ultimate question—who wins?—is answered. Notwithstanding the quirky success of the plaintiffs in the *Capital Duplicators* cases through serendipitous disaggregation, the usual corollary of limiting the issues to abstract questions of law—that is, the absence of comprehensive findings of fact—will often be an insurmountable obstacle for a plaintiff, as in *Kruger v Commonwealth* (1997).

Reflecting on the *Capital Duplicators* cases, David Bennett, who was **counsel** for the plaintiffs, concluded somewhat fatalistically (and, given his standpoint as victor, somewhat generously to the vanquished) that 'bearing in mind the difficulty of predicting results in constitutional cases, there is probably no moral'. It is true that counsel cannot generally be held to account for failing to predict the outcomes of High Court decisions—especially on **constitutional law**, and especially in view of the openness of most issues that now come before the Court, the endemic diversity of individual opinion, and the occasional tendency for a wrong prediction to embody the right view (or at least the preferable view) of the law. But it is also true that, in view of the extraordinary impact on outcomes of seemingly innocuous procedural choices, particularly in the Court's original jurisdiction, litigants and their advisers will ignore this fascinating field of study at their peril.

MICHAEL COPER

Further Reading
David Bennett, 'Does an ACT Ordinance Constitute an Invalid Excise Under s90 of the Constitution?' (1994) 68 *ALJ* 913

Overruling. The High Court has never regarded itself as bound to follow its previous decisions. The application by the Court of a strict rule of *stare decisis* (adherence to **precedent**) would be inappropriate, particularly since the Court has original **jurisdiction** in all matters arising under the Constitution or involving its interpretation, and is now, since the abolition of appeals to the **Privy Council**, a final court of appeal. However, the power to overrule previous decisions is generally treated by the Court as one to be exercised with great caution and restraint.

The principle of *stare decisis* serves the interests of continuity, predictability, and certainty in the law. Like most courts of ultimate appeal, however, the Court has recognised that too rigid an adherence to that principle can be counter-productive. By forcing Justices to distinguish, often on artificial and obscure grounds, earlier decisions perceived as unsatisfactory, a strict observance of *stare decisis* can lead to uncertainty and incoherence in underlying legal principles. Further, the principle may impede the proper development of the law to suit contemporary circumstances, and can potentially produce injustice in individual cases. Accordingly, the principle of *stare decisis* is moderated by the Court's ability to overrule or depart from such decisions in appropriate cases.

The Court has adopted a rule of practice requiring a party to obtain **leave** from the Court before arguing that an earlier decision of the Court should be departed from (*Evda Nominees v Victoria* (1984); *Allders International v Commissioner of State Revenue* (1996)). **Deane** disagreed with this requirement in *Evda Nominees* and thereafter, and **Kirby** has consistently taken a similar view (see, for example, *Re Colina; Ex parte Torney* (1999)). Although the requirement continues to be observed by the Court, it does not apply where the earlier decision involved a **tied vote**, as such decisions have no status as precedents (*FCT v St Helens Farm* (1981); *Re Wakim* (1999)).

The Court has not laid down any definite rule or principle governing the circumstances in which it will reconsider one of its earlier decisions. Various Justices have, however, identified a number of relevant factors. It has often been said that the Court will not follow a decision that is 'manifestly incorrect' or 'plainly wrong', and that in such circumstances the Court (or each individual Justice) has a responsibility to uphold the law (and in particular, the Constitution) rather than to perpetuate error. As **Isaacs** observed in the *Engine-Drivers Case* (1913), 'it is not … better that the Court should be persistently wrong than that it should be ultimately right'.

However, such statements are often somewhat rhetorical, and do not in themselves provide guidance as to when an earlier decision should be regarded as 'manifestly incorrect'. They also disguise the fact that past decisions of the Court should be taken into consideration in determining what view

is 'correct'. Although each individual Justice must ultimately form his or her own view of the law, departure from an earlier decision will not ordinarily be justified merely because the Justice regards the earlier decision as wrong, in the sense that he or she would have decided that case differently. This is particularly so where the issues are finely balanced, such that reasonable minds might reach different conclusions. In such cases, even if the individual Justice disagrees with the earlier decision, it may be more difficult to characterise it as plainly or manifestly incorrect (see **Stephen** in the *Second Territory Senators Case* (1977) and compare **Mason** in *Babaniaris v Lutony Fashions* (1987)).

Some of the core considerations to be addressed by the Court in deciding whether to reopen or depart from an earlier decision were referred to by **Gibbs** in *Commonwealth v Hospital Contribution Fund* (1982) and adopted by the Court in *John v FCT* (1989). Those considerations are: whether the earlier decision rested upon a principle carefully worked out in a succession of cases; whether there was a difference between the reasons of the majority Justices in the earlier decision; whether the earlier decision had achieved no useful result but instead had led to inconvenience; and whether it had been independently acted upon in a manner militating against reconsideration.

Reference is sometimes also made to other considerations of more indeterminate significance. Among them is the date of the earlier decision. A recent decision might be less likely to have been acted upon in a manner that militated against reconsideration, but unless the Court overlooked an **argument** or authority in the earlier case, it may be difficult to point to any factor justifying departure (other than perhaps a change in the composition of the Bench, which is generally acknowledged not to be a relevant consideration in itself). On the other hand, a long-standing decision is not immune from reconsideration—for example, where the principle adopted in the earlier decision is regarded as ill-suited to contemporary conditions in the light of later developments.

The number of Justices who sat on the Court in the earlier decision, and whether or not the decision was unanimous, are sometimes also regarded as relevant. In *John v FCT*, however, **Brennan** stressed that 'a decision of this Court has authority as a precedent precisely because it is the Court's decision, not because it is the decision of the participating justices or a majority of them'.

The Court generally adopts a different approach in constitutional cases from that taken in cases involving the **common law** or **statutory interpretation**. In constitutional cases, the principle of *stare decisis* applies with less force, particularly where the case involves a principle of 'vital constitutional importance' with potentially far-reaching implications for other cases (see *Street v Queensland Bar Association* (1989)). Thus, individual Justices often regard themselves as having a duty to act upon their own understanding of what the Constitution requires, although paying due regard to the opinions of other Justices past and present (see, for example, **Barwick** in the *Second Territory Senators Case*; Deane and **Gaudron** in *Stevens v Head* (1993) and *Re Tyler; Ex parte Foley* (1994)). In contrast to cases involving the common law or issues of statutory construction, the legislature cannot 'correct' a decision on a constitutional issue that is regarded as erroneous or inconvenient. This argument is often relied on to justify a departure from an earlier decision on a constitutional issue that is now seen as incorrect, whereas in a non-constitutional context the Court might simply affirm the legal status quo and leave it to the Parliament to take steps to change the law. There is, however, a parallel argument that incorrect or inconvenient constitutional decisions should be overturned only by the electorate voting at a referendum (see **Amendment of Constitution**). In any event, examples can be found of Justices electing to follow an earlier decision on a constitutional issue despite their belief that it was wrongly decided. Most famously, in the *Second Territory Senators Case*, Gibbs and Stephen refused to accept a change in the membership of the Bench as a reason for reversing a decision less than two years old.

The Court addresses two distinct questions when considering whether or not to reopen and depart from one of its previous decisions: whether or not the earlier decision is correct, and whether or not it should be followed. The order in which these inquiries are conducted is not settled. In practice, the Court often hears argument on an application for leave to reopen an earlier decision at the same time as it hears argument on the substantive issues. As a result, the considerations relevant to each stage of the inquiry can overlap. For example, the correctness or otherwise of the earlier decision may sometimes be taken into account in deciding whether or not to give leave to reopen that decision (see *Thompson v Byrne* (1999) and the majority judgments in *Newcrest Mining v Commonwealth* (1997)).

It is sometimes possible for the Court to overturn the reasoning that supports an earlier decision without overruling the actual decision itself. In *Esso v Commissioner of Taxation* (1999), a majority of the Court rejected the 'sole purpose' test for legal professional privilege adopted by the majority in *Grant v Downs* (1976) in favour of a more liberal 'dominant purpose' test. While it was not necessary to overrule the decision in *Grant*, since the result in that case would have been the same on either test, the Court indicated that any reconsideration of the majority reasoning in that case should be determined by similar considerations to those set out in *John v FCT*. In *Ha v NSW* (1997), the Court effectively abandoned the 'business franchise fee exception' to the prohibition on state and territory **excise duties** contained in section 90 of the Constitution. This exception had been founded on the decisions in **Dennis Hotels v Victoria** (1960) and *Dickenson's Arcade v Tasmania* (1974). However, instead of overruling those decisions, the majority confined them to their facts, treating them as authority only for the validity of the particular imposts that they upheld.

Sometimes, the effect of the Court's decision on earlier decisions is unclear. In **Cole v Whitfield** (1988), the Court reconsidered the proper construction of section 92 of the Constitution, potentially affecting some 140 previous decisions of the Court and of the Privy Council. The Court's jurisprudence on section 92 had been characterised by a number of differing approaches, producing 'neither clarity of meaning nor certainty of operation'. In the absence of any settled interpretation of the provision, the Court unanimously adopted a fresh construction based on the historical context and purpose of section 92. Without specifically overruling any of the previous decisions, the decision in *Cole v Whitfield*

meant that their authority became 'open to question to the extent to which [they] were decided by reference to an interpretation of [section 92] that could no longer be supported' (*Barley Marketing Board (NSW) v Norman* (1990)).

The fact that a decision has been overruled, or that a particular aspect of the reasoning supporting it has been disapproved, does not always prevent other aspects of the reasoning in that case from being applied in future cases. For example, the majority in the *Incorporation Case* (1990) relied on the judgments in *Huddart Parker v Moorehead* (1909) to support their conclusion that the **corporations power** is confined to corporations already in existence, notwithstanding that the decision in *Huddart Parker* had been overruled in *Strickland v Rocla Concrete Pipes* (1971). This reliance on *Huddart Parker*, 'disinterred and selectively dissected for the occasion', was criticised in a **dissenting judgment** by Deane, who rejected the 'attempt to restore partial validity' to the judgments in *Huddart Parker* that had been discredited by the **Engineers Case** (1920) and disapproved by *Strickland*.

Finally, the Court has rejected the practice adopted by the **United States Supreme Court**, of declaring that an overruling is to operate for the future only (see **Prospective overruling**). Despite some earlier flirtation with the practice, notably by Deane in *Oceanic Sun Line Co v Fay* (1988), the Court unanimously held in *Ha* that such a practice was inconsistent with the nature of **judicial power**.

David Bennett

Further Reading

Garfield Barwick, *Precedent in the Southern Hemisphere* (1970)
Bryan Horrigan, 'Towards a Jurisprudence of High Court Overruling' (1992) 66 *ALJ* 199
Anthony Mason, 'The Use and Abuse of Precedent' (1990) 4 *Aust Bar Rev* 93
Lyndel Prott, 'When Will a Superior Court Overrule its Own Decision?' (1978) 52 *ALJ* 304
RC Springall, 'Stare Decisis as Applied by the High Court to its Previous Decisions' (1978) 9 *FL Rev* 483

Owen, William Francis Langer (*b* 21 November 1899; *d* 31 March 1972; Justice 1961–72), was appointed to the High Court from the Supreme Court of NSW, where both his father (Langer Meade Loftus Owen) and grandfather (William Owen) had served. A contributor to the *Australian Law Journal* in 1961 described him as 'a conservative judge, preferring what in legal principle is well-established to that which savours of experiment: many an adventurous submission has been dispersed by the chill wind of his common sense and there is running through his judgments a sober realization that not everything novel in the law has proved of permanent value'. In a long judicial career, his most prominent role was, however, as Chairman of the Royal Commission on Espionage (1954–55), established by the Commonwealth government under **Prime Minister** Robert **Menzies** to investigate espionage activity after the defection of Vladimir and Evdokia Petrov, officials at the Soviet Embassy in Canberra.

Owen was born in Hunters Hill, Sydney, the youngest of three children and only son of Langer Owen, then a barrister, and Mary Louisa, née Dames Longworth. In December 1915 he ran away from school—the Sydney Church of England

William Owen, Justice 1961–72

Grammar School (Shore). Owen's father placed advertisements in the city newspapers seeking his return and promising forgiveness, and Owen's sister, working for the Red Cross, caught sight of him at the Sydney Showground among the new recruits to the Australian Imperial Force (AIF). Owen had claimed to be 18 years old in order to enlist. As a sapper in the 7th Field Company, Engineers, he was wounded in action in France in September 1917, and gassed in May 1918. He transferred to the Australian Flying Corps and was in training as a pilot in England when the war ended. He was commissioned in April 1919.

Leaving the AIF in November 1919 in Sydney, Owen turned to law, in the family tradition. He worked as an associate to Chief Justice William Cullen of the Supreme Court of NSW while studying for the Bar examinations, and was admitted on 2 August 1923. (Owen was one of the handful of High Court Justices not to have a university degree.) His practice was wide ranging, and included occasional appearances as **counsel** in the High Court from 1927. In 1924, he published a co-authored book of annotations on the *Mining Act* 1906 (NSW).

Briefly in the early 1930s, Owen dabbled in politics. Alarmed by the crises of the state government under Jack Lang, he joined the Old Guard, and stood, unsuccessfully, for preselection as a United Australia Party candidate for the 1932 state election.

Owen took silk in 1935 and was first appointed to the Supreme Court of NSW as an acting judge on 1 April 1936. He became a permanent member in October 1937. He presided over jury trials in both civil and criminal cases, and sat as a member of the Court in Banco for civil appeals, and

as a member of the Court of Criminal Appeal. He was also seconded to various non-judicial positions by the Commonwealth. John Curtin's Labor government appointed him Chairman of the Central Wool Committee (which administered the strategic wartime wool industry), a full-time occupation from 1942 to 1945, for which he declined salary. The Chifley Labor government sent him to London in 1945 as a member of the Australian delegation to the Imperial Wool Conference on disposal of wartime wool stocks. In 1950, the Menzies Liberal–Country Party government appointed him to chair a committee to investigate claims for payment of an allowance to ex-prisoners of war.

For the Petrov Commission, Menzies' first choice was **Dixon**. Dixon declined on the principle that Justices of the High Court ought not to serve as Royal Commissioners. Owen was then appointed as Chairman in May 1954. (The other Commissioners were Supreme Court Justices George Ligertwood from SA and RF Philp from Queensland; **Windeyer** was senior counsel assisting the Commission; **Barwick** represented the Australian Security Intelligence Organization.) An early preoccupation for the Commission was the intervention of **Evatt**, then Leader of the Opposition, to defend members of his staff who had been named in evidence and contend that the defections were the product of a political conspiracy against him and the Labor Party. In September 1954, the Commissioners responded to Evatt's excesses by terminating his right to appear. Ultimately, the Commission's inquiries proved inconsequential, but the Commissioners were rewarded with honours—Owen was made a KBE in 1957.

Owen endured later difficulties with Evatt when the Labor leader, then in physical and mental decline, became Chief Justice of the Supreme Court of NSW in 1960. Owen, as Senior Puisne Judge from 1955, had been expecting promotion, but the state Labor government appointed Evatt after complex political manoeuvres to ease him out of federal politics. As Geoffrey Bolton observed in the *Australian Dictionary of Biography*, Evatt's judicial colleagues shielded him from open scandal. Owen bore the brunt of this responsibility, including the writing of Evatt's judgments. The experience embittered him, and his elevation to the High Court in 1961 brought relief and the consolation of 'congenial company'. In 1962, he was appointed a member of the **Privy Council**.

According to the **Dixon diaries**, Owen was first considered by Menzies for **appointment** to the Court in 1940, and again in 1952 and 1958 (see **Appointments that might have been**). Once installed on the Bench, he was not conspicuous. He rarely dissented, and his judgments tended to be short—often in concurrence with a fellow Justice. **Chief Justice** Barwick spoke on Owen's death of his capacity for quiet consideration and sound judgment, his willingness to play his part, and his helpful contribution to discussion of matters both in and out of the courtroom.

In 1980, David Marr described Owen's 'unselfconscious presence' and 'appearance of natural authority for which his upbringing had groomed him'. Barwick himself remarked upon 'a certain shyness'. Yet Owen showed warmth and a sense of **humour** among family and colleagues. He was 'an enthusiastic clubman'—a member of the Union Club

(Sydney), the Royal Sydney Golf Club, and the Melbourne Club. His recreations were golf, fishing, and reading.

In 1967, an aneurism led to amputation of Owen's right leg. More surgery followed on his left leg, and thereafter he suffered constant discomfort and pain and anxiety about a further amputation. He continued his judicial duties with a commitment that fellow judges regarded as heroic. On 29 March 1972, during a Sydney court **sitting**, he fell ill, and two days later died in hospital of a ruptured aneurism and arteriosclerosis. He was survived by his wife Joan (daughter of NSW judge, Thomas Rolin), whom he married in 1923, and an only child, Pamela.

PHILLIPA WEEKS

Further Reading
Robert Manne, *The Petrov Affair: Politics and Espionage* (1987)

P

Papua and New Guinea gave Australia its nearest approximation to an experience of external **colonialism**. Appeals to the High Court were initially authorised (for Papua) by the *Papua Act* 1905 (Cth), and (for the former German New Guinea) by the Judiciary Ordinance 1922. Continuing until independence in 1975, they helped to shape the Court's approach to **sovereignty**, **criminal law**, the **external affairs power** and above all the **territories** power (section 122 of the Constitution).

Papua—a British Protectorate since 1884, and a British Crown Colony since 1888—was placed under Australian control by British Order in Council in 1902, and thus 'placed by the [King] under the authority of and accepted by the Commonwealth'. Hence the 1905 Papua Act was clearly within section 122. British Orders in Council continued to apply until 1905, with the Governor-General taking over the former supervisory role of the Queensland Governor (see *Strachan v Commonwealth* (1906)).

The position of the former German colony in north-eastern New Guinea was more complex. Captured by Australian forces at the outbreak of **World War I**, it remained under military control until 1921. By the Treaty of Versailles Germany renounced its claim to the territory, and the allied powers agreed that Australia should administer it under a League of Nations Mandate. The *New Guinea Act* 1920 (Cth) declared it to be 'a Territory under the authority of the Commonwealth', and authorised the Governor-General to accept the Mandate. King George V was also authorised to accept the Mandate by the *Treaty of Peace Act* 1919 (UK).

For **Isaacs** in *Mainka v Custodian of Expropriated Property* (1924), these arrangements showed 'a connected chain of authority' within the British Empire, starting with the UK legislation of 1919. Once the King accepted the Mandate, as authorised by that legislation, the Australian legislation had come into effect. Since the Mandate envisaged the territory being governed 'as an integral portion' of Australia, it was 'territory belonging to the King in right of the Commonwealth of Australia'. Hence (he implied) for New Guinea, as for Papua, section 122 was applicable, since New Guinea, too, had been placed under Commonwealth authority by the King. In *R v Bernasconi* (1915), he had asserted that if the 'recently conquered' area (meaning the German colony) became an Australian territory, section 122 would apply as the appropriate constitutional basis for 'the government of

territories, not as constituent parts of the self-governing body … but rather as parts annexed to the Commonwealth and subordinate to it'.

Evatt's analysis in *Jolley v Mainka* (1933) was very different. Taking an internationalist rather than an Imperial viewpoint, he concluded that section 122 could not possibly be the source of power. The mandated territory was never placed under Commonwealth authority 'by the King', but by the Mandate itself. Nor was the mandated territory ever 'acquired' by the Commonwealth: it 'is not part of, but outside, His Majesty's Dominions'. This was demonstrated, he said, by two Imperial Orders in Council—in 1923 under the *Merchant Shipping Act* 1894 (UK) and in 1928 under the *Fugitive Offenders Act* 1881 (UK)—each treating the mandated territory as 'a place "outside" or "out of" His Majesty's Dominions'. Besides, the scheme of section 122, envisaging 'a gradual approach' towards integration into the Commonwealth, was wholly inappropriate:

> In the Mandated Territory, the process … is exactly the reverse … Its development is to be not towards, but away from, absorption by the Commonwealth … It is improbable that sec 122 would ever have been regarded as relevant but for the fact that the word 'territory' is used in that section and in the mandate alike.

He concluded that the only source of legislative power was section 51(xxix) of the Constitution (external affairs). The New Guinea Act was valid 'as a law for the fulfilment of the duties imposed upon, and the exercise of the rights of administration committed to, the Commonwealth as mandatory power'. The analysis foreshadowed his expansive approach to 'external affairs' in *R v Burgess; Ex parte Henry* (1936); but it presupposed a detailed understanding of the Mandate system, and a broad conception of Parliament's capacity to implement international treaties, with which other judges would feel discomfort for another two generations.

In *Ffrost v Stevenson* (1937), **Latham** gave some support to Evatt's approach. Stevenson, a police officer from the mandated territory, had obtained a warrant in Rabaul for Ffrost's extradition from NSW on a charge of unlawfully killing a native. The question was whether the Australian extradition proceedings came under the Fugitive Offenders Act 1881 (UK) or the *Service and Execution of Process Act* 1901 (Cth).

The majority, including Evatt and Latham, held that both Acts applied.

Evatt again saw section 51(xxix) as 'the source of the Commonwealth's *legislative* power to govern New Guinea in pursuance of its *executive* power and international duty' under the Mandate. Latham relied on a combination of sections 51(xxix) and 122. He, too, read the Treaty of Versailles and the League of Nations Covenant as meaning 'that mandated territories did not become possessions, in the ordinary sense, of the mandatory powers', and agreed that in two vital respects—the initial steps bringing New Guinea under Australia's governmental authority, and the application of the Service and Execution of Process Act—validity must depend on the external affairs power, not on section 122. Yet in other respects he insisted that the source of legislative power *must* be section 122.

He did not adopt Isaacs' explanation. For Latham, the territory had been placed under Commonwealth authority not literally by the King, but 'by the concurrence' of the allied powers, the League of Nations, 'the Governor-General acting as the representative of His Majesty', and the Australian Parliament. The Governor-General had accepted the mandate as the King's representative. Alternatively, section 122 might apply because the territory was 'otherwise acquired by the Commonwealth'; or section 52(iii) of the Constitution might be relevant, since the governance of territories under section 122 was an exclusive Commonwealth power.

His real reason for continued reliance on section 122 was his anxiety that any move away from it might require an **overruling** of all the Court's 'territories' cases—not only *Bernasconi*, but *Porter v The King* (1926) and *Buchanan v Commonwealth* (1913), both Northern Territory cases. *Bernasconi* had held that section 80 of the Constitution (requiring **jury trial** for certain offences against 'any law of the Commonwealth') did not apply in 'the territories'. The actual decision related to Papua, but Isaacs had foreshadowed its extension to the 'recently conquered' area, too. Importantly, *Bernasconi* had helped to establish a view of the 'territories' power as set apart from the main constitutional framework, and hence not subject to its constraints—including Chapter III's delimitation of Commonwealth **judicial power**.

In *Porter*, the conception that 'the territories' lay wholly outside Chapter III had led **Knox** and **Gavan Duffy** (dissenting) to hold that they also lay outside the Court's appellate jurisdiction under section 73 of the Constitution. The majority in *Porter* had rejected that argument, holding that for appellate purposes the Northern Territory Supreme Court was a 'federal court' because of (or in spite of) its dependence on section 122. That had involved a tortured explanation by Isaacs of his judgments in *Bernasconi* and the first *Mainka* case, which appeared to suggest that a territory court both was and was not a 'federal court' for Chapter III purposes. That explanation, too, was part of what Latham in *Ffrost v Stevenson* perceived as being at risk.

As to the mandated territory of New Guinea, Latham's fears were legitimate. If the power to legislate for that territory did not depend on section 122, then the reasons for excluding that territory from Chapter III and other constitutional safeguards would no longer apply. But for Papua, and other territories to which section 122 clearly applied, the same result would not follow. Unaccountably, Latham had jumped from an argument that legislation for the mandated territory might depend on section 51(xxix) rather than section 122, to an argument that legislation for 'the territories'—considered as an undifferentiated whole—might so depend.

The separate arrangements for 'Papua' and 'New Guinea' continued until the Japanese invasion in 1942. Thereupon, civil government was suspended; both territories were treated as subject to Australian military administration throughout **World War II**. The *Papua-New Guinea Provisional Administration Act* 1945 (Cth) restored civil administration, combining the two territories for administrative purposes into 'the Territory of Papua-New Guinea', with appeals to the High Court as before.

Under the UN Charter, the Mandate system was replaced by a Trusteeship system. (Evatt, as one of the architects of the UN, had suggested the new terminology; his analysis in *Ffrost v Stevenson* had persuaded him that **trust** was the appropriate legal conception.) In 1946, the Australian government entered into a Trusteeship Agreement with the UN in respect of the formerly mandated territory. The General Assembly approved the Agreement in 1946. The Australian Parliament did so in the *Papua and New Guinea Act* 1949 (Cth), which continued the joint administrative arrangements for one combined 'Territory of Papua-New Guinea'.

In *Chow Hung Ching v The King* (1948) and *Wong Man On v Commonwealth* (1952), the effects of *Jolley v Mainka* and *Ffrost v Stevenson* were regarded as settled: the High Court's appellate jurisdiction 'cannot now be denied', and the mandated territory had never become a British dominion. But in *Fishwick v Cleland* (1960), the constitutional validity of the 1949 Act was challenged: it was argued that the Act was authorised neither by section 122 (since the Territory of New Guinea was never 'acquired' by the Commonwealth), nor by the external affairs power (since the combined administrative arrangements violated the Trusteeship Agreement).

Dixon dismissed these arguments. Speaking for a unanimous Court, he pointed out that the Trusteeship Agreement had expressly permitted Australia 'to bring the Territory into a customs, fiscal or administrative union … with other dependent territories'. But he added that, even if there had been a problem under the Trusteeship Agreement, it would not have affected 'the legislative validity of the enactment considered as a matter of municipal law'.

As to the relevant source of power, Dixon preferred 'on the whole' to rely on section 122. Its language, though 'perhaps not altogether appropriate', should be construed widely. It could probably be said that the territory had been placed under Commonwealth authority by the Crown; if not, it had been 'otherwise acquired' through the Mandate and the Trusteeship Agreement. In *Ffrost v Stevenson* he had left the issue open; even now he did not wholly resolve it. But his preference had been consistently clear from *Jolley v Mainka* onwards. The resistance to internationalism no longer depended on British imperialism, but on constitutional sovereignty.

The history of Papua, and especially of New Guinea, reflected the comings and goings of a diversity of peoples—not only the colonising or invading forces of the British, Germans, Japanese, and an army of Australian expatriates, but indigenous New Guinea Chinese (*Wong Man On*); the workforce despatched from the Republic of China to process surplus American war materials on Manus Island (*Chow Hung Ching*); and the skippers of island trading vessels (*Strachan v Commonwealth*; *Amess v Bremen* (1959)). But for all of them the principles and processes of legal reasoning applied by the Court were those of Australian law, and particularly of the **common law**.

The **reception of English law** in the mandated territory was prescribed by the Laws Repeal and Adopting Ordinance 1921, which applied specific statutes and Ordinances and 'the principles and rules of common law and equity' as in force in England on 9 May 1921. German law was expressly excluded; indigenous law was not mentioned. The Court did not hesitate to stretch these provisions. When a property dispute between husband and wife in *Booth v Booth* (1935) disclosed an apparent 'legal vacuum', with 'no law at all' on the legal capacity of **women**, **Rich** and Dixon held that the reception of 'the principles and rules of common law' must be given a very wide meaning, so that they were received 'subject to and together with the statutory modifications' in England prior to 1921—including the *Married Women's Property Acts*, even though the categories of applicable statutes specified in the Ordinance did not include those Acts. **Starke** went even further: 'the principles and rules of common law' must themselves *include* the Married Women's Property Acts, since the subject had undergone continuous development in which the common law, equity and statutes had all played a part.

The 1921 Ordinance did adopt the Queensland Criminal Code. The Court declined to apply its exculpation of 'an event which occurs by accident' in *Mamote-Kulang v The Queen* (1964), where a husband's blow to his wife's stomach fatally ruptured her spleen, which was enlarged by malaria; but **Kitto**, **Menzies**, and **Owen** accepted that formula in *Timbu Kolian v The Queen* (1968), where a husband striking at his wife in the darkness inadvertently killed their infant son. Barwick and McTiernan applied a different Code formula: the husband's act had occurred 'independently of the exercise of his will'. **Windeyer** adopted both grounds, but (citing *Booth v Booth*) ascribed them not to the Code but to the common law.

Any attempt by indigenous groups to assert their self-determination was usually brushed aside—sometimes by the blanket exclusion of 'the territories' from constitutional safeguards. Thus, when an indigenous kinship group in *Teori Tau v Commonwealth* (1969) asserted a claim to land occupied by the Bougainville copper mine, arguing that the absence of compensation had rendered the Mining Ordinance 1922 and its successors invalid, the Court rejected the argument without waiting to hear the respondents: speaking *ex tempore*, Barwick declared that the constitutional requirement of 'just terms' for **acquisition of property** does not apply in a territory (but see now *Newcrest Mining v Commonwealth* (1997)).

Occasionally an indigenous claim succeeded. In *Benggong v Bougainville Copper* (1971), the Court upheld a Mining Warden's award of compensation for the loss of 110 cocoa trees, destroyed by the Bougainville Copper company while constructing a road. The Court rejected the company's arguments that the Warden had ignored 'business hazards' such as fluctuating world prices for cocoa; had exceeded his jurisdiction because the road was not part of the mine; and had made an award 'so extravagant' as to be 'without jurisdiction'. Yet it did not question the Warden's judgment that 'land being worked by an indigene' should be valued less highly than land 'in the possession of expatriate owners', and that compensation should be limited to the actual value of the trees.

Other indigenous claims were accorded even less recognition, particularly when they involved what would now be called **native title**. In *Custodian of Expropriated Property v Tedep* (1964) and *Administration of Papua and New Guinea v Daera Guba* (1973), the **Barwick Court** rejected such claims, though in each case the Supreme Court of Papua and New Guinea had accepted them. In *Tedep*, the system of registered titles established for the mandated territory by the Lands Registration Ordinance 1924 had been subject to an express stipulation that no registration 'shall affect any system or custom of land tenure … in use among natives'; but this was construed as applicable only where an indigenous tenure had specifically been registered as such. In *Daera Guba*, a claim that land in Port Moresby was erroneously purchased in 1886 from the wrong traditional owners was dismissed as implausible: Barwick, evoking the **stereotype** of the primitive native, asserted that if such a transfer had occurred, the true owners—notoriously 'belligerent' and 'savage, at times quite inhuman'—would not have stood by without 'carnage'.

At least for the remote New Guinea highlands, a similar perception pervaded the Court's responses to criminal appeals. In cases involving 'primitive natives' in 'wild and inaccessible country', the Court was acutely conscious of the difficulties of maintaining law and order, and of working through interpreters with limited understanding of what they had to translate; and pragmatically adjusted the rules of **evidence** to ensure the admissibility of confessions (*Gaio v The Queen* (1960); *Wendo v The Queen* (1963)). Yet in *Smith v The Queen* (1957)—where the crime was not a massacre in a remote highland village but a murder on the golf course at Rabaul, the accused was not a 'primitive native' but a 19-year-old 'half-caste of very limited experience and education'; and the alleged confession was obtained not (as in *Wendo*) by a District Officer after an arduous two-week journey, but by police who seemed less concerned 'with investigating the crime [than] with incriminating the appellant'—the Court allowed an appeal, holding that the trial judge should have excluded the confession. The case was a landmark in the Court's approach to confessions (see **Criminal procedure**). Decided on general common law principles, it suggests that, as in the case of Australia's **Aboriginal peoples** (see *Tuckiar v The King* (1934)), indigenous defendants may benefit most from the even-handed application of the common law.

Yet, generally, the perception of the gulf between civilising expatriates and 'primitive natives' was pervasive. To ensure the effectiveness of the White Women's Protection Ordinance 1926 (Papua), the Court in *Ofu-Koloi v The Queen* (1956) dealt pragmatically with the semantic and evidentiary problems of the requirement that a victim be 'European': it was sufficient that 'upon inspection' the victim was 'a fair white child', and that her parents' appearance was 'that ordinarily borne by the white inhabitants of this country' (see **Race**). And preoccupation with law and order was nowhere more evident than in the insistence that expatriates should set a good example, and not undermine the authorities. When the defendant missionaries in *Foege v The King* (1936) and *Cranssen v The King*

(1936) were convicted of crimes arising from reprisals against indigenous tribesmen for attacks on the mission settlements, the whole Court was conscious of the 'significance of such actions' for 'the natives in uncontrolled areas'. Foege received two years imprisonment; Cranssen's imprisonment was reduced to six months. In dissent, Starke insisted on parity of sentencing with Foege, since Cranssen's actions had

> rendered the work of the Government 'more hard and more dangerous'. They might easily have led to loss of life and the rising of the treacherous and savage Kanakas … The appellant was guilty of a serious and dangerous breach of the law of the territory which should be firmly and sternly repressed so that others may be deterred from like conduct. The sentence was … a warning to persons in the uncivilized parts of New Guinea against taking the law into their own hands and doing acts which might excite dangerous savages and arouse them into action.

In 1915, when George Bernasconi was jailed for twelve months for assaulting a native, Isaacs emphasised the implications of such an assault 'in a region like New Guinea', insisting that a lesser penalty 'might easily detract from the influence of the law in protecting the islanders'. Such perceptions coloured the Court's response to appeals for the next six decades, and perhaps also helped to shape the conviction that 'the territories' stand outside the normal operation of Australian **constitutional law**.

TONY BLACKSHIELD
FRANCESCA DOMINELLO

Further Reading
HV Evatt, 'The British Dominions as Mandatories' (1935) 1 *ANZSILP* 27
JR Mattes, 'Sources of Law in Papua and New Guinea' (1963) 37 *ALJ* 148

Parker v The Queen (1963). In 1960, Frank Parker and his wife, Joan, with their six children, were visiting Joan's brother near Jerilderie, NSW, when Joan developed a relationship with a neighbour known as Dan Kelly. After several days of increasing tension, Joan announced that she was leaving with Dan. She and Dan set off on a bicycle. Frank followed, and ran them off the road in his car. Thinking he had killed Joan, he then attacked Dan with a knuckleduster and stabbed him in the throat.

Parker was convicted of Dan's murder. In 1961, the NSW Court of Criminal Appeal dismissed an appeal focused on the intention required under section 18 of the *Crimes Act* 1900 (NSW) (*R v Parker* (1961)). Ten months later, actively supported by NSW **Solicitor-General** Harold Snelling, Parker belatedly sought special **leave** for a High Court appeal on a different question: namely, whether the issue of provocation, reducing the offence from murder to manslaughter under section 23 of the Crimes Act, had been wrongly withheld from the jury.

In those days, section 23 required that the fatal act be done 'suddenly, in the heat of passion … without the intent to take life'. **Taylor**, **Owen**, and **Menzies** held that Parker could not possibly meet these conditions. **Dixon** and **Windeyer** dissented.

In 1964 (again with the Solicitor-General's support), Parker sought special leave to appeal to the **Privy Council**. This time, the appeal was allowed. The case was remitted to the Court of Criminal Appeal, which quashed the conviction, entered a verdict of manslaughter, and reduced the sentence to a six-year term dated from October 1960.

The 1961 appeal turned in part on the presumption that one intends the natural and probable consequences of one's acts. The High Court appeal touched more peripherally on the same presumption. In *Stapleton v The Queen* (1952), **Chief Justice** Dixon had treated that presumption as 'seldom helpful and always dangerous'. But in *DPP v Smith* (1960), the **House of Lords** had applied it strictly, with much subsequent controversy as to its 'subjective' or 'objective' basis.

In *Parker's Case*, this controversy led Dixon (speaking in this respect for the whole Court) to a momentous pronouncement. *Smith*, he said, confirmed 'only too unfortunately' his earlier caution in *Stapleton*:

> I say too unfortunately for I think it forces a critical situation in our (Dominion) relation to … decisions in England. Hitherto I have thought that we ought to follow decisions of the House of Lords, at the expense of our own opinions … but having carefully studied *Smith's Case* I think we cannot adhere to that view or policy. There are propositions laid down in the judgment which I believe to be misconceived and wrong. They are fundamental and they are propositions which I could never bring myself to accept … I wish there to be no misunderstanding on the subject. I shall not depart from the law on the matter as [laid down] … in this Court and I think *Smith's Case* should not be used as authority in Australia at all.

The pronouncement was a decisive landmark in the evolution of the High Court's independence in developing Australian law.

TONY BLACKSHIELD

Parliamentary process, intervention in. The **jurisdiction** of the High Court to grant relief that interferes with the parliamentary process is doubtful. Even if the jurisdiction exists, relief is discretionary and the Court will grant it only in the most exceptional circumstances. Central to the Court's reluctance to interfere is the fundamental Westminster principle that each House of Parliament has the exclusive privilege to control its own proceedings. This was recognised by the High Court in the early years of federation in *Osborne v Commonwealth* (1911), when **O'Connor**, referring to the requirement in section 55 of the Constitution that laws imposing **taxation** deal only with the imposition of taxation, contrasted the reference to 'laws' in that section with the references to 'proposed laws' in sections 53 and 54, and noted: 'This Court can have no cognizance of proposed laws, nor can it in any way interfere in questions of parliamentary procedure. Its jurisdiction arises only when the proposed law becomes a law.'

Nonetheless, judicial scrutiny of parliamentary proceedings is required by the Constitution to ensure compliance with the special law-making procedures in section 57 (the deadlock provision) and section 128 (the **amendment** provision). **Judicial review** of these provisions is an exception to the general principle established by the **House of Lords** in *Edinburgh and Dalkeith Railway v Wauchope* (1842) and *British Railways Board v Pickin* (1974) that irregularities in the passage of a Bill through Parliament are non-justiciable.

However, even in relation to special law-making procedures, the settled practice of the Court is to wait until after enactment of the relevant Bills before hearing any challenge to their validity based on non-compliance with those special procedures. This practice is based on at least three considerations: that adequate relief can usually be granted after the Bill is enacted; that the Court ought not to trespass on the exclusive privilege of each House to control its own proceedings; and that intervention before enactment may be premature if the Bill is never enacted.

Judicial intervention has been sought where a Bill is introduced into a parliament and those who oppose it wish to prevent either its further passage or its presentation for royal assent. The basis for seeking this relief is usually that the Bill has failed to satisfy one or more procedural requirements for its enactment prescribed by a manner and form provision such as section 57 or section 128 of the Constitution. Intervention might also be sought on the ground that the parliament lacks legislative power to enact the Bill or that it infringes an express or implied restriction on power. In *Re-diffusion (Hong Kong) v A-G (Hong Kong)* (1970), the **Privy Council** held that the Supreme Court of Hong Kong had jurisdiction to intervene to prevent the enactment of a Bill that would be repugnant to a law of the UK.

The High Court has been asked on only a few occasions to consider its jurisdiction to intervene in the parliamentary process. The most prominent was the application made in *Cormack v Cope* (1974) to prevent the 1974 joint sitting of the Commonwealth Parliament pursuant to section 57. All other occasions on which the Court was asked to intervene involved judicial intervention in a state parliamentary process. In none of them has the Court actually intervened by declaration or the grant of an injunction.

Indeed, the only instance of such relief being granted in Australia was the grant of an injunction by the Full Supreme Court of NSW in *Trethowan v Peden* (1930) to prevent the President of the NSW Legislative Council and certain government ministers from presenting two Bills to the Governor for royal assent without the referendum approval required by section 7A of the *Constitution Act* 1902 (NSW). The Court granted the declaration and injunction essentially on two grounds: section 7A contained an express negative prohibition on presenting such Bills for royal assent without satisfying the referendum requirement, so that their presentation would be strictly unlawful; and because the second of the Bills was to abolish the Legislative Council, the rights of its members would be 'injuriously affected'. In granting special **leave to appeal**, the High Court confined the issue to the question of whether section 7A was valid. In *A-G (NSW) v Trethowan* (1931), a majority (**Rich**, **Starke**, and **Dixon**) held that the section was valid; **Gavan Duffy** and **McTiernan** dissented.

Subsequently, in *Hughes & Vale v Gair* (1954), Dixon (with whom the rest of the Court agreed) expressed doubt as to the correctness of the Supreme Court decision in *Trethowan v Peden*. In this case, the High Court rejected a motion for an injunction to restrain the Speaker of the Queensland Legislative Assembly from presenting a Bill to the Governor for royal assent on the ground that if enacted, it would infringe section 92 of the Constitution. Dixon effectively denied the Court's jurisdiction to intervene: 'An application for an injunction restraining the presentation of a Bill for the Royal Assent is, I will say, not unprecedented but it is at least very exceptional. We do not think it should be granted on this occasion or later or *in any case*' (emphasis added).

In *Clayton v Heffron* (1960), the Court again heard an appeal from the NSW Full Supreme Court, again in relation to an attempt pursuant to section 7A of the Constitution Act to abolish the NSW Legislative Council. *Trethowan v Peden* was distinguished: in that case injunctive relief had been sought to prevent the presentation of Bills for royal assent, whereas in this case relief was sought to prevent submission of a Bill to a referendum, on the basis that the prerequisites for a referendum under section 7A had not been satisfied. The **joint judgment** of Dixon, McTiernan, **Taylor**, and **Windeyer** agreed with the NSW Full Court that the Bill had complied with all the mandatory requirements of section 7A. But they considered the issue only on the basis that the parties had agreed that injunctive relief would be available if section 7A had not been satisfied. The Court appeared to accept jurisdiction reluctantly, observing that by virtue of the parties' agreement, the Court 'must enter upon an inquiry into the lawfulness and regularity of the course pursued within the Parliament itself in the process of legislation and before its completion. It is an inquiry which according to the traditional view courts do not undertake'.

Fourteen years later, in *Cormack v Cope*, the position was no clearer. The circumstances of that case were closest to those of *Clayton v Heffron*, in that what was alleged was non-compliance with a manner and form provision. Declaratory and injunctive relief was sought to prevent the first joint sitting of the Commonwealth Parliament, on the basis that its prerequisites in section 57 of the Constitution had not been satisfied. On the eve of the joint sitting, the Court unanimously refused to grant any relief, and delivered its judgments orally. Only **Barwick** clearly accepted the Court's jurisdiction to grant the relief sought, but he declined to grant it on the ground that the appropriate time for the Court to enforce the requirements of section 57 would be after the enactment of any Bills that might be passed at the joint sitting. This discretionary ground was also relied on, with subtle shifts of emphasis, by **Gibbs**, **Menzies**, **Stephen**, and **Mason**. McTiernan regarded section 57 as non-justiciable, dealing with matters 'intrinsically of concern to the Senate and the House of Representatives'. While Gibbs was 'disposed to think' that the Court had jurisdiction to prevent a violation of the Constitution, Stephen clearly denied it, and Menzies virtually did so except in a case where the enactment of the Bill would leave the Court without jurisdiction. Mason expressly left the jurisdictional issue open.

It is extremely difficult to imagine a situation in which the High Court might lose jurisdiction after enactment of a Bill. Indeed, it would seem impossible. For the **state Supreme Courts**, the position might be different, since the state judicial systems do not enjoy the same security of tenure as the High Court—though the reasoning in *Kable v DPP* (1996) may suggest that some impairments of judicial integrity would be unconstitutional as incompatible with federal **judicial power**.

Following the decision in *Cormack v Cope*, six Bills were passed at the joint sitting on 7 August 1974; all were subsequently enacted. Of these, the *Petroleum and Minerals Authority Act* 1973 (Cth) and three electoral enactments were challenged. The former was held invalid in the *PMA Case* (1975) for not complying with the three-month interval required by section 57 between the Senate's failure to pass the Bill and its second passage through the House of Representatives. In rejecting the Commonwealth's submission that the law-making procedure of section 57 was non-justiciable, the majority emphasised the constitutional duty to comply with any special law-making procedure prescribed by the Constitution. The challenge to the three electoral enactments failed in the *First Territory Senators Case* (1975). Indeed, in that case, **Murphy** and **Jacobs** agreed with McTiernan's earlier view that the requirements of section 57 were not **justiciable**.

These authorities establish the principle that judicial intervention to prevent a Bill being enacted is justified only in the most exceptional circumstances: where the Court would be denied jurisdiction to declare the enacted Bill invalid; where adequate relief cannot be given after enactment; where the alleged irregularity has clear legal consequences on which the courts are bound to pronounce; or where there is a clear legislative directive requiring judicial intervention, such as (possibly) the express negative prohibition in *Trethowan v Peden*.

GERARD CARNEY

Patents and designs are important forms of intellectual property whose statutory protection has required the High Court to negotiate the complicated interface between law and technology. What is the appropriate balance between the public domain of ideas and science, and the encouragement of innovation and development?

Until the mid-1970s, the Court exercised direct control over the interpretation and development of Australian patent law through its original **jurisdiction** over such matters, as well as by hearing appeals from decisions of the Commissioner of Patents under the *Patents Acts* 1903 and 1952 (Cth). Since then, its **role** has been purely appellate. As the cases are usually technically complex, they camouflage profound issues of **policy** that only occasionally surface directly. In some instances, however, the Court's determinations have had considerable influence in other **common law** jurisdictions.

Among the most striking examples is the Court's seminal decision on the meaning of 'invention' in *National Research Development Corporation v Commissioner of Patents* (1959). Under each of the 1903, 1952, and 1990 Patents Acts, this term was defined by reference to whether there was a 'manner of new manufacture' within the meaning of section 6 of the *Statute of Monopolies* 1624 (UK). While the UK and Australian courts had traditionally interpreted this phrase in a flexible manner, covering both products and processes, its flexibility had been limited by the requirement that some kind of 'vendible product' should result from, or be involved in, the alleged invention (see the UK decision in *Re GEC's Application* (1942)). The High Court, however, viewed the phrase 'manner of new manufacture' in its historical context, noting that the purpose of section 6 of the Statute of Monopolies was to 'allow the use of the prerogative to encourage national development in a field which already, in 1623, was seen as excitingly unpredictable'. On this basis, the phrase 'manner of new manufacture' was capable of embracing almost all new developments in the industrial sphere: the word 'product' was to be understood as covering 'every end produced', and 'vendible' as pointing only 'to the requirement of utility in practical affairs'. Little, if anything, was now excluded from the scope of what might be patented, although **Dixon**, **Kitto**, and **Windeyer** hinted at possible exclusions for methods of human treatment and agricultural and horticultural methods. These suggestions, however, have not been taken up by the legislature, nor by lower courts (see, for example, the **Federal Court** decision in *Bristol-Meyers Squibb v FH Faulding* (2000)); and the range of patentable subject matter is now at large, subject to the specific exclusion of patents with respect to human beings under section 18(2) of the *Patents Act* 1990 (Cth).

A similar expansive approach is evident in *Grain Pool of WA v Commonwealth* (2000), where the Court interpreted the words 'patents of inventions' in section 51(xviii) of the Constitution broadly enough to embrace the novel concept of plant breeder's rights. In a significant **joint judgment**, **Gleeson**, **Gaudron**, **McHugh**, **Gummow**, **Hayne**, and **Callinan** (**Kirby** concurring in a separate judgment) held that the phrase did not carry with it such fixed concepts of inventiveness, novelty, or exclusive rights as to exclude the validity of the *Plant Breeder's Rights Act* 1994 (Cth). The criteria posited by those concepts had varied too greatly throughout the history of the patent system for the concept of 'patents of inventions' to be restricted to any fixed content. A necessary counterbalance, perhaps, to this expansive approach can be seen in the Court's insistence in *NV Philips Gloeilampenfabrieken v Mirabella International Co* (1995) and *Advanced Building Systems v Ramset Fasteners* (1999) that the concept of 'invention' imports certain threshold requirements of novelty and inventiveness (apart from those specifically required by statute), so that mere new uses of old materials will not be patentable (see also *Commissioner of Patents v Microcell* (1959)).

Patents are the heavy artillery of the intellectual property armoury, and there is a tension frequently apparent in High Court decisions, both at first instance and on appeal, between different conceptions of the conditions of patentability and the scope of the rights conferred. Matters of dry statutory and textual construction can have far-reaching economic and financial effects, and monopolies, interpreted too widely, can press harshly upon competitors and the general public alike. On the other hand, too strict an approach to criteria such as 'novelty' and 'inventiveness' may exclude otherwise worthy inventions from protection, and thus act as a disincentive to further investment by industrialists, both local and foreign.

One seldom finds any express or overt judicial acknowledgment of these matters, but High Court patent litigation has offered many examples. Thus, for many years, the Court struggled with the absence of inventiveness as a ground of objection under the original Patents Act of 1903, with the result that some aspects of lack of subject matter or inventiveness were embraced within the concept of novelty to ensure that 'mere workshop variations' and 'immaterial differences' were not accepted for registration (see, for example, *Linotype Co v Mounsey* (1909); *Gum v Stevens* (1923); *William Arnott v Peak Frean & Co* (1935); *Griffin v Isaacs* (1938); *Hume Pipe Co v Monier Industries* (1943); and the detailed examination of these cases by the Federal Court in *Werner & Co v Bailey Aluminium Products* (1989)). On the other hand, the two leading judgments of **Aickin** in relation to the requirement of inventiveness under the Patents Act 1952 in *Minnesota Mining & Manufacturing Co v Beiersdorf* (1980) and *Wellcome Foundation v VR Laboratories* (1981) had quite different implications. The concept of 'common general knowledge' enunciated in these decisions was much more favourable to patentees, since inventions were not to be excluded from protection simply because it might have been possible to piece them together from prior knowledge by a process of 'mosaicing' and with the benefit of hindsight. Henceforth, a broader range of inventions was potentially patentable.

Approaches that similarly favour patentees can be discerned in the tests for anticipation (*Meyers Taylor v Vicarr Industries* (1977)); utility (*Welch Perrin & Co v Worrel* (1961)); fair basis (*Palmer v Dunlop Perdriau Rubber Co* (1937); *Sami S Svendsen v Independent Products Canada* (1968); *Hoffman-La Roche & Co v Commissioner of Patents* (1970); *Montecatini Edison v Eastman Kodak* (1971); *Olin Corporation v Super Cartridge Co* (1977)); sufficiency of description (*Samuel Taylor v SA Brush Co* (1950); *AMP v Utilux* (1971)); and interpretation of claims (*Martin v Scribal* (1954); *Universal Oil Products Co v Monsanto* (1972)). However, it must be said that most of the cases show how easy it is for a patentee to win on one issue but lose on another, depending upon the facts, the drafting of the claims and specification, and the volume of prior art. Judicial emphasis on a common-sense approach to these issues can amount to very little if the patentee has locked itself out of protection through loose language or overambitious claims.

In the area of infringement, also, the Court has set itself against strict or literalist constructions, seeking to hold liable infringers who have tried to escape through colourable evasion and subterfuge (see *Shave v HV McKay* (1935); *Walker v Alemite Corporation* (1933); *Olin Corporation*; *Minnesota Mining*; *Commonwealth Industrial Gases v MWA Holdings* (1970)). Occasionally, however, patentees have been defeated when they failed to identify clearly the essential integers of their invention (see, for example, *Shave v HV McKay*).

More inexplicable, except by reference to some deep-seated anti-monopoly—even nationalistic—sentiment, was the Court's reluctance to grant extensions of term on the ground of inadequate remuneration, even when the patentee's invention appeared to have unusual merit and when exploitation had been delayed or deferred by circumstances outside the patentee's control. Thus, in *In re Robinson's Patent* (1918), **Isaacs** stressed the concessionary nature of the patent grant and the need for the patentee to show special circumstances if the patent was to continue after its term had expired. Many years later, the holders of an important patent in the area of colour television were at the mercy of government regulations that meant colour television could not be introduced into Australia until long after the patent had expired (*Re NV Philips Gloeilampenfabrieken's Patent (No 2)* (1967)). It was

only after the extension jurisdiction was transferred to **state Supreme Courts** in the late 1970s that petitioners obtained any degree of success (*ICI's Australian Patent Extensions* (1979); *Re Henri Vidal's Patent Extension Petition* (1980); *Re Sanofi's Patent Extension Petition* (1981); *Re Application of Eli Lilly & Co* (1982); *Bayer v Minister for Health* (1988)).

Registered designs have come far less frequently before the Court. When they have, the Court has had to wrestle with the question of how far this form of protection should extend. What is the protection of 'designs' intended to cover? How far can it capture the benefits of the real innovation or commercial value that the registered owner has made? Most importantly, to what extent is the scope of protection limited by the statutory language of the *Designs Act* 1906 (Cth)? In *In re Wolanski's Registered Design* (1953), the Court stressed the limited nature of the statutory protection: a 'monopoly for one thing only', for 'one particular individual and specific appearance'—a form of protection that may be of little, if any, assistance when the registered owner is really seeking protection for the broader innovative advance underlining the design. Thus, in *Firmagroup Australia v Byrne & Davidson* (1987), the real advance was embodied in the 'idea' of a recessed door handle in a flexible shutter door for a garage. But this could hardly be covered by the specific appearance of the rectangular locking plate that was the subject of the registered design, as that would take the subject matter of protection outside the statutory definition of 'design', extending it to a method or principle of construction. Even where the Court has sought to interpret the Designs Act generously, as in *Malleys v JW Tomlin* (1961), it has not been possible to extend the scope of protection to subject matter outside the statutory definition of 'design'. This is not a failure by the Court, but by the legislature, and subsequent expert inquiries on designs have seemed unable to come to grips with the innovation gap that is left by the statutory provisions. Possibly, new government proposals such as those of the Advisory Council on Industrial Property in its *Review of the Petty Patent System* (1995) will meet this demand.

Sam Ricketson

Patrick Stevedores Case (1998) cast the Court as an influential player in the drama of the waterfront dispute that occupied centre stage in Australian public life in the early months of 1998. The industrial and political, if not legal, significance and urgency of the case saw the convening of a unique seven-member Bench to hear a special leave application (including Chief Justice **Brennan**, who had stopped hearing new cases in preparation for **retirement**), the amalgamation of the special leave and appeal proceedings, and a remarkably expeditious disposition of the matter.

The factual background to the case was complex and, because of the interlocutory nature of the proceedings, some aspects were never tested. On the public record, the federal coalition government, elected in March 1996, promoted waterfront reform, specifically aimed at improved productivity and removal of the monopoly over employment and negotiation of working conditions exercised by the Maritime Union of Australia (MUA). A major container port operator, Patrick Stevedores (a group of companies), was prepared to take on the union.

Unionists protesting in the hard-fought waterfront dispute involving Patrick Stevedores

In September 1997, unknown to the employees and the union, Patrick carried out a corporate restructure. Four stevedoring companies that employed MUA workers (the Patrick employer companies) sold their stevedoring businesses to another company in the group (Patrick Operations) and entered into agreements to supply labour to it. Patrick Operations could terminate the agreements for any interruption to the labour supply. The employer companies used the sale funds to pay off intra-group debts and buy back shares from group companies, thereby retaining minimal assets. During this period, Patrick was also involved with various parties in a secret venture to train a new, non-union workforce. Former and current military personnel were recruited and transported to Dubai, but media exposure and the threat of international union action stymied the project.

The MUA launched industrial action in January 1998, when Patrick locked employees out of one of its Melbourne docks in order to lease the facilities to a new operator backed by the National Farmers' Federation, Producers and Consumers Stevedores (PCS), for training a new, non-union workforce. During January, February, and March, the MUA conducted strikes and bans at various ports, largely under the protection of provisions in the *Workplace Relations Act* 1996 (Cth) that rendered the action immune from legal lia-

bility. On 6 April, believing that Patrick was about to dismiss the union employees, the MUA applied to the **Federal Court** for temporary restraining orders, and Justice Anthony North fixed a hearing for 8 April.

Patrick made its move on 7 April. Patrick Operations cancelled the labour supply agreements on the ground of interruption through industrial action, locked out the union workers with the assistance of masked and armed security guards accompanied by guard dogs, and engaged one of the companies in the PCS group to provide a (non-union) workforce. The Patrick employer companies, stripped of their only significant asset, the labour supply agreements, and faced with insolvency, appointed administrators, and the union employees were advised that they were creditors. Thousands of supporters joined MUA members on sometimes-violent picket lines at Patrick docks. On 8 April, the MUA asked Justice North to issue injunctions requiring the Patrick employer companies to continue to employ the employees and Patrick Operations to use only those employees.

In the proceedings in the Federal Court over the next week, the MUA alleged that the Patrick group had breached the freedom of association provisions in the Workplace Relations Act that prohibited victimisation of employees on the ground of union membership, and that it had engaged with the National Farmers' Federation, the PCS companies, the Commonwealth, and the Minister for Workplace Relations and Small Business, Peter Reith, in an unlawful conspiracy actionable under **tort law**. PCS, Patrick, and the government mounted a challenge to the Federal Court's jurisdiction in the High Court, but failed to persuade **Gaudron**, who observed: 'I have a feeling I am being trifled with' (*PCS Operations v MUA* (1998)). On 21 April, Justice North issued interlocutory orders of the kind sought by the MUA, restoring the position as it had been prior to 7 April (*MUA v Patrick Stevedores No 1* (1998)).

On appeal, a Full Court of the Federal Court found, just two days later on 23 April, that Justice North's reasons for decision were 'free from appellable error' (*Patrick Stevedores Operations No 2 v MUA* (1998)). Public interest was so high that the presiding Justice Murray Wilcox read the decision in a live television and radio broadcast, the first for the Federal Court. Patrick immediately secured a stay order from **Hayne** of the High Court in advance of appeal proceedings set for 27 April. **Argument** in the High Court ran for three days, and judgment was delivered on 4 May (*Patrick Stevedores Operations No 2 v MUA* (1998)).

All members of the Court agreed to grant **leave to appeal**, though Gaudron expressed some inclination to refuse it. On the appeal proper, six members (**Callinan** dissenting) upheld Justice North's orders, but five (the majority minus Gaudron) revised the orders so as to avoid fettering the discretion of the administrators of the Patrick employer companies, leaving them free to determine whether or not it was commercially feasible to trade.

Observers attributed the unexpected level of consensus in the Court to this apparent compromise. The majority pointed out that it was not the orders made, but a decision to resume trading, that would see the employees return to work. And the majority took the opportunity, in such high-profile and controversial proceedings, to characterise the exercise of **judicial power**:

> The courts do not—indeed, they cannot—resolve disputes that involve issues wider than legal rights and obligations. They are confined to the ascertainment and declaration of legal rights and obligations and, when legal rights are in competition, the courts do no more than define which rights take priority over others.

Inevitably, however, the Court decision influenced the resolution of the wider dispute. The MUA did not pursue the substantive legal action, and the High Court's decision bolstered Patrick's position in the settlement negotiations.

PHILLIPA WEEKS

Further Reading
Graeme Orr, 'Conspiracy on the Waterfront' (1998) 11 *AJLL* 159
Helen Trinca and Anne Davies, *Waterfront: The Battle that Changed Australia* (2000)

Personal relations. Any human grouping has its own politics and its own complex network of interpersonal relationships. These relationships may affect the way the group discharges its collective task; and, conversely, the structures in place to facilitate the discharge of that task may affect group dynamics by fostering or inhibiting the development of personal relationships (see **Conferences**). The High Court—a small, collegial group with the dual **role** of deciding particular cases and, in so doing, of declaring the law for Australia—is no exception.

For obvious reasons, information about personal relations within the Court is necessarily incomplete, inevitably selective, and not entirely reliable, or at least not always conveyed or received in its proper context. Nevertheless, neither is it wholly irrelevant or gratuitous; interpersonal relationships bear upon the work of the Court both directly and indirectly, particularly upon the consensus-building aspects of the **decision-making process**. Facts, so far as they are known, can be reported, and readers—making due allowance for the subjectivity of the sources (which include diaries, letters, and other **private papers**, as well as interviews and other records)—may make their own assessments of any extrapolations or generalisations from those facts, or indeed may make extrapolations or generalisations of their own.

One easy generalisation is that personal relations in the Court have varied considerably over time. In the very beginning, they were good. The personal friendship of the foundation Justices, **Griffith**, **Barton**, and **O'Connor** is well documented, and is nicely illustrated by their unanimous reaction to **Attorney-General** Josiah Symon's attempt to create a permanent **seat** for the Court (see **Strike of 1905**). When Symon suggested a reduced allowance for the Justices when travelling together, Griffith told Symon that it had 'fortunately happened that we are on terms of personal friendship', and on most occasions had therefore been able to reside together while on **circuit**. But 'this is an accident which cannot be regarded as a permanent solution'.

At a **ceremonial sitting** to commemorate Griffith's **retirement** in 1919, Barton, who was unable to attend, forwarded a message to the Court testifying to Griffith's 'ceaseless devotion', 'unwearied labour', and 'matchless ability'. In his farewell speech, Griffith, in turn, could 'not refrain from mentioning' his 'especial regret' at the absence of Barton, his 'oldest, and always trusty, colleague'. Griffith and O'Connor also quickly developed an 'affectionate regard and confidence which was never broken or weakened'. Griffith said that their minds 'ran to a great extent in similar grooves', to which 'our early training at our common University of Sydney may have in some degree contributed'. Barton and O'Connor had been friends from boyhood; their friendship continued through years in state politics, and as proponents of federation. When Griffith announced that he was resigning in 1919, Barton wrote to him: 'Up to [1912] … the three original members of the Court remained—now there will be only one. The result is indescribable loneliness, and the sundering of the old companionship will make me feel the chill of isolation as I sit in the cases that are to come.'

When **Isaacs** and **Higgins** were appointed in 1906, there began, to use Barton's words, years of 'stirring up the peace'. In 1903, Isaacs had expressed a clear preference for Barton or O'Connor, rather than Griffith, for the Chief Justiceship: 'I look upon Griffith as a past number.' Letters from Griffith and Isaacs do not otherwise reveal much about the relationship between the two men. But their judgments reveal that they were far from comfortable colleagues. Their **judicial style** and judicial philosophy differed; Griffith sought a 'balanced' Constitution that **reserved state powers**, while Isaacs interpreted **Commonwealth legislative powers** widely. Both possessed dominant personalities; both were ambitious, highly intelligent, and self-assured. Consequently, they often expressed their opposing positions emphatically and dogmatically, sometimes with little tolerance of each other's views. Their 'exceedingly fierce brushes', **Evatt** wrote in 1940, 'delighted the law students, if they scandalized the public'.

Before federation, Barton, in Alfred **Deakin's** words, had 'cordially disliked' Isaacs. Barton had been irritated, during the **Convention Debates**, by Isaacs' combativeness, insults, and lengthy displays of erudition. Barton's letters show his unrestrained dislike of Isaacs after Isaacs' **appointment**. The two men did not merely interpret the Constitution differently—they differed temperamentally in almost every way. In 1913, Barton wrote to Griffith that Isaacs was 'trying to make such a big splash that he will make himself manifest as the right CJ … His judgments are swelling to bigger proportions than ever—in fact they are very weighty—in respect of paper; and he has assumed an oracular air in court that is quite laughable'.

Griffith's few letters to Higgins have a friendly, sometimes jocular, tone, and they sometimes visited each other's homes. Barton, however, appears to have had little regard for Higgins. He wrote to Griffith: 'You will see how little decency there is about [Isaacs and Higgins] … All the same, I think they hate each other, although they conspire. They had a little brush at consultation yesterday … [Higgins'] manner, in his annoyance with Isaacs, was most offensive to the rest of us.'

Isaacs and Higgins differed in many respects, but shared similar views of the Constitution, and were partners in the shift in **constitutional interpretation** ushered in by the *Engineers Case* (1920). They had had a long association at the Bar and in state and federal politics. When Higgins died, Isaacs said: 'There will ever live in my memory his individual kindness of spirit—I never knew him to utter an unkind word—his courtesy, his marvellous fortitude … his gentleness, his dignity under all circumstances.' Although there are often differences between public statements and private views, Isaacs' tribute to Higgins sits particularly oddly with Barton's description of the Justices' relationships; so too do Isaacs' public tributes to Griffith and Barton. In 1919, Isaacs spoke of Griffith's 'wisdom and capacity', 'great talents', 'ripe experience', and 'erudition'; and in 1920, of Barton's 'unfailing gentleness of disposition, his personal attraction and warm sympathy of soul—qualities that always endeared him to his colleagues'.

Of the 1913 appointees, Barton wrote to Griffith that he thought **Powers** behaved, in one case at least, 'more satisfactorily than either [**Gavan Duffy** or **Rich**]'. He thought Gavan Duffy, whose relationship with Griffith was sometimes strained, was 'honest', and is 'honestly sticking to the line of construction for which he argued at the Bar'. Barton said Rich 'followed Gavan Duffy in all things'. While Griffith was overseas, there had 'been no electricity in the judicial atmosphere', apart from the failure to consult in the *Engine-Driver's Case* (see **Conferences**), although Barton feared he 'may have said one or two unpleasant things'.

Griffith wrote to the Chief Justice of NZ, Robert Stout, that although differences between Griffith, Isaacs, Higgins, Gavan Duffy, Powers, and Rich occurred 'often', they did not 'affect our relationship'. However, in 1919—in what Barton described to Governor-General Munro Ferguson as Griffith's attempt to 'requite in deadly fashion the man [Isaacs] who had injured him', even if it meant that 'he killed the man [Barton] who had helped him'—Griffith secured **Knox's** appointment ahead of Isaacs and Barton as the next **Chief Justice**.

In the **Knox Court**, strong differences developed between **Starke** and Isaacs and Higgins. There were also tensions between other Justices and Isaacs. Rich recalled to **Latham** the acrimonious atmosphere that existed before Latham was appointed: 'My mind goes back to the time when Duffy opposed the acceptance of Isaacs' portrait, and with the aid of Knox and Starke prevented the Court having it.' According to the *Bulletin*, although Knox had been the strongest President the Australian Jockey Club had had, 'he has not been quite so assured on the Bench. The restless, questioning Isaacs who was the bane of old Samuel Griffith, is a continued menace to Griffith's successor also'.

A member of an old Sydney elite, Knox had nothing in common with Isaacs or Higgins, but would have been brought up in the company of Barton and would have found Gavan Duffy, an Irishman of the governing class, congenial. Knox was not as erudite as Isaacs or Higgins, nor did he share their passion for judicial work. In his retirement speech, Dixon said that he had known Knox 'to refuse to have anything to do with a judgment I wrote, on the ground that it sounded too philosophical for him'. Initially, Knox joined in judgments with Isaacs, but in general, his letters to Isaacs—who served with him for more than a decade—are courteous and polite, rather than friendly. His letter to Isaacs informing him of his intention to resign in 1930 ends: 'I am very grateful to you for the loyal support you have always given me, and hope to see you to thank you personally on my return from Canberra on Wednesday or Thursday next'. In contrast, when Barton died, Knox wrote to Lady Barton in emotional terms: 'I shall never forget his kindness to me on many occasions during my career and most of all on my appointment as CJ. I doubt if any other man in his position would have gone out of his way as he did to convince me of his gracious feelings towards me.'

There were tensions in the **Gavan Duffy Court** between Starke and **Evatt** and between Starke and **McTiernan** (partly because of the political nature of Evatt's and McTiernan's appointments), and between Gavan Duffy and Starke (who had married a daughter of Gavan Duffy's half-brother). According to Robert **Menzies**, Starke 'would not temper the wind to the shorn lamb'; and when Gavan Duffy 'chose to sting, he could sting like an adder'. On one occasion, after a series of insults from Starke, the recipient of which is unknown, Gavan Duffy adjourned the Court; but, due to a misunderstanding, Starke remained on the bench alone. According to the **Dixon diaries**, Gavan Duffy confronted Starke about the incident years later. He asked Starke: 'Is our misunderstanding to continue until I die?', to which Starke replied: 'I see no reason why it should not.' Starke and Dixon thought that Gavan Duffy—who was 78 when appointed Chief Justice—would have to leave the Court if personal relations were to improve. They encouraged Gavan Duffy to resign, which Gavan Duffy resented.

Latham inherited a difficult situation. Everybody in the early **Latham Court**, as Dixon recalled in 1964, seemed 'to dislike everybody else'. In 1939, Latham wrote to Evatt: 'What can be done in these circumstances which I found existing when I came to the Court? I have tried very hard to improve the personal relations of other members of the Court, but I confess without success … We ought to be able to enjoy our work and live happily together. Will you not help to bring this about?'

Starke was a particular problem. Latham had been Starke's pupil; now Latham was Starke's Chief Justice. When Latham tried to persuade Starke to travel on circuit in 1940, Starke responded: 'I resent your dirty insinuation that I stayed on in Sydney to make a bob out of the government, and also your silly schoolmaster attitude toward me. I think an apology is overdue and in future … keep your criticisms of me to yourself unless I ask for them.'

Although Dixon was often privately highly critical of Latham, he also recognised his abilities—Dixon praised Latham's judgment in the *Jehovah's Witnesses Case* (1943)— and recorded at least one occasion when he talked with Latham 'pleasantly about all sorts of things'. Evatt showed resentment about the way Gavan Duffy had been 'forced off the Bench'—to make way for Latham—'by a combination which included one member of the present Bench'. He also resented Latham's riding roughshod over him. In 1939, Evatt accused Latham of delivering *Moran's Case* (1939) 'without any consideration of my opinion, or even prior discussion of the great constitutional questions involved … If you persist in this mode of conduct to me, you leave me no alternative except to appeal to authority outside this court'. Evatt suspected that *Moran* had been expedited because of political pressure: 'Under these conditions, good work is rendered almost impossible. I regret to say that I think you have exacerbated feelings of unpleasantness, suspicion and even hostility among the Judges.'

Most of the Justices related well to Rich; but Starke could treat him harshly. Starke wrote to Latham in 1936 about Rich's appointment to the **Privy Council**: 'He will be like a dog with two tails … But I thought the Privy Councillorship was reserved for those who had rendered distinguished political, judicial or other services. It is a pity to degrade the rank by such an appointment.' Yet the Dixon diaries record that Evatt 'liked old Rich'. McTiernan, who served as Rich's **associate**, had certainly liked Rich initially. When McTiernan's appointment to the Court was announced, 'Rich phoned me and walked down from the Court to the city to have a cup of tea. He brought Dixon along. Dixon was quite friendly … Duffy was very friendly'. But over time, McTiernan began to think that Rich was a 'mean' man and a lazy Justice: 'If you said anything to Rich about a case, he'd grab … [the references] and you would find them in the judgment … He was a terror. If he did a little work and found a case, he'd say, "Well, I'm not going to circulate my judgments because if I do they'll bag my cases".'

Dixon socialised with Starke, and continued to do so after Starke's retirement. Starke, however, flatly refused to cooperate with Evatt. Evatt, in turn, refused to cooperate with Starke. When Latham was away, Starke was Acting Chief Justice. Evatt wrote to Latham in 1936 that Starke's behaviour as presiding Justice 'to his colleagues—and I refer to McTiernan and myself, has been disgraceful. It is only one's sense of duty to the Court that prevents grave public scandal'. In 1948, McTiernan withdrew from hearing *Henry Jones v Talbot* (1948) in protest at Starke's insults—'This conduct interferes with my placid consideration of a case and harasses me in the discharge of my duties. To mark my protest, I retire from any further part in the hearing of this case'. The *Commonwealth Parliamentary Debates* record that after the incident, an MP requested the government to consider giving the Chief Justice disciplinary power to ensure 'such incidents which detract from the standing of the court will not be allowed to recur'.

Writing to Latham in 1938, Starke derided Evatt's and McTiernan's tendency to follow Dixon uncritically: 'It is gravely detrimental to the High Court and its **independence** that whenever a grave difference of opinion is disclosed, the "parrots" always reach the same conclusion as Dixon.' Starke largely blamed Dixon. He wrote to Latham that Dixon 'angles for their support and shepherds them into the proper cage as he thinks fit'. Dixon rejected this, writing in his diary: 'Latham s[ai]d E[vatt] should not join in my judgments. I agreed but s[ai]d why should I refuse to let him when he asks.' Starke also disagreed with aspects of Dixon's judicial style and substance. Starke wrote to Latham: 'Dixon sent me his judgment which I think is a delightful exhibition of the logical method at which I often scoff.'

McTiernan valued his friendship with Dixon. McTiernan said that he and Dixon 'used to go for walks and chat about things' and have 'wonderful dinners'. They used to 'tell stories, and laugh at one another'. Dixon 'could be frivolous when he wanted to be' as, for example, when he proposed to put a hotel 'Do Not Disturb' sign in front of **Fullagar** when Fullagar fell asleep on the Bench (see **Humour**). McTiernan continued to visit Dixon after Dixon's retirement. McTiernan said that Dixon 'viewed a lot of people, including judges and barristers, with a sort of haughty contempt'; but, according to McTiernan, Dixon would not allow himself to show it.

Dixon thought Evatt's 'great fault was that he generated hostile feeling'. His main social intercourse with Evatt, and with Rich and McTiernan, was over afternoon tea. But by the time Evatt became Chief Justice of NSW, Dixon had little to do with Evatt. Dixon had respected many of Evatt's judgments, though he privately criticised him and collected stories of his 'misbehaviour'. On the other hand, Dixon thought that **Williams** and **Webb** were 'passengers', and that Webb should never have been appointed. As to Williams, Dixon persuaded him to retire; Williams regretted his retirement, and was inclined to blame Dixon.

From 1950, after Starke and Evatt had gone and after the congenial Fullagar and **Kitto** had been appointed, 'harmony and friendliness prevailed', to use Dixon's words in 1952. In 1950, Latham wrote that Fullagar and Kitto were 'great acquisitions and the appointments have given me great pleasure. They are both highly competent and cooperative'. Dixon and Fullagar were life-long friends; the two shared many interests. Dixon admired Kitto's ability and liked him as a person, but they were almost a generation apart. Kitto was not especially close to Fullagar, although they respected each other. There was some tension between Dixon and **Taylor**, but neither allowed this to interfere with the functioning of the Court. Dixon respected **Windeyer**, who greatly admired Dixon. Dixon had been very close to **Owen** since the 1930s. He arranged for Owen to succeed him as Chairman of the Central Wool Committee and often mentioned Owen for consideration for the High Court in the 1950s (see **Appointments that might have been**). But after Owen's appointment to the Court, Dixon was disappointed by both the quality of Owen's work and his attitude to it.

The character of the Court began to change part-way into the **Barwick Court**, when Justices who had been Barwick's contemporaries and had sat on the **Dixon Court** died or retired, and were replaced by younger Justices. Kitto was the first of the Dixon Court Justices to retire. He and Barwick had worked together closely as **counsel** in the *Bank Nationalisation Case* (1948), but they differed temperamentally and their relationship deteriorated. When Barwick was appointed, Dixon, who was upset by the appointment, encouraged Kitto to resign. Kitto reminded Dixon that he, Dixon, had been persuaded not to resign when Evatt and McTiernan were appointed. Kitto said that for the sake of the Court he would remain. Nevertheless, Kitto remained in the Barwick Court for only six years, during which time the two Justices occasionally expressed their differences of judicial opinion in very strong terms.

In 1969, a year before Kitto retired, Taylor died. In his eulogy, Barwick said that Taylor was 'a companionable man—kind, loyal and generous in his friendship'. Owen died in 1972, a month after Windeyer retired. Barwick told the Court that he had always had Owen's 'loyal co-operation and the benefit of his wise advice. Over all the years of our association we have been friends'. Douglas **Menzies** had been Barwick's closest friend on the Court; the two became close friends during their frequent visits to the Privy Council. In 1995, Barwick wrote that Menzies' friendship 'became a large part of my life, a part I shall ever cherish'. Menzies, renowned for his sense of humour, provided a valuable bridge between Barwick and the younger Justices. He organised social events for the Justices, such as trips to the races, when they were on circuit. He died in 1974 and was replaced by **Murphy**, with whom Barwick had a poor relationship, made worse by Barwick's role in the **dismissal of 1975**.

There were obvious tensions between Barwick and **Aickin** when Aickin appeared before the early Barwick Court. But once Aickin was appointed in 1976, his relationship with Barwick improved, and they became friendly. There were serious disputes between Barwick and some of the **puisne Justices** in the late 1970s and early 1980s about the Court's move to **Canberra** and Barwick's proposals for the **administration of the Court**. As part of the Court's move to Canberra, Barwick attempted to introduce a compound in which to house the Justices, in an attempt to foster collegiality, but the proposal failed to gain the support of the puisne Justices.

Personal relations improved when **Gibbs** was appointed Chief Justice in 1981. According to **Mason**, 'the more I saw of [Gibbs], the more I was impressed with him as a person and as a lawyer. He is, I think, in many respects, the most naturally courteous and considerate person I know'. The relative calm was interrupted by the '**Murphy affair**', when personal differences arose between Murphy and other Justices; the tensions led to some Justices having only formal contact with Murphy. The affair led to the publication of correspondence between Murphy and Gibbs, in relation to Murphy's right to sit, but even so, the relationship between Gibbs and Murphy was always civil.

An account of personal relations within the Court in more recent times remains to be provided, and awaits the passage and distance of time to yield memoirs, letters, oral histories, and other pieces of information. Even so, that account will share with the story of personal relations in earlier times the fragmentary and quite possibly unrepresentative nature of that story. In particular, poor relations, like bad news, inevitably attract more attention than good relations. Yet acknowledgment of this phenomenon should not be allowed to trivialise the point that there can be a connection with the Court's work. In general terms, strained relations may impede the collegial aspects of the Court's work, whereas relations that are too cosy may be thought to take the edge off the Justices' independence from each other and present a challenge for each Justice's individual responsibility for decision making. Fortunately, the overall quality and professional integrity of the Justices of the High Court appears largely to have rendered these dangers more theoretical than real (see **Personal relations: a personal reflection**); yet the true nature of the various connections between the Justices' personal relations and the Court's work awaits serious study.

AMELIA SIMPSON
TROY SIMPSON

Further Reading
Clem Lloyd, 'Not Peace but a Sword! The High Court under JG Latham' (1987) 11 *Adel L Rev* 175
Bob Woodward and Scott Armstrong, *The Brethren* (1979)

Personal relations: a personal reflection. Personal relationships between Justices, depending as they do upon so many diverse factors, vary considerably. Geographical propinquity, age, experience, shared experiences, common legal interests, ambition, and personality are among the many matters that shape the personal relationships between members of the Court. In earlier times, residence in different states inhibited the development of a close relationship between Justices, and sometimes even of a satisfactory working relationship. In modern times, the advent of new **information technology** has enabled Justices to develop a closer working relationship despite the tyranny of distance.

In the days of the **Barwick Court**, when I joined it, there were friendships between **Barwick** and Douglas **Menzies**, between **Walsh**, **Gibbs**, and **Stephen**, and between myself, Gibbs, and **Jacobs**. Although **Murphy** was not on close terms with other members and had many friends outside the Court, there was no difficulty in establishing a working relationship with him. His judicial methodology and **judicial style** made it very difficult to agree with his judgments. There was limited discussion of cases between Justices before circulation of a judgment (see **Conferences**). From time to time, I discussed cases with Jacobs (a continuation of our practice in the NSW Court of Appeal), Gibbs, and Stephen, and on occasions with Barwick, Menzies, **McTiernan**, and Murphy.

Discussion of this kind became more frequent during my later years on the Court.

In shaping the relations between Justices, of more potential importance than any of the matters already mentioned is identity or conflict of view about issues that are central to the work of the Court. That this should be so is not surprising when the burden of the Court's work is all-consuming. Two issues that have generated strongly expressed conflicts of opinion are the **role** of the Court in **constitutional interpretation**—especially questions relating to the balance of powers between the Commonwealth and the states—and judicial **law-making**. These issues raise fundamental questions concerning the use of **precedent** and judicial methodology. Disagreement about them goes not only to the core of the Court's **decision-making process** but also to the personal relationship between Justices. Such disagreements played a part in the well-known frictions that existed between the original members of the Court (especially **Griffith**) and **Isaacs** and **Higgins**, between **Starke** and **Evatt** and McTiernan (though this antagonism had more to do with the vagaries of Starke's disposition), and between Barwick and **Kitto** (and later Murphy).

The antagonism between Starke and Evatt and McTiernan found expression in derisive comments made by Starke in the course of **argument** and in his refusal to circulate a copy of his judgment for consideration by his colleagues before it was delivered. In these two respects, particularly the latter, it can be said that personal relations affected the Court's work. The refusal by a Justice to contribute to the deliberations of his colleagues was an extraordinary and exceptional step. We do not know precisely what prompted it. With this exception, friction between members of the Court does not appear to have significantly affected the Court's work.

In writing judgments, High Court Justices have generally conformed to the English tradition of refraining from criticising or attacking the judgments of colleagues in preference to the American tradition of launching a vigorous assault on the opinions of colleagues who hold a contrary view. The English tradition has much to commend it. A Justice can always exhibit his or her thinking to full advantage by canvassing and analysing the relevant arguments without descending to reflections on the judicial integrity, competence, or consistency of colleagues. The difference between the two traditions is to be explained partly by the difference in the target readership. The English judgment is written for the parties and the legal community. The American opinion is written with a view to persuading the **media**, as well as the parties and the legal community, of the correctness of the author's view on issues that often relate to human rights questions in which the public is very interested.

Nonetheless, one can point to High Court judgments on contentious issues that reflect authors' deep-seated and passionate conviction that they are right and that one or more of their colleagues are mired in error, if not recreant to their judicial responsibility. An illuminating example is the judgment of Kitto in *Samuels v Readers Digest* (1969), where he defended **Dixon's** section 92 reasoning against the criticisms of Barwick that the reasoning was excessively formalistic. Kitto said:

When such a precisely-worded statement of principle has been worked out by strenuous thought over a long period of years,

and has been made the basis of the Court's decisions in a succession of cases on the ground of its exactness in defining a complicated concept which the Constitution expresses with economy of language, the national interest is well served by a continuing acknowledgment that to that extent certainty as to the meaning of the Constitution has been achieved.

This strong affirmation of adherence to precedent in constitutional interpretation captures the philosophy and conviction of those Justices who resist the endeavours of others, such as Barwick, to undermine precedent when they consider it to reflect an incorrect or unsound interpretation of a constitutional provision. Judicial disagreement on such an issue has the potential to affect personal relations and to inhibit the prospect of closer cooperation in areas to which the disagreement relates.

Standing in sharp contrast to the judgment of Kitto in *Samuels* is the dissent of Barwick in the *Second Territory Senators Case* (1977) in which he sought to overturn the decision in the *First Territory Senators Case* (1975) upholding **territory** representation in the Senate. Like other Justices who have wanted to vindicate their interpretation of the Constitution in the face of contrary precedent, Barwick called in aid Isaacs' statement: 'Our sworn loyalty is to the law itself, and to the organic law of the Constitution' (*Engine-Drivers Case* (1913)). This citation was aimed at the majority judgments in the *Second Territory Senators Case*—particularly that of Stephen, who did not give effect to the interpretation Barwick preferred.

A similar tension exists between the divergent approaches to precedent in its application to **common law** principle. In this area, one can point to strongly expressed judgments counselling against judicial willingness to depart from precedent. The **dissenting judgments** in *Trident General Insurance v McNiece* (1988) fall into this category. Judicial disagreement about the force of precedent in its application to common law principle does not have the same potential to affect personal relations or to inhibit the prospect of judicial cooperation as judicial disagreement in its application to constitutional interpretation.

Why this should be so is not altogether clear. The answer seems to lie in the conviction of many, if not all, High Court Justices that constitutional interpretation is the most important aspect of the Court's work. In one respect, this conviction is soundly based. What the Court decides by way of constitutional interpretation can be undone only by constitutional **amendment** (or by judicial **overruling**), whereas common law principle as declared by the Court can be altered by legislation. The view that constitutional interpretation is of paramount importance is reflected in the attitude of some Justices who may view a newly appointed Justice as lacking depth in constitutional knowledge and experience. Obviously, any such assessment must depend upon the professional and judicial experience of the individual Justice concerned. In general, judges of **state Supreme Courts** and the **Federal Court** do not decide many constitutional cases, though this situation may be changing. In the vast majority of cases, a High Court Justice's views about the Constitution and the role of the Court will develop during the course of his or her judicial career. And it is to be expected that a Justice will have the capacity to master a constitutional question with the aid that skilful professional argument brings to consideration of the question.

In more than 22 years of service on the High Court—in the course of which there were disagreements between Barwick and other members of the Court over the move to **Canberra**, the part played by Barwick in the **dismissal of 1975**, and the '**Murphy Affair**'—I at no time felt that personal relations between Justices affected or had an impact upon the decisions made by the Court. The ingrained tradition of judicial responsibility that governs the decision-making process, and the fact that the decision is made on arguments presented by **counsel**, preserve the integrity of the process from impairment in consequence of any deterioration in personal relations.

It is inevitable that tensions will arise from time to time between seven Justices who come together not as a matter of choice, but as a result of external selection. From what we know from the correspondence, diaries, and statements of earlier Justices, the tensions between them were considerable, exceeding anything that has occurred in recent times. Whatever the difficulties may be, they are matters for the **Chief Justice** and the Justices themselves to resolve. What Evatt meant by his threat to Latham 'to appeal to authority outside the Court' is far from clear. The threat seems to have arisen out of **Latham's** conduct towards Evatt rather than Latham's alleged weakness in handling Starke. There are, of course, limits to what a Chief Justice can do in providing wise counsel. It is obvious that Starke would have been a problem for any Chief Justice. But it is equally obvious that the Chief Justice and the Justices should insist on an equal distribution of labour, including participation in **sittings** in capitals other than Canberra, Sydney, and Melbourne (see **Circuit system**).

ANTHONY MASON

Piddington, Albert Bathurst (*b* 9 September 1862; *d* 5 June 1945; Justice 1913) is unique among High Court Justices. He resigned before taking up his position.

After a rebellious childhood, Piddington discovered Greek and foreign literature. As a scholarship boy, he progressed triumphantly through Sydney Grammar School and the University of Sydney to win the University Medal in Classics on graduation in 1883. As a teacher on the first staff at Sydney (Boys) High School, his presence is still remembered in the AB Piddington Prize for English. After a tour of Europe in 1887, his interests turned to law. He was associate to Justice William Windeyer of the Supreme Court of NSW in 1889 and was called to the Bar in 1890. His early practice was in **common law**.

Piddington entered public life as independent Liberal MP for Tamworth in 1895. He was a brilliant orator with a set of radical opinions, supporting free trade, abolition of the Legislative Council, a preferential voting system, women's suffrage, and a public service based on merit, while opposing capital punishment, dismissal of married **women** teachers, and coal mining on the Sydney Harbour foreshore. His views on women's issues were influenced by the strong-minded Marion O'Reilly, whom he married in 1896.

Although a supporter of federation, he argued in the public campaign of 1898 against the proposed bicameral

Albert Piddington, appointed Justice in 1913 but never sat

system, especially where the Senate had a veto power. He warned that the Senate would develop along party, not state, lines. It would grow in power, insisting on having senators as ministers. It could influence **appointments** to the High Court. His prescience proved superior to that of **Evatt**, who stated in an essay on *Liberalism in Australia* (1915) that concern about the Senate's power 'was a fear that subsequent events have falsified in an extraordinary way'.

Piddington defied the warning of his friend **Barton** that those who opposed the Convention Bill in the referendum would be opposed at the next election. He linked with **Higgins**, who led the campaign against the Bill in Victoria. Piddington enjoyed victory when the first NSW vote in favour of the Bill did not reach the required threshold of 80 000 (though it did achieve a majority).

Defeated in the state elections in 1898 and 1901, Piddington turned again to law in the new state jurisdiction of industrial relations, appearing as **counsel** on behalf of trade unions in the NSW Arbitration Court (established in 1901), and in the High Court. From this experience and two inquiries as a Royal Commissioner into labour conditions and arbitration, by 1913 Piddington had become a fervent advocate of the need for a judicial arbiter in industrial disputes to provide industrial justice. It was his influence that shaped the form of the arbitration system in NSW.

At the same time, Piddington was building a favourable reputation in legal and academic circles in Sydney. He was elected unopposed as a Fellow of the Senate of the University in 1910—an honour 'perhaps unique, except in the case of judges'. The Fellows were mostly professors, judges, and barristers, and they welcomed Piddington as one of their own. Nor was he out of place in the literary world, publishing a number of books in the course of his career (for example, *Spanish Sketches* (1916) and *Worshipful Masters* (1929)).

While Piddington was returning from overseas in 1913, Labor **Attorney-General** WM Hughes needed two appointments to bring the High Court to its new strength of seven. One offer was made to **Powers**, the Commonwealth **Solicitor-General**, the other to Piddington. This was the first opportunity to appoint Justices likely to be more sympathetic to Labor viewpoints on **Commonwealth legislative powers**. Piddington was not a member of the Labor Party, nor a KC, but he was the most appropriate NSW barrister known to Hughes. Wanting to be sure of Piddington's stance on **Commonwealth–state relations**, Hughes asked Piddington's brother-in-law, the poet Dowell O'Reilly, to sound Piddington out. In an exchange of cables, Piddington replied that he was 'in sympathy with supremacy of Commonwealth powers'. He accepted Hughes' offer on 14 February 1913, on the understanding that he had 'complete independence'.

Congratulations flowed in from appreciative former pupils; from the son of Piddington's headmaster at Grammar, delighted that Piddington 'had so fully justified' his father's high opinion of his abilities; from William Holman, soon to be Premier of NSW; and from Jethro Brown, later President of the Industrial Court of SA. But the Sydney *Bulletin*, maintaining its low opinion of Piddington as a freetrader, dismissed him as 'a more or less obscure junior', with 'no sense of legal proportion'.

Arriving in Melbourne, Marion Piddington noted that 'the feeling here is not altogether pleasant'. Although **Isaacs** was 'very cordial', **Griffith** was 'not so, but still nice'. If Piddington had foreseen the general lack of cordiality, 'he would have stayed at home and taken silk'. The appointments brought intense **criticism** from the Victorian Bar; and although O'Reilly had expected that the Sydney Bar would support Piddington, it joined Melbourne in what the *Sydney Morning Herald* called 'an absolutely unprecedented course'. Hughes was accused of stacking the High Court.

Piddington was shattered by the strength of the criticism. He decided to resign on the ground that he had compromised himself. Feeling at first that his insistence on independence was adequate, he wrote: 'I finally saw that the offer ... was infected by that mistake and that nothing could undo it, so far as my peace of mind was concerned, but giving up an appointment.' Barton and William Cullen, Chief Justice of NSW, assured him that his position was 'completely unexceptionable'. Barton wrote to Marion Piddington that Piddington's determination to resign was not 'quixotic', but 'conduct worthy of a high mind'. Adamant, Piddington resigned on 5 April to the delight of the Melbourne and Sydney Bars. The politically thick-skinned Hughes accused him of cowardice. He was closer to the truth than Barton. Powers, whose appointment had also been trenchantly criticised (and perhaps with more justification) rode out the storm.

But Piddington recovered quickly. In August 1913, the new Liberal **Prime Minister**, Joseph Cook, appointed Piddington as Chief Commissioner of the constitutionally mandated but only newly established **Inter-State Commission**. Under section 101 of the Constitution, the Inter-State Commission was invested with 'such powers of adjudication and administration' as were needed to deal with the constitutional issues relating to trade and commerce. The concept of the Commission had evolved to make it potentially one of the most powerful Commonwealth institutions, overseeing the ramifications of Alfred **Deakin's** 'New Protection' policy for capital and labour. No wonder Hughes had himself been eager for the position of Chief Commissioner. Piddington gave NSW representation, and, as the Commissioner with legal expertise, he became Chief Commissioner. Cook chose Piddington on his favourable recollection of him as a parliamentarian and on his blossoming reputation from the Royal Commissions.

The Melbourne *Argus* now deemed him 'fully competent' for these judicial functions. Piddington was elated. While the reports of Royal Commissioners could be ignored, the Inter-State Commission had teeth. But Piddington's contact with the High Court had not ended. The Court, ready to defend its territory, was waiting in ambush.

The opportunity came in 1915. Outvoting Piddington, the other two Commissioners had determined that the *Wheat Acquisition Act* 1914 (NSW) was invalid because it infringed section 92 of the Constitution, and had made consequential orders (see **Interstate trade and commerce**). In the High Court, the NSW government challenged the Commission's capacity to exercise **judicial power** (the *Wheat Case* (1915)). Griffith, Isaacs, Powers, and **Rich** held that the Commission was not a court in a decision that could be described as saying that 'section 101 did not mean what it said'. Barton and **Gavan Duffy** dissented. Having demolished the Commission's judicial powers, the Court went on to hold that the Act was constitutional. Year after year, the Commonwealth government, with Hughes now Prime Minister, refused to restore the intended powers. Hughes did not forgive and forget. He would not give Piddington more judicial power than he had rejected.

When the Inter-State Commission came to an end in 1920 with the expiration of Piddington's seven-year term, Piddington had an unequalled knowledge of the functioning of the Australian **economy**. He had also become an expert on the living wage, gaining international recognition for his support of a system of child endowment. But he had become further radicalised. He envisioned a growing, democratic Australia. To him, heavy war casualties and the greed of capitalists were destroying that national future. For two years, 1923–25, he wrote colourful articles for *Smith's Weekly*, critical of the state of the nation and the world. As a result, he alienated the Nationalist governments and the commercial and legal establishments.

But he won support in the labour movement, becoming Labor Premier Jack Lang's first Industrial Commissioner in 1926. He used his position to have a system of child endowment introduced—albeit watered down—and to resist cuts in the basic wage as the **Depression** began to bite. He was seen by capital as biased and erratic and his power was reduced by the Nationalist government in 1927. He resigned from a major public position for the second time in his career, this time in protest at the dismissal of Lang by the state Governor in 1932. Thereafter, he spoke and wrote against the growth of fascism in Australia.

Piddington returned to the High Court in 1934, successfully defending the multilingual Czech communist, Egon Kisch, from deportation for failing a dictation test in Scottish Gaelic. In the aftermath of the *Kisch Case* (1934), he represented Dulcie Williams in her complaint against the Sydney *Sun* for **contempt** of the Court (*R v Dunbabin; Ex parte Williams* (1935)); and soon afterwards he represented her again in a test case challenging the Commonwealth's power to regulate radio (*R v Brislan; Ex parte Williams* (1935)). His last appearance before the Court, however, was as a plaintiff. In 1938, while attempting as a pedestrian to cross Phillip Street in Sydney, he was knocked down by a motorcycle and seriously injured. Although it seems he was ultimately unsuccessful in his litigation, the case raised important issues relating to **evidence law** and is still cited today (*Piddington v Bennett and Wood* (1940)). The only reference to Piddington's former status as a Justice of the Court a quarter of a century earlier came in an oblique but poignant remark by **Starke** in the course of a dissent from the majority view that a new trial should be ordered: 'Friendship and sympathy for an old and distinguished member of the legal profession should not sway the judgment of the court.' No doubt it did not. But it was ironic that Piddington came to be judged by those with whom, in other circumstances, he might well have been sitting. He died five years later, in 1945, at the age of 82.

In 1950, the year of Marion Piddington's death, their only child, Ralph Piddington (1906–74), then Professor of Anthropology at Auckland, NZ, dedicated his *An Introduction to Social Anthropology* to his father. That father and son shared a common opposition to injustice and a fearless outspokenness in expressing it had been shown in 1932. After researching the living conditions of **Aboriginal people** near Broome, WA, Ralph Piddington publicly condemned their working arrangements on cattle stations as slavery and denounced WA as 'a plague spot of European oppression'. He was disowned by the conservative anthropological establishment at the University of Sydney, fearful of the damage another untamed Piddington could cause. With continued support from the Rockefeller Foundation, he developed his career outside Australia. The dedication was a translation of a Pacific island dirge to a 'maru', a public official:

Broken is the shelter
Of my father
Lost to sight
You were the true maru, generous to the common folk.

Morris Graham

Further Reading
Laurence Fitzhardinge, *WM Hughes: A Political Biography* vols 1 and 2 (1964 and 1979)
Morris Graham, *AB Piddington: The Last Radical Liberal* (1995)
Michael Roe, *Nine Australian Progressives 1890–1960* (1984)

Policy considerations. '"Policy"' has become a hideously inexact word in legal discourse' (Neil MacCormick, *Legal Reasoning and Legal Theory* (1978)). In this respect, 'policy' is not unlike '**values**'. Each term is used from time to time in an all-embracing sense so as to include the other. The expression 'policy considerations' is generally reserved in the law for arguments or factors of a non-ethical kind, 'values' being a term used often to denote ethical values, though its use is by no means always so confined.

Policy considerations may become relevant to the making of a judicial decision when the decision cannot be made by reference to established rules, whether grounded in **precedent** or even in statute. The Court will then consider the values and policy arguments that are relevant to the articulation of the potential rule (or principle). The Court must make an evaluation of them as a preliminary to articulating the rule to be applied in the instant case. The rule will have an application that extends beyond the parties to the case. Just how far it will extend depends upon its terms, its nature, and subject matter.

In this context, policy arguments come into play as the rule to be adopted is shaped and evaluated by reference to its effect in producing a desirable state of affairs. A policy argument is not used to reach a decision in a particular case dissociated from the general rule to be applied, except in cases where the Court is exercising a statutory judicial discretion requiring the Court to take into account certain policy considerations. Even in such a case, a court will endeavour to deal with them in a principled way.

As **United States Supreme Court** Justice Oliver Wendell Holmes observed in 1881, 'every important principle which is developed by litigation is in fact and at bottom the result of more or less definitely understood views of public policy'. In this passage, Holmes was equating 'public policy' to 'public interest'. He was not referring to public policy in its technical sense—for example, as a ground for rejecting **evidence** (*Ridgeway v The Queen* (1995)) or for invalidating **contracts**. In relation to the invalidation of contracts, 'public policy' signifies 'some definite and governing principle which the community as a whole has already adopted either formally by law or tacitly by its general course of corporate life' (**Isaacs** in *Wilkinson v Osborne* (1915)). But notions of public policy in that limited sense are not fixed; they vary according to the state and development of society and conditions of life in a community (*Stevens v Keogh* (1946)).

Justices have been reticent about the role of policy in judicial decision making. Some judicial statements have been taken, perhaps erroneously, to minimise the relevance of policy considerations. Examples are **Dixon's** expositions of judicial method as involving 'strict logic and high technique', **Kitto's** dismissive references to 'judicial policy' and 'social expediency' in *Rootes v Shelton* (1967), and the statement of **Gaudron** and **McHugh** that a 'new' rule must be derived 'logically or analogically from other legal principles, rules and institutions' (*Breen v Williams* (1996)). Statements of this kind may have been made with the declaratory theory of law in mind. In 1972 that theory was rightly characterised by Lord Reid as a fairy tale.

Sometimes Justices refer to 'judicial policy' when they are discussing what the law ought to be. Goaded by this use of the expression 'judicial policy' in the NSW Court of Appeal in *Rootes v Shelton*, Kitto condemned its use. He was at pains, as many Justices have been, to draw a sharp distinction between determining what the law is (the Justice's central responsibility) and what the law ought to be (a responsibility said to be beyond the province of the Justice). The problem here is that no clear line can be drawn. The distinction fails to take account of the Justice's **law-making role**. An appellate court, in determining what the law is, cannot entirely exclude considerations of what the law ought to be. Ascertainment of the correct rule involves articulation of a rule that will be just and work well.

Judicial reticence about the role of policy considerations in judicial decision making has been associated with judicial reluctance to acknowledge that Justices engage in law making. Some Justices believe that if they are not circumspect about their law-making function, they will imperil public confidence in the law, notwithstanding that lack of candour about the judicial function will itself endanger public confidence in the law. That belief plays a part in judicial utterances made from time to time that any change in the law as it is understood to be is a matter for the legislature.

There are many instances of the Court's consideration of values that in some respects can be regarded equally as policy considerations. In defamation cases, for example, the Court has been confronted with the necessity of resolving the tension between freedom of expression and the need to protect the reputation of the individual. That tension underlies the rules governing aspects of **defamation law** such as fair comment and qualified privilege (see *Lange v ABC* (1997)). Yet another instance is the weight given by the Court to the policy of maintaining public confidence in the administration of justice when shaping rules relating to abuse of process (*Jago v District Court (NSW)* (1989)) and identifying the **non-judicial functions** that may be entrusted to federal judges (*Wilson v Minister for Aboriginal and Torres Strait Islander Affairs* (1996); *Grollo v Palmer* (1995); and see *Kable v DPP* (1996)).

A further example is *Trident General Insurance v McNiece* (1988), where **Mason** and **Wilson**, in departing from the privity of contract requirement (which in that case would have prevented a third party from enforcing an insurance contract) discussed three relevant policy considerations: the risk of double recovery; the barrier to potential plaintiffs presented by the privity requirement; and the impact of third party enforcement on the contracting parties' freedom of action.

The strongest example of the Court grappling with policy considerations is provided by the duty of care cases. It is widely recognised that the question whether a duty of care exists may entail examination of a complex of policy considerations, notably in claims for economic loss (*Caltex Oil v The Dredge 'Willemstad'* (1976) and *Perre v Apand* (1999)) and claims against public authorities (*Sutherland Shire Council v Heyman* (1985) and *Crimmins v Stevedoring Industry Finance Committee* (1999)). Perhaps the neatest illustration of how policy considerations permeate judicial determination of such an issue is to be seen in the closely divided and extremely debatable **House of Lords** decision in *Stovin v Wise* (1996).

The relevance of policy considerations to the determination of constitutional questions is a different and fundamental issue. Leslie Zines has identified an array of judgments in which the Court has taken account of policy arguments. The controversy over the meaning of duties of **excise** in section 90 of the Constitution involves an argument between those who see the object of the section as serving the purpose or

policy of giving the Commonwealth exclusive power to control levels of production (see *Parton v Milk Board* (1949)) and those who seek to preserve the effective powers of the states in the Australian federation. Likewise, in the interpretation of section 92 (see **Interstate trade and commerce**), policy considerations have been introduced, often in the name of attributing a purpose to the section. A well-known illustration is **Barwick's** statement that the object of section 92 was to preserve a common market (*Samuels v Readers Digest* (1969)). In the *Boilermakers Case* (1957), the **Privy Council** considered that conferring non-judicial as well as judicial functions on judges could 'sap their **independence** and impartiality'. And in *Kable*, the Court had regard to the need to maintain public confidence in the administration of justice in supporting the constitutional implication that state courts cannot be invested with functions incompatible with their exercise of federal **judicial power**.

Statements have been made, by Justices of high authority, which may suggest that courts do not have regard to policy considerations in interpreting the Constitution. In *Theophanous v Herald & Weekly Times* (1994), **Brennan** said: 'In the interpretation of the Constitution judicial policy has no role to play.' This statement, like others, is to be understood as saying that a policy argument is irrelevant unless a foundation for its relevance can be found in the Constitution itself. The difficulty is that Justices do not agree whether such a foundation exists in particular cases. From time to time, a Justice will identify a policy as the 'purpose' or 'object' of a provision, without providing reasons for that identification.

Policy considerations, it must be emphasised, are material to judicial decision making only to the extent that they inform the formulation of a relevant rule or the interpretation of a statutory or constitutional provision, and it is appropriate to take account of such policy considerations in the course of reaching an interpretation.

Anthony Mason

Political communication, freedom of. Freedom of speech is probably the most prized of the civil and political rights commonly recognised in the constitutions of Western democracies. It has been described by the **United States Supreme Court** as 'the matrix, the indispensable condition of nearly every other form of freedom' (*Palko v Connecticut* (1937)).

Despite its widespread recognition, freedom of speech receives no express recognition in the Australian Constitution which, in an increasingly marked contrast to related constitutional systems, contains very little rights protection. The High Court has, however, narrowed this gap, through the recognition of **implied constitutional rights**. In light of the pedigree of freedom of speech, it is not surprising that the first step in this direction was to recognise a free speech right: the freedom of political communication, an implication drawn from the text and structure of the Constitution.

The first decisions recognising the freedom, *Nationwide News v Wills* (1992) and *Australian Capital Television v Commonwealth* (1992) (see *Free Speech Cases*), were greeted, in **constitutional law** circles at least, with excitement and controversy. For a while, it seemed as if the Court might embark on the development of a highly protective free-speech regime—or even on the development of a broad range of implied rights. The influence of American free speech law (an extensive and fiercely protective free speech regime and part of an extensive rights system) on early High Court decisions after 1992 seemed to confirm this (see *Theophanous v Herald & Weekly Times* (1994)). However, in the end, the development has turned out to be relatively modest. The right created is constrained by several important factors.

First, the freedom of political communication is not a general freedom of speech or expression such as those conferred by many other constitutional and international instruments. Because the doctrine is founded on the notion that the Constitution establishes a system of **representative government** and **responsible government**, the freedom protects only discussion and communication necessary to ensure the proper operation of this form of government. This obviously excludes certain kinds of speech often protected in other constitutional systems, such as speech of purely artistic or commercial value. (However, because the freedom is a freedom of 'communication' rather than of 'speech', the freedom does extend to expressive conduct where it communicates a relevantly political message; see *Levy v Victoria* (1997).)

Secondly, the freedom is limited by the Court's reliance on textual interpretation. In *Lange v ABC* (1997), the Court held that the freedom does not exist to protect a broad or general concept of representative and responsible government, but only to protect specific aspects of that form of government that can be found in the constitutional text. Therefore, to claim the protection of the freedom of political communication, it is not enough to show that the communication concerned is political in some broad sense. It is necessary to show that the communication relates to specific institutions of the federal government such as the election of the House of Representatives or the Senate (established by sections 7 and 24), the referendum procedure of section 128, or the holding of ministers responsible to the Parliament (contemplated by, among others, the provision in section 64 of the Constitution that ministers be members of the Parliament).

This narrow reading of the doctrine means that not only does it not cover speech or expression generally, it does not even cover all discussion or communication that can be described as political. For example, despite some statements to the contrary (see *Australian Capital Television* and *Stephens v WA Newspapers* (1994)), it would seem to follow from *Lange* and *Levy* that the freedom does not automatically accord protection to discussion of matters relevant to the government of the states. The institutions that the freedom protects are aspects of the *federal* government and discussion of state political matters will be covered by the freedom only if a specific link can be shown between the matter discussed and government at a federal level.

The Court has also confined the freedom of political communication by holding that it limits only legislative and executive power. In *Lange*, contrary to its earlier decision in *Theophanous*, the Court held that the freedom does not render invalid rules of the **common law** that might interfere with freedom of political communication. It drew this limitation because, in its view, the freedom of political communication, like other aspects of the Constitution, limits only government action and not common law actions between individuals, which the Court characterises as private. However, although the characterisation of common law actions as private might be open to question (given the US Supreme Court's position, in cases such as *Shelley v Kraemer* (1948), that the enforcement of the common law involves an exercise of government power), the exclusion of the common law from direct constitutional scrutiny has relatively limited effect. It is much mitigated, if not entirely overcome, by the High Court's simultaneous finding that the rules of the common law should be developed consistently with the Constitution, including the constitutional doctrine of freedom of political communication (*Lange*).

Finally, there is a further limitation, which may turn out to be the most important limitation of all: the finding that the freedom of political communication is not 'absolute'. This means that communication can sometimes be regulated even if it meets all the other criteria just described. Thus the Court recognises that, sometimes, it is legitimate for the government to interfere with freedom of political communication in pursuit of other interests. Although the precise way the Court will go about distinguishing between valid and invalid laws remains unclear (compare the test announced in *Lange* with those applied by **Mason** and **McHugh** in *Australian Capital Television* and **Gaudron** and **Kirby** in *Levy*), this qualification has provided an important way for Justices to uphold laws challenged under the freedom (see, for example, *Levy*).

Predictions that the freedom of political communication heralded a new, rights-conscious era were overstated. On the other hand, it does seem safe to say that the freedom of political communication is here to stay. However, it is only a limited kind of right that protects only a narrow class of communication from certain kinds of laws. Although the same interpretive technique (implication from representative and responsible government) might give rise to some other implied constitutional rights such as a **freedom of movement** and association (as was suggested by Gaudron in *Kruger v Commonwealth* (1997)), it is likely that these rights would also be limited in scope. Comprehensive protection of rights in Australia awaits legislative action or constitutional reform.

Adrienne Stone

Further Reading
Nicholas Aroney, *Freedom of Speech in the Constitution* (1998)
Deborah Cass, 'Through the Looking Glass: The High Court and the Right to Speech' (1993) 4 *PLR* 229
Gerald Rosenberg and John Williams, 'Do not Go Gently into that Good Right: The First Amendment in the High Court of Australia' [1997] *Supreme Court Review* 439
Adrienne Stone, 'Freedom of Political Communication, the Constitution and the Common Law' (1998) 26 *FL Rev* 219
Symposium: Constitutional Rights for Australia? (1994) 16(2) *Syd LR*

Political impact of Court's decisions. The decisions of the High Court can have a direct and profound impact, particularly on the lives of the **litigants** (see, for example, the *Chamberlain Case* (1984), the *Irish Envoys Case* (1923), *Tait's Case* (1962), and *Marion's Case* (1992)), but also on the Australian **economy**. The Court's decisions can also have a direct and profound impact in a broader, political sense.

As the third branch of government, the judiciary in Australia is independent of the other two branches—the executive and the Parliament (see **Separation of powers**). That **independence** is vital, given the Court's continuing and frequent interaction with the other two branches, and its powers to determine the constitutional validity of Commonwealth (and state and territory) legislation and the legality of the actions of ministers and other officials. What is not always recognised is that, despite (or perhaps because of) this independence, the Court's decisions can impact on and affect the political process (see **Political institution**), even to the extent of helping or hindering the political standing in the community of a particular government (see **Political parties**).

There are numerous examples of High Court decisions having a political impact (see, for example, *Mabo* (1992); *Wik* (1996); *Patrick Stevedores Case* (1998)). These examples may help to explain why governments are often tempted to take into account political as well as legal factors when considering the **appointment** of Justices (see also **Appointments that might have been**), and in this way perhaps seek to influence the course of the Court's decision making.

The Court's decisions have had a considerable impact on Australian **federalism**. The relative legislative, executive, and financial powers of the Commonwealth vis-à-vis the states have been largely determined by decisions of the Court. Those decisions have helped to influence not only the actual powers of the Commonwealth and states, but also perceptions by voters of the relative importance of the different levels of government. For example, from the time of the *Tasmanian Dam Case* (1983), conservation and environmental issues had to be considered from a federal as well as a state perspective. In the early 1970s, the Whitlam government had tried, without much success, to assert some federal powers in this area (see **Whitlam era**). But as a result of the *Tasmanian Dam Case*, the Commonwealth was empowered to determine national environmental policies, so long as they could be linked to international treaties or concerns (see also **External affairs power; Environmental law**). Environmental issues were decisive in determining the outcome of federal elections in 1990 and 1993.

The Court's decisions have also occasionally affected the way party politics is conducted. An important example is the effect of the Court's decisions in 1908 to invalidate key legislation introduced by Alfred **Deakin's** Protectionist Party, with the active collaboration of the Labor Party, to advance what was called at the time the 'new protectionism'—essentially, a scheme to maintain tariff protection of Australian industries on condition that it improved conditions for workers in those industries. After the Court ruled the legislation invalid (*R v Barger* (1908)), the Labor Party withdrew its support from the Protectionists. Within months, there was a fusion of the two non-Labor parties and from that time on, Australian politics became a two-way battle between Labor and the principal conservative party (which underwent changes of name as it assimilated people breaking away from Labor). There is little doubt that *Barger* helped to precipitate an enduring change from a three-party system to a two-party system at the federal level.

Court decisions have also had a direct impact on the political fortunes of governing parties—though it is perhaps more accurate to say that various governments have suffered in electoral terms because of the way they have responded to High Court decisions. The perennial political tensions surrounding the **conciliation and arbitration** power were inevitably exacerbated by High Court decisions on the scope of the power, whether in any particular case the power was strengthened or weakened. The tensions reached a climax in 1929 when the Bruce–Page United Australia Party government in effect decided to opt out of industrial relations altogether, retaining a limited Commonwealth role based on the **trade and commerce power** but effectively returning control to the states. Among the particular grievances adduced to justify this radical reaction were the inability at Commonwealth level to establish a 'common rule' (*Whybrow's Case (No 2)* (1910)), the inclusion of state government instrumentalities within Commonwealth arbitral power (*Engineers Case* (1920)), and, ironically, the supremacy of Commonwealth awards over state laws through **inconsistency** (*Clyde Engineering v Cowburn* (1926)), since this was perceived as exacerbating the problem of duplication and overlap between state and federal systems. The political crisis induced by the government's proposals led immediately to a dissolution of Parliament, and the policy was roundly rejected by the electorate at the ensuing election.

Twenty years later, legislation of the Chifley Labor government intended to give a monopoly of all governmental banking in Australia to the government-owned Commonwealth bank (see *Melbourne Corporation Case* (1947)) was declared invalid, as was a subsequent law to nationalise the private banks (see *Bank Nationalisation Case* (1948); **Prime Ministers**). The decision on nationalisation struck at the heart of the Labor Party's electoral platform, which had long proclaimed the need to nationalise key industries. The decision led the Labor Party to distrust the Court and to advocate major **amendments** to the Constitution. It also affected Labor's policies for the 1949 election, which it lost.

A few years later, the new **Menzies** government suffered a major setback when legislation to outlaw the Communist Party was struck down by the High Court in the *Communist Party Case* (1951). The government sought to overturn the Court's decision through a referendum, but this failed to gain majority support. In a different way, the Court damaged the electoral prospects of the Fraser government in the late 1970s. For several years, decisions by the Court on **taxation law** had thwarted the government's attempts to tighten the law against tax evasion (see **Barwick Court**). One consequence was that the Fraser government gained the reputation of being soft on tax issues, and this was exploited by the Opposition.

Many decisions by the Court affect the conduct of government by forcing changes to institutional structures or policies. For example, in the 1950s, the government had to change the conciliation and arbitration system because the Court ruled in the *Boilermakers Case* (1956) that the Court of Conciliation and Arbitration could not exercise both the power to arbitrate industrial disputes and the power to judicially consider and enforce industrial awards and punish any breaches of them. In fact, that was the second time the arbitration system had to be changed. In 1918, in *Alexander's Case*, the Court ruled that the Arbitration Court could not exercise judicial functions because its judges were not proper judges, as they did not have life **tenure**.

The Court is conscious of the desirability of not disturbing long-standing institutional arrangements, and resists hearing appeals seeking to overturn its previous decisions where reliance has been placed on those decisions over a significant period. For example, in *Philip Morris v Commissioner of Business Franchises* (1989), **Mason** and **Deane** said that there were 'powerful considerations against **overruling**' the decisions in several cases concerning duties of **excise**. They pointed out that financial arrangements of great importance to the governments of the state and perhaps the national economy had been made for a long time on the faith of those decisions. 'The power of this Court to overrule its previous decisions would not be properly exercised to disturb those arrangements unless, in the light of later insights into the true meaning of the Constitution, obedience to its terms or the interests of certainty in those arrangements clearly demanded that those arrangements be reconsidered.' The Court reaffirmed in that case the ability of the states to raise taxes based on past sales of alcohol, tobacco, and petrol, even though these seemed to be excise duties that could be raised only by the Commonwealth. However, in *Ha v NSW* (1997), the Court held that these taxes were excises, even though the states had by then become even more reliant on them. The Commonwealth then had to establish a mechanism to collect taxes on a uniform basis and to recompense the states for the revenue they had lost. It meant a special arrangement in the case of Queensland, where there had previously been no petrol tax—the state had to pay the money it received from the Commonwealth back to oil companies to try to keep prices at pre-tax levels.

The Court has generally avoided making decisions that would involve interfering in the internal workings of the Parliament (see **Parliamentary process**). In *R v Richards; Ex parte Fitzpatrick and Browne* (1955), for example, it decided not to review a decision by the House of Representatives that two men had been guilty of a serious contempt of the Parliament and should be imprisoned for three months. The courts could not go behind the declaration made by the House. In *Cormack v Cope* (1974), the Court decided that it would not prevent the holding of a joint sitting of the two Houses to pass legislation whose rejection by the Senate had led to a double-dissolution election. However, the Court retained the power to decide whether, in the case of each Bill that was considered by the joint sitting and subsequently passed, the formal preconditions for its being a double dissolution Bill had been satisfied. In the *PMA Case* (1975), a majority held that one of the Bills did not meet the constitutional requirements set out in section 57.

The Court does not set out to make political decisions. Even when ex-politicians have been appointed to the Court, they have insisted that their decisions have been made on legal, not political grounds. But whether or not political considerations affect the **decision-making process** (see **Role of Court**), the decisions that are made can have definite political consequences, sometimes profound, often dramatic, and generally beyond the Court's control.

DAVID SOLOMON

Further Reading
David Solomon, *The Political High Court* (1999)

Political institution, Court as. The High Court is often said to be a 'political' institution, or to be an important part of the Australian political scene, or to be an important player in Australian politics. This is loose talk. The assertions deserve closer scrutiny.

One of the Court's major roles is to interpret and apply the Constitution. The Constitution is itself a political document: it divides power between the different levels and institutions of government, and it imposes restrictions on the exercise of that power. The Court's interpretations will therefore always have political consequences. But those interpretations are, to state the classical view, arrived at through the impartial application of legal doctrine and principle, by Justices with expertise and wisdom in the law, who exercise **judicial power** with complete **independence** from the executive government (see **Role of Court**).

The classical view is unimpeachably correct. Moreover, those who label the High Court as political frequently confuse the inevitability of the political consequences of its decisions with the quite different question of whether political considerations enter into or guide those decisions. Why, then, is this not the end of the matter?

To start with, the multitude of senses in which the High Court might be said to be a political institution—the rich variety of interactions between the Court and politics—should be clarified. There are at least four.

First, **appointments** to the Court are sometimes said to be political. The appointments are of course made by politicians, and it is sometimes former politicians who are appointed. Neither of these facts makes the Court a political institution in any important sense, or detracts from the classical view of the role of the Court. All of the first five High Court Justices had had political experience, as have many others since, and their practical understanding of the workings of government is often said to be a virtue. Whether or not this is so, the diversity of their records on the Court challenges any generalisation about the connection between their judicial decisions and the presence or absence of prior political experience. Former politician or not, appointees are expected to otherwise meet the necessary qualifications for judicial office and to conform to the classical view of the Court's role in the discharge of their duties.

The assertion that an appointment is political sometimes goes to the motivations of the appointers. The classical view of the role of the Court assumes that the Justices will have been appointed because of their outstanding legal qualifications and experience. But, from among the meritorious, it would not be surprising if the appointers gravitated towards appointees whose general **values** and social outlook, and perhaps general political leanings, were perceived to be similar to their own. In this respect, Labor appointments have often seemed the more overtly political (particularly those of **Evatt**, **McTiernan**, and **Murphy**), but appointments by conservative governments of evidently politically and socially conservative senior barristers are not qualitatively different. **Callinan's** appointment provoked unusual public discussion, but the focus of **criticism** was precisely on the motives of the appointers, who had called publicly for a 'capital C conservative' to be appointed, rather than on the merits of the appointee. Most other appointments by conservative governments have attracted little attention. In any event, the expectations of the appointers are often confounded, sometimes quite spectacularly; general values and social and political outlook, even if correctly perceived, translate uncertainly into the specifics of legal **decision making**.

The second sense in which the High Court might be said to be a political institution relates to judicial behaviour. There is of course a certain 'politics' of decision making, as the dynamics of **conferencing**, the negotiation of **joint judgments**, and other aspects of the internal operation of the Court work themselves out. But there is nothing remarkable about this; every group of decision makers, in every field of human endeavour, has its own internal politics.

More importantly, Justices of the High Court have over the years engaged in a range of extra-judicial activities, some of which might be seen as political or at least as involving, wittingly or unwittingly, forays into politics. Some have been outspoken on issues of public concern—most notably, **Kirby**. **Latham** and **Dixon** were respectively Australian Ministers in Tokyo and Washington before or during **World War II**, though Dixon later had second thoughts about the wisdom of undertaking that role. **Griffith** (in 1914) and **Barwick** (in 1975) advised the Governor-General on constitutional matters. Opinions vary on the appropriateness of these kinds of extra-judicial actions and activities (see **Dismissal of 1975; Non-judicial functions; Separation of powers**), but when a **Chief Justice** advises a Governor-General, it is not difficult to understand the perception of the High Court as a political institution. So far as the classical view of the role of the Court emphasises the complete independence of the Court from the executive, that view is eroded by inappropriate or unwise extra-judicial intrusions into the political process.

The third sense in which the Court might be said to be a political institution relates to the nature and impact of its work. In a broad sense, the Court is an integral part of our system of government, and judicial power is a part of the public power and governmental apparatus of the state. This would be so even if the Court's function were confined to the final determination of matters of private law; but when it extends to reviewing, under the Constitution, the legality of the actions of the other arms of government, its constitutional function is quintessentially political. Institutionally, the Court plays a key role in the political system, and its decisions have profound political consequences—affecting, for example, the balance of power between the Commonwealth and the states, and making possible or frustrating particular government policies or programs (see also **Commonwealth–state relations; Federalism**). The Court's decisions significantly shape the framework in which the politics of the day are played out.

The classical view of the role of the Court is not in any way threatened by the fact that the Court's decisions inevitably have political consequences. Indeed, that these consequences are but the accidental result of the impartial application of legal doctrine is sometimes said to be demonstrated by the even-handedness of the Court's dramatic invalidation of the Chifley Labor government's bank nationalisation legislation in 1948 (see *Bank Nationalisation Case*) and the Court's equally dramatic invalidation of the **Menzies** Liberal government's legislation banning the Communist Party three years later in 1951 (see *Communist Party Case*). That is not to say that individual Justices might not have had political views

about these matters, or that individual Justices might not have found the results of the cases to be politically congenial (Latham, dissenting in the *Communist Party Case*, made it clear that he found the majority result in that case distinctly uncongenial). According to the classical view, however, these views would have been irrelevant to the legal issues that the Court had to decide.

But the difficult question is, can it be fairly said that these and other like decisions were arrived at simply through the 'impartial application of legal doctrine'? This is the fourth and most contentious aspect of whether the Court is a political institution: its decisions have political consequences, but is it influenced or guided in making those decisions by political considerations?

It can be said with some confidence—and it would be unacceptable if it could not—that the Court is not influenced by immediate, short-term, party-political considerations. For one thing, to be so influenced would be inconsistent with the independence of the judiciary from the executive, and the **judicial oath** to do justice according to law. For another, the resolution of legal issues, especially in constitutional cases, calls for the application of general principles that transcend short-term political considerations and cut across other considerations relating to the immediate result of a case. The *Tasmanian Dam Case* (1983), for example, turned not on the politics of conservation (the policy of the federal Labor government) versus development (the policy of the state Liberal government) but on the antecedent question of whether the Commonwealth or Tasmania was constitutionally empowered to resolve that clash of policies. The legal doctrines and principles employed for the resolution of that question would have broad and long-term consequences for other cases and other situations and for Commonwealth and state power generally.

Yet the legal doctrines and principles were far from clear-cut. There were respectable arguments on both sides. The Justices had a choice. The choice would not be resolved by simple resort to legal principle because it was a choice between legal principles. The choice could not be determined by law; the choice determined the law.

What influences choice in these circumstances? It could conceivably be an unadorned intellectual conviction about the superiority of one **argument** over another, without regard to the consequences of those arguments. More likely, it is the subtle influence—conscious or unconscious—of values, **background**, life experience, and general social outlook (see **Jurimetrics**). It would be a mistake to think that the areas of discretionary choice are so large as to give free play to a Justice's personal values, unconstrained by legal principle. But it would equally be a mistake to think that the application of legal principle leaves no room for choice or that that choice is value-free and unaffected by factors external to the law. In this sense, political considerations—understood not narrowly as immediate short-term or party-political considerations but broadly as general social and political philosophy—play an irresistible role in judicial decision making.

The classical view of the role of the Court may be unimpeachably correct, but judging is different from political policy making. Politicians are elected and are answerable to the electors. Justices are appointed on the basis of their legal skills; their legitimacy resides in their commitment to legal doctrine and principle. Yet the classical view is incomplete. When legal doctrine and principle are found wanting, or competing doctrines and principles throw up difficult choices, broader considerations inevitably impinge.

Interestingly, in **constitutional interpretation** these broader considerations are themselves incorporated into and expressed in the form of legal principles. In the *Tasmanian Dam Case*, the close division of opinion reflected different views of the nature of the federal polity enshrined in the Constitution. These views were framed partly in terms of what the **framers of the Constitution** must have intended, though this was more a way of expressing a conclusion than a source of guidance towards it. The different views pitted the policy of a strong national voice in international affairs against the policy of a genuine federal division of powers. Those **policy considerations** were transmuted into legal conclusions.

Dixon, the Court's most often quoted proponent of 'strict and complete **legalism**', also famously observed that 'the Constitution is a political instrument ... It is not a question whether the considerations [providing the ground for restraining Commonwealth power] are political, for nearly every consideration arising from the Constitution can be so described, but whether they are compelling' (*Melbourne Corporation Case* (1947)). Nothing captures the complexity and subtlety of the nature of the Court's role as a 'political' institution better than this cryptic aphorism.

MICHAEL COPER

Further Reading
Michael Coper, *Encounters with the Australian Constitution* (1987, popular edn 1988) ch 3
Brian Galligan, *Politics of the High Court* (1987)
David Solomon, *The Political High Court* (1999)

Political parties. For more than a century, political parties have been dominant actors in Australian politics. Australia's parliamentary system of **responsible government** is effectively a system of party government, with the executive formed by the majority party in the lower House of Parliament. Instead of Parliament controlling the executive, as the democratic theory of parliamentary government would have it, the executive controls Parliament through iron discipline over its own party. The leader who wins elections and keeps the confidence of his or her party is the **Prime Minister**. Parliament provides the ritualised public forum for pronouncing policy and passing legislation, as well as the place for testing leadership and doing verbal battle with the Opposition. At least that is the case for the House of Representatives. The Senate's role is less clearly defined: to the extent that it functions as a 'house of review', its scrutiny of the conduct of government may sometimes be more effective—because, although a party House, it is usually not controlled by the government but by minor parties and independents, elected under the voting system of proportional representation introduced in 1949.

Party government in Australia has shaped the environment of **judicial review** and at particular times provided challenges for the High Court. Fusing the executive and legislature by means of disciplined parties reduces parliamentary scrutiny and heightens the need for judicial **independence**. At times,

Justices have defended a more **activist** role for the Court to compensate for executive dominance and the lack of parliamentary accountability. The Court's 1990s sortie into **implied constitutional rights** is a notable instance.

Partisanship in judicial **appointments** has occasionally been a contentious issue. For most of its history, however, the Court has professed a strict **legalism**, interpreting rather than making law, and has usually been taken at its word. In most of the 43 appointments to the High Court, governments have, without obvious political regard, chosen leading barristers and judges. Non-Labor governments have made 29 appointments, or just over two-thirds of all High Court judges, and Labor governments only 14. Such asymmetry parallels Labor's proportion of time in federal office, in part because of its earlier fractious history of party splits.

The appointment of prominent lawyer–politicians to the Court has become increasingly rare. The exception was the early 'Founders' Courts', where the first five appointees in 1903 and 1906 were all prominent **framers of the Constitution** and leading politicians. Federal politics had not yet crystallised into the enduring divide between Labor and the Liberal–Conservative coalition. Since 1906, there have been five practising politicians appointed to the Court. Labor made three of these appointments: **Evatt** and **McTiernan** in 1930 and **Murphy** in 1975. Evatt and McTiernan had both been active Labor politicians, while Murphy was a colourful federal Senator and **Attorney-General**. Non-Labor governments have made two appointments of leading conservative politicians: **Latham** as **Chief Justice** in 1935 and **Barwick** as Chief Justice in 1964. Both men had been outstanding lawyers as well as senior ministers so that, in contrast to the storms of **criticism** against the Labor appointments, there was no public controversy. A few other Justices, such as **Powers** and **Knox**, had some political experience or past identification with political parties (see **Background of Justices**).

The main political challenge to the Court has come from the Labor Party, a reformist party with a centralist bent that until the 1960s was formally pledged to abolish **federalism** and downgrade the states to administrative agencies. In 1957, rising Labor leader Gough **Whitlam** characterised Australia's political history as 'Labor versus the Constitution', with the Court pitted against Labor by its interpretations of the Constitution. This is hardly surprising, since Labor was a centralist and social reformist party (see **Socialism**) that had virtually no input into the making of the federal Constitution in the 1890s but won federal office in 1910. The Court had already overturned Alfred **Deakin**'s 'New Protection' policy of tying tariff protection for manufacturers to the payment by companies of higher wages, and emasculated the **corporations power** in *Huddart Parker v Moorehead* (1909). Labor's ambitious policies for controlling monopolies and trusts and setting up a national **conciliation and arbitration** system were problematical, so Labor began prefacing its major policy planks with proposals for sweeping constitutional change. When in office, Labor attempted to expand Commonwealth powers through constitutional referendums—but all of these were defeated except the social services **amendment** in 1946. Alternatively, it sought to change the direction of the High Court by increasing its size and appointing Justices more sympathetic to its policies, but with limited success.

Labor's first chance to shape the Court was after **O'Connor**'s death in 1912, when the Fisher government increased the size of the Court from five to seven Justices. Attorney-General WM Hughes, who masterminded the change, chose **Gavan Duffy**, Powers, and **Piddington** as the new bloc. Piddington's appointment was aborted when he resigned without sitting on the Bench after public controversy over his assurance to Hughes that he favoured the Commonwealth over the states. **Rich** was appointed instead. Controversy also surrounded the next brace of Labor appointments: Evatt and McTiernan. They were appointed at the insistence of the federal Labor caucus and against the wishes of Prime Minister James Scullin and Attorney-General Frank Brennan, who were overseas at the time. This time, the government and its appointees weathered the storm. The third incident of attempted Labor court packing was in late 1945; if successful, it could have changed the direction and legitimacy of the Court. Radical members of the Labor Cabinet pushed through a decision to make three new appointments in late 1945, one to fill the seventh place that had remained unfilled since **Isaacs'** retirement in 1931 and two new positions to increase the Court's size to nine. This was overturned by Evatt in a fiery Cabinet confrontation when he returned from overseas in early 1946. Consequently, **Webb** was the only Labor appointment during the long period of Labor rule during the 1940s (see **Appointments that might have been**). The next Labor appointment, that of **Jacobs** in 1974, was uncontroversial; but the same could not be said of Murphy's appointment in 1975. Thus until the extended period of 'New Labor' government under Bob Hawke and Paul Keating from 1983 to 1996, Labor governments had all experienced difficulty with the Court or made controversial appointments.

The Liberal–Conservative side of politics, under various Protectionist, Fusion, Liberal, Nationalist, and United Australia names, in coalition with the Country or National party, has routinely appointed the bulk of High Court Justices without public controversy. The **Menzies** Liberal–Country Party coalition government, for example, appointed seven Justices to the High Court including Barwick as Chief Justice, as well as elevating **Dixon** to the Chief Justiceship in 1952. All the Menzies appointees were leading barristers or judges from Sydney or Melbourne: **Kitto**, Douglas **Menzies**, **Windeyer**, and Barwick were leaders of the Bar, and **Fullagar**, **Taylor**, and **Owen** were already **state Supreme Court** judges. None except Barwick had political experience, and all shared the legal culture and constitutional jurisprudence espoused by Robert Menzies as leading **counsel** in the *Engineers Case* (1920) and championed by Menzies' mentor, Dixon, on the Court.

That is not to imply that Liberal–Conservative governments have not been astute in choosing Justices of broadly similar outlook, or that their appointees have always favoured their policies. Deakin admitted that his prime motive in expanding the **number of Justices** in 1906 to five, and appointing Isaacs and **Higgins**, was to enhance Commonwealth power. These two radical nationalists orchestrated the subsequent *Engineers* revolution in **constitutional interpretation** that has led inexorably to the expansion of Commonwealth power. On the other hand, the High Court, after

striking down the Chifley Labor government's attempt to nationalise banking in 1948 (see *Bank Nationalisation Case* (1948)), also quashed the Menzies government's illiberal attempt to ban the Communist Party in 1951 (see *Communist Party Case* (1951)).

The most intemperate stance of the non-Labor parties was during the 1990s in response to the decisions of the **Mason Court** and the **Brennan Court** on **native title** and implied constitutional rights. National and Liberal state premiers from Queensland and WA branded the Court as lawless and political. Deputy Prime Minister Tim Fischer accused the Court of manipulating the timing of its decisions for political purposes, and threatened that the government would make 'capital C conservative' appointments to change its direction. Not surprisingly, there was controversy over the ensuing appointment of **Callinan** from Queensland.

The taming of the Labor Party, and the expansive interpretation of **Commonwealth legislative powers** by the High Court, has changed the dynamics of Australia's constitutional politics. Labor is now a party committed to market solutions and corporate management practices, instead of nationalisation and government direction of the **economy**. Because of the Court's expansive interpretation of Commonwealth powers using the *Engineers* methodology, federal governments have more than ample scope to implement their policies. Hence, party has become a less contentious issue in Australian constitutional politics. Ironically, the Labor Party would expand the Court's **role** in public affairs by having a **Bill of Rights**, while the Liberal–National coalition is opposed on partisan grounds. Politicising the Court is now more likely to be provoked by the Justices' open profession of **realism** without giving a plausible, legitimating account for the activist role that such a profession implies.

BRIAN GALLIGAN

Further Reading
Brian Galligan, *Politics of the High Court: A Study of the Judicial Branch of Government in Australia* (1987)
Robert Menzies, *Central Power in the Australian Commonwealth* (1967)
Geoffrey Sawer, *Australian Federalism in the Courts* (1967)
Gough Whitlam, *On Australia's Constitution* (1977)

Popular culture. There are times when the facts and issues of a particular case bring judges directly into contact with manifestations of popular culture. At other times, awareness of the role of **values** in **decision-making** may prompt judges to resort to popular attitudes ('community beliefs and values') as a guide to decision making, on the basis that the **role** of the Court is to act as an institutional representative of those beliefs.

McHugh has recognised, however ('The Judicial Method' (1999) 73 *ALJ* 37), that in 'a multi-cultural society, which is constantly undergoing rapid social and economic change', any search for 'permanent or enduring community values' is in vain. (His perception of the present chaotic state of popular culture is drawn from Paul Kelly's book *The End of Certainty* (1992).) He concludes that, when popular culture is in transitional confusion and upheaval, judges are likely to rely primarily on the values secreted within the legal culture itself. He instances 'values such as freedom of the individual, **equality** before the law, certainty and predictability, **unconscionability**, good faith, **reasonableness** and, in recent years, fairness'. Such values may or may not resonate in popular culture; what is important is that they saturate the **authoritative legal materials**.

McHugh's analysis may appear to imply a dichotomy between popular culture and **legalism**, or at least between popular and legal values. This, however, would be too simple. Judges may react to popular culture in various ways: sometimes distancing themselves from it through legalism, sometimes appropriating it to support their own reasoning, and (rarely) seeking to apprehend it as part of the changing human experience to which the development of law should respond. It is understandable that judges may often be tempted to fall back on legalism when faced with the difficulty of coming to grips with a culture characterised by the implosion of meaning through the overproduction of images—a phenomenon Jean Baudrillard has described as 'hyperreality'. Moreover, even when they do try to come to terms with this culture and use it to support legal reasoning, they tend to resort to their own frames of reference to shape their presentation of reality. There is no suggestion that the images or experiences that the Justices draw upon might be problematic or contestable (see **Judicial notice**). Instead, in the context of legal discourse, these realities are invested with authority so that they come to shape the law. Transposing this event in Baudrillardian terms, these realities become more legal than real.

In *Dickenson's Arcade v Tasmania* (1974), **Barwick** waxed lyrical about the social experiences of shared cigarettes and tobacco. At one level, he invoked as the frame of reference for his decision a romantic image from his youth—a scene that was real in his experience. But his story featuring the old man on the wall also reads simply as a rhetorical and poetic fiction. By presenting it as real and therefore as fact, however, Barwick effectively used this fiction to demonstrate that the operation of Tasmania's consumption tax on tobacco was itself unrealistic.

In *Adamson's Case* (1979), conflicting popular attitudes divided the Court on state lines over whether Australian Rules football was subject to the *Trade Practices Act* 1974 (Cth). On the one hand, the commercial promotion of the game and its massive corporate earnings led **Mason** and other Sydney Justices to conclude that the participating clubs and leagues were 'trading corporations'. On the other hand, **Stephen** (from Melbourne) was eloquent in his explanation that such earnings simply showed how 'ardently' the game was supported by those 'content to find their reward in the satisfaction of their enthusiasm' for 'Australia's most popular spectator sport'. **Aickin**, also from Melbourne, expressed his 'complete agreement' with Stephen.

When civil libertarians challenged the censorship laws by producing magazines called *Censor* and *Obscenity* (*Crowe v Graham* (1968)), the whole Court held that the publication of such material to the world at large was an offence to 'community standards', but both Barwick and **Windeyer** were readily able to imagine subcultures in which such material would not have been offensive. For Barwick, 'sexual matters were referred to ... in a way that might pass muster in a tap room or smoke concert'; for Windeyer, with his military **background**, 'the

photographs ... are of a kind which might be found pinned up to decorate the wall of a barrack room or hut'.

In all these cases, the influence of the Justices' backgrounds is clearly apparent. When rival toymakers in *Day v Perrott* (1924) disputed the **patent** rights to a system using nuts and bolts to lock the parts of construction toys together, the manufacturers of Meccano construction sets were not parties to the proceedings; but the Justices were quick to demonstrate their familiarity with Meccano, and used their knowledge of Meccano as the frame of reference of the decision. For **Isaacs** and **Rich**, 'Meccano, or the elements of constructional toys, was well known'; for **Starke**, 'there was nothing novel in all this, for the well-known "Meccano" toy sets are constructed on the same principle'. It is obvious that this knowledge is derived from the fact that the Justices were **men**—or at least that they were once little boys. By contrast, in the *Berlei Bra Case* (1973), the Justices demonstrated a striking unfamiliarity with women's lingerie.

The influence of the Justices' religious or moral inclinations was evident in *Transport Publishing Co v Literature Board of Review* (1956). The proceedings concerned a range of love comics with titles such as 'Darling Romance', and the issue was whether these publications had an undue emphasis on **sex**, or were 'likely to be injurious to morality ... or encourage depravity', within the meaning of the *Objectionable Literature Act* 1954 (Qld). The majority Justices, **Dixon**, **Kitto**, and **Taylor**, allowing the publishers' appeal, appeared to be just as engrossed in the stories of romance as the feminine audience at whom they understood the publications to be aimed. Their account reads as much like a 'romance novel' as the romance novels in dispute. The majority Justices associated the images evoked with American culture and cinema, so that ultimately these American values were used to evaluate the publications and their impact on their readers:

> The stories and the pictures bear every mark of American origin. The drug store and the campus may be the place of meeting and the scenes through which the story takes the lovers thence are American and so is the idiom of the simple speech in which it is told. The whole atmosphere resembles that of American cinema.

Capturing here what Baudrillard was later to encapsulate in his aphorism that 'life is cinematic', the Justices found that there was no danger to the morality of the readers of the romance novels. At worst, the Justices opined, the content of the publications 'is an affront to the intelligence of the reader but hardly a real threat to her morals'. By contrast, **McTiernan** and **Webb**, the two Catholics on the Court, dissented. McTiernan, appalled by the publications, thundered: 'Some of the publications, of course, are less evil than others, but all of them are distinctly evil.'

Sometimes, the Justices are able to demonstrate their familiarity with popular culture by drawing on its resources for **metaphor**. Yet, typically, unlike the examples given above, these metaphorical invocations of phenomena in popular culture are purposely made to illuminate a sense of fiction rather than fact, though still for the ultimate purpose of supporting a process of legal reasoning. When Mason observed that the bungled Australian Security Intelligence Service training exercise in *A v Hayden* (1984) 'has the appearance of a Law School moot based on an episode taken from the adventures of Maxwell Smart', he was using this allusion to emphasise what he called the 'air of unreality' about the entire affair. McHugh had the same purpose when he wrote in *Yanner v Eaton* (1999)—and repeated in *Re Pacific Coal; Ex parte CFMEU* (2000)— that 'words in legislative instruments should not be read as if they were buildings on a movie set—structures with the appearance of reality but having no substance behind them'. This was no mere demonstration of familiarity with the backlots of Hollywood; it was a deliberate and effective invocation of the unreal.

When Justices have to deal with the technical or commercial aspects of popular culture, or when everyday cultural objects become the focus for claims to patent protection or allegations of patent infringement, they typically resort to an elaborate diction in which the technical process involved is described with a curious combination of particularity and detachment, making it more legal than real. No doubt, in patent cases, this diction reflects the conventions of painstaking detail in the writing of specifications for a patentable invention or improvement. Sometimes, the Court is conscious of the incongruity that the use of such language involves: for example, when Dixon in *Martin v Scribal* (1954) launched into an elaborate explanation of a ball with an 'inner revolving face … in contact with a column of viscous ink' contained in 'a capillary tube or duct the diameter of which should not exceed 4 mm', and having an air vent at the other end so that 'a concave meniscus is formed at the interface of the viscous fluid and the air', he was conscious that he was giving 'an abstract description … of an ordinary ball-point pen'. The use of such language has a double effect. Confronted with physical or mechanical processes in the real world, it appropriates them into the language of legal discourse and thus into the world of law, while at the same time effecting a self-conscious distancing from the real world—a fastidious refusal to engage with the world on its own terms.

Through this refusal, the Court is able to deal with the technological or commercial aspects of phenomena in popular culture without engaging with their cultural content. When JC Bancks, the creator of the comic strip character Ginger Meggs, complained that the technological change from colour newsprint to rotogravure in the production of Sunday comics was a fundamental breach of his **contract** (*Associated Newspapers v Bancks* (1951)), the Court was able to decide in his favour without considering the identity and significance of Ginger Meggs in Australian culture.

At one level, when the Court held in *Radio Corporation v Disney* (1937) that an Australian manufacturer of radio receivers was not entitled to give them the **trade marks** 'Mickey Mouse' and 'Minnie Mouse', the Justices' encounter with Mickey and Minnie evoked the usual stilted diction. Mickey and Minnie were 'fantastic and amusing cinema characters', whose 'grotesque forms and absurd antics' had given the public 'pleasure and amusement'. In this way, Mickey and Minnie Mouse are appropriated into legal formalism, and find themselves reinvented in legal discourse. At a deeper level, however, the cultural significance of Mickey and Minnie was the crux of the issue.

The applicants argued that Mickey and Minnie Mouse were 'simply the well-known names of highly popular characters in the fiction of the cinema … and that no one possesses an exclusive right to their use'. For the Court, however, the question whether Disney had any exclusive rights was irrelevant. It was an issue between the applicants and the 'public', relating to the unique cultural significance of Mickey Mouse in the minds of the public. **Latham** noted with an air of judicial objectivity that Mickey and Minnie had 'become very popular throughout the world', and held that because of the unique 'world-wide association of ideas' between Disney and Mickey Mouse, the registration of the trade mark would be 'likely to deceive'. Rich agreed, but found it less easy to reduce the cultural phenomenon to a dry statement of objective facts and logical consequences. For him, it was 'fruitless to inquire' how the association with Disney had arisen: it was simply a matter of 'the vague and indefinite impressions of the great mass of the public', perhaps analogous 'to the fame of some personage of fiction or history'. He saw no need to state 'in definite terms' precisely how the public might be confused, since by definition 'confusion involves indefiniteness of ideas'. For Dixon, it was not a question of deceiving the public at all, but of public enthusiasm being exploited 'improperly': the Court ought not to approve 'the unauthorised diversion' by the applicants of 'the celebrity and reputation' attaching to Mickey Mouse as an 'intangible advantage arising from public celebrity, widespread fame and interest'.

The Court's refusal to rule on the **property** rights to Mickey and Minnie Mouse, focusing instead on the cultural perception of the relationship between them and Disney as an object of consumption, represents a radical departure from the liberal underpinnings of property law. Mickey and Minnie are not the property of one, nor of the many. In terms of Baudrillard's theories of contemporary consumerism, 'the subject no longer provides the vantage point of reality': that is, possessive individualism in such a context has no meaning, and the cultural phenomena are the focus of attention. 'The privileged position has shifted to the object' (Mark Poster, *Jean Baudrillard: Selected Writings* (1988)).

What happens when the Court itself becomes dramatically swept up in the current of sensational public events? In the *Communist Party Case* (1951) and the *Tasmanian Dam Case* (1983), the Court reacted by emphasising the strict and complete legalism of its concerns, seeking to maintain the integrity of legal discourse even in the supercharged atmosphere of public excitation. The *Chamberlain Case* (1984) was more complex. Clearly, the majority Justices who dismissed Lindy Chamberlain's appeal were at pains to distance themselves from the trial by **media** hysteria surrounding the case: for example, **Gibbs** and Mason made it clear that they saw the Chamberlains' strong religious faith as supporting the hypothesis of innocence, rather than inviting suspicion. In dismissing the appeal on the ground that the jury could 'safely' or 'comfortably' have arrived at its guilty verdict, all three majority Justices made it clear that they were deferring to popular judgments only in the sense that the **common law** commitment to **jury trial** has always done: namely, that on questions of guilt or innocence it is the jury, not the court (and still less an appellate court) that truly represents the community. Yet in one respect the majority Justices may perhaps have shared in a widespread popular perception of the Chamberlains generated by media images: namely, the perception that Lindy Chamberlain's stoic composure in media interviews was inconsistent with the innocence of a bereaved and traumatised mother. **Brennan** said that 'the jury may have thought' that the Chamberlains' conduct when interviewed 'was inconsistent with the manifestations of shock and grief of the night before'. Gibbs and Mason thought that 'if she committed the crime she was extraordinarily self-possessed and a clever actress'. These echoes of media images were hypothetical and indirect; but they sit uncomfortably with the Court's own striving for detachment and objectivity in the circumstances of the case.

In rare instances, Justices have engaged with a cultural phenomenon on its own terms (as Rich did in *Disney*), rather than simply transposing it into legal terms or denying its potency. In *Phonographic Performance Co v Federation of Commercial Television Stations* (1998), the Court had to determine whether, when the soundtrack of a feature film shown on television included popular songs—and particularly when what was included was only a fleeting snatch of a commercially released recording—the **copyright** in the song or recording was infringed by the telecast of the film. By 3:2, the Court held that it was. The majority judgment of **Gaudron**, **Gummow**, and **Hayne** described the two specific examples before the Court with the usual fastidious detachment. By contrast, the **dissenting judgment** of McHugh and **Kirby** traced the problem to its roots 'in the history of cinema', going back 'at least to the advent of "talkies"'. They appreciated that the commercial and artistic interrelation between music and cinema soundtracks is more complex than the particular examples adduced in the litigation: for example, that the use of a recording in a soundtrack, 'far from disadvantaging the makers and later owners of copyright in sound recordings, [may] actually tend (in many cases at least) to promote the fame and fortune of the original sound recording, the artists involved in it and their other works'. They thought that this was particularly so in view of 'the modern expansion of broadcasting as a global phenomenon'. In a footnote, they added examples of music which had gained a lasting place in popular culture precisely because of its use in a soundtrack: 'the music from *Singing in the Rain*, *The Wizard of Oz*, *Star Wars*, *The Man From Snowy River* and *The Piano*, as well as songs embodied in the various Pink Panther and James Bond movies'. It was probably Kirby who, a few footnotes later, emphasised the limits of judicial development in response to new technologies, by saying: 'Courts cannot always, in the manner of Star Trek's Captain Jean-Luc Picard, say "Make it so!"'

In their dissent, McHugh and Kirby demonstrate sensitivity to the changing technologies of popular culture in a way that looks both backward and forward. On the one hand, their appreciation of the momentous change that came about 'once sound-tracks were added to moving films' recalls the dilemma that the **Latham Court** had faced in *JC Williamson v Metro-Goldwyn-Mayer* (1937). In 1924, JC Williamson, at that time perhaps the major theatrical entrepreneur in Australasia, had obtained the exclusive rights to produce the musical *Rose Marie* in Australasia and South Africa, with an exception for 'motion picture film rights'. At the time of that agreement, neither party had anticipated the development of sound films. Nevertheless, the Court held that the reservation covered sound films as well as silent films—with the result that the MGM film starring Jeanette McDonald and Nelson Eddy could be shown in Australia. On the other hand, the dissent in *Phonographic Performance* is particularly sensitive to the possibility that inappropriate copyright laws might impede the development of new forms of 'multimedia products (such as, perhaps, "interactive" movies)'. The degree of foresight shown here (and adduced as a reason for judicial caution) may prove comparable to that shown by Rich in *Victoria Park Racing v Taylor* (1937) (and used as a reason for judicial creativity):

The prospects of television make our present decision a very important one, and I venture to think that the advance of that art may force the courts to recognize that protection against the complete exposure of the doings of the individual may be a right indispensable to the enjoyment of life.

Francesca Dominello

Further Reading
Jean Baudrillard, *In the Shadow of the Silent Majorities* (1983)
Jean Baudrillard, *America* (1988)
Jean Baudrillard, *Fatal Strategies* (1990)

Popular images of Court. The High Court has rarely been represented to the public outside the news **media**, which themselves provide a vital machine in the production of popular images. Any depictions of the Court in the arts have tended to come from within the **legal profession**. Callinan's novel *The Lawyer and the Libertine* (1996) stands out as a work with a plot centred on the Court. Its two protagonists end the novel respectively as High Court **Chief Justice** and Commonwealth **Attorney-General**, and the story of their lifetime rivalry is a lawyer's *roman à clef*. However, the novel itself has not really appealed to a popular audience, and lawyers are probably more aware of its existence than most lay people.

Despite occasional documentaries about the Court in recent times, primarily on television, the general absence of images of the Court has assisted in conjuring up its contemporary popular image as inaccessible—either because it is perceived as affordable only to the wealthy and therefore as protecting their interests only, or because, as a final court of appeal, its focus is more on technical questions of law than on the factual issues arising from a particular case. Whatever the reason for the absence of images, the impression is left that whatever the Court does is of little interest to anyone other than lawyers and the media. Even when the Court takes centre stage in a dispute of popular interest (for example, the *Tasmanian Dam Case* (1983)), there is usually a perception that the Court's intervention is only ancillary to the unfolding of broader public issues.

This is evident in two Australian feature films, *Newsfront* (1978) and *Evil Angels* (1988), where the Court is referred to fleetingly in news items incorporated in each film. In the former, the reference is to the Court's decision in the *Communist Party Case* (1951); in the latter, it is to its decision in

Dennis Denuto (Tiriel Mora), Lawrence Hamill QC (Charles Tingwell) and Darryl Kerrigan (Michael Caton) approach the Court in *The Castle*

the *Chamberlain Case* (1984). Both films are based on real events; the news coverage of those events has a cinematic quality; and when that news coverage is then incorporated within the medium of film, the events themselves become cinematic. Yet in both films, the references to the Court are verbal only: a soundtrack voiceover reports the outcome of each decision as a remote event that happens off-screen.

Newsfront, directed by Phillip Noyce, is explicitly a film about the media, looking nostalgically at the history of Australian cinema newsreels from the end of **World War II** to the introduction of television in 1956. The reference to the Court is made in a voiceover which is being recorded for a newsreel being produced about the Australian anti-communist campaign (a theme that permeates the entire film). While the scene is set in the newsreel production room (constructed as part of the film set), and the voiceover is part of the film and constitutes part of the drama of the film, the accompanying visual images of Robert **Menzies** and of a protest march during the referendum campaign are real. Through a combination of narration and visual images, the continuity of events is established—moving swiftly from Menzies' condemnation of 'the Communist pressure all round the world' to the defeat of the *Communist Party Dissolution Act* in the High Court, to the Menzies government's referendum campaign after the Court's decision. While the absence of any visual image of the Court might go unnoticed by a lay person, it may be more obvious to a lawyer, who is likely to have a heightened sense of the **role** of the Court in the sequence of events. The visual images that have been used, however, may be more like what ordinary Australians associated with the events at the time: images of Menzies, who was an adamant opponent of communism, and images of the referendum campaign that divided the nation.

Evil Angels, directed by Fred Schepisi, is an Australian film based on the true story of Michael and Lindy Chamberlain (played by Sam Neill and Meryl Streep), and on the subsequent book by John Bryson in 1985 with the same title. In the book, the reference to the Court comes close to the end and simply reports: 'An appeal to the High Court of Australia was lost, three judges to two, on 22 February 1984.' The reference to the Court in the film is made in a voiceover commentary of a television newscast, announcing that the Chamberlains have lost their High Court appeal. The accompanying visual

images are of Lindy Chamberlain gardening in the prison grounds and of print media stories supporting the Chamberlains. The film cuts to what appears to be a re-enactment of a television interview given by Michael Chamberlain about the outcome of the appeal. The film then cuts to a household of people watching the broadcast who appear unsympathetic towards the Chamberlains. The television is switched off before the news item is finished.

The treatment of the High Court appeal in the film is minuscule when compared to the detailed depiction of the events leading up to the disappearance of Azaria Chamberlain, the Coroner's inquest into her death and the 1982 criminal trial. However, this allocation of time within the film is proportionate: in their different ways, both *Evil Angels* and *Newsfront* are films about the media, and both attribute to the media a role far overshadowing that of the Court. By the time of the appeal, the role of the media in generating public controversy has been well established. The film's reference to the Court's 3:2 division, while relating the outcome of the appeal and thus moving the story along, also symbolises the division in public opinion. Yet this entire sequence serves mainly as an occasion to present one of the many interviews given by Michael Chamberlain, and as a further depiction of divided public opinion. Throughout the film, the Chamberlains' interviews are portrayed as keeping their story alive and as feeding public divisiveness. But, while Michael Chamberlain also states during the interview that despite the Court's decision the drama is not over, the real drama of interest to the public has already been played out. As one member of the household watching the television interview exclaims: 'Talk about flogging a dead horse.' The film, like the book, ends soon after.

In contrast to *Newsfront* and *Evil Angels*, *The Castle* (1997), directed by Rob Sitch, is a comedy based on a fictional story, presented as if it were a true story in the form of a narrative by Dale Kerrigan (Stephen Curry) about the way his father Darryl Kerrigan (Michael Caton) took on a multi-million dollar corporation and won. The more significant contrast is that while in the docu-dramas of both *Newsfront* and *Evil Angels* the Court is given only a small role, in *The Castle* the Court has a starring role when, in successfully upholding Darryl's appeal, it saves the day for the Kerrigan family and their neighbours Farouk (Costas Kilias), Jack (Monty Maizels), and Evonne (Linda Gibson).

Inspired by the Court's decision in **Mabo** (1992), and poignantly linking the threat to the Kerrigans with the theft of lands belonging to **Aboriginal peoples**, *The Castle* presents an image of the Court as a place where ordinary Australians can go to vindicate their rights under the Constitution (and tell the government 'to shove it'). As a response to the controversy surrounding the *Mabo* decision, *The Castle* demonstrates the way the Court's judicial **activism** can recognise and protect the land rights of Aboriginal and non-Aboriginal peoples alike when their rights are threatened by large corporations interested only in making large profits.

However, apart from this highly idealised depiction of the Court (for if the case described in *The Castle* came before the Court in reality, it would probably fail), other aspects of the film simply confirm the image of the Court as inaccessible. Darryl did not know he could appeal to the High Court, as is evident when he exclaims: 'But we've been to the **Federal**

Court. How much further can we take it?' But implicit in the dialogue is his understanding that he must have a 'QC' to help him, that 'they're the lawyers rich people use' and that he would have had no hope of success if he had not found a friendly retired QC in Lawrence Hamill (Charles Tingwell), who was willing to help him 'gratis'. Before the High Court **building** in Canberra, the camera angle gives the Court the image of a monolithic deity, which the three characters, Darryl, Dennis, and even Hamill QC approach as meek subjects and humble supplicants. Furthermore, while the argument first made by Darryl as an unrepresented applicant before the Administrative Appeals Tribunal (AAT) becomes the basis for Hamill's closing argument before the High Court, it seems to have more authority coming from a barrister than from Darryl: the former can successfully combine legal argument and sentiment in a way that neither Darryl (in the AAT) nor Dennis Denuto (Tiriel Mora) (in the Federal Court), both lacking in legal knowledge, had the capacity to do.

Needless to say, the depiction of the Court is obviously a fairy-tale picture. Inside the **courtroom**, anyone who has visited the Court building would be aware that the setting is not in fact one of its courtrooms. The only aspect of the scene that appears real is that the respondent corporation has too many lawyers instructing **counsel**. Everything else in the scene is fictional: the **Court attire** of the three sitting Justices (Roger Neave, Tony Evans, and Robin Miller) wearing red robes and full-bottomed wigs looks more like something out of Gilbert and Sullivan than the Court dress of High Court Justices. Their appearance, including agedness, facial hair, and spectacles, suggests a caricature of High Court Justices (or at most is reminiscent of Justices long dead) rather than a realistic depiction of any members of the Court in 1997. The fact that Darryl and Dennis are allowed to sit at the Bar table with Hamill QC is quite contrary to the usual **etiquette** of the Court. The close shots of the Bar table, the Bench, and the characters give a sense of intimacy, while the *mise en scène* of the courtroom, the lighting, and the warm colours of the robes and of the wood finishes are antithetical to the initial perception of inaccessibility outside the High Court building. In fact, of the three legal institutions depicted in the film—the AAT, the Federal Court, and the High Court—the High Court in this scene is depicted as the most accessible, while the AAT, which in many cases is the first port of call for many claims of abuses of fairness and **natural justice**, and must deal with many more **litigants in person** like Darryl than either the Federal Court or the High Court, is depicted as the least accessible.

Straight from the courtroom scene, the film cuts to the evening's *National Nine News* with Ian Ross (playing himself) who reports: 'First tonight, a landmark decision in the High Court today has confirmed the age-old saying "a man's home is his castle"'. The news broadcast then cuts to footage shot earlier showing Darryl, Dennis, and Hamill QC leaving the High Court building and being greeted by a barrage of media representatives (a common sight nowadays when a landmark decision is handed down by the Court), while the footage is accompanied by a voiceover commentary. Their victory, broadcast 'all over the news that night', establishes Darryl Kerrigan not only as a 'notable litigant' but also as a national hero. Dale Kerrigan proudly reports in his voiceover

narrative that 'the victory was reported in all of the newspapers. It came to be known as the *Kerrigan* decision'.

Although *The Castle* is a work of fiction, its incorporation of narration, references to real High Court decisions such as *Mabo*, the *Tasmanian Dam Case*, *Grace Bros v Commonwealth* (1946), and *Georgiadis v Australian & Overseas Telecommunications Corporation* (1994), and media attention from Channel Nine, including an appearance by one of their better-known news anchormen, give the impression that events in the film actually took place—the film then is another example of life made cinematic just as in *Newsfront* and in *Evil Angels*.

Many of the film's messages ring true. The depiction of the relationship between the media and the Court demonstrates how, as in the case of Eddie Mabo, fame can be achieved virtually overnight. For all the perceptions of the Court as inaccessible, such accessibility as it has depends on the media, which has the resources (including assistance from **commentators**) to simplify and make comprehensible to its wide audience what would otherwise be incomprehensible. At times, coverage of the Court may be critical, at other times comical. Inevitably, as with any other news item, the information disseminated about the Court by the media may not be uniform or of equal interest to the public. It may be biased and selective, and it may give an unreliable picture of the Court. Yet, as *The Castle* illustrates, the contribution of media to images of the Court, including its image as a maker of news, cannot be ignored.

FRANCESCA DOMINELLO

Positivism. 'Legal positivism' is an ambiguous term that has been applied to a variety of philosophical theories of law. The elements common to most of them are the claims that law and morality are conceptually distinct, and that the identification of valid law depends fundamentally on factual rather than moral criteria. Legal positivists regard law as a human artefact, whose content depends on beliefs and practices that vary from one place to another, rather than on universal standards of justice or morality. It follows that the law in any jurisdiction may be just or unjust.

'Legal positivism' usually denotes theories of law, not theories of adjudication. At least since the time of John Austin (1790–1859), positivist theories of law have frequently been accompanied by theories of adjudication that concede and even emphasise the inevitability of a judicial **law-making role**, guided by moral and political value judgments (nowadays, often referred to in positivist theories as 'judicial discretion'). This is because, if the identification of law is fundamentally dependent on factual rather than moral criteria, it will sometimes be unclear, internally inconsistent, or incomplete, and consequently unable to provide judges with a determinate solution. In such cases, judges must go beyond the law, and exercise discretion guided by their own moral or political **values**. At the same time, legal positivists have frequently argued that such judicial discretion is confined to 'penumbral' or 'interstitial' areas, in relatively uncommon 'hard cases'.

Legal positivism is best understood by comparing it with its traditional adversary, **natural law**. Some natural law theories deny that law and morality are conceptually distinct, and assert that the identification of law necessarily depends partly on moral criteria, such as justice. They have therefore claimed that an extremely unjust norm cannot be a valid law: its injustice is inconsistent with its being regarded as law. They regard this as a universal truth that applies to all legal systems, by virtue of the very concept of 'law'.

'Exclusive' legal positivists hold that the identification of law depends exclusively on factual criteria, whereas 'inclusive' legal positivists argue that it may depend on moral criteria as well—but only if they are made legally relevant by their incorporation or authorisation through positive law. So long as that condition is satisfied, 'inclusive' legal positivists concede that the identification of valid law may sometimes depend on moral criteria—for example, when judges have to decide whether a statute is invalid because it violates a constitutionally protected right whose application requires moral judgment. Nevertheless, they insist that moral criteria are relevant to legal validity only if they have as a matter of fact been positively enacted in a legal document such as a Constitution. Only then are they legal as well as moral criteria, and so legal validity still depends ultimately on factual criteria.

'Exclusive' legal positivists deny even this. They argue that when a legal document requires judges to invalidate any law that violates stated moral criteria, it in effect requires them to exercise an essentially legislative power. Rather than ascertaining that the law is invalid according to legal criteria, the judges make the law invalid by applying extra-legal criteria.

Legal positivists, and especially exclusive legal positivists, have difficulty providing a plausible explanation of the way in which the **common law**, including **equity**, is identified and applied. In common law cases, judges seem to be guided by fundamental principles whose identification or application involves moral judgment. For example, any exercise of their powers of distinguishing **precedents**, or of **overruling** established doctrines, seems necessarily to be guided by moral judgment. The reasoning of most past and present members of the High Court exemplifies this kind of reasoning, most recently in cases such as *Mabo* (1992) and *Dietrich v The Queen* (1992). The common law appears to be a dynamic, continually evolving body of essentially moral judgments, in which nothing is immune from revision or repudiation. Indeed, some version of natural law theory may best explain statements such as Lord Esher's, that no wholly unreasonable or unjust proposition could possibly be part of the common law (*Emmens v Pottle* (1885)).

But legal positivism seems to provide a more persuasive account of statutes and constitutions in Australian law. Both their identification as valid law, and their content, seem to be matters of fact rather than morality. According to orthodox principles of interpretation, their content is determined by the meanings of their words, understood (to an extent that remains contested) in the light of admissible evidence of the intentions or purposes of the law makers who created them (see **Originalism**). A legal positivist would argue that these criteria are factual rather than moral, though perhaps conceding that when they are insufficient to fix a determinate meaning, judges must exercise a law-making discretion based on extra-legal criteria, and thereby in effect add new meaning to the text in question.

Even when constitutions require judges to invalidate statutes that they deem inconsistent with moral criteria, such

as those enshrined in a constitutional **Bill of Rights**, inclusive legal positivists provide a persuasive explanation: those criteria constitute legal criteria only because and insofar as they have in fact been positively enacted in a written constitution. This would also seem to be true of the Australian conception of **implied constitutional rights**. They are usually said to be 'implied' because they are practically necessary if constitutional provisions are to achieve their intended purposes. If so, their ultimate rationale must depend on the assumed intentions or purposes of those who made the Constitution.

The High Court might adopt a non-positivist theory of the Constitution if it were to accept the view expressed by a few of its members, that the Constitution should be interpreted in the light of contemporary moral values rather than the original intentions or purposes of its **framers**. But whether this would amount to a non-positivist theory would depend on how far it was taken. If it were limited to cases in which the meaning of the Constitution is unclear and must be supplemented by judicial 'discretion', it would be consistent with most contemporary versions of legal positivism. Only if the Court held that the meaning of the Constitution always depends partly on contemporary moral values would it clearly adopt a non-positivist theory. One such theory, defended by the legal philosopher Ronald Dworkin, is that a constitution should always be interpreted in the light of whatever principles of political morality best justify it, regardless of its founders' intentions.

No member of the High Court has ever expressly endorsed the natural law theory that extremely unjust statutes are necessarily invalid, although the Court has said that whether state legislative power 'is subject to some restraints by reference to rights deeply rooted in our democratic system of government and the common law … is another question which we need not explore' (*Union Steamship v King* (1988)). If legal positivism does not accurately account for the common law, and if the validity of statute law depends ultimately on the common law, then legal positivism does not accurately account for statute law either. But despite the Court's hesitation, the law on this question is clear: legislative power in Australia is subordinate only to limits contained, expressly or impliedly, in superior constitutional instruments, and not to the common law. Indeed, the common law is wholly subject to legislative alteration.

Presently, therefore, Australian law as recognised and enforced by the High Court seems to combine one part (the common law, including equity) that is best understood in non-positivist terms, with other parts (statutory and **constitutional law**) that are best understood in positivist terms. But the former is subordinate to the latter, rather than vice versa.

JEFFREY GOLDSWORTHY

Further Reading
HLA Hart, *The Concept of Law* (2nd edn 1994)
Joseph Raz, *The Authority of Law* (1979)
Wilfrid Waluchow, *Inclusive Legal Positivism* (1994)

Powers, Charles (*b* 3 March 1853; *d* 24 April 1939; Justice 1913–29) was a Justice whose substance did not match his distinguished, courteous mien. Appointed the day before **Piddington**, he demonstrated that it pays to tough it out. He

Charles Powers, Justice 1913–29

weathered the storm of professional disapproval and achieved modest acceptance.

The son of James Powers, wine and spirits merchant, and Mary Ann, née Marsden, Powers was educated at Brisbane Grammar School. As a young man, he was a capable cricketer, and once captained a Queensland eleven against an English side. In 1876, Powers was admitted to practice as a solicitor, and worked in that capacity in Bundaberg for six years. In 1878, he married Kate Ann Thorburn, the daughter of a Victorian solicitor. The marriage resulted in eleven children. Three of the sons were to enlist for service in **World War I**. One attained the rank of lieutenant, but suffered shellshock in France in June 1916 and had to leave the front.

At the age of 30, Powers became the mayor of Maryborough. Three years later, he became a member of the Burrum Divisional Board. He entered the Legislative Assembly of Queensland in 1888, and in the following years, he became Postmaster-General and Minister for Education in the Morehead ministry. He held those portfolios until August 1890. During these years, he pursued a number of business activities.

In 1891, he was appointed a member of a royal commission on the establishment of a university in Queensland, chaired by Chief Justice Charles Lilley. Powers was one of a strong minority urging that university education should be free. He also urged caution in the introduction of coeducation in Queensland schools, since he feared it might close off teaching opportunities for women—one of the few avenues of state employment open to them.

In 1894, Powers applied to the Supreme Court of Queensland to practise as a barrister and solicitor. The Court was presided over by **Griffith**, who was to become a colleague some two decades later. The application was granted on the basis of Powers having practised as a solicitor for at least three years, and also of having passed in Latin and French.

Powers was thus in formal terms a barrister, but he received minimal experience in advocacy over the next 20 years. At the time of his admission to the Bar, he was Leader of the Opposition in the Queensland Parliament. In 1899, he was appointed Crown Solicitor for Queensland, and four years later he became the first Commonwealth Crown Solicitor, at about the time of the High Court's **establishment**.

Powers is one of the few High Court Justices who had never appeared as **counsel** before the Court. His only experience prior to **appointment** was in the preparation of cases that advocates presented to the High Court. He was also the first High Court Justice not to have obtained a university degree.

As Crown Solicitor, Powers played a large part in preparing the successful prosecution in the *Coal Vend Case* (1911), which was heard by **Isaacs**. WM Hughes as **Attorney-General** congratulated Powers on his efforts. But the elation turned to disillusionment when the **Full Court** of the High Court allowed the appeal of the ship and colliery owners. Powers believed that Griffith displayed prejudice during the hearing of the appeal.

In 1913, on his appointment to the High Court, Powers was aged 60—two years older than Griffith had been at the time of his appointment. The path to judicial office had been plodding, and the achievements of Powers were far more pedestrian than those of Griffith.

The press did not pull any punches in its response to the announcement that Powers and Piddington had been appointed. On 20 February 1913, the *Bulletin* launched its assault under the heading: 'The Ghastly Error of WM Hughes.' The article said that the pair, regarded as High Court Justices, were 'not so much mistakes as grim tragedies'. It mentioned that Powers had been 'for six years a Bundaberg solicitor' and allowed that he had been 'a useful Crown Solicitor'. But the writer thought that Robert **Garran**, the departmental secretary, had probably done most of the work in preparing constitutional arguments for Hughes.

Powers remained unmoved. As Hughes' biographer Laurence Fitzhardinge has observed, Powers, less sensitive and more self-confident than Piddington (who resigned), braved the storm and was accepted.

Although he was accepted, Powers did nothing to excite enthusiasm. When he is mentioned in the literature, it is usually in terms of his stolidity—or, as Geoffrey Sawer put it, his 'mediocrity'. It is difficult to recall any notable contribution made by Powers to the jurisprudence of the Court. In the epoch-making *Engineers Case* (1920), he did not even sit—although **Brennan** has suggested he may have been on leave. He did, however, sit on the Court that rejected the application in that case for a certificate allowing appeal to the **Privy Council**. He dissented, considering, with **Gavan Duffy**, that a certificate should be granted (*Engineers Case* (1921)).

Nor did Powers do anything to add to the levity of the Court. He seems to have had a positive aversion to **humour**. Garran relates how Powers, on his appointment to the Arbitration Court, asked Garran to accompany him on an inspection of the proposed courtroom. The Navy had just vacated the building. Powers' first impression of the boardroom was favourable, but when Garran laughingly drew his attention to the motto on the scroll behind the dais: 'Strike first, strike hard, strike often', Powers reacted with horror. He said that the motto would have to be removed before the press saw it. Garran pleaded in vain that the retention of the motto would help to achieve a light-hearted atmosphere.

Powers' conservatism was reflected in his nineteenth-century hirsute style. In 1903, **Barton** had been the only clean-shaven Justice, but by 1906, Isaacs and **Higgins** had confined themselves to moustaches, and Powers was to be the last bearded High Court Justice in the twentieth century.

Powers' appointment as Deputy President of the Commonwealth Court of **Conciliation and Arbitration** reflected the policy, which prevailed until 1926, that the Arbitration Court should be given stature by staffing it with High Court Justices. In 1913, Powers was initially appointed as a Deputy President, to give additional support to Higgins as President; but their different approaches led to frequent discord. In *Waterside Workers Federation v Commonwealth Steamship Owners Association* (1915 and 1916), Higgins ruled that wharf labourers who refused to accept work had not been 'on strike'. Powers vehemently objected to the ruling, and threatened to resign. Gavan Duffy's intervention procured a truce: Powers abandoned his threat of resignation, and the issue was referred to the High Court, which unanimously endorsed Higgins' view. Both Higgins and Powers sat. Higgins was 'very glad to have the opinion of my learned brothers upon a matter which, to my mind, was obvious, but which unfortunately has been made the subject of frequent discussion and bitter controversy'. Powers simply concurred. In 1920, Powers did resign from the Arbitration Court; but when Higgins himself resigned as President in 1921, Powers replaced him, and continued as President until 1926.

Powers was proud of his conservatism in industrial matters, and when he wrote to the Attorney-General asking for a knighthood in 1925, he 'specifically mentioned his blocking of the Basic Wage Royal Commission's findings, his restoration of the forty-eight hour week and his cutting of the 12/- per week off fitters and turners' wages'. He did eventually receive a knighthood, but not until June 1929, a month before his **retirement**.

If Powers' appointment to the High Court attracted critical attention in the **media**, his departure was unlamented. The contrast in 1929 between the eulogies on the death of Higgins and the laconic references to Powers' retirement are striking. When he died, the most favourable observation an obituary writer was able to make about him related to his 'patience and courtesy'. That item appeared in the *Australian Law Journal*. No posthumous tribute to Powers appeared in the *Commonwealth Law Reports*.

In appointing Powers, Hughes probably wanted to harness the pro-Commonwealth attitudes Powers had developed in his 10 years as Commonwealth Crown Solicitor. It is hard to resist the conclusion that Hughes would have done better by accepting the advice of journalist Hector Lamond, who responded to Hughes' request for advice by suggesting the appointment of Garran.

GRAHAM FRICKE

Further Reading
Laurence Fitzhardinge, *That Fiery Particle 1862–1914* (1978)
Humphrey McQueen, 'Shoot the Bolshevik! Hang the Profiteer! Reconstructing Australian Capitalism 1918–21' in EL Wheelwright and Ken Buckley (eds), *Essays in the Political Economy of Australian Capitalism vol 2* (1978)

Practice directions. From time to time, the Court's Justices issue practice directions to regulate the practice and **procedure** to be adopted in matters before the Court. Normally, a practice direction will supplement or expand upon matters covered by the **High Court Rules**. In some cases, aspects of a practice direction, after having been in place for some time, become incorporated into the High Court Rules by amendment.

The issuing of a practice direction enables the Court to deal with emerging trends or developments without resorting to a change in the High Court Rules—for example, the implementation of video link hearings.

Before a practice direction is issued, the Court generally consults with interested parties such as the **Solicitors-General** for the states and Commonwealth, the Australian Bar Association, and the Law Council of Australia.

While there is no limit to the areas of practice and procedure that may be covered by a practice direction, matters that have been the subject of recent practice directions include the entitlement and publication of proceedings involving custody of **children**; applications for industrial **orders** *nisi* (that is, applications in the High Court for **writs** directed to the Industrial Relations Commission, where the application might be subject to **remittal** to another court); provision of authorities and statutory material in support of applications for **leave to appeal** or special leave to appeal, or for **removal** pursuant to section 40 of the *Judiciary Act* 1903 (Cth); use of initials or pseudonyms in applications for leave or special leave to appeal or for removal; and written submissions and **citations** of authorities for all **Full Court** matters except removal applications or leave or special leave applications.

The last-mentioned practice direction came into effect from June 2000. It is a comprehensive document that sets out the time frames prior to hearing for the filing of written submissions by all parties, including **interveners**, in a matter before the Full Court. It also deals with the content, structure, and length of written submissions and the provision of, or reference to, cases, textbooks, articles, legislation, and other authorities. It is the most frequently referred to and implemented practice direction, and compliance with it is essential to the orderly preparation of matters for hearing by the Full Court.

ELISA HARRIS

Precedent is the mechanism through which judges in **common law** countries such as Australia exercise their lawmaking role. It is also a constraint on that role.

In a loose sense, all of us follow precedent (as do judges in all legal systems) whenever we face a new problem and look for guidance in the way that others have handled similar problems. What is distinctive about the common law practice is that judges must sometimes follow a relevant precedent even if they disagree with it. The practice implies simultaneously that every past decision of a **superior court** has made law, but that every present decision merely applies pre-existing law. These contradictory implications result in a unique combination of stability and flexibility.

Generally the hierarchy of binding precedent follows the **hierarchy of courts**. A lower court must follow the decisions of a higher court, but not the reverse: it is only because the higher court can reverse the decision that an appellate **jurisdiction** makes sense. Conversely, it is partly because of this power of reversal that a lower court *must* follow the decisions of the court that reviews its decisions on appeal.

Thus, so long as the **Privy Council** could entertain appeals from High Court decisions, the Court was absolutely bound by Privy Council rulings; but once appeals to the Privy Council from the High Court were abolished, the Court was able to declare that it was no longer so bound (see *Viro v The Queen* (1978)). In the NSW Court of Appeal in *Hawkins v Clayton* (1986), **McHugh** went further: he suggested that, once the *Australia Acts* 1986 had excluded the Privy Council altogether from Australian appellate hierarchies, all Privy Council decisions had ceased to bind any Australian court. The better interpretation of *Viro*, however, is that past Privy Council decisions now have the same degree of authority as the High Court's own past decisions: they continue to bind the High Court unless the Court itself overrules them, and continue to bind other Australian courts until the High Court decides otherwise.

Historically, the power to lay down binding precedents was ascribed only to the superior courts. Yet in *Babaniaris v Lutony Fashions* (1987), the whole Court agreed that a 1953 decision by a state Workers Compensation Board should be treated as a precedent—because, as **Mason** explained, the Board had been exercising **judicial power**—and divided 3:2 on whether it should now be overruled. On the older view, a magistrate might not be bound by the ruling of a District Court or County Court—especially if no direct appellate link was involved. Yet in practice, no magistrate would hesitate to treat such a ruling as binding.

If appellate hierarchy is decisive, there may be other cases in which a lower court is not technically bound by a higher court. For example, a decision by a single Justice in the High Court's original jurisdiction may not be binding on **state Supreme Courts**, since such a decision stands outside the appellate structure affecting those Courts (see **Jacobs** in *Bone v Commissioner of Stamp Duties* (1972) in the NSW Court of Appeal). Again, it has been argued (see *Trade Practices Commission v Allied Mills (No 4)* (1981)) that judges in the **Federal Court of Australia** have never been bound by Privy Council decisions—since the Federal Court was created only after Privy Council appeals from the High Court had already been abolished, so that Federal Court and Privy Council never did coexist in the same appellate hierarchy. A question never finally settled was whether Australian courts were strictly bound by Privy Council decisions on appeal from other jurisdictions (see *Mayer v Coe* (1968)). At least three Justices in *Viro* (**Gibbs**, Jacobs and **Aickin**) expressly held that *all* Privy Council decisions had the same status, regardless of the jurisdiction appealed from; but it is unlikely that the point need ever be resolved.

From the linkage of the precedent hierarchy to the appellate hierarchy, it follows that the High Court was never bound by decisions of the **House of Lords**. Despite this, the Court at one stage adhered to a policy that it would invariably follow House of Lords decisions, even if this involved **overruling** a previous decision of its own that the Court continued to prefer. The high water mark of this policy came in *Piro v Foster* (1943), where *Bourke v Butterfield & Lewis* (1926)—a landmark decision of the **Knox Court**—was overruled by the **Latham Court** in deference to the more conservative view of the House of Lords. **Latham** ruled that 'it should now be formally decided' (though still only as 'a wise general rule of practice')

> that in cases of clear conflict between a decision of the House of Lords and of the High Court, this Court, and other courts in Australia, should follow a decision of the House of Lords upon matters of general principle.

The policy was sometimes explained as a pragmatic response to the overlapping membership of Appellate Committees of the House of Lords and Judicial Committees of the Privy Council—which meant that, once the House of Lords had spoken, the Privy Council was likely to agree. But the policy also reflected a strong belief in the system of precedent as a source of common law uniformity: the House of Lords had a uniquely authoritative role in determining the law of England, and acceptance of its decisions throughout the Empire would ensure that the common law developed uniformly in all British countries. At times, and with greater qualifications, this reasoning extended even to decisions of the English Court of Appeal (see especially **Dixon's** analysis and **McTiernan's** dissent in *Waghorn v Waghorn* (1942)). Latham's pronouncement in *Piro v Foster* quoted what the Privy Council had said in *Trimble v Hill* (1879): 'It is of the utmost importance that in all parts of the Empire where English law prevails the interpretation of that law by the courts should be as nearly as possible the same.' A later Privy Council decision, in *Robins v National Trust* (1927), had recognised that a 'Colonial Court' might sometimes legitimately decline to follow an English court, but had added:

> It is otherwise if the authority in England is that of the House of Lords. That is the supreme tribunal to settle English law, and that being settled, the Colonial Court, which is bound by English law, is bound to follow it.

On similar grounds, Privy Council decisions for all British jurisdictions, regardless of whether or not the strict doctrine of precedent required that they be treated as binding, were in practice accepted as binding; and the fact that High Court decisions were binding in all Australian jurisdictions was highly valued as an assurance of **national unity**. In *Waghorn v Waghorn*, **Rich** acknowledged that the uniformity thus achieved may sometimes be 'uniformity of error', but added complacently: 'In that event it is at least uniformity.' Be that as it may, the degree of uniformity throughout Australia achieved by the binding effect of High Court decisions has been substantial (see, for example, **Criminal law defences**).

However, while the emphasis on national unity remains an essential feature of the Court's approach to its precedents, the emphasis on Empire unity faded along with the Empire itself. *Robins v National Trust* was distinguished: since their Lordships were speaking only of the duty of 'an appellate Court in a colony which is regulated by English law', it was argued that this did not apply to jurisdictions such as those of Australia, where the legal system was based on a foundational **reception of English law**, but only to colonies such as Hong Kong, where English law might still be said to apply by its own direct force. In *Watts v Watts* (1953), the Court recognised that the House of Lords in *Preston-Jones v Preston-Jones* (1950) had subjected allegations of adultery to a more stringent standard of proof than the flexible standard spelled out by Dixon in *Briginshaw v Briginshaw* (1938), but managed to reconcile the two views (and hence to adhere to *Briginshaw*) by the rationalisation that in *Preston-Jones* the legitimacy of a child was at stake, so that even on the basis of *Briginshaw*, a higher standard of proof might be required. And in *Parker v The Queen* (1963), Dixon led the whole Court in announcing that the Lords' decision in *DPP v Smith* (1960) was so 'misconceived and wrong' in 'fundamental' respects that it 'should not be used as authority in Australia at all'. Thereafter, in *Australian Consolidated Press v Uren* (1967) (see **Defamation**), the Privy Council conceded that the common law of England and Australia might develop along separate lines.

Although the hierarchical principle gives general guidance to the operation of precedent as between higher and lower courts, it gives no guidance when questions of precedent arise at the same hierarchical level—as to whether a single judge is bound by the decision of another single judge in the same court, and (particularly) as to whether a superior court is bound by its own prior decisions. In *The Vera Cruz (No 2)* (1884), the great English judge William Balliol Brett (later Lord Esher) explained that, while the old common law courts had in practice accepted their own decisions and each other's decisions as binding, that practice was based on 'no statute or common law rule', but only on 'judicial comity'. It follows that the extent to which a court is bound by its own previous decisions depends on the practice adopted by that court. In Australia, the practice of the state Supreme Courts has varied from state to state, and sometimes within the same court over time.

Uniquely, during the latter part of the nineteenth century, the House of Lords adopted a practice of regarding itself as irreversibly bound by its own decisions. The practice became entrenched with the *London Tramways Case* (1898), and was only abandoned by a 'Practice Statement' in 1966. The Privy Council never adopted such a practice, and neither did the High Court. In the *Engine-Drivers Case* (1913) **Isaacs**—with typical dogmatic overstatement—insisted that in this respect the High Court was *bound* to follow the Privy Council's example. More persuasively, he invoked the **judicial oath**, by which each member of the Court is bound 'to do right to all manner of people *according to law*' (Isaacs' italics). This meant, said Isaacs, that the Court must give effect to its own present understanding of the law:

A prior decision does not constitute the law, but is only a judicial declaration as to what the law is … [If] we find the law to be plainly in conflict with what we or any of our predecessors

erroneously thought it to be, we have, as I conceive, no right to choose between giving effect to the law, and maintaining an incorrect interpretation. It is not, in my opinion, better that the Court should be persistently wrong than that it should ultimately be right.

For Isaacs, the test of when the Court should overrule its own prior decision was simple: it should do so whenever it thought the prior decision was 'manifestly wrong'. At the other extreme lies Jacobs' insistence in *HC Sleigh v SA* (1977) that the Court should overrule a prior decision only if it was 'leading to social, economic or political consequences which cannot be tolerated by the nation'. Between these two extremes most Justices have steered a middle course. Almost invariably, however, recognition of the power to overrule is accompanied by emphasis that it should be exercised cautiously and sparingly. In the *Second Territory Senators Case* (1977), Stephen noted that while the Court 'has always asserted its power to review its previous decisions', it would do so only in 'exceptional' cases, after 'most careful scrutiny' of the precedent case and 'full consideration' of what the consequences of overruling might be. If these propositions are (as Stephen put it) 'replete with adjectival qualifications', that serves only to emphasise the judicial commitment to the maxim *stare decisis* ('to stand by what has been decided'). Often understood as a general synonym for the whole doctrine of precedent, that maxim is in fact a specific enjoiner that a court should stand by its own decisions.

In the *Second Uniform Tax Case* (1957), for example, Dixon felt free to overrule the *First Uniform Tax Case* (1942) on a minor issue because he saw the decision on that point 'as isolated, as receiving no support from prior decisions and as forming no part of what in one **metaphor** is called a stream of authority and in another a *catena* of cases'. By contrast, on the larger question of Commonwealth grants to the states under section 96 of the Constitution (see **Economy, impact of Court's decisions on**), he held that, despite his own evident discomfort with the 1942 decision, it should be followed because it formed part of a trilogy of cases, beginning with the *Federal Roads Case* (1926), which 'combine to give to s 96 a consistent and coherent interpretation' whose 'cumulative authority' was 'impossible to disregard'.

In *Commonwealth v Hospital Contribution Fund* (1982), Gibbs took a similar approach, concluding that it was appropriate to overrule the decisions in *Kotsis v Kotsis* (1970) and *Knight v Knight* (1971) in part because 'they do not rest upon a principle that has been carefully worked out in a succession of cases … They stand alone and to overrule them will not unsettle the law in other respects.' He added, secondly, that there was no unanimity of reasoning among the majority Justices in *Kotsis*; thirdly, that the decisions 'achieve no useful result, but on the contrary lead to considerable inconvenience'; and, finally, that the decisions had not been acted upon in such a way that their overruling would be disruptive. In *John v FCT* (1989), these four criteria were adopted by five members of the Court.

Indeed, since the 1970s, attempts to articulate such criteria have become more elaborate (see **Overruling**). In *A-G (NSW) v Perpetual Trustee Co* (1952), Dixon remarked comfortably that the Court 'has adopted no very definite rule as to the circumstances in which it will reconsider an earlier decision'; certainly he doubted 'the wisdom or justice' of the highly restrictive limits on overruling which the English Court of Appeal had set for itself in *Young v Bristol Aeroplane Co* (1944). But more recently, the need for precise criteria has apparently been felt more keenly. Moreover, since *Evda Nominees v Victoria* (1984), **counsel** wishing to submit that a High Court decision should be reopened must seek leave to do so; and once such leave has been given, the submission is heard by a full Bench of all available Justices.

Ironically, in all of this the Court has continued to be influenced by the House of Lords—where the 1966 assertion of power to 'depart from' prior decisions was followed by a series of anxious attempts to define the conditions under which it might be appropriate to do so. Paradoxically, their Lordships' handling of precedent became more rigid than it had been before. A similar trend can be discerned in Australia.

Yet agreement on the factors that militate for or against overruling remains elusive. For example, the fact that a challenged precedent is of very recent vintage can be used both ways. Even the fact that a decision 'stands by itself' outside any 'stream of authority', which Dixon used in the *Second Uniform Tax Case* to support overruling, had been used by him in the *Perpetual Trustee* case to show that there was no compelling need to overrule (as there would have been if the challenged decision was in conflict with a 'stream of authority').

What has been clearly recognised is that the doctrine of precedent carries less weight in **constitutional law**, where judicial decisions perceived as errors, unlike those that occur in the development of the common law, are beyond simple legislative correction (see, for example, the *Engineers Case* (1920), *Strickland v Rocla Concrete Pipes* (1971), and *Cole v Whitfield* (1988)). Judges as different as **Barwick** and **Murphy** have insisted on the individual duty to give effect to the Constitution as each Justice understands it, even at the expense of precedent. 'Always the Constitution remains the text', said Barwick in *Damjanovic v Commonwealth* (1968). 'The task is to apply the Constitution, not the judicial decisions', said Murphy in *Buck v Bavone* (1976). And from opposite sides of the *Second Territory Senators Case*, each of their judgments reaffirmed that view.

In *Stevens v Head* (1993), **Deane** relied on those judgments to assert that, 'in matters of fundamental constitutional importance', individual Justices 'are obliged to adhere to what they see as the requirements of the Constitution of which the Court is both a creature and the custodian'. Despite the decision in *McKain v Miller* (1991), he adhered to his own view of section 118 of the Constitution. **Gaudron** agreed, asserting that, while some constitutional provisions may 'permit of different views as to their meaning', section 118 'is not one of them'. In a trilogy of cases on **military justice**—*Re Tracey; Ex parte Ryan* (1989), *Re Nolan; Ex parte Young* (1991), and *Re Tyler; Ex parte Foley* (1994)—the same two Justices took a similar stance.

Even when precedents are not overruled, the extent to which they constrain the Court's continuing re-evaluation of legal principles is limited. In *Tasmania v Victoria* (1935), for example, Dixon—following Brett's analysis in *The Vera Cruz*—concluded that a **tied vote** yields no binding precedent, since, even if the reasoning of the Justices whose view

prevails is unanimous, it has not been accepted by a majority of the Court.

Moreover, much of what is said in a precedent case can be set aside as *obiter dicta*, leaving only its *ratio decidendi* as binding; and debate as to what precisely is the *ratio decidendi* of a particular case serves often to limit its authority—especially if there is no agreed *ratio* at all, as Deane and Gaudron contended in the military justice cases. Even then, the formal doctrine remains that 'the actual decision' is binding; and while that confines the effect of precedent to a very narrow scope indeed, it means at least—as McHugh concluded in *Tyler*, quoting Lord Reid in *Midland Silicones v Scruttons* (1961)—that the Court must 'apply that decision where the circumstances of the instant case "are not reasonably distinguishable from those which gave rise to the decision"'.

Yet questions of hierarchical authority, of whether a precedent will be overruled, and of what exactly is its binding scope, are only a small part of the influence of precedent on common law **judicial reasoning**. Around the core of the strict doctrine of precedent, and the broader conception of the common law as made and remade by judges, the pattern of legal and judicial argument is dominated by review, comparison, analysis, synthesis, interpretation, and inductive restatement of *all* previous judicial pronouncements that might be relevant, whether technically binding or not. All such pronouncements are part of the **authoritative legal materials** which may or may not be decisive, but cannot be ignored. In common law cases, judicial reasoning is based almost wholly on such prior pronouncements; and in **statutory interpretation**—and even **constitutional interpretation**—particular provisions are encrusted, over time, with a body of case law supplying not only alternative methods and assumptions of interpretation, but judicially determined meanings. It is through this looser sense of the practice of precedent, rather than in strict determination of which precedents are binding, that the habits of thought characteristic of courts in common law countries are formed.

TONY BLACKSHIELD

Further Reading
Garfield Barwick, *Precedent in the Southern Hemisphere* (1970)
Alastair MacAdam and John Pyke, *Judicial Reasoning and the Doctrine of Precedent in Australia* (1998)
Anthony Mason, 'The Use and Abuse of Precedent' (1988) 4 *ABR* 93
Julius Stone, *Precedent and Law* (1985)

Presumption of constitutionality. The presumption of constitutionality has been referred to on a number of occasions by the High Court. It has, however, no clearly recognised place in Australian constitutional theory. It is used in a variety of senses. For instance, one use is to signify a degree of deference by the Court to other arms of government out of respect for the political process and **representative government**. It is rarely used in that way in Australia, although this is the main use of the term in the USA. In that context, it is an attempt to reconcile **judicial review** of the constitutional validity of legislation with the democratic majority represented in the legislature. In Australia, the presumption is used more often as a statement about the burden of proof where underlying questions of fact are relevant in the determination of constitutional questions. This means that the presumption has the greatest scope where questions of reasonable means or sufficient connection arise (see also **Proportionality**). However, its use in those contexts still remains limited, with the Court generally relying on matters of impression or public knowledge to establish **reasonableness** of the means adopted by the legislature to achieve a permissible end or the necessary connection between the subject of legislation and the ambit of constitutional power.

The presumption has been seen as even more limited in relation to issues concerning fundamental rights. There has been no obvious reliance on the presumption when balancing, for instance, the implied freedom of **political communication** with other social interests in order to determine whether the means are appropriate to a legitimate end. Even there, however, the insistence by **Brennan** in such contexts on a 'margin of appreciation' for the legislative judgment reflects similar underlying concerns.

The greatest proponent of the concept on the High Court was **Murphy**. He undertook an extended discussion of the concept, drawing on examples from other jurisdictions, in the *Tasmanian Dam Case* (1983). Other Justices have referred at times to the concept, to bolster a conclusion or approach to construction, but it appears more often as an afterthought than as a foundation principle of **constitutional interpretation**. Used in this limited way, it is little more than a principle or mechanism for 'reading down' a statute so as not to exceed power. **Isaacs** in *FCT v Munro* (1926) referred to 'an initial presumption that Parliament did not intend to pass beyond constitutional bounds. If the language of a statute is not so intractable as to be incapable of being consistent with the presumption, the presumption should prevail'.

The effect of the presumption is weakened by the fact that Parliament rarely articulates its reasons for thinking that a particular legislative measure is a reasonable means for achieving an end within power or has a sufficient connection with a head of power. The **United States Supreme Court** has often relied on 'legislative findings' as an aid to validity; but in Australia, when facts are relevant for constitutional purposes, the legislative consideration of the measure will rarely provide much assistance. There is also a reluctance to allow Parliament to recite itself into power, that is, to presume the existence of facts necessary to support a particular exercise of constitutional power (see *Communist Party Case* (1951)). The **fact finding** engaged in by the Court in constitutional cases is limited, and this also limits the usefulness of the concept.

HENRY BURMESTER

Further Reading
Henry Burmester, 'The Presumption of Constitutionality' (1983) 13 *FL Rev* 277

Prime Ministers are at the pinnacle of the Australian political system and have played a formative role in constitutional politics—not only through judicial **appointments** to the High Court and referendums to change the Constitution, but through controversial legislation that comes to the Court for decision and occasionally through innovative politics that become embedded without being challenged.

During the century since federation, Australia has had 25 different Prime Ministers heading 30 governments (Alfred **Deakin** and Andrew Fisher were each three times Prime Minister; Robert **Menzies** was twice Prime Minister). Federal politics have been more stable than these aggregate figures suggest, with half a dozen Prime Ministers serving for long periods. WM Hughes, Stanley Bruce, Joseph Lyons, Malcolm Fraser, and Bob Hawke all held office for terms of between six and eight years, while Menzies was Prime Minister for 18 years, including an unbroken spell of 16 years (to 1966). This has been balanced by periods of instability and rapid turnover. There were eight different governments in the decade before the emergence of the disciplined two-party system in 1910; three during 1939–41, when the United Australia Party was in decline; and four in 1966–72, when Menzies retired, and Harold Holt drowned. Three Prime Ministers have served for only a few weeks while the governing party chose a new leader following the death of a Prime Minister: Earle Page after Lyons died in 1937; Frank Forde after Ben Chifley died in 1945; and John McEwen after Holt died in 1967.

Australian constitutional politics have also been stable during the century, with the federal Constitution proving to be a flexible and robust instrument of government. While it has been developed through political practice, **judicial review**, and, to a lesser extent, through referendums, the Constitution has in turn shaped Australian political practice. The Constitution and its authoritative interpreter, the High Court, have allowed a good deal of innovative change while also restricting more radical centralist and **socialist** initiatives, especially those of federal Labor governments. Labor Prime Ministers until Hawke were associated with tempestuous constitutional politics and major tussles with the High Court. In contrast, non-Labor Prime Ministers and governments (in their various guises of Liberal, Nationalist, and United Australia Party) have usually enjoyed harmonious constitutional politics. Because they have dominated Australian politics, being in office for three-quarters of the time until the 1980s, they have largely set and consolidated the mould of Australian constitutional governance.

Two outstanding Liberal Prime Ministers, Deakin and Menzies, have had the greatest influence on the High Court and on constitutional politics. As **Attorney-General** in the first Commonwealth government of **Barton**, Deakin was the architect of the High Court, shaping its structure in the *Judiciary Act* 1903 (Cth) and orchestrating the appointment of the founding Justices, **Griffith**, Barton, and O'Connor. Succeeding Barton as Prime Minister in 1903, Deakin expanded the Court to five Justices in 1906, appointing Isaacs and **Higgins**. This consolidated the pre-eminence of the High Court at the pinnacle of Australian law and ensured its primary **role** in **constitutional interpretation**. As Deakin intended in appointing two ardent nationalists, the new Justices challenged the 'balancing' approach to **federalism** taken by the original Justices and helped to shift the Court's interpretive method to one that favoured the dominance of the Commonwealth over the states.

This occurred in the famous *Engineers Case* (1920), in which Menzies, although only a junior barrister at the time, was the catalyst, and in which Isaacs wrote the leading judgment. *Engineers* scrapped the **Griffith Court's** doctrines of

Prime Ministers of Australia

Name	Period in office	Government in office
Edmund Barton	1/01/01–24/9/03	Protectionist
Alfred Deakin	24/9/03–27/4/04	Protectionist
John Watson	27/4/04–17/8/04	ALP
George Reid	18/8/04–5/7/05	Free Trade–Protectionist Coalition
Alfred Deakin	5/7/05–13/11/08	Protectionist
Andrew Fisher	13/11/08–2/6/09	ALP
Alfred Deakin	2/6/09–28/4/10	Protectionist–Free Trade–Tariff Reform Coalition
Andrew Fisher	29/4/10–24/6/13	ALP
Joseph Cook	24/6/13–17/9/14	Liberal
Andrew Fisher	17/9/14–27/10/15	ALP
WM Hughes	27/10/15–9/2/23	ALP (27/10/15–14/11/16) National Labour/Nationalist (14/11/16–9/2/23)
Stanley Bruce	9/2/23–22/10/29	Nationalist–CP Coalition
James Scullin	22/10/29–6/1/32	ALP
Joseph Lyons	6/1/32–7/4/39	UAP (6/1/32–9/11/34) UAP–CP Coalition (9/11/34–7/4/39)
Earle Page	7/4/39–26/4/39	CP–UAP Coalition
Robert Menzies	26/4/39–29/8/41	UAP (26/4/39–14/3/40) UAP–CP Coalition (14/3/40–29/8/41)
Arthur Fadden	29/8/41–7/10/41	CP–UAP Coalition
John Curtin	7/10/41–5/7/45	ALP
Frank Forde	6/7/45–13/7/45	ALP
Ben Chifley	13/7/45–19/12/49	ALP
Robert Menzies	19/12/49–26/1/66	Liberal–CP Coalition
Harold Holt	26/1/66–19/12/67	Liberal–CP Coalition
John McEwen	19/12/67–10/1/68	Liberal–CP Coalition
John Gorton	10/1/68–10/3/71	Liberal–CP Coalition
William McMahon	10/3/71–5/12/72	Liberal–CP Coalition
Gough Whitlam	5/12/72–11/11/75	ALP
Malcolm Fraser	11/11/75–11/3/83	Liberal–NCP/NPA Coalition
Bob Hawke	11/3/83–20/12/91	ALP
Paul Keating	20/12/91–11/3/96	ALP
John Howard	11/3/96–	Liberal–NPA Coalition

implied **intergovernmental immunities** and **reserved state powers**, and enshrined the meta-constitutional doctrine of **literalism**. Henceforward, **Commonwealth legislative powers** were to be read in a full and plenary way, regardless of the impact on the states, with the inevitable consequence of ever-increasing centralisation. Menzies' move from Victorian to Commonwealth politics in 1934 also entailed Court politics: he replaced **Latham** in the blue ribbon seat of Kooyong and as Attorney-General, while Latham was appointed **Chief Justice**.

As Prime Minister, Menzies shaped the High Court by appointing leading lawyers and Justices in the mould of **Dixon**, his own great friend and mentor. Dixon himself had been appointed to the High Court in 1929 by Latham, then Attorney-General in the Lyons government. Menzies elevated Dixon to the Chief Justiceship in 1952, and appointed eight additional Justices—**Williams** in 1940, **Fullagar** and **Kitto** in 1950, **Taylor** in 1952, Douglas **Menzies** and **Windeyer** in 1958, **Owen** in 1961, and **Barwick** as Chief Justice to succeed Dixon in 1964. In all of these appointments, Menzies chose specialist lawyers who had been leaders of the Sydney and Melbourne Bars and were deeply committed to **legalism** and professional conservatism. Latham and Barwick had also been senior politicians, but were first and foremost leading lawyers. In many of these appointments, Menzies consulted Dixon (see **Appointments that might have been**).

Not surprisingly, given that he handpicked all of its members except one—**Webb** in 1946—for 30 years, Menzies enjoyed harmonious relations with the High Court. The single blot was his unsuccessful attempt to ban the Communist Party, overruled by the Court in 1951 and defeated in a subsequent referendum (see *Communist Party Case*).

By comparison with Deakin and Menzies, most other non-Labor Prime Ministers have had little impact on the High Court. Hughes (as a conservative Nationalist Party Prime Minister), John Gorton, and William McMahon each made two appointments to the Court. Hughes appointed **Knox** as Chief Justice to replace Griffith in 1919, and **Starke** to replace Barton in 1920. Gorton appointed **Walsh** and **Gibbs** in 1969 and 1970. McMahon appointed **Stephen** and **Mason** in 1972.

Prime Ministers in shorter-lived governments have limited capability for shaping the Court through appointments, unless they increase the size of the Court as Deakin did in 1906, and the Labor Cabinet threatened to do in 1945. Nine Prime Ministers, including John Curtin, have had no opportunity to make High Court appointments. Some Prime Ministers have little knowledge of or interest in such matters (only 10 of the 25 Prime Ministers since federation have had legal backgrounds). Some, like John Watson and Chifley, left court matters, including appointments, to such strong-minded Attorneys-General as Hughes and **Evatt**.

Non-Labor governments—with conservative policy agendas—are also less likely to expand the bounds of **Commonwealth legislative powers** through referendums or bold legislative initiatives that end up before the Court. Most noticeably, the Bruce–Page coalition government (1923–29) favoured private enterprise and a contraction of government intervention in the **economy**, so it did not exploit the enormous potential for expanding Commonwealth power that *Engineers* had opened up. Nor did it take advantage of the

Isaacs interpretation of section 92 in *McArthur v Queensland* (1920), which had that section applying only to the states (see **Interstate trade and commerce**).

Labor Prime Ministers and governments were quite different, at least for the first three-quarters of the century. As a reformist party pledged to the abolition of federalism, the Australian Labor Party was often at odds with the Constitution and the High Court. According to Gough Whitlam in his 1957 Chifley Memorial Lecture, Labor had been handicapped 'by a Constitution framed in such a way as to make it difficult to carry out Labor objectives and interpreted in such a way as to make it impossible to carry them out'. While somewhat exaggerated, this diagnosis reflected Labor's attitude, and summed up much of its experience with constitutional politics and judicial review.

As Attorney-General in the first majority Labor government under Fisher from 1910 to 1913, Hughes was at the centre of the struggle between Labor and the Constitution. He masterminded proposals to boost Commonwealth powers over **trade and commerce**, **corporations** and monopolies, and **labour relations**, put to referendum as a slate in 1911 and separately in 1913. Both referendums failed, as did legislative attempts to regulate trusts and monopolies using existing powers. These were overruled by the Griffith Court (*Adelaide Steamship Co v The King and A-G (Cth)* (1912); *Colonial Sugar Refining Co v A-G (Cth)* (1912)), and used by Hughes to further his campaign for constitutional change. This led to an acrimonious exchange with Griffith. When O'Connor died in November 1912, Hughes had the chance to change the Court (now evenly divided between Griffith and Barton on the one hand, and Isaacs and Higgins on the other). In a bold move that was publicly criticised as blatant court packing, Hughes rushed through amendments to the Judiciary Act to increase the Court's size to seven, and appointed **Gavan Duffy**, **Powers**, and **Piddington**. When Piddington resigned amid a storm of **criticism**, **Rich** was appointed in his stead.

Labor narrowly lost the 1913 election, but regained office in 1914 after Liberal Prime Minister Joseph Cook miscalculated in precipitating a double dissolution. Hughes succeeded Fisher as Labor Prime Minister in 1915, but was totally absorbed in fighting **World War I**. He precipitated a disastrous split in the Labor Party over conscription in 1916, and subsequently formed the Nationalist Party, which absorbed the old Liberal Party and kept him as Prime Minister until 1923. Because the High Court allowed enormous expansion of the **defence power** during the war, there was no further friction between Hughes and the Court.

Labor languished in Opposition for 13 years after the conscription split, winning federal office under James Scullin in October 1929, just as the **Depression** was beginning. The Bruce–Page Nationalist–Country Party government had been brought down through defections in its own ranks, orchestrated by the renegade Hughes. Because there was no Senate election, the Scullin Labor government never controlled the Senate. Labor's program for economic restructuring was more radical than Franklin D Roosevelt's New Deal in the USA, but there was no equivalent court crisis. The program included agricultural regulation and marketing schemes in depressed sectors such as wheat, the Theodore

Plan to control credit and interest rates while financing public works projects for the unemployed, and a referendum to delete section 128 of the Constitution altogether, leaving the Commonwealth Parliament with plenary power of constitutional **amendment**. All of these proposals were rejected by the Senate, and never reached the High Court. Forced to accept the conservative Premiers' Plan favoured by the banks, which led to a rift with the belligerent NSW Lang Labor government and a bitter split in the federal Labor Party, the Scullin government was brought down in early 1932 by defectors from its own ranks. One of the defectors was Lyons, who became Prime Minister at the head of the new United Australia Party (which absorbed the Nationalists) and held office until his death in 1939.

Although saved from confrontation with the Scullin government by the Opposition-controlled Senate, the High Court did not escape unscathed. Evatt and **McTiernan** were appointed to the Court during the December 1930 parliamentary recess while Scullin and Attorney-General Frank Brennan were overseas. Ironically, these two Labor Justices would divide in the *State Garnishee Cases* (1932), with McTiernan joining the majority upholding the Lyons government's tough financial measures that overrode Premier Lang in paying the interest on NSW public debt.

Curtin became Labor Prime Minister in October 1941, at the time of Australia's greatest crisis in **World War II**. He was primarily concerned with putting Australia on a total war footing and redirecting its defence alliance and efforts from Britain and Europe to the USA and the Asia-Pacific region. Curtin reversed Labor's traditional opposition to conscription, and put the Australian forces under General Douglas MacArthur's supreme control. Curtin consolidated Labor's grip on federal office by winning a landslide electoral victory in 1943, but died in July 1945 when victory in the war was in sight. Because the centralisation of power required by the war effort was sanctioned by expansive interpretation of the defence power, Curtin enjoyed harmonious relations with the Court, appointing Dixon as Australian Minister to Washington during 1942–44.

Chifley succeeded Curtin as Prime Minister in 1945, and presided over one of the most dramatic periods of confrontation between Labor and the High Court. Labor had won both Houses of Parliament in 1943 and consolidated its grip on legislative power in the 1946 election. As Treasurer in the Curtin government, Chifley had masterminded uniform **taxation** and effectively controlled banking through regulation. He was restrained towards the High Court, however, and did not push through the Calwell–Ward initiative to appoint three new Justices that Cabinet adopted in Evatt's absence in October 1945. Instead, he accepted Evatt's reversal of that decision and the single appointment of Webb to restore the Court's membership to seven Justices.

Chifley was the primary architect of Australia's post-war welfare state and its more centralised economy. That was constitutionally possible because of the High Court's sanctioning of uniform taxation in 1942 (see *Uniform Tax Cases*), and successful passage of the Social Services Referendum in 1946 that added a new section 51(xxiiiA) to the Constitution. Chifley's attempts to introduce a comprehensive pharmaceutical benefits scheme were overturned by the High Court in 1945 and, despite the 1946 referendum, again in 1949, because of the prohibition in the new section on 'civil conscription'. More dramatic were the Court's adverse decisions on airline nationalisation in 1945 (*Australian National Airways v Commonwealth*) and bank nationalisation in 1948 (*Bank Nationalisation Case*). Thus, the High Court was jointly responsible with the Chifley Labor government for shaping Australia's post-war political economy and its federal system of government.

Becoming leader of the federal Labor Party in 1967, Whitlam won office in 1972 after 23 years of Liberal Coalition government, but never controlled the Senate. Labor had become more like a social-democratic than a workers party, broadly supportive of market capitalism and dedicated to enhancing civic and suburban life. With Labor's traditional planks of nationalising industry and abolishing federalism discarded, Whitlam devised strategies for working with the federal Constitution. These included using section 81 (the appropriations power: see the *AAP Case* (1975)) and section 96 (the grants power). The Whitlam government's performance was poor, due to ministerial incompetence and the abrupt ending of the long boom of post-war prosperity. It was hamstrung by the Opposition-controlled Senate that triggered Governor-General John Kerr's unprecedented **dismissal** of Whitlam in 1975. In the **Whitlam era**, two judicial appointments were made—**Jacobs** and, more controversially, **Murphy**—that helped ensure a balanced High Court. Despite antagonism on some issues from Barwick, who sanctioned Kerr's action, the High Court was broadly accommodating of Labor's adventurous use of Commonwealth powers.

Fraser won office in the 1975 election and, despite some 'New Right' rhetoric, led a traditionalist Liberal Coalition government that continued protectionist policies and industrial wage fixing. Fraser championed a 'New Federalism' that was more accommodating of the states, but his attempt to devolve some modest control over income tax failed because of state opposition. The Fraser government implemented **Aboriginal** land rights in the Northern Territory, and Fraser took a leading role in isolating the South African apartheid regime. His government was also successful in having three machinery-of-government referendums passed in 1977. These addressed the Senate casual vacancies problem that had triggered the 1975 crisis, gave Commonwealth voting rights to territorians, and set the **retirement** age for Justices at 70 years. The Fraser government appointed four new Justices to the High Court—**Aickin, Wilson, Brennan**, and **Deane**—as well as elevating Gibbs to the Chief Justiceship. Deane and Brennan would play prominent roles in reshaping **native title** and **implied constitutional rights** in the 1990s.

Hawke succeeded Fraser and held office from 1983 to 1991, the longest term of any Labor Prime Minister. He was succeeded by Paul Keating, who kept Labor in office until 1996, making this the longest-ever period of federal Labor government. Apart from a residual concern with **social justice** and wage fixing, the Hawke government and its forceful treasurer, Keating, accepted modern neo-liberal orthodoxy and vigorously pursued microeconomic reform—phasing down tariff protection for manufacturing, adopting neo-corporate managerial practices for public administration, and streamlining **Commonwealth–state relations**. Labor's economic approach and agenda were now thoroughly neo-liberal, and modern Labor had broken both with the big-spending social policies of Whitlam and the traditional government interventionism of Fraser.

Constitutionally, the Hawke and Keating governments were moderately reconciled with federalism and the Constitution, albeit with a residual preference for centralism and uniformity. Two sets of referendums were put to the people in 1984 and 1988 that included reruns of old proposals, but would also, in preparation for an entrenched **Bill of Rights**, have extended limited existing **express constitutional rights** to apply to the states. All failed, as did Labor's various attempts at a statutory Bill of Rights. More fruitful was the 'new politics' of human rights and **environmental** protection. The landmark constitutional cases of the period, such as the *Tasmanian Dam Case* (1983), resulted from the Commonwealth's entering into international treaties and using its **external affairs power** to gain domestic jurisdiction over policy areas that otherwise came within state jurisdiction. The Court was broadly supportive of such globalisation and sanctioned the associated expansion in Commonwealth power.

For the first time in decades, Labor had the opportunity to reshape the High Court through appointments. **Toohey**, **Gaudron** (as the first woman), and **McHugh** were all appointed by the Hawke government, and Mason was elevated to the Chief Justiceship. On the retirement of Mason and Deane, the Keating government appointed **Gummow** and **Kirby**, as well as making Brennan Chief Justice. The **Mason Court** and, to a lesser extent, the **Brennan Court**, were activist in revolutionising native title and finding implied constitutional rights.

Winning office in 1996, the Howard government was critical of judicial **activism** and committed to changing the direction of the Court. It appointed **Hayne** and **Callinan**, as well as **Gleeson** to replace Brennan as Chief Justice. Despite some public controversy over Callinan's appointment, the Court itself has reverted to a more restrained public **role**. This is likely to continue for the foreseeable future, given the ideological bent of both the Liberal Coalition and Labor parties in contemporary Australia, and the now conservative character of the High Court.

BRIAN GALLIGAN

Further Reading
Michelle Grattan (ed), *Australian Prime Ministers* (2000)

Private papers. The term 'private papers' encompasses the personal and semi-official documentary records accumulated by individuals and families in the course of their lives. Letters usually form the core of personal archives and other categories include diaries, notebooks, speeches, drafts of published works, press cuttings, and photographs. In the period 1900 to 1950, a few Australian libraries slowly became aware of the research value of personal papers of public figures, but acquisitions were sporadic and their collections remained small. In the second half of the century, a growing number of research libraries and archives became interested in personal papers and the larger institutions started to undertake collecting in a far more systematic way.

Two of the earliest acquisitions were the papers of Justices of the High Court. In 1919, **Griffith** passed over many of his papers to the Sydney collector William Dixson, and a few years later they were lodged in the Public Library of NSW. In 1929, **Barton's** daughter donated the first instalment of his papers to the Commonwealth National Library. Both collections remain important sources for legal and constitutional historians. The Griffith Papers consist of an extensive official and private correspondence, diaries extending from 1862 to 1919, university notes, articles, and photographs. The Barton Papers document the federation movement and the drafting of the Australian Constitution at the 1897–98 Federal Conventions. In addition, there are letters dating from 1870 to 1920, a few diaries, photographs, cuttings, and Barton's 1903–04 judicial notebook. Living in different cities, Griffith and Barton often corresponded with each other. The letters that Barton wrote to Griffith in 1913, when Griffith was overseas, are especially useful in shedding light on the **personal relations** between the various Justices.

There are no surviving papers of O'Connor, but other early Justices such as Higgins, Isaacs, and Piddington left personal papers, now held in the National Library. To a large extent, they relate to their political and literary careers and contain relatively little on their judicial work. The Piddington Papers, however, deal with his brief **appointment** to the High Court in 1913. After this period, there is a decline in the number of judicial collections. Of the 13 Justices appointed to the Court between 1920 and 1960, only three are known to have been keepers of papers: **Dixon**, **Evatt**, and **Latham**. Dixon's papers are still in private possession, but his diaries have been used by a few historians, and are said to be of considerable historical value. The Evatt Papers at Flinders University Library are broad in their subject coverage, but they mainly deal with his political career and contain relatively little on the High Court.

The Latham Papers form one of the greatest collections of papers in Australia. They extend over a period of nearly 70 years and record in great detail Latham's academic, legal, political, and diplomatic career, as well as his private friendships and interests. He had a preference for written communication—he did not discard paper lightly—and his High Court papers range from minor administrative matters, such as arranging **sittings**, to discussions of judgments in major cases. The letters and notes from Evatt, **Starke**, and other Justices reveal many of the tensions and difficulties that Latham faced as **Chief Justice**, especially in the early part of the **Latham Court**. The correspondence also records the experiences and ideas of his fellow Justices. For instance, both Dixon and **Webb** wrote regularly to Latham during the periods they were overseas on diplomatic and judicial postings.

Several of the Justices who served on the Court in the period 1960–2000 have retained their papers, but others have already placed them in libraries and archives. As well as holding **judges' notebooks**, the National Archives of Australia has an extensive collection of papers of **Barwick** and a smaller group of papers of **Gibbs**. In size, the Barwick Papers are exceeded only by the Latham Papers. They comprise correspondence dating from 1942 to 1981, opinions, retainers, **appeal books**, notebooks, speeches, and articles. There are also papers of **Murphy** and **Kirby** in the National Archives, and of **Stephen** and **Gaudron** in the National Library. These collections are important biographical sources but, taken as a group, they contain only limited information on the operation of the High Court or the thoughts and ideas of the Justices during their years on the Bench.

It is not easy to explain why there are so few major collections of personal papers of Justices of the High Court. In the USA, there are huge archives of Justices of the **United States Supreme Court** in the Library of Congress and elsewhere and collections of similar size and significance are held in British archives. In Australia, many politicians have been assiduous accumulators of papers and other public figures, such as diplomats, journalists, and academics, have formed notable collections. A few academic lawyers have left good collections', but among Australian barristers and judges, the hoarding instinct seems to have been weak. It is worth noting that, as politicians, Griffith, Latham, and Barwick were accustomed to keeping papers long before they were appointed to the High Court.

Some Justices were good correspondents and their letters can be found in other collections of personal papers, in Australia and also overseas. The letters of Barton to his great friend and colleague Alfred **Deakin** extend over a period of 30 years, while his letters to his former secretary Thomas Bavin refer to the **establishment** of the Court in 1903. In their last years, both Barton and Griffith corresponded regularly with the Governor-General, Ronald Munro Ferguson, on political events such as the 1913 double dissolution and on many other matters of public policy. Higgins, Evatt, and Dixon were among the international correspondents of the American judge Felix Frankfurter, while Dixon was a long-time correspondent of Robert **Menzies**. The papers of the Victorian judge John Barry and the legal academic Geoffrey Sawer also contain letters from various High Court Justices.

The papers of early Commonwealth **Attorneys-General** contain information about the creation of the High Court, judicial appointments, and the administration of the Court. The National Library holds the papers of most of the Attorneys-General from 1901 until 1940. In particular, the papers of Alfred Deakin, Higgins, and Josiah Symon deal with the *Judiciary Act* 1903 (Cth), the funding and sittings of the Court in its early years, and the '**strike**' of the three Justices in 1905. The papers of Robert **Garran**, the first **Solicitor-General**, are also in the Library, but they contain very little on the Court. There are papers of his successors, George Knowles and Kenneth Bailey, in the National Archives.

A final category of personal papers are the artificial collections formed by the biographers of High Court Justices. Roger Joyce (Griffith), Geoffrey Bolton (Barton), Kylie Tennant (Evatt), David Marr (Barwick), and others obtained copies of papers from a great diversity of sources and, after their books were published, deposited the material in the National Library.

GRAEME POWELL

Further Reading

Roger Joyce, 'Samuel Griffith, the Biographer and the Matter of Sources' in James Walter and Raija Nugent, *Biographers at Work* (1984) 17

Sir John Latham: *A Guide to His Papers in the National Library of Australia* (1980)

Clem Lloyd 'Not Peace but a Sword!—the High Court under JG Latham' (1987) 11 *Adel L Rev* 175

Don Markwell, 'Griffith, Barton and the Early Governor-Generals: Aspects of Australia's Constitutional Development' (1999) 10 *PLR* 280

WG McMinn, 'The High Court Imbroglio and the Fall of the Reid–McLean Government' (1978) 64(1) *Journal of the Royal Australian Historical Society* 14

James Thomson, 'History, Justices and the High Court: An Institutional Perspective' (1995) 1 *Aust J of Legal Hist* 281

Privative clauses. A privative clause, also known variously as an 'ouster clause', a 'preclusive clause', and a 'no-review clause', represents an attempt by a legislature to insulate action of the executive government from **judicial review**. Considered from the perspective of the legislature, such clauses have largely been a failure, and their interpretation has placed under great strain the notion of parliamentary supremacy.

Privative clauses take various forms, but they typically involve an assertion that a decision is to be 'final and conclusive' or 'without appeal', that it 'may not be called into question in any court of law', or some similarly minded incantation. One of the more expansive privative clauses provided that a decision was 'final and may not be appealed against, reviewed, quashed or called into question by any court or tribunal'. It is difficult to conceive of a more clear expression of legislative intent. Yet neither in Australia nor abroad have courts ever accepted privative clauses as amounting to a complete bar against judicial review. As **Kirby** once put it, 'unreviewable administrative action is a contradiction in terms' (*Warringah Shire Council v Pittwater Provisional Council* (1992)). In essence, the **common law** position is that it is inconceivable that a parliament would grant authority to an administrative entity to define its own jurisdiction. It is through this inference of legislative intent that the courts have always—even in the face of the most explicitly phrased privative clause—been able to justify judicial review for jurisdictional error (such error being, of course, itself of considerable elasticity in definition: see **Administrative law**).

The High Court has a special view of privative clauses because of section 75(v) of the Constitution, which vests the Court with original **jurisdiction** in all matters 'in which a **writ** of mandamus or prohibition or an injunction is sought against an officer of the Commonwealth'. This provision makes it constitutionally impossible completely to preclude judicial review of Commonwealth administrative action. Much of the judicial discussion about the scope of section 75(v) has concerned the various versions of privative clause that have been included in Commonwealth industrial relations legislation. In a series of cases, the Court repeatedly rebuffed attempts to insulate the work of the old Commonwealth Court of **Conciliation and Arbitration** from judicial review (see, for example; *Ex parte Whybrow* (1910); *Allen Taylor's Case* (1912); *Ince Bros v Federated Clothing and Allied Trades Union* (1924)). In a typically colourful characterisation, Prime Minister WM Hughes described the interplay between the Court and the Parliament over the clause as a 'miserable battledore and shuttlecock business'. As to the resulting jurisprudence, **Higgins** (in his capacity as President of the Court of Conciliation and Arbitration) once described the High Court's holdings on the issue as 'a veritable Serbonian bog of technicalities' (see *Australian Boot Trade Employees v Whybrow & Co* (1910)).

While it will not permit a complete ouster of judicial review, the High Court has suggested on occasion that it will be prepared to read a privative clause as an indication that it should tread softly in the exercise of its review powers. As Mark Aronson and Bruce Dyer have put it, 'the trick is to increase the relevant tribunal's jurisdiction rather than to decrease the Court's'. This judicial 'compromise' stems from the judgment of **Dixon** in *R v Hickman; Ex parte Fox and Clinton* (1945). Stated at its simplest, the *Hickman* principle, as it is sometimes known, holds that provided a tribunal's decision represents a bona fide attempt to exercise its power, and provided that the decision relates to the subject matter of the legislation and is reasonably capable of reference to the power given to the tribunal, then the net of jurisdictional error should be narrowly cast. The *Hickman* principle has been cited by the Court several times. It was once described by Douglas **Menzies** as 'classical', and *Hickman* has been given contemporary currency through two recent decisions which relied upon it, *R v Coldham; Ex parte Australian Workers Union* (1983), and *O'Toole v Charles David* (1991). Yet it would be an exaggeration to say that it has been applied faithfully by Australian courts since 1945.

The High Court has been no less complicating in its approach to privative clauses than its counterparts in the UK or Canada. In the seminal case of *Anisminic v Foreign Compensation Commission* (1968), the **House of Lords** held that a provision of the *Foreign Compensation Act* 1950 (UK) that determinations by the Foreign Compensation Commission 'shall not be called in question in any court of law' did not operate to oust review for jurisdictional error. Significantly, their Lordships found the relevant jurisdictional error to be an error of law. In Canada, the bog of complexity around privative clauses is even more Serbonian, to use Higgins' words. In *Canadian Union of Public Employees v New Brunswick Liquor* (1979), the Supreme Court of Canada issued its own counterpart to the *Hickman* principle, stating the scope of review in the face of a privative clause in even more restrictive terms (for Canada does not have an analogue to section 75(v) of the Australian Constitution). Yet every year since, the Supreme Court has found it necessary to revisit the issue of privative clauses. Whether in its Australian, Canadian, or British form, the simple fact is that the common law will never permit a legislative injunction to totally insulate administrative injustice from review.

IAN HOLLOWAY

Further Reading

Mark Aronson and Bruce Dyer, *Judicial Review of Administrative Action* (1996) ch 18

Leslie Zines, 'Constitutional Aspects of Judicial Review of Administrative Action' (1998) 1 *Constitutional Law and Policy Review* 50

Privy Council, Judicial Committee of the. Although established by the Constitution as the highest court in Australia, the High Court became the final court of appeal for Australia

only when the **Australia Acts** 1986 abolished the last remaining appeals from state courts to the Privy Council in London. Appeals from the High Court to the Privy Council had been abolished successively by legislation introduced by the Gorton government in 1968 (abolishing appeals in federal and constitutional **matters**) and by the **Whitlam** government in 1975 (abolishing all remaining appeals).

The eleven years between 1975 and 1986 thus saw a bizarre situation of dualism—and potential conflict—at the apex of the Australian **hierarchy of courts**. Unsuccessful litigants in the **state Supreme Courts** could choose to appeal either to the High Court or to the Privy Council, each an ultimate court of appeal: thus, in different cases, both ultimate courts might decide the same issue, potentially with opposite results. This gave rise to delicate problems of **precedent** and judicial comity. In *Viro v The Queen* (1978), the High Court affirmed that it was no longer bound by Privy Council decisions, and most Justices—with varying qualifications—suggested that in case of conflict the state courts should invariably follow the High Court. But logically, as **Stephen** and **Aickin** recognised, the dilemma was insoluble.

Historically, the Privy Council was a council of advisers to the British monarch, which, over time, developed into the final court of appeal for courts in the British colonies. Appeals were formally expressed as petitions to the Queen in the exercise of her royal prerogative of justice, though considered on her behalf by the Judicial Committee of her Privy Council. The reasons for judgment were formally expressed as mere advice to the Queen, invariably ending with the formal recital: 'Their Lordships will humbly advise Her Majesty …'. It was for this reason that, until 1966 (when **Barwick** was instrumental in changing the practice), **dissenting judgments** were not permitted—since it was said that Her Majesty might be confused if she were advised in more than one voice—and its members were officially referred to as 'Privy Counsellors' rather than 'Privy Councillors'. Yet this concept of mere 'advice' was misleading. In *Hull v McKenna* (1923), Viscount Haldane explained:

> We have nothing to do with politics, or policies, or party considerations; we are really Judges, but in form and in name we are the Committee of the Privy Council. The Sovereign gives the judgment himself, and always acts upon the report which we make … so that you see, in substance, what takes place is a strictly judicial proceeding.

This distinction between **form and substance** was reaffirmed in *Ibralebbe v The Queen* (1963).

Since the jurisdiction had its foundation in royal prerogative power, it could be regulated—and even 'displaced' or 'extinguished'—by legislation (see Stephen's analysis in *A-G (Cth) v T & G Mutual Life* (1978)). It was regulated by the *Judicial Committee Acts* 1833 and 1844 (Imp). Arguably, these Acts could have been used to place Privy Council appeals on a purely statutory footing, but this approach was not taken and the prerogative was preserved. One consequence was that, although Orders in Council made under the 1844 Act authorised the state Supreme Courts to grant **leave to appeal** to the Privy Council, the Privy Council itself could also grant special leave to appeal.

Although it sat in London and its membership consisted largely of present and former law lords (that is, judicial members of the **House of Lords**), it was not part of the hierarchy of British domestic courts but rather the common apex of the hierarchy of courts of each colony. Occasionally its membership included colonial or Dominion judges (sitting only on appeals from other colonies or Dominions). Most of the early High Court Justices sat occasionally on the Privy Council, as did many members of the **Barwick Court**. But the predominance of law lords ensured that it applied the principles of English **common law**, and, as the common court of final appeal for all parts of the British Empire, it played a significant role in unifying the law throughout the Empire (see **Precedent**).

Given their status as British subjects and their identification as British, it was not surprising that many of the **framers of the Constitution** (including **Griffith**) wished to retain Privy Council appeals, especially as federation was to make no immediate difference to Australia's colonial status. Large sections of the colonial **legal professions** also supported their retention, while many of the colonies' Chief Justices saw the proposed High Court as a threat to their status. And British mercantile interests not only wanted uniform law throughout the Empire, but also feared that Australian judges might be less well disposed to their interests than English judges.

On the other hand, Privy Council appeals were expensive and thus unpopular with litigants, and many of the framers saw a local final **superior court** as more consistent with Australian **nationhood**, especially in relation to **constitutional interpretation**: it was said that English judges would not be familiar with a written federal constitution, and that colonial judges were just as competent as their English counterparts.

In the 1891 drafting committee, Andrew **Inglis Clark** conceded the political need to retain at least some Privy Council appeals. He foresaw, correctly, that the British government would wish to retain appeals. In fact, during the constitutional negotiations in London in 1900, British intransigence on the issue almost caused the Australian delegates to return home without securing approval to the Constitution. At the last minute, a compromise was reached at a private dinner party given by the Colonial Secretary, Joseph Chamberlain. This compromise was embodied in section 74 of the Constitution, which reflected the tension not only between the Australian delegation and the British government but also between the opposing viewpoints in Australia.

In its final form, the compromise was to preserve appeals to the Privy Council from state courts (by being silent on the matter); and to allow 'prerogative' appeals from the High Court by special leave of the Privy Council, subject to two qualifications. First, no appeal would be permitted from the High Court on any *inter se* question (that is, one involving competition or conflict between state and Commonwealth powers), unless the High Court certified that the question 'is one which ought to be determined' by the Privy Council. Secondly, the Commonwealth Parliament was empowered to make laws 'limiting' appeals from the High Court (by restricting the matters in which special leave might be asked).

Thus, the Constitution immediately excluded the Privy Council from the central constitutional question of the scope of **Commonwealth legislative powers** (subject only to

the High Court granting a 'section 74 certificate'), and looked ahead to the later development of further restrictions when that was judged desirable by the Australian democratic process. The concept of an '*inter se* question' was not entirely clear, and its boundaries would be much litigated; but some important constitutional questions fell outside those boundaries and could therefore be dealt with by the Privy Council so long as the legislative power to 'limit' appeals had not been exercised. After some initial doubt, the category of non–*inter se* questions was held to include the interpretation of section 92's guarantee of freedom of **interstate trade**; many aspects of the **separation of powers** at Commonwealth level, especially of **judicial power**; and questions of **inconsistency** under section 109 of the Constitution (though the status of these remained unclear until 1956). Geoffrey Sawer observed tartly in 1967 that the Privy Council never had a sufficient flow of Australian constitutional cases to develop a proper understanding of the Australian Constitution, but did have enough to do considerable damage.

The High Court has only once certified an *inter se* question for decision by the Privy Council. That was in *Colonial Sugar Refining Co v A-G (Cth)* (1912), where O'Connor's illness had left the Court evenly divided (see **Tied vote**) on the powers of Royal Commissions. Certificates were sought in many other cases, but invariably refused.

The legislative power to restrict appeals from the High Court to the Privy Council was exercised in two stages. Since the 1968 legislation excluded only federal and constitutional appeals, the Privy Council itself held, in *Kitano v Commonwealth* (1975), that it was a valid exercise of the power of 'limiting' appeals. When the 1975 legislation abolished all remaining appeals, it was challenged on the basis that the power to 'limit' did not extend to complete abolition. In *A-G (Cth) v T & G Mutual Life*, the High Court rejected this argument, thus avoiding the logical puzzle of how much, and what, would have to be preserved to make the limitation less than complete. And since the 1968 Act had already been held to be valid, there could be no appeal to the Privy Council in relation to the validity of the 1975 Act.

As the Constitution was silent in relation to appeals to the Privy Council direct from state courts, the possibility remained that through such appeals the Privy Council could adjudicate on *inter se* matters after all. At one stage in the final negotiations over section 74, the section would have provided explicitly that no *inter se* question 'shall be capable of final decision except by the High Court'. On that wording, even if such a question arose in a state Supreme Court, it would have been impossible for that Court to grant leave to appeal to the Privy Council. But late in the negotiations that wording was deleted—in response to a cabled suggestion from Griffith, who proposed that the blocking of such appeals should be left to legislative action in Australia. The *Judiciary Act* 1903 (Cth) attempted to deal with the problem by permitting **removal** of *inter se* matters into the High Court (section 40), and by making the Court's appellate jurisdiction in such matters exclusive (section 39(2)(a)). But in a series of cases involving the liability of Commonwealth officials to state income tax, the effectiveness of these provisions was challenged.

In *Wollaston's Case* (1902), the Supreme Court of Victoria had held that such taxes were valid. It reaffirmed that view in

In re the Income Tax Acts (No 4) (1904), this time in relation to **Deakin's** salary as a federal minister. **Isaacs**, appearing for Thomas Webb, the Victorian Commissioner of Taxes, asserted that the High Court's doctrine of **intergovernmental immunities**, formulated in *D'Emden v Pedder* (1904), had 'no application'—to which Chief Justice John Madden responded: 'We are entirely of that opinion.' There was no overt defiance of the High Court: the Court distinguished *D'Emden v Pedder*, but added that if the High Court took a different view, 'we will show it all the respect we are in duty bound to show it according as it may turn out to be the ultimate Court of Appeal, and its decision the final ascertainment of the law on the matter'. Whether the High Court was 'the ultimate Court of Appeal' was, of course, precisely what had to be determined.

On appeal, the High Court reversed the Supreme Court's decision (*Deakin v Webb* (1904)). Isaacs' request for a certificate under section 74 was unanimously refused, and the Privy Council refused special leave to appeal—having earlier acknowledged the High Court's 'great dignity' and 'supreme authority', and announced that special leave would be granted only with 'great caution' (*Daily Telegraph v McLaughlin* (1904)).

But that did not settle the taxation issue. By agreement with Deputy Postmaster-General Frank Outtrim, who was sympathetic to the state's cause, Webb (again represented by Isaacs) returned to the Supreme Court of Victoria, suing Outtrim for the tax on his salary. The Commonwealth government was not informed or given a chance to intervene. Counsel for both sides admitted that the case was governed by *Deakin v Webb*; but Isaacs explained that the proceedings 'had been instituted in order that an appeal might be taken to the Privy Council'. The Supreme Court duly followed *Deakin v Webb*; but, in a further Supreme Court hearing (*In re the Income Tax Acts* (1905)), Justice Henry Hodges granted leave to appeal to the Privy Council. He held that section 39(2)(a) of the Judiciary Act was invalid, and in any event that no Commonwealth enactment could affect the Imperial Orders in Council authorising the state Supreme Courts to grant leave to appeal.

The Privy Council allowed the appeal (*Webb v Outtrim* (1906))—agreeing with Hodges that section 39(2)(a) was invalid, and holding on the substantive point that *D'Emden v Pedder* was wrong: the Australian Constitution did not include the implied principles, such as immunity of instrumentalities, developed in the USA. Rather, the ordinary common law principles of **statutory interpretation** should govern statutes of all types, including the Constitution. Ironically, this was precisely the approach eventually adopted by the High Court in the **Engineers Case** (1920)—where the Court again refused to grant a section 74 certificate (and the Privy Council refused a patently untenable application for special leave to appeal).

Australian reaction to *Webb v Outtrim* was immediate and largely hostile—not because of the substantive issue, but because of the Privy Council's willingness to pronounce on what was clearly an *inter se* question. Almost immediately, a NSW District Court judge, Charles Murray, chose to follow *Webb v Outtrim* rather than *D'Emden v Pedder*; but in *Baxter v Commissioners of Taxation (NSW)* (1907), the High Court allowed an appeal, holding that the Privy Council had spoken without jurisdiction. The Justices—including Isaacs, who on the substantive issue of intergovernmental immunities joined **Higgins** in dissent—insisted that their normal obligation to follow Privy Council decisions did not apply to *inter se* questions. The strength of the High Court's reactions was an important step in the growth of Australian national identity; and perhaps in recognition of this, the Privy Council refused special leave to appeal.

Two decades after *Webb v Outtrim*, the Privy Council responded more cautiously to a new Victorian strategy devised by **Dixon** and Robert **Menzies**. The legislative response to *Webb v Outtrim* had been to bolster the original provision in the Judiciary Act *permitting* removal of *inter se* matters into the High Court by a new section 40A, which ensured their automatic removal. In *Pirrie v McFarlane* (1925)—where the issue was whether members of the Commonwealth armed forces had to comply with state road traffic and licensing laws—the Supreme Court of Victoria held that an *inter se* question was involved, and forwarded the papers to the High Court as section 40A required. Without waiting for the High Court to hear the matter, the Victorian government surreptitiously applied to the Privy Council for special leave to appeal from the Supreme Court decision. The Privy Council granted special leave, and informed the High Court by cable. A 'clearly disturbed' **Knox** told Edward Mitchell, counsel for the Commonwealth: 'We shall expect some explanation of this. It seems a most extraordinary procedure.' But Mitchell was equally surprised. He explained that the question should be addressed to Dixon; but when the matter came on for mention, Dixon blandly told the Court that no explanation was needed. It was left to Victoria's Attorney-General, FW Eggleston, to explain in a press release that the real objective was to secure a ruling that section 40A was invalid—and without its operation the High Court would have no jurisdiction.

Consistently with that argument, when the matter came on for hearing in the High Court, Dixon and Menzies failed to appear. Knox directed Mitchell to argue his case in their absence. Mitchell submitted that the matter should simply be struck out with an order for **costs**; but Knox replied: 'You have been told that we will hear you.' 'Not officially, your Honour', said Mitchell. 'I have said so just now', said Knox.

The High Court decision—affirming the validity of section 40A but, ironically, deciding the substantive issue in Victoria's favour—was handed down three months later. By then, the Court had received a full transcript of the Privy Council proceedings, and was reassured to find that their Lordships had said that it 'might materially assist' them to know the High Court's view. When the matter eventually came on for hearing in the Privy Council, their Lordships stopped the hearing, holding that the substantial question 'had already been determined ... the other questions becoming academic'.

Despite its early acknowledgment of the High Court's 'supreme authority', the Privy Council's membership fluctuated too often for any consistent policy of judicial comity towards the High Court to emerge. In *Victorian Railway Commissioners v Brown* (1906), the Privy Council announced that it would not normally allow litigants two bites at the cherry. A losing party in a state court who chose to appeal to the High Court, rather than to the Privy Council, would be bound by that election: if the same party was unsuccessful in the High Court, the Privy Council would not then grant special leave to appeal. Yet this principle was frequently ignored or forgotten, notably in *Hocking v Bell* (1947), a medical negligence case. Throughout the uneasy relationship between the two courts, there were mutual irritations—from the Privy Council decision in *Williams v Curator of Intestate Estates* (1909), which provoked Griffith to an unusual public complaint that 'in three out of the four cases in which the judgment of this Court has been reversed by the Judicial Committee … the decision has been based on materials not adverted to in Australia', to the High Court judgments in *Port Jackson Stevedoring v Salmond & Spraggon* (1978), where Stephen and **Murphy** suggested that the Privy Council decision in *NZ Shipping Co v Satterthwaite* (1974) should not be followed in Australia. Stephen even hinted that the *Satterthwaite* rule—enabling stevedores unloading cargo to obtain the benefit of exemption clauses in a bill of lading—was designed to serve British commercial interests at the expense of Australian. The Privy Council 'exceptionally' granted special leave to appeal, and emphatically reaffirmed *Satterthwaite* (*Port Jackson Stevedoring v Salmond & Spraggon* (1980)).

The Privy Council gave some important decisions on state constitutional law. In *McCawley v The King* (1920), reversing the High Court, it affirmed the continuing and unrestricted power of state Parliaments to amend their own **state constitutions**; but in *A-G (NSW) v Trethowan* (1932), it affirmed the High Court's decision that this power could validly be used to 'entrench' constitutional provisions in a way that would limit the power of future Parliaments. In federal constitutional matters as well, the Privy Council frequently affirmed views already expressed in the High Court—particularly in relation to the separation of powers and the freedom of interstate trade.

As to the separation of powers, the Privy Council based its opinion in the *Shell Case* (1930) on the judgment of Isaacs and **Rich** in *Alexander's Case* (1918), which held that 'the judicial power of the Commonwealth' could be vested only in courts established or given jurisdiction by Chapter III of the Constitution ('Chapter III courts'). In the *Boilermakers Case* (1956), a strong bench of seven upheld the High Court's majority view that the separation of powers precluded the vesting of non-judicial power in Chapter III courts.

As for section 92's guarantee of the freedom of interstate trade, the High Court's only clear view after *McArthur v Queensland* (1920) was that the section did not restrict Commonwealth actions, but applied only to the states. Isaacs, and later Dixon, took a very broad view of the guaranteed 'freedom', extending it beyond fiscal imposts to any type of government interference. In *James v Cowan* (1932), where the High Court had upheld compulsory acquisition under a primary products marketing scheme, their Lordships' reversal of that decision relied extensively on the dissenting judgment of Isaacs. In *James v Commonwealth* (1936), the Privy Council overruled the holding in *McArthur* that section 92 did not bind the Commonwealth, yet appeared nevertheless to endorse the broad view of the section for which the *McArthur* holding had been the underpinning.

In the *Bank Nationalisation Case* (1949), the Privy Council took a very wide view of the scope of section 92, endorsing Dixon's 'individual right' approach and thereby entrenching—at least until *Cole v Whitfield* (1988)—the view of the section as a guarantee of individual enterprise, rather than a provision essentially designed to ensure a national common market free from state protectionism. Their Lordships recognised that the underlying issue—the validity of the *Banking Act 1947* (Cth)—necessarily involved *inter se* questions, so that even though the section 92 issue was not an *inter se* question, they ought not to give any decision. Yet they thought it 'right to state their views upon the question', since counsel had come a long way and had made substantial arguments. In *Hughes & Vale v NSW* (1954), the Privy Council vindicated Dixon's substantive view of the operation of section 92 in the road transport area, overturning his poignant decision in the High Court (*Hughes & Vale v NSW (No 1)* (1953)) to abandon his personal view and to form a majority for the contrary view on the basis of precedent.

The Privy Council's jurisprudence of section 92 has not survived, and was in any event derivative of the views of selected High Court Justices. In other areas, too, the impact of its decisions is now greatly diminished. The first case in which it granted special leave to appeal from a High Court decision—*Colonial Bank v Marshall* (1906)—was also among the first Privy Council decisions overruled by the High Court after *Viro* (see *Commonwealth Trading Bank v Sydney Wide Stores* (1981)). In the area of **occupiers' liability**, a significant development in the High Court—beginning with *Thompson v Bankstown Corporation* (1953), and culminating in *Commissioner for Railways v Cardy* (1960)—had been cut short by the Privy Council in *Commissioner for Railways v Quinlan* (1964), where the Australian development was said to be 'in direct conflict with an inescapable weight of established rules of the common law'. Their Lordships took a less draconian view in *Southern Portland Cement v Cooper* (1973); but it was left to **Deane**, in *Hackshaw v Shaw* (1984), to take up the Australian development where *Cardy's Case* had left off (see now *Australian Safeway Stores v Zaluzna* (1987)).

The Privy Council's jurisdiction has steadily dwindled as former colonies have moved to independence and in due course judged the retention of Privy Council appeals to be inappropriate. Appeals now come primarily from the West Indies and from New Zealand, where indigenous demands for an arm's-length tribunal may have helped to preserve the appeal. The last Australian appeal (from a state court) was heard in 1987.

Together with other factors (see **Leave to appeal**), the final abolition of Privy Council appeals has had a dramatic effect on the High Court's own jurisprudence. Many commentators have observed that that abolition did more than formally make the High Court the final court of appeal for all Australian matters. It also contributed to the evolution of a new judicial mindset. Liberated first from correction by a higher court and then from competition in relation to appeals from state courts, the High Court became the true apex of the Australian hierarchy and undertook a new responsibility for shaping the law for Australia.

Theoretically, appeals to the Privy Council from the High Court are still possible if the High Court grants a certificate under section 74. It is ironic that the only remaining possibility for appeal survives in the area where it is least likely ever to be contemplated again.

Tony Blackshield
Michael Coper
John Goldring

Further Reading

Tony Blackshield, *The Abolition of Privy Council Appeals: Judicial Responsibility and The Law for Australia* (1978)

Tony Blackshield, 'The Last of England—Farewell to Their Lordships Forever' (1982) 36 *LIJ* 779

Almeric Fitz Roy, *The History of the Privy Council* (1928)

John Goldring, *The Privy Council and the Australian Constitution* (1996)

DB Swinfen, *Imperial Appeal: The Debate on the Appeal to the Privy Council, 1833–1986* (1987)

Procedure denotes the mode of proceeding by which a legal right is enforced, as distinguished from the substantive law that gives or defines the right (*Minister for Army v Parbury Henty* (1945)).

At the **establishment** of the Court, matters of procedure were to be found in both the *Judiciary Act* 1903 (Cth) and in the *High Court Procedure Act* 1903 (Cth). The **High Court Rules** appeared first in the Schedule to the High Court Procedure Act. Until 1928, amendments were made to those Rules by the Justices of the Court. In that year, the Justices made new Rules under both the Judiciary Act and the High Court Procedure Act. In 1937, the sections of the High Court Procedure Act under which the earlier Rules had been made were repealed, and all Rules made by the Justices were deemed to be Rules of Court made under section 86 of the Judiciary Act, so that the rule-making power was placed under one Act. Then, with effect from 1 January 1953, the Rules were remade under the Judiciary Act and it is these that form the basis of the current Rules (*Merribee Pastoral Industries v ANZ Banking Group* (1998)). There have been scores of amendments to the Rules since 1953, the Rules being kept under review by the Rules Committee with the assistance of the Registry. Less formally, procedure is prescribed by **practice directions** issued by the Court from time to time.

As a rationalisation measure, the balance of the High Court Procedure Act was repealed in 1980. Its substantive parts were incorporated into the Judiciary Act and the remainder, dealing with the **administration** of the Court, was re-enacted as the *High Court of Australia Act* 1979 (Cth).

The Rules were framed for a court with substantial trial work and so they have remained, although with increased attention to the efficient exercise of the Court's **role** as the ultimate appeal court for Australia. But the Rules still deal with such matters as discovery of documents, discovery by interrogatories, and notices to produce, and in those respects are finding increased use as the recent effects of Part 8 of the *Migration Act* 1958 (Cth) have increasingly added to the trial work of the Court (*Re Minister for Immigration; Ex parte Durairajasingham* (2000); *Herijanto v Refugee Review Tribunal* (2000); see also **Fact finding; Immigration law**).

From the early days of the Court until 1977, a substantial part of the Court's **jurisdiction** and work involved trials by single Justices, especially in the fields of revenue and intellectual property. These trials involved disputed questions of fact as well as of law. On occasion, a single Justice would find the facts in order for a **Full Court** to deal with a constitutional question: thus, for example, in March, April, and June 1979, **Murphy** sat in Melbourne hearing evidence in the *DOGS Case* (1981). Because of the workload of the Court, this practice has not been used since then. Now, in the event of disputed facts, the matter would be the subject of **remittal** to the **Federal Court** or to a state **Supreme Court** or a territory Supreme Court.

In the Court's original jurisdiction, **a matter** may be commenced by a writ of summons and statement of claim, or by application for the **remedies** referred to in section 75(v) of the Constitution. By Order 55 of the High Court Rules, such applications are initially for the grant of an **order** *nisi*, returnable before a Full Court. Proceedings may also come to the Court by **removal** under section 40 of the Judiciary Act.

The most common procedure for bringing a matter before the Full Court in its original jurisdiction is the stating of a case or reserving of a question under section 18 of the Judiciary Act. But the Court cannot draw inferences of fact under that procedure (*Johanson v Dixon* (1979)). This may be contrasted with the more rarely used special case under section 18 of the Judiciary Act in which, by Order 35 of the High Court Rules, the Court is specifically enabled to draw inferences. Under these procedures, it is primarily the parties who agree on the facts that should be put before the Court.

Less frequently used now is the demurrer provided for by Order 26 of the Rules whereby a party may raise a question of law for the determination of the Court. In such a case, the facts are to be collected from the pleadings. For the purpose of the demurrer, the demurring party admits those facts but contends that they do not show a cause of action or ground of defence, as the case may be. Most commonly, a demurrer is used in the Court to raise a constitutional question, but the procedure is not limited to those questions.

Under Order 55, the application for one or more of the prerogative **writs** must generally be for an order calling upon the proposed respondent to show cause why the writ or order should not be issued or made. The Justice who hears the application may, if satisfied that there is an arguable case, grant the order, in which case the order to show cause goes to a Full Court. Alternatively, the Justice may direct that the application be made by Notice of Motion to a Full Court. A third alternative is to make an order of remittal.

An appeal from a decision of a single Justice is provided for by section 34 of the Judiciary Act. Where the decision is interlocutory, such as the refusal of an application for orders *nisi* for prohibition and certiorari, then an appeal is by leave.

An appeal to the Court from the federal courts, other courts exercising federal jurisdiction, territory courts, and state Supreme Courts is by special leave and has been since 1984. This is a narrow gateway. There are approximately 300 civil and 100 criminal special leave applications filed each year, and leave is granted in approximately 45 civil and 20 criminal appeals.

By section 21 of the Judiciary Act, an application for special **leave to appeal** may be heard by a single Justice (an example is *A-G (Qld); Ex rel Kerr v T* (1983)), but generally such applications are heard by a Full Court of two or three Justices. It sometimes happens that a special leave application is heard by five or seven Justices. The criteria for special leave are to be found in section 35A of the Judiciary Act and the formal procedure is set out in Order 69A of the High Court Rules. Written summaries of **argument** are required, and any oral argument is limited to 20 minutes for each side with the applicant having five minutes in reply. This limitation was first made in 1994 following the introduction of Order 69A in its original form on 1 January 1987. The Court does not encourage parties to use these maximum times. Applications for special leave to appeal may be heard by video link from capital cities other than Canberra, Sydney, and Melbourne. This facility was first introduced in 1988. The hearing of applications in which either party is heard by video link takes place with the Court **sitting** in Canberra.

If leave to appeal is granted, a notice of appeal must be filed and served within 21 days of the grant. Other time limits are also prescribed by Order 70 for the compilation of the **appeal books** so that the hearing of each appeal may be brought on efficiently. A grant of special leave may be rescinded at the hearing of the appeal, or beforehand.

An appeal to the Court under section 73 of the Constitution is an appeal in the strict sense: its function is simply to determine whether the decision in question was right or wrong on the evidence and the law as it stood when that decision was given. The Court cannot receive further evidence, and its powers are limited to setting aside the decision under appeal and, if it be appropriate, to substituting the decision that should have been made at first instance (*Coal and Allied Operations v Australian Industrial Relations Commission* (2000)). In a complex matter, there will be one or more **directions hearings** before a Justice.

Argument before the Court in matters in which a Full Court sits, whether in the original or in the appellate jurisdiction, remains fundamentally oral, but full written submissions are required before the hearing. They are the subject of a lengthy practice direction, intended to ensure that the Justices may better understand the contentions of the parties before the hearing of the matter commences and to enhance the utility of oral argument. There is a timetable within which each party is to file and serve written submissions, of no more than 20 pages, signed by the senior legal practitioner who is to present the case in court. A chronology is also required. No supplementary written submission may be filed before the hearing except with the leave of the Court, a Justice, or the Registrar. Corresponding requirements are imposed in relation to **interveners**. Written submissions, limited to outlines, were first required by a practice direction as recently as 1982, when **counsel** was 'to hand up to the Bench at the beginning of his oral argument a typewritten outline of his submissions … A copy should then be handed to counsel for other parties … Ordinarily the outline should not exceed three pages'.

An important aspect of procedure is dictated by section 78B of the Judiciary Act, whereby a court is not to proceed in a cause that involves a matter arising under the Constitution or involving its interpretation unless reasonable notice of the nature of the matter has been given to the **Attorneys-General**. To this end, a notice under section 78B must be filed and served and a practice direction requires each party to certify that they have considered whether any notice or further notice should be given to Attorneys-General in compliance with that section. If an appropriate notice has not been given, the Court must adjourn that part of the matter and any part not severable from it, although urgent interlocutory relief may be granted.

A constitutional case, or one in which leave has been given to argue that the Court should **overrule** one of its own prior decisions, will generally be heard by all the available members of the Court. Other cases are normally heard by five of the seven Justices (see **Bench, composition of**). The decision of the Court will be accompanied by substantial written reasons. Occasionally, in cases of urgency, the decision of the Court will first be given and written reasons will follow some weeks afterwards.

It was held early in the Court's history that sections 15 and 16 of the Judiciary Act showed clearly an intention on the part of the legislature that the jurisdiction of the Court should be publicly exercised (*Dickason v Dickason* (1913); see also **Accountability**). Some of the Court's jurisdiction, mainly interlocutory matters, may by section 16 of the Judiciary Act be exercised by a Justice sitting in **chambers**—but with the prevalence of public chambers, the distinction between a hearing in **open court** and a Justice sitting in chambers to which the public did not have access has lost most of its significance (*Raybos Australia v Tectran Corporation* (1987)). There is, however, no requirement to robe for an application to be heard in chambers (see **Etiquette**). Also, where counsel attends at a Justice's chambers, **costs** of the attendance are not allowed unless the Justice certifies it to be a proper case for counsel to attend.

ALAN ROBERTSON

Further Reading
John Daley, 'Interlocutory Orders Pending High Court Litigation' (1995) 13 *Aust Bar Rev* 41
David Jackson, 'Practice in the High Court of Australia' (1996–97) 15 *Aust Bar Rev* 187
Frank Jones, 'High Court Procedure under the Judiciary Act' (1994) 68 *ALJ* 442
Anthony Mason, 'The Regulation of Appeals to the High Court of Australia: The Jurisdiction to Grant Special Leave to Appeal' (1996) 15 *U Tas LR* 1

Property. At **common law**, the concept of property has been the source of a wide variety of rights and **remedies** (see also **Acquisition of property; Land law**). Yet, despite the familiarity and usefulness of the concept, it has never been comprehensively defined. Neither the **connotation** nor the denotation of the term is fixed, and the High Court, in company with other **superior courts**, has both exploited and been confused by this uncertainty. In *Mabo* (1992), **Brennan** observed that 'Australian law is not only the historical successor of, but is an organic development from, the law of England'. The Court has been slow to draw on the law of countries other than England, and has also been relatively slow to extend the concept of property or to create new property interests, although it has shown considerable creativity in the areas of **native title, estoppel**, and constructive **trusts**.

Although it is difficult to identify a particularly characteristic approach, as many of the Court's important judgments are so diverse (see, for example, *Latec Investments v Hotel Terrigal* (1965)), the nebulous quality of the Court's concept of property does enable the Court to adjust its characterisation of rights as 'proprietary' to the factual and legal context in which the decision is made. **Murphy** recognised this in *Dorman v Rodgers* (1982), noting that 'the concept of property has been used to recognise the legitimacy of claims and to secure them by bringing them within the scope of legal remedies'. *Dorman v Rodgers* was an appeal by Dr George Dorman against a direction that his name be removed from the register of medical practitioners, thus depriving him of the right to practise his profession. Murphy held that the doctor's right to practise was a property right, citing numerous US and Canadian decisions that held property to include a calling, business, or profession. He also expressed the view that 'in modern legal systems, "property" embraces every possible interest recognised by law which a person can have in anything and includes practically all valuable rights'. The majority of the Court, however, followed previous authority on the nature of a barrister's profession (*Clyne v NSW Bar Association* (1960)) and perfunctorily rejected the assertion of a property interest in such circumstances.

Murphy's comment was out of step with the Court's usual approach, which has been relatively traditional and consistent with English common law. According to orthodoxy, property interests are generally, but not invariably, assignable and exclusive. Such an interest is enforceable, if not against the whole world, at least against a wider group than those from whom it is acquired, and the rights of others commonly limit its sphere of enforceability. It is not necessary that the interest be permanent, although it will be difficult to characterise a merely ephemeral right as proprietary. In *R v Toohey; Ex parte Meneling Station* (1982), **Mason** accepted Lord Wilberforce's statement in *National Provincial Bank v Ainsworth* (1965) that to be characterised as property, a right must be 'definable, identifiable by third parties, capable in its nature of assumption by third parties and have some degree of permanence or stability'. Mason recognised that some forms of property are expressed to be inalienable by statute and that assignability is not always essential, but accepted Lord Wilberforce's assertion that such a right must be 'capable in its nature of assumption by third parties'. In *Mabo*, Brennan stated that the inalienability of native title did not settle the question of whether native title was proprietary (see also *Georgiadis v Australian & Overseas Telecommunications Corporation* (1994)).

In *Australian Tape Manufacturers Association v Commonwealth* (1993), where a law had provided that the copying of recorded music onto blank tapes was not a breach of **copyright**, the Court held that the law did not amount to an acquisition of property for which just compensation was payable under section 51(xxxi) of the Constitution. **Dawson** and **Toohey** (with whom **McHugh** agreed) stated that although copyright is property, the immunity given by the statute was not: it was not of a permanent nature, was not exclusive, and could not be assigned. There is a fine line between this decision and the decision in *Commonwealth v WMC Resources* (1998), where the Court accepted that exploration permits for petroleum, which effectively granted immunity from prosecution, were proprietary because the immunity was identifiable, assignable, exclusive, and valuable.

Other cases on section 51(xxxi) also give insights into the Court's conception of property. The Court has accepted the traditional view that property in land consists of a bundle of rights exercisable with respect to the land (see **Rich** in *Minister for the Army v Dalziel* (1944)). This is also true of personal property such as shares. In the **Bank Nationalisation Case** (1948), the Court held that the bundle of rights that constitutes the property in a share includes the right of shareholders to vote in the election of directors. However, given that a particular bundle of rights is seen as proprietary, questions may still arise as to particular elements in the bundle. In *Commonwealth v WA* (1999), **Callinan** emphasised that every individual right in the bundle that constitutes the relevant property is itself a property right. Callinan's assertion provides no assistance, however, in determining the scope of the bundle. For example, the assignee of a lease acquires the right to enforce only some of the covenants in the lease, namely those that touch and concern the land. Similarly, an option to purchase contained in a lease is not an integral part of the lease—although, perhaps anomalously, an option to renew the lease is (see *Mercantile Credits v Shell* (1976)). In the same way, a covenant of guarantee contained in an instrument of mortgage is not integral to a mortgage (see *Consolidated Trust Co v Naylor* (1936)). On this issue, the Court's views have been largely consistent with the English common law.

The Court has also accepted that possession of land or chattels gives rise to a proprietary interest (see *Allen v Roughley* (1955); *Penfolds Wines v Elliott* (1946); *City Motors v Southern Aerial Super Service* (1961)), although 'possession' in this context means possession as a matter of law, carrying with it the right to exclude others (see *Willey v Synan* (1937)). In the case of land, possession must also be distinguished from sole occupation (see *Radaich v Smith* (1959) and the **Privy Council** decision in *Isaac v Hotel de Paris* (1959)). In *Mabo*, Brennan accepted this, commenting that where native title comprises an exclusive right to occupy, the interest is proprietary.

The Court has been cautious in extending the concept of property where the claim is apparently designed to avoid the limitations of another legal category such as nuisance, or the scope of **damages** in **contract**. In *Victoria Park Racing v Taylor* (1937), the appellant claimed to have a property interest in the spectacle it had created, namely horse racing. The respondent had been making a profit by broadcasting descriptions of the races from adjoining property without the appellant's permission and, pertinently, without making any payment. **Latham** declined to accept that there could be property in a spectacle. He rejected the appellant's 'bootstraps' argument, saying that even if there were a legal principle that prevented the respondent from gaining an advantage by describing the appellant's horse races, then the rights of the appellant could be described as 'property' only in a metaphorical sense. The principle itself could not be based on a **metaphor**.

The other members of the majority, **Dixon** and **McTiernan**, were equally cautious. Dixon held that only rights that fell within 'a recognized category to which legal or equitable protection attaches' could assume the exclusiveness of property. Rich and **Evatt**, who dissented, took a more expansive approach, focusing more on what the law should be rather than its existing limits; their solution, however, was to extend the scope of nuisance and, in Rich's words, 'to reconcile the free prospect from one piece of land with the right of profitable enjoyment of another'.

The description of a right as property in a metaphorical sense, rejected in *Victoria Park v Taylor*, has been used by the High Court in other contexts where there is an underlying principle to support the concept—for example, in the development of remedies for breach of confidence. In *Brent v FCT* (1971), **Gibbs**, citing Latham in *FCT v United Aircraft Corporation* (1943), commented that 'neither knowledge nor information is property in a strictly legal sense, although they can be said to be property in a loose metaphorical sense'. In *Breen v Williams* (1996), Brennan accepted Lord Upjohn's description (in *Phipps v Boardman* (1966)) of the sense in which confidential information can be characterised as property: 'In the end the real truth is that it is not property in any normal sense but equity will restrain its transmission to another if in breach of some confidential relationship.' The underlying principle relevant to these cases, which did not arise on the facts in *Victoria Park v Taylor*, is identified by **Deane** in *Moorgate Tobacco v Philip Morris (No 2)* (1984) as being 'an obligation of conscience arising from the circumstances in or through which the information was communicated or obtained' (see also **Williams** in *FCT v United Aircraft Corporation*).

The rights surrounding the production of a spectacle have also occupied the Court in cases where it has been invited to extend the property concept to a licence to enter land. The Court has accepted the well-established principle that a mere licence is not assignable and is not property (see *Cowell v Rosehill Racecourse* (1937); *Dalziel*; *Radaich v Smith*). Consequently, such a licence can be revoked even if to do so is a breach of contract (see *Heatley v Tasmanian Racing and Gaming Commission* (1977)). In England, *Hurst v Picture Theatres* (1914) had decided that a 'right to see a spectacle' was a proprietary interest capable of being granted, so that when coupled with a licence to go into a theatre or a racecourse the licence was irrevocable; but in *Cowell*, the Court refused to follow that case. The Court was sympathetic to the plight of the licensee, but did not accept that extension of the concept of property was appropriate. This view has not escaped **criticism** (see *Forbes v NSW Trotting Club* (1979)), but, in part, the solution came later in *Baltic Shipping Co v Dillon* (1993), where the Court was prepared to recognise a right to damages for disappointment and distress in circumstances where the contract involved a promise to provide enjoyment.

Mabo is undoubtedly one of the Court's most far-reaching decisions. On one view, the decision does not involve any novel concept of property. However, the decision to recognise native title has had a profound effect on the nature of property in land. Moreover, the Court's analysis involved some modification of the traditional doctrine of tenure, although, according to Brennan, that doctrine 'could not be overturned without fracturing the skeleton which gives our land law its shape and consistency'. The modification reconciled the theory of tenure with recognition of the native title of **Aboriginal peoples**, and was achieved by the familiar technique of describing the doctrine at a higher level of generality than in previous cases. The Court held that the tenurial title of the Crown affords the Crown radical title to all land over which it has **sovereignty**. This radical title enabled the Crown, by an exercise of sovereignty, to grant interests in land and to become absolute beneficial owner of unalienated land required for its purposes. However, in the absence of such an exercise of sovereign power, there was no reason why native title should not continue under the protection of the common law.

The question of whether native title itself is property has received much attention. In *Mabo*, Brennan was explicit that where native title entailed exclusive possession, even at the community level, it is proprietary. In Toohey's view, the nature of the interest was irrelevant to the threshold question of whether the interest existed. However, the issue may be relatively unimportant. Although the characterisation of an interest as proprietary is necessary at common law to determine its sphere of enforceability, the enforceability of native title is determined by customary law, by whether there has been a relevant exercise of sovereignty, and by the statutory protection afforded under native title legislation.

The concept of property is at its most flexible within the realm of **equity**. Before an equitable property interest can exist, there must be some separation of legal and equitable interests. The Court has accepted that where the legal owner of property is also entitled to the entire beneficial interest, there can be no separate equitable interest in that property (see *DKLR Holding Co (No 2) v Commissioner of Stamp Duties (NSW)* (1982)). This is a corollary of the established principle that one cannot be a trustee for oneself (see *In re Selous* (1901); *In re Cook* (1948)). Where there is a separation of legal and equitable interests, the separation is not always complete and there has been considerable controversy as to when, and to what extent, a separate equitable proprietary interest has been formed. The link between substantive rights and remedies has been more particularly marked in this area, particularly in the last two decades.

This link is seen in the consideration of whether a specifically enforceable contract renders the vendor a trustee for the purchaser. The notion has on occasion been explicitly rejected (see Deane in *Kern Corporation v Walter Reid Trading* (1987)). The Court has held that a purchaser cannot claim an equitable interest unless the contract is specifically enforceable, or at least able to be protected by injunction or other equitable remedies (see *Chan v Cresdon Pty Ltd* (1989); *Williams v Frayne* (1937)). Where this is the case, the purchaser's equitable interest is conditional on payment of the price and fulfilment of any other preconditions under the contract (*KLDE v Commissioner of Stamp Duties (Qld)* (1984), and see **Kitto** in *Haque v Haque (No 2)* (1965)). There has been some debate as to whether the equitable interest is commensurate with the rights of the purchaser under the contract (see *Brown v Heffer* (1967); *Ziel Nominees v VACC Insurance* (1975)) or with the purchaser's ability to protect the rights under the contract by injunction (*Legione v Hateley* (1983)). Generally, the Court has been willing to sidestep this largely fruitless debate, while at the same time recognising the distinction between being the equitable owner and having an equitable interest in the property (see Brennan in *KLDE v Commissioner of Stamp Duties*). However, the accepted position seems to be as stated by Deane in *Kern Corporation v Walter Reid Trading*, namely that 'the purchaser has an equitable interest in the land which reflects the extent to which equitable remedies are available to protect his contractual rights and ... the vendor is under obligations in equity which attach to the land'.

On the question of whether a contract is specifically enforceable, the Court has been prepared in some circumstances to order specific performance even where the plaintiff is in breach of the contract (see *Legione v Hateley*; *Stern v McArthur* (1988)), thus extending the sphere of property to the rights of the successful plaintiff. Other equitable interests may arise such as an equitable lien (*Hewett v Court* (1983)) or an option to purchase (*Commissioner of Taxes (Qld) v Camphin* (1937)).

Waltons Stores v Maher (1988) is a seminal decision of fundamental importance for the law of contract and property. In that case, the majority of the High Court accepted that promissory estoppel could apply outside an existing legal relationship between the parties. Three Justices (Mason, **Wilson**, and Brennan) relied on the English cases on proprietary estoppel and accepted that estoppel could be relied upon to create positive rights including property rights. The decision created a **precedent** on which lower courts could rely (in the **Federal Court**, see *S & E Promotions v Tobin Bros* (1994); in the NSW Court of Appeal, see *Austotel v Franklins Selfserve* (1989)). The Court was also creative, and similarly provided a stimulus to lower courts, in *Bahr v Nicolay (No 2)* (1988) in relation to the enforcement of a contract by a third party for whose benefit the contract was made.

During the 1950s, English and Australian courts were under pressure to recognise property rights claimed to arise from informal arrangements, especially within families and in de facto relationships. Led by Lord Denning, the English Court of Appeal took a robust approach to its power under section 17 of the *Married Women's Property Act* 1882 (UK) to make such orders as it saw fit. According to Denning, the jurisdiction over family assets was entirely discretionary: the Court was entitled to make 'such order as appears to be fair and just in all the circumstances' (*Hine v Hine* (1962)). The High Court rejected this 'palm-tree justice' and insisted that the equivalent Australian legislation be interpreted strictly in accordance with the rules of law and the traditional presumptions of equity.

This conservative approach also showed itself in the cases in which the Court rejected the argument that it was entitled, in its equitable jurisdiction, to impose a constructive trust whenever it thought that this would be a means of achieving a fair distribution of property between spouses or de facto partners. In *Muschinski v Dodds* (1985), Deane accepted that notions of fairness and justice are relevant to the equitable concept of **unconscionable** conduct, but specifically rejected the proposition that the Court could impose a trust on the basis of an individual judge's idiosyncratic notions of unconscionable conduct (confirmed in *Baumgartner v Baumgartner* (1987)). However, the Court's refusal to follow the more extreme English decisions should not be allowed to obscure the fact that, in a more modest way, the High Court has exercised considerable creativity. The Court's acceptance of the remedial nature of the constructive trust in *Muschinski v Dodds*, and its recognition of the equities arising out of informal arrangements in cases such as *Baumgartner* and

Calverley v Green (1984), have been followed in numerous lower court decisions.

Nevertheless, the nature of the constructive trust continues to raise problems. Most recently, **Gleeson**, McHugh, **Gummow**, and Callinan asserted in *Giumelli v Giumelli* (1999) that 'some constructive trusts create or recognise no proprietary interest. Rather there is the imposition of a personal liability to account in the same manner as that of an express trustee'. They gave as an example the imposition of personal liability upon a person who is dishonestly involved in a breach of trust or **fiduciary obligation**. This proposition appears to confuse the position before the imposition of a constructive trust (when there may be no proprietary interest) and after its imposition (when there must be something over which the trust is held). Alternatively, it would appear that the Justices are positing two categories of constructive trust: one that involves property, and one that does not. As they offered no explanation for a proposition that would seem to be a contradiction in terms, it is difficult to throw light on the matter.

Throughout its existence, the Court has taken a cautious attitude to the concept of property and has been wary of unnecessarily diluting the category of property interests. However, over the last two or three decades, the expansion of the constructive trust, the recognition of native title, and the preparedness to recognise proprietary interests arising from estoppel have demonstrated that the Court is moderately creative and responsive to the changing needs of society.

MARGARET STONE

Proportionality is a deceptively simple legal doctrine, intimately intertwined with the protection of individual rights, which the High Court came to apply in three public law contexts in the 1980s and 1990s. It is a form of analysis of the relationship between a legitimate governmental end and the means employed to achieve it. The core idea is captured by the aphorism that one should not use a sledgehammer to crack a nut. As a distinct legal doctrine, it appears to have been derived from jurisprudence of the European Court of Justice and the European Court of Human Rights.

The European understanding of the notion involves three overlapping aspects: that a governmental measure is a suitable means to achieve the relevant end; that it is necessary, in that no practical alternative means is available which is less restrictive of relevant protected interests; and that it represents an acceptable balance, such that the significance of achieving the governmental end outweighs the significance of any infringement of the protected interests. All three aspects played some role in the Australian decisions.

Proportionality was introduced in Australia by **Deane** in the *Tasmanian Dam Case* (1983). It was employed first as a **characterisation** test to assess whether a federal law was sufficiently connected to federal powers to be constitutionally valid, being employed in relation to those federal powers that had a purposive aspect (in particular, the **external affairs power**, the **defence power**, and the incidental aspect of other powers). This limited application appeared to manifest a misapprehension—namely, that proportionality is essentially a test of purpose. The doctrine was applied by a series of different Justices in *Richardson v Forestry Commission*

(1988), *Davis v Commonwealth* (1988), the *War Crimes Act Case* (1991), and *Nationwide News v Wills* (1992). A majority of the Court came to regard proportionality as synonymous with the traditional test for purposive characterisation—that is, that the measure be 'appropriate and adapted' to achieving the valid federal purpose.

In fact, the use of proportionality in this manner represented a significant change in approach. The effect of the doctrine is to protect particular interests or rights from what is deemed to be undue governmental regulation. The identification of such interests is presupposed by the necessity and balancing aspects of the doctrine. Thus in Australia, various High Court Justices employed the doctrine to protect freedom of communication (*Davis*; *Nationwide News*), **property** (*Tasmanian Dam*; *Richardson*), and freedom from retrospective criminal laws (*War Crimes Act Case*).

The high-water mark of this use of the doctrine was reached in **Mason's** judgment in *Nationwide News*, where he stated that the doctrine would protect 'fundamental **values** traditionally protected by the **common law**'. The application of proportionality in this manner effectively created a new, unspecified range of **implied constitutional rights** (protecting interests identified or chosen by the Justices), albeit rights that were only protected when certain types of federal power were relied upon by the Commonwealth. This qualitative protection of particular interests contrasted with what had been the orthodox approach to purposive characterisation, set out most clearly in *Burton v Honan* (1952) and *Herald & Weekly Times v Commonwealth* (1966). On that view, considerations of fairness and justice were regarded as matters for the Parliament to assess.

Characterisation tests invariably involve questions of degree, and some consideration of proportionality was probably implicit in the traditional 'appropriate and adapted' formula. On the orthodox approach, the assessments were inevitably made against the backdrop of the general social context, including the qualitative concerns and values inherent in that context. The change wrought by the introduction of a distinct doctrine of proportionality related to the specificity with which the particular interests deemed worthy of protection were articulated and taken into account, and in the relative weight attached to protection of those interests.

This qualitative use of proportionality in characterisation came under vehement attack from **Dawson** in *Nationwide News*, later joined by **Toohey** in *Cunliffe v Commonwealth* (1994). In the *Industrial Relations Act Case* (1996) and *Leask v Commonwealth* (1996), a majority of the Court retreated from the previous acceptance that proportionality could be deployed in a strong manner in the characterisation context to protect individual rights. The concept was not totally disavowed, however, and it is conceivable that the concept will maintain some role in characterisation.

The second context in which the High Court employed the concept of proportionality was as a test of the justifiability of laws infringing certain constitutional guarantees. Constitutionally protected interests can sometimes be regulated or restricted in order to achieve other legitimate governmental ends. For example, freedom of **interstate trade** may be tempered by genuine quarantine laws. It is necessary then to have some way of testing what types and degrees of restriction are permissible. Proportionality is employed by many courts around the world as one such test. The constitutionally protected interests in this context, unlike those in the characterisation context, are already identified, not chosen by the Justices.

The High Court first expressly employed proportionality in this role in *Castlemaine Tooheys v SA* (1990), in relation to the section 92 guarantee of freedom of interstate trade and commerce. Proportionality, or variants of it, were similarly invoked in relation to the newly recognised freedom of **political communication**, particularly in the *Free Speech Cases* (1992), *Theophanous v Herald & Weekly Times* (1994), *Cunliffe*, and *Levy v Victoria* (1997). Various Justices have also turned to proportionality in relation to the putative guarantee of **equality** of voting power (*McGinty v WA* (1996)), the section 117 prohibition of **discrimination** on the basis of state residence (*Street v Queensland Bar Association* (1989)), and the section 51(xxxi) requirement that the Commonwealth accord just terms when it compulsorily acquires property (*Mutual Pools v Commonwealth* (1994); *Airservices Australia v Canadian Airlines International* (1999); see **Acquisition of property**).

The core elements of the concept (necessity and balancing) had come to play a role in the section 92 case law well before the 'proportionality' label was introduced (for example, *North Eastern Dairy Case* (1975); *Uebergang v Australian Wheat Board* (1980)). These notions are recurring ones in relation to constitutional guarantees. Thus, the High Court noted in *Lange v ABC* (1997) that, at least in the context of the implied guarantee of free political communication, there was little difference between the 'proportionality' and the 'reasonably appropriate and adapted' tests.

The key virtue of employing proportionality in the guarantee context is that it enables variable standards of review depending on the importance of the competing interests at stake and the degree of restriction involved, while still allowing a structured form of analysis. The cost of this flexibility is a decrease in certainty. The approach contrasts with the type of approach generally taken by the **United States Supreme Court**, which involves different levels of review according to the particular category in which a restriction is seen to fall. In practice, the difference between the two approaches is less significant than first appears.

The third context in which proportionality was applied by the High Court was to test whether subordinate legislation (regulations) was made within statutory power (*SA v Tanner* (1989)). This usage is similar to the concept being employed as a characterisation test. A fourth possible usage, suggested by Deane in *Australian Broadcasting Tribunal v Bond* (1990), was as a ground of general review in **administrative law**. Although this possibility has not, as yet, become accepted law, there is little doubt that notions of proportionality are an element in the tests for **reasonableness** applied in that area of law.

The High Court's invocation of the doctrine of proportionality in the 1980s and 1990s illustrates two main points about the evolution of the Court. First, the doctrine's use in the characterisation context was an example of the Court's new-found readiness to recognise implied constitutional rights. Secondly, the fact that the doctrine appears to have been imported from Europe reflected a new willingness to look to a broader range of sources than had previously been evident. The difficulties associated with the Court's use of the doctrine illustrate the perils associated with seeking to import apparently simple doctrines from other legal systems. On the other hand, the fact that a substantially similar test had already evolved locally in the guarantee context illustrates that similar problems—and solutions—can be found in quite different legal systems.

JEREMY KIRK

Further Reading

Evelyn Ellis (ed), *The Principle of Proportionality in the Laws of Europe* (1999)

Brian Fitzgerald, 'Proportionality and Australian Constitutionalism' (1993) 12 *U Tas LR* 263

Jeremy Kirk, 'Constitutional Guarantees, Characterisation and the Concept of Proportionality' (1997) 21 *MULR* 1

Brad Selway, 'The Rise and Rise of the Reasonable Proportionality Test in Public Law' (1996) 7 *PLR* 212

Leslie Zines, 'Characterisation of Commonwealth Laws' in HP Lee and George Winterton (eds), *Australian Constitutional Perspectives* (1992)

Prospective overruling is a device whereby an appellate court overrules one of its earlier decisions—but in a manner that purports to operate only in relation to subsequent transactions. The device has frequently been used by the **United States Supreme Court** (see, for example, *Linkletter v Walker* (1965)). Where appropriate, the Supreme Court has even nominated some date other than that of its new decision as fixing the time from which its new ruling will operate. For a time, the device appeared to be looked on favourably by some members of the High Court.

The High Court may **overrule** decisions of lower courts or its own earlier decisions. When this happens, common assumptions may be disturbed or existing legal principles may be abrogated; that is, new law is created. In earlier times, the High Court tended to mask this process through emphasis on the declaratory theory of law. More recently, there has been frank acknowledgment of the **law-making role** of the High Court (see, for example, **Brennan** in *Giannarelli v Wraith* (1988) and **Mason** in the *War Crimes Act Case* (1991)).

A judicial declaration that a statute is invalid is a judgment that it was invalid *ab initio* (see *Residual Assco Group v Spalvins* (2000)). This may expose a person to civil or criminal liability for actions believed lawful when committed. Similarly, when an earlier judicial determination is overruled, the retroactive effect of judicial decision making is obvious. The law as 'reformulated' will be applied to the parties and other litigants even though the 'old law' was current when they entered into the transaction in question. In recent years, there have been several instances of earlier law being overturned by the High Court with retroactive effect (see, for example, *Northern Territory v Mengel* (1995); *Ha v NSW* (1997); *Esso v Commissioner of Taxation* (1999)). They include some relatively rare criminal decisions (for example, *R v L* (1991), abrogating the marital rape immunity rule).

At about the time the High Court began to acknowledge its law-making role, individual Justices suggested it might be open to the Court to overrule an earlier **precedent** in a way that would operate prospectively only (see Mason in *Baba-

niaris v Lutony Fashions (1987); Brennan in *John v FCT* (1989); **Deane** in *Oceanic Sun Line Co v Fay* (1988); **Toohey** in *Trident General Insurance v McNiece* (1988)).

However, in *Ha* the Court declared prospective overruling to be

> inconsistent with **judicial power** on the simple ground that the new regime that would be ushered in when the overruling took effect would alter existing rights and obligations. If an earlier case is erroneous and it is necessary to overrule it, it would be a perversion of judicial power to maintain in force that which is acknowledged not to be the law.

Whether prospective overruling is foreclosed to non-Chapter III courts would be decided in the event that such a court adopted this device.

In addition to the objection of principle expressed in *Ha*, prospective overruling has the further disadvantages of both drawing invidious distinctions between the positions of past litigants and of current and future litigants and—at least if the implementation of the new rule is deferred beyond the case then before the Court—of providing a serious disincentive to litigants to bring actions. On the other hand, prospective overruling is understandably aimed at avoiding the potentially alarming consequences of retrospective law-making. Thus, the High Court has at times limited the retroactive effect of ground-breaking decisions by methods other than prospective overruling (see, for example, *Bropho v WA* (1990), where earlier enactments were quarantined from a new rule of **statutory interpretation**, and *McKinney v The Queen* (1991), where the prospective requirement to give a warning to juries was justified by treating the law as a 'rule of practice'). Much earlier, when the Court held that a training farm for delinquent boys was a charitable institution, the **joint judgment** delivered by **Dixon** disapproved of earlier decisions giving undue weight when interpreting statutes to the popular meaning of 'charitable' rather than its legal meaning, and warned that 'our courts in the future should be slow to do this unless there is a clear indication of a contrary intention' (*Salvation Army v Fern Tree Gully Corporation* (1952)).

In *David Securities v Commonwealth Bank* (1992), the Court declared that a rule precluding recovery of moneys paid under a mistake of law does not form part of the law in Australia. It remains to be decided whether a payment made under a well-grounded assumption that a legal obligation existed may be treated as having occurred under mistake of law if a later judicial decision destroys the basis of the assumption (compare *Kleinwort Benson v Lincoln City Council* (1998) with *Esso Australia Resources*). An affirmative answer would not be inconsistent with *Ha*.

KEITH MASON

Further Reading

Tony Blackshield, '"Fundamental Rights" and the Economic Viability of the Indian Nation, Part III: Prospective Overruling' (1968) 10 *Journal of the Indian Law Institute* 183

Keith Mason, 'Prospective Overruling' (1989) 63 *ALJ* 526

Proximity. In *Donoghue v Stevenson* (1932), Lord Atkin formulated the 'neighbour' principle to explain and limit the extent to which **tort law** should impose liability on persons who negligently inflict harm on others. Having enunciated the principle in terms of 'reasonable foreseeability', he went on to elaborate his famous dictum and to apply it to the facts of the case, using the word 'proximity'. He did not clarify the relationship between the two concepts; and for many years, the resulting ambiguity bore no fruit. Increasingly from the 1960s, attempts were made to persuade courts to extend the scope of the tort of negligence from physical damage to mental injuries and purely economic loss, and from misfeasance to nonfeasance. But many felt that beyond the paradigm case of physical injury caused by misfeasance, the criterion of reasonable foreseeability was apt to cast the net of negligence liability too widely; and that it needed to be supplemented by some additional precondition to the existence of a duty of care. In *Hedley Byrne v Heller* (1963), the **House of Lords** found this in a 'special relationship' between the plaintiff and the defendant. The concept was adopted (and adapted) by several Justices in *Caltex Oil v The Dredge 'Willemstad'* (1976). On the other hand, **Stephen** in *Caltex*, focusing on the nexus between the alleged negligence and the damage suffered, opted for proximity as the necessary control device additional to reasonable foreseeability.

However, the real champion of proximity on the Court was **Deane**. He first expounded the concept in *Jaensch v Coffey* (1984). Deane was unable to accept that Atkin's requirement of proximity 'involved no more than the notion of reasonable foreseeability'. Proximity he said, was a 'touchstone for determining the existence and content' of the duty of care, and a 'continuing general limitation on the test of reasonable foreseeability'. It involved closeness of relationship between plaintiff and defendant, and between negligence and damage ('causal proximity'). Whether the requirement of proximity was satisfied was a question of law and legal **policy** to be answered with reference to categories of case, not the facts of individual cases.

Deane used the concept of proximity to rationalise limitations on liability for foreseeable nervous shock in *Jaensch v Coffey*; and on the liability of occupiers for foreseeable injury to trespassers in *Hackshaw v Shaw* (1984). In *Sutherland Shire Council v Heyman* (1985), he used it to set limits to the liability of local authorities for negligent performance of statutory functions; and in *Stevens v Brodribb Sawmilling* (1986), to explain the scope of the employer's duty of care to independent contractors. Other Justices were soon attracted to the concept. A majority adopted it as the basis for reformulation of the law governing negligent misstatement (*San Sebastian v Minister* (1986)), standard of care (*Cook v Cook* (1986)), and the defence of illegality (*Gala v Preston* (1991)). Proximity's triumph seemed complete when, in **Burnie Port Authority v General Jones** (1994) and *Bryan v Maloney* (1995), majorities described it as an 'overriding requirement', a 'conceptual determinant', and a 'unifying theme' for duties of care.

Deane resigned from the Court in November 1995; **Brennan**, who had consistently rejected the proximity idea, became **Chief Justice** in April 1995. In *Hill v Van Erp* (1997), **Gummow** expressed serious reservations about the usefulness of the concept, and even former supporters such as **Dawson**, **Toohey**, and **McHugh** pulled back somewhat. In *Caparo Industries v Dickman* (1990), the House of Lords

adopted a three-stage test of duty of care in which proximity played a less dominant part than in Deane's jurisprudence. By 1999, in cases such as *Perre v Apand* and *Crimmins v Stevedoring Industry Finance Committee*, even this approach attracted the disapproval of members of the Court, with the notable exception of **Kirby**.

Deane acknowledged that so vague a concept as proximity is suitable only to express conclusions about liability, not arguments for or against its imposition. In seeking a new approach, Justices emphasised the need to reason 'incrementally', 'by analogy' with 'relevant' precedents; and to provide 'policy arguments' to support results. The danger is that the Court may thus be led into a 'wilderness of single instances'. Deane was right about the need for a final appellate tribunal to paint with a broad brush. The challenge is to develop principles that are neither so abstract as to be vacuous, nor so narrow that they create the risk of divergent results in similar cases. This demands judicial creativity of the highest order.

PETER CANE

Public awareness. In November 1998, the federal **Attorney-General**, Daryl Williams, observed that Australia's remarkably stable **democracy** could be attributed in no small part 'to the community's acceptance of the legitimacy of our courts to maintain the balance between the executive, the legislature and the community'. When applied to the High Court, that observation is unarguable. Legally, the Court's authority derives from the Constitution; and the authority of the Constitution derives from the community. But in order to be truly effective, the Court needs the authority that comes from fighting and winning a continual battle for perceptions.

As the twenty-first century begins, the Court seems to be doing well on this front. Its rulings on **common law** and **statutory interpretation** are not often overturned by the federal Parliament, which suggests that politicians—the best judges of community sentiment—have identified no groundswell of discontent. Even after the intense debate that followed the landmark cases establishing **native title** to land, national governments from both sides of politics decided not to abolish what the Court had effectively created. Native title was tempered, confined, and qualified; but it survived. That is the strongest evidence that the Court is winning the battle of perceptions. Despite all the **criticism** that had been heaped upon the Justices after the *Mabo* (1992) decision, governments allowed the concept to stand.

On constitutional matters, the Court has been fortunate to avoid more criticism. Its 1999 decision in *Re Wakim* and its 2000 decision in *R v Hughes* struck down **cross-vesting** schemes that underpinned the national corporations law, creating major uncertainty for business. Logically, that should have unleashed a torrent of complaints about the Court from well-placed business leaders. Instead, those who found themselves being criticised were the state and federal governments, which had difficulty in agreeing on how to overcome the problems that had been caused by the Court.

But the Court will not always be so fortunate. The rules that govern the way it works make it very likely that it will increasingly find itself dealing with cases that have the potential to expose it to criticism. Chief Justice **Gleeson** has explained that the rules on special **leave** applications mean that most civil appeals before the Court now involve an argument aimed at modifying established common law principles or overturning **precedents**: 'A court whose **business** consists largely of dealing with cases of that character is more likely to take on the appearance of being radical, not necessarily by reason of the disposition of the members of the court, but by reason of the nature of its business.'

A degree of criticism is important in keeping the Court **accountable**. But if that criticism undermines community acceptance of the Court, its effectiveness will suffer. And if the High Court becomes less effective, so does Australian democracy. Moreover, if it became apparent that the Court no longer commanded respect, politicians might be more inclined to overturn rulings on common law and statute because those decisions would no longer be protected by the gloss of legitimacy. And in constitutional matters, it would probably not be long before the other branches of government were tempted to increase their constitutional territory; or more accurately, their unconstitutional territory.

The Court therefore has legitimate reasons for seeking to ensure that the community understands and accepts its **role** and respects its **independence**. But it does not follow that the Court needs to be populist or, indeed, popular. These are the hallmarks of politicians. Justices, on the other hand, are occasionally required to antagonise the community by protecting an unpopular minority—such as communists (see *Communist Party Case* (1951)) or bankers (see *Bank Nationalisation Case* (1948))—from the dictatorship of the majority.

In these circumstances, it should come as no surprise that the Court is occasionally unpopular—at least among those whose interests are adversely affected by its decisions. It would actually be of greater concern if the Court were universally popular, as that could suggest that it amounted to no real check on the excesses of the strong. So the challenge facing the Court is this: it is heading into more contentious territory that could expose it to criticism. It is frequently obliged to make unpopular decisions. Yet it needs to ensure that it retains community confidence. How is this to be done?

In 1997, former Chief Justice **Brennan** gave a speech in Ireland in which he recognised that the **rule of law** was not to be achieved by raw power, but by public acceptance of the law and public confidence in the institutions that administered it. He said the courts and the **media** performed 'disparate but interlocking functions' which, if properly performed, should create public confidence in the rule of law by the courts. This view is held by a number of judges and senior law makers.

But there is a problem here. Implicit in this view is the assumption that the Court's responsibility in this area is limited, and if there are problems in the way its work is understood by the public, those problems can be attributed to the media. It is difficult to imagine this passive approach to communications existing anywhere but inside a court. Consider what would happen if a public company produced complicated annual accounts and declined to explain them, summarise them, or illuminate them in any way on the grounds that the accounts could speak for themselves. Could such a company then be heard to complain if the media missed some vital point? While accountants and experienced business journalists probably understand accounts devoid of

commentary, sensible companies seek to minimise the chance of misreporting by explaining what their accounts mean.

If the public's perception of the High Court and its work is so important, surely the Court itself could legitimately play a more proactive role in providing information about itself to the media. Most senior courts—including the **Federal Court**, the Family Court, and the **state Supreme Courts** of Victoria and NSW—have public information officers to ease the flow of information to the media and the public. The High Court does not. So far, its luck has held.

CHRIS MERRITT

Further Reading
George Williams, 'The High Court and the Media' (1999) 1 *UTS Law Review* 136

Public opinion. When, in June 1983, the High Court handed down its decision in the *Tasmanian Dam Case* (1983), it took the extraordinary step of making a public statement about what the Justices did not take into account in reaching their decision. The statement said in part:

> The Court is in no way concerned with the question whether it is desirable or undesirable, either on the whole, or from any particular point of view, that the construction of the dam should proceed. The assessment of the possible advantages and disadvantages of constructing the dam, and the balancing of the one against the other, are not matters for the Court, and the Court's judgment does not reflect any view of the merits of the dispute.

Gibbs, **Wilson**, **Deane**, and **Brennan** made similar disclaimers in their judgments. The Court is not normally concerned about how the public at large interprets its decisions. But this was a special case. Governments were divided, the matter had been politically divisive, and public opinion was strongly aroused. The Court was intent on trying to persuade the public that it was making a legal decision, not one about the merits of the construction of the dam. It was notable that it concerned itself at all to inform the public about what it was doing, and why.

The Court's concern about public opinion can probably be traced to its move to **Canberra** in 1980. Before then, there had for many years been little continuity in the reporting of what the Court did, and in **reporting** the Court's decisions. The intense newspaper coverage of the earlier years had dwindled by the 1930s. The Court was an itinerant institution, **sitting** mainly in Sydney and Melbourne, but regularly travelling to other capital cities (see **Circuit system**). Cases heard in one city were frequently handed down in another. **Barwick**, the **Chief Justice** who oversaw the construction of the High Court **building** in Canberra, considered that the move to the national capital would increase **public awareness** of the Court. This would be achieved partly through its gaining a place on the tourist circuit, attracting hundreds of thousands of visitors a year. However, he also hoped that, like the Parliament, it would have its own press gallery, with specialist reporters assigned full time to cover its work. The Court provided office space for journalists, and they were well used for about a decade. However, most media organisations then decided to cover the Court more spasmodically, with journalists based in the parliamentary press gallery.

While Barwick and his successors have been keen to educate the public about the Court's work, they have resisted any suggestion that the Court might be influenced by public opinion. The Justices agreed with sentiments expressed in a special leave application by Chief Justice Gibbs. Responding to a comment by **counsel** for the Commissioner of Taxation that there had been 'a general hardening of public attitudes against tax avoidance' the Chief Justice said: 'We are not concerned with public attitudes, we are concerned with trying legal principles' (*Commissioner of Taxation v Insomnia*, 13 May 1983, **transcript**). In similar vein, **Griffith** observed as long ago as 1904, in *Deakin v Webb* that

> I hope the day will never come when this Court will strain its ear to catch the breath of public opinion before coming to a decision … If it does, it will perhaps be the practice, if ever there is a Court weak enough, to adjourn the argument in order that public meetings may be held, leading articles written in the newspapers, and pressure brought to bear to compel the Court to shirk its responsibility.

Nevertheless, the Justices like to think that they are conscious of community attitudes (received primarily through the media) and in particular the attitude of the **legal profession**, though that is not synonymous with the public generally or any part of it. As an American **commentator** observed in relation to the **United States Supreme Court**, they may respond to the climate of the age rather than the weather of the day (see also **Policy considerations; Values**). The Justices read legal journals and books as well as decisions by other courts. They find assistance from reading the work of legal academics (without necessarily agreeing with the views of critics). When the *Sydney Law Review* introduced a new section in which academics could comment on pending cases, Chief Justice **Mason** welcomed the move. He commented that 'it would be helpful if, from time to time, we had the advantage of reading a reasoned and critical appraisal of the judgment under appeal in the form of an article or note in a law journal. Not every case, even in the High Court, is argued with consummate skill and ability'. His invitation was widely applauded by academics, though the opportunity to publish such appraisals depends partly on how much time there is between the time special **leave to appeal** is granted and the hearing of an appeal. The Supreme Court of Canada has recently indicated that it will not receive unpublished manuscripts, on the ground that, as the parties would be unaware of their existence, and could not make submissions in relation to them, this would be a denial of **natural justice**.

The question of whether the Court is influenced by or responds to public opinion cannot wholly be separated from the equally intriguing question of whether the Court itself influences public opinion—as the US Supreme Court is sometimes said to do, for example in its landmark decision in *Brown v Board of Education* (1954) that racial segregation was unconstitutional. If it is ever possible to say that the Court has influenced public opinion, it is likely to be in conjunction with a response to public opinion; the two phenomena are likely to be intertwined rather than there being any simple cause and effect. Arguably, the *Engineers Case* in 1920 pushed along the development of Australian **nationhood**, though the Court may itself have been responding to changed perceptions following the experience of **World War I**. The decision in the *Communist Party Case* in 1951 that the **Menzies** government's ban of the Communist Party was unconstitutional may have fostered a view in the wider community that the ban was undesirable, and may thus have exerted some influence on the outcome of the subsequent failed referendum to permit the ban. However, to attribute to the Court a power to influence public opinion assumes in the public a degree of knowledge and understanding of High Court decisions that may not be warranted (see **Accountability; Media and the Court**).

Since the Court took up its residence in Canberra, Justices have been much more ready to make public speeches drawing attention to the need for judicial **independence** and calling attention to the problems faced by the judiciary in general. This probably should be seen as an attempt to educate the broader public against the specific public it confronts in Canberra—the government and the Parliament. An informed public opinion contributes to the maintenance of judicial independence.

DAVID SOLOMON

Puisne Justices refers to all Justices other than the **Chief Justice**. Pronounced 'puny', the term has survived into modern legal use from Law French, the hybrid Anglo-Norman language that remained in use in English courts until the seventeenth century. Literally *puis-né* ('later born'), the term simply came to mean 'junior', whether in age, or in seniority of appointment, and was used in each of the English **superior courts** administering the **common law**.

Although the term was still used, and precisely defined, in section 5 of the *Supreme Court of Judicature Act* 1877 (UK), it has dropped out of use in England, but remains current in those former British possessions whose legal professions were most heavily Anglicised, notably Australia and India. Its use in the Australian **state Supreme Courts** usually has a basis in the various state *Supreme Court Acts*. Its corresponding use in the High Court of Australia has no statutory foundation, but has been the established usage ever since the Court's inception. In the **United States Supreme Court**, the term 'Associate Justice' is used instead.

TONY BLACKSHIELD

Q

'Quick and Garran' is shorthand for *The Annotated Constitution of the Australian Commonwealth* (1901), written by John Quick and Robert **Garran**. Described by Geoffrey Sawer as 'the basic commentary from which many a contemporary search for relevant constitutional doctrine must start', it has been the most oft-cited and influential work on the Constitution written to date, and this despite its publication before any case law on the Constitution. To appreciate why that has been the case, it is necessary to say something about the book's qualities, its authors, and the High Court's attitude towards historical material.

Any account of Quick and Garran's influence must start with the status of its authors. Quick and Garran were both intimately involved with the process that led to establishment of the Commonwealth: the two of them had observed, or had participated in, the **Convention Debates** that settled on the text of the Constitution. Quick was a delegate in 1897–98, and Garran was Secretary of the Drafting Committee at the same period. This alone lent their book an authority in matters of constitutional exegesis that could not easily be matched by later writers. It goes some way to explaining the obvious popularity of their book at the Bar and Bench.

Another factor that has set Quick and Garran apart from other commentaries, even those written shortly after federation, has been the High Court's attitude to historical mater-

John Quick and Robert Garran, authors of *The Annotated Constitution of the Australian Commonwealth* (1901), at the Quick residence, Edelweiss

ial. Until *Cole v Whitfield* (1988), the High Court refused, by and large, to have resort to the Convention Debates in interpreting the Constitution (see **History**; **Originalism**). As it happened, Quick and Garran had not only been present at those debates, but they referred to and summarised those materials throughout their commentary. It was not surprising that, when faced with a self-imposed ban on accessing the debates themselves, the High Court turned to Quick and Garran as a substitute. The consequence was to render the interpretations that the authors placed on the debates even more authoritative, because there was hardly any other source of historical material to contradict them.

Perhaps the final reason for the influence of Quick and Garran, however, has been its comprehensiveness. Quick intended the book as an encyclopedia of anything that might be relevant to the interpretation of the Constitution, as '*The Compleat Angler*' to cover everything relating to the subject'. He achieved his aim in spite of Garran's wish for a slimmer volume. The outcome is a monumental book that canvasses the history of the federal movement; that focuses on each provision of the Constitution, drawing the reader's attention to similar provisions in the *British North America Act* 1867, the Constitution of the USA, and the basic laws of other nations; and that quotes from noted British and American **commentators**, cites the decisions of the **United States Supreme Court** and the **Privy Council**, and surveys the juristic history of certain concepts, such as 'citizen', from classical Athens onwards. To Justices who could not have been familiar with the background of constitutional provisions, and indeed to anyone interested in the Constitution, this comprehensiveness has given Quick and Garran an authority and a status almost unique in Australian **constitutional law**.

GIM DEL VILLAR

Further Reading
Robert Garran, *Prosper the Commonwealth* (1958)
Michele Matthews, 'A Forgotten "Father of Federation": Sir John Quick' (1998) 2 *The New Federalist* 55
Carl McCamish, 'The Use of Historical Materials in Interpreting the Commonwealth Constitution' (1996) 70 *ALJ* 638

R

Race. Prior to 1967, the races power (section 51(xxvi) of the Constitution) gave power to Parliament to make laws with respect to 'the people of any race, other than the aboriginal race in any State, for whom it is deemed necessary to make special laws'. According to **Quick and Garran**, its purpose was to give power to Parliament over persons newly migrated to Australia:

> This sub-section does not refer to immigration; that is covered by sub-sec xxvii. It enables the Parliament to deal with the people of any alien race after they have entered the Commonwealth; to localise them within defined areas, to restrict their migration, to confine them to certain occupations, or to give them special protection and secure their return after a certain period to the country whence they came.

The original version of the clause was drafted in 1891 by **Griffith**, who explained: 'What I have had more particularly in my own mind was the immigration of coolies from British India, or any eastern people subject to civilised powers … I maintain that no state should be [permitted] … to allow the state to be flooded by such people as I have referred to.' And in 1910 Harrison Moore saw the power as aimed at 'the Indian, Afghan and Syrian hawkers; the Chinese miners, laundrymen, market gardeners, and furniture manufacturers; the Japanese settlers and Kanaka plantation labourers of Queensland, and the various coloured races employed in the pearl fisheries of Queensland and Western Australia'.

In fact, however, it is not the races power that has been used for these purposes. Instead, consistently since the *Pacific Island Labourers Act* 1901 (Cth), the legislative control of immigrants or 'aliens' has depended on the **immigration power** (section 51(xxvii) of the Constitution) and increasingly on the naturalisation and aliens power (section 51(xix)).

The 1967 referendum amended the races power, by deleting the words 'other than the aboriginal race in any State'. In the *Hindmarsh Island Bridge Case* (1998), **Kirby** observed that the races power had apparently never been exercised at all before that **amendment**, and had since been used only to make laws for the benefit of **Aboriginal peoples**.

In the early cases under the *Immigration Restriction Act* 1901 (Cth), the High Court did not usually question Parliament's power to enact such a law, but often had to consider whether particular persons came within the power. The Act was not directly discriminatory on the basis of race, but discriminated indirectly by requiring the completion of a dictation test in any prescribed European language. The absurdity of this procedure is clearly evident in the *Kisch Case* (1934), where the Court, led by **Dixon**, found that Scottish Gaelic was not a European language for this purpose. For the Scots whom he offended, Dixon's comments reeked of ethnic prejudice (see **Colonialism**), though the result for Kisch, the Czechoslovakian communist, suggests otherwise.

Despite the obvious racist undertones in the circumstances of particular cases (for example, *O'Keefe v Calwell* (1949); *Koon Wing Lau v Calwell* (1949); and *Wong Man On v Commonwealth* (1952)), none of them called on the Court directly to consider 'race' as a concept or to make a finding on the underlying racism of Parliament's enactments. Nor were the Justices morally motivated to go beyond the immediate issues they had been asked to determine.

If High Court attitudes seem inhospitable in cases involving **immigration law**, it is partly because the Justices themselves were committed to the White Australia Policy that all Australian governments had maintained since the late nineteenth century. Not all Justices, however, displayed the same degree of inhospitability. In *Potter v Minahan* (1908), Griffith noted that because James Minahan's mother bore 'a British name', she was presumably 'of British race'; and that her relationship with James' Chinese father could not support a presumption of marriage, 'having regard to conditions in Victoria in 1876, and to the relations between Chinese [men] and European women at that time'. But this enabled Griffith to conclude that James had acquired his mother's Victorian domicile, so that on his return from China he was not an 'immigrant', but was merely returning to 'the part of the earth' that he was entitled to regard 'as his home'.

The most inhospitable Justice was **Isaacs**, who in the *Irish Envoys Case* (1923) coined the infamous dictum: 'Once an immigrant always an immigrant', to this day not expressly **overruled** by the Court. Isaacs justified his dictum by a lengthy, encomiastic account of the nineteenth-century history of opposition to 'colored labour', which he credited with having done 'much to arouse a sentiment … of paramount national significance, a determination to preserve a White Australia'. In *Ex parte Walsh and Johnson; In re Yates* (1925), where **Knox** and **Starke** repudiated Isaacs' dictum, he defended it with colourful hypothetical examples of 'anarchic and terroristic or treasonable' conduct by 'an Italian … or a Hindoo'.

The White Australia Policy was reflected not only in Commonwealth immigration policies, but also in state and territory laws regulating Aboriginal peoples. Again, despite the explicit racial classifications used in the statutes, the Court initially showed little interest in developing a jurisprudence of 'race'. In *Muramats v Commonwealth Electoral Officer (WA)* (1923), the Court considered a provision of the *Electoral Act* 1907 (WA), which disqualified any 'aboriginal native of Australia, Asia, Africa or the Islands of the Pacific, or a person of the half-blood' from voting. **Higgins** thought that the definition of 'aboriginal' was a matter of the 'vernacular meaning of the word as used in an Act addressed to inhabitants of Australia or Western Australia', to be determined simply by asking: 'Whom would Australians treat as aboriginal natives of Australia or of Asia?' Much later, in *Ofu-Koloi v The Queen* (1956), the Court had to determine whether an underage girl who had been sexually assaulted was a 'European' within the meaning of Papua's *White Women's Protection Ordinance* 1926–34. The Court thought that racial classifications in statutes 'do not call upon the courts to make an ethnological inquiry of a scientific, historical or scholarly character'. Dixon, **Fullagar**, and **Taylor** said:

> The fact that at, so to speak, the edges of the racial classification there is an uncertainty of definition cannot make it difficult to apply it in the common run of cases. There can be no doubt that it refers to the racial stock or stocks associated in ordinary understanding with the continent of Europe. People derived from European stocks without known admixture of African, Asian or other stocks are regarded as European.

These cases may be contrasted with *Dowling v Bowie* (1952), where the Court, again led by Dixon, quashed Dowling's conviction for selling wine to James Shannon, a man of Aboriginal descent. Under the Aboriginals Ordinance 1918–47 (NT), Aboriginal peoples were required to obtain an exemption before being permitted to buy alcohol. The Court found that the prosecution had not discharged the burden of proof that Shannon was a 'half-caste' within the meaning of the Ordinance. This was despite the fact that all parties 'knew' that Shannon was a 'half-caste'.

The contrast between the technical reading of the Ordinance in *Dowling v Bowie*, and the bluff assumption in *Muramats* and *Ofu-Koloi* that racial identity was simply a matter of obvious common sense, can perhaps be seen as an example of the tension between form and substance. Yet in each case, whether treated as a matter of form or of substance, the racial categories before the Court were accepted uncritically. By distinguishing indigenous peoples both from the rest of the 'white' community and from one another, the legislative use of artificial categories denied their equal status with the rest of their respective populations. Whether indigenous identity was treated as a construction of law (form) or community attitudes (substance), no room was left for indigenous peoples to define or assert their own identities (see also **Namatjira v Raabe** (1959)). Indeed, the racial categories used in the statutes—often defined by admixtures of blood (full-blood, half-caste, quadroon, octoroon)—carried

the underlying implication that indigenous peoples were an inferior form of humanity.

The Court was finally asked to adjudicate on whether the Northern Territory Ordinance had a genocidal intent in *Kruger v Commonwealth* (1997). The paternalistic protective purpose apparent on the face of the Ordinance defeated the plaintiffs' claim that the Ordinance had been made 'with intent to destroy' the identity of indigenous communities. Accordingly, the powers of removal and detention conferred by the Ordinance were valid; most judgments indicated, however, that this did not necessarily mean that particular exercises of those powers were valid. Thus, the question of whether the Ordinance operated substantively in a genocidal way is yet to be determined authoritatively.

The construction of Aboriginal identity as inferior—uncivilised, lacking laws and lacking social foundations—supported the doctrine of *terra nullius*. In *Milirrpum v Nabalco* (1971), Justice Richard Blackburn recognised that Yolngu occupation of the Gove Peninsula was under a 'system of laws', yet felt compelled to maintain the status quo. However, it was obvious that judicial perceptions of indigenous peoples were changing, largely in response to the initiative of indigenous people themselves (see **Litigants, notable, 1945–2001**). The High Court has demonstrated a distinct growth in awareness of indigenous culture, and indeed of the heterogeneity of Aboriginal cultures.

The original text of the Constitution had assumed the existence of a homogeneous 'aboriginal race', but those words had been deleted by the 1967 referendum and were ethnographically dubious. In the *Tasmanian Dam Case* (1983), one question concerned the validity of Commonwealth heritage protection regulations applying to sites that were of outstanding universal value, but also of particular significance to Aboriginal peoples. Moreover, the claim to significance was strongest not for all Aboriginal peoples, but only for some Tasmanian Aboriginal people. In determining whether the original Tasmanians were the people of a particular race, the Court needed a definition of race. The Australian case law was minimal, and cases on the *Race Relations Acts* in NZ and the UK offered only limited guidance. **Deane** thought the words 'people of any race' had 'a wide and non-technical meaning' which could include all Aboriginal peoples collectively, but could also be applied to any identifiable racial subgroup. **Brennan** said: '"Race" is not a term of art; it is not a precise concept.' He thought a biological element essential, but added other elements that might contribute to racial identity: physical similarities, common history, common religion or spiritual beliefs, and common culture. While genetic inheritance is fixed at birth, 'the historic, religious, spiritual and cultural heritage are acquired and are susceptible to influences for which a law may provide. The advancement of the people of any race in any of these aspects of their group life falls within the power'. A narrow majority upheld the validity of the legislation.

In *Mabo* (1992), the Court showed a willingness to accept that a particular Aboriginal subgroup may form 'an identifiable community, the members of whom are identified by one another as members of that community living under its laws and customs'. Yet the **native title** regime that emerged in response to *Mabo* has itself given rise to apprehensions—not only because the form in which native title is recognised does nothing for those whose dispossession or removal during the colonisation process has already extinguished their claims, but because the image now made operative of traditional indigenous communities, though a vast improvement on the earlier approach by classification of blood lines, is still a problematic construct, especially in view of the extensive anthropological evidence required to prove continuity or group identity and connection to the land. At worst, the evidentiary processes involved are at risk of reducing indigenous identity to a legal commodity.

It was only with the passage of the *Racial Discrimination Act* 1975 (Cth) that racial **discrimination** was directly addressed by Parliament, and the Court was called upon for the first time to consider the term 'race' in the context of Commonwealth legislation. In *Koowarta's Case* (1982), a majority of the Court accepted the view that the **external affairs power** (section 51(xxvi) of the Constitution) supported the validity of the Racial Discrimination Act as an implementation of the International Convention on the Elimination of All Forms of Racial Discrimination. An alternative argument based on the races power was unsuccessful. As **Gibbs** put it, 'a law which applies equally to the people of all races is not a special law for the people of any one race'. To be a 'special law' for the people of a particular race, **Stephen** suggested that there would be a need to demonstrate a special need, threat, or problem pertaining to that racial group.

In the *Tasmanian Dam Case*, the legislative use of the races power (along with other heads of **Commonwealth legislative power**) was upheld. As **Deane** expressed the majority view, the constitutional power was broad enough to include laws 'protecting the cultural and spiritual heritage' of a racially identified group 'by protecting property ... of particular significance to that spiritual and cultural heritage'. Later, in the *Native Title Act Case* (1995), the Court would state simply: 'A special quality appears when the law confers a right or benefit or imposes an obligation or disadvantage especially on the people of a particular race.'

In *Gerhardy v Brown* (1985), the Court had accepted that legislation (in that case the *Pitjantjatjara Land Rights Act* 1981 (SA)) might endow such a group with effective communal control of its territory, including (with certain exceptions) the power to exclude the entry of other persons. The state legislation was held to be compatible with the Racial Discrimination Act (thus avoiding any problem of **inconsistency** under section 109 of the Constitution) because it fell within Article 1.4 of the International Convention to which the Racial Discrimination Act gives effect. That article permits 'Special measures taken for the sole purpose of securing adequate advancement of certain racial or ethnic groups or individuals requiring such protection as may be necessary in order to ensure ... [their] equal enjoyment or exercise of human rights and fundamental freedoms.' Brennan quoted what the **United States Supreme Court** had said in *University of California Regents v Bakke* (1978): 'In order to get beyond racism, we must first take account of race. There is no other way. And in order to treat some persons equally, we must treat them differently.'

Yet, in other cases where the Racial Discrimination Act has given rise to problems of inconsistency with state legislation, the Court's analytical and doctrinal focus on those immedi-

ate problems has led it into a mode of reasoning oblivious to, and perhaps at times even subversive of, the underlying racial issues (see, for example, *Viskauskas v Niland* (1983); *University of Wollongong v Metwally* (1984); *Dao v Australian Postal Commission* (1987)). And, while *Gerhardy v Brown* recognises the legitimacy of 'positive' or 'benign' discrimination at the state level, the question of whether in relation to Aboriginal peoples the races power permits adverse discrimination at the Commonwealth level remains a live issue.

Originally, the delegates at the **Convention Debates** had thought that the primary use of the power would be to discriminate *against* persons of particular races. The 1967 referendum, however, was presented to the people as designed to remove any basis for suggesting that the Constitution 'discriminates in some ways against people of the Aboriginal race'. The Commonwealth's object was stated to be cooperation with the states 'to ensure that together we act in the best interests of the Aboriginal people of Australia'. Thus, despite the clear intention of the original section 51(xxvi), the argument has been advanced that, at least in relation to Aboriginal peoples, the 1967 referendum had rendered the power exercisable only for their benefit. For example, in the *Tasmanian Dam Case*, **Murphy** argued that 'for' means 'for the benefit of'. Brennan said the amendment was 'an affirmation of the will of the Australian people that the odious policies of oppression and neglect were to be at an end, and that the primary object of the power is beneficial'. Deane thought it had become 'increasingly clear that Australia, as a nation, must be diminished until acceptable laws be enacted to mitigate the effects of past barbarism'. Thus, he thought, the purpose of the 1967 referendum was to remove 'a fetter upon the legislative competence of the Commonwealth Parliament to pass necessary special laws for their benefit'.

In the *Hindmarsh Island Bridge Case*, the Court was asked to consider whether the races power could be used only to benefit Aboriginal peoples. Four Justices gave some consideration to this issue. **Gaudron** conceded that the power could be exercised either for the benefit or to the disadvantage of persons of a particular race. However, given that Parliament must make a political judgment deeming it 'necessary' to make such laws, she thought it 'difficult to conceive of circumstances in which a law presently operating to the disadvantage of a racial minority would be valid'. She concluded that 'prima facie, at least, [the power] presently only authorises laws which operate to the benefit of Aboriginal Australians'.

Gummow and **Hayne** were prepared to assume that what was intended by Parliament and the people in 1967 was the passage of beneficial legislation for Aboriginal peoples; but 'it does not follow that this was implemented by a change to the constitutional text', or that the scope of the power as it now stands can be 'hedged by limitations unexpressed therein'. The power is plenary, even though it was primarily intended for beneficial application. Kirby was alone in confining the power so that it 'does not extend to the enactment of detrimental and adversely discriminatory special laws by reference to a people's race'.

In the last few decades, though sometimes only by a small majority, the Court has undergone a teleological transformation in its approach to race, and in particular to the Aboriginal race. Some have seen this as a radical departure from the proper **role** of the Court. Others may turn to the Court's record on race as a crucial test of its successes and failures in delivering an acceptable degree of protection of human rights to the nation. If the Justices themselves have had mixed responses, this may partly reflect the inevitable mixture of judicial **appointments** and the irresistible pull of **legalism**: the application of avowedly neutral legal principles, in which positive or negative racial outcomes are seen as essentially accidental (see, for example, *Tuckiar v The King* (1934)).

It is also, however, a simple reflection of generational change. When Dixon wrote as **Chief Justice** in *Dowling v Bowie*, he was able to recognise that Aboriginal peoples classified as 'half-castes' might not welcome the classification, but was yet to form the judicial consciousness that the word 'half-caste' was inherently derogatory and demeaning. That at least would not be true of most Justices appointed to the Bench in recent times. And it may be that some Justices who are still committed to 'strict and complete legalism' can nevertheless find room in their judgments to condemn racist practices (see Brennan in *Wik* (1996)).

Frank Brennan
Francesca Dominello

Further Reading

Jennifer Clarke, 'Law and Race: The Position of Indigenous people' in Stephen Bottomley and Stephen Parker (eds), *Law in Context* (1997)

John McCorquodale, 'The Legal Classification of Race in Australia' (1986) 10 *Aboriginal History* 7

Sally Weaver, 'Struggles of the Nation-state to Define Aboriginal Ethnicity: Canada and Australia' in Gerald Gold (ed), *Minorities and Mother Country Imagery* (1984)

Ratio decidendi ('the reason for deciding') is the term used in the **common law** doctrine of **precedent** to identify the aspect of a judicial decision which later judges bound by that decision must accept as authoritative. The contrast is with *obiter dicta*, which are said to be merely persuasive. The idea that a later judge is not bound by 'a mere *gratis dictum*' is at least as old as *Bole v Horton* (1673); but the contrasting expression *ratio decidendi* became current only with John Austin's 1834 *Lectures on Jurisprudence* (published posthumously in 1863), and Lord Campbell's speech in the **House of Lords** in *A-G v Dean and Canons of Windsor* (1860).

Campbell's version of the *ratio decidendi*—the rule 'propounded and acted upon in giving judgment'—emphasised the binding effect of what was actually said. Austin emphasised the judges' **law-making role**: a *ratio decidendi* is 'a *new* ground or principle … *not previously law*', and its content depends on later analysis:

> Law made judicially must be found in the general *grounds* [of judicial decisions] … as detached or abstracted from the specific peculiarities of the decided [cases] … The general reasons or principles of a judicial decision (as thus abstracted from any peculiarities of the case) are commonly styled, by writers on jurisprudence, the *ratio decidendi*.

Similarly, the New Zealand jurist John Salmond, teaching in Adelaide from 1897 to 1906, insisted that the ratio of a case is its 'underlying principle': 'The concrete decision is binding between the parties to it, but it is the abstract *ratio decidendi* which alone has the force of law as regards the world at large' (*Jurisprudence* (1902)). Yet in *Quinn v Leathem* (1901), Lord Halsbury insisted that 'a case is only an authority for what it actually decides'; and in 1930, the Anglo-American jurist Arthur Goodhart proposed a formula for determining the *ratio decidendi* of a case by combining 'the facts treated by the judge as material' with the decision. The ratio would be a proposition in the form: 'Where *X* and *Y*, then *Z*' (or 'facts plus result'). Austin's insistence that the ratio be 'detached or abstracted' from the specificity of the facts was turned on its head.

In Australia after **World War II**, the ambiguities were carried further by the teachings of George Paton in Melbourne and Julius Stone in Sydney. For Paton, 'the classical view was that the *ratio* was the principle of law which the judge considered necessary to the decision' (*Jurisprudence* (1946)). This focus on what the judge considered necessary paralleled Goodhart's focus on the facts the judge treated as material; yet in practice, since in common law **judicial reasoning** a ratio is rarely spelled out explicitly, the analysis must shift to what later interpreters conclude that the judge *must logically* have considered necessary or treated as material. The judgment of necessity or materiality becomes that of the interpreter, limited only by logic. For Stone, this was no limit at all, since logically a case can yield 'as many general propositions' as it has 'possible combinations of distinguishable facts' (*The Province and Function of Law* (1946)).

As Stone developed his argument in 1959, it meant that the analytical ideal of a single uniquely authoritative ratio for any given case was unattainable by any of the suggested methods. Goodhart's focus on 'material facts', for example, requires not only a selective judgment of which facts are 'material', but a further judgment as to the level of generality at which they should be stated. Similarly, any inductive attempt to formulate an 'underlying principle' may be stated with different degrees of selectivity and levels of generality. It might not have seemed sensible to confine the ratio of *Donoghue v Stevenson* (1932) to dead snails in ginger beer bottles; but it might have been sensible to confine it to deleterious foreign matter, undetectable before consumption, in articles of food or drink. In fact it has been understood much more broadly, as a general foundation for the law of negligence.

Even exclusion of the 'dead snail' level of analysis depends on an element of evaluative judgment rather than objective necessity. The **Dixon Court** had limited the operation of section 92 of the Constitution by insisting that the production or manufacture of commodities destined for **interstate trade** is not itself part of interstate trade (*Grannall v Marrickville Margarine* (1955)). When **Barwick**, as **Chief Justice**, sought to give section 92 a wider operation, he suggested that the ratio of *Grannall* was inapplicable to a levy on the number of hens kept by poultry farmers (*Damjanovic v Commonwealth* (1968)). He saw no 'analogy between the manufacture of margarine and either the keeping of egg-producing hens, or the laying of eggs by hens so kept'; and insisted that, though later courts must accept the *ratio decidendi* of *Grannall*—'the fundamental conclusions on which the order of the Court is founded'—the Dixon Court's 'reasoning towards decision' should not be treated as binding. In *Samuels v Readers Digest Association* (1969), **Kitto** retorted that although the earlier cases involved manufacture, 'the principle for which they are authorities is missed if they are thought of as having been decided … because of some consideration applying exclusively to manufacture'.

For Barwick, the ratio of *Grannall* was limited to 'manufacture'. (He did not seriously try to confine it to the manufacture of margarine.) For Kitto, such cases were merely examples of a wider principle relating to processes 'preparatory or antecedent' to interstate trade. The disagreement could not be resolved by logical analysis; it reflected divergent **policy considerations** affecting both the regulation of the **economy** and the **role** of the Court in **constitutional interpretation**.

Nevertheless, Barwick had a point. The reason for limiting the ratio of a case to what was 'necessary to the decision'—to what the court *had to* decide that day to resolve the immediate issue—is that the binding pronouncement of an unnecessarily wide proposition might prematurely foreclose other issues on which there has been no opportunity to consider possible arguments. The differences between the economic circumstances of primary and secondary industry might conceivably affect the appropriate degree of freedom from regulatory control; and to limit the ratio of *Grannall* to manufacture would not preclude its later extension to cases of primary production, but would merely leave that issue to be determined when such a case arose.

This reasoning might also support **Mason's** suggestion, in *Kailis v WA* (1974), that the difficult *ratio decidendi* of **Dennis Hotels v Victoria** (1960)—exempting certain licence fees for the handling of goods from classification as **excise duties**—was limited to licences for the retail sale of goods, rather than for their production or processing. Since *Kailis* involved a processing licence, the ratio of *Dennis Hotels* could plausibly be distinguished, since a tax imposed directly on the production of goods might be closer to the traditional conception of 'excise' than a licence fee for retail sale—even if only one Justice (**Fullagar**) drew such a distinction in *Dennis Hotels* itself. By contrast, when Mason and **Deane** later suggested, in *Philip Morris v Commissioner of Business Franchises* (1989), that the ratio of *Dennis Hotels* could be limited to licences for the retail sale of alcohol and tobacco, the singling out of those commodities seemed comparable to an attempt to confine the ratio of *Donoghue v Stevenson* to 'snails', or that of *Grannall* to 'margarine'. Yet even that could be rationalised: in the context of traditional state regulation of alcohol and tobacco, a licence fee might be easier to classify as part of a genuine regulatory scheme, and therefore not an 'excise'. In *Dennis Hotels*, **Taylor** thought it significant—perhaps even 'material'—that a liquor licence was 'a traditionally accepted method of regulating a trade which the public interest demands shall be subject to strict supervision'.

In all such cases, what is important is not the mere presence of a factual difference, but whether it is *relevant*—or in Goodhart's word, 'material'. This was the point of Kitto's response to Barwick in *Readers Digest*: since primary and secondary modes of production were equally 'antecedent' to trade, the differences between them were irrelevant. Whether an acknowledged factual difference is relevant or 'material' is

a matter for persuasive argument, interpretation, and evaluative judgment.

For Stone, the impossibility of resolving such issues objectively was compounded by other ambiguities—including the proliferation of suggested techniques for ascertaining the *ratio decidendi*, none of them a proposition of law and none of them authoritative. Not only do arguments about *rationes decidendi* involve choices—between Paton's 'classical view' and Goodhart's emphasis on 'material facts', or between a rule actually 'propounded' and one that can be inferred as a 'necessary' basis for the decision—but the indeterminacy of the ratio notion leaves room for slippages and combinations among these diverse elements in any given case. And while all these ambiguities affect the attempt to ascribe one uniquely authoritative ratio even to a single judgment, they are vastly compounded, in a multi-member court such as the High Court, by the presence of separate judgments.

Yet it is precisely in relation to decisions by courts of final appeal that the need to identify what is binding is most of practical importance. When the High Court is divided 4:3— as it often is in a difficult case—it may be possible to construct a ratio on the 'Goodhart view' (material facts plus decision), but there will not be a ratio on the 'classical view' unless it is possible to formulate a principle on which all four majority Justices founded their decision. As the Supreme Court of South Africa concluded in *Fellner v Minister of the Interior* (1954), a principle or process of reasoning adopted only by 'the majority of the majority' cannot be a ratio unless those Justices also constitute a majority of the Court; and a principle accepted (for example) by two majority Justices and two dissenters cannot be a ratio, since the two dissenters did not rely on it as the basis for the Court's decision.

Similarly, the High Court ruled in *Federation Insurance v Wasson* (1987) that 'it would not be proper to seek to extract a binding authority from an opinion expressed in a dissenting judgment'. And in *Dickenson's Arcade v Tasmania* (1974), Barwick made the point even more firmly for the *Dennis Hotels* case. Stressing that *Dennis Hotels* should be followed only where its 'statutory and factual situation' was indistinguishable, since there was 'no reason for decision common to the majority', he rebuked Deane (as **counsel** in *Dickenson's Arcade*) for attempting to extract an authoritative rule by combining the views of **Dixon**, **McTiernan**, and **Windeyer** (who dissented on the relevant issue) with a passage from Kitto's judgment. Such a course, said Barwick, 'is inadmissible, just as a common reason for decision could not be constructed by adding views of single Justices to form a conglomerate … A composite reason so constructed does not furnish a reason for decision'. Besides, the principle Deane sought to construct ran contrary to the actual decision. 'The reason for the decision' cannot be provided by a principle that logically supports the opposite decision.

Equally unconvincing versions of previous *rationes decidendi* were advanced in the **Tasmanian Dam Case** (1983). On the one hand, Deane maintained that the ratio of *R v Burgess; Ex parte Henry* (1936) had already extended the **external affairs power** to legislation giving effect within Australia to any international treaty, regardless of subject matter. **Latham**, **Evatt**, and McTiernan had indeed taken that view in *Burgess*; but Dixon and **Starke** had suggested that the power might be limited to treaties with some inherent 'international' element, apart from the mere existence of the treaty. Since the subject matter in *Burgess*—air navigation—had obvious international significance, the disagreement was only obiter. The whole Court agreed that the external affairs power could be used *at least* if the qualifications suggested by Dixon and Starke were satisfied, and that was all the Court had to decide.

On the other hand, the dissenters in the *Dam Case* attempted to find a supportive ratio in *Koowarta's Case* (1982)—where Mason, **Murphy**, and **Brennan** held that the legislative power extended to *any* treaty; **Gibbs, Aickin,** and **Wilson** supported limits of the kind proposed by Dixon and Starke; and **Stephen**, agreeing with them that some limit was needed but finding their suggestions too restrictive, extended the power to treaties on matters 'of international concern'.

What the dissenting Justices in the *Dam Case* tried to extract from *Koowarta* was a binding *denial* that the power extends to any treaty whatsoever. On that, said Gibbs, 'four members of the Court' (Gibbs, Aickin, Wilson, and Stephen) had agreed. Moreover, they had agreed that the power must be limited *at least* by Stephen's requirement of 'international concern'. Wilson, who put this claim most boldly in terms of a *ratio decidendi*, emphasised that the subject of the treaty in *Koowarta*—racial **discrimination**—was 'of undeniable international importance': in effect, it was a 'material fact' in *Koowarta* that the test of 'international concern' was satisfied. Yet at least two members of the *Koowarta* majority, Mason and Murphy, did not treat this fact as 'material'; and in any event, the suggested ratio was supported by only one majority Justice in *Koowarta* (Stephen), and by three who dissented.

On one view, even the ratio of the *Dam Case* remained a limited one. Both Murphy and Brennan explicitly held that the subject of the treaty in that case—the protection of the world's cultural and natural heritage—was of 'international concern'. On that basis, the immediate issue in the *Dam Case*, as in *Koowarta*, would still be limited to the power to implement treaties of 'international concern'. It would follow that in the *Dam Case*, as in *Koowarta*, the majority assertions of a wider power were not necessary to the decision, and were merely obiter. Yet in the *Industrial Relations Act Case* (1996), that analysis was rejected. It was 'not to the point', said the Court, that the *Dam Case* would have had the same result if decided on the narrower basis, since the four majority Justices had in fact adopted the broader view as the basis for their decision:

> It is to seek to distort the principles of *stare decisis* and of *ratio decidendi* to contend that a decision lacks authority because it might have been reached upon a different path of legal reasoning from that which was actually followed. That would be to replace what was decided by that which might have been decided.

Historically, this principle was fundamental to the Court's early efforts to establish its authority over **state Supreme Courts**. In *Deakin v Webb* (1904), the Supreme Court of Victoria had accepted the result of the High Court decision in *D'Emden v Pedder* (1904), but purported to substitute its own rationale for that result. **Griffith's** condemnation was

scathing. To treat the High Court's actual reasoning as mere *obiter dicta* because the same result 'might have been reached by another road' was, he said, a direct assault on 'the value of judgments as expositions of the law'.

Recurring throughout the line of cases on implementation of treaties was the 'lowest common denominator' view of the *ratio decidendi*: if the relatively narrow principle relied on by one or more majority Justices can be seen as necessarily subsumed within a broader principle asserted by other majority Justices, then arguably those asserting the broader principle must necessarily have accepted at least the narrower principle, even though they were prepared to go further. In the *Dam Case*, for example, Mason accepted that Stephen's view was the ratio of *Koowarta*, because it was 'the narrowest expression of it by the justices who constituted the majority'. But this reasoning is acceptable only if the logical relationship between the differing majority views can appropriately be represented as one in which a broader conception encompasses a narrower conception. Whether that is so may often be open to dispute.

In *Theophanous v Herald & Weekly Times* (1994), the **joint judgment** of Mason, **Toohey**, and **Gaudron** asserted that, on certain conditions, the publication of political information or comment was constitutionally immune from liability for **defamation**. Deane asserted a much broader immunity. His position necessarily entailed that political publication should be immune *at least* when the conditions specified in the joint judgment were satisfied; and in an 'Addendum' to his judgment he expressly so held. Yet in *Lange v ABC* (1997), the Court was uncertain whether *Theophanous* had any *ratio decidendi* at all. Could the joint judgment be taken as 'the narrowest expression' of a conception on which all four majority Justices agreed? Or was Deane's conception so fundamentally different as to make such an approach unacceptable? In the end, the *Lange* Court felt free to reconsider the issue as one 'of principle and not of authority' (see **Concurring judgments**).

In some cases, competing but overlapping analyses in separate majority judgments make it difficult to discern any common ground. Notorious examples are the majority judgments in *Kirmani v Captain Cook Cruises* (1985), and the different explanations of liability for economic loss in *Caltex Oil v The Dredge 'Willemstad'* (1976) and *Perre v Apand* (1999). In *Caltex*, the reasons given were so diverse that the **Privy Council**, in *Candlewood Navigation Corporation v Mitsui* (1985), professed itself 'unable to extract from them any single *ratio decidendi*'. In 1988, Mason was provoked to an **extra-judicial** retort:

> Every decision has its *ratio decidendi*, even the decision for which no reasons are given. Then the case is only authority for what it actually decides, that is, for the proposition of law to be derived from the order of the court and the material facts.

He argued that this solution should also be used where, as in *Caltex*, the divergency of judgments yields 'no majority for a particular principle or reason'. If the Privy Council thought *Caltex* had no ratio, they were wrong: 'Every decision has its *ratio*.'

Shortly afterwards, Mason, Deane, and Gaudron asserted, in *Davis v Commonwealth* (1988), that even the *AAP Case*

(1975) had a ratio. In that case, the challenge to the AAP scheme was dismissed by McTiernan, **Jacobs**, Murphy, and Stephen. Stephen took the distinctive ground that Victoria, as the plaintiff state, lacked **standing** to raise the issue; but McTiernan and Murphy held that a Commonwealth parliamentary appropriation of money, for any purpose whatsoever, was necessarily valid. Mason's dissenting judgment agreed with that proposition so far as a bare appropriation was concerned; Jacobs also agreed, but, unlike Mason, went on to hold the scheme wholly valid. The ratio supposedly extracted in *Davis* relied on the judgments of McTiernan and Murphy, as supplemented by Mason's dissenting judgment and what was arguably only an *obiter dictum* by Jacobs. Whether this was an adequate basis for constructing a ratio is doubtful. In any event, the suggested ratio was singularly unhelpful: the *AAP Case* was said to be an authority

> for the proposition that the validity of an appropriation act is not ordinarily susceptible to effective legal challenge. It is unnecessary to consider whether there are extraordinary circumstances in which an appropriation of money by the Parliament may be susceptible to such challenge. It suffices to say that, if there be such cases, the present is not one of them.

A rule that operates 'ordinarily'—except when it operates 'extraordinarily'—is an extraordinarily indeterminate rule. In any event, the strategy adopted appeared to attract Barwick's censure of constructing 'a common reason for decision … by adding views of single Justices to form a conglomerate'. In such cases, it seems better to say that there is no *ratio decidendi* at all.

TONY BLACKSHIELD

Further Reading

Arthur Goodhart, 'Determining the Ratio Decidendi of a Case' (1930) 40 *Yale LJ* 161

Anthony Mason, 'The Use and Abuse of Precedent' (1988) 4 *Aust Bar Rev* 93

George Paton and Geoffrey Sawer, '*Ratio Decidendi* and *Obiter Dictum* in Appellate Courts' (1947) 63 *LQR* 461

Julius Stone, 'The *Ratio* of the *Ratio Decidendi*' (1959) 22 *Modern LR* 597

Realism, in legal discourse, usually refers to 'American legal realism', but sometimes to the 'Scandinavian legal realism' of Axel Hägerström, Karl Olivecrona and others. The Scandinavian version was a strong positivist rejection of metaphysical theories. The American version also had its roots in that aspect of **positivism** which conceives of law as that which is 'posited'—that is, laid down by determinate human beings at determinate historical moments. But where English positivism applied this conception primarily to enactments by Parliament, the American realists applied it primarily to decisions by judges—emphasising the judges' **law-making role**, and denying that their decisions were mere applications of pre-existing and objectively ascertainable rules. In later writing on **jurisprudence**, 'realism' has often been reduced to an extreme caricature of these concerns, enabling it to be counterposed diametrically to **legalism**.

Despite polemical overstatements, the realists never espoused the extreme views which such caricatures suggest. In their efforts to identify the 'real' reasons for judicial decisions, they repeatedly referred to judicial opinions as rationalisations, and occasionally as 'mere' rationalisations. Yet their attack was not on legal doctrine as such, but on absolutist conceptions of doctrine divorced from its social context. Primarily the realists were a group of law teachers, mostly at Yale and Columbia, who sought to transform legal education in the 1920s and early 1930s. In the USA, this was the era of Prohibition; and Karl Llewellyn (1893–1962), who formulated the realist slogan, took special delight in referring to the movement as a 'ferment'.

Until 1928, the 'ferment' was primarily at Columbia, but in that year a sustained attempt to reform the law school curriculum on realist principles collapsed when the realist Herman Oliphant was passed over for the deanship. Along with other realists—including William O Douglas, later the most **activist** Justice on the **United States Supreme Court**—Oliphant resigned in protest. Douglas and William Underhill Moore went to join the realist cadre at Yale. Oliphant joined Walter Wheeler Cook—who had previously taught at both Yale and Columbia—in establishing a new Institute for the Study of Law at Johns Hopkins University. Of the leading realists, only Llewellyn and Edwin Patterson remained at Columbia.

Not all of the realists were law teachers: indeed, some of those most vocal in the sceptical questioning of determinate legal doctrine were not. Joseph Hutcheson, whose writings emphasised the role of 'hunch' or 'intuition' in the judicial process, was a federal district court judge in Texas. Jerome Frank (1889–1957) was a New York legal practitioner (later a judge of the US Court of Appeals), who became a regular visitor at Yale after publishing his *Law and the Modern Mind* (1930)—which, in crudely Freudian terms, portrayed lawyers' preoccupation with 'rules' as reflecting a childish yearning for an authoritative father figure.

Yet the psychoanalysis of judges was not a pervasive concern. In their quest for the 'real' reasons for judicial decision, the realists recognised that individual personalities and idiosyncrasies must play a part; but their primary emphasis was on external factors, amenable to generalisation and to empirical observation and testing. Many stressed the need to understand judicial decisions in the context of their particular fact-situations. As Llewellyn pointed out in *The Bramble Bush* (1930), if the members of a collegiate bench reach the same result by different reasoning, their 'reactions to the facts' must be more significant than 'reactions to the forms of words we know as legal rules'. For Underhill Moore, the facts must themselves be understood in an institutional and behavioural context, reflecting 'the contemporary culture of the place where the facts happened and the decision was made'. Others sought a functional understanding of rules through attention to their practical operation in particular empirical contexts. Douglas sought to reconstitute **corporations law** on the basis of 'the phenomena observed in the organization and operation of a business', by 'observations of the things men attempt to do and are found doing when engaging in business'. Oliphant complained that a mastery of 'the technical legal definition of larceny', for example, shed no light on 'the criminal law's effective control of pawnbrokers as possible culpable receivers of stolen property'.

A significant factor at both Yale and Columbia was the rivalry of both schools with Harvard. A principal target of realist polemics was the Harvard 'case method' of teaching—not because of its focus on appellate decisions (which most realists shared), but because the goal of classroom analysis was simply to extract 'the rule of the case', a single authoritative *ratio decidendi* sufficient to explain the decision. Another target was the division of the law curriculum into neat doctrinal categories such as **contract and tort**: in real life, said the realists, legal problems are rarely confined to such boundaries. Like the Scandinavian realists, those at Yale and Columbia were fond of attacking legal 'theology'; but for them this meant the belief in an autonomous universe of authoritative legal doctrine. Thus, in 1929 Douglas called for a shift 'from a static theology to postulates stated in terms of human behavior'.

Ironically, much of this program drew on the writings of Roscoe Pound—on his 1907 call for a 'sociological jurisprudence', his 1908 attack on 'mechanical jurisprudence', and his contrast in 1910 between 'law in the books' and 'law in action'. But since 1916 Pound had been dean at Harvard, and the younger realists perceived him as having failed to fulfil his own program. Llewellyn charged that '"sociological jurisprudence" remains bare of most of what is significant in sociology' ('A Realistic Jurisprudence—The Next Step' (1930) 30 *Columbia LR* 431). Frank, in *Law and the Modern Mind*, implied that Pound had deliberately circumscribed his own insights to preserve a sphere of operation for Harvard conceptualism. Pound's response ('The Call for a Realist Jurisprudence' (1931) 44 *Harvard LR* 697) hit back—accusing the realists of exaggerating the unreliability of legal rules, pursuing mindless empiricism, overemphasising psychoanalysis, and neglecting the role of **values** in law. Llewellyn (assisted by Frank) refuted these charges ('Some Realism About Realism' (1931) 44 *Harvard LR* 1222). But the criticisms had a lasting impact.

There were other intellectual forebears. At Yale, the great **contracts** lawyer Arthur Corbin had as early as 1913 portrayed judging as an evolutionary process, resulting not in immutable rules but only in tentative generalisations always subject to further revision—so effectively that the younger realists claimed him as one of their own. At Harvard, John Chipman Gray (*The Nature and Sources of the Law* (1904)) had asserted that *all* law is judge-made law. Statutes are only 'sources' of law, since their practical operation depends on **statutory interpretation** by judges. Only the rules applied by the courts are 'law': 'there is no mysterious entity called "The Law" apart from these rules'.

Looming over all these progenitors of realism was the great American judge Oliver Wendell Holmes Jr, hailed by Frank in *Law and the Modern Mind* as the one 'completely adult jurist'. Already in *The Common Law* (1881), Holmes had proclaimed: 'The life of the law has not been logic; it has been experience'. His aphorisms in 'The Path of the Law' ((1897) 10 *Harvard LR* 457) were even more suggestive: he spoke of 'the fallacy of the logical form' and the need for judges in doubtful cases 'to exercise the sovereign prerogative of choice', albeit on 'disguised' or 'inarticulate and unconscious' grounds. Noting that 'certainty generally is illusion; and repose is not the destiny of man', he sketched a 'predictive' theory of law:

> A legal duty so called is nothing but a prediction that if a man does or omits certain things he will be made to suffer in this or that way by judgment of the court … The bad man … does not care two straws for the axioms or deductions, but … he does want to know what the Massachusetts or English courts are likely to do in fact … The prophecies of what the courts will do in fact, and nothing more pretentious, are what I mean by the law.

To increase the predictability of 'what the courts will do in fact'—not for Holmes' 'bad man', but for legal practitioners—was the realists' chief aspiration.

Born of and buffeted by law school politics, realism was buffeted by external forces as well. The **Depression** put an end to external funding for ambitious empirical studies of the effectiveness of legal rules in regulating human behaviour. The seconding of many realists to administrative roles in President Franklin Roosevelt's New Deal not only interrupted their scholarship, but antagonised conservatives in the **legal profession**, including influential alumni. The outbreak of **World War II** exposed the realists—and even Holmes—to charges that their ethical relativism might lead to totalitarianism. In the **Cold War** era, the condemnation of McCarthyism by unrepentant realists such as Yale's Fred Rodell led to accusations of communism.

None of this had much direct impact on the legal cultures of England and Australia. The Australian-born CK Allen, writing in England in 1939, dismissed it all as 'Jazz Jurisprudence'. Judges in both countries showed some concern with the social effects of decisions, but when English and Australian approaches diverged, the alignment might go either way. In *Waghorn v Waghorn* (1942), **Rich** saw the relevant English cases as 'influenced in some degree by considerations of convenience and social needs, whereas the decision of this court followed the traditional legal reasoning by deduction or induction from antecedent principles, and so was less "sociological"'. But in *Piro v Foster* (1943), that contrast was reversed.

In the 1940s, Australian law schools encountered American influence through the teachings of George Paton in Melbourne and Julius Stone in Sydney. Both were influenced by Pound. Stone had worked with Pound at Harvard (1931–36) and had personal links with many of the notable realists, including Frank and Llewellyn. Like them, he rejected the orthodox belief in uniquely correct judicial decisions derived from a predeterminate body of objectively knowable 'law', insisting that the pervasive indeterminacy of **authoritative legal materials** inescapably compels an element of creative judicial choice. Instead of provocative aphorisms and generalisations, Stone argued his case by a detailed analysis of 'categories of illusory reference' pervading and subverting the legal materials (*The Province and Function of Law* (1946)). For future High Court Justices who studied at Sydney—including **Mason, Jacobs, Murphy, Deane**, and **Kirby**—these teachings were deeply influential.

Dixon responded in a series of cases from 1952 onwards—sometimes accepting and exploiting Stone's 'categories of competing reference', as in *Thompson v Bankstown Corporation* (1953) (see **Occupiers' liability**); at other times resisting Stone's diagnosis of a 'category of meaningless reference', yet digging beneath the formal doctrine to articulate substantive grounds for a 'fair and reasonable' result (*Alford v Magee* (1952); *Dowling v Bowie* (1952); *Vines v Djordjevitch* (1955)).

More directly, Dixon's perception of realism was shaped by his friendships with Dean Acheson, secretary of state in the Truman administration, and with US Supreme Court Justice Felix Frankfurter. In the academic politics of realism, both men had been directly involved. Frankfurter had taught at Harvard from 1914 to 1939. Despite much intellectual and political common ground with the realists, he had ultimately attracted their unyielding hostility—initially for his role in the politics of Harvard Law School, and later for his advocacy, as a Supreme Court Justice, of 'judicial restraint'. Acheson, a member of the Yale Corporation from 1936 onwards, had strongly supported the realists, and in 1939 was almost appointed as law school dean. But in 1945, a bid by Acheson and Frankfurter to influence postwar recruitment at Yale (by recommending 'Harvard men') was savagely rebuffed. By the 1950s, Acheson's reports to Dixon on the US judicial scene were consistently disparaging.

In 1955, Dixon was honoured by Yale University with the Henry E Howland Memorial Prize, awarded biennially for 'marked distinction in the field of literature or fine arts, or the science of government', with an emphasis on 'the idealistic element in the recipient's work'. Accepting the honour, Dixon was conscious that at Yale he was speaking in the very heart of American legal realism. He characterised it initially (echoing Stone) as a movement in which 'categories … are viewed as unreal' and 'only as illusory guides'. He added (echoing Holmes) that 'the life of the law' was perceived to lie in 'the experience of judges, sharply distinguished no doubt from their logic'; and that 'the obsession of our ancestors with certainty in the law' had yielded to 'what the courts choose to say' and attempts 'to describe or even to define law in terms of predictability'. Against such views he set Frederic Maitland's belief in the 'strict logic and high technique' of the **common law** tradition.

He acknowledged that, in an age that no longer had faith in 'the immutability of ascertained and accepted truths', law too—by 'false analogy' and 'contagion of ideas'—might be thought to depend on 'the subjective notions' of the judges who expound it; but insisted that, as a judge, he found such theories 'peculiarly unreal and certainly unsatisfying'. 'Prophecies of what the courts will do in fact', he said, offer no assistance to the judges themselves, who 'do in fact proceed upon the assumption that the law provides a body of doctrine which governs the decision of a given case … It is a tacit assumption. But it is basal.'

> It is open to the realist … to attack the validity of such an assumption. But he cannot deny its existence … It is open to him to condemn it … [as responding] insufficiently or perhaps not at all to the actual or supposed demands of an ever-changing social order. It still remains true that it is the way in which the administration of justice proceeds.

Why, then, had the realists denied it? Perhaps, said Dixon, they gave too much weight to the special features of **judicial review** based on a **Bill of Rights**. Perhaps the English positivists' insistence on statute as 'the only source of law', denying *any* judicial role in legal development, had produced a reaction going 'so far in the contrary direction that it has overshot the truth'. Yet in England, said Dixon, even when the 'false doctrine' of judicial impotence was in its heyday, it did not in fact 'retard the development of the law under judicial hands':

> Principles were not only used, they were developed. There was a steady, if intuitive, attempt to develop the law as a science … not by an abandonment of the high technique and strict logic of the common law … [but by] apt and felicitous use of that very technique.

The same potential for judicial development, he argued, remains open today. But it must be 'gradual and evolutionary', avoiding 'abrupt and almost arbitrary change', and according no legitimate role to 'deliberate innovators'. There must be 'no violent break with traditional conceptions and methods of reasoning'. Ironically, his account paralleled that of Holmes in *Southern Pacific Co v Jensen* (1917):

> Judges do and must legislate, but they can do so only interstitially: they are confined from molar to molecular motions. A common-law judge could not say, 'I think the doctrine of consideration a bit of historical nonsense and shall not enforce it in my court.'

Although Dixon did not refer to this passage, he may well have had it in mind, for he went on to devote almost half of his lecture to illustrating how different judges might react to an intuitive 'feeling that there is something wrong' with the rule—described by WR Anson in 1879 as 'a necessary result of the doctrine of consideration'—that the payment of a smaller sum accepted in satisfaction of a larger does not discharge the debt. A court inspired by 'reforming zeal' and 'boldness of innovation' might simply reject this idea, perhaps acting 'merely on its conception of justice or social convenience'; but a similar result might also be reached by entirely traditional means. He proceeded to demonstrate how this might be done by using his own analysis of **estoppel** in *Grundt v Great Boulder Gold Mines* (1937). But he added that although traditional reasoning can meet the demands of 'changing conceptions of justice and convenience … it is of the very essence of the accepted judicial method that the result is not predetermined'. Moreover,

> the demands made in the name of justice must not be arbitrary or fanciful. They must proceed, not from political or sociological propensities, but from deeper, more ordered, more philosophical and perhaps more enduring conceptions of justice.

In short, the supposed dichotomy between legalism and realism is a false dichotomy. At one stage in the introduction to his *Cases and Materials on the Law of Sales* (1930), Llewellyn seemed to be telling his students that any case must have one of two outcomes: '*either* a triumph of the felt needs of the case, with a consequent ignoring or reshaping of doctrine to fit the result, *or* the triumph of mechanical, deductive reasoning from formulae which crush to death some needed, budding economic institution'. Dixon rejected these stark alternatives: for him the common law's 'strict logic and high technique' offered neither rationalisation nor exclusion of 'the felt needs of the case', but the medium through which those needs could be met. But when Llewellyn went on to emphasise 'the difference between doctrine as a causal factor in inducing a decision and doctrine as a mere *ex post facto* justification of a decision already reached', he was posing an issue to which Dixon could respond. For Dixon, doctrine was always 'a causal factor'; it was never the only factor.

TONY BLACKSHIELD

Further Reading

Tony Blackshield, 'The Legacy of Julius Stone' (1997) 20 *UNSWLJ* 215

Owen Dixon, 'Concerning Judicial Method' (1956) 29 *ALJ* 468, reprinted in *Jesting Pilate* (1965) 152

Laura Kalman, *Legal Realism at Yale, 1927–1960* (1986)

William Twining, *Karl Llewellyn and the Realist Movement* (1973, reissued 1985)

Reasonableness has been described by former Chief Justice **Mason** as providing 'a flexible but objective standard by which to fashion legal rules capable of application in a multitude of contexts'. In one sense, reasonableness is objective: it is judged by the standards of the reasonable person. But in another, it is subjective: the judgment is made by an individual (or group of individuals) whose notion of what is reasonable may not accord with that of other, no less reasonable, people. Nevertheless, the law endeavours to treat reasonableness as an objective concept.

The quoted statement reflects an increasing adoption by the High Court in recent years of reasonableness as a standard by which conduct should be judged. This has been a consequence of its greater concern to look for underlying community **values** and unifying themes. Over a similar period, there have been changes in those values that are reflected in the decisions of the Court: as to the appropriate balance between the risk of injury, damage or loss and the pursuit of profit; between imposing obligations upon parties to a relationship and leaving to them the allocation of their losses; between legal certainty and justice in individual cases; and between the judiciary on the one hand and the legislature and executive on the other.

The standard of reasonableness applies in many areas of law. It is relevant not only to conduct but also to legislation, although its increasing prevalence as a standard is greatest in **tort law**, **contract law**, and **estoppel**, and **administrative law** and **constitutional law**.

The question of what is reasonable may arise at two stages in the law of torts. The first is in measuring the conduct (act or omission) of a defendant. The second is in determining whether, assuming that the defendant is negligent, it is reasonable that the plaintiff should recover **damages** for that negligence—that is, 'in balancing against the interest of the injured party in recovering compensation the interest of the wrongdoer in avoiding subjection to a liability disproportionate to his negligent conduct' (Mason in *Caltex Oil v The Dredge 'Willemstad'* (1976)). In this context, 'reasonable' may be used interchangeably with 'fair' or 'just', and the question of what is reasonable or fair or just more clearly involves **policy considerations** in this second stage than at the first stage. However, both stages do involve policy to some extent.

At the first stage, the High Court has rationalised and simplified the law of torts by giving effect to what the Court has identified as a trend towards making liability dependent on either intentional or negligent infliction of harm (*Northern Territory v Mengel* (1995)). In the process, it has necessarily widened the scope of negligence. It has done this by eliminating the *Rylands v Fletcher* doctrine of **strict liability** (see *Burnie Port Authority v General Jones* (1994)); by eliminating the different categories of entrant for the purpose of **occupiers' liability** (*Australian Safeway Stores v Zaluzna* (1987)); and by **overruling** *Beaudesert Shire Council v Smith* (1966). The Court has also extended liability for negligence by elevating the standard of care that a reasonable person would adopt in a number of familiar situations including employer–employee, doctor–patient (see *Rogers v Whitaker* (1992)), and owner–occupier relationships. Policy considerations have affected decisions on this question both in extending and in limiting liability.

At the second stage, the Court has substantially widened liability for pure economic loss to include a number of new situations. In doing so, it has referred more openly to the policy considerations that affect a fair balance between compensating the victims of negligent acts or omissions and avoiding liability for loss disproportionate to the wrongful conduct.

Mason has also said that 'at least in a commercial environment, community morality may well demand that expectations reasonably held should be protected'. The law of contract had tended to conform to the **ideology** of economic rationalism and the free market, and hence to the belief that the certainty and predictability of contracts were the primary goals in contract law (see **Contract and tort**). It is only in recent times that courts in Australia and elsewhere have looked towards notions of reasonableness, good faith, and fair dealing in contract (but see *Astley v Austrust* (1999)). Equitable principles have played a major part in this development. But the renewed emphasis on the reasonable expectations of the parties has also played a part.

There are close similarities between obligations based on a duty of care and those based on the implied obligation of each party to a contract to do all things necessary to enable the other to have the benefit of, or secure performance of, the contract. While not importing a duty of care into contracts, the High Court has re-emphasised and applied this implied obligation in a variety of situations. And although **unconscionability** has perhaps had a greater influence on the development of contract law than this obligation has had, reasonableness may also be relevant to some aspects of unconscionability.

In the High Court's development of the principles of estoppel, unconscionability has been the 'driving force', but reasonableness has played a part. So in determining whether it is unconscientious for a party to depart from a representation or assumption, it may be relevant to inquire whether he or she might reasonably have expected that the representation would have induced action or forbearance by the other party (see *Waltons Stores v Maher* (1988)), and whether it was reasonable for the other party to act or forbear in reliance on the representation or assumption. Reasonableness may also be relevant to whether the remedy is proportionate to the detriment. The development of these principles can be seen to complement the **remedies** for negligent misstatement.

Reasonable **proportionality** has emerged in recent years as a touchstone of the constitutional validity of Commonwealth legislation and of delegated legislation generally. Traditionally, the constitutional validity of Commonwealth legislation was determined as a question of **characterisation**, considerable deference being accorded to legislative opinion. However, in cases where the impugned law was perceived as not falling directly within the 'core' of the relevant legislative power, it was said that, for validity, its connection with the power must be reasonable. In assessing the validity of delegated legislation (usually regulations), the traditional test was whether it could reasonably have been adopted as a means of attaining the ends of the delegated power. Here, too, considerable deference was accorded to legislative opinion. Reasonableness has long been a ground for **judicial review** of administrative action, though in this context it has traditionally been limited to '*Wednesbury* unreasonableness' (as defined in *Associated Provincial Picture Houses v Wednesbury Corporation* (1947)).

Since the *Tasmanian Dam Case* (1983), reasonable proportionality has frequently been used to determine the constitutional validity of Commonwealth legislation enacted under a purposive power (such as **defence** or the aspect of the **external affairs power** that relates to the legislative implementation of international treaties). According to *Nationwide News v Wills* (1992) (see *Free Speech Cases*), a similar purposive element arises in any case where validity depends on an express or implied incidental power. In such cases, the Court has considered whether the law is reasonably and appropriately adapted to (that is, reasonably proportionate to and not disproportionate to) the pursuit of an end within power. In determining this, the Court will consider whether, and to what extent, the law goes beyond what is reasonably necessary for the achievement of the legitimate object. It is relevant to ascertain for this purpose whether the law results in an infringement of any fundamental value traditionally protected by the **common law**. Such an infringement would be at least some indication that the legislation has gone beyond what is reasonably proportionate to the pursuit of the legitimate purpose.

Reasonable proportionality has been held to operate in much the same way as a touchstone of legislative validity in a separate but related context. Whenever an exercise of legislative power would infringe upon a right or freedom expressly or impliedly granted by the Constitution, its validity will depend on whether the interference with the right or freedom was more than reasonably necessary, or disproportionate, to the legitimate interest being pursued by the legislation.

In considering legislation, otherwise within power, that is said to infringe a right or freedom expressly guaranteed by the Constitution, the High Court has long, in effect, carried out a balancing exercise—although it has not often done so expressly. The history of section 92 (see **Interstate trade and commerce**) is an example of changes in that balance. The concept of reasonable proportionality in this context may do no more than state expressly what the Court was implicitly doing in any event. But by stating it expressly as a balancing exercise, the Court has drawn attention to—although rarely stating expressly—the factors that are or may be relevant to that balance. And by finding rights implied in the Constitution it has, of course, introduced an additional consideration.

In the application of the reasonable proportionality test in each of these contexts, the question will always arise as to the extent of deference that ought to be accorded to the apparent intention of the legislature. In the first situation, where the question is one of characterisation of the legislation, there being no constitutional limitation on power, it might be thought that considerable deference ought to be given to the legislative intention, provided it is made unmistakably clear. On the other hand, where there is an express or implied constitutional guarantee, the Court should feel freer to hold legislation invalid. However, where the constitutional guarantee is one found by the Court to be implied in the Constitution, a greater degree of deference to legislative intent might be expected than would be the case where it was expressly guaranteed. The process of identifying precise, formulaic 'levels of scrutiny' appropriate to these various contexts, well advanced in the **United States Supreme Court**, remains undeveloped in the High Court.

At about the same time as reasonable proportionality came to be accepted as a determinant of the constitutional validity of Commonwealth legislation, it also came to be accepted as a determinant of the validity of delegated legislation: that is, whether it is capable of being considered to be reasonably proportionate to the pursuit of the enabling purpose. And in determining that question, similar questions may arise: whether it infringes any fundamental value protected by the common law or whether it infringes any right or freedom expressly or impliedly granted by the Constitution.

Wednesbury unreasonableness remains a determinant of the validity of administrative decisions, proportionality not being a separate determinant. In England, however, proportionality has been applied in a way that equates it, at least in practical effect, with *Wednesbury* unreasonableness—the question being, on one view, whether on either approach the decision maker has struck a balance that was fairly and reasonably open.

GEOFFREY DAVIES

Reception of English law was first examined closely by the High Court in *Delohery v Permanent Trustee (NSW)* (1904). The issue was whether particular rules or doctrines of English law were 'received' into the Australian colonies. In 1765, William Blackstone, in his *Commentaries on the Laws of England*, had formulated the **common law** rule by asserting that in 'settled' colonies, which all Australian colonies were later presumed to be, 'all the English laws then in being … are immediately there in force'; but later he had qualified this by stating that the colonists carry with them 'only so much of the English law, as is applicable to their own situation and the condition of an infant colony'. Thus the common law rule involved a flexible test. As the **Privy Council** understood it in *Cooper v Stuart* (1889), in deciding whether the rule against perpetuities had been in force in NSW in 1823, the question was whether the particular rule would be 'beneficial' and consonant with 'public policy' in a developing colony.

In NSW, by the 1820s, the uncertain operation of the common law rule had led to difficulties. The doubts were resolved by section 24 of the *Australian Courts Act* 1828 (Imp), which itself applied in Australia not by reception but by 'paramount force'. That section, which also applies to Tasmania, Victoria, Queensland, and the ACT, provides that all laws and statutes in force in England on 25 July 1828 are to be applied 'so far as the same can be applied'.

The issue in *Delohery* concerned the common law doctrine of ancient lights, under which, by 20 years continuous usage, one may acquire an easement for uninterrupted access of air and light to one's windows. **Griffith**, speaking for the Court, held that the doctrine of ancient lights had been 'received' under section 24 of the 1828 Act.

The 1828 statutory formula, 'so far as the same can be applied', was capable of being read as reproducing the flexible common law test; but Griffith read it in a more rigid, mechanical sense, rejecting any inquiry into whether the law was beneficial or suitable to the colony. Instead, he emphasised the statutory word 'can', concluding that since the law of ancient lights 'can' be administered, it had necessarily been received.

On this approach, Australia was likely to adopt most of the laws of England (so far as they were in force in England in 1828). Although the mechanical test itself had **policy** implications (since it favoured uniformity of laws throughout the British Empire, rather than legal pluralism), it was essentially a test rooted in legal **positivism**. Griffith emphasised that 'whether a law is suitable or beneficial to a country … is a question for the legislature, and not for a Court of law'.

Yet colonial judges in NSW had previously taken a different view. When section 24 was first applied by the Supreme Court of NSW in *Macdonald v Levy* (1833), William Burton applied the mechanical test—but his was a minority view. Renowned for his belief that the only good law was an English law, Burton decided that the English usury laws 'can' be applied in the colony. The majority judges, Francis Forbes and James Dowling, rejected that conclusion, holding that the 1828 Act had merely provided a new date of reception, not a new rule. In this and other cases, Forbes used the test of whether the English law in question was applicable to the state and condition of the colony—often concluding that conditions (and thus appropriate laws) varied across the Empire. In particular, in *R v Maloney* (1836), he rejected the mechanical test because its tendency to apply the whole of English law 'without limitation or restraint' would be 'much too inconvenient in its consequences' to be just. The Supreme Court of Victoria took a similar view (see, for example, *M'Hugh v Robertson* (1885)).

To add to the confusion, only a year after *Delohery*, Griffith himself adopted the more flexible common law approach in *Quan Yick v Hinds* (1905). In that case, the High Court found that English statutory law concerning lotteries had not been 'received', Griffith stating that the test under section 24 was not whether those laws were 'capable' of application, but whether it could be said that they 'can reasonably be applied': that is, whether they were suitable to the needs of the colony at the date of reception. The Court confirmed this approach in *Mitchell v Scales* (1907), this time in relation to the statutory offence of fortune-telling.

In the complex jurisprudence of the reception of English law, inconsistency of approach is common; but in general, later courts have followed *Quan Yick v Hinds* in preference to *Delohery*, at least in relation to the reception of statutory law. At the same time—particularly where the reception of the unenacted common law was concerned, a distinction which may to some extent explain Griffith's divergent approaches— the general trend in the High Court and elsewhere has strongly favoured reception, even when the flexible approach to 'applicability' is taken.

This tendency was strikingly illustrated when the issue surfaced again in the High Court in the late 1970s. In *Dugan v Mirror Newspapers* (1978), the Court affirmed the reception into NSW law of the common law doctrine of 'civil death' or 'corruption of the blood', by which a person sentenced to death is rendered incapable of suing in the civil courts. **Barwick** and **Gibbs** relied on the test in *Quan Yick* rather than *Delohery*, but found that the doctrine had been suitable and reasonably applicable to colonial NSW. Only **Murphy** dissented, holding the doctrine to be anachronistic.

The Court took an even more deferential approach to English law in the following year, in *State Government Insurance Commission v Trigwell* (1979). This concerned the reception in SA of the English common law, as stated by the **House of Lords** in *Searle v Wallbank* (1946), giving an exemption from liability to the owners of animals straying onto a highway. Unlike the eastern states, SA and WA operate under the common law rules on reception of English law, rather than the statutory formula in section 24 of the Australian Courts Act. In *Trigwell*, the Court declared (Murphy again in dissent) that the rule in *Searle* was part of the law of SA, even though the rule had been abolished by statute in England and had been rejected in Scotland, Canada, the USA, and even WA. The High Court took the mechanical test used in *Delohery* and applied it to the common law rules on reception, apparently unaware that this mechanical test was itself invented as an interpretation of the word 'can' in section 24. **Mason** (who wrote the leading judgment) said that the test is not whether the English law is suitable or beneficial, but whether it is capable of application. *Quan Yick's* concern with 'reasonable' was forgotten, and its use of the adjective 'suitable' was rejected. The Court had returned to the strict test in *Delohery*, despite that test having been invented for reception under the Australian Courts Act, not under the common law.

Rather than the High Court taking an increasingly independent line in such cases, *Trigwell* showed that, until 1979 at least, it had become increasingly deferential to English authority. Elsewhere, the Court was tending to reassess the value of English precedents (see, for example, *Parker v The Queen* (1963); *Skelton v Collins* (1966)). In *Trigwell*, Mason (but not Gibbs) displayed some openness to the possibility of changing a common law rule once it was received: in very limited circumstances, the Court could alter the common law because of changed conditions, though generally this should be left to the legislature. He did not show the same independence on the initial reception of law.

Trigwell was decided not long before a dramatic change in the Court's attitude to English **precedent** and positivism. The *Australia Acts* 1986 freed the Australian courts from imperial control, and the **Mason Court** took advantage of that freedom to create (or rediscover) a distinctively Australian common law. This was nowhere more evident than in *Mabo* (1992), where the Court departed from previous decisions or *obiter dicta* that had ignored or refused to recognise **native title**. In doing so, it affirmed the 'settlement' theory on which the common law rules on reception of English law in Australia are based. In *Mabo*, the Court returned to the test of 'reasonably applicable' in deciding that the doctrine of tenure had been received in Australia. The finding that the Crown had only radical rather than beneficial title left room for the recognition of native title, and with it, a return to the pluralism that had been evident in early nineteenth century colonial courts such as that led by Forbes.

The reception of English common law (as distinct from English statutory law) is complicated by the question of whether the 'general body' of common law was received in 1828, and whether it was ambulatory in character, changing shape with new decisions over time. Moreover, the Court's attitude to the reception of English common law is difficult to disentangle from its attitude on two cognate and interrelated issues: whether courts create or simply discover and declare the common law, and whether English decisions should be followed as a matter of precedent. Attitudes on all three issues have changed over time, and all impinge on the further question of whether—or the extent to which—there is a distinctively Australian common law.

However, the new spirit of independence shown in *Mabo* may result in a much more critical attitude towards the reception of English law should that distinct question arise again. On that issue, *Trigwell* may prove to have been the last gasp of positivism and unquestioning deference to England.

BRUCE KERCHER

Further Reading
Alex Castles, 'The Reception and Status of English Law in Australia' (1963) 2 *Adel L Rev* 1
Michael Coper, *Encounters with the Australian Constitution* (1987, popular edn 1988) ch 2

Reform of Court. Despite its controversial beginnings (see **Establishment of Court**; **Deakin**), the High Court has, since its formation, been characterised by stability. As an institution, it has undergone little significant reform. Nevertheless, various proposals for reform have been advanced. Legal professional organisations, academics, political parties, members of parliament, and parliamentary committees have been the most prolific generators of reform proposals. At various times, specialist bodies have been established to review constitutional and legal arrangements; many of these have generated reform proposals relating to the Court's composition, **jurisdiction**, **procedure**, and **administration**.

Reform proposals concerning the composition of the Court have focused on four principal issues: the **number of Justices**; length of **tenure** and **retirement** age; criteria for **appointment**; and the mechanism of appointment. At its inception in 1903, the Court comprised three Justices. The appointment of additional Justices has been proposed for different reasons at different times. Early increases in number—to five in 1906, and then to seven in 1912—were justified principally by reference to the Court's workload and the demands of constant travel. Enhancement of the Court's standing and authority appeared on each occasion to be a subsidiary concern. At other times, proposals to appoint additional Justices have been motivated by political concerns. In 1945, Labor minister Arthur Calwell presented Cabinet with a proposal to increase the numbers of Justices to nine. This was an overtly political strategy, modelled on the court-packing plan by which US President Franklin D Roosevelt had proposed in 1937 to shore up his New Deal agenda. Calwell hoped that new Labor appointees might stem High Court resistance to the Curtin government's own radical reform agenda. In the face of impassioned opposition from the **Attorney-General**, former High Court Justice **Evatt**, the Calwell reform plan was ultimately defeated.

Issues concerning tenure have spawned numerous reform proposals, many relating to the age at which Justices should retire. In 1929, the Royal Commission on the Constitution recommended an **amendment** to the Constitution to set a retiring age of 72. Though acknowledging that opinion within the **legal profession** was divided on the issue, the Royal Commission emphasised that a similar reform had recently been proposed for judges in the UK. A Standing Committee of the Australian Constitutional Convention considered the issue again in 1974. That Committee specifically rejected the setting of a retirement age for High Court Justices in the Constitution itself. Rather, it suggested that the Constitution should include a provision empowering the Parliament to legislate on the subject. This suggestion, aimed at providing a measure of flexibility and parliamentary discretion, did not enjoy widespread support. Reformers ultimately reverted to the idea of making direct constitutional provision, and in 1977, the Australian people approved a proposal put at referendum to specify a retiring age of 70 in section 72 of the Constitution.

The process surrounding the appointment of Justices to the Court has attracted widespread **criticism** and prompted many reform proposals. The key concern has been the limited state involvement in the selection process. The states have always argued that, as partners in the federal compact, they should have a formal role in selecting the Justices who will interpret the Constitution. Some proposals have looked to the formation of a council, comprising representatives of all Australian parliaments, to make appointments; others have suggested that appointments be made by Australian governments or parliaments on a rotational basis. In 1979, in response to ongoing disquiet and to the particular controversy surrounding **Murphy's** appointment in 1975, the Commonwealth Parliament provided in section 6 of the *High Court of Australia Act* 1979 (Cth) that the Commonwealth Attorney-General must 'consult with the Attorneys-General of the States' before making appointments to the Court. This reform has not appeased the states, as it merely entitles them to express a view, with no guarantee that their views will be determinative or even influential.

In 1997, Attorney-General Daryl Williams proposed a widening of this consultative process to seek the opinions of existing judges of Commonwealth courts, former judges, leaders of the legal profession and members of the Opposition and minor parties. However, as with the opinions of the state Attorneys-General, there would be no guarantee that these additional opinions would influence the ultimate decision. More radical proposals to reform the selection process have at times been made. In 1993, Attorney-General Michael Lavarch canvassed several possibilities including popular election of Justices, parliamentary interrogation and ratification of proposed appointees, and the creation of a representative Commission to generate short lists of potential appointees. More radical still were the reforms mooted in February 1997 by Queensland Premier Rob Borbidge in the wake of the Court's decision in *Wik* (1996). Openly defying traditional conceptions of judicial **independence**, Borbidge suggested various changes to the High Court appointments process including ten-year fixed terms, ratification of appointments by popular vote, and provision for the removal of errant Justices by public initiative.

Some reform proposals have focused on the necessary qualifications for appointment. There are none entrenched in the Constitution, but section 7 of the High Court of Australia Act provides that appointees must either have served as a judge on another Australian court or have been enrolled as a legal practitioner for at least five years. Beyond these formal requirements, merit has always been the avowed principal criterion for appointment. Some **commentators** have criticised the opacity of this criterion and suggested—somewhat ambitiously—that the particular qualities and skills that go to defining merit should be prescribed. Related are proposals concerning the overall composition of the Bench, particularly the degree to which it reflects the composition of the general community in relation to gender, ethnicity, and other characteristics. Changing perceptions of the Court's **role**, and the recognition that it unavoidably draws upon **values** and **policy considerations** in its **decision making**, have highlighted the Court's overwhelming homogeneity and sparked calls for more diversity among Justices. These suggestions have typically encountered strong opposition from legal professional bodies, concerned that conscious efforts to create a more diverse Court might compromise its quality and impartiality.

As far as the Court's jurisdiction is concerned, significant actual and proposed reforms have included attempts to require or allow the Court to give **advisory opinions**; abolition of appeals to the **Privy Council**; the introduction of a requirement of special **leave to appeal**; refinement of the Court's original jurisdiction; and the provision of procedures allowing **removal** of cases into the Court and **remittal** of cases from the Court. The general theme of reform proposals relating to jurisdiction has been a desire to increase the Court's control over the volume and nature of its work.

The two provisions in the Constitution concerning the Court's original jurisdiction have been the subject of sustained criticism and reform suggestions. Critics suggest that the core part of that jurisdiction—which is conferred directly by the Constitution and thus entrenched—includes matters now having comparatively minor importance, such as those involving foreign diplomats (Constitution, section 75). By contrast, the Court's additional original jurisdiction provided for in section 76, which Parliament is able to bestow or take away at will, includes matters arising under the Constitution or involving its interpretation. Reform proposals have thus focused on a reshuffle of the heads of core and additional original jurisdiction to ensure that the vital parts of that jurisdiction are constitutionally protected, and that the other, relatively less important parts, are within the control of Parliament. Reform of this kind was recommended by the Royal Commission on the Constitution in 1929, by a Standing Committee of the Australian Constitutional Convention in 1974, and by the Constitutional Commission in 1988. However, no proposal to amend the text of sections 75 and 76 has ever been put to the Australian people.

With the creation of the **Federal Court** in 1976, the High Court was divested of much of the additional original jurisdiction it had had in respect of matters arising under Commonwealth statutes. This reform reduced significantly the amount of the Court's non-constitutional work. That same intention underpinned the introduction of new procedures for remittal of cases from the Court in 1976. Thus the Court's original jurisdiction became, from 1976 onward, more tightly focused on constitutional matters, and the Court enjoyed greater flexibility and discretion in managing its caseload. In the appellate jurisdiction, the introduction of the requirement for special leave to appeal further enhanced the Court's control of its own docket. Unlike most other proposals concerning the Court, these jurisdictional reforms of the 1970s and 1980s were actively supported—and indeed promoted—by members of the Court itself.

In relation to the procedure and administration of the Court, key reforms have been implemented concerning, among other things, aspects of **civil procedure**, the introduction of **directions hearings**, procedures relating to **fact finding**, and the way deadlocks are resolved when there is a **tied vote**. Other recent suggestions for reform, not yet taken up, have been the imposition of time limits on oral **argument** before the Court and the development of transparent criteria to guide the Court's discretion in allowing **interveners and *amici curiae***. Some reform proposals relating to procedure and administration have been surprisingly controversial. Addressing the Court in 1998 at the swearing-in of Chief Justice **Gleeson**, Attorney-General Daryl Williams strongly suggested that the Court should generate more **joint judgments**—a suggestion not warmly received by the Justices.

The Court's move in 1980 to a permanent home in **Canberra**, provided for in the High Court of Australia Act, was widely celebrated. This reform did, however, give rise to concerns in some of the more distant states that the Court would become less accessible—a concern partly alleviated by the Court's use of the **circuit system**. One of the significant changes that accompanied the move to Canberra was the creation of a single High Court Registry to oversee administration of the Court's **business**. The High Court of Australia Act also gave the Court an unprecedented measure of autonomy in the management of its financial affairs, staffing, and **building**. More recently, the Court has itself given consideration to the idea of appointing a media officer, to facilitate awareness and understanding of the Court's decisions by the **media** and the community.

In general, reform of the Court has been minimalist and incremental. Only a small number of relatively uncontroversial reform proposals have gained acceptance and been implemented. Proposals for more fundamental reform typically lose momentum quickly and are condemned to gather dust in long-forgotten reports.

AMELIA SIMPSON

Further Reading
Australian Constitutional Convention, *Official Record of Debates*: Perth (1978) 10–51, 165–74; Brisbane (1985) 170–204
Report of the Royal Commission on the Constitution (1929) 252–55
Final Report of the Constitutional Commission (1988) vol 1, 373–90, 398–403

Reform of Court: reflections. The Court is not in need of reform. It is efficient, and it enjoys the confidence of the public. Its hearings are conducted with the utmost dispatch. Its caseflow is managed by imposing time standards. Judgments, when delivered, are available immediately. Modern **information technology** (including video link and the Internet) is used to good advantage.

It is true that in some cases (a minority) a considerable time elapses between the date when a case is ready for hearing and the date when the decision is given. The delay between the time when a **matter** is ready for hearing and the time when it is listed for hearing may be explained in some cases for good reasons. Delay between hearing and decision may be a matter for greater concern, but is explicable because of the heavy caseload of the Court.

Some suggestions for change have been made, but none, if adopted, would be so significant as to amount to reform.

The suggestion that the **number of Justices** should be increased to enable the Court to give judgment more expeditiously should be rejected. It is the practice in important cases for all Justices to sit (see **Bench, composition of**), and the need to obtain the views of nine rather than seven Justices in important cases would be likely to increase delay rather than reduce it.

It is sometimes suggested that the Court should produce more **joint judgments**—not only to reduce delay, but also for convenience and clarity (see **Collective responsibility**). In some cases, a single judgment is desirable, but experience shows that such judgments lead to compromise and may inhibit fruitful expressions of opinion. It is a question for decision by the Justices in every case whether a joint judgment is appropriate.

No appeal may now be brought to the Court from a judgment of a **state Supreme Court** or of the **Federal Court** unless the Court grants special **leave to appeal**. In deciding whether to grant an application for special leave, the Court has in truth an unfettered discretion. It has been argued that it is inappropriate that its appellate **jurisdiction** should be undefined, and that it is impossible to know whether or not the Court will grant special leave in any particular case. However, it is necessary to confine the work of the Court within reasonable bounds, and the prescription of criteria for a right of appeal has proved unsatisfactory. A further suggestion is that the grounds on which special leave should be granted or refused should be more narrowly defined than is done by section 35A of the *Judiciary Act* 1903 (Cth). It would be difficult, if not impossible, to arrive at a more precise formula for the grant of special leave.

The consideration of applications for special leave involves a great deal of unproductive work for the Court, and the burden on the Court might be reduced if a procedure such as the following were provided. If a Supreme Court or the Federal Court granted a certificate that one or other of the conditions described in paragraphs (a) and (b) of section 35A were satisfied, an appeal could then be brought unless the High Court revoked the certificate. Parties refused a certificate could apply to the High Court for special leave, since a court that had given a judgment might be reluctant to recognise that the interests of the administration of justice required the High Court to consider the judgment.

Arguments by **litigants in person** are almost invariably no more than a waste of the Court's time. If the government will not provide legal aid in these cases, there should be a reversion to the rule that applications for special leave should be made only by a member of the **legal profession**.

It is undesirable that the Court should be obliged to hear in its original jurisdiction matters other than those properly commenced to raise a constitutional issue. However, the Court can, where necessary, usually direct the **remittal** of other matters to another court. There are exceptions to the power of remittal—for example, **electoral** petitions: the law should be changed so that the Court is not obliged to hear such matters at first instance.

In principle, **appointments** to the Court should not be made by the Commonwealth alone; the states should have a greater right than merely to be consulted.

HARRY GIBBS

Reform of Court: further reflections. Special **leave to appeal** is an area where reform should be considered. Applications are steadily increasing. In the financial year 1999/2000, the Court decided 387 applications and refused 321 of them. Earlier, in order to alleviate the problem, the Court introduced strict time limits on oral **argument** at special leave hearings and required presentation of written submissions. More recently, the Court constituted a **Bench** of two instead of three Justices to hear applications. Although these measures have resulted in a saving of judicial time, the burden on Justices is very considerable. It limits the time that would otherwise be available for constitutional questions and appeals.

Alternative solutions have shortcomings. Giving intermediate courts of appeal the power to grant special leave or a certificate to appeal, subject to review by the High Court, would be a retrograde step. The Court should be in control of the work that comes to it. The special leave requirement filters the cases coming to the Court. It ensures that only those cases worthy of attention obtain leave, and that the Court's workload is manageable. Although true comparisons between applications cannot be made, the object of the requirement is that applications will be allowed in the cases most deserving of the Court's attention.

The Justices of the Court have a more informed perspective on what are the critical questions of law requiring its attention than judges of intermediate appellate courts that are primarily concerned with matters of federal law and jurisdiction (the **Federal Court**) or the law in a particular state (the **state Supreme Courts**).

Section 93 of the *Family Law Act* 1973 (Cth) enables the Full Court of the Family Court to issue a certificate. The power has been rarely exercised. When exercised, it has given rise to difficulties. The experience has not been encouraging.

Perhaps consideration should be given to a substantial **costs** disincentive. The costs of a special leave application are insignificant when compared with the amount or subject matter at stake and the costs already incurred. So there is little to be lost by making a special leave application. A strong costs disincentive—even an order against legal representatives in extreme cases—may be worth considering. This approach might not be appropriate for criminal cases.

Another option is to increase the **number of Justices** to nine. Although that would reduce the burden of special leave applications and single-Justice cases, it would not necessarily enhance the capacity of the Court to deal with substantive appeals and constitutional questions. The larger the Court, the greater the difficulty of ensuring collegial consensus.

A growing problem is the greater incidence of applications presented by **litigants in person**, a high proportion of which are without merit. Formerly, the Rules required an application to be presented by **counsel**. Solicitors considered that the rule discriminated against them. Tempting though it might be to insist upon presentation of an application by a legal practitioner, such a requirement is unacceptable today.

Another problem arises from the restrictions imposed by the *Migration Act* 1958 (Cth) on the jurisdiction of the Federal Court to exercise **judicial review** of migration decisions accompanied by a restriction on the High Court's power to **remit** such cases to the Federal Court. Because Parliament cannot impose a like restriction on the High Court's **jurisdiction** under section 75(v) of the Constitution, a number of cases which, but for the restrictions, would have been heard in the Federal Court, are now heard in the High Court. The object of the legislation is to force applicants in certain migration cases—for example, those who complain of denial of **natural justice**—to go to the High Court. This needless burden on the High Court should be removed (see also **Fact finding**).

Another possible reform is abolition of the annual **sittings** in the state capitals. Here I agree with **Barwick**, who was strongly opposed to the practice. It is a very inefficient way of dealing with the Court's work. It is a flag-waving exercise, and its intangible benefits are outweighed by loss of efficiency (see **Circuit system**).

Otherwise, I see no strong case for reform of the Court. **Joint judgments** are to be applauded, and the Court is now delivering a higher percentage of joint judgments with less diversity of opinion. But I strongly oppose any compulsion in relation to joint judgments and any attempt to confine the Court to one majority and one minority judgment. Either step would constrain judicial integrity and the obligation of the individual Justice to express an opinion.

Finally, there is a case for greater use of written argument—but that is not a pressing matter unless pressure of work makes it so. There is a stronger case for improving the quality of written argument presented to the Court.

ANTHONY MASON

Remedies are the means by which the law responds to and attempts to redress the breach of a plaintiff's rights arising from the defendant's **tort**, breach of **contract**, or breach of statutory or equitable obligation. These responses take the form of a nominate remedy (principally **damages**, account of profits, specific performance, and injunction). In the Court's treatment of these nominate remedies, six basic points are discernible as applicable to remedies generally.

First, the remedy necessarily reflects the right breached. Thus, statutory remedies take their meaning and shape from the statutory rights to which they give effect. For example, damages under section 82 of the *Trade Practices Act* 1974 (Cth), and the remedies available under section 87, reflect the compensatory response appropriate to the breach in question; they are not limited by analogies from the general law (*Marks v GIO* (1998)). At general law, the **common law** remedy of damages is aimed at compensating plaintiffs for breach of their rights by restoring the position that existed before breach. In most cases, damages are an appropriate remedy either because compensation restores the pre-breach position where, in monetary terms, it is more or less equivalent to the right breached (as in injury to **property** cases: *Butler v Egg and Egg Pulp Marketing Board* (1966)), or because compensation is the only practical remedy in the circumstances (as in personal injury cases where pain and suffering and other non-economic losses have no monetary equivalent but the law is incapable of otherwise repairing them: **Dixon** in *Lee Transport v Watson* (1940)). By contrast, the **trust**-like nature of equitable obligations means that the remedies granted for their breach contain a more pronounced deterrent element, with the result that such obligations are protected as a matter of course by injunctive relief (*Red Book Case* (1948); *A-G (NSW) v Perpetual Trustee Co* (1940)) or by an account of profits (*Scott v Scott* (1963); *Warman International v Dwyer* (1995)). Further, equitable remedies can be moulded, case by case, to reflect as precisely as possible the nature of the obligation breached (*Maguire v Makaronis* (1997)).

Secondly, the fact that the remedy reflects the right breached means that the remedy granted is, generally, an appropriate remedy in the circumstances. However, the historical evolution of our legal system requires at least a theoretical qualification to this. Because **equity** developed as a supplement to the common law, the power to grant remedies of equitable origin—principally, injunctions, specific performance, and an account of profits—in support of common law rights is restricted to situations where the common law remedy (generally damages) is, in the circumstances, inadequate and where the discretion of the court favours the grant of the equitable remedy in question (see *Dougan v Ley* (1946)).

Thirdly, the remedy granted by a court is an integral part of the right it supports. There is no suggestion in the jurisprudence of the Court that, in the absence of statutory authority, a court has a general discretion to select whatever remedy is appropriate once it is satisfied that a right has been breached. This proposition is not compromised by the rule that equitable remedies in support of common law rights are granted only in the discretion of the court. In such cases, the discretion is narrowly curtailed: in the light of the circumstances of each case, the hardship that would result to the defendant and third parties from the grant of equitable relief must be weighed against the unfairness to the plaintiff of refusing such relief, which confines the plaintiff to the remedy at law (*Dowsett v Reid* (1912); *Gall v Mitchell* (1924); *Summers v Cocks* (1927); *Slee v Warke* (1949); *Blomley v Ryan* (1956); **Patrick Stevedores Case** (1998)).

Fourthly, where the plaintiff can establish a cause of action on more than one basis, or where the plaintiff has a choice of remedies, the choice is the plaintiff's. Thus, where the claim lies either in tort or for breach of contract, the plaintiff can choose to claim in contract—with the remedial consequence, for example, that damages will not be reduced for contributory negligence as they would be in tort (*Astley v Austrust* (1999); and see **Contract and tort**). The plaintiff's choice of remedies is limited only by the rule that there must be no double recovery (see *Warman v Dwyer*) and the rule that the plaintiff must not have elected irrevocably in favour of an inconsistent right. The court approaches this issue of inconsistency in a pragmatic way. For instance, a plaintiff who seeks or obtains an order for specific performance of a contract can later appear to act inconsistently, subject to the approval of the court, by terminating the contract—even where the defendant is not guilty of a fresh breach. The rationale is that the election involved in seeking or obtaining specific performance is, on its proper analysis, an election for the continuation of the contract under the control of the court (*Facey v Rawsthorne* (1925); *Ogle v Comboyuro Investments* (1976); *Sunbird Plaza v Maloney* (1988)).

Fifthly, principles applicable to nominate remedies are kept separate from one another to the extent necessary to ensure the integrity of the rights and remedies in question. Thus, the discretionary factors governing the availability of equitable relief are not necessarily appropriate to the determination of whether or not a declaration should be made in the exercise of a discretion conferred by statute (*Mayfair Trading v Dreyer* (1958)). Again, the Court has insisted that an injunction will go only to protect the breach, or threatened breach, of a recognised right of the plaintiff's. Thus, orders resembling injunctions but not satisfying this requirement—such as asset preservation (*Mareva*) orders—have to be justified on some basis other than the law of injunctions (*Cardile v LED Builders* (1999)). Of course, principles developed for one remedy may, where appropriate, be applied in another. Thus, for purposes of damages under section 82 of the Trade Practices Act, the principles to be applied in proving and quantifying probable losses are the same as those at general law (*Sellars v Adelaide Petroleum* (1994)).

Sixthly, while compensation in the form of damages is, in practice, the most important remedy, it is not the exclusive monetary remedy. In *Uren v John Fairfax & Sons* (1966), the Court, in an early demonstration of its independence of English law, refused to adopt the strictures on exemplary damages imposed by the **House of Lords** in *Rookes v Barnard* (1964). Exemplary damages continued to be available in Australia in circumstances in which they had traditionally been available. Unfortunately, those circumstances were so uncertain that Australian law was left in a state of incoherence until the Court, in *Gray v Motor Accident Commission* (1998), began to place exemplary damages on a principled basis by reference to their function. The importance of an approach rejecting compensation as the more or less exclusive objective of monetary relief is that it leaves open the possibility of such relief serving other objectives (such as **restitution**).

The Court's jurisprudence in remedies reflects strong concerns with **legalism**, principle, doctrinal consistency, and historical continuity. This is best illustrated in the Court's continued adherence to the traditional understanding, derived largely from nineteenth-century jurisprudence, of the relationship between legal and equitable remedies. In particular, the isolation of the inadequacy of damages as a factor independent of the court's discretion and relevant to its ability (jurisdiction) to grant equitable remedies (see *Mayfair Trading v Dreyer*) has resulted in the development of categories of cases, identified principally by subject matter, in which specific performance will and will not be granted in breach of contract cases. Thus, specific performance of land contracts is always appropriate, as the Court affirmed in *Pianta v National Finance & Trustees* (1964). Yet in *Coulls v Bagot's Executor & Trustee Co* (1967), **Windeyer** said that 'there is no reason today for limiting by particular categories, rather than by general principle, the cases in which orders for specific performance will be made'. The Court has heeded this opinion by effectively departing from the traditional rule excluding specific performance of contracts relating to the purchase and sale of goods—at least to the extent that it has recognised categories of goods for which such a remedy is appropriate: goods that are rare, commercially unique, or of some special value to the purchaser (*Dougan v Ley*). Yet the full import of Windeyer's statement has yet to be realised.

The danger of the Court's general approach is that rationality and the principled development of the law can suffer, or be delayed, at the hands of strict legalism and its handmaiden, subtle reasoning. Four leading examples occur in this context. First, in breach of contract cases, the plaintiff is allowed to recover as damages losses incurred in reliance on the contract ('reliance loss') where the potential gains from the contract are too uncertain to be assessed by the court ('expectation loss') unless the defendant can prove that the reliance loss would have been incurred in any event because the plaintiff had made a bad bargain (*McRae v Commonwealth Disposals Commission* (1951); compare *Commonwealth v Amann Aviation* (1991)). Yet the qualification is illusory: the uncertainty of the gains prevents the defendant from ever satisfying it. Secondly, an unwritten land contract is unenforceable by statute unless there are acts of part-performance justifying the specific enforcement of the contract. The Court has held out the possibility of an injunction also being a remedy after part-performance of such a contract, yet an injunction could never satisfy the stringent test of part-performance adopted by the Court (*Williamson v Lukey and Mulholland* (1931)). Thirdly, in personal injury cases, the loss of ability to act as a homemaker is identified as a 'need created', by a simplistic analysis equating the loss with the need for replacement domestic services (*Kars v Kars* (1996)). The failure to identify its true nature as a 'lost economic capacity' means that injured homemakers are invariably under-compensated (see **Murphy** in *Sharman v Evans* (1977)). Fourthly, the straightforward application of authority in refusing to evaluate the function of exemplary damages has led to the absurd rule that exemplary damages are awardable against a compulsory third-party insurer whose behaviour will be unaffected by their sting (*Lamb v Cotogno* (1987)).

Notwithstanding these reservations, the Court's contribution to the development of the law of remedies has generally been impressive—particularly in the application of (equitable) discretion in the administration of equitable remedies. The principled development of the law now requires the Court to build on *Uren v Fairfax* by recognising the appropriateness of a variety of remedial responses to breaches of obligations. In doing so, it should, as in *Gray v Motor Accident Commission*, determine the appropriateness of supporting the right in question by the identified function of the remedy in issue. It should also recognise that remedies derived from different sources (that is, common law, equity, or statute) are often functionally linked and ought to be governed by the same principles, so as to avoid unnecessary distinctions.

MICHAEL TILBURY

Further Reading

Robyn Carroll (ed), *Civil Remedies: Issues and Developments* (1996)

Bruce Kercher and Michael Noone, *Remedies* (2nd edn 1990)

RP Meagher, WMC Gummow, and JLR Lehane, *Equity: Doctrines and Remedies* (3rd edn 1992)

ICF Spry, *The Principles of Equitable Remedies* (5th edn 1997)

Michael Tilbury, *Civil Remedies* vol 1 (1990), vol 2 (1993)

Michael Tilbury, Michael Noone, and Bruce Kercher, *Remedies: Commentary and Materials* (3rd edn 2000)

Remittal of cases from Court. The remittal **procedure** enables the High Court to redirect cases to other courts. The remittal of a case from the High Court may be after a full hearing by the Court, either for the execution of the judgment of the Court under section 37 of the *Judiciary Act* 1903 (Cth), or as part of the disposition of an appeal under section 36 or otherwise. More commonly, remittal is for the purpose of the case being heard at first instance and for the first time by another court. It is then governed by two provisions of the Judiciary Act, the specific provision being section 42 and the general being section 44.

Section 42 deals with a cause that has been the subject of an order for **removal** into the Court. The Court may, at any stage of the proceedings, remit the cause to the court from which it was removed. The Court is required to remit the cause thus removed where it does not have original **jurisdiction**. But where a matter is removed under section 40 on the application of an **Attorney-General**, the absence of a discretion to refuse removal tells against the exercise of a discretion, if any, to remit (*A-G (NSW) v Commonwealth Savings Bank* (1986)).

The purpose of the general power to remit in section 44 of the Judiciary Act is to relieve the Court of the necessity to hear cases that have been commenced in the Court's original jurisdiction, but may more conveniently be heard elsewhere, particularly where the litigation involves the trial of issues of fact (see **Fact finding**). Prior to 1977, the power could be exercised only at the request of a party; now the Court can also remit on its own initiative. The section is designed to ensure that the Court is not diverted from its principal functions (*State Bank of NSW v Commonwealth Savings Bank* (1984); *Ravenor Overseas v Readhead* (1998)). It reflects the recognition by the Parliament of the need for the High Court to confine itself to constitutional and important appellate matters (*Re Minister for Immigration; Ex parte Durairajasingham* (2000)).

Section 44(1) empowers the Court to remit a matter pending before it, other than a matter referred to in paragraphs 38(a) to (d) of the Judiciary Act, to any court that has jurisdiction over the same kind of party and the same kind of subject matter as those in the proceedings in question (*Johnstone v Commonwealth* (1979)). Section 44(2) relates to the matters described in paragraphs 38(a) to (d) and permits remittal to the **Federal Court** or to any court of a state or territory. Section 44(2A) permits remittal to the Federal Court of **matters** to which the Commonwealth is a party and ensures that there is no gap caused by the *Administrative Decisions (Judicial Review) Act* 1977 (Cth) (*State Bank of NSW*).

On remitter, jurisdiction is conferred on the court by the Parliament rather than by the act of remitter. The Court should not, by remitting, alter the rights of the parties: remitter should be made to a court in which the law to be applied is the same as that applicable in the High Court. Where the relevant law is materially different, the safe course is to remit to the state whose law gave rise to the cause of action (*State Bank of NSW*; *Pozniak v Smith* (1982)). After the change to the choice of law rules effected by *John Pfeiffer v Rogerson* (2000), the significance of this factor may diminish, and considerations of practical convenience may predominate.

Some **commentators** have suggested that section 44 may be unconstitutional in that it allows the Court to avoid the exercise of its mandated original jurisdiction, but the section has never been challenged on this basis, and the point seems more theoretical than real. Together with the 1984 provision for special **leave to appeal**, section 44 is a key element in the efficient operation of the Court.

ALAN ROBERTSON

Removal of cases into Court. The removal **procedure** allows the High Court to hear cases commenced in, but not yet finally determined by, other courts. Removal is governed by section 40 of the *Judiciary Act* 1903 (Cth). The object of the procedure is to secure early determination by the Court of constitutional questions and other questions of public importance.

Section 40(1) deals with constitutional issues pending in another court. The High Court may **order** removal at any stage of the proceedings before final judgment. Where an application under section 40(1) is made by or on behalf of an **Attorney-General**, the order is to be made as of course.

Section 40(2) deals with causes pending in a court otherwise involving the exercise of federal jurisdiction by that court. Whoever makes the application, the Court retains a discretion to make or decline to make the order. The order may be made at any stage of the proceedings before final judgment. An order is not to be made under section 40(2) unless all parties consent, or the Court is satisfied that it is appropriate to make the order.

From 1903 to 1907, section 40 was limited to constitutional questions pending in any court of a state on appeal. Applicants had to show special cause. In the 1903 parliamentary debates, **Deakin** said the purpose of the provision was as a safeguard, in order that the class of cases for which the Court was specially created, and to decide which it would exist, might be brought before it when necessary, in the most summary and inexpensive manner.

In 1907, sections 38A and 40A were enacted so that *inter se* **questions** should be finally determined by the High Court. In such cases, the cause was, without any order of the High Court and by virtue of the Judiciary Act, removed to the High Court. Those provisions were enacted in response to the taking of appeals from the **state Supreme Courts** directly to the **Privy Council** without going to the High Court—thus circumventing section 74 of the Constitution (see *Webb v Outtrim* (1906)).

This second phase ended in 1976, when sections 38A and 40A were repealed by the *Judiciary Amendment Act* 1976 (Cth) as no longer necessary to prevent appeals to the Privy Council.

Section 40 provides for the removal of any extant judicial proceeding, including an appeal, but it does not enable the Court to remove an original action that stands dismissed by a valid curial order (*A-G (NSW) v Commonwealth Savings Bank* (1986)). The procedure for removal allows preliminary questions of law decided by a Full Court of the **Federal Court** to be reconsidered by the High Court (*O'Toole v Charles David* (1991)). An antecedent non-constitutional question should be decided before removal (*Richmond v Edelsten* (1986)).

The procedures for removal, **remittal**, and special **leave to appeal** together enable the Court to manage its caseload and to ensure that it hears only appropriate cases.

ALAN ROBERTSON

Removal of Justices of the High Court (and other federal judges) is strictly controlled by section 72(ii) of the Constitution, which seeks to balance judicial **independence** and judicial **accountability**. A Justice may be removed only by the Governor-General in Council, and only after 'an address from both Houses of the Parliament in the same session, praying for such removal on the ground of proved misbehaviour or incapacity'. No Justice has ever been removed, and although the possibility of removal was a subtext of the '**Murphy affair**' of 1984–86, the outcome served only to demonstrate the absence of any workable procedure for dealing with such an issue.

In England, after the turbulent events of the seventeenth century, section 3 of the *Act of Settlement* 1701 had sought to protect judicial independence by guaranteeing security of **tenure**. But it did so ambiguously. It provided that judges' commissions were conditional only on good behaviour; yet it added that 'upon the Address of both Houses of Parliament it may be lawful to remove them'.

At the 1897 **Convention Debates**, the **framers** of the Australian Constitution were troubled by this ambiguity. Most of them favoured continuation of the British practice—but what was that practice? How did the Act of Settlement's assurance of tenure during good behaviour fit in with its provision for Parliament to initiate removal by address? Were the two conceptions complementary, with the 'good behaviour' provision making misbehaviour the only ground for removal, but parliamentary address providing the procedure for adducing such a ground? Or were they independent alternatives, so that the Crown could remove a judge for misbehaviour (independently of parliamentary action), but alternatively a judge could be removed at the instance of Parliament (on any ground that it deemed sufficient)?

Isaacs in particular pressed the latter view as the correct interpretation of **history**, and insisted that in any event, an unrestricted parliamentary power of removal was essential. Initially, he argued that the word 'misbehaviour' should not be used at all; he was finally induced to accept it by assurances that the only 'judges of misbehaviour' would be 'the two Houses of Parliament'. **Higgins** was not satisfied even then; he thought the clause should provide for a Justice's removal whenever 'both Houses are *of opinion* that he has been guilty of misconduct or misbehaviour'. Otherwise, he appeared to think that any specification of grounds for removal would require the Parliament to establish them by proof in a court of law.

Some of the framers turned to the American model, in which Justices of the **United States Supreme Court** can be removed only by impeachment. (In the US practice, the House of Representatives frames 'articles of impeachment', which are then tried by the Senate.) Bernhard Wise, however, argued that the cumbrous and unfamiliar impeachment model would 'raise difficulties out of all proportion to [its] value'. Moreover, Justices might have 'very serious faults' that would justify removal but not impeachment, 'because they did not come into the category of criminal acts'. Eventually, these arguments prevailed.

Only SA's John Downer found the argument for impeachment compelling. Given the need for a definite finding 'of misbehaviour, or unfitness, or something else', he argued that the 'method' of trial must also be clearly prescribed:

> The Americans required two things to be done, and ... I think we had better do the same. They require an impeachment to be made by one House and a trial by the other ... We ought to surround the removal of the judge ... with all sorts of precautions. We ought to ensure him a trial, and not act upon the loose talk of the two popular Houses in a mere debate, to which he has no possible opportunity of replying.

He foreshadowed that he would 'probably, before the Convention is over, bring the matter up again', but he never did so.

The problems foreseen by Downer were graphically illustrated by the Murphy affair, and more fleetingly by the uncertainty of **Callinan's** position in 1998. The Murphy affair, despite its seemingly endless profusion of allegations, primarily revolved around two allegations of attempting to pervert the course of justice, arising from **Murphy's** alleged interference with criminal proceedings against the Sydney solicitor Morgan Ryan. The Callinan issue arose from a finding by Justice Alan Goldberg of the **Federal Court**, in *White Industries v Flower & Hart* (1998), that solicitors responsible for a statement of claim in December 1986 had been guilty of an abuse of process: they had issued the statement of claim knowing that its allegations of fraud were wholly unfounded, with the sole purpose of delaying or embarrassing litigation by the defendant. Callinan, as senior **counsel**, had signed the statement of claim; and Goldberg found that he was 'privy' to its improper purpose, 'and at the least acquiesced in it and approved of it'. The speculation abated when a Full Court of the Federal Court, while affirming the findings against the solicitors, found it unnecessary to express any opinion on Callinan's role (*Flower & Hart v White Industries* (1999)).

While the allegations that Murphy had tried to pervert the course of justice would presumably (if proven) have been relevant to his fitness for judicial office, the relevance (as well as the factual foundation) of many other allegations against him remained more uncertain. The same was true of the questions about Callinan. Whether in 1986 he breached the professional ethics of the Queensland Bar, and if so how seriously, were indeterminate questions. Who should determine them was equally unclear. In any event, the relevance of an incident in 1986 to his fitness for judicial office in 1998 was debatable. Assuming that conduct amounting to misbehaviour need not occur in the actual exercise of **judicial power**, nor even contemporaneously with the holding of judicial office, it must at least have some bearing upon *fitness* for judicial office. Would conduct by a practising barrister in 1986, even if it amounted to an abuse of judicial process, bear sufficiently on his role as a Justice, or his attitude to the judicial process, to affect his fitness for judicial office in 1998?

The earlier authorities (including **Quick and Garran**) had repeated ad nauseam the summation by Alpheus Todd (*On Parliamentary Government in England* (1867)) of the English meaning of 'misbehaviour':

> Misbehaviour includes, firstly, the improper exercise of judicial functions; secondly, wilful neglect of duty, or non-attendance; and thirdly, a conviction for any infamous offence, by which, although it be not connected with the duties of his office, the offender is rendered unfit to exercise any office or public franchise.

In the early stages of the Murphy affair, Murphy's lawyers argued that these categories were exhaustive; and on 24 February 1984, an opinion by Commonwealth **Solicitor-General** Gavan Griffith took a similar view. But a later opinion by Bill Pincus on 14 May 1984 went much further:

> I think it is for Parliament to decide whether any conduct alleged against a judge constitutes misbehaviour sufficient to justify removal from office. There is no 'technical' relevant meaning of misbehaviour and in particular it is not necessary … that an offence be proved.

The Parliamentary Commission of Inquiry established in the final phases of the Murphy affair agreed. In a ruling on 5 August 1986 (tabled in Parliament on 21 August 1986), the Commissioners doubted whether Todd had accurately stated the British position. But in any event, they held that the Australian provision should be treated as a distinctive fresh start.

This open-ended view of 'misbehaviour' is both convincing and paradoxical. If 'misbehaviour' has no 'technical' meaning, Parliament's power of removal cannot legally be defined at all. Yet Pincus and the Commissioners spoke as legal authorities expounding a legal opinion. They were simultaneously informing us of the legal meaning of section 72, and asserting that it has none.

Commissioner Andrew Wells spoke of section 72 as a 'code', and sought to emulate 'the approach that a Court should adopt' to 'construing' such a code. Commissioner Richard Blackburn spoke of 'solving this problem of construction'. Yet to give 'misbehaviour' a legal meaning would invite the very kind of **judicial review** that Isaacs and Higgins

thought inappropriate. Any Justice removed from office could appeal to the High Court forthwith, arguing that Parliament (and the Governor-General) had misunderstood or misapplied their legally circumscribed powers.

Commissioner George Lush was prepared to concede the **justiciability** of such an issue. Yet in 1897, the possibility that the phrase 'proved misbehaviour or incapacity' *might* be justiciable was precisely why some delegates resisted it. The 1897 debate had a double purpose: to ensure that no one but Parliament can remove a Justice from office, but also to ensure that Parliament *can*, and that its decision will be final.

Accordingly, any finding of 'proved misbehaviour' must be solely a matter for the Parliament. The constraints are political, not legal. The discussion by the 1986 Commissioners of what might or might not warrant removal was valid as political advice that members of Parliament might accept or reject, not as legal instruction by which Parliament or its members were bound.

All this demonstrates the need for an orderly deliberative procedure by which allegations can be tested. But the Murphy affair and the later speculation over Callinan exposed the absence of any such procedure. The experiments with **jury trial** in the Murphy affair, despite the eventual acquittals, showed only that the criminal trial process offers no solution. The relationship in the USA between the impeachment of judges and their prosecution on criminal charges has been deeply problematic; and the Murphy affair exposed similar problems. A parliamentary finding that 'misbehaviour' was proved beyond a reasonable doubt would so obviously be prejudicial to subsequent criminal proceedings that members of Parliament might be led—for that reason—to avoid such a finding, or to adopt a lesser standard of proof; while conversely, a *prior* acquittal on criminal charges might unduly inhibit a parliamentary finding of misbehaviour, even where that was appropriate. Besides, the attempt in the criminal proceedings to use evidence from the Senate inquiries raised questions of parliamentary privilege (*R v Murphy* (1986)).

The fact that in 1984 two successive Senate Committees were unable to resolve the issues in the Murphy affair is less conclusive, since both Committees were hampered by Murphy's refusal to submit to questioning. But his reasons for this refusal, especially in the case of the first Committee, raised difficult institutional issues, which any future Committee would need to resolve.

First, Murphy insisted that **natural justice** requires that a person accused of misbehaviour should be able to cross-examine witnesses. The fact that Senate standing orders excluded cross-examination may well have been a sufficient answer to this claim as a matter of law, but on more substantive considerations of fairness and probative value Murphy's argument seems clearly correct. The second Senate Committee, however, showed that this problem could be rectified.

Murphy's second argument invoked the **separation of powers**. He did not challenge the basic idea that the legislative branch can procure the removal of Justices; clearly, that is a good example of the checks and balances that a separation of powers makes possible. He argued only that a member of the judicial branch ought not to submit to interrogation by the legislative branch. Yet, as the Clerk of the Senate, Harry Evans, has pointed out, British parliamentary history offers ample precedents for the summoning of judges by the House of Commons; and even if Australia's separation of powers makes those precedents inapplicable, inquiries under section 72 present special problems—since without the testimony of the Justice in question (and perhaps of judicial colleagues), it may be impossible to conduct such an inquiry at all. Murphy's strongest argument was that a Justice cannot be *compelled* to appear. But for Evans, even that is debatable.

Thirdly, and most importantly, Murphy argued that the question whether grounds exist for a Justice's removal from office is entrusted exclusively to Parliament. Consistently with this, it *may* be possible for Parliament (or either House) to seek preliminary advice and guidance from a delegated Committee, or even from an external body so long as it remains firmly under Parliament's control. But any such inquiry must stop short of anything approaching an adjudicative role.

This argument seems clearly correct. While a House may be entitled to seek assistance in preliminary fact-finding processes, those processes cannot pre-empt the responsibilities of the House itself. To delegate the fact-finding task to an external body, such as the 1986 'Parliamentary Commission of Inquiry', involves problems both of principle and of practicality, which the 1986 precedent failed to resolve.

On the other hand, the reference of investigative and advisory tasks to a Committee—so long as the final judgment is reserved for the House itself—appears to fall comfortably within the authority of each House under section 50(i) of the Constitution to determine for itself 'the mode in which its powers … may be exercised'. Moreover, the use of such an internal committee has much to commend it. Whatever the practical difficulties relating to 'proved misbehaviour', it seems easier to deal with them initially in a small committee. Besides, this is likely to be less dramatic (and therefore less damaging) in cases where no misbehaviour is found.

For Evans, the final lesson of the Murphy affair was that in 1897, Downer may have been right: the American impeachment model may deserve further consideration. No doubt, as Evans concedes, its effectiveness in the USA may reflect the greater capacity of American politicians for 'devotion to constitutional principles and a willingness to perform their constitutional duties without allowing their activities to be distorted by partisan considerations'. Given the intensity of Australian politics, impeachment might work less well in Australia. Yet this is also a cause for concern in relation to the existing procedure. In any event, Evans argues that, here as elsewhere:

> The answer to party control … is to seek to lessen its stranglehold over the Parliament rather than to write off the Parliament as an institution because of it. One of the ways of mitigating its influence is to ensure that the Parliament retains its high constitutional responsibilities and is reminded of the need to exercise them properly.

Precisely because the impeachment model casts legislators in an explicitly judicial role, it might help to instil a sobering consciousness of solemn constitutional duty and the need for impartial judgment.

TONY BLACKSHIELD

Further Reading
Tony Blackshield, 'Appointment and Removal of Federal Judges' in Brian Opeskin and Fiona Wheeler (eds), *The Australian Federal Judicial System* (2000) 400
Michael Coper, *Encounters with the Australian Constitution* (1987, popular edn 1988) 132–40
Harry Evans, 'Parliament and the Judges: The Removal of Federal Judges under Section 72 of the Constitution' (1987) 2(2) *Legislative Studies* 17
Anthony Mason, 'The Appointment and Removal of Judges' in Helen Cunningham (ed), *Fragile Bastion: Judicial Independence in the Nineties and Beyond* (1997)
James Thomson, 'Removal of High Court and Federal Judges' (1984) *Australian Current Law* 36033, 36055

Remuneration of Justices. Judicial **independence** rests on two fundamental constitutional guarantees—security of **tenure** and security of remuneration—bolstered by the **separation** of **judicial power**. Section 72(iii) of the Constitution provides that High Court Justices and other federal judges 'shall receive such remuneration as the Parliament may fix; but the remuneration shall not be diminished during their continuance in office'. The Constitution does not guarantee increases in remuneration, but if these depend upon the executive's satisfaction with the Court's work, or are inadequate to attract judges of the highest calibre, both the independence and quality of the Court may be imperilled.

In an extreme case, a decline in the real value of judicial remuneration could conceivably contravene section 72(iii), as **Gleeson** suggested (while Chief Justice of NSW) in 1988. Such a claim, based upon a 36 per cent decline in the purchasing power of judicial salaries, was rejected in the USA in 1977, but the court suggested that a claim might succeed were Congress to discriminate against the judiciary in failing to respond to hyperinflation (*Atkins v US* (1977)). The imposition upon serving Justices of a non-discriminatory tax not levied specifically upon judicial remuneration would probably not contravene section 72(iii) (*Cooper v Commissioner of Income Tax (Qld)* (1907)). A similar view was taken by the **United States Supreme Court** in May 2001 (*US v Hatter*). Taxes levied specifically upon judicial remuneration, including pensions, run a greater risk of contravening section 72(iii); serving federal judges were exempted from the Commonwealth's superannuation contributions surcharge in 1997.

Remuneration of High Court Justices falls naturally into three periods. Between the Court's **establishment** in 1903 and 1947, the annual salary of a **puisne Justice** was £3000 ($6000) and that of the **Chief Justice** £3500 ($7000)—the same as that of the Chief Justice of NSW. Puisne judges of the NSW Supreme Court received £2600. Although considerably less than the salary of an English High Court judge (£5000), the remuneration of High Court Justices was handsome. In 1907, it was five times that of Commonwealth members of Parliament and 27 times the basic wage.

In addition to salary, section 47 of the *Judiciary Act* 1903 (Cth) authorised payment to each Justice of 'such sums as are considered reasonable by the Governor-General' for travelling expenses 'to discharge the duties of [the Justice's] office'. In 1905, the foundation Justices resisted **Attorney-General** Josiah Symon's attempts to reduce their travelling expenses and persuade them to abandon the **circuit system** (see **Strike of 1905**). The dispute was resolved to the Justices' satisfaction when Symon was succeeded by **Isaacs**. During the **Depression**, Parliament enacted legislation to reduce the salary of Commonwealth office-holders and public servants (the *Financial Emergency Act* 1931 (Cth)). The Act could not apply to federal judges because of section 72 of the Constitution, but **Prime Minister** James Scullin wrote to federal judges requesting them to accept a reduced salary. The High Court Justices declined on the ground that 'no encroachment should be allowed upon the independence of the judicial office and the immunity of its emoluments from reduction'. Nevertheless, in letters of 10 August 1931, all Justices accepted reductions: **Rich**, **Dixon**, and **McTiernan** by repaying 25 per cent of their annual salary, and **Gavan Duffy**, **Starke** and **Evatt** by forgoing travelling expenses ranging from £445 to £886. The voluntary reduction ended in 1935.

The second period runs from 1947, when the Justices' salaries were increased by £1000, to 1973. Notwithstanding these increases, judicial remuneration had declined by half in relative terms: after the 1947 rise, the salary of a High Court puisne Justice was two and a half times that of a Commonwealth member of Parliament and 14 times the basic wage. During this period, Parliament periodically amended the Judiciary Act by increasing judicial salaries to keep up with increasing wages and prices. On at least two occasions, the salary of a High Court Justice fell below that of some **state Supreme Court** judges—a situation Prime Minister Robert **Menzies** condemned as 'absurd' and Attorney-General **Barwick** as 'intolerable', although the salary of the Chief Justice of NSW had exceeded that of a High Court puisne Justice from 1903 to 1947. A major increase occurred in 1955, after **Dixon** became Chief Justice, with the Chief Justice's salary rising by 60 per cent and a puisne Justice's by 44 per cent. Parliamentary determination of judicial remuneration proved unsatisfactory because it was *ad hoc* and potentially impinged on judicial independence; in addition, Parliament inevitably faced political and trade union pressure to limit increases. Hence, Parliament delegated the task to an independent body, the Remuneration Tribunal, in 1973, ushering in the present period. The Tribunal also determines the remuneration of Commonwealth public officers and Commonwealth parliamentary and ministerial allowances.

The Remuneration Tribunal comprises three part-time members appointed for a five-year (renewable) term by the Governor-General, by whom they are removable for 'misbehaviour or physical or mental incapacity'. Its first two chairmen (1974–92) were state Supreme Court judges. Section 12 of the *High Court of Australia Act* 1979 (Cth) provides that the Justices shall receive such salary and annual and travelling allowances as Parliament fixes, salary and annual allowance being payable monthly. Pursuant to the *Remuneration Tribunal Act* 1973 (Cth), the Remuneration Tribunal's determinations come into effect subject to disallowance by either House of the Commonwealth Parliament. Remuneration Tribunal determinations can also be set aside by statute, as occurred in 1990 (*Remuneration and Allowances Act* 1990 (Cth)). The High Court has declined to make submissions to the Tribunal.

The Remuneration Tribunal operated reasonably satisfactorily until the mid-1980s. However, the High Court clashed with the government over remuneration on three occasions between 1988 and 1991. In November 1988, the Remuneration Tribunal recommended increases of more than 80 per cent in High Court salaries. Although statutorily bound to take account of then current industrial principles of wage restraint, the Tribunal reasoned that the increasing frequency of lengthy trials, greater complexity of commercial litigation, increasing use of case management and computers, and **cross-vesting** legislation had so 'fundamentally changed' the functions of federal judges that they were 'not relevantly comparable with the pre-existing offices'. It therefore recommended substantial increases for **Federal Court** judges, with consequential increases for High Court Justices. The government's submission to the Tribunal, noting difficulty in attracting senior barristers to the Bench, and its decision to increase the salaries of chief executives of government business enterprises to private sector levels, appear to have led the Tribunal to believe that the government favoured a substantial increase in judicial remuneration. However, this proved incorrect. The Tribunal's recommendation was condemned in the **media** and the government's wages accord with the trade unions appeared threatened. The government rejected the Tribunal's recommendation, instead granting increases of some 26 per cent, following a second recommendation by members of the Tribunal acting in their individual capacities. Chief Justice **Mason** expressed lack of confidence in 'the present procedures for determining judicial remuneration', remarking that the issue had become a 'political football'.

The government again rejected the Tribunal's determination in 1990, although the Tribunal had essentially adopted the government's own submission. A dispute was narrowly averted the following year when the Tribunal rejected the government's proposal to award a substantial 'displacement allowance' to the Commonwealth **Solicitor-General** and Chairman of the National Crime Authority, which would have given them a salary exceeding that of the Chief Justice of the High Court—traditionally the highest paid Commonwealth public officer. In a strongly worded letter to the Tribunal, Mason (with 'the unqualified concurrence' of the entire Court) condemned what he perceived as a deliberate governmental policy of 'downgrading the Commonwealth Judiciary'. He considered the procedures for determining judicial remuneration 'manifestly unsatisfactory'; remuneration and conditions of service had been so eroded that there was a 'distinct possibility, if not a likelihood, that the quality of the Federal Judiciary will be impaired'. In October 2000, High Court base salaries were $276 800 for the Chief Justice and $251 200 for puisne Justices.

The Judiciary Bill 1902 (Cth) would have provided a pension for High Court Justices (70 per cent of salary after 15 years service and attaining the age of 65 years), but the provision was deleted from the eventual Judiciary Act 1903 (Cth) for reasons of economy. Legislation was enacted in 1918 to grant Chief Justice **Griffith** the pension he would have received had he remained Chief Justice of Queensland (*Chief Justice's Pension Act* 1918 (Cth)), but High Court Justices received no pension until 1926, when a non-contributory pension of 50 per cent of salary after 15 years of service was introduced, with provision for a smaller pension for Justices retiring on account of disability or infirmity after five years service (*Judiciary Act* 1926 (Cth)). In introducing the Bill, Attorney-General **Latham** noted that the value of High Court salaries had declined by almost half since 1903, that the Justices were the only Commonwealth public officers without pensions, that judges in four states received pensions, and that 'when judges are appointed with a life tenure [as federal judges were until 1977], pensions are essential to efficiency'. The *Judges' Pensions Act* 1948 (Cth) varied entitlement to 27.5 per cent after 10 years service and attainment of the age of 60 years, with annual increases of 2.5 per cent, to a maximum of 40 per cent after 15 years service. This was liberalised to 50 per cent after 10 years service in 1958, and further to 60 per cent in 1973—the present entitlement. Provision is also made for surviving spouses. Since no pension is payable to those failing to qualify (unless the Attorney-General certifies that **retirement** was due to permanent disability or infirmity), there is a strong incentive for Justices to serve until the age of 60.

GEORGE WINTERTON

Further Reading
George Winterton, *Judicial Remuneration in Australia* (1995)

Reporting of decisions. The beginning of Australian law reports, before federation, has been traced by Professor Alex Castles. The reporters—practising barristers—attended court and took notes from which to write up **argument**, decisions, and often, for newspapers, evidence. Many lawyers were then proficient shorthand writers. Chief Justice James Dowling of NSW (1837–44) had begun as a typical English barrister–reporter (*Dowling & Ryland's Reports*). In the colony, as judge, he noted, and transcribed longhand, most significant Supreme Court cases: excerpts from his 237 notebooks have now been published electronically (see: www.law.mq.edu.au/scnsw/). Judicial notebooks and diaries, in 'Taylor's shorthand', by his successor, Chief Justice Alfred Stephen, still survive.

All Australian nineteenth-century law reports were products of private publishers or newspaper proprietors, whose requirements did not always correspond. PA Jacobs, of the Victorian Bar, was irritated at having to write 'news value' reports for the *Argus* newspaper: the companion *Argus Law Reports*, begun in 1895, were for lawyers' eyes. He described, thus, the method that would prevail in the High Court from its opening in 1903, the reporter necessarily being in court:

> After listening to **counsel's** argument, [the reporter] can generally, with such knowledge of the law as he has, tell whether the case is reportable. If in doubt, he takes a note and decides later whether to make a report. To complete his report … he gives a short summary of the relevant facts, and sometimes of counsel's argument … The judgments have to be faithfully and diligently reproduced.

The *Commonwealth Law Reports* (CLR) began, effectively from 1903, as the High Court's authorised reports, the Attorney-General's Department advising the private publishers that 'the **Chief Justice** has expressed his willingness, and that

of the other Justices, to revise the proofs of the reports, and to give any other assistance'. For decades, the Justices personally reviewed long galley proofs pulled from metallic type.

The amount of detail in earlier High Court **judges' notebooks**, and a few surviving **transcripts**, suggest that official shorthand reporting did not commence until about 1920. The introduction of official transcripts made legal reporters' tasks easier, obviating the need for court attendance. In 1939, experimental recording of NZ court proceedings by 'a dictaphone-telecord system' was noted in Australia with scepticism. Protests at overwork by the High Court manual reporting staff, from 1942, went unrecognised until, a decade later, electronic reporting was introduced at the Court's Sydney and Melbourne premises. Advanced systems were installed in the **Canberra** building, opened in 1980.

Paradoxically, until 1974 the CLRs eschewed federation's unifying influence by having separate state reporters, albeit directed by an editor and, occasionally, an assistant editor. The editors of those reports (to 2000) were: JC Anderson (1903–14); AH Hayball (1914–34); EF Healy (1933–41); Bernard Sugerman KC (1941–44); BP Macfarlan QC (1945–57); RA Howell (1958–69); and JD Merralls QC (1969–). The particular contribution of the Victorian barrister JD Merralls was recognised by Chief Justice **Mason** in a foreword to 180 CLR. Reporters to the series have invariably been barristers, many destined for the Bench. Editorial policy, throughout the history of these reports, has corresponded with the statement by Lord MacKinnon of the English Court of Appeal in *O'Grady v Saper* (1940), that 'a decided case is only worthy of report if it decides some principle of law'. Interlocutory matters, special **leave** applications, decisions on spent legislation, and matters going to quantum or to discretionary considerations are generally not reported in the CLRs. Distilling principle from judgments that have become lengthy, complicated, and often far from unanimous in reasoning, even if reaching a common conclusion, has increasingly taxed the reporter's skill and ingenuity.

The CLRs are published in arrears in the interests of accuracy and to allow the reported arguments to be condensed, though with a consistent flow only twice seriously interrupted. In 1941, there was a contretemps because the publisher, finding subscriptions in decline during **World War II**, proposed that the editor, EF Healy of the Victorian Bar, accept a reduced salary. He declined, relying on his interpretation of the relevant contract, and, on being dismissed, sued the publisher unsuccessfully in the Victorian County Court. His appeals to the Full Supreme Court and to the High Court (*Healy's Case* (1942)) were equally unavailing. Thereafter, the editorship moved to Sydney for nearly 30 years. In the 1970s, a different problem arose from the unwillingness of the printers, whose association with the series had been continuous from 1903, to adapt to more modern printing technology. Publication fell far behind, and there were three changes of printer over a short span. A noteworthy contribution was made by RA Sundberg QC (later a judge of the **Federal Court**) as a principal reporter in overtaking delays flowing from those difficulties.

Other sources for High Court decisions include the *Australian Law Reports* and the *Australian Law Journal Reports*: various 'advance' prints have diminished since the High

Court's publication of judgments in pamphlet and electronic form on delivery. Competition between private publishers to provide reports online has become fierce, and the Court itself has become the principal competitor, providing a similar but immediate service with catchwords and headnotes supplied. From the 1990s, the Court also adopted a policy of identifying each case by a neutral **citation** (one not beholden to any publisher), and incorporating numbered paragraphs. That procedure, with the provision of catchwords and headnotes, has been followed in most subordinate courts. As attempts by lower courts to act as their own reporters have not always been felicitous, it may fairly be assumed that the day of the traditional law reporter is not yet spent.

JM BENNETT

Further Reading
JM Bennett, *Keystone of the Federal Arch* (1980) 111, 113
Alex Castles, *An Australian Legal History* (1982)
Alex Castles, *Annotated Bibliography of Printed Materials on Australian Law* (1994)
'Court Reporting' (1939) 12 *ALJ* 369
JC Fox, *A Handbook of English Law Reports* (1913)
PA Jacobs, *A Lawyer Tells* (1949)
Bruce Kercher, 'Publication of Forgotten Case Law of the NSW Supreme Court' (1998) 72 *ALJ* 876

Representative government implies the transmission of the people's authority to elected representatives from among whom the government is formed. Periodic elections make for both the establishment and authorisation of governments, and their chastening through the threat of rejection at the polls. Since these procedures merely facilitate the formation and dissolution of governments, representative government as a democratic mechanism cannot be viewed in isolation from **responsible government**, which signifies the ongoing relationship between the government and the governed. Nevertheless, representative government can accommodate a system of supplementary representation including pressures applied to governments by lobbies and pressure groups, through which aspects of the will of constituents can be expressed.

Modern forms of **democracy** are sometimes distinguished from the 'direct democracy' evolved by ancient Athens through reference to representative systems. Athenian democracy was characterised by the competence of all (adult, male) citizens to vote in assembly on all matters, and to share directly in the **sovereignty** of the state. This system is said to be unrepeatable, largely because of the scale of the modern state, where an assembly of all citizens is held to be impracticable—although James Madison distanced representation from democracy, insisting that it had the capacity to 'refine and enlarge the public views' through the superior wisdom and commitment of chosen representatives.

Representation theory has to contend with the objections of Rousseau, who claimed that the transmission of the will of the people to representatives was an impossibility, and that as a democratic instrument, representation was a sham. The attempt to actualise direct democracy through representation is indeed vain, since such devices as proportional representation and multi-party systems resulting in 'assembly government' are arguably less effective in fixing responsibility than the two-party model typical of the English-speaking world. Viewing representation as a vehicle of popular consent may also encumber it with too heavy a load, and attempts to think of a 'pure' democracy should perhaps be discarded in favour of a frank recognition of the reality of government needing to be kept under watch. Some modern theorists would not wish us to return to direct democracy because of its inability to fix responsibility in any meaningful sense beyond placing it on an entire people. Representative government, in this view, has the advantage both of having a party to blame for failures in government and of nurturing an alternative government available for the smooth transfer of power. The representative system makes for effective surveillance of the government by the people, and places in their hands the means of punishing an incompetent or unpopular government. Besides these practical advantages, representation powerfully symbolises the subordination of the government to the governed, implying the chastening of power.

In the course of **constitutional interpretation**, the High Court has expressed pronounced views on the nature of representative government. While under the **separation of powers** it determines the constitutionality of legislation brought before it, the Court has been able to reconcile that function with deference to the **policy** judgments made by elected representatives on the basis that, provided a law does fall within an allocated area of power, a parliament may make any law within that area that it likes. The Court is not concerned with the 'justice, wisdom, morality and propriety of legislation' (*Burton v Honan* (1952)). By contrast, the majority in *Australian Capital Television v Commonwealth* (1992) did purport to sit in judgment on the policy choices made by the Parliament (see *Free Speech Cases*; **Political communication**). Even while the majority opinions claimed to be refining and protecting the mechanisms of representative government, they risked undermining the 'supremacy of Parliament' usually embraced by this term. The *Political Broadcasts and Political Disclosures Act* 1991 (Cth) had banned paid political advertisements on television and radio during election periods, but had left television reporting, editorial commentary, talk-back programs, and the other news media untouched. Chief Justice **Mason** declared: 'Freedom of communication, at least in relation to public affairs and political discussion, is so indispensable to the efficacy of the system of representative government for which the Constitution makes provision that it is necessarily implied in the making of that provision.' **McHugh** reasoned that citizens 'must have access to the information, ideas and arguments which are necessary to make an informed judgment'.

This ruling, in the writer's view, compromised the responsibility of Parliament to enhance the conditions of a democratic society. In his **dissenting judgment**, **Dawson** noted that the Constitution had not originally provided for universal suffrage—a building block of democracy that was established by Parliament itself. He rightly noted that the **framers of the Constitution** 'preferred to place their trust in Parliament to preserve the nature of our society and regarded as undemocratic guarantees which fettered its powers'. The government argued that it was its responsibility to protect political parties from the financial drain of endless expensive advertising and to protect the public from the undue influence of the rich.

The Parliament also had a duty to regulate the standards of public broadcasting—and, arguably, to shield the public from political bombardment. The Court's removal of this responsibility was perhaps a diminution, rather than an expansion, of the effectiveness of representative government.

GRAHAM MADDOX

Further Reading

Graham Maddox, *Australian Democracy in Theory and Practice* (4th edn 2000)

Bernard Manin, *The Principles of Representative Government* (1997)

Research assistance. The level of research assistance required by, and available to, the Justices of the Court has fluctuated over the Court's lifetime, most notably over the last 25 years.

Before the Court's move to **Canberra**, Justices either undertook their own research or delegated research tasks to their **associates**. The years 1976–79 stand as an exception, however, as during this period a legally qualified researcher was employed to assist the Justices. The Sydney-based appointment was initiated by **Barwick**. It was in this context that the first comparative research on other **common law** jurisdictions was carried out for a judgment (*Grant v Downs* (1976)). This research position was abolished when, in 1979, the Court upgraded the position of Court Librarian to one requiring legal qualifications.

Once the Court had established itself in Canberra, the need for greater research assistance again became a pressing concern. In 1982, on the recommendation of the Court's Library Committee (chaired by **Mason**), the Court appointed a full-time legal research officer to the Library. The Justices believed that the Court would benefit from the cross-fertilisation of the research officer's legal knowledge with the librarians' legal bibliographical knowledge. Increasing demand for research assistance led to the creation of a second research officer position in 1987.

At the time of the Court's move to Canberra, the personal staff of each Justice comprised a secretary, an associate, and a **tipstaff**. In response to growing workloads, several Justices elected (from 1987) to combine the associate and tipstaff roles, each recruiting two legally qualified people to fill this dual position. One effect of the restructuring has been an increase in the capacity for legal research within **chambers**.

During the period of the **Mason Court**, research officers worked on some complex constitutional matters, and for a short period prepared preliminary reports on cases listed to be heard. Many of the most notable judgments delivered during that time display strong historical, philosophical, or comparative emphases—in part, a reflection of the Justices' improved access to and ready utilisation of research assistance over that period. With the **retirement** of Mason and later **Brennan**, the research emphasis shifted from in-depth, case-related work to a wider variety of case research, speech drafting, and production of in-house publications to keep the Court informed of relevant legal developments. Further changes to the Bench coincided with **budget** cuts and an increasing emphasis on speedy delivery of judgments. Thus the second research position was left unfilled in 1999, and the savings were used to employ an additional **judgment production** officer.

Research officers work at the direction of the Justices and in collaboration with the Justices' associates, often being assigned the more substantial research tasks that Justices' associates would not have time to complete. Some Justices rely heavily on the library-based researchers, while others only rarely use them. Court research sometimes involves exploring the philosophical background to a particular issue, or investigating the historical origins of a principle of law. Comparative legal research is frequently required. Research officers have been asked to research such matters as the meaning and effect of a constitutional provision, the origin of the doctrine of fitness to plead, the principle of **proportionality** in the European Union, and non-delegable duties of care.

In addition to this assistance with specific tasks, Justices also benefit from ongoing research assistance of a more general nature. Research officers monitor legal developments in Australian and other jurisdictions, drawing to the attention of the Justices any notable decisions or other material of particular interest. This involves reading **transcripts** and reviewing all new journals received, as well as law reports from other common law appellate jurisdictions and parliamentary *Hansard*. For research on recent cases, research staff use Internet databases (see **Information technology**). This general research assistance is important to the Justices, as it ensures they are aware of new developments that may assist them in their judgment writing.

AMELIA SIMPSON

Reserved judgments. The opinions or reasons for the judgments, decrees, **orders**, and sentences of the High Court are commonly described as judgments (though formally, a judgment is merely the order of the Court determining the rights of the parties). Where reasons are not given in an *ex tempore* judgment, they are published in pamphlet form in **open court** on a date of which the parties and the public are given prior notice.

It is a convention of appellate courts, including the High Court, that if any participating Justice wishes to consider his or her reasons, the Court must reserve its decision. If there is a clear majority, the Court may proceed to pronounce its orders immediately. It will commonly do this if the orders will result in the provision of urgent relief such as release of a prisoner whose conviction and sentence is quashed or (if a new trial is ordered) to apply for bail; or where an order affects the status of a party or other pending litigation. Where there is a difference among the Justices immediately following the **argument** of an appeal or application, it is usual, but not invariable, to delay pronouncing orders until all reasons have been prepared and circulated, in case the reasons of one Justice might occasion a change of mind of others.

In the High Court, most decisions are reserved. Once reserved, the case 'stands for judgment'. The interval that follows is commonly described in the law reports as 'CAV' or '*cur adv vult*'. This is an abbreviation for the Latin *curia advisari vult*, signifying that the Court wishes to consider its decision. The length of time a decision stands reserved will depend upon a number of factors, including the number of participating Justices; the differences of view that emerge in the draft reasons; and discussions between the Justices designed to explore concurrence in draft reasons, or common holdings in separate reasons, or agreed orders for the Court. The delay can be as short as a day or as long as a year. The typical interval is approximately six months. It has become shorter in recent years. Details of the intervals between the hearing and the delivery of judgments are published in the **Annual Report** of the High Court, which must be tabled in federal Parliament.

It is normal practice in the Court for draft reasons, once prepared, to be circulated to all Justices who participated in the hearing of the proceeding, with a copy to the Chief Justice's **chambers** whether the Chief Justice participated or not. These arrangements have not always been observed. In the 1930s, **Starke's** personal relationships with all of the Justices except **Dixon** broke down so badly that he declined to exchange his draft judgments with them. He confined communication with them off the Bench to brief notes, usually curt and often offensive (see **Conferences; Personal relations**).

High security is attached to the draft judgments of the Justices before they are published. It is the duty of the Justices' **associates**, in cooperation with Court staff, to help in the preparation of pamphlets of reserved judgments for distribution (see **Judgment production**). Within minutes of the announcement of the order of the Court and publication of the reasons in Court, those reasons are available on the Internet (see **Information technology**). Before delivery, the Justices sign their opinions, the original copy being deposited in the Court's Registry as the authentic record of the reasons for disposing of the proceedings in terms of the Court's orders.

Virtually all reserved judgments of the High Court are **reported** in law reports available to the public and the **legal profession**. The more important judgments are selected for publication in the authorised reports of the Court, the *Commonwealth Law Reports*. Those reports have contained the reasons of the Justices from the **establishment** of the Court in October 1903.

MICHAEL KIRBY

Reserved state powers. The reserved state powers doctrine, as applied in early High Court cases, required the Constitution to be read as impliedly reserving certain areas of legislative power to the states. In consequence, some heads of **Commonwealth legislative power** were given a narrow construction to avoid encroachment on the reserved area of state power. The reserved state powers doctrine (or the doctrine of implied prohibitions, as it was sometimes called) was **overruled** in 1920 in the *Engineers Case*. The doctrine in its original form has not received any formal judicial support in the High Court since that time.

The concept of reserved state powers was particularly important in the interpretation of Commonwealth power over **trade and commerce** (section 51(i)), **taxation** (section 51(ii)), **trade marks** (section 51(xviii)), and **corporations** (section 51(xx)); it also influenced the meaning given to 'duties of excise' in section 90 of the Constitution. The crucial formative cases were *Peterswald v Bartley* (1904) (on section 90), *R v Barger* (1908) (on section 51(ii)), the *Union Label Case* (1908) (on section 51(xviii) with *obiter dicta* on section 51(i)), and *Huddart Parker v Moorehead* (1909) (on section 51(xx), with dicta on section 51(i)).

Peterswald v Bartley adopted a narrow meaning of excise duty in section 90, in part because the Court considered that a broader meaning would have reduced state power over internal state affairs perceived to be beyond Commonwealth power. The judgment asserted that 'the Constitution contains no provisions for enabling the Commonwealth Parliament to interfere with the private or internal affairs of the States, or to restrict the power of the State to regulate the carrying on of any businesses or trades within their boundaries, or even, if they think fit, to prohibit them altogether'. In other words, the perspective went beyond treating the federal context as merely a general interpretive factor, and indicated a preference for a restrictive interpretation of Commonwealth legislative powers.

In 1908, *R v Barger* decided that the *Excise Tariff Act* 1906 (Cth) was not in substance a law with respect to taxation. The law imposed an excise tariff on the manufacture of agricultural implements, but created an exemption for manufacturers engaging labour under prescribed conditions. The majority (**Griffith, Barton**, and **O'Connor; Isaacs** and **Higgins** dissenting) inferred from the general federal scheme of the Constitution (which they compared with the US constitutional scheme) an intention to reserve state powers. They found that intention expressed in section 107, and they described the Tenth Amendment of the US Constitution (which actually speaks of 'powers … reserved to the States') as a 'corresponding provision'. More specifically, the taxation power, on which the Excise Tariff Act relied, was said to be 'intended to be something entirely distinct from a power to directly regulate the domestic affairs of the States, which was denied to the Parliament'. The majority judgment lists paragraphs (xii), (xiii), (xv), (xvi), (xvii), and (xx) of section 51 as examples of paragraphs in which the express words indicate an intention to authorise power over the domestic affairs of the states. This curious list demonstrates the elusive character of the reserved state powers doctrine. The **dissenting judgments** of Isaacs and Higgins in *Barger* contain powerful attacks on the foundation logic of the doctrine.

During the arguments of **counsel** in *Barger*, Griffith made comments linking the idea of reserved powers specifically with the interpretation of section 51(i). The link was developed in *Union Label*, a decision on the meaning of trade marks in section 51(xviii). Once again, in the context of a choice between a narrow and a wide meaning of Commonwealth power, the narrow meaning was preferred, in part on the basis of the reserved state powers doctrine. Griffith reasoned that the express grant of power in section 51(i) over interstate and overseas trade and commerce indicated an intention to deny power to the Commonwealth over intrastate trade and commerce. He cited dicta about the US commerce clause in *US v De Witt* (1869) in support. It followed, Griffith argued, that 'the power to legislate as to internal trade and commerce is reserved to the State' by section 107. A narrow reading of 'trade marks' for section 51(xviii) purposes accorded with this implied intention about state powers over trade. An exception to the reservation of state power over trade within a state would be allowed, in the language of *US v De Witt*, 'as a necessary and proper means for carrying into execution some other power expressly granted'. Griffith considered that an exception could be made only if there were 'clear and unequivocal words'—a requirement not met by the power over trade marks. Barton and O'Connor delivered **concurring judgments**. Isaacs and Higgins dissented.

Huddart Parker held that the corporations power did not authorise Commonwealth laws over the intrastate trading activities of section 51(xx) corporations. The reserved powers interpretation of section 51(i), as developed in *Union Label* (especially by Griffith), with its consequential effect on section 51(xx), was central to the majority reasoning of Griffith, Barton, and O'Connor. Section 51(xx), like section 51(xviii), was not within the exception to the operation of the doctrine. Higgins, also in the majority, did not rely on reserved powers reasoning, while Isaacs dissented. Of all the early cases involving the reserved state powers doctrine, *Huddart Parker* had the most crippling effect on Commonwealth legislative power.

The *Engineers Case* overruled the reserved state powers doctrine with the blunt statement that 'it is a fundamental and fatal error to read sec 107 as reserving any power from the Commonwealth that falls fairly within the explicit terms of an express grant in sec 51, as that grant is reasonably construed, unless that reservation is as explicitly stated'. The effect and significance of *Engineers* in this regard was encapsulated by **Barwick** in *Strickland v Rocla Concrete Pipes* (1971):

> Section 107 of the Constitution so far from reserving anything to the States leaves them the then residue of power after full effect is given to the powers granted to the Commonwealth: and then subject to s 109. Section 51(i) contains no explicit or implicit prohibition and does not reserve the subject of intra-State trade to the States. It can thus be seen that the earlier doctrine virtually reversed the Constitution. The question in relation to the validity of a Commonwealth Act is whether it fairly falls within the scope of the subject matter granted to the Commonwealth by the Constitution. That subject matter will be determined by construing the words of the Constitution by which legislative power is given to the Commonwealth irrespective of what effect the construction may have upon the residue of power which the States may enjoy.

While cases after *Engineers* have not contemplated a revival of a fully fledged version of the reserved state powers doctrine, there is an ongoing debate about whether elements of the doctrine, or something akin to it, feature in **constitutional interpretation**. For example, **Murphy** in *A-G (WA); Ex rel Ansett Transport Industries v Australian National Airlines* (1976) considered that the orthodox interpretation of the scope of incidental power in relation to section 51(i) has kept the 'pre-*Engineers* ghosts walking'. The unsuccessful attempt by a minority of Justices to limit the **external affairs power** by reference to a notion of 'federal balance' also gives rise to this debate, as the comments on 'federal balance' in *Koowarta's Case* (1982) demonstrate.

Much of the reasoning on the reserved state powers doctrine in the foundation judgments seems loose and question-begging. However, whatever the deficiencies in logic and style in those judgments, there is much to be said for the view that ultimately the significant difference between *Engineers* and the earlier cases is, as Geoffrey Sawer has commented, a difference in 'political judgment about the nature of the Constitution'.

The wording of the Constitution permits both the reserved state powers doctrine and the contrary view adopted in *Engineers*. And it permits variations on those views. It may well permit understandings of the **Commonwealth–state** division of power not yet explored in the case law.

Keven Booker

Further Reading
Michael Coper and George Williams (eds), *How Many Cheers for Engineers?* (1997)
RD Lumb, 'Problems of Characterization of Federal Powers in the High Court' (1982) *Australian Current Law Digest* 45
Geoffrey Sawer, *Australian Federalism in the Courts* (1967)
Leslie Zines, *The High Court and the Constitution* (4th edn 1997) ch 1

Responsible government. The political doctrine of responsible government was developed in England in the eighteenth and nineteenth centuries to explain and justify the political changes that were then occurring. These changes included the increasing political importance and power of the House of Commons, the requirement that the monarch act only upon the advice of his or her ministers, the requirement that ministers be members of parliament, the development of the Cabinet, and the creation of a professional and impartial public service.

In accordance with the doctrine, the collective ministry must have the support of the popular (usually the lower) house of parliament, which is in turn responsible to the people. The ministry is required to take collective responsibility for the acts of the Crown. On the other hand, the Crown can only act upon the advice of a minister or the ministry. Another aspect of the doctrine is that individual ministers are accountable to the houses of parliament for the actions of the administration for which they are responsible. As **Mason** put it in *FAI Insurances v Winneke* (1982), 'ministerial responsibility means (1) the individual responsibility of Ministers to Parliament for the administration of their departments, and (2) the collective responsibility of Cabinet to Parliament (and the public) for the whole conduct of the administration'.

The doctrine, although not directly judicially enforceable, has been used and applied by the High Court as a fundamental assumption to be applied in **constitutional interpretation**, and more generally in the development of the **common law**.

The Australian Constitution assumes the existence—at least at the Commonwealth level—of a system of responsible government (see especially the *Engineers Case* (1920)). In *Lange v ABC* (1997), the Court identified sections 6, 49, 62, 64, and 83 of the Constitution as sections that assume or provide for responsible government. However, it is probably more correct to say, as did Isaacs in the *Skin Wool Case*, that responsible government is 'part of the fabric on which the written words of the Constitution are superimposed'—or, as the majority said in the *Boilermakers Case* (1956), that responsible government 'is a central feature of the Australian constitutional system'.

The doctrine has had two significant effects in the interpretation by the High Court of the Constitution. The first is in limiting the extent to which the Court has been prepared to rely upon decisions of the **United States Supreme Court** when interpreting the Constitution. This has been most obviously true in relation to the **separation of powers** doctrine as it applies to the relationship between the legislature and the executive (see *Victorian Stevedoring & General Contracting Co v Meakes and Dignan* (1931); *Boilermakers Case*). However, as the *Engineers Case* shows, the doctrine may also limit the relevance of US authorities in other contexts, such as whether the doctrine of **reserved state powers** should be incorporated into the Constitution.

The second effect in constitutional interpretation is as a source, together with the associated concept of **representative government**, of **implied constitutional rights**, particularly in the *Free Speech Cases* (1992). As the Court stated in *Lange*, 'those provisions which prescribe the system of responsible government necessarily imply a limitation on legislative and executive power to deny the electors and their [parliamentary] representatives information concerning the conduct of the executive branch of government'.

The Court has also applied the doctrine more generally as an anterior assumption both to the common law and to statutes. In this context, the doctrine has not been limited to the Commonwealth, but has applied to the states and the **territories**. For example, in *FAI Insurances*, several members of the Court referred to the doctrine in their analyses of whether the Victorian Governor in Council was amenable to **judicial review**. In *Commonwealth v Northern Land Council* (1993), the members of the Court referred to the principle of collective responsibility when determining the extent of public interest immunity for Commonwealth Cabinet documents. And in *Egan v Willis* (1998), the Court referred to and relied upon the doctrine in determining the extent to which the Legislative Council of NSW had the power to suspend a member who was a minister of the Crown for failing to produce documents that the Council had ordered to be produced.

The doctrine is based, in large part, upon historical practice and political convention (see **Dismissal of 1975**); when the Court has referred to the doctrine, it has usually acknowledged this, and has therefore recognised that the doctrine is capable of development and change. For example, in *Egan*, three Justices commented: 'It should not be assumed that the characteristics of a system of responsible government are fixed or that the principles of ministerial responsibility which developed in New South Wales after 1855 necessarily reflected closely those from time to time accepted at Westminster.' However, notwithstanding those comments, the Court has invariably analysed the doctrine in terms of political principle and theory, rather than factual historical practice. *Egan* is an example.

BRADLEY SELWAY

Further Reading
Rodney Brazier, *Ministers of the Crown* (1997)
Paul Finn, *Law and Government in Colonial Australia* (1987)
Geoffrey Lindell, 'Responsible Government', in Paul Finn (ed), *Essays on Law and Government: Principles and Values* (1995)
John Mackintosh, *The British Cabinet* (3rd edn 1977)
Henry Parris, *Constitutional Bureaucracy* (1969)
Diana Woodhouse, *Ministers and Parliament: Accountability in Theory and Practice* (1994)

Restitution. In a range of anomalous situations that did not fit neatly into the doctrinal categories of **contract** and **tort**, the **common law** allowed a plaintiff to be paid for benefits derived by the defendant at the plaintiff's expense. Traditionally, these cases were referred to as 'quasi-contract', because typically (though often artificially) the success of the claim depended on the willingness of the court to find an implied contract that the defendant would restore the benefit to the plaintiff. The notion of quasi-contract was reinforced by analogy with older forms of action (predating the development of contract law) in which a plaintiff sued simply on a debt. These were the common money counts, which asserted, for example, that money was owing to the plaintiff for: goods sold; money lent; money paid at the defendant's request; money had and received by the defendant to the plaintiff's use; or work and labour done by the plaintiff at the defendant's request. In most of these cases, it was reasonably easy to assume that the defendant had impliedly promised to pay. In cases of quasi-contract, however, the courts' willingness to imply a contract was a thinly veiled way of giving effect to judicial perceptions that the plaintiff *ought* to be reimbursed.

More recently, the rationale for such claims has depended on a more open recognition that the defendant should not be unjustly enriched at the plaintiff's expense. In Australia, the breakthrough came in *Pavey & Matthews v Paul* (1987), when a majority of the **Mason Court** rejected implied contract as the basis of the common money counts and as the explanation for 'quasi-contract'. **Deane** explained that unjust enrichment was a 'unifying legal concept which explains why the law recognizes, in a variety of distinct categories of case, an obligation on the part of a defendant to make fair and just restitution for a benefit derived at the expense of a plaintiff'. Prospectively, the unjust enrichment concept offered a framework for recognising new types of claim and 'defences' to claims. The obsolete English system of common law pleading preserved by Edward Bullen and Stephen Leake in their *Precedents of Pleadings in Personal Actions* (3rd edn 1868) ceased to be a primary point of reference, and the door was opened to the encyclopedia of the American *Restatement of Restitution*, to the pioneering work of Robert Goff and Gareth Jones, *The Law of Restitution* (5th edn 1998), and to other writings on restitution by scholars such as Peter Birks, Jack Beatson, Andrew Burrows, and George Palmer.

Before *Pavey*, the High Court had generally followed the lead of the English courts in this area. Early *obiter dicta* had echoed Lord Mansfield's explanation in terms of **natural justice** and **equity** (**Barton** in *Campbell v Kitchen & Sons* (1910); **Isaacs** in *Sargood Bros v Commonwealth* (1910); **Griffith** in *R v Brown* (1912)). But in the mid-twentieth century, the Court followed Lord Sumner in *Sinclair v Brougham* (1914), treating the notion of implied contract as determinative (see *Smith v William Charlick* (1924); *Turner v Bladin* (1951)). Nevertheless, unjust enrichment was occasionally adverted to as the basis of recovery (*Phillips v Ellinson Bros* (1941); **Latham** in *Burns Philp v Gillespie Bros* (1947)).

In *Pavey*, a claim to reasonable remuneration for work done pursuant to a contract rendered unenforceable by statute was based upon the concept of unjust enrichment. Restitution to reverse or prevent unjust enrichment was later recognised as the basis of claims to recover money paid under mistake (*ANZ Banking Group v Westpac* (1988) (mistake of fact) and **David Securities v Commonwealth Bank** (1992) (mistake of law)); recovery of money upon a total failure of consideration (*Baltic Shipping v Dillon* (1993)); and the recovery of illegally demanded imposts (*Commissioner of State Revenue (Vic) v Royal Insurance* (1994)).

There are also indications that the unjust enrichment concept will lead to further reconsideration of established principles, particularly in the context of ineffective contracts. Thus, unjust enrichment has provided a basis for questioning the traditional approach to illegality (**McHugh, Gummow,** and **Kirby** in *Fitzgerald v FJ Leonhardt* (1997)) as well as the law's insistence on total failure of consideration as a requirement for restitution of money paid under an ineffective contract (*David Securities*).

The Court has been cautious about adopting unjust enrichment as a conceptual basis for causes of action lying outside those formerly occupied by the common money counts or as the ground for explaining certain equitable doctrines (*Westpac Banking*). However, some Justices have been prepared to consider this (for example, **Toohey** in *Baumgartner v Baumgartner* (1987) on constructive **trusts**).

Various defences have been recognised as applicable to restitutionary claims, including payment for good consideration in discharge of an existing debt, payment to an intermediary who hands on the money before notification of the claim, and change of position (*Westpac Banking*; *David Securities*)—but not the passing on by the plaintiff to a third party of the burden of a recoverable payment (*Commissioner of State Revenue v Royal Insurance*).

JOHN CARTER
KEITH MASON

Retirement of Justices. The provisions of the Constitution relating to the **tenure** of Justices (sections 71 and 72) are an important aspect of their **independence**. Until 1977, when the Constitution was amended, section 72 was interpreted—ironically, but unavoidably, by the Justices themselves—to mean that the Justices had tenure for life, subject only to **removal** for proved misbehaviour or incapacity, so that Parliament could not validly legislate to impose a retirement age (*Alexander's Case* (1918)). In their **joint judgment**, Isaacs and **Rich** found it 'plain that the independence of the tribunal would be seriously weakened if the Commonwealth Parliament could fix any less permanent tenure than for life, subject to proved misbehaviour or incapacity'. **Higgins** and **Gavan Duffy** dissented.

The decision in *Alexander's Case* was not necessarily popular. In 1926, when **Latham** as **Attorney-General** introduced an amendment to the *Judiciary Act* 1903 (Cth) to provide for judicial pensions, many members spoke in favour of fixing a retirement age for federal judges. When Latham explained that this would be unconstitutional, other members suggested that the High Court should reconsider *Alexander*. However, over the ensuing years the Court only reconfirmed its holding in that case, as did the **Privy Council** in *Shell Co v FCT* (1930).

The issue of Justices' pensions had been controversial from the beginning (see **Remuneration of Justices**). In 1903, parliamentary factions hostile to the **establishment** of a High

Court had succeeded in deleting the pension provisions from the Judiciary Bill. Thus, until 1926, the Justices had no financial incentive for retirement—and indeed a financial disincentive. From 1907 onwards, **O'Connor** was unable to retire despite chronic illness; and in 1919, **Griffith** found it necessary to petition the Attorney-General personally for a pension after finding that he had insufficient funds on which to retire. In 1926, after lengthy debate and vehement opposition in Parliament, the amendment Bill introduced by Latham added section 48A to the Judiciary Act. It provided that a Justice who had served on the Court for not less than 15 years would, on retirement, be entitled to an annual pension at the rate of half of the salary. A pension was also provided in the case of disability or infirmity after five years of service. The amendment was supported as ensuring the continued efficiency of the judiciary, given the necessity of life tenure (see now *Judges' Pensions Act* 1968 (Cth)).

Following the 1926 debates, a proposal to amend the Constitution—retaining life tenure for existing High Court Justices, but imposing a retirement age of 72 years for future High Court **appointments**—was adopted by the 1929 Royal Commission on the Constitution, despite contrary submissions by **Dixon** and Andrew **Inglis Clark**. The proposal was taken up again by the Australian Constitutional Convention of the **Whitlam era**, which agreed 'that the Constitution be altered to provide that in the future all federal judges (including justices of the High Court) be appointed on the basis of a retiring age of 70 years'. The specific example that attracted comment at the time from conservatives was the Labor appointee **McTiernan**, who in 1975 at the age of 83 was in his forty-fifth year on the Court. But the move for a constitutional **amendment** was initiated, and most strongly supported, by Labor Attorney-General Kep Enderby (at the Melbourne session of the Convention in September 1975). The only strong contrary argument was offered by Liberal Senator Ivor Greenwood, who emphasised that the **United States Supreme Court** had no compulsory retirement age (at the Hobart session of the Convention in October 1976).

Despite Greenwood's opposition and that of the Law Council of Australia, the proposal received bipartisan support at the Convention, and thereafter in the Senate Standing Committee on Constitutional and Legal Affairs and in both Houses of Parliament. In the parliamentary debates, members referred to the growing acceptance in Australia of the need for a maximum retiring age for judges (such an age had been fixed for all **state Supreme Court** judges), and of the need to maintain vigorous and dynamic courts (the assumption being that younger judges would bring to the Bench new ideas and fresh social attitudes). By a 1977 referendum carried in every electorate in the country, and by 80 per cent of the electors, section 72 of the Constitution was amended to provide that the appointment of each Justice thereafter would be for a term expiring on the attainment of 70 years of age.

There are no written guidelines for what a Justice can or cannot do in retirement, or after resignation. During the debates surrounding the 1977 constitutional amendment, members of parliament spoke of the suitability of retired judges for positions as royal commissioners, members of boards and committees of inquiry, and as directors or commissioners of government authorities.

Of the 36 past Justices, ten (all appointed prior to 1977) have died in office. Sixteen, including **Piddington**, have resigned. Ten have retired. Most voluntary departures were related to ill-health or politics. Particularly before the 1977 constitutional amendment, there appear to have been a few cases of Justices remaining in office for partisan reasons. Most Justices, however, have wished to remain in office as long as physically and mentally capable, out of personal commitment and their sense of professional and institutional achievement and the status of the position.

Nevertheless, extra-judicial interests have led to several resignations. **Knox** resigned as **Chief Justice** in 1930 in order to take up the very considerable residuary estate of his friend John Brown, taking the view that his direct continuing interest in the business was incompatible with judicial office. Isaacs became the first Australian-born Governor-General upon his resignation in 1931. This path was later followed by both **Stephen** and **Deane**. **Evatt** resigned in 1940 in order to re-enter federal politics, recommencing an illustrious career involving positions such as the first President of the International Atomic Energy Commission and President of the Third Session of the United Nations General Assembly. Evatt also broke the unwritten rule (now more frequently broken, at least by lower-court judges) against moving back from Bench to Bar, appearing as **counsel** in such important cases as the *Bank Nationalisation Case* (1948) and the *Communist Party Case* (1951), and at the Petrov Royal Commission (1954). After holding the leadership of the Opposition from 1951 to 59, he became Chief Justice of NSW from 1960 to 62. **Jacobs** retired early because of ill-health and has been living in England as a bookbinder. Former Justices such as **Webb**, **Kitto**, **Gibbs**, **Wilson**, **Mason**, **Dawson**, **Toohey**, and **Brennan** have taken up positions including chairmanships and presidencies of state bodies, and chancellorships and fellowships of universities. More recently, Gibbs, Mason, and Dawson have also become judges of courts such as the Supreme Court of Fiji, the Hong Kong Court of Final Appeal, the Solomon Islands Court of Appeal, and the Permanent Court of Arbitration. Stephen, after 1989, has also taken up a number of chairmanships, and was also Australian Ambassador for the Environment and a Judge of the International Tribunal for the Former Yugoslavia and Rwanda. Some Justices, particularly those who retired late in life or due to illness, have pursued no public activities in their retirement.

REBECCA CRASKE

Rich, George Edward (*b* 3 May 1863; *d* 14 May 1956; Justice 1913–50) was regarded by his contemporaries as a man of humanity, urbanity, and wit—amiable, approachable, courteous, and considerate. In *Briginshaw v Briginshaw* (1938), the High Court held that the standard of proof in civil cases should be adjusted to the nature of the particular issue. Rich said: 'In a serious matter like a charge of adultery the satisfaction of a just and prudent mind cannot be produced by slender and exiguous proofs or circumstances pointing with a wavering finger to an affirmative conclusion.' His reputation rested on a talent for stating complex propositions clearly and concisely. Over his 37 years as a Justice of the High Court, he too rarely exploited this talent.

George Rich, Justice 1913–50, on his ninetieth birthday

Rich was born on 3 May 1863 at Braidwood in NSW. His father, Canon Charles Hamor Rich, was a highly respected and scholarly Anglican cleric in the district. His mother was Isabella Tempest Bird. Both had been born in London. Rich attended Sydney Grammar School and then the University of Sydney. He studied classics under Professor Charles Badham, whose scholarship cast a lifelong spell. Rich graduated as BA in 1883 and MA in 1885. On 10 March 1887, he was called to the Bar. From 1890, he was Challis lecturer in law at the University. He was the founder of the University Boat Club and a co-founder of the first undergraduate literary magazine, *Hermes*.

In 1891, he became a member and the secretary of the Council of the Women's College, which was established in 1892. The first principal, Louisa Macdonald, said 'he manages everything and his power of seeing the corny side of things cheers me up'. In 1919, Rich argued successfully for the appointment as the second principal of Susan Williams from Castlemaine, a gold town near Melbourne. He protested against incurring 'a grave responsibility in importing an unknown quantity when there is to say the least of it one suitable candidate here, if not two'. Rich remained on the Council of the College until 1937.

Rich was recognised as one of the most prominent and promising juniors at the **equity** Bar. He co-authored books on equity practice and company law. In 1911, he took silk; shortly afterwards, he was appointed an acting—and then permanent—Judge of the Supreme Court of NSW. In 1913, he was elevated to the High Court to replace **Piddington**. The **appointment** was widely welcomed.

On the Court, Rich became known, like Geoffrey Chaucer's 'Woman Unconstant', as a weathercock 'that turneth his face with every wind'. Three cases explain the sobriquet. In *Foggitt Jones v NSW* (1916), under a state law that required all stock in NSW to be kept for the disposal of the British government, NSW sought to prevent a company that cured ham and bacon sending 243 pigs from NSW to Queensland to make bacon. After a short **argument**, Rich— in the majority, with **Gavan Duffy** 'doubting'—held that the NSW Act infringed section 92 of the Constitution by preventing the pig owners 'from doing with their stock and chattels what the Constitution secures that they may do' (see **Interstate trade and commerce**).

Queensland legislation was identical. Yet in *Duncan v Queensland* (1916), after 13 days of argument, Rich was part of a majority, now including **Higgins** and **Powers**, that **overruled** *Foggitt Jones*. Rich, like **Griffith**, altered his opinion and joined in a judgment with Gavan Duffy. In dissent, **Barton** expressed his heavy sorrow at the majority decision. **Isaacs** felt no judicial regret at his inability to concur with it.

In *McArthur v Queensland* (1920), a majority, which included Rich and Isaacs, with two newcomers, **Knox** and **Starke**, held that *Duncan* was wrongly decided and *Foggitt Jones* rightly decided. Rich explained his twice-changed opinion in a judgment of one paragraph.

In the confusion that followed, Isaacs, dissenting with Powers, remarked in *James v SA* (1927): 'If this series of acts … is not an interference with interstate freedom of trade, it is difficult to imagine what would be.' In *James v Cowan* (1930), Rich lamented the absence of some hint or distant allusion 'from which the nature of the immunity intended could afterwards have been deduced by those whose lot it is to explain the elliptical and expound the unexpressed'. He reasoned that section 92 forbade state legislation that operated to restrict, regulate, fetter, or control trade or commerce 'immediately or directly as distinct from giving rise to some consequential impediment'. He awaited 'with a patience not entirely hopeless the powerful beacon light of complete authoritative exposition from those who can speak with finality' (see **Metaphor**).

This patience was to be sorely tested. According to one **commentator**, the **Privy Council** proceeded to obfuscate much and settle nothing in *James v Cowan* (1932). Another observed that the decisions of the Privy Council in that case and in *James v Commonwealth* (1936) contained between them suggestions for every conceivable construction of section 92. After 19 years, the Privy Council adopted Rich's test of directness in the *Bank Nationalisation Case* (1949).

The use of the expression 'industrial disputes' in the **conciliation and arbitration** power (section 51(xxxv) of the Constitution) to identify a basis of federal power offended the canons of interpretation familiar to the equity lawyer and philologist. In the *Municipalities Case* (1919), Rich joined with the expansionist Isaacs in formulating the criterion that 'industrial disputes' are those which occur

when, in relation to operations in which capital and labour are contributed in co-operation for the satisfaction of human wants or desires, those engaged in co-operation dispute as to the basis to be observed, by the parties engaged, respecting

either a share of the product or any other terms and conditions of their co-operation.

In the context of the *Municipalities Case*, this formula was meant to defend the Commonwealth power against narrower readings (in that case, against an attempt to limit 'industrial disputes' to those arising from operations carried on for profit or involving manual labour). Isaacs and Rich again applied their formula in that way in the *Insurance Staffs Case* (1923). But in the *School Teachers Case* (1929), Rich used the same formula to join the majority of the Court in holding that a dispute about the wages and conditions of state teachers employed in public education schemes was not an 'industrial dispute'. Isaacs was left in sole dissent. Rich equated the disquisitions of other Justices with the 'mystic experience and philosophy' which Frederick Pollock described in his book called, with some appropriateness, *Outside the Law*, and said: 'It is difficult to suppose that any person not indoctrinated by a long course of quasi-philosophic and quasi-economic dissertations would ever apply the term "industrial" to such a controversy.'

In the *ARU Case* (1935), in dissent along with Starke and **Dixon**, Rich remarked upon the attempts to press to an impossible extension the already very wide interpretation that section 51(xxxv) had received in the Court: 'Every constitutional power has limits, and however liberally it may be construed, the limits are at length reached and an attempt is then made to go beyond them.'

In *Victoria Park Racing v Taylor* (1937), a racecourse owner complained that the respondents were broadcasting the running of races from a platform on adjoining land. With **Evatt**, Rich would have allowed the appeal. With remarkable prescience, he said:

The prospects of television make our present decision a very important one, and I venture to think that the advance of that art may force the courts to recognise that protection against the complete exposure of the doings of the individual may be a right indispensable to the enjoyment of life.

Dixon wrote in his diaries that on occasion he helped Rich with his judgments. According to Robert **Menzies**, Rich was inclined to be indolent. Usually in the majority, Rich joined with others in the judgment or wrote a short statement of concurrence. He never felt the need, when agreeing, to express his reasoning process in different language. In *Hoyt's v Spencer* (1919) he said:

I have had the advantage of reading the judgments just delivered. As I agree with them, I consider it is inexpedient to add, and I refrain from adding, collateral matter which, at best, merely paraphrases and often blurs the clearness of the main judgments, and so increases the difficulty of the profession in interpreting the decision of the Court.

Few of his successors have followed this path (see **Collective responsibility; Concurring judgments; Joint judgments and separate judgments**).

On 3 May 1950, his eighty-seventh birthday and five months after the fall of the federal Labor government in

December 1949 and the election of a conservative government led by Menzies, Rich retired. Some said his timing was not coincidental. In Sydney in 1952, at his swearing in as **Chief Justice**, Dixon welcomed the presence of Rich 'who for so long, during I should think the greater part of my life as an advocate and as a judge, has given by example, a lesson in the place that humanity, urbanity and wit may take in a court of ultimate appeal'.

In 1894, Rich married Betha Steer Bowker. They had two sons, one of whom was killed in action in 1915, and one daughter. In 1945, Betha died. In the year of his **retirement**, Rich married Letitia Woodward, who survived him. In 1922, he was an Australian delegate to the League of Nations. He was knighted and appointed KCMG in 1932. In 1936, he became a Privy Counsellor, and in 1950 an Honorary Bencher of the Inner Temple. On 14 May 1956, shortly after his ninety-third birthday, he died. Addressing the Privy Council the next day, **Barwick** said: 'After so long and so distinguished an occupancy of the Bench, none could have been found to whom [Rich] had been discourteous or inconsiderate, none who had found him inattentive to duty or to the matter in hand.'

Simon Sheller

Rights, critique of. Australia has a written Constitution that does not include a comprehensive **Bill of Rights** or Charter of Rights. Various proposals for a Bill of Rights have been made (though unsuccessfully) over the decades, and the High Court has also, through case law, implied some rights into the Constitution (see **Implied constitutional rights**). But the opposition to such initiatives has not been merely conservative; it has also arisen from progressive critiques of reliance on the discourse of rights as a way of formulating political struggles. These critiques remain relevant to evaluating the Court's record in relation to rights, and to the larger question of whether the Court's **jurisdiction** in relation to rights should or should not be enlarged.

Some critics of rights have argued that rights are indeterminate, and even incoherent. For example, Fran Olsen has suggested that a right to family privacy cannot assist us in determining our response to particular issues. Is it a protection of family privacy or a breach of it if a law provides that the parents of a young woman must be told that she is being prescribed contraceptives? On one view, such a law could be described as reducing state intervention—and thus protecting family privacy—by preventing the state making decisions for families; on the other hand, she argues, this could be viewed as breaching family privacy 'by intrud[ing] into the parent–child relationship and passing along information that the parents have neglected to obtain in the old-fashioned way—by talking to their **children**'. While a 'right to privacy' might be attractive in the abstract, its precise content is always contestable, and has been used to protect violence in the home from public scrutiny (see Katherine O'Donovan, *Sexual Divisions in Law* (1985)).

The Court in *Marion's Case* (1992), when it was asked to determine whether the sterilisation of a teenage girl with an intellectual **disability** could be authorised by her parents or only by a court, avoided using the language of family privacy. By majority, the Court held that the decision could not be left to the parents because of the grave consequences the

decision would have for their child. The majority Justices chose to base their decision on the **common law** right to 'personal inviolability'. They were careful to refrain, however, from endorsing the notion of 'a basic human right ... to procreate', on which other courts had relied in similar contexts: 'an absolute right in a man to reproduce' might turn out to conflict with a woman's right to bodily integrity, while recognition of the latter right gave sufficient protection to a woman's 'right to reproduce'. Moreover, it was 'quite impossible to spell out all the implications which may flow from ... a right to reproduce'. The majority's unwillingness to do so reflects clear awareness of the potential dangers in incautious acceptance of absolute and unpredictable 'rights'.

It has also been argued that rights discourses treat people as isolated and autonomous individuals, when they are in fact embedded in a complex of relationships. Joel Bakan suggested in 1997 that the 'atomistic' model of rights persists even where it is recognised that groups are capable of possessing or claiming rights. The model 'constructs social conflict in dyadic terms, as an accumulation of discrete clashes between rights-bearers and duty-holders, each clash potentially resolved by adjusting the relationship between the two disputants. Power relations and social conditions beyond the rights/duty dyad are irrelevant'.

Some critics of rights are concerned that rights, or certainly constitutional rights, turn political questions into legal questions. This may make the resolution of an issue appear objective and value-free because it has been translated into the discourse of **legalism**, even when it remains fundamentally a political question. Moreover, 'legalisation' may narrow the terms of debate. Judy Fudge has argued that this has happened in Canada in relation to sexual violence against **women**:

> By resorting to the Charter [of Rights], feminists have focused on the law, particularly legislatively created law, as the source of the problem of sexual violence, with the result that the social construction of sexuality and the social relations of power in which sexual practices take place fade into the background.

Others, such as Peter Hanks, have argued against the legalisation of rights by emphasising the unelected nature of the judiciary, to whom the determination of claims to such rights is likely to be entrusted, and by emphasising the restrictions imposed by the **cost of litigation** on access to judicial relief. Hanks recognises that part of the desire for a written Bill of Rights arises out of dissatisfaction with unrepresentative and unresponsive political institutions, but asks:

> Why would we willingly increase the catalogue of economic and social issues which are seen as legal questions to be settled through litigation (with all the access problems, the random nature of the agenda and trivialisation of complex issues which litigation involves), rather than political questions for debate, development of policy, negotiation and compromise?

The implicit argument here that questions about rights should be treated as 'political questions', and thus not as 'legal questions', is of course the fundamental rationale on which High Court Justices have relied ever since **Isaacs'** proclamation in the *Engineers Case* (1920) that 'possible

607

abuse of powers … is a matter to be guarded against by the constituencies and not by the Courts'.

These criticisms of rights have not gone unanswered. US scholars of colour have argued that the language of rights has more to offer than these criticisms would suggest. In 1991, Patricia Williams pointed out that criticisms of rights are easy to make for those who have always had rights: 'Where one's experience is rooted not just in a sense of illegitimacy but in *being* illegitimate, in being raped, and in the fear of being murdered then the black adherence to a scheme of … rights—to the self, to the sanctity of one's own boundaries— makes sense.' And Elizabeth Schneider, an academic with an extensive background in legal practice, argues that 'rights' and political action are not antithetical, but rather interact with each other: 'Rights discourse can reinforce alienation and individualism, and can constrict political vision and debate. But, at the same time, it can help to affirm human values, enhance political growth, and assist in the development of collective identity.'

A standard criticism of rights is the observation that they can be set off against each other, with no clear answer as to whose rights 'win'. Issues of 'rights' are characteristically issues of *conflicts* of rights, so that the mere assertion of a right by one party will often be inconclusive. And the absence of a Bill of Rights in the Constitution has not meant that the Court has avoided 'rights talk', or the conflict of rights. This is not to enter the debate on implied rights, but rather to focus on common law rights. One of the most prominent—and well-litigated—of these common law rights is an accused person's right to a fair trial. This has frequently arisen in sexual assault cases, where the Court has often been asked to adjudicate on the meaning of legislative attempts to ameliorate the effect of discriminatory special **evidence** rules. In such cases—for example, *Bull v The Queen* (2000)—the court weighs in the balance the rights of the accused and the interests of complainants. Hence, in *Bull*, the Court persistently referred to the potential 'humiliation and embarrassment' of the complainant— the terms the WA legislature had used in enacting legislation restricting questioning on sexual history evidence. However, it would appear that the common law rights of the accused are very likely to 'trump' these interests of the victims of sexual assault (see also, for example, *Crofts v The Queen* (1996)).

The critiques of authors like Bakan and Fudge might suggest that if the Court were to focus on 'power relations and social conditions' beyond the 'rights' of the individual—for example, the fact that women are overwhelmingly the targets of rape, which is overwhelmingly perpetrated by **men**—the sterility of rights-balancing might be avoided. Alternatively, the critics of these authors encourage us to ask whether the entrenchment of the rights of complainants in some constitutional form—for example, a right to **equality**—might better meet the already well-entrenched common law right of the accused to a fair trial. In this context, it is instructive to compare the recent decisions of the Supreme Court of Canada in *R v Darrach* (2000) and *R v Mills* (1999) with the approach of the High Court. In these Canadian cases, the constitutional equality and privacy rights of complainants are balanced against the fair trial rights of the accused. It at least appears that a constitutional rights approach concedes more prominence to the interests of complainants than does the present Australian system.

One possible response to these arguments is to argue, as Frank Brennan has, for the constitutional entrenchment of some rights rather than a wholesale entrenchment of rights. He singles out the need for restrictions on governmental **discrimination** on the grounds of **race**, sex, and **sexual preference**. Yet it is also necessary to emphasise the importance of ensuring that any such non-discrimination principle is defined with enough specificity to prevent Justices understanding equality in merely formal terms.

In any event, it may be well to remember that, even if a judicially enforceable Bill of Rights were adopted, it would not be a panacea. As Bakan reminds us: 'The struggle for **social justice** is much larger than constitutional rights; it is waged through **political parties** and movements, demonstrations, protests, boycotts, strikes, civil disobedience, grassroots activism, and critical commentary and art.'

JENNY MORGAN

Further Reading

Frank Brennan, *Legislating Liberty: A Bill of Rights for Australia* (1998)

Wendy Brown, *States of Injury* (1995)

Judy Fudge, 'The Effect of Entrenching a Bill of Rights Upon Political Discourse: Feminist Demands and Sexual Violence in Canada' (1989) 17 *IJSL* 445

Peter Hanks, 'Moving Towards the Legalisation of Politics' (1988) 6(2) *LIC* 80

Fran Olsen, 'The Myth of State Intervention in the Family' (1985) 18 *University of Michigan Journal of Law Reform* 835

Elizabeth Schneider, 'The Dialectics of Rights and Politics: Perspectives from the Women's Movement' (1986) 61 *NYULR* 589

Rogers v Whitaker (1992) defined the fundamental principles of the liability of doctors to their patients (see also **Health law**). The case dealt with an ophthalmic surgeon's failure to warn a patient, who was undergoing elective surgery to restore sight in one bad eye, of a one-in-14 000 chance that she could lose sight in both eyes. A number of medical experts gave evidence that they considered the risk so low that the patient need not be warned of it. The risk materialised, and the patient was rendered blind, though there was nothing otherwise blameworthy in the doctor's treatment.

The general principle stated by the Court was that a doctor has a duty of care to a patient to observe the standard of reasonable care and skill of an ordinary doctor in the particular area of specialisation. But how to define what 'reasonable care' meant? In its judgment, the Court rejected the English *Bolam* principle (*Bolam v Friern Hospital* (1957)), which stated that it was appropriate for a doctor to follow standards accepted by one responsible group of the medical profession, even if another group of doctors disagreed with the practice. The Court said there was a fundamental distinction between the standard of care that doctors must observe in diagnosis and treatment, and the standard they must observe in the provision of information and advice. In the former situation, the general standard accepted by the medical profession as a whole will in most cases be an appropriate measure of 'reasonable care'. But in the context of providing information or warning of the risks inherent in surgical procedures, a doctor is required to warn a patient of all risks that a hypothetical reasonable patient would be likely to regard as significant. In addition, the doctor must warn of any risks that she or he is aware, or should reasonably be aware, are of significance to the particular patient.

Gaudron even said that the practice or practices of medical professionals should be treated as irrelevant to the determination of the relevant standard. She suggested that a doctor's duty to give advice should be judged no differently from the duty that may exist in non-medical contexts to warn of real and foreseeable risks.

The joint majority judgment recognised an exception for 'therapeutic privilege'. In Maree Whitaker's case, however, the whole Court agreed that the risk, though remote, was so important that Dr Christopher Rogers should have warned of it. Further, Whitaker's particular concern that her good eye be protected had been made clear to the doctor.

In *Chappel v Hart* (1998), the Court held that a doctor may be liable for failing to warn of a risk in circumstances where the plaintiff's condition made it unavoidable that the plaintiff would have to undergo the surgical procedure at some time. Surgeons may also be under a duty to advise the plaintiff of their level of experience. Of further significance is the Court's decision in the case of *Nagle v Rottnest Island Authority* (1993) that a risk may be foreseeable even if it is unlikely to occur, and even if the plaintiff has been foolhardy and in some way contributed to the risk occurring.

The responses to the decisions in *Rogers v Whitaker* and *Chappel v Hart* have been divided. By some, they are seen as tolling the end of medical paternalism and forcing doctors to improve their communications with patients. Subsequent cases in other courts have confirmed that doctors are required to explain the risks and consequences in terms understandable to the patient, and in language that is clear, comprehensible, and free of jargon. On the other hand, it is claimed that the decisions have raised the costs of health care by contributing to expensive insurance premiums and an increase in the number of clinical tests and medical investigations performed. Courts are accused of being too accepting of plaintiffs' claims that, had they been warned, they would never have consented to surgery. It is also claimed that leaving the question of materiality of risks to be decided by judges and juries fails to provide doctors with clear guidance as to which risks they are required to make known to their patients.

CATHERINE HENRY

Further Reading

Angus Corbett, 'A Reformulation of the Right to Recover Compensation for Medically Related Injuries in the Tort of Negligence' (1997) 19 *Syd LR* 141

Tony Honore, 'Medical Non-disclosure, Causation and Risk: *Chappel v Hart*' (1999) 7 *TLJ* 1

Bernadette McSherry, 'Failing to Advise and Warn of Risks Inherent in Medical Treatment' (1993) 1 *Journal of Law and Medicine* 5

Role of Court. The principal responsibilities of the High Court are to uphold the Constitution, maintain the **rule of law**, and act as the nation's final court of appeal in civil and criminal cases.

At the time of federation, each of the self-governing colonies that were to become states had its own Supreme Court. Chapter III of the Constitution established what is described in section 71 as a 'Federal Supreme Court, to be called the High Court of Australia', and defined the Court's original and appellate **jurisdiction**.

It is of the essence of a federal system of government that there is a formal allocation of governmental functions between the polities that make up the federation. This is effected by a written Constitution, which may also contain provisions regulating various aspects of the exercise of governmental power and protecting the **rights** of citizens. Divisions of responsibility, limitations upon power, and guarantees of rights necessarily give rise to controversies which, if not settled through the political process, require authoritative judicial resolution.

Legal disputes concerning the meaning and effect of the Constitution may arise between citizens, between citizens and governments, or between governments. Much of the constitutional litigation that has come before the Court has involved disputes between state and federal governments. The proper discharge of the Court's function as the ultimate interpreter of the Constitution requires manifest **independence** of the executive government. It also requires both the reality and the appearance of impartiality. The Court has consistently maintained that this can be achieved only through a commitment to **legalism**. The Court's first **Chief Justice** rightly said that 'it would be a lamentable thing if this Court should allow itself to be guided in its interpretation of the Constitution by its own notions of what it is expedient that the Constitution should contain or the Parliament should enact' (*Union Label Case* (1908)). In a parliamentary **democracy**, it is for the elected representatives of the people, acting through the political process, to determine contested issues of governmental policy. The task of **constitutional interpretation** is entrusted to a body of unelected lawyers, who qualify for **appointment** on the basis of their legal expertise, experience, and judgment. They exercise **judicial power** upon the faith of an understanding that they will do so according to law. The political legitimacy of parliamentarians rests upon the will of the electorate. Judicial legitimacy rests upon a commitment to the impartial application of legal doctrine and principle. The fact that so many of the cases, especially the constitutional cases, that come before the Court have political implications is not a reason to relax the constraints inherent in the judicial function or to doubt their application to constitutional decision making (see also **Political impact of Court's decisions; Political institution**).

Early in the history of federation, it was established that giving **advisory opinions** to governments is not part of the functions assigned to the Court by the Constitution. The Court exercises its judicial power by resolving **justiciable** controversies. This underlines the importance of judicial independence, and the right of the public to be assured that decisions are made free from the influence of governments or other powerful interests.

In its capacity as a federal Supreme Court, the High Court maintains the rule of law by enforcing observance of the

Constitution, and of the general law, by governments and their agencies, as well as by citizens and corporations. Section 75 of the Constitution gives the Court jurisdiction in suits against the Commonwealth, and confers upon the Court power to issue certain prerogative **writs** and injunctions against officers of the Commonwealth.

In its capacity as a national appellate court of general jurisdiction, the role of the High Court is different from that of the **United States Supreme Court**. From the beginning, the Court—subject to varying requirements of **leave to appeal**—has heard civil and criminal appeals from the Supreme Courts of the states and **territories**, and from the other federal **superior courts**, including (since their establishment) the **Federal Court** and the Family Court. Until the abolition of appeals to the Judicial Committee of the **Privy Council**, there was some ambiguity in the Court's position in the appellate **hierarchy**. Since that abolition, however, the position is clear. The Court stands at the apex of the national judicial system, state and federal.

A unified Australian **common law** has been made possible by this aspect of the Court's role. By the exercise of its civil and criminal appellate jurisdiction, the Court has the capacity to develop and refine the principles of the common law, adapting them to changing social and **economic** conditions. The Court declares the common law for the whole of Australia, seeking where necessary to resolve differences that may have arisen between Australian jurisdictions. It also settles issues as to the meaning and effect of state and federal legislation. All this is done in the exercise of its jurisdiction as a court, not as a legislative or policy-making body. The Court resolves issues presented to it by the parties to litigation. It has no agenda, and no constituency. When it alters or develops the common law, it does so constrained by settled principles as to the proper limits of the judicial function (see also **Activism; Law-making role**).

Appeals can no longer come to the Court as of right. All now require a grant of special leave to appeal. The introduction of the requirement of leave in 1984, together with the creation of the Federal Court in 1976—which relieved the High Court of a substantial part of the **business** that would otherwise come within its original jurisdiction—enabled the High Court to concentrate its attention upon its duties as the national court of appeal and the court with the ultimate responsibility of interpreting and enforcing the Constitution.

MURRAY GLEESON

Further Reading
Murray Gleeson, *The Rule of Law and the Constitution* (2000)
Anthony Mason, 'The Evolving Role and Function of the High
Court' in Brian Opeskin and Fiona Wheeler (eds), *The
Australian Federal Judicial System* (2000) 95

Rule of law. The rule of law is a central concept in most modern political philosophies, though its roots in **liberalism** and republicanism run deepest. As with many such concepts, it dates at least as far back as Aristotle, who famously expressed his preference for the rule of law to that of men. As Aristotle was aware, however, it is inevitably human agents who make and administer the law. The rule of law is thus a normative or regulative ideal that operates to constrain and

structure the activities of those making and implementing the law. While there may be disagreement between individual Justices of the High Court as to the doctrinal consequences of **Dixon's** declaration in the *Communist Party Case* (1951) that the rule of law is an unwritten, yet fundamental, assumption of the Constitution, there is little doubt that all would point to the concept as a—if not the—bedrock justification for the Court's work and its importance in the functioning of Australian **democracy**.

Notwithstanding the lineage and contemporary centrality of the rule of law, it remains a contested cluster of sometimes-conflicting principles. (An exasperated legal theorist, George Fletcher, recently opined, 'we are never quite sure of what we mean by the "rule of law".) But disputes over the content and relative importance of particular principles comprising the rule of law can work to obscure a developing consensus as to what, as a set of constraints on law, the ideal minimally includes. Modern **natural law** theorists (such as John Finnis and Lon Fuller) and legal **positivists** (such as Joseph Raz) seem in general agreement on the basic content of the rule of law, though differing, among other things, on the extent to which it is constitutive of law, the nature of its value, and its importance relative to other political ideals and values.

Where there are significant disagreements about the content of the ideal, these tend to concern the desirability of making more substantive additions to the formal or procedural principles that are acknowledged as its core focus. Laws must be prospective and exhibit a requisite degree of openness, clarity, stability, and coherence (at least in the minimal sense of being comprehensible and non-contradictory). 'Generality' is also commonly listed as an indicium of the rule of law, but usually in the Diceyan sense of requiring all, including government officials, to be subject to (potentially unequal) laws. In this sense, generality or 'formal legal **equality**' has more to do with the application of legal rules (that is, that there be *rules*) than their actual content. It picks up on the strand of rule of law thought that requires all government actions to be legally authorised; the constraints on law making and application will not avail if government is free to use alternative modes of regulation.

These so-called desiderata of the rule of law have been said to flow from the organising idea that the law should be capable of providing guidance. If law is to guide, then people must be able to rely on it; so the rule of law must be extended to encompass certain institutional safeguards and cultural mores instrumental to ensuring fidelity to the law (such as an independent judiciary, fair administrative and judicial procedures, and a general attitude that law matters and should normally be obeyed). Given the High Court's functional **role** (under the **separation of powers**) as the ultimate authority in the application and interpretation of the law, it is thus a key institution in the maintenance of the rule of law. Not only does it, in various ways, check that the other branches of government comply with the ideal, but the ideal plays a regulative role in its own work.

There is an obvious sense in which rule of law values are ubiquitous in the output of the High Court, as the Justices strive to uphold their **judicial oaths** of justice according to law. However, although explicit references to the ideal can be found in many doctrinal areas (for example, the interpretation of **privative clauses**, the availability of **remedies** for jurisdictional error, **common law** rights to fair trial, and **natural justice**), these references are rarely matched by careful examination of the rule of law's precise content, the way its elements interrelate, or the way doctrinal outcomes are thereby determined. Indeed, it is not uncommon to hear echoes of the ideal on both sides of a given doctrinal divide. For example, disputation on the issue of whether dissenting Justices should fall into line with an established majority view in constitutional cases can be seen to reflect different views on the importance of fidelity to the Constitution as against stability in the law.

So although the ideal is accepted as a constitutional assumption, and no doubt guides the Court in its roles of interpreting and making the law, the meaning and consequences of this remain inchoate in its jurisprudence. This would come as no surprise to legal philosophers, who recognise the difficulty of bringing the individually complex components of the rule of law into an architectonic ideal. 'With respect to the demands of legality,' wrote Fuller, 'the most we can expect of constitutions and courts is that they save us from the abyss; they cannot be expected to lay out very many compulsory steps towards truly significant accomplishment'. His point was not only that compliance with the rule of law is a matter of degree. What individual precepts require will often be unclear—for example, is clarity best served by pages of precision or a simple, though less precise, principle?—and compliance will often involve resolving conflicts internal to the ideal. It is thus a mistake to see *the* rule of law as approximate to *a* rule of law capable of simplistic statement and straightforward application.

In *Abebe v Commonwealth* (1999), **Gummow** and **Hayne** said the constitutional assumption means at least that it is the Court's role and duty 'to say what the law is' (quoting *Marbury v Madison* (1803))—and every person is entitled to liberty except as abridged by the due administration of law (compare Dicey's first principle of the rule of law: *Introduction to the Study of the Law of the Constitution* (1885)). This statement usefully highlights the significant contribution made by rule of law ideas to the interpretation of the nature and province of federal **judicial power**. Central to this, the Court's understanding of its role under Chapter III of the Constitution includes the image of itself at the apex of a robustly independent judiciary with powers of **judicial review**.

Section 75(v) of the Constitution is thought to entrench judicial review of administrative action. 'Judicial review', wrote **Brennan**, 'is neither more nor less than the enforcement of the rule of law over executive action' (*Church of Scientology v Woodward* (1982); see also **Gaudron** in *Enfield Corporation v Development Assessment Commission* (2000)). And the High Court has followed the **United States Supreme Court** in holding, despite the absence of express textual warrant, that judicial review of legislation is 'axiomatic'; if the legislature is to be ruled by the law of the Constitution, then the Court must have powers of review, lest there be a government of persons and not laws. (Or so the reasoning goes. Although the historical record indicates the **framers** so intended, nothing in logic compels the conclusion that constitutional or legal limits require judicial review—after all, though the High Court is itself bound by the law, its decisions are not review-

able. This is not to deny that judicial review may be practically or empirically necessary.) In Australia, therefore, judicial enforcement of the rule of law denies the British doctrine of parliamentary **sovereignty** at least insofar as the Court sees itself as duty-bound 'to see that the Constitution is not infringed and to preserve it inviolate' (*Cormack v Cope* (1974), quoting *Bribery Commissioner v Ranasinghe* (1964)).

The Court's unwavering protection of constitutional limits indicates the extent to which it sees itself as the primary institution for protecting the rule of law, though it tells little about the values protected in its name. Chapter III jurisprudence has supplied some content here, though the nature and extent of any implied rights or legislative disabilities in this area are very much under construction. In the *War Crimes Act Case* (1991), for example, a majority of Justices held that Bills of Attainder, by conclusively determining the guilt of named individuals, would involve a 'usurpation of the judicial power'. A minority, in judgments strongly resonant with rule of law ideals, thought that retroactive criminal laws were also such a usurpation. Another example is the strong support in *Chu Kheng Lim v Minister for Immigration* (1992) for the proposition that there is 'a constitutional immunity from being imprisoned … except pursuant to an order by a court', though it has been questioned whether acknowledged, yet uncertain, exceptions render this principle unsustainable (Gaudron in *Kruger v Commonwealth* (1997)).

A more ambitious attempt to extract individual rights from the rule of law ideal came in *Leeth v Commonwealth* (1992), where **Deane** and **Toohey** argued that Dicey's notion of legal equality extended to the 'theoretical equality of all persons under the law' and required grounds of **discrimination** to be capable of reasonable justification (to the Court). In essence, these Justices concluded that the generality requirement of the rule of law was a fundamental doctrine of the common law and that it was adopted by the Constitution by necessary implication. Although the basis for this implication is not entirely clear, the cadence of the argument is suggestive of a particular approach to the meaning and value of coherence: interpreting the Constitution in the suggested way would allegedly promote coherence in **constitutional law** in the sense of giving the best justification, consistent with the document, of the Constitution's authority and presumed legitimacy. This approach stretches the generality requirement of the rule of law well beyond Dicey's formal rendition of legal equality, to include substantive equality.

Philosophically speaking, the Deane and Toohey substantive (content-dependent) conception of the rule of law must meet the powerful objection that it collapses the ideal into a complete social philosophy, rendering it redundant as a distinct ideal. And to the extent that a substantive conception is thought to be a necessary implication of constitutional arrangements, any distinction between law *as it is* and law *as it ought to be* is dissolved. Moreover, the constitutional argument faces devastating objections based on specific constitutional provisions dealing with—and, in some instances, denying—equality. In any event, it is an argument that has been decisively lost, though some Justices have acknowledged (without fully articulating) a more limited guarantee of procedural equality or **due process** based on Chapter III that relies on a less controversial mode of deriving constitutional implications (see Gaudron in *Kruger*).

Thus, to the extent that the rule of law ideal will influence 'judicial power' jurisprudence, the Court is likely to be attuned to its formal or procedural conception. Further, the rejection of the 'theoretical' or substantive equality argument also makes it unlikely that particular components of the rule of law will be implied merely on the basis of its status as a constitutional assumption. While the assumption will no doubt illuminate the structure and text of the Constitution, it has not been conceived as a free-standing constitutional principle (compare *Lange v ABC* (1997)).

Of course, even procedural principles and institutions rest on substantive justifications. The formal rule of law can be defended not only on grounds of providing efficient guidance, but also by its contribution to the creation of social conditions whereby individuals can meaningfully chart their lives, even in the face of a degree of ineliminable legal uncertainty and vagueness. (Compare the arguments of the critical legal studies movement.) The formal ideal has also been given democratic justifications, and is reflective of the sense in which the rule of law is contrasted with the rule of persons, seen as particular forms of arbitrary rule or anarchy (no rule). Such defences of the rule of law do not mean that its pursuit will guarantee the moral worth of laws—only that it should be respected in any just society.

The value to be accorded to the Court's contribution to the furtherance of the rule of law in Australia is thus a matter of substance. However, exactly how the Court's contribution might be evaluated is unclear. Particular areas of law would each need to be evaluated to see the extent to which they foster the values underpinning the ideal. And given that the formal rule of law is not a sufficient condition for justice (albeit a necessary condition for justice), such considerations need to be weighed against other political ideals and aspirations—ideals and aspirations that may sometimes conflict with rule of law values.

What is clearer is that the Court's reluctance to mould the ideal into a specific constitutional doctrine cannot, of itself, constitute failure. First, we need to acknowledge that achieving rule of law values depends on an institutional, political, and cultural context that travels far beyond legal doctrine. Secondly, it may well be that the best way for the Court to further the rule of law, as a contested and fluid political ideal, is not to encrust a particular version of it as an implied constitutional guarantee, but to acknowledge it as a complex guiding assumption that will not yield simple answers. For example, the consensus as to the guidance function, assumed to unite the rule of law desiderata, might need rethinking in the context of a modern administrative state where effective regulation may prove incompatible with stable, pre-established rules. The dangerous temptation in utilising the concept—a temptation to which the Court has sometimes succumbed—is to invoke its rhetorically powerful language as an argument stopper, thus avoiding the substantive arguments that the ideal inevitably involves.

LEIGHTON MCDONALD

Further Reading

Gerard Brennan, 'The Parliament, the Executive and the Courts: Role and Immunities' (1997) 9 *Bond LR* 136

International Commission of Jurists, *The Rule of Law in a Free Society: Report of the International Congress of Jurists* (1959)

Geoffrey de Q Walker, *The Rule of Law: Foundation of Constitutional Democracy* (1988)

S

Sankey v Whitlam (1978) was a sequel to the **Whitlam era** and the so-called 'loans affair', which began on 13 December 1974 when Rex Connor, Minister for Minerals and Energy, was authorised by the Executive Council to negotiate with a middleman, Tirath Khemlani, for the possible borrowing of $4000 million in Arab petrodollars.

The Opposition contended that, under the Commonwealth–State Financial Agreement of 1928, the proposal needed Loan Council approval. But Attorney-General **Murphy** (appointed to the High Court two months later) had advised the Executive Council that no such approval was needed, since the loan, although repayable over 20 years, would be 'for temporary purposes' and thus within a specific exemption in the Financial Agreement.

On 11 November 1975, the loans affair culminated in the **dismissal** of the Whitlam government. On 20 November, in the midst of the ensuing election campaign, Sydney solicitor Danny Sankey initiated a private prosecution against Whitlam, Connor, Murphy, and Jim Cairns (Treasurer in 1974).

There were two informations against each defendant. The first ('the statutory charge') alleged that the loan proposal would have contravened the Financial Agreement, and had therefore involved a conspiracy 'to effect a purpose that is unlawful under a law of the Commonwealth', contrary to section 86(1)(c) of the *Crimes Act* 1914 (Cth). The crucial issue here was whether the Financial Agreement was 'a law of the Commonwealth'.

The second information against each defendant ('the **common law** charge') alleged that, at the Executive Council meeting, the four defendants had agreed to recommend the proposal to the Governor-General on the basis that the loan would be for temporary purposes; but that, since this was untrue, there had been a conspiracy to deceive the Governor-General in the performance of his duties. The crucial issue here was whether the 'temporary purposes' argument was correct, or at least legally tenable.

The case was heard in Queanbeyan by Stipendiary Magistrate Darcy Leo, with many interruptions and detours. In *Connor v Sankey* (1976), the NSW Court of Appeal, rejecting various challenges to Leo's jurisdiction, refused to interfere. On 1 April 1976, Labor member in the House of Representatives Bert James launched an attack under parliamentary privilege on Sankey, his counsel David Rofe, and Leo (imply-

ing that Leo was biased by personal association with Rofe). The gist of the attack was reported next day in the *Sydney Morning Herald*. Seven months later, Leo sued the *Herald* for **defamation**.

In January 1977, Leo attempted to disqualify himself from further involvement, lest his interest in the defamation proceedings attract imputations of bias. But when Chief Stipendiary Magistrate Murray Farquhar proposed to replace him, Rofe objected, and applied for a Supreme Court order that Leo continue to sit.

That order, made by Justice Jack Lee in March 1977, was confirmed by the NSW Court of Appeal in *Sankey v Whitlam* (1977). The Court found that Leo's withdrawal had been influenced by 'an unnamed officer of an unnamed government department', and that 'the integrity of the administration of justice' required that he continue to sit.

Throughout the proceedings, Sankey sought access to Executive Council and Loan Council documents, many of them already tabled in Parliament during the loans affair. In June 1976, to enable Sankey to prepare his case, the Fraser government allowed him limited access to the documents— as recommended by **Attorney-General** RJ Ellicott, who in 1975 (while in Opposition) had been among the most vigorous pursuers of the loans affair. On 9 November 1976, Sankey subpoenaed the documents for production in court, while Whitlam issued his own subpoenas for relevant Treasury documents. On 12 November, the Fraser government announced its objection to producing most of the documents—arguing that confidential, high-level government documents, especially Cabinet documents, should be shielded by 'Crown privilege'.

On 22 August 1977, Connor died. The Fraser government then tried to end the saga: Ellicott, as Attorney-General, was to take over the prosecution and terminate it. But on 6 September 1977, Ellicott resigned as Attorney-General in protest against this proposal, and the private prosecution went on.

In November 1977, Leo substantially upheld the government's claim to Crown privilege, ruling that most of the documents should *not* be produced. Sankey appealed to the Supreme Court of NSW. Whitlam entered a cross-appeal against *any* production of documents, and again denied that the Financial Agreement was 'a law of the Commonwealth'.

In February 1978, this appeal and cross-appeal were **removed**, at the instance of Attorney-General Peter Durack, into the High Court. Murphy did not sit. (To avoid embarrassment, his name was deleted from the record.) Chief Justice **Barwick** was on leave.

The five Justices who heard the case gave judgment on 9 November 1978. They accepted the view of Crown privilege established in England by cases such as *Conway v Rimmer* (1968)—treating the issue of privilege as one for the courts, not for the government, so that in doubtful cases the court should inspect the documents for itself. Moreover, going significantly beyond the English cases, they held that even Cabinet documents have no absolute claim to protection. On Whitlam's cross-appeal, they unanimously held that the Financial Agreement was not 'a law of the Commonwealth'. Thus the statutory charge was bad in law.

On 4 December 1978, Leo formally dismissed the statutory charges. On 16 February 1979, after two weeks of evidence, he dismissed the common law charges as well, holding that there was no case to answer. The central issue was whether Murphy's 'temporary purposes' argument had been advanced in good faith. There was evidence that the **Solicitor-General**, Maurice Byers, the Head of the Attorney-General's Department, Clarrie Harders, and a senior Departmental officer, Denis Rose, while expressing reservations about the argument, had all agreed that it was tenable. And both Harders and Rose expressed their belief that the defendants had acted in good faith.

For Leo, this meant that the prosecution must fail. The alleged offence was a conspiracy to 'deceive' the Governor-General; but once the Attorney-General gives an opinion in good faith, 'how can it be said it was deception if his opinion is later shown to be incorrect?'

Rofe conceded that the four defendants had been 'vindicated'. Sankey, he said, had acted 'for pious motives'; the prosecution had succeeded where the Parliament had failed, in bringing out at last the full facts of the loans affair. Whitlam told the press that the case had been 'a farce, and a protracted one'. Now, he said: 'The comedy is ended.'

TONY BLACKSHIELD

Seal of Court. The Great Seal and office seals of the High Court were introduced in 1903 to give authority to official documents of the new Court. The rules for use of the seals are laid down in the **High Court Rules**.

Following the creation of the Court, Chief Justice **Griffith** signed his approval of the first rubber seal on 5 October 1903. It featured a design using the Royal Coat of Arms. Seven days later, he signed his approval of the office seals for the Principal Registry in Victoria and the Registries of NSW, Queensland, SA, WA, and Tasmania.

On 17 November 1903, he approved a new design for the Great Seal in metal. The Great Seal was to be embossed with a screw press and kept and operated by the Principal Registry in Melbourne. Duplicates, modified to identify the location of each Registry, were issued to each High Court registry around the country.

On 4 June 1930, Chief Justice **Isaacs** approved an office seal for the new Canberra District Registry. Following the hiatus in the monarchy in 1936 caused by the abdication of King Edward VIII, on 4 February 1937 Chief Justice **Latham** approved the use of new office seals deleting the letters of the

sovereign and replacing them with the words 'Office Seal'. In May 1968, Chief Justice **Barwick** decided to use the Commonwealth Coat of Arms in place of the Royal Coat of Arms, and after some minor changes, approved a new design by the Government Printing Office in March 1969. Manufactured by the Royal Australian Mint in Canberra, the title 'Great' was dropped and the new Seal was introduced in 1970, with each High Court Registry having the name of its state added.

On 13 August 1973, the Seal followed the Principal Registry from Melbourne to Sydney, and arrived at its current home in Canberra on 26 May 1980.

The Seal was used with plain embossing (without the red overlay currently used) on Letters of Request, and to forward documents to the **Privy Council** in Great Britain, until Australia severed all remaining formal legal ties with Great Britain in March 1986 with the passing of the *Australia Acts*. From 7 September 1936, the Great Seal has been pressed into a red overlay on all certificates of practitioners on the Register of Practitioners of the High Court of Australia. Strictly speaking, this is the only current use of the Seal, although rubber stamps in the shape of the Seal are used to indicate that documents filed in the Court have been 'sealed'.

HAMISH LINDSAY

Seat of Court. The *Judiciary Act* 1903 (Cth) decreed that 'the principal seat of the High Court shall be at the seat of Government'. The *High Court of Australia Act* 1979 (Cth) makes a similar provision—no longer referring to the Court's 'principal seat', but simply to its 'seat'. Pursuant to that provision, Governor-General Zelman Cowen proclaimed on 1 September 1980 that as from that date 'the seat of the High Court of Australia shall be at the seat of Government'.

The preposition 'at' suggests a precise geographical location; yet no such location for the seat of government has ever been determined. Section 125 of the Constitution requires that the seat of government 'shall be determined by the Parliament'. But the *Seat of Government Act* 1908 (Cth) said only: 'It is hereby determined that the Seat of Government … shall be in the district of Yass–Canberra'. Commonwealth Parliamentary Draftsman John Ewens—after working in the **Attorney-General's** Department in Canberra since 1933—concluded in 1952 that no more precise legislative determination has ever been made. The assumption that the seat of government is the city of Canberra—or perhaps is located 'at' Canberra—has no clear legal foundation.

The *British North America Act* 1867 (Imp) provided that Canada's seat of government 'shall be Ottawa': the reference is to the city. As **Windeyer** observed in *Spratt v Hermes* (1965), 'the phrase "seat of government" has for centuries been used to describe a capital city'. The US Constitution referred to 'such District (not exceeding ten Miles square) as may … become the Seat of the Government'. Thus the whole of the District of Columbia is the seat of government. By contrast, the Australian section 125 required that the territory for the seat of government—referred to since 1938 as 'the Australian Capital Territory'—must be 'not less than one hundred square miles'. It is in fact some 900 square miles (2331 km^2). As Ewens argued, the seat of government can hardly extend to that entire area; and indeed section 125 stipulates that the seat of government shall be 'within' the chosen territory. In *Spratt v Hermes*, Ewen's argument was cited by **counsel** and accepted by the whole Court. **Taylor** concluded that the ACT and the seat of government 'are not synonymous terms'; Windeyer noted that they are 'not co-extensive in fact; nor could they be regarded as co-extensive in law'—since this would ignore the word 'within' and the geographical fact that the ACT extends far beyond the city of Canberra.

Section 125 provides, in its entirety:

> The seat of Government of the Commonwealth shall be determined by the Parliament, and shall be within territory which shall have been granted to or acquired by the Commonwealth, and shall be vested in and belong to the Commonwealth, and shall be in the State of New South Wales, and be distant not less than one hundred miles from Sydney.
>
> Such territory shall contain an area of not less than one hundred square miles, and such portion thereof as shall consist of Crown lands shall be granted to the Commonwealth without any payment therefor.
>
> The Parliament shall sit at Melbourne until it meet at the seat of Government.

Grammatically, it is unclear whether the last three stipulations in the first paragraph of section 125 relate to the word 'territory' or to the seat of government. Windeyer thought in *Spratt v Hermes* that the clause beginning 'shall be within territory …' was 'an inartistic interpolation', apparently assuming that the later clauses related to 'the seat of government'. On that reading, the section would require that the seat of government be both 'within' the territory referred to, and 'in' the state of NSW. Alternatively, the later clauses might relate to the word 'territory', thus requiring that the territory be 'in' NSW. Yet even that requirement is puzzling: if the designated territory has been carved out of the state of NSW, it no longer forms part of that state. The legislative mechanism that established the territory proceeded on that basis: the *Seat of Government Surrender Act* 1909 (NSW) and the *Seat of Government Acceptance Act* 1909 (Cth) provided for 'surrender' by the state, and 'acceptance' by the Commonwealth, of territory which had been part of the state.

This legislation followed the formula in section 111 of the Constitution, which provides:

> The Parliament of a State may surrender any part of the State to the Commonwealth; and upon such surrender, and the acceptance thereof by the Commonwealth, such part of the State shall become subject to the exclusive jurisdiction of the Commonwealth.

Yet whether this use of section 111 was appropriate is also unclear. As Bernard Sugerman pointed out in 1973, after his retirement as President of the NSW Court of Appeal, section 125 does not refer to 'a territory' or 'the territory', but to 'territory' and 'such territory'; and its formulae 'granted to or acquired by the Commonwealth' and 'vested in and belong to the Commonwealth' are not necessarily synonymous with surrender and acceptance under section 111. Those are legislative processes; yet the words 'granted' and 'acquired' suggest executive processes—a Crown grant or a Commonwealth **acquisition of property** under section 51(xxxi). In section 52(i),

which gives the Commonwealth exclusive power to legislate for 'the seat of government … and all places acquired by the Commonwealth for public purposes', the word 'acquired' undoubtedly refers to acquisition under section 51(xxxi). Alternatively, as **Menzies** suggested in *Worthing v Rowell & Muston* (1970), the words 'shall be vested in and belong to the Commonwealth' in section 125 might mean that, once the Parliament has determined the relevant territory, it automatically 'becomes the property of the Commonwealth by virtue of s 125 itself'.

In short, if section 125 is read as requiring that the seat of government shall itself be in NSW—and if 'in' is read as meaning something more than simply 'surrounded by'—the establishment of the separate territory of the ACT was in error. Equally, if section 125 is read as requiring the seat of government to be 'within territory which … shall be in' NSW, the establishment of a separate territory was in error. If the 'territory' was intended to be merely an example of 'a territory' carved out of a state under section 111—and if 'in' means simply 'surrounded by'—section 125 has been applied correctly.

The initial problem, therefore, centres on the word 'territory'. Sugerman argued that it should be read, as in sections 123 and 124, as 'merely a geographical term denoting a portion of the land surface' of a state. On that reading, the 'territory' referred to in section 125—unlike the Commonwealth territories envisaged by section 111—was never intended to be 'withdrawn from a state'.

Of course, the word 'territory' also appears in the heading to section 111 ('States may surrender territory') and in section 122. But for Sugerman the use of the word in this context only heightens the contrast with the way it is used in section 125. A territory surrendered under section 111 is followed into section 122, and assimilated for legislative purposes to the other **territories** described in that section. The power to legislate for 'the seat of government' is quite different. It is found in section 52(i), which, unlike section 122, is said to be 'subject to this Constitution'—as **Kirby** emphasised in *Re Governor, Goulburn Correctional Centre; Ex parte Eastman* (1999). Moreover, whereas section 122 gives power to make laws 'for the government of [the] territory', section 52(i) gives power to make laws 'for the peace, order, and good government of the Commonwealth' with respect to the seat of government. The emphasis is on the needs of the Commonwealth, not on the needs of community governance in a populated territory.

The two sources of power might overlap, or even be coextensive—since, if the appropriate starting point is the power in section 52(i) to legislate for the seat of government, the incidental power given by section 51(xxxix) might enable the Parliament to legislate for the surrounding territory as well. On either basis, the Commonwealth could legislate for the whole of the ACT. But whether section 122 or section 52(i) is the relevant source of power has repeatedly troubled the Court.

In Sugerman's view, if the territory for the seat of government is subject to section 122, no meaningful operation remains for section 52(i). He argued that the assimilation of the ACT to 'territories' under sections 111 and 122 had obscured a consistent constitutional design in which the seat of government would be determined by the Commonwealth Parliament, 'acquired' by the Commonwealth under section

51(xxxi), and assimilated to other 'places acquired by the Commonwealth' under section 52(i). Like those other places, it would be subject to the Commonwealth's exclusive legislative power, but would 'be and remain' within the state.

If Sugerman's argument is understood as a plea for **originalism**, in the sense of a return to what the **framers of the Constitution** intended, it may be answered by the original 1891 draft of section 52(i), which was closely examined by the Court in *Svikart v Stewart* (1994). It explicitly used the language of state 'surrender' and Commonwealth 'acceptance' of 'any territory which may … become the seat of government'. Yet the later shift to the language of 'grant and acquisition' is equivocal: does it show that the framers saw no difference between the two modes of expression? Or did they subsequently adopt the language of grant and acquisition precisely because they did see a difference? In a footnote to his judgment in *Svikart v Stewart*, **Brennan** acknowledged Sugerman's argument, and noted that, in a curious passage in *Paterson v O'Brien* (1978), the Court had referred to the ACT as 'vested in the Commonwealth by surrender or acquisition'. In *Paterson*—a sequel to the **Territory Senators Cases**—it was argued that, under section 123 of the Constitution, NSW's 'surrender' of the ACT should have been subject to approval by the people of NSW in a referendum. Rejecting that argument, the Court emphasised that although section 125 required that the territory 'should be geographically in' NSW, it also stipulated that 'the selection of that Territory was in the initiative of the Commonwealth'. Yet the Court appeared to accept that, once the Commonwealth had made its selection, what was then required was that the selected area be 'surrendered', rather than 'granted or acquired'.

In earlier years, individual Justices—**Dixon** in *Federal Capital Commission v Laristan Building & Investment* (1929) and *Australian National Airways v Commonwealth* (1945), **Evatt** in *Davies v Ryan* (1933)—assumed that the relevant legislative power was section 52(i). Perhaps Dixon was influenced in *Laristan* by the fact that the relevant legislation was entitled the *Seat of Government (Administration) Act* 1924 (Cth). At all events, as Menzies observed in *Rowell & Muston*, these early cases revealed 'an opinion that the generality of laws made for the government of the seat of government … are made under s 52'. The power was assumed to extend to the whole ACT and all of its needs: *Laristan*, for example, concerned kerbing and guttering on Canberra's Northbourne Avenue.

What led the Court to depart from these early assumptions was the issue of whether judicial appointments in the ACT must satisfy the requirements for exercise of federal **judicial power** under Chapter III of the Constitution, specifically section 72. If the ultimate source of the appointments lay in section 52(i)—or the incidental power in section 51(xxxix)—they would be 'subject to this Constitution', and section 72 would apply. But in *Spratt v Hermes*, and more recently when *Eastman* reaffirmed that decision, the Court held that the relevant source of power was section 122. It followed that the appointments need not comply with section 72. In both cases, the Court took care to disclaim any blanket exclusion of the ACT from the whole of Chapter III, since that would make Chapter III inapplicable to the seat of government, which in turn might mean that ministers of the Crown, performing their functions in the seat of govern-

ment, would not be amenable to constitutional **writs** under section 75(v). **Barwick**, in particular, found that prospect so disturbing as to be unacceptable.

If the source of power for the governance of the ACT is section 122, it is necessary to identify a more limited purpose for the power in section 52(i). That process began in *Spratt v Hermes*. Counsel suggested that section 52(i) was confined to laws 'in respect of government as such … Parliament, Government House, public servants and so on'. **Kitto** focused on 'the seat of government as a specific and separate topic … distinguished from more general topics which may affect a place in which the seat of government is or is to be'. **Taylor** discerned a power not 'to make general laws irrespective of their subject matter having an operation within the seat of government', but only on the very subject matter of the seat of government itself.

Later judgments have confirmed these suggestions. At one stage in *Rowell & Muston*, Kitto read the reference to the seat of government in section 52(i) very narrowly indeed, as picking up *only* the power to 'determine' the seat of government envisaged by section 125. He accepted, however, that the power extends to 'such other laws as can fairly be said to be with respect to that subject matter'. Barwick refused to limit the power to laws having 'the seat of government, as such, for their subject matter. Indeed, I am not sure that I comprehend what would be such a law.' But he held that the power is limited 'by relevance to the seat of government and the activities to be conducted there'. In *Svikart*, **Mason**, **Deane**, **Dawson**, and **McHugh** suggested that laws for the seat of government 'would seem to be concerned with its political or constitutional aspects, rather than with the government of the territory which it occupies'. In *Eastman*, that formula was accepted by **Gaudron**, and also (in dissent) by Kirby, who agreed that 'the making of a law with respect to health or education or most aspects of the criminal law in the ACT would appear unconnected with the seat of government *as such*'.

The acceptance that the power to legislate for the seat of government does not extend to general laws for a territorial area might suggest that the seat of government is not a territorial concept at all. (Kirby suggested during argument in *Eastman* that it might be 'a sort of **metaphor**'.) But the whole Court agreed in *Rowell & Muston* that it is a 'place' (and therefore, like the other 'places' specified in section 52(i), an exclusive Commonwealth 'place' to which state legislation could not apply). As Barwick observed, the expression 'seat of government' in the US Constitution 'clearly refers to a physical area of land'. He explained the relationship between sections 52(i) and 122 by suggesting that a 'place' and a 'territory' are different—and the difference may be 'more than one of degree or extent', since a 'territory' is not only larger than a 'place', but is usually 'subject to some political arrangements'.

Both Barwick and Menzies, in *Rowell & Muston*, held that the seat of government must be a 'place' because the stipulations in section 125 require that it be 'geographically situated'. Yet this returns us to the confused grammatical structure of section 125. Menzies relied on the words 'shall be in [NSW]', while both he and Barwick relied on the stipulated 100-mile distance from Sydney. Yet their reasoning only makes sense if those stipulations refer to the seat of government. If they refer to the territory, the argument falls apart.

In any event, while *Rowell & Muston* established that the seat of government must be a 'place', the Court has remained unable to determine its precise location, and has usually sidestepped the issue. Though Windeyer agreed in *Rowell & Muston* that the seat of government is a 'place, a locality', he also recalled his earlier view in *Spratt v Hermes* that it means 'a capital city'. As such, he said, it 'has never been taken to mean a precise area of the earth's surface delineated by metes and bounds, any more than has a seat of learning, meaning a university town, or a place described as the seat of a bishop'. He conceded that 'a power to make laws with respect to a place, if it be understood as a power to make laws for the conduct of people in that place, does postulate that the place can be precisely defined', but did not see this as a problem— since 'the seat of government, however it be spatially measured', would in any event be covered by legislation under section 122. The majority in *Svikart* noted again that the limits of the seat of government 'have not been precisely determined by the Parliament'; and that it is neither 'co-extensive with the Territory in which it is located nor, under s 125, is it intended to be'. In *Eastman*, this prompted Solicitor-General David Bennett to argue that the phrase 'seat of government' is after all 'non-geographical', referring only 'to the national capital, *qua* capital'.

In *Spratt v Hermes*, Menzies concluded 'that if there can be no seat of government of the Commonwealth unless and until some portion of the Australian Capital Territory has been specified as such by the Parliament, then there is at present no seat of government of the Commonwealth'. Given the apparent equanimity with which the Justices have accepted the indeterminate boundaries of the seat of government, and even its uncertain metaphysical status, one might wonder whether this matters. Yet the Court has insisted that the seat of government is important to the federal system. In *Spratt v Hermes*, after holding that section 52(i) did not extend to 'laws for the government of the Capital Territory', Windeyer added: 'That does not mean that the Capital Territory has not a special position in the polity of Australia. It has, for within it lies the seat of government.' In *R v Smithers; Ex parte Benson* (1912), **Griffith** and **Barton** saw freedom of **movement** as an inherent right of **citizenship** in a federation—in part because, as the **United States Supreme Court** held in *Crandall v Nevada* (1868), it includes 'the right to come to the seat of government'. In *Pioneer Express v Hotchkiss* (1958), where the Court upheld legislation preventing an interstate bus service from setting down passengers at Canberra, the judgments nevertheless acknowledged the special status of the ACT, and the need for unrestricted access to the federal capital. No one, said Dixon,

would wish to deny that the constitutional place of the Capital Territory in the federal system of government and the provision in the Constitution relating to it necessarily imply the most complete immunity from State interference with all that is involved in its existence as the centre of national government.

Yet the Court agreed that this was not the occasion to explore such a doctrine; judicial acknowledgment of the special position of the seat of government has not in fact had any special effect.

Barwick's reasoning in *Spratt v Hermes*—using the application of section 75(v) of the Constitution to decisions taken in the seat of government to exclude the conclusion that Chapter III does not apply in the territories—is perhaps an exception. In August 1999, when motorists passing the Indonesian Embassy repeatedly honked their horns in protest at violence in East Timor, it was suggested that, if prosecuted, they might invoke the constitutional freedom of **political communication** as a defence; and that idea, too, might gain weight from the fact that such protests are commonly directed to national embassies at the seat of government.

If the seat of government—whether as 'place' or as 'metaphor'—is of special constitutional significance, what is the significance of the directive that the High Court be 'at' the seat of government? Advocates of its location there, from Patrick Glynn to Barwick, have stressed its symbolic significance (see **Circuit System; Canberra, Court's move to**). The strong insistence on **open court**, and perhaps the Justices' general tolerance of **litigants in person**, might reflect the theme of citizen access to federal institutions sounded in *Re Smithers; Ex parte Benson* and *Pioneer Express v Hotchkiss*. Yet the Court's endorsement of a requirement of special **leave to appeal** as a restriction on access (see *Smith Kline & French Laboratories v Commonwealth* (1991)) may point in a different direction.

In any event, the Court's inability to define 'the seat of government' leaves it unclear whether the directive for its own location has been fulfilled. Perhaps the ambiguity reflects the confusion, in a system of **responsible government**, between 'parliament' and 'government'. The arguments in *Eastman* assumed that the 'seat of government' must at least include the precincts of Parliament House. Yet perhaps, if 'government' means 'executive government', the focus should be on Government House—the place where the Governor-General, as the Queen's representative, 'sits'. In that event, the High Court **building** may simply be in the wrong place.

TONY BLACKSHIELD
FRANCESCA DOMINELLO

Further Reading
JQ Ewens, 'Where is the Seat of Government?' (1951) 25 *ALJ* 532
Bernard Sugerman, Letter to the Editor (1973) 47 *ALJ* 344

Seniority. The **Chief Justice** is the most senior Justice. The *High Court of Australia Act* 1979 (Cth) provides that the other Justices—the **puisne Justices**—have seniority according to the dates of their commissions. Where two or more Justices have commissions with the same date, their relative seniorities are set out in their commissions. This was the case when **Toohey** and **Gaudron** were appointed on the same day in 1987 (Toohey was senior).

On only one other occasion has more than one puisne Justice been appointed on the same day: when the first **appointments** were made, in 1903. At that time, the relevant provision (in the *Judiciary Act* 1903 (Cth)) provided that, where the commissions did not make it clear, the relative seniorities were determined by the order in which the Justices took their **judicial oaths**. The commissions of the first two puisne Justices (**Barton** and **O'Connor**) did not set out their relative seniorities. No doubt it was understood that Barton would be the senior puisne Justice, and he took his oath before O'Connor.

The most senior available Justice acts as Chief Justice during the Chief Justice's absence from Australia, or if the Chief Justice is unable or unavailable to perform the duties of the office, or when a vacancy in the office occurs.

The Justices' seniority has its only substantive application when a **Full Court** is evenly divided in its opinion (see **Tied vote**). Normally, the Court's decision is that of the majority of Justices. However, if the Court is equally divided when exercising its original **jurisdiction**, the Judiciary Act provides that the Court's decision is that of the Chief Justice or, in his or her absence, that of the senior Justice present. (If the Court is equally divided when exercising its appellate jurisdiction, the general rule is that the decision appealed from is affirmed.)

The Chief Justice, or the most senior puisne Justice, presides over hearings and sits at the centre of the Bench. The seating of the other Justices is determined by their seniority (see also **Etiquette**). The most senior Justice after the presiding Justice sits on his or her right; the next most senior sits on the presiding Justice's left; the next sits two places to the presiding Justice's right; and so on. The recognition of this order of seniority was taken to extreme lengths by the practice of court officers in handing documents up to the bench in a zig-zag fashion, sequentially from the most senior to the most junior. Documents are now distributed in a slightly less complicated way, though it still takes account of seniority: documents are handed first to the Chief Justice (or presiding Justice), then to the next most senior Justice and all Justices on that side of the presiding Justice, and then to the next most senior Justice and all Justices on the other side. When judgments are handed down, the court officer still collects the judgments in the zig-zag way.

If separate reasons for judgment are given, they are published and reported in order of the seniority of the most senior Justice who joined in those reasons. When joint reasons for judgment are given or later referred to, the names of the Justices who joined in those reasons are listed in order of seniority.

Six of the eleven Chief Justices have been appointed from the High Court Bench. Each was the senior puisne Justice at the time of his appointment, though there is no statutory impediment to the appointment of any puisne Justice as Chief Justice, regardless of seniority.

JAMES POPPLE

Separation of powers. The Australian Constitution incorporates, as one of its basic elements, a separation of federal legislative, executive, and judicial powers. The High Court has held that this doctrine is implied from the text and structure of the Constitution, in particular from the words of sections 1, 61, and 71 and the nature of Chapters I, II, and III. The Court has also elaborated the constitutional constraints that flow from the separation of powers. As a result, the Court has had a profound impact on the functions, and general design, of a number of institutions of federal government. In turn, the separation of powers has played a major role in shaping the functions of the High Court and its Justices.

Despite some earlier references to the separation of powers, the Court, led in this respect by **Isaacs**, first clearly recognised and applied the doctrine in the *Wheat Case* (1915). There, it was found that only Chapter III courts (the High Court, federal courts created by Parliament, and courts invested with federal jurisdiction) could validly exercise the **judicial power** of the Commonwealth. On the facts of the case, this meant that the **Inter-State Commission**—dealt with in sections 101–104 of the Constitution—could not be empowered to issue an injunction, or other judicial remedy, in aid of its determination that a law of **trade or commerce** had been breached. Predictably, the *Wheat Case* hindered the activities of the Commission, contributing to its effective abolition in 1920 after a mere seven years of existence. Three years after the *Wheat Case*, in *Alexander's Case* (1918), the Court found that the other major federal tribunal envisaged by the framers—the Commonwealth Court of **Conciliation and Arbitration**—had not been validly established as a federal court because its President did not have life **tenure** in accordance with section 72 of the Constitution, as that section (as it then stood prior to its **amendment** in 1977) was interpreted by a majority. Thus, under the separation doctrine it could not validly discharge the judicial function of enforcing industrial awards.

The effect of these two cases was to ensure that courts, including the High Court, retained control over the exercise of federal judicial power. The proposition that only Chapter III courts can exercise federal judicial power is commonly described as the 'first limb' of the separation of federal judicial power. The 'second limb'—that the Commonwealth Parliament cannot ordinarily invest Chapter III courts with legislative or executive functions—was recognised by the High Court in the *Boilermakers Case* (1956) in a judgment generally attributed to **Dixon**. Once again, the institution immediately affected was the Court of Conciliation and Arbitration. In 1926, the Commonwealth had purportedly restructured the Arbitration Court as a federal court with judges appointed for life. It was empowered to exercise judicial and non-judicial functions, and in fact did so for the next 30 years. However, the holding in the *Boilermakers Case* that these functions had been invalidly combined meant that the Commonwealth was thenceforth required to maintain two separate institutions to administer its system of industrial arbitration: a non-court tribunal to participate in the quasi-legislative function of making industrial awards, and a Chapter III court to enforce those awards. This divided system, which at times has been strongly criticised, remains in place today.

The *Wheat Case*, *Alexander's Case*, and the *Boilermakers Case* indicate that, from its earliest days, the High Court was concerned to ensure that the judicial power of the Commonwealth was exercised independently and impartially by bodies meeting the traditional description of a court. The fact that enforcement of this principle disturbed settled institutional arrangements—or, in the case of the Inter-State Commission, undermined the viability of a body expressly contemplated by the Constitution—was no impediment. Admittedly, the *Wheat Case* and *Alexander's Case* also had the effect of protecting the High Court, and Chapter III courts generally, from challenges to their authority posed by rival institutions such as the Inter-State Commission at a time when governments were actively experimenting with quasi-judicial tribunals. However, whether the Court was influenced by these considerations is entirely speculative; there is no reason to suppose that the Court, in recognising the separation of federal judicial power, was influenced by anything other than a genuine intellectual conviction as to the requirements of the text and structure of the Constitution, in particular the need to preserve the **rule of law** within a federal system.

Nonetheless, whereas the Court has said that federal judicial power must be segregated from other federal governmental functions, it has not required a strict division between federal legislative and executive powers. The doctrine of **responsible government** clearly compels some blending of federal legislative and executive functions. Moreover, in *Victorian Stevedoring & General Contracting Co v Meakes and Dignan* (1931), the Court affirmed, in the face of a separation of powers challenge, that the Commonwealth Parliament could delegate wide-ranging law-making powers to the executive. The Court has never resiled from this view, and the Commonwealth government has always made extensive use of subordinate legislation. In this respect, the Court has interpreted the Constitution against the backdrop of an established Anglo-Australian tradition of parliamentary delegation to the executive and in light of the needs of practical governance.

The separation of federal judicial power is also, however, a potential impediment to practical governance in the sense that it constrains the choices elected governments can make in establishing administrative agencies and tribunals. Thus, as Geoffrey Sawer pointed out in *Australian Federalism in the Courts* (1967), a zealous approach to the separation of powers may have hindered the capacity of the Commonwealth to frame an effective system of federal **administrative law** and justice. However, the High Court has not applied the two limbs of the separation doctrine in a rigid or fundamentalist fashion. To the contrary, it has generally recognised—as Isaacs put it in *Le Mesurier v Connor* (1929)—that the Constitution must remain a 'working apparatus'. To this end, the Court has developed a pragmatic conception of judicial power. It has recognised that certain functions, like the trial of a criminal offence, are exclusively judicial in nature. Such functions, when arising in federal jurisdiction, must be exercised by a court. Other functions, however, have a flexible character, presenting as judicial when exercised by a court and non-judicial when exercised by a non-court body. In addition, the Court has declined to draw a sharp distinction between the enforcement of existing legal rights and the creation of fresh entitlements. This flexible approach to the identification of judicial power has featured in a number of prominent judgments upholding the validity of Commonwealth administrative tribunals such as the Taxation Boards of Review and the Trade Practices Tribunal (see, respectively, *FCT v Munro* (1926) and *R v Trade Practices Tribunal; Ex parte Tasmanian Breweries* (1970), but compare *Brandy v Human Rights and Equal Opportunity Commission* (1995)).

In its endeavour to promote a working framework of government, the Court has not only developed a flexible approach to the concept of judicial power, but has also recognised several exceptions to the separation principle itself. For example, defence tribunals established under Commonwealth authority—such as courts martial—may, at least in some situations, exercise judicial power despite their failure to satisfy the tenure requirements of a federal court (see *Re Tracey; Ex parte Ryan* (1989)). In *Harris v Caladine* (1991), the Court found that federal courts may be empowered to delegate certain of their judicial responsibilities to officers of the court such as registrars. Moreover, the Court accepts that federal judges may legitimately discharge certain executive functions, but only when clearly acting in their personal capacity—that is, when acting as 'designated persons' rather than as members of a court (see *Hilton v Wells* (1985); *Grollo v Palmer* (1995)). Thus, a person who is a federal judge may also be a member of the non-judicial Administrative Appeals Tribunal.

But despite these efforts to strike a balance between the values promoted by the separation of powers and the apparently conflicting demands of public administration, a series of recent decisions has extended the reach of the separation doctrine. Thus, in the 1990s, the Court held that the separation of federal judicial power, like the doctrine of **representative government**, gives rise to implied limitations on legislative power that are protective of individual rights (see **Due process**). In *Kable v DPP* (1996), the Court found that a doctrine of 'incompatibility' with federal judicial power operates as a restraint on state legislative power. And in *Re Wakim* (1999), the separation doctrine played an indirect role in the Court's finding that federal courts cannot validly exercise state judicial power—a controversial conclusion that undermined the unity of the national **cross-vesting** scheme. These decisions suggest that the balance is shifting towards a more vigorous assertion by the High Court of the rule of law objectives served by the separation doctrine.

The separation of powers has also directly moulded the functions of the High Court itself. Like all courts in the **common law** tradition, the High Court has consciously distanced itself from the political branches of government. It seeks to ensure that it operates in a manner that is strictly independent—both in actuality and appearance—from all public and private interests. Under the separation doctrine, it is bound to decide controversies brought before it according to law. Thus, it is not uncommon for members of the High Court to remark that the social or political merits of a claim have no bearing on the Court's legal responsibilities (see **Role of Court**; **Political institution**). At the same time, the Court has observed that it has neither the expertise nor the authority to resolve social or political disputes that do not present a legal issue for determination. In the words of **Brennan** in *Re Citizen Limbo* (1989): 'Courts perform one function and the political branches of government perform another … Unless one observes the separation of powers and unless the courts are restricted to the application of the domestic law of this country, there would be a state of confusion and chaos.'

The Court has recognised a number of specific legal rules and principles that flow from these limitations on its authority. Although these rules affect other federal courts as well, they reflect the High Court's vision of the proper domain of the federal judiciary. In addition, some of these rules necessarily have a special impact on the High Court as the nation's ultimate court of appeal. The Court has accepted, for example, that it cannot engage in **prospective overruling**. The practice was rejected in *Ha v NSW* (1997) on the basis that it involved the quasi-legislative creation of new entitlements, rather than the strict enforcement of existing legal rights. The High Court's steadfast refusal to deliver **advisory opinions** (see *Re Judiciary and Navigation Acts* (1921)) is also linked to the separation of federal judicial power. In a comprehensive review of the separation of powers in Australia, Cheryl Saunders has noted that these and other constitutional and general law doctrines developed or applied by the High Court should be understood against the backdrop of its reluctance to assume functions with a legislative or executive flavour or to interfere with matters legitimately the responsibility of another branch. Further illustrations given by Saunders include the rules governing the reading-down or severance of statutes, and the inability of courts to deal with the merits of administrative decisions that are the subject of **judicial review**.

The separation of powers has also shaped the functions undertaken by individual High Court Justices. Despite the general prohibition on the exercise by federal courts of legislative and executive functions, the Court has recognised that federal judges may undertake certain executive functions in their capacity as individuals. Thus, **Latham** and Dixon served in diplomatic posts during **World War II** without resigning from the Court. Although there are further examples of members of the High Court discharging executive functions in that way, it has not been the practice in recent decades (see **Non-judicial functions**). In that respect, there is a clear contrast with members of other federal courts, many of whom sit on federal tribunals.

FIONA WHEELER

Further Reading

Anthony Mason, 'A New Perspective on Separation of Powers' (1996) 82 *Canberra Bulletin of Public Administration* 1

Cheryl Saunders, 'The Separation of Powers' in Brian Opeskin and Fiona Wheeler (eds), *The Australian Federal Judicial System* (2000)

Geoffrey Sawer, *Australian Federalism in the Courts* (1967) ch 9

Leslie Zines, *The High Court and the Constitution* (4th edn 1997) chs 9–10

Sex. The High Court has addressed the topic of sexual conduct in a variety of legal contexts. In the first half of the twentieth century, the Court determined the boundaries between licit and illicit sex by reference to matrimony and marital status. For the purpose of obscenity laws and the crime of rape, 'illicit' sex was defined as sexual intercourse outside the marital relationship. A gradual shift in emphasis is evident from the 1960s onwards. The Court no longer viewed Christian moral standards—in particular, the sanctity of marriage—as the exclusive measure of sexual propriety and decency. In redrawing the boundaries of 'illicitness' for sexual conduct, the Court increasingly drew on liberal **values** of autonomy, **equality**, and privacy. Rather than resort to religious moral absolutes, secular notions of decency could 'objectively' be determined by reference to the prevailing community standards. While the legal construction of objectivity has not been challenged by the Court in the field of sexual offences, there is some dissenting opinion in other areas (for example, provocation) suggesting that the abstract standard of the reasonable, ordinary, or right-thinking person may operate unfairly or discriminate against minorities (see **Criminal law defences**).

In the 1950s, the legitimacy of sex was contingent upon the marital status of the parties. This is apparent in the reasoning in cases where the Court reviewed obscenity laws. In *Transport Publishing Co v Literature Board of Review* (1956), the Court considered whether a series of cartoon picture books was 'objectionable' within the meaning of the *Objectionable Literature Act* 1954 (Qld). **Dixon, Kitto,** and **Taylor** examined the publications and noted:

The theme of them [the publications] all really is love, courtship and marriage. Virtue never falters and right triumphs. Matrimony is the proper end and if you are not told that happiness ensues it is the constant assumption ... The pages contain nothing prurient, lewd or licentious ... Why then has this literature been considered unduly to emphasise matters of sex and exhibit a tendency to deprave? It is because the lovers are depicted as loving passionately. They embrace and they embrace closely. Their kisses, though pure are full and perhaps prolonged. Their feelings for one another are intense and joy and happiness are represented as coming from a love that is as deep and passionate as it is devoted. Moreover, the eyes of the heroine are drawn with lids either drooping or unduly raised and her lips, though drawn in black and white, are obviously as rosy as lipstick can make them. There is, too, an evident though crude attempt to infuse the subject with glamour, in the modern technical sense of that term.

The inherently subjective nature of the majority's judgment is apparent in **McTiernan's** dissent, where he said:

The publications debase courtship: the drawings in many cases are calculated to convey that courtship justifies conduct which appears to be bestial rather than a manifestation of love. Illicit intercourse is nowhere explicitly represented as a motive, but the pictures and the stories are likely to inflame the venereal passions of the classes of young persons likely to devour this trash.

The liberal result in this case was not achieved by the majority resorting to **civil liberties** arguments such as the importance of free speech. Unable to locate this dispute within the broader constitutional framework of a **Bill of Rights**, the majority used matrimony as the moral justification for legitimating these otherwise lewd depictions of sexual passion.

In *Crowe v Graham* (1968), the Court returned to the issue of the depictions of illicit sex. The Court heard appeals against convictions under the *Obscene and Indecent Publications Act* 1901 (NSW). The two publications in question—magazines called *Censor* and *Obscenity*—contained some material promoting reform of censorship laws, 'coarse and crude' jokes, excerpts from *Fanny Hill*, and 'voluptuous' photographs of naked and nearly naked **women** of 'alluring appearance'. The Court noted the importance of the context in which the publications were circulated, emphasising that material offensive in one context might be more acceptable in another. As **Barwick** noted:

Sexual matters were referred to in the issues of the magazines in a way which might pass muster in a tap room or smoke concert but which, displayed in print to the reader of the magazine, could, in my opinion, be held to offend the modesty of the ordinary man.

Although there was some material in the magazine that argued for law reform or against censorship, this was not sufficient to remove the indecency. As **Windeyer** remarked: 'If the Gospels were printed with indecent pictures interleaved, the indecency would be the greater.'

Notwithstanding this religious sentiment, the case marked a move away from Christian moral standards of measurement for indecency and obscenity. The earlier **common law** had examined this question by determining whether material had a tendency to 'deprave and corrupt' morals, or whether it was, as Windeyer put it, 'filthy, bawdy, lewd and disgusting'. The Court replaced this moral corruption test with an 'objective' test of indecency, based on community standards. As in *Transport Publishing Co*, the issue, at least for Windeyer, could not be resolved by reference to civil rights arguments, and US jurisprudence based on the right to free speech was no more than 'remotely relevant'.

In *Papadimitropoulos v The Queen* (1957), the Court (Dixon, McTiernan, **Webb**, Kitto, and Taylor) grappled with the problem of sexual deceit in the context of rape. In *Papadimitropoulos*, a young Greek woman, recently migrated to Australia, had sexual intercourse with her fiancé under the false belief that she was already married to him. This belief had been induced by the accused by a visit to the Melbourne Registry Office, where the couple had merely registered their intention to marry. The accused's appeal from his conviction on a charge of rape was dismissed by the Supreme Court of Victoria, which held that the consent obtained was vitiated because of his immoral motivation. The High Court was critical of this approach, and drew a clear distinction between immoral or 'wicked and heartless conduct', and the legal notions of rape and consent. What was at issue, according to the Court, was whether she consented to penetration:

Rape is carnal knowledge of a woman without her consent: carnal knowledge is the physical fact of penetration; it is the consent to that which is in question; such a consent demands a perception as to what is about to take place, as to the identity of the man and the character of what he is doing. But once the consent is comprehending and actual the inducing causes cannot destroy its reality and leave the man guilty of rape.

Although perhaps useful for separating immorality from illegality, this limited conception of the type of mistake that serves to vitiate consent has been criticised by **commentators**. Why should mistake as to 'what', and not as to 'why', be determinative? Should the accused's fraudulent motives be irrelevant to the question of consent? While the Court has adopted a narrow conception of autonomy, the categories where consent is negated have been expanded by legislation in most Australian jurisdictions. The Court's jurisprudence on the definition of consent appears relatively undeveloped compared to that of the Supreme Court of Canada. The Canadian court has recently held that serious forms of fraud, such as the accused's non-disclosure of HIV status to a sexual partner, will destroy consent and leave the accused guilty of sexual assault (*R v Cuerrier* (1998)). The Canadian court also held that juries should not be directed that consent may be 'implied' from conduct for the purpose of sexual assault (*R v Ewanchuk* (1999)).

Society's attitudes to marital sex undoubtedly changed with the sexual revolution and **feminist** movement in the 1960s and 1970s. The common law traditionally presumed an implied consent on the part of spouses that could be revoked only by divorce or judicial orders of separation. As **men** were not routinely prosecuted for acts of marital rape, there was limited judicial consideration of the scope of the common law immunity. To modernise the law, legislation was enacted in all Australian jurisdictions to abolish the immunity in the 1970s and 1980s. The status of the common law immunity arose for consideration much later in the case of *R v L* (1991).

Mason, Deane, and **Toohey** did not find it necessary to determine the historical existence of such consent in order to decide that it should not be the law now:

Without endeavouring to resolve the development of the common law in this regard, it is appropriate for this Court to reject the existence of such a rule as now part of the common law of Australia ... It is unnecessary for the Court to do more than to say that, if it was ever the common law that by marriage a wife gave irrevocable consent to sexual intercourse by her husband, it is no longer the common law.

Dawson adopted a similar position on this point. **Brennan**, after a learned discussion of the ecclesiastical law of marriage, concluded that if a 'right' to sexual intercourse existed in marriage, it was limited, and that, in ecclesiastical law at least, marriage implied rights inconsistent with an ability of a husband to force sexual intercourse:

Far from relegating a wife to the position of a sexual chattel, the status of wife created by marriage confers on a wife a right ... to live with her husband, to have him listen and talk to her, to be cherished, to be entertained at bed and board and treated with respect. These are not rights which can be enforced by decree but they are rights attached to the status of husband and wife. To jurists in the ecclesiastical courts, the attachment of these rights to the status of a wife distinguished the institution of marriage from the state of concubinage 'which degrades (a woman) as the object of loose desire and mere sensual gratification' ... Each spouse has a mutual right to sexual intercourse provided the right be exercised reasonably, subject to the health of the spouses and the exigencies of family life. It is a right to be exercised by consent.

The openly reformist nature of the judgments of Mason, Deane, and Toohey, and Dawson, stands in stark contrast to the equivalent English case of *R v R* (1991). In that case, the **House of Lords** did not acknowledge its change of the common law, preferring rather to consider that the judicial development over the previous centuries was in error and that the common law had never recognised such an immunity.

Another contrast may be drawn between the attitudes of the High Court and the House of Lords towards 'violent' or 'dangerous' sex. The issue of dangerous sadomasochistic practices (S&M) was examined by the High Court in *Boughey v The Queen* (1986). According to Mason, **Wilson**, and Deane, the accused 'claimed that he introduced the deceased to certain unconventional sexual activities including practices from which he derived masochistic pleasure and the particular practice or "technique" of applying pressure to the carotid arteries'. The deceased was cohabiting with the accused, a doctor residing in Hobart. She died as a result of pressure being applied to her throat. Boughey claimed that this erotic strangulation was designed to increase her sexual pleasure and that he had no intention to harm her.

The issue before the Court was Boughey's liability for murder. The case was important for its discussion of the requirements of intention and foresight. But the case also provides an illustration of the Court's relative lack of concern with the accused's sexual morals. Although classed as 'unconventional', it was not, except to the extent that it was harmful and resulted in her death, discussed in morally reproving or stigmatising terms. This may be contrasted with the review of the S&M activities by the House of Lords in *R v Brown* (1993). In that case, the majority speeches were deeply concerned with the immoral nature of the acts in question. The majority was clearly disgusted by the descriptions of the practices, which included genital piercing and buttock branding, though it was 'spared' the ordeal of viewing the videotaped **evidence**. In denying consent as a defence in the public interest, the majority highlighted what it perceived to be the perverted, predatory, and diseased nature of the homosexual subjects.

An examination of the High Court's judgments dealing with sex reveals a changed focus on the interests at stake. In early cases, the cultural reference point for distinguishing between licit and illicit sex was marriage and marital status. In later cases, the Court's attention shifts to protecting sexual autonomy. It is on the liberal concepts of consent and the prevention of sexual harm to others, rather than traditional Christian morals, that the Court's jurisprudence on sex now concentrates. The Court's capacity to continue to shape the law of sexual offences and obscenity by reference to those liberal concepts may, however, be constrained by legislative changes arising more as a response to the political demands of radical feminism or moral conservatism than by reference to legal principle.

SIMON BRONITT
HENRY MARES

Further Reading
Tony Blackshield, 'Censorship and the Law' in G Dutton and M Harris (eds), *Australia's Censorship Crisis* (1970)
Simon Bronitt and Bernadette McSherry, *Principles of Criminal Law* (2001) ch 12
Sangeetha Chandra-Shekeran, 'Theorising the Limits of the "Sadomasochistic Homosexual" Identity in *R v Brown*' (1997) 21 *MULR* 584
Patricia Easteal, 'Rape in Marriage: Has the License Lapsed?' in Patricia Easteal (ed), *Balancing the Scales: Rape Law Reform and Australian Culture* (1998)
Gail Mason, 'Reforming the Law of Rape: Incursion into the Masculinist Sanctum' in Diane Kirkby (ed), *Sex, Power and Justice: Historical Perspectives on Law in Australia* (1995)

Sexual preference. Lesbians and gay men still experience **discrimination** under the law in Australia, as well as at the hands of private individuals. Yet the High Court has had few opportunities to engage with issues concerning sexual preference. This is primarily because, with no **Bill of Rights** or relevant federal anti-discrimination legislation, and no general guarantee of **equality** of the kind envisaged in *Leeth v Commonwealth* (1992), there is no legal basis on which to challenge laws that discriminate on the basis of sexual preference. However, in *Croome v Tasmania* (1997), the High Court played an important role in the battle to change the Tasmanian law that had criminalised **sex** between **men**.

Until 1997, sex between men was a criminal offence in Tasmania, punishable by up to 21 years in prison under sections 122 and 123 of the *Criminal Code* 1924 (Tas). For many years, the Tasmanian Gay and Lesbian Rights Group had unsuccessfully lobbied the Tasmanian Parliament to reform the law. A breakthrough came in 1992, when Australia ratified the First Optional Protocol to the International Covenant on Civil and Political Rights ('the ICCPR')—a central element in the **International Bill of Rights**. The Protocol enabled individual Australians to complain about human rights violations to the United Nations Human Rights Committee. The first such communication, lodged on the day of the ratification, was by a Tasmanian gay activist, Nicholas Toonen. Toonen complained that the Tasmanian provisions violated his right to privacy, as protected by Article 17 of the ICCPR. The Human Rights Committee upheld Toonen's complaint and found that Australia, as a nation, was in breach of its international human rights obligations under the ICCPR.

Tasmania, however, refused to repeal its laws. After some lobbying, the federal Parliament intervened and, using the **external affairs power**, enacted the *Human Rights (Sexual Conduct) Act* 1994 (Cth), which provided that sexual conduct between consenting adults in private was not to be subject to any arbitrary interference with privacy within the meaning of Article 17 of the ICCPR.

Tasmania, however, still refused to repeal its laws, maintaining that they did not constitute an 'arbitrary interference with privacy'. In order to give effect to the Human Rights Committee's decision, Toonen and another Tasmanian activist, Rodney Croome, sued Tasmania in the original **jurisdiction** of the High Court, seeking a declaration that under section 109 of the Constitution, the Tasmanian law was invalid by reason of **inconsistency** with the Human Rights (Sexual Conduct) Act. Tasmania challenged the plaintiffs' claim on two grounds: first, that the Court had no jurisdiction because the case involved no '**matter**' within the meaning of section 76 of the Constitution; and secondly, that since no immediate right or duty of any person was involved, the claim amounted to a request for an **advisory opinion**. The basis for these arguments was that the plaintiffs had not been prosecuted or threatened with prosecution under the law.

The Court sat as a **Bench** of six to hear the case, **Kirby** having **disqualified** himself because of his previous support for the plaintiffs' cause. All six Justices held that the case did involve a 'matter' and did not constitute a request for an advisory opinion. They observed that the fact that the plaintiffs had engaged in sexual activity prohibited by the Criminal Code rendered them liable to prosecution, conviction, and punishment; thus they had a real interest in the case sufficient to give them **standing**. **Gaudron**, **McHugh**, and **Gummow** commented that 'the conduct by the plaintiffs of

Rodney Croome (centre) and Nicholas Toonen, who challenged Tasmania's anti-gay laws in the High Court

their personal lives in significant respects is overshadowed by the presence of sections 122 and 123 of the Code'.

Following the plaintiffs' decisive victory at this initial stage of the case, Tasmania repealed sections 122 and 123 of the Criminal Code in 1997. The Court thus never had to decide the substantive issue in *Croome*.

In the area of the **criminal law**, the High Court has considered the question of whether a 'homosexual advance' may operate to reduce a charge of murder to manslaughter under the doctrine of provocation (see **Criminal law defences**). In *Green v The Queen* (1997), the accused claimed that the deceased had made sexual advances towards him that had triggered in his mind a memory of his father sexually abusing his sisters, and had therefore caused him to lose control and kill the deceased. The trial judge ruled that evidence of the father's sexual abuse of the accused's sisters was inadmissible on the question of whether a defence of provocation could apply. The case thus involved something more than simply a claim that a homosexual advance constituted provocation under the law. Nonetheless, some members of the Court commented on this aspect of the case.

Kirby stated in the strongest terms that a non-violent homosexual advance should not be accepted as constituting provocation under Australian law. He held that:

> For the law to accept that a non-violent sexual advance, without more, by a man to a man could induce in an ordinary person such a reduction in self-control as to occasion the formation of an intent to kill, or to inflict grievous bodily harm, would sit ill with contemporary legal, educative, and policing

efforts designed to remove such violent responses from society, grounded as they are in irrational hatred and fear.

> In my view, the 'ordinary person' in Australian society today is not so homophobic as to respond to a non-violent sexual advance by a homosexual person [by forming] an intent to kill or to inflict grievous bodily harm.

Gummow also rejected the idea that a non-violent homosexual advance could constitute provocation.

In contrast, **Brennan** seemed to accept that a non-violent homosexual advance may constitute provocation, stating that:

> A reasonable jury might have come to the conclusion that an ordinary person, who was provoked to the degree the [accused] was provoked, could have formed an intent to kill or to inflict grievous bodily harm ... A juryman or woman would not be unreasonable because he or she might accept that the appellant found the deceased's conduct 'revolting' rather than 'amorous'.

Ultimately, a majority of the Court allowed the accused's appeal. Thus, at least in circumstances where an accused has experienced sexual abuse or grown up in a family where sexual abuse occurred, a non-violent homosexual advance may constitute provocation under Australian law. This sets a **precedent**, potentially allowing anti-gay prejudice to provide a partial justification for murder.

In two cases concerning **disability discrimination**, the Court, by majority, has held that complaints against discrimination based on HIV status should be dismissed (see *IW v*

City of Perth (1997); *X v Commonwealth* (1999)). In the former case, the Perth City Council had refused its approval (contrary to the recommendation of its Town Planning Committee) for the establishment of a support centre for people infected with HIV. The plaintiff was a member of the WA branch of the support group PLWA (People Living With AIDS), which had sought to establish the centre. He complained that the Council was in breach of section 66K of the *Equal Opportunity Act* 1984 (WA), which prohibits discrimination in the provision of 'goods or services' on the ground of a person's physical 'impairment'. The majority Justices held variously that the giving of planning approvals was not a 'service'; or that, if the relevant 'service' was deliberation upon whether to grant approval or not, the Council had not withheld that service. **Dawson** and Gaudron added that, in any event, the individual plaintiff was not an 'aggrieved person' within the meaning of the Act, since the application for planning approval had not been made by him. Gummow sharpened the point into a paradox: 'The appellant suffered impairment but did not seek the provision of services by the Council. Services were sought by PLWA, but it did not suffer impairment.' **Toohey** and Kirby dissented.

In other contexts, some members of the Court have made positive statements of potential importance to lesbians and gay men, albeit only in *obiter dicta*. First, in refugee law, McHugh and Kirby accepted in *Applicant A v Minister for Immigration* (1997) that lesbians and gay men may claim refugee status in Australia if they suffer persecution because of their sexual preference. Secondly, on the question of same-sex marriage, McHugh commented in *Re Wakim* (1999):

> In 1901 'marriage' was seen as meaning a voluntary union for life between one man and one woman to the exclusion of all others. If that level of abstraction were now accepted, it would deny the Parliament of the Commonwealth the power to legislate for same sex marriages, although arguably 'marriage' now means, or in the near future may mean, a voluntary union for life between two *people* to the exclusion of others.

This is an indication that the High Court may eventually accept that the federal Parliament has the power to legislate for recognition of same-sex marriage.

Little is known about the sexual preferences of previous Justices. However, mention must be made of the **appointment** of the first openly gay Justice of the High Court, Michael Kirby, in 1996. Kirby had been a long-time advocate of lesbian and gay rights prior to his appointment. In 1999, he included in his entry in *Who's Who in Australia* reference to his 30-year relationship with his partner, Johan van Vloten. This was noticed by the press some six months after it first appeared, and although most of the **media** reaction was muted, there was some negative reaction to his disclosure.

One media **commentator** expressed concern that Kirby might think that his partner was somehow equivalent to a married spouse. It should be noted, however, that the law certainly does not treat Kirby's partner as equivalent to a married spouse, notwithstanding the length of the relationship. Although ad hoc provision has been made for van Vloten to accompany Kirby on Court **sittings**, broader equality for Justices' same-sex partners has not yet been achieved. The *Judges' Pensions Act* 1968 (Cth), which provides for the payment of a judicial pension to the surviving heterosexual partner of a deceased judge, makes no provision for the domestic partner of a gay or lesbian judge.

KRISTEN WALKER

Further Reading
Eric Beecher, 'The Modern Judge', *Eye*, 7–20 October 1999
Nathan Hodge, 'Transgressive Sexualities and the Homosexual Advance' (1998) 23 *Alt LJ* 30
Michael Kirby, 'Same Sex Relationships: Some Australian Developments' (1999) 19 *Aust Bar Rev* 4
David Marr, *The High Price of Heaven* (1999)
Kristen Walker, 'International Human Rights Law and Sexuality: Strategies for Domestic Litigation' (1998) 3 *New York City Law Review* 115

Sittings of Court. The Court's first sitting, at 11.30 am on Tuesday 6 October 1903, was at Melbourne, the principal **seat** of the Court until 1973. From its **establishment**, the Court made annual visits to the states (see **Circuit system**). The Court first sat in Sydney on 15 October 1903. Its first scheduled sitting in Brisbane was on 26 October 1903, in Adelaide on 24 November 1903, in Perth on 2 December 1903, and in Hobart on 23 February 1904.

The *Judiciary Act* 1903 (Cth) provides that the Justices of the Court, or a majority of them, may make Rules of Court appointing and regulating the sittings of the Court and of Justices. Pursuant to the **High Court Rules**, the sittings of the **Full Court** are settled each calendar year and promulgated through a Rule of Court. The Court's sitting schedule is now published on the Court's web site; sitting schedules for earlier years are contained in the *Commonwealth Government Gazettes* and various legal periodicals.

One of the major interruptions to the Court's sitting schedule occurred in 1905, when the Court adjourned its sittings in protest at Josiah Symon's conduct as **Attorney-General** (see **Strike of 1905**). After the dispute with Symon had been resolved, the Court continued its itinerant sittings until 1931, when circuits were suspended as a result of the **Depression**. Full interstate sittings resumed in 1933. In 1927, Attorney-General **Latham** had secured an amendment to the

Admission ticket to the first sitting of the High Court; handwriting is of Walter Bingle, the Court's first Marshal

The Court's first sitting as anticipated by the *Argus*, 6 October 1903

Judiciary Act to prevent the automatic removal of the Court's seat to **Canberra**, since there was no adequate accommodation for the Court; but from 1933, individual Justices periodically sat in Canberra in exercise of the original **jurisdiction** in relation to the **territory**.

The **Dixon diaries** record that the Justices had to cope with uncomfortable train trips between states, and boat trips to Hobart and Perth. **Starke**, in particular, often cavilled at having to sit in what he called the 'outlying states'. **Barwick**, likewise, argued against the value of interstate sittings and unsuccessfully proposed that they be abandoned when the Court finally moved to Canberra in 1980.

Full Court sittings in each year are now set for approximately two consecutive weeks in each month except for January and July, when the Court is in recess. In addition, each year the Court appoints one week's sittings in each of Brisbane, Perth, Adelaide, and Hobart, subject to there being sufficient **business** in each of those locations.

In each of the Full Court sittings, a motion day is designated. On these days, the Court hears applications for special **leave to appeal** and motions for **removal** of causes. The Court sits in Sydney, Melbourne, or Canberra for hearings of these applications and motions. On those motion days when the Court sits in Canberra, a video link with Hobart, Adelaide, Perth, Darwin, or Brisbane, or a combination of these, is arranged to supplement the hearings of applications for special leave to appeal and motions for removal that take place during the circuit sittings in those locations.

The High Court Rules make provision for the sittings of single Justices in Court or in **chambers**, as appointed by a Rule of Court or as a Justice thinks fit. In practical terms, single-Justice sittings are arranged as is necessary from time to time both during and outside Full Court designated sittings. The Full Court usually sits from 10.30 am to 4.30 pm each sitting day, with single Justices hearing matters in chambers before and after those times.

There are two vacations during each calendar year. The long vacation (of seven weeks) begins on a day appointed in December, and the winter vacation (of five weeks) begins on a day appointed in June or July. The Full Court does not sit during this time, but the Justices and their staff often remain in chambers working on the **production of judgments**, and the Registry remains open. If the need arises, arrangements are made with a single Justice to deal with any matters of urgency.

ELISA HARRIS

Socialism. Australia did not begin as a community of free settlers. It began as a military establishment under the grasp of our first authorised entrepreneurs, the Rum Corps, who busied themselves selling grog and claiming grants of land. Within 30 years, **men** of **property** had gained title to their pastures; secured access to the magistracy; obtained convict labour at nominal expense; enforced the law of master and servant; and excluded emancipated convicts from social standing.

The merits and menace of socialism began to be recognised around 1875, with the agitation for the formation of a labour party asserting the social claims of the wage-dependent classes against those of the pastoral and merchant classes. The introduction of customs and **excise duties** showed that the law could serve the men of property and consumers and producers at the same time: set the source of revenue on the value of goods at the wharf or at the factory gate, and everything would follow satisfactorily from that. Some working men, whose earnings bore a disproportionate share of the duties, saw things differently and called for a land tax; others among them welcomed the new duties as a guarantee of employment, where competition from foreign goods might otherwise rage. Local manufacturers were also quite partisan upon the point. The 'fiscal issue' and 'Free Trade versus Protection' were two sides of the same penny.

By 1901, federation would offer new arenas for the contest—the federal Parliament, **conciliation and arbitration** in **labour relations**, and the High Court of Australia.

Initially, **O'Connor**, then **Higgins**, and later **Powers** sat in the Court of Conciliation and Arbitration to settle industrial disputes between employers and unions of employees (frequently led by socialists). Their work was subject to the High Court's rulings on the limits of their jurisdiction, which was frequently challenged by employers. In the first three decades of federation, an extensive body of rules about these matters grew rapidly.

One spur to federation had been a conservative fear of the new unionism, which had shown its militancy in the 1890s across Queensland, NSW, and Victoria, and at Broken Hill—that is, in common cause across the colonial borders in mining, shearing, and maritime employment. The workers had faced the squatters' guns, the colonial police, and the **criminal law**. They had political claims, and recent successes in colonial elections. They were making ground.

The new High Court swung quickly into action against unionism, at a time when the rate of recruitment was mounting feverishly. In the *Railway Servants Case* (1906), it refused to permit the Commonwealth Arbitration Court to accept an application under the *Conciliation and Arbitration Act* 1904 (Cth) for registration of a union of employees in the NSW railways: the mere registration, without more, of an association of railway employees was deemed to be a breach of the ramparts. Hold them out or there would soon be a national union of railway men! There soon was.

Given the developments against which the doctrine of **intergovernmental immunities** was deployed in this way, the decision was a belated rearguard action. Already a government had fallen on account of the issue. On 21 April 1904, in the Commonwealth Parliament, a Labor member had moved an amendment to Alfred **Deakin's** Bill for a federal conciliation and arbitration system to extend it to cover disputes affecting the public services of the Commonwealth and the states and any public authority. The amendment was carried, and the government resigned. The Watson Labor government succeeded it. The times were changing but the Court was not moving with them.

A union achieved an award by arbitration under the federal tribunal. It asked for the award to be declared as a 'common rule' throughout the industry. Notwithstanding the **common law** tradition of treating an individual **precedent** as the basis for a general rule of law, the Court rejected this concept (*Whybrow's Case (No 2)* (1910)). Earlier, in response to *Whybrow's Case (No 1)* (1910), where the Court had ruled that the federal arbitration power was confined by state law, Higgins

(in his role as President of the Arbitration Court) had been moved to denounce the High Court's rulings as a 'veritable Serbonian bog of technicalities' that would 'make it impracticable to make awards which would work' (*Australian Boot Trade Employees Federation v Whybrow* (1910)).

The rejection of the provision for a common rule was quickly circumvented by resort to the 'paper dispute'. The unions simply wrote to every conceivable employer in relevant industries making claims in advance of going into court, or afterwards for what they had won. Reluctant employers found themselves roped in. It was effective, but costly and inconvenient, and it did nothing for the prestige of the High Court that this bureaucratic task was required in the new world of widespread unionism that was coming into being. It was seen as a measure of harassment, aimed at the protection of employers.

Even more provocatively, the Court struck down a federal legislative scheme which had used the customs power to enforce 'fair and reasonable wages' in specified industries (*R v Barger* (1908)). John Watson, the parliamentary leader of the Labor Party, had declared it to be a 'socialist' measure. In the same year, in *Slayter v Daily Telegraph* (1908), an action in defamation, the Court held that to call a parliamentary candidate for election to the House of Representatives a 'socialistic candidate', was not, without more, to impute that he favoured the nationalisation of all industry or the confiscation of all property by the state.

A great many of these irritations were allayed in the new era that began with the *Engineers Case* (1920). Unionism was received warmly into the federal fold.

Salvation from socialism became the main task of section 92 of the Constitution (see **Interstate trade and commerce**). At the time of its promulgation to the voters in the referenda of 1898 and 1899, its critical declaration that, once uniform customs duties were imposed, 'trade, commerce and intercourse between the States ... shall be absolutely free' had been simply a bald statement of a fact in prospect. In NSW, in the decade before federation, 'free trade' and land tax were the most popular causes in the colony. There was high excitement about them. But there was no such excitement for federation. There was always doubt that the voters of that colony would vote for federation. In the first referendum of 3 June 1898, opposition to the Constitution Bill was strongest by far in NSW; and in the event, the turnout was low and inadequate. The majority for federation was a mere 5367 voters (3.9 per cent).

Because the total 'Yes' vote fell short of the special statutory requirement of 80 000 imposed by the NSW Parliament, the Bill was deemed to be rejected. George Reid, Premier, a 'free trader', and a leading participant in the work of the **Conventions**, was barely able to commit himself to the project. They called him 'Yes–No' Reid for his hesitations. A second referendum was projected. There was huge opposition to the 'Braddon clause' (now section 87 of the Constitution), which provided for a certain proportion of Commonwealth customs and excise revenue to be returned to the states. In August 1898, both Houses of the NSW Parliament asked for its removal altogether. The Premiers conferred in January 1899 and agreed to placate the colony by limiting its term to ten years.

This was one sop to the voters of NSW. Section 92 was another. That colony, more than any other, had a contingent of voters committed to free trade. The critical text of section 92 was nothing more than a reassurance, an inducement to the voters of NSW to fetch their endorsement of federation. The language adopted was emphatic, but brought nothing except votes to the customs and excise scheme already set by sections 86–95, into the middle of which the assurance of section 92 was set. The free traders would settle for nothing less than free trade. They would not suffer duties at the borders. That was all.

The limited scope of section 92 was recognised by **Piddington**, sitting as Chief Commissioner of the **Inter-State Commission** in the *Wheat Case* (1915). In finding that the *Wheat Acquisition Act* 1914 (NSW), a wartime measure for control of essential foodstuffs, did not breach section 92, he said:

> The Constitution of Australia is distinguished from that of the United States of America by the very fact that no attempt has been made anywhere to bind the electors to any prescribed course of economic action … If ever any Legislature in Australia … adopts in its legislation the policy of 'Socialism in our time', I do not believe it will be incumbent upon the Courts to point to section 92 as saying 'Never, in this Commonwealth'.

Nevertheless, in the High Court, section 92 soon came to be transformed from a statement of fact about customs houses into a proposition of law that severely inhibited any attempt to enact socialist policies. Initially, **discrimination** against out-of-state commodities other than by a customs provision was outlawed (*Fox v Robbins* (1909)). **Isaacs** in particular was determined that section 92 should not be 'a worthless scrap of paper' (*Duncan v Queensland* (1916)). He, especially, became a tribune for section 92 to be appreciated as a declaration of an unqualified private right, an omnibus legal entitlement of traders, at least against state laws. His argument, as a matter of history, even language, was gratuitous and unnecessary. The High Court should have left issues beyond customs duties to the market place and the ballot box.

Claims for trade without restraint across state borders were promoted by the High Court under staid common law rules of construction. The Court's response was not tailored to the context—and even went against the context—of laws made pursuant to constitutional power. In *James v Commonwealth* (1936), the **Privy Council** was unmoved by Robert **Menzies'** submission that striking down of a Commonwealth law creating a marketing scheme founded on prohibitions and regulation would mean 'that the totality of power in Australia will prove to be less than the totality of power in other civilised countries'. It opted for **literalism**. It was hardly the American way, but advocacy upon these premises obviated the need to raise a hue and cry against socialism at the Bar table.

When, in the marketing cases, in road transport and in banking, the readings given to section 92 of the Constitution transformed a freedom from imposts at the borders into a freedom from Parliaments, this was a triumph for free enterprise. The outcomes were justified as merely an imperative of literalism. Yet section 112 of the Constitution had made express provision against bad faith: in that section, the **framers** had recognised that the states might burden interstate trade by inspection laws and associated charges, and had made such measures subject to annulment by the Com-

monwealth Parliament if they went too far. But the literalists did not stoop to suffer the rule *expressio unius exclusio alterius* to fracture their cause. The culture of the men of affairs was at work. *Laissez-faire* had protected them for a century under English law.

Nothing underlines better the intellectual opportunism of these cases (for example, as it was brought into play in the **Bank Nationalisation Case** (1948 and 1949)) than the Privy Council's rider on the denial of Commonwealth power to prohibit privately owned capital from engaging in interstate trade and commerce:

> Every case must be judged on its own facts, in its own setting, time and circumstance, and it may be that, in regard to some economic activities and at some stage of social development, it might be maintained that prohibition, with a view to State monopoly, was the only practicable and reasonable manner of regulation.

The philosophy was clear: it was unsullied *laissez-faire*. The law of interstate trade and commerce was as long as the Chancellor's foot. Nevertheless, the High Court took its lead for some 40 years from the text of *Bank Nationalisation*, setting the capitalists free and the socialist tigers back in their cages. Eventually, the approach created such uncertainty, apparent inconsistency, and frustration for law and policy makers that the Court, acknowledging the ruins of its reasoning all round, threw everything from the past aside, and announced a new doctrine perhaps better suited to protect the traders from the people, even while the possibility of some degree of social control was in principle conceded (see *Cole v Whitfield* (1988)).

Although after **World War II** agitators for vested interest had continued to cry out against 'socialism' and to plead for 'states' rights'; by 1950, the dominant law makers were substantially on the side of business—out of conviction, indifference, or surrender, as the case may be. But at the same time as business—big, small, and foreign—was demanding salvation from the state, it was also pressing for active intervention by the state in their affairs, especially in the spheres of **taxation**, labour relations, and the public provision of industrial infrastructure. In these spheres and others, they clamoured for privileges and assistance. Amending the statutes for taxation and industrial relations has been almost an annual federal event, especially since World War II.

The **Cold War** gave international credibility to the campaign against socialism. Menzies, as leader of the Liberal Party, and Arthur Fadden, leader of the Country Party, formed an alliance to defeat the Chifley government, using the campaign against bank nationalisation as their vehicle. 'Their task is to rescue Australia from Socialism', proclaimed the new hardline journal *Hard Comment*. The ensuing struggles against the threat of socialism and communism tore the union movement and the Labor Party apart. Yet the High Court refused to allow the new government to outlaw the Communist party (see *Communist Party Case* (1951)); and when Frank and Denis Hursey vowed to 'split the union from top to bottom' by refusing to pay a union levy supporting the Labor Party, **Fullagar** responded by affirming the right of the workers to 'form associations for the furtherance of their …

interests'. Even in nineteenth-century England, he said, 'it was only if, and so far as, such an association offended against the sacred principle of freedom of trade, that it incurred the disfavour of the common law' (*Williams v Hursey* (1959)). It had been inevitable that the unions should seek direct representation in Parliament by supporting their own political party: 'The Labor Party was in its structure and in its essential character a product of trade unionism.' For a union to impose a financial levy on its members for party political purposes was clearly within its powers. The 'highly controversial' contrary decision of the **House of Lords** in *Amalgamated Society of Railway Servants v Osborne* (1909) should probably never have been regarded as 'applicable at all in Australia', and in any event could have no application to a union registered under the Commonwealth Conciliation and Arbitration Act.

The socialist era ended in 1975 with the **dismissal** of the Whitlam government from office. Although it enjoyed greater success in the High Court than had the Chifley government of the late 1940s—which had failed not only to nationalise the banks and the airlines but also to establish a pharmaceutical benefits scheme—the Whitlam government had lacked true power to enact its program, being a minority party in the Senate and ruthlessly opposed in the Parliament and the electorate (see **Whitlam era**).

Over time, the enthusiasm for socialist measures had abated. In their revenue laws, Labor governments had never sought to challenge the social utility of the concepts of income, capital, the corporation, or the trust; taxation expenditure; or the array of double-tax treaties of the Commonwealth—all of which were and are powerful segments of the legal armour of capitalists in Australia.

Federally, Labor's access to untrammelled power in the 75 years before the removal of the Whitlam government had been little available and little enjoyed. Labor formed governments for just one-quarter of the first 100 years of federation. It held power—a majority in both Houses—for only 11 years and seven months. It had terms in Opposition of 13 years (1916–29), ten years (1932–41), and 23 years (1949–72). None of this made for experience, briskness, or confidence in office when it came. The Labor governments of Hawke and Keating (1983–96), unlike that of Whitlam, made no pretence to a socialist purpose. The commitment of the political movement born in 1891 to socialism in law making had never provided an enduring task for the Court.

JIM STAPLES

Social justice in twentieth century Australia had many dimensions. Today, it is associated with **equality** of opportunity in access to law, education, employment, health, and community facilities. In the 1970s, other concepts justified state intervention in housing, health care, education, legal aid, and income support for the poor and disadvantaged. In the 1940s, the wider hope that post-war reconstruction would materially benefit the working class was reflected in the Catholic Bishops' vision for social justice through a new order of work and family life. In earlier decades, religious, charitable, progressive, and liberal values had to varying degrees incorporated the aspirations of **socialism**. Early twentieth-century Australians saw the state, in Meredith

Atkinson's words, as 'themselves in social community', and believed that its 'powers and resources … [were] properly utilised when … directed to the positive promotion of the welfare of the people as a whole'.

The pre-1970s High Court had few opportunities to engage with social justice, except perhaps indirectly—as when **Barton** observed in *R v Smithers; Ex parte Benson* (1912) that the federal union had assured to Australians 'the rights of access to the institutions, and of due participation in the activities of the nation', or when **Starke** acknowledged the contribution of cultural conflict to the wrongful conviction of an Aboriginal in *Tuckiar v The King* (1934). Social justice was an important background presence in the flow of cases on the arbitration power in the 1920s and 1930s, as it was when the *First Pharmaceutical Benefits Case* (1945) and the *Bank Nationalisation Case* (1948) defeated assertions of Commonwealth power to administer social welfare and regulate the **economy**. The absence of more frequent engagements with social justice, however, requires explanation.

According to Mauro Cappelletti and Bryant Garth, modern Western legal institutions initially concentrated upon 'formal, not effective, access to justice [and] formal, not effective equality'—upon liberal **legalism**. This tendency was reinforced in Australia by the **role** assigned to the Court. The designers of federation saw legislatures as the primary instruments of social justice (see **Democracy, Court's conception of**) and by 1914 governments, public administrators, and the Commonwealth Court of **Conciliation and Arbitration** had adapted the colonial legislative experiments in social welfare to establish the foundations of the wage earners' welfare state.

The High Court thus had only limited opportunities to mandate social justice concerns. The Constitution served primarily to allocate governmental powers and functions, creating few **justiciable** rights of social **citizenship**. Until mid-century, federal social welfare powers were confined to invalid and old age pensions, and resort to the grants power was negligible. These limitations were compounded by judicial attitudes to **constitutional interpretation**: neither **literalism** nor the countervailing sense of broad constitutional vision is attuned to practical considerations conducive to the development of social justice jurisprudence. The relative infrequency of constitutional litigation was a further restriction.

The primary constraint was the **common law** itself. Legal modernisation had seen the causes of the poor gradually excluded from judge-made law. By the late nineteenth century, most litigation was, as Alan Hunt put it in 1978, 'profoundly bourgeois'—concerned primarily 'with the mutual regulation of the propertied classes'. The rapid evolution of the welfare state diversified civil litigation, without necessarily raising the judicial profile of the poor. Moreover, in modern Anglo-American societies, as Harry Arthurs observed in 1985, the **ideology** giving paramountcy to judge-made law had engineered an omnipresent conception of law as 'unsullied by close identification with contending interests or classes or political philosophies'. This apolitical conception of law formed a powerful barrier to the Court engaging with social justice issues.

Nor did section 69(3) of the *Judiciary Act* 1903 (Cth) or the *High Court Procedure Act* 1903 (Cth) expand the Court's role, since their legal aid provisions made no real attempt to improve access to justice for the poor. The former emerged from a belated parliamentary amendment, and the first **High Court Rules** merely incorporated the anachronistic *in forma pauperis* procedures (the old form of action available to a pauper). The perfunctory **reform** of the High Court Rules in 1952 did nothing to improve legal representation for poor parties. In its criminal **jurisdiction**, the Court conducted very few trials, and in appeals it concentrated on issues of process and doctrinal review.

The gap between the Court and social justice was not always reflected in the lives of its members. **Higgins'** work in the Conciliation and Arbitration Court in ensuring that workers received 'wages sufficient for the essentials of human existence' is well known. **Evatt** had lifelong connections with working-class causes—warning, even while a Justice, that trade unions risked extinction unless their 'members throughout the world are always ready to sacrifice their personal interests, their safety, or even their lives for the amelioration of the lot of the poor'. As an aspiring young politician in Queensland, **Griffith** had, as Douglas Graham put it in 1939, 'boldly declared himself … as a man who would steadily resist class domination, and work hard [for] fair and equitable representation for the people'. Even **Latham** told the Australian Legal Convention in 1935 that law 'should be regarded, as it is, as a powerful social instrument for the advancement of the people'.

Other early Justices shared these reformist sentiments, and like others in public life, were influenced by American progressivism. Moreover, radical and conservative judges alike were united by the public service ideals of the **legal profession**. As Latham told the Australian Legal Convention in 1935, it 'should never be forgotten by the members of the legal profession that the justification for [their] existence … as a profession is to be found in the value of the service they render to the people'. But the institutional constraints prevailed.

The global 'awakening of interest in effective access to justice' from the 1950s onwards in part reflected the growing influence of liberal ideals of equal justice, as Cappelletti and Garth maintain, but was also a product of what DA Rustow calls 'the revolution of modernisation' that 'entered its most intensive worldwide phase' in the 1950s. The emergence of global cultures and an **international Bill of Rights** meant that national responses to the social problems of law were more comparable than ever before.

Moreover, significant changes had occurred within Australian society itself. Australians emerged from their postwar stupor to confront a period of great social change. It became increasingly evident that not everyone had an equal share in the prosperity of postwar society. Middle-class radicalism gave new urgency to issues of social justice, the **environment**, poverty, **health**, and education. The functions and scope of government were changing. **Trade practices** legislation and other regulatory reforms signalled a new stage in Australian welfare capitalism. The expanded role of federal governments as financiers of social welfare services further hybridised the wage-earners' welfare state. All this, together with the emphasis on law reform, human rights legislation, and policies of multiculturalism, stimulated popular expectations of the rights of social citizenship. Institutional reforms such as the end of **Privy Council** appeals, the 1984

special **leave** provisions, the 1981 reforms to section 15 of the *Acts Interpretation Act* 1901, and the establishment of the **Federal Court** contributed to the climate of reform.

By the mid-1980s, it seemed that everyone—governments, interest groups, citizens, and the national **media**—was complaining of the **cost of litigation**, and of inefficiency and ineffectiveness in the legal system. In 1989, the Senate Standing Committee on Legal and Constitutional Affairs announced an inquiry into the 'Cost of Justice', and in 1993 the Access to Justice Advisory Committee was directed to consider reforms 'to enhance access to justice and render the system fairer, more efficient and more effective'.

Yet the pressure for 'access to justice' coincided with a profound shift of public policy. The expansion of federal social welfare functions had coincided with the end of the post-war expansion in Western economies. Governments began to reassess the direction of public policy, the role of the state, and commitments to social expenditure. By the 1980s, governments had decided, as FG Castles has noted, that the 'public generosity' of the social welfare state was 'no longer economically practicable' and that the new challenge was the way in which 'regulative activities … impeded economic competition'. The policies that had underpinned the wage-earners' welfare state were abandoned. In their place came policies dictating business deregulation, mandating the retreat of the state from public functions, shaping national competition policies, and creating an Australian Competition and Consumer Commission to oversee the new socio-economic order.

The changed political economy of the welfare state had significant implications for law. Commercialisation, privatisation, and corporatisation reorganised ownership and service delivery in the public sector. In Anna Yeatman's words, the maxims of New Public Management were antithetical to the socio-legal ideal of a public administration committed to 'substantive public service obligations like maintaining the **rule of "law"** [and] upholding citizens' rights of access to fair and equitable government administration'.

The ideological innovations in the public sector, and the increased emphasis on self-regulation by industry and business, restored the social significance of contract, and generated new styles of **administrative law** not always sympathetic to liberal legalist ideals. Negative government attitudes towards publicly funded intervention diluted the promises of social citizenship, encouraging instead new ideals of self-reliant citizens capable of managing their own social well-being. National competition policy, competition in the market for legal services, and an expanding business clientele, reshaped the modern alliance between the legal profession and the state, and reduced the economic incentives for its members to fulfil social justice obligations. The policies of the new 'market' welfare state fractured the established configurations of law and government, while also affecting the timing and significance of the 'access to justice' phenomenon.

After 1980, demands for the courts to display greater social **accountability** and responsiveness grew progressively more insistent. Judges, and the processes and functions of the courts, were subjected to unfamiliar—and often critical—public scrutiny. The new dynamics increased the High Court's exposure to social justice, and it also had new opportunities to engage with such issues. The poor and disadvantaged had attained a new and unprecedented national legal profile. A national legal aid scheme was introduced and a network of community legal centres sprang up. Federal public inquiries by the Commissioner for Law and Poverty, the Human Rights and Equal Opportunity Commission, and the Australian Law Reform Commission highlighted the problems encountered by the poor, **children**, **women**, and **Aboriginal peoples** in negotiating the legal system.

The growing 'rights' consciousness was another factor. The hybridised social welfare state, the surfacing of social citizenship, and the growing social prominence of human rights, fostered diverse popular expectations of legally effective, state-mandated social justice. The disappearance of the wage-earners' welfare state pierced the legal fabric protecting the collective social well-being to which Australians had grown accustomed. The 'access to justice' phenomenon, and the appearance of the legally proactive consumer citizen, produced different versions of popular rights in relation to legal institutions. With a new frequency, the courts and lawyers' organisations asserted the role of judge-administered law and its institutions against the challenges presented by New Public Management and by the emerging new administrative technologies.

Yet the newly acquired 'rights' of social citizenship and 'access to justice' were subjected to a cruel paradox, emerging as the commitment of the state to liberal legalist ideals of social governance was fading. Governments in the market welfare state were inherently less disposed to guarantee social well-being or attach material benefits to citizenship, and progressively more reluctant to do so. Australians began to look to other institutions for social protection, and to vent their frustrated expectations of effective legal citizenship. The Court, its Justices, and its law were obvious targets.

There was no dramatic reversal of the Court's historical disengagement from social justice. The expansion of federal social welfare functions produced some relevant cases: in the *DOGS Case* (1981), a majority of the Court upheld a Commonwealth legislative scheme financially assisting non-government schools notwithstanding its indirect support to the promotion of religion, while the *AAP Case* (1975) saw the dismissal of a challenge to a Commonwealth scheme providing integrated, Australia-wide welfare programs to complement public income support and the welfare-related aspects of federal social policies. In *Green v Daniels* (1977), the Court held that applicants for payments under the *Social Security Act* 1947 (Cth) could not merely be regarded as supplicants, but possessed 'a substantial interest recognised by law' that was enforceable in the courts.

The growing expectations of social citizenship and human rights were a more significant source of cases. In *Koowarta's Case* (1982), a majority of the Court upheld provisions in the *Racial Discrimination Act* 1975 (Cth) for equal access to human rights and fundamental freedoms regardless of race, colour, descent, or national or ethnic origins. In *Mabo (No 1)* (1988), the Court held that these freedoms extended to the exercise of property rights by indigenous Australians. Fundamental issues of social justice for indigenous Australians also arose in *Mabo* (1992), *Wik* (1996), and other **native title** cases. Social justice considerations were also at stake in the dispute resolved by the *Tasmanian Dam Case* (1983) over

Commonwealth laws protecting the natural environment. First in *McInnis v The Queen* (1979), and later more responsively in *Dietrich v The Queen* (1992), the Court considered the rights of poor defendants in criminal cases to legal aid and to legal representation at trial.

Nevertheless, cases directly involving the rights of the poor and disadvantaged remained the exception. The Court's **business** was increasingly dominated by the causes of government, business, and economic regulation. Ironically, it is in the Court's response to these causes that we find the most significant increase in sensitivity to social justice issues.

New, socially aware judicial approaches to decision making were submerging literalism, and adapting the pragmatism of earlier periods to a changed institutional context. While **Murphy** drew openly on the 'deeper heritage of humane and egalitarian principles' within the orthodox legal tradition, his tenure coincided in any event with 'the last period of the ascendancy of the declaratory theory'. Justices such as **Stephen** and **Jacobs** had already begun to leaven the orthodoxy with new versions of pragmatism, gradually incorporating socially responsive judicial techniques.

Related to the shift in **judicial reasoning** was the Court's emergence as a political actor. Haig Patapan has said that to 'an unprecedented extent', its Justices are now prepared 'to decide the character and shape the contours of democracy in Australia'. Ultimately, it was the interaction between the new politics of the Court and the changing politics of law that gave the Court its greater exposure to social justice issues.

The Court now finds itself exposed to expectations of social justice and judicial intervention and innovation in a way unknown to its predecessors. Yet its institutional capacity to satisfy such expectations has not been correspondingly enlarged. Its constitutional warrant remains limited, as cases such as *Kruger v Commonwealth* (1997) illustrate. So too does its capacity to 'create new rules ... to mould the [common] law to correspond with the contemporary **values** of society'—even when, as **Brennan's** judgment in *Dietrich* demonstrates, that may be the preference of individual Justices. Similar constraints restrict its role in administrative justice, as the Court reminded us in *Minister for Immigration v Wu* (1996) and *A-G (NSW) v Quin* (1990).

The challenge for the Court is to develop social justice jurisprudence within these constraints, while conforming to the goal of the **Attorney-General's** 1995 *Justice Statement* that Australians should 'reap the benefits of living in a democratic society governed by the rule of law'. Its acceptance of this challenge is not uncontested, and is made doubly difficult by the fact that the concept of social justice itself is among the liberal legalist ideals imperilled by the new politics of law in Australian society.

DON FLEMING

Further Reading

Meredith Atkinson, *The New Social Order: A Study of Post-War Reconstruction* (1919)

Mauro Cappelletti and Bryant Garth, *Access to Justice: A World Survey* (1978)

FG Castles, 'The Dynamics of Policy Change: What Happened to the English-speaking Nations in the 1980s' (1990) 18 *European Journal of Political Research* 491

DA Rustow, 'Man or Citizen? Global Modernisation and Human Rights' in PR Newberg (ed), *The Politics of Human Rights* (1980)

Anna Yeatman, 'The Concept of Public Management and the Australian State in the 1980s' (1987) 46 *Australian Journal of Public Administration* 339

Solicitors-General. Unlike the concurrent office in England, in Australia, Solicitors-General—as Second Law Officers to the **Attorneys-General** of the Commonwealth, the states, and the **territories**—are neither members of Parliament nor politically partisan.

The Commonwealth office was combined with that of Secretary to the Attorney-General's Department until 1964. The first Solicitor-General (indeed, the first employee of the Commonwealth) was Robert **Garran**, who held office until 1932. He was succeeded by George Knowles, who remained in office until 1946. Then followed Kenneth Bailey, former Dean of the University of Melbourne Law School. On his retirement as Secretary in 1963, Bailey continued for 12 months in the separate office of Solicitor-General. The position was reconstituted as the statutory office of Second Law Officer for the Commonwealth by the *Law Officers Act* 1964 (Cth), with the principal functions of acting as **counsel** for the Commonwealth and giving advice. The statutory office has been held successively by **Mason** (1964–69); RJ Ellicott (1969–72); Maurice Byers (1973–83); Gavan Griffith (1984–97); and David Bennett (since 1998). As an evolutionary aspect of **nationhood**, the Commonwealth Solicitor-General has come to be designated as the Solicitor-General of Australia.

Maurice Byers, Commonwealth Solicitor-General 1973–83

Commonwealth Attorneys-General may or may not be counsel with the capacity to conduct constitutional litigation in person. In either event, nowadays the other demands of their senior political office make it necessary that the Solicitor-General act for the Attorney-General as senior counsel appearing for the Commonwealth's interest, particularly in the High Court. As the Second Law Officer, the principal function of the Commonwealth Solicitor-General is to be the leading counsel and legal adviser for the Commonwealth, particularly in constitutional matters.

There has also been an international role. Bailey joined with **Evatt**, when the latter was Foreign Minister, in the establishment of the UN. Between 1966 and 1987, the Solicitor-General was Australia's Delegate to the UN International Trade Law Organisation (UNCITRAL), and continues as Delegate to The Hague Conference on Private International Law. Solicitors-General have appeared as counsel and agent for the Commonwealth in the International Court of Justice, notably in the *Nuclear Test Cases* against France in 1973–74 and extensively into the 1990s, defending the *Nauru Case* in 1989 and the *East Timor Case* in 1995, as well as in the *Nuclear Weapons Advisory Opinions* in 1996. In 1994–95, Griffith, as Solicitor-General, was seconded as special counsel to the Under Secretary-General of Legal Affairs at the UN in New York.

The offices of Solicitor-General in the states also have a statutory basis. As well as being involved in **constitutional law** and public law issues, the state office holders tend to have a more active role in **criminal law** issues.

There is an unbroken tradition that Solicitors-General render dispassionate and non-political advice to their governments, including those of the contrary complexion to those under whom they took office. To some extent, the concept that the office is non-political is more clearly understood by the holders of office than by incoming governments. Byers served three successive administrations with affection and distinction. Professional satisfaction has compensated for the absence of the greater financial rewards from the highest level of practice as counsel.

It has been suggested that the American counterpart is the tenth Justice of the **United States Supreme Court**. Similar influence cannot be claimed for the office in Australia, although as the senior counsel for each government in the federation, the Solicitors-General enhance the quality of practice in public law, and contribute to the depth and continuity of constitutional arguments presented for governments to the High Court. A number of Solicitors-General have subsequently been appointed as Justices of the High Court: Mason (Commonwealth), **Webb** (Queensland), **Wilson** (WA), **Dawson** (Victoria), and **Gaudron** (NSW).

In their emanation as the Special Committee of Solicitors-General, the Solicitors-General have worked collectively, under the direction of the Standing Committee of Attorneys-General, to advise all governments and to develop statutory and constitutional structures at the national level. Their enduring achievement was to negotiate and agree upon the terms of the *Australia Acts* 1986—which, on the statutory request of the states, were enacted by the Commonwealth and UK Parliaments to sever the last of the states' residual links to the UK, thus establishing Australia as

Table of Commonwealth Solicitors-General

Name	Period in office
Robert Garran	1916–32
George Knowles	1932–46
Kenneth Bailey	1946–64
Anthony Mason	1964–69
Robert Ellicott	1969–73
Maurice Byers	1973–83
Gavan Griffith	1984–97
David Bennett	1998–

an independent state in form as well as in fact. The Special Committee also devised the **cross-vesting** scheme, which unfortunately endured for only 12 years before being fractured by the High Court's decision in *Re Wakim* (1999). The Committee also works together to evolve a cooperative approach to constitutional issues in the High Court, although at times some or all of the states and territories join in opposition to the Commonwealth.

GAVAN GRIFFITH

Sovereignty, as **Gummow** and **Kirby** observed in *Commonwealth v Mewett* (1997), was described in 1833 by the great American judge Joseph Story as a term used in different senses in different contexts—leading to 'confusion of ideas, and sometimes to very mischievous and unfounded conclusions'. Externally, the description of a nation as 'sovereign' imports its recognition as an independent political entity, with what Story called 'the absolute right to govern' within its own territory. Internally, questions of sovereignty are concerned with where exactly, among the institutions of government, this absolute power is located, or how it is allocated among them.

'Sovereignty' in the external sense is an attribute of the nation itself as a single entity—in **international law**, a 'juristic person'. Sovereignty in the internal sense may well be fragmented or disputed. **Federalism** and **separation of powers** are ways of distributing or apportioning the components of sovereignty among different organisational structures. Logically, while the allocated components may add up to 'sovereignty', none of the entities involved can be 'sovereign', unless perhaps one has ultimate priority over the others. In Britain, external sovereignty was symbolically vested in the Crown; yet the senses in which the Crown was internally sovereign were politically contested and legally confused. In particular, the monarch had no independent power of legislation—arguably the primary attribute of internal sovereignty. British constitutional theory developed a basic postulate of 'parliamentary sovereignty', to which the executive and the courts are subordinate.

Assertions of sovereignty often depend on logical circularity. For example, international law was traditionally understood as the *product* of national sovereignty—the rules and practices that sovereign nations had agreed to accept. Yet the sovereignty of a nation was also perceived as the product of international law, depending on recognition by the international community according to its rules and criteria. Thus national sovereignty depends on recognition by an international community made up of nation states which both seek and confer that recognition.

At the time of Britain's acquisition of 'sovereignty' over the Australian continent—initially as a result of its 'discovery' by Captain James Cook in 1770—the closed self-supporting structure of circularity upon which sovereignty depends was confined to consensual relationships among European nations. Though Cook had been instructed to obtain the consent of the inhabitants in taking possession of 'convenient situations in the country in the name of the King in Great Britain', Australia's **Aboriginal peoples** were neither asked for their consent nor informed that a declaration of British sovereignty had been made. Under the international law of the time, indigenous peoples outside the circle of recognition were simply deemed to be subject to it. The acquisition by European nations of lands occupied by indigenous peoples, and its consequences in **colonialism**, were sanctioned by the evolving understanding of international law. As Emeric de Vattel wrote in his *Law of Nations* (1758): 'The people of Europe, too closely pent up at home, finding land of which the savages stood in no particular need, and of which they made no actual and constant use, were lawfully entitled to take possession of it.'

The belated recognition in *Mabo* (1992) that the acquisition of British sovereignty did not necessarily extinguish **native title** did nothing to displace the successive forms of British and Australian sovereignty that flowed from Cook's declaration and from subsequent occupation. On the contrary, the decision was reached by painstaking reappraisal of the legal effects of the acquisition of British sovereignty on the rights of an existing population. After *Mabo*, though the content of native title rights is determined by Aboriginal custom, their recognition and enforceability depends on the **common law** and on subsequent Commonwealth legislation: that is, on laws that derive their authority ultimately from the acquisition of British sovereignty. As Kirby explained in *Wik* (1996), *Mabo* created 'no dual system of law': any Aboriginal rights enforced in Australian courts must be grounded in the Australian legal system, in common law or statute. The position might be different in other countries, 'where indigenous peoples have been recognised, in effect, as nations with inherent powers of a limited sovereignty that have never been extinguished'; but that was not the case in Australia. Accordingly, arguments that the Court should recognise 'Aboriginal sovereignty' have repeatedly been rebuffed (see *Coe v Commonwealth (Nos 1 and 2)* (1979 and 1993); *Walker v NSW* (1994)).

In part, the Court's refusal to entertain such issues depends on the distribution of internal sovereignty: issues of sovereign acquisition or recognition are for the executive government, not for the courts. As **Brennan** explained in *Mabo*, 'the acquisition of a territory by a sovereign state for the first time is an act of state which cannot be challenged, controlled or interfered with by the courts of that state'. In part, the Court's attitude reflects a perception that competing claims to 'sovereignty' are mutually incompatible: decision-making bodies that derive their own validity from one power system cannot logically acknowledge the possibility of an alternative power system. Yet that argument makes sense only if the Aboriginal claim is conceived of as a claim to 'sovereignty' in the external sense—and, as **Gibbs** understood it in *Coe (No 1)*, as a claim by 'the Aboriginal people of Australia' as a single political entity. Understood as a claim by particular Aboriginal tribes or nations or 'peoples' to a degree of autonomous political control of their own communities and traditional lands, its acceptance within a national system poses no logical difficulties.

The attempt to formulate international norms on such issues is part of a wider effort, since **World War II**, to set universal standards for acceptable government treatment of individuals and subject peoples—particularly through the instruments comprised in the **International Bill of Rights**. The UN Charter declares that nothing in its provisions permits the UN to intervene in matters 'essentially within the domestic jurisdiction of any state'—a formula suggested by **Evatt** and inspired by the issues in *R v Burgess; Ex parte Henry* (1936). But, as concern for human rights has deepened, the understanding of what matters remain purely 'domestic' has changed.

Such developments do not themselves undermine or compromise national sovereignty, since the system of international law and the various systems of national law remain separate legal systems: a rule of international law has no necessary legal consequences within the Australian legal system, any more than a rule of French law would do. In *Triquet v Bath* (1764), Lord Mansfield remembered earlier judges as saying that international law 'was part of the law of England', automatically accepted and applied as part of the common law. But both common law and international law were still evolving; international law drew heavily on **natural law** and state practice ('customary international law'). Even if Mansfield's view still applied, international law 'incorporated' as he supposed would have only the status of common law, which can always be overridden by statute. In *Polites v Commonwealth* (1945)—where the plaintiff argued that under international law his Greek nationality precluded liability to military service in Australia—the Court held that, even if that were so, the clear provisions of the *National Security Act 1939* (Cth) would prevail.

At most, the common law could incorporate only customary international law. As international legal obligations have increasingly depended on treaties, Australian courts have consistently denied that they can have any direct effect for domestic legal purposes unless a deliberate law-making act by the proper law-making authority has 'transformed' the international rule into a domestic rule. Already in *Brown v Lizars* (1905), the **Griffith Court** had held that neither the courts nor the Crown could give effect to an extradition treaty in the absence of legislation. In *Chow Hung Ching v The King* (1948), **Dixon** emphasised that treaty ratification is effective only externally, with no internal effect on the rights and duties of 'subjects of the Crown'. Other Justices, including Gibbs in *Kioa v West* (1985) and **Mason** and **McHugh** in *Dietrich v The Queen* (1992), have repeatedly reaffirmed the point.

In the USA, the ratification of treaties requires 'the Advice and Consent of the Senate', by a two-thirds majority; but after that legislative input the treaty becomes, along with the Constitution itself, 'the supreme Law of the Land'. In Australia, as the Court explained in the *Industrial Relations Act Case* (1996), the internal division of sovereignty is different. The signing and ratifying of treaties is a purely executive process; their domestic implementation requires legislation under the **external affairs power** (section 51(xxix) of the Constitution).

The idea that **judicial reasoning** can be influenced or guided by international law—in development of the common law (*Mabo*), **statutory interpretation** (*Polites*), or **constitutional interpretation** (Kirby in *Newcrest Mining v Commonwealth* (1997))—does not detract from the basic principle. In any event, as Brennan emphasised in *Mabo* and Kirby in *Newcrest*, such questions arise primarily in response to the international concern with fundamental human values that flourished in the 1960s ('globalism'). Later pressures for internationalisation of the **economy** and removal of barriers to international trade ('globalisation') may threaten national sovereignty more directly—as Mason recognised in **retirement** through his public opposition to a proposed Multilateral Agreement on Investment (MAI). In *Project Blue Sky v Australian Broadcasting Authority* (1998), the Court struck down requirements for Australian content in television programming as inconsistent with a 1988 protocol to the Closer Economic Trade Agreement with New Zealand. Yet even then, it was not the treaty itself that compelled this conclusion, but a statutory provision in the *Broadcasting Services Act* 1992 (Cth) requiring conformity to 'Australia's obligations under any convention to which Australia is a party or any agreement between Australia and a foreign country'.

The British origins of Australia's federal polity compromised its internal sovereignty well into the twentieth century—primarily through the *Colonial Laws Validity Act* 1865 (Imp), which declared colonial laws inconsistent with certain Imperial statutes 'absolutely void and inoperative'. In the *Union Steamship Case* (1925), the Court held that this restricted the exercise even of **Commonwealth legislative powers**. In the *Limerick Steamship Case* (1924) and the *Skin Wool Case* (1926)), the Court struggled to reconcile its deference to Imperial sovereignty with insistence that **Privy Council** appeals were 'wholly concerned with Australian affairs, the local administration of justice'. In the end, the Court managed to avoid the operation of the Imperial legislation, and uphold the Australian legislation, by focusing on the fact that the Imperial legislation required implementation by British Orders in Council 'on the advice of Imperial Ministers responsible only to the Imperial Parliament'. This, said the Court, was incompatible with the principle of **responsible government** (see **Nationhood, Court's role in building**).

For the Commonwealth, such problems were finally solved by the *Statute of Westminster* 1931 (Imp), which declared that the Colonial Laws Validity Act could no longer restrict the legislative powers of the Dominions. But that declaration did not extend to the states. The result, as a series of High Court cases showed in the 1970s, was that the Commonwealth was sovereign and independent, but its component states were not. The problems were resolved only by the *Australia Acts* 1986.

An earlier attempt to show that the evolution of independence at the national level had effectively severed state links with the UK as well was rejected in *China Ocean v SA*

(1979). But for external purposes, what **Callinan** in *Sue v Hill* (1999) called 'the evolutionary theory' was accepted much sooner. Already in 1908, as the *Industrial Relations Act Case* noted, UK officials recognised that in Australia's relations with foreign nations, 'the Government of the Commonwealth alone can speak'.

Indeed, for this purpose, it seems that Australia's external sovereignty was established by the Constitution on 1 January 1901. In *R v Burgess; Ex parte Henry*, **Latham** held not only that 'international recognition and constitutional convention' had established Dominion independence quite apart from the Statute of Westminster, but that the Constitution itself had established Australia 'as a new political entity' controlling its own external affairs: the reference in section 61 to 'execution and maintenance of the Constitution' must include 'the establishment of relations at any time with other countries, including the acquisition of rights and obligations upon the international plane'. In *Barton v Commonwealth* (1974), Mason took a similar view.

In the *Seas and Submerged Lands Case* (1975), the Court upheld Commonwealth legislation asserting sovereignty over Australia's territorial sea and continental shelf. The Court held that the Commonwealth was the appropriate political entity to do this; **Barwick**, in particular, saw it as an exercise of inherent **nationhood power**. Even Gibbs and **Stephen**, who dissented as to the territorial sea, agreed that the continental shelf was properly claimed by the Commonwealth: the idea of the continental shelf had developed in international law, and made sense only in that context. The majority took that view for the territorial sea as well: both the legal concepts and the resource interests involved were the subject of mutual recognition and adjustment among the community of nations. The Commonwealth was a member of that community; the states were not. As Barwick explained, 'the important thing is that whatever the extent of the power or jurisdiction sovereignty or sovereign rights embraces, that power, jurisdiction or authority is conceded internationally to the nation state and depends on international mutuality'.

As an issue of external sovereignty, the case was simple enough; but issues of internal sovereignty were also involved. In *Bonser v La Macchia* (1969), Barwick and **Windeyer** had held that, before federation, sovereignty over Australia's territorial sea was vested in the Imperial Crown. That sovereignty had now devolved on the Commonwealth; but state powers, as in colonial times, still stopped at low water mark. In *Seas and Submerged Lands* McTiernan, Mason, and **Jacobs** accepted that theory; of the five majority Justices, only **Murphy** conceded that the colonies (now states) had begun to develop relevant powers before 1900, at least in an incipient way.

Because the Australian settlements went straight from colonial status into union as states of a federation, ideas of state 'sovereignty' differ from those in the USA—where the colonies had fought a war of independence against the British, and at least the thirteen original states had achieved independence as 'sovereign states' before joining in the pact of 1789 to form 'a more perfect union'. The Australian history was legally and emotionally different. There was no revolution; the Australian settlements had grown up as colonies of Great Britain, from which they had never separated. Rather, they had asked the Imperial Parliament to pass legis-

lation uniting them as a nation. The US Constitution could be understood as a compact to which the original states, in the exercise of their sovereignty, had agreed. In Australia, as Barwick emphasised in the *Payroll Tax Case* (1971), no such analysis was possible.

The Griffith Court did not immediately recognise the difference. Its decisions on the validity of state legislation affecting the Commonwealth (*D'Emden v Pedder* (1904)), and of Commonwealth legislation affecting the states (the *Railway Servants Case* (1906)), assumed—though the *Steel Rails Case* (1908) soon showed the need for exceptions—that each level of government was absolutely immune from legislative interference by the other. In adapting this doctrine of **intergovernmental immunities** and the related doctrine of **reserved state powers** from decisions of the **United States Supreme Court**, the Court was tailoring Australian federalism to the US pattern. It was also greatly influenced by the **jurisprudence** of John Austin (1790–1859), which dominated legal thought at the time. For Austin, the sovereign is a 'determinate human superior' to whom the bulk of the community habitually owe obedience, but who does not in turn owe obedience to any other superior. It followed from that conception that if one Australian government could make laws binding on another, that other could not truly be sovereign.

This view of the states as Austinian sovereigns affected other issues as well. In *Potter v BHP* (1906), the Court held that an action in Victoria based on a **patent** granted in NSW, in which the defendant challenged the patent's validity, could not be entertained. The grant of a patent is an 'exercise of the sovereign power of the State', and the courts of a state cannot examine the validity of acts 'by the supreme authority of another State in the exercise of its sovereign or quasi-sovereign powers'. The Court saw no distinction between the sovereignty of the states and that of foreign powers.

As a legal concept, 'sovereignty' remains artificial and malleable, open to reinterpretation by the legal imagination. The **joint judgment** in the *Engineers Case* (1920) did just this. Rejecting the American model, the Court found instead that the Commonwealth and states were formed in the image of Great Britain: that as sovereignty resided in the Crown and the Crown was indivisible, the sovereignty of the Commonwealth and that of each state were merely manifestations of the one and indivisible Crown. Although it made sense to speak of sovereignty in right of the Commonwealth and in right of each state, there was no reason why these separate 'rights' should be immune from each other's laws.

The US conception of 'sovereign states' carried with it a doctrine of 'sovereign immunity', apparently derived from the royal prerogative. Since 1997, a series of controversial decisions, including *Alden v Maine* (1999) and *University of Alabama v Garrett* (2001), has extended the sovereign immunity of American states to increasingly diverse areas. The primary effect of such an immunity is that a sovereign government cannot be sued except with its consent, particularly in **tort law**.

Such doctrines have had relatively little effect in Australia. The Constitution itself envisages litigation by and against the Commonwealth, and by and against the states; and the *Claims against the Commonwealth Act* 1902 (Cth), passed by the first federal Parliament, provided that in such cases the rights of the parties 'shall as nearly as possible be the same … as in an ordinary case between subject and subject'. The precise effect of that provision—as re-enacted in the *Judiciary Act* 1903 (Cth) and extended to claims against the states—has not been fully determined; but *Maguire v Simpson* (1977) decided that it deals with substantive as well as procedural rights.

The tort liability of Australian governments was established well before federation (see *Farnell v Bowman* (1887)). Yet 'sovereign immunity' dies hard. In *Enever v The King* (1906), a Tasmanian plaintiff sued under the *Crown Redress Act* 1891 (Tas) for wrongful arrest by a constable. But at common law the Crown would not have been liable for wrongful action by the police, and the Court held that the 1891 Act had not clearly changed that situation. The plaintiff argued that, because the constable was acting under the *Police Act* 1865 (Tas), he had acted with state authority. Since 'the state' meant 'the government as a whole', its legislative, executive, and judicial power were 'one and indivisible'; the constable's *legislative* authority meant that the state in its *executive* capacity was responsible for his actions. **Barton** found this 'a bold and novel proposition' which, if accepted, 'would involve the whole fabric of the State in confusion and disaster'.

In the Supreme Court of Tasmania, Andrew **Inglis Clark** had dissented (*Enever v The King* (1905)). For him, the state of Tasmania was simply 'a politically organised community, the juristic personality of which is located by the common law in the Crown'. Every servant of the Crown was a servant of the state; and the Crown enjoyed its powers and privileges 'as the supreme executive organ of the State, and for the purpose and welfare of the State'. The language was that of the Crown, but the functional ideas were those of the state as a politically organised community; the maintenance and enforcement of its law; and the welfare of its people.

In the High Court, a similar focus seems to be emerging. The shift, in British history, from the personal power of the monarch to the abstract symbolism of 'the Crown' had already reflected the tendency for political power to become depersonalised and then transpersonalised (NS Timasheff, *Introduction to the Sociology of Law* (1939)). Dixon carried that tendency further. In *Uther's Case* (1947), he explained his view of Commonwealth immunity from state legislation by invoking 'the prerogatives of the Crown' and the Commonwealth's special relationship with 'subjects of the Crown'. In the *Cigamatic Case* (1962), he found it better 'in modern times' to speak simply of 'the legal rights of the Commonwealth in relation to its subjects'.

More recently, in *Bropho v WA* (1990), a joint judgment of six Justices held that the controversial presumption that the Crown is not bound by statutes was 'largely inapplicable to conditions in this country', since government activities now reach 'into almost all aspects of commercial, industrial and developmental endeavour' on the same basis as private enterprise. And in *Bass v Permanent Trustee Co* (1999), another joint judgment suggested that it might be time to abandon 'inappropriate and potentially misleading' expressions such as 'shield of the Crown', 'binding the Crown', or 'the Crown in right of the Commonwealth', and instead to ask simply whether a statute is intended to regulate the conduct 'of the members, servants and agents of the executive government of the polity concerned'.

In a footnote to his **concurring judgment** in *Bass*, Kirby wondered whether 'at this stage in the understanding of the nature of a State of the Commonwealth, as provided for in the Constitution, it is appropriate to continue to treat it as an emanation of the Crown' at all. He cited the Irish decision in *Byrne v Ireland* (1971), where a defence of 'sovereign immunity' was dismissed because the Constitution proclaimed that all powers of government derive from the people. A written constitution whose sovereign authority is the people had no room for a 'sovereign immunity'—nor for any immunities not expressly conferred by the Constitution itself.

The High Court's understanding of 'sovereignty' has moved in a similar direction (see **Free Speech Cases**). In *Australian Capital Television v Commonwealth* (1992), Mason noted that the Australia Act 'marked the end of the legal sovereignty of the Imperial Parliament and recognized that ultimate sovereignty resided in the Australian people'. In *Nationwide News v Wills* (1992), the joint judgment of **Deane** and **Toohey** proclaimed that 'the legislative, executive or judicial powers of government … are ultimately derived from the people themselves'.

Yet theories of popular sovereignty rest on a final circularity. The Constitution is valid because it is a people's constitution; but it is a people's constitution because the Court reads it that way. To escape this circularity, the Court may have to fall back on another: while the law derives its validity from its grounding in 'sovereignty', what is 'sovereign' under the **rule of law** may be simply the law itself.

Tony Blackshield
Francesca Dominello

Further Reading
James Crawford, *The Creation of States in International Law* (1979)
EI Daes, 'Some Considerations on the Right of Indigenous Peoples to Self-Determination' (1993) 3 *Transnational Law and Contemporary Problems* 1
Elizabeth Evatt, 'The Acquisition of Territory in Australia and New Zealand' in CH Alexandrowicz (ed), *Grotian Society Papers* 1968 (1970) 16
Anthony Mason, 'International Law as a Source of Domestic Law', in Brian Opeskin and Donald Rothwell (eds), *International Law and Australian Federalism* (1997) 210
Michael Wait, 'The Slumbering Sovereign: Sir Owen Dixon's Common Law Constitution Revisited' (2001) 29 *FLRev* 57
Leslie Zines, *Constitutional Change in the Commonwealth* (1991)

Standing (or *locus standi*) is concerned with access to the courts and whether the person initiating proceedings is an appropriate person to do so. In public law, particularly **constitutional law**, the approach taken to standing is linked to what is seen as the appropriate judicial **role**. A view that the courts should primarily adjudicate on the rights of individuals when directly raised in a justiciable controversy would lead to a narrow approach to standing. By contrast, in both constitutional and non-constitutional cases, the High Court has generally taken a broad view of standing. This reflects its view that access to justice should not be unnecessarily denied because of narrow rules of standing, particularly where the actions of the executive are at issue. It is the courts that the Constitution principally entrusts with ensuring that the executive and legislature act within power. The approach of the High Court sets it apart from the **United States Supreme Court**, where the rules of standing are increasingly restrictive. The Supreme Court of Canada, by contrast, has adopted liberal rules of standing.

Standing is related to other judicial control devices such as **justiciability**, and the requirement for there to be a '**matter**', both of which limit the circumstances where the exercise of **judicial power** is appropriate. The relief being sought, and the context in which the action arises, are therefore relevant in determining whether the person bringing an action has the necessary standing.

The High Court has required a member of the public challenging the validity of a law or executive act to have a 'special interest' establishing that they are affected more particularly than is the public at large. This is, however, a flexible requirement, as is evident from *Shop Distributive & Allied Employees Association v Minister for Industrial Affairs (SA)* (1995). There it was held that the union had standing to challenge the validity of certain exemptions from shop trading hours on the basis that its members were shop assistants who had a special interest in the trading hours of shops in which they were employed. The Court said that the generally accepted rule remains that stated in *Australian Conservation Foundation v Commonwealth* (1980) and *Onus v Alcoa* (1981)—that a plaintiff has no standing to bring an action to prevent the violation of a public right if he or she has no interest in the subject matter beyond that of any other member of the public. However, the Court stated that 'the rule is flexible, and the nature and subject matter of the litigation will dictate what amounts to a special interest'.

The earlier general rule of British law—that only the **Attorney-General** may institute proceedings for a public wrong—has been regarded by the High Court as inappropriate for Australia. The difference in the roles of Australian and British Attorneys-General in relation to enforcing the law was emphasised in *Bateman's Bay Local Aboriginal Land Council v Aboriginal Community Benefit Fund* (1998) as a reason for allowing wider rules of standing, in order to allow an interested person to seek equitable or other relief to ensure the enforcement of the law. This does not, however, mean that in all circumstances any person will be accorded standing. Some members of the Court recognised that there are arguments for leaving the general enforcement of the law to the political process. Mere busybodies should not have standing. If, however, a person can show a special interest of their own, the High Court will regard that as sufficient.

The special interest must, however, arise in relation to a justiciable controversy capable of being a 'matter' in the constitutional sense. Thus, in *Croome v Tasmania* (1997), the fact that the plaintiffs faced possible criminal prosecution sufficed to enable them to seek a declaration that certain provisions of the Tasmanian Criminal Code were invalid because of **inconsistency** with Commonwealth law. However, the fact that a person desires to act in contravention of a law may not by itself suffice to confer standing to seek a declaration as to the validity of the law.

One area that has not been finally determined is the standing of a taxpayer to challenge **taxation** laws or expenditure of money by government. The High Court in *Davis v Common-*

wealth (1988) left open the issue whether a taxpayer has standing in that capacity to bring such a challenge.

In the *Truth About Motorways Case* (2000), the Court unanimously confirmed the ability of Parliament as part of a law on a subject matter otherwise within power to confer standing on 'any person' to bring an action for judicial enforcement of the law. The concept of judicial power does not dictate that a person must have a direct or special interest in the subject matter of the proceedings, if the requirements for a matter are otherwise met.

In taking this approach, the Court rejected the view of the US Supreme Court—expressed in the 1990s, under the influence of Justice Antonin Scalia—that Congress has limited power to provide for enforcement of the law by what amount to actions by 'private attorneys-general'. This approach leads to a significant restriction on the power of the US Congress to confer on 'any person' a right of enforcement of federal laws. In *Truth About Motorways*, the High Court considered that **responsible government** and the absence of the American version of **separation of powers** meant that the Australian context is different. The Australian Constitution did not require the adoption of the restrictive American approach. Examples in which any person has standing to enforce the law already existed in **criminal law** and in relation to certain prerogative **writs**. Parliament, it was held, should not be precluded from conferring broad standing on persons as part of a regulatory scheme.

The relaxed approach to the standing of private individuals has also been reflected in the Court's willingness to allow the states to challenge Commonwealth laws on the ground that they infringe the Constitution, whether or not any state law or direct state interest is affected. In the USA, the attitude to the standing of states to bring constitutional challenges is much more restrictive than in Australia. Much frustration at the inability to obtain **advisory opinions** has been overcome in Australia by the High Court's willingness to determine challenges by the states to the validity of Commonwealth laws that have been enacted but have not yet come into force. No direct state interest has to be shown to establish standing. There have been occasional contrary narrow views expressed by individual Justices. For instance, in the *AAP Case* (1975), **Stephen** held that the states did not have standing to challenge an appropriation, but the rest of the Court either found to the contrary or did not finally decide the point. In the *Union Label Case* (1908), **Higgins** tried to establish that a state Attorney-General had no right to represent the citizens of that state and needed, in order to have standing, to show some distinct injury to the state itself. These narrow views have not prevailed. The view stated by **Gibbs** in the *AAP Case*—that the Constitution, by defining the limits *inter se* of the powers of the Commonwealth and the states—has given each state a right to the observance of constitutional limits and a standing to obtain such remedy as may be necessary, has generally been endorsed.

HENRY BURMESTER

Further Reading

Henry Burmester, 'Locus Standi in Constitutional Litigation' in HP Lee and George Winterton (eds), *Australian Constitutional Perspectives* (1992)

Elizabeth Fisher and Jeremy Kirk, 'Still Standing: An Argument for Open Standing in Australia and England' (1997) 71 *ALJ* 370

PW Johnson, 'Governmental Standing under the Constitution' in L Stein (ed), *Locus Standi* (1979)

Starke, Hayden Erskine (*b* 22 February 1871; *d* 14 May 1958; Justice 1920–50) was a blunt individualist who resembled **Barwick** in his espousal of the practical effect of legislation, **Taylor** in his direct and sometimes discourteous style, and **Knox** in his detestation of philosophy.

Starke was born in Creswick, Victoria, the second of four children, to Dr Anthony George Hayden Starke and Elizabeth Jemima, née Mattingly. It is not clear why Starke senior, who had graduated in medicine at St Andrews, chose the name Erskine, but the invocation of the name of one of Britain's greatest and most courageous advocates was certainly appropriate. The practice was followed when Hayden's son John, also to become a fearless advocate, was born.

Starke's **background** of privation seems to have shaped his personality. When he was only six years old, his father died of typhoid, leaving his widow, two sons, and two daughters in straitened circumstances. Hayden's mother obtained work as postmistress in several country towns, and finally at the Melbourne suburb of Clifton Hill. For many years, she supported the family.

The young Starke won a scholarship to Scotch College, where he completed his last year at school. He then became an articled clerk while working at the office of Weigall & Dobson. It was his practice to walk from Clifton Hill to the office and back in order to save the penny fare. He demonstrated brilliance as a student and in 1892 became the first person to complete the articled clerks' course.

Although Starke did not care much for working on committees, he was an active member and secretary of the Law Students' Society. He liked rowing—although not competitively—and became president of the Rowing Association.

When Starke joined the Bar, the land-boom bubble was bursting, and he had to continue his practice of walking to work for a while. But inevitably, given his intellect, industry, determination, and presence, he prospered. He was able before long to purchase a home for the family in Toorak. He felt indebted to his mother for her years of struggle, and was devastated when she and her sister were lost in the *Waratah* during a voyage to South Africa in 1909. For years, he refused to abandon hope that the ship would be found. (The wreck was not discovered until the late 1990s.)

By the turn of the century, Starke was well established at the Victorian Bar. When the High Court began **sitting**, he was soon chosen to argue both constitutional and appellate cases before it. In the first three years of the Court, Starke appeared before it 13 times, including appearances with **Isaacs** in *Alexander Cowan & Sons v Lockyer* (1904) and *Duke of Wellington Gold Mining v Armstrong* (1906), with **Gavan Duffy** in *Austin v Austin* (1906), and with Edward Mitchell in *Melbourne Corporation v A-G (Vic)* (1906) and *McLean Bros v Grice* (1906). He also appeared on his own—initially, in *Christie v Permewan Wright & Co* (1904), and most audaciously in *Musgrove v McDonald* (1905), where he argued unsuccessfully that the Court could hear an appeal against a civil jury verdict notwithstanding the contrary practice of

Hayden Starke, Justice 1920–50

the **Privy Council**, since 'this Court is bound by sec 73 [of the Constitution], which must be interpreted without reference to the procedure of any other Court not controlled by a similar section'.

From 1908 onwards, as his reputation as an advocate grew, so too did the frequency of his appearances before the Court. In *Whybrow's Case (No 1)* (1910), Starke (again appearing as a junior to Mitchell) developed the argument on behalf of the states that the state legislation 'covered the ground' to the exclusion of Commonwealth law. Isaacs was obviously impressed by the argument, and later used it as the basis for his 'cover the field' test of section 109 **inconsistency** resulting in the supremacy of Commonwealth law.

By 1909, when he was aged 38, Starke felt sufficiently established to marry Margaret May Duffy, a daughter of John Gavan Duffy and a niece of Frank Gavan Duffy. In later years, however, when Starke and Gavan Duffy sat together on the High Court Bench, the **personal relations** between them were to become increasingly strained.

In 1912, the Chief Justice of Victoria, John Madden, invited Starke to apply for silk. It has sometimes been suggested that Starke declined the invitation because he did not want to take advantage of the active service of other members of the Bar (for, unlike his son, Starke did not go to war). But this would not explain Starke's failure to apply in 1912 or in 1918 (on the prompting of Chief Justice William Irvine), the year in which **World War I** ended. It was uncommon for leaders of the Bar to take silk in those days, although most High Court appointees had done so.

Starke continued to be busy during the second decade of the twentieth century, writing as many as 20 short opinions over a weekend. At the same time, he had a heavy load of court appearances, in the Supreme Court of Victoria, the Court of **Conciliation and Arbitration**, and the High Court. Between 1913 and 1917, his appearances as **counsel** before the High Court averaged 20 a year. By the time of his appointment in 1920, he had made at least 210 appearances before the High Court.

Even before his **appointment** to the High Court, Starke was a formidable figure. When Robert **Menzies** responded to Starke's belated command to propose a toast to the chief guest, **Barton**, at a Melbourne Bar dinner, Menzies recalled, 'with an instinct of obedience that has never deserted me in Starke's presence, I promptly did so'. A year later, when Menzies, then 25 years old, appeared before the High Court in the *Engineers Case* (1920), he again revealed his apprehension. 'Mr Justice Starke, who was a very distinguished common lawyer, and whose blunt habits of expression made no exception in favour of a very young man, looking at me in a grumbling way, said, "This argument is a lot of nonsense!"'

Starke's most pugnacious shafts, however, were usually reserved for his colleagues. By 1924, his judgments were showing signs of testiness. When Isaacs and Gavan Duffy held that a new way of flavouring sausages had sufficient originality to justify the grant of a **patent**, Starke wrote: 'I deplore the legal ingenuity which enables the applicants to obtain the grant of a patent … but there is, in my opinion, no other ingenuity, or invention, or novelty, in the case' (*Henry Berry & Co v Potter* (1924)). He adapted the language of Lord Justice Lindley in *Blakey & Co v Latham & Co* (1889): 'My opinion is that this is a very rubbishy and mischievous patent, and I think we ought to say so.' Again, when **Higgins** suggested that the industrial dispute in *Australian Commonwealth Shipping Board v Federated Seamen's Union (No 1)* (1925) was a one-state dispute in which the Court of Conciliation and Arbitration would have had no jurisdiction, Starke retorted that 'only a misunderstanding of facts or a misapplication of law' could lead to such a conclusion.

It was only when **McTiernan** and **Evatt** joined the Court in 1930 that Starke's relations with his colleagues settled into sustained and undisguised hostility. His inability to work amicably with the rest of the Court meant that he often refused to attend **conferences** with other Justices, and refused to exchange draft judgments with Evatt, whom Starke described in correspondence as one of Dixon's 'parrots' (on another occasion, he described his fellow Justices as 'worms', 'not men'). On one occasion, Evatt and Starke were members of a court being addressed by Evatt's brother, Clive. At the end of the exchange, Starke, having pushed Clive Evatt into a logical corner, leant back and said: 'There, let's see Brother Bert get you out of *that* one!'

Years after Evatt left the Bench, the acrimonious relationship between Starke and Evatt remained for all to see during the *Bank Nationalisation Case* (1948), in which Evatt, as **Attorney-General**, appeared for the Commonwealth. At the outset, Starke made an angry public pronouncement that the **Solicitor-General**, Kenneth Bailey, had called on him to express concern about the fact that his wife held shares in the National Bank. He said he had no intention of **disqualifying** himself from the case. Evatt's objection to Starke and **Williams** hearing the case was overruled.

From 1935, Starke sat on a Court presided over by his former pupil, **Latham**. Latham had read with Starke at a time when Starke was beginning to establish one of the busiest High Court practices. The role reversal of a former pupil becoming the headmaster and attempting to discipline his older and more experienced former master created perpetual problems.

When Latham suggested that Starke should travel on **circuit** to what Starke described as the 'outlying' states (all but Victoria and NSW), Starke's response was frequently obstructive. He suggested that these visits should be undertaken by Evatt and McTiernan and offered a variety of reasons for his own refusal. When Starke discovered that his son John had failed in **conflict of laws**, for example, he used that as a reason for not going on circuit. He did not want to leave his 'boy' alone in the house and wanted to help him get through a supplementary exam. In a letter to Latham informing him of this development, Starke added: 'It is most annoying when a proper attention to the work would have given him a pass'.

Starke's concern about leaving his 'boy' on his own in the house may have stemmed less from protective feelings for John's welfare than from concern about what John would get up to if left alone. An entry in the **Dixon diaries** for 27 August 1936 explains Starke's concern: 'Latham … told me that John Starke in the absence of all his people had used the housekeeping money for a drinking party & had dismissed all the servants.'

Despite his rebellious nature, or perhaps because of it, John went on to become a much-loved Victorian Supreme Court judge, after a colourful career at the Bar that included his vigorous role as defence counsel in *Tait's Case* (1962).

The Dixon diaries also contain several references to a judgment Starke wrote—which was never delivered—for *Nassoor v Nette* (1937), a bankruptcy appeal. In April 1937, **Rich** and Dixon had repeated anxious discussions with Latham and with each other over what to do about Starke's draft judgment, which apparently complained that the case had received 'insufficient consideration' from the Court, and particularly from Evatt. Dixon suggested to Latham that Starke was 'irrational': 'His inhibitions had gone & his old obsessions governed him. [He] ought not ever to come back to bench if his judgment was published.' Latham called on Starke 'to relent', while Rich and Dixon discussed what other action to take. Rich asked Attorney-General Menzies to get Starke to resign or go on leave. Eventually, although Dixon considered it 'quite wrong & unjust to the parties', it was agreed that for Evatt's protection the only solution was to have the case reargued without Starke's participation. The precise content of Starke's undelivered judgment will probably never be known.

Consistently with his rugged individualism, Starke had an antipathy towards authority. When the SA government claimed that the production of documents would be prejudicial to the public interest, he alone thought that the Court should exercise its power of inspecting the documents to determine for itself whether the claim was justified (*Griffin v SA* (1925); see now *Sankey v Whitlam* (1978)). If he had had his way, the Commonwealth would not have succeeded in monopolising the income tax field during **World War II**. He reacted to the Commonwealth's arguments in the *Uniform Tax Case* (1942) with characteristic cynicism, describing the contention that the legislation offered the states a mere inducement that the states could accept or reject, as 'specious but unreal'. He condemned the transfer of state **taxation** departments to the Commonwealth as 'wholly inconsistent' with the powers and functions of the states 'as self-governing bodies'. He insisted that the wartime **defence power** could not be used for such a purpose, and that nothing in the *Engineers Case* had excluded a proper judicial concern for **intergovernmental immunities**—pausing only for a sarcastic sideswipe at Evatt, who in *West's Case* (1937) had 'happily assure[d] us that the decision [in *Engineers*] was inevitable and a wise one'. He continued to inveigh against this aspect of the *Uniform Tax Case* in *R v Commonwealth Court of Conciliation and Arbitration; Ex parte Victoria* (1942):

> I must leave to those who were responsible for the decision ... the task of expounding and explaining it. I do not profess to understand that part of it which relates to the *Income Tax (War-time Arrangements) Act* ... The ascertainment of the nature and character of an Act must often prove difficult ... But if all legal standards be abandoned and the Court surrender to the principle that the defence power extends to anything that can be conceived, imagined or thought of as aiding the safety and defence of the Commonwealth, then those difficulties will be multiplied and the Court launched upon inquiries that cannot be described as judicial.

It was on this basis that Starke repeatedly dissented from the decisions upholding the extensive use of the defence power during World War II. Dixon had persuaded the rest of the Court that the defence power was a 'purpose' power (so that any law conducive to the purpose of defence would be valid); Starke alone insisted that it was a 'subject matter' power (so that only laws on the topic of defence would be valid; see **Characterisation**). In the *Women's Employment Case* (1943), he insisted that 'the real question' was one of the limits of constitutional power:

> But to substitute ... some other vague and meaningless collection of words does not aid a solution ... as may be gathered from the decisions of this Court. The real question is difficult enough in itself without these vague phrases and the imaginative efforts of the judicial mind.

In *de Mestre v Chisholm* (1944), he said that he had 'abandoned the hope of deciding any case [involving the defence power] upon grounds that are intelligible, satisfactory or convincing'. Rejecting the majority reasoning as 'mere conjecture and guesswork', he dismissed an order for the compulsory opening of licensed premises as 'one of those irritating orders and restrictions upon freedom of action which is arbitrary and capricious, serves no useful purpose, and has no connection whatever with defence'. He later referred to the 'atmosphere of make-believe' that surrounded the defence power (*Australian Textiles v Commonwealth* (1945)).

Despite his acerbity towards his colleagues and often towards counsel, Starke could be conspicuously humane in his attitude towards litigants—as in the gentleness with which he sentenced a public servant to prison for **contempt** in *James v Cowan; In re Botten* (1929), or in his response to the mentally disturbed adulterous wife in *Johnson v Johnson* (1923): 'The case is a painful one, and much, in my opinion, ought to be forgiven the unfortunate woman.' During World War II, the Court assumed an unusual administrative responsibility for the wives and children of enemy aliens interned under the *Trading with the Enemy Act* 1939 (Cth). Usually, the internees had been employed in Australia by alien enemy companies. A Court-appointed controller was empowered to collect the assets of the companies, wind up their Australian business, and pay the proceeds into a Court fund used for 'sustenance payments' for the wives and children. Starke assumed the responsibility for this scheme and administered it with paternalistic vigour. For example, when Mr Joklik, a senior manager with an Austrian company trading in Australia, was interned, Starke wrote: 'It is clear that Joklik must have sustenance for his wife and children if they are not to suffer hardship. The scale of military allowances for privates is not appropriate to a man of Joklik's position.' He estimated that the family would need £481 a year, including £7 a week for each of the two boys to attend Cranbook School. He acknowledged that the school fees were open to question, but wrote: 'It is important I think that the education of the boys should not be prejudiced by the war conditions if it can be reasonably avoided.'

One of Starke's idiosyncrasies was that in an age in which High Court Justices normally wore wigs, he generally did not do so. As an individualist, he detested **socialism**. To avoid giving his old enemy Evatt the opportunity to appoint his successor, Starke, together with Rich, refused to retire until the Menzies government was installed in 1949. They then retired in 1950, aged 78 and 87 respectively.

Because of his gruff, quintessential Australian personality, Starke was sometimes underestimated as a lawyer. Nonetheless, he combined outstanding abilities as an advocate and cross-examiner with profound scholarship. He was, according to Dixon, an advocate of great power and capacity to get to the heart of a case.

GRAHAM FRICKE

Further Reading
Arthur Dean, 'Sir Hayden Starke' (1959) 2 *MULR* 1
Clem Lloyd, 'Not Peace but a Sword! The High Court under JG Latham' (1987) 11 *Adel L Rev* 175

State constitutions were left largely untouched by the Australian Constitution. The **framers of the Constitution** generally confined themselves to the creation of the new federal level of government and the few express limits that had to be imposed on the states to achieve the purposes of federation (such as the guarantee of freedom of **interstate trade and commerce**). This approach could have given the state constitutions a strong independent life, as their counterparts have had in the USA. But they had been written in the British tradition, allowing easy amendment and avoiding limitations on parliament that could be enforced in the courts. They gave rise more to political disputes than legal ones. Until the abolition of appeals to the **Privy Council**, it was even possible for state constitutional cases to bypass the High Court altogether, as in *Cobb & Co v Kropp* (1966).

Despite the framers' general emphasis on the independence of state constitutions, they adopted what Andrew **Inglis**

Clark called the 'wholesome innovation' of allowing the High Court to hear appeals in all cases, not just those involving federal questions. This brought to the Court appeals not only in **criminal law**, **land law**, and other areas of private law, but also in cases concerning the interpretation of state constitutions. The **United States Supreme Court**, on the other hand, reviews only federal questions, making state courts the final courts of appeal in many state constitutional cases.

The state constitutions do impose some limitations on parliament, particularly in the form of procedures for the enactment of legislation and the amendment of the constitutions themselves. In *Taylor v A-G (Qld)* (1917) and *Clayton v Heffron* (1960), the High Court upheld the calling of (unsuccessful) referendums for the abolition of upper houses in Queensland and NSW under provisions governing disagreements between the two houses; the Queensland upper house later agreed to its own abolition. The decision in *A-G (NSW) v Trethowan* (1931) upheld NSW legislation requiring that abolition of the upper house be submitted to referendum, even if the upper house had agreed to its own demise. Other questions about the 'manner and form' of state legislation occupied the Court, with sometimes cryptic results, in *Clydesdale v Hughes* (1934), *South-Eastern Drainage Board (SA) v Savings Bank of SA* (1939), and *WA v Wilsmore* (1982). The extent to which these special legislative procedures are binding remains the most difficult question of state **constitutional law**.

Other issues to have reached the Court include the location of state borders (*Boundary Dispute Case* (1911); *A Raptis & Son v SA* (1977)), the territorial limits of state legislative power (*Broken Hill South v Commissioner of Taxation* (1937); *Pearce v Florenca* (1976); *Union Steamship v King* (1988); *Port MacDonnell Professional Fishermen's Association v SA* (1989)), the powers and privileges of houses of state parliament (*Willis and Christie v Perry* (1912); *Egan v Willis* (1998)), and the power of state governments to enter into contracts (*NSW v Bardolph* (1934)). The Court described the working of the conventions of **responsible government**, not spelled out in state constitutions, while dealing with **judicial review** of state executive decisions in *FAI Insurances v Winneke* (1982) and *SA v O'Shea* (1987).

Section 106 of the Australian Constitution expressly continued the state constitutions, prompting **Quick and Garran** to speculate that they should be seen as 'incorporated into the new Constitution, and should be read as if they formed parts or chapters of the new Constitution', thus producing 'a national plan of government having a Federal structure'. *Cooper v Commissioner of Income Tax (Qld)* (1907) treated state constitutions as fundamental laws amendable only by express words. Such talk perhaps came to be seen as tainted by the doctrine of **reserved state powers**, fundamental to the **Griffith Court** and rejected in the *Engineers Case* (1920). By the time of *McCawley v The King* (1918), **Higgins** was suggesting in **argument** that the Queensland constitution could be amended 'as if it were a Dog Act'. On appeal, the Privy Council adopted his description, at least for the parts of state constitutions that are not entrenched by special requirements for amendment.

This line of thinking likened state constitutions to ordinary Acts of Parliament, but more recent decisions hint at a higher status, although without any suggestion of reviving reserved powers. In *WA v Wilsmore*, **Murphy** concluded that the constitution of WA derived its authority from section 106, and that therefore 'a contravention of a State Constitution is a contravention of the Australian Constitution'. Though his disagreements with Murphy on other issues could hardly have been greater, **Barwick** apparently agreed, at least about the source of the state constitutions' authority. On this basis, the powers of state parliaments would also come from the Australian Constitution, thanks to section 106 and the related section 107. **Dixon** said flatly that state legislative power is not granted by the Constitution, but recent decisions contain some support, albeit inconclusive, for the proposition that the Australian Constitution is the source of state legislative power, if not also the basis of the state constitutions themselves.

The Court's **jurisdiction** to hear state constitutional cases emphasises its **role** as a national, rather than just a federal, court of appeal—one that deals not only with federal questions but also with matters of purely state concern. This power draws state constitutions into a more integrated national constitutional framework. But the Court's fragmentary pronouncements make their position in that framework ambiguous. Addition of new entrenched guarantees would increase their significance and raise their profile in the High Court, but for the moment they remain somewhere between Higgins' Dog Acts, amended and interpreted on appeal like any other legislation, and Quick and Garran's chapters of the Australian Constitution.

JOHN WAUGH

Further Reading
RD Lumb, *The Constitutions of the Australian States* (5th edn 1991)
Special Issue, 'State Constitutional Law' (1990) 20 *UWALR* 203
'State and Territory Constitutional Law: A Symposium' (1992) 3 *PLR* 3

State Supreme Courts. At the time of federation in 1901, each of the states of Australia had a **superior court** of record named the Supreme Court. The oldest state Supreme Court is that of NSW, established by the *Third Charter of Justice* in 1824. Prior to the **appointment** of the first Bench of the High Court, the only avenue of appeal from a decision of a state Supreme Court was to the Judicial Committee of the **Privy Council** in London. Due to factors such as the time and expense involved in travelling to England to address the Privy Council, this right of appeal was infrequently used prior to the onset of the jet age. Effectively, this meant that the decision of the Full Court of a state Supreme Court was often final. With the **establishment** of the High Court, a local alternative avenue of appeal from decisions of state Supreme Courts became available.

Since the High Court's inception, its Justices have been drawn from the Bar, the Benches of state Supreme Courts (and more recently the **Federal Court**), the ranks of federal and state parliaments and (occasionally) the executive government. The first **Chief Justice** of the High Court, **Griffith**, was Chief Justice of the Supreme Court of Queensland before taking his position on the High Court Bench. Of the 43 Justices of the High Court, 15 have been drawn directly from state Supreme Court Benches and a further four served on a

Supreme Court at some time prior to their High Court appointments (see **Background of Justices**). Given the wealth of judicial experience that former state Supreme Court judges have brought to the High Court, it is somewhat surprising that the number of such appointments has been so few.

Appeals from state Supreme Courts to the High Court are governed by section 73 of the Constitution. The first reported case of this kind was *Hannah v Dalgarno* (1903). In that case, the Court adopted the rule laid down by the Privy Council in *Prince v Gagnon* (1882) regarding the requirement of special **leave to appeal** from state Supreme Court decisions. However, it was the second reported case, *Bond v Commonwealth* (1903), that first considered the relationship between the High Court and the Supreme Courts of the states beyond the criteria for special leave. The decision in that case indicated the extent to which the High Court was willing to pay deference to the judgments of state Supreme Courts—at least as far as the interpretation of state legislation was concerned (but see **National unity**). It was held that, as a general rule, the High Court would be reluctant to put a different construction upon a state Act from that decided by the relevant Supreme Court, unless its opinion was directly invited by appeal from that Court.

Even apart from the High Court's appellate function, decisions of the Court can have a significant impact upon the role and functioning of state Supreme Courts. A notable example is the decision in *Kable v DPP* (1996). It was held in *Kable* that state Supreme Courts are prohibited from exercising a non-judicial function where such function is incompatible with the exercise of federal **judicial power** vested in the Supreme Courts under Chapter III of the Constitution. The High Court thus extended to state Supreme Courts the practical effect of the doctrine of **separation of powers**, though continuing to assert that the doctrine does not formally apply to the states. As a result of this decision, state legislatures are effectively prohibited from imposing any non-judicial function on the judicial officers of a Supreme Court.

Re Wakim (1999) reveals the potential for decisions of the High Court to have an indirect impact on the functions of state Supreme Courts. In that case, the High Court invalidated the cooperative state and federal **cross-vesting** legislation. This legislation was enacted to avoid the inconvenience, expense, and uncertainty caused in cases where state and federal jurisdictional boundaries were unclear. The legislation was widely regarded as having been successful in achieving its aims. It is perhaps too soon to assess the effect of the High Court decision in *Re Wakim* upon the business of state Supreme Courts. However, it is possible that the inability of states to invest jurisdiction in federal courts will result in an increase in the cases heard at state Supreme Court level.

Some may have thought that the status of the state Supreme Courts would be diminished as a consequence of the establishment of the High Court as the ultimate court of appeal. Certainly, there appeared to be less opportunity for state Supreme Courts to develop the **common law** as it pertains to Australia. However, though the decisions of the High Court have resulted in the overruling of many state Supreme Court decisions, the role of the state courts in the development of the common law remains significant. One of the reasons for this is the 1984 amendments to the *Judiciary Act 1903 (Cth)* requiring prospective appellants to obtain special leave to appeal to the High Court.

Prior to 1984, unsuccessful litigants in civil matters had a right of appeal to the High Court from the Full Court or Court of Appeal of any state, subject to a monetary qualification. In 1984, this right of appeal was effectively abolished, and appellants now have a right of appeal only by way of special leave. Only a very small proportion of the total number of civil and criminal appeals decided by the Court of Appeal or the Full Court of the Supreme Court of a state are the subject of applications for special leave to appeal to the High Court. In the 1990s, the criteria for the grant of special leave became more stringent. About 80 per cent of applications for special leave to appeal are refused. As a result, the Court of Appeal, Court of Criminal Appeal, or Full Court of a state Supreme Court, although technically an intermediate appeal court, is in reality a final court of appeal for most litigants (see also **Hierarchy of courts**).

DAVID MALCOLM

Statutory interpretation is the process of ascertaining the meaning of the words used in legislation. The **separation of powers** doctrine entrusts this task to the judiciary while recognising that a court's conclusion on the meaning of legislation may be overturned by the parliament. The **role** of the High Court in the interpretation of legislation is one of the more significant of its functions. As a result of statutes becoming the primary source of law, the majority of cases that come before the Court involve some element of interpretation.

From its beginning, the Court recognised the two broad approaches to statutory interpretation adopted in **common law** jurisdictions: the literal approach (in the USA, the 'plain meaning' approach) and the purposive approach (or, as it was originally called, the mischief rule).

One of the earliest statements of the literal approach is provided by **Higgins** in the *Engineers Case* (1920). Higgins referred to meaning having to be derived from the language of the statute as a whole and added that 'when we find what the language means in its ordinary and natural sense, it is our duty to obey that meaning, even if we think the result to be inconvenient, impolitic or improbable'. This preoccupation with the text of the legislation, justified as avoiding judicial consideration of **policy** issues, was still being enunciated in the 1970s (see, for example, *Phosphate Cooperative v Environment Protection Agency* (1977), where **Stephen** and **Mason** endorsed an interpretation of an Act while noting that such an interpretation 'remorselessly pursued must lead to curious and perhaps unforeseen consequences of considerable detriment to the community as a whole').

Concurrently with this adherence to **literalism**, endorsement can be found for the purposive approach—without acknowledgment that the two are not always compatible. Early in the life of the Court, in the *Engine-Drivers Case* (1911), **O'Connor** expressly endorsed the famous statement in *Heydon's Case* (1584) that, after ascertaining the 'mischief' with which a statute is concerned and the nature of the intended remedy, 'the office of all the Judges is always to make such construction as shall suppress the mischief, and advance the remedy'. Use of this approach can be found in High Court cases running through to the 1980s.

The purposive approach gave rise to the issue for the Court—how was the purpose of the legislation to be ascertained? Again, there was considerable jurisprudence from other countries that could be drawn on. The Court followed the common law tradition: purpose was primarily to be ascertained by reading the Act, though by reading it as a whole. Assistance could also be obtained from other associated legislation. Material **extrinsic** to the Act, such as law reform committee reports and international conventions, could be looked at to ascertain the problem with which the legislation was concerned but not to identify the remedy adopted. Parliamentary materials relevant to the Act in question could generally not be taken into account.

This traditional approach, whether literal or purposive, continued until the 1980s. But two decisions provoked a radical change. First, in *Commissioner for Prices and Consumer Affairs v Charles Moore* (1977), the Court reaffirmed that it would not look at parliamentary materials in the form of speeches and amendments to draft Bills to ascertain the meaning of legislation. The Court then interpreted the legislation in a way that ignored the fact that an amendment to avoid that interpretation had been expressly made to the Bill in its passage through the Parliament. (It is interesting to note that the two former parliamentarians on the Court, **Barwick** and **Murphy**, dissented.) The second factor of importance was that the Court, in a series of cases that culminated in the decision in *FCT v Westraders* (1980), adopted a literal approach to the interpretation of tax legislation, resulting in persons avoiding payment of tax by using a number of well-publicised tax-avoidance schemes (see **Taxation law; Ideology**).

In 1981, the Court gave hint of being prepared to take a more flexible approach to the ascertainment of meaning of legislation (see *Cooper Brookes v FCT* (1981); *Wacando v Commonwealth* (1981))—but it was too late for an exasperated executive. In 1981 and 1984, provisions reacting to the approach of the Court were included in the Commonwealth *Acts Interpretation Act* 1901 and later replicated in most of the states and **territories**. The first required the adoption of a purposive approach to statutory interpretation, thus ostensibly spelling the end of the literal approach. The second permitted regard to be paid, in the case of ambiguity, to a wide range of **extrinsic materials**, including parliamentary materials of the kind that the Court had declined to look at in the *Charles Moore* case.

With the enactment of these provisions, the jurisprudence of eight decades was swept aside. The Court was effectively told that its approach to statutory interpretation was wrong.

The Court has embraced the first of these changes without apparent difficulty (see particularly **Dawson** in *Mills v Meeking* (1990)). This is not surprising, as the purposive approach had always been available to it (and the intended purpose was often said to be discoverable only in the literal meaning). The Court has been less comfortable with the direction to have regard to extrinsic materials in ascertaining that purpose. It has stated on a number of occasions that the materials cannot be substituted for the words of the Act and can only be used where there is an ambiguity in the legislation. However, it is doubtful that the outcome of the *Charles Moore* case will be replicated. The changes have had a con-

siderable effect on High Court reasoning and practice. They were logical developments in the law of statutory interpretation but they were not able to be achieved by the Court.

Many 'rules' of interpretation have been recognised by the High Court and other courts over the years. They take many different forms. Some are grammatical—for example, the *noscitur a sociis* rule (words are to be interpreted in their context); some are syntactical—for example, the *expressio unius inclusio alterius* rule (an express reference to one matter indicates that other matters are to be excluded); some are founded on apparent common sense—for example, that re-enactment after interpretation preserves the previous interpretation (but see *Melbourne Corporation v Barry* (1922)). Some are based on earlier ideologies—for example, that tax Acts should be construed in favour of the taxpayer. Some are based on social circumstances that no longer exist—for example, that penal statutes should be strictly construed (which was said to have been adopted to ameliorate the wide application of the death penalty).

The High Court has relegated such rules to a supportive role only. The primary issue is the intention of the legislation. The various rules may assist in divining that intent but they are guides at best.

A recent example of this attitude concerned the issue of whether compliance with the terms of a statute is mandatory or directory; that is to say, whether a failure to comply strictly leads to an act being invalid or a sanction being attracted, or whether substantial compliance is enough. The High Court has rejected the validity of this distinction and indeed the language itself, despite its long history (*Project Blue Sky v Australian Broadcasting Authority* (1998)). In similar vein is the abandonment of the presumption against the Crown being bound by legislation in the absence of a clear indication (*Bropho v WA* (1990)).

This refusal to recognise constraints on the way legislation is interpreted is defensible to the extent that ascertainment of legislative intent is the sole purpose of statutory interpretation. But downgrading the value of the so-called 'rules' may lead to anarchy—and statutory interpretation *has* become anarchic. In this situation, drafters of legislation cannot follow the traditional guidelines in expectation of a certain outcome. Interpreters likewise are left to guess at meaning.

The Court clearly cannot endorse an interpretation of legislation that it considers to be wrong. However, the refusal to give weight to the traditional aids to interpretation results in the self-fulfilling outcome that the aids are valueless. The Court has provided minimal assistance to those engaged in the practical tasks of drafting and interpreting legislation.

While the Court has demonstrated an unwillingness to follow traditional common law rules of interpretation, it has had no such reservations about applying common law presumptions to interpretation. Principles that might be found in a **Bill of Rights**—such as freedom of religion, **property** not to be alienated without compensation, no self-incrimination, habeas corpus and so on—have been given de facto recognition by the Court. This has been achieved through the Court requiring that the principles be clearly displaced if they are not to limit the application of legislation. The Court expressed this requirement early in its existence in *Potter v Minahan* (1908), and more recently and most cogently in

Coco v The Queen (1994), where Mason, **Brennan**, **Gaudron**, and **McHugh** said: 'The courts should not impute to the legislature an intention to interfere with fundamental rights. Such an intention must be clearly manifested by unmistakable and unambiguous language. General words will rarely be sufficient for the purpose.'

Whether such an approach has always given full recognition to the actual intent of legislation is questionable, particularly in regard to legislation purporting to exclude **judicial review** (see **Privative clauses**). However, 'curial insistence on a clear expression of an unmistakable and unambiguous intention to abrogate or curtail a fundamental freedom will enhance the parliamentary process by securing a greater measure of attention to the impact of legislative proposals on fundamental rights' (*Coco's Case*). It is difficult to disagree with this as an appropriate guiding principle of statutory interpretation.

The 'intention of the legislature' is not the sum total of the subjective intentions of individual legislators, but is rather an abstract construct that seeks to give a single, objective meaning to a set of words. Given the ambiguity of language, it is not surprising that there may be a tension between a court's interpretation of that meaning and the views of individual legislators, particularly those sponsoring the legislation, on what was 'really' meant. As Bishop Hoadly said in 1717, 'whosoever hath the power to interpret the law hath the power to make it'.

The High Court's approach has been conservative, and is one factor that has led to the often-criticised practice of legislative drafting in Australia being very detailed and overly prescriptive. In developing rules to assist the task of statutory interpretation and to make the meaning of legislation more easily ascertainable and predictable, the High Court cannot be said to have made a significant contribution to the law of statutory interpretation.

DENNIS PEARCE

Stephen, Ninian Martin (*b* 15 June 1923; Justice 1972–82) was the only child of Barbara, née Cruickshank, and Frederick Stephen. His father, a Scots poultry farmer, died when Stephen was only a few weeks old, after being gassed in **World War I**. His mother worked as a companion to a wealthy Queensland woman, Nina Beatrice Mylne, after whom Stephen was named. Mylne took a considerable interest in the young boy and sent him to the Edinburgh Academy and then to St Paul's School in London. As a teenager, he attended Chillon College on Lake Geneva in Switzerland. Mylne decided to return to Australia after war was declared, and Stephen and his mother accompanied her in 1940. On arrival, Stephen attended Scotch College, Melbourne, for two terms. He began his legal career as a five-year articled law clerk with Arthur Robinson & Co in Melbourne and at the University of Melbourne in late 1940, but this was interrupted after one year by war service in the Australian Imperial Forces from 1941 to 1946. On discharge, Stephen completed his law course and articles and was admitted to practice in Victoria in 1949.

On discharge, Stephen met Valery Sinclair, a University of Melbourne arts graduate. They were married in 1949 and have five daughters. The long, close, and happy marriage has no doubt contributed to Stephen's famous equanimity and charm. And perhaps because he has always been surrounded

Ninian Stephen, Justice 1972–82

by **women** at home, Stephen was unmarked by the sometimes patronising attitude towards women encountered in the culture of the Bar and judiciary in Australia.

In 1952, Stephen left Arthur Robinson & Co and joined the Melbourne Bar, developing a specialised practice in **equity**, company law, **constitutional law**, and **taxation law**. He read with DM Little, later a Victorian Supreme Court judge. Stephen developed a reputation as an outstanding junior **counsel** to Aickin, and indeed postponed taking silk to continue in this role. He was appointed QC in 1966, became a Justice of the Supreme Court of Victoria in 1970, and was **appointed** to the High Court on 1 March 1972.

Stephen's approach to High Court cases is not easily categorised. While he was personally a liberal and progressive thinker, these views are not consistently reflected in his judgments, which reveal a cautious attitude to **judicial review** and no particular social or political agenda or judicial philosophy. He was not obviously a supporter of states' rights, nor of the federal government. On his **retirement**, he remarked that he had no burning interest in the **outcomes** of cases, such as might have led other Justices to seek in different ways to persuade the Court to their point of view. He rather saw his duty as to decide each case as he thought appropriate, and to let the result of the case take care of itself. His judgment in *Simsek v Macphee* (1982), on the rights of applicants for refugee status, is a clear example of his syllogistic method.

Early in his High Court career, Stephen was a dissenting voice for a broad interpretation of a constitutional guarantee in *Henry v Boehm* (1973). This case concerned the interpretation of section 117 of the Constitution, which prohibits

discrimination on the basis of state residence. While the majority of the Court read section 117 very narrowly, Stephen was concerned with the practical effect of a South Australian Rule of Court applying to lawyers admitted in other Australian jurisdictions, which required three months residence in SA before admission as a legal practitioner. He pointed out that SA residents would not be affected by the rule, but a resident of another state would be forced to give up legal practice elsewhere for three months in order to meet the SA requirements. Stephen's common sense approach to section 117 was endorsed by the High Court in *Street v Queensland Bar Association* (1989).

This 'common sense' approach continued to display itself. In *Adamson's Case* (1979), Stephen had the 'misfortune of disagreeing with other members of the Court' on whether the South Australian National Football League was a 'trading corporation' for the purposes of the *Trade Practices Act* 1974 (Cth). In an impressive essay on Australian Rules Football, by a person who had no interest at all in the sport, Stephen said that 'the fact that it is Australia's most popular spectator sport … which is in question is … of great importance' (see **Popular culture**). It would not, he believed,

> occur to many Australians to describe this Club as a trading corporation, and this for the good reason that both its predominant object and its sole activity is remote from trade and from profit-making. It does what it does to promote football, the income that comes its way being no doubt eagerly gathered in, but only as a means of better promoting its predominant purpose, the fostering of football.

In *Clark King & Co v Australian Wheat Board* (1978), *Permewan Wright v Trewhitt* (1979), and *Uebergang v Australian Wheat Board* (1980), Stephen contributed to the acceptance of a more generous approach to 'reasonable regulation' of **interstate trade and commerce**. In *Permewan Wright*, he said that the 'guaranteed freedom should … be qualified in the interests of the community at large' and provided a whimsical meditation on the nature of eggs. In that case, the testing and grading of eggs was held to be reasonably necessary to protect consumers of eggs (and therefore not to infringe section 92), since, as Stephen put it,

> eggs are so notoriously perishable a foodstuff that in their deteriorated state they have much enriched the English language in a number of picturesque phrases. There are, perhaps, few other foodstuffs which combine the qualities of being so dependent for their wholesomeness upon freshness, of being so prone to deterioration and the freshness of which at the time of purchase it is so difficult for the consumer to determine from outward appearance. They are not merely perishable but are enigmatic to the ordinary shopper; nor is this quality confined to their state of freshness, it can be no easy matter to distinguish by eye alone between the various weight-related grades of egg.

Stephen often found himself occupying a singular position in major cases, sitting apart from both majority and minority. For example, in the *AAP Case* (1975), Victoria challenged a Commonwealth appropriation as outside Commonwealth power. While all the other members of the Court decided the case by determining the substantive meaning and effect of the relevant constitutional provisions (with the six Justices equally divided on the result), Stephen took a completely different tack by denying that Victoria had **standing** to bring the action.

In *Koowarta's Case* (1982), Stephen also took a position somewhere between the majority and minority Justices by presenting a narrower view of the scope of the **external affairs power** than the rest of the majority but a wider view than the minority. He insisted that, in order for a treaty to give rise to an external affair so as to activate the power of the Commonwealth to implement it by domestic legislation, its subject matter had to be a genuine matter of international concern.

Stephen's approach also differed from that of the other majority Justices, as well as from that of the minority Justices, in *Ansett Transport Industries v Wardley* (1980). **Mason**, one of the majority, reasoned that the Commonwealth law in question did not 'confer a substantive right of dismissal' on Ansett, but rather prescribed 'the procedure … whereby the right to terminate may be effected'. Since the Commonwealth law assumed the right of dismissal provided by the general law, and Victorian legislation prohibiting dismissal from employment on the grounds of sex had modified that general law, there was no **inconsistency** under section 109. The minority Justices, on the other hand, took the view that the Commonwealth law *did* intend to deal exhaustively with all aspects of dismissal—substantive and procedural—and that the Victorian law intruded into a 'field' covered by the Commonwealth law. Stephen differed by saying that the Commonwealth law conferred a right of dismissal, but one that must be read in the context of the ends to which the Commonwealth law was directed: 'the settlement of an industrial dispute', not the entirely different purpose of preventing the 'socially evil' practice of sexual discrimination, with which the Victorian law was concerned. The two laws 'intermeshed'; but there was no inconsistency.

Among Stephen's other noteworthy judgments are those in *Russell v Russell* (1976), where he and Mason provided the pivotal judgments that substantially upheld the validity of the *Family Law Act* 1975 (Cth), and in the *Seas and Submerged Lands Case* (1975), where he agreed with the majority that the Commonwealth's assertion of **sovereignty** over Australia's continental shelf was valid, but (dissenting with **Gibbs**) would have recognised state powers over the territorial sea. Another pivotal judgment was in *A-G (WA); Ex rel Ansett Transport Industries v Australian National Airlines* (1976), where he agreed with **Barwick** and Gibbs that the **trade and commerce power** does not authorise the regulation of intrastate trade when the only relationship with interstate trade is economic, but also agreed with Mason and **Murphy** that a similar economic justification was sufficient to bring the legislation within the **territories** power. In the *Territory Senators Cases* (1975 and 1977), Stephen joined with Gibbs in differing from the majority view, but also in adhering to it in the second case because they saw no sufficient reason for **overruling** the earlier decision. His tentative exploration in *Caltex Oil v The Dredge 'Willemstad'* (1976) of 'the need … for some control mechanism based upon notions of **proximity**' between tortious act and resultant detriment' was subsequently to be picked up and substantially extended by **Deane**, while his eloquent essay on **characterisation** in *Actors Equity v Fontana Films* (1982) remains perhaps the clearest and most thoughtful exposition of the modern approach to that task.

Stephen maintained good **personal relations** with all his fellow Justices and never allowed jurisprudential differences to interfere in this. In the 2000 Sir Ninian Stephen Lecture at the University of Newcastle, **Brennan** observed that 'collegiality in a numerically small court can be a fragile thing, especially when issues of great moment fall for decision. Sir Ninian's scholarship and experience, his urbanity and especially his openness of mind made professional association as easy and agreeable as personal friendship'. Brennan also recalled some memories of the one year the two men sat together on the Court:

I witnessed the working of an incisive and cultivated mind responding with seeming ease to an unrelenting caseload. There were moments of apprehension when, immediately before walking through the court door to take his seat on the Bench, Sir Ninian would tuck a fuming pipe into the pocket of his bar jacket. A sense of relief grew only with the passing minutes, although there was never a sign of conflagration.

In 1982, **Prime Minister** Malcolm Fraser appointed Stephen as Governor-General to succeed Zelman Cowen, a move that took most of Australia by surprise because Stephen had little public profile. The idea also surprised Stephen, but he accepted it with alacrity, perhaps as an antidote to ten rather solitary years on the High Court. At the time of the appointment, Gough **Whitlam** predicted that Stephen 'would not frighten the horses' as Governor-General. The comment significantly understated the energy, perspicacity, and curiosity both Stephen and his wife brought to the role. Stephen's relaxed manner and cheerful, self-deprecating **humour** dissipated much of the vice-regal pomp and ceremony. He would willingly admit to being true to the Scottish **stereotype** of being mean with money—although, he would point out, not successfully mean. The pipe-smoking, tall, urbane figure was known for his interest in others and his sudden uproarious laugh. He was much happier asking questions than speaking about himself or his views. Stephen quickly established cordial relations with both Prime Ministers with whom he worked, Fraser and Bob Hawke.

Stephen's term as Governor-General will also be remembered for his special interest in indigenous issues, particularly his participation in the grand gesture of the handing back of Uluru to its indigenous owners in 1985. Stephen was respected by Australian republicans such as Manning Clark, who declared that he would make an ideal Australian President. The particular regard in which Stephen was also held by his royal principal is indicated by his induction as a Knight of the Garter, a rare honour bestowed personally by the Queen, in June 1994. While in office, Stephen spoke of the constitutional role of Governor-General as a '*fait accompli*' and 'no use railing against'. In 1976, during his time on the High Court, he gave a subtle speech in the wake of the **dismissal of 1975** in which he displayed rare insight into the role of the Governor-General and the intricate operation of the conventions of the Constitution—all couched in characteristically elegant and teasingly allusive prose.

After his term as Governor-General, Stephen has enjoyed the occasional controversial excursion into public affairs, including on one occasion calling for the abolition of the states. Stephen has taken on a wide range of international positions. He was appointed Australia's first Ambassador on the Environment in 1989. In 1992, the UK and Republic of Ireland governments appointed Stephen to chair Strand Two of the Talks on Northern Ireland. In 1993, he was elected, on Australia's nomination, for a four-year term as a judge on the International Criminal Tribunal for the Former Yugoslavia (ICTY). Stephen was subsequently elected to the appeal division of the ICTY and of the International Criminal Tribunal for Rwanda. His strong commitment to the values of the **common law** is evident in an opinion in the controversial *Tadic Case* (1995). At issue was whether witnesses in sexual assault cases could remain anonymous because of the trauma and danger involved in giving evidence. The majority of the Trial Chamber accepted that witness anonymity could be justified in certain exceptional circumstances. Stephen dissented, arguing that a fair trial required that the accused always know in advance the identity of all witnesses.

In 1995, Stephen was nominated by Australia as its ad hoc judge on the International Court of Justice in the *Case Concerning East Timor* and joined with the majority of the Court in dismissing on technical grounds Portugal's claim that the 1989 bilateral treaty between Australia and Indonesia dividing up resources in the Timor Gap was invalid. In 1998, the Secretary-General of the UN, Kofi Annan, asked Stephen to chair a commission on the establishment of a tribunal to deal with war crimes in Cambodia. He has also held a Commonwealth of Nations appointment as facilitator of discussion between government and Opposition in Bangladesh, has chaired a number of Australian government inquiries, and serves on the Ethics Commission of the International Olympics Committee.

Stephen is inevitably likely to be remembered more for his public role as Governor-General and internationally eminent person than for his ten-year term on the High Court. However, although his national judicial career has been overshadowed by his later achievements, Stephen's High Court legacy is a distinguished one. He was a wise, courteous, and insightful judicial figure with an elegant **judicial style** and a truly independent mind.

HILARY CHARLESWORTH

Further Reading
Ninian Stephen, 'Address to Mark the 75th Anniversary of the Constitution' in David Marr, *Barwick* (1980) 302
Ninian Stephen, 'Judicial Independence: A Fragile Bastion' (1982) 13 *MULR* 334

Stereotypes are a form of perceptual **discrimination**. They impose on individuals of a particular class—identified by **race**, ethnicity, or gender—a generalised set of attributes (often superficial and condescending) assumed to apply to all members of that class. When used in **popular culture**, they may constitute 'group libel', as a story in the fiction section of *Woman's Day* did when it implied that Arab airlines were liable to be hijacked by Israelis (*Sungravure v Middle East Airlines* (1975)). While it was an airline company that complained, the comment could equally have been offensive to Israelis.

On one view, the image of law as objective and neutral is essential to its authority, and the striving to maintain this authority is often translated into an effort to establish objective tests against which human behaviour may be judged. Yet the objectivity of such tests is not always what it seems. They are formulated by processes of generalisation and categorisation from what is assumed to be common human experience: yet while such processes may be unavoidable and indispensable to human communication, their application to human beings inevitably lapses into the use of stereotypes. The classic examples are the 'reasonable man' and 'ordinary man' tests (see **Men**).

Such tests have been rightly criticised for their exclusivity. Nevertheless, standards of '**reasonableness**' or 'ordinariness' may sometimes facilitate legal adaptation to judicial perceptions of social change. Yet this adaptation depends not so much on the immediate fact of change as on the gradual emergence of a generalised perception that change has occurred. By tailoring their reasoning to such perceptions, judges are able to sustain what they consider to be objective moral standards. Furthermore, for judges bombarded constantly with images present in popular culture, resort to generalisations or stereotypical fact situations to make sense of a complicated factual history is a more attractive alternative than trying to come to terms with the reality on its own terms.

The High Court has been quite inhospitable when it comes to accommodating **cultural diversity**; and even when it has done so, it has not escaped stereotyping. The Court has accepted that age is a relevant characteristic when assessing liability in **tort law** (*McHale v Watson* (1966)) and in **criminal law** (*Stingel v The Queen* (1990)). In *Moffa v The Queen* (1977), **Barwick** and **Murphy** acknowledged the ethnicity of the accused as relevant to the **criminal law defence** of provocation, by which murder is reduced to manslaughter. However, in doing so they did not appear to rely on evidence as to how 'typical' Italian men would behave. Rather they implied a stereotype of the values, behaviour, and sense of honour to be imputed to Italian men.

In *Stingel*, the attempt to accommodate ethnic profiles was abandoned, though this in turn provoked widespread **criticisms**, by which **McHugh** declared himself in *Masciantonio v The Queen* (1995) to be persuaded. He insisted that without some allowance for 'the general characteristics of an ordinary person of the same age, race, culture and background as the accused',

the law of provocation is likely to result in discrimination and injustice. In a multicultural society such as Australia, the notion of an ordinary person is pure fiction. Worse still, its invocation in cases heard by juries of predominantly Anglo-Saxon-Celtic origin almost certainly results in the accused being judged by the standard of self-control attributed to a middle class Australian of Anglo-Saxon-Celtic heritage, that being the stereotype of the ordinary person with which the jurors are most familiar.

There is still a danger (as *Moffa* illustrates) that to focus on essentialist identity traits may contribute to the creation and sustenance of stereotypes. Using stereotypes reduces the fluidity of human identity formation, and the multitude of intersections of identities in the one identity, to a static, unchanging typecast, incapable of capturing what **Stephen** recognised in *Gronow v Gronow* (1979) as the 'infinite variability of human beings'. In that case, despite some ambivalence as to how far the stereotyped roles of **women** and men in the family were changing, Stephen considered that

even in a community of unchanging social conditions, hard and fast rules or presumptions, based only upon matters of common but not invariable experience, provide a poor basis for the assessment of human behaviour compared with detailed investigation of the individuals in question. In times of rapid social change their inadequacy will be the greater.

Often, however, faced with what **Hayne** in *AMS v AIF* (1999) called 'the complexity of real life', the Court has preferred either to ignore it or to simplify it by stereotypes.

In *Water Conservation and Irrigation Commission v Browning* (1947), the appellant Commission refused to approve the transfer of a Murrumbidgee irrigation lease to Antonio Carbone because 'it was found from experience that as a general rule Italians are not good farmers under irrigation methods'. The Supreme Court of NSW overturned the decision, holding that although the matter was 'entirely in the discretion of the Commission', this was not an 'arbitrary and unlimited' discretion: the Commission could not take 'extraneous considerations' into account. The various reasons given by the Commission were 'irrelevant' or 'none of its business'. The High Court, however, unanimously restored the Commission's decision. **Dixon** took refuge in strict and complete **legalism**, refusing to 'take into account the wisdom or unwisdom of the Commission's opinions, or the justness or unjustness of their views about Italians as irrigation farmers'. **Rich**, on the other hand, responded colourfully to the view that Italians were not good farmers:

Some of the answers appear to be erroneous or irrelevant, as the Supreme Court has suggested; for instance, the statement that Italians as a general rule are not good farmers under irrigation. One remembers that during the centuries BC the Romans were farmers and that in the Augustan period Virgil in the Georgics wrote a treatise or sort of handbook on agriculture and husbandry. We also know that during this war the Italians transformed very unpromising land in this country into flourishing gardens.

As against the stereotype that Italians were terrible farmers he set up a stereotype that Italians were terrific farmers!

Stereotypes relating to women are pervasive in legal discourse. In cases of sexual assault, stereotypical images of complainants (usually, as the High Court has accepted, women and **children**) as likely to fabricate stories of their abuse have been difficult to dispel, especially when the complainant can adduce no corroboration or has delayed making a complaint. These stereotypes have led to an emphasis on scrutiny of the complainant's behaviour, rather than that of the accused, which in turn reinforces the stereotypes. The underlying prejudice was already entrenched when William Blackstone wrote in his *Commentaries on the Laws of England* (1765) that if a woman 'be of good fame; if she presently discovered the offence, and made search for the offender', she might readily be believed; but that 'if she be of evil fame' and lacks corroboration, if she delayed in making her complaint 'for any considerable time' or failed to cry out when she could have done, 'these and the like circumstances carry a strong, but not conclusive, presumption that her testimony is false or feigned'. When **Barwick** affirmed the need for a jury warning in cases of delayed complaint (*Kilby v The Queen* (1973)), he noted that *Wigmore on Evidence* had traced the underlying idea to 'old tradition and practice', going back 'by a continuous thread to the primitive rule of hue-and-cry'.

Where a complaint has been delayed or is uncorroborated, the usual course had been for judges to warn juries of the dangers of convicting on the basis of the testimony of the complainant. This general rule depended on the perception that complainants as a class are dangerous and unreliable witnesses. In *R v Henry* (1968), Lord Justice Salmon stated the rationale underlying the need for jury warnings: 'Human experience has shown that in these courts girls and women do sometimes tell an entirely false story which is very easy to fabricate, but extremely difficult to refute. Such stories are fabricated for all sorts of reasons … and sometimes for no reason at all.'

The **common law** position in Australia developed consistently with the English **precedents**. More recently, the absolute need for a warning of the danger of convicting on the basis of a complaint that has been delayed, or that lacks corroboration, or both, has been the subject of legislative amendments (and sometimes repeated amendments) in every state. The Court, however, has had difficulty in letting go of the warning (see, for example, *Longman v The Queen* (1989); *Crofts v The Queen* (1996)). In interpreting the new provisions, the Court has been careful to disturb the common law as little as possible. At best, the statutory amendments have been interpreted as rejecting the stereotype that *all* complainants, as a category of witnesses, are unreliable, which had required the full warning to be given in every case. Rather, the warning is now to be given only if it is justified in the circumstances of a particular case.

According to the Court, the rationale no longer depends on the stereotype of the deceitful complainant. In *Crofts*, **Toohey**, **Gaudron**, **Gummow**, and **Kirby** insisted that the absolute abolition of the warning would create an imbalance between the position of the complainant and that of the accused: the legislature could not have intended to tilt the balance so far in favour of the complainant as to override the interests of fairness to the accused. They recognised that the general legislative intent was 'to rid the law of … stereotypes', and that complainants should no longer be assigned to a class of their own as inherently suspect witnesses—yet insisted that 'the purpose was not to convert complainants in sexual misconduct cases into an especially trustworthy class of witnesses' either. In practice, as the results in *Longman* and *Crofts* make clear, the focus on the individual case turns out

still to evoke the same old stereotypical impressions of complainants. Both cases involved either lack of corroboration, or delay, or both; and on that basis, the Court found that a warning was required in each case.

Stereotypical images of women and men pervade other legal contexts also, though the stereotypes are far from uniform. The portrayals of women vary considerably, especially when their relationships with men are involved. The judicial impressions of women evident in *Yerkey v Jones* (1939) and *Louth v Diprose* (1992) form a striking contrast. Implicit in Dixon's judgment in *Yerkey* is the notion that wives lack financial experience (an impression to which he still adhered 25 years later in *Taylor v White* (1964)), and are therefore vulnerable to exploitation by their husbands. Explicit in Rich's judgment is the notion that the husband should have acted with more chivalry, 'not to say propriety', towards his wife's interests. It may be true that the respondent wife did in fact fit into Dixon's implicit perception of wives in general, but this is not self-evident from his judgment. Kirby in *Garcia v National Australia Bank* (1998), criticising Dixon in *Yerkey*, made the point that: 'The stereotype underlying *Yerkey* may hold true for some, perhaps even a significant number of, wives. But this Court should, where possible, refuse to "classify unnecessarily and overbroadly by gender when more accurate and impartial" principles can be stated.' To overcome the image of the stereotypical wife in *Yerkey*, he proposed to expand the category of persons who may be vulnerable in their personal relations, requiring the Court to examine the actual relationship before it in each case for any vulnerability. However, Kirby may be somewhat naïve to think that a resort to 'impartial principles' can somehow overcome the use of stereotypes.

While wives in the eyes of the Court may be stereotypically vulnerable, a woman presented as a man's ex-lover evokes almost the opposite reaction. Lisa Sarmas has shown how the majority judgments in *Louth v Diprose* reduced the parties' relationship to one in which the man, a fond and foolish romantic, was 'manipulated' by a younger woman who 'played upon' his 'susceptibility', but was 'quite indifferent' to his feelings though she had 'deliberately created' his emotional dependence by 'her own deceit'; and how, even on the subtler interpretation in Toohey's **dissenting judgment**, 'the stereotype is reversed rather than eliminated', as the woman 'turns from undeserving whore into pitiful victim'. Sarmas offers another version in which the man's 'unrequited love' is seen as sexual harassment; but this, too, reduces the facts to a stereotypical situation, though one less readily accepted by mainstream society.

Although the example is a powerful one, the Justices in *Louth v Diprose* were more conscious of the dangers of stereotyping than Sarmas's account makes out. **Dawson**, Gaudron, and McHugh began their judgment by noting that 'ordinary expectations … [and] assumptions' about professional men and 'the relationships between men and women' would predispose one to sympathy with the woman in such a case, so that the man bore 'a substantial evidentiary burden' in undertaking to show that he was unconscionably exploited. They noted also that anyone determining the facts in such cases 'brings to bear his or her experience of life and, perhaps, his or her personal predilections'. For them, however, this became a reason for reluctance to disturb the trial judge's findings. Toohey, for his part, was conscious that there were 'precedents in history and in literature for the sort of relationship that existed here', but that any attempt to fit this particular history into the framework of those precedents would be purely 'speculation'. He was conscious that 'certain expressions used by the trial judge' ('unrequited love', 'pathetic devotion', 'utter infatuation', and the like) 'tend to give an unbalanced picture of the relationship between the parties'; but conscious also that any assumption of 'a "normal" standard of conduct in such circumstances' would itself be 'questionable'. A peculiar feature of this case is the struggle, within both judicial views, between stereotypes of inequality (the man or the woman as victim), and the distinctive stereotype of legal **liberalism** that relationships between consenting adults are conducted on a basis of **equality**. Dawson, Gaudron, and McHugh did acknowledge the appellant's attempt to point out 'the differences' between the parties, 'he being a professionally qualified person with a measure of economic security and she being a person of most unfortunate circumstances'; yet, counter-intuitively, they could see in this only an attempt to show that the relationship was one 'of relative equality'. Toohey, for his part, emphasised that 'they were both adults' and experienced adults, since 'each had been married before'.

The avoidance of stereotypes in such a case is not made any easier by the fact that the parties themselves may resort to conflicting stereotypes, as each tries to deal with the bitterness of the soured relationship by reinterpreting the course of events in terms of one or another 'stock story', so as to represent his or her own role in the best possible light. The truth is that while the competing stereotypes (the woman's self-serving exploitation of the man's romantic infatuation, or the man's persistent sexual harassment although the woman 'had made her position … quite clear') may both capture elements of such a relationship, neither is an adequate representation of a complex human situation.

In recent times, McHugh and Kirby have explicitly turned their minds to the misuse of stereotypes, seeking either to dispel the stereotypes or to suggest alternative approaches to their use. Their insight has led to some powerful dissents, such as McHugh's dissents in *M v The Queen* (1994) and *Masciantonio* or Kirby's dissent in *X v Commonwealth* (1999) and his repudiation of gender categories in *Garcia*.

Such insights are a welcome change, especially when they demonstrate awareness of societal changes that challenge outdated stereotypes. In *M v The Queen* (a father–daughter sex abuse case), McHugh made the pertinent observation that

> I do not think that it is open to this Court to set aside the convictions of M because K did not act in accordance with some perceived stereotype of a victim of sexual assault … Attitudes towards sexual matters and the behaviour of young people have changed so much in recent years that in many instances the views of appellate judges about how teenagers behave, derived from their own past contact with teenagers, may well be out of date.

However, there is still a danger that efforts to dispel stereotypes lead only to the manufacture of others. In *Osland v The*

Queen (1998), Kirby quoted a decision from the Supreme Court of Canada in *R v Malott* (1998) relating to battered women:

> It is possible that those women who are unable to fit themselves within the stereotype of a victimized, passive, helpless, dependent, battered woman will not have their claims to self-defence fairly decided. For instance, women who have demonstrated too much strength or initiative, women of colour, women who are professionals, or women who might have fought back against their abusers on previous occasions, should not be penalized for failing to accord with the stereotypical image of the archetypal battered woman.

Remarkably, this attempt to avoid stereotypes depends on a list of women who do not fit the stereotype, which is itself a list of stereotypes.

Dixon probably grappled best with the difficulties posed by stereotyping in *Guise v Kouvelis* (1947) (a **defamation** case between two Greek men), by acknowledging both the possibilities and the dangers of generalised cultural differentiation, and leaving the problem unresolved:

> In deciding this question, we should not, I think, allow ourselves to be affected by the canons of social conduct and the standards of discretion and restraint in such matters which we may suppose to be accepted in graver and more sedate, if not more select, bodies than the Hellenic Club. I do not mean that it is a matter to be treated according to Greek usage and custom, even if we knew what they demand. But we should recognize that in such matters conceptions of social duty or of interest and of propriety of conduct are not uniform.

FRANCESCA DOMINELLO

Further Reading
Lisa Sarmas, 'Storytelling and the Law: A Case Study of *Louth v Diprose*' (1994) 19 *MULR* 701

Strict liability refers to liability for wrongful actions without proof of intention or negligence. Strict liability is recognised in both **tort law** and **criminal law**. In criminal law, it refers to statutory offences that do not require proof of any form of *mens rea* (criminal intention) or recklessness in order for the offence to be proved. In tort law, the concept applies to specified categories of liability that do not require evidence of negligence or intent in order for the plaintiff to succeed in an action for **damages**.

In both tort law and criminal law, the High Court has progressively moved away from strict liability. The trend in tort law was explicitly recognised by a majority of the Court in *Stevens v Brodribb Sawmilling* (1986), where **Wilson** and **Dawson** noted the existence of a 'preference for [the] view which is more in harmony with the ordinary principles governing liability for negligence'. **Mason's** view in *Stevens* was that 'the traditional **common law** response to the creation of a special danger is not to impose strict liability but to insist on a higher standard of care'.

The decision in **Burnie Port Authority v General Jones** (1994) marked a complete departure, at least in theory, from strict liability in tort. In *Burnie Port*, a majority rejected the rule in *Rylands v Fletcher* (1866 and 1868), which had held that a defendant will be strictly liable for damage caused by the escape of dangerous goods or agencies (such as fire) from the defendant's property. In the Court's view, the rule in *Rylands v Fletcher* had been so eroded by judicial reinterpretation, and the domain covered by negligence so expanded, that the rule in *Rylands v Fletcher* had been absorbed within the principles of negligence, so as to render it 'highly unlikely' that any case falling within the rule in *Rylands* would not now be covered by the principles of ordinary negligence. The 'perception of underlying antithesis' between strict liability and negligence had been 'deprived … of some of its theoretical validity and most of its practical significance'.

The Court's aversion to strict liability is particularly pronounced in criminal law. In respect of common law offences, liability requires proof of *mens rea*. However, it is open to the legislature to remove this requirement. In response to legislative attempts to exclude the *mens rea* requirement the Court held in *Proudman v Dayman* (1941) that it was to be presumed that an accused would not be criminally liable under a statute imposing strict liability where the accused acted under an 'honest and reasonable mistake' as to the existence of facts which, if true, would have made the act innocent. Furthermore, the Court held that it was for the prosecution to establish the absence of such an honest and reasonable mistake. In this way, the Court reimported a *mens rea* requirement (albeit in a lesser form) into the application of strict liability offences. In reaching these conclusions, **Dixon** built on the judgments in *Maher v Musson* (1934) and *Thomas v The King* (1937).

In *He Kaw Teh v The Queen* (1985), a majority of the Court declared that there is a presumption that the legislature does not intend to abrogate the requirement of *mens rea* in respect of serious offences. Although the decision concerned the serious offence of importing prohibited drugs, many **commentators** have suggested that it represents a new direction in the construction of statutory offences—specifically, that courts should be reluctant to construe a statutory offence as one of strict liability.

The trend away from strict liability in common law jurisdictions had begun many years before the **establishment** of the High Court. In the USA, for example, the trend in tort was evident as early as *Brown v Kendall* (1850), where it was held that if the defendant was 'free from blame', no tortious liability arose. Similarly, in England, it was held as early as *Sherras v de Rutzen* (1895) that there is a 'presumption that *mens rea* is an essential ingredient of every offence'.

In its movement away from strict liability, the High Court has both influenced, and been influenced by, the courts of other jurisdictions. In *Burnie Port*, for example, the Court was influenced to a large degree by the restrictions that the **House of Lords** had already placed on the *Rylands v Fletcher* rule in *Read v Lyons* (1946). In turn, the English Court of Appeal in *R v Gould* (1968) placed much emphasis on the High Court's decision in *Thomas v The King* concerning honest mistake of fact. The Court of Appeal paid particular regard to the judgment of Dixon, describing him as having 'earned a world-wide reputation as a common lawyer which is outstanding in the 20th century'.

Nonetheless, despite the concurrence of other common law jurisdictions in the development away from strict liability, the legislatures in most jurisdictions have tended towards an increased use of strict liability, particularly in tort law. Product liability and **environmental** liability are two examples. In both of these areas, governments at both state and federal level have enacted statutory regimes of strict liability in respect of environmental damage and damage caused by faulty goods (see, for example, the *Trade Practices Act* 1974 (Cth)).

This apparent divergence in judicial and legislative approaches is not as marked in practice as in theory. Some continuing judicial support for strict liability, especially in the area of tort, can be identified. In *Benning v Wong* (1969), for example, **Windeyer** argued strongly that to view strict liability as an unjust anomaly is to 'mistake present **values** as well as past **history**'. Specifically, he argued that the prevalence of insurance in modern times justified the imposition of strict liability. In his view, where such insurance was commonplace, it could not be 'unjust' for the law to hold persons carrying on hazardous activities liable for harm that is caused by those activities. **Murphy**, dissenting in *Cartwright v McLaine* (1979), had justified the imposition of strict liability on the defendants as the 'solution suggested by the balancing of the social values' in certain cases, because of the chances of harm arising even if a high standard of care is observed. He went on to say that 'what is reasonable care often becomes such a high standard that it amounts virtually to strict liability'.

Furthermore, while the theoretical basis of liability has moved towards the fault-based notions of negligence and away from strict liability, the standard of care applied has been raised to levels approaching strict liability, as foreshadowed by Murphy. In *Rogers v Whitaker* (1992), for example, a surgeon who was specifically held not to be negligent in his conduct of an eye operation was held negligent for failing to warn the patient of a one in 14 000 chance of a particular complication occurring. In addition, various decisions of the late 1990s have indicated a willingness to extend the imposition of the duty of care into novel areas, demonstrating the continuing expansion of negligence. Examples are in the realm of liability for causing pure economic loss (*Perre v Apand* (1999); *Hill v Van Erp* (1997)), and increased duties imposed on statutory authorities in regard to nonfeasance rather than misfeasance (*Pyrenees Shire Council v Day* (1998); *Crimmins v Stevedoring Industry Finance Committee* (1999)).

This approach gives scope to judicial discretion and responsiveness to changing social requirements more readily than imposing strict liability, but may ultimately produce very little difference in outcome in particular cases. In *Burnie Port* itself, the Court found that, although strict liability did not apply, the defendant Port Authority was subject to a 'non-delegable duty', which required it not merely to exercise due care itself, but also to ensure that care was taken, even by a qualified independent contractor. In the result, the defendant was held liable in negligence, the abolition of the rule of strict liability failing to change its responsibility to the plaintiff.

BELINDA BAKER
PENELOPE WATSON

Strike of 1905. The decision by the **Griffith Court** to adjourn its proceedings in Melbourne at the beginning of May 1905 was the only time when any of the Court's Justices threatened not to sit and actually did not sit. The details of this incident, variously described as a 'strike', a 'High Court deadlock', and as a 'trial of strength' between Chief Justice **Griffith** and **Attorney-General** Josiah Symon, remain unique in the Court's history. It was also an event that shaped the future operation of the Court.

By the time Symon, an eminent lawyer and politician from SA, became Attorney-General in August 1904, the likelihood of his being appointed to the Bench had never gone beyond speculation (see **Appointments that might have been**), and the judicial concepts he had entertained at the time of federation—that the original High Court be the final Court of Appeal and be created with a permanent **seat**, like the **United States Supreme Court**—had been crushed. His arguments against **Privy Council** appeals had been met with resistance by Griffith in 1900 and the Court's practice of undertaking regular **sittings** in the state capitals had been facilitated by the *Judiciary Act* 1903 (Cth), which Griffith had also drafted. Perhaps not surprisingly, Symon had disapproved of Griffith's **appointment** as **Chief Justice** and had commented on it with 'ominous reserve' when it was announced in the Senate.

These factors combined to provide the impetus for what was to become an escalating and ultimately public confrontation between Symon and the Court. The feud concerned the Court's travelling expenses and accommodation and the provision of staff. It was fought out through reams of correspondence, primarily between Symon and Griffith, and involved an exchange of regular telegrams and letters that were eloquent, frequently long, and, according to Gavin Souter, 'marked on both sides by suppressed fury, and deadly icy courtesy'.

On 2 December 1904, Griffith wrote to Symon as a mere formality, indicating 'with some reluctance' his intention to move from his home in Brisbane and take up permanent residence in Sydney, where the other Justices lived, so that his travelling expenses would be reduced. He requested that his **chambers** in Darlinghurst be furnished with an extra 300 feet of bookshelves to accommodate his law **library**. He had also written to **Prime Minister** George Reid a few weeks earlier exhorting him to seriously consider making Sydney the principal seat of the Court, on the understanding that all three Justices would continue to live there.

When Symon replied to Griffith's requests three weeks later, he reminded him of the Court's earlier and unsuccessful attempts to obtain additional finances for travelling purposes, particularly for **associates**, from Attorney-General **Higgins**, and indicated that travelling expenses accrued by the Bench had 'attained a magnitude which ... has occasioned remark and evoked sharp criticism'. He appealed to the Justices to consider his views on the matter of economy, emphasising that **circuits** were unnecessary and that 'the High Court *qua* **Full Court** ought not, unless under very exceptional circumstances, to incur any travelling expenses'. He also insisted that the proper seat of the Court was Melbourne, because it was also the seat of the Commonwealth government, and proposed that from 1 January 1905, all expenses were to be calculated from Melbourne, and not from the Justices' residences. Further, he added that each Jus-

A central figure in the strike of 1905, Josiah Symon, Commonwealth Attorney-General 1904–05

tice would receive a maximum of three guineas a day for travelling costs including those of his associate. The request for shelving was deferred.

Griffith, in a prompt response on behalf of the Court, repeated his request for shelving; interpreting Symon's stance not just as one of economy but also as an intrusion by the executive into the Court's discretionary powers, he leapt to the defence of circuits as a policy 'adopted after full consideration and with warm concurrence of the Federal Government' which, as far as he had been able to observe, had 'received the approval of **public opinion** throughout the Commonwealth'.

Symon's reply on 13 January 1905 persisted with the economic focus of his previous correspondence, but this time targeted the wording of Griffith's latest letter, and suggested that questions of 'policy' were not for the judiciary to consider but for the executive and Parliament alone. He dismissed the request for shelving: 'In my experience, the domicile of the Court and not the Judge's residence or place of an occasional circuit determines the situation of his furnished **chambers** ... I shall ... be most happy to sanction whatever shelving may be required for your chambers in Melbourne.'

In January, the government also suggested a compromise: that the circuit system be simplified so that NSW and Queensland appeals be heard in Sydney and all others 'at the principal seat of the Court in Melbourne'. However, the Justices made no formal response to the government's suggestion and by February opposition from the states and the **legal profession** to the possibility of curtailing the practice of circuits began to emerge in the newspapers.

Griffith threatened to go public with the dispute if his library had not reached Sydney before the law term opened in February 1905. Symon, on the defensive, remained unmoved, believing that what he was doing in his official capacity was correct.

In the middle of February, responding with the same defiance as the Attorney-General, the Justices left for circuit in Hobart before moving to Melbourne in the first week of March. Symon wrote to Griffith immediately.

In a long letter dated 22 February, he reminded the Justices of the 'excessive' sum of £2285 that the Court's sittings had cost the Commonwealth since October 1903 and indicated, as a 'trustee for the public in relation to High Court expenditure', that he had every intention of continuing with his economic measures in order to 'prevent its recurrence', and draw in the purse strings accordingly. Symon regretted the attitude of antagonism and unwillingness the Justices had adopted in the matter of circuits, and once more emphasised that it was 'circuits which gave occasion for swollen travelling expenses'. He was unable to understand how the Chief Justice could doubt that 'Parliament, rightly following the Constitution, never contemplated circuits of any sort' and continued throughout his written discourse with the same theme.

The confrontation was now absolute. The Justices refused to comply with Symon's view by abandoning circuits; nor would they allow him to make any changes to High Court expenditure. Symon, for his part, refused to exercise any tempered measures of self-restraint or to reconsider his position. In March, Alfred **Deakin** wrote to Littleton Groom about the 'extraordinary action of the Government—or is it the A-G only paying off old scores? In any case the action taken is more than indefensible no matter from what point of view it is regarded. It is indeed to me perhaps the most regrettable incident that has occurred outside the legislature since the Commonwealth began to be'.

The High Court continued sitting. Griffith wrote to Symon on 17 April to inform him that the Court intended to go to Brisbane and asked for a **courtroom** to be placed at the High Court's disposal. In a calculated attempt to escalate the dispute, Symon refused to give his consent. Furthermore, he notified Griffith that travelling costs would be limited to the provision of one associate and one **tipstaff**, rather than the customary three associates and three tipstaves. This was a deft move because, as WG McMinn has noted, both Griffith and **Barton** had sons, Percy Griffith and Edmund Barton, for associates. The number of telephones in the rooms of the Justices and their associates in Sydney would be reduced from five to one, and payment for telephones in the private residences of the Justices would be discontinued. Moreover, Symon refused reimbursement for the cost of direct steamer fares from Sydney to Hobart and back to Melbourne. He argued that when visiting Hobart, the Justices should have travelled only between Melbourne and Launceston by sea, using their government-issued railway passes for the rest of the journey. He also requested additional information about the cost of the Court's visit to Melbourne.

The time had come for the Court to bring the details of the crisis to public attention. **O'Connor** was due to hear a case in Melbourne on 1 May, but the Justices had met in Sydney on the preceding Saturday and decided to suspend the sitting.

The decision made newspaper headlines. On hearing about the adjournment, Symon, in absolute dismay, sent an urgent telegram to O'Connor: 'I shall, therefore, be obliged if you will state to me the reason for the adjournment of the Court, and also whether you propose to proceed with the trials next Tuesday … forgive my pointing out the importance of an immediate reply.'

Griffith's response was short and to the point. He defended the High Court's action as an imperative of judicial **independence**. 'We cannot recognise your right to demand the reasons for any judicial action taken by the Court, except such request as may be made by any litigant in open Court.' Symon, in a frustrated response, is reported to have scribbled on a scrap of paper: 'How can any Ct. because of disagreement as to Hotel expenses go on strike? … no wharflabourers union do such thing.'

On 5 July 1905, Deakin was sworn in as Prime Minister and **Isaacs** as Attorney-General. Isaacs wrote to Griffith less than a week later. In further correspondence throughout August, the government was able to offer a 'satisfactory and permanent solution of the matters agitated'. The Court would continue its practice of sitting in each state capital 'as may be required', the government would have full confidence in 'their Honours' wisdom' with regards to travelling expenses, the numbers of associates and tipstaves would not be reduced, and the 'trivial matter' of shelving was attended to. The affair had ended. Griffith was delighted: 'On behalf of my learned colleagues and myself I have pleasure in saying that we concur in the opinion of the Government that the conclusions set out in your letter constitute a satisfactory, and, as we trust, a permanent solution of the matters in question.'

Nearly a century later, it could be said that although neither of the parties in the dispute can be 'aquitted of all blame', the strike of 1905 remains an early demonstration of judicial authority and independence. It also consolidated the pattern of the Court's sitting practice which, in a modified form, remains to this day.

SUSAN PRIEST

Further Reading
Roger Joyce, *Samuel Walker Griffith* (1984)
Anthony Mason, 'The High Court in Sir Samuel Griffith's Time: Contemporary Parallels and Contrasts' (1994) 3 *GLR* 179
WG McMinn, 'The High Court Imbroglio and the Fall of the Reid–McLean Government' (1978) 64 *Journal of the Royal Australian Historical Society* 14
Gavin Souter, *Lion and Kangaroo* (1976)
DI Wright, 'Sir Josiah Symon, Federation and the High Court' (1978) 64 *Journal of the Royal Australian Historical Society* 73

Succession law. The High Court has had few occasions in recent years to consider issues of inheritance and devolution of **property** on death, since succession law is mainly articulated through first-instance decisions. The Court has left its mark, however, not only through the resolution of problems, but also through the variety of opinions voiced and the interpretive possibilities left open.

One key issue is the very nature of a will itself, which in part involves a distinction between lifetime and testamentary transactions. This has arisen principally when a person now deceased has made dispositions by a document that was not signed with the formalities required for wills. In *Russell v Scott* (1936), a unanimous High Court held that a joint banking account that benefited the survivor, although he had contributed nothing to the account, was effective as a lifetime transaction: it was not an invalid will. Although the decision has not gone uncriticised, its significance lies in the primacy given to the donor's intention.

The Court has not yet had an opportunity to revisit the so-called 'rule against delegation of testamentary power', which prevents a testator from delegating to another person the responsibility for decisions affecting the disposition of the estate. The rule was confirmed by the Court in *Tatham v Huxtable* (1950). But since then, a related rule affecting the validity of powers of appointment and **trusts**—requiring the potential beneficiaries to be designated with sufficient certainty (the 'certainty of objects rule')—has been rendered more flexible by the **House of Lords** decision in *McPhail v Doulton* (1970). The High Court has not yet squarely considered whether the certainty of objects rule and the non-delegation rule are in effect the same. Until it does, the possible range of beneficiaries under a power of appointment in a will may be narrower than is now permitted in a lifetime transaction.

In the interrelationship between probate law and **equity**, two decisions of the High Court stand out: *Birmingham v Renfrew* (1937) and *Palmer v Bank of NSW* (1975). In these cases, the Court held that a pre-existing **contract** made by the testator could affect the disposition of an estate: while probate of the will would not be overturned or upset, equity would intervene by means of constructive trusts to ensure the fulfilment of the contract. Both cases concerned the freedom of action during lifetime of a promisor who had previously promised to leave his or her estate by will in a particular manner. *Birmingham* was a 'mutual wills' case in which **Dixon** gave expression to the idea of a 'floating obligation' that would govern the surviving party once the first will had taken effect. Although the precise nature of this obligation has been questioned, the significance of the case is in the power of constructive trusts to give effect to lifetime promises independent of the will. In *Palmer*, the Court was called upon to consider more precisely the extent of the relationship between the contract and the promisor's freedom of action. The Court required the contract to be very specific in its terms before it could control the extent of lifetime giving by the promisor.

The rules as to testamentary capacity go to the heart of probate law in that they define the minimum mental element required to make a will. The leading nineteenth-century English case of *Banks v Goodfellow* (1870) has consistently been applied (see *Tipper v Moore* (1911); *Landers v Landers* (1914); *Bailey v Bailey* (1924); *Worth v Clasohm* (1952)). The Court has asked whether the testator understands the extent of the property being disposed of; comprehends and appreciates the claims to which effect should be given; and is not affected by insane delusions that might influence the will. In *Derrett v Hall* (1942), the Court identified an insane delusion as 'a fixed and incorrigible false belief which the victim could not be reasoned out of'. In *Timbury v Coffee* (1941), the Court was able to find, despite the absence of medical evidence, that the testator's beliefs about his wife's infidelity

were a characteristic symptom of his alcoholism. The Justices would not be drawn on whether the beliefs were rational or not. *Bull v Fulton* (1942) revealed an interesting divergence of view in the case of a testator who died at 91 years of age and whose hobbies had included will-making. At a certain time, her pattern of benefaction had altered: her nephews, who had also acted as her solicitors and had been the executors and principal beneficiaries of her earlier wills, were wholly excluded. It was alleged this was the result of delusions and that therefore the wills thereafter could not stand. For **Latham** and **Williams**, the claim succeeded on the basis of irrational false beliefs (that her nephews had forged her signature on transfers of land and shares, and had misapplied or misappropriated her income). **McTiernan** disagreed. He considered that the testator, when challenged to admit the authenticity of the documents, had refused to do so, preferring to protect her pride and dignity by maligning her nephews. The issue of 'rationality' here is a challenging one. The majority decision might suggest a slightly patronising attitude to **women**, particularly elderly women, but such an interpretation must be very guarded.

In the absence of a statutory power to rectify a will, the Court's **jurisdiction** to do so is limited. The Court may not add words to a will, nor may it delete words from a will if to do so will alter the meaning and effect of the words that remain. In *Osborne v Smith* (1960), the High Court affirmed a decision of the Supreme Court of NSW refusing a grant of probate or letters of administration. **Kitto** stated the principles strictly. The case was one where legacies to a hospital were expressed in a form that would give to the hospital more than the testator intended; yet omission of the legacies would give to the residuary beneficiary more than the testator intended. In that situation, the Court was unable to rectify the will. Accordingly, the entire document could not be admitted to probate. Such limitations on the powers of the Court have led in some Australian jurisdictions to the introduction of statutory rectification powers—though not, as in NZ, to the extension to wills of the equitable doctrine of rectification (*Re Jensen* (1991)).

In the days before the introduction of 'dispensing powers' —that is, powers to relax the strict formalities in favour of documents clearly intended to be wills—a perplexing issue was the location of the 'foot or end' of the will, where the testator was required to sign. In *Cinnamon v Public Trustee for Tasmania* (1934), the Court endorsed a broadly liberal approach to the problem, moving the emphasis away from attempts to locate the literal or physical 'foot or end' of the will. In a document folded into four pages, and signed on the first page only, the writing on the third page was deemed to be incorporated into the first page. Such questions have now been overtaken by the introduction of dispensing powers, though their exercise has led to a fresh divergence of view between conceptions of a will as a document, and conceptions of it as a series of dispositions (*Estate of Masters* (1994); *Will of Lobato* (1991)). This is an area that is ripe for resolution by the High Court.

An important aspect of succession law is the body of doctrine concerning failure of gifts ('ademption'). One such decision—puzzling in some respects—is *Fairweather v Fair-*

weather (1944), set in the context of the moratorium legislation during the **Depression of the 1930s**. The house in which the appellant lived had been left to him in his father's will, subject to a mortgage. The father then entered into a contract for the sale of the house to the son, whereupon the gift in the will was adeemed (by the equitable doctrine of conversion). The son defaulted on his payment of instalments under the contract, but the moratorium legislation relieved him of liability to pay the instalments. By successive codicils, both before and after the legislation, the testator had effectively republished the will. The Court held by majority that the republication did not revive the gift that had been adeemed by the contract of sale. The decision leaves open exactly how far republication of a will might act to 'save' gifts by enabling the will to be read as at the date of republishing.

The Court has added a new chapter to **tort law** by expanding the liability of solicitors where they held a will as custodians (*Hawkins v Clayton* (1988)), or where their negligence in drafting the will caused beneficiaries to miss out on their intended gifts (*Hill v Van Erp* (1997)). In this area, there is much opportunity for development, though **McHugh's** strong dissents may be a reason for caution in predicting its future course.

None of this reveals much about the High Court as an institution, apart from the recurrent emphasis on the role of the testator as property owner and the importance of giving effect to his or her intention. Greater insight into the Justices' philosophical viewpoints is afforded by cases under family provision legislation, as the focus there is principally on broad concepts, rather than technical points of law. Those cases exhibit strong elements of nineteenth-century **liberalism**—not only interwoven in the fabric of the legislation but also in the judgments by which it is applied—and allow glimpses of differing judicial attitudes: frequently the decisions are split, with many separate judgments.

The task of assessing whether the testator has made adequate provision for the proper maintenance, education, and advancement in life of claimants (initially, spouses and **children**) has been translated into an assessment of the testator's 'moral duty' (endorsed by the **Privy Council** in *Bosch v Perpetual Trustee Co* (1938)). At the same time, the decisions have reaffirmed the importance of testamentary freedom—by reiterating that the court must not rewrite the will of the testator (for example, *Pontifical Society v Scales* (1962)), and by holding that the adequacy of provision for a particular applicant must be determined as at the date of death of the testator (*Coates v National Trustees Executors & Agency* (1956)). We see also the responsibility expected of husbands and fathers for their widows and dependent children, along with an emphasis on the self-reliance of adults, especially **men**.

We also find, at times, a recognition of the limitations of the legislation (expressed as it is in terms of maintenance), particularly in the case of widows. The Court has struggled—sometimes consciously but often seemingly unconsciously—to overcome this limitation. Divergences between the judgments in different cases and at different times reflect a tension between recognition of the limitations of the legislation, particular judicial understandings of family responsibilities, and a desire to provide some restitution for contributions and services. This is evident especially in relation to claims by adult sons and by widows.

For example, in *Boyce v Humphreys* (1974), **Barwick** led a majority judgment against the provision of a lump sum to an elderly widow on the basis that it went beyond the provision of maintenance, while McTiernan dissented. In *White v Barron* (1980) and *Goodman v Windeyer* (1980), the Court shifted its position. In *White*, Barwick was now in the minority, while the majority of the Court supported a lump sum **order** and considered that provision for an annuity terminating on remarriage was itself an indication of failure to make proper provision for the widow. (An earlier Court had considered that the obligation towards a widow should ordinarily be confined to widowhood: *Worladge v Doddridge* (1957).)

Some Justices have also seen the claimant's good conduct as relevant to the assessment of the moral duty of the deceased (**Gibbs** in *Goodman v Windeyer*)—although this view was strongly resisted by **Murphy**, who regarded the concept of 'moral duty' as a gloss on the legislation. This approach points towards a sense of entitlement rather than of maintenance. It suggests the germ of a 'contribution' approach, although constrained by the legislation into a framework of needs for maintenance. However, in *Singer v Berghouse* (1994), an emphasis on needs appeared predominant again. The case also revealed a striking divergence of attitudes towards the claims of widows.

The applicant widow had married the deceased only a year before he died; each had been married before and had children by the previous marriage. They had agreed at the time of their marriage not to make claims on each other's estates. They had plans for the acquisition of property together. The deceased's will provided nothing for his widow and everything to his son. The widow's claim was rejected both at first instance and on appeal in NSW; it was held that as both parties had comparable assets and had married on the basis of a written agreement about their respective future interests, in the absence of any case based on need, the widow's claim should fail. Her appeal to the High Court also failed. The majority judgment of **Mason**, **Deane**, and McHugh stressed that the courts must not 'disregard or discount the non-financial contributions made to the property and finances of the parties to a marriage' but nevertheless dismissed the appeal. **Gaudron** delivered a strong dissent, emphasising the value of '**women's work**', which, she stated, was often overlooked or undervalued.

A shift is also evident in the analysis of claims by adult sons. The self-reliant individual of nineteenth-century liberalism is seen most clearly in the form of the applicant son. So in *McCosker v McCosker* (1957), Dixon and Williams thought that an adult, able-bodied son should be relegated to a low order of priority. The third Justice in that case, Kitto, would have allowed the testator to have made his own judgment as to provision for his 'hale and hearty, and long-independent, 49-year-old son'. A similar analysis was made in *Stott v Cook* (1960) and *Pontifical Society v Scales*. *Hughes v National Trustees Executors & Agency Co* (1979) revealed a shift in thinking. The need for an adult son to establish a 'special claim' was expressly rejected; and an adult son—able-bodied but rather a 'lame duck'—was allowed virtually the entire estate. Barwick's **dissenting judgment** strongly reflects the earlier view.

The questions for the future analysis of this legislation will concern the standard to be applied generally to adult children, male and female, and the extent to which the contributions of spouses, particularly women, can be recognised in the orders allowable under the legislation.

The Court has also played a significant **role** in marking out the relationship between the jurisdiction under family provision legislation, and agreements made during lifetime not to claim under such legislation. All of the High Court cases have concerned an agreement by a wife to make no application for provision out of her husband's estate. The earlier cases supported the contract against the legislation; *Lieberman v Morris* (1944) upheld the legislation over the contract.

The public interest was seen as assuring proper maintenance to the family by investing the Court with a discretionary jurisdiction to review wills. A contract not to make an application was not valid because it attempted 'to oust or fetter the discretion of the court', and prevented or tended to prevent the Act from fulfilling its objective. *Lieberman* and *Easterbrook v Young* (1977) reveal a benevolent approach to the legislation, giving it its maximum operation. Both were widows' cases that reflected the protective, paternal, approach that underlay the introduction of the legislation in the early twentieth century.

ROSALIND ATHERTON

Further Reading

Rosalind Atherton and Prue Vines, *Australian Succession Law Commentary and Materials: Families, Property and Death* (1996)

John De Groot and Bruce Nickel, *Family Provision in Australia and New Zealand* (1993)

Anthony Dickey, *Family Provision After Death* (1992)

Ian Hardingham, Marcia Neave, and Harold Ford, *Wills and Intestacy in Australia and New Zealand* (2nd edn 1989)

Ken Mackie and Mark Burton, *Outline of Succession* (2nd edn 2000)

Superior court. The notion of a superior court is rooted in the antiquity of the **common law**—and, while the notion is not capable of precise definition, broadly speaking it signifies three related properties. First, a superior court's **jurisdiction** was unlimited by reference to person, place, or subject matter. Secondly, such a court was not liable to have any other court exercise a supervisory jurisdiction over it by use of prerogative **writs**. Thirdly, a superior court was always presumed to act within jurisdiction, so that even acts that turned out to be in excess of jurisdiction were nevertheless regarded as valid until set aside on appeal.

Section 71 of the Constitution creates the High Court as a 'Federal Supreme Court'. This was probably enough in itself to make the High Court a superior court, but the *Judiciary Act* 1903 (Cth) expressly provided that the High Court was 'a superior court of record' (section 4, continued in section 5 of the *High Court of Australia Act* 1979 (Cth)).

There is tension between the limited nature of the High Court's jurisdiction set out in sections 75 and 76 of the Constitution and the common law's conception of a superior court as one of unlimited jurisdiction. Nevertheless, the Court has confirmed that it is a superior court, that it has the jurisdiction to determine its own jurisdiction, and that its members, when acting in their capacity as Justices of the High Court, are not susceptible to prerogative relief (*Re Brennan; Ex parte Muldowney* (1993); *Re Toohey; Ex parte Gunter* (1996)).

More conceptual difficulty has been occasioned by the creation of statutory courts of limited jurisdiction such as the **Federal Court** and the Family Court (see, in relation to the Federal Court of Bankruptcy, *Cameron v Cole* (1944)). These courts are not only of limited jurisdiction by definition but are also subject to the supervisory jurisdiction of the High Court under section 75(v) of the Constitution. The residual significance of their status as superior courts would appear to be that their acts made in excess of jurisdiction are voidable rather than void (that is, valid until set aside).

NYE PERRAM

Symbolism of Court building. Perhaps the most significant symbol of the High Court is the building itself. It is listed on the Royal Australian Institute of Architects (RAIA) Register of Significant Twentieth Century Buildings for its 'monumental character in keeping with the power and standing of the High Court'. It is considered to be of 'architectural significance as a large scale Brutalist style public building, which is rare in Australia' (see **Architecture of Court building**).

The site was allocated in 1970 in accordance with the 1964 Holford Plan for the Parliamentary Zone, which supported the constitutional relationship between Parliament and the judiciary by placing the High Court next to Parliament House (at that time, beside the foreshore of Lake Burley Griffin). John Overall, chairman of the National Capital Development Commission, said that 'it was always in my mind that under the British Constitution and countries influenced by that Constitution, the High Court was second to the Parliament, and should be located there. It was certainly reflected in the siting of the various buildings in the Parliamentary Triangle'. The High Court **building** site was then moved slightly north towards the lake, to express judicial **independence** by separating it from the line of the neighbouring buildings.

The national competition conditions for the design of the building specified that 'in the siting and in its form the High Court building should impart a sense of strength and security. The visitor should be made to feel aware of the rights, privileges and responsibilities of the Australian judicial system'. The overwhelming space of the main entrance foyer was to echo these terms, as well as to impress the majesty of the law on the country's citizens.

The detailed internal design of the building and its ornamentation, furnishings, and fittings, are rich in symbolism, much of it carefully planned by the architects and the design team (and sometimes by **Barwick**). As with Walter Burley Griffin's original design for **Canberra** itself (see Peter Proudfoot, *The Secret Plan of Canberra* (1994)), it is possible to interpret features of the building or its ornamentation as allusions to the mystical lore of Freemasonry or of ancient

The Public Hall features many of the Court's symbols, including murals reflecting the history and role of the Court

Egypt; and as in Burley Griffin's case—or for that matter with **originalism** as a guide to the interpretation of the constitutional text—these interpretations may or may not reflect an original conscious intention. The original design work, assigned by Colin **Madigan** to Christopher Kringas (until Kringas's death in March 1975), embodied three fundamental concepts.

First, Kringas saw the Court as a 'bridge' joining the Constitution to the citizen. Thus, standing in front of or behind the building, the visitor can see right through it as one can see through a bridge.

Secondly, Kringas perceived the Australian landscape as that of a spacious country, allowing for freedom of **movement**, with lots of natural sunlight. The public areas of the building symbolise this, with floors and pedestrian ramps leading visitors through varying angles and aspects from which to appreciate the grand space of the foyer, backed by vistas of panoramic views through trees, to the surrounding grassed areas of the Parliamentary Triangle.

Thirdly, to relate the old with the new, Kringas drew a building of contemporary design of the times, but the ceiling of the foyer has a pattern that can readily be interpreted as symbolic of ancient Egypt.

The building has many other symbolic features. The first symbol a visitor encounters is the fountain beside the ceremonial ramp. Made of South Australian imperial black granite, the fountain is representative of a trout stream with a pattern of jets at the top to symbolise a sheaf of grain or corn.

A sheaf of grain with running water, required to grow the grain, represents 'plenty' in the Freemasonry society.

The Commonwealth of Australia coat of arms is mounted on the glass south wall of the building facing the ceremonial ramp. Made of sand-blasted glass and acrylic, the window mullions dictated that the kangaroo and emu could not support the shield, so they are depicted separately. The emu is in the act of taking a step forward towards the shield. A carved wooden version is mounted in **Courtroom** No 2 and a copper rod version presides over Courtroom No 3.

The British coat of arms is mounted on the glass north wall. Barwick wanted Lake Burley Griffin and Mount Ainslie to be viewed through the British coat of arms as the High Court of Australia was founded upon the Westminster system of law.

On the northern and western walls of the foyer are murals in aluminium to reflect the history, function, and aspirations of the High Court. The straight-lined, angular design and construction of the murals complements the design of the building.

The first mural, on the western or States Wall, symbolises the role of the states in federation and the significance of the High Court at the apex of the judicial **hierarchy** in Australia. The six double panels show stylised state flags and images associated with each state.

On the first of the six panels dominating the top of the second mural, on the northern or Constitutional Wall, a lighthouse throws beams of light to represent the search for knowledge and justice, and is a symbol for the Constitution that set the framework for the new Commonwealth in 1901. The remaining five panels illustrate elements of the coming together as a nation that the Constitution effected: the Australian flag and the Southern Cross flag (representing the two sides of constitutional debate); a montage of historical figures involved with federation and the **establishment** of the High Court; the rising of the seas and oceans that isolated Australia as a continent and led to the rise of **Aboriginal** culture; the arrival of Parliament and **nationhood**; and the coming together of the colonies (symbolised by the River Murray, the rail link at Albury, and the warship HMS *Cerberus*).

The layout of the black leather lounge settees in the foyer areas is based on Aboriginal art concepts—the two semicircular ends represent two people sitting cross-legged in discussion, separated by circular white marble tables symbolising water holes between. This also reflects the arrangement of the courtrooms, with the Bar facing the Bench for debate.

The dual doors of silver and glass leading to each of the three courtrooms celebrate the origins and traditions of the judicial system. The shield motif symbolises the High Court's function as a protector of the Constitution and liberties of the citizen. The heraldic divisions within the shields acknowledge the tradition of the Westminster system of law.

The ribbons, derived from the tapes binding legal documents, unify the individual emblems and visually unite each door as a single unit, while their implied flexible movement refers to the changes and developments of society from one era to another. They also represent the final tying up of the case; after passing through these doors, there is no higher judicial authority to turn to.

The airlock between the doors has the functional purpose of sound insulation; but the pause in brief isolation before entering the courtroom encourages a mood of contemplation, and a consciousness of **etiquette** and protocol.

Behind the bench in Courtrooms No 1 and No 2, the panels of red tulip oak are separated by vertical slots, with colours ranging from rich purple (behind the **Chief Justice** in the centre) to light red at both ends of the bench (for the least senior **puisne Justices**). Traditionally associated with royalty (see Meyer Reinhold, *History of Purple as a Status Symbol in Antiquity* (1970)), purple or deep red had also acquired particular associations of judicial solemnity and independence from the 'purple curtain' through which Justices enter the **United States Supreme Court.**

The 4.3 metre by 2.5 metre tapestry hanging on the western wall of Courtroom No 1 was designed by Ron Brooks. The colours of blue and gold used liberally in the design are the prescribed livery colours of the Commonwealth coat of arms. In the form of a banner, the tapestry incorporates the badges of the states and the shield of arms of the Commonwealth, surmounted by the crest of the Commonwealth.

Hamish Lindsay

T

Tait's Case (1962) ignited passionate debate about capital punishment and involved a bitter collision between the executive and the judiciary. Robert Peter Tait was convicted of a brutal murder and sentenced to death. His defence of insanity was rejected by the jury. There was widespread opposition to the hanging—opposition directed at capital punishment generally, and the hanging of Tait in particular. Even the victim's son, a Christian minister, publicly vowed to 'do everything [he could] to prevent ... Tait from being hanged'. Victorian Premier Henry Bolte, however, was determined to have Tait executed.

Following the end of a long and unsuccessful appeal process, during which Tait's execution was postponed twice, the Victorian government scheduled Tait's hanging for Monday 22 October 1962.

Two matters were brought before the Full Court of the Supreme Court of Victoria in an attempt to save Tait's life. They were based on the **common law** rule that it was unlawful to hang an insane person. The issue was no longer whether Tait had been insane at the time of the murder, but whether he was insane now.

In the first matter, the Associate Director of the Brotherhood of St Laurence, David Scott, had applied for an order under the *Mental Hygiene Act* 1958 (Vic) seeking an inquiry into Tait's sanity. Justice Gregory Gowans rejected that application on 15 October, a week before the planned hanging. Scott appealed to the Full Supreme Court, which began to hear the appeal two days later.

The second matter arose from an application by Tait's **counsel** to Justice Arthur Dean (the presiding judge at Tait's trial) for a respite of execution on the grounds of insanity. Dean referred that application to the Full Court, which was hearing the Scott appeal. The Court heard the two matters together.

Pressure on the government had mounted to stay Tait's execution so that the Court would have time to consider the case properly. The state Opposition leader, Clive Stoneham, accused the government of holding the Court 'up to ridicule by ... disregard[ing] entirely the legal processes that are being worked out there'. Tait's counsel pleaded for 'something to be done' to allow the Court more time to reach a reasoned decision. One judge referred to the 'acute embarrassment' to which he was being subjected. Reluctantly, the government postponed Tait's execution to 'a date to be fixed'.

On 30 October, the Court dismissed the first appeal (*Re Tait* (1962)) and referred the second matter back to Justice Dean (*Tait v R* (1962)). Later that day, before Dean had a chance to hear the case, and despite its knowledge that an appeal to the High Court was imminent, the government announced that Tait would be executed at 8.00 am on 1 November. The *Mental Health Act* 1959 (Vic) was to come into force on that day (having apparently been proclaimed by accident). Because that Act would allow government psychiatrists to certify that Tait was mentally ill, it was believed that his execution would be impossible once the Act was in force.

The decision to execute Tait although judicial processes were still pending provoked outrage. There were heated exchanges in Parliament; newspapers around the country ran front-page stories attacking the decision; community and religious groups were appalled. 'No longer [did] it seem a matter of capital punishment, but of getting rid of Tait in spite of any possible legal processes still open.'

Dean brought the case forward to the evening of 30 October. He sat late into the night. He referred to the 'very embarrassing and unfortunate' situation in which he found himself, having to decide the case so close to Tait's planned execution. At about 10.30 pm, he ruled that he had no power to intervene, on the ground that the common law power of judges to grant a reprieve had been superseded by the *Crimes Act* 1958 (Vic). Tait's grave had been prepared at Pentridge Prison at least an hour before.

With less than 24 hours remaining before Tait was due to hang, and with the Court not in session, three High Court Justices flew down from Sydney to join two others in Melbourne. The convening of the Court was so rapid that **Dixon** had time only to thumb through the Full Court judgments while he was being driven to town.

John Starke (son of High Court Justice **Starke**), acting for Scott, argued for a stay of Tait's execution so that the High Court could fully consider the arguments made before it. He protested that 'we have been bundled through this court to keep an appointment with the hangman at 8 o'clock tomorrow morning'. The state government treated the High Court as it had the lower courts before: it attempted to pressure the Court into deciding the case quickly, allowing it no time to consider properly the complex issues involved.

Chief Justice Dixon was angered. When the prosecution suggested that the executive would not resile from its decision

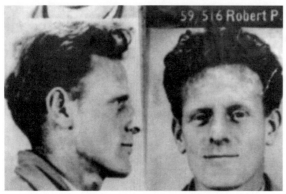

Convicted murderer Robert Peter Tait, who avoided the death penalty by a last-minute appeal to the High Court

to execute Tait as planned, he responded: 'When you say it to this Court, you are saying it to a court which has supreme **jurisdiction** in Australia, and in effect saying "Well, even if you want time to consider the case we will not give it"'. He announced that the case would be adjourned and Tait's execution postponed 'entirely so that the authority of this Court may be maintained'.

Victorian **Solicitor-General** Henry Winneke, who had been embarrassed by the government's instructions to him, was unable to give an undertaking that the execution would be postponed. Dixon, after Winneke had drawn the Court's attention to the possibility, then ordered that the Chief Secretary, the Sheriff, and his deputies 'be restrained accordingly'. Newspapers reported that for the first time in Australian history, the Court had issued an injunction against a state government. The adjournment and stay of execution effectively forced the government to commute Tait's sentence. Tait was sentenced to life imprisonment with the endorsement 'never to be released'. He died in prison in 1985.

Ironically, in 1967 John Starke, by then himself a judge, presided over the trial of Ronald Ryan, the last person hanged in Australia. In 1991, Starke told Jon Faine in a radio interview that he used to see Tait from time to time when he came before the Victorian Parole Board: 'One time he came in before the Board, and I said, "How are you going, Peter?". And he said, "… Don't worry Mr Starke, I've never really blamed you for this". Blame me? For God's sake, I saved his bloody life.' Despite occupying the High Court for less than three hours, *Tait's Case* stands as one of the clearest demonstrations of the authority and **independence** of the Court.

TROY SIMPSON

Further Reading

Creighton Burns, *The Tait Case* (1962)

Jon Faine, *Taken on Oath: A Generation of Lawyers* (1992) ch 4

JD Feltham, 'The Common Law and the Execution of Insane Criminals' (1964) 4 *MULR* 434

Colin Howard, 'An Australian Letter: The Principle of Fair Trial' [1963] *Crim LR* 603

Peter Ryan, *Lines of Fire* (1997)

Tasmanian Dam Case (1983). By the *Gordon River Hydro-Electric Power Development Act* 1982 (Tas), the Tasmanian Hydro-Electric Commission was authorised to dam the Gordon River below its junction with the Franklin. In response to environmental protests, the Commonwealth (in March 1983) promulgated the World Heritage (Western Tasmania Wilderness) Regulations 1983 (under the *National Parks and Wildlife Conservation Act* 1975). Later (in May 1983) the Commonwealth enacted the *World Heritage Properties Conservation Act* 1983.

The dam site fell within national parklands which in December 1982 had been entered at Australia's request (after an initial request by Tasmania was withdrawn) on a 'World Heritage List' compiled under the 1972 UNESCO Convention for the Protection of the World Cultural and Natural Heritage.

The Commonwealth brought separate High Court actions (based respectively on the Act and the Regulations) for orders restraining further work on the dam. Tasmania sought declarations that the Regulations and Act were invalid. The issues involved a wide-ranging exploration of **Commonwealth legislative powers**. The main Commonwealth arguments were accepted by **Mason**, **Murphy**, **Brennan**, and **Deane**, but rejected by **Gibbs**, **Wilson**, and **Dawson**.

The Regulations, and sections 6 and 9 of the Act, relied for their validity on section 51(xxix) of the Constitution (the **external affairs power**). The different paragraphs of section 6(2) were drafted to attract several different aspects of 'external affairs', but the majority focused only on paragraph (b), which assumed that this power extends to legislation fulfilling within Australia an international 'obligation'. The majority held that the World Heritage Convention did impose a legal 'obligation'; Gibbs, Wilson, and Dawson dissented.

Despite the limited focus on 'obligations', the case resolved a long-standing doubt about the scope of the power to implement international treaties. The majority held clearly, for the first time, that the mere existence of a treaty necessarily provides the requisite international element; there is no superadded requirement that the *subject matter* be 'international' or of 'international concern'.

Despite this, Deane voted with Gibbs, Wilson and Dawson to hold the Regulations *invalid*, since in his view their effect on the state's control of its bushlands entailed an **acquisition of property** without adequate provision for the 'just terms' required by section 51(xxxi) of the Constitution. Moreover, both he and Brennan held that most of the detailed prohibitions in section 9 of the Act were invalid. In the first clear articulation of the idea that treaty implementation is subject to a requirement of **proportionality**, they held that only the particular precise prohibitions envisaged by section 9(1)(h) were sufficiently closely tailored to the needs of the World Heritage Convention. Thus, the actual result on this branch of the case was limited to section 6(2)(b) and section 9(1)(h).

Sections 7 and 10 of the Act relied on section 51(xx) of the Constitution (the **corporations power**). The four majority Justices accepted (with Gibbs and Dawson dissenting) that, because the Hydro-Electric Commission 'traded' in electricity supplies, it was a 'trading corporation' in the constitutional sense. On that assumption, section 10 imposed a wide range of prohibitions, for example against felling trees or using explosives. This sharpened another unresolved issue: once a 'trading corporation' exists, will *any* regulation of its conduct be valid? Or must the regulation have some

Protesters demonstrate against the building of a dam on the Gordon River below the Franklin

what is now an authoritative reading of the *Melbourne Corporation Case* (1947) as having two 'limbs': one forbidding Commonwealth discrimination against the states, the other forbidding substantial interference with their 'capacity to function'. The further evolution of this bifurcation is a key to current understandings of **intergovernmental immunities**. Yet in the *Dam Case*, the potential impact of Commonwealth legislation on 11 per cent of the state's land mass was not enough to attract the second 'limb'.

Other 'states' rights' arguments received short shrift. For example, section 100 of the Constitution, which specifically protects 'the right of a State … to the reasonable use of 'the waters of rivers' was brushed aside because the protection is only against laws enacted under the Commonwealth's **trade and commerce power**.

All this may help to explain the common perception that the decision encroached too far on 'states' rights'. 'A heavy blow to state sovereignty' thundered the *Australian* editorial next day. In Tasmania, there was a widespread perception that the building of future dams was essential to the state's economy and employment levels; elsewhere, there was an equal conviction of the need for environmental protection of the south-west Tasmanian wilderness. It was therefore easy to depict the case as pitting state majority interests against national majority interests.

The controversy persists to this day. Its focus has been mainly on the majority view of the external affairs power, though some of the majority observations on the corporations power were potentially much more far-reaching.

Tony Blackshield

Further Reading
Michael Coper, *The Franklin Dam Case* (1983)
M Sornarajah (ed), *The South-West Dam Dispute* (1983)

connection with its trading activities (as Gibbs had repeatedly insisted)?

Despite the support of Mason, Murphy, and Deane for the former view, the issue remained unresolved. Section 10(4) prohibited acts such as felling trees or using explosives *if they were undertaken by a trading corporation for the purposes of its trading activities*. Brennan held (and Gibbs agreed) that even on Gibbs' narrower view, this limited prohibition was valid. Thus the actual result was confined to the validity of section 10(4).

Sections 8 and 11 of the Act relied on section 51(xxvi) of the Constitution (the races power). The argument was that once the valley was flooded, an elaborate system of riverbank caves (which *might* contain irreplaceable Aboriginal art and relics) would be lost forever. Thus a law to prevent that loss was a 'special law' for the benefit of the Aboriginal **race**. The dissenters argued that since preservation of this heritage would benefit all mankind, it could not be a 'special law' for Aboriginal people. The majority answered that beyond their significance for humanity in general, such relics would have sufficient *particular* significance for **Aboriginal peoples** to justify a 'special law'.

Pervading all these issues were competing conceptions of **federalism**. The dissenters were anxious to interpret all Commonwealth legislative powers so as to preserve a 'federal balance', whereas Mason spoke dismissively of 'ritual invocations of the federal balance' and Murphy saw any such balance as 'a balance between fallacies'. Mason did crystallise

Taxation law. The **role** of the High Court in shaping the essential concepts and impact of Australian taxation law is possibly greater than its role in any other area of **commercial law**. In relation to income tax, the legislature has found it prudent to delegate to the judiciary the responsibility of defining the key operative terms. The income tax legislation defined the tax base—taxable income—as gross income minus allowable deductions, but included no definition of 'gross income' or 'allowable deductions'. In the absence of legislative guidance, the courts turned to **precedents** from other areas, particularly the law of **trusts**, to identify a narrow subset of income in the real world as constituting the 'gross income' (referred to in the case law as 'income according to ordinary concepts') that was assessable for tax purposes. The courts played a similar role in relation to deductions, first by establishing judicial tests of the nexus between allowable deductions and the relevant corresponding income, and secondly by defining the characteristics of so-called 'capital outgoings' that the taxpayer was not entitled to claim as immediate deductions when they were incurred.

By the time the first income tax cases reached the High Court, the judicial concept of 'income' had already been established, with the Court's role limited to cementing the relatively narrow judicial concept by confirming the artificial distinction between enterprising realisations of profit (which fell outside the concept of income) and business realisations (within the concept) in cases such as *Scottish Australian Mining v FCT* (1950).

Rather than replace the narrow judicial concept of income with a sounder base such as accounting profits, the legislature responded to judicial base-defining initiatives in a piecemeal and ad hoc manner—time and again inserting narrow inclusion provisions often intended only to respond to the factual situations raised in particular cases.

Much of the Court's impact on taxation law has resulted from consideration of these base-broadening amendments, particularly of provisions intended to do no more than to codify existing concepts. Under the stewardship of Chief Justice **Barwick** in particular, the Court often read down the amendments so that their effect was one of base narrowing, not base broadening. The narrow and literal interpretations offered taxpayers considerable scope to avoid tax on gains from the disposal of assets, for example by interposing inter-family transfers (*FCT v Williams* (1972)) or corporate shareholder transfers (*Steinberg v FCT* (1975)) prior to realisation of gains.

The judicial concept of income, built upon subjective criteria such as taxpayers' motives and objectives, afforded considerable scope for base-narrowing interpretations of the legislation. However, the judicial concepts proved to be sufficiently ambiguous and inflexible to provide opportunities for base-broadening after Barwick's departure from the Court. For example, not long after his **retirement**, the Court creatively imputed the motive of new shareholders to the company they controlled, enabling the Commissioner to succeed in characterising a gain derived by the company as ordinary income (*FCT v Whitfords Beach* (1982)). This trend continued in the late 1980s when, through a substantial broadening of the judicial concept of income, the Court foiled an ingenious scheme devised by a bank to enable its customer to deduct the interest and principal on a loan (*FCT v Myer Emporium* (1987)). A similar trend developed with respect to statutory inclusion measures, resulting, in the late 1990s, in a somewhat bizarre finding that a taxpayer was assessable on a hypothetical profit in a transaction that yielded no gain to the taxpayer (*Commissioner of Taxation v Orica* (1998)).

The ambiguous deduction provisions in the tax legislation afforded the Court as many opportunities to define the deduction side of the taxable income equation as it enjoyed on the income side. Questions reaching the Court concerning expenses generally involved one of two issues. The first was the nexus required, if an expense was to be deductible, between the expense and the derivation of income. In some ways, the Court's early views of the requisite connection between outgoings and income were flexible and unrealistic—with the Court denying taxpayers' deductions, for example, if there was a significant interval between the time of the expenditure and the derivation of income to which it was related (*Amalgamated Zinc v FCT* (1935)). At the same time, the Court took a liberal view of the appropriateness of different types of expenditure that were clearly related to, though not directly part of, business operations—finding a sufficient nexus between outgoings and income production to allow deductions for expenses such as **damages** due to negligent behaviour on the taxpayer's part in the course of

business (*Herald & Weekly Times v FCT* (1932)) or theft losses (*Charles Moore & Co v FCT* (1956)).

The second deduction issue often considered by the Court was the distinction between capital and current outgoings. The legislation denied taxpayers an immediate deduction for capital expenses where an expense did not actually yield an economic loss to a taxpayer but rather resulted in the substitution of a long life benefit for the cash spent to acquire the benefit. Early jurisprudence taken from UK precedents looked primarily at the longevity of a benefit to determine the character of the expense incurred to acquire the benefit. In *Sun Newspapers v FCT* (1938)—a case that was to become one of the leading precedents in Australian tax jurisprudence—**Dixon** proposed a new test based on whether an expense was related to the 'process' of a business (in which case, he viewed it as a current expense), or to its 'structure' (in which case, he considered it to be a capital outgoing). The test was initially rejected by the rest of the Court (*Hallstroms v FCT* (1946)), but once Dixon became **Chief Justice**, he resurrected his dissenting view, cementing it as the basis for post-war jurisprudence in this area (*Broken Hill Theatres v FCT* (1952)).

One consequence of the new test—which had no basis in tax policy, accounting, or **economic** theory—was the denial of deductions for a wide range of business outgoings that became known as 'nothings' or 'black hole' expenses. The problem was partly addressed in 1985, when the government allowed taxpayers to recognise some black hole expenses under capital gains provisions; but most black hole expenses remained in a state of tax limbo. The need to overcome the effect of the test adopted by Dixon was treated as a priority in the 1999 final report of the Review of Business Taxation, whose recommendations, if implemented, would have allowed an immediate deduction for many expenses that were labelled non-deductible capital outgoings under the Dixon test.

The shift between the base-narrowing decisions of the **Barwick Court** and the base-broadening decisions of the post-Barwick Court paralleled an ongoing tension between the **legalism** of so-called 'black letter law' analysis, in which provisions were construed literally, narrowly, and almost inevitably in favour of the taxpayer, and what was labelled purposive analysis, in which provisions were read with a view to giving effect to the supposed purpose of the legislature. The highly restrictive approach adopted by the Barwick Court spawned an era of unprecedented tax avoidance, and rampant exploitation of schemes devised to attract the Court's base-narrowing precedents. In this era, the Court endorsed a range of blatant avoidance schemes, including arrangements to transfer Australian company profits overseas for tax avoidance purposes (*FCT v Commonwealth Aluminium* (1980)), and schemes to disguise the non-deductible purchase price of **property** as deductible rent (*FCT v SA Battery Makers* (1978)). Among the most infamous of the tax avoidance cases heard by the Court during this period were those in *Curran v FCT* (1974), *FCT v Westraders* (1980), and *Slutzkin v FCT* (1977)—cases involving schemes to strip profits from companies free of any tax. The Court's endorsement of the schemes—particularly the *Slutzkin* scheme—led to an explosion of similar arrangements, and ultimately to the illegal 'bottom-of-the-harbour' tax evasion phenomenon.

The Court's conduct during this period was the subject of considerable **criticism** by **commentators**, and, within the Court, by **Murphy**. In *Westraders*, in a famous exchange with Barwick, Murphy argued strongly that the Court's narrow and literal interpretation techniques, which had the effect of endorsing blatant tax avoidance schemes, were an abdication of the Court's responsibility to uphold the intention of the legislature when interpreting the law. Barwick responded by expressing the view that a strict and literal approach was the best guarantee of consistency in **statutory interpretation**, honouring the words of the legislation as passed by the Parliament.

At the time, Barwick's approach attracted strong criticism by those concerned about the perceived threatened disintegration of much of the income tax base. With the benefit of hindsight, however, Barwick's analysis seems almost prescient. Murphy's assertion that the Court has a responsibility to interpret legislation to achieve its intended purpose is no doubt correct. However, in the income tax sphere, there was no obvious purpose in much of the law. In all the key policy areas, the legislature had abdicated responsibility entirely to the judiciary. In effect, the legislature had implicitly endorsed wholly irrational distinctions, such as the reliance on trust law notions to determine which profits should bear tax and which expenses should be deductible. Moreover, when it moved to change the tax base, it often incorporated judicial notions into the law, regardless of how irrational they might seem from a policy perspective.

The leading example of this phenomenon was the adoption of the capital gains tax regime in 1985. The capital gains measures maintained and built upon the judicial concepts, relying on an array of highly artificial and complicated deeming provisions to bring into the tax base some amounts excluded from the judicial notion of income. When the first case involving the new legislation reached the Court, the judgments exposed the shortcomings of the legislative approach of piling deeming provision on top of deeming provision. Six of the seven Justices agreed that the gains were assessable, but were evenly divided as to which artificial deeming provision applied (*Hepples v FCT (No 1)* (1991)). In the end, they concluded that with no clear majority in favour of any one provision, the taxpayer should escape tax completely (*Hepples v FCT (No 2)* (1992)).

Badly drafted and poorly planned legislation introduced in the 1980s made the Court's task more difficult, and also made the Court itself somewhat reluctant to continue its intervention into the tax law-making process. For a brief period after *Hepples (No 1)* and *Hepples (No 2)*, the Court decided to treat the Full **Federal Court** as the final court of appeal for most tax matters, by using its power to deny special **leave to appeal**. The retreat proved relatively short-lived, however. Throughout the 1980s and continuing into the 1990s, the pendulum had clearly swung away from the strict **literalism** of the Barwick Court to a willingness to frustrate those who rely on artificial and contrived arrangements that apparently meet the technical words of the law.

That process is well illustrated by the Court's treatment of the general anti-avoidance provision. Australia's income tax legislation has always contained such a provision, originally copied from NZ. For six decades, the provision appeared to work moderately well—until dismembered by the Barwick Court in cases such as *Mullens v FCT* (1976) and *Cridland v FCT* (1977), through the development of earlier doctrines into a so-called 'choice principle' that effectively offered taxpayers the option of minimising tax if the scheme were sufficiently clever to fit within a literal reading of the legislation.

The emasculation of the general anti-avoidance provision in the mid-1970s led to its replacement by a comprehensive set of provisions in the early 1980s. Coincidentally with the introduction of the new anti-avoidance legislation, the **Gibbs Court** signalled that it was prepared to adopt a more purposive approach to analysing tax legislation (*Cooper Brookes v FCT* (1981)); and by the mid-1980s, the Court had actually revived the effectiveness of the original (and by then repealed) anti-avoidance provision (*FCT v Gulland* (1985)). By the late 1980s, cases such as *John v FCT* (1989) had repudiated and **overruled** the worst decisions of the tax avoidance era. Although the Court was not prepared to give the Commissioner of Taxation carte blanche to apply the new anti-avoidance provision whenever the underlying legislation might be flawed, it has nevertheless viewed with sympathy the application of the provision to contrived and artificial arrangements (see, for example, *Commissioner of Taxation v Spotless Services* (1996)).

Michael Kobetsky
Rick Krever

Taylor, Alan Russell (*b* 25 November 1901; *d* 3 August 1969; Justice 1952–69), was born at Newcastle, NSW, the fifth son of Walter Durham Taylor, customs officer from York, England, and his native-born wife Lilias Martha, née Hewitt.

In about 1911, the family moved to Sydney. Taylor attended Fort Street Boys High School, leaving at the age of 14. He joined the federal public service in Sydney in November 1917 as a clerk in the Postmaster General's Department, where he remained until 1921. While studying law at the University of Sydney, he worked in the Commonwealth Crown Solicitor's Office until January 1924. He graduated in 1926 with second-class honours and was admitted to the Bar on 2 June of the same year. Although he was to practise mainly in **equity**, **common law**, and company law, he also built up a considerable practice in **admiralty**. In Chancery Chambers from 1926, with friends Bernard Sugerman and David Roper, he moved in 1939 to University Chambers and in 1942 to Chalfont Chambers.

On 25 July 1933, Taylor married Ceinwen Gertrude Williams, a public servant whom he had met while working in the Crown Solicitor's Office. He was Challis lecturer in legal interpretation between 1936 and 1942 at the University of Sydney Law School. By the late 1930s, he had a large and wide-ranging general practice and was sharing the leading junior work at the Bar with Jack Shand and with **Barwick**. In October 1943, he took silk; he was president of the NSW Bar Association in 1948 and 1949.

Between 1926 and 1952, Taylor increasingly appeared as **counsel** before the High Court in a number of leading constitutional cases (see, for example, *Kisch Case* (1934); the *First Uniform Tax Case* (1942); *Jehovah's Witnesses Case* (1943); *Grace Bros v Commonwealth* (1946); and *Chaff and Hay Acquisition Committee v Hemphill* (1947)). His incisive mind was gaining him a reputation as a formidable cross-examiner;

Alan Taylor, Justice 1952–69

Rae Else-Mitchell noticed that, while his first question often seemed harmless, the last could be unanswerable.

In 1948, appearing for the English-controlled Bank of Australasia and others, Taylor was a member of the legal team led by Barwick that successfully challenged the Chifley government's legislation to nationalise the trading banks in the High Court (see *Bank Nationalisation Case*). He had resigned his brief to defend Tasmania's pea marketing laws in the *Field Peas Case* (1948), so as not to jeopardise the banks' case on freedom of **interstate trade** by using arguments that might weaken it or possibly prematurely settle the issue.

Described by the *Sydney Morning Herald* as 'one of the great appellate advocates', Taylor's skills continued to be very much in demand. He was briefed by the Commonwealth in 1950 to defend the High Court's decisions in three cases (*Grace Bros v Commonwealth*, *Nelungaloo v Commonwealth* (1948), and *Bonython v Commonwealth* (1948)) before the **Privy Council** in London; he was accompanied by Else-Mitchell as his junior. He won them all (*Nelungaloo* and *Grace Bros* because the Privy Council detected an *inter se* **question**)—much to the displeasure of Barwick, the opposing counsel in all but *Bonython*. While in London, he was asked to appear before the Privy Council to oppose a grant of special leave to appeal against the High Court's decision in the *Whose Baby Case* (1949)) and also succeeded in that case. Back home, in 1951 he was second to Barwick in the team of ten counsel unsuccessfully defending the validity of the *Communist Party Dissolution Act* 1950 (Cth) in the High Court (see *Communist Party Case* (1951)). During the subsequent referendum campaign, Barwick and Taylor provided the **Menzies** government with a joint opinion that the proposed legislation would not authorise the making of a law dealing with persons other than communists.

On Taylor's elevation to the Supreme Court Bench on 5 May 1952, Norman Cowper, a Sydney solicitor, congratulated him, but lamented the loss to the Bar of the 'quiet persuasiveness' of his advocacy, 'the effortless flow, the apt phrase, the pleasant voice and manner, the patience, ready wit and genial **humour**, the ability to draw a fine distinction with convincing lucidity, the wealth of learning at immediate command'.

On 3 September the same year, Taylor was appointed to the High Court, after **Dixon** became **Chief Justice**. Both Else-Mitchell and Ray Reynolds believed that Taylor was appointed at the personal behest of **Prime Minister** Menzies (see also **Appointments that might have been**). Under Dixon, who set very high standards, the High Court was widely respected in other **common law** countries and, as the *Australian Law Journal* noted in 1972, 'attained a standard of excellence that gained for it the reputation of being the finest court of law in the English-speaking world'. The **personal relations** between the Justices, reflecting their similarity of outlook, were amicable. Possessing a 'capacity for felicitous and clear expression of his judicial views', as Barwick observed in 1969, Taylor was 'co-operative and self-effacing', an 'indefatigable worker who liked to write his judgments the same day'. As the *Sydney Morning Herald* recorded at the time of his death, he 'undertook more than his share of the burdensome task of producing' the many **joint judgments** of the Court and willingly undertook the constant travelling with the Court from state to state (see **Circuit system**).

In the 1930s, the states' efforts to protect the railways by imposing charges and taxes on interstate road carriers had been upheld in a series of 'transport cases' in the High Court; but in 1954, those cases were **overruled**. A new series of transport cases ensued in which such legislation was frequently held to be unconstitutional. An adherent of free enterprise doctrines, Taylor believed with Dixon that section 92 of the Constitution guaranteed that each individual had a constitutional right to engage in interstate trade. Indeed, Taylor's view was more unyielding than Dixon's. In *Hughes & Vale v NSW (No 2)* (1955), where the Dixon majority conceded in principle that the states might impose a charge on interstate road transport as a 'reasonable recompense or compensation for the use of the highway' and for wear and tear on the roads, Taylor protested that in such a context he had 'great difficulty in giving any real meaning' to the use of concepts like compensation or **reasonableness**. He concluded categorically 'that any impost or tax, or so-called charge, whether levied upon a limited class for special purposes or by way of contribution to a tax for general purposes, which is made payable as a condition of engaging in or carrying on inter-State trade, must offend against s 92'. In *Armstrong v Victoria (No 2)* (1957), where the Dixon majority held that Victoria had in fact succeeded in devising a reasonable wear and tear charge, Webb, **Kitto**, and Taylor dissented. And in *Commonwealth Freighters v Sneddon* (1959), while accepting the authority of *Armstrong (No 2)*, he continued to protest that the expression 'reasonable' in this context 'was an abstract and not a practical concept'.

A down-to-earth, no-nonsense man—a common lawyer in the NSW mould—Taylor had little time for excessive legalism. He was more robust in manner and outlook than Dixon, **Fullagar**, and Kitto, and did not share their intellectual approach. He preferred, in JD Merralls' words, to 'decide the case in hand according to accepted principles and was not greatly interested in the organic development of the law'. He was more attuned intellectually to his friends Douglas **Menzies** and **Owen**. On Taylor's death, Barwick paid tribute to the breadth of Taylor's 'general knowledge and experience of the law and his mastery of constitutional principle and **precedent**' and noted that his colleagues had found him 'wise in conference, confident and practical in decision and gentle in dissent'.

As a KC, Taylor had taken extreme care in preparing his arguments. He did not believe that obviously fallacious propositions should be adumbrated in the hope that the majority of the Court might be erroneously attracted, but rather that counsel should so frame their **argument** that it formed a basis of a favourable judgment. On the Bench, he expected the same standards from counsel appearing before him. When faced with what he considered 'a plethora of irrelevancies' he was forthright, and could at times be impatient and curt with counsel.

A big, bluff, craggy man, and physically fit (until suffering a heart attack in 1968), Taylor was an expert tennis player when young and, later, a golfer. He belonged to the Australian and Royal Sydney golf clubs, and the Elanora Country Club, and enjoyed playing snooker at the University Club. In 1955, he was appointed KBE. Sworn in as a Privy Counsellor by the Queen at Government House, Canberra, on 19 February 1963, he was to sit on the Judicial Committee of the Privy Council for three months in 1967 (see *Aik Hoe & Co v Superintendent of Lands* (1967) and *Peiris v Appu* (1968)).

Suffering from coronary sclerosis, Taylor died suddenly on 3 August 1969 at his home in Wentworth Road, Vaucluse. His wife, son, and daughter survived him. Barwick considered Taylor to have been 'a most distinguished judge, one of the ablest this country has produced', and mourned the loss of 'the warmth of his friendship, his unfailing good humour, and his ready turn of wit and phrase on all occasions, making our daily association with him pleasant and memorable … Indeed he was a companionable man—kind, loyal and generous in his friendship'.

MARTHA RUTLEDGE

Televising of proceedings. There are few if any attributes of justice more important than that it be administered openly, its processes available to public scrutiny. The principle of open justice is of such importance that failure to accord it will, in the absence of well-recognised exceptions that require proceedings to be held in camera (that is, in closed court), vitiate the entire proceedings.

Until very recently, the concept of proceedings being in **open court** involved the **courtroom** being freely open to the public and the press and court records also being generally available. It did not extend to the public or the press taking photographs or making sound recordings of proceedings.

With the arrival of television, a whole new medium for informing the public of the work of the courts has arisen— one capable of reaching the widest of audiences instead of the relatively few members of the public who ever choose to attend the courts. It can also bring court proceedings to the viewer at firsthand rather than through journalists' accounts appearing in the print medium.

Courts and governments worldwide have responded in very different ways to this new medium. A number of overseas countries of the **common law** have set up committees to consider—some have undertaken pilot studies—the televising of court proceedings, among them England and Wales, Ireland, Scotland, and NZ. Canada has gone rather further; in some of its federal and certain of its provincial courts, a degree of routine televising of selected cases has occurred. In the USA, the federal courts and the courts of all but two of the states—though not the **United States Supreme Court**— had, by 1999, permitted very substantial access to court proceedings by television, subject to a range of varying restrictions and guidelines, while in 2000 a controversial Bill was introduced to permit televising of the Supreme Court itself. Other countries have differed widely in their reaction: from absolute prohibition in Sweden and Denmark to liberal access in India and Thailand.

In Australia, the High Court's own installed closed-circuit cameras record proceedings for the Court's own purposes, and occasional public televising of the handing down of decisions and of **ceremonial sittings** has taken place. It is understood that the whole question of public televising of proceedings is under review by the Court.

The **Federal Court** has gone rather further. It commissioned a detailed report by Daniel Stepniak in 1998, which gives an account of the extent of television broadcasting of court proceedings around the world and discusses the advantages and disadvantages of using the medium. The principal argument in favour of televising court proceedings has been that it enhances public access to court proceedings and so makes 'the principle of open justice more of a reality. A closely related argument is that of the educative value of showing court cases on television'.

The major overriding contrary argument is that the presence of cameras in a courtroom 'would affect proceedings in a way that would be antithetical to the defendant receiving a fair trial. In the main, this argument rests on trial participants behaving differently because of cameras'.

Portions of a number of hearings before the Federal Court and the handing down of judgments in certain cases have been televised and broadcast in recent years. Full details of these occasions appear in the report, including information about the as yet quite limited extent to which the proceedings of some state courts in Australia have been televised.

A major question in considering the televising of court proceedings is how the results would be shown to the public. Court proceedings are necessarily conducted without any regard to their attractiveness to an audience, and experience overseas suggests that there is very limited interest on the part of the general public in viewing court cases in their entirety. This may mean that in the general run of cases decided in the courts throughout Australia it is unlikely, even if the future lies in multiple channels, that they will be televised and screened in full. To this extent, television may have relatively little to contribute to the concept of openness of the courts. The televising and screening of no more than the occasional sensational incident or the particular behaviour of a witness or an accused at a moment of tension may not be thought either to advance that concept or to greatly assist in the public's better understanding of the justice system.

The case of proceedings in the High Court is, however, rather special. A dedicated channel devoted to a coverage of all **Full Court** hearings on television or on the Internet would seem likely to attract a small group of regular viewers in universities and legal circles around Australia, together with a scattering of the general public, and would be a useful educative tool; it would also be free of the difficulties some envisage in the televising of cases involving juries and witnesses. Its viewing audience would no doubt considerably expand for constitutional and other cases of great public interest, and the screening of the proceedings would greatly enlarge the opportunity of interested members of the public to follow the arguments and reasoning of the parties.

NINIAN STEPHEN

Further Reading
Daniel Stepniak, *Electronic Media Coverage of Courts: A Report Prepared for the Federal Court of Australia* (1998)

Tenure. Security of tenure is an important aspect of judicial **independence**. Under the Constitution, Justices can be removed only in particular circumstances, and their **remuneration** cannot be diminished. This is vital, given their function of determining the limits of power under the Constitution of the other branches of government.

For most of the High Court's history, its Justices have been appointed for life. However, in 1977, the Constitution was amended to provide for the **retirement** of all High Court Justices when they reach the age of 70.

It was once thought that it might be possible for Parliament to introduce a compulsory retiring age for High Court Justices without amending the Constitution. In its original form, section 72, which deals with the **appointment** of judges, provided simply that Justices of the High Court (and other courts created by federal Parliament) could not be removed unless both Houses of Parliament voted for their removal on the ground of proved misbehaviour or incapacity (see **Removal of Justices**). The section did not explicitly preclude the possibility that judges might be appointed only until they reached a certain age; but in *Alexander's Case* (1918), the Court (by a 5:2 majority) construed it as requiring that all federal judges be appointed for life.

Although some continued to argue that a compulsory retiring age for High Court Justices could be provided for by legislation, it was generally accepted after 1918 that it would require a constitutional **amendment**. Such an amendment was proposed, in 1929, by the Royal Commission on the Constitution. The Commission recommended a compulsory retiring age of 72. However, the suggestion was not taken further, and the matter then seems to have lain dormant for nearly half a century.

It came into public prominence again during the deliberations of the Australian Constitutional Convention in the 1970s. The issue was raised in 1975, and in October 1976 the Convention proposed a constitutional amendment making retirement at age 70 compulsory for High Court Justices. In the same month, the Senate Standing Committee on Legal and Constitutional Affairs handed down a report with the same recommendation. The Committee gave four reasons for introducing a compulsory retiring age for federal judges. First, it would help to maintain vigorous and dynamic courts, which require the input of new and younger judges who could be expected to bring to the bench new ideas and fresh social attitudes. Secondly, the relatively high average age of federal judges limited the opportunity for able legal practitioners to serve on the Bench while at the peak of their professional abilities and before their health began to decline. Thirdly, there was an acceptance by the community of the need for a compulsory retiring age for judges. Fourthly, it would avoid the unfortunate necessity of having to remove a judge who ought not to continue in office because of declining health, but who was unwilling to resign.

In its report, the Committee also considered two alternative ways to encourage judges to retire early—allowing them to retire on full pay, or—more controversially—instituting a system that reduced their annual pensions for every year after age 70 that they stayed on the Bench. Both of these options were rejected.

In February 1977, all major political parties voted in favour of a provision instituting a compulsory retiring age of 70 for High Court Justices (and allowing Parliament to set a retirement age of 70 or lower for judges of other federal courts). In May, it was put to the electorate as part of a package of four constitutional amendments—three of which were successfully adopted. The proposal received a majority in all states, and was supported by 80 per cent of voters, making it the third most popular referendum proposal in Australia's history. The argument favoured by some that a similar amendment in the USA would have deprived the **United States Supreme Court** of much of the wisdom and many of the enduring insights of Oliver Wendell Holmes, who retired from the Court at the age of 92, was evidently unpersuasive in the Australian context.

The 1977 amendment affected all Justices appointed to the High Court or elevated to the position of Chief Justice after that date. After the death of **Murphy** in 1986, all members of the Bench were subject to the compulsory retiring age provision.

Prior to the constitutional amendment, few Justices had retired before they turned 70. Of the 31 Justices appointed with life tenure, only four retired below this age—**Knox** (at age 66), **Evatt** (at age 46), **Williams** (at age 68), and **Kitto** (at age 67).

Yet the main factor affecting the average tenure of High Court Justices has not been the introduction of a compulsory retiring age. Rather, it has been the steady increase in the average age of appointees. With the exception of the period 1903–20, when the appointment of several former politicians pushed the average age up to 55, the average age of appointees has risen from 45 (1921–40), to 46 (1941–60), to 52 (1961–80), to 54 (1981–2000).

Thus, while the average tenure of High Court Justices has fluctuated somewhat, the general trend has been downwards. The average tenure for Justices appointed between 1903 and 1920 was 19 years (though this is skewed somewhat by the appointment of **Piddington** for just 30 days). Since then, it has gone from 25 years (1921–40), to 15 years (1941–60), to 11 years (1961–80), to 14 years (1981–2000, not including the current Bench).

In all this, one thing is clear. Never again will we see a Justice like **McTiernan**, who served for 46 years—longer than any other judge of a final appellate court in the **common law** world.

ANDREW LEIGH

Teoh's Case (1995) was the high-water mark in the **Mason Court**'s application of **international law** to Australian law. It showed a High Court that was aware of the reality that actions by Australian governments on the international stage have ramifications on the national stage, and that the Australian public is alert to this. However, it created significant tensions between the High Court and successive governments over the national consequences of international actions.

The circumstances that gave rise to this case were not ones that might be considered to merit a case of such controversy. Ah Hin Teoh applied for residency status on the basis that he was married to an Australian and was the main carer of seven Australian children. His application was refused because, while his application was pending, he had been convicted for importing and possessing heroin and sentenced to six years imprisonment. He appealed against the refusal of his residency application on the basis that the minister had failed to give consideration to the best interests of the children, as required by Article 3 of the United Nations Convention on the Rights of the Child 1989. The Australian government argued that while Australia had ratified this treaty (and so had clear international legal obligations under it), it had not been implemented by legislation so as to become part of Australian law; thus, under the rules relating to international law in Australia, the treaty—being unincorporated—could not create rights or obligations available as the subject of a claim in an Australian court.

While the High Court accepted this argument, the majority did not think it conclusive. In a decision that asserted the need to link international and national legal obligations, **Mason**, **Deane**, and **Toohey** drew a distinction between a claim based on a substantive right arising from a treaty and a procedural right. While the former could not arise in relation to an unincorporated treaty, the latter would arise, as a matter of procedural fairness, where a **legitimate expectation** had arisen that the treaty's provisions would be applied. If that were not to be the case, the decision maker should provide the applicant with a hearing.

In this case, such a legitimate expectation had arisen by virtue of the Australian government's ratification of the Convention. As Mason and Deane expressed it:

Ratification by Australia of an international convention is not to be dismissed as a merely platitudinous or ineffectual act, particularly when the instrument evidences internationally accepted standards to be applied by courts and administrative authorities in dealing with basic human rights affecting the family and children. Rather, ratification of a convention is a positive statement by the Executive Government of this country to the world and to the Australian people that the Executive Government and its agencies will act in accordance with the Convention.

This was a strong recognition that there should be consistency between an international act and its national consequences, especially in relation to human rights issues. However, the majority recognised the limits on the remedial capacity of the **common law**: there could be no legitimate expectation where there was a statutory or executive indication to the contrary.

The sole dissent was by **McHugh**. In his view, if the majority's decision was correct, it would mean that the executive government could change any laws in Australia simply by ratifying a treaty. That would cause appalling consequences for administrative decision making in Australia, including decisions at state government level.

The decision elicited immediate outrage from the government and many administrative lawyers, and great delight from international lawyers. Barely one month after the decision, the Labor government issued a press release from the Minister for Foreign Affairs and the **Attorney-General** rejecting the majority's decision. The government largely adopted the views of McHugh and gave priority to efficient administrative decision making and cost savings.

Because of the uncertainty as to whether such an executive statement was sufficient to overturn the legitimate expectation articulated by the High Court, the government introduced the Administrative Decisions (Effect of International Instruments) Bill 1995 expressly to overturn the decision in *Teoh*. The Bill was referred to a Senate Committee, which, largely along party lines, upheld it. However, with elections, the Bill lapsed. The new Coalition government wasted little time in introducing an almost identical Bill. It also went to a Senate Committee, at which the **political parties** reversed their previous positions, but it then lapsed with new elections. On the re-election of the Coalition government, it was expected that, as nearly five years had passed since the *Teoh* decision without apparent adverse effect to administrative decision making, the matter would be allowed to rest. However, the Bill was reintroduced to Parliament in 2000 and again met with opposition in the Senate.

The decision in *Teoh*, while ostensibly about the relationship of international to national law, became a touchstone for the relationship between the High Court and the executive. The Mason Court had attempted to bring the government to some limited account for its international actions. However, successive governments showed that they were not only unwilling to have their **external affairs power** limited in any way, but that they would pass legislation specifically aimed at overturning a 4:1 decision of the High Court. Indeed, there was speculation in some quarters that Deane had been invited to be Governor-General to remove him from the High Court because of this and other controversial decisions. It may be that the views of McHugh, which were so fully adopted by the various governments, were a harbinger of changes to the balance in the Court after the departure of Deane and Mason. Above all, *Teoh* highlights the dilemma at the heart of the High Court's **role** in clarifying domestic legal obligations in an era of increasing globalisation of law.

ROBERT MCCORQUODALE

Further Reading

Margaret Allars, 'One Small Step for Legal Doctrine, One Giant Leap Towards Integrity in Government: *Teoh's* Case and the Internationalisation of Administrative Law' (1995) 17 *Syd LR* 204

Hilary Charlesworth, 'Australia's Split Personality: Implementation of Human Rights Treaty Obligations in Australia' in Phillip Alston and Madeleine Chiam (eds), *Treaty-Making and Australia: Globalisation versus Sovereignty* (1995)

Senate Legal and Constitutional References Committee, *Trick or Treaty? Commonwealth Power to Make and Implement Treaties* (1995)

Senate Legal and Constitutional References Committee, *Administrative Decisions (Effect of International Instruments) Bill* (1995 and 1997)

Teoh's Case: some quandaries. The constitutional significance of *Teoh's Case* (1995) lay in the significance it attached to Australia's international obligations subscribed to by the executive government. In an era of globalisation and a heightened focus on human rights protection, Australia's international commitments were not, according to the majority, to be treated as merely 'platitudinous and ineffectual'. So much can be agreed; but other issues remain. Did *Teoh* enunciate a sensible standard for evaluating validity under **administrative law**? Can domestic and **international law** be harmonised better in another way? Did the Court usurp Parliament's role?

Teoh confronts a decision maker with two options: either exercise a discretionary power in conformity with any relevant international treaty standard or, in accordance with **natural justice**, notify a person in advance that the government's treaty commitment is to be disregarded, and conduct a hearing on whether that should be so. It is unlikely as a practical matter that a decision maker will avowedly choose to disregard the international standard—to do so could invite criticism, lead to a complaint to an ombudsman or human rights agency, and possibly trigger a legal challenge on another ground, such as failure to approach the merits of the case with an open mind.

The prudent alternative of acting in accordance with Australia's international obligations unlocks a different range of problems. Which international treaties (and which clauses in those treaties) will be relevant to any particular decision, and how do they mesh with domestic legislation and other executive policies? To take the facts of *Teoh* as an example, in making a decision to deport a person for drug offences in Australia, how does the treaty stipulation that the best interests of a child are 'a primary consideration' mesh with the detailed provisions of the *Migration Act* 1958 (Cth) and with executive policy on deportation of drug offenders? It will not be enough for the decision maker to consider the impact of deportation on a child; unless the interests of the child are treated as 'a primary consideration', a hearing must be given on the separate issue of whether to honour Australia's international obligations. Quite likely, the decision maker cannot gauge whether the treaty has been implemented until the decision has already been made and the reasons prepared. Should all decisions be regarded as provisional, followed by an additional hearing 'just in case'?

Those quandaries are not imaginary and are illustrated by decisions of the Administrative Appeals Tribunal that have been declared invalid by the **Federal Court** because the Tribunal mistakenly thought it had decided consistently with a treaty, and had therefore omitted to conduct a *Teoh*-style hearing (for example, *Vaitaiki v Minister for Immigration* (1998); *Lam v Minister for Immigration* (1998); *Hui v Minister for Immigration* (1998)). The difficulties are compounded by the fact that Australia is a signatory to more than 900 treaties, many of them containing a multiplicity of principles expressed in indeterminate and aspirational language.

The difficulty with *Teoh* stems from the Court's choice of the imprecise concepts of **natural justice** and **legitimate expectation** to harmonise domestic and international law. An alternative and less problematic approach would have been to require that consideration be given by a decision maker to the values articulated in a treaty, rather than to the treaty itself. It is questionable, too, whether consideration of international law obligations should be a criterion of administrative validity. An alternative is to consign principal responsibility for developing and monitoring the standards for decision making to the ombudsman, administrative tribunals, and the Human Rights and Equal Opportunity Commission.

Teoh, as these points illustrate, also touched on deeper constitutional issues. Although the Court affirmed the orthodox principle that a treaty entered into by the executive is binding only internationally and does not, in the absence of implementing legislation, change the law domestically, treaty commitments were still accorded a significance they did not formerly have. The established principle that a treaty has no legal effect upon the rights and duties of the public until adoption by Parliament (*Chow Hung Ching v The King* (1948); *Simsek v Macphee* (1982)) was, if nothing else, undermined. This was shown by *Teoh* itself. Although the deportation order against Ah Hin Teoh had been made fully in compliance with the criteria and procedures expressly defined in the Migration Act, the decision was invalid because of the meaning and effect to be attributed to an additional body of international criteria. In effect, though the formal holding of the Court stopped short of saying so, the statute was no longer a self-evident code for administrative decision making: the government's international undertakings, embodied in the treaties it had ratified, had become part of the legal matrix.

Some may feel that a transformation of the Australian legal framework of that dimension should not be undertaken by judicial decision, but in a democratic parliamentary context (see in particular **McHugh's** powerful dissent in *Teoh*). Although the choices made by Parliament and the executive often coincide in a system of **responsible government**, disagreement often occurs, particularly if the government does not control the Upper House. Moreover, Parliament provides a public forum for debate and consideration of whether undertakings made by the executive in the international domain should be subordinated to competing principles of public policy. This point has added weight in a federal system if *Teoh* means that a treaty commitment undertaken by the Commonwealth executive creates a legitimate expectation in relation to decision making under state legislation (a matter that is unresolved).

Ultimately, *Teoh* illustrates the growing complexity of administrative decision making, and the shifting balance of power between the courts and Parliament. Whether it is now too complex, and whether the balance is tilted too far one way or another, are issues that will continue to enliven debate and on which reasonable minds will differ.

JOHN MCMILLAN

Further Reading

John McMillan and Neil Williams, 'Administrative Law and Human Rights' in David Kinley (ed), *Human Rights in Australian Law* (1998)

Richard Piotriwicz, 'Unincorporated Treaties in Australian Law' [1996] *Public Law* 190

Territories. As well as limiting the power of the Commonwealth vis-à-vis the states, the Constitution gives the Commonwealth general power in relation to federal 'territories'— areas of land that have been acquired by the Commonwealth at various times since federation, on surrender by a state or otherwise. This gives the Commonwealth a dual personality: on the one hand, a body limited by federal considerations when legislating in relation to the states and, on the other, a quasi-unitary body when legislating or acting in relation to the territories. Yet many constitutional restrictions on the Commonwealth's powers are expressed in general terms, and the Court has had to decide whether those restrictions apply even when the Commonwealth is legislating for the territories, or whether those restrictions are so intimately connected to the federal framework that they do not apply outside that framework.

The Court's decisions on this constitutional dilemma reveal a range of competing approaches. Notwithstanding earlier authorities treating the territories as a 'disparate and non-federal matter', subsequent decisions of the Court have to some extent attempted to 'integrate' the territories (and particularly the mainland or 'internal' territories) into the Constitution as a whole. Nevertheless, a consensus has not yet emerged on any general approach to questions involving the application and operation of constitutional provisions in and to the territories.

The decisions of the Court in the early decades after federation viewed the Commonwealth's power in relation to its territories as divorced from the federal relationship and unrestricted by other provisions of the Constitution. In *Buchanan v Commonwealth* (1913), the Court held that a law enacted for the territories by the Commonwealth Parliament did not have to comply with section 55 of the Constitution, which limits the matters that may be dealt with in Commonwealth laws imposing **taxation**, on the basis that the requirements imposed by section 55 were designed to protect the interests of the states. Shortly thereafter, in *R v Bernasconi* (1915), the Court held that the requirement of trial by **jury** (contained in section 80 of the Constitution)—which is applicable to Commonwealth indictable offences—does not apply to offences against Commonwealth laws enacted for the territories under section 122 of the Constitution.

Particularly in *Bernasconi*, the Court appears to have been influenced by the perceived inappropriateness and potential impracticality of imposing the full rigour of constitutional

protections in territories that were in an early stage of development (see **Papua and New Guinea**). Isaacs, for example, described the territories as 'parts annexed to the Commonwealth and subordinate to it', and noted that territories within the scope of the legislative power conferred by section 122 were 'not yet in a condition to enter into the full participation of Commonwealth constitutional rights and powers'. These early decisions represent the high-water mark of the 'disparate and non-federal' approach, treating the territories and their government as separate and distinct from 'the Commonwealth proper'.

The beginnings of a shift in the attitude of the Court were revealed in the judgment of **Dixon** in *Australian National Airways v Commonwealth* (1945), whose approach was subsequently adopted by a majority of the Court in *Lamshed v Lake* (1958). In *Lamshed*, the Court rejected an argument that the Commonwealth Parliament acted merely as a local legislature when exercising its powers in relation to territories under section 122. Rather, the Court concluded that a law enacted for the government of a territory was a law of the national Parliament, capable of extending beyond the boundaries of the relevant territory and overriding state laws pursuant to section 109 of the Constitution.

The Court has since taken a broad view of the concept of a law for the government of a territory under section 122, not requiring that the law operate on matters or things wholly within the territory. In *A-G (WA); Ex rel Ansett Transport Industries v Australian National Airlines* (1976), the majority of the Court held that a law authorising an intrastate air service between Perth and Port Hedland was supported by the territories power because it facilitated the provision of air services for the Northern Territory.

In both *ANA v Commonwealth* and *Lamshed*, Dixon emphasised that the territories were not 'disjoined' from the rest of the Constitution. **Kitto** agreed, noting in *Lamshed* that it was necessary to treat the Constitution 'as one coherent instrument for the government of the federation, and not as two constitutions, one for the federation and the other for its territories'. This theme was picked up by **Barwick** in *Spratt v Hermes* (1965), who commented that it was an error to 'compartmentalize' the Constitution—a sentiment that was later endorsed by **Gaudron**, **Gummow**, and **Kirby** in *Newcrest Mining v Commonwealth* (1997). Gaudron and Kirby have also stated (in *Kruger v Commonwealth* (1997) and *Newcrest Mining* respectively) that the Constitution does not empower the Commonwealth to govern the territories as federal 'fiefdoms'.

Consequently, it is accepted that many constitutional provisions are clearly capable of application in relation to the territories (see Dixon in *Lamshed*). Whether and to what extent the **Commonwealth legislative power** in relation to territories is subject to any particular constitutional provision or limitation will generally be determined case by case (see Barwick in *Spratt*).

Nevertheless, in *Teori Tau v Commonwealth* (1969), the Court was prepared to reject the application to the territories of the constitutional guarantee of just terms for the **acquisition of property** (derived from section 51(xxxi) of the Constitution), delivering a unanimous *ex tempore* judgment without even hearing **argument** from the Commonwealth in support of this position. The Court emphasised that the legislative power conferred by section 122 of the Constitution was non-federal in nature, and was plenary and unlimited in terms of subject matter.

The future status of the decision in *Teori Tau* is now questionable after the decision in *Newcrest Mining*. While a majority of the Court in the latter case either affirmed *Teori Tau* or declined to **overrule** it, three Justices (Gaudron, Gummow, and Kirby) concluded that the earlier decision was incorrect and should now be departed from. Further, together with **Toohey**, these Justices accepted an alternative approach, which precludes reliance on the legislative power conferred by section 122 to avoid the 'just terms' guarantee in circumstances where the law also derives support from one of the Commonwealth's 'federal' legislative powers that are qualified by section 51(xxxi).

In two cases during the 1970s, the Court upheld Commonwealth legislation that provided for the representation of the Northern Territory and the ACT in the Commonwealth Parliament. In the *First Territory Senators Case* (1975), a majority held that the power conferred by section 122 to 'allow the representation of [a] territory in either House of the Parliament to the extent and on the terms which it thinks fit' should not be read down in the light of other provisions of the Constitution—in particular section 7, which provides that the Senate 'shall be composed of' senators for each state. This decision was followed, and extended to territory representation in the House of Representatives, by a differently constituted majority in the *Second Territory Senators Case* (1977).

While the two territory representation decisions turned on a construction of section 122 as independent of other constitutional provisions, in one sense they reinforced integrationist tendencies by enabling the representation of the people of the territories in the national legislature. However, the absence of any *constitutional* right to political representation for territory residents has been viewed as significant by some Justices—for example, in the application of the implied constitutional freedom of **political communication** (see, for example, McHugh in *Kruger*—but note that other Justices have taken a contrary view) or even as an additional reason for the extension to the territories of other constitutional guarantees and limitations (see Gaudron in *Kruger*).

In similar vein, the Court has upheld the power of the Commonwealth Parliament to bestow self-government arrangements on its territories (as has been done in the Northern Territory, the ACT, and Norfolk Island). Thus, section 122 authorises the Parliament 'to endow a Territory with separate political, representative and administrative institutions, having control of its own fiscus' (**Mason** in *Berwick v Gray* (1976)). In *Capital Duplicators v ACT (No 1)* (1992), a majority of the Court (comprising **Brennan, Deane**, Toohey, and Gaudron) adopted the view that the legislature of a self-governing territory (in that case, the Legislative Assembly of the ACT) can be established as an independent legislature with its own general legislative authority, rather than as a mere delegate of the Commonwealth Parliament. However, the majority held that the legislative power bestowed upon the territorial legislature was subject to section 90 of the Constitution, so as to preclude laws imposing **excise duties** in the territory.

In recent years, many Justices have been critical of the complexity and uncertainty surrounding the relationship between Chapter III of the Constitution and the territories (see Gaudron in *Northern Territory v GPAO* (1999); **Gleeson**, McHugh, **Callinan**, and Kirby in *Re Governor, Goulburn Correctional Centre; Ex parte Eastman* (1999)). Several important decisions had established and maintained a separation between territory courts and **judicial power** on the one hand, and federal courts and the judicial power of the Commonwealth on the other. In *Spratt*, the Court held that territory courts established by the Commonwealth Parliament were not subject to the requirements imposed by section 72 of the Constitution relating to the appointment of judges, security of **tenure**, and the protection of **remuneration**. In *Capital TV & Appliances v Falconer* (1971), the Court held that there was no constitutional right to appeal from a territory court to the High Court under section 73 of the Constitution, on the basis that territory courts were neither federal courts nor courts exercising federal **jurisdiction**. However, the Court has upheld the power of the Parliament to confer on federal courts (including the High Court) appellate jurisdiction—and possibly also original jurisdiction—in relation to the territories, even if such jurisdiction does not fall within Chapter III (see *Porter v The King; Ex parte Chin Man Yee* (1926)).

Despite coming under some pressure in recent cases, a majority of the Court has affirmed the holding in *Spratt* that territory courts are not 'federal courts' and therefore need not be constituted in accordance with the requirements of section 72 of the Constitution (*Eastman*). However, the Court has held that a matter arising under a law enacted by the Commonwealth Parliament for the territories falls within section 76(ii) of the Constitution and therefore involves federal jurisdiction, at least when exercised by a federal court (*GPAO*). Further, some Justices have indicated that it is possible for territory courts to be invested with, and to exercise, 'federal jurisdiction' with respect to matters falling within sections 75 and 76 of the Constitution (for example, see Gaudron in *GPAO*; Gaudron, Gummow, and **Hayne** in *Eastman*). Such a conclusion would bring some, if not all, decisions by territory courts within section 73 of the Constitution, attracting a right of appeal to the High Court that is not dependent on Commonwealth legislation. Further, this approach may render territory courts subject to the principles applied in *Kable v DPP* (1996), which limit the conferral of non-judicial functions on courts invested with federal jurisdiction.

The Court has generally avoided drawing any material distinctions between different kinds of territories for constitutional purposes (see, for example, *Teori Tau*). However, there have been some suggestions that the 'internal' territories that formed part of the area of the original states at federation may stand in a different position in some respects from other territories (see, for example, Gaudron in *Capital Duplicators (No 1)*). And it appears to have been accepted that the ACT, which contains the **seat** of government, is unique in that it cannot be admitted as a new state (Brennan, Deane, and Toohey in *Capital Duplicators (No 1)*).

The evolution of the Court's approach to the territories has undoubtedly been influenced by, among other things, developments in the status and importance of territories such as the ACT and the Northern Territory. The tension between the 'disparate and non-federal' approach and the attempt to integrate the territories into the Constitution as a whole is not yet fully resolved. To some extent, the development of a coherent theory concerning the constitutional position of the territories may have been hampered by an unwillingness to disturb decisions in previous cases. In any event, the applicable principles in many areas remain unsettled.

CHRISTOPHER HORAN

Further Reading

A Hopper, 'Territories and Commonwealth Places: The Constitutional Position' (1999) 73 *ALJ* 181

Chris Horan, 'Section 122 of the Constitution: A "Disparate and Non-federal" Power?' (1997) 25 *FL Rev* 97

Leslie Zines, 'Laws for the Government of any Territory: Section 122 of the Constitution' (1966) 2 *FL Rev* 72

Leslie Zines, 'The Nature of the Commonwealth' (1998) 20 *Adel L Rev* 83

Territory Senators Cases (1975 and 1977). The two *Territory Senators Cases*—*WA v Commonwealth* (1975) and *Queensland v Commonwealth* (1977)—required the High Court to pass judgment not only on the powers of the federal Parliament but on its very composition—a politically sensitive issue at the best of times. The first case arose in the highly charged political atmosphere of the **Whitlam era**, and was part of the chain of events that led to the **dismissal** of the **Prime Minister** in November 1975. The second case raised exquisite questions of **precedent** and *stare decisis*. Both cases vividly illustrate the challenge posed by **constitutional interpretation**, when constitutional provisions are seemingly in irreconcilable conflict and interpreters face a rich array of evenly balanced arguments and counter arguments clamouring to aid the resolution of that conflict.

The dilemma of having to choose between the two conflicting provisions reflected a deeper conflict between the competing principles underlying them. On the one hand, section 7 of the Constitution provided that the Senate was to be composed of (not merely 'include') senators for each state. This reflected—indeed embodied—the notion of the Senate as the 'states' House', the legislative chamber in which (unlike the House of Representatives that is elected on a population basis) the states would be equally represented—as states. On the other hand, section 122 provided that the Parliament could allow the representation of a **territory** in either House, to the extent and on the terms it thought fit. This section pitted **democracy** against the **federalism** principle embedded in section 7. As the federal Parliament was, under section 122, the body that made laws for the territories (and remained ultimately responsible even for those territories on which it had conferred a measure of self-government), it would be anti-democratic to deny the people of the territories a say in the body that governed them.

So thought the Whitlam Labor government when it introduced legislation in 1973 to provide for four territory senators: two for the Northern Territory and two for the ACT. But the government lacked a majority in the Senate, and the Senate—whether it was acting as a states' House or merely as a House of review or even as an opportunistic opposition—rejected the legislation, which was ultimately passed, pursuant to the deadlock procedure in section 57 of the Constitution and against the wishes of the Senate, at the joint sitting of 1974 (see *Cormack v Cope* (1974)).

In the High Court, three states (WA, Queensland, and NSW) argued that section 7 of the Constitution should prevail, and that representation in section 122 had to be taken to be something less than full membership with full voting rights. The Commonwealth argued that section 122 should prevail, and that any fear of the Senate being 'swamped' by territory senators was unrealistic and, if used as a reason to read section 122 down, would not reflect the trust and respect that the courts should extend to Parliament and the political process. Neither side was obviously right. The plain meanings of the words of the two sections were in flat opposition; the historical intentions were ambivalent, disclosing concerns both for the Senate as the states' House and for proper representation for federal territories that might develop appropriately; and resort to contemporary **policy considerations** or **values** did nothing to resolve the inherent tension between federalism and democracy.

Reflecting the fine balance of these arguments, the Court split 4:3, the majority—**McTiernan, Mason, Jacobs**, and **Murphy**—holding the creation of the territory senators to be valid. **Barwick, Gibbs**, and **Stephen** dissented. The decision was handed down on 10 October 1975. The prospect that Labor might win a majority of the new seats—which would be filled immediately—and thus gain a majority in the Senate, galvanised the Liberal–National Party Opposition into taking a firm decision to block the government's budget in the Senate, thereby precipitating the endgame of the political crisis that culminated in the dismissal of the Prime Minister just four weeks later, on 11 November 1975.

Closely divided decisions of the High Court are always vulnerable to being **overruled**, and changes in the composition of the Bench often invite fresh challenges. The optimal timing of such a challenge is a tricky thing. If it is made too soon, it may be seen as an opportunistic attempt to exploit the change in membership of the Court, and subversive of a proper respect for precedent. If the challenge is too long delayed, the passage of time may bestow on the earlier decision an aura of being settled, making it difficult to dislodge, particularly if there has been a degree of reliance on it (compare *Dennis Hotels v Victoria* (1960)).

The membership of the Court changed in the year following the first *Territory Senators Case*. After 46 years on the Bench, McTiernan retired in 1976 and was replaced by **Aickin**. It was widely perceived that Aickin would have sided with the minority in the first case. Encouraged by what was seen as an invitation by Barwick in *A-G (NSW); Ex rel McKellar v Commonwealth* (1977) to reopen the issue, two states (Queensland and WA) brought a second challenge.

The perception of Aickin's inclination proved to be correct. He held that the territories were not entitled to representation in the Senate. Barwick adhered to the same view. Both would have overruled the first *Territory Senators Case*. Moreover, the other two dissenters in the first case, Gibbs and Stephen, had not changed their minds on the substance of the constitutional issue. So a majority of Justices were of the view that territory representation in the Senate was unconstitutional.

That was not, however, the end of the story. Gibbs and Stephen now opted to follow the earlier decision as a matter of precedent, even though they thought it was wrong (see **Law-making role**). Thus, with Gibbs and Stephen now joining Mason, Jacobs, and Murphy (who stuck to their earlier views), the challenge failed for the second time—this time by a margin of 5:2, with only Barwick and Aickin in dissent.

The second *Territory Senators Case* presented a poignant choice between principle and precedent for those Justices who thought that the first *Territory Senators Case* was wrongly decided. The second case contains a wealth of discussion of the factors that might guide such a choice—none of which can ever compel a particular result, as the difference of opinion in the application of those factors to the case at hand so emphatically illustrates. In the result, territory representation survives. The Senate has not been flooded with senators from Norfolk Island or the Antarctic. Whether it can justly be described as the states' House—and indeed whether it could ever have justly been so described—depends on factors, such as the operation of the party system, that extend well beyond the question of territory representation.

MICHAEL COPER

Further Reading
Michael Coper, 'Commentary' in Gareth Evans (ed), *Labor and the Constitution 1972–1975* (1977) 209
Peter Hanks, 'Parliamentarians and the Electorate' in Gareth Evans (ed), *Labor and the Constitution 1972–1975* (1977) 178

Theory and legitimacy. If courts, like bodies, have constitutions, then legal theories are the very bowels of judgment. Everyone has them, and they serve a vital function of processing inputs and sorting use from waste. But at the dinner table or on the Bench, it is considered bad form to talk about it. Theories, like innards, are meant to get on with the job, well away from prying eyes and the offensive drawing and divining of entrails that constitutes scholarship.

A legal theory is the internal structure of thought that allows judges to discriminate—between fact and law, 'is' and 'ought', law and politics—and so to choose among the many contradictory arguments advanced before them. Theory makes judgment possible. In particular, judgment is dependent on a theory of origin or legitimacy (*Where does law come from?*) and a theory of interpretation (*What does law mean?*). On both these questions, the High Court has largely followed the conventional philosophical wisdom of **positivism**—though not, particularly in recent times, without dissent and reflection. As the Court appears to be becoming an increasingly important forum in the articulation of social conflict in Australian life, it seems likely that the theories used to justify and define the Court's **role** will also have to develop and diversify. As that happens, the Court may increasingly find itself faced with a third fundamental issue of legal theory: *What is a High Court for?*

The question of legitimacy cannot simply be referred to the Constitution, for it is precisely the bounds of the Constitution that the Court is called on to judge. Justification of its power in those terms raises a logical paradox referred to in writings on the **conflict of laws** as *renvoi*, and in some philosophical circles as *aporia*. A theory of the legitimate exercise

of judgment must draw on some source above the stream. But what?

For many judges, the need for **judicial independence** and the **separation of powers** is inherent in the fundamental structure of government, at a level logically prior, and historically antecedent, to the enactment of the Constitution. And although this fundamental conception of the role and importance of judges was well articulated by Edward Coke in the early seventeenth century (*Prohibitions del Roy* (1607); *Dr Bonham's Case* (1610)), he himself referred it to even more fundamental arguments of necessity, nature, and tradition. It is this necessary judicial independence that has surely grounded the great constitution-building cases of the High Court—particularly the *Boilermakers Case* (1956)—enabling the Court both to expand its own interpretive role and to supervise the role of the Parliament. *Boilermakers*, in particular, offered little textual support for its dual propositions that *only judges* can judge, and that judges can *judge only*. The Court drew instead on ancient intuitions of what it is to *be* a judge.

Yet the Court has continually emphasised the *textual* authority that gives rise to, and delimits, its power according to interpretive theories of **legalism** and **literalism** (*Engineers Case* (1920)). This textual basis for the Court's authority originally found support in the **sovereignty** of the Imperial Parliament (**Dixon**, 'The Law and the Constitution' (1935) 51 *LQR* 590) and more recently in the sovereignty of the Australian nation itself (*McGinty v WA* (1996); *Australia Act 1986* (Cth)). The argument for a legitimacy based on the inherent imperatives of national sovereignty reaches its highest point in relation to the **defence power**, and in relation to the concept of a **nationhood power** as an independent source of Commonwealth legislative capacity. The gradual move away from reliance on an external and therefore transcendent source of the Court's power—its *grundnorm* (Hans Kelsen, *The Pure Theory of Law* (1967))—has ushered in a radical change, for it has led the Court to draw on theories of **democracy** rather than sovereignty or **history** to ground its normative authority.

The theoretical perspective adopted has a profound impact on the Justices' decisions. The *Free Speech Cases* (1992) drew upon the Court's new theory of legitimacy to justify the 'implied rights' that most Justices found not in the sovereign text itself but in the theory that gives it force. *Kruger v Commonwealth* (1997) is a dramatic contrast. Confronted with allegations of genocide committed in pursuance of a Northern Territory Ordinance made by the Commonwealth under the **territories** power, **Dawson** drew on a theory of 'sovereign power' to argue that 'there is nothing which places rights of any description beyond its reach'. **Gaudron's** theory of democracy, on the other hand, led her to protect more carefully the rights of Territorians from laws which, until self-government, they had no direct say in enacting. One might ask whether this theory of legitimacy might have led her to protect even more steadfastly the rights of **Aboriginal peoples**, who at the time had no rights to participate in civil society at all.

Conversely, in many of his judgments, **Brennan** relied on a theory of the judicial office that Coke might have found congenial four centuries earlier. In *Mabo* (1992), it gave Brennan the authority to overturn the settled law; in *Dietrich v The*

Queen (1992), it forced him to declare that a judge cannot decline the honour and onus of judgment. Here, too, theory is the guts of law. And it provides us with a model of judicial responsibility that denies any transcendent abdication to the power of the people or of the Crown, and may yet repay further thought.

The question of meaning, likewise, cannot be reduced to any simple pattern. Undoubtedly, under the flag of Dixon's celebrated approbation of 'a strict and complete legalism', the Court has eschewed, on the one hand, any naïve faith in our ability to divine the 'original intention' of the **framers of the Constitution**, of the kind that has bedevilled the **United States Supreme Court** under the banner of **originalism**; and on the other, any cynical disregard for the texts that the Court must interpret in favour of a swingeing **activism** based on **policy considerations**. It is an approach to meaning which has found its inspiration in *Marbury v Madison* (1803), its imprimatur in *Engineers*, its apologist in Dixon, and its apotheosis in **Latham**. But it has not been without its critics. Some would condemn the Court for its abstract logical reasoning removed from any consideration of purposes or consequences. The mischief that has followed the Court's various interpretations of the meaning of **excise duties** may be cited in evidence. But there has been an increasing chorus of theoretical argument on the impossibility of ever determining, on logical or objective grounds alone, the meaning of words at all. And though the academic argument has become increasingly complex, it probably has not advanced beyond Lon Fuller's 1958 repudiation of HLA Hart, and certainly not beyond the work of Julius Stone. Together they establish that judgment is and must be an articulation of **values**, discursively governed but not substantively limited by the form and language of law.

In that light, the work of a range of Justices including **Evatt**, **Murphy**, and **Kirby** forms a powerful voice of conscience against the positivist orthodoxy, reminding the judiciary of its responsibility to the values that lie behind, and the consequences that flow from, all the Court's decisions. For the real criticism of the theory of legalism is that it can so easily become a cipher by which to conceal the real choices that judges make in every act of interpretation. The claim of logic or plain meaning operates as a dogma to estop further inquiry. When **McHugh**, for example, castigates his brethren for allowing, under the guise of 'common sense', the expression of 'subjective, unexpressed, and undefined extra-legal values' (*March v Stramare* (1991)), it is perhaps not that values themselves have no place in the law, but rather the fact that they are hidden by a theory which, against all the evidence, denies them any legitimate voice.

Alternative theories of interpretation, of which in recent years that of Ronald Dworkin is the best known (see, for example, *Law's Empire* (1986)), also come back to the notion of legitimacy. In the 1990s, interpretive legalism appears to command less support than ever before. At the same time, the role of the High Court is becoming both even more important and even more contentious. If the Court cannot anchor its responsibility either to a transcendent text or to a comforting past, what then? The contention in which the Court was embroiled over *Wik* (1996) came from populist rhetoric that equated 'strict legalism' with simple-minded **literalism**, and would deny the Court any greater legitimacy. Contemporary denials of a judicial **law-making role** echo the viewpoint of James I, who in 1616 told the judges: 'You are no makers of Law, but Interpretours of Law … [by] bookes and presidents [precedents]'. Such a view is, as Lord Reid put it in 1974, 'a fairy tale'—but, as Kirby added in his 1983 Boyer Lectures, 'the public, and especially newspaper editorialists, hate to see it doubted'.

Yet judges have by and large done little to articulate the more sophisticated theories of interpretation and legitimacy which in fact guide their endeavours. They have been hoist by their own silence. Theory implies that judges must look inside themselves to explain not only how they decide, but also why they decide how they decide. Theoretical reflection and explanation may reduce what Jacques Derrida has wrestled with as the 'mystical *authority* of law'; and indeed may replace our image of the infallible judge with that of a more imperfect being altogether. But if theory provides instead a more genuine portrayal of the difficulties of judgment, and highlights the role of the Court not just as the final arbiter of disputes but as an important and thoughtful participant in the ongoing discourse of social issues, the *legitimacy* of the High Court will have been immeasurably enhanced. (See also **Constitutional interpretation**; **Judicial reasoning**; **Jurisprudence**; **Natural law**; **Realism**).

DESMOND MANDERSON

Further Reading

Jacques Derrida, 'Force of Law: The Mystical Foundation of Authority' (1990) 11 *Cardozo Law Review* 919, reprinted in D Cornell, M Rosenfeld and D Carlson (eds), *Deconstruction and the Possibility of Justice* (1992)

Lon Fuller, 'Positivism and Fidelity to Law' (1958) 71 *Harvard Law Review* 630

HLA Hart, *The Concept of Law* (1961)

Lord Reid, 'The Judge as Law Maker' (1972) 12 *JSPTL* 22

Julius Stone, *Legal System and Lawyers' Reasonings* (1964)

Tied vote. When the High Court speaks with one voice (see **Joint judgments and separate judgments**), there can be little doubt about the outcome of a case. When the Court speaks with many voices, the outcome is determined by the opinion of the majority. But what happens when the Court is evenly divided?

This situation is best avoided in the first place, by ensuring that, for **Full Court** hearings, an odd number of Justices sit. Given the practice of assigning all available Justices to major cases, especially constitutional cases, this will generally be achieved, so long as the Court continues to comprise its traditional and current complement of seven. However, there have been times in the Court's history when the full complement has fallen below seven. When **Isaacs** resigned in 1931 to become Governor-General, a Labor government stung by the hostile reaction to the **appointments** of **Evatt** and **McTiernan** in 1930 failed to appoint a replacement, and in 1933, during the **Depression**, the *Judiciary Act* 1903 (Cth) was amended to officially reduce the number of Justices to six, not to be restored to seven until 1946. The Court was also reduced to six in 1985, when **Murphy** stood down to respond to the charges brought against him (see **Murphy affair**). At other times, a Justice may be unavailable because of illness, conflict of interest, other duties, leave, or impending **retirement**. Consequently, evenly divided decisions are not uncommon. Notable examples include *Ex parte Nelson (No 1)* (1928), *Field Peas Case* (1948), *Logan Downs v Queensland* (1977), and *Gould v Brown* (1998).

Apart from ensuring that it does not arise in the first place, a range of solutions to the problem of the evenly divided **Bench** can be proposed. The case might be reheard before the full complement of Justices, if that has not already occurred. One Justice, perhaps the most junior, might withdraw his or her judgment. One Justice, perhaps the most senior, might be given a casting vote. Or, arguably, the evenly divided Bench might be taken to yield no decision, so that the status quo would be preserved.

The solution adopted for the High Court is set out in the Judiciary Act. If the case has come on appeal—at least if the appeal is from a single Justice of the High Court or from a court of sufficient status such as a **state Supreme Court** or the **Federal Court** or Family Court—then the appeal fails and the decision appealed from is affirmed (section 23(2)(a)). In any other case, the opinion of the **Chief Justice** (or, if the Chief Justice is absent, that of the next most senior Justice) prevails (section 23(2)(b)).

These provisions have not been uncontroversial, for two reasons. First, there is no ideal solution other than avoidance. If the Justices are taken to be equals, what is the rationale for giving the Chief Justice a casting vote? The Chief Justice is symbolically the first among equals—*primus inter pares*—but the casting vote confers significant power. Similarly, if the Justices are taken to be equals, what is the rationale for the most junior to withdraw? (In fact, there are instances of a different practice: in *Perpetual Trustee Co v Tindal* (1940), **Starke**, although not the most junior Justice, withdrew his judgment, for reasons that are unclear.) Rehearing before all of the Justices will rarely suffice, as the problem will have come precisely from the fact that the full complement is an even number, or that only an even number is available; and rehearing before an odd number that can be achieved only by the withdrawal of one Justice simply revives the problem of who should withdraw, and also subverts the principle that in important cases all available Justices should sit.

Preservation of the status quo, although frustrating for the losing applicant or appellant, is probably the best of a bad lot of solutions, and it is this idea that underlies the rule in relation to appeals. However, the second reason for controversy, which attaches particularly to the casting vote rule, is that there is a serious doubt about whether legislative rules of this kind are constitutionally valid.

The doubt stems from the **separation of powers** in the Constitution between the judiciary and the other branches of government. As Murphy observed in *FCT v St Helens Farm* (1981), 'how the individual opinions or votes of the justices should be transformed into judgments of the Court … seems to be well within the sphere of the judicial branch'. If Parliament can give the Chief Justice a casting vote, Murphy asked, then why not the most junior Justice or some other particular Justice? And if (as section 23(1) of the Judiciary Act provides) Parliament can direct that three Justices must concur in a decision affecting the constitutional power of the Commonwealth, can it direct that such a decision be unanimous? At some point, purported exercises by the federal Parliament of its undoubted power to regulate the exercise of federal **jurisdiction** may be seen to cross the line and trespass into the forbidden territory of **judicial power**.

Murphy was particularly disturbed by the possibility that, if the Court were to invalidate an Act, not by a genuine majority but by the Judiciary Act's so-called 'statutory' majority (as it did in *Logan Downs*), it would run counter to his notion of the 'presumption of validity'. His attack was directed primarily at the casting vote rule; the rule that affirmed a decision appealed from conformed to a 'widespread convention'. Yet others have been more disturbed by the rule about appeals, as the court at first instance, whose opinion will ultimately be decisive, is said to be unlikely to have considered the matter in the same depth and refined it to the same degree as the appellate court.

The value that should be attached to the decision of an equally divided Bench as a precedent is a further issue. The accepted view is that of **Dixon** in *Tasmania v Victoria* (1935), affirmed in *Re Wakim* (1999): it has none. The High Court is not strictly bound to follow its earlier decisions in any event, but a decision by a statutory majority is said to carry no weight.

This has been held to be so even in relation to equal divisions of opinion on an appeal from a single Justice of the High Court itself (*St Helens Farm*), though it might be argued—and a minority in that case thought—that if the single Justice's view were added to that of the statutory majority on appeal, there was at the end of the day a view that was supported by a genuine majority of the Justices, and that view should carry weight. That argument was, however, outweighed by the counter argument that the judge at first instance did not have the benefit of the argument on appeal, and that it was therefore a matter of speculation whether, had the first instance judge been a part of the appellate Bench, his or her decision would have been the same. Ironically, this is precisely the argument seen by some as undermining the wisdom of the rule that affirms the decision appealed from in the first place.

Whether, as a matter of policy, the Chief Justice should have a casting vote goes to the very heart of our conception of the role and status of the Chief Justice. If the Chief Justice of the day is the intellectual leader of the Court, as has been the case perhaps three or four times, then the casting vote rule seems more palatable. But is intellectual leadership an appropriate or sufficient criterion by which to decide the outcome of a closely divided case? The casting vote really is a mere expedient, as is any other method of resolving the problem of the evenly divided Bench—and all come a distant second to ensuring that the full complement of Justices is an odd number.

Whether, as a matter of **constitutional law**, it is possible for the Parliament to dictate the casting vote rule, and perhaps the rule affirming the original decision on an appeal, is, although the dictation is of long standing, unresolved. The Judiciary Act purports to lay down even the standard rule that when an odd number of Justices are divided in opinion, the majority view prevails (section 23(2)); no doubt this unimpeachable edict would govern in any case, and is scarcely open to legislative variation. There is much to be said for simply repealing section 23 altogether, and leaving it to the judicial branch to work out its own solution. If, in a particular case, all attempts at resolution were to fail and the Court were to remain evenly divided, then, in effect, no decision could be given and, of necessity, the relevant application or appeal must fail. The **criticism** that this situation would attract is likely to ensure that its occurrence would be rare.

MICHAEL COPER

Tipstaves. The term 'tipstaff' was defined in 1899 in Arthur English's *A Dictionary of Words and Phrases used in Ancient and Modern Law* as an 'officer attendant on judges of the King's Courts to arrest those committed. He carries a staff tipped with silver. An officer of a court who preserves order, attends juries and jurors, serves processes, &c'. The more recent *Butterworths Australian Legal Dictionary* defines tipstaff as a 'member of the personal staff of the judge with the function of assisting the judge and retrieving legal materials required by the judge'.

Griffith, **Barton**, and **O'Connor** each had tipstaves. However, in 1905, **Symon**, then **Attorney-General**, decided to abolish the tipstaves' positions because the Justices refused to allow their tipstaves to carry out the duties of **Court Crier**. He proposed that instead of three tipstaves there would be an officer designated 'High Court Usher', who would perform the duties of Court Crier and Court Attendant, and keep order in court. Fortunately for the Justices and their tipstaves, **Isaacs**, who replaced Symon as Attorney-General, did not consider that the interests of the community would be served by the abolition of tipstaves (see **Strike of 1905**).

The designation of tipstaff was used for some years, until it was changed to 'Justice's Assistant', apparently for public service administrative purposes. In 1945, there was ongoing debate between the Attorney-General's Department and the Justices as to whether Justices' Assistants should in future be selected from within the public service and be under the *Public Service Act*, or continue to be personal appointments of the Justices. **Starke** urged **Latham** to retain the right of the Justices to appoint persons of their choice from outside the public service. At the same time, he suggested that the nomenclature of 'Justices' Assistants' be changed back to the 'old legal term tipstaff'. This had taken place by 1950.

Tipstaves were recruited on the recommendation of other judicial acquaintances or friends of the Justices. Usually, they came from a background in the armed services or the police force. They were exclusively male until 1976, when **Murphy** appointed the first female tipstaff. Tipstaves were appointed at the pleasure of the Justice. When a Justice retired or died in office, the tipstaff offered his or her services to the new Justice, which was usually accepted.

The duties of the personal staff of the Justices varied between the **chambers**. Traditionally, the tipstaff would attend to the personal needs of the Justice. This involved providing refreshments for the Justice and guests, running errands, and assisting the Justice to robe. The tipstaff was also responsible for ensuring that all relevant authorities listed for **citation** by **counsel** were in court for hearings. When counsel referred to the cited case, the tipstaff would hand the report to the Justice, open at the relevant page. On **circuit**, the tipstaff had the responsibility of transporting perhaps five or six suitcases containing the Justice's personal luggage and judicial robes, and the **appeal books** for the cases to be heard. As Justices invariably worked on judgments while they were on circuit, any material that a Justice was using in the preparation of judgments was also packed in a suitcase.

Gaudron on her **appointment** chose to have two legally qualified **associates** to share the duties with the Justice's personal assistant, instead of the traditional chambers of associate, personal assistant, and tipstaff. This practice has been adopted by all Justices except **Gummow**, who retained Russell Slatter, a tipstaff with over 20 years service, and previously with **Mason**.

REBECCA CRASKE
FRANK JONES

Toohey, John Leslie (*b* 4 March 1930; Justice 1987–98), was a Justice greatly concerned to develop the law to reflect justice and morality within the boundaries of the **rule of law**. He was born in countryside WA to publicans Albert and Sylvia Toohey. He grew up in the country (Meekatharra, Kojonup, and Lake Grace) and was the eldest child in his family, with two younger sisters and one younger brother.

Toohey undertook his secondary schooling at a Catholic college, St Louis (now John XXIII) College, and his tertiary education at the University of WA. He excelled in law and graduated in 1950 (later completing his BA in 1956) with first-class honours, winning the FE Parsons Prize (for the most outstanding graduate) and the HCF Keall Prize (for the best fourth-year student). Toohey undertook articles of clerkship with David Walsh and then with John Lavan. Following a short period at Lavan & Walsh, at only 24 he founded Ilbery & Toohey with John Ilbery.

Toohey rapidly established his pre-eminence in the Perth legal profession, particularly in **taxation** and **land law**. His first appearance in the High Court, as leading **counsel** in *Commissioner of Taxation v Finn* (1961), came at the age of only 31. In 1967, at the age of 38, he joined the WA Independent Bar and was appointed a QC the following year. Appointments as President of the Bar Association of WA and President of the Law Society of WA followed very shortly thereafter.

By 1973, Toohey was established as one of the leading QCs at the WA Bar, appearing often in the High Court in areas including **criminal law**, **contract law**, and **restitution**. His interest and strength in **property** law saw him keen to pass on that knowledge and he taught Real Property at the University of WA while practising. He was also the obvious choice to argue one of the best known WA property law cases before the High Court, *Adamson v Hayes* (1973), involving the vexed section 34 of the *Property Law Act* 1969 (WA).

His compassion and strong sense of civic duty saw him, in 1974, leave Perth and his lucrative work as a senior silk to establish the inaugural Aboriginal Legal Office in Port Hedland. His interests in Aboriginal law and society were powerfully forged from this time onwards. His work often involved representing Aboriginal plaintiffs and defendants (including his appearance as senior counsel for **Aboriginal peoples** at a Royal Commission inquiring into relations between Aboriginal people and police), so that when on 7 April 1977 Toohey was appointed the first Aboriginal Land Commissioner for

John Toohey, Justice 1987–98

tice', his 'genuine interest', and 'great patience'. He wrote that 'it was hard not to be impressed by the Judge's negotiating cheerfully with an old man to share the trunk of the only tree as a back rest'.

On 6 February 1987, Toohey was sworn in as a Justice of the High Court. At the same ceremony, **Mason** was sworn in as **Chief Justice** and **Gaudron** as another **puisne Justice**. His **appointment** followed those of **Deane** and **Brennan**, both of whom had sat regularly with him on the Federal Court, particularly after Toohey finished as Aboriginal Land Commissioner in 1982. Toohey's appointment was not unexpected. There had been much speculation in the **media** that he would be appointed, and when it happened it was widely applauded. One consequence was that he had to resign from his position as a member of the Constitutional Commission, which had only recently begun its work.

On the High Court, Toohey's judgments on the **common law** reflected a judicial philosophy of common law development consonant with notions of justice and morality. He was a member of the majority in *Dietrich v The Queen* (1992), concerning the common law right to a fair trial; *Cheatle v The Queen* (1993), affirming jury unanimity as an essential element in the constitutional guarantee of **jury trial** in Commonwealth cases; and *R v Swaffield* (1998), reviewing the exclusion of **evidence** for 'unfairness', particularly in relation to an accused person's right to silence. He dissented in *Carter v Managing Partner Northmore Hale Davy & Leake* (1995), where he and Gaudron would have held that the right of accused persons to documents that might fairly exculpate them prevails over legal professional privilege.

However, Toohey was always aware of the constraints of **precedent** and the rule of law. In *Newcrest Mining v Commonwealth* (1997), Gaudron, **Gummow**, and **Kirby** would have been prepared to overrule *Teori Tau v Commonwealth* (1969), which had held that section 51(xxxi) of the Constitution (requiring 'just terms' for a governmental **acquisition of property**) did not apply in the **territories**. Toohey agreed with their reasoning but declined to **overrule** the decision, recognising that it would be 'a serious step to overrule a [High Court] decision which has stood for nearly 30 years and which reflects an approach which may have been relied on in earlier years'. Yet he pointed out also that the primary holding in *Newcrest* (that a Northern Territory acquisition was also a Commonwealth acquisition, to which the requirement of 'just terms' did apply) made it unlikely that *Teori Tau* would ever again have any practical impact.

The pinnacle of Toohey's work on the High Court came with his judgments in *Mabo* (1992) and *Wik* (1996). They afforded an opportunity to develop the common law in an area never before directly considered by the High Court. They concerned legal issues of property and issues of fundamental importance to indigenous people. Toohey brought to these judgments not only a wealth of knowledge of property law but also a lifetime of experience and understanding of Aboriginal people. His judgments are powerful and compelling. In concluding in *Mabo* that the traditional native title of indigenous people, and in particular the Meriam people, was recognised by the common law of this country, Toohey was joined by five other members of the Court in the most momentous decision of the High Court during his

the Northern Territory (concurrently with an appointment as a judge of the **Federal Court** and of the Supreme Court of the Northern Territory), he brought with him an acute understanding of Aboriginal issues.

During his term as Aboriginal Land Commissioner (1977–82), Toohey heard 15 claims under the *Aboriginal Land Rights (Northern Territory) Act* 1976 (Cth) extending over country north to the Finnis River, east to the Gulf of Carpentaria and south to Uluru. At the time, these claims were controversial; the legislation governing land hearings and **native title** claims in the Northern Territory was unique. As Commissioner, Toohey had wide statutory powers and appeals from his decisions went straight to the **Full Court** of the High Court. A number of such appeals were made during Toohey's time as Commissioner, and in the *Commonwealth Law Reports* these cases bear his name (*R v Toohey; Ex parte A-G (NT)* (1980); the ***Northern Land Council Case*** (1981); *R v Toohey; Ex parte Meneling Station* (1982); *R v Toohey; Ex parte Stanton* (1982)). Only one of these decisions was reversed. Even then, in the High Court, **Wilson** said there was 'good ground for saying that the Commissioner faithfully applied the relevant law so far as it has been expressed previously in Australia'.

As Aboriginal Land Commissioner, Toohey was widely respected. Ian Barker QC described one occasion in the harsh Northern Territory heat with Toohey 'leading us like Moses who led the 12 tribes of Israel through the wilderness with a cheerful fortitude which did not ever leave him'. At the conclusion of his term as Aboriginal Land Commissioner, Ross Howie, a barrister who often appeared for Aboriginal claimants, wrote of Toohey's 'sensitivity to historical injus-

time. In some respects, still not fully resolved, his judgment (supported by Deane and Gaudron) went further than that of Brennan (supported by Mason and **McHugh**; see **Fiduciary obligations**). In *Kruger v Commonwealth* (1997), he agreed with Gaudron that the history of the 'stolen generations' of Aboriginal children might in substance raise issues of an **implied constitutional right** to freedom of **movement** and association, and of the **express constitutional right** to freedom of religion; and he added a reference to the possible relevance of the implied guarantee of **equality** that he and Deane had adumbrated in *Leeth v Commonwealth* (1992). But unlike Gaudron, who felt able by invoking the freedoms of movement and association to hold invalid the relevant provisions of the Aboriginals Ordinance 1918 (NT), he did not feel able to make a conclusive finding of invalidity on the basis of the limited materials before the High Court.

The decisions in *Mabo* and *Wik*, together with his judgments in constitutional decisions recognising 'implied rights' (or, more properly, 'freedoms') in the Constitution (see, for example, *Free Speech Cases* (1992); *Cunliffe v Commonwealth* (1994); *McGinty v WA* (1996)) led to **criticism** of Toohey from sections of the media for judicial 'activism'. In particular, in *McGinty*, he and Gaudron held that, although the conception of **democracy** implied in the electoral provisions of the Constitution could have no impact on electoral distributions for purposes of state elections, a similar conception implied in the state *Constitution Act* 1889 had evolved, by 1987, to a point where continued inequalities in electoral districts could no longer be valid. In *Leeth*, his **joint judgment** with Deane had propounded a far-reaching view of 'equality' that proved particularly controversial; and at a conference in Darwin on 4–6 October 1992, within days of the handing down of judgments in the *Free Speech Cases*, he had argued (in a speech later published in 1993) that a court 'established as guardian of a written constitution within the context of a liberal-democratic society' might need to act more vigorously 'to protect core liberal-democratic values' and the rule of law, in an age when 'parliaments are increasingly seen to be the de facto agents or facilitators of executive power, rather than bulwarks against it'. Moreover, he had linked this possibility expressly with 'a revival of **natural law** jurisprudence—that for law to be law it must conform with fundamental principles of justice'.

Shortly before his **retirement**, Toohey was asked what his reaction was to the media references to him as an 'activist'. Toohey replied 'almost none'. He stated that judges must 'create law', and that this is done every time a judge changes or develops the law (see **Law-making role**); but that 'references to activism use the word "change" … as a pejorative term'. Toohey argued that a decision *not* to change or *not* to develop the law is just as 'activist' as a decision to change the law and can have consequences just as dramatic.

In retrospect, it is this very 'activism' that is Toohey's legacy to the law. If Toohey had to be described in a single word, the most fitting would be 'compassionate'. If it were necessary to point to one area of his work in which he had the most impact during his career as a lawyer, Commissioner, and Justice, it would be the legacy his compassion created for Aboriginal people.

JAMES EDELMAN
NATALIE GRAY

Further Reading

James Edelman and Natalie Gray, 'A Short Biography of John Leslie Toohey AC: Justice of the High Court of Australia 1987–1998' (1998) 8 *JJA* 109

Ross Howie, 'Mr Justice Toohey Ends Term as Aboriginal Land Commissioner' (1982) 4 *ALB* 14

John Toohey, 'A Government of Laws and Not of Men?' (1993) 4 *PLR* 158

John Toohey, '"Without Fear or Favour, Affection or Ill Will": The Role of Courts in the Community' (1999) 28 *UWAL Rev* 1

Tort law. Australia enjoys the benefit of having a single **common law**, not separate common laws in each of its states (*Lange v ABC* (1997)). Much of the credit for this is due to the High Court, which has since the abolition of appeals to the **Privy Council** acted as the ultimate court of appeal for the whole country. It entertains many appeals in private law matters. Among these, cases on the law of torts have been prominent. The very first case to appear in the *Commonwealth Law Reports*, *Hannah v Dalgarno* (1903), though on a jurisdictional issue, arose out of an ordinary negligence claim against the Commonwealth.

When the **House of Lords** decided *Donoghue v Stevenson* (1932), the High Court did not immediately embrace the case with any enthusiasm (*Australian Knitting Mills v Grant* (1933)). Only **Evatt** dissented. But on further appeal, the Privy Council in 1935 recognised that the House of Lords had treated 'negligence, where there is a duty to take care, as a specific tort in itself, and not simply as an element in some more complex relationship or in some specialized breach of duty'. Since then, as with common law courts everywhere, negligence cases have predominated in appeals to the High Court.

In an address to the National Press Club in 1976, **Barwick** complained that the monetary threshold (then $3000) allowing appeals as of right from state courts to the High Court under section 35 of the *Judiciary Act* 1903 (Cth) had become too low and that the Court should not have to deal with the many personal injury appeals with which it was faced (see also *Leotta v Public Transport Commission of NSW* (1976)). The Judiciary Act was then amended not only to increase the threshold to $20 000 but also to require special **leave** from the Court in the case of appeals relating only to the quantum of **damages** in respect of death or personal injury. This immediately reduced the number of appeals in this area. Subsequently, appeals as of right from state courts were abolished altogether, and the special leave procedure was extended to all such appeals by section 3 of the *Judiciary Amendment Act (No 2)* 1984 (Cth). Similar provisions were made applicable to appeals from federal courts. Notwithstanding these changes, the High Court has continued to find issues of sufficient importance or principle, or sufficient disagreement among the different state courts, to warrant special leave to appeal in many tort cases each year.

One aspect of Barwick's antipathy to having the Court's time wasted by appeals on negligence and damages was the Justices' attitude during that time to findings of negligence (or of no negligence) by trial judges. In this context, Barwick and several of the members of his Court were advocates of judicial restraint—appellate courts should not reverse trial decisions if the findings were reasonably open to the trial judges (see, for example, *Da Costa v Cockburn Salvage & Trading* (1970); *Edwards v Noble* (1971)). A similar attitude was manifested to the assessment of damages. However, in *Warren v Coombes* (1979), some other members took advantage of Barwick's temporary absence from the Court to reassert the orthodox rule that appeals are a rehearing on all issues. On this view, while allowance must be made for the advantages a trial judge enjoys in assessing the credibility of witnesses, it is for the appellate court to determine for itself whether on the facts found by the trial judge the conduct was or was not negligent.

Until the 1960s, the High Court regarded itself as bound to apply the law of England as enunciated by the House of Lords. This led it, in *Piro v Foster* (1943), to reverse its own previous decision in *Bourke v Butterfield & Lewis* (1926) out of deference to *Caswell v Powell Duffryn Associated Collieries* (1939) and to hold that contributory negligence is a defence to breach of statutory duty. This decision proved unpopular with the NSW legislature, which restored the *Bourke v Butterfield* position in the *Statutory Duties (Contributory Negligence) Act* 1945 (NSW), though it has since reneged in cases of industrial accidents (*Workers Compensation Act* 1987 (NSW), section 151N).

Although foreshadowed in a criminal case, *Parker v The Queen* (1963), a refusal by the High Court to follow a decision of the House of Lords came first in a personal injuries damages action, *Skelton v Collins* (1966). The Privy Council itself gave approval to this course in another torts damages case, *Australian Consolidated Press v Uren* (1967). It was in a torts case involving the standard of care of a learner driver, *Cook v Cook* (1986), that the High Court took the opportunity to state definitively that precedents from England should no longer be regarded as binding by lower courts and would not necessarily be more persuasive than those from other common law systems. Since then, the Court and the Supreme Court of Canada have often considered each other's opinions in the area of torts, though not necessarily agreeing upon outcomes (see, for example, *Bryan v Maloney* (1995) on the liability of builders for pure economic loss). US courts have seldom provided the High Court with inspiration in tort law, though **Murphy**, who was not averse to seizing on **precedent** wherever he could find it, in one of his many **dissenting judgments** in favour of tort plaintiffs once cited as persuasive a statement 'from the Supreme Court of the famous horse state of Wyoming' (see *Eather v Jones* (1975)).

The earliest case the High Court was called on to decide on the law of torts raised for consideration the doctrines of **occupiers' liability** (*Mountney v Smith* (1904)). **Dixon**, using traditional common law methods, later stated these doctrines with clarity (*Lipman v Clendinnen* (1932)) and did what he could to alleviate some of their absurdities (for example, *Commissioner for Railways (NSW) v Cardy* (1960)). Years later, under the influence of **Deane**, who had advocated the absorption of these doctrines into the general law of negligence in *Hackshaw v Shaw* (1984), the Court swept away the traditional distinctions in *Australian Safeway Stores v Zaluzna* (1987). This brought the remaining states into line with Victoria, WA, and SA, which had previously enacted legislation to achieve the same end. The legislation has been largely, though not wholly, ignored since then, courts generally preferring to look to the High Court's exposition of principle in *Zaluzna*.

In another area, the Court was undoubtedly influenced by Deane to sweep away subtle distinctions and absorb a discrete area of tort law into the law of negligence. In **Burnie Port Authority v General Jones** (1994), it became the first court in the common law world to reject the rule of **strict liability** laid down in *Rylands v Fletcher* (1866 and 1868). The success of this enterprise awaits the verdict of history.

It is probably not too soon to know that Deane's repeated claims for the concept of **proximity** as the 'touchstone and control (or unifying theme) of the categories of case in which the common law of negligence will admit the existence of a duty of care' have proved illusory and the concept has been all but buried. Although Deane—in his earlier highly original analyses of the law of negligence (*Jaensch v Coffey* (1984); *Sutherland Shire Council v Heyman* (1985))—acknowledged a role for rules operating to preclude the implication of a duty of care at a stage later than the investigation into proximity, his preference for deciding issues of policy under the rubric of proximity led the majority of the Court in *Gala v Preston* (1991) into its peculiar use of that concept to deny that a duty of care was owed to a passenger in a motor car by the driver with whom he had stolen the car. The strong protests from **Brennan** and **Dawson** against the burden that 'proximity' was required to bear in this case have proved unanswerable. But whatever the method of reasoning, the gyrations of the High Court in relation to the effects of illegality on the right to recover damages in tort have not inspired confidence in its ability to guide lower courts (compare *Henwood v Municipal Tramways Trust* (1938); *Smith v Jenkins* (1970); *Progress & Properties Ltd v Craft* (1976); *Jackson v Harrison* (1978)).

Ironically, Deane dissented in the one tort case where the Court most clearly applied **policy considerations** to deny recovery without mention of the notion of proximity. This was in *Giannarelli v Wraith* (1988), where the majority followed the House of Lords decision in *Rondel v Worsley* (1967) in conferring an immunity from claims in negligence on advocates actually engaged in court proceedings and in matters intimately related thereto. **Kirby** has since shown dissatisfaction with this decision, though the rest of the Court has been much less enthusiastic about revisiting the area (*Boland v Yates Property Corporation* (1999)). This may change in the light of the decision of the House of Lords itself to depart from *Rondel* in *Arthur JS Hall & Co v Simons* (2000).

The role of insurance as a policy factor in imposing or denying a duty of care is another possible area of disagreement among the present High Court. In *Kars v Kars* (1996), it openly influenced a majority, including Kirby and **McHugh**, to allow an injured plaintiff (a wife) to recover damages in respect of the value of services that had been voluntarily provided by the defendant (her husband). In so deciding, the Court refused to follow the House of Lords in *Hunt v Severs* (1994). Dawson preferred to decide the same way on other grounds. The majority did say that a review of the relevance of insurance to the development of common law liability in tort may indeed be timely. Subsequently, McHugh has declared insurance to be irrelevant in determining the existence of a duty of a care to avoid pure economic loss (*Perre v*

Apand (1999)). Kirby, on the other hand, appears to consider it relevant, declining to take it into account only because of the absence of evidence in particular cases as to its incidence and availability (for example, *Pyrenees Shire Council v Day* (1998)).

The High Court has been in the forefront of the common law world in admitting duties of care relating to pure economic loss caused by negligent acts. *Caltex Oil v The Dredge 'Willemstad'* (1976) unanimously allowed recovery in such a case probably for the first time anywhere at the highest appellate level. The decision was plagued by a common occurrence in the High Court—agreement on the result but disagreement in the reasoning by which the result was reached. The Privy Council declined to follow it because it could not find in it a *ratio decidendi* (*Candlewood Navigation Corporation v Mitsui OSK Lines* (1985)). The problem was aggravated by the seven different judgments, all in favour of allowing recovery to at least some of the plaintiffs, in *Perre v Apand*.

The law of torts has also proved to be fertile ground for disagreement on the Court as to when it is appropriate to develop the law and when it is better to leave matters to legislatures to remedy. The conservative line taken by **Mason** in *State Government Insurance Commission v Trigwell* (1979) in refusing to bring the rule in *Searle v Wallbank* (1946) into the general principles of negligence (Murphy dissenting), was quoted against him by McHugh in *Burnie Port* when the majority of the Court took the more radical step of abolishing *Rylands v Fletcher* liability. McHugh did acknowledge, however, that the intervening years had seen a greater readiness in the Court to alter the rules of the common law.

In two areas where tort law overlaps with **constitutional law** issues, initial disagreement among the members of the Court was eventually resolved by authoritative judgments. In **defamation**, the Court was bitterly divided over the extent, if any, of constitutional protection for freedom of speech in the cases of *Theophanous v Herald & Weekly Times* (1994) and *Stephens v WA Newspapers* (1994). The disagreements were overcome and the Court unanimously resolved the issue in *Lange*. Similarly, the law to be applied when a plaintiff was injured in one state but sued in another led to sharp differences in cases such as *Breavington v Godleman* (1988) and *Stevens v Head* (1993). A definitive ruling was finally given by a **joint judgment** of five members of the Court in *John Pfeiffer v Rogerson* (2000) (see **Conflict of laws**).

The Court has also employed the law of torts to protect **civil liberties** other than free speech. **Fullagar**, Mason, Brennan, and Deane all expressed strong views in the course of judgments on the importance of preserving the liberty of the subject. But the record of the Court on appeals relating to the tort of false imprisonment appears to be a spotty one. There are three such appeals reported in the first volume of the *Commonwealth Law Reports* alone, two holding against plaintiffs and one in favour. Certainly, the decision in *Enever v The King* (1906), denying vicarious liability for wrongful arrests carried out by constables, would have deprived many victims of a real remedy and was long subjected to **criticism** until reversed by statute in some, though not all, Australian jurisdictions. The decision against the arrogant barrister plaintiff in the same year in *Balmain New Ferry Co v Robert-son* (1906) has entertained many a law student, but represents an early example of the Court's frequent inability to agree on a single line of reasoning for its decision, aggravated in this instance by a further interpretation by the Privy Council in upholding the decision of the High Court that false imprisonment had not been committed. More consistent has been the tendency of the High Court to read down **privative clauses**, which would at least on their face have given protection to government authorities of various sorts in their interference with the civil rights of ordinary citizens (see, for example, *Hazelton v Potter* (1907); *Board of Fire Commissioners of NSW v Ardouin* (1961); *Webster v Lampard* (1993); *Puntoriero v Water Administration Ministerial Corporation* (1999)). Cases such as *Healing v Inglis Electrix* (1968) and *Plenty v Dillon* (1991) have by means of the trespass action protected both commercial enterprises and private occupiers of land from unwarranted invasions, perhaps excessively so (see Matthew Goode, 'Trespass to Land by Police Attempting to Serve a Summons' (1993) 1 *TLJ* 1). Privacy, on the other hand, at least when claimed by commerce, still escapes protection as a result of the decision of the majority of the Court in **Victoria Park Racing v Taylor** (1937) that no tort of any sort had been committed in broadcasting a description of races from a tower situated on neighbouring land. Another case that can be seen as strongly protective of civil liberty is **Marion's Case** (1992). Although not strictly a tort case, in holding that an intellectually disabled child could not be sterilised without the approval of the Family Court, the judgments emphasised the tort **remedies** that would be available for any unjustified interference with bodily integrity. A similar theme permeates *Rogers v Whitaker* (1992) on the duty of a medical practitioner to disclose risks in proposed treatment.

Two torts cases that provoked passionate dissenting judgments can be seen with hindsight to have raised **feminist** issues. In *Wright v Cedzich* (1930), the majority adhered to the traditional view of the action of enticement being founded on the husband's proprietary rights over the wife and so refused to extend the action to the wife. At the time, **Isaacs'** dissent, ranging Shakespeare's Petruchio alongside Jeremy Bentham, may have been the more progressive, but the subsequent abolition of the action altogether by section 120 of the *Family Law Act 1975* (Cth) is more in keeping with modern ideas. Similarly, Deane was provoked to remark in *Jaensch v Coffey* that the 'judgments of the majority in *Chester's Case* have not worn well with time'. He was referring to *Chester v Waverley Corporation* (1939), which denied a mother damages for 'nervous shock' when she had spent hours searching for her drowned child and seen the body retrieved. Subsequently, in *Bourhill v Young* (1942), Lord Wright remarked that it was Evatt's powerful dissenting judgment in that case which would 'demand the consideration of any judge who is called on to consider these questions'. Recent years have seen the adoption by all members of the High Court of gender-neutral language in sharp contrast to the continued use by the House of Lords of male-oriented pronouns.

In Australia, where industrial action is generally not protected from common law suits, disputes on the waterfront have several times been played out all the way up to the High Court on the tort of conspiracy. These have usually involved demarcation and membership disputes among unions (see *Brisbane Shipwrights Provident Union v Heggie* (1906); *McKernan v Fraser* (1931); *Williams v Hursey* (1959)). Most recently, the tort of conspiracy was the ostensible cause of action that occupied the Court over several days in an urgent hearing of an application for special leave to appeal against an injunction granted against the employers in the *Patrick Stevedores Case* (1998).

Finally, mention should be made of an ill-judged attempt by a Court of three (which nowadays never sits to hear full appeals) to develop the 'action on the case' so as to permit a remedy independently of trespass, nuisance, or negligence for a person who suffers harm or loss as the inevitable consequence of the unlawful, intentional, and positive acts of another (*Beaudesert Shire Council v Smith* (1966)). After much academic criticism, the case was **overruled** by *Northern Territory v Mengel* (1995).

Harold Luntz

Further Reading
Harold Luntz, 'Throwing off the Chains: English Precedent and the Law of Torts in Australia' in MP Ellinghaus, AJ Bradbrook, and AJ Duggan (eds), *The Emergence of Australian Law* (1989) ch 4

Trade and commerce power. The trade and commerce power in section 51(i) of the Constitution authorises Commonwealth legislation with respect to 'trade and commerce with other countries, and among the States'. Trade and commerce with other countries is usually referred to as foreign or overseas trade and commerce. Trade and commerce among the states is usually referred to as **interstate trade and commerce**.

'Trade and commerce' for constitutional purposes is treated as a composite expression without a sharp distinction being made between 'trade' and 'commerce'. As **Dixon** explained in the *Bank Nationalisation Case* (1948), 'trade' includes, but is not confined to, the buying and selling of goods. The primary meaning, as Dixon noted, 'is much wider, covering as it does the pursuit of a calling or handicraft, and its **history** emphasises rather use, regularity and course of conduct, than concern with commodities'. As was said in *McArthur v Queensland* (1920), the words 'trade and commerce' carry their ordinary or plain meaning: 'The mutual communings, the negotiations, verbal and by correspondence, the bargain, the transport and the delivery are all, but not exclusively, parts of that class of relations between mankind which the world calls "trade and commerce".'

Transportation, at least where it is for reward, is a form of trade, as well as being a means for conducting trade (*Australian National Airways v Commonwealth* (1945)). That case also held that the trade and commerce power permits the Commonwealth to create and control its own trading instrumentalities as well as legislating for the conduct of trade by others.

The Court has drawn a distinction between interstate trade, centred on a flow or movement from one state to another, and trade that merely occurs in or loosely involves more than one state. The latter has not been regarded as interstate trade in the relevant sense (see *Hospital Provident Fund v Victoria* (1953)). However, many of the authorities on the ambit of interstate trade, including the *Hospital Provi-*

dent Fund case, dealt with the issue for the purposes of applying section 92 of the Constitution before the fundamental shift in doctrine effected by *Cole v Whitfield* (1988). It seems that overseas trade at its heart also requires a flow or movement in a trading context, although there is very little authority on the point.

The implied incidental power that forms part of every head of power permits the Commonwealth to reach into activities that may, in isolation, not be regarded as part of the core subject matter of section 51(i). For example, in *O'Sullivan v Noarlunga Meat* (1954), it was assumed, in line with earlier authority, that production is antecedent to trade—but Commonwealth control over production processes for the slaughtering of stock for export was nevertheless upheld as an exercise of the implied incidental power. **Fullagar** explained that the Commonwealth's 'legitimate concern' with Australian exports must include

> not only grade and quality of goods but packing, get-up, description, labelling, handling, and anything at all that may reasonably be considered likely to affect an export market ... It may very reasonably be thought necessary to go further back, and even to enter the factory or the field or the mine.

At the same time, the Court has repeatedly insisted that the specific grants of power in relation to 'trade and commerce with other countries' and 'trade and commerce ... among the States' must be limited by the *absence* of any grant of Commonwealth power in relation to intrastate trade and commerce: that is, the scope of legislative power in the former two areas must be strictly confined so as not to permit encroachment into the latter. In *Airlines of NSW v NSW (No 2)* (1965), **Kitto** insisted in this connection that the Court 'is entrusted with the preservation of constitutional distinctions, and it both fails in its task and exceeds its authority if it discards them, however out of touch with practical conceptions or with modern conditions they may appear to be in some or all of their applications'. Similarly, in *A-G (WA); Ex rel Ansett Transport Industries v Australian National Airlines* (1976), **Gibbs** insisted that the contrast between interstate and intrastate trade 'must be maintained however much interdependence may now exist between those two divisions of trade and however artificial the distinction may be thought to be'. According to the oft-cited view of Dixon in *Wragg v NSW* (1953), not even the incidental aspect of section 51(i) can be used to obliterate this distinction. Despite all this, in particular contexts and with suitably framed laws, the Commonwealth has been able to use its trade and commerce power to control considerable areas of intrastate trade. *Airlines of NSW*, for example, upheld a Commonwealth law dealing with the licensing of intrastate air operations throughout Australia.

The decisions the Court has made in pursuit of this distinction seem arbitrary. In *Airlines of NSW*, it considered that the Commonwealth could exercise authority over intrastate air operations where physical factors such as safety affected foreign and interstate air operations, but not where the influence was merely a matter of the economic interaction between intrastate and other air services. This distinction between physical and economic factors was applied by the majority in the *Australian National Airlines* case in relation to the trade and commerce power (though not the **territories** power).

Before the *Engineers Case* (1920), the scope of the trade and commerce power was at the heart of the **reserved state powers** doctrine: under that doctrine, the express grant of power over foreign and interstate trade was perceived to be an implied prohibition against Commonwealth laws on intrastate trade. The limits placed on incidental power as it attaches to section 51(i) arguably keep alive a truncated, but powerful, notion that some matters are assumed to be within the exclusive power of the states, although some decisions may simply reflect a cautious view of judicially manageable criteria of validity.

The trade and commerce power is not purposive. This means that, in accordance with standard **characterisation** doctrine, laws may operate directly on the subject matter and be within power even though the main purpose of those laws is not directed to trading policies or purposes. In *Murphyores v Commonwealth* (1976), for example, a law placing a conditional prohibition on the export of mineral sands was upheld as a valid use of the trade and commerce power despite the fact that it was clear that the purpose of the export ban was to pursue an ecological purpose unrelated to the export trade. This aspect of doctrine allows the Commonwealth to influence behaviour over activities that would not be regarded as part of the subject matter of the power, even as aided by a generous interpretation of implied incidental power—a point to be borne in mind in assessing the extent to which the Court is influenced by some notion of federal balance.

The trade and commerce power is modelled on the Commerce Clause of the US Constitution, which (relevantly) provides that Congress has power 'to regulate Commerce with foreign Nations, and among the several States'. On a literal interpretation, the Australian trade and commerce power could be regarded as according more power than the US provision, for the latter is only a power to 'regulate'. The reality is that the American clause, especially in the second half of the twentieth century, has been given a far broader interpretation than the High Court has applied to or suggested for section 51(i). The exception is **Murphy**, who in *Australian National Airlines* said the Australian power 'is at least as wide as, if not wider than, the United States power'.

In terms of judicial elucidation and also (perhaps consequently) in the extent of legislative reliance, the trade and commerce power has tended in recent decades to be overshadowed by the **corporations power** and the **external affairs power**. As **Mason** has observed, 'the existing interpretation of [the trade and commerce power] may be anchored in the artifices of legal formalism'. While the style of reasoning in many of the key cases now seems dated, it is unclear how fundamentally the Court would be prepared to shift the content of doctrine on the trade and commerce power in the future. The interpretive imagination will be tested only by a bold legislative initiative.

KEVEN BOOKER

Further Reading

Anthony Mason, 'The Role of a Constitutional Court in a Federation' (1986) 16 *FL Rev* 1

Trade marks are critical elements in the conduct of any business undertaking. They provide the badge or banner under which traders distribute their goods and services in the marketplace, and can become an enormously valuable business asset. The power to regulate them by legislation was included in section 51(xviii) of the Constitution, and a registered trade marks system at Commonwealth level was introduced by the *Trade Marks Act* 1905 (Cth).

Part VII of that Act made controversial provision for the registration of 'workers' marks', to be used to indicate that goods were produced by a particular worker or by members of a particular union. Under section 74 of the Act, it was an offence to apply the mark to goods that were not so produced, although unlike other trade marks, these workers' marks could be applied only by or with the authority of the employer for whom the goods were produced. There were American **precedents** for such provisions and, in the Australian context, it appears that their inclusion in the Act was crucial to the Labor Party's continued support for the **Deakin** government and its 'New Protection' policy.

When a NSW union of brewery employees registered a workers' mark, the NSW **Attorney-General**, at the relation of several brewery companies, instituted a suit in the High Court against the union and the Registrar of Trade Marks for a declaration that the provisions concerning workers' marks were invalid, and for an injunction restraining the Registrar from keeping a register of such marks (*Union Label Case* (1908)). **Griffith**, **Barton**, and **O'Connor** held that a workers' mark was not a 'trade mark', and was thus beyond **Commonwealth legislative power** under section 51(xviii) of the Constitution. In their view, it was necessary to ascertain the meaning the term 'trade mark' bore in 1900, by considering the statutory and non-statutory law concerning trade marks both in the UK and in the Australian colonies up to that time. On that basis, these three Justices concluded that in 1900 the term 'trade mark', whether as a term of art or in popular language, was limited, in Griffith's words, to 'the visible symbol of a particular kind of incorporeal or industrial property consisting in the right of a person engaged in trade to distinguish by a special mark goods in which he deals, or with which he has dealt, from the goods of other persons'.

On these criteria, the workers' mark was not a trade mark. It could not be said that the right to prevent others from using it conferred a right of **property** in its exclusive use. A trade union could not engage in trade, though its individual members might do so. Furthermore, at no stage did the union have any 'independent dominion' over the goods to which the mark was to be affixed: while the union might perhaps stipulate that only union members should be employed in the production of the goods, this was an 'entirely different concept from the right of dominion involved in the concept of a trade mark', since the mark was still applied by or with the authority of the employer. Finally, the workers' mark did not purport to distinguish a product as that of a particular trader, but merely indicated that certain persons—unionists—had been engaged in its production.

Not surprisingly, **Isaacs** and **Higgins** dissented. They argued that the 'workers' trade mark' did, in fact, have all the essential characteristics of a 'trade mark' as understood in 1900. Higgins added that, even if this were not the case, the

Constitution had given the federal Parliament full power to make laws on the whole subject of 'trade marks', that is, to say what marks should be enforceable and what should not. The meaning of the expression in 1900 was 'the centre, not the circumference, of the power.'

The problem of the *Union Label Case*—the interpretation of ongoing grants of power in an instrument enacted in 1900—is now a familiar one. The expression '**patents** of inventions', also included in section 51(xviii), has now been construed as capable of extending to 'plant breeder's rights' (*Grain Pool of WA v Commonwealth* (2000)); and although for a long time the *Union Label* decision inhibited the extension of trade marks protection to 'service marks'(marks used in relation to the provision of services, as distinct from goods) there is now no suggestion that such a mark does not fall within section 51(xviii). Unlike 'workers' marks', service marks still have the necessary connection with the trader who applies them.

The scope of registered trade mark protection, and the conditions for such protection, have been regularly raised in the High Court, both in its original and appellate **jurisdiction**, with respect to infringement and rectification proceedings, and in its **role** as the appeal tribunal from decisions of the Registrar of Trade Marks. Only since the introduction of the *Trade Marks Amendment Act 1976* (Cth), has the Court's jurisdiction been restricted to a purely appellate one. In each capacity, however, the Court has added significantly to the corpus of traditional British trade mark jurisprudence, and there is now a large and freestanding body of Australian case law that reflects and extends the British law.

Trade mark exploitation and litigation often has an international character. In *Radio Corporation v Disney* (1937), the High Court accorded de facto recognition to an unregistered famous mark by refusing registration of the words 'Mickey Mouse' in respect of radio receiving sets and kits on the ground that this would be confusing and deceptive, given the wide popularity and public recognition of the cartoon character of that name. Later, in *Smith Kline & French v Registrar of Trade Marks* (1967), **Windeyer** upheld the Registrar's refusal to register as a trade mark the 'total appearance' of the capsules of a pharmaceutical company, where this comprised 'a capsule of which one half was coloured, the other half colourless, containing pellets of two or more colours, one of which may be white'. In Windeyer's view, it was fundamental that a trade mark should be 'something distinct from the goods in relation to which it is used or proposed to be used'. It is clear that he was also concerned at the incidental monopoly registration might confer over the sale of part-coloured capsules containing pellets of different colours. It is noteworthy that in relation to the same mark the **House of Lords** took a different approach (see *Smith Kline & French v Sterling-Winthrop Group* (1975)), but later refused a similar application by Coca-Cola to register the shape of its well-known bottle (*In re Coca-Cola Co* (1986)), distinguishing its earlier *Smith Kline* decision and expressing similar anti-monopoly sentiments to those of Windeyer. Subsequently, registration of 'shape' marks has been permitted by legislation in both Australia and the UK (*Trade Marks Acts* 1994 (UK) and 1995 (Cth)).

Over the course of nearly a century, the High Court has built up a solid body of case law on the requirement of dis-

tinctiveness, and what is required for the purposes of registration. Many of its judgments contain masterly exegeses on such crucial matters as invented words (*Howard Auto-Cultivators v Webb Industries* (1946)); descriptive words (the *Tub Happy Case* (1956)); geographical designations (*Clark Equipment v Registrar of Trade Marks* (1964)); and the overall concept of distinctiveness (*Burger King v Registrar of Trade Marks* (1973); *Registrar of Trade Marks v Muller* (1980)). The Court's exploration of issues such as deception and confusion still remains relevant under the 1995 Act (see, for example, *Jafferjee v Scarlett* (1937); *Reckitt & Colman v Boden* (1945); *Sym Choon v Gordon Choons Nuts* (1949); *Southern Cross Refrigerating v Toowoomba Foundry* (1954); *Bayer Pharma v FBA* (1965)) and all these decisions continue to inform and guide Trade Marks Office practice.

In other areas, High Court decisions continue to exert great influence on the daily operation of trade marks law. **Aickin's** decision in *Pioneer Electronic Corporation v Registrar of Trade Marks* (1978) is something of a tour de force; his examination of the connection required to maintain the registration of a trade mark where the mark is licensed still remains relevant under the 1995 Act. The concept of 'ownership' of a trade mark, as the basis of entitlement to apply for registration, remains embedded in a number of decisions under the earlier legislation (including *Aston v Harlee Manufacturing* (1960); *Moorgate Tobacco v Philip Morris (No 2)* (1984)), and is untouched by the 1995 Act. In the area of infringement, several earlier decisions, including the *Tub Happy Case* and *Shell Co v Esso* (1963), have explained the concept of 'use as a trade mark', although the 1995 Act may have gone too far in incorporating this phrase as part of the statutory definition of infringement.

The law of trade marks represents a difficult balancing of opposing interests: those of traders, their competitors, and consumers. This tension has been strongly evident in cases involving applications to remove marks from the register on the ground that they were confusing or deceptive when registered, or have subsequently become so. The legislation has always allowed for the possibility of a certain degree of deception or confusion between marks—for example, where there has been honest concurrent use. At the same time, sympathy can be felt for a registered trade mark owner who finds that its mark has become deceptive or confusing through the 'assiduous efforts of an infringer' (see *Berlei Bra Case* (1973)). In several cases, although with some division of judicial opinion, the High Court has inclined towards UK authority to the effect that a mark should be removed from the register only where there has been some 'blameworthy act' on the part of the registered owner. This has now been enshrined in legislative form in the 1995 Act, but in another tour de force decision, the Court has revisited the prior law and held that this was an unnecessary gloss. The decision in *Campomar v Nike International* (2000), which bears the unmistakable imprint of **Gummow**, ranges widely across trade marks law, passing off, and section 52 of the *Trade Practices Act* 1974 (Cth), and is now required reading for those who want to trace and understand the roots and rationales of these different forms of protection for traders and their marks.

SAM RICKETSON

Trade practices law. Australia struggled to introduce a comprehensive competition policy from the time of federation. The Commonwealth's first attempt, in the form of the *Australian Industries Preservation Act* 1906 (Cth), was a disaster. Influenced by the **reserved state powers** doctrine, the Court in *Huddart Parker v Moorehead* (1909) held that those provisions of the Act dependent on the **corporations power** were unconstitutional. It was not until the later decision in *Strickland v Rocla Concrete Pipes* (1971) that the High Court **overruled** *Huddart Parker* and allowed a more expansive approach. With the **Barwick Court** moving away from a states' rights approach to the Constitution, the way was paved for the introduction of the modern *Trade Practices Act*. As **Attorneys-General**, first **Barwick** and later **Murphy** had been instrumental in the introduction of this legislation.

Trade practices law is the law embodied in the *Trade Practices Act* 1974 (Cth), its 'fair trading' counterparts in the states and **territories**, and the judicial decisions and tribunal rulings on these Acts. In essence, the Act prohibits a variety of anti-competitive practices, mainly by corporations, and also prohibits misleading, false, or deceptive conduct. In preventing anti-competitive practices and providing for consumer protection, the Act seeks to ensure fair, competitive, and informed markets for the benefit of **consumers**.

Robert Bork noted in 1978 that 'antitrust is necessarily a hybrid policy science, a cross between law and **economics** that produces a mode of reasoning somewhat different from that of either alone'. Perhaps less kindly, RK Eassie has written that 'as disciplines go, the two (law and economics) generally regard themselves as would two strange dogs with nothing in common, not liking each other, but not needing to fight because there are two lamp posts in the street'. Trade practices law removes the lamp posts and requires both disciplines to work together for the benefit of consumers. Adjudication of trade practices issues requires tribunals to approach the Act and competition policy with skills that go beyond orthodox legal reasoning.

Until its decision in *Queensland Wire Industries v BHP* (1989), the High Court's approach to the different mode of reasoning required by trade practices law was marked by **legalism** and a concern to achieve doctrinal consistency. The few cases that came to the Court were concerned either with threshold issues of **constitutional interpretation** or with relatively narrow issues of **statutory interpretation**. In these cases, the Court was preoccupied with two issues: the constitutional validity of the Trade Practices Act or specific provisions of the Act, and then, once it became clear that the Act would survive constitutional challenge, the meaning and scope of its provisions.

This somewhat skewed development of trade practices law has largely been a function of the limited **role** of the High Court in this area. The High Court is not the primary adjudicator of trade practices cases; that is the role of the **Federal Court**. The role of the High Court is primarily appellate, and only a few cases involving substantive trade practices issues have reached the High Court. Moreover, as there is no explicit or comprehensive power in the Constitution for the direct regulation by the Commonwealth of restrictive trading practices, the Act has had to rely on a combination of other powers (mainly the interstate **trade and commerce power** in section 51(i) and the corporations power in section 51(xx)), which entail limits on the Act's scope. Thus, it is not surprising that many cases have concerned issues of constitutional validity and, to a lesser extent, statutory interpretation. The resolution of these issues did not require an exploration of the economic and **policy** concerns underlying the Act. Instead, the Court relied on traditional modes of legal reasoning developed to ensure interpretive consistency. Decisions until the 1980s on the meaning of the Act indicate the Court's preoccupation with the text of the legislation; a **literalist** approach that enabled the Court to avoid a consideration of the underlying policy issues. Accordingly, the decisions provided little scope for the development of meaningful guidance about deeper competition law principles.

The literalist approach to the Act was indicated by the Court's emphasis on formal deductions from fixed legal categories, often at the expense of the competition policy underlying the section under consideration. In *Castlemaine Tooheys v Williams & Hodgson Transport* (1986), the Court interpreted section 47(6) of the Act, which prohibits 'exclusive dealing', as having no application if the customer was presented with a 'packaged' product (in that case, a combination of beer and transport services). All of the Justices adopted a literal approach that completely defied the purpose of the section. This highly restricted construction created a 'loophole' that has since been vigorously exploited.

Paradoxically, the Court's approach to the consumer protection provisions of the Act has tended to be expansive. Section 52 was inserted into the Act to provide for a standard of conduct; corporations were prohibited from engaging in conduct that was misleading or deceptive or likely to mislead or deceive. It was originally intended as a remedy for consumers against the misleading conduct of large corporations. However, the decisions in *Hornsby Building Information Centre v Sydney Building Information Centre* (1978) and *Parkdale Custom Built Furniture v Puxu* (1982) established that section 52 was not limited to cases involving consumers and could be employed in commercial litigation. The practical consequence has been the explosion of commercial litigation involving section 52 as an alternative to other forms of commercial causes of action. This was a consequence that Attorney-General Murphy had not intended in 1974, and despite an attempt by the Court in *Concrete Constructions v Nelson* (1990) to give a more restricted interpretation of section 52, its use remains unabated.

The willingness of the Court to respond to societal **values** was evidenced during the 1980s under Chief Justice **Mason**, especially in developing the field of **unconscionable** conduct. Looking past the strict form of a guarantee, the Court's celebrated decision in *Amadio's Case* (1983) looked to the substance of the transaction in finding that the Commercial Bank had engaged in unconscionable conduct. Similarly, the treatment of the consumer protection provisions of the Trade Practices Act throughout the 1980s and early 1990s indicated the High Court's willingness to emphasise the substance of a transaction rather than its strict form (see **Form and substance**). This attitude corresponded to the Court's willingness to adopt a purposive approach to the Act, recognising the limitations of interpreting a statute by reference to its words alone without regard to underlying values.

The purposive approach reached its peak in the *Queensland Wire* decision. The appellant in that case, Queensland Wire Industries, was a manufacturer of fencing wire (using steel bought from BHP), which it used to supply rural fencing in Queensland and northern NSW. But the most popular form of wire fencing in rural Australia used 'star picket posts', cut from lengths of a product known as Y-bar. Although BHP was the only manufacturer of Y-bar in Australia, it did not offer the product for general sale. Apart from some exports to a subsidiary in NZ and a former subsidiary in Papua New Guinea, it supplied Y-bar exclusively to its wholly owned subsidiary Australian Wire Industries. Both BHP and Australian Wire Industries used Y-bar to make star picket posts.

When Queensland Wire Industries sought supplies of Y-bar from BHP and Australian Wire Industries so that it too could make star picket posts, they initially refused to supply the product, and then offered to do so at a very high price. The question was whether BHP had breached section 46 of the Act, which prohibits a corporation with 'a substantial degree of power in a market' from taking advantage of that power for anti-competitive purposes, including the purpose of 'preventing the entry of a person into that market or into any other market', or 'deterring or preventing a person from engaging in competitive conduct in that market'.

The comparative under-consideration of the anti-competitive provisions of the Act had left the federal courts attempting to grapple with the unfamiliar concepts of 'a substantial degree of market power' and 'taking advantage of market power'. This analytical void made it difficult for courts to differentiate between genuinely competitive conduct that might disadvantage a competitor and conduct calculated to eliminate that competitor. It was little wonder that the primary judge and the Full Federal Court in their 1987 judgments produced wildly different and unsatisfactory results. Lawyers are more comfortable arguing about intent and motives than about economic efficiency, and at first instance Justice CW Pincus had imported these notions into the Act and had therefore dismissed the case. An attempt by the Full Federal Court to grapple with 'market definition' produced absurd results: since the only sales of Y-bar were between BHP and Australian Wire Industries, there *was* no relevant market.

It was only on appeal in the *Queensland Wire Case* that the High Court had its first opportunity to confront the economic principles that underpinned the Act. The Court held that the words 'take advantage of' did not import notions of intention or motives, but simply meant 'use'. Most judges solved the problem of market definition by concluding that the relevant market was the rural fencing market (or alternatively, the star picket post market). The Court found that BHP had breached section 46 of the Act. In short, the Court rejected a legalistic approach and explored the Act's purpose. In this way, the case provided the Court with its long-awaited opportunity to develop a meaningful exegesis of the economic concepts behind the legislation. A literalist approach would have seen the Court fragment the elements of section 46 and approach each element as a separable integer in the overall definition of the prohibited practice. Instead, the Court displayed considerable sophistication in adopting a purposive approach that accommodated the different mode of reasoning necessitated by a blending of economics and law. A part of that process was the Court's rejection of the idea that intent or motive played a role in the resolution of essentially economic questions.

Those who had hoped that the Court would articulate a definitive set of interpretive principles, capable of repeated mechanical application, were disappointed. However, the Court's decision clarified the economic basis of the Act and brought new levels of sophistication to the analysis of its underlying economic concepts.

Although *Queensland Wire* is probably the Court's most important trade practices decision to date, it has not been universally acclaimed. Fears were expressed that the principles developed by the Court would be applied in a mechanistic way without regard to the economic subtleties required by a purposive approach. The decisions of the Federal and Full Federal Courts in *Melway Publishing v Robert Hicks* (1999) suggested that these fears were not without foundation.

In refusing to supply Melbourne street directories to Robert Hicks, Melway Publishing was found to have contravened section 46 of the Act. At first instance, and on appeal, the Federal Court assumed that in a competitive market, Melway would not have refused to supply the directories because it would have lost sales. Since Melway could refuse supply only because there was a lack of competition, the Federal Court assumed that Melway must therefore have 'taken advantage' of its market power.

However, in allowing Melway's appeal (*Melway Publishing v Robert Hicks* (2001)), the High Court employed the purposive approach it had outlined in *Queensland Wire*. Such an approach requires each case to be considered on its own merits, devoid of economic assumptions. When Melway's conduct in refusing to supply was examined in context of its overall distribution system, the High Court concluded that the assumptions underlying the Federal Court's decisions were not warranted. The decision confirmed the High Court's use of purposive analysis to distinguish between legitimate but potentially harmful conduct and illegal anti-competitive conduct.

ALEX BRUCE

Further Reading
Michael Coper, 'Constitutional Imponderables in the Path of a National Competition Policy' (1994) 2 *TPLJ* 68

Transcripts of argument now provide a complete and accurate record of the oral proceedings in the Court. They record counsels' **arguments**, exchanges between **counsel** and the Bench, and exchanges between Justices. The way the Court uses and produces transcripts characterises the Court as a modern and efficient institution. But it was not always thus.

Official transcripts were introduced in about 1920 when official Court reporters were employed to record Court proceedings by writing notes in shorthand. The fullness and accuracy of these transcripts were often deficient: 'The law reporter … heard only half of what went on in court and reported the other half'. To the editor of the *Australian Law Journal* in 1939, in which the preceding quotation appears, the reporter's discretion to omit minor or irrelevant matters may at times have constituted 'a distinct benefit'.

Manual shorthand recording imposed heavy burdens upon reporting staff, especially during **World War II**. The Court's Chief Reporter wrote to the Attorney-General's Department in 1942: 'The branch has been under-staffed and over-worked during the past two years or more … This branch staff is the hardest worked reporting staff in Australia.'

Tape recording facilities replaced manual reporting in Sydney and Melbourne during the time of the **Dixon Court**. Deficiencies persisted, epitomised by the transcription of *Tait's Case* (1962). To correct any errors in the transcript, **Dixon** painstakingly compared the tape recording of the case to the official, typed transcript. After several attempts, Dixon realised that the reporter misheard: when Dixon said 'Court of Common Pleas' the reporter thought he said '*causa complit*', two words the reporter assumed to be technical Latin terms.

Proceedings during this time were recorded by microphone contained in a back room. Runners collected the tapes used to record the proceedings and delivered them to a transcription department located some distance away. In 1964, on **Barwick's** initiative, the transcribing officer was relocated to the **courtroom** itself. Under this system, the transcribing officer could see the speaker and avoid incorrectly attributing the recording. This system could not be replicated when the Court moved to **Canberra**, however, because of the design of the Canberra courtrooms. So Barwick then introduced a system that has since been adopted in other Australian courts.

Today, no court reporters are present in the courtrooms during hearings. Rather, microphones and closed-circuit **television** cameras capture the audio and video of the proceedings. Signals are sent to television monitors and recording devices in a special room in another part of the building. There, an employee dubs each speaker's name onto the audio tape of proceedings, using the television pictures from the courtroom to identify the speaker. The audio is recorded onto a digital master tape (for archive purposes) and also onto a series of short cassette tapes. A team of Court Reporting Officers transcribe the proceedings from the cassette tapes onto word processors. Two senior reporting officers then proofread these 'bites' of the proceedings before amalgamating them into one continuous transcript, which is then distributed.

Another major feature of the High Court's reporting service is that anything quoted from an outside source (legislation, court decisions, legal articles, and so on) by counsel during the proceedings is checked against the source document, thereby ensuring the accuracy of the quotation. This checking is done by the Court Reporting Officers during the transcription process.

Working at a level of constant intensity, and with rigorous adherence to set procedures, Court reporting staff are generally able to have the transcript of a full day's proceedings (about 120 A4 pages) ready for distribution within an hour of the Court rising. Paper copies are placed in the Court's **archives** for permanent preservation, provided to each Justice involved in the case, given to each of the parties, and made available for sale to the public from offices of the Court registry throughout Australia. Electronic versions are filed on the Court's internal computer network, and since 1997 published on the AUSTLII web site (www.austlii.edu.au), usually the following day. The master audio tapes of both constitutional cases and important appeals are archived permanently. The tapes of other cases are returned to the system for eventual reuse. Facilities are also available to videotape proceedings if required.

Apart from providing a permanent record of every day's proceedings, transcripts are a valuable resource in the Justices' judgment-writing process. The electronic file can be searched rapidly for particular references, and important parts of counsel's argument easily consolidated. In addition, in longer cases it is the practice of some Justices to read over the day's transcript before argument continues the following day, in order to prepare further questions for counsel from the Bench. The transcript is also a valuable reference tool for legal practitioners. Not only does it allow counsel in a long case to review their argument from the previous day, it is also useful in the provision of legal advice and in preparation for other cases. The comments made by the Justices by way of interjection during argument are sometimes examined for hints of emerging views, but are not an **authoritative** or even reliable guide to later opinion.

The changes that have occurred over time in the Court's production and use of transcripts have led to an increase in the immediacy, accuracy, and accessibility of transcripts and legal information, and have improved the judgment-writing process and presentation of argument before the Court (see also **Information technology**).

LEX HOWARD

Trident General Insurance v McNiece (1988) exposed differing attitudes in the **Mason Court** towards the Court's law-making role. At issue was the doctrine of **contract law** known as 'privity of contract', which treats contract as a private arrangement between the parties, incapable of conferring any legal benefit on a 'third party'. If A promises B to do something for C and fails to do so, B may have a legal remedy against A, but C has none. One reason is that C has given nothing to A that might constitute 'consideration' for a contractual right.

In 1937, an English Law Revision Committee recommended that this doctrine be abolished, as 'lacking any reason in logic or public **policy**'. Thereafter, for many reformist lawyers, the desirability of abolishing the doctrine was axiomatic. In *Wilson v Darling Island Stevedoring* (1956), **Fullagar** and **Kitto** explored possible ways of mitigating the rigours of the doctrine, as did **Windeyer** in *Coulls v Bagot's Executor & Trustee Co* (1967). But both cases reaffirmed 'privity' as fundamental to Anglo-Australian contract law.

Over the years, various statutory provisions enabled a third party to sue on a contract in particular circumstances. In particular, section 48 of the *Insurance Contracts Act 1984* (Cth) provided that where an insurance policy is expressed to cover third parties, they may claim the benefit of it. This was the very situation at issue in the *Trident* case. But *Trident* concerned a policy made in 1977, in its application to an accident in 1979. Section 48 came into force in 1986, and was not retrospective.

The accident happened when a crane overturned on a construction site. The injured crane driver recovered **damages** from the contractor, McNiece Bros, who thereupon invoked the insurance policy that the site owner, Blue Circle Southern Cement, had taken out with the Trident insurance company. The policy was expressed to cover 'all contractors and sub-contractors'; but the contract was only between Blue Circle and Trident.

Successive courts upheld McNiece's claim. The trial judge, David Yeldham, held that the premiums paid by Blue Circle must have reflected its financial arrangements with its contractors, so that some consideration could be treated as coming from McNiece. He also held that by seeking to enforce the policy, McNiece had 'ratified' it, thus becoming a party.

In 1987, the NSW Court of Appeal found these arguments too artificial, but declared, through a powerful judgment by **McHugh**, that a **common law** exception to the 'privity' doctrine had evolved for liability insurance. McHugh noted that other common law exceptions to privity (for instance, as to commercial letters of credit) had reflected commercial necessity and usage, and argued that similar reasoning should apply to liability insurance. He relied partly on the general practice of the insurance industry; partly on the 1984 statutory provision (which he treated as 'only giving effect to the common law' as it had already developed); and partly on the contemporary interplay between common law and **equity**. In equity, a contract for the benefit of third parties is usually enforceable under the law of **trusts**. The contracting party to whom the promise is made is treated as receiving it as a trustee for the beneficiaries, who can therefore sue to enforce the trust, joining their 'trustee' as a defendant. That solution was not available in the *Trident* case because McNiece had raised it too late: the Court of Appeal had excluded the argument because Trident had had no opportunity to call **evidence** negating a trust. Nevertheless, McHugh held that the position in equity could properly be considered in developing the common law.

In the High Court, **Mason** and **Wilson** went further, seizing the opportunity to argue that the privity doctrine should be abolished altogether. They asserted 'the responsibility of this Court to reconsider in appropriate cases common law rules which operate unsatisfactorily and unjustly', adding that the recent statutory change was no reason 'for continuing to insist on the application of an unjust rule'. Yet in the end, their actual decision was confined to the insurance issue: they noted that 'in the ultimate analysis the limited question we have to decide is whether the old rules apply to a policy of insurance'.

Conversely, **Toohey** emphasised throughout that the Court was not concerned with the privity doctrine 'in all its aspects', but only with a limited exception for insurance policies. Yet he recognised that to formulate such an exception would inevitably 'have implications for privity of contract in other situations'. Like Mason and Wilson, he formally confined his actual decision to an insurance exception, while clearly contemplating that this might entail a wholesale abolition of the doctrine.

Indeed, it was to this equivocation that **Brennan** and **Dawson** responded most emphatically in their dissents. For Dawson, the proposed exception 'could not be restricted upon any conceptual basis to contracts of insurance'; for Brennan, 'to admit such an exception involves the overthrow of the doctrine'. For both of them, such a frontal assault on a basic common law axiom went beyond any legitimate conception of the High Court's law-making role. 'The invitation

was not so much to engage in judicial creativity as to engage in the destruction of accepted principle, which is a very different thing.'

As to the NSW Court of Appeal, Brennan and Dawson insisted that the doctrine of **precedent**, and its place in the **hierarchy of courts**, should have obliged it unquestioningly to apply the privity doctrine. For the High Court, however, they acknowledged some scope for judicial creativity. They recognised that the law of agency and **estoppel**, as well as the law of trusts, had been used to minimise or avoid the injustices of the privity rule, and envisaged the further expansion of these devices to eliminate any remaining hardship. Mason, Wilson, and Toohey had also acknowledged these devices, but doubted their sufficiency, and argued that acceptable outcomes should not (for instance) 'be made to depend on the vagaries of such an intricate doctrine' as estoppel.

Deane essentially agreed with Brennan and Dawson. He thought that 'accepted processes of legal reasoning' might *sometimes* require an appellate court 'to reverse the development of the law by disowning established principle', but that for a principle as 'entrenched' as privity, only 'precisely defined and compelling reasons' could justify such a course. Here there were no such reasons. He emphasised that the privity doctrine operates only 'within the confines of the law of contract', and that outside those confines its 'practical effect' had been 'confined and qualified', and its potential injustices 'precluded', by the development of other principles. For him, the solution to the *Trident* case lay in a trust. He would have adjourned the proceedings to enable Blue Circle to be joined as a respondent trustee, and Trident to adduce any evidence negating the existence of a trust. Assuming there was no such evidence, he would then have dismissed the appeal.

Gaudron expressed 'general agreement' with Mason and Wilson. Yet she too held back from wholesale rejection of the privity doctrine. For her, the decisive fact was that Trident had received full consideration (through appropriate premiums) for its promise to benefit third parties, and should not therefore be allowed to avoid its part of the bargain. The fundamental principle thus attracted was the avoidance of unjust enrichment (see **Restitution**). That principle imposed on Trident a legal obligation to keep its part of the bargain, and correlatively entitled McNiece to enforce that obligation.

She emphasised, however, that on this analysis, 'the right of the third party is not a right to sue on the contract'. Like Deane, she was affirming the continued hegemony of the privity doctrine within the domain of contract law, but confining it strictly within that domain, and allowing its unjust consequences to be avoided by another route.

TONY BLACKSHIELD

Trusts. The trust is the relationship that arises when a person (the 'trustee') holds legal title to **property** for the benefit of other persons (the 'beneficiaries'). The creation and administration of trusts are governed by state and **territory** legislation. The bulk of Australian trust law has been developed in the **state Supreme Courts**. Nevertheless, through the exercise of appellate **jurisdiction**, the High Court has created a distinctive palimpsest of Australian doctrine written over the original English law. In its first 50 years, the Court provided a steady flow of illuminating decisions on difficult points of trust law. The second 50 years, commencing with the elevation of **Dixon** to **Chief Justice** in 1952, and continuing through the **Mason Court** of the 1980s and early 1990s, has generated a flowering of impressive **equity** and trusts jurisprudence, notable for its emerging flexibility and the willingness of the Court to mould existing trust concepts to provide relief in new situations.

Much of the High Court's contribution in the area of express trusts has stressed the importance of ascertaining the intention of the creator of the trust, thus reflecting the trust as a principal vehicle through which an intention to dispose of property is effected. To this end, in *Commissioner of Stamp Duties (Qld) v Jolliffe* (1920), **Knox** and **Gavan Duffy** decided that whatever words are used, what is essential is that those words manifest an intention by the settlor or declarant to create a trust. Similarly, in the abstruse jurisprudence of the secret trust, Dixon, in *Voges v Monaghan* (1954), confirmed the intention of the testator as the key to the validity of this type of trust. The pre-eminence of intention was reflected more recently, albeit following a rather strewn pathway, in *Corin v Patton* (1990), where the Court took an undemanding view of what is necessary for the complete constitution of trusts. In that case, the Court finally gave effect to the view expressed by **Griffith** in *Anning v Anning* (1907) that, to give effect to their intentions, transferors must complete only those acts required of them—rather than requiring them to complete every single step in the transfer.

The Court, in the process of determining and giving effect to intention, has consistently adopted a constructionist rather than a formulaic approach to the creation of trusts. Thus it has not been constrained by the presence or absence of the word 'trust' in the purported disposition. For instance, in *Dean v Cole* (1921), the Court concluded that a testator's will 'trusting' his wife 'divide in fair, just and equal shares between [the] **children**' amounted to words of precation rather than obligatory trust.

Yet it is in the context of inferring an intention to create a trust that the Court has most highlighted the express trust as a vehicle of immense flexibility. The Court has not been deterred from finding an intention to create an express trust even when the parties have expressed themselves in the language of **contract** rather than trust. A striking example is *Bahr v Nicolay (No 2)* (1988), where **Mason** and **Dawson** gave effect, through the lens of an express trust, to a clause in a contract for the sale of land acknowledging a pre-existing entitlement to repurchase by the original owner of the land. They held that where a person has shown an intention for another person to benefit from specific property and the appropriate legal mechanism to give effect to this intention is a trust, the Court will infer such an intention. This flexibility was echoed in the same year in *Trident General Insurance v McNiece* (1988), where **Deane** inferred an intention to create a trust through which the benefit of an insurance policy was secured to a person named as an 'insured' but not in a relationship of privity with the insurer.

Thus the Court has shown a willingness to use the express trust as a vehicle to provide relief in circumstances where common law relief is unavailable or inadequate and the parties' expectations and obligations can be explained—though not necessarily expressed—as a trust. Although this some-times appears to go beyond what can be properly described as the true intention of the settlor, the Court has steadfastly refused to cross the line into imputing an intention to create a trust.

In circumstances where the facts demanded relief but the inference of an intention to create a trust could not properly be made, the Court has been willing to adopt the resulting or constructive trust as a means of granting relief. This has particular, though not exclusive, relevance in the context of breakdown of de facto relationships. Faced with the breakdown of quasi-marriage relationships, and unable to resort to a statutory scheme whereby property division could be effected, the Court resorted to the trust. Thus the trust was moulded to give legal recognition to aspects of a relationship otherwise lacking that recognition. In so doing, the Court addressed a growing social trend.

Initially, the resulting trust was employed to provide relief. In an effort to generate an equitable outcome in *Calverley v Green* (1984), the Court held that a signature on a mortgage document had constituted a contribution to property sufficient to generate a corresponding equitable interest under a resulting trust. This, however, was not an adequate remedy. The scope of a resulting trust had traditionally been limited to financial contributions, and in any event, the use of the device in this context was patently artificial. Accordingly, the Court proceeded to shape a new role for the doctrine of constructive trust—a vehicle previously used chiefly to make fiduciaries (and those associated with them) accountable for gains and losses resulting from a breach of **fiduciary** duty.

This process commenced in *Muschinski v Dodds* (1985) and bore fruit two years later in *Baumgartner v Baumgartner* (1987), where the Court imposed a constructive trust on a man who asserted complete beneficial ownership of property after the breakdown of a de facto union in which both parties had pooled their income. The basis of the Court's intervention by way of constructive trusteeship was to prevent the man unconscionably denying the woman an interest in the property to which she had made a substantial, albeit indirect and partly non-financial, contribution. Again, the Court favoured an approach of a most flexible kind—so much so that, despite judicial protestations against unbridled discretion and 'idiosyncratic' notions of justice, the Court's concept of **unconscionability** may not be too far removed from Lord Denning's trust of a 'new model' based on fairness. What *Baumgartner* also heralded was a broad approach to the concept of the constructive trust—one not limited by the institutional character of express and resulting trusts, but able to provide a remedy in circumstances lacking a pre-existing legal relationship.

The shifting boundaries between the institutional trust and the remedial trust have also been explored by the Court in contexts other than de facto unions. In a family dispute over farming property in *Giumelli v Giumelli* (1999), the Court vacillated between the constructive trust and the doctrine of **estoppel** as the foundation for relief. In the context of constructive trusts effecting accountability for breaches of fiduciary duty—a principal form of so-called 'institutional constructive trust'—it is the typically erudite judgments of Mason in *Hospital Products v US Surgical Corporation* (1984) and Deane in *Chan v Zacharia* (1984) that provide the guiding lights. Yet the Court has not, despite an opportunity to do so in *Consul Development v DPC Estates* (1975), made a definitive statement as to constructive trusteeship in 'knowing receipt' cases, an increasingly important area especially in view of the multiple directorships of the new Australian management class.

The movement to the widespread use of the discretionary trust in family and commercial settings in Australia was preceded by—and required—an adumbration of the differences between the power and the trust. In Australia, this adumbration was predicated on decisions such as *Hourigan v Trustees Executors & Agency Co* (1934) and *Kinsela v Caldwell* (1975). In *Kinsela*, the Court, contemporaneously with the English decision in *Re Manisty's Settlements* (1973), confirmed that a trust does not fail for uncertainty merely because the actual persons to whom the distribution will be made cannot be known in advance of the date of distribution. This decision was in line with the earlier **House of Lords** decision in *McPhail v Doulton* (1970), which upheld the validity of a discretionary trust the beneficiaries of which could not be listed, but could be identified by way of a criterion capable of certain application.

This loosening of the strictures of certainty of object for discretionary trusts, coupled with the very lax approach to tax avoidance of the **Barwick Court**, signalled the 1960s and 1970s as the heyday of tax avoidance in Australia. In *Cridland v FCT* (1977), for example, a university student successfully relied on the holding of units in a primary production unit trust to attain the benefits of income averaging available to primary producers. The Court's reasoning was that taxpayers were entitled to arrange their affairs so as to attract tax consequences for which the tax legislation makes specific provision. The 1980s saw not only legislative change but also a judicial tightening of the trust as a vehicle for tax minimisation, as evidenced by *FCT v Gulland* (1985).

Consistent with its foregoing disposition to flexibility, the Court has, in dealing with the legality of trusts, eschewed an approach that defers too slavishly to rules and presumptions. In *Nelson v Nelson* (1995), faced with an attempt by a plaintiff to recover property transferred for an illegal purpose, the Court refused to be limited by the rule that denies assistance to a person to recover property transferred for an illegal purpose if he or she cannot establish title thereto without relying on the illegality. The Court was concerned that an inflexible application of the general rule could generate a result achieved at the expense of substance, and cast upon a claimant a burden disproportionate with the nature of the wrong.

Like the Court's application of the constructive trust in de facto cases, the Court's judgments in the area of charitable trusts reflect the nature of Australian society. This is perhaps nowhere better illustrated than in the context of religious charitable purposes. Reflecting the multicultural nature of that society, coupled with the valued constitutional guarantees of freedom of religion that have secured religious tolerance in this country, the Court in *Church of the New Faith v Commissioner of Pay-roll Tax (Vic)* (1983) adopted a legal meaning of 'religion' that broke free from the boundaries of Christianity. The judgment of Mason and **Brennan**, described by an expert witness in a corresponding NZ case as an excellent theological essay, identified a religion as requiring belief in a supernatural being, thing, or principle and an acceptance of canons of conduct (see **Church and state**).

In the English law of charitable trusts, particular questions about the Roman Catholic religion have encountered two recurring difficulties. The first was the view that a gift for the repose of a soul for a particular person could not be 'charitable', since it conferred no benefit on the community generally. The High Court rejected that interpretation as early as *Nelan v Downes* (1917), in part because a restrictive statute dating from the reign of Edward VI was not part of Australian law (see **Reception of English law**).

The second difficulty was the notion that a gift that might extend to the support of a purely contemplative order of nuns could not be 'charitable' since such orders did no good works. The High Court has had little opportunity to deal with this problem, in part because mid-century litigants in such cases preferred to appeal directly to the **Privy Council** (see, for example, *Davies v Perpetual Trustee Co* (1959)). However, in *A-G (NSW) v Donnelly* (1958), the Court held that a general gift for 'such order of nuns' as the executors might select was a valid charitable trust. **Williams, Webb,** and **Kitto** held that the possible selection of a contemplative order presented no problem; Dixon and **McTiernan** thought that there was a problem but that it could be solved by the reading-down provision in section 37D of the *Conveyancing Act* 1919 (NSW). On appeal, the Privy Council adopted the view of Dixon and McTiernan (see *Leahy v A-G (NSW)* (1959)).

In *Roman Catholic Archbishop of Melbourne v Lawlor* (1934), the Court was evenly divided on the question whether a gift for the establishment of a Roman Catholic newspaper was valid. (The appellants included the Pope; see **Litigants, notable, 1903–1945.**) **Evatt** joined the Roman Catholics, Gavan Duffy and McTiernan, in holding that the gift was valid. **Rich, Starke,** and Dixon took the opposite view (which prevailed, since that had been the view taken by the Supreme Court of Victoria; see **Tied vote**). However, in *Trustees of Church Property v Ebbeck* (1960), Dixon and **Windeyer** (with Kitto dissenting) struck down as contrary to public **policy** a condition on a gift that the gift be forfeited if the intended donees married **women** who did not profess the Protestant faith.

Other characteristics of Australian society have been reflected in the Court upholding certain trusts as charitable. For example, the **nationhood** of Australia was evident in the Court's validation of a trust 'for the benefit of Australia' in *Way v Commissioner of Stamp Duties (NSW)* (1949), notwithstanding its apparent vagueness. In *Downing v FCT* (1971), a trust for the amelioration of the conditions of ex-members of the armed forces was held to be charitable, despite the fact that its beneficiaries could no longer defend Australia. The decision presumably reflected the importance Australian society attaches to the freedom that its armed forces secure.

By the close of the century, the imported English oak had been well pruned. An autochthonous equity and trusts jurisprudence was apparent. The Court has demonstrated its conceptual flexibility by shaping the trust to an ever-increasing variety of situations and social institutions to better serve the needs of modern Australian society.

DONALD CHALMERS
GINO DAL PONT

Tuckiar v The King (1934) is a case still regularly cited on the duty of **counsel** to a client, but it has a wider significance in the history both of the High Court and of white–black relations (see **Colonialism**). The case was the Court's first encounter with issues of Aboriginal rights. By unanimously quashing a conviction for murder and sentence of death, and expressing grave disquiet at the whole Northern Territory system of justice, the Court established a pattern of broad sympathy for the rights of **Aboriginal peoples**, to which it has increasingly returned.

Tuckiar was a traditional Yolngu man from Caledon Bay in north-eastern Arnhem Land. He spoke no English and had little or no contact with white men. In 1932, five Japanese fishermen were killed by Aboriginal people in the area; and in mid-1933, four policemen, with Aboriginal trackers, came in search of the culprits. They found a group of Aboriginal women, whom they handcuffed together. While the women were being questioned, a tracker saw other Aboriginals in a canoe, and all but one of the police set off in pursuit. The women were unfettered and left behind with the remaining policeman, Albert McColl, and two trackers. When the other police returned, the two trackers were there, but the women and McColl had disappeared. McColl's body was found the next morning about 400 metres away, with a spear wound in the chest and a bloodied spear alongside. His revolver had been fired three times.

Although the High Court judgments did not refer to it, the killing led to demands from police, Territorians, and even senior Northern Territory bureaucrats for a 'punitive expedition'. It was said that unless the natives were taught a lesson, they would become emboldened, and the lives of all the whites, including missionaries, in the area would be endangered. The demands for revenge prompted a counter reaction from groups sympathetic to Aboriginal people. Eventually, a church organisation brought to Darwin a group of Aboriginals thought to be implicated in the Japanese deaths and in that of McColl. One of them, Tuckiar, was charged with killing McColl, and appeared before Justice Thomas Wells of the Supreme Court of the Northern Territory and a jury of 12 white men.

The Crown relied almost entirely on two pieces of confessional evidence given by Aboriginal men who had accompanied Tuckiar in the boat to Darwin. One witness, Parriner, whose evidence was translated into pidgin English by one of the original trackers, Paddy, told the Court that Tuckiar had told him that three of the women in the police camp had been his wives. When the main police party left, he had signalled to one of the women by sign language that he was nearby. When McColl walked behind her, Tuckiar had signalled to his wife to move away, and had then thrown his spear at him. McColl had clutched the spear with one hand and drawn his revolver and fired three times before dying. According to Parriner, Tuckiar had said that he threw his spear because he was frightened the policeman would kill him.

Another Aboriginal witness, Harry, told the Court that Tuckiar had told him he had at first hidden when he saw the police, but that later, hearing a baby cry, he had looked and seen McColl with one of his wives and a baby. McColl was said to have had sexual intercourse with the woman, after which the woman had walked on to open ground. Tuckiar had communicated by signs to her, but McColl had seen him, whereupon Tuckiar had asked McColl for tobacco. McColl was said then to have fired at him three times and reloaded; Tuckiar said he was behind a tree but that as McColl had fired again, he had thrown his spear at him and hit him. Then, he said, he had run away.

Counsel for Tuckiar, instructed by the Protector for Aborigines, had no interpreter through whom to communicate with Tuckiar, who had no English. After Parriner had given evidence, the judge asked Tuckiar's counsel whether he had discussed Parriner's story with his client, and (when counsel said no) whether he thought it proper to do so to find out whether the story was correct. On counsel agreeing, the judge adjourned for a consultation between Tuckiar and his counsel, arranging for Paddy to act as interpreter.

When the Court resumed, counsel, in the presence of the jury, asked if he could discuss something important with the judge, adding that he was in the worst predicament he had encountered in all his legal career. In chambers, counsel told the judge that he had put both confessional statements to Tuckiar and that Tuckiar had told him that the story told to Parriner was correct, and that he had told the other story to Harry because he had been worried. Counsel asked the judge's advice about what to do. The judge told him that in the ordinary course, the thing to do once a confession of guilt was made would be to withdraw; but that

> as your client was an Aboriginal and there might be some remnant of doubt as to whether his confession of guilt to you was any more reliable than any other confession he had made, the better course would be to continue to appear, because if you retired from the case it would be left open to ignorant, malicious and irresponsible persons to say that this Aboriginal had been abandoned and left without any proper defence.

The case continued, with no real cross-examination of the only two witnesses. Evidence from the other police, the trackers, or the woman was not given. Then the prosecutor was given leave, without objection, to call a witness to give evidence about the good character of Constable McColl, directed at refuting any suggestion of a propensity to have **sex** with Aboriginal women. Before the Crown had completed its case, the jury asked what it should do if it was satisfied that there was not enough evidence to convict. The judge (saying later, in his report to the High Court, that he understood them to mean that they thought the Crown had not adduced all the evidence it could have) told the jury that they should not be swayed by the fact that the Crown had not done its duty. A verdict of not guilty would mean that Tuckiar would be freed, and could not be tried again, even if further evidence was found, and that could be a miscarriage of justice. Moreover, he told the jury that he was troubled by the fact that reflections had been made about Constable McColl, and that a not guilty verdict might suggest that they believed it, which would be a serious slander on that man.

The defence gave no evidence, and the judge's directions to the jury were focused on a guilty verdict. No directions were given about the possibility of a manslaughter verdict, and Harry's account, which clearly raised that possibility, was dismissed. The judge also told the jury that they were entitled to take into account the fact that Tuckiar had not given evidence, a direction clearly at variance with the operative South Australian Criminal Code.

Tuckiar was convicted and sentenced to death. During the sentencing, defence counsel told the Court that Tuckiar had informed him that his statement to Harry was a lie and that 'this clears Constable McColl'. The judge congratulated him for saying so.

All five High Court Justices were scathing about the conduct of the case, and of the trial judge and defence counsel. Chief Justice **Gavan Duffy** and **Dixon**, **Evatt**, and **McTiernan** thought the judge's comment on the failure to give evidence was itself enough to make the case miscarry. Moreover, the evidence as to McColl's character should not have been admitted. They were also highly critical of the judge's answer to the question from the jury. The High Court could not understand why counsel for the defence had seen himself in a predicament: he had 'a plain duty to press such rational considerations as the evidence fairly gave rise to in favour of complete acquittal or conviction of manslaughter only'. Even if counsel was satisfied that the version of events obtained with Paddy's assistance was

the truth (and 'misgiving on this point would have been pardonable'), the argument that the homicide amounted only to manslaughter was by no means hopeless; and even if counsel knew that his client was guilty, he was entitled to argue that the Crown had failed to prove its case. There was no point in ordering a new trial, particularly after counsel's public statement during the sentencing process.

Starke was more generally critical of the trial, the conduct of the judge, and defence counsel, and the judge's charge to the jury. The substance of a fair trial had been denied the accused, he said.

As a triumph for Tuckiar, it was short-lived. Shortly after being released from custody, he disappeared. As the historian Henry Reynolds comments, 'it was widely believed in Darwin that he was shot by police and his body dumped in the harbour'.

JACK WATERFORD

Further Reading
Ted Egan, *Justice All Their Own* (1996)
Henry Reynolds, *This Whispering in Our Hearts* (1998)

U

Unconscionability. Although most cases raising issues in **equity** are decided in state courts, the High Court has made a significant contribution to our understanding of unconscionability.

The concepts of 'unconscionability', 'unconscientious behaviour', or 'unconscionable conduct' originated in, and were based on, the prevention of equitable fraud. While 'fraud' at **common law** referred to wilful deceit or an intentional disregard for the truth, 'equitable fraud' or 'constructive fraud' was much broader and was defined as a breach by one party (albeit an innocent breach) of an obligation to another.

Today, while unconscionability has outgrown its historical origins, it still rests on the prevention of equitable wrongdoing. An analysis of unconscionability involves the recognition of three distinct but interrelated tiers of complexity. On the first level is the overarching theme of unconscionability under which equitable jurisprudence is subsumed. It is an abstract but convenient shorthand for the principal focus of equitable intervention. At the second level are five generic descriptors of the unconscionable conduct at which equitable intervention is directed: exploitation of vulnerability or weakness; abuse of a position of trust or confidence; oppressive insistence upon rights; inequitable denial of obligations; and unjust retention of **property**. On the third and lowest level, specific equitable doctrines such as **undue influence** or **fiduciary obligations** inform the two higher tiers; upon these any cause of action will be based.

The High Court has made a significant contribution to our understanding of unconscionability in four major ways. First, as the highest appellate court in the land, it decides contentious and ground-breaking cases that resolve conflicting authorities and thereby set the boundaries for equitable intervention. The Court has taken the opportunity to refashion equitable principle in response to modern conditions (see, for example, *Muschinski v Dodds* (1985)).

Secondly, the Court has retained unconscionability as the touchstone of equity jurisprudence, whereas other jurisdictions—notably, NZ and Canada—have adopted another frame of reference: unjust enrichment. The extent to which unconscionability and unjust enrichment overlap remains unclear.

Thirdly, the Court has made it abundantly clear that recourse to arguments based on unconscionability as an abstract concept will not be a sufficient foundation for equitable intervention (see, for example, *Muschinski*; *Stern v McArthur* (1988)). Instead, any reference to unconscionability must be informed by specific equitable doctrines and **precedent** as well as the factual content of the case.

Finally, the Court has responded to changing community attitudes towards the excesses of commercial self-interest. Whereas in the past the pursuit of self-interest was lauded as a desirable objective, there has been a sober realisation that untrammelled commercialism can lead to the unacceptable exploitation of vulnerable persons. The Court has been at the forefront of this significant shift in **ideology**, and has effectively used the concept of unconscionability to develop more rigorous standards of conduct in commercial transactions—such as requiring fair dealing in precontractual negotiations (see, for example, *Waltons Stores v Maher* (1988)) and greater disclosure of relevant commercial information together with independent and impartial advice (see, for example, *Amadio's Case* (1983); *Garcia v National Australia Bank* (1998)); and refusing to permit unconscionable exploitation of strict contractual rights (see, for example, *Legione v Hateley* (1983); *Stern v McArthur*) or unjust retention of benefits on the breakdown of a joint endeavour (see, for example, *Muschinksi*). In so doing, the Court has extended the boundaries of long-established doctrines and infused them with new meaning (see, for example, *Commonwealth v Verwayen* (1990); *Louth v Diprose* (1992); *Garcia*). Moreover, it has remedied not only procedural unconscionability—where the problem lies in the process by which one party gained a benefit (see, for example, *Amadio*)—but also substantive unconscionability, where equitable intervention is based on the prevention of an unjust outcome (see, for example, *Muschinski*).

However, the Court has undertaken its expansion of unconscionability cautiously. For example, it has resisted attempts to extend the protection and **remedies** afforded by fiduciary obligations to a manufacturer under a distribution agreement (see, for example, *Hospital Products v US Surgical Corporation* (1984)) or to a patient seeking access to her medical file from her doctor (see, for example, *Breen v Williams* (1996)). In that respect, the Court has been concerned to retain the significant divide between rights and remedies in common law and equity.

FIONA BURNS

Further Reading

Paul Finn, 'Unconscionable Conduct' (1994) 8 *JCL* 37

Patrick Parkinson, 'The Conscience of Equity' in Patrick Parkinson (ed), *The Principles of Equity* (1996) 28

CJ Rossiter and Margaret Stone, 'The Chancellor's New Shoe' (1988) 11 *UNSWLJ* 11

Undue influence. In order to chart the future course of undue influence as a doctrine that informs the wider framework of **unconscionability**, it will be necessary for the Court to choose a well-reasoned conceptual basis as a benchmark for judicial **decision making**.

Under the doctrine of undue influence, **equity** has developed the jurisdiction to set aside transactions procured by the unconscientious use of pressure or presumed to have resulted from an improper exercise of influence by one party over the other. Actual undue influence arises where a claimant can prove that a party has exerted undue influence in order to procure a transaction. Presumed undue influence arises where a claimant proves that there is a relationship of influence so that it may be presumed that the wrongdoer has exerted influence in order to procure the transaction. Presumed undue influence is further divided into established relations of influence—such as solicitor and client—and relationships which, by their nature, make undue influence likely. The presumption may be rebutted by evidence that the transaction was the free and independent act of the claimant.

It is evident that the High Court has drawn on the English **common law** heritage when applying and elaborating undue influence in the Australian context (see, for example, *Spong v Spong* (1914); *Watkins v Combes* (1921); *Jenyns v Public Curator (Qld)* (1953)). In so doing, the Court has indicated that undue influence of any kind will make the transaction voidable.

Where appropriate, the Court will find that a special relationship of influence exists in the absence of actual influence or an established relationship of influence. For example, in *Johnson v Buttress* (1936), an illiterate and commercially ignorant elderly man made a gift of his home to a friend upon whom he had become emotionally dependent after the death of his wife. A majority of the Court held that the circumstances indicated that there was a special relationship of influence that had not been rebutted.

In *Bank of NSW v Rogers* (1941), the Court made it clear that third parties may be assumed to be aware of the existence of undue influence. It was held that the bank had sufficient notice of the circumstances giving rise to a presumption of undue influence to put it on inquiry; and the absence of further investigations meant that the bank had constructive notice of the undue influence. The transaction in its favour was set aside. In this case, the Court foreshadowed the need for higher standards of commercial dealing.

In recent times in England, unconscionable bargains and spousal guarantees have been considered within the framework of undue influence, requiring a careful adjustment of the doctrine (see, for example, *Barclays Bank v O'Brien* (1993)). However, as the High Court has been eager to redress these situations and precisely define the doctrinal basis of equitable intervention, it has actively and consistently developed the separate and alternative doctrines of unconscionable dealings (see, for example, *Blomley v Ryan*

(1956); *Wilton v Farnworth* (1948); **Amadio's Case** (1983)) and the wife's special equity (see, for example; **Yerkey v Jones** (1939); **Garcia v National Australia Bank** (1998)).

Notwithstanding the Court's progressive approach to undue influence, two important matters need to be determined in the future. First, the relationship between common law duress and actual undue influence needs to be considered. These doctrines significantly overlap and it may be preferable to meld them into a single principle.

Secondly, at present, there are two influential conceptual justifications for findings of undue influence evident in the cases. In *Johnson v Buttress*, **Dixon** held that undue influence would arise 'whenever one party occupies or assumes towards another a position naturally involving an ascendancy or influence over that other, or a dependence or trust on his part'. He emphasised the quasi-**fiduciary** nature of undue influence, which constituted the abuse of a relationship of trust and confidence. The alternative interpretation can be found in later cases concerned with unconscionable dealing (see, for example, *Amadio*; *Bridgewater v Leahy* (1998)). The Court suggested that the key indicator of undue influence was the absence of a 'free, voluntary and independent act of the weaker party'.

FIONA BURNS

Further Reading

Malcolm Cope, 'Undue Influence' in *The Laws of Australia* (1993) 35.8

Tony Duggan, 'Undue Influence' in Patrick Parkinson (ed), *The Principles of Equity* (1996) 379

RP Meagher, WMC Gummow, and JRF Lehane, *Equity: Doctrines and Remedies* (3rd edn 1992) 381

Uniform Tax Cases (1942 and 1957). The *First Uniform Tax Case* (*SA v Commonwealth* (1942)) facilitated the start of a reconstruction of the federal system. The *Second Uniform Tax Case* (*Victoria v Commonwealth* (1957)) **overruled** the earlier case in one largely immaterial respect, and affirmed that the reconstruction that occurred between 1942 and 1957 had a sound constitutional base.

The uniform **taxation** scheme in question in the *First Uniform Tax Case* comprised four elements, each contained in a separate law. Speaking of the first three laws, Chief Justice **Latham** acknowledged the clarity of 'the intention to get rid of State income tax and of State income tax departments'. The first was the *Income Tax Act* 1942 (Cth) that imposed a rate 'such that there is left little practical room for State income tax'. But although the rate was such that it was 'politically impossible for the States to impose further income tax', the Act did not prohibit a state from so doing. Nor did it infringe any of the limitations the Constitution placed on the taxation power in section 51(ii). Latham insisted that the validity of legislation was not to be determined by the motives of the Parliament or the end sought to be achieved by the law. In this way, he followed the reasoning of the *Engineers Case* (1920) in its implied rejection of *R v Barger* (1908).

The second element of the scheme, the *States Grants (Income Tax Reimbursement) Act* 1942 (Cth), gave a state an incentive not to levy any income tax. If it abstained from doing so, it would receive a grant roughly equal to the revenue it would thereby lose. This was attacked on a number of grounds, the most fundamental being that 'the Commonwealth cannot direct its legislative powers towards destroying or weakening the constitutional functions or capacities of a State'—at least in respect of its 'essential governmental functions'. Latham reasoned that while the Commonwealth could not make a law with respect to the capacity and functions of a state legislature, this was not such a law. It provided an inducement to the states to refrain from exercising the power to levy income tax, but it did not require them to do so.

This reading of the scope of the power to make grants to the states under section 96 was upheld in the *Second Uniform Tax Case*, albeit with some reluctance, by Chief Justice **Dixon**. He said:

> While others asked where the limits of what could be done in virtue of the power the section conferred were to be drawn, the [High] Court has said that none are drawn; that any enactment is valid if it can be brought within the literal meaning of the words of the section and as to the words 'financial assistance' even that is unnecessary. For it may be said that a very extended meaning has been given to the words 'grant financial assistance to any State' and that they have received an application beyond that suggested by a literal interpretation.

The third law—the *Income Tax (War-Time Arrangements) Act* 1942 (Cth)—was said by Latham to show an intention that the Commonwealth 'should take over the officers and the physical means which are necessary for administering any system of State taxation upon income. As soon as a State which refused to abandon income tax formed a department to collect the tax the Commonwealth could take it over'. The validity of this law was upheld under the **defence power** (section 51(vi) of the Constitution) by a majority of 3:2. In any event, the validity of this law may not have been crucial, given the effects of the other three laws.

The fourth law was a new provision in the *Income Tax Assessment Act* 1942 (Cth), which, in Latham's words, was 'manifestly designed to make sure that the Government collects Commonwealth income tax, whatever may happen to any claim of a State for income tax'. This provision for Commonwealth priority was upheld unanimously in the *First Uniform Tax Case*, and overruled by a majority of 4:3 in the *Second Uniform Tax Case*. By implication rejecting the approach taken by Latham in the first case, Dixon said in the second case that 'it would be absurd to ignore the place the section takes in the plan for uniform taxation and examine it as if it were appurtenant to nothing and possessed no context'. That was so because

> when you are considering what is incidental to a power not only must you take into account the nature and subject of the power but you must pay regard to the context in which you find the power. Here we are dealing with powers of taxation in a federal system of government. Further, you must look at the purpose disclosed by the law said to be incidental to the main power. Here the purpose is to make it more difficult for the States to impose an income tax.

In this context, it was not incidental to the federal power of taxation 'to forbid the subjects of a State to pay the tax imposed by the State until that imposed upon them by the Commonwealth is paid and, moreover, to do that as a measure assisting to exclude the States from the same field of taxation'.

The legal reasoning employed in the *First Uniform Tax Case* justifies Geoffrey Sawer's observation that 'the decision is the high-water mark of the *Engineers Case* techniques'. In the first place, the Justices employed a technique for **characterisation** that, in Latham's words, looked to what a law did, and not to 'the effect in relation to other matters of what the law does'. 'The true nature of a law is to be ascertained by examining its terms and, speaking generally, ascertaining what it does in relation to duties, rights or powers which it creates, abolishes or regulates.' By this technique, the Court was able to dispose of the main arguments relied on to challenge the laws—namely, that they amounted to a scheme to prohibit the states from exercising their powers of taxation, and that the differential use of the grants power had effectively undermined the requirement that taxation laws should be framed 'so as not to discriminate between States or parts of States'. It was held that the Commonwealth could do indirectly what it could not do directly.

In the second place, and more directly reflecting the influence of the *Engineers Case*, the reasoning in the *First Uniform Tax Case* paid no regard to any conception that the states were immune from the operation of Commonwealth law (see **Intergovernmental immunities**). The most that was conceded was that the Commonwealth did not have power to make laws with respect to the functions and capacities of the states. The retreat from that position in the **Melbourne Corporation Case** (1947) is reflected in the overruling in the *Second Uniform Tax Case* of that aspect of the *First Uniform Tax Case* that had upheld the provision for Commonwealth priority in the Income Tax Assessment Act.

The legal reasoning in the *First Uniform Tax Case* may now be judged by some to be unsatisfactory. In terms of the character of the federal system of government, however—and indeed the quality of life of all Australians—Kenneth Bailey's view in 1942 that the *First Uniform Tax Case* was 'probably the most far-reaching judgment ever handed down by the High Court' holds true today. While he may have overstated the point in saying that in time the states would become 'primarily administrative agencies', we are close to a position in which 'the main lines of policy in all major matters [are] nationally determined', at least so far as economic and social policy is concerned. The 'constitutional reconstruction' presaged by the *First Uniform Tax Case* has come about.

Bailey maintained that the 1942 scheme sprang in essentials from 'the requirements of war finance' during **World War II**. There have always been those who query this view of the matter. According to Rodney Maddock, the scheme 'yielded just the same aggregate revenue as the existing schemes'. On other evidence, too, Maddock suggests that this result—and the decision to enact four separate Acts—may have been designed to ensure that the High Court did not rest the validity of the scheme on the defence power in section 51(vi). In this way, the Labor government used the opportunity presented by the war to resolve an issue of public policy that had intermittently occupied politicians of all major parties since 1916, when the Commonwealth had first enacted an income tax law. Over that time, there had been bipartisan support for a resolution that placed the Commonwealth in a pre-eminent position, although state-based politicians, including those from the Labor Party, had not favoured that outcome. The uniform tax scheme of 1942 was, as Maddock says, 'a unilateral assertion of commonwealth powers'—and, moreover, one designed to achieve a social policy of alleviating the tax burden on lower income persons. The scheme was, nevertheless, supported by some leading figures on the Opposition side of the Commonwealth Parliament. They may have perceived, as did Latham, that just what use was made of the scheme would be played out in the field of politics.

It is ironic that Robert **Menzies**, who opposed the 1942 scheme on the ground that it was unconstitutional, was, as **Prime Minister** from 1949 to 1966, able to make use of the Commonwealth's monopoly of the power to levy income tax, and the power to make grants to the states, to reconstruct the character of Australian **federalism**. His governments employed these powers to finance and control social and economic policy in a way that sustained him in office for so long as Prime Minister. The *First Uniform Tax Case* was a genuine attempt to force the Commonwealth to find some other means (and such there were) to finance the war. The *Second Uniform Tax Case* was more in the nature of a bargaining ploy in the attempts by the states to gain more of the revenue raised by the Commonwealth. Dixon may have understood—as a query raised by him in his judgment suggests—that his holding that Commonwealth taxes could no longer have priority would be of no practical importance in relation to the system of uniform taxation. By 1957, the scheme of uniform taxation was well entrenched. Within two more years, the law was changed to remove the provision of the Grants Act that the states not levy income tax—and that was abandoned even as an informal stipulation by 1976. In 1978, Commonwealth law permitted the states to levy income tax again, but none did so.

PETER BAYNE

Further Reading

Kenneth Bailey, 'The Uniform Tax Plan' [1944] *Economic Record* 170

Rodney Maddock, 'Unification of Income Taxes in Australia' (1982) 23 *Australian J of Pol & Hist* 354

Geoffrey Sawer, 'The Second Uniform Tax Case' (1957) 31 *ALJ* 347

Geoffrey Sawer, *Australian Federal Politics and Law 1929–1949* (1963)

United States Supreme Court. In language similar to Chapter III of the Australian Constitution, Article III of the US Constitution vests the national **judicial power** in a Supreme Court and in such inferior federal courts as Congress chooses to create. The Constitution further establishes that federal judges are nominated by the President, with the advice and consent of the Senate. Like the Justices of the High Court, American federal judges hold office during good behaviour, and the Constitution guarantees that their **remuneration** may not be diminished during their continuance in office. Unlike the High Court, there is no mandatory **retirement** age for American federal judges.

There have always been personal connections between Justices of the High Court and those of the Supreme Court. **Dixon**, for instance, developed a strong personal friendship with Felix Frankfurter while the former was in the USA during **World War II**. **Brennan's** friendship with the American William Brennan began with a newspaper clipping that confused one for the other. There is regular amicable contact between the two courts.

The US Constitution is silent on the Supreme Court's **number of Justices**. There has always been a **Chief Justice**, though the number of associate Justices (in Australia, **puisne Justices**) has ranged from four to nine; since 1870, the Court has comprised nine members. Although some recent Senate Judiciary Committee confirmation hearings have garnered substantial public attention, most are not controversial.

Oral arguments before the Court are limited to one hour per case. The current Chief Justice, William H Rehnquist, is known for being especially punctilious. The time limit had been strictly maintained, regardless of the significance of the issue, until the unprecedented litigation arising from the 2000 presidential election, when on two successive occasions an extra half-hour was allowed (*Bush v Palm Beach County Canvassing Board* (2000); *Bush v Gore* (2000)). By contrast, there is no time limit for **argument** before the Court in the High Court, and arguments can and often do last for days. As in Australia, the American Justices are well prepared for each argument, and often engage in sharp and lively questioning with the attorneys—and sometimes with each other. Oral arguments are open to the public, although seating is quite limited. After argument, the Justices discuss the cases in **conference** among themselves; deliberations are strictly confidential. During the conference, preliminary votes are taken. Each Justice has one vote, and the Chief Justice (or the senior associate Justice in the majority) assigns the writing of the majority opinion. Unlike the Australian practice, the Supreme Court has since the early 1800s issued an opinion of the Court, which is signed by one Justice but which four or more others join. Justices may also write **concurring** or **dissenting** opinions.

Some **commentators** have noticed changes in the Court's practice in recent years, with the effect that the American and

Owen Dixon with Felix Frankfurter, in front of portrait of Oliver Wendell Holmes, Harvard Law Library, 1955

Australian practices seem to be converging. Just as the High Court is developing the use of a conference procedure, for instance, some have suggested that the American conference is devolving into just a brief vote and the assignment of the majority opinion. In addition, the Supreme Court's opinions are now longer and more fragmented, so that it is becoming increasingly challenging to discern the *ratio decidendi*—a difficulty with which Americans have not previously had to contend. As in Australia, Justices develop their own personal **judicial style** and, eventually, reputations for certain types of writing; whereas Anthony Kennedy, for instance, has a florid and sometimes philosophical style, Antonin Scalia is known for his polemic and acerbic wit. In her early years on the Court, Sandra Day O'Connor (the first female Justice) was said to have a distinctly feminine style, a charge she vigorously disavows. Robert Jackson is considered by many to be the Court's finest writer, though Oliver Wendell Holmes was renowned for his strikingly aphoristic literary style.

Article III delineates federal court **jurisdiction** and defines the Supreme Court's original and appellate jurisdiction in language similar, but not identical, to Chapter III of the Australian Constitution. Beyond that, the Constitution says very little about the Supreme Court's powers. In *Marbury v Madison* (1803), Chief Justice John Marshall held that the federal judiciary has the power of **judicial review**, enabling it to review and if necessary invalidate legislative or executive acts of federal or state governments. Although criticisms of Marshall's logic abound, the opinion is a mainstay of both American and Australian constitutional jurisprudence. In Australia, it was cited as early as 1905 (see *Ah Yick v Lehmert*). Indeed, the High Court has referred to Australia's acceptance of the *Marbury* principle as 'axiomatic' (see *Communist Party Case* (1951); *Commonwealth v Mewett* (1997)). Because it departs from the principle of parliamentary **sovereignty**, it may be said to give extraordinary power to judges who are neither elected nor **accountable**. This counter-majoritarian difficulty has been a central feature of commentary about the Supreme Court since *Marbury* was decided.

The Supreme Court decides only federal questions—defined as questions arising under federal laws or treaties or the federal Constitution (see *Murdock v Memphis* (1875)). Thus, it will not hear cases from either lower federal courts or state courts if the decision rests on state law grounds independent of federal law and adequate to support the judgment (see *Michigan v Long* (1983)). The Supreme Court's jurisdiction is therefore much more limited than that of the High Court, which has general appellate jurisdiction over all civil and criminal cases from both state and federal courts. Furthermore, limited by concerns about **separation of powers** and federalism, the Supreme Court has refused to create a general federal **common law** (see *Erie Railroad v Tompkins* (1938)). Thus, the Court prefers to present its decisions as having been compelled by the statute or constitutional provision at issue. Compare, for example, *New York Times v Sullivan* (1964) (holding that the First Amendment limits certain **defamation** actions) with *Lange v ABC* (1997) (finding common law limitations on a similar class of defamation actions). These same concerns have also led the Court to develop a reasonably sophisticated 'political question' doctrine under which, for jurisprudential reasons, it will refuse to hear a case if it believes that the decision is more appropri-

ately left to another branch of government (see *Nixon v US* (1993), holding that the US Senate and not the Court should determine the correct procedures for impeachment).

Since *McCulloch v Maryland* (1819), the US Supreme Court has been committed to interpreting the Constitution relatively broadly to give the text meaning. In sharp contrast to the High Court, which generally applies tools of **statutory interpretation** to **constitutional interpretation** (see *Engineers Case* (1920)), the Supreme Court routinely refers not just to the words and the structure of the Constitution, but to the intent of the **framers** (as evidenced in the *Federalist Papers* or other writings), **history**, traditions, or any other factor that may appear relevant. As a result, implications from the text are not at all uncommon; arguably, American constitutional interpretation would be unthinkable without judicial power to make or uncover implications. Indeed, in recent years, the Court has repeatedly adverted to the maxim that 'behind the words of the constitutional provisions are postulates which limit and control' (*Monaco v Mississippi* (1934)). In *Saenz v Roe* (1999), for instance, the Court implied a right to travel simply from the fact of union and from the privileges and immunities clauses; in *Printz v US* (1997), state immunity from certain federal obligations was implied from various constitutional provisions regarding the states. In some instances, in fact, the Court's jurisprudence runs directly contrary to the constitutional text (see, for example, *Near v Minnesota* (1931), applying the First Amendment to the states though its prohibition of laws abridging freedom of speech is addressed only to 'Congress'; *Hans v Louisiana* (1890), holding that the Eleventh Amendment precludes virtually all federal court suits against states, notwithstanding the more specific and limited constitutional language; and *Alden v Maine* (1999), extending the prohibition to similar suits in a state court).

One source that the Supreme Court rarely consults, however, is the decisional law of other nations, including opinions of the High Court. This is in marked contrast to the Australian practice of regarding relevant American constitutional interpretation 'not as an infallible guide, but as a most welcome aid and assistance' (*D'Emden v Pedder* (1904); see also, **Foreign precedents**; **Citations by Court** and for an extended discussion of the extent to which American defamation law should be followed in Australia, *Theophanous v Herald & Weekly Times* (1994)).

Many of the enduring principles of the Court's constitutional jurisprudence were initially laid down by John Marshall during his 34-year **tenure** as Chief Justice. In addition to the rules of judicial review and of broad constitutional interpretation, Marshall also established broad federal court jurisdiction (*Osborn v Bank of US* (1824) and broad legislative commerce power (*Gibbons v Ogden* (1824)). Marshall also established foundational principles relating to native Americans, asserting that Indian tribes constitute 'domestic dependent nations' that enjoy some degree of sovereignty, but that lost their claim to **native title** through European discovery of their land (see *Johnson v McIntosh* (1823); *Cherokee Nation v Georgia* (1831)).

Throughout the nineteenth century, most of the Supreme Court's constitutional cases concerned state power to regulate interstate commerce. After the Civil War, when the Constitution was amended to protect individual (and, by

Unreported judgments

implication, corporate) equal protection and **due process** rights, the Court's attention began to shift towards economic and personal rights.

From the 1880s to 1937, the Court's jurisprudence was **activist** and conservative. In *Lochner v New York* (1905), for instance, the Court held that a state law regulating the working hours of bakers violated due process. In the period immediately following, the Court became more deferential to the political branches (see, for instance, *US v Carolene Products* (1938)), though in mid-century, the Court again began actively to protect individual rights (see, for example, *Brown v Board of Education* (1954); *Miranda v Arizona* (1966); *Roe v Wade* (1973)). In recent years, the Court has limited the reach of some prior decisions protecting individual rights (see, for example, *Planned Parenthood v Casey* (1992); *Employment Division v Smith* (1990)), although the freedoms of speech and association continue to be robustly protected (see *Texas v Johnson* (1989); *Board of Regents of the University of Wisconsin v Southworth* (2000); *Boy Scouts of America v Dale* (2000)).

Although much of the Court's twentieth-century jurisprudence focused on the individual rights that are enumerated or implied in the **Bill of Rights** and the Reconstruction Amendments, the focus now seems to be shifting to the structure of the Constitution (see *City of Boerne v Flores* (1997); *Kimel v Florida Board of Regents* (2000)). This may also suggest a convergence with the Australian practice. As the High Court is experimenting with individual rights implied from the very nature of **democracy** (see *Free Speech Cases* (1992)), the Supreme Court is increasingly finding that the structure of the Constitution is the primary protector of individual rights (see, for example, *New York v US* (1992), holding that **federalism**-based limits on federal power protect individual liberty, and *Clinton v City of New York* (1998), Justice Anthony Kennedy arguing in concurrence that separation of powers protects individual liberty).

The US Supreme Court has figured prominently in the popular imagination of many Americans. There are scores of monographs about the Supreme Court's practice, history, current jurisprudence, and membership, intended for both lay and professional readers. One of the most famous is *The Brethren* (1979) by Bob Woodward and Scott Armstrong, which chronicles the 1973 term. The Court's willingness to confront controversial issues throughout most of the twentieth century has earned it a particularly high profile among American institutions yielding both praise and, as the protests on each anniversary of *Roe v Wade* attest, scorn. 'Equal justice under law'—the inscription on the Supreme Court building—is a familiar phrase to many Americans.

ERIN DALY

Further Reading
Kermit Hall (ed), *The Oxford Companion to the Supreme Court of the United States* (1992)

Unreported judgments. The **reporting of decisions** of the High Court has taken various forms during the life of the Court. The authorised reports have always been the *Commonwealth Law Reports*, commonly referred to as the CLRs. The editors of those reports have always been selective about the particular cases they choose to report. Cases involving **constitutional interpretation** have always been reported; the

choice of other cases has usually been the responsibility of the editor. In 1992, a special volume of the CLRs (volume 180) was published to include previously unreported judgments that were now considered to have assisted in the development of the law.

The *Australian Law Journal* published brief notes of High Court and **Privy Council** decisions from its inception in 1927. Gradually, these notes became more extensive, until in 1951 they were reformatted as verbatim reports. In Melbourne, the *Argus Law Reports*, which had begun publication in 1895, began extensive reporting of High Court decisions as soon as the Court was established in 1903. With the death of the *Argus*, the series was taken over by Butterworths in 1959. It was renamed the *Australian Argus Law Reports* and then, in 1973, began a new series under the name of the *Australian Law Reports*. Both the *Australian Law Journal Reports* and the *Australian Law Reports* have consistently reported many cases omitted from the more authoritative CLRs; but these, too, are selective, and each year a number of cases remain unreported altogether.

During the period when the appellate **jurisdiction** of the Court allowed appeals as of right in cases where a civil right involving a specified monetary amount was involved, it was common for the **Full Court** to deliver *ex tempore* judgments in appeals that involved no question of law. These judgments were usually written by the presiding Justice during a brief recess of the Court, or, in cases presided over by Chief Justice **Barwick**, during the **argument**. Judgments of Justices sitting in the original jurisdiction of the Court were often not reported. In both cases, however, an original copy of the reasons was placed on the court file.

The practice of delivering *ex tempore* judgments flourished in the period of the **Barwick Court**, and was expanded to include the giving of brief reasons for refusing special **leave to appeal** in criminal applications. The abolition of the appeal as of right, and the introduction of the screening processes introduced by the Court in civil and criminal special leave applications, has meant that only those cases involving important questions of law are now considered by the Court. This has led to the virtual demise of the *ex tempore* judgment, as the importance and difficulty of the questions raised in appeals requires a considered judgment by the Court.

David Solomon, a legally qualified and respected political **commentator**, began a monthly publication called *The Legal Reporter* in 1980. Solomon reported every judgment, whether it was of the Full Court or of a single Justice sitting in court or in **chambers**, thus picking up judgments that would otherwise have been unreported. *The Legal Reporter* was made available on subscription and soon found a niche within the **legal profession**, particularly the Bar. The profession for the first time had ready access to, commentary on, and extracts from, judgments that had been delivered by the Court, without having to purchase a copy of the entire judgment from the Court registry or having to await the published report, if the case was to be reported at all. The significance of this was that **counsel** could have readily available a recital of the relevant facts, usually together with the majority judgment, which they could cite to a court. Since 1997, all judgments of the Court have been made available on the Internet (see **Information technology**).

FRANK JONES

694

V

Values. For many years, the Court's judicial methodology was what **Dixon** designated as 'strict and complete **legalism**'. Its application was not limited to constitutional cases. In *Rootes v Shelton* (1967), a **common law** case, **Kitto** rejected discussions of 'judicial **policy**' and 'social expediency' which, in his view, would 'introduce deleterious foreign matter into the waters of the common law—in which, after all, we have no more than riparian rights'. The method was congruent with the theory that there is a body of ascertained principles or doctrine sufficient by itself to govern the determination of concrete cases. With the passing of that theory, the methodology has been questioned. **Mason** thought it to be 'a cloak for undisclosed and unidentified policy values' that underlie a judgment. If the underlying values are not discussed, they are difficult to debate; and the doctrine of **precedent** may perpetuate their influence even when community values have changed. If an existing rule, principle, or practice is rejected or modified in response to a change in community values, the change should be acknowledged in the judgment and its influence on the judgment should be stated.

Since the High Court asserted its independent authority to declare the law for Australia and appeals to the **Privy Council** were finally abolished, the development of Australian law has sometimes invited consideration of whether existing principles and precedents are consistent with the values of the Australian community. In cases in which the Court has developed the law for Australia during the last two decades, there has been a more overt acknowledgment of the role that values and policy play in the formulation of new rules or principles or the reformulation of old ones.

Different kinds of values have varying degrees of significance. Some values relate to standards of conduct or of worth and govern the application, but not the expression, of legal rules or principles. Thus contemporary community standards of conduct determine what is '**reasonable**' in cases of negligence, and determine what is obscene or indecent (*Crowe v Graham* (1968)). Community standards show a sentencing judge the degree of seriousness to be attributed to criminal conduct. Standards of worth affect the assessment of general **damages** in **tort**: such assessments 'give weight to current general ideas of fairness and moderation' (*Planet Fisheries v La Rosa* (1968)), and involve 'an element of value judgment' that 'may properly be influenced by local community circumstances and standards' (*Coyne v Citizen Finance* (1991); see also *Sharman v Evans* (1977); *Carson v John Fairfax & Sons* (1993)). Contemporary community standards can affect the findings or assessments to be made in determining factual issues, without affecting the operation of established rules or principles. Other kinds of values can warrant the modification or rejection of a legal rule or principle, or a change in an existing practice.

The principal source from which courts derive the values that affect the development of the law is the existing body of the law itself. The concepts of the law—not always articulated—are the frames of reference for professional thinking. Judges who have spent their professional lives working within those frames of reference are imbued with the values to which the existing body of law gives effect. In approaching a problem, a Justice's starting point is necessarily that body of law. The values that inhere in existing legal principles are the basis from which any reformulation of principle must proceed—provided they are consistent with the enduring values of the community. Lord Atkin's speech in *Donoghue v Stevenson* (1932) is an example.

In a community ruled by law, a basic value is the law's certainty, consistency, and predictability—a value that the policy of *stare decisis* (adherence to precedent) protects. The importance of this basic value tends to suppress or delay the influence of shifts in community values on the judicial development of the law. Although 'courts necessarily reflect community values and beliefs', as **Stephen** said in *Onus v Alcoa* (1981), he thought that 'quite major changes in accepted community values would seem to be required' to change a principle governing the exercise of a judicial discretion. The occasions for reconsidering a principle or practice established by precedent are few, and good cause for reconsideration must be shown. Not every shift in values warrants reconsideration of the existing body of law: 'The contemporary values which justify judicial development of the law are not the transient notions which emerge in reaction to a particular event or which are inspired by a publicity campaign conducted by an interest group. They are the relatively permanent values of the Australian community' (*Dietrich v The Queen* (1992)).

But if there be a change in the enduring values of the community, or if the current formulation of the law is incompatible with what are perceived to be those values, reconsideration of established precedent or the formulation of a new rule, principle, or practice may be needed to keep the law in a serviceable state and thereby improve the curial administration of justice (see, for example, *R v L* (1991)). The object is 'to serve the contemporary needs and aspirations of society and to reflect society's contemporary values' in a way that 'ensures or enhances the administration of justice' (*McKinney v The Queen* (1991)).

Values in this context must be distinguished from more ephemeral attitudes formed with respect to social, **economic**, or political topics. Such attitudes are often the product of self-interest, prejudicial publicity, and temporary emotion rather than an expression of enduring values. Enduring values can affect the development of the law; transient attitudes cannot. Indeed, although a court might perceive that a principle or rule of the common law is consistent with an attitude prevalent in the community, the court may modify or reject the existing principle or rule if it is found to be inconsistent with the enduring values of that community. In *Mabo* (1992), the High Court rejected the rules based on the commonly held notion that the interest **Aboriginal peoples** had in their traditional lands did not survive European settlement. Instead, the Court gave effect to the enduring community value of non-**discrimination**, that is, the **equality** of all people before the law. This value founded the recognition of **native title**.

Judicial changes in rules, principles, or practices are sometimes the result of curial policy rather than new perceptions of, or shifts in, values. For example, a policy of simplification in the formulation of legal principle led to the subsuming of the several categories of **occupiers' liability** under the general principles of negligence (*Australian Safeway Stores v Zaluzna* (1987)). Policy has a given result as its end or object, and may be adopted by judges in order to improve the efficiency or utility of the common law. But a value need have no end or object; it provides a criterion against which the morality of laws and conduct can be judged. In a 1996 public lecture, Mason identified 'personal liberty, freedom of expression, no imprisonment without trial, [and] procedural fairness ... as values which inform legal principle and require an unambiguous expression of statutory intention to override them'. That is not to say that the precise content of a new legal rule, principle, or practice flows directly from the informing value.

Judicial amendment of the law to give effect to enduring values and judicial policies is constrained by several factors. First, the adversary system focuses on fact and precedent. Relatively little **argument** is, or usefully could be, devoted to the explicit examination of values and policies. Generally speaking, there is no dispute about the existence of an enduring community value. Secondly, any new rule, principle, or practice must be integrated with the existing body of law. No judicial development can 'fracture the skeleton of principle which gives the body of our law its shape and internal consistency' (*Mabo*). Thirdly, the reasons for judgment must show the necessity for developing the law despite the consequent detriment to its certainty and predictability. Fourthly, no judicial development of the law can override the Constitution or the provisions of a statute.

However, the interpretation of the Constitution or of a statute is not immutable. Written instruments take their original meaning from the time and circumstances in which they came into force. Changing circumstances (including changes in community values) may call for new applications of the unchanging text when it is looked at in the light of contemporary conditions—as **Deane** argued forcefully in *Theophanous v Herald & Weekly Times* (1994). The denotation of terms may be expanded (see **Connotation and denotation**), and past errors in interpretation revealed. The expansion of materials admissible to assist interpretation may show some presumptions to be ill-founded or obsolete (see, for example, *Bropho v WA* (1990)). But the effect of changing values on **constitutional interpretation** and **statutory interpretation** is more indirect than their effect on the substantive rules or principles of the common law.

Rapid advances in technology, especially medical technology, may sometimes present the courts with problems for which neither guiding precedent nor clear community values can show the path to judgment. Perhaps the chief example is *Marion's Case* (1992), where the question was the authority of the parents of an intellectually retarded girl to consent to her sterilisation. The judgments reveal an attempt to find and give effect to values, whether inhering in the existing body of law or accepted by the contemporary community. An enduring value may require expression in a new legal norm, but the precise formulation of the new rule, principle, or practice evokes the experience, knowledge, and wisdom of the court.

The effect of enduring values on the development of the law should not be overstated; neither can that effect be denied.

Gerard Brennan

Further Reading
John Braithwaite, 'Community Values and Australian Jurisprudence' (1995) 17 *Syd LR* 351
Gerard Brennan, 'A Critique of Criticism' (1993) 19 *Mon LR* 213
Anthony Mason, 'The Role of a Constitutional Court in a Federation' (1986) 16 *FL Rev* 1

Veterans' entitlements. Australia has participated in every major world conflict since the Boer War, and a higher proportion of the population than in most other Western democracies has served in the armed forces. The special place of veterans in Australian history is reflected in the generosity, by world standards, of their entitlements. Since 1914, the legislation granting financial and other assistance has enjoyed bipartisan political support, underpinned by a strong lobby of ex-service bodies. Nowhere is that support reflected more strongly than in the evidentiary provisions determining onus and standard of proof. Yet the favourable treatment of veterans' claims by those provisions has come at a cost, as **Murphy** reflected in his **dissenting judgment** in *Repatriation Commission v Law* (1981):

The Australian solution to the problem of ensuring that the costs of war-related losses were borne by society rather than fall on the injured persons or their dependants was the adoption (along with other measures) of the 'onus of proof' section in war veterans legislation which requires the Commonwealth or its agency to disprove a claim rather than to require the claimant to prove it. It has been obvious that this remedial section would result and has resulted in many claims being allowed which in truth were not well-founded. This was the price of ensuring that no valid claim was rejected because of insufficiency of proof.

The nation's willingness to acknowledge its debt remained undiminished for the first three-quarters of the twentieth century, but began to wane with distance from conflict and pressures on government to expend funds on a wider range of social problems. Generally, however, the courts, including the High Court, have continued to interpret the legislation in a way that benefits the veterans' community, while the Parliament, particularly since the Vietnam War, has taken a more fiscally stringent stance. The interplay is a reflection of the volatility of the legislative solution, so well described by Murphy, and has involved the High Court on at least five occasions, some of which have been followed by specific legislative action to overturn the effect of the Court's decision.

A statutory scheme for payments to returned members of the services was introduced in 1914. For many years, the legislation was skeletal, its details being found only in policy manuals. From 1929, the onus was on the veteran to make a *prima facie* or presumptive case for entitlement. During **World War II**, the legislation abolished the need for a veteran to furnish proof and the onus of proof was shifted to those contending that the claim should not be granted—a curious reversal of the normal practice. Since this raised the spectre that the determination process was adversary in character, in 1977 the reference to onus of proof was removed, and from 1986 the legislation has specifically provided that there is no onus on either party.

The anomalies do not end there. Proof of entitlement to benefits from government is usually on the balance of probabilities—or civil—standard. However, in 1935, amendments provided that, on entitlement questions, war veterans were to be given 'the benefit of any reasonable doubt', later amended in 1943 to provide that those deciding claims were to draw 'all reasonable inferences' in favour of the veteran. According to successive **Attorneys-General**—John Spicer in 1953 and **Barwick** in 1960—the statutory formula invoked the criminal, not the civil, standard. Since these were administrative proceedings, their opinions were controversial. The matter was settled in 1977 with an amendment specifically providing that a body was to allow an entitlement claim 'unless it is satisfied, beyond reasonable doubt, that there are insufficient grounds for granting the claim'. The complexity of the unusual combination of the criminal standard, a burden of disproof, and the double negative—a claim will be successful only if the decision maker cannot be satisfied beyond reasonable doubt that the death or medical condition was not due to service—has meant that these tests have been at issue in half the veterans' cases before the High Court.

The Court was first asked to rule on the evidentiary provisions in *Repatriation Commission v Law* (1981). James Law had enlisted in 1940 and served in the Middle East before being taken as a prisoner of war (POW) by the Japanese in Java. He was a POW for more than three years and when he returned 'was in a wretched physical condition and remained in poor health for the remainder of his life'. He died from lung cancer, aged 67. Edward (Weary) Dunlop, a notable Australian patriot, ex-serviceman and himself a POW, gave evidence in support of the claim by Law's widow that her husband's death from lung cancer, a disease of unknown aetiology, was probably due to his smoking, a habit he acquired on service. As Dunlop noted, the causes of diseases such as cancers are subtle, long-acting and may not be observable. Hence, the benefit of any reasonable doubt should favour the veteran. **Aickin**, with whom **Gibbs**, **Stephen**, and **Mason** agreed, upheld the claim, noting that the introduction of the criminal standard must have been intended to expand, rather than reduce, the likelihood of ex-service personnel succeeding. The outcome led to a flood of applications and the acceptance of pension entitlement by veterans for smoking-related diseases to an extent unparalleled in Western countries. Amendments in 1997 finally precluded Commonwealth liability for diseases related to smoking where the smoking commenced or increased after 31 December 1997.

The test, as Aickin warned, created 'a heavy onus' of disproof on the Commission—so heavy that the High Court, by majority, in *Repatriation Commission v O'Brien* (1985), found that if there was no evidence of the cause of the veteran's disease or death, or the evidence was in equipoise, the burden could not be overcome. The result, as the minister noted when introducing amending legislation in 1985, brought **disability** pension claims close to 'automatic acceptance'.

John O'Brien had claimed that his essential hypertension was related to his war-caused anxiety neurosis. Since 1975, the claim had been unsuccessful on 12 of 16 occasions before the Repatriation Board, the Repatriation Commission, the War Pensions Entitlement Appeal Tribunal, the Repatriation Review Tribunal, and the Administrative Appeals Tribunal. On appeal, the High Court split 3:2, upholding the claim. Senator Peter Walsh, in a famous diatribe against the *Law* and *O'Brien* cases, fulminated:

> The award … for presenting big bills to taxpayers which no government intended they should receive goes to another case which started in an administrative appeal body and finished in the High Court.
>
> A majority of the learned Justices decreed that the widow of a former serviceman who started smoking as a POW and who died of lung cancer nearly 40 years later was a war widow, indistinguishable from the widow of a serviceman killed in action. That preposterous conclusion was hung on an extrapolation of a (possibly ill-considered) reference in section 47 of the *Repatriation Act* (as it stood then) to 'beyond reasonable doubt' …
>
> When enriched by another decision [*O'Brien's* case] the out-year cost of that judgment would have been round $400M a year. I submit that only the conscious decision of a government which has the responsibility to levy taxes to pay the bills should be allowed to control outlays of that magnitude.

Brennan and Murphy vigorously dissented in *O'Brien*. Brennan said the majority view need not be given 'so absurd an operation', and suggested that the burden of proof section—a provision he described as 'legislative legerdemain'—should be interpreted to require that there be at least a reasonable hypothesis connecting service and the claimed condition before a claim could be successful. His view formed the basis for the revised statutory test—the 'reasonable hypothesis' test—introduced in 1985, and substantially retained in the legislative overhaul in 1986. The new test, introduced pointedly to negate the High Court's interpretation in *O'Brien*, was intended to ensure that a pension would be payable only if there was more than a theoretical connection between disease, injury, or death and service.

As *Bushell v Repatriation Commission* (1992) indicated, the hoped-for improvement in the standard of proof was not achieved. Allen Bushell's claim, which involved similar medical issues to those in *O'Brien's* case, had earlier been rejected by the Repatriation Commission, the Veterans' Review Board, the Administrative Appeals Tribunal, and the Full **Federal Court**. The High Court concluded there must be *some* evidence if a claim was to meet the 'reasonable hypothesis' test. However, in words that served to undo the expected benefits of the new test, the majority added: 'The case must be rare where it can be said that a hypothesis based on the raised facts, is unreasonable when it is put forward by a medical practitioner who is eminent in the relevant field of knowledge.'

Following *Bushell*, claims again increased. As the minister commented when introducing the 1994 amendments, if the High Court's interpretation had been permitted to stand, by the year 2001–02, it was estimated claims would cost $235 to $440 million a year, and the cumulative costs over ten years would be $1.2 to $2.2 billion. The government again responded, with legislation avowedly designed to reverse the effect of the decision in *Bushell*. A new body, the Repatriation Medical Authority (RMA), comprising a panel of medical experts, was to set out in legislative form the exclusive circumstances in which particular diseases, injuries, or death could be linked to service. If a claim did not fall within the legislative template it failed. The Court has not yet commented on these provisions although, in November 2000, it refused special **leave to appeal** aspects of the scheme in *Repatriation Commission v Keeley*.

What is apparent from this chronicle is that the evidentiary provisions in the veterans' legislation are sacrosanct. Even when a government inquiry in 1994 recommended that the civil standard be substituted and the negative burden of proof on the Commission abandoned, the Parliament, faced with the probable backlash from veterans' groups, chose a less contentious route, the RMA scheme. The privileged position of its veterans' community was not to be eroded—at least in any overt fashion. **Toohey** provided the epitaph for this story in *Bushell* when he said: 'Most of the problems have arisen through attempts to provide a scheme for veterans which is beneficial but which, at the same time, excludes claims that are fanciful. This accommodation has proved most difficult where the aetiology of a disease is unknown or uncertain.'

ROBIN CREYKE

Further Reading

Catriona Cook and Robin Creyke, 'Repatriation Claims and the Burden of Proof of the Negative' (1984) 58 *ALJ* 263

Robin Creyke and Peter Sutherland, *Veterans' Entitlements Law* (2000)

Report of the Independent Enquiry into the Repatriation System (*Toose Report*) (1975) vol 1

Reports of the Veterans' Entitlements Act Monitoring Committee (1988) and *Government Response to the Veterans' Entitlements Act Monitoring Committee* (1988)

Vexatious litigants. It is evident from the original **High Court Rules** that the Justices did not anticipate that there would be a large number of vexatious litigants. It was not until 9 March 1943 that a specific Rule entitled 'Prevention of Vexatious Proceedings' was inserted.

This Rule had its genesis in events that began with the issue of a number of **writs** out of the Hobart District Registry in 1942 by one Angus Dean against Dr EJ Hanly. Hanly was the warden of the Tasman Council responsible for collecting rates in the Hobart area. Dean was later joined in his activities by Horace Benjafield. Dean and Benjafield were members of a group that believed there should be reform of the monetary system. They also contended that war expenditure could and should be met by the issue of the necessary funds by the Commonwealth Bank, and accordingly that war loans with their burden of interest were entirely unnecessary. Their activities led to a Board of Inquiry being established under the National Securities (Inquiries) Legislation.

The Court began to take their activities seriously when writs were issued against **Latham**, **Starke**, and **McTiernan**, and the litigants began writing privately to Starke. A draft of the proposed Rule was circulated by Starke. On 3 September 1942, Latham had a conversation with **Evatt**, who by then had become Commonwealth **Attorney-General**, at which he stated his reluctance to suggest any legislation, whether by statute or by Rule of Court, which would be regarded as designed to give some special protection to judges against proceedings directed against them. Evatt thought it might have a salutary effect if a Rule of Court were made empowering a Justice, if the Justice thought fit, to stay proceedings on a writ issued by a person who had failed to pay any **costs** incurred in litigation previously instituted by that person in the High Court. Starke and **Rich** did not support Evatt's proposal. Rich, commenting on the proposal, wrote: 'I think this cannot or should not be inserted. We are not a debt collecting agency. Action in the Bankruptcy Court is available.' The Justices had no such inhibition in signing the new proposed order. Curiously, neither Dean nor Benjafield was declared a vexatious litigant by the Court.

On 13 June 1952, Goldsmith Collins became the first person to be declared a vexatious litigant pursuant to an order made by **Williams**. This did not stop Collins' activities. He successfully argued that the lodging or giving notice of appeal was not instituting a 'proceeding' within the meaning of the order made by Williams. Collins, buoyed by his success, went too far when he issued a writ out of the Supreme Court of Victoria, the endorsement of which alleged that Williams and three other named persons had conspired against him. The Commonwealth Attorney-General obtained an order from **Taylor** committing Collins to Pentridge Prison for one month for **contempt**. Collins purged his contempt by apologising unreservedly to the Court and Williams. He subsequently served a number of terms of imprisonment for contempt of the Supreme Court of Victoria.

Constance May Bienvenu was the next person to be declared vexatious by the High Court on 19 August 1971. Bienvenu had taken the Victorian branch of the Royal Society for the Prevention of Cruelty to Animals (RSPCA) to court over its by-laws. She succeeded in the case but, in a curious decision, Starke awarded costs against her. The RSPCA bankrupted her in an attempt to obtain its costs. This action set in motion a trail of litigation that had her declared vexatious in the Supreme Court of Victoria. Bienvenu then turned her attention to the High Court. A writ was issued by Frank Jones, then Deputy Registrar at the Principal Registry, on the direction of **Barwick**, naming Jones and the Principal Registrar, Neil Gamble, as defendants. The alleged cause of action was that they had conspired to deny Bienvenu her constitutional rights by refusing to supply her free of charge with a copy of the Constitution. The matter was heard by way of demurrer before a **Full Court**, which dismissed the action. Bienvenu continued to issue proceedings, which ultimately led the Commonwealth Crown Solicitor to take the proceedings that led to her being declared a vexatious litigant.

The Court has an inherent power to restrict vexatious applications, but only in proceedings that are already before it. The High Court Rules provide two separate mechanisms for preventing the commencement of vexatious proceedings. First, if a person seeks to file a document that a Registrar considers to be, on its face, 'an abuse of the process of the Court or a frivolous or vexatious proceeding', the Registrar must seek a direction from a Justice. The Justice can direct that the process be issued (that is, that the document be accepted for filing), or that it not be issued without the leave of a Justice. Secondly, if the Court or a Justice is satisfied that a person 'frequently and without reasonable ground has instituted vexatious legal proceedings', it may order that the person not be allowed to institute any proceeding without leave. The first mechanism restricts the issuing only of the process that is the subject of the direction; the second restricts the person named in the order from having any process issued without leave.

These mechanisms are not lightly invoked. As **McHugh** explained in *Re Davison's Application* (1997), it is only in 'very clear cases' that Registrars approach Justices for directions or that Justices refuse leave to proceed. 'If, on the face of the "process", there is a possibility that it is not frivolous, vexatious or an abuse of the process of the Court, the matter will be left to be dealt with in accordance with the ordinary curial processes of the Court.'

Between 1996 and 1999, an average of only eight applications a year were made for leave to issue process after a direction had been made under the first mechanism. Such applications have usually been unsuccessful, but not always: in *Re Davison's Application (No 2)* (1997), **Gaudron** granted the applicant leave to issue a process that **Gummow** had earlier directed the Registrar not to issue without leave.

Orders under the second mechanism are rarer still. As **Toohey** explained in *Jones v Skyring* (1992), the power to make such orders reinforces the Court's power 'to protect its own process against unwarranted usurpation of its time and resources and to avoid the loss caused to those who have to face actions which lack any substance'. Because of the nature of such an order (restricting a person's access to the Court), it can be made only in limited circumstances: upon the application of the Commonwealth or a state Attorney-General or **Solicitor-General**, the Australian Government Solicitor, or the Principal Registrar of the Court.

An order made under the second mechanism in the High Court Rules is the only way the Court can restrict a particular person from commencing any action in the Court. In *Commonwealth Trading Bank v Inglis* (1974), the Court decided that, although it has an inherent power to exercise control over the making of unwarranted and vexatious applications in actions that are pending in the Court, it has no inherent jurisdiction to make an order 'impeding a particular person in the exercise of the right of access to the court'.

Importantly, as explained in *Jones v Skyring*, it is not relevant whether the person is acting maliciously or in bad faith. The question is not whether legal proceedings have been instituted vexatiously but whether the proceedings are in fact vexatious. A person who frequently, and without reasonable ground, institutes vexatious legal proceedings can be prohibited from instituting any further proceeding regardless of his or her motives. Strictly speaking, it is the proceedings, not the litigants, that are vexatious.

FRANK JONES
JAMES POPPLE

Victoria Park Racing v Taylor (1937). In this case, a majority of the Court refused to stop a radio station from broadcasting the results of horse races observed from a tower erected on the front lawn of a house across the road from the racecourse. In the process, the Court considered principles of nuisance, **copyright**, privacy, the nature of **property** rights, and the **role** of the Court in developing the **common law**.

The judgments reflect what **Dixon** referred to as a distinction between founding liability on the infliction of unjustified damage or on breach of a specific legal duty. **Rich** and **Evatt**, in separate **dissenting judgments**, relied on the former. While they each acknowledged that there was no general right to privacy in Australia, they argued that the general principles of the **tort** of nuisance encompassed what they considered to be the illegitimate interference with the rights of the property owner in this case. The rights of the property owner should include a right to profitable enjoyment, undiminished by the non-natural use of neighbouring land. Evatt adopted the language of the **United States Supreme Court** in *International News Service v Associated Press* (1918) to assert that in endeavouring 'to reap where it has not sown', the broadcasting company was doing more than merely looking over its neighbour's fence. Both Evatt and Rich decided that common law principles such as nuisance could adapt to changing social contexts to provide protection against the broadcaster's actions.

The other three members of the Court—Dixon, **Latham**, and **McTiernan**—each rejected the US position and refused to extend the notion of property to prevent the conduct in this case. Any copyright in the racing guide or the results of the race did not protect the information conveyed, but only the original manner in which that information was expressed. To be protected, any compilation of information required some originality beyond the mere presentation of facts. Thus, to draw on the information in the racing guide when describing the running of the races did not constitute an infringement of copyright. Nor was there any property in the spectacle of each race. These Justices emphasised that intellectual property does not protect all the intangible elements of value that flow from the use of ingenuity, knowledge, skill, or labour—an emphasis that has continued to determine the

Court's approach to extending the scope of intellectual property in cases such as *Moorgate Tobacco v Philip Morris (No 2)* (1984) and *Breen v Williams* (1996).

There was also no general right to privacy established by the common law. As Latham stated, the law could not be used to erect fences, nor, as he and the other members of the majority decided, could it be used to extend any existing fences. To establish nuisance required an interference with some right incident to the ownership or possession of land. While the categories of the tort of negligence were not closed, the basis of that cause of action required something more than mere competition that could affect the profits to be earned from the use of the land. The only effect in this case was on those people who listened to the broadcast and may as a consequence have decided not to attend the race. As there was no effect on the activities being conducted on the land, nor any interference with the comfort or enjoyment of those attending, there was no intrusion on the bundle of rights of the property owner recognised by the common law.

None of the Justices in the majority was therefore willing to create a new basis of liability reliant on generalisations cutting across existing categories. Perceived gaps in the common law could only be filled by the Court consistently with the principles established by those existing categories. This aspect of the case was referred to by **Gummow** in *Perre v Apand* (1999) in considering whether to expand recovery for negligence causing purely economic loss. It highlights the difficulty of a court shaking off the bounds of **precedent** and trying to establish for itself principles by which the common law may be expanded.

However, the case also illustrates a more fundamental conception of the role of the Court. By refusing to extend protection beyond the established rights of action, the majority helped to orient the Court towards protection of individual autonomy. It is for the Court to justify any interference with that autonomy. Notions of property and privacy may be used by the courts to protect the individual from government authority, but they would not be used to extend the reach of the court into the decisions of individuals beyond the restrictions firmly established by the common law.

DANIEL STEWART

Viro v The Queen (1978) is now generally regarded as an unsatisfactory attempt to clarify the effect of a plea of self-defence by a person accused of murder (see **Criminal defences**). But the case remains important as the High Court's declaration of independence from the **Privy Council**.

Frederick Viro was a heroin addict. He and his companions had an agreement to supply heroin to John Rellis, but decided to rob him. The party were travelling by car, with Rellis in the back seat and Viro in the front passenger seat, when Viro turned around and attacked Rellis with a jack handle in order to stun him. The car stopped. Rellis produced a knife and fought back. Viro took a steak knife from the glove box and stabbed Rellis repeatedly. One wound penetrated the heart. Viro was convicted of murder and the NSW Court of Criminal Appeal dismissed his appeal.

The High Court appeal was heard initially by **Gibbs**, **Stephen**, **Jacobs**, **Murphy**, and **Aickin**, all of whom ultimately allowed the appeal because the jury had not been directed on whether Viro was so affected by drugs as to be incapable of forming a criminal intent. However, another issue emerged that required reargument before a Full Bench of seven.

In *R v Howe* (1958), the **Dixon Court** had held that, if a person accused of murder was acting in self-defence but used excessive force, the charge of murder must be reduced to manslaughter, and that juries should be instructed accordingly. But in *Palmer v The Queen* (1971), the Privy Council disagreed. Thus the threshold question in *Viro* was whether the Court was bound to follow *Palmer*. The Court unanimously held that it was not so bound.

The *Privy Council (Appeals from the High Court) Act* 1975 (Cth) had effectively abolished appeals to the Privy Council from the High Court. For **Barwick**, the 'essential basis' of the doctrine of **precedent** was that a lower court must accept the rulings of a higher court that 'can correct' its decisions. Since the Privy Council could no longer 'correct' the High Court, its rulings were no longer binding. Gibbs (with **Mason's** concurrence) drew the same conclusion from reflection upon the Court's new status as 'an ultimate court of appeal, with the responsibility of deciding finally and conclusively every question that it is called upon to consider'. It followed, he said,

> that we should discharge that responsibility for ourselves, and that we should have the power and the duty to determine whether the decision of any other court, however eminent, should be followed in Australia … It is for this Court to assess the needs of Australian society and to expound and develop the law for Australia in the light of that assessment. It would be an impediment to the proper performance of that function, and inconsistent with the Court's new function, if we were bound to defer, without question, to … the Privy Council.

Stephen, too, spoke of the Court's 'assumption of the **role of a final court of appeal** and with it of the responsibility which that involves ultimately to determine for itself the true state of the law'. Aickin based his concurrence on the functional needs of the Court's new place in the **hierarchy of courts**, and Murphy on 'an orderly approach to precedent'. Jacobs argued that 'there is no longer a hierarchy', and accordingly that the previous view of precedent 'cannot be applied'.

In short, the whole Court agreed that it was no longer bound by Privy Council decisions. As authoritative pronouncements of the highest court in the precedent system, the existing Privy Council decisions would continue to be binding unless overruled, and only the highest court in the system had power to overrule them. But that was now the High Court. For the future, the only Privy Council decisions affecting Australia would be those on appeal from **state Supreme Courts**. To these, the High Court would show the courtesy due to a coordinate court, not the subservience due to a superior court.

There was less agreement on what should be done by a state Supreme Court faced with a conflict between High Court and Privy Council. Barwick insisted that the High Court's view must now always be preferred, since 'it is for this Court alone to decide whether its decision is correct'. Jacobs agreed on the basis that the 1975 Act had perfected the Australian hierarchy envisaged by section 73 of the Constitution. Gibbs, Mason, and Murphy gave more qualified answers, which in practice would usually have meant that, as between conflicting High Court and Privy Council decisions, whichever was more recent should prevail. Stephen and Aickin argued persuasively that the problem was an insoluble one—and it remained unsolved until the final abolition of appeals from state Supreme Courts to the Privy Council in 1986.

As to the immediate conflict concerning the law of self-defence, there was still less agreement. The issue was not only whether (as *Howe* had affirmed and *Palmer* had denied) a verdict of manslaughter, as a 'halfway house' between conviction of murder and outright acquittal, should be used when a plea of self-defence fails because the force used was disproportionate. There was also a question of 'subjective' and 'objective' standards: if the accused had an honest subjective belief in the need to resist attack and in the proportionality of the resistance, should those beliefs (or the prosecution's failure to disprove them beyond a reasonable doubt) entitle the accused to acquittal? Or should a conclusion that those beliefs were objectively unreasonable deprive the accused of that entitlement? On either view, why should a verdict of manslaughter be used as a halfway house? Through their own variations on these questions, Barwick and Gibbs preferred *Palmer* to *Howe*, and would therefore have treated the trial judge's direction in *Viro* as correct; while Jacobs (who favoured only a limited threshold requirement of objective '**reasonableness**') and Murphy (who favoured no such requirement at all) would also have treated the trial judge's direction as correct. On the other hand, Stephen, Mason, and Aickin expressed a clear preference for **Dixon's** analysis in *Howe*.

In this situation, Gibbs, Jacobs, and Murphy all subordinated their own opinions to a reaffirmation of *Howe*. Gibbs stated his reasons most fully:

> It seems to me that we would be failing in our function if we did not make it clear what principle commands the support of the majority of the Court. The task of judges presiding at criminal trials becomes almost impossible if they are left in doubt what this Court has decided on a question of **criminal law**. In the present case the view which appears to have more support

than any other is that we should accept as correct the statement of Dixon CJ in *Reg v Howe*. Contrary to my personal opinion, but in a desire to achieve a measure of certainty, I am prepared to agree.

Jacobs and Murphy made similar concessions. But Gibbs went further. Stephen and Aickin had specifically agreed not only with Mason's reasoning, but also with his suggestion of a six-point formula as the basis for directions to juries. Gibbs, unlike Jacobs and Murphy, agreed that this formula 'should be accepted as correct'.

The absence of doubt at trial level sought by these concessions proved elusive. In *Zecevic v DPP* (1987), Mason himself conceded that his six-point formula had 'rendered the jury's already difficult task even more complex', and 'imposes an onerous burden on trial judges and juries'. While protesting that the difficulties encountered by trial judges were 'not wholly to be accounted for by the complexity of the summary formulation at the end of my judgment', he joined **Wilson**, **Dawson**, and **Toohey** (in a **joint judgment**) and **Brennan** (in a **concurring judgment**) in returning to *Palmer v The Queen*. Only **Deane** and **Gaudron** sought to retain essential elements of *Viro*; and even Deane conceded that 'with the benefit of hindsight' its six-point formula was:

> open to legitimate **criticism** on two distinct grounds. The first is that … the formulation fails adequately to distinguish between factual considerations and legal principle. The result is unduly to complicate legal principle. This complication … is heightened by the synthesis of the constituents of a defence of self-defence and the operation of the onus of proof in relation to such a defence. The result … is an unavoidable use of negatives and one double negative which makes overall comprehension somewhat difficult even for a lawyer.

TONY BLACKSHIELD

Further Reading
Tony Blackshield, '*Viresne ex Virone Virent an Virus*? Some Thoughts on *Viro v R*' (1978) 2 *UNSWLJ* 277

W

Walsh, Cyril Ambrose (*b* 15 June 1909; *d* 29 November 1973; Justice 1969–73) was born in Sydney, the sixth child and fourth son of Michael John Walsh, labourer with the Water and Sewerage Board, and Mary Ellen, née Murphy. Despite humble family origins, at least three of those children achieved distinction in their chosen careers. Cyril grew up at Werrington, on the western outskirts of Sydney, where his father had acquired a small dairy farm.

The early indications of academic ability that Walsh manifested during his primary education at St Joseph's Convent School at St Mary's and his secondary education at Parramatta High School were more than fulfilled at the University of Sydney, where throughout his university studies Walsh was a resident at St John's College.

Cyril Walsh, Justice 1969–73

His undergraduate achievements have been neither equalled nor surpassed by any lawyer graduating from the University of Sydney. Graduating BA in 1930 with first-class honours and the University Medal in English, first-class honours and the University Medal in Philosophy, and first-class honours in Latin, he was awarded the James Coutts Scholarship for English. In 1934, he graduated LLB with first-class honours and the University Medal, and shared the John George Dalley Prize.

The award of first-class honours and the University Medal in Philosophy was a tribute no less to the outstanding scholarship and intellectual abilities of Walsh—a devout and loyal member of the Catholic Church throughout his life—than to the rigorous academic honesty of John Anderson, Challis Professor of Philosophy, whose reputation as a free-thinking materialist made him a controversial figure in the University of Sydney for more than 30 years.

Although never a lecturer at the University of Sydney Law School, Walsh maintained his academic interests throughout his life. Shortly after his graduation in law, he became an assistant editor of the *Australian Digest 1825–1933*. In 1950, he wrote (with RE Walker, Prothonotary of the Supreme Court of NSW) the annotated *Married Women's Property Act 1901 (NSW)*.

Walsh was admitted to the NSW Bar on 26 May 1934, and shortly thereafter acquired chambers on the fifth floor of Chalfont Chambers, where his colleagues included William Sheehan (a future NSW Attorney-General), **Barwick** (another product of humble origins who attained the greatest achievements in law and politics entirely through his own efforts, and whose career touched that of Walsh at a number of significant points), Hugh Maguire, John McKeon, Col Bowie, Eric Clegg, Gerald Donovan, and Joe Bannon (all of whom later attained judicial office).

Although he developed a substantial practice, especially in the **equity** jurisdiction, an innate diffidence and a reluctance for self-promotion prevented Walsh from attaining the public recognition his outstanding intellectual abilities and academic achievements more than justified. However, the *NSW State Reports* and the *NSW Weekly Notes* throughout the 1940s and early 1950s frequently record his appearances in reported cases in the Supreme Court of NSW, especially in equity proceedings before the then Chief Judge in Equity, David Roper. Throughout that period, Walsh also appeared as **counsel** before the High Court in ten matters reported in the *Commonwealth Law Reports*. Those cases were mainly, but not exclusively, appeals from decisions of the Supreme Court of NSW in its equity jurisdiction. In subject matter, they included will construction, company law, death duty, specific performance of a **contract**, extension of a **patent**, and liability for injury to a seaman.

That his professional competence entitled him to judicial office was never doubted by his colleagues at the Bar. In January 1954, he was appointed a judge of the Supreme Court of NSW, at the relatively young age of 44, and not having been a QC. Yet it may be queried whether, had it not been for the fortunate concordance of the former leader of his chambers, William Sheahan, being Attorney-General of NSW, and one of Walsh's older brothers, Louis Andrew Walsh, being a member of the state Parliament in the party then in government, his appointment to the Bench would have occurred as early in his career as it did. Neither then, however, nor upon his elevation to the High Court (by a federal government of a different political complexion), was there the slightest hint that the appointment had any political flavour. Indeed, Walsh's own political views were never divulged.

His appointment to the Supreme Court more than fulfilled the high expectations of the legal profession, by which it had been acclaimed. As a trial judge, Walsh was outstanding. He was courteous, patient, and fair. His judgments and charges to juries were models of lucidity. He had the dubious distinction of being the last judge in NSW to pronounce the death sentence.

When a separate Commercial Causes List was established in 1958, Walsh was appointed the judge in charge of that list. Among the many cases of commercial significance he heard in that capacity was *The Wagon Mound (No 2)* (1963). From that decision, an appeal was taken directly to the Judicial Committee of the **Privy Council**. In the course of delivering the decision of the Board in 1966, Lord Reid said:

Their Lordships are indebted to that learned Judge [Walsh] for the full and careful survey of the evidence which is set out in his judgment. Few of his findings of fact have been attacked, and their Lordships do not find it necessary to set out or deal with the evidence at any length.

Upon the establishment of a Court of Appeal in NSW on 1 January 1966, Walsh was one of the original appointees as a Judge of Appeal. His membership greatly enhanced the reputation and prestige of that court (the first such appellate court to be established in Australia). Previously, he had very often sat upon the hearing of appeals to the Full Court of the Supreme Court. The Court of Appeal and the Full Court gave him further scope for the exercise of his outstanding judicial capacity.

Walsh remained a Judge of Appeal until his **appointment** to the High Court on 3 October 1969 (filling the vacancy occasioned by the death of **Taylor**). On 29 September 1969, he was appointed a KBE, and on 1 January 1971, a Privy Counsellor. His appointment to the highest court of the nation and the honours he then received were a fitting recognition of his overwhelming capacity as one of the greatest appellate judges of his generation.

With the transition to the High Court, Walsh assumed new and, in some respects, different judicial responsibilities, especially in the field of **constitutional law**. Among the significant cases in which he participated in his tragically short period on the High Court were *Ward v Williams* (1969) on the freedom of **interstate trade and commerce**, in which Walsh delivered the leading judgment; the *Payroll Tax Case* (1971), in which the Commonwealth payroll tax was held to be valid in its application to the states; *Strickland v Rocla Concrete Pipes* (1971) on the constitutional foundation for modern **trade practices law**; and *SOS (Mowbray) v Mead* (1972) on the freedom of interstate trade and commerce.

Of his abilities as an appellate judge, both in the High Court and in the Supreme Court, Barwick later said of him:

In **argument** he was patient, courteous and painstaking, ever anxious to understand the submissions of counsel, ever alert to see that all aspects of the problem in hand received attention. His judgments betray the intense and unremitting research into the subject matter which he always undertook and the calm, penetrating and dispassionate consideration from which his decision resulted. He was completely independent of mind. He understood and spoke of the task of deciding 'as one for which one is personally responsible and as an anxious and lonely one'.

From his undergraduate days, Walsh maintained a close and active connection with St John's College within the University of Sydney. He lived there throughout his seven years as a student, from his arrival at the university in 1927. He participated in such college activities as debating and football. His manifest abilities and his capacity for conscientious service, as well as his popularity with his fellow students, were recognised in his election as secretary, and later president, of the students' club of the College. He won various prizes and scholarships during his undergraduate courses, and these were of considerable assistance financially. On 3 May 1955, he became a Fellow of the Council of the College—a position he held until his death 18 years later. He was the deputy chairman of the Council for the years 1969 and 1972. In the late 1960s, he was responsible for the rewriting of the by-laws of the College. His portrait hangs in the College.

In 1962, while a judge of the Supreme Court of NSW, Walsh was appointed (upon the recommendation of the then Australian Foreign Minister, Barwick) to represent Australia at the meeting in Bangkok of the Working Party of the UN Economic Commission for Asia and the Far East on the subject of international commercial arbitration.

Before the establishment of the NSW Law Reform Commission, Walsh was a member of its predecessor, the Chief Justice's Law Reform Committee. He was conscious of the need for changes in the law, both procedural and substantive, but always so that the law retained its coherence as a legal system upon the foundations of which human relations, personal and commercial, could reliably be formed and conducted.

A foundation member of the St Thomas More Society in 1945, Walsh was actively involved in that organisation for the remainder of his life, holding various offices on its Council, including that of president from 1955 to 1958 and from 1962 to 1964.

Walsh died in office on 29 November 1973, at the relatively early age of 64, from multiple myeloma. He was survived by Lady (Mary Agnes) Walsh, née Smyth, whom he had married at St Joseph's Catholic Church, Burwood Heights, on 28 November 1942, and their three sons. At the time of his death, he and Lady Walsh were living at Mosman, but for most of their married life they resided in Prospect Road, Summer Hill.

Upon his death, a special sitting of the High Court was held on 30 November 1973, at which the eulogy was delivered by **Chief Justice** Barwick, whose admiration of Walsh as a lawyer and as a judge was without bounds. Of Walsh he said: 'He had not reached his zenith. The Court has lost a Justice from whom increasingly distinguished service was confidently expected.'

Although by nature gentle and unassuming, Walsh greatly enjoyed social occasions with friends and colleagues (especially at the University Club in Phillip Street, Sydney, after court had adjourned for the day). He derived the utmost pleasure from a close-knit family life and from the professional and academic achievements of his three sons, of whom he was intensely proud. It was Walsh who happily assumed the role of barbecue chef at family gatherings and who played the piano at parties. His Irish ancestry was apparent in his tall and lanky frame (six feet, three inches (190 cm) in height), broad and lofty forehead, dark hair, and hazel eyes. As a result of an early injury to his right forefinger, Walsh became ambidextrous.

It was a tragedy for the administration of justice in Australia that Walsh occupied his position as a member of the highest court in the land for only four years, and died long before his potential as an outstanding constitutionalist had been fulfilled.

JOHN KENNEDY MCLAUGHLIN

Waltons Stores v Maher (1988) is a prominent example of the **Mason Court's** willingness to extend to new situations the principles of **equity** affecting dealings between individuals. The Court abandoned restrictions on the availability of promissory **estoppel**, and thus expanded the range of situations in which individuals must take responsibility for harm caused by their inconsistent conduct.

Waltons Stores had negotiated to lease land from Terrence and Patricia Maher on terms that required the Mahers to demolish a building on their land and construct a new one to Waltons' specifications. Time was short, and the terms of the lease needed to be finalised quickly so the Mahers could begin construction. When negotiations were essentially complete, Waltons' solicitors sent the lease to the Mahers' solicitors for signing, undertaking to inform them the following day if any of the final amendments requested by the Mahers were not acceptable to Waltons. The Mahers signed the lease and returned it to Waltons' solicitors, expecting that it would be signed by Waltons. Waltons delayed signing pending a review of its retailing strategy, knowing that the Mahers had commenced the demolition and construction work. When construction of the new building was well underway, Waltons informed the Mahers that they did not intend to proceed with the lease.

No **contract** existed between the parties because Waltons had not executed the lease. **Deane** and **Gaudron** found that the Mahers had acted on the assumption that a binding agreement for lease had been made. This was an assumption of existing fact which, when relied upon, established an estoppel *in pais* (**common law** estoppel). The effect of that estoppel was to prevent Waltons from denying that they had signed the lease. **Mason**, **Wilson**, and **Brennan** had a different analysis: they found that the Mahers had acted on the assumption that Waltons would complete the transaction. This was an assumption as to Waltons' future conduct, which could give rise only to a promissory estoppel.

In England, there had been—and remains—a reluctance to allow promissory estoppel to be used for the positive enforcement of a representation that a person would do something in the future. This reluctance arises out of a fear that a broadly applicable doctrine of promissory estoppel would undermine the law of contract by making promises enforceable whenever they are relied upon. Accordingly, before *Waltons Stores*, it was thought that a promissory estoppel could arise only where the parties were in a pre-existing legal relationship—and even then, that it could operate only as a defence, preventing the enforcement of rights that the plaintiff had promised not to enforce. In the USA, on the other hand, the principle of promissory estoppel operates as an independent source of rights arising from the making of a promise which the promisor could reasonably expect to induce reliance, and which does in fact induce reliance by the promisee.

Mason and Wilson held that a promissory estoppel could arise between parties involved in precontractual negotiations, and could be used to support a cause of action in contract. Here, they said, Waltons' inaction encouraged the Mahers to continue to act on the assumption that the completion of the transaction was merely a formality. It was **unconscionable** for Waltons to act as it did, and Waltons was estopped from retreating from its implied promise to complete the contract. While Mason and Wilson attempted to chart a middle course between the English and American approaches, Brennan recognised that promissory estoppel could operate as an independent source of rights. He found that Waltons' unconscionable conduct raised an equity in favour of the Mahers, which the Court had to satisfy by granting appropriate relief. The appropriate relief was to treat Waltons as though it had signed and exchanged the lease.

The decision in *Waltons Stores* was an important development in Australian law because it involved a significant departure from the classical idea that a promise creates a legal obligation only when consideration has been given in return for the promise and a contract has been formed. The decision greatly expanded the range of situations in which liability can result from reliance on non-contractual promises. That liability arises from the notion that it is unconscionable to refuse to perform a promise which the promisee has acted upon in such a way as to suffer detriment if the promise is not fulfilled. The Court expanded the scope of the relevant equitable principle to provide more consistent protection against the harmful consequences of this type of unconscionable conduct.

ANDREW ROBERTSON

War Crimes Act Case (1991). In the *War Crimes Act Case* (*Polyukhovich v Commonwealth* (1991)), the High Court decided by a narrow majority that the *War Crimes Amendment Act* 1988 (Cth) was valid. The decision paved the way for three prosecutions in the 1990s relating to atrocities that had occurred in Europe during **World War II**. Evidentiary problems were a significant barrier, and none of the prosecutions succeeded. In the end, the Special Investigations Unit established to investigate alleged Nazi war criminals in Australia was wound up, leaving lingering doubts about Australia's willingness to prosecute such crimes. However, the *War Crimes Act Case* is interesting for what it says about the relevance of international legal principles to Australia's jurisdictional competence, the protection afforded by the Australian Constitution to international human rights, and the High Court's **role** in scrutinising action by the legislature on both these counts.

Facing trial under the Act for war crimes allegedly committed in the Ukraine in 1942–43, Ivan Polyukhovich argued that the legislation was invalid, lacking any sufficient connection with either Australian **defence** or Australian **external affairs** (respectively under section 51(vi) and (xxix) of the Constitution). His challenge was based on the fact that the legislation did not introduce the international legal concept of war crimes as such into Australian law. Rather, the legislation sought to extend the reach of Australian **criminal law** applicable during World War II to include acts committed in Europe by persons who were then non-nationals but presently resident in Australia. When the case was first argued in September 1990, **Brennan** and **Deane** expressed particular concern at the idea that a criminal law should operate in this selective and retrospective way, and accordingly the case was reargued in November.

The challenge was unsuccessful. Apart from Brennan, who concluded that the legislation was *not* within power, the Court held that it was valid as a law with respect to external affairs simply because it concerned matters geographically external to Australia. The decision highlights the paramountcy of the legislature's role in shaping the interplay between **international law** and Australian law.

Since Brennan did not accept mere geographical externality as a sufficient basis for legislation with respect to 'external affairs', he alone gave any detailed consideration to the alternative argument based on 'defence'. The strongest version of that argument was that, by helping to establish an effective international regime against war crimes, the legislation might give stronger protection to Australian men and women who might have to fight in future wars. Brennan rejected this argument because 'respect for the laws and customs of war cannot be secured by a law having such an oppressive and discriminatory operation'. For similar reasons, it was only Brennan who gave detailed consideration to a number of alternative arguments for regarding the legislation as a valid exercise of the external affairs power. For example, international law permits universal jurisdiction in relation to war crimes: any state may try a war criminal regardless of the nationality of the accused or the fact that the crime was committed outside state territory, and a prosecution for war crimes by Australian authorities might plausibly have been justified as an assertion of this jurisdiction.

But universal jurisdiction is available only for international crimes such as war crimes, crimes against humanity, or genocide—and only to the extent that they are defined according to international law. In the case of other offences or other definitions, the international community may view a state's assertion of jurisdiction as exorbitant in the absence of a real link between the state and the offender or the crime. Except for Brennan and **Toohey**, the Court gave little, if any, weight to these issues.

It was also only Brennan and Toohey who held that matters geographically external to Australia must have some demonstrable link with Australia in order for legislation on those matters to come within the external affairs power. (**Gaudron** also discussed the necessity of a link, but thought the existence of legislation was sufficient to show the necessary interest or concern on the part of Australia. Toohey thought the link was established simply by the fact that Australia had been a belligerent in World War II.) Subsequently, in a unanimous ruling in *Horta v Commonwealth* (1994), the Court held that legislation implementing the Timor Gap Treaty could not be challenged on the basis of the invalidity of the treaty at international law: whether or not the treaty was valid, the fact that the legislation related to matters geographically external to Australia was sufficient for its **characterisation** as a law with respect to external affairs.

The retrospectivity issue provoked a range of responses from the Bench. Since Australia does not have a constitutional **Bill of Rights** that spells out a prohibition on retrospective criminal punishment, nor a constitutional provision for the general applicability within Australia of treaty provisions on the subject (such as those in the **International Bill of Rights**), the argument was framed in terms of the **separation of powers**. **Counsel** for Polyukhovich argued that imposition of retrospective criminal punishment would undermine **judicial power**:

> Parliament cannot require a court to act in a way which betrays the judicial power of the Commonwealth. There is no proper investiture of judicial power where a court is required to deal with matters which involve inevitable unfairness … What is invested is then something less than judicial power … The retroactive operation of the Act is obnoxious to Ch III which guarantees a fair trial of offences against Commonwealth law.

Three Justices—**Mason**, **Dawson**, and **McHugh**—held that since the judiciary would still be responsible for determining guilt, there was no breach of the separation of powers. They rejected the suggestion that the Constitution imports any general prohibition on retrospective laws. (They agreed, however, that the Constitution would not permit a Bill of Attainder, by which the legislature itself would convict and sentence a named individual.) On this issue, **Deane** and Gaudron dissented: as Deane put it, judicial power under Chapter III of the Constitution must be exercised by courts 'acting as courts with all that that notion essentially requires', and it is 'basic to our penal jurisprudence that a person who has disobeyed no relevant law is not guilty of a crime'.

With Deane and Gaudron holding the legislation invalid on the retrospectivity ground, and Brennan holding it invalid on the ground that it was not within power, the balance was tipped in favour of its validity by Toohey's judgment. He found that, at least in the context of the Polyukhovich prosecution, the legislation was not retroactive in any troublesome sense, because the offences with which Polyukhovich was charged had in any event been universally outlawed by national criminal codes.

If international law had been not simply the stimulus but the basis for the War Crimes Amendment Act, it would have been easier to rebut the allegations of retrospectivity in the *War Crimes Act Case* on the basis of the Nuremberg precedent. The Nuremberg Tribunal had dismissed similar arguments concerning retrospectivity about 40 years earlier. The legislation itself, and the Court's generous approach to the geographic limb of the external affairs power, are testimony to the dualist approach to the relationship between international and domestic law that prevails in Australia.

Moreover, as the Court's ruling on the retrospectivity issue demonstrates, municipal Australian law gives only limited protection to rights protected by international law. In some contexts, the Court itself has been prepared to use international law indirectly to further the protection of human rights: at the least, the Court attempts to construe legislation in conformity with international law. The impressive familiarity with international law of some members of the Court is evident in many cases, including the *War Crimes Act Case*. However, while the purpose of the War Crimes Amendment Act itself is to punish human rights violations, the literal interpretation of legislative power in relation to external affairs supports an outmoded conception of the state as an insular entity possessing unlimited **sovereignty**. This conception of the state ignores the existence of international law, and is directly opposed to the conception of human rights as a constraint on and a source of obligation for the legislature.

Of course, the High Court is constrained by the Constitution. But a committed internationalist cannot help but question whether there are untapped links between the external affairs power and international law that would give the Court a greater role in scrutinising legislative power. Does the Court's interpretive approach constrain its own power, becoming a self-fulfilling prophecy?

PENELOPE MATHEW

Further Reading

Russell Blackford, 'Judicial Power, Political Liberty and the Post-industrial State' (1997) 71 *ALJ* 267

Irene Nemes, 'Punishing Nazi War Criminals in Australia: Issues of Law and Morality' (1992) 4 *CICJ* 141

James Thomson, 'Is it a Mess? The High Court and the War Crimes Case: External Affairs, Defence, Judicial Power and the Australian Constitution' (1992) 22 *UWAL Rev* 197

Gillian Triggs, 'Australia's War Crimes Trials: All Pity Choked' in Gerry Simpson and Timothy McCormack, *The Law of War Crimes: National and International Approaches* (1997) 123

Webb, William Flood (*b* 21 January 1887; *d* 11 August 1972; Justice 1946–58). To participate in public affairs is to attract attention and inevitable criticism. Webb's career provides no exception to this general rule. Although he served as a Justice of the High Court from 16 May 1946 to 11 August 1958, his

William Webb, Justice 1946–58, pictured as a judge of the Supreme Court of Queensland

many other public roles must have been a source of great—perhaps even greater—interest to him.

Webb was born in Brisbane in 1887 during an event to which he owes one of his given names—a flood that had recently inundated a large part of the city. The son of an Anglican father and a Roman Catholic mother, who both died when Webb was young, he was raised by relatives in circumstances of great poverty and educated at a number of small parochial Catholic schools.

In the early years of the twentieth century, the public service offered an opportunity for ambitious and impoverished young men to enter a profession that might otherwise be unavailable to them. In 1904, at the age of 17, Webb became a public servant, initially working for the Commissioner of Police and then in the Crown Solicitor's Office. He studied while working, and qualified for the Queensland Bar in 1913. Two years later, he was selected as Official Solicitor to the Public Curator of Queensland. In 1916, he became Public Defender—at that time, a unique office for Australia—and the following year, at the age of 30, he became Crown Solicitor for the state. He remained in that office until 1922, when he was appointed as Queensland's first **Solicitor-General**.

Webb's comparatively young age at the time of his various appointments attracted attention. He was unfairly accused of conniving with the government of the day to obtain exemption from army service during **World War I**. The truth was that he suffered from a permanent back injury disqualifying him from military service.

One of his most interesting duties as Crown Solicitor was the preparation of the government case in defence of the appointment of Thomas McCawley in October 1917 as a judge of the Supreme Court of Queensland, nine months after McCawley's appointment as President of Queensland's new Industrial Court. Throughout the long litigation that followed, it was assumed that the Supreme Court appointment was unconstitutional, because the Industrial Court appointment was only for a seven-year term. In the Supreme Court of Queensland (in *Re McCawley* (1918)) and the High Court (*McCawley v The King* (1918)), the government's defence of the appointment failed; but in the **Privy Council** (*McCawley v The King* (1920)), it succeeded. Even though the appointment did not comply with the **state Constitution**, their Lordships held that it was valid because the Queensland Parliament had unlimited power expressly or impliedly to amend its own Constitution.

Over the next two decades, Webb's career successes continued. He was elevated to the Supreme Court of Queensland on 24 April 1925, and simultaneously appointed President of the Industrial Court (McCawley's term having expired). On 26 November 1926, he was also appointed as chairman of the Central Sugar Cane Prices Board, a position he was to occupy for the next 16 years. It is easy now to overlook the historical importance of the sugar industry to Queensland. The chairmanship of the Board was traditionally regarded as an appropriate position for a Supreme Court Judge, and a sign of great executive confidence. In addition, Webb was a Royal Commissioner on three occasions—inquiring into the railway disaster at Traveston in 1925, transport in Queensland in 1936, and the sugar industry in 1938.

In May 1940, Webb succeeded Hugh Macrossan as Chief Justice of Queensland, and in 1942 the state Labor government, contrary to its long-standing policy, recommended him for a knighthood. In the same year, the Commonwealth government established an Australian Industrial Relations Council, composed of representatives of industry and labour and intended to further the Australian war effort through a harmonious and fruitful partnership between employers and employees. Webb was appointed as its chairman.

In 1943, the Commonwealth appointed Webb as a commissioner to investigate allegations of atrocities by Japanese soldiers and breaches of the rules of warfare. He gathered evidence from soldiers, many still on active service. Then, in 1944, reportedly on his own recommendation, his term as commissioner was extended and the ambit of his commission widened in 1945 to cover any matter within the charter of the UN War Crimes Commission. Later that year, he visited England to appear before the UN Commission, and subsequently served on the Committee drafting instructions for UK commanders on the conduct of war crimes trials. In the same year, at the age of 58, he was appointed as Communications Censorship Commissioner, and became a member of the Senate of the University of Queensland.

In early 1946, Webb was appointed as President of the International Military Tribunal for the Far East, sitting in Tokyo to try Japanese war criminals including General Hideki Tojo. A few months later, at the instance of Australia's wartime Foreign Minister, **Evatt**, Webb was appointed to the High Court. According to Bruce McPherson, Evatt was 'keen to maintain a high profile for Australia in the international sphere', though it has been suggested that at least in part the **appointment** was intended 'to dissuade him from returning to Queensland to devote himself to his duties as Chief Justice' (see also **Appointments that might have been**).

Webb's obligations as a member of the High Court conflicted with the sittings of the War Crimes Tribunal, and initially he was unable to perform his duties as a Justice. In November 1947, he briefly returned to Australia as a result of intervention from **Prime Minister** Ben Chifley and Evatt, who were anxious that there not be a **tied vote** in important constitutional cases in a court of six. Initially, their request for Webb's return was resisted by General Douglas MacArthur, who insisted that Webb's absence at that stage of the Tribunal's proceedings 'would amount to an international calamity' and 'demoralize the entire proceedings'. But Chifley and Evatt were insistent. As it turned out, Webb sat only in *Nelungaloo v Commonwealth* (1948)—a case concerning compensation on two different bases for the compulsory acquisition of a wheat harvest (see *Inter se* **questions**). Ironically, in a Court of six (since **Williams** had sat at first instance), Webb's participation produced a tied vote, so that Williams' decision to award compensation on the more limited basis was upheld. If Webb had not sat, the plaintiff's appeal would have succeeded.

After the *Nelungaloo* hearing, Webb returned to Tokyo and resumed his duties as President of the International Military Tribunal. His work there did not end until late 1948. When the final judgments of the Tribunal were drafted, Webb was among those who differed from the majority. In the end, in a separate statement stopping short of formal dissent, he adhered to his strongly held view that the execution of those found guilty was an excessive punishment, especially in view of the Allies' refusal to implicate the Emperor.

Graham Fricke has suggested, unkindly and not entirely fairly, that although up to this point in his career Webb had 'amassed a plenitude of distinctions', culminating in a KBE in 1954, his ten years on the High Court from 1949 onwards were 'a period of personal decrescendo' (see also **Dixon diaries**). In October 1949, as the most junior **puisne Justice**, he played a critical role in the *Whose Baby Case* (1949)—a protracted dispute over the parentage and custody of a four-year-old girl. The other Justices divided 2:2 (Chief Justice **Latham** and **McTiernan** for the Morrison family; **Rich** and **Dixon** for the Jenkins family), leaving the outcome to be determined by Webb. In a judgment described as characteristically 'straight to the point', he decided in favour of the Jenkins family. **Barwick** then took the Morrisons' case to the Privy Council; but (with **Taylor** representing the Jenkins family) the Morrisons were denied special leave to appeal.

Like other members of the **Dixon Court**, especially in the great cases of the 1950s on freedom of **interstate trade**, Webb frequently agreed with Dixon, sometimes in brief separate judgments, as in *Hospital Provident Fund v Victoria* (1953) and *Hughes & Vale v NSW (No 1)* (1953). At other times, he simply joined in Dixon's judgment, as in *Hughes & Vale v NSW (No 2)* (1955), *Grannall v Marrickville Margarine* (1955), and *R v Richards; Ex parte Fitzpatrick and Browne* (1955).

In the *Boilermakers Case* (1956), however, he dissented, primarily on the basis of a strong view of parliamentary **sovereignty** (and hence of minimal constitutional restraints) that may have reflected his earlier experience in *McCawley's Case*—since he heavily relied, as the Privy Council had done in *McCawley*, on the older Privy Council expositions of colonial legislative power in *R v Burah* (1878), *Hodge v The Queen* (1883), and *Powell v Apollo Candle Co* (1885). He added that, in any event, the long-standing assumptions that the majority was overturning 'should be allowed to stand'; and predicted that if the majority view prevailed, it could readily be circumvented by the *personae designatae* device. In fact, that device was only to emerge as a significant exception to the *Boilermakers* doctrine in the 1980s (see *Hilton v Wells* (1985); **Judicial power**).

His professional career was interesting and sometimes controversial. There were some who criticised his acceptance of office in the wartime Australian Industrial Relations Council on grounds of its apparent incompatibility with the holding of judicial office. It was also suggested that, having investigated Japanese atrocities during wartime, he should not thereafter have presided over the Tribunal by which Japanese war criminals were tried. The Tribunal itself has also been criticised, not least because it was constituted exclusively by appointees from the victorious belligerent nations, with none from neutral countries. Much remains to be written and explained about the activities of the Tribunal, which has never received the same attention as the Nuremburg War Crimes Tribunal. While Webb, in his role as President, was sometimes accused of brusqueness, his conscientiousness was never doubted.

In his history of the Supreme Court of Queensland, McPherson suggests that in some respects, Webb's career was the result of a happy combination of timing, opportunity, good fortune, and a proven ability to persuade colleagues to work together in harmony. Yet this criticism, like that of his work in Tokyo, does less than justice to him. In retrospect, his professional life can be seen as a remarkable record of public service in many areas, during war times, hard times, and good times. No person without formidable abilities could have occupied so many offices and performed so many different tasks as did Webb during his long public life.

Malcolm Morris, in his account of the War Crimes Tribunal in his book *The Wise Bamboo* (1954), described Webb as 'a quiet, soft-spoken, amiable man to meet socially', but added that 'when presiding over the Court he could be a terror. When he let an attorney know that he was out of line, he did it in a way that the man did not wilt, he withered'. One of the defendants, Kenryo Sato, recalled Webb as 'an imposing figure with a brilliant mind, a man of strong will who did not want to be a loser'. Dayle Smith portrays him as conservative by nature, 'courteous and compassionate on occasions'. Barwick remembered him as 'equable and friendly, thoughtful and generous in his attitudes'. His commitment and courage are put beyond doubt by his final statement in the War Crimes Tribunal, in which he took the independent and unpopular view that no Japanese should be sentenced to death for conspiring to wage war, or for planning, preparing, initiating, or waging aggressive war.

Webb married Beatrice Agnew in 1917. He survived his wife, who died in 1970. There were six children of the marriage: two sons and four daughters. He retired from the High Court in 1958, two months before Williams. Thereafter, he

and his wife lived in Coorparoo, Brisbane. From 1958, he served as chairman of the Electric Power Transmission Corporation in Queensland. In 1960, and again in 1963, he was appointed chairman of a committee of inquiry into Queensland parliamentary salaries. His long and varied life ended in 1972, at the age of 85.

IAN CALLINAN

Further Reading
Arnold Brackman, *The Other Nuremberg* (1989)
Colin Duck and Martin Thomas, *Whose Baby?* (1984)
BH McPherson, *The Supreme Court of Queensland 1859–1960* (1989)
Dayle Smith, *MacArthur's Kangaroo Court* (2000)

Whitlam era (2 December 1972 to 11 November 1975). In the 1940s, the acts and actions of the Curtin and Chifley Labor governments were successfully challenged in many cases before the **Latham Court**. When the Australian Labor Party, led by me, next won government in 1972 and 1974, I was determined that my governments should anticipate challenges in the High Court. I consulted with Attorneys-General **Murphy** and Kep Enderby, **Solicitors-General** RJ Ellicott and Maurice Byers, Secretary of the Attorney-General's Department Clarrie Harders, and First Parliamentary Counsel Charles Comans, before any legislation was introduced or other action was taken which, in the view of any of us, might come before the courts. This was the basis of the exceptional success of my governments in the High Court. No governments have had so many of their acts and actions challenged during and after their terms of office. No other governments have had so many of their acts and actions upheld. Only the *Petroleum and Mineral Authority Act* 1973 (Cth) was struck down, and then for procedural reasons rather than for a lack of power.

My government took prompt steps to raise the status of the High Court. During the Commonwealth Law Ministers Conference in London in January 1973, Murphy raised the abolition of appeals to the **Privy Council**. On 24 April, I discussed it with Prime Minister Edward Heath, the Lord Chancellor Lord Hailsham, and Attorney-General Peter Rawlinson. On 31 May, I introduced the Privy Council Appeals Abolition Bill to abolish all remaining rights of appeal.

On 9 May 1973, Australia and NZ had lodged applications in the International Court of Justice at The Hague requesting interim measures to restrain France from further atmospheric nuclear tests in the Pacific. On 10 May, I announced that after consultation with NZ, **Barwick** had been appointed as an ad hoc judge for the hearing of the case. Australia was represented by Murphy, Ellicott, and Byers. On 22 June, the Court made an order for interim measures to restrain France.

On 31 May, the Coalition government of Queensland and the Labor government of Tasmania had lodged petitions at the office of the Privy Council in London concerning the Seas and Submerged Lands Bill that my government had introduced on 10 May 1973. The petition asked the Queen to refer the matter to the Privy Council under the *Judicial Committee Act* 1833 (Imp) on the ground that it was a territorial dispute between British colonies. I wrote to Heath. When the Queen opened the Parliament on 28 February 1974 she said:

Gough Whitlam, Prime Minister 1972–75

I have decided not to refer to the Privy Council petitions addressed to me by the State of Queensland and the State of Tasmania concerning rights to the seabed. My Australian and United Kingdom ministers were agreed that the High Court of Australia is the appropriate tribunal to determine the issues raised in the petitions.

In Sydney on 6 September 1973, during the first session of the Australian Constitutional Convention, Barwick took me in his car to introduce me to his mother in her flat in Macleay Street. He wanted to discuss the future of the High Court. He wished to be reassured that my government would proceed with the abolition of appeals to the Privy Council, the construction of the High Court **building** in **Canberra**, and the establishment of a **superior court**. I reassured him on all counts. On 8 October, he and I announced that the architects who were designing the National Gallery had won the competition to design the High Court (see **Architecture of Court building**; **Madigan**).

Of the six **puisne Justices** of the **Barwick Court**, **McTiernan** had been appointed by the Scullin government, Douglas **Menzies** by the Menzies government, **Walsh** and **Gibbs** by the Gorton government, and **Stephen** and **Mason** by the McMahon government. Walsh died on 29 November 1973.

In the House of Representatives, as early as June 1955, I had recalled the irresponsible conduct of the two oldest Justices, **Rich** and **Starke**, in the *BMA Case* (1949). Starke sat throughout the hearing on 10–12 August 1949, but then, learning that a solid majority of his brethren would find against the government, took leave and did not write a judgment; he resigned on 31 January 1950, a month before his

seventy-ninth birthday. Rich delivered his judgment with his brethren on 7 October 1949 and then took leave. The delayed resignations (now made impossible by the introduction of a retiring age for federal judges following the 1977 referendum to amend the Constitution) deprived the Chifley government of the opportunity to appoint their replacements. The **Menzies** government appointed **Fullagar** on 8 February and **Kitto** on 10 May 1950.

On my visit on 6 September 1973, Barwick had given me a list of NSW and Victorian barristers whom he thought worthy of consideration for **appointment** to the High Court, the Commonwealth Industrial Court, and the Northern Territory and ACT Supreme Courts. He expressly advised me against appointing judges from the **state Supreme Courts** to the High Court: 'It has taken me four years to train Cyril.' There was no discussion. After Walsh's unexpected death, a Labor government had to make an appointment to the High Court for the first time in more than 27 years. In 1945, during Attorney-General **Evatt's** absence overseas, the Chifley government had decided to enlarge the High Court and appoint three new Justices. On his return, Evatt (with great difficulty) persuaded his colleagues to make only one appointment (**Webb**)—albeit an inadequate one (see also **Appointments that might have been**). I was determined that Labor would not again squander an opportunity.

Murphy proposed to me that Professor Colin Howard of the University of Melbourne should be appointed. I told him that Australians were not yet prepared for an academic lawyer to be appointed to the High Court. We agreed to appoint **Jacobs**, who, like Walsh, had been an initial member of the NSW Court of Appeal. He was now its President. He had to take his place on the Court when it sat in February 1974. Because I had to be overseas from mid-January, I telephoned Barwick well ahead. He let me know clearly that he was not at all pleased. On 23 January, Paul Hasluck signed Jacobs' commission and Murphy announced his appointment.

I had proposed a federal circuit court in a lecture at the University of Melbourne in July 1957. I developed the idea on two occasions in the House, and at the Eleventh Australian Legal Convention in 1959. At the Thirteenth Convention in 1963, it was announced that the Menzies government had authorised Barwick to design a new federal superior court. In December 1973, in response to Barwick's 6 September 1973 agenda, Murphy reintroduced the Superior Court of Australia Bill. It lapsed when Parliament was prorogued on the occasion of the Queen's visit in February 1974. Murphy introduced the Bill in March, but the Senate rejected it on party lines in April.

Six other Bills that had been passed by the House of Representatives were twice rejected by the Senate. Governor-General Hasluck accepted my advice to dissolve both Houses and to hold elections on 18 May 1974.

The International Court of Justice heard the *Nuclear Tests Case* over ten days in July 1974. Ellicott having been elected as a Liberal member of the House of Representatives, Australia was represented by Murphy and Byers.

The new Parliament assembled on 9 July 1974. On 11 July, John Kerr was installed as Governor-General. The House of Representatives again passed the six Bills but the Senate again failed to pass them. On 30 July, Kerr convened the first joint sitting of both Houses to deliberate on all six Bills. The President of the former Senate issued a writ in the High Court claiming that Kerr's proclamation was invalid, and that a joint sitting could deliberate on only one Bill. In *Cormack v Cope* (1974), the High Court unanimously held that a joint sitting could deliberate and vote on any number of Bills and, with Barwick alone dissenting, that the proclamation was not invalid. At the joint sitting on 6 and 7 August, all the Bills were enacted. As a result, the House of Representatives became the first legislative body in Australia to be elected on the principle of one vote, one value; the Northern Territory and the ACT secured representation in the Senate; and Medibank was established.

On 29 November 1974, Douglas Menzies died at the annual dinner of the NSW Bar Association. Murphy, who was present, promptly made a telephone call to Barwick at The Hague. Shortly before I left for Europe on 14 December, my Deputy, Jim Cairns, told me of Murphy's wish to succeed Menzies. I agreed that Murphy had been a great reform **Attorney-General**; in particular, he had been able to persuade the Senate, which we did not control, to pass the Trade Practices Bill and the Family Law Bill, superseding the inadequate *Trade Practices Act* 1965 (Cth) and outdated *Matrimonial Causes Act* 1959 (Cth). We proposed to make the appointment before the Parliament and High Court resumed their sittings in the second week of February. Contrary to the assertion of Barwick in his autobiography, Murphy did not seek, nor did I give, any assurance that he would be appointed **Chief Justice** when the opportunity arose. Nor had there been any pre-existing decision to appoint Byers, whose advocacy was central to my government's success in the High Court.

On 20 December, the International Court delivered its judgments. After further atmospheric tests in July, August, and September, the French Ministers of Foreign Affairs and Defence had announced that they would carry out no more atmospheric tests but would proceed to underground testing. The Court, by nine votes to six, found that Australia's objective had been accomplished and that the Court needed to make no further pronouncement. The six dissenting judges, including Barwick, dissented on the ground that Australia had the right to have the case adjudicated.

I returned from Europe on 20 January 1975. I invited Barwick to the Lodge for dinner on 24 January. Over dinner, he accepted my invitation to chair the Council for the Order of Australia. I thanked him for his participation at The Hague and applauded, with respect, the lucid and cogent terms of his dissenting judgment. I proposed that Australia should withdraw its long-winded and over-cautious 1954 instrument accepting the Court's compulsory jurisdiction with reservations, and substitute a more succinct and wholehearted instrument. He agreed. Australia's new instrument accepting the compulsory jurisdiction of the International Court was deposited on 17 March.

The Cabinet held its first meeting in 1975 on the afternoon of Sunday, 9 February. Cairns, Murphy, and I met before the meeting and Murphy accepted our proposal to appoint him to the vacancy on the High Court. The Cabinet endorsed our proposal. It took me some hours to inform Barwick, for he was travelling in Tasmania. He was most upset and peremptorily closed the conversation. Murphy was appointed on 10 February.

Early in January, McTiernan had informed Cairns, the Acting Prime Minister, that he wished to resign from the High Court. On Sunday, 23 February, McTiernan and I dined with our wives at the Windsor Hotel in Melbourne. We discussed the timing of his resignation. He had not divulged his intentions to Barwick. He wanted a Catholic to succeed him.

My government, however, never had an opportunity to appoint another Justice to the High Court. The Chief Justice is merely *primus inter pares* (first among equals), but he or she effectively determines when the Court will commence hearings and deliver judgments. During 1975, new cases were invariably commenced while judgments were pending in earlier cases. Between 11 March and 16 April, the Court heard the challenge by all the states to the *Seas and Submerged Lands Act* 1973 (Cth). The Justices, with Gibbs and Stephen alone dissenting, handed down their judgments upholding the Act on 17 December. Barwick had effectively prevented McTiernan from resigning.

The chronology is convoluted. Between 24 and 27 February, the Court heard a challenge by NSW, Queensland, and WA to the Petroleum and Minerals Authority Act passed at the joint sitting. From 6 to 8 May, it heard the *AAP Case*, a challenge by Victoria to the appropriation for the Australian Assistance Plan. From 19 to 21 May, it heard my government's challenge to the Queensland Act purporting to expand the Queen's title to 'Queen of Queensland' and to allow appeals to the Privy Council on any law in force in Queensland.

The Senate referred the eligibility of Country Party Senator Jim Webster to the **Court of Disputed Returns** (see **Electoral law**). On 19 May, the matter was mentioned before Barwick, who remarked that he would probably refer it to the **Full Court**. When the hearing was resumed on 2 June, he decided to take the case himself. The case proceeded for two days. On 24 June, he ruled that Webster was not ineligible (*In re Webster* (1975)).

On 21 and 22 May, the Court heard the challenges by WA, NSW, and Queensland to the *Senate (Representation of Territories) Act* 1973 (Cth) passed at the joint sitting.

On 24 June, Barwick announced that he and Gibbs, Stephen, and Mason held that Hasluck should not have referred the PMA Bill to the Joint Sitting since the Senate had not twice rejected it. The Justices' reasons were to be published later.

While High Court judgments were being held up, Barwick was out of Australia for some seven weeks in July and August on the way to and from the Privy Council. He wanted to end appeals to the Privy Council from Australia but to sit on appeals from other countries. Between 14 and 24 July, he sat on a tax appeal from the NZ Court of Appeal (*Europa Oil v Inland Revenue Commissioner* (1976)).

On 29 September, my wife and I invited the seven Justices and their wives to lunch with us at the Lodge before I unveiled a plaque to commemorate the start of construction of the High Court building. Since the rain was falling in torrents, I was able to compliment the Justices on nobly fulfilling one of their tenets, *fiat justitia ruat coelum* ('Let justice be done though the heavens are falling'). On 30 September, the

Justices delivered their written reasons for judgment in the *PMA Case* (1975).

On 10 October, the Court handed down its unanimous judgment that the 'Queen of Queensland' Act was invalid (*Queen of Queensland Case* (1975)). On the same day, in the *First Territory Senators Case* (1975), the Court, by a majority (McTiernan, Mason, Jacobs, and Murphy), declared that the Senate (Representation of Territories) Act was valid. In dissent, Barwick, Gibbs, and Stephen held that senators from the **territories** were not entitled to the same powers as senators from the states.

On 16 October, the Senate deferred the Appropriation Bills. On the next day, the Court handed down the reasons for judgment in the *Territory Senators Case*. On the same day, the Court pronounced in favour of the government in the *AAP Case* but did not state the names of the Justices in favour or publish their reasons.

On 29 October, the Court handed down seven different judgments in the *AAP Case*. Barwick, Gibbs, and Mason held the appropriation invalid but McTiernan, Jacobs, and Murphy held it valid. Stephen held that a state did not have **standing** to impugn an appropriation. The Chief Justice was again in a minority.

On Sunday evening, 19 October, Kerr telephoned me at Kirribilli House from Admiralty House next door, to ask whether I would agree to his seeking advice from Barwick on the dispute between the House of Representatives and the Senate. I immediately gave him my reasons against such a consultation. RC Munro Ferguson was the last Governor-General to consult a Chief Justice on an election. He did so in 1914, at a much earlier stage of Australia's constitutional development, and the then Chief Justice was one of the founding fathers. In 1921, the High Court had said that it would not give **advisory opinions** (*In re Judiciary and Navigation Acts* (1921)); if the Court as a whole could not give such opinions, still less could a single Justice of the Court do so. In cases where the Court had been divided since my government came to office, Barwick had usually been in the minority. In any event, the matter upon which the Chief Justice or any other Justice might be asked to give advice could come before another Justice and almost certainly before the Full Court for argument and decision. Kerr did not demur in any way to my response.

On Monday, 10 November, the High Court was sitting in Sydney. Kerr asked Barwick to call at Admiralty House before going to the Court, and sought his advice. Barwick delivered a letter of advice to him at lunch time. At Kerr's request, he showed the letter to Mason and Stephen. At lunch time the next day, Kerr dismissed me and my ministers. He told me that Barwick had agreed with this course of action. He did not tell me that he had a letter from Barwick. He released the letter a week later.

Earlier in 1975, Attorney-General Enderby and I had sought to enhance Australia's judicial system. After the Superior Court of Australia Bill was twice defeated in the Senate, Enderby prepared a new Bill that took into account the creation of the Family Court by the *Family Law Act* 1975 (Cth), which had received assent on 12 June 1975. His Bill received assent under a new name, the **Federal Court** of Australia Bill, on 9 December 1976. This had been the third item on the agenda adopted by Barwick and me in September 1973.

Construction of the new High Court building proceeded, and it was opened by the Queen on 26 May 1980. This had been the second item on my agenda with Barwick.

Under the *Australia Acts*, which came into operation on 3 March 1986, all remaining appeals to the Privy Council were abolished. That had been the first item on our agenda.

GOUGH WHITLAM

Further Reading
Gough Whitlam, *Abiding Interests* (1997)

Wik (1996). The plaintiffs in *Wik Peoples v Queensland* claimed lands and waters on the western side of the Cape York Peninsula on the basis of **native title** and possessory title. The Thayorre People were later joined as respondents; they cross-claimed, seeking similar relief in respect of lands that partly overlapped with those claimed by the Wik Peoples.

The areas claimed included land over which the Queensland government had granted pastoral leases and mining leases. The plaintiffs argued that the mining leases were invalid and that the pastoral leases did not extinguish native title.

The effect of the pastoral leases was unclear. In *Mabo* (1992), while affirming the survival of native title over most of the Murray Islands, the Court as a whole had expressed no concluded determination in relation to three small areas that had previously been the subject of leasehold interests, thus suggesting that the mere grant of a lease does not necessarily distinguish native title. On the other hand, a passage in the leading judgment of **Brennan** had suggested that a lease did have that effect:

> If a lease be granted, the lessee acquires possession and the Crown acquires the reversion expectant on the expiry of the term. The Crown's title is thus expanded from the mere radical title and, on the expiry of the term, becomes a plenum dominium.

In other words, both the lessee's entitlement to exclusive possession, and the fact that at the end of the lease the beneficial ownership would revert to the Crown, were inconsistent with the survival of any native title claim.

Yet, assuming that this accurately stated the effect of a standard **common law** lease, it was still an open question whether the same analysis would apply to the 'pastoral leases' that had been widely used to implement colonial land policy. Especially in cases where the lease was never taken up, or was only minimally developed, the mere grant of such a lease might not necessarily be inconsistent with the continued enjoyment of native title rights and interests. In that event, a later sentence from Brennan's judgment in *Mabo* might apply: 'Where the Crown has not granted interests ... inconsistently with the right to continued enjoyment of native title by the indigenous inhabitants, native title survives and is legally enforceable.' On this view, the question was not to be determined by reference to the traditional incidents of a common law lease. 'Pastoral leases' were a novel form of tenure created by Australian statutes, and their incidents and effects were to be determined by reference to the relevant statutes.

In *Re Waanyi Peoples Native Title Application* (1994), Justice Robert French, as President of the Native Title Tribunal, had

The Bar table, overflowing for the hearing of the Wik Case

held that, having regard to the terms of the relevant Queensland legislation, certain pastoral leases granted in 1883 and 1904 had necessarily operated to grant exclusive possession to the lessee, and that this was inconsistent with the survival of native title. On appeal from that decision, in the *Waanyi Case* (1995), the **Federal Court** held that Justice French's ruling had been premature; but two of the three judges (Justices Kenneth Jenkinson and Graham Hill) held that the ruling had in fact been correct. The third judge, Justice Malcolm Lee, dissented. The division of opinion served only to emphasise that the question whether native title was extinguished by the mere grant of a pastoral lease was still unresolved. When the *Waanyi Case* reached the High Court, the uncertainty was prolonged: in judgments handed down in March 1996, the Court ruled that since Justice French had exceeded his powers by ruling on the question at that preliminary stage, there was no properly constituted proceeding in which the High Court could properly express a judicial opinion on the question.

Meanwhile, in January 1996, Justice Douglas Drummond, in the Federal Court, had ruled on a number of preliminary questions of law in the *Wik Case* (*Wik Peoples v Queensland* (1996)). Following the majority view in the Federal Court in the *Waanyi Case*, he determined that Queensland pastoral leases extinguish native title. An appeal to the Full Federal Court against that ruling was **removed** into the High Court under section 40 of the *Judiciary Act* 1903 (Cth). The case was argued in June 1996, and judgments were handed down on 23 December that year.

The Court unanimously rejected an argument that two special bauxite mining leases were invalid for breach of a **fiduciary obligation** owed by the government to **Aboriginal peoples**, or for failure to accord **natural justice**. That argument was rejected primarily for the reason that the leases had specifically been authorised by Queensland statutes. What attracted national attention, however, was the decision about the effect of pastoral leases.

The *Native Title Act* 1993 (Cth), in providing for the validation of 'past acts', had placed pastoral leases in Category A, with the consequence that validation would wholly extinguish native title. But these provisions operated only in respect of past acts that would have been invalid because of the existence of native title—such as leases granted after the commencement of the *Racial Discrimination Act* 1975 (Cth) in cases where native title had survived until that time. If native title had already been extinguished before that time, there would be no problem. After the *Mabo* decision, some governments had proceeded on the assumption that, on any land that had ever been the subject of pastoral leases, native title had been wholly extinguished; they had therefore dealt

with the land in other ways (particularly by the granting of mining leases) without pausing to consider the possible survival of native title.

By a 4:3 majority, the High Court decided that the Queensland pastoral leases under consideration in *Wik* did not confer a right of exclusive possession, and hence did not necessarily extinguish all native title rights that may otherwise have survived. (There was as yet no determination whether any native title rights had survived or, if so, what those rights might be.) However, in the event of any inconsistency between native title rights and the rights of the pastoralists, the rights of the pastoralists would prevail.

The majority Justices, **Toohey, Gaudron, Gummow**, and **Kirby**, delivered separate judgments, though they did express their concurrence in the 'Postscript' to the judgment of Toohey, which summarised the majority's decision in clear and simple terms (see **Collective responsibility**). By contrast, **Dawson** and **McHugh** confined themselves to brief **concurrences** with the **dissenting judgment** of **Chief Justice** Brennan.

For Brennan, a pastoral lease was to be treated as a lease in the generally understood common law sense to which he had alluded in *Mabo*. It granted a right of exclusive possession, and this was inconsistent with the survival of any native title rights. Nor could native title rights revive on the expiry of a lease; a Crown grant of any estate, freehold or leasehold, would remove the land in question permanently from the domain of native title into the domain of Crown-granted tenures. Accordingly, when a lease expired, the reversion would go to the Crown.

The majority Justices rejected that analysis, but did not find it necessary to decide whether native title might revive on the expiry of a pastoral lease. They found no evidence in the Queensland legislation or in the particular leases of a clear and plain intention that native title holders were to be totally excluded. The use of the term 'lease' did not conclude the matter.

Pastoral leases cover some 42 per cent of the Australian land mass. The *Wik* decision immediately attracted hostile **criticism** from the pastoral industry and from a number of politicians and **commentators**. The Howard government's proposed amendments to the Native Title Act were withdrawn and subsequently re-presented with other amendments designed specifically to reduce the impact of the Court's decision. The entire package became known as 'the *Wik* Bill'. After the Bill was twice amended in the Senate in ways the government found to be unacceptable, a compromise was reached, and the *Native Title Amendment Act* 1998 (Cth) was ultimately enacted.

Brennan's dissenting judgment had hinted at a different legislative response. While adhering to his view that as a matter of law native title in such cases was extinguished, he adopted a comment by Justice French in the *Waanyi Case* that this outcome entailed 'a significant moral shortcoming in the principles by which native title is recognised'. He suggested that such a 'shortcoming' could be 'rectified only by legislation or by the acquisition of an estate which would allow the traditions and customs of the Wik and Thayorre peoples to be preserved and observed'.

In other words, the appropriate response was to give the applicants' claims a more secure basis, in the form of 'proprietary rights', which 'unlike … native title, are not liable to extinguishment by subsequent executive action'.

The High Court decision did not determine the merits of the Wik Peoples' claim; it determined only that the mere grant of pastoral leases had not barred the claim. The substantive issues were **remitted** to the Federal Court. On 3 October 2000, the Federal Court made a consent determination in respect of about one-fifth of the claim area, and negotiations continue in relation to the remainder.

GARTH NETTHEIM

Further Reading
Tony Abrahams (ed), 'Forum. Wik: The Aftermath and Implications' (1997) 20 *UNSWLJ* 487
Richard Bartlett, *Native Title in Australia* (2000) ch 4
Graham Hiley (ed), *The Wik Case: Issues and Implications* (1997)

Williams, Dudley (*b* 7 December 1889; *d* 8 January 1963; Justice 1940–58) was the product of an education in the late Victorian and Edwardian age; of front-line service in France during **World War I**; of pupillage with Frederick Jordan, later Chief Justice of NSW and one of Australia's foremost **equity** lawyers and judges; and of practice at the Equity Bar in NSW, then steeped in the tradition and practice of the English Chancery Court. In many ways, Williams was as qualified an equity judge as has ever sat on the High Court. But this did not necessarily prepare him well for High Court service.

Third child of Prosper Williams—a solicitor, and a descendant of the first American consul to Australia—and Florence Milson, a granddaughter of the first settler in North Sydney, Williams was educated at Sydney Church of England Grammar School and at the University of Sydney. Upon graduating in arts and law, he began active service in World War I. He rose to the rank of captain, received the Military Cross, and was mentioned twice in dispatches.

Following his discharge, Williams married Rua Webster, a daughter of businessman HC Webster and Catherine Fairfax. He served as associate to Chief Justice William Cullen of the Supreme Court of NSW until 1921, when he commenced practice at the Sydney Bar.

His appearances in the High Court both as a junior and senior **counsel** were mostly in equity-related matters—including cases about companies, wills, intellectual property, and revenue. Only twice did he appear in constitutional appeals: once as junior in an **excise** duty case, *John Fairfax & Sons v NSW* (1927), and once as senior counsel in an **inconsistency** case, *Tasmanian Steamers v Lang* (1938).

Williams received an acting appointment to the Supreme Court of NSW when he was almost 50, four years after he took silk. The appointment was made permanent in the following year, and soon afterwards he was appointed to the High Court.

In **background**, Williams was closest to **Rich**. Like Rich, he adopted a low profile, though he was much more conscientious in the writing of judgments. Rich not infrequently concurred with Williams and joined in a judgment in the *Bank Nationalisation Case* (1948), which Williams almost certainly wrote.

In personality, Williams was probably closer to the Justices later appointed by Robert **Menzies**, including **Fullagar**,

Dudley Williams, Justice 1940–58

Kitto, **Taylor**, and Douglas **Menzies**, than he was to the members of the Court he joined in 1940. But he shared the conservative approach of senior members such as Rich and **Starke**, and fitted in with the life of the Court.

Williams' construction of the **defence power** tended to occupy the middle ground between **Latham's** expansive view of that power and Starke's gruff dissents. The validity of the Women's Employment Regulations was challenged in a series of cases about the employment of **women** in industry during **World War II**, and government attempts to secure them reasonable working conditions and wages. Initially, the regulations were fairly closely confined to women who, when the **men** left to fight overseas, had moved into the jobs that had until that time normally been performed by men. Williams agreed that the industrial employment of these women had directly arisen from the war, so that regulations concerning them had a sufficient connection with defence. (In the very first case, **Barwick** referred to these women as 'the new women'—a phrase Williams seized upon and used in every relevant judgment thereafter.) Increasingly, as the cases went on, however, and the regulations extended to wider classes of women, Williams joined the original dissenters to argue that the extensions were invalid. In some of the crucial cases, Williams' view became the majority view.

Williams joined his brethren in rejecting the attempt by Labor governments to nationalise aviation and banking. Like Starke, he had announced at the outset of the *Bank Nationalisation Case* that his family had shareholdings in the private banks—indeed, his ancestors on both sides had been involved in banking interests for many decades. But, again, like Starke, he refused to **disqualify** himself from hearing the challenge to the legislation.

Williams found life on the High Court demanding. He served initially under **Latham**, who worked hard to achieve harmony among the Justices (see **Personal relations**). That process was assisted by the **retirement** of Evatt, whom Williams replaced, and who had suffered a bitter relationship with his colleague Starke. The work was arduous, and was made even harder by the fact that the Court had managed its **business** with six members since 1930. In 1946, that changed when a seventh Justice, **Webb**, was appointed, though he did not take up his seat on the Court until 1948. In the next decade, following the retirement of the elderly Rich and Starke, Williams began to find himself surrounded by men of similar backgrounds and interests to himself. When **Dixon** was elevated to the position of **Chief Justice** in 1952, the new Chief was able to bring out the best in the members of his team, including Williams.

Williams had to learn to deal in a practical sense with constitutional problems, which in large measure at that time concerned the defence power, industrial disputes, and the guaranteed freedom of **interstate trade and commerce**. He approached all his work by applying the analytical technique then the mark of the equity lawyer: logic and precision were its hallmarks.

In his eulogy to Williams, Dixon spoke of the energy and unremitting application that characterised Williams' work and the careful, methodical, and thorough investigation he applied in addressing the heaviest case (but see **Dixon diaries**). These techniques did not necessarily sit comfortably with the broader considerations necessary for the working of a living Constitution. He relished equity appeals and intellectual property appeals in which, like other Justices at that time, he sat at first instance. His experience in valuation law was well recognised. His reasoning in *Murdoch's Case* (1942), *McCathie v FCT* (1944), and *Abrahams v FCT* (1944) influenced valuation law for many years.

In *McCarter v Brodie* (1950), a road transport case, Williams—perhaps defensively—explained his reasoning in *Australian National Airways v Commonwealth* (1945), the first section 92 case in which he had sat. He said that he had attempted to reconcile the conflicting statements by which at various times the **Privy Council** had seemed to approve both what **Isaacs** had written in *James v Cowan* (1930) and what Evatt had written in *R v Vizzard; Ex parte Hill* (1933). In the *Bank Nationalisation Case*, regulation of interstate trade and commerce had been accepted by the Privy Council as compatible with its absolute freedom. Thus, in *McCarter*, Williams concluded that a state could enact all legislation reasonably required for the safety, maintenance, and preservation of public roads and could make a reasonable charge for their use. With the majority, he upheld legislation designed to protect the state's railways. He said, adopting the words of Lord Porter in the *Bank Nationalisation Case*, that whether an enactment was regulatory although it included prohibition presented a problem often 'not so much legal as political, social and **economic**'.

In *Hughes & Vale v NSW (No 1)* (1953), Fullagar retorted that the new ground that had emerged in *McCarter* (which Williams had foreshadowed in *Australian National Air-*

ways)—that the states, because they provided facilities for transport, must have power to control the use of such facilities in any manner thought fit—had no real foundation 'except expediency'. While a Constitution must be interpreted against a political, social, and economic background, this could not mean that it was proper to give to a particular provision one meaning where bankers and airline operators are concerned and another where carriers by land are concerned.

The exchange reflected the growing refinement of artificial doctrine relating to section 92, which finally collapsed in *Cole v Whitfield* (1988). The contrasting approaches of Williams and Fullagar perhaps reflect a contrast between the views of those (like Dixon and Fullagar) who were masterly exponents of the then-emergent doctrine, and the approach of a Justice attempting to apply ordinary principles of reasoning and accepted methods of **statutory interpretation** and **precedent**.

Dixon and Fullagar were classical Greek scholars. Williams, who was a Latin scholar but knew no Greek, in his later years on the Court sat beside Dixon, often with Fullagar on his other side. Williams was not impressed by the habit that Dixon and Fullagar developed of passing notes to each other across him in Greek. He also deplored the persistent practice of the Privy Council, for instance in the *Bank Nationalisation Case*, of continuing to sit with only five judges even when hearing an appeal from the High Court consisting of five or more Justices. He was proud of the fact that from May to August 1952, when both Dixon and McTiernan were absent, he was Acting Chief Justice of the Court.

Williams was knighted in 1954. Thereafter, his health began to fail, and in 1958, at the age of 68, he retired. He had set himself modest targets on his **appointment**, and he had met these aims. He had been a conscientious craftsman who had helped to maintain the prestige of the Court and its reputation as a civilised institution. Dixon set the tone of the Court, but Williams had always displayed an equable temperament. He died shortly after his seventy-fourth birthday.

When **Windeyer** was sworn in to replace Williams, he said that 'all who practised before [Williams] as a judge gratefully appreciated his considerate courtesy, recognised the range of his learning, especially of the doctrines of equity, and respected the thorough care and scholarship which his judgments reflect'. But Williams did not find the work on the High Court particularly congenial. Towards the end of his career, he expressed regret that he had left the NSW Equity Court.

GRAHAM FRICKE
SIMON SHELLER

Wilson, Ronald Darling (*b* 23 August 1922; Justice 1979–89), born in Geraldton, WA, was the first Western Australian to be appointed a Justice of the High Court. His father was an English-trained solicitor who migrated to Australia in about 1912 and set up practice in Geraldton. There were only two or three competitors in the town at that stage. His was a typical country practice of those days—creaking staircase and old leather chairs. Unfortunately, he suffered a stroke in 1929 or 1930, when Wilson was only seven, and was thereafter totally disabled and confined to a nursing home in Perth until he died five years later. He took in a partner, but the practice disintegrated and the bank foreclosed on the Wilson

Ronald Wilson, Justice 1979–89

home in 1936. Wilson remembers helping to bury his father's library in the backyard of their home (including a complete set of English law reports) before the house was sold. Wilson has often wondered if the new owners of the house ever tried to start a garden in the backyard and what fertiliser they needed to overcome the learning buried therein. It would have been hopeless to try to sell a law library in the aftermath of the **Depression**.

Wilson left school in 1936, having completed what was then described as the Junior Certificate (equivalent to about year ten in today's schools). He started work as a messenger in the Geraldton courthouse, becoming a permanent public servant as a junior clerk on his fifteenth birthday in August 1937. He transferred to Perth in 1939 and continued in the state Public Service (Crown Law Department) until he enlisted for war service in November 1941. In the meantime, he had acquired enough Leaving Certificate subjects to enable him to matriculate into the university on his return to civilian life in February 1946, although not into law, as he did not have Latin among his certificates.

As far as he recalls, Wilson did not have a strong sense of commitment to law. He had enjoyed flying in the RAAF in England during the war, where he flew spitfires. He thought of training to join the clergy, so long as he could then work as a flying padre in the north. He enquired of the Church if it had any plans to establish such a ministry. The answer was negative, so his thoughts turned to law.

As he could not enrol as a law student, he enrolled in arts and then transferred into law at the end of 1946, when he had completed first year. It was a great period to be at university, and the law school had more than its usual number of mature, bright, and hard-working students. Wilson was one of the brightest, and ultimately its most distinguished, graduates when he became a High Court Justice in 1979.

Wilson continued his employment in the Crown Law Department, and on completion of his LLB honours degree in December 1949 was articled to the Crown Solicitor. On admission, he moved into the state prosecuting section, addressing his first jury in a criminal case in April 1951. Thereafter, he never thought seriously of leaving the Crown service and entering private practice, although he was urged to do so by more than one judge. The reason was simple: he enjoyed advocacy—and many good briefs in WA, including many constitutional briefs, were to be got from the Crown. During his years with the Department, he obtained a wide experience both as a Crown Prosecutor—ultimately becoming the Chief Crown Prosecutor—and as Crown Counsel. He accordingly acquired a great knowledge of both **criminal law** and civil law. In 1956, he was awarded a Fulbright Scholarship, which enabled him to complete an LLM degree at the University of Pennsylvania. He was appointed QC in 1963. He remained a member of the Department for the next 20 years until his appointment as **Solicitor-General** of WA in 1969.

Wilson's ten years as the Solicitor-General of WA were rewarding for him. As the leading **counsel** for the state in the High Court, he acquired a sound knowledge of **constitutional law** and was prominent among the counsel appearing before the Court. The study of constitutional law had always been an interest for him; in 1967, he wrote, with Peter Durack, a paper entitled 'Do We Need a New Constitution?' It was presented to the Law Council Convention in that year with a negative answer. It was a controversial period for the future of the federal system, and Wilson addressed the conference with great verve and confidence.

At the end of 1975, the High Court decided the *Seas and Submerged Lands Case*. It immediately engaged the attention of all the states as it held that their **sovereignty** did not extend to the territorial sea and sea bed. Negotiations were set in train to restore the interests of the states and the Northern Territory. The negotiations were long and difficult, and Wilson played an important role. He was appointed to the High Court before they were successfully completed.

In addition to his demanding legal career, Wilson devoted considerable time to the affairs of the Presbyterian Church and later the Uniting Church. From 1951 to 1956, he was Honorary Secretary of the WA Council of Churches. In 1964–65 he was Moderator of the Assembly of the Presbyterian Church in WA and Moderator of the WA Synod of the Uniting Church from 1977 to 1979.

In May 1979, Wilson was sworn in as a Justice of the High Court. It was not unexpected, as he had been considered for some time (see **Appointments that might have been**). He had never been in private practice, nor a member of an independent Bar. His was the first **appointment** after the introduction of the requirement for consultation between the Commonwealth and state **Attorneys-General** about a High Court appointment. His name had been put forward by the WA Attorney-General and was supported by **Barwick**. The appointment was widely applauded.

Wilson joined an experienced and strong-minded Bench, though he did so at a time of some tension between Barwick and the **puisne Justices** about the expectation that, with the Court's move to **Canberra**, the Justices would also move their homes there. Wilson became entangled in this when Cabinet decided to support Barwick at the end of 1979. The difficulty was soon resolved, and Wilson was able to retain his home in Perth, from which he travelled to **sittings** of the Court. He was assisted by the provision of **chambers** for him in the Perth Supreme Court building.

The operation of the Court during Wilson's time appears to have been free of voting blocs, although some Justices were more conservative than others, and Wilson was frequently in the minority on issues relating to the scope of **Commonwealth legislative power**. There also seems to have been a lack of tension in the Justices' **personal relations** after the issues surrounding the move to Canberra were resolved. There were many **joint judgments**, though the Justices who chose to participate in them varied greatly. Wilson was often a party to a joint judgment, including the unanimous judgment of *Cole v Whitfield* (1988), which has largely cured the long-running sore of section 92 of the Constitution as to freedom of **interstate trade**. He also participated in a large number of criminal appeals.

In addition to *Cole v Whitfield*, the Court dealt with a number of important constitutional cases during Wilson's term. In *Queensland Electricity Commission v Commonwealth* (1985), another unanimous decision, the Court struck down a Commonwealth law that discriminated against Queensland by singling out its electricity authorities for special treatment in relation to the settlement of industrial disputes (see **Intergovernmental immunities**).

Both *Koowarta's Case* (1982) and the *Tasmanian Dam Case* (1983) raised a major issue for the future of **federalism**. They concerned the scope of the **external affairs power**.

Koowarta was the last High Court decision on this issue which, in the writer's view, had any semblance of restraint in its interpretation. The case concerned the application of sections 9 and 12 of the *Racial Discrimination Act* 1975 (Cth) to actions occurring only in Australia. It was decided 4:3, with **Stephen** the only member of the majority who did not go so far as to hold that the existence of any treaty obligation gave rise to an external affair. Stephen rather held that the particular matter of racial **discrimination** was a matter of international concern. Wilson dissented, and relied on the forceful view of **Dixon** that federal legislation giving effect to a treaty must be based on some matter 'indisputably international in character' such as a convention on international civil aviation (*R v Burgess; Ex parte Henry* (1936)). Wilson wrote: 'In my opinion, the power in Section 51(xxix) does not extend to enable the Parliament to implement every obligation which Australia assumes in its international relations.'

The *Tasmanian Dam Case* put an end to the restrained view of the external affairs power. Again, the Court was divided 4:3, but this time the majority Justices all adopted the broadest view of the power, and again Wilson dissented. In doing so, he gave a strong warning that

> an expansive reading of section 51(xxix) so as to bring the implementation of any treaty within Commonwealth legislative power poses a serious threat to the basic federal polity of the Constitution. Such an interpretation, if adopted, would result in

the Commonwealth Parliament acquiring power over practically the whole range of domestic concerns within Australia.

He then cited the many treaties that were ripe for the picking. His views have been prophetic.

One of Wilson's last cases was *Mabo (No 1)* (1988). It decided, again 4:3, that section 10 of the *Racial Discrimination Act* overrode a Queensland law purporting to extinguish **native title** rights being sought by the plaintiffs. Whether such rights actually existed was not determined until *Mabo* (1992). Nevertheless, the first decision has had great significance for the growth of native title. Wilson dissented. He did so on a more restricted interpretation of section 10 than that of the majority.

Wilson took part in a number of other important judgments, including *Todorovic v Waller* (1981) (**damages**); *R v O'Connor* (1980) (effect of intoxication on criminal intent); *Williams v The Queen* (1986) (arrest); the *Northern Land Council Case* (1981) (limit of Crown immunity); and *Actors Equity v Fontana Films* (1982) (**corporations power**). His judgments were well crafted, displaying in particular, unusually careful attention to the **argument** of counsel. This feature of his **judicial style** reflected not merely his conservatism but also his lack of affectation.

Wilson retired in February 1989, shortly after he became the National President of the Uniting Church of Australia for a three-year term. He was Chancellor of Murdoch University from 1980 to 1995. In 1990, he became President of the Human Rights and Equal Opportunity Commission (HREOC) for a term of seven years. He was Deputy Chairman of the Council for **Aboriginal** Reconciliation (1991–94), and President of the Australian Branch of the World Conference on Religion and Peace (1991–95). In 1997, he was elected President of the Australian Council for Overseas Aid. His report for HREOC on the stolen generation of Aboriginal children, *Bringing Them Home*, was a profoundly moving experience both for him and for many members of the community. Freed of the constraints of judicial office, Wilson has displayed a passion and commitment far removed from the conservatism of his judicial opinions.

He has been married to Leila since 1950. They have five children and nine grandchildren. He has received a number of honorary degrees and honours (CMG, KBE, and AC) for his extensive services to the law and the community.

PETER DURACK

Windeyer, (William John) Victor (*b* 28 July 1900; *d* 23 November 1987; Justice 1958–72). Of Australian families which boast a strong tradition in the law, one outstanding family is the Windeyers. Of Swiss origin (the first Windeyer going to England in about 1735), Charles Windeyer (1780–1855) arrived in Australia in 1828. He had been a London law reporter—the first recognised reporter of the **House of Lords**—and in NSW became Senior Police Magistrate and the first Mayor of Sydney. Each generation since has served the community in the law and other fields. Richard Windeyer (1806–47), the son of Charles, had been admitted to the English Bar before he migrated; he became a leading barrister in Sydney and a Member of the NSW Legislative Council. His son William Charles Windeyer (1834–97) was a

Victor Windeyer, Justice 1958–72

a Major three months earlier, he rapidly regained his peacetime rank, and on 9 August 1940 he took command of the 2/48 Infantry Battalion, which consisted predominantly of South Australians and was the most decorated battalion of the second AIF. It was not usual for an infantry commanding officer to be brought in from another state, but Windeyer quickly won the confidence and affection of the South Australians. Windeyer commanded his battalion during the siege at Tobruk. In January 1942, he was promoted to the rank of Brigadier, taking command of the Twentieth Brigade and leading it through the rest of the war in campaigns in North Africa, New Guinea, and Borneo, notably at El Alamein and at the capture of Finschhafen in New Guinea. Described as a versatile and outstanding commander, he was three times mentioned in dispatches, awarded the DSO and Bar in 1942, and appointed CBE in 1944.

Windeyer continued his military service after the war, serving in the Citizen Military Forces. In 1950, he was promoted to the rank of Major-General, and from 1950 to 1953 sat on the Military Board. He commanded the Second Division until 1952. From 1956 to 1966, he was Honorary Colonel of the Sydney University Regiment. He was appointed CB in 1953.

Admitted as a barrister in NSW in 1925, he quickly established a wide-ranging practice which, in later years, was predominantly in **equity** and **commercial law**. As junior **counsel**, he appeared in two constitutional cases, *Moran's Case* (1939) and *R v Connare* (1939), in the latter for the NSW government whose lottery laws were held not to infringe section 92. He was appointed a KC in 1949. As silk, he appeared in a number of cases in the High Court and **Privy Council**, including the *Melbourne Corporation Case* (1947) (a forerunner to the *Bank Nationalisation Case* (1948)).

Probably the best known of Windeyer's cases was the controversial Royal Commission on Espionage in 1954, popularly called the Petrov Royal Commission. It was a forensic exercise quite removed from his usual practice. He was senior counsel assisting the Commission. His description of Exhibit J, one of the more notorious exhibits, as 'a farrago of fact, falsity and filth' has endured.

Windeyer's interests in the law were academic and historical, as well as professional. He was lecturer in legal history at the University of Sydney from 1929 to 1936 and lecturer in equity from 1937 to 1940. He wrote *The Law of Wagers, Gaming and Lotteries* (1929) and *Lectures on Legal History* (1938), the latter becoming a standard text well known to generations of law students. All of his writing, legal and historical, displays a careful if not painstaking erudition. His interest in and knowledge of history extended beyond legal history. His high reputation was acknowledged in his appointment as Vice-President of the Selden Society (London) and as Honorary Fellow of the Royal Australian Historical Society. He was also made an honorary member of the Society of Public Teachers of Law (UK).

His interest in education was not limited to lecturing and writing. From 1943 to 1970, he was a member of the Board of Trustees of Sydney Grammar School. He was a Fellow of the Senate of the University of Sydney (1949–59) and Deputy Chancellor (1955–58). From 1951 to 1955, he was a member of the Council for the Australian National University. He

judge of the Supreme Court of NSW from 1879 to 1896; William's eldest son Richard was a leading barrister who frequently appeared before the High Court (see **Counsel, notable**), while another son, William Archibald (the Justice's father), was a prominent Sydney solicitor who later became Mayor of Hunters Hill.

It was there that Windeyer was born. His mother, Ruby, was a sister of John LeGay Brereton who, in 1921, became Professor of English Literature at the University of Sydney. This **background** plainly equipped Windeyer with an interest in the law, legal **history**, and literature. He had two brothers, also lawyers.

After attending Sydney Grammar School, Windeyer entered the University of Sydney in 1919 where he graduated BA and LLB, obtaining in 1922 the University Medal for History. Later, he obtained an MA. University of Sydney later awarded him an honorary LLD.

In 1918, he left school to enlist in the first AIF, but the war finished before he could be sent overseas. Then, in 1919, Windeyer began a distinguished career as a soldier. Liable for military service under the military training scheme introduced during **World War I**, he joined the Sydney University Regiment. In February 1922, he was commissioned with the rank of Lieutenant. On 1 July 1937, he was appointed commanding officer of the regiment with the rank of Lieutenant Colonel.

During **World War II**, he served with great distinction in the Ninth Australian Division of the AIF. Having enlisted as

was, for some time, Chairman of the Gowrie Scholarship Trust Fund.

He held directorships in the Colonial Sugar Refinery Company (1953–58) and in the Mutual Life and Citizens Assurance Company (1954–58). He also served on the Board of Royal Prince Alfred Hospital and was President of the NSW Boy Scouts Association. In 1949, after he had been appointed a KC, he made an unsuccessful bid for Senate pre-selection as a member of the Liberal Party. Later, he sat as a member of the Judicial Committee of the Privy Council.

On 10 July 1934, he married Margaret Vicars. They enjoyed 53 years of married life. Two of their sons are lawyers, their eldest son a judge of the Supreme Court of NSW. Two grandchildren are also lawyers.

Windeyer was appointed to the High Court to replace **Williams**. Noting the appointment, the *Australian Law Journal* referred to his 'personal qualities which command the respect of his colleagues in the law. He brings to the High Court bench not only legal knowledge but also wide experience and a cultivated mind'. Windeyer's detractors attributed his **appointment** to his role in the Petrov Commission. They overlooked his busy practice, his wide legal knowledge, his cultivated mind, and the broadness of his intellect.

Some may have judged Windeyer as a conservative. It is futile, if not misleading, to ascribe such epithets. In personal life and beliefs, he may have been conservative but as a Justice he was far less conservative and traditional than many of his colleagues. He was a member of a particularly strong Court.

As a legal historian, Windeyer was particularly conscious of the dynamism of the **common law** 'to grow and develop as the needs of men change'. He was concerned to link law with the development of society. After his **retirement**, he said, 'the law of a people is not an aggregate of abstract concepts, it governs their lives and reflects their history'—a view expressed some 40 years earlier in the early pages of his *Legal History*: 'Law is not, in essence, a body of technical rules, uncouth formulae and inexorable commands … It is really a simpler and a grander thing. It is that which makes it possible for men to live together in communities, to lead a peaceful, organised, social life.'

As Henry Burmester has noted, this sounds like Oliver Wendell Holmes, reflecting the pragmatic approach of American jurisprudence in the early twentieth century. Not infrequently, he quoted Holmes. He did so in his preface to *Legal History*—'a page of history is worth a volume of logic'—Windeyer adding that a detailed knowledge of the history of a rule is necessary for an understanding of the living law.

The concept of the common law evolving to meet changed circumstances applied also in **constitutional law**, where he advocated the need for an appreciation that '**legalism** there demands rather that kind of consistency that is the product of the application of a constant principle to contemporary needs in developing circumstances'.

Some instances of his brilliance in the elucidation of historical aspects include *Norman v FCT* (1963) on choses in action; *Olsson v Dyson* (1969) and *Coulls v Bagot's Executor & Trustee Co* (1967) on **contracts** for the benefit of third parties; *Randwick Municipal Council v Rutledge* (1959) on uses consistent with the exemption from rating of a public reserve, applied later by the High Court in *Storey v North*

Sydney Municipal Council (1970); *R v District Court; Ex parte White* (1966) on the law relating to conscientious objection to compulsory military service; *Crowe v Graham* (1968), a discussion of what constitutes obscene and indecent material; and *Brickworks v Warringah Shire Council* (1963) on **estoppel** and local authorities. Instances of his vision of a common law for Australian conditions pragmatically applying the inherited English common law are *Skelton v Collins* (1966) and *Gartner v Kidman* (1962). His pragmatism is evident in *Nominal Defendant v Clements* (1960) concerning prior consistent statements and *Jones v Dunkel* (1959) on the use to be made of an unexplained failure to call a witness. As a student, he had a particular interest in philosophy, later reflected in his discussion of **causation** in *National Insurance of New Zealand v Espagne* (1961).

In constitutional matters, he was usually in respectable company, either as part of the majority or in a sizeable dissenting minority. In **Dennis Hotels v Victoria** (1960), he wrote a dissent agreeing with **Dixon**—a view **Barwick** later expressed to be correct. When he wrote individual judgments, his reasoning was distinct from that of other Justices who, for the most part, were more traditional, relying on **precedent** and abstract principles. His judgments indicate a nationalist approach and a concern to ensure a single nation, united economically. They reflect the pragmatism identified earlier.

His constitutional judgments therefore offer an alternative to the legalism and narrow **positivism** often associated with the **Dixon Court** and perhaps reflected by Justices such as **Kitto** and **Taylor**. Thus, as Burmester has noted, he saw a need to accommodate law to changing facts, and so in the *Professional Engineers Case* (1959) rejected an approach to whether a matter was an industrial dispute by reference to a distinction between governmental and non-governmental functions. His willingness to accommodate constitutional principle with practical considerations is seen in the *Tasmanian Breweries Case* (1970) in his attitude to the **separation of powers** and the need to avoid extending needlessly the ambit of **judicial power**. Unlike **Murphy** and **Deane**, however, he did not seek to find in the Constitution safeguards of individual rights and liberties.

Windeyer did not interpret **Commonwealth legislative powers** with a narrow **literalism** (see *Worthing v Rowell & Muston* (1970); *R v Phillips* (1970)) but, in the *Marriage Act Case* (1962), while prepared to give the **marriage power** a broad interpretation, he dissented from the view that it extended to regulating legitimacy. Windeyer's conclusion in *Bonser v La Macchia* (1969) that it was appropriate for the Commonwealth to control all waters beyond the low water mark was later reflected in the majority judgments in the *Seas and Submerged Lands Case* (1975). He did not see section 92 as protecting individual rights but as a provision primarily designed to ensure a common market. So in cases such as *Chapman v Suttie* (1963), he held that laws that did not discriminate between interstate transactions and intrastate transactions did not infringe section 92—a view not shared by his colleagues, but later accepted in *Cole v Whitfield* (1988) (see also **Interstate trade and commerce**). In the *Payroll Tax Case* (1971), he saw the limits to Commonwealth legislative power as fixed by implications relating to the use of the powers, not to the inherent nature of the subject matter of the law. A Commonwealth law could not, therefore, prevent the states from carrying out their functions as part of the Commonwealth.

He also took the opportunity to place the *Engineers Case* (1920) in the broader context of historical development. After observing that with the growth of Australian **nationhood**, the position of the Commonwealth had waxed and that of the states had waned, and that the *Engineers Case* had played a significant part in that process, he eloquently observed:

I have never thought it right to regard the discarding of the [pre-*Engineers* doctrines] as the correction of antecedent errors or as the uprooting of heresy. To return today to the discarded theories would indeed be an error and the adoption of a heresy. But that is because in 1920 the Constitution was read in a new light, a light reflected from events that had, over twenty years, led to a growing realization that Australians were now one people and Australia one country … The *Engineers Case* looked at as an event in legal and constitutional history, was a consequence of developments that had occurred outside the law courts as well as a cause of further developments there.

His contribution to law and legal literature is summarised by two colleagues. **Mason** has said:

His judgments … have been acclaimed, not only in Australia but elsewhere in the common law world. He brought to his work in this Court a profound understanding of the law, stemming from his appreciation of its historical development. His sense of history and his knowledge of literature and the classics strengthened his capacity to articulate the law and explain its place in society.

Stephen has added that Windeyer's 'great scholarship and mastery of the written word have long turned law into literature … while losing nothing in the process'.

BRUCE DEBELLE

Further Reading

Henry Burmester, 'Justice Windeyer and the Constitution' (1987) 17 *FL Rev* 65

John Coates, *Bravery Above Blunder* (1999)

John Glenn, *Tobruk to Tarakan* (1960)

Barton Maughan, *Tobruk and El Alamein* (Australian War Memorial, *Australia in the War of 1939–1945*, series I, vol 3, 1966)

Victor Windeyer, *Lectures in Legal History* (2nd edn 1949)

Women. It is not without irony that a consideration of the construction of 'women' by the High Court must begin with some observations about the absence of women.

An arguably trite observation concerns the lack of women on the Court itself. **Gaudron**, appointed as the first woman Justice in 1987, remains the Court's only woman member. **Kirby** has lamented the relative absence of other women with 'speaking parts': even when women barristers do appear, it is usually only in a silent role as junior **counsel** (see **Women practitioners**).

A different kind of absence is characterised by *Dietrich v The Queen* (1992). Despite the devastating effect of this deci-

sion on women as participants in the formal legal system, women were completely absent from the case as parties (or even as **interveners**). In *Dietrich*, the Court decided that in cases involving serious criminal offences, the right to a fair trial may require the state to provide the accused with legal representation. The Court had heard an argument that this 'would impose an unsustainable financial burden on government', and concluded that it 'may require no more than a re-ordering of the priorities according to which legal aid funds are presently allocated'. No reference was made to the gendered distribution of legal aid funding—that is, to the well-documented fact that legal aid in criminal cases overwhelmingly goes to men, while women are more likely to seek legal aid in family or civil matters. Partly because of the *Dietrich* decision, the availability of aid in the latter categories continues to decline (see Attorney-General's Department, *Gender Bias in Litigation Legal Aid* (1994)).

When women do appear as parties in reported cases, they mostly appear in disputes about relationships. They are presented in **stereotype** roles as wives, or mothers, or carers of others. It is in such contexts, and by reference to such roles, that the Court's construction of women emerges.

Women's choices to be mothers. In *A-G (Qld); Ex rel Kerr v T* (1983), **Gibbs** refused to grant special **leave to appeal** to a man who, in the Supreme Court of Queensland, had failed in a relator action (see **Attorney-General**) against a woman with whom he had had **sex**; he had sought an injunction to prevent her from terminating a pregnancy. Gibbs found that 'a foetus has no right of its own until it is born and has a separate existence from its mother', and concluded: 'There are limits to the extent to which the law should intrude upon personal liberty and personal privacy in the pursuit of moral and religious aims. These limits would be overstepped if an injunction were to be granted in this case.' While this decision appears to support a woman's right to choose to terminate a pregnancy, it is only a decision of a single Justice on a special leave application. The Court as a whole has had no opportunity to consider the legality of abortion.

That opportunity nearly arose in the appeal against the NSW Court of Appeal decision in *CES v Superclinics* (1995). This case concerned a young woman suing a medical clinic for its negligent failure to detect her pregnancy, which was eventually diagnosed too late for her to consider the option of a termination. It would have been possible for the Court to confine its consideration of the appeal to the issues directly in dispute, without pronouncing on the legality or otherwise of what was a hypothetical abortion. There were, however, indications that the Court, or at least some Justices, may have been anxious to decide the broader question.

On the first day of the hearing, the Court was confronted with an application from the Catholic Bishops Conference and the Catholic Health Care Association for leave to intervene. Chief Justice **Brennan** revealed that he was personally acquainted with members of the Bishops Conference, but chose not to **disqualify** himself from hearing their application. The Court proceeded to consider whether the Conference should be allowed to intervene. Unlike courts in the USA and Canada, Australian courts have been reluctant to allow intervention by *amici curiae* or 'friends of the court' (see, for example, *Bropho v Tickner* (1993)); but in this instance, the Court divided 3:3 and the intervention was allowed on the **Chief Justice's** casting vote (see **Tied vote**).

Once the Catholic Church was allowed to participate, the nature of the case seemed about to change dramatically, to become what the **media** described as the first major 'abortion test case'. However, the case was settled after the second day of the hearing, before the Court could decide whether the Women's Electoral Lobby (WEL) should also have leave to intervene. Such leave had been granted to the Abortion Providers Federation, and the question whether WEL would have been seen as representing separate interests remains unanswered.

Issues concerning human reproduction have been considered in other contexts. A majority of the Court in *Marion's Case* (1992) held that the decision to sterilise a young woman with an intellectual **disability** is one to be made by a court rather than parents. The majority refused to base its decision on a 'right to reproduce', noting:

> There cannot be said to be an absolute right in a man to reproduce (except where a woman consents to bear a child), unless it be contended that the right to bodily integrity yield to the former right, and that cannot be so. That is to say, if there is an absolute right to reproduce, is there a duty to bear **children**?

Women as mothers. One of the Court's most infamous decisions on 'mothers' is *Chester v Waverley Corporation* (1939). There, the Court dismissed a claim for nervous shock by a woman whose child was drowned through the negligence of the local council. The council had dug a trench in the street; it had been left exposed, and became filled with water. Janet Chester went to look for her child after he had been missing for a time, became distressed on failing to find him, and suffered severe nervous shock when, some time later, the child's body was removed from the ditch. The majority rejected her claim, apparently dismissing any notion of something distinctive about the relationship between a woman and her child. **Latham** (who was later to suffer the loss of two of his three children) stated:

> The question which must be asked … is whether the defendant should have foreseen that a mother would suffer from nervous shock amounting to illness if she saw the dead body of her child … This mode of formulating the question is very favourable to the plaintiff … The question should probably be put in a form which substituted the words 'person' and 'another person' for 'mother' and 'child'.

Evatt, in a strong dissent, drew on William Blake's poetry and Joseph Furphy's novel *Such is Life* (1903) to stress the reality of Chester's agony. His dissent has been almost universally preferred by subsequent courts (see *Jaensch v Coffey* (1984)).

In *Gronow v Gronow* (1979), the Court firmly rejected the 'tender years' doctrine—the notion that in the event of parental divorce or separation young children, and particularly girls, were best looked after by their mothers because women were somehow innately suited to motherhood. However, in doing so, it managed to entrench another common judicial fallacy—that women and **men** now share the work in the home. **Mason** and **Wilson** stated:

There has come a radical change in the division of responsibilities between parents and in the ability of the mother to devote the whole of her time and attention to the household and to the family. As frequently as not, the mother works, thereby reducing the time which she can devote to her children. A corresponding development has been that the father gives more of his time to the household and to the family.

No evidence was given for this conclusion. The data show exactly the opposite: that as more women work outside the home, they continue to carry the major responsibility for household work and child care (see Australian Bureau of Statistics, *How Australians Use Their Time 1997* (1998)).

One recent example of willingness to acknowledge the empirical context of a dispute is *AMS v AIF* (1999). The Court (**Callinan** dissenting) rejected the requirement that a parent with care of a child had to provide 'compelling reasons' before she could move with the child interstate. As Kirby put it:

> The need to demonstrate 'compelling reasons' imposes on a custodial parent an unreasonable inhibition. It effectively ties that parent to an obligation of physical proximity to a person with whom, by definition, the personal relationship which gave rise to the birth of the child has finished or at least significantly altered.

He recognised not only that the welfare of the child could not be viewed separately from the circumstances of the residence parent, but that to insist on 'compelling reasons' before a move was justified would set a standard that few custodial parents could meet. He recognised that most custodial (now residence) parents were women: 'The result would be a very serious inhibition upon the freedom of custodial parents, *mostly women*, without any commensurate or equivalent inhibition upon the freedom of movement of non-custodial parents' (emphasis added). Obvious as this may seem, it is one of the few occasions when there has been recognition on the Bench of the gendered effect of its decisions.

Women as wives. Only as late as its decision in *R v L* (1991) has the Court been prepared to declare that the so-called marital rape immunity was no longer part of the **common law** of Australia. In that case Mason, **Deane**, and **Toohey** stated:

> Even if the respondent could, by reference to compelling early authority, support the proposition … that by reason of marriage there is an irrevocable consent to sexual intercourse, this Court would be justified in refusing to accept a notion that is so out of keeping with the view society now takes of the relationship between the parties to a marriage … It is unnecessary for the Court to do more than to say that, if it was ever the common law that by marriage a wife gave irrevocable consent to sexual intercourse by her husband, it is no longer the common law.

Without any reference to the extensive **feminist** literature critical of the marital rape immunity, they instead endeavoured to rehabilitate the common law—taking the view that either we had all misread the common law, as it had never really provided an immunity to husband rapists, or that if it had provided such an immunity, it should now be rejected.

The notion of wives as appendages of (or indeed as one with) their husbands has not been wholly rejected. The **criminal law defence** of provocation has offered a fertile field for the judicial construction of wives. Provocation broadly provides a partial defence to murder, reducing the offence to manslaughter, if the accused was so provoked by the actions of the victim (and occasionally others) as to lose his (or her) self-control where an 'ordinary person' could have done so (see *Stingel v The Queen* (1990)). Almost all the appeals on this doctrine have been in the context of domestic homicide, often where a man has killed his wife (or his wife's new lover) because she has said she is leaving, or has started a relationship with someone else. As the NSW Law Reform Commission succinctly put it, 'men use the provocation defence when they kill their partners or ex-partners in a jealous rage and … women use it … where they have been the victims of long term domestic abuse' (*Provocation, Diminished Responsibility and Infanticide*, Discussion Paper No 31 (1993)).

The High Court's **role** in the development of this pattern has been decisive, beginning with its decision in *Moffa v The Queen* (1977). Michele Moffa was alleged to have killed his wife because she no longer loved him, was engaging in sexual activity with other men, had shown him nude photos of herself (taken by him), had thrown a telephone at him (it did not hit him), and called him a 'black bastard'. The majority (Gibbs dissenting) concluded that the issue of provocation should have been left to the jury: in other words, that it is 'ordinary' and excusable for a man to react with homicidal violence on learning that his wife wants to leave him. While the later decision in *Stingel*, apparently tightening the provocation defence, might indicate some reassessment of the separate subjectivity of women, the case did not concern a wife, but rather a former girlfriend (and her new partner). Whether married men's assertion of a 'proprietary interest' in their wives (see Justice JC Major in the Canadian case of *R v Thibert* (1996)) will be similarly restrained is unclear.

A range of assumptions about the value of **women's work** in the home and in the paid labour market emerge from cases involving the assessment of **damages** for personal injury. The cumulative effect of the Court's decisions in *Griffiths v Kerkemeyer* (1977) and *Van Gervan v Fenton* (1992) has entitled injured plaintiffs to claim as damages the market cost of caring services arising from an injury. While each case gave the Court the opportunity to consider the value of the work that women do as carers of accident victims, only **Stephen** in *Griffiths* acknowledged the fact that most carers of accident victims are women, while only Gaudron in *Van Gervan* referred to literature relating to the historical devaluation of women's work. Her observation that a wife is not an 'indentured domestic servant' appears to be a direct response to Deane and **Dawson**, who took the view (in dissent) that these damages should be awarded only where a plaintiff has no wife to care for him.

In *Wynn v NSW Insurance Ministerial Corporation* (1995), the Court allowed (in part) an appeal against a substantial reduction of the damages awarded to a female senior executive for loss of earning capacity. The NSW Court of Appeal had reduced the award on two grounds: that the plaintiff would no longer incur the cost of childcare, and that she would not have continued her employment until the age of 60. The High Court lowered the reduction on both counts, holding that childcare costs should not be deducted from women's damages awards and finding that there was no evidence to suggest that the plaintiff could not 'successfully combine a demanding career and family responsibilities'.

In other cases, however, the Court has done little to dispel the image of a wife as her husband's property or appendage. Traditionally, only a husband has been entitled to sue for loss of consortium (see *Wright v Cedzich* (1930); *Toohey v Hollier* (1955)). The inequality has been addressed only by statute—in Queensland and SA by allowing either spouse to sue for loss of consortium of the other, in most other states by abolishing the husband's cause of action as obsolete.

Perhaps the clearest example of an antiquated approach to the status of woman 'as wife' is *Garcia v National Australia Bank* (1998), where the Court affirmed the principle of *Yerkey v Jones* (1939) providing a special defence for wives who have guaranteed debts for their husbands. While this led to Jean Garcia (long since divorced from the husband whose debts she had guaranteed) being relieved of liability, the majority judgments—Kirby took a different approach but agreed in the outcome—did little to clarify a complex issue that affects a much broader range of relationships than that of husband and wife. (The Court did leave open the possibility that the principle might be extended in the future.) Just as this decision provides no clear guidance on how to deal with such cases, it also shows that the Court has no clear understanding of how women are affected by legal doctrines, nor of some of the important theoretical work on gender and **equality** that might assist it in developing a clear and principled approach to such issues.

There are other areas of law (for example, sexual assault cases in **criminal law**) where women appear before the Court as witnesses or as parties. Across a variety of doctrinal areas, the Court has indeed constructed 'women', though not necessarily in a coherent way. Sometimes, the Court has recognised that women are overwhelmingly the carers of children and the ill; at other times, Justices have suggested, contrary to all data, that women and men now share the work in the home. Sometimes, the Court has decided that women should have a subjectivity independent of their husbands (for example, in relation to marital rape); at other times, that separate interest seems to disappear (for example, in *Moffa*). Thus, even if there was an opening up of opportunities for women's groups to intervene in important litigation (as may have been suggested in *CES*), it remains unclear what approach they should adopt, or what reception they would be given. The Court's ability to create its own truth about women will not be easy to influence, particularly if any intervention by women's groups should endeavour to take account of the diversity of women in the Australian community.

Even when women are absent from litigation, that does not necessarily imply that the decision will have no gendered effect. Yet explicit recognition that a decision may have a particular impact on women is comparatively rare.

Regina Graycar
Jenny Morgan

Further Reading
Regina Graycar and Jenny Morgan, *The Hidden Gender of Law* (2nd edn 2000)

Women practitioners were notably absent from the High Court for much of its history. They began to make appearances before the Court spasmodically, in the late 1930s. The frequency of these appearances increased from the 1970s, but they remain minuscule compared with those of **men**. As the Court approaches its centenary, the proportion of **women** appearing as **counsel** is less than 3 per cent, although women constitute approximately 50 per cent of law graduates and 30 per cent of practitioners, of whom approximately 12 per cent are barristers.

The absence of women needs to be understood in light of the long history of resistance towards their becoming citizens of the jurisprudential community. When the Court opened its doors in 1903, not one woman had been admitted to practise law in Australia, but the exclusion was under challenge from first-wave **feminism**. Ada Evans graduated in 1902 from the University of Sydney after a struggle to be accepted as a law student, but was refused admission to practice by the Supreme Court of NSW solely on the ground of her sex. Although she campaigned for many years to be admitted, this did not occur until 1921, following the passage of the *Women's Legal Status Act* 1918 (NSW). Not one of the **state Supreme Courts** was prepared to admit women of its own volition, despite having the power to determine fitness to practise. Enabling legislation had to be enacted in each jurisdiction separately.

The contemporary judicial belief that women were unfit to practise law by virtue of their sex is underscored by *In re Edith Haynes* (1904). The Supreme Court of WA found that Edith Haynes had no right to be admitted under the *Legal Practitioners Act* 1893 (WA) because a woman was not a 'person' for the purposes of the Act. Neither the gender-neutral language nor the well-established principles of **statutory interpretation** sufficed to overcome the prejudice towards the idea of women as legal practitioners.

In 1905, Grata Flos Greig became the first woman to be admitted to legal practice in Australia when the *Women's Disabilities Removal Act* 1903 (Vic) was passed especially for her benefit. Only a handful of women satisfied the requirements for admission to practise before the Court over the next 30 years. Women tended to play roles as solicitors, or research assistants and editors behind the scenes, rather than as advocates, but low visibility was not necessarily a matter of choice. Joan Rosanove, the first woman to sign the Bar Roll in Victoria, was offered a room in Selborne Chambers by a friend in 1925, but the directors threatened to cancel his lease if he let the room to a woman. Chagrined, Rosanove left the Bar to become an amalgam in suburban practice and did not formally return as a barrister for more than two decades.

Perhaps unsurprisingly, given these inauspicious beginnings, it was not until 1937 that a woman practitioner is recorded as first appearing before the Court, when Roma Mitchell acted as junior counsel in *Maeder v Busch* (1938). One woman in a visible, albeit non-speaking, role before the High Court over 35 years—a period that encompasses 59 volumes of the *Commonwealth Law Reports*—highlights the overwhelmingly masculinist character of the Court, a factor that has shaped both its jurisprudence and its practice. Rosanove followed in Mitchell's footsteps, appearing in *Briginshaw v Briginshaw* (1938), a case that was to become an important **precedent** for the civil standard of proof. She appeared as junior counsel with her father, Mark Lazarus, a familial relationship that facilitated the launch of her career, as it did for a number of other women practitioners. Unusually for junior counsel, Rosanove is recorded as having addressed the Court, albeit briefly. Also unusual is the fact that Rosanove subsequently appeared as either sole or leading counsel in a number of appeals, which enabled her to present **argument** before the Court.

Leading counsel have frequently been either KCs or QCs (now generally SCs), but very few women have been appointed to the senior Bar. The resistance to women practitioners has been most marked in respect of authoritative positions. Rosanove was not made a QC until 11 years after her first application and 46 years after her admission to practise, despite her undisputed leadership at the Bar in matrimonial matters. The women practitioners who appeared before the Court invariably occupied the position of junior counsel, which affirmed and perpetuated the **stereotype** that women in public life should be subordinate to men. Mitchell, the first woman to be made a QC, appeared on several occasions before the Court in the early 1960s, but only once as 'Miss RF Mitchell QC', shortly before her appointment to the Supreme Court of SA as Australia's first woman judge in 1965.

Prior to 1970, women practitioners before the Court featured in no more than two dozen reported cases. Almost all of them involved women from the less populous states, notably SA, which did not have a separate Bar. The absence of a formally divided profession—with independent barristers briefed by solicitors—removed a barrier that continues to constitute an impediment for women at the Bar. Thus, in Mitchell's first appeal, 'Nelligan (with him Roma Mitchell)' are reported as having been instructed by 'Nelligan, Angas Parsons, and Mitchell'; in *Stuart v The Queen* (1959), 'JD O'Sullivan and Miss H Devaney' appeared for the applicant, while the instructing solicitors were 'O'Sullivan and Devaney'. In Rosanove's appearances before **World War II**, she too was the instructing solicitor. A fused profession also facilitated appearances by Miss SM McClemans from WA in the 1940s and Miss NW Levis from Tasmania in the 1950s. In contrast, NSW, a jurisdiction with a rigidly separate Bar, did not have a woman practitioner appear before the Court until 1966, when Miss Janet Coombs is reported as appearing. Miss NJ Haxton, from Queensland, a state that sought to emulate NSW, appeared in 1970.

From the 1970s, women practitioners were less of a curiosity, but they continued to appear overwhelmingly as junior counsel. Nevertheless, in one striking role reversal, Miss CC Simpson appeared as leading counsel with CR Evatt QC as her junior (*Johnstone v Commonwealth* (1978–79)). Also of interest are the first husband and wife team: 'DMJ Bennett QC (with him Mrs AC Bennett)' in *Datt v Law Society of NSW* (1981), and the first all-women team, 'MG **Gaudron** QC, **Solicitor-General** for the State of New South Wales (with her RS McColl)' in *Actors Equity v Fontana Films* (1982). Nevertheless, it was not until the end of the century that women practitioners appeared in all capacities for the first time. In *Osland v The Queen* (1998), Dr Jocelynne Scutt, with Hilary Bonney, appeared on the application for **leave to appeal** for the appellant wife; Dr Scutt, with Anne Thacker and Fiona Phillips, appeared at the appeal; the instructing solicitor for Heather Osland was Susan Wakeling of Hale & Wakeling.

Roma Mitchell, the first woman to appear before the High Court

Until the 1980s, women practitioners were designated in the Reports as 'Miss' or 'Mrs'. The practice of including only the name and initials of counsel, in addition to professional rather than marital status, began to be applied to women practitioners from the early 1980s, particularly with appearances by Mary Gaudron QC and Catherine Branson, Crown Solicitor for SA and later a judge of the **Federal Court**. In contrast, the gender-specific practice of identifying counsel as either 'Mr' or 'Ms' has been adopted in the Court's **transcripts of argument**.

Women practitioners have appeared in a wide range of matters, despite a reluctance by most solicitors to brief them in anything other than **family law**, if prepared to brief them at all. During the 1980s and 1990s, a small group of women, including Susan Kenny (later a Federal Court judge) and Susan Crennan, appeared regularly in constitutional and public law cases. Indeed, government solicitors appear to have been somewhat more amenable than corporate law firms to the idea of briefing women .

A focus on a small number of very visible women can obscure the continuing disproportionality between men and women practitioners. The significant increase in the overall percentage of women practitioners, as well as the expansion in matters before the Court, has exacerbated the disparity. Its starkness is encapsulated by the pattern of representation even in cases such as *Rainsong Holdings v ACT* (1993), where scattered among the 23 counsel appearing were five women, all in supporting roles representing their respective **Attorneys-General**: Genevieve Ebbeck (SA), Susan Kenny (Victoria), Katherine Guilfoyle and Madeleine Marty (NSW), and Christine Wheeler (WA—later a judge of the Supreme Court of WA). Clearly, there have been positive changes over the century, given that there were no women practitioners at all at the outset, but change has occurred at a snail's pace. The fact that women constitute less than 3 per cent of practitioners appearing before the Court in all matters, including special leave applications, falls well short of the societal norm of gender **equality**. That the preponderance of these women appear in the less-authoritative role of junior counsel, which usually precludes them from being heard, underscores the inequality.

MARGARET THORNTON

Further Reading

Isabel Carter, *Woman in a Wig: Joan Rosanove QC* (1970)

Mary Gaudron, Speech to launch Australian Women Lawyers (1998) 72 *ALJ* 119

Michael Kirby, 'Women Lawyers: Making a Difference' (1998) 10 *AFLJ* 125

Margaret Thornton, *Dissonance and Distrust* (1996)

Women's work. When judges assess **damages** for **women** who have been injured through the negligence of others, they often tell us stories about their conceptions of women's work. Both the work women do in the paid labour market, and the work they do at home, come under scrutiny in relation to various heads of damages. The High Court has had several opportunities to consider the value of women's work in these contexts. These cases resonate with analogous cases in other areas such as **succession law** (testators' family maintenance or 'family provision'—see, for example, *Goodman v Windeyer* (1980); *Singer v Berghouse* (1994)) and **family law** (see, for example, *Mallet v Mallet* (1984); *Baumgartner v Baumgartner* (1987); *Muschinski v Dodds* (1985)). Looking at work outside the context of **labour law** provides a rare insight into the continuing marginalisation of women's paid work, and the undervaluation of their work in the home, as carers and contributors to household management.

In one of the best-known damages cases, *Sharman v Evans* (1977), the High Court considered how to value the loss of earning capacity for a young woman who had been catastrophically injured and would be unable to work again. She had been in paid work, and was engaged to be married at the time of the accident. It is not uncommon for courts to apply a considerable reduction to a damages assessment to take account of the possibility that a woman may cease paid work once she marries and has **children**. As **Gibbs** and **Stephen** noted: 'Despite recent changes in patterns of employment of married women this [cessation of paid work] remains a not unusual situation, the woman in effect exchanging the exercise of her earning capacity for such financial security as her marriage may provide.' In this instance, the Court decided to disregard the prospect of marriage, emphasising that what is compensated for is the loss of capacity, rather than the exercise of it. It was in the course of his judgment in this case that **Murphy** most clearly articulated the economic basis of the work that women do in their homes:

> A woman who loses her capacity to make the usual contributions of a wife and mother in a household suffers great economic deprivation. Actions for loss of services correctly treat this as economic injury, but as a loss to the husband on the archaic view of the husband as master or owner of his wife. The economic loss is one to the wife or mother. It is her capacity to work, either in the household or outside, which is affected.

Unfortunately, courts do not always recognise women's economic contributions so clearly. In 1994, the NSW Court of Appeal had reduced a trial judge's award for loss of earning capacity made in favour of a female senior executive injured in an accident. The trial judge had held that the plaintiff 'would have worked ... at least until the age of sixty years' and found that it was improbable that she would 'simply have retired to the laudable but limited role of housewife and mother and abandoned her business career'. In the Court of Appeal, Justice Kenneth Handley seemed unaware that it was possible (nay, common) for a woman to juggle work and family responsibilities, holding that had the plaintiff tried to do so, it would have been necessary to engage 'a

full time nanny for the children and substantial household help during the week'. Accordingly, the Court of Appeal reduced the award, partly to allow for the substantial child-care costs that she would no longer incur, and partly on the basis that she would not have worked until retirement age, since to do so 'would have placed ... heavy demands on her time, energy and health and the love and patience of her husband'. When the High Court heard the special **leave** application, **McHugh** asked: 'Supposing the applicant had been a male, could you imagine a judge making a finding like this?'

The High Court partially upheld the appeal (*Wynn v NSW Insurance Ministerial Corporation* (1995)). The Court refused to discount the award to allow for the costs of child care. **Dawson, Toohey, Gaudron,** and **Gummow** pointed out in a **joint judgment** that such costs may be incurred by **men** or women whether or not the child's mother is in the paid workforce, and added that there was 'nothing in the evidence to suggest that the appellant was any less able than any other career oriented person, whether male or female, to successfully combine a demanding career and family responsibilities'.

A related, but quite different, issue is how to calculate an award for the cost of services an injured plaintiff requires. In *Griffiths v Kerkemeyer* (1977), the High Court held that an accident victim can recover the costs of care from a defendant, even where the care is provided 'gratuitously'— that is, at no cost to the plaintiff (and see the analogous *Nguyen v Nguyen* (1990) dealing with fatal accidents). Stephen expressly noted that most carers of accident victims are women: a rare acknowledgment of context that stands in contrast to Gibbs' use of gender-neutral language to refer to the services provided by 'a relative or friend' to the 'plaintiff'.

Even after the decision in *Griffiths*, state courts continued to discount damages awards where family members provided care, suggesting that such work was merely part of the 'ordinary currency of family life and obligation' (see, for example, *Kovac v Kovac* (1980)). The issue came before the High Court again in *Van Gervan v Fenton* (1992). There, the question was how to place a value on the cost of such care. The judgment under review had affirmed the trial court's decision that the appropriate measure of damages was what Mrs Lambertus Van Gervan had previously earned while working as a nurse's aide in a nursing home. A majority of the Court decided that the cost of care is generally the market or replacement cost for those services, rather than the opportunity cost (that is, what the provider of the services had forgone by undertaking that work).

Deane and **Dawson** dissented: in their view, while if the plaintiff had not been married, it might have been reasonable to award him the market cost of purchasing the services he needed, the fact that he had a wife available to undertake that care meant that 'the ordinary incidents of a particular continuing relationship' ought not be transformed into 'services' for which a market cost is to be paid. They failed to acknowledge that there was no guarantee that Van Gervan, or any family member in a similar situation, would remain available to provide that type of care. And they also glossed over the disparity between work outside the home (usually, about 35 hours per week if it is 'full time'), and virtually 24 hours a day, seven days a week caring work—though they did note that the plaintiff could be left alone for periods of 'up to one hour'.

Only Gaudron noted the 'degree of controversy as to the true nature of work that is usually perceived as "women's work", whether … in the home or in the paid work force' and reminded us that a wife is not an 'indentured domestic servant'. She echoed those sentiments in the family provision case of *Singer v Berghouse* (1994) where, in a minority judgment, she noted: 'The tendency of the courts to overlook or undervalue women's work, whether in the home or in the paid work force, has often been remarked upon.'

Notwithstanding these occasional judicial acknowledgments, that tendency to undervalue or ignore women's work continues. By naming the problem, and describing it as a broader issue about the valuation of women's work, whether it emerges in a succession case or a damages case, Gaudron, like Murphy before her, has at least acknowledged its existence.

REGINA GRAYCAR

Further Reading
Regina Graycar, 'Hoovering as a Hobby and Other Stories: Gendered Assessments of Personal Injury Damages' (1997) 31 *UBCLR* 17

Workers' compensation, as it developed in Australia, was just as much 'a new province of law and order' as **conciliation and arbitration** in the field of **labour relations**.

Appeals to the High Court on the interpretation of the various state and Commonwealth schemes have come from **state Supreme Courts**, and decisions relating to Commonwealth employees. The early state compensation schemes largely followed the UK legislation, and the Court, particularly before the *Workers Compensation Act* 1926 (NSW), relied extensively on English precedents.

The NSW Act introduced a far more comprehensive scheme than any previous legislation, with new benefits and major extensions of the circumstances under which compensation was payable and the class of persons entitled to claim. It departed materially from the schemes then in force in the UK and in other states, and has since been subject to progressive and extensive amendment.

In the UK, the progressive updating of the *Workmens Compensation Acts* 1925–45 ceased in 1945. For the most part, the Acts were simply repealed when the whole field of disability, whether resulting from illness or injury, was taken over by the *National Insurance (Industrial Injuries) Act* 1946 (UK). Consequently, all the English cases to which the High Court has frequently referred became less relevant to the Australian provisions—in which the basic definition of 'injury', for instance, has been changed in ways that make it totally different from the English provisions.

All the early Australian statutes, following the English legislation, provided that the payment of compensation by employers depended upon the worker having suffered an 'injury by accident arising out of and in the course of employment'. The 1926 NSW Act omitted the requirement that the injury be 'by accident', though the Commonwealth and many of the other states retained it until late into the twentieth century.

The retention by some states of the requirement of 'injury by accident' influenced the Court in its approach to the question of whether or not an injury arose in the course of employment. Moreover, most states retained for a significant time the requirement that an injury 'in the course of' employment must also arise 'out of' the employment. In determining whether an injury occurred in the course of the employment, the Court frequently imported a requirement that it must also be causally connected with the employment—even after the relevant legislation required that the injury need only be one 'arising out of *or* in the course of employment'. NSW had adopted this alternative form in 1942. (In WA a similar change, though still in relation to 'injury by accident', had been made in 1924.)

On its face, this statutory construction appears to give rise to two alternative bases for compensation. While an injury 'arising out of' the employment must have some causal connection with the employment, the requirement of an injury 'in the course of employment' is 'satisfied if the accident happens *while* the workman is doing something in the exercise of his functions' (emphasis added) (*Pearson v Fremantle Harbour Trust* (1929)). The connection with the employment is purely temporal; no causal link is required. Yet the idea that an injury 'in the course of employment' must have some causal connection with the employment has repeatedly reasserted itself. The reasons include the continuing influence of the English cases on 'injury by accident'; the diversity of statutory provisions in different Australian jurisdictions, exacerbated by the sometimes confusing effect of repeated statutory amendments; and the interplay of cases where the alleged injury occurs at work (that is, 'in the course of employment') with those arising from the statutory provision (introduced in NSW in 1942) for compensation where the injury is suffered during the 'daily or other periodic journey' to and from work. In *Hume Steel v Peart* (1947), for example, the Court held that, while a causal connection was required for injuries 'in the course of employment', in the 'journey' cases only a temporal connection was required.

The difficulty is most acute in those cases (of which *Peart* was one) where the alleged 'injury' is attributable to the natural progression of a pre-existing 'disease'. The English cases had made it clear that the consequences of a systemic disease could not be regarded as an 'accident', and, as **Latham** pointed out in *Peart*, there is an obvious difference 'between getting hurt and becoming sick'. Nevertheless, a disablement arising from 'disease' might be regarded as an 'injury' in at least two types of case: those where the disablement arises not merely from gradual deterioration but from a sudden traumatic breakage or rupture; and those where the disease is contracted because the worker's body is invaded by a virus during the course of employment.

Peart was a case of the former kind. The worker had died as a result of a coronary occlusion suffered while pedalling a bicycle uphill in the rain on his way to work. Part of the coronary artery had come loose and blocked the artery, enabling Latham to observe that he saw no difference between a broken leg and a broken artery. The difficulty was that, at least for injuries arising 'in the course of employment', the NSW Act had defined 'injury' to include a disease, but only one 'to which the employment was a contributing factor'. The question was whether the word 'injury' in the 'journey' provision was governed by this limiting definition, or was open to a broader interpretation. The Court took the broader view.

This appeared to imply, however, that, outside the special context of the 'journey' provision, 'arising out of or in the course of the employment' was still to be treated as a composite phrase, so that causal connection with the employment would still be necessary where the alleged injury was suffered at work. A worker suffering a heart attack on a journey to or from work would be entitled to compensation, but a worker who collapsed from such an attack immediately before leaving work would not be so entitled. Latham thought this a 'remarkable' anomaly, but one to be left 'for the consideration of the legislature'.

In *Slazengers v Burnett* (1950), the **Privy Council** rejected the reasoning in *Peart's Case*, holding that the word 'injury' must have the same meaning in the journey provisions as elsewhere in the Act; a heart attack suffered during the journey to work would be compensable only if the employment (including the journey) was a contributing factor. Lord Simonds agreed with Latham that the consequences of the interpretation in *Peart's Case* were anomalous, and took 'the clue' to a coherent construction from **Dixon's** observation in *Peart's Case* that 'in a general way … injury received in the course of [the] journey is to stand in the same position as injury in the course of employment'. He concluded that 'the result of this construction is to displace the reasoning on which the decision in *Peart's Case* was largely based'.

When the High Court, in *Darling Island Stevedoring v Hussey* (1959), considered the effect of the Privy Council's decision, **Fullagar** held flatly that *Peart's Case* must be treated as **overruled**. Dixon understood the Privy Council as holding that the 'journey' provisions did not cover a case of disease, unless, as required by the definition of 'injury', it was a disease 'contracted by the worker in the course of his employment … and to which the employment was a contributing factor'.

Peart, Slazengers and *Hussey* all involved heart attacks. In *Peart*, a majority of the Court accepted that, even if the requirement of causal connection applied, it was satisfied by the effort of pedalling up hill in the rain. In *Slazengers*, where the heart attack was suffered during a tram ride to work, any causative element of 'physical effort' had been expressly negated. In *Hussey*, the heart attack occurred while the worker was waiting to sign on for work after climbing two flights of stairs. An argument that the heart attack had been triggered by the effort of climbing the stairs was offered, but rejected.

The *Workers Compensation (Amendment) Act* 1960 (NSW) removed some of the effects of the decision in *Hussey*, but implicitly accepted its correctness. In the new definition of injury, 'disease' was expressed to include 'the aggravation, acceleration, exacerbation or deterioration of any disease, where the employment was a contributing factor to such aggravation'. This statutory change would appear to have ruled out, once and for all, any argument that a temporal connection alone would suffice.

However, the controversy was revived in *Kavanagh v Commonwealth* (1960), where a widow claimed compensation under the *Commonwealth Employees Compensation Act* 1930 (Cth) for the death of her husband, which resulted from pneumonia and heart failure supervening upon a rupture of the oesophagus during working hours at his place of employment. The Commonwealth Act at that time still required an injury to be suffered as a result of accident.

Dixon had no difficulty in classifying the rupture as an injury by accident. He also held that it did occur in the course of the employment, since this included visits to the toilet and pauses in the actual performance of work activities. The real difficulty was whether it was necessary for the injury to have anything more than a temporal connection with the employment. The vomiting attack that caused the rupture had no known connection with the employment: it could have occurred at any time. The Commonwealth relied on the Court's earlier decision in *Commonwealth v Ockenden* (1958), where a valvular regurgitation happening while at work was held not to be an 'injury by accident', because it was the natural progressive consequence of an attack of rheumatic fever in childhood. In that case, the Court had held:

> In cases where it must be established that the so-called injury by accident arose in the course of the worker's employment … the traditional view must still prevail that a physiological change, sudden or otherwise, is not an injury by accident arising in the course of the employment unless it is associated with some incident of the employment.

In *Kavanagh*, however, Dixon considered that this statement of the law could not be pressed further than applying to events that were the inevitable consequences of non-employment-related diseases. He considered it significant that the Commonwealth Act had originally followed the English legislation, but like other state Acts, had been amended to make the two elements of the definition of injury alternative: the legislative change could not be ignored. An injury that did not arise out of the employment could still be suffered in the course of the employment, even where there was no causal connection with the employment. Furthermore, he held that the expression 'in the course of the employment' did not require an element of causation. No longer could the statutory alternatives be regarded as cumulative.

Taylor and **Windeyer** dissented. For Taylor, it was enough that at the time the oesophagus ruptured, the worker was not in the course of performing the work he was employed to do, nor anything incidental to that work. The rupture had not the remotest connection or association either with the work, or with any activity incidental to it.

In short, the division of opinion re-echoed the earlier uncertainty in the journey cases. On the one hand, full effect is given to the temporal nature of the expression 'in the course of', while on the other, some element of causal connection is still insisted upon.

In *Favelle Mort v Murray* (1976), the whole Court held that meningo-encephalitis contracted by an Australian worker during the construction of the World Trade Centre in New York was a disease to which his employment was a contributing factor. He was therefore entitled to compensation. Again, however, the reasoning accepted the need for a causal connection. While **Jacobs** agreed on the simpler basis that 'the entry of the virus into the human body' is itself a physical 'injury'—an invasive event—he, too, accepted that the employment must be a 'contributing factor'. He distinguished the decisions in *Slazengers* and *Hussey* as dealing only with autogenous disease. **Barwick** agreed with this approach in principle, but thought that it entailed a degree of departure from *Slazengers* that could not be entertained until 'the Court as a whole' had determined the extent to which it remained bound by Privy Council authority. That determination came only in **Viro v The Queen** (1978).

In *Hockey v Yelland* (1984)—a case of cerebral haemorrhage under the Queensland legislation—the leading judgments of **Gibbs** and **Wilson** both reaffirmed *Slazengers* and *Hussey*, though they left open the possibility of confining those precedents to cases of autogenous disease. Even when the issue surfaced again in *Zickar v MGH Plastic Industries* (1996), only **Kirby** held flatly that *Slazengers* should be overruled. **Toohey**, **McHugh**, and **Gummow** joined him, however, in holding that the rupture of a cerebral aneurism could be treated as an 'injury arising … in the course of employment', entitling the worker to compensation without any need to demonstrate a causal connection with the employment. They conceded that, although the rupture of the arterial wall was an injury, 'the aneurism itself, that is the swelling of the blood vessel, was a disease'; but denied that this necessarily attracted the statutory category of 'disease … to which the employment was a contributing factor'.

The problem was that the *Workers Compensation Act* 1987 (NSW), replacing the 1926 Act, had elaborately divided the definition of compensable injury into paragraphs and subparagraphs—with the general definition of 'injury arising out of or in the course of employment' re-enacted as paragraph (a), and the formula about 'disease … to which the employment was a contributing factor' as paragraph (b)(ii). The majority held that paragraphs (a) and (b) were not mutually exclusive: so long as the rupture of the aneurism satisfied the definition of 'injury' in paragraph (a), the presence of the underlying disease did not shift the case into paragraph (b). **Brennan**, **Dawson**, and **Gaudron**, however, took the opposite view—so that even then, on the underlying issue of the need for a causal connection with the employment, the Court remained divided.

A broader approach has been taken by the Court in relation to injuries suffered during many of the permitted breaks or pauses in the performance of active duties in the employment. The Workers Compensation Commission, which had judicial functions prior to the creation of the Compensation Court of NSW in 1984, had taken the view that a worker who sustained an injury during any of these periods was entitled to compensation if acting reasonably, and not engaging in a 'frolic of his own'. The High Court supported this approach against a more restrictive approach by the NSW Supreme Court. In *Commonwealth v Oliver* (1962), as summarised by CP Mills,

> Dixon CJ himself said that 'the course of the employment has doubtless widened its practical boundaries with the enlarged conception of what belongs to the factory or other organized industrial unit in the amenities and welfare of the staff or labour force'. In particular, he would regard lunch-time cricket now 'as more regularly and commonly accepted as a concomitant or incident' of the employment.

There are many other respects in which the Australian workers' compensation legislation has created a totally new province of law and order. The legislation is mainly concerned with compensation for workers who are injured. However, the category of 'worker' has been expanded to cover 'deemed workers', who do not work under traditional contracts of service and, on the old definition of 'worker' in the master and servant sense, could under no circumstances be regarded as workers (see **Employment law**). Further, new statutory rules have been introduced to fix liability to pay compensation on particular persons and entities. Provisions have been introduced in relation to compulsory insurance for the purpose of ensuring that, where compensation has been ordered, there will always be some viable entity capable of paying workers' benefits. The Court has been involved in extensive litigation involving the interpretation of all these expansive and novel provisions. In addition, the tendency of the various Commonwealth and state legislatures to introduce a degree of retrospectivity into changes in compensation legislation has raised novel and complex problems (see, for example, *Nash v Sunshine Porcelain Potteries* (1959)).

Workers' compensation has become an infinitely expanding field, which has in many ways taken over large parts of the area formerly covered by **common law** actions for **damages** for personal injury arising out of negligence and breach of statutory duty by employers. The overlapping of these two fields gives rise to questions of adjustments between them, double benefits, and double insurance, which have added to the flood of litigation, frequently ending up in the High Court. What were originally simple provisions designed to tide a worker over for a limited period until he recovered his work capacity have developed into a whole galaxy of provisions involving adjudication upon difficult issues of insurance law, licensing, and the administration of quite new machinery erected to insure the proper behaviour and solvency of insurers providing workers' compensation cover, or upon the operation of the various administrative schemes which have, in many areas, taken over the provision of insurance cover for workers' compensation.

Frank McGrath

Further Reading
CP Mills, *Workers Compensation (New South Wales)* (2nd edn 1979)

World War I broke out in August 1914, when the High Court had already shared in the experience of nation-building for over a decade. The Commonwealth itself had come to birth during the Imperial struggle in South Africa (1898–1902), and the challenge of war was not new. But the Great War was different, both in size and significance, from anything since the French Revolution and the advent of Napoleon.

In every country, the war intensified the uncertainties of a changing society: in Australia, it did so through the ambiguous relationship between nationalism and **federalism**, the unprecedented strain on civil rights, and the economic and community tensions arising from an all-out war effort. The Court, like other Commonwealth institutions, was on trial for its relevance, efficiency, and capacity to maintain social coherence and balance. Inevitably, the rhythms of the Court's life changed.

The Australian plenipotentiaries and staff at the peace conference in Paris, 1919. Pictured in the first row (first, third, and fourth, respectively) are Latham, WM Hughes, and Robert Garran

The **appointments** of Isaacs and **Higgins** in 1906 had already disrupted the harmony of the early **Griffith Court**, and in 1913 the advent of **Gavan Duffy**, **Powers**, and **Rich** had further diluted Griffith's influence. The war added urgent new 'national' pressure on all Australian institutions, from which the Court was not immune. As Griffith's biographer, Roger Joyce, writes: 'Relationships on the High Court bench were strained after 1914, with the strong differences on commonwealth–state powers being accentuated' (see **Intergovernmental immunities**).

All the Justices were personally affected by the war. Rich's son was killed at Anzac Cove. Higgins had travelled overseas in August 1914, 'a strange and unsettling odyssey of anxiety and disruption', fully participating in the social and political life of a London preparing for war, and returning in May 1915. His only son survived Gallipoli, only to be killed in Egypt in 1916. **Griffith** had spent most of 1913 abroad, and his health was clearly deteriorating by 1914. In March 1917, he had a stroke and was forced to leave the Bench until February 1918. **Barton** was in England at the **Privy Council** during 1915, and spent some time with his soldier son. The course of the war, the drastic legislation, and the erratic behaviour of WM Hughes as **Prime Minister** all affected the Court.

Initially, the war's influence on the Court's decisions was unpredictable. In the *Wheat Case* (1915), the Court effectively upheld a Commonwealth scheme for the wartime control of essential foodstuffs; but the decision itself concerned the validity of cooperative state legislation, and Griffith did not think it necessary to deal with 'the arguments founded upon the actual conditions' of war.

Yet, only a day earlier, the Court had disposed *ex tempore* of *Corbet v Lovekin* (1915), in which **military** arguments and the *War Precautions Act* 1914 (Cth) were crucial. The WA chief censor had charged the proprietors of the Perth *Daily News* with publishing information about the Suez Canal that might be 'useful to the enemy'. A Perth magistrate dismissed the complaint. The whole Court refused to hear the censor's appeal. Isaacs protested, however, that since the Canal's strategic importance was 'common knowledge', the information 'could not but be of immense importance to the enemy'; he regretted that technical constraints on the grant of special **leave to appeal** had prevented the Court's intervention, 'not merely for the safety of the Empire but for the defence of our fellow Australians'. Griffith leapt to distance himself from these comments, declaring that the publication 'was not, in any rational sense of the words, one which was calculated to be or which might be advantageous to the enemy'.

Thereafter, the Court repeatedly accepted the need to curtail peacetime legal rights in the interests of the war effort. In *Lloyd v Wallach* (1915), the Court upheld regulations made under the War Precautions Act and returned Franz Wallach to military custody. Initially interned on suspicion of being 'disaffected or disloyal', he had been discharged by the Supreme Court of Victoria because the minister refused to divulge his reasons for believing Wallach disloyal. Even Higgins agreed that the Parliament was entitled to entrust the minister with 'extraordinary powers during the present extraordinary war'. In *Sickerdick v Ashton* (1918), a Victorian magistrate had acquitted the respondent of a charge that his pamphlet calling for a truce 'while the Peace Conference is sitting' might prejudice recruiting efforts; but the Court allowed the informant's appeal. Again affirming the validity of the regulations, Barton stressed that the Court's role was purely legal: 'Questions of propriety and wisdom are for the Parliament.' Isaacs also stressed that he had 'nothing to do as a Judge with the **policy** of the regulation', but went on to complain that the pamphlet 'elevates Germany as a country seeking peace', despite that country's pursuit of 'world mastery' through 'terrorism' and 'ruthless and cynical disregard of all human rights and … national honour'.

Deference to the government on sensitive 'enemy alien' questions persisted well after the cessation of hostilities, as the Court's 1920 decisions regarding Father Charles Jerger indicate. This popular, outspoken Catholic priest was interned during the war on account of his German heritage, and was ultimately deported. In May 1920, in *Jerger v Pearce (No 1)*, his challenge to a deportation order failed, the Court construing the relevant legislation strictly to negate his claim to British **citizenship**. In July 1920, in *Jerger v Pearce (No 2)*, **Starke**, sitting alone, rejected Jerger's argument that the valid operation of the wartime regulations had been terminated by peace with Germany, because there was still no formal proclamation of peace with Austria–Hungary.

Deference also characterised the Court's approach to the Commonwealth's **defence power**, most clearly in *Farey v Burvett* (1916). The War Precautions Act had authorised the making of regulations 'for the more effectual prosecution of the war', and the Commonwealth had used that power to set maximum prices for flour and bread. A Victorian magistrate had convicted WA Farey of overcharging for bread. Upholding the conviction, Griffith described the defence power as 'a paramount power', since 'the best security of Australia lies in the success of the British arms'. So long as a particular exercise of the power 'could be warranted', it was up to the executive, not the Court, to identify the measures necessary to meet the defence objective.

Similarly, the Court accepted the defence power as underpinning the War Precautions (Moratorium) Regulations, which placed restrictions on mortgagees and other creditors wishing to call up loans. In *In re Allen* (1917), Isaacs accepted that 'having regard to the general dislocation of affairs directly and indirectly occasioned by the War, it is *prima facie* contrary to the public welfare to permit mortgagees to rigidly enforce their strict rights against their debtors'. Other Justices proved equally resistant to the demands of nervous creditors (see, for example, *In re Hynds* (1917)).

The success of wartime measures adopted by the states was less predictable, in part due to the shadow of section 92 of the Constitution, guaranteeing free **interstate trade**. In the *Wheat Case*, the *Wheat Acquisition Act* 1914 (NSW) survived constitutional challenge; but in *Foggitt Jones v NSW* (1916) the *Meat Supply for Imperial Uses Act* 1915 (NSW) fell foul of section 92. A bacon manufacturer in Queensland owning pigs in NSW wished to take them over the border. NSW refused permission, since under the Act, all stock was to be held for the Imperial war effort. In finding that this infringed section 92, the Court distinguished the *Wheat Case* by saying that the legislation in that case dealt only with the ownership of the wheat, divesting the wheat growers of their property *before* its entry into interstate trade. The legislation in *Foggitt*

Jones had operated to prevent the interstate movement of stock *before* the state government acquired it.

Yet within six months, Griffith changed his mind. In a case involving equivalent Queensland legislation, *Duncan v Queensland* (1916), he held that the impact on interstate trade, regardless of the timing of the acquisition, was 'merely incidental' to the Act's 'main purpose' of conserving meat for Imperial Forces. 'The Court is bound to take **judicial notice** of the War, and of the fact that an adequate supply of meat to the Forces is essential to the effectual prosecution of the War.'

Despite its ready acceptance of 'special measures', the Court was not prepared to tolerate the erosion of **due process** by reason only of the war. In *McDonnell v Smith* (1918), the Commonwealth argued that the War Precautions Act permitted the commencement of certain prosecutions before the necessary ministerial consent had been granted. In a unanimous *ex tempore* decision, the Court rejected that construction, favouring a much stricter reading to preserve the usual procedural protections for accused persons. Rather than justifying a loosening of safeguards, the Court saw the wartime context as a reason for additional vigilance. As Rich explained, 'the necessity for getting the prescribed consent to a prosecution is a check on irresponsible persons who might heatedly, although from patriotic motives, institute proceedings'.

While due process was defended valiantly during the war, the **separation of powers** doctrine was not implemented anywhere near as rigorously as it is today. Griffith, in particular, willingly dispensed advice to the Governor-General and the Hughes government on highly sensitive issues—sometimes on his own initiative. In May 1916, Griffith wrote to the Governor-General to convey his concerns that a challenge to wartime regulations (apparently *Farey v Burvett*) was imminent, and might succeed. This letter concluded with the astonishing assurance that: 'Any help I can give in planning any necessary legislation is, as I told Mr Hughes before he left for England, at the service of the Government.' Griffith's disregard for the traditional constraints of judicial office was again evident in December 1917, around the time of the second conscription plebiscite. He provided ongoing advice to the Governor-General concerning the scope of the latter's reserve powers, as well as the legal effect of Hughes' pledge to resign if the plebiscite went against conscription. Yet all of this occurred behind closed doors, Griffith's public persona remaining one of distance from the political fray. So successfully did he maintain this appearance that he was entrusted with the sensitive 1918 Royal Commission into soldier numbers and projected recruitment needs.

In his judgments, at any rate, Griffith appeared fully cognisant of the important distinction between the **role** of the Court and that of the legislature under a separation of powers. In *R v Snow* (1915), an Adelaide merchant had been indicted, under the *Trading with the Enemy Act* 1914 (Cth), for attempting to procure a consignment of copper for supply to a German manufacturer. The trial judge directed the jury to find him not guilty, and by 4:2 (Isaacs and Higgins dissenting) the Court declined to review the decision. Isaacs stressed that the alleged offence would be 'one of unparalleled gravity in the history of Australia'; 'an unpardonable act' that would enable 'our enemies to sow death and destruction in our ranks and those of our Allies'; 'a deliberate and sustained and sordid disregard … of the ties of allegiance to the Sovereign, and the most sacred bonds of honour and fidelity and natural sentiment towards his fellow subjects'. Powers, with Griffith's endorsement, responded that the Court 'had no right to adopt one practice in time of war and another in time of peace. It is for Parliament, not this Court, during time of war to take any exceptional and extreme steps necessary for the defence of Australia and its people; and all Parliaments are doing so'.

Isaacs was undeterred. In *Farey v Burvett*, his patriotic fervour was in full flight:

> A war imperilling our very existence, involving not the internal development of progress, but the array of the whole community in mortal combat with the common enemy, is a fact of such transcendent and dominating character as to take precedence of every other fact of life. It is the *ultima ratio* of the nation … When we see before us a mighty and unexampled struggle in which we as a people, as an indivisible people, are not spectators but actors … the Court has then reached the limit of its jurisdiction.

Barton did not share this hysteria and was clearly suspicious of the various wartime restrictions on **civil liberties**. In *Pankhurst v Porter* (1917), he quashed on a technicality the convictions of Melbourne anti-war activist Adela Pankhurst, daughter of famous suffragette Emmeline, and two others. Addressing a Melbourne rally, they had urged the crowd to march on Parliament House to accost Prime Minister Hughes. Each was charged, under the War Precautions Regulations, with unlawfully assembling 'on the pretext of making known their grievances'. Barton's leading judgment insisted that the women had assembled not on the 'pretext' but for the express 'purpose' of making their grievances known. On this nice distinction, all three were freed.

Rich brought a poignant humaneness to his **non-judicial function** as Royal Commissioner into the administration of a military camp at Liverpool. After spending 14 days resident at the camp, collecting evidence and examining conditions at first hand, Rich delivered a damning report in August 1915. In addition to exposing a catalogue of particular inadequacies, his report was also critical of the entire pedagogy of the camp. In Rich's view, 'the Spartan-like method of exposing soft recruits to unnecessary privations and hardships is not only cruel, but calculated to endanger their lives'.

Higgins had long been recognised as an eminent jurist and confident, modern politician. He had been the **Attorney-General** and solitary non-Labor member of the first federal Labor government, and as President of the Arbitration Court was inured to the vituperation of capitalists offended by his form of social activism. Yet although he had from the time of the Boer War hated conflict—at the outbreak of hostilities, he was president of the Australian Peace Alliance—he was as patriotic as the next man. The war was a turbulent time for Higgins, not helped by Hughes' dynamic and controversial role as wartime Prime Minister. Such a paladin of tolerance, the 'fair go' and modern civilisation was not to be stampeded into trampling on conscientious objectors or maximising grandiosely the powers of the servile state. Yet neither he nor Isaacs could withstand the enormity of war, or the injustices wrought upon enemy aliens in detention.

Even in a time of global conflict, the Court did not shirk its role as 'keystone of the federal arch'. When the Court sat on 13 November 1918, Griffith spoke movingly of the signing of the armistice as 'an occasion without precedent in the recorded annals of the world. After being oppressed for more than four years by the most savage war, conducted with most unbridled outrage, we can look forward with confidence to a period comparatively free from anxiety'—a time of national 'recasting of conditions and … revision of doctrines that have long been regarded by multitudes as axiomatic and fundamental'. He called for an end to the warfare of class against class as well as among the nations, and for the forging of a 'sense of equality and of the paramount duty of every man to bear his part of the load of his neighbours' burdens as well as of his own'.

It would be easier said than done. The first fine and innocent days of the youthful federation during the decade of 'colonial nationalism' had yielded to the harsh experience of an emerging nation, gravely disillusioned by its blooding at the Dardanelles and the Western Front.

JOHN EDDY
AMELIA SIMPSON

World War II demonstrated that Australia's Constitution is a sufficiently flexible instrument of government to allow a virtually complete concentration of power in the federal executive for purposes of war. This was achieved by a strong national government using a greatly expanded **defence power** sanctioned by a compliant High Court. World War II was the occasion of Australia's achieving effective independence as a nation in international affairs, as well as greater consolidation of national power for domestic governance.

Australia entered the war as a loyal British dominion with its foreign and defence policies still entrusted to the British government. **Prime Minister** Robert Menzies announced, on 3 September 1939, his 'melancholy duty' of officially informing Australians that Great Britain had declared war on Germany and that 'as a result Australia is also at war'. As had been the case in **World War I**, Australian volunteer forces were soon fighting thousands of miles from home in the Battle for Britain and around the Mediterranean. Over the next two years, however, both the national government and the international situation changed dramatically, with Australia having to fight for its own survival against Japanese aggression in the Pacific.

During the first year of the war, Australia was ruled by a fractious United Australia (UAP) and Country Party coalition government. The election of 21 September 1940 had resulted in a deadlock with two independents—Arthur Coles and Alex Wilson—holding the balance of power. Menzies continued as Prime Minister, but he was replaced by Arthur Fadden on 29 August 1941. Such instability was the final straw for the two independents, who switched their support to Labor. On 7 October 1941, the Curtin government was sworn in. Labor provided the strong government Australia needed during wartime and remained in federal office until the end of 1949, winning national elections with decisive

Dixon, Australian Minister in Washington during World War II, and Lady Dixon, speaking to an Australian audience on a short wave Anzac broadcast, New York, 26 December 1943

majorities in both Houses of Parliament in August 1943 and September 1946.

Besides waging war, the Curtin (1941–45) and Chifley (1945–49) governments used war powers and the war environment to advance Labor's political agenda during this 'Golden Era' of federal Labor rule. The main strands of Labor's policy were greater national independence in international affairs, increased centralisation of power in the Commonwealth, a more extensive welfare state, and, most controversial of all, the nationalisation of key industries. Such an ambitious program required substantial constitutional change, some of which occurred: Australia became a more independent and more centralised nation. However, Labor's more extreme postwar attempts at concentrating power in Canberra and nationalising industries such as airlines and banking were defeated—either by the Australian people voting in referendums, or by the High Court in its exercise of **judicial review** (see *Bank Nationalisation Case* (1948)).

Evatt had resigned from the High Court after ten years of service to enter federal Parliament in the September 1940 election. As both **Attorney-General** and Minister for External Affairs from 1941 to 1949, he was prominent in public affairs and in the constitutional battles of the decade.

The Labor government signalled a more independent stance in foreign affairs by making Australia's own declaration of war on Japan on 8 December 1941, after the treacherous bombing of Pearl Harbour. This was Australia's first assertion of equal status with Britain in external affairs. In principle, the British dominions had won that status by their military contributions in World War I. It was formally acknowledged by the Balfour Declaration of 1926, and was put on a legislative basis by the *Statute of Westminster* 1931 (Imp). For dominions to which that statute applied, it repealed the *Colonial Laws Validity Act* 1865 (UK) and provided that British laws no longer had Imperial paramountcy in the dominions. Its operation was subject to adoption by individual member countries, however, and conservative Australian governments were opposed to the breaking of legal links with Britain. The Labor government passed the *Statute of Westminster Adoption Act* 1942 (Cth), with retrospective effect to the beginning of the war, to ensure the Commonwealth's authority over its own naval forces and foreign shipping in Australian ports.

Faced with the Japanese threat to national survival, Australia reoriented its outlook to the Asia–Pacific region and switched its main strategic alliance to the USA. Australia built up its own diplomatic service through the Department of External Affairs, with senior High Court Justices serving as interim ambassadors: **Latham** to Japan (1940–41) and **Dixon** to the USA (1942–44). Evatt contributed significantly to the founding conference of the UN in 1945 and was president of the General Assembly for its third session (1948–49). But his efforts to give smaller countries such as Australia a larger voice in international affairs foundered on the Great Power politics that divided spheres of influence in the latter stages of the war, and on the **Cold War** that divided West and East in the postwar period.

During the war, and only gradually tapering off during postwar reconstruction, power was centralised in the Commonwealth executive, governing mainly through National Security Regulations. Under the *National Security Act 1939* (Cth), the executive was given sweeping powers for securing public safety and defence and could prescribe 'all matters' deemed necessary for the 'more effectual prosecution of the war'. Labor's strong central government received minimal parliamentary scrutiny and was endorsed by the High Court. The mood of the Court was summed up by veteran Justice **Rich**, who allowed that the nation's survival required 'what is in effect a dictatorship with power to do anything which can contribute to defence' (*Dawson v Commonwealth* (1946)).

Accordingly, the Court upheld the provision in the National Security Act empowering the executive to govern by regulation (*Wishart v Fraser* (1941)). It subsequently allowed broad regulations controlling prices, the workforce, and the production and distribution of goods, as well as regulations controlling landlord and tenant relations and rents, fixing maximum and minimum share prices, prohibiting advertising for special occasions such as Christmas, and adjusting contracts to take account of war conditions. Labor used its war power to regulate industrial relations, including regulating the wages and conditions of **women** and limiting the holidays of state employees engaged in industry. Some regulatory schemes had only tenuous links with defence: one example was a national marketing scheme for apples and pears (*Andrews v Howell* (1941)); another was restricting drinking hours in hotels (*de Mestre v Chisholm* (1944)). In gruff dissents, **Starke** rejected the effective suspension of **federalism** and the Commonwealth's seizure of power over 'the whole social, industrial and economic conditions of Australia' (*Women's Employment Case* (1943)). However, Latham spoke for a majority of Justices in professing to find it 'difficult to think of a modern State conducting a large-scale war without the power of controlling the industry of the country' (*Australian Woollen Mills v Commonwealth* (1944)).

There were some limits to what the defence power allowed. The Court struck down the federal government's attempt to regulate the working conditions of state public servants engaged in routine administrative work. It disallowed the regulation of admissions to universities (*R v University of Sydney; Ex parte Drummond* (1943)), controls over the making of insect sprays (*Wertheim v Commonwealth* (1945)), and setting standards for artificial lighting in factories (*Industrial Lighting Case* (1943)). While allowing a generous transitional phase of regulation for postwar reconstruction, the Court began pegging back the scope of the defence power for central regulation of the **economy** in 1947 and 1948.

More enduring for peacetime was the High Court's endorsement of Labor's uniform tax scheme (*Uniform Tax Case* (1942)). Although the case was decided at the height of the war, only one element of the scheme—the Commonwealth's takeover of state tax offices—depended on the defence power. The more important parts of the scheme depended on the Commonwealth's taxing and grants powers. Despite a challenge by four states, the Court refused to consider the argument that the various Acts constituted a Commonwealth scheme to monopolise income tax and exclude the states from the field. Because it did not depend crucially on the defence power, the Commonwealth's income tax monopoly was easily made a permanent feature of Australian federalism after the war, and was endorsed by the Court in 1957 without any reliance on the defence power (*Second Uniform Tax Case* (1957)). As a result, Australian federalism became more fiscally centralised than that of any comparable federal country.

During the war, Labor began laying the foundations for postwar economic management and social welfare. When the states refused to transfer postwar reconstruction powers to Canberra after a 1942 conference, Evatt proposed a sweeping constitutional **amendment** instead. The Commonwealth was to be given 14 new heads of power, including power over employment, production, companies, national **health**, and **Aboriginal people**, as well as guaranteeing freedom of speech and religion. The package was defeated in the referendum of 19 August 1944. A proposal for bolstering the Commonwealth's power over social services—maternity allowances, widow's pensions, child endowment, unemployment, pharmaceutical, sickness and hospital benefits and dental services, benefits to students, and family allowances—was approved at a referendum on 28 September 1946; but other proposals for expanding **Commonwealth legislative power** over marketing of primary production and industrial relations were again defeated. The social services amendment was necessary because the High Court had struck down Labor's pharmaceutical scheme in 1945 (*First Pharmaceutical Benefits Case* (1945)), throwing into doubt Labor's strategy of using the Commonwealth's spending power to implement social welfare programs.

The High Court was instrumental in restricting Labor's social welfare and socialisation objectives, striking down airline nationalisation in 1945, bank nationalisation in 1948, and a second pharmaceutical benefits scheme in 1949. Ironically, it was able to do so because Evatt had headed off an attempt to pack the Court. The Labor Cabinet had decided to appoint three new Justices in 1945 (thereby increasing the size of the Court to nine) while Evatt was overseas, but on his return in early 1946, Evatt had had the decision reversed in a stormy Cabinet confrontation. Labor consequently made only one **appointment** to the Court—that of **Webb** in 1946—and that was a conservative appointment (see **Appointments that might have been**).

While Labor was constrained in its more radical attempts at centralising power and socialising key industries, Australia did become a more independent nation during World War II, with more centralised domestic governance and an extended welfare state.

BRIAN GALLIGAN

Writs issued by the High Court in its original **jurisdiction** under section 75(v) of the Constitution against 'officers of the Commonwealth' are prohibition and mandamus. Although it is not expressly mentioned in section 75(v), the Court may also issue the writ of certiorari as an ancillary remedy. **Remedies** that are not strictly writs are injunctions, expressly mentioned in section 75(v), and declarations, issued by the Court in its accrued jurisdiction. Section 75(v) vests in the High Court a constitutional jurisdiction to ensure observance of the **rule of law** by the executive branch and by courts of limited jurisdiction (*Enfield Corporation v Development Assessment Commission* (2000); *Coal and Allied Operations v Australian Industrial Relations Commission* (2000); *Re Refugee Review Tribunal; Ex parte Aala* (2000)).

Pursuant to section 77 of the Constitution, this jurisdiction of the High Court has been made exclusive of state courts. However, since 1983 a broadly parallel jurisdiction has been vested in the **Federal Court**. When a **matter** is pending before the High Court in which a writ is sought, the High Court may **remit** it to the Federal Court if that Court has jurisdiction with respect to the subject matter and parties (*Judiciary Act* 1903 (Cth), sections 38(e), 44(1); *Re Jarman; Ex parte Cook* (1997)). The power to issue the writs is distinct from jurisdiction under section 75(v), and has been conferred by federal legislation (Judiciary Act, section 33(1)); see *Ex parte Aala*).

The expression 'officer of the Commonwealth' includes judges of federal courts and members of federal tribunals, but excludes state judicial and administrative officers (*R v Gray; Ex parte Marsh* (1985); *R v Ross-Jones; Ex parte Green* (1984); *Re McJannet; Ex parte Minister for Employment (Queensland)* (1995); *R v Trade Practices Tribunal; Ex parte Tasmanian Breweries* (1970)). Statutory corporations are not officers of the Commonwealth because there must be an office with some tenure, involving an appointment and usually a salary, with power that is limited or subject to supervision (*R v Murray and Cormie; Ex parte Commonwealth* (1916); *Re McJannet*; *Re Jarman*). The applicant may also invoke the High Court's pendent jurisdiction over parties additional to the officer of the Commonwealth, such as the other party to the proceedings before the court or tribunal.

The early **common law** conception of the wide jurisdiction of **superior courts** is not readily applied to federal courts in Australia, whose jurisdiction is limited by the Constitution and federal Acts (*Re McJannet*). Thus, the High Court may issue prohibition against a superior court such as the Federal Court because it is a court of limited jurisdiction (*R v Gray; Re McJannet*). However, the writs are non-reflexive in the sense that the High Court cannot under section 75(v) issue a writ directed towards itself (*Federated Engine Drivers v Colonial Sugar Refining Co* (1916); *R v Murray and Cormie*; *Re Jarman*).

The writs have an ancient history in English law. They have been called 'prerogative writs' because the rationale for their issue is that a court or tribunal that acts unlawfully by exceeding its jurisdiction encroaches upon the royal prerogative. For this reason, the writs are sought nominally by the Crown and directed at the court or tribunal rather than at the other contender in the litigation (*R v Hibble; Ex parte BHP* (1920); *Re Wakim* (1999)—see **Cross-vesting**). However, the expressions 'prohibition' and 'jurisdiction' in the context of section 75(v) are constitutional expressions (*Ex parte Aala*). Since the Crown is not an element of the Judicature established by Chapter III of the Constitution, the expression 'constitutional writ' is preferable to 'prerogative writ'.

In 2000, the High Court rejected the view that the term 'prohibition' in section 75(v) imports the law relating to the grant of prohibition by the Court of King's Bench in Eng-land at the time of federation. The different position in Australia is demonstrated, said the Court in *Aala*, by the availability under section 75(v) of prohibition directed to a judge of a superior court, or to action taken under legislation that is invalid on constitutional grounds. Nonetheless, **Gleeson**, **Gaudron**, and **Gummow** acknowledged that the essential characteristics of prohibition as a constitutional writ are appreciated by referring to legal scholarship of the past, including English common law at the time of commencement of the Constitution, without the Court being tied to past constitutional interpretation or automatically transposing those English principles to the Australian constitutional context. By contrast, **Kirby** took the view that the essential characteristics are to be derived having regard to the constitutional purposes for which the words appear in the text of the Constitution, historical limitations upon availability of the writs in English law being constitutionally irrelevant.

As a superior court, the High Court supervises tribunals, other administrators and courts of limited jurisdiction on grounds of jurisdictional error, error of law on the face of the record, and denial of **natural justice**. Issued to prevent a tribunal from proceeding to exceed its jurisdiction, prohibition is not granted unless something remains to be done by the court or tribunal (*R v Spicer; Ex parte Waterside Workers' Federation (No 2)* (1958)); *Re Wakim*). For this purpose, prohibition is available under section 75(v) to restrain an officer of the Commonwealth from denying a party natural justice, because such a decision would not be a true exercise of jurisdiction (*Ex parte Aala*). Once the court or tribunal has completed its task and is therefore *functus officio*, the appropriate writ is certiorari, which lies to bring a decision up to the superior court to be quashed.

Jurisdictional error attracting the High Court's jurisdiction to issue the writs occurs where a court or tribunal mistakenly asserts or denies the existence of jurisdiction or misapprehends the nature or limits of its powers (*Ex parte Marsh*; *Re McJannet*; *Craig v SA* (1995); *Abebe v Commonwealth* (1999)). The writs do not lie in respect of an error of law made by the court or tribunal in the course of exercising a jurisdiction that it truly has (*Re Queensland Electricity Commission; Ex parte Electrical Trades Union* (1987)). If the empowering Act of the court or tribunal, properly interpreted, makes an occurrence or circumstance a condition upon which jurisdiction depends, the Court may issue the writs if it concludes that the court or tribunal wrongly determined this jurisdictional fact (*R v Gray; Re McJannet*). The Court makes its own assessment of whether the jurisdictional fact objectively exists but gives considerable weight to the view of the facts taken by a specialist court or tribunal (*R v Ludeke; Ex parte Queensland Electricity Commission* (1985); *Enfield Corporation*). The writs do not lie to a court or tribunal that is expressly empowered to reach its own opinion regarding the existence of the jurisdictional fact, provided the opinion is formed reasonably upon the material before it (*Adamson's Case* (1979); *Enfield Corporation*).

However, where power to determine a jurisdictional fact marks the constitutional limits of the power to confer jurisdiction on the court or tribunal, the writs are available to ensure those limits are not exceeded (*R v Blakeley; Ex parte Association of Architects* (1950); *Re McJannet*).

The High Court's original jurisdiction to issue prohibition and mandamus to officers of the Commonwealth implies the conferral of an ancillary jurisdiction to grant certiorari (*Pitfield v Franki* (1970); *R v Cook; Ex parte Twigg* (1980); *Re Coldham; Ex parte Brideson* (1989); *R v Ross-Jones*). Doubts have been expressed as to whether the Court may issue certiorari when it is sought independently of a claim for relief for which section 75(v) makes provision (*R v Dunphy; Ex parte Maynes* (1978); *R v Cook; Re Coldham; Re East; Ex parte Nguyen* (1998)). However, in such cases a matter may arise under section 76(i) of the Constitution, founding jurisdiction to issue certiorari (*Re McJannet*).

Certiorari is issued to quash a decision affected by jurisdictional error, failure to observe procedural fairness, fraud or non-jurisdictional error appearing on the face of the record of the court or tribunal (*Craig v SA*).

Obtaining the writs involves difficulties that are not associated with the availability of the equitable remedies of injunction and declaration in public law (*Abebe; Enfield Corporation*). According to the classic test, prohibition and certiorari lie where a body of persons having legal authority to determine questions affecting the rights of subjects, and having the duty to act judicially, acts in excess of its legal authority (*R v Electricity Commissioners; Ex parte London Electricity Joint Committee* (1923)).

Applying this test, it has sometimes been held that the writs are not available in relation to merely recommendatory or preliminary decisions. For example, there is authority that certiorari does not lie in respect of a royal commissioner's report, which is purely recommendatory, not directly affecting rights (*R v Collins; Ex parte ACTU-Solo Enterprises* (1976)). However, the High Court is progressively extending the availability of the writs: they may now be issued where the decision challenged is a step in a process capable of altering rights, interests or liabilities, or operates as a precondition or as a bar to a course of action in the sense that the final decision maker has a legal duty to take the recommendatory decision into account (*Ainsworth v Criminal Justice Commission* (1992); *Hot Holdings v Creasy* (1996)).

The writ of mandamus is issued by the High Court to a subordinate officer, commanding the performance of a public duty the officer has wrongly refused or neglected to perform (*Re Jarman*). For example, the Court issues mandamus to compel a court or tribunal to exercise jurisdiction where it has erroneously decided that the conditions for its jurisdiction do not exist (*R v Blakeley*, **Northern Land Council Case** (1981)). Mandamus also lies where the exercise of power or jurisdiction is bad—for example, because the court or tribunal's misinterpretation of a statutory provision or abuse of its power results in its misconceiving the nature of its task to such an extent that it fails to perform it. This is sometimes called a 'constructive' refusal to exercise power or jurisdiction (*R v War Pensions Entitlement Appeal Tribunal; Ex parte Bott* (1933); *R v Connell; Ex parte Hetton Bellbird Collieries* (1944); *Ex parte Hebburn* (1947); *Re Coldham; Coal and Allied Operations*).

Mandamus compels the exercise of an administrative discretion rather than its exercise in a particular manner (*Randall v Northcote Corporation* (1910); *Re Coldham*). However, mandamus may be issued to compel an administrator to take particular action where there is no discretion to exercise because there is only one decision that can lawfully be made (*R v Anderson; Ex parte Ipec-Air* (1965)).

When sought by a stranger to the proceedings in the court or tribunal, the Court has a discretion to issue prohibition (*Re Grimshaw; Ex parte Australian Telephone and Phonogram Officers' Association* (1986); *Ex parte Aala*). When sought by an aggrieved party, prohibition issues almost as of right (*R v Ross-Jones; Ex parte Green* (1984); *Ex parte Aala*). However, in all cases the Court has a discretion to issue the writs (*Ex parte Aala*). They may be refused where the unlawful action had no effect on the decision; where the application is not made in good faith, is made for some ulterior motive or is premature; where relief would be futile; or on the ground of delay (*R v Commonwealth Court of Conciliation and Arbitration; Ex parte Ozone Theatres* (1949); *Ex parte Aala*). Where there is another remedy that is equally convenient, beneficial and effective, mandamus may be refused (*Tooth & Co v Parramatta City Council* (1955)).

Some statutes attempt to oust the writs by providing that the decisions of a court or tribunal shall not be challenged, appealed against, reviewed or called into question or be subject to prohibition, mandamus or injunction in any court on any account whatever. These '**privative clauses**' cannot affect the High Court's jurisdiction under section 75(v) of the Constitution (*R v Hickman; Ex parte Fox and Clinton* (1945)). Often there is an apparent inconsistency between such privative clauses and other provisions in the same statute limiting the ambit of the jurisdiction of the court or tribunal. This is to be reconciled according to principles of **statutory interpretation**. Provided the decision is a *bona fide* attempt to exercise statutory power, relates to the subject matter of the statute and is reasonably capable of reference to the power given to the court or tribunal, the privative clause will protect the decision from supervision by means of the writs (*R v Hickman; Darling Casino v NSW Casino Control Authority* (1997)).

A writ not expressly mentioned in section 75(v) is habeas corpus, by which a court orders the release of a person unlawfully held in custody. The High Court may issue habeas corpus in exercise of its original jurisdiction with respect to matters arising under the Constitution and involving its interpretation (Constitution, section 76(i)); Judiciary Act, sections 30(a), 33(1)(f); *Re Governor, Goulburn Correctional Centre; Ex parte Eastman* (1999)).

Margaret Allars

Further Reading

David Clark and Gerard McCoy, *Habeas Corpus: Australia, New Zealand, The South Pacific* (2000)

X

X v Commonwealth (1999). Public **health, disability discrimination** in **employment**, and the function of the **military** were all bound up in the High Court's decision in 1999 to uphold the Commonwealth's appeal from a finding that it had discriminated against a soldier on the ground of disability when he was discharged from the Australian Regular Army, part of the Australian Defence Forces. 'X' was discharged when he was found, shortly after enlistment, to have HIV—the virus that causes AIDS.

The case came to the Court some 17 years into the HIV/AIDS epidemic in Australia. The epidemic presented new challenges to public health that are still being explored. AIDS symptoms do not appear in every case; when they do appear, it is usually after a 'silent' infection period of some ten years, during which the person with HIV is completely able-bodied. In the absence of treatment, the disease is eventually fatal. By 1999, however, treatments had turned the disease into a chronic, manageable condition for many with HIV infection. The problem for public health authorities was that disease prevention was made difficult by the taboos involved in the modes of transmission: sexual intercourse and sharing drug injecting equipment.

Transfusion of infected blood products, however, is just as effective a mode of HIV transmission as sharing needles. When HIV testing was introduced for Defence Force members in the late 1980s, one of the rationales was the risk of infection caused by the need for emergency 'battlefield transfusions'.

By the mid-1990s, Australia's multifaceted legal response to HIV/AIDS had been held up overseas as a model for other countries and was considered to have contributed to Australia's position as one of the few countries that had successfully contained the epidemic. The Commonwealth *Disability Discrimination Act* had been passed in 1992, in part to protect people with HIV and AIDS from undue **discrimination**.

After he was discharged from the Army, 'X' had complained to the Human Rights and Equal Opportunity Commission of discrimination contrary to the Disability Discrimination Act. The Commonwealth conceded that the soldier had been discriminated against on the ground of disability but contended that, because he was a member of the Defence Forces, the discrimination was not unlawful. The Commission disagreed, and upheld the complaint. The Commonwealth applied to the **Federal Court** for **judicial review**, claiming the Commission erred in law. At first instance, Justice Richard Cooper dismissed the Commonwealth's application, but that decision was reversed by a Full Court of the Federal Court.

By majority (**Kirby** dissenting), the High Court agreed with the Full Court. However, contrary to domestic and international **media** accounts of the case, the High Court did not finally determine whether the discrimination was a breach of the Act. Rather, the Court focused on the meaning of the statutory defence that the worker 'would be unable to carry out the inherent requirements of the particular employment' without assistance that it would be unjustifiably harsh to expect the employer to provide. This defence is generally provided by anti-discrimination law for employers who sack or prejudice a worker on the ground of an attribute such as disability. The Court held that the defence extends beyond the immediate issue of the worker's ability to do the job. 'Inherent requirements' also covers issues external to the worker—the circumstances in which the work is to be carried out.

In this case, the Court held that the question to be decided was whether workplace safety would be adversely affected. An employee must be able to perform the inherent requirements of the job with reasonable safety not only to the individual, but also to others with whom he or she will come into contact in the course of employment.

The Commonwealth argued that, because of the conditions in which they might need suddenly to be deployed, soldiers need to be able to 'bleed safely'. Bleeding, and the exigencies and discipline of military service, loomed large in this litigation. Justice Charles Burchett, in the Federal Court's Full Court decision, evoked the struggle of Horatius and his companions to hold a bridge, cumbered with corpses:

> … the narrow way
> Where, wallowing in a pool of blood,
> The bravest Tuscans lay.

Callinan in the High Court cited Charles Clode's *The Military Forces of the Crown* (1869) to show that military service is of a special nature, having no obligations that compete with the personal and strict obligation of service to the Crown.

There was a division of opinion on the extent to which infection with blood-borne disease might mean an inability to perform military duties without risking the health or life of others, particularly in circumstances of overseas or battle-field deployment. Callinan did not think a narrow view of such an inability was possible. The rest of the majority, **Gleeson**, **McHugh**, **Gummow**, and **Hayne**, together with Kirby in dissent, would require close scrutiny of the army's reasons for being unwilling or unable to deploy an HIV-positive soldier as the exigencies of the service require, particularly given the second leg of the defence—that the risk to others cannot be eliminated or nullified by facilities that can be provided without unjustifiable hardship.

The decision of the Court, therefore, was that the Full Court of the Federal Court's decision was correct—the matter needed to be remitted to the Commissioner to determine the Commonwealth's defence in accordance with the broader scope of the term 'inherent requirements of the job'. The Full Court of the Federal Court was also right in identifying error in the approach to judicial review taken by Justice Cooper in the Federal Court, as to whether the Commissioner's narrow construction of 'inherent requirements of the job' *would* have, rather than *could* have, led to a different result in the initial appeal.

In his **dissenting judgment**, Kirby disagreed with the appeal judges' reading of the Commissioner's original decision. Off the Bench, Kirby was and is a prominent international advocate for a rational approach to the HIV/AIDS pandemic. His 'AIDS paradox' had been adopted and proven in many countries: the most effective way to promote the behaviour modification essential to reduce transmission of HIV is not quarantine or punishment—it is protection of the vulnerable who are at risk and defence of their basic human rights; only then will they be receptive to the messages and means necessary for their self-protection and the protection of others. Kirby was instrumental in the promulgation in 1998 of the UN's International Guidelines on HIV/AIDS and Human Rights.

In his reasons in *X v Commonwealth*, Kirby underlined the demand of the legislation to attend to the inherent requirements of the 'particular' employment. This was in contrast to the fact that 'X' had been discharged without consideration of how his disability of having HIV infection could be accommodated, and simply in the implementation of a general policy to discharge Defence Force members with HIV.

It was this feature of the case that provided its public health ramifications. Kirby pointed out that the whole purpose of anti-discrimination legislation is to achieve social change by removing **stereotypes**. It was not as if the High Court was unfamiliar with the stigma surrounding HIV/AIDS (see *IW v City of Perth* (1997)). Yet here the army was compounding the public health problems of addressing the epidemic by sending a message—in contradiction of the Disability Discrimination Act—that HIV infection was an automatic disqualification from any sort of military service.

It is for this reason that, on a close reading, public health authorities would welcome the Court's decision in *X*. The Court held that the Disability Discrimination Act mandates an inquiry into the circumstances and requirements of the particular case, not as it impacts across the board for every employee in the organisation. Further, the majority made it clear that employers must not, in the way they organise their business, disguise unlawful discrimination. Finally, the defence of 'inherent requirements' must be read as a whole. That is, consideration must be given to whether the employer can provide services and facilities to the worker so that the inherent requirements test can be satisfied.

As it happened, the question of whether the army's conduct could be supported on a fuller analysis of the circumstances of *X*'s case was never answered. Observers thought it was telling that the Commonwealth subsequently settled its litigation with 'X' on terms not to be disclosed.

DAVID BUCHANAN

Further Reading
Kevin Farrell, 'Human Immunodeficiency Virus (HIV) Testing in the Australian Defence Force' (1992) 94 *Australian Defence Force Journal* 19
Eric Feldman, *Testing the Force: HIV and Discrimination in the Australian Military*, Center for Interdisciplinary Research into AIDS, Yale University School of Medicine, vol 1(2), 15 July 1998
Michael Flynn, 'HIV in the Australian Defence Force 1985–1993' (1993) 9 *Australian HIV Surveillance Report* 1
Michael Kirby, 'AIDS Legislation: Turning Up the Heat?' (1986) 60 *ALJ* 324
Michael Kirby, 'AIDS and Human Rights' (1992) 1 *Australasian Gay & Lesbian Law Journal* 1

Yerkey v Jones (1939), decided in the year that Australia entered **World War II**, epitomises the style of **judicial reasoning** and social attitudes of the period. The issue was whether Florence Jones was bound by a mortgage she gave over her property to secure the purchase by her husband of a poultry farm. The High Court unanimously held that she was not entitled to be relieved of her obligations under the mortgage, since her decision to grant the mortgage was a 'free and voluntary act' accompanied by an understanding of the nature and consequences of the transaction. Despite this outcome, **Dixon's** judgment became the leading Australian authority affirming the protection given by **equity** to married **women** in financial transactions for the benefit of their husbands.

Only **Latham** and Dixon delivered full reasons and Dixon's are by far the more extensive. Dixon impressively and painstakingly traced the development of equity's recognition of the ability of a married woman to deal with her **property**, beginning with case law in the early seventeenth century. He concluded that although there was no automatic presumption of **undue influence** between husband and wife, the marriage relationship had 'never been divested completely of what may be called equitable presumptions of an invalidating tendency'.

It is typical of the judicial reasoning of the period that Dixon reached his conclusions without admitting to any creative **law-making role**. His judgment is cast in terms of deducing the legal principles from the authorities, even though he acknowledged that the state of the law was 'somewhat indefinite, if not uncertain', and engaged in extensive organisation and reformulation of the confusing and conflicting authorities. Similarly, there is no normative discussion of the equitable principles involved. His sole reference to **policy considerations** is in justifying the established doctrinal position that large gifts by a woman to her husband do not attract the presumption of undue influence, whereas those by a woman to her fiancé will do so. He stated that the presumption is a rule of policy 'and, upon a balance, policy is against applying it to husband and wife'.

Yerkey v Jones also illustrates the social attitudes of the time. Implicit in the judgments is an assumption that women were vulnerable to exploitation and pressure from their husbands, and did not make independent financial decisions. The absence of discussion is a powerful indication that the proposition was taken to be self-evident. One also gains a sense of the distinction between legal and moral standards of behaviour. Latham, **Rich**, and Dixon each noted the ungentlemanly conduct of Mr Jones. Rich commented: 'He acted with less consideration for her interests than chivalry, not to say propriety, demanded.' And in Dixon's view: 'She was placed in a dilemma, a dilemma unfair to a woman, but not in a situation rendering the course she chose to take one from which afterwards she was entitled to be relieved.'

Yerkey v Jones became controversial in the 1980s when economic conditions led to increasing reliance on the decision by guarantors. The social attitudes implicit in the judgments were criticised as anachronistic and discriminatory, and the extent to which financial institutions should be regulated in their dealings with guarantors was questioned. Nonetheless, Dixon's treatment of the law remains impressive, and ultimately his judgment was endorsed by a majority of the Court in *Garcia v National Australia Bank* (1998).

PAULINE RIDGE

Further Reading

Paula Baron, 'The Free Exercise of Her Will: Women and Emotionally Transmitted Debt' (1995) 13 *LIC* 23

Belinda Fehlberg, 'Women in "Family" Companies: English and Australian Experiences' (1997) 15 *C&SLJ* 348

Janine Pascoe, 'Wives, Business Debts and Guarantees' (1997) 9 *Bond LR* 58

George Williams, 'Equitable Principles for the Protection of Vulnerable Guarantors: Is the Principle in *Yerkey v Jones* Still Needed?' (1994) 8 *JCL* 67

Z

Ziems v Prothonotary of the Supreme Court of NSW (1957) is a leading case on legal professional conduct in which the High Court elaborated the principles applicable to the requirement that a lawyer be a fit and proper person to practise, particularly where there has been a conviction for a criminal offence. The case is not only of major importance among the comparatively few in which the High Court has dealt with these principles; it is also notable because of its unusual facts.

Trevor Ziems was admitted as a barrister of the Supreme Court of NSW in 1936 and practised at the Bar in Sydney. From 1948 onwards, he occasionally appeared as **counsel** in the High Court—for instance, in *Peter Turnbull & Co v Mundus Trading Co* (1954) and *Basto v The Queen* (1954). One evening in 1955, after he had appeared as counsel in a case at Newcastle, NSW, there was an incident at a local hotel where he intended to stay. Ziems remonstrated with a drunken seaman, who had thrown beer bottles and had used disgusting expressions to two young women. The seaman, a younger and bigger man, punched Ziems about the head and upper body, knocking Ziems' spectacles off and then striking Ziems' head against a brick wall. Police were called; they arrested the seaman. A police sergeant advised Ziems to go to the hospital to have his head injuries, which were considerable, treated. Ziems drove off in his own car. Veering erratically onto the wrong side of the road, he collided with an oncoming motorcyclist. Some witnesses suggested Ziems was under the influence of alcohol, but at the coronial inquiry the police sergeant conceded that Ziems' condition could have been due to the blows he received from the seaman. Ziems was indicted for manslaughter. The police sergeant was not called by the prosecutor at the trial, and although Ziems said he was suffering shock and concussion from the attack, he was convicted of manslaughter and sentenced to two years imprisonment with hard labour. The Supreme Court ordered that his name be removed from the roll of barristers.

The true cause of Ziems' erratic driving was never established, as no direct evidence was available. The trial judge had evidently been convinced that Ziems was intoxicated at the time of his accident, as he imposed a sentence that Ziems' counsel described as unusually heavy. In any case, Ziems did not appeal against his conviction and sentence, choosing instead to challenge his striking off.

The High Court, by a majority (**Fullagar**, **Kitto**, and **Taylor**; **Dixon** and **McTiernan** dissenting), allowed Ziems' appeal against that removal, and instead ordered that he be suspended from practice only during the continuance of his imprisonment. The judgments exhibit a tension between, on the one hand, the need to protect the integrity of the **legal profession** and the legal system and, on the other, the need to protect individual lawyers against unjustified persecution and loss of livelihood.

While Dixon pointed to the undoubted need for counsel to 'command the confidence and respect of the court, of his fellow counsel and of his professional and lay clients', he was clearly in dissent upon the ultimate disposition of the appeal. Dixon noted that the Supreme Court's disciplinary jurisdiction is not a punitive one. Nevertheless, he said:

> When a barrister is justly convicted of a serious crime and imprisoned the law has pronounced a judgment upon him which must ordinarily mean the loss by him of the standing before the court and the public which, as it seems to me, should belong to those to whom are entrusted the privileges, duties and responsibilities of an advocate.

The majority was of a different mind. After a detailed examination of the evidence and directions at the trial, Fullagar said:

> When one looks at the evidence apart from the verdict, it seems to me impossible to say that it justifies a finding that [Ziems] is not a fit and proper person to practise at the Bar. One must be very sure of the facts before making so serious a finding.

Kitto and Taylor also focused on the facts and circumstances of the case, rather than the felony conviction. Kitto indicated it was not enough that some fellow barristers or judges *might* disdain contact with a barrister so convicted; especially in the present case, 'since no one has come forward to say a word against the appellant, and he has been called upon to answer nothing but the fact of his conviction'. He was, on this score, more charitable than Ziems' colleagues of the NSW Bar Association, the Council of which was represented at Ziems' appeal. The Court was informed that the Council supported Ziems' position by majority, but not unanimously.

On one view, the majority's cautious approach is justified. Malice, unjust **discrimination**, professional rivalries, political unpopularity, grudges, or the like, can result in improper attempts to exclude or remove persons from legal practice. It is precisely because of the importance of an independent and robust legal profession in maintaining the **rule of law** in civil society that courts have a duty to examine very stringently any claim to exclude persons from the practice of the law.

To some minds, decisions such as that in *Ziems* raise questions about the ability of judges objectively to rule upon the conduct of other lawyers. Others will say that judges are well qualified to make such rulings. Similar views have been expressed about the Court's approach to professional negligence. In recent years, the Court has upheld the immunity of advocates against suits in negligence in relation to their curial functions (*Giannarelli v Wraith* (1988); *Boland v Yates Property Corporation* (1999)). The Court's position on advocates' immunity is in contrast to its increasing tendency to recognise actionable negligence among other professionals (see, for example, *Chappel v Hart* (1998)).

Other leading High Court decisions on issues of legal professional conduct and fitness to practise as a lawyer include *Re Davis* (1947); *Ex parte Lenehan* (1948); and *NSW Bar Association v Evatt* (1968). Previous convictions are one thing; failure to disclose them, or other matters relevant to fitness to practise, has been viewed particularly seriously, as those things bear upon honesty and candour. Generally speaking, however, issues of professional conduct are a rarity before the Court. The territory and **state Supreme Courts** have general supervisory jurisdiction over their respective legal professions, and few litigants have been willing to challenge the judgment of those courts by appeal in such matters. This deference has been shared by the High Court, which in recent times has been reluctant to grant special **leave to appeal** from decisions relating to lawyers' professional conduct.

As for Ziems, he served his sentence, returned to the Sydney Bar, and continued in practice for a number of years. His last appearance before the High Court was, ironically, made as junior counsel (led by **Murphy**) for the respondent plaintiff in a case arising from a fatal head-on road collision (*Transport & General Insurance Co v Edmondson* (1961)).

DOUGLAS HASSALL

Further Reading
Gino Dal Pont, *Lawyers' Professional Responsibility in Australia and New Zealand* (1996)
Julian Disney *et al.*, *Lawyers* (2nd edn 1986)

Civil honours awarded to High Court Justices

Aickin, Sir Keith Arthur	KBE (1976), QC (1957)
Barton, Sir Edmund	GCMG (1902), QC (1889)
Barwick, Sir Garfield Edward John	PC (1964), AK (1981), GCMG (1965), Kt (1953), KC (1941)
Brennan, Sir Francis Gerard	AC (1988), KBE (1981), QC (1965)
Callinan, Ian David	QC (1978)
Dawson, Sir Daryl Michael	AC (1988), KBE (1982), CB (1980), QC (1971)
Deane, Sir William Patrick	AC (1988), KBE (1982), QC (1966)
Dixon, Sir Owen	OM (1963), PC (1951), GCMG (1954), KCMG (1941), KC (1922)
Evatt, Herbert Vere	KC (1929)
Fullagar, Sir Wilfred Kelsham	KBE (1954) KC (1933)
Gaudron, Mary Genevieve	QC (1981)
Gavan Duffy, Sir Frank	PC (1932), KCMG (1929), KC (1901)
Gibbs, Sir Harry Talbot	PC (1972), AC (1987), GCMG (1981), KBE (1970), QC (1957)
Gleeson, (Anthony) Murray	AC (1992), QC (1974)
Griffith, Sir Samuel Walker	PC (1901), GCMG (1895), KCMG (1886), QC (1876)
Gummow, William Montague	AC (1997), QC (1986)
Hayne, Kenneth Madison	QC (1984)
Higgins, Henry Bourne	KC (1903)
Isaacs, Sir Isaac Alfred	GCB (1937), GCMG (1932), KCMG (1928), QC (1899)
Jacobs, Sir Kenneth Sydney	KBE (1976), QC (1958)
Kirby, Michael Donald	AC (1991), CMG (1983)
Kitto, Sir Frank Walters	PC (1963), AC (1983), KBE (1955), KC (1942)
Knox, Sir Adrian	PC (1920), KCMG (1921), KC (1906)
Latham, Sir John Grieg	PC (1933), GCMG (1935), CMG (1920), KC (1922)
Mason, Sir Anthony Frank	AC (1988), KBE (1972), CBE (1969), QC (1964)
McHugh, Michael Hudson	AC (1989), QC (1973)
McTiernan, Sir Edward Aloysius	PC (1963), KBE (1951)
Menzies, Sir Douglas	PC (1963), KBE (1958), KC (1948)
Murphy, Lionel Keith	QC (1960)
O'Connor, Richard Edward	QC (1896)
Owen, Sir William Francis Langer	PC (1963), KBE (1957), KC (1935)
Piddington, Albert Bathurst	KC (1943)

Powers, Sir Charles	KCMG (1929)
Rich, Sir George Edward	PC (1936), KCMG (1932), KC (1911)
Starke, Sir Hayden Erskine	KCMG (1939)
Stephen, Sir Ninian Martin	PC (1979), KG (1994), AK (1982), GCMG (1982), CGVO (1982), KBE (1972), QC (1966)
Taylor, Sir Alan Russell	PC (1963), KBE (1955), KC (1943)
Toohey, John Leslie	AC (1988), QC (1968)
Walsh, Sir Cyril Ambrose	PC (1971), KBE (1969)
Webb, Sir William Flood	KBE (1954), Kt (1942)
Williams, Sir Dudley	KBE (1954), KC (1935)
Wilson, Sir Ronald Darling	AC (1988), KBE (1979), CMG (1978), QC (1963)
Windeyer, Sir William John Victor	PC (1963), KBE (1958), CBE (1944), KC (1949)

Note

For convenience of reference, the list above includes the dates upon which Justices took silk (accepted their commissions as QC or KC), although this is a professional rank rather than a civil honour, despite being granted by commission from the Crown. On retirement, Justices revert to use of KC or QC (or SC, Senior Counsel), which are not used while they hold judicial office. In formal address, High Court Justices are accorded the distinction 'The Honourable' while in office, and are usually permitted to retain it afterwards (see **Etiquette**); Privy Counsellors (an office conferred for life) are addressed as 'The Right Honourable'. The Order of Merit is a distinguished order, limited to 24 members, ranking in precedence immediately after Knights Grand Cross of the Order of the Bath.

The list does not include honorary degrees. In addition to Australian civil honours the Justices of the High Court have been accorded various academic and other honours.

The current Justices have had conferred on them honorary degrees of Australian and overseas universities: **Gleeson** (2), **Gaudron** (2), **McHugh** (1), **Gummow** (1) and **Kirby** (7). Among living past Justices the position is similar: **Brennan** (7), **Deane** (9), **Gibbs** (2), **Mason** (7), **Stephen** (4), **Toohey** (1), and **Wilson** (4).

Kirby, Mason, and Stephen have been elected Honorary Fellows of the Academy of the Social Sciences in Australia. In the international sphere, Gleeson was elected an Honorary Bencher of the Middle Temple (1989). Gummow (1997) and Kirby J (2000) were elected members of the American Law Institute. Kirby, while a Justice, was named Laureate of the biennial UNESCO Prize for Human Rights Education (1998). Stephen was appointed an Honorary Commander of the Légion d'honneur of France (1993).

Distinguished honours conferred upon earlier Justices include **Dixon's** Henry E Howland Memorial Prize, awarded to him by Yale University in 1955 for 'marked distinction in the field of literature or fine arts, or the science of government', with an emphasis on 'the idealistic element in the recipient's work'.

Illustration acknowledgments

The authors and publisher would like to thank the following for giving us permission to reproduce their material. The words in **bold** refer to the entry where the illustration appears.

Aickin, Keith Arthur Photo by Robert Pearce. Fairfax Photo Library. **Appointments that might have been** Courtesy of the State Library of South Australia. **Architecture of Court building** Photo by Hamish Lindsay. **Architecture of Court building** Courtesy of Colin Madigan and Jennifer Taylor. **Artworks of Court** Photo by Hamish Lindsay. **Australia Acts** NAA: KN18/3/86/33. Commonwealth of Australia copyright. Reproduced by permission. **Barton, Edmund** MS51/1273. By permission of the National Library of Australia. **Barwick, Garfield Edward John** High Court Collection. **Brennan, (Francis) Gerard** Photo by Heide Smith. **Brennan Court** Photo by David Coward. High Court Collection. **Buildings, Court** High Court Collection. **Buildings, Court** NAA: A6180/5, 19/8/74/9. Commonwealth of Australia copyright. Reproduced by permission. **Callinan, Ian David Francis** Photo by Ray Strange. By permission of Newspix. **Canberra, Court's move to** NAA: A8746/1, KN6/6/80/20. Commonwealth of Australia copyright. Reproduced by permission. **Canberra, Court's move to** NAA: A8746/1, KN6/6/80/31. Commonwealth of Australia copyright. Reproduced by permission. **Ceremonial sittings** By permission of the National Library of Australia. *Chamberlain's Case* (1984) *The Canberra Times*, February 1981. By permission of the National Library of Australia. **Chambers.** High Court Collection. **Convention debates** By permission of the National Library of Australia. **Counsel, notable** Photo by Harold Cazneaux. By permission of the National Library of Australia and Cazneaux family. **Court officials** High Court collection. **Courtrooms** NAA: A8746/1, KN1/9/80/9. Commonwealth of Australia copyright Reproduced by permission. **Courtrooms** NAA: A6180/13, 9/6/82/9. Commonwealth of Australia copyright. Reproduced by permission. **Courtrooms** NAA: A6180/13, 9/6/82/8. Commonwealth of Australia copyright. Reproduced by permission. **Dawson, Daryl Michael** Photo by David Coward. High Court collection. **Deakin, Alfred** Photo by Elliott & Fry, London. By permission of the National Library of Australia. **Deane, William Patrick** Courtesy of Government House, Canberra. **Dismissal of 1975** By permission of the National Library of Australia. **Dixon, Owen** La Trobe Picture Collection, State Library of Victoria. **Dixon Court** By permission of the National Library of Australia. **Dixon diaries** Photo by Ken Chandler, Monash University. **Evatt, Herbert Vere** By permission of Newspix. **Framers of the Consti-**

tution Shakespeare Collection. By permission of the National Library of Australia. **Fullagar, Wilfred Kelsham** Australian Information Service. High Court Collection. **Garran, Robert Randolph** Photo by Roslyn Poignant. By permission of the National Library of Australia and Roslyn Poignant. **Gaudron, Mary.** Photo by Hamish Lindsay. **Gavan Duffy, Frank** High Court collection. **Gibbs, Harry Talbot** Photo by Australian Information Service (19/3/80). By permission of the National Library of Australia. **Gleeson, (Anthony) Murray** Photo by Hamish Lindsay. **Gleeson Court** Photo by David Coward. High Court collection. **Griffith, Samuel Walker** Dwyer Collection. By permission of the National Library of Australia. **Griffith Court** NAA: CP207/1. Commonwealth of Australia copyright. Reproduced by permission. **Gummow, William Montague Charles** Photo by Hamish Lindsay. **Hayne, Kenneth Madison** Photo by Hamish Lindsay. **Higgins, Henry Bournes** Palmer Collection. By permission of the National Library of Australia. **Inglis Clark, Andrew** Photo by Vandyck. By permission of the National Library of Australia. *Irish Envoys Case* (1923) O'Farrell Collection. By permission of the National Library of Australia. **Isaacs, Isaac Alfred** Photograph Album 893A. By permission of the National Library of Australia. **Jacobs, Kenneth Sydney** Photo by Lipman. Fairfax Photo Library. **Kirby, Michael Donald** Photo by Hamish Lindsay. *Kisch Case* (1934) Image Library, State Library of New South Wales. **Kitto, Frank Walters** By permission of Margaret Connor. **Knox, Adrian** High Court collection. **Latham, John Greig** Photograph by Spencer Shier La Trobe Picture Collection, State Library of Victoria. **Litigants, notable 1903–1945** Image Library, State Library of New South Wales. **Litigants, notable 1945–2001** Photo by Alan Funnell. By permission of Newspix. *Mabo* (1992) By permission of Newspix. **Mabo: counsel's perspective** Photo by Francis Reiss. By permission of the National Library of Australia. **Madigan, Colin** Courtesy of *The Canberra Times*. **Mason, Anthony Frank** University of New South Wales Archives. **Mason Court** NAA: A8746/5, KN30/6/87/1. Commonwealth of Australia copyright. Reproduced by permission. **McHugh, Michael Hudson** Photo by Hamish Lindsay. **McTiernan, Edward Aloysius** Photo by May Moore. By permission of the National Library of Australia. **Menzies, Douglas Ian** High Court Collection. **Menzies, Robert Gordon** Menzies' Papers, MS4936. By permission of the National Library of Australia. **Murphy, Lionel Keith** Photo by Attila Kiraly. High Court Collection. **Murphy affair** Photo by Robert Pearce. Fairfax Photo Library. *Namatjira v Raabe* (1959) Photo by News and Information Bureau. By permission of the National Library

Illustration acknowledgments

of Australia. **Non-judicial functions** MS 6923. By permission of the National Library of Australia. **O'Connor, Richard Edward.** By permission of the National Library of Australia. **Owen, William Francis Langer.** By permission of the National Library of Australia. *Patrick Stevedores Case* (1998) Photo by Francis Reiss and June Orford. By permission of the National Library of Australia. **Piddington, Albert Bathurst.** Courtesy of Morris Graham. **Popular images of Court** Courtesy of Working Dog. **Powers, Charles** Australian Information Service. High Court Collection. **Quick and Garran** Courtesy of Richard Snedden. **Rich, George** Photo by RL Stewart. Fairfax Photo Library. **Sexual preference** Photo courtesy of Roger Lovell, *Frontpage Photography*. **Sittings of Court** By permission of the Manuscript Section, National Library of Australia. **Sittings of Court** By permission of the National Library of Australia. **Solicitors-General** Courtesy of *The Canberra Times*. **Starke, Hayden Erskine** High Court Collection. . **Stephen, Ninian Martin** NAA: A8746/5, KN3/6/85/8. Commonwealth of Australia copyright. Reproduced by permission. **Strike of 1905** By permission of the State Library of South Australia. **Symbolism of Court building** Photo by Hamish Lindsay. *Tait's Case* (1962) Courtesy of Victorian Police Department. *Tasmanian Dam Case* (1983) NAA: A6135/8, K18/2/83/15. Commonwealth of Australia copyright. Reproduced by permission. **Taylor, Alan Russell** High Court Collection. **Toohey, John Leslie** High Court Collection. **United States Supreme Court** Photo by Verner Reed. **Walsh, Cyril Ambrose.** High Court Collection. **Webb, William Flood** Negative number 62055. John Oxley Library Photograph collection. **Whitlam era** Photo by Luoi Seselja. By permission of the National Library of Australia. *Wik* (1996) Photo by Hamish Lindsay. **Williams, Dudley.** High Court Collection. **Wilson, Ronald Darling** Courtesy of *The Canberra Times*. **Windeyer, (William John) Victor** Negative Number 016473. Australian War Memorial. **Women practitioners** By permission of *Advertiser* newspapers and State Library of South Australia. **World War I** Australian War Memorial. Negative Number A02615. **World War II** Negative Number 106111. Australian War Memorial.

Abbreviations used in table of cases

Australian

ACL Rep	Australian Current Law Reporter
A Crim R	Australian Criminal Reports
ALD	Administrative Law Decisions
ALJ	Australian Law Journal
ALJR	Australian Law Journal Reports
ALR	Australian Law Reports
AOJP	Australian Official Journal of Patents
Aust Torts Rep	Australian Torts Reports
CAR	Conciliation and Arbitration Reports
CLR	Commonwealth Law Reports
Fam LR	Family Law Reports
FCR	Federal Court Reports
FLR	Federal Law Reports
Hore	Hore's Digest of Cases Decided in Tasmania (1856–1896)
IPR	Intellectual Property Reports
Legge	Legge's Reports (NSW) (1825–62)
NSWR	New South Wales Reports (1960–70)
NSWLR	New South Wales Law Reports (since 1971; also 1880–1900)
Qd LJ Rep	Queensland Law Journal Reports
Qd R	Queensland Reports (since 1958)
QWN	Queensland Weekly Notes (annexed to State Reports (Queensland))
SASR	South Australian State Reports
SCR (NSW)	Supreme Court Reports (New South Wales) (1862–79)
SR (NSW)	State Reports (New South Wales) (1901–70)
St R Qld	State Reports (Queensland) (1902–57)
Tas LR	Tasmanian Law Reports
VLR	Victorian Law Reports (1875–1956)
VR	Victorian Reports (since 1957)
WAR	Western Australian Reports (since 1961)
WALR	Western Australian Law Reports (1899–1959)
WN (NSW)	Weekly Notes (NSW) (1884–1970)

United Kingdom

AC	Appeal Cases (since 1891)
App Cas	Appeal Cases (1875–90)
Burr	Burrow's Reports (now in English Reports)
Ch	Chancery Reports (since 1891)
Cl & F	Clarke & Finnelly's Reports (now in English Reports)
Co Rep	Coke's Reports (now in English Reports)
Cr App R	Criminal Appeal Reports
ER	English Reports (compilation)
H & C	Hurlstone & Coltman's Reports (now in English Reports)
HL	House of Lords
HLC	House of Lords Cases (1847–66)
KB	King's Bench (1901–52)
LJ (PC)	Law Journal Reports (Privy Council)
Lloyd's Rep	Lloyd's Law Reports
LQR	*Law Quarterly Review*
LR … CP	Law Reports (Common Pleas) (1865–75)
LR … Ex	Law Reports (Exchequer) (1865–75)
LR … HL	Law Reports (House of Lords) (1865–75)
LR … P & D	Law Reports (Probate and Divorce) (1865–75)
M & W	Meeson & Welsby's Reports (now in English Reports)
Mac & G	M'Naghten & Gordon's Reports (now in English Reports)
PD	Probate Division (1875–90)
QB	Queen's Bench (1891–1901, 1952—)
QBD	Queen's Bench Division (1875–90)
R	The Reports (1893–95)
RPC	Reports of Patent, Design and Trade Mark Cases
SC (HL)	Session Cases (House of Lords) (Scotland)
St Tr	State Trials (1163–1820)
Vaughan	Vaughan's Reports (now in English Reports)
WLR	Weekly Law Reports

Other

Cranch	Cranch's Supreme Court Reports (now in US Reports)
Cush	Cushing's Massachusetts Reports
DLR	Dominion Law Reports (Canada)
Eur Court HR	European Court of Human Rights, Reports of Judgments and Decisions
F 2d	Federal Reporter (Second Series) (US)
Fed Cas	Federal Cases (US)
Gall	Gallinson's United States Circuit Court Reports

Abbreviations used in table of cases

Howard	Howard's Supreme Court Reports (now in US Reports)
ICJ Reports	International Court of Justice, Reports of Judgments, Advisory Opinions and Orders
Int LR	International Law Reports
IR	Irish Reports (Ireland)
Mass	Massachusetts Reports
NE	Northeastern Reporter (US)
NY	New York Reports
NZLR	New Zealand Law Reports
Peters	Peters' Supreme Court Reports (now in US Reports)
SALR	South African Law Reports
SCR	Supreme Court Reports (Canada)
S Ct	Supreme Court Reporter (US)
Serg & Rawle	Sergeant & Rawles' Reports (Pennsylvania)
US	United States Reports
Wall	Wallace's Supreme Court Reports (now in US Reports)
Wheat	Wheaton's Supreme Court Reports (now in US Reports)

Table of cases

Index of names

Index of names

Index of names

Index of names

Subject index

Page numbers in plain type refer to the main references to a subject; those in bold refer to the main article on the subject; and those in italics refer to illustrations.